Collins

BESTSELLING BILINGUAL DICTIONARIES

Italian Dictionary

HarperCollins Publishers
Westerhill Road
Bishopbriggs
Glasgow
G64 2QT
Great Britain

Second Edition 2010

Reprint 10 9 8 7 6 5 4 3 2 1 0

ISBN 978-0-00-732318-0

www.collinslanguage.com

A catalogue record for this book is available from the British Library

HarperCollins Publishers, 10 East 53rd Street, New York, NY 10022

COLLINS ITALIAN CONCISE DICTIONARY
Fifth US Edition 2010

ISBN 978-0-06-199865-2

www.harpercollins.com

HarperCollins books may be purchased for educational, business, or sales promotional use. For information, please write to: Special Markets Department, HarperCollins Publishers, 10 East 53rd Street, New York, NY 10022

Typeset by Davidson Publishing Solutions, Glasgow

Printed in Italy by LEGO S.p.A., Lavis (Trento), Italy

Acknowledgements
We would like to thank those authors and publishers who kindly gave permission for copyright material to be used in the Collins Word Web. We would also like to thank Times Newspapers Ltd for providing valuable data.

MANAGING EDITOR
Gaëlle Amiot-Cadey

PROJECT MANAGEMENT
Maggie Seaton
Rachel Smith

CONTRIBUTORS
Gabriella Bacchelli
Donatella Boi
Michela Clari
Daphne Day
Genevieve Gerrard
Angela Jack
[illegible] Littlejohn
Val McNulty
Elizabeth Potter
Caroline Smart
Jill Williams

TECHNICAL SUPPORT
Thomas Callan

SERIES EDITOR
Rob Scriven

Indice

Contents

William Collins' dream of knowledge for all began with the publication of his first book in 1819. A self-educated mill worker, he not only enriched millions of lives, but also founded a flourishing publishing house. Today, staying true to this spirit, Collins books are packed with inspiration, innovation, and practical expertise. They place you at the centre of a world of possibility and give you exactly what you need to explore it.

Language is the key to this exploration, and at the heart of Collins Dictionaries is language as it is really used. New words, phrases, and meanings spring up every day, and all of them are captured and analysed by the Collins Word Web. Constantly updated, and with over 2.5 billion entries, this living language resource is unique to our dictionaries.

Words are tools for life. And a Collins Dictionary makes them work for you.

Collins. Do more.

Introduzione

Se desiderate imparare l'inglese o approfondire le conoscenze già acquisite, se volete leggere o redigere dei testi in inglese, oppure conversare con interlocutori di madrelingua inglese, se siete studenti, turisti, uomini o donne d'affari avete scelto il compagno di viaggio ideale per esprimervi e comunicare in inglese sia a voce che per iscritto. Strumento pratico e moderno, il vostro dizionario dà largo spazio al linguaggio quotidiano in campi quali l'attualità, gli affari, la gestione d'ufficio, l'informatica e il turismo. Come in tutti i nostri dizionari, grande importanza è stata data alla lingua contemporanea e alle espressioni idiomatiche.

Come usare il dizionario

Troverete qui di seguito alcune spiegazioni sul modo in cui le informazioni sono state presentate nel testo. L'obiettivo del dizionario è quello di darvi il maggior numero possible di informazioni senza tuttavia sacrificare la chiarezza all'interno delle voci.

Le voci

Qui di seguito verranno descritti i vari elementi di cui si compone una voce tipo del vostro dizionario.

La trascrizione fonetica

Come regola generale è stata data la pronuncia di tutte le parole inglesi e quella delle parole italiane che potevano presentare qualche difficoltà per il parlante inglese. Nella parte inglese-italiano, tuttavia, per la pronuncia di nomi composti formati da due parole non unite dal trattino si dovrà cercare la trascrizione di ciascuna di queste parole alla rispettiva posizione alfabetica. La pronuncia si trova tra parentesi quadra, subito dopo il lemma. Come nella maggior parte dei dizionari moderni è stato adottato il sistema noto come "alfabeto fonetico internazionale". Troverete qui di seguito, a pagina xiii e xiv, un elenco completo dei caratteri utilizzati in questo sistema.

Le categorie grammaticali

Tutte le parole appartengono ad una categoria grammaticale, cioè possono essere sostantivi, verbi, aggettivi, avverbi, pronomi, articolio o congiunzioni.

I sostantivi possono essere singolari o plurali, sia in italiano che in inglese, e maschili o femminili in italiano. I verbi possono essere transitivi o intransitivi in entrambe le lingue, ma anche riflessivi o impersonali in italiano. La categoria grammaticale è stata introdotta in *corsivo* subito dopo la pronuncia ed eventuali informazioni di tipo morfologico (plurali irregolari ecc.).

Numerose voci sono state suddivise in varie categorie grammaticali. Per esempio la parola italiana **bene** può essere sia un avverbio che un aggettivo o un sostantivo, e la parola inglese **sneeze** può essere sia un sostantivo ("starnuto") che un verbo intransitivo ("starnutire"). Analogamente il verbo italiano **correre** può essere usato sia come verbo intransitivo ("correre alla stazione") che come transitivo ("correre un rischio"). Per presentare la voce con maggiore chiarezza e permettervi di trovare rapidamente la traduzione che cercate, è stato introdotto il simbolo ■ per contrassegnare il passaggio da una categoria grammaticale ad un'altra.

Suddivisioni semantiche

La maggior parte delle parole ha più di un significato. Per esempio, la parola **fiocco** può essere sia un'annodatura di un nastro che una falda di neve. Molte parole si traducono in modo diverso a seconda del contesto in cui sono usate: per esempio **scala** si tradurrà in inglese con "staircase" o "stairs" se si tratta di una scala con gradini, con "ladder" se è una scala a pioli. Per permettervi di scegliere la traduzione giusta per ciascuno dei contesti in cui la parola si può trovare, le voci sono state suddivise in categorie di significato. Ciascuna suddivisione è introdotta da un "indicatore d'uso" tra parentesi in *corsivo*. Le voci **fiocco** e **scala** compariranno quindi nel testo nel modo seguente:

> **fiocco, chi** *sm* (*di nastro*) bow; (*di stoffa, lana*) flock; (*di neve*) flake
> **scala** *sf* (*a gradini etc*) staircase, stairs *pl*; (*a pioli, di corda*) ladder

Per segnalare la traduzione appropriata sono stati introdotti anche degli indicatori d'ambito d'uso in *corsivo* con la prima lettera maiuscola, tra parentesi, spesso in forma abbreviata, come per esempio nel caso della voce **tromba**:

> **tromba** *sf* (*Mus*) trumpet; (*Aut*) horn

L'elenco completo delle abbreviazioni adottate nel dizionario è riportato alle pagine xiii e xiv.

Le traduzioni

Per la maggior parte delle parole inglesi ed italiane ci sono traduzioni precise a seconda del significato o del contesto, come risulta dagli esempi riportati fin qui. A volte, tuttavia, le parole non hanno un preciso equivalente nella lingua d'arrivo: in questi casi è stato fornito un equivalente approssimativo, preceduto dal segno ≈, come ad esempio per l'abbreviazione **RAC**, per cui è stato dato l'equivalente italiano "A.C.I.", dato che le due associazioni svolgono nei due paesi funzioni analoghe:

> **RAC** *n abbr* (*Brit*: = *Royal Automobile Club*) ≈ *A.C.I. m* (= *Automobile Club d'Italia*)

A volte è persino impossibile trovare un equivalente approssimativo. Questo è il caso, per esempio, di piatti tipici di un certo paese, come ad esempio **pandoro**:

> **pandoro** *sm type of sponge cake eaten at Christmas*

In questi casi, al posto della traduzione, che non esiste, comparirà una spiegazione: per maggiore chiarezza, questa spiegazione o glossa è stata messa in *corsivo*.

Molto spesso la traduzione di una parola può non funzionare all'interno di una data locuzione. Ad esempio alla voce **dare**, verbo spesso tradotto con "to give" in inglese, troviamo varie locuzioni per alcune delle quali la traduzione fornita all'inizio della voce non si può utilizzare: **quanti anni mi dai?** "how old do you think I am?" **danno ancora quel film?** "is that film still showing?", **dare per certo qc** "to consider sth certain", e così via. Ed è proprio in questi casi che potrete verificare l'utilità e la completezza del dizionario, che contiene una ricca gamma di composti, locuzioni e frasi idiomatiche.

Il registro linguistico

In italiano sapete istintivamente scegliere l'espressione corretta da usare a seconda del contesto in cui vi esprimete. Per esempio saprete quando dire **Non me ne importa!** e quando invece potete dire **Chi se ne frega?** Più difficile sarà farlo in inglese, dove avete minore consapevolezza delle sfumature di registro linguistico. Per questo motivo nella parte inglese-italiano le parole ed espressioni inglesi di uso più familiare sono segnalate dall'abbreviazione (*col*), mentre (*col!*) segnala le parole ed espressioni volgari. Nella parte italiano-inglese (*!*) dopo una traduzione segnala che si tratta di una parola od espressione volgare.

Parole chiave

Come vedrete, ad alcune voci è stato riservato un trattamento particolare sia dal punto di vista grafico che da quello linguistico. Si tratta di voci come **essere** o **fare**, o dei loro equivalenti inglesi **be** e **do**, che per la loro importanza e complessità meritano una strutturazione più articolata ed un maggior numero di locuzioni illustrative. Queste voci sono strutturate in diverse categorie di significato contrassegnate da numeri, e le costruzioni sintattiche e locuzioni che illustrano quel particolare significato sono riportate all'interno della relativa categoria.

Informazioni culturali

Le voci affiancate da una riga verticale di punti approfondiscono aspetti della cultura italiana o di quella dei paesi di lingua inglese in argomenti quali la politica, la scuola, i mass media e le festività nazionali.

Introduction

You may be starting to learn Italian, or you may wish to extend your knowledge of the language. Perhaps you want to read and study Italian books, newspapers and magazines, or perhaps simply have a conversation with Italian speakers. Whatever the reason, whether you're a student, a tourist or want to use Italian for business, this is the ideal book to help you understand and communicate. This modern, user-friendly dictionary gives priority to everyday vocabulary and the language of current affairs, business and tourism. As in all Collins dictionaries, the emphasis is firmly placed on contemporary language and expressions.

How to use the dictionary

Below you will find an outline of how information is presented in your dictionary. Our aim is to give you the maximum amount of detail in the clearest and most helpful way.

Entries

A typical entry in your dictionary will be made up of the following elements:

Phonetic transcription

Phonetics appear in square brackets immediately after the headword. They are shown using the International Phonetic Alphabet (IPA), and a complete list of the symbols used in this system can be found on pages xiii and xiv.

Grammatical information

All words belong to one of the following parts of speech: noun, verb, adjective, adverb, pronoun, article, conjunction, preposition.

Nouns can be singular or plural and, in Italian, masculine or feminine. Verbs can be transitive, intransitive, reflexive or impersonal. Parts of speech appear in *italics* immediately after the phonetic spelling of the headword.

Often a word can have more than one part of speech. Just as the English word **chemical** can be an adjective or a noun, the Italian word **fondo** can be an adjective ("deep") or a masculine noun ("bottom"). In the same way the verb **to walk** is sometimes transitive, ie it takes an object ("to walk the dog") and sometimes intransitive, ie it doesn't take an object ("to walk to school"). To help you find the meaning you are looking for quickly and for clarity of presentation, the different part of speech categories are separated by the symbol ■.

Meaning divisions

Most words have more than one meaning. Take, for example, **punch** which can be, amongst other things, a blow with the fist or an object used for making holes. Other words are translated differently depending on the context in which they are used.

The transitive verb **to roll up**, for example, can be translated by "arrotolare" or "rimboccare" depending on what it is you are rolling up. To help you select the most appropriate translation in every context, entries are divided according to meaning. Each different meaning is introduced by an "indicator" in *italics* and in brackets. Thus, the examples given above will be shown as follows:

punch *n* (*blow*) pugno; (*tool*) punzone *m*
roll up *vt* (*carpet, cloth, map*) arrotolare; (*sleeves*) rimboccare

Likewise, some words can have a different meaning when used to talk about a specific subject area or field. For example, **bishop**, which is generally used to mean a high-ranking clergyman, is also the name of a chess piece. To show English speakers which translation to use, we have added "subject field labels" in *italics*, starting with a capital letter, and in brackets, in this case (*Chess*):

bishop *n* vescovo; (*Chess*) alfiere *m*

Field labels are often shortened to save space. You will find a complete list of abbreviations used in the dictionary on pages xiii and xiv.

Translations

Most English words have a direct translation in Italian and vice versa, as shown in the examples given above. Sometimes, however, no exact equivalent exists in the target language. In such cases we have given an approximate equivalent, indicated by the sign ≈. Such is the case of **National Insurance**, the Italian equivalent of which is "Previdenza Sociale". This is not an exact translation since the systems of the two countries in question are quite different:

National Insurance *n* (*Brit*) ≈ Previdenza Sociale

On occasion it is impossible to find even an approximate equivalent. This may be the case, for example, with the names of types of food:

cottage pie *n piatto a base di carne macinata in sugo e purè di patate*

Here the translation (which doesn't exist) is replaced by an explanation. For increased clarity the explanation, or "gloss", is shown in *italics*.

It is often the case that a word, or a particular meaning of a word, cannot be translated in isolation. The translation of **Dutch**, for example, is "olandese". However, the phrase **to go Dutch** is rendered by "fare alla romana". Even an expression as simple as **washing powder** needs a separate translation since it translates as "detersivo (in polvere)", not "polvere per lavare". This is where your dictionary will prove to be particularly informative and useful since it contains an abundance of compounds, phrases and idiomatic expressions.

Levels of formality and familiarity

In English you instinctively know when to say **I'm broke** *or* **I'm a bit short of cash** and when to say **I don't have any money**. When you are trying to understand someone who is speaking Italian, however, or when you yourself try to speak Italian, it is important to know what is polite and what is less so, and what you can say in a relaxed situation but not in a formal context. To help you with this, on the Italian-English side we have added the label (*fam*) to show that an Italian word or expression is colloquial, while those words or expressions which are vulgar are given an exclamation mark (*fam!*), warning you they can cause serious offence. Note also that on the English-Italian side, translations which are vulgar are followed by an exclamation mark in brackets.

Keywords

Words labelled in the text as **KEYWORDS**, such as **be** and **do** or their Italian equivalents **essere** and **fare**, have been given special treatment because they form the basic elements of the language. This extra help will ensure that you know how to use these complex words with confidence.

Cultural information

Entries which appear distinguished in the text by a column of dots explain aspects of culture in Italy and English-speaking countries. Subject areas covered include politics, education, media and national festivals.

Abbreviazioni		Abbreviations
abbreviazione	*abbr*	abbreviation
aggettivo	*adj*	adjective
amministrazione	*Admin*	administration
avverbio	*adv*	adverb
aeronautica, viaggi aerie	*Aer*	flying, air travel
aggettivo	*ag*	adjective
agricoltura	*Agr*	agriculture
amministrazione	*Amm*	administration
anatomia	*Anat*	anatomy
architettura	*Archit*	architecture
astronomia, astrologia	*Astr*	astronomy, astrology
l'automobile	*Aut*	the motor car and motoring
verbo ausiliare	*aux vb*	auxiliary verb
avverbio	*av*	adverb
aeronautica, viaggi aerei	*Aviat*	flying, air travel
biologia	*Biol*	biology
botanica	*Bot*	botany
inglese della Gran Bretagna	*Brit*	British English
consonante	*C*	consonant
chimica	*Chim, Chem*	chemistry
familiare (! da evitare)	*col(!)*	colloquial usage (! particularly offensive)
commercio, finanza, banca	*Comm*	commerce, finance, banking
informatica	*Comput*	computing
congiunzione	*cong*	conjunction
congiunzione	*conj*	conjunction
edilizia	*Constr*	building
sostantivo usato come aggettivo, non può essere usato nè come attributo, nè dopo il sostantivo qualificato	*cpd*	compound element: noun used as adjective and which cannot follow the noun it qualifies
cucina	*Cus, Culin*	cookery
davanti a	*dav*	before
determinante: articolo, aggettivo dimostrativo o indefinito etc	*det*	determiner: article, demonstrative etc
diritto	*Dir*	law
economia	*Econ*	economics
edilizia	*Edil*	building
elettricità, elettronica	*Elettr, Elec*	electricity, electronics
esclamazione, interiezione	*escl, excl*	exclamation, interjection
specialmente	*esp*	especially
femminile	*f*	feminine
familiare (! da evitare)	*fam(!)*	colloquial usage (! particularly offensive)
ferrovia	*Ferr*	railways
figurato	*fig*	figurative use
fisiologia	*Fisiol*	physiology
fotografia	*Fot*	photography
(verbo inglese) la cui particella è inseparabile dal verbo	*vt fus*	(phrasal verb) where the particle cannot be separated from main verb
nella maggior parte dei sensi; generalmente	*gen*	in most or all senses; generally
geografia, geologia	*Geo*	geography, geology
geometria	*Geom*	geometry
impersonale	*impers*	impersonal
informatica	*Inform*	computing

insegnamento, sistema scolastico e universitario	*Ins*	schooling, schools and universities
invariabile	*inv*	invariable
irregolare	*irreg*	irregular
grammatica, linguistica	*Ling*	grammar, linguistics
maschile	*m*	masculine
matematica	*Mat(h)*	mathematics
termine medico, medicina	*Med*	medical term, medicine
il tempo, meteorologia	*Meteor*	the weather, meteorology
maschile o femminile	*m/f*	either masculine or feminine depending on sex
esercito, linguaggio militare	*Mil*	military matters
musica	*Mus*	music
sostantivo	*n*	noun
nautical	*Naut*	sailing, navigation
sostantivo che non si usa al plurale	*no pl*	uncountable noun: not used in the plural
numerale (aggettivo, sostantivo)	*num*	numeral adjective or noun
	o.s.	oneself
peggiorativo	*peg, pej*	derogatory, pejorative
fotografia	*Phot*	photography
fisiologia	*Physiol*	physiology
plurale	*pl*	plural
politica	*Pol*	politics
participio passato	*pp*	past participle
preposizione	*prep*	preposition
pronome	*pron*	pronoun
psicologia, psichiatria	*Psic, Psych*	psychology, psychiatry
tempo passato	*pt*	past tense
qualcosa	*qc*	
qualcuno	*qn*	
religione, liturgia	*Rel*	religions, church service
sostantivo	*s*	noun
	sb	somebody
insegnamento, sistema scolastico e universitario	*Scol*	schooling, schools and universities
singolare	*sg*	singular
soggetto (grammaticale)	*sog*	(grammatical) subject
	sth	something
congiuntivo	*sub*	subjunctive
soggetto (grammaticale)	*subj*	(grammatical) subject
termine tecnico, tecnologia	*Tecn, Tech*	technical term, technology
telecomunicazioni	*Tel*	telecommunications
tipografia	*Tip*	typography, printing
televisione	*TV*	television
tipografia	*Typ*	typography, printing
inglese degli Stati Uniti	*US*	American English
vocale	*v*	vowel
verbo (ausiliare)	*vb (aus)*	(auxiliary) verb
verbo o gruppo verbale con funzione intransitiva	*vi*	verb or phrasal verb used intransitively
verbo riflessivo	*vr*	reflexive verb
verbo o gruppo verbale con funzione transitiva	*vt*	verb or phrasal verb used transitively
zoologia	*Zool*	zoology
marchio registrato	®	registered trademark
introduce un'equivalenza culturale	≈	introduces a cultural equivalent

Trascrizione Fonetica

Consonanti		Consonants
NB. **p, b, t, d, k, g** sono seguite da un'aspirazione in inglese.		NB. **p, b, t, d, k, g** are not aspirated in Italian.
padre	p	puppy
bambino	b	baby
tutto	t	tent
dado	d	daddy
cane che	k	cork kiss chord
gola ghiro	g	gag guess
sano	s	so rice kiss
svago esame	z	cousin buzz
scena	ʃ	sheep sugar
	ʒ	pleasure beige
pece lanciare	tʃ	church
giro gioco	dʒ	judge general
afa faro	f	farm raffle
vero bravo	v	very rev
	θ	thin maths
	ð	that other
letto ala	l	little ball
gli	ʎ	
rete arco	r	rat brat
ramo madre	m	mummy comb
no fumante	n	no ran
gnomo	ɲ	
	ŋ	singing bank
	h	hat reheat
buio piacere	j	yet
uomo guaio	w	wall bewail
	x	loch

Varie		Miscellaneous
per l'inglese: la "r" finale viene pronunciata se seguita da una vocale	ʳ	
precede la sillaba accentata	ˈ	precedes the stressed syllable

Come regola generale, in tutte le voci la trascrizione fonetica in parentesi quadra segue il termine cui si riferisce. Tuttavia, dalla parte inglese-italiano del dizionario, per la pronuncia di composti che sono formati da più parole non unite da trattino che appaiono comunque nel dizionario, si veda la trascrizione fonetica di ciascuna di queste parole alla rispettiva posizione alfabetica.

Phonetic Transcription

Vocali		Vowels
NB. La messa in equivalenza di certi suoni indica solo una rassomiglianza approssimativa.		NB. The pairing of some vowel sounds only indicates approximate equivalence.
vino idea	i iː	heel bead
	ɪ	hit pity
stella edera	e	
epoca eccetto	ɛ	set tent
mamma amore	a æ	apple bat
	ɑː	after car calm
	ʌ	fun cousin
	ə	over above
	əː	urn fern work
rosa occhio	ɔ	wash pot
	ɔː	born cork
ponte ognuno	o	
utile zucca	u	full soot
	uː	boon lewd

Dittonghi		Diphthongs
	ɪə	beer tier
	ɛə	tear fair there
	eɪ	date plaice day
	aɪ	life buy cry
	au	owl foul now
	əu	low no
	ɔɪ	boil boy oily
	uə	poor tour

In general, we give the pronunciation of each entry in square brackets after the word in question. However, on the English-Italian side, where the entry is composed of two or more unhyphenated words, each of which is given elsewhere in this dictionary, you will find the pronunciation of each word in its alphabetical position.

Italian Pronunciation

Vowels

Where the vowel **e** or the vowel **o** appears in a stressed syllable it can be either open [ɛ], [ɔ] or closed [e], [o]. As the open or closed pronunciation of these vowels is subject to regional variation, the distinction is of little importance to the user of this dictionary. Phonetic transcription for headwords containing these vowels will therefore only appear where other pronunciation difficulties are present.

Consonants

c before "e" or "i" is pronounced *tch*.
ch is pronounced like the "k" in "kit".
g before "e" or "i" is pronounced like the "j" in "jet".
gh is pronounced like the "g" in "get".
gl before "e" or "i" is normally pronounced like the "lli" in "million", and in a few cases only like the "gl" in "glove".
gn is pronounced like the "ny" in "canyon".
sc before "e" or "i" is pronounced *sh*.
z is pronounced like the "ts" in "stetson", or like the "d's" in "bird's eye".

Headwords containing the above consonants and consonantal groups have been given full phonetic transcription in this dictionary.

NB. All double written consonants in Italian are fully sounded: e.g. the *tt* in "tutto" is pronounced as in "*hat trick*".

Italian Verbs

1 Gerund **2** Past participle **3** Present **4** Imperfect **5** Past historic **6** Future **7** Conditional **8** Present subjunctive **9** Imperfect subjunctive **10** Imperative

accadere *like* **cadere**
accedere *like* **concedere**
accendere **2** acceso **5** accesi, accendesti
accludere *like* **alludere**
accogliere *like* **cogliere**
accondiscendere *like* **scendere**
accorgersi *like* **scorgere**
accorrere *like* **correre**
accrescere *like* **crescere**
addirsi *like* **dire**
addurre *like* **ridurre**
affiggere **2** affisso **5** affissi, affiggesti
affliggere **2** afflitto **5** afflissi, affliggesti
aggiungere *like* **giungere**
alludere **2** alluso **5** allusi, alludesti
ammettere *like* **mettere**
andare **3** vado, vai, va, andiamo, andate, vanno **6** andrò *etc* **8** vada **10** va'!, vada!, andate!, vadano!
annettere **2** annesso **5** annessi *o* annettei, annettesti
apparire **2** apparso **3** appaio, appari *o* apparisci, appare *o* apparisce, appaiono *o* appariscono **5** apparvi *o* apparsi, appariste, apparve *o* apparì *o* apparse, apparvero *o* apparirono *o* apparsero **8** appaia *o* apparisca
appartenere *like* **tenere**
appendere **2** appeso **5** appesi, appendesti
apporre *like* **porre**
apprendere *like* **prendere**
aprire **2** aperto **3** apro **5** aprii *o* apersi, apristi **8** apra
ardere **2** arso **5** arsi, ardesti
ascendere *like* **scendere**
aspergere **2** asperso **5** aspersi, aspergesti
assalire *like* **salire**
assistere **2** assistito
assolvere **2** assolto **5** assolsi *o* assolvei *o* assolvetti, assolvesti
assumere **2** assunto **5** assunsi, assumesti
astenersi *like* **tenere**
attendere *like* **tendere**
attingere *like* **tingere**
AVERE **3** ho, hai, ha, abbiamo, avete, hanno **5** ebbi, avesti, ebbe, avemmo, aveste, ebbero **6** avrò *etc* **8** abbia *etc* **10** abbi!, abbia!, abbiate!, abbiano!
avvedersi *like* **vedere**
avvenire *like* **venire**
avvincere *like* **vincere**
avvolgere *like* **volgere**
benedire *like* **dire**
bere **1** bevendo **2** bevuto **3** bevo *etc* **4** bevevo *etc* **5** bevvi *o* bevetti, bevesti **6** berrò *etc* **8** beva *etc* **9** bevessi *etc*
cadere **5** caddi, cadesti **6** cadrò *etc*
chiedere **2** chiesto **5** chiesi, chiedesti
chiudere **2** chiuso **5** chiusi, chiudesti
cingere **2** cinto **5** cinsi, cingesti
cogliere **2** colto **3** colgo, colgono **5** colsi, cogliesti **8** colga
coincidere **2** coinciso **5** coincisi, coincidesti
coinvolgere *like* **volgere**
commettere *like* **mettere**
commuovere *like* **muovere**
comparire *like* **apparire**
compiacere *like* **piacere**
compiangere *like* **piangere**
comporre *like* **porre**
comprendere *like* **prendere**
comprimere **2** compresso **5** compressi, comprimesti
compromettere *like* **mettere**
concedere **2** concesso *o* conceduto **5** concessi *o* concedei *o* concedetti, concedesti
concludere *like* **alludere**
concorrere *like* **correre**
condurre *like* **ridurre**
confondere *like* **fondere**
congiungere *like* **giungere**
connettere *like* **annettere**
conoscere **2** conosciuto **5** conobbi, conoscesti
consistere *like* **assistere**
contendere *like* **tendere**
contenere *like* **tenere**
contorcere *like* **torcere**
contraddire *like* **dire**
contraffare *like* **fare**
contrarre *like* **trarre**
convenire *like* **venire**
convincere *like* **vincere**
coprire *like* **aprire**
correggere *like* **reggere**
correre **2** corso **5** corsi, corresti
corrispondere *like* **rispondere**
corrompere *like* **rompere**
costringere *like* **stringere**
costruire **5** costrussi, costruisti
crescere **2** cresciuto **5** crebbi, crescesti
cuocere **2** cotto **3** cuocio, cociamo, cuociono **5** cossi, cocesti
dare **3** do, dai, dà, diamo, date, danno **5** diedi *o* detti, desti **6** darò *etc* **8** dia *etc* **9** dessi *etc* **10** da'!, dai!, date!, diano!

decidere **2** deciso **5** decisi, decidesti
decrescere *like* **crescere**
dedurre *like* **ridurre**
deludere *like* **alludere**
deporre *like* **porre**
deprimere *like* **comprimere**
deridere *like* **ridere**
descrivere *like* **scrivere**
desumere *like* **assumere**
detergere *like* **tergere**
devolvere **2** devoluto
difendere **2** difeso **5** difesi, difendesti
diffondere *like* **fondere**
dipendere *like* **appendere**
dipingere *like* **tingere**
dire **1** dicendo **2** detto **3** dico, dici, dice, diciamo, dite, dicono **4** dicevo *etc* **5** dissi, dicesti **6** dirò *etc* **8** dica, diciamo, diciate, decano **9** dicessi *etc* **10** di'!, dica!, dite!, dicano!
dirigere **2** diretto **5** diressi, dirigesti
discendere *like* **scendere**
dischiudere *like* **chiudere**
disciogliere *like* **sciogliere**
discorrere *like* **correre**
discutere **2** discusso **5** discussi, discutesti
disfare *like* **fare**
disilludere *like* **alludere**
disperdere *like* **perdere**
dispiacere *like* **piacere**
disporre *like* **porre**
dissolvere **2** dissolto *o* disoluto **5** dissolsi *o* dissolvetti *o* dissolvei, dissolvesti
dissuadere *like* **persuadere**
distendere *like* **tendere**
distinguere **2** distinto **5** distinsi, distinguesti
distogliere *like* **togliere**
distrarre *like* **trarre**
distruggere *like* **struggere**
divenire *like* **venire**
dividere **2** diviso **5** divisi, dividesti
dolere **3** dolgo, duoli, duole, dolgono **5** dolsi, dolesti **6** dorrò *etc* **8** dolga
DORMIRE **1** GERUND dormendo
2 PAST PARTICIPLE dormito
3 PRESENT dormo, dormi, dorme, dormiamo, dormite, dormono
4 IMPERFECT dormivo, dormivi, dormiva, dormivamo, dormivate, dormivano
5 PAST HISTORIC dormii, dormisti, dormì, dormimmo, dormiste, dormirono
6 FUTURE dormirò, dormirai, dormirà, dormiremo, dormirete, dormiranno
7 CONDITIONAL dormirei, dormiresti, dormirebbe, dormiremmo, dormireste, dormirebbero
8 PRESENT SUBJUNCTIVE dorma, dorma, dorma, dormiamo, dormiate, dormano
9 IMPERFECT SUBJUNCTIVE dormissi, dormissi, dormisse, dormissimo, dormiste, dormissero
10 IMPERATIVE dormi!, dorma!, dormite!, dormano!
dovere **3** devo *o* debbo, devi, deve, dobbiamo, dovete, devono *o* debbono **6** dovrò *etc*
8 debba, dobbiamo, dobbiate, devano *o* debbano
eccellere **2** eccelso **5** eccelsi, eccellesti
eludere *like* **alludere**
emergere **2** emerso **5** emersi, emergesti
emettere *like* **mettere**
erigere *like* **dirigere**
escludere *like* **alludere**
esigere **2** esatto
esistere **2** esistito
espellere **2** espulso **5** espulsi, espellesti
esplodere **2** esploso **5** esplosi, esplodesti
esporre *like* **porre**
esprimere *like* **comprimere**
ESSERE **2** stato **3** sono, sei, è, siamo, siete, sono **4** ero, eri, era, eravamo, eravate, erano **5** fui, fosti, fu, fummo, foste, furono **6** sarò *etc* **8** sia *etc* **9** fossi, fossi, fosse, fossimo, foste, fossero **10** sii!, sia!, siate!, siano!
estendere *like* **tendere**
estinguere *like* **distinguere**
estrarre *like* **trarre**
evadere **2** evaso **5** evasi, evadesti
evolvere **2** evoluto
fare **1** facendo **2** fatto **3** faccio, fai, fa, facciamo, fate, fanno **4** facevo *etc* **5** feci, facesti **6** farò *etc* **8** faccia *etc* **9** facessi *etc* **10** fa'!, faccia!, fate!, facciano!
fingere *like* **cingere**
FINIRE **1** GERUND finendo
2 PAST PARTICIPLE finito
3 PRESENT finisco, finisci, finisce, finiamo, finite, finiscono
4 IMPERFECT finivo, finivi, finiva, finivamo, finivate, finivano
5 PAST HISTORIC finii, finisti, finì, finimmo, finiste, finirono
6 FUTURE finirò, finirai, finirà, finiremo, finirete, finiranno
7 CONDITIONAL finirei, finiresti, finirebbe, finiremmo, finireste, finirebbero
8 PRESENT SUBJUNCTIVE finisca, finisca, finisca, finiamo, finiate, finiscano
9 IMPERFECT SUBJUNCTIVE finissi, finissi, finisse, finissimo, finiste, finissero
10 IMPERATIVE finisci!, finisca!, finite!, finiscano!
flettere **2** flesso
fondere **2** fuso **5** fusi, fondesti
friggere **2** fritto **5** frissi, friggesti

fungere **2** funto **5** funsi, fungesti
giacere **3** giaccio, giaci, giace, giac(c)iamo, giacete, giacciono **5** giacqui, giacesti **8** giaccia *etc* **10** giaci!, giaccia!, giac(c)iamo!, giacete!, giacciano!
giungere **2** giunto **5** giunsi, giungesti
godere **6** godrò *etc*
illudere *like* **alludere**
immergere *like* **emergere**
immettere *like* **mettere**
imporre *like* **porre**
imprimere *like* **comprimere**
incidere *like* **decidere**
includere *like* **alludere**
incorrere *like* **correre**
incutere *like* **discutere**
indulgere **2** indulto **5** indulsi, indulgesti
indurre *like* **ridurre**
inferire[1] **2** inferto **5** infersi, inferisti
inferire[2] **2** inferito **5** inferii, inferisti
infliggere *like* **affliggere**
infrangere **2** infranto **5** infransi, infrangesti
infondere *like* **fondere**
insistere *like* **assistere**
intendere *like* **tendere**
interdire *like* **dire**
interporre *like* **porre**
interrompere *like* **rompere**
intervenire *like* **venire**
intraprendere *like* **prendere**
introdurre *like* **ridurre**
invadere *like* **evadere**
irrompere *like* **rompere**
iscrivere *like* **scrivere**
istruire *like* **costruire**
ledere **2** leso **5** lesi, ledesti
leggere **2** letto **5** lessi, leggesti
maledire *like* **dire**
mantenere *like* **tenere**
mettere **2** messo **5** misi, mettesti
mordere **2** morso **5** morsi, mordesti
morire **2** morto **3** muoio, muori, muore, moriamo, morite, muoiono **6** morirò *o* morrò *etc* **8** muoia
mungere **2** munto **5** munsi, mungesti
muovere **2** mosso **5** mossi, movesti
nascere **2** nato **5** nacqui, nascesti
nascondere **2** nascosto **5** nascosi, nascondesti
nuocere **2** nuociuto **3** nuoccio, nuoci, nuoce, nociamo *o* nuociamo, nuocete, nuocciono **4** nuocevo *etc* **5** nocqui, nuocesti **6** nuocerò *etc* **7** nuoccia
occorrere *like* **correre**
offendere *like* **difendere**
offrire **2** offerto **3** offro **5** offersi *o* offrii, offristi **8** offra
omettere *like* **mettere**
opporre *like* **porre**
opprimere *like* **comprimere**
ottenere *like* **tenere**
parere **2** parso **3** paio, paiamo, paiono **5** parvi *o* parsi, paresti **6** parrò *etc* **8** paia, paiamo, paiate, paiano
PARLARE **1** GERUND parlando
2 PAST PARTICIPLE parlato
3 PRESENT parlo, parli, parla, parliamo, parlate, parlano
4 IMPERFECT parlavo, parlavi, parlava, parlavamo, parlavate, parlavano
5 PAST HISTORIC parlai, parlasti, parlò, parlammo, parlaste, parlarono
6 FUTURE parlerò, parlerai, parlerà, parleremo, parlerete, parleranno
7 CONDITIONAL parlerei, parleresti, parlerebbe, parleremmo, parlereste, parlerebbero
8 PRESENT SUBJUNCTIVE parli, parli, parli, parliamo, parliate, parlino
9 IMPERFECT SUBJUNCTIVE parlassi, parlassi, parlasse, parlassimo, parlaste, parlassero
10 IMPERATIVE parla!, parli!, parlate!, parlino!
percorrere *like* **correre**
percuotere **2** percosso **5** percossi, percotesti
perdere **2** perso *o* perduto **5** persi *o* perdei *o* perdetti, perdesti
permettere *like* **mettere**
persuadere **2** persuaso **5** persuasi, persuadesti
pervenire *like* **venire**
piacere **2** piaciuto **3** piaccio, piacciamo, piacciono **5** piacqui, piacesti **8** piaccia *etc*
piangere **2** pianto **5** piansi, piangesti
piovere **5** piovve
porgere **2** porto **5** porsi, porgesti
porre **1** ponendo **2** posto **3** pongo, poni, pone, poniamo, ponete, pongono **4** ponevo *etc* **5** posi, ponesti **6** porrò *etc* **8** ponga, poniamo, poniate, pongano **9** ponessi *etc*
posporre *like* **porre**
possedere *like* **sedere**
potere **3** posso, puoi, può, possiamo, potete, possono **6** potrò *etc* **8** possa, possiamo, possiate, possano
prediligere **2** prediletto **5** predilessi, prediligesti
predire *like* **dire**
prefiggersi *like* **affiggere**
preludere *like* **alludere**
prendere **2** preso **5** presi, prendesti
preporre *like* **porre**
prescrivere *like* **scrivere**
presiedere *like* **sedere**
presumere *like* **assumere**
pretendere *like* **tendere**

prevalere *like* **valere**
prevedere *like* **vedere**
prevenire *like* **venire**
produrre *like* **ridurre**
proferire *like* **inferire**[2]
profondere *like* **fondere**
promettere *like* **mettere**
promuovere *like* **muovere**
proporre *like* **porre**
prorompere *like* **rompere**
proscrivere *like* **scrivere**
proteggere **2** protetto **5** protessi, proteggesti
provenire *like* **venire**
provvedere *like* **vedere**
pungere **2** punto **5** punsi, pungesti
racchiudere *like* **chiudere**
raccogliere *like* **cogliere**
radere **2** raso **5** rasi, radesti
raggiungere *like* **giungere**
rapprendere *like* **prendere**
ravvedersi *like* **vedere**
recidere *like* **decidere**
redigere **2** redatto
redimere **2** redento **5** redensi, redimesti
reggere **2** retto **5** ressi, reggesti
rendere **2** reso **5** resi, rendesti
reprimere *like* **comprimere**
rescindere *like* **scindere**
respingere *like* **spingere**
restringere *like* **stringere**
ricadere *like* **cadere**
richiedere *like* **chiedere**
riconoscere *like* **conoscere**
ricoprire *like* **coprire**
ricorrere *like* **correre**
ridere **2** riso **5** risi, ridesti
ridire *like* **dire**
ridurre **1** riducendo **2** ridotto **3** riduco *etc* **4** riducevo *etc* **5** ridussi, riducesti **6** ridurrò *etc* **8** riduca *etc* **9** riducessi *etc*
riempire **1** riempiendo **3** riempio, riempi, riempie, riempiono
rifare *like* **fare**
riflettere **2** riflettuto *o* riflesso
rifrangere *like* **infrangere**
rimanere **2** rimasto **3** rimango, rimangono **5** rimasi, rimanesti **6** rimarrò *etc* **8** rimanga
rimettere *like* **mettere**
rimpiangere *like* **piangere**
rinchiudere *like* **chiudere**
rincrescere *like* **crescere**
rinvenire *like* **venire**
ripercuotere *like* **percuotere**
riporre *like* **porre**
riprendere *like* **prendere**
riprodurre *like* **ridurre**
riscuotere *like* **scuotere**
risolvere *like* **assolvere**
risorgere *like* **sorgere**
rispondere **2** risposto **5** risposi, rispondesti
ritenere *like* **tenere**
ritrarre *like* **trarre**
riuscire *like* **uscire**
rivedere *like* **vedere**
rivivere *like* **vivere**
rivolgere *like* **volgere**
rodere **2** roso **5** rosi, rodesti
rompere **2** rotto **5** ruppi, rompesti
salire **3** salgo, sali, salgono **8** salga
sapere **3** so, sai, sa, sappiamo, sapete, sanno **5** seppi, sapesti **6** saprò *etc* **8** sappia *etc* **10** sappi!, sappia!, sappiate!, sappiano!
scadere *like* **cadere**
scegliere **2** scelto **3** scelgo, scegli, sceglie, scegliamo, scegliete, scelgono **5** scelsi, scegliesti **8** scelga, scegliamo, scegliate, scelgano **10** scegli!, scelga!, scegliamo!, scegliete!, scelgano!
scendere **2** sceso **5** scesi, scendesti
schiudere *like* **chiudere**
scindere **2** scisso **5** scissi, scindesti
sciogliere **2** sciolto **3** sciolgo, sciolgi, scioglie, sciogliamo, sciogliete, sciolgono **5** sciolsi, sciogliesti **8** sciolga, sciogliamo, sciogliate, sciolgano **10** sciogli!, sciolga!, sciogliamo!, sciogliete!, sciolgano!
scommettere *like* **mettere**
scomparire *like* **apparire**
scomporre *like* **porre**
sconfiggere **2** sconfitto **5** sconfissi, sconfiggesti
sconvolgere *like* **volgere**
scoprire *like* **aprire**
scorgere **2** scorto **5** scorsi, scorgesti
scorrere *like* **correre**
scrivere **2** scritto **5** scrissi, scrivesti
scuotere **2** scosso **3** scuoto, scuoti, scuote, scotiamo, scotete, scuotono **5** scossi, scotesti **6** scoterò *etc* **8** scuota, scotiamo, scotiate, scuotano **10** scuoti!, scuota!, scotiamo!, scotete!, scuotano!
sedere **3** siedo, siedi, siede, siedono **8** sieda
seppellire **2** sepolto
smettere *like* **mettere**
smuovere *like* **muovere**
socchiudere *like* **chiudere**
soccorrere *like* **correre**
soddisfare *like* **fare**
soffriggere *like* **friggere**
soffrire **2** sofferto **5** soffersi *o* soffrii, soffristi
soggiungere *like* **giungere**
solere **2** solito **3** soglio, suoli, suole, sogliamo, solete, sogliono **8** soglia, sogliamo, sogliate, sogliano
sommergere *like* **emergere**

sopprimere *like* **comprimere**
sorgere **2** sorto **3** sorsi, sorgesti
sorprendere *like* **prendere**
sorreggere *like* **reggere**
sorridere *like* **ridere**
sospendere *like* **appendere**
sospingere *like* **spingere**
sostenere *like* **tenere**
sottintendere *like* **tendere**
spandere **2** spanto
spargere **2** sparso **5** sparsi, spargesti
sparire **5** sparii *o* sparvi, sparisti
spegnere **2** spento **3** spengo, spengono **5** spensi, spegnesti **8** spenga
spendere **2** speso **5** spesi, spendesti
spingere **2** spinto **5** spinsi, spingesti
sporgere *like* **porgere**
stare **2** stato **3** sto, stai, sta, stiamo, state, stanno **5** stetti, stesti **6** starò *etc* **8** stia *etc* **9** stessi *etc* **10** sta'!, stia!, state!, stiano!
stendere *like* **tendere**
storcere *like* **torcere**
stringere **2** stretto **5** strinsi, stringesti
struggere **2** strutto **5** strussi, struggesti
succedere *like* **concedere**
supporre *like* **porre**
svenire *like* **venire**
svolgere *like* **volgere**
tacere **2** taciuto **3** taccio, tacciono **5** tacqui, tacesti **8** taccia
tendere **2** teso **5** tesi, tendesti *etc*
tenere **3** tengo, tieni, tiene, tengono **5** tenni, tenesti **6** terrò *etc* **8** tenga
tingere **2** tinto **5** tinsi, tingesti
togliere **2** tolto **3** tolgo, togli, toglie, togliamo, togliete, tolgono **5** tolsi, togliesti **8** tolga, togliamo, togliate, tolgano **10** togli!, tolga!, togliamo!, togliete!, tolgano!
torcere **2** torto **5** torsi, torcesti
tradurre *like* **ridurre**
trafiggere *like* **sconfiggere**
transigere *like* **esigere**
trarre **1** traendo **2** tratto **3** traggo, trai, trae, traiamo, traete, traggono **4** traevo *etc* **5** trassi, traesti **6** trarrò *etc* **8** tragga **9** traessi *etc*
trascorrere *like* **correre**
trascrivere *like* **scrivere**
trasmettere *like* **mettere**
trasparire *like* **apparire**
trattenere *like* **tenere**
uccidere **2** ucciso **5** uccisi, uccidesti
udire **3** odo, odi, ode, odono **8** oda
ungere **2** unto **5** unsi, ungesti
uscire **3** esco, esci, esce, escono **8** esca
valere **2** valso **3** valgo, valgono **5** valsi, valesti **6** varrò *etc* **8** valga
vedere **2** visto *o* veduto **5** vidi, vedesti **6** vedrò *etc*
VENDERE **1** GERUND vendendo
2 PAST PARTICIPLE venduto
3 PRESENT vendo, vendi, vende, vendiamo, vendete, vendono
4 IMPERFECT vendevo, vendevi, vendeva, vendevamo, vendevate, vendevano
5 PAST HISTORIC vendei *o* vendetti, vendesti, vendé *o* vendette, vendemmo, vendeste, venderono *o* vendettero
6 FUTURE venderò, venderai, venderà, venderemo, venderete, venderanno
7 CONDITIONAL venderei, venderesti, venderebbe, venderemmo, vendereste, venderebbero
8 PRESENT SUBJUNCTIVE venda, venda, venda, vendiamo, vendiate, vendano
9 IMPERFECT SUBJUNCTIVE vendessi, vendessi, vendesse, vendessimo, vendeste, vendessero
10 IMPERATIVE vendi!, venda!, vendete!, vendano!
venire **2** venuto **3** vengo, vieni, viene, vengono **5** venni, venisti **6** verrò *etc* **8** venga
vincere **2** vinto **5** vinsi, vincesti
vivere **2** vissuto **5** vissi, vivesti
volere **3** voglio, vuoi, vuole, vogliamo, volete, vogliono **5** volli, volesti **6** vorrò *etc* **8** voglia *etc* **10** vogli!, voglia!, vogliate!, vogliano!
volgere **2** volto **5** volsi, volgesti

For additional information on Italian verb formation, see pp6-125 of the Grammar section.

Verbi inglesi

present	pt	pp
arise	arose	arisen
awake	awoke	awoken
be (am, is, are; being)	was, were	been
bear	bore	born(e)
beat	beat	beaten
become	became	become
befall	befell	befallen
begin	began	begun
behold	beheld	beheld
bend	bent	bent
beset	beset	beset
bet	bet, betted	bet, betted
bid *(at auction, cards)*	bid	bid
bid *(say)*	bade	bidden
bind	bound	bound
bite	bit	bitten
bleed	bled	bled
blow	blew	blown
break	broke	broken
breed	bred	bred
bring	brought	brought
build	built	built
burn	burnt, burned	burnt, burned
burst	burst	burst
buy	bought	bought
can	could	(been able)
cast	cast	cast
catch	caught	caught
choose	chose	chosen
cling	clung	clung
come	came	come
cost	cost	cost
cost *(work out price of)*	costed	costed
creep	crept	crept
cut	cut	cut
deal	dealt	dealt
dig	dug	dug
do *(3rd person:* **he/she/it does)**	did	done
draw	drew	drawn
dream	dreamed, dreamt	dreamed, dreamt
drink	drank	drunk
drive	drove	driven
dwell	dwelt	dwelt
eat	ate	eaten
fall	fell	fallen
feed	fed	fed
feel	felt	felt
fight	fought	fought
find	found	found
flee	fled	fled
fling	flung	flung
fly	flew	flown
forbid	forbad(e)	forbidden
forecast	forecast	forecast
forget	forgot	forgotten
forgive	forgave	forgiven
forsake	forsook	forsaken
freeze	froze	frozen
get	got	got, (US) gotten
give	gave	given
go (goes)	went	gone
grind	ground	ground
grow	grew	grown
hang	hung	hung
hang *(execute)*	hanged	hanged
have	had	had
hear	heard	heard
hide	hid	hidden
hit	hit	hit
hold	held	held
hurt	hurt	hurt
keep	kept	kept
kneel	knelt, kneeled	knelt, kneeled
know	knew	known
lay	laid	laid
lead	led	led
lean	leant, leaned	leant, leaned
leap	leapt, leaped	leapt, leaped
learn	learnt, learned	learnt, learned
leave	left	left
lend	lent	lent
let	let	let

present	pt	pp
lie (lying)	lay	lain
light	lit, lighted	lit, lighted
lose	lost	lost
make	made	made
may	might	—
mean	meant	meant
meet	met	met
mistake	mistook	mistaken
mow	mowed	mown, mowed
must	(had to)	(had to)
pay	paid	paid
put	put	put
quit	quit, quitted	quit, quitted
read	read	read
rid	rid	rid
ride	rode	ridden
ring	rang	rung
rise	rose	risen
run	ran	run
saw	sawed	sawed, sawn
say	said	said
see	saw	seen
seek	sought	sought
sell	sold	sold
send	sent	sent
set	set	set
sew	sewed	sewn
shake	shook	shaken
shear	sheared	shorn, sheared
shed	shed	shed
shine	shone	shone
shoot	shot	shot
show	showed	shown
shrink	shrank	shrunk
shut	shut	shut
sing	sang	sung
sink	sank	sunk
sit	sat	sat
slay	slew	slain
sleep	slept	slept
slide	slid	slid
sling	slung	slung
slit	slit	slit
smell	smelt, smelled	smelt, smelled

present	pt	pp
sow	sowed	sown, sowed
speak	spoke	spoken
speed	sped, speeded	sped, speeded
spell	spelt, spelled	spelt, spelled
spend	spent	spent
spill	spilt, spilled	spilt, spilled
spin	spun	spun
spit	spat	spat
spoil	spoiled, spoilt	spoiled, spoilt
spread	spread	spread
spring	sprang	sprung
stand	stood	stood
steal	stole	stolen
stick	stuck	stuck
sting	stung	stung
stink	stank	stunk
stride	strode	stridden
strike	struck	struck
strive	strove	striven
swear	swore	sworn
sweep	swept	swept
swell	swelled	swollen, swelled
swim	swam	swum
swing	swung	swung
take	took	taken
teach	taught	taught
tear	tore	torn
tell	told	told
think	thought	thought
throw	threw	thrown
thrust	thrust	thrust
tread	trod	trodden
wake	woke, waked	woken, waked
wear	wore	worn
weave	wove	woven
weave (*wind*)	weaved	weaved
wed	wedded, wed	wedded, wed
weep	wept	wept
win	won	won
wind	wound	wound
wring	wrung	wrung
write	wrote	written

I numeri		Numbers
uno(a)	1	one
due	2	two
tre	3	three
quattro	4	four
cinque	5	five
sei	6	six
sette	7	seven
otto	8	eight
nove	9	nine
dieci	10	ten
undici	11	eleven
dodici	12	twelve
tredici	13	thirteen
quattordici	14	fourteen
quindici	15	fifteen
sedici	16	sixteen
diciassette	17	seventeen
diciotto	18	eighteen
diciannove	19	nineteen
venti	20	twenty
ventuno	21	twenty-one
ventidue	22	twenty-two
ventitré	23	twenty-three
ventotto	28	twenty-eight
trenta	30	thirty
quaranta	40	forty
cinquanta	50	fifty
sessanta	60	sixty
settanta	70	seventy
ottanta	80	eighty
novanta	90	ninety
cento	100	a hundred, one hundred
centouno	101	a hundred and one
duecento	200	two hundred
mille	1 000	a thousand, one thousand
milleduecentodue	1 202	one thousand two hundred and two
cinquemila	5 000	five thousand
un milione	1 000 000	a million, one million

I numeri	Numbers
primo(a), 1°	first, 1st
secondo(a), 2°	second, 2nd
terzo(a), 3°	third, 3rd
quarto(a)	fourth, 4th
quinto(a)	fifth, 5th
sesto(a)	sixth, 6th
settimo(a)	seventh
ottavo(a)	eighth
nono(a)	ninth
decimo(a)	tenth
undicesimo(a)	eleventh
dodicesimo(a)	twelfth
tredicesimo(a)	thirteenth
quattordicesimo(a)	fourteenth
quindicesimo(a)	fifteenth
sedicesimo(a)	sixteenth
diciassettesimo(a)	seventeenth
diciottesimo(a)	eighteenth
diciannovesimo(a)	nineteenth
ventesimo(a)	twentieth
ventunesimo(a)	twenty-first
ventiduesimo(a)	twenty-second
ventitreesimo(a)	twenty-third
ventottesimo(a)	twenty-eighth
trentesimo(a)	thirtieth
centesimo(a)	hundredth
centunesimo(a)	hundred-and-first
millesimo(a)	thousandth
milionesimo(a)	millionth

## L'ora	## The time
che ora è ?, che ore sono?	***what time is it?***
è …, sono …	***it's …***
mezzanotte	midnight
l'una (del mattino)	one o'clock (in the morning), one (am)
l'una e cinque	five past one
l'una e dieci	ten past one
l'una e un quarto, l'una e quindici	a quarter past one, one fifteen
l'una e venticinque	twenty-five past one, one twenty-five
l'una e mezzo *o* mezza, l'una e trenta	half past one, one thirty
l'una e trentacinque	twenty-five to two, one thirty-five
le due meno venti, l'una e quaranta	twenty to two, one forty
le due meno un quarto, l'una e quarantacinque	a quarter to two, one forty-five
le due meno dieci, l'una e cinquanta	ten to two, one fifty
mezzogiorno	twelve o'clock, midday, noon
le tre (del pomeriggio), le quindici	three o'clock (in the afternoon), three (pm)
le sette (di sera), le diciannove	seven o'clock (in the evening), seven (pm)
a che ora?	***at what time?***
a mezzanotte	at midnight
alle sette at	seven o'clock
fra venti minuti	in twenty minutes
venti minuti fa	twenty minutes ago

## La data	## The date
oggi	today
domani	tomorrow
dopodomani	the day after tomorrow
ieri	yesterday
l'altro ieri	the day before yesterday
il giorno prima	the day before, the previous day
il giorno dopo	the next *or* following day
la mattina	morning
la sera	evening
stamattina	this morning
stasera	this evening
questo pomeriggio	this afternoon
ieri mattina	yesterday morning
ieri sera	yesterday evening
domani mattina	tomorrow morning

domani sera	tomorrow evening
nella notte tra sabato e domenica	during Saturday night, during the night of Saturday to Sunday
viene sabato	he's coming on Saturday
il sabato	on Saturdays
tutti i sabati	every Saturday
sabato scorso, lo scorso sabato	last Saturday
il prossimo sabato	next Saturday
fra due sabati	a week on Saturday
fra tre sabati	a fortnight *or* two weeks on Saturday
da lunedý a sabato	from Monday to Saturday
tutti i giorni	every day
una volta alla settimana	once a week
una volta al mese	once a month
due volte alla settimana	twice a week
una settimana fa	a week ago
quindici giorni fa	a fortnight *or* two weeks ago
l'anno scorso *or* passato	last year
fra due giorni	in two days
fra una settimana	in a week
fra quindici giorni	in a fortnight *or* two weeks
il mese prossimo	next month
l'anno prossimo	next year
che giorno è oggi?	***what day is it?***
il primo/24 ottobre 2010	the 1st/24th of October 2010, October 1st/24th 2010
nel 2011	in 2011
il millenovecentonovantacinque	nineteen ninety-five
44 a.C.	44 BC
14 d.C.	14 AD
nel diciannovesimo secolo, nel XIX secolo, nell'Ottocento	in the nineteenth century
negli anni trenta	in the thirties
c'era una volta ...	once upon a time ...

A, a [a] *sf o m inv* (*lettera*) A, a; **A come Ancona** ≈ A for Andrew (*Brit*), ≈ A for Able (*US*); **dalla a alla z** from a to z

A *abbr* (= *altezza*) h; (= *area*) A; (= *autostrada*) ≈ M (*Brit*)

PAROLA CHIAVE

a (*a* + *il* = **al**, *a* + *lo* = **allo**, *a* + *l'* = **all'**, *a* + *la* = **alla**, *a* + *i* = **ai**, *a* + *gli* = **agli**, *a* + *le* = **alle**) *prep* **1** (*stato in luogo*) at; (: *in*) in; **essere alla stazione** to be at the station; **essere a casa/a scuola/a Roma** to be at home/at school/in Rome; **è a 10 km da qui** it's 10 km from here, it's 10 km away; **restare a cena** to stay for dinner
2 (*moto a luogo*) to; **andare a casa/a scuola/alla stazione** to go home/to school/to the station; **andare a Roma/al mare** to go to Rome/to the seaside
3 (*tempo*) at; (*epoca, stagione*) in; **alle cinque** at five (o'clock); **a mezzanotte/Natale** at midnight/Christmas; **al mattino** in the morning; **a maggio/primavera** in May/spring; **a cinquant'anni** at fifty (years of age); **a domani!** see you tomorrow!; **a lunedì!** see you on Monday!; **a giorni** within (a few) days
4 (*complemento di termine*) to; **dare qc a qn** to give sb sth, give sth to sb; **l'ho chiesto a lui** I asked him
5 (*mezzo, modo*) with, by; **a piedi/cavallo** on foot/horseback; **viaggiare a 100 km all'ora** to travel at 100 km an *o* per hour; **alla televisione/radio** on television/the radio; **fatto a mano** made by hand, handmade; **una barca a motore** a motorboat; **una stufa a gas** a gas heater; **a uno a uno** one by one; **a fatica** with difficulty; **all'italiana** the Italian way, in the Italian fashion
6 (*rapporto*) a, per; (: *con prezzi*) at; **due volte al giorno/mese** twice a day/month; **prendo 2000 euro al mese** I get 2000 euro a *o* per month; **pagato a ore** paid by the hour; **vendere qc a 2 euro il chilo** to sell sth at 2 euro a *o* per kilo; **cinque a zero** (*punteggio*) five nil

AA *sigla* = **Alto Adige**
AAST *sigla f* = **Azienda Autonoma di Soggiorno e Turismo**
AA.VV. *abbr* = **autori vari**
ab. *abbr* = **abitante**
a'bate *sm* abbot
abbacchi'ato, -a [abbak'kjato] *ag* downhearted, in low spirits
abbacin'are [abbatʃi'nare] *vt* to dazzle
abbagli'ante [abbaʎ'ʎante] *ag* dazzling; **abbaglianti** *smpl* (*Aut*): **accendere gli abbaglianti** to put one's headlights on full (*Brit*) *o* high (*US*) beam
abbagli'are [abbaʎ'ʎare] *vt* to dazzle; (*illudere*) to delude
ab'baglio [ab'baʎʎo] *sm* blunder; **prendere un ~** to blunder, make a blunder
abbai'are *vi* to bark
abba'ino *sm* dormer window; (*soffitta*) attic room
abbando'nare *vt* to leave, abandon, desert; (*trascurare*) to neglect; (*rinunciare a*) to abandon, give up; **abbandonarsi** *vr* to let o.s. go; **~ il campo** (*Mil*) to retreat; **~ la presa** to let go; **abbandonarsi a** (*ricordi, vizio*) to give o.s. up to
abbando'nato, -a *ag* (*casa*) deserted; (*miniera*) disused; (*trascurato: terreno, podere*) neglected; (*bambino*) abandoned
abban'dono *sm* abandoning; neglecting; (*stato*) abandonment; neglect; (*Sport*) withdrawal; (*fig*) abandon; **in ~** (*edificio, giardino*) neglected
abbarbi'carsi *vr*: **~ (a)** (*anche fig*) to cling (to)
abbassa'mento *sm* lowering; (*di pressione, livello dell'acqua*) fall; (*di prezzi*) reduction; **~ di temperatura** drop in temperature
abbas'sare *vt* to lower; (*radio*) to turn down; **abbassarsi** *vr* (*chinarsi*) to stoop; (*livello, sole*)

to go down; (*fig: umiliarsi*) to demean o.s.; **~ i fari** (*Aut*) to dip (*Brit*) *o* dim (*US*) one's lights; **~ le armi** (*Mil*) to lay down one's arms

ab'basso *escl*: **~ il re!** down with the king!

abbas'tanza [abbas'tantsa] *av* (*a sufficienza*) enough; (*alquanto*) quite, rather, fairly; **non è ~ furbo** he's not shrewd enough; **un vino ~ dolce** quite a sweet wine, a fairly sweet wine; **averne ~ di qn/qc** to have had enough of sb/sth

ab'battere *vt* (*muro, casa, ostacolo*) to knock down; (*albero*) to fell; (*: vento*) to bring down; (*bestie da macello*) to slaughter; (*cane, cavallo*) to destroy, put down; (*selvaggina, aereo*) to shoot down; (*fig: malattia, disgrazia*) to lay low; **abbattersi** *vr* (*avvilirsi*) to lose heart; **abbattersi a terra** *o* **al suolo** to fall to the ground; **abbattersi su** (*maltempo*) to beat down on; (*disgrazia*) to hit, strike

abbatti'mento *sm* knocking down; felling; (*di casa*) demolition; (*prostrazione: fisica*) exhaustion; (*: morale*) despondency

abbat'tuto, -a *ag* despondent, depressed

abba'zia [abbat'tsia] *sf* abbey

abbece'dario [abbetʃe'darjo] *sm* primer

abbelli'mento *sm* embellishment

abbel'lire *vt* to make beautiful; (*ornare*) to embellish

abbeve'rare *vt* to water; **abbeverarsi** *vr* to drink

abbevera'toio *sm* drinking trough

'abbi *vb vedi* **avere**

'abbia *vb vedi* **avere**

abbi'amo *vb vedi* **avere**

'abbiano *vb vedi* **avere**

abbi'ate *vb vedi* **avere**

abbiccì [abbit'tʃi] *sm inv* alphabet; (*sillabario*) primer; (*fig*) rudiments *pl*

abbi'ente *ag* well-to-do, well-off

abbi'etto, -a *ag* = **abietto**

abbiezi'one [abbjet'tsjone] *sf* = **abiezione**

abbiglia'mento [abbiʎʎa'mento] *sm* dress *no pl*; (*indumenti*) clothes *pl*; (*industria*) clothing industry

abbigli'are [abbiʎ'ʎare] *vt* to dress up

abbina'mento *sm* combination; linking; matching

abbi'nare *vt*: **~ (con** *o* **a)** (*gen*) to combine (with); (*nomi*) to link (with); **~ qc a qc** (*colori etc*) to match sth with sth

abbindo'lare *vt* (*fig*) to cheat, trick

abbocca'mento *sm* (*colloquio*) talks *pl*, meeting; (*Tecn: di tubi*) connection

abboc'care *vt* (*tubi, canali*) to connect, join up ■ *vi* (*pesce*) to bite; (*tubi*) to join; **~ (all'amo)** (*fig*) to swallow the bait

abboc'cato, -a *ag* (*vino*) sweetish

abbona'mento *sm* subscription; (*alle ferrovie etc*) season ticket; **in ~** for subscribers only; for season ticket holders only; **fare l'~ (a)** to take out a subscription (to); to buy a season ticket (for)

abbo'nare *vt* (*cifra*) to deduct; (*fig: perdonare*) to forgive; **abbonarsi** *vr*: **abbonarsi a un giornale** to take out a subscription to a newspaper; **abbonarsi al teatro/alle ferrovie** to take out a season ticket for the theatre/the train

abbo'nato, -a *sm/f* subscriber; season-ticket holder; **elenco degli abbonati** telephone directory

abbon'dante *ag* abundant, plentiful; (*giacca*) roomy

abbon'danza [abbon'dantsa] *sf* abundance; plenty

abbon'dare *vi* to abound, be plentiful; **~ in** *o* **di** to be full of, abound in

abbor'dabile *ag* (*persona*) approachable; (*prezzo*) reasonable

abbor'dare *vt* (*nave*) to board; (*persona*) to approach; (*argomento*) to tackle; **~ una curva** to take a bend

abbotto'nare *vt* to button up, do up; **abbottonarsi** *vr* to button (up)

abbotto'nato, -a *ag* (*camicia etc*) buttoned (up); (*fig*) reserved

abbottona'tura *sf* buttons *pl*; **questo cappotto ha l'~ da uomo/da donna** this coat buttons on the man's/woman's side

abboz'zare [abbot'tsare] *vt* to sketch, outline; (*Scultura*) to rough-hew; **~ un sorriso** to give a hint of a smile

ab'bozzo [ab'bɔttso] *sm* sketch, outline; (*Dir*) draft

abbracci'are [abbrat'tʃare] *vt* to embrace; (*persona*) to hug, embrace; (*professione*) to take up; (*contenere*) to include; **abbracciarsi** *vr* to hug *o* embrace (one another)

ab'braccio [ab'brattʃo] *sm* hug, embrace

abbrevi'are *vt* to shorten; (*parola*) to abbreviate, shorten

abbreviazi'one [abbrevjat'tsjone] *sf* abbreviation

abbron'zante [abbron'dzante] *ag* tanning, sun *cpd*

abbron'zare [abbron'dzare] *vt* (*pelle*) to tan; (*metalli*) to bronze; **abbronzarsi** *vr* to tan, get a tan

abbron'zato, -a [abbron'dzato] *ag* (sun)tanned

abbronza'tura [abbrondza'tura] *sf* tan, suntan

abbrusto'lire *vt* (*pane*) to toast; (*caffè*) to roast

abbruti'mento *sm* exhaustion; degradation

abbru'tire *vt* (*snervare, stancare*) to exhaust; (*degradare*) to degrade; **essere abbrutito dall'alcool** to be ruined by drink
abbuf'farsi *vr* (*fam*): ~ **(di qc)** to stuff o.s. (with sth)
abbuf'fata *sf* (*fam*) nosh-up; (*fig*) binge; **farsi un'~** to stuff o.s.
abbuo'nare *vt* = **abbonare**
abbu'ono *sm* (*Comm*) allowance, discount; (*Sport*) handicap
abdi'care *vi* to abdicate; ~ **a** to give up, renounce
abdicazi'one [abdikat'tsjone] *sf* abdication
aberrazi'one [aberrat'tsjone] *sf* aberration
abe'taia *sf* fir wood
a'bete *sm* fir (tree); ~ **bianco** silver fir; ~ **rosso** spruce
abi'etto, -a *ag* despicable, abject
abiezi'one [abjet'tsjone] *sf* abjection
'abile *ag* (*idoneo*): ~ **(a qc/a fare qc)** fit (for sth/ to do sth); (*capace*) able; (*astuto*) clever; (*accorto*) skilful; ~ **al servizio militare** fit for military service
abilità *sf inv* ability; cleverness; skill
abili'tante *ag* qualifying; **corsi abilitantei** (*Ins*) ≈ teacher training *sg*
abili'tare *vt*: ~ **qn a qc/a fare qc** to qualify sb for sth/to do sth; **è stato abilitato all'insegnamento** he has qualified as a teacher
abili'tato, -a *ag* qualified; (*Tel*) which has an outside line
abilitazi'one [abilitat'tsjone] *sf* qualification
abis'sale *ag* abysmal; (*fig: senza limiti*) profound
abis'sino, -a *ag, sm/f* Abyssinian
a'bisso *sm* abyss, gulf
abitabilità *sf*: **licenza di** ~ *document stating that a property is fit for habitation*
abi'tacolo *sm* (*Aer*) cockpit; (*Aut*) inside; (*di camion*) (driver's) cab
abi'tante *sm/f* inhabitant
abi'tare *vt* to live in, dwell in ▪ *vi*: ~ **in campagna/a Roma** to live in the country/ in Rome
abi'tato, -a *ag* inhabited; lived in ▪ *sm* (*anche*: **centro abitato**) built-up area
abitazi'one [abitat'tsjone] *sf* residence; house
'abito *sm* dress *no pl*; (*da uomo*) suit; (*da donna*) dress; (*abitudine, disposizione, Rel*) habit; **abiti** *smpl* (*vestiti*) clothes; **in ~ da cerimonia** in formal dress; **in ~ da sera** in evening dress; **"è gradito l'~ scuro"** "dress formal"; ~ **mentale** way of thinking
abitu'ale *ag* usual, habitual; (*cliente*) regular
abitual'mente *av* usually, normally
abitu'are *vt*: ~ **qn a** to get sb used *o* accustomed to; **abituarsi a** to get used to, accustom o.s. to
abitudi'nario, -a *ag* of fixed habits ▪ *sm/f* creature of habit
abi'tudine *sf* habit; **aver l'~ di fare qc** to be in the habit of doing sth; **d'~** usually; **per ~** from *o* out of habit
abiu'rare *vt* to renounce
abla'tivo *sm* ablative
abnegazi'one [abnegat'tsjone] *sf* (self-) abnegation, self-denial
ab'norme *ag* (*enorme*) extraordinary; (*anormale*) abnormal
abo'lire *vt* to abolish; (*Dir*) to repeal
abolizi'one [abolit'tsjone] *sf* abolition; repeal
abomi'nevole *ag* abominable
abo'rigeno [abo'ridʒeno] *sm* aborigine
abor'rire *vt* to abhor, detest
abor'tire *vi* (*Med: accidentalmente*) to miscarry, have a miscarriage; (*: deliberatamente*) to have an abortion; (*fig*) to miscarry, fail
abor'tista, -i, e *ag* pro-choice, pro-abortion ▪ *sm/f* pro-choicer
a'borto *sm* miscarriage; abortion; (*fig*) freak; ~ **clandestino** backstreet abortion
abrasi'one *sf* abrasion
abra'sivo, -a *ag, sm* abrasive
abro'gare *vt* to repeal, abrogate
abrogazi'one [abrogat'tsjone] *sf* repeal
abruz'zese [abrut'tsese] *ag* of (*o* from) the Abruzzi
A'bruzzo [a'bruttso] *sm*: **l'~, gli Abruzzi** the Abruzzi
ABS [abi'ɛsse] *sigla m* ABS (= *anti-lock braking system*)
'abside *sf* apse
'Abu 'Dhabi *sf* Abu Dhabi
a'bulico, -a, ci, che *ag* lacking in willpower
abu'sare *vi*: ~ **di** to abuse, misuse; (*approfittare, violare*) to take advantage of; ~ **dell'alcool/ dei cibi** to drink/eat to excess
abusi'vismo *sm* (*anche*: **abusivismo edilizio**) unlawful building, building without planning permission (*Brit*)
abu'sivo, -a *ag* unauthorized, unlawful; **(occupante)** ~ (*di una casa*) squatter
a'buso *sm* abuse, misuse; excessive use; **fare ~ di** (*stupefacenti, medicine*) to abuse
a.C. *abbr* (= *avanti Cristo*) BC
a'cacia, -cie [a'katʃa] *sf* acacia
'acca *sf* letter H; **non capire un'~** not to understand a thing
ac'cadde *vb vedi* **accadere**
acca'demia *sf* (*società*) learned society; (*scuola: d'arte, militare*) academy; ~ **di Belle Arti** art school

acca'demico, -a, ci, che *ag* academic ■ *sm* academician
acca'dere *vi* to happen, occur
acca'duto *sm* event; **raccontare l'~** to describe what has happened
accalappia'cani *sm inv* dog-catcher
accalappi'are *vt* to catch; (*fig*) to trick, dupe
accal'care *vt*, **accal'carsi** *vr* to crowd, throng
accal'darsi *vr* to grow hot
accalo'rarsi *vr* (*fig*) to get excited
accampa'mento *sm* camp
accam'pare *vt* to encamp; (*fig*) to put forward, advance; **accamparsi** *vr* to camp; **~ scuse** to make excuses
accani'mento *sm* fury; (*tenacia*) tenacity, perseverance
acca'nirsi *vr* (*infierire*) to rage; (*ostinarsi*) to persist
accanita'mente *av* fiercely; assiduously
acca'nito, -a *ag* (*odio, gelosia*) fierce, bitter; (*lavoratore*) assiduous; (*giocatore*) inveterate; (*tifoso, sostenitore*) keen; **fumatore ~** chain smoker
ac'canto *av* near, nearby; **~ a** *prep* near, beside, close to; **la casa ~** the house next door
accanto'nare *vt* (*problema*) to shelve; (*somma*) to set aside
accaparra'mento *sm* (*Comm*) cornering, buying up
accapar'rare *vt* (*Comm*) to corner, buy up; (*versare una caparra*) to pay a deposit on; **accaparrarsi** *vr*: **accaparrarsi qc** (*fig*: *simpatia, voti*) to secure sth (for o.s.)
accapigli'arsi [akkapiʎ'ʎarsi] *vr* to come to blows; (*fig*) to quarrel
accappa'toio *sm* bathrobe
accappo'nare *vi*: **far ~ la pelle a qn** (*fig*) to bring sb out in goosepimples
accarez'zare [akkaret'tsare] *vt* to caress, stroke, fondle; (*fig*) to toy with
accartocci'are [akkartot'tʃare] *vt* (*carta*) to roll up, screw up; **accartocciarsi** *vr* (*foglie*) to curl up
acca'sarsi *vr* to set up house; to get married
accasci'arsi [akkaʃ'ʃarsi] *vr* to collapse; (*fig*) to lose heart
accatas'tare *vt* to stack, pile
accatto'naggio [akkatto'naddʒo] *sm* begging
accat'tone, -a *sm/f* beggar
accaval'lare *vt* (*gambe*) to cross; **accavallarsi** *vr* (*sovrapporsi*) to overlap; (*addensarsi*) to gather
acce'care [attʃe'kare] *vt* to blind ■ *vi* to go blind
ac'cedere [at'tʃɛdere] *vi*: **~ a** to enter; (*richiesta*) to grant, accede to; (*fonte*) to gain access to
accele'rare [attʃele'rare] *vt* to speed up ■ *vi* (*Aut*) to accelerate; **~ il passo** to quicken one's pace
accele'rato, -a [attʃele'rato] *ag* quick, rapid ■ *sm* (*Ferr*) local train, stopping train
accelera'tore [attʃelera'tore] *sm* (*Aut*) accelerator
accelerazi'one [attʃelerat'tsjone] *sf* acceleration
ac'cendere [at'tʃɛndere] *vt* (*fuoco, sigaretta*) to light; (*luce, televisione*) to put *o* switch *o* turn on; (*Aut*: *motore*) to switch on; (*Comm*: *conto*) to open; (: *debito*) to contract; (: *ipoteca*) to raise; (*fig*: *suscitare*) to inflame, stir up; **accendersi** *vr* (*luce*) to come *o* go on; (*legna*) to catch fire, ignite; (*fig*: *lotta, conflitto*) to break out
accen'dino [attʃen'dino], **accendi'sigaro** [attʃendi'sigaro] *sm* (cigarette) lighter
accen'nare [attʃen'nare] *vt* to indicate, point out; (*Mus*) to pick out the notes of; to hum ■ *vi*: **~ a** (*fig*: *alludere a*) to hint at; (: *far atto di*) to make as if; **~ un saluto** (*con la mano*) to make as if to wave; (*col capo*) to half nod; **~ un sorriso** to half smile; **accenna a piovere** it looks as if it's going to rain
ac'cenno [at'tʃenno] *sm* (*cenno*) sign; nod; (*allusione*) hint
accensi'one [attʃen'sjone] *sf* (*vedi accendere*) lighting; switching on; opening; (*Aut*) ignition
accen'tare [attʃen'tare] *vt* (*parlando*) to stress; (*scrivendo*) to accent
accentazi'one [attʃentat'tsjone] *sf* accentuation; stressing
ac'cento [at'tʃɛnto] *sm* accent; (*Fonetica, fig*) stress; (*inflessione*) tone (of voice)
accentra'mento [attʃentra'mento] *sm* centralization
accen'trare [attʃen'trare] *vt* to centralize
accentra'tore, -trice [attʃentra'tore] *ag* (*persona*) unwilling to delegate; **politica accentratrice** policy of centralization
accentu'are [attʃentu'are] *vt* to stress, emphasize; **accentuarsi** *vr* to become more noticeable
accerchi'are [attʃer'kjare] *vt* to surround, encircle
accerta'mento [attʃerta'mento] *sm* check; assessment
accer'tare [attʃer'tare] *vt* to ascertain; (*verificare*) to check; (*reddito*) to assess; **accertarsi** *vr*: **accertarsi (di qc/che)** to make sure (of sth/that)

ac'ceso, -a [at'tʃeso] *pp di* **accendere** ■ *ag* lit; on; open; (*colore*) bright; **~ di** (*ira, entusiasmo etc*) burning with
acces'sibile [attʃes'sibile] *ag* (*luogo*) accessible; (*persona*) approachable; (*prezzo*) reasonable; (*idea*): **~ a qn** within the reach of sb
ac'cesso [at'tʃɛsso] *sm* (*anche Inform*) access; (*Med*) attack, fit; (*impulso violento*) fit, outburst; **programmi dell'~** (*TV*) educational programmes; **tempo di ~** (*Inform*) access time; **~ casuale/seriale/sequenziale** (*Inform*) random/serial/sequential access
accessori'ato, -a [attʃesso'rjato] *ag* with accessories
acces'sorio, -a [attʃes'sɔrjo] *ag* secondary, of secondary importance; **accessori** *smpl* accessories
ac'cetta [at'tʃetta] *sf* hatchet
accet'tabile [attʃet'tabile] *ag* acceptable
accet'tare [attʃet'tare] *vt* to accept; **~ di fare qc** to agree to do sth
accettazi'one [attʃettat'tsjone] *sf* acceptance; (*locale di servizio pubblico*) reception; **~ bagagli** (*Aer*) check-in (desk); **~ con riserva** qualified acceptance
ac'cetto, -a [at'tʃɛtto] *ag* (*persona*) welcome; **(ben) ~ a tutti** well-liked by everybody
accezi'one [attʃet'tsjone] *sf* meaning
acchiap'pare [akkjap'pare] *vt* to catch; (*afferrare*) to seize
ac'chito [ak'kito] *sm*: **a primo ~** at first sight
acciac'cato, -a [attʃak'kato] *ag* (*persona*) full of aches and pains; (*abito*) crushed
acci'acco, -chi [at'tʃakko] *sm* ailment; **acciacchi** *smpl* aches and pains
acciaie'ria [attʃaje'ria] *sf* steelworks *sg*
acci'aio [at'tʃajo] *sm* steel; **~ inossidabile** stainless steel
acciden'tale [attʃiden'tale] *ag* accidental
accidental'mente [attʃidental'mente] *av* (*per caso*) by chance; (*non deliberatamente*) accidentally, by accident
acciden'tato, -a [attʃiden'tato] *ag* (*terreno etc*) uneven
acci'dente [attʃi'dɛnte] *sm* (*caso imprevisto*) accident; (*disgrazia*) mishap; **accidenti!** (*fam: per rabbia*) damn (it)!; (*: per meraviglia*) good heavens!; **accidenti a lui!** damn him!; **non vale un ~** it's not worth a damn; **non capisco un ~** it's as clear as mud to me; **mandare un ~ a qn** to curse sb
ac'cidia [at'tʃidja] *sf* (*Rel*) sloth
accigli'ato, -a [attʃiʎ'ʎato] *ag* frowning
ac'cingersi [at'tʃindʒersi] *vr*: **~ a fare** to be about to do
acciotto'lato [attʃotto'lato] *sm* cobbles *pl*
acciuf'fare [attʃuf'fare] *vt* to seize, catch
acci'uga, -ghe [at'tʃuga] *sf* anchovy; **magro come un'~** as thin as a rake
accla'mare *vt* (*applaudire*) to applaud; (*eleggere*) to acclaim
acclamazi'one [akklamat'tsjone] *sf* applause; acclamation
acclima'tare *vt* to acclimatize; **acclimatarsi** *vr* to become acclimatized
acclimatazi'one [akklimatat'tsjone] *sf* acclimatization
ac'cludere *vt* to enclose
ac'cluso, -a *pp di* **accludere** ■ *ag* enclosed
accocco'larsi *vr* to crouch
acco'darsi *vr* to follow, tag on (behind)
accogli'ente [akkoʎ'ʎɛnte] *ag* welcoming, friendly
accogli'enza [akkoʎ'ʎɛntsa] *sf* reception; welcome; **fare una buona ~ a qn** to welcome sb
ac'cogliere [ak'kɔʎʎere] *vt* (*ricevere*) to receive; (*dare il benvenuto*) to welcome; (*approvare*) to agree to, accept; (*contenere*) to hold, accommodate
ac'colgo *etc vb vedi* **accogliere**
accol'lare *vt* (*fig*): **~ qc a qn** to force sth on sb; **accollarsi** *vr*: **accollarsi qc** to take sth upon o.s., shoulder sth
accol'lato, -a *ag* (*vestito*) high-necked
ac'colsi *etc vb vedi* **accogliere**
accoltel'lare *vt* to knife, stab
ac'colto, -a *pp di* **accogliere**
accoman'dita *sf* (*Dir*) limited partnership
accomia'tare *vt* to dismiss; **accomiatarsi** *vr*: **accomiatarsi (da)** to take one's leave (of)
accomoda'mento *sm* agreement, settlement
accomo'dante *ag* accommodating
accomo'dare *vt* (*aggiustare*) to repair, mend; (*riordinare*) to tidy; (*sistemare: questione, lite*) to settle; **accomodarsi** *vr* (*sedersi*) to sit down; (*fig: risolversi: situazione*) to work out; **si accomodi!** (*venga avanti*) come in!; (*si sieda*) take a seat!
accompagna'mento [akkompaɲɲa'mento] *sm* (*Mus*) accompaniment; (*Comm*): **lettera di ~** accompanying letter
accompa'gnare [akkompaɲ'ɲare] *vt* to accompany, come *o* go with; (*Mus*) to accompany; (*unire*) to couple; **accompagnarsi** *vr* (*armonizzarsi*) to go well together; **~ qn a casa** to see sb home; **~ qn alla porta** to show sb out; **~ un regalo con un biglietto** to put in *o* send a card with a present; **~ qn con lo sguardo** to follow sb with one's eyes; **~ la porta** to close the door

gently; **accompagnarsi a** (*frequentare*) to frequent; (*colori*) to go with, match; (*cibi*) to go with
accompagna'tore, -'trice [akkompaɲɲa'tore] *sm/f* companion, escort; **~ turistico** courier; tour guide; (*Mus*) accompanist; (*Sport*) team manager
accomu'nare *vt* to pool, share; (*avvicinare*) to unite
acconcia'tura [akkontʃa'tura] *sf* hairstyle
accondiscen'dente [akkondiʃʃen'dɛnte] *ag* affable
accondi'scendere [akkondiʃʃendere] *vi*: **~ a** to agree *o* consent to
accondi'sceso, -a [akkondiʃʃeso] *pp di* **accondiscendere**
acconsen'tire *vi*: **~ (a)** to agree *o* consent (to); **chi tace acconsente** silence means consent
acconten'tare *vt* to satisfy; **accontentarsi** *vr*: **accontentarsi di** to be satisfied with, content o.s. with; **chi si accontenta gode** there's no point in complaining
ac'conto *sm* part payment; **pagare una somma in ~** to pay a sum of money as a deposit; **~ di dividendo** interim dividend
accoppia'mento *sm* pairing off; mating; (*Elettr, Inform*) coupling
accoppi'are *vt* to couple, pair off; (*Biol*) to mate; **accoppiarsi** *vr* to pair off; to mate
accoppia'tore *sm* (*Tecn*) coupler; **~ acustico** (*Inform*) acoustic coupler
acco'rato, -a *ag* heartfelt
accorci'are [akkor'tʃare] *vt* to shorten; **accorciarsi** *vr* to become shorter; (*vestiti: nel lavaggio*) to shrink
accor'dare *vt* to reconcile; (*colori*) to match; (*Mus*) to tune; (*Ling*): **~ qc con qc** to make sth agree with sth; (*Dir*) to grant; **accordarsi** *vr* to agree, come to an agreement; (*colori*) to match
ac'cordo *sm* agreement; (*armonia*) harmony; (*Mus*) chord; **essere d'~** to agree; **andare d'~** to get on well together; **d'~!** all right!, agreed!; **mettersi d'~ (con qn)** to agree *o* come to an agreement with sb; **prendere accordi con** to reach an agreement with; **~ commerciale** trade agreement; **A~ generale sulle tariffe ed il commercio** General Agreement on Tariffs and Trade, GATT
ac'corgersi [ak'kɔrdʒersi] *vr*: **~ di** to notice; (*fig*) to realize
accorgi'mento [akkordʒi'mento] *sm* shrewdness *no pl*; (*espediente*) trick, device
ac'correre *vi* to run up
ac'corsi *vb vedi* **accorgersi**; **accorrere**
ac'corso, -a *pp di* **accorrere**
accor'tezza [akkor'tettsa] *sf* (*avvedutezza*) good sense; (*astuzia*) shrewdness
ac'corto, -a *pp di* **accorgersi** ■ *ag* shrewd; **stare ~** to be on one's guard
accosta'mento *sm* (*di colori etc*) combination
accos'tare *vt* (*avvicinarsi a*) to approach; (*socchiudere: imposte*) to half-close; (*: porta*) to leave ajar ■ *vi*: **~ (a)** (*Naut*) to come alongside; (*Aut*) to draw up (at); **accostarsi** *vr*: **accostarsi a** to draw near, approach; (*somigliare*) to be like, resemble; (*fede, religione*) to turn to; (*idee politiche*) to come to agree with; **~ qc a** (*avvicinare*) to bring sth near to, put sth near to; (*colori, stili*) to match sth with; (*appoggiare: scala etc*) to lean sth against
accovacci'arsi [akkovat'tʃarsi] *vr* to crouch
accoz'zaglia [akkot'tsaʎʎa] *sf* (*peg: di idee, oggetti*) jumble, hotchpotch; (*: di persone*) odd assortment
ac'crebbi *etc vb vedi* **accrescere**
accredi'tare *vt* (*notizia*) to confirm the truth of; (*Comm*) to credit; (*diplomatico*) to accredit; **accreditarsi** *vr* (*fig*) to gain credit
ac'credito *sm* (*Comm: atto*) crediting; (*: effetto*) credit
ac'crescere [ak'kreʃʃere] *vt* to increase; **accrescersi** *vr* to increase, grow
accresci'mento [akkreʃʃi'mento] *sm* increase, growth
accresci'tivo, -a [akkreʃʃi'tivo] *ag, sm* (*Ling*) augmentative
accresci'uto, -a [akkreʃʃuto] *pp di* **accrescere**
accucci'arsi [akkut'tʃarsi] *vr* (*cane*) to lie down; (*persona*) to crouch down
accu'dire *vi*: **~ a** to attend to ■ *vt* to look after
acculturazi'one [akkulturat'tsjone] *sf* (*Sociologia*) integration
accumu'lare *vt* to accumulate; **accumularsi** *vr* to accumulate; (*Finanza*) to accrue
accumula'tore *sm* (*Elettr*) accumulator
accumulazi'one [akkumulat'tsjone] *sf* accumulation
ac'cumulo *sm* accumulation
accurata'mente *av* carefully
accura'tezza [akkura'tettsa] *sf* care; accuracy
accu'rato, -a *ag* (*diligente*) careful; (*preciso*) accurate
ac'cusa *sf* accusation; (*Dir*) charge; **l'~, la pubblica ~** (*Dir*) the prosecution; **mettere qn sotto ~** to indict sb; **in stato di ~** committed for trial
accu'sare *vt* (*sentire: dolore*) to feel; **~ qn di qc** to accuse sb of sth; (*Dir*) to charge sb with sth; **~ ricevuta di** (*Comm*) to acknowledge receipt of; **~ la fatica** to show signs of exhaustion; **ha accusato il colpo** (*anche fig*) you could see that he had felt the blow

accusa'tivo *sm* accusative
accu'sato, -a *sm/f* accused
accusa'tore, -'trice *ag* accusing ■ *sm/f* accuser ■ *sm* (*Dir*) prosecutor
a'cerbo, -a [a'tʃɛrbo] *ag* bitter; (*frutta*) sour, unripe; (*persona*) immature
'acero ['atʃero] *sm* maple
a'cerrimo, -a [a'tʃɛrrimo] *ag* very fierce
ace'tato [atʃe'tato] *sm* acetate
a'ceto [a'tʃeto] *sm* vinegar; **mettere sotto ~** to pickle
ace'tone [atʃe'tone] *sm* nail varnish remover
'A.C.I. ['atʃi] *sigla m* (= *Automobile Club d'Italia*) ≈ AA (*Brit*), ≈ AAA (*US*)
acidità [atʃidi'ta] *sf* acidity; sourness; **~ (di stomaco)** heartburn
'acido, -a ['atʃido] *ag* (*sapore*) acid, sour; (*Chim, colore*) acid ■ *sm* (*Chim*) acid
a'cidulo, -a [a'tʃidulo] *ag* slightly sour, slightly acid
'acino ['atʃino] *sm* berry; **~ d'uva** grape
'ACLI *sigla fpl* (= *Associazioni Cristiane dei Lavoratori Italiani*) *Christian Trade Union Association*
'acme *sf* (*fig*) acme, peak; (*Med*) crisis
'acne *sf* acne
ACNUR *sigla m* (= *Alto Commissariato delle Nazioni Unite per i Rifugiati*) UNHCR
'acqua *sf* water; (*pioggia*) rain; **acque** *sfpl* waters; **fare ~** (*Naut*) to leak, take in water; **essere con** *o* **avere l'~ alla gola** to be in great difficulty; **tirare ~ al proprio mulino** to feather one's own nest; **navigare in cattive acque** (*fig*) to be in deep water; **~ in bocca!** mum's the word!; **~ corrente** running water; **~ dolce** fresh water; **~ di mare** sea water; **~ minerale** mineral water; **~ ossigenata** hydrogen peroxide; **~ piovana** rain water; **~ potabile** drinking water; **~ salata** *o* **salmastra** salt water; **~ tonica** tonic water
acqua'forte (*pl* **acqueforti**) *sf* etching
a'cquaio *sm* sink
acqua'ragia [akkwa'radʒa] *sf* turpentine
a'cquario *sm* aquarium; (*dello zodiaco*): **A~** Aquarius; **essere dell'A~** to be Aquarius
acquartie'rare *vt* (*Mil*) to quarter
acqua'santa *sf* holy water
acquas'cooter [akkwas'cuter] *sm inv* Jet Ski®
a'cquatico, -a, ci, che *ag* aquatic; (*sport, sci*) water *cpd*
acquat'tarsi *vr* to crouch (down)
acqua'vite *sf* brandy
acquaz'zone [akkwat'tsone] *sm* cloudburst, heavy shower
acque'dotto *sm* aqueduct; waterworks *pl*, water system
'acqueo, -a *ag*: **vapore ~** water vapour (*Brit*) *o* vapor (*US*); **umore ~** aqueous humour (*Brit*) *o* humor (*US*)
acque'rello *sm* watercolour (*Brit*), watercolor (*US*)
acque'rugiola [akkwe'rudʒola] *sf* drizzle
acquie'tare *vt* to appease; (*dolore*) to ease; **acquietarsi** *vr* to calm down
acqui'rente *sm/f* purchaser, buyer
acqui'sire *vt* to acquire
acquisizi'one [akkwizit'tsjone] *sf* acquisition
acquis'tare *vt* to purchase, buy; (*fig*) to gain ■ *vi* to improve; **~ in bellezza** to become more beautiful; **ha acquistato in salute** his health has improved
a'cquisto *sm* purchase; **fare acquisti** to go shopping; **ufficio acquisti** (*Comm*) purchasing department; **~ rateale** instalment purchase, hire purchase (*Brit*)
acqui'trino *sm* bog, marsh
acquo'lina *sf*: **far venire l'~ in bocca a qn** to make sb's mouth water
a'cquoso, -a *ag* watery
'acre *ag* acrid, pungent; (*fig*) harsh, biting
a'credine *sf* (*fig*) bitterness
a'crilico, -a, ci, che *ag, sm* acrylic
a'critico, -a, ci, che *ag* uncritical
a'crobata, -i, e *sm/f* acrobat
acro'batico, -a, ci, che *ag* (*ginnastica*) acrobatic; (*Aer*) aerobatic ■ *sf* acrobatics *sg*
acroba'zia [akrobat'tsia] *sf* acrobatic feat; **acrobazie aeree** aerobatics
a'cronimo *sm* acronym
a'cropoli *sf inv*: **l'A~** the Acropolis
acu'ire *vt* to sharpen; **acuirsi** *vr* (*gen*) to increase; (*crisi*) to worsen
a'culeo *sm* (*Zool*) sting; (*Bot*) prickle
a'cume *sm* acumen, perspicacity
acumi'nato, -a *ag* sharp
a'custico, -a, ci, che *ag* acoustic ■ *sf* (*scienza*) acoustics *sg*; (*di una sala*) acoustics *pl*; **apparecchio ~** hearing aid; **cornetto ~** ear trumpet
acu'tezza [aku'tettsa] *sf* sharpness; shrillness; acuteness; high pitch; intensity; keenness
acutiz'zare [akutid'dzare] *vt* (*fig*) to intensify; **acutizzarsi** *vr* (*fig: crisi, malattia*) to become worse, worsen
a'cuto, -a *ag* (*appuntito*) sharp, pointed; (*suono, voce*) shrill, piercing; (*Mat, Ling, Med*) acute; (*Mus*) high-pitched; (*fig: dolore, desiderio*) intense; (*: perspicace*) acute, keen ■ *sm* (*Mus*) high note
ad *prep* (*dav V*) = **a**
adagi'are [ada'dʒare] *vt* to lay *o* set down carefully; **adagiarsi** *vr* to lie down, stretch out

a'dagio [a'dadʒo] *av* slowly ■ *sm* (*Mus*) adagio; (*proverbio*) adage, saying
ada'mitico, -a, ci, che *ag*: **in costume ~** in one's birthday suit
adat'tabile *ag* adaptable
adattabilità *sf* adaptability
adatta'mento *sm* adaptation; **avere spirito di ~** to be adaptable
adat'tare *vt* to adapt; (*sistemare*) to fit; **adattarsi** *vr*: **adattarsi (a)** (*ambiente, tempi*) to adapt (to); (*essere adatto*) to be suitable (for); (*accontentarsi*): **adattarsi a qc/a fare qc** to make the best of sth/of doing sth
adatta'tore *sm* (*Elettr*) adapter, adaptor
a'datto, -a *ag*: **~ (a)** suitable (for), right (for)
addebi'tare *vt*: **~ qc a qn** to debit sb with sth; (*fig: incolpare*) to blame sb for sth
ad'debito *sm* (*Comm*) debit
addensa'mento *sm* thickening; gathering
adden'sare *vt* to thicken; **addensarsi** *vr* to thicken; (*nuvole*) to gather
adden'tare *vt* to bite into
adden'trarsi *vr*: **~ in** to penetrate, go into
ad'dentro *av* (*fig*): **essere molto ~ in qc** to be well-versed in sth
addestra'mento *sm* training; **~ aziendale** company training
addes'trare *vt*, **addes'trarsi** *vr* to train; **addestrarsi in qc** to practise (*Brit*) *o* practice (*US*) sth
ad'detto, -a *ag*: **~ a** (*persona*) assigned to; (*oggetto*) intended for ■ *sm* employee; (*funzionario*) attaché; **~ commerciale/ stampa** commercial/press attaché; **~ al telex** telex operator; **gli addetti ai lavori** authorized personnel; (*fig*) those in the know; **"vietato l'ingresso ai non addetti ai lavori"** "authorized personnel only"
addì *av* (*Amm*): **~ 3 luglio 1989** on the 3rd of July 1989 (*Brit*), on July 3rd 1989 (*US*)
addi'accio [ad'djattʃo] *sm* (*Mil*) bivouac; **dormire all'~** to sleep in the open
addi'etro *av* (*indietro*) behind; (*nel passato, prima*) before, ago
ad'dio *sm, escl* goodbye, farewell
addirit'tura *av* (*veramente*) really, absolutely; (*perfino*) even; (*direttamente*) directly, right away
ad'dirsi *vr*: **~ a** to suit, be suitable for
'Addis A'beba *sf* Addis Ababa
addi'tare *vt* to point out; (*fig*) to expose
addi'tivo *sm* additive
addizio'nale [addittsjo'nale] *ag* additional ■ *sf* (*anche*: **imposta addizionale**) surtax
addizio'nare [addittsjo'nare] *vt* (*Mat*) to add (up)
addizi'one [addit'tsjone] *sf* addition
addob'bare *vt* to decorate
ad'dobbo *sm* decoration
addol'cire [addol'tʃire] *vt* (*caffè etc*) to sweeten; (*acqua, fig: carattere*) to soften; **addolcirsi** *vr* (*fig*) to mellow, soften; **~ la pillola** (*fig*) to sugar the pill
addolo'rare *vt* to pain, grieve; **addolorarsi** *vr*: **addolorarsi (per)** to be distressed (by)
addolo'rato, -a *ag* distressed, upset; **l'Addolorata** (*Rel*) Our Lady of Sorrows
ad'dome *sm* abdomen
addomesti'care *vt* to tame
addomi'nale *ag* abdominal; **(muscoli) addominali** stomach muscles
addormen'tare *vt* to put to sleep; **addormentarsi** *vr* to fall asleep, go to sleep
addormen'tato, -a *ag* sleeping, asleep; (*fig: tardo*) stupid, dopey
addos'sare *vt* (*appoggiare*): **~ qc a qc** to lean sth against sth; (*fig*): **~ la colpa a qn** to lay the blame on sb; **addossarsi** *vr*: **addossarsi qc** (*responsabilità etc*) to shoulder sth
ad'dosso *av* (*sulla persona*) on; **~ a** *prep* (*sopra*) on; (*molto vicino*) right next to; **mettersi ~ il cappotto** to put one's coat on; **andare (*o* venire) ~ a** (*Aut: altra macchina*) to run into; (*: pedone*) to run over; **non ho soldi ~** I don't have any money on me; **stare ~ a qn** (*fig*) to breathe down sb's neck; **dare ~ a qn** (*fig*) to attack sb; **mettere gli occhi ~ a qn/qc** to take quite a fancy to sb/sth; **mettere le mani ~ a qn** (*picchiare*) to hit sb; (*catturare*) to seize sb; (*molestare: donna*) to touch sb up
ad'dotto, -a *pp di* **addurre**
ad'duco *etc vb vedi* **addurre**
ad'durre *vt* (*Dir*) to produce; (*citare*) to cite
ad'dussi *etc vb vedi* **addurre**
adegu'are *vt*: **~ qc a** to adjust sth to; **adeguarsi** *vr* to adapt
adegua'tezza [adegwa'tettsa] *sf* adequacy; suitability; fairness
adegu'ato, -a *ag* adequate; (*conveniente*) suitable; (*equo*) fair
a'dempiere *vt* to fulfil (*Brit*), fulfill (*US*), carry out; (*comando*) to carry out
adempi'mento *sm* fulfilment (*Brit*), fulfillment (*US*); carrying out; **nell'~ del proprio dovere** in the performance of one's duty
adem'pire *vt* = **adempiere**
'Aden: **il golfo di ~** *sm* the Gulf of Aden
ade'noidi *sfpl* adenoids
a'depto *sm* disciple, follower
ade'rente *ag* adhesive; (*vestito*) close-fitting ■ *sm/f* follower
ade'renza [ade'rɛntsa] *sf* adhesion; **aderenze** *sfpl* (*fig*) connections, contacts

heavy; *(fig: pena)* to make worse; **aggravarsi** *vr (fig)* to worsen, become worse
ag'gravio *sm:* ~ **di costi** increase in costs
aggrazi'ato, -a [aggrat'tsjato] *ag* graceful
aggre'dire *vt* to attack, assault
aggre'gare *vt:* ~ **qn a qc** to admit sb to sth; **aggregarsi** *vr* to join; **aggregarsi a** to join, become a member of
aggre'gato, -a *ag* associated ■ *sm* aggregate; ~ **urbano** built-up area
aggressi'one *sf* aggression; *(atto)* attack; ~ **a mano armata** armed assault
aggressività *sf* aggressiveness
aggres'sivo, -a *ag* aggressive
aggres'sore *sm* aggressor, attacker
aggrot'tare *vt:* ~ **le sopracciglia** to frown
aggrovigli'are [aggroviʎ'ʎare] *vt* to tangle; **aggrovigliarsi** *vr (fig)* to become complicated
agguan'tare *vt* to catch, seize
aggu'ato *sm* trap; *(imboscata)* ambush; **tendere un ~ a qn** to set a trap for sb
agguer'rito, -a *ag (sostenitore, nemico)* fierce
agia'tezza [adʒa'tettsa] *sf* prosperity
agi'ato, -a [a'dʒato] *ag (vita)* easy; *(persona)* well-off, well-to-do
'agile ['adʒile] *ag* agile, nimble
agilità [adʒili'ta] *sf* agility, nimbleness
'agio ['adʒo] *sm* ease, comfort; **agi** *smpl* comforts; **mettersi a proprio ~** to make o.s. at home *o* comfortable; **dare ~ a qn di fare qc** to give sb the chance of doing sth
a'gire [a'dʒire] *vi* to act; *(esercitare un'azione)* to take effect; *(Tecn)* to work, function; ~ **contro qn** *(Dir)* to take action against sb
agi'tare [adʒi'tare] *vt (bottiglia)* to shake; *(mano, fazzoletto)* to wave; *(fig: turbare)* to disturb; *(: incitare)* to stir (up); **agitarsi** *vr (mare)* to be rough; *(malato, dormitore)* to toss and turn; *(bambino)* to fidget; *(emozionarsi)* to get upset; *(Pol)* to agitate
agi'tato, -a [adʒi'tato] *ag* rough; restless; fidgety; upset, perturbed
agita'tore, -'trice [adʒita'tore] *sm/f (Pol)* agitator
agitazi'one [adʒitat'tsjone] *sf* agitation; *(Pol)* unrest, agitation; **mettere in ~ qn** to upset *o* distress sb
'agli ['aʎʎi] *prep + det vedi* **a**
'aglio ['aʎʎo] *sm* garlic
a'gnello [aɲ'ɲɛllo] *sm* lamb
a'gnostico, -a, ci, che [aɲ'ɲɔstiko] *ag, sm/f* agnostic
'ago *(pl* **aghi***)* *sm* needle; ~ **da calza** knitting needle
ago. *abbr (= agosto)* Aug.
ago'nia *sf* agony

ago'nistico, -a, ci, che *ag* athletic; competitive
agoniz'zante [agonid'dzante] *ag* dy
agoniz'zare [agonid'dzare] *vi* to be d
agopun'tura *sf* acupuncture
agorafo'bia *sf* agoraphobia
a'gosto *sm* August; *vedi anche* **luglio**
a'grario, -a *ag* agrarian, agricultural; land *cpd* ■ *sm* landowner ■ *sf* agric
a'gricolo, -a *ag* agricultural, farm *cpd*
agricol'tore *sm* farmer
agricol'tura *sf* agriculture, farming
agri'foglio [agri'fɔʎʎo] *sm* holly
agrimen'sore *sm* land surveyor
agritu'rismo *sm* farm holidays *pl*
agritu'ristico, -a, ci, che *ag* farm holi
'agro, -a *ag* sour, sharp
agro'dolce [agro'doltʃe] *ag* bittersweet; *(salsa)* sweet and sour
agrono'mia *sf* agronomy
a'gronomo *sm* agronomist
a'grume *sm (spesso al pl: pianta)* citrus; *(:* citrus fruit
agru'meto *sm* citrus grove
aguz'zare [agut'tsare] *vt* to sharpen; ~ **g orecchi** to prick up one's ears; ~ **l'inge** to use one's wits
aguz'zino, -a [agud'dzino] *sm/f* jailer; *(f* tyrant
a'guzzo, -a [a'guttso] *ag* sharp
'ahi *escl (dolore)* ouch!
ahimè *escl* alas!
'ai *prep + det vedi* **a**
'Aia *sf:* **L'~** The Hague
'aia *sf* threshing floor
AIDDA *sigla f (= Associazione Imprenditrici Don Dirigenti d'Azienda) association of women entrepreneurs and managers*
AIDS ['aids] *abbr m o f* AIDS
AIE *sigla f (= Associazione Italiana degli Editori) publishers' association*
AIEA *sigla f* = **Agenzia Internazionale per l'Energia Atomica**
AIED *sigla f (= Associazione Italiana Educazione Demografica)* ≈ FPA *(= Family Planning Associati*
AIG *sigla f (= Associazione Italiana Alberghi per la Gioventù)* ≈ YHA *(Brit)*
ai'ola *sf* = **aiuola**
airbag *sm inv* air bag
AIRC *abbr f* = **Associazione Italiana per la Ricerca sul Cancro**
ai'rone *sm* heron
ai'tante *ag* robust
aiu'ola *sf* flower bed
aiu'tante *sm/f* assistant ■ *sm (Mil)* adjutant; *(Naut)* master-at-arms; ~ **di campo** aide-de-camp

ade'rire *vi (stare attaccato)* to adhere, stick; ~ **a** to adhere to, stick to; *(fig: società, partito)* to join; *(: opinione)* to support; *(richiesta)* to agree to
ades'care *vt (attirare)* to lure, entice; *(Tecn: pompa)* to prime
adesi'one *sf* adhesion; *(fig: assenso)* agreement, acceptance; *(appoggio)* support
ade'sivo, -a *ag, sm* adhesive
a'desso *av (ora)* now; *(or ora, poco fa)* just now; *(tra poco)* any moment now; **da ~ in poi** from now on; **per ~** for the moment, for now
adia'cente [adja'tʃɛnte] *ag* adjacent
adi'bire *vt (usare):* ~ **qc a** to turn sth into
'Adige ['adidʒe] *sm:* **l'~** the Adige
'adipe *sm* fat
adi'poso, -a *ag (tessuto, zona)* adipose
adi'rarsi *vr:* ~ **(con** *o* **contro qn per qc)** to get angry (with sb over sth)
adi'rato, -a *ag* angry
a'dire *vt (Dir):* ~ **le vie legali** to take legal proceedings; ~ **un'eredità** to take legal possession of an inheritance
'adito *sm:* **dare ~ a** *(sospetti)* to give rise to
adocchi'are [adok'kjare] *vt (scorgere)* to catch sight of; *(occhieggiare)* to eye
adole'scente [adoleʃ'ʃɛnte] *ag, sm/f* adolescent
adole'scenza [adoleʃ'ʃɛntsa] *sf* adolescence
adolescenzi'ale [adoleʃʃen'tsjale] *ag* adolescent
adom'brarsi *vr (cavallo)* to shy; *(persona)* to grow suspicious; *(: aversene a male)* to be offended
adope'rare *vt* to use; **adoperarsi** *vr* to strive; **adoperarsi per qn/qc** to do one's best for sb/sth
ado'rabile *ag* adorable
ado'rare *vt* to adore; *(Rel)* to adore, worship
adorazi'one [adorat'tsjone] *sf* adoration; worship
ador'nare *vt* to adorn
a'dorno, -a *ag:* ~ **(di)** adorned (with)
adot'tare *vt* to adopt; *(decisione, provvedimenti)* to pass
adot'tivo, -a *ag (genitori)* adoptive; *(figlio, patria)* adopted
adozi'one [adot'tsjone] *sf* adoption; ~ **a distanza** child sponsorship
adrena'linico, -a, ci, che *ag (fig: vivace, eccitato)* charged-up
adri'atico, -a, ci, che *ag* Adriatic ■ *sm:* **l'A~, il mare A~** the Adriatic, the Adriatic Sea
ADSL *sigla m* ADSL *(= asymmetric digital subscriber line)*
adu'lare *vt* to flatter
adula'tore, -'trice *sm/f* flatterer

adula'torio, -a *ag* flattering
adulazi'one [adulat'tsjone] *sf* flattery
adulte'rare *vt* to adulterate
adul'terio *sm* adultery
a'dultero, -a *ag* adulterous ■ *sm/f* adulterer/adulteress
a'dulto, -a *ag* adult; *(fig)* mature ■ *sm* adult, grown-up
adu'nanza [adu'nantsa] *sf* assembly, meeting
adu'nare *vt,* **adu'narsi** *vr* to assemble, gather
adu'nata *sf (Mil)* parade, muster
a'dunco, -a, chi, che *ag* hooked
aerazi'one [aerat'tsjone] *sf* ventilation; *(Tecn)* aeration
a'ereo, -a *ag* air *cpd*; *(radice)* aerial ■ *sm* aerial; *(aeroplano)* plane; ~ **da caccia** fighter (plane); ~ **di linea** airliner; ~ **a reazione** jet (plane)
ae'robica *sf* aerobics *sg*
aerodi'namico, -a, ci, che *ag* aerodynamic; *(affusolato)* streamlined ■ *sf* aerodynamics *sg*
aeromo'dello *sm* model aircraft
aero'nautica *sf (scienza)* aeronautics *sg*; ~ **militare** air force
aerona'vale *ag (forze, manovre)* air and sea *cpd*
aero'plano *sm* (aero)plane *(Brit)*, (air)plane *(US)*
aero'porto *sm* airport
aeroportu'ale *ag* airport *cpd*
aeros'calo *sm* airstrip
aero'sol *sm inv* aerosol
aerospazi'ale [aerospat'tsjale] *ag* aerospace
aeros'tatico, -a, ci, che *ag* aerostatic; **pallone ~** air balloon
ae'rostato *sm* aerostat
A.F. *abbr (= alta frequenza)* HF; *(Amm)* = **assegni familiari**
'afa *sf* sultriness
af'fabile *ag* affable
affabilità *sf* affability
affaccen'darsi [affattʃen'darsi] *vr:* ~ **intorno a qc** to busy o.s. with sth
affaccen'dato, -a [affattʃen'dato] *ag* busy
affacci'arsi [affat'tʃarsi] *vr:* ~ **(a)** to appear (at); ~ **alla vita** to come into the world
affa'mato, -a *ag* starving; *(fig):* ~ **(di)** eager (for)
affan'nare *vt* to leave breathless; *(fig)* to worry; **affannarsi** *vr:* **affannarsi per qn/qc** to worry about sb/sth
af'fanno *sm* breathlessness; *(fig)* anxiety, worry
affannosa'mente *av* with difficulty; anxiously
affan'noso, -a *ag (respiro)* difficult; *(fig)* troubled, anxious

afˈfare *sm* (*faccenda*) matter, affair; (*Comm*) piece of business, (business) deal; (*occasione*) bargain; (*Dir*) case; (*fam: cosa*) thing; **affari** *smpl* (*Comm*) business *sg*; **~ fatto!** done!, it's a deal!; **sono affari miei** that's my business; **bada agli affari tuoi!** mind your own business!; **uomo d'affari** businessman; **ministro degli Affari Esteri** Foreign Secretary (*Brit*), Secretary of State (*US*)

affaˈrista, -i *sm* profiteer, unscrupulous businessman

affasciˈnante [affaʃʃi'nante] *ag* fascinating

affasciˈnare [affaʃʃi'nare] *vt* to bewitch; (*fig*) to charm, fascinate

affaticaˈmento *sm* tiredness

affatiˈcare *vt* to tire; **affaticarsi** *vr* (*durar fatica*) to tire o.s. out

afˈfatto *av* completely; **non ... ~** not ... at all; **niente ~** not at all

afferˈmare *vi* (*dire di sì*) to say yes ■ *vt* (*dichiarare*) to maintain, affirm; **affermarsi** *vr* to assert o.s., make one's name known

affermativaˈmente *av* in the affirmative, affirmatively

affermaˈtivo, -a *ag* affirmative

afferˈmato, -a *ag* established, well-known

affermaziˈone [affermat'tsjone] *sf* affirmation, assertion; (*successo*) achievement

afferˈrare *vt* to seize, grasp; (*fig: idea*) to grasp; **afferrarsi** *vr*: **afferrarsi a** to cling to

Aff. Est. *abbr* = **Affari Esteri**

affetˈtare *vt* (*tagliare a fette*) to slice; (*ostentare*) to affect

affetˈtato, -a *ag* sliced; affected ■ *sm* sliced cold meat

affettaˈtrice [affetta'tritʃe] *sf* meat slicer

affettaziˈone [affettat'tsjone] *sf* affectation

affetˈtivo, -a *ag* emotional, affective

afˈfetto, -a *ag*: **essere ~ da** to suffer from ■ *sm* affection; **gli affetti familiari** one's nearest and dearest

affettuosaˈmente *av* affectionately; (*nelle lettere*): **(ti saluto) ~, Maria** love, Maria

affettuosità *sf inv* affection; **affettuosità** *sfpl* (*manifestazioni*) demonstrations of affection

affettuˈoso, -a *ag* affectionate

affezioˈnarsi [affettsjo'narsi] *vr*: **~ a** to grow fond of

affezioˈnato, -a [affettsjo'nato] *ag*: **~ a qn/qc** fond of sb/sth; (*attaccato*) attached to sb/sth

affeziˈone [affet'tsjone] *sf* (*affetto*) affection; (*Med*) ailment, disorder

affianˈcare *vt* to place side by side; (*Mil*) to flank; (*fig*) to support; **~ qc a qc** to place sth next to *o* beside sth; **affiancarsi** *vr*: **affiancarsi a qn** to stand beside sb

affiataˈmento *sm* understanding

affiaˈtato, -a *ag*: **essere affiatati** to work well together *o* get on; **formano una squadra affiatata** they make a good team

affibbiˈare *vt* to buckle, do up; (*fig: dare*) to give

affiˈdabile *ag* reliable

affidabilità *sf* reliability

affidaˈmento *sm* (*Dir: di bambino*) custody; (*fiducia*): **fare ~ su qn** to rely on sb; **non dà nessun ~** he's not to be trusted

affiˈdare *vt*: **~ qc** *o* **qn a qn** to entrust sth *o* sb to sb; **affidarsi** *vr*: **affidarsi a** to place one's trust in

affievoˈlirsi *vr* to grow weak

afˈfiggere [af'fiddʒere] *vt* to stick up, post up

affiˈlare *vt* to sharpen

affiˈlato, -a *ag* (*gen*) sharp; (*volto, naso*) thin

affiliˈare *vt* to affiliate; **affiliarsi** *vr*: **affiliarsi a** to become affiliated to

affiˈnare *vt* to sharpen

affinché [affin'ke] *cong* in order that, so that

afˈfine *ag* similar

affinità *sf inv* affinity

affioˈrare *vi* to emerge

afˈfissi *etc vb vedi* **affiggere**

affissiˈone *sf* billposting

afˈfisso, -a *pp di* **affiggere** ■ *sm* bill, poster; (*Ling*) affix

affittaˈcamere *sm/f inv* landlord/landlady

affitˈtare *vt* (*dare in affitto*) to let, rent (out); (*prendere in affitto*) to rent

afˈfitto *sm* rent; (*contratto*) lease; **dare in ~** to rent (out), let; **prendere in ~** to rent

affittuˈario *sm* lessee

afˈfliggere [af'fliddʒere] *vt* to torment; **affliggersi** *vr* to grieve

afˈflissi *etc vb vedi* **affliggere**

afˈflitto, -a *pp di* **affliggere**

afflizi'one [afflit'tsjone] *sf* distress, torment

affloscˈiarsi [afflo∫'∫arsi] *vr* to go limp; (*frutta*) to go soft

affluˈente *sm* tributary

affluˈenza [afflu'ɛntsa] *sf* flow; (*di persone*) crowd

affluˈire *vi* to flow; (*fig: merci, persone*) to pour in

afˈflusso *sm* influx

affoˈgare *vt, vi* to drown; **affogarsi** *vr* to drown; (*deliberatamente*) to drown o.s.

affoˈgato, -a *ag* drowned; (*Cuc: uova*) poached

affollaˈmento *sm* crowding; (*folla*) crowd

affolˈlare *vt*, **affolˈlarsi** *vr* to crowd

affolˈlato, -a *ag* crowded

affondaˈmento *sm* (*di nave*) sinking

affonˈdare *vt* to sink

[af]franˈcare *vt* to free, liberate; (*Amm*) to [r]edeem; (*lettera*) to stamp; (*: meccanicamente*) [t]o frank (*Brit*), meter (*US*); **affrancarsi** *vr* to [f]ree o.s.

[af]francaˈtrice [affranka'tritʃe] *sf* franking [m]achine (*Brit*), postage meter (*US*)

[af]francaˈtura *sf* (*di francobollo*) stamping; [f]ranking (*Brit*), metering (*US*); (*tassa di* [s]*pedizione*) postage; **~ a carico del [d]estinatario** postage paid

[af]ˈfranto, -a *ag* (*esausto*) worn out; (*abbattuto*) [o]vercome

[af]ˈfresco, -schi *sm* fresco

[a]ffretˈtare *vt* to quicken, speed up; **affrettarsi** *vr* to hurry; **affrettarsi a fare qc** to hurry *o* hasten to do sth

[a]ffretˈtato, -a *ag* (*veloce: passo, ritmo*) quick, fast; (*frettoloso: decisione*) hurried, hasty; (*: lavoro*) rushed

[a]ffronˈtare *vt* (*pericolo etc*) to face; (*assalire:* *nemico*) to confront; **affrontarsi** *vr* (*reciproco*) to confront each other

[a]fˈfronto *sm* affront, insult; **fare un ~ a qn** to insult sb

[a]ffumiˈcare *vt* to fill with smoke; to blacken with smoke; (*alimenti*) to smoke

[a]ffusoˈlato, -a *ag* tapering

afˈgano, -a *ag, sm/f* Afghan

Afˈghanistan [af'ganistan] *sm*: **l'~** Afghanistan

afˈghano, -a *ag, sm/f* = **afgano**

afoˈrisma, -i *sm* aphorism

aˈfoso, -a *ag* sultry, close

Africa *sf*: **l'~** Africa

afriˈcano, -a *ag, sm/f* African

afroasiˈatico, -a, ci, che *ag* Afro-Asian

afrodiˈsiaco, -a, ci, che *ag, sm* aphrodisiac

AG *sigla* = **Agrigento**

aˈgenda [a'dʒɛnda] *sf* diary; **~ tascabile/da tavolo** pocket/desk diary

aˈgente [a'dʒɛnte] *sm* agent; **~ di cambio** stockbroker; **~ di custodia** prison officer; **~ marittimo** shipping agent; **~ di polizia** police officer; **~ provocatore** agent provocateur; **~ delle tasse** tax inspector; **~ di vendita** sales agent; **resistente agli agenti atmosferici** weather-resistant

agenˈzia [adʒen'tsia] *sf* agency; (*succursale*) branch; **~ di collocamento** employment agency; **~ immobiliare** estate agent's (office) (*Brit*), real estate office (*US*); **A~ Internazionale per l'Energia Atomica** International Atomic Energy Agency; **~ matrimoniale** marriage bureau; **~ pubblicitaria** advertising agency; **~ di stampa** press agency; **~ viaggi** travel agency

agevoˈlare [adʒevo'lare] *vt* to facilitate, make easy

agevolaziˈone [adʒevolat'tsjone] *sf* (*facilitazione economica*) facility; **~ di pagamento** payment on easy terms; **agevolazioni creditizie** credit facilities; **agevolazioni fiscali** tax concessions

aˈgevole [a'dʒevole] *ag* easy; (*strada*) smooth

agganciˈare [aggan'tʃare] *vt* to hook up; (*Ferr*) to couple; **agganciarsi** *vr*: **agganciarsi a** to hook up to; (*fig: pretesto*) to seize on

agˈgancio [ag'gantʃo] *sm* (*Tecn*) coupling; (*fig: conoscenza*) contact

agˈgeggio [ad'dʒeddʒo] *sm* gadget, contraption

aggetˈtivo [addʒet'tivo] *sm* adjective

agghiacciante [aggjat'tʃante] *ag* (*fig*) chilling

agghiacciˈare [aggjat'tʃare] *vt* to freeze; (*fig*) to make one's blood run cold; **agghiacciarsi** *vr* to freeze

agghinˈdarsi [aggin'darsi] *vr* to deck o.s. out

aggiornaˈmento [addʒorna'mento] *sm* updating; revision; postponement; **corso di ~** refresher course

aggiorˈnare [addʒor'nare] *vt* (*opera, manuale*) to bring up-to-date; (*: rivedere*) to revise; (*listino*) to maintain, up-date; (*seduta etc*) to postpone; **aggiornarsi** *vr* to bring (*o* keep) o.s. up-to-date

aggiorˈnato, -a [addʒor'nato] *ag* up-to-date

aggioˈtaggio [addʒo'taddʒo] *sm* (*Econ*) rigging the market

aggiˈrare [addʒi'rare] *vt* to go round; (*fig: ingannare*) to trick; **aggirarsi** *vr* to wander about; **il prezzo s'aggira sul milione** the price is around the million mark

aggiudiˈcare [addʒudi'kare] *vt* to award; (*all'asta*) to knock down; **aggiudicarsi qc** to win sth

aggiˈungere [ad'dʒundʒere] *vt* to add; (*Inform* **grazie per avermi aggiunto (come amico)** thanks for the add

aggiˈunsi *etc* [ad'dʒunsi] *vb vedi* **aggiunger**

aggiˈunto, -a [ad'dʒunto] *pp di* **aggiunger** ■ *ag* assistant *cpd* ■ *sm* assistant ■ *sf* addition; **sindaco ~** deputy mayor; **in aggiunta ...** what's more ...

aggiusˈtare [addʒus'tare] *vt* (*accomodar* mend, repair; (*riassettare*) to adjust; (*f* to settle; **aggiustarsi** *vr* (*arrangiarsi*) t do; (*con senso reciproco*) to come to an agreement; **ti aggiusto io!** I'll fix y

agglomeˈrato *sm* (*di rocce*) conglom (*di legno*) chipboard; **~ urbano** buil

aggrapˈparsi *vr*: **~ a** to cling to

aggravaˈmento *sm* worsening

aggraˈvante *ag* (*Dir*) aggravatin aggravation

aggraˈvare *vt* (*aumentare*) to inc (*appesantire: anche fig*) to weigh

ade'rire *vi* (*stare attaccato*) to adhere, stick; **~ a** to adhere to, stick to; (*fig: società, partito*) to join; (*: opinione*) to support; (*richiesta*) to agree to
ades'care *vt* (*attirare*) to lure, entice; (*Tecn: pompa*) to prime
adesi'one *sf* adhesion; (*fig: assenso*) agreement, acceptance; (*appoggio*) support
ade'sivo, -a *ag, sm* adhesive
a'desso *av* (*ora*) now; (*or ora, poco fa*) just now; (*tra poco*) any moment now; **da ~ in poi** from now on; **per ~** for the moment, for now
adia'cente [adja'tʃɛnte] *ag* adjacent
adi'bire *vt* (*usare*): **~ qc a** to turn sth into
'Adige ['adidʒe] *sm*: **l'~** the Adige
'adipe *sm* fat
adi'poso, -a *ag* (*tessuto, zona*) adipose
adi'rarsi *vr*: **~ (con** *o* **contro qn per qc)** to get angry (with sb over sth)
adi'rato, -a *ag* angry
a'dire *vt* (*Dir*): **~ le vie legali** to take legal proceedings; **~ un'eredità** to take legal possession of an inheritance
'adito *sm*: **dare ~ a** (*sospetti*) to give rise to
adocchi'are [adok'kjare] *vt* (*scorgere*) to catch sight of; (*occhieggiare*) to eye
adole'scente [adoleʃ'ʃɛnte] *ag, sm/f* adolescent
adole'scenza [adoleʃ'ʃɛntsa] *sf* adolescence
adolescenzi'ale [adoleʃʃen'tsjale] *ag* adolescent
adom'brarsi *vr* (*cavallo*) to shy; (*persona*) to grow suspicious; (*: aversene a male*) to be offended
adope'rare *vt* to use; **adoperarsi** *vr* to strive; **adoperarsi per qn/qc** to do one's best for sb/sth
ado'rabile *ag* adorable
ado'rare *vt* to adore; (*Rel*) to adore, worship
adorazi'one [adorat'tsjone] *sf* adoration; worship
ador'nare *vt* to adorn
a'dorno, -a *ag*: **~ (di)** adorned (with)
adot'tare *vt* to adopt; (*decisione, provvedimenti*) to pass
adot'tivo, -a *ag* (*genitori*) adoptive; (*figlio, patria*) adopted
adozi'one [adot'tsjone] *sf* adoption; **~ a distanza** child sponsorship
adrena'linico, -a, ci, che *ag* (*fig: vivace, eccitato*) charged-up
adri'atico, -a, ci, che *ag* Adriatic ■ *sm*: **l'A~, il mare A~** the Adriatic, the Adriatic Sea
ADSL *sigla m* ADSL (= *asymmetric digital subscriber line*)
adu'lare *vt* to flatter
adula'tore, -'trice *sm/f* flatterer
adula'torio, -a *ag* flattering
adulazi'one [adulat'tsjone] *sf* flattery
adulte'rare *vt* to adulterate
adul'terio *sm* adultery
a'dultero, -a *ag* adulterous ■ *sm/f* adulterer/adulteress
a'dulto, -a *ag* adult; (*fig*) mature ■ *sm* adult, grown-up
adu'nanza [adu'nantsa] *sf* assembly, meeting
adu'nare *vt*, **adu'narsi** *vr* to assemble, gather
adu'nata *sf* (*Mil*) parade, muster
a'dunco, -a, chi, che *ag* hooked
aerazi'one [aerat'tsjone] *sf* ventilation; (*Tecn*) aeration
a'ereo, -a *ag* air *cpd*; (*radice*) aerial ■ *sm* aerial; (*aeroplano*) plane; **~ da caccia** fighter (plane); **~ di linea** airliner; **~ a reazione** jet (plane)
ae'robica *sf* aerobics *sg*
aerodi'namico, -a, ci, che *ag* aerodynamic; (*affusolato*) streamlined ■ *sf* aerodynamics *sg*
aeromo'dello *sm* model aircraft
aero'nautica *sf* (*scienza*) aeronautics *sg*; **~ militare** air force
aerona'vale *ag* (*forze, manovre*) air and sea *cpd*
aero'plano *sm* (aero)plane (*Brit*), (air)plane (*US*)
aero'porto *sm* airport
aeroportu'ale *ag* airport *cpd*
aeros'calo *sm* airstrip
aero'sol *sm inv* aerosol
aerospazi'ale [aerospat'tsjale] *ag* aerospace
aeros'tatico, -a, ci, che *ag* aerostatic; **pallone ~** air balloon
ae'rostato *sm* aerostat
A.F. *abbr* (= *alta frequenza*) HF; (*Amm*) = **assegni familiari**
'afa *sf* sultriness
af'fabile *ag* affable
affabilità *sf* affability
affaccen'darsi [affattʃen'darsi] *vr*: **~ intorno a qc** to busy o.s. with sth
affaccen'dato, -a [affattʃen'dato] *ag* busy
affacci'arsi [affat'tʃarsi] *vr*: **~ (a)** to appear (at); **~ alla vita** to come into the world
affa'mato, -a *ag* starving; (*fig*): **~ (di)** eager (for)
affan'nare *vt* to leave breathless; (*fig*) to worry; **affannarsi** *vr*: **affannarsi per qn/qc** to worry about sb/sth
af'fanno *sm* breathlessness; (*fig*) anxiety, worry
affannosa'mente *av* with difficulty; anxiously
affan'noso, -a *ag* (*respiro*) difficult; (*fig*) troubled, anxious

af'fare *sm* (*faccenda*) matter, affair; (*Comm*) piece of business, (business) deal; (*occasione*) bargain; (*Dir*) case; (*fam: cosa*) thing; **affari** *smpl* (*Comm*) business *sg*; **~ fatto!** done!, it's a deal!; **sono affari miei** that's my business; **bada agli affari tuoi!** mind your own business!; **uomo d'affari** businessman; **ministro degli Affari Esteri** Foreign Secretary (*Brit*), Secretary of State (*US*)
affa'rista, -i *sm* profiteer, unscrupulous businessman
affasci'nante [affaʃʃi'nante] *ag* fascinating
affasci'nare [affaʃʃi'nare] *vt* to bewitch; (*fig*) to charm, fascinate
affatica'mento *sm* tiredness
affati'care *vt* to tire; **affaticarsi** *vr* (*durar fatica*) to tire o.s. out
af'fatto *av* completely; **non ... ~** not ... at all; **niente ~** not at all
affer'mare *vi* (*dire di sì*) to say yes ■ *vt* (*dichiarare*) to maintain, affirm; **affermarsi** *vr* to assert o.s., make one's name known
affermativa'mente *av* in the affirmative, affirmatively
afferma'tivo, -a *ag* affirmative
affer'mato, -a *ag* established, well-known
affermazi'one [affermat'tsjone] *sf* affirmation, assertion; (*successo*) achievement
affer'rare *vt* to seize, grasp; (*fig: idea*) to grasp; **afferrarsi** *vr*: **afferrarsi a** to cling to
Aff. Est. *abbr* = **Affari Esteri**
affet'tare *vt* (*tagliare a fette*) to slice; (*ostentare*) to affect
affet'tato, -a *ag* sliced; affected ■ *sm* sliced cold meat
affetta'trice [affetta'tritʃe] *sf* meat slicer
affettazi'one [affettat'tsjone] *sf* affectation
affet'tivo, -a *ag* emotional, affective
af'fetto, -a *ag*: **essere ~ da** to suffer from ■ *sm* affection; **gli affetti familiari** one's nearest and dearest
affettuosa'mente *av* affectionately; (*nelle lettere*): **(ti saluto) ~, Maria** love, Maria
affettuosità *sf inv* affection; **affettuosità** *sfpl* (*manifestazioni*) demonstrations of affection
affettu'oso, -a *ag* affectionate
affezio'narsi [affettsjo'narsi] *vr*: **~ a** to grow fond of
affezio'nato, -a [affettsjo'nato] *ag*: **~ a qn/qc** fond of sb/sth; (*attaccato*) attached to sb/sth
affezi'one [affet'tsjone] *sf* (*affetto*) affection; (*Med*) ailment, disorder
affian'care *vt* to place side by side; (*Mil*) to flank; (*fig*) to support; **~ qc a qc** to place sth next to *o* beside sth; **affiancarsi** *vr*: **affiancarsi a qn** to stand beside sb
affiata'mento *sm* understanding
affia'tato, -a *ag*: **essere affiatati** to work well together *o* get on; **formano una squadra affiatata** they make a good team
affibbi'are *vt* to buckle, do up; (*fig: dare*) to give
affi'dabile *ag* reliable
affidabilità *sf* reliability
affida'mento *sm* (*Dir: di bambino*) custody; (*fiducia*): **fare ~ su qn** to rely on sb; **non dà nessun ~** he's not to be trusted
affi'dare *vt*: **~ qc** *o* **qn a qn** to entrust sth *o* sb to sb; **affidarsi** *vr*: **affidarsi a** to place one's trust in
affievo'lirsi *vr* to grow weak
af'figgere [af'fiddʒere] *vt* to stick up, post up
affi'lare *vt* to sharpen
affi'lato, -a *ag* (*gen*) sharp; (*volto, naso*) thin
affili'are *vt* to affiliate; **affiliarsi** *vr*: **affiliarsi a** to become affiliated to
affi'nare *vt* to sharpen
affinché [affin'ke] *cong* in order that, so that
af'fine *ag* similar
affinità *sf inv* affinity
affio'rare *vi* to emerge
af'fissi *etc vb vedi* **affiggere**
affissi'one *sf* billposting
af'fisso, -a *pp di* **affiggere** ■ *sm* bill, poster; (*Ling*) affix
affitta'camere *sm/f inv* landlord/landlady
affit'tare *vt* (*dare in affitto*) to let, rent (out); (*prendere in affitto*) to rent
af'fitto *sm* rent; (*contratto*) lease; **dare in ~** to rent (out), let; **prendere in ~** to rent
affittu'ario *sm* lessee
af'fliggere [af'fliddʒere] *vt* to torment; **affliggersi** *vr* to grieve
af'flissi *etc vb vedi* **affliggere**
af'flitto, -a *pp di* **affliggere**
afflizi'one [afflit'tsjone] *sf* distress, torment
afflosci'arsi [affloʃ'ʃarsi] *vr* to go limp; (*frutta*) to go soft
afflu'ente *sm* tributary
afflu'enza [afflu'ɛntsa] *sf* flow; (*di persone*) crowd
afflu'ire *vi* to flow; (*fig: merci, persone*) to pour in
af'flusso *sm* influx
affo'gare *vt, vi* to drown; **affogarsi** *vr* to drown; (*deliberatamente*) to drown o.s.
affo'gato, -a *ag* drowned; (*Cuc: uova*) poached
affolla'mento *sm* crowding; (*folla*) crowd
affol'lare *vt*, **affol'larsi** *vr* to crowd
affol'lato, -a *ag* crowded
affonda'mento *sm* (*di nave*) sinking
affon'dare *vt* to sink

affran'care *vt* to free, liberate; (*Amm*) to redeem; (*lettera*) to stamp; (: *meccanicamente*) to frank (*Brit*), meter (*US*); **affrancarsi** *vr* to free o.s.
affranca'trice [affranka'tritʃe] *sf* franking machine (*Brit*), postage meter (*US*)
affranca'tura *sf* (*di francobollo*) stamping; franking (*Brit*), metering (*US*); (*tassa di spedizione*) postage; **~ a carico del destinatario** postage paid
af'franto, -a *ag* (*esausto*) worn out; (*abbattuto*) overcome
af'fresco, -schi *sm* fresco
affret'tare *vt* to quicken, speed up; **affrettarsi** *vr* to hurry; **affrettarsi a fare qc** to hurry *o* hasten to do sth
affret'tato, -a *ag* (*veloce*: *passo, ritmo*) quick, fast; (*frettoloso*: *decisione*) hurried, hasty; (: *lavoro*) rushed
affron'tare *vt* (*pericolo etc*) to face; (*assalire*: *nemico*) to confront; **affrontarsi** *vr* (*reciproco*) to confront each other
af'fronto *sm* affront, insult; **fare un ~ a qn** to insult sb
affumi'care *vt* to fill with smoke; to blacken with smoke; (*alimenti*) to smoke
affuso'lato, -a *ag* tapering
af'gano, -a *ag, sm/f* Afghan
Af'ghanistan [af'ganistan] *sm*: **l'~** Afghanistan
af'ghano, -a *ag, sm/f* = **afgano**
afo'risma, -i *sm* aphorism
a'foso, -a *ag* sultry, close
'Africa *sf*: **l'~** Africa
afri'cano, -a *ag, sm/f* African
afroasi'atico, -a, ci, che *ag* Afro-Asian
afrodi'siaco, -a, ci, che *ag, sm* aphrodisiac
AG *sigla* = **Agrigento**
a'genda [a'dʒɛnda] *sf* diary; **~ tascabile/da tavolo** pocket/desk diary
a'gente [a'dʒɛnte] *sm* agent; **~ di cambio** stockbroker; **~ di custodia** prison officer; **~ marittimo** shipping agent; **~ di polizia** police officer; **~ provocatore** agent provocateur; **~ delle tasse** tax inspector; **~ di vendita** sales agent; **resistente agli agenti atmosferici** weather-resistant
agen'zia [adʒen'tsia] *sf* agency; (*succursale*) branch; **~ di collocamento** employment agency; **~ immobiliare** estate agent's (office) (*Brit*), real estate office (*US*); **A~ Internazionale per l'Energia Atomica** International Atomic Energy Agency; **~ matrimoniale** marriage bureau; **~ pubblicitaria** advertising agency; **~ di stampa** press agency; **~ viaggi** travel agency
agevo'lare [adʒevo'lare] *vt* to facilitate, make easy
agevolazi'one [adʒevolat'tsjone] *sf* (*facilitazione economica*) facility; **~ di pagamento** payment on easy terms; **agevolazioni creditizie** credit facilities; **agevolazioni fiscali** tax concessions
a'gevole [a'dʒevole] *ag* easy; (*strada*) smooth
agganci'are [aggan'tʃare] *vt* to hook up; (*Ferr*) to couple; **agganciarsi** *vr*: **agganciarsi a** to hook up to; (*fig*: *pretesto*) to seize on
ag'gancio [ag'gantʃo] *sm* (*Tecn*) coupling; (*fig*: *conoscenza*) contact
ag'geggio [ad'dʒeddʒo] *sm* gadget, contraption
agget'tivo [addʒet'tivo] *sm* adjective
agghiacciante [aggjat'tʃante] *ag* (*fig*) chilling
agghiacci'are [aggjat'tʃare] *vt* to freeze; (*fig*) to make one's blood run cold; **agghiacciarsi** *vr* to freeze
agghin'darsi [aggin'darsi] *vr* to deck o.s. out
aggiorna'mento [addʒorna'mento] *sm* updating; revision; postponement; **corso di ~** refresher course
aggior'nare [addʒor'nare] *vt* (*opera, manuale*) to bring up-to-date; (: *rivedere*) to revise; (*listino*) to maintain, up-date; (*seduta etc*) to postpone; **aggiornarsi** *vr* to bring (*o* keep) o.s. up-to-date
aggior'nato, -a [addʒor'nato] *ag* up-to-date
aggio'taggio [addʒo'taddʒo] *sm* (*Econ*) rigging the market
aggi'rare [addʒi'rare] *vt* to go round; (*fig*: *ingannare*) to trick; **aggirarsi** *vr* to wander about; **il prezzo s'aggira sul milione** the price is around the million mark
aggiudi'care [addʒudi'kare] *vt* to award; (*all'asta*) to knock down; **aggiudicarsi qc** to win sth
aggi'ungere [ad'dʒundʒere] *vt* to add; (*Inform*): **grazie per avermi aggiunto (come amico)** thanks for the add
aggi'unsi *etc* [ad'dʒunsi] *vb vedi* **aggiungere**
aggi'unto, -a [ad'dʒunto] *pp di* **aggiungere** ■ *ag* assistant *cpd* ■ *sm* assistant ■ *sf* addition; **sindaco ~** deputy mayor; **in aggiunta ...** what's more ...
aggius'tare [addʒus'tare] *vt* (*accomodare*) to mend, repair; (*riassettare*) to adjust; (*fig*: *lite*) to settle; **aggiustarsi** *vr* (*arrangiarsi*) to make do; (*con senso reciproco*) to come to an agreement; **ti aggiusto io!** I'll fix you!
agglome'rato *sm* (*di rocce*) conglomerate; (*di legno*) chipboard; **~ urbano** built-up area
aggrap'parsi *vr*: **~ a** to cling to
aggrava'mento *sm* worsening
aggra'vante *ag* (*Dir*) aggravating ■ *sf* aggravation
aggra'vare *vt* (*aumentare*) to increase; (*appesantire*: *anche fig*) to weigh down, make

heavy; (*fig: pena*) to make worse; **aggravarsi** *vr* (*fig*) to worsen, become worse
ag'gravio *sm*: **~ di costi** increase in costs
aggrazi'ato, -a [aggrat'tsjato] *ag* graceful
aggre'dire *vt* to attack, assault
aggre'gare *vt*: **~ qn a qc** to admit sb to sth; **aggregarsi** *vr* to join; **aggregarsi a** to join, become a member of
aggre'gato, -a *ag* associated ■ *sm* aggregate; **~ urbano** built-up area
aggressi'one *sf* aggression; (*atto*) attack; **~ a mano armata** armed assault
aggressività *sf* aggressiveness
aggres'sivo, -a *ag* aggressive
aggres'sore *sm* aggressor, attacker
aggrot'tare *vt*: **~ le sopracciglia** to frown
aggrovigli'are [aggroviʎ'ʎare] *vt* to tangle; **aggrovigliarsi** *vr* (*fig*) to become complicated
agguan'tare *vt* to catch, seize
aggu'ato *sm* trap; (*imboscata*) ambush; **tendere un ~ a qn** to set a trap for sb
agguer'rito, -a *ag* (*sostenitore, nemico*) fierce
agia'tezza [adʒa'tettsa] *sf* prosperity
agi'ato, -a [a'dʒato] *ag* (*vita*) easy; (*persona*) well-off, well-to-do
'agile ['adʒile] *ag* agile, nimble
agilità [adʒili'ta] *sf* agility, nimbleness
'agio ['adʒo] *sm* ease, comfort; **agi** *smpl* comforts; **mettersi a proprio ~** to make o.s. at home *o* comfortable; **dare ~ a qn di fare qc** to give sb the chance of doing sth
a'gire [a'dʒire] *vi* to act; (*esercitare un'azione*) to take effect; (*Tecn*) to work, function; **~ contro qn** (*Dir*) to take action against sb
agi'tare [adʒi'tare] *vt* (*bottiglia*) to shake; (*mano, fazzoletto*) to wave; (*fig: turbare*) to disturb; (*: incitare*) to stir (up); **agitarsi** *vr* (*mare*) to be rough; (*malato, dormitore*) to toss and turn; (*bambino*) to fidget; (*emozionarsi*) to get upset; (*Pol*) to agitate
agi'tato, -a [adʒi'tato] *ag* rough; restless; fidgety; upset, perturbed
agita'tore, -'trice [adʒita'tore] *sm/f* (*Pol*) agitator
agitazi'one [adʒitat'tsjone] *sf* agitation; (*Pol*) unrest, agitation; **mettere in ~ qn** to upset *o* distress sb
'agli ['aʎʎi] *prep + det vedi* **a**
'aglio ['aʎʎo] *sm* garlic
a'gnello [aɲ'ɲɛllo] *sm* lamb
a'gnostico, -a, ci, che [aɲ'ɲɔstiko] *ag, sm/f* agnostic
'ago (*pl* **aghi**) *sm* needle; **~ da calza** knitting needle
ago. *abbr* (= *agosto*) Aug.
ago'nia *sf* agony
ago'nistico, -a, ci, che *ag* athletic; (*fig*) competitive
agoniz'zante [agonid'dzante] *ag* dying
agoniz'zare [agonid'dzare] *vi* to be dying
agopun'tura *sf* acupuncture
agorafo'bia *sf* agoraphobia
a'gosto *sm* August; *vedi anche* **luglio**
a'grario, -a *ag* agrarian, agricultural; (*riforma*) land *cpd* ■ *sm* landowner ■ *sf* agriculture
a'gricolo, -a *ag* agricultural, farm *cpd*
agricol'tore *sm* farmer
agricol'tura *sf* agriculture, farming
agri'foglio [agri'fɔʎʎo] *sm* holly
agrimen'sore *sm* land surveyor
agritu'rismo *sm* farm holidays *pl*
agritu'ristico, -a, ci, che *ag* farm holiday *cpd*
'agro, -a *ag* sour, sharp
agro'dolce [agro'doltʃe] *ag* bittersweet; (*salsa*) sweet and sour
agrono'mia *sf* agronomy
a'gronomo *sm* agronomist
a'grume *sm* (*spesso al pl: pianta*) citrus; (*: frutto*) citrus fruit
agru'meto *sm* citrus grove
aguz'zare [agut'tsare] *vt* to sharpen; **~ gli orecchi** to prick up one's ears; **~ l'ingegno** to use one's wits
aguz'zino, -a [agud'dzino] *sm/f* jailer; (*fig*) tyrant
a'guzzo, -a [a'guttso] *ag* sharp
'ahi *escl* (*dolore*) ouch!
ahimè *escl* alas!
'ai *prep + det vedi* **a**
'Aia *sf*: **L'~** The Hague
'aia *sf* threshing floor
AIDDA *sigla f* (= *Associazione Imprenditrici Donne Dirigenti d'Azienda*) *association of women entrepreneurs and managers*
AIDS ['aids] *abbr m o f* AIDS
AIE *sigla f* (= *Associazione Italiana degli Editori*) *publishers' association*
AIEA *sigla f* = **Agenzia Internazionale per l'Energia Atomica**
AIED *sigla f* (= *Associazione Italiana Educazione Demografica*) ≈ FPA (= *Family Planning Association*)
AIG *sigla f* (= *Associazione Italiana Alberghi per la Gioventù*) ≈ YHA (*Brit*)
ai'ola *sf* = **aiuola**
airbag *sm inv* air bag
AIRC *abbr f* = **Associazione Italiana per la Ricerca sul Cancro**
ai'rone *sm* heron
ai'tante *ag* robust
aiu'ola *sf* flower bed
aiu'tante *sm/f* assistant ■ *sm* (*Mil*) adjutant; (*Naut*) master-at-arms; **~ di campo** aide-de-camp

aiu'tare *vt* to help; **~ qn (a fare)** to help sb (to do)
ai'uto *sm* help, assistance, aid; (*aiutante*) assistant; **venire in ~ di qn** to come to sb's aid; **~ chirurgo** assistant surgeon
aiz'zare [ait'tsare] *vt* to incite; **~ i cani contro qn** to set the dogs on sb
al *prep + det vedi* **a**
a.l. *abbr* = **anno luce**
'ala (*pl* **ali**) *sf* wing; **fare ~** to fall back, make way; **~ destra/sinistra** (*Sport*) right/left wing
ala'bastro *sm* alabaster
'alacre *ag* quick, brisk
alacrità *sf* promptness, speed
alam'bicco, -chi *sm* still (*Chim*)
a'lano *sm* Great Dane
a'lare *ag* wing *cpd*; **alari** *smpl* firedogs
A'laska *sf*: **l'~** Alaska
a'lato, -a *ag* winged
'alba *sf* dawn; **all'~** at dawn
alba'nese *ag, sm/f, sm* Albanian
Alba'nia *sf*: **l'~** Albania
'albatro *sm* albatross
albeggi'are [albed'dʒare] *vi, vb impers* to dawn
albe'rato, -a *ag* (*viale, piazza*) lined with trees, tree-lined
albera'tura *sf* (*Naut*) masts *pl*
alber'gare *vt* (*dare albergo*) to accommodate ■ *vi* (*poetico*) to dwell
alberga'tore, -'trice *sm/f* hotelier, hotel owner
alberghi'ero, -a [alber'gjɛro] *ag* hotel *cpd*
al'bergo, -ghi *sm* hotel; **~ diurno** *public toilets with washing and shaving facilities etc*; **~ della gioventù** youth hostel
'albero *sm* tree; (*Naut*) mast; (*Tecn*) shaft; **~ a camme** camshaft; **~ genealogico** family tree; **~ a gomiti** crankshaft; **~ maestro** mainmast; **~ di Natale** Christmas tree; **~ di trasmissione** transmission shaft
albi'cocca, -che *sf* apricot
albi'cocco, -chi *sm* apricot tree
al'bino, -a *ag, sm/f* albino
'albo *sm* (*registro*) register, roll; (*Amm*) notice board
'album *sm* album; **~ da disegno** sketch book
al'bume *sm* albumen; (*bianco d'uovo*) egg white
albu'mina *sf* albumin
'alce ['altʃe] *sm* elk
al'chimia [al'kimja] *sf* alchemy
alchi'mista, -i [alki'mista] *sm* alchemist
'alcol *sm inv* = **alcool**
alcolicità [alkolitʃi'ta] *sf* alcohol(ic) content
al'colico, -a, ci, che *ag* alcoholic ■ *sm* alcoholic drink
alco'lismo *sm* alcoholism
alco'lista, -i, e *sm/f* alcoholic
alcoliz'zato, -a [alkolid'dzato] *sm/f* alcoholic
'alcool *sm inv* alcohol; **~ denaturato** methylated spirits *pl* (*Brit*), wood alcohol (*US*); **~ etilico** ethyl alcohol; **~ metilico** methyl alcohol
alco'olico *etc vedi* **alcolico** *etc*
alco'test *sm inv* Breathalyser® (*Brit*), Breathalyzer® (*US*)
al'cova *sf* alcove
al'cuno, -a *det* (*dav sm:* **alcun** + *C, V,* **alcuno** + *s impura, gn, pn, ps, x, z; dav sf:* **alcuna** + *C,* **alcun'** + *V: nessuno*): **non ... ~** no, not any; **alcuni, e** *det pl, pron pl* some, a few; **non c'è alcuna fretta** there's no hurry, there isn't any hurry; **senza alcun riguardo** without any consideration
aldilà *sm inv*: **l'~** the next life, the after-life
alea'torio, -a *ag* (*incerto*) uncertain
aleggi'are [aled'dʒare] *vi* (*fig: profumo, sospetto*) to be in the air
Ales'sandria *sf* (*anche*: **Alessandria d'Egitto**) Alexandria
a'letta *sf* (*Tecn*) fin; tab
alet'tone *sm* (*Aer*) aileron
Aleu'tine *sfpl*: **le isole ~** the Aleutian Islands
alfa'betico, -a, ci, che *ag* alphabetical
alfa'beto *sm* alphabet
alfanu'merico, -a, ci, che *ag* alphanumeric
alfi'ere *sm* standard-bearer; (*Scacchi*) bishop
al'fine *av* finally, in the end
'alga, -ghe *sf* seaweed *no pl*, alga
'algebra ['aldʒebra] *sf* algebra
Al'geri [al'dʒeri] *sf* Algiers
Alge'ria [aldʒe'ria] *sf*: **l'~** Algeria
alge'rino, -a [aldʒe'rino] *ag, sm/f* Algerian
algo'ritmo *sm* algorithm
ALI *sigla f* (= *Associazione Librai Italiani*) *booksellers' association*
ali'ante *sm* (*Aer*) glider
'alibi *sm inv* alibi
a'lice [a'litʃe] *sf* anchovy
alie'nare *vt* (*Dir*) to transfer; (*rendere ostile*) to alienate; **alienarsi qn** to alienate sb
alie'nato, -a *ag* alienated; transferred; (*fuor di senno*) insane ■ *sm* lunatic, insane person
alienazi'one [aljenat'tsjone] *sf* alienation; transfer; insanity
ali'eno, -a *ag* (*avverso*): **~ (da)** opposed (to), averse (to) ■ *sm/f* alien
alimen'tare *vt* to feed; (*Tecn*) to feed, supply; (*fig*) to sustain ■ *ag* food *cpd*; **alimentari** *smpl* foodstuffs; (*anche*: **negozio di alimentari**) grocer's shop; **regime ~** diet
alimenta'tore *sm* (*Elettr*) feeder

alimentazi'one [alimentat'tsjone] *sf* feeding; (*cibi*) diet; **~ di fogli** (*Inform*) sheet feed
ali'mento *sm* food; **alimenti** *smpl* food *sg*; (*Dir*) alimony
a'liquota *sf* share; **~ d'imposta** tax rate; **~ minima** (*Fisco*) basic rate
alis'cafo *sm* hydrofoil
'alito *sm* breath
all. *abbr* (= *allegato*) enc., encl.
'alla *prep + det vedi* **a**
allaccia'mento [allattʃa'mento] *sm* (*Tecn*) connection
allacci'are [allat'tʃare] *vt* (*scarpe*) to tie, lace (up); (*cintura*) to do up, fasten; (*due località*) to link; (*luce, gas*) to connect; (*amicizia*) to form; **allacciarsi** *vr* (*vestito*) to fasten; **~ o allacciarsi la cintura** to fasten one's belt
allaccia'tura [allattʃa'tura] *sf* fastening
allaga'mento *sm* flooding *no pl*; flood
alla'gare *vt*, **alla'garsi** *vr* to flood
allampa'nato, -a *ag* lanky
allar'gare *vt* to widen; (*vestito*) to let out; (*aprire*) to open; (*fig: dilatare*) to extend; **allargarsi** *vr* (*gen*) to widen; (*scarpe, pantaloni*) to stretch; (*fig: problema, fenomeno*) to spread
allar'mare *vt* to alarm; **allarmarsi** *vr* to become alarmed
al'larme *sm* alarm; **mettere qn in ~** to alarm sb; **~ aereo** air-raid warning
allar'mismo *sm* scaremongering
allar'mista, -i, e *sm/f* scaremonger, alarmist
allat'tare *vt* (*donna*) to (breast-)feed; (*: animale*) to suckle; **~ artificialmente** to bottle-feed
'alle *prep + det vedi* **a**
alle'anza [alle'antsa] *sf* alliance; **A~ Democratica** (*Pol*) *moderate centre-left party*; **A~ Nazionale** (*Pol*) *party on the far right*
alle'arsi *vr* to form an alliance
alle'ato, -a *ag* allied ■ *sm/f* ally
alleg. *abbr* = **all.**
alle'gare *vt* (*accludere*) to enclose; (*Dir: citare*) to cite, adduce; (*denti*) to set on edge
alle'gato, -a *ag* enclosed ■ *sm* enclosure; (*di e-mail*) attachment; **in ~** enclosed; **in ~ Vi inviamo ...** please find enclosed ...
allegge'rire [alleddʒe'rire] *vt* to lighten, make lighter; (*fig: sofferenza*) to alleviate, lessen; (*: lavoro, tasse*) to reduce
allego'ria *sf* allegory
alle'gorico, -a, ci, che *ag* allegorical
alle'gria *sf* gaiety, cheerfulness
al'legro, -a *ag* cheerful, merry; (*un po' brillo*) merry, tipsy; (*vivace: colore*) bright ■ *sm* (*Mus*) allegro
allena'mento *sm* training
alle'nare *vt*, **alle'narsi** *vr* to train
allena'tore *sm* (*Sport*) trainer, coach
allen'tare *vt* to slacken; (*disciplina*) to relax; **allentarsi** *vr* to become slack; (*ingranaggio*) to work loose
aller'gia, -'gie [aller'dʒia] *sf* allergy
al'lergico, -a, ci, che [al'lɛrdʒiko] *ag* allergic
allesti'mento *sm* preparation, setting up; **in ~** in preparation
alles'tire *vt* (*cena*) to prepare; (*esercito, nave*) to equip, fit out; (*spettacolo*) to stage
allet'tante *ag* attractive, alluring
allet'tare *vt* to lure, entice
alleva'mento *sm* breeding, rearing; (*luogo*) stock farm; **pollo d'~** battery hen
alle'vare *vt* (*animale*) to breed, rear; (*bambino*) to bring up
alleva'tore *sm* breeder
allevi'are *vt* to alleviate
alli'bire *vi* to turn pale; (*essere turbato*) to be disconcerted
alli'bito, -a *ag* pale; disconcerted
allibra'tore *sm* bookmaker
allie'tare *vt* to cheer up, gladden
alli'evo *sm* pupil; (*apprendista*) apprentice; **~ ufficiale** cadet
alliga'tore *sm* alligator
allinea'mento *sm* alignment
alline'are *vt* (*persone, cose*) to line up; (*Tip*) to align; (*fig: economia, salari*) to adjust, align; **allinearsi** *vr* to line up; (*fig: a idee*): **allinearsi a** to come into line with
alline'ato, -a *ag* aligned, in line; **paesi non allineati** (*Pol*) non-aligned countries
'allo *prep + det vedi* **a**
allo'care *vt* to allocate
al'locco, -a, chi, che *sm/f* oaf ■ *sm* tawny owl
allocuzi'one [allokut'tsjone] *sf* address, solemn speech
al'lodola *sf* (sky)lark
alloggi'are [allod'dʒare] *vt* to accommodate ■ *vi* to live
al'loggio [al'lɔddʒo] *sm* lodging, accommodation (*Brit*), accommodations (*US*); (*appartamento*) flat (*Brit*), apartment (*US*)
allontana'mento *sm* removal; dismissal; estrangement
allonta'nare *vt* to send away, send off; (*impiegato*) to dismiss; (*pericolo*) to avert, remove; (*estraniare*) to alienate; **allontanarsi** *vr*: **allontanarsi (da)** to go away (from); (*estraniarsi*) to become estranged (from)
al'lora *av* (*in quel momento*) then ■ *cong* (*in questo caso*) well then; (*dunque*) well then, so; **la gente d'~** people then *o* in those days; **da ~ in poi** from then on; **e ~?** (*che fare?*) what now?; (*e con ciò?*) so what?

allor'ché [allor'ke] *cong* (*formale*) when, as soon as
al'loro *sm* laurel; **riposare** *o* **dormire sugli allori** to rest on one's laurels
'alluce ['allutʃe] *sm* big toe
alluci'nante [allutʃi'nante] *ag* (*scena, spettacolo*) awful, terrifying; (*fam: incredibile*) amazing
alluci'nato, -a [allutʃi'nato] *ag* terrified; (*fuori di sé*) bewildered, confused
allucinazi'one [allutʃinat'tsjone] *sf* hallucination
al'ludere *vi*: **~ a** to allude to, hint at
allu'minio *sm* aluminium (*Brit*), aluminum (*US*)
allu'naggio [allu'naddʒo] *sm* moon landing
allu'nare *vi* to land on the moon
allun'gare *vt* to lengthen; (*distendere*) to prolong, extend; (*diluire*) to water down; **allungarsi** *vr* to lengthen; (*ragazzo*) to stretch, grow taller; (*sdraiarsi*) to lie down, stretch out; **~ le mani** (*rubare*) to pick pockets; **gli allungò uno schiaffo** he took a swipe at him
al'lusi *etc vb vedi* **alludere**
allusi'one *sf* hint, allusion
al'luso, -a *pp di* **alludere**
alluvi'one *sf* flood
alma'nacco, -chi *sm* almanac
al'meno *av* at least ■ *cong*: **(se) ~** if only; **(se) ~ piovesse!** if only it would rain!
a'logeno, -a [a'lɔdʒeno] *ag*: **lampada alogena** halogen lamp
a'lone *sm* halo
al'pestre *ag* (*delle alpi*) alpine; (*montuoso*) mountainous
'Alpi *sfpl*: **le ~** the Alps
alpi'nismo *sm* mountaineering, climbing
alpi'nista, -i, e *sm/f* mountaineer, climber
al'pino, -a *ag* Alpine; mountain *cpd*; **alpini** *smpl* (*Mil*) Italian Alpine troops
al'quanto *av* rather, a little ■ *det*: **~(-a)** a certain amount of, some ■ *pron* a certain amount, some; **alquanti, e** *det pl, pron pl* several, quite a few
Al'sazia [al'sattsja] *sf* Alsace
alt *escl* halt!, stop! ■ *sm*: **dare l'~** to call a halt
alta'lena *sf* (*a funi*) swing; (*in bilico, anche fig*) seesaw
alta'mente *av* extremely, highly
al'tare *sm* altar
alte'rare *vt* to alter, change; (*cibo*) to adulterate; (*registro*) to falsify; (*persona*) to irritate; **alterarsi** *vr* to alter; (*cibo*) to go bad; (*persona*) to lose one's temper
alterazi'one [alterat'tsjone] *sf* alteration, change; adulteration; falsification; annoyance
al'terco, -chi *sm* altercation, wrangle
alter'nanza [alter'nantsa] *sf* alternation; (*Agr*) rotation
alter'nare *vt*, **alter'narsi** *vr* to alternate
alterna'tivo, -a *ag* alternative ■ *sf* alternative; **non abbiamo alternative** we have no alternative
alter'nato, -a *ag* alternate; (*Elettr*) alternating
alterna'tore *sm* alternator
al'terno, -a *ag* alternate; **a giorni alterni** on alternate days, every other day; **circolazione a targhe alterne** (*Aut*) *system of restricting vehicle use to odd/even registrations on alternate days*
al'tero, -a *ag* proud
al'tezza [al'tettsa] *sf* (*di edificio, persona*) height; (*di tessuto*) width, breadth; (*di acqua, pozzo*) depth; (*di suono*) pitch; (*Geo*) latitude; (*titolo*) highness; (*fig: nobiltà*) greatness; **essere all'~ di** to be on a level with; (*fig*) to be up to *o* equal to; **all'~ della farmacia** near the chemist's
altez'zoso, -a [altet'tsoso] *ag* haughty
al'ticcio, -a, ci, ce [al'tittʃo] *ag* tipsy
altipi'ano *sm* = **altopiano**
altiso'nante *ag* (*fig*) high-sounding, pompous
alti'tudine *sf* altitude
'alto, -a *ag* high; (*persona*) tall; (*tessuto*) wide, broad; (*sonno, acque*) deep; (*suono*) high (-pitched); (*Geo*) upper; (*: settentrionale*) northern ■ *sm* top (part) ■ *av* high; (*parlare*) aloud, loudly; **il palazzo è ~ 20 metri** the building is 20 metres high; **il tessuto è ~ 70 cm** the material is 70 cm wide; **ad alta voce** aloud; **a notte alta** in the dead of night; **in ~** up, upwards; at the top; **mani in ~!** hands up!; **dall'~ in** *o* **al basso** up and down; **degli alti e bassi** (*fig*) ups and downs; **andare a testa alta** (*fig*) to carry one's head high; **essere in ~ mare** (*fig*) to be far from a solution; **alta definizione** (*TV*) high definition; **alta fedeltà** high fidelity, hi-fi; **alta moda** haute couture; **l'A~ Medioevo** the Early Middle Ages; **l'~ Po** the upper reaches of the Po; **alta velocità** (*Ferr*) high speed rail system
altoate'sino, -a *ag* of (*o* from) the Alto Adige
alto'forno *sm* blast furnace
altolo'cato, -a *ag* of high rank, highly placed
altopar'lante *sm* loudspeaker
altopi'ano (*pl* **altipiani**) *sm* upland plain, plateau
'Alto 'Volta *sm*: **l'~** Upper Volta
altret'tanto, -a *ag, pron* as much; (*pl*) as many ■ *av* equally; **tanti auguri! — grazie, ~** all the best! — thank you, the same to you

ˈ**altri** *pron inv* (*qualcuno*) somebody; (*: in espressioni negative*) anybody; (*un'altra persona*) another (person)
altriˈmenti *av* otherwise

 PAROLA CHIAVE

ˈ**altro, -a** *det* **1** (*diverso*) other, different; **questa è un'altra cosa** that's another *o* a different thing; **passami l'altra penna** give me the other pen
2 (*supplementare*) other; **prendi un altro cioccolatino** have another chocolate; **hai avuto altre notizie?** have you had any more *o* any other news?; **hai altro pane?** have you got any more bread?
3 (*nel tempo*): **l'altro giorno** the other day; **l'altr'anno** last year; **l'altro ieri** the day before yesterday; **domani l'altro** the day after tomorrow; **quest'altro mese** next month
4: **d'altra parte** on the other hand
■ *pron* **1** (*persona, cosa diversa o supplementare*): **un altro, un'altra** another (one); **lo farà un altro** someone else will do it; **altri, e** others; **gli altri** (*la gente*) others, other people; **l'uno e l'altro** both (of them); **aiutarsi l'un l'altro** to help one another; **prendine un altro** have another (one); **da un giorno all'altro** from day to day; (*nel giro di 24 ore*) from one day to the next; (*da un momento all'altro*) any day now
2 (*sostantivato: solo maschile*) something else; (*: in espressioni interrogative*) anything else; **non ho altro da dire** I have nothing else *o* I don't have anything else to say; **desidera altro?** do you want anything else?; **più che altro** above all; **se non altro** if nothing else, at least; **tra l'altro** among other things; **ci mancherebbe altro!** that's all we need!; **non faccio altro che lavorare** I do nothing but work; **contento? — altro che!** are you pleased? — I certainly am!; *vedi anche* **senza**; **noialtri**; **voialtri**; **tutto**

altroché [altro'ke] *escl* certainly!, and how!
alˈtronde *av*: **d'~** on the other hand
alˈtrove *av* elsewhere, somewhere else
alˈtrui *ag inv* other people's ■ *sm*: **l'~** other people's belongings *pl*
altruˈismo *sm* altruism
altruˈista, -i, e *ag* altruistic ■ *sm/f* altruist
alˈtura *sf* (*rialto*) height, high ground; (*alto mare*) open sea; **pesca d'~** deep-sea fishing
aˈlunno, -a *sm/f* pupil
alveˈare *sm* hive
ˈ**alveo** *sm* riverbed
alzabandiˈera [altsaban'djera] *sm inv* (*Mil*): **l'~** the raising of the flag
alˈzare [al'tsare] *vt* to raise, lift; (*issare*) to hoist; (*costruire*) to build, erect; **alzarsi** *vr* to rise; (*dal letto*) to get up; (*crescere*) to grow tall (*o* taller); **~ le spalle** to shrug one's shoulders; **~ le carte** to cut the cards; **~ il gomito** to drink too much; **~ le mani su qn** to raise one's hand to sb; **~ i tacchi** to take to one's heels; **alzarsi in piedi** to stand up, get to one's feet; **alzarsi col piede sbagliato** to get out of bed on the wrong side
alˈzata [al'tsata] *sf* lifting, raising; **un'~ di spalle** a shrug
A.M. *abbr* = **aeronautica militare**
aˈmabile *ag* lovable; (*vino*) sweet
ˈ**AMAC** *sigla f* = **Aeronautica Militare-Aviazione Civile**
aˈmaca, -che *sf* hammock
amalgaˈmare *vt*, **amalgaˈmarsi** *vr* to amalgamate
aˈmante *ag*: **~ di** (*musica etc*) fond of ■ *sm/f* lover/mistress
amaraˈmente *av* bitterly
amaˈranto *sm* (*Bot*) love-lies-bleeding ■ *ag inv*: **color ~** reddish purple
aˈmare *vt* to love; (*amico, musica, sport*) to like
amareggiˈare [amared'dʒare] *vt* to sadden, upset; **amareggiarsi** *vr* to get upset; **amareggiarsi la vita** to make one's life a misery
amareggiˈato, -a [amared'dʒato] *ag* upset, saddened
amaˈrena *sf* sour black cherry
amaˈretto *sm* (*dolce*) macaroon; (*liquore*) *bitter liqueur made with almonds*
amaˈrezza [ama'rettsa] *sf* bitterness
aˈmaro, -a *ag* bitter ■ *sm* bitterness; (*liquore*) bitters *pl*
amaˈrognolo, -a [ama'roɲɲolo] *ag* slightly bitter
aˈmato, -a *ag* beloved, loved, dear ■ *sm/f* loved one
amaˈtore, -ˈtrice *sm/f* (*amante*) lover; (*intenditore: di vini etc*) connoisseur; (*dilettante*) amateur
aˈmazzone [a'maddzone] *sf* (*Mitologia*) Amazon; (*cavallerizza*) horsewoman; (*abito*) riding habit; **cavalcare all'~** to ride sidesaddle; **il Rio delle Amazzoni** the (river) Amazon
Amazˈzonia [amad'dzonja] *sf* Amazonia
amazˈzonico, -a, ci, che [amad'dzɔniko] *ag* Amazonian; Amazon *cpd*
ambasceˈria [ambaʃʃe'ria] *sf* embassy
ambasciˈata [ambaʃ'ʃata] *sf* embassy; (*messaggio*) message

ambascia'tore, -'trice [ambaʃʃa'tore] *sm/f* ambassador/ambassadress
ambe'due *ag inv*: **~ i ragazzi** both boys ■ *pron inv* both
ambi'destro, -a *ag* ambidextrous
ambien'tale *ag* (*temperatura*) ambient *cpd*; (*problemi, tutela*) environmental
ambienta'lismo *sm* environmentalism
ambienta'lista, -i, e *ag* environmental ■ *sm/f* environmentalist
ambien'tare *vt* to acclimatize; (*romanzo, film*) to set; **ambientarsi** *vr* to get used to one's surroundings
ambientazi'one [ambjentat'tsjone] *sf* setting
ambi'ente *sm* environment; (*fig: insieme di persone*) milieu; (*stanza*) room
ambiguità *sf inv* ambiguity
am'biguo, -a *ag* ambiguous; (*persona*) shady
am'bire *vt* (*anche: vi: ambire a*) to aspire to; **un premio molto ambito** a much sought-after prize
'ambito *sm* sphere, field
ambiva'lente *ag* ambivalent; **questo apparecchio è ~** this is a dual-purpose device
ambizi'one [ambit'tsjone] *sf* ambition
ambizi'oso, -a [ambit'tsjoso] *ag* ambitious
'ambo *ag inv* both
'ambra *sf* amber; **~ grigia** ambergris
ambu'lante *ag* travelling, itinerant
ambu'lanza [ambu'lantsa] *sf* ambulance
ambulatori'ale *ag* (*Med*) outpatients *cpd*; **operazione ~** operation as an outpatient; **visita ~** visit to the doctor's surgery (*Brit*) *o* office (*US*)
ambula'torio *sm* (*studio medico*) surgery (*Brit*), doctor's office (*US*)
'AMDI *sigla f* = **Associazione Medici Dentisti Italiani**
a'meba *sf* amoeba (*Brit*), ameba (*US*)
amenità *sf inv* pleasantness *no pl*; (*facezia*) pleasantry
a'meno, -a *ag* pleasant; (*strano*) funny, strange; (*spiritoso*) amusing
A'merica *sf*: **l'~** America; **l'~ latina** Latin America; **l'~ del sud** South America
america'nata *sf* (*peg*): **le Olimpiadi sono state una vera ~** the Olympics were a typically vulgar American extravaganza
america'nismo *sm* Americanism; (*ammirazione*) love of America
ameri'cano, -a *ag, sm/f* American
ame'tista *sf* amethyst
ami'anto *sm* asbestos
a'mica *sf vedi* **amico**
ami'chevole [ami'kevole] *ag* friendly
ami'cizia [ami'tʃittsja] *sf* friendship; **amicizie** *sfpl* (*amici*) friends; **fare ~ con qn** to make friends with sb
a'mico, -a, ci, che *sm/f* friend; (*amante*) boyfriend/girlfriend; **~ del cuore** *o* **intimo** bosom friend; **~ d'infanzia** childhood friend; (*Internet*): **aggiungere come ~** to friend
'amido *sm* starch
ammac'care *vt* (*pentola*) to dent; (*persona*) to bruise; **ammaccarsi** *vr* to bruise
ammacca'tura *sf* dent; bruise
ammaes'trare *vt* (*animale*) to train; (*persona*) to teach
ammai'nare *vt* to lower, haul down
amma'larsi *vr* to fall ill
amma'lato, -a *ag* ill, sick ■ *sm/f* sick person; (*paziente*) patient
ammali'are *vt* (*fig*) to enchant, charm
ammalia'tore, -'trice *sm/f* enchanter/enchantress
am'manco, -chi *sm* (*Econ*) deficit
ammanet'tare *vt* to handcuff
ammani'cato, -a, ammanigli'ato, -a [ammaniʎ'ʎato] *ag* (*fig*) with friends in high places
amman'sire *vt* (*animale*) to tame; (*fig: persona*) to calm down, placate
amman'tarsi *vr*: **~ di** (*persona*) to wrap o.s. in; (*fig: prato etc*) to be covered in
amma'raggio [amma'raddʒo] *sm* (sea) landing; splashdown
amma'rare *vi* (*Aer*) to make a sea landing; (*astronave*) to splash down
ammas'sare *vt* (*ammucchiare*) to amass; (*raccogliere*) to gather together; **ammassarsi** *vr* to pile up; to gather
am'masso *sm* mass; (*mucchio*) pile, heap; (*Econ*) stockpile
ammat'tire *vi* to go mad
ammaz'zare [ammat'tsare] *vt* to kill; **ammazzarsi** *vr* (*uccidersi*) to kill o.s.; (*rimanere ucciso*) to be killed; **ammazzarsi di lavoro** to work o.s. to death
am'menda *sf* amends *pl*; (*Dir, Sport*) fine; **fare ~ di qc** to make amends for sth
am'messo, -a *pp di* **ammettere** ■ *cong*: **~ che** supposing that
am'mettere *vt* to admit; (*riconoscere: fatto*) to acknowledge, admit; (*permettere*) to allow, accept; (*supporre*) to suppose; **ammettiamo che ...** let us suppose that ...
ammez'zato [ammed'dzato] *sm* (*anche*: **piano ammezzato**) entresol, mezzanine
ammic'care *vi*: **~ (a)** to wink (at)
amminis'trare *vt* to run, manage; (*Rel, Dir*) to administer
amministra'tivo, -a *ag* administrative

amministra'tore *sm* administrator; (*Comm*) director; **~ aggiunto** associate director; **~ delegato** managing director; **~ fiduciario** trustee; **~ unico** sole director
amministrazi'one [amministrat'tsjone] *sf* management; administration; **consiglio d'~** board of directors; **l'~ comunale** local government; **~ fiduciaria** trust
ammi'raglia [ammi'raʎʎa] *sf* flagship
ammiragli'ato [ammiraʎ'ʎato] *sm* admiralty
ammi'raglio [ammi'raʎʎo] *sm* admiral
ammi'rare *vt* to admire
ammira'tore, -'trice *sm/f* admirer
ammirazi'one [ammirat'tsjone] *sf* admiration
am'misi *etc vb vedi* **ammettere**
ammis'sibile *ag* admissible, acceptable
ammissi'one *sf* admission; (*approvazione*) acknowledgment
Amm.ne *abbr* = **amministrazione**
ammobili'are *vt* to furnish
ammobili'ato, -a *ag* (*camera, appartamento*) furnished
ammoder'nare *vt* to modernize
am'modo, a'modo *av* properly *ag inv* respectable, nice
ammogli'are [ammoʎ'ʎare] *vt* to find a wife for; **ammogliarsi** *vr* to marry, take a wife
am'mollo *sm*: **lasciare in ~** to leave to soak
ammo'niaca *sf* ammonia
ammoni'mento *sm* warning; admonishment
ammo'nire *vt* (*avvertire*) to warn; (*rimproverare*) to admonish; (*Dir*) to caution
ammonizi'one [ammonit'tsjone] *sf* (*monito: anche Sport*) warning; (*rimprovero*) reprimand; (*Dir*) caution
ammon'tare *vi*: **~ a** to amount to ▪ *sm* (total) amount
ammonticchi'are [ammontik'kjare] *vt* to pile up, heap up
ammor'bare *vt* (*diffondere malattia*) to infect; (*odore*) to taint, foul
ammorbi'dente *sm* fabric softener
ammorbi'dire *vt* to soften
ammorta'mento *sm* redemption; amortization; **~ fiscale** capital allowance
ammor'tare *vt* (*Finanza: debito*) to pay off, redeem; (*: spese d'impianto*) to write off
ammortiz'zare [ammortid'dzare] *vt* (*Finanza*) to pay off, redeem; (*: spese d'impianto*) to write off; (*Aut, Tecn*) to absorb, deaden
ammortizza'tore [ammortiddza'tore] *sm* (*Aut, Tecn*) shock absorber
ammucchi'are [ammuk'kjare] *vt*, **ammucchi'arsi** *vr* to pile up, accumulate
ammuf'fire *vi* to go mouldy (*Brit*) *o* moldy (*US*)
ammutina'mento *sm* mutiny
ammuti'narsi *vr* to mutiny
ammuti'nato, -a *ag* mutinous ▪ *sm* mutineer
ammuto'lire *vi* to be struck dumb
amne'sia *sf* amnesia
amnis'tia *sf* amnesty
'amo *sm* (*Pesca*) hook; (*fig*) bait
amo'rale *ag* amoral
a'more *sm* love; **amori** *smpl* love affairs; **il tuo bambino è un ~** your baby's a darling; **fare l'~** *o* **all'~** to make love; **andare d'~ e d'accordo con qn** to get on like a house on fire with sb; **per ~ o per forza** by hook or by crook; **amor proprio** self-esteem, pride
amoreggi'are [amored'dʒare] *vi* to flirt
amo'revole *ag* loving, affectionate
a'morfo, -a *ag* amorphous; (*fig: persona*) lifeless
amo'rino *sm* cupid
amo'roso, -a *ag* (*affettuoso*) loving, affectionate; (*d'amore: sguardo*) amorous; (*: poesia, relazione*) love *cpd*
am'pere ['pɛr] *sm inv* amp(ère)
ampi'ezza [am'pjettsa] *sf* width, breadth; spaciousness; (*fig: importanza*) scale, size; **~ di vedute** broad-mindedness
'ampio, -a *ag* wide, broad; (*spazioso*) spacious; (*abbondante: vestito*) loose; (*: gonna*) full; (*: spiegazione*) ample, full
am'plesso *sm* (*sessuale*) intercourse
amplia'mento *sm* (*di strada*) widening; (*di aeroporto*) expansion; (*fig*) broadening
ampli'are *vt* (*allargare*) to widen; (*fig: discorso*) to enlarge on; **ampliarsi** *vr* to grow, increase; **~ la propria cultura** to broaden one's mind
amplifi'care *vt* to amplify; (*magnificare*) to extol
amplifica'tore *sm* (*Tecn, Mus*) amplifier
amplificazi'one [amplifikat'tsjone] *sf* amplification
am'polla *sf* (*vasetto*) cruet
ampol'loso, -a *ag* bombastic, pompous
ampu'tare *vt* (*Med*) to amputate
amputazi'one [amputat'tsjone] *sf* amputation
'Amsterdam *sf* Amsterdam
amu'leto *sm* lucky charm
AN *sigla* = **Ancona**
A.N. *sigla f* (*Pol*) = **Alleanza Nazionale**
anabbagli'ante [anabbaʎ'ʎante] *ag* (*Aut*) dipped (*Brit*), dimmed (*US*); **anabbaglianti** *smpl* dipped *or* dimmed headlights
anaboliz'zante [anabolid'dzante] *sm* anabolic steroid ▪ *ag* anabolic
anacro'nismo *sm* anachronism

a'nagrafe *sf* (*registro*) register of births, marriages and deaths; (*ufficio*) registry office (*Brit*), office of vital statistics (*US*)
ana'grafico, -a, ci, che *ag* (*Amm*): **dati anagrafici** personal data; **comune di residenza anagrafica** district where resident
ana'gramma, -i *sm* anagram
anal'colico, -a, ci, che *ag* non-alcoholic ■ *sm* soft drink; **bevanda analcolica** soft drink
a'nale *ag* anal
analfa'beta, -i, e *ag, sm/f* illiterate
analfabe'tismo *sm* illiteracy
anal'gesico, -a, ci, che [anal'dʒɛziko] *ag, sm* analgesic
a'nalisi *sf inv* analysis; (*Med: esame*) test; **in ultima ~** in conclusion, in the final analysis; **~ grammaticale** parsing; **~ del sangue** blood test; **~ dei sistemi/costi** systems/cost analysis
ana'lista, -i, e *sm/f* analyst; (*Psic*) (psycho)analyst; **~ finanziario** financial analyst; **~ di sistemi** systems analyst
ana'litico, -a, ci, che *ag* analytic(al)
analiz'zare [analid'dzare] *vt* to analyse (*Brit*), analyze (*US*); (*Med*) to test
analo'gia, -'gie [analo'dʒia] *sf* analogy
ana'logico, -a, ci, che [ana'lɔdʒiko] *ag* analogical; (*calcolatore, orologio*) analog(ue)
a'nalogo, -a, ghi, ghe *ag* analogous
'ananas *sm inv* pineapple
anar'chia [anar'kia] *sf* anarchy
a'narchico, -a, ci, che [a'narkiko] *ag* anarchic(al) ■ *sm/f* anarchist
anarco-insurreziona'lista [anarko,insurrettsjona'lista] *ag* anarcho-revolutionary
'A.N.A.S. *sigla f* (= *Azienda Nazionale Autonoma delle Strade*) *national roads department*
ana'tema, -i *sm* anathema
anato'mia *sf* anatomy
ana'tomico, -a, ci, che *ag* anatomical; (*sedile*) contoured
'anatra *sf* duck; **~ selvatica** mallard
ana'troccolo *sm* duckling
'ANCA *sigla f* = **Associazione Nazionale Cooperative Agricole**
'anca, -che *sf* (*Anat*) hip; (*Zool*) haunch
ANCC *sigla f* = **Associazione Nazionale Carabinieri**
'anche ['anke] *cong* also; (*perfino*) even; **vengo anch'io!** I'm coming too!; **~ se** even if; **~ volendo, non finiremmo in tempo** even if we wanted to, we wouldn't finish in time
ancheggi'are [anked'dʒare] *vi* to wiggle (one's hips)
anchilo'sato, -a [ankilo'zato] *ag* stiff
'ANCI ['antʃi] *sigla f* (= *Associazione Nazionale dei Comuni Italiani*) *national confederation of local authorities*
ancone'tano, -a *ag* of (*o* from) Ancona
an'cora *av* still; (*di nuovo*) again; (*di più*) some more; (*persino*): **~ più forte** even stronger; **non ~** not yet; **~ una volta** once more, once again; **~ un po'** a little more; (*di tempo*) a little longer
'ancora *sf* anchor; **gettare/levare l'~** to cast/weigh anchor; **~ di salvezza** (*fig*) last hope
anco'raggio [anko'raddʒo] *sm* anchorage
anco'rare *vt*, **anco'rarsi** *vr* to anchor
ANCR *sigla f* (= *Associazione Nazionale Combattenti e Reduci*) *servicemen's and ex-servicemen's association*
Andalu'sia *sf*: **l'~** Andalusia
anda'luso, -a *ag, sm/f* Andalusian
anda'mento *sm* (*di strada, malattia*) course; (*del mercato*) state
an'dante *ag* (*corrente*) current; (*di poco pregio*) cheap, second-rate ■ *sm* (*Mus*) andante
an'dare *sm*: **a lungo ~** in the long run; **con l'andar del tempo** with the passing of time; **racconta storie a tutto ~** she's forever talking rubbish ■ *vi* (*gen*) to go; (*essere adatto*): **~ a** to suit; (*piacere*): **il suo comportamento non mi va** I don't like the way he behaves; **ti va di ~ al cinema?** do you feel like going to the cinema?; **~ a cavallo** to ride; **~ in macchina/aereo** to go by car/plane; **~ a fare qc** to go and do sth; **~ a pescare/sciare** to go fishing/skiing; **andarsene** to go away; **vado e vengo** I'll be back in a minute; **~ per i 50** (*età*) to be getting on for 50; **~ a male** to go bad; **~ fiero di qc/qn** to be proud of sth/sb; **~ perduto** to be lost; **come va?** (*lavoro, progetto*) how are things?; **come va? — bene, grazie!** how are you? — fine, thanks!; **va fatto entro oggi** it's got to be done today; **ne va della nostra vita** our lives are at stake; **se non vado errato** if I'm not mistaken; **le mele vanno molto** apples are selling well; **va da sé** (*è naturale*) it goes without saying; **per questa volta vada** let's say no more about it this time
an'data *sf* (*viaggio*) outward journey; **biglietto di sola ~** single (*Brit*) *o* one-way ticket; **biglietto di ~ e ritorno** return (*Brit*) *o* round-trip (*US*) ticket
anda'tura *sf* (*modo di andare*) walk, gait; (*Sport*) pace; (*Naut*) tack
an'dazzo [an'dattso] *sm* (*peg*): **prendere un brutto ~** to take a turn for the worse
'Ande *sfpl*: **le ~** the Andes
an'dino, -a *ag* Andean

andirivi'eni *sm inv* coming and going
'andito *sm* corridor, passage
An'dorra *sf* Andorra
andrò *etc vb vedi* **andare**
an'drone *sm* entrance hall
a'neddoto *sm* anecdote
ane'lare *vi*: **~ a** *(fig)* to long for, yearn for
a'nelito *sm (fig)*: **~ di** longing *o* yearning for
a'nello *sm* ring; *(di catena)* link
ane'mia *sf* anaemia *(Brit)*, anemia *(US)*
a'nemico, -a, ci, che *ag* anaemic *(Brit)*, anemic *(US)*
a'nemone *sm* anemone
aneste'sia *sf* anaesthesia *(Brit)*, anesthesia *(US)*
aneste'sista, -i, e *sm/f* anaesthetist *(Brit)*, anesthetist *(US)*
anes'tetico, -a, ci, che *ag, sm* anaesthetic *(Brit)*, anesthetic *(US)*
anestetiz'zare [anestetid'dzare] *vt* to anaesthetize *(Brit)*, anesthetize *(US)*
anfeta'mina *sf* amphetamine
anfeta'minico, -a, ci, che *ag (fig)* hyper
an'fibio, -a *ag* amphibious ■ *sm* amphibian; *(Aut)* amphibious vehicle
anfite'atro *sm* amphitheatre *(Brit)*, amphitheater *(US)*
anfitri'one *sm* host
'anfora *sf* amphora
an'fratto *sm* ravine
an'gelico, -a, ci, che [an'dʒɛliko] *ag* angelic(al)
'angelo ['andʒelo] *sm* angel; **~ custode** guardian angel; **l'~ del focolare** *(fig)* the perfect housewife
anghe'ria [ange'ria] *sf* vexation
an'gina [an'dʒina] *sf* tonsillitis; **~ pectoris** angina
angli'cano, -a *ag* Anglican
angli'cismo [angli'tʃizmo] *sm* anglicism
an'glofilo, -a *ag* anglophilic ■ *sm/f* anglophile
anglo'sassone *ag* Anglo-Saxon
An'gola *sf*: **l'~** Angola
ango'lano, -a *ag, sm/f* Angolan
ango'lare *ag* angular
angolazi'one [angolat'tsjone] *sf (di angolo)* angulation; *(Fot, Cine, TV, fig)* angle
'angolo *sm* corner; *(Mat)* angle; **~ cottura** *(di appartamento etc)* cooking area; **fare ~ con** *(strada)* to run into; **dietro l'~** *(anche fig)* round the corner
ango'loso, -a *ag (oggetto)* angular; *(volto, corpo)* angular, bony
'angora *sf*: **lana d'~** angora
an'goscia, -sce [an'gɔʃʃa] *sf* deep anxiety, anguish *no pl*
angosci'are [angoʃ'ʃare] *vt* to cause anguish to; **angosciarsi** *vr*: **angosciarsi (per)** *(preoccuparsi)* to become anxious (about); *(provare angoscia)* to get upset (about *o* over)
angosci'oso, -a [angoʃ'ʃoso] *ag (d'angoscia)* anguished; *(che dà angoscia)* distressing, painful
angu'illa *sf* eel
an'guria *sf* watermelon
an'gustia *sf (ansia)* anguish, distress; *(povertà)* poverty, want
angusti'are *vt* to distress; **angustiarsi** *vr*: **angustiarsi (per)** to worry (about)
an'gusto, -a *ag (stretto)* narrow; *(fig)* mean, petty
'anice ['anitʃe] *sm (Cuc)* aniseed; *(Bot)* anise; *(liquore)* anisette
ani'dride *sf (Chim)*: **~ carbonica/solforosa** carbon/sulphur dioxide
'anima *sf* soul; *(abitante)* inhabitant; **~ gemella** soul mate; **un'~ in pena** *(anche fig)* a tormented soul; **non c'era ~ viva** there wasn't a living soul; **volere un bene dell'~ a qn** to be extremely fond of sb; **rompere l'~ a qn** to drive sb mad; **il nonno buon'~ ...** Grandfather, God rest his soul ...
ani'male *sm, ag* animal
anima'lesco, -a, schi, sche *ag (gesto, atteggiamento)* animal-like
anima'lista, -i, e *ag* animal rights *cpd* ■ *sm/f* animal rights activist
ani'mare *vt* to give life to, liven (up); *(incoraggiare)* to encourage; **animarsi** *vr* to become animated, come to life
ani'mato, -a *ag* animate; *(vivace)* lively, animated; (: *strada)* busy
anima'tore, -'trice *sm/f* guiding spirit; *(Cine)* animator; *(di festa)* life and soul
animazi'one [animat'tsjone] *sf* liveliness; *(di strada)* bustle; *(Cine)* animation; **~ teatrale** amateur dramatics
'animo *sm (mente)* mind; *(cuore)* heart; *(coraggio)* courage; *(disposizione)* character, disposition; **avere in ~ di fare qc** to intend *o* have a mind to do sth; **farsi ~** to pluck up courage; **fare qc di buon/mal ~** to do sth willingly/unwillingly; **perdersi d'~** to lose heart
animosità *sf* animosity
A'NITA *sigla f* = **Associazione Naturista Italiana**
'anitra *sf* = **anatra**
'Ankara *sf* Ankara
ANM *sigla f (= Associazione Nazionale dei Magistrati) national association of Magistrates*
anna'cquare *vt* to water down, dilute
annaffi'are *vt* to water

annaffia'toio *sm* watering can
an'nali *smpl* annals
annas'pare *vi* (*nell'acqua*) to flounder; (*fig: nel buio, nell'incertezza*) to grope
an'nata *sf* year; (*importo annuo*) annual amount; **vino di ~** vintage wine
annebbi'are *vt* (*fig*) to cloud; **annebbiarsi** *vr* to become foggy; (*vista*) to become dim
annega'mento *sm* drowning
anne'gare *vt, vi* to drown; **annegarsi** *vr* (*accidentalmente*) to drown; (*deliberatamente*) to drown o.s.
anne'rire *vt* to blacken ■ *vi* to become black
annessi'one *sf* (*Pol*) annexation
an'nesso, -a *pp di* **annettere** ■ *ag* attached; (*Pol*) annexed; **... e tutti gli annessi e connessi** ... and so on and so forth
an'nettere *vt* (*Pol*) to annex; (*accludere*) to attach
annichi'lire [anniki'lire] *vt* to annihilate
anni'darsi *vr* to nest
annienta'mento *sm* annihilation, destruction
annien'tare *vt* to annihilate, destroy
anniver'sario *sm* anniversary
'anno *sm* year; **quanti anni hai? — ho 40 anni** how old are you? — I'm 40 (years old); **gli anni 20** the 20s; **porta bene gli anni** she doesn't look her age; **porta male gli anni** she looks older than she is; **~ commerciale** business year; **~ giudiziario** legal year; **~ luce** light year; **gli anni di piombo** *the Seventies in Italy, characterized by terrorist attacks and killings*
anno'dare *vt* to knot, tie; (*fig: rapporto*) to form
annoi'are *vt* to bore; (*seccare*) to annoy; **annoiarsi** *vr* to be bored; to be annoyed
an'noso, -a *ag* (*albero*) old; (*fig: problema etc*) age-old
anno'tare *vt* (*registrare*) to note, note down (*Brit*); (*commentare*) to annotate
annotazi'one [annotat'tsjone] *sf* note; annotation
annove'rare *vt* to number
annu'ale *ag* annual
annual'mente *av* annually, yearly
annu'ario *sm* yearbook
annu'ire *vi* to nod; (*acconsentire*) to agree
annulla'mento *sm* annihilation, destruction; cancellation; annulment; quashing
annul'lare *vt* to annihilate, destroy; (*contratto, francobollo*) to cancel; (*matrimonio*) to annul; (*sentenza*) to quash; (*risultati*) to declare void
annunci'are [annun'tʃare] *vt* to announce; (*dar segni rivelatori*) to herald
annuncia'tore, -'trice [annuntʃa'tore] *sm/f* (*Radio, TV*) announcer
Annunciazi'one [annuntʃat'tsjone] *sf* (*Rel*): **l'~** the Annunciation
an'nuncio [an'nuntʃo] *sm* announcement; (*fig*) sign; **~ pubblicitario** advertisement; **annunci economici** classified advertisements, small ads; **piccoli annunci** small ads, classified ads; **annunci mortuari** (*colonna*) obituary column
'annuo, -a *ag* annual, yearly
annu'sare *vt* to sniff, smell; **~ tabacco** to take snuff
annuvola'mento *sm* clouding (over)
annuvo'lare *vt* to cloud; **annuvolarsi** *vr* to become cloudy, cloud over
'ano *sm* anus
'anodo *sm* anode
anoma'lia *sf* anomaly
a'nomalo, -a *ag* anomalous
anoni'mato *sm* anonymity; **conservare l'~** to remain anonymous
a'nonimo, -a *ag* anonymous ■ *sm* (*autore*) anonymous writer (*o* painter *etc*); **un tipo ~** (*peg*) a colourless (*Brit*) *o* colorless (*US*) character
anores'sia *sf* anorexia; **~ nervosa** anorexia nervosa
ano'ressico, -a, ci, che *ag* anorexic
anor'male *ag* abnormal ■ *sm/f* subnormal person; (*eufemismo*) homosexual
anormalità *sf inv* abnormality
'ANSA *sigla f* (= *Agenzia Nazionale Stampa Associata*) *national press agency*
'ansa *sf* (*manico*) handle; (*di fiume*) bend, loop
an'sante *ag* out of breath, panting
'ANSEA *sigla f* (= *Associazione delle Nazioni del Sud-Est asiatico*) ASEAN
'ansia *sf* anxiety; **stare in ~ (per qn/qc)** to be anxious (about sb/sth)
ansietà *sf* anxiety
ansi'mare *vi* to pant
ansi'oso, -a *ag* anxious
'anta *sf* (*di finestra*) shutter; (*di armadio*) door
antago'nismo *sm* antagonism
antago'nista, -i, e *sm/f* antagonist
an'tartico, -a, ci, che *ag* Antarctic ■ *sm*: **l'A~** the Antarctic
An'tartide *sf*: **l'~** Antarctica
ante'bellico, -a, ci, che *ag* prewar *cpd*
antece'dente [antetʃe'dɛnte] *ag* preceding, previous
ante'fatto *sm* previous events *pl*; previous history
ante'guerra *sm* pre-war period
ante'nato *sm* ancestor, forefather

an'tenna *sf* (*Radio, TV*) aerial; (*Zool*) antenna, feeler; **rizzare le antenne** (*fig*) to prick up one's ears; **~ parabolica** (*TV*) satellite dish
ante'porre *vt*: **~ qc a qc** to place *o* put sth before sth
ante'posto, -a *pp di* **anteporre**
ante'prima *sf* preview; **~ di stampa** (*Inform*) print preview
anteri'ore *ag* (*ruota, zampa*) front *cpd*; (*fatti*) previous, preceding
antesi'gnano [antesiɲ'ɲano] *sm* (*Storia*) standard-bearer; (*fig*) forerunner
antiade'rente *ag* non-stick
antia'ereo, -a *ag* anti-aircraft *cpd*
antial'lergico, -a [antial'lɛrdʒiko] *ag, sm* hypoallergenic
antia'tomico, -a, ci, che *ag* anti-nuclear; **rifugio ~** fallout shelter
antibi'otico, -a, ci, che *ag, sm* antibiotic
anti'caglia [anti'kaʎʎa] *sf* junk *no pl*
antical'care *ag* (*prodotto, detersivo*) anti-limescale
anti'camera *sf* anteroom; **fare ~** to be kept waiting; **non mi passerebbe neanche per l'~ del cervello** it wouldn't even cross my mind
anti'carie *ag inv* which fights tooth decay
antichità [antiki'ta] *sf inv* antiquity; (*oggetto*) antique
antici'clone [antitʃi'klone] *sm* anticyclone
antici'pare [antitʃi'pare] *vt* (*consegna, visita*) to bring forward, anticipate; (*somma di denaro*) to pay in advance; (*notizia*) to disclose ■ *vi* to be ahead of time
antici'pato, -a [antitʃi'pato] *ag* (*prima del previsto*) early; **pagamento ~** payment in advance
anticipazi'one [antiʃipat'tsjone] *sf* anticipation; (*di notizia*) advance information; (*somma di denaro*) advance
an'ticipo [an'titʃipo] *sm* anticipation; (*di denaro*) advance; **in ~** early, in advance; **con un sensibile ~** well in advance
anti'clan *ag inv* (*magistrato, processo*) anti-Mafia
an'tico, -a, chi, che *ag* (*quadro, mobili*) antique; (*dell'antichità*) ancient; **all'antica** old-fashioned
anticoncezio'nale [antikontʃettsjo'nale] *sm* contraceptive
anticonfor'mista, -i, e *ag, sm/f* nonconformist
anticonge'lante [antikondʒe'lante] *ag, sm* antifreeze
anticongiuntu'rale [antikondʒuntu'rale] *ag* (*Econ*): **misure anticongiunturali** measures to remedy the economic situation
anti'corpo *sm* antibody
anticostituzio'nale [antikostituttsjo'nale] *ag* unconstitutional
antidepres'sivo, -a *ag, sm* antidepressant
antidiluvi'ano, -a *ag* (*fig: antiquato*) ancient
antidolo'rifico, -ci *sm* painkiller
anti'doping *sm inv* (*Sport*) dope test ■ *ag inv* drug testing; **test ~** drugs (*Brit*) *o* drug (*US*) test
an'tidoto *sm* antidote
anti'droga *ag inv* anti-drugs *cpd*
antie'stetico, -a, ci, che *ag* unsightly
an'tifona *sf* (*Mus, Rel*) antiphon; **capire l'~** (*fig*) to take the hint
anti'forfora *ag inv* anti-dandruff
anti'furto *sm* anti-theft device
anti'gelo [anti'dʒɛlo] *ag inv* antifreeze *cpd* ■ *sm* (*per motore*) antifreeze; (*per cristalli*) de-icer
an'tigene [an'tidʒene] *sm* antigen
antigi'enico, -a, ci, che [anti'dʒɛniko] *ag* unhygienic
antiglobalizza'zione [antiglobaliddza'tsjone] *ag* anti-globalization
An'tille *sfpl*: **le ~** the West Indies
an'tilope *sf* antelope
anti'mafia *ag inv* anti-mafia *cpd*
antin'cendio [antin'tʃɛndjo] *ag inv* fire *cpd*; **bombola ~** fire extinguisher
anti'nebbia *sm inv* (*anche*: **faro antinebbia**: *Aut*) fog lamp
antine'vralgico, -a, ci, che [antine'vraldʒiko] *ag* painkilling ■ *sm* painkiller
antin'fiammatorio, -a *ag, sm* anti-inflammatory
antio'rario *ag*: **in senso ~** in an anticlockwise (*Brit*) *o* counterclockwise (*US*) direction, anticlockwise, counterclockwise
anti'pasto *sm* hors d'œuvre
antipa'tia *sf* antipathy, dislike
anti'patico, -a, ci, che *ag* unpleasant, disagreeable
anti'placca *ag inv* (*dentifricio*) anti-plaque
an'tipodi *smpl*: **essere agli ~** (*fig: di idee opposte*) to be poles apart
antipro'iettile *ag inv* bulletproof
antiquari'ato *sm* antique trade; **un pezzo d'~** an antique
anti'quario *sm* antique dealer
anti'quato, -a *ag* antiquated, old-fashioned
antirici'claggio [antiritʃi'kladdʒo] *ag* (*attività, operazioni*) anti-laundering
antiri'flesso *ag inv* (*schermo*) non-glare *cpd*
anti'ruggine [anti'ruddʒine] *ag* anti-rust *cpd* ■ *sm inv* rust-preventer
anti'rughe [anti'ruge] *ag inv* anti-wrinkle
antise'mita, -i, e *ag* anti-semitic

antisemi'tismo *sm* anti-semitism
anti'settico, -a, ci, che *ag, sm* antiseptic
antista'minico, -a, ci, che *ag, sm* antihistamine
anti'stante *ag* opposite
anti'tartaro *ag inv* anti-tartar
antiterro'rismo *sm* anti-terrorist measures *pl*
an'titesi *sf* antithesis
antitraspi'rante *ag* antiperspirant
anti'vipera *ag inv*: **siero ~** remedy for snake bites
antivi'rale *adj* antiviral
anti'virus [anti'virus] *sm inv* antivirus software *no pl*
antolo'gia, -'gie [antolo'dʒia] *sf* anthology
antono'masia *sf* antonomasia; **per ~** par excellence
antra'cite [antra'tʃite] *sf* anthracite
'antro *sm* cavern
antro'pofago, -gi *sm* cannibal
antropolo'gia [antropolo'dʒia] *sf* anthropology
antropo'logico, -a, ci, che [antropo'lɔdʒiko] *ag* anthropological
antro'pologo, -a, gi, ghe *sm/f* anthropologist
anu'lare *ag* ring *cpd* ■ *sm* ring finger
An'versa *sf* Antwerp
'anzi ['antsi] *av* (*invece*) on the contrary; (*o meglio*) or rather, or better still
anzianità [antsjani'ta] *sf* old age; (*Amm*) seniority
anzi'ano, -a [an'tsjano] *ag* old; (*Amm*) senior ■ *sm/f* old person; senior member
anziché [antsi'ke] *cong* rather than
anzi'tempo [antsi'tɛmpo] *av* (*in anticipo*) early
anzi'tutto [antsi'tutto] *av* first of all
AO *sigla* = **Aosta**
a'orta *sf* aorta
aos'tano, -a *ag* of (*o* from) Aosta
AP *sigla* = **Ascoli Piceno**
apar'titico, -a, ci, che *ag* (*Pol*) non-party *cpd*
apa'tia *sf* apathy, indifference
a'patico, -a, ci, che *ag* apathetic, indifferent
a.p.c. *abbr* = **a pronta cassa**
'ape *sf* bee
aperi'tivo *sm* apéritif
aperta'mente *av* openly
a'perto, -a *pp di* **aprire** ■ *ag* open ■ *sm*: **all'~** in the open (air); **rimanere a bocca aperta** (*fig*) to be taken aback
aper'tura *sf* opening; (*ampiezza*) width, spread; (*Pol*) approach; (*Fot*) aperture; **~ alare** wing span; **~ mentale** open-mindedness; **~ di credito** (*Comm*) granting of credit
API *sigla f* = **Associazione Piccole e Medie Industrie**
'apice ['apitʃe] *sm* apex; (*fig*) height
apicol'tore *sm* beekeeper
apicol'tura *sf* beekeeping
ap'nea *sf*: **immergersi in ~** to dive without breathing apparatus
apoca'lisse *sf* apocalypse
apo'geo [apo'dʒɛo] *sm* (*Astr*) apogee; (*fig: culmine*) zenith
a'polide *ag* stateless
apo'litico, -a, ci, che *ag* (*neutrale*) nonpolitical; (*indifferente*) apolitical
apolo'gia, -gie [apolo'dʒia] *sf* (*difesa*) apologia; (*esaltazione*) praise; **~ di reato** attempt to defend criminal acts
apoples'sia *sf* (*Med*) apoplexy
apop'lettico, -a, ci, che *ag* apoplectic; **colpo ~** apoplectic fit
a'postolo *sm* apostle
apostro'fare *vt* (*parola*) to write with an apostrophe; (*persona*) to address
a'postrofo *sm* apostrophe
app. *abbr* (= *appendice*) app.
appaga'mento *sm* satisfaction; fulfilment
appa'gare *vt* to satisfy; (*desiderio*) to fulfil; **appagarsi** *vr*: **appagarsi di** to be satisfied with
appa'gato, -a *ag* satisfied
appai'are *vt* to couple, pair
ap'paio *etc vb vedi* **apparire**
appallotto'lare *vt* (*carta, foglio*) to screw into a ball; **appallottolarsi** *vr* (*gatto*) to roll up into a ball
appalta'tore *sm* contractor
ap'palto *sm* (*Comm*) contract; **dare/prendere in ~ un lavoro** to let out/undertake a job on contract
appan'naggio [appan'naddʒo] *sm* (*compenso*) annuity; (*fig*) privilege, prerogative
appan'nare *vt* (*vetro*) to mist; (*metallo*) to tarnish; (*vista*) to dim; **appannarsi** *vr* to mist over; to tarnish; to grow dim
appa'rato *sm* equipment, machinery; (*Anat*) apparatus; **~ scenico** (*Teat*) props *pl*
apparecchi'are [apparek'kjare] *vt* to prepare; (*tavola*) to set ■ *vi* to set the table
apparecchia'tura [apparekkja'tura] *sf* equipment; (*macchina*) machine, device
appa'recchio [appa'rekkjo] *sm* piece of apparatus, device; (*aeroplano*) aircraft *inv*; **apparecchi sanitari** bathroom *o* sanitary appliances; **~ televisivo/telefonico** television set/telephone
appa'rente *ag* apparent
apparente'mente *av* apparently
appa'renza [appa'rɛntsa] *sf* appearance; **in** *o* **all'~** apparently, to all appearances
appa'rire *vi* to appear; (*sembrare*) to seem, appear

a

appari'scente [appariʃʃɛnte] *ag* (*colore*) garish, gaudy; (*bellezza*) striking
apparizi'one [apparit'tsjone] *sf* apparition
ap'parso, -a *pp di* **apparire**
apparta'mento *sm* flat (*Brit*), apartment (*US*)
appar'tarsi *vr* to withdraw
appar'tato, -a *ag* (*luogo*) secluded
apparte'nenza [apparte'nɛntsa] *sf*: **~ (a)** (*gen*) belonging (to); (*a un partito, club*) membership (of)
apparte'nere *vi*: **~ a** to belong to
ap'parvi *etc vb vedi* **apparire**
appassio'nante *ag* thrilling, exciting
appassio'nare *vt* to thrill; (*commuovere*) to move; **appassionarsi** *vr*: **appassionarsi a qc** to take a great interest in sth; to be deeply moved by sth
appassio'nato, -a *ag* passionate; (*entusiasta*): **~ (di)** keen (on)
appas'sire *vi* to wither
appel'larsi *vr* (*ricorrere*): **~ a** to appeal to; (*Dir*): **~ contro** to appeal against
ap'pello *sm* roll-call; (*implorazione, Dir*) appeal; (*sessione d'esame*) exam session; **fare ~ a** to appeal to; **fare l'~** (*Ins*) to call the register *o* roll; (*Mil*) to call the roll
ap'pena *av* (*a stento*) hardly, scarcely; (*solamente, da poco*) just ■ *cong* as soon as; **(non) ~ furono arrivati ...** as soon as they had arrived ...; **basta ~ a sfamarli** it's scarcely enough to feed them; **ho ~ finito** I've just finished
ap'pendere *vt* to hang (up)
appendi'abiti *sm inv* hook, peg; (*mobile*) hall stand (*Brit*), hall tree (*US*)
appen'dice [appen'ditʃe] *sf* appendix; **romanzo d'~** popular serial
appendi'cite [appendi'tʃite] *sf* appendicitis
appen'dino *sm* (coat) hook
Appen'nini *smpl*: **gli ~** the Apennines
appesan'tire *vt* to make heavy; **appesantirsi** *vr* to grow stout
ap'peso, -a *pp di* **appendere**
appe'tito *sm* appetite
appeti'toso, -a *ag* appetising; (*fig*) attractive, desirable
appezza'mento [appettsa'mento] *sm* (*anche*: **appezzamento di terreno**) plot, piece of ground
appia'nare *vt* to level; (*fig*) to smooth away, iron out; **appianarsi** *vr* (*divergenze*) to be ironed out
appiat'tire *vt* to flatten; **appiattirsi** *vr* to become flatter; (*farsi piatto*) to flatten o.s.; **appiattirsi al suolo** to lie flat on the ground
appic'care *vt*: **~ il fuoco a** to set fire to, set on fire
appicci'care [appittʃi'kare] *vt* to stick; (*fig*): **~ qc a qn** to palm sth off on sb; **appiccicarsi** *vr* to stick; (*fig: persona*) to cling
appiccica'ticcio, -a, ci, ce [appittʃika'tittʃo], **appicci'coso, -a** [appittʃi'koso] *ag* sticky; (*fig: persona*): **essere ~** to cling like a leech
appie'dato, -a *ag*: **rimanere ~** to be left without means of transport
appi'eno *av* fully
appigli'arsi [appiʎ'ʎarsi] *vr*: **~ a** (*afferrarsi*) to take hold of; (*fig*) to cling to
ap'piglio [ap'piʎʎo] *sm* hold; (*fig*) pretext
appiop'pare *vt*: **~ qc a qn** (*nomignolo*) to pin sth on sb; (*compito difficile*) to saddle sb with sth; **gli ha appioppato un pugno sul muso** he punched him in the face
appiso'larsi *vr* to doze off
applau'dire *vt, vi* to applaud
ap'plauso *sm* applause *no pl*
appli'cabile *ag*: **~ (a)** applicable (to)
appli'care *vt* to apply; (*regolamento*) to enforce; **applicarsi** *vr* to apply o.s.
appli'cato, -a *ag* (*arte, scienze*) applied ■ *sm* (*Amm*) clerk
applica'tore *sm* applicator
applicazi'one [applikat'tsjone] *sf* application; enforcement; **applicazioni tecniche** (*Ins*) practical subjects
appoggi'are [appod'dʒare] *vt* (*mettere contro*): **~ qc a qc** to lean *o* rest sth against sth; (*fig: sostenere*) to support; **appoggiarsi** *vr*: **appoggiarsi a** to lean against; (*fig*) to rely upon
ap'poggio [ap'pɔddʒo] *sm* support
appollai'arsi *vr* (*anche fig*) to perch
ap'pongo, ap'poni *etc vb vedi* **apporre**
ap'porre *vt* to affix
appor'tare *vt* to bring
ap'porto *sm* (*gen, Finanza*) contribution
ap'posi *etc vb vedi* **apporre**
apposita'mente *av* (*apposta*) on purpose; (*specialmente*) specially
ap'posito, -a *ag* appropriate
ap'posta *av* on purpose, deliberately; **neanche a farlo ~, ...** by sheer coincidence, ...
appos'tarsi *vr* to lie in wait
ap'posto, -a *pp di* **apporre**
ap'prendere *vt* (*imparare*) to learn; (*comprendere*) to grasp
apprendi'mento *sm* learning
appren'dista, -i, e *sm/f* apprentice
apprendi'stato *sm* apprenticeship
apprensi'one *sf* apprehension
appren'sivo, -a *ag* apprehensive
ap'preso, -a *pp di* **apprendere**
ap'presso *av* (*accanto, vicino*) close by, near; (*dietro*) behind; (*dopo, più tardi*) after, later

■ *ag inv* (*dopo*): **il giorno ~** the next day; **~ a** *prep* (*vicino a*) near, close to
appres'tare *vt* to prepare, get ready; **apprestarsi** *vr*: **apprestarsi a fare qc** to prepare *o* get ready to do sth
ap'pretto *sm* starch
apprez'zabile [appret'tsabile] *ag* (*notevole*) noteworthy, significant; (*percepibile*) appreciable
apprezza'mento [apprettsa'mento] *sm* appreciation; (*giudizio*) opinion; (*commento*) comment
apprez'zare [appret'tsare] *vt* to appreciate
ap'proccio [ap'prɔttʃo] *sm* approach
appro'dare *vi* (*Naut*) to land; (*fig*): **non ~ a nulla** to come to nothing
ap'prodo *sm* landing; (*luogo*) landing place
approfit'tare *vi*: **~ di** (*persona, situazione*) to take advantage of; (*occasione, opportunità*) to make the most of, profit by
approfon'dire *vt* to deepen; (*fig*) to study in depth; **approfondirsi** *vr* (*gen, fig*) to deepen; (*peggiorare*) to get worse
appron'tare *vt* to prepare, get ready
appropri'arsi *vr*: **~ di qc** to appropriate sth, take possession of sth; **~ indebitamente di** to embezzle
appropri'ato, -a *ag* appropriate
appropriazi'one [approprjat'tsjone] *sf* appropriation; **~ indebita** (*Dir*) embezzlement
approssi'mare *vt* (*cifra*): **~ per eccesso/per difetto** to round up/down; **approssimarsi** *vr*: **approssimarsi a** to approach, draw near
approssima'tivo, -a *ag* approximate, rough; (*impreciso*) inexact, imprecise
approssimazi'one [approssimat'tsjone] *sf* approximation; **per ~** approximately, roughly
appro'vare *vt* (*condotta, azione*) to approve of; (*candidato*) to pass; (*progetto di legge*) to approve
approvazi'one [approvat'tsjone] *sf* approval
approvvigiona'mento [approvvidʒona'mento] *sm* supplying; stocking up; **approvvigionamenti** *smpl* (*Mil*) supplies
approvvigio'nare [approvvidʒo'nare] *vt* to supply; **approvvigionarsi** *vr* to lay in provisions, stock up; **~ qn di qc** to supply sb with sth
appunta'mento *sm* appointment; (*amoroso*) date; **darsi ~** to arrange to meet (one another)
appun'tare *vt* (*rendere aguzzo*) to sharpen; (*fissare*) to pin, fix; (*annotare*) to note down
appun'tato *sm* (*Carabinieri*) corporal
appun'tino *av* perfectly
appun'tire *vt* to sharpen
ap'punto *sm* note; (*rimprovero*) reproach; (*Inform*): **Appunti** Clipboard *sg* ■ *av* (*proprio*) exactly, just; **per l'~!, ~!** exactly!
appu'rare *vt* to check, verify
apr. *abbr* (= *aprile*) Apr.
apribot'tiglie [apribot'tiʎʎe] *sm inv* bottleopener
a'prile *sm* April; **pesce d'~!** April Fool!; *vedi anche* **luglio**
a'prire *vt* to open; (*via, cadavere*) to open up; (*gas, luce, acqua*) to turn on ■ *vi* to open; **aprirsi** *vr* to open; **~ le ostilità** (*Mil*) to start up *o* begin hostilities; **~ una sessione** (*Inform*) to log on; **aprirsi a qn** to confide in sb, open one's heart to sb; **mi si è aperto lo stomaco** I feel rather peckish; **apriti cielo!** heaven forbid!
apris'catole *sm inv* tin (*Brit*) *o* can opener
APT *sigla f* (= *Azienda di Promozione*) ≈ tourist board
AQ *sigla* = **L'Aquila**
aquagym [akwa'dʒim] *sf* aquarobics
a'quario *sm* = **acquario**
'aquila *sf* (*Zool*) eagle; (*fig*) genius
aqui'lino, -a *ag* aquiline
aqui'lone *sm* (*giocattolo*) kite; (*vento*) North wind
AR *sigla* = **Arezzo**
A/R *abbr* (= *andata e ritorno*) return
ara'besco *sm* (*decorazione*) arabesque
A'rabia Sau'dita *sf*: **l'~** Saudi Arabia
a'rabico, -a, ci, che *ag*: **il Deserto ~** the Arabian Desert
a'rabile *ag* arable
'arabo, -a *ag, sm/f* Arab ■ *sm* (*Ling*) Arabic; **parlare ~** (*fig*) to speak double Dutch (*Brit*)
a'rachide [a'rakide] *sf* peanut
ara'gosta *sf* spiny lobster
a'raldica *sf* heraldry
a'raldo *sm* herald
aran'ceto [aran'tʃeto] *sm* orange grove
a'rancia, -ce [a'rantʃa] *sf* orange
aranci'ata [aran'tʃata] *sf* orangeade
a'rancio [a'rantʃo] *sm* (*Bot*) orange tree; (*colore*) orange ■ *ag inv* (*colore*) orange; **fiori di ~** orange blossom *sg*
aranci'one [aran'tʃone] *ag inv*: **(color) ~** bright orange
a'rare *vt* to plough (*Brit*), plow (*US*)
ara'tore *sm* ploughman (*Brit*), plowman (*US*)
a'ratro *sm* plough (*Brit*), plow (*US*)
ara'tura *sf* ploughing (*Brit*), plowing (*US*)
a'razzo [a'rattso] *sm* tapestry
arbi'traggio [arbi'traddʒo] *sm* (*Sport*) refereeing; umpiring; (*Dir*) arbitration; (*Comm*) arbitrage

arbi'trare *vt* (*Sport*) to referee; to umpire; (*Dir*) to arbitrate
arbi'trario, -a *ag* arbitrary
arbi'trato *sm* arbitration
ar'bitrio *sm* will; (*abuso, sopruso*) arbitrary act
'arbitro *sm* arbiter, judge; (*Dir*) arbitrator; (*Sport*) referee; (: *Tennis, Cricket*) umpire
ar'busto *sm* shrub
'arca, -che *sf* (*sarcofago*) sarcophagus; **l'~ di Noè** Noah's ark
ar'caico, -a, ci, che *ag* archaic
arca'ismo *sm* (*Ling*) archaism
ar'cangelo [ar'kandʒelo] *sm* archangel
ar'cano, -a *ag* arcane, mysterious ■ *sm* mystery
ar'cata *sf* (*Archit, Anat*) arch; (*ordine di archi*) arcade
archeolo'gia [arkeolo'dʒia] *sf* arch(a)eology
archeo'logico, -a, ci, che [arkeo'lɔdʒiko] *ag* arch(a)eological
arche'ologo, -a, gi, ghe [arke'ɔlogo] *sm/f* arch(a)eologist
ar'chetipo [ar'kɛtipo] *sm* archetype
ar'chetto [ar'ketto] *sm* (*Mus*) bow
architet'tare [arkitet'tare] *vt* (*fig: ideare*) to devise; (: *macchinare*) to plan, concoct
archi'tetto [arki'tetto] *sm* architect
architet'tonico, -a, ci, che [arkitet'tɔniko] *ag* architectural
architet'tura [arkitet'tura] *sf* architecture
archivi'are [arki'vjare] *vt* (*documenti*) to file; (*Dir*) to dismiss
archiviazi'one [arkivjat'tsjone] *sf* filing; dismissal
ar'chivio [ar'kivjo] *sm* archives *pl*; (*Inform*) file; **~ principale** (*Inform*) master file
archi'vista, -i, e [arki'vista] *sm/f* (*Amm*) archivist; (*in ufficio*) filing clerk
'ARCI ['artʃi] *sigla f* (*= Associazione Ricreativa Culturale Italiana*) *cultural society*
arci'duca, -chi [artʃi'duka] *sm* archduke
arci'ere [ar'tʃɛre] *sm* archer
ar'cigno, -a [ar'tʃiɲɲo] *ag* grim, severe
arci'pelago, -ghi [artʃi'pɛlago] *sm* archipelago
arci'vescovo [artʃi'veskovo] *sm* archbishop
'arco, -chi *sm* (*arma, Mus*) bow; (*Archit*) arch; (*Mat*) arc; **nell'~ di 3 settimane** within the space of 3 weeks; **~ costituzionale** *political parties involved in formulating Italy's post-war constitution*
arcoba'leno *sm* rainbow
arcu'ato, -a *ag* curved, bent; **dalle gambe arcuate** bow-legged
ar'dente *ag* burning; (*fig*) burning, ardent
'ardere *vt, vi* to burn; **legna da ~** firewood
ar'desia *sf* slate
ardi'mento *sm* daring
ar'dire *vi* to dare ■ *sm* daring
ar'dito, -a *ag* brave, daring, bold; (*sfacciato*) bold
ar'dore *sm* blazing heat; (*fig*) ardour, fervour
'arduo, -a *ag* arduous, difficult
'area *sf* area; (*Edil*) land, ground; **nell'~ dei partiti di sinistra** among the parties of the left; **~ fabbricabile** building land; **~ di rigore** (*Sport*) penalty area; **~ di servizio** (*Aut*) service area
a'rena *sf* arena; (*per corride*) bullring; (*sabbia*) sand
are'naria *sf* sandstone
are'narsi *vr* to run aground; (*fig: trattative*) to come to a standstill
areo'plano *sm* = **aeroplano**
are'tino, -a *ag* of (*o* from) Arezzo
'argano *sm* winch
argen'tato, -a [ardʒen'tato] *ag* silver-plated; (*colore*) silver, silvery; (*capelli*) silver(-grey)
ar'genteo, -a [ar'dʒɛnteo] *ag* silver, silvery
argente'ria [ardʒente'ria] *sf* silverware, silver
Argen'tina [ardʒen'tina] *sf*: **l'~** Argentina
argen'tino, -a [ardʒen'tino] *ag, sm/f* (*dell'Argentina*) Argentinian ■ *sf* crewneck sweater
ar'gento [ar'dʒɛnto] *sm* silver; **~ vivo** quicksilver; **avere l'~ (vivo) addosso** (*fig*) to be fidgety
ar'gilla [ar'dʒilla] *sf* clay
argil'loso, -a [ardʒil'loso] *ag* (*contenente argilla*) clayey; (*simile ad argilla*) clay-like
argi'nare [ardʒi'nare] *vt* (*fiume, acque*) to embank; (: *con diga*) to dyke up; (*fig: inflazione, corruzione*) to check; (: *spese*) to limit
'argine ['ardʒine] *sm* embankment, bank; (*diga*) dyke, dike; **far ~ a, porre un ~ a** (*fig*) to check, hold back
argomen'tare *vi* to argue
argo'mento *sm* argument; (*materia, tema*) subject; **tornare sull'~** to bring the matter up again
argu'ire *vt* to deduce
ar'guto, -a *ag* sharp, quick-witted; (*spiritoso*) witty
ar'guzia [ar'guttsja] *sf* wit; (*battuta*) witty remark
'aria *sf* air; (*espressione, aspetto*) air, look; (*Mus: melodia*) tune; (: *di opera*) aria; **all'~ aperta** in the open (air); **manca l'~** it's stuffy; **andare all'~** (*piano, progetto*) to come to nothing; **mandare all'~ qc** to ruin *o* upset sth; **darsi delle arie** to put on airs and graces; **ha la testa per ~** his head is in the clouds; **che ~ tira?** (*fig: atmosfera*) what's the atmosphere like?

aridità *sf* aridity, dryness; *(fig)* lack of feeling
'arido, -a *ag* arid
arieggi'are [arjed'dʒare] *vt (cambiare aria)* to air; *(imitare)* to imitate
ari'ete *sm* ram; *(Mil)* battering ram; *(dello zodiaco)*: **A~** Aries; **essere dell'A~** to be Aries
a'ringa, -ghe *sf* herring *inv*; **~ affumicata** smoked herring, kipper; **~ marinata** pickled herring
ari'oso, -a *ag (ambiente, stanza)* airy; *(Mus)* ariose
'arista *sf (Cuc)* chine of pork
aristo'cratico, -a, ci, che *ag* aristocratic
aristocra'zia [aristokrat'tsia] *sf* aristocracy
arit'metica *sf* arithmetic
arit'metico, -a, ci, che *ag* arithmetical
arlec'chino [arlek'kino] *sm* harlequin
'arma, -i *sf* weapon, arm; *(parte dell'esercito)* arm; **alle armi!** to arms!; **chiamare alle armi** to call up *(Brit)*, draft *(US)*; **sotto le armi** in the army *(o forces)*; **combattere ad armi pari** *(anche fig)* to fight on equal terms; **essere alle prime armi** *(fig)* to be a novice; **passare qn per le armi** to execute sb; **~ a doppio taglio** *(anche fig)* double-edged weapon; **~ da fuoco** firearm; **armi convenzionali/non convenzionali** conventional/unconventional weapons; **armi di distruzione de massa** weapons of mass destruction
ar'madio *sm* cupboard; *(per abiti)* wardrobe; **~ a muro** built-in cupboard
armamen'tario *sm* equipment, instruments *pl*
arma'mento *sm (Mil)* armament; *(: materiale)* arms *pl*, weapons *pl*; *(Naut)* fitting out; manning; **la corsa agli armamenti** the arms race
ar'mare *vt* to arm; *(arma da fuoco)* to cock; *(Naut: nave)* to rig, fit out; to man; *(Edil: volta, galleria)* to prop up, shore up; **armarsi** *vr* to arm o.s.; *(Mil)* to take up arms
ar'mato, -a *ag*: **~ (di)** *(anche fig)* armed (with) ■ *sf (Mil)* army; *(Naut)* fleet; **rapina a mano armata** armed robbery
arma'tore *sm* shipowner
arma'tura *sf (struttura di sostegno)* framework; *(impalcatura)* scaffolding; *(Storia)* armour *no pl (Brit)*, armor *no pl (US)*
armeggi'are [armed'dʒare] *vi (affaccendarsi)*: **~ (intorno a qc)** to mess about (with sth)
ar'meno, -a *ag, sm/f, sm* Armenian
arme'ria *sf (deposito)* armoury *(Brit)*, armory *(US)*; *(collezione)* collection of arms
armis'tizio [armis'tittsjo] *sm* armistice
armo'nia *sf* harmony
ar'monico, -a, ci, che *ag* harmonic; *(fig)* harmonious ■ *sf (Mus)* harmonica; **armonica a bocca** mouth organ
armoni'oso, -a *ag* harmonious
armoniz'zare [armonid'dzare] *vt* to harmonize; *(colori, abiti)* to match ■ *vi* to be in harmony; to match
ar'nese *sm* tool, implement; *(oggetto indeterminato)* thing, contraption; **male in ~** *(malvestito)* badly dressed; *(di salute malferma)* in poor health; *(di condizioni economiche)* down-at-heel
'arnia *sf* hive
a'roma, -i *sm* aroma; fragrance; **aromi** *smpl* herbs and spices; **aromi naturali/ artificiali** natural/artificial flavouring *sg (Brit) o* flavoring *sg (US)*
aromatera'pia *sf* aromatherapy
aro'matico, -a, ci, che *ag* aromatic; *(cibo)* spicy
aromatiz'zare [aromatid'dzare] *vt* to season, flavour *(Brit)*, flavor *(US)*
'arpa *sf (Mus)* harp
ar'peggio [ar'peddʒo] *sm (Mus)* arpeggio
ar'pia *sf (anche fig)* harpy
arpi'one *sm (gancio)* hook; *(cardine)* hinge; *(Pesca)* harpoon
arrabat'tarsi *vr* to do all one can, strive
arrabbi'are *vi (cane)* to be affected with rabies; **arrabbiarsi** *vr (essere preso dall'ira)* to get angry, fly into a rage
arrabbi'ato, -a *ag (cane)* rabid, with rabies; *(persona)* furious, angry
arrabbia'tura *sf*: **prendersi un'~ (per qc)** to become furious (over sth)
arraf'fare *vt* to snatch, seize; *(sottrarre)* to pinch
arrampi'carsi *vr* to climb (up); **~ sui vetri** *o* **sugli specchi** *(fig)* to clutch at straws
arrampi'cata *sf* climb
arrampica'tore, -'trice *sm/f (gen, Sport)* climber; **~ sociale** *(fig)* social climber
arran'care *vi* to limp, hobble; *(fig)* to struggle along
arrangia'mento [arrandʒa'mento] *sm (Mus)* arrangement
arran'giare [arran'dʒare] *vt* to arrange; **arrangiarsi** *vr* to manage, do the best one can
arre'care *vt* to bring; *(causare)* to cause
arreda'mento *sm (studio)* interior design; *(mobili etc)* furnishings *pl*
arre'dare *vt* to furnish
arreda'tore, -'trice *sm/f* interior designer
ar'redo *sm* fittings *pl*, furnishings *pl*; **~ per uffici** office furnishings
arrem'baggio [arrem'baddʒo] *sm (Naut)* boarding

ar'rendersi *vr* to surrender; **~ all'evidenza (dei fatti)** to face (the) facts
arren'devole *ag* (*persona*) yielding, compliant
arrendevo'lezza [arrendevo'lettsa] *sf* compliancy
ar'reso, -a *pp di* **arrendersi**
arres'tare *vt* (*fermare*) to stop, halt; (*catturare*) to arrest; **arrestarsi** *vr* (*fermarsi*) to stop
arres'tato, -a *sm/f* person under arrest
ar'resto *sm* (*cessazione*) stopping; (*fermata*) stop; (*cattura, Med*) arrest; (*Comm: in produzione*) stoppage; **subire un ~** to come to a stop *o* standstill; **mettere agli arresti** to place under arrest; **arresti domiciliari** (*Dir*) house arrest
arre'trare *vt, vi* to withdraw
arre'trato, -a *ag* (*lavoro*) behind schedule; (*paese, bambino*) backward; (*numero di giornale*) back *cpd*; **arretrati** *smpl* arrears; **gli arretrati dello stipendio** back pay *sg*
arricchi'mento [arrikki'mento] *sm* enrichment
arric'chire [arrik'kire] *vt* to enrich; **arricchirsi** *vr* to become rich
arric'chito, -a [arrik'kito] *sm/f* nouveau riche
arricci'are [arrit'tʃare] *vt* to curl; **~ il naso** to turn up one's nose
ar'ridere *vi*: **~ a qn** (*fortuna, successo*) to smile on sb
ar'ringa, -ghe *sf* harangue; (*Dir*) address by counsel
arrischi'are [arris'kjare] *vt* to risk; **arrischiarsi** *vr* to venture, dare
arrischi'ato, -a [arris'kjato] *ag* risky; (*temerario*) reckless, rash
ar'riso, -a *pp di* **arridere**
arri'vare *vi* to arrive; (*avvicinarsi*) to come; (*accadere*) to happen, occur; **~ a** (*livello, grado etc*) to reach; **lui arriva a Roma alle 7** he gets to *o* arrives at Rome at 7; **~ a fare qc** to manage to do sth, succeed in doing sth; **non ci arrivo** I can't reach it; (*fig: non capisco*) I can't understand it
arri'vato, -a *ag* (*persona: di successo*) successful ■ *sm/f*: **essere un ~** to have made it; **nuovo ~** newcomer; **ben ~!** welcome!; **non sono l'ultimo ~!** (*fig*) I'm no fool!
arrive'derci [arrive'dertʃi] *escl* goodbye!
arrive'derla *escl* (*forma di cortesia*) goodbye!
arri'vismo *sm* (*ambizione*) ambitiousness; (*sociale*) social climbing
arri'vista, -i, e *sm/f* go-getter
ar'rivo *sm* arrival; (*Sport*) finish, finishing line
arro'gante *ag* arrogant
arro'ganza [arro'gantsa] *sf* arrogance
arro'gare *vt*: **arrogarsi il diritto di fare qc** to assume the right to do sth; **arrogarsi il merito di qc** to claim credit for sth
arrossa'mento *sm* reddening
arros'sare *vt* (*occhi, pelle*) to redden, make red; **arrossarsi** *vr* to go *o* become red
arros'sire *vi* (*per vergogna, timidezza*) to blush; (*per gioia*) to flush, blush
arros'tire *vt* to roast; (*pane*) to toast; (*ai ferri*) to grill
ar'rosto *sm, ag inv* roast; **~ di manzo** roast beef
arro'tare *vt* to sharpen; (*investire con un veicolo*) to run over
arro'tino *sm* knife-grinder
arroto'lare *vt* to roll up
arroton'dare *vt* (*forma, oggetto*) to round; (*stipendio*) to add to; (*somma*) to round off
arrovel'larsi *vr* (*anche*: **arrovellarsi il cervello**) to rack one's brains
arroven'tato, -a *ag* red-hot
arruf'fare *vt* to ruffle; (*fili*) to tangle; (*fig: questione*) to confuse
arruggi'nire [arruddʒi'nire] *vt* to rust; **arrugginirsi** *vr* to rust; (*fig*) to become rusty
arruola'mento *sm* (*Mil*) enlistment
arruo'lare *vt* (*Mil*) to enlist; **arruolarsi** *vr* to enlist, join up
arse'nale *sm* (*Mil*) arsenal; (*cantiere navale*) dockyard
ar'senico *sm* arsenic
'arsi *vb vedi* **ardere**
'arso, -a *pp di* **ardere** ■ *ag* (*bruciato*) burnt; (*arido*) dry
ar'sura *sf* (*calore opprimente*) burning heat; (*siccità*) drought
art. *abbr* (= *articolo*) art.
'arte *sf* art; (*abilità*) skill; **a regola d'~** (*fig*) perfectly; **senz'~ né parte** penniless and out of a job; **arti figurative** visual arts
arte'fatto, -a *ag* (*stile, modi*) affected; (*cibo*) adulterated
ar'tefice [ar'tefitʃe] *sm/f* craftsman(-woman); (*autore*) author
ar'teria *sf* artery
arterioscle'rosi *sf* arteriosclerosis, hardening of the arteries
arteri'oso, -a *ag* arterial
'artico, -a, ci, che *ag* Arctic ■ *sm*: **l'A~** the Arctic; **il Circolo polare ~** the Arctic Circle; **l'Oceano ~** the Arctic Ocean
artico'lare *ag* (*Anat*) of the joints, articular ■ *vt* to articulate; (*suddividere*) to divide, split up; **articolarsi** *vr*: **articolarsi in** (*discorso, progetto*) to be divided into
artico'lato, -a *ag* (*linguaggio*) articulate; (*Aut*) articulated

articolazi'one [artikolat'tsjone] *sf* (*Anat, Tecn*) joint; (*di voce, concetto*) articulation
ar'ticolo *sm* article; **~ di fondo** (*Stampa*) leader, leading article; **articoli di marca** branded goods; **un bell'~** (*fig*) a real character
'Artide *sm*: **l'~** the Arctic
artifici'ale [artifi'tʃale] *ag* artificial
artifici'ere [artifi'tʃɛre] *sm* (*Mil*) artificer; (*: per disinnescare bombe*) bomb-disposal expert
arti'ficio [arti'fitʃo] *sm* (*espediente*) trick, artifice; (*ricerca di effetto*) artificiality
artifici'oso, -a [artifi'tʃoso] *ag* cunning; (*non spontaneo*) affected
artigia'nale [artidʒa'nale] *ag* craft *cpd*
artigia'nato [artidʒa'nato] *sm* craftsmanship; craftsmen *pl*
artigi'ano, -a [arti'dʒano] *sm/f* craftsman(-woman)
artigli'ere [artiʎ'ʎɛre] *sm* artilleryman
artiglie'ria [artiʎʎe'ria] *sf* artillery
ar'tiglio [ar'tiʎʎo] *sm* claw; (*di rapaci*) talon; **sfoderare gli artigli** (*fig*) to show one's claws
ar'tista, -i, e *sm/f* artist; **un lavoro da ~** (*fig*) a professional piece of work
ar'tistico, -a, ci, che *ag* artistic
'arto *sm* (*Anat*) limb
ar'trite *sf* (*Med*) arthritis
ar'trosi *sf* osteoarthritis
arzigogo'lato, -a [ardzigogo'lato] *ag* tortuous
ar'zillo, -a [ar'dzillo] *ag* lively, sprightly
a'scella [aʃ'ʃɛlla] *sf* (*Anat*) armpit
ascen'dente [aʃʃen'dɛnte] *sm* ancestor; (*fig*) ascendancy; (*Astr*) ascendant
a'scendere [aʃ'ʃendere] *vi*: **~ al trono** to ascend the throne
ascensi'one [aʃʃen'sjone] *sf* (*Alpinismo*) ascent; (*Rel*): **l'A~** the Ascension; **isola dell'A~** Ascension Island
ascen'sore [aʃʃen'sore] *sm* lift
a'scesa [aʃ'ʃesa] *sf* ascent; (*al trono*) accession; (*al potere*) rise
a'scesi [aʃ'ʃɛzi] *sf* asceticism
a'sceso, -a [aʃ'ʃeso] *pp di* **ascendere**
a'scesso [aʃ'ʃɛsso] *sm* (*Med*) abscess
a'sceta, -i [aʃ'ʃɛta] *sm* ascetic
'ascia ['aʃʃa] (*pl* **asce**) *sf* axe
asciugaca'pelli [aʃʃugaka'pelli] *sm* hair dryer
asciuga'mano [aʃʃuga'mano] *sm* towel
asciu'gare [aʃʃu'gare] *vt* to dry; **asciugarsi** *vr* to dry o.s.; (*diventare asciutto*) to dry
asciuga'trice [aʃʃuga'tritʃe] *sf* spin-dryer
asciut'tezza [aʃʃut'tettsa] *sf* dryness; leanness; curtness
asci'utto, -a [aʃ'ʃutto] *ag* dry; (*fig: magro*) lean; (*: burbero*) curt ■ *sm*: **restare all'~** (*fig*) to be left penniless; **restare a bocca asciutta** (*fig*) to be disappointed
asco'lano, -a *ag* of (*o* from) Ascoli
ascol'tare *vt* to listen to; **~ il consiglio di qn** to listen to *o* heed sb's advice
ascolta'tore, -'trice *sm/f* listener
as'colto *sm*: **essere** *o* **stare in ~** to be listening; **dare** *o* **prestare ~ (a)** to pay attention (to); **indice di ~** (*TV, Radio*) audience rating
AS. COM. *sigla f* = **Associazione Commercianti**
as'critto, -a *pp di* **ascrivere**
as'crivere *vt* (*attribuire*): **~ qc a qn** to attribute sth to sb; **~ qc a merito di qn** to give sb credit for sth
a'settico, -a, ci, che *ag* aseptic
asfal'tare *vt* to asphalt
as'falto *sm* asphalt
asfis'sia *sf* asphyxia, asphyxiation
asfissi'ante *ag* (*gas*) asphyxiating; (*fig: calore, ambiente*) stifling, suffocating; (*: persona*) tiresome
asfissi'are *vt* to asphyxiate, suffocate; (*fig: opprimere*) to stifle; (*: infastidire*) to get on sb's nerves ■ *vi* to suffocate, asphyxiate
'Asia *sf*: **l'~** Asia
asi'atico, -a, ci, che *ag, sm/f* Asiatic, Asian
a'silo *sm* refuge, sanctuary; **~ (d'infanzia)** nursery(-school); **~ nido** day nursery, crèche (*for children aged 0 to 3*); **~ politico** political asylum
asim'metrico, -a, ci, che *ag* asymmetric(al)
'asino *sm* donkey, ass; **la bellezza dell'~** (*fig: di ragazza*) the beauty of youth; **qui casca l'~!** there's the rub!
ASL [azl] *sigla f* (*= Azienda Sanitaria Locale*) local health centre
'asma *sf* asthma
as'matico, -a, ci, che *ag, sm/f* asthmatic
asoci'ale [aso'tʃale] *ag* antisocial
'asola *sf* buttonhole
as'parago, -gi *sm* asparagus *no pl*
as'pergere [as'pɛrdʒere] *vt*: **~ (di** *o* **con)** to sprinkle (with)
asperità *sf inv* roughness *no pl*; (*fig*) harshness *no pl*
as'persi *etc vb vedi* **aspergere**
as'perso, -a *pp di* **aspergere**
aspet'tare *vt* to wait for; (*anche Comm*) to await; (*aspettarsi*) to expect; (*essere in serbo: notizia, evento etc*) to be in store for, lie ahead of ■ *vi* to wait; **aspettarsi qc** to expect sth; **~ un bambino** to be expecting (a baby); **questo non me l'aspettavo** I wasn't

expecting this; **me l'aspettavo!** I thought as much!

aspettaˈtiva *sf* expectation; **inferiore all'~** worse than expected; **essere/mettersi in ~** (*Amm*) to be on/take leave of absence

asˈpetto *sm* (*apparenza*) aspect, appearance, look; (*punto di vista*) point of view; **di bell'~** good-looking

aspiˈrante *ag* (*attore etc*) aspiring ■ *sm/f* candidate, applicant

aspiraˈpolvere *sm inv* vacuum cleaner

aspiˈrare *vt* (*respirare*) to breathe in, inhale; (*apparecchi*) to suck (up) ■ *vi*: **~ a** to aspire to

aspiraˈtore *sm* extractor fan

aspiraziˈone [aspiratˈtsjone] *sf* (*Tecn*) suction; (*anelito*) aspiration

aspiˈrina *sf* aspirin

asporˈtare *vt* (*anche Med*) to remove, take away

asˈprezza [asˈprettsa] *sf* sourness, tartness; pungency; harshness; roughness; rugged nature

ˈaspro, -a *ag* (*sapore*) sour, tart; (*odore*) acrid, pungent; (*voce, clima, fig*) harsh; (*superficie*) rough; (*paesaggio*) rugged

Ass. *abbr* = **assicurazione**; **assicurata**; **assegno**

assaggiˈare [assadˈdʒare] *vt* to taste

assagˈgini [assadˈdʒini] *smpl* (*Cuc*) *selection of first courses*

asˈsaggio [asˈsaddʒo] *sm* tasting; (*piccola quantità*) taste; (*campione*) sample

asˈsai *av* (*molto*) a lot, much; (: *con ag*) very; (*a sufficienza*) enough ■ *ag inv* (*quantità*) a lot of, much; (*numero*) a lot of, many; **~ contento** very pleased

asˈsalgo *etc vb vedi* **assalire**

assaˈlire *vt* to attack, assail

assaliˈtore, -ˈtrice *sm/f* attacker, assailant

assalˈtare *vt* (*Mil*) to storm; (*banca*) to raid; (*treno, diligenza*) to hold up

asˈsalto *sm* attack, assault; **prendere d'~** (*fig*: *negozio, treno*) to storm; (: *personalità*) to besiege; **d'~** (*editoria, giornalista etc*) aggressive

assapoˈrare *vt* to savour (*Brit*), savor (*US*)

assassiˈnare *vt* to murder; (*Pol*) to assassinate; (*fig*) to ruin

assasˈsinio *sm* murder; assassination

assasˈsino, -a *ag* murderous ■ *sm/f* murderer; assassin

ˈasse *sm* (*Tecn*) axle; (*Mat*) axis ■ *sf* board; **~ da stiro** ironing board

asseconˈdare *vt*: **~ qn (in qc)** to go along with sb (in sth); **~ i desideri di qn** to go along with sb's wishes; **~ i capricci di qn** to give in to sb's whims

assediˈare *vt* to besiege

asˈsedio *sm* siege

asseˈgnare [assenˈɲare] *vt* to assign, allot; (*premio*) to award

assegnaˈtario [asseɲɲaˈtarjo] *sm* (*Dir*) assignee; (*Comm*) recipient; **l'~ del premio** the person awarded the prize

assegnaziˈone [asseɲɲatˈtsjone] *sf* (*di casa, somma*) allocation; (*di carica*) assignment; (*di premio, borsa di studio*) awarding

asˈsegno [asˈseɲɲo] *sm* allowance; (*anche*: **assegno bancario**) cheque (*Brit*), check (*US*); **contro ~** cash on delivery; **~ circolare** bank draft; **~ di invalidità** *o* **di malattia** injury *o* sickness benefit; **~ post-datato** post-dated cheque; **~ sbarrato** crossed cheque; **~ non sbarrato** uncrossed cheque; **~ di studio** study grant; **"~ non trasferibile"** "account payee only"; **~ di viaggio** travel(l)er's cheque; **~ a vuoto** dud cheque; **assegni alimentari** alimony *sg*; **assegni familiari** ≈ child benefit *sg*

assemˈblaggio [assemˈbladdʒo] *sm* (*Industria*) assembly

assemˈblare *vt* to assemble

assemˈblea *sf* assembly; (*raduno, adunanza*) meeting

assembraˈmento *sm* public gathering; **divieto di ~** ban on public meetings

assenˈnato, -a *ag* sensible

asˈsenso *sm* assent, consent

assenˈtarsi *vr* to go out

asˈsente *ag* absent; (*fig*) faraway, vacant ■ *sm/f* absentee

assenteˈismo *sm* absenteeism

assenteˈista, -i, e *sm/f* (*dal lavoro*) absentee

assenˈtire *vi*: **~ (a)** to agree (to), assent (to)

asˈsenza [asˈsɛntsa] *sf* absence

asseˈrire *vt* to maintain, assert

asserragliˈarsi [asserraʎˈʎarsi] *vr*: **~ (in)** to barricade o.s. (in)

asserˈvire *vt* to enslave; (*fig*: *animo, passioni*) to subdue; **asservirsi** *vr*: **asservirsi (a)** to submit (to)

asserziˈone [asserˈtsjone] *sf* assertion

assessoˈrato *sm* councillorship

assesˈsore *sm* councillor

assestaˈmento *sm* (*sistemazione*) arrangement; (*Edil, Geo*) settlement

assesˈtare *vt* (*mettere in ordine*) to put in order, arrange; **assestarsi** *vr* to settle in; (*Geo*) to settle; **~ un colpo a qn** to deal sb a blow

asseˈtato, -a *ag* thirsty, parched

asˈsetto *sm* order, arrangement; (*Naut, Aer*) trim; **in ~ di guerra** on a war footing; **~ territoriale** country planning

assicuˈrare *vt* (*accertare*) to ensure; (*infondere certezza*) to assure; (*fermare, legare*) to make

fast, secure; (*fare un contratto di assicurazione*) to insure; **assicurarsi** *vr* (*accertarsi*): **assicurarsi (di)** to make sure (of); (*contro il furto etc*): **assicurarsi (contro)** to insure o.s. (against)
assicu'rato, -a *ag* insured ■ *sf* (*anche*: **lettera assicurata**) registered letter
assicura'tore, -'trice *ag* insurance *cpd* ■ *sm/f* insurance agent; **società assicuratrice** insurance company
assicurazi'one [assikurat'tsjone] *sf* assurance; insurance; **~ multi-rischio** comprehensive insurance
assidera'mento *sm* exposure
asside'rare *vt* to freeze; **assiderarsi** *vr* to freeze; **morire assiderato** to die of exposure
as'siduo, -a *ag* (*costante*) assiduous; (*regolare*) regular
assi'eme *av* (*insieme*) together ■ *prep*: **~ a** (together) with
assil'lante *ag* (*dubbio, pensiero*) nagging; (*creditore*) pestering
assil'lare *vt* to pester, torment
as'sillo *sm* (*fig*) worrying thought
assimi'lare *vt* to assimilate
assimilazi'one [assimilat'tsjone] *sf* assimilation
assi'oma, -i *sm* axiom
assio'matico, -a, ci, che *ag* axiomatic
as'sise *sfpl* (*Dir*) assizes (*Brit*); **corte d'~** court of assizes, ≈ crown court (*Brit*); *vedi anche* **Corte d'Assise**
assis'tente *sm/f* assistant; **~ sociale** social worker; **~ universitario** (assistant) lecturer; **~ di volo** (*Aer*) steward/stewardess
assis'tenza [assis'tentsa] *sf* assistance; **~ legale** legal aid; **~ ospedaliera** free hospital treatment; **~ sanitaria** health service; **~ sociale** welfare services *pl*
assistenzi'ale [assisten'tsjale] *ag* (*ente, organizzazione*) welfare *cpd*; (*opera*) charitable
assistenzia'lismo [assistentsja'lizmo] *sm* (*peg*) excessive state aid
as'sistere *vt* (*aiutare*) to assist, help; (*curare*) to treat ■ *vi*: **~ (a qc)** (*essere presente*) to be present (at sth), attend (sth)
assis'tito, -a *pp di* **assistere**
'asso *sm* ace; **piantare qn in ~** to leave sb in the lurch
associ'are [asso'tʃare] *vt* to associate; (*rendere partecipe*): **~ qn a** (*affari*) to take sb into partnership in; (*partito*) to make sb a member of; **associarsi** *vr* to enter into partnership; **associarsi a** to become a member of, join; (*dolori, gioie*) to share in; **~ qn alle carceri** to take sb to prison
associazi'one [assotʃat'tsjone] *sf* association; **~ di categoria** trade association; **~ a** *o* **per delinquere** (*Dir*) criminal association; **A~ Europea di Libero Scambio** European Free Trade Association, EFTA; **~ in partecipazione** (*Comm*) joint venture
asso'dare *vt* (*muro, posizione*) to strengthen; (*fatti, verità*) to ascertain
asso'dato, -a *ag* well-founded
assogget'tare [assoddʒet'tare] *vt* to subject, subjugate; **assoggettarsi** *vr*: **assoggettarsi a** to submit to
asso'lato, -a *ag* sunny
assol'dare *vt* to recruit
as'solsi *etc vb vedi* **assolvere**
as'solto, -a *pp di* **assolvere**
assoluta'mente *av* absolutely
asso'luto, -a *ag* absolute
assoluzi'one [assolut'tsjone] *sf* (*Dir*) acquittal; (*Rel*) absolution
as'solvere *vt* (*Dir*) to acquit; (*Rel*) to absolve; (*adempiere*) to carry out, perform
assomigli'are [assomiʎ'ʎare] *vi*: **~ a** to resemble, look like
asson'nato, -a *ag* sleepy
asso'pirsi *vr* to doze off
assor'bente *ag* absorbent ■ *sm*: **~ igienico** sanitary towel; **~ interno** tampon
assor'bire *vt* to absorb; (*fig: far proprio*) to assimilate
assor'dante *ag* (*rumore, musica*) deafening
assor'dare *vt* to deafen
assorti'mento *sm* assortment
assor'tire *vt* (*disporre*) to arrange
assor'tito, -a *ag* assorted; (*colori*) matched, matching
as'sorto, -a *ag* absorbed, engrossed
assottigli'are [assottiʎ'ʎare] *vt* to make thin, thin; (*aguzzare*) to sharpen; (*ridurre*) to reduce; **assottigliarsi** *vr* to grow thin; (*fig: ridursi*) to be reduced
assue'fare *vt* to accustom; **assuefarsi** *vr*: **assuefarsi a** to get used to, accustom o.s. to
assue'fatto, -a *pp di* **assuefare**
assuefazi'one [assuefat'tsjone] *sf* (*Med*) addiction
as'sumere *vt* (*impiegato*) to take on, engage; (*responsabilità*) to assume, take upon o.s.; (*contegno, espressione*) to assume, put on; (*droga*) to consume
as'sunsi *etc vb vedi* **assumere**
as'sunto, -a *pp di* **assumere** ■ *sm* (*tesi*) proposition
assunzi'one [assun'tsjone] *sf* (*di impiegati*) employment, engagement; (*Rel*): **l'A~** the Assumption

assurdità *sf inv* absurdity; **dire delle ~** to talk nonsense
as'surdo, -a *ag* absurd
'asta *sf* pole; (*modo di vendita*) auction
as'tante *sm* bystander
astante'ria *sf* casualty department
as'temio, -a *ag* teetotal ■ *sm/f* teetotaller
aste'nersi *vr*: **~ (da)** to abstain (from), refrain (from); (*Pol*) to abstain (from)
astensi'one *sf* abstention
astensio'nista, -i, e *sm/f* (*Pol*) abstentionist
aste'risco, -schi *sm* asterisk
aste'roide *sm* asteroid
'astice ['astitʃe] *sm* lobster
astigi'ano, -a [asti'dʒano] *ag* of (*o* from) Asti
astig'matico, -a, ci, che *ag* astigmatic
asti'nenza [asti'nɛntsa] *sf* abstinence; **essere in crisi di ~** to suffer from withdrawal symptoms
'astio *sm* rancour, resentment
asti'oso, -a *ag* resentful
astrat'tismo *sm* (*Arte*) abstract art
as'tratto, -a *ag* abstract
astrin'gente [astrin'dʒɛnte] *ag, sm* astringent
'astro *sm* star
astrolo'gia [astrolo'dʒia] *sf* astrology
astro'logico, -a, ci, che [astro'lɔdʒiko] *ag* astrological
as'trologo, -a, ghi, ghe *sm/f* astrologer
astro'nauta, -i, e *sm/f* astronaut
astro'nautica *sf* astronautics *sg*
astro'nave *sf* space ship
astrono'mia *sf* astronomy
astro'nomico, -a, ci, che *ag* astronomic(al)
as'tronomo *sm* astronomer
as'truso, -a *ag* (*discorso, ragionamento*) abstruse
as'tuccio [as'tuttʃo] *sm* case, box, holder
as'tuto, -a *ag* astute, cunning, shrewd
as'tuzia [as'tuttsja] *sf* astuteness, shrewdness; (*azione*) trick
AT *sigla* = **Asti**
ATA *sigla f* = **Associazione Turistica Albergatori**
a'tavico, -a, ci, che *ag* atavistic
ate'ismo *sm* atheism
atelier [atə'lje] *sm inv* (*laboratorio*) workshop; (*studio*) studio; (*sartoria*) fashion house
A'tene *sf* Athens
ate'neo *sm* university
ateni'ese *ag, sm/f* Athenian
'ateo, -a *ag, sm/f* atheist
a'tipico, -a, ci, che *ag* atypical
at'lante *sm* atlas; **i Monti dell'A~** the Atlas Mountains
at'lantico, -a, ci, che *ag* Atlantic ■ *sm*: **l'A~, l'Oceano A~** the Atlantic, the Atlantic Ocean
at'leta, -i, e *sm/f* athlete
at'letica *sf* athletics *sg*; **~ leggera** track and field events *pl*; **~ pesante** weightlifting and wrestling
atmos'fera *sf* atmosphere
atmos'ferico, -a, ci, che *ag* atmospheric
a'tollo *sm* atoll
a'tomico, -a, ci, che *ag* atomic; (*nucleare*) atomic, atom *cpd*, nuclear
atomizza'tore [atomiddza'tore] *sm* (*di acqua, lacca*) spray; (*di profumo*) atomizer
'atomo *sm* atom
'atono, -a *ag* (*Fonetica*) unstressed
'atrio *sm* entrance hall, lobby
a'troce [a'trotʃe] *ag* (*che provoca orrore*) dreadful; (*terribile*) atrocious
atrocità [atrotʃi'ta] *sf inv* atrocity
atro'fia *sf* atrophy
attacca'brighe [attakka'brige] *sm/f inv* quarrelsome person
attacca'mento *sm* (*fig*) attachment, affection
attacca'panni *sm* hook, peg; (*mobile*) hall stand
attac'care *vt* (*unire*) to attach; (*cucire*) to sew on; (*far aderire*) to stick (on); (*appendere*) to hang (up); (*assalire: anche fig*) to attack; (*iniziare*) to begin, start; (*fig: contagiare*) to pass on ■ *vi* to stick, adhere; **attaccarsi** *vr* to stick, adhere; (*trasmettersi per contagio*) to be contagious; (*afferrarsi*): **attaccarsi (a)** to cling (to); (*fig: affezionarsi*): **attaccarsi (a)** to become attached (to); **~ discorso** to start a conversation; **con me non attacca!** that won't work with me!
attacca'ticcio, -a, ci, ce [attakka'tittʃo] *ag* sticky
attacca'tura *sf* (*di manica*) join; **~ (dei capelli)** hairline
at'tacco, -chi *sm* (*azione offensiva: anche fig*) attack; (*Med*) attack, fit; (*Sci*) binding; (*Elettr*) socket
attanagli'are [attanaʎ'ʎare] *vt* (*anche fig*) to grip
attar'darsi *vr*: **~ a fare qc** (*fermarsi*) to stop to do sth; (*stare più a lungo*) to stay behind to do sth
attec'chire [attek'kire] *vi* (*pianta*) to take root; (*fig*) to catch on
atteggia'mento [atteddʒa'mento] *sm* attitude
atteggi'arsi [atted'dʒarsi] *vr*: **~ a** to pose as
attem'pato, -a *ag* elderly
atten'dente *sm* (*Mil*) orderly, batman
at'tendere *vt* to wait for, await ■ *vi*: **~ a** to attend to
atten'dibile *ag* (*scusa, storia*) credible; (*fonte, testimone, notizia*) reliable; (*persona*) trustworthy

atte'nersi *vr*: **~ a** to keep *o* stick to
atten'tare *vi*: **~ a** to make an attempt on
atten'tato *sm* attack; **~ alla vita di qn** attempt on sb's life
attenta'tore, -'trice *sm/f* bomber; **~ suicida** suicide bomber
at'tento, -a *ag* attentive; (*accurato*) careful, thorough ■ *escl* be careful!; **stare ~ a qc** to pay attention to sth; **attenti!** (*Mil*) attention!; **attenti al cane** beware of the dog
attenu'ante *sf* (*Dir*) extenuating circumstance
attenu'are *vt* to alleviate, ease; (*diminuire*) to reduce; **attenuarsi** *vr* to ease, abate
attenuazi'one [attenuat'tsjone] *sf* alleviation; easing; reduction
attenzi'one [atten'tsjone] *sf* attention ■ *escl* watch out!, be careful!; **coprire qn di attenzioni** to lavish attention on sb
atter'raggio [atter'raddʒo] *sm* landing; **~ di fortuna** emergency landing
atter'rare *vt* to bring down ■ *vi* to land
atter'rire *vt* to terrify
at'tesa *sf vedi* **atteso**
at'tesi *etc vb vedi* **attendere**
at'teso, -a *pp di* **attendere** ■ *sf* waiting; (*tempo trascorso aspettando*) wait; **essere in attesa di qc** to be waiting for sth; **in attesa di una vostra risposta** (*Comm*) awaiting your reply; **restiamo in attesa di Vostre ulteriori notizie** (*Comm*) we look forward to hearing (further) from you
attes'tare *vt*: **~ qc/che** to testify to sth/(to the fact) that
attes'tato *sm* certificate
attestazi'one [attestat'tsjone] *sf* (*certificato*) certificate; (*dichiarazione*) statement
'attico, -ci *sm* attic
at'tiguo, -a *ag* adjacent, adjoining
attil'lato, -a *ag* (*vestito*) close-fitting, tight; (*persona*) dressed up
'attimo *sm* moment; **in un ~** in a moment
atti'nente *ag*: **~ a** relating to, concerning
atti'nenza [atti'nɛntsa] *sf* connection
at'tingere [at'tindʒere] *vt*: **~ a** *o* **da** (*acqua*) to draw from; (*denaro, notizie*) to obtain from
at'tinto, -a *pp di* **attingere**
atti'rare *vt* to attract; **attirarsi delle critiche** to incur criticism
atti'tudine *sf* (*disposizione*) aptitude; (*atteggiamento*) attitude
atti'vare *vt* to activate; (*far funzionare*) to set going, start
atti'vista, -i, e *sm/f* activist
attività *sf inv* activity; (*Comm*) assets *pl*; **~ liquide** (*Comm*) liquid assets
at'tivo, -a *ag* active; (*Comm*) profit-making ■ *sm* (*Comm*) assets *pl*; **in ~** in credit; **chiudere in ~** to show a profit; **avere qc al proprio ~** (*fig*) to have sth to one's credit
attiz'zare [attit'tsare] *vt* (*fuoco*) to poke; (*fig*) to stir up
attizza'toio [attittsa'tojo] *sm* poker
'atto, -a *ag*: **~ a** fit for, capable of ■ *sm* act; (*azione, gesto*) action, act, deed; (*Dir: documento*) deed, document; **atti** *smpl* (*di congressi etc*) proceedings; **essere in ~** to be under way; **mettere in ~** to put into action; **fare ~ di fare qc** to make as if to do sth; **all'~ pratico** in practice; **dare ~ a qn di qc** to give sb credit for sth; **~ di nascita/morte** birth/death certificate; **~ di proprietà** title deed; **~ pubblico** official document; **~ di vendita** bill of sale; **atti osceni (in luogo pubblico)** (*Dir*) indecent exposure; **atti verbali** transactions
at'tonito, -a *ag* dumbfounded, astonished
attorcigli'are [attortʃiʎ'ʎare] *vt*, **attorcigli'arsi** *vr* to twist
at'tore, -'trice *sm/f* actor/actress
attorni'are *vt* (*circondare*) to surround; **attorniarsi** *vr*: **attorniarsi di** to surround o.s. with
at'torno *av* round, around, about ■ *prep*: **~ a** round, around, about
attrac'care *vt, vi* (*Naut*) to dock, berth
at'tracco, -chi *sm* (*Naut: manovra*) docking, berthing; (*luogo*) berth
at'trae *etc vb vedi* **attrarre**
attra'ente *ag* attractive
at'traggo *etc vb vedi* **attrarre**
at'trarre *vt* to attract
at'trassi *etc vb vedi* **attrarre**
attrat'tiva *sf* attraction, charm
at'tratto, -a *pp di* **attrarre**
attraversa'mento *sm* crossing; **~ pedonale** pedestrian crossing
attraver'sare *vt* to cross; (*città, bosco, fig: periodo*) to go through; (*fiume*) to run through
attra'verso *prep* through; (*da una parte all'altra*) across
attrazi'one [attrat'tsjone] *sf* attraction
attrez'zare [attret'tsare] *vt* to equip; (*Naut*) to rig
attrezza'tura [attrettsa'tura] *sf* equipment *no pl*; rigging; **attrezzature per uffici** office equipment
at'trezzo [at'trettso] *sm* tool, instrument; (*Sport*) piece of equipment
attribu'ire *vt*: **~ qc a qn** (*assegnare*) to give *o* award sth to sb; (*quadro etc*) to attribute sth to sb
attri'buto *sm* attribute

at'trice [at'tritʃe] *sf vedi* **attore**
at'trito *sm* (*anche fig*) friction
attu'abile *ag* feasible
attuabilità *sf* feasibility
attu'ale *ag* (*presente*) present; (*di attualità*) topical; (*che è in atto*) actual
attualità *sf inv* topicality; (*avvenimento*) current event; **notizie d'~** (*TV*) the news *sg*
attualiz'zare [attualid'dzare] *vt* to update, bring up to date
attual'mente *av* at the moment, at present
attu'are *vt* to carry out; **attuarsi** *vr* to be realized
attuazi'one [attuat'tsjone] *sf* carrying out
attu'tire *vt* to deaden, reduce; **attutirsi** *vr* to die down
A.U. *abbr* = **allievo ufficiale**
au'dace [au'datʃe] *ag* audacious, daring, bold; (*provocante*) provocative; (*sfacciato*) impudent, bold
au'dacia [au'datʃa] *sf* audacity, daring; boldness; provocativeness; impudence
'audio *sm* (*TV, Radio, Cine*) sound
audiocas'setta *sf* (audio) cassette
audio'leso, -a *sm/f* person who is hard of hearing
audiovi'sivo, -a *ag* audiovisual
audi'torio *sm*, **audi'torium** *sm inv* auditorium
audizi'one [audit'tsjone] *sf* hearing; (*Mus*) audition
'auge ['audʒe] *sf* (*della gloria, carriera*) height, peak; **essere in ~** to be at the top
augu'rale *ag*: **messaggio ~** greeting; **biglietto ~** greetings card
augu'rare *vt* to wish; **augurarsi qc** to hope for sth
au'gurio *sm* (*presagio*) omen; (*voto di benessere etc*) (good) wish; **essere di buon/cattivo ~** to be of good omen/be ominous; **fare gli auguri a qn** to give sb one's best wishes; **tanti auguri!** all the best!
'aula *sf* (*scolastica*) classroom; (*universitaria*) lecture theatre; (*di edificio pubblico*) hall; **~ magna** main hall; **~ del tribunale** courtroom
aumen'tare *vt, vi* to increase; **~ di peso** (*persona*) to put on weight; **la produzione è aumentata del 50%** production has increased by 50%
au'mento *sm* increase
'aureo, -a *ag* (*di oro*) gold *cpd*; (*fig: colore, periodo*) golden
au'reola *sf* halo
au'rora *sf* dawn
ausili'are *ag, sm, sm/f* auxiliary
au'silio *sm* aid
auspi'cabile *ag* desirable
auspi'care *vt* to call for, express a desire for
aus'picio [aus'pitʃo] *sm* omen; (*protezione*) patronage; **sotto gli auspici di** under the auspices of; **è di buon ~** it augurs well
austerità *sf inv* austerity
aus'tero, -a *ag* austere
aus'trale *ag* southern
Aus'tralia *sf*: **l'~** Australia
australi'ano, -a *ag, sm/f* Australian
'Austria *sf*: **l'~** Austria
aus'triaco, -a, ci, che *ag, sm/f* Austrian
au'tarchico, -a, ci, che [au'tarkiko] *ag* (*sistema*) self-sufficient, autarkic; (*prodotto*) home *cpd*, home-produced
'aut 'aut *sm inv* ultimatum
autenti'care *vt* to authenticate
autenticità [autentitʃi'ta] *sf* authenticity
au'tentico, -a, ci, che *ag* (*quadro, firma*) authentic, genuine; (*fatto*) true, genuine
au'tista, -i *sm* driver; (*personale*) chauffeur
'auto *sf inv* car; **~ blu** official car
autoabbron'zante *ag* self-tanning
autoade'sivo, -a *ag* self-adhesive ■ *sm* sticker
autoartico'lato *sm* articulated lorry (*Brit*), semi (trailer) (*US*)
autobiogra'fia *sf* autobiography
autobio'grafico, -a, ci, che *ag* autobiographic(al)
auto'blinda *sf* armoured (*Brit*) *o* armored (*US*) car
auto'bomba *sf inv* car carrying a bomb; **l'~ si trovava a pochi metri** the car bomb was a few metres away
auto'botte *sf* tanker
'autobus *sm inv* bus
autocari'cabile *ag*: **scheda ~** top-up card
auto'carro *sm* lorry (*Brit*), truck
autocertificazi'one [autotʃertifikat'tsjone] *sf* self-declaration
autocis'terna [autotʃis'tɛrna] *sf* tanker
autoco'lonna *sf* convoy
autocon'trollo *sm* self-control
autocopia'tivo, -a *ag*: **carta autocopiativa** carbonless paper
autocorri'era *sf* coach, bus
auto'cratico, -a, ci, che *ag* autocratic
auto'critica, -che *sf* self-criticism
au'toctono, -a *ag, sm/f* native
autodemolizi'one [autodemolit'tsjone] *sf* breaker's yard (*Brit*)
autodi'datta, -i, e *sm/f* autodidact, self-taught person
autodi'fesa *sf* self-defence
autoferrotranvi'ario, -a *ag* public transport *cpd*

autogesti'one [autodʒes'tjone] *sf* worker management
autoges'tito, -a [autodʒes'tito] *ag* under worker management
au'tografo, -a *ag, sm* autograph
auto'grill *sm inv* motorway café (*Brit*), roadside restaurant (*US*)
autoim'mune *ag* autoimmune
autolesio'nismo *sm* (*fig*) self-destruction
auto'linea *sf* bus route
au'toma, -i *sm* automaton
auto'matico, -a, ci, che *ag* automatic ■ *sm* (*bottone*) snap fastener; (*fucile*) automatic; **selezione automatica** (*Tel*) direct dialling
automazi'one [automat'tsjone] *sf*: **~ delle procedure d'ufficio** office automation
automedicazi'one [automedikat'tsjone] *sf* (*medicine, farmaci*): **medicinale di ~** self-medication
auto'mezzo [auto'mɛddzo] *sm* motor vehicle
auto'mobile *sf* (motor) car; **~ da corsa** racing car (*Brit*), race car (*US*)
automobi'lismo *sm* (*gen*) motoring; (*Sport*) motor racing
automobi'lista, -i, e *sm/f* motorist
automobi'listico, -a, ci, che *ag* car *cpd* (*Brit*), automobile *cpd* (*US*); (*sport*) motor *cpd*
autono'leggio [autono'leddʒo] *sm* car hire (*Brit*), car rental
autono'mia *sf* autonomy; (*di volo*) range
au'tonomo, -a *ag* autonomous; (*sindacato, pensiero*) independent
auto'parco, -chi *sm* (*parcheggio*) car park (*Brit*), parking lot (*US*); (*insieme di automezzi*) transport fleet
auto'pompa *sf* fire engine
autop'sia *sf* post-mortem (examination), autopsy
auto'radio *sf inv* (*apparecchio*) car radio; (*autoveicolo*) radio car
au'tore, -'trice *sm/f* author; **l'~ del furto** the person who committed the robbery; **diritti d'~** copyright *sg*; (*compenso*) royalties
autoregolamentazi'one [autoregolamentat'tsjone] *sf* self-regulation
auto'revole *ag* authoritative; (*persona*) influential
autori'messa *sf* garage
autorità *sf inv* authority
autori'tratto *sm* self-portrait
autoriz'zare [autorid'dzare] *vt* to authorize, give permission for
autorizzazi'one [autoriddzat'tsjone] *sf* authorization; **~ a procedere** (*Dir*) authorization to proceed
autos'catto *sm* (*Fot*) timer
autos'contro *sm* dodgem car (*Brit*), bumper car (*US*)
autoscu'ola *sf* driving school
autosno'dato *sm* articulated vehicle
autos'top *sm* hitchhiking
autostop'pista, -i, e *sm/f* hitchhiker
autos'trada *sf* motorway (*Brit*), highway (*US*); **~ informatica** information superhighway
autosuffici'ente [autosuffi'tʃɛnte] *ag* self-sufficient
autosuffici'enza [autosuffi'tʃɛntsa] *sf* self-sufficiency
auto'treno *sm* articulated lorry (*Brit*), semi (trailer) (*US*)
autove'icolo *sm* motor vehicle
auto'velox® *sm inv* (police) speed camera
autovet'tura *sf* (motor) car
autun'nale *ag* (*di autunno*) autumn *cpd*; (*da autunno*) autumnal
au'tunno *sm* autumn
AV *sigla* = **Avellino**
aval'lare *vt* (*Finanza*) to guarantee; (*fig: sostenere*) to back; (*: confermare*) to confirm
a'vallo *sm* (*Finanza*) guarantee
avam'braccio [avam'brattʃo] (*pl*(*f*) **avambraccia**) *sm* forearm
avam'posto *sm* (*Mil*) outpost
A'vana *sf*: **l'~** Havana
a'vana *sm inv* (*sigaro*) Havana (cigar); (*colore*) Havana brown
avangu'ardia *sf* vanguard; (*Arte*) avant-garde
avansco'perta *sf* (*Mil*) reconnaissance; **andare in ~** to reconnoitre
a'vanti *av* (*stato in luogo*) in front; (*moto: andare, venire*) forward; (*tempo: prima*) before ■ *prep* (*luogo*): **~ a** before, in front of; (*tempo*): **~ Cristo** before Christ ■ *escl* (*entrate*) come (*o* go) in!; (*Mil*) forward!; (*coraggio*) come on! ■ *sm inv* (*Sport*) forward; **il giorno ~** the day before; **~ e indietro** backwards and forwards; **andare ~** to go forward; (*continuare*) to go on; (*precedere*) to go (on) ahead; (*orologio*) to be fast; **essere ~ negli studi** to be well advanced with one's studies; **mandare ~ la famiglia** to provide for one's family; **mandare ~ un'azienda** to run a business; **~ il prossimo!** next please!
avan'treno *sm* (*Aut*) front chassis
avanza'mento [avantsa'mento] *sm* (*gen*) advance; (*fig*) progress; promotion
avan'zare [avan'tsare] *vt* (*spostare in avanti*) to move forward, advance; (*domanda*) to put forward; (*promuovere*) to promote; (*essere creditore*): **~ qc da qn** to be owed sth by sb ■ *vi* (*andare avanti*) to move forward, advance; (*fig: progredire*) to make progress; (*essere d'avanzo*) to

be left, remain; **basta e avanza** that's more than enough
avan'zato, -a [avan'tsato] *ag* (*teoria, tecnica*) advanced ■ *sf* (*Mil*) advance; **in età avanzata** advanced in years, up in years
a'vanzo [a'vantso] *sm* (*residuo*) remains *pl*, left-overs *pl*; (*Mat*) remainder; (*Comm*) surplus; (*eccedenza di bilancio*) profit carried forward; **averne d'~ di qc** to have more than enough of sth; **~ di cassa** cash in hand; **~ di galera** (*fig*) jailbird
ava'ria *sf* (*guasto*) damage; (: *meccanico*) breakdown
avari'ato, -a *ag* (*merce*) damaged; (*cibo*) off
ava'rizia [ava'rittsja] *sf* avarice; **crepi l'~!** to hang with the expense!
a'varo, -a *ag* avaricious, miserly ■ *sm* miser
a'vena *sf* oats *pl*

 PAROLA CHIAVE

a'vere *sm* (*Comm*) credit; **gli averi** (*ricchezze*) wealth *sg*, possessions
■ *vt* **1** (*possedere*) to have; **ha due bambini/una bella casa** she has (got) two children/a lovely house; **ha i capelli lunghi** he has (got) long hair; **non ho da mangiare/bere** I've (got) nothing to eat/drink, I don't have anything to eat/drink
2 (*indossare*) to wear, have on; **aveva una maglietta rossa** he was wearing *o* he had on a red T-shirt; **ha gli occhiali** he wears *o* has glasses
3 (*ricevere*) to get; **hai avuto l'assegno?** did you get *o* have you had the cheque?
4 (*età, dimensione*) to be; **ha 9 anni** he is 9 (years old); **la stanza ha 3 metri di lunghezza** the room is 3 metres in length; *vedi* **fame**; **paura**; **sonno** *etc*
5 (*tempo*): **quanti ne abbiamo oggi?** what's the date today?; **ne hai per molto?** will you be long?
6 (*fraseologia*): **avercela con qn** to be angry with sb; **cos'hai?** what's wrong *o* what's the matter (with you)?; **non ha niente a che vedere** *o* **fare con me** it's got nothing to do with me
■ *vb aus* **1** to have; **aver bevuto/mangiato** to have drunk/eaten; **l'ho già visto** I have seen it already; **l'ho visto ieri** I saw it yesterday; **ci ha creduto?** did he believe it?
2 (*+ da + infinito*): **avere da fare qc** to have to do sth; **non ho niente da dire** I have nothing to say; **non hai che da chiederlo** you only have to ask him

avia'tore, -'trice *sm/f* aviator, pilot
avi'ario, -a *ag* bird *cpd*; **influenza aviaria** bird flu
aviazi'one [avjat'tsjone] *sf* aviation; (*Mil*) air force; **~ civile** civil aviation
avicol'tura *sf* bird breeding; (*di pollame*) poultry farming
avidità *sf* eagerness; greed
'avido, -a *ag* eager; (*peg*) greedy
avi'ere *sm* (*Mil*) airman
avitami'nosi *sf* vitamin deficiency
'avo *sm* (*antenato*) ancestor; **i nostri avi** our ancestors
avo'cado *sm* avocado
a'vorio *sm* ivory
a'vulso, -a *ag*: **parole avulse dal contesto** words out of context; **~ dalla società** (*fig*) cut off from society
Avv. *abbr* = **avvocato**
avva'lersi *vr*: **~ di** to avail o.s. of
avvalla'mento *sm* sinking *no pl*; (*effetto*) depression
avvalo'rare *vt* to confirm
avvantaggi'are [avvantad'dʒare] *vt* to favour (*Brit*), favor (*US*); **avvantaggiarsi** *vr* (*trarre vantaggio*): **avvantaggiarsi di** to take advantage of; (*prevalere*): **avvantaggiarsi negli affari/sui concorrenti** to get ahead in business/of one's competitors
avve'dersi *vr*: **~ di qn/qc** to notice sb/sth
avve'duto, -a *ag* (*accorto*) prudent; (*scaltro*) astute
avvelena'mento *sm* poisoning
avvele'nare *vt* to poison
avve'nente *ag* attractive, charming
avve'nenza [avve'nɛntsa] *sf* good looks *pl*
av'vengo *etc vb vedi* **avvenire**
avveni'mento *sm* event
avve'nire *vi, vb impers* to happen, occur ■ *sm* future
av'venni *etc vb vedi* **avvenire**
avven'tarsi *vr*: **~ su** *o* **contro qn/qc** to hurl o.s. *o* rush at sb/sth
avven'tato, -a *ag* rash, reckless
avven'tizio, -a [avven'tittsjo] *ag* (*impiegato*) temporary; (*guadagno*) casual
av'vento *sm* advent, coming; (*Rel*): **l'A~** Advent
avven'tore *sm* customer
avven'tura *sf* adventure; (*amorosa*) affair; **avere spirito d'~** to be adventurous
avventu'rarsi *vr* to venture
avventuri'ero, -a *sm/f* adventurer/adventuress
avventu'roso, -a *ag* adventurous
avve'nuto, -a *pp di* **avvenire**
avve'rarsi *vr* to come true
av'verbio *sm* adverb

avverrò *etc vb vedi* **avvenire**
avver'sare *vt* to oppose
avver'sario, -a *ag* opposing ▪ *sm* opponent, adversary
avversi'one *sf* aversion
avversità *sf inv* adversity, misfortune
av'verso, -a *ag* (*contrario*) contrary; (*sfavorevole*) unfavourable (*Brit*), unfavorable (*US*)
avver'tenza [avver'tɛntsa] *sf* (*ammonimento*) warning; (*cautela*) care; (*premessa*) foreword; **avvertenze** *sfpl* (*istruzioni per l'uso*) instructions
avverti'mento *sm* warning
avver'tire *vt* (*avvisare*) to warn; (*rendere consapevole*) to inform, notify; (*percepire*) to feel
av'vezzo, -a [av'vettso] *ag*: **~ a** used to
avvia'mento *sm* (*atto*) starting; (*effetto*) start; (*Aut*) starting; (*: dispositivo*) starter; (*Comm*) goodwill
avvi'are *vt* (*mettere sul cammino*) to direct; (*impresa, trattative*) to begin, start; (*motore*) to start; **avviarsi** *vr* to set off, set out
avvicenda'mento [avvitʃenda'mento] *sm* alternation; (*Agr*) rotation; **c'è molto ~ di personale** there is a high turnover of staff
avvicen'dare [avvitʃen'dare] *vt*, **avvicen'darsi** *vr* to alternate
avvicina'mento [avvitʃina'mento] *sm* approach
avvici'nare [avvitʃi'nare] *vt* to bring near; (*trattare con: persona*) to approach; **avvicinarsi** *vr*: **avvicinarsi (a qn/qc)** to approach (sb/sth), draw near (to sb/sth); (*somigliare*) to be similar (to sb/sth), be close (to sb/sth)
avvi'lente *ag* (*umiliante*) humiliating; (*scoraggiante*) discouraging, disheartening
avvili'mento *sm* humiliation; disgrace; discouragement
avvi'lire *vt* (*umiliare*) to humiliate; (*degradare*) to disgrace; (*scoraggiare*) to dishearten, discourage; **avvilirsi** *vr* (*abbattersi*) to lose heart
avvilup'pare *vt* (*avvolgere*) to wrap up; (*ingarbugliare*) to entangle
avvinaz'zato, -a [avvinat'tsato] *ag* drunk
avvin'cente [avvin'tʃɛnte] *ag* (*film, racconto*) enthralling
av'vincere [av'vintʃere] *vt* to charm, enthral
avvinghi'are [avvin'gjare] *vt* to clasp; **avvinghiarsi** *vr*: **avvinghiarsi a** to cling to
av'vinsi *etc vb vedi* **avvincere**
av'vinto, -a *pp di* **avvincere**
av'vio *sm* start, beginning; **dare l'~ a qc** to start sth off; **prendere l'~** to get going, get under way
avvi'saglia [avvi'zaʎʎa] *sf* (*sintomo: di temporale etc*) sign; (*di malattia*) manifestation, sign, symptom; (*scaramuccia*) skirmish
avvi'sare *vt* (*far sapere*) to inform; (*mettere in guardia*) to warn
avvisa'tore *sm* (*apparecchio d'allarme*) alarm; **~ acustico** horn; **~ d'incendio** fire alarm
av'viso *sm* warning; (*annuncio*) announcement; (*affisso*) notice; (*inserzione pubblicitaria*) advertisement; **a mio ~** in my opinion; **mettere qn sull'~** to put sb on their guard; **fino a nuovo ~** until further notice; **~ di chiamata** (*servizio*) call waiting; (*segnale*) call waiting signal; **~ di consegna/spedizione** (*Comm*) delivery/consignment note; **~ di garanzia** (*Dir*) notification (*of impending investigation and of the right to name a defence laywer*); **~ di pagamento** (*Comm*) payment advice
avvista'mento *sm* sighting
avvis'tare *vt* to sight
avvi'tare *vt* to screw down (*o* in)
avviz'zire [avvit'tsire] *vi* to wither
avvo'cato, -'essa *sm/f* (*Dir*) barrister (*Brit*), lawyer; (*fig*) defender, advocate; **~ del diavolo**: **fare l'~ del diavolo** to play devil's advocate; **~ difensore** counsel for the defence; **~ di parte civile** counsel for the plaintiff
av'volgere [av'vɔldʒere] *vt* to roll up; (*bobina*) to wind up; (*avviluppare*) to wrap up; **avvolgersi** *vr* (*avvilupparsi*) to wrap o.s. up
avvol'gibile [avvol'dʒibile] *sm* roller blind (*Brit*), blind
avvolgi'mento [avvoldʒi'mento] *sm* winding
av'volsi *etc vb vedi* **avvolgere**
av'volto, -a *pp di* **avvolgere**
avvol'toio *sm* vulture
aza'lea [addza'lɛa] *sf* azalea
Azerbaigi'an [addzɛrbai'dʒan] *sm* Azerbaijan
azerbaig'iano, -a [addzɛrbai'dʒano] *ag* Azerbaijani ▪ *sm/f* (*abitante*) Azerbaijani ▪ *sm* (*Ling*) Azerbaijani
a'zero, -a [ad'dzɛro] *sm/f* Azeri
azi'enda [ad'dzjɛnda] *sf* business, firm, concern; **~ agricola** farm; **~ (autonoma) di soggiorno** tourist board; **~ a partecipazione statale** *business in which the State has a financial interest*; **aziende pubbliche** public corporations
azien'dale [addzjen'dale] *ag* company *cpd*; **organizzazione ~** business administration
azio'nare [attsjo'nare] *vt* to activate
azio'nario, -a [attsjo'narjo] *ag* share *cpd*; **capitale ~** share capital; **mercato ~** stock market
azi'one [at'tsjone] *sf* action; (*Comm*) share; **~ sindacale** industrial action; **azioni preferenziali** preference shares (*Brit*), preferred stock *sg* (*US*)

azioˈnista, -i, e [attsjoˈnista] *sm/f* (*Comm*) shareholder
aˈzoto [adˈdzɔto] *sm* nitrogen
azˈteco, -a, ci, che [asˈtɛko] *ag, sm/f* Aztec
azzanˈnare [attsanˈnare] *vt* to sink one's teeth into
azzarˈdare [addzarˈdare] *vt* (*soldi, vita*) to risk, hazard; (*domanda, ipotesi*) to hazard, venture; **azzardarsi** *vr*: **azzardarsi a fare** to dare (to) do
azzarˈdato, -a [addzarˈdato] *ag* (*impresa*) risky; (*risposta*) rash
azˈzardo [adˈdzardo] *sm* risk; **gioco d'~** game of chance
azzecˈcare [attsekˈkare] *vt* (*bersaglio*) to hit, strike; (*risposta, pronostico*) to get right; (*fig: indovinare*) to guess
azzeraˈmento [addzeraˈmento] *sm* (*Inform*) reset
azzeˈrare [addzeˈrare] *vt* (*Mat, Fisica*) to make equal to zero, reduce to zero; (*Tecn: strumento*) to (re)set to zero
ˈazzimo, -a [ˈaddzimo] *ag* unleavened ■ *sm* unleavened bread
azzopˈpare [attsopˈpare] *vt* to lame, make lame
Azˈzorre [adˈdzorre] *sfpl*: **le ~** the Azores
azzufˈfarsi [attsufˈfarsi] *vr* to come to blows
azˈzurro, -a [adˈdzurro] *ag* blue ■ *sm* (*colore*) blue; **gli azzurri** (*Sport*) the Italian national team
azzurˈrognolo, -a [addzurˈroɲɲolo] *ag* bluish

Bb

B, b [bi] *sf o m inv* (*lettera*) B, b; **B come Bologna** ≈ B for Benjamin (*Brit*), ≈ B for Baker (*US*)
BA *sigla* = **Bari**
ba'bau *sm inv* ogre, bogey man
bab'beo *sm* simpleton
'babbo *sm* (*fam*) dad, daddy; **B~ Natale** Father Christmas
bab'buccia, -ce [bab'buttʃa] *sf* slipper; (*per neonati*) bootee
babbu'ino *sm* baboon
babilo'nese *ag, sm/f* Babylonian
Babi'lonia *sf* Babylonia
ba'bordo *sm* (*Naut*) port side
baby'sitter ['beibisitə^r] *sm/f inv* baby-sitter
ba'cato, -a *ag* worm-eaten, rotten; (*fig: mente*) diseased; (*: persona*) corrupt
'bacca, -che *sf* berry
baccalà *sm* dried salted cod; (*fig: peg*) dummy
bac'cano *sm* din, clamour (*Brit*), clamor (*US*)
bac'cello [bat'tʃɛllo] *sm* pod
bac'chetta [bak'ketta] *sf* (*verga*) stick, rod; (*di direttore d'orchestra*) baton; (*di tamburo*) drumstick; **comandare a ~** to rule with a rod of iron; **~ magica** magic wand
ba'checa, -che [ba'kɛka] *sf* (*mobile*) showcase, display case; (*Università, in ufficio*) notice board (*Brit*), bulletin board (*US*)
bacia'mano [batʃa'mano] *sm*: **fare il ~ a qn** to kiss sb's hand
baci'are [ba'tʃare] *vt* to kiss; **baciarsi** *vr* to kiss (one another)
ba'cillo [ba'tʃillo] *sm* bacillus, germ
baci'nella [batʃi'nɛlla] *sf* basin
ba'cino [ba'tʃino] *sm* basin; (*Mineralogia*) field, bed; (*Anat*) pelvis; (*Naut*) dock; **~ carbonifero** coalfield; **~ di carenaggio** dry dock; **~ petrolifero** oilfield; **~ d'utenza** catchment area
'bacio ['batʃo] *sm* kiss
'baco, -chi *sm* worm; **~ da seta** silkworm
'bada *sf*: **tenere qn a ~** (*tener d'occhio*) to keep an eye on sb; (*tenere a distanza*) to hold sb at bay
ba'dante *sm/f* care worker
ba'dare *vi* (*fare attenzione*) to take care, be careful; **~ a** (*occuparsi di*) to look after, take care of; (*dar ascolto*) to pay attention to; **è un tipo che non bada a spese** money is no object to him; **bada ai fatti tuoi!** mind your own business!
ba'dia *sf* abbey
ba'dile *sm* shovel
'baffi *smpl* moustache *sg*, mustache *sg* (*US*); (*di animale*) whiskers; **leccarsi i ~** to lick one's lips; **ridere sotto i ~** to laugh up one's sleeve
bagagli'aio [bagaʎ'ʎajo] *sm* luggage van (*Brit*) *o* car (*US*); (*Aut*) boot (*Brit*), trunk (*US*)
ba'gaglio [ba'gaʎʎo] *sm* luggage *no pl*, baggage *no pl*; **fare/disfare i bagagli** to pack/unpack; **~ a mano** hand luggage
bagat'tella *sf* trifle, trifling matter
Bag'dad *sf* Baghdad
baggia'nata [baddʒa'nata] *sf* foolish action; **dire baggianate** to talk nonsense
bagli'ore [baʎ'ʎore] *sm* flash, dazzling light; **un ~ di speranza** a sudden ray of hope
ba'gnante [baɲ'ɲante] *sm/f* bather
ba'gnare [baɲ'ɲare] *vt* to wet; (*inzuppare*) to soak; (*innaffiare*) to water; (*fiume*) to flow through; (*: mare*) to wash, bathe; (*brindare*) to drink to, toast; **bagnarsi** *vr* (*al mare*) to go swimming *o* bathing; (*in vasca*) to have a bath
ba'gnato, -a [baɲ'ɲato] *ag* wet; **era come un pulcino ~** he looked like a drowned rat
ba'gnino [baɲ'ɲino] *sm* lifeguard
'bagno ['baɲɲo] *sm* bath; (*locale*) bathroom; **bagni** *smpl* (*stabilimento*) baths; **fare il ~** to have a bath; (*nel mare*) to go swimming *o* bathing; **fare il ~ a qn** to give sb a bath; **mettere a ~** to soak
bagnoma'ria [baɲɲoma'ria] *sm*: **cuocere a ~** to cook in a double saucepan (*Brit*) *o* double boiler (*US*)
bagnoschi'uma [baɲɲoskj'uma] *sm inv* bubble bath
Ba'hama [ba'ama] *sfpl*: **le ~** the Bahamas

Bah'rein [ba'rein] *sm*: **il ~** Bahrain *o* Bahrein
'baia *sf* bay
baio'netta *sf* bayonet
'baita *sf* mountain hut
balaus'trata *sf* balustrade
balbet'tare *vi* to stutter, stammer; (*bimbo*) to babble ■ *vt* to stammer out
bal'buzie [bal'buttsje] *sf* stammer
balbuzi'ente [balbut'tsjɛnte] *ag* stuttering, stammering
Bal'cani *smpl*: **i ~** the Balkans
bal'canico, -a, ci, che *ag* Balkan
bal'cone *sm* balcony
baldac'chino [baldak'kino] *sm* canopy; **letto a ~** four-poster (bed)
bal'danza [bal'dantsa] *sf* self-confidence; boldness
'baldo, -a *ag* bold, daring
bal'doria *sf*: **fare ~** to have a riotous time
Bale'ari *sfpl*: **le isole ~** the Balearic Islands
ba'lena *sf* whale
bale'nare *vb impers*: **balena** there's lightning ■ *vi* to flash; **mi balenò un'idea** an idea flashed through my mind
baleni'era *sf* (*per la caccia*) whaler, whaling ship
ba'leno *sm* flash of lightning; **in un ~** in a flash
ba'lera *sf* (*locale*) dance hall; (*pista*) dance floor
ba'lestra *sf* crossbow
'balia *sf* wet-nurse; **~ asciutta** nanny
ba'lia *sf*: **in ~ di** at the mercy of; **essere lasciato in ~ di se stesso** to be left to one's own devices
ba'lilla *sm inv* (*Storia*) *member of Fascist youth group*
ba'listico, -a, ci, che *ag* ballistic ■ *sf* ballistics *sg*; **perito ~** ballistics expert
'balla *sf* (*di merci*) bale; (*fandonia*) (tall) story
bal'labile *sm* dance number, dance tune
bal'lare *vt, vi* to dance
bal'lata *sf* ballad
balla'toio *sm* (*terrazzina*) gallery
balle'rina *sf* dancer; ballet dancer; (*scarpa*) pump; **~ di rivista** chorus girl
balle'rino *sm* dancer; ballet dancer
bal'letto *sm* ballet
'ballo *sm* dance; (*azione*) dancing *no pl*; **~ in maschera** *o* **mascherato** fancy-dress ball; **essere in ~** (*fig: persona*) to be involved; (*: cosa*) to be at stake; **tirare in ~ qc** to bring sth up, raise sth
ballot'taggio [ballot'taddʒo] *sm* (*Pol*) second ballot
balne'are *ag* seaside *cpd*; (*stagione*) bathing
ba'locco, -chi *sm* toy
ba'lordo, -a *ag* stupid, senseless
bal'samico, -a, ci, che *ag* (*aria, brezza*) balmy; **pomata balsamica** balsam
'balsamo *sm* (*aroma*) balsam; (*lenimento, fig*) balm; (*per capelli*) (hair) conditioner
'baltico, -a, ci, che *ag* Baltic; **il (mar) B~** the Baltic (Sea)
balu'ardo *sm* bulwark
'balza ['baltsa] *sf* (*dirupo*) crag; (*di stoffa*) frill
bal'zano, -a [bal'tsano] *ag* (*persona, idea*) queer, odd
bal'zare [bal'tsare] *vi* to bounce; (*lanciarsi*) to jump, leap; **la verità balza agli occhi** the truth of the matter is obvious
'balzo ['baltso] *sm* bounce; jump, leap; (*del terreno*) crag; **prendere la palla al ~** (*fig*) to seize one's opportunity
bam'bagia [bam'badʒa] *sf* (*ovatta*) cotton wool (*Brit*), absorbent cotton (*US*); (*cascame*) cotton waste; **tenere qn nella ~** (*fig*) to mollycoddle sb
bam'bina *sf vedi* **bambino**
bambi'naia *sf* nanny, nurse(maid)
bam'bino, -a *sm/f* child; **fare il ~** to behave childishly
bam'boccio [bam'bɔttʃo] *sm* plump child; (*pupazzo*) rag doll
'bambola *sf* doll
bambo'lotto *sm* male doll
bambù *sm* bamboo
ba'nale *ag* banal, commonplace
banalità *sf inv* banality
ba'nana *sf* banana
ba'nano *sm* banana tree
'banca, -che *sf* bank; **~ d'affari** merchant bank; **~ (di) dati** data bank
banca'rella *sf* stall
ban'cario, -a *ag* banking, bank *cpd* ■ *sm* bank clerk
banca'rotta *sf* bankruptcy; **fare ~** to go bankrupt
bancarotti'ere *sm* bankrupt
ban'chetto [ban'ketto] *sm* banquet
banchi'ere [ban'kjɛre] *sm* banker
ban'china [ban'kina] *sf* (*di porto*) quay; (*per pedoni, ciclisti*) path; (*di stazione*) platform; **~ cedevole** (*Aut*) soft verge (*Brit*) *o* shoulder (*US*); **~ spartitraffico** (*Aut*) central reservation (*Brit*), median (strip) (*US*)
ban'chisa [ban'kiza] *sf* pack ice
'banco, -chi *sm* bench; (*di negozio*) counter; (*di mercato*) stall; (*di officina*) (work)bench; (*Geo, banca*) bank; **sotto ~** (*fig*) under the counter; **tenere il ~** (*nei giochi*) to be (the) banker; **tener ~** (*fig*) to monopolize the conversation; **medicinali da ~** over-the-counter medicines; **~ di chiesa** pew; **~ di corallo** coral reef; **~ degli imputati** dock; **~ del Lotto** lottery-ticket office; **~ di prova** (*fig*) testing ground; **~ dei testimoni** witness box (*Brit*) *o* stand (*US*)

b

banco'giro [banko'dʒiro] *sm* credit transfer
'Bancomat® *sm inv* (*tessera*) cash card; (*sportello*) cashpoint (*Brit*), ATM (*US*)
banco'nota *sf* banknote
'banda *sf* band; (*di stoffa*) band, stripe; (*lato, parte*) side; (*di calcolatore*) tape; **~ larga** broadband; **~ perforata** punch tape
banderu'ola *sf* (*Meteor*) weathercock, weathervane; **essere una ~** (*fig*) to be fickle
bandi'era *sf* flag, banner; **battere ~ italiana** (*nave etc*) to fly the Italian flag; **cambiare ~** (*fig*) to change sides; **~ di comodo** flag of convenience
ban'dire *vt* to proclaim; (*esiliare*) to exile; (*fig*) to dispense with
ban'dito *sm* outlaw, bandit
bandi'tore *sm* (*di aste*) auctioneer
'bando *sm* proclamation; (*esilio*) exile, banishment; **mettere al ~ qn** to exile sb; (*fig*) to freeze sb out; **~ alle ciance!** that's enough talk!
'bandolo *sm* (*di matassa*) end; **trovare il ~ della matassa** (*fig*) to find the key to the problem
Bang'kok [ban'kɔk] *sf* Bangkok
Bangla'desh [bangla'dɛʃ] *sm*: **il ~** Bangladesh
bar *sm inv* bar
'bara *sf* coffin
ba'racca, -che *sf* shed, hut; (*peg*) hovel; **mandare avanti la ~** to keep things going; **piantare ~ e burattini** to throw everything up
barac'cato, -a *sm/f person living in temporary camp*
barac'chino [barak'kino] *sm* (*chiosco*) stall; (*apparecchio*) CB radio
barac'cone *sm* booth, stall; **baracconi** *smpl* (*luna park*) funfair *sg* (*Brit*), amusement park; **fenomeno da ~** circus freak
barac'copoli *sf inv* shanty town
bara'onda *sf* hubbub, bustle
ba'rare *vi* to cheat
'baratro *sm* abyss
barat'tare *vt*: **~ qc con** to barter sth for, swap sth for
ba'ratto *sm* barter
ba'rattolo *sm* (*di latta*) tin; (*di vetro*) jar; (*di coccio*) pot
'barba *sf* beard; **farsi la ~** to shave; **farla in ~ a qn** (*fig*) to fool sb; **servire qn di ~ e capelli** (*fig*) to teach sb a lesson; **che ~!** what a bore!
barbabi'etola *sf* beetroot (*Brit*), beet (*US*); **~ da zucchero** sugar beet
Bar'bados *sf* Barbados
bar'barico, -a, ci, che *ag* (*invasione*) barbarian; (*usanze, metodi*) barbaric
bar'barie *sf* barbarity
'barbaro, -a *ag* barbarous ■ *sm* barbarian; **i Barbari** the Barbarians
'barbecue ['ba:bikju:] *sm inv* barbecue
barbi'ere *sm* barber
barbi'turico, -a, ci, che *ag* barbituric ■ *sm* barbiturate
bar'bone *sm* (*cane*) poodle; (*vagabondo*) tramp
bar'buto, -a *ag* bearded
'barca, -che *sf* boat; **una ~ di** (*fig*) heaps of, tons of; **mandare avanti la ~** (*fig*) to keep things going; **~ a remi** rowing boat (*Brit*), rowboat (*US*); **~ a vela** sailing boat (*Brit*), sailboat (*US*)
barcai'olo *sm* boatman
barcame'narsi *vr* (*nel lavoro*) to get by; (*a parole*) to beat about the bush
Barcel'lona [bartʃel'lona] *sf* Barcelona
barcol'lare *vi* to stagger
bar'cone *sm* (*per ponti di barche*) pontoon
ba'rella *sf* (*lettiga*) stretcher
'Barents: il mar di ~ *sm* the Barents Sea
ba'rese *ag* of (*o* from) Bari
bari'centro [bari'tʃɛntro] *sm* centre (*Brit*) *o* center (*US*) of gravity
ba'rile *sm* barrel, cask
ba'rista, -i, e *sm/f* barman/barmaid; bar owner
ba'ritono *sm* baritone
bar'lume *sm* glimmer, gleam
'baro *sm* (*Carte*) cardsharp
ba'rocco, -a, chi, che *ag, sm* baroque
ba'rometro *sm* barometer
ba'rone *sm* baron; **i baroni della medicina** (*fig peg*) the top brass in the medical faculty
baro'nessa *sf* baroness
'barra *sf* bar; (*Naut*) helm; (*segno grafico*) stroke
bar'rare *vt* to bar
barri'care *vt* to barricade
barri'cata *sf* barricade; **essere dall'altra parte della ~** (*fig*) to be on the other side of the fence
barri'era *sf* barrier; (*Geo*) reef; **la Grande B~ Corallina** the Great Barrier Reef
bar'roccio [bar'rɔttʃo] *sm* cart
ba'ruffa *sf* scuffle; **fare ~** to squabble
barzel'letta [bardzel'letta] *sf* joke, funny story
basa'mento *sm* (*parte inferiore, piedestallo*) base; (*Tecn*) bed, base plate
ba'sare *vt* to base, found; **basarsi** *vr*: **basarsi su** (*fatti, prove*) to be based *o* founded on; (*: persona*) to base one's arguments on
'basco, -a, schi, sche *ag* Basque ■ *sm/f* Basque ■ *sm* (*lingua*) Basque; (*copricapo*) beret
bas'culla *sf* weighing machine, weighbridge
'base *sf* base; (*fig: fondamento*) basis; (*Pol*) rank and file; **di ~** basic; **in ~ a** on the basis of,

according to; **in ~ a ciò ...** on that basis ...; **a ~ di caffè** coffee-based; **essere alla ~ di qc** to be at the root of sth; **gettare le basi per qc** to lay the basis *o* foundations for sth; **avere buone basi** (*Ins*) to have a sound educational background

'**baseball** ['beisbɔ:l] *sm* baseball

ba'setta *sf* sideburn

basi'lare *ag* basic, fundamental

Basi'lea *sf* Basle

ba'silica, -che *sf* basilica

ba'silico *sm* basil

bas'sezza [bas'settsa] *sf* (*d'animo, di sentimenti*) baseness; (*azione*) base action

bas'sista, -i, e *sm/f* bass player

'**basso, -a** *ag* low; (*di statura*) short; (*meridionale*) southern ■ *sm* bottom, lower part; (*Mus*) bass; **a occhi bassi** with eyes lowered; **a ~ prezzo** cheap; **scendere da ~** to go downstairs; **cadere in ~** (*fig*) to come down in the world; **la bassa Italia** southern Italy; **il ~ Medioevo** the late Middle Ages

basso'fondo (*pl* **bassifondi**) *sm* (*Geo*) shallows *pl*; **i bassifondi (della città)** the seediest parts of the town

bassorili'evo *sm* bas-relief

bas'sotto, -a *ag* squat ■ *sm* (*cane*) dachshund

bas'tardo, -a *ag* (*animale, pianta*) hybrid, crossbreed; (*persona*) illegitimate, bastard (*peg*) ■ *sm/f* illegitimate child, bastard (*peg*); (*cane*) mongrel

bas'tare *vi, vb impers* to be enough, be sufficient; **~ a qn** to be enough for sb; **~ a se stesso** to be self-sufficient; **basta chiedere** *o* **che chieda a un vigile** you have only to *o* need only ask a policeman; **basti dire che ...** suffice it to say that ...; **basta!** that's enough!, that will do!; **basta così?** (*al bar etc*) will that be all?; **punto e basta!** and that's that!

basti'an *sm*: **~ contrario** awkward customer

basti'mento *sm* ship, vessel

basti'one *sm* bastion

basto'nare *vt* to beat, thrash; **avere l'aria di un cane bastonato** to look crestfallen

basto'nata *sf* blow (with a stick); **prendere qn a bastonate** to give sb a good beating

baston'cino [baston'tʃino] *sm* (*piccolo bastone*) small stick; (*Tecn*) rod; (*Sci*) ski pole; **bastoncini di pesce** (*Cuc*) fish fingers (*Brit*), fish sticks (*US*)

bas'tone *sm* stick; **bastoni** *smpl* (*Carte*) *suit in Neapolitan pack of cards*; **~ da passeggio** walking stick; **mettere i bastoni fra le ruote a qn** to put a spoke in sb's wheel

bat'tage [ba'taʒ] *sm inv*: **~ promozionale** *o* **pubblicitario** publicity campaign

bat'taglia [bat'taʎʎa] *sf* battle

bat'taglio [bat'taʎʎo] *sm* (*di campana*) clapper; (*di porta*) knocker

battagli'one [battaʎ'ʎone] *sm* battalion

bat'tello *sm* boat

bat'tente *sm* (*imposta: di porta*) wing, flap; (*: di finestra*) shutter; (*per bussare*) knocker; (*di orologio*) hammer; **chiudere i battenti** (*fig*) to shut up shop

'**battere** *vt* to beat; (*grano*) to thresh; (*percorrere*) to scour; (*rintoccare: le ore*) to strike ■ *vi* (*bussare*) to knock; (*urtare*): **~ contro** to hit *o* strike against; (*pioggia, sole*) to beat down; (*cuore*) to beat; (*Tennis*) to serve; **battersi** *vr* to fight; **~ le mani** to clap; **~ i piedi** to stamp one's feet; **~ su un argomento** to hammer home an argument; **~ a macchina** to type; **~ il marciapiede** (*peg*) to walk the streets, be on the game; **~ un rigore** (*Calcio*) to take a penalty; **~ in testa** (*Aut*) to knock; **in un batter d'occhio** in the twinkling of an eye; **senza ~ ciglio** without batting an eyelid; **battersela** to run off

batte'ria *sf* battery; (*Mus*) drums *pl*; **~ da cucina** pots and pans *pl*

bat'terio *sm* bacterium; **batteri** *smpl* bacteria

batteriolo'gia [batterjolo'dʒia] *sf* bacteriology

bat'tesimo *sm* (*sacramento*) baptism; (*rito*) baptism, christening; **tenere qn a ~** to be godfather (*o* godmother) to sb

battez'zare [batted'dzare] *vt* to baptize; to christen

battiba'leno *sm*: **in un ~** in a flash

batti'becco, -chi *sm* squabble

batticu'ore *sm* palpitations *pl*; **avere il ~** to be frightened to death

bat'tigia [bat'tidʒa] *sf* water's edge

batti'mano *sm* applause

batti'panni *sm inv* carpet-beater

battis'tero *sm* baptistry

battis'trada *sm inv* (*di pneumatico*) tread; (*di gara*) pacemaker

battitap'peto *sm inv* upright vacuum cleaner

'**battito** *sm* beat, throb; **~ cardiaco** heartbeat; **~ della pioggia/dell'orologio** beating of the rain/ticking of the clock

batti'tore *sm* (*Cricket*) batsman; (*Baseball*) batter; (*Caccia*) beater

batti'tura *sf* (*anche*: **battitura a macchina**) typing; (*del grano*) threshing

bat'tuta *sf* blow; (*di macchina da scrivere*) stroke; (*Mus*) bar; beat; (*Teat*) cue; (*di caccia*) beating; (*Polizia*) combing, scouring; (*Tennis*) service; **fare una ~** to crack a joke, make a witty remark; **aver la ~ pronta** (*fig*) to have a

ready answer; **è ancora alle prime battute** it's just started
ba'tuffolo *sm* wad
ba'ule *sm* trunk; (*Aut*) boot (*Brit*), trunk (*US*)
bau'xite [bauk'site] *sf* bauxite
'bava *sf* (*di animale*) slaver, slobber; (*di lumaca*) slime; (*di vento*) breath
bava'glino [bavaʎ'ʎino] *sm* bib
ba'vaglio [ba'vaʎʎo] *sm* gag
bava'rese *ag, sm/f* Bavarian
'bavero *sm* collar
Bavi'era *sf* Bavaria
ba'zar [bad'dzar] *sm inv* bazaar
baz'zecola [bad'dzekola] *sf* trifle
bazzi'care [battsi'kare] *vt* (*persona*) to hang about with; (*posto*) to hang about ■ *vi*: **~ in/con** to hang about/hang about with
BCE *sigla f* (= *Banca centrale europea*) ECB
be'arsi *vr*: **~ di qc/a fare qc** to delight in sth/in doing sth; **~ alla vista di** to enjoy looking at
beati'tudine *sf* bliss
be'ato, -a *ag* blessed; (*fig*) happy; **~ te!** lucky you!
bebè *sm inv* baby
bec'caccia, -ce [bek'kattʃa] *sf* woodcock
bec'care *vt* to peck; (*fig: raffreddore*) to pick up, catch; **beccarsi** *vr* (*fig*) to squabble
bec'cata *sf* peck
beccheggi'are [bekked'dʒare] *vi* to pitch
beccherò *etc* [bekke'rɔ] *vb vedi* **beccare**
bec'chime [bek'kime] *sm* birdseed
bec'chino [bek'kino] *sm* gravedigger
'becco, -chi *sm* beak, bill; (*di caffettiera etc*) spout; lip; (*fig fam*) cuckold; **mettere ~** (*fam*) to butt in; **chiudi il ~!** (*fam*) shut your mouth!, shut your trap!; **non ho il ~ di un quattrino** (*fam*) I'm broke
Be'fana *sf old woman who, according to legend, brings children their presents at the Epiphany;* (*Epifania*) Epiphany; (*donna brutta*): **befana** hag, witch; *see note*

BEFANA

Marking the end of the traditional 12 days of Christmas on 6 January, the *Befana*, or the feast of the Epiphany, is a national holiday in Italy. It is named after the old woman who, legend has it, comes down the chimney the night before, bringing gifts to children who have been good during the year and leaving lumps of coal for those who have not.

'beffa *sf* practical joke; **farsi ~** *o* **beffe di qn** to make a fool of sb
bef'fardo, -a *ag* scornful, mocking
bef'fare *vt* (*anche*: **beffarsi di**) to make a fool of, mock
'bega, -ghe *sf* quarrel
'begli ['bɛʎʎi], **'bei** *ag vedi* **bello**
beige [bɛʒ] *ag inv* beige
Bei'rut *sf* Beirut
bel *ag vedi* **bello**
be'lare *vi* to bleat
be'lato *sm* bleating
'belga, -gi, ghe *ag, sm/f* Belgian
'Belgio ['bɛldʒo] *sm*: **il ~** Belgium
Bel'grado *sf* Belgrade
'bella *sf vedi* **bello**
bel'lezza [bel'lettsa] *sf* beauty; **chiudere** *o* **finire qc in ~** to finish sth with a flourish; **che ~!** fantastic!; **ho pagato la ~ di 300 euro** I paid 300 euro, no less
belli'coso, -a *ag* warlike
bellige'rante [bellidʒe'rante] *ag* belligerent
bellim'busto *sm* dandy

PAROLA CHIAVE

'bello, -a (*ag: dav sm* **bel** + *C*, **bell'** + *V*, **bello** + *s impura, gn, pn, ps, x, z, pl* **bei** + *C*, **begli** + *s impura etc o V*) *ag* **1** (*oggetto, donna, paesaggio*) beautiful; (*uomo*) handsome; (*tempo*) beautiful, fine, lovely; **farsi bello di qc** to show off about sth; **fare la bella vita** to have an easy life; **le belle arti** fine arts

2 (*quantità*): **una bella cifra** a considerable sum of money; **un bel niente** absolutely nothing

3 (*rafforzativo*): **è una truffa bella e buona!** it's a real fraud!; **oh bella!, anche questa è bella!** (*ironico*) that's nice!; **è bell'e finito** it's already finished

■ *sm/f* (*innamorato*) sweetheart

■ *sm* **1** (*bellezza*) beauty; (*tempo*) fine weather

2: **adesso viene il bello** now comes the best bit; **sul più bello** at the crucial point; **cosa fai di bello?** are you doing anything interesting?

■ *sf* (*anche*: **bella copia**) fair copy; (*Sport, Carte*) decider

■ *av*: **fa bello** the weather is fine, it's fine; **alla bell'e meglio** somehow or other

bellu'nese *ag* of (*o* from) Belluno
'belva *sf* wild animal
belve'dere *sm inv* panoramic viewpoint
benché [ben'ke] *cong* although
'benda *sf* bandage; (*per gli occhi*) blindfold
ben'dare *vt* to bandage; to blindfold
bendis'posto, -a *ag*: **~ a qn/qc** well disposed towards sb/sth

'**bene** *av* well; (*completamente, affatto*): **è ben difficile** it's very difficult ■ *ag inv*: **gente ~** well-to-do people ■ *sm* good; (*Comm*) asset; **beni** *smpl* (*averi*) property *sg*, estate *sg*; **io sto ~/poco ~** I'm well/not very well; **va ~** all right; **ben più lungo/caro** much longer/ more expensive; **lo spero ~** I certainly hope so; **volere un ~ dell'anima a qn** to love sb very much; **un uomo per ~** a respectable man; **fare ~** to do the right thing; **fare ~ a** (*salute*) to be good for; **fare del ~ a qn** to do sb a good turn; **di ~ in meglio** better and better; **beni ambientali** environmental assets; **beni di consumo** consumer goods; **beni di consumo durevole** consumer durables; **beni culturali** cultural heritage; **beni immateriali** immaterial *o* intangible assets; **beni patrimoniali** fixed assets; **beni privati** private property *sg*; **beni pubblici** public property *sg*; **beni reali** tangible assets

bene'detto, -a *pp di* **benedire** ■ *ag* blessed, holy

bene'dire *vt* to bless; to consecrate; **l'ho mandato a farsi ~** (*fig*) I told him to go to hell

benedizi'one [benedit'tsjone] *sf* blessing

benedu'cato, -a *ag* well-mannered

benefat'tore, -'trice *sm/f* benefactor/ benefactress

benefi'cenza [benefi'tʃɛntsa] *sf* charity

benefici'are [benefi'tʃare] *vi*: **~ di** to benefit by, benefit from

benefici'ario, -a [benefi'tʃarjo] *ag, sm/f* beneficiary

bene'ficio [bene'fitʃo] *sm* benefit; **con ~ d'inventario** (*fig*) with reservations

be'nefico, -a, ci, che *ag* beneficial; charitable

'**Benelux** *sm*: **il ~** Benelux, the Benelux countries

beneme'renza [beneme'rɛntsa] *sf* merit

bene'merito, -a *ag* meritorious

bene'placito [bene'platʃito] *sm* (*approvazione*) approval; (*permesso*) permission

be'nessere *sm* well-being

benes'tante *ag* well-to-do

benes'tare *sm* consent, approval

benevo'lenza [benevo'lɛntsa] *sf* benevolence

be'nevolo, -a *ag* benevolent

ben'godi *sm* land of plenty

benia'mino, -a *sm/f* favourite (*Brit*), favorite (*US*)

be'nigno, -a [be'niɲɲo] *ag* kind, kindly; (*critica etc*) favourable (*Brit*), favorable (*US*); (*Med*) benign

benintenzio'nato, -a [benintentsjo'nato] *ag* well-meaning

benin'teso *av* of course; **~ che** *cong* provided that

benpen'sante *sm/f* conformist

benser'vito *sm*: **dare il ~ a qn** (*sul lavoro*) to give sb the sack, fire sb; (*fig*) to send sb packing

bensì *cong* but (rather)

benve'nuto, -a *ag, sm* welcome; **dare il ~ a qn** to welcome sb

ben'visto, -a *ag*: **essere ~ (da)** to be well thought of (by)

benvo'lere *vt*: **farsi ~ da tutti** to win everybody's affection; **prendere a ~ qn/qc** to take a liking to sb/sth

ben'zina [ben'dzina] *sf* petrol (*Brit*), gas (*US*); **fare ~** to get petrol *o* gas; **rimanere senza ~** to run out of petrol *o* gas; **~ verde** unleaded petrol, lead-free petrol

benzi'naio [bendzi'najo] *sm* petrol (*Brit*) *o* gas (*US*) pump attendant

be'one *sm* heavy drinker

'**bere** *vt* to drink; (*assorbire*) to soak up; **questa volta non me la dai a ~!** I won't be taken in this time!

berga'masco, -a, schi, sche *ag* of (*o* from) Bergamo

'**Bering** ['beriŋ]: **il mar di ~** *sm* the Bering Sea

ber'lina *sf* (*Aut*) saloon (car) (*Brit*), sedan (*US*); **mettere alla ~** (*fig*) to hold up to ridicule

Ber'lino *sf* Berlin; **~ est/ovest** East/West Berlin

Ber'muda *sfpl*: **le ~** Bermuda *sg*

ber'muda *smpl* (*calzoncini*) Bermuda shorts

'**Berna** *sf* Bern

ber'noccolo *sm* bump; (*inclinazione*) flair

ber'retto *sm* cap

berrò *etc vb vedi* **bere**

bersagli'are [bersaʎ'ʎare] *vt* to shoot at; (*colpire ripetutamente, fig*) to bombard; **bersagliato dalla sfortuna** dogged by ill fortune

bersagli'ere [bersaʎ'ʎɛre] *sm member of rifle regiment in Italian army*

ber'saglio [ber'saʎʎo] *sm* target

bes'temmia *sf* curse; (*Rel*) blasphemy

bestemmi'are *vi* to curse, swear; to blaspheme ■ *vt* to curse, swear at; to blaspheme; **~ come un turco** to swear like a trooper

'**bestia** *sf* animal; **lavorare come una ~** to work like a dog; **andare in ~** (*fig*) to fly into a rage; **una ~ rara** (*fig: persona*) an oddball; **~ da soma** beast of burden

besti'ale *ag* bestial, brutish; (*fam*): **fa un caldo ~** it's terribly hot; **fa un freddo ~** it's bitterly cold

bestialità *sf inv* (*qualità*) bestiality; **dire/fare una ~ dopo l'altra** to say/do one idiotic thing after another
besti'ame *sm* livestock; (*bovino*) cattle *pl*
Bet'lemme *sf* Bethlehem
betoni'era *sf* cement mixer
'bettola *sf* (*peg*) dive
be'tulla *sf* birch
be'vanda *sf* drink, beverage
bevi'tore, -'trice *sm/f* drinker
'bevo *etc vb vedi* **bere**
be'vuto, -a *pp di* **bere** ■ *sf* drink
'bevvi *etc vb vedi* **bere**
BG *sigla* = **Bergamo**
BI *sigla f* = **Banca d'Italia** ■ *sigla* = **Biella**
bi'ada *sf* fodder
bianche'ria [bjanke'ria] *sf* linen; **~ intima** underwear; **~ da donna** ladies' underwear, lingerie
bi'anco, -a, chi, che *ag* white; (*non scritto*) blank ■ *sm* white; (*intonaco*) whitewash ■ *sm/f* white, white man/woman; **in ~** (*foglio, assegno*) blank; **in ~ e nero** (*TV, Fot*) black and white; **mangiare in ~** to follow a bland diet; **pesce in ~** boiled fish; **andare in ~** (*non riuscire*) to fail; (*in amore*) to be rejected; **notte bianca** *o* **in ~** sleepless night; **voce bianca** (*Mus*) treble (voice); **votare scheda bianca** to return a blank voting slip; **~ dell'uovo** egg-white
bianco'segno [bjanko'seɲɲo] *sm* signature to a blank document
biancos'pino *sm* hawthorn
biasci'care [bjaʃʃi'kare] *vt* to mumble
biasi'mare *vt* to disapprove of, censure
bi'asimo *sm* disapproval, censure
'bibbia *sf* bible
bibe'ron *sm inv* feeding bottle
'bibita *sf* (soft) drink
bibliogra'fia *sf* bibliography
biblio'teca, -che *sf* library; (*mobile*) bookcase
bibliote'cario, -a *sm/f* librarian
bicame'rale *ag* (*Pol*) two-chamber *cpd*
bicarbo'nato *sm*: **~ (di sodio)** bicarbonate (of soda)
bicchi'ere [bik'kjɛre] *sm* glass; **è (facile) come bere un bicchier d'acqua** it's as easy as pie
bici'cletta [bitʃi'kletta] *sf* bicycle; **andare in ~** to cycle
bi'cipite [bi'tʃipite] *sm* bicep
bidè *sm inv* bidet
bi'dello, -a *sm/f* (*Ins*) janitor
bi'det *sm inv* = **bidè**
bidirezio'nale [bidirettsjo'nale] *ag* bidirectional
bido'nare *vt* (*fam: piantare in asso*) to let down; (*: imbrogliare*) to cheat, swindle
bido'nata *sf* (*fam*) swindle
bi'done *sm* drum, can; (*anche*: **bidone dell'immondizia**) (dust)bin; (*fam: truffa*) swindle; **fare un ~ a qn** (*fam*) to let sb down; to cheat sb
bidon'ville [bidɔ̃'vil] *sf inv* shanty town
bi'eco, -a, chi, che *ag* sinister
bi'ella *sf* (*Tecn*) connecting rod
Bielo'russia *sf* Belarus, Belorussia
bielo'russo, -a *ag, sm/f* Belarussian, Belorussian
bien'nale *ag* biennial ■ *sf*: **la B~ di Venezia** the Venice Arts Festival; *see note*

BIENNALE

Dating back to 1895, the *Biennale di Venezia* is an international festival of the contemporary arts. It takes place every two years in the "Giardini Pubblici". The various countries taking part each put on exhibitions in their own pavilions. There is a section dedicated to the work of young artists, as well as a special exhibition organized around a specific theme for that year.

bi'ennio *sm* period of two years
bi'erre *sm/f* *member of the Red Brigades*
bi'etola *sf* beet
bifami'liare *ag* (*villa, casetta*) semi-detached
bifo'cale *ag* bifocal
bi'folco, -a, chi, che *sm/f* (*peg*) bumpkin
'bifora *sf* (*Archit*) mullioned window
bifor'carsi *vr* to fork
biforcazi'one [biforkat'tsjone] *sf* fork
bifor'cuto, -a *ag* (*anche fig*) forked
biga'mia *sf* bigamy
'bigamo, -a *ag* bigamous ■ *sm/f* bigamist
bighello'nare [bigello'nare] *vi* to loaf (about)
bighel'lone, -a [bigel'lone] *sm/f* loafer
bigiotte'ria [bidʒotte'ria] *sf* costume jewellery (*Brit*) *o* jewelry (*US*); (*negozio*) jeweller's (shop) (*Brit*) *o* jewelry store (*US*) (*selling only costume jewellery*)
bigli'ardo [biʎ'ʎardo] *sm* = **biliardo**
bigliet'taio, -a [biʎʎet'tajo] *sm/f* (*nei treni*) ticket inspector; (*in autobus etc*) conductor/conductress; (*Cine, Teat*) box-office attendant
bigliette'ria [biʎʎette'ria] *sf* (*di stazione*) ticket office; booking office; (*di teatro*) box office
bigli'etto [biʎ'ʎetto] *sm* (*per viaggi, spettacoli etc*) ticket; (*cartoncino*) card; **~ di banca** (bank)note; (*anche*: **biglietto d'auguri/da visita**) greetings/visiting card; **~ d'andata e**

ritorno return (*Brit*) *o* round-trip (*US*) ticket; **~ elettronico** e-ticket; **~ omaggio** complimentary ticket
bignè [biɲ'ɲɛ] *sm inv* cream puff
bigo'dino *sm* roller, curler
bi'gotto, -a *ag* over-pious ■ *sm/f* church fiend
bi'kini *sm inv* bikini
bi'lancia, -ce [bi'lantʃa] *sf* (*pesa*) scales *pl*; (: *di precisione*) balance; (*dello zodiaco*): **B~** Libra; **essere della B~** to be Libra; **~ commerciale/dei pagamenti** balance of trade/payments
bilanci'are [bilan'tʃare] *vt* (*pesare*) to weigh; (: *fig*) to weigh up; **~ le uscite e le entrate** (*Comm*) to balance expenditure and revenue
bi'lancio [bi'lantʃo] *sm* (*Comm*) balance (sheet); (*statale*) budget; **far quadrare il ~** to balance the books; **chiudere il ~ in attivo/passivo** to make a profit/loss; **fare il ~ di** (*fig*) to assess; **~ consolidato** consolidated balance; **~ consuntivo** (final) balance; **~ preventivo** budget; **~ pubblico** national budget; **~ di verifica** trial balance
bilate'rale *ag* bilateral
'bile *sf* bile; (*fig*) rage, anger
bili'ardo *sm* billiards *sg*; (*tavolo*) billiard table
'bilico, -chi *sm*: **essere in ~** to be balanced; (*fig*) to be undecided; **tenere qn in ~** to keep sb in suspense
bi'lingue *ag* bilingual
bili'one *sm* (*mille milioni*) thousand million, billion (*US*); (*milione di milioni*) billion (*Brit*), trillion (*US*)
bilo'cale *sm* two-room flat (*Brit*) *o* apartment (*US*)
'bimbo, -a *sm/f* little boy/girl
bimen'sile *ag* fortnightly
bimes'trale *ag* two-monthly, bimonthly
bi'mestre *sm* two-month period; **ogni ~** every two months
bi'nario, -a *ag* binary ■ *sm* (railway) track *o* line; (*piattaforma*) platform; **~ morto** dead-end track
bi'nocolo *sm* binoculars *pl*
bio'chimica [bio'kimika] *sf* biochemistry
biodegra'dabile *ag* biodegradable
biodiversità *sf* biodiversity
bio'etica *sf* bioethics *sg*
bio'etico, -a, ci, che *ag* bioethical
bio'fabbrica *sf* *factory producing biological control agents*
bio'fisica *sf* biophysics *sg*
biogra'fia *sf* biography
bio'grafico, -a, ci, che *ag* biographical
bi'ografo, -a *sm/f* biographer
biolo'gia [biolo'dʒia] *sf* biology
bio'logico, -a, ci, che [bio'lɔdʒiko] *ag* (*scienze, fenomeni etc*) biological; (*agricoltura, prodotti*) organic
bi'ologo, -a, ghi, ghe *sm/f* biologist
bi'ondo, -a *ag* blond, fair
bi'onico, -a, ci, che *ag* bionic
biop'sia *sf* biopsy
bio'ritmo *sm* biorhythm
bios'fera *sf* biosphere
biotecnolo'gia [bioteknolo'dʒia] *sf* biotechnology
bipar'tito, -a *ag* (*Pol*) two-party *cpd* ■ *sm* (*Pol*) two-party alliance
'birba *sf* rascal, rogue
bir'bante *sm* rascal, rogue
birbo'nata *sf* naughty trick
bir'bone, -a *ag* (*bambino*) naughty ■ *sm/f* little rascal
biri'chino, -a [biri'kino] *ag* mischievous ■ *sm/f* scamp, little rascal
bi'rillo *sm* skittle (*Brit*), pin (*US*); **birilli** *smpl* (*gioco*) skittles *sg* (*Brit*), bowling *no pl* (*US*)
Bir'mania *sf*: **la ~** Burma
bir'mano, -a *ag, sm/f* Burmese (*inv*)
'biro® *sf inv* biro®
'birra *sf* beer; **~ scura** stout; **a tutta ~** (*fig*) at top speed
birre'ria *sf* (*locale*) ≈ bierkeller; (*fabbrica*) brewery
bis *escl, sm inv* encore ■ *ag inv* (*treno, autobus*) relief *cpd* (*Brit*), additional; (*numero*): **12 ~** 12a
bi'saccia, -ce [bi'zattʃa] *sf* knapsack
Bi'sanzio [bi'zantsjo] *sf* Byzantium
bis'betico, -a, ci, che *ag* ill-tempered, crabby
bisbigli'are [bizbiʎ'ʎare] *vt, vi* to whisper
bis'biglio [biz'biʎʎo] *sm* whisper; (*notizia*) rumour (*Brit*), rumor (*US*)
bisbi'glio [bizbiʎ'ʎio] *sm* whispering
bis'boccia, -ce [biz'bɔttʃa] *sf* binge, spree; **fare ~** to have a binge
'bisca, -sche *sf* gambling house
Bis'caglia [bis'kaʎʎa] *sf*: **il golfo di ~** the Bay of Biscay
'bischero ['biskero] *sm* (*Mus*) peg; (*fam: toscano*) fool, idiot
'biscia, -sce ['biʃʃa] *sf* snake; **~ d'acqua** water snake
biscot'tato, -a *ag* crisp; **fette biscottate** rusks
bis'cotto *sm* biscuit
bisessu'ale *ag, sm/f* bisexual
bises'tile *ag*: **anno ~** leap year
bisezi'one [biset'tsjone] *sf* dichotomy
bis'lacco, -a, chi, che *ag* odd, weird
bis'lungo, -a, ghi, ghe *ag* oblong
biso'gnare [bizoɲ'ɲare] *vb impers*: **bisogna che tu parta/lo faccia** you'll have to go/do

it; **bisogna parlargli** we'll (*o* I'll) have to talk to him ▪ *vi* (*esser utile*) to be necessary
bi'sogno [bi'zoɲɲo] *sm* need; **bisogni** *smpl* (*necessità corporali*): **fare i propri bisogni** to relieve o.s.; **avere ~ di qc/di fare qc** to need sth/to do sth; **al ~, in caso di ~** if need be
biso'gnoso, -a [bizoɲ'ɲoso] *ag* needy, poor; **~ di** in need of, needing
bi'sonte *sm* (*Zool*) bison
bis'tecca, -che *sf* steak, beefsteak; **~ al sangue/ai ferri** rare/grilled steak
bisticci'are [bistit'tʃare] *vi*, **bisticci'arsi** *vr* to quarrel, bicker
bis'ticcio [bis'tittʃo] *sm* quarrel, squabble; (*gioco di parole*) pun
bistrat'tare *vt* to maltreat
'bisturi *sm inv* scalpel
bi'sunto, -a *ag* very greasy
bi'torzolo [bi'tortsolo] *sm* (*sulla testa*) bump; (*sul corpo*) lump
'bitter *sm inv* bitters *pl*
bi'tume *sm* bitumen
bivac'care *vi* (*Mil*) to bivouac; (*fig*) to bed down
bi'vacco, -chi *sm* bivouac
'bivio *sm* fork; (*fig*) dilemma
bizan'tino, -a [biddzan'tino] *ag* Byzantine
'bizza ['biddza] *sf* tantrum; **fare le bizze** to throw a tantrum
biz'zarro, -a [bid'dzarro] *ag* bizarre, strange
biz'zeffe [bid'dzɛffe]: **a ~** *av* in plenty, galore
BL *sigla* = **Belluno**
blan'dire *vt* to soothe; to flatter
'blando, -a *ag* mild, gentle
blas'femo, -a *ag* blasphemous ▪ *sm/f* blasphemer
bla'sone *sm* coat of arms
blate'rare *vi* to chatter
'blatta *sf* cockroach
blin'dare *vt* to armour (*Brit*), armor (*US*)
blin'data *sf* (*macchina*) armoured car *o* limousine
blin'dato, -a *ag* armoured (*Brit*), armored (*US*); **camera blindata** strongroom; **mezzo ~** armoured vehicle; **porta blindata** reinforced door; **vita blindata** life amid maximum security; **vetro ~** bulletproof glass
bloc'care *vt* to block; (*isolare*) to isolate, cut off; (*porto*) to blockade; (*prezzi, beni*) to freeze; (*meccanismo*) to jam; **bloccarsi** *vr* (*motore*) to stall; (*freni, porta*) to jam, stick; (*ascensore*) to get stuck, stop; **ha bloccato la macchina** (*Aut*) he jammed on the brakes
bloccas'terzo [blokkas'tɛrtso] *sm* (*Aut*) steering lock
bloccherò *etc* [blokke'rɔ] *vb vedi* **bloccare**
bloc'chetto [blok'ketto] *sm* notebook; (*di biglietti*) book
'blocco, -chi *sm* block; (*Mil*) blockade; (*dei fitti*) restriction; (*quadernetto*) pad; (*fig: unione*) coalition; (*il bloccare*) blocking; isolating, cutting-off; blockading; freezing; jamming; **in ~** (*nell'insieme*) as a whole; (*Comm*) in bulk; **~ cardiaco** cardiac arrest
bloc-'notes [blɔk'nɔt] *sm inv* notebook, notepad
blog [blog] *sm inv* blog
'bloggare *vi* to blog
blu *ag inv, sm inv* dark blue
bluff [blɛf] *sm inv* bluff
bluf'fare *vi* (*anche fig*) to bluff
'blusa *sf* (*camiciotto*) smock; (*camicetta*) blouse
BN *sigla* = **Benevento**
BO *sigla* = **Bologna**
'boa *sm inv* (*Zool*) boa constrictor; (*sciarpa*) feather boa ▪ *sf* buoy
bo'ato *sm* rumble, roar
bob [bɔb] *sm inv* bobsleigh
bo'bina *sf* reel, spool; (*di pellicola*) spool; (*di film*) reel; (*Elettr*) coil
'bocca, -che *sf* mouth; **essere di buona ~** to be a hearty eater; (*fig*) to be easily satisfied; **essere sulla ~ di tutti** (*persona, notizia*) to be the talk of the town; **rimanere a ~ asciutta** to have nothing to eat; (*fig*) to be disappointed; **in ~ al lupo!** good luck!; **~ di leone** (*Bot*) snapdragon
boc'caccia, -ce [bok'kattʃa] *sf* (*malalingua*) gossip; (*smorfia*): **fare le boccacce** to pull faces
boc'caglio [bok'kaʎʎo] *sm* (*Tecn*) nozzle; (*di respiratore*) mouthpiece
boc'cale *sm* jug; **~ da birra** tankard
bocca'scena [bokkaʃʃena] *sm inv* proscenium
boc'cata *sf* mouthful; (*di fumo*) puff; **prendere una ~ d'aria** to go out for a breath of (fresh) air
boc'cetta [bot'tʃetta] *sf* small bottle
boccheggi'are [bokked'dʒare] *vi* to gasp
boc'chino [bok'kino] *sm* (*di sigaretta, sigaro: cannella*) cigarette-holder; cigar-holder; (*di pipa, strumenti musicali*) mouthpiece
'boccia, -ce ['bottʃa] *sf* bottle; (*da vino*) decanter, carafe; (*palla di legno, metallo*) bowl; **gioco delle bocce** bowls *sg*
bocci'are [bot'tʃare] *vt* (*proposta, progetto*) to reject; (*Ins*) to fail; (*Bocce*) to hit
boccia'tura [bottʃa'tura] *sf* failure
bocci'olo [bot'tʃɔlo] *sm* bud
'boccolo *sm* curl
boccon'cino [bokkon'tʃino] *sm* (*pietanza deliziosa*) delicacy
boc'cone *sm* mouthful, morsel; **mangiare un ~** to have a bite to eat
boc'coni *av* face downwards

Bo'emia *sf* Bohemia
bo'emo, -a *ag, sm/f* Bohemian
bofonchi'are [bofon'kjare] *vi* to grumble
Bogotá *sf* Bogotá
'boia *sm inv* executioner; hangman; **fa un freddo ~** (*fam*) it's cold as hell; **mondo ~!, ~ d'un mondo ladro!** (*fam*) damn!, blast!
boi'ata *sf* botch
boicot'taggio [boikot'taddʒo] *sm* boycott
boicot'tare *vt* to boycott
'bolgia, -ge ['bɔldʒa] *sf* (*fig*): **c'era una tale ~ al cinema** the cinema was absolutely mobbed
'bolide *sm* (*Astr*) meteor; (*macchina: da corsa*) racing car (*Brit*), race car (*US*); (*: elaborata*) performance car; **come un ~** like a flash, at top speed; **entrare/uscire come un ~** to charge in/out
Bo'livia *sf*: **la ~** Bolivia
bolivi'ano, -a *ag, sm/f* Bolivian
'bolla *sf* bubble; (*Med*) blister; (*Comm*) bill, receipt; **finire in una ~ di sapone** (*fig*) to come to nothing; **~ di accompagnamento** waybill; **~ di consegna** delivery note; **~ papale** papal bull
bol'lare *vt* to stamp; (*fig*) to brand
bol'lente *ag* boiling; boiling hot; **calmare i bollentei spiriti** to sober up, calm down
bol'letta *sf* bill; (*ricevuta*) receipt; **essere in ~** to be hard up; **~ di consegna** delivery note; **~ doganale** clearance certificate; **~ di trasporto aereo** air waybill
bollet'tino *sm* bulletin; (*Comm*) note; **~ meteorologico** weather forecast; **~ di ordinazione** order form; **~ di spedizione** consignment note
bolli'cina [bolli'tʃina] *sf* bubble; **acqua con le ~** fizzy water
bol'lire *vt, vi* to boil; **qualcosa bolle in pentola** (*fig*) there's something brewing
bol'lito *sm* (*Cuc*) boiled meat
bolli'tore *sm* (*Tecn*) boiler; (*Cuc: per acqua*) kettle; (*: per latte*) milk pan
bolli'tura *sf* boiling
'bollo *sm* stamp; **imposta di ~** stamp duty; **~ auto** road tax; **~ per patente** driving licence tax; **~ postale** postmark
bol'lore *sm*: **dare un ~ a qc** to bring sth to the boil (*Brit*) *o* a boil (*US*); **i bollori della gioventù** youthful enthusiasm *sg*
Bo'logna [bo'lɔɲɲa] *sf* Bologna
bolo'gnese [boloɲ'ɲese] *ag* Bolognese; **spaghetti alla ~** spaghetti bolognese
'bomba *sf* bomb; **tornare a ~** (*fig*) to get back to the point; **sei stato una ~!** you were tremendous!; **~ atomica** atom bomb; **~ a mano** hand grenade; **~ ad orologeria** time bomb
bombarda'mento *sm* bombardment; bombing
bombar'dare *vt* to bombard; (*da aereo*) to bomb
bombardi'ere *sm* bomber
bom'betta *sf* bowler (hat) (*Brit*), derby (*US*)
'bombola *sf* cylinder; **~ del gas** gas cylinder
bombo'letta *sf* spray can
bomboni'era *sf* box of sweets (*as souvenir at weddings, first communions etc*)
bo'naccia, -ce [bo'nattʃa] *sf* dead calm
bonacci'one, -a [bonat'tʃone] *ag* good-natured ■ *sm/f* good-natured sort
bo'nario, -a *ag* good-natured, kind
bo'nifica, -che *sf* reclamation; reclaimed land
bo'nifico, -ci *sm* (*riduzione, abbuono*) discount; (*versamento a terzi*) credit transfer
Bonn *sf* Bonn
bontà *sf* goodness; (*cortesia*) kindness; **aver la ~ di fare qc** to be good *o* kind enough to do sth
'bonus-'malus *sm inv* ≈ no-claims bonus
bor'bonico, -a, ci, che *ag* Bourbon; (*fig*) backward, out of date
borbot'tare *vi* to mumble; (*stomaco*) to rumble
borbot'tio, -ii *sm* mumbling; rumbling
'borchia ['borkja] *sf* stud
borda'tura *sf* (*Sartoria*) border, trim
bor'deaux [bor'dɔ] *sm* (*colore*) burgundy, maroon; (*vino*) Bordeaux
bor'dello *sm* brothel
'bordo *sm* (*Naut*) ship's side; (*orlo*) edge; (*striscia di guarnizione*) border, trim; **a ~ di** (*nave, aereo*) aboard, on board; (*macchina*) in; **sul ~ della strada** at the roadside; **persona d'alto ~** VIP
bor'dura *sf* border
bor'gata *sf* hamlet; (*a Roma*) working-class suburb
bor'ghese [bor'geze] *ag* (*spesso peg*) middle-class; bourgeois; **abito ~** civilian dress; **poliziotto in ~** plainclothes policeman
borghe'sia [borge'zia] *sf* middle classes *pl*; bourgeoisie
'borgo, -ghi *sm* (*paesino*) village; (*quartiere*) district; (*sobborgo*) suburb
'boria *sf* self-conceit, arrogance
bori'oso, -a *ag* arrogant
bor'lotto *sm* kidney bean
'Borneo *sm*: **il ~** Borneo
boro'talco *sm* talcum powder
bor'raccia, -ce [bor'rattʃa] *sf* canteen, water-bottle
'borsa *sf* bag; (*anche*: **borsa da signora**) handbag; (*Econ*): **la B~ (valori)** the Stock

Exchange; **~ dell'acqua calda** hot-water bottle; **B~ merci** commodity exchange; **~ nera** black market; **~ della spesa** shopping bag; **~ di studio** grant

borsai'olo *sm* pickpocket

bor'seggio [bor'seddʒo] *sm* pickpocketing

borsel'lino *sm* purse

bor'sello *sm* gent's handbag

bor'setta *sf* handbag

bor'sista, -i, e *sm/f* (*Econ*) speculator; (*Ins*) grant-holder

bos'caglia [bos'kaʎʎa] *sf* woodlands *pl*

boscai'olo, boscaiu'olo *sm* woodcutter; forester

bos'chetto [bos'ketto] *sm* copse, grove

'bosco, -schi *sm* wood

bos'coso, -a *ag* wooded

bos'niaco, -a, ci, che *ag, sm/f* Bosnian

'Bosnia-Erze'govina ['bɔsnja erdze'govina] *sf*: **la ~** Bosnia-Herzegovina

'bossolo *sm* cartridge case

Bot, bot *sigla m inv vedi* **buono ordinario del Tesoro**

bo'tanico, -a, ci, che *ag* botanical ■ *sm* botanist ■ *sf* botany

'botola *sf* trap door

Bots'wana [bots'vana] *sm*: **il ~** Botswana

'botta *sf* blow; (*rumore*) bang; **dare (un sacco di) botte a qn** to give sb a good thrashing; **~ e risposta** (*fig*) cut and thrust

'botte *sf* barrel, cask; **essere in una ~ di ferro** (*fig*) to be as safe as houses; **volere la ~ piena e la moglie ubriaca** to want to have one's cake and eat it

bot'tega, -ghe *sf* shop; (*officina*) workshop; **stare a ~ da qn** to serve one's apprenticeship (with sb); **le Botteghe Oscure** *headquarters of the DS, Italian left-wing party*

botte'gaio, -a *sm/f* shopkeeper

botte'ghino [botte'gino] *sm* ticket office; (*del lotto*) public lottery office

bot'tiglia [bot'tiʎʎa] *sf* bottle

bottiglie'ria [bottiʎʎe'ria] *sf* wine shop

bot'tino *sm* (*di guerra*) booty; (*di rapina, furto*) loot; **fare ~ di qc** (*anche fig*) to make off with sth

'botto *sm* bang; crash; **di ~** suddenly; **d'un ~** (*fam*) in a flash

bot'tone *sm* button; (*Bot*) bud; **stanza dei bottoni** control room; (*fig*) nerve centre; **attaccare (un) ~ a qn** to buttonhole sb

bo'vino, -a *ag* bovine; **bovini** *smpl* cattle

box [bɔks] *sm inv* (*per cavalli*) horsebox; (*per macchina*) lock-up; (*per macchina da corsa*) pit; (*per bambini*) playpen

boxe [bɔks] *sf* boxing

'boxer ['bɔkser] *sm inv* (*cane*) boxer ■ *smpl* (*mutande*): **un paio di ~** a pair of boxer shorts

'bozza ['bɔttsa] *sf* draft; (*Tip*) proof; **~ di stampa/impaginata** galley/page proof

boz'zetto [bot'tsetto] *sm* sketch

'bozzolo ['bɔttsolo] *sm* cocoon

BR *sigla fpl* = **Brigate Rosse** ■ *sigla* = **Brindisi**

'braca, -che *sf* (*gamba di pantalone*) trouser leg; **brache** *sfpl* (*fam*) trousers, pants (*US*); (*mutandoni*) drawers; **calare le brache** (*fig fam*) to chicken out

brac'care *vt* to hunt

brac'cetto [brat'tʃetto] *sm*: **a ~** arm in arm

braccherò *etc* [brakke'rɔ] *vb vedi* **braccare**

bracci'ale [brat'tʃale] *sm* bracelet; (*per nuotare, anche distintivo*) armband

braccia'letto [brattʃa'letto] *sm* bracelet, bangle

bracci'ante [brat'tʃante] *sm* (*Agr*) day labourer

bracci'ata [brat'tʃata] *sf* armful; (*nel nuoto*) stroke

'braccio ['brattʃo] *sm* (*Anat*) (*pl(f)* **braccia**) arm; (*di gru, fiume*) (*pl* **bracci**) arm; (*: di edificio*) wing; **camminare sotto ~** to walk arm in arm; **è il suo ~ destro** he's his right-hand man; **~ di ferro** (*anche fig*) trial of strength; **~ di mare** sound

bracci'olo [brat'tʃɔlo] *sm* (*appoggio*) arm

'bracco, -chi *sm* hound

bracconi'ere *sm* poacher

'brace ['bratʃe] *sf* embers *pl*

braci'ere [bra'tʃɛre] *sm* brazier

braci'ola [bra'tʃɔla] *sf* (*Cuc*) chop

'bradipo *sm* (*Zool*) sloth

'brado, -a *ag*: **allo stato ~** in the wild *o* natural state

'brama *sf*: **~ (di/di fare)** longing (for/to do), yearning (for/to do)

bra'mare *vt*: **~ (qc/di fare qc)** to long (for sth/ to do sth), yearn (for sth/to do sth)

bramo'sia *sf*: **~ (di)** longing (for), yearning (for)

'branca, -che *sf* branch

'branchia ['brankja] *sf* (*Zool*) gill

'branco, -chi *sm* (*di cani, lupi*) pack; (*di uccelli, pecore*) flock; (*peg: di persone*) gang, pack

branco'lare *vi* to grope, feel one's way

'branda *sf* camp bed

bran'dello *sm* scrap, shred; **a brandelli** in tatters, in rags; **fare a brandelli** to tear to shreds

bran'dina *sf* camp bed (*Brit*), cot (*US*)

bran'dire *vt* to brandish

'brano *sm* piece; (*di libro*) passage

bra'sare *vt* to braise

bra'sato *sm* braised beef

Bra'sile *sm*: **il ~** Brazil

Bra'silia *sf* Brasilia

brasili'ano, -a *ag, sm/f* Brazilian
bra'vata *sf* (*azione spavalda*) act of bravado
'bravo, -a *ag* (*abile*) clever, capable, skilful; (*buono*) good, honest; (*: bambino*) good; (*coraggioso*) brave; **~!** well done!; (*al teatro*) bravo!; **su da ~!** (*fam*) there's a good boy!; **mi sono fatto le mie brave 8 ore di lavoro** I put in a full 8 hours' work
bra'vura *sf* cleverness, skill
'breccia, -ce ['brettʃa] *sf* breach; **essere sulla ~** (*fig*) to be going strong; **fare ~ nell'animo** *o* **nel cuore di qn** to find the way to sb's heart
'Brema *sf* Bremen
bre'saola *sf kind of dried salted beef*
bresci'ano, -a [breʃʃano] *ag* of (*o* from) Brescia
Bre'tagna [bre'taɲɲa] *sf*: **la ~** Brittany
bre'tella *sf* (*Aut*) link; **bretelle** *sfpl* braces
brettone, 'bret(t)one *ag, sm/f* Breton
'breve *ag* brief, short; **in ~** in short; **per farla ~** to cut a long story short; **a ~** (*Comm*) short-term
brevet'tare *vt* to patent
bre'vetto *sm* patent; **~ di pilotaggio** pilot's licence (*Brit*) *o* license (*US*)
brevità *sf* brevity
'brezza ['breddza] *sf* breeze
'bricco, -chi *sm* jug; **~ del caffè** coffeepot
bricco'nata *sf* mischievous trick
bric'cone, -a *sm* rogue, rascal
'briciola ['britʃola] *sf* crumb
'briciolo ['britʃolo] *sm* (*specie fig*) bit
bridge [bridʒ] *sm* bridge
'briga, -ghe *sf* (*fastidio*) trouble, bother; **attaccar ~** to start a quarrel; **pigliarsi la ~ di fare qc** to take the trouble to do sth
brigadi'ere *sm* (*dei carabinieri etc*) ≈ sergeant
bri'gante *sm* bandit
bri'gata *sf* (*Mil*) brigade; (*gruppo*) group, party; **le Brigate Rosse** (*Pol*) the Red Brigades
briga'tismo *sm phenomenon of the Red Brigades*
briga'tista, -i, e *sm/f* (*Pol*) *member of the Red Brigades*
'briglia ['briʎʎa] *sf* rein; **a ~ sciolta** at full gallop; (*fig*) at full speed
bril'lante *ag* bright; (*anche fig*) brilliant; (*che luccica*) shining ■ *sm* diamond
brillan'tina *sf* brilliantine
bril'lare *vi* to shine; (*mina*) to blow up ■ *vt* (*mina*) to set off
'brillo, -a *ag* merry, tipsy
'brina *sf* hoarfrost
brin'dare *vi*: **~ a qn/qc** to drink to *o* toast sb/sth
'brindisi *sm inv* toast
'brio *sm* liveliness, go
bri'oche [bri'ɔʃ] *sf inv* brioche (bun)
bri'oso, -a *ag* lively
'briscola *sf type of card game*; (*seme vincente*) trump(s); (*carta*) trump card
bri'tannico, -a, ci, che *ag* British ■ *sm/f* Briton; **i Britannici** the British *pl*
'brivido *sm* shiver; (*di ribrezzo*) shudder; (*fig*) thrill; **racconti del ~** suspense stories
brizzo'lato, -a [brittso'lato] *ag* (*persona*) going grey; (*barba, capelli*) greying
'brocca, -che *sf* jug
broc'cato *sm* brocade
'broccolo *sm* broccoli *no pl*
bro'daglia [bro'daʎʎa] *sf* (*peg*) dishwater
'brodo *sm* broth; (*per cucinare*) stock; **~ ristretto** consommé; **lasciare (cuocere) qn nel suo ~** to let sb stew (in his own juice); **tutto fa ~** every little bit helps
'broglio ['brɔʎʎo] *sm*: **~ elettorale** gerrymandering; **brogli** *smpl* (*Dir*) malpractices
'bromo *sm* (*Chim*) bromine
bron'chite [bron'kite] *sf* (*Med*) bronchitis
'broncio ['brontʃo] *sm* sulky expression; **tenere il ~** to sulk
'bronco, -chi *sm* bronchial tube
bronto'lare *vi* to grumble; (*tuono, stomaco*) to rumble
bronto'lio *sm* grumbling, mumbling
bronto'lone, -a *ag* grumbling ■ *sm/f* grumbler
bron'zina [bron'dzina] *sf* (*Tecn*) bush
'bronzo ['brondzo] *sm* bronze; **che faccia di ~!** what a brass neck!
bross. *abbr* = **in brossura**
bros'sura *sf*: **in ~** (*libro*) limpback
'browser ['brauzer] *sm inv* (*Inform*) browser
bru'care *vt* to browse on, nibble at
brucherà *etc* [bruke'ra] *vb vedi* **brucare**
bruciacchi'are [brutʃak'kjare] *vt* to singe, scorch; **bruciacchiarsi** *vr* to become singed *o* scorched
brucia'pelo [brutʃa'pelo]: **a ~** *av* point-blank
bruci'are [bru'tʃare] *vt* to burn; (*scottare*) to scald ■ *vi* to burn; **~ gli avversari** (*Sport, fig*) to leave the rest of the field behind; **~ le tappe** *o* **i tempi** (*Sport, fig*) to shoot ahead; **bruciarsi la carriera** to put an end to one's career
brucia'tore [brutʃa'tore] *sm* burner
brucia'tura [brutʃa'tura] *sf* (*atto*) burning *no pl*; (*segno*) burn; (*scottatura*) scald
bruci'ore [bru'tʃore] *sm* burning *o* smarting sensation
'bruco, -chi *sm* grub; (*di farfalla*) caterpillar
'brufolo *sm* pimple, spot
brughi'era [bru'gjɛra] *sf* heath, moor

bruli'care *vi* to swarm
bruli'chio, -ii [bruli'kio] *sm* swarming
'brullo, -a *ag* bare, bleak
'bruma *sf* mist
'bruno, -a *ag* brown, dark; (*persona*) dark(-haired)
brusca'mente *av* (*frenare, fermarsi*) suddenly; (*rispondere, reagire*) sharply
'brusco, -a, schi, sche *ag* (*sapore*) sharp; (*modi, persona*) brusque, abrupt; (*movimento*) abrupt, sudden
bru'sio *sm* buzz, buzzing
bru'tale *ag* brutal
brutalità *sf inv* brutality
'bruto, -a *ag* (*forza*) brute *cpd* ■ *sm* brute
'brutta *sf vedi* **brutto**
brut'tezza [brut'tettsa] *sf* ugliness
'brutto, -a *ag* ugly; (*cattivo*) bad; (*malattia, strada, affare*) nasty, bad ■ *sm*: **guardare qn di ~** to give sb a nasty look ■ *sf* rough copy, first draft; **~ tempo** bad weather; **passare un ~ quarto d'ora** to have a nasty time of it; **vedersela brutta** (*per un attimo*) to have a nasty moment; (*per un periodo*) to have a bad time of it
brut'tura *sf* (*cosa brutta*) ugly thing; (*sudiciume*) filth; (*azione meschina*) mean action
Bru'xelles [bry'sɛl] *sf* Brussels
BS *sigla* = **Brescia**
BSE *sigla f* BSE (= *bovine spongiform encephalopathy*)
B.T. *abbr* (= *bassa tensione*) LT ■ *sigla m inv* = **buono del Tesoro**
btg *abbr* = **battaglione**
Btp *sigla m* = **buono del Tesoro poliennale**; *vedi* **buono**
bub'bone *sm* swelling
'buca, -che *sf* hole; (*avvallamento*) hollow; **~ delle lettere** letterbox
buca'neve *sm inv* snowdrop
bu'care *vt* (*forare*) to make a hole (*o* holes) in; (*pungere*) to pierce; (*biglietto*) to punch; **bucarsi** *vr* (*con eroina*) to mainline; **~ una gomma** to have a puncture; **avere le mani bucate** (*fig*) to be a spendthrift
'Bucarest *sf* Bucharest
bu'cato *sm* (*operazione*) washing; (*panni*) wash, washing
'buccia, -ce ['buttʃa] *sf* skin, peel; (*corteccia*) bark
bucherel'lare [bukerel'lare] *vt* to riddle with holes
bucherò *etc* [buke'rɔ] *vb vedi* **bucare**
'buco, -chi *sm* hole; **fare un ~ nell'acqua** to fail, draw a blank; **farsi un ~** (*fam: drogarsi*) to have a fix; **~ nero** (*anche fig*) black hole
'Budapest *sf* Budapest
'Budda *sm inv* Buddha
bud'dismo *sm* Buddhism
bu'dello *sm* intestine; (*fig: tubo*) tube; (*vicolo*) alley; **budella** *sfpl* bowels, guts
bu'dino *sm* pudding
'bue (*pl* **buoi**) *sm* ox; (*anche*: **carne di bue**) beef; **uovo all'occhio di ~** fried egg
Bu'enos 'Aires *sf* Buenos Aires
'bufalo *sm* buffalo
bu'fera *sf* storm
buf'fetto *sm* flick
'buffo, -a *ag* funny; (*Teat*) comic
buffo'nata *sf* (*azione*) prank, jest; (*parola*) jest
buf'fone *sm* buffoon
bugge'rare [buddʒe'rare] *vt* to swindle, cheat
bu'gia, -'gie [bu'dʒia] *sf* lie; (*candeliere*) candleholder
bugi'ardo, -a [bu'dʒardo] *ag* lying, deceitful ■ *sm/f* liar
bugi'gattolo [budʒi'gattolo] *sm* poky little room
'buio, -a *ag* dark ■ *sm* dark, darkness; **fa ~ pesto** it's pitch-dark
'bulbo *sm* (*Bot*) bulb; **~ oculare** eyeball
Bulga'ria *sf*: **la ~** Bulgaria
'bulgaro, -a *ag, sm/f, sm* Bulgarian
buli'mia *sf* bulimia
bullismo [bul'lizmo] *sm* bullying
'bullo *sm* (*persona*) tough
bul'lone *sm* bolt
bu'oi *smpl di* **bue**
buona'fede *sf* good faith
buon'anima *sf* = **buon'anima**; *vedi* **anima**
buona'notte *escl* good night! ■ *sf*: **dare la ~ a** to say good night to
buona'sera *escl* good evening!
buoncos'tume *sm* public morality; **la (squadra del) ~** (*Polizia*) the vice squad
buondì *escl* hello!
buongi'orno [bwon'dʒorno] *escl* good morning (*o* afternoon)!
buon'grado *av*: **di ~** willingly
buongus'taio, -a *sm/f* gourmet
buon'gusto *sm* good taste

 PAROLA CHIAVE

bu'ono, -a (*ag: dav sm* **buon** + *C o V*, **buono** + *s impura, gn, pn, ps, z; dav sf* **buon'** + *V*) *ag* **1** (*gen*) good; **un buon pranzo/ristorante** a good lunch/restaurant; **(stai) buono!** behave!; **che buono!** (*cibo*) this is nice!
2 (*benevolo*): **buono (con)** good (to), kind (to)
3 (*giusto, valido*) right; **al momento buono** at the right moment
4 (*adatto*): **buono a/da** fit for/to; **essere buono a nulla** to be no good *o* use at anything

5 (*auguri*): **buon compleanno!** happy birthday!; **buon divertimento!** have a nice time!; **buona fortuna!** good luck!; **buon riposo!** sleep well!; **buon viaggio!** have a good trip!
6: **ad ogni buon conto** in any case; **tante buone cose!** all the best!; **di buon cuore** (*persona*) goodhearted; **di buon grado** willingly; **le buone maniere** good manners; **di buon mattino** early in the morning; **a buon mercato** cheap; **di buon'ora** early; **mettere una buona parola** to put in a good word; **di buon passo** at a good pace; **buon pro ti faccia!** much good may it do you!; **buon senso** common sense; **la buona società** the upper classes; **una buona volta** once and for all; **alla buona** simple
■ *av* in a simple way, without any fuss; **un tipo alla buona** an easy-going sort
■ *sm/f*: **essere un buono/una buona** to be a good person; **buono a nulla** good for nothing; **i buoni e i cattivi** (*in storia, film*) the goodies and the baddies; **accetterà con le buone o con le cattive** one way or another he's going to agree to it
■ *sm* **1** (*bontà*) goodness, good
2 (*Comm*) voucher, coupon; **buono d'acquisto** credit note; **buono di cassa** cash voucher; **buono di consegna** delivery note; **buono fruttifero** interest-bearing bond; **buono ordinario del Tesoro** short-term Treasury bond; **buono postale fruttifero** interest-bearing bond (*issued by Italian Post Office*); **buono del Tesoro** Treasury bill

buon'senso *sm* = **buon senso**
buontem'pone, -a *sm/f* jovial person
buonu'scita [bwonuʃʃita] *sf* (*Industria*) golden handshake; (*di affitti*) *sum paid for the relinquishing of tenancy rights*
buratti'naio *sm* puppeteer, puppet master
burat'tino *sm* puppet
'burbero, -a *ag* surly, gruff
'burla *sf* prank, trick
bur'lare *vt*: **~ qc/qn, burlarsi di qc/qn** to make fun of sth/sb
bu'rocrate *sm* bureaucrat
buro'cratico, -a, ci, che *ag* bureaucratic
burocra'zia [burokrat'tsia] *sf* bureaucracy
bur'rasca, -sche *sf* storm
burras'coso, -a *ag* stormy
'burro *sm* butter
bur'rone *sm* ravine
bus'care *vt* (*anche*: **buscarsi**: *raffreddore*) to get, catch; **buscarle** (*fam*) to get a hiding
buscherò *etc* [buske'rɔ] *vb vedi* **buscare**
bus'sare *vi* to knock; **~ a quattrini** (*fig*) to ask for money
'bussola *sf* compass; **perdere la ~** (*fig*) to lose one's bearings
'busta *sf* (*da lettera*) envelope; (*astuccio*) case; **in ~ aperta/chiusa** in an unsealed/sealed envelope; **~ paga** pay packet
busta'rella *sf* bribe, backhander
bus'tina *sf* (*piccola busta*) envelope; (*di cibi, farmaci*) sachet; (*Mil*) forage cap; **~ di tè** tea bag
'busto *sm* bust; (*indumento*) corset, girdle; **a mezzo ~** (*fotografia, ritratto*) half-length
bu'tano *sm* butane
but'tare *vt* to throw; (*anche*: **buttare via**) to throw away; **buttarsi** *vr* (*saltare*) to jump; **~ giù** (*scritto*) to scribble down, dash off; (*cibo*) to gulp down; (*edificio*) to pull down, demolish; (*pasta, verdura*) to put into boiling water; **ho buttato là una frase** I mentioned it in passing; **buttiamoci!** (*saltiamo*) let's jump!; (*rischiamo*) let's have a go!; **buttarsi dalla finestra** to jump out of the window
'buzzo ['buddzo] *sm* (*fam*: *pancia*) belly, paunch; **di ~ buono** (*con impegno*) with a will

Cc

C, c [tʃi] *sf o m inv* (*lettera*) C, c ■ *abbr* (*Geo*) = **capo**; (= *Celsius, centigrado*) C; (= *conto*) a/c; **C come Como** ≈ C for Charlie
CA *sigla* = **Cagliari**
c.a. *abbr* (*Elettr*) *vedi* **corrente alternata**; (*Comm*) = **corrente anno**
caba'ret [kaba'rɛ] *sm inv* cabaret
ca'bina *sf* (*di nave*) cabin; (*da spiaggia*) beach hut; (*di autocarro, treno*) cab; (*di aereo*) cockpit; (*di ascensore*) cage; **~ di proiezione** (*Cine*) projection booth; **~ di registrazione** recording booth; **~ telefonica** callbox, (tele)phone box *o* booth
cabi'nato *sm* cabin cruiser
ca'blaggio [ka'bladdʒo] *sm* wiring
cablo'gramma *sm* cable(gram)
ca'cao *sm* cocoa
'cacca *sf* (*fam: anche fig*) shit (*!*)
'caccia ['kattʃa] *sf* hunting; (*con fucile*) shooting; (*inseguimento*) chase; (*cacciagione*) game ■ *sm inv* (*aereo*) fighter; (*nave*) destroyer; **andare a ~** to go hunting; **andare a ~ di guai** to be asking for trouble; **~ grossa** big-game hunting; **~ all'uomo** manhunt
cacciabombardi'ere [kattʃabombar'djɛre] *sm* fighter-bomber
cacciagi'one [kattʃa'dʒone] *sf* game
cacci'are [kat'tʃare] *vt* to hunt; (*mandar via*) to chase away; (*ficcare*) to shove, stick ■ *vi* to hunt; **cacciarsi** *vr* (*fam: mettersi*): **cacciarsi tra la folla** to plunge into the crowd; **dove s'è cacciata la mia borsa?** where has my bag got to?; **cacciarsi nei guai** to get into trouble; **~ fuori qc** to whip *o* pull sth out; **~ un urlo** to let out a yell
caccia'tora [kattʃa'tora] *sf* (*giacca*) hunting jacket; (*Cuc*): **pollo** *etc* **alla ~** chicken *etc* chasseur
caccia'tore [kattʃa'tore] *sm* hunter; **~ di frodo** poacher; **~ di dote** fortune-hunter
cacciatorpedini'ere [kattʃatorpedi'njɛre] *sm* destroyer
caccia'vite [kattʃa'vite] *sm inv* screwdriver
cache'mire [kaʃmir] *sm inv* cashmere
ca'chet [ka'ʃɛ] *sm* (*Med*) capsule; (*: compressa*) tablet; (*compenso*) fee; (*colorante per capelli*) rinse
'cachi ['kaki] *sm inv* (*albero, frutto*) persimmon; (*colore*) khaki ■ *ag inv* khaki
'cacio ['katʃo] *sm* cheese; **essere come il ~ sui maccheroni** (*fig*) to turn up at the right moment
'cactus *sm inv* cactus
ca'davere *sm* (dead) body, corpse
cada'verico, -a, ci, che *ag* (*fig*) deathly pale
'caddi *etc vb vedi* **cadere**
ca'dente *ag* falling; (*casa*) tumbledown; (*persona*) decrepit
ca'denza [ka'dɛntsa] *sf* cadence; (*andamento ritmico*) rhythm; (*Mus*) cadenza
ca'dere *vi* to fall; (*denti, capelli*) to fall out; (*tetto*) to fall in; **questa gonna cade bene** this skirt hangs well; **lasciar ~** (*anche fig*) to drop; **~ dal sonno** to be falling asleep on one's feet; **~ ammalato** to fall ill; **~ dalle nuvole** (*fig*) to be taken aback
ca'detto *sm* cadet
cadrò *etc vb vedi* **cadere**
ca'duto, -a *ag* (*morto*) dead ■ *sm* dead soldier ■ *sf* fall; **monumento ai caduti** war memorial; **caduta di temperatura** drop in temperature; **la caduta dei capelli** hair loss; **caduta del sistema** (*Inform*) system failure
caffè *sm inv* coffee; (*locale*) café; **~ corretto** coffee with liqueur; **~ in grani** coffee beans; **~ macchiato** coffee with a dash of milk; **~ macinato** ground coffee
caffe'ina *sf* caffeine
caffel'latte *sm inv* white coffee
caffette'ria *sf* coffee shop
caffetti'era *sf* coffeepot
ca'fone *sm* (*contadino*) peasant; (*peg*) boor
cagio'nare [kadʒo'nare] *vt* to cause, be the cause of
cagio'nevole [kadʒo'nevole] *ag* delicate, weak

cagli'are [kaʎ'ʎare] *vi* to curdle
cagliari'tano, -a [kaʎʎari'tano] *ag* of (*o* from) Cagliari
'cagna ['kaɲɲa] *sf* (*Zool, peg*) bitch
ca'gnara [kaɲ'ɲara] *sf* (*fig*) uproar
ca'gnesco, -a, schi, sche [kaɲ'ɲesko] *ag* (*fig*): **guardare qn in ~** to scowl at sb
CAI *sigla m* = **Club Alpino Italiano**
'Cairo *sm*: **il ~** Cairo
cala'brese *ag, sm/f* Calabrian
cala'brone *sm* hornet
Cala'hari [kala'ari]: **il Deserto di ~** *sm* the Kalahari Desert
cala'maio *sm* inkpot; inkwell
cala'maro *sm* squid
cala'mita *sf* magnet
calamità *sf inv* calamity, disaster; **~ naturale** natural disaster
ca'lare *vt* (*far discendere*) to lower; (*Maglia*) to decrease ■ *vi* (*discendere*) to go (*o* come) down; (*tramontare*) to set, go down; **~ di peso** to lose weight
ca'lata *sf* (*invasione*) invasion
'calca *sf* throng, press
cal'cagno [kal'kaɲɲo] *sm* heel
cal'care *sm* limestone; (*incrostazione*) (lime)scale ■ *vt* (*premere coi piedi*) to tread, press down; (*premere con forza*) to press down; (*mettere in rilievo*) to stress; **~ la mano** to overdo it, exaggerate; **~ le scene** (*fig*) to be on the stage; **~ le orme di qn** (*fig*) to follow in sb's footsteps
'calce ['kaltʃe] *sm*: **in ~** at the foot of the page ■ *sf* lime; **~ viva** quicklime
calces'truzzo [kaltʃes'truttso] *sm* concrete
cal'cetto [kal'tʃetto] *sm* (*calcio-balilla*) table football; (*calcio a cinque*) five-a-side (football)
calcherò *etc* [kalke'rɔ] *vb vedi* **calcare**
calci'are [kal'tʃare] *vt, vi* to kick
calcia'tore [kaltʃa'tore] *sm* footballer (*Brit*), (football) player
cal'cina [kal'tʃina] *sf* (lime) mortar
'calcio ['kaltʃo] *sm* (*pedata*) kick; (*sport*) football, soccer; (*di pistola, fucile*) butt; (*Chim*) calcium; **~ d'angolo** (*Sport*) corner (kick); **~ di punizione** (*Sport*) free kick
'calco, -chi *sm* (*Arte*) casting, moulding (*Brit*), molding (*US*); cast, mo(u)ld
calco'lare *vt* to calculate, work out, reckon; (*ponderare*) to weigh (up)
calcola'tore, -'trice *ag* calculating ■ *sm* calculator; (*fig*) calculating person ■ *sf* (*anche*: **macchina calcolatrice**) calculator; **~ digitale** digital computer; **~ elettronico** computer; **~ da tavolo** desktop computer
'calcolo *sm* (*anche Mat*) calculation; (*infinitesimale etc*) calculus; (*Med*) stone; **fare il ~ di qc** to work sth out; **fare i propri calcoli** (*fig*) to weigh the pros and cons; **per ~** out of self-interest
cal'daia *sf* boiler
caldar'rosta *sf* roast chestnut
caldeggi'are [kalded'dʒare] *vt* to support
'caldo, -a *ag* warm; (*molto caldo*) hot; (*fig: appassionato*) keen ■ *sm* heat; **ho ~** I'm warm; I'm hot; **fa ~** it's warm; it's hot; **non mi fa né ~ né freddo** I couldn't care less; **a ~** (*fig*) in the heat of the moment
caleidos'copio *sm* kaleidoscope
calen'dario *sm* calendar
ca'lende *sfpl* calends; **rimandare qc alle ~ greche** to put sth off indefinitely
ca'lesse *sm* gig
'calibro *sm* (*di arma*) calibre, bore; (*Tecn*) callipers *pl*; (*fig*) calibre; **di grosso ~** (*fig*) prominent
'calice ['kalitʃe] *sm* goblet; (*Rel*) chalice
Cali'fornia *sf* California
californi'ano, -a *ag* Californian
ca'ligine [ka'lidʒine] *sf* fog; (*mista con fumo*) smog
calligra'fia *sf* (*scrittura*) handwriting; (*arte*) calligraphy
'callo *sm* callus; (*ai piedi*) corn; **fare il ~ a qc** to get used to sth
'calma *sf* calm; **faccia con ~** take your time
cal'mante *sm* sedative, tranquillizer
cal'mare *vt* to calm; (*lenire*) to soothe; **calmarsi** *vr* to grow calm, calm down; (*vento*) to abate; (*dolori*) to ease
calmi'ere *sm* controlled price
'calmo, -a *ag* calm, quiet
'calo *sm* (*Comm: di prezzi*) fall; (*: di volume*) shrinkage; (*: di peso*) loss
ca'lore *sm* warmth; (*intenso, Fisica*) heat; **essere in ~** (*Zool*) to be on heat
calo'ria *sf* calorie
calo'rifero *sm* radiator
calo'roso, -a *ag* warm; **essere ~** not to feel the cold
calpes'tare *vt* to tread on, trample on; **"è vietato ~ l'erba"** "keep off the grass"
ca'lunnia *sf* slander; (*scritta*) libel
calunni'are *vt* to slander
cal'vario *sm* (*fig*) affliction, cross
cal'vizie [kal'vittsje] *sf* baldness
'calvo, -a *ag* bald
'calza ['kaltsa] *sf* (*da donna*) stocking; (*da uomo*) sock; **fare la ~** to knit
calza'maglia [kaltsa'maʎʎa] *sf* tights *pl*; (*per danza, ginnastica*) leotard
cal'zare [kal'tsare] *vt* (*scarpe, guanti: mettersi*) to put on; (*: portare*) to wear ■ *vi* to fit; **~ a pennello** to fit like a glove

calza'tura [kaltsa'tura] *sf* footwear
calzaturi'ficio [kaltsaturi'fitʃo] *sm* shoe *o* footwear factory
cal'zetta [kal'tsetta] *sf* ankle sock; **una mezza ~** (*fig*) a nobody
calzet'tone [kaltset'tone] *sm* heavy knee-length sock
cal'zino [kal'tsino] *sm* sock
calzo'laio [kaltso'lajo] *sm* shoemaker; (*che ripara scarpe*) cobbler
calzole'ria [kaltsole'ria] *sf* (*negozio*) shoe shop; (*arte*) shoemaking
calzon'cini [kaltson'tʃini] *smpl* shorts; **~ da bagno** (swimming) trunks
cal'zone [kal'tsone] *sm* trouser leg; (*Cuc*) *savoury turnover made with pizza dough*; **calzoni** *smpl* trousers (*Brit*), pants (*US*)
camale'onte *sm* chameleon
cambi'ale *sf* bill (of exchange); (*pagherò cambiario*) promissory note; **~ di comodo** *o* **di favore** accommodation bill
cambia'mento *sm* change; **cambiamenti climatici** climate change *sg*
cambi'are *vt* to change; (*modificare*) to alter, change; (*barattare*): **~ (qc con qn/qc)** to exchange (sth with sb/for sth) ■ *vi* to change, alter; **cambiarsi** *vr* (*variare abito*) to change; **~ casa** to move (house); **~ idea** to change one's mind; **~ treno** to change trains; **~ le carte in tavola** (*fig*) to change one's tune; **~ (l')aria in una stanza** to air a room; **è ora di ~ aria** (*andarsene*) it's time to move on
cambiava'lute *sm inv* exchange office
'cambio *sm* change; (*modifica*) alteration, change; (*scambio, Comm*) exchange; (*corso dei cambi*) rate (of exchange); (*Tecn, Aut*) gears *pl*; **in ~ di** in exchange for; **dare il ~ a qn** to take over from sb; **fare il** *o* **un ~** to change (over); **~ a termine** (*Comm*) forward exchange
'Cambital *sigla m* = **Ufficio Italiano dei Cambi**
Cam'bogia [kam'bɔdʒa] *sf*: **la ~** Cambodia
cambogi'ano, -a [kambo'dʒano] *ag, sm/f* Cambodian
cam'busa *sf* storeroom
'camera *sf* room; (*anche*: **camera da letto**) bedroom; (*Pol*) chamber, house; **~ ardente** mortuary chapel; **~ d'aria** inner tube; (*di pallone*) bladder; **~ blindata** strongroom; **C~ di Commercio** Chamber of Commerce; **C~ dei Deputati** Chamber of Deputies, ≈ House of Commons (*Brit*), ≈ House of Representatives (*US*); *see note*; **~ a gas** gas chamber; **~ del lavoro** trades union centre (*Brit*), labor union center (*US*); **~ a un letto/a due letti/matrimoniale** single/twin-bedded/double room; **~ oscura** (*Fot*) dark room; **~ da pranzo** dining room

CAMERA DEI DEPUTATI

The *Camera dei deputati* is the lower house of the Italian Parliament and is presided over by the "Presidente della Camera" who is chosen by the "deputati". Elections to the Chamber are normally held every 5 years. Since the electoral reform of 1993 members have been voted in via a system which combines a first-past-the-post element with proportional representation; *see also* "Parlamento".

came'rata, -i, e *sm/f* companion, mate ■ *sf* dormitory
camera'tismo *sm* comradeship
cameri'era *sf* (*domestica*) maid; (*che serve a tavola*) waitress; (*che fa le camere*) chambermaid
cameri'ere *sm* (man)servant; (*di ristorante*) waiter
came'rino *sm* (*Teat*) dressing room
'Camerun *sm*: **il ~** Cameroon
'camice ['kamitʃe] *sm* (*Rel*) alb; (*per medici etc*) white coat
cami'cetta [kami'tʃetta] *sf* blouse
ca'micia, -cie [ka'mitʃa] *sf* (*da uomo*) shirt; (*da donna*) blouse; **nascere con la ~** (*fig*) to be born lucky; **sudare sette camicie** (*fig*) to have a hell of a time; **~ di forza** straitjacket; **~ da notte** (*da donna*) nightdress; (*da uomo*) nightshirt; **C~ nera** (*fascista*) Blackshirt
camici'aio, -a [kami'tʃajo] *sm/f* (*sarto*) shirtmaker; (*che vende camicie*) shirtseller
camici'ola [kami'tʃɔla] *sf* vest
camici'otto [kami'tʃɔtto] *sm* casual shirt; (*per operai*) smock
cami'netto *sm* hearth, fireplace
ca'mino *sm* chimney; (*focolare*) fireplace, hearth
'camion *sm inv* lorry (*Brit*), truck (*US*)
camion'cino [kamjon'tʃino] *sm* van
camio'netta *sf* jeep
camio'nista, -i *sm* lorry driver (*Brit*), truck driver (*US*)
'camma *sf* cam; **albero a camme** camshaft
cam'mello *sm* (*Zool*) camel; (*tessuto*) camel hair
cam'meo *sm* cameo
cammi'nare *vi* to walk; (*funzionare*) to work, go; **~ a carponi** *o* **a quattro zampe** to go on all fours
cammi'nata *sf* walk; **fare una ~** to go for a walk

C

cam'mino *sm* walk; (*sentiero*) path; (*itinerario, direzione, tragitto*) way; **mettersi in ~** to set *o* start off; **cammin facendo** on the way; **riprendere il ~** to continue on one's way
camo'milla *sf* camomile; (*infuso*) camomile tea
ca'morra *sf* Camorra; (*fig*) racket
camor'rista, -i, e *sm/f* member of the Camorra; (*fig*) racketeer
ca'moscio [ka'moʃʃo] *sm* chamois
cam'pagna [kam'paɲɲa] *sf* country, countryside; (*Pol, Comm, Mil*) campaign; **in ~** in the country; **andare in ~** to go to the country; **fare una ~** to campaign; **~ promozionale vendite** sales campaign
campa'gnolo, -a [kampaɲ'ɲɔlo] *ag* country *cpd* ■ *sf* (*Aut*) cross-country vehicle
cam'pale *ag* field *cpd*; (*fig*): **una giornata ~** a hard day
cam'pana *sf* bell; (*anche*: **campana di vetro**) bell jar; **sordo come una ~** as deaf as a doorpost; **sentire l'altra ~** (*fig*) to hear the other side of the story; **~ (per la raccolta del vetro)** bottle bank
campa'nella *sf* small bell; (*di tenda*) curtain ring
campa'nello *sm* (*all'uscio, da tavola*) bell
campa'nile *sm* bell tower, belfry
campani'lismo *sm* parochialism
cam'pano, -a *ag* of (*o* from) Campania
cam'pare *vi* to live; (*tirare avanti*) to get by, manage; **~ alla giornata** to live from day to day
cam'pato, -a *ag*: **~ in aria** unsound, unfounded
campeggi'are [kamped'dʒare] *vi* to camp; (*risaltare*) to stand out
campeggia'tore, -'trice [kampeddʒa'tore] *sm/f* camper
cam'peggio [kam'peddʒo] *sm* camping; (*terreno*) camp site; **fare (del) ~** to go camping
cam'pestre *ag* country *cpd*, rural; **corsa ~** cross-country race
Campi'doglio [kampi'dɔʎʎo] *sm*: **il ~** the Capitol; *see note*

Campidoglio

The *Campidoglio*, one of the Seven Hills of Rome, is the home of the "Comune di Roma".

'camping ['kæmpiŋ] *sm inv* camp site
campiona'mento *sm* sampling
campio'nario, -a *ag*: **fiera campionaria** trade fair ■ *sm* collection of samples
campio'nato *sm* championship
campiona'tura *sf* (*Comm*) production of samples; (*Statistica*) sampling
campi'one, -'essa *sm/f* (*Sport*) champion ■ *sm* (*Comm*) sample; **~ gratuito** free sample; **prelievi di ~** product samples
'campo *sm* (*gen*) field; (*Mil*) field; (: *accampamento*) camp; (*spazio delimitato*: *sportivo etc*) ground; field; (*di quadro*) background; **i campi** (*campagna*) the countryside; **padrone del ~** (*fig*) victor; **~ da aviazione** airfield; **~ di concentramento** concentration camp; **~ di golf** golf course; **~ lungo** (*Cine, TV, Fot*) long shot; **~ nomadi** travellers' camp; **~ da tennis** tennis court; **~ visivo** field of vision
campobas'sano, -a *ag* of (*o* from) Campobasso
campo'santo (*pl* **campisanti**) *sm* cemetery
camuf'fare *vt* to disguise; **camuffarsi** *vr*: **camuffarsi (da)** to disguise o.s. (as); (*per ballo in maschera*) to dress up (as)
CAN *abbr* (= *Costo, Assicurazione e Nolo*) CIF
Can. *abbr* (*Geo*) = **canale**
'Canada *sm*: **il ~** Canada
cana'dese *ag, sm/f* Canadian ■ *sf* (*anche*: **tenda canadese**) ridge tent
ca'naglia [ka'naʎʎa] *sf* rabble, mob; (*persona*) scoundrel, rogue
ca'nale *sm* (*anche fig*) channel; (*artificiale*) canal
'canapa *sf* hemp; **~ indiana** cannabis
Ca'narie *sfpl*: **le (isole) ~** the Canary Islands, the Canaries
cana'rino *sm* canary
Can'berra *sf* Canberra
cancel'lare [kantʃel'lare] *vt* (*con la gomma*) to rub out, erase; (*con la penna*) to strike out; (*annullare*) to annul, cancel; (*disdire*) to cancel
cancel'lata [kantʃel'lata] *sf* railing(s) *pl*
cancelle'ria [kantʃelle'ria] *sf* chancery; (*quanto necessario per scrivere*) stationery
cancelli'ere [kantʃel'ljɛre] *sm* chancellor; (*di tribunale*) clerk of the court
can'cello [kan'tʃɛllo] *sm* gate
cance'rogeno, -a [kantʃe'rɔdʒeno] *ag* carcinogenic ■ *sm* carcinogen
cance'rologo, -a, gi, ghe [kantʃe'rɔlogo] *sm/f* cancer specialist
cance'roso, -a [kantʃe'roso] *ag* cancerous ■ *sm/f* cancer patient
can'crena *sf* gangrene
'cancro *sm* (*Med*) cancer; (*dello zodiaco*): **C~** Cancer; **essere del C~** to be Cancer
candeggi'are [kanded'dʒare] *vt* to bleach
candeg'gina [kanded'dʒina] *sf* bleach
can'deggio [kan'deddʒo] *sm* bleaching
can'dela *sf* candle; **~ (di accensione)** (*Aut*) spark(ing) plug; **una lampadina da 100**

candele (*Elettr*) a 100 watt bulb; **a lume di ~** by candlelight; **tenere la ~** (*fig*) to play gooseberry (*Brit*), act as chaperone
cande'labro *sm* candelabra
candeli'ere *sm* candlestick
cande'lotto *sm* candle; **~ di dinamite** stick of dynamite; **~ lacrimogeno** tear gas grenade
candi'dare *vt* to present as candidate; **candidarsi** *vr* to present o.s. as candidate
candi'dato, -a *sm/f* candidate; (*aspirante a una carica*) applicant
candida'tura *sf* candidature; application
'candido, -a *ag* white as snow; (*puro*) pure; (*sincero*) sincere, candid
can'dito, -a *ag* candied
can'dore *sm* brilliant white; purity; sincerity, candour (*Brit*), candor (*US*)
'cane *sm* dog; (*di pistola, fucile*) cock; **fa un freddo ~** it's bitterly cold; **non c'era un ~** there wasn't a soul; **quell'attore è un ~** he's a rotten actor; **~ da caccia** hunting dog; **~ da guardia** guard dog; **~ lupo** alsatian; **~ da salotto** lap dog; **~ da slitta** husky
ca'nestro *sm* basket; **fare un ~** (*Sport*) to shoot a basket
'canfora *sf* camphor
cangi'ante [kan'dʒante] *ag* iridescent; **seta ~** shot silk
can'guro *sm* kangaroo
ca'nicola *sf* scorching heat
ca'nile *sm* kennel; (*di allevamento*) kennels *pl*; **~ municipale** dog pound
ca'nino, -a *ag, sm* canine
'canna *sf* (*pianta*) reed; (*: da zucchero*) cane; (*bastone*) stick, cane; (*di fucile*) barrel; (*di organo*) pipe; (*Droga*) joint; **~ fumaria** chimney flue; **~ da pesca** (fishing) rod; **~ da zucchero** sugar cane
can'nella *sf* (*Cuc*) cinnamon; (*di conduttura, botte*) tap
cannel'loni *smpl pasta tubes stuffed with sauce and baked*
can'neto *sm* bed of reeds
can'nibale *sm* cannibal
cannocchi'ale [kannok'kjale] *sm* telescope
canno'nata *sf*: **è una vera ~!** (*fig*) it's (*o* he's *etc*) fantastic!
can'none *sm* (*Mil*) gun; (*: Storia*) cannon; (*tubo*) pipe, tube; (*piega*) box pleat; (*fig*) ace; **donna ~** fat woman
cannoni'ere *sm* (*Naut*) gunner; (*Calcio*) goal scorer
can'nuccia, -ce [kan'nuttʃa] *sf* (drinking) straw
'canone *sm* canon, criterion; (*mensile, annuo*) rent; fee; **legge dell'equo ~** fair rent act
ca'nonica, -che *sf* presbytery
ca'nonico, -ci *sm* (*Rel*) canon
canoniz'zare [kanonid'dzare] *vt* to canonize
ca'noro, -a *ag* (*uccello*) singing, song *cpd*
ca'notta *sf* vest
canot'taggio [kanot'taddʒo] *sm* rowing
canotti'era *sf* vest (*Brit*), undershirt (*US*)
ca'notto *sm* small boat, dinghy; canoe
cano'vaccio [kano'vattʃo] *sm* (*tela*) canvas; (*strofinaccio*) duster; (*trama*) plot
can'tante *sm/f* singer
can'tare *vt, vi* to sing; **~ vittoria** to crow; **fare ~ qn** (*fig*) to make sb talk
cantas'torie *sm/f inv* storyteller
cantau'tore, -'trice *sm/f* singer-composer
canterel'lare *vt, vi* to hum, sing to o.s.
canticchi'are [kantik'kjare] *vt, vi* to hum, sing to o.s.
canti'ere *sm* (*Edil*) (building) site; (*anche*: **cantiere navale**) shipyard
canti'lena *sf* (*filastrocca*) lullaby; (*fig*) singsong voice
can'tina *sf* (*locale*) cellar; (*bottega*) wine shop
'canto *sm* song; (*arte*) singing; (*Rel*) chant; chanting; (*Poesia*) poem, lyric; (*parte di una poesia*) canto; (*parte, lato*): **da un ~** on the one hand; **d'altro ~** on the other hand
canto'nata *sf* (*di edificio*) corner; **prendere una ~** (*fig*) to blunder
can'tone *sm* (*in Svizzera*) canton
cantoni'era *ag*: **(casa) ~** road inspector's house
can'tuccio [kan'tuttʃo] *sm* corner, nook
ca'nuto, -a *ag* white, whitehaired
canzo'nare [kantso'nare] *vt* to tease
canzona'tura [kantsona'tura] *sf* teasing; (*beffa*) joke
can'zone [kan'tsone] *sf* song; (*Poesia*) canzone
canzoni'ere [kantso'njɛre] *sm* (*Mus*) songbook; (*Letteratura*) collection of poems
'caos *sm inv* chaos
ca'otico, -a, ci, che *ag* chaotic
CAP *sigla m* = **codice di avviamento postale**
cap. *abbr* (= *capitolo*) ch.
ca'pace [ka'patʃe] *ag* able, capable; (*ampio, vasto*) large, capacious; **sei ~ di farlo?** can you *o* are you able to do it?; **~ d'intendere e di volere** (*Dir*) in full possession of one's faculties
capacità [kapatʃi'ta] *sf inv* ability; (*Dir, di recipiente*) capacity; **~ produttiva** production capacity
capaci'tarsi [kapatʃi'tarsi] *vr*: **~ di** to make out, understand
ca'panna *sf* hut
capan'nello *sm* knot (of people)

ca'panno *sm* (*di cacciatori*) hide; (*da spiaggia*) bathing hut
capan'none *sm* (*Agr*) barn; (*fabbricato industriale*) (factory) shed
caparbietà *sf* stubbornness
ca'parbio, -a *ag* stubborn
ca'parra *sf* deposit, down payment
capa'tina *sf*: **fare una ~ da qn/in centro** to pop in on sb/into town
capeggi'are [kaped'dʒare] *vt* (*rivolta etc*) to head, lead
ca'pello *sm* hair; **capelli** *smpl* (*capigliatura*) hair *sg*; **averne fin sopra i capelli di qc/qn** to be fed up to the (back) teeth with sth/sb; **mi ci hanno tirato per i capelli** (*fig*) they dragged me into it; **tirato per i capelli** (*spiegazione*) far-fetched
capel'lone, -a *sm/f* hippie
capel'luto, -a *ag*: **cuoio ~** scalp
capez'zale [kapet'tsale] *sm* bolster; (*fig*) bedside
ca'pezzolo [ka'pettsolo] *sm* nipple
capi'ente *ag* capacious
capi'enza [ka'pjɛntsa] *sf* capacity
capiglia'tura [kapiʎʎa'tura] *sf* hair
capil'lare *ag* (*fig*) detailed ■ *sm* (*Anat*: *anche*: **vaso capillare**) capillary
ca'pire *vt* to understand; **~ al volo** to catch on straight away; **si capisce!** (*certamente!*) of course!, certainly!
capi'tale *ag* (*mortale*) capital; (*fondamentale*) main *cpd*, chief *cpd* ■ *sf* (*città*) capital ■ *sm* (*Econ*) capital; **~ azionario** equity capital, share capital; **~ d'esercizio** working capital; **~ fisso** capital assets, fixed capital; **~ immobile** real estate; **~ liquido** cash assets *pl*; **~ mobile** movables *pl*; **~ di rischio** risk capital; **~ sociale** (*di società*) authorized capital; (*di club*) funds *pl*; **~ di ventura** venture capital, risk capital
capita'lismo *sm* capitalism
capita'lista, -i, e *ag, sm/f* capitalist
capitaliz'zare [kapitalid'dzare] *vt* to capitalize
capitalizzazi'one [kapitaliddzat'tsjone] *sf* capitalization
capita'nare *vt* to lead; (*Calcio*) to captain
capitane'ria *sf*: **~ (di porto)** port authorities *pl*
capi'tano *sm* captain; **~ di lungo corso** master mariner; **~ di ventura** (*Storia*) mercenary leader
capi'tare *vi* (*giungere casualmente*) to happen to go, find o.s.; (*accadere*) to happen; (*presentarsi*: *cosa*) to turn up, present itself ■ *vb impers* to happen; **~ a proposito/bene/male** to turn up at the right moment/at a good time/at a bad time; **mi è capitato un guaio** I've had a spot of trouble
capi'tello *sm* (*Archit*) capital
capito'lare *vi* to capitulate
capitolazi'one [kapitolat'tsjone] *sf* capitulation
ca'pitolo *sm* chapter; **capitoli** *smpl* (*Comm*) items; **non ho voce in ~** (*fig*) I have no say in the matter
capi'tombolo *sm* headlong fall, tumble
'capo *sm* (*Anat*) head; (*persona*) head, leader; (*: in ufficio*) head, boss; (*: in tribù*) chief; (*estremità*: *di tavolo, scale*) head, top; (*: di filo*) end; (*Geo*) cape; **andare a ~** to start a new paragraph; **"punto a ~"** "full stop — new paragraph"; **da ~** over again; **in ~ a** (*tempo*) within; **da un ~ all'altro** from one end to the other; **fra ~ e collo** (*all'improvviso*) out of the blue; **un discorso senza né ~ né coda** a senseless *o* meaningless speech; **~ d'accusa** (*Dir*) charge; **~ di bestiame** head *inv* of cattle; **C~ di Buona Speranza** Cape of Good Hope; **~ di vestiario** item of clothing
capo'banda (*pl* **capibanda**) *sm* (*Mus*) bandmaster; (*di malviventi, fig*) gang leader
ca'poccia [ka'pɔttʃa] *sm inv* (*di lavoranti*) overseer; (*peg*: *capobanda*) boss
capo'classe (*mpl* **capiclasse**, *fpl* **~**) *sm/f* (*Ins*) ≈ form captain (*Brit*), class president (*US*)
capocu'oco, -chi *sm* head cook
Capo'danno *sm* New Year
capofa'miglia [kapofa'miʎʎa] (*mpl* **capifamiglia**, *fpl* **~**) *sm/f* head of the family
capo'fitto; **a ~** *av* headfirst, headlong
capo'giro [kapo'dʒiro] *sm* dizziness *no pl*; **da ~** (*fig*) astonishing, staggering
capo'gruppo (*mpl* **capigruppo**, *fpl* **~**) *sm/f* group leader
capola'voro, -i *sm* masterpiece
capo'linea (*pl* **capilinea**) *sm* terminus; (*fig*) end of the line
capo'lino *sm*: **far ~** to peep out (*o* in *etc*)
capo'lista (*mpl* **capilista**, *fpl* **~**) *sm/f* (*Pol*) *top candidate on electoral list*
capolu'ogo (*pl* **capoluoghi** *o* **capiluoghi**) *sm* chief town, administrative centre (*Brit*) *o* center (*US*)
capo'mastro (*pl* **capomastri** *o* **capimastri**) *sm* master builder
capo'rale *sm* (*Mil*) lance corporal (*Brit*), private first class (*US*)
capore'parto (*mpl* **capireparto**, *fpl* **~**) *sm/f* (*di operai*) foreman; (*di ufficio, negozio*) head of department
capo'sala *sf inv* (*Med*) ward sister
capo'saldo (*pl* **capisaldi**) *sm* stronghold; (*fig*: *fondamento*) basis, cornerstone
capo'squadra (*pl* **capisquadra**) *sm* (*di operai*) foreman, ganger; (*Mil*) squad leader; (*Sport*) team captain

capostazi'one (*pl* **capistazione**) [kapostat'tsjone] *sm* station master
capos'tipite *sm* progenitor; (*fig*) earliest example
capo'tavola (*mpl* **capitavola**, *fpl* **~**) *sm/f* (*persona*) head of the table; **sedere a ~** to sit at the head of the table
ca'pote [ka'pɔt] *sf inv* (*Aut*) hood (*Brit*), soft top
capo'treno (*pl* **capitreno** *o* **capotreni**) *sm* guard
capouf'ficio [kapouf'fitʃo] *sm/f inv* head clerk
'Capo 'Verde *sm*: **il ~** Cape Verde
capo'verso *sm* (*di verso, periodo*) first line; (*Tip*) indent; (*paragrafo*) paragraph; (*Dir: comma*) section
capo'volgere [kapo'voldʒere] *vt* to overturn; (*fig*) to reverse; **capovolgersi** *vr* to overturn; (*barca*) to capsize; (*fig*) to be reversed
capovolgi'mento [kapovoldʒi'mento] *sm* (*fig*) reversal, complete change
capo'volto, -a *pp di* **capovolgere** ■ *ag* upside down; (*barca*) capsized
'cappa *sf* (*mantello*) cape, cloak; (*del camino*) hood
cap'pella *sf* (*Rel*) chapel
cappel'lano *sm* chaplain
cap'pello *sm* hat; **Tanto di ~!** (*fig*) I take my hat off to you!; **~ a bombetta** bowler (hat), derby (*US*); **~ a cilindro** top hat; **~ di paglia** straw hat
'cappero *sm* caper
cap'pone *sm* capon
cappot'tare *vi* (*Aut*) to overturn
cap'potto *sm* (over)coat
cappuc'cino [kapput'tʃino] *sm* (*frate*) Capuchin monk; (*bevanda*) cappuccino
cap'puccio [kap'puttʃo] *sm* (*copricapo*) hood; (*della biro*) cap
'capra *sf* (she-)goat
ca'prese *ag* from (*o* of) Capri
ca'pretto *sm* kid
ca'priccio [ka'prittʃo] *sm* caprice, whim; (*bizza*) tantrum; **fare i capricci** to be very naughty; **~ della sorte** quirk of fate
capricci'oso, -a [kaprit'tʃoso] *ag* capricious, whimsical; naughty
Capri'corno *sm* Capricorn; **essere del ~** (*dello zodiaco*) to be Capricorn
capri'foglio [kapri'fɔʎʎo] *sm* honeysuckle
capri'ola *sf* somersault
capri'olo *sm* roe deer
'capro *sm* billy-goat; **~ espiatorio** (*fig*) scapegoat
ca'prone *sm* billy-goat
'capsula *sf* capsule; (*di arma, per bottiglie*) cap
cap'tare *vt* (*Radio, TV*) to pick up; (*cattivarsi*) to gain, win
CAR *sigla m* = **Centro Addestramento Reclute**
cara'bina *sf* rifle
carabini'ere *sm* *member of Italian military police force; see note*

CARABINIERI

Originally part of the armed forces, the *Carabinieri* are police who now have civil as well as military duties, such as maintaining public order. They include paratroop units and mounted divisions and report to either the Minister of the Interior or the Minister of Defence, depending on the function they are performing.

Ca'racas *sf* Caracas
ca'raffa *sf* carafe
Ca'raibi *smpl*: **il mar dei ~** the Caribbean (Sea)
cara'ibico, -a, ci, che *ag* Caribbean
cara'mella *sf* sweet
cara'mello *sm* caramel
ca'rato *sm* (*di oro, diamante etc*) carat
ca'rattere *sm* character; (*caratteristica*) characteristic, trait; **avere un buon ~** to be good-natured; **informazione di ~ tecnico/confidenziale** information of a technical/confidential nature; **essere in ~ con qc** (*intonarsi*) to be in harmony with sth; **~ jolly** wild card
caratte'rino *sm* difficult nature *o* character
caratte'ristico, -a, ci, che *ag* characteristic ■ *sf* characteristic, feature; **segni caratteristici** (*su passaporto etc*) distinguishing marks
caratteriz'zare [karatterid'dzare] *vt* to characterize, distinguish
carboi'drato *sm* carbohydrate
carbo'naio *sm* (*chi fa carbone*) charcoal-burner; (*commerciante*) coalman, coal merchant
car'bone *sm* coal; **~ fossile** (pit) coal; **essere** *o* **stare sui carboni ardenti** to be like a cat on hot bricks
car'bonio *sm* (*Chim*) carbon
carboniz'zare [karbonid'dzare] *vt* (*legna*) to carbonize; (*: parzialmente*) to char; **morire carbonizzato** to be burned to death
carbu'rante *sm* (motor) fuel
carbura'tore *sm* carburettor
car'cassa *sf* carcass; (*fig: peg: macchina etc*) (old) wreck
carce'rato, -a [kartʃe'rato] *sm/f* prisoner
'carcere ['kartʃere] *sm* prison; (*pena*) imprisonment; **~ di massima sicurezza** top-security prison
carceri'ere, -a [kartʃe'rjɛre] *sm/f* (*anche fig*) jailer

carci'ofo [kar'tʃɔfo] *sm* artichoke
cardel'lino *sm* goldfinch
car'diaco, -a, ci, che *ag* cardiac, heart *cpd*
cardi'nale *ag, sm* cardinal
'cardine *sm* hinge
cardiolo'gia [kardjolo'dʒia] *sf* cardiology
cardi'ologo, -gi *sm* heart specialist, cardiologist
'cardo *sm* thistle
ca'rente *ag*: **~ di** lacking in
ca'renza [ka'rɛntsa] *sf* lack, scarcity; (*vitaminica*) deficiency
cares'tia *sf* famine; (*penuria*) scarcity, dearth
ca'rezza [ka'rettsa] *sf* caress; **dare** *o* **fare una ~ a** (*persona*) to caress; (*animale*) to stroke, pat
carez'zare [karet'tsare] *vt* to caress, stroke, fondle
carez'zevole [karet'tsevole] *ag* sweet, endearing
'cargo, -ghi *sm* (*nave*) cargo boat, freighter; (*aereo*) freighter
cari'are *vt*, **cari'arsi** *vr* (*denti*) to decay
'carica *sf vedi* **carico**
caricabatte'rie *sm inv* (*Elettr*) battery charger
cari'care *vt* to load; (*aggravare: anche fig*) to weigh down; (*orologio*) to wind up; (*batteria, Mil*) to charge; (*Inform*) to load; **caricarsi** *vr*: **caricarsi di** to burden *o* load o.s. with; (*fig: di responsabilità, impegni*) to burden o.s. with
carica'tura *sf* caricature
'carico, -a, chi, che *ag* (*che porta un peso*): **~ di** loaded *o* laden with; (*fucile*) loaded; (*orologio*) wound up; (*batteria*) charged; (*colore*) deep; (*caffè, tè*) strong ■ *sm* (*il caricare*) loading; (*ciò che si carica*) load; (*Comm*) shipment; (*fig: peso*) burden, weight ■ *sf* (*mansione ufficiale*) office, position; (*Mil, Tecn, Elettr*) charge; **~ di debiti** up to one's ears in debt; **persona a ~** dependent; **essere a ~ di qn** (*spese etc*) to be charged to sb; (*accusa, prova*) to be against sb; **testimone a ~** witness for the prosecution; **farsi ~ di** (*problema, responsabilità*) to take on; **a ~ del cliente** at the customer's expense; **~ di lavoro** (*di ditta, reparto*) workload; **~ utile** payload; **capacità di ~** cargo capacity; **entrare/essere in carica** to come into/be in office; **ricoprire** *o* **rivestire una carica** to hold a position; **uscire di carica** to leave office; **dare la carica a** (*orologio*) to wind up; (*fig: persona*) to back up; **tornare alla carica** (*fig*) to insist, persist; **ha una forte carica di simpatia** he's very likeable
'carie *sf* (*dentaria*) decay
ca'rino, -a *ag* lovely, pretty, nice; (*simpatico*) nice
ca'risma [ka'rizma] *sm* charisma
caris'matico, -a, ci, che *ag* charismatic
carità *sf* charity; **per ~!** (*escl di rifiuto*) good heavens, no!
carita'tevole *ag* charitable
carnagi'one [karna'dʒone] *sf* complexion
car'nale *ag* (*amore*) carnal; (*fratello*) blood *cpd*
'carne *sf* flesh; (*bovina, ovina etc*) meat; **in ~ e ossa** in the flesh, in person; **essere (bene) in ~** to be well padded, be plump; **non essere né ~ né pesce** (*fig*) to be neither fish nor fowl; **~ di manzo/maiale/pecora** beef/pork/mutton; **~ in scatola** tinned *o* canned meat; **~ tritata** mince (*Brit*), hamburger meat (*US*), minced (*Brit*) *o* ground (*US*) meat
car'nefice [kar'nefitʃe] *sm* executioner; hangman
carnefi'cina [karnefi'tʃina] *sf* carnage; (*fig*) disaster
carne'vale *sm* carnival; **C~** *see note*

CARNEVALE

Carnevale is the name given to the period between Epiphany (6 January) and the beginning of Lent, when people throw parties, put on processions with spectacular floats, build bonfires in the "piazze" and dress up in fabulous costumes and masks. Building to a peak just before Lent, *Carnevale* culminates in the festivities of Martedì grasso (Shrove Tuesday).

car'nivoro, -a *ag* carnivorous
car'noso, -a *ag* fleshy; (*pianta, frutto, radice*) pulpy; (*labbra*) full
'caro, -a *ag* (*amato*) dear; (*costoso*) dear, expensive; **se ti è cara la vita** if you value your life
ca'rogna [ka'roɲɲa] *sf* carrion; (*fig fam*) swine
caro'sello *sm* merry-go-round
ca'rota *sf* carrot
caro'vana *sf* caravan
caro'vita *sm* high cost of living
'carpa *sf* carp
Car'pazi [kar'patsi] *smpl*: **i ~** the Carpathian Mountains
carpente'ria *sf* carpentry
carpenti'ere *sm* carpenter
car'pire *vt*: **~ qc a qn** (*segreto etc*) to get sth out of sb
car'poni *av* on all fours
car'rabile *ag* suitable for vehicles; **"passo ~"** "keep clear"
car'raio, -a *ag*: **passo ~** vehicle entrance
carré *sm* (*acconciatura*) bob
carreggi'ata [karred'dʒata] *sf* carriageway (*Brit*), roadway; **rimettersi in ~** (*fig:*

recuperare) to catch up; **tenersi in ~** (*fig*) to keep to the right path
carrel'lata *sf* (*Cine, TV: tecnica*) tracking; (*: scena*) running shot; **~ di successi** medley of hit tunes
car'rello *sm* trolley; (*Aer*) undercarriage; (*Cine*) dolly; (*di macchina da scrivere*) carriage
car'retta *sf*: **tirare la ~** (*fig*) to plod along
car'retto *sm* handcart
carri'era *sf* career; **fare ~** to get on; **ufficiale di ~** (*Mil*) regular officer; **a gran ~** at full speed
carri'ola *sf* wheelbarrow
'carro *sm* cart, wagon; **il Gran/Piccolo C~** (*Astr*) the Great/Little Bear; **mettere il ~ avanti ai buoi** (*fig*) to put the cart before the horse; **~ armato** tank; **~ attrezzi** (*Aut*) breakdown van (*Brit*), tow truck (*US*); **~ funebre** hearse; **~ merci/bestiame** (*Ferr*) goods/animal wagon
car'roccio [kar'rɔttʃo] *sm* (*Pol*): **il C~** *symbol of Lega Nord*
car'rozza [kar'rɔttsa] *sf* carriage, coach; **~ letto** (*Ferr*) sleeper; **~ ristorante** (*Ferr*) dining car
carroz'zella [karrot'tsɛlla] *sf* (*per bambini*) pram (*Brit*), baby carriage (*US*); (*per invalidi*) wheelchair
carrozze'ria [karrottse'ria] *sf* body, coachwork (*Brit*); (*officina*) coachbuilder's workshop (*Brit*), body shop
carrozzi'ere [karrot'tsjɛre] *sm* (*Aut: progettista*) car designer; (*: meccanico*) coachbuilder
carroz'zina [karrot'tsina] *sf* pram (*Brit*), baby carriage (*US*)
carroz'zone [karrot'tsone] *sm* (*da circo, di zingari*) caravan
car'rucola *sf* pulley
'carta *sf* paper; (*al ristorante*) menu; (*Geo*) map; plan; (*documento, da gioco*) card; (*costituzione*) charter; **carte** *sfpl* (*documenti*) papers, documents; **alla ~** (*al ristorante*) à la carte; **cambiare le carte in tavola** (*fig*) to shift one's ground; **fare carte false** (*fig*) to go to great lengths; **~ assegni** bank card; **~ assorbente** blotting paper; **~ bollata** *o* **da bollo** (*Amm*) official stamped paper; **~ di credito** credit card; **~ di debito** cash card; **~ fedeltà** loyalty card; **~ (geografica)** map; **~ d'identità** identity card; **~ igienica** toilet paper; **~ d'imbarco** (*Aer, Naut*) boarding card, boarding pass; **~ da lettere** writing paper; **~ libera** (*Amm*) unstamped paper; **~ millimetrata** graph paper; **~ oleata** waxed paper; **~ da pacchi, ~ da imballo** wrapping paper, brown paper; **~ da parati** wallpaper; **~ verde** (*Aut*) green card; **~ vetrata** sandpaper; **~ da visita** visiting card
cartacar'bone (*pl* **cartecarbone**) *sf* carbon paper
car'taccia, -ce [kar'tattʃa] *sf* waste paper
cartamo'dello *sm* (*Cucito*) paper pattern
cartamo'neta *sf* paper money
carta'pecora *sf* parchment
carta'pesta *sf* papier-mâché
cartas'traccia [kartas'trattʃa] *sf* waste paper
car'teggio [kar'teddʒo] *sm* correspondence
car'tella *sf* (*scheda*) card; (*custodia: di cartone, Inform*) folder; (*: di uomo d'affari etc*) briefcase; (*: di scolaro*) schoolbag, satchel; **~ clinica** (*Med*) case sheet
cartel'lino *sm* (*etichetta*) label; (*su porta*) notice; (*scheda*) card; **timbrare il ~** (*all'entrata*) to clock in; (*all'uscita*) to clock out; **~ di presenza** clock card, timecard
car'tello *sm* sign; (*pubblicitario*) poster; (*stradale*) sign, signpost; (*in dimostrazioni*) placard; (*Econ*) cartel
cartel'lone *sm* (*pubblicitario*) advertising poster; (*della tombola*) scoring frame; (*Teat*) playbill; **tenere il ~** (*spettacolo*) to have a long run
carti'era *sf* paper mill
carti'lagine [karti'ladʒine] *sf* cartilage
car'tina *sf* (*Aut, Geo*) map
car'toccio [kar'tɔttʃo] *sm* paper bag; **cuocere al ~** (*Cuc*) to bake in tinfoil
cartogra'fia *sf* cartography
carto'laio, -a *sm/f* stationer
cartolarizzazi'one [kartolariddza'tsjone] *sf* securitization
cartole'ria *sf* stationer's (shop (*Brit*))
carto'lina *sf* postcard; **~ di auguri** greetings card; **~ precetto** *o* **rosa** (*Mil*) call-up card
carto'mante *sm/f* fortune-teller (*using cards*)
carton'cino [karton'tʃino] *sm* (*materiale*) thin cardboard; (*biglietto*) card; **~ della società** compliments slip
car'tone *sm* cardboard; (*del latte, dell'aranciata*) carton; (*Arte*) cartoon; **cartoni animati** (*Cine*) cartoons
car'tuccia, -ce [kar'tuttʃa] *sf* cartridge; **~ a salve** blank cartridge; **mezza ~** (*fig: persona*) good-for-nothing
'casa *sf* house; (*specialmente la propria casa*) home; (*Comm*) firm, house; **essere a ~** to be at home; **vado a ~ mia/tua** I'm going home/ to your house; **~ di correzione** ≈ community home (*Brit*), reformatory (*US*); **~ di cura** nursing home; **~ editrice** publishing house; **C~ delle Libertà** House of Liberties, *centre-right coalition*; **~ di riposo** (old people's) home, care home; **~ dello studente** student hostel; **~ di tolleranza, ~ d'appuntamenti** brothel; **case popolari** ≈ council houses (*o* flats) (*Brit*), ≈ public housing units (*US*)
ca'sacca, -che *sf* military coat; (*di fantino*) blouse

ca'sale *sm* (*gruppo di case*) hamlet; (*casa di campagna*) farmhouse
casa'lingo, -a, ghi, ghe *ag* household, domestic; (*fatto a casa*) home-made; (*semplice*) homely; (*amante della casa*) home-loving ■ *sf* housewife; **casalinghi** *smpl* (*oggetti*) household articles; **cucina casalinga** plain home cooking
ca'sata *sf* family lineage
ca'sato *sm* family name
casca'morto *sm* woman-chaser; **fare il ~** to chase women
cas'care *vi* to fall; **~ bene/male** (*fig*) to land lucky/unlucky; **~ dalle nuvole** (*fig*) to be taken aback; **~ dal sonno** to be falling asleep on one's feet; **caschi il mondo** no matter what; **non cascherà il mondo se ...** it won't be the end of the world if ...
cas'cata *sf* fall; (*d'acqua*) cascade, waterfall
cascherò *etc* [kaske'rɔ] *vb vedi* **cascare**
ca'scina [kaʃʃina] *sf* farmstead
casci'nale [kaʃʃi'nale] *sm* (*casolare*) farmhouse; (*cascina*) farmstead
'casco (*pl* **caschi**) *sm* helmet; (*del parrucchiere*) hair-dryer; (*di banane*) bunch; **~ blu** (*Mil*) blue helmet (*UN soldier*)
caseggi'ato [kased'dʒato] *sm* (*edificio*) large block of flats (*Brit*) *o* apartment building (*US*); (*gruppo di case*) group of houses
casei'ficio [kazei'fitʃo] *sm* creamery
ca'sella *sf* pigeonhole; **~ email** mailbox; **~ postale** post office box
casel'lario *sm* (*mobile*) filing cabinet; (*raccolta di pratiche*) files *pl*; **~ giudiziale** court records *pl*; **~ penale** police files *pl*
ca'sello *sm* (*di autostrada*) tollgate
case'reccio, -a, ci, ce [kase'rettʃo] *ag* home-made
ca'serma *sf* barracks
caser'tano, -a *ag* of (*o* from) Caserta
ca'sino *sm* (*confusione*) row, racket; (*casa di prostituzione*) brothel
casinò *sm inv* casino
ca'sistica *sf* (*Med*) record of cases; **secondo la ~ degli incidenti stradali** according to road accident data
'caso *sm* chance; (*fatto, vicenda*) event, incident; (*possibilità*) possibility; (*Med, Ling*) case; **a ~** at random; **per ~** by chance, by accident; **in ogni ~, in tutti i casi** in any case, at any rate; **in ~ contrario** otherwise; **al ~** should the opportunity arise; **nel ~ che** in case; **~ mai** if by chance; **far ~ a qc/qn** to pay attention to sth/sb; **fare** *o* **porre** *o* **mettere il ~ che** to suppose that; **fa proprio al ~ nostro** it's just what we need; **guarda ~ ...** strangely enough ...; **è il ~ che ce ne andiamo** we'd better go; **~ limite** borderline case
caso'lare *sm* cottage
'Caspio *sm*: **il mar ~** the Caspian Sea
'caspita *escl* (*di sorpresa*) good heavens!; (*di impazienza*) for goodness' sake!
'cassa *sf* case, crate, box; (*bara*) coffin; (*mobile*) chest; (*involucro: di orologio etc*) case; (*macchina*) cash register; (*luogo di pagamento*) cash desk, checkout (counter); (*fondo*) fund; (*istituto bancario*) bank; **battere ~** (*fig*) to come looking for money; **~ automatica prelievi** automatic telling machine, cash dispenser; **~ continua** night safe; **mettere in ~ integrazione** ≈ to lay off; **C~ del Mezzogiorno** *development fund for the South of Italy*; **~ mutua** *o* **malattia** health insurance scheme; **~ di risonanza** (*Mus*) soundbox; (*fig*) platform; **~ di risparmio** savings bank; **~ rurale e artigiana** credit institution (*serving farmers and craftsmen*); **~ toracica** (*Anat*) chest
cassa'forte (*pl* **casseforti**) *sf* safe
cassa'panca (*pl* **cassapanche** *o* **cassepanche**) *sf* settle
casseru'ola, casse'rola *sf* saucepan
cas'setta *sf* box; (*per registratore*) cassette; (*Cine, Teat*) box-office takings *pl*; **pane a** *o* **in ~** toasting loaf; **film di ~** (*commerciale*) box-office draw; **far ~** to be a box-office success; **~ delle lettere** letterbox; **~ di sicurezza** strongbox
cas'setto *sm* drawer
casset'tone *sm* chest of drawers
cassi'ere, -a *sm/f* cashier; (*di banca*) teller
cassinte'grato, -a *sm/f* *person who has been laid off*
cas'sone *sm* (*cassa*) large case, large chest
'casta *sf* caste
cas'tagna [kas'taɲɲa] *sf* chestnut; **prendere qn in ~** (*fig*) to catch sb in the act
cas'tagno [kas'taɲɲo] *sm* chestnut (tree)
cas'tano, -a *ag* chestnut (brown)
cas'tello *sm* castle; (*Tecn*) scaffolding
casti'gare *vt* to punish
casti'gato, -a *ag* (*casto, modesto*) pure, chaste; (*emendato: prosa, versione*) expurgated, amended
cas'tigo, -ghi *sm* punishment; **mettere/essere in ~** to punish/be punished
castità *sf* chastity
'casto, -a *ag* chaste, pure
cas'toro *sm* beaver
cas'trante *ag* frustrating
cas'trare *vt* to castrate; to geld; to doctor (*Brit*), fix (*US*); (*fig: iniziativa*) to frustrate
castrone'ria *sf* (*fam*): **dire castronerie** to talk rubbish

casu'ale *ag* chance *cpd*
ca'supola *sf* simple little cottage
catac'lisma, -i *sm* (*fig*) catastrophe
cata'comba *sf* catacomb
cata'fascio [kata'faʃʃo] *sm*: **andare a ~** to collapse; **mandare a ~** to wreck
cata'litico, -a, ci, che *ag*: **marmitta catalitica** (*Aut*) catalytic converter
cataliz'zare [katalid'dzare] *vt* (*fig*) to act as a catalyst (up)on
cataliz'zato, -a [katalid'dzato] *ag* (*Aut*) with catalytic converter
catalizza'tore [kataliddza'tore] *sm* (*anche fig*) catalyst; (*Aut*) catalytic converter
Cata'logna [kata'loɲɲa] *sf*: **la ~** Catalonia
ca'talogo, -ghi *sm* catalogue; **~ dei prezzi** price list
cata'nese *ag* of (*o* from) Catania
catanza'rese [katandza'rese] *ag* of (*o* from) Catanzaro
cata'pecchia [kata'pekkja] *sf* hovel
cata'pulta *sf* catapult
catarifran'gente [katarifran'dʒɛnte] *sm* (*Aut*) reflector
ca'tarro *sm* catarrh
ca'tarsi *sf inv* catharsis
ca'tasta *sf* stack, pile
ca'tasto *sm* land register; land registry office
ca'tastrofe *sf* catastrophe, disaster
catas'trofico, -a, ci, che *ag* (*evento*) catastrophic; (*persona, previsione*) pessimistic
catastro'fista, -i, e *ag, sm/f* doom-monger; **non fare il ~** don't be so pessimistic
cate'chismo [kate'kizmo] *sm* catechism
catego'ria *sf* category; (*di albergo*) class
cate'gorico, -a, ci, che *ag* categorical
ca'tena *sf* chain; **reazione a ~** chain reaction; **susseguirsi a ~** to happen in quick succession; **~ alimentare** food chain; **~ di montaggio** assembly line; **~ montuosa** mountain range; **catene da neve** (*Aut*) snow chains
cate'naccio [kate'nattʃo] *sm* bolt
cate'nella *sf* (*ornamento*) chain; (*di orologio*) watch chain; (*di porta*) door chain
cate'ratta *sf* cataract; (*chiusa*) sluice gate
ca'terva *sf* (*di cose*) loads *pl*, heaps *pl*; (*di persone*) horde
cate'tere *sm* (*Med*) catheter
cati'nella *sf*: **piovere a catinelle** to pour, rain cats and dogs
ca'tino *sm* basin
ca'todico, -a, ci, che *ag*: **tubo a raggi catodici** cathode-ray tube
ca'torcio [ka'tɔrtʃo] *sm* (*peg*) old wreck
ca'trame *sm* tar
'cattedra *sf* teacher's desk; (*di università*) chair; **salire** *o* **montare in ~** (*fig*) to pontificate
catte'drale *sf* cathedral
catte'dratico, -a, ci, che *ag* (*insegnamento*) university *cpd*; (*ironico*) pedantic ■ *sm/f* professor
catti'veria *sf* (*qualità*) wickedness; (*di bambino*) naughtiness; (*azione*) wicked action; **fare una ~** to do something wicked; to be naughty
cattività *sf* captivity
cat'tivo, -a *ag* bad; (*malvagio*) bad, wicked; (*turbolento: bambino*) bad, naughty; (*: mare*) rough; (*odore, sapore*) nasty, bad ■ *sm/f* bad *o* wicked person; **farsi ~ sangue** to worry, get in a state; **farsi un ~ nome** to earn o.s. a bad reputation; **i cattivi** (*nei film*) the baddies (*Brit*), the bad guys (*US*)
cattocomu'nista, -i, e *ag combining Catholic and communist ideas*
cattoli'cesimo [kattoli'tʃezimo] *sm* Catholicism
cat'tolico, -a, ci, che *ag, sm/f* (Roman) Catholic
cat'tura *sf* capture
cattu'rare *vt* to capture
cau'casico, -a, ci, che *ag, sm/f* Caucasian
'Caucaso *sm*: **il ~** the Caucasus
caucciù [kaut'tʃu] *sm* rubber
'causa *sf* cause; (*Dir*) lawsuit, case, action; **a ~ di** because of; **per ~ sua** because of him; **fare** *o* **muovere ~ a qn** to take legal action against sb; **parte in ~** litigant
cau'sale *ag* (*Ling*) causal ■ *sf* cause, reason
cau'sare *vt* to cause
'caustico, -a, ci, che *ag* caustic
cau'tela *sf* caution, prudence
caute'lare *vt* to protect; **cautelarsi** *vr*: **cautelarsi (da** *o* **contro)** to take precautions (against)
'cauto, -a *ag* cautious, prudent
cauzio'nare [kauttsjo'nare] *vt* to guarantee
cauzi'one [kaut'tsjone] *sf* security; (*Dir*) bail; **rilasciare dietro ~** to release on bail
cav. *abbr* = **cavaliere**
'cava *sf* quarry
caval'care *vt* (*cavallo*) to ride; (*muro*) to sit astride; (*ponte*) to span
caval'cata *sf* ride; (*gruppo di persone*) riding party
cavalca'via *sm inv* flyover
cavalci'oni [kaval'tʃoni]: **a ~ di** *prep* astride
cavali'ere *sm* rider; (*feudale, titolo*) knight; (*soldato*) cavalryman; (*al ballo*) partner
cavalleg'gero [kavalled'dʒɛro] *sm* (*Mil*) light cavalryman

cavalle'resco, -a, schi, sche *ag* chivalrous
cavalle'ria *sf* chivalry; (*milizia a cavallo*) cavalry
cavalle'rizzo, -a [kavalle'rittso] *sm/f* riding instructor; circus rider
caval'letta *sf* grasshopper; (*dannosa*) locust
caval'letto *sm* (*Fot*) tripod; (*da pittore*) easel
caval'lina *sf* (*Ginnastica*) horse; (*gioco*) leap-frog; **correre la ~** (*fig*) to sow one's wild oats
ca'vallo *sm* horse; (*Scacchi*) knight; (*Aut*: *anche*: **cavallo vapore**) horsepower; (*dei pantaloni*) crotch; **a ~** on horseback; **a ~ di** astride, straddling; **siamo a ~** (*fig*) we've made it; **da ~** (*fig*: *dose*) drastic; (: *febbre*) raging; **vivere a ~ tra due periodi** to straddle two periods; **~ di battaglia** (*Teat*) tour de force; (*fig*) hobbyhorse; **~ da corsa** racehorse; **~ a dondolo** rocking horse; **~ da sella** saddle horse; **~ da soma** packhorse
ca'vare *vt* (*togliere*) to draw out, extract, take out; (: *giacca, scarpe*) to take off; (: *fame, sete, voglia*) to satisfy; **cavarsi** *vr*: **cavarsi da** (*guai, problemi*) to get out of; **cavarsela** to get away with it; to manage, get on all right; **non ci caverà un bel nulla** you'll get nothing out of it (*o* him *etc*)
cava'tappi *sm inv* corkscrew
ca'verna *sf* cave
caver'noso, -a *ag* (*luogo*) cavernous; (*fig*: *voce*) deep; (: *tosse*) raucous
ca'vezza [ka'vettsa] *sf* halter
'cavia *sf* guinea pig
cavi'ale *sm* caviar
ca'viglia [ka'viʎʎa] *sf* ankle
cavil'lare *vi* to quibble
ca'villo *sm* quibble
cavil'loso, -a *ag* quibbling, hair-splitting
cavità *sf inv* cavity
'cavo, -a *ag* hollow ▪ *sm* (*Anat*) cavity; (*grossa corda*) rope, cable; (*Elettr, Tel*) cable
cavo'lata *sf* (*fam*) stupid thing
cavolfi'ore *sm* cauliflower
'cavolo *sm* cabbage; **non m'importa un ~** (*fam*) I don't give a hoot; **che ~ vuoi?** (*fam*) what the heck do you want?; **~ di Bruxelles** Brussels sprout
caz'zata [kat'tsata] *sf* (*fam!*: *stupidaggine*) stupid thing, something stupid
'cazzo ['kattso] *sm* (*fam!*: *pene*) prick (*!*); **non gliene importa un ~** (*fig fam!*) he doesn't give a damn about it; **fatti i cazzi tuoi** (*fig fam!*) mind your own damn business
caz'zotto [kat'tsɔtto] *sm* punch; **fare a cazzotti** to have a punch-up
cazzu'ola [kat'tswɔla] *sf* trowel
CB *sigla* = **Campobasso**
CC *abbr* = **Carabinieri**
cc *abbr* (= *centimetro cubico*) cc
C.C. *abbr* = **codice civile**
c.c. *abbr* (= *conto corrente*) c/a, a/c; (*Elettr*) *vedi* **corrente continua**
c/c *abbr* (= *conto corrente*) c/a, a/c
C.C.D. *sigla m* (*Pol*: = *Centro Cristiano Democratico*) *party originating from Democrazia Cristiana*
CCI *sigla f* (= *Camera di Commercio Internazionale*) ICC (= *International Chamber of Commerce*)
CCIAA *abbr* = **Camera di Commercio Industria, Agricoltura e Artigianato**
CCT *sigla m* = **certificato di credito del Tesoro**
C.D. *abbr* (= *Corpo Diplomatico*) CD ▪ *sm inv* (= *compact disc*) CD
c.d. *abbr* = **cosiddetto**
C.d.A. *abbr* = **Consiglio di Amministrazione**
c.d.d. *abbr* (= *come dovevasi dimostrare*) QED (= *quod erat demonstrandum*)
C.d.M. *abbr* = **Cassa del Mezzogiorno**
CD-Rom [tʃidi'rɔm] *sigla m inv* (= *Compact Disc Read Only Memory*) CD-Rom
C.d.U. [tʃidi'u] *sigla m* (= *Cristiano Democratici Uniti*) United Christian Democrats (*Italian centre-right political party*)
CE *sigla* = **Caserta**
ce [tʃe] *pron, av vedi* **ci**
C.E. *sigla* = **Consiglio d'Europa**
cec'chino [tʃek'kino] *sm* sniper; (*Pol*) *member of parliament who votes against his own party*
'cece ['tʃetʃe] *sm* chickpea, garbanzo (US)
Ce'cenia [tʃe'tʃenja] *sf* Chechnya
ce'ceno, -a [tʃe'tʃeno] *ag, sm/f* Chechen
cecità [tʃetʃi'ta] *sf* blindness
'ceco, -a, chi, che ['tʃɛko] *ag, sm/f, sm* Czech; **la Repubblica Ceca** the Czech Republic
Cecoslo'vacchia [tʃekozlo'vakkja] *sf*: **la ~** Czechoslovakia
cecoslo'vacco, -a, chi, che [tʃekozlo'vakko] *ag, sm/f* Czechoslovakian
CED [tʃɛd] *sigla m* = **centro elaborazione dati**
'cedere ['tʃɛdere] *vt* (*concedere*: *posto*) to give up; (*Dir*) to transfer, make over ▪ *vi* (*cadere*) to give way, subside; **~ (a)** to surrender (to), yield (to), give in (to); **~ il passo (a qn)** to let (sb) pass in front; **~ il passo a qc** (*fig*) to give way to sth; **~ la parola (a qn)** to hand over (to sb)
ce'devole [tʃe'devole] *ag* (*terreno*) soft; (*fig*) yielding
'cedola ['tʃɛdola] *sf* (*Comm*) coupon; voucher
ce'drata [tʃe'drata] *sf* citron juice
'cedro ['tʃɛdro] *sm* cedar; (*albero da frutto, frutto*) citron
'CEE ['tʃɛe] *sigla f* = **Comunità Economica Europea**
'ceffo ['tʃɛffo] *sm* (*peg*) ugly mug
cef'fone [tʃef'fone] *sm* slap, smack
'ceko, -a ['tʃɛko] *ag, sm/f, sm* = **ceco**

ce'lare [tʃe'lare] *vt* to conceal; **celarsi** *vr* to hide
cele'brare [tʃele'brare] *vt* to celebrate; (*cerimonia*) to hold; **~ le lodi di qc/qn** to sing the praises of sth/sb
celebrazi'one [tʃelebrat'tsjone] *sf* celebration
'celebre ['tʃɛlebre] *ag* famous, celebrated
celebrità [tʃelebri'ta] *sf inv* fame; (*persona*) celebrity
'celere ['tʃɛlere] *ag* fast, swift; (*corso*) crash *cpd* ■ *sf* (*Polizia*) riot police
ce'leste [tʃe'lɛste] *ag* celestial; heavenly; (*colore*) sky-blue
'celia [tʃɛlja] *sf* joke; **per ~** for a joke
celi'bato [tʃeli'bato] *sm* celibacy
'celibe ['tʃɛlibe] *ag* single, unmarried ■ *sm* bachelor
'cella ['tʃɛlla] *sf* cell; **~ di rigore** punishment cell
cello'phane® [sɛlo'fan] *sm* cellophane®
'cellula ['tʃɛllula] *sf* (*Biol, Elettr, Pol*) cell
cellu'lare [tʃellu'lare] *ag* cellular ■ *sm* (*furgone*) police van; (*telefono*) cellphone; **segregazione ~** (*Dir*) solitary confinement
cellu'lite [tʃellu'lite] *sf* cellulitis
'celta ['tʃɛlta] *sm/f* Celt
'celtico, -a, ci, che ['tʃɛltiko] *ag, sm* Celtic
'cembalo ['tʃembalo] *sm* (*Mus*) harpsichord
cemen'tare [tʃemen'tare] *vt* (*anche fig*) to cement
ce'mento [tʃe'mento] *sm* cement; **~ armato** reinforced concrete
'cena ['tʃena] *sf* dinner; (*leggera*) supper
ce'nacolo [tʃe'nakolo] *sm* (*circolo*) coterie, circle; (*Rel, dipinto*) Last Supper
ce'nare [tʃe'nare] *vi* to dine, have dinner
'cencio ['tʃentʃo] *sm* piece of cloth, rag; (*per spolverare*) duster; **essere bianco come un ~** to be as white as a sheet
'cenere ['tʃenere] *sf* ash
Cene'rentola [tʃene'rɛntola] *sf* (*anche fig*) Cinderella
'cenno ['tʃenno] *sm* (*segno*) sign, signal; (*gesto*) gesture; (*col capo*) nod; (*con la mano*) wave; (*allusione*) hint, mention; (*breve esposizione*) short account; **far ~ di sì/no** to nod (one's head)/shake one's head; **~ d'intesa** sign of agreement; **cenni di storia dell'arte** an outline of the history of art
censi'mento [tʃensi'mento] *sm* census
cen'sire [tʃen'sire] *vt* to take a census of
'CENSIS ['tʃensis] *sigla m* (= *Centro Studi Investimenti Sociali*) *independent institute carrying out research on Italy's social and cultural welfare*
cen'sore [tʃen'sore] *sm* censor
cen'sura [tʃen'sura] *sf* censorship; censor's office; (*fig*) censure
censu'rare [tʃensu'rare] *vt* to censor; to censure
cent. *abbr* = **centesimo**
centelli'nare [tʃentelli'nare] *vt* to sip; (*fig*) to savour (*Brit*), savor (*US*)
cente'nario, -a [tʃente'narjo] *ag* (*che ha cento anni*) hundred-year-old; (*che ricorre ogni cento anni*) centennial, centenary *cpd* ■ *sm/f* centenarian ■ *sm* centenary
cen'tesimo, -a [tʃen'tɛzimo] *ag, sm* hundredth; (*di euro, dollaro*) cent; **essere senza un ~** to be penniless
cen'tigrado, -a [tʃen'tigrado] *ag* centigrade; **20 gradi centigradi** 20 degrees centigrade
cen'tilitro [tʃen'tilitro] *sm* centilitre
cen'timetro [tʃen'timetro] *sm* centimetre (*Brit*), centimeter (*US*); (*nastro*) measuring tape (*in centimetres*)
centi'naio [tʃenti'najo] (*pl*(*f*) **centinaia**) *sm*: **un ~ (di)** a hundred; about a hundred
'cento ['tʃɛnto] *num* a hundred, one hundred; **per ~** per cent; **al ~ per ~** a hundred per cent; **~ di questi giorni!** many happy returns (of the day)!
centodi'eci [tʃento'djɛtʃi] *num* one hundred and ten; **~ e lode** (*Università*) ≈ first-class honours
cento'mila [tʃento'mila] *num* a *o* one hundred thousand; **te l'ho detto ~ volte** (*fig*) I've told you a thousand times
Cen'trafrica [tʃen'trafrika] *sm*: **il ~** the Central African Republic
cen'trale [tʃen'trale] *ag* central ■ *sf*: **~ elettrica** electric power station; **~ eolica** wind farm; **~ del latte** dairy; **~ di polizia** police headquarters *pl*; **~ telefonica** (telephone) exchange; **sede ~** head office
centrali'nista [tʃentrali'nista] *sm/f* operator
centra'lino [tʃentra'lino] *sm* (telephone) exchange; (*di albergo etc*) switchboard
centraliz'zare [tʃentralid'dzare] *vt* to centralize
cen'trare [tʃen'trare] *vt* to hit the centre (*Brit*) *o* center (*US*) of; (*Tecn*) to centre; **~ una risposta** to get the right answer; **ha centrato il problema** you've hit the nail on the head
centra'vanti [tʃentra'vanti] *sm inv* centre forward
cen'trifuga [tʃen'trifuga] *sf* spin-dryer
centrifu'gare [tʃentrifu'gare] *vt* (*Tecn*) to centrifuge; (*biancheria*) to spin-dry
'centro ['tʃɛntro] *sm* centre (*Brit*), center (*US*); **fare ~** to hit the bull's eye; (*Calcio*) to score; (*fig*) to hit the nail on the head; **~ balneare** seaside resort; **~ commerciale** shopping centre; (*città*) commercial centre; **~ di costo**

cost centre; **~ elaborazione dati** data-processing unit; **~ ospedaliero** hospital complex; **~ di permanenza temporanea** reception centre; **~ sociale** community centre; **centri vitali** (*anche fig*) vital organs

centro'destra [tʃentro'dɛstra] *sm* (*Pol*) centre right

centromedi'ano [tʃentrome'djano] *sm* (*Calcio*) centre half

centrosi'nistra [tʃentrosi'nistra] *sm* (*Pol*) centre left

'ceppo ['tʃeppo] *sm* (*di albero*) stump; (*pezzo di legno*) log

'cera ['tʃera] *sf* wax; (*aspetto*) appearance, look; **~ per pavimenti** floor polish

cera'lacca [tʃera'lakka] *sf* sealing wax

ce'ramica [tʃe'ramika] (*pl* **ceramiche**) *sf* ceramic; (*Arte*) ceramics *sg*

cerbi'atto [tʃer'bjatto] *sm* fawn

'cerca ['tʃerka] *sf*: **in** *o* **alla ~ di** in search of

cercaper'sone [tʃerkaper'sone] *sm inv* bleeper

cer'care [tʃer'kare] *vt* to look for, search for ■ *vi*: **~ di fare qc** to try to do sth

cercherò *etc* [tʃerke'rɔ] *vb vedi* **cercare**

'cerchia ['tʃerkja] *sf* circle

cerchi'ato, -a [tʃer'kjato] *ag*: **occhiali cerchiati d'osso** horn-rimmed spectacles; **avere gli occhi cerchiati** to have dark rings under one's eyes

'cerchio ['tʃerkjo] *sm* circle; (*giocattolo, di botte*) hoop; **dare un colpo al ~ e uno alla botte** (*fig*) to keep two things going at the same time

cerchi'one [tʃer'kjone] *sm* (wheel)rim

cere'ale [tʃere'ale] *sm* cereal

cere'brale [tʃere'brale] *ag* cerebral

ceri'monia [tʃeri'mɔnja] *sf* ceremony; **senza tante cerimonie** (*senza formalità*) informally; (*bruscamente*) unceremoniously, without so much as a by-your-leave

cerimoni'ale [tʃerimo'njale] *sm* etiquette; ceremonial

cerimoni'ere [tʃerimo'njɛre] *sm* master of ceremonies

cerimoni'oso, -a [tʃerimo'njoso] *ag* formal, ceremonious

ce'rino [tʃe'rino] *sm* wax match

CERN [tʃern] *sigla m* (*= Comitato Europeo di Ricerche Nucleari*) CERN

'cernia ['tʃɛrnja] *sf* (*Zool*) stone bass

cerni'era [tʃer'njɛra] *sf* hinge; **~ lampo** zip (fastener) (*Brit*), zipper (*US*)

'cernita ['tʃɛrnita] *sf* selection; **fare una ~ di** to select

'cero ['tʃero] *sm* (church) candle

ce'rone [tʃe'rone] *sm* (*trucco*) greasepaint

ce'rotto [tʃe'rɔtto] *sm* sticking plaster

certa'mente [tʃerta'mente] *av* certainly, surely

cer'tezza [tʃer'tettsa] *sf* certainty

certifi'care [tʃertifi'kare] *vt* to certify

certifi'cato [tʃertifi'kato] *sm* certificate; **~ medico/di nascita** medical/birth certificate; **~ di credito del Tesoro** treasury bill

certificazi'one [tʃertifikat'tsjone] *sf* certification; **~ di bilancio** (*Comm*) external audit

 PAROLA CHIAVE

'certo, -a ['tʃɛrto] *ag* (*sicuro*): **certo (di/che)** certain *o* sure (of/that)
■ *det* **1** (*tale*) certain; **un certo signor Smith** a (certain) Mr Smith
2 (*qualche; con valore intensivo*) some; **dopo un certo tempo** after some time; **un fatto di una certa importanza** a matter of some importance; **di una certa età** past one's prime, not so young
■ *pron*: **certi, e** (*pl*) some
■ *av* (*certamente*) certainly; (*senz'altro*) of course; **di certo** certainly; **no (di) certo!**, **certo che no!** certainly not!; **sì certo** yes indeed, certainly

certo'sino [tʃerto'zino] *sm* Carthusian monk; (*liquore*) chartreuse; **è un lavoro da ~** it's a pernickety job

cer'tuni [tʃer'tuni] *pron pl* some (people)

ce'rume [tʃe'rume] *sm* (ear) wax

'cerva ['tʃɛrva] *sf* (female) deer, doe

cer'vello [tʃer'vɛllo] (*pl* **cervelli**, *pl(f)* **cervella** *o* **cervelle**) *sm* brain; **~ elettronico** computer; **avere il** *o* **essere un ~ fino** to be sharp-witted; **è uscito di ~, gli è dato di volta il ~** he's gone off his head

cervi'cale [tʃervi'kale] *ag* cervical

'cervo, -a ['tʃɛrvo] *sm/f* stag/hind ■ *sm* deer; **~ volante** stag beetle

cesel'lare [tʃezel'lare] *vt* to chisel; (*incidere*) to engrave

ce'sello [tʃe'zɛllo] *sm* chisel

ce'soie [tʃe'zoje] *sfpl* shears

ces'puglio [tʃes'puʎʎo] *sm* bush

ces'sare [tʃes'sare] *vi, vt* to stop, cease; **~ di fare qc** to stop doing sth; **"cessato allarme"** "all clear"

ces'sate il fu'oco [tʃes'sate-] *sm* ceasefire

cessazi'one [tʃessat'tsjone] *sf* cessation; (*interruzione*) suspension

cessi'one [tʃes'sjone] *sf* transfer

'cesso ['tʃɛsso] *sm* (*fam: gabinetto*) bog

'cesta ['tʃesta] *sf* (large) basket

ces'tello [tʃes'tɛllo] *sm* *(per bottiglie)* crate; *(di lavatrice)* drum
cesti'nare [tʃesti'nare] *vt* to throw away; *(fig: proposta)* to turn down; *(: romanzo)* to reject
ces'tino [tʃes'tino] *sm* basket; *(per la carta straccia)* wastepaper basket; **~ da viaggio** (*Ferr*) packed lunch (*o* dinner)
'cesto ['tʃesto] *sm* basket
ce'sura [tʃe'zura] *sf* caesura
ce'taceo [tʃe'tatʃeo] *sm* sea mammal
'ceto ['tʃɛto] *sm* (social) class
'cetra ['tʃetra] *sf* zither; *(fig: di poeta)* lyre
cetrio'lino [tʃetrio'lino] *sm* gherkin
cetri'olo [tʃetri'ɔlo] *sm* cucumber
Cf., Cfr. *abbr (= confronta)* cf.
CFC [tʃiɛffe'tʃi] *abbr mpl (= clorofluorocarburi)* CFC
CFS *sigla m (= Corpo Forestale dello Stato) body responsible for the planting and management of forests*
cg *abbr (= centigrammo)* cg
C.G.I.L. [tʃidʒi'ɛlle] *sigla f (= Confederazione Generale Italiana del Lavoro) trades union organization*
CH *sigla* = **Chieti**
cha'let [ʃa'lɛ] *sm inv* chalet
cham'pagne [ʃã'paɲ] *sm inv* champagne
chance [ʃãs] *sf inv* chance
charme [ʃarm] *sm* charm
'charter ['tʃa:tər] *ag inv* (*volo*) charter *cpd*; (*aereo*) chartered ■ *sm inv* chartered plane
chat'tare [tʃat'tare] *vi* to chat; (*online*) to chat
centrosi'nistra [tʃentrosi'nistra] *sm* (*Pol*) centre left

PAROLA CHIAVE

che [ke] *pron* **1** *(relativo: persona: soggetto)* who; *(: oggetto)* whom, that; *(: cosa, animale)* which, that; **il ragazzo che è venuto** the boy who came; **l'uomo che io vedo** the man (whom) I see; **il libro che è sul tavolo** the book which *o* that is on the table; **il libro che vedi** the book (which *o* that) you see; **la sera che ti ho visto** the evening I saw you
2 *(interrogativo, esclamativo)* what; **che (cosa) fai?** what are you doing?; **a che (cosa) pensi?** what are you thinking about?; **non sa che (cosa) fare** he doesn't know what to do; **sai di che si tratta?** do you know what it's about?; **che (cosa) succede?** what's happening?; **ma che dici!** what are you saying!
3 *(indefinito)*: **quell'uomo ha un che di losco** there's something suspicious about that man; **un certo non so che** an indefinable something; **non è un gran che** it's nothing much
■ *det* **1** *(interrogativo: tra tanti)* what; *(: tra pochi)* which; **che tipo di film preferisci?** what sort of film do you prefer?; **che vestito ti vuoi mettere?** what (*o* which) dress do you want to put on?
2 *(esclamativo: seguito da aggettivo)* how; *(: seguito da sostantivo)* what; **che buono!** how delicious!; **che bel vestito!** what a lovely dress!; **che macchina!** what a car!
■ *cong* **1** *(con proposizioni subordinate)* that; **credo che verrà** I think he'll come; **voglio che tu studi** I want you to study; **so che tu c'eri** I know (that) you were there; **non che sia sbagliato, ma ...** not that it's wrong, but ...
2 *(finale)* so that; **vieni qua, che ti veda** come here, so (that) I can see you; **stai attento che non cada** mind it doesn't fall
3 *(temporale)*: **arrivai che eri già partito** you had already left when I arrived; **sono anni che non lo vedo** I haven't seen him for years
4 *(in frasi imperative, concessive)*: **che venga pure!** let him come by all means!; **che tu sia benedetto!** may God bless you!; **che tu venga o no partiamo lo stesso** we're going whether you come or not
5 *(comparativo: con più, meno)* than; **è più lungo che largo** it's longer than it's wide; **più bella che mai** more beautiful than ever; *vedi anche* **più**; **meno**; **così** *etc*

'checca, -che ['kekka] *sf* *(fam: omosessuale)* fairy
chef [ʃɛf] *sm inv* chef
chemiotera'pia [kemjotera'pia] *sf* chemotherapy
chero'sene [kero'zɛne] *sm* kerosene
cheru'bino [keru'bino] *sm* cherub
che'tare [ke'tare] *vt* to hush, silence; **chetarsi** *vr* to quieten down, fall silent
cheti'chella [keti'kɛlla]: **alla ~** *av* stealthily, unobtrusively; **andarsene alla ~** to slip away
'cheto, -a ['keto] *ag* quiet, silent

PAROLA CHIAVE

chi [ki] *pron* **1** *(interrogativo: soggetto)* who; *(: oggetto)* who, whom; **chi è?** who is it?; **di chi è questo libro?** whose book is this?, whose is this book?; **con chi parli?** who are you talking to?; **a chi pensi?** who are you thinking about?; **chi di voi?** which of you?; **non so a chi rivolgermi** I don't know who to ask

2 (*relativo*) whoever, anyone who; **dillo a chi vuoi** tell whoever you like; **portate chi volete** bring anyone you like; **so io di chi parlo** I know who I'm talking about; **lo riferirò a chi di dovere** I'll pass it on to the relevant person
3 (*indefinito*): **chi ... chi ...** some ... others ...; **chi dice una cosa, chi dice un'altra** some say one thing, others say another

chiacchie'rare [kjakkje'rare] *vi* to chat; (*discorrere futilmente*) to chatter; (*far pettegolezzi*) to gossip
chiacchie'rata [kjakkje'rata] *sf* chat; **farsi una ~** to have a chat
chi'acchiere ['kjakkjere] *sfpl* chatter *no pl*; gossip *no pl*; **fare due** *o* **quattro ~** to have a chat; **perdersi in ~** to waste time talking
chiacchie'rone, -a [kjakkje'rone] *ag* talkative, chatty gossipy ■ *sm/f* chatterbox; gossip
chia'mare [kja'mare] *vt* to call; (*rivolgersi a qn*) to call (in), send for; **chiamarsi** *vr* (*aver nome*) to be called; **mi chiamo Paolo** my name is Paolo, I'm called Paolo; **mandare a ~ qn** to send for sb, call sb in; **~ alle armi** to call up; **~ in giudizio** to summon; **~ qn da parte** to take sb aside
chia'mata [kja'mata] *sf* (*Tel*) call; (*Mil*) call-up; **~ interurbana** long-distance call; **~ con preavviso** person-to-person call; **~ alle urne** (*Pol*) election
chi'appa ['kjappa] *sf* (*fam: natica*) cheek; **chiappe** *sfpl* bottom *sg*
chi'ara ['kjara] *sf* egg white
chia'rezza [kja'rettsa] *sf* clearness; clarity
chiarifi'care [kjarifi'kare] *vt* (*anche fig*) to clarify
chiarificazi'one [kjarifikat'tsjone] *sf* clarification
chiari'mento [kjari'mento] *sm* clarification *no pl*, explanation
chia'rire [kja'rire] *vt* to make clear; (*fig: spiegare*) to clear up, explain; **chiarirsi** *vr* to become clear; **si sono chiariti** they've sorted things out
chi'aro, -a ['kjaro] *ag* clear; (*luminoso*) clear, bright; (*colore*) pale, light ■ *av* (*parlare, vedere*) clearly; **si sta facendo ~** the day is dawning; **sia chiara una cosa** let's get one thing straight; **mettere in ~ qc** (*fig*) to clear sth up; **parliamoci ~** let's be frank; **trasmissione in ~** (*TV*) uncoded broadcast
chia'rore [kja'rore] *sm* (diffuse) light
chiaroveg'gente [kjaroved'dʒɛnte] *sm/f* clairvoyant

chi'asso ['kjasso] *sm* uproar, row; **far ~** to make a din; (*fig*) to make a fuss; (*: notizia*) to cause a stir
chias'soso, -a [kjas'soso] *ag* noisy, rowdy; (*vistoso*) showy, gaudy
'chiatta ['kjatta] *sf* barge
chi'ave ['kjave] *sf* key ■ *ag inv* key *cpd*; **chiudere a ~** to lock; **~ d'accensione** (*Aut*) ignition key; **~ a forcella** fork spanner; **~ inglese** monkey wrench; **in ~ politica** in political terms; **~ di volta** (*anche fig*) keystone; **chiavi in mano** (*contratto*) turn-key *cpd*; **prezzo chiavi in mano** (*di macchina*) on-the-road price; **~ USB** (*Inform*) USB key
chiavis'tello [kjavis'tɛllo] *sm* bolt
chi'azza ['kjattsa] *sf* stain, splash
chiaz'zare [kjat'tsare] *vt* to stain, splash
chic [ʃik] *ag inv* chic, elegant
chicches'sia [kikkes'sia] *pron* anyone, anybody
'chicco, -chi ['kikko] *sm* (*di cereale, riso*) grain; (*di caffè*) bean; **~ di grandine** hailstone; **~ d'uva** grape
chi'edere ['kjɛdere] *vt* (*per sapere*) to ask; (*per avere*) to ask for ■ *vi*: **~ di qn** to ask after sb; (*al telefono*) to ask for *o* want sb; **chiedersi** *vr*: **chiedersi (se)** to wonder (whether); **~ qc a qn** to ask sb sth; to ask sb for sth; **~ scusa a qn** to apologize to sb; **~ l'elemosina** to beg; **non chiedo altro** that's all I want
chieri'chetto [kjeri'ketto] *sm* altar boy
chi'erico, -ci ['kjɛriko] *sm* cleric; altar boy
chi'esa ['kjɛza] *sf* church
chi'esi *etc* ['kjɛzi] *vb vedi* **chiedere**
chi'esto, -a ['kjɛsto] *pp di* **chiedere**
'Chigi ['kidʒi]: **palazzo ~** *sm* (*Pol*) *offices of the Italian Prime Minister*
'chiglia ['kiʎʎa] *sf* keel
'chilo ['kilo] *sm* kilo
chilo'grammo [kilo'grammo] *sm* kilogram(me)
chilome'traggio [kilome'traddʒo] *sm* (*Aut*) ≈ mileage
chilo'metrico, -a, ci, che [kilo'mɛtriko] *ag* kilometric; (*fig*) endless
chi'lometro [ki'lɔmetro] *sm* kilometre (*Brit*), kilometer (*US*)
'chimico, -a, ci, che ['kimiko] *ag* chemical ■ *sm/f* chemist ■ *sf* chemistry
chi'mono [ki'mɔno] *sm inv* kimono
'china ['kina] *sf* (*pendio*) slope, descent; (*Bot*) cinchona; **(inchiostro di) ~** Indian ink; **risalire la ~** (*fig*) to be on the road to recovery
chi'nare [ki'nare] *vt* to lower, bend; **chinarsi** *vr* to stoop, bend

chincaglie'ria [kinkaʎʎe'ria] *sf* fancy-goods shop; **chincaglierie** *sfpl* fancy goods, knick-knacks
chi'nino [ki'nino] *sm* quinine
'chino, -a ['kino] *ag*: **a capo ~, a testa china** head bent *o* bowed
chi'occia, -ce ['kjɔttʃa] *sf* brooding hen
chi'occio, -a, ci, ce ['kjɔttʃo] *ag* (*voce*) clucking
chi'occiola ['kjɔttʃola] *sf* snail; (*di indirizzo e-mail*) at; **scala a ~** spiral staircase
chi'odo ['kjɔdo] *sm* nail; (*fig*) obsession; **~ scaccia ~** (*proverbio*) one problem drives away another; **roba da chiodi!** it's unbelievable!; **~ di garofano** (*Cuc*) clove
chi'oma ['kjɔma] *sf* (*capelli*) head of hair; (*di albero*) foliage
chi'osco, -schi ['kjɔsko] *sm* kiosk, stall
chi'ostro ['kjɔstro] *sm* cloister
chiro'mante [kiro'mante] *sm/f* palmist; (*indovino*) fortune-teller
chirur'gia [kirur'dʒia] *sf* surgery
chi'rurgico, -a, ci, che [ki'rurdʒiko] *ag* (*anche fig*) surgical
chi'rurgo, -ghi *o* **gi** [ki'rurgo] *sm* surgeon
chissà [kis'sa] *av* who knows, I wonder
chi'tarra [ki'tarra] *sf* guitar
chitar'rista, -i, e [kitar'rista] *sm/f* guitarist, guitar player
chi'udere ['kjudere] *vt* to close, shut; (*luce, acqua*) to put off, turn off; (*definitivamente: fabbrica*) to close down, shut down; (*strada*) to close; (*recingere*) to enclose; (*porre termine*) to end ■ *vi* to close, shut; to close down, shut down; to end; **chiudersi** *vr* to shut, close; (*ritirarsi: anche fig*) to shut o.s. away; (*ferita*) to close up; **~ un occhio su** (*fig*) to turn a blind eye to; **chiudi la bocca!** *o* **il becco!** (*fam*) shut up!
chi'unque [ki'unkwe] *pron* (*relativo*) whoever; (*indefinito*) anyone, anybody; **~ sia** whoever it is
'chiusi *etc* ['kjusi] *vb vedi* **chiudere**
chi'uso, -a ['kjuso] *pp di* **chiudere** ■ *ag* (*porta*) shut, closed; (*: a chiave*) locked; (*senza uscita: strada etc*) blocked off; (*rubinetto*) off; (*persona*) uncommunicative; (*ambiente, club*) exclusive ■ *sm*: **stare al ~** (*fig*) to be shut up ■ *sf* (*di corso d'acqua*) sluice, lock; (*recinto*) enclosure; (*di discorso etc*) conclusion, ending; **"~"** (*negozio etc*) "closed"; **"~ al pubblico"** "no admittance to the public"
chiu'sura [kju'sura] *sf* closing; shutting; closing *o* shutting down; enclosing; putting *o* turning off; ending; (*dispositivo*) catch; fastening; fastener; **orario di ~** closing time; **~ lampo**® zip (fastener) (*Brit*), zipper (*US*)

 PAROLA CHIAVE

ci [tʃi] (*dav lo, la, li, le, ne diventa* **ce**) *pron*
1 (*personale: complemento oggetto*) us; (*: a noi: complemento di termine*) (to) us; (*: riflessivo*) ourselves; (*: reciproco*) each other, one another; (*impersonale*): **ci si veste** we get dressed; **ci ha visti** he's seen us; **non ci ha dato niente** he gave us nothing; **ci vestiamo** we get dressed; **ci amiamo** we love one another *o* each other; **ci siamo divertiti** we had a good time
2 (*dimostrativo: di ciò, su ciò, in ciò etc*) about (*o* on *o* of) it; **non ci capisco nulla** I can't make head nor tail of it; **non so cosa farci** I don't know what to do about it; **che ci posso fare?** what can I do about it?; **che c'entro io?** what have I got to do with it?; **ci puoi giurare** you can bet on it; **ci puoi contare** you can depend on it; **ci sei?** (*sei pronto?*) are you ready?; (*hai capito?*) are you with me?
■ *av* (*qui*) here; (*lì*) there; (*moto attraverso luogo*): **ci passa sopra un ponte** a bridge passes over it; **non ci passa più nessuno** nobody comes this way any more; **qui ci abito da un anno** I've been living here for a year; **esserci** *vedi* **essere**

C.I. *abbr* = **carta d'identità**
CIA ['tʃia] *sigla f* (= *Central Intelligence Agency*) CIA
C.ia *abbr* (= *compagnia*) Co
cia'batta [tʃa'batta] *sf* mule, slipper
ciabat'tino [tʃabat'tino] *sm* cobbler
ciac [tʃak] *sm* (*Cine*) clapper board; **~, si gira!** action!
Ci'ad [tʃad] *sm*: **il ~** Chad
ci'alda ['tʃalda] *sf* (*Cuc*) wafer
cial'trone [tʃal'trone] *sm* good-for-nothing
ciam'bella [tʃam'bɛlla] *sf* (*Cuc*) ring-shaped cake; (*salvagente*) rubber ring
ci'ancia, -ce ['tʃantʃa] *sf* gossip *no pl*, tittle-tattle *no pl*
cianfru'saglie [tʃanfru'zaʎʎe] *sfpl* bits and pieces
cia'nuro [tʃa'nuro] *sm* cyanide
ci'ao ['tʃao] *escl* (*all'arrivo*) hello!; (*alla partenza*) cheerio! (*Brit*), bye!
ciar'lare [tʃar'lare] *vi* to chatter; (*peg*) to gossip
ciarla'tano [tʃarla'tano] *sm* charlatan
cias'cuno, -a [tʃas'kuno] (*dav sm:* **ciascun** + *C, V,* **ciascuno** + *s impura, gn, pn, ps, x, z; dav sf:* **ciascuna** + *C,* **ciascun'** + *V*) *det, pron* each
ci'bare [tʃi'bare] *vt* to feed; **cibarsi** *vr*: **cibarsi di** to eat
ci'barie [tʃi'barje] *sfpl* foodstuffs

ciber'netica [tʃiber'nɛtika] *sf* cybernetics *sg*
'cibo ['tʃibo] *sm* food
ci'cala [tʃi'kala] *sf* cicada
cica'trice [tʃika'tritʃe] *sf* scar
cicatriz'zarsi [tʃikatrid'dzarsi] *vr* to form a scar, heal (up)
'cicca, -che ['tʃikka] *sf* cigarette end; (*fam: sigaretta*) fag; **non vale una ~** (*fig*) it's worthless
'ciccia ['tʃittʃa] *sf* (*fam: carne*) meat; (*: grasso umano*) fat, flesh
cicci'one, -a [tʃit'tʃone] *sm/f* (*fam*) fatty
cice'rone [tʃitʃe'rone] *sm* guide
cicla'mino [tʃikla'mino] *sm* cyclamen
ci'clismo [tʃi'klizmo] *sm* cycling
ci'clista, -i, e [tʃi'klista] *sm/f* cyclist
'ciclo ['tʃiklo] *sm* cycle; (*di malattia*) course
ciclomo'tore [tʃiklomo'tore] *sm* moped
ci'clone [tʃi'klone] *sm* cyclone
ciclos'tile [tʃiklos'tile] *sm* cyclostyle (*Brit*)
ci'cogna [tʃi'koɲɲa] *sf* stork
ci'coria [tʃi'kɔrja] *sf* chicory
ci'eco, -a, chi, che ['tʃɛko] *ag* blind ■ *sm/f* blind man(-woman); **alla cieca** (*anche fig*) blindly
ciel'lino, -a [tʃiel'lino] *sm/f* (*Pol*) *member of CL movement*
ci'elo ['tʃɛlo] *sm* sky; (*Rel*) heaven; **toccare il ~ con un dito** (*fig*) to walk on air; **per amor del ~!** for heavens' sake!
'cifra ['tʃifra] *sf* (*numero*) figure, numeral; (*somma di denaro*) sum, figure; (*monogramma*) monogram, initials *pl*; (*codice*) code, cipher
ci'frare [tʃi'frare] *vt* (*messaggio*) to code; (*lenzuola etc*) to embroider with a monogram
'ciglio ['tʃiʎʎo] *sm* (*margine*) edge, verge; (*pl(f)* **ciglia**: *delle palpebre*) (eye)lash; (*sopracciglio*) eyebrow; **non ha battuto ~** (*fig*) he didn't bat an eyelid
'cigno ['tʃiɲɲo] *sm* swan
cigo'lante [tʃigo'lante] *ag* squeaking, creaking
cigo'lare [tʃigo'lare] *vi* to squeak, creak
'Cile ['tʃile] *sm*: **il ~** Chile
ci'lecca [tʃi'lekka] *sf*: **far ~** to fail
ci'leno, -a [tʃi'lɛno] *ag, sm/f* Chilean
cili'egia, -gie *o* **ge** [tʃi'ljɛdʒa] *sf* cherry
cilie'gina [tʃiljɛ'dʒina] *sf* glacé cherry; **la ~ sulla torta** (*fig*) the icing *o* cherry on the cake
cili'egio [tʃi'ljɛdʒo] *sm* cherry tree
cilin'drata [tʃilin'drata] *sf* (*Aut*) (cubic) capacity; **una macchina di grossa ~** a big-engined car
ci'lindro [tʃi'lindro] *sm* cylinder; (*cappello*) top hat
CIM [tʃim] *sigla m* = **centro d'igiene mentale**
'cima ['tʃima] *sf* (*sommità*) top; (*di monte*) top, summit; (*estremità*) end; (*fig: persona*) genius; **in ~ a** at the top of; **da ~ a fondo** from top to bottom; (*fig*) from beginning to end
ci'melio [tʃi'mɛljo] *sm* relic
cimen'tarsi [tʃimen'tarsi] *vr*: **~ in** (*atleta, concorrente*) to try one's hand at
'cimice ['tʃimitʃe] *sf* (*Zool*) bug; (*puntina*) drawing pin (*Brit*), thumbtack (*US*)
cimini'era [tʃimi'njɛra] *sf* chimney; (*di nave*) funnel
cimi'tero [tʃimi'tɛro] *sm* cemetery
ci'murro [tʃi'murro] *sm* (*di cani*) distemper
'Cina ['tʃina] *sf*: **la ~** China
cin'cin, cin cin [tʃin'tʃin] *escl* cheers!
cincischi'are [tʃintʃis'kjare] *vi* to mess about
'cine ['tʃine] *sm inv* (*fam*) cinema
cine'asta, -i, e [tʃine'asta] *sm/f* person in the film industry; film-maker
cinegior'nale [tʃinedʒor'nale] *sm* newsreel
'cinema ['tʃinema] *sm inv* cinema; **~ muto** silent films; **~ d'essai** (*locale*) avant-garde cinema, experimental cinema
cinemato'grafico, -a, ci, che [tʃinemato'grafiko] *ag* (*attore, critica*) movie *cpd*, film *cpd*; (*festival*) film *cpd*; **sala cinematografica** cinema; **successo ~** box-office success
cinema'tografo [tʃinema'tɔgrafo] *sm* cinema
cine'presa [tʃine'presa] *sf* cine-camera
ci'nese [tʃi'nese] *ag, sm/f, sm* Chinese *inv*
cine'teca, -che [tʃine'tɛka] *sf* (*collezione*) film collection; (*locale*) film library
ci'netico, -a, ci, che [tʃi'nɛtiko] *ag* kinetic
'cingere ['tʃindʒere] *vt* (*attorniare*) to surround, encircle; **~ la vita con una cintura** to put a belt round one's waist; **~ d'assedio** to besiege, lay siege to
'cinghia ['tʃingja] *sf* strap; (*cintura, Tecn*) belt; **tirare la ~** (*fig*) to tighten one's belt
cinghi'ale [tʃin'gjale] *sm* wild boar
cinguet'tare [tʃingwet'tare] *vi* to twitter
'cinico, -a, ci, che ['tʃiniko] *ag* cynical ■ *sm/f* cynic
ci'nismo [tʃi'nizmo] *sm* cynicism
cin'quanta [tʃin'kwanta] *num* fifty
cinquante'nario [tʃinkwante'narjo] *sm* fiftieth anniversary
cinquan'tenne [tʃinkwan'tɛnne] *sm/f* fifty-year-old man/woman
cinquan'tesimo, -a [tʃinkwan'tɛzimo] *num* fiftieth
cinquan'tina [tʃinkwan'tina] *sf* (*serie*): **una ~ (di)** about fifty; (*età*): **essere sulla ~** to be about fifty

'**cinque** ['tʃinkwe] *num* five; **avere ~ anni** to be five (years old); **il ~ dicembre 1988** the fifth of December 1988; **alle ~** *(ora)* at five (o'clock); **siamo in ~** there are five of us
cinquecen'tesco, -a, schi, sche [tʃinkwetʃen'tesko] *ag* sixteenth-century
cinque'cento [tʃinkwe'tʃɛnto] *num* five hundred ■ *sm*: **il C~** the sixteenth century
cinque'mila [tʃinkwe'mila] *num* five thousand
'**cinsi** *etc* ['tʃinsi] *vb vedi* **cingere**
'**cinta** ['tʃinta] *sf* (*anche*: **cinta muraria**) city walls *pl*; **muro di ~** *(di giardino etc)* surrounding wall
cin'tare [tʃin'tare] *vt* to enclose
'**cinto, -a** ['tʃinto] *pp di* **cingere**
'**cintola** ['tʃintola] *sf (cintura)* belt; *(vita)* waist
cin'tura [tʃin'tura] *sf* belt; **~ di salvataggio** lifebelt *(Brit)*, life preserver *(US)*; **~ di sicurezza** *(Aut, Aer)* safety *o* seat belt
cintu'rino [tʃintu'rino] *sm* strap; **~ dell'orologio** watch strap
CIO *sigla m (= Comitato Internazionale Olimpico)* IOC *(= International Olympic Committee)*
ciò [tʃɔ] *pron* this; that; **ciò che** what; **ciò nonostante** *o* **nondimeno** nevertheless, in spite of that; **con tutto ciò** for all that, in spite of everything
ci'occa, -che ['tʃɔkka] *sf (di capelli)* lock
ciocco'lata [tʃokko'lata] *sf* chocolate; *(bevanda)* (hot) chocolate; **~ al latte/ fondente** milk/plain chocolate
cioccola'tino [tʃokkola'tino] *sm* chocolate
ciocco'lato [tʃokko'lato] *sm* chocolate
cio'è [tʃo'ɛ] *av* that is (to say)
ciondo'lare [tʃondo'lare] *vt (far dondolare)* to dangle, swing ■ *vi* to dangle; *(fig)* to loaf (about)
ci'ondolo ['tʃondolo] *sm* pendant; **~ portafortuna** charm
ciondo'loni [tʃondo'loni] *av*: **con le braccia/ gambe ~** with arms/legs dangling
ciononos'tante [tʃononos'tante] *av* nonetheless, nevertheless
ci'otola ['tʃɔtola] *sf* bowl
ci'ottolo ['tʃɔttolo] *sm* pebble; *(di strada)* cobble(stone)
C.I.P. [tʃip] *sigla m* = **comitato interministeriale prezzi**; *vedi* **comitato**
Cipe ['tʃipe] *sigla m* = **comitato interministeriale per la programmazione economica**; *vedi* **comitato**
'**Cipi** ['tʃipi] *sigla m* = **comitato interministeriale per lo sviluppo industriale**; *vedi* **comitato**
ci'piglio [tʃi'piʎʎo] *sm* frown
ci'polla [tʃi'polla] *sf* onion; *(di tulipano etc)* bulb
cipol'lina [tʃipol'lina] *sf* onion; **cipolline sottaceto** pickled onions; **cipolline sottolio** baby onions in oil
ci'presso [tʃi'prɛsso] *sm* cypress (tree)
'**cipria** ['tʃiprja] *sf* (face) powder
cipri'ota, -i, e [tʃipri'ɔta] *ag, sm/f* Cypriot
'**Cipro** ['tʃipro] *sm* Cyprus
'**circa** ['tʃirka] *av* about, roughly ■ *prep* about, concerning; **a mezzogiorno ~** about midday
'**circo, -chi** ['tʃirko] *sm* circus
circo'lare [tʃirko'lare] *vi* to circulate; *(Aut)* to drive (along), move (along) ■ *ag* circular ■ *sf (Amm)* circular; *(di autobus)* circle (line); **circola voce che ...** there is a rumour going about that ...; **assegno ~** banker's draft
circolazi'one [tʃirkolat'tsjone] *sf* circulation; *(Aut)*: **la ~** (the) traffic; **libretto di ~** log book, registration book; **tassa di ~** road tax; **~ a targhe alterne** *see note*

CIRCOLAZIONE A TARGHE ALTERNE

Circolazione a targhe alterne was introduced by some town councils to combat the increase in traffic and pollution in town centres. It stipulates that on days with an even date, only cars whose number plate ends in an even number or a zero may be on the road; on days with an odd date, only cars with odd registration numbers may be used. Public holidays are generally, but not always, exempt.

'**circolo** ['tʃirkolo] *sm* circle; **entrare in ~** *(Anat)* to enter the bloodstream
circoncisi'one [tʃirkontʃi'zjone] *sf* circumcision
circon'dare [tʃirkon'dare] *vt* to surround
circondari'ale [tʃirkonda'rjale] *ag*: **casa di pena ~** district prison
circon'dario [tʃirkon'darjo] *sm (Dir)* administrative district; *(zona circostante)* neighbourhood *(Brit)*, neighborhood *(US)*
circonfe'renza [tʃirkonfe'rɛntsa] *sf* circumference
circonvallazi'one [tʃirkonvallat'tsjone] *sf* ring road *(Brit)*, beltway *(US)*; *(per evitare una città)* by-pass
circos'critto, -a [tʃirkos'kritto] *pp di* **circoscrivere**
circos'crivere [tʃirkos'krivere] *vt* to circumscribe; *(fig)* to limit, restrict
circoscrizi'one [tʃirkoskrit'tsjone] *sf (Amm)* district, area; **~ elettorale** constituency
circos'petto, -a [tʃirkos'pɛtto] *ag* circumspect, cautious

circos'tante [tʃirkos'tante] *ag* surrounding, neighbouring (*Brit*), neighboring (*US*)
circos'tanza [tʃirkos'tantsa] *sf* circumstance; (*occasione*) occasion; **parole di ~** words suited to the occasion
circu'ire [tʃirku'ire] *vt* (*fig*) to fool, take in
cir'cuito [tʃir'kuito] *sm* circuit; **andare in** *o* **fare corto ~** to short-circuit; **~ integrato** integrated circuit
ci'rillico, -a, ci, che [tʃi'rilliko] *ag* Cyrillic
cir'rosi [tʃir'rɔzi] *sf*: **~ epatica** cirrhosis (of the liver)
'C.I.S.A.L. ['tʃizal] *sigla f* (= *Confederazione Italiana Sindacati Autonomi dei Lavoratori*) *trades union organization*
C.I.S.L. [tʃizl] *sigla f* (= *Confederazione Italiana Sindacati Lavoratori*) *trades union organization*
'C.I.S.N.A.L. ['tʃiznal] *sigla f* (= *Confederazione Italiana Sindacati Nazionali dei Lavoratori*) *trades union organization*
'ciste ['tʃiste] *sf* = **cisti**
cis'terna [tʃis'tɛrna] *sf* tank, cistern
'cisti ['tʃisti] *sf inv* cyst
cis'tite [tʃis'tite] *sf* cystitis
C.I.T. [tʃit] *sigla f* = **Compagnia Italiana Turismo**
cit. *abbr* (= *citato, citata*) cit.
ci'tare [tʃi'tare] *vt* (*Dir*) to summon; (*autore*) to quote; (*a esempio, modello*) to cite; **~ qn per danni** to sue sb
citazi'one [tʃitat'tsjone] *sf* summons *sg*; quotation; (*di persona*) mention
ci'tofono [tʃi'tɔfono] *sm* entry phone; (*in uffici*) intercom
cito'logico, -a, ci, che [tʃito'lɔdʒiko] *ag*: **esame ~** *test for detection of cancerous cells*
'citrico, -a, ci, che ['tʃitriko] *ag* citric
città [tʃit'ta] *sf inv* town; (*importante*) city; **~ giardino** garden city; **~ mercato** shopping centre, mall; **~ universitaria** university campus; **C~ del Capo** Cape Town
citta'della [tʃitta'dɛlla] *sf* citadel, stronghold
cittadi'nanza [tʃittadi'nantsa] *sf* citizens *pl*, inhabitants *pl* of a town (*o* city); (*Dir*) citizenship
citta'dino, -a [tʃitta'dino] *ag* town *cpd*; city *cpd* ■ *sm/f* (*di uno Stato*) citizen; (*abitante di città*) town dweller, city dweller
ci'uccio ['tʃuttʃo] *sm* (*fam*) comforter, dummy (*Brit*), pacifier (*US*)
ci'uco, -a, chi, che ['tʃuko] *sm/f* ass
ci'uffo ['tʃuffo] *sm* tuft
ci'urma ['tʃurma] *sf* (*di nave*) crew
ci'vetta [tʃi'vetta] *sf* (*Zool*) owl; (*fig: donna*) coquette, flirt ■ *ag inv*: **auto/nave ~** decoy car/ship; **fare la ~ con qn** to flirt with sb
civet'tare [tʃivet'tare] *vt* to flirt
civette'ria [tʃivette'ria] *sf* coquetry, coquettishness
civettu'olo, -a [tʃivet'twɔlo] *ag* flirtatious
'civico, -a, ci, che ['tʃiviko] *ag* civic; (*museo*) municipal, town *cpd*; **guardia civica** town policeman; **senso ~** public spirit
ci'vile [tʃi'vile] *ag* civil; (*non militare*) civilian; (*nazione*) civilized ■ *sm* civilian; **stato ~** marital status; **abiti civili** civvies
civi'lista, -i, e [tʃivi'lista] *sm/f* (*avvocato*) civil lawyer; (*studioso*) expert in civil law
civiliz'zare [tʃivilid'dzare] *vt* to civilize
civilizzazi'one [tʃiviliddzat'tsjone] *sf* civilization
civiltà [tʃivil'ta] *sf* civilization; (*cortesia*) civility
ci'vismo [tʃi'vizmo] *sm* public spirit
CL [tʃi'ɛlle] *sigla f* (*Pol*: = *Comunione e Liberazione*) *Catholic youth movement* ■ *sigla* = **Caltanissetta**
cl *abbr* (= *centilitro*) cl
'clacson *sm inv* (*Aut*) horn
cla'more *sm* (*frastuono*) din, uproar, clamour (*Brit*), clamor (*US*); (*fig*) outcry
clamo'roso, -a *ag* noisy; (*fig*) sensational
clan *sm inv* clan
clandestinità *sf* (*di attività*) secret nature; **vivere nella ~** to live in hiding; (*ricercato politico*) to live underground
clandes'tino, -a *ag* clandestine; (*Pol*) underground, clandestine ■ *sm/f* stowaway; (*anche*: **immigrato clandestino**) illegal immigrant
clari'netto *sm* clarinet
'classe *sf* class; **di ~** (*fig*) with class; of excellent quality; **~ turistica** (*Aer*) economy class
classi'cismo [klassi'tʃizmo] *sm* classicism
'classico, -a, ci, che *ag* classical; (*tradizionale: moda*) classic(al) ■ *sm* classic; classical author; (*anche*: **liceo classico**) *secondary school with emphasis on the humanities*
clas'sifica, -che *sf* classification; (*Sport*) placings *pl*; (*di dischi*) charts *pl*, hit parade
classifi'care *vt* to classify; (*candidato, compito*) to grade; **classificarsi** *vr* to be placed
classifica'tore *sm* filing cabinet
classificazi'one [klassifikat'tsjone] *sf* classification; grading
clas'sista, -i, e *ag* class-conscious ■ *sm/f* class-conscious person
claudi'cante *ag* (*zoppo*) lame; (*fig: prosa*) halting
'clausola *sf* (*Dir*) clause
claustro'fobico, -a, ci, che *ag* claustrophobic
clau'sura *sf* (*Rel*): **monaca di ~** nun belonging to an enclosed order; **fare una vita di ~** (*fig*) to lead a cloistered life

ˈclava *sf* club
claviˈcembalo [klaviˈtʃembalo] *sm* harpsichord
claˈvicola *sf* (*Anat*) collarbone
cleˈmente *ag* merciful; (*clima*) mild
cleˈmenza [kleˈmɛntsa] *sf* mercy, clemency; mildness
clepˈtomane *sm/f* kleptomaniac
creriˈcale *ag* clerical
ˈclero *sm* clergy
clesˈsidra *sf* (*a sabbia*) hourglass; (*ad acqua*) water clock
clicˈcare *vi* (*Inform*): **~ su** to click on
cliché [kliˈʃe] *sm inv* (*Tip*) plate; (*fig*) cliché
cliˈente *sm/f* customer, client
clienˈtela *sf* customers *pl*, clientèle
clienteˈlismo *sm*: **~ politico** political nepotism
ˈclima, -i *sm* climate
cliˈmatico, -a, ci, che *ag* climatic; **stazione climatica** health resort
climatizzaˈtore [klimatiddzaˈtore] *sm* air conditioner
climatizzaziˈone [klimatiddzatˈtsjone] *sf* air conditioning
ˈclinico, -a, ci, che *ag* clinical ▪ *sm* (*medico*) clinician ▪ *sf* (*scienza*) clinical medicine; (*casa di cura*) clinic, nursing home; (*settore d'ospedale*) clinic; **quadro ~** anamnesis; **avere l'occhio ~** (*fig*) to have an expert eye
clisˈtere *sm* (*Med*) enema; (*: apparecchio*) *device used to give an enema*
cloˈaca, -che *sf* sewer
cloche [klɔʃ] *sf inv* control stick, joystick; **cambio a ~** (*Aut*) floor-mounted gear lever
cloˈnare *vt* to clone
clonaˈzione [clonatˈtsjone] *sf* (*Biol, fig*) cloning
ˈcloro *sm* chlorine
cloroˈfilla *sf* chlorophyll
cloroˈformio *sm* chloroform
club *sm inv* club
cm *abbr* (= *centimetro*) cm
c.m. *abbr* (= *corrente mese*) inst.
CN *sigla* = **Cuneo**
c/n *abbr* = **conto nuovo**
CNEN *sigla m* (= *Comitato Nazionale per l'Energia Nucleare*) ≈ AEA (*Brit*), AEC (*US*)
CNIOP *sigla m* = **Centro Nazionale per l'Istruzione e l'Orientamento Professionale**
CNR *sigla m* (= *Consiglio Nazionale delle Ricerche*) *science research council*
CNRN *sigla m* = **Comitato Nazionale Ricerche Nucleari**
CO *sigla* = **Como**
Co. *abbr* (= *compagnia*) Co.
c/o *abbr* (= *care of*) c/o
coabiˈtare *vi* to live together, live under the same roof
coaguˈlare *vt* to coagulate ▪ *vi*, **coagularsi** *vr* to coagulate; (*latte*) to curdle
coaliziˈone [koalitˈtsjone] *sf* coalition
coˈatto, -a *ag* (*Dir*) compulsory, forced; **condannare al domicilio ~** to place under house arrest
ˈCOBAS *sigla mpl* (= *Comitati di base*) *independent trades unions*
ˈcobra *sm inv* cobra
ˈcoca ˈcola® *sf* coca cola®
cocaˈina *sf* cocaine
cocˈcarda *sf* cockade
cocchiˈere [kokˈkjɛre] *sm* coachman
ˈcocchio [ˈkɔkkjo] *sm* (*carrozza*) coach; (*biga*) chariot
cocciˈnella [kottʃiˈnɛlla] *sf* ladybird (*Brit*), ladybug (*US*)
ˈcoccio [ˈkɔttʃo] *sm* earthenware; (*vaso*) earthenware pot; **cocci** *smpl* fragments (of pottery)
cocciuˈtaggine [kottʃuˈtaddʒine] *sf* stubbornness, pig-headedness
cocciˈuto, -a [kotˈtʃuto] *ag* stubborn, pigheaded
ˈcocco, -chi *sm* (*pianta*) coconut palm; (*frutto*): **noce di ~** coconut ▪ *sm/f* (*fam*) darling; **è il ~ della mamma** he's mummy's darling
coccoˈdrillo *sm* crocodile
coccoˈlare *vt* to cuddle, fondle
coˈcente [koˈtʃɛnte] *ag* (*anche fig*) burning
cocerò *etc* [kotʃeˈrɔ] *vb vedi* **cuocere**
coˈcomero *sm* watermelon
coˈcuzzolo [koˈkuttsolo] *sm* top; (*di capo, cappello*) crown
cod. *abbr* = **codice**
ˈcoda *sf* tail; (*fila di persone, auto*) queue (*Brit*), line (*US*); (*di abiti*) train; **con la ~ dell'occhio** out of the corner of one's eye; **mettersi in ~** to queue (up) (*Brit*), line up (*US*); to join the queue *o* line; **~ di cavallo** (*acconciatura*) ponytail; **avere la ~ di paglia** (*fig*) to have a guilty conscience; **~ di rospo** (*Cuc*) frogfish tail
codarˈdia *sf* cowardice
coˈdardo, -a *ag* cowardly ▪ *sm/f* coward
coˈdesto, -a *ag, pron* (*poetico*) this; that
ˈcodice [ˈkɔditʃe] *sm* code; (*manoscritto antico*) codex; **~ di avviamento postale** postcode (*Brit*), zip code (*US*); **~ a barre** bar code; **~ civile** civil code; **~ fiscale** tax code; **~ penale** penal code; **~ segreto** (*di tessera magnetica*) PIN (number); **~ della strada** highway code
coˈdifica *sf* codification; (*Inform: di programma*) coding
codifiˈcare *vt* (*Dir*) to codify; (*cifrare*) to code

codificazi'one [kodifikat'tsjone] *sf* coding
coercizi'one [koertʃit'tsjone] *sf* coercion
coe'rente *ag* coherent
coe'renza [koe'rɛntsa] *sf* coherence
coesi'one *sf* cohesion
coe'sistere *vi* to coexist
coe'taneo, -a *ag, sm/f* contemporary; **essere ~ di qn** to be the same age as sb
cofa'netto *sm* casket; **~ dei gioielli** jewel case
'cofano *sm* (*Aut*) bonnet (*Brit*), hood (*US*); (*forziere*) chest
'coffa *sf* (*Naut*) top
'cogli ['koʎʎi] *prep + det vedi* **con**
'cogliere ['kɔʎʎere] *vt* (*fiore, frutto*) to pick, gather; (*sorprendere*) to catch, surprise; (*bersaglio*) to hit; (*fig: momento opportuno etc*) to grasp, seize, take; (*: capire*) to grasp; **~ l'occasione (per fare)** to take the opportunity (to do); **~ sul fatto** *o* **in flagrante/alla sprovvista** to catch red-handed/unprepared; **~ nel segno** (*fig*) to hit the nail on the head
cogli'one [koʎ'ʎone] *sm* (*fam!: testicolo*): **coglioni** balls (*!*); (*: fig: persona sciocca*) jerk; **rompere i coglioni a qn** to get on sb's tits (*!*)
co'gnac [kɔ'ɲak] *sm inv* cognac
co'gnato, -a [koɲ'ɲato] *sm/f* brother-(-sister)-in-law
cognizi'one [koɲɲit'tsjone] *sf* knowledge; **con ~ di causa** with full knowledge of the facts
co'gnome [koɲ'ɲome] *sm* surname
'coi *prep + det vedi* **con**
coi'bente *ag* insulating
coinci'denza [kointʃi'dɛntsa] *sf* coincidence; (*Ferr, Aer, di autobus*) connection
coin'cidere [koin'tʃidere] *vi* to coincide
coin'ciso, -a [koin'tʃizo] *pp di* **coincidere**
coinqui'lino *sm* fellow tenant
cointeres'senza [kointeres'sɛntsa] *sf* (*Comm*): **avere una ~ in qc** to own shares in sth; **~ dei lavoratori** profit-sharing
coin'volgere [koin'vɔldʒere] *vt*: **~ in** to involve in
coinvolgi'mento [koinvoldʒi'mento] *sm* involvement
coin'volto, -a *pp di* **coinvolgere**
col *prep + det vedi* **con**
Col. *abbr* (*= colonnello*) Col.
colà *av* there
cola'brodo *sm inv* strainer
cola'pasta *sm inv* colander
co'lare *vt* (*liquido*) to strain; (*pasta*) to drain; (*oro fuso*) to pour ■ *vi* (*sudore*) to drip; (*botte*) to leak; (*cera*) to melt; **~ a picco** (*nave*) to sink
co'lata *sf* (*di lava*) flow; (*Fonderia*) casting
colazi'one [kolat'tsjone] *sf* (*anche*: **prima colazione**) breakfast; (*anche*: **seconda colazione**) lunch; **fare ~** to have breakfast (*o* lunch); **~ di lavoro** working lunch
Coldi'retti *abbr f* (*= Confederazione nazionale coltivatori diretti*) *federation of Italian farmers*
co'lei *pron vedi* **colui**
co'lera *sm* (*Med*) cholera
coleste'rolo *sm* cholesterol
colf *abbr f* = **collaboratrice familiare**
'colgo *etc vb vedi* **cogliere**
colibrì *sm* hummingbird
'colica *sf* (*Med*) colic
co'lino *sm* strainer
'colla *prep + det vedi* **con** ■ *sf* glue; (*di farina*) paste
collabo'rare *vi* to collaborate; (*con la polizia*) to co-operate; **~ a** to collaborate on; (*giornale*) to contribute to
collabora'tore, -'trice *sm/f* collaborator; (*di giornale, rivista*) contributor; **~ esterno** freelance; **collaboratrice familiare** home help; **~ di giustizia** = **pentito, a**
collaborazi'one [kollaborat'tsjone] *sf* collaboration; contribution
col'lana *sf* necklace; (*collezione*) collection, series
col'lant [kɔ'lã] *sm inv* tights *pl*
col'lare *sm* collar
col'lasso *sm* (*Med*) collapse
collate'rale *ag* collateral; **effetti collaterali** side effects
col'laudo *sm* testing *no pl*; test
'colle *prep + det vedi* **con** ■ *sm* hill
col'lega, -ghi, ghe *sm/f* colleague
collega'mento *sm* connection; (*Mil*) liaison; (*Radio*) link(-up); (*Inform*) link; **ufficiale di ~** liaison officer; **~ ipertestuale** hyperlink
colle'gare *vt* to connect, join, link; **collegarsi** *vr* (*Radio, TV*) to link up; **collegarsi con** (*Tel*) to get through to
collegi'ale [kolle'dʒale] *ag* (*riunione, decisione*) collective; (*Ins*) boarding school *cpd* ■ *sm/f* boarder; (*fig: persona timida e inesperta*) schoolboy(-girl)
col'legio [kol'lɛdʒo] *sm* college; (*convitto*) boarding school; **~ elettorale** (*Pol*) constituency
'collera *sf* anger; **andare in ~** to get angry
col'lerico, -a, ci, che *ag* quick-tempered, irascible
col'letta *sf* collection
collettività *sf* community
collet'tivo, -a *ag* collective; (*interesse*) general, everybody's; (*biglietto, visita etc*) group *cpd* ■ *sm* (*Pol*) (political) group; **società in nome ~** (*Comm*) partnership

col'letto *sm* collar; **colletti bianchi** (*fig*) white-collar workers
collezio'nare [kollettsjo'nare] *vt* to collect
collezi'one [kollet'tsjone] *sf* collection
collezio'nista [kollettsjo'nista] *sm/f* collector
colli'mare *vi* to correspond, coincide
col'lina *sf* hill
colli'nare *ag* hill *cpd*
col'lirio *sm* eyewash
collisi'one *sf* collision
'collo *prep+det vedi* **con** ■ *sm* neck; (*di abito*) neck, collar; (*pacco*) parcel; **~ del piede** instep
colloca'mento *sm* (*impiego*) employment; (*disposizione*) placing, arrangement; **ufficio di ~** ≈ Jobcentre (*Brit*), state (*o* federal) employment agency (*US*); **~ a riposo** retirement
collo'care *vt* (*libri, mobili*) to place; (*persona: trovare un lavoro per*) to find a job for, place; (*Comm: merce*) to find a market for; **~ qn a riposo** to retire sb
collocazi'one [kollokat'tsjone] *sf* placing; (*di libro*) classification
colloqui'ale *ag* (*termine etc*) colloquial; (*tono*) informal
col'loquio *sm* conversation, talk; (*ufficiale, per un lavoro*) interview; (*Ins*) preliminary oral exam; **avviare un ~ con qn** (*Pol etc*) to start talks with sb
col'loso, -a *ag* sticky
col'lottola *sf* nape *o* scruff of the neck; **afferrare qn per la ~** to grab sb by the scruff of the neck
collusi'one *sf* (*Dir*) collusion
colluttazi'one [kolluttat'tsjone] *sf* scuffle
col'mare *vt*: **~ di** (*anche fig*) to fill with; (*dare in abbondanza*) to load *o* overwhelm with; **~ un divario** (*fig*) to bridge a gap
'colmo, -a *ag*: **~ (di)** full (of) ■ *sm* summit, top; (*fig*) height; **al ~ della disperazione** in the depths of despair; **è il ~!** it's the last straw!; **e per ~ di sfortuna ...** and to cap it all ...
co'lomba *sf vedi* **colombo**
Co'lombia *sf*: **la ~** Colombia
colombi'ano, -a *ag, sm/f* Colombian
co'lombo, -a *sm/f* dove; pigeon; **colombi** (*fig fam*) lovebirds
Co'lonia *sf* Cologne
co'lonia *sf* colony; (*per bambini*) holiday camp; **(acqua di) ~** (eau de) cologne
coloni'ale *ag* colonial ■ *sm/f* colonist, settler
co'lonico, -a, ci, che *ag*: **casa colonica** farmhouse
coloniz'zare [kolonid'dzare] *vt* to colonize
co'lonna *sf* column; **~ sonora** (*Cine*) sound track; **~ vertebrale** spine, spinal column
colon'nello *sm* colonel
co'lono *sm* (*coltivatore*) tenant farmer
colo'rante *sm* colouring (*Brit*), coloring (*US*)
colo'rare *vt* to colour (*Brit*), color (*US*); (*disegno*) to colo(u)r in
co'lore *sm* colour (*Brit*), color (*US*); (*Carte*) suit; **a colori** in colo(u)r, colo(u)r *cpd*; **la gente di ~** colo(u)red people; **diventare di tutti i colori** to turn scarlet; **farne di tutti i colori** to get up to all sorts of mischief; **passarne di tutti i colori** to go through all sorts of problems
colo'rito, -a *ag* coloured (*Brit*), colored (*US*); (*viso*) rosy, pink; (*linguaggio*) colourful (*Brit*), colorful (*US*) ■ *sm* (*tinta*) colour (*Brit*), color (*US*); (*carnagione*) complexion
co'loro *pron pl vedi* **colui**
colos'sale *ag* colossal, enormous
co'losso *sm* colossus
'colpa *sf* fault; (*biasimo*) blame; (*colpevolezza*) guilt; (*azione colpevole*) offence; (*peccato*) sin; **di chi è la ~?** whose fault is it?; **è ~ sua** it's his fault; **per ~ di** through, owing to; **senso di ~** sense of guilt; **dare la ~ a qn di qc** to blame sb for sth
col'pevole *ag* guilty
colpevoliz'zare [kolpevolid'dzare] *vt*: **~ qn** to make sb feel guilty
col'pire *vt* to hit, strike; (*fig*) to strike; **rimanere colpito da qc** to be amazed *o* struck by sth; **è stato colpito da ordine di cattura** there is a warrant out for his arrest; **~ nel segno** (*fig*) to hit the nail on the head, be spot on (*Brit*)
'colpo *sm* (*urto*) knock; (*fig: affettivo*) blow, shock; (*: aggressivo*) blow; (*di pistola*) shot; (*Med*) stroke; (*furto*) raid; **di ~, tutto d'un ~** suddenly; **fare ~** to make a strong impression; **il motore perde colpi** (*Aut*) the engine is misfiring; **è morto sul ~** he died instantly; **mi hai fatto venire un ~!** what a fright you gave me!; **ti venisse un ~!** (*fam*) drop dead!; **~ d'aria** chill; **~ in banca** bank job *o* raid; **~ basso** (*Pugilato, fig*) punch below the belt; **~ di fulmine** love at first sight; **~ di grazia** coup de grâce; (*fig*) finishing blow; **a ~ d'occhio** at a glance; **~ di scena** (*Teat*) coup de théâtre; (*fig*) dramatic turn of events; **~ di sole** sunstroke; **colpi di sole** (*nei capelli*) highlights; **~ di Stato** coup d'état; **~ di telefono** phone call; **~ di testa** (sudden) impulse *o* whim; **~ di vento** gust (of wind)
col'poso, -a *ag*: **omicidio ~** manslaughter
'colsi *etc vb vedi* **cogliere**
coltel'lata *sf* stab

col'tello *sm* knife; **avere il ~ dalla parte del manico** (*fig*) to have the whip hand; **~ a serramanico** clasp knife
colti'vare *vt* to cultivate; (*verdura*) to grow, cultivate
coltiva'tore *sm* farmer; **~ diretto** small independent farmer
coltivazi'one [koltivat'tsjone] *sf* cultivation; growing; **~ intensiva** intensive farming
'colto, -a *pp di* **cogliere** ■ *ag* (*istruito*) cultured, educated
'coltre *sf* blanket
col'tura *sf* cultivation; **~ alternata** crop rotation
co'lui, co'lei (*pl* **co'loro**) *pron* the one; **~ che parla** the one *o* the man *o* the person who is speaking; **colei che amo** the one *o* the woman *o* the person (whom) I love
com. *abbr* = **comunale; commissione**
'coma *sm inv* coma
comanda'mento *sm* (*Rel*) commandment
coman'dante *sm* (*Mil*) commander, commandant; (*di reggimento*) commanding officer; (*Naut, Aer*) captain
coman'dare *vi* to be in command ■ *vt* to command; (*imporre*) to order, command; **~ a qn di fare** to order sb to do
co'mando *sm* (*ingiunzione*) order, command; (*autorità*) command; (*Tecn*) control; **~ generale** general headquarters *pl*; **~ a distanza** remote control
co'mare *sf* (*madrina*) godmother; (*donna pettegola*) gossip
co'masco, -a, schi, sche *ag* of (*o* from) Como
combaci'are [komba'tʃare] *vi* to meet; (*fig: coincidere*) to coincide, correspond
combat'tente *ag* fighting ■ *sm* combatant; **ex-~** ex-serviceman
com'battere *vt* to fight; (*fig*) to combat, fight against ■ *vi* to fight
combatti'mento *sm* fight; fighting *no pl*; (*di pugilato*) match; **mettere fuori ~** to knock out
combat'tivo, -a *ag* pugnacious
combat'tuto, -a *ag* (*incerto: persona*) uncertain, undecided; (*gara, partita*) hard fought
combi'nare *vt* to combine; (*organizzare*) to arrange; (*fam: fare*) to make, cause ■ *vi* (*corrispondere*): **~ (con)** to correspond (with)
combinazi'one [kombinat'tsjone] *sf* combination; (*caso fortuito*) coincidence; **per ~** by chance
com'briccola *sf* (*gruppo*) party; (*banda*) gang
combus'tibile *ag* combustible ■ *sm* fuel
combusti'one *sf* combustion
com'butta *sf* (*peg*) gang; **in ~** in league

PAROLA CHIAVE

'come *av* **1** (*alla maniera di*) like; **ti comporti come lui** you behave like him *o* like he does; **bianco come la neve** (as) white as snow; **come se** as if, as though; **com'è vero Dio!** as God is my witness!
2 (*in qualità di*) as a; **lavora come autista** he works as a driver
3 (*interrogativo*) how; **come ti chiami?** what's your name?; **come sta?** how are you?; **com'è il tuo amico?** what is your friend like?; **come?** (*prego?*) pardon?, sorry?; **come mai?** how come?; **come mai non ci hai avvertiti?** how come you didn't warn us?
4 (*esclamativo*): **come sei bravo!** how clever you are!; **come mi dispiace!** I'm terribly sorry!
■ *cong* **1** (*in che modo*) how; **mi ha spiegato come l'ha conosciuto** he told me how he met him; **non so come sia successo** I don't know how it happened; **attento a come parli!** watch your mouth!
2 (*correlativo*) as; (*con comparativi di maggioranza*) than; **non è bravo come pensavo** he isn't as clever as I thought; **è meglio di come pensassi** it's better than I thought
3 (*quasi se*) as; **è come se fosse ancora qui** it's as if he was still here; **come se niente fosse** as if nothing had happened; **come non detto!** let's forget it!
4 (*appena che, quando*) as soon as; **come arrivò, iniziò a lavorare** as soon as he arrived, he set to work; *vedi anche* **così**; **oggi**; **ora**

'COMECON *abbr m* (= *Consiglio di Mutua Assistenza Economica*) COMECON
come'done *sm* blackhead
co'meta *sf* comet
'comico, -a, ci, che *ag* (*Teat*) comic; (*buffo*) comical ■ *sm* (*attore*) comedian, comic actor; (*comicità*) comic spirit, comedy
co'mignolo [ko'miɲɲolo] *sm* chimney top
cominci'are [komin'tʃare] *vt, vi* to begin, start; **~ a fare/col fare** to begin to do/by doing; **cominciamo bene!** (*ironico*) we're off to a fine start!
comi'tato *sm* committee; **~ direttivo** steering committee; **~ di gestione** works council; **~ interministeriale prezzi** interdepartmental committee on prices; **~ interministeriale per la programmazione economica** interdepartmental committee for economic planning; **~ interministeriale per lo sviluppo industriale** interdepartmental committee for industrial development

comi'tiva *sf* party, group
co'mizio [ko'mittsjo] *sm* (*Pol*) meeting, assembly; **~ elettorale** election rally
'comma, -i *sm* (*Dir*) subsection
com'mando *sm inv* commando (squad)
com'media *sf* comedy; (*opera teatrale*) play; (*: che fa ridere*) comedy; (*fig*) playacting *no pl*
commedi'ante *sm/f* (*peg*) third-rate actor(-actress); (*: fig*) sham
commedi'ografo, -a *sm/f* (*autore*) comedy writer
commemo'rare *vt* to commemorate
commemorazi'one [kommemorat'tsjone] *sf* commemoration
commenda'tore *sm official title awarded for services to one's country*
commen'sale *sm/f* table companion
commen'tare *vt* to comment on; (*testo*) to annotate; (*Radio, TV*) to give a commentary on
commenta'tore, -'trice *sm/f* commentator
com'mento *sm* comment; (*a un testo, Radio, TV*) commentary; **~ musicale** (*Cine*) background music
commerci'ale [kommer'tʃale] *ag* commercial, trading; (*peg*) commercial
commercia'lista, -i, e [kommertʃa'lista] *sm/f* (*laureato*) graduate in economics and commerce; (*consulente*) business consultant
commercializ'zare [kommertʃalid'dzare] *vt* to market
commercializzazi'one [kommertʃaliddzat-tsjone] *sf* marketing
commerci'ante [kommer'tʃante] *sm/f* trader, dealer; (*negoziante*) shopkeeper; **~ all'ingrosso** wholesaler; **~ in proprio** sole trader
commerci'are [kommer'tʃare] *vi*: **~ in** to deal *o* trade in ▪ *vt* to deal *o* trade in
com'mercio [kom'mɛrtʃo] *sm* trade, commerce; **essere in ~** (*prodotto*) to be on the market *o* on sale; **essere nel ~** (*persona*) to be in business; **~ all'ingrosso/al minuto** wholesale/retail trade
com'messo, -a *pp di* **commettere** ▪ *sm/f* shop assistant (*Brit*), sales clerk (*US*) ▪ *sm* (*impiegato*) clerk ▪ *sf* (*Comm*) order; **~ viaggiatore** commercial traveller
commes'tibile *ag* edible; **commestibili** *smpl* foodstuffs
com'mettere *vt* to commit; (*ordinare*) to commission, order
commi'ato *sm* leave-taking; **prendere ~ da qn** to take one's leave of sb
commi'nare *vt* (*Dir*) to make provision for
commise'rare *vt* to sympathize with, commiserate with
commiserazi'one [kommizerat'tsjone] *sf* commiseration
com'misi *etc vb vedi* **commettere**
commissaria'mento *sm* temporary receivership
commissari'are *vt* to put under temporary receivership
commissari'ato *sm* (*Amm*) commissionership; (*: sede*) commissioner's office; (*: di polizia*) police station
commis'sario *sm* commissioner; (*di pubblica sicurezza*) ≈ (police) superintendent (*Brit*), ≈ (police) captain (*US*); (*Sport*) steward; (*membro di commissione*) member of a committee *o* board; **alto ~** high commissioner; **~ di bordo** (*Naut*) purser; **~ d'esame** member of an examining board; **~ di gara** race official; **~ tecnico** (*Sport*) national coach
commissio'nare *vt* to order, place an order for
commissio'nario *sm* (*Comm*) agent, broker
commissi'one *sf* (*incarico*) errand; (*comitato, percentuale*) commission; (*Comm: ordinazione*) order; **commissioni** *sfpl* (*acquisti*) shopping *sg*; **~ d'esame** examining board; **~ d'inchiesta** committee of enquiry; **~ permanente** standing committee; **commissioni bancarie** bank charges
commit'tente *sm/f* (*Comm*) purchaser, customer
com'mosso, -a *pp di* **commuovere**
commo'vente *ag* moving
commozi'one [kommot'tsjone] *sf* emotion, deep feeling; **~ cerebrale** (*Med*) concussion
commu'overe *vt* to move, affect; **commuoversi** *vr* to be moved
commu'tare *vt* (*pena*) to commute; (*Elettr*) to change *o* switch over
commutazi'one [kommutat'tsjone] *sf* (*Dir, Elettr*) commutation
comò *sm inv* chest of drawers
como'dino *sm* bedside table
comodità *sf inv* comfort; convenience
'comodo, -a *ag* comfortable; (*facile*) easy; (*conveniente*) convenient; (*utile*) useful, handy ▪ *sm* comfort; convenience; **con ~** at one's convenience *o* leisure; **fare il proprio ~** to do as one pleases; **far ~** to be useful *o* handy; **stia ~!** don't bother to get up!
'compact disc *sm inv* compact disc
compae'sano, -a *sm/f* fellow-countryman(-woman); person from the same town
com'pagine [kom'padʒine] *sf* (*squadra*) team
compa'gnia [kompaɲ'ɲia] *sf* company; (*gruppo*) gathering; **fare ~ a qn** to keep sb company; **essere di ~** to be sociable

com'pagno, -a [kom'paɲɲo] *sm/f* (*di classe, gioco*) companion; (*Pol*) comrade; **~ di lavoro** workmate; **~ di scuola** schoolfriend; **~ di viaggio** fellow traveller
com'paio *etc vb vedi* **comparire**
compa'rare *vt* to compare
compara'tivo, -a *ag, sm* comparative
comparazi'one [komparat'tsjone] *sf* comparison
com'pare *sm* (*padrino*) godfather; (*complice*) accomplice; (*fam: amico*) old pal, old mate
compa'rire *vi* to appear; **~ in giudizio** (*Dir*) to appear before the court
comparizi'one [komparit'tsjone] *sf* (*Dir*) appearance; **mandato di ~** summons *sg*
com'parso, -a *pp di* **comparire** ■ *sf* appearance; (*Teat*) walk-on; (*Cine*) extra
comparteci'pare [kompartetʃi'pare] *vi* (*Comm*): **~ a** to have a share in
compartecipazi'one [kompartetʃipat'tsjone] *sf* sharing; (*quota*) share; **~ agli utili** profit-sharing; **in ~** jointly
comparti'mento *sm* compartment; (*Amm*) district
com'parvi *etc vb vedi* **comparire**
compas'sato, -a *ag* (*persona*) composed; **freddo e ~** cool and collected
compassi'one *sf* compassion, pity; **avere ~ di qn** to feel sorry for sb, pity sb; **fare ~** to arouse pity
compassio'nevole *ag* compassionate
com'passo *sm* (pair of) compasses *pl*; callipers *pl*
compa'tibile *ag* (*scusabile*) excusable; (*conciliabile, Inform*) compatible
compati'mento *sm* compassion; indulgence; **con aria di ~** with a condescending air
compa'tire *vt* (*aver compassione di*) to sympathize with, feel sorry for; (*scusare*) to make allowances for
compatri'ota, -i, e *sm/f* compatriot
compat'tezza [kompat'tettsa] *sf* (*solidità*) compactness; (*fig: unità*) solidarity
com'patto, -a *ag* compact; (*roccia*) solid; (*folla*) dense; (*fig: gruppo, partito*) united, close-knit
com'pendio *sm* summary; (*libro*) compendium
compen'sare *vt* (*equilibrare*) to compensate for, make up for; **compensarsi** *vr* (*reciproco*) to balance each other out; **~ qn di** (*rimunerare*) to pay *o* remunerate sb for; (*risarcire*) to pay compensation to sb for; (*fig fatiche, dolori*) to reward sb for
compen'sato *sm* (*anche*: **legno compensato**) plywood
com'penso *sm* compensation; payment, remuneration; reward; **in ~** (*d'altra parte*) on the other hand
'compera *sf* purchase; **fare le compere** to do the shopping
compe'rare *vt* = **comprare**
compe'tente *ag* competent; (*mancia*) apt, suitable; (*capace*) qualified; **rivolgersi all'ufficio ~** to apply to the office concerned
compe'tenza [kompe'tɛntsa] *sf* competence; (*Dir: autorità*) jurisdiction; (*Tecn, Comm*) expertise; **competenze** *sfpl* (*onorari*) fees; **definire le competenze** to establish responsibilities
com'petere *vi* to compete, vie; (*Dir: spettare*): **~ a** to lie within the competence of
competitività *sf inv* competitiveness
competi'tivo, -a *ag* competitive
competi'tore, -'trice *sm/f* competitor
competizi'one [kompetit'tsjone] *sf* competition; **spirito di ~** competitive spirit
compia'cente [kompja'tʃɛnte] *ag* courteous, obliging
compia'cenza [kompja'tʃɛntsa] *sf* courtesy
compia'cere [kompja'tʃere] *vi*: **~ a** to gratify, please ■ *vt* to please; **compiacersi** *vr* (*provare soddisfazione*): **compiacersi di** *o* **per qc** to be delighted at sth; (*rallegrarsi*): **compiacersi con qn** to congratulate sb; (*degnarsi*): **compiacersi di fare** to be so good as to do
compiaci'mento [kompjatʃi'mento] *sm* satisfaction
compiaci'uto, -a [kompja'tʃuto] *pp di* **compiacere**
compi'angere [kom'pjandʒere] *vt* to sympathize with, feel sorry for
compi'anto, -a *pp di* **compiangere** ■ *ag*: **il ~ presidente** the late lamented president ■ *sm* mourning, grief
'compiere *vt* (*concludere*) to finish, complete; (*adempiere*) to carry out, fulfil; **compiersi** *vr* (*avverarsi*) to be fulfilled, come true; **~ gli anni** to have one's birthday
compi'lare *vt* to compile; (*modulo*) to complete, fill in (*Brit*), fill out (*US*)
compila'tore, -'trice *sm/f* compiler
compilazi'one [kompilat'tsjone] *sf* compilation; completion
compi'mento *sm* (*termine, conclusione*) completion, fulfilment; **portare a ~ qc** to conclude sth, bring sth to a conclusion
com'pire *vb* = **compiere**
'compito *sm* (*incarico*) task, duty; (*dovere*) duty; (*Ins*) exercise; (*: a casa*) piece of homework; **fare i compiti** to do one's homework
com'pito, -a *ag* well-mannered, polite

compiu'tezza [kompju'tettsa] *sf* (*completezza*) completeness; (*perfezione*) perfection
compi'uto, -a *pp di* **compiere** ■ *ag*: **a 20 anni compiuti** at 20 years of age, at age 20; **un fatto ~** a fait accompli
comple'anno *sm* birthday
complemen'tare *ag* complementary; (*Ins: materia*) subsidiary
comple'mento *sm* complement; (*Mil*) reserve (troops); **~ oggetto** (*Ling*) direct object
comples'sato, -a *ag, sm/f*: **essere (un) ~** to be full of complexes *o* hang-ups (*fam*)
complessità *sf* complexity
complessiva'mente *av* (*nell'insieme*) on the whole; (*in tutto*) altogether
comples'sivo, -a *ag* (*globale*) comprehensive, overall; (*totale: cifra*) total; **visione complessiva** overview
com'plesso, -a *ag* complex ■ *sm* (*Psic, Edil*) complex; (*Mus: corale*) ensemble; (*: orchestrina*) band; (*: di musica pop*) group; **in** *o* **nel ~** on the whole
completa'mento *sm* completion
comple'tare *vt* to complete
com'pleto, -a *ag* complete; (*teatro, autobus*) full ■ *sm* suit; **al ~** full; (*tutti presenti*) all present; **essere al ~** (*teatro*) to be sold out; **~ da sci** ski suit
compli'care *vt* to complicate; **complicarsi** *vr* to become complicated
complicazi'one [komplikat'tsjone] *sf* complication; **salvo complicazioni** unless any difficulties arise
'complice ['kɔmplitʃe] *sm/f* accomplice
complicità [komplitʃi'ta] *sf inv* complicity; **un sorriso/uno sguardo di ~** a knowing smile/look
complimen'tarsi *vr*: **~ con** to congratulate
compli'mento *sm* compliment; **complimenti** *smpl* (*cortesia eccessiva*) ceremony *sg*; **complimenti!** congratulations!; **senza complimenti!** don't stand on ceremony!; make yourself at home!; help yourself!
complot'tare *vi* to plot, conspire
com'plotto *sm* plot, conspiracy
com'pone *etc vb vedi* **comporre**
compo'nente *sm/f* member ■ *sm* component
com'pongo *etc vb vedi* **comporre**
compo'nibile *ag* (*mobili, cucina*) fitted
componi'mento *sm* (*Dir*) settlement; (*Ins*) composition; (*poetico, teatrale*) work
com'porre *vt* (*musica, testo*) to compose; (*mettere in ordine*) to arrange; (*Dir: lite*) to settle; (*Tip*) to set; (*Tel*) to dial; **comporsi** *vr*: **comporsi di** to consist of, be composed of
comportamen'tale *ag* behavioural (*Brit*), behavioral (*US*)
comporta'mento *sm* behaviour (*Brit*), behavior (*US*); (*di prodotto*) performance
compor'tare *vt* (*implicare*) to involve, entail; (*consentire*) to permit, allow (of); **comportarsi** *vr* (*condursi*) to behave
com'posi *etc vb vedi* **comporre**
composi'tore, -'trice *sm/f* composer; (*Tip*) compositor, typesetter
composizi'one [kompozit'tsjone] *sf* composition; (*Dir*) settlement
com'posta *sf vedi* **composto**
compos'tezza [kompos'tettsa] *sf* composure; decorum
com'posto, -a *pp di* **comporre** ■ *ag* (*persona*) composed, self-possessed; (*: decoroso*) dignified; (*formato da più elementi*) compound *cpd* ■ *sm* compound; (*Cuc etc*) mixture ■ *sf* (*Cuc*) stewed fruit *no pl*; (*Agr*) compost
com'prare *vt* to buy; (*corrompere*) to bribe
compra'tore, -'trice *sm/f* buyer, purchaser
compra'vendita *sf* (*Comm*) (contract of) sale; **un atto di ~** a deed of sale
com'prendere *vt* (*contenere*) to comprise, consist of; (*capire*) to understand
compren'donio *sm*: **essere duro di ~** to be slow on the uptake
compren'sibile *ag* understandable
comprensi'one *sf* understanding
compren'sivo, -a *ag* (*prezzo*): **~ di** inclusive of; (*indulgente*) understanding
compren'sorio *sm* area, territory; (*Amm*) district
com'preso, -a *pp di* **comprendere** ■ *ag* (*incluso*) included; **tutto ~** all included, all-in (*Brit*)
com'pressa *sf vedi* **compresso**
compressi'one *sf* compression
com'presso, -a *pp di* **comprimere** ■ *ag* (*vedi comprimere*) pressed; compressed; repressed ■ *sf* (*Med: garza*) compress; (*: pastiglia*) tablet
compres'sore *sm* compressor; (*anche*: **rullo compressore**) steamroller
compri'mario, -a *sm/f* (*Teat*) supporting actor(-actress)
com'primere *vt* (*premere*) to press; (*Fisica*) to compress; (*fig*) to repress
compro'messo, -a *pp di* **compromettere** ■ *sm* compromise
compro'mettere *vt* to compromise; **compromettersi** *vr* to compromise o.s.
comproprietà *sf* (*Dir*) joint ownership
compro'vare *vt* to confirm
com'punto, -a *ag* contrite; **con fare ~** with a solemn air
compunzi'one [kompun'tsjone] *sf* contrition; solemnity

C

compu'tare *vt* to calculate; (*addebitare*): **~ qc a qn** to debit sb with sth
com'puter [kəm'pju:tər] *sm inv* computer
computeriz'zato, -a [komputerid'dzato] *ag* computerized
computerizzazi'one [komputeriddzat'tsjone] *sf* computerization
computiste'ria *sf* accounting, book-keeping
'computo *sm* calculation; **fare il ~ di** to count
comu'nale *ag* municipal, town *cpd*; **consiglio/palazzo ~** town council/hall; **è un impiegato ~** he works for the local council
Co'mune *sm* (*Amm*) town council; (*sede*) town hall; *see note*

> **COMUNE**
>
> The *Comune* is the smallest autonomous political and administrative unit. It keeps records of births, marriages and deaths and has the power to levy taxes and vet proposals for public works and town planning. It is run by a "Giunta comunale", which is elected by the "Consiglio Comunale". The *Comune* is headed by the "sindaco" (mayor) who since 1993 has been elected directly by the citizens.

co'mune *ag* common; (*consueto*) common, everyday; (*di livello medio*) average; (*ordinario*) ordinary ■ *sf* (*di persone*) commune; **fuori del ~** out of the ordinary; **avere in ~** to have in common, share; **mettere in ~** to share; **un nostro ~ amico** a mutual friend of ours; **fare cassa ~** to pool one's money
comuni'care *vt* (*notizia*) to pass on, convey; (*malattia*) to pass on; (*ansia etc*) to communicate; (*trasmettere: calore etc*) to transmit, communicate; (*Rel*) to administer communion to ■ *vi* to communicate; **comunicarsi** *vr* (*propagarsi*): **comunicarsi a** to spread to; (*Rel*) to receive communion
comunica'tivo, -a *ag* (*sentimento*) infectious; (*persona*) communicative ■ *sf* communicativeness
comuni'cato *sm* communiqué; **~ stampa** press release
comunicazi'one [komunikat'tsjone] *sf* communication; (*annuncio*) announcement; (*Tel*): **~ (telefonica)** (telephone) call; **dare la ~ a qn** to put sb through; **ottenere la ~** to get through; **salvo comunicazioni contrarie da parte Vostra** unless we hear from you to the contrary
comuni'one *sf* communion; **~ dei beni** (*Dir: tra coniugi*) joint ownership of property
comu'nismo *sm* communism
comu'nista, -i, e *ag, sm/f* communist
comunità *sf inv* community; **C~ Economica Europea** European Economic Community; **~ terapeutica** *rehabilitation centre run by voluntary organizations for people with drug, alcohol etc dependency*
comuni'tario, -a *ag* community *cpd*
co'munque *cong* however, no matter how ■ *av* (*in ogni modo*) in any case; (*tuttavia*) however, nevertheless
con *prep* (*nei seguenti casi* **con** *può fondersi con l'articolo definito: con + il =* **col**, *con + la =* **colla**, *con + gli =* **cogli**, *con + I =* **coi**, *con + le =* **colle**) with; **partire col treno** to leave by train; **~ mio grande stupore** to my great astonishment; **~ la forza** by force; **~ questo freddo** in this cold weather; **~ il 1° di ottobre** as of October 1st; **~ tutto ciò** in spite of that, for all that; **~ tutto che era arrabbiato** even though he was angry, in spite of the fact that he was angry; **e ~ questo?** so what?
co'nato *sm*: **~ di vomito** retching
'conca, -che *sf* (*Geo*) valley
concate'nare *vt* to link up, connect; **concatenarsi** *vr* to be connected
'concavo, -a *ag* concave
con'cedere [kon'tʃɛdere] *vt* (*accordare*) to grant; (*ammettere*) to admit, concede; **concedersi qc** to treat o.s. to sth, allow o.s. sth
concentra'mento [kontʃentra'mento] *sm* concentration
concen'trare [kontʃen'trare] *vt*, **concen'trarsi** *vr* to concentrate
concen'trato [kontʃen'trato] *sm* concentrate; **~ di pomodoro** tomato purée
concentrazi'one [kontʃentrat'tsjone] *sf* concentration; **~ orizzontale/verticale** (*Econ*) horizontal/vertical integration
con'centrico, -a, ci, che [kon'tʃɛntriko] *ag* concentric
conce'pibile [kontʃe'pibile] *ag* conceivable
concepi'mento [kontʃepi'mento] *sm* conception
conce'pire [kontʃe'pire] *vt* (*bambino*) to conceive; (*progetto, idea*) to conceive (of); (*metodo, piano*) to devise; (*situazione*) to imagine, understand
con'cernere [kon'tʃɛrnere] *vt* to concern; **per quanto mi concerne** as far as I'm concerned
concer'tare [kontʃer'tare] *vt* (*Mus*) to harmonize; (*ordire*) to devise, plan; **concertarsi** *vr* to agree
concer'tista, -i, e [kontʃer'tista] *sm/f* (*Mus*) concert performer
con'certo [kon'tʃɛrto] *sm* (*Mus*) concert; (*: componimento*) concerto
con'cessi *etc* [kon'tʃɛssi] *vb vedi* **concedere**

concessio'nario [kontʃessjo'narjo] *sm* (*Comm*) agent, dealer; **~ esclusivo (di)** sole agent (for)
concessi'one [kontʃes'sjone] *sf* concession
con'cesso, -a [kon'tʃɛsso] *pp di* **concedere**
con'cetto [kon'tʃɛtto] *sm* (*pensiero, idea*) concept; (*opinione*) opinion; **è un impiegato di ~** ≈ he's a white-collar worker
concezi'one [kontʃet'tsjone] *sf* conception; (*idea*) view, idea
con'chiglia [kon'kiʎʎa] *sf* shell
'concia ['kontʃa] *sf* (*di pelli*) tanning; (*di tabacco*) curing; (*sostanza*) tannin
conci'are [kon'tʃare] *vt* (*pelli*) to tan; (*tabacco*) to cure; (*fig: ridurre in cattivo stato*) to beat up; **conciarsi** *vr* (*sporcarsi*) to get in a mess; (*vestirsi male*) to dress badly; **ti hanno conciato male** *o* **per le feste!** they've really beaten you up!
concili'abile [kontʃi'ljabile] *ag* compatible
concili'abolo [kontʃi'ljabolo] *sm* secret meeting
concili'ante [kontʃi'ljante] *ag* conciliatory
concili'are [kontʃi'ljare] *vt* to reconcile; (*contravvenzione*) to pay on the spot; (*favorire: sonno*) to be conducive to, induce; (*procurare: simpatia*) to gain; **conciliarsi qc** to gain *o* win sth (for o.s.); **conciliarsi qn** to win sb over; **conciliarsi con** to be reconciled with
conciliazi'one [kontʃiljat'tsjone] *sf* reconciliation; (*Dir*) settlement; **la C~** (*Storia*) the Lateran Pact
con'cilio [kon'tʃiljo] *sm* (*Rel*) council
conci'mare [kontʃi'mare] *vt* to fertilize; (*con letame*) to manure
con'cime [kon'tʃime] *sm* manure; (*chimico*) fertilizer
concisi'one [kontʃi'zjone] *sf* concision, conciseness
con'ciso, -a [kon'tʃizo] *ag* concise, succinct
conci'tato, -a [kontʃi'tato] *ag* excited, emotional
concitta'dino, -a [kontʃitta'dino] *sm/f* fellow citizen
con'clave *sm* conclave
con'cludere *vt* to conclude; (*portare a compimento*) to conclude, finish, bring to an end; (*operare positivamente*) to achieve ■ *vi* (*essere convincente*) to be conclusive; **concludersi** *vr* to come to an end, close
conclusi'one *sf* conclusion; (*risultato*) result
conclu'sivo, -a *ag* conclusive; (*finale*) final
con'cluso, -a *pp di* **concludere**
concomi'tanza [konkomi'tantsa] *sf* (*di circostanze, fatti*) combination
concor'danza [konkor'dantsa] *sf* (*anche Ling*) agreement
concor'dare *vt* (*prezzo*) to agree on; (*Ling*) to make agree ■ *vi* to agree; **~ una tregua** to agree to a truce
concor'dato *sm* agreement; (*Rel*) concordat
con'corde *ag* (*d'accordo*) in agreement; (*simultaneo*) simultaneous
con'cordia *sf* harmony, concord
concor'rente *ag* competing; (*Mat*) concurrent ■ *sm/f* (*Sport, Comm*) competitor; (*a un concorso di bellezza*) contestant
concor'renza [konkor'rɛntsa] *sf* competition; **~ sleale** unfair competition; **a prezzi di ~** at competitive prices
concorrenzi'ale [konkorren'tsjale] *ag* competitive
con'correre *vi*: **~ (in)** (*Mat*) to converge *o* meet (in); **~ (a)** (*competere*) to compete (for); (*: Ins: a una cattedra*) to apply (for); (*partecipare: a un'impresa*) to take part (in), contribute (to)
con'corso, -a *pp di* **concorrere** ■ *sm* competition; (*esame*) competitive examination; **~ di bellezza** beauty contest; **~ di circostanze** combination of circumstances; **~ di colpa** (*Dir*) contributory negligence; **un ~ ippico** a showjumping event; **~ in reato** (*Dir*) complicity in a crime; **~ per titoli** competitive examination for qualified candidates
con'creto, -a *ag* concrete ■ *sm*: **in ~** in reality
concu'bina *sf* concubine ■ *sm*: **sono concubini** they are living together
concussi'one *sf* (*Dir*) extortion
con'danna *sf* condemnation; sentence; conviction; **~ a morte** death sentence
condan'nare *vt* (*disapprovare*) to condemn; (*Dir*): **~ a** to sentence to; **~ per** to convict of
condan'nato, -a *sm/f* convict
con'densa *sf* condensation
conden'sare *vt*, **conden'sarsi** *vr* to condense
condensa'tore *sm* capacitor
condensazi'one [kondensat'tsjone] *sf* condensation
condi'mento *sm* seasoning; dressing
con'dire *vt* to season; (*insalata*) to dress
condiscen'dente [kondiʃʃen'dɛnte] *ag* obliging; compliant
condiscen'denza [kondiʃʃen'dɛntsa] *sf* (*disponibilità*) obligingness; (*arrendevolezza*) compliance
condi'scendere [kondiʃʃendere] *vi*: **~ a** to agree to
condi'sceso, -a [kondiʃʃeso] *pp di* **condiscendere**
condi'videre *vt* to share
condi'viso, -a *pp di* **condividere**
condizio'nale [kondittsjo'nale] *ag* conditional ■ *sm* (*Ling*) conditional ■ *sf* (*Dir*) suspended sentence

condiziona'mento [kondittsjona'mento] *sm* conditioning; **~ d'aria** air conditioning
condizio'nare [kondittsjo'nare] *vt* to condition; **ad aria condizionata** air-conditioned
condiziona'tore [kondittsjona'tore] *sm* air conditioner
condizi'one [kondit'tsjone] *sf* condition; **condizioni** *sfpl* (*di pagamento etc*) terms, conditions; **a ~ che** on condition that, provided that; **a nessuna** ~ on no account; **condizioni a convenirsi** terms to be arranged; **condizioni di lavoro** working conditions; **condizioni di vendita** sales terms
condogli'anze [kondoʎ'ʎantse] *sfpl* condolences
condomini'ale *ag*: **riunione** ~ residents' meeting; **spese condominiali** common charges
condo'minio *sm* joint ownership; (*edificio*) jointly-owned building
con'domino *sm* joint owner
condo'nare *vt* (*Dir*) to remit
con'dono *sm* remission; **~ fiscale** *conditional amnesty for people evading tax*
con'dotta *sf vedi* **condotto**
con'dotto, -a *pp di* **condurre** ■ *ag*: **medico ~** local authority doctor (*in country district*) ■ *sm* (*canale, tubo*) pipe, conduit; (*Anat*) duct ■ *sf* (*modo di comportarsi*) conduct, behaviour (*Brit*), behavior (*US*); (*di un affare etc*) handling; (*di acqua*) piping; (*incarico sanitario*) *country medical practice controlled by a local authority*
condu'cente [kondu'tʃɛnte] *sm* driver
con'duco *etc vb vedi* **condurre**
con'durre *vt* to conduct; (*azienda*) to manage; (*accompagnare*: *bambino*) to take; (*automobile*) to drive; (*trasportare*: *acqua, gas*) to convey, conduct; (*fig*) to lead ■ *vi* to lead; **condursi** *vr* to behave, conduct o.s.; **~ a termine** to conclude
con'dussi *etc vb vedi* **condurre**
condut'tore, -'trice *ag*: **filo ~** (*fig*) thread; **motivo** ~ leitmotiv ■ *sm* (*di mezzi pubblici*) driver; (*Fisica*) conductor
condut'tura *sf* (*gen*) pipe; (*di acqua, gas*) main
conduzi'one [kondut'tsjone] *sf* (*di affari, ditta*) management; (*Dir*: *locazione*) lease; (*Fisica*) conduction
confabu'lare *vi* to confab
confa'cente [konfa'tʃɛnte] *ag*: **~ a qn/qc** suitable for sb/sth; **clima ~ alla salute** healthy climate
CONFAGRICOL'TURA *abbr f* (= *Confederazione generale dell'Agricoltura Italiana*) *confederation of Italian farmers*
CON'FAPI *sigla f* = **Confederazione Nazionale della Piccola Industria**
con'farsi *vr*: **~ a** to suit, agree with
CONFARTIGIA'NATO [konfartidʒa'nato] *abbr f* = **Confederazione Generale dell'Artigianato Italiano**
con'fatto, -a *pp di* **confarsi**
CONFCOM'MERCIO [konfkom'mɛrtʃo] *abbr f* = **Confederazione Generale del Commercio**
confederazi'one [konfederat'tsjone] *sf* confederation; **~ imprenditoriale** employers' association
confe'renza [konfe'rɛntsa] *sf* (*discorso*) lecture; (*riunione*) conference; **~ stampa** press conference
conferenzi'ere, -a [konferen'tsjɛre] *sm/f* lecturer
conferi'mento *sm* conferring, awarding
confe'rire *vt*: **~ qc a qn** to give sth to sb, confer sth on sb ■ *vi* to confer
con'ferma *sf* confirmation
confer'mare *vt* to confirm
confes'sare *vt*, **confes'sarsi** *vr* to confess; **andare a confessarsi** (*Rel*) to go to confession
confessio'nale *ag, sm* confessional
confessi'one *sf* confession; (*setta religiosa*) denomination
con'fesso, -a *ag*: **essere reo ~** to have pleaded guilty
confes'sore *sm* confessor
con'fetto *sm* sugared almond; (*Med*) pill
confet'tura *sf* (*gen*) jam; (*di arance*) marmalade
confezio'nare [konfettsjo'nare] *vt* (*vestito*) to make (up); (*merci, pacchi*) to package
confezi'one [konfet'tsjone] *sf* (*di abiti*: *da uomo*) tailoring; (: *da donna*) dressmaking; (*imballaggio*) packaging; **~ regalo** gift pack; **~ risparmio** economy size; **~ da viaggio** travel pack; **confezioni per signora** ladies' wear *no pl*; **confezioni da uomo** menswear *no pl*
confic'care *vt*: **~ qc in** to hammer *o* drive sth into; **conficcarsi** *vr* to stick
confi'dare *vi*: **~ in** to confide in, rely on ■ *vt* to confide; **confidarsi con qn** to confide in sb
confi'dente *sm/f* (*persona amica*) confidant/confidante; (*informatore*) informer
confi'denza [konfi'dɛntsa] *sf* (*familiarità*) intimacy, familiarity; (*fiducia*) trust, confidence; (*rivelazione*) confidence; **prendersi (troppe) confidenze** to take liberties; **fare una ~ a qn** to confide something to sb
confidenzi'ale [konfiden'tsjale] *ag* familiar, friendly; (*segreto*) confidential; **in via ~** confidentially

configu'rare *vt* (*Inform*) to set; **configurarsi** *vr*: **configurarsi a** to assume the shape *o* form of

configurazi'one [konfigurat'tsjone] *sf* configuration; (*Inform*) setting

confi'nante *ag* neighbouring (*Brit*), neighboring (*US*)

confi'nare *vi*: **~ con** to border on ■ *vt* (*Pol*) to intern; (*fig*) to confine; **confinarsi** *vr* (*isolarsi*): **confinarsi in** to shut o.s. up in

confi'nato, -a *ag* interned ■ *sm/f* internee

CONFIN'DUSTRIA *sigla f* (= *Confederazione Generale dell'Industria Italiana*) *employers' association*, ≈ CBI (*Brit*)

con'fine *sm* boundary; (*di paese*) border, frontier; **territorio di ~** border zone

con'fino *sm* internment

con'fisca *sf* confiscation

confis'care *vt* to confiscate

conflagrazi'one [konflagrat'tsjone] *sf* conflagration

con'flitto *sm* conflict; **essere in ~ con qc** to clash with sth; **essere in ~ con qn** to be at loggerheads with sb; **~ d'interessi** conflict of interests

conflittu'ale *ag*: **rapporto ~** relationship based on conflict

conflittualità *sf* conflicts *pl*

conflu'enza [konflu'ɛntsa] *sf* (*di fiumi*) confluence; (*di strade*) junction

conflu'ire *vi* (*fiumi*) to flow into each other, meet; (*strade*) to meet

con'fondere *vt* to mix up, confuse; (*imbarazzare*) to embarrass; **confondersi** *vr* (*mescolarsi*) to mingle; (*turbarsi*) to be confused; (*sbagliare*) to get mixed up; **~ le idee a qn** to mix sb up, confuse sb

confor'mare *vt* (*adeguare*): **~ a** to adapt *o* conform to; **conformarsi** *vr*: **conformarsi (a)** to conform (to)

con'forme *ag*: **~ a** (*simile*) similar to; (*corrispondente*) in keeping with

conforme'mente *av* accordingly; **~ a** in accordance with

confor'mismo *sm* conformity

confor'mista, -i, e *sm/f* conformist

conformità *sf* conformity; **in ~ a** in conformity with

confor'tare *vt* to comfort, console

confor'tevole *ag* (*consolante*) comforting; (*comodo*) comfortable

con'forto *sm* (*consolazione, sollievo*) comfort, consolation; (*conferma*) support; **a ~ di qc** in support of sth; **i conforti (religiosi)** the last sacraments

confra'ternita *sf* brotherhood

confron'tare *vt* to compare; **confrontarsi** *vr* (*scontrarsi*) to have a confrontation

con'fronto *sm* comparison; (*Dir, Mil, Pol*) confrontation; **in** *o* **a ~ di** in comparison with, compared to; **nei miei (***o* **tuoi** *etc***) confronti** towards me (*o* you *etc*)

con'fusi *etc vb vedi* **confondere**

confusi'one *sf* confusion; (*imbarazzo*) embarrassment; **far ~** (*disordine*) to make a mess; (*chiasso*) to make a racket; (*confondere*) to confuse things

con'fuso, -a *pp di* **confondere** ■ *ag* (*vedi confondere*) confused; embarrassed

confu'tare *vt* to refute

conge'dare [kondʒe'dare] *vt* to dismiss; (*Mil*) to demobilize; **congedarsi** *vr* to take one's leave

con'gedo [kon'dʒedo] *sm* (*anche Mil*) leave; **prendere ~ da qn** to take one's leave of sb; **~ assoluto** (*Mil*) discharge

conge'gnare [kondʒeɲ'ɲare] *vt* to construct, put together

con'gegno [kon'dʒeɲɲo] *sm* device, mechanism

congela'mento [kondʒela'mento] *sm* (*gen*) freezing; (*Med*) frostbite; **~ salariale** wage freeze

conge'lare [kondʒe'lare] *vt*, **conge'larsi** *vr* to freeze

congela'tore [kondʒela'tore] *sm* freezer

con'genito, -a [kon'dʒɛnito] *ag* congenital

con'gerie [kon'dʒɛrje] *sf inv* (*di oggetti*) heap; (*di idee*) muddle, jumble

congestio'nare [kondʒestjo'nare] *vt* to congest; **essere congestionato** (*persona, viso*) to be flushed; (*zona: per traffico*) to be congested

congesti'one [kondʒes'tjone] *sf* congestion

conget'tura [kondʒet'tura] *sf* conjecture, supposition

con'giungere [kon'dʒundʒere] *vt*, **con'giungersi** *vr* to join (together)

congiunti'vite [kondʒunti'vite] *sf* conjunctivitis

congiun'tivo [kondʒun'tivo] *sm* (*Ling*) subjunctive

congi'unto, -a [kon'dʒunto] *pp di* **congiungere** ■ *ag* (*unito*) joined ■ *sm/f* (*parente*) relative

congiun'tura [kondʒun'tura] *sf* (*giuntura*) junction, join; (*Anat*) joint; (*circostanza*) juncture; (*Econ*) economic situation

congiuntu'rale [kondʒuntu'rale] *ag* of the economic situation; **crisi ~** economic crisis

congiunzi'one [kondʒun'tsjone] *sf* (*Ling*) conjunction

congi'ura [kon'dʒura] *sf* conspiracy

congiu'rare [kondʒu'rare] *vi* to conspire

conglome'rato *sm* (*Geo*) conglomerate; (*fig*) conglomeration; (*Edil*) concrete
'Congo *sm*: **il ~** the Congo
congo'lese *ag, sm/f* Congolese *inv*
congratu'larsi *vr*: **~ con qn per qc** to congratulate sb on sth
congratulazi'oni [kongratulat'tsjoni] *sfpl* congratulations
con'grega, -ghe *sf* band, bunch
congregazi'one [kongregat'tsjone] *sf* congregation
congres'sista, -i, e *sm/f* participant at a congress
con'gresso *sm* congress
'congruo, -a *ag* (*prezzo, compenso*) adequate, fair; (*ragionamento*) coherent, consistent
conguagli'are [kongwaʎ'ʎare] *vt* to balance; (*stipendio*) to adjust
congu'aglio [kon'gwaʎʎo] *sm* balancing; adjusting; (*somma di denaro*) balance; **fare il ~ di** to balance; to adjust
coni'are *vt* to mint, coin; (*fig*) to coin
coniazi'one [konjat'tsjone] *sf* mintage
'conico, -a, ci, che *ag* conical
co'nifere *sfpl* conifers
conigli'era [koniʎ'ʎɛra] *sf* (*gabbia*) rabbit hutch; (*più grande*) rabbit run
conigli'etta [koniʎ'ʎetta] *sf* bunny girl
conigli'etto [koniʎ'ʎetto] *sm* bunny
co'niglio [ko'niʎʎo] *sm* rabbit; **sei un ~!** (*fig*) you're chicken!
coniu'gale *ag* (*amore, diritti*) conjugal; (*vita*) married, conjugal
coniu'gare *vt* to combine; (*Ling*) to conjugate; **coniugarsi** *vr* to get married
coniu'gato, -a *ag* (*Amm*) married
coniugazi'one [konjugat'tsjone] *sf* (*Ling*) conjugation
'coniuge ['kɔnjudʒe] *sm/f* spouse
connatu'rato, -a *ag* inborn
connazio'nale [konnattsjo'nale] *sm/f* fellow-countryman(-woman)
connessi'one *sf* connection
con'nesso, -a *pp di* **connettere**
con'nettere *vt* to connect, join ▪ *vi* (*fig*) to think straight
connet'tore *sm* (*Elettr*) connector
conni'vente *ag* conniving
conno'tati *smpl* distinguishing marks; **rispondere ai ~** to fit the description; **cambiare i ~ a qn** (*fam*) to beat sb up
con'nubio *sm* (*matrimonio*) marriage; (*fig*) union
'cono *sm* cone; **~ gelato** ice-cream cone
co'nobbi *etc vb vedi* **conoscere**
cono'scente [konoʃ'ʃɛnte] *sm/f* acquaintance
cono'scenza [konoʃ'ʃɛntsa] *sf* (*il sapere*) knowledge *no pl*; (*persona*) acquaintance; (*facoltà sensoriale*) consciousness *no pl*; **essere a ~ di qc** to know sth; **portare qn a ~ di qc** to inform sb of sth; **per vostra ~** for your information; **fare la ~ di qn** to make sb's acquaintance; **perdere ~** to lose consciousness; **~ tecnica** know-how
co'noscere [ko'noʃʃere] *vt* to know; **ci siamo conosciuti a Firenze** we (first) met in Florence; **~ qn di vista** to know sb by sight; **farsi ~** (*fig*) to make a name for o.s.
conosci'tore, -'trice [konoʃʃi'tore] *sm/f* connoisseur
conosci'uto, -a [konoʃ'ʃuto] *pp di* **conoscere** ▪ *ag* well-known
con'quista *sf* conquest
conquis'tare *vt* to conquer; (*fig*) to gain, win
conquista'tore, -'trice *sm/f* (*in guerra*) conqueror ▪ *sm* (*seduttore*) lady-killer
cons. *abbr* = **consiglio**
consa'crare *vt* (*Rel*) to consecrate; (*: sacerdote*) to ordain; (*dedicare*) to dedicate; (*fig: uso etc*) to sanction; **consacrarsi a** to dedicate o.s. to
consangu'ineo, a *sm/f* blood relation
consa'pevole *ag*: **~ di** aware of
consapevo'lezza [konsapevo'lettsa] *sf* awareness, consciousness
conscia'mente [konʃa'mente] *av* consciously
'conscio, -a, sci, sce ['kɔnʃo] *ag*: **~ di** aware *o* conscious of
consecu'tivo, -a *ag* consecutive; (*successivo: giorno*) following, next
con'segna [kon'seɲɲa] *sf* delivery; (*merce consegnata*) consignment; (*custodia*) care, custody; (*Mil: ordine*) orders *pl*; (*: punizione*) confinement to barracks; **alla ~** on delivery; **dare qc in ~ a qn** to entrust sth to sb; **passare le consegne a qn** to hand over to sb; **~ a domicilio** home delivery; **~ in contrassegno**, **pagamento alla ~** cash on delivery; **~ sollecita** prompt delivery
conse'gnare [konseɲ'ɲare] *vt* to deliver; (*affidare*) to entrust, hand over; (*Mil*) to confine to barracks
consegna'tario [konseɲɲa'tarjo] *sm* consignee
consegu'ente *ag* consequent
conseguente'mente *av* consequently
consegu'enza [konse'gwɛntsa] *sf* consequence; **per** *o* **di ~** consequently
consegui'mento *sm* (*di scopo, risultato etc*) achievement, attainment; **al ~ della laurea** on graduation
consegu'ire *vt* to achieve ▪ *vi* to follow, result; **~ la laurea** to graduate, obtain one's degree
con'senso *sm* approval, consent
consensu'ale *ag* (*Dir*) by mutual consent

consen'tire *vi*: **~ a** to consent *o* agree to ■ *vt* to allow, permit; **mi si consenta di ringraziare ...** I would like to thank ...
consenzi'ente [konsen'tsjɛnte] *ag* (*gen, Dir*) consenting
con'serto, -a *ag*: **a braccia conserte** with one's arms folded
con'serva *sf* (*Cuc*) preserve; **~ di frutta** jam; **~ di pomodoro** tomato purée; **conserve alimentari** tinned (*o* canned *o* bottled) foods
conser'vante *sm* (*per alimenti*) preservative
conser'vare *vt* (*Cuc*) to preserve; (*custodire*) to keep; (*: dalla distruzione etc*) to preserve, conserve; **conservarsi** *vr* to keep
conserva'tore, -'trice *ag, sm/f* (*Pol*) conservative
conserva'torio *sm* (*di musica*) conservatory
conservato'rismo *sm* (*Pol*) conservatism
conservazi'one [konservat'tsjone] *sf* preservation; conservation; **istinto di ~** instinct for self-preservation; **a lunga ~** (*latte, panna*) long-life *cpd*
con'sesso *sm* (*assemblea*) assembly; (*riunione*) meeting
conside'rabile *ag* worthy of consideration
conside'rare *vt* to consider; (*reputare*) to consider, regard; **~ molto qn** to think highly of sb
conside'rato, -a *ag* (*prudente*) cautious, careful; (*stimato*) highly thought of, esteemed
considerazi'one [konsiderat'tsjone] *sf* (*esame, riflessione*) consideration; (*stima*) regard, esteem; (*pensiero, osservazione*) observation; **prendere in ~** to take into consideration
conside'revole *ag* considerable
consigli'abile [konsiʎ'ʎabile] *ag* advisable
consigli'are [konsiʎ'ʎare] *vt* (*persona*) to advise; (*metodo, azione*) to recommend, advise, suggest; **consigliarsi** *vr*: **consigliarsi con qn** to ask sb for advice
consigli'ere, -a [konsiʎ'ʎɛre] *sm/f* adviser ■ *sm*: **~ d'amministrazione** board member; **~ comunale** town councillor; **~ delegato** (*Comm*) managing director
con'siglio [kon'siʎʎo] *sm* (*suggerimento*) advice *no pl*, piece of advice; (*assemblea*) council; **~ d'amministrazione** board; **C~ d'Europa** Council of Europe; **~ di fabbrica** works council; **il C~ dei Ministri** (*Pol*) ≈ the Cabinet; **C~ di stato** *advisory body to the Italian government on administrative matters and their legal implications*; **C~ superiore della magistratura** *state body responsible for judicial appointments and regulations*; *see note*

CONSIGLI

The *Consiglio dei Ministri*, the Italian Cabinet, is headed by the "Presidente del Consiglio", the Prime Minister, who is the leader of the Government. The *Consiglio superiore della Magistratura*, the magistrates' governing body, ensures their autonomy and independence as enshrined in the Constitution. Chaired by the "Presidente della Repubblica", it mainly deals with appointments and transfers, and can take disciplinary action as required. Of the 30 magistrates elected to the *Consiglio* for a period of four years, 20 are chosen by their fellow magistrates and 10 by Parliament. The "Presidente della Repubblica" and the "Vicepresidente" are ex-officio members.

con'simile *ag* similar
consis'tente *ag* solid; (*fig*) sound, valid
consis'tenza [konsis'tɛntsa] *sf* (*di impasto*) consistency; (*di stoffa*) texture; **senza ~** (*sospetti, voci*) ill-founded, groundless; **~ di cassa/di magazzino** cash/stock in hand; **~ patrimoniale** financial solidity
con'sistere *vi*: **~ in** to consist of
consis'tito, -a *pp di* **consistere**
'CONSOB *sigla f* (*= Commissione nazionale per le società e la borsa*) *regulatory body for the Italian Stock Exchange*
consoci'arsi [konso'tʃarsi] *vr* to go into partnership
consociati'vismo [konsotʃati'vizmo] *sm* (*Pol*) pact-building
consocia'tivo, -a [konsotʃa'tivo] *ag* (*Pol: democrazia*) based on pacts
consoci'ato, -a [konso'tʃato] *ag* associated ■ *sm/f* associate
conso'lante *ag* consoling, comforting
conso'lare *ag* consular ■ *vt* (*confortare*) to console, comfort; (*rallegrare*) to cheer up; **consolarsi** *vr* to be comforted; to cheer up
conso'lato *sm* consulate
consolazi'one [konsolat'tsjone] *sf* consolation, comfort
'console[1] *sm* consul
console[2] [kɔ̃'sɔl] *sf* (*quadro di comando*) console
consolida'mento *sm* strengthening; consolidation
consoli'dare *vt* to strengthen, reinforce; (*Mil, terreno*) to consolidate; **consolidarsi** *vr* to consolidate
consolidazi'one [konsolidat'tsjone] *sf* strengthening; consolidation
consommé [kɔ̃sɔ'me] *sm inv* consommé

C

conso'nante *sf* consonant
conso'nanza [konso'nantsa] *sf* consonance
'consono, -a *ag*: **~ a** consistent with, consonant with
con'sorte *sm/f* consort
con'sorzio [kon'sɔrtsjo] *sm* consortium; **~ agrario** farmers' cooperative; **~ di garanzia** (*Comm*) underwriting syndicate
con'stare *vi*: **~ di** to consist of ■ *vb impers*: **mi consta che** it has come to my knowledge that, it appears that; **a quanto mi consta** as far as I know
consta'tare *vt* to establish, verify; (*notare*) to notice, observe
constatazi'one [konstatat'tsjone] *sf* observation; **~ amichevole** (*in incidenti*) *jointly-agreed statement for insurance purposes*
consu'eto, -a *ag* habitual, usual ■ *sm*: **come di ~** as usual
consuetudi'nario, -a *ag*: **diritto ~** (*Dir*) common law
consue'tudine *sf* habit; (*usanza*) custom
consu'lente *sm/f* consultant; **~ aziendale/tecnico** management/technical consultant
consu'lenza [konsu'lɛntsa] *sf* consultancy; **~ medica/legale** medical/legal advice; **ufficio di ~ fiscale** tax consultancy office; **~ tecnica** technical consultancy *o* advice
consul'tare *vt* to consult; **consultarsi** *vr*: **consultarsi con qn** to seek the advice of sb
consultazi'one [konsultat'tsjone] *sf* consultation; **consultazioni** *sfpl* (*Pol*) talks, consultations; **libro di ~** reference book
consul'tivo, -a *ag* consultative
consul'torio *sm*: **~ familiare** *o* **matrimoniale** marriage guidance centre; **~ pediatrico** children's clinic
consu'mare *vt* (*logorare*: *abiti, scarpe*) to wear out; (*usare*) to consume, use up; (*mangiare, bere*) to consume; (*Dir*) to consummate; **consumarsi** *vr* to wear out; to be used up; (*anche fig*) to be consumed; (*combustibile*) to burn out
consu'mato, -a *ag* (*vestiti, scarpe, tappeto*) worn; (*persona*: *esperto*) accomplished
consuma'tore *sm* consumer
consumazi'one [konsumat'tsjone] *sf* (*bibita*) drink; (*spuntino*) snack; (*Dir*) consummation
consu'mismo *sm* consumerism
con'sumo *sm* consumption; wear; use; **generi** *o* **beni di ~** consumer goods; **beni di largo ~** basic commodities; **imposta sui consumi** tax on consumer goods
consun'tivo *sm* (*Econ*) final balance
con'sunto, -a *ag* worn-out; (*viso*) wasted
'conta *sf* (*nei giochi*): **fare la ~** to see who is going to be "it"
con'tabile *ag* accounts *cpd*, accounting ■ *sm/f* accountant
contabilità *sf* (*attività, tecnica*) accounting, accountancy; (*insieme dei libri etc*) books *pl*, accounts *pl*; **(ufficio) ~** accounts department; **~ finanziaria** financial accounting; **~ di gestione** management accounting
contachi'lometri [kontaki'lɔmetri] *sm inv* ≈ mileometer
conta'dino, -a *sm/f* countryman(-woman); farm worker; (*peg*) peasant
contagi'are [konta'dʒare] *vt* to infect
con'tagio [kon'tadʒo] *sm* infection; (*per contatto diretto*) contagion; (*epidemia*) epidemic
contagi'oso, -a [konta'dʒoso] *ag* infectious; contagious
conta'giri [konta'dʒiri] *sm inv* (*Aut*) rev counter
conta'gocce [konta'gottʃe] *sm inv* dropper
contami'nare *vt* to contaminate
contaminazi'one [kontaminat'tsjone] *sf* contamination
con'tante *sm* cash; **pagare in contanti** to pay cash
con'tare *vt* to count; (*considerare*) to consider ■ *vi* to count, be of importance; **~ su qn** to count *o* rely on sb; **~ di fare qc** to intend to do sth; **ha i giorni contati, ha le ore contate** his days are numbered; **la gente che conta** people who matter
contas'catti *sm inv* telephone meter
conta'tore *sm* meter
contat'tare *vt* to contact
con'tatto *sm* contact; **essere in ~ con qn** to be in touch with sb; **fare ~** (*Elettr*: *fili*) to touch
'conte *sm* count
con'tea *sf* (*Storia*) earldom; (*Amm*) county
conteggi'are [konted'dʒare] *vt* to charge, put on the bill
con'teggio [kon'teddʒo] *sm* calculation
con'tegno [kon'teɲɲo] *sm* (*comportamento*) behaviour (*Brit*), behavior (*US*); (*atteggiamento*) attitude; **darsi un ~** (*ostentare disinvoltura*) to act nonchalant; (*ricomporsi*) to pull o.s. together
conte'gnoso, -a [konteɲ'ɲoso] *ag* reserved, dignified
contem'plare *vt* to contemplate, gaze at; (*Dir*) to make provision for
contempla'tivo, -a *ag* contemplative
contemplazi'one [kontemplat'tsjone] *sf* contemplation
con'tempo *sm*: **nel ~** meanwhile, in the meantime
contemporanea'mente *av* simultaneously; at the same time

contempo'raneo, -a *ag, sm/f* contemporary
conten'dente *sm/f* opponent, adversary
con'tendere *vi* (*competere*) to compete; (*litigare*) to quarrel ■ *vt*: **~ qc a qn** to contend with *o* be in competition with sb for sth
conte'nere *vt* to contain; **contenersi** *vr* to contain o.s.
conteni'tore *sm* container
conten'tabile *ag*: **difficilmente ~** difficult to please
conten'tare *vt* to please, satisfy; **contentarsi** *vr*: **contentarsi di** to be satisfied with, content o.s. with; **si contenta di poco** he is easily satisfied
conten'tezza [konten'tettsa] *sf* contentment
conten'tino *sm* sop
con'tento, -a *ag* pleased, glad; **~ di** pleased with
conte'nuto *ag* (*ira, entusiasmo*) restrained, suppressed; (*forza*) contained ■ *sm* contents *pl*; (*argomento*) content
contenzi'oso, -a [konten'tsjɔso] *ag* (*Dir*) contentious ■ *sm* (*Amm: ufficio*) legal department
con'teso, -a *pp di* **contendere** ■ *sf* dispute, argument
con'tessa *sf* countess
contes'tare *vt* (*Dir*) to notify; (*fig*) to dispute; **~ il sistema** to protest against the system
contesta'tore, -'trice *ag* anti-establishment ■ *sm/f* protester
contestazi'one [kontestat'tsjone] *sf* (*Dir: disputa*) dispute; (*: notifica*) notification; (*Pol*) anti-establishment activity; **in caso di ~** if there are any objections
con'testo *sm* context
con'tiguo, -a *ag*: **~ (a)** adjacent (to)
continen'tale *ag* continental
conti'nente *ag* continent ■ *sm* (*Geo*) continent; (*: terra ferma*) mainland
conti'nenza [konti'nɛntsa] *sf* continence
contin'gente [kontin'dʒɛnte] *ag* contingent ■ *sm* (*Comm*) quota; (*Mil*) contingent
contin'genza [kontin'dʒɛntsa] *sf* circumstance; **(indennità di) ~** cost-of-living allowance
continua'mente *av* (*senza interruzione*) continuously, nonstop; (*ripetutamente*) continually
continu'are *vt* to continue (with), go on with ■ *vi* to continue, go on; **~ a fare qc** to go on *o* continue doing sth; **continua a nevicare/a fare freddo** it's still snowing/cold
continua'tivo, -a *ag* (*occupazione*) permanent; (*periodo*) consecutive
continuazi'one [kontinuat'tsjone] *sf* continuation
continuità *sf* continuity
con'tinuo, -a *ag* (*numerazione*) continuous; (*pioggia*) continual, constant; (*Elettr: corrente*) direct; **di ~** continually
'conto *sm* (*calcolo*) calculation; (*Comm, Econ*) account; (*di ristorante, albergo*) bill; (*fig: stima*) consideration, esteem; **avere un ~ in sospeso (con qn)** to have an outstanding account (with sb); (*fig*) to have a score to settle (with sb); **fare i conti con qn** to settle one's account with sb; **fare ~ su qn** to count *o* rely on sb; **fare ~ che** (*supporre*) to suppose that; **rendere ~ a qn di qc** to be accountable to sb for sth; **rendersi ~ di qc/che** to realize sth/that; **tener ~ di qn/qc** to take sb/sth into account; **tenere qc da ~** to take great care of sth; **ad ogni buon ~** in any case; **di poco/nessun ~** of little/no importance; **per ~ di** on behalf of; **per ~ mio** as far as I'm concerned; (*da solo*) on my own; **a conti fatti, in fin dei conti** all things considered; **mi hanno detto strane cose sul suo ~** I've heard some strange things about him; **~ capitale** capital account; **~ cifrato** numbered account; **~ corrente** current account (*Brit*), checking account (*US*); **~ corrente postale** Post Office account; **~ economico** profit and loss account; **~ in partecipazione** joint account; **~ passivo** account payable; **~ profitti e perdite** profit and loss account; **~ alla rovescia** countdown; **~ valutario** foreign currency account
con'torcere [kon'tɔrtʃere] *vt* to twist; (*panni*) to wring (out); **contorcersi** *vr* to twist, writhe
contor'nare *vt* to surround; **contornarsi** *vr*: **contornarsi di** to surround o.s. with
con'torno *sm* (*linea*) outline, contour; (*ornamento*) border; (*Cuc*) vegetables *pl*; **fare da ~ a** to surround
contorsi'one *sf* contortion
con'torto, -a *pp di* **contorcere**
contrabban'dare *vt* to smuggle
contrabbandi'ere, -a *sm/f* smuggler
contrab'bando *sm* smuggling, contraband; **merce di ~** contraband, smuggled goods *pl*
contrab'basso *sm* (*Mus*) (double) bass
contraccambi'are *vt* (*favore etc*) to return; **vorrei ~** I'd like to show my appreciation
contraccet'tivo, -a [kontrattʃet'tivo] *ag, sm* contraceptive
contrac'colpo *sm* rebound; (*di arma da fuoco*) recoil; (*fig*) repercussion
con'trada *sf* street, district; *vedi anche* **Palio**
contrad'detto, -a *pp di* **contraddire**
contrad'dire *vt* to contradict; **contraddirsi** *vr* to contradict o.s.; (*uso reciproco: persone*) to

contradict each other *o* one another; (: *testimonianze etc*) to be contradictory
contraddis'tinguere *vt* (*merce*) to mark; (*fig*: *atteggiamento, persona*) to distinguish
contraddis'tinto, -a *pp di* **contraddistinguere**
contraddit'torio, -a *ag* contradictory; (*sentimenti*) conflicting ■ *sm* (*Dir*) cross-examination
contraddizi'one [kontraddit'tsjone] *sf* contradiction; **cadere in ~** to contradict o.s.; **essere in ~** (*tesi, affermazioni*) to contradict one another; **spirito di ~** argumentativeness
con'trae *etc vb vedi* **contrarre**
contra'ente *sm* contractor
contra'erea *sf* (*Mil*) anti-aircraft artillery
contra'ereo, -a *ag* anti-aircraft
contraf'fare *vt* (*persona*) to mimic; (*voce*) to disguise; (*firma*) to forge, counterfeit
contraf'fatto, -a *pp di* **contraffare** ■ *ag* counterfeit
contraffazi'one [kontraffat'tsjone] *sf* mimicking *no pl*; disguising *no pl*; forging *no pl*; (*cosa contraffatta*) forgery
contraf'forte *sm* (*Archit*) buttress; (*Geo*) spur
con'traggo *etc vb vedi* **contrarre**
con'tralto *sm* (*Mus*) contralto
contrap'pello *sm* (*Mil*) second roll call
contrappe'sare *vt* to counterbalance; (*fig*: *decisione*) to weigh up
contrap'peso *sm* counterbalance, counterweight
contrap'porre *vt*: **~ qc a qc** to counter sth with sth; (*paragonare*) to compare sth with sth; **contrapporsi** *vr*: **contrapporsi a qc** to contrast with sth, be opposed to sth
contrap'posto, -a *pp di* **contrapporre**
contraria'mente *av*: **~ a** contrary to
contrari'are *vt* (*contrastare*) to thwart, oppose; (*irritare*) to annoy, bother; **contrariarsi** *vr* to get annoyed
contrari'ato, -a *ag* annoyed
contrarietà *sf* adversity; (*fig*) aversion
con'trario, -a *ag* opposite; (*sfavorevole*) unfavourable (*Brit*), unfavorable (*US*) ■ *sm* opposite; **essere ~ a qc** (*persona*) to be against sth; **al ~** on the contrary; **in caso ~** otherwise; **avere qualcosa in ~** to have some objection; **non ho niente in ~** I have no objection
con'trarre *vt* (*malattia, debito*) to contract; (*muscoli*) to tense; (*abitudine, vizio*) to pick up; (*accordo, patto*) to enter into; **contrarsi** *vr* to contract; **~ matrimonio** to marry
contrasse'gnare [kontrassen'ɲare] *vt* to mark
contras'segno [kontras'seɲɲo] *sm* (*distintivo*) distinguishing mark; **spedire in ~** (*Comm*) to send COD
con'trassi *etc vb vedi* **contrarre**
contras'tante *ag* contrasting
contras'tare *vt* (*avversare*) to oppose; (*impedire*) to bar; (*negare*: *diritto*) to contest, dispute ■ *vi*: **~ (con)** (*essere in disaccordo*) to contrast (with); (*lottare*) to struggle (with)
con'trasto *sm* contrast; (*conflitto*) conflict; (*litigio*) dispute
contrat'tacco *sm* counterattack; **passare al ~** (*fig*) to fight back
contrat'tare *vt, vi* to negotiate
contrat'tempo *sm* hitch
con'tratto, -a *pp di* **contrarre** ■ *sm* contract; **~ di acquisto** purchase agreement; **~ di affitto, ~ di locazione** lease; **~ collettivo di lavoro** collective agreement; **~ di lavoro** contract of employment; **~ a termine** forward contract
contrattu'ale *ag* contractual; **forza ~** (*di sindacato*) bargaining power
contravve'nire *vi*: **~ a** (*legge*) to contravene; (*obbligo*) to fail to meet
contravven'tore, -'trice *sm/f* offender
contravve'nuto, -a *pp di* **contravvenire**
contravvenzi'one [kontravven'tsjone] *sf* contravention; (*ammenda*) fine
contrazi'one [kontrat'tsjone] *sf* contraction; (*di prezzi etc*) reduction
contribu'ente *sm/f* taxpayer; ratepayer (*Brit*), property tax payer (*US*)
contribu'ire *vi* to contribute
contribu'tivo, -a *ag* contributory
contri'buto *sm* contribution; (*sovvenzione*) subsidy, contribution; (*tassa*) tax; **contributi previdenziali** ≈ national insurance (*Brit*) *o* welfare (*US*) contributions; **contributi sindacali** trade union dues
con'trito, -a *ag* contrite, penitent
'contro *prep* against; **~ di me/lui** against me/him; **pastiglie ~ la tosse** throat lozenges; **~ pagamento** (*Comm*) on payment; **~ ogni mia aspettativa** contrary to my expectations; **per ~** on the other hand
contro'battere *vt* (*fig*: *a parole*) to answer back; (: *confutare*) to refute
controbilanci'are [kontrobilan'tʃare] *vt* to counterbalance
controcor'rente *av*: **andare ~** (*anche fig*) to swim against the tide
controcul'tura *sf* counterculture
contro'esodo *sm* return from holiday
contro'fax *sm inv* reply to a fax
controffen'siva *sf* counteroffensive
controfi'gura *sf* (*Cine*) double

controfir'mare *vt* to countersign
control'lare *vt* (*accertare*) to check; (*sorvegliare*) to watch, control; (*tenere nel proprio potere, fig: dominare*) to control; **controllarsi** *vr* to control o.s.
control'lato, -a *ag* (*persona*) self-possessed; (*reazioni*) controlled ■ *sf* (*Comm: società*) associated company
con'trollo *sm* check; watch; control; **base di ~** (*Aer*) ground control; **telefono sotto ~** tapped telephone; **visita di ~** (*Med*) checkup; **~ doganale** customs inspection; **~ di gestione** management control; **~ delle nascite** birth control; **~ di qualità** quality control
control'lore *sm* (*Ferr, Autobus*) (ticket) inspector; **~ di volo** *o* **del traffico aereo** air traffic controller
contro'luce [kontro'lutʃe] *sf inv* (*Fot*) backlit shot ■ *av*: **(in) ~** against the light; (*fotografare*) into the light
contro'mano *av*: **guidare ~** to drive on the wrong side of the road; (*in un senso unico*) to drive the wrong way up a one-way street
contropar'tita *sf* (*fig: compenso*): **come ~** in return
contropi'ede *sm* (*Sport*): **azione di ~** sudden counter-attack; **prendere qn in ~** (*fig*) to catch sb off his (*o* her) guard
controprodu'cente [kontroprodu'tʃɛnte] *ag* counterproductive
con'trordine *sm* counter-order; **salvo ~** unless I (*o* you *etc*) hear to the contrary
contro'senso *sm* (*contraddizione*) contradiction in terms; (*assurdità*) nonsense
controspio'naggio [kontrospio'naddʒo] *sm* counterespionage
controva'lore *sm* equivalent (value)
contro'vento *av* against the wind; **navigare ~** (*Naut*) to sail to windward
contro'versia *sf* controversy; (*Dir*) dispute; **~ sindacale** industrial dispute
contro'verso, -a *ag* controversial
contro'voglia [kontro'vɔʎʎa] *av* unwillingly
contu'mace [kontu'matʃe] *ag* (*Dir*): **rendersi ~** to default, fail to appear in court ■ *sm/f* (*Dir*) defaulter
contu'macia [kontu'matʃa] *sf* (*Dir*) default
contun'dente *ag*: **corpo ~** blunt instrument
contur'bante *ag* (*sguardo, bellezza*) disturbing
contur'bare *vt* to disturb, upset
contusi'one *sf* (*Med*) bruise
convale'scente [konvaleʃ'ʃɛnte] *ag, sm/f* convalescent
convale'scenza [konvaleʃ'ʃɛntsa] *sf* convalescence
con'valida *sf* (*Dir*) confirmation; (*di biglietto*) stamping
convali'dare *vt* (*Amm*) to validate; (*fig: sospetto, dubbio*) to confirm
con'vegno [kon'veɲɲo] *sm* (*incontro*) meeting; (*congresso*) convention, congress; (*luogo*) meeting place
conve'nevoli *smpl* civilities
conveni'ente *ag* suitable; (*vantaggioso*) profitable; (*: prezzo*) cheap
conveni'enza [konve'njɛntsa] *sf* suitability; advantage; cheapness; **convenienze** *sfpl* social conventions
conve'nire *vt* to agree upon ■ *vi* (*riunirsi*) to gather, assemble; (*concordare*) to agree; (*tornare utile*) to be worthwhile ■ *vb impers*: **conviene fare questo** it is advisable to do this; **conviene andarsene** we should go; **ne convengo** I agree; **come convenuto** as agreed; **in data da ~** on a date to be agreed; **come (si) conviene ad una signorina** as befits a young lady
conven'ticola *sf* (*cricca*) clique; (*riunione*) secret meeting
con'vento *sm* (*di frati*) monastery; (*di suore*) convent
conve'nuto, -a *pp di* **convenire** ■ *sm* (*cosa pattuita*) agreement ■ *sm/f* (*Dir*) defendant; **i convenuti** (*i presenti*) those present
convenzio'nale [konventsjo'nale] *ag* conventional
convenzio'nato, -a [konventsjo'nato] *ag* (*ospedale, clinica*) providing free health care, ≈ National Health Service *cpd* (*Brit*)
convenzi'one [konven'tsjone] *sf* (*Dir*) agreement; (*nella società*) convention; **le convenzioni (sociali)** social conventions
conver'gente [konver'dʒɛnte] *ag* convergent
conver'genza [konver'dʒɛntsa] *sf* convergence
con'vergere [kon'verdʒere] *vi* to converge
con'versa *sf* (*Rel*) lay sister
conver'sare *vi* to have a conversation, converse
conversazi'one [konversat'tsjone] *sf* conversation; **fare ~** (*chiacchierare*) to chat, have a chat
conversi'one *sf* conversion; **~ ad U** (*Aut*) U-turn
con'verso, -a *pp di* **convergere**; **per ~** *av* conversely
conver'tire *vt* (*trasformare*) to change; (*Inform, Pol, Rel*) to convert; **convertirsi** *vr*: **convertirsi (a)** to be converted (to)
conver'tito, -a *sm/f* convert
converti'tore *sm* (*Elettr*) converter
con'vesso, -a *ag* convex
convin'cente [konvin'tʃɛnte] *ag* convincing

con'vincere [kon'vintʃere] *vt* to convince; **~ qn di qc** to convince sb of sth; (*Dir*) to prove sb guilty of sth; **~ qn a fare qc** to persuade sb to do sth
con'vinto, -a *pp di* **convincere** ■ *ag*: **reo ~** (*Dir*) convicted criminal
convinzi'one [konvin'tsjone] *sf* conviction, firm belief
convis'suto, -a *pp di* **convivere**
convi'tato, -a *sm/f* guest
con'vitto *sm* (*Ins*) boarding school
convi'venza [konvi'vɛntsa] *sf* living together; (*Dir*) cohabitation
con'vivere *vi* to live together
convivi'ale *ag* convivial
convo'care *vt* to call, convene; (*Dir*) to summon
convocazi'one [konvokat'tsjone] *sf* meeting; summons *sg*; **lettera di ~** (letter of) notification to appear *o* attend
convogli'are [konvoʎ'ʎare] *vt* to convey; (*dirigere*) to direct, send
con'voglio [kon'vɔʎʎo] *sm* (*di veicoli*) convoy; (*Ferr*) train; **~ funebre** funeral procession
convo'lare *vi*: **~ a (giuste) nozze** (*scherzoso*) to tie the knot
convulsi'one *sf* convulsion
con'vulso, -a *ag* (*pianto*) violent, convulsive; (*attività*) feverish
COOP *abbr f* = **cooperativa**
coope'rare *vi*: **~ (a)** to cooperate (in)
coopera'tiva *sf* cooperative
cooperazi'one [kooperat'tsjone] *sf* cooperation
coordina'mento *sm* coordination
coordi'nare *vt* to coordinate
coordi'nato, -a *ag* (*movimenti*) coordinated ■ *sf* (*Ling, Geo, Mat*) coordinate ■ *smpl*: **coordinati** (*Moda*) coordinates
coordinazi'one [koordinat'tsjone] *sf* coordination
co'perchio [ko'pɛrkjo] *sm* cover; (*di pentola*) lid
co'perta *sf* cover; (*di lana*) blanket; (*da viaggio*) rug; (*Naut*) deck
coper'tina *sf* (*Stampa*) cover, jacket
co'perto, -a *pp di* **coprire** ■ *ag* covered; (*cielo*) overcast ■ *sm* place setting; (*posto a tavola*) place; (*al ristorante*) cover charge; **~ di** covered in *o* with
coper'tone *sm* (*telo impermeabile*) tarpaulin; (*Aut*) rubber tyre
coper'tura *sf* (*anche Econ, Mil*) cover; (*di edificio*) roofing; **fare un gioco di ~** (*Sport*) to play a defensive game; **~ assicurativa** insurance cover
'copia *sf* copy; (*Fot*) print; **brutta/bella ~** rough/final copy; **~ conforme** (*Dir*) certified copy; **~ omaggio** presentation copy
copi'are *vt* to copy
copia'trice [kopja'tritʃe] *sf* copier, copying machine
copincol'lare *vt* to copy and paste
copi'one *sm* (*Cine, Teat*) script
'coppa *sf* (*bicchiere*) goblet; (*per frutta, gelato*) dish; (*trofeo*) cup, trophy; **coppe** *sfpl* (*Carte*) *suit in Neapolitan pack of cards*
'coppia *sf* (*di persone*) couple; (*di animali, Sport*) pair
cop'rente *ag* (*colore, cosmetico*) covering; (*calze*) opaque
copri'capo *sm* headgear; (*cappello*) hat
coprifu'oco, -chi *sm* curfew
copri'letto *sm* bedspread
copripiu'mino *sm inv* duvet cover
co'prire *vt* to cover; (*occupare: carica, posto*) to hold; **coprirsi** *vr* (*cielo*) to cloud over; (*vestirsi*) to wrap up, cover up; (*Econ*) to cover o.s.; **coprirsi di** (*macchie, muffa*) to become covered in; **~ qn di baci** to smother sb with kisses; **~ le spese** to break even; **coprirsi le spalle** (*fig*) to cover o.s.
coque [kɔk] *sf*: **uovo alla ~** boiled egg
co'raggio [ko'raddʒo] *sm* courage, bravery; **~!** (*forza!*) come on!; (*animo!*) cheer up!; **farsi ~** to pluck up courage; **hai un bel ~!** (*sfacciataggine*) you've got a nerve *o* a cheek!
coraggi'oso, -a [korad'dʒoso] *ag* courageous, brave
co'rale *ag* choral; (*approvazione*) unanimous
co'rallo *sm* coral; **il mar dei Coralli** the Coral Sea
co'rano *sm* (*Rel*) Koran
co'razza [ko'rattsa] *sf* armour (*Brit*), armor (*US*); (*di animali*) carapace, shell; (*Mil*) armo(u)r(-plating)
coraz'zato, -a [korat'tsato] *ag* (*Mil*) armoured (*Brit*), armored (*US*) ■ *sf* battleship
corazzi'ere [korat'tsjɛre] *sm* (*Storia*) cuirassier; (*guardia presidenziale*) *carabiniere of the President's guard*
corbelle'ria *sf* stupid remark; **corbellerie** *sfpl* (*sciocchezze*) nonsense *no pl*
'corda *sf* cord; (*fune*) rope; (*spago, Mus*) string; **dare ~ a qn** (*fig*) to let sb have his (*o* her) way; **tenere sulla ~ qn** (*fig*) to keep sb on tenterhooks; **tagliare la ~** (*fig*) to slip away, sneak off; **essere giù di ~** to feel down; **corde vocali** vocal cords
cor'data *sf* (*Alpinismo*) roped party; (*fig*) *alliance system in financial and business world*
cordi'ale *ag* cordial, warm ■ *sm* (*bevanda*) cordial
cordialità *sf inv* warmth, cordiality ■ *sfpl* (*saluti*) best wishes

cor'doglio [kor'dɔʎʎo] *sm* grief; (*lutto*) mourning
cor'done *sm* cord, string; (*linea: di polizia*) cordon; **~ ombelicale** umbilical cord; **~ sanitario** quarantine line
Co'rea *sf*: **la ~** Korea; **la ~ del Nord/Sud** North/South Korea
core'ano, -a *ag, sm/f* Korean
coreogra'fia *sf* choreography
core'ografo, -a *sm/f* choreographer
cori'aceo, -a [ko'rjatʃeo] *ag* (*Bot, Zool*) coriaceous; (*fig*) tough
cori'andolo *sm* (*Bot*) coriander; **coriandoli** *smpl* (*per carnevale etc*) confetti *no pl*
cori'care *vt* to put to bed; **coricarsi** *vr* to go to bed
coricherò *etc* [korike'rɔ] *vb vedi* **coricare**
Co'rinto *sf* Corinth
co'rista, -i, e *sm/f* (*Rel*) choir member, chorister; (*Teat*) member of the chorus
'corna *sfpl vedi* **corno**
cor'nacchia [kor'nakkja] *sf* crow
corna'musa *sf* bagpipes *pl*
'cornea *sf* (*Anat*) cornea
'corner *sm inv* (*Calcio*) corner (kick); **salvarsi in ~** (*fig: in gara, esame etc*) to get through by the skin of one's teeth
cor'netta *sf* (*Mus*) cornet; (*Tel*) receiver
cor'netto *sm* (*Cuc*) croissant; **~ acustico** ear trumpet
cor'nice [kor'nitʃe] *sf* frame; (*fig*) background, setting
cornici'one [korni'tʃone] *sm* (*di edificio*) ledge; (*Archit*) cornice
'corno *sm* (*Zool: pl(f) corna, Mus*) horn; (*fam*): **fare le corna a qn** to be unfaithful to sb; **dire peste e corna di qn** to call sb every name under the sun; **un ~!** not on your life!
Corno'vaglia [korno'vaʎʎa] *sf*: **la ~** Cornwall
cor'nuto, -a *ag* (*con corna*) horned; (*fam!: marito*) cuckolded ■ *sm* (*fam!*) cuckold; (*: insulto*) bastard (*!*)
'coro *sm* chorus; (*Rel*) choir
corol'lario *sm* corollary
co'rona *sf* crown; (*di fiori*) wreath
corona'mento *sm* (*di impresa*) completion; (*di carriera*) crowning achievement; **il ~ dei propri sogni** the fulfilment of one's dreams
coro'nare *vt* to crown
coro'naria *sf* coronary artery
'corpo *sm* body; (*cadavere*) (dead) body; (*militare, diplomatico*) corps *inv*; (*di opere*) corpus; **prendere ~** to take shape; **darsi anima e ~ a** to give o.s. heart and soul to; **a ~ a ~** hand-to-hand; **~ d'armata** army corps; **~ di ballo** corps de ballet; **~ dei carabinieri** ≈ police force; **~ celeste** heavenly body; **~ di guardia** (*soldati*) guard; (*locale*) guardroom; **~ insegnante** teaching staff; **~ del reato** material evidence
corpo'rale *ag* bodily; (*punizione*) corporal
corpora'tura *sf* build, physique
corporazi'one [korporat'tsjone] *sf* corporation
cor'poreo, -a *ag* bodily, physical
cor'poso, -a *ag* (*vino*) full-bodied
corpu'lento, -a *ag* stout, corpulent
corpu'lenza [korpu'lɛntsa] *sf* stoutness, corpulence
cor'puscolo *sm* corpuscle
corre'dare *vt*: **~ di** to provide *o* furnish with; **domanda corredata dai seguenti documenti** application accompanied by the following documents
cor'redo *sm* equipment; (*di sposa*) trousseau
cor'reggere [kor'rɛddʒere] *vt* to correct; (*compiti*) to correct, mark
cor'rente *ag* (*fiume*) flowing; (*acqua del rubinetto*) running; (*moneta, prezzo*) current; (*comune*) everyday ■ *sm*: **essere al ~ (di)** to be well-informed (about) ■ *sf* (*movimento di liquido*) current, stream; (*spiffero*) draught; (*Elettr, Meteor*) current; (*fig*) trend, tendency; **mettere al ~ (di)** to inform (of); **la vostra lettera del 5 ~ mese** (*in lettere commerciali*) in your letter of the 5th inst.; **articoli di qualità ~** average-quality products; **~ alternata (c.a.)** alternating current (AC); **~ continua (c.c.)** direct current (DC)
corrente'mente *av* (*comunemente*) commonly; **parlare una lingua ~** to speak a language fluently
corren'tista, -i, e *sm/f* (current (*Brit*) *o* checking (*US*)) account holder
cor'reo, -a *sm/f* (*Dir*) accomplice
'correre *vi* to run; (*precipitarsi*) to rush; (*partecipare a una gara*) to race, run; (*fig: diffondersi*) to go round ■ *vt* (*Sport: gara*) to compete in; (*rischio*) to run; (*pericolo*) to face; **~ dietro a qn** to run after sb; **corre voce che ...** it is rumoured that ...
corresponsabilità *sf* joint responsibility; (*Dir*) joint liability
corresponsi'one *sf* payment
cor'ressi *etc vb vedi* **correggere**
corret'tezza [korret'tettsa] *sf* (*di comportamento*) correctness; (*Sport*) fair play
cor'retto, -a *pp di* **correggere** ■ *ag* (*comportamento*) correct, proper; **caffè ~ al cognac** coffee laced with brandy
corret'tore, -'trice *sm/f*: **~ di bozze** proofreader ■ *sm*: **(liquido) ~** correction fluid
correzi'one [korret'tsjone] *sf* correction; marking; **~ di bozze** proofreading

cor'rida *sf* bullfight
corri'doio *sm* corridor; **manovre di ~** *(Pol)* lobbying *sg*
corri'dore *sm* *(Sport)* runner; (: *su veicolo*) racer
corri'era *sf* coach *(Brit)*, bus
corri'ere *sm* *(diplomatico, di guerra)* courier; *(posta)* mail, post; *(spedizioniere)* carrier
corri'mano *sm* handrail
corrispet'tivo *sm* amount due; **versare a qn il ~ di una prestazione** to pay sb the amount due for his (*o* her) services
corrispon'dente *ag* corresponding ■ *sm/f* correspondent
corrispon'denza [korrispon'dɛntsa] *sf* correspondence; **~ in arrivo/partenza** incoming/outgoing mail
corris'pondere *vi* *(equivalere)*: **~ (a)** to correspond (to); *(per lettera)*: **~ con** to correspond with ■ *vt* *(stipendio)* to pay; *(fig: amore)* to return
corris'posto, -a *pp di* **corrispondere**
corrobo'rare *vt* to strengthen, fortify; *(fig)* to corroborate, bear out
cor'rodere *vt*, **cor'rodersi** *vr* to corrode
cor'rompere *vt* to corrupt; *(comprare)* to bribe
corrosi'one *sf* corrosion
corro'sivo, -a *ag* corrosive
cor'roso, -a *pp di* **corrodere**
corrotta'mente *av* corruptly
cor'rotto, -a *pp di* **corrompere** ■ *ag* corrupt
corrucci'arsi [korrut'tʃarsi] *vr* to grow angry *o* vexed
corru'gare *vt* to wrinkle; **~ la fronte** to knit one's brows
cor'ruppi *etc vb vedi* **corrompere**
corrut'tela *sf* corruption, depravity
corruzi'one [korrut'tsjone] *sf* corruption; bribery; **~ di minorenne** *(Dir)* corruption of a minor
'corsa *sf* running *no pl*; *(gara)* race; *(di autobus, taxi)* journey, trip; **fare una ~** to run, dash; *(Sport)* to run a race; **andare** *o* **essere di ~** to be in a hurry; **~ automobilistica/ciclistica** motor/cycle racing; **~ campestre** cross-country racing; **~ ad ostacoli** *(Ippica)* steeplechase; *(Atletica)* hurdles race
cor'saro, -a *ag*: **nave corsara** privateer ■ *sm* privateer
'corsi *etc vb vedi* **correre**
cor'sia *sf* *(Aut, Sport)* lane; *(di ospedale)* ward; **~ di emergenza** *(Aut)* hard shoulder; **~ preferenziale** ≈ bus lane; *(fig)* fast track; **~ di sorpasso** *(Aut)* overtaking lane
'Corsica *sf*: **la ~** Corsica
cor'sivo *sm* cursive (writing); *(Tip)* italics *pl*
'corso, -a *pp di* **correre** ■ *ag, sm/f* Corsican ■ *sm* course; *(strada cittadina)* main street; *(di unità monetaria)* circulation; *(di titoli, valori)* rate, price; **dar libero ~ a** to give free expression to; **in ~** in progress, under way; *(annata)* current; **~ d'acqua** river; stream; *(artificiale)* waterway; **~ serale** evening class; **aver ~ legale** to be legal tender
'corte *sf* (court)yard; *(Dir, regale)* court; **fare la ~ a qn** to court sb; **~ d'appello** court of appeal; **~ di cassazione** final court of appeal; **C~ dei Conti** *State audit court*; **C~ Costituzionale** *special court dealing with constitutional and ministerial matters*; **~ marziale** court-martial; *see note*

CORTE

The *Corte d'Appello* hears appeals against sentences passed by courts in both civil and criminal cases and can modify sentences where necessary. The *Corte d'Assise* tries serious crimes such as manslaughter and murder; its judges include both legal professionals and members of the public. Similar in structure, the *Corte d'Assise d'Appello* hears appeals imposed by these two courts. The *Corte di Cassazione* is the highest judicial authority and ensures that the law is correctly applied by the other courts; it may call for a re-trial if required. The politically independent *Corte Costituzionale* decides whether laws comply with the principles of the Constitution, and has the power to impeach the "Presidente della Repubblica". The *Corte dei Conti* ensures the Government's compliance with the law and the Constitution. Reporting directly to Parliament, it oversees the financial aspects of the state budget.

cor'teccia, -ce [kor'tettʃa] *sf* bark
corteggia'mento [korteddʒa'mento] *sm* courtship
corteggi'are [korted'dʒare] *vt* to court
corteggia'tore [korteddʒa'tore] *sm* suitor
cor'teo *sm* procession; **~ funebre** funeral cortège
cor'tese *ag* courteous
corte'sia *sf* courtesy; **fare una ~ a qn** to do sb a favour; **per ~, dov'è ...?** excuse me, please, where is ...?
cortigi'ano, -a [korti'dʒano] *sm/f* courtier ■ *sf* courtesan
cor'tile *sm* (court)yard
cor'tina *sf* curtain; *(anche fig)* screen
corti'sone *sm* cortisone

ˈ**corto, -a** *ag* short ▪ *av*: **tagliare ~** to come straight to the point; **essere a ~ di qc** to be short of sth; **essere a ~ di parole** to be at a loss for words; **la settimana corta** the 5-day week; **~ circuito** short-circuit
cortocirˈcuito [kortotʃirˈkuito] *sm* = **corto circuito**
cortomeˈtraggio [kortomeˈtraddʒo] *sm* short (feature film)
corˈvino, -a *ag* (*capelli*) jet-black
ˈ**corvo** *sm* raven
ˈ**cosa** *sf* thing; (*faccenda*) affair, matter, business *no pl*; **(che) ~?** what?; **(che) cos'è?** what is it?; **a ~ pensi?** what are you thinking about?; **tante belle cose!** all the best!; **ormai è ~ fatta!** (*positivo*) it's in the bag!; (*negativo*) it's done now!; **a cose fatte** when it's all over
ˈ**Cosa ˈNostra** *sf* Cosa Nostra
ˈ**cosca, -sche** *sf* (*di mafiosi*) clan
ˈ**coscia, -sce** [ˈkɔʃʃa] *sf* thigh; **~ di pollo** (*Cuc*) chicken leg
cosciˈente [koʃˈʃɛnte] *ag* conscious; **~ di** conscious *o* aware of
cosciˈenza [koʃˈʃɛntsa] *sf* conscience; (*consapevolezza*) consciousness; **~ politica** political awareness
coscienziˈoso, -a [koʃʃenˈtsjoso] *ag* conscientious
cosciˈotto [koʃˈʃɔtto] *sm* (*Cuc*) leg
cosˈcritto *sm* (*Mil*) conscript
coscriziˈone [koskritˈtsjone] *sf* conscription

PAROLA CHIAVE

così *av* **1** (*in questo modo*) like this, (in) this way; (*in tal modo*) so; **le cose stanno così** this is the way things stand; **non ho detto così!** I didn't say that!; **come stai? — (e) così** how are you? — so-so; **e così via** and so on; **per così dire** so to speak; **così sia** amen
2 (*tanto*) so; **così lontano** so far away; **un ragazzo così intelligente** such an intelligent boy
▪ *ag inv* (*tale*): **non ho mai visto un film così** I've never seen such a film
▪ *cong* **1** (*perciò*) so, therefore; **e così ho deciso di lasciarlo** so I decided to leave him
2: **così ... come** as ... as; **non è così bravo come te** he's not as good as you; **così ... che** so ... that

cosicché [kosikˈke] *cong* so (that)
cosidˈdetto, -a *ag* so-called
cosˈmesi *sf* (*scienza*) cosmetics *sg*; (*prodotti*) cosmetics *pl*; (*trattamento*) beauty treatment
cosˈmetico, -a, ci, che *ag, sm* cosmetic
ˈ**cosmico, -a, ci, che** *ag* cosmic
ˈ**cosmo** *sm* cosmos
cosmoˈnauta, -i, e *sm/f* cosmonaut
cosmopoˈlita, -i, e *ag* cosmopolitan
ˈ**coso** *sm* (*fam: oggetto*) thing, thingumajig; (*: aggeggio*) contraption; (*: persona*) what's his name, thingumajig
cosˈpargere [kosˈpardʒere] *vt*: **~ di** to sprinkle with
cosˈparso, -a *pp di* **cospargere**
cosˈpetto *sm*: **al ~ di** in front of; in the presence of
cospicuità *sf* vast quantity
cosˈpicuo, -a *ag* considerable, large
cospiˈrare *vi* to conspire
cospiraˈtore, -ˈtrice *sm/f* conspirator
cospiraziˈone [kospiratˈtsjone] *sf* conspiracy
ˈ**cossi** *etc vb vedi* **cuocere**
Cost. *abbr* = **costituzione**
ˈ**costa** *sf* (*tra terra e mare*) coast(line); (*litorale*) shore; (*pendio*) slope; (*Anat*) rib; **navigare sotto ~** to hug the coast; **la C~ Azzurra** the French Riviera; **la C~ d'Avorio** the Ivory Coast; **velluto a coste** corduroy
costà *av* there
cosˈtante *ag* constant; (*persona*) steadfast ▪ *sf* constant
cosˈtanza [kosˈtantsa] *sf* (*gen*) constancy; (*fermezza*) constancy, steadfastness; **il Lago di C~** Lake Constance
cosˈtare *vi, vt* to cost; **~ caro** to be expensive, cost a lot; **~ un occhio della testa** to cost a fortune; **costi quel che costi** no matter what
ˈ**Costa ˈRica** *sf*: **la ~** Costa Rica
cosˈtata *sf* (*Cuc: di manzo*) large chop
cosˈtato *sm* (*Anat*) ribs *pl*
costeggiˈare [kostedˈdʒare] *vt* to be close to; to run alongside
cosˈtei *pron vedi* **costui**
costellaziˈone [kostellatˈtsjone] *sf* constellation
costerˈnare *vt* to dismay
costerˈnato, -a *ag* dismayed
costernaziˈone [kosternatˈtsjone] *sf* dismay, consternation
costiˈero, -a *ag* coastal, coast *cpd* ▪ *sf* stretch of coast
costiˈpato, -a *ag* (*stitico*) constipated
costituˈire *vt* (*comitato, gruppo*) to set up, form; (*collezione*) to put together, build up; (*elementi, parti: comporre*) to make up, constitute; (*rappresentare*) to constitute; (*Dir*) to appoint; **costituirsi** *vr*: **costituirsi (alla polizia)** to give o.s. up (to the police), **costituirsi parte civile** (*Dir*) *to associate in an action with the public prosecutor for damages*; **il fatto non costituisce reato** this is not a crime

costitu'tivo, -a *ag* constituent, component; **atto ~** (*Dir: di società*) memorandum of association
costituzio'nale [kostituttsjo'nale] *ag* constitutional
costituzi'one [kostitut'tsjone] *sf* setting up; building up; constitution
'costo *sm* cost; **sotto ~** for less than cost price; **a ogni** *o* **qualunque ~, a tutti i costi** at all costs; **costi di esercizio** running costs; **costi fissi** fixed costs; **costi di gestione** operating costs; **costi di produzione** production costs
'costola *sf* (*Anat*) rib; **ha la polizia alle costole** the police are hard on his heels
costo'letta *sf* (*Cuc*) cutlet
cos'toro *pron pl vedi* **costui**
cos'toso, -a *ag* expensive, costly
cos'tretto, -a *pp di* **costringere**
cos'tringere [kos'trindʒere] *vt*: **~ qn a fare qc** to force sb to do sth
costrit'tivo, -a *ag* coercive
costrizi'one [kostrit'tsjone] *sf* coercion
costru'ire *vt* to construct, build
costrut'tivo, -a *ag* (*Edil*) building *cpd*; (*fig*) constructive
costruzi'one [kostrut'tsjone] *sf* construction, building; **di ~ inglese** British-made
cos'tui, cos'tei (*pl* **cos'toro**) *pron* (*soggetto*) he/she; (*pl*) they; (*complemento*) him/her; (*pl*) them; **si può sapere chi è ~?** (*peg*) just who is that fellow?
cos'tume *sm* (*uso*) custom; (*foggia di vestire, indumento*) costume; **il buon ~** public morality; **donna di facili costumi** woman of easy morals; **~ da bagno** bathing *o* swimming costume (*Brit*), swimsuit; (*da uomo*) bathing *o* swimming trunks *pl*
costu'mista, -i, e *sm/f* costume maker, costume designer
co'tenna *sf* bacon rind
co'togna [ko'toɲɲa] *sf* quince
coto'letta *sf* (*di maiale, montone*) chop; (*di vitello, agnello*) cutlet
coto'nare *vt* (*capelli*) to backcomb
co'tone *sm* cotton; **~ idrofilo** cotton wool (*Brit*), absorbent cotton (*US*)
cotoni'ficio [kotoni'fitʃo] *sm* cotton mill
'cotta *sf* (*Rel*) surplice; (*fam: innamoramento*) crush
'cottimo *sm*: **lavorare a ~** to do piecework
'cotto, -a *pp di* **cuocere** ■ *ag* cooked; (*fam: innamorato*) head-over-heels in love ■ *sm* brickwork; **~ a puntino** cooked to perfection; **dirne di cotte e di crude a qn** to call sb every name under the sun; **farne di cotte e di crude** to get up to all kinds of mischief; **mattone di ~** fired brick; **pavimento in ~** tile floor
cot'tura *sf* cooking; (*in forno*) baking; (*in umido*) stewing; **~ a fuoco lento** simmering; **angolo (di) ~** cooking area
co'vare *vt* to hatch; (*fig: malattia*) to be sickening for; (*: odio, rancore*) to nurse ■ *vi* (*fuoco, fig*) to smoulder (*Brit*), smolder (*US*)
co'vata *sf* (*anche fig*) brood
'covo *sm* den; **~ di terroristi** terrorist base
co'vone *sm* sheaf
'cozza ['kɔttsa] *sf* mussel
coz'zare [kot'tsare] *vi*: **~ contro** to bang into, collide with
'cozzo ['kɔttso] *sm* collision
C.P. *abbr* (*= cartolina postale*) pc; (*Posta*) *vedi* **casella postale**; (*Naut*) = **capitaneria (di porto)**; (*Dir*) = **codice penale**
CPT *sigla m inv* = **Centro di Permanenza Temporanea**
crac'care *vt* (*Inform*) to crack
crack *sm inv* (*droga*) crack
Cra'covia *sf* Cracow
'crampo *sm* cramp
'cranio *sm* skull
cra'tere *sm* crater
cra'vatta *sf* tie; **~ a farfalla** bow tie
cravat'tino *sm* bow tie
cre'anza [kre'antsa] *sf* manners *pl*; **per buona ~** out of politeness
cre'are *vt* to create
creatività *sf* creativity
cre'ato *sm* creation
crea'tore, -'trice *ag* creative ■ *sm/f* creator; **un ~ di alta moda** fashion designer; **andare al C~** to go to meet one's maker
crea'tura *sf* creature; (*bimbo*) baby, infant
creazi'one [kreat'tsjone] *sf* creation; (*fondazione*) foundation, establishment
'crebbi *etc vb vedi* **crescere**
cre'dente *sm/f* (*Rel*) believer
cre'denza [kre'dɛntsa] *sf* belief; (*armadio*) sideboard
credenzi'ali [kreden'tsjali] *sfpl* credentials
'credere *vt* to believe ■ *vi*: **~ in, ~ a** to believe in; **~ qn onesto** to believe sb (to be) honest; **~ che** to believe *o* think that; **credersi furbo** to think one is clever; **lo credo bene!** I can well believe it!; **fai quello che credi** *o* **come credi** do as you please
cre'dibile *ag* credible, believable
credibilità *sf* credibility
credi'tizio, -a [kredi'tittsjo] *ag* credit
'credito *sm* (*anche Comm*) credit; (*reputazione*) esteem, repute; **comprare a ~** to buy on credit; **~ agevolato** easy credit terms; **~ d'imposta** tax credit

credi'tore, -'trice *sm/f* creditor
'credo *sm inv* creed
'credulo, -a *ag* credulous
credu'lone, -a *sm/f* simpleton, sucker (*fam*)
'crema *sf* cream; (*con uova, zucchero etc*) custard; **~ idratante** moisturizing cream; **~ pasticciera** confectioner's custard; **~ solare** sun cream
cre'mare *vt* to cremate
crema'torio *sm* crematorium
cremazi'one [kremat'tsjone] *sf* cremation
'cremisi *ag inv, sm inv* crimson
Crem'lino *sm*: **il ~** the Kremlin
cremo'nese *ag* of (*o* from) Cremona
cre'moso, -a *ag* creamy
'crepa *sf* crack
cre'paccio [kre'pattʃo] *sm* large crack, fissure; (*di ghiacciaio*) crevasse
crepacu'ore *sm* broken heart
crepa'pelle *av*: **ridere a ~** to split one's sides laughing
cre'pare *vi* (*fam: morire*) to snuff it (*Brit*), kick the bucket; **~ dalle risa** to split one's sides laughing; **~ dall'invidia** to be green with envy
crepi'tare *vi* (*fuoco*) to crackle; (*pioggia*) to patter
crepi'tio, -ii *sm* crackling; pattering
cre'puscolo *sm* twilight, dusk
cre'scendo [kreʃʃɛndo] *sm* (*Mus*) crescendo
cre'scente [kreʃʃɛnte] *ag* (*gen*) growing, increasing; (*luna*) waxing
'crescere ['kreʃʃere] *vi* to grow ■ *vt* (*figli*) to raise
cre'scione [kreʃʃone] *sm* watercress
'crescita ['kreʃʃita] *sf* growth
cresci'uto, -a [kreʃʃuto] *pp di* **crescere**
'cresima *sf* (*Rel*) confirmation
cresi'mare *vt* to confirm
'crespo, -a *ag* (*capelli*) frizzy; (*tessuto*) puckered ■ *sm* crêpe
'cresta *sf* crest; (*di polli, uccelli*) crest, comb; **alzare la ~** (*fig*) to become cocky; **abbassare la ~** (*fig*) to climb down; **essere sulla ~ dell'onda** (*fig*) to be riding high
'Creta *sf* Crete
'creta *sf* (*gesso*) chalk; (*argilla*) clay
cre'tese *ag, sm/f* Cretan
creti'nata *sf* (*fam*): **dire/fare una ~** to say/do a stupid thing
cre'tino, -a *ag* stupid ■ *sm/f* idiot, fool
CRI *sigla f* = **Croce Rossa Italiana**
cric *sm inv* (*Tecn*) jack
'cricca, -che *sf* clique
'cricco, -chi *sm* = **cric**
cri'ceto [kri'tʃɛto] *sm* hamster
crimi'nale *ag, sm/f* criminal
criminalità *sf* crime; **~ organizzata** organized crime
'Criminalpol *abbr* = **polizia criminale**
'crimine *sm* (*Dir*) crime
criminolo'gia [kriminolo'dʒia] *sf* criminology
crimi'noso, -a *ag* criminal
cri'nale *sm* ridge
'crine *sm* horsehair
crini'era *sf* mane
'cripta *sf* crypt
crip'tare *vt* (*TV: programma*) to encrypt
crip'tato, -a *ag* (*programma, messaggio*) encrypted
crisan'temo *sm* chrysanthemum; *vedi anche* **Giorno dei Morti**
'crisi *sf inv* crisis; (*Med*) attack, fit; **essere in ~** (*partito, impresa etc*) to be in a state of crisis; **~ energetica** energy crisis; **~ di nervi** attack *o* fit of nerves
cristalle'ria *sf* (*fabbrica*) crystal glassworks *sg*; (*oggetti*) crystalware
cristal'lino, -a *ag* (*Mineralogia*) crystalline; (*fig: suono, acque*) crystal clear ■ *sm* (*Anat*) crystalline lens
cristalliz'zare [kristallid'dzare] *vi*, **cristalliz'zarsi** *vr* to crystallize; (*fig*) to become fossilized
cris'tallo *sm* crystal
cristia'nesimo *sm* Christianity
cristianità *sf* Christianity; (*i cristiani*) Christendom
cristi'ano, -a *ag, sm/f* Christian; **un povero ~** (*fig*) a poor soul *o* beggar; **comportarsi da ~** (*fig*) to behave in a civilized manner
'cristo *sm*: **C~** Christ; **(un) povero ~** (a) poor beggar
cri'terio *sm* criterion; (*buon senso*) (common) sense
'critica, -che *sf vedi* **critico**
criti'care *vt* to criticize
'critico, -a, ci, che *ag* critical ■ *sm* critic ■ *sf* criticism; **la critica** (*attività*) criticism; (*persone*) the critics *pl*
criti'cone, -a *sm/f* faultfinder
crivel'lare *vt*: **~ (di)** to riddle (with)
cri'vello *sm* riddle
cro'ato, -a *ag, sm/f* Croatian, Croat
Cro'azia [kro'attsja] *sf*: **la ~** Croatia
croc'cante *ag* crisp, crunchy ■ *sm* (*Cuc*) almond crunch
'crocchia ['krɔkkja] *sf* chignon, bun
'crocchio ['krɔkkjo] *sm* (*di persone*) small group, cluster
'croce ['krotʃe] *sf* cross; **in ~** (*di traverso*) crosswise; (*fig*) on tenterhooks; **mettere in ~** (*anche fig: criticare*) to crucify; (*: tormentare*) to nag to death; **la C~ Rossa** the Red Cross; **~ uncinata** swastika

croce'figgere *etc* [krotʃe'fiddʒere] = **crocifiggere** *etc*
croceros'sina [krotʃeros'sina] *sf* Red Cross nurse
croce'via [krotʃe'via] *sm inv* crossroads *sg*
croci'ato, -a [kro'tʃato] *ag* cross-shaped ■ *sm* (*anche fig*) crusader ■ *sf* crusade
cro'cicchio [kro'tʃikkjo] *sm* crossroads *sg*
croci'era [kro'tʃɛra] *sf* (*viaggio*) cruise; (*Archit*) transept; **altezza di ~** (*Aer*) cruising height; **velocità di ~** (*Aer, Naut*) cruising speed
croci'figgere [krotʃi'fiddʒere] *vt* to crucify
crocifissi'one [krotʃifis'sjone] *sf* crucifixion
croci'fisso, -a [krotʃi'fisso] *pp di* **crocifiggere** ■ *sm* crucifix
crogio'larsi [krodʒo'larsi] *vr*: **~ al sole** to bask in the sun
crogi'olo [kro'dʒɔlo], **crogiu'olo** [kro'dʒwɔlo] *sm* crucible; (*fig*) melting pot
crol'lare *vi* to collapse
'crollo *sm* collapse; (*di prezzi*) slump, sudden fall
'croma *sf* (*Mus*) quaver (*Brit*), eighth note (*US*)
cro'mato, -a *ag* chromium-plated
'cromo *sm* chrome, chromium
cromo'soma, -i *sm* chromosome
'cronaca, -che *sf* chronicle; (*Stampa*) news *sg*; (: *rubrica*) column; (*TV, Radio*) commentary; **fatto** *o* **episodio di ~** news item; **~ nera** crime news *sg*; crime column
'cronico, -a, ci, che *ag* chronic
cro'nista, -i *sm* (*Stampa*) reporter, columnist
cronis'toria *sf* chronicle; (*fig: ironico*) blow-by-blow account
cro'nografo *sm* (*strumento*) chronograph
cronolo'gia [kronolo'dʒia] *sf* chronology
cronome'trare *vt* to time
cro'nometro *sm* chronometer; (*a scatto*) stopwatch
'crosta *sf* crust; (*Med*) scab; (*Zool*) shell; (*di ghiaccio*) layer; (*fig peg: quadro*) daub
cros'tacei [kros'tatʃei] *smpl* shellfish
cros'tata *sf* (*Cuc*) tart
cros'tino *sm* (*Cuc*) croûton; (: *da antipasto*) canapé
crucci'are [krut'tʃare] *vt* to torment, worry; **crucciarsi** *vr*: **crucciarsi per** to torment o.s. over
'cruccio ['kruttʃo] *sm* worry, torment
cruci'ale [kru'tʃale] *ag* crucial
cruci'verba [krutʃi'vɛrba] *sm inv* crossword (puzzle)
cru'dele *ag* cruel
crudeltà *sf* cruelty
'crudo, -a *ag* (*non cotto*) raw; (*aspro*) harsh, severe
cru'ento, -a *ag* bloody
cru'miro *sm* (*peg*) blackleg (*Brit*), scab
'cruna *sf* eye (of a needle)
'crusca *sf* bran
crus'cotto *sm* (*Aut*) dashboard
CS *sigla* = **Cosenza**
c.s. *abbr* = **come sopra**
CSI [tʃi'ɛsse'i] *sigla f* (= *Comunità di Stati Indipendenti*) CIS
CSM [tʃiɛsse'ɛmme] *sigla m* (= *consiglio superiore della magistratura*) Magistrates' Board of Supervisors
CT *sigla* = **Catania**
c.t. *abbr* = **commissario tecnico**
'Cuba *sf* Cuba
cu'bano, -a *ag, sm/f* Cuban
cu'betto *sm* (small) cube; **~ di ghiaccio** ice cube
'cubico, -a, ci, che *ag* cubic
cu'bista *sf* podium dancer, *dancer who performs on stage in a club*
'cubo, -a *ag* cubic ■ *sm* cube; **elevare al ~** (*Mat*) to cube
cuc'cagna [kuk'kaɲɲa] *sf*: **paese della ~** land of plenty; **albero della ~** greasy pole (*fig*)
cuc'cetta [kut'tʃetta] *sf* (*Ferr*) couchette; (*Naut*) berth
cucchiai'ata [kukkja'jata] *sf* spoonful; tablespoonful
cucchia'ino [kukkja'ino] *sm* teaspoon; coffee spoon
cucchi'aio [kuk'kjajo] *sm* spoon; (*da tavola*) tablespoon; (*cucchiaiata*) spoonful; tablespoonful
'cuccia, -ce ['kuttʃa] *sf* dog's bed; **a ~!** down!
cuccio'lata [kuttʃo'lata] *sf* litter
'cucciolo ['kuttʃolo] *sm* cub; (*di cane*) puppy
cu'cina [ku'tʃina] *sf* (*locale*) kitchen; (*arte culinaria*) cooking, cookery; (*le vivande*) food, cooking; (*apparecchio*) cooker; **di ~** (*libro, lezione*) cookery *cpd*; **~ componibile** fitted kitchen; **~ economica** kitchen range
cuci'nare [kutʃi'nare] *vt* to cook
cuci'nino [kutʃi'nino] *sm* kitchenette
cu'cire [ku'tʃire] *vt* to sew, stitch; **~ la bocca a qn** (*fig*) to shut sb up
cu'cito, -a [ku'tʃito] *sm* sewing; (*Ins*) sewing, needlework
cuci'trice [kutʃi'tritʃe] *sf* (*Tip: per libri*) stitching machine; (*per fogli*) stapler
cuci'tura [kutʃi'tura] *sf* sewing, stitching; (*costura*) seam
cucù *sm inv*, **cu'culo** *sm* cuckoo
'cuffia *sf* bonnet, cap; (*da infermiera*) cap; (*da bagno*) (bathing) cap; (*per ascoltare*) headphones *pl*, headset
cu'gino, -a [ku'dʒino] *sm/f* cousin

PAROLA CHIAVE

'cui *pron* **1** (*nei complementi indiretti: persona*) whom; (*: oggetto, animale*) which; **la persona/le persone a cui accennavi** the person/people you were referring to *o* to whom you were referring; **la penna con cui scrivo** the pen I'm writing with; **il paese da cui viene** the country he comes from; **i libri di cui parlavo** the books I was talking about *o* about which I was talking; **parla varie lingue, fra cui l'inglese** he speaks several languages, including English; **il quartiere in cui abito** the district where I live; **visto il modo in cui ti ha trattato ...** considering how he treated you ...; **la ragione per cui** the reason why; **per cui non so più che fare** that's why I don't know what to do
2 (*inserito tra articolo e sostantivo*) whose; **la donna i cui figli sono scomparsi** the woman whose children have disappeared; **il signore, dal cui figlio ho avuto il libro** the man from whose son I got the book

culi'naria *sf* cookery
culi'nario, -a *ag* culinary
'culla *sf* cradle
cul'lare *vt* to rock; (*fig: idea, speranza*) to cherish; **cullarsi** *vr* (*gen*) to sway; **cullarsi in vane speranze** (*fig*) to cherish fond hopes; **cullarsi nel dolce far niente** (*fig*) to sit back and relax
culmi'nante *ag*: **posizione ~** (*Astr*) highest point; **punto** *o* **momento ~** (*fig*) climax
culmi'nare *vi*: **~ in** *o* **con** to culminate in
'culmine *sm* top, summit
'culo *sm* (*fam!*) arse (*Brit!*), ass (*US!*); (*: fig: fortuna*): **aver ~** to have the luck of the devil; **prendere qn per il ~** to take the piss out of sb (*!*)
'culto *sm* (*religione*) religion; (*adorazione*) worship, adoration; (*venerazione: anche fig*) cult
cul'tura *sf* (*gen*) culture; (*conoscenza*) education, learning; **di ~** (*persona*) cultured; (*istituto*) cultural, of culture; **~ generale** general knowledge; **~ di massa** mass culture
cultu'rale *ag* cultural
cultu'rismo *sm* body-building
cumu'lare *vt* to accumulate, amass
cumula'tivo, -a *ag* cumulative; (*prezzo*) inclusive; (*biglietto*) group *cpd*
'cumulo *sm* (*mucchio*) pile, heap; (*Meteor*) cumulus; **~ dei redditi** (*Fisco*) combined incomes; **~ delle pene** (*Dir*) consecutive sentences

'cuneo *sm* wedge
cu'netta *sf* (*di strada etc*) bump; (*scolo: nelle strade di città*) gutter; (*: di campagna*) ditch
cu'nicolo *sm* (*galleria*) tunnel; (*di miniera*) pit, shaft; (*di talpa*) hole
cu'oca *sf vedi* **cuoco**
cu'ocere ['kwɔtʃere] *vt* (*alimenti*) to cook; (*mattoni etc*) to fire ■ *vi* to cook; **~ in umido/a vapore/in padella** to stew/steam/fry; **~ al forno** (*pane*) to bake; (*arrosto*) to roast
cu'oco, -a, chi, che *sm/f* cook; (*di ristorante*) chef
cuoi'ame *sm* leather goods *pl*
cu'oio *sm* leather; **~ capelluto** scalp; **tirare le cuoia** (*fam*) to kick the bucket
cu'ore *sm* heart; **cuori** *smpl* (*Carte*) hearts; **avere buon ~** to be kind-hearted; **stare a ~ a qn** to be important to sb; **un grazie di ~** heartfelt thanks; **ringraziare di ~** to thank sincerely; **nel profondo del ~** in one's heart of hearts; **avere la morte nel ~** to be sick at heart; **club dei cuori solitari** lonely hearts club
cupi'digia [kupi'didʒa] *sf* greed, covetousness
'cupo, -a *ag* dark; (*suono*) dull; (*fig*) gloomy, dismal
'cupola *sf* dome; (*più piccola*) cupola; (*fig*) Mafia high command
'cura *sf* care; (*Med: trattamento*) (course of) treatment; **aver ~ di** (*occuparsi di*) to look after; **a ~ di** (*libro*) edited by; **fare una ~** to follow a course of treatment; **~ dimagrante** diet
cu'rabile *ag* curable
cu'rante *ag*: **medico ~** doctor (in charge of a patient)
cu'rare *vt* (*malato, malattia*) to treat; (*: guarire*) to cure; (*aver cura di*) to take care of; (*testo*) to edit; **curarsi** *vr* to take care of o.s.; (*Med*) to follow a course of treatment; **curarsi di** to pay attention to; (*occuparsi di*) to look after
cu'rato *sm* parish priest; (*protestante*) vicar, minister
cura'tore, -'trice *sm/f* (*Dir*) trustee; (*di antologia etc*) editor; **~ fallimentare** (official) receiver
'curdo, -a *ag* Kurdish ■ *sm/f* Kurd
'curia *sf* (*Rel*): **la ~ romana** the Roman curia; **~ notarile** notaries' association *o* guild
curio'saggine [kurjo'saddʒine] *sf* nosiness
curio'sare *vi* to look round, wander round; (*tra libri*) to browse; **~ nei negozi** to look *o* wander round the shops; **~ nelle faccende altrui** to poke one's nose into other people's affairs
curiosità *sf inv* curiosity; (*cosa rara*) curio, curiosity

C

curi'oso, -a *ag* (*che vuol sapere*) curious, inquiring; (*ficcanaso*) curious, inquisitive; (*bizzarro*) strange, curious ■ *sm/f* busybody, nosy parker; **essere ~ di** to be curious about; **una folla di curiosi** a crowd of onlookers
cur'riculum *sm inv*: **~ (vitae)** curriculum vitae
cur'sore *sm* (*Inform*) cursor
'curva *sf* curve; (*stradale*) bend, curve
cur'vare *vt* to bend ■ *vi* (*veicolo*) to take a bend; (*strada*) to bend, curve; **curvarsi** *vr* to bend; (*legno*) to warp
'curvo, -a *ag* curved; (*piegato*) bent
CUS *sigla m* = **Centro Universitario Sportivo**
cusci'netto [kuʃʃi'netto] *sm* pad; (*Tecn*) bearing ■ *ag inv*: **stato ~** buffer state; **~ a sfere** ball bearing
cu'scino [kuʃʃino] *sm* cushion; (*guanciale*) pillow
'cuspide *sf* (*Archit*) spire
cus'tode *sm/f* (*di museo*) keeper, custodian; (*di parco*) warden; (*di casa*) concierge; (*di fabbrica, carcere*) guard
cus'todia *sf* care; (*Dir*) custody; (*astuccio*) case, holder; **avere qc in ~** to look after sth; **dare qc in ~ a qn** to entrust sth to sb's care; **agente di ~** prison warder; **~ delle carceri** prison security; **~ cautelare** (*Dir*) remand
custo'dire *vt* (*conservare*) to keep; (*assistere*) to look after, take care of; (*fare la guardia*) to guard
customiz'zare [kustomid'dzare] *vt* (*Inform*) to customize
'cute *sf* (*Anat*) skin
cu'ticola *sf* cuticle
C.V. *abbr* = **cavallo vapore**
c.v.d. *abbr* (= *come volevasi dimostrare*) QED (= *quod erat demonstrandum*)
c.vo *abbr* = **corsivo**
cy'clette® [si'klɛt] *sf inv* exercise bike
CZ *sigla* = **Catanzaro**

Dd

D, d [di] *sf o m inv* (*lettera*) D, d; **D come Domodossola** ≈ D for David (*Brit*), D for Dog (*US*)

D *abbr* (= *destra*) R; (*Ferr*) = **diretto**

 PAROLA CHIAVE

da (*da + il* = **dal**, *da + lo* = **dallo**, *da + l'* = **dall'**, *da + la* = **dalla**, *da + i* = **dai**, *da + gli* = **dagli**, *da + le* = **dalle**) *prep* **1** (*agente*) by; **dipinto da un grande artista** painted by a great artist
2 (*causa*) with; **tremare dalla paura** to tremble with fear
3 (*stato in luogo*) at; **abito da lui** I'm living at his house *o* with him; **sono dal giornalaio** I'm at the newsagent's; **era da Francesco** she was at Francesco's (house)
4 (*moto a luogo*) to; (*moto per luogo*) through; **vado da Pietro/dal giornalaio** I'm going to Pietro's (house)/to the newsagent's; **sono passati dalla finestra** they came in through the window
5 (*provenienza, allontanamento*) from; **da ... a** from ... to; **arrivare/partire da Milano** to arrive/depart from Milan; **scendere dal treno/dalla macchina** to get off the train/out of the car; **viene da una famiglia povera** he comes from a poor background; **viene dalla Scozia** he comes from Scotland; **ti chiamo da una cabina** I'm phoning from a call box; **si trova a 5 km da qui** it's 5 km from here
6 (*tempo: durata*) for; (*: a partire da: nel passato*) since; (*: nel futuro*) from; **vivo qui da un anno** I've been living here for a year; **è dalle 3 che ti aspetto** I've been waiting for you since 3 (o'clock); **da mattina a sera** from morning till night; **da oggi in poi** from today onwards; **da bambino** as a child, when I (*o* he *etc*) was a child
7 (*modo, maniera*) like; **comportarsi da uomo** to behave like a man; **l'ho fatto da me** I did it (by) myself; **non è da lui** it's not like him
8 (*descrittivo*): **una macchina da corsa** a racing car; **è una cosa da poco** it's nothing special; **una ragazza dai capelli biondi** a girl with blonde hair; **sordo da un orecchio** deaf in one ear; **abbigliamento da uomo** menswear; **un vestito da 100 euro** a 100 euro dress; **qualcosa da bere/mangiare** something to drink/eat

dà *vb vedi* **dare**

dab'bene *ag inv* honest, decent

'Dacca *sf* Dacca

dac'capo, da'capo *av* (*di nuovo*) (once) again; (*dal principio*) all over again, from the beginning

dacché [dak'ke] *cong* since

'dado *sm* (*da gioco*) dice *o* die; (*Cuc*) stock cube (*Brit*), bouillon cube (*US*); (*Tecn*) (screw) nut; nut; **dadi** *smpl* (game of) dice

daf'fare, da'fare *sm* work, toil; **avere un gran ~** to be very busy

'dagli ['daʎʎi], **'dai** *prep + det vedi* **da**

'daino *sm* (fallow) deer *inv*; (*pelle*) buckskin

Da'kar *sf* Dakar

dal *prep + det vedi* **da**

dal *abbr* (= *decalitro*) dal

dall', 'dalla, 'dalle, 'dallo *prep + det vedi* **da**

dal'tonico, -a, ci, che *ag* colour-blind (*Brit*), colorblind (*US*)

dam *abbr* (= *decametro*) dam

'dama *sf* lady; (*nei balli*) partner; (*gioco*) draughts *sg* (*Brit*), checkers *sg* (*US*); **far ~** (*nel gioco*) to make a crown; **~ di compagnia** lady's companion; **~ di corte** lady-in-waiting

Da'masco *sf* Damascus

dami'gella [dami'dʒɛlla] *sf* (*Storia*) damsel; (*: titolo*) mistress; **~ d'onore** (*di sposa*) bridesmaid

damigi'ana [dami'dʒana] *sf* demijohn

dam'meno *ag inv*: **per non essere ~ di qn** so as not to be outdone by sb

DAMS *sigla m*: **Disciplina delle Arti, della musica, dello spettacolo** *study of the performing arts*
da'naro *sm* = **denaro**
dana'roso, -a *ag* wealthy
da'nese *ag* Danish ■ *sm/f* Dane ■ *sm* (*Ling*) Danish
Dani'marca *sf*: **la ~** Denmark
dan'nare *vt* (*Rel*) to damn; **dannarsi** *vr*: **dannarsi per** (*fig*: *tormentarsi*) to be worried to death (by); **far ~ qn** to drive sb mad; **dannarsi l'anima per qc** (*affannarsi*) to work o.s. to death for sth; (*tormentarsi*) to worry o.s. to death over sth
dan'nato, -a *ag* damned
dannazi'one [dannat'tsjone] *sf* damnation
danneggi'are [danned'dʒare] *vt* to damage; (*rovinare*) to spoil; (*nuocere*) to harm; **la parte danneggiata** (*Dir*) the injured party
'danno *vb vedi* **dare** ■ *sm* damage; (*a persona*) harm, injury; **danni** *smpl* (*Dir*) damages; **a ~ di qn** to sb's detriment; **chiedere/risarcire i danni** to sue for/pay damages
dan'noso, -a *ag*: **~ (a** *o* **per)** harmful (to), bad (for)
dan'tesco, -a, schi, sche *ag* Dantesque; **l'opera dantesca** Dante's work
Da'nubio *sm*: **il ~** the Danube
'danza ['dantsa] *sf*: **la ~** dancing; **una ~** a dance
dan'zante [dan'tsante] *ag* dancing; **serata ~** dance
dan'zare [dan'tsare] *vt, vi* to dance
danza'tore, -'trice [dantsa'tore] *sm/f* dancer
dapper'tutto *av* everywhere
dap'poco *ag inv* inept; worthless
dap'prima *av* at first
Darda'nelli *smpl*: **i ~** the Dardanelles
'dardo *sm* dart
'dare *sm* (*Comm*) debit ■ *vt* to give; (*produrre*: *frutti, suono*) to produce ■ *vi* (*guardare*): **~ su** to look (out) onto; **darsi** *vr*: **darsi a** to dedicate o.s. to; **quanti anni mi dai?** how old do you think I am?; **danno ancora quel film?** is that film still showing?; **~ da mangiare a qn** to give sb something to eat; **~ per certo qc** to consider sth certain; **~ ad intendere a qn che ...** to lead sb to believe that ...; **~ per morto qn** to give sb up for dead; **~ qc per scontato** to take sth for granted; **darsi ammalato** to report sick; **darsi alla bella vita** to have a good time; **darsi al bere** to take to drink; **darsi al commercio** to go into business; **darsi da fare per fare qc** to go to a lot of bother to do sth; **darsi per vinto** to give in; **può darsi** maybe, perhaps; **si dà il caso che ...** it so happens that ...; **darsela a gambe** to take to one's heels; **il ~ e l'avere** (*Econ*) debits and credits *pl*
Dar-es-Sa'laam *sf* Dar-es-Salaam
'darsena *sf* dock
'data *sf* date; **in ~ da destinarsi** on a date still to be announced; **in ~ odierna** as of today; **amicizia di lunga** *o* **vecchia ~** long-standing friendship; **~ di emissione** date of issue; **~ di nascita** date of birth; **~ di scadenza** expiry date; **~ limite d'utilizzo** *o* **di consumo** (*Comm*) best-before date
da'tare *vt* to date ■ *vi*: **~ da** to date from
da'tato, -a *ag* dated
da'tivo *sm* dative
'dato, -a *ag* (*stabilito*) given ■ *sm* datum; **dati** *smpl* data *pl*; **~ che** given that; **in dati casi** in certain cases; **è un ~ di fatto** it's a fact; **dati sensibili** sense data
da'tore, -'trice *sm/f*: **~ di lavoro** employer
'dattero *sm* date (*Bot*)
dattilogra'fare *vt* to type
dattilogra'fia *sf* typing
datti'lografo, -a *sm/f* typist
dattilos'critto *sm* typescript
da'vanti *av* in front; (*dirimpetto*) opposite ■ *ag inv* front ■ *sm* front; **~ a** *prep* in front of; (*dirimpetto a*) facing, opposite; (*in presenza di*) before, in front of
davan'zale [davan'tsale] *sm* windowsill
da'vanzo, d'a'vanzo [da'vantso] *av* more than enough
dav'vero *av* really, indeed; **dico ~** I mean it
dazi'ario, -a [dat'tsjarjo] *ag* excise *cpd*
'dazio ['dattsjo] *sm* (*somma*) duty; (*luogo*) customs *pl*; **~ d'importazione** import duty
db *abbr* (= *decibel*) dB
DC *sigla f* = **Democrazia Cristiana** (*former political party*)
d.C. *abbr* (= *dopo Cristo*) A.D.
D.D.T. *abbr m* (= *dicloro-difenil-tricloroetano*) D.D.T.
'dea *sf* goddess
'debbo *etc vb vedi* **dovere**
debel'lare *vt* to overcome, conquer
debili'tare *vt* to debilitate
debita'mente *av* duly, properly
'debito, -a *ag* due, proper ■ *sm* debt; (*Comm*: *dare*) debit; **a tempo ~** at the right time; **portare a ~ di qn** to debit sb with; **~ consolidato** consolidated debt; **~ d'imposta** tax liability; **~ pubblico** national debt
debi'tore, -'trice *sm/f* debtor
'debole *ag* weak, feeble; (*suono*) faint; (*luce*) dim ■ *sm* weakness
debo'lezza [debo'lettsa] *sf* weakness
debut'tante *sm/f* (*gen*) beginner, novice; (*Teat*) actor/actress at the beginning of his (*o* her) career

debut'tare *vi* to make one's début
de'butto *sm* début
'decade *sf* period of ten days
deca'dente *ag* decadent
deca'denza [deka'dɛntsa] *sf* decline; (*Dir*) loss, forfeiture
deca'dere *vi* to decline
deca'duto, -a *ag* (*persona*) impoverished; (*norma*) lapsed
decaffei'nato, -a *ag* decaffeinated
de'calogo *sm* (*fig*) rulebook
de'cano *sm* (*Rel*) dean
decan'tare *vt* (*virtù, bravura etc*) to praise; (*persona*) to sing the praises of
decapi'tare *vt* to decapitate, behead
decappot'tabile *ag, sf* convertible
dece'duto, -a [detʃe'duto] *ag* deceased
decele'rare [detʃele'rare] *vt, vi* to decelerate, slow down
decen'nale [detʃen'nale] *ag* (*che dura 10 anni*) ten-year *cpd*; (*che ricorre ogni 10 anni*) ten-yearly, every ten years ■ *sm* (*ricorrenza*) tenth anniversary
de'cenne [de'tʃɛnne] *ag*: **un bambino ~** a ten-year-old child, a child of ten
de'cennio [de'tʃɛnnjo] *sm* decade
de'cente [de'tʃɛnte] *ag* decent, respectable, proper; (*accettabile*) satisfactory, decent
decentraliz'zare [detʃentralid'dzare] *vt* (*Amm*) to decentralize
decentra'mento [detʃentra'mento] *sm* decentralization
decen'trare [detʃen'trare] *vt* to decentralize, move out of *o* away from the centre
de'cenza [de'tʃɛntsa] *sf* decency, propriety
de'cesso [de'tʃɛsso] *sm* death; **atto di ~** death certificate
de'cidere [de'tʃidere] *vi* to decide, make up one's mind ■ *vt*: **~ qc** to decide on sth; (*questione, lite*) to settle sth; **decidersi** *vr*: **decidersi (a fare)** to decide (to do), make up one's mind (to do); **~ di fare/che** to decide to do/that; **~ di qc** (*cosa*) to determine sth
deci'frare [detʃi'frare] *vt* to decode; (*fig*) to decipher, make out
de'cilitro [de'tʃilitro] *sm* decilitre (*Brit*), deciliter (*US*)
deci'male [detʃi'male] *ag* decimal
deci'mare [detʃi'mare] *vt* to decimate
de'cimetro [de'tʃimetro] *sm* decimetre
'decimo, -a ['dɛtʃimo] *num* tenth
de'cina [de'tʃina] *sf* ten; (*circa dieci*): **una ~ (di)** about ten
de'cisi *etc* [de'tʃizi] *vb vedi* **decidere**
decisio'nale [detʃizjo'nale] *ag* decision-making *cpd*
decisi'one [detʃi'zjone] *sf* decision; **prendere una ~** to make a decision; **con ~** decisively, resolutely
deci'sivo, -a [detʃi'zivo] *ag* (*gen*) decisive; (*fattore*) deciding
de'ciso, -a [de'tʃizo] *pp di* **decidere** ■ *ag* (*persona, carattere*) determined; (*tono*) firm, resolute
declas'sare *vt* to downgrade; to lower in status; **1a declassata** (*Ferr*) *first-class carriage which may be used by second-class passengers*
decli'nare *vi* (*pendio*) to slope down; (*fig: diminuire*) to decline; (*tramontare*) to set, go down ■ *vt* to decline; **~ le proprie generalità** (*fig*) to give one's particulars; **~ ogni responsabilità** to disclaim all responsibility
declinazi'one [deklinat'tsjone] *sf* (*Ling*) declension
de'clino *sm* decline
de'clivio *sm* (downward) slope
decodifi'care *vt* to decode
decodifica'tore *sm* decoder
decol'lare *vi* (*Aer*) to take off
décolleté [dekol'te] *ag inv* (*abito*) low-necked, low-cut ■ *sm* (*di abito*) low neckline; (*di donna*) cleavage
de'collo *sm* take-off
decolo'rare *vt* to bleach
decom'porre *vt*, **decomporsi** *vr* to decompose
decomposizi'one [dekompozit'tsjone] *sf* decomposition
decom'posto, -a *pp di* **decomporre**
decompressi'one *sf* decompression
deconge'lare [dekondʒe'lare] *vt* to defrost
decongestio'nare [dekondʒestjo'nare] *vt* (*Med, traffico*) to relieve congestion in
deco'rare *vt* to decorate
decora'tivo, -a *ag* decorative
decora'tore, -trice *sm* (interior) decorator
decorazi'one [dekorat'tsjone] *sf* decoration
de'coro *sm* decorum
deco'roso, -a *ag* decorous, dignified
decor'renza [dekor'rɛntsa] *sf*: **con ~ da** (as) from
de'correre *vi* to pass, elapse; (*avere effetto*) to run, have effect
de'corso, -a *pp di* **decorrere** ■ *sm* (*evoluzione: anche Med*) course
de'crebbi *etc vb vedi* **decrescere**
de'crepito, -a *ag* decrepit
de'crescere [de'kreʃʃere] *vi* (*diminuire*) to decrease, diminish; (*acque*) to subside, go down; (*prezzi*) to go down
decresci'uto, -a [dekreʃ'ʃuto] *pp di* **decrescere**
decre'tare *vt* (*norma*) to decree; (*mobilitazione*) to order; **~ lo stato d'emergenza** to declare a

d

state of emergency; **~ la nomina di qn** to decide on the appointment of sb
de'creto *sm* decree; **~ legge** *decree with the force of law*; **~ di sfratto** eviction order
decur'tare *vt* (*debito, somma*) to reduce
decurtazi'one [dekurtat'tsjone] *sf* reduction
'dedalo *sm* maze, labyrinth
'dedica, -che *sf* dedication
dedi'care *vt* to dedicate; **dedicarsi** *vr*: **dedicarsi a** (*votarsi*) to devote o.s. to
dedicherò *etc* [dedike'rɔ] *vb vedi* **dedicare**
'dedito, -a *ag*: **~ a** (*studio etc*) dedicated *o* devoted to; (*vizio*) addicted to
de'dotto, -a *pp di* **dedurre**
de'duco *etc vb vedi* **dedurre**
de'durre *vt* (*concludere*) to deduce; (*defalcare*) to deduct
de'dussi *etc vb vedi* **dedurre**
deduzi'one [dedut'tsjone] *sf* deduction
defal'care *vt* to deduct
defenes'trare *vt* to throw out of the window; (*fig*) to remove from office
defe'rente *ag* respectful, deferential
defe'rire *vt* (*Dir*): **~ a** to refer to
defezi'one [defet'tsjone] *sf* defection, desertion
defici'ente [defi'tʃɛnte] *ag* (*mancante*): **~ di** deficient in; (*insufficiente*) insufficient ■ *sm/f* mental defective; (*peg: cretino*) idiot
defici'enza [defi'tʃɛntsa] *sf* deficiency; (*carenza*) shortage; (*fig: lacuna*) weakness
'deficit ['dɛfitʃit] *sm inv* (*Econ*) deficit
defi'nire *vt* to define; (*risolvere*) to settle; (*questione*) to finalize
defini'tivo, -a *ag* definitive, final ■ *sf*: **in definitiva** (*dopotutto*) when all is said and done; (*dunque*) well then
defi'nito, -a *ag* definite; **ben ~** clear, clear cut
definizi'one [definit'tsjone] *sf* (*gen*) definition; (*di disputa, vertenza*) settlement; (*di tempi, obiettivi*) establishment
deflagrazi'one [deflagrat'tsjone] *sf* explosion
deflazi'one [deflat'tsjone] *sf* (*Econ*) deflation
deflet'tore *sm* (*Aut*) quarterlight (*Brit*), deflector (*US*)
deflu'ire *vi*: **~ da** (*liquido*) to flow away from; (*fig: capitali*) to flow out of
de'flusso *sm* (*della marea*) ebb
defor'mare *vt* (*alterare*) to put out of shape; (*corpo*) to deform; (*pensiero, fatto*) to distort; **deformarsi** *vr* to lose its shape
deformazi'one [deformat'tsjone] *sf* (*Med*) deformation; **questa è ~ professionale!** that's force of habit because of your (*o* his *etc*) job!
de'forme *ag* deformed; disfigured
deformità *sf inv* deformity
defrau'dare *vt*: **~ qn di qc** to defraud sb of sth, cheat sb out of sth
de'funto, -a *ag* late *cpd* ■ *sm/f* deceased
degene'rare [dedʒene'rare] *vi* to degenerate
degenerazi'one [dedʒenerat'tsjone] *sf* degeneration
de'genere [de'dʒɛnere] *ag* degenerate
de'gente [de'dʒɛnte] *sm/f* bedridden person; (*ricoverato in ospedale*) in-patient
de'genza [de'dʒɛntsa] *sf* confinement to bed; **~ ospedaliera** period in hospital
'degli ['deʎʎi] *prep + det vedi* **di**
deglu'tire *vt* to swallow
de'gnare [deɲ'ɲare] *vt*: **~ qn della propria presenza** to honour sb with one's presence; **degnarsi** *vr*: **degnarsi di fare qc** to deign *o* condescend to do sth; **non mi ha degnato di uno sguardo** he wouldn't even look at me
'degno, -a ['deɲɲo] *ag* dignified; **~ di** worthy of; **~ di lode** praiseworthy
degra'dare *vt* (*Mil*) to demote; (*privare della dignità*) to degrade; **degradarsi** *vr* to demean o.s.
de'grado *sm*: **~ urbano** urban decline
degus'tare *vt* to sample, taste
degustazi'one [degustat'tsjone] *sf* sampling, tasting; **~ di vini** (*locale*) specialist wine bar; **~ di caffè** (*locale*) specialist coffee shop
'dei *smpl di* **dio** ■ *prep + det vedi* **di**
del *prep + det vedi* **di**
dela'tore, -'trice *sm/f* police informer
delazi'one [delat'tsjone] *sf* informing
'delega, -ghe *sf* (*procura*) proxy; **per ~ notarile** ≈ through a solicitor (*Brit*) *o* lawyer
dele'gare *vt* to delegate
dele'gato *sm* delegate
delegazi'one [delegat'tsjone] *sf* delegation
delegherò *etc* [delege'rɔ] *vb vedi* **delegare**
dele'terio, -a *ag* deleterious, noxious
del'fino *sm* (*Zool*) dolphin; (*Storia*) dauphin; (*fig*) probable successor
'Delhi ['dɛli] *sf* Delhi
de'libera *sf* decision
delibe'rare *vt* to come to a decision on ■ *vi* (*Dir*): **~ (su qc)** to rule (on sth)
delica'tezza [delika'tettsa] *sf* delicacy; frailty; thoughtfulness; tactfulness
deli'cato, -a *ag* delicate; (*salute*) delicate, frail; (*fig: gentile*) thoughtful, considerate; (*: che dimostra tatto*) tactful
delimi'tare *vt* (*anche fig*) to delimit
deline'are *vt* to outline; **delinearsi** *vr* to be outlined; (*fig*) to emerge
delin'quente *sm/f* criminal, delinquent

delin'quenza [delin'kwɛntsa] *sf* criminality, delinquency; **~ minorile** juvenile delinquency

de'liquio *sm* (*Med*) swoon; **cadere in ~** to swoon

deli'rante *ag* (*Med*) delirious; (*fig: folla*) frenzied; (*: discorso, mente*) insane

deli'rare *vi* to be delirious, rave; (*fig*) to rave

de'lirio *sm* delirium; (*ragionamento insensato*) raving; (*fig*): **andare/mandare in ~** to go/send into a frenzy

de'litto *sm* crime; **~ d'onore** *crime committed to avenge one's honour*

delittu'oso, -a *ag* criminal

de'lizia [de'littsja] *sf* delight

delizi'are [delit'tsjare] *vt* to delight; **deliziarsi** *vr*: **deliziarsi di qc/a fare qc** to take delight in sth/in doing sth

delizi'oso, -a [delit'tsjoso] *ag* delightful; (*cibi*) delicious

dell', 'della, 'delle, 'dello *prep + det vedi* **di**

'delta *sm inv* delta

delta'plano *sm* hang-glider; **volo col ~** hang-gliding

delucidazi'one [delutʃidat'tsjone] *sf* clarification *no pl*

delu'dente *ag* disappointing

de'ludere *vt* to disappoint

delusi'one *sf* disappointment

de'luso, -a *pp di* **deludere** ■ *ag* disappointed

dema'gogico, -a, ci, che [dema'gɔdʒiko] *ag* popularity-seeking, demagogic

dema'gogo, -ghi *sm* demagogue

de'manio *sm* state property

de'mente *ag* (*Med*) demented, mentally deranged; (*fig*) crazy, mad

de'menza [de'mɛntsa] *sf* dementia; madness; **~ senile** senile dementia

demenzi'ale [demen'tsjale] *ag* (*fig*) off-the-wall

'demmo *vb vedi* **dare**

demo'cratico, -a, ci, che *ag* democratic

democra'zia [demokrat'tsia] *sf* democracy; **la D~ Cristiana** the Christian Democrat Party

democristi'ano, -a *ag, sm/f* Christian Democrat

demogra'fia *sf* demography

demo'grafico, -a, ci, che *ag* demographic; **incremento ~** increase in population

demo'lire *vt* to demolish

demolizi'one [demolit'tsjone] *sf* demolition

'demone *sm* demon

de'monio *sm* demon, devil; **il D~** the Devil

demoniz'zare [demonid'dzare] *vt* to make a monster of

demonizzazi'one [demoniddzat'tsjone] *sf* demonizing, demonization

demoraliz'zare [demoralid'dzare] *vt* to demoralize; **demoralizzarsi** *vr* to become demoralized

de'mordere *vi*: **non ~ (da)** to refuse to give up

demoti'vare *vt*: **~ qn** to take away sb's motivation

demoti'vato, -a *ag* unmotivated, lacking motivation

de'naro *sm* money; **denari** *smpl* (*Carte*) *suit in Neapolitan pack of cards*

denatu'rato, -a *ag vedi* **alcool**

deni'grare *vt* to denigrate, run down

denomi'nare *vt* to name; **denominarsi** *vr* to be named *o* called

denomina'tore *sm* (*Mat*) denominator

denominazi'one [denominat'tsjone] *sf* name; denomination; **~ di origine controllata** *label guaranteeing the quality and origin of a wine*

deno'tare *vt* to denote, indicate

densità *sf inv* density; (*di nebbia*) thickness, denseness; **ad alta/bassa ~ di popolazione** densely/sparsely populated

'denso, -a *ag* thick, dense

den'tale *ag* dental

den'tario, -a *ag* dental

denta'tura *sf* set of teeth, teeth *pl*; (*Tecn: di ruota*) serration

'dente *sm* tooth; (*di forchetta*) prong; (*Geo: cima*) jagged peak; **al ~** (*Cuc: pasta*) *cooked so as to be firm when eaten*; **mettere i denti** to teethe; **mettere qc sotto i denti** to have a bite to eat; **avere il ~ avvelenato contro** *o* **con qn** to bear sb a grudge; **~ di leone** (*Bot*) dandelion; **denti del giudizio** wisdom teeth

'dentice ['dɛntitʃe] *sm* (*Zool*) sea bream

denti'era *sf* (set of) false teeth *pl*

denti'fricio [denti'fritʃo] *sm* toothpaste

den'tista, -i, e *sm/f* dentist

'dentro *av* inside; (*in casa*) indoors; (*fig: nell'intimo*) inwardly ■ *prep*: **~ (a)** in; **piegato in ~** folded over; **qui/là ~** in here/there; **~ di sé** (*pensare, brontolare*) to oneself; **tenere tutto ~** to keep everything bottled up (inside o.s.); **darci ~** (*fig fam*) to slog away, work hard

denucleariz'zato, -a [denuklearid'dzato] *ag* denuclearized, nuclear-free

denu'dare *vt* (*persona*) to strip; (*parte del corpo*) to bare; **denudarsi** *vr* to strip

de'nuncia [de'nuntʃa] (*pl* **denunce** *o* **denuncie**), **de'nunzia** [de'nuntsja] *sf* denunciation; declaration; **fare una ~** *o* **sporgere ~ contro qn** (*Dir*) to report sb to the police; **~ del reddito** (income) tax return

denunci'are [denun'tʃare], **denunzi'are** [denun'tsjare] *vt* to denounce; (*dichiarare*) to

declare; **~ qn/qc (alla polizia)** to report sb/sth to the police
denu'trito, -a *ag* undernourished
denutrizi'one [denutrit'tsjone] *sf* malnutrition
deodo'rante *sm* deodorant
deontolo'gia [deontolo'dʒia] *sf* (*professionale*) professional code of conduct
depenalizzazi'one [depenaliddzat'tsjone] *sf* decriminalization
dépen'dance [depɑ̃'dɑ̃s] *sf inv* outbuilding
depe'ribile *ag* perishable; **merce ~** perishables *pl*, perishable goods *pl*
deperi'mento *sm* (*di persona*) wasting away; (*di merci*) deterioration
depe'rire *vi* to waste away
depi'lare *vt* to depilate
depila'torio, -a *ag* hair-removing, depilatory ■ *sm* hair remover, depilatory
depilazi'one [depilat'tsjone] *sf* hair removal, depilation
depis'taggio [depis'taddʒo] *sm* diversion
depis'tare *vt* to set on the wrong track
dépli'ant [depli'ɑ̃] *sm inv* leaflet; (*opuscolo*) brochure
deplo'rare *vt* to deplore; to lament
deplo'revole *ag* deplorable
de'pone, de'pongo *etc vb vedi* **deporre**
de'porre *vt* (*depositare*) to put down; (*rimuovere: da una carica*) to remove; (*: re*) to depose; (*Dir*) to testify; **~ le armi** (*Mil*) to lay down arms; **~ le uova** to lay eggs
depor'tare *vt* to deport
depor'tato, -a *sm/f* deportee
deportazi'one [deportat'tsjone] *sf* deportation
de'posi *etc vb vedi* **deporre**
deposi'tante *sm* (*Comm*) depositor
deposi'tare *vt* (*gen, Geo, Econ*) to deposit; (*lasciare*) to leave; (*merci*) to store; **depositarsi** *vr* (*sabbia, polvere*) to settle
deposi'tario *sm* (*Comm*) depository
de'posito *sm* deposit; (*luogo*) warehouse; depot; (*: Mil*) depot; **~ bagagli** left-luggage office; **~ di munizioni** ammunition dump
deposizi'one [depozit'tsjone] *sf* deposition; (*da una carica*) removal; **rendere una falsa ~** to perjure o.s.
de'posto, -a *pp di* **deporre**
depra'vare *vt* to corrupt, pervert
depra'vato, -a *ag* depraved ■ *sm/f* degenerate
depre'care *vt* to deprecate, deplore
depre'dare *vt* to rob, plunder
depressi'one *sf* depression; **area** *o* **zona di ~** (*Meteor*) area of low pressure; (*Econ*) depressed area
de'presso, -a *pp di* **deprimere** ■ *ag* depressed
deprezza'mento [deprettsa'mento] *sm* depreciation
deprez'zare [depret'tsare] *vt* (*Econ*) to depreciate
depri'mente *ag* depressing
de'primere *vt* to depress
depu'rare *vt* to purify
depura'tore *sm*: **~ d'acqua** water purifier; **~ di gas** scrubber
depu'tato, -a *sm/f* (*Pol*) deputy, ≈ Member of Parliament (*Brit*), ≈ Congressman(-woman (*US*)); *vedi anche* **Camera dei Deputati**
deputazi'one [deputat'tsjone] *sf* deputation; (*Pol*) position of deputy, ≈ parliamentary seat (*Brit*), ≈ seat in Congress (*US*)
deraglia'mento [deraʎʎa'mento] *sm* derailment
deragli'are [deraʎ'ʎare] *vi* to be derailed; **far ~** to derail
dera'pare *vi* (*veicolo*) to skid; (*Sci*) to sideslip
derattizzazi'one [derattiddzat'tsjone] *sf* rodent control
deregolamen'tare *vt* to deregulate
deregolamentazi'one [deregolamentat'tsjone] *sf* deregulation
dere'litto, -a *ag* derelict
dere'tano *sm* (*fam*) bottom, buttocks *pl*
de'ridere *vt* to mock, deride
de'risi *etc vb vedi* **deridere**
derisi'one *sf* derision, mockery
de'riso, -a *pp di* **deridere**
deri'sorio, -a *ag* (*gesto, tono*) mocking
de'riva *sf* (*Naut, Aer*) drift; (*dispositivo: Aer*) fin; (*: Naut*) centre-board (*Brit*), centerboard (*US*); **andare alla ~** (*anche fig*) to drift
deri'vare *vi*: **~ da** to derive from ■ *vt* to derive; (*corso d'acqua*) to divert
deri'vato, -a *ag* derived ■ *sm* (*Chim, Ling*) derivative; (*prodotto*) by-product
derivazi'one [derivat'tsjone] *sf* derivation; diversion
derma'tite *sf* dermatitis
dermatolo'gia [dermatolo'dʒia] *sf* dermatology
derma'tologo, -a, gi, ghe *sm/f* dermatologist
dermoprotet'tivo, -a *ag* (*crema, azione*) protecting the skin
'deroga, -ghe *sf* (special) dispensation; **in ~ a** as a (special) dispensation to
dero'gare *vi*: **~ a** (*Dir*) to repeal in part
der'rate *sfpl* commodities; **~ alimentari** foodstuffs
deru'bare *vt* to rob
des'critto, -a *pp di* **descrivere**
des'crivere *vt* to describe
descrizi'one [deskrit'tsjone] *sf* description

de'serto, -a *ag* deserted ■ *sm* (*Geo*) desert; **isola deserta** desert island

deside'rabile *ag* desirable

deside'rare *vt* to want, wish for; (*sessualmente*) to desire; **~ fare/che qn faccia** to want *o* wish to do/sb to do; **desidera fare una passeggiata?** would you like to go for a walk?; **farsi ~** (*fare il prezioso*) to play hard to get; (*farsi aspettare*) to take one's time; **lascia molto a ~** it leaves a lot to be desired

desi'derio *sm* wish; (*più intenso, carnale*) desire

deside'roso, -a *ag*: **~ di** longing *o* eager for

desi'gnare [desiɲ'ɲare] *vt* to designate, appoint; (*data*) to fix; **la vittima designata** the intended victim

designazi'one [desiɲɲat'tsjone] *sf* designation, appointment

desi'nare *vi* to dine, have dinner ■ *sm* dinner

desi'nenza [dezi'nɛntsa] *sf* (*Ling*) ending, inflexion

de'sistere *vi*: **~ da** to give up, desist from

desis'tito, -a *pp di* **desistere**

deso'lante *ag* distressing

deso'lato, -a *ag* (*paesaggio*) desolate; (*persona: spiacente*) sorry

desolazi'one [dezolat'tsjone] *sf* desolation

'despota, -i *sm* despot

'dessi *etc vb vedi* **dare**

destabiliz'zare [destabilid'dzare] *vt* to destabilize

des'tare *vt* to wake (up); (*fig*) to awaken, arouse; **destarsi** *vr* to wake (up)

'deste *etc vb vedi* **dare**

desti'nare *vt* to destine; (*assegnare*) to appoint, assign; (*indirizzare*) to address; **~ qc a qn** to intend to give sth to sb, intend sb to have sth

destina'tario, -a *sm/f* (*di lettera*) addressee; (*di merce*) consignee; (*di mandato*) payee

destinazi'one [destinat'tsjone] *sf* destination; (*uso*) purpose

des'tino *sm* destiny, fate

destitu'ire *vt* to dismiss, remove

destituzi'one [destitut'tsjone] *sf* dismissal, removal

'desto, -a *ag* (wide) awake

'destra *sf vedi* **destro**

destreggi'arsi [destred'dʒarsi] *vr* to manoeuvre (*Brit*), maneuver (*US*)

des'trezza [des'trettsa] *sf* skill, dexterity

'destro, -a *ag* right, right-hand; (*abile*) skilful (*Brit*), skillful (*US*), adroit ■ *sf* (*mano*) right hand; (*parte*) right (side); (*Pol*): **la destra** the right ■ *sm* (*Boxe*) right; **a destra** (*essere*) on the right; (*andare*) to the right; **tenere la destra** to keep to the right

de'sumere *vt* (*dedurre*) to infer, deduce; (*trarre: informazioni*) to obtain

de'sunto, -a *pp di* **desumere**

detas'sare *vt* to remove the duty (*o* tax) from

dete'nere *vt* (*incarico, primato*) to hold; (*proprietà*) to have, possess; (*in prigione*) to detain, hold

de'tengo, de'tenni *etc vb vedi* **detenere**

deten'tivo, -a *ag*: **mandato ~** imprisonment order; **pena detentiva** prison sentence

deten'tore, -'trice *sm/f* (*di titolo, primato etc*) holder

dete'nuto, -a *sm/f* prisoner

detenzi'one [deten'tsjone] *sf* holding; possession; detention

deter'gente [deter'dʒɛnte] *ag* detergent; (*crema, latte*) cleansing ■ *sm* detergent

de'tergere [de'tɛrdʒere] *vt* (*gen*) to clean; (*pelle, viso*) to cleanse; (*sudore*) to wipe (away)

deteriora'mento *sm*: **~ (di)** deterioration (in)

deterio'rare *vt* to damage; **deteriorarsi** *vr* to deteriorate

deteri'ore *ag* (*merce*) second-rate; (*significato*) pejorative; (*tradizione letteraria*) lesser, minor

determi'nante *ag* decisive, determining

determi'nare *vt* to determine

determina'tivo, -a *ag* determining; **articolo ~** (*Ling*) definite article

determi'nato, -a *ag* (*gen*) certain; (*particolare*) specific; (*risoluto*) determined, resolute

determinazi'one [determinat'tsjone] *sf* determination; (*decisione*) decision

deter'rente *ag, sm* deterrent

deterrò *etc vb vedi* **detenere**

deter'sivo *sm* detergent; (*per bucato: in polvere*) washing powder (*Brit*), soap powder

de'terso, -a *pp di* **detergere**

detes'tare *vt* to detest, hate

deti'ene *etc vb vedi* **detenere**

deto'nare *vi* to detonate

detona'tore *sm* detonator

detonazi'one [detonat'tsjone] *sf* (*di esplosivo*) detonation, explosion; (*di arma*) bang; (*di motore*) pinking (*Brit*), knocking

de'trae, de'traggo *etc vb vedi* **detrarre**

de'trarre *vt*: **~ (da)** to deduct (from), take away (from)

de'trassi *etc vb vedi* **detrarre**

de'tratto, -a *pp di* **detrarre**

detrazi'one [detrat'tsjone] *sf* deduction; **~ d'imposta** tax allowance

detri'mento *sm* detriment, harm; **a ~ di** to the detriment of

de'trito *sm* (*Geo*) detritus

detroniz'zare [detronid'dzare] *vt* to dethrone

'detta *sf*: **a ~ di** according to

dettagli'ante [dettaʎ'ʎante] *sm/f* (*Comm*) retailer

dettagli'are [dettaʎ'ʎare] *vt* to detail, give full details of
dettagliata'mente [dettaʎʎata'mente] *av* in detail
det'taglio [det'taʎʎo] *sm* detail; (*Comm*): **il ~** retail; **al ~** (*Comm*) retail; separately
det'tame *sm* dictate, precept
det'tare *vt* to dictate; **~ legge** (*fig*) to lay down the law
det'tato *sm* dictation
detta'tura *sf* dictation
'**detto, -a** *pp di* **dire** ▪ *ag* (*soprannominato*) called, known as; (*già nominato*) above-mentioned ▪ *sm* saying; **~ fatto** no sooner said than done; **presto ~!** it's easier said than done!
detur'pare *vt* to disfigure; (*moralmente*) to sully
devas'tante *ag* (*anche fig*) devastating
devas'tare *vt* to devastate; (*fig*) to ravage
devastazi'one [devastat'tsjone] *sf* devastation, destruction
devi'are *vi*: **~ (da)** to turn off (from) ▪ *vt* to divert
devi'ato, -a *ag* (*fig: persona, organizzazione*) corrupt, bent (*col*)
deviazi'one [devjat'tsjone] *sf* (*anche Aut*) diversion; **fare una ~** to make a detour
'**devo** *etc vb vedi* **dovere**
devo'luto, -a *pp di* **devolvere**
devoluzi'one [devolut'tsjone] *sf* (*Dir*) devolution, transfer
de'volvere *vt* (*Dir*) to transfer, devolve; **~ qc in beneficenza** to give sth to charity
de'voto, -a *ag* (*Rel*) devout, pious; (*affezionato*) devoted
devozi'one [devot'tsjone] *sf* devoutness; (*anche Rel*) devotion
dezip'pare [dedzip'pare] *vt* (*Comput*) to unzip
dg *abbr* (= *decigrammo*) dg

PAROLA CHIAVE

di (*di + il* = **del**, *di + lo* = **dello**, *di + l'* = **dell'**, *di + la* = **della**, *di + i* = **dei**, *di + gli* = **degli**, *di + le* = **delle**) *prep* **1** (*possesso, specificazione*) of; (*composto da, scritto da*) by; **la macchina di Paolo/di mio fratello** Paolo's/my brother's car; **un amico di mio fratello** a friend of my brother's, one of my brother's friends; **la grandezza della casa** the size of the house; **le foto delle vacanze** the holiday photos; **la città di Firenze** the city of Florence; **il nome di Maria** the name Mary; **un quadro di Botticelli** a painting by Botticelli
2 (*caratterizzazione, misura*) of; **una casa di mattoni** a brick house, a house made of bricks; **un orologio d'oro** a gold watch; **un bimbo di 3 anni** a child of 3, a 3-year-old child; **una trota di un chilo** a trout weighing a kilo; **una strada di 10 km** a road 10 km long; **un quadro di valore** a valuable picture
3 (*causa, mezzo, modo*) with; **tremare di paura** to tremble with fear; **morire di cancro** to die of cancer; **spalmare di burro** to spread with butter
4 (*argomento*) about, of; **discutere di sport** to talk about sport; **parlare di politica/lavoro** to talk about politics/work
5 (*luogo: provenienza*) from; out of; **essere di Roma** to be from Rome; **uscire di casa** to come out of *o* leave the house
6 (*tempo*) in; **d'estate/d'inverno** in (the) summer/winter; **di notte** by night, at night; **di mattina/sera** in the morning/evening; **di lunedì** on Mondays; **di ora in ora** by the hour
7 (*partitivo*) of; **alcuni di voi/noi** some of you/us; **il più bravo di tutti** the best of all; **il migliore del mondo** the best in the world; **non c'è niente di peggio** there's nothing worse
8 (*paragone*) than; **più veloce di me** faster than me; **guadagna meno di me** he earns less than me
▪ *det* (*una certa quantità di*) some; (*: negativo*) any; (*: interrogativo*) any, some; **del pane** (some) bread; **delle caramelle** (some) sweets; **degli amici miei** some friends of mine; **vuoi del vino?** do you want some *o* any wine?

dì *sm* day; **buon dì!** hallo!; **a dì** = **addì**
DIA *sigla f* = **Direzione investigativa antimafia**
dia'bete *sm* diabetes *sg*
dia'betico, -a, ci, che *ag, sm/f* diabetic
dia'bolico, -a, ci, che *ag* diabolical
di'acono *sm* (*Rel*) deacon
dia'dema, -i *sm* diadem; (*di donna*) tiara
di'afano, -a *ag* (*trasparente*) diaphanous; (*pelle*) transparent
dia'framma, -i *sm* (*divisione*) screen; (*Anat, Fot, contraccettivo*) diaphragm
di'agnosi [di'aɲɲozi] *sf* diagnosis *sg*
diagnosti'care [diaɲɲosti'kare] *vt* to diagnose
dia'gnostico, -a, ci, che [diaɲ'ɲɔstiko] *ag* diagnostic; **aiuti diagnostici** (*Inform*) debugging aids
diago'nale *ag, sf* diagonal
dia'gramma, -i *sm* diagram; **~ a barre** bar chart; **~ di flusso** flow chart
dialet'tale *ag* dialectal; **poesia ~** poetry in dialect

dia'letto *sm* dialect
di'alisi *sf* dialysis
dialo'gante *ag*: **unità ~** (*Inform*) interactive terminal
dialo'gare *vi*: **~ (con)** to have a dialogue (with); (*conversare*) to converse (with) ■ *vt* (*scena*) to write the dialogue for
di'alogo, -ghi *sm* dialogue
dia'mante *sm* diamond
di'ametro *sm* diameter
di'amine *escl*: **che ~ ...?** what on earth ...?
diaposi'tiva *sf* transparency, slide
di'aria *sf* daily (expense) allowance
di'ario *sm* diary; **~ di bordo** (*Naut*) log(book); **~ di classe** (*Ins*) class register; **~ degli esami** (*Ins*) exam timetable
diar'rea *sf* diarrhoea
dia'triba *sf* diatribe
diavole'ria *sf* (*azione*) act of mischief; (*aggeggio*) weird contraption
di'avolo *sm* devil; **è un buon ~** he's a good sort; **avere un ~ per capello** to be in a foul temper; **avere una fame/un freddo del ~** to be ravenously hungry/frozen stiff; **mandare qn al ~** (*fam*) to tell sb to go to hell; **fare il ~ a quattro** to kick up a fuss
di'battere *vt* to debate, discuss; **dibattersi** *vr* to struggle
dibatti'mento *sm* (*dibattito*) debate, discussion; (*Dir*) hearing
di'battito *sm* debate, discussion
dic. *abbr* (= *dicembre*) Dec
dicas'tero *sm* ministry
'dice ['ditʃe] *vb vedi* **dire**
di'cembre [di'tʃɛmbre] *sm* December; *vedi anche* **luglio**
dice'ria [ditʃe'ria] *sf* rumour (*Brit*), rumor (*US*), piece of gossip
dichia'rare [dikja'rare] *vt* to declare; **dichiararsi** *vr* to declare o.s.; (*innamorato*) to declare one's love; **si dichiara che ...** it is hereby declared that ...; **dichiararsi vinto** to admit defeat
dichia'rato, -a [dikja'rato] *ag* (*nemico, ateo*) avowed
dichiarazi'one [dikjarat'tsjone] *sf* declaration; **~ dei redditi** statement of income; (*modulo*) tax return
dician'nove [ditʃan'nɔve] *num* nineteen
dicianno'venne [ditʃanno'vɛnne] *ag, sm/f* nineteen-year-old
dicias'sette [ditʃas'sɛtte] *num* seventeen
diciasset'tenne [ditʃasset'tɛnne] *ag, sm/f* seventeen-year-old
diciot'tenne [ditʃot'tɛnne] *ag, sm/f* eighteen-year-old
dici'otto [di'tʃɔtto] *num* eighteen ■ *sm inv* (*Ins*) *minimum satisfactory mark awarded in Italian universities*
dici'tura [ditʃi'tura] *sf* words *pl*, wording
'dico *etc vb vedi* **dire**
didasca'lia *sf* (*di illustrazione*) caption; (*Cine*) subtitle; (*Teat*) stage directions *pl*
di'dattico, -a, ci, che *ag* didactic; (*metodo, programma*) teaching; (*libro*) educational ■ *sf* didactics *sg*; teaching methodology
di'dentro *av* inside, indoors
didi'etro *av* behind ■ *ag inv* (*ruota, giardino*) back, rear *cpd* ■ *sm* (*di casa*) rear; (*fam: sedere*) backside
di'eci ['djɛtʃi] *num* ten
dieci'mila [djɛtʃi'mila] *num* ten thousand
die'cina [dje'tʃina] *sf* = **decina**
di'edi *etc vb vedi* **dare**
di'eresi *sf* dieresis *sg*
'diesel ['di:zəl] *sm inv* diesel engine
dies'sino, -a *ag* (*Pol*) of *o* belonging to the Democrats of the Left (*Italian left-wing party*)
di'eta *sf* diet; **essere a ~** to be on a diet
die'tetica *sf* dietetics *sg*
die'tologo, -a, gi, ghe *sm/f* dietician
di'etro *av* behind; (*in fondo*) at the back ■ *prep* behind; (*tempo: dopo*) after ■ *sm* (*di foglio, giacca*) back; (*di casa*) back, rear ■ *ag inv* back *cpd*; **le zampe di ~** the hind legs; **~ ricevuta** against receipt; **~ richiesta** on demand; (*scritta*) on application; **andare ~ a** (*anche fig*) to follow; **stare ~ a qn** (*sorvegliare*) to keep an eye on sb; (*corteggiare*) to hang around sb; **portarsi ~ qn/qc** to bring sb/sth with one, bring sb/sth along; **gli hanno riso/parlato ~** they laughed at/talked about him behind his back
di'etro 'front *escl* about turn! (*Brit*), about face! (*US*) ■ *sm* (*Mil*) about-turn, about-face; (*fig*) volte-face, about-turn, about-face; **fare ~** (*Mil, fig*) to about-turn, about-face; (*tornare indietro*) to turn round
di'fatti *cong* in fact, as a matter of fact
di'fendere *vt* to defend; **difendersi** *vr* (*cavarsela*) to get by; **difendersi da/contro** to defend o.s. from/against; **difendersi dal freddo** to protect o.s. from the cold; **sapersi ~** to know how to look after o.s.
difen'sivo, -a *ag* defensive ■ *sf*: **stare sulla difensiva** (*anche fig*) to be on the defensive
difen'sore, -a *sm/f* defender; **avvocato ~** counsel for the defence (*Brit*) *o* defense (*US*)
di'fesa *sf vedi* **difeso**
di'fesi *etc vb vedi* **difendere**
di'feso, -a *pp di* **difendere** ■ *sf* defence (*Brit*), defense (*US*); **prendere le difese di qn** to defend sb, take sb's part

difet'tare *vi* to be defective; **~ di** to be lacking in, lack
difet'tivo, -a *ag* defective
di'fetto *sm* (*mancanza*): **~ di** lack of; (*di fabbricazione*) fault, flaw, defect; (*morale*) fault, failing, defect; (*fisico*) defect; **far ~** to be lacking; **in ~** at fault; in the wrong
difet'toso, -a *ag* defective, faulty
diffa'mare *vt* (*a parole*) to slander; (*per iscritto*) to libel
diffama'torio, -a *ag* slanderous; libellous
diffamazi'one [diffamat'tsjone] *sf* slander; libel
diffe'rente *ag* different
diffe'renza [diffe'rɛntsa] *sf* difference; **a ~ di** unlike; **non fare ~ (tra)** to make no distinction (between)
differenzi'ale [differen'tsjale] *ag, sm* differential; **classi differenziali** (*Ins*) special classes (*for backward children*)
differenzi'are [differen'tsjare] *vt* to differentiate; **differenziarsi da** to differentiate o.s. from; to differ from
diffe'rire *vt* to postpone, defer ■ *vi* to be different
diffe'rita *sf*: **in ~** (*trasmettere*) prerecorded
dif'ficile [dif'fitʃile] *ag* difficult; (*persona*) hard to please, difficult (to please); (*poco probabile*): **è ~ che sia libero** it is unlikely that he'll be free ■ *sm/f*: **fare il(la) ~** to be difficult, be awkward ■ *sm* difficult part; difficulty; **essere ~ nel mangiare** to be fussy about one's food
difficil'mente [diffitʃil'mente] *av* (*con difficoltà*) with difficulty; **~ verrà** he's unlikely to come
difficoltà *sf inv* difficulty
difficol'toso, -a *ag* (*compito*) difficult, hard; (*persona*) difficult, hard to please; **digestione difficoltosa** poor digestion
dif'fida *sf* (*Dir*) warning, notice
diffi'dare *vi*: **~ di** to be suspicious *o* distrustful of ■ *vt* (*Dir*) to warn; **~ qn dal fare qc** to warn sb not to do sth, caution sb against doing sth
diffi'dente *ag* suspicious, distrustful
diffi'denza [diffi'dɛntsa] *sf* suspicion, distrust
dif'fondere *vt* (*luce, calore*) to diffuse; (*notizie*) to spread, circulate; **diffondersi** *vr* to spread
dif'fusi *etc vb vedi* **diffondere**
diffusi'one *sf* diffusion; spread; (*anche di giornale*) circulation; (*Fisica*) scattering
dif'fuso, -a *pp di* **diffondere** ■ *ag* (*Fisica*) diffuse; (*notizia, malattia etc*) widespread; **è opinione diffusa che ...** it's widely held that ....

difi'lato *av* (*direttamente*) straight, directly; (*subito*) straight away
difte'rite *sf* diphtheria
'diga, -ghe *sf* dam; (*portuale*) breakwater
dige'rente [didʒe'rɛnte] *ag* (*apparato*) digestive
dige'rire [didʒe'rire] *vt* to digest
digesti'one [didʒes'tjone] *sf* digestion
diges'tivo, -a [didʒes'tivo] *ag* digestive ■ *sm* (after-dinner) liqueur
Digi'one [di'dʒone] *sf* Dijon
digi'tale [didʒi'tale] *ag* digital; (*delle dita*) finger *cpd*, digital ■ *sf* (*Bot*) foxglove
digi'tare [didʒi'tare] *vt* (*dati*) to key (in); (*tasto*) to press
digiu'nare [didʒu'nare] *vi* to starve o.s.; (*Rel*) to fast
digi'uno, -a [di'dʒuno] *ag*: **essere ~** not to have eaten ■ *sm* fast; **a ~** on an empty stomach
dignità [diɲɲi'ta] *sf inv* dignity
digni'tario [diɲɲi'tarjo] *sm* dignitary
digni'toso, -a [diɲɲi'toso] *ag* dignified
'DIGOS *sigla f* (= *Divisione Investigazioni Generali e Operazioni Speciali*) *police department dealing with political security*
digressi'one *sf* digression
digri'gnare [digriɲ'ɲare] *vt*: **~ i denti** to grind one's teeth
dila'gare *vi* to flood; (*fig*) to spread
dilani'are *vt* to tear to pieces
dilapi'dare *vt* to squander, waste
dila'tare *vt* to dilate; (*gas*) to cause to expand; (*passaggio, cavità*) to open (up); **dilatarsi** *vr* to dilate; (*Fisica*) to expand
dilatazi'one [dilatat'tsjone] *sf* (*Anat*) dilation; (*di gas, metallo*) expansion
dilazio'nare [dilattsjo'nare] *vt* to delay, defer
dilazi'one [dilat'tsjone] *sf* deferment
dileggi'are [diled'dʒare] *vt* to mock, deride
dilegu'are *vi*, **dilegu'arsi** *vr* to vanish, disappear
di'lemma, -i *sm* dilemma
dilet'tante *sm/f* dilettante; (*anche Sport*) amateur
dilet'tare *vt* to give pleasure to, delight; **dilettarsi** *vr*: **dilettarsi di** to take pleasure in, enjoy
dilet'tevole *ag* delightful
di'letto, -a *ag* dear, beloved ■ *sm* pleasure, delight
dili'gente [dili'dʒɛnte] *ag* (*scrupoloso*) diligent; (*accurato*) careful, accurate
dili'genza [dili'dʒɛntsa] *sf* diligence; care; (*carrozza*) stagecoach
dilu'ire *vt* to dilute
dilun'garsi *vr* (*fig*): **~ su** to talk at length on *o* about

diluvi'are *vb impers* to pour (down)
di'luvio *sm* downpour; (*inondazione, fig*) flood; **il ~ universale** the Flood
dima'grante *ag* slimming *cpd*
dima'grire *vi* to get thinner, lose weight
dime'nare *vt* to wave, shake; **dimenarsi** *vr* to toss and turn; (*fig*) to struggle; **~ la coda** (*cane*) to wag its tail
dimensi'one *sf* dimension; (*grandezza*) size; **considerare un discorso nella sua ~ politica** to look at a speech in terms of its political significance
dimenti'canza [dimenti'kantsa] *sf* forgetfulness; (*errore*) oversight, slip; **per ~** inadvertently
dimenti'care *vt* to forget; **dimenticarsi** *vr*: **dimenticarsi di qc** to forget sth
dimentica'toio *sm* (*scherzoso*): **cadere/ mettere nel ~** to sink into/consign to oblivion
di'mentico, -a, chi, che *ag*: **~ di** (*che non ricorda*) forgetful of; (*incurante*) oblivious of, unmindful of
di'messo, -a *pp di* **dimettere** ■ *ag* (*voce*) subdued; (*uomo, abito*) modest, humble
dimesti'chezza [dimesti'kettsa] *sf* familiarity
di'mettere *vt*: **~ qn da** to dismiss sb from; (*dall'ospedale*) to discharge sb from; **dimettersi** *vr*: **dimettersi (da)** to resign (from)
dimez'zare [dimed'dzare] *vt* to halve
diminu'ire *vt* to reduce, diminish; (*prezzi*) to bring down, reduce ■ *vi* to decrease, diminish; (*rumore*) to die down, die away; (*prezzi*) to fall, go down
diminu'tivo, -a *ag, sm* diminutive
diminuzi'one [diminut'tsjone] *sf* decreasing, diminishing; **in ~** on the decrease; **~ della produttività** fall in productivity
di'misi *etc vb vedi* **dimettere**
dimissio'nario, -a *ag* outgoing, resigning
dimissi'oni *sfpl* resignation *sg*; **dare** *o* **presentare le ~** to resign, hand in one's resignation
di'mora *sf* residence; **senza fissa ~** of no fixed address *o* abode
dimo'rare *vi* to reside
dimos'trante *sm/f* (*Pol*) demonstrator
dimos'trare *vt* to demonstrate, show; (*provare*) to prove, demonstrate; **dimostrarsi** *vr*: **dimostrarsi molto abile** to show o.s. *o* prove to be very clever; **non dimostra la sua età** he doesn't look his age; **dimostra 30 anni** he looks about 30 (years old)
dimostra'tivo, -a *ag* (*anche Ling*) demonstrative
dimostrazi'one [dimostrat'tsjone] *sf* demonstration; proof
di'namico, -a, ci, che *ag* dynamic ■ *sf* dynamics *sg*
dina'mismo *sm* dynamism
dinami'tardo, -a *ag*: **attentato ~** dynamite attack ■ *sm/f* dynamiter
dina'mite *sf* dynamite
'dinamo *sf inv* dynamo
di'nanzi [di'nantsi]: **~ a** *prep* in front of
dinas'tia *sf* dynasty
dini'ego, -ghi *sm* (*rifiuto*) refusal; (*negazione*) denial
dinocco'lato, -a *ag* lanky; **camminare ~** to walk with a slouch
dino'sauro *sm* dinosaur
din'torno *av* round, (round) about; **dintorni** *smpl* outskirts; **nei dintorni di** in the vicinity *o* neighbourhood of
'dio (*pl* **dei**) *sm* god; **D~** God; **gli dei** the gods; **si crede un ~** he thinks he's wonderful; **D~ mio!** my God!; **D~ ce la mandi buona** let's hope for the best; **D~ ce ne scampi e liberi!** God forbid!
di'ocesi [di'ɔtʃezi] *sf inv* diocese
dios'sina *sf* dioxin
dipa'nare *vt* (*lana*) to wind into a ball; (*fig*) to disentangle, sort out
diparti'mento *sm* department
dipen'dente *ag* dependent ■ *sm/f* employee
dipen'denza [dipen'dɛntsa] *sf* dependence; **essere alle dipendenze di qn** to be employed by sb *o* in sb's employ
di'pendere *vi*: **~ da** to depend on; (*finanziariamente*) to be dependent on; (*derivare*) to come from, be due to
di'pesi *etc vb vedi* **dipendere**
di'peso, -a *pp di* **dipendere**
di'pingere [di'pindʒere] *vt* to paint
di'pinsi *etc vb vedi* **dipingere**
di'pinto, -a *pp di* **dipingere** ■ *sm* painting
di'ploma, -i *sm* diploma
diplo'mare *vt* to award a diploma to, graduate (*US*) ■ *vi* to obtain a diploma, graduate (*US*)
diplo'matico, -a, ci, che *ag* diplomatic ■ *sm* diplomat
diplo'mato, -a *ag* qualified ■ *sm/f* qualified person, holder of a diploma
diploma'zia [diplomat'tsia] *sf* diplomacy
di'porto *sm*: **imbarcazione da ~** pleasure craft
dira'dare *vt* to thin (out); (*visite*) to reduce, make less frequent; **diradarsi** *vr* to disperse; (*nebbia*) to clear (up)
dira'mare *vt* to issue; ■ *vi*, **diramarsi** ■ *vr* (*strade*) to branch

d

ˈdire *vt* to say; (*segreto, fatto*) to tell; **~ qc a qn** to tell sb sth; **~ a qn di fare qc** to tell sb to do sth; **~ di sì/no** to say yes/no; **si dice che ...** they say that ...; **mi si dice che ...** I am told that ...; **si direbbe che ...** it looks (*o* sounds) as though ...; **dica, signora?** (*in un negozio*) yes, Madam, can I help you?; **sa quello che dice** he knows what he's talking about; **lascialo ~** (*esprimersi*) let him have his say; (*ignoralo*) just ignore him; **come sarebbe a ~?** what do you mean?; **che ne diresti di andarcene?** how about leaving?; **chi l'avrebbe mai detto!** who would have thought it!; **si dicono esperti** they say they are experts; **per così ~** so to speak; **a dir poco** to say the least; **non c'è che ~** there's no doubt about it; **non dico di no** I can't deny it; **il che è tutto ~** need I say more?

diˈressi *etc vb vedi* **dirigere**

diˈretta *sf vedi* **diretto**

direttaˈmente *av* (*immediatamente*) directly, straight; (*personalmente*) directly; (*senza intermediari*) direct, straight

diretˈtissima *sf* (*tragitto*) most direct route; (*Dir*): **processo per ~** summary trial

diretˈtissimo *sm* (*Ferr*) fast (through) train

diretˈtivo, -a *ag* (*Pol, Amm*) executive; (*Comm*) managerial, executive ▪ *sm* leadership, leaders *pl* ▪ *sf* directive, instruction

diˈretto, -a *pp di* **dirigere** ▪ *ag* direct ▪ *sm* (*Ferr*) through train ▪ *sf*: **in (linea) diretta** (*Radio, TV*) live; **il mio ~ superiore** my immediate superior

diretˈtore, -ˈtrice *sm/f* (*di azienda*) director, manager(-manageress); (*di scuola elementare*) head (teacher) (*Brit*), principal (*US*); **~ amministrativo** company secretary (*Brit*), corporate executive secretary (*US*); **~ del carcere** prison governor (*Brit*) *o* warden (*US*); **~ di filiale** branch manager; **~ d'orchestra** conductor; **~ di produzione** (*Cine*) producer; **~ sportivo** team manager; **~ tecnico** (*Sport*) trainer, coach

direziˈone [diretˈtsjone] *sf* (*senso: anche fig*) direction; (*conduzione: gen*) running; (*: di partito*) leadership; (*: di società*) management; (*: di giornale*) editorship; (*direttori*) management; **in ~ di** in the direction of, towards

diriˈgente [diriˈdʒɛnte] *ag* managerial ▪ *sm/f* executive; (*Pol*) leader; **classe ~** ruling class

diriˈgenza [diriˈdʒɛntsa] *sf* management; (*Pol*) leadership

dirigenziˈale [diridʒenˈtsjale] *ag* managerial

diˈrigere [diˈridʒere] *vt* to direct; (*impresa*) to run, manage; (*Mus*) to conduct; **dirigersi** *vr*: **dirigersi verso** *o* **a** to make *o* head for; **~ i propri passi verso** to make one's way towards; **il treno era diretto a Pavia** the train was heading for Pavia

diriˈgibile [diriˈdʒibile] *sm* airship

dirimˈpetto *av* opposite; **~ a** *prep* opposite, facing

diˈritto, -a *ag* straight; (*onesto*) straight, upright ▪ *av* straight, directly ▪ *sm* right side; (*Tennis*) forehand; (*Maglia*) plain stitch, knit stitch; (*prerogativa*) right; (*leggi, scienza*): **il ~** law; **stare ~** to stand up straight; **aver ~ a qc** to be entitled to sth; **punto ~** plain (stitch); **andare ~** to go straight on; **a buon ~** quite rightly; **diritti (d'autore)** royalties; **~ di successione** right of succession

diritˈtura *sf* (*Sport*) straight; (*fig*) rectitude

dirocˈcato, -a *ag* tumbledown, in ruins

diromˈpente *ag* (*anche fig*) explosive

dirottaˈmento *sm*: **~ (aereo)** hijack

dirotˈtare *vt* (*nave, aereo*) to change the course of; (*aereo: sotto minaccia*) to hijack; (*traffico*) to divert ▪ *vi* (*nave, aereo*) to change course

dirottaˈtore, -ˈtrice *sm/f* hijacker

diˈrotto, -a *ag* (*pioggia*) torrential; (*pianto*) unrestrained; **piovere a ~** to pour, rain cats and dogs; **piangere a ~** to cry one's heart out

diˈrupo *sm* crag, precipice

diˈsabile *sm/f* disabled person

disabiˈtato, -a *ag* uninhabited

disabituˈarsi *vr*: **~ a** to get out of the habit of

disacˈcordo *sm* disagreement

disadatˈtato, -a *ag* (*Psic*) maladjusted

disaˈdorno, -a *ag* plain, unadorned

disaffeziˈone [dizaffetˈtsjone] *sf* disaffection

disaˈgevole [disaˈdʒevole] *ag* (*scomodo*) uncomfortable; (*difficile*) difficult

disagiˈato, -a [dizaˈdʒato] *ag* poor, needy; (*vita*) hard

diˈsagio [diˈzadʒo] *sm* discomfort; (*disturbo*) inconvenience; (*fig: imbarazzo*) embarrassment; **disagi** *smpl* hardship *sg*, poverty *sg*; **essere a ~** to be ill at ease

diˈsamina *sf* close examination

disapproˈvare *vt* to disapprove of

disapprovaziˈone [dizapprovatˈtsjone] *sf* disapproval

disapˈpunto *sm* disappointment

disarcioˈnare [dizartʃoˈnare] *vt* to unhorse

disarˈmante *ag* (*fig*) disarming

disarˈmare *vt, vi* to disarm

diˈsarmo *sm* (*Mil*) disarmament

diˈsastro *sm* disaster

disasˈtroso, -a *ag* disastrous

disatˈtento, -a *ag* inattentive

disattenziˈone [dizattenˈtsjone] *sf* carelessness, lack of attention

disattiˈvare *vt* (*bomba*) to de-activate, defuse

disa'vanzo [diza'vantso] *sm* (*Econ*) deficit
disavven'tura *sf* misadventure, mishap
dis'brigo, -ghi *sm* (prompt) clearing up *o* settlement
dis'capito *sm*: **a ~ di** to the detriment of
dis'carica, -che *sf* (*di rifiuti*) rubbish tip *o* dump
discen'dente [diʃʃen'dɛnte] *ag* descending ▪ *sm/f* descendant
di'scendere [diʃʃɛndere] *vt* to go (*o* come) down ▪ *vi* to go (*o* come) down; (*smontare*) to get off; **~ da** (*famiglia*) to be descended from; **~ dalla macchina/dal treno** to get out of the car/out of *o* off the train; **~ da cavallo** to dismount, get off one's horse
di'scepolo, -a [diʃʃepolo] *sm/f* disciple
di'scernere [diʃʃɛrnere] *vt* to discern
discerni'mento [diʃʃerni'mento] *sm* discernment
disce'sista [diʃʃe'sista] *sm/f* downhill skier
di'sceso, -a [diʃʃeso] *pp di* **discendere** ▪ *sf* descent; (*pendio*) slope; **in discesa** (*strada*) downhill *cpd*, sloping; **discesa libera** (*Sci*) downhill race
dischi'udere [dis'kjudere] *vt* (*aprire*) to open; (*fig: rivelare*) to disclose, reveal
dischi'usi *etc* [dis'kjusi] *vb vedi* **dischiudere**
dischi'uso, -a [dis'kjuso] *pp di* **dischiudere**
di'scinto, -a [diʃʃinto] *ag* (*anche*: **in abiti discinti**) half-undressed
disci'ogliere [diʃʃɔʎʎere] *vt*, **disci'ogliersi** *vr* to dissolve; (*fondere*) to melt
disci'plina [diʃʃi'plina] *sf* discipline
discipli'nare [diʃʃipli'nare] *ag* disciplinary ▪ *vt* to discipline
'disco, -schi *sm* disc, disk; (*Sport*) discus; (*fonografico*) record; (*Inform*) disk; **~ magnetico** (*Inform*) magnetic disk; **~ orario** (*Aut*) parking disc; **~ rigido** (*Inform*) hard disk; **~ volante** flying saucer
discogra'fia *sf* (*tecnica*) recording, record-making; (*industria*) record industry
disco'grafico, -a, ci, che *ag* record *cpd*, recording *cpd* ▪ *sm* record producer; **casa discografica** record(ing) company
'discolo, -a *ag* (*bambino*) undisciplined, unruly ▪ *sm/f* rascal
discol'pare *vt* to clear of blame; **discolparsi** *vr* to clear o.s., prove one's innocence; (*giustificarsi*) to excuse o.s.
disco'noscere [disko'noʃʃere] *vt* (*figlio*) to disown; (*meriti*) to ignore, disregard
disconosci'uto, -a [diskonoʃʃuto] *pp di* **disconoscere**
discon'tinuo, -a *ag* (*linea*) broken; (*rendimento, stile*) irregular; (*interesse*) sporadic
dis'corde *ag* conflicting, clashing
dis'cordia *sf* discord; (*dissidio*) disagreement, clash
dis'correre *vi*: **~ (di)** to talk (about)
dis'corso, -a *pp di* **discorrere** ▪ *sm* speech; (*conversazione*) conversation, talk
dis'costo, -a *ag* faraway, distant ▪ *av* far away; **~ da** *prep* far from
disco'teca, -che *sf* (*raccolta*) record library; (*luogo di ballo*) disco(theque)
discre'panza [diskre'pantsa] *sf* discrepancy
dis'creto, -a *ag* discreet; (*abbastanza buono*) reasonable, fair
discrezi'one [diskret'tsjone] *sf* discretion; (*giudizio*) judgment, discernment; **a ~ di** at the discretion of
discrimi'nante *ag* (*fattore, elemento*) decisive ▪ *sf* (*Dir*) extenuating circumstance
discrimi'nare *vt* to discrimate
discriminazi'one [diskriminat'tsjone] *sf* discrimination
dis'cussi *etc vb vedi* **discutere**
discussi'one *sf* discussion; (*litigio*) argument; **mettere in ~** to bring into question; **fuori ~** out of the question
dis'cusso, -a *pp di* **discutere**
dis'cutere *vt* to discuss, debate; (*contestare*) to question, dispute ▪ *vi* (*conversare*): **~ (di)** to discuss; (*litigare*) to argue
discu'tibile *ag* questionable
disde'gnare [dizdeɲ'ɲare] *vt* to scorn
dis'degno [diz'deɲɲo] *sm* scorn, disdain
disde'gnoso, -a [dizdeɲ'ɲoso] *ag* disdainful, scornful
dis'detto, -a *pp di* **disdire** ▪ *sf* cancellation; (*sfortuna*) bad luck
disdi'cevole [dizdi'tʃevole] *ag* improper, unseemly
dis'dire *vt* (*prenotazione*) to cancel; **~ un contratto d'affitto** (*Dir*) to give notice (to quit)
dise'gnare [diseɲ'ɲare] *vt* to draw; (*progettare*) to design; (*fig*) to outline
disegna'tore, -'trice [diseɲɲa'tore] *sm/f* designer
di'segno [di'zeɲɲo] *sm* drawing; (*su stoffa etc*) design; (*fig: schema*) outline; **~ industriale** industrial design; **~ di legge** (*Dir*) bill
diser'bante *sm* weedkiller
disere'dare *vt* to disinherit
diser'tare *vt, vi* to desert
diser'tore *sm* (*Mil*) deserter
diserzi'one [dizer'tsjone] *sf* (*Mil*) desertion
disfaci'mento [disfatʃi'mento] *sm* (*di cadavere*) decay; (*fig: di istituzione, impero, società*) decline, decay; **in ~** in decay
dis'fare *vt* to undo; (*valigie*) to unpack; (*meccanismo*) to take to pieces; (*lavoro, paese*)

to destroy; (*neve*) to melt; **disfarsi** *vr* to come undone; (*neve*) to melt; ~ **il letto** to strip the bed; **disfarsi di qn** (*liberarsi*) to get rid of sb
dis'fatta *sf vedi* **disfatto**
disfat'tista, -i, e *sm/f* defeatist
dis'fatto, -a *pp di* **disfare** ■ *ag* (*gen*) undone, untied; (*letto*) unmade; (*persona*: *sfinito*) exhausted, worn-out; (: *addolorato*) grief-stricken ■ *sf* (*sconfitta*) rout
disfunzi'one [disfun'tsjone] *sf* (*Med*) dysfunction; ~ **cardiaca** heart trouble
disge'lare [dizdʒe'lare] *vt, vi*, **disge'larsi** *vr* to thaw
dis'gelo [diz'dʒɛlo] *sm* thaw
dis'grazia [diz'grattsja] *sf* (*sventura*) misfortune; (*incidente*) accident, mishap
disgrazi'ato, -a [dizgrat'tsjato] *ag* unfortunate ■ *sm/f* wretch
disgre'gare *vt*, **disgre'garsi** *vr* to break up
disgu'ido *sm* hitch; ~ **postale** error in postal delivery
disgus'tare *vt* to disgust; **disgustarsi** *vr*: **disgustarsi di** to be disgusted by
dis'gusto *sm* disgust
disgus'toso, -a *ag* disgusting
disidra'tare *vt* to dehydrate
disidra'tato, -a *ag* dehydrated
disil'ludere *vt* to disillusion, disenchant
disillusi'one *sf* disillusion, disenchantment
disimpa'rare *vt* to forget
disimpe'gnare [dizimpeɲ'ɲare] *vt* (*persona*: *da obblighi*): ~ **da** to release from; (*oggetto dato in pegno*) to redeem, get out of pawn; **disimpegnarsi** *vr*: **disimpegnarsi da** (*obblighi*) to release o.s. from, free o.s. from
disincagli'are [dizinkaʎ'ʎare] *vt* (*barca*) to refloat; **disincagliarsi** *vr* to get afloat again
disincan'tato, -a *ag* disenchanted, disillusioned
disincenti'vare [dizintʃenti'vare] *vt* to discourage
disinfes'tare *vt* to disinfest
disinfestazi'one [dizinfestat'tsjone] *sf* disinfestation
disinfet'tante *ag, sm* disinfectant
disinfet'tare *vt* to disinfect
disinfezi'one [dizinfet'tsjone] *sf* disinfection
disingan'nare *vt* to disillusion
disin'ganno *sm* disillusion
disini'bito, -a *ag* uninhibited
disinnes'care *vt* to defuse
disinnes'tare *vt* (*marcia*) to disengage
disinqui'nare *vt* to free from pollution
disinte'grare *vt, vi* to disintegrate
disinteres'sarsi *vr*: ~ **di** to take no interest in
disinte'resse *sm* indifference; (*generosità*) unselfishness
disintossi'care *vt* (*alcolizzato, drogato*) to treat for alcoholism (*o* drug addiction); **disintossicarsi** *vr* to clear out one's system; (*alcolizzato, drogato*) to be treated for alcoholism (*o* drug addiction)
disintossicazi'one [dizintossikat'tsjone] *sf* treatment for alcoholism (*o* drug addiction)
disin'volto, -a *ag* casual, free and easy
disinvol'tura *sf* casualness, ease
disles'sia *sf* dyslexia
disli'vello *sm* difference in height; (*fig*) gap
dislo'care *vt* to station, position
dismi'sura *sf* excess; **a** ~ to excess, excessively
disobbe'dire *etc* = **disubbidire** *etc*
disoccu'pato, -a *ag* unemployed ■ *sm/f* unemployed person
disoccupazi'one [dizokkupat'tsjone] *sf* unemployment
disonestà *sf* dishonesty
diso'nesto, -a *ag* dishonest
disono'rare *vt* to dishonour (*Brit*), dishonor (*US*), bring disgrace upon
diso'nore *sm* dishonour (*Brit*), dishonor (*US*), disgrace
di'sopra *av* (*con contatto*) on top; (*senza contatto*) above; (*al piano superiore*) upstairs ■ *ag inv* (*superiore*) upper ■ *sm inv* top, upper part; **la gente** ~ the people upstairs; **il piano** ~ the floor above
disordi'nare *vt* to mess up, disarrange; (*Mil*) to throw into disorder
disordi'nato, -a *ag* untidy; (*privo di misura*) irregular, wild
di'sordine *sm* (*confusione*) disorder, confusion; (*sregolatezza*) debauchery; **disordini** *smpl* (*Pol etc*) disorder *sg*; (*tumulti*) riots
disor'ganico, -a, ci, che *ag* incoherent, disorganized
disorganiz'zato, -a [dizorganid'dzato] *ag* disorganized
disorienta'mento *sm* (*fig*) confusion, bewilderment
disorien'tare *vt* to disorientate; **disorientarsi** *vr* (*fig*) to get confused, lose one's bearings
disorien'tato, -a *ag* disorientated
disos'sare *vt* (*Cuc*) to bone
di'sotto *av* below, underneath; (*in fondo*) at the bottom; (*al piano inferiore*) downstairs ■ *ag inv* (*inferiore*) lower; bottom *cpd* ■ *sm inv* (*parte inferiore*) lower part; bottom; **la gente** ~ the people downstairs; **il piano** ~ the floor below
dis'paccio [dis'pattʃo] *sm* dispatch
dispa'rato, -a *ag* disparate
'dispari *ag inv* odd, uneven
disparità *sf inv* disparity

dis'parte: **in ~** *av* (*da lato*) aside, apart; **tenersi** *o* **starsene in ~** to keep to o.s., hold aloof
dis'pendio *sm* (*di denaro, energie*) expenditure; (*: spreco*) waste
dispendi'oso, -a *ag* expensive
dis'pensa *sf* pantry, larder; (*mobile*) sideboard; (*Dir*) exemption; (*Rel*) dispensation; (*fascicolo*) number, issue
dispen'sare *vt* (*elemosine, favori*) to distribute; (*esonerare*) to exempt
dispe'rare *vi*: **~ (di)** to despair (of); **disperarsi** *vr* to despair
dispe'rato, -a *ag* (*persona*) in despair; (*caso, tentativo*) desperate
disperazi'one [disperat'tsjone] *sf* despair
dis'perdere *vt* (*disseminare*) to disperse; (*Mil*) to scatter, rout; (*fig: consumare*) to waste, squander; **disperdersi** *vr* to disperse; to scatter
dispersi'one *sf* dispersion, dispersal; (*Fisica, Chim*) dispersion
disper'sivo, -a *ag* (*lavoro etc*) disorganized
dis'perso, -a *pp di* **disperdere** ■ *sm/f* missing person; (*Mil*) missing soldier
dis'petto *sm* spite *no pl*, spitefulness *no pl*; **fare un ~ a qn** to play a (nasty) trick on sb; **a ~ di** in spite of; **con suo grande ~** much to his annoyance
dispet'toso, -a *ag* spiteful
dispia'cere [dispja'tʃere] *sm* (*rammarico*) regret, sorrow; (*dolore*) grief ■ *vi*: **~ a** to displease ■ *vb impers*: **mi dispiace (che)** I am sorry (that); **dispiaceri** *smpl* (*preoccupazioni*) troubles, worries; **se non le dispiace, me ne vado adesso** if you don't mind, I'll go now
dispiaci'uto, -a [dispja'tʃuto] *pp di* **dispiacere** ■ *ag* sorry
dis'pone, dis'pongo *etc vb vedi* **disporre**
dispo'nibile *ag* available; (*persona: solerte, gentile*) helpful
disponibilità *sf inv* availability; (*solerzia, gentilezza*) helpfulness; **disponibilità** *sfpl* (*economiche*) resources
dis'porre *vt* (*sistemare*) to arrange; (*preparare*) to prepare; (*Dir*) to order; (*persuadere*): **~ qn a** to incline *o* dispose sb towards ■ *vi* (*decidere*) to decide; (*usufruire*): **~ di** to use, have at one's disposal; (*essere dotato*): **~ di** to have; **disporsi** *vr* (*ordinarsi*) to place o.s., arrange o.s.; **disporsi a fare** to get ready to do; **disporsi all'attacco** to prepare for an attack; **disporsi in cerchio** to form a circle
dis'posi *etc vb vedi* **disporre**
disposi'tivo *sm* (*meccanismo*) device; (*Dir*) pronouncement; **~ di controllo** *o* **di comando** control device; **~ di sicurezza** (*gen*) safety device; (*di arma da fuoco*) safety catch
disposizi'one [dispozit'tsjone] *sf* arrangement, layout; (*stato d'animo*) mood; (*tendenza*) bent, inclination; (*comando*) order; (*Dir*) provision, regulation; **a ~ di qn** at sb's disposal; **per ~ di legge** by law; **~ testamentaria** provisions of a will
dis'posto, -a *pp di* **disporre** ■ *ag* (*incline*): **~ a fare** disposed *o* prepared to do
dis'potico, -a, ci, che *ag* despotic
dispo'tismo *sm* despotism
disprez'zare [dispret'tsare] *vt* to despise
dis'prezzo [dis'prettso] *sm* contempt; **con ~ del pericolo** with a total disregard for the danger involved
'disputa *sf* dispute, quarrel
dispu'tare *vt* (*contendere*) to dispute, contest; (*Sport: partita*) to play; (*: gara*) to take part in ■ *vi* to quarrel; **~ di** to discuss; **disputarsi qc** to fight for sth
disqui'sire *vi* to discourse on
disquisizi'one [diskwizit'tsjone] *sf* detailed analysis
dissa'crare *vt* to desecrate
dissangua'mento *sm* loss of blood
dissangu'are *vt* (*fig: persona*) to bleed white; (*: patrimonio*) to suck dry; **dissanguarsi** *vr* (*Med*) to lose blood; (*fig*) to ruin o.s.; **morire dissanguato** to bleed to death
dissa'pore *sm* slight disagreement
'disse *vb vedi* **dire**
disse'care *vt* to dissect
dissec'care *vt*, **dissec'carsi** *vr* to dry up
dissemi'nare *vt* to scatter; (*fig: notizie*) to spread
dissenna'tezza [dissenna'tettsa] *sf* foolishness
dis'senso *sm* dissent; (*disapprovazione*) disapproval
dissente'ria *sf* dysentery
dissen'tire *vi*: **~ (da)** to disagree (with)
disseppel'lire *vt* (*esumare: cadavere*) to disinter, exhume; (*dissotterrare: anche fig*) to dig up, unearth; (*: rancori*) to resurrect
dissertazi'one [dissertat'tsjone] *sf* dissertation
disser'vizio [disser'vittsjo] *sm* inefficiency
disses'tare *vt* (*Econ*) to ruin
disses'tato, -a *ag* (*fondo stradale*) uneven; (*economia, finanze*) shaky; **"strada dissestata"** (*per lavori in corso*) "road up" (*Brit*), "road out" (*US*)
dis'sesto *sm* (*financial*) ruin
disse'tante *ag* refreshing
disse'tare *vt* to quench the thirst of; **dissetarsi** *vr* to quench one's thirst

dissezi'one [disset'tsjone] *sf* dissection
'dissi *vb vedi* **dire**
dissi'dente *ag, sm/f* dissident
dis'sidio *sm* disagreement
dis'simile *ag* different, dissimilar
dissimu'lare *vt* (*fingere*) to dissemble; (*nascondere*) to conceal
dissimula'tore, -'trice *sm/f* dissembler
dissimulazi'one [dissimulat'tsjone] *sf* dissembling; concealment
dissi'pare *vt* to dissipate; (*scialacquare*) to squander, waste
dissipa'tezza [dissipa'tettsa] *sf* dissipation
dissi'pato, -a *ag* dissolute, dissipated
dissipazi'one [dissipat'tsjone] *sf* squandering
dissoci'are [disso'tʃare] *vt* to dissociate
dis'solto, -a *pp di* **dissolvere**
disso'lubile *ag* soluble
dissolu'tezza [dissolu'tettsa] *sf* dissoluteness
dissolu'tivo, -a *ag* (*forza*) divisive; **processo ~** (*anche fig*) process of dissolution
disso'luto, -a *pp di* **dissolvere** ■ *ag* dissolute, licentious
dissol'venza [dissol'vɛntsa] *sf* (*Cine*) fading
dis'solvere *vt* to dissolve; (*neve*) to melt; (*fumo*) to disperse; **dissolversi** *vr* to dissolve; to melt; to disperse
disso'nante *ag* discordant
disso'nanza [disso'nantsa] *sf* (*fig*: *di opinioni*) clash
dissotter'rare *vt* (*cadavere*) to disinter, exhume; (*tesori, rovine*) to dig up, unearth; (*fig*: *sentimenti, odio*) to bring up again, resurrect
dissu'adere *vt*: **~ qn da** to dissuade sb from
dissuasi'one *sf* dissuasion
dissu'aso, -a *pp di* **dissuadere**
dissua'sore *sm*: **~ di velocità** (*Aut*) speed bump
distacca'mento *sm* (*Mil*) detachment
distac'care *vt* to detach, separate; (*Sport*) to leave behind; **distaccarsi** *vr* to be detached; (*fig*) to stand out; **distaccarsi da** (*fig*: *allontanarsi*) to grow away from
dis'tacco, -chi *sm* (*separazione*) separation; (*fig*: *indifferenza*) detachment; (*Sport*): **vincere con un ~ di ...** to win by a distance of ...
dis'tante *av* far away ■ *ag* distant, far away; **essere ~ (da)** to be a long way (from); **è ~ da qui?** is it far from here?; **essere ~ nel tempo** to be in the distant past
dis'tanza [dis'tantsa] *sf* distance; **comando a ~** remote control; **a ~ di 2 giorni** 2 days later; **tener qn a ~** to keep sb at arm's length; **prendere le distanze da qc/qn** to dissociate o.s. from sth/sb; **tenere** *o* **mantenere le distanze** to keep one's distance; **~ focale** focal length; **~ di sicurezza** safe distance; (*Aut*) braking distance; **~ di tiro** range; **~ di visibilità** visibility
distanzi'are [distan'tsjare] *vt* to space out, place at intervals; (*Sport*) to outdistance; (*fig*: *superare*) to outstrip, surpass
dis'tare *vi*: **distiamo pochi chilometri da Roma** we are only a few kilometres (away) from Rome; **dista molto da qui?** is it far (away) from here?; **non dista molto** it's not far (away)
dis'tendere *vt* (*coperta*) to spread out; (*gambe*) to stretch (out); (*mettere a giacere*) to lay; (*rilassare*: *muscoli, nervi*) to relax; **distendersi** *vr* (*rilassarsi*) to relax; (*sdraiarsi*) to lie down
distensi'one *sf* stretching; relaxation; (*Pol*) détente
disten'sivo, -a *ag* (*gen*) relaxing, restful; (*farmaco*) tranquillizing; (*Pol*) conciliatory
dis'teso, -a *pp di* **distendere** ■ *ag* (*allungato*: *persona, gamba*) stretched out; (*rilassato*: *persona, atmosfera*) relaxed ■ *sf* expanse, stretch; **avere un volto ~** to look relaxed
distil'lare *vt* to distil
distil'lato *sm* distillate
distillazi'one [distillat'tsjone] *sf* distillation
distille'ria *sf* distillery
dis'tinguere *vt* to distinguish; **distinguersi** *vr* (*essere riconoscibile*) to be distinguished; (*emergere*) to stand out, be conspicuous, distinguish o.s.; **un vino che si distingue per il suo aroma** a wine with a distinctive bouquet
dis'tinguo *sm inv* distinction
dis'tinta *sf* (*nota*) note; (*elenco*) list; **~ di pagamento** receipt; **~ di versamento** pay-in slip
distin'tivo, -a *ag* distinctive; distinguishing ■ *sm* badge
dis'tinto, -a *pp di* **distinguere** ■ *ag* (*dignitoso ed elegante*) distinguished; **distinti saluti** (*in lettera*) yours faithfully
distinzi'one [distin'tsjone] *sf* distinction; **non faccio distinzioni** (*tra persone*) I don't discriminate; (*tra cose*) it's all one to me; **senza ~ di razza/religione ...** no matter what one's race/creed ...
dis'togliere [dis'tɔʎʎere] *vt*: **~ da** to take away from; (*fig*) to dissuade from
dis'tolto, -a *pp di* **distogliere**
dis'torcere [dis'tɔrtʃere] *vt* to twist; (*fig*) to twist, distort; **distorcersi** *vr* (*contorcersi*) to twist

distorsi'one *sf* (*Med*) sprain; (*Fisica, Ottica*) distortion
dis'torto, -a *pp di* **distorcere**
dis'trarre *vt* to distract; (*divertire*) to entertain, amuse; **distrarsi** *vr* (*non fare attenzione*) to be distracted, let one's mind wander; (*svagarsi*) to amuse *o* enjoy o.s.; **~ lo sguardo** to look away; **non distrarti!** pay attention!
distratta'mente *av* absent-mindedly, without thinking
dis'tratto, -a *pp di* **distrarre** ■ *ag* absent-minded; (*disattento*) inattentive
distrazi'one [distrat'tsjone] *sf* absent-mindedness; inattention; (*svago*) distraction, entertainment; **errori di ~** careless mistakes
dis'tretto *sm* district
distribu'ire *vt* to distribute; (*Carte*) to deal (out); (*consegnare: posta*) to deliver; (*lavoro*) to allocate, assign; (*ripartire*) to share out
distribu'tore *sm* (*di benzina*) petrol (*Brit*) *o* gas (*US*) pump; (*Aut, Elettr*) distributor; (*automatico*) vending machine
distribuzi'one [distribut'tsjone] *sf* distribution; delivery; allocation, assignment; sharing out
distri'care *vt* to disentangle, unravel; **districarsi** *vr* (*tirarsi fuori*): **districarsi da** to get out of, disentangle o.s. from; (*fig: cavarsela*) to manage, get by
dis'truggere [dis'truddʒere] *vt* to destroy
distrut'tivo, -a *ag* destructive
dis'trutto, -a *pp di* **distruggere**
distruzi'one [distrut'tsjone] *sf* destruction
distur'bare *vt* to disturb, trouble; (*sonno, lezioni*) to disturb, interrupt; **disturbarsi** *vr* to put o.s. out; **non si disturbi** please don't bother
dis'turbo *sm* trouble, bother, inconvenience; (*indisposizione*) (slight) disorder, ailment; **disturbi** *smpl* (*Radio, TV*) static *sg*; **~ della quiete pubblica** (*Dir*) disturbance of the peace; **disturbi di stomaco** stomach trouble *sg*
disubbidi'ente *ag* disobedient
disubbidi'enza [dizubbi'djɛntsa] *sf* disobedience; **~ civile** civil disobedience
disubbi'dire *vi*: **~ (a qn)** to disobey (sb)
disuguagli'anza [dizugwaʎ'ʎantsa] *sf* inequality
disugu'ale *ag* unequal; (*diverso*) different; (*irregolare*) uneven
disumanità *sf* inhumanity
disu'mano, -a *ag* inhuman; **un grido ~** a terrible cry
disuni'one *sf* disunity
disu'nire *vt* to divide, disunite
di'suso *sm*: **andare** *o* **cadere in ~** to fall into disuse
'dita *sfpl di* **dito**
di'tale *sm* thimble
di'tata *sf* (*colpo*) jab (with one's finger); (*segno*) fingermark
'dito (*pl(f)* **dita**) *sm* finger; (*misura*) finger, finger's breadth; **~ (del piede)** toe; **mettersi le dita nel naso** to pick one's nose; **mettere il ~ sulla piaga** (*fig*) to touch a sore spot; **non ha mosso un ~ (per aiutarmi)** he didn't lift a finger (to help me); **ormai è segnato a ~** everyone knows about him now
'ditta *sf* firm, business; **macchina della ~** company car
dit'tafono *sm* Dictaphone®
ditta'tore *sm* dictator
ditta'tura *sf* dictatorship
dit'tongo, -ghi *sm* diphthong
di'urno, -a *ag* day *cpd*, daytime *cpd*; **ore diurne** daytime *sg*; **spettacolo ~** matinee; **turno ~** day shift; *vedi anche* **albergo**
'diva *sf vedi* **divo**
diva'gare *vi* to digress
divagazi'one [divagat'tsjone] *sf* digression; **divagazionei sul tema** variations on a theme
divam'pare *vi* to flare up, blaze up
di'vano *sm* sofa; (*senza schienale*) divan; **~ letto** bed settee, sofa bed
divari'care *vt* to open wide
di'vario *sm* difference
di'vengo *etc vb vedi* **divenire**
dive'nire *vi* = **diventare**
di'venni *etc vb vedi* **divenire**
diven'tare *vi* to become; **~ famoso/professore** to become famous/a teacher; **~ vecchio** to grow old; **c'è da ~ matti** it's enough to drive you mad
dive'nuto, -a *pp di* **divenire**
di'verbio *sm* altercation
diver'gente [diver'dʒɛnte] *ag* divergent
diver'genza [diver'dʒɛntsa] *sf* divergence; **~ d'opinioni** difference of opinion
di'vergere [di'vɛrdʒere] *vi* to diverge
diverrò *etc vb vedi* **divenire**
diversa'mente *av* (*in modo differente*) differently; (*altrimenti*) otherwise; **~ da quanto stabilito** contrary to what had been decided
diversifi'care *vt* to diversify, vary; **diversificarsi** *vr*: **diversificarsi (per)** to differ (in)
diversificazi'one [diversifikat'tsjone] *sf* diversification; difference
diversi'one *sf* diversion
diversità *sf inv* difference, diversity; (*varietà*) variety

diver'sivo, -a *ag* diversionary ■ *sm* diversion, distraction; **fare un'azione diversiva** to create a diversion
di'verso, -a *ag* (*differente*): ~ **(da)** different (from) ■ *sm* (*omosessuale*) homosexual; **diversi, e** *det pl* several, various; (*Comm*) sundry ■ *pron pl* several people, many (people)
diver'tente *ag* amusing
diverti'mento *sm* amusement, pleasure; (*passatempo*) pastime, recreation; **buon ~!** enjoy yourself!, have a nice time!
diver'tire *vt* to amuse, entertain; **divertirsi** *vr* to amuse *o* enjoy o.s.; **divertiti!** enjoy yourself, have a good time!; **divertirsi alle spalle di qn** to have a laugh at sb's expense
diver'tito, -a *ag* amused
divi'dendo *sm* dividend
di'videre *vt* (*anche Mat*) to divide; (*distribuire, ripartire*) to divide (up), split (up); **dividersi** *vr* (*persone*) to separate, part; (*coppia*) to separate; **dividersi (in)** (*scindersi*) to divide (into), split up (into); (*ramificarsi*) to fork; **è diviso dalla moglie** he's separated from his wife; **si divide tra casa e lavoro** he divides his time between home and work
divi'eto *sm* prohibition; **"~ di accesso"** "no entry"; **"~ di caccia"** "no hunting"; **"~ di parcheggio"** "no parking"; **"~ di sosta"** (*Aut*) "no waiting"
divinco'larsi *vr* to wriggle, writhe
divinità *sf inv* divinity
di'vino, -a *ag* divine
di'visa *sf* (*Mil etc*) uniform; (*Comm*) foreign currency
di'visi *etc vb vedi* **dividere**
divisi'one *sf* division; **~ in sillabe** syllable division; (*a fine riga*) hyphenation
di'vismo *sm* (*esibizionismo*) playing to the crowd
di'viso, -a *pp di* **dividere**
divi'sorio, -a *ag* (*siepe, muro esterno*) dividing; (*muro interno*) dividing, partition *cpd* ■ *sm* (*in una stanza*) partition
'divo, -a *sm/f* star; **come una diva** like a prima donna
divo'rare *vt* to devour; **~ qc con gli occhi** to eye sth greedily
divorzi'are [divor'tsjare] *vi*: **~ (da qn)** to divorce (sb)
divorzi'ato, -a [divor'tsjato] *ag* divorced ■ *sm/f* divorcee
di'vorzio [di'vɔrtsjo] *sm* divorce
divul'gare *vt* to divulge, disclose; (*rendere comprensibile*) to popularize; **divulgarsi** *vr* to spread
divulgazi'one [divulgat'tsjone] *sf* (*vedi vb*) disclosure; popularization; spread
dizio'nario [dittsjo'narjo] *sm* dictionary
dizi'one [dit'tsjone] *sf* diction; pronunciation
Dja'karta [dʒa'karta] *sf* Djakarta
dl *abbr* (= *decilitro*) dl
dm *abbr* (= *decimetro*) dm
DNA [di'ennɛa] *sigla m* (*Biol*: = *acido deossiribonucleico*) DNA ■ *sigla f* = **direzione nazionale antimafia**
do *sm* (*Mus*) C; (: *solfeggiando la scala*) do(h)
dobbi'amo *vb vedi* **dovere**
D.O.C. [dɔk] *sigla* = **denominazione di origine controllata**
doc. *abbr* = **documento**
'doccia, -ce ['dottʃa] *sf* (*bagno*) shower; (*condotto*) pipe; **fare la ~** to have a shower; **~ fredda** (*fig*) slap in the face
docciaschi'uma [dottʃas'kjuma] *sm inv* shower gel
do'cente [do'tʃɛnte] *ag* teaching ■ *sm/f* teacher; (*di università*) lecturer; **personale non ~** non-teaching staff
do'cenza [do'tʃɛntsa] *sf* university teaching *o* lecturing; **ottenere la libera ~** to become a lecturer
D.O.C.G. *sigla* (= *denominazione di origine controllata e garantita*) *label guaranteeing the quality and origin of a wine*
'docile ['dɔtʃile] *ag* docile
docilità [dotʃili'ta] *sf* docility
documen'tare *vt* to document; **documentarsi** *vr*: **documentarsi (su)** to gather information *o* material (about)
documen'tario, -a *ag, sm* documentary
documentazi'one [dokumentat'tsjone] *sf* documentation
docu'mento *sm* document; **documenti** *smpl* (*d'identità etc*) papers
Dodecan'neso *sm*: **le Isole del ~** the Dodecanese Islands
dodi'cenne [dodi'tʃɛnne] *ag, sm/f* twelve-year-old
dodi'cesimo, -a [dodi'tʃɛzimo] *num* twelfth
'dodici ['doditʃi] *num* twelve
do'gana *sf* (*ufficio*) customs *pl*; (*tassa*) (customs) duty; **passare la ~** to go through customs
doga'nale *ag* customs *cpd*
dogani'ere *sm* customs officer
'doglie ['dɔʎʎe] *sfpl* (*Med*) labour *sg* (*Brit*), labor *sg* (*US*), labo(u)r pains
'dogma, -i *sm* dogma
dog'matico, -a, ci, che *ag* dogmatic
'dolce ['doltʃe] *ag* sweet; (*colore*) soft; (*carattere, persona*) gentle, mild; (*fig: mite: clima*) mild; (*non ripido: pendio*) gentle ■ *sm* (*sapore dolce*)

sweetness, sweet taste; (*Cuc: portata*) sweet, dessert; (*: torta*) cake; **il ~ far niente** sweet idleness
dolcemente *av* (*baciare, trattare*) gently; (*sorridere, cantare*) sweetly; (*parlare*) softly
dol'cezza [dol'tʃettsa] *sf* sweetness; softness; mildness; gentleness
dolci'ario, -a [dol'tʃarjo] *ag* confectionery *cpd*
dolci'astro, -a [dol'tʃastro] *ag* (*sapore*) sweetish
dolcifi'cante [doltʃifi'kante] *ag* sweetening ■ *sm* sweetener
dolci'umi [dol'tʃumi] *smpl* sweets
do'lente *ag* sorrowful, sad
do'lere *vi* to be sore, hurt, ache; **dolersi** *vr* to complain; (*essere spiacente*): **dolersi di** to be sorry for; **mi duole la testa** my head aches, I've got a headache
'dolgo *etc vb vedi* **dolere**
'dollaro *sm* dollar
'dolo *sm* (*Dir*) malice; (*frode*) fraud, deceit
Dolo'miti *sfpl*: **le ~** the Dolomites
dolo'rante *ag* aching, sore
do'lore *sm* (*fisico*) pain; (*morale*) sorrow, grief; **se lo scoprono sono dolori!** if they find out there'll be trouble!
dolo'roso, -a *ag* painful; sorrowful, sad
do'loso, -a *ag* (*Dir*) malicious; **incendio ~** arson
'dolsi *etc vb vedi* **dolere**
dom. *abbr* (*= domenica*) Sun
do'manda *sf* (*interrogazione*) question; (*richiesta*) demand; (*: cortese*) request; (*Dir: richiesta scritta*) application; (*Econ*): **la ~** demand; **fare una ~ a qn** to ask sb a question; **fare ~ (per un lavoro)** to apply (for a job); **far regolare ~ (di qc)** to apply through the proper channels (for sth); **fare ~ all'autorità giudiziaria** to apply to the courts; **~ di divorzio** divorce petition; **~ di matrimonio** proposal
doman'dare *vt* (*per avere*) to ask for; (*per sapere*) to ask; (*esigere*) to demand; **domandarsi** *vr* to wonder, ask o.s.; **~ qc a qn** to ask sb for sth; to ask sb sth
do'mani *av* tomorrow ■ *sm* (*l'indomani*) next day, following day; **il ~** (*il futuro*) the future; (*il giorno successivo*) the next day; **un ~** some day; **~ l'altro** the day after tomorrow; **~ (a) otto** tomorrow week, a week tomorrow; **a ~!** see you tomorrow!
do'mare *vt* to tame
doma'tore, -'trice *sm/f* (*gen*) tamer; **~ di cavalli** horsebreaker; **~ di leoni** lion tamer
domat'tina *av* tomorrow morning
do'menica, -che *sf* Sunday; *vedi anche* **martedì**
domeni'cale *ag* Sunday *cpd*
domeni'cano, -a *ag, sm/f* Dominican
do'mestica, -che *sf vedi* **domestico**
do'mestico, -a, ci, che *ag* domestic ■ *sm/f* servant, domestic; **le pareti domestiche** one's own four walls; **animale ~** pet; **una domestica a ore** a daily (woman)
domicili'are [domitʃi'ljare] *ag vedi* **arresto**
domicili'arsi [domitʃi'ljarsi] *vr* to take up residence
domi'cilio [domi'tʃiljo] *sm* (*Dir*) domicile, place of residence; **visita a ~** (*Med*) house call; **"recapito a ~"** "deliveries"; **violazione di ~** (*Dir*) breaking and entering
domi'nante *ag* (*colore, nota*) dominant; (*opinione*) prevailing; (*idea*) main *cpd*, chief *cpd*; (*posizione*) dominating *cpd*; (*classe, partito*) ruling *cpd*
domi'nare *vt* to dominate; (*fig: sentimenti*) to control, master ■ *vi* to be in the dominant position; **dominarsi** *vr* (*controllarsi*) to control o.s.; **~ su** (*fig*) to surpass, outclass
domina'tore, -'trice *ag* ruling *cpd* ■ *sm/f* ruler
dominazi'one [dominat'tsjone] *sf* domination
domini'cano, -a *ag*: **la Repubblica Dominicana** the Dominican Republic
do'minio *sm* dominion; (*fig: campo*) field, domain; **domini coloniali** colonies; **essere di ~ pubblico** (*notizia etc*) to be common knowledge
don *sm* (*Rel*) Father
do'nare *vt* to give, present; (*per beneficenza etc*) to donate ■ *vi* (*fig*): **~ a** to suit, become; **~ sangue** to give blood
dona'tore, -'trice *sm/f* donor; **~ di sangue/di organi** blood/organ donor
donazi'one [donat'tsjone] *sf* donation; **atto di ~** (*Dir*) deed of gift
'donde *av* (*poetico*) whence
dondo'lare *vt* (*cullare*) to rock; **dondolarsi** *vr* to swing, sway
'dondolo *sm*: **sedia/cavallo a ~** rocking chair/horse
dongio'vanni [dondʒo'vanni] *sm* Don Juan, ladies' man
'donna *sf* woman; (*titolo*) Donna; (*Carte*) queen; **figlio di buona ~!** (*fam*) son of a bitch!; **~ di casa** housewife; **~ a ore** daily (help *o* woman); **~ delle pulizie** cleaning lady, cleaner; **~ di servizio** maid; **~ di vita** *o* **di strada** prostitute, streetwalker
donnai'olo *sm* ladykiller
'donnola *sf* weasel
'dono *sm* gift
'doping *sm* doping

'**dopo** *av* (*tempo*) afterwards; (: *più tardi*) later; (*luogo*) after, next ■ *prep* after ■ *cong* (*temporale*): **~ aver studiato** after having studied ■ *ag inv*: **il giorno ~** the following day; **~ mangiato va a dormire** after having eaten *o* after a meal he goes for a sleep; **un anno ~** a year later; **~ di me/lui** after me/him; **~ che** = **dopoché**
dopo'barba *sm inv* after-shave
dopoché [dopo'ke] *cong* after, when
dopodiché [dopodi'ke] *av* after which
dopodo'mani *av* the day after tomorrow
dopogu'erra *sm* postwar years *pl*
dopola'voro *sm* recreational club
dopo'pranzo [dopo'prandzo] *av* after lunch (*o* dinner)
doposcì [dopoʃʃi] *sm inv* après-ski outfit
doposcu'ola *sm inv school club offering extra tuition and recreational facilities*
dopo'sole *sm inv, ag inv*: **(lozione/crema) ~** aftersun (lotion/cream)
dopo'tutto *av* after all
doppi'aggio [dop'pjaddʒo] *sm* (*Cine*) dubbing
doppi'are *vt* (*Naut*) to round; (*Sport*) to lap; (*Cine*) to dub
doppia'tore, -'trice *sm/f* dubber
doppi'etta *sf* (*fucile*) double-barrelled (*Brit*) *o* double-barreled (*US*) shotgun; (*sparo*) shot from both barrels; (*Calcio*) double; (*Pugilato*) one-two; (*Aut*) double-declutch (*Brit*), double-clutch (*US*)
doppi'ezza [dop'pjettsa] *sf* (*fig: di persona*) duplicity, double-dealing
'**doppio, -a** *ag* double; (*fig: falso*) double-dealing, deceitful ■ *sm* (*quantità*): **il ~ (di)** twice as much (*o* many), double the amount (*o* number) of; (*Sport*) doubles *pl* ■ *av* double; **battere una lettera in doppia copia** to type a letter with a carbon copy; **fare il ~ gioco** (*fig*) to play a double game; **chiudere a doppia mandata** to double-lock; **~ senso** double entendre; **frase a ~ senso** sentence with a double meaning; **un utensile a ~ uso** a dual-purpose utensil
doppio'fondo *sm* (*di valigia*) false bottom; (*Naut*) double hull
doppi'one *sm* duplicate (copy)
doppio'petto *sm* double-breasted jacket
dop'pista *sm/f* (*Tennis*) doubles player
do'rare *vt* to gild; (*Cuc*) to brown; **~ la pillola** (*fig*) to sugar the pill
do'rato, -a *ag* golden; (*ricoperto d'oro*) gilt, gilded
dora'tura *sf* gilding
dormicchi'are [dormik'kjare] *vi* to doze
dormi'ente *ag* sleeping ■ *sm/f* sleeper
dormigli'one, -a [dormiʎ'ʎone] *sm/f* sleepyhead
dor'mire *vi* to sleep; (*essere addormentato*) to be asleep, be sleeping; **il caffè non mi fa ~** coffee keeps me awake; **~ come un ghiro** to sleep like a log; **~ della grossa** to sleep soundly, be dead to the world; **~ in piedi** (*essere stanco*) to be asleep on one's feet
dor'mita *sf*: **farsi una ~** to have a good sleep
dormi'torio *sm* dormitory; **~ pubblico** doss house (*Brit*) *o* flophouse (*US*) (*run by local authority*)
dormi'veglia [dormi'veʎʎa] *sm* drowsiness
dorrò *etc vb vedi* **dolere**
dor'sale *ag*: **spina ~** backbone, spine
'**dorso** *sm* back; (*di montagna*) ridge, crest; (*di libro*) spine; (*Nuoto*) backstroke; **a ~ di cavallo** on horseback
do'saggio [do'zaddʒo] *sm* (*atto*) measuring out; **sbagliare il ~** to get the proportions wrong
do'sare *vt* to measure out; (*Med*) to dose
'**dose** *sf* quantity, amount; (*Med*) dose
dossi'er [do'sje] *sm inv* dossier, file
'**dosso** *sm* (*rilievo*) rise; (: *di strada*) bump; (*dorso*): **levarsi di ~ i vestiti** to take one's clothes off; **levarsi un peso di ~** (*fig*) to take a weight off one's mind
do'tare *vt*: **~ di** to provide *o* supply with; (*fig*) to endow with
do'tato, -a *ag*: **~ di** (*attrezzature*) equipped with; (*bellezza, intelligenza*) endowed with; **un uomo ~** a gifted man
dotazi'one [dotat'tsjone] *sf* (*insieme di beni*) endowment; (*di macchine etc*) equipment; **dare qc in ~ a qn** to issue sb with sth, issue sth to sb; **i macchinari in ~ alla fabbrica** the machinery in use in the factory
'**dote** *sf* (*di sposa*) dowry; (*assegnata a un ente*) endowment; (*fig*) gift, talent
Dott. *abbr* (= *dottore*) Dr
'**dotto, -a** *ag* (*colto*) learned ■ *sm* (*sapiente*) scholar; (*Anat*) duct
dotto'rato *sm* degree; **~ di ricerca** doctorate, doctor's degree
dot'tore, -'essa *sm/f* doctor
dot'trina *sf* doctrine
Dott.ssa *abbr* (= *dottoressa*) Dr
double-'face [dubl'fas] *ag inv* reversible
'**dove** *av* where; (*in cui*) where, in which; (*dovunque*) wherever ■ *sm*: **per ogni ~** everywhere; **di dov'è?** where are you from?; **da ~ abito vedo tutta la città** I can see the whole city from where I live; **per ~ si passa?** which way should we go?; **le dò una mano fin ~ posso** I'll help you as much as I can
do'vere *sm* (*obbligo*) duty ■ *vt* (*essere debitore*): **~ qc (a qn)** to owe (sb) sth ■ *vi* (*obbligo*) to have to; **devo partire domani** (*intenzione*) I'm

(due) to leave tomorrow; **dev'essere tardi** (*probabilità*) it must be late; **lui deve farlo** he has to do it, he must do it; **è dovuto partire** he had to leave; **ha dovuto pagare** he had to pay; **doveva accadere** it was bound to happen; **avere il senso del ~** to have a sense of duty; **rivolgersi a chi di ~** to apply to the appropriate authority *o* person; **a ~** (*bene*) properly; (*debitamente*) as he (*o* she *etc*) deserves; **come si deve** (*bene*) properly; (*meritatamente*) properly, as he (*o* she *etc*) deserves; **una persona come si deve** a respectable person

dove'roso, -a *ag* (right and) proper

do'vizia [do'vittsja] *sf* abundance

dovrò *etc vb vedi* **dovere**

do'vunque *av* (*in qualunque luogo*) wherever; (*dappertutto*) everywhere; **~ io vada** wherever I go

dovuta'mente *av* (*debitamente*: *redigere, compilare*) correctly; (: *rimproverare*) as he (*o* she *etc*) deserves

do'vuto, -a *ag* (*causato*): **~ a** due to ■ *sm* due; **nel modo ~** in the proper way; **ho lavorato più del ~** I worked more than was necessary

doz'zina [dod'dzina] *sf* dozen; **una ~ di uova** a dozen eggs; **di** *o* **da ~** (*scrittore, spettacolo*) second-rate

dozzi'nale [doddzi'nale] *ag* cheap, second-rate

DP *sigla f* (= *Democrazia Proletaria*) *political party*

'draga, -ghe *sf* dredger

dra'gare *vt* to dredge

dragherò *etc* [drage'rɔ] *vb vedi* **dragare**

'drago, -ghi *sm* dragon; (*fig fam*) genius

'dramma, -i *sm* drama; **fare un ~ di qc** to make a drama out of sth

dram'matico, -a, ci, che *ag* dramatic

drammatiz'zare [drammatid'dzare] *vt* to dramatize

dramma'turgo, -ghi *sm* playwright

drappeggi'are [drapped'dʒare] *vt* to drape

drap'peggio [drap'peddʒo] *sm* (*tessuto*) drapery; (*di abito*) folds

drap'pello *sm* (*Mil*) squad; (*gruppo*) band, group

'drappo *sm* cloth

'drastico, -a, ci, che *ag* drastic

dre'naggio [dre'naddʒo] *sm* drainage

dre'nare *vt* to drain

'Dresda *sf* Dresden

drib'blare *vi* (*Calcio*) to dribble ■ *vt* (*avversario*) to dodge, avoid

'dritto, -a *ag, av* = **diritto** ■ *sm/f* (*fam*: *furbo*): **è un ~** he's a crafty *o* sly one ■ *sf* (*destra*) right, right hand; (*Naut*) starboard; **a dritta e a manca** (*fig*) on all sides, right, left and centre

driz'zare [drit'tsare] *vt* (*far tornare diritto*) to straighten; (*volgere*: *sguardo, occhi*) to turn, direct; (*innalzare*: *antenna, muro*) to erect; **drizzarsi** *vr* to stand up; **~ le orecchie** to prick up one's ears; **drizzarsi in piedi** to rise to one's feet; **drizzarsi a sedere** to sit up

'droga, -ghe *sf* (*sostanza aromatica*) spice; (*stupefacente*) drug; **droghe pesanti/leggere** hard/soft drugs

dro'gare *vt* to drug, dope; **drogarsi** *vr* to take drugs

dro'gato, -a *sm/f* drug addict

droghe'ria [droge'ria] *sf* grocer's (shop) (*Brit*), grocery (store) (*US*)

drogherò *etc* [droge'rɔ] *vb vedi* **drogare**

droghi'ere, -a [dro'gjɛre] *sm/f* grocer

drome'dario *sm* dromedary

DS [di'ɛsse] *smpl* (= *Democratici di Sinistra*) Democrats of the Left (*Italian left-wing party*)

'dubbio, -a *ag* (*incerto*) doubtful, dubious; (*ambiguo*) dubious ■ *sm* (*incertezza*) doubt; **avere il ~ che** to be afraid that, suspect that; **essere in ~ fra** to hesitate between; **mettere in ~ qc** to question sth; **nutrire seri dubbi su qc** to have grave doubts about sth; **senza ~** doubtless, no doubt

dubbi'oso, -a *ag* doubtful, dubious

dubi'tare *vi*: **~ di** (*onestà*) to doubt; (*risultato*) to be doubtful of; **~ di qn** to mistrust sb; **~ di sé** to be unsure of o.s.

Du'blino *sf* Dublin

'duca, -chi *sm* duke

'duce ['dutʃe] *sm* (*Storia*) captain; (: *del fascismo*) duce

du'chessa [du'kessa] *sf* duchess

'due *num* two; **a ~ a ~** two at a time, two by two; **dire ~ parole** to say a few words; **ci metto ~ minuti** I'll have it done in a jiffy

duecen'tesco, -a, schi, sche [duetʃen'tesko] *ag* thirteenth-century

due'cento [due'tʃɛnto] *num* two hundred ■ *sm*: **il D~** the thirteenth century

duel'lare *vi* to fight a duel

du'ello *sm* duel

due'mila *num* two thousand ■ *sm inv*: **il ~** the year two thousand

due'pezzi [due'pɛttsi] *sm* (*costume da bagno*) two-piece swimsuit; (*abito femminile*) two-piece suit

du'etto *sm* duet

'dulcis in 'fundo ['dultʃisin'fundo] *av* to cap it all

'duna *sf* dune

'dunque *cong* (*perciò*) so, therefore; (*riprendendo il discorso*) well (then) ■ *sm inv*: **venire al ~** to come to the point

'duo *sm inv* (*Mus*) duet; (*Teat, Cine, fig*) duo

d

du'ole *etc vb vedi* **dolere**
du'omo *sm* cathedral
'duplex *sm inv* (*Tel*) party line
dupli'cato *sm* duplicate
'duplice ['duplitʃe] *ag* double, twofold; **in ~ copia** in duplicate
duplicità [duplitʃi'ta] *sf* (*fig*) duplicity
du'rante *prep* during; **vita natural ~** for life
du'rare *vi* to last; **non può ~!** this can't go on any longer!; **~ fatica a** to have difficulty in; **~ in carica** to remain in office
du'rata *sf* length (of time); duration; **per tutta la ~ di** throughout; **~ media della vita** life expectancy
dura'turo, -a *ag*, **du'revole** *ag* (*ricordo*) lasting; (*materiale*) durable
du'rezza [du'rettsa] *sf* hardness; stubbornness; harshness; toughness
'duro, -a *ag* (*pietra, lavoro, materasso, problema*) hard; (*persona: ostinato*) stubborn, obstinate; (*: severo*) harsh, hard; (*voce*) harsh; (*carne*) tough ■ *sm/f* (*persona*) tough one ■ *av*: **tener ~** (*resistere*) to stand firm, hold out; **avere la pelle dura** (*fig: persona*) to be tough; **fare il ~** to act tough; **~ di comprendonio** slow-witted; **~ d'orecchi** hard of hearing
du'rone *sm* hard skin
'duttile *ag* (*sostanza*) malleable; (*fig: carattere*) docile, biddable; (*: stile*) adaptable
DVD [divu'di] *sm inv* DVD; (*lettore*) DVD player

Ee

e

E, e [e] *sf o m inv* (*lettera*) E, e; **E come Empoli** ≈ E for Edward (*Brit*), E for Easy (*US*)
E *abbr* (= *est*) E; (*Aut*) = **itinerario europeo**
e (*dav V spesso* **ed**) *cong* and; (*avversativo*) but; (*eppure*) and yet; **e lui?** what about him?; **e compralo!** well buy it then!
è *vb vedi* **essere**
E.A.D. *sigla f* = **elaborazione automatica dei dati**
ebaniste'ria *sf* cabinet-making; (*negozio*) cabinet-maker's shop
'ebano *sm* ebony
eb'bene *cong* well (then)
'ebbi *etc vb vedi* **avere**
eb'brezza [eb'brettsa] *sf* intoxication
'ebbro, -a *ag* drunk; **~ di** (*gioia etc*) beside o.s. *o* wild with
'ebete *ag* stupid, idiotic
ebe'tismo *sm* stupidity
ebollizi'one [ebollit'tsjone] *sf* boiling; **punto di ~** boiling point
e'braico, -a, ci, che *ag* Hebrew, Hebraic ■ *sm* (*Ling*) Hebrew
e'breo, -a *ag* Jewish ■ *sm/f* Jew/Jewess
'Ebridi *sfpl*: **le (isole) ~** the Hebrides
e'burneo, -a *ag* ivory *cpd*
E/C *abbr* = **estratto conto**
eca'tombe *sf* (*strage*) slaughter, massacre
ecc. *abbr* (= *eccetera*) etc
ecce'dente [ettʃe'dɛnte] *sm* surplus
ecce'denza [ettʃe'dɛntsa] *sf* excess, surplus; (*Inform*) overflow
ec'cedere [et'tʃɛdere] *vt* to exceed ■ *vi* to go too far; **~ nel bere/mangiare** to indulge in drink/food to excess
eccel'lente [ettʃel'lɛnte] *ag* excellent; (*cadavere, arresto*) of a prominent person
eccel'lenza [ettʃe'lɛntsa] *sf* excellence; (*titolo*): **Sua E~** His Excellency
ec'cellere [et'tʃɛllere] *vi*: **~ (in)** to excel (at); **~ su tutti** to surpass everyone
ec'celso, -a [et'tʃɛlso] *pp di* **eccellere** ■ *ag* (*cima, montagna*) high; (*fig: ingegno*) great, exceptional
ec'centrico, -a, ci, che [et'tʃɛntriko] *ag* eccentric
ecces'sivo, -a [ettʃes'sivo] *ag* excessive
ec'cesso [et'tʃɛsso] *sm* excess; **all'~** (*gentile, generoso*) to excess, excessively; **dare in eccessi** to fly into a rage; **~ di velocità** (*Aut*) speeding; **~ di zelo** overzealousness
ec'cetera [et'tʃɛtera] *av* et cetera, and so on
ec'cetto [et'tʃɛtto] *prep* except, with the exception of; **~ che** *cong* except, other than; **~ che (non)** unless
eccettu'are [ettʃettu'are] *vt* to except; **eccettuati i presenti** present company excepted
eccezio'nale [ettʃettsjo'nale] *ag* exceptional; **in via del tutto ~** in this instance, exceptionally
eccezi'one [ettʃet'tsjone] *sf* exception; (*Dir*) objection; **a ~ di** with the exception of, except for; **d'~** exceptional; **fare un'~ alla regola** to make an exception to the rule
ec'chimosi [ek'kimozi] *sf inv* bruise
ec'cidio [et'tʃidjo] *sm* massacre
ecci'tante [ettʃi'tante] *ag* (*gen*) exciting; (*sostanza*) stimulating ■ *sm* stimulant
ecci'tare [ettʃi'tare] *vt* (*curiosità, interesse*) to excite, arouse; (*folla*) to incite; **eccitarsi** *vr* to get excited; (*sessualmente*) to become aroused
eccitazi'one [ettʃitat'tsjone] *sf* excitement
ecclesi'astico, -a, ci, che *ag* ecclesiastical, church *cpd*; clerical ■ *sm* ecclesiastic
'ecco *av* (*per dimostrare*): **~ il treno!** here's *o* here comes the train!; (*dav pronome*): **eccomi!** here I am!; **eccone uno!** here's one (of them)!; (*dav pp*): **~ fatto!** there, that's it done!
ec'come *av* rather; **ti piace? — ~!** do you like it? — I'll say! *o* and how! *o* rather! (*Brit*)
ECG *sigla m* = **elettrocardiogramma**
echeggi'are [eked'dʒare] *vi* to echo
e'clettico, -a, ci, che *ag, sm/f* eclectic
eclet'tismo *sm* eclecticism

eclis'sare *vt* to eclipse; (*fig*) to eclipse, overshadow; **eclissarsi** *vr* (*persona: scherzoso*) to slip away
e'clissi *sf* eclipse
'eco (*pl(m)* **echi**) *sm o f* echo; **suscitò** *o* **ebbe una profonda ~** it caused quite a stir
ecogra'fia *sf* (*Med*) ultrasound
ecolo'gia [ekolo'dʒia] *sf* ecology
eco'logico, -a, ci, che [eko'lɔdʒiko] *ag* ecological
ecolo'gista, -i, e [ekolo'dʒista] *ag* ecological ■ *sm/f* ecologist, environmentalist
e'cologo, -a, gi, ghe *sm/f* ecologist
eco'mafia *sf mafia involved in crimes related to the environment, in particular the illegal disposal of waste*
econo'mato *sm* (*Ins*) bursar's office
econo'mia *sf* economy; (*scienza*) economics *sg*; (*risparmio: azione*) saving; **fare ~** to economize, make economies; **l'~ sommersa** the black (*Brit*) *o* underground (*US*) economy; **~ di mercato** market economy; **~ pianificata** planned economy
eco'nomico, -a, ci, che *ag* economic; (*poco costoso*) economical; **edizione economica** economy edition
econo'mista, -i *sm* economist
economiz'zare [ekonomid'dzare] *vt, vi* to save
e'conomo, -a *ag* thrifty ■ *sm/f* (*Ins*) bursar
ecosis'tema, -i *sm* ecosystem
'ecstasy ['ɛkstasi] *sf inv* ecstasy
'Ecuador *sm*: **l'~** Ecuador
ec'zema [ek'dzɛma] *sm* eczema
ed *cong vedi* **e**
Ed. *abbr* = **editore**
ed. *abbr* = **edizione**
'edera *sf* ivy
e'dicola *sf* newspaper kiosk *o* stand (*US*)
edico'lante *sm/f* news vendor (*in kiosk*)
edifi'cante *ag* edifying
edifi'care *vt* to build; (*fig: teoria, azienda*) to establish; (*indurre al bene*) to edify
edi'ficio [edi'fitʃo] *sm* building; (*fig*) structure
e'dile *ag* building *cpd*
edi'lizio, -a [edi'littsjo] *ag* building *cpd* ■ *sf* building, building trade
Edim'burgo *sf* Edinburgh
'edito, -a *ag* published
edi'tore, -'trice *ag* publishing *cpd* ■ *sm/f* publisher; (*curatore*) editor
edito'ria *sf* publishing
editori'ale *ag* publishing *cpd* ■ *sm* (*articolo di fondo*) editorial, leader
e'ditto *sm* edict
edizi'one [edit'tsjone] *sf* edition; (*tiratura*) printing; **~ a tiratura limitata** limited edition
edo'nismo *sm* hedonism
e'dotto, -a *ag* informed; **rendere qn ~ su qc** to inform sb about sth
edu'canda *sf* boarder
edu'care *vt* to educate; (*gusto, mente*) to train; **~ qn a fare** to train sb to do
educa'tivo, -a *ag* educational
edu'cato, -a *ag* polite, well-mannered
educazi'one [edukat'tsjone] *sf* education; (*familiare*) upbringing; (*comportamento*) (good) manners *pl*; **per ~** out of politeness; **questa è pura mancanza d'~!** this is sheer bad manners!; **~ fisica** (*Ins*) physical training *o* education
educherò *etc* [eduke'rɔ] *vb vedi* **educare**
E.E.D. *sigla f* = **elaborazione elettronica dei dati**
EEG *sigla m* = **elettroencefalogramma**
e'felide *sf* freckle
effemi'nato, -a *ag* effeminate
effe'rato, -a *ag* brutal, savage
efferve'scente [effervef'ʃɛnte] *ag* effervescent
effettiva'mente *av* (*in effetti*) in fact; (*a dire il vero*) really, actually
effet'tivo, -a *ag* (*reale*) real, actual; (*impiegato, professore*) permanent; (*Mil*) regular ■ *sm* (*Mil*) strength; (*di patrimonio etc*) sum total
ef'fetto *sm* effect; (*Comm: cambiale*) bill; (*fig: impressione*) impression; **far ~** (*medicina*) to take effect, (start to) work; **cercare l'~** to seek attention; **in effetti** in fact; **effetti attivi** (*Comm*) bills receivable; **effetti passivi** (*Comm*) bills payable; **effetti personali** personal effects, personal belongings; **~ serra** greenhouse effect; **effetti speciali** (*Cine*) special effects
effettu'are *vt* to effect, carry out
effi'cace [effi'katʃe] *ag* effective
effi'cacia [effi'katʃa] *sf* effectiveness
effici'ente [effi'tʃɛnte] *ag* efficient
efficien'tismo [effitʃen'tizmo] *sm* maximum efficiency
effici'enza [effi'tʃɛntsa] *sf* efficiency
effigi'are [effi'dʒare] *vt* to represent, portray
ef'figie [ef'fidʒe] *sf inv* effigy
ef'fimero, -a *ag* ephemeral
ef'fluvio *sm* (*anche peg, ironico*) scent, perfume
effusi'one *sf* effusion
e.g. *abbr* (= *exempli gratia*) e.g.
egemo'nia [edʒemo'nia] *sf* hegemony
E'geo [e'dʒɛo] *sm*: **l'~, il mare ~** the Aegean (Sea)
'egida ['ɛdʒida] *sf*: **sotto l'~ di** under the aegis of
E'gitto [e'dʒitto] *sm*: **l'~** Egypt
egizi'ano, -a [edʒit'tsjano] *ag, sm/f* Egyptian
e'gizio, -a [e'dʒittsjo] *ag, sm/f* (ancient) Egyptian

'egli ['eʎʎi] *pron* he; **~ stesso** he himself
'ego *sm inv* (*Psic*) ego
ego'centrico, -a, ci, che [ego'tʃɛntriko] *ag* egocentric(al) ■ *sm/f* self-centred (*Brit*) *o* self-centered (*US*) person
egocen'trismo [egotʃen'trizmo] *sm* egocentricity
ego'ismo *sm* selfishness, egoism
ego'ista, -i, e *ag* selfish, egoistic ■ *sm/f* egoist
ego'istico, -a, ci, che *ag* egoistic, selfish
ego'tismo *sm* egotism
ego'tista, -i, e *ag* egotistic ■ *sm/f* egotist
Egr. *abbr* = **Egregio**
e'gregio, -a, gi, gie [e'grɛdʒo] *ag* distinguished; (*nelle lettere*): **E~ Signore** Dear Sir
eguagli'anza *etc* [egwaʎ'ʎantsa] *vedi* **uguaglianza** *etc*
eguali'tario, -a *ag, sm/f* egalitarian
E.I. *abbr* = **Esercito Italiano**
eiaculazi'one [ejakulat'tsjone] *sf* ejaculation; **~ precoce** premature ejaculation
elabo'rare *vt* (*progetto*) to work out, elaborate; (*dati*) to process; (*digerire*) to digest
elabora'tore *sm* (*Inform*): **~ elettronico** computer
elaborazi'one [elaborat'tsjone] *sf* elaboration; processing; digestion; **~ automatica dei dati** (*Inform*) automatic data processing; **~ elettronica dei dati** (*Inform*) electronic data processing; **~ testi** (*Inform*) text processing
elar'gire [elar'dʒire] *vt* to hand out
elargizi'one [elardʒit'tsjone] *sf* donation
elasticiz'zato, -a [elastitʃid'dzato] *ag* (*tessuto*) stretch *cpd*
e'lastico, -a, ci, che *ag* elastic; (*fig: andatura*) springy; (*: decisione, vedute*) flexible ■ *sm* (*gommino*) rubber band; (*per il cucito*) elastic *no pl*
ele'fante *sm* elephant
ele'gante *ag* elegant
ele'ganza [ele'gantsa] *sf* elegance
e'leggere [e'lɛddʒere] *vt* to elect
elemen'tare *ag* elementary; **le (scuole) elementari** *vedi* **scuola elementare**; **prima ~** first year of primary school, ≈ infants' class (*Brit*), ≈ 1st grade (*US*)
ele'mento *sm* element; (*parte componente*) element, component, part; **elementi** *smpl* (*della scienza etc*) elements, rudiments
ele'mosina *sf* charity, alms *pl*; **chiedere l'~** to beg
elemosi'nare *vt* to beg for, ask for ■ *vi* to beg
elen'care *vt* to list
elencherò *etc* [elenke'rɔ] *vb vedi* **elencare**
e'lenco, -chi *sm* list; **~ nominativo** list of names; **~ telefonico** telephone directory
e'lessi *etc vb vedi* **eleggere**
elet'tivo, -a *ag* (*carica etc*) elected
e'letto, -a *pp di* **eleggere** ■ *sm/f* (*nominato*) elected member
eletto'rale *ag* electoral, election *cpd*
eletto'rato *sm* electorate
elet'tore, -'trice *sm/f* voter, elector
elet'trauto *sm inv* workshop for car electrical repairs; (*tecnico*) car electrician
elettri'cista, -i [elettri'tʃista] *sm* electrician
elettricità [elettritʃi'ta] *sf* electricity
e'lettrico, -a, ci, che *ag* electric(al)
elettrifi'care *vt* to electrify
elettriz'zante [elettrid'dzante] *ag* (*fig*) electrifying, thrilling
elettriz'zare [elettrid'dzare] *vt* to electrify; **elettrizzarsi** *vr* to become charged with electricity; (*fig: persona*) to be thrilled
e'lettro... *prefisso* electro...
elettrocardio'gramma, -i *sm* electrocardiogram
e'lettrodo *sm* electrode
elettrodo'mestico, -a, ci, che *ag*: **apparecchi elettrodomestici** domestic (electrical) appliances
elettroencefalo'gramma, -i [elettroen-tʃefalo'gramma] *sm* electroencephalogram
elet'trogeno, -a [elet'trɔdʒeno] *ag*: **gruppo ~** generator
elet'trolisi *sf* electrolysis
elettroma'gnetico, -a, ci, che [elettromaɲ'ɲɛtiko] *ag* electromagnetic
elettromo'trice [elettromo'tritʃe] *sf* electric train
elet'trone *sm* electron
elet'tronico, -a, ci, che *ag* electronic ■ *sf* electronics *sg*
elettro'shock [elettroʃ'ʃɔk] *sm inv* (electro)shock treatment
elettro'tecnico, -a, ci, che *ag* electrotechnical ■ *sm* electrical engineer
ele'vare *vt* to raise; (*edificio*) to erect; (*multa*) to impose; **~ un numero al quadrato** to square a number
eleva'tezza [eleva'tettsa] *sf* (*altezza*) elevation; (*di animo, pensiero*) loftiness
ele'vato, -a *ag* (*gen*) high; (*cime*) high, lofty; (*fig: stile, sentimenti*) lofty
elevazi'one [elevat'tsjone] *sf* elevation; (*l'elevare*) raising
elezi'one [elet'tsjone] *sf* election; **elezioni** *sfpl* (*Pol*) election(s); **patria d'~** chosen country
'elica, -che *sf* propeller

eli'cottero *sm* helicopter
e'lidere *vt* (*Fonetica*) to elide; **elidersi** *vr* (*forze*) to cancel each other out, neutralize each other
elimi'nare *vt* to eliminate
elimina'toria *sf* eliminating round
eliminazi'one [eliminat'tsjone] *sf* elimination
'elio *sm* helium
eli'porto *sm* heliport
elisabetti'ano, -a *ag* Elizabethan
eli'sir *sm inv* elixir
e'liso, -a *pp di* **elidere**
elisoc'corso *sm* helicoper ambulance
eli'tario, -a *ag* elitist
é'lite [e'lit] *sf inv* élite
'ella *pron* she; (*forma di cortesia*) you; **~ stessa** she herself; you yourself
el'lisse *sf* ellipse
el'littico, -a, ci, che *ag* elliptic(al)
el'metto *sm* helmet
'elmo *sm* helmet
elogi'are [elo'dʒare] *vt* to praise
elogia'tivo, -a [elodʒa'tivo] *ag* laudatory
e'logio [e'lɔdʒo] *sm* (*discorso, scritto*) eulogy; (*lode*) praise; **~ funebre** funeral oration
elo'quente *ag* eloquent; **questi dati sono eloquentei** these facts speak for themselves
elo'quenza [elo'kwɛntsa] *sf* eloquence
e'loquio *sm* speech, language
elucu'brare *vt* to ponder about *o* over
elucubrazi'oni [elukubrat'tsjoni] *sfpl* (*anche ironico*) cogitations, ponderings
e'ludere *vt* to evade
e'lusi *etc vb vedi* **eludere**
elusi'one *sf*: **~ d'imposta** tax evasion
elu'sivo, -a *ag* evasive
e'luso, -a *pp di* **eludere**
el'vetico, -a, ci, che *ag* Swiss
emaci'ato, -a [ema'tʃato] *ag* emaciated
e-'mail, e'mail [e'mail] *sf inv, ag inv* email; **indirizzo ~** email address
ema'nare *vt* to send out, give off; (*fig: leggi*) to promulgate; (*: decreti*) to issue ■ *vi*: **~ da** to come from
emanazi'one [emanat'tsjone] *sf* (*di raggi, calore*) emanation; (*di odori*) exhalation; (*di legge*) promulgation; (*di ordine, circolare*) issuing
emanci'pare [emantʃi'pare] *vt* to emancipate; **emanciparsi** *vr* (*fig*) to become liberated *o* emancipated
emancipazi'one [emantʃipat'tsjone] *sf* emancipation
emargi'nare [emardʒi'nare] *vt* (*fig: socialmente*) to cast out
emargi'nato, -a [emardʒi'nato] *sm/f* outcast
ematolo'gia [ematolo'dʒia] *sf* haematology (*Brit*), hematology (*US*)
ema'toma, -i *sm* haematoma (*Brit*), hematoma (*US*)
em'blema, -i *sm* emblem
emble'matico, -a, ci, che *ag* emblematic; (*fig: atteggiamento, parole*) symbolic
embo'lia *sf* embolism
embrio'nale, -i, e *ag* embryonic, embryo *cpd*; **allo stadio ~** at the embryo stage
embri'one *sm* embryo
emenda'mento *sm* amendment
emen'dare *vt* to amend
emer'gente [emer'dʒɛnte] *ag* emerging
emer'genza [emer'dʒɛntsa] *sf* emergency; **in caso di ~** in an emergency
e'mergere [e'mɛrdʒere] *vi* to emerge; (*sommergibile*) to surface; (*fig: distinguersi*) to stand out
e'merito, -a *ag* (*insigne*) distinguished; **è un ~ cretino!** he's a complete idiot!
e'mersi *etc vb vedi* **emergere**
e'merso, -a *pp di* **emergere** ■ *ag* (*Geo*): **terre emerse** lands above sea level
e'messo, -a *pp di* **emettere**
e'mettere *vt* (*suono, luce*) to give out, emit; (*onde radio*) to send out; (*assegno, francobollo, ordine*) to issue; (*fig: giudizio*) to express, voice; **~ la sentenza** (*Dir*) to pass sentence
emi'crania *sf* migraine
emi'grante *ag, sm/f* emigrant
emi'grare *vi* to emigrate
emi'grato, -a *ag* emigrant ■ *sm/f* emigrant; (*Storia*) émigré
emigrazi'one [emigrat'tsjone] *sf* emigration
emili'ano, -a *ag* of (*o* from) Emilia
emi'nente *ag* eminent, distinguished
emi'nenza [emi'nɛntsa] *sf* eminence; **~ grigia** (*fig*) éminence grise
emi'rato *sm* emirate; **gli Emirati Arabi Uniti** the United Arab Emirates
e'miro *sm* emir
emis'fero *sm* hemisphere; **~ boreale/australe** northern/southern hemisphere
e'misi *etc vb vedi* **emettere**
emis'sario *sm* (*Geo*) outlet, effluent; (*inviato*) emissary
emissi'one *sf* (*vedi emettere*) emission; sending out; issue; (*Radio*) broadcast
emit'tente *ag* (*banca*) issuing; (*Radio*) broadcasting, transmitting ■ *sf* (*Radio*) transmitter
emofi'lia *sf* haemophilia (*Brit*), hemophilia (*US*)
emofi'liaco, -a, ci, che *ag, sm/f* haemophiliac (*Brit*), hemophiliac (*US*)

emoglo'bina *sf* haemoglobin (*Brit*), hemoglobin (*US*)
emolli'ente *ag* soothing
emorra'gia, -'gie [emorra'dʒia] *sf* haemorrhage (*Brit*), hemorrhage (*US*)
emor'roidi *sfpl* haemorrhoids (*Brit*), hemorrhoids (*US*)
emos'tatico, -a, ci, che *ag* haemostatic (*Brit*), hemostatic (*US*); **laccio ~** tourniquet; **matita emostatica** styptic pencil
emotività *sf* emotionalism
emo'tivo, -a *ag* emotional
emozio'nante [emottsjo'nante] *ag* exciting, thrilling
emozio'nare [emottsjo'nare] *vt* (*appassionare*) to thrill, excite; (*commuovere*) to move; (*innervosire*) to upset; **emozionarsi** *vr* to be excited; to be moved; to be upset
emozi'one [emot'tsjone] *sf* emotion; (*agitazione*) excitement
'empio, -a *ag* (*sacrilego*) impious; (*spietato*) cruel, pitiless; (*malvagio*) wicked, evil
em'pirico, -a, ci, che *ag* empirical
em'porio *sm* general store
emu'lare *vt* to emulate
'emulo, -a *sm/f* imitator
emulsi'one *sf* emulsion
EN *sigla* = **Enna**
en'ciclica, -che [en'tʃiklika] *sf* (*Rel*) encyclical
enciclope'dia [entʃiklope'dia] *sf* encyclop(a)edia
encomi'abile *ag* commendable, praiseworthy
encomi'are *vt* to commend, praise
en'comio *sm* commendation; **~ solenne** (*Mil*) mention in dispatches
endove'noso, -a *ag* (*Med*) intravenous ■ *sf* intravenous injection
E'NEA *sigla f* = **Comitato nazionale per la ricerca e lo sviluppo dell'Energia Nucleare e delle Energie Alternative**
'E.N.E.L. *sigla m* (= *Ente Nazionale per l'Energia Elettrica*) *national electricity company*
ener'getico, -a, ci, che [ener'dʒɛtiko] *ag* (*risorse, crisi*) energy *cpd*; (*sostanza, alimento*) energy-giving
ener'gia, -'gie [ener'dʒia] *sf* (*Fisica*) energy; (*fig*) energy, strength, vigour (*Brit*), vigor (*US*)
e'nergico, -a, ci, che [e'nɛrdʒiko] *ag* energetic, vigorous
'enfasi *sf* emphasis; (*peg*) bombast, pomposity
en'fatico, -a, ci, che *ag* emphatic; pompous
enfatiz'zare [enfatid'dzare] *vt* to emphasize, stress
enfi'sema *sm* emphysema
'ENI *sigla m* = **Ente Nazionale Idrocarburi**
e'nigma, -i *sm* enigma
enig'matico, -a, ci, che *ag* enigmatic
'ENIT *sigla m* (= *Ente Nazionale Italiano per il Turismo*) *Italian tourist authority*
en'nesimo, -a *ag* (*Mat, fig*) nth; **per l'ennesima volta** for the umpteenth time
enolo'gia [enolo'dʒia] *sf* oenology (*Brit*), enology (*US*)
e'nologo, -gi *sm* wine expert
e'norme *ag* enormous, huge
enormità *sf inv* enormity, huge size; (*assurdità*) absurdity; **non dire enormità!** don't talk nonsense!
eno'teca, -che *sf* (*negozio*) wine bar
'E.N.P.A. *sigla m* (= *Ente Nazionale Protezione Animali*) ≈ RSPCA (*Brit*), ≈ SPCA (*US*)
'E.N.P.A.S. *sigla m* (= *Ente Nazionale di Previdenza e Assistenza per i Dipendenti Statali*) *welfare organization for State employees*
'ente *sm* (*istituzione*) body, board, corporation; (*Filosofia*) being; **~ locale** local authority (*Brit*), local government (*US*); **~ pubblico** public body; **~ di ricerca** research organization
ente'rite *sf* enteritis
entità *sf* (*Filosofia*) entity; (*di perdita, danni, investimenti*) extent; (*di popolazione*) size; **di molta/poca ~** (*avvenimento, incidente*) of great/little importance
en'trambi, -e *pron pl* both (of them) ■ *ag pl*: **~ i ragazzi** both boys, both of the boys
en'trante *ag* (*prossimo: mese, anno*) next, coming
en'trare *vi* to enter, go (*o* come) in; **~ in** (*luogo*) to enter, go (*o* come) into; (*trovar posto, poter stare*) to fit into; (*essere ammesso a: club etc*) to join, become a member of; **~ in automobile** to get into the car; **far ~ qn** (*visitatore etc*) to show sb in; **~ in società/in commercio con qn** to go into partnership/business with sb; **questo non c'entra** (*fig*) that's got nothing to do with it
en'trata *sf* entrance, entry; **entrate** *sfpl* (*Comm*) receipts, takings; (*Econ*) income *sg*; **"~ libera"** "admission free"; **con l'~ in vigore dei nuovi provvedimenti ...** once the new measures come into effect ...; **entrate tributarie** tax revenue *sg*
'entro *prep* (*temporale*) within; **~ domani** by tomorrow; **~ e non oltre il 25 aprile** no later than 25th April
entro'terra *sm inv* hinterland
entusias'mante *ag* exciting
entusias'mare *vt* to excite, fill with enthusiasm; **entusiasmarsi** *vr*: **entusiasmarsi (per qc/qn)** to become enthusiastic (about sth/sb)

entusi'asmo *sm* enthusiasm
entusi'asta, -i, e *ag* enthusiastic ■ *sm/f* enthusiast
entusi'astico, -a, ci, che *ag* enthusiastic
enucle'are *vt* (*formale: chiarire*) to explain
enume'rare *vt* to enumerate, list
enunci'are [enun'tʃare] *vt* (*teoria*) to enunciate, set out
en'zima, -i *sm* enzyme
e'patico, -a, ci, che *ag* hepatic; **cirrosi epatica** cirrhosis of the liver
epa'tite *sf* hepatitis
'epico, -a, ci, che *ag* epic
epide'mia *sf* epidemic
epi'dermico, -a, ci, che *ag* (*Anat*) skin *cpd*; (*fig: interesse, impressioni*) superficial
epi'dermide *sf* skin, epidermis
Epifa'nia *sf* Epiphany
e'pigono *sm* imitator
e'pigrafe *sf* epigraph; (*su libro*) dedication
epiles'sia *sf* epilepsy
epi'lettico, -a, ci, che *ag, sm/f* epileptic
e'pilogo, -ghi *sm* conclusion
epi'sodico, -a, ci, che *ag* (*romanzo, narrazione*) episodic; (*fig: occasionale*) occasional
epi'sodio *sm* episode; **sceneggiato a episodi** serial
e'pistola *sf* epistle
episto'lare *ag* epistolary; **essere in rapporto** *o* **relazione ~ con qn** to correspond *o* be in correspondence with sb
e'piteto *sm* epithet
'epoca, -che *sf* (*periodo storico*) age, era; (*tempo*) time; (*Geo*) age; **mobili d'~** period furniture; **fare ~** (*scandalo*) to cause a stir; (*cantante, moda*) to mark a new era
epo'pea *sf* (*anche fig*) epic
ep'pure *cong* and yet, nevertheless
EPT *sigla m* (= *Ente Provinciale per il Turismo*) *district tourist bureau*
epu'rare *vt* (*Pol*) to purge
equ'anime *ag* (*imparziale*) fair, impartial
equa'tore *sm* equator
equazi'one [ekwat'tsjone] *sf* (*Mat*) equation
e'questre *ag* equestrian
equi'latero, -a *ag* equilateral
equili'brare *vt* to balance
equili'brato, -a *ag* (*carico, fig: giudizio*) balanced; (*vita*) well-regulated; (*persona*) stable, well-balanced
equi'librio *sm* balance, equilibrium; **perdere l'~** to lose one's balance; **stare in ~ su** (*persona*) to balance on; (*oggetto*) to be balanced on
equili'brismo *sm* tightrope walking; (*fig*) juggling
e'quino, -a *ag* horse *cpd*, equine
equi'nozio [ekwi'nɔttsjo] *sm* equinox
equipaggia'mento [ekwipaddʒa'mento] *sm* (*operazione: di nave*) equipping, fitting out; (*: di spedizione, esercito*) equipping, kitting out; (*attrezzatura*) equipment
equipaggi'are [ekwipad'dʒare] *vt* to equip; **equipaggiarsi** *vr* to equip o.s.
equi'paggio [ekwi'paddʒo] *sm* crew
equipa'rare *vt* to make equal
é'quipe [e'kip] *sf* (*Sport, gen*) team
equità *sf* equity, fairness
equitazi'one [ekwitat'tsjone] *sf* (horse-) riding
equiva'lente *ag, sm* equivalent
equiva'lenza [ekwiva'lɛntsa] *sf* equivalence
equiva'lere *vi*: **~ a** to be equivalent to; **equivalersi** *vr* (*forze etc*) to counterbalance each other; (*soluzioni*) to amount to the same thing; **equivale a dire che ...** that is the same as saying that ...
equi'valso, -a *pp di* **equivalere**
equivo'care *vi* to misunderstand
e'quivoco, -a, ci, che *ag* equivocal, ambiguous; (*sospetto*) dubious ■ *sm* misunderstanding; **a scanso di equivoci** to avoid any misunderstanding; **giocare sull'~** to equivocate
'equo, -a *ag* fair, just
'era *sf* era
'era *etc vb vedi* **essere**
erari'ale *ag*: **ufficio ~** ≈ tax office; **imposte erariali** revenue taxes; **spese erariali** public expenditure *sg*
e'rario *sm*: **l'~** ≈ the Treasury
'erba *sf* grass; (*aromatica, medicinale*) herb; **in ~** (*fig*) budding; **fare di ogni ~ un fascio** (*fig*) to lump everything (*o* everybody) together
er'baccia, -ce [er'battʃa] *sf* weed
er'bivoro, -a *ag* herbivorous ■ *sm/f* herbivore
erbo'rista, -i, e *sm/f* herbalist
erboriste'ria *sf* (*scienza*) study of medicinal herbs; (*negozio*) herbalist's (shop)
er'boso, -a *ag* grassy
e'rede *sm/f* heir; **~ legittimo** heir-at-law
eredità *sf* (*Dir*) inheritance; (*Biol*) heredity; **lasciare qc in ~ a qn** to leave *o* bequeath sth to sb
eredi'tare *vt* to inherit
eredi'tario, -a *ag* hereditary
erediti'era *sf* heiress
ere'mita, -i *sm* hermit
eremi'taggio [eremi'taddʒo] *sm* hermitage
'eremo *sm* hermitage; (*fig*) retreat
ere'sia *sf* heresy
e'ressi *etc vb vedi* **erigere**

e'retico, -a, ci, che *ag* heretical ■ *sm/f* heretic
e'retto, -a *pp di* **erigere** ■ *ag* erect, upright
erezi'one [eret'tsjone] *sf* (*Fisiol*) erection
ergasto'lano, -a *sm/f* prisoner serving a life sentence, lifer (*fam*)
er'gastolo *sm* (*Dir: pena*) life imprisonment; (*: luogo di pena*) prison (*for those serving life sentences*)
ergono'mia *sf* ergonomics *sg*
ergo'nomico, -a, ci, che *ag* ergonomic(al)
'erica *sf* heather
e'rigere [e'ridʒere] *vt* to erect, raise; (*fig: fondare*) to found
eri'tema *sm* (*Med*) inflammation, erythema; **~ solare** sunburn
Eri'trea *sf* Eritrea
ermel'lino *sm* ermine
er'metico, -a, ci, che *ag* hermetic
'ernia *sf* (*Med*) hernia; **~ del disco** slipped disc
'ero *vb vedi* **essere**
e'rodere *vt* to erode
e'roe *sm* hero
ero'gare *vt* (*somma*) to distribute; (*gas, servizi*) to supply
erogazi'one [erogat'tsjone] *sf* distribution; supply
e'roico, -a, ci, che *ag* heroic
ero'ina *sf* heroine; (*droga*) heroin
ero'ismo *sm* heroism
'eros *sm* Eros
erosi'one *sf* erosion
e'roso, -a *pp di* **erodere**
e'rotico, -a, ci, che *ag* erotic
ero'tismo *sm* eroticism
'erpete *sm* herpes *sg*
'erpice ['erpitʃe] *sm* (*Agr*) harrow
er'rare *vi* (*vagare*) to wander, roam; (*sbagliare*) to be mistaken
er'roneo, -a *ag* erroneous, wrong
er'rore *sm* error, mistake; (*morale*) error; **per ~** by mistake; **~ giudiziario** miscarriage of justice
'erto, -a *ag* (very) steep ■ *sf* steep slope; **stare all'erta** to be on the alert
eru'dire *vt* to teach, educate
eru'dito, -a *ag* learned, erudite
erut'tare *vt* (*vulcano*) to throw out, belch
eruzi'one [erut'tsjone] *sf* eruption; (*Med*) rash
es. *abbr* (= *esempio*) e.g.
E.S. *sigla m* (= *elettroshock*) ECT
E.S.A. ['eza] *sigla m* (= *European Space Agency*) ESA
esacer'bare [ezatʃer'bare] *vt* to exacerbate
esage'rare [ezadʒe'rare] *vt* to exaggerate ■ *vi* to exaggerate; (*eccedere*) to go too far; **senza ~** without exaggeration
esage'rato, -a [ezadʒe'rato] *ag* (*notizia, proporzioni*) exaggerated; (*curiosità, pignoleria*) excessive; (*prezzo*) exorbitant ■ *sm/f*: **sei il solito ~** you are exaggerating as usual
esagerazi'one [esadʒerat'tsjone] *sf* exaggeration
esago'nale *ag* hexagonal
e'sagono *sm* hexagon
esa'lare *vt* (*odori*) to give off ■ *vi*: **~ (da)** to emanate (from); **~ l'ultimo respiro** (*fig*) to breathe one's last
esalazi'one [ezalat'tsjone] *sf* (*emissione*) exhalation; (*odore*) fumes *pl*
esal'tante *ag* exciting
esal'tare *vt* to exalt; (*entusiasmare*) to excite, stir; **esaltarsi** *vr*: **esaltarsi (per qc)** to grow excited (about sth)
esal'tato, -a *sm/f* fanatic
esaltazi'one [ezaltat'tsjone] *sf* (*elogio*) extolling, exalting; (*nervosa*) intense excitement; (*mistica*) exaltation
e'same *sm* examination; (*Ins*) exam, examination; **fare** *o* **dare un ~** to sit *o* take an exam; **fare un ~ di coscienza** to search one's conscience; **~ di guida** driving test; **~ del sangue** blood test
esami'nare *vt* to examine
e'sangue *ag* bloodless; (*fig: pallido*) pale, wan; (*: privo di vigore*) lifeless
e'sanime *ag* lifeless
esaspe'rare *vt* to exasperate; (*situazione*) to exacerbate; **esasperarsi** *vr* to become annoyed *o* exasperated
esasperazi'one [ezasperat'tsjone] *sf* exasperation
esatta'mente *av* exactly; accurately, precisely
esat'tezza [ezat'tettsa] *sf* exactitude, accuracy, precision; **per l'~** to be precise
e'satto, -a *pp di* **esigere** ■ *ag* (*calcolo, ora*) correct, right, exact; (*preciso*) accurate, precise; (*puntuale*) punctual
esat'tore *sm* (*di imposte etc*) collector
esatto'ria *sf*: **~ comunale** district rates office (*Brit*) *o* assessor's office (*US*)
esau'dire *vt* to grant, fulfil (*Brit*), fulfill (*US*)
esauri'ente *ag* exhaustive
esauri'mento *sm* exhaustion; **~ nervoso** nervous breakdown; **svendita (fino) ad ~ della merce** clearance sale
esau'rire *vt* (*stancare*) to exhaust, wear out; (*provviste, miniera*) to exhaust; **esaurirsi** *vr* to exhaust o.s., wear o.s. out; (*provviste*) to run out
esau'rito, -a *ag* exhausted; (*merci*) sold out; (*libri*) out of print; **essere ~** (*persona*) to be run down; **registrare il tutto ~** (*Teat*) to have a full house

e'sausto, -a *ag* exhausted
esauto'rare *vt* (*dirigente, funzionario*) to deprive of authority
esazi'one [ezat'tsjone] *sf* collection (of taxes)
'esca (*pl* **esche**) *sf* bait
escamo'tage [ɛskamɔ'taʒ] *sm* subterfuge
escande'scenza [eskandeʃ'ʃɛntsa] *sf*: **dare in escandescenze** to lose one's temper, fly into a rage
'esce ['ɛʃʃe] *vb vedi* **uscire**
eschi'mese [eski'mese] *ag, sm/f, sm* Eskimo
'esci ['ɛʃʃi] *vb vedi* **uscire**
escl. *abbr* (= *escluso*) excl
escla'mare *vi* to exclaim, cry out
esclama'tivo, -a *ag*: **punto ~** exclamation mark
esclamazi'one [esklamat'tsjone] *sf* exclamation
es'cludere *vt* to exclude
es'clusi *etc vb vedi* **escludere**
esclusi'one *sf* exclusion; **a ~ di, fatta ~ per** except (for), apart from; **senza ~ (alcuna)** without exception; **procedere per ~** to follow a process of elimination; **senza ~ di colpi** (*fig*) with no holds barred
esclu'siva *sf vedi* **esclusivo**
esclusiva'mente *av* exclusively, solely
esclu'sivo, -a *ag* exclusive ■ *sf* (*Dir, Comm*) exclusive *o* sole rights *pl*
es'cluso, -a *pp di* **escludere** ■ *ag*: **nessuno ~** without exception; **IVA esclusa** excluding VAT, exclusive of VAT
'esco *vb vedi* **uscire**
escogi'tare [eskodʒi'tare] *vt* to devise, think up
'escono *vb vedi* **uscire**
escoriazi'one [eskorjat'tsjone] *sf* abrasion, graze
escre'menti *smpl* excrement *sg*, faeces
escursi'one *sf* (*gita*) excursion, trip; (*a piedi*) hike, walk; (*Meteor*): **~ termica** temperature range
escursio'nista, -i, e *sm/f* (*gitante*) (day) tripper; (*a piedi*) hiker, walker
ese'crare *vt* to loathe, abhor
esecu'tivo, -a *ag, sm* executive
esecu'tore, -'trice *sm/f* (*Mus*) performer; (*Dir*) executor
esecuzi'one [ezekut'tsjone] *sf* execution, carrying out; (*Mus*) performance; **~ capitale** execution
ese'geta, -i [eze'dʒɛta] *sm* commentator
esegu'ire *vt* to carry out, execute; (*Mus*) to perform, execute
e'sempio *sm* example; **per ~** for example, for instance; **fare un ~** to give an example
esem'plare *ag* exemplary ■ *sm* example; (*copia*) copy; (*Bot, Zool, Geo*) specimen
esemplifi'care *vt* to exemplify
esen'tare *vt*: **~ qn/qc da** to exempt sb/sth from
esen'tasse *ag inv* tax-free
e'sente *ag*: **~ da** (*dispensato da*) exempt from; (*privo di*) free from
esenzi'one [ezen'tsjone] *sf* exemption
e'sequie *sfpl* funeral rites; funeral service *sg*
eser'cente [ezer'tʃɛnte] *sm/f* trader, dealer; shopkeeper
eserci'tare [ezertʃi'tare] *vt* (*professione*) to practise (*Brit*), practice (*US*); (*allenare: corpo, mente*) to exercise, train; (*diritto*) to exercise; (*influenza, pressione*) to exert; **esercitarsi** *vr* to practise; **esercitarsi nella guida** to practise one's driving
esercitazi'one [ezertʃitat'tsjone] *sf* (*scolastica, militare*) exercise; **esercitazioni di tiro** target practice *sg*
e'sercito [e'zɛrtʃito] *sm* army
eser'cizio [ezer'tʃittsjo] *sm* practice; (*compito, movimento*) exercise; (*azienda*) business, concern; (*Econ*): **~ finanziario** financial year; **in ~** (*medico etc*) practising (*Brit*), practicing (*US*); **nell'~ delle proprie funzioni** in the execution of one's duties
esfoli'ante *sm* exfoliator
esi'bire *vt* to exhibit, display; (*documenti*) to produce, present; **esibirsi** *vr* (*attore*) to perform; (*fig*) to show off
esibizi'one [ezibit'tsjone] *sf* exhibition; (*di documento*) presentation; (*spettacolo*) show, performance
esibizio'nista, -i, e [ezibittsjo'nista] *sm/f* exhibitionist
esi'gente [ezi'dʒɛnte] *ag* demanding
esi'genza [ezi'dʒɛntsa] *sf* demand, requirement
e'sigere [e'zidʒere] *vt* (*pretendere*) to demand; (*richiedere*) to demand, require; (*imposte*) to collect
esi'gibile [ezi'dʒibile] *ag* payable
e'siguo, -a *ag* small, slight
esila'rante *ag* hilarious; **gas ~** laughing gas
'esile *ag* (*persona*) slender, slim; (*stelo*) thin; (*voce*) faint
esili'are *vt* to exile
esili'ato, -a *ag* exiled ■ *sm/f* exile
e'silio *sm* exile
e'simere *vt*: **~ qn/qc da** to exempt sb/sth from; **esimersi** *vr*: **esimersi da** to get out of
esis'tente *ag* existing; (*attuale*) present, current
esis'tenza [ezis'tɛntsa] *sf* existence
esistenzia'lismo [ezistentsja'lizmo] *sm* existentialism

e'sistere *vi* to exist; **esiste più di una versione dell'opera** there is more than one version of the work; **non esiste!** (*fam*) no way!
esis'tito, -a *pp di* **esistere**
esi'tante *ag* hesitant; (*voce*) faltering
esi'tare *vi* to hesitate
esitazi'one [ezitat'tsjone] *sf* hesitation
'esito *sm* result, outcome
'eskimo *sm* (*giaccone*) parka
'esodo *sm* exodus
e'sofago, -gi *sm* oesophagus (*Brit*), esophagus (*US*)
esone'rare *vt*: **~ qn da** to exempt sb from
esorbi'tante *ag* exorbitant, excessive
esor'cismo [ezor'tʃizmo] *sm* exorcism
esor'cista, -i [ezor'tʃista] *sm* exorcist
esorciz'zare [ezortʃid'dzare] *vt* to exorcize
esordi'ente *sm/f* beginner
e'sordio *sm* debut
esor'dire *vi* (*nel teatro*) to make one's debut; (*fig*) to start out, begin (one's career); **esordì dicendo che ...** he began by saying (that) ...
esor'tare *vt*: **~ qn a fare** to urge sb to do
esortazi'one [ezortat'tsjone] *sf* exhortation
e'soso, -a *ag* (*prezzo*) exorbitant; (*persona: avido*) grasping
eso'terico, -a, ci, che *ag* esoteric
e'sotico, -a, ci, che *ag* exotic
es'pandere *vt* to expand; (*confini*) to extend; (*influenza*) to extend, spread; **espandersi** *vr* to expand
espansi'one *sf* expansion
espansività *sf* expansiveness
espan'sivo, -a *ag* expansive, communicative
es'panso, -a *pp di* **espandere**
espatri'are *vi* to leave one's country
es'patrio *sm* expatriation; **permesso di ~** authorization to leave the country
espedi'ente *sm* expedient; **vivere di espedienti** to live by one's wits
es'pellere *vt* to expel
esperi'enza [espe'rjɛntsa] *sf* experience; (*Sci: prova*) experiment; **parlare per ~** to speak from experience
esperi'mento *sm* experiment; **fare un ~** to carry out *o* do an experiment
es'perto, -a *ag, sm/f* expert
espi'anto *sm* (*Med*) removal
espi'are *vt* to atone for
espiazi'one [espiat'tsjone] *sf*: **~ (di)** expiation (of), atonement (for)
espi'rare *vt, vi* to breathe out
espleta'mento *sm* (*Amm*) carrying out
esple'tare *vt* (*Amm*) to carry out
espli'care *vt* (*attività*) to carry out, perform
esplica'tivo, -a *ag* explanatory
es'plicito, -a [es'plitʃito] *ag* explicit
es'plodere *vi* (*anche fig*) to explode ■ *vt* to fire
esplo'rare *vt* to explore
esplora'tore, -'trice *sm/f* explorer; (*anche:* **giovane esploratore**) (boy) scout/(girl) guide (*Brit*) *o* scout (*US*) ■ *sm* (*Naut*) scout (ship)
esplorazi'one [esplorat'tsjone] *sf* exploration; **mandare qn in ~** (*Mil*) to send sb to scout ahead
esplosi'one *sf* (*anche fig*) explosion
esplo'sivo, -a *ag, sm* explosive
es'ploso, -a *pp di* **esplodere**
es'pone *etc vb vedi* **esporre**
espo'nente *sm/f* (*rappresentante*) representative
esponenzi'ale [esponen'tsjale] *ag* (*Mat*) exponential
es'pongo, es'poni *vb vedi* **esporre**
es'porre *vt* (*merci*) to display; (*quadro*) to exhibit, show; (*fatti, idee*) to explain, set out; (*porre in pericolo, Fot*) to expose; **esporsi** *vr*: **esporsi a** (*sole, pericolo*) to expose o.s. to; (*critiche*) to lay o.s. open to
espor'tare *vt* to export
esporta'tore, -'trice *ag* exporting ■ *sm* exporter
esportazi'one [esportat'tsjone] *sf* (*azione*) exportation, export; (*insieme di prodotti*) exports *pl*
es'pose *etc vb vedi* **esporre**
espo'simetro *sm* exposure meter
esposizi'one [espozit'tsjone] *sf* displaying; exhibiting; setting out; (*anche Fot*) exposure; (*mostra*) exhibition; (*narrazione*) explanation, exposition
es'posto, -a *pp di* **esporre** ■ *ag*: **~ a nord** facing north, north-facing ■ *sm* (*Amm*) statement, account; (*: petizione*) petition
espressi'one *sf* expression
espres'sivo, -a *ag* expressive
es'presso, -a *pp di* **esprimere** ■ *ag* express ■ *sm* (*lettera*) express letter; (*anche:* **treno espresso**) express train; (*anche:* **caffè espresso**) espresso
es'primere *vt* to express; **esprimersi** *vr* to express o.s.
espropri'are *vt* (*terreni, edifici*) to place a compulsory purchase order on; (*persona*) to dispossess
espropriazi'one [esproprjat'tsjone] *sf*, **es'proprio** *sm* expropriation; **~ per pubblica utilità** compulsory purchase
espu'gnare [espuɲ'ɲare] *vt* to take by force, storm
es'pulsi *etc vb vedi* **espellere**
espulsi'one *sf* expulsion
es'pulso, -a *pp di* **espellere**

e

'essa *pron f*, **'esse** *pron fpl vedi* **esso**
es'senza [es'sɛntsa] *sf* essence
essenzi'ale [essen'tsjale] *ag* essential; (*stile, linea*) simple ■ *sm*: **l'~** the main *o* most important thing

PAROLA CHIAVE

'essere *sm* being; **essere umano** human being
■ *vb copulativo* **1** (*con attributo, sostantivo*) to be; **sei giovane/simpatico** you are *o* you're young/nice; **è medico** he is *o* he's a doctor
2 (*+ di: appartenere*) to be; **di chi è la penna?** whose pen is it?; **è di Carla** it is *o* it's Carla's, it belongs to Carla
3 (*+ di: provenire*) to be; **è di Venezia** he is *o* he's from Venice
4 (*data, ora*): **è il 15 agosto** it is *o* it's the 15th of August; **è lunedì** it is *o* it's Monday; **che ora è?, che ore sono?** what time is it?; **è l'una** it is *o* it's one o'clock; **sono le due** it is *o* it's two o'clock
5 (*costare*): **quant'è?** how much is it?; **sono 20 euro** it's 20 euros
■ *vb aus* **1** (*attivo*): **essere arrivato/venuto** to have arrived/come; **è già partita** she has already left
2 (*passivo*) to be; **essere fatto da** to be made by; **è stata uccisa** she has been killed
3 (*riflessivo*): **si sono lavati** they washed, they got washed
4 (*+ da + infinito*): **è da farsi subito** it must be done *o* is to be done immediately
■ *vi* **1** (*esistere, trovarsi*) to be; **sono a casa** I'm at home; **essere in piedi/seduto** to be standing/sitting
2 (*succedere*): **sarà quel che sarà** what will be will be; **sia quel che sia, io me ne vado** come what may, I'm going now
3: **esserci**: **c'è** there is; **ci sono** there are; **che c'è?** what's the matter?, what is it?; **non c'è niente da fare** there's nothing we can do; **c'è da sperare che ...** one can only hope that ...; **ci sono!** (*sono pronto*) I'm ready; (*ho capito*) I get it!; *vedi* **ci**
■ *vb impers*: **è tardi/Pasqua** it's late/Easter; **è mezzanotte** it's midnight; **è bello/caldo/freddo** it's nice/hot/cold; **è possibile che venga** he may come; **è così** that's the way it is

'essi *pron mpl vedi* **esso**
essic'care *vt* (*gen*) to dry; (*legname*) to season; (*cibi*) to desiccate; (*bacino, palude*) to drain; **essiccarsi** *vr* (*fiume, pozzo*) to dry up; (*vernice*) to dry (out)
'esso, -a *pron* it; (*riferito a persona: soggetto*) he/she; (: *complemento*) him/her; **essi, e** *pron pl* (*complemento*) them
est *sm* east; **i paesi dell'E~** the Eastern bloc *sg*
'estasi *sf* ecstasy
estasi'are *vt* to send into raptures; **estasiarsi** *vr*: **estasiarsi (davanti a)** to go into ecstasies (over), go into raptures (over)
es'tate *sf* summer
es'tatico, -a, ci, che *ag* ecstatic
estempo'raneo, -a *ag* (*discorso*) extempore, impromptu; (*brano musicale*) impromptu
es'tendere *vt* to extend; **estendersi** *vr* (*diffondersi*) to spread; (*territorio, confini*) to extend
estensi'one *sf* extension; (*di superficie*) expanse; (*di voce*) range
estenu'ante *ag* wearing, tiring
estenu'are *vt* (*stancare*) to wear out, tire out
esteri'ore *ag* outward, external
esteriorità *sf inv* outward appearance
esterioriz'zare [esterjorid'dzare] *vt* (*gioia etc*) to show
ester'nare *vt* to express; **~ un sospetto** to voice a suspicion
es'terno, -a *ag* (*porta, muro*) outer, outside; (*scala*) outside; (*alunno, impressione*) external ■ *sm* outside, exterior ■ *sm/f* (*allievo*) day pupil; **"per uso ~"** "for external use only"; **gli esterni sono stati girati a Glasgow** (*Cine*) the location shots were taken in Glasgow
'estero, -a *ag* foreign ■ *sm*: **all'~** abroad; **Ministero degli Esteri, gli Esteri** Ministry for Foreign Affairs, ≈ Foreign Office (*Brit*), ≈ State Department (*US*)
esterofi'lia *sf excessive love of foreign things*
esterre'fatto, -a *ag* (*costernato*) horrified; (*sbalordito*) astounded
es'tesi *etc vb vedi* **estendere**
es'teso, -a *pp di* **estendere** ■ *ag* extensive, large; **scrivere per ~** to write in full
estetica'mente *av* aesthetically
es'tetico, -a, ci, che *ag* aesthetic ■ *sf* (*disciplina*) aesthetics *sg*; (*bellezza*) attractiveness; **chirurgia estetica** cosmetic surgery; **cura estetica** beauty treatment
este'tista, -i, e *sm/f* beautician
'estimo *sm* valuation; (*disciplina*) surveying
es'tinguere *vt* to extinguish, put out; (*debito*) to pay off; (*conto*) to close; **estinguersi** *vr* to go out; (*specie*) to become extinct
es'tinsi *etc vb vedi* **estinguere**
es'tinto, -a *pp di* **estinguere**
estin'tore *sm* (fire) extinguisher
estinzi'one [estin'tsjone] *sf* putting out; (*di specie*) extinction; (*di debito*) payment; (*di conto*) closing

estir'pare *vt* (*pianta*) to uproot, pull up; (*dente*) to extract; (*tumore*) to remove; (*fig: vizio*) to eradicate
es'tivo, -a *ag* summer *cpd*
'estone *ag, sm/f, sm* Estonian
Es'tonia *sf*: **l'~** Estonia
es'torcere [es'tɔrtʃere] *vt*: **~ qc (a qn)** to extort sth (from sb)
estorsi'one *sf* extortion
es'torto, -a *pp di* **estorcere**
estra'dare *vt* to extradite
estradizi'one [estradit'tsjone] *sf* extradition
es'trae, es'traggo *vb vedi* **estrarre**
es'traneo, -a *ag* foreign; (*discorso*) extraneous, unrelated ■ *sm/f* stranger; **rimanere ~ a qc** to take no part in sth; **sentirsi ~ a** (*famiglia, società*) to feel alienated from; **"ingresso vietato agli estranei"** "no admittance to unauthorized personnel"
estrani'arsi *vr*: **~ (da)** to cut o.s. off (from)
es'trarre *vt* to extract; (*minerali*) to mine; (*sorteggiare*) to draw; **~ a sorte** to draw lots
es'trassi *etc vb vedi* **estrarre**
es'tratto, -a *pp di* **estrarre** ■ *sm* extract; (*di documento*) abstract; **~ conto** (bank) statement; **~ di nascita** birth certificate
estrazi'one [estrat'tsjone] *sf* extraction; mining; drawing *no pl*; draw
estrema'mente *av* extremely
estre'mismo *sm* extremism
estre'mista, -i, e *sm/f* extremist
estremità *sf inv* extremity, end ■ *sfpl* (*Anat*) extremities
es'tremo, -a *ag* extreme; (*ultimo: ora, tentativo*) final, last ■ *sm* extreme; (*di pazienza, forza*) limit, end; **estremi** *smpl* (*Dir*) essential elements; (*Amm: dati essenziali*) details, particulars; **l'E~ Oriente** the Far East
estrinse'care *vt* to express, show
'estro *sm* (*capriccio*) whim, fancy; (*ispirazione creativa*) inspiration
estro'messo, -a *pp di* **estromettere**
estro'mettere *vt*: **~ (da)** (*partito, club etc*) to expel (from); (*discussione*) to exclude (from)
estromissi'one *sf* expulsion
es'troso, -a *ag* whimsical, capricious; inspired
estro'verso, -a *ag, sm* extrovert
estu'ario *sm* estuary
esube'rante *ag* exuberant; (*Comm*) redundant (*Brit*)
esube'ranza [ezube'rantsa] *sf* (*di persona*) exuberance; **~ di personale** (*Comm*) overmanning (*Brit*), over-staffing (*US*)
e'subero *sm*: **~ di personale** surplus staff; **in ~** redundant, due to be laid off
esu'lare *vi*: **~ da** (*competenza*) to be beyond; (*compiti*) not to be part of
'esule *sm/f* exile
esul'tanza [ezul'tantsa] *sf* exultation
esul'tare *vi* to exult
esu'mare *vt* (*salma*) to exhume, disinter; (*fig*) to unearth
età *sf inv* age; **all'età di 8 anni** at the age of 8, at 8 years of age; **ha la mia età** he (*o* she) is the same age as me *o* as I am; **di mezza età** middle-aged; **raggiungere la maggiore età** to come of age; **essere in età minore** to be under age; **in età avanzata** advanced in years
eta'nolo *sm* ethanol
etc. *abbr* etc.
'etere *sm* ether; **via ~** on the airwaves
e'tereo, -a *ag* ethereal
eternità *sf* eternity
e'terno, -a *ag* eternal; (*interminabile: lamenti, attesa*) never-ending; **in ~** for ever, eternally
etero'geneo, -a [etero'dʒɛneo] *ag* heterogeneous
eterosessu'ale *ag, sm/f* heterosexual
'etica *sf vedi* **etico**
eti'chetta [eti'ketta] *sf* label; (*cerimoniale*): **l'~** etiquette
'etico, -a, ci, che *ag* ethical ■ *sf* ethics *sg*
eti'lometro *sm* Breathalyzer®
etimolo'gia, -'gie [etimolo'dʒia] *sf* etymology
etimo'logico, -a, ci, che [etimo'lɔdʒiko] *ag* etymological
e'tiope *ag, sm/f* Ethiopian
Eti'opia *sf*: **l'~** Ethiopia
eti'opico, -a, ci, che *ag, sm* (*Ling*) Ethiopian
'Etna *sm*: **l'~** Etna
'etnico, -a, ci, che *ag* ethnic
e'trusco, -a, schi, sche *ag, sm/f* Etruscan
'ettaro *sm* hectare (= 10,000 m²)
'etto *abbr m* = **ettogrammo**
etto'grammo *sm* hectogram(me) (= 100 grams)
et'tolitro *sm* hectolitre (*Brit*), hectoliter (*US*)
et'tometro *sm* hectometre
EU *abbr* = **Europa**
euca'lipto *sm* eucalyptus
Eucaris'tia *sf*: **l'~** the Eucharist
eufe'mismo *sm* euphemism
eufe'mistico, -a, ci, che *ag* euphemistic
eufo'ria *sf* euphoria
eu'forico, -a, ci, che *ag* euphoric
Eu'rasia *sf* Eurasia
eurasi'atico, -a, ci, che *ag, sm/f* Eurasian
Eura'tom *sigla f* (= *Comunità Europea dell'Energia Atomica*) Euratom
eu'ristico, -a, ci, che *ag* heuristic
'euro *sm inv* (*divisa*) euro

euro'corpo *sm* European force
eurodepu'tato *sm* Euro MP
eurodi'visa *sf* Eurocurrency
euro'dollaro *sm* Eurodollar
Euro'landia *sf* Euroland
euromer'cato *sm* Euromarket
euro'missile *sm* Euro-missile
Eu'ropa *sf*: **l'~** Europe
europarlamen'tare *sm/f* Member of the European Parliament, MEP
euro'peo, -a *ag, sm/f* European
euro'scettico, -a, ci, che [euroʃʃɛttiko] *sm/f* Euro-sceptic
eutana'sia *sf* euthanasia
E.V. *abbr* = **Eccellenza Vostra**
evacu'are *vt* to evacuate
evacuazi'one [evakuat'tsjone] *sf* evacuation
e'vadere *vi* (*fuggire*): **~ da** to escape from ■ *vt* (*sbrigare*) to deal with, dispatch; (*tasse*) to evade
evan'gelico, -a, ci, che [evan'dʒɛliko] *ag* evangelical
evange'lista, -i [evandʒe'lista] *sm* evangelist
evapo'rare *vi* to evaporate
evaporazi'one [evaporat'tsjone] *sf* evaporation
e'vasi *etc vb vedi* **evadere**
evasi'one *sf* (*vedi evadere*) escape; dispatch; **dare ~ ad un ordine** to carry out *o* execute an order; **letteratura d'~** escapist literature; **~ fiscale** tax evasion
eva'sivo, -a *ag* evasive
e'vaso, -a *pp di* **evadere** ■ *sm* escapee
eva'sore *sm*: **~ (fiscale)** tax evader
eveni'enza [eve'njɛntsa] *sf*: **nell'~ che ciò succeda** should that happen; **essere pronto ad ogni ~** to be ready for anything *o* any eventuality
e'vento *sm* event
eventu'ale *ag* possible
eventualità *sf inv* eventuality, possibility; **nell'~ di** in the event of
eventual'mente *av* if need be, if necessary
'Everest *sm*: **l'~, il Monte ~** (Mount) Everest
eversi'one *sf* subversion
ever'sivo, -a *ag* subversive
evi'dente *ag* evident, obvious
evidente'mente *av* evidently; (*palesemente*) obviously, evidently
evi'denza [evi'dɛntsa] *sf* obviousness; **mettere in ~** to point out, highlight; **tenere in ~ qc** to bear sth in mind
evidenzi'are [eviden'tsjare] *vt* (*sottolineare*) to emphasize, highlight; (*con evidenziatore*) to highlight
evidenzia'tore [evidentsja'tore] *sm* (*penna*) highlighter
evi'rare *vt* to castrate
evi'tabile *ag* avoidable
evi'tare *vt* to avoid; **~ di fare** to avoid doing; **~ qc a qn** to spare sb sth
'evo *sm* age, epoch
evo'care *vt* to evoke
evoca'tivo, -a *ag* evocative
evocherò *etc* [evoke'rɔ] *vb vedi* **evocare**
evolu'tivo, -a *ag* (*gen, Biol*) evolutionary; (*Med*) progressive
evo'luto, -a *pp di* **evolversi** ■ *ag* (*popolo, civiltà*) (highly) developed, advanced; (*persona: emancipato*) independent; (*: senza pregiudizi*) broad-minded
evoluzi'one [evolut'tsjone] *sf* evolution
e'volversi *vr* to evolve; **con l'~ della situazione** as the situation develops
ev'viva *escl* hurrah!; **~ il re!** long live the king!, hurrah for the king!
ex *prefisso* ex-, former ■ *sm/f inv* ex-boyfriend/girlfriend
ex 'aequo [ɛg'zɛkwo] *av*: **classificarsi primo ~** to come joint first, come equal first
'extra *ag inv, sm inv* extra
extracomuni'tario, -a *ag* non-EEC ■ *sm/f* non-EEC national (*often referring to non-European immigrant*)
extraconiu'gale *ag* extramarital
extraparlamen'tare *ag* extraparliamentary
extrasensori'ale *ag*: **percezione ~** extrasensory perception
extrater'restre *ag, sm/f* extraterrestrial
extraur'bano, -a *ag* suburban

F, f ['ɛffe] *sf o m inv* (*lettera*) F, f; **F come Firenze** ≈ F for Frederick (*Brit*), F for Fox (*US*)
F *abbr* (= *Fahrenheit*) F
F. *abbr* (= *fiume*) R
fa *vb vedi* **fare** ■ *sm inv* (*Mus*) F; (*: solfeggiando la scala*) fa ■ *av*: **10 anni fa** 10 years ago
fabbi'sogno [fabbi'zoɲɲo] *sm* needs *pl*, requirements *pl*; **il ~ nazionale di petrolio** the country's oil requirements; **~ del settore pubblico** public sector borrowing requirement (*Brit*), government debt borrowing (*US*)
'fabbrica *sf* factory
fabbri'cante *sm* manufacturer, maker
fabbri'care *vt* to build; (*produrre*) to manufacture, make; (*fig*) to fabricate, invent
fabbri'cato *sm* building
fabbricazi'one [fabbrikat'tsjone] *sf* building, fabrication; making, manufacture, manufacturing
'fabbro *sm* (black)smith
fac'cenda [fat'tʃɛnda] *sf* matter, affair; (*cosa da fare*) task, chore; **le faccende domestiche** the housework *sg*
faccendi'ere [fattʃen'djɛre] *sm* wheeler-dealer, (shady) operator
fac'cetta [fat'tʃetta] *sf* (*di pietra preziosa*) facet
fac'chino [fak'kino] *sm* porter
'faccia, -ce ['fattʃa] *sf* face; (*di moneta, medaglia*) side; **~ a ~** face to face; **di ~ a** opposite, facing; **avere la ~ (tosta) di dire/fare qc** to have the cheek *o* nerve to say/do sth; **fare qc alla ~ di qn** to do sth to spite sb; **leggere qc in ~ a qn** to see sth written all over sb's face
facci'ata [fat'tʃata] *sf* façade; (*di pagina*) side
'faccio *etc* ['fattʃo] *vb vedi* **fare**
fac'cina [fat'tʃina] *sf* (*Comput*) emoticon
fa'cente [fa'tʃente]: **~ funzione** *sm* (*Amm*) deputy
fa'cessi *etc* [fa'tʃessi] *vb vedi* **fare**
fa'ceto, -a [fa'tʃeto] *ag* witty, humorous
fa'cevo *etc* [fa'tʃevo] *vb vedi* **fare**
fa'cezia [fa'tʃɛttsja] *sf* witticism, witty remark
fa'chiro [fa'kiro] *sm* fakir
'facile ['fatʃile] *ag* easy; (*affabile*) easy-going; (*disposto*): **~ a** inclined to, prone to; (*probabile*): **è ~ che piova** it's likely to rain; **donna di facili costumi** woman of easy virtue, loose woman
facilità [fatʃili'ta] *sf* easiness; (*disposizione, dono*) aptitude
facili'tare [fatʃili'tare] *vt* to make easier
facilitazi'one [fatʃilitat'tsjone] *sf* (*gen*) facilities *pl*; **facilitazioni di pagamento** easy terms, credit facilities
facil'mente [fatʃil'mente] *av* (*gen*) easily; (*probabilmente*) probably
faci'lone, -a [fatʃi'lone] *sm/f* (*peg*) happy-go-lucky person
facino'roso, -a [fatʃino'roso] *ag* violent
facoltà *sf inv* faculty; (*Chim*) property; (*autorità*) power
facolta'tivo, -a *ag* optional; (*fermata d'autobus*) request *cpd*
facol'toso, -a *ag* wealthy, rich
fac'simile *sm* facsimile
'faggio ['faddʒo] *sm* beech
fagi'ano [fa'dʒano] *sm* pheasant
fagio'lino [fadʒo'lino] *sm* French (*Brit*) *o* string bean
fagi'olo [fa'dʒɔlo] *sm* bean; **capitare a ~** to come at the right time
fagoci'tare [fagotʃi'tare] *vt* (*fig: industria etc*) to absorb, swallow up; (*scherzoso: cibo*) to devour
fa'gotto *sm* bundle; (*Mus*) bassoon; **far ~** (*fig*) to pack up and go
'fai *vb vedi* **fare**
'faida *sf* feud
fai-da-'te *sm inv* DIY, do-it-yourself
fa'ina *sf* (*Zool*) stone marten
'Fahrenheit ['fa:rənheit] *sm* Fahrenheit
fa'lange [fa'landʒe] *sf* (*Anat, Mil*) phalanx
fal'cata *sf* stride

'falce ['faltʃe] *sf* scythe; **~ e martello** (*Pol*) hammer and sickle
fal'cetto [fal'tʃetto] *sm* sickle
falci'are [fal'tʃare] *vt* to cut; (*fig*) to mow down
falcia'trice [faltʃa'tritʃe] *sf* (*per fieno*) reaping machine; (*per erba*) mowing machine
'falco, -chi *sm* (*anche fig*) hawk
fal'cone *sm* falcon
'falda *sf* (*Geo*) layer, stratum; (*di cappello*) brim; (*di cappotto*) tails *pl*; (*di monte*) lower slope; (*di tetto*) pitch; (*di neve*) flake; **abito a falde** tails *pl*
fale'gname [faleɲ'ɲame] *sm* joiner
fa'lena *sf* (*Zool*) moth
'Falkland ['fɔːlklənd] *sfpl*: **le isole ~** the Falkland Islands
fal'lace [fal'latʃe] *ag* misleading, deceptive
'fallico, -a, ci, che *ag* phallic
fallimen'tare *ag* (*Comm*) bankruptcy *cpd*; **bilancio ~** negative balance, deficit; **diritto ~** bankruptcy law
falli'mento *sm* failure; bankruptcy
fal'lire *vi* (*non riuscire*): **~ (in)** to fail (in); (*Dir*) to go bankrupt ■ *vt* (*colpo, bersaglio*) to miss
fal'lito, -a *ag* unsuccessful; bankrupt ■ *sm/f* bankrupt
'fallo *sm* error, mistake; (*imperfezione*) defect, flaw; (*Sport*) foul; fault; (*Anat*) phallus; **senza ~** without fail; **cogliere qn in ~** to catch sb out; **mettere il piede in ~** to slip
fal'locrate *sm* male chauvinist
falò *sm inv* bonfire
fal'sare *vt* to distort, misrepresent
falsa'riga, -ghe *sf* lined page, ruled page; **sulla ~ di ...** (*fig*) along the lines of ...
fal'sario *sm* forger; counterfeiter
falsifi'care *vt* to forge; (*monete*) to forge, counterfeit
falsità *sf inv* (*di persona, notizia*) falseness; (*bugia*) falsehood, lie
'falso, -a *ag* false; (*errato*) wrong; (*falsificato*) forged; fake; (*: oro, gioielli*) imitation *cpd* ■ *sm* forgery; **essere un ~ magro** to be heavier than one looks; **giurare il ~** to commit perjury; **~ in atto pubblico** forgery (of a legal document)
'fama *sf* fame; (*reputazione*) reputation, name
'fame *sf* hunger; **aver ~** to be hungry; **fare la ~** (*fig*) to starve, exist at subsistence level
fa'melico, -a, ci, che *ag* ravenous
famige'rato, -a [famidʒe'rato] *ag* notorious, ill-famed
fa'miglia [fa'miʎʎa] *sf* family
famili'are *ag* (*della famiglia*) family *cpd*; (*ben noto*) familiar; (*rapporti, atmosfera*) friendly; (*Ling*) informal, colloquial ■ *sm/f* relative, relation; **una vettura ~** a family car
familiarità *sf* familiarity; friendliness; informality
familiariz'zare [familjarid'dzare] *vi*: **~ con qn** to get to know sb; **abbiamo familiarizzato subito** we got on well together from the start
fa'moso, -a *ag* famous, well-known
fa'nale *sm* (*Aut*) light, lamp (*Brit*); (*luce stradale, Naut*) light; (*di faro*) beacon
fa'natico, -a, ci, che *ag* fanatical; (*del teatro, calcio etc*): **~ di** *o* **per** mad *o* crazy about ■ *sm/f* fanatic; (*tifoso*) fan
fana'tismo *sm* fanaticism
fanciul'lezza [fantʃul'lettsa] *sf* childhood
fanci'ullo, -a [fan'tʃullo] *sm/f* child
fan'donia *sf* tall story; **fandonie** *sfpl* nonsense *sg*
fan'fara *sf* brass band; (*musica*) fanfare
fanfa'rone *sm* braggart
fan'ghiglia [fan'giʎʎa] *sf* mire, mud
'fango, -ghi *sm* mud; **fare i fanghi** (*Med*) to take a course of mud baths
fan'goso, -a *ag* muddy
'fanno *vb vedi* **fare**
fannul'lone, -a *sm/f* idler, loafer
fantasci'enza [fantaʃ'ʃentsa] *sf* science fiction
fanta'sia *sf* fantasy, imagination; (*capriccio*) whim, caprice ■ *ag inv*: **vestito ~** patterned dress
fantasi'oso, -a *ag* (*dotato di fantasia*) imaginative; (*bizzarro*) fanciful, strange
fan'tasma, -i *sm* ghost, phantom
fantasti'care *vi* to daydream
fantastiche'ria [fantastike'ria] *sf* daydream
fan'tastico, -a, ci, che *ag* fantastic; (*potenza, ingegno*) imaginative
'fante *sm* infantryman; (*Carte*) jack, knave (*Brit*)
fante'ria *sf* infantry
fan'tino *sm* jockey
fan'toccio [fan'tɔttʃo] *sm* puppet
fanto'matico, -a, ci, che *ag* (*nave, esercito*) phantom *cpd*; (*personaggio*) mysterious
FAO *sigla f* FAO (= *Food and Agriculture Organization*)
fara'butto *sm* crook
fara'ona *sf* guinea fowl
fara'one *sm* (*Storia*) Pharaoh
fara'onico, -a, ci, che *ag* of the Pharaohs; (*fig*) enormous, huge
far'cire [far'tʃire] *vt* (*carni, peperoni etc*) to stuff; (*torte*) to fill
fard [far] *sm inv* blusher
far'dello *sm* bundle; (*fig*) burden

PAROLA CHIAVE

'fare *sm* **1** (*modo di fare*): **con fare distratto** absent-mindedly; **ha un fare simpatico** he has a pleasant manner
2: **sul far del giorno/della notte** at daybreak/nightfall
■ *vt* **1** (*fabbricare, creare*) to make; (: *casa*) to build; (: *assegno*) to make out; **fare una promessa/un film** to make a promise/a film; **fare rumore** to make a noise
2 (*effettuare*: *lavoro, attività, studi*) to do; (: *sport*) to play; **cosa fa?** (*adesso*) what are you doing?; (*di professione*) what do you do?; **fare psicologia/italiano** to do psychology/ Italian; **fare tennis** to play tennis; **fare un viaggio** to go on a trip *o* journey; **fare una passeggiata** to go for a walk; **fare la spesa** to do the shopping
3 (*funzione*) to be; (*Teat*) to play; **fare il medico** to be a doctor; **fare il malato** (*fingere*) to act the invalid
4 (*suscitare*: *sentimenti*): **fare paura a qn** to frighten sb; **mi fa rabbia** it makes me angry; **(non) fa niente** (*non importa*) it doesn't matter
5 (*ammontare*): **3 più 3 fa 6** 3 and 3 are *o* make 6; **fanno 6 euro** that's 6 euros; **Roma fa oltre 2.000.000 di abitanti** Rome has over 2,000,000 inhabitants; **che ora fai?** what time do you make it?
6 (*+ infinito*): **far fare qc a qn** (*obbligare*) to make sb do sth; (*permettere*) to let sb do sth; **fare piangere/ridere qn** to make sb cry/ laugh; **fare venire qn** to send for sb; **fammi vedere** let me see; **far partire il motore** to start (up) the engine; **far riparare la macchina/costruire una casa** to get *o* have the car repaired/a house built
7: **farsi**: **farsi una gonna** to make o.s. a skirt; **farsi un nome** to make a name for o. s.; **farsi la permanente** to get a perm; **farsi notare** to get o.s. noticed; **farsi tagliare i capelli** to get one's hair cut; **farsi operare** to have an operation
8 (*fraseologia*): **farcela** to succeed, manage; **non ce la faccio più** I can't go on; **ce la faremo** we'll make it; **me l'hanno fatta!** I've been done!; **lo facevo più giovane** I thought he was younger; **fare sì/no con la testa** to nod/shake one's head
■ *vi* **1** (*agire*) to act, do; **fate come volete** do as you like; **fare presto** to be quick; **fare da** to act as; **non c'è niente da fare** it's no use; **saperci fare con qn/qc** to know how to deal with sb/sth; **ci sa fare** she's very good at it; **faccia pure!** go ahead!
2 (*dire*) to say; **"davvero?" fece** "really?" he said
3: **fare per** (*essere adatto*) to be suitable for; **fare per fare qc** to be about to do sth; **fece per andarsene** he made as if to leave
4: **farsi**: **si fa così** you do it like this, this is the way it's done; **non si fa così!** (*rimprovero*) that's no way to behave!; **la festa non si fa** the party is off
5: **fare a gara con qn** to compete with sb; **fare a pugni** to come to blows; **fare in tempo a fare** to be in time to do
■ *vb impers*: **fa bel tempo** the weather is fine; **fa caldo/freddo** it's hot/cold; **fa notte** it's getting dark
■ **farsi** *vr* **1** (*diventare*) to become; **farsi prete** to become a priest; **farsi grande/vecchio** to grow tall/old
2 (*spostarsi*): **farsi avanti/indietro** to move forward/back; **fatti più in là** move along a bit
3 (*fam*: *drogarsi*) to be a junkie

fa'retra *sf* quiver
far'falla *sf* butterfly
farfugli'are [farfuʎ'ʎare] *vt, vi* to mumble, mutter
fa'rina *sf* flour; **~ gialla** maize (*Brit*) *o* corn (*US*) flour; **~ integrale** wholemeal (*Brit*) *o* whole-wheat (*US*) flour; **questa non è ~ del tuo sacco** (*fig*) this isn't your own idea (*o* work)
fari'nacei [fari'natʃei] *smpl* starches
fa'ringe [fa'rindʒe] *sf* (*Anat*) pharynx
farin'gite [farin'dʒite] *sf* pharyngitis
fari'noso, -a *ag* (*patate*) floury; (*neve, mela*) powdery
farma'ceutico, -a, ci, che [farma'tʃeutiko] *ag* pharmaceutical
farma'cia, -cie [farma'tʃia] *sf* pharmacy; (*negozio*) chemist's (shop) (*Brit*), pharmacy
farma'cista, -i, e [farma'tʃista] *sm/f* chemist (*Brit*), pharmacist
'farmaco (*pl* **farmaci** *o* **farmachi**) *sm* drug, medicine
farneti'care *vi* to rave, be delirious
'faro *sm* (*Naut*) lighthouse; (*Aer*) beacon; (*Aut*) headlight, headlamp (*Brit*)
farragi'noso, -a [farradʒi'noso] *ag* (*stile*) muddled, confused
'farsa *sf* farce
far'sesco, -a, schi, sche *ag* farcical
fasc. *abbr* = **fascicolo**
'fascia, -sce ['faʃʃa] *sf* band, strip; (*Med*) bandage; (*di sindaco, ufficiale*) sash; (*parte di territorio*) strip, belt; (*di contribuenti etc*) group, band; **essere in fasce** (*anche fig*) to be in one's infancy; **~ oraria** time band

fasci'are [faʃʃare] *vt* to bind; *(Med)* to bandage; *(bambino)* to put a nappy *(Brit)* *o* diaper *(US)* on
fascia'tura [faʃʃa'tura] *sf (azione)* bandaging; *(fascia)* bandage
fa'scicolo [faʃʃikolo] *sm (di documenti)* file, dossier; *(di rivista)* issue, number; *(opuscolo)* booklet, pamphlet
'fascino ['faʃʃino] *sm* charm, fascination
'fascio ['faʃʃo] *sm* bundle, sheaf; *(di fiori)* bunch; *(di luce)* beam; *(Pol)*: **il F~** the Fascist Party
fa'scismo [faʃʃizmo] *sm* fascism
fa'scista, -i, e [faʃʃista] *ag, sm/f* fascist
'fase *sf* phase; *(Tecn)* stroke; **in ~ di espansione** in a period of expansion; **essere fuori ~** *(motore)* to be rough *(Brit)*, run roughly; *(fig)* to feel rough *(Brit)* *o* rotten
fas'tidio *sm* bother, trouble; **dare ~ a qn** to bother *o* annoy sb; **sento ~ allo stomaco** my stomach's upset; **avere fastidi con la polizia** to have trouble *o* bother with the police
fastidi'oso, -a *ag* annoying, tiresome; *(schifiltoso)* fastidious
'fasto *sm* pomp, splendour *(Brit)*, splendor *(US)*
fas'toso, -a *ag* sumptuous, lavish
fa'sullo, -a *ag (gen)* fake; *(dichiarazione, persona)* false; *(pretesto)* bogus
'fata *sf* fairy
fa'tale *ag* fatal; *(inevitabile)* inevitable; *(fig)* irresistible
fata'lismo *sm* fatalism
fatalità *sf inv* inevitability; *(avversità)* misfortune; *(fato)* fate, destiny
fa'tato, -a *ag (spada, chiave)* magic; *(castello)* enchanted
fa'tica, -che *sf* hard work, toil; *(sforzo)* effort; *(di metalli)* fatigue; **a ~** with difficulty; **respirare a ~** to have difficulty (in) breathing; **fare ~ a fare qc** to find it difficult to do sth; **animale da ~** beast of burden
fati'caccia, -ce [fati'kattʃa] *sf*: **fu una ~** it was hard work, it was a hell of a job *(fam)*
fati'care *vi* to toil; **~ a fare qc** to have difficulty doing sth
fati'cata *sf* hard work
fa'tichi *etc* [fa'tiki] *vb vedi* **faticare**
fati'coso, -a *ag (viaggio, camminata)* tiring, exhausting; *(lavoro)* laborious
fa'tidico, -a, ci, che *ag* fateful
'fato *sm* fate, destiny
Fatt. *abbr (= fattura)* inv
fat'taccio [fat'tattʃo] *sm* foul deed
fat'tezze [fat'tettse] *sfpl* features
fat'tibile *ag* feasible, possible
fattis'pecie [fattis'pεtʃe] *sf*: **nella** *o* **in ~** in this case *o* instance
'fatto, -a *pp di* **fare** ■ *ag*: **un uomo ~** a grown man ■ *sm* fact; *(azione)* deed; *(avvenimento)* event, occurrence; *(di romanzo, film)* action, story; **~ a mano/in casa** hand-/home-made; **è ben fatta** she has a nice figure; **cogliere qn sul ~** to catch sb red-handed; **il ~ sta** *o* **è che** the fact remains *o* is that; **in ~ di** as for, as far as ... is concerned; **fare i fatti propri** to mind one's own business; **è uno che sa il ~ suo** he knows what he's about; **gli ho detto il ~ suo** I told him what I thought of him; **porre qn di fronte al ~ compiuto** to present sb with a fait accompli; **coppia/unione di ~** long-standing relationship
fat'tore *sm (Agr)* farm manager; *(Mat: elemento costitutivo)* factor
fatto'ria *sf* farm; *(casa)* farmhouse
fatto'rino *sm* errand boy; *(di ufficio)* office boy; *(d'albergo)* porter
fattucchi'era [fattuk'kjεra] *sf* witch
fat'tura *sf (Comm)* invoice; *(di abito)* tailoring; *(malia)* spell; **pagamento contro presentazione ~** payment on invoice
fattu'rare *vt (Comm)* to invoice; *(prodotto)* to produce; *(vino)* to adulterate
fattu'rato *sm (Comm)* turnover
fatturazi'one [fatturat'tsjone] *sf* billing, invoicing
'fatuo, -a *ag* vain, fatuous; **fuoco ~** *(anche fig)* will-o'-the-wisp
'fauci ['fautʃi] *sfpl (di leone etc)* jaws; *(di vulcano)* mouth *sg*
'fauna *sf* fauna
'fausto, -a *ag (formale)* happy; **un ~ presagio** a good omen
fau'tore, -'trice *sm/f* advocate, supporter
'fava *sf* broad bean
fa'vella *sf* speech
fa'villa *sf* spark
'favo *sm (di api)* honeycomb
'favola *sf (fiaba)* fairy tale; *(d'intento morale)* fable; *(fandonia)* yarn; **essere la ~ del paese** *(oggetto di critica)* to be the talk of the town; *(zimbello)* to be a laughing stock
favo'loso, -a *ag* fabulous; *(incredibile)* incredible
fa'vore *sm* favour *(Brit)*, favor *(US)*; **per ~** please; **prezzo/trattamento di ~** preferential price/treatment; **condizioni di ~** *(Comm)* favo(u)rable terms; **fare un ~ a qn** to do sb a favo(u)r; **col ~ delle tenebre** under cover of darkness
favoreggia'mento [favoreddʒa'mento] *sm (Dir)* aiding and abetting

favo'revole *ag* favourable (*Brit*), favorable (*US*)
favo'rire *vt* to favour (*Brit*), favor (*US*); (*il commercio, l'industria, le arti*) to promote, encourage; **vuole ~?** won't you help yourself?; **favorisca in salotto** please come into the sitting room; **mi favorisca i documenti** please may I see your papers?
favori'tismo *sm* favouritism (*Brit*), favoritism (*US*)
favo'rito, -a *ag, sm/f* favourite (*Brit*), favorite (*US*)
fax *sm inv* fax; **mandare qc via ~** to fax sth
fa'xare *vt* to fax
fazi'one [fat'tsjone] *sf* faction
faziosità [fattsjosi'ta] *sf* sectarianism
fazzo'letto [fattso'letto] *sm* handkerchief; (*per la testa*) (head)scarf
F.B.I. *sigla f* (= *Federal Bureau of Investigation*) FBI
F.C. *abbr* = **fuoricorso**
f.co *abbr* = **franco**
FE *sigla* = **Ferrara**
febb. *abbr* (= *febbraio*) Feb
feb'braio *sm* February; *vedi anche* **luglio**
'febbre *sf* fever; **aver la ~** to have a high temperature; **~ da fieno** hay fever
feb'brile *ag* (*anche fig*) feverish
'feccia, -ce ['fettʃa] *sf* dregs *pl*
'feci ['fɛtʃi] *sfpl* faeces, excrement *sg*
'feci *etc* ['fetʃi] *vb vedi* **fare**
'fecola *sf* potato flour
fecon'dare *vt* to fertilize
fecondazi'one [fekondat'tsjone] *sf* fertilization; **~ artificiale** artificial insemination
fecondità *sf* fertility
fe'condo, -a *ag* fertile
'Fedcom *sigla m* = **Fondo Europeo di Cooperazione Monetaria**
'fede *sf* (*credenza*) belief, faith; (*Rel*) faith; (*fiducia*) faith, trust; (*fedeltà*) loyalty; (*anello*) wedding ring; (*attestato*) certificate; **aver ~ in qn** to have faith in sb; **tener ~ a** (*ideale*) to remain loyal to; (*giuramento, promessa*) to keep; **in buona/cattiva ~** in good/bad faith; **"in ~"** (*Dir*) "in witness whereof"
fe'dele *ag* (*leale*): **~ (a)** faithful (to); (*veritiero*) true, accurate ■ *sm/f* follower; **i fedeli** (*Rel*) the faithful
fedeltà *sf* faithfulness; (*coniugale*) fidelity; (*esattezza: di copia, traduzione*) accuracy; **alta ~** (*Radio*) high fidelity
'federa *sf* pillowslip, pillowcase
fede'rale *ag* federal
federa'lismo *sm* (*Pol*) federalism
federa'lista, -i, e *ag, sm/f* (*Pol*) federalist
federazi'one [federat'tsjone] *sf* federation
Feder'caccia [feder'kattʃa] *abbr f* (= *Federazione Italiana della Caccia*) *hunting federation*
Feder'calcio [feder'kaltʃo] *abbr m* (= *Federazione Italiana Gioco Calcio*) *Italian football association*
Federcon'sorzi [federkon'sɔrtsi] *abbr f* (= *Federazione Italiana dei Consorzi Agrari*) *federation of farmers' cooperatives*
fe'difrago, -a, ghi, ghe *ag* faithless, perfidious
fe'dina *sf* (*Dir*): **~ (penale)** record; **avere la ~ penale sporca** to have a police record
'fegato *sm* liver; (*fig*) guts *pl*, nerve; **mangiarsi** *o* **rodersi il ~** to be consumed with rage
'felce ['feltʃe] *sf* fern
fe'lice [fe'litʃe] *ag* happy; (*fortunato*) lucky
felicità [felitʃi'ta] *sf* happiness
felici'tarsi [felitʃi'tarsi] *vr* (*congratularsi*): **~ con qn per qc** to congratulate sb on sth
felicitazi'oni [felitʃitat'tsjoni] *sfpl* congratulations
fe'lino, -a *ag, sm* feline
'felpa *sf* sweatshirt
fel'pato, -a *ag* (*tessuto*) brushed; (*passo*) stealthy; **con passo ~** stealthily
'feltro *sm* felt
'femmina *sf* (*Zool, Tecn*) female; (*figlia*) girl, daughter; (*spesso peg*) woman
femmi'nile *ag* feminine; (*sesso*) female; (*lavoro, giornale*) woman's, women's; (*moda*) women's ■ *sm* (*Ling*) feminine
femminilità *sf* femininity
femmi'nismo *sm* feminism
femmi'nista, -i, e *ag, sm/f* feminist
'femore *sm* thighbone, femur
'fendere *vt* to cut through
fendi'nebbia *sm* (*Aut*) fog lamp
fendi'tura *sf* (*gen*) crack; (*di roccia*) cleft, crack
fe'nomeno *sm* phenomenon
'feretro *sm* coffin
feri'ale *ag*: **giorno ~** weekday, working day
'ferie *sfpl* holidays (*Brit*), vacation *sg* (*US*); **andare in ~** to go on holiday *o* vacation; **25 giorni di ~ pagate** 25 days' holiday *o* vacation with pay
feri'mento *sm* wounding
fe'rire *vt* to injure; (*deliberatamente: Mil etc*) to wound; (*colpire*) to hurt; **ferirsi** *vr* to hurt o.s., injure o.s.
fe'rito, -a *sm/f* wounded *o* injured man/woman ■ *sf* injury; wound
feri'toia *sf* slit
'ferma *sf* (*Mil*) (period of) service; (*Caccia*): **cane da ~** pointer
ferma'carte *sm inv* paperweight
fermacra'vatta *sm inv* tiepin (*Brit*), tie tack (*US*)

fer'maglio [fer'maʎʎo] *sm* clasp; (*gioiello*) brooch; (*per documenti*) clip

ferma'mente *av* firmly

fer'mare *vt* to stop, halt; (*Polizia*) to detain, hold; (*bottone etc*) to fasten, fix ■ *vi* to stop; **fermarsi** *vr* to stop, halt; **fermarsi a fare qc** to stop to do sth

fer'mata *sf* stop; **~ dell'autobus** bus stop

fermen'tare *vi* to ferment; (*fig*) to be in a ferment

fermentazi'one [fermentat'tsjone] *sf* fermentation

fer'mento *sm* (*anche fig*) ferment; (*lievito*) yeast; **fermenti lattici** probiotics, probiotic bacteria

fer'mezza [fer'mettsa] *sf* (*fig*) firmness, steadfastness

'fermo, -a *ag* still, motionless; (*veicolo*) stationary; (*orologio*) not working; (*saldo*: *anche fig*) firm; (*voce, mano*) steady ■ *escl* stop!; keep still! ■ *sm* (*chiusura*) catch, lock; (*Dir*): **~ di polizia** police detention; **~ restando che ...** it being understood that ...

'fermo 'posta *av, sm inv* poste restante (*Brit*), general delivery (*US*)

fe'roce [fe'rotʃe] *ag* (*animale*) wild, fierce, ferocious; (*persona*) cruel, fierce; (*fame, dolore*) raging

fe'rocia, -cie [fe'rotʃa] *sf* ferocity

Ferr. *abbr* = **ferrovia**

fer'raglia [fer'raʎʎa] *sf* scrap iron

ferra'gosto *sm* (*festa*) feast of the Assumption; (*periodo*) August holidays *pl* (*Brit*) *o* vacation (*US*); *see note*

Ferragosto

Ferragosto, 15 August, is a national holiday. Marking the feast of the Assumption, its origins are religious but in recent years it has simply become the most important public holiday of the summer season. Most people take some extra time off work and head out of town to the holiday resorts. Consequently, most of industry and commerce grinds to a standstill.

ferra'menta *sfpl* ironmongery *sg* (*Brit*), hardware *sg*; **negozio di ~** ironmonger's (*Brit*), hardware shop *o* store (*US*)

fer'rare *vt* (*cavallo*) to shoe

fer'rato, -a *ag* (*Ferr*): **strada ferrata** railway line (*Brit*), railroad line (*US*); (*fig*): **essere ~ in** (*materia*) to be well up in

ferra'vecchio [ferra'vɛkkjo] *sm* scrap merchant

'ferreo, -a *ag* iron *cpd*

ferri'era *sf* ironworks *inv*

'ferro *sm* iron; **una bistecca ai ferri** a grilled steak; **mettere a ~ e fuoco** to put to the sword; **essere ai ferri corti** (*fig*) to be at daggers drawn; **tocca ~!** touch wood!; **~ battuto** wrought iron; **~ di cavallo** horseshoe; **~ da stiro** iron; **ferri da calza** knitting needles; **i ferri del mestiere** the tools of the trade

ferrotranvi'ario, -a *ag* public transport *cpd*

Ferrotranvi'eri *abbr f* (= *Federazione Nazionale Lavoratori Autoferrotranvieri e Internavigatori*) *transport workers' union*

ferro'vecchio [ferro'vɛkkjo] *sm* = **ferravecchio**

ferro'via *sf* railway (*Brit*), railroad (*US*)

ferrovi'ario, -a *ag* railway *cpd* (*Brit*), railroad *cpd* (*US*)

ferrovi'ere *sm* railwayman (*Brit*), railroad man (*US*)

'fertile *ag* fertile

fertilità *sf* fertility

fertiliz'zante [fertilid'dzante] *sm* fertilizer

fertiliz'zare [fertilid'dzare] *vt* to fertilize

fer'vente *ag* fervent, ardent

'fervere *vi*: **fervono i preparativi per ...** they are making feverish preparations for ...

'fervido, -a *ag* fervent, ardent

fer'vore *sm* fervour (*Brit*), fervor (*US*), ardour (*Brit*), ardor (*US*); (*punto culminante*) height

'fesa *sf* (*Cuc*) rump of veal

fesse'ria *sf* stupidity; **dire fesserie** to talk nonsense

'fesso, -a *pp di* **fendere** ■ *ag* (*fam*: *sciocco*) crazy, cracked

fes'sura *sf* crack, split; (*per gettone, moneta*) slot

'festa *sf* (*religiosa*) feast; (*pubblica*) holiday; (*compleanno*) birthday; (*onomastico*) name day; (*ricevimento*) celebration, party; **far ~** to have a holiday; (*far baldoria*) to live it up; **far ~ a qn** to give sb a warm welcome; **essere vestito a ~** to be dressed up to the nines; **~ comandata** (*Rel*) holiday of obligation; **la ~ della mamma/del papà** Mother's/Father's Day; **la F~ della Repubblica** *see note*

Festa della Repubblica

The *Festa della Repubblica*, 2 June, celebrates the founding of the Italian Republic after the fall of the monarchy and the subsequent referendum in 1946. It is marked by military parades and political speeches.

festeggia'menti [festeddʒa'menti] *smpl* celebrations

festeggi'are [fested'dʒare] *vt* to celebrate; (*persona*) to have a celebration for

fes'tino *sm* party; (*con balli*) ball

fes'tivo, -a *ag* (*atmosfera*) festive; **giorno ~** holiday

fes'toso, -a *ag* merry, joyful

fe'tente *ag* (*puzzolente*) fetid; (*comportamento*) disgusting ■ *sm/f* (*fam*) stinker, rotter (*Brit*)

fe'ticcio [fe'tittʃo] *sm* fetish

'feto *sm* foetus (*Brit*), fetus (*US*)

fe'tore *sm* stench, stink

'fetta *sf* slice

fet'tuccia, -ce [fet'tuttʃa] *sf* tape, ribbon

fettuc'cine [fettut'tʃine] *sfpl* (*Cuc*) ribbon-shaped pasta

feu'dale *ag* feudal

'feudo *sm* (*Storia*) fief; (*fig*) stronghold

ff *abbr* (*Amm*) = **facente funzione**; (= *fogli*) pp

FF.AA *abbr* = **forze armate**

FG *sigla* = **Foggia**

FI *sigla* = **Firenze** ■ *abbr* = **Forza Italia**

fi'aba *sf* fairy tale

fia'besco, -a, schi, sche *ag* fairy-tale *cpd*

fi'acca *sf* weariness; (*svogliatezza*) listlessness; **battere la ~** to shirk

fiac'care *vt* to weaken

fiaccherò *etc* [fjakke'rɔ] *vb vedi* **fiaccare**

fi'acco, -a, chi, che *ag* (*stanco*) tired, weary; (*svogliato*) listless; (*debole*) weak; (*mercato*) slack

fi'accola *sf* torch

fiacco'lata *sf* torchlight procession

fi'ala *sf* phial

fi'amma *sf* flame; (*Naut*) pennant

fiam'mante *ag* (*colore*) flaming; **nuovo ~** brand new

fiam'mata *sf* blaze

fiammeggi'are [fjammed'dʒare] *vi* to blaze

fiam'mifero *sm* match

fiam'mingo, -a, ghi, ghe *ag* Flemish ■ *sm/f* Fleming ■ *sm* (*Ling*) Flemish; (*Zool*) flamingo; **i Fiamminghi** the Flemish

fian'cata *sf* (*di nave etc*) side; (*Naut*) broadside

fiancheggi'are [fjanked'dʒare] *vt* to border; (*fig*) to support, back (up); (*Mil*) to flank

fi'anco, -chi *sm* side; (*di persona*) hip; (*Mil*) flank; **di ~** sideways, from the side; **a ~ a ~** side by side; **prestare il proprio ~ alle critiche** to leave o.s. open to criticism; **~ destr/sinistr!** (*Mil*) right/left turn!

Fi'andre *sfpl*: **le ~** Flanders *sg*

fiaschette'ria [fjaskette'ria] *sf* wine shop

fi'asco, -schi *sm* flask; (*fig*) fiasco; **fare ~** to be a fiasco

fia'tare *vi* (*fig: parlare*): **senza ~** without saying a word

fi'ato *sm* breath; (*resistenza*) stamina; **fiati** *smpl* (*Mus*) wind instruments; **avere il ~ grosso** to be out of breath; **prendere ~** to catch one's breath; **bere qc tutto d'un ~** to drink sth in one go *o* gulp

'fibbia *sf* buckle

'fibra *sf* fibre, fiber (*US*); (*fig*) constitution; **~ ottica** optical fibre; **~ di vetro** fibreglass (*Brit*), fiberglass (*US*)

ficca'naso (*mpl* **ficcanasi**, *fpl* **~**) *sm/f* busybody, nos(e)y parker

fic'care *vt* to push, thrust, drive; **ficcarsi** *vr* (*andare a finire*) to get to; **~ il naso negli affari altrui** (*fig*) to poke *o* stick one's nose into other people's business; **ficcarsi nei pasticci** *o* **nei guai** to get into hot water *o* a fix

ficcherò *etc* [fikke'rɔ] *vb vedi* **ficcare**

fiche [fiʃ] *sf inv* (*nei giochi d'azzardo*) chip

'fico, -chi *sm* (*pianta*) fig tree; (*frutto*) fig; **~ d'India** prickly pear; **~ secco** dried fig

fiction ['fikʃon] *sf inv* TV drama

fidanza'mento [fidantsa'mento] *sm* engagement

fidan'zarsi [fidan'tsarsi] *vr* to get engaged

fidan'zato, -a [fidan'tsato] *sm/f* fiancé/fiancée

fi'darsi *vr*: **~ di** to trust; **~ è bene non ~ è meglio** (*proverbio*) better safe than sorry

fi'dato, -a *ag* reliable, trustworthy

fide'ismo *sm* unquestioning belief

fide'istico, -a, ci, che *ag* (*atteggiamento, posizione*) totally uncritical

fideius'sore *sm* (*Dir*) guarantor

fideliz'zare [fidelid'dzare] *vt*: **~ la clientela** to build customer loyalty; **fidelizzarsi** *vr* to stay loyal

'fido, -a *ag* faithful, loyal ■ *sm* (*Comm*) credit

fi'ducia [fi'dutʃa] *sf* confidence, trust; **incarico di ~** position of trust, responsible position; **persona di ~** reliable person; **è il mio uomo di ~** he is my right-hand man; **porre la questione di ~** (*Pol*) to ask for a vote of confidence

fiduci'oso, -a [fidu'tʃoso] *ag* trusting

fi'ele *sm* (*Med*) bile; (*fig*) bitterness

fie'nile *sm* hayloft

fi'eno *sm* hay

fi'era *sf* fair; (*animale*) wild beast; **~ di beneficenza** charity bazaar; **~ campionaria** trade fair

fie'rezza [fje'rettsa] *sf* pride

fi'ero, -a *ag* proud; (*crudele*) fierce, cruel; (*audace*) bold

fi'evole *ag* (*luce*) dim; (*suono*) weak

F.I.F.A. *sigla f* (= *Féderation Internationale de Football Association*) FIFA

'fifa *sf* (*fam*): **aver ~** to have the jitters

fi'fone, -a *sm/f* (*fam, scherzoso*) coward

fig. *abbr* (*= figura*) fig
FIGC *sigla f* (*= Federazione Italiana Gioco Calcio*) *Italian football association*
'**Figi** ['fidʒi] *sfpl*: **le isole ~** Fiji, the Fiji Islands
'**figlia** ['fiʎʎa] *sf* daughter; (*Comm*) counterfoil (*Brit*), stub
figli'are [fiʎ'ʎare] *vi* to give birth
figli'astro, -a [fiʎ'ʎastro] *sm/f* stepson(-daughter)
'**figlio** ['fiʎʎo] *sm* son; (*senza distinzione di sesso*) child; **~ d'arte**: **essere ~ d'arte** to come from a theatrical (*o* musical *etc*) family; **~ di puttana** (*fam!*) son of a bitch (*!*); **~ unico** only child
figli'occio, -a, ci, ce [fiʎ'ʎɔttʃo] *sm/f* godchild, godson(-daughter)
figli'ola [fiʎ'ʎɔla] *sf* daughter; (*fig: ragazza*) girl
figli'olo [fiʎ'ʎɔlo] *sm* (*anche fig: ragazzo*) son
fi'gura *sf* figure; (*forma, aspetto esterno*) form, shape; (*illustrazione*) picture, illustration; **far ~** to look smart; **fare una brutta ~** to make a bad impression; **che ~!** how embarrassing!
figu'raccia, -ce [figu'rattʃa] *sf*: **fare una ~** to create a bad impression
figu'rare *vi* to appear ■ *vt*: **figurarsi qc** to imagine sth; **figurarsi** *vr*: **figurati!** imagine that!; **ti do noia? — ma figurati!** am I disturbing you? — not at all!
figura'tivo, -a *ag* figurative
figu'rina *sf* (*statuetta*) figurine; (*cartoncino*) picture card
figuri'nista, -i, e *sm/f* dress designer
figu'rino *sm* fashion sketch
fi'guro *sm*: **un losco ~** a suspicious character
figu'rone *sm*: **fare un ~** (*persona, oggetto*) to look terrific; (*persona: con un discorso etc*) to make an excellent impression
'**fila** *sf* row, line; (*coda*) queue; (*serie*) series, string; **di ~** in succession; **fare la ~** to queue; **in ~ indiana** in single file
fila'mento *sm* filament
fi'lanca® *sf stretch material*
fi'landa *sf* spinning mill
fi'lante *ag*: **stella ~** (*stella cadente*) shooting star; (*striscia di carta*) streamer
filantro'pia *sf* philanthropy
filan'tropico, -a, ci, che *ag* philanthropic(al)
fi'lantropo *sm* philanthropist
fi'lare *vt* to spin; (*Naut*) to pay out ■ *vi* (*baco, ragno*) to spin; (*formaggio fuso*) to go stringy; (*liquido*) to trickle; (*discorso*) to hang together; (*fam: amoreggiare*) to go steady; (*muoversi a forte velocità*) to go at full speed; (*andarsene lestamente*) to make o.s. scarce ■ *sm* (*di alberi etc*) row, line; **~ diritto** (*fig*) to toe the line
filar'monico, -a, ci, che *ag* philharmonic
filas'trocca, -che *sf* nursery rhyme
filate'lia *sf* philately, stamp collecting
fi'lato, -a *ag* spun ■ *sm* yarn ■ *av*: **vai dritto ~ a casa** go straight home; **3 giorni filati** 3 days running *o* on end
fila'tura *sf* spinning; (*luogo*) spinning mill
fi'letto *sm* (*ornamento*) braid, trimming; (*di vite*) thread; (*di carne*) fillet
fili'ale *ag* filial ■ *sf* (*di impresa*) branch
filibusti'ere *sm* pirate; (*fig*) adventurer
fili'grana *sf* (*in oreficeria*) filigree; (*su carta*) watermark
fi'lippica *sf* invective
Filip'pine *sfpl*: **le ~** the Philippines
filip'pino, -a *ag, sm/f* Filipino
film *sm inv* film
fil'mare *vt* to film
fil'mato *sm* short film
fil'mina *sf* film strip
'**filo** *sm* (*anche fig*) thread; (*filato*) yarn; (*metallico*) wire; (*di lama, rasoio*) edge; **con un ~ di voce** in a whisper; **un ~ d'aria** (*fig*) a breath of air; **dare del ~ da torcere a qn** to create difficulties for sb, make life difficult for sb; **fare il ~ a qn** (*corteggiare*) to be after sb, chase sb; **per ~ e per segno** in detail; **~ d'erba** blade of grass; **~ interdentale** dental floss; **~ di perle** string of pearls; **~ di Scozia** fine cotton yarn; **~ spinato** barbed wire
filoameri'cano, -a *ag* pro-American
'**filobus** *sm inv* trolley bus
filodiffusi'one *sf* rediffusion
filodram'matico, -a, ci, che *ag*: **(compagnia) filodrammatica** amateur dramatic society ■ *sm/f* amateur actor/actress
filon'cino [filon'tʃino] *sm* ≈ French stick
fi'lone *sm* (*di minerali*) seam, vein; (*pane*) ≈ Vienna loaf; (*fig*) trend
filoso'fia *sf* philosophy
filo'sofico, -a, ci, che *ag* philosophical
fi'losofo, -a *sm/f* philosopher
filosovi'etico, -a, ci, che *ag* pro-Soviet
filo'via *sf* (*linea*) trolley line; (*bus*) trolley bus
fil'trare *vt, vi* to filter
'**filtro** *sm* filter; (*pozione*) potion; **~ dell'olio** (*Aut*) oil filter
'**filza** ['filtsa] *sf* (*anche fig*) string
FIN *sigla f* **= Federazione Italiana Nuoto**
fin *av, prep* **= fino**
fi'nale *ag* final ■ *sm* (*di libro, film*) end, ending; (*Mus*) finale ■ *sf* (*Sport*) final
fina'lista, -i, e *sm/f* finalist
finalità *sf* (*scopo*) aim, purpose
finaliz'zare [finalid'dzare] *vt*: **~ a** to direct towards
final'mente *av* finally, at last

fi'nanza [fi'nantsa] *sf* finance; **finanze** *sfpl* (*di individuo, Stato*) finances; **(Guardia di) ~** (*di frontiera*) ≈ Customs and Excise (*Brit*), ≈ Customs Service (*US*); **(Intendenza di) ~** ≈ Inland Revenue (*Brit*), ≈ Internal Revenue Service (*US*); **Ministro delle finanze** Minister of Finance, ≈ Chancellor of the Exchequer (*Brit*), ≈ Secretary of the Treasury (*US*)

finanzia'mento [finantsja'mento] *sm* (*azione*) financing; (*denaro fornito*) funds *pl*

finanzi'are [finan'tsjare] *vt* to finance, fund

finanzi'ario, -a [finan'tsjarjo] *ag* financial ▪ *sf* (*anche*: **società finanziaria**) investment company; (*anche*: **legge finanziaria**) finance act, ≈ budget (*Brit*)

finanzia'tore, -'trice *ag*: **ente ~, società finanziatrice** backer ▪ *sm/f* backer

finanzi'ere [finan'tsjɛre] *sm* financier; (*guardia di finanza: doganale*) customs officer; (: *tributaria*) Inland Revenue official (*Brit*), Internal Revenue official (*US*)

finché [fin'ke] *cong* (*per tutto il tempo che*) as long as; (*fino al momento in cui*) until; **~ vorrai** as long as you like; **aspetta ~ non esca** wait until he goes (*o* comes) out

'fine *ag* (*lamina, carta*) thin; (*capelli, polvere*) fine; (*vista, udito*) keen, sharp; (*persona: raffinata*) refined, distinguished; (*osservazione*) subtle ▪ *sf* end ▪ *sm* aim, purpose; (*esito*) result, outcome; **in** *o* **alla ~** in the end, finally; **alla fin ~** at the end of the day, in the end; **che ~ ha fatto?** what became of him?; **buona ~ e buon principio!** (*augurio*) happy New Year!; **a fin di bene** with the best of intentions; **al ~ di fare qc** (in order) to do sth; **condurre qc a buon ~** to bring sth to a successful conclusion; **secondo ~** ulterior motive

'fine setti'mana *sm o f inv* weekend

fi'nestra *sf* window

fines'trino *sm* (*di treno, auto*) window

fi'nezza [fi'nettsa] *sf* thinness; fineness; keenness, sharpness; refinement; subtlety

'fingere ['findʒere] *vt* to feign; (*supporre*) to imagine, suppose; **fingersi** *vr*: **fingersi ubriaco/pazzo** to pretend to be drunk/crazy; **~ di fare** to pretend to do

fini'menti *smpl* (*di cavallo etc*) harness *sg*

fini'mondo *sm* pandemonium

fi'nire *vt* to finish ▪ *vi* to finish, end ▪ *sm*: **sul ~ della festa** towards the end of the party; **~ di fare** (*compiere*) to finish doing; (*smettere*) to stop doing; **~ in galera** to end up *o* finish up in prison; **farla finita** (*con la vita*) to put an end to one's life; **farla finita con qc** to have done with sth; **com'è andata a ~?** what happened in the end?; **finiscila!** stop it!

fini'tura *sf* finish

finlan'dese *ag* Finnish ▪ *sm/f* Finn ▪ *sm* (*Ling*) Finnish

Fin'landia *sf*: **la ~** Finland

'fino, -a *ag* (*capelli, seta*) fine; (*oro*) pure; (*fig: acuto*) shrewd ▪ *av* (*spesso troncato in fin: pure, anche*) even ▪ *prep* (*spesso troncato in fin: tempo*): **fin quando?** till when?; (: *luogo*): **fin qui** as far as here; **~ a** (*tempo*) until, till; (*luogo*) as far as, (up) to; **fin da domani** from tomorrow onwards; **fin da ieri** since yesterday; **fin dalla nascita** from *o* since birth

fi'nocchio [fi'nɔkkjo] *sm* fennel; (*fam peg: pederasta*) queer

fi'nora *av* up till now

'finsi *etc vb vedi* **fingere**

'finto, -a *pp di* **fingere** ▪ *ag* (*capelli, dente*) false; (*fiori*) artificial; (*cuoio, pelle*) imitation *cpd*; (*fig: simulato: pazzia etc*) feigned, sham ▪ *sf* pretence (*Brit*), pretense (*US*), sham; (*Sport*) feint; **far finta (di fare)** to pretend (to do); **l'ho detto per finta** I was only pretending; (*per scherzo*) I was only kidding

finzi'one [fin'tsjone] *sf* pretence (*Brit*), pretense (*US*), sham

fioc'care *vi* (*neve*) to fall; (*fig: insulti etc*) to fall thick and fast

fi'occo, -chi *sm* (*di nastro*) bow; (*di stoffa, lana*) flock; (*di neve*) flake; (*Naut*) jib; **coi fiocchi** (*fig*) first-rate; **fiocchi di granoturco** cornflakes

fi'ocina ['fjɔtʃina] *sf* harpoon

fi'oco, -a, chi, che *ag* faint, dim

fi'onda *sf* catapult

fio'raio, -a *sm/f* florist

fiorda'liso *sm* (*Bot*) cornflower

fi'ordo *sm* fjord

fi'ore *sm* flower; **fiori** *smpl* (*Carte*) clubs; **nel ~ degli anni** in one's prime; **a fior d'acqua** on the surface of the water; **a fior di labbra** in a whisper; **aver i nervi a fior di pelle** to be on edge; **fior di latte** cream; **è costato fior di soldi** it cost a pretty penny; **il fior ~ della società** the cream of society; **~ all'occhiello** feather in the cap; **fiori di campo** wild flowers

fio'rente *ag* (*industria, paese*) flourishing; (*salute*) blooming; (*petto*) ample

fioren'tino, -a *ag, sm/f* Florentine ▪ *sf* (*Cuc*) T-bone steak

fio'retto *sm* (*Scherma*) foil

fio'rino *sm* florin

fio'rire *vi* (*rosa*) to flower; (*albero*) to blossom; (*fig*) to flourish

fio'rista, -i, e *sm/f* florist

fiori'tura *sf* (*di pianta*) flowering, blooming; (*di albero*) blossoming; (*fig: di commercio, arte*)

flourishing; (*insieme dei fiori*) flowers *pl*; (*Mus*) fioritura
fi'otto *sm* (*di lacrime*) flow, flood; (*di sangue*) gush, spurt
'FIPE *sigla f* = **Federazione Italiana Pubblici Esercizi**
Fi'renze [fi'rɛntse] *sf* Florence
'firma *sf* signature; (*reputazione*) name
firma'mento *sm* firmament
fir'mare *vt* to sign
firma'tario, -a *sm/f* signatory
fisar'monica, -che *sf* accordion
fis'cale *ag* fiscal, tax *cpd*; (*meticoloso*) punctilious; **medico ~** *doctor employed by Social Security to verify cases of sick leave*
fisca'lista, -i, e *sm/f* tax consultant
fiscaliz'zare [fiskalid'dzare] *vt* to exempt from taxes
fischi'are [fis'kjare] *vi* to whistle ■ *vt* to whistle; (*attore*) to boo, hiss; **mi fischian le orecchie** my ears are singing; (*fig*) my ears are burning
fischiet'tare [fiskjet'tare] *vi, vt* to whistle
fischi'etto [fis'kjetto] *sm* (*strumento*) whistle
'fischio ['fiskjo] *sm* whistle; **prendere fischi per fiaschi** to get hold of the wrong end of the stick
'fisco *sm* tax authorities *pl*, ≈ Inland Revenue (*Brit*), ≈ Internal Revenue Service (*US*)
'fisica *sf vedi* **fisico**
fisica'mente *av* physically
'fisico, -a, ci, che *ag* physical ■ *sm/f* physicist ■ *sm* physique ■ *sf* physics *sg*
'fisima *sf* fixation
fisiolo'gia [fizjolo'dʒia] *sf* physiology
fisiono'mia *sf* face, physiognomy
fisiotera'pia *sf* physiotherapy
fisiotera'pista *sm/f* physiotherapist
fis'saggio [fis'saddʒo] *sm* (*Fot*) fixing
fis'sante *ag* (*spray, lozione*) holding
fis'sare *vt* to fix, fasten; (*guardare intensamente*) to stare at; (*data, condizioni*) to fix, establish, set; (*prenotare*) to book; **fissarsi** *vr*: **fissarsi su** (*sguardo, attenzione*) to focus on; (*fig: idea*) to become obsessed with
fissazi'one [fissat'tsjone] *sf* (*Psic*) fixation
fissi'one *sf* fission
'fisso, -a *ag* fixed; (*stipendio, impiego*) regular ■ *av*: **guardar ~ qn/qc** to stare at sb/sth; **avere un ragazzo ~** to have a steady boyfriend; **senza fissa dimora** of no fixed abode; **telefono ~** landline
fitoterma'lismo *sm* herbal hydrotherapy
'fitta *sf vedi* **fitto**
fit'tavolo *sm* tenant
fit'tizio, -a [fit'tittsjo] *ag* fictitious, imaginary
'fitto, -a *ag* thick, dense; (*pioggia*) heavy ■ *sm* (*affitto, pigione*) rent ■ *sf* sharp pain; **una fitta al cuore** (*fig*) a pang of grief; **nel ~ del bosco** in the heart *o* depths of the wood
fiu'mana *sf* torrent; (*fig*) stream, flood
fi'ume *sm* river ■ *ag inv*: **processo ~** long-running trial; **scorrere a fiumi** (*acqua, sangue*) to flow in torrents
fiu'tare *vt* to smell, sniff; (*animale*) to scent; (*fig: inganno*) to get wind of, smell; **~ tabacco** to take snuff; **~ cocaina** to snort cocaine
fi'uto *sm* (sense of) smell; (*fig*) nose
'flaccido, -a ['flattʃido] *ag* flabby
fla'cone *sm* bottle
flagel'lare [fladʒel'lare] *vt* to flog, scourge; (*onde*) to beat against
fla'gello [fla'dʒɛllo] *sm* scourge
fla'grante *ag* flagrant; **cogliere qn in ~** to catch sb red-handed
fla'nella *sf* flannel
flash [flaʃ] *sm inv* (*Fot*) flash; (*giornalistico*) newsflash
flau'tista, -i *sm/f* flautist
'flauto *sm* flute
'flebile *ag* faint, feeble
fle'bite *sf* phlebitis
'flemma *sf* (*calma*) coolness, phlegm; (*Med*) phlegm
flem'matico, -a, ci, che *ag* phlegmatic, cool
fles'sibile *ag* pliable; (*fig: che si adatta*) flexible
flessi'one *sf* (*gen*) bending; (*Ginnastica: a terra*) sit-up; (*: in piedi*) forward bend; (*: sulle gambe*) knee-bend; (*diminuzione*) slight drop, slight fall; (*Ling*) inflection; **fare una ~** to bend; **una ~ economica** a downward trend in the economy
'flesso, -a *pp di* **flettere**
flessu'oso, -a *ag* supple, lithe; (*andatura*) flowing, graceful
'flettere *vt* to bend
'flipper ['flipper] *sm inv* pinball machine
flirt [flə:t] *sm inv* brief romance, flirtation
flir'tare *vi* to flirt
F.lli *abbr* (= *fratelli*) Bros
'flora *sf* flora
'florido, -a *ag* flourishing; (*fig*) glowing with health
'floscio, -a, sci, sce ['flɔʃʃo] *ag* (*cappello*) floppy, soft; (*muscoli*) flabby
'flotta *sf* fleet
flot'tante *sm* (*Econ*): **titoli a largo ~** blue chips, stocks on the market
'fluido, -a *ag, sm* fluid
flu'ire *vi* to flow
fluore'scente [fluoreʃʃɛnte] *ag* fluorescent
flu'oro *sm* fluorine
fluo'ruro *sm* fluoride

'**flusso** *sm* flow; (*Fisica, Med*) flux; **~ e riflusso** ebb and flow; **~ di cassa** (*Comm*) cash flow
'**flutti** *smpl* waves
fluttu'are *vi* to rise and fall; (*Econ*) to fluctuate
fluvi'ale *ag* river *cpd*, fluvial
FM *abbr vedi* **modulazione di frequenza**
FMI *sigla m* = **Fondo Monetario Internazionale**
FO *sigla* = **Forlì**
fo'bia *sf* phobia
'**foca, -che** *sf* (*Zool*) seal
fo'caccia, -ce [fo'kattʃa] *sf kind of pizza*; (*dolce*) bun; **rendere pan per ~** to get one's own back, give tit for tat
fo'cale *ag* focal
focaliz'zare [fokalid'dzare] *vt* (*Fot: immagine*) to get into focus; (*fig: situazione*) to get into perspective; **~ l'attenzione su** to focus one's attention on
'**foce** ['fotʃe] *sf* (*Geo*) mouth
fo'chista, -i [fo'kista] *sm* (*Ferr*) stoker, fireman
foco'laio *sm* (*Med*) centre (*Brit*) *o* center (*US*) of infection; (*fig*) hotbed
foco'lare *sm* hearth, fireside; (*Tecn*) furnace
fo'coso, -a *ag* fiery; (*cavallo*) mettlesome, fiery
'**fodera** *sf* (*di vestito*) lining; (*di libro, poltrona*) cover
fode'rare *vt* to line; to cover
'**fodero** *sm* (*di spada*) scabbard; (*di pugnale*) sheath; (*di pistola*) holster
'**foga** *sf* enthusiasm, ardour (*Brit*), ardor (*US*)
'**foggia, -ge** ['fɔddʒa] *sf* (*maniera*) style; (*aspetto*) form, shape; (*moda*) fashion, style
foggi'are [fod'dʒare] *vt* to shape; to style
'**foglia** ['fɔʎʎa] *sf* leaf; **ha mangiato la ~** (*fig*) he's caught on; **~ d'argento/d'oro** silver/gold leaf
fogli'ame [foʎ'ʎame] *sm* foliage, leaves *pl*
fogli'etto [foʎ'ʎetto] *sm* (*piccolo foglio*) slip of paper, piece of paper; (*manifestino*) leaflet, handout
'**foglio** ['fɔʎʎo] *sm* (*di carta*) sheet (of paper); (*di metallo*) sheet; (*documento*) document; (*banconota*) (bank)note; **~ di calcolo** spreadsheet; **~ rosa** (*Aut*) provisional licence; **~ di via** (*Dir*) expulsion order; **~ volante** pamphlet
'**fogna** ['foɲɲa] *sf* drain, sewer
fogna'tura [foɲɲa'tura] *sf* drainage, sewerage
föhn [fø:n] *sm inv* hair-dryer
fo'lata *sf* gust
fol'clore *sm* folklore
folclo'ristico, -a, ci, che *ag* folk *cpd*
folgo'rare *vt* (*fulmine*) to strike down; (*: alta tensione*) to electrocute
folgorazi'one [folgorat'tsjone] *sf* electrocution; **ebbe una ~** (*fig: idea*) he had a brainwave
'**folgore** *sf* thunderbolt
folksono'mia *sf* (*Inform*) folksonomy
'**folla** *sf* crowd, throng
'**folle** *ag* mad, insane; (*Tecn*) idle; **in ~** (*Aut*) in neutral
folleggi'are [folled'dʒare] *vi* (*divertirsi*) to paint the town red
fol'letto *sm* elf
fol'lia *sf* folly, foolishness; foolish act; (*pazzia*) madness, lunacy; **amare qn alla ~** to love sb to distraction; **costare una ~** to cost the earth
'**folto, -a** *ag* thick
fomen'tare *vt* to stir up, foment
fon *sm inv* = **föhn**
fon'dale *sm* (*del mare*) bottom; (*Teat*) backdrop; **il ~ marino** the sea bed
fondamen'tale *ag* fundamental, basic
fondamenta'lista, -i, e *ag, sm/f* (*Rel*) fundamentalist
fonda'mento *sm* foundation; **fondamenta** *sfpl* (*Edil*) foundations
fon'dare *vt* to found; (*fig: dar base*): **~ qc su** to base sth on; **fondarsi** *vr* (*teorie*): **fondarsi (su)** to be based (on)
fonda'tezza [fonda'tettsa] *sf* (*di ragioni*) soundness; (*di dubbio, sospetto*) basis in fact
fon'dato, -a *ag* (*ragioni*) sound; (*dubbio, sospetto*) well-founded
fondazi'one [fondat'tsjone] *sf* foundation
fon'dente *ag*: **cioccolato ~** plain *o* dark chocolate
'**fondere** *vt* (*neve*) to melt; (*metallo*) to fuse, melt; (*fig: colori*) to merge, blend; (*: imprese, gruppi*) to merge ■ *vi* to melt; **fondersi** *vr* to melt; (*fig: partiti, correnti*) to unite, merge
fonde'ria *sf* foundry
fondi'ario, -a *ag* land *cpd*
fon'dina *sf* (*piatto fondo*) soup plate; (*portapistola*) holster
'**fondo, -a** *ag* deep ■ *sm* (*di recipiente, pozzo*) bottom; (*di stanza*) back; (*quantità di liquido che resta, deposito*) dregs *pl*; (*sfondo*) background; (*unità immobiliare*) property, estate; (*somma di denaro*) fund; (*Sport*) long-distance race; **fondi** *smpl* (*denaro*) funds; **a notte fonda** at dead of night; **in ~ a** at the bottom of; at the back of; (*strada*) at the end of; **laggiù in ~** (*lontano*) over there; (*in profondità*) down there; **in ~** (*fig*) after all, all things considered; **andare fino in ~ a** (*fig*) to examine thoroughly; **andare a ~** (*nave*) to sink; **conoscere a ~** to know inside out; **dar ~ a**

(*fig: provvisti, soldi*) to use up; **toccare il ~** (*fig*) to plumb the depths; **a ~ perduto** (*Comm*) without security; **~ comune di investimento** investment trust; **F~ Monetario Internazionale** International Monetary Fund; **~ di previdenza** social insurance fund; **~ di riserva** reserve fund; **~ urbano** town property; **fondi di caffè** coffee grounds; **fondi d'esercizio** working capital *sg*; **fondi liquidi** ready money *sg*, liquid assets; **fondi di magazzino** old *o* unsold stock *sg*; **fondi neri** slush fund *sg*
fondo'tinta *sm inv* (*cosmetico*) foundation
fo'nema *sm* phoneme
fo'netica *sf* phonetics *sg*
fo'netico, -a, ci, che *ag* phonetic
fon'tana *sf* fountain
fonta'nella *sf* drinking fountain
'fonte *sf* spring, source; (*fig*) source ■ *sm*: **~ battesimale** (*Rel*) font
fon'tina *sm* *full fat hard, sweet cheese*
'footing ['futiŋ] *sm* jogging
forag'giare [forad'dʒare] *vt* (*cavalli*) to fodder; (*fig: partito etc*) to bankroll
fo'raggio [fo'raddʒo] *sm* fodder, forage
fo'rare *vt* to pierce, make a hole in; (*pallone*) to burst; (*pneumatico*) to puncture; (*biglietto*) to punch; **forarsi** *vr* (*gen*) to develop a hole; (*Aut, pallone, timpano*) to burst; **~ una gomma** to burst a tyre (*Brit*) *o* tire (*US*)
fora'tura *sf* piercing; bursting; puncturing; punching
'forbici ['fɔrbitʃi] *sfpl* scissors
forbi'cina [forbi'tʃina] *sf* earwig
for'bito, -a *ag* (*stile, modi*) polished
'forca, -che *sf* (*Agr*) fork, pitchfork; (*patibolo*) gallows *sg*
for'cella [for'tʃɛlla] *sf* (*Tecn*) fork; (*di monte*) pass
for'chetta [for'ketta] *sf* fork; **essere una buona ~** to enjoy one's food
for'cina [for'tʃina] *sf* hairpin
'forcipe ['fɔrtʃipe] *sm* forceps *pl*
for'cone *sm* pitchfork
fo'rense *ag* (*linguaggio*) legal; **avvocato ~** barrister (*Brit*), lawyer
fo'resta *sf* forest; **la F~ Nera** the Black Forest
fores'tale *ag* forest *cpd*; **guardia ~** forester
foreste'ria *sf* (*di convento, palazzo etc*) guest rooms *pl*, guest quarters *pl*
foresti'ero, -a *ag* foreign ■ *sm/f* foreigner
for'fait [fɔr'fɛ] *sm inv*: **(prezzo a) ~** fixed price, set price; **dichiarare ~** (*Sport*) to withdraw; (*fig*) to give up
forfe'tario, -a *ag*: **prezzo ~** (*da pagare*) fixed *o* set price; (*da ricevere*) lump sum
'forfora *sf* dandruff
'forgia, -ge ['fɔrdʒa] *sf* forge
forgi'are [for'dʒare] *vt* to forge
'forma *sf* form; (*aspetto esteriore*) form, shape; (*Dir: procedura*) procedure; (*per calzature*) last; (*stampo da cucina*) mould (*Brit*), mold (*US*); **forme** *sfpl* (*del corpo*) figure, shape; **le forme** (*convenzioni*) appearances; **errori di ~** stylistic errors; **essere in ~** to be in good shape; **mantenersi in ~** to keep fit; **in ~ ufficiale/privata** officially/privately; **una ~ di formaggio** a (whole) cheese
format'gino [formad'dʒino] *sm* processed cheese
for'maggio [for'maddʒo] *sm* cheese
for'male *ag* formal
formalità *sf inv* formality
formaliz'zare [formalid'dzare] *vt* to formalize
for'mare *vt* to form, shape, make; (*numero di telefono*) to dial; (*fig: carattere*) to form, mould (*Brit*), mold (*US*); **formarsi** *vr* to form, take shape; **il treno si forma a Milano** the train starts from Milan
for'mato *sm* format, size
format'tare *vt* (*Inform*) to format
formattazi'one [formattat'tsjone] *sf* (*Inform*) formatting
formazi'one [format'tsjone] *sf* formation; (*fig: educazione*) training; **~ continua** continuing education; **~ permanente** lifelong learning; **~ professionale** vocational training
for'mica, -che *sf* ant
formi'caio *sm* anthill
formico'lare *vi* (*gamba, braccio*) to tingle; (*brulicare: anche fig*): **~ di** to be swarming with; **mi formicola la gamba** I've got pins and needles in my leg, my leg's tingling
formico'lio *sm* pins and needles *pl*; swarming
formi'dabile *ag* powerful, formidable; (*straordinario*) remarkable
for'moso, -a *ag* shapely
'formula *sf* formula; **~ di cortesia** (*nelle lettere*) letter ending
formu'lare *vt* to formulate
for'nace [for'natʃe] *sf* (*per laterizi etc*) kiln; (*per metalli*) furnace
for'naio *sm* baker
for'nello *sm* (*elettrico, a gas*) ring; (*di pipa*) bowl
for'nire *vt*: **~ qn di qc, fornire qc a qn** to provide *o* supply sb with sth, supply sth to sb; **fornirsi** *vr*: **fornirsi di** (*procurarsi*) to provide o.s. with
for'nito, -a *ag*: **ben ~** (*negozio*) well-stocked
forni'tore, -'trice *ag*: **ditta fornitrice di ...** company supplying ... ■ *sm/f* supplier
forni'tura *sf* supply

'forno *sm* (*di cucina*) oven; (*panetteria*) bakery; (*Tecn*: *per calce etc*) kiln; (: *per metalli*) furnace; **fare i forni** (*Med*) to undergo heat treatment
'foro *sm* (*buco*) hole; (*Storia*) forum; (*tribunale*) (law) court
'forse *av* perhaps, maybe; (*circa*) about; **essere in ~** to be in doubt
forsen'nato, -a *ag* mad, crazy, insane
'forte *ag* strong; (*suono*) loud; (*spesa*) considerable, great ■ *av* strongly; (*velocemente*) fast; (*a voce alta*) loud(ly); (*violentemente*) hard ■ *sm* (*edificio*) fort; (*specialità*) forte, strong point; **piatto ~** (*Cuc*) main dish; **avere un ~ mal di testa/raffreddore** to have a bad headache/cold; **essere ~ in qc** to be good at sth; **farsi ~ di qc** to make use of sth; **dare man ~ a qn** to back sb up, support sb; **usare le maniere forti** to use strong-arm tactics
for'tezza [for'tettsa] *sf* (*morale*) strength; (*luogo fortificato*) fortress
fortifi'care *vt* to fortify, strengthen
for'tuito, -a *ag* fortuitous, chance *cpd*
for'tuna *sf* (*destino*) fortune, luck; (*buona sorte*) success, fortune; (*eredità, averi*) fortune; **per ~** luckily, fortunately; **di ~** makeshift, improvised; **atterraggio di ~** emergency landing
fortu'nale *sm* storm
fortunata'mente *av* luckily, fortunately
fortu'nato, -a *ag* lucky, fortunate; (*coronato da successo*) successful
fortu'noso, -a *ag* (*vita*) eventful; (*avvenimento*) unlucky
fo'runcolo *sm* (*Med*) boil
forvi'are *vt, vi* **= fuorviare**
'forza ['fɔrtsa] *sf* strength; (*potere*) power; (*Fisica*) force ■ *escl* come on!; **forze** *sfpl* (*fisiche*) strength *sg*; (*Mil*) forces; **per ~** against one's will; (*naturalmente*) of course; **per ~ di cose** by force of circumstances; **a viva ~** by force; **a ~ di** by dint of; **farsi ~** (*coraggio*) to pluck up one's courage; **bella ~!** (*ironico*) how clever of you (*o* him *etc*)!; **~ lavoro** work force, manpower; **per causa di ~ maggiore** (*Dir*) by reason of an act of God; (*per estensione*) due to circumstances beyond one's control; **la ~ pubblica** the police *pl*; **~ di pace** peacekeeping force; **~ di vendita** (*Comm*) sales force; **~ di volontà** willpower; **le forze armate** the armed forces; **F~ Italia** (*Pol*) *moderate right-wing party*
for'zare [for'tsare] *vt* to force; (*cassaforte, porta*) to force (open); (*voce*) to strain; **~ qn a fare** to force sb to do
for'zato, -a [for'tsato] *ag* forced ■ *sm* (*Dir*) prisoner sentenced to hard labour (*Brit*) *o* labor (*US*)
forzi'ere [for'tsjɛre] *sm* strongbox; (*di pirati*) treasure chest
for'zista, -i, e [for'tsista] *ag* of Forza Italia ■ *sm/f* member (*o* supporter) of Forza Italia
for'zuto, -a [for'tsuto] *ag* big and strong
fos'chia [fos'kia] *sf* mist, haze
'fosco, -a, schi, sche *ag* dark, gloomy; **dipingere qc a tinte fosche** (*fig*) to paint a gloomy picture of sth
fos'fato *sm* phosphate
fosfore'scente [fosforeʃʃɛnte] *ag* phosphorescent; (*lancetta dell'orologio etc*) luminous
'fosforo *sm* phosphorous
'fossa *sf* pit; (*di cimitero*) grave; **~ comune** mass grave
fos'sato *sm* ditch; (*di fortezza*) moat
fos'setta *sf* dimple
'fossi *etc vb vedi* **essere**
'fossile *ag, sm* fossil (*cpd*)
'fosso *sm* ditch; (*Mil*) trench
'foste *etc vb vedi* **essere**
'foto *sf inv* photo; **~ ricordo** souvenir photo; **~ tessera** passport(-type) photo
foto... *prefisso* photo...
foto'camera *sf*: **~ digitale** digital camera
fotocomposi'tore *sm* filmsetter
foto'copia *sf* photocopy
fotocopi'are *vt* to photocopy
fotocopiste'ria *sf* photocopy shop
fotofo'nino *sm* camera phone
foto'genico, -a, ci, che [foto'dʒɛniko] *ag* photogenic
fotogra'fare *vt* to photograph
fotogra'fia *sf* (*procedimento*) photography; (*immagine*) photograph; **fare una ~** to take a photograph; **una ~ a colori/in bianco e nero** a colour/black and white photograph
foto'grafico, -a, ci, che *ag* photographic; **macchina fotografica** camera
fo'tografo, -a *sm/f* photographer
foto'gramma, -i *sm* (*Cine*) frame
fotomo'dello, -a *sm/f* fashion model
fotomon'taggio [fotomon'taddʒo] *sm* photomontage
fotore'porter *sm/f inv* newspaper (*o* magazine) photographer
fotoro'manzo [fotoro'mandzo] *sm* romantic picture story
foto'sintesi *sf* photosynthesis
fotovol'taico, -a, ci, che *ag* (*sistema, pannello*) photovoltaic
'fottere *vt* (*fam!*: *avere rapporti sessuali*) to fuck (*!*), screw (*!*); (: *rubare*) to pinch, swipe; (: *fregare*): **mi hanno fottuto** they played a dirty trick on me; **vai a farti ~!** fuck off! (*!*)
fot'tuto, -a *ag* (*fam!*) bloody, fucking (*!*)
fou'lard [fu'lar] *sm inv* scarf

FR *sigla* = **Frosinone**
fra *prep* = **tra**
fracas'sare *vt* to shatter, smash; **fracassarsi** *vr* to shatter, smash; (*veicolo*) to crash
fra'casso *sm* smash; crash; (*baccano*) din, racket
'fradicio, -a, ci, ce ['fraditʃo] *ag* (*guasto*) rotten; (*molto bagnato*) soaking (wet); **ubriaco ~** blind drunk
'fragile ['fradʒile] *ag* fragile; (*salute*) delicate; (*nervi, vetro*) brittle
fragilità [fradʒili'ta] *sf* (*vedi ag*) fragility; delicacy; brittleness
'fragola *sf* strawberry
fra'gore *sm* (*di cascate, carro armato*) roar; (*di tuono*) rumble
frago'roso, -a *ag* deafening; **ridere in modo ~** to roar with laughter
fra'grante *ag* fragrant
fraintendi'mento *sm* misunderstanding
frain'tendere *vt* to misunderstand
frain'teso, -a *pp di* **fraintendere**
fram'mento *sm* fragment
fram'misto, -a *ag*: **~ a** interspersed with
'frana *sf* landslide; (*fig: persona*): **essere una ~** to be useless, be a walking disaster area
fra'nare *vi* to slip, slide down
franca'mente *av* frankly
fran'cese [fran'tʃeze] *ag* French ■ *sm/f* Frenchman(-woman) ■ *sm* (*Ling*) French; **i Francesi** the French
fran'chezza [fran'kettsa] *sf* frankness, openness
fran'chigia, -gie [fran'kidʒa] *sf* (*Amm*) exemption; (*Dir*) franchise; (*Naut*) shore leave; **~ doganale** exemption from customs duty
'Francia ['frantʃa] *sf*: **la ~** France
'franco, -a, chi, che *ag* (*Comm*) free; (*sincero*) frank, open, sincere ■ *sm* (*moneta*) franc; **farla franca** (*fig*) to get off scot-free; **~ a bordo** free on board; **~ di dogana** duty-free; **~ a domicilio** delivered free of charge; **~ fabbrica** ex factory, ex works; **prezzo ~ fabbrica** ex-works price; **~ magazzino** ex warehouse; **~ di porto** carriage free; **~ vagone** free on rail; **~ tiratore** sniper; (*Pol*) *member of parliament who votes against his own party*
franco'bollo *sm* (postage) stamp
franco-cana'dese *ag, sm/f* French Canadian
Franco'forte *sf* Frankfurt
fran'gente [fran'dʒɛnte] *sm* (*onda*) breaker; (*scoglio emergente*) reef; (*circostanza*) situation, circumstance
frangia, -ge ['frandʒa] *sf* fringe
frangi'flutti [frandʒi'flutti] *sm inv* breakwater
frangi'vento [frandʒi'vɛnto] *sm* windbreak
fran'toio *sm* (*Agr*) olive press; (*Tecn*) crusher
frantu'mare *vt*, **frantu'marsi** *vr* to break into pieces, shatter
fran'tumi *smpl* pieces, bits; (*schegge*) splinters; **andare in ~, mandare in ~** to shatter, smash to pieces *o* smithereens
frappé *sm* (*Cuc*) milk shake
fra'sario *sm* (*gergo*) vocabulary, language
'frasca, -sche *sf* (leafy) branch; **saltare di palo in ~** to jump from one subject to another
'frase *sf* (*Ling*) sentence; (*locuzione, espressione, Mus*) phrase; **~ fatta** set phrase
fraseolo'gia [frazeolo'dʒia] *sf* phraseology
'frassino *sm* ash (tree)
frastagli'ato, -a [frastaʎ'ʎato] *ag* (*costa*) indented, jagged
frastor'nare *vt* (*intontire*) to daze; (*confondere*) to bewilder, befuddle
frastor'nato, -a *ag* dazed; bewildered
frastu'ono *sm* hubbub, din
'frate *sm* friar, monk
fratel'lanza [fratel'lantsa] *sf* brotherhood; (*associazione*) fraternity
fratel'lastro *sm* stepbrother; (*con genitore in comune*) half brother
fra'tello *sm* brother; **fratelli** *smpl* brothers; (*nel senso di fratelli e sorelle*) brothers and sisters
fra'terno, -a *ag* fraternal, brotherly
fratri'cida, -i, e [fratri'tʃida] *ag* fratricidal ■ *sm/f* fratricide; **guerra ~** civil war
frat'taglie [frat'taʎʎe] *sfpl* (*Cuc: gen*) offal *sg*; (*: di pollo*) giblets
frat'tanto *av* in the meantime, meanwhile
frat'tempo *sm*: **nel ~** in the meantime, meanwhile
frat'tura *sf* fracture; (*fig*) split, break
frattu'rare *vt* to fracture
fraudo'lento, -a *ag* fraudulent
fraziona'mento [frattsjona'mento] *sm* division, splitting up
frazio'nare [frattsjo'nare] *vt* to divide, split up
frazi'one [frat'tsjone] *sf* fraction; (*borgata*): **~ di comune** hamlet
'freccia, -ce ['frettʃa] *sf* arrow; **~ di direzione** (*Aut*) indicator
frec'ciata [fret'tʃata] *sf*: **lanciare una ~** to make a cutting remark
fred'dare *vt* to shoot dead
fred'dezza [fred'dettsa] *sf* coldness
'freddo, -a *ag, sm* cold; **fa ~** it's cold; **aver ~** to be cold; **soffrire il ~** to feel the cold; **a ~** (*fig*) deliberately

freddo'loso, -a *ag* sensitive to the cold
fred'dura *sf* pun
'freezer ['frizer] *sm inv* fridge-freezer
fre'gare *vt* to rub; (*fam: truffare*) to take in, cheat; (*: rubare*) to swipe, pinch; **fregarsene** (*fam!*): **chi se ne frega?** who gives a damn (about it)?
fre'gata *sf* rub; (*fam*) swindle; (*Naut*) frigate
frega'tura *sf* (*fam: imbroglio*) rip-off; (*: delusione*) let-down
fregherò *etc* [frege'rɔ] *vb vedi* **fregare**
'fregio ['fredʒo] *sm* (*Archit*) frieze; (*ornamento*) decoration
'fremere *vi*: **~ di** to tremble *o* quiver with; **~ d'impazienza** to be champing at the bit
'fremito *sm* tremor, quiver
fre'nare *vt* (*veicolo*) to slow down; (*cavallo*) to rein in; (*lacrime*) to restrain, hold back ■ *vi* to brake; **frenarsi** *vr* (*fig*) to restrain o.s., control o.s.
fre'nata *sf*: **fare una ~** to brake
frene'sia *sf* frenzy
fre'netico, -a, ci, che *ag* frenetic
'freno *sm* brake; (*morso*) bit; **tenere a ~** (*passioni etc*) to restrain; **tenere a ~ la lingua** to hold one's tongue; **~ a disco** disc brake; **~ a mano** handbrake
'freon® *sm inv* (*Chim*) Freon®
frequen'tare *vt* (*scuola, corso*) to attend; (*locale, bar*) to go to, frequent; (*persone*) to see (often)
frequen'tato, -a *ag* (*locale*) busy
fre'quente *ag* frequent; **di ~** frequently
fre'quenza [fre'kwɛntsa] *sf* frequency; (*Ins*) attendance
fre'sare *vt* (*Tecn*) to mill
fres'chezza [fres'kettsa] *sf* freshness
'fresco, -a, schi, sche *ag* fresh; (*temperatura*) cool; (*notizia*) recent, fresh ■ *sm*: **godere il ~** to enjoy the cool air; **~ di bucato** straight from the wash, newly washed; **stare ~** (*fig*) to be in for it; **mettere al ~** to put in a cool place; (*fig: in prigione*) to put inside *o* in the cooler
fres'cura *sf* cool
'fresia *sf* freesia
'fretta *sf* hurry, haste; **in ~** in a hurry; **in ~ e furia** in a mad rush; **aver ~** to be in a hurry; **far ~ a qn** to hurry sb
frettolosa'mente *av* hurriedly, in a rush
fretto'loso, -a *ag* (*persona*) in a hurry; (*lavoro etc*) hurried, rushed
fri'abile *ag* (*terreno*) friable; (*pasta*) crumbly
'friggere ['friddʒere] *vt* to fry ■ *vi* (*olio etc*) to sizzle; **vai a farti ~!** (*fam*) get lost!
frigidità [fridʒidi'ta] *sf* frigidity
'frigido, -a ['fridʒido] *ag* (*Med*) frigid
fri'gnare [friɲ'ɲare] *vi* to whine, snivel
fri'gnone, -a [friɲ'ɲone] *sm/f* whiner, sniveller
'frigo, -ghi *sm* fridge
frigo'bar *sm inv* minibar
frigo'rifero, -a *ag* refrigerating ■ *sm* refrigerator; **cella frigorifera** cold store
fringu'ello *sm* chaffinch
'frissi *etc vb vedi* **friggere**
frit'tata *sf* omelet(te); **fare una ~** (*fig*) to make a mess of things
frit'tella *sf* (*Cuc*) pancake; (*: ripiena*) fritter
'fritto, -a *pp di* **friggere** ■ *ag* fried ■ *sm* fried food; **ormai siamo fritti!** (*fig fam*) now we've had it!; **è un argomento ~ e rifritto** that's old hat; **~ misto** mixed fry
frit'tura *sf* (*cibo*) fried food; **~ di pesce** mixed fried fish
friu'lano, -a *ag* of (*o* from) Friuli
frivo'lezza [frivo'lettsa] *sf* frivolity
'frivolo, -a *ag* frivolous
frizi'one [frit'tsjone] *sf* friction; (*di pelle*) rub, rub-down; (*Aut*) clutch
friz'zante [frid'dzante] *ag* (*anche fig*) sparkling
'frizzo ['friddzo] *sm* witticism
fro'dare *vt* to defraud, cheat
'frode *sf* fraud; **~ fiscale** tax evasion
'frodo *sm*: **di ~** illegal, contraband; **pescatore di ~, cacciatore di ~** poacher
'frogia, -gie ['frɔdʒa] *sf* (*di cavallo etc*) nostril
'frollo, -a *ag* (*carne*) tender; (*: selvaggina*) high; (*fig: persona*) soft; **pasta frolla** short(crust) pastry
'fronda *sf* (leafy) branch; (*di partito politico*) internal opposition; **fronde** *sfpl* (*di albero*) foliage *sg*
fron'tale *ag* frontal; (*scontro*) head-on
'fronte *sf* (*Anat*) forehead; (*di edificio*) front, façade ■ *sm* (*Mil, Pol, Meteor*) front; **a ~, di ~** facing, opposite; **di ~ a** (*posizione*) opposite, facing, in front of; (*a paragone di*) compared with; **far ~ a** (*nemico, problema*) to confront; (*responsabilità*) to face up to; (*spese*) to cope with
fronteggi'are [fronted'dʒare] *vt* (*avversari, difficoltà*) to face, stand up to; (*spese*) to cope with
frontes'pizio [frontes'pittsjo] *sm* (*Archit*) frontispiece; (*di libro*) title page
fronti'era *sf* border, frontier
fron'tone *sm* pediment
'fronzolo ['frondzolo] *sm* frill
'frotta *sf* crowd; **in ~, a frotte** in their hundreds, in droves
'frottola *sf* fib; **raccontare un sacco di frottole** to tell a pack of lies
fru'gale *ag* frugal
fru'gare *vi* to rummage ■ *vt* to search
frugherò *etc* [fruge'rɔ] *vb vedi* **frugare**

frui'tore *sm* user
fruizi'one [fruit'tsjone] *sf* use
frul'lare *vt* (*Cuc*) to whisk ■ *vi* (*uccelli*) to flutter; **cosa ti frulla in mente?** what is going on in that mind of yours?
frul'lato *sm* (*Cuc*) milk shake; (: *con solo frutta*) fruit drink
frulla'tore *sm* electric mixer
frul'lino *sm* whisk
fru'mento *sm* wheat
frusci'are [fruʃ'ʃare] *vi* to rustle
fru'scio [fruʃ'ʃio] *sm* rustle; rustling
'frusta *sf* whip; (*Cuc*) whisk
frus'tare *vt* to whip
frus'tata *sf* lash
frus'tino *sm* riding crop
frus'trare *vt* to frustrate
frus'trato, -a *ag* frustrated
frustrazi'one [frustrat'tsjone] *sf* frustration
'frutta *sf* fruit; (*portata*) dessert; **~ candita/secca** candied/dried fruit
frut'tare *vi* (*investimenti, deposito*) to bear dividends, give a return; **il mio deposito in banca (mi) frutta il 10%** my bank deposits bring (me) in 10%; **quella gara gli fruttò la medaglia d'oro** he won the gold medal in that competition
frut'teto *sm* orchard
frutticol'tura *sf* fruit growing
frut'tifero, -a *ag* (*albero etc*) fruit-bearing; (*fig: che frutta*) fruitful, profitable; **deposito ~** interest-bearing deposit
frutti'vendolo, -a *sm/f* greengrocer (*Brit*), produce dealer (*US*)
'frutto *sm* fruit; (*fig: risultato*) result(s); (*Econ: interesse*) interest; (: *reddito*) income; **è ~ della tua immaginazione** it's a figment of your imagination; **frutti di mare** seafood *sg*
fruttu'oso, -a *ag* fruitful, profitable
FS *abbr* (= *Ferrovie dello Stato*) *Italian railways*
f.t. *abbr* = **fuori testo**
f.to *abbr* (= *firmato*) signed
fu *vb vedi* **essere** ■ *ag inv*: **il fu Paolo Bianchi** the late Paolo Bianchi
fuci'lare [futʃi'lare] *vt* to shoot
fuci'lata [futʃi'lata] *sf* rifle shot
fucilazi'one [futʃilat'tsjone] *sf* execution (by firing squad)
fu'cile [fu'tʃile] *sm* rifle, gun; (*da caccia*) shotgun, gun; **~ a canne mozze** sawn-off shotgun
fu'cina [fu'tʃina] *sf* forge
'fuco, -chi *sm* drone
'fucsia *sf* fuchsia
'fuga, -ghe *sf* escape, flight; (*di gas, liquidi*) leak; (*Mus*) fugue; **mettere qn in ~** to put sb to flight; **~ di cervelli** brain drain
fu'gace [fu'gatʃe] *ag* fleeting, transient
fu'gare *vt* (*dubbi, incertezze*) to dispel, drive out
fug'gevole [fud'dʒevole] *ag* fleeting
fuggi'asco, -a, schi, sche [fud'dʒasko] *ag, sm/f* fugitive
fuggi'fuggi [fuddʒi'fuddʒi] *sm* scramble, stampede
fug'gire [fud'dʒire] *vi* to flee, run away; (*fig: passar veloce*) to fly ■ *vt* to avoid
fuggi'tivo, -a [fuddʒi'tivo] *sm/f* fugitive, runaway
'fui *vb vedi* **essere**
'fulcro *sm* (*Fisica*) fulcrum; (*fig: di teoria, questione*) central *o* key point
ful'gore *sm* brilliance, splendour (*Brit*), splendor (*US*)
fu'liggine [fu'liddʒine] *sf* soot
fulmi'nare *vt* (*elettricità*) to electrocute; (*con arma da fuoco*) to shoot dead; **fulminarsi** *vr* (*lampadina*) to go, blow; (*fig: con lo sguardo*): **mi fulminò (con uno sguardo)** he looked daggers at me
'fulmine *sm* bolt of lightning; **fulmini** *smpl* lightning *sg*; **~ a ciel sereno** bolt from the blue
ful'mineo, -a *ag* (*fig: scatto*) rapid; (: *minaccioso*) threatening
'fulvo, -a *ag* tawny
fumai'olo *sm* (*di nave*) funnel; (*di fabbrica*) chimney
fu'mante *ag* (*piatto etc*) steaming
fu'mare *vi* to smoke; (*emettere vapore*) to steam ■ *vt* to smoke
fu'mario, -a *ag*: **canna fumaria** flue
fu'mata *sf* (*segnale*) smoke signal; **farsi una ~** to have a smoke; **~ bianca/nera** (*in Vaticano*) *signal that a new pope has/has not been elected*
fuma'tore, -'trice *sm/f* smoker
fu'metto *sm* comic strip; **giornale a fumetti** comic
'fummo *vb vedi* **essere**
'fumo *sm* smoke; (*vapore*) steam; (*il fumare tabacco*) smoking; **fumi** *smpl* (*industriali etc*) fumes; **vendere ~** to deceive, cheat; **è tutto ~ e niente arrosto** it has no substance to it; **i fumi dell'alcool** (*fig*) the after-effects of drink; **~ passivo** passive smoking
fu'mogeno, -a [fu'mɔdʒeno] *ag* (*candelotto*) smoke *cpd* ■ *sm* smoke bomb; **cortina fumogena** smoke screen
fu'moso, -a *ag* smoky; (*fig*) muddled
fu'nambolo, -a *sm/f* tightrope walker
'fune *sf* rope, cord; (*più grossa*) cable
'funebre *ag* (*rito*) funeral; (*aspetto*) gloomy, funereal
fune'rale *sm* funeral

fu'nesto, -a *ag* (*incidente*) fatal; (*errore, decisione*) fatal, disastrous; (*atmosfera*) gloomy, dismal
'fungere ['fundʒere] *vi*: **~ da** to act as
'fungo, -ghi *sm* fungus; (*commestibile*) mushroom; **~ velenoso** toadstool; **crescere come i funghi** (*fig*) to spring up overnight
funico'lare *sf* funicular railway
funi'via *sf* cable railway
'funsi *etc vb vedi* **fungere**
'funto, -a *pp di* **fungere**
funzio'nare [funtsjo'nare] *vi* to work, function; (*fungere*): **~ da** to act as
funzio'nario [funtsjo'narjo] *sm* official; **~ statale** civil servant
funzi'one [fun'tsjone] *sf* function; (*carica*) post, position; (*Rel*) service; **in ~** (*meccanismo*) in operation; **in ~ di** (*come*) as; **vive in ~ dei figli** he lives for his children; **far ~ di** to act as; **fare la ~ di qn** (*farne le veci*) to take sb's place
fu'oco, -chi *sm* fire; (*fornello*) ring; (*Fot, Fisica*) focus; **dare ~ a qc** to set fire to sth; **far ~** (*sparare*) to fire; **prendere ~** to catch fire; **~ d'artificio** firework; **~ di paglia** flash in the pan; **~ sacro** *o* **di Sant'Antonio** (*Med: fam*) shingles *sg*
fuorché [fwor'ke] *cong, prep* except
FU'ORI *sigla m* (= *Fronte Unitario Omosessuale Rivoluzionario Italiano*) *gay liberation movement*
fu'ori *av* outside; (*all'aperto*) outdoors, outside; (*fuori di casa, Sport*) out; (*esclamativo*) get out! ■ *prep*: **~ (di)** out of, outside ■ *sm* outside; **essere in ~** (*sporgere*) to stick out; **lasciar ~ qc/qn** to leave sth/sb out; **far ~** (*fam: soldi*) to spend; (*: cioccolatini*) to eat up; (*: rubare*) to nick; **far ~ qn** (*fam*) to kill sb, do sb in; **essere tagliato ~** (*da un gruppo, ambiente*) to be excluded; **essere ~ di sé** to be beside oneself; **~ luogo** (*inopportuno*) out of place, uncalled for; **~ mano** out of the way, remote; **~ pasto** between meals; **~ pericolo** out of danger; **~ dai piedi!** get out of the way!; **~ servizio** out of order; **~ stagione** out of season; **illustrazione ~ testo** (*Stampa*) plate; **~ uso** out of use
fuori'bordo *sm inv* speedboat (with outboard motor); outboard motor
fuori'busta *sm inv* unofficial payment
fuori'classe *sm/f inv* (undisputed) champion
fuori'corso *ag inv* (*moneta*) no longer in circulation; (*Ins*): **(studente)** ~ *undergraduate who has not completed a course in due time*
fuorigi'oco [fwori'dʒɔko] *sm* offside
fuori'legge [fwori'leddʒe] *sm/f inv* outlaw
fuoriprog'ramma *sm inv* (*TV, Radio*) unscheduled programme; (*fig*) change of plan *o* programme
fuori'serie *ag inv* (*auto etc*) custom-built ■ *sf* custom-built car
fuoris'trada *sm* (*Aut*) cross-country vehicle
fuoru'scito, -a [fworuʃʃito], **fuoriu'scito, -a** [fworiuʃʃito] *sm/f* exile ■ *sf* (*di gas*) leakage, escape; (*di sangue, linfa*) seepage
fuorvi'are *vt* to mislead; (*fig*) to lead astray ■ *vi* to go astray
furbacchi'one, -a [furbak'kjone] *sm/f* cunning old devil
fur'bizia [fur'bittsja] *sf* (*vedi ag*) cleverness; cunning; **una ~** a cunning trick
'furbo, -a *ag* clever, smart; (*peg*) cunning ■ *sm/f*: **fare il ~** to (try to) be clever *o* smart; **fatti ~!** show a bit of sense!
fu'rente *ag*: **~ (contro)** furious (with)
fure'ria *sf* (*Mil*) orderly room
fu'retto *sm* ferret
fur'fante *sm* rascal, scoundrel
furgon'cino [furgon'tʃino] *sm* small van
fur'gone *sm* van
'furia *sf* (*ira*) fury, rage; (*fig: impeto*) fury, violence; (*fretta*) rush; **a ~ di** by dint of; **andare su tutte le furie** to fly into a rage
furi'bondo, -a *ag* furious
furi'ere *sm* quartermaster
furi'oso, -a *ag* furious; (*mare, vento*) raging
'furono *vb vedi* **essere**
fu'rore *sm* fury; (*esaltazione*) frenzy; **far ~** to be all the rage
furtiva'mente *av* furtively
fur'tivo, -a *ag* furtive
'furto *sm* theft; **~ con scasso** burglary
'fusa *sfpl*: **fare le ~** to purr
fu'scello [fuʃʃɛllo] *sm* twig
fu'seaux *smpl inv* leggings
'fusi *etc vb vedi* **fondere**
fu'sibile *sm* (*Elettr*) fuse
fusi'one *sf* (*di metalli*) fusion, melting; (*colata*) casting; (*Comm*) merger; (*fig*) merging
'fuso, -a *pp di* **fondere** ■ *sm* (*Filatura*) spindle; **diritto come un ~** as stiff as a ramrod; **~ orario** time zone
fusoli'era *sf* (*Aer*) fusillage
fus'tagno [fus'taɲɲo] *sm* corduroy
fus'tella *sf* (*su scatola di medicinali*) tear-off tab
fusti'gare *vt* (*frustare*) to flog; (*fig: costumi*) to censure, denounce
fus'tino *sm* (*di detersivo*) tub
'fusto *sm* stem; (*Anat, di albero*) trunk; (*recipiente*) drum, can; (*fam*) he-man
'futile *ag* vain, futile
futilità *sf inv* futility
futu'rismo *sm* futurism

Gg

G, g [dʒi] *sf o m inv* (*lettera*) G, g; **G come Genova** ≈ G for George
g *abbr* (= *grammo*) g
G8 [dʒi'otto] *smpl* G8 (= *Group of Eight*)
G20 [dʒi'venti] *smpl* G20 (= *Group of Twenty*)
gabar'dine [gabar'din] *sm* (*tessuto*) gabardine; (*soprabito*) gabardine raincoat
gab'bare *vt* to take in, dupe; **gabbarsi** *vr*: **gabbarsi di qn** to make fun of sb
'gabbia *sf* cage; (*Dir*) dock; (*da imballaggio*) crate; **la ~ degli accusati** (*Dir*) the dock; **~ dell'ascensore** lift (*Brit*) *o* elevator (*US*) shaft; **~ toracica** (*Anat*) rib cage
gabbi'ano *sm* (sea)gull
gabi'netto *sm* (*Med etc*) consulting room; (*Pol*) ministry; (*di decenza*) toilet, lavatory; (*Ins: di fisica etc*) laboratory
Ga'bon *sm*: **il ~** Gabon
ga'elico, -a, ci, che *ag, sm* Gaelic
gaffe [gaf] *sf inv* blunder, boob (*fam*)
gagli'ardo, -a [gaʎ'ʎardo] *ag* strong, vigorous
gai'ezza [ga'jettsa] *sf* gaiety, cheerfulness
'gaio, -a *ag* cheerful
'gala *sf* (*sfarzo*) pomp; (*festa*) gala
ga'lante *ag* gallant, courteous; (*avventura, poesia*) amorous
galante'ria *sf* gallantry
galantu'omo (*pl* **galantuomini**) *sm* gentleman
Ga'lapagos *sfpl*: **le (isole) ~** the Galapagos Islands
ga'lassia *sf* galaxy
gala'teo *sm* (good) manners *pl*, etiquette
gale'otto *sm* (*rematore*) galley slave; (*carcerato*) convict
ga'lera *sf* (*Naut*) galley; (*prigione*) prison
'galla *sf*: **a ~** afloat; **venire a ~** to surface, come to the surface; (*fig: verità*) to come out
galleggia'mento [galleddʒa'mento] *sm* floating; **linea di ~** (*di nave*) waterline
galleggi'ante [galled'dʒante] *ag* floating ■ *sm* (*natante*) barge; (*di pescatore, lenza, Tecn*) float
galleggi'are [galled'dʒare] *vi* to float
galle'ria *sf* (*traforo*) tunnel; (*Archit, d'arte*) gallery; (*Teat*) circle; (*strada coperta con negozi*) arcade; **~ del vento** *o* **aerodinamica** (*Aer*) wind tunnel
'Galles *sm*: **il ~** Wales
gal'lese *ag* Welsh ■ *sm/f* Welshman(-woman) ■ *sm* (*Ling*) Welsh; **i Gallesi** the Welsh
gal'letta *sf* cracker; (*Naut*) ship's biscuit
gal'letto *sm* young cock, cockerel; (*fig*) cocky young man; **fare il ~** to play the gallant
'Gallia *sf*: **la ~** Gaul
gal'lina *sf* hen; **andare a letto con le galline** to go to bed early
gal'lismo *sm* machismo
'gallo *sm* cock; **al canto del ~** at daybreak, at cockcrow; **fare il ~** to play the gallant
gal'lone *sm* piece of braid; (*Mil*) stripe; (*unità di misura*) gallon
galop'pare *vi* to gallop
galop'pino *sm* errand boy; (*Pol*) canvasser
ga'loppo *sm* gallop; **al** *o* **di ~** at a gallop
galvaniz'zare [galvanid'dzare] *vt* to galvanize
'gamba *sf* leg; (*asta: di lettera*) stem; **in ~** (*in buona salute*) well; (*bravo, sveglio*) bright, smart; **prendere qc sotto ~** (*fig*) to treat sth too lightly; **scappare a gambe levate** to take to one's heels; **gambe!** scatter!
gam'bale *sm* legging
gambe'retto *sm* shrimp
'gambero *sm* (*di acqua dolce*) crayfish; (*di mare*) prawn
'Gambia *sf*: **la ~** the Gambia
gambiz'zare [gambid'dzare] *vt* to kneecap
'gambo *sm* stem; (*di frutta*) stalk
ga'mella *sf* mess tin
'gamma *sf* (*Mus*) scale; (*di colori, fig*) range; **~ di prodotti** product range
ga'nascia, -sce [ga'naʃʃa] *sf* jaw; **ganasce del freno** (*Aut*) brake shoes
'gancio ['gantʃo] *sm* hook
'Gange ['gandʒe] *sm*: **il ~** the Ganges

'gangheri ['gangeri] *smpl*: **uscire dai ~** (*fig*) to fly into a temper
gan'grena *sf* = **cancrena**
'gara *sf* competition; (*Sport*) competition; contest; match; (*: corsa*) race; **fare a ~** to compete, vie; **~ d'appalto** (*Comm*) tender
ga'rage [ga'raʒ] *sm inv* garage
ga'rante *sm/f* guarantor
garan'tire *vt* to guarantee; (*debito*) to stand surety for; (*dare per certo*) to assure
garan'tismo *sm* protection of civil liberties
garan'tista, -i, e *ag* concerned with civil liberties
garan'zia [garan'tsia] *sf* guarantee; (*pegno*) security; **in ~** under guarantee
gar'bare *vi*: **non mi garba** I don't like it (*o* him *etc*)
garba'tezza [garba'tettsa] *sf* courtesy, politeness
gar'bato, -a *ag* courteous, polite
'garbo *sm* (*buone maniere*) politeness, courtesy; (*di vestito etc*) grace, style
gar'buglio [gar'buʎʎo] *sm* tangle; (*fig*) muddle, mess
gareggi'are [gared'dʒare] *vi* to compete
garga'nella *sf*: **a ~** from the bottle
garga'rismo *sm* gargle; **fare i gargarismi** to gargle
ga'ritta *sf* (*di caserma*) sentry box
ga'rofano *sm* carnation; **chiodo di ~** clove
gar'retto *sm* hock
gar'rire *vi* to chirp
'garrulo, -a *ag* (*uccello*) chirping; (*persona: loquace*) garrulous, talkative
'garza ['gardza] *sf* (*per bende*) gauze
gar'zone [gar'dzone] *sm* (*di negozio*) boy
gas *sm inv* gas; **a tutto ~** at full speed; **dare ~** (*Aut*) to accelerate; **~ lacrimogeno** tear gas; **~ naturale** natural gas
ga'sare *etc* = **gassare** *etc*
ga'sato, -a *sm/f* (*fam: persona*) freak
gas'dotto *sm* gas pipeline
ga'solio *sm* diesel (oil)
ga's(s)are *vt* to aerate, carbonate; (*asfissiare*) to gas; **gas(s)arsi** *vr* (*fam*) to get excited
ga's(s)ato, -a *ag* (*bibita*) aerated, fizzy
gas'soso, -a *ag* gaseous; gassy ▪ *sf* fizzy drink
'gastrico, -a, ci, che *ag* gastric
gast'rite *sf* gastritis
gastroente'rite *sf* gastroenteritis
gastrono'mia *sf* gastronomy
gas'tronomo, -a *sm/f* gourmet, gastronome
G.A.T.T. *sigla m* (= *General Agreement on Tariffs and Trade*) GATT
'gatta *sf* cat, she-cat; **una ~ da pelare** (*fam*) a thankless task; **qui ~ ci cova!** I smell a rat!, there's something fishy going on here!
gatta'buia *sf* (*fam scherzoso: prigione*) clink
gat'tino *sm* kitten
'gatto *sm* cat, tomcat; **~ delle nevi** (*Aut, Sci*) snowcat; **~ a nove code** cat-o'-nine-tails; **~ selvatico** wildcat
gatto'pardo *sm*: **~ africano** serval; **~ americano** ocelot
gat'tuccio [gat'tuttʃo] *sm* dogfish
gau'dente *sm/f* pleasure-seeker
'gaudio *sm* joy, happiness
ga'vetta *sf* (*Mil*) mess tin; **venire dalla ~** (*Mil, fig*) to rise from the ranks
'gazza ['gaddza] *sf* magpie
gaz'zarra [gad'dzarra] *sf* racket, din
gaz'zella [gad'dzɛlla] *sf* gazelle; (*dei carabinieri*) (high-speed) police car
gaz'zetta [gad'dzetta] *sf* news sheet; **G~ Ufficiale** *official publication containing details of new laws*
gaz'zoso, -a [gad'dzoso] *ag* = **gassoso**
Gazz. Uff. *abbr* = **Gazzetta Ufficiale**
GB *sigla* (= *Gran Bretagna*) GB
G.C. *abbr* = **genio civile**
G.d.F. *abbr* = **guardia di finanza**
GE *sigla* = **Genova**
gel [dʒɛl] *sm inv* gel
ge'lare [dʒe'lare] *vt, vi, vb impers* to freeze; **mi ha gelato il sangue** (*fig*) it made my blood run cold
ge'lata [dʒe'lata] *sf* frost
gela'taio, -a [dʒela'tajo] *sm/f* ice-cream vendor
gelate'ria [dʒelate'ria] *sf* ice-cream shop
gela'tina [dʒela'tina] *sf* gelatine; **~ esplosiva** gelignite; **~ di frutta** fruit jelly
gelati'noso, -a [dʒelati'noso] *ag* gelatinous, jelly-like
ge'lato, -a [dʒe'lato] *ag* frozen ▪ *sm* ice cream
'gelido, -a ['dʒɛlido] *ag* icy, ice-cold
'gelo ['dʒɛlo] *sm* (*temperatura*) intense cold; (*brina*) frost; (*fig*) chill
ge'lone [dʒe'lone] *sm* chilblain
gelo'sia [dʒelo'sia] *sf* jealousy
ge'loso, -a [dʒe'loso] *ag* jealous
'gelso ['dʒɛlso] *sm* mulberry (tree)
gelso'mino [dʒelso'mino] *sm* jasmine
gemel'laggio [dʒemel'laddʒo] *sm* twinning
gemel'lare [dʒemel'lare] *ag* twin *cpd* ▪ *vt* (*città*) to twin
ge'mello, -a [dʒe'mɛllo] *ag, sm/f* twin; **gemelli** *smpl* (*di camicia*) cufflinks; (*dello zodiaco*): **Gemelli** Gemini *sg*; **essere dei Gemelli** to be Gemini
'gemere ['dʒɛmere] *vi* to moan, groan; (*cigolare*) to creak; (*gocciolare*) to drip, ooze
'gemito ['dʒɛmito] *sm* moan, groan

g

'**gemma** ['dʒɛmma] *sf* (*Bot*) bud; (*pietra preziosa*) gem
Gen. *abbr* (*Mil*: = *generale*) Gen
gen. *abbr* (= *generale, generalmente*) gen
gen'darme [dʒen'darme] *sm* policeman; (*fig*) martinet
'**gene** ['dʒɛne] *sm* gene
genealo'gia, -'gie [dʒenealo'dʒia] *sf* genealogy
genea'logico, -a, ci, che [dʒenea'lɔdʒiko] *ag* genealogical; **albero** ~ family tree
gene'rale [dʒene'rale] *ag, sm* general; **in** ~ (*per sommi capi*) in general terms; (*di solito*) usually, in general; **a ~ richiesta** by popular request
generalità [dʒenerali'ta] *sfpl* (*dati d'identità*) particulars
generaliz'zare [dʒeneralid'dzare] *vt, vi* to generalize
generalizzazi'one [dʒeneraliddzat'tsjone] *sf* generalization
general'mente [dʒeneral'mente] *av* generally
gene'rare [dʒene'rare] *vt* (*dar vita*) to give birth to; (*produrre*) to produce; (*causare*) to arouse; (*Tecn*) to produce, generate
genera'tore [dʒenera'tore] *sm* (*Tecn*) generator
generazi'one [dʒenerat'tsjone] *sf* generation
'**genere** ['dʒɛnere] *sm* kind, type, sort; (*Biol*) genus; (*merce*) article, product; (*Ling*) gender; (*Arte, Letteratura*) genre; **in** ~ generally, as a rule; **cose del** *o* **di questo** ~ such things; **il ~ umano** mankind; **generi alimentari** foodstuffs; **generi di consumo** consumer goods; **generi di prima necessità** basic essentials
ge'nerico, -a, ci, che [dʒe'nɛriko] *ag* generic; (*vago*) vague, imprecise; **medico** ~ general practitioner
'**genero** ['dʒɛnero] *sm* son-in-law
generosità [dʒenerosi'ta] *sf* generosity
gene'roso, -a [dʒene'roso] *ag* generous
'**genesi** ['dʒɛnezi] *sf* genesis
ge'netico, -a, ci, che [dʒe'nɛtiko] *ag* genetic ■ *sf* genetics *sg*
gen'giva [dʒen'dʒiva] *sf* (*Anat*) gum
ge'nia [dʒe'nia] *sf* (*peg*) mob, gang
geni'ale [dʒe'njale] *ag* (*persona*) of genius; (*idea*) ingenious, brilliant
'**genio** ['dʒɛnjo] *sm* genius; (*attitudine, talento*) talent, flair, genius; **andare a ~ a qn** to be to sb's liking, appeal to sb; **~ civile** civil engineers *pl*; **il ~ (militare)** the Engineers
geni'tale [dʒeni'tale] *ag* genital; **genitali** *smpl* genitals
geni'tore [dʒeni'tore] *sm* parent, father *o* mother; **genitori** *smpl* parents
genn. *abbr* (= *gennaio*) Jan
gen'naio [dʒen'najo] *sm* January; *vedi anche* **luglio**
geno'cidio [dʒeno'tʃidjo] *sm* genocide
'**Genova** ['dʒɛnova] *sf* Genoa
geno'vese [dʒeno'vese] *ag, sm/f* Genoese (*pl inv*)
gen'taglia [dʒen'taʎʎa] *sf* (*peg*) rabble
'**gente** ['dʒɛnte] *sf* people *pl*
gentil'donna [dʒentil'dɔnna] *sf* lady
gen'tile [dʒen'tile] *ag* (*persona, atto*) kind; (: *garbato*) courteous, polite; (*nelle lettere*): **G~ Signore** Dear Sir; (: *sulla busta*): **G~ Signor Fernando Villa** Mr Fernando Villa
genti'lezza [dʒenti'lettsa] *sf* kindness; courtesy, politeness; **per** ~ (*per favore*) please
gentilu'omo [dʒenti'lwɔmo] (*pl* **gentiluomini**) *sm* gentleman
genuflessi'one [dʒenufles'sjone] *sf* genuflection
genu'ino, -a [dʒenu'ino] *ag* (*prodotto*) natural; (*persona, sentimento*) genuine, sincere
geogra'fia [dʒeogra'fia] *sf* geography
geo'grafico, -a, ci, che [dʒeo'grafiko] *ag* geographical
ge'ografo, -a [dʒe'ɔgrafo] *sm/f* geographer
geolo'gia [dʒeolo'dʒia] *sf* geology
geo'logico, -a, ci, che [dʒeo'lɔdʒiko] *ag* geological
ge'ometra, -i, e [dʒe'ɔmetra] *sm/f* (*professionista*) surveyor
geome'tria [dʒeome'tria] *sf* geometry
geo'metrico, -a, ci, che [dʒeo'mɛtriko] *ag* geometric(al)
geopo'litico, -a, ci, che [dʒeopo'litiko] *ag* geopolitical
Ge'orgia [dʒe'ɔrdʒa] *sf* Georgia
geor'giano, -a [dʒeor'dʒano] *ag, sm/f* Georgian
ge'ranio [dʒe'ranjo] *sm* geranium
ge'rarca, -chi [dʒe'rarka] *sm* (*Storia: nel fascismo*) party official
gerar'chia [dʒerar'kia] *sf* hierarchy
ge'rarchico, -a, ci, che [dʒe'rarkiko] *ag* hierarchical
ge'rente [dʒe'rɛnte] *sm/f* manager/ manageress
ge'renza [dʒe'rɛntsa] *sf* management
ger'gale [dʒer'gale] *ag* slang *cpd*
'**gergo, -ghi** ['dʒɛrgo] *sm* jargon; slang
geria'tria [dʒerja'tria] *sf* geriatrics *sg*
geri'atrico, -a, ci, che [dʒe'rjatriko] *ag* geriatric
'**gerla** ['dʒɛrla] *sf* conical wicker basket
Ger'mania [dʒer'manja] *sf*: **la** ~ Germany; **la ~ occidentale/orientale** West/East Germany

'**germe** ['dʒɛrme] *sm* germ; (*fig*) seed
germinazi'one [dʒerminat'tsjone] *sf* germination
germogli'are [dʒermoʎ'ʎare] *vi* (*emettere germogli*) to sprout; (*germinare*) to germinate
ger'moglio [dʒer'moʎʎo] *sm* shoot; (*gemma*) bud
gero'glifico, -ci [dʒero'glifiko] *sm* hieroglyphic
geron'tologo, -a, gi, ghe [dʒeron'tɔlogo] *sm/f* specialist in geriatrics
ge'rundio [dʒe'rundjo] *sm* gerund
Gerusa'lemme [dʒeruza'lɛmme] *sf* Jerusalem
'**gesso** ['dʒɛsso] *sm* chalk; (*Scultura, Med, Edil*) plaster; (*statua*) plaster figure; (*minerale*) gypsum
'**gesta** ['dʒɛsta] *sfpl* (*letterario*) deeds, feats
ges'tante [dʒes'tante] *sf* expectant mother
gestazi'one [dʒestat'tsjone] *sf* gestation
gestico'lare [dʒestiko'lare] *vi* to gesticulate
gestio'nale [dʒestjo'nale] *ag* administrative, management *cpd*
gesti'one [dʒes'tjone] *sf* management; **~ di magazzino** stock control; **~ patrimoniale** investment management
ges'tire [dʒes'tire] *vt* to run, manage
'**gesto** ['dʒɛsto] *sm* gesture
ges'tore [dʒes'tore] *sm* manager
Gesù [dʒe'zu] *sm* Jesus; **~ bambino** the Christ Child
gesu'ita, -i [dʒezu'ita] *sm* Jesuit
get'tare [dʒet'tare] *vt* to throw; (*anche*: **gettare via**) to throw away *o* out; (*Scultura*) to cast; (*Edil*) to lay; (*acqua*) to spout; (*grido*) to utter; **gettarsi** *vr*: **gettarsi in** (*impresa*) to throw o.s. into; (*mischia*) to hurl o.s. into; (*fiume*) to flow into; **~ uno sguardo su** to take a quick look at
get'tata [dʒet'tata] *sf* (*di cemento, gesso, metalli*) cast; (*diga*) jetty
'**gettito** ['dʒɛttito] *sm* revenue
'**getto** ['dʒɛtto] *sm* (*di gas, liquido, Aer*) jet; (*Bot*) shoot; **a ~ continuo** uninterruptedly; **di ~** (*fig*) straight off, in one go
get'tone [dʒet'tone] *sm* token; (*per giochi*) counter; (: *roulette etc*) chip; **~ di presenza** attendance fee; **~ telefonico** telephone token
gettoni'era [dʒetto'njɛra] *sf* telephone-token dispenser
'**geyser** ['gaizə] *sm inv* geyser
'**Ghana** ['gana] *sm*: **il ~** Ghana
'**ghenga, -ghe** ['gɛnga] *sf* (*fam*) gang, crowd
ghe'pardo [ge'pardo] *sm* cheetah
gher'mire [ger'mire] *vt* to grasp, clasp, clutch
'**ghetta** ['getta] *sf* (*gambale*) gaiter
ghettiz'zare [gettid'dzare] *vt* to segregate
'**ghetto** ['getto] *sm* ghetto
ghiacci'aia [gjat'tʃaja] *sf* (*anche fig*) icebox
ghiacci'aio [gjat'tʃajo] *sm* glacier
ghiacci'are [gjat'tʃare] *vt* to freeze; (*fig*): **~ qn** to make sb's blood run cold ■ *vi* to freeze, ice over
ghiacci'ato, -a [gjat'tʃato] *ag* frozen; (*bevanda*) ice-cold
ghi'accio ['gjattʃo] *sm* ice
ghiacci'olo [gjat'tʃɔlo] *sm* icicle; (*tipo di gelato*) ice lolly (*Brit*), popsicle (*US*)
ghi'aia ['gjaja] *sf* gravel
ghi'anda ['gjanda] *sf* (*Bot*) acorn
ghi'andola ['gjandola] *sf* gland
ghiando'lare [gjando'lare] *ag* glandular
ghigliot'tina [giʎʎot'tina] *sf* guillotine
ghi'gnare [giɲ'ɲare] *vi* to sneer
'**ghigno** ['giɲɲo] *sm* (*espressione*) sneer; (*risata*) mocking laugh
'**ghingheri** ['gingeri] *smpl*: **in ~** all dolled up; **mettersi in ~** to put on one's Sunday best
ghi'otto, -a ['gjotto] *ag* greedy; (*cibo*) delicious, appetizing
ghiot'tone, -a [gjot'tone] *sm/f* glutton
ghiottone'ria [gjottone'ria] *sf* greed, gluttony; (*cibo*) delicacy, titbit (*Brit*), tidbit (*US*)
ghiri'goro [giri'gɔro] *sm* scribble, squiggle
ghir'landa [gir'landa] *sf* garland, wreath
'**ghiro** ['giro] *sm* dormouse
'**ghisa** ['giza] *sf* cast iron
G.I. *abbr* = **giudice istruttore**
già [dʒa] *av* already; (*ex, in precedenza*) formerly ■ *escl* of course!, yes indeed!; **già che ci sei ...** while you are at it ...
gi'acca, -che ['dʒakka] *sf* jacket; **~ a vento** windcheater (*Brit*), windbreaker (*US*)
giacché [dʒak'ke] *cong* since, as
giac'chetta [dʒak'ketta] *sf* (light) jacket
'**giaccio** *etc* ['dʒattʃo] *vb vedi* **giacere**
giac'cone [dʒak'kone] *sm* heavy jacket
gia'cenza [dʒa'tʃɛntsa] *sf*: **merce in ~** goods in stock; **capitale in ~** uninvested capital; **giacenze di magazzino** unsold stock
gia'cere [dʒa'tʃere] *vi* to lie
giaci'mento [dʒatʃi'mento] *sm* deposit
gia'cinto [dʒa'tʃinto] *sm* hyacinth
giaci'uto, -a [dʒa'tʃuto] *pp di* **giacere**
gi'acqui *etc* ['dʒakkwi] *vb vedi* **giacere**
gi'ada ['dʒada] *sf* jade
giaggi'olo [dʒad'dʒɔlo] *sm* iris
giagu'aro [dʒa'gwaro] *sm* jaguar
gial'lastro, -a [dʒal'lastro] *ag* yellowish; (*carnagione*) sallow
gi'allo ['dʒallo] *ag* yellow; (*carnagione*) sallow ■ *sm* yellow; (*anche*: **romanzo giallo**) detective novel; (*anche*: **film giallo**) detective

g

film; ~ **dell'uovo** yolk; **il mar G~** the Yellow Sea
gial'lognolo, -a [dʒal'loɲɲolo] *ag* yellowish, dirty yellow
Gia'maica [dʒa'maika] *sf*: **la** ~ Jamaica
giamai'cano, -a [dʒamai'kano] *ag, sm/f* Jamaican
giam'mai [dʒam'mai] *av* never
Giap'pone [dʒap'pone] *sm*: **il** ~ Japan
giappo'nese [dʒappo'nese] *ag, sm/f, sm* Japanese *inv*
gi'ara ['dʒara] *sf* jar
giardi'naggio [dʒardi'naddʒo] *sm* gardening
giardi'netta [dʒardi'netta] *sf* estate car (*Brit*), station wagon (*US*)
giardini'ere, -a [dʒardi'njɛre] *sm/f* gardener ▪ *sf* (*misto di sottaceti*) mixed pickles *pl*; (*automobile*) = **giardinetta**
giar'dino [dʒar'dino] *sm* garden; ~ **d'infanzia** nursery school; ~ **pubblico** public gardens *pl*, (public) park; ~ **zoologico** zoo
giarretti'era [dʒarret'tjɛra] *sf* garter
Gi'ava ['dʒava] *sf* Java
giavel'lotto [dʒavel'lɔtto] *sm* javelin
gib'boso, -a [dʒib'boso] *ag* (*superficie*) bumpy; (*naso*) crooked
Gibil'terra [dʒibil'tɛrra] *sf* Gibraltar
gi'gante, -'essa [dʒi'gante] *sm/f* giant ▪ *ag* giant, gigantic; (*Comm*) giant-size
gigan'tesco, -a, schi, sche [dʒigan'tesko] *ag* gigantic
gigantogra'fia [dʒigantogra'fia] *sf* (*Fot*) blow-up
'giglio ['dʒiʎʎo] *sm* lily
gilè [dʒi'lɛ] *sm inv* waistcoat
gin [dʒin] *sm inv* gin
gin'cana [dʒin'kana] *sf* gymkhana
ginecolo'gia [dʒinekolo'dʒia] *sf* gynaecology (*Brit*), gynecology (*US*)
gine'cologo, -a, gi, ghe [dʒine'kɔlogo] *sm/f* gynaecologist (*Brit*), gynecologist (*US*)
gi'nepro [dʒi'nepro] *sm* juniper
gi'nestra [dʒi'nɛstra] *sf* (*Bot*) broom
Gi'nevra [dʒi'nevra] *sf* Geneva; **il Lago di** ~ Lake Geneva
gingil'larsi [dʒindʒil'larsi] *vr* to fritter away one's time; (*giocare*): ~ **con** to fiddle with
gin'gillo [dʒin'dʒillo] *sm* plaything
gin'nasio [dʒin'nazjo] *sm* *the 4th and 5th year of secondary school in Italy*
gin'nasta, -i, e [dʒin'nasta] *sm/f* gymnast
gin'nastica [dʒin'nastika] *sf* gymnastics *sg*; (*esercizio fisico*) keep-fit exercises *pl*; (*Ins*) physical education
'ginnico, -a, ci, che ['dʒinnko] *ag* gymnastic
gi'nocchio [dʒi'nɔkkjo] (*pl(f)* **ginocchi,** *pl(m)* **ginocchia**) *sm* knee; **stare in** ~ to kneel, be on one's knees; **mettersi in** ~ to kneel (down)
ginocchi'oni [dʒinok'kjoni] *av* on one's knees
gio'care [dʒo'kare] *vt* to play; (*scommettere*) to stake, wager, bet; (*ingannare*) to take in ▪ *vi* to play; (*a roulette etc*) to gamble; (*fig*) to play a part, be important; (*Tecn: meccanismo*) to be loose; ~ **a** (*gioco, sport*) to play; (*cavalli*) to bet on; ~ **d'astuzia** to be crafty; **giocarsi la carriera** to put one's career at risk; **giocarsi tutto** to risk everything; **a che gioco giochiamo?** what are you playing at?
gioca'tore, -'trice [dʒoka'tore] *sm/f* player; gambler
gio'cattolo [dʒo'kattolo] *sm* toy
giocherel'lare [dʒokerel'lare] *vi*: ~ **con** (*giocattolo*) to play with; (*distrattamente*) to fiddle with
giocherò *etc* [dʒoke'rɔ] *vb vedi* **giocare**
gio'chetto [dʒo'ketto] *sm* (*gioco*) game; (*tranello*) trick; (*fig*): **è un** ~ it's child's play
gi'oco, -chi ['dʒɔko] *sm* game; (*divertimento, Tecn*) play; (*al casinò*) gambling; (*Carte*) hand; (*insieme di pezzi etc necessari per un gioco*) set; **per** ~ for fun; **fare il doppio** ~ **con qn** to double-cross sb; **prendersi** ~ **di qn** to pull sb's leg; **stare al** ~ **di qn** to play along with sb; **è in** ~ **la mia reputazione** my reputation is at stake; ~ **d'azzardo** game of chance; ~ **della palla** ball game; ~ **degli scacchi** chess set; **i Giochi Olimpici** the Olympic Games
gioco'forza [dʒoko'fɔrtsa] *sm*: **essere** ~ to be inevitable
giocoli'ere [dʒoko'ljɛre] *sm* juggler
gio'coso, -a [dʒo'koso] *ag* playful, jesting
gio'gaia [dʒo'gaja] *sf* (*Geo*) range of mountains
gi'ogo, -ghi ['dʒogo] *sm* yoke
gi'oia ['dʒɔja] *sf* joy, delight; (*pietra preziosa*) jewel, precious stone
gioielle'ria [dʒojelle'ria] *sf* jeweller's (*Brit*) *o* jeweler's (*US*) craft; (*negozio*) jewel(l)er's (shop)
gioielli'ere, -a [dʒojel'ljɛre] *sm/f* jeweller (*Brit*), jeweler (*US*)
gioi'ello [dʒo'jɛllo] *sm* jewel, piece of jewellery (*Brit*) *o* jewelry (*US*); **gioielli** *smpl* (*gioie*) jewel(l)ery *sg*
gioi'oso, -a [dʒo'joso] *ag* joyful
Gior'dania [dʒor'danja] *sf*: **la** ~ Jordan
Gior'dano [dʒor'dano] *sm*: **il** ~ the Jordan
gior'dano, -a [dʒor'dano] *ag, sm/f* Jordanian
giorna'laio, -a [dʒorna'lajo] *sm/f* newsagent (*Brit*), newsdealer (*US*)
gior'nale [dʒor'nale] *sm* (news)paper; (*diario*) journal, diary; (*Comm*) journal; ~ **di bordo** (*Naut*) ship's log; ~ **radio** radio news *sg*

giorna'letto [dʒorna'letto] *sm* (children's) comic
giornali'ero, -a [dʒorna'ljɛro] *ag* daily; (*che varia: umore*) changeable ■ *sm* day labourer (*Brit*) *o* laborer (*US*)
giorna'lino [dʒorna'lino] *sm* children's comic
giorna'lismo [dʒorna'lizmo] *sm* journalism
giorna'lista, -i, e [dʒorna'lista] *sm/f* journalist
giorna'listico, -a, ci, che [dʒorna'listiko] *ag* journalistic; **stile ~** journalese
giornal'mente [dʒornal'mente] *av* daily
gior'nata [dʒor'nata] *sf* day; (*paga*) day's wages, day's pay; **durante la ~ di ieri** yesterday; **fresco di ~** (*uovo*) freshly laid; **vivere alla ~** to live from day to day; **~ lavorativa** working day
gi'orno ['dʒorno] *sm* day; (*opposto alla notte*) day, daytime; (*luce del giorno*) daylight; **al ~** per day; **di ~** by day; **~ per ~** day by day; **al ~ d'oggi** nowadays; **tutto il santo ~** all day long; **il G~ dei Morti** *see note*

IL GIORNO DEI MORTI

Il Giorno dei Morti, All Souls' Day, falls on 2 November. At this time of year people visit cemeteries to lay flowers on the graves of their loved ones.

gi'ostra ['dʒɔstra] *sf* (*per bimbi*) merry-go-round; (*torneo storico*) joust
gios'trare [dʒos'trare] *vi* (*Storia*) to joust, tilt; **giostrarsi** *vr* to manage
giov. *abbr* (= *giovedì*) Thur(s)
giova'mento [dʒova'mento] *sm* benefit, help
gi'ovane ['dʒovane] *ag* young; (*aspetto*) youthful ■ *sm/f* youth/girl, young man(-woman); **i giovani** young people; **è ~ del mestiere** he's new to the job
giova'netto, -a [dʒova'netto] *sm/f* young man(-woman)
giova'nile [dʒova'nile] *ag* youthful; (*scritti*) early; (*errore*) of youth
giova'notto [dʒova'nɔtto] *sm* young man
gio'vare [dʒo'vare] *vi*: **~ a** (*essere utile*) to be useful to; (*far bene*) to be good for ■ *vb impers* (*essere bene, utile*) to be useful; **giovarsi** *vr*: **giovarsi di qc** to make use of sth; **a che giova prendersela?** what's the point of getting upset?
Gi'ove ['dʒɔve] *sm* (*Mitologia*) Jove; (*Astr*) Jupiter
giovedì [dʒove'di] *sm inv* Thursday; *vedi anche* **martedì**
gio'venca, -che [dʒo'vɛnka] *sf* heifer
gioventù [dʒoven'tu] *sf* (*periodo*) youth; (*i giovani*) young people *pl*, youth
gio'vi'ale [dʒo'vjale] *ag* jovial, jolly
giovi'nastro [dʒovi'nastro] *sm* young thug
giovin'cello [dʒovin'tʃɛllo] *sm* young lad
giovi'nezza [dʒovi'nettsa] *sf* youth
gip [dʒip] *sigla m inv* (= *giudice per le indagini preliminari*) judge for preliminary enquiries
gira'dischi [dʒira'diski] *sm inv* record player
gi'raffa [dʒi'raffa] *sf* giraffe; (*TV, Cine, Radio*) boom
gira'mento [dʒira'mento] *sm*: **~ di testa** fit of dizziness
gira'mondo [dʒira'mondo] *sm/f inv* globetrotter
gi'randola [dʒi'randola] *sf* (*fuoco d'artificio*) Catherine wheel; (*giocattolo*) toy windmill; (*banderuola*) weather vane, weathercock
gi'rante [dʒi'rante] *sm/f* (*di assegno*) endorser
gi'rare [dʒi'rare] *vt* (*far ruotare*) to turn; (*percorrere, visitare*) to go round; (*Cine*) to shoot; (*: film: come regista*) to make; (*Comm*) to endorse ■ *vi* to turn; (*più veloce*) to spin; (*andare in giro*) to wander, go around; **girarsi** *vr* to turn; **~ attorno a** to go round; to revolve round; **si girava e rigirava nel letto** he tossed and turned in bed; **far ~ la testa a qn** to make sb dizzy; (*fig*) to turn sb's head; **gira al largo** keep your distance; **girala come ti pare** (*fig*) look at it whichever way you like; **gira e rigira ...** after a lot of driving (*o* walking) about ...; (*fig*) whichever way you look at it; **cosa ti gira?** (*fam*) what's got into you?; **mi ha fatto ~ le scatole** (*fam*) he drove me crazy
girar'rosto [dʒirar'rɔsto] *sm* (*Cuc*) spit
gira'sole [dʒira'sole] *sm* sunflower
gi'rata [dʒi'rata] *sf* (*passeggiata*) stroll; (*con veicolo*) drive; (*Comm*) endorsement
gira'tario, -a [dʒira'tarjo] *sm/f* endorsee
gira'volta [dʒira'vɔlta] *sf* twirl, turn; (*curva*) sharp bend; (*fig*) about-turn
gi'rello [dʒi'rɛllo] *sm* (*di bambino*) Babywalker® (*Brit*), go-cart (*US*); (*taglio di carne*) topside (*Brit*), top round (*US*)
gi'retto [dʒi'retto] *sm* (*passeggiata*) walk, stroll; (*: in macchina*) drive, spin; (*: in bicicletta*) ride
gi'revole [dʒi'revole] *ag* revolving, turning
gi'rino [dʒi'rino] *sm* tadpole
'giro ['dʒiro] *sm* (*circuito, cerchio*) circle; (*di chiave, manovella*) turn; (*viaggio*) tour, excursion; (*passeggiata*) stroll, walk; (*in macchina*) drive; (*in bicicletta*) ride; (*Sport: della pista*) lap; (*di denaro*) circulation; (*Carte*) hand; (*Tecn*) revolution; **fare un ~** to go for a walk (*o* a drive *o* a ride); **fare il ~ di** (*parco, città*) to go round; **andare in ~** (*a piedi*) to go about,

walk around; **guardarsi in ~** to look around; **prendere in ~ qn** (*fig*) to take sb for a ride; **a stretto ~ di posta** by return of post; **nel ~ di un mese** in a month's time; **essere nel ~** (*fig*) to belong to a circle (of friends); **~ d'affari** (*viaggio*) business tour; (*Comm*) turnover; **~ di parole** circumlocution; **~ di prova** (*Aut*) test drive; **~ turistico** sightseeing tour; **~ vita** waist measurement

giro'collo [dʒiro'kɔllo] *sm*: **a ~** crewneck *cpd*

giro'conto [dʒiro'konto] *sm* (*Econ*) credit transfer

gi'rone [dʒi'rone] *sm* (*Sport*) series of games; **~ di andata/ritorno** (*Calcio*) first/second half of the season

gironzo'lare [dʒirondzo'lare] *vi* to stroll about

giro'tondo [dʒiro'tondo] *sm* ring-a-ring-o'roses (*Brit*), ring-around-the-rosey (*US*); **in ~** in a circle

girova'gare [dʒirova'gare] *vi* to wander about

gi'rovago, -a, ghi, ghe [dʒi'rɔvago] *sm/f* (*vagabondo*) tramp; (*venditore*) peddler; **una compagnia di girovaghi** (*attori*) a company of strolling actors

'gita ['dʒita] *sf* excursion, trip; **fare una ~** to go for a trip, go on an outing

gi'tano, -a [dʒi'tano] *sm/f* gipsy

gi'tante [dʒi'tante] *sm/f* member of a tour

giù [dʒu] *av* down; (*dabbasso*) downstairs; **in giù** downwards, down; **la mia casa è un po' più in giù** my house is a bit further on; **giù di lì** (*pressappoco*) thereabouts; **bambini dai 6 anni in giù** children aged 6 and under; **cadere giù per le scale** to fall down the stairs; **giù le mani!** hands off!; **essere giù** (*fig*: *di salute*) to be run down; (: *di spirito*) to be depressed; **quel tipo non mi va giù** I can't stand that guy

gi'ubba ['dʒubba] *sf* jacket

giub'botto [dʒub'bɔtto] *sm* jerkin; **~ antiproiettile** bulletproof vest

giubi'lare [dʒubi'lare] *vi* to rejoice

gi'ubilo ['dʒubilo] *sm* rejoicing

giudi'care [dʒudi'kare] *vt* to judge; (*accusato*) to try; (*lite*) to arbitrate in; **~ qn/qc bello** to consider sb/sth (to be) beautiful

giudi'cato [dʒudi'kato] *sm* (*Dir*): **passare in ~** to pass final judgment

gi'udice ['dʒuditʃe] *sm* judge; **~ collegiale** member of the court; **~ conciliatore** justice of the peace; **~ istruttore** examining (*Brit*) *o* committing (*US*) magistrate; **~ popolare** member of a jury

giudizi'ale [dʒudit'tsjale] *ag* judicial

giudizi'ario, -a [dʒudit'tsjarjo] *ag* legal, judicial

giu'dizio [dʒu'dittsjo] *sm* judgment; (*opinione*) opinion; (*Dir*) judgment, sentence; (: *processo*) trial; (: *verdetto*) verdict; **aver ~** to be wise *o* prudent; **essere in attesa di ~** to be awaiting trial; **citare in ~** to summons; **l'imputato è stato rinviato a ~** the accused has been committed for trial

giudizi'oso, -a [dʒudit'tsjoso] *ag* prudent, judicious

gi'uggiola ['dʒuddʒola] *sf*: **andare in brodo di giuggiole** (*fam*) to be over the moon

gi'ugno ['dʒuɲɲo] *sm* June; *vedi anche* **luglio**

giu'livo, -a [dʒu'livo] *ag* merry

giul'lare [dʒul'lare] *sm* jester

giu'menta [dʒu'menta] *sf* mare

gi'unco, -chi ['dʒunko] *sm* (*Bot*) rush

gi'ungere ['dʒundʒere] *vi* to arrive ■ *vt* (*mani etc*) to join; **~ a** to arrive at, reach; **~ nuovo a qn** to come as news to sb; **~ in porto** to reach harbour; (*fig*) to be brought to a successful outcome

gi'ungla ['dʒungla] *sf* jungle

gi'unsi *etc* ['dʒunsi] *vb vedi* **giungere**

gi'unto, -a ['dʒunto] *pp di* **giungere** ■ *sm* (*Tecn*) coupling, joint ■ *sf* addition; (*organo esecutivo, amministrativo*) council, board; **per giunta** into the bargain, in addition; **giunta militare** military junta; *vedi anche* **Comune**; **Provincia**; **Regione**

giun'tura [dʒun'tura] *sf* joint

giuo'care [dʒwo'kare] *vt, vi* = **giocare**

giu'oco ['dʒwɔko] *sm* = **gioco**

giura'mento [dʒura'mento] *sm* oath; **~ falso** perjury

giu'rare [dʒu'rare] *vt* to swear ■ *vi* to swear, take an oath; **gliel'ho giurata** I swore I would get even with him

giu'rato, -a [dʒu'rato] *ag*: **nemico ~** sworn enemy ■ *sm/f* juror, juryman(-woman)

giu'ria [dʒu'ria] *sf* jury

giu'ridico, -a, ci, che [dʒu'ridiko] *ag* legal

giurisdizi'one [dʒurizdit'tsjone] *sf* jurisdiction

giurispru'denza [dʒurispru'dɛntsa] *sf* jurisprudence

giu'rista, -i, e [dʒu'rista] *sm/f* jurist

giustap'porre [dʒustap'porre] *vt* to juxtapose

giustapposizi'one [dʒustappozit'tsjone] *sf* juxtaposition

giustap'posto, -a [dʒustap'posto] *pp di* **giustappore**

giustifi'care [dʒustifi'kare] *vt* to justify; **giustificarsi** *vr*: **giustificarsi di** *o* **per qc** to justify *o* excuse o.s. for sth

giustifica'tivo, -a [dʒustifika'tivo] *ag* (*Amm*): **nota** *o* **pezza giustificativa** receipt

giustificazi'one [dʒustifikat'tsjone] *sf* justification; *(Ins)* (note of) excuse
gius'tizia [dʒus'tittsja] *sf* justice; **farsi ~ (da sé)** *(vendicarsi)* to take the law into one's own hands
giustizi'are [dʒustit'tsjare] *vt* to execute, put to death
giustizi'ere [dʒustit'tsjɛre] *sm* executioner
gi'usto, -a ['dʒusto] *ag* *(equo)* fair, just; *(vero)* true, correct; *(adatto)* right, suitable; *(preciso)* exact, correct ■ *av* *(esattamente)* exactly, precisely; *(per l'appunto, appena)* just; **arrivare ~** to arrive just in time; **ho ~ bisogno di te** you're just the person I need
'glabro, -a *ag* hairless
glaci'ale [gla'tʃale] *ag* glacial
gla'diolo *sm* gladiolus
'glandola *sf* = **ghiandola**
'glassa *sf* *(Cuc)* icing
glau'coma *sm* glaucoma
gli [ʎi] *det mpl (dav V, s impura, gn, pn, ps, x, z)* the ■ *pron (a lui)* to him; *(a esso)* to it; *(in coppia con lo, la, li, le, ne: a lui, a lei, a loro etc)*: **gliele do** I'm giving them to him (*o* her *o* them); **gliene ho parlato** I spoke to him (*o* her *o* them) about it; *vedi anche* **il**
glice'mia [glitʃe'mia] *sf* glycaemia
glice'rina [glitʃe'rina] *sf* glycerine
'glicine ['glitʃine] *sm* wistaria
gli'ela *etc* ['ʎela] *vedi* **gli**
glo'bale *ag* overall; *(vista)* global
'globo *sm* globe
'globulo *sm* *(Anat)*: **~ rosso/bianco** red/white corpuscle
glocalizzazi'one [glokaliddza'tsjone] *sf* glocalization
'gloria *sf* glory; **farsi ~ di qc** to pride o.s. on sth, take pride in sth
glori'arsi *vr*: **~ di qc** to pride o.s. on sth, glory *o* take pride in sth
glorifi'care *vt* to glorify
glori'oso, -a *ag* glorious
glos'sario *sm* glossary
glu'cosio *sm* glucose
'gluteo *sm* gluteus; **glutei** *smpl* buttocks
GM *abbr* = **genio militare**
'gnocchi ['ɲɔkki] *smpl* *(Cuc)* *small dumplings made of semolina pasta or potato*
'gnomo ['ɲɔmo] *sm* gnome
'gnorri ['ɲɔrri] *sm/f inv*: **non fare lo ~!** stop acting as if you didn't know anything about it!
GO *sigla* = **Gorizia**
'goal ['goul] *sm inv* *(Sport)* goal
'gobba *sf* *(Anat)* hump; *(protuberanza)* bump
'gobbo, -a *ag* hunchbacked; *(ricurvo)* round-shouldered ■ *sm/f* hunchback
'Gobi *smpl*: **il Deserto dei ~** the Gobi Desert
'goccia, -ce ['gottʃa] *sf* drop; **~ di rugiada** dewdrop; **somigliarsi come due gocce d'acqua** to be as like as two peas in a pod; **è la ~ che fa traboccare il vaso!** it's the last straw!
'goccio ['gottʃo] *sm* drop, spot
goccio'lare [gottʃo'lare] *vi, vt* to drip
goccio'lio [gottʃo'lio] *sm* dripping
go'dere *vi* *(compiacersi)*: **~ (di)** to be delighted (at), rejoice (at); *(trarre vantaggio)*: **~ di** to enjoy, benefit from ■ *vt* to enjoy; **godersi la vita** to enjoy life; **godersela** to have a good time, enjoy o.s.
godi'mento *sm* enjoyment
godrò *etc vb vedi* **godere**
gof'faggine [gof'faddʒine] *sf* clumsiness
'goffo, -a *ag* clumsy, awkward
'gogna ['goɲɲa] *sf* pillory
gol *sm inv* = **goal**
'gola *sf* *(Anat)* throat; *(golosità)* gluttony, greed; *(di camino)* flue; *(di monte)* gorge; **fare ~** *(anche fig)* to tempt; **ricacciare il pianto** *o* **le lacrime in ~** to swallow one's tears
go'letta *sf* *(Naut)* schooner
golf *sm inv* *(Sport)* golf; *(maglia)* cardigan
'golfo *sm* gulf
goli'ardico, -a, ci, che *ag* *(canto, vita)* student *cpd*
go'loso, -a *ag* greedy
'golpe *sm inv* *(Pol)* coup
gomi'tata *sf*: **dare una ~ a qn** to elbow sb; **farsi avanti a (forza** *o* **furia di) gomitate** to elbow one's way through; **fare a gomitate per qc** to fight to get sth
'gomito *sm* elbow; *(di strada etc)* sharp bend
go'mitolo *sm* ball
'gomma *sf* rubber; *(colla)* gum; *(per cancellare)* rubber, eraser; *(di veicolo)* tyre *(Brit)*, tire *(US)*; **~ da masticare** chewing gum; **~ a terra** flat tyre
gommapi'uma® *sf* foam rubber
gom'mino *sm* rubber tip; *(rondella)* rubber washer
gom'mista, -i, e *sm/f* tyre *(Brit)* *o* tire *(US)* specialist; *(rivenditore)* tyre *o* tire merchant
gom'mone *sm* rubber dinghy
gom'moso, -a *ag* rubbery
'gondola *sf* gondola
gondoli'ere *sm* gondolier
gonfa'lone *sm* banner
gonfi'are *vt* *(pallone)* to blow up, inflate; *(dilatare, ingrossare)* to swell; *(fig: notizia)* to exaggerate; **gonfiarsi** *vr* to swell; *(fiume)* to rise
'gonfio, -a *ag* swollen; *(stomaco)* bloated; *(palloncino, gomme)* inflated, blown up; *(con pompa)* pumped up; *(vela)* full; **occhi gonfi di**

pianto eyes swollen with tears; **~ di orgoglio** (*persona*) puffed up (with pride); **avere il portafoglio ~** to have a bulging wallet
gonfi'ore *sm* swelling
gongo'lare *vi* to look pleased with o.s.; **~ di gioia** to be overjoyed
'gonna *sf* skirt; **~ pantalone** culottes *pl*
'gonzo ['gondzo] *sm* simpleton, fool
googlare [gu'glare] *vt* (*Inform*) to google
gorgheggi'are [gorged'dʒare] *vi* to warble; to trill
gor'gheggio [gor'geddʒo] *sm* (*Mus, di uccello*) trill
'gorgo, -ghi *sm* whirlpool
gorgogli'are [gorgoʎ'ʎare] *vi* to gurgle
gorgo'glio [gorgoʎ'ʎio] *sm* gurgling
go'rilla *sm inv* gorilla; (*guardia del corpo*) bodyguard
'Gotha *sm inv* (*del cinema, letteratura, industria*) leading lights *pl*
'gotico, -a, ci, che *ag, sm* Gothic
'gotta *sf* gout
gover'nante *sm/f* ruler ■ *sf* (*di bambini*) governess; (*donna di servizio*) housekeeper
gover'nare *vt* (*stato*) to govern, rule; (*pilotare, guidare*) to steer; (*bestiame*) to tend, look after
governa'tivo, -a *ag* (*politica, decreto*) government *cpd*, governmental; (*stampa*) pro-government
governa'tore *sm* governor
go'verno *sm* government; **~ ombra** shadow cabinet
'gozzo ['gottso] *sm* (*Zool*) crop; (*Med*) goitre; (*fig fam*) throat
gozzovigli'are [gottsoviʎ'ʎare] *vi* to make merry, carouse
GPL [dʒipi'ɛlle] *sigla m* (= *Gas di Petrolio Liquefatto*) LPG (= *Liquefied Petroleum Gas*)
gpm *abbr* (= *giri per minuto*) rpm
GPS [dʒipi'ɛsse] *sigla m* GPS (= *Global Positioning System*)
GR [dzi'erre] *sigla* = **Grosseto** ■ *sigla m* (= *giornale radio*) radio news
gracchi'are [grak'kjare] *vi* to caw
graci'dare [gratʃi'dare] *vi* to croak
graci'dio, -ii [gratʃi'dio] *sm* croaking
'gracile ['gratʃile] *ag* frail, delicate
gra'dasso *sm* boaster
gradata'mente *av* gradually, by degrees
gradazi'one [gradat'tsjone] *sf* (*sfumatura*) gradation; **~ alcolica** alcoholic content
gra'devole *ag* pleasant, agreeable
gradi'mento *sm* pleasure, satisfaction; **essere di mio (o tuo etc) ~** to be to my (*o* your *etc*) liking
gradi'nata *sf* flight of steps; (*in teatro, stadio*) tiers *pl*
gra'dino *sm* step; (*Alpinismo*) foothold
gra'dire *vt* (*accettare con piacere*) to accept; (*desiderare*) to wish, like; **gradisce una tazza di tè?** would you like a cup of tea?
gra'dito, -a *ag* welcome
'grado *sm* (*Mat, Fisica etc*) degree; (*stadio*) degree, level; (*Mil, sociale*) rank; **essere in ~ di fare** to be in a position to do; **di buon ~** willingly; **per gradi** by degrees; **un cugino di primo/secondo ~** a first/second cousin; **subire il terzo ~** (*anche fig*) to be given the third degree
gradu'ale *ag* gradual
gradu'are *vt* to grade
gradu'ato, -a *ag* (*esercizi*) graded; (*scala, termometro*) graduated ■ *sm* (*Mil*) non-commissioned officer
gradua'toria *sf* (*di concorso*) list; (*per la promozione*) order of seniority
'graffa *sf* (*gancio*) clip; (*segno grafico*) brace
graf'fetta *sf* paper clip
graffi'are *vt* to scratch
graffia'tura *sf* scratch
'graffio *sm* scratch
graf'fiti *smpl* graffiti
gra'fia *sf* spelling; (*scrittura*) handwriting
'grafico, -a, ci, che *ag* graphic ■ *sm* graph; (*persona*) graphic designer ■ *sf* graphic arts *pl*; **~ a torta** pie chart
gra'migna [gra'miɲɲa] *sf* weed; couch grass
gram'matica, -che *sf* grammar
grammati'cale *ag* grammatical
'grammo *sm* gram(me)
gram'mofono *sm* gramophone
'gramo, -a *ag* (*vita*) wretched
gran *ag vedi* **grande**
'grana *sf* (*granello, di minerali, corpi spezzati*) grain; (*fam: seccatura*) trouble; (*: soldi*) cash ■ *sm inv* *cheese similar to Parmesan*
gra'naglie [gra'naʎʎe] *sfpl* corn *sg*, seed *sg*
gra'naio *sm* granary, barn
gra'nata *sf* (*frutto*) pomegranate; (*pietra preziosa*) garnet; (*proiettile*) grenade
granati'ere *sm* (*Mil*) grenadier; (*fig*) fine figure of a man
Gran Bre'tagna [granbre'taɲɲa] *sf*: **la ~** Great Britain
gran'cassa *sf* (*Mus*) bass drum
'granchio ['grankjo] *sm* crab; (*fig*) blunder; **prendere un ~** (*fig*) to blunder
grandango'lare *sm* wide-angle lens *sg*
gran'dangolo *sm* (*Fot*) wide-angle lens *sg*
'grande *ag* (*qualche volta* **gran** + C, **grand'** + V) (*grosso, largo, vasto*) big, large; (*alto*) tall; (*lungo*) long; (*in sensi astratti*) great ■ *sm/f* (*persona adulta*) adult, grown-up; (*chi ha ingegno e potenza*) great man(-woman); **mio fratello più ~** my big *o* older brother; **il gran**

pubblico the general public; **di gran classe** (*prodotto*) high-class; **cosa farai da ~?** what will you be *o* do when you grow up?; **fare le cose in ~** to do things in style; **fare il ~** (*strafare*) to act big; **una gran bella donna** a very beautiful woman; **non è una gran cosa** *o* **un gran che** it's nothing special; **non ne so gran che** I don't know very much about it

grandeggi'are [granded'dʒare] *vi* (*emergere per grandezza*): **~ su** to tower over; (*darsi arie*) to put on airs

gran'dezza [gran'dettsa] *sf* (*dimensione*) size; (*fig*) greatness; **in ~ naturale** lifesize; **manie di ~** delusions of grandeur

grandi'nare *vb impers* to hail

'grandine *sf* hail

grandi'oso, -a *ag* grand, grandiose

gran'duca, -chi *sm* grand duke

grandu'cato *sm* grand duchy

grandu'chessa [grandu'kessa] *sf* grand duchess

gra'nello *sm* (*di cereali, uva*) seed; (*di frutta*) pip; (*di sabbia, sale etc*) grain

gra'nita *sf* *kind of water ice*

gra'nito *sm* granite

'grano *sm* (*in quasi tutti i sensi*) grain; (*frumento*) wheat; (*di rosario, collana*) bead; **~ di pepe** peppercorn

gran'turco *sm* maize

'granulo *sm* granule; (*Med*) pellet

'grappa *sf* *rough, strong brandy*

'grappolo *sm* bunch, cluster

'graspo *sm* bunch (of grapes)

gras'setto *sm* (*Tip*) bold (type) (*Brit*), bold face

'grasso, -a *ag* fat; (*cibo*) fatty; (*pelle*) greasy; (*terreno*) rich; (*fig: guadagno, annata*) plentiful; (*: volgare*) coarse, lewd ■ *sm* (*di persona, animale*) fat; (*sostanza che unge*) grease

gras'soccio, -a, ci, ce [gras'sɔttʃo] *ag* plump

gras'sone, -a *sm/f* (*fam: persona*) dumpling

'grata *sf* grating

gra'ticcio [gra'tittʃo] *sm* trellis; (*stuoia*) mat

gra'ticola *sf* grill

gra'tifica, -che *sf* bonus; **~ natalizia** Christmas bonus

gratificazi'one [gratifikat'tsjone] *sf* (*soddisfazione*) satisfaction, reward

grati'nare *vt* (*Cuc*) to cook au gratin

'gratis *av* free, for nothing

grati'tudine *sf* gratitude

'grato, -a *ag* grateful

gratta'capo *sm* worry, headache

grattaci'elo [gratta'tʃɛlo] *sm* skyscraper

gratta e 'sosta *sm inv* *scratch card used to pay for parking*

gratta e 'vinci [grattae'vintʃi] *sm* (*lotteria*) lottery; (*biglietto*) scratchcard

grat'tare *vt* (*pelle*) to scratch; (*raschiare*) to scrape; (*pane, formaggio, carote*) to grate; (*fam: rubare*) to pinch ■ *vi* (*stridere*) to grate; (*Aut*) to grind; **grattarsi** *vr* to scratch o.s.; **grattarsi la pancia** (*fig*) to twiddle one's thumbs

grat'tata *sf* scratch; **fare una ~** (*Aut: fam*) to grind the gears

grat'tugia, -gie [grat'tudʒa] *sf* grater

grattugi'are [grattu'dʒare] *vt* to grate; **pane grattugiato** breadcrumbs *pl*

gratuità *sf* (*fig*) gratuitousness

gra'tuito, -a *ag* free; (*fig*) gratuitous

gra'vame *sm* tax; (*fig*) burden, weight

gra'vare *vt* to burden ■ *vi*: **~ su** to weigh on

'grave *ag* (*danno, pericolo, peccato etc*) grave, serious; (*responsabilità*) heavy, grave; (*contegno*) grave, solemn; (*voce, suono*) deep, low-pitched; (*Ling*): **accento ~** grave accent ■ *sm* (*Fisica*) (heavy) body; **un malato ~** a person who is seriously ill

grave'mente *av* (*ammalato, ferito*) seriously

gravi'danza [gravi'dantsa] *sf* pregnancy

'gravido, -a *ag* pregnant

gravità *sf* seriousness; (*anche Fisica*) gravity

gravi'tare *vi* (*Fisica*): **~ intorno a** to gravitate round

gra'voso, -a *ag* heavy, onerous

'grazia ['grattsja] *sf* grace; (*favore*) favour (*Brit*), favor (*US*); (*Dir*) pardon; **di ~** (*ironico*) if you please; **troppa ~!** (*ironico*) you're too generous!; **quanta ~ di Dio!** what abundance!; **entrare nelle grazie di qn** to win sb's favour; **Ministero di G~ e Giustizia** Ministry of Justice, ≈ Lord Chancellor's Office (*Brit*), ≈ Department of Justice (*US*)

grazi'are [grat'tsjare] *vt* (*Dir*) to pardon

'grazie ['grattsje] *escl* thank you!; **~ mille!** *o* **tante!** *o* **infinite!** thank you very much!; **~ a** thanks to

grazi'oso, -a [grat'tsjoso] *ag* charming, delightful; (*gentile*) gracious

'Grecia ['grɛtʃa] *sf*: **la ~** Greece

'greco, -a, ci, che *ag, sm/f, sm* Greek

gre'gario *sm* (*Ciclismo*) supporting rider

'gregge ['greddʒe] (*pl(f)* **greggi**) *sm* flock

'greggio, -a, gi, ge ['greddʒo] *ag* raw, unrefined; (*diamante*) rough, uncut; (*tessuto*) unbleached ■ *sm* (*anche*: **petrolio greggio**) crude (oil)

grembi'ule *sm* apron; (*sopravveste*) overall

'grembo *sm* lap; (*ventre della madre*) womb

gre'mito, -a *ag*: **~ (di)** packed *o* crowded (with)

'greto *sm* (exposed) gravel bed of a river

'gretto, -a *ag* mean, stingy; (*fig*) narrow-minded

g

'greve *ag* heavy
'grezzo, -a ['greddzo] *ag* = **greggio**
gri'dare *vi* (*per chiamare*) to shout, cry (out); (*strillare*) to scream, yell ■ *vt* to shout (out), yell (out); ~ **aiuto** to cry *o* shout for help
'grido (*pl(m)* **gridi**, *pl(f)* **grida**) *sm* shout, cry; scream, yell; (*di animale*) cry; **di** ~ famous; **all'ultimo** ~ in the latest style
'grigio, -a, gi, gie ['gridʒo] *ag, sm* grey (*Brit*), gray (*US*)
'griglia ['griʎʎa] *sf* (*per arrostire*) grill; (*Elettr*) grid; (*inferriata*) grating; **alla** ~ (*Cuc*) grilled
grigli'ata [griʎ'ʎata] *sf* (*Cuc*) grill
gril'letto *sm* trigger
'grillo *sm* (*Zool*) cricket; (*fig*) whim; **ha dei grilli per la testa** his head is full of nonsense
grimal'dello *sm* picklock
'grinfia *sf*: **cadere nelle grinfie di qn** (*fig*) to fall into sb's clutches
'grinta *sf* grim expression; (*Sport*) fighting spirit; **avere molta** ~ to be very determined
grintoso, -a *ag* forceful
'grinza ['grintsa] *sf* crease, wrinkle; (*ruga*) wrinkle; **il tuo ragionamento non fa una** ~ your argument is faultless
grin'zoso, -a [grin'tsoso] *ag* wrinkled; creased
grip'pare *vi* (*Tecn*) to seize
gris'sino *sm* bread-stick
groenlan'dese *ag* Greenland *cpd* ■ *sm/f* Greenlander
Groen'landia *sf*: **la** ~ Greenland
'gronda *sf* eaves *pl*
gron'daia *sf* gutter
gron'dante *ag* dripping
gron'dare *vi* to pour; (*essere bagnato*): ~ **di** to be dripping with ■ *vt* to drip with
'groppa *sf* (*di animale*) back, rump; (*fam: dell'uomo*) back, shoulders *pl*
'groppo *sm* tangle; **avere un** ~ **alla gola** (*fig*) to have a lump in one's throat
'grossa *sf* (*unità di misura*) gross
gros'sezza [gros'settsa] *sf* size; thickness
gros'sista, -i, e *sm/f* (*Comm*) wholesaler
'grosso, -a *ag* big, large; (*di spessore*) thick; (*grossolano: anche fig*) coarse; (*grave, insopportabile*) serious, great; (*tempo, mare*) rough ■ *sm*: **il** ~ **di** the bulk of; **un pezzo** ~ (*fig*) a VIP, a bigwig; **farla grossa** to do something very stupid; **dirle grosse** to tell tall stories (*Brit*) *o* tales (*US*); **questa è grossa!** that's a good one!; **sbagliarsi di** ~ to be completely wrong; **dormire della grossa** to sleep like a log
grossolanità *sf* coarseness
grosso'lano, -a *ag* rough, coarse; (*fig*) coarse, crude; (*: errore*) stupid
grosso'modo *av* roughly
'grotta *sf* cave; grotto
grot'tesco, -a, schi, sche *ag* grotesque
grovi'era *sm o f* gruyère (cheese)
gro'viglio [gro'viʎʎo] *sm* tangle; (*fig*) muddle
gru *sf inv* crane
'gruccia, -ce ['gruttʃa] *sf* (*per camminare*) crutch; (*per abiti*) coat-hanger
gru'gnire [gruɲ'ɲire] *vi* to grunt
gru'gnito [gruɲ'ɲito] *sm* grunt
'grugno ['gruɲɲo] *sm* snout; (*fam: faccia*) mug
'grullo, -a *ag* silly, stupid
'grumo *sm* (*di sangue*) clot; (*di farina etc*) lump
gru'moso, -a *ag* lumpy
'gruppo *sm* group; ~ **sanguigno** blood group
gruvi'era *sm o f* = **groviera**
'gruzzolo ['gruttsolo] *sm* (*di denaro*) hoard
GT *abbr* (*Aut: = gran turismo*) GT
G.U. *abbr* = **Gazzetta Ufficiale**
guada'gnare [gwadaɲ'ɲare] *vt* (*ottenere*) to gain; (*soldi, stipendio*) to earn; (*vincere*) to win; (*raggiungere*) to reach; **tanto di guadagnato!** so much the better!
gua'dagno [gwa'daɲɲo] *sm* earnings *pl*; (*Comm*) profit; (*vantaggio, utile*) advantage, gain; ~ **di capitale** capital gains *pl*; ~ **lordo/netto** gross/net earnings *pl*
gu'ado *sm* ford; **passare a** ~ to ford
gu'ai *escl*: ~ **a te (o lui** *etc*)**!** woe betide you (*o* him *etc*)!
gua'ina *sf* (*fodero*) sheath; (*indumento per donna*) girdle
gu'aio *sm* trouble, mishap; (*inconveniente*) trouble, snag
gua'ire *vi* to whine, yelp
gua'ito *sm* (*di cane*) yelp, whine; (*il guaire*) yelping, whining
gu'ancia, -ce ['gwantʃa] *sf* cheek
guanci'ale [gwan'tʃale] *sm* pillow; **dormire fra due guanciali** (*fig*) to sleep easy, have no worries
gu'anto *sm* glove; **trattare qn con i guanti** (*fig*) to handle sb with kid gloves; **gettare/raccogliere il** ~ (*fig*) to throw down/take up the gauntlet
guan'tone *sm* boxing glove
guarda'boschi [gwarda'bɔski] *sm inv* forester
guarda'caccia [gwarda'kattʃa] *sm inv* gamekeeper
guarda'coste *sm inv* coastguard; (*nave*) coastguard patrol vessel
guarda'linee *sm inv* (*Sport*) linesman
guarda'macchine [gwarda'makkine] *sm/f inv* car-park (*Brit*) *o* parking lot (*US*) attendant
guar'dare *vt* (*con lo sguardo: osservare*) to look at; (*film, televisione*) to watch; (*custodire*) to look after, take care of ■ *vi* to look; (*badare*): ~ **a** to

pay attention to; (*luoghi: esser orientato*): **~ a** to face; **guardarsi** *vr* to look at o.s.; **~ di** to try to; **guardarsi da** (*astenersi*) to refrain from; (*stare in guardia*) to beware of; **guardarsi dal fare** to take care not to do; **ma guarda un po'!** good heavens!; **e guarda caso ...** as if by coincidence ...; **~ qn dall'alto in basso** to look down on sb; **non ~ in faccia a nessuno** (*fig*) to have no regard for anybody; **~ di traverso** to scowl *o* frown at; **~ a vista qn** to keep a close watch on sb

guarda'roba *sm inv* wardrobe; (*locale*) cloakroom

guardarobi'ere, -a *sm/f* cloakroom attendant

guardasi'gilli [gwardasi'dʒilli] *sm inv* ≈ Lord Chancellor (*Brit*), ≈ Attorney General (*US*)

gu'ardia *sf* (*individuo, corpo*) guard; (*sorveglianza*) watch; **fare la ~ a qc/qn** to guard sth/sb; **stare in ~** (*fig*) to be on one's guard; **il medico di ~** the doctor on call; **il fiume ha raggiunto il livello di ~** the river has reached the high-water mark; **~ carceraria** (prison) warder (*Brit*) *o* guard (*US*); **~ del corpo** bodyguard; **~ di finanza** (*corpo*) customs *pl*; (*persona*) customs officer; *see note*; **~ forestale** forest ranger; **~ giurata** security guard; **~ medica** emergency doctor service; **~ municipale** town policeman; **~ notturna** night security guard; **~ di pubblica sicurezza** policeman

Guardia di finanza

The *Guardia di Finanza* is a military body which deals with infringements of the laws governing income tax and monopolies. It reports to the Ministers of Finance, Justice or Agriculture, depending on the function it is performing.

guardia'caccia [gwardja'kattʃa] *sm inv* = **guardacaccia**

guardi'ano, -a *sm/f* (*di carcere*) warder (*Brit*), guard (*US*); (*di villa etc*) caretaker; (*di museo*) custodian; (*di zoo*) keeper; **~ notturno** night watchman

guar'dina *sf* cell

guar'dingo, -a, ghi, ghe *ag* wary, cautious

guardi'ola *sf* porter's lodge; (*Mil*) look-out tower

guarigi'one [gwari'dʒone] *sf* recovery

gua'rire *vt* (*persona, malattia*) to cure; (*ferita*) to heal ■ *vi* to recover, be cured; to heal (up)

guarnigi'one [gwarni'dʒone] *sf* garrison

guar'nire *vt* (*ornare: abiti*) to trim; (*Cuc*) to garnish

guarnizi'one [gwarnit'tsjone] *sf* trimming; garnish; (*Tecn*) gasket

guasta'feste *sm/f inv* spoilsport

guas'tare *vt* to spoil, ruin; (*meccanismo*) to break; **guastarsi** *vr* (*cibo*) to go bad; (*meccanismo*) to break down; (*tempo*) to change for the worse; (*amici*) to quarrel, fall out

gu'asto, -a *ag* (*non funzionante*) broken; (*: telefono etc*) out of order; (*andato a male*) bad, rotten; (*: dente*) decayed, bad; (*fig: corrotto*) depraved ■ *sm* breakdown; (*avaria*) failure; **~ al motore** engine failure

Guate'mala *sm*: **il ~** Guatemala

guatemal'teco, -a, ci, che *ag, sm/f* Guatemalan

gu'ercio, -a, ci, ce ['gwertʃo] *ag* cross-eyed

gu'erra *sf* war; (*tecnica: atomica, chimica etc*) warfare; **fare la ~ (a)** to wage war (against); **la ~ fredda** the Cold War; **~ mondiale** world war; **~ preventiva** preventive war; **la prima/seconda ~ mondiale** the First/Second World War

guerrafon'daio *sm* warmonger

guerreggi'are [gwerred'dʒare] *vi* to wage war

guer'resco, -a, schi, sche *ag* (*di guerra*) war *cpd*; (*incline alla guerra*) warlike

guerri'ero, -a *ag* warlike ■ *sm* warrior

guer'riglia [gwer'riʎʎa] *sf* guerrilla warfare

guerrigli'ero [gwerriʎ'ʎɛro] *sm* guerrilla

'gufo *sm* owl

'guglia ['guʎʎa] *sf* (*Archit*) spire; (*di roccia*) needle

Gui'ana *sf*: **la ~ francese** French Guiana

gu'ida *sf* (*persona*) guide; (*libro*) guide(book); (*comando, direzione*) guidance, direction; (*Aut*) driving; (*: sterzo*) steering; (*tappeto*) runner; **~ a destra/sinistra** (*Aut*) right-/left-hand drive; **essere alla ~ di** (*governo*) to head; (*spedizione, paese*) to lead; **far da ~ a qn** (*mostrare la strada*) to show sb the way; (*in una città*) to show sb (a)round; **~ telefonica** telephone directory

gui'dare *vt* to guide; (*condurre a capo*) to lead; (*auto*) to drive; (*aereo, nave*) to pilot; **sa ~?** can you drive?

guida'tore, -'trice *sm/f* (*conducente*) driver

Gui'nea *sf*: **la Repubblica di ~** the Republic of Guinea; **la ~ Equatoriale** Equatorial Guinea

guin'zaglio [gwin'tsaʎʎo] *sm* leash, lead

gu'isa *sf*: **a ~ di** like, in the manner of

guiz'zare [gwit'tsare] *vi* to dart; to flicker; to leap; **~ via** (*fuggire*) to slip away

gu'izzo ['gwittso] *sm* (*di animali*) dart; (*di fulmine*) flash

'guru *sm inv* (*Rel, anche fig*) guru

'guscio ['guʃʃo] *sm* shell

gus'tare *vt* (*cibi*) to taste; (*: assaporare con piacere*) to enjoy, savour (*Brit*), savor (*US*); (*fig*) to enjoy, appreciate ■ *vi*: **~ a** to please; **non mi gusta affatto** I don't like it at all
gusta'tivo, -a *ag*: **papille gustative** taste buds
'gusto *sm* (*senso*) taste; (*sapore*) taste, flavour (*Brit*), flavor (*US*); (*godimento*) enjoyment; **al ~ di fragola** strawberry-flavo(u)red; **di ~ barocco** in the baroque style; **mangiare di ~** to eat heartily; **prenderci ~**: **ci ha preso ~** he's acquired a taste for it, he's got to like it
gus'toso, -a *ag* tasty; (*fig*) agreeable
guttu'rale *ag* guttural
Gu'yana [gu'jana] *sf*: **la ~** Guyana

H, h ['akka] *sf o m inv (lettera)* H, h ■ *abbr* (= *ora*) hr; (= *etto, altezza*) h; **H come hotel** ≈ H for Harry (*Brit*), H for How (*US*)
ha[1], **'hai** [a, ai] *vb vedi* **avere**
ha[2] *abbr* (= *ettaro*) ha
Ha'iti [a'iti] *sf* Haiti
haiti'ano, -a [ai'tjano] *ag, sm/f* Haitian
hall [hɔːl] *sf inv* hall, foyer
'handicap ['handikap] *sm inv* handicap
handicap'pato, -a [andikap'pato] *ag* handicapped ■ *sm/f* handicapped person, disabled person
'hanno ['anno] *vb vedi* **avere**
ha'scisc [aʃʃiʃ] *sm* hashish
hawai'ano, -a [ava'jano] *ag, sm/f* Hawaiian
Ha'waii [a'vai] *sfpl*: **le ~** Hawaii *sg*
'Helsinki ['ɛlsinki] *sf* Helsinki
'herpes ['ɛrpes] *sm* (*Med*) herpes *sg*; **~ zoster** shingles *sg*
hg *abbr* (= *ettogrammo*) hg
'hi-fi ['haifai] *sm inv, ag inv* hi-fi
Hima'laia [ima'laja] *sm*: **l'~** the Himalayas *pl*
hl *abbr* (= *ettolitro*) hl
ho [ɔ] *vb vedi* **avere**
'hobby ['hɔbi] *sm inv* hobby
'hockey ['hɔki] *sm* hockey; **~ su ghiaccio** ice hockey
'holding ['houldiŋ] *sf inv* holding company
Hon'duras [on'duras] *sm* Honduras
'Hong Kong ['ɔ̃kɔ̃g] *sf* Hong Kong
Hono'lulu [ono'lulu] *sf* Honolulu
'hostess ['houstis] *sf inv* air hostess (*Brit*) *o* stewardess
ho'tel [o'tɛl] *sm inv* hotel
Hz *abbr* (= *hertz*) Hz

I, i [i] *sf o m inv* (*lettera*) I, i; **I come Imola** ≈ I for Isaac (*Brit*), I for Item (*US*)
i *det mpl* the; *vedi anche* **il**
IACP *sigla m* (= *Istituto Autonomo per le Case Popolari*) *public housing association*
i'ato *sm* hiatus
i'berico, -a, ci, che *ag* Iberian; **la Penisola Iberica** the Iberian Peninsula
iber'nare *vi* to hibernate ■ *vt* (*Med*) to induce hypothermia in
ibernazi'one [ibernat'tsjone] *sf* hibernation
ibid. *abbr* (= *ibidem*) ib(id)
'ibrido, -a *ag, sm* hybrid
IC *abbr* = **intercity**
'ICE ['itʃe] *sigla m* (= *Istituto nazionale per il Commercio Estero*) *overseas trade board*
i'cona *sf* icon
id *abbr* (= *idem*) do.
Id'dio *sm* God
i'dea *sf* idea; (*opinione*) opinion, view; (*ideale*) ideal; **avere le idee chiare** to know one's mind; **cambiare ~** to change one's mind; **dare l'~ di** to seem, look like; **neanche** *o* **neppure per ~!** certainly not!, no way!; **~ fissa** obsession
ide'ale *ag, sm* ideal
idea'lismo *sm* idealism
idea'lista, -i, e *sm/f* idealist
idea'listico, -a, ci, che *ag* idealistic
idealiz'zare [idealid'dzare] *vt* to idealize
ide'are *vt* (*immaginare*) to think up, conceive; (*progettare*) to plan
idea'tore, -'trice *sm/f* author
i'dentico, -a, ci, che *ag* identical
identifi'care *vt* to identify
identificazi'one [identifikat'tsjone] *sf* identification
identità *sf inv* identity
ideolo'gia, -'gie [ideolo'dʒia] *sf* ideology
ideo'logico, -a, ci, che [ideo'lɔdʒiko] *ag* ideological
idil'liaco, -a, ci, che *ag* = **idillico**
i'dillico, -a, ci, che *ag* idyllic
i'dillio *sm* idyll; **tra di loro è nato un ~** they have fallen in love
idi'oma, -i *sm* idiom, language
idio'matico, -a, ci, che *ag* idiomatic; **frase idiomatica** idiom
idiosincra'sia *sf* idiosyncrasy
idi'ota, -i, e *ag* idiotic ■ *sm/f* idiot
idio'zia [idjot'tsia] *sf* idiocy; (*atto, discorso*) idiotic thing to do (*o* say)
ido'latra, -i, e *ag* idolatrous ■ *sm/f* idolater
idola'trare *vt* to worship; (*fig*) to idolize
idola'tria *sf* idolatry
'idolo *sm* idol
idoneità *sf* suitability; **esame** *m* **di ~** qualifying examination
i'doneo, -a *ag*: **~ a** suitable for, fit for; (*Mil*) fit for; (*qualificato*) qualified for
i'drante *sm* hydrant
idra'tante *ag* (*crema*) moisturizing ■ *sm* moisturizer
idra'tare *vt* (*pelle*) to moisturize
idratazi'one [idratat'tsjone] *sf* moisturizing
i'draulico, -a, ci, che *ag* hydraulic ■ *sm* plumber ■ *sf* hydraulics *sg*
'idrico, -a, ci, che *ag* water *cpd*
idrocar'buro *sm* hydrocarbon
idroe'lettrico, -a, ci, che *ag* hydroelectric
i'drofilo, -a *ag*: **cotone ~** cotton wool (*Brit*), absorbent cotton (*US*)
idrofo'bia *sf* rabies *sg*
i'drofobo, -a *ag* rabid; (*fig*) furious
i'drogeno [i'drɔdʒeno] *sm* hydrogen
idroli'pidico, -a, ci, che *ag* hydrolipid
idro'porto *sm* (*Aer*) seaplane base
idrorepel'lente *ag* water-repellent
idros'calo *sm* = **idroporto**
idrovo'lante *sm* seaplane
i'ella *sf* bad luck
iel'lato, -a *ag* plagued by bad luck
i'ena *sf* hyena
ie'ratico, -a, ci, che *ag* (*Rel: scrittura*) hieratic; (*fig: atteggiamento*) solemn

i'eri *av, sm* yesterday; **il giornale di ~** yesterday's paper; **~ l'altro** the day before yesterday; **~ sera** yesterday evening
ietta'tore, -'trice *sm/f* jinx
igi'ene [i'dʒɛne] *sf* hygiene; **norme d'~** sanitary regulations; **ufficio d'~** public health office; **~ mentale** mental health; **~ pubblica** public health
igi'enico, -a, ci, che [i'dʒɛniko] *ag* hygienic; (*salubre*) healthy
igloo [i'glu] *sm inv* igloo; (*tenda*) dome tent
IGM *sigla m* (*= Ispettorato Generale della Motorizzazione*) *road traffic inspectorate*
i'gnaro, -a [iɲ'ɲaro] *ag*: **~ di** unaware of, ignorant of
i'gnifugo, -a, ghi, ghe [iɲ'ɲifugo] *ag* flame-resistant, fireproof
i'gnobile [iɲ'ɲɔbile] *ag* despicable, vile
igno'minia [iɲɲo'minja] *sf* ignominy
igno'rante [iɲɲo'rante] *ag* ignorant
igno'ranza [iɲɲo'rantsa] *sf* ignorance
igno'rare [iɲɲo'rare] *vt* (*non sapere, conoscere*) to be ignorant *o* unaware of, not to know; (*fingere di non vedere, sentire*) to ignore
i'gnoto, -a [iɲ'ɲɔto] *ag* unknown ■ *sm/f*: **figlio di ignoti** child of unknown parentage; **il Milite I~** the Unknown Soldier

PAROLA CHIAVE

il (*pl(m)* **i**; *diventa* **lo** (*pl* **gli**) *davanti a s impura, gn, pn, ps, x, z; f* **la** (*pl* **le**)) *det m* **1** the; **il libro/lo studente/l'acqua** the book/the student/the water; **gli scolari** the pupils
2 (*astrazione*): **il coraggio/l'amore/la giovinezza** courage/love/youth
3 (*tempo*): **il mattino/la sera** in the morning/evening; **il venerdì** (*abitualmente*) on Fridays; (*quel giorno*) on (the) Friday; **la settimana prossima** next week
4 (*distributivo*) a, an; **2 euro il chilo/paio** 2 euros a *o* per kilo/pair
5 (*partitivo*) some, any; **hai messo lo zucchero?** have you added sugar?; **hai comprato il latte?** did you buy (some *o* any) milk?
6 (*possesso*): **aprire gli occhi** to open one's eyes; **rompersi la gamba** to break one's leg; **avere i capelli neri/il naso rosso** to have dark hair/a red nose; **mettiti le scarpe** put your shoes on
7 (*con nomi propri*): **il Petrarca** Petrarch; **il Presidente Bush** President Bush; **dov'è la Francesca?** where's Francesca?
8 (*con nomi geografici*): **il Tevere** the Tiber; **l'Italia** Italy; **il Regno Unito** the United Kingdom; **l'Everest** Everest

'ilare *ag* cheerful
ilarità *sf* hilarity, mirth
ill. *abbr* (*= illustrazione, illustrato*) ill.
illangui'dire *vi* to grow weak *o* feeble
illazi'one [illat'tsjone] *sf* inference, deduction
il'lecito, -a [il'letʃito] *ag* illicit
ille'gale *ag* illegal
illegalità *sf* illegality
illeg'gibile [illed'dʒibile] *ag* illegible
illegittimità [illedʒittimi'ta] *sf* illegitimacy
ille'gittimo, -a [ille'dʒittimo] *ag* illegitimate
il'leso, -a *ag* unhurt, unharmed
illette'rato, -a *ag* illiterate
illiba'tezza [illiba'tettsa] *sf* (*di donna*) virginity
illi'bato, -a *ag*: **donna illibata** virgin
illimi'tato, -a *ag* boundless; unlimited
illivi'dire *vi* (*volto, mani*) to turn livid; (*cielo*) to grow leaden
ill.mo *abbr* = **illustrissimo**
il'logico, -a, ci, che [il'lɔdʒiko] *ag* illogical
il'ludere *vt* to deceive, delude; **illudersi** *vr* to deceive o.s., delude o.s.
illumi'nare *vt* to light up, illuminate; (*fig*) to enlighten; **illuminarsi** *vr* to light up; **~ a giorno** (*con riflettori*) to floodlight
illumi'nato, -a *ag* (*fig*: *sovrano, spirito*) enlightened
illuminazi'one [illuminat'tsjone] *sf* lighting; illumination; floodlighting; (*fig*) flash of inspiration
illumi'nismo *sm* (*Storia*): **l'I~** the Enlightenment
il'lusi *etc vb vedi* **illudere**
illusi'one *sf* illusion; **farsi delle illusioni** to delude o.s.
illusio'nismo *sm* conjuring
illusio'nista, -i, e *sm/f* conjurer
il'luso, -a *pp di* **illudere**
illu'sorio, -a *ag* illusory
illus'trare *vt* to illustrate
illustra'tivo, -a *ag* illustrative
illustrazi'one [illustrat'tsjone] *sf* illustration
il'lustre *ag* eminent, renowned
illus'trissimo, -a *ag* (*negli indirizzi*) very revered
'ILOR *sigla f* = **imposta locale sui redditi**
IM *sigla* = **Imperia**
imbacuc'care *vt*, **imbacuc'carsi** *vr* to wrap up
imbaldan'zire [imbaldan'tsire] *vt* to give confidence to; **imbaldanzirsi** *vr* to grow bold
imbal'laggio [imbal'laddʒo] *sm* packing *no pl*
imbal'lare *vt* to pack; (*Aut*) to race; **imballarsi** *vr* (*Aut*) to race
imbalsa'mare *vt* to embalm
imbalsa'mato, -a *ag* embalmed
imbambo'lato, -a *ag* (*sguardo, espressione*) vacant, blank

imban'dire *vt*: **~ un banchetto** to prepare a lavish feast
imban'dito, -a *ag*: **tavola imbandita** lavishly *o* sumptuously decked table
imbaraz'zante [imbarat'tsante] *ag* embarrassing, awkward
imbaraz'zare [imbarat'tsare] *vt* (*mettere a disagio*) to embarrass; (*ostacolare: movimenti*) to hamper; (*: stomaco*) to lie heavily on; **imbarazzarsi** *vr* to become embarrassed
imbaraz'zato, -a [imbarat'tsato] *ag* embarrassed; **avere lo stomaco ~** to have an upset stomach
imba'razzo [imba'rattso] *sm* (*disagio*) embarrassment; (*perplessità*) puzzlement, bewilderment; **essere** *o* **trovarsi in ~** to be in an awkward situation *o* predicament; **mettere in ~** to embarrass; **~ di stomaco** indigestion
imbarbari'mento *sm* (*di civiltà, costumi*) barbarization
imbarca'dero *sm* landing stage
imbar'care *vt* (*passeggeri*) to embark; (*merci*) to load; **imbarcarsi** *vr*: **imbarcarsi su** to board; **imbarcarsi per l'America** to sail for America; **imbarcarsi in** (*fig: affare*) to embark on
imbarcazi'one [imbarkat'tsjone] *sf* (small) boat, (small) craft *inv*; **~ di salvataggio** lifeboat
im'barco, -chi *sm* embarkation; loading; boarding; (*banchina*) landing stage; **carta d'~** boarding pass (*Brit*), boarding card
imbastar'dire *vt* to bastardize, debase; **imbastardirsi** *vr* to degenerate, become debased
imbas'tire *vt* (*cucire*) to tack; (*fig: abbozzare*) to sketch, outline
im'battersi *vr*: **~ in** (*incontrare*) to bump *o* run into
imbat'tibile *ag* unbeatable, invincible
imbavagli'are [imbavaʎ'ʎare] *vt* to gag
imbec'care *vt* (*uccelli*) to feed; (*fig*) to prompt, put words into sb's mouth
imbec'cata *sf* (*Teat*) prompt; **dare l'~ a qn** to prompt sb; (*fig*) to give sb their cue
imbe'cille [imbe'tʃille] *ag* idiotic ■ *sm/f* idiot; (*Med*) imbecile
imbecillità [imbetʃilli'ta] *sf inv* (*Med, fig*) imbecility, idiocy; **dire ~** to talk nonsense
imbellet'tare *vt* (*viso*) to make up, put make-up on; **imbellettarsi** *vr* to make o.s. up, put on one's make-up
imbel'lire *vt* to adorn, embellish ■ *vi* to grow more beautiful
im'berbe *ag* beardless; **un giovanotto ~** a callow youth
imbestia'lire *vt* to infuriate; **imbestialirsi** *vr* to become infuriated, fly into a rage
im'bevere *vt* to soak; **imbeversi** *vr*: **imbeversi di** to soak up, absorb
imbe'vuto, -a *ag*: **~ (di)** soaked (in)
imbian'care *vt* to whiten; (*muro*) to whitewash ■ *vi* to become *o* turn white
imbianca'tura *sf* (*di muro: con bianco di calce*) whitewashing; (*: con altre pitture*) painting
imbian'chino [imbjan'kino] *sm* (house) painter, painter and decorator
imbion'dire *vt* (*capelli*) to lighten; (*Cuc: cipolla*) to brown; **imbiondirsi** *vr* (*capelli*) to lighten, go blonde, go fair; (*messi*) to turn golden, ripen
imbizzar'rirsi [imbiddzar'rirsi] *vr* (*cavallo*) to become frisky
imboc'care *vt* (*bambino*) to feed; (*entrare: strada*) to enter, turn into ■ *vi*: **~ in** (*strada*) to lead into; (*: fiume*) to flow into
imbocca'tura *sf* mouth; (*di strada, porto*) entrance; (*Mus, del morso*) mouthpiece
im'bocco, -chi *sm* entrance
imboni'tore *sm* (*di spettacolo, circo*) barker
imborghe'sire [imborge'zire] *vi*, **imborghe'sirsi** *vr* to become bourgeois
imbos'care *vt* to hide; **imboscarsi** *vr* (*Mil*) to evade military service
imbos'cata *sf* ambush
imbos'cato *sm* draft dodger (*US*)
imboschi'mento [imboski'mento] *sm* afforestation
imbottigli'are [imbottiʎ'ʎare] *vt* to bottle; (*Naut*) to blockade; (*Mil*) to hem in; **imbottigliarsi** *vr* to be stuck in a traffic jam
imbot'tire *vt* to stuff; (*giacca*) to pad; **imbottirsi** *vr*: **imbottirsi di** (*rimpinzarsi*) to stuff o.s. with
imbot'tito, -a *ag* (*sedia*) upholstered; (*giacca*) padded ■ *sf* quilt
imbotti'tura *sf* stuffing; padding
imbracci'are [imbrat'tʃare] *vt* (*fucile*) to shoulder; (*scudo*) to grasp
imbra'nato, -a *ag* clumsy, awkward ■ *sm/f* clumsy person
imbratta'carte *sm/f* (*peg*) scribbler
imbrat'tare *vt* to dirty, smear, daub; **imbrattarsi** *vr*: **imbrattarsi (di)** to dirty o.s. (with)
imbratta'tele *sm/f* (*peg*) dauber
imbrigli'are [imbriʎ'ʎare] *vt* to bridle
imbroc'care *vt* (*fig*) to guess correctly
imbrogli'are [imbroʎ'ʎare] *vt* to mix up; (*fig: raggirare*) to deceive, cheat; (*: confondere*) to confuse, mix up; **imbrogliarsi** *vr* to get tangled; (*fig*) to become confused

im'broglio [im'brɔʎʎo] *sm* (*groviglio*) tangle; (*situazione confusa*) mess; (*truffa*) swindle, trick
imbrogli'one, -a [imbroʎ'ʎone] *sm/f* cheat, swindler
imbronci'ato, -a [imbron'tʃato] *ag* (*persona*) sulky; (*cielo*) cloudy, threatening
imbru'nire *vi, vb impers* to grow dark; **all'~** at dusk
imbrut'tire *vt* to make ugly ■ *vi* to become ugly
imbu'care *vt* to post
imbur'rare *vt* to butter
imbuti'forme *ag* funnel-shaped
im'buto *sm* funnel
I.M.C.T.C. *sigla* (= *Ispettorato Generale della Motorizzazione Civile e dei Trasporti in Concessione*) ≈ DVLA
i'mene *sm* hymen
imi'tare *vt* to imitate; (*riprodurre*) to copy; (*assomigliare*) to look like
imita'tore, -'trice *sm/f* (*gen*) imitator; (*Teat*) impersonator, impressionist
imitazi'one [imitat'tsjone] *sf* imitation
immaco'lato, -a *ag* spotless; immaculate
immagazzi'nare [immagaddzi'nare] *vt* to store
immagi'nabile [immadʒi'nabile] *ag* imaginable
immagi'nare [immadʒi'nare] *vt* to imagine; (*supporre*) to suppose; (*inventare*) to invent; **s'immagini!** don't mention it!, not at all!
immagi'nario, -a [immadʒi'narjo] *ag* imaginary
immagina'tiva [immadʒina'tiva] *sf* imagination
immaginazi'one [immadʒinat'tsjone] *sf* imagination; (*cosa immaginata*) fancy
im'magine [im'madʒine] *sf* image; (*rappresentazione grafica, mentale*) picture
immagi'noso, -a [immadʒi'noso] *ag* (*linguaggio, stile*) fantastic
immalinco'nire *vt* to sadden, depress; **immalinconirsi** *vr* to become depressed, become melancholy
imman'cabile *ag* unfailing
immancabil'mente *av* without fail, unfailingly
im'mane *ag* (*smisurato*) huge; (*spaventoso, inumano*) terrible
imma'nente *ag* (*Filosofia*) inherent, immanent
immangi'abile [imman'dʒabile] *ag* inedible
immatrico'lare *vt* to register; **immatricolarsi** *vr* (*Ins*) to matriculate, enrol
immatricolazi'one [immatrikolat'tsjone] *sf* registration; matriculation; enrolment
immaturità *sf* immaturity
imma'turo, -a *ag* (*frutto*) unripe; (*persona*) immature; (*prematuro*) premature
immedesi'marsi *vr*: **~ in** to identify with
immediata'mente *av* immediately, at once
immedia'tezza [immedja'tettsa] *sf* immediacy
immedi'ato, -a *ag* immediate
immemo'rabile *ag* immemorial; **da tempo ~** from time immemorial
im'memore *ag*: **~ di** forgetful of
immensità *sf* immensity
im'menso, -a *ag* immense
im'mergere [im'mɛrdʒere] *vt* to immerse, plunge; **immergersi** *vr* to plunge; (*sommergibile*) to dive, submerge; (*dedicarsi a*): **immergersi in** to immerse o.s. in
immeri'tato, -a *ag* undeserved
immeri'tevole *ag* undeserving, unworthy
immersi'one *sf* immersion; (*di sommergibile*) submersion, dive; (*di palombaro*) dive; **linea di ~** (*Naut*) water line
im'merso, -a *pp di* **immergere**
im'messo, -a *pp di* **immettere**
im'mettere *vt*: **~ (in)** to introduce (into); **~ dati in un computer** to enter data on a computer
immi'grante *ag, sm/f* immigrant
immi'grare *vi* to immigrate
immi'grato, -a *sm/f* immigrant
immigrazi'one [immigrat'tsjone] *sf* immigration
immi'nente *ag* imminent
immi'nenza [immi'nɛntsa] *sf* imminence
immischi'are [immis'kjare] *vt*: **~ qn in** to involve sb in; **immischiarsi** *vr*: **immischiarsi in** to interfere *o* meddle in
immiseri'mento *sm* impoverishment
immise'rire *vt* to impoverish
immis'sario *sm* (*Geo*) affluent, tributary
immissi'one *sf* (*gen*) introduction; (*di aria, gas*) intake; **~ di dati** (*Inform*) data entry
im'mobile *ag* motionless, still; **(beni) immobili** real estate *sg*
immobili'are *ag* (*Dir*) property *cpd*; **patrimonio ~** real estate; **società ~** property company
immobi'lismo *sm* inertia
immobilità *sf* immobility
immobiliz'zare [immobilid'dzare] *vt* to immobilize; (*Econ*) to lock up
immobi'lizzo [immobi'liddzo] *sm*: **spese d'~** capital expenditure
immo'destia *sf* immodesty
immo'desto, -a *ag* immodest
immo'lare *vt* to sacrifice
immondez'zaio [immondet'tsajo] *sm* rubbish dump

i

immon'dizia [immon'dittsja] *sf* dirt, filth; (*spesso al pl*: *spazzatura, rifiuti*) rubbish *no pl*, refuse *no pl*
immo'rale *ag* immoral
immoralità *sf* immorality
immorta'lare *vt* to immortalize
immor'tale *ag* immortal
immortalità *sf* immortality
im'mune *ag* (*esente*) exempt; (*Med, Dir*) immune
immunità *sf* immunity; **~ diplomatica** diplomatic immunity; **~ parlamentare** parliamentary privilege
immuniz'zare [immunid'dzare] *vt* (*Med*) to immunize
immunizzazi'one [immuniddzat'tsjone] *sf* immunization
immunodefi'cienza [immunodefi'tʃɛntsa] *sf*: **~ acquisita** acquired immunodeficiency
immuno'logico, -a, ci, che [immuno'lɔdʒiko] *ag* immunological
immu'tabile *ag* immutable; unchanging
impac'care *vt* to pack
impacchet'tare [impakket'tare] *vt* to pack up
impacci'are [impat'tʃare] *vt* to hinder, hamper
impacci'ato, -a [impat'tʃato] *ag* awkward, clumsy; (*imbarazzato*) embarrassed
im'paccio [im'pattʃo] *sm* obstacle; (*imbarazzo*) embarrassment; (*situazione imbarazzante*) awkward situation
im'pacco, -chi *sm* (*Med*) compress
impadro'nirsi *vr*: **~ di** to seize, take possession of; (*fig*: *apprendere a fondo*) to master
impa'gabile *ag* priceless
impagi'nare [impadʒi'nare] *vt* (*Tip*) to paginate, page (up)
impaginazi'one [impadʒinat'tsjone] *sf* pagination
impagli'are [impaʎ'ʎare] *vt* to stuff (with straw)
impa'lato, -a *ag* (*fig*) stiff as a board
impalca'tura *sf* scaffolding; (*anche fig*) framework
impalli'dire *vi* to turn pale; (*fig*) to fade
impalli'nare *vt* to riddle with shot
impal'pabile *ag* impalpable
impa'nare *vt* (*Cuc*) to dip (*o* roll) in breadcrumbs, bread (*US*)
impanta'narsi *vr* to sink (in the mud); (*fig*) to get bogged down
impape'rarsi *vr* to stumble over a word
impappi'narsi *vr* to stammer, falter
impa'rare *vt* to learn; **così impari!** that'll teach you!
impara'ticcio [impara'tittʃo] *sm* half-baked notions *pl*
impareggi'abile [impared'dʒabile] *ag* incomparable
imparen'tarsi *vr*: **~ con** (*famiglia*) to marry into
'impari *ag inv* (*disuguale*) unequal; (*dispari*) odd
impar'tire *vt* to bestow, give
imparzi'ale [impar'tsjale] *ag* impartial, unbiased
imparzialità [impartsjali'ta] *sf* impartiality
impas'sibile *ag* impassive
impas'tare *vt* (*pasta*) to knead; (*colori*) to mix
impastic'carsi *vr* to pop pills
im'pasto *sm* (*l'impastare*: *di pane*) kneading; (: *di cemento*) mixing; (*pasta*) dough; (*anche fig*) mixture
im'patto *sm* impact; **~ ambientale** impact on the environment
impau'rire *vt* to scare, frighten ■ *vi* (*anche*: **impaurirsi**) to become scared *o* frightened
im'pavido, -a *ag* intrepid, fearless
impazi'ente [impat'tsjɛnte] *ag* impatient
impazi'enza [impat'tsjɛntsa] *sf* impatience
impaz'zata [impat'tsata] *sf*: **all'~** (*precipitosamente*) at breakneck speed; (*colpire*) wildly
impaz'zire [impat'tsire] *vi* to go mad; **~ per qn/qc** to be crazy about sb/sth
impec'cabile *ag* impeccable
impedi'mento *sm* obstacle, hindrance
impe'dire *vt* (*vietare*): **~ a qn di fare** to prevent sb from doing; (*ostruire*) to obstruct; (*impacciare*) to hamper, hinder
impe'gnare [impeɲ'ɲare] *vt* (*dare in pegno*) to pawn; (*onore etc*) to pledge; (*prenotare*) to book, reserve; (*obbligare*) to oblige; (*occupare*) to keep busy; (*Mil*: *nemico*) to engage; **impegnarsi** *vr* (*vincolarsi*): **impegnarsi a fare** to undertake to do; (*mettersi risolutamente*): **impegnarsi in qc** to devote o.s. to sth; **impegnarsi con qn** (*accordarsi*) to come to an agreement with sb
impegna'tivo, -a [impeɲɲa'tivo] *ag* binding; (*lavoro*) demanding, exacting
impe'gnato, -a [impeɲ'ɲato] *ag* (*occupato*) busy; (*fig*: *romanzo, autore*) committed, engagé
im'pegno [im'peɲɲo] *sm* (*obbligo*) obligation; (*promessa*) promise, pledge; (*zelo*) diligence, zeal; (*compito*: *d'autore*) commitment; **impegni di lavoro** business commitments
impego'larsi *vr* (*fig*): **~ in** to get heavily involved in
impela'garsi *vr* = **impegolarsi**
impel'lente *ag* pressing, urgent
impene'trabile *ag* impenetrable
impen'narsi *vr* (*cavallo*) to rear up; (*Aer*) to go into a climb; (*fig*) to bridle

impen'nata *sf* (*di cavallo*) rearing up; (*di aereo*) climb, nose-up; (*fig: scatto d'ira*) burst of anger; (*: di prezzi etc*) sudden increase
impen'sabile *ag* (*inaccettabile*) unthinkable; (*difficile da concepire*) inconceivable
impen'sato, -a *ag* unforeseen, unexpected
impensie'rire *vt*, **impensie'rirsi** *vr* to worry
impe'rante *ag* prevailing
impe'rare *vi* (*anche fig*) to reign, rule
impera'tivo, -a *ag, sm* imperative
impera'tore, -'trice *sm/f* emperor/empress
impercet'tibile [impertʃet'tibile] *ag* imperceptible
imperdo'nabile *ag* unforgivable, unpardonable
imper'fetto, -a *ag* imperfect ■ *sm* (*Ling*) imperfect (tense)
imperfezi'one [imperfet'tsjone] *sf* imperfection
imperi'ale *ag* imperial
imperia'lismo *sm* imperialism
imperia'lista, -i, e *ag* imperialist
imperi'oso, -a *ag* (*persona*) imperious; (*motivo, esigenza*) urgent, pressing
imperi'turo, -a *ag* everlasting
impe'rizia [impe'rittsja] *sf* lack of experience
imperma'lirsi *vr* to take offence
imperme'abile *ag* waterproof ■ *sm* raincoat
imperni'are *vt*: **~ qc su** to hinge sth on; (*fig: discorso, relazione etc*) to base sth on; **imperniarsi** *vr* (*fig*): **imperniarsi su** to be based on
im'pero *sm* empire; (*forza, autorità*) rule, control
imperscru'tabile *ag* inscrutable
imperso'nale *ag* impersonal
imperso'nare *vt* to personify; (*Teat*) to play, act (the part of); **impersonarsi** *vr*: **impersonarsi in un ruolo** to get into a part, live a part
imper'territo, -a *ag* unperturbed
imperti'nente *ag* impertinent
imperti'nenza [imperti'nɛntsa] *sf* impertinence
impertur'babile *ag* imperturbable
imperver'sare *vi* to rage
im'pervio, -a *ag* (*luogo*) inaccessible; (*strada*) impassable
'impeto *sm* (*moto, forza*) force, impetus; (*assalto*) onslaught; (*fig: impulso*) impulse; (*: slancio*) transport; **con ~** (*parlare*) forcefully, energetically
impet'tito, -a *ag* stiff, erect; **camminare ~** to strut
impetu'oso, -a *ag* (*vento*) strong, raging; (*persona*) impetuous
impian'tare *vt* (*motore*) to install; (*azienda, discussione*) to establish, start
impian'tistica *sf* plant design and installation
impi'anto *sm* (*installazione*) installation; (*apparecchiature*) plant; (*sistema*) system; **~ elettrico** wiring; **~ sportivo** sports complex; **impianti di risalita** (*Sci*) ski lifts
impias'trare, impiastricci'are [impjastrit'tʃare] *vt* to smear, dirty
impi'astro *sm* poultice; (*fig fam: persona*) nuisance
impiccagi'one [impikka'dʒone] *sf* hanging
impic'care *vt* to hang; **impiccarsi** *vr* to hang o.s.
impicci'are [impit'tʃare] *vt* to hinder, hamper; **impicciarsi** *vr* to meddle, interfere; **impicciati degli affari tuoi!** mind your own business!
im'piccio [im'pittʃo] *sm* (*ostacolo*) hindrance; (*seccatura*) trouble, bother; (*affare imbrogliato*) mess; **essere d'~** to be in the way; **cavare** *o* **togliere qn dagli impicci** to get sb out of trouble
impicci'one, -a [impit'tʃone] *sm/f* busybody
impie'gare *vt* (*usare*) to use, employ; (*assumere*) to employ, take on; (*spendere: denaro, tempo*) to spend; (*investire*) to invest; **impiegarsi** *vr* to get a job, obtain employment; **impiego un quarto d'ora per andare a casa** it takes me *o* I take a quarter of an hour to get home
impiega'tizio, -a [impjega'tittsjo] *ag* clerical, white-collar *cpd*; **lavoro/ceto ~** clerical *o* white-collar work/workers *pl*
impie'gato, -a *sm/f* employee; **~ statale** state employee
impi'ego, -ghi *sm* (*uso*) use; (*occupazione*) employment; (*posto di lavoro*) (regular) job, post; (*Econ*) investment; **~ pubblico** job in the public sector
impieto'sire *vt* to move to pity; **impietosirsi** *vr* to be moved to pity
impie'toso, -a *ag* pitiless, cruel
impie'trire *vt* (*anche fig*) to petrify
impigli'are [impiʎ'ʎare] *vt* to catch, entangle; **impigliarsi** *vr* to get caught up *o* entangled
impi'grire *vt* to make lazy ■ *vi* (*anche*: **impigrirsi**) to grow lazy
impingu'are *vt* (*maiale etc*) to fatten; (*fig: tasche, casse dello Stato*) to stuff with money
impiom'bare *vt* (*pacco*) to seal (with lead); (*dente*) to fill
impla'cabile *ag* implacable
implemen'tare *vt* to implement
impli'care *vt* to imply; (*coinvolgere*) to involve; **implicarsi** *vr*: **implicarsi (in)** to become involved (in)

implicazi'one [implikat'tsjone] *sf* implication
im'plicito, -a [im'plitʃito] *ag* implicit
implo'rare *vt* to implore
implorazi'one [implorat'tsjone] *sf* plea, entreaty
impolli'nare *vt* to pollinate
impollinazi'one [impollinat'tsjone] *sf* pollination
impolve'rare *vt* to cover with dust; **impolverarsi** *vr* to get dusty
impoma'tare *vt* (*pelle*) to put ointment on; (*capelli*) to pomade; (*baffi*) to wax; **impomatarsi** *vr* (*fam*) to get spruced up
imponde'rabile *ag* imponderable
im'pone *etc vb vedi* **imporre**
impo'nente *ag* imposing, impressive
im'pongo *etc vb vedi* **imporre**
impo'nibile *ag* taxable ■ *sm* taxable income
impopo'lare *ag* unpopular
impopolarità *sf* unpopularity
im'porre *vt* to impose; (*costringere*) to force, make; (*far valere*) to impose, enforce; **imporsi** *vr* (*persona*) to assert o.s.; (*cosa: rendersi necessario*) to become necessary; (*aver successo: moda, attore*) to become popular; **~ a qn di fare** to force sb to do, make sb do
impor'tante *ag* important
impor'tanza [impor'tantsa] *sf* importance; **dare ~ a qc** to attach importance to sth; **darsi ~** to give o.s. airs
impor'tare *vt* (*introdurre dall'estero*) to import ■ *vi* to matter, be important ■ *vb impers* (*essere necessario*) to be necessary; (*interessare*) to matter; **non importa!** it doesn't matter!; **non me ne importa!** I don't care!
importa'tore, -'trice *ag* importing ■ *sm/f* importer
importazi'one [importat'tsjone] *sf* importation; (*merci importate*) imports *pl*
im'porto *sm* (total) amount
importu'nare *vt* to bother
impor'tuno, -a *ag* irksome, annoying
im'posi *etc vb vedi* **imporre**
imposizi'one [impozit'tsjone] *sf* imposition; (*ordine*) order, command; (*onere, imposta*) tax
imposses'sarsi *vr*: **~ di** to seize, take possession of
impos'sibile *ag* impossible; **fare l'~** to do one's utmost, do all one can
impossibilità *sf* impossibility; **essere nell'~ di fare qc** to be unable to do sth
impossibili'tato, -a *ag*: **essere ~ a fare qc** to be unable to do sth
im'posta *sf* (*di finestra*) shutter; (*tassa*) tax; **~ indiretta sui consumi** excise duty *o* tax; **~ locale sui redditi (ILOR)** tax on unearned income; **~ patrimoniale** property tax; **~ sul reddito** income tax; **~ sul reddito delle persone fisiche** personal income tax; **~ di successione** capital transfer tax (*Brit*), inheritance tax (*US*); **~ sugli utili** tax on profits; **~ sul valore aggiunto** value added tax (*Brit*), sales tax (*US*)
impos'tare *vt* (*imbucare*) to post; (*servizio, organizzazione*) to set up; (*lavoro*) to organize, plan; (*resoconto, rapporto*) to plan; (*problema*) to set out, formulate; (*Tip: pagina*) to lay out; **~ la voce** (*Mus*) to pitch one's voice
impostazi'one [impostat'tsjone] *sf* (*di lettera*) posting (*Brit*), mailing (*US*); (*di problema, questione*) formulation, statement; (*di lavoro*) organization, planning; (*di attività*) setting up; (*Mus: di voce*) pitch
im'posto, -a *pp di* **imporre**
impos'tore, -a *sm/f* impostor
impo'tente *ag* weak, powerless; (*anche Med*) impotent
impo'tenza [impo'tɛntsa] *sf* weakness, powerlessness; impotence
impove'rire *vt* to impoverish ■ *vi* (*anche*: **impoverirsi**) to become poor
imprati'cabile *ag* (*strada*) impassable; (*campo da gioco*) unplayable
imprati'chire [imprati'kire] *vt* to train; **impratichirsi** *vr*: **impratichirsi in qc** to practise (*Brit*) *o* practice (*US*) sth
impre'care *vi* to curse, swear; **~ contro** to hurl abuse at
imprecazi'one [imprekat'tsjone] *sf* abuse, curse
impreci'sato, -a [impretʃi'zato] *ag* (*non preciso: quantità, numero*) indeterminate
imprecisi'one [impretʃi'zjone] *sf* imprecision; inaccuracy
impre'ciso, -a [impre'tʃizo] *ag* imprecise, vague; (*calcolo*) inaccurate
impre'gnare [impreɲ'ɲare] *vt*: **~ (di)** (*imbevere*) to soak *o* impregnate (with); (*riempire: anche fig*) to fill (with)
imprendi'tore *sm* (*industriale*) entrepreneur; (*appaltatore*) contractor; **piccolo ~** small businessman
imprendito'ria *sf* enterprise; (*imprenditori*) entrepreneurs *pl*
imprenditori'ale *ag* (*ceto, classe*) entrepreneurial
imprepa'rato, -a *ag*: **~ (a)** (*gen*) unprepared (for); (*lavoratore*) untrained (for); **cogliere qn ~** to catch sb unawares
impreparazi'one [impreparat'tsjone] *sf* lack of preparation
im'presa *sf* (*iniziativa*) enterprise; (*azione*) exploit; (*azienda*) firm, concern; **~ familiare**

family firm; **~ pubblica** state-owned enterprise

impre'sario *sm* (*Teat*) manager, impresario; **~ di pompe funebri** funeral director

imprescin'dibile [impreʃʃin'dibile] *ag* not to be ignored

im'pressi *etc vb vedi* **imprimere**

impressio'nante *ag* impressive; upsetting

impressio'nare *vt* to impress; (*turbare*) to upset; (*Fot*) to expose; **impressionarsi** *vr* to be easily upset

impressi'one *sf* impression; (*fig: sensazione*) sensation, feeling; (*stampa*) printing; **fare ~** (*colpire*) to impress; (*turbare*) to frighten, upset; **fare buona/cattiva ~ a** to make a good/bad impression on

im'presso, -a *pp di* **imprimere**

impres'tare *vt*: **~ qc a qn** to lend sth to sb

impreve'dibile *ag* unforeseeable; (*persona*) unpredictable

imprevi'dente *ag* lacking in foresight

imprevi'denza [imprevi'dɛntsa] *sf* lack of foresight

impre'visto, -a *ag* unexpected, unforeseen ■ *sm* unforeseen event; **salvo imprevisti** unless anything unexpected happens

imprezio'sire [imprettsjo'sire] *vt*: **~ di** to embellish with

imprigiona'mento [impridʒona'mento] *sm* imprisonment

imprigio'nare [impridʒo'nare] *vt* to imprison

im'primere *vt* (*anche fig*) to impress, stamp; (*comunicare: movimento*) to transmit, give

impro'babile *ag* improbable, unlikely

'improbo, -a *ag* (*fatica, lavoro*) hard, laborious

improdut'tivo, -a *ag* (*investimento*) unprofitable; (*terreno*) unfruitful; (*fig: sforzo*) fruitless

im'pronta *sf* imprint, impression, sign; (*di piede, mano*) print; (*fig*) mark, stamp; **~ digitale** fingerprint; **~ di carbonio** carbon footprint; **rilevamento delle impronte genetiche** genetic fingerprinting

impro'perio *sm* insult

impropo'nibile *ag* which cannot be proposed *o* suggested

im'proprio, -a *ag* improper; **arma impropria** offensive weapon

improro'gabile *ag* (*termine*) that cannot be extended

improvvisa'mente *av* suddenly; unexpectedly

improvvi'sare *vt* to improvise; **improvvisarsi** *vr*: **improvvisarsi cuoco** to (decide to) act as cook

improvvi'sata *sf* (pleasant) surprise

improvvisazi'one [improvvizat'tsjone] *sf* improvisation; **spirito d'~** spirit of invention

improv'viso, -a *ag* (*imprevisto*) unexpected; (*subitaneo*) sudden; **all'~** unexpectedly; suddenly

impru'dente *ag* foolish, imprudent; (*osservazione*) unwise

impru'denza [impru'dɛntsa] *sf* foolishness, imprudence; **è stata un'~** that was a foolish *o* an imprudent thing to do

impu'dente *ag* impudent

impu'denza [impu'dɛntsa] *sf* impudence

impudi'cizia [impudi'tʃittsja] *sf* immodesty

impu'dico, -a, chi, che *ag* immodest

impu'gnare [impuɲ'ɲare] *vt* to grasp, grip; (*Dir*) to contest

impugna'tura [impuɲɲa'tura] *sf* grip, grasp; (*manico*) handle; (*: di spada*) hilt

impulsività *sf* impulsiveness

impul'sivo, -a *ag* impulsive

im'pulso *sm* impulse; **dare un ~ alle vendite** to boost sales

impune'mente *av* with impunity

impunità *sf* impunity

impun'tarsi *vr* to stop dead, refuse to budge; (*fig*) to be obstinate

impun'tura *sf* stitching

impurità *sf inv* impurity

im'puro, -a *ag* impure

impu'tare *vt* (*ascrivere*): **~ qc a** to attribute sth to; (*Dir: accusare*): **~ qn di** to charge sb with, accuse sb of

impu'tato, -a *sm/f* (*Dir*) accused, defendant

imputazi'one [imputat'tsjone] *sf* (*Dir*) charge; (*di spese*) allocation

imputri'dire *vi* to rot

PAROLA CHIAVE

in (*in + il* = **nel**, *in + lo* = **nello**, *in + l'* = **nell'**, *in + la* = **nella**, *in + i* = **nei**, *in + gli* = **negli**, *in + le* = **nelle**) *prep* **1** (*stato in luogo*) in; **vivere in Italia/città** to live in Italy/town; **essere in casa/ufficio** to be at home/the office; **è nel cassetto/in salotto** it's in the drawer/in the sitting room; **se fossi in te** if I were you

2 (*moto a luogo*) to; (*: dentro*) into; **andare in Germania/città** to go to Germany/town; **andare in ufficio** to go to the office; **entrare in macchina/casa** to get into the car/go into the house

3 (*tempo*) in; **nel 1989** in 1989; **in giugno/estate** in June/summer; **l'ha fatto in sei mesi** he did it in six months; **in gioventù, io ...** when I was young, I ...

4 (*modo, maniera*) in; **in silenzio** in silence; **parlare in tedesco** to speak (in) German; **in abito da sera** in evening dress; **in guerra** at war; **in vacanza** on holiday; **Maria Bianchi**

in Rossi Maria Rossi née Bianchi
5 (*mezzo*) by; **viaggiare in autobus/treno** to travel by bus/train
6 (*materia*) made of; **in marmo** made of marble, marble *cpd*; **una collana in oro** a gold necklace
7 (*misura*) in; **siamo in quattro** there are four of us; **in tutto** in all
8 (*fine*): **dare in dono** to give as a gift; **spende tutto in alcool** he spends all his money on drink; **in onore di** in honour of

i'nabile *ag*: ~ **a** incapable of; (*fisicamente, Mil*) unfit for
inabilità *sf*: ~ **(a)** unfitness (for)
inabis'sare *vt* (*nave*) to sink; **inabissarsi** *vr* to go down
inabi'tabile *ag* uninhabitable
inabi'tato, -a *ag* uninhabited
inacces'sibile [inattʃes'sibile] *ag* (*luogo*) inaccessible; (*persona*) unapproachable; (*mistero*) unfathomable
inaccet'tabile [inattʃet'tabile] *ag* unacceptable
inacer'bire [inatʃer'bire] *vt* to exacerbate; **inacerbirsi** *vr* (*persona*) to become embittered
inaci'dire [inatʃi'dire] *vt* (*persona, carattere*) to embitter; **inacidirsi** *vr* (*latte*) to go sour; (*fig: persona, carattere*) to become sour, become embittered
ina'datto, -a *ag*: ~ **(a)** unsuitable *o* unfit (for)
inadegu'ato, -a *ag* inadequate
inadempi'ente *ag* defaulting ■ *sm/f* defaulter
inadempi'enza [inadem'pjɛntsa] *sf*: ~ **a un contratto** non-fulfilment of a contract; **dovuto alle inadempienze dei funzionari** due to negligence on the part of the officials
inadempi'mento *sm* non-fulfilment
inaffer'rabile *ag* elusive; (*concetto, senso*) difficult to grasp
'INAIL *sigla m* (*= Istituto Nazionale per l'Assicurazione contro gli Infortuni sul Lavoro*) *state body providing sickness benefit in the event of accidents at work*
ina'lare *vt* to inhale
inala'tore *sm* inhaler
inalazi'one [inalat'tsjone] *sf* inhalation
inalbe'rare *vt* (*Naut*) to hoist, raise; **inalberarsi** *vr* (*fig*) to flare up, fly off the handle
inalte'rabile *ag* unchangeable; (*colore*) fast, permanent; (*affetto*) constant
inalte'rato, -a *ag* unchanged
inami'dare *vt* to starch
inami'dato, -a *ag* starched
inammis'sibile *ag* inadmissible
inani'mato, -a *ag* inanimate; (*senza vita: corpo*) lifeless
inappa'gabile *ag* insatiable
inappel'labile *ag* (*decisione*) final, irrevocable; (*Dir*) final, not open to appeal
inappe'tenza [inappe'tɛntsa] *sf* (*Med*) lack of appetite
inappun'tabile *ag* irreproachable, flawless
inar'care *vt* (*schiena*) to arch; (*sopracciglia*) to raise; **inarcarsi** *vr* to arch
inaridi'mento *sm* (*anche fig*) drying up
inari'dire *vt* to make arid, dry up ■ *vi* (*anche:* **inaridirsi**) to dry up, become arid
inarres'tabile *ag* (*processo*) irreversible; (*emorragia*) that cannot be stemmed; (*corsa del tempo*) relentless
inascol'tato, -a *ag* unheeded, unheard
inaspettata'mente *av* unexpectedly
inaspet'tato, -a *ag* unexpected
inas'prire *vt* (*disciplina*) to tighten up, make harsher; (*carattere*) to embitter; (*rapporti*) to make worse; **inasprirsi** *vr* to become harsher; to become bitter; to become worse
inattac'cabile *ag* (*anche fig*) unassailable; (*alibi*) cast-iron
inatten'dibile *ag* unreliable
inat'teso, -a *ag* unexpected
inat'tivo, -a *ag* inactive, idle; (*Chim*) inactive
inattu'abile *ag* impracticable
inau'dito, -a *ag* unheard of
inaugu'rale *ag* inaugural
inaugu'rare *vt* to inaugurate, open; (*monumento*) to unveil
inaugurazi'one [inaugurat'tsjone] *sf* inauguration; unveiling
inavve'duto, -a *ag* careless, inadvertent
inavver'tenza [inavver'tɛntsa] *sf* carelessness, inadvertence
inavvertita'mente *av* inadvertently, unintentionally
inavvici'nabile [inavvitʃi'nabile] *ag* unapproachable
'Inca *ag inv, sm/f inv* Inca
incagli'are [inkaʎ'ʎare] *vi* (*Naut: anche:* **incagliarsi**) to run aground
incalco'labile *ag* incalculable
incal'lito, -a *ag* calloused; (*fig*) hardened, inveterate; (*: insensibile*) hard
incal'zante [inkal'tsante] *ag* urgent, insistent; (*crisi*) imminent
incal'zare [inkal'tsare] *vt* to follow *o* pursue closely; (*fig*) to press ■ *vi* (*urgere*) to be pressing; (*essere imminente*) to be imminent
incame'rare *vt* (*Dir*) to expropriate
incammi'nare *vt* (*fig: avviare*) to start up; **incamminarsi** *vr* to set off

incana'lare *vt* (*anche fig*) to channel; **incanalarsi** *vr* (*folla*): **incanalarsi verso** to converge on

incancre'nire *vi*, **incancre'nirsi** *vi* to become gangrenous

incande'scente [inkandeʃʃɛnte] *ag* incandescent, white-hot

incan'tare *vt* to enchant, bewitch; **incantarsi** *vr* (*rimanere intontito*) to be spellbound; to be in a daze; (*meccanismo: bloccarsi*) to jam

incanta'tore, -'trice *ag* enchanting, bewitching ■ *sm/f* enchanter/enchantress

incan'tesimo *sm* spell, charm

incan'tevole *ag* charming, enchanting

in'canto *sm* spell, charm, enchantment; (*asta*) auction; **come per ~** as if by magic; **ti sta d'~!** (*vestito etc*) it really suits you!; **mettere all'~** to put up for auction

incanu'tire *vi* to go white

inca'pace [inka'patʃe] *ag* incapable

incapacità [inkapatʃi'ta] *sf* inability; (*Dir*) incapacity; **~ d'intendere e di volere** diminished responsibility

incapo'nirsi *vr* to be stubborn, be determined

incap'pare *vi*: **~ in qc/qn** (*anche fig*) to run into sth/sb

incappucci'are [inkapput'tʃare] *vt* to put a hood on; **incappucciarsi** *vr* (*persona*) to put on a hood

incapricci'arsi [inkaprit'tʃarsi] *vr*: **~ di** to take a fancy to *o* for

incapsu'lare *vt* (*dente*) to crown

incarce'rare [inkartʃe'rare] *vt* to imprison

incari'care *vt*: **~ qn di fare** to give sb the responsibility of doing; **incaricarsi** *vr*: **incaricarsi di** to take care *o* charge of

incari'cato, -a *ag*: **~ (di)** in charge (of), responsible (for) ■ *sm/f* delegate, representative; **docente ~** (*di università*) lecturer without tenure; **~ d'affari** (*Pol*) chargé d'affaires

in'carico, -chi *sm* task, job; (*Ins*) temporary post

incar'nare *vt* to embody; **incarnarsi** *vr* to be embodied; (*Rel*) to become incarnate

incarnazi'one [inkarnat'tsjone] *sf* incarnation; (*fig*) embodiment

incarta'mento *sm* dossier, file

incartapeco'rito, -a *ag* (*pelle*) wizened, shrivelled (*Brit*), shriveled (*US*)

incar'tare *vt* to wrap (in paper)

incasel'lare *vt* (*posta*) to sort; (*fig: nozioni*) to pigeonhole

incas'sare *vt* (*merce*) to pack (in cases); (*gemma: incastonare*) to set; (*Econ: riscuotere*) to collect; (*Pugilato: colpi*) to take, stand up to

in'casso *sm* cashing, encashment; (*introito*) takings *pl*

incasto'nare *vt* to set

incastona'tura *sf* setting

incas'trare *vt* to fit in, insert; (*fig: intrappolare*) to catch; **incastrarsi** *vr* (*combaciare*) to fit together; (*restare bloccato*) to become stuck

in'castro *sm* slot, groove; (*punto di unione*) joint; **gioco a ~** interlocking puzzle

incate'nare *vt* to chain up

incatra'mare *vt* to tar

incatti'vire *vt* to make wicked; **incattivirsi** *vr* to turn nasty

in'cauto, -a *ag* imprudent, rash

inca'vare *vt* to hollow out

inca'vato, -a *ag* hollow; (*occhi*) sunken

in'cavo *sm* hollow; (*solco*) groove

incavo'larsi *vr* (*fam*) to lose one's temper, get annoyed

incaz'zarsi [inkat'tsarsi] *vr* (*fam!*) to get steamed up

in'cedere [in'tʃɛdere] *vi* (*poetico*) to advance solemnly ■ *sm* solemn gait

incendi'are [intʃen'djare] *vt* to set fire to; **incendiarsi** *vr* to catch fire, burst into flames

incendi'ario, -a [intʃen'djarjo] *ag* incendiary ■ *sm/f* arsonist

in'cendio [in'tʃɛndjo] *sm* fire

incene'rire [intʃene'rire] *vt* to burn to ashes, incinerate; (*cadavere*) to cremate; **incenerirsi** *vr* to be burnt to ashes

inceneri'tore [intʃeneri'tore] *sm* incinerator

in'censo [in'tʃɛnso] *sm* incense

incensu'rato, -a [intʃensu'rato] *ag* (*Dir*): **essere ~** to have a clean record

incenti'vare [intʃenti'vare] *vt* (*produzione, vendite*) to boost; (*persona*) to motivate

incen'tivo [intʃen'tivo] *sm* incentive

incen'trarsi [intʃen'trarsi] *vr*: **~ su** (*fig*) to centre (*Brit*) *o* center (*US*) on

incep'pare [intʃep'pare] *vt* to obstruct, hamper; **incepparsi** *vr* to jam

ince'rata [intʃe'rata] *sf* (*tela*) tarpaulin; (*impermeabile*) oilskins *pl*

incer'tezza [intʃer'tettsa] *sf* uncertainty

in'certo, -a [in'tʃɛrto] *ag* uncertain; (*irresoluto*) undecided, hesitating ■ *sm* uncertainty; **gli incerti del mestiere** the risks of the job

incespi'care [intʃespi'kare] *vi*: **~ (in qc)** to trip (over sth)

inces'sante [intʃes'sante] *ag* incessant

in'cesto [in'tʃɛsto] *sm* incest

incestu'oso, -a [intʃestu'oso] *ag* incestuous

in'cetta [in'tʃetta] *sf* buying up; **fare ~ di qc** to buy up sth

inchi'esta [in'kjɛsta] *sf* investigation, inquiry

inchi'nare [inki'nare] *vt* to bow; **inchinarsi** *vr* to bend down; (*per riverenza*) to bow; (: *donna*) to curtsy
in'chino [in'kino] *sm* bow; curtsy
inchio'dare [inkjo'dare] *vt* to nail (down); **~ la macchina** (*Aut*) to jam on the brakes
inchi'ostro [in'kjɔstro] *sm* ink; **~ simpatico** invisible ink
inciam'pare [intʃam'pare] *vi* to trip, stumble
inci'ampo [in'tʃampo] *sm* obstacle; **essere d'~ a qn** (*fig*) to be in sb's way
inciden'tale [intʃiden'tale] *ag* incidental
incidental'mente [intʃidental'mente] *av* (*per caso*) by chance; (*per inciso*) incidentally, by the way
inci'dente [intʃi'dɛnte] *sm* accident; (*episodio*) incident; **e con questo l'~ è chiuso** and that is the end of the matter; **~ d'auto** car accident; **~ diplomatico** diplomatic incident
inci'denza [intʃi'dɛntsa] *sf* incidence; **avere una forte ~ su qc** to affect sth greatly
in'cidere [in'tʃidere] *vi*: **~ su** to bear upon, affect ■ *vt* (*tagliare incavando*) to cut into; (*Arte*) to engrave; to etch; (*canzone*) to record
in'cinta [in'tʃinta] *ag f* pregnant
incipi'ente [intʃi'pjɛnte] *ag* incipient
incipri'are [intʃi'prjare] *vt* to powder
in'circa [in'tʃirka] *av*: **all'~** more or less, very nearly
in'cisi *etc* [in'tʃizi] *vb vedi* **incidere**
incisi'one [intʃi'zjone] *sf* cut; (*disegno*) engraving; etching; (*registrazione*) recording; (*Med*) incision
inci'sivo, -a [intʃi'zivo] *ag* incisive; (*Anat*): **(dente) ~** incisor
in'ciso, -a [in'tʃizo] *pp di* **incidere** ■ *sm*: **per ~** incidentally, by the way
inci'sore [intʃi'zore] *sm* (*Arte*) engraver
incita'mento [intʃita'mento] *sm* incitement
inci'tare [intʃi'tare] *vt* to incite
inci'vile [intʃi'vile] *ag* uncivilized; (*villano*) impolite
incivi'lire [intʃivi'lire] *vt* to civilize
inciviltà [intʃivil'ta] *sf* (*di popolazione*) barbarism; (*fig: di trattamento*) barbarity; (: *maleducazione*) incivility, rudeness
incl. *abbr* (= *incluso*) encl.
incle'mente *ag* (*giudice, sentenza*) severe, harsh; (*fig: clima*) harsh; (: *tempo*) inclement
incle'menza [inkle'mɛntsa] *sf* severity; harshness; inclemency
incli'nabile *ag* (*schienale*) reclinable
incli'nare *vt* to tilt ■ *vi* (*fig*): **~ a qc/a fare** to incline towards sth/doing; to tend towards sth/to do; **inclinarsi** *vr* (*barca*) to list; (*aereo*) to bank
incli'nato, -a *ag* sloping
inclinazi'one [inklinat'tsjone] *sf* slope; (*fig*) inclination, tendency
in'cline *ag*: **~ a** inclined to
in'cludere *vt* to include; (*accludere*) to enclose
inclusi'one *sf* inclusion
inclu'sivo, -a *ag*: **~ di** inclusive of
in'cluso, -a *pp di* **includere** ■ *ag* included; enclosed
incoe'rente *ag* incoherent; (*contraddittorio*) inconsistent
incoe'renza [inkoe'rɛntsa] *sf* incoherence; inconsistency
in'cognito, -a [in'kɔɲɲito] *ag* unknown ■ *sm*: **in ~** incognito ■ *sf* (*Mat, fig*) unknown quantity
incol'lare *vt* to glue, gum; (*unire con colla*) to stick together; **~ gli occhi addosso a qn** (*fig*) to fix one's eyes on sb
incolla'tura *sf* (*Ippica*): **vincere/perdere di un'~** to win/lose by a head
incolon'nare *vt* to draw up in columns
inco'lore *ag* colourless (*Brit*), colorless (*US*)
incol'pare *vt*: **~ qn di** to charge sb with
in'colto, -a *ag* (*terreno*) uncultivated; (*trascurato: capelli*) neglected; (*persona*) uneducated
in'colume *ag* safe and sound, unhurt
incolumità *sf* safety
incom'bente *ag* (*pericolo*) imminent, impending
incom'benza [inkom'bɛntsa] *sf* duty, task
in'combere *vi* (*sovrastare minacciando*): **~ su** to threaten, hang over
incominci'are [inkomin'tʃare] *vi, vt* to begin, start
incomo'dare *vt* to trouble, inconvenience; **incomodarsi** *vr* to put o.s. out
in'comodo, -a *ag* uncomfortable; (*inopportuno*) inconvenient ■ *sm* inconvenience, bother
incompa'rabile *ag* incomparable
incompa'tibile *ag* incompatible
incompatibilità *sf* incompatibility; **~ di carattere** (mutual) incompatibility
incompe'tente *ag* incompetent
incompe'tenza [inkompe'tɛntsa] *sf* incompetence
incompi'uto, -a *ag* unfinished, incomplete
incom'pleto, -a *ag* incomplete
incompren'sibile *ag* incomprehensible
incomprensi'one *sf* incomprehension
incom'preso, -a *ag* not understood; misunderstood
inconce'pibile [inkontʃe'pibile] *ag* inconceivable
inconcili'abile [inkontʃi'ljabile] *ag* irreconcilable

inconclu'dente *ag* inconclusive; (*persona*) ineffectual
incondizio'nato, -a [inkondittsjo'nato] *ag* unconditional
inconfes'sabile *ag* (*pensiero, peccato*) unmentionable
inconfon'dibile *ag* unmistakable
inconfu'tabile *ag* irrefutable
incongru'ente *ag* inconsistent
incongru'enza [inkongru'ɛntsa] *sf* inconsistency
in'congruo, -a *ag* incongruous
inconsa'pevole *ag*: **~ di** unaware of, ignorant of
inconsapevo'lezza [inkonsapevo'lettsa] *sf* ignorance, lack of awareness
in'conscio, -a, sci, sce [in'kɔnʃo] *ag* unconscious ■ *sm* (*Psic*): **l'~** the unconscious
inconsis'tente *ag* (*patrimonio*) insubstantial; (*dubbio*) unfounded; (*ragionamento, prove*) tenuous, flimsy
inconsis'tenza [inkonsis'tɛntsa] *sf* insubstantial nature; lack of foundation; flimsiness
inconso'labile *ag* inconsolable
inconsu'eto, -a *ag* unusual
incon'sulto, -a *ag* rash
inconte'nibile *ag* (*rabbia*) uncontrollable; (*entusiasmo*) irrepressible
inconten'tabile *ag* (*desiderio, avidità*) insatiable; (*persona: capriccioso*) hard to please, very demanding
incontes'tabile *ag* incontrovertible, indisputable
incontes'tato, -a *ag* undisputed
inconti'nenza [inkonti'nɛntsa] *sf* incontinence
incon'trare *vt* to meet; (*difficoltà*) to meet with; **incontrarsi** *vr* to meet
incon'trario *av*: **all'~** (*sottosopra*) upside down; (*alla rovescia*) back to front; (*all'indietro*) backwards; (*nel senso contrario*) the other way round
incontras'tabile *ag* incontrovertible, indisputable
incontras'tato, -a *ag* (*successo, vittoria, verità*) uncontested, undisputed
in'contro *av*: **~ a** (*verso*) towards ■ *sm* meeting; (*Sport*) match; meeting; (*fortuito*) encounter; **venire ~ a** (*richieste, esigenze*) to comply with; **~ di calcio** football match (*Brit*), soccer game (*US*)
incontrol'labile *ag* uncontrollable
inconveni'ente *sm* drawback, snag
incoraggia'mento [inkoraddʒa'mento] *sm* encouragement; **premio d'~** consolation prize
incoraggi'are [inkorad'dʒare] *vt* to encourage
incor'nare *vt* to gore
incornici'are [inkorni'tʃare] *vt* to frame
incoro'nare *vt* to crown
incoronazi'one [inkoronat'tsjone] *sf* coronation
incorpo'rare *vt* to incorporate; (*fig: annettere*) to annex
incorreg'gibile [inkorred'dʒibile] *ag* incorrigible
in'correre *vi*: **~ in** to meet with, run into
incorrut'tibile *ag* incorruptible
in'corso, -a *pp di* **incorrere**
incosci'ente [inkoʃ'ʃɛnte] *ag* (*inconscio*) unconscious; (*irresponsabile*) reckless, thoughtless
incosci'enza [inkoʃ'ʃɛntsa] *sf* unconsciousness; recklessness, thoughtlessness
incos'tante *ag* (*studente, impiegato*) inconsistent; (*carattere*) fickle, inconstant; (*rendimento*) sporadic
incos'tanza [inkos'tantsa] *sf* inconstancy, fickleness
incostituzio'nale [inkostituttsjo'nale] *ag* unconstitutional
incre'dibile *ag* incredible, unbelievable
incredulità *sf* incredulity
in'credulo, -a *ag* incredulous, disbelieving
incremen'tare *vt* to increase; (*dar sviluppo a*) to promote
incre'mento *sm* (*sviluppo*) development; (*aumento numerico*) increase, growth
incresci'oso, -a [inkreʃ'ʃoso] *ag* (*spiacevole*) unpleasant; regrettable
incres'pare *vt* (*capelli*) to curl; (*acque*) to ripple; **incresparsi** *vr* (*vedi vt*) to curl; to ripple
incrimi'nare *vt* (*Dir*) to charge
incriminazi'one [inkriminat'tsjone] *sf* (*atto d'accusa*) indictment, charge
incri'nare *vt* to crack; (*fig: rapporti, amicizia*) to cause to deteriorate; **incrinarsi** *vr* to crack; to deteriorate
incrina'tura *sf* crack; (*fig*) rift
incroci'are [inkro'tʃare] *vt* to cross; (*incontrare*) to meet ■ *vi* (*Naut, Aer*) to cruise; **incrociarsi** *vr* (*strade*) to cross, intersect; (*persone, veicoli*) to pass each other; **~ le braccia/le gambe** to fold one's arms/cross one's legs
incrocia'tore [inkrotʃa'tore] *sm* cruiser
in'crocio [in'krotʃo] *sm* (*anche Ferr*) crossing; (*di strade*) crossroads
incrol'labile *ag* (*fede*) unshakeable, firm
incros'tare *vt* to encrust; **incrostarsi** *vr*: **incrostarsi di** to become encrusted with

incrostazi'one [inkrostat'tsjone] *sf* encrustation; (*di calcare*) scale; (*nelle tubature*) fur (*Brit*), scale
incru'ento, -a *ag* (*battaglia*) without bloodshed, bloodless
incuba'trice [inkuba'tritʃe] *sf* incubator
incubazi'one [inkubat'tsjone] *sf* incubation
'incubo *sm* nightmare
in'cudine *sf* anvil; **trovarsi** *o* **essere tra l'~ e il martello** (*fig*) to be between the devil and the deep blue sea
incul'care *vt*: **~ qc in** to inculcate sth into, instill sth into
incune'are *vt* to wedge
incu'pire *vt* (*rendere scuro*) to darken; (*fig*: *intristire*) to fill with gloom ▪ *vi* (*vedi vt*) to darken; to become gloomy
incu'rabile *ag* incurable
incu'rante *ag*: **~ (di)** heedless (of), careless (of)
in'curia *sf* negligence
incurio'sire *vt* to make curious; **incuriosirsi** *vr* to become curious
incursi'one *sf* raid
incur'vare *vt*, **incur'varsi** *vr* to bend, curve
in'cusso, -a *pp di* **incutere**
incusto'dito, -a *ag* unguarded, unattended; **passaggio a livello ~** unmanned level crossing
in'cutere *vt* to arouse; **~ timore/rispetto a qn** to strike fear into sb/command sb's respect
'indaco *sm* indigo
indaffa'rato, -a *ag* busy
inda'gare *vt* to investigate
indaga'tore, -'trice *ag* (*sguardo, domanda*) searching; (*mente*) inquiring
in'dagine [in'dadʒine] *sf* investigation, inquiry; (*ricerca*) research, study; **~ di mercato** market survey
indebita'mente *av* (*immeritatamente*) undeservedly; (*erroneamente*) wrongfully
indebi'tare *vt*: **~ qn** to get sb into debt; **indebitarsi** *vr* to run *o* get into debt
in'debito, -a *ag* undeserved; wrongful
indeboli'mento *sm* weakening; (*debolezza*) weakness
indebo'lire *vt, vi* (*anche*: **indebolirsi**) to weaken
inde'cente [inde'tʃɛnte] *ag* indecent
inde'cenza [inde'tʃɛntsa] *sf* indecency; **è un'~!** (*vergogna*) it's scandalous!, it's a disgrace!
indeci'frabile [indetʃi'frabile] *ag* indecipherable
indecisi'one [indetʃi'zjone] *sf* indecisiveness; indecision
inde'ciso, -a [inde'tʃizo] *ag* indecisive; (*irresoluto*) undecided
indeco'roso, -a *ag* (*comportamento*) indecorous, unseemly
inde'fesso, -a *ag* untiring, indefatigable
indefi'nibile *ag* indefinable
indefi'nito, -a *ag* (*anche Ling*) indefinite; (*impreciso, non determinato*) undefined
indefor'mabile *ag* crushproof
in'degno, -a [in'deɲɲo] *ag* (*atto*) shameful; (*persona*) unworthy
inde'lebile *ag* indelible
indelica'tezza [indelika'tettsa] *sf* tactlessness
indeli'cato, -a *ag* (*domanda*) indiscreet, tactless
indemoni'ato, -a *ag* possessed (by the devil)
in'denne *ag* unhurt, uninjured
indennità *sf inv* (*rimborso*: *di spese*) allowance; (: *di perdita*) compensation, indemnity; **~ di contingenza** cost-of-living allowance; **~ di fine rapporto** severance payment (*on retirement, redundancy or when taking up other employment*); **~ di trasferta** travel expenses *pl*
indenniz'zare [indennid'dzare] *vt* to compensate
inden'nizzo [inden'niddzo] *sm* (*somma*) compensation, indemnity
indero'gabile *ag* binding
indescri'vibile *ag* indescribable
indeside'rabile *ag* undesirable
indeside'rato, -a *ag* unwanted
indetermina'tezza [indetermina'tettsa] *sf* vagueness
indetermina'tivo, -a *ag* (*Ling*) indefinite
indetermi'nato, -a *ag* indefinite, indeterminate
in'detto, -a *pp di* **indire**
'India *sf*: **l'~** India; **le Indie occidentali** the West Indies
indi'ano, -a *ag* Indian ▪ *sm/f* (*d'India*) Indian; (*d'America*) Red Indian; **l'Oceano I~** the Indian Ocean
indiavo'lato, -a *ag* possessed (by the devil); (*vivace, violento*) wild
indi'care *vt* (*mostrare*) to show, indicate; (: *col dito*) to point to, point out; (*consigliare*) to suggest, recommend
indica'tivo, -a *ag* indicative ▪ *sm* (*Ling*) indicative (mood)
indi'cato, -a *ag* (*consigliato*) advisable; (*adatto*): **~ per** suitable for, appropriate for
indica'tore, -'trice *ag* indicating ▪ *sm* (*elenco*) guide; directory; (*Tecn*) gauge; indicator; **cartello ~** sign; **~ della benzina** petrol (*Brit*) *o* gas (*US*) gauge, fuel gauge; **~ di velocità** (*Aut*) speedometer; (*Aer*) airspeed indicator

indicazi'one [indikat'tsjone] *sf* indication; (*informazione*) piece of information; **indicazioni per l'uso** instructions for use
'indice ['inditʃe] *sm* (*Anat: dito*) index finger, forefinger; (*lancetta*) needle, pointer; (*fig: indizio*) sign; (*Tecn, Mat, nei libri*) index; **~ azionario** share index; **~ di gradimento** (*Radio, TV*) popularity rating; **~ dei prezzi al consumo** ≈ retail price index
indicherò *etc* [indike'rɔ] *vb vedi* **indicare**
indi'cibile [indi'tʃibile] *ag* inexpressible
indiciz'zare [inditʃid'dzare] *vt*: **~ al costo della vita** to index-link (*Brit*), index (*US*)
indiciz'zato, -a [inditʃid'dzato] *ag* (*polizza, salario etc*) index-linked (*Brit*), indexed (*US*)
indicizzazi'one [inditʃiddzat'tsjone] *sf* indexing
indietreggi'are [indjetred'dʒare] *vi* to draw back, retreat
indi'etro *av* back; (*guardare*) behind, back; (*andare, cadere: anche:* **all'indietro**) backwards; **rimanere ~** to be left behind; **essere ~** (*col lavoro*) to be behind; (*orologio*) to be slow; **rimandare qc ~** to send sth back; **non vado né avanti né ~** (*fig*) I'm not getting anywhere, I'm getting nowhere
indi'feso, -a *ag* (*città, confine*) undefended; (*persona*) defenceless (*Brit*), defenseless (*US*), helpless
indiffe'rente *ag* indifferent ■ *sm*: **fare l'~** to pretend to be indifferent, be *o* act casual; (*fingere di non vedere o sentire*) to pretend not to notice
indiffe'renza [indiffe'rɛntsa] *sf* indifference
in'digeno, -a [in'didʒeno] *ag* indigenous, native ■ *sm/f* native
indi'gente [indi'dʒɛnte] *ag* poverty-stricken, destitute
indi'genza [indi'dʒɛntsa] *sf* extreme poverty
indigesti'one [indidʒes'tjone] *sf* indigestion
indi'gesto, -a [indi'dʒɛsto] *ag* indigestible
indi'gnare [indiɲ'ɲare] *vt* to fill with indignation; **indignarsi** *vr* to be (*o* get) indignant
indignazi'one [indiɲɲat'tsjone] *sf* indignation
indimenti'cabile *ag* unforgettable
'indio, -a *ag, sm/f* (South American) Indian
indipen'dente *ag* independent
indipendente'mente *av* independently; **~ dal fatto che gli piaccia o meno, verrà!** he's coming, whether he likes it or not!
indipen'denza [indipen'dɛntsa] *sf* independence
in'dire *vt* (*concorso*) to announce; (*elezioni*) to call
indi'retto, -a *ag* indirect
indiriz'zare [indirit'tsare] *vt* (*dirigere*) to direct; (*mandare*) to send; (*lettera*) to address; **~ la parola a qn** to address sb
indiriz'zario [indirit'tsarjo] *sm* mailing list
indi'rizzo [indi'rittso] *sm* address; (*direzione*) direction; (*avvio*) trend, course; **~ Internet** web address
indisci'plina [indiʃʃi'plina] *sf* indiscipline
indiscipli'nato, -a [indiʃʃipli'nato] *ag* undisciplined, unruly
indis'creto, -a *ag* indiscreet
indiscrezi'one [indiskret'tsjone] *sf* indiscretion
indiscrimi'nato, -a *ag* indiscriminate
indis'cusso, -a *ag* unquestioned
indiscu'tibile *ag* indisputable, unquestionable
indispen'sabile *ag* indispensable, essential
indispet'tire *vt* to irritate, annoy ■ *vi* (*anche:* **indispettirsi**) to get irritated *o* annoyed
indispo'nente *ag* irritating, annoying
indis'porre *vt* to antagonize
indisposizi'one [indispozit'tsjone] *sf* (slight) indisposition
indis'posto, -a *pp di* **indisporre** ■ *ag* indisposed, unwell
indisso'lubile *ag* indissoluble
indissolubil'mente *av* indissolubly
indistinta'mente *av* (*senza distinzioni*) indiscriminately, without exception; (*in modo indefinito: vedere, sentire*) vaguely, faintly
indis'tinto, -a *ag* indistinct
indistrut'tibile *ag* indestructible
in'divia *sf* endive
individu'ale *ag* individual
individua'lismo *sm* individualism
individua'lista, -i, e *sm/f* individualist
individualità *sf* individuality
individual'mente *av* individually
individu'are *vt* (*dar forma distinta a*) to characterize; (*determinare*) to locate; (*riconoscere*) to single out
indi'viduo *sm* individual
indivi'sibile *ag* indivisible; **quei due sono indivisibili** (*fig*) those two are inseparable
indizi'are [indit'tsjare] *vt*: **~ qn di qc** to cast suspicion on sb for sth
indizi'ato, -a [indit'tsjato] *ag* suspected ■ *sm/f* suspect
in'dizio [in'dittsjo] *sm* (*segno*) sign, indication; (*Polizia*) clue; (*Dir*) piece of evidence
Indo'cina [indo'tʃina] *sf*: **l'~** Indochina
'indole *sf* nature, character
indo'lente *ag* indolent
indo'lenza [indo'lɛntsa] *sf* indolence
indolen'zire [indolen'tsire] *vt* (*gambe, braccia etc*) to make stiff, cause to ache; (*: intorpidire*)

to numb; **indolenzirsi** *vr* to become stiff; to go numb
indolen'zito, -a [indolen'tsito] *ag* stiff, aching; (*intorpidito*) numb
indo'lore *ag* (*anche fig*) painless
indo'mani *sm*: **l'~** the next day, the following day
Indo'nesia *sf*: **l'~** Indonesia
indonesi'ano, -a *ag, sm/f, sm* Indonesian
indo'rare *vt* (*rivestire in oro*) to gild; (*Cuc*) to dip in egg yolk; **~ la pillola** (*fig*) to sugar the pill
indos'sare *vt* (*mettere indosso*) to put on; (*avere indosso*) to have on
indossa'tore, -'trice *sm/f* model
in'dotto, -a *pp di* **indurre**
indottri'nare *vt* to indoctrinate
indovi'nare *vt* (*scoprire*) to guess; (*immaginare*) to imagine, guess; (*il futuro*) to foretell; **tirare a ~** to make a shot in the dark
indovi'nato, -a *ag* successful; (*scelta*) inspired
indovi'nello *sm* riddle
indo'vino, -a *sm/f* fortuneteller
indù *ag, sm/f* Hindu
indubbia'mente *av* undoubtedly
in'dubbio, -a *ag* certain, undoubted
in'duco *etc vb vedi* **indurre**
indugi'are [indu'dʒare] *vi* to take one's time, delay
in'dugio [in'dudʒo] *sm* (*ritardo*) delay; **senza ~** without delay
indul'gente [indul'dʒɛnte] *ag* indulgent; (*giudice*) lenient
indul'genza [indul'dʒɛntsa] *sf* indulgence; leniency
in'dulgere [in'duldʒere] *vi*: **~ a** (*accondiscendere*) to comply with; (*abbandonarsi*) to indulge in
in'dulto, -a *pp di* **indulgere** ■ *sm* (*Dir*) pardon
indu'mento *sm* article of clothing, garment; **indumenti** *smpl* (*vestiti*) clothes; **indumenti intimi** underwear *sg*
induri'mento *sm* hardening
indu'rire *vt* to harden ■ *vi* (*anche*: **indurirsi**) to harden, become hard
in'durre *vt*: **~ qn a fare qc** to induce *o* persuade sb to do sth; **~ qn in errore** to mislead sb; **~ in tentazione** to lead into temptation
in'dussi *etc vb vedi* **indurre**
in'dustria *sf* industry; **la piccola/grande ~** small/big business
industri'ale *ag* industrial ■ *sm* industrialist
industrializ'zare [industrjalid'dzare] *vt* to industrialize
industrializzazi'one [industrjaliddzat'tsjone] *sf* industrialization
industri'arsi *vr* to do one's best, try hard
industri'oso, -a *ag* industrious, hard-working
induzi'one [indut'tsjone] *sf* induction
inebe'tito, -a *ag* dazed, stunned
inebri'are *vt* (*anche fig*) to intoxicate; **inebriarsi** *vr* to become intoxicated
inecce'pibile [inettʃe'pibile] *ag* unexceptionable
i'nedia *sf* starvation
i'nedito, -a *ag* unpublished
inef'fabile *ag* ineffable
ineffi'cace [ineffi'katʃe] *ag* ineffective
ineffi'cacia [ineffi'katʃa] *sf* inefficacy, ineffectiveness
inefficī'ente [ineffi'tʃɛnte] *ag* inefficient
inefficī'enza [ineffi'tʃɛntsa] *sf* inefficiency
ineguagli'abile [inegwaʎ'ʎabile] *ag* incomparable, matchless
ineguagli'anza [inegwaʎ'ʎantsa] *sf* (*sociale*) inequality; (*di superficie, livello*) unevenness
inegu'ale *ag* unequal; (*irregolare*) uneven
inelut'tabile *ag* inescapable
ineluttabilità *sf* inescapability
inenar'rabile *ag* unutterable
inequivo'cabile *ag* unequivocal
ine'rente *ag*: **~ a** concerning, regarding
i'nerme *ag* unarmed, defenceless (*Brit*), defenseless (*US*)
inerpi'carsi *vr*: **~ (su)** to clamber (up)
i'nerte *ag* inert; (*inattivo*) indolent, sluggish
i'nerzia [i'nɛrtsja] *sf* inertia; indolence, sluggishness
inesat'tezza [inezat'tettsa] *sf* inaccuracy
ine'satto, -a *ag* (*impreciso*) inaccurate, inexact; (*erroneo*) incorrect; (*Amm: non riscosso*) uncollected
inesau'ribile *ag* inexhaustible
inesis'tente *ag* non-existent
ineso'rabile *ag* inexorable, relentless
inesorabil'mente *av* inexorably
inesperi'enza [inespe'rjɛntsa] *sf* inexperience
ines'perto, -a *ag* inexperienced
inespli'cabile *ag* inexplicable
inesplo'rato, -a *ag* unexplored
ines'ploso, -a *ag* unexploded
inespres'sivo, -a *ag* (*viso*) expressionless, inexpressive
ines'presso, -a *ag* unexpressed
inespri'mibile *ag* inexpressible
inespu'gnabile [inespuɲ'ɲabile] *ag* (*fortezza, torre etc*) impregnable
ineste'tismo *sm* beauty problem
inesti'mabile *ag* inestimable; (*valore*) incalculable

inestir'pabile *ag* ineradicable
inestri'cabile *ag* (*anche fig*) impenetrable
inetti'tudine *sf* ineptitude
i'netto, -a *ag* (*incapace*) inept; (*che non ha attitudine*): **~ (a)** unsuited (to)
ine'vaso, -a *ag* (*ordine, corrispondenza*) outstanding
inevi'tabile *ag* inevitable
inevitabil'mente *av* inevitably
i'nezia [i'nɛttsja] *sf* trifle, thing of no importance
infagot'tare *vt* to bundle up, wrap up; **infagottarsi** *vr* to wrap up
infal'libile *ag* infallible
infallibilità *sf* infallibility
infa'mante *ag* (*accusa*) defamatory, slanderous
infa'mare *vt* to defame
in'fame *ag* infamous; (*fig: cosa, compito*) awful, dreadful
in'famia *sf* infamy
infan'gare *vt* (*sporcare*) to cover with mud; (*nome, reputazione*) to sully; **infangarsi** *vr* to get covered in mud; to be sullied
infan'tile *ag* child *cpd*, childlike; (*adulto, azione*) childish; **letteratura ~** children's books *pl*
in'fanzia [in'fantsja] *sf* childhood; (*bambini*) children *pl*; **prima ~** babyhood, infancy
infari'nare *vt* to cover with (*o* sprinkle with *o* dip in) flour; **~ di zucchero** to sprinkle with sugar
infarina'tura *sf* (*fig*) smattering
in'farto *sm* (*Med*): **~ (cardiaco)** coronary
infasti'dire *vt* to annoy, irritate; **infastidirsi** *vr* to get annoyed *o* irritated
infati'cabile *ag* tireless, untiring
in'fatti *cong* as a matter of fact, in fact, actually
infatu'arsi *vr*: **~ di** *o* **per** to become infatuated with, fall for
infatuazi'one [infatuat'tsjone] *sf* infatuation
in'fausto, -a *ag* unpropitious, unfavourable (*Brit*), unfavorable (*US*)
infecondità *sf* infertility
infe'condo, -a *ag* infertile
infe'dele *ag* unfaithful
infedeltà *sf* infidelity
infe'lice [infe'litʃe] *ag* unhappy; (*sfortunato*) unlucky, unfortunate; (*inopportuno*) inopportune, ill-timed; (*mal riuscito: lavoro*) bad, poor
infelicità [infelitʃi'ta] *sf* unhappiness
infel'trire *vi*, **infeltrirsi** *vr* (*lana*) to become matted
infe'renza [infe'rɛntsa] *sf* inference
inferi'ore *ag* lower; (*per intelligenza, qualità*) inferior ■ *sm/f* inferior; **~ a** (*numero, quantità*) less *o* smaller than; (*meno buono*) inferior to; **~ alla media** below average
inferiorità *sf* inferiority
infe'rire *vt* (*dedurre*) to infer, deduce
inferme'ria *sf* infirmary; (*di scuola, nave*) sick bay
infermi'ere, -a *sm/f* nurse
infermità *sf inv* illness; infirmity; **~ di mente** mental illness
in'fermo, -a *ag* (*ammalato*) ill; (*debole*) infirm; **~ di mente** mentally ill
infer'nale *ag* infernal; (*proposito, complotto*) diabolical; **un tempo ~** (*fam*) hellish weather
in'ferno *sm* hell; **soffrire le pene dell'~** (*fig*) to go through hell
infero'cire [infero'tʃire] *vt* to make fierce ■ *vi*, **inferocirsi** *vr* to become fierce
inferri'ata *sf* grating
infervo'rare *vt* to arouse enthusiasm in; **infervorarsi** *vr* to get excited, get carried away
infes'tare *vt* to infest
infet'tare *vt* to infect; **infettarsi** *vr* to become infected
infet'tivo, -a *ag* infectious
in'fetto, -a *ag* infected; (*acque*) polluted, contaminated
infezi'one [infet'tsjone] *sf* infection
infiac'chire [infjak'kire] *vt* to weaken ■ *vi* (*anche*: **infiacchirsi**) to grow weak
infiam'mabile *ag* inflammable
infiam'mare *vt* to set alight; (*fig, Med*) to inflame; **infiammarsi** *vr* to catch fire; (*Med*) to become inflamed; (*fig*): **infiammarsi di** to be fired with
infiammazi'one [infjammat'tsjone] *sf* (*Med*) inflammation
infias'care *vt* to bottle
infici'are [infi'tʃare] *vt* (*Dir: atto, dichiarazione*) to challenge
in'fido, -a *ag* unreliable, treacherous
infie'rire *vi*: **~ su** (*fisicamente*) to attack furiously; (*verbalmente*) to rage at; (*epidemia*) to rage over
in'figgere [in'fiddʒere] *vt*: **~ qc in** to thrust *o* drive sth into
infi'lare *vt* (*ago*) to thread; (*mettere: chiave*) to insert; (*: vestito*) to slip *o* put on; (*strada*) to turn into, take; **infilarsi** *vr*: **infilarsi in** to slip into; (*indossare*) to slip on; **~ un anello al dito** to slip a ring on one's finger; **~ l'uscio** to slip in; to slip out; **infilarsi la giacca** to put on one's jacket
infil'trarsi *vr* to penetrate, seep through; (*Mil*)

i

to infiltrate
infil'trato, -a *sm/f* infiltrator
infiltrazi'one [infiltrat'tsjone] *sf* infiltration
infil'zare [infil'tsare] *vt* (*infilare*) to string together; (*trafiggere*) to pierce
'infimo, -a *ag* lowest; **un albergo di ~ ordine** a third-rate hotel
in'fine *av* finally; (*insomma*) in short
infin'gardo, -a *ag* lazy ■ *sm/f* slacker
infinità *sf* infinity; (*in quantità*): **un'~ di** an infinite number of
infinitesi'male *ag* infinitesimal
infi'nito, -a *ag* infinite; (*Ling*) infinitive ■ *sm* infinity; (*Ling*) infinitive; **all'~** (*senza fine*) endlessly; (*Ling*) in the infinitive
infinocchi'are [infinok'kjare] *vt* (*fam*) to hoodwink
infiore'scenza [infjoreʃ'ʃɛntsa] *sf* inflorescence
infir'mare *vt* (*Dir*) to invalidate
infischi'arsi [infis'kjarsi] *vr*: **~ di** not to care about
in'fisso, -a *pp di* **infiggere** ■ *sm* fixture; (*di porta, finestra*) frame
infit'tire *vt, vi* (*anche*: **infittirsi**) to thicken
inflazio'nare [inflattsjo'nare] *vt* to inflate
inflazi'one [inflat'tsjone] *sf* inflation
inflazio'nistico, -a, ci, che [inflattsjo'nistiko] *ag* inflationary
infles'sibile *ag* inflexible; (*ferreo*) unyielding
inflessi'one *sf* inflexion
in'fliggere [in'fliddʒere] *vt* to inflict
in'flissi *etc vb vedi* **infliggere**
in'flitto, -a *pp di* **infliggere**
influ'ente *ag* influential
influ'enza [influ'ɛntsa] *sf* influence; (*Med*) influenza, flu; **~ aviaria** bird flu; **~ suina** swine flu
influen'zare [influen'tsare] *vt* to influence, have an influence on
influ'ire *vi*: **~ su** to influence
in'flusso *sm* influence
INFN *sigla m* = **Istituto Nazionale di Fisica Nucleare**
info'cato, -a *ag* = **infuocato**
info'gnarsi [infoɲ'ɲarsi] *vr* (*fam*) to get into a mess; **~ in un mare di debiti** to be up to one's *o* the eyes in debt
infol'tire *vt, vi* to thicken
infon'dato, -a *ag* unfounded, groundless
in'fondere *vt*: **~ qc in qn** to instill sth in sb; **~ fiducia in qn** to inspire sb with confidence
infor'care *vt* to fork (up); (*bicicletta, cavallo*) to get on; (*occhiali*) to put on
infor'male *ag* informal
infor'mare *vt* to inform, tell; **informarsi** *vr*: **informarsi (di *o* su)** to inquire (about); **tenere informato qn** to keep sb informed
infor'matico, -a, ci, che *ag* (*settore*) computer *cpd* ■ *sf* computer science
informa'tivo, -a *ag* informative; **a titolo ~** for information only
informatiz'zare [informatid'dzare] *vt* to computerize
infor'mato, -a *ag* informed; **tenersi ~** to keep o.s. (well-)informed
informa'tore *sm* informer
informazi'one [informat'tsjone] *sf* piece of information; **informazioni** *sfpl* information *sg*; **chiedere un'~** to ask for (some) information; **~ di garanzia** (*Dir*) = **avviso di garanzia**
in'forme *ag* shapeless
informico'larsi, informico'lirsi *vr*: **mi si è informicolata una gamba** I've got pins and needles in my leg
infor'nare *vt* to put in the oven
infor'nata *sf* (*anche fig*) batch
infortu'narsi *vr* to injure o.s., have an accident
infortu'nato, -a *ag* injured, hurt ■ *sm/f* injured person
infor'tunio *sm* accident; **~ sul lavoro** industrial accident, accident at work
infortu'nistica *sf* study of (industrial) accidents
infos'sarsi *vr* (*terreno*) to sink; (*guance*) to become hollow
infos'sato, -a *ag* hollow; (*occhi*) deep-set; (*: per malattia*) sunken
infradici'are [infradi'tʃare] *vt* (*inzuppare*) to soak, drench; (*marcire*) to rot; **infradiciarsi** *vr* to get soaked, get drenched; to rot
infra'dito *sm inv* (*calzatura*) flip flop (*Brit*), thong (*US*)
in'frangere [in'frandʒere] *vt* to smash; (*fig: legge, patti*) to break; **infrangersi** *vr* to smash, break
infran'gibile [infran'dʒibile] *ag* unbreakable
in'franto, -a *pp di* **infrangere** ■ *ag* broken
infra'rosso, -a *ag, sm* infrared
infrasettima'nale *ag* midweek *cpd*
infrastrut'tura *sf* infrastructure
infrazi'one [infrat'tsjone] *sf*: **~ a** breaking of, violation of
infredda'tura *sf* slight cold
infreddo'lito, -a *ag* cold, chilled
infre'quente *ag* infrequent, rare
infrol'lire *vi*, **infrol'lirsi** *vr* (*selvaggina*) to become high
infruttu'oso, -a *ag* fruitless
infuo'cato, -a *ag* (*metallo*) red-hot; (*sabbia*) burning; (*fig: discorso*) heated, passionate
infu'ori *av* out; **all'~** outwards; **all'~ di** (*eccetto*) except, with the exception of

infuri'are *vi* to rage; **infuriarsi** *vr* to fly into a rage
infusi'one *sf* infusion
in'fuso, -a *pp di* **infondere** ■ *ag*: **scienza infusa** (*anche ironico*) innate knowledge ■ *sm* infusion; **~ di camomilla** camomile tea
Ing. *abbr* = **ingegnere**
ingabbi'are *vt* to (put in a) cage
ingaggi'are [ingad'dʒare] *vt* (*assumere con compenso*) to take on, hire; (*Sport*) to sign on; (*Mil*) to engage
in'gaggio [in'gaddʒo] *sm* hiring; signing on
ingagliar'dire [ingaʎʎar'dire] *vt* to strengthen, invigorate ■ *vi* (*anche*: **ingagliardirsi**) to grow stronger
ingan'nare *vt* to deceive; (*coniuge*) to be unfaithful to; (*fisco*) to cheat; (*eludere*) to dodge, elude; (*fig*: *tempo*) to while away ■ *vi* (*apparenza*) to be deceptive; **ingannarsi** *vr* to be mistaken, be wrong
inganna'tore, -'trice *ag* deceptive; (*persona*) deceitful
ingan'nevole *ag* deceptive
in'ganno *sm* deceit, deception; (*azione*) trick; (*menzogna, frode*) cheat, swindle; (*illusione*) illusion
ingarbugli'are [ingarbuʎ'ʎare] *vt* to tangle; (*fig*) to confuse, muddle; **ingarbugliarsi** *vr* to become confused *o* muddled
ingarbu'gliato, -a [ingarbuʎ'ʎato] *ag* tangled; confused, muddled
inge'gnarsi [indʒeɲ'ɲarsi] *vr* to do one's best, try hard; **~ per vivere** to live by one's wits; **basta ~ un po'** you just need a bit of ingenuity
inge'gnere [indʒeɲ'ɲɛre] *sm* engineer; **~ civile/navale** civil/naval engineer
ingegne'ria [indʒeɲɲe'ria] *sf* engineering
in'gegno [in'dʒeɲɲo] *sm* (*intelligenza*) intelligence, brains *pl*; (*capacità creativa*) ingenuity; (*disposizione*) talent
ingegnosità [indʒeɲɲosi'ta] *sf* ingenuity
inge'gnoso, -a [indʒeɲ'ɲoso] *ag* ingenious, clever
ingelo'sire [indʒelo'sire] *vt* to make jealous ■ *vi* (*anche*: **ingelosirsi**) to become jealous
in'gente [in'dʒɛnte] *ag* huge, enormous
ingenti'lire [indʒenti'lire] *vt* to refine, civilize; **ingentilirsi** *vr* to become more refined, become more civilized
ingenuità [indʒenui'ta] *sf* ingenuousness
in'genuo, -a [in'dʒɛnuo] *ag* ingenuous, naïve
inge'renza [indʒe'rɛntsa] *sf* interference
inge'rire [indʒe'rire] *vt* to ingest
inges'sare [indʒes'sare] *vt* (*Med*) to put in plaster
ingessa'tura [indʒessa'tura] *sf* plaster
Inghil'terra [ingil'tɛrra] *sf*: **l'~** England
inghiot'tire [ingjot'tire] *vt* to swallow
in'ghippo [in'gippo] *sm* trick
ingial'lire [indʒal'lire] *vi* to go yellow
ingigan'tire [indʒigan'tire] *vt* to enlarge, magnify ■ *vi* to become gigantic *o* enormous
inginocchi'arsi [indʒinok'kjarsi] *vr* to kneel (down)
inginocchia'toio [indʒinokkja'tojo] *sm* prie-dieu
ingioiel'lare [indʒojel'lare] *vt* to bejewel, adorn with jewels
ingiù [in'dʒu] *av* down, downwards
ingi'ungere [in'dʒundʒere] *vt*: **~ a qn di fare qc** to enjoin *o* order sb to do sth
ingi'unto, -a [in'dʒunto] *pp di* **ingiungere**
ingiunzi'one [indʒun'tsjone] *sf* injunction, command; **~ di pagamento** final demand
ingi'uria [in'dʒurja] *sf* insult; (*fig*: *danno*) damage
ingiuri'are [indʒu'rjare] *vt* to insult, abuse
ingiuri'oso, -a [indʒu'rjoso] *ag* insulting, abusive
ingiusta'mente [indʒusta'mente] *av* unjustly
ingiustifi'cabile [indʒustifi'kabile] *ag* unjustifiable
ingiustifi'cato, -a [indʒustifi'kato] *ag* unjustified
ingius'tizia [indʒus'tittsja] *sf* injustice
ingi'usto, -a [in'dʒusto] *ag* unjust, unfair
in'glese *ag* English ■ *sm/f* Englishman(-woman) ■ *sm* (*Ling*) English; **gli Inglesi** the English; **andarsene** *o* **filare all'~** to take French leave
inglori'oso, -a *ag* inglorious
ingob'bire *vi*, **ingob'birsi** *vr* to become stooped
ingoi'are *vt* to gulp (down); (*fig*) to swallow (up); **ha dovuto ~ il rospo** (*fig*) he had to accept the situation
ingol'fare *vt*, **ingol'farsi** *vr* (*motore*) to flood
ingolo'sire *vt*: **~ qn** to make sb's mouth water; (*fig*) to attract sb ■ *vi* (*anche*: **ingolosirsi**): **~ (di)** (*anche fig*) to become greedy (for)
ingom'brante *ag* cumbersome
ingom'brare *vt* (*strada*) to block; (*stanza*) to clutter up
in'gombro, -a *ag*: **~ di** (*strada*) blocked by; (*stanza*) cluttered up with ■ *sm* obstacle; **essere d'~** to be in the way; **per ragioni di ~** for reasons of space
ingor'digia [ingor'didʒa] *sf*: **~ (di)** greed (for); avidity (for)
in'gordo, -a *ag*: **~ di** greedy for; (*fig*) greedy *o* avid for ■ *sm/f* glutton

i

ingor'gare *vt* to block; **ingorgarsi** *vr* to be blocked up, be choked up
in'gorgo, -ghi *sm* blockage, obstruction; (*anche*: **ingorgo stradale**) traffic jam
ingoz'zare [ingot'tsare] *vt* (*animali*) to fatten; (*fig*: *persona*) to stuff; **ingozzarsi** *vr*: **ingozzarsi (di)** to stuff o.s. (with)
ingra'naggio [ingra'naddʒo] *sm* (*Tecn*) gear; (*di orologio*) mechanism; **gli ingranaggi della burocrazia** the bureaucratic machinery
ingra'nare *vi* to mesh, engage ■ *vt* to engage; **~ la marcia** to get into gear
ingrandi'mento *sm* enlargement; extension; magnification; growth; expansion
ingran'dire *vt* (*anche Fot*) to enlarge; (*estendere*) to extend; (*Ottica, fig*) to magnify ■ *vi* (*anche*: **ingrandirsi**) to become larger *o* bigger; (*aumentare*) to grow, increase; (*espandersi*) to expand
ingrandi'tore *sm* (*Fot*) enlarger
ingras'saggio [ingras'saddʒo] *sm* greasing
ingras'sare *vt* to make fat; (*animali*) to fatten; (*Agr*: *terreno*) to manure; (*lubrificare*) to grease ■ *vi* (*anche*: **ingrassarsi**) to get fat, put on weight
ingrati'tudine *sf* ingratitude
in'grato, -a *ag* ungrateful; (*lavoro*) thankless, unrewarding
ingrazi'are [ingrat'tsjare] *vt*: **ingraziarsi qn** to ingratiate o.s. with sb
ingredi'ente *sm* ingredient
in'gresso *sm* (*porta*) entrance; (*atrio*) hall; (*l'entrare*) entrance, entry; (*facoltà di entrare*) admission; **"~ libero"** "admission free"; **~ principale** main entrance; **~ di servizio** tradesmen's entrance
ingros'sare *vt* to increase; (*folla, livello*) to swell ■ *vi* (*anche*: **ingrossarsi**) to increase; to swell
in'grosso *av*: **all'~** (*Comm*) wholesale; (*all'incirca*) roughly, about
ingru'gnato, -a [ingruɲ'ɲato] *ag* grumpy
inguai'arsi *vr* to get into trouble
inguai'nare *vt* to sheathe
ingual'cibile [ingwal'tʃibile] *ag* crease-resistant
ingua'ribile *ag* incurable
'inguine *sm* (*Anat*) groin
ingurgi'tare [ingurdʒi'tare] *vt* to gulp down
ini'bire *vt* to forbid, prohibit; (*Psic*) to inhibit
ini'bito, -a *ag* inhibited ■ *sm/f* inhibited person
inibi'torio, -a *ag* (*Psic*) inhibitory, inhibitive; (*provvedimento, misure*) restrictive
inibizi'one [inibit'tsjone] *sf* prohibition; inhibition
iniet'tare *vt* to inject; **iniettarsi** *vr*: **iniettarsi di sangue** (*occhi*) to become bloodshot
iniet'tore *sm* injector
iniezi'one [injet'tsjone] *sf* injection
inimi'care *vt* to alienate, make hostile; **inimicarsi** *vr*: **inimicarsi con qn** to fall out with sb; **si è inimicato gli amici di un tempo** he has alienated his old friends
inimi'cizia [inimi'tʃittsja] *sf* animosity
inimi'tabile *ag* inimitable
inimmagi'nabile [inimmadʒi'nabile] *ag* unimaginable
ininfiam'mabile *ag* non-flammable
inintelli'gibile [inintelli'dʒibile] *ag* unintelligible
ininterrotta'mente *av* non-stop, continuously
ininter'rotto, -a *ag* (*fila*) unbroken; (*rumore*) uninterrupted
iniquità *sf inv* iniquity; (*atto*) wicked action
i'niquo, -a *ag* iniquitous
inizi'ale [init'tsjale] *ag, sf* initial
inizializ'zare [inittsjalid'dzare] *vt* (*Inform*) to boot
inizial'mente [inittsjal'mente] *av* initially, at first
inizi'are [init'tsjare] *vi, vt* to begin, start; **~ qn a** to initiate sb into; (*pittura etc*) to introduce sb to; **~ a fare qc** to start doing sth
inizia'tiva [inittsja'tiva] *sf* initiative; **~ privata** private enterprise
inizia'tore, -'trice [inittsja'tore] *sm/f* initiator
i'nizio [i'nittsjo] *sm* beginning; **all'~** at the beginning, at the start; **dare ~ a qc** to start sth, get sth going; **essere agli inizi** (*progetto, lavoro etc*) to be in the initial stages
innaffi'are *etc* = **annaffiare** *etc*
innal'zare [innal'tsare] *vt* (*sollevare, alzare*) to raise; (*rizzare*) to erect; **innalzarsi** *vr* to rise
innamora'mento *sm* falling in love
innamo'rare *vt* to enchant, charm; **innamorarsi** *vr*: **innamorarsi (di qn)** to fall in love (with sb)
innamo'rato, -a *ag* (*che nutre amore*): **~ (di)** in love (with); (*appassionato*): **~ di** very fond of ■ *sm/f* lover; (*anche scherzoso*) sweetheart
in'nanzi [in'nantsi] *av* (*stato in luogo*) in front, ahead; (*moto a luogo*) forward, on; (*tempo*: *prima*) before ■ *prep* (*prima*) before; **~ a** in front of; **d'ora ~** from now on; **farsi ~** to step forward; **~ tempo** ahead of time
innanzi'tutto [innantsi'tutto] *av* above all; (*per prima cosa*) first of all
in'nato, -a *ag* innate
innatu'rale *ag* unnatural

inne'gabile *ag* undeniable
inneggi'are [inned'dʒare] *vi*: **~ a** to sing hymns to; (*fig*) to sing the praises of
innervo'sire *vt*: **~ qn** to get on sb's nerves; **innervosirsi** *vr* to get irritated *o* upset
innes'care *vt* to prime
in'nesco, -schi *sm* primer
innes'tare *vt* (*Bot, Med*) to graft; (*Tecn*) to engage; (*inserire: presa*) to insert
in'nesto *sm* graft; grafting *no pl*; (*Tecn*) clutch; (*Elettr*) connection
'inno *sm* hymn; **~ nazionale** national anthem
inno'cente [inno'tʃɛnte] *ag* innocent
inno'cenza [inno'tʃɛntsa] *sf* innocence
in'nocuo, -a *ag* innocuous, harmless
innomi'nato, -a *ag* unnamed
inno'vare *vt* to change, make innovations in
innova'tivo, -a *ag* innovative
innovazi'one [innovat'tsjone] *sf* innovation
innume'revole *ag* innumerable
inocu'lare *vt* (*Med*) to inoculate
ino'doro, -a *ag* odourless (*Brit*), odorless (*US*)
inoffen'sivo, -a *ag* harmless
inol'trare *vt* (*Amm*) to pass on, forward; **inoltrarsi** *vr* (*addentrarsi*) to advance, go forward
inol'trato, -a *ag*: **a notte inoltrata** late at night; **a primavera inoltrata** late in the spring
i'noltre *av* besides, moreover
i'noltro *sm* (*Amm*) forwarding
inon'dare *vt* to flood
inondazi'one [inondat'tsjone] *sf* flooding *no pl*; flood
inope'roso, -a *ag* inactive, idle
inopi'nato, -a *ag* unexpected
inoppor'tuno, -a *ag* untimely, ill-timed; (*poco adatto*) inappropriate; (*momento*) inopportune
inoppu'gnabile [inoppuɲ'ɲabile] *ag* incontrovertible
inor'ganico, -a, ci, che *ag* inorganic
inorgo'glire [inorgoʎ'ʎire] *vt* to make proud ■ *vi* (*anche*: **inorgoglirsi**) to become proud; **inorgoglirsi di qc** to pride o.s. on sth
inorri'dire *vt* to horrify ■ *vi* to be horrified
inospi'tale *ag* inhospitable
inosser'vante *ag*: **essere ~ di** to fail to comply with
inosser'vato, -a *ag* (*non notato*) unobserved; (*non rispettato*) not observed, not kept; **passare ~** to go unobserved, escape notice
inossi'dabile *ag* stainless
INPS *sigla m* (= *Istituto Nazionale Previdenza Sociale*) *social security service*
inqua'drare *vt* (*foto, immagine*) to frame; (*fig*) to situate, set

inquadra'tura *sf* (*Cine, Fot: atto*) framing; (*: immagine*) shot; (*: sequenza*) sequence
inqualifi'cabile *ag* unspeakable
inquie'tante *ag* disturbing, worrying
inquie'tare *vt* (*turbare*) to disturb, worry; **inquietarsi** *vr* to worry, become anxious; (*impazientirsi*) to get upset
inqui'eto, -a *ag* restless; (*preoccupato*) worried, anxious
inquie'tudine *sf* anxiety, worry
inqui'lino, -a *sm/f* tenant
inquina'mento *sm* pollution
inqui'nare *vt* to pollute
inqui'rente *ag* (*Dir*): **magistrato ~** examining (*Brit*) *o* committing (*US*) magistrate; **commissione ~** commission of inquiry
inqui'sire *vt, vi* to investigate
inqui'sito, -a *ag* (*persona*) under investigation
inquisi'tore, -'trice *ag* (*sguardo*) inquiring
inquisizi'one [inkwizit'tsjone] *sf* inquisition
insabbia'mento *sm* (*fig*) shelving
insabbi'are *vt* (*fig: pratica*) to shelve; **insabbiarsi** *vr* (*barca*) to run aground; (*fig: pratica*) to be shelved
insac'care *vt* (*grano, farina etc*) to bag, put into sacks; (*carne*) to put into sausage skins
insac'cati *smpl* (*Cuc*) sausages
insa'lata *sf* salad; (*pianta*) lettuce; **~ mista** mixed salad
insalati'era *sf* salad bowl
insa'lubre *ag* unhealthy
insa'nabile *ag* (*piaga*) which cannot be healed; (*situazione*) irremediable; (*odio*) implacable
insangui'nare *vt* to stain with blood
in'sania *sf* insanity
in'sano, -a *ag* (*pazzo, folle*) insane
insapo'nare *vt* to soap; **insaponarsi le mani** to soap one's hands
insapo'nata *sf*: **dare un'~ a qc** to give sth a (quick) soaping
insapo'rire *vt* to flavour (*Brit*), flavor (*US*); (*con spezie*) to season; **insaporirsi** *vr* to acquire flavo(u)r
insa'poro, -a *ag* tasteless, insipid
insa'puta *sf*: **all'~ di qn** without sb knowing
insazi'abile [insat'tsjabile] *ag* insatiable
inscato'lare *vt* (*frutta, carne*) to can
insce'nare [inʃe'nare] *vt* (*Teat*) to stage, put on; (*fig*) to stage
inscin'dibile [inʃin'dibile] *ag* (*fattori*) inseparable; (*legame*) indissoluble
insec'chire [insek'kire] *vt* (*seccare*) to dry up; (*: piante*) to wither ■ *vi* to dry up, become dry; to wither
insedia'mento *sm* (*Amm: in carica, ufficio*) installation; (*villaggio, colonia*) settlement

insedi'are *vt* (*Amm*) to install; **insediarsi** *vr* (*Amm*) to take up office; (*colonia, profughi etc*) to settle; (*Mil*) to take up positions
in'segna [in'seɲɲa] *sf* sign; (*emblema*) sign, emblem; (*bandiera*) flag, banner; **insegne** *sfpl* (*decorazioni*) insignia *pl*
insegna'mento [inseɲɲa'mento] *sm* teaching; **trarre ~ da un'esperienza** to learn from an experience, draw a lesson from an experience; **che ti serva da ~** let this be a lesson to you
inse'gnante [inseɲ'ɲante] *ag* teaching ■ *sm/f* teacher
inse'gnare [inseɲ'ɲare] *vt, vi* to teach; **~ a qn qc** to teach sb sth; **~ a qn a fare qc** to teach sb (how) to do sth; **come lei ben m'insegna ...** (*ironico*) as you will doubtless be aware ...
insegui'mento *sm* pursuit, chase; **darsi all'~ di qn** to give chase to sb
insegu'ire *vt* to pursue, chase
insegui'tore, -'trice *sm/f* pursuer
insel'lare *vt* to saddle
inselvati'chire [inselvati'kire] *vt* (*persona*) to make unsociable ■ *vi* (*anche*: **inselvatichirsi**) to grow wild; (*persona*) to become unsociable
inseminazi'one [inseminat'tsjone] *sf* insemination
insena'tura *sf* inlet, creek
insen'sato, -a *ag* senseless, stupid
insen'sibile *ag* (*anche fig*) insensitive
insensibilità *sf* insensitivity, insensibility
insepa'rabile *ag* inseparable
inse'polto, -a *ag* unburied
inseri'mento *sm* (*gen*) insertion; **problemi di ~** (*di persona*) adjustment problems
inse'rire *vt* to insert; (*Elettr*) to connect; (*allegare*) to enclose; **inserirsi** *vr* (*fig*): **inserirsi in** to become part of; **~ un annuncio sul giornale** to put *o* place an advertisement in the newspaper
in'serto *sm* (*pubblicazione*) insert; **~ filmato** (film) clip
inser'vibile *ag* useless
inservi'ente *sm/f* attendant
inserzi'one [inser'tsjone] *sf* insertion; (*avviso*) advertisement; **fare un'~ sul giornale** to put an advertisement in the newspaper
inserzio'nista, -i, e [insertsjo'nista] *sm/f* advertiser
insetti'cida, -i [insetti'tʃida] *sm* insecticide
in'setto *sm* insect
insicu'rezza [insiku'rettsa] *sf* insecurity
insi'curo, -a *ag* insecure
in'sidia *sf* snare, trap; (*pericolo*) hidden danger; **tendere un'~ a qn** to lay *o* set a trap for sb
insidi'are *vt* (*Mil*) to harass; **~ la vita di qn** to make an attempt on sb's life
insidi'oso, -a *ag* insidious
insi'eme *av* together; (*contemporaneamente*) at the same time ■ *prep*: **~ a** *o* **con** together with ■ *sm* whole; (*Mat, servizio, assortimento*) set; (*Moda*) ensemble, outfit; **tutti ~** all together; **tutto ~** all together; (*in una volta*) at one go; **nell'~** on the whole; **d'~** (*veduta etc*) overall
in'signe [in'siɲɲe] *ag* (*persona*) famous, distinguished, eminent; (*città, monumento*) notable
insignifi'cante [insiɲɲifi'kante] *ag* insignificant
insi'gnire [insiɲ'ɲire] *vt*: **~ qn di** to honour (*Brit*) *o* honor (*US*) sb with, decorate sb with
insin'cero, -a [insin'tʃɛro] *ag* insincere
insinda'cabile *ag* unquestionable
insinu'ante *ag* (*osservazione, sguardo*) insinuating; (*maniere*) ingratiating
insinu'are *vt* (*introdurre*): **~ qc in** to slip *o* slide sth into; (*fig*) to insinuate, imply; **insinuarsi** *vr*: **insinuarsi in** to seep into; (*fig*) to creep into; to worm one's way into
insinuazi'one [insinuat'tsjone] *sf* (*fig*) insinuation
in'sipido, -a *ag* insipid
insis'tente *ag* insistent; (*pioggia, dolore*) persistent
insistente'mente *av* repeatedly
insis'tenza [insis'tɛntsa] *sf* insistence; persistence
in'sistere *vi*: **~ su qc** to insist on sth; **~ in qc/a fare** (*perseverare*) to persist in sth/in doing
insis'tito, -a *pp di* **insistere**
'insito, -a *ag*: **~ (in)** inherent (in)
insoddis'fatto, -a *ag* dissatisfied
insoddisfazi'one [insoddisfat'tsjone] *sf* dissatisfaction
insoffe'rente *ag* intolerant
insoffe'renza [insoffe'rɛntsa] *sf* impatience
insolazi'one [insolat'tsjone] *sf* (*Med*) sunstroke
inso'lente *ag* insolent
insolen'tire *vi* to grow insolent ■ *vt* to insult, be rude to
inso'lenza [inso'lɛntsa] *sf* insolence
in'solito, -a *ag* unusual, out of the ordinary
inso'lubile *ag* insoluble
inso'luto, -a *ag* (*non risolto*) unsolved; (*non pagato*) unpaid, outstanding
insol'vente *ag* (*Dir*) insolvent
insol'venza [insol'vɛntsa] *sf* (*Dir*) insolvency
insol'vibile *ag* insolvent
in'somma *av* (*in breve, in conclusione*) in short; (*dunque*) well ■ *escl* for heaven's sake!

inson'dabile *ag* unfathomable
in'sonne *ag* sleepless
in'sonnia *sf* insomnia, sleeplessness
insonno'lito, -a *ag* sleepy, drowsy
insonorizzazi'one [insonoriddzat'tsjone] *sf* soundproofing
insoppor'tabile *ag* unbearable
insoppri'mibile *ag* insuppressible
insor'genza [insor'dʒɛntsa] *sf* (*di malattia*) onset
in'sorgere [in'sordʒere] *vi* (*ribellarsi*) to rise up, rebel; (*apparire*) to come up, arise
insormon'tabile *ag* (*ostacolo*) insurmountable, insuperable
in'sorsi *etc vb vedi* **insorgere**
in'sorto, -a *pp di* **insorgere** ■ *sm/f* rebel, insurgent
insospet'tabile *ag* (*al di sopra di ogni sospetto*) above suspicion; (*inatteso*) unsuspected
insospet'tire *vt* to make suspicious ■ *vi* (*anche*: **insospettirsi**) to become suspicious
insoste'nibile *ag* (*posizione, teoria*) untenable; (*dolore, situazione*) intolerable, unbearable; **le spese di manutenzione sono insostenibili** the maintenance costs are excessive
insostitu'ibile *ag* (*persona*) irreplaceable; (*aiuto, presenza*) invaluable
insoz'zare [insot'tsare] *vt* (*pavimento*) to make dirty; (*fig*: *reputazione, memoria*) to tarnish, sully; **insozzarsi** *vr* to get dirty
inspe'rabile *ag*: **la guarigione/salvezza era** ~ there was no hope of a cure/of rescue; **abbiamo ottenuto risultati insperabilei** the results we achieved were far better than we had hoped
inspe'rato, -a *ag* unhoped-for
inspie'gabile *ag* inexplicable
inspi'rare *vt* to breathe in, inhale
in'stabile *ag* (*carico, indole*) unstable; (*tempo*) unsettled; (*equilibrio*) unsteady
instabilità *sf* instability; (*di tempo*) changeability
instal'lare *vt* to install; **installarsi** *vr* (*sistemarsi*): **installarsi in** to settle in
installazi'one [installat'tsjone] *sf* installation
instan'cabile *ag* untiring, indefatigable
instau'rare *vt* to establish
instaurazi'one [instaurat'tsjone] *sf* establishment
instil'lare *vt* to instil
instra'dare *vt* = **istradare**
insù *av* up, upwards; **guardare all'~** to look up *o* upwards; **naso all'~** turned-up nose
insubordinazi'one [insubordinat'tsjone] *sf* insubordination
insuc'cesso [insut'tʃɛsso] *sm* failure, flop
insudici'are [insudi'tʃare] *vt* to dirty; **insudiciarsi** *vr* to get dirty
insuffici'ente [insuffi'tʃɛnte] *ag* insufficient; (*compito, allievo*) inadequate
insuffici'enza [insuffi'tʃɛntsa] *sf* insufficiency; inadequacy; (*Ins*) fail; ~ **di prove** (*Dir*) lack of evidence
insu'lare *ag* insular
insu'lina *sf* insulin
in'sulso, -a *ag* (*sciocco*) inane, silly; (*persona*) dull, insipid
insul'tare *vt* to insult, affront
in'sulto *sm* insult, affront
insupe'rabile *ag* (*ostacolo, difficoltà*) insuperable, insurmountable; (*eccellente*: *qualità, prodotto*) unbeatable; (: *persona, interpretazione*) unequalled
insuper'bire *vt* to make proud, make arrogant; **insuperbirsi** *vr* to become arrogant
insurrezi'one [insurret'tsjone] *sf* revolt, insurrection
insussis'tente *ag* non-existent
intac'care *vt* (*fare tacche*) to cut into; (*corrodere*) to corrode; (*fig*: *cominciare ad usare*: *risparmi*) to break into; (: *ledere*) to damage
intagli'are [intaʎ'ʎare] *vt* to carve
intaglia'tore, -'trice [intaʎʎa'tore] *sm/f* engraver
in'taglio [in'taʎʎo] *sm* carving
intan'gibile [intan'dʒibile] *ag* (*bene, patrimonio*) untouchable; (*fig*: *diritto*) inviolable
in'tanto *av* (*nel frattempo*) meanwhile, in the meantime; (*per cominciare*) just to begin with; ~ **che** *cong* while
intarsi'are *vt* to inlay
in'tarsio *sm* inlaying *no pl*, marquetry *no pl*; inlay
intasa'mento *sm* (*ostruzione*) blockage, obstruction; (*Aut*: *ingorgo*) traffic jam
inta'sare *vt* to choke (up), block (up); (*Aut*) to obstruct, block; **intasarsi** *vr* to become choked *o* blocked
intas'care *vt* to pocket
in'tatto, -a *ag* intact; (*puro*) unsullied
intavo'lare *vt* to start, enter into
inte'gerrimo, -a [inte'dʒɛrrimo] *ag* honest, upright
inte'grale *ag* complete; (*pane, farina*) wholemeal (*Brit*), wholewheat (*US*); **film in versione** ~ uncut version of a film; **calcolo** ~ (*Mat*) integral calculus; **edizione** ~ unabridged edition
inte'grante *ag*: **parte** ~ integral part
inte'grare *vt* to complete; (*Mat*) to integrate; **integrarsi** *vr* (*persona*) to become integrated

integra'tivo, -a *ag* (*assegno*) supplementary; (*Ins*): **esame ~** *assessment test sat when changing schools*
integra'tore *sm*: **integratori alimentari** nutritional supplements
integrazi'one [integrat'tsjone] *sf* integration
integrità *sf* integrity
'integro, -a *ag* (*intatto, intero*) complete, whole; (*retto*) upright
intelaia'tura *sf* frame; (*fig*) structure, framework
intel'letto *sm* intellect
intellettu'ale *ag, sm/f* intellectual
intellettua'loide (*peg*) *ag* pseudo-intellectual ■ *sm/f* pseudo-intellectual, would-be intellectual
intelli'gente [intelli'dʒɛnte] *ag* intelligent
intelli'genza [intelli'dʒɛntsa] *sf* intelligence
intelli'ghenzia [intelli'gɛntsja] *sf* intelligentsia
intelli'gibile [intelli'dʒibile] *ag* intelligible
inteme'rato, -a *ag* (*persona, vita*) blameless, irreproachable; (*coscienza*) clear; (*fama*) unblemished
intempe'rante *ag* intemperate, immoderate
intempe'ranza [intempe'rantsa] *sf* intemperance; **intemperanze** *sfpl* (*eccessi*) excesses
intem'perie *sfpl* bad weather *sg*
intempes'tivo, -a *ag* untimely
inten'dente *sm*: **~ di Finanza** inland (*Brit*) *o* internal (*US*) revenue officer
inten'denza [inten'dɛntsa] *sf*: **~ di Finanza** inland (*Brit*) *o* internal (*US*) revenue office
in'tendere *vt* (*avere intenzione*): **~ fare qc** to intend *o* mean to do sth; (*comprendere*) to understand; (*udire*) to hear; (*significare*) to mean; **intendersi** *vr* (*conoscere*): **intendersi di** to know a lot about, be a connoisseur of; (*accordarsi*) to get on (well); **intendersi con qn su qc** to come to an agreement with sb about sth; **intendersela con qn** (*avere una relazione amorosa*) to have an affair with sb; **mi ha dato a ~ che ...** he led me to believe that ...; **non vuole ~ ragione** he won't listen to reason; **s'intende!** naturally!, of course!; **intendiamoci** let's get it quite clear; **ci siamo intesi?** is that clear?, is that understood?
intendi'mento *sm* (*intelligenza*) understanding; (*proposito*) intention
intendi'tore, -'trice *sm/f* connoisseur, expert; **a buon intenditor poche parole** (*proverbio*) a word is enough to the wise
intene'rire *vt* (*fig*) to move (to pity); **intenerirsi** *vr* (*fig*) to be moved
intensifi'care *vt*, **intensifi'carsi** *vr* to intensify
intensità *sf* intensity; (*del vento*) force, strength
inten'sivo, -a *ag* intensive
in'tenso, -a *ag* (*luce, profumo*) strong; (*colore*) intense, deep
inten'tare *vt* (*Dir*): **~ causa contro qn** to start *o* institute proceedings against sb
inten'tato, -a *ag*: **non lasciare nulla d'~** to leave no stone unturned, try everything
in'tento, -a *ag* (*teso, assorto*): **~ (a)** intent (on), absorbed (in) ■ *sm* aim, purpose; **fare qc con l'~ di** to do sth with the intention of; **riuscire nell'~** to achieve one's aim
intenzio'nale [intentsjo'nale] *ag* intentional; (*Dir: omicidio*) premeditated; **fallo ~** (*Sport*) deliberate foul
intenzio'nato, -a [intentsjo'nato] *ag*: **essere ~ a fare qc** to intend to do sth, have the intention of doing sth; **ben ~** well-meaning, well-intentioned; **mal ~** ill-intentioned
intenzi'one [inten'tsjone] *sf* intention; (*Dir*) intent; **avere ~ di fare qc** to intend to do sth, have the intention of doing sth
intera'gire [intera'dʒire] *vi* to interact
intera'mente *av* entirely, completely
interat'tivo, -a *ag* interactive
interazi'one [interat'tsjone] *sf* interaction
interca'lare *sm* pet phrase, stock phrase ■ *vt* to insert
interca'pedine *sf* gap, cavity
inter'cedere [inter'tʃɛdere] *vi* to intercede
intercessi'one [intertʃes'sjone] *sf* intercession
intercetta'mento [intertʃetta'mento] *sm* = **intercettazione**
intercet'tare [intertʃet'tare] *vt* to intercept
intercettazi'one [intertʃettat'tsjone] *sf*: **~ telefonica** telephone tapping
intercity [inter'siti] *sm inv* (*Ferr*) ≈ intercity (train)
intercon'nettere *vt* to interconnect
inter'correre *vi* (*esserci*) to exist; (*passare: tempo*) to elapse
inter'corso, -a *pp di* **intercorrere**
inter'detto, -a *pp di* **interdire** ■ *ag* forbidden, prohibited; (*sconcertato*) dumbfounded ■ *sm* (*Rel*) interdict; **rimanere ~** to be taken aback
inter'dire *vt* to forbid, prohibit, ban; (*Rel*) to interdict; (*Dir*) to deprive of civil rights
interdizi'one [interdit'tsjone] *sf* prohibition, ban
interessa'mento *sm* interest; (*intervento*) intervention, good offices *pl*
interes'sante *ag* interesting; **essere in stato ~** to be expecting (a baby)
interes'sare *vt* to interest; (*concernere*) to concern, be of interest to; (*far intervenire*): **~ qn**

a to draw sb's attention to ■ *vi*: ~ **a** to interest, matter to; **interessarsi** *vr* (*mostrare interesse*): **interessarsi a** to take an interest in, be interested in; (*occuparsi*): **interessarsi di** to take care of; **precipitazioni che interessano le regioni settentrionali** rainfall affecting the north; **si è interessato di farmi avere quei biglietti** he took the trouble to get me those tickets

interes'sato, -a *ag* (*coinvolto*) interested, involved; (*peg*): **essere ~** to act out of pure self-interest ■ *sm/f* (*coinvolto*) person concerned; **a tutti gli interessati** to all those concerned, to all interested parties

inte'resse *sm* (*anche Comm*) interest; (*tornaconto*): **fare qc per ~** to do sth out of self-interest; **~ maturato** (*Econ*) accrued interest; **~ privato in atti di ufficio** (*Amm*) abuse of public office

interes'senza [interes'sɛntsa] *sf* (*Econ*) profit-sharing

inter'faccia, -ce [inter'fattʃa] *sf* (*Inform*) interface; **~ utente** user interface

interfacci'are [interfat'tʃare] *vt* (*Inform*) to interface

interfe'renza [interfe'rɛntsa] *sf* interference

interfe'rire *vi* to interfere

inter'fono *sm* intercom; (*apparecchio*) internal phone

interiezi'one [interjet'tsjone] *sf* exclamation, interjection

'interim *sm inv* (*periodo*) interim, interval; **ministro ad ~** acting *o* interim minister; (*incarico*) temporary appointment

interi'nale *ag*: **lavoro ~** temporary work (*through an agency*); **lavoratore ~** temporary worker

interi'ora *sfpl* entrails

interi'ore *ag* inner *cpd*; **parte ~** inside

interiorità *sf* inner being

interioriz'zare [interjorid'dzare] *vt* to internalize

inter'linea *sf* (*Dattilografia*) spacing; (*Tip*) leading; **doppia ~** double spacing

interlocu'tore, -'trice *sm/f* speaker

interlocu'torio, -a *ag* interlocutory

inter'ludio *sm* (*Mus*) interlude

intermedi'ario, -a *ag, sm/f* intermediary

intermediazi'one [intermedjat'tsjone] *sf* mediation

inter'medio, -a *ag* intermediate

inter'mezzo [inter'mɛddzo] *sm* (*intervallo*) interval; (*breve spettacolo*) intermezzo

intermi'nabile *ag* interminable, endless

intermit'tente *ag* intermittent

intermit'tenza [intermit'tɛntsa] *sf*: **ad ~** intermittent

interna'mento *sm* internment; confinement (to a mental hospital)

inter'nare *vt* (*arrestare*) to intern; (*Med*) to confine to a mental hospital

inter'nato, -a *ag* interned; confined (to a mental hospital) ■ *sm/f* internee; inmate (of a mental hospital) ■ *sm* (*collegio*) boarding school; (*Med*) period as a houseman (*Brit*) *o* an intern (*US*)

internazio'nale [internattsjo'nale] *ag* international

'Internet ['internet] *sf* internet; **in ~** on the internet

inter'nista, -i, e *sm/f* specialist in internal medicine

in'terno, -a *ag* (*di dentro*) internal, interior, inner; (*: mare*) inland; (*nazionale*) domestic; (*allievo*) boarding ■ *sm* inside, interior; (*di paese*) interior; (*fodera*) lining; (*di appartamento*) flat (*Brit*) *o* apartment (*US*) (number); (*Tel*) extension ■ *sm/f* (*Ins*) boarder; **interni** *smpl* (*Cine*) interior shots; **commissione interna** (*Ins*) internal examination board; **"per uso ~"** (*Med*) "to be taken internally"; **all'~** inside; **Ministero degli Interni** Ministry of the Interior, ≈ Home Office (*Brit*), ≈ Department of the Interior (*US*); **notizie dall'~** (*Stampa*) home news

in'tero, -a *ag* (*integro, intatto*) whole, entire; (*completo, totale*) complete; (*numero*) whole; (*non ridotto: biglietto*) full

interpel'lanza [interpel'lantsa] *sf*: **presentare un'~** (*Pol*) to ask a (parliamentary) question; **~ parlamentare** interpellation

interpel'lare *vt* to consult; (*Pol*) to question

INTER'POL *sigla f* (= *International Criminal Police Organization*) INTERPOL

inter'porre *vt* (*ostacolo*): **~ qc a qc** to put sth in the way of sth; (*influenza*) to use; **interporsi** *vr* to intervene; **~ appello** (*Dir*) to appeal; **interporsi fra** (*mettersi in mezzo*) to come between

inter'posto, -a *pp di* **interporre**

interpre'tare *vt* (*spiegare, tradurre*) to interpret; (*Mus, Teat*) to perform; (*personaggio, sonata*) to play; (*canzone*) to sing

interpretari'ato *sm* interpreting

interpretazi'one [interpretat'tsjone] *sf* interpretation

in'terprete *sm/f* interpreter; (*Teat*) actor/actress, performer; (*Mus*) performer; **farsi ~ di** to act as a spokesman for

interpunzi'one [interpun'tsjone] *sf* punctuation; **segni di ~** punctuation marks

inter'rare *vt* (*seme, pianta*) to plant; (*tubature etc*) to lay underground; (*Mil: pezzo d'artiglieria*) to dig in; (*riempire di terra: canale*) to fill in

interregio'nale [interredʒo'nale] *sm train that travels between two or more regions of Italy*

interro'gare *vt* to question; (*Ins*) to test

interroga'tivo, -a *ag* (*occhi, sguardo*) questioning, inquiring; (*Ling*) interrogative ■ *sm* question; (*fig*) mystery

interroga'torio, -a *ag* interrogatory, questioning ■ *sm* (*Dir*) questioning *no pl*

interrogazi'one [interrogat'tsjone] *sf* questioning *no pl*; (*Ins*) oral test; (*Pol*): ~ **(parlamentare)** question

inter'rompere *vt* to interrupt; (*studi, trattative*) to break off, interrupt; **interrompersi** *vr* to break off, stop

inter'rotto, -a *pp di* **interrompere**

interrut'tore *sm* switch

interruzi'one [interrut'tsjone] *sf* (*vedi interrompere*) interruption; break; ~ **di gravidanza** termination of pregnancy

interse'care *vt*, **interse'carsi** *vr* to intersect

inter'stizio [inter'stittsjo] *sm* interstice, crack

interur'bano, -a *ag* inter-city; (*Tel: chiamata*) trunk *cpd* (*Brit*), long-distance; (*: telefono*) long-distance ■ *sf* trunk call (*Brit*), long-distance call

inter'vallo *sm* interval; (*spazio*) space, gap; ~ **pubblicitario** (*TV*) commercial break

interve'nire *vi* (*partecipare*): ~ **a** to take part in; (*intromettersi: anche Pol*) to intervene; (*Med: operare*) to operate

interven'tista, -i, e *ag, sm/f* interventionist

inter'vento *sm* participation; (*intromissione*) intervention; (*Med*) operation; (*breve discorso*) speech; **fare un ~ nel corso di** (*dibattito, programma*) to take part in

interve'nuto, -a *pp di* **intervenire** ■ *sm*: **gli intervenuti** those present

inter'vista *sf* interview

intervis'tare *vt* to interview

intervista'tore, -'trice *sm/f* interviewer

in'teso, -a *pp di* **intendere** ■ *ag* agreed ■ *sf* understanding; (*accordo*) agreement, understanding; **resta ~ che ...** it is understood that ...; **non darsi per ~ di qc** to take no notice of sth; **uno sguardo d'intesa** a knowing look

in'tessere *vt* to weave together; (*fig: trama, storia*) to weave

intes'tare *vt* (*lettera*) to address; (*proprietà*): ~ **a** to register in the name of; ~ **un assegno a qn** to make out a cheque to sb

intesta'tario, -a *sm/f* holder

intestato, -a *ag* (*proprietà, casa, conto*) in the name of; (*assegno*) made out to; **carta intestata** headed paper

intestazi'one [intestat'tsjone] *sf* heading; (*su carta da lettere*) letterhead; (*registrazione*) registration

intesti'nale *ag* intestinal

intes'tino, -a *ag* (*lotte*) internal, civil ■ *sm* (*Anat*) intestine

intiepi'dire *vt* (*riscaldare*) to warm (up); (*raffreddare*) to cool (down); (*fig: amicizia etc*) to cool; **intiepidirsi** *vr* to warm (up); to cool (down); to cool

Inti'fada *sf* Intifada

intima'mente *av* intimately; **sono ~ convinto che ...** I'm firmly *o* deeply convinced that ...; **i due fatti sono ~ connessi** the two events are closely connected

inti'mare *vt* to order, command; **~ la resa a qn** (*Mil*) to call upon sb to surrender

intimazi'one [intimat'tsjone] *sf* order, command

intimida'torio, -a *ag* threatening

intimidazi'one [intimidat'tsjone] *sf* intimidation

intimi'dire *vt* to intimidate ■ *vi* (*anche*: **intimidirsi**) to grow shy

intimità *sf* intimacy; privacy; (*familiarità*) familiarity

'intimo, -a *ag* intimate; (*affetti, vita*) private; (*fig: profondo*) inmost ■ *sm* (*persona*) intimate *o* close friend; (*dell'animo*) bottom, depths *pl*; **parti intime** (*Anat*) private parts; **rapporti intimi** (*sessuali*) intimate relations

intimo'rire *vt* to frighten; **intimorirsi** *vr* to become frightened

in'tingere [in'tindʒere] *vt* to dip

in'tingolo *sm* sauce; (*pietanza*) stew

in'tinto, -a *pp di* **intingere**

intiriz'zire [intirid'dzire] *vt* to numb ■ *vi*, **intirizzirsi** *vr* to go numb

intiriz'zito, -a [intirid'dzito] *ag* numb (with cold)

intito'lare *vt* to give a title to; (*dedicare*) to dedicate; **intitolarsi** *vr* (*libro, film*) to be called

intolle'rabile *ag* intolerable

intolle'rante *ag* intolerant

intolle'ranza [intolle'rantsa] *sf* intolerance

intona'care *vt* to plaster

in'tonaco (*mpl* **intonaci** *o* **intonachi**) *sm* plaster

into'nare *vt* (*canto*) to start to sing; (*armonizzare*) to match; **intonarsi** *vr* (*colori*) to go together; **intonarsi a** (*carnagione*) to suit; (*abito*) to go with, match

intonazi'one [intonat'tsjone] *sf* intonation

inton'tire *vt* to stun, daze ■ *vi*, **intontirsi** *vr* to be stunned *o* dazed
inton'tito, -a *ag* stunned, dazed; **~ dal sonno** stupid with sleep
in'toppo *sm* stumbling block, obstacle
intorbi'dire *vt* (*liquido*) to make turbid; (*mente*) to cloud; **~ le acque** (*fig*) to muddy the waters
in'torno *av* around; **~ a** *prep* (*attorno a*) around; (*riguardo, circa*) about
intorpi'dire *vt* to numb; (*fig*) to make sluggish ■ *vi* (*anche*: **intorpidirsi**) to grow numb; (*fig*) to become sluggish
intossi'care *vt* to poison
intossicazi'one [intossikat'tsjone] *sf* poisoning
intradu'cibile [intradu'tʃibile] *ag* untranslatable
intralci'are [intral'tʃare] *vt* to hamper, hold up
in'tralcio [in'traltʃo] *sm* hitch
intrallaz'zare [intrallat'tsare] *vi* to intrigue, scheme
intral'lazzo [intral'lattso] *sm* (*Pol*) intrigue, manoeuvre (*Brit*), maneuver (*US*); (*traffico losco*) racket
intramon'tabile *ag* timeless
intramusco'lare *ag* intramuscular
'Intranet ['intranet] *sf* Intranet
intransi'gente [intransi'dʒɛnte] *ag* intransigent, uncompromising
intransi'genza [intransi'dʒɛntsa] *sf* intransigence
intransi'tivo, -a *ag, sm* intransitive
intrappo'lare *vt* to trap; **rimanere intrappolato** to be trapped; **farsi ~** to get caught
intrapren'dente *ag* enterprising, go-ahead; (*con le donne*) forward, bold
intrapren'denza [intrapren'dɛntsa] *sf* audacity, initiative; (*con le donne*) boldness
intra'prendere *vt* to undertake; (*carriera*) to embark (up)on
intra'preso, -a *pp di* **intraprendere**
intrat'tabile *ag* intractable
intratte'nere *vt* (*divertire*) to entertain; (*chiacchierando*) to engage in conversation; (*rapporti*) to have, maintain; **intrattenersi** *vr* to linger; **intrattenersi su qc** to dwell on sth
intratteni'mento *sm* entertainment
intrave'dere *vt* to catch a glimpse of; (*fig*) to foresee
intrecci'are [intret'tʃare] *vt* (*capelli*) to plait, braid; (*intessere: anche fig*) to weave, interweave, intertwine; **intrecciarsi** *vr* to intertwine, become interwoven; **~ le mani** to clasp one's hands; **~ una relazione amorosa** (*fig*) to begin an affair
in'treccio [in'trettʃo] *sm* (*fig: trama*) plot, story
in'trepido, -a *ag* fearless, intrepid
intri'care *vt* (*fili*) to tangle; (*fig: faccenda*) to complicate; **intricarsi** *vr* to become tangled; to become complicated
in'trico, -chi *sm* (*anche fig*) tangle
intri'gante *ag* scheming ■ *sm/f* schemer, intriguer
intri'gare *vi* to manoeuvre (*Brit*), maneuver (*US*), scheme
in'trigo, -ghi *sm* plot, intrigue
in'trinseco, -a, ci, che *ag* intrinsic
in'triso, -a *ag*: **~ (di)** soaked (in)
intris'tire *vi* (*persona: diventare triste*) to grow sad; (*pianta*) to wilt
intro'dotto, -a *pp di* **introdurre**
intro'durre *vt* to introduce; (*chiave etc*): **~ qc in** to insert sth into; (*persona: far entrare*) to show in; **introdursi** *vr* (*moda, tecniche*) to be introduced; **introdursi in** (*persona: penetrare*) to enter; (*: entrare furtivamente*) to steal *o* slip into
in'troito *sm* income, revenue
intro'messo, -a *pp di* **intromettersi**
intro'mettersi *vr* to interfere, meddle; (*interporsi*) to intervene
intromissi'one *sf* interference, meddling; intervention
introspezi'one [introspet'tsjone] *sf* introspection
intro'vabile *ag* (*persona, oggetto*) who (*o* which) cannot be found; (*libro etc*) unobtainable
intro'verso, -a *ag* introverted ■ *sm/f* introvert
intrufo'larsi *vr*: **~ (in)** (*stanza*) to sneak (into), slip (into); (*conversazione*) to butt in (on)
in'truglio [in'truʎʎo] *sm* concoction
intrusi'one *sf* intrusion; interference
in'truso, -a *sm/f* intruder
intu'ire *vt* to perceive by intuition; (*rendersi conto*) to realize
in'tuito *sm* intuition; (*perspicacia*) perspicacity
intuizi'one [intuit'tsjone] *sf* intuition
inturgi'dire [inturdʒi'dire] *vi*, **inturgi'dirsi** *vr* to swell
inumanità *sf inv* inhumanity
inu'mano, -a *ag* inhuman
inu'mare *vt* (*seppellire*) to bury, inter
inumazi'one [inumat'tsjone] *sf* burial, interment
inumi'dire *vt* to dampen, moisten; **inumidirsi** *vr* to become damp *o* wet
inurba'mento *sm* urbanization
inusi'tato, -a *ag* unusual
i'nutile *ag* useless; (*superfluo*) pointless, unnecessary; **è stato tutto ~!** it was all in vain!

inutilità *sf* uselessness; pointlessness
inutiliz'zabile [inutilid'dzabile] *ag* unusable
inutil'mente *av* (*senza risultato*) fruitlessly; (*senza utilità, scopo*) unnecessarily, needlessly; **l'ho cercato ~** I looked for him in vain; **ti preoccupi ~** there's nothing for you to worry about, there's no need for you to worry
inva'dente *ag* (*fig*) intrusive
inva'denza [inva'dɛntsa] *sf* intrusiveness
in'vadere *vt* to invade; (*affollare*) to swarm into, overrun; (*acque*) to flood
invadi'trice [invadi'tritʃe] *ag f vedi* **invasore**
inva'ghirsi [inva'girsi] *vr*: **~ di** to take a fancy to
invali'cabile *ag* (*montagna*) impassable
invali'dare *vt* to invalidate
invalidità *sf* infirmity; disability; (*Dir*) invalidity
in'valido, -a *ag* (*infermo*) infirm; (*al lavoro*) disabled; (*Dir: nullo*) invalid ■ *sm/f* invalid; disabled person; **~ di guerra** disabled ex-serviceman; **~ del lavoro** industrially disabled person
in'valso, -a *ag* (*diffuso*) established
in'vano *av* in vain
invari'abile *ag* invariable
invari'ato, -a *ag* unchanged
inva'sare *vt* (*pianta*) to pot
inva'sato, -a *ag* possessed (by the devil) ■ *sm/f* person possessed by the devil; **urlare come un ~** to shout like a madman
invasi'one *sf* invasion
in'vaso, -a *pp di* **invadere**
inva'sore, invadi'trice [invadi'tritʃe] *ag* invading ■ *sm/f* invader
invecchia'mento [invekkja'mento] *sm* growing old; ageing; **questo whisky ha un ~ di 12 anni** this whisky has been matured for 12 years
invecchi'are [invek'kjare] *vi* (*persona*) to grow old; (*vino, popolazione*) to age; (*moda*) to become dated ■ *vt* to age; (*far apparire più vecchio*) to make look older; **lo trovo invecchiato** I find he has aged
in'vece [in'vetʃe] *av* instead; (*al contrario*) on the contrary; **~ di** *prep* instead of
inve'ire *vi*: **~ contro** to rail against
invele'nire *vt* to embitter; **invelenirsi** *vr* to become bitter
inven'duto, -a *ag* unsold
inven'tare *vt* to invent; (*pericoli, pettegolezzi*) to make up, invent
inventari'are *vt* to make an inventory of, inventory
inven'tario *sm* inventory; (*Comm*) stocktaking *no pl*
inven'tivo, -a *ag* inventive ■ *sf* inventiveness
inven'tore, -'trice *sm/f* inventor
invenzi'one [inven'tsjone] *sf* invention; (*bugia*) lie, story
invere'condia *sf* shamelessness, immodesty
inver'nale *ag* winter *cpd*; (*simile all'inverno*) wintry
in'verno *sm* winter; **d'~** in (the) winter
invero'simile *ag* unlikely ■ *sm*: **ha dell'~** it's hard to believe, it's incredible
inversi'one *sf* inversion; **"divieto d'~"** (*Aut*) "no U-turns"
in'verso, -a *ag* opposite; (*Mat*) inverse ■ *sm* contrary, opposite; **in senso ~** in the opposite direction; **in ordine ~** in reverse order
inverte'brato, -a *ag, sm* invertebrate
inver'tire *vt* to invert; (*disposizione, posti*) to change; (*ruoli*) to exchange; **~ la marcia** (*Aut*) to do a U-turn; **~ la rotta** (*Naut*) to go about; (*fig*) to do a U-turn
inver'tito, -a *sm/f* homosexual
investi'gare *vt, vi* to investigate
investiga'tivo, -a *ag*: **squadra investigativa** detective squad
investiga'tore, -'trice *sm/f* investigator, detective
investigazi'one [investigat'tsjone] *sf* investigation, inquiry
investi'mento *sm* (*Econ*) investment; (*di veicolo*) crash, collision; (*di pedone*) knocking down
inves'tire *vt* (*denaro*) to invest; (*veicolo: pedone*) to knock down; (*: altro veicolo*) to crash into; (*apostrofare*) to assail; (*incaricare*): **~ qn di** to invest sb with; **investirsi** *vr* (*fig*): **investirsi di una parte** to enter thoroughly into a role
investi'tore, -'trice *sm/f* driver responsible for an accident
investi'tura *sf* investiture
invete'rato, -a *ag* inveterate
invet'tiva *sf* invective
invi'are *vt* to send
invi'ato, -a *sm/f* envoy; (*Stampa*) correspondent
in'vidia *sf* envy; **fare ~ a qn** to make sb envious
invidi'abile *ag* enviable
invidi'are *vt*: **~ qn (per qc)** to envy sb (for sth); **~ qc a qn** to envy sb sth; **non aver nulla da ~ a nessuno** to be as good as the next one
invidi'oso, -a *ag* envious
invin'cibile [invin'tʃibile] *ag* invincible
in'vio, -'vii *sm* sending; (*insieme di merci*) consignment; (*tasto*) Return (key), Enter (key)
invio'labile *ag* inviolable

invio'lato, -a *ag* (*diritto, segreto*) inviolate; (*foresta*) virgin *cpd*; (*montagna, vetta*) unscaled

invipe'rire *vi*, **invipe'rirsi** *vr* to become furious, fly into a temper

invipe'rito, -a *ag* furious

invis'chiare [invis'kjare] *vt* (*fig*): **~ qn in qc** to involve sb in sth, mix sb up in sth; **invischiarsi** *vr*: **invischiarsi (con qn/in qc)** to get mixed up *o* involved (with sb/in sth)

invi'sibile *ag* invisible

in'viso, -a *ag*: **~ a** unpopular with

invi'tante *ag* (*proposta, odorino*) inviting; (*sorriso*) appealing, attractive

invi'tare *vt* to invite; **~ qn a fare** to invite sb to do

invi'tato, -a *sm/f* guest

in'vito *sm* invitation; **dietro ~ del sig. Rossi** at Mr Rossi's invitation

invo'care *vt* (*chiedere: aiuto, pace*) to cry out for; (*appellarsi: la legge, Dio*) to appeal to, invoke

invogli'are [invoʎ'ʎare] *vt*: **~ qn a fare** to tempt sb to do, induce sb to do

involon'tario, -a *ag* (*errore*) unintentional; (*gesto*) involuntary

invol'tino *sm* (*Cuc*) roulade

in'volto *sm* (*pacco*) parcel; (*fagotto*) bundle

in'volucro *sm* cover, wrapping

involu'tivo, -a *ag*: **subire un processo ~** to regress

invo'luto, -a *ag* involved, intricate

involuzi'one [involut'tsjone] *sf* (*di stile*) convolutedness; (*regresso*): **subire un'~** to regress

invulne'rabile *ag* invulnerable

inzacche'rare [intsakke'rare] *vt* to spatter with mud; **inzaccherarsi** *vr* to get muddy

inzup'pare [intsup'pare] *vt* to soak; **inzupparsi** *vr* to get soaked; **inzuppò i biscotti nel latte** he dipped the biscuits in the milk

'io *pron* I ■ *sm inv*: **l'io** the ego, the self; **io stesso(a)** I myself; **sono io** it's me

i'odio *sm* iodine

i'ogurt *sm inv* = **yoghurt**

i'one *sm* ion

I'onio *sm*: **lo ~, il mar ~** the Ionian (Sea)

ionizza'tore [joniddza'tore] *sm* ioniser

'iosa; **a ~** *av* in abundance, in great quantity

'IPAB *sigla fpl* (= *Istituzioni pubbliche di Assistenza e Beneficenza*) *charitable institutions*

i'perbole *sf* (*Letteratura*) hyperbole; (*Mat*) hyperbola

iper'bolico, -a, ci, che *ag* (*Letteratura, Mat*) hyperbolic(al); (*fig: esagerato*) exaggerated

ipermer'cato *sm* hypermarket

ipersen'sibile *ag* (*persona*) hypersensitive; (*Fot: lastra, pellicola*) hypersensitized

ipertecno'logico, -a, ci, che [ipertekno'lɔdʒiko] *ag* hi-tech

ipertensi'one *sf* high blood pressure, hypertension

iper'testo *sm* hypertext

ipertestu'ale *ag* (*Comput*): **collegamento ~, link ~** hyperlink

ip'nosi *sf* hypnosis

ip'notico, -a, ci, che *ag* hypnotic

ipno'tismo *sm* hypnotism

ipnotiz'zare [ipnotid'dzare] *vt* to hypnotize

ipoaller'genico, -a, ci, che [ipoaller'dʒɛniko] *ag* hypoallergenic

ipocon'dria *sf* hypochondria

ipocon'driaco, -a, ci, che *ag, sm/f* hypochondriac

ipocri'sia *sf* hypocrisy

i'pocrita, -i, e *ag* hypocritical ■ *sm/f* hypocrite

ipo'sodico, -a, ci, che *ag* low sodium *cpd*

ipo'teca, -che *sf* mortgage

ipote'care *vt* to mortgage

ipote'nusa *sf* hypotenuse

i'potesi *sf inv* hypothesis; **facciamo l'~ che ..., ammettiamo per ~ che ...** let's suppose *o* assume that ...; **nella peggiore/migliore delle ~** at worst/best; **nell'~ che venga** should he come, if he comes; **se per ~ io partissi ...** just supposing I were to leave ....

ipo'tetico, -a, ci, che *ag* hypothetical

ipotiz'zare [ipotid'dzare] *vt*: **~ che** to form the hypothesis that

'ippico, -a, ci, che *ag* horse *cpd* ■ *sf* horseracing

ippocas'tano *sm* horse chestnut

ip'podromo *sm* racecourse

ippo'potamo *sm* hippopotamus

'ipsilon *sf o m inv* (*lettera*) Y, y; (: *dell'alfabeto greco*) epsilon

IP'SOA *sigla m* (= *Istituto Post-Universitario per lo Studio dell'Organizzazione Aziendale*) *postgraduate institute of business administration*

IR *abbr* (*Ferr*) = **interregionale**

IRA *sigla f* (= *Irish Republican Army*) IRA

'ira *sf* anger, wrath

ira'cheno, -a [ira'kɛno] *ag, sm/f* Iraqi

I'ran *sm*: **l'~** Iran

irani'ano, -a *ag, sm/f* Iranian

I'raq *sm*: **l'~** Iraq

iras'cibile [iraʃ'ʃibile] *ag* quick-tempered

'IRCE ['irtʃe] *sigla m* = **Istituto per le relazioni culturali con l'Estero**

'IRI *sigla m* (= *Istituto per la Ricostruzione Industriale*) *state-controlled industrial investment office*

'iride *sf* (*arcobaleno*) rainbow; (*Anat, Bot*) iris

'iris *sm inv* iris

Ir'landa *sf*: **l'~** Ireland; **l'~ del Nord** Northern Ireland, Ulster; **la Repubblica d'~** Eire, the Republic of Ireland; **il mar d'~** the Irish Sea
irlan'dese *ag* Irish ■ *sm/f* Irishman(-woman); **gli Irlandesi** the Irish
iro'nia *sf* irony
i'ronico, -a, ci, che *ag* ironic(al)
ironiz'zare [ironid'dzare] *vt, vi*: **~ su** to be ironical about
i'roso, -a *ag* (*sguardo, tono*) angry, wrathful; (*persona*) irascible
'IRPEF *sigla f* = **imposta sul reddito delle persone fisiche**
ir'pino, -a *ag* of (*o* from) Irpinia
irradi'are *vt* to radiate; (*raggi di luce*: *illuminare*) to shine on ■ *vi* (*diffondersi*: *anche*: **irradiarsi**) to radiate
irradiazi'one [irradjat'tsjone] *sf* radiation
irraggiun'gibile [irraddʒun'dʒibile] *ag* unreachable; (*fig*: *meta*) unattainable
irragio'nevole [irradʒo'nevole] *ag* (*privo di ragione*) irrational; (*fig*: *persona, pretese, prezzo*) unreasonable
irrazio'nale [irrattsjo'nale] *ag* irrational
irre'ale *ag* unreal
irrealiz'zabile [irrealid'dzabile] *ag* (*sogno, desiderio*) unattainable, unrealizable; (*progetto*) unworkable, impracticable
irrealtà *sf* unreality
irrecupe'rabile *ag* (*gen*) irretrievable; (*fig*: *persona*) irredeemable
irrecu'sabile *ag* (*offerta*) not to be refused; (*prova*) irrefutable
irreden'tista, -i, e *ag, sm/f* (*Storia*) Irredentist
irrefre'nabile *ag* uncontrollable
irrefu'tabile *ag* irrefutable
irrego'lare *ag* irregular; (*terreno*) uneven
irregolarità *sf inv* irregularity; unevenness *no pl*
irremo'vibile *ag* (*fig*) unshakeable, unyielding
irrepa'rabile *ag* irreparable; (*fig*) inevitable
irrepe'ribile *ag* nowhere to be found
irrepren'sibile *ag* irreproachable
irrequi'eto, -a *ag* restless
irresis'tibile *ag* irresistible
irreso'luto, -a *ag* irresolute
irrespi'rabile *ag* (*aria*) unbreathable; (*fig*: *opprimente*) stifling, oppressive; (*: malsano*) unhealthy
irrespon'sabile *ag* irresponsible
irrestrin'gibile [irrestrin'dʒibile] *ag* unshrinkable, non-shrink (*Brit*)
irre'tire *vt* to seduce
irrever'sibile *ag* irreversible
irrevo'cabile *ag* irrevocable
irricono'scibile [irrikonoʃ'ʃibile] *ag* unrecognizable
irridu'cibile [irridu'tʃibile] *ag* irreducible; (*fig*) unshakeable
irrifles'sivo, -a *ag* thoughtless
irri'gare *vt* (*annaffiare*) to irrigate; (*fiume etc*) to flow through
irrigazi'one [irrigat'tsjone] *sf* irrigation
irrigidi'mento [irridʒidi'mento] *sm* stiffening; hardening; tightening
irrigi'dire [irridʒi'dire] *vt* to stiffen; (*disciplina*) to tighten; **irrigidirsi** *vr* to stiffen; (*posizione, atteggiamento*) to harden
irriguar'doso, -a *ag* disrespectful
irrile'vante *ag* (*trascurabile*) insignificant
irrimedi'abile *ag*: **un errore ~** a mistake which cannot be rectified; **non è ~!** we can do something about it!
irrinunci'abile [irrinun'tʃabile] *ag* vital; which cannot be abandoned
irripe'tibile *ag* unrepeatable
irri'solto, -a *ag* (*problema*) unresolved
irri'sorio, -a *ag* derisory
irrispet'toso, -a *ag* disrespectful
irri'tabile *ag* irritable
irri'tante *ag* (*atteggiamento*) irritating, annoying; (*Med*) irritant
irri'tare *vt* (*mettere di malumore*) to irritate, annoy; (*Med*) to irritate; **irritarsi** *vr* (*stizzirsi*) to become irritated *o* annoyed; (*Med*) to become irritated
irritazi'one [irritat'tsjone] *sf* irritation; annoyance
irrive'rente *ag* irreverent
irrobus'tire *vt* (*persona*) to make stronger, make more robust; (*muscoli*) to strengthen; **irrobustirsi** *vr* to become stronger
ir'rompere *vi*: **~ in** to burst into
irro'rare *vt* to sprinkle; (*Agr*) to spray
ir'rotto, -a *pp di* **irrompere**
irru'ente *ag* (*fig*) impetuous, violent
irru'enza [irru'ɛntsa] *sf* impetuousness; **con ~** impetuously
ir'ruppi *etc vb vedi* **irrompere**
irruvi'dire *vt* to roughen ■ *vi* (*anche*: **irruvidirsi**) to become rough
irruzi'one [irrut'tsjone] *sf*: **fare ~ in** to burst into; (*polizia*) to raid
ir'suto, -a *ag* (*petto*) hairy; (*barba*) bristly
'irto, -a *ag* bristly; **~ di** bristling with
Is. *abbr* (= *isola*) I
ISBN *abbr* (= *International Standard Book Number*) ISBN
is'crissi *etc vb vedi* **iscrivere**
is'critto, -a *pp di* **iscrivere** ■ *sm/f* member; **gli iscritti alla gara** the competitors; **per** *o* **in ~** in writing
is'crivere *vt* to register, enter; (*persona*): **~ (a)** to register (in), enrol (in); **iscriversi** *vr*:

iscriversi (a) *(club, partito)* to join; *(università)* to register *o* enrol (at); *(esame, concorso)* to register *o* enter (for)
iscrizi'one [iskrit'tsjone] *sf (epigrafe etc)* inscription; *(a scuola, società etc)* enrolment; registration
'ISEF *sigla m* = **Istituto Superiore di Educazione Fisica**
Is'lam *sm*: **l'~** Islam
is'lamico, -a, ci, che *ag* Islamic
Is'landa *sf*: **l'~** Iceland
islan'dese *ag* Icelandic ■ *sm/f* Icelander ■ *sm (Ling)* Icelandic
'isola *sf* island; **~ pedonale** *(Aut)* pedestrian precinct
isola'mento *sm* isolation; *(Tecn)* insulation; **essere in cella di ~** to be in solitary confinement; **~ acustico** soundproofing; **~ termico** thermal insulation
iso'lano, -a *ag* island *cpd* ■ *sm/f* islander
iso'lante *ag* insulating ■ *sm* insulator
iso'lare *vt* to isolate; *(Tecn)* to insulate; *(: acusticamente)* to soundproof
iso'lato, -a *ag* isolated; insulated ■ *sm (edificio)* block
isolazio'nismo [isolattsjo'nismo] *sm* isolationism
i'sotopo *sm* isotope
ispessi'mento *sm* thickening
ispes'sire *vt* to thicken; **ispessirsi** *vr* to get thicker, thicken
ispetto'rato *sm* inspectorate
ispet'tore, -'trice *sm/f* inspector; *(Comm)* supervisor; **~ di zona** *(Comm)* area supervisor *o* manager; **~ di reparto** shop walker *(Brit)*, floor walker *(US)*
ispezio'nare [ispettsjo'nare] *vt* to inspect
ispezi'one [ispet'tsjone] *sf* inspection
'ispido, -a *ag* bristly, shaggy
ispi'rare *vt* to inspire; **ispirarsi** *vr*: **ispirarsi a** to draw one's inspiration from; *(conformarsi)* to be based on; **l'idea m'ispira** the idea appeals to me
ispira'tore, -'trice *ag* inspiring ■ *sm/f* inspirer; *(di ribellione)* instigator
ispirazi'one [ispirat'tsjone] *sf* inspiration; **secondo l'~ del momento** according to the mood of the moment
israeli'ano, -a *ag, sm/f* Israeli
israe'lita, -i, e *sm/f* Jew/Jewess; *(Storia)* Israelite
israe'litico, -a, ci, che *ag* Jewish
is'sare *vt* to hoist; **~ l'ancora** to weigh anchor
'Istanbul *sf* Istanbul
istan'taneo, -a *ag* instantaneous ■ *sf (Fot)* snapshot
is'tante *sm* instant, moment; **all'~, sull'~** instantly, immediately
is'tanza [is'tantsa] *sf* petition, request; **giudice di prima ~** *(Dir)* judge of the court of first instance; **giudizio di seconda ~** judgment on appeal; **in ultima ~** *(fig)* finally; **~ di divorzio** petition for divorce
'ISTAT *sigla m* = **Istituto Centrale di Statistica**
'ISTEL *sigla f* = **Indagine sull'ascolto delle televisioni in Italia**
is'terico, -a, ci, che *ag* hysterical
isteri'lire *vt (terreno)* to render infertile; *(fig: fantasia)* to dry up; **isterilirsi** *vr* to become infertile; to dry up
iste'rismo *sm* hysteria
isti'gare *vt* to incite
istigazi'one [istigat'tsjone] *sf* instigation; **~ a delinquere** *(Dir)* incitement to crime
istin'tivo, -a *ag* instinctive
is'tinto *sm* instinct
istitu'ire *vt (fondare)* to institute, found; *(porre: confronto)* to establish; *(intraprendere: inchiesta)* to set up
isti'tuto *sm* institute; *(di università)* department; *(ente, Dir)* institution; **~ di bellezza** beauty salon; **~ di credito** bank, banking institution; **~ tecnico commerciale** ≈ commercial college; **~ tecnico industriale statale** ≈ technical college
istitu'tore, -'trice *sm/f (fondatore)* founder; *(precettore)* tutor, governess
istituzi'one [istitut'tsjone] *sf* institution; **istituzioni** *sfpl (Dir)* institutes; **lotta alle istituzioni** struggle against the Establishment
'istmo *sm (Geo)* isthmus
isto'gramma, -i *sm* histogram
istra'dare *vt (fig: persona)*: **~ (a/verso)** to direct (to/towards)
istri'ano, -a *ag, sm/f* Istrian
'istrice ['istritʃe] *sm* porcupine
istri'one *sm (peg)* ham (actor)
istru'ire *vt (insegnare)* to teach; *(ammaestrare)* to train; *(informare)* to instruct, inform; *(Dir)* to prepare
istru'ito, -a *ag* educated
istrut'tivo, -a *ag* instructive
istrut'tore, -'trice *sm/f* instructor ■ *ag*: **giudice ~** examining *(Brit) o* committing *(US)* magistrate
istrut'toria *sf (Dir)* (preliminary) investigation and hearing; **formalizzare un'~** to proceed to a formal hearing
istruzi'one [istrut'tsjone] *sf (gen)* training; *(Ins, cultura)* education; *(direttiva)* instruction; *(Dir)* = **istruttoria**; **Ministero della Pubblica I~** Ministry of Education; **istruzioni di spedizione** forwarding

i

instructions; **istruzioni per l'uso** instructions (for use)

istupi'dire *vt* (*colpo*) to stun, daze; (: *droga, stanchezza*) to stupefy; **istupidirsi** *vr* to become stupid

'ISVE *sigla m* (= *Istituto di Studi per lo Sviluppo Economico*) *institute for research into economic development*

I'talia *sf*: **l'~** Italy

itali'ano, -a *ag* Italian ■ *sm/f* Italian ■ *sm* (*Ling*) Italian; **gli Italiani** the Italians

ITC *sigla m* = **istituto tecnico commerciale**

'iter *sm* passage, course; **l'~ burocratico** the bureaucratic process

itine'rante *ag* wandering, itinerant; **mostra ~** touring exhibition; **spettacolo ~** travelling (*Brit*) *o* traveling (*US*) show, touring show

itine'rario *sm* itinerary

'ITIS *sigla m* = **istituto tecnico industriale statale**

itte'rizia [itte'rittsja] *sf* (*Med*) jaundice

'ittico, -a, ci, che *ag* fish *cpd*; fishing *cpd*

IUD *sigla m inv* (= *intra-uterine device*) IUD

Iugos'lavia *sf* = **Jugoslavia**

iugos'lavo, -a *ag, sm/f* = **jugoslavo, a**

i'uta *sf* jute

'I.V.A. *sigla f* = **imposta sul valore aggiunto**

'ivi *av* (*formale, poetico*) therein; (*nelle citazioni*) ibid

Jj

J, j [i'lunga] *sm o f inv* (*lettera*) J, j; **J come Jersey** ≈ J for Jack (*Brit*), J for Jig (*US*)
jazz [dʒaz] *sm* jazz
jaz'zista, -i [dʒad'dzista] *sm* jazz player
jeans [dʒinz] *smpl* jeans
jeep [dʒip] *sm inv* jeep
'jersey ['dʒɛrzi] *sm inv* jersey (cloth)
'jockey ['dʒɔki] *sm inv* (*Carte*) jack; (*fantino*) jockey
'jogging ['dʒɔgiŋ] *sm* jogging; **fare ~** to go jogging
'jolly ['dʒɔli] *sm inv* joker
jr. *abbr* (= *junior*) Jr., jr.
ju'do [dʒu'dɔ] *sm* judo
Jugos'lavia [jugoz'lavja] *sf*: **la ~** Yugoslavia
jugos'lavo, -a *ag, sm/f* Yugoslav(ian)
'juke 'box ['dʒuk'bɔks] *sm inv* jukebox

K, k ['kappa] *sf o m inv* (*lettera*) K, k ■ *abbr* (= *kilo-*, *chilo-*) k; (*Inform*) K; **K come Kursaal** ≈ K for King

Kam'pala *sf* Kampala

kara'oke [kara'oke] *sm inv* karaoke

karatè [kara'tɛ] *sm* karate

'Kashmir ['kaʃmir] *sm*: **il ~** Kashmir

ka'yak [ka'jak] *sm inv* kayak

Ka'zakistan [ɪa'dzakistan] *sm* Kazakhstan

ka'zako, -a [ka'dzako] *ag, sm/f* Kazakh

'Kenia ['kenja] *sm*: **il ~** Kenya

keni'ano, -a *ag, sm/f* Kenyan

keni'ota, -i, e *ag, sm/f* Kenyan

'Kenya ['kenja] *sm*: **il ~** Kenya

kero'sene [kero'zɛne] *sm* = **cherosene**

kg *abbr* (= *chilogrammo*) kg

kib'butz [kib'buts] *sm inv* kibbutz

Kilimangi'aro [kiliman'dʒaro] *sm*: **il ~** Kilimanjaro

'killer ['killer] *sm inv* gunman, hired gun

'kilo *etc* = **chilo** *etc*

kilt [kilt] *sm inv* kilt

ki'mono [ki'mɔno] *sm* = **chimono**

Kir'ghizistan [kir'gidzistan] *sm* Kyrgyzstan

kir'ghiso, -a [kir'gizo] *ag, sm/f* Kyrgyz

kitsch [kitʃ] *sm* kitsch

'kiwi ['kiwi] *sm inv* kiwi (fruit)

km *abbr* (= *chilometro*) km

kmq *abbr* (= *chilometro quadrato*) km^2

ko'ala [ko'ala] *sm inv* koala (bear)

koso'varo, -a *ag, sm/f* Kosovan

'Kosovo *sm* Kosovo

KR *sigla* = **Crotone**

'krapfen ['krapfən] *sm inv* doughnut

Ku'ala Lum'par *sf* Kuala Lumpur

Ku'wait [ku'vait] *sm*: **il ~** Kuwait

kW *abbr* (= *kilowatt, chilowatt*) kW

kWh *abbr* (= *kilowattora*) kW/h

L, l ['ɛlle] *sf o m inv* (*lettera*) L, l ■ *abbr* (= *lira*) L; (= *L come Livorno*) ≈ L for Lucy (*Brit*), L for Love (*US*)
l *abbr* (= *litro*) l
l' *det vedi* **la; lo**
la *det f* (*dav V* **l'**) the ■ *pron* (*dav V* **l'**) (*oggetto: persona*) her; (*: cosa*) it; (*: forma di cortesia*) you ■ *sm inv* (*Mus*) A; (*: solfeggiando la scala*) la; *vedi anche* **il**
là *av* there; **di là** (*da quel luogo*) from there; (*in quel luogo*) in there; (*dall'altra parte*) over there; **di là di** beyond; **per di là** that way; **più in là** further on; (*tempo*) later on; **là dentro/sopra/sotto** in/up (*o* on) /under there; **là per là** (*sul momento*) there and then; **essere in là con gli anni** to be getting on (in years); **essere più di là che di qua** to be more dead than alive; **va' là!** come off it!; **stavolta è andato troppo in là** this time he's gone too far; *vedi anche* **quello**
'labbro *sm* (*Anat: pl(f)* **labbra**) lip
'labile *ag* fleeting, ephemeral
labi'rinto *sm* labyrinth, maze
labora'torio *sm* (*di ricerca*) laboratory; (*di arti, mestieri*) workshop; **~ linguistico** language laboratory
labori'oso, -a *ag* (*faticoso*) laborious; (*attivo*) hard-working
labu'rista, -i, e *ag* Labour *cpd* (*Brit*) ■ *sm/f* Labour Party member (*Brit*)
'lacca, -che *sf* lacquer; (*per unghie*) nail varnish (*Brit*), nail polish
lac'care *vt* (*mobili*) to varnish, lacquer
'laccio ['lattʃo] *sm* noose; (*legaccio, tirante*) lasso; (*di scarpa*) lace; **~ emostatico** (*Med*) tourniquet
lace'rante [latʃe'rante] *ag* (*suono*) piercing, shrill
lace'rare [latʃe'rare] *vt* to tear to shreds, lacerate; **lacerarsi** *vr* to tear
lacerazi'one [latʃerat'tsjone] *sf* (*anche Med*) tear
'lacero, -a ['latʃero] *ag* (*logoro*) torn, tattered; (*Med*) lacerated; **ferita ~-contusa** injury with lacerations and bruising
la'conico, -a, ci, che *ag* laconic, brief
'lacrima *sf* tear; (*goccia*) drop; **in lacrime** in tears
lacri'mare *vi* to water
lacri'mevole *ag* heartrending, pitiful
lacri'mogeno, -a [lakri'mɔdʒeno] *ag*: **gas ~** tear gas
lacri'moso, -a *ag* tearful
la'cuna *sf* (*fig*) gap
la'custre *ag* lake *cpd*
lad'dove *cong* whereas
'ladro *sm* thief; **al ~!** stop thief!
ladro'cinio [ladro'tʃinjo] *sm* theft, robbery
la'druncolo, -a *sm/f* petty thief
laggiù [lad'dʒu] *av* down there; (*di là*) over there
'lagna ['laɲɲa] *sf* (*fam: persona, cosa*) drag, bore; **fare la ~** to whine, moan
la'gnanza [laɲ'ɲantsa] *sf* complaint
la'gnarsi [laɲ'ɲarsi] *vr*: **~ (di)** to complain (about)
'lago, -ghi *sm* lake
'Lagos ['lagos] *sf* Lagos
'lagrima *etc* = **lacrima** *etc*
la'guna *sf* lagoon
lagu'nare *ag* lagoon *cpd*
'laico, -a, ci, che *ag* (*apostolato*) lay; (*vita*) secular; (*scuola*) non-denominational ■ *sm/f* layman(-woman) ■ *sm* lay brother
'laido, -a *ag* filthy, foul; (*fig: osceno*) obscene, filthy
'lama *sf* blade ■ *sm inv* (*Zool*) llama; (*Rel*) lama
lambic'care *vt* to distil; **lambiccarsi il cervello** to rack one's brains
lam'bire *vt* (*fig: fiamme*) to lick; (*acqua*) to lap
lam'bretta® *sf* scooter
la'mella *sf* (*di metallo etc*) thin sheet, thin strip; (*di fungo*) gill
lamen'tare *vt* to lament; **lamentarsi** *vr* (*emettere lamenti*) to moan, groan;

(*rammaricarsi*): **lamentarsi (di)** to complain (about)
lamen'tela *sf* complaining *no pl*
lamen'tevole *ag* (*voce*) complaining, plaintive; (*stato*) lamentable, pitiful
la'mento *sm* moan, groan; (*per la morte di qn*) lament
lamen'toso, -a *ag* plaintive
la'metta *sf* razor blade
lami'era *sf* sheet metal
'lamina *sf* (*lastra sottile*) thin sheet (*o* layer *o* plate); **~ d'oro** gold leaf; gold foil
lami'nare *vt* to laminate
lami'nato, -a *ag* laminated; (*tessuto*) lamé ■ *sm* laminate
'lampada *sf* lamp; **~ a petrolio/a gas** oil/gas lamp; **~ a spirito** blowlamp (*Brit*), blowtorch; **~ a stelo** standard lamp (*Brit*), floor lamp; **~ da tavolo** table lamp
lampa'dario *sm* chandelier
lampa'dina *sf* light bulb; **~ tascabile** pocket torch (*Brit*), flashlight (*US*)
lam'pante *ag* (*fig: evidente*) crystal clear, evident
lam'para *sf* fishing lamp; (*barca*) boat for fishing by lamplight (*in Mediterranean*)
lampeggi'are [lamped'dʒare] *vi* (*luce, fari*) to flash ■ *vb impers*: **lampeggia** there's lightning
lampeggia'tore [lampeddʒa'tore] *sm* (*Aut*) indicator
lampi'one *sm* street light *o* lamp (*Brit*)
'lampo *sm* (*Meteor*) flash of lightning; (*di luce, fig*) flash ■ *ag inv*: **cerniera ~** zip (fastener) (*Brit*), zipper (*US*); **guerra ~** blitzkrieg; **lampi** *smpl* (*Meteor*) lightning *no pl*; **passare come un ~** to flash past *o* by
lam'pone *sm* raspberry
'lana *sf* wool; **~ d'acciaio** steel wool; **pura ~ vergine** pure new wool; **~ di vetro** glass wool
lan'cetta [lan'tʃetta] *sf* (*indice*) pointer, needle; (*di orologio*) hand
'lancia, -ce ['lantʃa] *sf* (*arma*) lance; (*: picca*) spear; (*di pompa antincendio*) nozzle; (*imbarcazione*) launch; **partire ~ in resta** (*fig*) to set off ready for battle; **spezzare una ~ in favore di qn** (*fig*) to come to sb's defence; **~ di salvataggio** lifeboat
lancia'bombe [lantʃa'bombe] *sm inv* (*Mil*) mortar
lanciafi'amme [lantʃa'fjamme] *sm inv* flamethrower
lancia'missili [lantʃa'missili] *ag inv* missile-launching ■ *sm inv* missile launcher
lancia'razzi [lantʃa'raddzi] *ag inv* rocket-launching ■ *sm inv* rocket launcher
lanci'are [lan'tʃare] *vt* to throw, hurl, fling; (*Sport*) to throw; (*far partire: automobile*) to get up to full speed; (*bombe*) to drop; (*razzo, prodotto, moda*) to launch; (*emettere: grido*) to give out; **lanciarsi** *vr*: **lanciarsi contro/su** to throw *o* hurl *o* fling o.s. against/on; **lanciarsi in** (*fig*) to embark on; **~ un cavallo** to give a horse his head; **~ il disco** (*Sport*) to throw the discus; **~ il peso** (*Sport*) to put the shot; **lanciarsi all'inseguimento di qn** to set off in pursuit of sb; **lanciarsi col paracadute** to parachute
lanci'ato, -a [lan'tʃato] *ag* (*affermato: attore, prodotto*) well-known, famous; (*veicolo*) speeding along, racing along
lanci'nante [lantʃi'nante] *ag* (*dolore*) shooting, throbbing; (*grido*) piercing
'lancio ['lantʃo] *sm* throwing *no pl*; throw; dropping *no pl*; drop; launching *no pl*; launch; **~ del disco** (*Sport*) throwing the discus; **~ del peso** (*Sport*) putting the shot
'landa *sf* (*Geo*) moor
'languido, -a *ag* (*fiacco*) languid, weak; (*tenero, malinconico*) languishing
langu'ire *vi* to languish; (*conversazione*) to flag
langu'ore *sm* weakness, languor
lani'ero, -a *ag* wool *cpd*, woollen (*Brit*), woolen (*US*)
lani'ficio [lani'fitʃo] *sm* woollen (*Brit*) *o* woolen (*US*) mill
lano'lina *sf* lanolin(e)
la'noso, -a *ag* woolly
lan'terna *sf* lantern; (*faro*) lighthouse
lanter'nino *sm*: **cercarsele col ~** to be asking for trouble
la'nugine [la'nudʒine] *sf* down
'Laos *sm* Laos
lapalissi'ano, -a *ag* self-evident
La 'Paz [la'pas] *sf* La Paz
lapi'dare *vt* to stone
lapi'dario, -a *ag* (*fig*) terse
'lapide *sf* (*di sepolcro*) tombstone; (*commemorativa*) plaque
la'pin [la'pɛ̃] *sm inv* coney
'lapis *sm inv* pencil
'lappone *ag, sm/f, sm* Lapp
Lap'ponia *sf*: **la ~** Lapland
'lapsus *sm inv* slip
laptop ['læp tɔp] *sm inv* laptop (computer)
'lardo *sm* bacon fat, lard
lar'ghezza [lar'gettsa] *sf* width; breadth; looseness; generosity; **~ di vedute** broad-mindedness
lar'gire [lar'dʒire] *vt* to give generously
'largo, -a, ghi, ghe *ag* wide, broad; (*maniche*) wide; (*abito: troppo ampio*) loose; (*fig*) generous ■ *sm* width; breadth; (*mare aperto*): **il ~** the

open sea ■ *sf*: **stare** *o* **tenersi alla larga (da qn/qc)** to keep one's distance (from sb/sth), keep away (from sb/sth); **~ due metri** two metres wide; **~ di spalle** broad-shouldered; **di larghe vedute** broad-minded; **in larga misura** to a great *o* large extent; **su larga scala** on a large scale; **di manica larga** generous, open-handed; **al ~ di Genova** off (the coast of) Genoa; **farsi ~ tra la folla** to push one's way through the crowd

'larice ['laritʃe] *sm* (*Bot*) larch

la'ringe [la'rindʒe] *sf* larynx

larin'gite [larin'dʒite] *sf* laryngitis

laringoi'atra, -i, e *sm/f* (*medico*) throat specialist

'larva *sf* larva; (*fig*) shadow

la'sagne [la'zaɲɲe] *sfpl* lasagna *sg*

lasciapas'sare [laʃʃapas'sare] *sm inv* pass, permit

lasci'are [laʃʃare] *vt* to leave; (*abbandonare*) to leave, abandon, give up; (*cessare di tenere*) to let go of ■ *vb aus*: **~ qn fare qc** to let sb do sth ■ *vi*: **~ di fare** (*smettere*) to stop doing; **lasciarsi andare/truffare** to let o.s. go/be cheated; **~ andare** *o* **correre** *o* **perdere** to let things go their own way; **~ stare qc/qn** to leave sth/sb alone; **~ qn erede** to make sb one's heir; **~ la presa** to lose one's grip; **~ il segno (su qc)** to leave a mark (on sth); (*fig*) to leave one's mark (on sth); **~ (molto) a desiderare** to leave much to be desired; **ci ha lasciato la vita** it cost him his life

'lascito ['laʃʃito] *sm* (*Dir*) legacy

la'scivia [laʃʃivja] *sf* lust, lasciviousness

la'scivo, -a [laʃʃivo] *ag* lascivious

'laser ['lazer] *ag, sm inv*: **(raggio) ~** laser (beam)

lassa'tivo, a *ag, sm* laxative

las'sismo *sm* laxity

'lasso *sm*: **~ di tempo** interval

lassù *av* up there

'lastra *sf* (*di pietra*) slab; (*di metallo, Fot*) plate; (*di ghiaccio, vetro*) sheet; (*radiografica*) X-ray (plate)

lastri'care *vt* to pave

lastri'cato *sm* paving

'lastrico (*mpl* **lastrici** *o* **lastrichi**) *sm* paving; **essere sul ~** (*fig*) to be penniless; **gettare qn sul ~** (*fig*) to leave sb destitute

las'trone *sm* (*Alpinismo*) sheer rock face

la'tente *ag* latent

late'rale *ag* lateral, side *cpd*; (*uscita, ingresso etc*) side *cpd* ■ *sm* (*Calcio*) half-back

lateral'mente *av* sideways

late'rizio [late'rittsjo] *sm* (perforated) brick

latifon'dista, -i, e *sm/f* large agricultural landowner

lati'fondo *sm* large estate

la'tino, -a *ag, sm* Latin

la'tinoameri'cano, -a *ag, sm/f* Latin-American

lati'tante *ag*: **essere ~** to be on the run ■ *sm/f* fugitive (from justice)

lati'tanza [lati'tantsa] *sf*: **darsi alla ~** to go into hiding

lati'tudine *sf* latitude

'lato, -a *ag*: **in senso ~** broadly speaking ■ *sm* side; (*fig*) aspect, point of view; **d'altro ~** (*d'altra parte*) on the other hand

la'trare *vi* to bark

lat'rato *sm* howling

la'trina *sf* public lavatory

latro'cinio [latro'tʃinjo] *sm* = **ladrocinio**

'latta *sf* tin (plate); (*recipiente*) tin, can

lat'taio, -a *sm/f* (*distributore*) milkman(-woman); (*commerciante*) dairyman(-woman)

lat'tante *ag* unweaned ■ *sm/f* breast-fed baby

'latte *sm* milk; **fratello di ~** foster brother; **avere ancora il ~ alla bocca** (*fig*) to be still wet behind the ears; **tutto ~ e miele** (*fig*) all smiles; **~ detergente** cleansing milk *o* lotion; **~ intero** full-cream milk; **~ a lunga conservazione** UHT milk; **~ magro** *o* **scremato** skimmed milk; **~ secco** *o* **in polvere** dried *o* powdered milk

'latteo, -a *ag* milky; (*dieta, prodotto*) milk *cpd*

latte'ria *sf* dairy

latti'cini [latti'tʃini] *smpl* dairy *o* milk products

lat'tina *sf* (*di birra etc*) can

lat'tuga, -ghe *sf* lettuce

'laurea *sf* ≈ degree; **~ breve** *university degree awarded at the end of a three-year course*; **avere una ~ in chimica** to have a degree in chemistry *o* a chemistry degree; *see note*

LAUREA

The *Laurea* is awarded to students who successfully complete their degree courses. Traditionally, this takes between four and six years; a major element of the final examinations is the presentation and discussion of a dissertation. A shorter, more vocational course of study, taking from two to three years, is also available; at the end of this time students receive a diploma called the *Laurea breve*.

laure'ando, -a *sm/f* final-year student

laure'are *vt* to confer a degree on; **laurearsi** *vr* to graduate

laure'ato, -a *ag, sm/f* graduate
'lauro *sm* laurel
'lauto, -a *ag* *(pranzo, mancia)* lavish; **lauti guadagni** handsome profits
'lava *sf* lava
lavabianche'ria [lavabjanke'ria] *sf inv* washing machine
la'vabo *sm* washbasin
la'vaggio [la'vaddʒo] *sm* washing *no pl*; **~ del cervello** brainwashing *no pl*
la'vagna [la'vaɲɲa] *sf* *(Geo)* slate; *(di scuola)* blackboard; **~ luminosa** overhead projector
la'vanda *sf* *(anche Med)* wash; *(Bot)* lavender; **fare una ~ gastrica a qn** to pump sb's stomach
lavan'daia *sf* washerwoman
lavande'ria *sf* *(di ospedale, caserma etc)* laundry; **~ automatica** launderette; **~ a secco** dry-cleaner's
lavan'dino *sm* sink; *(del bagno)* washbasin
lavapi'atti *sm/f* dishwasher
la'vare *vt* to wash; **lavarsi** *vr* to wash, have a wash; **~ a secco** to dry-clean; **~ i panni sporchi in pubblico** *(fig)* to wash one's dirty linen in public; **lavarsi le mani/i denti** to wash one's hands/clean one's teeth
lava'secco *sm o f inv* dry-cleaner's
lavasto'viglie [lavasto'viʎʎe] *sm o f inv* *(macchina)* dishwasher
la'vata *sf* wash; *(fig)*: **dare una ~ di capo a qn** to give sb a good telling-off
lava'tivo *sm* *(clistere)* enema; *(buono a nulla)* good-for-nothing, idler
lava'toio *sm* (public) washhouse
lava'trice [lava'tritʃe] *sf* washing machine
lava'tura *sf* washing *no pl*; **~ di piatti** dishwater
la'vello *sm* (kitchen) sink
la'vina *sf* snowslide
lavo'rante *sm/f* worker
lavo'rare *vi* to work; *(fig: bar, studio etc)* to do good business ■ *vt* to work; **~ a** to work on; **~ a maglia** to knit; **~ di fantasia** *(suggestionarsi)* to imagine things; *(fantasticare)* to let one's imagination run free; **lavorarsi qn** *(fig: convincere)* to work on sb
lavora'tivo, -a *ag* working
lavora'tore, -'trice *sm/f* worker ■ *ag* working
lavorazi'one [lavorat'tsjone] *sf* *(gen)* working; *(di legno, pietra)* carving; *(di film)* making; *(di prodotto)* manufacture; *(modo di esecuzione)* workmanship
lavo'rio *sm* intense activity
la'voro *sm* work; *(occupazione)* job, work *no pl*; *(opera)* piece of work, job; *(Econ)* labour *(Brit)*, labor *(US)*; **Ministero del L~** Department of Employment *(Brit)*, Department of Labor *(US)*; **(fare) i lavori di casa** (to do) the housework *sg*; **lavori forzati** hard labour *sg*; **i lavori del parlamento** the parliamentary session *sg*; **lavori pubblici** public works
lazi'ale [lat'tsjale] *ag* of (*o* from) Lazio
lazza'retto [laddza'retto] *sm* leper hospital
lazza'rone [laddza'rone] *sm* scoundrel
'lazzo ['laddzo] *sm* jest
LC *sigla* = **Lecco**
LE *sigla* = **Lecce**
le *det fpl* the ■ *pron* *(oggetto)* them; *(: a lei, a essa)* (to) her; *(: forma di cortesia)* (to) you; *vedi anche* **il**
le'ale *ag* loyal; *(sincero)* sincere; *(onesto)* fair
lea'lista, -i, e *sm/f* loyalist
lealtà *sf* loyalty; sincerity; fairness
'leasing ['li:ziŋ] *sm* leasing; lease
'lebbra *sf* leprosy
'lecca 'lecca *sm inv* lollipop
leccapi'edi *sm/f inv* *(peg)* toady, bootlicker
lec'care *vt* to lick; *(gatto: latte etc)* to lick *o* lap up; *(fig)* to flatter; **leccarsi** *vr* *(fig)* to preen o.s.; **leccarsi i baffi** to lick one's lips
lec'cato, -a *ag* affected ■ *sf* lick
leccherò *etc* [lekke'rɔ] *vb vedi* **leccare**
'leccio ['lettʃo] *sm* holm oak, ilex
leccor'nia *sf* titbit, delicacy
'lecito, -a ['letʃito] *ag* permitted, allowed; **se mi è ~** if I may; **mi sia ~ far presente che ...** may I point out that ...
'ledere *vt* to damage, injure; **~ gli interessi di qn** to be prejudicial to sb's interests
'lega, -ghe *sf* *(anche Pol)* league; *(di metalli)* alloy; **metallo di bassa ~** base metal; **gente di bassa ~** common *o* vulgar people; **Llega Nord** *(Pol)* *federalist party*
le'gaccio [le'gattʃo] *sm* string, lace
le'gale *ag* legal ■ *sm* lawyer; **corso ~ delle monete** official exchange rate; **medicina ~** forensic medicine; **studio ~** lawyer's office
legalità *sf* legality, lawfulness
legaliz'zare [legalid'dzare] *vt* to legalize; *(documento)* to authenticate
legalizzazi'one [legaliddzat'tsjone] *sf* *(vedi vt)* legalization; authentication
le'game *sm* *(corda, fig: affettivo)* tie, bond; *(nesso logico)* link, connection; **~ di sangue** *o* **di parentela** family tie
lega'mento *sm* *(Anat)* ligament
le'gare *vt* *(prigioniero, capelli, cane)* to tie (up); *(libro)* to bind; *(Chim)* to alloy; *(fig: collegare)* to bind, join ■ *vi* *(far lega)* to unite; *(fig)* to get on well; **è pazzo da ~** *(fam)* he should be locked up
lega'tario, -a *sm/f* *(Dir)* legatee

le'gato *sm* (*Rel*) legate; (*Dir*) legacy, bequest
legato'ria *sf* (*attività*) bookbinding; (*negozio*) bookbinder's
lega'tura *sf* (*di libro*) binding; (*Mus*) ligature
legazi'one [legat'tsjone] *sf* legation
le'genda [le'dʒɛnda] *sf* (*di carta geografica etc*) = **leggenda**
'legge ['leddʒe] *sf* law; **~ procedurale** procedural law
leg'genda [led'dʒɛnda] *sf* (*narrazione*) legend; (*di carta geografica etc*) key, legend
leggen'dario, -a [leddʒen'darjo] *ag* legendary
'leggere ['lɛddʒere] *vt, vi* to read; **~ il pensiero di qn** to read sb's mind *o* thoughts
legge'rezza [leddʒe'rettsa] *sf* lightness; thoughtlessness; fickleness
leg'gero, -a [led'dʒɛro] *ag* light; (*agile, snello*) nimble, agile, light; (*tè, caffè*) weak; (*fig: non grave, piccolo*) slight; (*: spensierato*) thoughtless; (*: incostante*) fickle; free and easy; **una ragazza leggera** (*fig*) a flighty girl; **alla leggera** thoughtlessly
leggi'adro, -a [led'dʒadro] *ag* pretty, lovely; (*movimenti*) graceful
leg'gibile [led'dʒibile] *ag* legible; (*libro*) readable, worth reading
leg'gio, -'gii [led'dʒio] *sm* lectern; (*Mus*) music stand
legherò *etc* [lege'rɔ] *vb vedi* **legare**
le'ghismo [le'gismo] *sm* *political movement with federalist tendencies*
le'ghista, -i, e [le'gista] *ag* (*Pol*) of a "lega" (*especially Lega Nord*) ■ *sm/f* member (*o* supporter) of a "lega" (*especially Lega Nord*)
legife'rare [ledʒife'rare] *vi* to legislate
legio'nario [ledʒo'narjo] *sm* (*romano*) legionary; (*volontario*) legionnaire
legi'one [le'dʒone] *sf* legion; **~ straniera** foreign legion
legisla'tivo, -a [ledʒizla'tivo] *ag* legislative
legisla'tore [ledʒizla'tore] *sm* legislator
legisla'tura [ledʒizla'tura] *sf* legislature
legislazi'one [ledʒizlat'tsjone] *sf* legislation
legitti'mare [ledʒitti'mare] *vt* (*figlio*) to legitimize; (*comportamento etc*) to justify
legittimità [ledʒittimi'ta] *sf* legitimacy
le'gittimo, -a [le'dʒittimo] *ag* legitimate; (*fig: giustificato, lecito*) justified, legitimate; **legittima difesa** (*Dir*) self-defence (*Brit*), self-defense (*US*)
'legna ['leɲɲa] *sf* firewood
le'gnaia [leɲ'ɲaja] *sf* woodshed
legnai'olo [leɲɲa'jɔlo] *sm* woodcutter
le'gname [leɲ'ɲame] *sm* wood, timber
le'gnata [leɲ'ɲata] *sf* blow with a stick; **dare a qn un sacco di legnate** to give sb a good hiding
'legno ['leɲɲo] *sm* wood; (*pezzo di legno*) piece of wood; **di ~** wooden; **~ compensato** plywood
le'gnoso, -a [leɲ'ɲoso] *ag* (*di legno*) wooden; (*come il legno*) woody; (*carne*) tough
le'gume *sm* (*Bot*) pulse; **legumi** *smpl* (*fagioli, piselli etc*) pulses
'lei *pron* (*soggetto*) she; (*oggetto: per dare rilievo, con preposizione*) her; (*forma di cortesia: anche*: **Lei**) you ■ *sf inv*: **la mia ~** my beloved ■ *sm*: **dare del ~ a qn** to address sb as "lei"; **~ stessa** she herself; you yourself; **è ~** it's her
'lembo *sm* (*di abito, strada*) edge; (*striscia sottile: di terra*) strip
'lemma, -i *sm* headword
'lemme 'lemme *av* (very) very slowly
'lena *sf* (*fig*) energy, stamina; **di buona ~** (*lavorare, camminare*) at a good pace
Lenin'grado *sf* Leningrad
le'nire *vt* to soothe
lenta'mente *av* slowly
'lente *sf* (*Ottica*) lens *sg*; **~ d'ingrandimento** magnifying glass; **lenti a contatto, lenti corneali** contact lenses; **lenti (a contatto) morbide** soft lenses; **lenti (a contatto) rigide** hard lenses
len'tezza [len'tettsa] *sf* slowness
len'ticchia [len'tikkja] *sf* (*Bot*) lentil
len'tiggine [len'tiddʒine] *sf* freckle
'lento, -a *ag* slow; (*molle: fune*) slack; (*non stretto: vite, abito*) loose ■ *sm* (*ballo*) slow dance
'lenza ['lɛntsa] *sf* fishing line
lenzu'olo [len'tswɔlo] *sm* sheet; **lenzuola** *sfpl* pair of sheets; **~ funebre** shroud
leon'cino [leon'tʃino] *sm* lion cub
le'one *sm* lion; (*dello zodiaco*): **L~** Leo; **essere del L~** to be Leo
leo'pardo *sm* leopard
lepo'rino, -a *ag*: **labbro ~** harelip
'lepre *sf* hare
'lercio, -a, ci, ce ['lɛrtʃo] *ag* filthy
lerci'ume [ler'tʃume] *sm* filth
'lesbico, -a, ci, che *ag, sf* lesbian
'lesi *etc vb vedi* **ledere**
lesi'nare *vt* to be stingy with ■ *vi*: **~ (su)** to skimp (on), be stingy (with)
lesi'one *sf* (*Med*) lesion; (*Dir*) injury, damage; (*Edil*) crack
le'sivo, -a *ag*: **~ (di)** damaging (to), detrimental (to)
'leso, -a *pp di* **ledere** ■ *ag* (*offeso*) injured; **parte lesa** (*Dir*) injured party; **lesa maestà** lese-majesty
Le'sotho [le'soto] *sm* Lesotho
les'sare *vt* (*Cuc*) to boil
'lessi *etc vb vedi* **leggere**
lessi'cale *ag* lexical

'lessico, -ci *sm* vocabulary; *(dizionario)* lexicon
lessicogra'fia *sf* lexicography
lessi'cografo, -a *sm/f* lexicographer
'lesso, -a *ag* boiled ■ *sm* boiled meat
'lesto, -a *ag* quick; *(agile)* nimble; **~ di mano** *(per rubare)* light-fingered; *(per picchiare)* free with one's fists
lesto'fante *sm* swindler, con man
le'tale *ag* lethal, deadly
leta'maio *sm* dunghill
le'tame *sm* manure, dung
le'targo, -ghi *sm* lethargy; *(Zool)* hibernation
le'tizia [le'tittsja] *sf* joy, happiness
'letta *sf*: **dare una ~ a qc** to glance *o* look through sth
'lettera *sf* letter; **lettere** *sfpl* *(letteratura)* literature *sg*; *(studi umanistici)* arts (subjects); **alla ~** literally; **in lettere** in words, in full; **diventar ~ morta** *(legge)* to become a dead letter; **restar ~ morta** *(consiglio, invito)* to go unheeded; **~ di accompagnamento** accompanying letter; **~ assicurata** registered letter; **~ di cambio** *(Comm)* bill of exchange; **~ di credito** *(Comm)* letter of credit; **~ di intenti** letter of intent; **~ di presentazione** *o* **raccomandazione** letter of introduction; **~ raccomandata** recorded delivery *(Brit)* *o* certified *(US)* letter; **~ di trasporto aereo** *(Comm)* air waybill
lette'rale *ag* literal
letteral'mente *av* literally
lette'rario, -a *ag* literary
lette'rato, -a *ag* well-read, scholarly
lettera'tura *sf* literature
let'tiga, -ghe *sf* *(portantina)* litter; *(barella)* stretcher
let'tino *sm* cot *(Brit)*, crib *(US)*; *(per il sole)* sun lounger
'letto, -a *pp di* **leggere** ■ *sm* bed; **andare a ~** to go to bed; **~ a castello** bunk beds *pl*; **~ a una piazza/a due piazze** *o* **matrimoniale** single/double bed
'lettone *ag, sm/f* Latvian ■ *sm* *(Ling)* Latvian
Let'tonia *sf*: **la ~** Latvia
lettorato *sm* *(Ins)* lectorship, assistantship; *(Rel)* lectorate
let'tore, -'trice *sm/f* reader; *(Ins)* (foreign language) assistant *(Brit)*, (foreign) teaching assistant *(US)* ■ *sm*: **~ ottico (di caratteri)** optical character reader; **~ CD/DVD** CD/DVD player; **~ MP3/MP4** MP3/MP4 player
let'tura *sf* reading
leuce'mia [leutʃe'mia] *sf* leukaemia
'leva *sf* lever; *(Mil)* conscription; **far ~ su qn** to work on sb; **essere di ~** to be due for call-up; **~ del cambio** *(Aut)* gear lever
le'vante *sm* east; *(vento)* East wind; **il L~** the Levant
le'vare *vt* *(occhi, braccio)* to raise; *(sollevare, togliere: tassa, divieto)* to lift; *(: indumenti)* to take off, remove; *(rimuovere)* to take away; *(: dal di sopra)* to take off; *(: dal di dentro)* to take out; **levarsi** *vr* to get up; *(sole)* to rise; **~ le tende** *(fig)* to pack up and leave; **levarsi il pensiero** to put one's mind at rest; **levati di mezzo** *o* **di lì** *o* **di torno!** get out of my way!
le'vata *sf* *(di posta)* collection
leva'taccia, -ce [leva'tattʃa] *sf* early rise
leva'toio, -a *ag*: **ponte ~** drawbridge
leva'trice [leva'tritʃe] *sf* midwife
leva'tura *sf* intelligence, mental capacity
levi'gare *vt* to smooth; *(con carta vetrata)* to sand
levi'gato, -a *ag* *(superficie)* smooth; *(fig: stile)* polished; *(: viso)* flawless
levità *sf* lightness
levri'ere *sm* greyhound
lezi'one [let'tsjone] *sf* lesson; *(all'università, sgridata)* lecture; **fare ~** to teach; to lecture
lezi'oso, -a [let'tsjoso] *ag* affected; simpering
'lezzo ['leddzo] *sm* stench, stink
LI *sigla* = **Livorno**
li *pron pl* *(oggetto)* them
lì *av* there; **di** *o* **da lì** from there; **per di lì** that way; **di lì a pochi giorni** a few days later; **lì per lì** there and then; at first; **essere lì (lì) per fare** to be on the point of doing, be about to do; **lì dentro** in there; **lì sotto** under there; **lì sopra** on there; up there; **tutto lì** that's all; *vedi anche* **quello**
libagi'one [liba'dʒone] *sf* libation
liba'nese *ag, sm/f* Lebanese *inv*
Li'bano *sm*: **il ~** the Lebanon
'libbra *sf* *(peso)* pound
li'beccio [li'bettʃo] *sm* south-west wind
li'bello *sm* libel
li'bellula *sf* dragonfly
libe'rale *ag, sm/f* liberal
liberaliz'zare [liberalid'dzare] *vt* to liberalize
libe'rare *vt* *(rendere libero: prigioniero)* to release; *(: popolo)* to free, liberate; *(sgombrare: passaggio)* to clear; *(: stanza)* to vacate; *(produrre: energia)* to release; **liberarsi** *vr*: **liberarsi di qc/qn** to get rid of sth/sb
libera'tore, -'trice *ag* liberating ■ *sm/f* liberator
liberazi'one [liberat'tsjone] *sf* *(di prigioniero)* release; *(di popolo)* liberation; **che ~!** what a relief!; **la L~** *see note*

LIBERAZIONE

The *Liberazione* is a national holiday which falls on 25 April. It commemorates the liberation of Italy in 1945 from German forces and Mussolini's government and marks the end of the war on Italian soil.

li'bercolo *sm* (*peg*) worthless book
Li'beria *sf*: **la ~** Liberia
liberi'ano, -a *ag, sm/f* Liberian
libe'rismo *sm* (*Econ*) laissez-faire
'libero, -a *ag* free; (*strada*) clear; (*non occupato*: *posto etc*) vacant, free; (*Tel*) not engaged; **~ di fare qc** free to do sth; **~ da** free from; **una donna di liberi costumi** a woman of loose morals; **avere via libera** to have a free hand; **dare via libera a qn** to give sb the go-ahead; **via libera!** all clear!; **~ arbitrio** free will; **~ professionista** self-employed professional person; **~ scambio** free trade; **libera uscita** (*Mil*) leave
liberoscam'bismo *sm* (*Econ*) free trade
libertà *sf inv* freedom; (*tempo disponibile*) free time ■ *sfpl* (*licenza*) liberties; **essere in ~ provvisoria/vigilata** to be released without bail/be on probation; **~ di riunione** right to hold meetings
liber'tario, -a *ag* libertarian
liber'tino, -a *ag, sm/f* libertine
'liberty ['liberti] *ag inv, sm* art nouveau
'Libia *sf*: **la ~** Libya
'libico, -a, ci, che *ag, sm/f* Libyan
li'bidine *sf* lust
libidi'noso, -a *ag* lustful, libidinous
li'bido *sf* libido
li'braio *sm* bookseller
li'brario, -a *ag* book *cpd*
li'brarsi *vr* to hover
libre'ria *sf* (*bottega*) bookshop; (*stanza*) library; (*mobile*) bookcase
li'bretto *sm* booklet; (*taccuino*) notebook; (*Mus*) libretto; **~ degli assegni** chequebook (*Brit*), checkbook (*US*); **~ di circolazione** (*Aut*) logbook; **~ di deposito** (bank) deposit book; **~ di risparmio** (savings) bankbook, passbook; **~ universitario** student's report book
'libro *sm* book; **~ bianco** (*Pol*) white paper; **~ di cassa** cash book; **~ di consultazione** reference book; **~ mastro** ledger; **~ paga** payroll; **~ tascabile** paperback; **~ di testo** textbook; **libri contabili** (account) books; **libri sociali** company records
li'cantropo *sm* werewolf
lice'ale [litʃe'ale] *ag* secondary school *cpd* (*Brit*), high school *cpd* (*US*) ■ *sm/f* secondary school *o* high school pupil
li'cenza [li'tʃɛntsa] *sf* (*permesso*) permission, leave; (*di pesca, caccia, circolazione*) permit, licence (*Brit*), license (*US*); (*Mil*) leave; (*Ins*) school-leaving certificate; (*libertà*) liberty; (*sfrenatezza*) licentiousness; **andare in ~** (*Mil*) to go on leave; **su ~ di ...** (*Comm*) under licence from ...; **~ di esportazione** export licence; **~ di fabbricazione** manufacturer's licence; **~ poetica** poetic licence
licenzia'mento [litʃentsja'mento] *sm* dismissal
licenzi'are [litʃen'tsjare] *vt* (*impiegato*) to dismiss; (*Ins*) to award a certificate to; **licenziarsi** *vr* (*impiegato*) to resign, hand in one's notice; (*Ins*) to obtain one's school-leaving certificate
licenziosità [litʃentsjosi'ta] *sf* licentiousness
licenzi'oso, -a [litʃen'tsjoso] *ag* licentious
li'ceo [li'tʃɛo] *sm* (*Ins*) secondary (*Brit*) *o* high (*US*) school (*for 14- to 19-year-olds*); **~ classico/scientifico** *secondary or high school specializing in classics/scientific subjects*
li'chene [li'kɛne] *sm* (*Bot*) lichen
'lido *sm* beach, shore
'Liechtenstein ['liktənstain] *sm*: **il ~** Liechtenstein
li'eto, -a *ag* happy, glad; **"molto ~"** (*nelle presentazioni*) "pleased to meet you"; **a ~ fine** with a happy ending
li'eve *ag* light; (*di poco conto*) slight; (*sommesso*: *voce*) faint, soft
lievi'tare *vi* (*anche fig*) to rise ■ *vt* to leaven
li'evito *sm* yeast; **~ di birra** brewer's yeast
'ligio, -a, gi, gie ['lidʒo] *ag* faithful, loyal
li'gnaggio [liɲ'ɲaddʒo] *sm* descent, lineage
'ligure *ag* Ligurian; **la Riviera L~** the Italian Riviera
Li'kud [li'kud] *sm* Likud
'lilla, lillà *sm inv* lilac
'Lima *sf* Lima
'lima *sf* file; **~ da unghie** nail file
limacci'oso, -a [limat'tʃoso] *ag* muddy
li'mare *vt* to file (down); (*fig*) to polish
'limbo *sm* (*Rel*) limbo
li'metta *sf* nail file
limi'tare *vt* to limit, restrict; (*circoscrivere*) to bound, surround
limitata'mente *av* to a limited extent; **~ alle mie possibilità** in so far as I am able
limi'tato, -a *ag* limited, restricted
limitazi'one [limitat'tsjone] *sf* limitation, restriction
'limite *sm* limit; (*confine*) border, boundary ■ *ag inv*: **caso ~** extreme case; **al ~** if the worst comes to the worst (*Brit*), if worst comes to worst (*US*); **~ di velocità** speed limit
li'mitrofo, -a *ag* neighbouring (*Brit*), neighboring (*US*)
'limo *sm* mud, slime; (*Geo*) silt

limo'nata *sf* lemonade (*Brit*), (lemon) soda (*US*); (*spremuta*) lemon squash (*Brit*), lemonade (*US*)
li'mone *sm* (*pianta*) lemon tree; (*frutto*) lemon
limpi'dezza [limpi'dettsa] *sf* clearness; (*di discorso*) clarity
'limpido, -a *ag* (*acqua*) limpid, clear; (*cielo*) clear; (*fig*: *discorso*) clear, lucid
'lince ['lintʃe] *sf* lynx
linci'aggio [lin'tʃaddʒo] *sm* lynching
linci'are [lin'tʃare] *vt* to lynch
'lindo, -a *ag* tidy, spick and span; (*biancheria*) clean
'linea *sf* (*gen*) line; (*di mezzi pubblici di trasporto*: *itinerario*) route; (: *servizio*) service; (*di prodotto*: *collezione*) collection; (: *stile*) style; **a grandi linee** in outline; **mantenere la ~** to look after one's figure; **è caduta la ~** (*Tel*) I (*o* you *etc*) have been cut off; **di ~**: **aereo di ~** airliner; **nave di ~** liner; **volo di ~** scheduled flight; **in ~ diretta da** (*TV*, *Radio*) coming to you direct from; **~ aerea** airline; **~ continua** solid line; **~ di partenza/d'arrivo** (*Sport*) starting/finishing line; **~ punteggiata** dotted line; **~ di tiro** line of fire
linea'menti *smpl* features; (*fig*) outlines
line'are *ag* linear; (*fig*) coherent, logical
line'etta *sf* (*trattino*) dash; (*d'unione*) hyphen
'linfa *sf* (*Bot*) sap; (*Anat*) lymph; **~ vitale** (*fig*) lifeblood
lin'gotto *sm* ingot, bar
'lingua *sf* (*Anat*, *Cuc*) tongue; (*idioma*) language; **mostrare la ~** to stick out one's tongue; **di ~ italiana** Italian-speaking; **~ madre** mother tongue; **una ~ di terra** a spit of land
lingu'accia [lin'gwattʃa] *sf* (*fig*) spiteful gossip
linguacci'uto, -a [lingwat'tʃuto] *ag* gossipy
lingu'aggio [lin'gwaddʒo] *sm* language; **~ giuridico** legal language; **~ macchina** (*Inform*) machine language; **~ di programmazione** (*Inform*) programming language
lingu'etta *sf* (*di strumento*) reed; (*di scarpa*, *Tecn*) tongue; (*di busta*) flap
lingu'ista, -i, e *sm/f* linguist
lingu'istico, -a, ci, che *ag* linguistic ■ *sf* linguistics *sg*
lini'mento *sm* liniment
'lino *sm* (*pianta*) flax; (*tessuto*) linen
li'noleum *sm inv* linoleum, lino
liofiliz'zare [liofilid'dzare] *vt* to freeze-dry
liofiliz'zati [liofilid'dzati] *smpl* freeze-dried foods
Li'one *sf* Lyons
liposuzi'one [liposut'tsjone] *sf* liposuction
'LIPU *sigla f* (= *Lega Italiana Protezione Uccelli*) *society for the protection of birds*
liqu'ame *sm* liquid sewage
lique'fare *vt* (*render liquido*) to liquefy; (*fondere*) to melt; **liquefarsi** *vr* to liquefy; to melt
lique'fatto, -a *pp di* **liquefare**
liqui'dare *vt* (*società, beni, persona*: *uccidere*) to liquidate; (*persona*: *sbarazzarsene*) to get rid of; (*conto, problema*) to settle; (*Comm*: *merce*) to sell off, clear
liquidazi'one [likwidat'tsjone] *sf* (*di società, persona*) liquidation; (*di conto*) settlement; (*di problema*) settling; (*Comm*: *di merce*) clearance sale; (*Amm*) severance pay (*on retirement, redundancy, or when taking up other employment*)
liquidità *sf* liquidity
'liquido, -a *ag, sm* liquid; **denaro ~** cash, ready money; **~ per freni** brake fluid
liqui'gas® *sm inv* Calor gas® (*Brit*), butane
liqui'rizia [likwi'rittsja] *sf* liquorice
li'quore *sm* liqueur
liquo'roso, -a *ag*: **vino ~** dessert wine
'lira *sf* (*unità monetaria*) lira; (*Mus*) lyre; **~ sterlina** pound sterling
'lirico, -a, ci, che *ag* lyric(al); (*Mus*) lyric ■ *sf* (*poesia*) lyric poetry; (*componimento poetico*) lyric; (*Mus*) opera; **cantante/teatro ~** opera singer/house
li'rismo *sm* lyricism
Lis'bona *sf* Lisbon
'lisca, -sche *sf* (*di pesce*) fishbone
lisci'are [liʃʃare] *vt* to smooth; (*fig*) to flatter; **lisciarsi i capelli** to straighten one's hair
'liscio, -a, sci, sce ['liʃʃo] *ag* smooth; (*capelli*) straight; (*mobile*) plain; (*bevanda alcolica*) neat; (*fig*) straightforward, simple ■ *av*: **andare ~** to go smoothly; **passarla liscia** to get away with it
'liso, -a *ag* worn out, threadbare
'lista *sf* (*striscia*) strip; (*elenco*) list; **~ elettorale** electoral roll; **~ delle vivande** menu
lis'tare *vt*: **~ (di)** to edge (with), border (with)
lis'tato *sm* (*Inform*) list, listing
lis'tino *sm* list; **~ di borsa** the Stock Exchange list; **~ dei cambi** (foreign) exchange rate; **~ dei prezzi** price list
lita'nia *sf* litany
'lite *sf* quarrel, argument; (*Dir*) lawsuit
liti'gare *vi* to quarrel; (*Dir*) to litigate
li'tigio [li'tidʒo] *sm* quarrel
litigi'oso, -a [liti'dʒoso] *ag* quarrelsome; (*Dir*) litigious
litogra'fia *sf* (*sistema*) lithography; (*stampa*) lithograph
lito'grafico, -a, ci, che *ag* lithographic
lito'rale *ag* coastal, coast *cpd* ■ *sm* coast
lito'raneo, -a *ag* coastal

'litro *sm* litre (*Brit*), liter (*US*)
lit'torio, -a *ag* (*Storia*) lictorial; **fascio ~** fasces *pl*
Litu'ania *sf*: **la ~** Lithuania
litu'ano, -a *ag, sm/f, sm* Lithuanian
litur'gia, -'gie [litur'dʒia] *sf* liturgy
li'uto *sm* lute
li'vella *sf* level; **~ a bolla d'aria** spirit level
livel'lare *vt* to level, make level; **livellarsi** *vr* to become level; (*fig*) to level out, balance out
livella'trice [livella'tritʃe] *sf* steamroller
li'vello *sm* level; (*fig*) level, standard; **ad alto ~** (*fig*) high-level; **a ~ mondiale** world-wide; **a ~ di confidenza** confidentially; **~ di magazzino** stock level; **~ del mare** sea level; **sul ~ del mare** above sea level; **~ occupazionale** level of employment; **~ retributivo** salary level
'livido, -a *ag* livid; (*per percosse*) bruised, black and blue; (*cielo*) leaden ■ *sm* bruise
li'vore *sm* malice, spite
Li'vorno *sf* Livorno, Leghorn
li'vrea *sf* livery
'lizza ['littsa] *sf* lists *pl*; **essere in ~ per** (*fig*) to compete for; **scendere in ~** (*anche fig*) to enter the lists
LO *sigla* = **Lodi**
lo *det m* (*dav s impura, gn, pn, ps, x, z; dav V* **l'**) the ■ *pron* (*dav V* **l'**: *oggetto: persona*) him; (*: cosa*) it; **lo sapevo** I knew it; **lo so** I know; **sii buono, anche se lui non lo è** be good, even if he isn't; *vedi anche* **il**
lob'bista, -i, e *sm/f* lobbyist
'lobby *sf inv* lobby
'lobo *sm* lobe; **~ dell'orecchio** ear lobe
lo'cale *ag* local ■ *sm* room; (*luogo pubblico*) premises *pl*; **~ notturno** nightclub
località *sf inv* locality
localiz'zare [lokalid'dzare] *vt* (*circoscrivere*) to confine, localize; (*accertare*) to locate, place
lo'canda *sf* inn
locandi'ere, -a *sm/f* innkeeper
locan'dina *sf* (*Teat*) poster
lo'care *vt* (*casa*) to rent out, let; (*macchina*) to hire out (*Brit*), rent (out)
loca'tario, -a *sm/f* tenant
loca'tivo, -a *ag* (*Dir*) rentable
loca'tore, -'trice *sm/f* landlord/lady
locazi'one [lokat'tsjone] *sf* (*da parte del locatario*) renting *no pl*; (*da parte del locatore*) renting out *no pl*, letting *no pl*; **(contratto di) ~** lease; **(canone di) ~** rent; **dare in ~** to rent out, let
locomo'tiva *sf* locomotive
locomo'tore *sm* electric locomotive
locomot'rice [lokomo'tritʃe] *sf* = **locomotore**
locomozi'one [lokomot'tsjone] *sf* locomotion; **mezzi di ~** vehicles, means of transport
'loculo *sm* burial recess
lo'custa *sf* locust
locuzi'one [lokut'tsjone] *sf* phrase, expression
lo'dare *vt* to praise
'lode *sf* praise; (*Ins*): **laurearsi con 110 e ~** ≈ to graduate with first-class honours (*Brit*), ≈ to graduate summa cum laude (*US*)
'loden *sm inv* (*stoffa*) loden; (*cappotto*) loden overcoat
lo'devole *ag* praiseworthy
loga'ritmo *sm* logarithm
log'garsi *vr* (*Inform*) to log in
'loggia, -ge ['lɔddʒa] *sf* (*Archit*) loggia; (*circolo massonico*) lodge
loggi'one [lod'dʒone] *sm* (*di teatro*): **il ~** the Gods *sg*
logica'mente [lodʒika'mente] *av* naturally, obviously
logicità [lodʒitʃi'ta] *sf* logicality
'logico, -a, ci, che ['lɔdʒiko] *ag* logical ■ *sf* logic
lo'gistica [lo'dʒistika] *sf* logistics *sg*
'logo *sm inv* logo
logora'mento *sm* (*di vestiti etc*) wear
logo'rante *ag* exhausting
logo'rare *vt* to wear out; (*sciupare*) to waste; **logorarsi** *vr* to wear out; (*fig*) to wear o.s. out
logo'rio *sm* wear and tear; (*fig*) strain
'logoro, -a *ag* (*stoffa*) worn out, threadbare; (*persona*) worn out
'Loira *sf*: **la ~** the Loire
lom'baggine [lom'baddʒine] *sf* lumbago
Lombar'dia *sf*: **la ~** Lombardy
lom'bardo, -a *ag, sm/f* Lombard
lom'bare *ag* (*Anat, Med*) lumbar
lom'bata *sf* (*taglio di carne*) loin
'lombo *sm* (*Anat*) loin
lom'brico, -chi *sm* earthworm
londi'nese *ag* London *cpd* ■ *sm/f* Londoner
'Londra *sf* London
lon'ganime *ag* forbearing
longevità [londʒevi'ta] *sf* longevity
lon'gevo, -a [lon'dʒevo] *ag* long-lived
longi'lineo, -a [londʒi'lineo] *ag* long-limbed
longi'tudine [londʒi'tudine] *sf* longitude
lontana'mente *av* remotely; **non ci pensavo neppure ~** it didn't even occur to me
lonta'nanza [lonta'nantsa] *sf* distance; absence
lon'tano, -a *ag* (*distante*) distant, faraway; (*assente*) absent; (*vago: sospetto*) slight, remote; (*tempo: remoto*) far-off, distant; (*parente*) distant, remote ■ *av* far; **è lontana la casa?** is it far to the house?, is the house far from here?; **è ~ un chilometro** it's a kilometre

away *o* a kilometre from here; **più ~** farther; **da** *o* **di ~** from a distance; **~ da** a long way from; **alla lontana** slightly, vaguely
'lontra *sf* otter
lo'quace [lo'kwatʃe] *ag* talkative, loquacious; (*fig: gesto etc*) eloquent
loquacità [lokwatʃi'ta] *sf* talkativeness, loquacity
'lordo, -a *ag* dirty, filthy; (*peso, stipendio*) gross; **~ d'imposta** pre-tax
Lo'rena *sf* (*Geo*) Lorraine
'loro *pron pl* (*oggetto, con preposizione*) them; (*complemento di termine*) to them; (*soggetto*) they; (*forma di cortesia: anche:* **Loro**) you; to you; **il(la) ~, i(le) ~** their; (*forma di cortesia: anche:* **Loro**) your ■ *pron* theirs; (*forma di cortesia: anche:* **Loro**) yours ■ *sm inv:* **il ~** their (*o* your) money ■ *sf inv:* **la ~** (*opinione*) their (*o* your) view; **i ~** (*famiglia*) their (*o* your) family; (*amici etc*) their (*o* your own people; **un ~ amico** a friend of theirs; **è dalla ~** he's on their (*o* your) side; **ne hanno fatto un'altra** they've (*o* you've) done it again; **~ stessi(e)** they themselves; you yourselves
lo'sanga, -ghe *sf* diamond, lozenge
Lo'sanna *sf* Lausanne
'losco, -a, schi, sche *ag* (*fig*) shady, suspicious
'lotta *sf* struggle, fight; (*Sport*) wrestling; **essere in ~ (con)** to be in conflict (with); **fare la ~ (con)** to wrestle (with); **~ armata** armed struggle; **~ di classe** (*Pol*) class struggle; **~ libera** (*Sport*) all-in wrestling (*Brit*), freestyle
lot'tare *vi* to fight, struggle; to wrestle
lotta'tore, -'trice *sm/f* wrestler
lotte'ria *sf* lottery; (*di gara ippica*) sweepstake
lottiz'zare [lottid'dzare] *vt* to divide into plots; (*fig*) to share out
lottizzazi'one [lottiddzat'tsjone] *sf* division into plots; (*fig*) share-out
'lotto *sm* (*gioco*) (state) lottery; (*parte*) lot; (*Edil*) site; **vincere un terno al ~** (*anche fig*) to hit the jackpot
lozi'one [lot'tsjone] *sf* lotion
LT *sigla* = **Latina**
LU *sigla* = **Lucca**
lubrifi'cante *sm* lubricant
lubrifi'care *vt* to lubricate
lu'cano, -a *ag* of (*o* from) Lucania
luc'chetto [luk'ketto] *sm* padlock
lucci'care [luttʃi'kare] *vi* to sparkle; (*oro*) to glitter; (*stella*) to twinkle; (*occhi*) to glisten
lucci'chio [luttʃi'kio] *sm* sparkling; glittering; twinkling; glistening
lucci'cone [luttʃi'kone] *sm:* **avere i lucciconi agli occhi** to have tears in one's eyes
'luccio ['luttʃo] *sm* (*Zool*) pike
'lucciola ['luttʃola] *sf* (*Zool*) firefly; glow-worm; (*fam, fig: prostituta*) girl (*o* woman) on the game
'luce ['lutʃe] *sf* light; (*finestra*) window; **alla ~ di** by the light of; **fare qc alla ~ del sole** (*fig*) to do sth in the open; **dare alla ~** (*bambino*) to give birth to; **fare ~ su qc** (*fig*) to shed *o* throw light on sth; **~ del sole/della luna** sun/moonlight
lu'cente [lu'tʃɛnte] *ag* shining
lucen'tezza [lutʃen'tettsa] *sf* shine
lu'cerna [lu'tʃɛrna] *sf* oil lamp
lucer'nario [lutʃer'narjo] *sm* skylight
lu'certola [lu'tʃɛrtola] *sf* lizard
luci'dare [lutʃi'dare] *vt* to polish; (*ricalcare*) to trace
lucida'trice [lutʃida'tritʃe] *sf* floor polisher
lucidità [lutʃidi'ta] *sf* lucidity
'lucido, -a ['lutʃido] *ag* shining, bright; (*lucidato*) polished; (*fig*) lucid ■ *sm* shine, lustre (*Brit*), luster (*US*); (*per scarpe etc*) polish; (*disegno*) tracing
lu'cignolo [lu'tʃiɲɲolo] *sm* wick
luc'rare *vt* to make money out of
lucra'tivo, -a *ag* lucrative; **a scopo ~** for gain
'lucro *sm* profit, gain; **a scopo di ~** for gain; **organizzazione senza scopo di ~** non-profit-making (*Brit*) *o* non-profit (*US*) organization
lu'croso, -a *ag* lucrative, profitable
luculli'ano, -a *ag* (*pasto*) sumptuous
lu'dibrio *sm* mockery *no pl*; (*oggetto di scherno*) laughing stock
'lue *sf* syphilis
'luglio ['luʎʎo] *sm* July; **nel mese di ~** in July, in the month of July; **il primo ~** the first of July; **arrivare il 2 ~** to arrive on the 2nd of July; **all'inizio/alla fine di ~** at the beginning/at the end of July; **durante il mese di ~** during July; **a ~ del prossimo anno** in July of next year; **ogni anno a ~** every July; **che fai a ~?** what are you doing in July?; **ha piovuto molto a ~ quest'anno** July was very wet this year
'lugubre *ag* gloomy
'lui *pron* (*soggetto*) he; (*oggetto: per dare rilievo, con preposizione*) him ■ *sm inv:* **il mio ~** my beloved; **~ stesso** he himself; **è ~** it's him
lu'maca, -che *sf* slug; (*chiocciola*) snail
luma'cone *sm* (large) slug; (*fig*) slowcoach (*Brit*), slowpoke (*US*)
'lume *sm* light; (*lampada*) lamp; **~ a olio** oil lamp; **chiedere lumi a qn** (*fig*) to ask sb for advice; **a ~ di naso** (*fig*) by rule of thumb
lumi'cino [lumi'tʃino] *sm* small *o* faint light; **essere (ridotto) al ~** (*fig*) to be at death's door
lumi'era *sf* chandelier

lumi'nare *sm* luminary
lumi'naria *sf* (*per feste*) illuminations *pl*
lumine'scente [lumineʃʃɛnte] *ag* luminescent
lu'mino *sm* small light; **~ da notte** night-light; **~ per i morti** candle for the dead
luminosità *sf* brightness; (*fig: di sorriso, volto*) radiance
lumi'noso, -a *ag* (*che emette luce*) luminous; (*cielo, colore, stanza*) bright; (*sorgente*) of light, light *cpd*; (*fig: sorriso*) bright, radiant; **insegna luminosa** neon sign
lun. *abbr* (= *lunedì*) Mon.
'luna *sf* moon; **~ nuova/piena** new/full moon; **avere la ~** to be in a bad mood; **~ di miele** honeymoon
'luna park *sm inv* amusement park, funfair
lu'nare *ag* lunar, moon *cpd*
lu'nario *sm* almanac; **sbarcare il ~** to make ends meet
lu'natico, -a, ci, che *ag* whimsical, temperamental
lunedì *sm inv* Monday; *vedi anche* **martedì**
lun'gaggine [lun'gaddʒine] *sf* slowness; **lungaggini della burocrazia** red tape
lunga'mente *av* (*a lungo*) for a long time; (*estesamente*) at length
lun'garno *sm* embankment along the Arno
lun'ghezza [lun'gettsa] *sf* length; **~ d'onda** (*Fisica*) wavelength
'lungi ['lundʒi]: **~ da** *prep* far from
lungimi'rante [lundʒimi'rante] *ag* far-sighted
'lungo, -a, ghi, ghe *ag* long; (*lento: persona*) slow; (*diluito: caffè, brodo*) weak, watery, thin ■ *sm* length ■ *prep* along; **~ 3 metri** 3 metres long; **avere la barba lunga** to be unshaven; **a ~** for a long time; **a ~ andare** in the long run; **di gran lunga** (*molto*) by far; **andare in ~ o per le lunghe** to drag on; **saperla lunga** to know what's what; **in ~ e in largo** far and wide, all over; **~ il corso dei secoli** throughout the centuries; **navigazione di ~ corso** ocean-going navigation
lungofi'ume *sm* embankment
lungo'lago *sm* road round a lake
lungo'mare *sm* promenade
lungome'traggio [lungome'traddʒo] *sm* (*Cine*) feature film
lungo'tevere *sm* embankment along the Tiber
lu'notto *sm* (*Aut*) rear *o* back window; **~ termico** heated rear window
lu'ogo, -ghi *sm* place; (*posto: di incidente etc*) scene, site; (*punto, passo di libro*) passage; **in ~ di** instead of; **in primo ~** in the first place; **aver ~** to take place; **dar ~ a** to give rise to; **~ comune** commonplace; **~ del delitto** scene of the crime; **~ geometrico** locus; **~ di nascita** birthplace; (*Amm*) place of birth; **~ di pena** prison, penitentiary; **~ di provenienza** place of origin
luogote'nente *sm* (*Mil*) lieutenant
lupacchi'otto [lupak'kjɔtto] *sm* (*Zool*) (wolf) cub
lu'para *sf* sawn-off shotgun
lu'petto *sm* (*Zool*) (wolf) cub; (*negli scouts*) cub scout
'lupo, -a *sm/f* wolf/she-wolf; **cane ~** alsatian (dog) (*Brit*), German shepherd (dog); **tempo da lupi** filthy weather
'luppolo *sm* (*Bot*) hop
'lurido, -a *ag* filthy
luri'dume *sm* filth
lu'singa, -ghe *sf* (*spesso al pl*) flattery *no pl*
lusin'gare *vt* to flatter
lusinghi'ero, -a [luzin'gjɛro] *ag* flattering, gratifying
lus'sare *vt* (*Med*) to dislocate
lussazi'one [lussat'tsjone] *sf* (*Med*) dislocation
lussembur'ghese [lussembur'gese] *ag* of (*o* from) Luxembourg ■ *sm/f* native (*o* inhabitant) of Luxembourg
Lussem'burgo *sm* (*stato*): **il ~** Luxembourg ■ *sf* (*città*) Luxembourg
'lusso *sm* luxury; **di ~** luxury *cpd*
lussu'oso, -a *ag* luxurious
lussureggi'are [lussured'dʒare] *vi* to be luxuriant
lus'suria *sf* lust
lussuri'oso, -a *ag* lascivious, lustful
lus'trare *vt* to polish, shine
lustras'carpe *sm/f inv* shoeshine
lus'trino *sm* sequin
'lustro, -a *ag* shiny; (*pelliccia*) glossy ■ *sm* shine, gloss; (*fig*) prestige, glory; (*quinquennio*) five-year period
lute'rano, -a *ag, sm/f* Lutheran
'lutto *sm* mourning; **essere in/portare il ~** to be in/wear mourning

l

Mm

M, m ['ɛmme] *sf o m inv* (*lettera*) M, m; **M come Milano** M for Mary (*Brit*), M for Mike (*US*)
m. *abbr* = **mese; metro; miglia; monte**
ma *cong* but; **ma insomma!** for goodness sake!; **ma no!** of course not!
'macabro, -a *ag* gruesome, macabre
ma'caco, -chi *sm* (*Zool*) macaque
macché [mak'ke] *escl* not at all!, certainly not!
macche'roni [makke'roni] *smpl* macaroni *sg*
'macchia ['makkja] *sf* stain, spot; (*chiazza di diverso colore*) spot splash, patch; (*tipo di boscaglia*) scrub; **~ d'inchiostro** ink stain; **estendersi a ~ d'olio** (*fig*) to spread rapidly; **darsi/vivere alla ~** (*fig*) to go into/live in hiding
macchi'are [mak'kjare] *vt* (*sporcare*) to stain, mark; **macchiarsi** *vr* (*persona*) to get o.s. dirty; (*stoffa*) to stain; to get stained *o* marked; **macchiarsi di un delitto** to be guilty of a crime
macchi'ato, -a [mak'kjato] *ag* (*pelle, pelo*) spotted; **~ di** stained with; **caffè ~** coffee with a dash of milk
macchi'etta [mak'kjetta] *sf* (*disegno*) sketch, caricature; (*Teat*) caricature; (*fig: persona*) character
'macchina ['makkina] *sf* machine; (*motore, locomotiva*) engine; (*automobile*) car; (*fig: meccanismo*) machinery; **andare in ~** (*Aut*) to go by car; (*Stampa*) to go to press; **salire in ~** to get into the car; **venire in ~** to come by car; **sala macchine** (*Naut*) engine room; **~ da cucire** sewing machine; **~ fotografica** camera; **~ da presa** cine *o* movie camera; **~ da scrivere** typewriter; **~ utensile** machine tool; **~ a vapore** steam engine
macchinal'mente [makkinal'mente] *av* mechanically
macchi'nare [makki'nare] *vt* to plot
macchi'nario [makki'narjo] *sm* machinery
macchinazi'one [makkinat'tsjone] *sf* plot, machination
macchi'netta [makki'netta] *sf* (*fam: caffettiera*) percolator; (*: accendino*) lighter
macchi'nista, -i [makki'nista] *sm* (*di treno*) engine-driver; (*di nave*) engineer; (*Teat, TV*) stagehand
macchi'noso, -a [makki'noso] *ag* complex, complicated
ma'cedone [ma'tʃɛdone] *ag, sm/f* Macedonian
Mace'donia [matʃe'dɔnja] *sm* Macedonia
mace'donia [matʃe'dɔnja] *sf* fruit salad
macel'laio [matʃel'lajo] *sm* butcher
macel'lare [matʃel'lare] *vt* to slaughter, butcher
macellazi'one [matʃellat'tsjone] *sf* slaughtering, butchering
macelle'ria [matʃelle'ria] *sf* butcher's (shop)
ma'cello [ma'tʃɛllo] *sm* (*mattatoio*) slaughterhouse, abattoir (*Brit*); (*fig*) slaughter, massacre; (*: disastro*) shambles *sg*
mace'rare [matʃe'rare] *vt* to macerate; (*Cuc*) to marinate; **macerarsi** *vr* to waste away; (*fig*): **macerarsi in** to be consumed with
macerazi'one [matʃerat'tsjone] *sf* maceration
ma'cerie [ma'tʃɛrje] *sfpl* rubble *sg*, debris *sg*
'macero ['matʃero] *sm* (*operazione*) pulping; (*stabilimento*) pulping mill; **carta da ~** paper for pulping
machia'vellico, -a, ci, che [makja'vɛlliko] *ag* (*anche fig*) Machiavellian
ma'cigno [ma'tʃiɲɲo] *sm* (*masso*) rock, boulder
maci'lento, -a [matʃi'lɛnto] *ag* emaciated
'macina ['matʃina] *sf* (*pietra*) millstone; (*macchina*) grinder
macinacaffè [matʃinakaf'fɛ] *sm inv* coffee grinder
macina'pepe [matʃina'pepe] *sm inv* peppermill
maci'nare [matʃi'nare] *vt* to grind; (*carne*) to mince (*Brit*), grind (*US*)
maci'nato [matʃi'nato] *sm* meal, flour; (*carne*) minced (*Brit*) *o* ground (*US*) meat

maci'nino [matʃi'nino] *sm* (*per caffè*) coffee grinder; (*per pepe*) peppermill; (*scherzoso: macchina*) old banger (Brit), clunker (US)
maciul'lare [matʃul'lare] *vt* (*canapa, lino*) to brake; (*fig: braccio etc*) to crush
'macro... *prefisso* macro...
macrobi'otico, -a *ag* macrobiotic ■ *sf* macrobiotics *sg*
macu'lato, -a *ag* (*pelo*) spotted
Ma'dama: **palazzo ~** *sm* (*Pol*) *seat of the Italian Chamber of Senators*
made in Italy [meɪdɪ'nɪtəlɪ] *sm*: **il ~** Italian exports *pl* (*especially fashion goods*)
Ma'dera *sf* (*Geo*) Madeira ■ *sm inv* (*vino*) Madeira
'madido, -a *ag*: **~ (di)** wet *o* moist (with)
Ma'donna *sf* (*Rel*) Our Lady
mador'nale *ag* enormous, huge
'madre *sf* mother; (*matrice di bolletta*) counterfoil ■ *ag inv* mother *cpd*; **ragazza ~** unmarried mother; **scena ~** (*Teat*) principal scene; (*fig*) terrible scene
madre'lingua *sf* mother tongue, native language
madre'patria *sf* mother country, native land
madre'perla *sf* mother-of-pearl
Ma'drid *sf* Madrid
madri'gale *sm* madrigal
madri'leno, -a *ag* of (*o* from) Madrid ■ *sm/f* person from Madrid
ma'drina *sf* godmother
maestà *sf inv* majesty; **Sua M~ la Regina** Her Majesty the Queen
maestosità *sf* majesty
maes'toso, -a *ag* majestic
ma'estra *sf vedi* **maestro**
maes'trale *sm* north-west wind
maes'tranze [maes'trantse] *sfpl* workforce *sg*
maes'tria *sf* mastery, skill
ma'estro, -a *sm/f* (*Ins: anche:* **maestro di scuola** *o* **elementare**) primary (Brit) *o* grade school (US) teacher; (*esperto*) expert ■ *sm* (*artigiano, fig: guida*) master; (*Mus*) maestro ■ *ag* (*principale*) main; (*di grande abilità*) masterly, skilful (Brit), skillful (US); **un colpo da ~** (*fig*) a masterly move; **muro ~** main wall; **strada maestra** main road; **maestra d'asilo** nursery teacher; **~ di ballo** dancing master; **~ di cerimonie** master of ceremonies; **~ d'orchestra** conductor, director (US); **~ di scherma** fencing master; **~ di sci** ski instructor
'mafia *sf* Mafia
mafi'oso *sm* member of the Mafia
'maga, -ghe *sf* sorceress
ma'gagna [ma'gaɲɲa] *sf* defect, flaw, blemish; (*noia, guaio*) problem
ma'gari *escl* (*esprime desiderio*): **~ fosse vero!** if only it were true!; **ti piacerebbe andare in Scozia? — ~!** would you like to go to Scotland? — I certainly would! ■ *av* (*anche*) even; (*forse*) perhaps
magazzi'naggio [magaddzi'naddʒo] *sm*: **(spese di) ~** storage charges *pl*, warehousing charges *pl*
magazzini'ere [magaddzi'njɛre] *sm* warehouseman
magaz'zino [magad'dzino] *sm* warehouse; **grande ~** department store; **~ doganale** bonded warehouse
'maggio ['maddʒo] *sm* May; *vedi anche* **luglio**
maggio'rana [maddʒo'rana] *sf* (*Bot*) (sweet) marjoram
maggio'ranza [maddʒo'rantsa] *sf* majority; **nella ~ dei casi** in most cases
maggio'rare [maddʒo'rare] *vt* to increase, raise
maggiorazi'one [maddʒorat'tsjone] *sf* (*Comm*) rise, increase
maggior'domo [maddʒor'dɔmo] *sm* butler
maggi'ore [mad'dʒore] *ag* (*comparativo: più grande*) bigger, larger; taller; greater; (*: più vecchio: sorella, fratello*) older, elder; (*: di grado superiore*) senior; (*: più importante, Mil, Mus*) major; (*superlativo*) biggest, largest; tallest; greatest; oldest, eldest ■ *sm/f* (*di grado*) superior; (*di età*) elder; (*Mil*) major; (*: Aer*) squadron leader; **la maggior parte** the majority; **andare per la ~** (*cantante, attore etc*) to be very popular, be "in"
maggio'renne [maddʒo'rɛnne] *ag* of age ■ *sm/f* person who has come of age
maggiori'tario, -a [maddʒori'tarjo] *ag* majority *cpd*; (*Pol: anche:* **sistema maggioritario**) first-past-the-post system
maggior'mente [maddʒor'mente] *av* much more; (*con senso superlativo*) most
ma'gia [ma'dʒia] *sf* magic
'magico, -a, ci, che ['madʒiko] *ag* magic; (*fig*) fascinating, charming, magical
'magio ['madʒo] *sm* (*Rel*): **i re Magi** the Magi, the Three Wise Men
magis'tero [madʒis'tɛro] *sm* teaching; (*fig: maestria*) skill; (*Ins*): **Facoltà di M~** ≈ teachers' training college
magis'trale [madʒis'trale] *ag* primary (Brit) *o* grade school (US) teachers', primary (Brit) *o* grade school (US) teaching; (*abile*) skilful (Brit), skillful (US); **istituto ~** *secondary school for the training of primary teachers*
magis'trato [madʒis'trato] *sm* magistrate
magistra'tura [madʒistra'tura] *sf* magistrature; (*magistrati*): **la ~** the Bench

'**maglia** ['maʎʎa] *sf* stitch; (*lavoro ai ferri*) knitting *no pl*; (*tessuto, Sport*) jersey; (*maglione*) jersey, sweater; (*di catena*) link; (*di rete*) mesh; **avviare/diminuire le maglie** to cast on/cast off; **lavorare a ~, fare la ~** to knit; **~ diritta/ rovescia** plain/purl

maglie'ria [maʎʎe'ria] *sf* knitwear; (*negozio*) knitwear shop; **macchina per ~** knitting machine

magli'etta [maʎ'ʎetta] *sf* (*canottiera*) vest; (*tipo camicia*) T-shirt

magli'ficio [maʎʎi'fitʃo] *sm* knitwear factory

ma'glina [maʎ'ʎina] *sf* (*tessuto*) jersey

'**maglio** ['maʎʎo] *sm* mallet; (*macchina*) power hammer

magli'one [maʎ'ʎone] *sm* jersey, sweater

'**magma** *sm* magma; (*fig*) mass

ma'gnaccia [maɲ'ɲattʃa] *sm inv* (*peg*) pimp

magnanimità [maɲɲanimi'ta] *sf* magnanimity

ma'gnanimo, -a [maɲ'ɲanimo] *ag* magnanimous

ma'gnate [maɲ'ɲate] *sm* tycoon, magnate

ma'gnesia [maɲ'ɲɛzja] *sf* (*Chim*) magnesia

ma'gnesio [maɲ'ɲɛzjo] *sm* (*Chim*) magnesium; **al ~** (*lampada, flash*) magnesium *cpd*

ma'gnete [maɲ'ɲɛte] *sm* magnet

ma'gnetico, -a, ci, che [maɲ'ɲɛtiko] *ag* magnetic

magne'tismo [maɲɲe'tizmo] *sm* magnetism

magnetiz'zare [maɲɲetid'dzare] *vt* (*Fisica*) to magnetize; (*fig*) to mesmerize

magne'tofono [maɲɲe'tɔfono] *sm* tape recorder

magnifica'mente [maɲɲifika'mente] *av* magnificently, extremely well

magnifi'cenza [maɲɲifi'tʃɛntsa] *sf* magnificence, splendour (*Brit*), splendor (*US*)

ma'gnifico, -a, ci, che [maɲ'ɲifiko] *ag* magnificent, splendid; (*ospite*) generous

'**magno, -a** ['maɲɲo] *ag*: **aula magnoa** main hall

ma'gnolia [maɲ'ɲɔlja] *sf* magnolia

'**mago, -ghi** *sm* (*stregone*) magician, wizard; (*illusionista*) magician

ma'grezza [ma'grettsa] *sf* thinness

'**magro, -a** *ag* (very) thin, skinny; (*carne*) lean; (*formaggio*) low-fat; (*fig: scarso,*) meagre (*Brit*), meager (*US*), poor; (*: meschino: scusa*) poor, lame; **mangiare di ~** not to eat meat

'**mai** *av* (*nessuna volta*) never; (*talvolta*) ever; **non ... ~** never; **~ più** never again; **come ~?** why (*o* how) on earth?; **chi/dove/quando ~?** whoever/wherever/whenever?

mai'ale *sm* (*Zool*) pig; (*carne*) pork

mail ['meil] *sf inv* = **e-mail**

mai'olica *sf* majolica

maio'nese *sf* mayonnaise

Mai'orca *sf* Majorca

'**mais** *sm* maize (*Brit*), corn (*US*)

mai'uscolo, -a *ag* (*lettera*) capital ■ *sf* capital letter ■ *sm* capital letters *pl*; (*Tip*) upper case; **scrivere tutto (in) ~** to write everything in capitals *o* in capital letters

mal *av, sm vedi* **male**

'**mala** *sf* (*gergo*) underworld

malac'corto, -a *ag* rash, careless

mala'fede *sf* bad faith

malaf'fare; **di ~** *ag* (*gente*) shady, dishonest; **donna di ~** prostitute

mala'gevole [mala'dʒevole] *ag* difficult, hard

mala'grazia [mala'grattsja] *sf*: **con ~** with bad grace, impolitely

mala'lingua (*pl* **malelingue**) *sf* gossip (*person*)

mala'mente *av* badly; (*sgarbatamente*) rudely

malan'dato, -a *ag* (*persona: di salute*) in poor health; (*: di condizioni finanziarie*) badly off; (*trascurato*) shabby

ma'lanimo *sm* ill will, malevolence; **di ~** unwillingly

ma'lanno *sm* (*disgrazia*) misfortune; (*malattia*) ailment

mala'pena *sf*: **a ~** hardly, scarcely

ma'laria *sf* malaria

ma'larico, -a, ci, che *ag* malarial

mala'sorte *sf* bad luck

mala'ticcio, -a [mala'tittʃo] *ag* sickly

ma'lato, -a *ag* ill, sick; (*gamba*) bad; (*pianta*) diseased ■ *sm/f* sick person; (*in ospedale*) patient; **darsi ~** (*sul lavoro etc*) to go sick

malat'tia *sf* (*infettiva etc*) illness, disease; (*cattiva salute*) illness, sickness; (*di pianta*) disease; **mettersi in ~** to go on sick leave; **fare una ~ di qc** (*fig: disperarsi*) to get in a state about sth

malaugu'rato, -a *ag* ill-fated, unlucky

malau'gurio *sm* bad *o* ill omen; **uccello del ~** bird of ill omen

mala'vita *sf* underworld

malavi'toso, -a *sm/f* gangster

mala'voglia [mala'vɔʎʎa]: **di ~** *av* unwillingly, reluctantly

Ma'lawi [ma'lavi] *sm*: **il ~** Malawi

Mala'ysia *sf* Malaysia

malaysi'ano, -a *ag, sm/f* Malaysian

malcapi'tato, -a *ag* unlucky, unfortunate ■ *sm/f* unfortunate person

mal'concio, -a, ci, ce [mal'kontʃo] *ag* in a sorry state

malcon'tento *sm* discontent

malcos'tume *sm* immorality

mal'destro, -a *ag* (*inabile*) inexpert, inexperienced; (*goffo*) awkward

maldi'cente [maldi'tʃɛnte] *ag* slanderous
maldi'cenza [maldi'tʃɛntsa] *sf* malicious gossip
maldis'posto, -a *ag*: **~ (verso)** ill-disposed (towards)
Mal'dive *sfpl*: **le ~** the Maldives
'male *av* badly ■ *sm* (*ciò che è ingiusto,*) evil; (*danno, svantaggio*) harm; (*sventura*) misfortune; (*dolore fisico,*) pain, ache; **sentirsi ~** to feel ill; **aver mal di cuore/fegato** to have a heart/liver complaint; **aver mal di denti/d'orecchi/di testa** to have toothache/earache/a headache; **aver mal di gola** to have a sore throat; **aver ~ ai piedi** to have sore feet; **far ~** (*dolere*) to hurt; **far ~ alla salute** to be bad for one's health; **far del ~ a qn** to hurt *o* harm sb; **parlar ~ di qn** to speak ill of sb; **restare** *o* **rimanere ~** to be sorry; to be disappointed to be hurt; **trattar ~ qn** to ill-treat sb; **andare a ~** to go off *o* bad; **come va? — non c'è ~** how are you? — not bad; **di ~ in peggio** from bad to worse; **per ~ che vada** however badly things go; **non avertene a ~, non prendertela a ~** don't take it to heart; **mal comune mezzo gaudio** (*proverbio*) a trouble shared is a trouble halved; **mal d'auto** carsickness; **mal di mare** seasickness
male'detto, -a *pp di* **maledire** ■ *ag* cursed, damned; (*fig fam*) damned, blasted
male'dire *vt* to curse
maledizi'one [maledit'tsjone] *sf* curse; **~!** damn it!
maledu'cato, -a *ag* rude, ill-mannered
maleducazi'one [maledukat'tsjone] *sf* rudeness
male'fatta *sf* misdeed
male'ficio [male'fitʃo] *sm* witchcraft
ma'lefico, -a, ci, che *ag* (*aria, cibo*) harmful, bad; (*influsso, azione*) evil
ma'lese *ag, sm/f* Malay(an) ■ *sm* (*Ling*) Malay
Ma'lesia *sf* Malaya
ma'lessere *sm* indisposition, slight illness; (*fig*) uneasiness
malevo'lenza [malevo'lɛntsa] *sf* malevolence
ma'levolo, -a *ag* malevolent
malfa'mato, -a *ag* notorious
mal'fatto, -a *ag* (*persona*) deformed; (*oggetto*) badly made; (*lavoro*) badly done
malfat'tore, -'trice *sm/f* wrongdoer
mal'fermo, -a *ag* unsteady, shaky; (*salute*) poor, delicate
malformazi'one [malformat'tsjone] *sf* malformation
'malga, -ghe *sf* Alpine hut
malgo'verno *sm* maladministration
mal'grado *prep* in spite of, despite ■ *cong* although; **mio** *o* **tuo** *etc* **~** against my (*o* your *etc*) will
ma'lia *sf* spell; (*fig: fascino*) charm
mali'ardo, -a *ag* (*occhi, sorriso*) bewitching ■ *sf* enchantress
maligna'mente [maliɲɲa'mente] *av* maliciously
mali'gnare [maliɲ'ɲare] *vi*: **~ su** to malign, speak ill of
malignità [maliɲɲi'ta] *sf inv* (*qualità*) malice, spite; (*osservazione*) spiteful remark; **con ~** spitefully, maliciously
ma'ligno, -a [ma'liɲɲo] *ag* (*malvagio*) malicious, malignant; (*Med*) malignant
malinco'nia *sf* melancholy, gloom
malin'conico, -a, ci, che *ag* melancholy
malincu'ore: **a ~** *av* reluctantly, unwillingly
malinfor'mato, -a *ag* misinformed
malintenzio'nato, -a [malintentsjo'nato] *ag* ill-intentioned
malin'teso, -a *ag* misunderstood; (*riguardo, senso del dovere*) mistaken, wrong ■ *sm* misunderstanding
ma'lizia [ma'littsja] *sf* (*malignità*) malice; (*furbizia*) cunning; (*espediente*) trick
malizi'oso, -a [malit'tsjoso] *ag* malicious; cunning; (*vivace, birichino*) mischievous
malle'abile *ag* malleable
mal'loppo *sm* (*fam: refurtiva*) loot
malme'nare *vt* to beat up; (*fig*) to ill-treat
mal'messo, -a *ag* shabby
malnu'trito, -a *ag* undernourished
malnutrizi'one [malnutrit'tsjone] *sf* malnutrition
'malo, -a *ag*: **in ~ modo** badly
ma'locchio [ma'lɔkkjo] *sm* evil eye
ma'lora *sf* (*fam*): **andare in ~** to go to the dogs; **va in ~!** go to hell!
ma'lore *sm* (sudden) illness
malri'dotto, -a *ag* (*abiti, scarpe, persona*) in a sorry state; (*casa, macchina*) dilapidated, in a poor state of repair
mal'sano, -a *ag* unhealthy
malsi'curo, -a *ag* unsafe
'Malta *sf* Malta
'malta *sf* (*Edil*) mortar
mal'tempo *sm* bad weather
'malto *sm* malt
mal'tolto *sm* ill-gotten gains *pl*
maltratta'mento *sm* ill treatment
maltrat'tare *vt* to ill-treat
malu'more *sm* bad mood; (*irritabilità*) bad temper; (*discordia*) ill feeling; **di ~** in a bad mood
'malva *sf* (*Bot*) mallow ■ *ag, sm inv* mauve

M

mal'vagio, -a, gi, gie [mal'vadʒo] *ag* wicked, evil
malvagità [malvadʒi'ta] *sf inv* (*qualità*) wickedness; (*azione*) wicked deed
malva'sia *sf Italian dessert wine*
malversazi'one [malversat'tsjone] *sf* (*Dir*) embezzlement
malves'tito, -a *ag* badly dressed, ill-clad
mal'visto, -a *ag*: **~ (da)** disliked (by), unpopular (with)
malvi'vente *sm* criminal
malvolenti'eri *av* unwillingly, reluctantly
malvo'lere *vt*: **farsi ~ da qn** to make o.s. unpopular with sb ■ *sm*: **prendere qn a ~** to take a dislike to sb
'mamma *sf* mum(my) (*Brit*), mom (*US*); **~ mia!** my goodness!
mam'mario, -a *ag* (*Anat*) mammary
mam'mella *sf* (*Anat*) breast; (*di vacca, capra etc*) udder
mam'mifero *sm* mammal
mam'mismo *sm excessive attachment to one's mother*
'mammola *sf* (*Bot*) violet
'manager ['mænidʒə] *sm inv* manager
manageri'ale [manadʒe'rjale] *ag* managerial
ma'nata *sf* (*colpo*) slap; (*quantità*) handful
'manca *sf* left (hand); **a destra e a ~** left, right and centre, on all sides
manca'mento *sm* (*di forze*) (feeling of) faintness, weakness
man'canza [man'kantsa] *sf* lack; (*carenza*) shortage, scarcity; (*fallo*) fault; (*imperfezione*) failing, shortcoming; **per ~ di tempo** through lack of time; **in ~ di meglio** for lack of anything better; **sentire la ~ di qc/qn** to miss sth/sb
man'care *vi* (*essere insufficiente*) to be lacking; (*venir meno*) to fail; (*sbagliare*) to be wrong, make a mistake; (*non esserci*) to be missing, not to be there; (*essere lontano*): **~ (da)** to be away (from) ■ *vt* to miss; **~ di** to lack; **~ a** (*promessa*) to fail to keep; **tu mi manchi** I miss you; **mancò poco che morisse** he very nearly died; **mancano ancora 10 sterline** we're still £10 short; **manca un quarto alle 6** it's a quarter to 6; **non mancherò** I won't forget, I'll make sure I do; **ci mancherebbe altro!** of course I (*o* you *etc*) will!; **~ da casa** to be away from home; **~ di rispetto a** *o* **verso qn** to be lacking in respect towards sb, be disrespectful towards sb; **~ di parola** not to keep one's word, go back on one's word; **sentirsi ~** to feel faint
man'cato, -a *ag* (*tentativo*) unsuccessful; (*artista*) failed
manche [mɑ̃ʃ] *sf inv* (*Sport*) heat
mancherò *etc* [manke'rɔ] *vb vedi* **mancare**
man'chevole [man'kevole] *ag* (*insufficiente*) inadequate, insufficient
manchevo'lezza [mankevo'lettsa] *sf* (*scorrettezza*) fault, shortcoming
'mancia, -ce ['mantʃa] *sf* tip; **~ competente** reward
manci'ata [man'tʃata] *sf* handful
man'cino, -a [man'tʃino] *ag* (*braccio*) left; (*persona*) left-handed; (*fig*) underhand
'manco *av* (*nemmeno*): **~ per sogno** *o* **per idea!** not on your life!
man'dante *sm/f* (*Dir*) principal; (*istigatore*) instigator
manda'rancio [manda'rantʃo] *sm* clementine
man'dare *vt* to send; (*far funzionare*: *macchina*) to drive; (*emettere*) to send out; (: *grido*) to give, utter, let out; **~ avanti** (*persona*) to send ahead; (*fig*: *famiglia*) to provide for; (*ditta*) to look after, run; (: *pratica*) to attend to; **~ a chiamare qn** to send for sb; **~ giù** to send down; (*anche fig*) to swallow; **~ in onda** (*Radio, TV*) to broadcast; **~ in rovina** to ruin; **~ via** to send away; (*licenziare*) to fire
manda'rino *sm* mandarin (orange); (*cinese*) mandarin
man'data *sf* (*quantità*) lot, batch; (*di chiave*) turn; **chiudere a doppia ~** to double-lock
manda'tario *sm* (*Dir*) representative, agent
man'dato *sm* (*incarico*) commission; (*Dir*: *provvedimento*) warrant; (*di deputato etc*) mandate; (*ordine di pagamento*) postal *o* money order; **~ d'arresto, ~ di cattura** warrant for arrest; **~ di comparizione** summons *sg*; **~ di perquisizione** search warrant
man'dibola *sf* mandible, jaw
mando'lino *sm* mandolin(e)
'mandorla *sf* almond
mandor'lato *sm* nut brittle
'mandorlo *sm* almond tree
'mandria *sf* herd
mandri'ano *sm* cowherd, herdsman
man'drino *sm* (*Tecn*) mandrel
maneg'gevole [maned'dʒevole] *ag* easy to handle
maneggi'are [maned'dʒare] *vt* (*creta, cera*) to mould (*Brit*), mold (*US*), work, fashion; (*arnesi, utensili*) to handle; (: *adoperare*) to use; (*fig*: *persone, denaro*) to handle, deal with
ma'neggio [ma'neddʒo] *sm* moulding (*Brit*), molding (*US*); handling use; (*intrigo*) plot, scheme; (*per cavalli*) riding school
ma'nesco, -a, schi, sche *ag* free with one's fists
ma'nette *sfpl* handcuffs
manga'nello *sm* club

manga'nese *sm* manganese
mange'reccio, -a, ci, ce [mandʒe'rettʃo] *ag* edible
mangi'abile [man'dʒabile] *ag* edible, eatable
mangia'dischi [mandʒa'diski] *sm inv* record player
mangia'nastri [mandʒa'nastri] *sm inv* cassette-recorder
mangi'are [man'dʒare] *vt* to eat; (*intaccare*) to eat into *o* away; (*Carte, Scacchi etc*) to take ■ *vi* to eat ■ *sm* eating; (*cibo*) food; (*cucina*) cooking; **fare da ~** to do the cooking; **mangiarsi le parole** to mumble; **mangiarsi le unghie** to bite one's nails
mangia'soldi [mandʒa'sɔldi] *ag inv* (*fam*): **macchinetta ~** one-armed bandit
mangia'toia [mandʒa'toja] *sf* feeding-trough
man'gime [man'dʒime] *sm* fodder
mangiucchi'are [mandʒuk'kjare] *vt* to nibble
'mango, -ghi *sm* mango
ma'nia *sf* (*Psic*) mania; (*fig*) obsession, craze; **avere la ~ di fare qc** to have a habit of doing sth; **~ di persecuzione** persecution complex *o* mania
mania'cale *ag* (*Psic*) maniacal; (*fanatico*) fanatical
ma'niaco, -a, ci, che *ag* suffering from a mania; **~ (di)** obsessed (by), crazy (about)
'manica, -che *sf* sleeve; (*fig: gruppo*) gang, bunch; (*Geo*): **la M~, il Canale della M~** the (English) Channel; **senza maniche** sleeveless; **essere in maniche di camicia** to be in one's shirt sleeves; **essere di ~ larga/stretta** to be easy-going/strict; **~ a vento** (*Aer*) wind sock
manica'retto *sm* titbit (*Brit*), tidbit (*US*)
mani'chetta [mani'ketta] *sf* (*Tecn*) hose
mani'chino [mani'kino] *sm* (*di sarto, vetrina*) dummy
'manico, -ci *sm* handle; (*Mus*) neck; **~ di scopa** broomstick
mani'comio *sm* mental hospital; (*fig*) madhouse
mani'cotto *sm* muff; (*Tecn*) coupling; sleeve
mani'cure *sm o f inv* manicure ■ *sf inv* manicurist
mani'era *sf* way, manner; (*stile*) style, manner; **maniere** *sfpl* manners; **in ~ che** so that; **in ~ da** so as to; **alla ~ di** in *o* after the style of; **in una ~ o nell'altra** one way or another; **in tutte le maniere** at all costs; **usare buone maniere con qn** to be polite to sb; **usare le maniere forti** to use strong-arm tactics
manie'rato, -a *ag* affected
mani'ero *sm* manor
manifat'tura *sf* (*lavorazione*) manufacture; (*stabilimento*) factory
manifatturi'ero, -a *ag* manufacturing
manifes'tante *sm/f* demonstrator
manifes'tare *vt* to show, display; (*esprimere*) to express; (*rivelare*) to reveal, disclose ■ *vi* to demonstrate; **manifestarsi** *vr* to show o.s.; **manifestarsi amico** to prove o.s. (to be) a friend
manifestazi'one [manifestat'tsjone] *sf* show, display expression; (*sintomo*) sign, symptom; (*dimostrazione pubblica*) demonstration; (*cerimonia*) event
manifes'tino *sm* leaflet
mani'festo, -a *ag* obvious, evident ■ *sm* poster, bill; (*scritto ideologico*) manifesto
ma'niglia [ma'niʎʎa] *sf* handle; (*sostegno: negli autobus etc*) strap
Ma'nila *sf* Manila
manipo'lare *vt* to manipulate; (*alterare: vino*) to adulterate
manipolazi'one [manipolat'tsjone] *sf* manipulation; adulteration
ma'nipolo *sm* (*drappello*) handful
manis'calco, -chi *sm* blacksmith, farrier (*Brit*)
'manna *sf* (*Rel*) manna
man'naia *sf* (*del boia*) (executioner's) axe *o* ax (*US*); (*per carni*) cleaver
man'naro, -a *ag*: **lupo ~** werewolf
'mano, -i *sf* hand; (*strato: di vernice etc*) coat; **a ~** by hand; **cucito a ~** hand-sewn; **fatto a ~** handmade; **alla ~** (*persona*) easy-going; **fuori ~** out of the way; **di prima ~** (*notizia*) first-hand; **di seconda ~** second-hand; **man ~** little by little, gradually; **man ~ che** as; **a piene mani** (*fig*) generously; **avere le mani bucate** to spend money like water; **aver le mani in pasta** to be in the know; **avere qc per le mani** (*progetto, lavoro*) to have sth in hand; **dare una ~ a qn** to lend sb a hand; **dare una ~ di vernice a qc** to give sth a coat of paint; **darsi** *o* **stringersi la ~** to shake hands; **forzare la ~** to go too far; **mettere ~ a qc** to have a hand in sth; **mettere le mani avanti** (*fig*) to safeguard o.s.; **restare a mani vuote** to be left empty-handed; **venire alle mani** to come to blows; **mani in alto!** hands up!; **mani pulite** *see note*

MANI PULITE

Mani pulite ("clean hands") is a term used to describe the judicial operation of the early 1990s to gather evidence against politicians and industrialists who were implicated in bribery and corruption scandals.

m

mano'dopera *sf* labour (*Brit*), labor (*US*)
mano'messo, -a *pp di* **manomettere**
ma'nometro *sm* gauge, manometer
mano'mettere *vt* (*alterare*) to tamper with; (*aprire indebitamente*) to break open illegally
manomissi'one *sf* (*di prove etc*) tampering; (*di lettera*) opening
ma'nopola *sf* (*dell'armatura*) gauntlet; (*guanto*) mitt; (*di impugnatura*) hand-grip; (*pomello*) knob
manos'critto, -a *ag* handwritten ■ *sm* manuscript
manova'lanza [manova'lantsa] *sf* unskilled workers *pl*
mano'vale *sm* labourer (*Brit*), laborer (*US*)
mano'vella *sf* handle; (*Tecn*) crank
ma'novra *sf* manoeuvre (*Brit*), maneuver (*US*); (*Ferr*) shunting; **manovre di corridoio** palace intrigues
mano'vrare *vt* (*veicolo*) to manoeuvre (*Brit*), maneuver (*US*); (*macchina, congegno*) to operate; (*fig: persona*) to manipulate ■ *vi* to manoeuvre
manro'vescio [manro'vɛʃʃo] *sm* slap (*with back of hand*)
man'sarda *sf* attic
mansi'one *sf* task, duty, job
mansu'eto, -a *ag* (*animale*) tame; (*persona*) gentle, docile
mansue'tudine *sf* tameness gentleness, docility
man'tello *sm* cloak; (*fig: di neve etc*) blanket, mantle; (*Tecn: involucro*) casing, shell; (*Zool*) coat
mante'nere *vt* to maintain; (*adempiere: promesse*) to keep, abide by; (*provvedere a*) to support, maintain; **mantenersi** *vr*: **mantenersi calmo/giovane** to stay calm/ young; **~ i contatti con qn** to keep in touch with sb
manteni'mento *sm* maintenance
mante'nuto, -a *sm/f* gigolo/kept woman
'mantice ['mantitʃe] *sm* bellows *pl*; (*di carrozza, automobile*) hood
'manto *sm* cloak; **~ stradale** road surface
'Mantova *sf* Mantua
manto'vano, -a *ag* of (*o* from) Mantua
manu'ale *ag* manual ■ *sm* (*testo*) manual, handbook
manua'listico, -a, ci, che *ag* textbook *cpd*
manual'mente *av* manually, by hand
ma'nubrio *sm* handle; (*di bicicletta etc*) handlebars *pl*; (*Sport*) dumbbell
manu'fatto *sm* manufactured article; **manufatti** *smpl* manufactured goods
manutenzi'one [manuten'tsjone] *sf* maintenance, upkeep; (*d'impianti*) maintenance, servicing
'manzo ['mandzo] *sm* (*Zool*) steer; (*carne*) beef
Mao'metto *sm* Mohammed
'mappa *sf* (*Geo*) map
mappa'mondo *sm* map of the world; (*globo girevole*) globe
ma'rasma, -i *sm* (*fig*) decay, decline
mara'tona *sf* marathon
'marca, -che *sf* mark; (*bollo*) stamp; (*Comm: di prodotti*) brand; (*contrassegno, scontrino*) ticket, check; **prodotti di (gran) ~** high-class products; **~ da bollo** official stamp
mar'care *vt* (*munire di contrassegno*) to mark; (*a fuoco*) to brand; (*Sport: gol*) to score; (*: avversario*) to mark; (*accentuare*) to stress; **~ visita** (*Mil*) to report sick
mar'cato, -a *ag* (*lineamenti, accento etc*) pronounced
'Marche ['marke] *sfpl*: **le ~** the Marches (*region of central Italy*)
marcherò *etc* [marke'rɔ] *vb vedi* **marcare**
mar'chese, -a [mar'keze] *sm/f* marquis *o* marquess/marchioness
marchi'ano, -a [mar'kjano] *ag* (*errore*) glaring, gross
marchi'are [mar'kjare] *vt* to brand
marchigi'ano, -a [marki'dʒano] *ag* of (*o* from) the Marches
'marchio ['markjo] *sm* (*di bestiame, Comm: fig*) brand; **~ depositato** registered trademark; **~ di fabbrica** trademark
'marcia, -ce ['martʃa] *sf* (*anche Mus, Mil*) march; (*funzionamento*) running; (*il camminare*) walking; (*Aut*) gear; **mettere in ~** to start; **mettersi in ~** to get moving; **far ~ indietro** (*Aut*) to reverse; (*fig*) to back-pedal; **~ forzata** forced march; **~ funebre** funeral march
marciapi'ede [martʃa'pjɛde] *sm* (*di strada*) pavement (*Brit*), sidewalk (*US*); (*Ferr*) platform
marci'are [mar'tʃare] *vi* to march; (*andare: treno, macchina*) to go; (*funzionare*) to run, work
'marcio, -a, ci, ce ['martʃo] *ag* (*frutta, legno*) rotten, bad; (*Med*) festering; (*fig*) corrupt, rotten ■ *sm*: **c'è del ~ in questa storia** (*fig*) there's something fishy about this business; **avere torto ~** to be utterly wrong
mar'cire [mar'tʃire] *vi* (*andare a male*) to go bad, rot; (*suppurare*) to fester; (*fig*) to rot
marci'ume [mar'tʃume] *sm* (*parte guasta: di cibi etc*) rotten part, bad part; (*di radice, pianta*) rot; (*fig: corruzione*) rottenness, corruption
'marco, -chi *sm* (*unità monetaria*) mark
'mare *sm* sea; **di ~** (*brezza, acqua, uccelli, pesce*) sea *cpd*; **in ~** at sea; **per ~** by sea; **sul ~** (*barca*) on the sea; (*villaggio, località*) by *o* beside the

sea; **andare al ~** *(in vacanza etc)* to go to the seaside; **il mar Caspio** the Caspian Sea; **il mar Morto** the Dead Sea; **il mar Nero** the Black Sea; **il ~ del Nord** the North Sea; **il mar Rosso** the Red Sea; **il mar dei Sargassi** the Sargasso Sea; **i marei del Sud** the South Seas

ma'rea *sf* tide; **alta/bassa ~** high/low tide

mareggi'ata [mared'dʒata] *sf* heavy sea

ma'remma *sf (Geo)* maremma, swampy coastal area

marem'mano, -a *ag (zona, macchia)* swampy; *(della Maremma)* of *o* from the Maremma

mare'moto *sm* seaquake

maresci'allo [mareʃ'ʃallo] *sm (Mil)* marshal; *(sottufficiale)* warrant officer

marez'zato, -a [mared'dzato] *ag (seta etc)* watered, moiré; *(legno)* veined; *(carta)* marbled

marga'rina *sf* margarine

marghe'rita [marge'rita] *sf* (ox-eye) daisy, marguerite; *(di stampante)* daisy wheel

margheri'tina [margeri'tina] *sf* daisy

margi'nale [mardʒi'nale] *ag* marginal

'margine ['mardʒine] *sm* margin; *(di bosco, via)* edge, border; **avere un buon ~ di tempo/denaro** to have plenty of time/money; **~ di guadagno** *o* **di utile** profit margin; **~ di sicurezza** safety margin

mariju'ana [mæri'wa:nə] *sf* marijuana

ma'rina *sf* navy; *(costa)* coast; *(quadro)* seascape; **~ mercantile** merchant navy *(Brit) o* marine *(US)*; **~ militare** ≈ Royal Navy *(Brit)*, ≈ Navy *(US)*

mari'naio *sm* sailor

mari'nare *vt (Cuc)* to marinate; **~ la scuola** to play truant

mari'naro, -a *ag (tradizione, popolo)* seafaring; *(Cuc)* with seafood; **alla marinara** *(vestito, cappello)* sailor *cpd*; **borgo ~** district where fishing folk live

mari'nata *sf* marinade

ma'rino, -a *ag* sea *cpd*, marine

mario'netta *sf* puppet

mari'tare *vt* to marry; **maritarsi** *vr*: **maritarsi a** *o* **con qn** to marry sb, get married to sb

mari'tato, -a *ag* married

ma'rito *sm* husband; **prendere ~** to get married; **ragazza (in età) da ~** girl of marriageable age

ma'rittimo, -a *ag* maritime, sea *cpd*

mar'maglia [mar'maʎʎa] *sf* mob, riff-raff

marmel'lata *sf* jam; *(di agrumi)* marmalade

mar'mitta *sf (recipiente)* pot; *(Aut)* silencer; **~ catalitica** catalytic converter

'marmo *sm* marble

mar'mocchio [mar'mɔkkjo] *sm (fam)* (little) kid

mar'motta *sf (Zool)* marmot

maroc'chino, -a [marok'kino] *ag, sm/f* Moroccan

Ma'rocco *sm*: **il ~** Morocco

ma'roso *sm* breaker

'marra *sf* hoe

Marra'kesh [marra'keʃ] *sf* Marrakesh

mar'rone *ag inv* brown ■ *sm (Bot)* chestnut

mar'sala *sm inv (vino)* Marsala (wine)

Mar'siglia [mar'siʎʎa] *sf* Marseilles

mar'sina *sf* tails *pl*, tail coat

mar'supio *sm (Zool)* pouch, marsupium

mart. *abbr (= martedì)* Tue(s)

'Marte *sm (Astr, Mitologia)* Mars

marte'dì *sm inv* Tuesday; **di** *o* **il ~** on Tuesdays; **oggi è ~ 3 aprile** (the date) today is Tuesday 3rd April; **~ stavo male** I wasn't well on Tuesday; **il giornale di ~** Tuesday's newspaper; **~ grasso** Shrove Tuesday

martel'lante *ag (fig: dolore)* throbbing

martel'lare *vt* to hammer ■ *vi (pulsare)* to throb; *(cuore)* to thump

martel'letto *sm (di pianoforte)* hammer; *(di macchina da scrivere)* typebar; *(di giudice, nelle vendite all'asta)* gavel; *(Med)* percussion hammer

mar'tello *sm* hammer; *(di uscio)* knocker; **suonare a ~** *(fig: campane)* to sound the tocsin; **~ pneumatico** pneumatic drill

marti'netto *sm (Tecn)* jack

martin'gala *sf (di giacca)* half-belt; *(di cavallo)* martingale

'martire *sm/f* martyr

mar'tirio *sm* martyrdom; *(fig)* agony, torture

martori'are *vt* to torment, torture

mar'xismo *sm* Marxism

mar'xista, -i, e *ag, sm/f* Marxist

marza'pane [martsa'pane] *sm* marzipan

marzi'ale [mar'tsjale] *ag* martial

'marzo ['martso] *sm* March; *vedi* **luglio**

marzo'lino, -a [martso'lino] *ag* March *cpd*

mascalzo'nata [maskaltso'nata] *sf* dirty trick

mascal'zone [maskal'tsone] *sm* rascal, scoundrel

mas'cara *sm inv* mascara

mascar'pone *sm soft cream cheese often used in desserts*

ma'scella [maʃ'ʃɛlla] *sf (Anat)* jaw

'maschera ['maskera] *sf* mask; *(travestimento)* disguise; *(per un ballo etc)* fancy dress; *(Teat, Cine)* usher/usherette; *(personaggio del teatro)* stock character; **in ~** *(mascherato)* masked; **ballo in ~** fancy-dress ball; **gettare la ~** *(fig)* to reveal o.s.;

m

~ antigas/subacquea gas/diving mask; **~ di bellezza** face pack
masche'rare [maske'rare] *vt* to mask; (*travestire*) to disguise; to dress up; (*fig: celare*) to hide, conceal; (*Mil*) to camouflage; **mascherarsi** *vr*: **mascherarsi da** to disguise o.s. as; to dress up as; (*fig*) to masquerade as
masche'rina [maske'rina] *sf* (*piccola maschera*) mask; (*di animale*) patch; (*di scarpe*) toe-cap; (*Aut*) radiator grill
mas'chile [mas'kile] *ag* masculine; (*sesso, popolazione*) male; (*abiti*) men's; (*per ragazzi: scuola*) boys'
'maschio, -a ['maskjo] *ag* (*Biol*) male; (*virile*) manly ■ *sm* (*anche Zool, Tecn*) male; (*uomo*) man; (*ragazzo*) boy; (*figlio*) son
masco'lino, -a *ag* masculine
mas'cotte [mas'kɔt] *sf inv* mascot
maso'chismo [mazo'kizmo] *sm* masochism
maso'chista, -i, e [mazo'kista] *ag* masochistic ■ *sm/f* masochist
'massa *sf* mass; (*di errori etc*): **una ~ di** heaps of, masses of; (*di gente*) mass, multitude; (*Elettr*) earth; **in ~** (*Comm*) in bulk; (*tutti insieme*) en masse; **adunata in ~** mass meeting; **manifestazione/cultura di ~** mass demonstration/culture; **produrre in ~** to mass-produce; **la ~ (del popolo)** the masses *pl*
massa'crante *ag* exhausting, gruelling
massa'crare *vt* to massacre, slaughter
mas'sacro *sm* massacre, slaughter; (*fig*) mess, disaster
massaggi'are [massad'dʒare] *vt* to massage
massaggia'tore, -'trice [massaddʒa'tore] *sm/f* masseur/masseuse
mas'saggio [mas'saddʒo] *sm* massage
mas'saia *sf* housewife
masse'ria *sf* large farm
masse'rizie [masse'rittsje] *sfpl* (household) furnishings
massicci'ata [massit'tʃata] *sf* (*di strada, ferrovia*) ballast
mas'siccio, -a, ci, ce [mas'sittʃo] *ag* (*oro, legno*) solid; (*palazzo*) massive; (*corporatura*) stout ■ *sm* (*Geo*) massif
'massima *sf vedi* **massimo**
massi'male *sm* maximum; (*Comm*) ceiling, limit
'massimo, -a *ag, sm* maximum ■ *sf* (*sentenza, regola*) maxim; (*Meteor*) maximum temperature; **in linea di massima** generally speaking; **arrivare entro il tempo ~** to arrive within the time limit; **al ~** at (the) most; **sfruttare qc al ~** to make full use of sth; **arriverò al ~ alle 5** I'll arrive at 5 at the latest; **erano presenti le massimoe autorità** all the most important dignitaries were there; **il ~ della pena** (*Dir*) the maximum penalty
mas'sivo, -a *ag* (*intervento*) en masse; (*emigrazione*) mass; (*emorragia*) massive
'masso *sm* rock, boulder
mas'sone *sm* freemason
massone'ria *sf* freemasonry
mas'sonico, -a, ci, che *ag* masonic
mas'tello *sm* tub
masteriz'zare [masterid'dzare] *vt* to burn
masterizza'tore [masteriddza'tore] *sm* CD burner *o* writer
masti'care *vt* to chew
'mastice ['mastitʃe] *sm* mastic; (*per vetri*) putty
mas'tino *sm* mastiff
masto'dontico, -a, ci, che *ag* gigantic
mastur'barsi *vr* to masturbate
masturbazi'one [masturbat'tsjone] *sf* masturbation
ma'tassa *sf* skein
mate'matico, -a, ci, che *ag* mathematical ■ *sm/f* mathematician ■ *sf* mathematics *sg*
materas'sino *sm* mat; **~ gonfiabile** air bed
mate'rasso *sm* mattress; **~ a molle** spring *o* interior-sprung mattress
ma'teria *sf* (*Fisica*) matter; (*Tecn, Comm*) material, matter *no pl*; (*disciplina*) subject; (*argomento*) subject matter, material; **prima di entrare in ~ ...** before discussing the matter in hand ...; **un esperto in ~ (di musica etc)** an expert on the subject (of music etc); **sono ignorante in ~** I know nothing about it; **~ cerebrale** cerebral matter; **~ grassa** fat; **~ grigia** (*anche fig*) grey matter; **materie plastiche** plastics; **materie prime** raw materials
materi'ale *ag* material; (*fig: grossolano*) rough, rude ■ *sm* material; (*insieme di strumenti etc*) equipment *no pl*, materials *pl*; **~ da costruzione** building materials *pl*
materia'lista, -i, e *ag* materialistic ■ *sm/f* materialist
materializ'zarsi [materjalid'dzarsi] *vr* to materialize
material'mente *av* (*fisicamente*) materially; (*economicamente*) financially
maternità *sf* motherhood, maternity; (*clinica*) maternity hospital; **in (congedo di) ~** on maternity leave
ma'terno, -a *ag* (*amore, cura etc*) maternal, motherly; (*nonno*) maternal; (*lingua, terra*) mother *cpd*; *vedi anche* **scuola**
ma'tita *sf* pencil; **matite colorate** crayons; **~ per gli occhi** eyeliner (pencil)
ma'trice [ma'tritʃe] *sf* matrix; (*Comm*) counterfoil; (*fig: origine*) background

ma'tricola *sf (registro)* register; *(numero)* registration number; *(nell'università)* freshman, fresher *(Brit fam)*
ma'trigna [ma'triɲɲa] *sf* stepmother
matrimoni'ale *ag* matrimonial, marriage *cpd*; **camera/letto ~** double room/bed
matri'monio *sm* marriage, matrimony; *(durata)* marriage, married life; *(cerimonia)* wedding
ma'trona *sf (fig)* matronly woman
matta'toio *sm* abattoir *(Brit)*, slaughterhouse
mat'tina *sf* morning; **la** *o* **alla** *o* **di ~** in the morning; **di prima ~, la ~ presto** early in the morning; **dalla ~ alla sera** *(continuamente)* from morning to night; *(improvvisamente: cambiare)* overnight
matti'nata *sf* morning; *(spettacolo)* matinée, afternoon performance; **in ~** in the course of the morning; **nella ~** in the morning; **nella tarda ~** at the end of the morning; **nella tarda ~ di sabato** late on Saturday morning
mattini'ero, -a *ag*: **essere ~** to be an early riser
mat'tino *sm* morning; **di buon ~** early in the morning
'matto, -a *ag* mad, crazy; *(fig: falso)* false, imitation; *(opaco)* matt, dull ■ *sm/f* madman/woman; **avere una voglia matta di qc** to be dying for sth; **far diventare ~ qn** to drive sb mad *o* crazy; **una gabbia di matti** *(fig)* a madhouse
mat'tone *sm* brick; *(fig)*: **questo libro/film è un ~** this book/film is heavy going
matto'nella *sf* tile
mattu'tino, -a *ag* morning *cpd*
matu'rare *vi (anche:* **maturarsi**: *frutta, grano)* to ripen; *(ascesso)* to come to a head; *(fig: persona, idea, Econ)* to mature ■ *vt* to ripen, to (make) mature; **~ una decisione** to come to a decision
maturità *sf* maturity; *(di frutta)* ripeness, maturity; *(Ins)* school-leaving examination, ≈ GCE A-levels *(Brit)*
ma'turo, -a *ag* mature; *(frutto)* ripe, mature
ma'tusa *sm/f inv (scherzoso)* old fogey
Mauri'tania *sf*: **la ~** Mauritania
Mau'rizio [mau'rittsjo] *sf*: **(l'isola di) ~** Mauritius
mauso'leo *sm* mausoleum
max. *abbr (= massimo)* max
'maxi... *prefisso* maxi...
maxipro'cesso [maksipro'tʃɛsso] *sm see note*

MAXIPROCESSO

A *maxiprocesso* is a criminal trial which is characterized by the large number of co-defendants. These people are usually members of terrorist or criminal organizations. The trials are often lengthy and many witnesses may be called to give evidence.

maxis'chermo [maksis'kermo] *sm* giant screen
'mazza ['mattsa] *sf (bastone)* club; *(martello)* sledge-hammer; *(Sport: da golf)* club; *(: da baseball, cricket)* bat
maz'zata [mat'tsata] *sf (anche fig)* heavy blow
maz'zetta [mat'tsetta] *sf (di banconote etc)* bundle; *(fig)* rake-off
'mazzo ['mattso] *sm (di fiori, chiavi etc)* bunch; *(di carte da gioco)* pack
MC *sigla* = **Macerata**
m.c.d. *abbr (= minimo comune denominatore)* lcd
m.c.m. *abbr (= minimo comune multiplo)* lcm
ME *sigla* = **Messina**
me *pron* me; **sei bravo quanto me** you are as clever as I (am) *o* as me
me'andro *sm* meander
M.E.C. [mɛk] *abbr m* = **Mercato Comune Europeo**
'Mecca *sf (anche fig)*: **La ~** Mecca
meccanica'mente *av* mechanically
mec'canico, -a, ci, che *ag* mechanical ■ *sm* mechanic ■ *sf* mechanics *sg*; *(attività tecnologica)* mechanical engineering; *(meccanismo)* mechanism; **officina meccanica** garage
mecca'nismo *sm* mechanism
meccaniz'zare [mekkanid'dzare] *vt* to mechanize
meccanizzazi'one [mekkaniddzat'tsjone] *sf* mechanization
meccanogra'fia *sf* (mechanical) data processing
meccano'grafico, -a, ci, che *ag*: **centro ~** data processing department
mece'nate [metʃe'nate] *sm* patron
mèche [mɛʃ] *sf inv* streak; **farsi le ~** to have one's hair streaked
me'daglia [me'daʎʎa] *sf* medal; **~ d'oro** *(oggetto)* gold medal; *(persona)* gold medallist *(Brit) o* medalist *(US)*
medagli'one [medaʎ'ʎone] *sm (Archit)* medallion; *(gioiello)* locket
me'desimo, -a *ag* same; *(in persona)*: **io ~** I myself
'media *sf vedi* **medio**
media'mente *av* on average
medi'ano, -a *ag* median; *(valore)* mean ■ *sm (Calcio)* half-back
medi'ante *prep* by means of
medi'are *vt (fare da mediatore)* to act as mediator in; *(Mat)* to average

m

medi'ato, -a *ag* indirect
media'tore, -'trice *sm/f* mediator; (*Comm*) middle man, agent; **fare da ~ fra** to mediate between
mediazi'one [medjat'tsjone] *sf* mediation; (*Comm: azione, compenso*) brokerage
medica'mento *sm* medicine, drug
medi'care *vt* to treat; (*ferita*) to dress
medi'cato, -a *ag* (*garza, shampoo*) medicated
medicazi'one [medikat'tsjone] *sf* treatment, medication dressing; **fare una ~ a qn** to dress sb's wounds
medi'cina [medi'tʃina] *sf* medicine; **~ legale** forensic medicine
medici'nale [meditʃi'nale] *ag* medicinal ■ *sm* drug, medicine
'medico, -a, ci, che *ag* medical ■ *sm* doctor; **~ di bordo** ship's doctor; **~ di famiglia** family doctor; **~ fiscale** *doctor who examines patients signed off sick for a lengthy period by their private doctor*; **~ generico** general practitioner, GP
medie'vale *ag* medieval
'medio, -a *ag* average; (*punto, ceto*) middle; (*altezza, statura*) medium ■ *sm* (*dito*) middle finger ■ *sf* average; (*Mat*) mean; (*Ins: voto*) end-of-term average; **medie** *sfpl vedi* **scuola media inferiore**; **licenza media** *leaving certificate awarded at the end of 3 years of secondary education*; **in media** on average; **al di sopra/sotto della media** above/below average; **viaggiare ad una media di ...** to travel at an average speed of ...; **il M~ Oriente** the Middle East
medi'ocre *ag* (*gen*) mediocre; (*qualità, stipendio*) poor
mediocrità *sf* mediocrity; poorness
medioe'vale *ag* = **medievale**
Medio'evo *sm* Middle Ages *pl*
medita'bondo, -a *ag* thoughtful
medi'tare *vt* to ponder over, meditate on; (*progettare*) to plan, think out ■ *vi* to meditate
medi'tato, -a *ag* (*gen*) meditated; (*parole*) carefully-weighed; (*vendetta*) premeditated; **ben ~** (*piano*) well worked-out, neat
meditazi'one [meditat'tsjone] *sf* meditation
mediter'raneo, -a *ag* Mediterranean; **il (mare) M~** the Mediterranean (Sea)
'medium *sm/f inv* medium
me'dusa *sf* (*Zool*) jellyfish
me'gafono *sm* megaphone
mega'lomane *ag, sm/f* megalomaniac
me'gera [me'dʒɛra] *sf* (*peg: donna*) shrew
'meglio ['mɛʎʎo] *av, ag inv* better; (*con senso superlativo*) best ■ *sm* (*la cosa migliore*): **il ~** the best (thing); **faresti ~ ad andartene** you had better leave; **alla ~** as best one can; **andar di bene in ~** to get better and better; **fare del proprio ~** to do one's best; **per il ~** for the best; **aver la ~ su qn** to get the better of sb
'mela *sf* apple; **~ cotogna** quince
mela'grana *sf* pomegranate
melan'zana [melan'dzana] *sf* aubergine (*Brit*), eggplant (*US*)
me'lassa *sf* molasses *sg*, treacle
me'lenso, -a *ag* dull, stupid
me'lissa *sf* (*Bot*) balm
mel'lifluo, -a *ag* (*peg*) sugary, honeyed
'melma *sf* mud, mire
'melo *sm* apple tree
melo'dia *sf* melody
me'lodico, -a, ci, che *ag* melodic
melodi'oso, -a *ag* melodious
melo'dramma, -i *sm* melodrama
me'lone *sm* (musk) melon
'membra *sfpl vedi* **membro**
mem'brana *sf* membrane
'membro *sm* (*person*) (*pl(m)* **membri**) member; (*arto*) (*pl(f)* **membra**) limb
memo'rabile *ag* memorable
memo'randum *sm inv* memorandum
'memore *ag*: **~ di** (*ricordando*) mindful of; (*riconoscente*) grateful for
me'moria *sf* (*anche Inform*) memory; **memorie** *sfpl* (*opera autobiografica*) memoirs; **a ~** (*imparare, sapere*) by heart; **a ~ d'uomo** within living memory; **~ di sola lettura** (*Inform*) read-only memory; **~ tampone** (*Inform*) buffer
memori'ale *sm* (*raccolta di memorie*) memoirs *pl*; (*Dir*) memorial
memoriz'zare [memorid'dzare] *vt* (*gen*) to memorize; (*Inform*) to store
memorizzazi'one [memoriddzat'tsjone] *sf* memorization; storage
'mena *sf* scheme
mena'dito; **a ~** *av* perfectly, thoroughly; **sapere qc a ~** to have sth at one's fingertips
mena'gramo *sm/f inv* jinx, Jonah
me'nare *vt* to lead; (*picchiare*) to hit, beat; (*dare: colpi*) to deal; **~ la coda** (*cane*) to wag its tail; **~ qc per le lunghe** to drag sth out; **~ il can per l'aia** (*fig*) to beat about (*Brit*) *o* around (*US*) the bush
mendi'cante *sm/f* beggar
mendi'care *vt* to beg for ■ *vi* to beg
menefre'ghismo [menefre'gizmo] *sm* (*fam*) couldn't-care-less attitude
me'ninge [me'nindʒe] *sf* (*Med*) meninx; **spremersi le meningi** to rack one's brains
menin'gite [menin'dʒite] *sf* meningitis
me'nisco *sm* (*Anat, Mat, Fisica*) meniscus

PAROLA CHIAVE

'meno *av* **1** (*in minore misura*) less; **dovresti mangiare meno** you should eat less, you shouldn't eat so much; **è sempre meno facile** it's getting less and less easy; **ne voglio di meno** I don't want so much
2 (*comparativo*): **meno ... di** not as ... as, less ... than; **sono meno alto di te** I'm not as tall as you (are), I'm less tall than you (are); **meno ... che** not as ... as, less ... than; **meno che mai** less than ever; **è meno intelligente che ricco** he's more rich than intelligent; **meno fumo più mangio** the less I smoke the more I eat; **meno di quanto pensassi** less than I thought
3 (*superlativo*) least; **il meno dotato degli studenti** the least gifted of the students; **è quello che compro meno spesso** it's the one I buy least often
4 (*Mat*) minus; **8 meno 5** 8 minus 5, 8 take away 5; **sono le 8 meno un quarto** it's a quarter to 8; **meno 5 gradi** 5 degrees below zero, minus 5 degrees; **mille euro in meno** a thousand euros less; **ha preso 6 meno** (*a scuola*) he scraped a pass; **cento euro meno le spese** a hundred euros minus *o* less expenses
5 (*fraseologia*): **quanto meno poteva telefonare** he could at least have phoned; **non so se accettare o meno** I don't know whether to accept or not; **non essere da meno di** not to be outdone by; **fare a meno di qc/qn** to do without sth/sb; **non potevo fare a meno di ridere** I couldn't help laughing; **meno male!** thank goodness!; **meno male che sei arrivato** it's a good job that you've come
■ *ag inv* (*tempo, denaro*) less; (*errori, persone*) fewer; **ha fatto meno errori di tutti** he made fewer mistakes than anyone, he made the fewest mistakes of all
■ *sm inv* **1**: **il meno** (*il minimo*) the least; **parlare del più e del meno** to talk about this and that; **era il meno che ti potesse succedere** it was the least you could have expected
2 (*Mat*) minus
■ *prep* (*eccetto*) except (for), apart from; **tutti meno lui** everybody apart from *o* except him; **a meno che, a meno di** unless; **a meno che non piova** unless it rains; **non posso, a meno di prendere ferie** I can't, unless I take some leave; *vedi anche* **più**

meno'mare *vt* (*danneggiare*) to maim, disable
meno'mato, -a *ag* (*persona*) disabled ■ *sm/f* disabled person
menomazi'one [menomat'tsjone] *sf* disablement
meno'pausa *sf* menopause
'mensa *sf* (*locale*) canteen; (*Mil*) mess; (: *nelle università*) refectory
men'sile *ag* monthly ■ *sm* (*periodico*) monthly (magazine); (*stipendio*) monthly salary
mensil'mente *av* (*ogni mese*) every month; (*una volta al mese*) monthly
'mensola *sf* bracket; (*ripiano*) shelf; (*Archit*) corbel
'menta *sf* mint; (*anche*: **menta piperita**) peppermint; (*bibita*) peppermint cordial; (*caramella*) mint, peppermint
men'tale *ag* mental
mentalità *sf inv* mentality
mental'mente *av* mentally
'mente *sf* mind; **imparare/sapere qc a ~** to learn/know sth by heart; **avere in ~ qc** to have sth in mind; **avere in ~ di fare qc** to intend to do sth; **fare venire in ~ qc a qn** to remind sb of sth; **mettersi in ~ di fare qc** to make up one's mind to do sth; **passare di ~ a qn** to slip sb's mind; **tenere a ~ qc** to bear sth in mind; **a ~ fredda** objectively; **lasciami fare ~ locale** let me think
mente'catto, -a *ag* half-witted ■ *sm/f* halfwit, imbecile
men'tire *vi* to lie
men'tito, -a *ag*: **sotto mentite spoglie** under false pretences (*Brit*) *o* pretenses (*US*)
'mento *sm* chin; **doppio ~** double chin
men'tolo *sm* menthol
'mentre *cong* (*temporale*) while; (*avversativo*) whereas ■ *sm*: **in quel ~** at that very moment
menù *sm inv* (set) menu; **~ turistico** standard *o* tourists' menu
menzio'nare [mentsjo'nare] *vt* to mention
menzi'one [men'tsjone] *sf* mention; **fare ~ di** to mention
men'zogna [men'tsoɲɲa] *sf* lie
menzo'gnero, -a [mentsoɲ'ɲɛro] *ag* false, untrue
mera'viglia [mera'viʎʎa] *sf* amazement, wonder; (*persona, cosa*) marvel, wonder; **a ~** perfectly, wonderfully
meravigli'are [meraviʎ'ʎare] *vt* to amaze, astonish; **meravigliarsi** *vr*: **meravigliarsi (di)** to marvel (at); (*stupirsi*) to be amazed (at), be astonished (at); **mi meraviglio di te!** I'm surprised at you!; **non c'è da meravigliarsi** it's not surprising
meravigli'oso, -a [meraviʎ'ʎoso] *ag* wonderful, marvellous (*Brit*), marvelous (*US*)

merc. *abbr* (= *mercoledì*) Wed
mer'cante *sm* merchant; **~ d'arte** art dealer; **~ di cavalli** horse dealer
mercanteggi'are [merkanted'dʒare] *vt* (*onore, voto*) to sell ■ *vi* to bargain, haggle
mercan'tile *ag* commercial, mercantile; (*nave, marina*) merchant *cpd* ■ *sm* (*nave*) merchantman
mercan'zia [merkan'tsia] *sf* merchandise, goods *pl*
merca'tino *sm* (*rionale*) local street market; (*Econ*) unofficial stock market
mer'cato *sm* market; **di ~** (*economia, prezzo, ricerche*) market *cpd*; **mettere** *o* **lanciare qc sul ~** to launch sth on the market; **a buon ~** cheap; **~ dei cambi** exchange market; **M~ Comune (Europeo)** (European) Common Market; **~ del lavoro** labour market, job market; **~ nero** black market; **~ al rialzo/al ribasso** (*Borsa*) sellers'/buyers' market
'merce ['mɛrtʃe] *sf* goods *pl*, merchandise; **~ deperibile** perishable goods *pl*
mercé [mer'tʃe] *sf* mercy; **essere alla ~ di qn** to be at sb's mercy
merce'nario, -a [mertʃe'narjo] *ag, sm* mercenary
merce'ria [mertʃe'ria] *sf* (*articoli*) haberdashery (*Brit*), notions *pl* (*US*); (*bottega*) haberdasher's shop (*Brit*), notions store (*US*)
mercoledì *sm inv* Wednesday; **~ delle Ceneri** Ash Wednesday; *see note*; *vedi anche* **martedì**

MERCOLEDÌ DELLE CENERI

In the Catholic church, *Mercoledì delle Ceneri* signals the beginning of Lent. Churchgoers are marked on the forehead with ash from the burning of the olive branch. Ash Wednesday is traditionally a day of fasting, abstinence and repentance.

mer'curio *sm* mercury
'merda *sf* (*fam!*) shit (*!*)
me'renda *sf* afternoon snack
meren'dina *sf* snack
meridi'ano, -a *ag* (*di mezzogiorno*) midday *cpd*, noonday ■ *sm* meridian ■ *sf* (*orologio*) sundial
meridio'nale *ag* southern ■ *sm/f* southerner
meridi'one *sm* south
me'ringa, -ghe *sf* (*Cuc*) meringue
meri'tare *vt* to deserve, merit ■ *vb impers* (*valere la pena*): **merita andare** it is worth going; **non merita neanche parlarne** it's not worth talking about; **per quel che merita** for what it's worth
meri'tevole *ag* worthy
'merito *sm* merit; (*valore*) worth; **dare ~ a qn di** to give sb credit for; **finire a pari ~** to finish joint first (*o* second *etc*); to tie; **in ~ a** as regards, with regard to; **entrare nel ~ di una questione** to go into a matter; **non so niente in ~** I don't know anything about it
meritocra'zia [meritokrat'tsia] *sf* meritocracy
meri'torio, -a *ag* praiseworthy
mer'letto *sm* lace
'merlo *sm* (*Zool*) blackbird; (*Archit*) battlement
mer'luzzo [mer'luttso] *sm* (*Zool*) cod
'mescere ['meʃʃere] *vt* to pour (out)
meschinità [meskini'ta] *sf* wretchedness; meagreness; meanness; narrow-mindedness
mes'chino, -a [mes'kino] *ag* wretched; (*scarso*) meagre (*Brit*), meager (*US*); (*persona: gretta*) mean; (*limitata*) narrow-minded, petty; **fare una figura meschina** to cut a poor figure
'mescita ['meʃʃita] *sf* wine shop
mesci'uto, -a [meʃʃuto] *pp di* **mescere**
mesco'lanza [mesko'lantsa] *sf* mixture
mesco'lare *vt* to mix; (*vini, colori*) to blend; (*mettere in disordine*) to mix up, muddle up; (*carte*) to shuffle; **mescolarsi** *vr* to mix; to blend; to get mixed up; (*fig*): **mescolarsi in** to get mixed up in, meddle in
'mese *sm* month; **il ~ scorso** last month; **il corrente ~** this month
'messa *sf* (*Rel*) mass; (*il mettere*): **~ a fuoco** focusing; **~ in moto** starting; **~ in piega** (*acconciatura*) set; **~ a punto** (*Tecn*) adjustment; (*Aut*) tuning; (*fig*) clarification; **~ in scena** = **messinscena**
messagge'rie [messaddʒe'rie] *sfpl* (*ditta: di distribuzione*) distributors; (*di trasporto*) freight company
messag'gero [messad'dʒɛro] *sm* messenger
messaggi'arsi [messad'dʒarsi] *vr*: **messaggiamoci** we'll text each other
messag'gino [messad'dʒino] *sm* (*di telefonino*) text (message)
mes'saggio [mes'saddʒo] *sm* message
messag'gistica [messad'dʒistica] *sf*: **~ immediata** (*Inform*) instant messaging; **programma di ~ immediata** instant messenger
mes'sale *sm* (*Rel*) missal
'messe *sf* harvest
Mes'sia *sm inv* (*Rel*): **il ~** the Messiah
messi'cano, -a *ag, sm/f* Mexican
'Messico *sm*: **il ~** Mexico; **Città del ~** Mexico City
messin'scena [messin'ʃɛna] *sf* (*Teat*) production

ˈ**messo, -a** *pp di* **mettere** ■ *sm* messenger
mestieˈrante *sm/f (peg)* money-grubber; (*: scrittore*) hack
mestiˈere *sm (professione)* job; *(manuale)* trade; *(artigianale)* craft; (*fig: abilità nel lavoro*) skill, technique; **di ~** by *o* to trade; **essere del ~** to know the tricks of the trade
mesˈtizia [mesˈtittsja] *sf* sadness, melancholy
ˈ**mesto, -a** *ag* sad, melancholy
ˈ**mestolo** *sm (Cuc)* ladle
mestruˈale *ag* menstrual
mestruaziˈone [mestruatˈtsjone] *sf* menstruation; **avere le mestruazioni** to have one's period
ˈ**meta** *sf* destination; *(fig)* aim, goal
metà *sf inv* half; *(punto di mezzo)* middle; **dividere qc a** *o* **per ~** to divide sth in half, halve sth; **fare a ~ (di qc con qn)** to go halves (with sb in sth); **a ~ prezzo** at half price; **a ~ settimana** midweek; **a ~ strada** halfway; **verso la ~ del mese** halfway through the month, towards the middle of the month; **dire le cose a ~** to leave some things unsaid; **fare le cose a ~** to leave things half-done; **la mia dolce ~** (*fam scherzoso*) my better half
metaboˈlismo *sm* metabolism
metaˈdone *sm* methadone
metaˈfisica *sf* metaphysics *sg*
meˈtafora *sf* metaphor
metaˈforico, -a, ci, che *ag* metaphorical
meˈtallico, -a, ci, che *ag (di metallo)* metal *cpd*; *(splendore, rumore etc)* metallic
metallizˈzato, -a [metallidˈdzato] *ag (verniciatura)* metallic
meˈtallo *sm* metal; **di ~** metal *cpd*
metallurˈgia [metallurˈdʒia] *sf* metallurgy
metalmecˈcanico, -a, ci, che *ag* engineering *cpd* ■ *sm* engineering worker
metaˈmorfosi *sf* metamorphosis
meˈtano *sm* methane
meˈteora *sf* meteor
meteoˈrite *sm* meteorite
meteoroloˈgia [meteoroloˈdʒia] *sf* meteorology
meteoroˈlogico, -a, ci, che [meteoroˈlɔdʒiko] *ag* meteorological, weather *cpd*
meteoˈrologo, -a, ghi, ghe *sm/f* meteorologist
meˈticcio, -a, ci, ce [meˈtittʃo] *sm/f* half-caste, half-breed
meticolosità *sf* meticulousness
meticoˈloso, -a *ag* meticulous
meˈtodico, -a, ci, che *ag* methodical
ˈ**metodo** *sm* method; *(manuale)* tutor *(Brit)*, manual; **far qc con/senza ~** to do sth methodically/unmethodically
meˈtraggio [meˈtraddʒo] *sm (Sartoria)* length; *(Cine)* footage; **film a lungo ~** feature film; **film a corto ~** short film
metraˈtura *sf* length
ˈ**metrico, -a, ci, che** *ag* metric; *(Poesia)* metrical ■ *sf* metrics *sg*
ˈ**metro** *sm* metre *(Brit)*, meter *(US)*; *(nastro)* tape measure; *(asta)* (metre) rule
metrò *sm inv* underground *(Brit)*, subway *(US)*
metroˈnotte *sm inv* night security guard
meˈtropoli *sf* metropolis
metropoliˈtano, -a *ag* metropolitan ■ *sf* underground *(Brit)*, subway *(US)*; **metropolitana leggera** metro (*mainly on the surface*)
metrosesˈsuale *ag* metrosexual
ˈ**mettere** *vt* to put; *(abito)* to put on; (*: portare*) to wear; (*installare: telefono*) to put in; (*fig: provocare*): **~ fame/allegria a qn** to make sb hungry/happy; *(supporre)*: **mettiamo che ...** let's suppose *o* say that ...; **mettersi** *vr (persona)* to put o.s.; *(oggetto)* to go; (*disporsi: faccenda*) to turn out; **mettersi a piangere/ridere** to start crying/laughing, start *o* begin to cry/laugh; **mettersi a sedere** to sit down; **mettersi al lavoro** to set to work; **mettersi a letto** to get into bed; (*per malattia*) to take to one's bed; **mettersi il cappello** to put on one's hat; **mettersi sotto** to get down to things; **mettersi in società** to set up in business; **si sono messi insieme** *(coppia)* they've started going out together *(Brit)* *o* dating *(US)*; **metterci**: **metterci molta cura/molto tempo** to take a lot of care/a lot of time; **mettercela tutta** to do one's best; **ci ho messo 3 ore per venire** it's taken me 3 hours to get here; **~ un annuncio sul giornale** to place an advertisement in the paper; **~ a confronto** to compare; **~ in conto** (*somma etc*) to put on account; **~ in luce** (*problemi, errori*) to stress, highlight; **~ a tacere qn/qc** to keep sb/sth quiet; **~ su casa** to set up house; **~ su un negozio** to start a shop; **~ su peso** to put on weight; **~ via** to put away
mezˈzadro [medˈdzadro] *sm (Agr)* sharecropper
mezzaˈluna [meddzaˈluna] (*pl* **mezzelune**) *sf* half-moon; (*dell'islamismo*) crescent; *(coltello)* (semicircular) chopping knife
mezzaˈnino [meddzaˈnino] *sm* mezzanine (floor)
mezˈzano, -a [medˈdzano] *ag (medio)* average, medium; *(figlio)* middle *cpd* ■ *sm/f (intermediario)* go-between; *(ruffiano)* pimp
mezzaˈnotte [meddzaˈnɔtte] *sf* midnight

m

ˈ**mezzo, -a** [ˈmɛddzo] *ag* half; **un ~ litro/ panino** half a litre/roll ■ *av* half-; **~ morto** half-dead ■ *sm* (*metà*) half; (*parte centrale: di strada etc*) middle; (*per raggiungere un fine*) means *sg*; (*veicolo*) vehicle; (*nell'indicare l'ora*): **le nove e ~** half past nine; **mezzogiorno e ~** half past twelve ■ *sf*: **la mezza** half-past twelve (in the afternoon); **mezzi** *smpl* (*possibilità economiche*) means; **di mezza età** middle-aged; **aver una mezza idea di fare qc** to have half a mind to do sth; **è stato un ~ scandalo** it almost caused a scandal; **un soprabito di mezza stagione** a spring (*o* autumn) coat; **a mezza voce** in an undertone; **una volta e ~ più grande** one and a half times bigger; **di ~** middle, in the middle; **andarci di ~** (*patir danno*) to suffer; **esserci di ~** (*ostacolo*) to be in the way; **levarsi** *o* **togliersi di ~** to get out of the way; **mettersi di ~** to interfere; **togliere di ~** (*persona, cosa*) to get rid of; (*fam: uccidere*) to bump off; **non c'è una via di ~** there's no middle course; **in ~ a** in the middle of; **nel bel ~ (di)** right in the middle (of); **per** *o* **a ~ di** by means of; **a ~ corriere** by carrier; **mezzi di comunicazione di massa** mass media *pl*; **mezzi pubblici** public transport *sg*; **mezzi di trasporto** means of transport

mezzogiˈorno [meddzoˈdʒorno] *sm* midday, noon; (*Geo*) south; **a ~** at 12 (o'clock) *o* midday *o* noon; **il ~ d'Italia** southern Italy

mezzˈora [medˈdzora] *sf* half-hour, half an hour

MI *sigla* = **Milano**

mi *pron* (*dav lo, la, li, le, ne diventa* **me**) (*oggetto*) me; (*complemento di termine*) (to) me; (*riflessivo*) myself ■ *sm* (*Mus*) E; (: *solfeggiando la scala*) mi; **mi aiuti?** will you help me?; **me ne ha parlato** he spoke to me about it, he told me about it; **mi servo da solo** I'll help myself

ˈ**mia** *vedi* **mio**

miagoˈlare *vi* to miaow, mew

Mib *sigla m, ag* (= *indice borsa Milano*) Milan Stock Exchange Index

ˈ**mica** *sf* (*Chim*) mica ■ *av* (*fam*): **non ... ~** not ... at all; **non sono ~ stanco** I'm not a bit tired; **non sarà ~ partito?** he wouldn't have left, would he?; **~ male** not bad

ˈ**miccia, -ce** [ˈmittʃa] *sf* fuse

micidiˈale [mitʃiˈdjale] *ag* fatal; (*dannosissimo*) deadly

ˈ**micio, -a, ci, cie** [ˈmitʃo] *sm/f* pussy (cat)

microbioloˈgia [mikrobioloˈdʒia] *sf* microbiology

ˈ**microbo** *sm* microbe

microcirˈcuito [mikrotʃirˈkuito] *sm* microcircuit

microˈfibra *sf* microfibre

microˈfilm *sm inv* microfilm

miˈcrofono *sm* microphone

microinforˈmatica *sf* microcomputing

microˈonda *sf* microwave

microprocesˈsore [mikroprotʃesˈsore] *sm* microprocessor

microsˈcopico, -a, ci, che *ag* microscopic

microsˈcopio *sm* microscope

microˈsolco, -chi *sm* (*solco*) microgroove; (*disco: a 33 giri*) long-playing record, LP; (: *a 45 giri*) extended-play record, EP

microsˈpia *sf* hidden microphone, bug (*fam*)

miˈdollo (*pl(f)* **midolla**) *sm* (*Anat*) marrow; **~ spinale** spinal cord

ˈ**mie** (*pl* **miei**) *vedi* **mio**

miˈele *sm* honey

miˈetere *vt* (*Agr*) to reap, harvest; (*fig: vite*) to take, claim

mietitrebbiaˈtrice [mjetitrebbjaˈtritʃe] *sf* combine harvester

mietiˈtrice [mjetiˈtritʃe] *sf* (*macchina*) harvester

mietiˈtura *sf* (*raccolto*) harvest; (*lavoro*) harvesting; (*tempo*) harvest-time

ˈ**miglia** [ˈmiʎʎa] *sfpl di* **miglio**

migliˈaio [miʎˈʎajo] (*pl(f)* **migliaia**) *sm* thousand; **un ~ (di)** about a thousand; **a migliaia** by the thousand, in thousands

ˈ**miglio**[1] [ˈmiʎʎo] (*pl(f)* **miglia**) *sm* (*unità di misura*) mile; **~ marino** *o* **nautico** nautical mile

ˈ**miglio**[2] [ˈmiʎʎo] *sm* (*Bot*) millet

miglioraˈmento [miʎʎoraˈmento] *sm* improvement

miglioˈrare [miʎʎoˈrare] *vt, vi* to improve

migliˈore [miʎˈʎore] *ag* (*comparativo*) better; (*superlativo*) best ■ *sm*: **il ~** the best (thing) ■ *sm/f*: **il(la) ~** the best (person); **il miglior vino di questa regione** the best wine in this area; **i migliori auguri** best wishes

miglioˈria [miʎʎoˈria] *sf* improvement

ˈ**mignolo** [ˈmiɲɲolo] *sm* (*Anat*) little finger, pinkie; (: *dito del piede*) little toe

miˈgrare *vi* to migrate

migraziˈone [migratˈtsjone] *sf* migration

ˈ**mila** *pl di* **mille**

milaˈnese *ag* Milanese ■ *sm/f* person from Milan; **i milanesi** the Milanese; **cotoletta alla ~** (*Cuc*) Wiener schnitzel; **risotto alla ~** (*Cuc*) *risotto with saffron*

Miˈlano *sf* Milan

miliarˈdario, -a *ag, sm/f* millionaire

miliˈardo *sm* thousand million (*Brit*), billion (*US*)

miliˈare *ag*: **pietra ~** milestone

milioˈnario, -a *ag, sm/f* millionaire

mili'one *sm* million; **un ~ di euro** a million euros
mili'tante *ag, sm/f* militant
mili'tanza [mili'tantsa] *sf* militancy
mili'tare *vi* (*Mil*) to be a soldier, serve; (*fig: in un partito*) to be a militant ■ *ag* military ■ *sm* serviceman; **fare il ~** to do one's military service; **~ di carriera** regular (soldier)
milita'resco, -a, schi, sche *ag* (*portamento*) military *cpd*
'**milite** *sm* soldier
mi'lizia [mi'littsja] *sf* (*corpo armato*) militia
milizi'ano [milit'tsjano] *sm* militiaman
millanta'tore, -'trice *sm/f* boaster
millante'ria *sf* (*qualità*) boastfulness
'**mille** (*pl* **mila**) *num* a *o* one thousand; **diecimila** ten thousand
mille'foglie [mille'fɔʎʎe] *sm inv* (*Cuc*) cream *o* vanilla slice
mil'lennio *sm* millennium
millepi'edi *sm inv* centipede
mil'lesimo, -a *ag, sm* thousandth
milli'grammo *sm* milligram(me)
mil'lilitro *sm* millilitre (*Brit*), milliliter (*US*)
mil'limetro *sm* millimetre (*Brit*), millimeter (*US*)
'**milza** ['miltsa] *sf* (*Anat*) spleen
mi'metico, -a, ci, che *ag* (*arte*) mimetic; **tuta mimetica** (*Mil*) camouflage
mime'tismo *sm* camouflage
mimetiz'zare [mimetid'dzare] *vt* to camouflage; **mimetizzarsi** *vr* to camouflage o.s.
'**mimica** *sf* (*arte*) mime
'**mimo** *sm* (*attore, componimento*) mime
mi'mosa *sf* mimosa
min. *abbr* (= *minuto, minimo*) min
'**mina** *sf* (*esplosiva*) mine; (*di matita*) lead
mi'naccia, -ce [mi'nattʃa] *sf* threat; **sotto la ~ di** under threat of
minacci'are [minat'tʃare] *vt* to threaten; **~ qn di morte** to threaten to kill sb; **~ di fare qc** to threaten to do sth; **minaccia di piovere** it looks like rain
minacci'oso, -a [minat'tʃoso] *ag* threatening
mi'nare *vt* (*Mil*) to mine; (*fig*) to undermine
mina'tore *sm* miner
mina'torio, -a *ag* threatening
minchi'one, -a [min'kjone] *ag* (*fam*) idiotic ■ *sm/f* idiot
mine'rale *ag, sm* mineral
mineralo'gia [mineralo'dʒia] *sf* mineralogy
mine'rario, -a *ag* (*delle miniere*) mining; (*dei minerali*) ore *cpd*
mi'nestra *sf* soup; **~ in brodo** noodle soup; **~ di verdura** vegetable soup
mines'trone *sm* thick vegetable and pasta soup
mingher'lino, -a [minger'lino] *ag* thin, slender
'**mini** *ag inv* mini ■ *sf inv* miniskirt
minia'tura *sf* miniature
mini'bar *sm inv* minibar
minielabora'tore *sm* minicomputer
mini'era *sf* mine; **~ di carbone** coalmine; (*impresa*) colliery (*Brit*), coalmine
mini'gonna *sf* miniskirt
minima'lista, -i, e *ag, sm/f* minimalist
minimiz'zare [minimid'dzare] *vt* to minimize
'**minimo, -a** *ag* minimum, least, slightest; (*piccolissimo*) very small, slight; (*il più basso*) lowest, minimum ■ *sm* minimum; **al ~** at least; **girare al ~** (*Aut*) to idle; **il ~ indispensabile** the bare minimum; **il ~ della pena** the minimum sentence
minis'tero *sm* (*Pol, Rel*) ministry; (*governo*) government; (*Dir*): **Pubblico M~** State Prosecutor; **M~ delle Finanze** Ministry of Finance, ≈ Treasury
mi'nistro *sm* (*Pol, Rel*) minister; **M~ delle Finanze** Minister of Finance, ≈ Chancellor of the Exchequer (*Brit*)
mino'ranza [mino'rantsa] *sf* minority; **essere in ~** to be in the minority
mino'rato, -a *ag* handicapped ■ *sm/f* physically (*o* mentally) handicapped person
minorazi'one [minorat'tsjone] *sf* handicap
Mi'norca *sf* Minorca
mi'nore *ag* (*comparativo*) less; (*più piccolo*) smaller; (*numero*) lower; (*inferiore*) lower, inferior; (*meno importante*) minor; (*più giovane*) younger; (*superlativo*) least; smallest; lowest; least important; youngest ■ *sm/f* (*minorenne*) minor, person under age; **in misura ~** to a lesser extent; **questo è il male ~** this is the lesser evil
mino'renne *ag* under age ■ *sm/f* minor, person under age
mino'rile *ag* juvenile; **carcere ~** young offenders' institution; **delinquenza ~** juvenile delinquency
minori'tario, -a *ag* minority *cpd*
mi'nuscolo, -a *ag* (*scrittura, carattere*) small; (*piccolissimo*) tiny ■ *sf* small letter ■ *sm* small letters *pl*; (*Tip*) lower case; **scrivere tutto (in) ~** to write everything in small letters
mi'nuta *sf* rough copy, draft
mi'nuto, -a *ag* tiny, minute; (*pioggia*) fine; (*corporatura*) delicate, fine; (*lavoro*) detailed ■ *sm* (*unità di misura*) minute; **al ~** (*Comm*) retail; **avere i minuti contati** to have very little time

m

mi'nuzia [mi'nuttsja] *sf* (*cura*) meticulousness; (*particolare*) detail
minuziosa'mente [minuttsjosa'mente] *av* meticulously; in minute detail
minuzi'oso, -a [minut'tsjoso] *ag* (*persona, descrizione*) meticulous; (*esame*) minute
'mio, 'mia, mi'ei, 'mie *det*: **il ~, la mia** *etc* my *pron*: **il ~, la mia** *etc* mine ■ *sm*: **ho speso del** ~ I spent my own money ■ *sf*: **la mia** (*opinione*) my view; **i miei** my family; **un ~ amico** a friend of mine; **per amor ~** for my sake; **è dalla mia** he is on my side; **anch'io ho avuto le mie** (*disavventure*) I've had my problems too; **ne ho fatta una delle mie!** (*sciocchezze*) I've done it again!; **cerco di stare sulle mie** I try to keep myself to myself
'miope *ag* short-sighted
mio'pia *sf* short-sightedness, myopia; (*fig*) short-sightedness
'mira *sf* (*anche fig*) aim; **avere una buona/cattiva ~** to be a good/bad shot; **prendere la ~** to take aim; **prendere di ~ qn** (*fig*) to pick on sb
mi'rabile *ag* admirable, wonderful
mi'racolo *sm* miracle
miraco'loso, -a *ag* miraculous
mi'raggio [mi'raddʒo] *sm* mirage
mi'rare *vi*: **~ a** to aim at
mi'rato, -a *ag* targetted
mi'riade *sf* myriad
mi'rino *sm* (*Tecn*) sight; (*Fot*) viewer, viewfinder
mir'tillo *sm* bilberry (*Brit*), blueberry (*US*), whortleberry
'mirto *sm* myrtle
mi'santropo, -a *sm/f* misanthropist
mi'scela [miʃ'ʃɛla] *sf* mixture; (*di caffè*) blend
miscel'lanea [miʃʃel'lanea] *sf* miscellany
'mischia ['miskja] *sf* scuffle; (*Rugby*) scrum, scrummage
mischi'are [mis'kjare] *vt*, **mischi'arsi** *vr* to mix, blend
misco'noscere [misko'noʃʃere] *vt* (*qualità, coraggio etc*) to fail to appreciate
miscre'dente *ag* (*Rel*) misbelieving; (: *incredulo*) unbelieving ■ *sm/f* misbeliever; unbeliever
mis'cuglio [mis'kuʎʎo] *sm* mixture, hotchpotch, jumble
'mise *vb vedi* **mettere**
mise'rabile *ag* (*infelice*) miserable, wretched; (*povero*) poverty-stricken; (*di scarso valore*) miserable
mi'seria *sf* extreme poverty; (*infelicità*) misery; **miserie** *sfpl* (*del mondo etc*) misfortunes, troubles; **costare una ~** to cost next to nothing; **piangere ~** to plead poverty; **ridursi in ~** to be reduced to poverty; **porca ~!** (*fam*) (bloody) hell!
miseri'cordia *sf* mercy, pity
misericordi'oso, -a *ag* merciful
'misero, -a *ag* miserable, wretched; (*povero*) poverty-stricken; (*insufficiente*) miserable
mis'fatto *sm* misdeed, crime
'misi *vb vedi* **mettere**
mi'sogino [mi'zɔdʒino] *sm* misogynist
'missile *sm* missile; **~ cruise** *o* **di crociera** cruise missile; **~ terra-aria** surface-to-air missile
missio'nario, -a *ag, sm/f* missionary
missi'one *sf* mission
misteri'oso, -a *ag* mysterious
mis'tero *sm* mystery; **fare ~ di qc** to make a mystery out of sth; **quanti misteri!** why all the mystery?
'mistico, -a, ci, che *ag* mystic(al) ■ *sm* mystic
mistifi'care *vt* to fool, bamboozle
'misto, -a *ag* mixed; (*scuola*) mixed, coeducational ■ *sm* mixture; **un tessuto in ~ lino** a linen mix
mis'tura *sf* mixture
mi'sura *sf* measure; (*misurazione, dimensione*) measurement; (*taglia*) size; (*provvedimento*) measure, step; (*moderazione*) moderation; (*Mus*) time; (: *divisione*) bar; (*fig*: *limite*) bounds *pl*, limit; **in ~ di** in accordance with, according to; **nella ~ in cui** inasmuch as, insofar as; **in giusta ~** moderately; **oltre ~** beyond measure; **su ~** made to measure; **in ugual ~** equally, in the same way; **a ~ d'uomo** on a human scale; **passare la ~** to overstep the mark, go too far; **prendere le misure a qn** to take sb's measurements, measure sb; **prendere le misure di qc** to measure sth; **ho preso le mie misure** I've taken the necessary steps; **non ha il senso della ~** he doesn't know when to stop; **~ di lunghezza/capacità** measure of length/capacity; **misure di sicurezza/prevenzione** safety/precautionary measures
misu'rare *vt* (*ambiente, stoffa*) to measure; (*terreno*) to survey; (*abito*) to try on; (*pesare*) to weigh; (*fig*: *parole etc*) to weigh up; (: *spese, cibo*) to limit ■ *vi* to measure; **misurarsi** *vr*: **misurarsi con qn** to have a confrontation with sb; (*competere*) to compete with sb
misu'rato, -a *ag* (*ponderato*) measured; (*prudente*) cautious; (*moderato*) moderate
misurazi'one [mizurat'tsjone] *sf* measuring; (*di terreni*) surveying
'mite *ag* mild; (*prezzo*) moderate, reasonable
'mitico, -a, ci, che *ag* mythical

miti'gare *vt* to mitigate, lessen; (*lenire*) to soothe, relieve; **mitigarsi** *vr* (*odio*) to subside; (*tempo*) to become milder
'mitilo *sm* mussel
'mito *sm* myth
mitolo'gia, -'gie [mitolo'dʒia] *sf* mythology
mito'logico, -a, ci, che [mito'lɔdʒiko] *ag* mythological
'mitra *sf* (*Rel*) mitre (*Brit*), miter (*US*) ■ *sm inv* (*arma*) sub-machine gun
mitragli'are [mitraʎ'ʎare] *vt* to machine-gun
mitraglia'tore, -'trice [mitraʎʎa'tore] *ag*: **fucile ~** sub-machine gun ■ *sf* machine gun
mitteleuro'peo, -a *ag* Central European
mit'tente *sm/f* sender
ml *abbr* (= *millilitro*) ml
MLD *sigla m* = **Movimento per la Liberazione della Donna**
MM *abbr* = **Metropolitana Milanese**
mm *abbr* (= *millimetro*) mm
M.M. *abbr* = **marina militare**
mms *sigla m inv* (= *multimedia messaging service*) (*servizio*) MMS (= *multimedia messaging service*); (*messaggio*) MMS message
MN *sigla* = **Mantova**
M/N, m/n *abbr* (= *motonave*) MV
MO *sigla* = **Modena**
M.O. *abbr* = **Medio Oriente**
mo ' *sm*: **a ~ di** *prep* like; **a ~ di esempio** by way of example
'mobile *ag* mobile; (*parte di macchina*) moving; (*Dir: bene*) movable, personal ■ *sm* (*arredamento*) piece of furniture; **mobili** *smpl* furniture *sg*
mo'bilia *sf* furniture
mobili'are *ag* (*Dir*) personal, movable
mo'bilio *sm* = **mobilia**
mobilità *sf* mobility
mobili'tare *vt* to mobilize; **~ l'opinione pubblica** to rouse public opinion
mobilitazi'one [mobilitat'tsjone] *sf* mobilization
mocas'sino *sm* moccasin
mocci'oso, -a [mot'tʃoso] *sm/f* (*bambino piccolo*) little kid; (*peg*) snotty-nosed kid
'moccolo *sm* (*di candela*) candle end; (*fam: bestemmia*) oath; (*moccio*) snot; **reggere il ~** to play gooseberry (*Brit*) act as chaperon(e)
'moda *sf* fashion; **alla ~, di ~** fashionable, in fashion
modalità *sf inv* formality; **seguire attentamente le ~ d'uso** to follow the instructions carefully; **~ giuridiche** legal procedures; **~ di pagamento** method of payment
mo'della *sf* model
model'lare *vt* (*creta*) to model, shape; **modellarsi** *vr*: **modellarsi su** to model o.s. on
mo'dello *sm* model; (*stampo*) mould (*Brit*), mold (*US*) ■ *ag inv* model *cpd*
'modem *sm inv* modem
mode'nese *ag* of (*o* from) Modena
mode'rare *vt* to moderate; **moderarsi** *vr* to restrain o.s.; **~ la velocità** to reduce speed; **~ i termini** to weigh one's words
mode'rato, -a *ag* moderate
modera'tore, -'trice *sm/f* moderator
moderazi'one [moderat'tsjone] *sf* moderation
moderniz'zare [modernid'dzare] *vt* to bring up to date, modernize; **modernizzarsi** *vr* to get up to date
mo'derno, -a *ag* modern
mo'destia *sf* modesty; **~ a parte ...** in all modesty ..., though I say it myself ...
mo'desto, -a *ag* modest
'modico, -a, ci, che *ag* reasonable, moderate
mo'difica, -che *sf* modification; **subire delle modifiche** to undergo some modifications
modifi'cabile *ag* modifiable
modifi'care *vt* to modify, alter; **modificarsi** *vr* to alter, change
mo'dista *sf* milliner
'modo *sm* way, manner; (*mezzo*) means, way; (*occasione*) opportunity; (*Ling*) mood; (*Mus*) mode; **modi** *smpl* (*maniere*) manners; **a suo ~, a ~ suo** in his own way; **ad** *o* **in ogni ~** anyway; **di** *o* **in ~ che** so that; **in ~ da** so as to; **in tutti i modi** at all costs; (*comunque sia*) anyway; (*in ogni caso*) in any case; **in un certo qual ~** in a way, in some ways; **in qualche ~** somehow or other; **oltre ~** extremely; **~ di dire** turn of phrase; **per ~ di dire** so to speak; **fare a ~ proprio** to do as one likes; **fare le cose a ~** to do things properly; **una persona a ~** a well-mannered person; **c'è ~ e ~ di farlo** there's a right way and a wrong way of doing it
modu'lare *vt* to modulate ■ *ag* modular
modulazi'one [modulat'tsjone] *sf* modulation; **~ di frequenza FM** frequency modulation (FM)
'modulo *sm* (*modello*) form; (*Archit: lunare, di comando*) module; **~ di domanda** application form; **~ d'iscrizione** enrolment form; **~ di versamento** deposit slip
Moga'discio [moga'diʃʃo] *sm* Mogadishu
'mogano *sm* mahogany
'mogio, -a, gi, gie ['mɔdʒo] *ag* down in the dumps, dejected
'moglie ['moʎʎe] *sf* wife

m

mo'hair [mɔ'ɛr] *sm* mohair
mo'ine *sfpl* cajolery *sg*; (*leziosità*) affectation *sg*; **fare le ~ a qn** to cajole sb
'mola *sf* millstone; (*utensile abrasivo*) grindstone
mo'lare *vt* to grind ■ *ag* (*pietra*) mill *cpd* ■ *sm* (*dente*) molar
'mole *sf* mass; (*dimensioni*) size; (*edificio grandioso*) massive structure; **una ~ di lavoro** masses (*Brit*) *o* loads of work
mo'lecola *sf* molecule
moles'tare *vt* to bother, annoy
mo'lestia *sf* annoyance, bother; **recar ~ a qn** to bother sb; **molestie sessuali** sexual harassment *sg*
mo'lesto, -a *ag* annoying
moli'sano, -a *ag* of (*o* from) Molise
'molla *sf* spring; **molle** *sfpl* (*per camino*) tongs; **prendere qn con le molle** to treat sb with kid gloves
mol'lare *vt* to release, let go; (*Naut*) to ease; (*fig: ceffone*) to give ■ *vi* (*cedere*) to give in; **~ gli ormeggi** (*Naut*) to cast off; **~ la presa** to let go
'molle *ag* soft; (*muscoli*) flabby; (*fig: debole*) weak, feeble
molleggi'ato, -a [molled'dʒato] *ag* (*letto*) sprung; (*auto*) with good suspension
mol'leggio [mol'leddʒo] *sm* (*per veicoli*) suspension; (*elasticità*) springiness; (*Ginnastica*) knee-bends *pl*
mol'letta *sf* (*per capelli*) hairgrip; (*per panni stesi*) clothes peg (*Brit*) *o* pin (*US*); **mollette** *sfpl* (*per zucchero*) tongs
mol'lezza [mol'lettsa] *sf* softness flabbiness weakness, feebleness; **mollezze** *sfpl*: **vivere nelle mollezze** to live in the lap of luxury
mol'lica, -che *sf* crumb, soft part
mol'liccio, -a, ci, ce [mol'littʃo] *ag* (*terreno, impasto*) soggy; (*frutta*) soft; (*floscio: mano*) limp; (*muscolo*) flabby
mol'lusco, -schi *sm* mollusc
'molo *sm* jetty, pier
mol'teplice [mol'teplitʃe] *ag* (*formato di più elementi*) complex; **molteplici** *pl* (*svariati: interessi, attività*) numerous, various
molteplicità [molteplitʃi'ta] *sf* multiplicity
moltipli'care *vt* to multiply; **moltiplicarsi** *vr* to multiply; (*richieste*) to increase in number
moltiplicazi'one [moltiplikat'tsjone] *sf* multiplication
molti'tudine *sf* multitude; **una ~ di** a vast number *o* a multitude of
'molto, -a *det* (*quantità*) a lot of, much; (*numero*) a lot of, many; **~ pane/carbone** a lot of bread/coal; **molta gente** a lot of people, many people; **molti libri** a lot of books, many books; **non ho ~ tempo** I haven't got much time; **per ~ (tempo)** for a long time; **ci vuole ~ (tempo)?** will it take long?; **arriverà fra non ~** he'll arrive soon; **ne hai per ~?** will you be long? ■ *av* a lot, (very) much; **viaggia ~** he travels a lot; **non viaggia ~** he doesn't travel much *o* a lot (*intensivo con aggettivi, avverbi*), very; (*: con participio passato*) (very) much; **~ buono** very good; **~ migliore, ~ meglio** much *o* a lot better ■ *pron* much, a lot; **molti, e** (*pl*) many, a lot; **molti pensano che ...** many (people) think that ...; **molte sono rimaste a casa** a lot of them stayed at home; **c'era gente, ma non molta** there were people there, but not many
momentanea'mente *av* at the moment, at present
momen'taneo, -a *ag* momentary, fleeting
mo'mento *sm* moment; **da un ~ all'altro** at any moment; (*all'improvviso*) suddenly; **al ~ di fare** just as I was (*o* you were *o* he was *etc*) doing; **a momenti** (*da un mo'mento all'altro*) any time *o* moment now; (*quasi*) nearly; **per il ~** for the time being; **dal ~ che** ever since; (*dato che*) since; **~ culminante** climax
'monaca, -che *sf* nun
'Monaco *sf* Monaco; **~ (di Baviera)** Munich
'monaco, -ci *sm* monk
mo'narca, -chi *sm* monarch
monar'chia [monar'kia] *sf* monarchy
mo'narchico, -a, ci, che [mo'narkiko] *ag* (*stato, autorità*) monarchic; (*partito, fede*) monarchist ■ *sm/f* monarchist
monas'tero *sm* (*di monaci*) monastery; (*di monache*) convent
mo'nastico, -a, ci, che *ag* monastic
'monco, -a, chi, che *ag* maimed; (*fig*) incomplete; **~ d'un braccio** one-armed
mon'cone *sm* stump
mon'dana *sf* prostitute
mondanità *sf* (*frivolezza*) worldliness; **le ~** (*piaceri*) the pleasures of the world
mon'dano, -a *ag* (*anche fig*) worldly; (*dell'alta società*) society *cpd*; fashionable
mon'dare *vt* (*frutta, patate*) to peel; (*piselli*) to shell; (*pulire*) to clean
mondez'zaio [mondet'tsajo] *sm* rubbish (*Brit*) *o* garbage (*US*) dump
mondi'ale *ag* (*campionato, popolazione*) world *cpd*; (*influenza*) world-wide; **di fama ~** world famous
'mondo *sm* world; (*grande quantità*): **un ~ di** lots of, a host of; **il gran** *o* **bel ~** high society; **per niente al ~, per nessuna cosa al ~** not for all the world; **da che ~ è ~** since time *o*

the world began; **mandare qn all'altro ~** to kill sb; **mettere/venire al ~** to bring/come into the world; **vivere fuori dal ~** to be out of touch with the real world; **(sono) cose dell'altro ~!** it's incredible!; **com'è piccolo il ~!** it's a small world!

mone'gasco, -a, schi, sche *ag, sm/f* Monegasque

monelle'ria *sf* prank, naughty trick

mo'nello, -a *sm/f* street urchin; (*ragazzo vivace*) scamp, imp

mo'neta *sf* coin; (*Econ: valuta*) currency; (*denaro spicciolo*) (small) change; **~ estera** foreign currency; **~ legale** legal tender

mone'tario, -a *ag* monetary

Mon'golia *sf*: **la ~** Mongolia

mon'golico, -a, ci, che *ag* Mongolian

mongo'lismo *sm* Down's syndrome

'mongolo, -a *ag* Mongolian ■ *sm/f, sm* Mongol, Mongolian

mongo'loide *ag, sm/f* (*Med*) mongol

'monito *sm* warning

'monitor *sm inv* (*Tecn, TV*) monitor

monito'raggio [monito'raddʒo] *sm* monitoring

monito'rare *vt* to monitor

mo'nocolo *sm* (*lente*) monocle, eyeglass

monoco'lore *ag* (*Pol*): **governo ~** one-party government

monoga'mia *sf* monogamy

mo'nogamo, -a *ag* monogamous ■ *sm* monogamist

monogra'fia *sf* monograph

mono'gramma, -i *sm* monogram

mono'lingue *ag* monolingual

monolo'cale *sm* ≈ studio flat

mo'nologo, -ghi *sm* monologue

mono'pattino *sm* scooter

mono'polio *sm* monopoly; **~ di stato** government monopoly

monopoliz'zare [monopolid'dzare] *vt* to monopolize

mono'sillabo, -a *ag* monosyllabic ■ *sm* monosyllable

monoto'nia *sf* monotony

mo'notono, -a *ag* monotonous

mono'uso *ag inv* disposable

monovo'lume *sf inv* people carrier, people mover

Mons. *abbr* (= *Monsignore*) Mgr

monsi'gnore [monsiɲ'ɲore] *sm* (*Rel: titolo*) Your (*o* His) Grace

mon'sone *sm* monsoon

monta'carichi [monta'kariki] *sm inv* hoist, goods lift

mon'taggio [mon'taddʒo] *sm* (*Tecn*) assembly; (*Cine*) editing

mon'tagna [mon'taɲɲa] *sf* mountain; (*zona montuosa*): **la ~** the mountains *pl*; **andare in ~** to go to the mountains; **aria/strada di ~** mountain air/road; **casa di ~** house in the mountains; **montagne russe** roller coaster *sg*

monta'gnoso, -a [montaɲ'ɲoso] *ag* mountainous

monta'naro, -a *ag* mountain *cpd* ■ *sm/f* mountain dweller

mon'tano, -a *ag* mountain *cpd*

mon'tante *sm* (*di porta*) jamb; (*di finestra*) upright; (*Calcio: palo*) post; (*Pugilato*) upper cut; (*Comm*) total amount

mon'tare *vt* to go (*o* come) up; (*cavallo*) to ride; (*apparecchiatura*) to set up, assemble; (*Cuc*) to whip; (*Zool*) to cover; (*incastonare*) to mount, set; (*Cine*) to edit; (*Fot*) to mount ■ *vi* to go (*o* come) up; (*a cavallo*): **~ bene/male** to ride well/badly; (*aumentare di livello, volume*) to rise; **montarsi** *vr* to become big-headed; **~ qc** to exaggerate sth; **~ qn** *o* **la testa a qn** to turn sb's head; **montarsi la testa** to become big-headed; **~ in bicicletta/macchina/treno** to get on a bicycle/ into a car/on a train; **~ a cavallo** to get on *o* mount a horse; **~ la guardia** (*Mil*) to mount guard

monta'tura *sf* assembling *no pl*; (*di occhiali*) frames *pl*; (*di gioiello*) mounting, setting; (*fig*): **~ pubblicitaria** publicity stunt

montavi'vande *sm inv* dumbwaiter

'monte *sm* mountain; **a ~** upstream; **andare a ~** (*fig*) to come to nothing; **mandare a ~ qc** (*fig*) to upset sth, cause sth to fail; **il M~ Bianco** Mont Blanc; **il M~ Everest** Mount Everest; **~ di pietà** pawnshop; **~ premi** prize

Monteci'torio [montetʃi'tɔrjo] *sm*: **palazzo ~** (*Pol*) *seat of the Italian Chamber of Deputies*

montene'grino, -a *ag, sm/f* Montenegrin

monte'negro *sm* Montenegro

mont'gomery [mənt'gʌməri] *sm inv* duffel coat

mon'tone *sm* (*Zool*) ram; (*anche*: **giacca di montone**) sheepskin (jacket); **carne di ~** mutton

montuosità *sf* mountainous nature

montu'oso, -a *ag* mountainous

monu'mento *sm* monument

mo'quette [mɔ'kɛt] *sf* fitted carpet

'mora *sf* (*del rovo*) blackberry; (*del gelso*) mulberry; (*Dir*) delay; (*somma*) arrears *pl*

mo'rale *ag* moral ■ *sf* (*scienza*) ethics *sg*, moral philosophy; (*complesso di norme*) moral standards *pl*, morality; (*condotta*) morals *pl*; (*insegnamento morale*) moral ■ *sm* morale; **la ~ della favola** the moral of the tale; **essere giù di ~** to be feeling down; **aver il ~ alto/a terra** to be in good/low spirits

m

mora'lista, -i, e *ag* moralistic ■ *sm/f* moralist
moralità *sf* morality; (*condotta*) morals *pl*
moraliz'zare [moralid'dzare] *vt* (*costumi, vita pubblica*) to set moral standards for
moralizzazi'one [moraliddzat'tsjone] *sf* setting of moral standards
mora'toria *sf* (*Dir*) moratorium
morbi'dezza [morbi'dettsa] *sf* softness; smoothness; tenderness
'morbido, -a *ag* soft; (*pelle*) soft, smooth; (*carne*) tender
mor'billo *sm* (*Med*) measles *sg*
'morbo *sm* disease
mor'boso, -a *ag* (*fig*) morbid
'morchia ['mɔrkja] *sf* (*residuo grasso*) dregs *pl*; oily deposit
mor'dente *sm* (*fig: di satira, critica*) bite; (*di persona*) drive
'mordere *vt* to bite; (*addentare*) to bite into; (*corrodere*) to eat into
mordicchi'are [mordik'kjare] *vt* (*gen*) to chew at
mo'rente *ag* dying ■ *sm/f* dying man/ woman
mor'fina *sf* morphine
mo'ria *sf* high mortality
mori'bondo, -a *ag* dying, moribund
morige'rato, -a [moridʒe'rato] *ag* of good morals
mo'rire *vi* to die; (*abitudine, civiltà*) to die out; **~ di dolore** to die of a broken heart; **~ di fame** to die of hunger; (*fig*) to be starving; **~ di freddo** to freeze to death; (*fig*) to be frozen; **~ d'invidia** to be green with envy; **~ di noia/ paura** to be bored/scared to death; **~ dalla voglia di fare qc** to be dying to do sth; **fa un caldo da ~** it's terribly hot
mormo'rare *vi* to murmur; (*brontolare*) to grumble; **si mormora che ...** it's rumoured (*Brit*) *o* rumored (*US*) that ...; **la gente mormora** people are talking
mormo'rio *sm* murmuring; grumbling
'moro, -a *ag* dark(-haired), dark(- complexioned); **i Mori** *smpl* (*Storia*) the Moors
mo'roso, -a *ag* in arrears ■ *sm/f* (*fam: innamorato*) sweetheart
'morsa *sf* (*Tecn*) vice (*Brit*), vise (*US*); (*fig: stretta*) grip
mor'setto *sm* (*Tecn*) clamp; (*Elettr*) terminal
morsi'care *vt* to nibble (at), gnaw (at); (*insetto*) to bite
'morso, -a *pp di* **mordere** ■ *sm* bite; (*di insetto*) sting; (*parte della briglia*) bit; **dare un ~ a qc/ qn** to bite sth/sb; **i morsi della fame** pangs of hunger
morta'della *sf* (*Cuc*) mortadella (*type of salted pork meat*)
mor'taio *sm* mortar
mor'tale *ag, sm* mortal
mortalità *sf* mortality; (*Statistica*) mortality, death rate
'morte *sf* death; **in punto di ~** at death's door; **ferito a ~** (*soldato*) mortally wounded; (*in incidente*) fatally injured; **essere annoiato a ~** to be bored to death *o* to tears; **avercela a ~ con qn** to be bitterly resentful of sb; **avere la ~ nel cuore** to have a heavy heart
mortifi'care *vt* to mortify
'morto, -a *pp di* **morire** ■ *ag* dead ■ *sm/f* dead man/woman; **i morti** the dead; **fare il ~** (*nell'acqua*) to float on one's back; **un ~ di fame** (*fig peg*) a down-and-out; **le campane suonavano a ~** the funeral bells were tolling; *vedi anche* **Giorno dei Morti**
mor'torio *sm* (*anche fig*) funeral
mo'saico, -ci *sm* mosaic; **l'ultimo tassello del ~** (*fig*) the last piece of the puzzle
'Mosca *sf* Moscow
'mosca, -sche *sf* fly; **rimanere** *o* **restare con un pugno di mosche** (*fig*) to be left empty-handed; **non si sentiva volare una ~** (*fig*) you could have heard a pin drop; **~ cieca** blind-man's buff
mos'cato *sm* muscatel (wine)
mosce'rino [moʃʃe'rino] *sm* midge, gnat
mos'chea [mos'kɛa] *sf* mosque
mos'chetto [mos'ketto] *sm* musket
moschet'tone [mosket'tone] *sm* (*gancio*) spring clip; (*Alpinismo*) karabiner, snaplink
moschi'cida, -i, e [moski'tʃida] *ag* fly *cpd*; **carta ~** flypaper
'moscio, -a, sci, sce ['moʃʃo] *ag* (*fig*) lifeless; **ha la "r" moscia** he can't roll his "r"s
mos'cone *sm* (*Zool*) bluebottle; (*barca*) pedalo; (*: a remi*) *kind of pedalo with oars*
mosco'vita, -i, e *ag, sm/f* Muscovite
'mossa *sf* movement; (*nel gioco*) move; **darsi una ~** (*fig*) to give o.s. a shake; **prendere le mosse da qc** to come about as the result of sth
'mossi *etc vb vedi* **muovere**
'mosso, -a *pp di* **muovere** ■ *ag* (*mare*) rough; (*capelli*) wavy; (*Fot*) blurred; (*ritmo, prosa*) animated
mos'tarda *sf* mustard
'mosto *sm* must
'mostra *sf* exhibition, show; (*ostentazione*) show; **in ~** on show; **far ~ di** (*fingere*) to pretend; **far ~ di sé** to show off; **mettersi in ~** to draw attention to o.s.
mos'trare *vt* to show ■ *vi*: **~ di fare** to pretend to do; **mostrarsi** *vr* to appear; **~ la lingua** to stick out one's tongue

'mostro *sm* monster
mostru'oso, -a *ag* monstrous
mo'tel *sm inv* motel
moti'vare *vt* (*causare*) to cause; (*giustificare*) to justify, account for
motivazi'one [motivat'tsjone] *sf* justification; (*Psic*) motivation
mo'tivo *sm* (*causa*) reason, cause; (*movente*) motive; (*letterario*) (central) theme; (*disegno*) motif, design, pattern; (*Mus*) motif; **per quale ~?** why?, for what reason?; **per motivi di salute** for health reasons, on health grounds; **motivi personali** personal reasons
'moto *sm* (*anche Fisica*) motion; (*movimento, gesto*) movement; (*esercizio fisico*) exercise; (*sommossa*) rising, revolt; (*commozione*) feeling, impulse ■ *sf inv* (*motocicletta*) motorbike; **fare del ~** to take some exercise; **un ~ d'impazienza** an impatient gesture; **mettere in ~** to set in motion; (*Aut*) to start up; **~ d'acqua** Jet Ski®
moto'carro *sm* three-wheeler van
motoci'cletta [mototʃi'kletta] *sf* motorcycle
motoci'clismo [mototʃi'klizmo] *sm* motorcycling, motorcycle racing
motoci'clista, -i, e [mototʃi'klista] *sm/f* motorcyclist
moto'nave *sf* motor vessel
motopeschereccio [motopeske'rettʃo] *sm* motor fishing vessel
mo'tore, -'trice *ag* motor; (*Tecn*) driving ■ *sm* engine, motor ■ *sf* (*Tecn*) engine, motor; **albero ~** drive shaft; **forza motrice** driving force; **a ~** motor *cpd*, power-driven; **~ a combustione interna/a reazione** internal combustion/jet engine; **~ di ricerca** (*Inform*) search engine
moto'rino *sm* moped; **~ di avviamento** (*Aut*) starter
motoriz'zato, -a [motorid'dzato] *ag* (*truppe*) motorized; (*persona*) having a car *o* transport
motorizzazi'one [motoriddzat'tsjone] *sf* (*ufficio tecnico e organizzativo*): **(ufficio della) ~** road traffic office
motos'cafo *sm* motorboat
motove'detta *sf* motor patrol vessel
mo'trice [mo'tritʃe] *sf vedi* **motore**
mot'teggio [mot'teddʒo] *sm* banter
'motto *sm* (*battuta scherzosa*) witty remark; (*frase emblematica*) motto, maxim
mountain bike *sf inv* mountain bike
'mouse ['maus] *sm inv* (*Inform*) mouse
mo'vente *sm* motive
mo'venza [mo'vɛntsa] *sf* movement
movimen'tare *vt* to liven up
movimen'tato, -a *ag* (*festa, partita*) lively; (*riunione*) animated; (*strada, vita*) busy; (*soggiorno*) eventful
movi'mento *sm* movement; (*fig*) activity, hustle and bustle; (*Mus*) tempo, movement; **essere sempre in ~** to be always on the go; **fare un po' di ~** (*esercizio fisico*) to take some exercise; **c'è molto ~ in città** the town is very busy; **~ di capitali** movement of capital; **M~ per la Liberazione della Donna** Women's Movement
movi'ola *sf* moviola; **rivedere qc alla ~** to see an action (*Brit*) *o* instant (*US*) replay of sth
Mozam'bico [moddzam'biko] *sm*: **il ~** Mozambique
mozi'one [mot'tsjone] *sf* (*Pol*) motion; **~ d'ordine** (*Pol*) point of order
mozzafi'ato [mottsa'fjato] *ag inv* breathtaking
moz'zare [mot'tsare] *vt* to cut off; (*coda*) to dock; **~ il fiato** *o* **il respiro a qn** (*fig*) to take sb's breath away
mozza'rella [mottsa'rɛlla] *sf* mozzarella
mozzi'cone [mottsi'kone] *sm* stub, butt, end; (*anche*: **mozzicone di sigaretta**) cigarette end
'mozzo[1] ['mɔddzo] *sm* (*Meccanica*) hub
'mozzo[2] ['mottso] *sm* (*Naut*) ship's boy; **~ di stalla** stable boy
mq *abbr* (= *metro quadro*) sq.m
MS *sigla* = **Massa Carrara**
M.S.I. *sigla m* (= *Movimento Sociale Italiano*) *former right-wing political party*
Mti *abbr* = **monti**
'mucca, -che *sf* cow; **~ pazza** BSE; **(morbo della) ~ pazza** mad cow disease, BSE; **l'emergenza ~ pazza** the mad cow crisis
'mucchio ['mukkjo] *sm* pile, heap; (*fig*): **un ~ di** lots of, heaps of
mucil'lagine [mutʃil'ladʒine] *sf* (*Bot*) mucilage (*green slime produced by plants growing in water*)
'muco, -chi *sm* mucus
mu'cosa *sf* mucous membrane
'muesli ['mjusli] *sm* muesli
'muffa *sf* mould (*Brit*), mold (*US*), mildew; **fare la ~** to go mouldy (*Brit*) *o* moldy (*US*)
mugghi'are [mug'gjare] *vi* (*fig: mare, tuono*) to roar; (*vento*) to howl
mug'gire [mud'dʒire] *vi* (*vacca*) to low, moo; (*toro*) to bellow; (*fig*) to roar
mug'gito [mud'dʒito] *sm* moo; bellow; roar
mu'ghetto [mu'getto] *sm* lily of the valley
mu'gnaio, -a [muɲ'ɲajo] *sm/f* miller
mugo'lare *vi* (*cane*) to whimper, whine; (*fig: persona*) to moan
mugu'gnare [muguɲ'ɲare] *vi* (*fam*) to mutter, mumble

mulatti'era *sf* mule track
mu'latto, -a *ag, sm/f* mulatto
muli'nare *vi* to whirl, spin round (and round)
muli'nello *sm* (*moto vorticoso*) eddy, whirl; (*di canna da pesca*) reel; (*Naut*) windlass
mu'lino *sm* mill; **~ a vento** windmill
'mulo *sm* mule
'multa *sf* fine
mul'tare *vt* to fine
multico'lore *ag* multicoloured (*Brit*), multicolored (*US*)
multi'etnico, -a, ci, che *ag* multiethnic
multi'forme *ag* (*paesaggio, attività, interessi*) varied; (*ingegno*) versatile
multimedi'ale *ag* multimedia *cpd*
multinazio'nale [multinattsjo'nale] *ag, sf* multinational; **forza ~ di pace** multinational peace-keeping force
'multiplo, -a *ag, sm* multiple
multiu'tenza [multiu'tɛntsa] *sf* (*Inform*) time sharing
'mummia *sf* mummy
'mungere ['mundʒere] *vt* (*anche fig*) to milk
mungi'tura [mundʒi'tura] *sf* milking
munici'pale [munitʃi'pale] *ag* (*gen*) municipal; **palazzo ~** town hall; **autorità municipali** local authorities (*Brit*), local government *sg*
muni'cipio [muni'tʃipjo] *sm* town council; (*edificio*) town hall; **sposarsi in ~** ≈ to get married in a registry office (*Brit*), have a civil marriage
munifi'cenza [munifi'tʃɛntsa] *sf* munificence
mu'nifico, -a, ci, che *ag* munificent, generous
mu'nire *vt*: **~ qc/qn di** to equip sth/sb with; **~ di firma** (*documento*) to sign
munizi'oni [munit'tsjoni] *sfpl* (*Mil*) ammunition *sg*
'munsi *etc vb vedi* **mungere**
'munto, -a *pp di* **mungere**
mu'oio *etc vb vedi* **morire**
mu'overe *vt* to move; (*ruota, macchina*) to drive; (*sollevare: questione, obiezione*) to raise, bring up; (*accusa*) to make, bring forward; **muoversi** *vr* to move; **~ causa a qn** (*Dir*) to take legal action against sb; **~ a compassione** to move to pity; **~ guerra a** *o* **contro qn** to wage war against sb; **~ mari e monti** to move heaven and earth; **~ al pianto** to move to tears; **~ i primi passi** to take one's first steps; (*fig*) to be starting out; **muoviti!** hurry up!, get a move on!
'mura *sfpl vedi* **muro**
mu'raglia [mu'raʎʎa] *sf* (high) wall
mu'rale *ag* wall *cpd*; mural
mu'rare *vt* (*persona, porta*) to wall up
mu'rario, -a *ag* building *cpd*; **arte muraria** masonry
mura'tore *sm* (*con pietre*) mason; (*con mattoni*) bricklayer
mura'tura *sf* (*lavoro murario*) masonry; **casa in ~** (*di pietra*) stonebuilt house; (*di mattoni*) brick house
'muro *sm* wall; **mura** *sfpl* (*cinta cittadina*) walls; **a ~** wall *cpd*; (*armadio etc*) built-in; **mettere al ~** (*fucilare*) to shoot *o* execute (by firing squad); **~ di cinta** surrounding wall; **~ divisorio** dividing wall; **~ del suono** sound barrier
'musa *sf* muse
'muschio ['muskjo] *sm* (*Zool*) musk; (*Bot*) moss
musco'lare *ag* muscular, muscle *cpd*
muscola'tura *sf* muscle structure
'muscolo *sm* (*Anat*) muscle
musco'loso, -a *ag* muscular
mu'seo *sm* museum
museru'ola *sf* muzzle
'musica *sf* music; **~ da ballo/camera** dance/ chamber music
musi'cale *ag* musical
musicas'setta *sf* (pre-recorded) cassette
musi'cista, -i, e [muzi'tʃista] *sm/f* musician
musi'comane *sm/f* music lover
'muso *sm* muzzle; (*di auto, aereo*) nose; **tenere il ~** to sulk
mu'sone, -a *sm/f* sulky person
'mussola *sf* muslin
mus(s)ul'mano, -a *ag, sm/f* Muslim, Moslem
'muta *sf* (*di animali*) moulting (*Brit*), molting (*US*); (*di serpenti*) sloughing; (*per immersioni subacquee*) diving suit; (*gruppo di cani*) pack
mu'tabile *ag* changeable
muta'mento *sm* change
mu'tande *sfpl* (*da uomo*) (under)pants
mutan'dine *sfpl* (*da donna, bambino*) pants (*Brit*), briefs; **~ di plastica** plastic pants
mu'tare *vt, vi* to change, alter
mutazi'one [mutat'tsjone] *sf* change, alteration; (*Biol*) mutation
mu'tevole *ag* changeable
muti'lare *vt* to mutilate, maim; (*fig*) to mutilate, deface
muti'lato, -a *sm/f* disabled person; (*through loss of limbs*): **~ di guerra** disabled ex-serviceman (*Brit*) *o* war veteran (*US*)
mutilazi'one [mutilat'tsjone] *sf* mutilation
mu'tismo *sm* (*Med*) mutism; (*atteggiamento*) (stubborn) silence
'muto, -a *ag* (*Med*) dumb; (*emozione, dolore, Cine*) silent; (*Ling*) silent, mute; (*carta geografica*) blank; **~ per lo stupore** *etc* speechless with amazement *etc*; **ha fatto scena muta** he didn't utter a word

'**mutua** *sf* (*anche*: **cassa mutua**) health insurance scheme; **medico della ~** ≈ National Health Service doctor (*Brit*)
mutu'are *vt* (*fig*) to borrow
mutu'ato, -a *sm/f* member of a health insurance scheme
'**mutuo, -a** *ag* (*reciproco*) mutual ▪ *sm* (*Econ*) (long-term) loan; **~ ipotecario** mortgage

m

Nn

N, n ['ɛnne] *sf o m* (*lettera*) N, n; **N come Napoli** ≈ N for Nellie (*Brit*), N for Nan (*US*)
N *abbr* (= *nord*) N
n *abbr* (= *numero*) no
NA *sigla* = **Napoli**
na'babbo *sm* (*anche fig*) nabob
'nacchere ['nakkere] *sfpl* castanets
NAD *sigla m* = **nucleo anti-droga**
na'dir *sm* (*Astr*) nadir
'nafta *sf* naphtha; (*per motori diesel*) diesel oil
nafta'lina *sf* (*Chim*) naphthalene; (*tarmicida*) mothballs *pl*
'naia *sf* (*Zool*) cobra; (*Mil*) *slang term for national service*
na'ïf [na'if] *ag inv* naïve
'nailon *sm* = **nylon**
Nai'robi *sf* Nairobi
'nanna *sf* (*linguaggio infantile*): **andare a ~** to go to beddy-byes
'nano, -a *ag, sm/f* dwarf
napole'tano, -a *ag, sm/f* Neapolitan ■ *sf* (*macchinetta da caffè*) Neapolitan coffee pot
'Napoli *sf* Naples
'nappa *sf* tassel
nar'ciso [nar'tʃizo] *sm* narcissus
'narcos *sm inv* (*colombiano*) Colombian drug trafficker
narco'dollari *smpl* drug money *sg*
nar'cosi *sf* general anaesthesia, narcosis
nar'cotico, -ci *sm* narcotic
narcotraffi'cante *sm/f* drug trafficker
narco'traffico *sm* drug trade
na'rice [na'ritʃe] *sf* nostril
nar'rare *vt* to tell the story of, recount
narra'tivo, -a *ag* narrative ■ *sf* (*branca*) fiction
narra'tore, -'trice *sm/f* narrator
narrazi'one [narrat'tsjone] *sf* narration; (*racconto*) story, tale
N.A.S.A. ['naza] *sigla f* (= *National Aeronautics and Space Administration*) NASA
na'sale *ag* nasal
na'scente [naʃ'ʃɛnte] *ag* (*sole, luna*) rising
'nascere ['naʃʃere] *vi* (*bambino*) to be born; (*pianta*) to come *o* spring up; (*fiume*) to rise, have its source; (*sole*) to rise; (*dente*) to come through; (*fig: derivare, conseguire*): **~ da** to arise from, be born out of; **è nata nel 1952** she was born in 1952; **da cosa nasce cosa** one thing leads to another
'nascita ['naʃʃita] *sf* birth
nasci'turo, -a [naʃʃi'turo] *sm/f* future child; **come si chiamerà il ~?** what's the baby going to be called?
nas'condere *vt* to hide, conceal; **nascondersi** *vr* to hide
nascon'diglio [naskon'diʎʎo] *sm* hiding place
nascon'dino *sm* (*gioco*) hide-and-seek
nas'cosi *etc vb vedi* **nascondere**
nas'costo, -a *pp di* **nascondere** ■ *ag* hidden; **di ~** secretly
na'sello *sm* (*Zool*) hake
'naso *sm* nose
Nas'sau *sf* Nassau
'nastro *sm* ribbon; (*magnetico, isolante, Sport*) tape; **~ adesivo** adhesive tape; **~ trasportatore** conveyor belt
nas'turzio [nas'turtsjo] *sm* nasturtium
na'tale *ag* of one's birth ■ *sm* (*Rel*): **N~** Christmas; (*giorno della nascita*) birthday; **natali** *smpl*: **di illustri/umili natali** of noble/humble birth
natalità *sf* birth rate
nata'lizio, -a [nata'littsjo] *ag* (*del Natale*) Christmas *cpd*
na'tante *sm* craft *inv*, boat
'natica, -che *sf* (*Anat*) buttock
na'tio, -a, tii, tie *ag* native
Natività *sf* (*Rel*) Nativity
na'tivo, -a *ag, sm/f* native
'nato, -a *pp di* **nascere** ■ *ag*: **un attore ~** a born actor; **nata Pieri** née Pieri
'N.A.T.O. *sigla f* NATO (= *North Atlantic Treaty Organization*)
na'tura *sf* nature; **pagare in ~** to pay in kind; **~ morta** still life

natu'rale *ag* natural ■ *sm*: **al ~** (*alimenti*) served plain; (*ritratto*) life-size; **(ma) è ~!** (*in risposte*) of course!; **a grandezza ~** life-size; **acqua ~** spring water
natura'lezza [natura'lettsa] *sf* naturalness
natura'lista, -i, e *sm/f* naturalist
naturaliz'zare [naturalid'dzare] *vt* to naturalize
natural'mente *av* naturally; (*certamente, sì*) of course
natu'rismo *sm* naturism, nudism
natu'rista, -i, e *ag, sm/f* naturist, nudist
naufra'gare *vi* (*nave*) to be wrecked; (*persona*) to be shipwrecked; (*fig*) to fall through
nau'fragio [nau'fradʒo] *sm* shipwreck; (*fig*) ruin, failure
'naufrago, -ghi *sm* castaway, shipwreck victim
'nausea *sf* nausea; **avere la ~** to feel sick (*Brit*) *o* ill (*US*); **fino alla ~** ad nauseam
nausea'bondo, -a *ag*; **nause'ante** *ag* nauseating, sickening
nause'are *vt* to nauseate, make (feel) sick (*Brit*) *o* ill (*US*)
'nautico, -a, ci, che *ag* nautical ■ *sf* (art of) navigation; **salone ~** (*mostra*) boat show
na'vale *ag* naval; **battaglia ~** naval battle; (*gioco*) battleships *pl*
na'vata *sf* (*anche*: **navata centrale**) nave; (*anche*: **navata laterale**) aisle
'nave *sf* ship, vessel; **~ da carico** cargo ship, freighter; **~ cisterna** tanker; **~ da guerra** warship; **~ di linea** liner; **~ passeggeri** passenger ship; **~ portaerei** aircraft carrier; **~ spaziale** spaceship
na'vetta *sf* shuttle; (*servizio di collegamento*) shuttle (service)
navi'cella [navi'tʃɛlla] *sf* (*di aerostato*) gondola; **~ spaziale** spaceship
navi'gabile *ag* navigable
navi'gante *sm* sailor, seaman
navi'gare *vi* to sail; **~ in cattive acque** (*fig*) to be in deep water; **~ in Internet** to surf the Net
navi'gato, -a *ag* (*fig: esperto*) experienced
naviga'tore, -'trice *sm/f* (*gen*) navigator; **~ solitario** single-handed sailor; **~ satellite** satellite navigator
navigazi'one [navigat'tsjone] *sf* navigation; **dopo una settimana di ~** after a week at sea
na'viglio [na'viʎʎo] *sm* fleet, ships *pl*; (*canale artificiale*) canal; **~ da pesca** fishing fleet
nazio'nale [nattsjo'nale] *ag* national ■ *sf* (*Sport*) national team
naziona'lismo [nattsjona'lizmo] *sm* nationalism
naziona'lista, -i, e [nattsjona'lista] *ag, sm/f* nationalist
nazionalità [nattsjonali'ta] *sf inv* nationality
nazionaliz'zare [nattsjonalid'dzare] *vt* to nationalize
nazionalizzazi'one [nattsjonaliddzat'tsjone] *sf* nationalization
nazi'one [nat'tsjone] *sf* nation
naziskin ['na:tsiskin] *sm inv* Nazi skinhead
na'zismo [nat'tsizmo] *sm* Nazism
na'zista, -i, e [nat'tsista] *ag, sm/f* Nazi
NB *abbr* (= *nota bene*) NB
N.d.A. *abbr* (= *nota dell'autore*) author's note
N.d.D. *abbr* = **nota della direzione**
N.d.E. *abbr* (= *nota dell'editore*) publisher's note
N.d.R. *abbr* (= *nota della redazione*) editor's note
'nd'rangheta [nd'rangeta] *sf* Calabrian Mafia
N.d.T. *abbr* (= *nota del traduttore*) translator's note

 PAROLA CHIAVE

ne *pron* **1** (*di lui, lei, loro*) of him/her/them; about him/her/them; **ne riconosco la voce** I recognize his (*o* her) voice
2 (*di questa, quella cosa*) of it; about it; **ne voglio ancora** I want some more (of it *o* them); **non parliamone più!** let's not talk about it any more!
3 (*da ciò*) from this; **ne deduco che l'avete trovato** I gather you've found it; **ne consegue che ...** it follows therefore, that ...
4 (*con valore partitivo*): **hai dei libri? — sì, ne ho** have you any books? — yes, I have (some); **hai del pane? — no, non ne ho** have you any bread? — no, I haven't any; **quanti anni hai? — ne ho 17** how old are you? — I'm 17
■ *av* (*moto da luogo: da lì*) from there; **ne vengo ora** I've just come from there

né *cong*: **né ... né** neither ... nor; **né l'uno né l'altro lo vuole** neither of them wants it; **né più né meno** no more no less; **non parla né l'italiano né il tedesco** he speaks neither Italian nor German, he doesn't speak either Italian or German; **non piove né nevica** it isn't raining or snowing
N.E. *abbr* (= *nordest*) NE
ne'anche [ne'anke] *av, cong* not even; **non ... ~** not even; **~ se volesse potrebbe venire** he couldn't come even if he wanted to; **non l'ho visto — neanch'io** I didn't see him — neither did I *o* I didn't either; **~ per idea** *o* **sogno!** not on your life!; **non ci penso ~!** I wouldn't dream of it!; **~ a pagarlo lo farebbe** he wouldn't do it even if you paid him

n

'**nebbia** *sf* fog; (*foschia*) mist
nebbi'oso, -a *ag* foggy; misty
nebulizza'tore [nebuliddza'tore] *sm* atomizer
nebu'losa *sf* nebula
nebulosità *sf* haziness
nebu'loso, -a *ag* (*atmosfera, cielo*) hazy; (*fig*) hazy, vague
néces'saire [nese'sɛr] *sm inv*: **~ da viaggio** overnight case *o* bag
necessaria'mente [netʃessarja'mente] *av* necessarily
neces'sario, -a [netʃes'sarjo] *ag* necessary ■ *sm*: **fare il ~** to do what is necessary; **lo stretto ~** the bare essentials *pl*
necessità [netʃessi'ta] *sf inv* necessity; (*povertà*) need, poverty; **trovarsi nella ~ di fare qc** to be forced *o* obliged to do sth, have to do sth
necessi'tare [netʃessi'tare] *vt* to require ■ *vi* (*aver bisogno*): **~ di** to need
necro'logio [nekro'lɔdʒo] *sm* obituary notice; (*registro*) register of deaths
ne'fando, -a *ag* infamous, wicked
ne'fasto, -a *ag* inauspicious, ill-omened
ne'gare *vt* to deny; (*rifiutare*) to deny, refuse; **~ di aver fatto/che** to deny having done/ that
negativa'mente *av* negatively; **rispondere ~** to give a negative response
nega'tivo, -a *ag, sf, sm* negative
negazi'one [negat'tsjone] *sf* negation
negherò *etc* [nege'rɔ] *vb vedi* **negare**
ne'gletto, -a [ne'glɛtto] *ag* (*trascurato*) neglected
'**negli** ['neʎʎi] *prep + det vedi* **in**
négli'gé [negli'ʒe] *sm inv* negligee
negli'gente [negli'dʒɛnte] *ag* negligent, careless
negli'genza [negli'dʒɛntsa] *sf* negligence, carelessness
negozi'abile [negot'tsjabile] *ag* negotiable
negozi'ante [negot'tsjante] *sm/f* trader, dealer; (*bottegaio*) shopkeeper (*Brit*), storekeeper (*US*)
negozi'are [negot'tsjare] *vt* to negotiate ■ *vi*: **~ in** to trade *o* deal in
negozi'ato [negot'tsjato] *sm* negotiation
negozia'tore, -'trice [negottsja'tore] *sm/f* negotiator
ne'gozio [ne'gɔttsjo] *sm* (*locale*) shop (*Brit*), store (*US*); (*affare*) (piece of) business *no pl*; (*Dir*): **~ giuridico** legal transaction
negri'ere, -a, negri'ero, -a *sm/f* slave trader; (*fig*) slave driver
'**negro, -a** *ag, sm/f* Negro
negro'mante *sm/f* necromancer
negroman'zia [negroman'tsia] *sf* necromancy
'**nei, nel, nell', 'nella, 'nelle, 'nello** *prep + det vedi* **in**
'**nembo** *sm* (*Meteor*) nimbus
ne'mico, -a, ci, che *ag* hostile; (*Mil*) enemy *cpd* ■ *sm/f* enemy; **essere ~ di** to be strongly averse *o* opposed to
nem'meno *av, cong* = **neanche**
'**nenia** *sf* dirge; (*motivo monotono*) monotonous tune
'**neo** *sm* mole; (*fig*) (slight) flaw
'**neo...** *prefisso* neo...
neofa'scista, -i, e [neofaʃ'ʃista] *sm/f* neofascist
neolo'gismo [neolo'dʒizmo] *sm* neologism
'**neon** *sm* (*Chim*) neon
neo'nato, -a *ag* newborn ■ *sm/f* newborn baby
neozelan'dese [neoddzelan'dese] *ag* New Zealand *cpd* ■ *sm/f* New Zealander
Ne'pal *sm*: **il ~** Nepal
nepo'tismo *sm* nepotism
nep'pure *av, cong* = **neanche**
ner'bata *sf* (*colpo*) blow; (*sferzata*) whiplash
'**nerbo** *sm* lash; (*fig*) strength, backbone
nerbo'ruto, -a *ag* muscular; robust
ne'retto *sm* (*Tip*) bold type
'**nero, -a** *ag* black; (*scuro*) dark ■ *sm* black; **nella miseria più nera** in utter *o* abject poverty; **essere di umore ~, essere ~** to be in a filthy mood; **mettere qc ~ su bianco** to put sth down in black and white; **vedere tutto ~** to look on the black side (of things)
nero'fumo *sm* lampblack
nerva'tura *sf* (*Anat*) nervous system; (*Bot*) veining; (*Archit, Tecn*) rib
'**nervo** *sm* (*Anat*) nerve; (*Bot*) vein; **avere i nervi** to be on edge; **dare sui nervi a qn** to get on sb's nerves; **tenere/avere i nervi saldi** to keep/be calm; **che nervi!** damn (it)!
nervo'sismo *sm* (*Psic*) nervousness; (*irritazione*) irritability
ner'voso, -a *ag* nervous; (*irritabile*) irritable ■ *sm* (*fam*): **far venire il ~ a qn** to get on sb's nerves; **farsi prendere dal ~** to let o.s. get irritated
'**nespola** *sf* (*Bot*) medlar; (*fig*) blow, punch
'**nespolo** *sm* medlar tree
'**nesso** *sm* connection, link

 PAROLA CHIAVE

nes'suno, -a (*det: dav sm* **nessun** *+ C, V,* **nessuno** *+ s impura, gn, pn, ps, x, z; dav sf* **nessuna** *+ C,* **nessun'** *+ V*) *det* **1** (*non uno*) no; (*espressione negativa*) + any; **non c'è nessun libro** there

isn't any book, there is no book; **nessun altro** no one else, nobody else; **nessun'altra cosa** nothing else; **in nessun luogo** nowhere
2 (*qualche*) any; **hai nessuna obiezione?** do you have any objections?
■ *pron* **1** (*non uno*) no one, nobody; (*espressione negativa* +) any(one); (*: cosa*) none; (*espressione negativa*) + any; **nessuno è venuto, non è venuto nessuno** nobody came
2 (*qualcuno*) anyone, anybody; **ha telefonato nessuno?** did anyone phone?

netta'mente *av* clearly
net'tare¹ *vt* to clean
'nettare² ['nɛttare] *sm* nectar
net'tezza [net'tettsa] *sf* cleanness, cleanliness; **~ urbana** cleansing department (*Brit*), department of sanitation (*US*)
'netto, -a *ag* (*pulito*) clean; (*chiaro*) clear, clear-cut; (*deciso*) definite; (*Econ*) net; **tagliare qc di ~** to cut sth clean off; **taglio ~ col passato** (*fig*) clean break with the past
nettur'bino *sm* dustman (*Brit*), garbage collector (*US*)
'neuro... *prefisso* neuro...
neurochirur'gia [neurokirur'dʒia] *sf* neurosurgery
neurolo'gia [neurolo'dʒia] *sf* neurology
neuro'logico, -a, ci, che [neuro'lɔdʒiko] *ag* neurological
neu'rologo, -a, gi, ghe *sm/f* neurologist
neu'rosi *sf inv* = **nevrosi**
neu'trale *ag* neutral
neutralità *sf* neutrality
neutraliz'zare [neutralid'dzare] *vt* to neutralize
'neutro, -a *ag* neutral; (*Ling*) neuter ■ *sm* (*Ling*) neuter
neu'trone *sm* neutron
ne'vaio *sm* snowfield
'neve *sf* snow; **montare a ~** (*Cuc*) to whip up; **~ carbonica** dry ice
nevi'care *vb impers* to snow
nevi'cata *sf* snowfall
ne'vischio [ne'viskjo] *sm* sleet
ne'voso, -a *ag* snowy; snow-covered
nevral'gia [nevral'dʒia] *sf* neuralgia
ne'vralgico, -a, ci, che [ne'vraldʒiko] *ag*: **punto ~** (*Med*) nerve centre; (*fig*) crucial point
nevras'tenico, -a, ci, che *ag* (*Med*) neurasthenic; (*fig*) hot-tempered ■ *sm/f* neurasthenic; hot-tempered person
ne'vrosi *sf inv* neurosis
ne'vrotico, -a, ci, che *ag, sm/f* (*anche fig*) neurotic

Nia'gara *sm*: **le cascate del ~** the Niagara Falls
'nibbio *sm* (*Zool*) kite
Nica'ragua *sm*: **il ~** Nicaragua
nicaragu'ense *ag, sm/f* Nicaraguan
'nicchia ['nikkja] *sf* niche; (*naturale*) cavity, hollow; **~ di mercato** (*Comm*) niche market
nicchi'are [nik'kjare] *vi* to shilly-shally, hesitate
'nichel ['nikel] *sm* nickel
nichi'lismo [niki'lizmo] *sm* nihilism
Nico'sia *sf* Nicosia
nico'tina *sf* nicotine
nidi'ata *sf* (*di uccelli, fig: di bambini*) brood; (*di altri animali*) litter
nidifi'care *vi* to nest
'nido *sm* nest ■ *ag inv*: **asilo ~** day nursery, crèche (*for children aged 0 to 3*); **a ~ d'ape** (*tessuto etc*) honeycomb *cpd*

 PAROLA CHIAVE

ni'ente *pron* **1** (*nessuna cosa*) nothing; **niente può fermarlo** nothing can stop him; **niente di niente** absolutely nothing; **grazie! — di niente!** thank you! — not at all!; **nient'altro** nothing else; **nient'altro che** nothing but; **niente affatto** not at all, not in the least; **come se niente fosse** as if nothing had happened; **cose da niente** trivial matters; **per niente** (*gratis, invano*) for nothing; **non per niente, ma ...** not for any particular reason, but ...; **poco o niente** next to nothing; **un uomo da niente** a man of no consequence
2 (*qualcosa*): **hai bisogno di niente?** do you need anything?
3: **non ... niente** nothing; (*espressione negativa*) anything; **non ho visto niente** I saw nothing, I didn't see anything; **non può farci niente** he can't do anything about it; **(non) fa niente** (*non importa*) it doesn't matter; **non ho niente da dire** I have nothing *o* haven't anything to say
■ *ag inv*: **niente paura!** never fear!; **e niente scuse!** and I don't want to hear excuses!
■ *sm* nothing; **un bel niente** absolutely nothing; **basta un niente per farla piangere** the slightest thing is enough to make her cry; **finire in niente** to come to nothing
■ *av* (*in nessuna misura*): **non ... niente** not ... at all; **non è (per) niente buono** it isn't good at all; **non ci penso per niente** (*non ne ho nessuna intenzione*) I wouldn't think of it; **niente male!** not bad at all!

n

nientedi'meno, niente'meno *av* actually, even ▪ *escl* really!, I say!
'Niger ['nidʒer] *sm*: **il ~** Niger; (*fiume*) the Niger
Ni'geria [ni'dʒɛrja] *sf* Nigeria
nigeri'ano, -a [nidʒe'rjano] *ag, sm/f* Nigerian
'Nilo *sm*: **il ~** the Nile
'nimbo *sm* halo
'ninfa *sf* nymph
nin'fea *sf* water lily
nin'fomane *sf* nymphomaniac
ninna'nanna *sf* lullaby
'ninnolo *sm* (*balocco*) plaything; (*gingillo*) knick-knack
ni'pote *sm/f* (*di zii*) nephew/niece; (*di nonni*) grandson/daughter, grandchild
nip'ponico, -a, ci, che *ag* Japanese
niti'dezza [niti'dettsa] *sf* (*gen*) clearness; (*di stile*) clarity; (*Fot, TV*) sharpness
'nitido, -a *ag* clear; (*immagine*) sharp
ni'trato *sm* nitrate
'nitrico, -a, ci, che *ag* nitric
ni'trire *vi* to neigh
ni'trito *sm* (*di cavallo*) neighing *no pl*; neigh; (*Chim*) nitrite
nitroglice'rina [nitroglitʃe'rina] *sf* nitroglycerine
'niveo, -a *ag* snow-white
'Nizza ['nittsa] *sf* Nice
nn *abbr* (= *numeri*) nos
NO *sigla* = **Novara**
no *av* (*risposta*) no; **vieni o no?** are you coming or not?; **come no!** of course!, certainly!; **perché no?** why not?
N.O. *abbr* (= *nordovest*) NW
nobil'donna *sf* noblewoman
'nobile *ag* noble ▪ *sm/f* noble, nobleman/woman
nobili'are *ag* noble
nobili'tare *vt* (*anche fig*) to ennoble; **nobilitarsi** *vr* (*rendersi insigne*) to distinguish o.s.
nobiltà *sf* nobility; (*di azione etc*) nobleness
nobilu'omo (*pl* **nobiluomini**) *sm* nobleman
'nocca, -che *sf* (*Anat*) knuckle
'noccio *etc* ['nɔttʃo] *vb vedi* **nuocere**
nocci'ola [not'tʃɔla] *sf* hazelnut ▪ *ag inv* (*anche*: **color nocciola**) hazel, light brown
noccio'lina [nottʃo'lina] *sf* (*anche*: **nocciolina**) peanut
'nocciolo[1] ['nɔttʃolo] *sm* (*di frutto*) stone; (*fig*) heart, core
'nocciolo[2] [not'tʃɔlo] *sm* (*albero*) hazel
'noce ['notʃe] *sm* (*albero*) walnut tree ▪ *sf* (*frutto*) walnut; **una ~ di burro** (*Cuc*) a knob of butter (*Brit*), a dab of butter (*US*); **~ di cocco** coconut; **~ moscata** nutmeg
noce'pesca, -sche [notʃe'pɛska] *sf* nectarine
no'cevo *etc* [no'tʃevo] *vb vedi* **nuocere**
noci'uto [no'tʃuto] *pp di* **nuocere**
no'civo, -a [no'tʃivo] *ag* harmful, noxious
'nocqui *etc vb vedi* **nuocere**
'nodo *sm* (*di cravatta, legname, Naut*) knot; (*Aut, Ferr*) junction; (*Med, Astr, Bot*) node; (*fig: legame*) bond, tie; (*: punto centrale*) heart, crux; **avere un ~ alla gola** to have a lump in one's throat; **tutti i nodi vengono al pettine** (*proverbio*) your sins will find you out
no'doso, -a *ag* (*tronco*) gnarled
'nodulo *sm* (*Anat, Bot*) nodule
no-'global [no-'global] *ag inv* anti-globalization *cpd*
'noi *pron* (*soggetto*) we; (*oggetto: per dare rilievo, con preposizione*) us; **~ stessi(e)** we ourselves; (*oggetto*) ourselves; **da ~** (*nel nostro paese*) in our country, where we come from; (*a casa nostra*) at our house
'noia *sf* boredom; (*disturbo, impaccio*) bother *no pl*, trouble *no pl*; **avere qn/qc a ~** not to like sb/sth; **mi è venuto a ~** I'm tired of it; **dare ~ a** to annoy; **avere delle noie con qn** to have trouble with sb
noi'altri *pron* we
noi'oso, -a *ag* boring; (*fastidioso*) annoying, troublesome
noleggi'are [noled'dʒare] *vt* (*prendere a noleggio*) to hire (*Brit*), rent; (*dare a noleggio*) to hire out (*Brit*), rent out; (*aereo, nave*) to charter
noleggia'tore, -'trice [noleddʒa'tore] *sm/f* hirer (*Brit*), renter; charterer
no'leggio [no'leddʒo] *sm* hire (*Brit*), rental charter
no'lente *ag*: **volente o ~** whether one likes it or not, willy-nilly
'nolo *sm* hire (*Brit*), rental charter; (*per trasporto merci*) freight; **prendere/dare a ~ qc** to hire/hire out sth (*Brit*), rent/rent out sth
'nomade *ag* nomadic ▪ *sm/f* nomad
noma'dismo *sm* nomadism
'nome *sm* name; (*Ling*) noun; **in** *o* **a ~ di** in the name of; **di** *o* **per ~** (*chiamato*) called, named; **conoscere qn di ~** to know sb by name; **fare il ~ di qn** to name sb; **faccia pure il mio ~** feel free to mention my name; **~ d'arte** stage name; **~ di battesimo** Christian name; **~ depositato** trade name; **~ di famiglia** surname; **~ da ragazza** maiden name; **~ da sposata** married name; **~ utente** login
no'mea *sf* notoriety
nomencla'tura *sf* nomenclature
nomenkla'tura *sf* (*di partito, stato*) nomenklatura
no'mignolo [no'miɲɲolo] *sm* nickname
'nomina *sf* appointment

nomi'nale *ag* nominal; (*Ling*) noun *cpd*
nomi'nare *vt* to name; (*eleggere*) to appoint; (*citare*) to mention; **non l'ho mai sentito ~** I've never heard of it (*o* him)
nomination [nomi'neʃʃon] *sf inv* (*in reality show*) nomination
nomina'tivo, -a *ag* (*intestato: titolo*) registered; (*libretto*) personal; (*Ling*) nominative ■ *sm* (*nome*) name; (*Ling*) nominative; **elenco ~** list of names
non *av* not ■ *prefisso* non-; **grazie — ~ c'è di che** thank you — don't mention it; **i ~ credenti** the unbelievers; **~ autosufficiente** (*persona anziana*) needing care; *vedi anche* **affatto**; **appena** *etc*
nonché [non'ke] *cong* (*tanto più, tanto meno*) let alone; (*e inoltre*) as well as
nonconfor'mista, -i, e *ag, sm/f* nonconformist
noncu'rante *ag*: **~ (di)** careless (of), indifferent (to); **con fare ~** with a nonchalant air
noncu'ranza [nonku'rantsa] *sf* carelessness, indifference; **un'aria di ~** a nonchalant air
nondi'meno *cong* (*tuttavia*) however; (*nonostante*) nevertheless
'nonno, -a *sm/f* grandfather/mother; (*in senso più familiare*) grandma/grandpa; **nonni** *smpl* grandparents
non'nulla *sm inv*: **un ~** nothing, a trifle
'nono, -a *num* ninth
nonos'tante *prep* in spite of, notwithstanding ■ *cong* although, even though
non plus 'ultra *sm inv*: **il ~ (di)** the last word (in)
nontiscordardimé *sm inv* (*Bot*) forget-me-not
nord *sm* north ■ *ag inv* north; (*regione*) northern; **verso ~** north, northwards; **l'America del N~** North America
nor'dest *sm* north-east
'nordico, -a, ci, che *ag* nordic, northern European
nor'dista, -i, e *ag, sm/f* Yankee
nor'dovest *sm* north-west
Norim'berga *sf* Nuremberg
'norma *sf* (*principio*) norm; (*regola*) regulation, rule; (*consuetudine*) custom, rule; **di ~** normally; **a ~ di legge** according to law, as laid down by law; **al di sopra della ~** above average, above the norm; **per sua ~ e regola** for your information; **proporsi una ~ di vita** to set o.s. rules to live by; **norme di sicurezza** safety regulations; **norme per l'uso** instructions for use
nor'male *ag* normal
normalità *sf* normality
normaliz'zare [normalid'dzare] *vt* to normalize, bring back to normal
normal'mente *av* normally
Norman'dia *sf*: **la ~** Normandy
nor'manno, -a *ag, sm/f* Norman
norma'tivo, -a *ag* normative ■ *sf* regulations *pl*
norve'gese [norve'dʒese] *ag, sm/f, sm* Norwegian
Nor'vegia [nor'vɛdʒa] *sf*: **la ~** Norway
noso'comio *sm* hospital
nostal'gia [nostal'dʒia] *sf* (*di casa, paese*) homesickness; (*del passato*) nostalgia
nos'talgico, -a, ci, che [nos'taldʒiko] *ag* homesick; nostalgic ■ *sm/f* (*Pol*) *person who hopes for the return of Fascism*
nos'trano, -a *ag* local; (*pianta, frutta*) home-produced
'nostro, -a *det*: **il(la) ~(a)** *etc* our ■ *pron*: **il(la) ~(a)** *etc* ours ■ *sm*: **abbiamo speso del ~** we spent our own money ■ *sf*: **la nostra** (*opinione*) our view; **i nostri** our family; our own people; **è dei nostri** he's one of us; **è dalla nostra** (*parte*) he's on our side; **anche noi abbiamo avuto le nostre** (*disavventure*) we've had our problems too; **alla nostra!** (*brindisi*) to us!
nos'tromo *sm* boatswain
'nota *sf* (*segno*) mark; (*comunicazione scritta, Mus*) note; (*fattura*) bill; (*elenco*) list; **prendere ~ di qc** to note sth, make a note of sth, write sth down; (*fig: fare attenzione*) to note sth, take note of sth; **degno di ~** noteworthy, worthy of note; **note caratteristiche** distinguishing marks *o* features; **note a piè di pagina** footnotes
no'tabile *ag* notable; (*persona*) important ■ *sm* prominent citizen
no'taio *sm* notary
no'tare *vt* (*segnare: errori*) to mark; (*registrare*) to note (down), write down; (*rilevare, osservare*) to note, notice; **farsi ~** to get o.s. noticed
nota'rile *ag*: **atto ~** legal document (*authorized by a notary*); **studio ~** notary's office
notazi'one [notat'tsjone] *sf* (*Mus*) notation
no'tevole *ag* (*talento*) notable, remarkable; (*peso*) considerable
no'tifica, -che *sf* notification
notifi'care *vt* (*Dir*): **~ qc a qn** to notify sb of sth, give sb notice of sth
notificazi'one [notifikat'tsjone] *sf* notification
no'tizia [no'tittsja] *sf* (piece of) news *sg*; (*informazione*) piece of information; **notizie** *sfpl* news *sg*; information *sg*
notizi'ario [notit'tsjarjo] *sm* (*Radio, TV, Stampa*) news *sg*

'noto, -a *ag* (well-)known
notorietà *sf* fame; notoriety
no'torio, -a *ag* well-known; (*peg*) notorious
not'tambulo, -a *sm/f* night-bird (*fig*)
not'tata *sf* night
'notte *sf* night; **di ~** at night; (*durante la notte*) in the night, during the night; **questa ~** (*passata*) last night; (*che viene*) tonight; **nella ~ dei tempi** in the mists of time; **come va? — peggio che andar di ~** how are things? — worse than ever; **~ bianca** sleepless night
notte'tempo *av* at night; during the night
'nottola *sf* (*Zool*) noctule
not'turno, -a *ag* nocturnal; (*servizio, guardiano*) night *cpd* ■ *sf* (*Sport*) evening fixture (*Brit*) *o* match
nov. *abbr* (= *novembre*) Nov
no'vanta *num* ninety
novan'tenne *ag, sm/f* ninety-year-old
novan'tesimo, -a *num* ninetieth
novan'tina *sf*: **una ~ (di)** about ninety
'nove *num* nine
novecen'tesco, -a, schi, sche [novetʃen'tesko] *ag* twentieth-century
nove'cento [nove'tʃɛnto] *num* nine hundred ■ *sm*: **il N~** the twentieth century
no'vella *sf* (*Letteratura*) short story
novel'lino, -a *ag* (*pivello*) green, inexperienced
novel'lista, -i, e *sm/f* short-story writer
novel'listica *sf* (*arte*) short-story writing; (*insieme di racconti*) short stories *pl*
no'vello, -a *ag* (*piante, patate*) new; (*insalata, verdura*) early; (*sposo*) newly-married
no'vembre *sm* November; *vedi anche* **luglio**
novem'brino, -a *ag* November *cpd*
nove'mila *num* nine thousand
noven'nale *ag* (*che dura 9 anni*) nine-year *cpd*; (*ogni 9 anni*) nine-yearly
novi'lunio *sm* (*Astr*) new moon
novità *sf inv* novelty; (*innovazione*) innovation; (*cosa originale, insolita*) something new; (*notizia*) (piece of) news *sg*; **le ~ della moda** the latest fashions
novizi'ato [novit'tsjato] *sm* (*Rel*) novitiate; (*tirocinio*) apprenticeship
no'vizio, -a [no'vittsjo] *sm/f* (*Rel*) novice; (*tirocinante*) beginner, apprentice
nozi'one [not'tsjone] *sf* notion, idea; **nozioni** *sfpl* (*rudimenti*) basic knowledge *sg*, rudiments
nozio'nismo [nottsjo'nizmo] *sm* superficial knowledge
nozio'nistico, -a, ci, che [nottsjo'nistiko] *ag* superficial
'nozze ['nɔttse] *sfpl* wedding *sg*, marriage *sg*; **~ d'argento/d'oro** silver/golden wedding *sg*
ns. *abbr* (*Comm*) = **nostro**
NU *sigla* = **Nuoro**
N.U. *sigla* (= *Nazioni Unite*) UN
'nube *sf* cloud
nubi'fragio [nubi'fradʒo] *sm* cloudburst
'nubile *ag* (*donna*) unmarried, single
'nuca, -che *sf* nape of the neck
nucle'are *ag* nuclear ■ *sm*: **il ~** nuclear energy
'nucleo *sm* nucleus; (*gruppo*) team, unit, group; (*Mil, Polizia*) squad; **~ antidroga** anti-drugs squad; **il ~ familiare** the family unit
nu'dismo *sm* nudism
nu'dista, -i, e *sm/f* nudist
nudità *sf inv* nudity, nakedness; (*di paesaggio*) bareness ■ *sfpl* (*parti nude del corpo*) nakedness *sg*
'nudo, -a *ag* (*persona*) bare, naked, nude; (*membra*) bare, naked; (*montagna*) bare ■ *sm* (*Arte*) nude; **a occhio ~** to the naked eye; **a piedi nudi** barefoot; **mettere a ~** (*cuore, verità*) to lay bare; **gli ha detto ~ e crudo che ...** he told him bluntly that ...
'nugolo *sm*: **un ~ di** a whole host of
'nulla *pron, av* = **niente** ■ *sm*: **il ~** nothing; **svanire nel ~** to vanish into thin air; **basta un ~ per farlo arrabbiare** he gets annoyed over the slightest thing
nulla'osta *sm inv* authorization
nullate'nente *ag*: **essere ~** to own nothing ■ *sm/f* person with no property
nullità *sf inv* nullity; (*persona*) nonentity
'nullo, -a *ag* useless, worthless; (*Dir*) null (and void); (*Sport*): **incontro ~** draw
nume'rale *ag, sm* numeral
nume'rare *vt* to number
numera'tore *sm* (*Mat*) numerator; (*macchina*) numbering device
numerazi'one [numerat'tsjone] *sf* numbering; (*araba, decimale*) notation
nu'merico, -a, ci, che *ag* numerical
'numero *sm* number; (*romano, arabo*) numeral; (*di spettacolo*) act, turn; **dare i numeri** (*farneticare*) not to be all there; **tanto per fare ~ invitiamo anche lui** why don't we invite him to make up the numbers?; **ha tutti i numeri per riuscire** he's got what it takes to succeed; **che ~ tuo fratello!** your brother is a real character!; **~ civico** house number; **~ chiuso** (*Università*) selective entry system; **~ doppio** (*di rivista*) issue with supplement; **~ di scarpe** size of shoe; **~ verde** (*Tel*) ≈ Freephone®
nume'roso, -a *ag* numerous, many; (*folla, famiglia*) large
numis'matica *sf* numismatics *sg*, coin collecting
'nunzio ['nuntsjo] *sm* (*Rel*) nuncio
nu'occio *etc* ['nwɔttʃo] *vb vedi* **nuocere**

nu'ocere ['nwɔtʃere] *vi*: ~ **a** to harm, damage; **il tentar non nuoce** (*proverbio*) there's no harm in trying
nuoci'uto, -a [nwo'tʃuto] *pp di* **nuocere**
nu'ora *sf* daughter-in-law
nuo'tare *vi* to swim; (*galleggiare: oggetti*) to float; ~ **a rana/sul dorso** to do the breast stroke/backstroke
nuo'tata *sf* swim
nuota'tore, -'trice *sm/f* swimmer
nu'oto *sm* swimming
nu'ova *sf vedi* **nuovo**
nuova'mente *av* again
Nu'ova York *sf* New York
Nu'ova Ze'landa [-dze'landa] *sf*: **la** ~ New Zealand
nu'ovo, -a *ag* new ■ *sf* (*notizia*) (piece of) news *sg*; **come** ~ as good as new; **di** ~ again; **fino a** ~ **ordine** until further notice; **il suo volto non mi è** ~ I know his face; **rimettere a** ~ (*cosa, macchina*) to do up like new; **anno** ~, **vita nuova!** it's time to turn over a new leaf!; ~ **fiammante** *o* **di zecca** brand-new; **la Nuova Guinea** New Guinea; **la Nuova Inghilterra** New England; **la Nuova Scozia** Nova Scotia
nu'trice [nu'tritʃe] *sf* wet nurse
nutri'ente *ag* nutritious, nourishing; (*crema, balsamo*) nourishing
nutri'mento *sm* food, nourishment
nu'trire *vt* to feed; (*fig: sentimenti*) to harbour (*Brit*), harbor (*US*), nurse
nutri'tivo, -a *ag* nutritional; (*alimento*) nutritious
nu'trito, -a *ag* (*numeroso*) large; (*fitto*) heavy; **ben/mal** ~ well/poorly fed
nutrizi'one [nutrit'tsjone] *sf* nutrition
'nuvolo, -a *ag* cloudy ■ *sf* cloud
nuvolosità *sf* cloudiness
nuvo'loso, -a *ag* cloudy
nuzi'ale [nut'tsjale] *ag* nuptial; wedding *cpd*
'nylon ['nailən] *sm* nylon

Oo

O, o [ɔ] *sf o m inv* (*lettera*) O, o; **O come Otranto** ≈ O for Oliver (*Brit*), O for Oboe (*US*)
o *cong* (*dav V spesso*): **od** or; **o ... o** either ... or; **o l'uno o l'altro** either (of them); **o meglio** or rather
O. *abbr* (= *ovest*) W
ˈ**oasi** *sf inv* oasis
obbediˈente *etc vedi* **ubbidiente** *etc*
obbietˈtare *etc vedi* **obiettare** *etc*
obbliˈgare *vt* (*costringere*): **~ qn a fare** to force *o* oblige sb to do; (*Dir*) to bind; **obbligarsi** *vr*: **obbligarsi a fare** to undertake to do; **obbligarsi per qn** (*Dir*) to stand surety for sb, act as guarantor for sb
obbligaˈtissimo, -a *ag* (*ringraziamento*): **~!** much obliged!
obbliˈgato, -a *ag* (*costretto, grato*) obliged; (*percorso, tappa*) set, fixed; **passaggio ~** (*fig*) essential requirement
obbligaˈtorio, -a *ag* compulsory, obligatory
obbligaziˈone [obbligat'tsjone] *sf* obligation; (*Comm*) bond, debenture; **~ dello Stato** government bond; **obbligazioni convertibili** convertible loan stock, convertible debentures
obbligazioˈnista, -i, e [obbligattsjo'nista] *sm/f* bond-holder
ˈ**obbligo, -ghi** *sm* obligation; (*dovere*) duty; **avere l'~ di fare, essere nell'~ di fare** to be obliged to do; **essere d'~** (*discorso, applauso*) to be called for; **avere degli obblighi con** *o* **verso qn** to be under an obligation to sb, be indebted to sb; **le formalità d'~** the necessary formalities
obb.mo *abbr* = **obbligatissimo**
obˈbrobrio *sm* disgrace; (*fig*) mess, eyesore
obeˈlisco, -schi *sm* obelisk
obeˈrato, -a *ag*: **~ di** (*lavoro*) overloaded *o* overburdened with; (*debiti*) crippled with
obesità *sf* obesity
oˈbeso, -a *ag* obese
obietˈtare *vt*: **~ che** to object that; **~ su** to object to sth, raise objections concerning sth
obiettivaˈmente *av* objectively
obiettività *sf* objectivity
obietˈtivo, -a *ag* objective ■ *sm* (*Ottica, Fot*) lens *sg*, objective; (*Mil*) *fig*, objective
obietˈtore *sm* objector; **~ di coscienza** conscientious objector
obieziˈone [objet'tsjone] *sf* objection
obiˈtorio *sm* morgue
oˈbliquo, -a *ag* oblique; (*inclinato*) slanting; (*fig*) devious, underhand; **sguardo ~** sidelong glance
obliteˈrare *vt* (*francobollo*) to cancel; (*biglietto*) to stamp
obliteraˈtrice [oblitera'tritʃe] *sf* (*anche*: **macchina obliteratrice**) cancelling machine; stamping machine
oblò *sm inv* porthole
oˈblungo, -a, ghi, ghe *ag* oblong
ˈ**oboe** *sm* oboe
ˈ**obolo** *sm* (*elemosina*) (small) offering, mite
obsoleˈscenza [obsoleʃʃɛntsa] *sf* (*Econ*) obsolescence
obsoˈleto, -a *ag* obsolete
OC *abbr* (= *onde corte*) SW
ˈ**oca** (*pl* **oche**) *sf* goose
oˈcaggine [o'kaddʒine] *sf* silliness, stupidity
occasioˈnale *ag* (*incontro*) chance; (*cliente, guadagni*) casual, occasional
occasiˈone *sf* (*caso favorevole*) opportunity; (*causa, motivo, circostanza*) occasion; (*Comm*) bargain; **all'~** should the need arise; **alla prima ~** at the first, opportunity; **d'~** (*a buon prezzo*) bargain *cpd*; (*usato*) secondhand
occhiˈaia [ok'kjaja] *sf* eye socket; **occhiaie** *sfpl* (*sotto gli occhi*) shadows (under the eyes)
occhiˈali [ok'kjali] *smpl* glasses, spectacles; **~ da sole** sunglasses
occhiˈata [ok'kjata] *sf* look, glance; **dare un'~ a** to have a look at
occhieggiˈare [okkjed'dʒare] *vi* (*apparire qua e là*) to peep (out)
occhiˈello [ok'kjɛllo] *sm* buttonhole; (*asola*) eyelet

'**occhio** ['ɔkkjo] *sm* eye; **~!** careful!, watch out!; **a ~ nudo** with the naked eye; **a quattr'occhii** privately, in private; **avere ~** to have a good eye; **chiudere un ~ (su)** *(fig)* to turn a blind eye (to), shut one's eyes (to); **costare un ~ della testa** to cost a fortune; **dare all'~** *o* **nell'~ a qn** to catch sb's eye; **fare l'~ a qc** to get used to sth; **tenere d'~ qn** to keep an eye on sb; **vedere di buon/mal ~ qc** to look favourably/unfavourably on sth
occhio'lino [okkjo'lino] *sm*: **fare l'~ a qn** to wink at sb
occiden'tale [ottʃiden'tale] *ag* western ■ *sm/f* Westerner
occi'dente [ottʃi'dɛnte] *sm* west; *(Pol)*: **l'O~** the West; **a ~** in the west
oc'cipite [ot'tʃipite] *sm* back of the head, occiput *(Anat)*
oc'cludere *vt* to block
occlusi'one *sf* blockage, obstruction
oc'cluso, -a *pp di* **occludere**
occor'rente *ag* necessary ■ *sm* all that is necessary
occor'renza [okkor'rɛntsa] *sf* necessity, need; **all'~** in case of need
oc'correre *vi* to be needed, be required ■ *vb impers*: **occorre farlo** it must be done; **occorre che tu parta** you must leave, you'll have to leave; **mi occorrono i soldi** I need the money
oc'corso, -a *pp di* **occorrere**
occulta'mento *sm* concealment
occul'tare *vt* to hide, conceal
oc'culto, -a *ag* hidden, concealed; *(scienze, forze)* occult
occu'pante *sm/f* *(di casa)* occupier, occupant; **~ abusivo** squatter
occu'pare *vt* to occupy; *(manodopera)* to employ; *(ingombrare)* to occupy, take up; **occuparsi** *vr* to occupy o.s., keep o.s. busy; *(impiegarsi)* to get a job; **occuparsi di** *(interessarsi)* to take an interest in; *(prendersi cura di)* to look after, take care of
occu'pato, -a *ag* *(Mil, Pol)* occupied; *(persona: affaccendato)* busy; *(posto, sedia)* taken; *(toilette, Tel)* engaged
occupazio'nale [okkupattsjo'nale] *ag* employment *cpd*, of employment
occupazi'one [okkupat'tsjone] *sf* occupation; *(impiego, lavoro)* job; *(Econ)* employment
Oce'ania [otʃe'anja] *sf*: **l'~** Oceania
o'ceano [o'tʃɛano] *sm* ocean
'**ocra** *sf* ochre
'**OCSE** *sigla f* (= *Organizzazione per la Cooperazione e lo Sviluppo Economico*) OECD (= *Organization for Economic Cooperation and Development*)
ocu'lare *ag* ocular, eye *cpd*; **testimone ~** eye witness
ocula'tezza [okula'tettsa] *sf* caution; shrewdness
ocu'lato, -a *ag* *(attento)* cautious, prudent; *(accorto)* shrewd
ocu'lista, -i, e *sm/f* eye specialist, oculist
od *cong vedi* **o**
'**ode** *sf* ode
'**ode** *etc vb vedi* **udire**
odi'are *vt* to hate, detest
odi'erno, -a *ag* today's, of today; *(attuale)* present; **in data odierna** *(formale)* today
'**odio** *sm* hatred; **avere in ~ qc/qn** to hate *o* detest sth/sb
odi'oso, -a *ag* hateful, odious; **rendersi ~ (a)** to make o.s. unpopular (with)
'**odo** *etc vb vedi* **udire**
odontoi'atra, -i, e *sm/f* dentist, dental surgeon
odontoia'tria *sf* dentistry
odonto'tecnico, -ci *sm* dental technician
odo'rare *vt* *(annusare)* to smell; *(profumare)* to perfume, scent ■ *vi*: **~ (di)** to smell (of)
odo'rato *sm* sense of smell
o'dore *sm* smell; **gli odori** *(Cuc)* (aromatic) herbs; **sentire ~ di qc** to smell sth; **morire in ~ di santità** *(Rel)* to die in the odour *(Brit)* *o* odor *(US)* of sanctity
odo'roso, -a *ag* sweet-smelling
of'fendere *vt* to offend; *(violare)* to break, violate; *(insultare)* to insult; *(ferire)* to hurt; **offendersi** *vr* *(con senso reciproco)* to insult one another; *(risentirsi)*: **offendersi (di)** to take offence (at), be offended (by)
offen'sivo, -a *ag, sf* offensive
offen'sore *sm* offender; *(Mil)* aggressor
offe'rente *sm* *(in aste)*: **al migliore ~** to the highest bidder
of'ferto, -a *pp di* **offrire** ■ *sf* offer; *(donazione, anche: Rel)* offering; *(in gara d'appalto)* tender; *(in aste)* bid; *(Econ)* supply; **fare un'offerta** to make an offer; *(per appalto)* to tender; *(ad un'asta)* to bid; **offerta pubblica d'acquisto** takeover bid; **offerta pubblica di vendita** public offer for sale; **offerta reale** tender; **"offerte d'impiego"** *(Stampa)* "situations vacant" *(Brit)*, "help wanted" *(US)*
of'feso, -a *pp di* **offendere** ■ *ag* offended; *(fisicamente)* hurt, injured ■ *sm/f* offended party ■ *sf* insult, affront; *(Mil)* attack; *(Dir)* offence *(Brit)*, offense *(US)*; **essere ~ con qn** to be annoyed with sb; **parte offesa** *(Dir)* plaintiff
offi'ciare [offi'tʃare] *vi* *(Rel)* to officiate
offi'cina [offi'tʃina] *sf* workshop
of'frire *vt* to offer; **offrirsi** *vr* *(proporsi)* to offer (o.s.), volunteer; *(occasione)* to present itself;

(*esporsi*): **offrirsi a** to expose o.s. to; **ti offro da bere** I'll buy you a drink; **"offresi posto di segretaria"** "secretarial vacancy", "vacancy for secretary"; **"segretaria offresi"** "secretary seeks post"

offus'care *vt* to obscure, darken; (*fig*: *intelletto*) to dim, cloud; (*fama*) to obscure, overshadow; **offuscarsi** *vr* to grow dark to cloud, grow dim to be obscured

of'talmico, -a, ci, che *ag* ophthalmic

oggettività [oddʒettivi'ta] *sf* objectivity

ogget'tivo, -a [oddʒet'tivo] *ag* objective

og'getto [od'dʒɛtto] *sm* object; (*materia, argomento*) subject (matter); (*in lettere commerciali*): **~ ...** re ...; **essere ~ di** (*critiche, controversia*) to be the subject of; (*odio, pietà etc*) to be the object of; **essere ~ di scherno** to be a laughing stock; **in ~ a quanto detto** (*in lettere*) as regards the matter mentioned above; **oggetti preziosi** valuables, articles of value; **oggetti smarriti** lost property *sg* (*Brit*), lost and found *sg* (*US*)

'oggi ['ɔddʒi] *av, sm* today; **~ stesso** today, this very day; **~ come ~** at present, as things stand; **dall' ~ al domani** from one day to the next; **a tutt'~** up till now, till today; **le spese a tutt'~ sono ...** expenses to date are ...; **~ a otto** a week today

oggigi'orno [oddʒi'dʒorno] *av* nowadays

o'giva [o'dʒiva] *sf* ogive, pointed arch

OGM [ɔddʒi'ɛmme] *sigla mpl* (= *organismi geneticamente modificati*) GMO (= *genetically modified organisms*)

'ogni ['oɲɲi] *det* every, each; (*tutti*) all; (*con valore distributivo*) every; **~ uomo è mortale** all men are mortal; **viene ~ due giorni** he comes every two days; **~ cosa** everything; **ad ~ costo** at all costs, at any price; **in ~ luogo** everywhere; **~ tanto** every so often; **~ volta che** every time that

Ognis'santi [oɲɲis'santi] *sm* All Saints' Day

o'gnuno [oɲ'ɲuno] *pron* everyone, everybody

'ohi *escl* oh!; (*esprimente dolore*) ow!

ohimè *escl* oh dear!

'OIL *sigla f* (= *Organizzazione Internazionale del Lavoro*) ILO

OL *abbr* (= *onde lunghe*) LW

O'landa *sf*: **l'~** Holland

olan'dese *ag* Dutch ■ *sm* (*Ling*) Dutch ■ *sm/f* Dutchman/woman; **gli Olandesi** the Dutch

ole'andro *sm* oleander

ole'ato, -a *ag*: **carta oleata** greaseproof paper (*Brit*), wax paper (*US*)

oleo'dotto *sm* oil pipeline

ole'oso, -a *ag* oily; (*che contiene olio*) oil *cpd*

o'lezzo [o'leddzo] *sm* fragrance

ol'fatto *sm* sense of smell

oli'are *vt* to oil

olia'tore *sm* oil can, oiler

oli'era *sf* oil cruet

oligar'chia [oligar'kia] *sf* oligarchy

olim'piadi *sfpl* Olympic Games

o'limpico, -a, ci, che *ag* Olympic

'olio *sm* oil; (*Pittura*): **un (quadro a) ~** an oil painting; **sott'~** (*Cuc*) in oil; **oli essenziali** essential oils; **~ di fegato di merluzzo** cod liver oil; **~ d'oliva** olive oil; **~ santo** holy oil; **~ di semi** vegetable oil; **~ solare** suntan oil

o'liva *sf* olive

oli'vastro, -a *ag* olive(-coloured) (*Brit*), olive(-colored) (*US*); (*carnagione*) sallow

oli'veto *sm* olive grove

o'livo *sm* olive tree

'olmo *sm* elm

olo'causto *sm* holocaust

OLP *sigla f* (= *Organizzazione per la Liberazione della Palestina*) PLO

oltraggi'are [oltrad'dʒare] *vt* to offend, insult

ol'traggio [ol'traddʒo] *sm* offence (*Brit*), offense (*US*), insult; (*Dir*): **~ al pudore** indecent behaviour (*Brit*) *o* behavior (*US*); **~ alla corte** contempt of court

oltraggi'oso, -a [oltrad'dʒoso] *ag* offensive

ol'tralpe *av* beyond the Alps

ol'tranza [ol'trantsa] *sf*: **a ~** to the last, to the bitter end; **sciopero ad ~** all-out strike

oltran'zismo [oltran'tsizmo] *sm* (*Pol*) extremism

oltran'zista, -i, e [oltran'tsista] *sm/f* (*Pol*) extremist

'oltre *av* (*più in là*) further; (*di più*: *aspettare*) longer, more ■ *prep* (*di là da*) beyond, over, on the other side of; (*più di*) more than, over; (*in aggiunta a*) besides; (*eccetto*): **~ a** except, apart from; **~ a tutto** on top of all that

oltrecor'tina *av* behind the Iron Curtain; **paesi d'~** Iron Curtain countries

oltre'manica *av* across the Channel

oltre'mare *av* overseas

oltre'modo *av* extremely, greatly

oltreo'ceano [oltreo'tʃɛano] *av* overseas ■ *sm*: **paesi d'~** overseas countries

oltrepas'sare *vt* to go beyond, exceed

oltre'tomba *sm inv*: **l'~** the hereafter

OM *abbr* (= *onde medie*) MW; (*Mil*) = **ospedale militare**

o'maggio [o'maddʒo] *sm* (*dono*) gift; (*segno di rispetto*) homage, tribute; **omaggi** *smpl* (*complimenti*) respects; **in ~** (*copia, biglietto*) complimentary; **rendere ~ a** to pay homage *o* tribute to; **presentare i propri omaggi a qn** (*formale*) to pay one's respects to sb

'Oman *sm*: **l'~** Oman

ombeli'cale *ag* umbilical
ombe'lico, -chi *sm* navel
'ombra *sf* (*zona non assolata, fantasma*) shade; (*sagoma scura*) shadow ■ *ag inv*: **bandiera ~** flag of convenience; **governo ~** (*Pol*) shadow cabinet; **sedere all'~** to sit in the shade; **nell'~** (*tramare, agire*) secretly; **restare nell'~** (*fig: persona*) to remain in obscurity; **senza ~ di dubbio** without the shadow of a doubt
ombreggi'are [ombred'dʒare] *vt* to shade
om'brello *sm* umbrella; **~ da sole** parasol, sunshade
ombrel'lone *sm* beach umbrella
om'bretto *sm* eyeshadow
om'broso, -a *ag* shady, shaded; (*cavallo*) nervous, skittish; (*persona*) touchy, easily offended
ome'lette [ɔmə'lɛt] *sf inv* omelet(te)
ome'lia *sf* (*Rel*) homily, sermon
ome'opata *sm/f* hom(o)eopath
omeopa'tia *sf* hom(o)eopathy
omeo'patico, -a, ci, che *ag* hom(o)eopathic ■ *sm* hom(o)eopath
omertà *sf* conspiracy of silence
o'messo, -a *pp di* **omettere**
o'mettere *vt* to omit, leave out; **~ di fare** to omit *o* fail to do
omi'cida, -i, e [omi'tʃida] *ag* homicidal, murderous ■ *sm/f* murderer/murderess
omi'cidio [omi'tʃidjo] *sm* murder; **~ colposo** (*Dir*) culpable homicide; **~ premeditato** (*Dir*) murder
o'misi *etc vb vedi* **omettere**
omissi'one *sf* omission; **reato d'~** criminal negligence; **~ di atti d'ufficio** negligence; (*by a public employee*): **~ di denuncia** failure to report a crime; **~ di soccorso** (*Dir*) failure to stop and give assistance
omogeneiz'zato [omodʒeneid'dzato] *sm* baby food
omo'geneo, -a [omo'dʒɛneo] *ag* homogeneous
omolo'gare *vt* (*Dir*) to approve, recognize; (*ratificare*) to ratify
omologazi'one [omologat'tsjone] *sf* approval; ratification
o'mologo, -a, ghi, ghe *ag* homologous, corresponding ■ *sm/f* opposite number
o'monimo, a *sm/f* namesake *sm* (*Ling*) homonym
omosessu'ale *ag, sm/f* homosexual
O.M.S. *sigla f* = **Organizzazione Mondiale della Sanità**
On. *abbr* (*Pol*) = **onorevole**
'oncia, -ce ['ontʃa] *sf* ounce
'onda *sf* wave; **mettere** *o* **mandare in ~** (*Radio, TV*) to broadcast; **andare in ~** (*Radio, TV*) to go on the air; **onde corte/medie/lunghe** short/medium/long wave *sg*; **l'~ verde** (*Aut*) synchronized traffic lights *pl*
on'data *sf* wave, billow; (*fig*) wave, surge; **a ondate** in waves; **~ di caldo** heatwave; **~ di freddo** cold spell *o* snap
'onde *cong* (*affinché: con il congiuntivo*) so that, in order that; (: *con l'infinito*) so as to, in order to
ondeggi'are [onded'dʒare] *vi* (*acqua*) to ripple; (*muoversi sulle onde: barca*) to rock, roll; (*fig: muoversi come le onde, barcollare*) to sway; (*essere incerto*) to waver
on'doso, -a *ag* (*moto*) of the waves
ondu'lato, -a *ag* (*capelli*) wavy; (*terreno*) undulating; **cartone ~** corrugated paper; **lamiera ondulata** sheet of corrugated iron
ondula'torio, -a *ag* undulating; (*Fisica*) undulatory, wave *cpd*
ondulazi'one [ondulat'tsjone] *sf* undulation; (*acconciatura*) wave
one'rato, -a *ag*: **~ di** burdened with, loaded with
'onere *sm* burden; **~ finanziario** financial charge; **oneri fiscali** taxes
one'roso, -a *ag* (*fig*) heavy, onerous
onestà *sf* honesty
onesta'mente *av* honestly; fairly, virtuously; (*in verità*) honestly, frankly
o'nesto, -a *ag* (*probo, retto*) honest; (*giusto*) fair; (*casto*) chaste, virtuous
'onice ['ɔnitʃe] *sf* onyx
o'nirico, -a, ci, che *ag* dreamlike, dream *cpd*
onnipo'tente *ag* omnipotent
onnipre'sente *ag* omnipresent; (*scherzoso*) ubiquitous
onnisci'ente [onniʃ'ʃɛnte] *ag* omniscient
onniveg'gente [onnived'dʒɛnte] *ag* all-seeing
ono'mastico, -ci *sm* name day
onomato'pea *sf* onomatopoeia
onomato'peico, -a, ci, che *ag* onomatopoeic
ono'ranze [ono'rantse] *sfpl* honours (*Brit*), honors (*US*)
ono'rare *vt* to honour (*Brit*), honor (*US*); (*far onore a*) to do credit to; **onorarsi** *vr*: **onorarsi di qc/di fare** to feel hono(u)red by sth/to do
ono'rario, -a *ag* honorary ■ *sm* fee
onora'tissimo, -a *ag* (*in presentazioni*): **~!** delighted to meet you!
ono'rato, -a *ag* (*reputazione, famiglia, carriera*) distinguished; **essere ~ di fare qc** to have the honour to do sth *o* of doing sth; **~ di conoscerla!** (it is) a pleasure to meet you!
o'nore *sm* honour (*Brit*), honor (*US*); **in ~ di** in hono(u)r of; **fare gli onori di casa** to play host (*o* hostess); **fare ~ a** to hono(u)r; (*pranzo*) to do justice to; (*famiglia*) to be a credit to;

O

farsi ~ to distinguish o.s.; **posto d'~** place of hono(u)r; **a onor del vero ...** to tell the truth ...

ono'revole *ag* honourable (*Brit*), honorable (*US*) ■ *sm/f* (*Pol*) ≈ Member of Parliament (*Brit*), ≈ Congressman/woman (*US*)

onorifi'cenza [onorifi'tʃɛntsa] *sf* honour (*Brit*), honor (*US*); decoration

ono'rifico, -a, ci, che *ag* honorary

'onta *sf* shame, disgrace; **ad ~ di** despite, notwithstanding

on'tano *sm* alder

'O.N.U. *sigla f* (= *Organizzazione delle Nazioni Unite*) UN, UNO

'OPA *sigla f* = **offerta pubblica d'acquisto**

o'paco, -a, chi, che *ag* (*vetro*) opaque; (*metallo*) dull, matt

o'pale *sm o f* opal

'O.P.E.C. *sigla f* (= *Organization of Petroleum Exporting Countries*) OPEC

'opera *sf* (*gen*) work; (*azione rilevante*) action, deed, work; (*Mus*) work; opus; (*melodramma*) opera; (*teatro*) opera house; (*ente*) institution, organization; **per ~ sua** thanks to him; **fare ~ di persuasione presso qn** to try to convince sb; **mettersi/essere all'~** to get down to/be at work; **~ d'arte** work of art; **~ buffa** comic opera; **~ lirica** (grand) opera; **~ pia** religious charity; **opere pubbliche (OO. PP.)** public works; **opere di restauro/di scavo** restoration/excavation work *sg*

ope'raio, -a *ag* working-class; workers'; (*Zool: ape, formica*) worker *cpd* ■ *sm/f* worker; **classe operaia** working class; **~ di fabbrica** factory worker; **~ a giornata** day labourer (*Brit*) *o* laborer (*US*); **~ specializzato** *o* **qualificato** skilled worker; **~ non specializzato** semi-skilled worker

ope'rare *vt* to carry out, make; (*Med*) to operate on ■ *vi* to operate, work; (*rimedio*) to act, work; (*Med*) to operate; **operarsi** *vr* to occur, take place; (*Med*) to have an operation; **operarsi d'appendicite** to have one's appendix out; **~ qn d'urgenza** to perform an emergency operation on sb

opera'tivo, -a *ag* operative, operating; **piano ~** (*Mil*) plan of operations

ope'rato *sm* (*comportamento*) actions *pl*

opera'tore, -'trice *sm/f* operator; (*TV, Cine*) cameraman; **aperto solo agli operatori** (*Comm*) open to the trade only; **~ di borsa** dealer on the stock exchange; **~ ecologico** refuse collector; **~ economico** agent, broker; **~ del suono** sound recordist; **~ turistico** tour operator

opera'torio, -a *ag* (*Med*) operating

operazi'one [operat'tsjone] *sf* operation

ope'retta *sf* (*Mus*) operetta, light opera

operosità *sf* industry

ope'roso, -a *ag* industrious, hard-working

opi'ficio [opi'fitʃo] *sm* factory, works *pl*

opi'nabile *ag* (*discutibile*) debatable, questionable; **è ~** it is a matter of opinion

opini'one *sf* opinion; **avere il coraggio delle proprie opinioni** to have the courage of one's convictions; **l'~ pubblica** public opinion

opinio'nista, -i, e *sm/f* (political) columnist

op là *escl* (*per far saltare*) hup!; (*a bimbo che è caduto*) upsy-daisy!

'oppio *sm* opium

oppi'omane *sm/f* opium addict

oppo'nente *ag* opposing ■ *sm/f* opponent

op'pongo *etc vb vedi* **opporre**

op'porre *vt* to oppose; **opporsi** *vr*: **opporsi (a qc)** to oppose (sth); to object (to sth); **~ resistenza/un rifiuto** to offer resistance/to refuse

opportu'nista, -i, e *sm/f* opportunist

opportunità *sf inv* opportunity; (*convenienza*) opportuneness, timeliness

oppor'tuno, -a *ag* timely, opportune; (*giusto*) right, appropriate; **a tempo ~** at the right *o* the appropriate time

op'posi *etc vb vedi* **opporre**

opposi'tore, -'trice *sm/f* opposer, opponent

opposizi'one [oppozit'tsjone] *sf* opposition; (*Dir*) objection; **essere in netta ~** (*idee, opinioni*) to clash, be in complete opposition; **fare ~ a qn/qc** to oppose sb/sth

op'posto, -a *pp di* **opporre** ■ *ag* opposite; (*opinioni*) conflicting ■ *sm* opposite, contrary; **all'~** on the contrary

oppressi'one *sf* oppression

oppres'sivo, -a *ag* oppressive

op'presso, -a *pp di* **opprimere**

oppres'sore *sm* oppressor

oppri'mente *ag* (*caldo, noia*) oppressive; (*persona*) tiresome; (*deprimente*) depressing

op'primere *vt* (*premere, gravare*) to weigh down; (*estenuare: caldo*) to suffocate, oppress; (*tiranneggiare: popolo*) to oppress

oppu'gnare [oppuɲ'ɲare] *vt* (*fig*) to refute

op'pure *cong* or (else)

op'tare *vi*: **~ per** (*scegliere*) to opt for, decide upon; (*Borsa*) to take (out) an option on

'optimum *sm inv* optimum

opu'lento, -a *ag* (*ricco*) rich, wealthy, affluent; (*arredamento etc*) opulent

opu'lenza [opu'lɛntsa] *sf* (*vedi ag*) richness, wealth, affluence; opulence

o'puscolo *sm* booklet, pamphlet

OPV *sigla f* = **offerta pubblica di vendita**

opzio'nale [optsjo'nale] *ag* optional

opzi'one [op'tsjone] *sf* option
OR *sigla* = **Oristano**
'ora *sf* (*60 minuti*) hour; (*momento*) time ■ *av* (*adesso*) now; (*poco fa*): **è uscito proprio ~** he's just gone out; (*tra poco*) presently, in a minute; (*correlativo*): **~ ..., ~** now ... now; **che ~ è?, che ore sono?** what time is it?; **domani a quest'~** this time tomorrow; **non veder l'~ di fare** to long to do, look forward to doing; **fare le ore piccole** to stay up till the early hours (of the morning) *o* the small hours; **è ~ di partire** it's time to go; **di buon' ~** early; **alla buon'~!** at last!; **~ legale** *o* **estiva** summer time (*Brit*), daylight saving time (*US*); **~ locale** local time; **~ di pranzo** lunchtime; **~ di punta** (*Aut*) rush hour; **d'~ in avanti** *o* **poi** from now on; **or ~** just now, a moment ago; **~ come ~** right now, at present; **10 anni or sono** 10 years ago
o'racolo *sm* oracle
'orafo *sm* goldsmith
o'rale *ag, sm* oral
oral'mente *av* orally
ora'mai *av* = **ormai**
o'rario, -a *ag* hourly; (*fuso, segnale*) time *cpd*; (*velocità*) per hour ■ *sm* timetable, schedule; (*di visite etc*) hours *pl*; time(s) (*pl*); **~ di apertura/chiusura** opening/closing time; **~ di apertura degli sportelli** bank opening hours; **~ elastico** *o* **flessibile** (*Industria*) flexitime; **~ ferroviario** railway timetable; **~ di lavoro/d'ufficio** working/office hours
o'rata *sf* sea bream
ora'tore, -'trice *sm/f* speaker; orator
ora'torio, -a *ag* oratorical ■ *sm* (*Rel*) oratory; (*Mus*) oratorio ■ *sf* (*arte*) oratory
orazi'one [orat'tsjone] *sf* (*Rel*) prayer; (*discorso*) speech, oration
or'bene *cong* so, well (then)
'orbita *sf* (*Astr, Fisica*) orbit; (*Anat*) (eye-)socket
orbi'tare *vi* to orbit
'orbo, -a *ag* blind
'Orcadi *sfpl*: **le (isole) ~** the Orkney Islands, the Orkneys
or'chestra [or'kɛstra] *sf* orchestra
orches'trale [orkes'trale] *ag* orchestral ■ *sm/f* orchestra player
orches'trare [orkes'trare] *vt* to orchestrate; (*fig*) to stage-manage
orchi'dea [orki'dɛa] *sf* orchid
'orcio ['ortʃo] *sm* jar
'orco, -chi *sm* ogre
'orda *sf* horde
or'digno [or'diɲɲo] *sm*: **~ esplosivo** explosive device
ordi'nale *ag, sm* ordinal
ordina'mento *sm* order, arrangement; (*regolamento*) regulations *pl*, rules *pl*; **~ scolastico/giuridico** education/legal system
ordi'nanza [ordi'nantsa] *sf* (*Dir, Mil*) order; (*Amm: decreto*) decree; (*persona: Mil*) orderly, batman; **d'~** (*Mil*) regulation *cpd*; **ufficiale d'~** orderly; **~ municipale** by(e)-law
ordi'nare *vt* (*mettere in ordine*) to arrange, organize; (*Comm*) to order; (*prescrivere: medicina*) to prescribe; (*comandare*): **~ a qn di fare qc** to order *o* command sb to do sth; (*Rel*) to ordain
ordi'nario, -a *ag* (*comune*) ordinary; (*grossolano*) coarse, common ■ *sm* ordinary; (*di università*) full professor
ordina'tivo, -a *ag* regulating, governing ■ *sm* (*Comm*) order
ordi'nato, -a *ag* tidy, orderly
ordinazi'one [ordinat'tsjone] *sf* (*Comm*) order; (*Rel*) ordination; **fare un'~ di qc** to put in an order for sth, order sth; **eseguire qc su ~** to make sth to order
'ordine *sm* order; (*carattere*): **d'~ pratico** of a practical nature; **all'~** (*Comm: assegno*) to order; **di prim'~** first-class; **fino a nuovo ~** until further notice; **essere in ~** (*documenti*) to be in order; (*persona, stanza*) to be tidy; **mettere in ~** to put in order, tidy (up); **richiamare all'~** to call to order; **le forze dell'~** the forces of law and order; **~ d'acquisto** purchase order; **l'~ degli avvocati** ≈ the Bar; **~ del giorno** (*di seduta*) agenda; (*Mil*) order of the day; **l'~ dei medici** ≈ the Medical Association; **~ di pagamento** standing order (*Brit*), automatic payment (*US*); **l'~ pubblico** law and order; **ordini (sacri)** (*Rel*) holy orders
or'dire *vt* (*fig*) to plot, scheme
or'dito *sm* (*di tessuto*) warp
orecchi'abile [orek'kjabile] *ag* (*canzone*) catchy
orec'chino [orek'kino] *sm* earring
o'recchio [o'rekkjo] (*pl(f)* **orecchie**) *sm* (*Anat*) ear; **avere ~** to have a good ear (for music); **venire all'~ di qn** to come to sb's attention; **fare orecchie da mercante (a)** to turn a deaf ear (to)
orecchi'oni [orek'kjoni] *smpl* (*Med*) mumps *sg*
o'refice [o'refitʃe] *sm* goldsmith; jeweller (*Brit*), jeweler (*US*)
orefice'ria [orefitʃe'ria] *sf* (*arte*) goldsmith's art; (*negozio*) jeweller's (shop) (*Brit*), jewelry store (*US*)
'orfano, -a *ag* orphan(ed) ■ *sm/f* orphan; **~ di padre/madre** fatherless/motherless
orfano'trofio *sm* orphanage

O

orga'netto *sm* barrel organ; (*fam: armonica a bocca*) mouth organ; (*fisarmonica*) accordion
or'ganico, -a, ci, che *ag* organic ■ *sm* personnel, staff
organi'gramma, -i *sm* organization chart; (*Inform*) computer flow chart
orga'nismo *sm* (*Biol*) organism; (*Anat, Amm*) body, organism
orga'nista, -i, e *sm/f* organist
organiz'zare [organid'dzare] *vt* to organize; **organizzarsi** *vr* to get organized
organizza'tivo, -a [organiddza'tivo] *ag* organizational
organizza'tore, -'trice [organiddza'tore] *ag* organizing ■ *sm/f* organizer
organizzazi'one [organiddzat'tsjone] *sf* (*azione*) organizing, arranging; (*risultato*) organization; **O~ Mondiale della Sanità** World Health Organization
'organo *sm* organ; (*di congegno*) part; (*portavoce*) spokesman/woman, mouthpiece; **organi di trasmissione** (*Tecn*) transmission (unit) *sg*
or'gasmo *sm* (*Fisiol*) orgasm; (*fig*) agitation, anxiety
'orgia, -ge ['ɔrdʒa] *sf* orgy
or'goglio [or'goʎʎo] *sm* pride
orgogli'oso, -a [orgoʎ'ʎoso] *ag* proud
orien'tabile *ag* adjustable
orien'tale *ag* (*paese, regione*) eastern; (*tappeti, lingua, civiltà*) oriental
orienta'mento *sm* positioning; orientation; direction; **senso di ~** sense of direction; **perdere l'~** to lose one's bearings; **~ professionale** careers guidance
orien'tare *vt* (*situare*) to position; (*carta, bussola*) to orientate; (*fig*) to direct; **orientarsi** *vr* to find one's bearings; (*fig: tendere*) to tend, lean; (*indirizzarsi*): **orientarsi verso** to take up, go in for
orienta'tivo, -a *ag* indicative, for guidance; **a scopo ~** for guidance
ori'ente *sm* east; **l'O~** the East, the Orient; **il Medio/l'Estremo O~** the Middle/Far East; **a ~** in the east
ori'ficio [ori'fitʃo], **ori'fizio** [ori'fittsjo] *sm* (*apertura*) opening; (*di tubo*) mouth; (*Anat*) orifice
o'rigano *sm* oregano
origi'nale [oridʒi'nale] *ag* original; (*bizzarro*) eccentric ■ *sm* original
originalità [oridʒinali'ta] *sf* originality; eccentricity
origi'nare [oridʒi'nare] *vt* to bring about, produce ■ *vi*: **~ da** to arise *o* spring from
origi'nario, -a [oridʒi'narjo] *ag* original; **essere ~ di** to be a native of; (*animale, pianta*) to be indigenous to, be native to
o'rigine [o'ridʒine] *sf* origin; **all'~** originally; **d'~ inglese** of English origin; **avere ~ da** to originate from; **dare ~ a** to give rise to
origli'are [oriʎ'ʎare] *vi*: **~ (a)** to eavesdrop (on)
o'rina *sf* urine
ori'nale *sm* chamberpot
ori'nare *vi* to urinate ■ *vt* to pass
orina'toio *sm* (public) urinal
ori'undo, -a *ag*: **essere ~ di Milano** *etc* to be of Milanese *etc* extraction *o* origin ■ *sm/f* person of foreign extraction *o* origin
orizzon'tale [oriddzon'tale] *ag* horizontal
oriz'zonte [orid'dzonte] *sm* horizon
ORL *sigla f* (*Med: = otorinolaringoiatria*) ENT
or'lare *vt* to hem
orla'tura *sf* (*azione*) hemming *no pl*; (*orlo*) hem
'orlo *sm* edge, border; (*di recipiente*) rim, brim; (*di vestito etc*) hem; **pieno fino all'~** full to the brim, brimful; **sull'~ della pazzia/della rovina** on the brink *o* verge of madness/ruin; **~ a giorno** hemstitch
'orma *sf* (*di persona*) footprint; (*di animale*) track; (*impronta, traccia*) mark, trace; **seguire** *o* **calcare le orme di qn** to follow in sb's footsteps
or'mai *av* by now, by this time; (*adesso*) now; (*quasi*) almost, nearly
ormeggi'are [ormed'dʒare] *vt*, **ormeggi'arsi** *vr* (*Naut*) to moor
or'meggio [or'meddʒo] *sm* (*atto*) mooring *no pl*; (*luogo*) moorings *pl*; **posto d'~** berth
ormo'nale *ag* hormonal; (*disfunzione, cura*) hormone *cpd*; **terapia ~** hormone therapy
or'mone *sm* hormone
ornamen'tale *ag* ornamental, decorative
orna'mento *sm* ornament, decoration
or'nare *vt* to adorn, decorate; **ornarsi** *vr*: **ornarsi (di)** to deck o.s. (out) (with)
or'nato, -a *ag* ornate
ornitolo'gia [ornitolo'dʒia] *sf* ornithology
orni'tologo, -a, gi, ghe *sm/f* ornithologist
'oro *sm* gold; **d'~, in ~** gold *cpd*; **d'~** (*colore, occasione*) golden; (*persona*) marvellous (*Brit*), marvelous (*US*); **un affare d'~** a real bargain; **prendere qc per ~ colato** to take sth as gospel (truth); **~ nero** black gold; **~ zecchino** pure gold
orologe'ria [orolodʒe'ria] *sf* watchmaking *no pl*; watchmaker's (shop), clockmaker's (shop); **bomba a ~** time bomb
orologi'aio [orolo'dʒajo] *sm* watchmaker; clockmaker
oro'logio [oro'lɔdʒo] *sm* clock; (*da tasca, da polso*) watch; **~ biologico** biological clock; **~ da polso** wristwatch; **~ al quarzo** quartz watch; **~ a sveglia** alarm clock

o'roscopo *sm* horoscope
or'rendo, -a *ag* (*spaventoso*) horrible, awful; (*bruttissimo*) hideous
or'ribile *ag* horrible
'orrido, -a *ag* fearful, horrid
orripi'lante *ag* hair-raising, horrifying
or'rore *sm* horror; **avere in ~ qn/qc** to loathe *o* detest sb/sth; **mi fanno ~** I loathe *o* detest them
orsacchi'otto [orsak'kjɔtto] *sm* teddy bear
'orso *sm* bear; **~ bruno/bianco** brown/polar bear
orsù *escl* come now!
or'taggio [or'taddʒo] *sm* vegetable
or'tensia *sf* hydrangea
or'tica, -che *sf* (stinging) nettle
orti'caria *sf* nettle rash
orticol'tura *sf* horticulture
'orto *sm* vegetable garden, kitchen garden; (*Agr*) market garden (*Brit*), truck farm (*US*); **~ botanico** botanical garden(s) (*pl*)
orto'dosso, -a *ag* orthodox
ortofrut'ticolo, -a *ag* fruit and vegetable *cpd*
ortogo'nale *ag* perpendicular
ortogra'fia *sf* spelling
orto'lano, -a *sm/f* (*venditore*) greengrocer (*Brit*), produce dealer (*US*)
ortope'dia *sf* orthopaedics *sg* (*Brit*), orthopedics *sg* (*US*)
orto'pedico, -a, ci, che *ag* orthopaedic (*Brit*), orthopedic (*US*) ■ *sm* orthopaedic specialist (*Brit*), orthopedist (*US*)
orzai'olo [ordza'jɔlo], **orzaiu'olo** [ordza'jwɔlo] *sm* (*Med*) stye
or'zata [or'dzata] *sf* barley water
'orzo ['ɔrdzo] *sm* barley
'OSA *sigla f* (= *Organizzazione degli Stati Americani*) OAS (= *Organization of American States*)
o'sare *vt, vi* to dare; **~ fare** to dare (to) do; **come osi?** how dare you?
oscenità [oʃʃeni'ta] *sf inv* obscenity
o'sceno, -a [oʃ'ʃɛno] *ag* obscene; (*ripugnante*) ghastly
oscil'lare [oʃʃil'lare] *vi* (*pendolo*) to swing; (*dondolare: al vento etc*) to rock; (*variare*) to fluctuate; (*Tecn*) to oscillate; (*fig*): **~ fra** to waver between
oscillazi'one [oʃʃillat'tsjone] *sf* oscillation; (*di prezzi, temperatura*) fluctuation
oscura'mento *sm* darkening; obscuring; (*in tempo di guerra*) blackout
oscu'rare *vt* to darken, obscure; (*fig*) to obscure; **oscurarsi** *vr* (*cielo*) to darken, cloud over; (*persona*): **si oscurò in volto** his face clouded over
oscurità *sf* (*vedi ag*) darkness; obscurity; gloominess
os'curo, -a *ag* dark; (*fig: incomprensibile*) obscure; (*umile: vita, natali*) humble, obscure; (*triste: pensiero*) gloomy, sombre ■ *sm*: **all'~** in the dark; **tenere qn all'~ di qc** to keep sb in the dark about sth
'Oslo *sf* Oslo
ospe'dale *sm* hospital
ospedali'ero, -a *ag* hospital *cpd*
ospi'tale *ag* hospitable
ospitalità *sf* hospitality
ospi'tare *vt* to give hospitality to; (*albergo*) to accommodate
'ospite *sm/f* (*persona che ospita*) host/hostess; (*persona ospitata*) guest
os'pizio [os'pittsjo] *sm* (*per vecchi etc*) home
'ossa *sfpl vedi* **osso**
os'sario *sm* (*Mil*) war memorial (*with burial place*)
ossa'tura *sf* (*Anat*) skeletal structure, frame; (*Tecn, fig*) framework
'osseo, -a *ag* bony; (*tessuto etc*) bone *cpd*
osse'quente *ag*: **~ alla legge** law-abiding
os'sequio *sm* deference, respect; **ossequi** *smpl* (*saluto*) respects, regards; **porgere i propri ossequi a qn** (*formale*) to pay one's respects to sb; **ossequi alla signora!** (give my) regards to your wife!
ossequi'oso, -a *ag* obsequious
osser'vanza [osser'vantsa] *sf* observance
osser'vare *vt* to observe, watch; (*esaminare*) to examine; (*notare, rilevare*) to notice, observe; (*Dir: la legge*) to observe, respect; (*mantenere: silenzio*) to keep, observe; **far ~ qc a qn** to point sth out to sb
osserva'tore, -'trice *ag* observant, perceptive ■ *sm/f* observer
osserva'torio *sm* (*Astr*) observatory; (*Mil*) observation post
osservazi'one [osservat'tsjone] *sf* observation; (*di legge etc*) observance; (*considerazione critica*) observation, remark; (*rimprovero*) reproof; **in ~** under observation; **fare un'~** to make a remark; to raise an objection; **fare un'~ a qn** to criticize sb
ossessio'nare *vt* to obsess, haunt; (*tormentare*) to torment, harass
ossessi'one *sf* obsession; (*seccatura*) nuisance
osses'sivo, -a *ag* obsessive, haunting troublesome
os'sesso, -a *ag* (*spiritato*) possessed
os'sia *cong* that is, to be precise
ossi'buchi [ossi'buki] *smpl di* **ossobuco**
ossi'dare *vt*, **ossi'darsi** *vr* to oxidize
ossidazi'one [ossidat'tsjone] *sf* oxidization, oxidation
'ossido *sm* oxide; **~ di carbonio** carbon monoxide

O

ossige'nare [ossidʒe'nare] *vt* to oxygenate; (*decolorare*) to bleach; **acqua ossigenata** hydrogen peroxide
os'sigeno [os'sidʒeno] *sm* oxygen
'osso *sm* (*Anat*: *pl(f)* **ossa**) bone; **d'~** (*bottone etc*) of bone, bone *cpd*; **avere le ossa rotte** to be dead *o* dog tired; **bagnato fino all'~** soaked to the skin; **essere ridotto all'~** (*fig*: *magro*) to be just skin and bone; (*senza soldi*) to be in dire straits; **rompersi l'~ del collo** to break one's neck; **rimetterci l'~ del collo** (*fig*) to ruin o.s., lose everything; **un ~ duro** (*persona, impresa*) a tough number; **~ di seppia** cuttlebone
osso'buco (*pl* **ossibuchi**) *sm* (*Cuc*) marrowbone; (*piatto*) *stew made with knuckle of veal in tomato sauce*
os'suto, -a *ag* bony
ostaco'lare *vt* to block, obstruct
os'tacolo *sm* obstacle; (*Equitazione*) hurdle, jump; **essere di ~ a qn/qc** (*fig*) to stand in the way of sb/sth
os'taggio [os'taddʒo] *sm* hostage
'oste, ostessa *sm/f* innkeeper
osteggi'are [osted'dʒare] *vt* to oppose, be opposed to
os'tello *sm* hostel; **~ della gioventù** youth hostel
osten'sorio *sm* (*Rel*) monstrance
osten'tare *vt* to make a show of, flaunt
ostentazi'one [ostentat'tsjone] *sf* ostentation, show
oste'ria *sf* inn
os'tessa *sf vedi* **oste**
os'tetrico, -a, ci, che *ag* obstetric ■ *sm* obstetrician ■ *sf* midwife
'ostia *sf* (*Rel*) host; (*per medicinali*) wafer
'ostico, -a, ci, che *ag* difficult, tough
os'tile *ag* hostile
ostilità *sf* hostility ■ *sfpl* (*Mil*) hostilities
osti'narsi *vr* to insist, dig one's heels in; **~ a fare** to persist (obstinately) in doing
osti'nato, -a *ag* (*caparbio*) obstinate; (*tenace*) persistent, determined
ostinazi'one [ostinat'tsjone] *sf* obstinacy; persistence
ostra'cismo [ostra'tʃizmo] *sm* ostracism
'ostrica, -che *sf* oyster
ostru'ire *vt* to obstruct, block
ostruzi'one [ostrut'tsjone] *sf* obstruction, blockage
ostruzio'nismo [ostruttsjo'nizmo] *sm* (*Pol*) obstructionism; (*Sport*) obstruction; **fare dell'~ a** (*progetto, legge*) to obstruct; **~ sindacale** work-to-rule (*Brit*), slowdown (*US*)
o'tite *sf* ear infection
otorinolaringoiatra, oto'rino(laringoi'atra), -i, e *sm/f* ear, nose and throat specialist
'otre *sm* (*recipiente*) goatskin
ott. *abbr* (= *ottobre*) Oct
ottago'nale *ag* octagonal
ot'tagono *sm* octagon
ot'tano *sm* octane; **numero di ottani** octane rating
ot'tanta *num* eighty
ottan'tenne *ag* eighty-year-old ■ *sm/f* octogenarian
ottan'tesimo, -a *num* eightieth
ottan'tina *sf*: **una ~ (di)** about eighty
ot'tavo, -a *num* eighth ■ *sf* octave
ottempe'ranza [ottempe'rantsa] *sf*: **in ~ a** (*Amm*) in accordance with, in compliance with
ottempe'rare *vi*: **~ a** to comply with, obey
ottene'brare *vt* to darken; (*fig*) to cloud
otte'nere *vt* to obtain, get; (*risultato*) to achieve, obtain
'ottico, -a, ci, che *ag* (*della vista*: *nervo*) optic; (*dell'ottica*) optical ■ *sm* optician ■ *sf* (*scienza*) optics *sg*; (*Fot*: *lenti, prismi etc*) optics *pl*
otti'male *ag* optimal, optimum
ottima'mente *av* excellently, very well
otti'mismo *sm* optimism
otti'mista, -i, e *sm/f* optimist
ottimiz'zare [ottimid'dzare] *vt* to optimize
ottimizzazi'one [ottimiddzat'tsjone] *sf* optimization
'ottimo, -a *ag* excellent, very good
'otto *num* eight
ot'tobre *sm* October; *vedi anche* **luglio**
otto'brino, -a *ag* October *cpd*
ottocen'tesco, -a, schi, sche [ottotʃen'tesko] *ag* nineteenth-century
otto'cento [otto'tʃɛnto] *num* eight hundred ■ *sm*: **l'O~** the nineteenth century
otto'mila *num* eight thousand
ot'tone *sm* brass; **gli ottoni** (*Mus*) the brass
ottuage'nario, -a [ottuadʒe'narjo] *ag, sm/f* octogenarian
ot'tundere *vt* (*fig*) to dull
ottu'rare *vt* to close (up); (*dente*) to fill
ottura'tore *sm* (*Fot*) shutter; (*nelle armi*) breechblock
otturazi'one [otturat'tsjone] *sf* closing (up); (*dentaria*) filling
ottusità *sf* (*vedi ag*) obtuseness; dullness
ot'tuso, -a *pp di* **ottundere** ■ *ag* (*Mat, fig*) obtuse; (*suono*) dull
o'vaia *sf*, **o'vaio** *sm* (*Anat*) ovary
o'vale *ag, sm* oval
o'varico, -a *ag* ovarian
o'vatta *sf* cotton wool; (*per imbottire*) padding, wadding

ovat'tare *vt* (*imbottire*) to pad; (*fig: smorzare*) to muffle
ovazi'one [ovat'tsjone] *sf* ovation
'**ovest** *sm* west; **a ~ (di)** west (of); **verso ~** westward(s)
o'**vile** *sm* pen, enclosure; **tornare all'~** (*fig*) to return to the fold
o'**vino, -a** *ag* sheep *cpd*, ovine
'**O.V.N.I.** *sigla m* (= *oggetto volante non identificato*) UFO
ovulazi'one [ovulat'tsjone] *sf* ovulation
'**ovulo** *sm* (*Fisiol*) ovum
o'**vunque** *av* = **dovunque**
ov'vero *cong* (*ossia*) that is, to be precise; (*oppure*) or (else)
ovvi'are *vi*: **~ a** to obviate
'**ovvio, -a** *ag* obvious
ozi'are [ot'tsjare] *vi* to laze around
'**ozio** ['ɔttsjo] *sm* idleness; (*tempo libero*) leisure; **ore d'~** leisure time; **stare in ~** to be idle
ozi'oso, -a [ot'tsjoso] *ag* idle
o'**zono** [od'dzɔno] *sm* ozone; **lo strato d'~** the ozone layer
ozonos'fera [oddzonos'fɛra] *sf* ozone layer

Pp

P, p [pi] *sf o m inv* (*lettera*) P, p; **P come Padova** ≈ P for Peter
P *abbr* (= *peso*) wt (= *parcheggio*); P
p. *abbr* (= *pagina*) p
P2 *abbr f* (= *la (loggia) P2*) the P2 masonic lodge
PA *sigla* = **Palermo**
P.A. *abbr* = **pubblica amministrazione**
pa'care *vt* to calm; **pacarsi** *vr* (*tempesta, disordini*) to subside
paca'tezza [paka'tettsa] *sf* quietness, calmness
pa'cato, -a *ag* quiet, calm
'pacca, -che *sf* slap
pac'chetto [pak'ketto] *sm* packet; **~ applicativo** (*Inform*) applications package; **~ azionario** (*Finanza*) shareholding; **~ software** (*Inform*) software package; **~ turistico** package holiday (*Brit*) *o* tour
pacchi'ano, -a [pak'kjano] *ag* (*colori*) garish; (*abiti, arredamento*) vulgar, garish
'pacco, -chi *sm* parcel; (*involto*) bundle; **~ postale** parcel
paccot'tiglia [pakkot'tiʎʎa] *sf* trash, junk
'pace ['patʃe] *sf* peace; **darsi ~** to resign o.s.; **fare (la) ~ con qn** to make it up with sb
pachis'tano, -a [pakis'tano] *ag, sm/f* Pakistani
pacifi'care [patʃifi'kare] *vt* (*riconciliare*) to reconcile, make peace between; (*mettere in pace*) to pacify
pacificazi'one [patʃifikat'tsjone] *sf* (*vedi vt*) reconciliation; pacification
pa'cifico, -a, ci, che [pa'tʃifiko] *ag* (*persona*) peaceable; (*vita*) peaceful; (*fig: indiscusso*) indisputable; (*ovvio*) obvious, clear ■ *sm*: **il P~, l'Oceano P~** the Pacific (Ocean)
paci'fismo [patʃi'fizmo] *sm* pacifism
paci'fista, -i, e [patʃi'fista] *sm/f* pacifist
PACS [paks] *sigla mpl* civil partnerships
pa'dano, -a *ag* of the Po; **la pianura padana** the Lombardy plain
pa'della *sf* frying pan; (*per infermi*) bedpan
padigli'one [padiʎ'ʎone] *sm* pavilion
'Padova *sf* Padua
pado'vano, -a *ag* of (*o* from) Padua
'padre *sm* father; **padri** *smpl* (*antenati*) forefathers
Padre'terno *sm*: **il ~** God the Father
pa'drino *sm* godfather
padro'nale *ag* (*scala, entrata*) main, principal; **casa ~** country house
padro'nanza [padro'nantsa] *sf* command, mastery
padro'nato *sm*: **il ~** the ruling class
pa'drone, -a *sm/f* master/mistress; (*proprietario*) owner; (*datore di lavoro*) employer; **essere ~ di sé** to be in control of o.s.; **~/a di casa** master/mistress of the house; (*per gli inquilini*) landlord/lady
padroneggi'are [padroned'dʒare] *vt* (*fig: sentimenti*) to master, control; (*materia*) to master, know thoroughly; **padroneggiarsi** *vr* to control o.s.
pae'saggio [pae'zaddʒo] *sm* landscape
paesag'gista, -i, e [paezad'dʒista] *sm/f* (*pittore*) landscape painter
pae'sano, -a *ag* country *cpd* ■ *sm/f* villager, countryman/woman
pa'ese *sm* (*nazione*) country, nation; (*terra*) country, land; (*villaggio*) village; **~ di provenienza** country of origin; **i Paesi Bassi** the Netherlands
paf'futo, -a *ag* chubby, plump
'paga, -ghe *sf* pay, wages *pl*; **giorno di ~** pay day
pa'gabile *ag* payable; **~ alla consegna/a vista** payable on delivery/on demand
pa'gaia *sf* paddle
paga'mento *sm* payment; **~ anticipato** payment in advance; **~ alla consegna** payment on delivery; **~ all'ordine** cash with order; **la TV a ~** pay TV
pa'gano, -a *ag, sm/f* pagan
pa'gare *vt* to pay; (*acquisto, fig: colpa*) to pay for; (*contraccambiare*) to repay, pay back ■ *vi* to pay; **quanto l'ha pagato?** how much did

you pay for it?; **~ con carta di credito** to pay by credit card; **~ in contanti** to pay cash; **~ di persona** (*fig*) to suffer the consequences; **l'ho pagata cara** (*fig*) I paid dearly for it

pa'gella [pa'dʒɛlla] *sf* (*Ins*) school report (*Brit*), report card (*US*)

'paggio ['paddʒo] *sm* page(boy)

pagherò [page'rɔ] *vb vedi* **pagare** ■ *sm inv* IOU; **~ cambiario** promissory note

'pagina ['padʒina] *sf* page; **Pagine bianche** phone book, telephone directory; **Pagine Gialle®** Yellow Pages®

'paglia ['paʎʎa] *sf* straw; **avere la coda di ~** (*fig*) to have a guilty conscience; **fuoco di ~** (*fig*) flash in the pan

pagliac'cetto [paʎʎat'tʃetto] *sm* (*per bambini*) rompers *pl*

pagliac'ciata [paʎʎat'tʃata] *sf* farce

pagli'accio [paʎ'ʎattʃo] *sm* clown

pagli'aio [paʎ'ʎajo] *sm* haystack

paglie'riccio [paʎʎe'rittʃo] *sm* straw mattress

paglie'rino, -a [paʎʎe'rino] *ag*: **giallo ~** pale yellow

pagli'etta [paʎ'ʎetta] *sf* (*cappello per uomo*) (straw) boater; (*per tegami etc*) steel wool

pagli'uzza [paʎ'ʎuttsa] *sf* (blade of) straw; (*d'oro etc*) tiny particle, speck

pa'gnotta [paɲ'ɲɔtta] *sf* round loaf

'pago, -a, ghi, ghe *ag*: **~ (di)** satisfied (with)

pa'goda *sf* pagoda

pail'lette [pa'jɛt]] *sf inv* sequin

'paio (*pl(f)* **paia**) *sm* pair; **un ~ di occhiali** a pair of glasses; **un ~ di** (*alcuni*) a couple of; **è un altro ~ di maniche** (*fig*) that's another kettle of fish

'paio *etc vb vedi* **parere**

pai'olo, paiu'olo *sm* (copper) pot

'Pakistan *sm*: **il ~** Pakistan

pakis'tano, -a *ag, sm/f* = **pachistano**

pal. *abbr* = **palude**

'pala *sf* shovel; (*di remo, ventilatore, elica*) blade; (*di ruota*) paddle

palan'drana *sf* (*scherzoso: abito lungo e largo*) tent

pa'lata *sf* shovelful; **fare soldi a palate** to make a mint

pala'tale *ag* (*Anat, Ling*) palatal

pa'lato *sm* palate

pa'lazzo [pa'lattso] *sm* (*reggia*) palace; (*edificio*) building; **~ di giustizia** courthouse; **~ dello sport** sports stadium; *see note*

PALAZZI

Several of the Roman *palazzi* now have political functions. The sixteenth-century *Palazzo Chigi*, in Piazza Colonna, was acquired by the state in 1919 and became the seat of the Ministry of Foreign Affairs; since 1961 it has housed the Prime Minister's office and hosted Cabinet meetings. *Palazzo Madama*, another sixteenth-century building which was originally built for the Medici family, has been the home of the Senate since 1871. *Palazzo di Montecitorio*, completed in 1694, has housed the "Camera dei deputati" since 1870.

pal'chetto [pal'ketto] *sm* shelf

'palco, -chi *sm* (*Teat*) box; (*tavolato*) platform, stand; (*ripiano*) layer

palco'scenico, -ci [palkoʃ'ʃɛniko] *sm* (*Teat*) stage

palermi'tano, -a *ag* of (*o* from) Palermo ■ *sm/f* person from Palermo

Pa'lermo *sf* Palermo

pale'sare *vt* to reveal, disclose; **palesarsi** *vr* to reveal *o* show o.s.

pa'lese *ag* clear, evident

Pales'tina *sf*: **la ~** Palestine

palesti'nese *ag, sm/f* Palestinian

pa'lestra *sf* gymnasium; (*esercizio atletico*) exercise, training; (*fig*) training ground, school

paletot [pal'to] *sm inv* overcoat

pa'letta *sf* spade; (*per il focolare*) shovel; (*del capostazione*) signalling disc

pa'letto *sm* stake, peg; (*spranga*) bolt

palin'sesto *sm* (*Storia*) palimpsest; (*TV, Radio*) programme (*Brit*) *o* program (*US*) schedule

'palio *sm* (*gara*): **il P~** *horse race run at Siena*; **mettere qc in ~** to offer sth as a prize; *see note*

PALIO

The *Palio* is a horse race which takes place in a number of Italian towns, the most famous being the "Palio di Siena". The Tuscan race dates back to the thirteenth century; nowadays it is usually held twice a year, on 2 July and 16 August, in the Piazza del Campo. 10 of the 17 city districts or "contrade" take part; the winner is the first horse to complete the course, whether or not it still has its rider. The race is preceded by a procession of "contrada" members in historical dress.

palis'sandro *sm* rosewood

paliz'zata [palit'tsata] *sf* palisade

'palla *sf* ball; (*pallottola*) bullet; **prendere** (*fig*) to seize one's opportunity

pallaca'nestro *sf* basketball
pallanu'oto *sf* water polo
palla'volo *sf* volleyball
palleggi'are [palled'dʒare] *vi* (*Calcio*) to practise (*Brit*) *o* practice (*US*) with the ball; (*Tennis*) to knock up
pallia'tivo *sm* palliative; (*fig*) stopgap measure
'pallido, -a *ag* pale
pal'lina *sf* (*bilia*) marble
pal'lino *sm* (*Biliardo*) cue ball; (*Bocce*) jack; (*proiettile*) pellet; (*pois*) dot; **bianco a pallini blu** white with blue dots; **avere il ~ di** (*fig*) to be crazy about
pallon'cino [pallon'tʃino] *sm* balloon; (*lampioncino*) Chinese lantern
pal'lone *sm* (*palla*) ball; (*Calcio*) football; (*aerostato*) balloon; **gioco del ~** ball game
pal'lore *sm* pallor, paleness
pal'lottola *sf* pellet; (*proiettile*) bullet
'palma *sf* (*Anat*) = **palmo**; (*Bot*) palm; **~ da datteri** date palm
pal'mato, -a *ag* (*Zool: piede*) webbed; (*Bot*) palmate
pal'mipede *ag* web-footed
pal'mizio [pal'mittsjo] *sm* (*palma*) palm tree; (*ramo*) palm
'palmo *sm* (*Anat*) palm; **essere alto un ~** (*fig*) to be tiny; **restare con un ~ di naso** (*fig*) to be badly disappointed
'palo *sm* (*legno appuntito*) stake; (*sostegno*) pole; **fare da** *o* **il ~** (*fig*) to act as look-out; **saltare di ~ in frasca** (*fig*) to jump from one topic to another
palom'baro *sm* diver
pa'lombo *sm* (*pesce*) dogfish
pal'pare *vt* to feel, finger
'palpebra *sf* eyelid
palpi'tare *vi* (*cuore, polso*) to beat; (*più forte*) to pound, throb; (*fremere*) to quiver
palpitazi'one [palpitat'tsjone] *sf* palpitation
'palpito *sm* (*del cuore*) beat; (*fig: d'amore etc*) throb
paltò *sm inv* overcoat
pa'lude *sf* marsh, swamp
palu'doso, -a *ag* marshy, swampy
pa'lustre *ag* marsh *cpd*, swamp *cpd*
'pampino *sm* vine leaf
pana'cea [pana'tʃɛa] *sf* panacea
'Panama *sf* Panama; **il canale di ~** the Panama Canal
pana'mense *ag, sm/f* Panamanian
'panca, -che *sf* bench
pancarrè *sm* sliced bread
pan'cetta [pan'tʃetta] *sf* (*Cuc*) bacon
pan'chetto [pan'ketto] *sm* stool; footstool
pan'china [pan'kina] *sf* garden seat; (*di giardino pubblico*) (park) bench
'pancia, -ce ['pantʃa] *sf* belly, stomach; **mettere** *o* **fare ~** to be getting a paunch; **avere mal di ~** to have stomach ache *o* a sore stomach
panci'era [pan'tʃɛra] *sf* corset
panci'olle [pan'tʃɔlle] *av*: **stare in ~** to lounge about (*Brit*) *o* around
panci'otto [pan'tʃɔtto] *sm* waistcoat
pan'ciuto, -a [pan'tʃuto] *ag* (*persona*) potbellied; (*vaso, bottiglia*) rounded
'pancreas *sm inv* pancreas
'panda *sm inv* panda
pande'mia *sf* pandemic
pande'monio *sm* pandemonium
pan'doro *sm* *type of sponge cake eaten at Christmas*
'pane *sm* bread; (*pagnotta*) loaf (of bread); (*forma*): **un ~ di burro/cera** *etc* a pat of butter/bar of wax *etc*; **guadagnarsi il ~** to earn one's living; **dire ~ al ~, vino al vino** (*fig*) to call a spade a spade; **rendere pan per focaccia** (*fig*) to give tit for tat; **~ casereccio** homemade bread; **~ a cassetta** sliced bread; **~ integrale** wholemeal bread; **~ di segale** rye bread; **pan di Spagna** sponge cake; **~ tostato** toast
pane'girico [pane'dʒiriko] *sm* (*fig*) panegyric
panette'ria *sf* (*forno*) bakery; (*negozio*) baker's (shop), bakery
panetti'ere, -a *sm/f* baker
panet'tone *sm* *a kind of spiced brioche with sultanas (eaten at Christmas)*
'panfilo *sm* yacht
pan'forte *sm* *Sienese nougat-type delicacy*
pangrat'tato *sm* breadcrumbs *pl*
'panico, -a, ci, che *ag, sm* panic; **essere in preda al ~** to be panic-stricken; **lasciarsi prendere dal ~** to panic
pani'ere *sm* basket
panifica'tore, -'trice *sm/f* bread-maker, baker
pani'ficio [pani'fitʃo] *sm* (*forno*) bakery; (*negozio*) baker's (shop), bakery
pa'nino *sm* roll; **~ imbottito** filled roll; sandwich
panino'teca, -che *sf* sandwich bar
'panna *sf* (*Cuc*) cream; (*Aut*) = **panne**; **~ di cucina** cooking cream; **~ montata** whipped cream
'panne [pan] *sf inv* (*Aut*) breakdown; **essere in ~** to have broken down
pan'nello *sm* panel; **~ di controllo** control panel; **~ solare** solar panel
'panno *sm* cloth; **panni** *smpl* (*abiti*) clothes; **mettiti nei miei panni** (*fig*) put yourself in my shoes
pan'nocchia [pan'nɔkkja] *sf* (*di mais etc*) ear
panno'lino *sm* (*per bambini*) nappy (*Brit*), diaper (*US*)

panno'lone *sm* incontinence pad
pano'rama, -i *sm* panorama
pano'ramico, -a, ci, che *ag* panoramic; **strada panoramica** scenic route
pantacol'lant *smpl* leggings
panta'loni *smpl* trousers (*Brit*), pants (*US*), pair *sg* of trousers *o* pants
pan'tano *sm* bog
pan'tera *sf* panther
'pantheon ['panteon] *sm inv* pantheon
pan'tofola *sf* slipper
panto'mima *sf* pantomime
pan'zana [pan'tsana] *sf* fib, tall story
pao'nazzo, -a [pao'nattso] *ag* purple
'papa, -i *sm* pope
papà *sm inv* dad(dy); **figlio di ~** spoilt young man
pa'pale *ag* papal
pa'pato *sm* papacy
pa'pavero *sm* poppy
'papero, -a *sm/f* (*Zool*) gosling ■ *sf* (*fig*) slip of the tongue, blunder
papil'lon [papi'jɔ̃] *sm inv* bow tie
pa'piro *sm* papyrus
'pappa *sf* baby cereal
pappa'gallo *sm* parrot; (*fig*: *uomo*) Romeo
pappa'gorgia, -ge [pappa'gɔrdʒa] *sf* double chin
pappar'della *sf* (*fig*) rigmarole
pap'pare *vt* (*fam*: *anche*: **papparsi**) to gobble up
par. *abbr* (= *paragrafo*) par
'para *sf*: **suole di ~** crepe soles
parà *abbr m inv* (= *paracadutista*) para
pa'rabola *sf* (*Mat*) parabola; (*Rel*) parable
para'bolico, -a, ci, che *ag* (*Mat*) parabolic; *vedi anche* **antenna**
para'brezza [para'breddza] *sm inv* (*Aut*) windscreen (*Brit*), windshield (*US*)
paracadu'tare *vt*, **paracadu'tarsi** *vr* to parachute
paraca'dute *sm inv* parachute
paracadu'tismo *sm* parachuting
paracadu'tista, -i, e *sm/f* parachutist; (*Mil*) paratrooper
para'carro *sm* kerbstone (*Brit*), curbstone (*US*)
paradi'siaco, -a, ci, che *ag* heavenly
para'diso *sm* paradise; **~ fiscale** tax haven
parados'sale *ag* paradoxical
para'dosso *sm* paradox
para'fango, -ghi *sm* mudguard
paraf'fina *sf* paraffin, paraffin wax
parafra'sare *vt* to paraphrase
pa'rafrasi *sf inv* paraphrase
para'fulmine *sm* lightning conductor
pa'raggi [pa'raddʒi] *smpl*: **nei ~** in the vicinity, in the neighbourhood (*Brit*) *o* neighborhood (*US*)
parago'nare *vt*: **~ con/a** to compare with/to
para'gone *sm* comparison; (*esempio analogo*) analogy, parallel; **reggere al ~** to stand comparison
pa'ragrafo *sm* paragraph
paraguai'ano, -a *ag, sm/f* Paraguayan
Paragu'ay [para'gwai] *sm*: **il ~** Paraguay
pa'ralisi *sf inv* paralysis
para'litico, -a, ci, che *ag, sm/f* paralytic
paraliz'zare [paralid'dzare] *vt* to paralyze
parallela'mente *av* in parallel
paralle'lismo *sm* (*Mat*) parallelism; (*fig*: *corrispondenza*) similarities *pl*
paral'lelo, -a *ag* parallel ■ *sm* (*Geo*) parallel; (*comparazione*): **fare un ~ tra** to draw a parallel between ■ *sf* parallel (line); **parallele** *sfpl* (*attrezzo ginnico*) parallel bars
para'lume *sm* lampshade
para'medico, -a, ci, che *ag* paramedical
para'menti *smpl* (*Rel*) vestments
pa'rametro *sm* parameter
paramili'tare *ag* paramilitary
pa'ranco, -chi *sm* hoist
para'noia *sf* paranoia; **andare/mandare in ~** (*fam*) to freak/be freaked out
para'noico, -a, ci, che *ag, sm/f* paranoid, (*fam*: *angosciato*) freaked (out)
paranor'male *ag* paranormal
para'occhi [para'ɔkki] *smpl* blinkers (*Brit*), blinders (*US*)
paraolim'piadi *sfpl* paralympics
para'petto *sm* parapet
para'piglia [para'piʎʎa] *sm* commotion
parapsicolo'gia [parapsikolo'dʒia] *sf* parapsychology
pa'rare *vt* (*addobbare*) to adorn, deck; (*proteggere*) to shield, protect; (*scansare*: *colpo*) to parry; (*Calcio*) to save ■ *vi*: **dove vuole andare a ~?** what are you driving at?; **pararsi** *vr* (*presentarsi*) to appear, present o.s.
parasco'lastico, -a, ci, che *ag* (*attività*) extracurricular
para'sole *sm inv* parasol, sunshade
paras'sita, -i *sm* parasite
parassi'tario, -a *ag* parasitic
parasta'tale *ag* state-controlled
paras'tato *sm* *employees in the state-controlled sector*
pa'rata *sf* (*Sport*) save; (*Mil*) review, parade
pa'rati *smpl* hangings *pl*; **carta da ~** wallpaper
para'tia *sf* (*di nave*) bulkhead
para'urti *sm inv* (*Aut*) bumper
para'vento *sm* folding screen; **fare da ~ a qn** (*fig*) to shield sb
par'cella [par'tʃɛlla] *sf* fee
parcheggi'are [parked'dʒare] *vt* to park

P

parcheggia'tore, -'trice [parkeddʒa'tore] *sm/f* parking attendant
par'cheggio [par'keddʒo] *sm* parking *no pl*; (*luogo*) car park (*Brit*), parking lot (*US*); (*singolo posto*) parking space
par'chimetro [par'kimetro] *sm* parking meter
'parco, -chi *sm* park; (*spazio per deposito*) depot; (*complesso di veicoli*) fleet
'parco, -a, chi, che *ag*: **~ (in)** (*sobrio*) moderate (in); (*avaro*) sparing (with)
par'cometro *sm* (*Aut*) (Pay and Display) ticket machine
pa'recchio, -a [pa'rekkjo] *det* quite a lot of; (*tempo*) quite a lot of, a long ■ *pron* quite a lot, quite a bit; (*tempo*) quite a while, a long time ■ *av* (*con ag*) quite, rather; (*con vb*) quite a lot, quite a bit; **parecchi, e** *det pl* quite a lot of, several ■ *pron pl* quite a lot, several
pareggi'are [pared'dʒare] *vt* to make equal; (*terreno*) to level, make level; (*bilancio, conti*) to balance ■ *vi* (*Sport*) to draw
pa'reggio [pa'reddʒo] *sm* (*Econ*) balance; (*Sport*) draw
paren'tado *sm* relatives *pl*, relations *pl*
pa'rente *sm/f* relative, relation
paren'tela *sf* (*vincolo di sangue: fig*) relationship; (*insieme dei parenti*) relations *pl*, relatives *pl*
pa'rentesi *sf* (*segno grafico*) bracket, parenthesis; (*frase incisa*) parenthesis; (*digressione*) parenthesis, digression; **tra ~** in brackets; (*fig*) incidentally
pa'rere *sm* (*opinione*) opinion; (*consiglio*) advice, opinion; **a mio ~** in my opinion ■ *vi* to seem, appear ■ *vb impers*: **pare che** it seems *o* appears that, they say that; **mi pare che** it seems to me that; **mi pare di sì/no** I think so/don't think so; **fai come ti pare** do as you like; **che ti pare del mio libro?** what do you think of my book?
pa'rete *sf* wall
'pargolo, -a *sm/f* child
'pari *ag inv* (*uguale*) equal, same; (*in giochi*) equal drawn, tied; (*Mat*) even ■ *sm inv* (*Pol: di Gran Bretagna*) peer ■ *sm/f inv* peer, equal; **copiato ~ ~** copied word for word; **siamo ~** (*fig*) we are quits *o* even; **alla ~** on the same level; (*Borsa*) at par; **ragazza alla ~** au pair (girl); **mettersi alla ~ con** to place o.s. on the same level as; **mettersi in ~ con** to catch up with; **andare di ~ passo con qn** to keep pace with sb
parifi'care *vt* (*scuola*) to recognize officially
parifi'cato, -a *ag*: **scuola parificata** *officially recognized private school*
Pa'rigi [pa'ridʒi] *sf* Paris
pari'gino, -a [pari'dʒino] *ag, sm/f* Parisian
pa'riglia [pa'riʎʎa] *sf* pair; **rendere la ~** to give tit for tat
parità *sf* parity, equality; (*Sport*) draw, tie
pari'tetico, -a, ci, che *ag*: **commissione paritetica** joint committee; **rapporto ~** equal relationship
parlamen'tare *ag* parliamentary ■ *sm/f* ≈ Member of Parliament (*Brit*), ≈ Congressman/woman (*US*) ■ *vi* to negotiate, parley
parla'mento *sm* parliament; *see note*

PARLAMENTO

The Italian constitution, which came into force on 1 January 1948, states that the *Parlamento* has legislative power. It is made up of two chambers, the "Camera dei deputati" and the "Senato". Parliamentary elections are held every 5 years.

parlan'tina *sf* (*fam*) talkativeness; **avere una buona ~** to have the gift of the gab
par'lare *vi* to speak, talk; (*confidare cose segrete*) to talk ■ *vt* to speak; **~ (a qn) di** to speak *o* talk (to sb) about; **~ chiaro** to speak one's mind; **~ male di qn/qc** to speak ill of sb/sth; **~ del più e del meno** to talk of this and that; **ne ho sentito ~** I have heard it mentioned; **non parliamone più** let's just forget about it; **i dati parlano** (*fig*) the facts speak for themselves
par'lata *sf* (*dialetto*) dialect
parla'tore, -'trice *sm/f* speaker
parla'torio *sm* (*di carcere etc*) visiting room; (*Rel*) parlour (*Brit*), parlor (*US*)
parlot'tare *vi* to mutter
parmigi'ano, -a [parmi'dʒano] *ag* Parma *cpd* of (*o* from) Parma ■ *sm* (*grana*) Parmesan (cheese); **alla parmigiana** (*Cuc*) with Parmesan cheese
paro'dia *sf* parody
parodi'are *vt* to parody
pa'rola *sf* word; (*facoltà*) speech; **parole** *sfpl* (*chiacchiere*) talk *sg*; **chiedere la ~** to ask permission to speak; **dare la ~ a qn** to call on sb to speak; **dare la propria ~ a qn** to give sb one's word; **mantenere la ~** to keep one's word; **mettere una buona ~ per qn** to put in a good word for sb; **passare dalle parole ai fatti** to get down to business; **prendere la ~** to take the floor; **rimanere senza parole** to be speechless; **rimangiarsi la ~** to go back on one's word; **non ho parole per ringraziarla** I don't know how to thank you; **rivolgere la ~ a qn** to speak to sb; **non è**

detta l'ultima ~ that's not the end of the matter; **è una persona di ~** he is a man of his word; **in parole povere** in plain English; **~ d'onore** word of honour; **~ d'ordine** (*Mil*) password; **parole incrociate** crossword (puzzle) *sg*

paro'laccia, -ce [paro'lattʃa] *sf* bad word, swearword

paros'sismo *sm* paroxysm

par'quet [par'kɛ] *sm* parquet (flooring)

parrò *etc vb vedi* **parere**

par'rocchia [par'rɔkkja] *sf* parish; (*chiesa*) parish church

parrocchi'ano, -a [parrok'kjano] *sm/f* parishioner

'parroco, -ci *sm* parish priest

par'rucca, -che *sf* wig

parrucchi'ere, -a [parruk'kjɛre] *sm/f* hairdresser ■ *sm* barber

parruc'cone *sm* (*peg*) old fogey

parsi'monia *sf* frugality, thrift

parsimoni'oso, -a *ag* frugal, thrifty

'parso, -a *pp di* **parere**

'parte *sf* part; (*lato*) side; (*quota spettante a ciascuno*) share; (*direzione*) direction; (*Pol*) party; faction; (*Dir*) party; **a ~** *ag* separate ■ *av* separately; **scherzi a ~** joking aside; **a ~ ciò** apart from that; **inviare a ~** (*campioni etc*) to send under separate cover; **da ~** (*in disparte*) to one side, aside; **mettere/prendere da ~** to put/take aside; **d'altra ~** on the other hand; **da ~ di** (*per conto di*) on behalf of; **da ~ mia** as far as I'm concerned, as for me; **da ~ di madre** on his (*o* her *etc*) mother's side; **essere dalla ~ della ragione** to be in the right; **da ~ a ~** right through; **da qualche ~** somewhere; **da nessuna ~** nowhere; **da questa ~** (*in questa direzione*) this way; **da ogni ~** on all sides, everywhere; (*moto da luogo*) from all sides; **fare ~ di qc** to belong to sth; **prendere ~ a qc** to take part in sth; **prendere le parti di qn** to take sb's side; **mettere qn a ~ di qc** to inform sb of sth; **costituirsi ~ civile contro qn** (*Dir*) to associate in an action with the public prosecutor against sb; **la ~ lesa** (*Dir*) the injured party; **le parti in causa** the parties concerned; **parti sociali** representatives of workers and employers

parteci'pante [partetʃi'pante] *sm/f*: **~ (a)** (*a riunione, dibattito*) participant (in); (*a gara sportiva*) competitor (in); (*a concorso*) entrant (to)

parteci'pare [partetʃi'pare] *vi*: **~ a** to take part in, participate in; (*utili etc*) to share in; (*spese etc*) to contribute to; (*dolore, successo di qn*) to share (in) ■ *vt*: **~ le nozze (a)** to announce one's wedding (to)

partecipazi'one [partetʃipat'tsjone] *sf* participation; sharing; (*Econ*) interest; **~ a banda armata** (*Dir*) belonging to an armed gang; **~ di maggioranza/minoranza** controlling/minority interest; **~ agli utili** profit-sharing; **partecipazioni di nozze** *wedding announcement card*; **ministro delle Partecipazioni statali** *minister responsible for companies in which the state has a financial interest*

par'tecipe [par'tetʃipe] *ag* participating; **essere ~ di** to take part in, participate in; (*gioia, dolore*) to share (in); (*consapevole*) to be aware of

parteggi'are [parted'dʒare] *vi*: **~ per** to side with, be on the side of

par'tenza [par'tɛntsa] *sf* departure; (*Sport*) start; **essere in ~** to be about to leave, be leaving; **passeggeri in ~ per** passengers travelling (*Brit*) *o* traveling (*US*) to; **siamo tornati al punto di ~** (*fig*) we are back where we started; **falsa ~** (*anche fig*) false start

parti'cella [parti'tʃɛlla] *sf* particle

parti'cipio [parti'tʃipjo] *sm* participle

partico'lare *ag* (*specifico*) particular; (*proprio*) personal, private; (*speciale*) special, particular; (*caratteristico*) distinctive; (*fuori dal comune*) peculiar ■ *sm* detail, particular; **in ~** in particular, particularly; **entrare nei particolari** to go into details

particolareggi'ato, -a [partikolared'dʒato] *ag* (extremely) detailed

particolarità *sf inv* (*carattere eccezionale*) peculiarity; (*dettaglio*) particularity, detail; (*caratteristica*) characteristic, feature

partigi'ano, -a [parti'dʒano] *ag* partisan ■ *sm* (*fautore*) supporter, champion; (*Mil*) partisan

par'tire *vi* to go, leave; (*allontanarsi*) to go (*o* drive *etc*) away *o* off; (*petardo, colpo*) to go off; (*fig: avere inizio, Sport*) to start; **sono partita da Roma alle 7** I left Rome at 7; **il volo parte da Ciampino** the flight leaves from Ciampino; **a ~ da** from; **la seconda a ~ da destra** the second from the right; **~ in quarta** to drive off at top speed; (*fig*) to be very enthusiastic

par'tita *sf* (*Comm*) lot, consignment; (*Econ: registrazione*) entry, item; (*Carte, Sport: gioco*) game; (*competizione*) match, game; **~ di caccia** hunting party; **~ IVA** VAT account; **~ semplice/doppia** (*Comm*) single-/double-entry book-keeping

par'tito *sm* (*Pol*) party; (*decisione*) decision, resolution; (*persona da maritare*) match; **per ~ preso** on principle; **mettere la testa a ~** to settle down

partitocra'zia [partitokrat'tsia] *sf hijacking of institutions by the party system*

P

parti'tura *sf* (*Mus*) score
'**parto** *sm* (*Med*) labour (*Brit*), labor (*US*); **sala ~** labo(u)r room; **morire di ~** to die in childbirth
partori'ente *sf* woman in labour (*Brit*) *o* labor (*US*)
parto'rire *vt* to give birth to; (*fig*) to produce
par'venza [par'vɛntsa] *sf* semblance
'**parvi** *etc vb vedi* **parere**
parzi'ale [par'tsjale] *ag* (*limitato*) partial; (*non obiettivo*) biased, partial
parzialità [partsjali'ta] *sf*: **~ a favore di** partiality (for), bias (towards); **~ contro** bias (against)
'**pascere** ['paʃʃere] *vi* to graze ■ *vt* (*brucare*) to graze on; (*far pascolare*) to graze, pasture
pasci'uto, -a [paʃʃuto] *pp di* **pascere** ■ *ag*: **ben ~** plump
pasco'lare *vt, vi* to graze
'**pascolo** *sm* pasture
'**Pasqua** *sf* Easter; **isola di ~** Easter Island
pas'quale *ag* Easter *cpd*
pasqu'etta *sf* Easter Monday
pas'sabile *ag* fairly good, passable
pas'saggio [pas'saddʒo] *sm* passing *no pl*, passage; (*traversata*) crossing *no pl*, passage; (*luogo, prezzo della traversata, brano di libro etc*) passage; (*su veicolo altrui*) lift (*Brit*), ride; (*Sport*) pass; **di ~** (*persona*) passing through; **~ pedonale/a livello** pedestrian/level (*Brit*) *o* grade (*US*) crossing; **~ di proprietà** transfer of ownership
passamane'ria *sf* braid, trimming
passamon'tagna [passamon'taɲɲa] *sm inv* balaclava
pas'sante *sm/f* passer-by ■ *sm* loop
passa'porto *sm* passport
pas'sare *vi* (*andare*) to go; (*veicolo, pedone*) to pass (by), go by; (*fare una breve sosta: postino etc*) to come, call; (*amico: per fare una visita*) to call *o* drop in; (*sole, aria, luce*) to get through; (*trascorrere: giorni, tempo*) to pass, go by; (*fig: proposta di legge*) to be passed; (*dolore*) to pass, go away; (*Carte*) to pass ■ *vt* (*attraversare*) to cross; (*trasmettere: messaggio*): **~ qc a qn** to pass sth on to sb; (*dare*): **~ qc a qn** to pass sth to sb, give sb sth; (*trascorrere: tempo*) to spend; (*superare: esame*) to pass; (*triturare: verdura*) to strain; (*approvare*) to pass, approve; (*oltrepassare, sorpassare: anche fig*) to go beyond, pass; (*fig: subire*) to go through; **~ da ... a** to pass from ... to; **~ di padre in figlio** to be handed down *o* to pass from father to son; **~ per** (*anche fig*) to go through; **~ per stupido/un genio** to be taken for a fool/a genius; **~ sopra** (*anche fig*) to pass over; **~ attraverso** (*anche fig*) to go through; **~ ad altro** to change the subject; (*in una riunione*) to discuss the next item; **~ in banca/ufficio** to call (in) at the bank/office; **~ alla storia** to pass into history; **~ a un esame** to go up (to the next class) after an exam; **~ di moda** to go out of fashion; **~ a prendere qc/qn** to call and pick sth/sb up; **le passo il Signor X** (*al telefono*) here is Mr X, I'm putting you through to Mr X; **farsi ~ per** to pass o.s. off as, pretend to be; **lasciar ~ qn/qc** to let sb/sth through; **col ~ degli anni** (*riferito al presente*) as time goes by; (*riferito al passato*) as time passed *o* went by; **il peggio è passato** the worst is over; **30 anni e passa** well over 30 years ago; **~ una mano di vernice su qc** to give sth a coat of paint; **passarsela**: **come te la passi?** how are you getting on *o* along?
pas'sata *sf*: **dare una ~ di vernice a qc** to give sth a coat of paint; **dare una ~ al giornale** to have a look at the paper, skim through the paper
passa'tempo *sm* pastime, hobby
pas'sato, -a *ag* (*scorso*) last; (*finito: gloria, generazioni*) past; (*usanze*) out of date; (*sfiorito*) faded ■ *sm* past; (*Ling*) past (tense); **l'anno ~** last year; **nel corso degli anni passati** over the past years; **nei tempi passati** in the past; **sono le 8 passate** it's past *o* after 8 o'clock; **è acqua passata** (*fig*) it's over and done with; **~ prossimo** (*Ling*) present perfect; **~ remoto** (*Ling*) past historic; **~ di verdura** (*Cuc*) vegetable purée
passa'tutto *sm inv*, **passaver'dura** *sm inv* vegetable mill
passeg'gero, -a [passed'dʒɛro] *ag* passing ■ *sm/f* passenger
passeggi'are [passed'dʒare] *vi* to go for a walk; (*in veicolo*) to go for a drive
passeggi'ata [passed'dʒata] *sf* walk; drive; (*luogo*) promenade; **fare una ~** to go for a walk (*o* drive)
passeg'gino [passed'dʒino] *sm* pushchair (*Brit*), stroller (*US*)
pas'seggio [pas'seddʒo] *sm* walk, stroll; (*luogo*) promenade; **andare a ~** to go for a walk *o* a stroll
passe'rella *sf* footbridge; (*di nave, aereo*) gangway; (*pedana*) catwalk
'**passero** *sm* sparrow
pas'sibile *ag*: **~ di** liable to
passio'nale *ag* (*temperamento*) passionate; **delitto ~** crime of passion
passi'one *sf* passion
passività *sf* (*qualità*) passivity, passiveness; (*Comm*) liability
pas'sivo, -a *ag* passive ■ *sm* (*Ling*) passive; (*Econ*) debit; (*complesso dei debiti*) liabilities *pl*

ˈ**passo** *sm* step; (*andatura*) pace; (*rumore*) (foot)step; (*orma*) footprint; (*passaggio*: *fig*: *brano*) passage; (*valico*) pass; **a ~ d'uomo** at walking pace; (*Aut*) dead slow; **~ (a) ~** step by step; **fare due** *o* **quattro passi** to go for a walk *o* a stroll; **andare al ~ coi tempi** to keep up with the times; **di questo ~** (*fig*) at this rate; **fare i primi passi** (*anche fig*) to take one's first steps; **fare il gran ~** (*fig*) to take the plunge; **fare un ~ falso** (*fig*) to make the wrong move; **tornare sui propri passi** to retrace one's steps; **"~ carraio"** "vehicle entrance — keep clear"

ˈ**pasta** *sf* (*Cuc*) dough; (*impasto per dolce*) pastry; (*anche*: **pasta alimentare**) pasta; (*massa molle di materia*) paste; (*fig*: *indole*) nature; **paste** *sfpl* (*pasticcini*) pastries; **~ in brodo** noodle soup; **~ sfoglia** puff pastry *o* paste (US)

pastasciˈutta [pastaʃˈʃutta] *sf* pasta

pasteggiˈare [pastedˈdʒare] *vi*: **~ a vino/ champagne** to have wine/champagne with one's meal

pasˈtella *sf* batter

pasˈtello *sm* pastel

pasˈtetta *sf* (*Cuc*) = **pastella**

pasˈticca, -che *sf* = **pastiglia**

pasticceˈria [pastittʃeˈria] *sf* (*pasticcini*) pastries *pl*, cakes *pl*; (*negozio*) cake shop; (*arte*) confectionery

pasticciˈare [pastitˈtʃare] *vt* to mess up, make a mess of ■ *vi* to make a mess

pasticciˈere, -a [pastitˈtʃɛre] *sm/f* pastrycook confectioner

pasticˈcino [pastitˈtʃino] *sm* petit four

pasˈticcio [pasˈtittʃo] *sm* (*Cuc*) pie; (*lavoro disordinato, imbroglio*) mess; **trovarsi nei pasticci** to get into trouble

pastiˈficio [pastiˈfitʃo] *sm* pasta factory

pasˈtiglia [pasˈtiʎʎa] *sf* pastille, lozenge

pasˈtina *sf small pasta shapes used in soup*

pastiˈnaca, -che *sf* parsnip

ˈ**pasto** *sm* meal; **vino da ~** table wine

pasˈtoia *sf* (*fig*): **~ burocratica** red tape

pasˈtone *sm* (*per animali*) mash; (*peg*) overcooked stodge

pastoˈrale *ag* pastoral

pasˈtore *sm* shepherd; (*Rel*) pastor, minister; (*anche*: **cane pastore**) sheepdog; **~ scozzese** (*Zool*) collie; **~ tedesco** (*Zool*) Alsatian (dog) (*Brit*) German shepherd (dog)

pastoˈrizia [pastoˈrittsja] *sf* sheep-rearing, sheep farming

pastorizˈzare [pastoridˈdzare] *vt* to pasteurize

pasˈtoso, -a *ag* doughy; pasty; (*fig*: *voce, colore*) mellow, soft

pasˈtrano *sm* greatcoat

paˈtacca, -che *sf* (*distintivo*) medal, decoration; (*fig*: *macchia*) grease spot, grease mark; (*articolo scadente*) bit of rubbish

paˈtata *sf* potato; **patate fritte** chips (*Brit*), French fries

pataˈtine *sfpl* (potato) crisps (*Brit*) *o* chips (*US*)

pataˈtrac *sm* (*crollo*: *anche fig*) crash

pâté [paˈte] *sm inv* pâté; **~ di fegato d'oca** pâté de foie gras

paˈtella *sf* (*Zool*) limpet

paˈtema, -i *sm* anxiety, worry

patenˈtato, -a *ag* (*munito di patente*) licensed, certified; (*fig scherzoso*: *qualificato*) utter, thorough

paˈtente *sf* licence (*Brit*), license (*US*); (*anche*: **patente di guida**) driving licence (*Brit*), driver's license (*US*); **~ a punti** *driving licence with penalty points*

patenˈtino *sm* temporary licence (*Brit*) *o* license (*US*)

paternaˈlismo *sm* paternalism

paternaˈlista *sm* paternalist

paternaˈlistico, -a, ci, che *ag* paternalistic

paternità *sf* paternity, fatherhood

paˈterno, -a *ag* (*affetto, consigli*) fatherly; (*casa, autorità*) paternal

paˈtetico, -a, ci, che *ag* pathetic; (*commovente*) moving, touching

ˈ**pathos** [ˈpatos] *sm* pathos

paˈtibolo *sm* gallows *sg*, scaffold

patiˈmento *sm* suffering

ˈ**patina** *sf* (*su rame etc*) patina; (*sulla lingua*) fur, coating

paˈtire *vt, vi* to suffer

paˈtito, -a *sm/f* enthusiast, fan, lover

patoloˈgia [patoloˈdʒia] *sf* pathology

patoˈlogico, -a, ci, che [patoˈlɔdʒiko] *ag* pathological

paˈtologo, -a, gi, ghe *sm/f* pathologist

ˈ**patria** *sf* homeland; **amor di ~** patriotism

patriˈarca, -chi *sm* patriarch

paˈtrigno [paˈtriɲɲo] *sm* stepfather

patrimoniˈale *ag* (*rendita*) from property ■ *sf* (*anche*: **imposta patrimoniale**) property tax

patriˈmonio *sm* estate, property; (*fig*) heritage; **mi è costato un ~** (*fig*) it cost me a fortune, I paid a fortune for it; **~ spirituale/ culturale** spiritual/cultural heritage; **~ ereditario** (*fig*) hereditary characteristics *pl*; **~ pubblico** public property

ˈ**patrio, -a, ii, ie** *ag* (*di patria*) native *cpd*, of one's country; (*Dir*): **patria potestà** parental authority; **amor ~** love of one's country

patriˈota, -i, e *sm/f* patriot

patriˈottico, -a, ci, che *ag* patriotic

patriotˈtismo *sm* patriotism

P

patroci'nare [patrotʃi'nare] *vt* (*Dir: difendere*) to defend; (*sostenere*) to sponsor, support
patro'cinio [patro'tʃinjo] *sm* defence (*Brit*), defense (*US*); support, sponsorship
patro'nato *sm* patronage; (*istituzione benefica*) charitable institution *o* society
pa'trono *sm* (*Rel*) patron saint; (*socio di patronato*) patron; (*Dir*) counsel
'patta *sf* flap; (*dei pantaloni*) fly
patteggia'mento [patteddʒa'mento] *sm* (*Dir*) plea bargaining
patteggi'are [patted'dʒare] *vt, vi* to negotiate
patti'naggio [patti'naddʒo] *sm* skating
patti'nare *vi* to skate; **~ sul ghiaccio** to ice-skate
pattina'tore, -'trice *sm/f* skater
'pattino *sm* skate; (*di slitta*) runner; (*Aer*) skid; (*Tecn*) sliding block; **pattini (da ghiaccio)** (ice) skates; **pattini in linea** rollerblades; **pattini a rotelle** roller skates
pat'tino *sm* (*barca*) *kind of pedalo with oars*
pat'tista, -i, e *ag* (*Pol*) of Patto per l'Italia ■ *sm/f* (*Pol*) member (*o* supporter) of Patto per l'Italia
'patto *sm* (*accordo*) pact, agreement; (*condizione*) term, condition; **a ~ che** on condition that; **a nessun ~** under no circumstances; **venire** *o* **scendere a patti (con)** to come to an agreement (with); **P~ per l'Italia** (*Pol*) *centrist party*
pat'tuglia [pat'tuʎʎa] *sf* (*Mil*) patrol
pattugli'are [pattuʎ'ʎare] *vt* to patrol
pattu'ire *vt* to reach an agreement on
pattumi'era *sf* (dust)bin (*Brit*), ashcan (*US*)
pa'ura *sf* fear; **aver ~ di/di fare/che** to be frightened *o* afraid of/of doing/that; **far ~ a** to frighten; **per ~ di/che** for fear of/that; **ho ~ di sì/no** I am afraid so/not
pau'roso, -a *ag* (*che fa paura*) frightening; (*che ha paura*) fearful, timorous
'pausa *sf* (*sosta*) break; (*nel parlare, Mus*) pause
paven'tato, -a *ag* much-feared
pa'vese *ag* of (*o* from) Pavia
'pavido, -a *ag* (*letterario*) fearful
pavimen'tare *vt* (*stanza*) to floor; (*strada*) to pave
pavimentazi'one [pavimentat'tsjone] *sf* flooring; paving
pavi'mento *sm* floor
pa'vone *sm* peacock
pavoneggi'arsi [pavoned'dʒarsi] *vr* to strut about, show off
pazien'tare [pattsjen'tare] *vi* to be patient
pazi'ente [pat'tsjɛnte] *ag, sm/f* patient
pazi'enza [pat'tsjɛntsa] *sf* patience; **perdere la ~** to lose (one's) patience
pazza'mente [pattsa'mente] *av* madly; **essere ~ innamorato** to be madly in love
paz'zesco, -a, schi, sche [pat'tsesko] *ag* mad, crazy
paz'zia [pat'tsia] *sf* (*Med*) madness, insanity; (*di azione, decisione*) madness, folly; **è stata una ~!** it was sheer madness!
'pazzo, -a ['pattso] *ag* (*Med*) mad, insane; (*strano*) wild, mad ■ *sm/f* madman/woman; **~ di** (*gioia, amore etc*) mad *o* crazy with; **~ per qc/qn** mad *o* crazy about sth/sb; **essere ~ da legare** to be raving mad *o* a raving lunatic
PC *sigla* = **Piacenza** ■ *sigla m inv* [pi'tʃi] (= *personal computer*) PC
p.c. *abbr* = **per condoglianze; per conoscenza**
p.c.c. *abbr* (= *per copia conforme*) cc
P.C.I. *sigla m* (= *Partito Comunista Italiano*) *former political party*
PCUS *sigla m* = **Partito Comunista dell'Unione Sovietica**
PD *sigla* = **Padova**
P.D . *abbr* = **partita doppia**
PE *sigla* = **Pescara**
'pecca, -che *sf* defect, flaw, fault
peccami'noso, -a *ag* sinful
pec'care *vi* to sin; (*fig*) to err
pec'cato *sm* sin; **è un ~ che** it's a pity that; **che ~!** what a shame *o* pity!; **un ~ di gioventù** (*fig*) a youthful error *o* indiscretion
pecca'tore, -'trice *sm/f* sinner
peccherò *etc* [pekke'rɔ] *vb vedi* **peccare**
'pece ['petʃe] *sf* pitch
pechi'nese [peki'nese] *ag, sm/f* Pekin(g)ese *inv* ■ *sm* (*anche*: **cane pechinese**) Pekin(g)ese *inv*, Peke
Pe'chino [pe'kino] *sf* Beijing, Peking
'pecora *sf* sheep; **~ nera** (*fig*) black sheep
peco'raio *sm* shepherd
peco'rella *sf* lamb; **la ~ smarrita** the lost sheep; **cielo a pecorelle** (*fig: nuvole*) mackerel sky
peco'rino *sm* sheep's milk cheese
pecu'lato *sm* (*Dir*) embezzlement
peculi'are *ag*: **~ di** peculiar to
peculiarità *sf* peculiarity
pecuni'ario, -a *ag* financial, money *cpd*
pe'daggio [pe'daddʒo] *sm* toll
pedago'gia [pedago'dʒia] *sf* pedagogy, educational methods *pl*
peda'gogico, -a, ci, che [peda'gɔdʒiko] *ag* pedagogic(al)
peda'gogo, -a, ghi, ghe *sm/f* pedagogue
peda'lare *vi* to pedal; (*andare in bicicletta*) to cycle
pe'dale *sm* pedal
pe'dana *sf* footboard; (*Sport: nel salto*) springboard; (*: nella scherma*) piste
pe'dante *ag* pedantic ■ *sm/f* pedant
pedante'ria *sf* pedantry

pe'data *sf (impronta)* footprint; *(colpo)* kick; **prendere a pedate qn/qc** to kick sb/sth
pede'rasta, -i *sm* pederast
pe'destre *ag* prosaic, pedestrian
pedi'atra, -i, e *sm/f* paediatrician *(Brit)* pediatrician *(US)*
pedia'tria *sf* paediatrics *sg (Brit)*, pediatrics *sg (US)*
pedi'atrico, -a, ci, che *ag* pediatric
pedi'cure *sm/f inv* chiropodist *(Brit)*, podiatrist *(US)*
pedigree *sm inv* pedigree
pedi'luvio *sm* footbath
pe'dina *sf (della dama)* draughtsman *(Brit)*, draftsman *(US)*; *(fig)* pawn
pedi'nare *vt* to shadow, tail
pe'dofilo, -a *ag, sm/f* paedophile
pedo'nale *ag* pedestrian
pe'done, -a *sm/f* pedestrian ■ *sm (Scacchi)* pawn
peeling ['piling] *sm inv (Cosmesi)* facial scrub
'peggio ['pɛddʒo] *av, ag inv* worse ■ *sm o f*: **il** *o* **la ~** the worst; **cambiare in ~** to get *o* become worse; **alla ~** at worst, if the worst comes to the worst; **tirare avanti alla meno ~** to get along as best one can; **avere la ~** to come off worse, get the worst of it
peggiora'mento [peddʒora'mento] *sm* worsening
peggio'rare [peddʒo'rare] *vt* to make worse, worsen ■ *vi* to grow worse, worsen
peggiora'tivo, -a [peddʒora'tivo] *ag* pejorative
peggi'ore [ped'dʒore] *ag (comparativo)* worse; *(superlativo)* worst ■ *sm/f*: **il(la) ~** the worst (person); **nel ~ dei casi** if the worst comes to the worst
'pegno ['peɲɲo] *sm (Dir)* security, pledge; *(nei giochi di società)* forfeit; *(fig)* pledge, token; **dare in ~ qc** to pawn sth; **in ~ d'amicizia** as a token of friendship; **banco dei pegni** pawnshop
pelapa'tate *sm inv* potato peeler
pe'lare *vt (spennare)* to pluck; *(spellare)* to skin; *(sbucciare)* to peel; *(fig)* to make pay through the nose; **pelarsi** *vr* to go bald
pe'lato, -a *ag (sbucciato)* peeled; *(calvo)* bald; **(pomodori) pelati** peeled tomatoes
pel'lame *sm* skins *pl*, hides *pl*
'pelle *sf* skin; *(di animale)* skin, hide; *(cuoio)* leather; **essere ~ ed ossa** to be skin and bone; **avere la ~ d'oca** to have goose pimples *o* goose flesh; **avere i nervi a fior di ~** to be edgy; **non stare più nella ~ dalla gioia** to be beside o.s. with delight; **lasciarci la ~** to lose one's life; **amici per la ~** firm *o* close friends
pellegri'naggio [pellegri'naddʒo] *sm* pilgrimage
pelle'grino, -a *sm/f* pilgrim
pelle'rossa *(pl* **pellirosse***)* *sm/f* Red Indian
pellette'ria *sf (articoli)* leather goods *pl*; *(negozio)* leather goods shop
pelli'cano *sm* pelican
pellicce'ria [pellittʃe'ria] *sf (negozio)* furrier's (shop); *(quantità di pellicce)* furs *pl*
pel'liccia, -ce [pel'littʃa] *sf (mantello di animale)* coat, fur; *(indumento)* fur coat; **~ ecologica** fake fur
pellicci'aio [pellit'tʃajo] *sm* furrier
pel'licola *sf (membrana sottile)* film, layer; *(Fot, Cine)* film
pelli'rossa *sm/f* = **pellerossa**
'pelo *sm* hair; *(pelame)* coat, hair; *(pelliccia)* fur; *(di tappeto)* pile; *(di liquido)* surface; **per un ~**: **per un ~ non ho perduto il treno** I very nearly missed the train; **c'è mancato un ~ che affogasse** he narrowly escaped drowning; **cercare il ~ nell'uovo** *(fig)* to pick holes, split hairs; **non aver peli sulla lingua** *(fig)* to speak one's mind
pe'loso, -a *ag* hairy
'peltro *sm* pewter
pe'luche [pə'lyʃ] *sm* plush; **giocattoli di ~** soft toys
pe'luria *sf* down
'pelvi *sf inv* pelvis
'pelvico, -a, ci, che *ag* pelvic
'pena *sf (Dir)* sentence; *(punizione)* punishment; *(sofferenza)* sadness *no pl*, sorrow; *(fatica)* trouble *no pl*, effort; *(difficoltà)* difficulty; **far ~** to be pitiful; **mi fai ~** I feel sorry for you; **essere** *o* **stare in ~ (per qc/qn)** to worry *o* be anxious (about sth/sb); **prendersi** *o* **darsi la ~ di fare** to go to the trouble of doing; **vale la ~ farlo** it's worth doing, it's worth it; **non ne vale la ~** it's not worth the effort, it's not worth it; **~ di morte** death sentence; **~ pecuniaria** fine
pe'nale *ag* penal ■ *sf (anche*: **clausola penale***)* penalty clause; **causa ~** criminal trial; **diritto ~** criminal law; **pagare la ~** to pay the penalty
pena'lista, -i, e *sm/f (avvocato)* criminal lawyer
penalità *sf inv* penalty
penaliz'zare [penalid'dzare] *vt (Sport)* to penalize
penalizzazi'one [penaliddzat'tsjone] *sf (Sport)* penalty
pe'nare *vi (patire)* to suffer; *(faticare)* to struggle
pen'dente *ag* hanging; leaning ■ *sm (ciondolo)* pendant; *(orecchino)* drop earring

P

pen'denza [pen'dɛntsa] *sf* slope, slant; (*grado d'inclinazione*) gradient; (*Econ*) outstanding account
'pendere *vi* (*essere appeso*): **~ da** to hang from; (*essere inclinato*) to lean; (*fig: incombere*): **~ su** to hang over
pen'dice [pen'ditʃe] *sf* (*di monte*) slope
pen'dio, -ii *sm* slope, slant; (*luogo in pendenza*) slope
'pendola *sf* pendulum clock
pendo'lare *ag* pendulum *cpd*, pendular ■ *sm/f* commuter
pendola'rismo *sm* commuting
'pendolo *sm* (*peso*) pendulum; (*anche:* **orologio a pendolo**) pendulum clock
'pene *sm* penis
pene'trante *ag* piercing, penetrating
pene'trare *vi* to come *o* get in ■ *vt* to penetrate; **~ in** to enter; (*proiettile*) to penetrate; (*acqua, aria*) to go *o* come into
penetrazi'one [penetrat'tsjone] *sf* penetration
penicil'lina [penitʃil'lina] *sf* penicillin
peninsu'lare *ag* peninsular; **l'Italia ~** mainland Italy
pe'nisola *sf* peninsula
peni'tente *sm/f* penitent
peni'tenza [peni'tɛntsa] *sf* penitence; (*punizione*) penance
penitenzi'ario [peniten'tsjarjo] *sm* prison
'penna *sf* (*di uccello*) feather; (*per scrivere*) pen; **penne** *sfpl* (*Cuc*) quills (*type of pasta*); **~ a feltro/stilografica/a sfera** felt-tip/ fountain/ballpoint pen
pen'nacchio [pen'nakkjo] *sm* (*ornamento*) plume; **un ~ di fumo** (*fig*) a plume *o* spiral of smoke
penna'rello *sm* felt(-tip) pen
pennel'lare *vi* to paint
pennel'lata *sf* brushstroke
pen'nello *sm* brush; (*per dipingere*) (paint)brush; **a ~** (*perfettamente*) to perfection, perfectly; **~ per la barba** shaving brush
Pen'nini *smpl*: **i ~** the Pennines
pen'nino *sm* nib
pen'none *sm* (*Naut*) yard; (*stendardo*) banner, standard
pen'nuto *sm* bird
pe'nombra *sf* half-light, dim light
pe'noso, -a *ag* painful, distressing; (*faticoso*) tiring, laborious
pen'sare *vi* to think ■ *vt* to think; (*inventare, escogitare*) to think out; **~ a** to think of; (*amico, vacanze*) to think of *o* about; (*problema*) to think about; **~ di fare qc** to think of doing sth; **~ bene/male di qn** to think well/badly of sb, have a good/bad opinion of sb; **penso di sì** I think so; **penso di no** I don't think so; **a pensarci bene ...** on second thoughts (*Brit*) *o* thought (*US*) ...; **non voglio nemmeno pensarci** I don't even want to think about it; **ci penso io** I'll see to *o* take care of it
pen'sata *sf* (*trovata*) idea, thought
pensa'tore, -'trice *sm/f* thinker
pensie'rino *sm* (*dono*) little gift; (*pensiero*): **ci farò un ~** I'll think about it
pensi'ero *sm* thought; (*modo di pensare, dottrina*) thinking *no pl*; (*preoccupazione*) worry, care, trouble; **darsi ~ per qc** to worry about sth; **stare in ~ per qn** to be worried about sb; **un ~ gentile** (*anche fig: dono etc*) a kind thought
pensie'roso, -a *ag* thoughtful
'pensile *ag* hanging ■ *sm* (*in cucina*) wall cupboard
pensi'lina *sf* (*in stazione*) platform roof
pensiona'mento *sm* retirement; **~ anticipato** early retirement
pensio'nante *sm/f* (*presso una famiglia*) lodger; (*di albergo*) guest
pensio'nato, -a *sm/f* pensioner ■ *sm* (*istituto*) hostel
pensi'one *sf* (*al prestatore di lavoro*) pension; (*vitto e alloggio*) board and lodging; (*albergo*) boarding house; **andare in ~** to retire; **mezza ~** half board; **~ completa** full board; **~ d'invalidità** disablement pension; **~ per la vecchiaia** old-age pension
pensio'nistico, -a, ci, che *ag* pension *cpd*
pen'soso, -a *ag* thoughtful, pensive, lost in thought
pen'tagono *sm* pentagon; **il P~** the Pentagon
pentag'ramma, -i *sm* (*Mus*) staff, stave
pentapar'tito *sm* (*Pol*) five-party coalition government
'pentathlon ['pɛntatlon] *sm* (*Sport*) pentathlon
Pente'coste *sf* Pentecost, Whit Sunday (*Brit*)
penti'mento *sm* repentance, contrition
pen'tirsi *vr*: **~ di** to repent of; (*rammaricarsi*) to regret, be sorry for
penti'tismo *sm* *confessions from terrorists and members of organized crime rackets*; *see note*

PENTITISMO

The practice of *pentitismo* first emerged in Italy during the 1970s, a period marked by major terrorist activity. Once arrested, some members of terrorist groups would collaborate with the authorities by providing information in return for a reduced sentence, or indeed for their own reasons. In recent years it has become common practice for members of Mafia organizations to become "pentiti", and special legislation has had to be introduced to provide for the sentencing and personal protection of these informants.

pen'tito, -a *sm/f* ≈ supergrass (*Brit*), *terrorist/criminal who turns police informer*
'pentola *sf* pot; **~ a pressione** pressure cooker
pe'nultimo, -a *ag* last but one (*Brit*), next to last, penultimate
pe'nuria *sf* shortage
penzo'lare [pendzo'lare] *vi* to dangle, hang loosely
penzo'loni [pendzo'loni] *av* dangling, hanging down; **stare ~** to dangle, hang down
pe'pato, -a *ag* (*condito con pepe*) peppery, hot; (*fig: pungente*) sharp
'pepe *sm* pepper; **~ macinato/in grani/nero** ground/whole/black pepper
pepero'nata *sf stewed peppers, tomatoes and onions*
peperon'cino [peperon'tʃino] *sm* chilli pepper
pepe'rone *sm*: **~ (rosso)** red pepper, capsicum; **~ (verde)** green pepper, capsicum; **rosso come un ~** as red as a beetroot (*Brit*), fire-engine red (*US*); **peperoni ripieni** stuffed peppers
pe'pita *sf* nugget

 PAROLA CHIAVE

per *prep* **1** (*moto attraverso luogo*) through; **i ladri sono passati per la finestra** the thieves got in (*o* out) through the window; **l'ho cercato per tutta la casa** I've searched the whole house *o* all over the house for it
2 (*moto a luogo*) for, to; **partire per la Germania/il mare** to leave for Germany/the sea; **il treno per Roma** the Rome train, the train for *o* to Rome; **proseguire per Londra** to go on to London
3 (*stato in luogo*): **seduto/sdraiato per terra** sitting/lying on the ground
4 (*tempo*) for; **per anni/tanto tempo** for years/a long time; **per tutta l'estate** throughout the summer, all summer long; **lo rividi per Natale** I saw him again at Christmas; **lo faccio per lunedì** I'll do it for Monday
5 (*mezzo, maniera*) by; **per lettera/ferrovia/via aerea** by letter/rail/airmail; **prendere qn per un braccio** to take sb by the arm
6 (*causa, scopo*) for; **assente per malattia** absent because of *o* through *o* owing to illness; **ottimo per il mal di gola** excellent for sore throats; **per abitudine** out of habit, from habit
7 (*limitazione*) for; **è troppo difficile per lui** it's too difficult for him; **per quel che mi riguarda** as far as I'm concerned; **per poco che sia** however little it may be; **per questa volta ti perdono** I'll forgive you this time
8 (*prezzo, misura*) for; (*distributivo*) a, per; **venduto per 3 milioni** sold for 3 million; **la strada continua per 3 km** the street goes on for 3 km; **15 euro per persona** 15 euros a *o* per person; **uno per volta** one at a time; **uno per uno** one by one; **giorno per giorno** day by day; **due per parte** two either side; **5 per cento** 5 per cent; **3 per 4 fa 12** 3 times 4 equals 12; **dividere/moltiplicare 12 per 4** to divide/multiply 12 by 4
9 (*in qualità di*) as; (*al posto di*) for; **avere qn per professore** to have sb as a teacher; **ti ho preso per Mario** I mistook you for Mario, I thought you were Mario; **dare per morto qn** to give sb up for dead; **lo prenderanno per pazzo** they'll think he's crazy
10 (*seguito da vb: finale*): **per fare qc** (so as) to do sth, in order to do sth; (*causale*): **per aver fatto qc** for having done sth; **studia per passare l'esame** he's studying in order to *o* (so as) to pass his exam; **l'hanno punito per aver rubato i soldi** he was punished for having stolen the money; **è abbastanza grande per andarci da solo** he's big enough to go on his own

'pera *sf* pear
pe'raltro *av* moreover, what's more
per'bacco *escl* by Jove!
per'bene *ag inv* respectable, decent ■ *av* (*con cura*) properly, well
perbe'nismo *sm* (so-called) respectability
percentu'ale [pertʃentu'ale] *sf* percentage; (*commissione*) commission
perce'pire [pertʃe'pire] *vt* (*sentire*) to perceive; (*ricevere*) to receive
percet'tibile [pertʃet'tibile] *ag* perceptible
percezi'one [pertʃet'tsjone] *sf* perception

perché [per'ke] *av* why; **perché no?** why not?; **perché non vuoi andarci?** why don't you want to go?; **spiegami perché l'hai fatto** tell me why you did it
■ *cong* (*causale*) **1** because; **non posso uscire**

perché ho da fare I can't go out because *o* as I've a lot to do
2 (*finale*) in order that, so that; **te lo do perché tu lo legga** I'm giving it to you so (that) you can read it
3 (*consecutivo*): **è troppo forte perché si possa batterlo** he's too strong to be beaten ■ *sm inv* reason; **il perché di** the reason for; **non c'è un vero perché** there's no real reason for it

perciò [per'tʃɔ] *cong* so, for this (*o* that) reason
per'correre *vt* (*luogo*) to go all over; (*paese*) to travel up and down, go all over; (*distanza*) to cover
percor'ribile *ag* (*strada*) which can be followed
per'corso, -a *pp di* **percorrere** ■ *sm* (*tragitto*) journey; (*tratto*) route
per'cosso, -a *pp di* **percuotere** ■ *sf* blow
percu'otere *vt* to hit, strike
percussi'one *sf* percussion; **strumenti a ~** (*Mus*) percussion instruments
per'dente *ag* losing ■ *sm/f* loser
'perdere *vt* to lose; (*lasciarsi sfuggire*) to miss; (*sprecare: tempo, denaro*) to waste; (*mandare in rovina: persona*) to ruin ■ *vi* to lose; (*serbatoio etc*) to leak; **perdersi** *vr* (*smarrirsi*) to get lost; (*svanire*) to disappear, vanish; **saper ~** to be a good loser; **lascia ~!** forget it!, never mind!; **non ho niente da ~** (*fig*) I've got nothing to lose; **è un'occasione da non ~** it's a marvellous opportunity; (*affare*) it's a great bargain; **è fatica persa** it's a waste of effort; **~ al gioco** to lose money gambling; **~ di vista qn** (*anche fig*) to lose sight of sb; **perdersi di vista** to lose sight of each other; (*fig*) to lose touch; **perdersi alla vista** to disappear from sight; **perdersi in chiacchiere** to waste time talking
perdifi'ato; **a ~** *av* (*correre*) at breathtaking speed; (*gridare*) at the top of one's voice
perdigi'orno [perdi'dʒorno] *sm/f inv* idler, waster
'perdita *sf* loss; (*spreco*) waste; (*fuoriuscita*) leak; **siamo in ~** (*Comm*) we are running at a loss; **a ~ d'occhio** as far as the eye can see
perdi'tempo *sm/f inv* waster, idler
perdizi'one [perdit'tsjone] *sf* (*Rel*) perdition, damnation; **luogo di ~** place of ill repute
perdo'nare *vt* to pardon, forgive; (*scusare*) to excuse, pardon; **per farsi ~** in order to be forgiven; **perdona la domanda ...** if you don't mind my asking ...; **vogliate ~ il (mio) ritardo** my apologies for being late; **un male che non perdona** an incurable disease
per'dono *sm* forgiveness; (*Dir*) pardon; **chiedere ~ a qn (per)** to ask for sb's forgiveness (for); (*scusarsi*) to apologize to sb (for)
perdu'rare *vi* to go on, last; (*perseverare*) to persist
perduta'mente *av* desperately, passionately
per'duto, -a *pp di* **perdere** ■ *ag* (*gen*) lost; **sentirsi** *o* **vedersi ~** (*fig*) to realize the hopelessness of one's position; **una donna perduta** (*fig*) a fallen woman
peregri'nare *vi* to wander, roam
pe'renne *ag* eternal, perpetual, perennial; (*Bot*) perennial
peren'torio, -a *ag* peremptory; (*definitivo*) final
perfetta'mente *av* perfectly; **sai ~ che ...** you know perfectly well that ...
per'fetto, -a *ag* perfect ■ *sm* (*Ling*) perfect (tense)
perfeziona'mento [perfettsjona'mento] *sm*: **~ (di)** improvement (in), perfection (of); **corso di ~** proficiency course
perfezio'nare [perfettsjo'nare] *vt* to improve, perfect; **perfezionarsi** *vr* to improve
perfezi'one [perfet'tsjone] *sf* perfection
perfezio'nismo [perfettsjo'nizmo] *sm* perfectionism
perfezio'nista, -i, e [perfettsjo'nista] *sm/f* perfectionist
per'fidia *sf* perfidy
'perfido, -a *ag* perfidious, treacherous
per'fino *av* even
perfo'rare *vt* to pierce; (*Med*) to perforate; (*banda, schede*) to punch; (*trivellare*) to drill
perfora'tore, -'trice *sm/f* punch-card operator ■ *sm* (*utensile*) punch; (*Inform*): **~ di schede** card punch ■ *sf* (*Tecn*) boring *o* drilling machine; (*Inform*) card punch
perforazi'one [perforat'tsjone] *sf* piercing; perforation; punching drilling
perga'mena *sf* parchment
'pergola *sf* pergola
pergo'lato *sm* pergola
perico'lante *ag* precarious
pe'ricolo *sm* danger; **essere fuori ~** to be out of danger; (*Med*) to be off the danger list; **mettere in ~** to endanger, put in danger
perico'loso, -a *ag* dangerous
perife'ria *sf* (*anche fig*) periphery; (*di città*) outskirts *pl*
peri'ferico, -a, ci, che *ag* (*Anat, Inform*) peripheral; (*zona*) outlying
pe'rifrasi *sf inv* circumlocution
pe'rimetro *sm* perimeter
peri'odico, -a, ci, che *ag* periodic(al); (*Mat*) recurring ■ *sm* periodical

pe'riodo *sm* period; **~ contabile** accounting period; **~ di prova** trial period
peripe'zie [peripet'tsie] *sfpl* ups and downs, vicissitudes
'periplo *sm* circumnavigation
pe'rire *vi* to perish, die
peris'copio *sm* periscope
pe'rito, -a *ag* expert, skilled ■ *sm/f* expert; (*agronomo, navale*) surveyor; **un ~ chimico** a qualified chemist
perito'nite *sf* peritonitis
pe'rizia [pe'rittsja] *sf* (*abilità*) ability; (*giudizio tecnico*) expert opinion; expert's report; **~ psichiatrica** psychiatrist's report
peri'zoma, -i [peri'dzoma] *sm* G-string
'perla *sf* pearl
per'lina *sf* bead
perli'nato *sm* matchboarding
perlo'meno *av* (*almeno*) at least
perlopiù *av* (*quasi sempre*) in most cases, usually
perlus'trare *vt* to patrol
perlustrazi'one [perlustrat'tsjone] *sf* patrol, reconnaissance; **andare in ~** to go on patrol
perma'loso, -a *ag* touchy
perma'nente *ag* permanent ■ *sf* permanent wave, perm
perma'nenza [perma'nɛntsa] *sf* permanence; (*soggiorno*) stay; **buona ~!** enjoy your stay!
perma'nere *vi* to remain
per'mango *vb vedi* **permanere**
per'masi *vb vedi* **permanere**
perme'abile *ag* permeable
perme'are *vt* to permeate
per'messo, -a *pp di* **permettere** ■ *sm* (*autorizzazione*) permission, leave; (*dato a militare, impiegato*) leave; (*licenza*) licence (*Brit*), license (*US*), permit; (*Mil: foglio*) pass; **~?, è ~?** (*posso entrare?*) may I come in?; (*posso passare?*) excuse me; **~ di lavoro/pesca** work/fishing permit
per'mettere *vt* to allow, permit; **~ a qn qc/di fare qc** to allow sb sth/to do sth; **permettersi** *vr*: **permettersi qc/di fare qc** (*concedersi*) to allow o.s. sth/to do sth; (*avere la possibilità*) to afford sth/to do sth; **permettete che mi presenti** let me introduce myself, may I introduce myself?; **mi sia permesso di sottolineare che ...** may I take the liberty of pointing out that ...
per'misi *etc vb vedi* **permettere**
permis'sivo, -a *ag* permissive
'permuta *sf* (*Dir*) transfer; (*Comm*) trade-in; **accettare qc in ~** to take sth as a trade-in; **valore di ~** (*di macchina etc*) trade-in value
permu'tare *vt* to exchange; (*Mat*) to permute
per'nacchia [per'nakkja] *sf* (*fam*): **fare una ~** to blow a raspberry
per'nice [per'nitʃe] *sf* partridge
'perno *sm* pivot
pernotta'mento *sm* overnight stay
pernot'tare *vi* to spend the night, stay overnight
'pero *sm* pear tree
però *cong* (*ma*) but; (*tuttavia*) however, nevertheless
pero'rare *vt* (*Dir: fig*): **~ la causa di qn** to plead sb's case
perpendico'lare *ag, sf* perpendicular
perpen'dicolo *sm*: **a ~** perpendicularly
perpe'trare *vt* to perpetrate
perpetu'are *vt* to perpetuate
per'petuo, -a *ag* perpetual
perplessità *sf inv* perplexity
per'plesso, -a *ag* perplexed, puzzled
perqui'sire *vt* to search
perquisizi'one [perkwizit'tsjone] *sf* (police) search; **mandato di ~** search warrant
'perse *etc vb vedi* **perdere**
persecu'tore *sm* persecutor
persecuzi'one [persekut'tsjone] *sf* persecution
persegu'ibile *ag* (*Dir*): **essere ~ per legge** to be liable to prosecution
persegu'ire *vt* to pursue; (*Dir*) to prosecute
persegui'tare *vt* to persecute
perseve'rante *ag* persevering
perseve'ranza [perseve'rantsa] *sf* perseverance
perseve'rare *vi* to persevere
'persi *etc vb vedi* **perdere**
'Persia *sf*: **la ~** Persia
persi'ano, -a *ag, sm/f* Persian ■ *sf* shutter; **persiana avvolgibile** roller blind
'persico, -a, ci, che *ag*: **il golfo P~** the Persian Gulf; **pesce ~** perch
per'sino *av* = **perfino**
persis'tente *ag* persistent
persis'tenza [persis'tɛntsa] *sf* persistence
per'sistere *vi* to persist; **~ a fare** to persist in doing
persis'tito, -a *pp di* **persistere**
'perso, -a *pp di* **perdere** ■ *ag* (*smarrito: anche fig*) lost; (*sprecato*) wasted; **fare qc a tempo ~** to do sth in one's spare time; **~ per ~** I've (*o* we've *etc*) got nothing further to lose
per'sona *sf* person; (*qualcuno*): **una ~** someone, somebody; (*espressione*) anyone *o* anybody; **persone** *sfpl* people *pl*; **non c'è ~ che ...** there's nobody who ..., there isn't anybody who ...; **in ~, di ~** in person; **per interposta ~** through an intermediary *o* a third party; **~ giuridica** (*Dir*) legal person

P

perso'naggio [perso'naddʒo] *sm* (*persona ragguardevole*) personality, figure; (*tipo*) character, individual; (*Letteratura*) character
perso'nale *ag* personal ■ *sm* staff, personnel; (*figura fisica*) build ■ *sf* (*mostra*) one-man *o* one-woman exhibition
personalità *sf inv* personality
personaliz'zare [personalid'dzare] *vt* (*arredamento, stile*) to personalize; (*adattare*) to customize
personaliz'zato, -a [personalid'dzato] *ag* personalized
personal'mente *av* personally
personifi'care *vt* to personify; (*simboleggiare*) to embody
personificazi'one [personifikat'tsjone] *sf* (*vedi vb*) personification; embodiment
perspi'cace [perspi'katʃe] *ag* shrewd, discerning
perspi'cacia [perspi'katʃa] *sf* perspicacity, shrewdness
persu'adere *vt*: **~ qn (di qc/a fare)** to persuade sb (of sth/to do)
persuasi'one *sf* persuasion
persua'sivo, -a *ag* persuasive
persu'aso, -a *pp di* **persuadere**
per'tanto *cong* (*quindi*) so, therefore
'pertica, -che *sf* pole
perti'nace [perti'natʃe] *ag* determined; persistent
perti'nente *ag*: **~ (a)** relevant (to), pertinent (to)
perti'nenza [perti'nɛntsa] *sf* (*attinenza*) pertinence, relevance; (*competenza*): **essere di ~ di qn** to be sb's business
per'tosse *sf* whooping cough
per'tugio [per'tudʒo] *sm* hole, opening
pertur'bare *vt* to disrupt; (*persona*) to disturb, perturb
perturbazi'one [perturbat'tsjone] *sf* disruption; disturbance
Perù *sm*: **il ~** Peru
peru'gino, -a [peru'dʒino] *ag* of (*o* from), Perugia
peruvi'ano, -a *ag, sm/f* Peruvian
per'vadere *vt* to pervade
per'vaso, -a *pp di* **pervadere**
perve'nire *vi*: **~ a** to reach, arrive at, come to; (*venire in possesso*): **gli pervenne una fortuna** he inherited a fortune; **far ~ qc a** to have sth sent to
perve'nuto, -a *pp di* **pervenire**
perversi'one *sf* perversion
perversità *sf* perversity
per'verso, -a *ag* perverted
perver'tire *vt* to pervert
perver'tito, -a *sm/f* pervert
pervi'cace [pervi'katʃe] *ag* stubborn, obstinate
pervi'cacia [pervi'katʃa] *sf* stubbornness, obstinacy
per'vinca, -che *sf* periwinkle ■ *sm inv* (*colore*) periwinkle (blue)
p.es. *abbr* (*= per esempio*) e.g.
'pesa *sf* weighing *no pl* weighbridge
pe'sante *ag* heavy; (*fig: noioso*) dull, boring
pesan'tezza [pesan'tettsa] *sf* (*anche fig*) heaviness; **avere ~ di stomaco** to feel bloated
pesaper'sone *ag inv*: **(bilancia) ~** (weighing) scales *pl*; (*automatica*) weighing machine
pe'sare *vt* to weigh ■ *vi* (*avere un peso*) to weigh; (*essere pesante*) to be heavy; (*fig*) to carry weight; **~ su** (*fig*) to lie heavy on; to influence to hang over; **mi pesa sgridarlo** I find it hard to scold him; **tutta la responsabilità pesa su di lui** all the responsibility rests on his shoulders; **è una situazione che mi pesa** it's a difficult situation for me; **il suo parere pesa molto** his opinion counts for a lot; **~ le parole** to weigh one's words
'pesca (*pl* **pesche**) *sf* (*frutto*) peach; (*il pescare*) fishing; **andare a ~** to go fishing; **~ di beneficenza** (*lotteria*) lucky dip; **~ con la lenza** angling; **~ subacquea** underwater fishing
pes'caggio [pes'kaddʒo] *sm* (*Naut*) draught (*Brit*), draft (*US*)
pes'care *vt* (*pesce*) to fish for; to catch; (*qc nell'acqua*) to fish out; (*fig: trovare*) to get hold of, find
pesca'tore *sm* fisherman; (*con lenza*) angler
'pesce ['peʃʃe] *sm* fish *gen inv*; **Pesci** (*dello zodiaco*) Pisces; **essere dei Pesci** to be Pisces; **non saper che pesci prendere** (*fig*) not to know which way to turn; **~ d'aprile!** April Fool!; *see note*; **~ martello** hammerhead; **~ rosso** goldfish; **~ spada** swordfish

IL PESCE D'APRILE

Il pesce d'aprile is a sort of April Fool's joke, played on 1 April. Originally it took its name from a paper fish which was secretly attached to a person's back but nowadays all sorts of practical jokes are popular.

pesce'cane [peʃʃe'kane] *sm* shark
pesche'reccio [peske'rettʃo] *sm* fishing boat
pesche'ria [peske'ria] *sf* fishmonger's (shop) (*Brit*), fish store (*US*)
pescherò *etc* [peske'rɔ] *vb vedi* **pescare**

peschi'era [pes'kjɛra] *sf* fishpond
pesci'vendolo, -a [peʃʃi'vendolo] *sm/f* fishmonger (*Brit*), fish merchant (*US*)
'pesco, -schi *sm* peach tree
pes'coso, -a *ag* teeming with fish
pe'seta *sf* peseta
'peso *sm* weight; (*Sport*) shot; **dar ~ a qc** to attach importance to sth; **essere di ~ a qn** (*fig*) to be a burden to sb; **rubare sul ~** to give short weight; **lo portarono via di ~** they carried him away bodily; **avere due pesi e due misure** (*fig*) to have double standards; **~ lordo/netto** gross/net weight; **~ piuma/mosca/gallo/medio/massimo** (*Pugilato*) feather/fly/bantam/middle/heavyweight
pessi'mismo *sm* pessimism
pessi'mista, -i, e *ag* pessimistic ■ *sm/f* pessimist
'pessimo, -a *ag* very bad, awful; **di pessima qualità** of very poor quality
pes'tare *vt* to tread on, trample on; (*sale, pepe*) to grind; (*uva, aglio*) to crush; (*fig: picchiare*): **~ qn** to beat sb up; **~ i piedi** to stamp one's feet; **~ i piedi a qn** (*anche fig*) to tread on sb's toes
'peste *sf* plague; (*persona*) nuisance, pest
pes'tello *sm* pestle
pesti'cida, -i [pesti'tʃida] *sm* pesticide
pes'tifero, -a *ag* (*anche fig*) pestilential, pestiferous; (*odore*) noxious
pesti'lenza [pesti'lɛntsa] *sf* pestilence; (*fetore*) stench
'pesto, -a *ag*: **c'è buio ~** it's pitch dark ■ *sm* (*Cuc*) *sauce made with basil, garlic, cheese and oil*; **occhio ~** black eye
'petalo *sm* (*Bot*) petal
pe'tardo *sm* firecracker, banger (*Brit*)
petizi'one [petit'tsjone] *sf* petition; **fare una ~ a** to petition
'peto *sm* (*fam!*) fart (*!*)
petro'dollaro *sm* petrodollar
petrol'chimica [petrol'kimika] *sf* petrochemical industry
petroli'era *sf* (*nave*) oil tanker
petroli'ere *sm* (*industriale*) oilman; (*tecnico*) worker in the oil industry
petroli'ero, -a *ag* oil *cpd*
petro'lifero, -a *ag* oil *cpd*
pe'trolio *sm* oil, petroleum; (*per lampada, fornello*) paraffin (*Brit*), kerosene (*US*); **lume a ~** oil *o* paraffin *o* kerosene lamp; **~ grezzo** crude oil
pettego'lare *vi* to gossip
pettego'lezzo [pettego'leddzo] *sm* gossip *no pl*; **fare pettegolezzi** to gossip
pet'tegolo, -a *ag* gossipy ■ *sm/f* gossip
petti'nare *vt* to comb (the hair of); **pettinarsi** *vr* to comb one's hair
pettina'tura *sf* (*acconciatura*) hairstyle
'pettine *sm* comb; (*Zool*) scallop
petti'rosso *sm* robin
'petto *sm* chest; (*seno*) breast, bust; (*Cuc: di carne bovina*) brisket; (*di pollo etc*) breast; **prendere qn/qc di ~** to face up to sb/sth; **a doppio ~** (*abito*) double-breasted
petto'rale *ag* pectoral
petto'rina *sf* (*di grembiule*) bib
petto'ruto, -a *ag* broad-chested; full-breasted
petu'lante *ag* insolent
pe'tunia *sf* petunia
'pezza ['pɛttsa] *sf* piece of cloth; (*toppa*) patch; (*cencio*) rag, cloth; (*Amm*): **~ d'appoggio** *o* **giustificativa** voucher; **trattare qn come una ~ da piedi** to treat sb like a doormat
pez'zato, -a [pet'tsato] *ag* piebald
pez'zente [pet'tsɛnte] *sm/f* beggar
'pezzo ['pɛttso] *sm* (*gen*) piece; (*brandello, frammento*) piece, bit; (*di macchina, arnese etc*) part; (*Stampa*) article; (*di tempo*): **aspettare un ~** to wait quite a while *o* some time; **andare a pezzi** to break into pieces; **essere a pezzi** (*oggetto*) to be in pieces *o* bits; (*fig: persona*) to be shattered; **un bel ~ d'uomo** a fine figure of a man; **abito a due pezzi** two-piece suit; **essere tutto d'un ~** (*fig*) to be a man (*o* woman) of integrity; **~ di cronaca** (*Stampa*) report; **~ grosso** (*fig*) bigwig; **~ di ricambio** spare part
PG *sigla* = **Perugia**
P.G. *abbr* = **procuratore generale**
pH [pi'akka] *sm inv* (*Chim*) pH
PI *sigla* = **Pisa**
P.I. *abbr* = **Pubblica Istruzione**
pi'accio *etc* ['pjattʃo] *vb vedi* **piacere**
pia'cente [pja'tʃɛnte] *ag* attractive, pleasant
pia'cere [pja'tʃere] *vi* to please ■ *sm* pleasure; (*favore*) favour (*Brit*), favor (*US*); **una ragazza che piace** (*piacevole*) a likeable girl; (*attraente*) an attractive girl; **~ a**: **mi piace** I like it; **quei ragazzi non mi piacciono** I don't like those boys; **gli piacerebbe andare al cinema** he would like to go to the cinema; **il suo discorso è piaciuto molto** his speech was well received; **"~!"** (*nelle presentazioni*) "pleased to meet you!"; **con ~** certainly, with pleasure; **per ~** please; **fare un ~ a qn** to do sb a favour; **mi fa ~ per lui** I am pleased for him; **mi farebbe ~ rivederlo** I would like to see him again
pia'cevole [pja'tʃevole] *ag* pleasant, agreeable
piaci'mento [pjatʃi'mento] *sm*: **a ~** (*a volontà*) as much as one likes, at will; **lo farà a suo ~** he'll do it when it suits him

P

piaci'uto, -a [pja'tʃuto] *pp di* **piacere**
pi'acqui *etc vb vedi* **piacere**
pi'aga, -ghe *sf* (*lesione*) sore; (*ferita: anche fig*) wound; (*fig: flagello*) scourge, curse; (*persona*) pest, nuisance
piagnis'teo [pjaɲɲis'tɛo] *sm* whining, whimpering
piagnuco'lare [pjaɲɲuko'lare] *vi* to whimper
piagnuco'lio, -ii [pjaɲɲuko'lio] *sm* whimpering
piagnuco'loso, -a [pjaɲɲuko'loso] *ag* whiny, whimpering, moaning
pi'alla *sf* (*arnese*) plane
pial'lare *vt* to plane
pialla'trice [pjalla'tritʃe] *sf* planing machine
pi'ana *sf* stretch of level ground; (*più esteso*) plain
pianeggi'ante [pjaned'dʒante] *ag* flat, level
piane'rottolo *sm* landing
pia'neta *sm* (*Astr*) planet
pi'angere ['pjandʒere] *vi* to cry, weep; (*occhi*) to water ■ *vt* to cry, weep; (*lamentare*) to bewail, lament; **~ la morte di qn** to mourn sb's death
pianifi'care *vt* to plan
pianificazi'one [pjanifikat'tsjone] *sf* (*Econ*) planning; **~ aziendale** corporate planning
pia'nista, -i, e *sm/f* pianist
pi'ano, -a *ag* (*piatto*) flat, level; (*Mat*) plane; (*facile*) straightforward, simple; (*chiaro*) clear, plain ■ *av* (*adagio*) slowly; (*a bassa voce*) softly; (*con cautela*) slowly, carefully ■ *sm* (*Mat*) plane; (*Geo*) plain; (*livello*) level, plane; (*di edificio*) floor; (*programma*) plan; (*Mus*) piano; **pian ~** very slowly; (*poco a poco*) little by little; **una casa di 3 piani** a 3-storey (*Brit*) *o* 3-storied (*US*) house; **al ~ di sopra/di sotto** on the floor above/below; **all'ultimo ~** on the top floor; **al ~ terra** on the ground floor; **in primo/secondo ~** (*Fot, Cine etc*) in the foreground/background; **fare un primo ~** (*Fot, Cine*) to take a close-up; **di primo ~** (*fig*) prominent, high-ranking; **un fattore di secondo ~** a secondary *o* minor factor; **passare in secondo ~** to become less important; **mettere tutto sullo stesso ~** to lump everything together, give equal importance to everything; **tutto secondo i piani** all according to plan; **~ di lavoro** (*superficie*) worktop; (*programma*) work plan; **~ regolatore** (*Urbanistica*) town-planning scheme; **~ stradale** road surface
piano'forte *sm* piano, pianoforte
piano'terra *sm inv* = **piano terra**
pi'ansi *etc vb vedi* **piangere**
pi'anta *sf* (*Bot*) plant; (*Anat: anche:* **pianta del piede**) sole (of the foot); (*grafico*) plan; (*cartina topografica*) map; **ufficio a ~ aperta** open-plan office; **in ~ stabile** on the permanent staff; **~ stradale** street map, street plan
piantagi'one [pjanta'dʒone] *sf* plantation
pianta'grane *sm/f inv* troublemaker
pian'tare *vt* to plant; (*conficcare*) to drive *o* hammer in; (*tenda*) to put up, pitch; (*fig: lasciare*) to leave, desert; **piantarsi** *vr:* **piantarsi davanti a qn** to plant o.s. in front of sb; **~ qn in asso** to leave sb in the lurch; **~ grane** (*fig*) to cause trouble; **piantala!** (*fam*) cut it out!
pian'tato, -a *ag:* **ben ~** (*persona*) well-built
pianta'tore *sm* planter
pianter'reno *sm* ground floor
pian'tina *sf* (*di edificio, città*) (small) map; (*Bot*) (small) plant
pi'anto, -a *pp di* **piangere** ■ *sm* tears *pl*, crying
pianto'nare *vt* to guard, watch over
pian'tone *sm* (*vigilante*) sentry, guard; (*soldato*) orderly; (*Aut*) steering column
pia'nura *sf* plain
pi'astra *sf* plate; (*di pietra*) slab; (*di fornello*) hotplate; **panino alla ~** ≈ toasted sandwich; **~ di registrazione** tape deck
pias'trella *sf* tile
piastrel'lare *vt* to tile
pias'trina *sf* (*Anat*) platelet; (*Mil*) identity disc (*Brit*) *o* tag (*US*)
piatta'forma *sf* (*anche fig*) platform; **~ continentale** (*Geo*) continental shelf; **~ girevole** (*Tecn*) turntable; **~ di lancio** (*Mil*) launching pad *o* platform; **~ rivendicativa** *document prepared by the unions in an industry, setting out their claims*
piat'tello *sm* clay pigeon; **tiro al ~** clay-pigeon shooting (*Brit*), trapshooting
piat'tino *sm* (*di tazza*) saucer
pi'atto, -a *ag* flat; (*fig: scialbo*) dull ■ *sm* (*recipiente, vivanda*) dish; (*portata*) course; (*parte piana*) flat (part); **piatti** *smpl* (*Mus*) cymbals; **un ~ di minestra** a plate of soup; **~ fondo** soup dish; **~ forte** main course; **~ del giorno** dish of the day, plat du jour; **~ del giradischi** turntable; **piatti già pronti** (*Cuc*) ready-cooked dishes
pi'azza ['pjattsa] *sf* square; (*Comm*) market; (*letto, lenzuolo*): **a una ~** single; **a due piazze** double; **far ~ pulita** to make a clean sweep; **mettere in ~** (*fig: rendere pubblico*) to make public; **scendere in ~** (*fig*) to take to the streets, demonstrate; **~ d'armi** (*Mil*) parade ground
piazza'forte [pjattsa'forte] *pl*, **piazze'forti** *sf* (*Mil*) stronghold
piaz'zale [pjat'tsale] *sm* (large) square
piazza'mento [pjattsa'mento] *sm* (*Sport*) place, placing

piaz'zare [pjat'tsare] *vt* to place; (*Comm*) to market, sell; **piazzarsi** *vr* (*Sport*) to be placed; **piazzarsi bene** to finish with the leaders *o* in a good position
piaz'zista, -i [pjat'tsista] *sm* (*Comm*) commercial traveller
piaz'zola [pjat'tsɔla] *sf* (*Aut*) lay-by (*Brit*), (roadside) stopping place; (*di tenda*) pitch
'picca, -che *sf* pike; **picche** *sfpl* (*Carte*) spades; **rispondere picche a qn** (*fig*) to give sb a flat refusal
pic'cante *ag* hot, pungent; (*fig*) racy
pic'carsi *vr*: **~ di fare** to pride o.s. on one's ability to do; **~ per qc** to take offence (*Brit*) *o* offense (*US*) at sth
picchet'taggio [pikket'taddʒo] *sm* picketing
picchet'tare [pikket'tare] *vt* to picket
pic'chetto [pik'ketto] *sm* (*Mil, di scioperanti*) picket
picchi'are [pik'kjare] *vt* (*persona: colpire*) to hit, strike; (*prendere a botte*) to beat (up); (*battere*) to beat; (*sbattere*) to bang ■ *vi* (*bussare*) to knock; (*: con forza*) to bang; (*colpire*) to hit, strike; (*sole*) to beat down
picchi'ata [pik'kjata] *sf* knock; bang; blow; (*percosse*) beating, thrashing; (*Aer*) dive; **scendere in ~** to (nose-)dive
picchiet'tare [pikkjet'tare] *vt* (*punteggiare*) to spot, dot; (*colpire*) to tap
'picchio ['pikkjo] *sm* woodpecker
pic'cino, -a [pit'tʃino] *ag* tiny, very small
picci'olo [pit'tʃɔlo] *sm* (*Bot*) stalk
piccio'naia [pittʃo'naja] *sf* pigeon-loft; (*Teat*): **la ~** the gods *sg* (*Brit*), the gallery
picci'one [pit'tʃone] *sm* pigeon; **pigliare due piccioni con una fava** (*fig*) to kill two birds with one stone
'picco, -chi *sm* peak; **a ~** vertically; **colare a ~** (*Naut, fig*) to sink
picco'lezza [pikko'lettsa] *sf* (*dimensione*) smallness; (*fig: grettezza*) meanness, pettiness; (*inezia*) trifle
'piccolo, -a *ag* small; (*oggetto, mano, di età: bambino*) small, little; (*dav sostantivo: di breve durata: viaggio*) short; (*fig*) mean, petty ■ *sm/f* child, little one ■ *sm*: **nel mio ~** in my own small way; **piccoli** *smpl* (*di animale*) young *pl*; **in ~** in miniature; **la piccola borghesia** the lower middle classes; (*peg*) the petty bourgeoisie
pic'cone *sm* pick(-axe)
pic'cozza [pik'kɔttsa] *sf* ice-axe
pic'nic *sm inv* picnic; **fare un ~** to have a picnic
pidies'sino, -a *ag* (*Pol*) of P.D.S. ■ *sm/f* member (*o* supporter) of P.D.S.
pi'docchio [pi'dɔkkjo] *sm* louse
pidocchi'oso, -a [pidok'kjoso] *ag* (*infestato*) lousy; (*fig: taccagno*) mean, stingy, tight
pidu'ista, -i, e *ag* P2 *cpd* (*masonic lodge*) ■ *sm* member of the P2 masonic lodge
piè *sm inv*: **a ogni piè sospinto** (*fig*) at every step; **saltare a piè pari** (*omettere*) to skip; **a piè di pagina** at the foot of the page; **note a piè di pagina** footnotes
pi'ede *sm* foot; (*di mobile*) leg; **in piedi** standing; **a piedi** on foot; **a piedi nudi** barefoot; **su due piedi** (*fig*) at once; **mettere qc in piedi** (*azienda etc*) to set sth up; **prendere ~** (*fig*) to gain ground, catch on; **puntare i piedi** (*fig*) to dig one's heels in; **sentirsi mancare la terra sotto i piedi** to feel lost; **non sta in piedi** (*persona*) he can't stand; (*fig: scusa etc*) it doesn't hold water; **tenere in piedi** (*persona*) to keep on his (*o* her) feet; (*fig: ditta etc*) to keep going; **a ~ libero** (*Dir*) on bail; **sul ~ di guerra** (*Mil*) ready for action; **~ di porco** crowbar
piedipi'atti *sm inv* (*peg: poliziotto*) cop
piedis'tallo, piedes'tallo *sm* pedestal
pi'ega, -ghe *sf* (*piegatura, Geo*) fold; (*di gonna*) pleat; (*di pantaloni*) crease; (*grinza*) wrinkle, crease; **prendere una brutta** *o* **cattiva ~** (*fig: persona*) to get into bad ways; (*situazione*) to take a turn for the worse; **non fa una ~** (*fig: ragionamento*) it's faultless; **non ha fatto una ~** (*fig: persona*) he didn't bat an eye(lid) (*Brit*) *o* an eye(lash) (*US*)
piega'mento *sm* folding; bending; **~ sulle gambe** (*Ginnastica*) kneebend
pie'gare *vt* to fold; (*braccia, gambe, testa*) to bend ■ *vi* to bend; **piegarsi** *vr* to bend; (*fig*): **piegarsi (a)** to yield (to), submit (to)
piega'tura *sf* folding *no pl*; bending *no pl*; fold bend
piegherò *etc* [pjege'rɔ] *vb vedi* **piegare**
pieghet'tare [pjeget'tare] *vt* to pleat
pie'ghevole [pje'gevole] *ag* pliable, flexible; (*porta*) folding; (*fig*) yielding, docile
Pie'monte *sm*: **il ~** Piedmont
piemon'tese *ag, sm/f* Piedmontese
pi'ena *sf vedi* **pieno**
pie'nezza [pje'nettsa] *sf* fullness
pi'eno, -a *ag* full; (*muro, mattone*) solid ■ *sm* (*colmo*) height, peak; (*carico*) full load ■ *sf* (*di fiume*) flood, spate; (*gran folla*) crowd, throng; **~ di** full of; **a piene mani** abundantly; **a tempo ~** full-time; **a pieni voti** (*eleggere*) unanimously; **laurearsi a pieni voti** *to graduate with full marks*; **in ~ giorno** in broad daylight; **in ~ inverno** in the depths of winter; **in piena notte** in the middle of the night; **in piena stagione** at the height of the season; **in ~** (*completamente: sbagliare*)

P

completely; (*colpire, centrare*) bang *o* right in the middle; **avere pieni poteri** to have full powers; **nel ~ possesso delle sue facoltà** in full possession of his faculties; **fare il ~ (di benzina)** to fill up (with petrol)

pie'none *sm*: **c'era il ~ al cinema/al teatro** the cinema/the theatre was packed

'piercing ['pirsing] *sm*: **farsi il ~ all'ombelico** to have one's navel pierced

pietà *sf* pity; (*Rel*) piety; **senza ~** (*agire*) ruthlessly; (*persona*) pitiless, ruthless; **avere ~ di** (*compassione*) to pity, feel sorry for; (*misericordia*) to have pity *o* mercy on; **far ~** to arouse pity; (*peg*) to be terrible

pie'tanza [pje'tantsa] *sf* dish, course

pie'toso, -a *ag* (*compassionevole*) pitying, compassionate; (*che desta pietà*) pitiful

pi'etra *sf* stone; **mettiamoci una ~ sopra** (*fig*) let bygones be bygones; **~ preziosa** precious stone, gem; **~ dello scandalo** (*fig*) cause of scandal

pie'traia *sf* (*terreno*) stony ground

pietrifi'care *vt* to petrify; (*fig*) to transfix, paralyze

piet'rina *sf* (*per accendino*) flint

pie'trisco, -schi *sm* crushed stone, road metal

pi'eve *sf* parish church

'piffero *sm* (*Mus*) pipe

pigi'ama [pi'dʒama] *sm* pyjamas *pl*

'pigia 'pigia ['pidʒa'pidʒa] *sm* crowd, press

pigi'are [pi'dʒare] *vt* to press

pigia'trice [pidʒa'tritʃe] *sf* (*macchina*) wine press

pigi'one [pi'dʒone] *sf* rent

pigli'are [piʎ'ʎare] *vt* to take, grab; (*afferrare*) to catch

'piglio ['piʎʎo] *sm* look, expression

pig'mento *sm* pigment

pig'meo, -a *sm/f* pygmy

'pigna ['piɲɲa] *sf* pine cone

pignole'ria [piɲɲole'ria] *sf* fastidiousness, fussiness

pi'gnolo, -a [piɲ'ɲɔlo] *ag* pernickety

pigno'rare [piɲɲo'rare] *vt* (*Dir*) to distrain

pigo'lare *vi* to cheep, chirp

pigo'lio *sm* cheeping, chirping

pigra'mente *av* lazily

pi'grizia [pi'grittsja] *sf* laziness

'pigro, -a *ag* lazy; (*fig: ottuso*) slow, dull

PIL *sigla m* = **prodotto interno lordo**

'pila *sf* (*catasta, di ponte*) pile; (*Elettr*) battery; (*fam: torcia*) torch (*Brit*), flashlight; **a ~, a pile** battery-operated

pi'lastro *sm* pillar

'pile ['pail] *sm inv* fleece

'pillola *sf* pill; **prendere la ~** (*contraccettivo*) to be on the pill; **~ del giorno dopo** morning-after pill

pi'lone *sm* (*di ponte*) pier; (*di linea elettrica*) pylon

pi'lota, -i, e *sm/f* pilot; (*Aut*) driver ■ *ag inv* pilot *cpd*; **~ automatico** automatic pilot

pilo'taggio [pilo'taddʒo] *sm*: **cabina di ~** flight deck

pilo'tare *vt* to pilot; to drive

piluc'care *vt* to nibble at

pi'mento *sm* pimento, allspice

pim'pante *ag* lively, full of beans

pinaco'teca, -che *sf* art gallery

pi'neta *sf* pinewood

ping-'pong [pɪŋ'pɔŋ] *sm* table tennis

'pingue *ag* fat, corpulent

pingu'edine *sf* corpulence

pingu'ino *sm* (*Zool*) penguin

'pinna *sf* fin; (*di pinguino, spatola di gomma*) flipper

pin'nacolo *sm* pinnacle

'pino *sm* pine (tree)

pi'nolo *sm* pine kernel

'pinta *sf* pint

'pinza ['pintsa] *sf* pliers *pl*; (*Med*) forceps *pl*; (*Zool*) pincer

pinzette [pin'tsette] *sfpl* tweezers

'pio, -a, 'pii, 'pie *ag* pious; (*opere, istituzione*) charitable, charity *cpd*

piogge'rella [pjoddʒe'rɛlla] *sf* drizzle

pi'oggia, -ge ['pjɔddʒa] *sf* rain; (*fig: di regali, fiori*) shower; (*di insulti*) hail; **sotto la ~** in the rain; **~ acida** acid rain

pi'olo *sm* peg; (*di scala*) rung

piom'bare *vi* to fall heavily; (*gettarsi con impeto*): **~ su** to fall upon, assail ■ *vt* (*dente*) to fill

piomba'tura *sf* (*di dente*) filling

piom'bino *sm* (*sigillo*) (lead) seal; (*del filo a piombo*) plummet; (*Pesca*) sinker

pi'ombo *sm* (*Chim*) lead; (*sigillo*) (lead) seal; (*proiettile*) (lead) shot; **a ~** (*cadere*) straight down; (*muro etc*) plumb; **andare con i piedi di ~** (*fig*) to tread carefully; **senza ~** (*benzina*) unleaded, lead-free; **anni di ~** (*fig*) *era of terrorist outrages*

pioni'ere, -a *sm/f* pioneer

pi'oppo *sm* poplar

pio'vano, -a *ag*: **acqua piovana** rainwater

pi'overe *vb impers* to rain ■ *vi* (*fig: scendere dall'alto*) to rain down; (*affluire in gran numero*): **~ in** to pour into; **non ci piove sopra** (*fig*) there's no doubt about it

pioviggi'nare [pjoviddʒi'nare] *vb impers* to drizzle

piovosità *sf* rainfall

pio'voso, -a *ag* rainy

pi'ovra *sf* octopus

pi'ovve *etc vb vedi* **piovere**

'pipa *sf* pipe

pipì *sf (fam)*: **fare ~** to have a wee (wee)
pipis'trello *sm (Zool)* bat
pi'ramide *sf* pyramid
pi'ranha *sm inv* piranha
pi'rata, -i *sm* pirate; **~ informatico** hacker; **~ della strada** hit-and-run driver
Pire'nei *smpl*: **i ~** the Pyrenees
pi'retro *sm* pyrethrum
'pirico, -a, ci, che *ag*: **polvere pirica** gunpowder
pi'rite *sf* pyrite
piro'etta *sf* pirouette
pi'rofilo, -a *ag* heat-resistant ■ *sf* heat-resistant glass; *(tegame)* heat-resistant dish
pi'roga, -ghe *sf* dug-out canoe
pi'romane *sm/f* arsonist
pi'roscafo *sm* steamer, steamship
'Pisa *sf* Pisa
pi'sano, -a *ag* Pisan
pisci'are [piʃʃare] *vi (fam!)* to piss *(!)*, pee *(!)*
pi'scina [piʃʃina] *sf* (swimming) pool
pi'sello *sm* pea
piso'lino *sm* nap; **fare un ~** to have a nap
'pista *sf (traccia)* track, trail; *(di stadio)* track; *(di pattinaggio)* rink; *(da sci)* run; *(Aer)* runway; *(di circo)* ring; **~ da ballo** dance floor; **~ ciclabile** cycle lane; **~ di lancio** launch(ing) pad; **~ di rullaggio** *(Aer)* taxiway; **~ di volo** *(Aer)* runway
pis'tacchio [pis'takkjo] *sm* pistachio (tree), pistachio (nut)
pis'tillo *sm (Bot)* pistil
pis'tola *sf* pistol, gun; **~ a spruzzo** spray gun; **~ a tamburo** revolver
pis'tone *sm* piston
pi'tocco, -chi *sm* skinflint, miser
pi'tone *sm* python
'pittima *sf (fig)* bore
pit'tore, -'trice *sm/f* painter
pitto'resco, -a, schi, sche *ag* picturesque
pit'torico, -a, ci, che *ag* of painting, pictorial
pit'tura *sf* painting; **~ fresca** wet paint
pittu'rare *vt* to paint

PAROLA CHIAVE

più *av* **1** *(in maggiore quantità)* more; **più del solito** more than usual; **in più, di più** more; **ne voglio di più** I want some more; **ci sono 3 persone in** *o* **di più** there are 3 more *o* extra people; **costa di più** it's more expensive; **una volta di più** once more; **più o meno** more or less; **né più né meno** no more, no less; **per di più** *(inoltre)* what's more, moreover; **è sempre più difficile** it is getting more and more difficult; **chi più chi meno hanno tutti contribuito** everybody made a contribution of some sort; **più dormo e più dormirei** the more I sleep the more I want to sleep
2 *(comparativo)* more; *(se monosillabo, spesso)*: + ...er; **più ... di/che** more ... than; **più intelligente di lui** more intelligent than him; **più furbo di te** smarter than you; **più tardi di ...** later than ...; **lavoro più di te/di Paola** I work harder than you/than Paola; **è più fortunato che bravo** he is lucky rather than skilled; **più di quanto pensassi** more than I thought; **più che altro** mainly; **più che mai** more than ever
3 *(superlativo)* most; *(se monosillabico, spesso)*: + ...est; **il più grande/intelligente** the biggest/most intelligent; **è quello che compro più spesso** that's the one I buy most often; **al più presto** as soon as possible; **al più tardi** at the latest
4 *(negazione)*: **non ... più** no more, no longer; **non ho più soldi** I've got no more money, I don't have any more money; **non lavoro più** I'm no longer working, I don't work any more; **non ce n'è più** there isn't any left; **non c'è più nessuno** there's no one left; **non c'è più niente da fare** there's nothing more to be done; **a più non posso** *(gridare)* at the top of one's voice; *(correre)* as fast as one can
5 *(Mat)* plus; **4 più 5 fa 9** 4 plus 5 equals 9; **più 5 gradi** 5 degrees above freezing, plus 5; **6 più** *(a scuola)* just above a pass
■ *prep* plus; **500.000 più le spese** 500,000 plus expenses; **siamo in quattro più il nonno** there are four of us, plus grandpa
■ *ag inv* **1**: **più ... (di)** more ... (than); **più denaro/tempo** more money/time; **più persone di quante ci aspettassimo** more people than we expected
2 *(numerosi, diversi)* several; **l'aspettai per più giorni** I waited for it for several days
■ *sm* **1** *(la maggior parte)*: **il più è fatto** most of it is done; **il più delle volte** more often than not, generally; **parlare del più e del meno** to talk about this and that
2 *(Mat)* plus (sign)
3: **i più** the majority

piuccheper'fetto [pjukkeper'fɛtto] *sm (Ling)* pluperfect, past perfect
pi'uma *sf* feather; **piume** *sfpl* down *sg*; *(piumaggio)* plumage *sg*, feathers
piu'maggio [pju'maddʒo] *sm* plumage, feathers *pl*
piu'mino *sm* (eider)down; *(per letto)* eiderdown; *(tipo danese)* duvet, continental quilt; *(giacca)* quilted jacket; *(with goose-*

feather padding: per cipria) powder puff; (*per spolverare*) feather duster
piut'tosto *av* rather; ~ **che** (*anziché*) rather than
'**piva** *sf*: **con le pive nel sacco** (*fig*) empty-handed
pi'vello, -a *sm/f* greenhorn
'**pizza** ['pittsa] *sf* (*Cuc*) pizza; (*Cine*) reel
pizze'ria [pittse'ria] *sf place where pizzas are made, sold or eaten*
pizzi'cagnolo, -a [pittsi'kaɲɲolo] *sm/f* specialist grocer
pizzi'care [pittsi'kare] *vt* (*stringere*) to nip, pinch; (*pungere*) to sting; to bite; (*Mus*) to pluck ■ *vi* (*prudere*) to itch, be itchy; (*cibo*) to be hot *o* spicy
pizziche'ria [pittsike'ria] *sf* delicatessen (shop)
'**pizzico, chi** ['pittsiko] *sm* (*pizzicotto*) pinch, nip; (*piccola quantità*) pinch, dash; (*d'insetto*) sting; bite
pizzi'cotto [pittsi'kɔtto] *sm* pinch, nip
'**pizzo** ['pittso] *sm* (*merletto*) lace; (*barbetta*) goatee beard; (*tangente*) protection money
pla'care *vt* to placate, soothe; **placarsi** *vr* to calm down
'**placca, -che** *sf* plate; (*con iscrizione*) plaque; (*anche*: **placca dentaria**) (dental) plaque
plac'care *vt* to plate; **placcato in oro/ argento** gold-/silver-plated
pla'centa [pla'tʃɛnta] *sf* placenta
placidità [platʃidi'ta] *sf* calm, peacefulness
'**placido, -a** ['platʃido] *ag* placid, calm
plafoni'era *sf* ceiling light
plagi'are [pla'dʒare] *vt* (*copiare*) to plagiarize; (*Dir: influenzare*) to coerce
'**plagio** ['pladʒo] *sm* plagiarism; (*Dir*) duress
plaid [plɛd] *sm inv* (travelling) rug (*Brit*), lap robe (*US*)
pla'nare *vi* (*Aer*) to glide
'**plancia, -ce** ['plantʃa] *sf* (*Naut*) bridge; (*Aut: cruscotto*) dashboard
'**plancton** *sm inv* plankton
plane'tario, -a *ag* planetary ■ *sm* (*locale*) planetarium
planis'fero *sm* planisphere
plan'tare *sm* arch support
'**plasma** *sm* plasma
plas'mare *vt* to mould (*Brit*), mold (*US*), shape
'**plastico, -a, ci, che** *ag* plastic ■ *sm* (*rappresentazione*) relief model; (*esplosivo*): **bomba al** ~ plastic bomb ■ *sf* (*arte*) plastic arts *pl*; (*Med*) plastic surgery; (*sostanza*) plastic; **in materiale** ~ plastic
plasti'lina® *sf* plasticine®
'**platano** *sm* plane tree
pla'tea *sf* (*Teat*) stalls *pl* (*Brit*), orchestra (*US*)
plate'ale *ag* (*gesto, atteggiamento*) theatrical
plateal'mente *av* theatrically
'**platino** *sm* platinum
pla'tonico, -a, ci, che *ag* platonic
plau'dire *vi*: ~ **a** to applaud
plau'sibile *ag* plausible
'**plauso** *sm* (*fig*) approval
'**playback** ['plei bæk] *sm*: **cantare in** ~ to mime
'**playboy** ['pleibɔi] *sm inv* playboy
'**playmaker** ['pleimeikə[r]] *sm/f inv* (*Sport*) playmaker
'**play-off** ['pleɪɔf] *sm inv* (*Sport*) play-off
ple'baglia [ple'baʎʎa] *sf* (*peg*) rabble, mob
'**plebe** *sf* common people
ple'beo, -a *ag* plebeian; (*volgare*) coarse, common
plebi'scito [plebiʃʃito] *sm* plebiscite
ple'nario, -a *ag* plenary
pleni'lunio *sm* full moon
plenipotenzi'ario, -a [plenipoten'tsjarjo] *ag* plenipotentiary
'**plenum** *sm inv* plenum
'**plettro** *sm* plectrum
'**pleura** *sf* (*Anat*) pleura
pleu'rite *sf* pleurisy
P.L.I. *sigla m* (= *Partito Liberale Italiano*) *former political party*
'**plico, -chi** *sm* (*pacco*) parcel; **in ~ a parte** (*Comm*) under separate cover
plissé [pli'se] *ag inv* plissé *cpd* ■ *sm inv* (*anche*: **tessuto plissé**) plissé
plisset'tato, -a *ag* plissé *cpd*
plo'tone *sm* (*Mil*) platoon; ~ **d'esecuzione** firing squad
'**plumbeo, -a** *ag* leaden
plu'rale *ag, sm* plural
plura'lismo *sm* pluralism
pluralità *sf* plurality; (*maggioranza*) majority
plusva'lenza [pluzva'lɛntsa] *sf* capital gain
plusva'lore *sm* (*Econ*) surplus
plu'tonio *sm* plutonium
pluvi'ale *ag* rain *cpd*
pluvi'ometro *sm* rain gauge
P.M. *abbr* (*Pol*) = **Pubblico Ministero**; (= *Polizia Militare*) MP (= *Military Police*)
pm *abbr* = **peso molecolare**
PMI *sigla fpl* (= *Piccole e Medie Imprese*) SME (= *Small and Medium-sized Enterprises*)
PN *sigla* = **Pordenone**
pneu'matico, -a, ci, che *ag* inflatable; (*Tecn*) pneumatic ■ *sm* (*Aut*) tyre (*Brit*), tire (*US*)
PNL *sigla m* = **prodotto nazionale lordo**
PO *sigla* = **Prato**
Po *sm*: **il Po** the Po
po' *av, sm vedi* **poco**
P.O. *abbr* = **posta ordinaria**

po'chezza [po'kettsa] *sf* insufficiency, shortage; (*fig: meschinità*) meanness, smallness

 PAROLA CHIAVE

'poco, -a, chi, che *ag* (*quantità*) little, not much; (*numero*) few, not many; **poco pane/denaro/spazio** little *o* not much bread/money/space; **con poca spesa** without spending much; **a poco prezzo** at a low price, cheap; **poco (tempo) fa** a short time ago; **poche persone/idee** few *o* not many people/ideas; **è un tipo di poche parole** he's a man of few words

■ *av* **1** (*in piccola quantità*) little, not much; (*numero limitato*) few, not many; **guadagna poco** he doesn't earn much, he earns little

2 (*con ag, av*) (a) little, not very; **è poco più vecchia di lui** she's a little *o* slightly older than him; **è poco socievole** he's not very sociable; **sta poco bene** he isn't very well

3 (*tempo*): **poco dopo/prima** shortly afterwards/before; **il film dura poco** the film doesn't last very long; **ci vediamo molto poco** we don't see each other very often, we hardly ever see each other

4: **un po'** a little, a bit; **è un po' corto** it's a little *o* a bit short; **arriverà fra un po'** he'll arrive shortly *o* in a little while

5: **a dir poco** to say the least; **a poco a poco** little by little; **per poco non cadevo** I nearly fell; **è una cosa da poco** it's nothing, it's of no importance; **una persona da poco** a worthless person

■ *pron* (a) little; **pochi, poche** (*pl: persone*) few (people); (*cose*) few; **ci vediamo tra poco** see you soon; **pochi lo sanno** not many people know it; **ci vuole tempo ed io ne ho poco** it takes time, and I haven't got much to spare

■ *sm* **1** little; **vive del poco che ha** he lives on the little he has

2: **un po'** a little; **un po' di zucchero** a little sugar; **un bel po' di denaro** quite a lot of money; **un po' per ciascuno** a bit each

podcast [pɔdkast] *sm* podcast
po'dere *sm* (*Agr*) farm
pode'roso, -a *ag* powerful
podestà *sm inv* (*nel fascismo*) podestà, mayor
'podio *sm* dais, platform; (*Mus*) podium
po'dismo *sm* (*Sport: marcia*) walking; (*corsa*) running
po'dista, -i, e *sm/f* walker; runner
po'ema, -i *sm* poem
poe'sia *sf* (*arte*) poetry; (*componimento*) poem
po'eta, -'essa *sm/f* poet/poetess
poe'tare *vi* to write poetry
po'etico, -a, ci, che *ag* poetic(al)
poggi'are [pod'dʒare] *vt* to lean, rest; (*posare*) to lay, place
poggia'testa [poddʒa'tɛsta] *sm inv* (*Aut*) headrest
'poggio ['pɔddʒo] *sm* hillock, knoll
poggi'olo [pod'dʒɔlo] *sm* balcony
'poi *av* then; (*alla fine*) finally, at last ■ *sm*: **pensare al ~** to think of the future; **e ~** (*inoltre*) and besides; **questa ~ (è bella)** (*ironico*) that's a good one!; **d'ora in ~** from now on; **da domani in ~** from tomorrow onwards
poi'ana *sf* buzzard
poiché [poi'ke] *cong* since, as
pois [pwa] *sm inv* spot, (polka) dot; **a ~** spotted, polka-dot *cpd*
'poker *sm* poker
po'lacco, -a, chi, che *ag* Polish ■ *sm/f* Pole
po'lare *ag* polar
polariz'zare [polarid'dzare] *vt* (*anche fig*) to polarize
'polca, -che *sf* polka
po'lemico, -a, ci, che *ag* polemical, controversial ■ *sf* controversy; **fare polemiche** to be contentious
polemiz'zare [polemid'dzare] *vi*: **~ (su qc)** to argue (about sth)
po'lenta *sf* (*Cuc*) *sort of thick porridge made with maize flour*
polen'tone, -a *sm/f* slowcoach (*Brit*), slowpoke (*US*)
pole'sano, -a *ag* of (*o* from) Polesine (*area between the Po and the Adige*)
POL'FER *abbr f* = **Polizia Ferroviaria**
'poli... *prefisso* poly...
poliambula'torio *sm* (*Med*) health clinic
poli'clinico, -ci *sm* general hospital, polyclinic
poli'edro *sm* polyhedron
poli'estere *sm* polyester
poliga'mia *sf* polygamy
polig'lotta, -i, e *ag, sm/f* polyglot
po'ligono *sm* polygon; **~ di tiro** rifle range
Poli'nesia *sf*: **la ~** Polynesia
polinesi'ano, -a *ag, sm/f* Polynesian
poliomielite, 'polio(mie'lite) *sf* polio(myelitis)
'polipo *sm* polyp
polisti'rolo *sm* polystyrene
poli'tecnico, -ci *sm* postgraduate technical college
po'litica, -che *sf vedi* **politico**
politi'cante *sm/f* (*peg*) petty politician
politiciz'zare [polititʃid'dzare] *vt* to politicize
po'litico, -a, ci, che *ag* political ■ *sm/f* politician ■ *sf* politics *sg*; (*linea di condotta*)

P

policy; **elezioni politiche** parliamentary (*Brit*) *o* congressional (*US*) election(s); **uomo ~** politician; **darsi alla politica** to go into politics; **fare politica** (*militante*) to be a political activist; (*come professione*) to be in politics; **la politica del governo** the government's policies; **politica aziendale** company policy; **politica estera** foreign policy; **politica dei prezzi** prices policy; **politica dei redditi** incomes policy

poliva'lente *ag* multi-purpose

poli'zia [polit'tsia] *sf* police; **~ giudiziaria** ≈ Criminal Investigation Department (CID) (*Brit*), Federal Bureau of Investigation (FBI) (*US*); **~ sanitaria/tributaria** health/tax inspectorate; **~ stradale** traffic police; **~ di stato** *see note*

POLIZIA DI STATO

The remit of the *polizia di stato* is to maintain public order, to uphold the law, and to prevent and investigate crime. This is a civilian branch of the police force; male and female officers perform similar duties. The *polizia di stato* reports to the Minister of the Interior.

polizi'esco, -a, schi, sche [polit'tsjesko] *ag* police *cpd*; (*film, romanzo*) detective *cpd*

polizi'otto [polit'tsjɔtto] *sm* policeman; **cane ~** police dog; **donna ~** policewoman; **~ di quartiere** local police officer

'polizza ['pɔlittsa] *sf* (*Comm*) bill; **~ di assicurazione** insurance policy; **~ di carico** bill of lading

pol'laio *sm* henhouse

pollai'olo, -a *sm/f* poulterer (*Brit*), poultryman

pol'lame *sm* poultry

pol'lastra *sf* pullet; (*fig: ragazza*) chick, wench

pol'lastro *sm* (*Zool*) cockerel

'pollice ['pɔllitʃe] *sm* thumb; (*unità di*) inch

'polline *sm* pollen

'pollo *sm* chicken; **far ridere i polli** (*situazione, persona*) to be utterly ridiculous

polmo'nare *ag* lung *cpd*, pulmonary

pol'mone *sm* lung

polmo'nite *sf* pneumonia; **~ atipica** SARS

'Polo *sm* (*Pol*) *centre-right coalition*

'polo *sm* (*Geo, Fisica*) pole; (*gioco*) polo ■ *sf inv* (*maglia*) polo shirt; **il P~ sud/nord** the South/North Pole

Po'lonia *sf*: **la ~** Poland

'polpa *sf* flesh, pulp; (*carne*) lean meat

pol'paccio [pol'pattʃo] *sm* (*Anat*) calf

polpas'trello *sm* fingertip

pol'petta *sf* (*Cuc*) meatball

polpet'tone *sm* (*Cuc*) meatloaf

'polpo *sm* octopus

pol'poso, -a *ag* fleshy

pol'sino *sm* cuff

'polso *sm* (*Anat*) wrist; (*pulsazione*) pulse; (*fig: forza*) drive, vigour (*Brit*), vigor (*US*); **avere ~** (*fig*) to be strong; **un uomo di ~** a man of nerve

pol'tiglia [pol'tiʎʎa] *sf* (*composto*) mash, mush; (*di fango e neve*) slush

pol'trire *vi* to laze about

pol'trona *sf* armchair; (*Teat: posto*) seat in the front stalls (*Brit*) *o* the orchestra (*US*)

poltron'cina [poltron'tʃina] *sf* (*Teat*) seat in the back stalls (*Brit*) *o* the orchestra (*US*)

pol'trone *ag* lazy, slothful

'polvere *sf* dust; (*anche*: **polvere da sparo**) (gun)powder; (*sostanza ridotta minutissima*) powder, dust; **caffè in ~** instant coffee; **latte in ~** dried *o* powdered milk; **sapone in ~** soap powder; **~ d'oro** gold dust; **~ pirica** *o* **da sparo** gunpowder; **polveri sottili** particulates

polveri'era *sf* powder magazine

polve'rina *sf* (*gen, Med*) powder; (*gergo: cocaina*) snow

polveriz'zare [polverid'dzare] *vt* to pulverize; (*nebulizzare*) to atomize; (*fig*) to crush, pulverize; (*record*) to smash

polve'rone *sm* thick cloud of dust

polve'roso, -a *ag* dusty

po'mata *sf* ointment, cream

po'mello *sm* knob

pomeridi'ano, -a *ag* afternoon *cpd*; **nelle ore pomeridiane** in the afternoon

pome'riggio [pome'riddʒo] *sm* afternoon; **nel primo/tardo ~** in the early/late afternoon

'pomice ['pomitʃe] *sf* pumice

pomici'are [pomi'tʃare] *vi* (*fam*) to neck

'pomo *sm* (*mela*) apple; (*ornamentale*) knob; (*di sella*) pommel; **~ d'Adamo** (*Anat*) Adam's apple

pomo'doro *sm* tomato

'pompa *sf* pump; (*sfarzo*) pomp (and ceremony); **~ antincendio** fire hose; **~ di benzina** petrol (*Brit*) *o* gas (*US*) pump; (*distributore*) filling *o* gas (*US*) station; **impresa di pompe funebri** funeral parlour *sg* (*Brit*), undertaker's *sg*, mortician's (*US*)

pom'pare *vt* to pump; (*trarre*) to pump out; (*gonfiare d'aria*) to pump up

pompei'ano, -a *ag* of (*o* from) Pompei

pom'pelmo *sm* grapefruit

pompi'ere *sm* fireman

pom'pon [pom'pɔn] *sm inv* pompom, pompon

pom'poso, -a *ag* pompous

ponde'rare *vt* to ponder over, consider carefully
ponde'roso, -a *ag* (*anche fig*) weighty
po'nente *sm* west
'pongo *vb vedi* **porre**
'poni *vb vedi* **porre**
'ponte *sm* bridge; (*di nave*) deck; (*: anche*: **ponte di comando**) bridge; (*impalcatura*) scaffold; **vivere sotto i ponti** to be a tramp; **fare il ~** (*fig*) to take the extra day off; (*between 2 public holidays*): **governo ~** interim government; **~ aereo** airlift; **~ di barche** (*Mil*) pontoon bridge; **~ di coperta** (*Naut*) upper deck; **~ levatoio** drawbridge; **~ radio** radio link; **~ sospeso** suspension bridge
pon'tefice [pon'tefitʃe] *sm* (*Rel*) pontiff
ponti'cello [ponti'tʃɛllo] *sm* (*di occhiali, Mus*) bridge
pontifi'care *vi* (*anche fig*) to pontificate
pontifi'cato *sm* pontificate
ponti'ficio, -a, ci, cie [ponti'fitʃo] *ag* papal; **Stato P~** Papal State
pon'tile *sm* jetty
'pony ['pɔni] *sm inv* pony
pool [pu:l] *sm inv* (*consorzio*) consortium; (*organismo internazionale*) pool; (*di esperti, ricercatori*) team; (*antimafia, antidroga*) working party
pop [pɔp] *ag inv* pop *cpd*
'popcorn ['pɔpkɔ:n] *sm inv* popcorn
'popeline ['pɔpelin] *sm* poplin
popò *sm inv* (*sedere*) botty
popo'lano, -a *ag* popular, of the people ▪ *sm/f* man/woman of the people
popo'lare *ag* popular; (*quartiere, clientela*) working-class; (*Pol*) of P.P.I. ▪ *sm/f* (*Pol*) member (*o* supporter) of P.P.I. ▪ *vt* (*rendere abitato*) to populate; **popolarsi** *vr* to fill with people, get crowded; **manifestazione ~** mass demonstration; **repubblica ~** people's republic
popolarità *sf* popularity
popolazi'one [popolat'tsjone] *sf* population
'popolo *sm* people
popo'loso, -a *ag* densely populated
po'pone *sm* melon
'poppa *sf* (*di nave*) stern; (*fam: mammella*) breast; **a ~** aft, astern
pop'pante *sm/f* unweaned infant; (*fig*) whippersnapper
pop'pare *vt* to suck
pop'pata *sf* (*allattamento*) feed
poppa'toio *sm* (feeding) bottle
popu'lista, -i, e *ag* populist
por'caio *sm* (*anche fig*) pigsty
por'cata *sf* (*libro, film etc*) load of rubbish; **fare una ~ a qn** to play a dirty trick on sb
porcel'lana [portʃel'lana] *sf* porcelain, china; (*oggetto*) piece of porcelain
porcel'lino, -a [portʃel'lino] *sm/f* piglet; **~ d'India** guinea pig
porche'ria [porke'ria] *sf* filth, muck; (*fig: oscenità*) obscenity; (*azione disonesta*) dirty trick; (*cosa mal fatta*) rubbish
por'chetta [por'ketta] *sf* roast sucking pig
por'cile [por'tʃile] *sm* pigsty
por'cino, -a [por'tʃino] *ag* of pigs, pork *cpd* ▪ *sm* (*fungo*) *type of edible mushroom*
'porco, -ci *sm* pig; (*carne*) pork
porcos'pino *sm* porcupine
'porfido *sm* porphyry
'porgere ['pɔrdʒere] *vt* to hand, give; (*tendere*) to hold out
'porno *ag inv* porn, porno
pornogra'fia *sf* pornography
porno'grafico, -a, ci, che *ag* pornographic
'poro *sm* pore
po'roso, -a *ag* porous
'porpora *sf* purple
'porre *vt* (*mettere*) to put; (*collocare*) to place; (*posare*) to lay (down), put (down); (*fig: supporre*): **poniamo (il caso) che ...** let's suppose that ...; **porsi** *vr* (*mettersi*): **porsi a sedere/in cammino** to sit down/, set off; **~ le basi di** (*fig*) to lay the foundations of, establish; **~ una domanda a qn** to ask sb a question, put a question to sb; **~ la propria fiducia in** to place one's trust in sb; **~ fine** *o* **termine a qc** to put an end *o* a stop to sth; **posto che ...** supposing that ..., on the assumption that ...; **porsi in salvo** to save o.s.
'porro *sm* (*Bot*) leek; (*Med*) wart
'porsi *etc vb vedi* **porgere**
'porta *sf* door; (*Sport*) goal; (*Inform*) port; **porte** *sfpl* (*di città*) gates; **mettere qn alla ~** to throw sb out; **sbattere** *o* **chiudere la ~ in faccia a qn** (*anche fig*) to slam the door in sb's face; **trovare tutte le porte chiuse** (*fig*) to find the way barred; **a porte chiuse** (*Dir*) in camera; **l'inverno è alle porte** (*fig*) winter is upon us; **vendita ~ a ~** door-to-door selling; **~ di servizio** tradesmen's entrance; **~ di sicurezza** emergency exit; **~ stagna** watertight door
portaba'gagli [portaba'gaʎʎi] *sm inv* (*facchino*) porter; (*Aut, Ferr*) luggage rack
portabandi'era *sm inv* standard bearer
porta'borse *sm inv* (*peg*) lackey
portabot'tiglie [portabot'tiʎʎe] *sm inv* bottle rack
porta-'CD [portatʃi'di] *sm inv* CD rack; (*astuccio*) CD holder
porta'cenere [porta'tʃenere] *sm inv* ashtray

P

portachi'avi [porta'kjavi] *sm inv* keyring
porta'cipria [porta'tʃiprja] *sm inv* powder compact
porta'erei *sf inv* (*nave*) aircraft carrier ■ *sm inv* (*aereo*) aircraft transporter
portafi'nestra (*pl* **portefinestre**) *sf* French window
porta'foglio [porta'fɔʎʎo] *sm* (*busta*) wallet; (*cartella*) briefcase; (*Pol, Borsa*) portfolio; ~ **titoli** investment portfolio
portagi'oie [porta'dʒɔje], **portagioi'elli** [portadʒo'jɛlli] *sm inv* jewellery (*Brit*) *o* jewelry (*US*) box
por'tale *sm* portal
porta'lettere *sm/f inv* postman/woman (*Brit*), mailman/woman (*US*)
porta'mento *sm* carriage, bearing
portamo'nete *sm inv* purse
por'tante *ag* (*muro etc*) supporting, load-bearing
portan'tina *sf* sedan chair; (*per ammalati*) stretcher
portaog'getti [portaod'dʒɛtti] *ag inv*: **vano** ~ (*in macchina*) glove compartment
portaom'brelli *sm inv* umbrella stand
porta'pacchi [porta'pakki] *sm inv* (*di moto, bicicletta*) luggage rack
porta'penne [porta'penne] *sm inv* pen holder; (*astuccio*) pencil case
por'tare *vt* (*sostenere, sorreggere: peso, bambino, pacco*) to carry; (*indossare: abito, occhiali*) to wear; (*capelli lunghi*) to have; (*avere: nome, titolo*) to have, bear; (*recare*): ~ **qc a qn** to take (*o* bring) sth to sb; (*fig: sentimenti*) to bear; **portarsi** *vr* (*recarsi*) to go; ~ **avanti** (*discorso, idea*) to pursue; ~ **via** to take away; (*rubare*) to take; ~ **i bambini a spasso** to take the children for a walk; ~ **fortuna** to bring good luck; ~ **qc alla bocca** to lift *o* put sth to one's lips; **porta bene i suoi anni** he's wearing well; **dove porta questa strada?** where does this road lead?, where does this road take you?; **il documento porta la tua firma** the document has *o* bears your signature; **non gli porto rancore** I don't bear him a grudge; **la polizia si è portata sul luogo del disastro** the police went to the scene of the disaster
portarit'ratti *sm inv* photo(graph) frame
portari'viste *sm inv* magazine rack
portasa'pone *sm inv* soap dish
portasiga'rette *sm inv* cigarette case
portas'pilli *sm inv* pincushion
por'tata *sf* (*vivanda*) course; (*Aut*) carrying (*o* loading) capacity; (*di arma*) range; (*volume d'acqua*) (rate of) flow; (*fig: limite*) scope, capability; (*: importanza*) impact, import; **alla** ~ **di tutti** (*conoscenza*) within everybody's capabilities; (*prezzo*) within everybody's means; **a/fuori** ~ **(di)** within/out of reach (of); **a** ~ **di mano** within (arm's) reach; **di grande** ~ of great importance
por'tatile *ag* portable
por'tato, -a *ag* (*incline*): ~ **a** inclined *o* apt to
porta'tore, -'trice *sm/f* (*anche Comm*) bearer; (*Med*) carrier; **pagabile al** ~ payable to the bearer; ~ **di handicap** disabled person
portatovagli'olo [portatovaʎ'ʎɔlo] *sm* napkin ring
portau'ovo *sm inv* eggcup
porta'voce [porta'votʃe] *sm/f inv* spokesman/woman
por'tello *sm* (*di portone*) door; (*Naut*) hatch
portel'lone *sm* (*Naut, Aer*) hold door
por'tento *sm* wonder, marvel
porten'toso, -a *ag* wonderful, marvellous (*Brit*), marvelous (*US*)
porti'cato *sm* portico
'portico, -ci *sm* portico; (*riparo*) lean-to
porti'era *sf* (*Aut*) door
porti'ere *sm* (*portinaio*) concierge, caretaker; (*di hotel*) porter; (*nel calcio*) goalkeeper
porti'naio, -a *sm/f* concierge, caretaker
portine'ria *sf* caretaker's lodge
'porto, -a *pp di* **porgere** ■ *sm* (*Naut*) harbour (*Brit*), harbor (*US*), port; (*spesa di trasporto*) carriage ■ *sm inv* port (wine); **andare** *o* **giungere in** ~ (*fig*) to come to a successful conclusion; **condurre qc in** ~ to bring sth to a successful conclusion; ~ **d'armi** gun licence (*Brit*) *o* license (*US*); ~ **fluviale** river port; ~ **franco** free port; ~ **marittimo** seaport; ~ **militare** naval base; ~ **pagato** carriage paid, post free *o* paid; ~ **di scalo** port of call
Porto'gallo *sm*: **il** ~ Portugal
porto'ghese [porto'gese] *ag, sm/f, sm* Portuguese *inv*
por'tone *sm* main entrance, main door
portori'cano, -a *ag, sm/f* Puerto Rican
Porto'rico *sf* Puerto Rico
portu'ale *ag* harbour *cpd* (*Brit*), harbor *cpd* (*US*), port *cpd* ■ *sm* dock worker
porzi'one [por'tsjone] *sf* portion, share; (*di cibo*) portion, helping
'posa *sf* (*Fot*) exposure; (*atteggiamento, di modello*) pose; (*riposo*): **lavorare senza** ~ to work without a break; **mettersi in** ~ to pose; **teatro di** ~ photographic studio
posa'cenere [posa'tʃenere] *sm inv* ashtray
po'sare *vt* to put (down), lay (down) ■ *vi* (*ponte, edificio, teoria*): ~ **su** to rest on; (*Fot: atteggiarsi*) to pose; **posarsi** *vr* (*ape, aereo*) to land; (*uccello*) to alight; (*sguardo*) to settle
po'sata *sf* piece of cutlery; **posate** *sfpl* cutlery *sg*

posa'tezza [posa'tettsa] *sf* (*di persona*) composure; (*di discorso*) balanced nature
po'sato, -a *ag* steady; (*discorso*) balanced
pos'critto *sm* postscript
'posi *etc vb vedi* **porre**
positiva'mente *av* positively; (*rispondere*) in the affirmative, affirmatively
posi'tivo, -a *ag* positive
posizi'one [pozit'tsjone] *sf* position; **farsi una ~** to make one's way in the world; **prendere ~** (*fig*) to take a stand; **luci di ~** (*Aut*) sidelights
posolo'gia, -'gie [pozolo'dʒia] *sf* dosage, directions *pl* for use
pos'porre *vt* to place after; (*differire*) to postpone, defer
pos'posto, -a *pp di* **posporre**
posse'dere *vt* to own, possess; (*qualità, virtù*) to have, possess; (*conoscere a fondo: lingua etc*) to have a thorough knowledge of; (*ira etc*) to possess
possedi'mento *sm* possession
pos'sente *ag* strong, powerful
posses'sivo, -a *ag* possessive
pos'sesso *sm* possession; **essere in ~ di** to be in possession of sth; **prendere ~** to take possession of sth; **entrare in ~** to come into one's inheritance
posses'sore *sm* owner
pos'sibile *ag* possible ■ *sm*: **fare tutto il ~** to do everything possible; **nei limiti del ~** as far as possible; **al più tardi ~** as late as possible; **vieni prima ~** come as soon as possible
possibi'lista, -i, e *ag*: **essere ~** to keep an open mind
possibilità *sf inv* possibility ■ *sfpl* (*mezzi*) means; **aver la ~ di fare** to be in a position to do; to have the opportunity to do; **nei limiti delle nostre ~** in so far as we can
possibil'mente *av* if possible
possi'dente *sm/f* landowner
possi'edo *etc vb vedi* **possedere**
'posso *etc vb vedi* **potere**
post ... *prefisso* post...
'posta *sf* (*servizio*) post, postal service; (*corrispondenza*) post, mail; (*ufficio postale*) post office; (*nei giochi d'azzardo*) stake; (*Caccia*) hide (*Brit*), blind (*US*); **poste** *sfpl* (*amministrazione*) post office; **fare la ~ a qn** (*fig*) to lie in wait for sb; **la ~ in gioco è troppo alta** (*fig*) there's too much at stake; **a bella ~** (*apposta*) on purpose; **piccola ~** (*su giornale*) letters to the editor, letters page; **~ aerea** airmail; **~ elettronica** electronic mail; **~ ordinaria** ≈ second-class mail; **~ prioritaria** first class (post); **Poste e Telecomunicazioni** *postal and telecommunications service*; **ministro delle Poste e Telecomunicazioni** Postmaster General
posta'giro [posta'dʒiro] *sm* post office cheque (*Brit*) *o* check (*US*), postal giro (*Brit*)
pos'tale *ag* postal, post office *cpd* ■ *sm* (*treno*) mail train; (*nave*) mail boat; (*furgone*) mail van; **timbro ~** postmark
postazi'one [postat'tsjone] *sf* (*Mil*) emplacement
post'bellico, -a, ci, che *ag* postwar
postda'tare *vt* to postdate
posteggi'are [posted'dʒare] *vt, vi* to park
posteggia'tore, -'trice [posteddʒa'tore] *sm/f* car-park attendant (*Brit*), parking-lot attendant (*US*)
pos'teggio [pos'teddʒo] *sm* car park (*Brit*), parking lot (*US*); (*di taxi*) rank (*Brit*), stand (*US*)
postelegra'fonico, -a, ci, che *ag* postal and telecommunications *cpd*
'poster *sm inv* poster
'posteri *smpl* posterity *sg*; **i nostri ~** our descendants
posteri'ore *ag* (*dietro*) back; (*dopo*) later ■ *sm* (*fam: sedere*) behind
posteri'ori: a ~ *ag inv* after the event; (*dopo sostantivo*) *av* looking back
pos'ticcio, -a, ci, ce [pos'tittʃo] *ag* false ■ *sm* hairpiece
postici'pare [postitʃi'pare] *vt* to defer, postpone
pos'tilla *sf* marginal note
pos'tino *sm* postman (*Brit*), mailman (*US*)
'posto, -a *pp di* **porre** ■ *sm* (*sito, posizione*) place; (*impiego*) job; (*spazio libero*) room, space; (*di parcheggio*) space; (*sedile: al teatro, in treno etc*) seat; (*Mil*) post; **a ~** (*in ordine*) in place, tidy; (*fig*) settled; (*: persona*) reliable; **mettere a ~** (*riordinare*) to tidy (up), put in order; (*faccende: sistemare*) to straighten out; **prender ~** to take a seat; **al ~ di** in place of; **sul ~** on the spot; **~ di blocco** roadblock; **~ di lavoro** job; **~ di polizia** police station; **~ telefonico pubblico** public telephone; **~ di villeggiatura** holiday (*Brit*) *o* tourist spot; **posti in piedi** (*Teat: in autobus*) standing room
postopera'torio, -a *ag* (*Med*) postoperative
pos'tribolo *sm* brothel
post'scriptum *sm inv* postscript
'postumo, -a *ag* posthumous; (*tardivo*) belated; **postumi** *smpl* (*conseguenze*) after-effects, consequences
po'tabile *ag* drinkable; **acqua ~** drinking water
po'tare *vt* to prune

P

po'tassio *sm* potassium
pota'tura *sf* pruning
po'tente *ag* (*nazione*) strong, powerful; (*veleno, farmaco*) potent, strong
poten'tino, -a *ag* of (*o* from) Potenza
Po'tenza [po'tɛntsa] *sf* Potenza
po'tenza [po'tɛntsa] *sf* power; (*forza*) strength; **all'ennesima** ~ to the nth degree; **le Grandi Potenze** the Great Powers; ~ **militare** military might *o* strength
potenzi'ale [poten'tsjale] *ag, sm* potential
potenzia'mento [potentsja'mento] *sm* development
potenzi'are [poten'tsjare] *vt* to develop

 PAROLA CHIAVE

po'tere *sm* power; **al potere** (*partito etc*) in power; **potere d'acquisto** purchasing power; **potere esecutivo** executive power; **potere giudiziario** legal power; **potere legislativo** legislative power
■ *vb aus* **1** (*essere in grado di*) can, be able to; **non ha potuto ripararlo** he couldn't *o* he wasn't able to repair it; **non è potuto venire** he couldn't *o* he wasn't able to come; **spiacente di non poter aiutare** sorry not to be able to help
2 (*avere il permesso*) can, may, be allowed to; **posso entrare?** can *o* may I come in?; **posso chiederti, dove sei stato?** where, may I ask, have you been?
3 (*eventualità*) may, might, could; **potrebbe essere vero** it might *o* could be true; **può aver avuto un incidente** he may *o* might *o* could have had an accident; **può darsi** perhaps; **può darsi** *o* **può essere che non venga** he may *o* might not come
4 (*augurio*): **potessi almeno parlargli!** if only I could speak to him!
5 (*suggerimento*): **potresti almeno scusarti!** you could at least apologize!
■ *vt* can, be able to; **può molto per noi** he can do a lot for us; **non ne posso più** (*per stanchezza*) I'm exhausted; (*per rabbia*) I can't take any more

potestà *sf* (*potere*) power; (*Dir*) authority
potrò *etc vb vedi* **potere**
pove'raccio, -a, ci, ce [pove'rattʃo] *sm/f* poor devil
'povero, -a *ag* poor; (*disadorno*) plain, bare
■ *sm/f* poor man/woman; **i poveri** the poor; ~ **di** lacking in, having little; **minerale ~ di ferro** ore with a low iron content; **paese ~ di risorse** country short of *o* lacking in resources
povertà *sf* poverty; ~ **energetica** fuel poverty
pozi'one [pot'tsjone] *sf* potion
'pozza ['pottsa] *sf* pool
poz'zanghera [pot'tsangera] *sf* puddle
'pozzo ['pottso] *sm* well; (*cava: di carbone*) pit; (*di miniera*) shaft; ~ **nero** cesspit; ~ **petrolifero** oil well
pp. *abbr* (= *pagine*) pp
p.p. *abbr* (= *per procura*) pp
P.P.I. *sigla m* (*Pol: Partito Popolare Italiano*) *party originating from D.C.*
PP.TT. *abbr* = **Poste e Telecomunicazioni**
PR *sigla* = **Parma** ■ *sigla m* (*Pol*) = **Partito Radicale**
P.R. *abbr* = **piano regolatore; procuratore della Repubblica**
'Praga *sf* Prague
prag'matico, -a, ci, che *ag* pragmatic
pram'matica *sf* custom; **essere di** ~ to be customary
pranotera'pia *sf* pranotherapy
pran'zare [pran'dzare] *vi* to dine, have dinner; to lunch, have lunch
'pranzo ['prandzo] *sm* dinner; (*a mezzogiorno*) lunch
'prassi *sf* usual procedure
'pratica, -che *sf* practice; (*esperienza*) experience; (*conoscenza*) knowledge, familiarity; (*tirocinio*) training, practice; (*Amm: affare*) matter, case; (*:incartamento*) file, dossier; **in ~** (*praticamente*) in practice; **mettere in ~** to put into practice; **fare le pratiche per** (*Amm*) to do the paperwork for; ~ **restrittiva** restrictive practice; **pratiche illecite** dishonest practices
prati'cabile *ag* (*progetto*) practicable, feasible; (*luogo*) passable, practicable
pratica'mente *av* (*in modo pratico*) in a practical way, practically; (*quasi*) practically, almost
prati'cante *sm/f* apprentice, trainee; (*Rel*) (regular) churchgoer
prati'care *vt* to practise (*Brit*), practice (*US*); (*Sport: tennis etc*) to play; (*nuoto, scherma etc*) to go in for; (*eseguire: apertura, buco*) to make; ~ **uno sconto** to give a discount
praticità [pratitʃi'ta] *sf* practicality, practicalness; **per ~** for practicality's sake
'pratico, -a, ci, che *ag* practical; ~ **di** (*esperto*) experienced *o* skilled in; (*familiare*) familiar with; **all'atto ~** in practice; **è ~ del mestiere** he knows his trade; **mi è più ~ venire di pomeriggio** it's more convenient for me to come in the afternoon
'prato *sm* meadow; (*di giardino*) lawn
preal'larme *sm* warning (signal)
Pre'alpi *sfpl*: **le ~** (the) Pre-Alps

preal'pino, -a *ag* of the Pre-Alps
pre'ambolo *sm* preamble; **senza tanti preamboli** without beating about (*Brit*) *o* around (*US*) the bush
preannunci'are [preannun'tʃare], **preannunzi'are** [preannun'tsjare] *vt* to give advance notice of
preavvi'sare *vt* to give advance notice of
preav'viso *sm* notice; **telefonata con ~** personal *o* person to person call
pre'bellico, -a, ci, che *ag* prewar *cpd*
precari'ato *sm* temporary employment
precarietà *sf* precariousness
pre'cario, -a *ag* precarious; (*Ins*) temporary, without tenure
precauzio'nale [prekauttsjo'nale] *ag* precautionary
precauzi'one [prekaut'tsjone] *sf* caution, care; (*misura*) precaution; **prendere precauzioni** to take precautions
prece'dente [pretʃe'dɛnte] *ag* previous ■ *sm* precedent; **il discorso/film ~** the previous *o* preceding speech/film; **senza precedenti** unprecedented; **precedenti penali** (*Dir*) criminal record *sg*
precedente'mente [pretʃedente'mente] *av* previously
prece'denza [pretʃe'dɛntsa] *sf* priority, precedence; (*Aut*) right of way; **dare ~ assoluta a qc** to give sth top priority
pre'cedere [pre'tʃedere] *vt* to precede, go *o* (come) before
precet'tare [pretʃet'tare] *vt* (*lavoratori*) to order back to work (*via an injunction*)
precettazi'one [pretʃettat'tsjone] *sf* (*di lavoratori*) order to resume work
pre'cetto [pre'tʃɛtto] *sm* precept; (*Mil*) call-up notice
precet'tore [pretʃet'tore] *sm* (private) tutor
precipi'tare [pretʃipi'tare] *vi* (*cadere*) to fall headlong; (*fig: situazione*) to get out of control ■ *vt* (*gettare dall'alto in basso*) to hurl, fling; (*fig: affrettare*) to rush; **precipitarsi** *vr* (*gettarsi*) to hurl *o* fling o.s.; (*affrettarsi*) to rush
precipi'tato, -a [pretʃipi'tato] *ag* hasty ■ *sm* (*Chim*) precipitate
precipitazi'one [pretʃipitat'tsjone] *sf* (*Meteor*) precipitation; (*fig*) haste
precipi'toso, -a [pretʃipi'toso] *ag* (*caduta, fuga*) headlong; (*fig: avventato*) rash, reckless; (*affrettato*) hasty, rushed
preci'pizio [pretʃi'pittsjo] *sm* precipice; **a ~** (*fig: correre*) headlong
pre'cipuo, -a [pre'tʃipuo] *ag* principal, main
precisa'mente [pretʃiza'mente] *av* (*gen*) precisely; (*con esattezza*) exactly
preci'sare [pretʃi'zare] *vt* to state, specify; (*spiegare*) to explain (in detail); **vi preciseremo la data in seguito** we'll let you know the exact date later; **tengo a ~ che ...** I must point out that ...
precisazi'one [pretʃizat'tsjone] *sf* clarification
precisi'one [pretʃi'zjone] *sf* precision; accuracy; **strumenti di ~** precision instruments
pre'ciso, -a [pre'tʃizo] *ag* (*esatto*) precise; (*accurato*) accurate, precise; (*deciso: idea*) precise, definite; (*uguale*): **2 vestiti precisi** 2 dresses exactly the same; **sono le 9 precise** it's exactly 9 o'clock
pre'cludere *vt* to block, obstruct
pre'cluso, -a *pp di* **precludere**
pre'coce [pre'kɔtʃe] *ag* early; (*bambino*) precocious; (*vecchiaia*) premature
precocità [prekotʃi'ta] *sf* (*di morte*) untimeliness; (*di bambino*) precociousness
precon'cetto, -a [prekon'tʃɛtto] *ag* preconceived ■ *sm* preconceived idea, prejudice
pre'correre *vt* to anticipate; **~ i tempi** to be ahead of one's time
precorri'tore, -'trice *sm/f* precursor, forerunner
pre'corso, -a *pp di* **precorrere**
precur'sore *sm* forerunner, precursor
'preda *sf* (*bottino*) booty; (*animale: fig*) prey; **essere ~ di** to fall prey to; **essere in ~ a** to be prey to
pre'dare *vt* to plunder
preda'tore *sm* predator
predeces'sore, -a [predetʃes'sore] *sm/f* predecessor
pre'della *sf* platform, dais; altar-step
predesti'nare *vt* to predestine
predestinazi'one [predestinat'tsjone] *sf* predestination
pre'detto, -a *pp di* **predire** ■ *ag* aforesaid, aforementioned
'predica, -che *sf* sermon; (*fig*) lecture, talking-to
predi'care *vt, vi* to preach
predica'tivo, -a *ag* predicative
predi'cato *sm* (*Ling*) predicate
predi'letto, -a *pp di* **prediligere** ■ *ag, sm/f* favourite (*Brit*), favorite (*US*)
predilezi'one [predilet'tsjone] *sf* fondness, partiality; **avere una ~ per qc/qn** to be partial to sth/fond of sb
predi'ligere [predi'lidʒere] *vt* to prefer, have a preference for
pre'dire *vt* to foretell, predict
predis'porre *vt* to get ready, prepare; **~ qn a qc** to predispose sb to sth

P

predisposizi'one [predispozit'tsjone] *sf* (*Med*) predisposition; (*attitudine*) bent, aptitude; **avere ~ alla musica** to have a bent for music
predis'posto, -a *pp di* **predisporre**
predizi'one [predit'tsjone] *sf* prediction
predomi'nante *ag* predominant
predomi'nare *vi* (*prevalere*) to predominate; (*eccellere*) to excel
predo'minio *sm* predominance; supremacy
preesis'tente *ag* pre-existent
pree'sistere *vi* to pre-exist
preesis'tito, -a *pp di* **preesistere**
prefabbri'cato, -a *ag* (*Edil*) prefabricated
prefazi'one [prefat'tsjone] *sf* preface, foreword
prefe'renza [prefe'rɛntsa] *sf* preference; **a ~ di** rather than; **di ~** preferably, by preference; **non ho preferenze** I have no preferences either way, I don't mind
preferenzi'ale [preferen'tsjale] *ag* preferential; **corsia ~** (*Aut*) bus and taxi lane
prefe'ribile *ag*: **~ (a)** preferable (to), better (than); **sarebbe ~ andarsene** it would be better to go
preferibil'mente *av* preferably
prefe'rire *vt* to prefer, like better; **~ il caffè al tè** to prefer coffee to tea, like coffee better than tea
pre'fetto *sm* prefect
prefet'tura *sf* prefecture
pre'figgersi [pre'fiddʒersi] *vr*: **~ uno scopo** to set o.s. a goal
prefigu'rare *vt* (*simboleggiare*) to foreshadow; (*prevedere*) to foresee
pre'fisso, -a *pp di* **prefiggersi** ■ *sm* (*Ling*) prefix; (*Tel*) dialling (*Brit*) *o* dial (*US*) code
Preg. *abbr* = **pregiatissimo**
pre'gare *vi* to pray ■ *vt* (*Rel*) to pray to; (*implorare*) to beg; (*chiedere*): **~ qn di fare** to ask sb to do; **farsi ~** to need coaxing *o* persuading
pre'gevole [pre'dʒevole] *ag* valuable
pregherò *etc* [prege'rɔ] *vb vedi* **pregare**
preghi'era [pre'gjɛra] *sf* (*Rel*) prayer; (*domanda*) request
pregi'arsi [pre'dʒarsi] *vr*: **mi pregio di farle sapere che ...** I am pleased to inform you that ...
pregia'tissimo, -a [predʒa'tissimo] *ag* (*in lettere*): **~ Signor G. Agnelli** G. Agnelli Esquire
pregi'ato, -a [pre'dʒato] *ag* (*opera*) valuable; (*tessuto*) fine; (*valuta*) strong; **vino ~** vintage wine
'pregio ['prɛdʒo] *sm* (*stima*) esteem, regard; (*qualità*) (good) quality, merit; (*valore*) value, worth; **il ~ di questo sistema è ...** the merit of this system is ...; **oggetto di ~** valuable object
pregiudi'care [predʒudi'kare] *vt* to prejudice, harm, be detrimental to
pregiudi'cato, -a [predʒudi'kato] *sm/f* (*Dir*) previous offender
pregiu'dizio [predʒu'dittsjo] *sm* (*idea errata*) prejudice; (*danno*) harm *no pl*
preg'nante [preɲ'ɲante] *ag* (*fig*) pregnant, meaningful
'pregno, -a ['preɲɲo] *ag* (*saturo*): **~ di** full of, saturated with
'prego *escl* (*a chi ringrazia*) don't mention it!; (*invitando qn ad accomodarsi*) please sit down!; (*invitando qn ad andare prima*) after you!
pregus'tare *vt* to look forward to
preis'toria *sf* prehistory
preis'torico, -a, ci, che *ag* prehistoric
pre'lato *sm* prelate
prela'vaggio [prela'vaddʒo] *sm* pre-wash
prelazi'one [prelat'tsjone] *sf* (*Dir*) pre-emption; **avere il diritto di ~ su qc** to have the first option on sth
preleva'mento *sm* (*Banca*) withdrawal; (*di merce*) picking up, collection
prele'vare *vt* (*denaro*) to withdraw; (*campione*) to take; (*merce*) to pick up, collect; (*polizia*) to take, capture
preli'evo *sm* (*Banca*) withdrawal; (*Med*): **fare un ~ (di)** to take a sample (of)
prelimi'nare *ag* preliminary; **preliminari** *smpl* preliminary talks; preliminaries
pre'ludere *vi*: **~ a** (*preannunciare: crisi, guerra, temporale*) to herald, be a sign of; (*introdurre: dibattito etc*) to introduce, be a prelude to
pre'ludio *sm* prelude
pre'luso, -a *pp di* **preludere**
pre-ma'man [prema'mã] *sm inv* maternity dress
prematrimoni'ale *ag* premarital
prema'turo, -a *ag* premature
premedi'tare *vt* to premeditate, plan
premeditazi'one [premeditat'tsjone] *sf* (*Dir*) premeditation; **con ~** *ag* premeditated ■ *av* with intent
'premere *vt* to press ■ *vi*: **~ su** to press down on; (*fig*) to put pressure on; **~ a** (*fig: importare*) to matter to; **~ il grilletto** to pull the trigger
pre'messo, -a *pp di* **premettere** ■ *sf* introductory statement, introduction; **mancano le premesse per una buona riuscita** we lack the basis for a successful outcome
pre'mettere *vt* to put before; (*dire prima*) to start by saying, state first; **premetto che ...** I must say first of all that ...; **premesso**

che ... given that ...; **ciò premesso ...** that having been said ...
premi'are *vt* to give a prize to; (*fig: merito, onestà*) to reward
premiazi'one [premjat'tsjone] *sf* prize giving
'**premier** ['prɛmjer] *sm inv* premier
premi'nente *ag* pre-eminent
'**premio** *sm* prize; (*ricompensa*) reward; (*Comm*) premium; (*Amm: indennità*) bonus; **in ~ per** as a prize (*o* reward) for; **~ d'ingaggio** (*Sport*) signing-on fee; **~ di produzione** productivity bonus
pre'misi *etc vb vedi* **premettere**
premoni'tore, -'trice *ag* premonitory
premonizi'one [premonit'tsjone] *sf* premonition
premu'nirsi *vr*: **~ di** to provide o.s. with; **~ contro** to protect o.s. from, guard o.s. against
pre'mura *sf* (*fretta*) haste, hurry; (*riguardo*) attention, care; **aver ~** to be in a hurry; **far ~ a qn** to hurry sb; **usare ogni ~ nei riguardi di qn, circondare qn di premure** to be very attentive to sb
premu'roso, -a *ag* thoughtful, considerate
prena'tale *ag* antenatal
'**prendere** *vt* to take; (*andare a prendere*) to get, fetch; (*ottenere*) to get; (*guadagnare*) to get, earn; (*catturare: ladro, pesce*) to catch; (*collaboratore, dipendente*) to take on; (*passeggero*) to pick up; (*chiedere: somma, prezzo*) to charge, ask; (*trattare: persona*) to handle ■ *vi* (*colla, cemento*) to set; (*pianta*) to take; (*fuoco: nel camino*) to catch; (*voltare*): **~ a destra** to turn (to the) right; **prendersi** *vr* (*azzuffarsi*): **prendersi a pugni** to come to blows; **prende qualcosa?** (*da bere, da mangiare*) would you like something to eat (*o* drink)?; **prendo un caffè** I'll have a coffee; **~ a fare qc** to start doing sth; **~ qn/qc per** (*scambiare*) to take sb/sth for; **~ l'abitudine di** to get into the habit of; **~ fuoco** to catch fire; **~ le generalità di qn** to take down sb's particulars; **~ nota di** to take note of; **~ parte a** to take part in; **prendersi cura di qn/qc** to look after sb/sth; **prendersi un impegno** to take on a commitment; **prendersela** (*adirarsi*) to get annoyed; (*preoccuparsi*) to get upset, worry
prendi'sole *sm inv* sundress
preno'tare *vt* to book, reserve
prenotazi'one [prenotat'tsjone] *sf* booking, reservation
'**prensile** *ag* prehensile
preoccu'pante *ag* worrying
preoccu'pare *vt* to worry; **preoccuparsi** *vr*: **preoccuparsi di qn/qc** to worry about sb/sth; **preoccuparsi per qn** to be anxious for sb
preoccupazi'one [preokkupat'tsjone] *sf* worry, anxiety
preordi'nato, -a *ag* preordained
prepa'rare *vt* to prepare; (*esame, concorso*) to prepare for; **prepararsi** *vr* (*vestirsi*) to get ready; **prepararsi a qc/a fare** to get ready *o* prepare (o.s.) for sth/to do; **~ da mangiare** to prepare a meal
prepara'tivi *smpl* preparations
prepa'rato, -a *ag* (*gen*) prepared; (*pronto*) ready ■ *sm* (*prodotto*) preparation
prepara'torio, -a *ag* preparatory
preparazi'one [preparat'tsjone] *sf* preparation; **non ha la necessaria ~ per svolgere questo lavoro** he lacks the qualifications necessary for the job
prepensiona'mento *sm* early retirement
preponde'rante *ag* predominant
pre'porre *vt* to place before; (*fig*) to prefer
preposizi'one [prepozit'tsjone] *sf* (*Ling*) preposition
pre'posto, -a *pp di* **preporre**
prepo'tente *ag* (*persona*) domineering, arrogant; (*bisogno, desiderio*) overwhelming, pressing ■ *sm/f* bully
prepo'tenza [prepo'tɛntsa] *sf* arrogance; (*comportamento*) arrogant behaviour (*Brit*) *o* behavior (*US*)
pre'puzio [pre'puttsjo] *sm* (*Anat*) foreskin
preroga'tiva *sf* prerogative
'**presa** *sf* taking *no pl*; catching *no pl*; (*di città*) capture; (*indurimento: di cemento*) setting; (*appiglio, Sport*) hold; (*di acqua, gas*) (supply) point; (*Elettr*): **~ (di corrente)** socket; (*al muro*) point; (*piccola quantità: di sale etc*) pinch; (*Carte*) trick; **far ~** (*colla*) to set; **ha fatto ~ sul pubblico** (*fig*) it caught the public's imagination; **a ~ rapida** (*cemento*) quick-setting; **di forte ~** (*fig*) with wide appeal; **essere alle prese con qc** (*fig*) to be struggling with sth; **macchina da ~** (*Cine*) cine camera (*Brit*), movie camera (*US*); **~ d'aria** air inlet; **~ diretta** (*Aut*) direct drive; **~ in giro** leg-pull (*Brit*), joke; **~ di posizione** stand
pre'sagio [pre'zadʒo] *sm* omen
presa'gire [preza'dʒire] *vt* to foresee
presa'lario *sm* (*Ins*) grant
'**presbite** *ag* long-sighted
presbiteri'ano, -a *ag, sm/f* Presbyterian
presbi'terio *sm* presbytery
pre'scindere [preʃ'ʃindere] *vi*: **~ da** to leave out of consideration; **a ~ da** apart from
pre'scisso, -a [preʃ'ʃisso] *pp di* **prescindere**
presco'lastico, -a, ci, che *ag* pre-school *cpd*
pres'critto, -a *pp di* **prescrivere**
pres'crivere *vt* to prescribe

P

prescrizi'one [preskrit'tsjone] *sf* (*Med, Dir*) prescription; (*norma*) rule, regulation; **cadere in ~** (*Dir*) to become statute-barred

'**prese** *etc vb vedi* **prendere**

presen'tare *vt* to present; (*far conoscere*): **~ qn (a)** to introduce sb (to); (*Amm: inoltrare*) to submit; **presentarsi** *vr* (*recarsi, farsi vedere*) to present o.s., appear; (*farsi*) to introduce o.s.; (*occasione*) to arise; **~ qc in un'esposizione** to show *o* display sth at an exhibition; **~ qn in società** to introduce sb into society; **presentarsi come candidato** (*Pol*) to stand (*Brit*) *o* run (*US*) as a candidate; **presentarsi bene/male** to have a good/poor appearance; **la situazione si presenta difficile** things aren't looking too good, things look a bit tricky

presentazi'one [prezentat'tsjone] *sf* presentation; introduction

pre'sente *ag* present; (*questo*) this ■ *sm* present ■ *sf* (*lettera*): **con la ~ vi comunico ...** this is to inform you that ... ■ *sm/f* person present; **i presenti** those present; **aver ~ qc/qn** to remember sth/sb; **essere ~ a una riunione** to be present at *o* attend a meeting; **tener ~ qn/qc** to keep sb/sth in mind; **esclusi i presenti** present company excepted

presenti'mento *sm* premonition

pre'senza [pre'zɛntsa] *sf* presence; (*aspetto esteriore*) appearance; **in ~ di** in (the) presence of; **di bella ~** of good appearance; **~ di spirito** presence of mind

presenzi'are [prezen'tsjare] *vi*: **~ a** to be present at, attend

pre'sepe, pre'sepio *sm* crib

preser'vare *vt* to protect

preserva'tivo *sm* sheath, condom

'**presi** *etc vb vedi* **prendere**

'**preside** *sm/f* (*Ins*) head (teacher) (*Brit*), principal (*US*); (*di facoltà universitaria*) dean

presi'dente *sm* (*Pol*) president; (*di assemblea, Comm*) chairman; **il P~ della Camera** (*Pol*) ≈ the Speaker; **P~ del Consiglio (dei Ministri)** ≈ Prime Minister; **P~ della Repubblica** President of the Republic; *see note*

PRESIDENTE

The *Presidente del Consiglio*, the Italian Prime Minister, is the leader of the Government. He or she submits nominations for ministerial posts to the *Presidente della Repubblica*, who then appoints them if approved. The *Presidente del Consiglio* is appointed by the *Presidente della Repubblica*, in consultation with the leaders of the parliamentary parties, former heads of state, the *Presidente della Camera* and the *Presidente del Senato*. The *Presidente della Repubblica* is the head of state. He or she must be an Italian citizen of at least 50 years of age, and is elected by Parliament and by three delegates from each of the Italian regions. He or she has the power to suspend the implementation of legislation and to dissolve one or both chambers of Parliament, and presides over the magistrates' governing body (the "Consiglio Superiore della Magistratura").

presiden'tessa *sf* president; (*moglie*) president's wife; (*di assemblea, Comm*) chairwoman

presi'denza [presi'dɛntsa] *sf* presidency; office of president; chairmanship; **assumere la ~** to become president; to take the chair; **essere alla ~** to be president (*o* chairman); **candidato alla ~** presidential candidate; candidate for the chairmanship

presidenzi'ale [presidɛn'tsjale] *ag* presidential

presidi'are *vt* to garrison

pre'sidio *sm* garrison

presi'edere *vt* to preside over ■ *vi*: **~ a** to direct, be in charge of

'**preso, -a** *pp di* **prendere**

'**pressa** *sf* (*Tecn*) press

pres'sante *ag* (*bisogno, richiesta*) urgent, pressing

pressap'poco *av* about, roughly, approximately

pres'sare *vt* (*anche fig*) to press; **~ qn con richieste** to pursue sb with demands

pressi'one *sf* pressure; **far ~ su qn** to put pressure on sb; **subire forti pressioni** to be under strong pressure; **~ sanguigna** blood pressure

'**presso** *av* (*vicino*) nearby, close at hand ■ *prep* (*vicino a*) near; (*accanto a*) beside, next to; (*in casa di*): **~ qn** at sb's home; (*nelle lettere*) care of; (*alle dipendenza di*): **lavora ~ di noi** he works for *o* with us ■ *smpl*: **nei pressi di** near, in the vicinity of; **ha avuto grande successo ~ i giovani** it has been a hit with young people

pressoché [presso'ke] *av* nearly, almost

pressuriz'zare [pressurid'dzare] *vt* to pressurize

prestabi'lire *vt* to arrange beforehand, arrange in advance

presta'nome *sm/f inv* (*peg*) figurehead

pres'tante *ag* good-looking

pres'tanza [pres'tantsa] *sf* (robust) good looks *pl*

pres'tare *vt*: **~ (qc a qn)** to lend (sb sth *o* sth to sb); **prestarsi** *vr* (*offrirsi*): **prestarsi a fare** to offer to do; (*essere adatto*): **prestarsi a** to lend itself to, be suitable for; **~ aiuto** to lend a hand; **~ ascolto** *o* **orecchio** to listen; **~ attenzione** to pay attention; **~ fede a qc/qn** to give credence to sth/sb; **~ giuramento** to take an oath; **la frase si presta a molteplici interpretazioni** the phrase lends itself to numerous interpretations

prestazi'one [prestat'tsjone] *sf* (*Tecn, Sport*) performance; **prestazioni** *sfpl* (*di persona: servizi*) services

prestigia'tore, -'trice [prestidʒa'tore] *sm/f* conjurer

pres'tigio [pres'tidʒo] *sm* (*potere*) prestige; (*illusione*): **gioco di ~** conjuring trick

prestigi'oso, -a [presti'dʒoso] *ag* prestigious

'prestito *sm* lending *no pl*; loan; **dar in ~** to lend; **prendere in ~** to borrow; **~ bancario** bank loan; **~ pubblico** public borrowing

'presto *av* (*tra poco*) soon; (*in fretta*) quickly; (*di buon'ora*) early; **a ~** see you soon; **~ o tardi** sooner or later; **fare ~ a fare qc** to hurry up and do sth; (*non costare fatica*) to have no trouble doing sth; **si fa ~ a criticare** it's easy to criticize; **è ancora ~ per decidere** it's still too early *o* too soon to decide

pre'sumere *vt* to presume, assume

presu'mibile *ag* (*dati, risultati*) likely

pre'sunsi *etc vb vedi* **presumere**

pre'sunto, -a *pp di* **presumere** ■ *ag*: **il ~ colpevole** the alleged culprit

presuntu'oso, -a *ag* presumptuous

presunzi'one [prezun'tsjone] *sf* presumption

presup'porre *vt* to suppose; to presuppose

presup'posto, -a *pp di* **presupporre** ■ *sm* (*premessa*) supposition, premise; **partendo dal ~ che ...** assuming that ...; **mancano i presupposti necessari** the necessary conditions are lacking

'prete *sm* priest

preten'dente *sm/f* pretender ■ *sm* (*corteggiatore*) suitor

pre'tendere *vt* (*esigere*) to demand, require; (*sostenere*): **~ che** to claim that; **pretende di aver sempre ragione** he thinks he's always right

pretenzi'oso, -a [preten'tsjoso] *ag* pretentious

preterintenzio'nale [preterintentsjo'nale] *ag* (*Dir*): **omicidio ~** manslaughter

pre'teso, -a *pp di* **pretendere** ■ *sf* (*esigenza*) claim, demand; (*presunzione, sfarzo*) pretentiousness; **avanzare una pretesa** to put forward a claim *o* demand; **senza pretese** *ag* unpretentious ■ *av* unpretentiously

pre'testo *sm* pretext, excuse; **con il ~ di** on the pretext of

pretestu'oso, -a *ag* (*data, motivo*) used as an excuse

pre'tore *sm* magistrate

pre'tura *sf* (*Dir: sede*) magistrate's court (*Brit*), circuit *o* superior court (*US*); (*: magistratura*) magistracy

preva'lente *ag* prevailing

prevalente'mente *av* mainly, for the most part

preva'lenza [preva'lɛntsa] *sf* predominance

preva'lere *vi* to prevail

pre'valso, -a *pp di* **prevalere**

prevari'care *vi* (*abusare del potere*) to abuse one's power

prevaricazi'one [prevarikat'tsjone] *sf* (*abuso di potere*) abuse of power

preve'dere *vt* (*indovinare*) to foresee; (*presagire*) to foretell; (*considerare*) to make provision for; **nulla lasciava ~ che ...** there was nothing to suggest *o* to make one think that ...; **come previsto** as expected; **spese previste** anticipated expenditure; **previsto per martedì** scheduled for Tuesday

prev'edibile *ag* predictable; **non era assolutamente ~ che ...** no one could have foreseen that ...

prevedibil'mente *av* as one would expect

preve'nire *vt* (*anticipare: obiezione*) to forestall; (*domanda*) to anticipate; (*evitare*) to avoid, prevent; (*avvertire*): **~ qn (di)** to warn sb (of); to inform sb (of)

preventi'vare *vt* (*Comm*) to estimate

preven'tivo, -a *ag* preventive ■ *sm* (*Comm*) estimate; **fare un ~** to give an estimate; **bilancio ~** budget; **carcere ~** custody; (*pending trial*)

preve'nuto, -a *ag* (*mal disposto*): **~ (contro qc/qn)** prejudiced (against sth/sb)

prevenzi'one [preven'tsjone] *sf* prevention; (*preconcetto*) prejudice

previ'dente *ag* showing foresight; prudent

previ'denza [previ'dɛntsa] *sf* foresight; **istituto di ~** provident institution; **~ sociale** social security (*Brit*), welfare (*US*)

pre'vidi *etc vb vedi* **prevedere**

'previo, -a *ag* (*Comm*): **~ avviso** upon notice; **~ pagamento** upon payment

previsi'one *sf* forecast, prediction; **previsioni meteorologiche** *o* **del tempo** weather forecast *sg*

pre'visto, -a *pp di* **prevedere** ■ *sm*: **piú/meno del ~** more/less than expected; **prima del ~** earlier than expected

P

prezi'oso, -a [pret'tsjoso] *ag* precious; (*aiuto, consiglio*) invaluable ■ *sm* jewel; valuable

prez'zemolo [pret'tsemolo] *sm* parsley

'prezzo ['prɛttso] *sm* price; **a ~ di costo** at cost, at cost price (*Brit*); **tirare sul ~** to bargain, haggle; **il ~ pattuito è 1000 di euro** the agreed price is 1000 euros; **~ d'acquisto/di vendita** buying/selling price; **~ di fabbrica** factory price; **~ di mercato** market price; **~ scontato** reduced price; **~ unitario** unit price

P.R.I. *sigla m* (= *Partito Repubblicano Italiano*) *former political party*

prigi'one [pri'dʒone] *sf* prison

prigio'nia [pridʒo'nia] *sf* imprisonment

prigioni'ero, -a [pridʒo'njɛro] *ag* captive ■ *sm/f* prisoner

'prima *sf vedi* **primo** ■ *av* before; (*in anticipo*) in advance, beforehand; (*per l'addietro*) at one time, formerly; (*più presto*) sooner, earlier; (*in primo luogo*) first ■ *cong*: **~ di fare/che parta** before doing/he leaves; **~ di** *prep* before; **~ o poi** sooner or later; **due giorni ~** two days before *o* earlier; **~ d'ora** before now

pri'mario, -a *ag* primary; (*principale*) chief, leading, primary ■ *sm/f* (*medico*) head physician, chief physician

pri'mate *sm* (*Rel, Zool*) primate

prima'tista, -i, e *sm/f* (*Sport*) record holder

pri'mato *sm* supremacy; (*Sport*) record

prima'vera *sf* spring

primave'rile *ag* spring *cpd*

primeggi'are [primed'dʒare] *vi* to excel, be one of the best

primi'tivo, -a *ag* (*gen*) primitive; (*significato*) original

pri'mizie [pri'mittsje] *sfpl* early produce *sg*

'primo, -a *ag* first; (*fig*) initial; basic; prime ■ *sm/f* first (one) ■ *sm* (*Cuc*) first course; (*in date*): **il ~ luglio** the first of July ■ *sf* (*Teat*) first night; (*Cine*) première; (*Aut*) first (gear); **le prime ore del mattino** the early hours of the morning; **di prima mattina** early in the morning; **in prima pagina** (*Stampa*) on the front page; **ai primi freddi** at the first sign of cold weather; **ai primi di maggio** at the beginning of May; **i primi del Novecento** the early twentieth century; **viaggiare in prima** to travel first-class; **per prima cosa** firstly; **in ~ luogo** first of all, in the first place; **di prim'ordine** *o* **prima qualità** first-class, first-rate; **in un ~ tempo** *o* **momento** at first; **prima donna** leading lady; (*di opera lirica*) prima donna

primo'genito, -a [primo'dʒɛnito] *ag, sm/f* firstborn

pri'mordi *smpl* beginnings

primordi'ale *ag* primordial

'primula *sf* primrose

princi'pale [printʃi'pale] *ag* main, principal ■ *sm* manager, boss; **sede ~** head office

principal'mente [printʃipal'mente] *av* mainly, principally

princi'pato [printʃi'pato] *sm* principality

'principe ['printʃipe] *sm* prince; **~ ereditario** crown prince

princi'pesco, -a, schi, sche [printʃi'pesko] *ag* (*anche fig*) princely

princi'pessa [printʃi'pessa] *sf* princess

principi'ante [printʃi'pjante] *sm/f* beginner

principi'are [printʃi'pjare] *vt, vi* to start, begin

prin'cipio [prin'tʃipjo] *sm* (*inizio*) beginning, start; (*origine*) origin, cause; (*concetto, norma*) principle; **al** *o* **in ~** at first; **fin dal ~** right from the start; **per ~** on principle; **una questione di ~** a matter of principle; **una persona di sani principi morali** a person of sound moral principles; **~ attivo** active ingredient

pri'ore *sm* (*Rel*) prior

pri'ori: **a ~** *ag inv* prior; a priori *av* at first glance; initially; a priori

priorità *sf* priority; **avere la ~ (su)** to have priority (over)

priori'tario, -a *ag* (*scelta*) first; (*interesse*) overriding; **posta prioritaria** first class (post)

'prisma, -i *sm* prism

pri'vare *vt*: **~ qn di** to deprive sb of; **privarsi** *vr*: **privarsi di** to go *o* do without

priva'tiva *sf* (*Econ*) monopoly

privatiz'zare [privatid'dzare] *vt* to privatize

privatizzazi'one [privatiddzat'tsjone] *sf* privatization

pri'vato, -a *ag* private ■ *sm/f* (*anche*: **privato cittadino**) private citizen; **in ~** in private; **diritto ~** (*Dir*) civil law; **ritirarsi a vita privata** to withdraw from public life; **"non vendiamo a privati"** "wholesale only"

privazi'one [privat'tsjone] *sf* privation, hardship

privilegi'are [privile'dʒare] *vt* to favour (*Brit*), favor (*US*)

privilegi'ato, -a [privile'dʒato] *ag* (*individuo, classe*) privileged; (*trattamento, Comm: credito*) preferential; **azioni privilegiate** preference shares (*Brit*), preferred stock (*US*)

privi'legio [privi'lɛdʒo] *sm* privilege; **avere il ~ di fare** to have the privilege of doing, be privileged to do

'privo, -a *ag*: **~ di** without, lacking

pro *prep* for, on behalf of ■ *sm inv* (*utilità*) advantage, benefit; **a che ~?** what's the use?; **il ~ e il contro** the pros and cons

pro'babile *ag* probable, likely
probabilità *sf inv* probability; **con molta ~** very probably, in all probability
probabil'mente *av* probably
pro'bante *ag* convincing
pro'blema, -i *sm* problem
proble'matico, -a, ci, che *ag* problematic; (*incerto*) doubtful ■ *sf* problems *pl*
pro'boscide [pro'bɔʃʃide] *sf* (*di elefante*) trunk
procacci'are [prokat'tʃare] *vt* to get, obtain
procaccia'tore [prokattʃa'tore] *sm*: **~ d'affari** sales executive
pro'cace [pro'katʃe] *ag* (*donna, aspetto*) provocative
pro'cedere [pro'tʃɛdere] *vi* to proceed; (*comportarsi*) to behave; (*iniziare*): **~ a** to start; **~ contro** (*Dir*) to start legal proceedings against; **~ oltre** to go on ahead; **prima di ~ oltre** before going any further; **gli affari procedono bene** business is going well; **bisogna ~ con cautela** we have to proceed cautiously; **non luogo a ~** (*Dir*) nonsuit
procedi'mento [protʃedi'mento] *sm* (*modo di condurre*) procedure; (*di avvenimenti*) course; (*Tecn*) process; **~ penale** (*Dir*) criminal proceedings *pl*
proce'dura [protʃe'dura] *sf* (*Dir*) procedure
proces'sare [protʃes'sare] *vt* (*Dir*) to try
processi'one [protʃes'sjone] *sf* procession
pro'cesso [pro'tʃɛsso] *sm* (*Dir*) trial; proceedings *pl*; (*metodo*) process; **essere sotto ~** to be on trial; **mettere sotto ~** (*anche fig*) to put on trial; **~ di fabbricazione** manufacturing process; **~ di pace** peace process
processu'ale [protʃessu'ale] *ag* (*Dir*): **atti processuali** records of a trial; **spese processuali** legal costs
Proc. Gen. *abbr* = **procuratore generale**
pro'cinto [pro'tʃinto] *sm*: **in ~ di fare** about to do, on the point of doing
pro'clama, -i *sm* proclamation
procla'mare *vt* to proclaim
proclamazi'one [proklamat'tsjone] *sf* proclamation, declaration
procrasti'nare *vt* (*data*) to postpone; (*pagamento*) to defer
procre'are *vt* to procreate
pro'cura *sf* (*Dir*) proxy, power of attorney; (*ufficio*) attorney's office; **per ~** by proxy; **la P~ della Repubblica** the Public Prosecutor's Office
procu'rare *vt*: **~ qc a qn** (*fornire*) to get *o* obtain sth for sb; (*causare: noie etc*) to bring *o* give sb sth
procura'tore, -'trice *sm/f* (*Dir*) ≈ solicitor; (*: chi ha la procura*) holder of power of attorney; **~ generale** (*in corte d'appello*) public prosecutor; (*in corte di cassazione*) Attorney General; **~ legale** ≈ solicitor (*Brit*), lawyer; **~ della Repubblica** (*in corte d'assise, tribunale*) public prosecutor
prodi'gare *vt* to be lavish with; **prodigarsi** *vr*: **prodigarsi per qn** to do all one can for sb
pro'digio [pro'didʒo] *sm* marvel, wonder; (*persona*) prodigy
prodigi'oso, -a [prodi'dʒoso] *ag* prodigious; phenomenal
'prodigo, -a, ghi, ghe *ag* lavish, extravagant
pro'dotto, -a *pp di* **produrre** ■ *sm* product; **~ di base** primary product; **~ finale** end product; **~ interno lordo** gross domestic product; **~ nazionale lordo** gross national product; **prodotti agricoli** farm produce *sg*; **prodotti di bellezza** cosmetics; **prodotti chimici** chemicals
pro'duco *etc vb vedi* **produrre**
pro'durre *vt* to produce
pro'dussi *etc vb vedi* **produrre**
produttività *sf* productivity
produt'tivo, -a *ag* productive
produt'tore, -'trice *ag* producing *cpd* ■ *sm/f* producer; **paese ~ di petrolio** oil-producing country
produzi'one [produt'tsjone] *sf* production; (*rendimento*) output; **~ in serie** mass production
pro'emio *sm* introduction, preface
Prof. *abbr* (= *professore*) Prof
profa'nare *vt* to desecrate
pro'fano, -a *ag* (*mondano*) secular, profane; (*sacrilego*) profane
profe'rire *vt* to utter
profes'sare *vt* to profess; (*medicina etc*) to practise (*Brit*), practice (*US*)
professio'nale *ag* professional; **scuola ~** training college
professi'one *sf* profession; **di ~** professional, by profession; **libera ~** profession
professio'nista, -i, e *sm/f* professional
profes'sore, -'essa *sm/f* (*Ins*) teacher; (*: di università*) lecturer; (*titolare di cattedra*) professor; **~ d'orchestra** member of an orchestra
pro'feta, -i *sm* prophet
pro'fetico, -a, ci, che *ag* prophetic
profetiz'zare [profetid'dzare] *vt* to prophesy
profe'zia [profet'tsia] *sf* prophecy
pro'ficuo, -a *ag* useful, profitable
profi'lare *vt* to outline; (*ornare: vestito*) to edge; **profilarsi** *vr* to stand out, be silhouetted; to loom up
profi'lassi *sf* (*Med*) preventive treatment, prophylaxis

profi'lattico, -a, ci, che *ag* prophylactic ■ *sm* (*anticoncezionale*) sheath, condom
pro'filo *sm* profile; (*breve descrizione*) sketch, outline; **di ~** in profile
profit'tare *vi*: **~ di** (*trarre profitto*) to profit by; (*approfittare*) to take advantage of
pro'fitto *sm* advantage, profit, benefit; (*fig: progresso*) progress; (*Comm*) profit; **ricavare un ~ da** to make a profit from *o* out of; **vendere con ~** to sell at a profit; **conto profitti e perdite** profit and loss account
pro'fondere *vt* (*lodi*) to lavish; (*denaro*) to squander; **profondersi** *vr*: **profondersi in** to be profuse in
profondità *sf inv* depth
pro'fondo, -a *ag* deep; (*rancore, meditazione*) profound ■ *sm* depth(s) (*pl*), bottom; **~ 8 metri** 8 metres deep
pro'forma *ag* routine *cpd* ■ *sm inv* formality ■ *av*: **fare qc ~** to do sth as a formality
'profugo, -a, ghi, ghe *sm/f* refugee
profu'mare *vt* to perfume ■ *vi* to be fragrant; **profumarsi** *vr* to put on perfume *o* scent
profumata'mente *av*: **pagare qc ~** to pay through the nose for sth
profu'mato, -a *ag* (*fiore, aria*) fragrant; (*fazzoletto, saponetta*) scented; (*pelle*) sweet-smelling; (*persona*) with perfume on
profume'ria *sf* perfumery; (*negozio*) perfume shop
pro'fumo *sm* (*prodotto*) perfume, scent; (*fragranza*) scent, fragrance
profusi'one *sf* profusion; **a ~** in plenty
pro'fuso, -a *pp di* **profondere**
progeni'tore, -'trice [prodʒeni'tore] *sm/f* ancestor
proget'tare [prodʒet'tare] *vt* to plan; (*Tecn: edificio*) to plan, design; **~ di fare qc** to plan to do sth
progettazi'one [prodʒettat'tsjone] *sf* planning; **in corso di ~** at the planning stage
proget'tista, -i, e [prodʒet'tista] *sm/f* designer
pro'getto [pro'dʒɛtto] *sm* plan; (*idea*) plan, project; **avere in ~ di fare qc** to be planning to do sth; **~ di legge** (*Pol*) bill
'prognosi ['prɔɲɲozi] *sf* (*Med*) prognosis; **essere in ~ riservata** to be on the danger list
pro'gramma, -i *sm* programme (*Brit*), program (*US*); (*TV, Radio*) program(me)s *pl*; (*Ins*) syllabus, curriculum; (*Inform*) program; **avere in ~ di fare qc** to be planning to do sth; **~ applicativo** (*Inform*) application program
program'mare *vt* (*TV, Radio*) to put on; (*Inform*) to program; (*Econ*) to plan
programma'tore, -'trice *sm/f* (*Inform*) computer programmer (*Brit*) *o* programer (*US*)
programmazi'one [programmat'tsjone] *sf* programming (*Brit*), programing (*US*); planning
progre'dire *vi* to progress, make progress
progressi'one *sf* progression
progres'sista, -i, e *ag, sm/f* progressive
progressiva'mente *av* progressively
progres'sivo, -a *ag* progressive
pro'gresso *sm* progress *no pl*; **fare progressi** to make progress
proi'bire *vt* to forbid, prohibit; **~ a qn di fare qc** (*vietare*) to forbid sb to do sth; (*impedire*) to prevent sb from doing sth
proibi'tivo, -a *ag* prohibitive
proi'bito, -a *ag* forbidden; **"è ~ l'accesso"** "no admittance"; **"è ~ fumare"** "no smoking"
proibizi'one [proibit'tsjone] *sf* prohibition
proibizio'nismo [proibittsjo'nizmo] *sm* prohibition
proiet'tare *vt* (*gen, Geom, Cine*) to project; (*presentare*) to show, screen; (*luce, ombra*) to throw, cast, project
proi'ettile *sm* projectile, bullet *o* shell *etc*
proiet'tore *sm* (*Cine*) projector; (*Aut*) headlamp; (*Mil*) searchlight
proiezi'one [projet'tsjone] *sf* (*Cine*) projection; showing
'prole *sf* children *pl*, offspring
proletari'ato *sm* proletariat
prole'tario, -a *ag, sm/f* proletarian
prolife'rare *vi* (*fig*) to proliferate
pro'lifico, -a, ci, che *ag* prolific
pro'lisso, -a *ag* verbose
'prologo, -ghi *sm* prologue
pro'lunga, -ghe *sf* (*di cavo elettrico etc*) extension
prolunga'mento *sm* (*gen*) extension; (*di strada*) continuation
prolun'gare *vt* (*discorso, attesa*) to prolong; (*linea, termine*) to extend
prome'moria *sm inv* memorandum
pro'messa *sf* promise; **fare/mantenere una ~** to make/keep a promise
pro'messo, -a *pp di* **promettere**
promet'tente *ag* promising
pro'mettere *vt* to promise ■ *vi* to be *o* look promising; **~ a qn di fare** to promise sb that one will do
promi'nente *ag* prominent
promi'nenza [promi'nɛntsa] *sf* prominence
promiscuità *sf* promiscuousness
pro'miscuo, -a *ag*: **matrimonio ~** mixed marriage; **nome ~** (*Ling*) common-gender noun
pro'misi *etc vb vedi* **promettere**

promon'torio *sm* promontory, headland
pro'mosso, -a *pp di* **promuovere**
promo'tore, -'trice *sm/f* promoter, organizer
promozio'nale [promottsjo'nale] *ag* promotional; **"vendita ~"** "special offer"
promozi'one [promot'tsjone] *sf* promotion; **~ delle vendite** sales promotion
promul'gare *vt* to promulgate
promulgazi'one [promulgat'tsjone] *sf* promulgation
promu'overe *vt* to promote
proni'pote *sm/f* (*di nonni*) great-grandchild, great-grandson/granddaughter; (*di zii*) great-nephew/niece; **pronipoti** *smpl* (*discendenti*) descendants
pro'nome *sm* (*Ling*) pronoun
pronomi'nale *ag* pronominal
pronosti'care *vt* to foretell, predict
pro'nostico, -ci *sm* forecast
pron'tezza [pron'tettsa] *sf* readiness; quickness, promptness; **~ di riflessi** quick reflexes; **~ di spirito/mente** readiness of wit/mind
'pronto, -a *ag* ready; (*rapido*) fast, quick, prompt; **~!** (*Tel*) hello!; **essere ~ a fare qc** to be ready to do sth; **~ all'ira** quick-tempered; **a pronta cassa** (*Comm*) cash (*Brit*) *o* collect (*US*) on delivery; **pronta consegna** (*Comm*) prompt delivery; **~ soccorso** (*trattamento*) first aid; (*reparto*) A&E (*Brit*), ER (*US*)
prontu'ario *sm* manual, handbook
pro'nuncia [pro'nuntʃa] *sf* pronunciation
pronunci'are [pronun'tʃare] *vt* (*parola, sentenza*) to pronounce; (*dire*) to utter; (*discorso*) to deliver; **pronunciarsi** *vr* to declare one's opinion; **pronunciarsi a favore di/contro** to pronounce o.s. in favour of/against; **non mi pronuncio** I'm not prepared to comment
pronunci'ato, -a [pronun'tʃato] *ag* (*spiccato*) pronounced, marked; (*sporgente*) prominent
pro'nunzia *etc* [pro'nuntsja] = **pronuncia** *etc*
propa'ganda *sf* propaganda
propagan'dare *vt* (*idea*) to propagandize; (*prodotto, invenzione*) to push, plug (*fam*)
propa'gare *vt* (*Fisica, Biol*) to propagate; (*notizia, idea, malattia*) to spread; **propagarsi** *vr* to propagate; to spread
propagaz'ione [propagat'tsjone] *sf* (*vedi vb*) propagation; spreading
prope'deutico, -a, ci, che *ag* (*corso, trattato*) introductory
pro'pendere *vi*: **~ per** to favour (*Brit*), favor (*US*), lean towards
propensi'one *sf* inclination, propensity; **avere ~ a credere che ...** to be inclined to think that ...
pro'penso, -a *pp di* **propendere** ■ *ag*: **essere ~ a qc** to be in favour (*Brit*) *o* favor (*US*) of sth; **essere ~ a fare qc** to be inclined to do sth
propi'nare *vt* to administer
pro'pizio, a [pro'pittsjo] *ag* favourable (*Brit*), favorable (*US*)
pro'porre *vt* (*suggerire*): **~ qc (a qn)** to suggest sth (to sb); (*candidato*) to put forward; (*legge, brindisi*) to propose; **~ di fare** to suggest *o* propose doing; **proporsi di fare** to propose *o* intend to do; **proporsi una meta** to set o.s. a goal
proporzio'nale [proportsjo'nale] *ag* proportional; **(sistema) ~** (*Pol*) proportional representation system
proporzio'nato, -a [proportsjo'nato] *ag*: **~ a** proportionate to, proportional to; **ben ~** well-proportioned
proporzi'one [propor'tsjone] *sf* proportion; **in ~ a** in proportion to
pro'posito *sm* (*intenzione*) intention, aim; (*argomento*) subject, matter; **a ~ di** regarding, with regard to; **a questo ~** on this subject; **di ~** (*apposta*) deliberately, on purpose; **a ~** by the way; **capitare a ~** (*cosa, persona*) to turn up at the right time
proposizi'one [propozit'tsjone] *sf* (*Ling*) clause; (*periodo*) sentence
pro'posto, -a *pp di* **proporre** ■ *sf* proposal; (*suggerimento*) suggestion; **fare una proposta** to put forward a proposal; to make a suggestion; **proposta di legge** (*Pol*) bill
propria'mente *av* (*correttamente*) properly, correctly; (*in modo specifico*) specifically; **~ detto** in the strict sense of the word
proprietà *sf inv* (*ciò che si possiede*) property *gen no pl*, estate; (*caratteristica*) property; (*correttezza*) correctness; **essere di ~ di qn** to belong to sb; **~ edilizia** (developed) property; **~ privata** private property
proprie'tario, -a *sm/f* owner; (*di albergo etc*) proprietor, owner; (*per l'inquilino*) landlord/lady; **~ terriero** landowner
'proprio, -a *ag* (*possessivo*) own; (*: impersonale*) one's; (*esatto*) exact, correct, proper; (*senso, significato*) literal; (*Ling: nome*) proper; (*particolare*): **~ di** characteristic of, peculiar to ■ *av* (*precisamente*) just, exactly; (*davvero*) really; (*affatto*): **non ... ~** not ... at all ■ *sm* (*Comm*): **mettersi in ~** to set up on one's own; **l'ha visto con i (suoi) propri occhi** he saw it with his own eyes
propu'gnare [propuɲ'ɲare] *vt* to support
propulsi'one *sf* propulsion; **a ~ atomica** atomic-powered
propul'sore *sm* (*Tecn*) propeller
'prora *sf* (*Naut*) bow(s) (*pl*), prow

P

'**proroga, -ghe** *sf* extension; postponement
proro'gare *vt* to extend; (*differire*) to postpone, defer
pro'rompere *vi* to burst out
pro'rotto, -a *pp di* **prorompere**
pro'ruppi *etc vb vedi* **prorompere**
'**prosa** *sf* prose; (*Teat*): **la stagione della ~** the theatre season; **attore di ~** theatre actor; **compagnia di ~** theatrical company
pro'saico, -a, ci, che *ag* (*fig*) prosaic, mundane
pro'sciogliere [proʃ'ʃɔʎʎere] *vt* to release; (*Dir*) to acquit
proscioglì'mento [proʃʃoʎʎi'mento] *sm* acquittal
prosci'olto, -a [proʃ'ʃɔlto] *pp di* **prosciogliere**
prosciu'gare [proʃʃu'gare] *vt* (*terreni*) to drain, reclaim; **prosciugarsi** *vr* to dry up
prosci'utto [proʃ'ʃutto] *sm* ham
pros'critto, -a *pp di* **proscrivere** ■ *sm/f* exile; outlaw
pros'crivere *vt* to exile, banish
proscrizi'one [proskrit'tsjone] *sf* (*esilio*) banishment, exile
prosecuzi'one [prosekut'tsjone] *sf* continuation
prosegui'mento *sm* continuation; **buon ~!** all the best!; (*a chi viaggia*) enjoy the rest of your journey!
prosegu'ire *vt* to carry on with, continue ■ *vi* to carry on, go on
pro'selito *sm* (*Rel, Pol*) convert
prospe'rare *vi* to thrive
prosperità *sf* prosperity
'**prospero, -a** *ag* (*fiorente*) flourishing, thriving, prosperous
prospe'roso, -a *ag* (*robusto*) hale and hearty; (*ragazza*) buxom
prospet'tare *vt* (*esporre*) to point out, show; (*ipotesi*) to advance; (*affare*) to outline; **prospettarsi** *vr* to look, appear
prospet'tiva *sf* (*Arte*) perspective; (*veduta*) view; (*fig: previsione, possibilità*) prospect
pros'petto *sm* (*Disegno*) elevation; (*veduta*) view, prospect; (*facciata*) façade, front; (*tabella*) table; (*sommario*) summary
prospici'ente [prospi'tʃente] *ag*: **~ qc** facing *o* overlooking sth
prossima'mente *av* soon
prossimità *sf* nearness, proximity; **in ~ di** near (to), close to; **in ~ delle feste natalizie** as Christmas approaches
'**prossimo, -a** *ag* (*vicino*): **~ a** near (to), close to; (*che viene subito dopo*) next; (*parente*) close ■ *sm* neighbour (*Brit*), neighbor (*US*), fellow man; **nei prossimi giorni** in the next few days; **in un ~ futuro** in the near future; **~ venturo (pv)** (*Amm*): **venerdì ~ venturo** next Friday
'**prostata** *sf* prostate (gland)
prostitu'irsi *vr* to prostitute o.s.
prosti'tuta *sf* prostitute
prostituzi'one [prostitut'tsjone] *sf* prostitution
pros'trare *vt* (*fig*) to exhaust, wear out; **prostrarsi** *vr* (*fig*) to humble o.s.; **prostrato dal dolore** overcome *o* prostrate with grief
prostrazi'one [prostrat'tsjone] *sf* prostration
protago'nista, -i, e *sm/f* protagonist
pro'teggere [pro'tɛddʒere] *vt* to protect
proteggi'slip [protɛddʒi'slip] *sm inv* panty liner
pro'teico, -a, ci, che *ag* protein *cpd*; **altamente ~** high in protein
prote'ina *sf* protein
pro'tendere *vt* to stretch out
'**protesi** *sf inv* (*Med*) prosthesis
pro'teso, -a *pp di* **protendere**
pro'testa *sf* protest
protes'tante *ag, sm/f* Protestant
protes'tare *vt, vi* to protest; **protestarsi** *vr*: **protestarsi innocente** *etc* to protest one's innocence *o* that one is innocent *etc*
pro'testo *sm* (*Dir*) protest; **mandare una cambiale in ~** to dishonour (*Brit*) *o* dishonor (*US*) a bill
protet'tivo, -a *ag* protective
pro'tetto, -a *pp di* **proteggere**
protetto'rato *sm* protectorate
protet'tore, -'trice *sm/f* protector; (*sostenitore*) patron ■ *ag* (*Rel*): **santo ~** patron saint; **società protettrice dei consumatori** consumer protection society
protezi'one [protet'tsjone] *sf* protection; (*patrocinio*) patronage; **misure di ~** protective measures; **~ civile** civil defence (*Brit*) *o* defense (*US*)
protezio'nismo [protettsjo'nizmo] *sm* protectionism
protocol'lare *vt* to register ■ *ag* formal; of protocol
proto'collo *sm* protocol; (*registro*) register of documents ■ *ag inv*: **foglio ~** foolscap; **numero di ~** reference number
pro'tone *sm* proton
pro'totipo *sm* prototype
pro'trarre *vt* (*prolungare*) to prolong; **protrarsi** *vr* to go on, continue
pro'tratto, -a *pp di* **protrarre**
protube'ranza [protube'rantsa] *sf* protuberance, bulge
Prov. *abbr* (= *provincia*) Prov
'**prova** *sf* (*esperimento, cimento*) test, trial; (*tentativo*) attempt, try; (*Mat*) proof *no pl*; (*Dir*)

evidence *no pl*, proof *no pl*; (*Ins*) exam, test; (*Teat*) rehearsal; (*di abito*) fitting; **a ~ di** (*in testimonianza di*) as proof of; **a ~ di fuoco** fireproof; **assumere in ~** (*per lavoro*) to employ on a trial basis; **essere in ~** (*persona*: *per lavoro*) to be on trial; **mettere alla ~** to put to the test; **giro di ~** test *o* trial run; **fino a ~ contraria** until (it's) proved otherwise; **~ a carico/a discarico** (*Dir*) evidence for the prosecution/for the defence; **~ documentale** (*Dir*) documentary evidence; **~ generale** (*Teat*) dress rehearsal; **~ testimoniale** (*Dir*) testimonial evidence

pro'vare *vt* (*sperimentare*) to test; (*tentare*) to try, attempt; (*assaggiare*) to try, taste; (*sperimentare in sé*) to experience; (*sentire*) to feel; (*cimentare*) to put to the test; (*dimostrare*) to prove; (*abito*) to try on; **provarsi** *vr*: **provarsi (a fare)** to try *o* attempt (to do); **~ a fare** to try *o* attempt to do

proveni'enza [prove'njɛntsa] *sf* origin, source

prove'nire *vi*: **~ da** to come from

pro'venti *smpl* revenue *sg*

prove'nuto, -a *pp di* **provenire**

Pro'venza [pro'ventsa] *sf*: **la ~** Provence

proven'zale [proven'tsale] *ag* Provençal

pro'verbio *sm* proverb

pro'vetta *sf* test tube; **bambino in ~** test-tube baby

pro'vetto, -a *ag* skilled, experienced

pro'vider [pro'vaider] *sm inv* (*Inform*) service provider

pro'vincia [pro'vintʃa] (*fpl* **province** *o* **provincie**) *sf* province; *see note*

PROVINCIA

A *Provincia* is the autonomous political and administrative unit which is on a level between a "Comune" and a "Regione"; there are 103 in the whole of Italy. The *Provincia* is responsible for public health and sanitation, for the maintenance of major roads and public buildings such as schools, and for agriculture and fisheries. Situated in the "capoluogo", or chief town, each *Provincia* is run by a "Giunta provinciale", which is elected by the "Consiglio Provinciale"; both of these bodies are presided over by a "Presidente".

provinci'ale [provin'tʃale] *ag* provincial; **(strada) ~** main road (*Brit*), highway (*US*)

pro'vino *sm* (*Cine*) screen test; (*campione*) specimen

provo'cante *ag* (*attraente*) provocative

provo'care *vt* (*causare*) to cause, bring about; (*eccitare*: *riso, pietà*) to arouse; (*irritare, sfidare*) to provoke

provoca'tore, -'trice *sm/f* agitator ■ *ag*: **agente ~** agent provocateur

provoca'torio, -a *ag* provocative

provocazi'one [provokat'tsjone] *sf* provocation

provve'dere *vi* (*disporre*): **~ (a)** to provide (for); (*prendere un provvedimento*) to take steps, act ■ *vt*: **~ qc a qn** to supply sth to sb; **provvedersi** *vr*: **provvedersi di** to provide o.s. with

provvedi'mento *sm* measure; (*di previdenza*) precaution; **~ disciplinare** disciplinary measure

provvedito'rato *sm* (*Amm*): **~ agli studi** divisional education offices *pl*

provvedi'tore *sm* (*Amm*): **~ agli studi** divisional director of education

provvi'denza [provvi'dɛntsa] *sf*: **la ~** providence

provvidenzi'ale [provviden'tsjale] *ag* providential

provvigi'one [provvi'dʒone] *sf* (*Comm*) commission; **lavoro/stipendio a ~** job/salary on a commission basis

provvi'sorio, -a *ag* temporary; (*governo*) temporary, provisional

prov'vista *sf* (*riserva*) supply, stock; **fare ~ di** to stock up with

prov'visto, -a *pp di* **provvedere** ■ *sf* provision, supply

pro'zia [prot'tsia] *sf* great-aunt

pro'zio, -zii [prot'tsio] *sm* great-uncle

'prua *sf* (*Naut*) = **prora**

pru'dente *ag* cautious, prudent; (*assennato*) sensible, wise

pru'denza [pru'dɛntsa] *sf* prudence, caution; wisdom; **per ~** as a precaution, to be on the safe side

'prudere *vi* to itch, be itchy

'prugna ['pruɲɲa] *sf* plum; **~ secca** prune

prurigi'noso, -a [pruridʒi'noso] *ag* itchy

pru'rito *sm* itchiness *no pl*; itch

PS *sigla* = **Pesaro**

P.S. *abbr* (= *postscriptum*) PS; (*Comm*) = **partita semplice** ■ *sigla f* = **Pubblica Sicurezza**

P.S.D.I. *sigla m* (= *Partito Socialista Democratico Italiano*) *former political party*

pseu'donimo *sm* pseudonym

PSI *sigla m* (*Pol*) = **Partito Socialista Italiano**

psica'nalisi *sf* psychoanalysis

psicana'lista, -i, e *sm/f* psychoanalyst

psicanaliz'zare [psikanalid'dzare] *vt* to psychoanalyse

P

ˈ**psiche** [ˈpsike] *sf* psyche
psicheˈdelico, -a, ci, che [psikeˈdɛliko] *ag* psychedelic
psichiˈatra, -i, e [psiˈkjatra] *sm/f* psychiatrist
psichiaˈtria [psikjaˈtria] *sf* psychiatry
psichiˈatrico, -a, ci, che [psiˈkjatriko] *ag* (*caso*) psychiatric; (*reparto, ospedale*) psychiatric, mental
ˈ**psichico, -a, ci, che** [ˈpsikiko] *ag* psychological
psicoˈfarmaco, -ci *sm* (*Med*) *drug used in treatment of mental conditions*
psicoloˈgia [psikoloˈdʒia] *sf* psychology
psicoˈlogico, -a, ci, che [psikoˈlɔdʒiko] *ag* psychological
psiˈcologo, -a, gi, ghe *sm/f* psychologist
psicoˈpatico, -a, ci, che *ag* psychopathic ■ *sm/f* psychopath
psiˈcosi *sf inv* (*Med*) psychosis; (*fig*) obsessive fear
psicosoˈmatico, -a, ci, che *ag* psychosomatic
PT *sigla* = **Pistoia**
Pt. *abbr* (*Geo: = punta*) Pt
P.T. *abbr* (= *Posta e Telegrafi*) ≈ PO (= *Post Office*); (*Fisco*) = **polizia tributaria**
P.ta *abbr* = **porta**
pubbliˈcare *vt* to publish
pubblicaziˈone [pubblikatˈtsjone] *sf* publication; **~ periodica** periodical; **pubblicazioni (matrimoniali)** (*pl*) (marriage) banns
pubbliˈcista, -i, e [pubbliˈtʃista] *sm/f* (*Stampa*) freelance journalist
pubblicità [pubblitʃiˈta] *sf* (*diffusione*) publicity; (*attività*) advertising; (*annunci nei giornali*) advertisements *pl*; **fare ~ a qc** to advertise sth
pubbliciˈtario, -a [pubblitʃiˈtarjo] *ag* advertising *cpd*; (*trovata, film*) publicity *cpd* ■ *sm* advertising agent; **annuncio** *o* **avviso ~** advertisement
ˈ**pubblico, -a, ci, che** *ag* public; (*statale: scuola etc*) state *cpd* ■ *sm* public; (*spettatori*) audience; **in ~** in public; **la pubblica amministrazione** public administration; **un ~ esercizio** a catering (*o* hotel *o* entertainment) business; **~ funzionario** civil servant; **Ministero della Pubblica Istruzione** ≈ Department of Education and Science (*Brit*), ≈ Department of Health, Education and Welfare (*US*); **P~ Ministero** Public Prosecutor's Office; **la Pubblica Sicurezza** the police
ˈ**pube** *sm* (*Anat*) pubis
pubertà *sf* puberty
ˈ**pudico, -a, ci, che** *ag* modest
puˈdore *sm* modesty
puericulˈtura *sf* infant care
pueˈrile *ag* childish
puˈerpera *sf woman who has just given birth*
pugiˈlato [pudʒiˈlato] *sm* boxing
ˈ**pugile** [ˈpudʒile] *sm* boxer
pugliˈese [puʎˈʎese] *ag* of (*o* from) Puglia
pugnaˈlare [puɲɲaˈlare] *vt* to stab
puˈgnale [puɲˈɲale] *sm* dagger
ˈ**pugno** [ˈpuɲɲo] *sm* fist; (*colpo*) punch; (*quantità*) fistful; **avere qn in ~** to have sb in the palm of one's hand; **tenere la situazione in ~** to have control of the situation; **scrivere qc di proprio ~** to write sth in one's own hand
ˈ**pulce** [ˈpultʃe] *sf* flea
pulˈcino [pulˈtʃino] *sm* chick
puˈledro, -a *sm/f* colt/filly
puˈleggia, -ge [puˈleddʒa] *sf* pulley
puˈlire *vt* to clean; (*lucidare*) to polish; **far ~ qc** to have sth cleaned; **~ a secco** to dry-clean
puˈlito, -a *ag* (*anche fig*) clean; (*ordinato*) neat, tidy ■ *sf* quick clean; **avere la coscienza pulita** to have a clear conscience
puliˈtura *sf* cleaning; **~ a secco** dry-cleaning
puliˈzia [pulitˈtsia] *sf* (*atto*) cleaning; (*condizione*) cleanness; **fare le pulizie** to do the cleaning, do the housework; **~ etnica** ethnic cleansing
ˈ**pullman** *sm inv* coach (*Brit*), bus
pulˈlover *sm inv* pullover, jumper
pulluˈlare *vi* to swarm, teem
pulˈmino *sm* minibus
ˈ**pulpito** *sm* pulpit
pulˈsante *sm* (push-)button
pulˈsare *vi* to pulsate, beat
pulsaziˈone [pulsatˈtsjone] *sf* beat
pulˈviscolo *sm* fine dust
ˈ**puma** *sm inv* puma
punˈgente [punˈdʒɛnte] *ag* prickly; stinging; (*anche fig*) biting
ˈ**pungere** [ˈpundʒere] *vt* to prick; (*insetto, ortica*) to sting; (*freddo*) to bite; **~ qn sul vivo** (*fig*) to cut sb to the quick
pungigliˈone [pundʒiʎˈʎone] *sm* sting
pungoˈlare *vt* to goad
puˈnire *vt* to punish
puniˈtivo, -a *ag* punitive
puniziˈone [punitˈtsjone] *sf* punishment; (*Sport*) penalty
ˈ**punsi** *etc vb vedi* **pungere**
ˈ**punta** *sf* point; (*parte terminale*) tip, end; (*di monte*) peak; (*di costa*) promontory; (*minima parte*) touch, trace; **in ~ di piedi** on tiptoe; **ore di ~** peak hours; **uomo di ~** (*Sport, Pol*) front-rank *o* leading man; **doppie punte** split ends

pun'tare *vt* (*piedi a terra, gomiti sul tavolo*) to plant; (*dirigere: pistola*) to point; (*scommettere*): **~ su** to bet on ■ *vi* (*mirare*): **~ a** to aim at; (*avviarsi*): **~ su** to head *o* make for; (*fig: contare*): **~ su** to count *o* rely on
puntas'pilli *sm inv* = **portaspilli**
pun'tata *sf* (*gita*) short trip; (*scommessa*) bet; (*parte di opera*) instalment (*Brit*), installment (*US*); **farò una ~ a Parigi** I'll pay a flying visit to Paris; **romanzo a puntate** serial
punteggi'are [punted'dʒare] *vt* to punctuate
punteggia'tura [punteddʒa'tura] *sf* punctuation
pun'teggio [pun'teddʒo] *sm* score
puntel'lare *vt* to support
pun'tello *sm* prop, support
punteru'olo *sm* (*Tecn*) punch; (*per stoffa*) bodkin
pun'tiglio [pun'tiʎʎo] *sm* obstinacy, stubbornness
puntigli'oso, -a [puntiʎ'ʎoso] *ag* punctilious
pun'tina *sf*: **~ da disegno** drawing pin (*Brit*), thumb tack (*US*); **puntine** *sfpl* (*Aut*) points
pun'tino *sm* dot; **fare qc a ~** to do sth properly; **arrivare a ~** to arrive just at the right moment; **cotto a ~** cooked to perfection; **mettere i puntini sulle "i"** (*fig*) to dot the i's and cross the t's
'**punto, -a** *pp di* **pungere** ■ *sm* (*segno, macchiolina*) dot; (*Ling*) full stop; (*Mat, momento, di punteggio: fig: argomento*) point; (*di indirizzo e-mail*) dot; (*posto*) spot; (*a scuola*) mark; (*nel cucire, nella maglia, Med*) stitch ■ *av*: **non ... ~** not ... at all; **due punti** (*inv: Ling*) colon; **ad un certo ~** at a certain point; **fino ad un certo ~** (*fig*) to a certain extent; **sul ~ di fare** (just) about to do; **fare il ~** (*Naut*) to take a bearing; **fare il ~ della situazione** (*analisi*) to take stock of the situation; (*riassunto*) to sum up the situation; **alle 6 in ~** at 6 o'clock sharp *o* on the dot; **essere a buon ~** to have reached a satisfactory stage; **mettere a ~** to adjust; (*motore*) to tune; (*cannocchiale*) to focus; (*fig*) to settle; **venire al ~** to come to the point; **vestito di tutto ~** all dressed up; **di ~ in bianco** point-blank; **~ d'arrivo** arrival point; **~ cardinale** point of the compass, cardinal point; **~ debole** weak point; **~ esclamativo/interrogativo** exclamation/question mark; **~ d'incontro** meeting place, meeting point; **~ morto** standstill; **~ nero** (*comedone*) blackhead; **~ nevralgico** (*anche fig*) nerve centre (*Brit*) *o* center (*US*); **~ di partenza** (*anche fig*) starting point; **~ di riferimento** landmark; (*fig*) point of reference; **~ di vendita** retail outlet; **~ e virgola** semicolon; **~ di vista** (*fig*) point of view; **punti di sospensione** suspension points
puntu'ale *ag* punctual
puntualità *sf* punctuality
puntualiz'zare [puntualid'dzare] *vt* to make clear
puntual'mente *av* (*gen*) on time; (*ironico: al solito*) as usual
pun'tura *sf* (*di ago*) prick; (*di insetto*) sting, bite; (*Med*) puncture; (*iniezione*) injection; (*dolore*) sharp pain
punzecchi'are [puntsek'kjare] *vt* to prick; (*fig*) to tease
punzo'nare [puntso'nare] *vt* (*Tecn*) to stamp
pun'zone [pun'tsone] *sm* (*per metalli*) stamp, die
può *vb vedi* **potere**
puoi *vb vedi* **potere**
'**pupa** *sf* doll
pu'pazzo [pu'pattso] *sm* puppet
pu'pillo, -a *sm/f* (*Dir*) ward; (*prediletto*) favourite (*Brit*), favorite (*US*), pet ■ *sf* (*Anat*) pupil
purché [pur'ke] *cong* provided that, on condition that
'**pure** *cong* (*tuttavia*) and yet, nevertheless; (*anche se*) even if ■ *av* (*anche*) too, also; **pur di** (*al fine di*) just to; **faccia ~!** go ahead!, please do!
purè *sm*, **pu'rea** *sf* (*Cuc*) purée; (*di patate*) mashed potatoes
pu'rezza [pu'rettsa] *sf* purity
'**purga, -ghe** *sf* purging *no pl*; purge
pur'gante *sm* (*Med*) purgative, purge
pur'gare *vt* (*Med, Pol*) to purge; (*pulire*) to clean
purga'torio *sm* purgatory
purifi'care *vt* to purify; (*metallo*) to refine
purificazi'one [purifikat'tsjone] *sf* purification; refinement
puri'tano, -a *ag, sm/f* puritan
'**puro, -a** *ag* pure; (*acqua*) clear, limpid; (*vino*) undiluted; **di razza pura** thoroughbred; **per ~ caso** by sheer chance, purely by chance
puro'sangue *sm/f inv* thoroughbred
pur'troppo *av* unfortunately
pus *sm* pus
pusil'lanime *ag* cowardly
'**pustola** *sf* pimple
puta'caso *av* just supposing, suppose
puti'ferio *sm* rumpus, row
putre'fare *vi* to putrefy, rot
putre'fatto, -a *pp di* **putrefare**
putrefazi'one [putrefat'tsjone] *sf* putrefaction
'**putrido, -a** *ag* putrid, rotten
put'tana *sf* (*fam!*) whore (*!*)
'**putto** *sm* cupid

P

'**puzza** ['puttsa] *sf* = **puzzo**
puz'zare [put'tsare] *vi* to stink; **la faccenda puzza (d'imbroglio)** the whole business stinks
'**puzzo** ['puttso] *sm* stink, foul smell
'**puzzola** ['puttsola] *sf* polecat
puzzo'lente [puttso'lɛnte] *ag* stinking
PV *sigla* = **Pavia**
pv *abbr* = **prossimo venturo**
P.V.C. [pivi'tʃi] *sigla m* (= *polyvinyl chloride*) PVC
PZ *sigla* = **Potenza**
p. za *abbr* = **piazza**

Qq

Q, q [ku] *sf o m inv* (*lettera*) Q, q; **Q come Quarto** ≈ Q for Queen
q *abbr* (= *quintale*) q
Qa'tar [ka'tar] *sm*: **il ~** Qatar
q.b. *abbr* (= *quanto basta*) as needed; (= *zucchero q.b.*) sugar to taste
Q.G. *abbr* = **quartier generale**
Q.I. *abbr* = **quoziente d'intelligenza**
qua *av* here; **in ~** (*verso questa parte*) this way; **~ dentro/sotto** *etc* in/under here *etc*; **da un anno in ~** for a year now; **da quando in ~?** since when?; **per di ~** (*passare*) this way; **al di ~ di** (*fiume, strada*) on this side of; *vedi* **questo**
'quacchero, -a ['kwakkero] *sm/f* Quaker
qua'derno *sm* notebook; (*per scuola*) exercise book
qua'drangolo *sm* quadrangle
qua'drante *sm* quadrant; (*di orologio*) face
qua'drare *vi* (*bilancio*) to balance, tally; (*fig: corrispondere*): **~ (con)** to correspond (with) ■ *vt* (*Mat*) to square; **far ~ il bilancio** to balance the books; **non mi quadra** I don't like it
qua'drato, -a *ag* square; (*fig: equilibrato*) level-headed, sensible; (*peg*) square ■ *sm* (*Mat*) square; (*Pugilato*) ring; **5 al ~** 5 squared
quadret'tato, -a *ag* (*foglio*) squared; (*tessuto*) checked
qua'dretto *sm*: **a quadretti** (*tessuto*) checked; (*foglio*) squared
quadrien'nale *ag* (*che dura 4 anni*) four-year *cpd*; (*che avviene ogni 4 anni*) four-yearly
quadri'foglio [kwadri'fɔʎʎo] *sm* four-leaf clover
quadri'mestre *sm* (*periodo*) four-month period; (*Ins*) term
'quadro *sm* (*pittura*) painting, picture; (*quadrato*) square; (*tabella*) table, chart; (*Tecn*) board, panel; (*Teat*) scene; (*fig: scena, spettacolo*) sight; (*descrizione*) outline, description; **quadri** *smpl* (*Pol*) party organizers; (*Comm*) managerial staff; (*Mil*) cadres; (*Carte*) diamonds; **a quadri** (*disegno*) checked; **fare un ~ della situazione** to outline the situation; **~ clinico** (*Med*) case history; **~ di comando** control panel; **quadri intermedi** middle management *sg*
qua'drupede *sm* quadruped
quadrupli'care *vt* to quadruple
'quadruplo, -a *ag, sm* quadruple
quaggiù [kwad'dʒu] *av* down here
'quaglia ['kwaʎʎa] *sf* quail

PAROLA CHIAVE

'qualche ['kwalke] *det* **1** some, a few; (*in interrogative*) any; **ho comprato qualche libro** I've bought some *o* a few books; **~ volta** sometimes; **hai qualche sigaretta?** have you any cigarettes?
2 (*uno*): **c'è qualche medico?** is there a doctor?; **in qualche modo** somehow
3 (*un certo, parecchio*) some; **un personaggio di qualche rilievo** a figure of some importance
4: **qualche cosa** = **qualcosa**

qualche'duno [kwalke'duno] *pron* = **qualcuno**
qual'cosa *pron* something; (*in espressioni interrogative*) anything; **qualcos'altro** something else; anything else; **~ di nuovo** something new; anything new; **~ da mangiare** something to eat; anything to eat; **c'è ~ che non va?** is there something *o* anything wrong?
qual'cuno *pron* (*persona*) someone, somebody; (*in espressioni interrogative*) anyone, anybody; (*alcuni*) some; **~ è favorevole a noi** some are on our side; **qualcun altro** someone *o* somebody else; anyone *o* anybody else

PAROLA CHIAVE

'quale (*spesso troncato in* **qual**) *det* **1** (*interrogativo*) what; (*scegliendo tra due o più cose o persone*) which; **quale uomo/denaro?** what man/

money?; which man/money?; **quali sono i tuoi programmi?** what are your plans?; **quale stanza preferisci?** which room do you prefer?
2 (*relativo: come*): **il risultato fu quale ci si aspettava** the result was as expected
3 (*in elenchi*) such as, like; **piante quali l'edera** plants such as *o* like ivy
4 (*esclamativo*) what; **quale disgrazia!** what bad luck!
5: **in un certo qual modo** in a way, in some ways; **per la qual cosa** for which reason
■ *pron* 1 (*interrogativo*) which; **quale dei due scegli?** which of the two do you want?
2 (*relativo*): **il(la) quale** (*persona: soggetto*) who; (*oggetto, con preposizione*) whom; (*cosa*) which; (*possessivo*) whose; **suo padre, il quale è avvocato, ...** his father, who is a lawyer, ...; **a tutti coloro i quali fossero interessati ...** to whom it may concern ...; **il signore con il quale parlavo** the gentleman to whom I was speaking; **l'albergo al quale ci siamo fermati** the hotel where we stayed *o* which we stayed at; **la signora della quale ammiriamo la bellezza** the lady whose beauty we admire
■ *av* (*in qualità di, come*) as; **quale sindaco di questa città** as mayor of this town

qua'lifica, -che *sf* qualification; (*titolo*) title
qualifi'care *vt* to qualify; (*definire*): **~ qn/qc come** to describe sb/sth as; **qualificarsi** *vr* (*Sport*) to qualify; **qualificarsi a un concorso** to pass a competitive exam
qualifica'tivo, -a *ag* qualifying
qualifi'cato, -a *ag* (*dotato di qualifica*) qualified; (*esperto, abile*) skilled; **non mi ritengo ~ per questo lavoro** I don't think I'm qualified for this job; **è un medico molto ~** he is a very distinguished doctor
qualificazi'one [kwalifikat'tsjone] *sf* qualification; **gara di ~** (*Sport*) qualifying event
qualità *sf inv* quality; **di ottima** *o* **prima ~** top quality; **in ~ di** in one's capacity as; **in ~ di amica** as a friend; **articoli di ogni ~** all sorts of goods; **controllo (di) ~** quality control; **prodotto di ~** quality product
qualita'tivo, -a *ag* qualitative
qua'lora *cong* in case, if
qual'siasi, qua'lunque *det inv* any; (*quale che sia*) whatever; (*discriminativo*) whichever; (*posposto: mediocre*) poor, indifferent; ordinary; **mettiti un vestito ~** put on any old dress; **~ cosa** anything; **~ cosa accada** whatever happens; **a ~ costo** at any cost, whatever the cost; **l'uomo ~** the man in the street; **~ persona** anyone, anybody

qualunqu'ista, -i, e *sm/f person indifferent to politics*
'quando *cong, av* when; **~ sarò ricco** when I'm rich; **da ~** (*dacché*) since; (*interrogativo*): **da ~ sei qui?** how long have you been here?; **di ~ in ~** from time to time; **quand'anche** even if
quantifi'care *vt* to quantify
quantità *sf inv* quantity; (*gran numero*): **una ~ di** a great deal of; a lot of; **in grande ~** in large quantities
quantita'tivo, -a *ag* quantitative ■ *sm* (*Comm: di merce*) amount, quantity

 PAROLA CHIAVE

'quanto, -a *det* 1 (*interrogativo: quantità*) how much; (*numero*) how many; **quanto pane/denaro?** how much bread/money?; **quanti libri/ragazzi?** how many books/boys?; **quanto tempo?** how long?; **quanti anni hai?** how old are you?
2 (*esclamativo*): **quante storie!** what a lot of nonsense!; **quanto tempo sprecato!** what a waste of time!
3 (*relativo: quantità*) as much ... as; (*: numero*) as many ... as; **ho quanto denaro mi occorre** I have as much money as I need; **prendi quanti libri vuoi** take as many books as you like
■ *pron* 1 (*interrogativo: quantità*) how much; (*: numero*) how many; (*tempo*) how long; **quanto mi dai?** how much will you give me?; **quanti me ne hai portati?** how many did you bring me?; **quanto starai via?** how long will you be away (for)?; **da quanto sei qui?** how long have you been here?; **quanti ne abbiamo oggi?** what's the date today?
2 (*relativo: quantità*) as much as; (*: numero*) as many as; **farò quanto posso** I'll do as much as I can; **a quanto dice lui** according to him; **in risposta a quanto esposto nella sua lettera ...** in answer to the points raised in your letter; **possono venire quanti sono stati invitati** all those who have been invited can come
■ *av* 1 (*interrogativo: con ag, av*) how; (*con vb*) how much; **quanto stanco ti sembrava?** how tired did he seem to you?; **quanto corre la tua moto?** how fast can your motorbike go?; **quanto costa?** how much does it cost?; **quant'è?** how much is it?
2 (*esclamativo: con ag, av*) how; (*con vb*) how much; **quanto sono felice!** how happy I am!; **sapessi quanto abbiamo camminato!** if you knew how far we've walked!; **studierò quanto posso** I'll study as much as

o all I can; **quanto prima** as soon as possible; **quanto più ... tanto meno** the more ... the less; **quanto più ... tanto più** the more ... the more
3: **in quanto** (*in qualità di*) as; (*perché, per il fatto che*) as, since; **in quanto legale della signora** as the lady's lawyer; **non è possibile in quanto non possiamo permettercelo** it isn't possible, since we can't afford it; **(in) quanto a** (*per ciò che riguarda*) as for, as regards; **(in) quanto a lui** as far as he's concerned
4: **per quanto** (*nonostante, anche se*) however; **per quanto si sforzi, non ce la farà** try as he may, he won't manage it; **per quanto sia brava, fa degli errori** however good she may be, she makes mistakes; **per quanto io sappia** as far as I know

quan'tunque *cong* although, though
qua'ranta *num* forty
quaran'tena *sf* quarantine
quaran'tenne *ag, sm/f* forty-year-old
quaran'tennio *sm* (period of) forty years
quaran'tesimo, -a *num* fortieth
quaran'tina *sf*: **una ~ (di)** about forty
quaran'totto *sm inv* forty-eight; **fare un ~** (*fam*) to raise hell
Qua'resima *sf*: **la ~** Lent
'quarta *sf vedi* **quarto**
quar'tetto *sm* quartet(te)
quarti'ere *sm* district, area; (*Mil*) quarters *pl*; **~ generale** headquarters *pl*; **~ residenziale** residential area *o* district; **i quartieri alti** the smart districts
'quarto, -a *ag* fourth ■ *sm* fourth; (*quarta parte*) quarter ■ *sf* (*Aut*) fourth (gear); (*Ins: elementare*) *fourth year of primary school*; (*:superiore*) *seventh year of secondary school*; **un ~ di vino** a quarter-litre (*Brit*) *o* quarter-liter (*US*) bottle of wine; **le 6 e un ~** a quarter past (*Brit*) *o* after (*US*) 6; **~ d'ora** quarter of an hour; **tre quarti d'ora** three quarters of an hour; **le otto e tre quarti, le nove meno un ~** (a) quarter to (*Brit*) *o* of (*US*) nine; **passare un brutto ~ d'ora** (*fig*) to have a bad *o* nasty time of it; **quarti di finale** (*Sport*) quarter finals
'quarzo ['kwartso] *sm* quartz
'quasi *av* almost, nearly ■ *cong* (*anche*: **quasi che**) as if; **(non) ... ~ mai** hardly ever; **~ ~ me ne andrei** I've half a mind to leave
quassù *av* up here
'quatto, -a *ag* crouched, squatting; (*silenzioso*) silent; **~ ~** very quietly; stealthily
quattordi'cenne [kwattordi'tʃɛnne] *ag, sm/f* fourteen-year-old
quat'tordici [kwat'torditʃi] *num* fourteen
quat'trini *smpl* money *sg*, cash *sg*
'quattro *num* four; **in ~ e quattr'otto** in less than no time; **dirne ~ a qn** to give sb a piece of one's mind; **fare il diavolo a ~** to kick up a rumpus; **fare ~ chiacchiere** to have a chat; **farsi in ~ per qn** to go out of one's way for sb, put o.s. out for sb
quat'trocchi [kwat'trɔkki] *sm inv* (*fig fam: persona con occhiali*) four-eyes; **a ~** *av* (*tra 2 persone*) face to face; (*privatamente*) in private
quattrocen'tesco, -a, schi, sche [kwattrotʃen'tesko] *ag* fifteenth-century
quattro'cento [kwattro'tʃɛnto] *num* four hundred ■ *sm*: **il Q~** the fifteenth century
quattro'mila *num* four thousand

PAROLA CHIAVE

'quello, -a (*dav sm* **quel** + *C*, **quell'** + *V*, **quello** + *s impura, gn, pn, ps, x, z; pl quei* + *C*, **quegli** + *V o s impura, gn, pn, ps, x, z; dav sf* **quella** + *C*, **quell'** + *V*; *pl* **quelle**) *det* that; those *pl*; **quella casa** that house; **quegli uomini** those men; **voglio quella camicia (lì *o* là)** I want that shirt; **quello è mio fratello** that's my brother
■ *pron* **1** (*dimostrativo*) that one, those ones *pl*; (*ciò*) that; **conosci quella?** do you know her?; **prendo quello bianco** I'll take the white one; **chi è quello?** who's that?; **prendiamo quello (lì *o* là)** let's take that one (there); **in quel di Milano** in the Milan area *o* region
2 (*relativo*): **quello(a) che** (*persona*) the one (who); (*cosa*) the one (which), the one (that); **quelli(e) che** (*persone*) those who; (*cose*) those which; **è lui quello che non voleva venire** he's the one who didn't want to come; **ho fatto quello che potevo** I did what I could; **è quella che ti ho prestato** that's the one I lent you; **è proprio quello che gli ho detto** that's exactly what I told him; **da quello che ho sentito** from what I've heard

'quercia, -ce ['kwɛrtʃa] *sf* oak (tree); (*legno*) oak; **la Q~** (*Pol*) *symbol of P.D.S.*
que'rela *sf* (*Dir*) (legal) action
quere'lare *vt* to bring an action against
que'sito *sm* question, query; problem
'questi *pron* (*poetico*) this person
questio'nario *sm* questionnaire
questi'one *sf* problem, question; (*controversia*) issue; (*litigio*) quarrel; **in ~** in question; **il caso in ~** the matter at hand; **la persona in ~** the person involved; **non voglio essere chiamato in ~** I don't want to be dragged into the argument; **fuor di ~** out of the question; **è ~ di tempo** it's a matter *o* question of time

q

 PAROLA CHIAVE

'questo, -a **1** *det* (*dimostrativo*) this; these *pl*; **~ libro (qui** *o* **qua)** this book; **io prendo questo cappotto, tu quello** I'll take this coat, you take that one; **quest'oggi** today; **questa sera** this evening
2 (*enfatico*): **non fatemi più prendere di queste paure** don't frighten me like that again ■ *pron* (*dimostrativo*) this (one), these (ones) *pl*; (*ciò*) this; **prendo questo (qui** *o* **qua)** I'll take this one; **preferisci questi o quelli?** do you prefer these (ones) or those (ones)?; **questo intendevo io** this is what I meant; **questo non dovevi dirlo** you shouldn't have said that; **e con questo?** so what?; **e con questo se n'è andato** and with that he left; **con tutto questo** in spite of this, despite all this; **questo è quanto** that's all

ques'tore *sm public official in charge of the police in the provincial capital, reporting to the prefetto*, ≈ chief constable (*Brit*), ≈ police commissioner (*US*)
'questua *sf* collection (of alms)
ques'tura *sf* police headquarters *pl*
questu'rino *sm* (*fam*: *poliziotto*) cop
qui *av* here; **da** *o* **di ~** from here; **di ~ in avanti** from now on; **di ~ a poco/una settimana** in a little while/a week's time; **~ dentro/sopra/vicino** in/up/near here; *vedi* **questo**
quie'scenza [kwjeʃ'ʃɛntsa] *sf* (*Amm*): **porre qn in ~** to retire sb
quie'tanza [kwje'tantsa] *sf* receipt
quie'tare *vt* to calm, soothe
qui'ete *sf* quiet, quietness; calmness; stillness; peace; **turbare la ~ pubblica** (*Dir*) to disturb the peace
qui'eto, -a *ag* quiet; (*notte*) calm, still; (*mare*) calm; **l'ho fatto per il ~ vivere** I did it for a quiet life
'quindi *av* then ■ *cong* therefore, so
quindi'cenne [kwindi'tʃɛnne] *ag, sm/f* fifteen-year-old
'quindici ['kwinditʃi] *num* fifteen; **~ giorni** a fortnight (*Brit*), two weeks
quindi'cina [kwindi'tʃina] *sf* (*serie*): **una ~ (di)** about fifteen; **fra una ~ di giorni** in a fortnight (*Brit*) *o* two weeks
quindici'nale [kwinditʃi'nale] *ag* fortnightly (*Brit*), semimonthly (*US*) ■ *sm* (*rivista*) fortnightly magazine (*Brit*), semimonthly (*US*)
quinquen'nale *ag* (*che dura 5 anni*) five-year *cpd*; (*che avviene ogni 5 anni*) five-yearly
quin'quennio *sm* period of five years
quinta *sf vedi* **quinto**
quin'tale *sm* quintal (*100 kg*)
quin'tetto *sm* quintet(te)
'quinto, -a *num* fifth ■ *sf* (*Aut*) fifth (gear); (*Ins*: *elementare*) *fifth year of primary school*; (:*superiore*) *final year of secondary school*; (*Teat*) wing; **un ~ della popolazione** a fifth of the population; **tre quinti** three fifths; **in quinta pagina** on the fifth page, on page five
qui pro quo *sm inv* misunderstanding
Quiri'nale *sm see note*

QUIRINALE

The *Quirinale* takes its name from one of the Seven Hills of Rome on which it stands. It is the official residence of the "Presidente della Repubblica".

'Quito *sf* Quito
quiz [kwidz] *sm inv* (*domanda*) question; (*anche*: **gioco a quiz**) quiz game
'quorum *sm* quorum
'quota *sf* (*parte*) quota, share; (*Aer*) height, altitude; (*Ippica*) odds *pl*; **prendere/perdere ~** (*Aer*) to gain/lose height *o* altitude; **~ imponibile** taxable income; **~ d'iscrizione** (*Ins*) enrolment fee; (*ad una gara*) entry fee; (*ad un club*) membership fee; **~ di mercato** market share; **quote rosa** (*Pol*) quota for women
quo'tare *vt* (*Borsa*) to quote; (*valutare*: *anche fig*) to value; **è un pittore molto quotato** he is rated highly as a painter
quotazi'one [kwotat'tsjone] *sf* quotation
quotidiana'mente *av* daily, every day
quotidi'ano, -a *ag* daily; (*banale*) everyday ■ *sm* (*giornale*) daily (paper)
quozi'ente [kwot'tsjɛnte] *sm* (*Mat*) quotient; **~ di crescita zero** zero growth rate; **~ d'intelligenza** intelligence quotient

Rr

R, r ['ɛrre] *sf o m* (*lettera*) R, r; **R come Roma** ≈ R for Robert (*Brit*), R for Roger (*US*)

R *abbr* (*Posta*) = **raccomandata**; (*Ferr*) = **rapido**

RA *sigla* = **Ravenna**

ra'barbaro *sm* rhubarb

Ra'bat *sf* Rabat

rabberci'are [rabber'tʃare] *vt* (*anche fig*) to patch up

'rabbia *sf* (*ira*) anger, rage; (*accanimento, furia*) fury; (*Med: idrofobia*) rabies *sg*

rab'bino *sm* rabbi

rabbi'oso, -a *ag* angry, furious; (*facile all'ira*) quick-tempered; (*forze, acqua etc*) furious, raging; (*Med*) rabid, mad

rabbo'nire *vt*, **rabbo'nirsi** *vr* to calm down

rabbrivi'dire *vi* to shudder, shiver

rabbui'arsi *vr* to grow dark

rabdo'mante *sm* water diviner

racc. *abbr* (*Posta*) = **raccomandata**

raccapez'zarsi [rakkapet'tsarsi] *vr*: **non ~** to be at a loss

raccapricci'ante [rakkaprit'tʃante] *ag* horrifying

racca'priccio [rakka'prittʃo] *sm* horror

raccatta'palle *sm inv* (*Sport*) ballboy

raccat'tare *vt* to pick up

rac'chetta [rak'ketta] *sf* (*per tennis*) racket; (*per ping-pong*) bat; **~ da neve** snowshoe; **~ da sci** ski stick

'racchio, -a ['rakkjo] *ag* (*fam*) ugly

racchi'udere [rak'kjudere] *vt* to contain

racchi'uso, -a [rak'kjuso] *pp di* **racchiudere**

rac'cogliere [rak'kɔʎʎere] *vt* to collect; (*raccattare*) to pick up; (*frutti, fiori*) to pick, pluck; (*Agr*) to harvest; (*approvazione: voti*) to win; (*profughi*) to take in; (*vele*) to furl; (*capelli*) to put up; **raccogliersi** *vr* to gather; (*fig*) to gather one's thoughts; to meditate; **non ha raccolto** (*allusione*) he didn't take the hint; (*frecciata*) he took no notice of it; **~ i frutti del proprio lavoro** (*fig*) to reap the benefits of one's work; **~ le idee** (*fig*) to gather one's thoughts

raccogli'mento [rakkoʎʎi'mento] *sm* meditation

raccogli'tore [rakkoʎʎi'tore] *sm* (*cartella*) folder, binder; **~ a fogli mobili** loose-leaf binder

rac'colto, -a *pp di* **raccogliere** ■ *ag* (*persona: pensoso*) thoughtful; (*luogo: appartato*) secluded, quiet ■ *sm* (*Agr*) crop, harvest ■ *sf* collecting *no pl*; collection; (*Agr*) harvesting *no pl*, gathering *no pl*; harvest, crop; **fare la raccolta di qc** to collect sth; **chiamare a raccolta** to gather together; **raccolta differenziata** (*dei rifiuti*) *separate collection of different kinds of household waste*

raccoman'dabile *ag* (highly) commendable; **è un tipo poco ~** he is not to be trusted

raccoman'dare *vt* to recommend; (*affidare*) to entrust; **raccomandarsi** *vr*: **raccomandarsi a qn** to commend o.s. to sb; **~ a qn di fare qc** to recommend that sb does sth; **~ a qn di non fare qc** to tell *o* warn sb not to do sth; **~ qn a qn/alle cure di qn** to entrust sb to sb/to sb's care; **mi raccomando!** don't forget!

raccoman'dato, -a *ag* (*lettera, pacco*) recorded-delivery (*Brit*), certified (*US*); (*candidato*) recommended ■ *sm/f*: **essere un(a) ~(a) di ferro** to have friends in high places ■ *sf* (*anche*: **lettera raccomandata**) recorded-delivery letter; **raccomandata con ricevuta di ritorno (Rr)** recorded-delivery letter with advice of receipt

raccomandazi'one [rakkomandat'tsjone] *sf* recommendation; **lettera di ~** letter of introduction

raccomo'dare *vt* (*riparare*) to repair, mend

raccon'tare *vt*: **~ (a qn)** (*dire*) to tell (sb); (*narrare*) to relate (to sb), tell (sb) about; **a me non la racconti** don't try and kid me; **cosa mi racconti di nuovo?** what's new?

rac'conto *sm* telling *no pl*, relating *no pl*; (*fatto raccontato*) story, tale; (*genere letterario*) short story; **racconti per bambini** children's stories

raccorci'are [rakkor'tʃare] *vt* to shorten
raccor'dare *vt* to link up, join
rac'cordo *sm* (*Tecn*: *giunzione*) connection, joint; (: *di autostrada*) slip road (*Brit*) entrance (*o* exit) ramp (*US*); **~ anulare** (*Aut*) ring road (*Brit*), beltway (*US*)
ra'chitico, -a, ci, che [ra'kitiko] *ag* suffering from rickets; (*fig*) scraggy, scrawny
rachi'tismo [raki'tizmo] *sm* (*Med*) rickets *sg*
racimo'lare [ratʃimo'lare] *vt* (*fig*) to scrape together, glean
'rada *sf* (natural) harbour (*Brit*) *o* harbor (*US*)
'radar *sm inv* radar
raddol'cire [raddol'tʃire] *vt* (*persona*: *carattere*) to soften; **raddolcirsi** *vr* (*tempo*) to grow milder; (*persona*) to soften, mellow
raddoppia'mento *sm* doubling
raddoppi'are *vt, vi* to double
rad'doppio *sm* (*gen*) doubling; (*Biliardo*) double; (*Equitazione*) gallop
raddriz'zare [raddrit'tsare] *vt* to straighten; (*fig*: *correggere*) to put straight, correct
'radere *vt* (*barba*) to shave off; (*mento*) to shave; (*fig*: *rasentare*) to graze; to skim; **radersi** *vr* to shave (o.s.); **~ al suolo** to raze to the ground
radi'ale *ag* radial
radi'ante *ag* (*calore, energia*) radiant
radi'are *vt* to strike off
radia'tore *sm* radiator
radiazi'one [radjat'tsjone] *sf* (*Fisica*) radiation; (*cancellazione*) striking off
'radica *sf* (*Bot*): **~ di noce** walnut (wood)
radi'cale *ag* radical ■ *sm* (*Ling*) root; (*Mat, Pol*) radical; **radicali liberi** free radicals
radi'cato, -a *ag* (*pregiudizio, credenza*) deep-seated, deeply-rooted
ra'dicchio [ra'dikkjo] *sm variety of chicory*
ra'dice [ra'ditʃe] *sf* root; **segno di ~** (*Mat*) radical sign; **colpire alla ~** (*fig*) to strike at the root; **mettere radici** (*idee, odio etc*) to take root; (*persona*) to put down roots; **~ quadrata** (*Mat*) square root
'radio *sf inv* radio ■ *sm* (*Chim*) radium; **trasmettere per ~** to broadcast; **stazione/ponte ~** radio station/link; **~ ricevente/trasmittente** receiver/transmitter
radioabbo'nato, -a *sm/f* radio subscriber
radioama'tore, -'trice *sm/f* amateur radio operator, ham (*fam*)
radioascolta'tore, -'trice *sm/f* (radio) listener
radioattività *sf* radioactivity
radioat'tivo, -a *ag* radioactive
radiocoman'dare *vt* to operate by remote control
radiocoman'dato, -a *ag* remote-controlled
radioco'mando *sm* remote control
radiocomunicazi'one [radjokomunikat'tsjone] *sf* radio message
radio'cronaca, -che *sf* radio commentary
radiocro'nista, -i, e *sm/f* radio commentator
radiodiffusi'one *sf* (radio) broadcasting
radio'fonico, -a, ci, che *ag* radio *cpd*
radiogra'fare *vt* to X-ray
radiogra'fia *sf* radiography; (*foto*) X-ray photograph
radio'lina *sf* portable radio, transistor (radio)
radiolo'gia [radjolo'dʒia] *sf* radiology
radi'ologo, -a, gi, ghe *sm/f* radiologist
radiorice'vente [radjoritʃe'vɛnte] *sf* (*anche*: **apparecchio radioricevente**) receiver
radi'oso, -a *ag* radiant
radiostazi'one [radjostat'tsjone] *sf* radio station
radios'veglia [radjoz'veʎʎa] *sf* radio alarm
radio'taxi *sm inv* radio taxi
radio'tecnico, -a, ci, che *ag* radio engineering *cpd* ■ *sm* radio engineer
radiotelegra'fista, -i, e *sm/f* radiotelegrapher
radiotera'pia *sf* radiotherapy
radiotrasmit'tente *ag* (radio) broadcasting *cpd* ■ *sf* (radio) broadcasting station
'rado, -a *ag* (*capelli*) sparse, thin; (*visite*) infrequent; **di ~** rarely; **non di ~** not uncommonly
radu'nare *vt,* **radu'narsi** *vr* to gather, assemble
radu'nata *sf* (*Mil*) muster
ra'duno *sm* gathering, meeting
ra'dura *sf* clearing
'rafano *sm* horseradish
raffazzo'nare [raffattso'nare] *vt* to patch up
raf'fermo, -a *ag* stale
'raffica, -che *sf* (*Meteor*) gust (of wind); **~ di colpi** (*di fucile*) burst of gunfire
raffigu'rare *vt* to represent
raffigurazi'one [raffigurat'tsjone] *sf* representation, depiction
raffi'nare *vt* to refine
raffina'tezza [raffina'tettsa] *sf* refinement
raffi'nato, -a *ag* refined
raffinazi'one [raffinat'tsjone] *sf* (*di sostanza*) refining; **~ del petrolio** oil refining
raffine'ria *sf* refinery
raffor'zare [raffor'tsare] *vt* to reinforce
rafforza'tivo, -a [raffortsa'tivo] *ag* (*Ling*) intensifying ■ *sm* (*Ling*) intensifier
raffredda'mento *sm* cooling
raffred'dare *vt* to cool; (*fig*) to dampen, have a cooling effect on; **raffreddarsi** *vr* to grow cool *o* cold; (*prendere un raffreddore*) to catch a cold; (*fig*) to cool (off)

raffred'dato, -a *ag* (*Med*): **essere ~** to have a cold
raffred'dore *sm* (*Med*) cold
raffron'tare *vt* to compare
raf'fronto *sm* comparison
'rafia *sf* (*fibra*) raffia
raga'nella *sf* (*Zool*) tree frog
ra'gazzo, -a [ra'gattso] *sm/f* boy/girl; (*fam*: *fidanzato*) boyfriend/girlfriend; **nome da ragazza** maiden name; **ragazza madre** unmarried mother; **ragazza squillo** call girl
ragge'lare [raddʒe'lare] *vt, vi*, **ragge'larsi** *vr* to freeze
raggi'ante [rad'dʒante] *ag* radiant, shining; **~ di gioia** beaming *o* radiant with joy
raggi'era [rad'dʒɛra] *sf* (*di ruota*) spokes *pl*; **a ~** with a sunburst pattern
'raggio ['raddʒo] *sm* (*di sole etc*) ray; (*Mat*: *distanza*) radius; (*di ruota etc*) spoke; **nel ~ di 20 km** within a radius of 20 km *o* a 20-km radius; **a largo ~** (*esplorazione, incursione*) wide-ranging; **~ d'azione** range; **~ laser** laser beam; **raggi X** X-rays
raggi'rare [raddʒi'rare] *vt* to take in, trick
rag'giro [rad'dʒiro] *sm* trick
raggi'ungere [rad'dʒundʒere] *vt* to reach; (*persona*: *riprendere*) to catch up (with); (*bersaglio*) to hit; (*fig*: *meta*) to achieve; **~ il proprio scopo** to reach one's goal, achieve one's aim; **~ un accordo** to come to *o* reach an agreement
raggi'unto, -a [rad'dʒunto] *pp di* **raggiungere**
raggomito'larsi *vr* to curl up
raggranel'lare *vt* to scrape together
raggrin'zare [raggrin'tsare] *vt, vi* (*anche*: **raggrinzarsi**) to wrinkle
raggrin'zire [raggrin'tsire] *vt* = **raggrinzare**
raggru'mare *vt*, **raggru'marsi** *vr* (*sangue, latte*) to clot
raggruppa'mento *sm* (*azione*) grouping; (*gruppo*) group; (*Mil*) unit
raggrup'pare *vt* to group (together)
ragguagli'are [raggwaʎ'ʎare] *vt* (*paragonare*) to compare; (*informare*) to inform
raggu'aglio [rag'gwaʎʎo] *sm* comparison; (*informazione, relazione*) piece of information
ragguar'devole *ag* (*degno di riguardo*) distinguished, notable; (*notevole*: *somma*) considerable
'ragia ['radʒa] *sf*: **acqua ~** turpentine
ragiona'mento [radʒona'mento] *sm* reasoning *no pl*; argument
ragio'nare [radʒo'nare] *vi* (*usare la ragione*) to reason; (*discorrere*): **~ (di)** to argue (about); **cerca di ~** try and be reasonable
ragi'one [ra'dʒone] *sf* reason; (*dimostrazione, prova*) argument, reason; (*diritto*) right; **aver ~** to be right; **aver ~ di qn** to get the better of sb; **dare ~ a qn** (*persona*) to side with sb; (*fatto*) to prove sb right; **farsi una ~ di qc** to accept sth, come to terms with sth; **in ~ di** at the rate of; **a** *o* **con ~** rightly, justly; **perdere la ~** to become insane; (*fig*) to take leave of one's senses; **a ragion veduta** after due consideration; **per ragioni di famiglia** for family reasons; **~ di scambio** terms of trade; **~ sociale** (*Comm*) corporate name; **ragion di stato** reason of State
ragione'ria [radʒone'ria] *sf* accountancy; (*ufficio*) accounts department
ragio'nevole [radʒo'nevole] *ag* reasonable
ragioni'ere, -a [radʒo'njɛre] *sm/f* accountant
ragli'are [raʎ'ʎare] *vi* to bray
ragna'tela [raɲɲa'tela] *sf* cobweb, spider's web
'ragno ['raɲɲo] *sm* spider; **non cavare un ~ dal buco** (*fig*) to draw a blank
ragù *sm inv* (*Cuc*) meat sauce (*for pasta*)
RAI-TV [raiti'vu] *sigla f* (= *Radio televisione italiana*) *Italian Broadcasting Company*
rallegra'menti *smpl* congratulations
ralle'grare *vt* to cheer up; **rallegrarsi** *vr* to cheer up; (*provare allegrezza*) to rejoice; **rallegrarsi con qn** to congratulate sb
rallenta'mento *sm* slowing down; slackening
rallen'tare *vt, vi* to slow down; **~ il passo** to slacken one's pace
rallenta'tore *sm* (*Cine*) slow-motion camera; **al ~** (*anche fig*) in slow motion
raman'zina [raman'dzina] *sf* lecture, telling-off
ra'mare *vt* (*superficie*) to copper, coat with copper; (*Agr*: *vite*) to spray with copper sulphate
ra'marro *sm* green lizard
ra'mato, -a *ag* (*oggetto*: *rivestito di rame*) copper coated, coppered; (*capelli, barba*) coppery, copper-coloured (*Brit*), copper-colored (*US*)
'rame *sm* (*Chim*) copper; **di ~** copper *cpd*; **incisione su ~** copperplate
ramifi'care *vi* (*Bot*) to put out branches; **ramificarsi** *vr* (*diramarsi*) to branch out; (*Med*: *tumore, vene*) to ramify; **ramificarsi in** (*biforcarsi*) to branch into
ramificazi'one [ramifikat'tsjone] *sf* ramification
ra'mingo, -a, ghi, ghe *ag* (*poetico*): **andare ~** to go wandering, wander
ra'mino *sm* (*Carte*) rummy
rammari'carsi *vr*: **~ (di)** (*rincrescersi*) to be sorry (about), regret; (*lamentarsi*) to complain (about)
ram'marico, -chi *sm* regret

rammen'dare *vt* to mend; (*calza*) to darn
ram'mendo *sm* mending *no pl*; darning *no pl*; mend darn
rammen'tare *vt* to remember, recall; **rammentarsi** *vr*: **rammentarsi (di qc)** to remember (sth); **~ qc a qn** to remind sb of sth
rammol'lire *vt* to soften ▪ *vi* (*anche*: **rammollirsi**) to go soft
rammol'lito, -a *ag* weak ▪ *sm/f* weakling
'ramo *sm* branch; (*di commercio*) field; **non è il mio ~** it's not my field *o* line
ramo'scello [ramoʃʃɛllo] *sm* twig
'rampa *sf* flight (of stairs); **~ di lancio** launching pad
rampi'cante *ag* (*Bot*) climbing
ram'pino *sm* (*gancio*) hook; (*Naut*) grapnel
ram'pollo *sm* (*di acqua*) spring; (*Bot: germoglio*) shoot; (*fig: discendente*) descendant
ram'pone *sm* harpoon; (*Alpinismo*) crampon
'rana *sf* frog; **~ pescatrice** angler fish
'rancido, -a ['rantʃido] *ag* rancid
'rancio ['rantʃo] *sm* (*Mil*) mess; **ora del ~** mess time
ran'core *sm* rancour (*Brit*), rancor (*US*), resentment; **portare ~ a qn, provare ~ per** *o* **verso qn** to bear sb a grudge
ran'dagio, -a, gi, gie *o* **ge** [ran'dadʒo] *ag* (*gatto, cane*) stray
ran'dello *sm* club, cudgel
'rango, -ghi *sm* (*grado*) rank; (*condizione sociale*) station, social standing; **persone di ~ inferiore** people of lower standing; **uscire dai ranghi** to fall out; (*fig*) to step out of line
Ran'gun *sf* Rangoon
rannicchi'arsi [rannik'kjarsi] *vr* to crouch, huddle
rannuvo'larsi *vr* to cloud over, become overcast
ra'nocchio [ra'nɔkkjo] *sm* (edible) frog
ranto'lare *vi* to wheeze
ranto'lio *sm* (*il respirare affannoso*) wheezing; (*di agonizzante*) death rattle
'rantolo *sm* wheeze; death rattle
ra'nuncolo *sm* (*Bot*) buttercup
'rapa *sf* (*Bot*) turnip
ra'pace [ra'patʃe] *ag* (*animale*) predatory; (*fig*) rapacious, grasping ▪ *sm* bird of prey
ra'pare *vt* (*capelli*) to crop, cut very short
'rapida *sf vedi* **rapido**
rapida'mente *av* quickly, rapidly
rapidità *sf* speed
'rapido, -a *ag* fast; (*esame, occhiata*) quick, rapid ▪ *sm* (*Ferr*) express (train) ▪ *sf* (*di fiume*) rapid
rapi'mento *sm* kidnapping; (*fig*) rapture
ra'pina *sf* robbery; **~ in banca** bank robbery; **~ a mano armata** armed robbery
rapi'nare *vt* to rob
rapina'tore, -'trice *sm/f* robber
ra'pire *vt* (*cose*) to steal; (*persone*) to kidnap; (*fig*) to enrapture, delight
ra'pito, -a *ag* (*persona*) kidnapped; (*fig: in estasi*): **ascoltare ~ qn** to be captivated by sb's words ▪ *sm/f* kidnapped person
rapi'tore, -'trice *sm/f* kidnapper
rappacifi'care [rappatʃifi'kare] *vt* (*riconciliare*) to reconcile; **rappacificarsi** *vr* (*uso*) to be reconciled, make it up (*fam*)
rappacificazi'one [rappatʃifikat'tsjone] *sf* reconciliation
rappez'zare [rappet'tsare] *vt* to patch
rappor'tare *vt* (*confrontare*) to compare; (*riprodurre*) to reproduce
rap'porto *sm* (*resoconto*) report; (*legame*) relationship; (*Mat, Tecn*) ratio; **rapporti** *smpl* (*fra persone, paesi*) relations; **in ~ a quanto è successo** with regard to *o* in relation to what happened; **fare ~ a qn su qc** to report sth to sb; **andare a ~ da qn** to report to sb; **chiamare qn a ~** (*Mil*) to summon sb; **essere in buoni/cattivi rapporti con qn** to be on good/bad terms with sb; **~ d'affari, ~ di lavoro** business relations; **~ di compressione** (*Tecn*) pressure ratio; **~ coniugale** marital relationship; **~ di trasmissione** (*Tecn*) gear; **rapporti sessuali** sexual intercourse *sg*
rap'prendersi *vr* to coagulate, clot; (*latte*) to curdle
rappre'saglia [rappre'saʎʎa] *sf* reprisal, retaliation
rappresen'tante *sm/f* representative; **~ di commercio** sales representative, sales rep; (*fam*): **~ sindacale** union delegate *o* representative
rappresen'tanza [rapprezen'tantsa] *sf* delegation, deputation; (*Comm: ufficio, sede*) agency; **in ~ di qn** on behalf of sb; **spese di ~** entertainment expenses; **macchina di ~** official car; **avere la ~ di** to be the agent for; **~ esclusiva** sole agency; **avere la ~ esclusiva** to be sole agent
rappresen'tare *vt* to represent; (*Teat*) to perform; **farsi ~ dal proprio legale** to be represented by one's lawyer
rappresenta'tivo, -a *ag* representative ▪ *sf* (*di partito, sindacale*) representative group; (*Sport: squadra*) representative (team)
rappresentazi'one [rapprezentat'tsjone] *sf* representation; performing *no pl*; (*spettacolo*) performance; **prima ~ assoluta** world première
rap'preso, -a *pp di* **rapprendere**
rapso'dia *sf* rhapsody

'raptus *sm inv*: **~ di follia** fit of madness
rara'mente *av* seldom, rarely
rare'fare *vt*, **rare'farsi** *vr* to rarefy
rare'fatto, -a *pp di* **rarefare** ■ *ag* rarefied
rarefazi'one [rarefat'tsjone] *sf* rarefaction
rarità *sf inv* rarity
'raro, -a *ag* rare
ra'sare *vt* (*barba etc*) to shave off; (*siepi, erba*) to trim, cut; **rasarsi** *vr* to shave (o.s.)
ra'sato, -a *ag* (*erba*) trimmed, cut; (*tessuto*) smooth; **avere la barba rasata** to be clean-shaven
rasa'tura *sf* shave
raschia'mento [raskja'mento] *sm* (*Med*) curettage; **~ uterino** D and C
raschi'are [ras'kjare] *vt* to scrape; (*macchia, fango*) to scrape off ■ *vi* to clear one's throat
rasen'tare *vt* (*andar rasente*) to keep close to; (*sfiorare*) to skim along (*o* over); (*fig*) to border on
ra'sente *prep*: **~ (a)** close to, very near
'raso, -a *pp di* **radere** ■ *ag* (*barba*) shaved; (*capelli*) cropped; (*con misure di capacità*) level; (*pieno: bicchiere*) full to the brim ■ *sm* (*tessuto*) satin; **~ terra** close to the ground; **volare ~ terra** to hedgehop; **un cucchiaio ~** a level spoonful
ra'soio *sm* razor; **~ elettrico** electric shaver *o* razor
ras'pare *vt* (*levigare*) to rasp; (*grattare*) to scratch
'raspo *sm* (*di uva*) grape stalk
ras'segna [ras'seɲɲa] *sf* (*Mil*) inspection, review; (*esame*) inspection; (*resoconto*) review, survey; (*pubblicazione letteraria etc*) review; (*mostra*) exhibition, show; **passare in ~** (*Mil: fig*) to review
rasse'gnare [rasseɲ'ɲare] *vt*: **~ le dimissioni** to resign, hand in one's resignation; **rassegnarsi** *vr* (*accettare*): **rassegnarsi (a qc/a fare)** to resign o.s. (to sth/to doing)
rassegnazi'one [rasseɲɲat'tsjone] *sf* resignation
rassere'nare *vt* (*persona*) to cheer up; **rasserenarsi** *vr* (*tempo*) to clear up
rasset'tare *vt* to tidy, put in order; (*aggiustare*) to repair, mend
rassicu'rante *ag* reassuring
rassicu'rare *vt* to reassure; **rassicurarsi** *vr* to take heart, recover one's confidence
rassicurazi'one [rassikurat'tsjone] *sf* reassurance
rasso'dare *vt* to harden, stiffen; (*fig*) to strengthen, consolidate
rassomigli'anza [rassomiʎ'ʎantsa] *sf* resemblance
rassomigli'are [rassomiʎ'ʎare] *vi*: **~ a** to resemble, look like
rastrella'mento *sm* (*Mil: di polizia*) (thorough) search
rastrel'lare *vt* to rake; (*fig: perlustrare*) to comb
rastrelli'era *sf* rack; (*per piatti*) dish rack
ras'trello *sm* rake
'rata *sf* (*quota*) instalment, installment (*US*); **pagare a rate** to pay by instal(l)ments *o* on hire purchase (*Brit*); **comprare/vendere a rate** to buy/sell on hire purchase (*Brit*) *o* on the installment plan (*US*)
rate'ale *ag*: **pagamento ~** payment by instal(l)ments; **vendita ~** hire purchase (*Brit*), installment plan (*US*)
rate'are *vt* to divide into instal(l)ments
rateazi'one [rateat'tsjone] *sf* division into instal(l)ments
rateiz'zare [rateid'dzare] *vt* = **rateare**
'rateo *sm* (*Comm*) accrual
ra'tifica, -che *sf* ratification
ratifi'care *vt* (*Dir*) to ratify
'ratto *sm* (*Dir*) abduction; (*Zool*) rat
rattop'pare *vt* to patch
rat'toppo *sm* patching *no pl*; patch
rattrap'pire *vt* to make stiff; **rattrappirsi** *vr* to be stiff
rattris'tare *vt* to sadden; **rattristarsi** *vr* to become sad
rau'cedine [rau'tʃɛdine] *sf* hoarseness
'rauco, -a, chi, che *ag* hoarse
rava'nello *sm* radish
raven'nate *ag* of (*o* from) Ravenna
ravi'oli *smpl* ravioli *sg*
ravve'dersi *vr* to mend one's ways
ravvi'are *vt* (*capelli*) to tidy; **ravviarsi i capelli** to tidy one's hair
ravvicina'mento [ravvitʃina'mento] *sm* (*tra persone*) reconciliation; (*Pol: tra paesi etc*) rapprochement
ravvici'nare [ravvitʃi'nare] *vt* (*avvicinare*): **~ qc a** to bring sth nearer to; (*oggetti*) to bring closer together; (*fig: persone*) to reconcile, bring together; **ravvicinarsi** *vr* to be reconciled
ravvi'sare *vt* to recognize
ravvi'vare *vt* to revive; (*fig*) to brighten up, enliven; **ravvivarsi** *vr* to revive; to brighten up
Rawal'pindi [raval'pindi] *sf* Rawalpindi
razio'cinio [rattsjo'tʃinjo] *sm* reasoning *no pl*; reason; (*buon senso*) common sense
razio'nale [rattsjo'nale] *ag* rational
razionalità [rattsjonali'ta] *sf* rationality; (*buon senso*) common sense
razionaliz'zare [rattsjonalid'dzare] *vt* (*metodo, lavoro, programma*) to rationalize; (*problema, situazione*) to approach rationally

r

raziona'mento [rattsjona'mento] *sm* rationing
razio'nare [rattsjo'nare] *vt* to ration
razi'one [rat'tsjone] *sf* ration; (*porzione*) portion, share
'razza ['rattsa] *sf* race; (*Zool*) breed; (*discendenza, stirpe*) stock, race; (*sorta*) sort, kind
raz'zia [rat'tsia] *sf* raid, foray
razzi'ale [rat'tsjale] *ag* racial
raz'zismo [rat'tsizmo] *sm* racism, racialism
raz'zista, -i, e [rat'tsista] *ag, sm/f* racist, racialist
'razzo ['raddzo] *sm* rocket; **~ di segnalazione** flare; **~ vettore** vector rocket
razzo'lare [rattso'lare] *vi* (*galline*) to scratch about
RC *sigla* = **Reggio Calabria**
RDT *sigla f vedi* **Repubblica Democratica Tedesca**
RE *sigla* = **Reggio Emilia**
re *sm inv* (*sovrano*) king; (*Mus*) D; (*: solfeggiando la scala*) re; **i Re Magi** the Three Wise Men, the Magi
rea'gente [rea'dʒɛnte] *sm* reagent
rea'gire [rea'dʒire] *vi* to react
re'ale *ag* real; (*di, da re*) royal ■ *sm*: **il ~** reality; **i Reali** the Royal family
rea'lismo *sm* realism
rea'lista, -i, e *sm/f* realist; (*Pol*) royalist
rea'listico, -a, ci, che *ag* realistic
reality [ri'aliti] *sm inv* reality show
realiz'zare [realid'dzare] *vt* (*progetto etc*) to realize, carry out; (*sogno, desiderio*) to realize, fulfil; (*scopo*) to achieve; (*Comm: titoli etc*) to realize; (*Calcio etc*) to score; **realizzarsi** *vr* to be realized
realizzazi'one [realiddzat'tsjone] *sf* realization; fulfilment; achievement; **~ scenica** stage production
rea'lizzo [rea'liddzo] *sm* (*conversione in denaro*) conversion into cash; (*vendita forzata*) clearance sale
real'mente *av* really, actually
realtà *sf inv* reality; **in ~** (*in effetti*) in fact; (*a dire il vero*) really
re'ame *sm* kingdom, realm; (*fig*) realm
re'ato *sm* offence (*Brit*), offense (*US*)
reat'tore *sm* (*Fisica*) reactor; (*Aer: aereo*) jet; (*motore*) jet engine
reazio'nario, -a [reattsjo'narjo] *ag, sm/f* (*Pol*) reactionary
reazi'one [reat'tsjone] *sf* reaction; **motore/aereo a ~** jet engine/plane; **forze della ~** reactionary forces; **~ a catena** (*anche fig*) chain reaction
'rebbio *sm* prong
'rebus *sm inv* rebus; (*fig*) puzzle; enigma
recapi'tare *vt* to deliver
re'capito *sm* (*indirizzo*) address; (*consegna*) delivery; **ha un ~ telefonico?** do you have a telephone number where you can be reached?; **~ a domicilio** home delivery (service)
re'care *vt* (*portare*) to bring; (*avere su di sé*) to carry, bear; (*cagionare*) to cause, bring; **recarsi** *vr* to go; **recarsi in città/a scuola** to go into town/to school; **~ danno a qn** to harm sb, cause harm to sb
re'cedere [re'tʃɛdere] *vi* to withdraw
recensi'one [retʃen'sjone] *sf* review
recen'sire [retʃen'sire] *vt* to review
recen'sore, -a [retʃen'sore] *sm/f* reviewer
re'cente [re'tʃɛnte] *ag* recent; **di ~** recently; **più ~** latest, most recent
recente'mente [retʃente'mente] *av* recently
rece'pire [retʃe'pire] *vt* to understand, take in
recessi'one [retʃes'sjone] *sf* (*Econ*) recession
re'cesso [re'tʃɛsso] *sm* (*azione*) recession, receding; (*Dir*) withdrawal; (*luogo*) recess
recherò *etc* [reke'rɔ] *vb vedi* **recare**
re'cidere [re'tʃidere] *vt* to cut off, chop off
reci'divo, -a [retʃi'divo] *sm/f* (*Dir*) second (*o* habitual) offender, recidivist ■ *sf* recidivism
recin'tare [retʃin'tare] *vt* to enclose, fence off
re'cinto [re'tʃinto] *sm* enclosure; (*ciò che recinge*) fence; surrounding wall
recinzi'one [retʃin'tsjone] *sf* (*azione*) enclosure, fencing-off; (*recinto: di legno*) fence; (*: di mattoni*) wall; (*reticolato*) wire fencing; (*a sbarre*) railings *pl*
recipi'ente [retʃi'pjɛnte] *sm* container
re'ciproco, -a, ci, che [re'tʃiproko] *ag* reciprocal
re'ciso, -a [re'tʃizo] *pp di* **recidere**
'recita ['rɛtʃita] *sf* performance
'recital ['rɛtʃital] *sm inv* recital
reci'tare [retʃi'tare] *vt* (*poesia, lezione*) to recite; (*dramma*) to perform; (*ruolo*) to play *o* act (the part of)
recitazi'one [retʃitat'tsjone] *sf* recitation; (*di attore*) acting; **scuola di ~** drama school
recla'mare *vi* to complain ■ *vt* (*richiedere*) to demand
réclame [re'klam] *sf inv* advertising *no pl*; advertisement, advert (*Brit*), ad (*fam*)
reclamiz'zare [reklamid'dzare] *vt* to advertise
re'clamo *sm* complaint; **sporgere ~ a** to complain to, make a complaint to
recli'nabile *ag* (*sedile*) reclining
recli'nare *vt* (*capo*) to bow, lower; (*sedile*) to tilt
reclusi'one *sf* (*Dir*) imprisonment
re'cluso, -a *sm/f* prisoner
'recluta *sf* recruit

reclutaˈmento *sm* recruitment
recluˈtare *vt* to recruit
reˈcondito, -a *ag* secluded; (*fig*) secret, hidden
ˈ**record** *ag inv* record *cpd* ■ *sm inv* record; **in tempo ~, a tempo di ~** in record time; **detenere il ~ di** to hold the record for; **~ mondiale** world record
recrimiˈnare *vi*: **~ (su qc)** to complain (about sth)
recriminaziˈone [rekriminatˈtsjone] *sf* recrimination
recrudeˈscenza [rekrudeʃˈʃɛntsa] *sf* fresh outbreak
recupeˈrare *etc* = **ricuperare** *etc*
redarguˈire *vt* to rebuke
reˈdassi *etc vb vedi* **redigere**
reˈdatto, -a *pp di* **redigere**
redatˈtore, -ˈtrice *sm/f* (*Stampa*) editor; (*: di articolo*) writer; (*di dizionario etc*) compiler; **~ capo** chief editor
redaziˈone [redatˈtsjone] *sf* editing; writing; (*sede*) editorial office(s); (*personale*) editorial staff; (*versione*) version
reddiˈtizio, a [reddiˈtittsjo] *ag* profitable
ˈ**reddito** *sm* income; (*dello Stato*) revenue; (*di un capitale*) yield; **~ complessivo** gross income; **~ disponibile** disposable income; **~ fisso** fixed income; **~ imponibile/non imponibile** taxable/non-taxable income; **~ da lavoro** earned income; **~ nazionale** national income; **~ pubblico** public revenue
reˈdensi *etc vb vedi* **redimere**
reˈdento, -a *pp di* **redimere**
redenˈtore *sm*: **il R~** the Redeemer
redenziˈone [redenˈtsjone] *sf* redemption
reˈdigere [reˈdidʒere] *vt* to write; (*contratto*) to draw up
reˈdimere *vt* to deliver; (*Rel*) to redeem
ˈ**redini** *sfpl* reins
rediˈvivo, -a *ag* returned to life, reborn
ˈ**reduce** [ˈrɛdutʃe] *ag* (*gen*): **~ da** returning from, back from ■ *sm/f* survivor; (*veterano*) veteran; **essere ~ da** (*esame, colloquio*) to have been through; (*malattia*) to be just over
ˈ**refe** *sm* thread
refeˈrendum *sm inv* referendum
refeˈrenza [refeˈrɛntsa] *sf* reference
reˈferto *sm* medical report
refetˈtorio *sm* refectory
refeziˈone [refetˈtsjone] *sf* (*Ins*) school meal
refratˈtario, -a *ag* refractory; (*fig*): **essere ~ alla matematica** to have no aptitude for mathematics
refrigeˈrante [refridʒeˈrante] *ag* (*Tecn*) cooling, refrigerating; (*bevanda*) refreshing ■ *sm* (*Chim: fluido*) coolant; (*Tecn: apparecchio*) refrigerator
refrigeˈrare [refridʒeˈrare] *vt* to refrigerate; (*rinfrescare*) to cool, refresh
refrigeraziˈone [refridʒeratˈtsjone] *sf* refrigeration; (*Tecn*) cooling; **~ ad acqua** (*Aut*) water-cooling
refriˈgerio [refriˈdʒɛrjo] *sm*: **trovare ~** to find somewhere cool
refurˈtiva *sf* stolen goods *pl*
Reg. *abbr* (= *reggimento*) Regt; (*Amm*) = **regolamento**
regaˈlare *vt* to give (as a present), make a present of
reˈgale *ag* regal
reˈgalo *sm* gift, present ■ *ag inv*: **confezione ~** gift pack; **fare un ~ a qn** to give sb a present; **"articoli da ~"** "gifts"
reˈgata *sf* regatta
regˈgente [redˈdʒɛnte] *ag* (*proposizione*) main; (*sovrano*) reigning ■ *sm/f* regent; **principe ~** prince regent
regˈgenza [redˈdʒɛntsa] *sf* regency
ˈ**reggere** [ˈrɛddʒere] *vt* (*tenere*) to hold; (*sostenere*) to support, bear, hold up; (*portare*) to carry, bear; (*resistere*) to withstand; (*dirigere: impresa*) to manage, run; (*governare*) to rule, govern; (*Ling*) to take, be followed by ■ *vi* (*resistere*): **~ a** to stand up to, hold out against; (*sopportare*): **~ a** to stand; (*durare*) to last; (*fig: teoria etc*) to hold water; **reggersi** *vr* (*stare ritto*) to stand; (*fig: dominarsi*) to control o.s.; **reggersi sulle gambe** *o* **in piedi** to stand up
ˈ**reggia, -ge** [ˈrɛddʒa] *sf* royal palace
reggiˈcalze [reddʒiˈkaltse] *sm inv* suspender belt
reggiˈmento [reddʒiˈmento] *sm* (*Mil*) regiment
reggiˈpetto [reddʒiˈpɛtto], **reggiˈseno** [reddʒiˈseno] *sm* bra
reˈgia, -ˈgie [reˈdʒia] *sf* (*TV, Cine etc*) direction
reˈgime [reˈdʒime] *sm* (*Pol*) regime; (*Dir: aureo, patrimoniale etc*) system; (*Med*) diet; (*Tecn*) (engine) speed; **~ di giri** (*di motore*) revs *pl* per minute; **~ vegetariano** vegetarian diet
reˈgina [reˈdʒina] *sf* queen
ˈ**regio, -a, gi, gie** [ˈrɛdʒo] *ag* royal
regioˈnale [redʒoˈnale] *ag* regional
regiˈone [reˈdʒone] *sf* (*gen*) region; (*territorio*) region, area; *see note*

REGIONE

The *Regione* is the biggest administrative unit in Italy. Each of the 20 *Regioni* consists of a variable number of "Province", which in turn are subdivided into "Comuni". Each of the regions has a "capoluogo", its chief province (for example, Florence is the chief province of the region of Tuscany). Five regions have special status and wider powers: Val d'Aosta, Friuli-Venezia Giulia, Trentino-Alto Adige, Sicily and Sardinia. A *Regione* is run by the "Giunta regionale", which is elected by the "Consiglio regionale"; both are presided over by a "Presidente". The "Giunta" has legislative powers within the region over the police, public health, schools, town planning and agriculture.

re'gista, -i, e [re'dʒista] *sm/f* (*TV, Cine etc*) director

regis'trare [redʒis'trare] *vt* (*Amm*) to register; (*Comm*) to enter; (*notare*) to report, note; (*canzone, conversazione: strumento di misura*) to record; (*mettere a punto*) to adjust, regulate; **~ i bagagli** (*Aer*) to check in one's luggage; **~ i freni** (*Tecn*) to adjust the brakes

registra'tore [redʒistra'tore] *sm* (*strumento*) recorder, register; (*magnetofono*) tape recorder; **~ di cassa** cash register; **~ a cassette** cassette recorder; **~ di volo** (*Aer*) flight recorder, black box (*fam*)

registrazi'one [redʒistrat'tsjone] *sf* registration; entry; reporting recording adjustment; **~ bagagli** (*Aer*) check-in

re'gistro [re'dʒistro] *sm* (*libro: Mus, Tecn, Ling*) register; (*Dir*) registry; (*Comm*): **~ (di cassa)** ledger; **ufficio del ~** registrar's office; **~ di bordo** logbook; **registri contabili** (account) books

re'gnante [reɲ'ɲante] *ag* reigning, ruling ■ *sm/f* ruler

re'gnare [reɲ'ɲare] *vi* to reign, rule; (*fig*) to reign

'regno ['reɲɲo] *sm* kingdom; (*periodo*) reign; (*fig*) realm; **il ~ animale/vegetale** the animal/vegetable kingdom; **il R~ Unito** the United Kingdom

'regola *sf* rule; **a ~ d'arte** duly; perfectly; **essere in ~** (*dipendente*) to be a registered employee; (*fig: essere pulito*) to be clean; **fare le cose in ~** to do things properly; **avere le carte in ~** (*gen*) to have one's papers in order; (*fig: essere adatto*) to be the right person; **per tua (norma e) ~** for your information; **un'eccezione alla ~** an exception to the rule

rego'labile *ag* adjustable

regolamen'tare *ag* (*distanza, velocità*) regulation *cpd*, proper; (*disposizione*) statutory ■ *vt* (*gen*) to control; **entro il tempo ~** within the time allowed, within the prescribed time

regola'mento *sm* (*complesso di norme*) regulations *pl*; (*di debito*) settlement; **~ di conti** (*fig*) settling of scores

rego'lare *ag* regular; (*velocità*) steady; (*superficie*) even; (*passo*) steady, even; (*in regola: documento*) in order ■ *vt* to regulate, control; (*apparecchio*) to adjust, regulate; (*questione, conto, debito*) to settle; **regolarsi** *vr* (*moderarsi*): **regolarsi nel bere/nello spendere** to control one's drinking/spending; (*comportarsi*) to behave, act; **presentare ~ domanda** to apply through the proper channels; **~ i conti** (*fig*) to settle old scores

regolarità *sf inv* regularity; steadiness; evenness; (*nel pagare*) punctuality

regolariz'zare [regolarid'dzare] *vt* (*posizione*) to regularize; (*debito*) to settle

rego'lata *sf*: **darsi una ~** to pull o.s. together

regola'tezza [regola'tettsa] *sf* (*ordine*) orderliness; (*moderazione*) moderation

rego'lato, -a *ag* (*ordinato*) orderly; (*moderato*) moderate

regola'tore *sm* (*Tecn*) regulator; **~ di frequenza/di volume** frequency/volume control

'regolo *sm* ruler; **~ calcolatore** slide rule

regre'dire *vi* to regress

regressi'one *sf* regression

re'gresso *sm* (*fig: declino*) decline

rei'etto, -a *sm/f* outcast

reincarnazi'one [reinkarnat'tsjone] *sf* reincarnation

reinte'grare *vt* (*produzione*) to restore; (*energie*) to recover; (*dipendente*) to reinstate

reintegrazi'one [reintegrat'tsjone] *sf* (*di produzione*) restoration; (*di dipendente*) reinstatement

relativa'mente *av* relatively

relatività *sf* relativity

rela'tivo, -a *ag* relative; (*attinente*) relevant; (*rispettivo*) respective; **~ a** (*che concerne*) relating to, concerning; (*proporzionato*) in proportion to

rela'tore, -'trice *sm/f* (*gen*) spokesman/woman; (*Ins: di tesi*) supervisor

re'lax [re'laks] *sm* relaxation

relazi'one [relat'tsjone] *sf* (*fra cose, persone*) relation(ship); (*resoconto*) report, account; **relazioni** *sfpl* (*conoscenze*) connections; **essere in ~** to be connected; **mettere in ~** (*fatti, elementi*) to make the connection between; **in ~ a quanto detto prima** with regard to what has already been said; **essere in buone relazioni con qn** to be on good terms with sb; **fare una ~** to make a report, give an account; **relazioni pubbliche (RP)** public relations (PR)

rele'gare *vt* to banish; (*fig*) to relegate

religi'one [reli'dʒone] *sf* religion

religi'oso, -a [reli'dʒoso] *ag* religious ■ *sm/f* monk/nun
re'liquia *sf* relic
re'litto *sm* wreck; (*fig*) down-and-out
re'mainder [ri'meindər] *sm inv* (*libro*) remainder
're'make ['ri:'meik] *sm inv* (*Cine*) remake
re'mare *vi* to row
remini'scenze [reminiʃ'ʃɛntse] *sfpl* reminiscences
remissi'one *sf* remission; (*deferenza*) submissiveness, compliance; **~ del debito** remission of debt; **~ di querela** (*Dir*) withdrawal of an action
remissività *sf* submissiveness
remis'sivo, -a *ag* submissive, compliant
'remo *sm* oar
'remora *sf* (*poetico: indugio*) hesitation
re'moto, -a *ag* remote
remune'rare *etc* = **rimunerare** *etc*
'rena *sf* sand
re'nale *ag* kidney *cpd*
'rendere *vt* (*ridare*) to return, give back; (*: saluto etc*) to return; (*produrre*) to yield, bring in; (*esprimere, tradurre*) to render; (*far diventare*): **~ qc possibile** to make sth possible ■ *vi* (*fruttare: ditta*) to be profitable; (*: investimento, campo*) to yield, be productive; **~ grazie a qn** to thank sb; **~ omaggio a qn** to honour sb; **~ un servizio a qn** to do sb a service; **~ una testimonianza** to give evidence; **~ la visita** to pay a return visit; **non so se rendo l'idea** I don't know whether I'm making myself clear; **rendersi utile** to make o.s. useful; **rendersi conto di qc** to realize sth
rendi'conto *sm* (*rapporto*) report, account; (*Amm, Comm*) statement of account
rendi'mento *sm* (*reddito*) yield; (*di manodopera, Tecn*) efficiency; (*capacità*) output; (*di studenti*) performance
'rendita *sf* (*di individuo*) private *o* unearned income; (*Comm*) revenue; **~ annua** annuity; **~ vitalizia** life annuity
'rene *sm* kidney
'reni *sfpl* back *sg*
reni'tente *ag* reluctant, unwilling; **~ ai consigli di qn** unwilling to follow sb's advice; **essere ~ alla leva** (*Mil*) to fail to report for military service
'renna *sf* reindeer *inv*
'Reno *sm*: **il ~** the Rhine
'reo, -a *sm/f* (*Dir*) offender
re'parto *sm* department, section; (*Mil*) detachment; **~ acquisti** purchasing office
repel'lente *ag* repulsive; (*Chim: insettifugo*): **liquido ~** (liquid) repellent
repen'taglio [repen'taʎʎo] *sm*: **mettere a ~** to jeopardize, risk
repen'tino, -a *ag* sudden, unexpected
repe'ribile *ag* available
repe'rire *vt* to find, trace
re'perto *sm* (*Archeologia*) find; (*Med*) report; (*anche*: **reperto giudiziario**) exhibit
reper'torio *sm* (*Teat*) repertory; (*elenco*) index, (alphabetical) list
'replica, -che *sf* repetition reply, answer; (*obiezione*) objection; (*Teat, Cine*) repeat performance; (*copia*) replica
repli'care *vt* (*ripetere*) to repeat; (*rispondere*) to answer, reply
repor'tage [rəpɔr'taʒ] *sm inv* (*Stampa*) report
repressi'one *sf* repression
repres'sivo, -a *ag* repressive
re'presso, -a *pp di* **reprimere**
re'primere *vt* to suppress, repress
re'pubblica, -che *sf* republic; **la R~ Democratica Tedesca (RDT)** the German Democratic Republic (GDR); **la R~ Federale Tedesca (RFT)** the Federal Republic of Germany (FRG); **la Prima/la Seconda R~** *terms used to refer to Italy before and after the political changes resulting from the 1994 elections; vedi anche* **Festa della Repubblica**; **Seconda Repubblica**
repubbli'cano, -a *ag, sm/f* republican
repu'tare *vt* to consider, judge
reputazi'one [reputat'tsjone] *sf* reputation; **farsi una cattiva ~** to get o.s. a bad name
'requie *sf* rest; **dare ~ a qn** to give sb some peace; **senza ~** unceasingly
'requiem *sm inv* (*preghiera*) requiem, prayer for the dead; (*fig: ufficio funebre*) requiem
requi'sire *vt* to requisition
requi'sito *sm* requirement; **avere i requisiti necessari per un lavoro** to have the necessary qualifications for a job
requisi'toria *sf* (*Dir*) closing speech (for the prosecution)
requisizi'one [rekwizit'tsjone] *sf* requisition
'resa *sf* (*l'arrendersi*) surrender; (*restituzione, rendimento*) return; **~ dei conti** rendering of accounts; (*fig*) day of reckoning
re'scindere [reʃ'ʃindere] *vt* (*Dir*) to rescind, annul
re'scisso, -a [reʃ'ʃisso] *pp di* **rescindere**
reset'tare *vt* (*Inform*) to reset
'resi *etc vb vedi* **rendere**
resi'dente *ag* resident
resi'denza [resi'dɛntsa] *sf* residence
residenzi'ale [residen'tsjale] *ag* residential
residu'ale *ag* residual
re'siduo, -a *ag* residual, remaining ■ *sm* remainder; (*Chim*) residue; **residui industriali** industrial waste *sg*

r

'**resina** *sf* resin
resis'tente *ag* (*che resiste*): **~ a** resistant to; (*forte*) strong; (*duraturo*) long-lasting, durable; **~ all'acqua** waterproof; **~ al caldo** heat-resistant; **~ al fuoco** fireproof; **~ al gelo** frost-resistant
resis'tenza [resis'tɛntsa] *sf* (*gen, Elettr*) resistance; (*di persona: fisica*) stamina, endurance; (*: mentale*) endurance, resistance; **opporre ~ (a)** to offer *o* put up resistance (to); (*decisione, scelta*) to show opposition (to); **la R~** *see note*

RESISTENZA

The Italian *Resistenza* fought against both the Nazis and the Fascists during the Second World War. It was particularly active after the fall of the Fascist government on 25 July 1943, throughout the German occupation and during the period of Mussolini's Republic of Salò in northern Italy. Resistance members spanned the whole political spectrum and played a vital role in the Liberation and in the formation of the new democratic government.

re'sistere *vi* to resist; **~ a** (*assalto, tentazioni*) to resist; (*dolore: pianta*) to withstand; (*non patir danno*) to be resistant to
resis'tito, -a *pp di* **resistere**
'**reso, -a** *pp di* **rendere**
reso'conto *sm* report, account
respin'gente [respin'dʒɛnte] *sm* (*Ferr*) buffer
res'pingere [res'pindʒere] *vt* to drive back, repel; (*rifiutare: pacco, lettera*) to return; (*: invito*) to refuse; (*: proposta*) to reject, turn down; (*Ins: bocciare*) to fail
res'pinto, -a *pp di* **respingere**
respi'rare *vi* to breathe; (*fig*) to get one's breath; to breathe again ▪ *vt* to breathe (in), inhale
respira'tore *sm* respirator
respira'torio, -a *ag* respiratory
respirazi'one [respirat'tsjone] *sf* breathing; **~ artificiale** artificial respiration; **~ bocca a bocca** mouth-to-mouth resuscitation, kiss of life; (*fam*)
res'piro *sm* breathing *no pl*; (*singolo atto*) breath; (*fig*) respite, rest; **mandare un ~ di sollievo** to give a sigh of relief; **trattenere il ~** to hold one's breath; **lavorare senza ~** to work non-stop; **di ampio ~** (*opera, lavoro*) far-reaching
respon'sabile *ag* responsible ▪ *sm/f* person responsible; (*capo*) person in charge; **~ di** responsible for; (*Dir*) liable for
responsabilità *sf inv* responsibility; (*legale*) liability; **assumere la ~ di** to take on the responsibility for; **affidare a qn la ~ di qc** to make sb responsible for sth; **~ patrimoniale** debt liability; **~ penale** criminal liability
responsabiliz'zare [responsabilid'dzare] *vt*: **~ qn** to make sb feel responsible
res'ponso *sm* answer; (*Dir*) verdict
'**ressa** *sf* crowd, throng
'**ressi** *etc vb vedi* **reggere**
res'tare *vi* (*rimanere*) to remain, stay; (*diventare*): **~ orfano/cieco** to become *o* be left an orphan/become blind; (*trovarsi*): **~ sorpreso** to be surprised; (*avanzare*) to be left, remain; **~ d'accordo** to agree; **non resta più niente** there's nothing left; **restano pochi giorni** there are only a few days left; **che resti tra di noi** this is just between ourselves; **~ in buoni rapporti** to remain on good terms; **~ senza parole** to be left speechless
restau'rare *vt* to restore
restaura'tore, -'trice *sm/f* restorer
restaurazi'one [restaurat'tsjone] *sf* (*Pol*) restoration
res'tauro *sm* (*di edifici etc*) restoration; **in ~** under repair; **sotto ~** (*dipinto*) being restored; **chiuso per restauri** closed for repairs
res'tio, -a, 'tii, 'tie *ag* restive; (*persona*): **~ a** reluctant to
restitu'ire *vt* to return, give back; (*energie, forze*) to restore
restituzi'one [restitut'tsjone] *sf* return; (*di soldi*) repayment
'**resto** *sm* remainder, rest; (*denaro*) change; (*Mat*) remainder; **resti** *smpl* leftovers; (*di città*) remains; **del ~** moreover, besides; **resti mortali** (mortal) remains
res'tringere [res'trindʒere] *vt* to reduce; (*vestito*) to take in; (*stoffa*) to shrink; (*fig*) to restrict, limit; **restringersi** *vr* (*strada*) to narrow; (*stoffa*) to shrink
restrit'tivo, -a *ag* restrictive
restrizi'one [restrit'tsjone] *sf* restriction
resurrezi'one [resurret'tsjone] *sf* = **risurrezione**
resusci'tare [resuʃʃi'tare] *vt, vi* = **risuscitare**
re'tata *sf* (*Pesca*) haul, catch; **fare una ~ di** (*fig: persone*) to round up
'**rete** *sf* net; (*di recinzione*) wire netting; (*Aut, Ferr, di spionaggio etc*) network; (*fig*) trap, snare; **segnare una ~** (*Calcio*) to score a goal; **~ ferroviaria/stradale/di distribuzione** railway/road/distribution network; **~ del letto** (sprung) bed base; **~ da pesca** fishing net; **~ sociale** social network; **~ (televisiva)** (*sistema*) network; (*canale*) channel; **la R~** the web; **calze a ~** fishnet tights *o* stockings

reti'cente [reti'tʃɛnte] *ag* reticent
reti'cenza [reti'tʃɛntsa] *sf* reticence
retico'lato *sm* grid; (*rete metallica*) wire netting; (*di filo spinato*) barbed wire fence
'retina *sf* (*Anat*) retina
re'torico, -a, ci, che *ag* rhetorical ■ *sf* rhetoric
retribu'ire *vt* to pay; (*premiare*) to reward; **un lavoro mal retribuito** a poorly paid job
retribu'tivo, -a *ag* pay *cpd*
retribuzi'one [retribut'tsjone] *sf* payment; reward
re'trivo, -a *ag* (*fig*) reactionary
'retro *sm inv* back ■ *av* (*dietro*): **vedi ~** see over(leaf)
retroattività *sf* retroactivity
retroat'tivo, -a *ag* (*Dir: legge*) retroactive; (*Amm: salario*) backdated
retrobot'tega, -ghe *sf* back shop
retro'cedere [retro'tʃɛdere] *vi* to withdraw ■ *vt* (*Calcio*) to relegate; (*Mil*) to degrade; (*Amm*) to demote
retrocessi'one [retrotʃes'sjone] *sf* (*di impiegato*) demotion
retro'cesso, -a [retro'tʃɛsso] *pp di* **retrocedere**
retroda'tare *vt* (*Amm*) to backdate
re'trogrado, -a *ag* (*fig*) reactionary, backward-looking
retrogu'ardia *sf* (*anche fig*) rearguard
retro'marcia [retro'martʃa] *sf* (*Aut*) reverse; (*dispositivo*) reverse gear
retro'scena [retroʃʃɛna] *sf inv* (*Teat*) backstage ■ *sm inv* (*fig*) behind-the-scenes activity
retrospet'tivo, -a *ag* retrospective ■ *sf* (*Arte*) retrospective (exhibition)
retros'tante *ag*: **~ (a)** at the back (of)
retro'terra *sm* hinterland
retro'via *sf* (*Mil*) zone behind the front; **mandare nelle retrovie** to send to the rear
retrovi'sore *sm* (*Aut*) (rear-view) mirror
'retta *sf* (*Mat*) straight line; (*di convitto*) charge for bed and board; (*fig: ascolto*): **dar ~ a** to listen to, pay attention to
rettango'lare *ag* rectangular
ret'tangolo, -a *ag* right-angled ■ *sm* rectangle
ret'tifica, -che *sf* rectification, correction
rettifi'care *vt* (*curva*) to straighten; (*fig*) to rectify, correct
'rettile *sm* reptile
retti'lineo, -a *ag* rectilinear
retti'tudine *sf* rectitude, uprightness
'retto, -a *pp di* **reggere** ■ *ag* straight; (*Mat*): **angolo ~** right angle; (*onesto*) honest, upright; (*giusto, esatto*) correct, proper, right
ret'tore *sm* (*Rel*) rector; (*di università*) ≈ chancellor
reuma'tismo *sm* rheumatism
Rev. *abbr* (= *Reverendo*) Rev(d)
reve'rendo, -a *ag*: **il ~ padre Belli** the Reverend Father Belli
reve'rente *ag* = **riverente**
reve'renza [reve'rɛntsa] *sf* = **riverenza**
rever'sibile *ag* reversible
revisio'nare *vt* (*conti*) to audit; (*Tecn*) to overhaul, service; (*Dir: processo*) to review; (*componimento*) to revise
revisi'one *sf* auditing *no pl*; audit servicing *no pl*; overhaul review revision; **~ di bilancio** audit; **~ di bozze** proofreading; **~ contabile interna** internal audit
revi'sore *sm*: **~ di conti/bozze** auditor/ proofreader
'revoca *sf* revocation
revo'care *vt* to revoke
re'volver *sm inv* revolver
revolve'rata *sf* revolver shot
'Reykjavik ['reikjavik] *sf* Reykjavik
RFT *sigla f vedi* **Repubblica Federale Tedesca**
ri'abbia *etc vb vedi* **riavere**
riabili'tare *vt* to rehabilitate; (*fig*) to restore to favour (*Brit*) *o* favor (*US*)
riabilitazi'one [riabilitat'tsjone] *sf* rehabilitation
riac'cendere [riat'tʃɛndere] *vt* (*sigaretta, fuoco, gas*) to light again; (*luce, radio, TV*) to switch on again; (*fig: sentimenti: interesse*) to rekindle, revive; **riaccendersi** *vr* (*fuoco*) to catch again; (*luce, radio, TV*) to come back on again; (*fig: sentimenti*) to revive, be rekindled
riac'ceso, -a [riat'tʃeso] *pp di* **riaccendere**
riacqui'stare *vt* (*gen*) to buy again; (*ciò che si era venduto*) to buy back; (*fig: buonumore, sangue freddo, libertà*) to regain; **~ la salute** to recover (one's health); **~ le forze** to regain one's strength
Ri'ad *sf* Riyadh
riaddormen'tare *vt* to put to sleep again; **riaddormentarsi** *vr* to fall asleep again
riallac'ciare [riallat'tʃare] *vt* (*cintura, cavo etc*) to refasten, tie up *o* fasten again; (*fig: rapporti, amicizia*) to resume, renew; **riallacciarsi** *vr*: **riallacciarsi a** (*fig: a discorso, tema*) to resume, take up again
rial'zare [rial'tsare] *vt* to raise, lift; (*alzare di più*) to heighten, raise; (*aumentare: prezzi*) to increase, raise ■ *vi* (*prezzi*) to rise, increase
rial'zato, -a [rial'tsato] *ag*: **piano ~** mezzanine, entresol
rial'zista, -i [rial'tsista] *sm* (*Borsa*) bull
ri'alzo [ri'altso] *sm* (*di prezzi*) increase, rise; (*sporgenza*) rise; **giocare al ~** (*Borsa*) to bull

rian'dare *vi*: **~ (in), ~ (a)** to go back (to), return (to)
riani'mare *vt* (*Med*) to resuscitate; (*fig: rallegrare*) to cheer up; (*dar coraggio*) to give heart to; **rianimarsi** *vr* to recover consciousness; to cheer up; to take heart
rianimazi'one [rianimat'tsjone] *sf* (*Med*) resuscitation; **centro di ~** intensive care unit
ria'perto, -a *pp di* **riaprire**
riaper'tura *sf* reopening
riappa'rire *vi* to reappear
riap'parso, -a *pp di* **riapparire**
riap'pendere *vt* to rehang; (*Tel*) to hang up
ria'prire *vt*, **ria'prirsi** *vr* to reopen, open again
ri'armo *sm* (*Mil*) rearmament
ri'arso, -a *ag* (*terreno*) arid; (*gola*) parched; (*labbra*) dry
riasset'tare *vt* (*vedi sm*) to rearrange; to reorganize
rias'setto *sm* (*di stanza etc*) rearrangement; (*ordinamento*) reorganization
rias'sumere *vt* (*riprendere*) to resume; (*impiegare di nuovo*) to re-employ; (*sintetizzare*) to summarize
rias'sunto, -a *pp di* **riassumere** ■ *sm* summary
riattac'care *vt* (*attaccare di nuovo*): **~ (a)** (*manifesto, francobollo*) to stick back (on); (*bottone*) to sew back (on); (*quadro, chiavi*) to hang back up (on); **~ (il telefono** *o* **il ricevitore)** to hang up (the receiver)
riatti'vare *vt* to reactivate
ria'vere *vt* to have again; (*avere indietro*) to get back; (*riacquistare*) to recover; **riaversi** *vr* to recover; (*da svenimento, stordimento*) to come round
riba'dire *vt* (*fig*) to confirm
ri'balta *sf* (*sportello*) flap; (*Teat: proscenio*) front of the stage; (*apparecchio d'illuminazione*) footlights *pl*; (*fig*) limelight; **tornare alla ~** (*personaggio*) to make a comeback; (*problema*) to come up again
ribal'tabile *ag* (*sedile*) tip-up
ribal'tare *vt, vi* (*anche*: **ribaltarsi**) to turn over, tip over
ribas'sare *vt* to lower, bring down ■ *vi* to come down, fall
ribas'sista, -i *sm* (*Borsa*) bear
ri'basso *sm* reduction, fall; **essere in ~** (*azioni, prezzi*) to be down; (*fig: popolarità*) to be on the decline; **giocare al ~** (*Borsa*) to bear
ri'battere *vt* (*battere di nuovo*) to beat again; (*con macchina da scrivere*) to type again; (*palla*) to return; (*confutare*) to refute; **~ che** to retort that
ribattez'zare [ribatted'dzare] *vt* to rename
ribel'larsi *vr*: **~ (a)** to rebel (against)
ri'belle *ag* (*soldati*) rebel; (*ragazzo*) rebellious ■ *sm/f* rebel
ribelli'one *sf* rebellion
'ribes *sm inv* currant; **~ nero** blackcurrant; **~ rosso** redcurrant
ribol'lire *vi* (*fermentare*) to ferment; (*fare bolle*) to bubble, boil; (*fig*) to seethe
ri'brezzo [ri'breddzo] *sm* disgust, loathing; **far ~ a** to disgust
ribut'tante *ag* disgusting, revolting
ricacci'are [rikat'tʃare] *vt* (*respingere*) to drive back; **~ qn fuori** to throw sb out
rica'dere *vi* to fall again; (*scendere a terra: fig: nel peccato etc*) to fall back; (*vestiti, capelli etc*) to hang (down); (*riversarsi: fatiche, colpe*): **~ su** to fall on
rica'duta *sf* (*Med*) relapse
rical'care *vt* (*disegni*) to trace; (*fig*) to follow faithfully
ricalci'trare [rikaltʃi'trare] *vi* (*cavalli, asini, muli*) to kick
rica'mare *vt* to embroider
ricambi'are *vt* to change again; (*contraccambiare*) to return
ri'cambio *sm* exchange, return; (*Fisiol*) metabolism; **ricambi** *smpl*: **pezzi di ~** spare parts; **~ della manodopera** labour turnover
ri'camo *sm* embroidery; **senza ricami** (*fig*) without frills
ricapito'lare *vt* to recapitulate, sum up
ricapitolazi'one [rikapitolat'tsjone] *sf* recapitulation, summary
ricari'care *vt* (*arma, macchina fotografica*) to reload; (*penna*) to refill; (*orologio, giocattolo*) to rewind; (*Elettr*) to recharge
ricat'tare *vt* to blackmail
ricatta'tore, -'trice *sm/f* blackmailer
ri'catto *sm* blackmail; **fare un ~ a qn** to blackmail sb; **subire un ~** to be blackmailed
rica'vare *vt* (*estrarre*) to draw out, extract; (*ottenere*) to obtain, gain
rica'vato *sm* (*di vendite*) proceeds *pl*
ri'cavo *sm* proceeds *pl*; (*Contabilità*) revenue
ric'chezza [rik'kettsa] *sf* wealth; (*fig*) richness; **ricchezze** *sfpl* (*beni*) wealth *sg*, riches; **ricchezze naturali** natural resources
'riccio, -a, ci, ce ['rittʃo] *ag* curly ■ *sm* (*Zool*) hedgehog; (*anche*: **riccio di mare**) sea urchin
'ricciolo ['rittʃolo] *sm* curl
ricci'uto, -a [rit'tʃuto] *ag* curly
'ricco, -a, chi, che *ag* rich; (*persona, paese*) rich, wealthy ■ *sm/f* rich man/woman; **i ricchi** the rich; **~ di** (*idee, illustrazioni etc*) full of; (*risorse, fauna etc*) rich in

riˈcerca, -che [riˈtʃerka] *sf* search; (*indagine*) investigation, inquiry; (*studio*): **la ~** research; **una ~** piece of research; **mettersi alla ~ di** to go in search of, look *o* search *o* hunt for; **essere alla ~ di** to be searching for, be looking for; **~ di mercato** market research; **~ operativa** operational research
ricerˈcare [ritʃerˈkare] *vt* (*motivi, cause*) to look for, try to determine; (*successo, piacere*) to pursue; (*onore, gloria*) to seek
ricercaˈtezza [ritʃerkaˈtettsa] *sf* (*raffinatezza*) refinement; (*peg*) affectation
ricerˈcato, -a [ritʃerˈkato] *ag* (*apprezzato*) much sought-after; (*affettato*) studied, affected ■ *sm/f* (*Polizia*) wanted man/woman
ricercaˈtore, -ˈtrice [ritʃerkaˈtore] *sm/f* (*Ins*) researcher
ricetrasmitˈtente [ritʃetrazmitˈtɛnte] *sf* two-way radio, transceiver
riˈcetta [riˈtʃɛtta] *sf* (*Med*) prescription; (*Cuc*) recipe; (*fig: antidoto*): **~ contro** remedy for
ricetˈtacolo [ritʃetˈtakolo] *sm* (*peg: luogo malfamato*) den
ricetˈtario [ritʃetˈtarjo] *sm* (*Med*) prescription pad; (*Cuc*) recipe book
ricettaˈtore, -ˈtrice [ritʃettaˈtore] *sm/f* (*Dir*) receiver (of stolen goods)
ricettaziˈone [ritʃettatˈtsjone] *sf* (*Dir*) receiving (stolen goods)
ricetˈtivo, -a [ritʃetˈtivo] *ag* receptive
riceˈvente [ritʃeˈvɛnte] *ag* (*Radio, TV*) receiving ■ *sm/f* (*Comm*) receiver
riˈcevere [riˈtʃevere] *vt* to receive; (*stipendio, lettera*) to get, receive; (*accogliere: ospite*) to welcome; (*vedere: cliente, rappresentante etc*) to see; **"confermiamo di aver ricevuto tale merce"** (*Comm*) "we acknowledge receipt of these goods"
riceviˈmento [ritʃeviˈmento] *sm* receiving *no pl*; (*trattenimento*) reception; **al ~ della merce** on receipt of the goods
riceviˈtore [ritʃeviˈtore] *sm* (*Tecn*) receiver; **~ delle imposte** tax collector
ricevitoˈria [ritʃevitoˈria] *sf* (*Fisco*): **~ (delle imposte)** Inland Revenue (*Brit*) *o* Internal Revenue (*US*) Office; **~ del lotto** lottery office
riceˈvuta [ritʃeˈvuta] *sf* receipt; **accusare ~ di qc** (*Comm*) to acknowledge receipt of sth; **~ fiscale** official receipt (for tax purposes); **~ di ritorno** (*Posta*) advice of receipt; **~ di versamento** receipt of payment
riceziˈone [ritʃetˈtsjone] *sf* (*Radio, TV*) reception
richiaˈmare [rikjaˈmare] *vt* (*chiamare indietro, ritelefonare*) to call back; (*ambasciatore, truppe*) to recall; (*rimproverare*) to reprimand; (*attirare*) to attract, draw; **richiamarsi** *vr*: **richiamarsi a** (*riferirsi a*) to refer to; **~ qn all'ordine** to call sb to order; **desidero ~ la vostra attenzione su ...** I would like to draw your attention to ...
richiˈamo [riˈkjamo] *sm* call; recall reprimand; attraction
richieˈdente [rikjeˈdɛnte] *sm/f* applicant
richiˈedere [riˈkjɛdere] *vt* to ask again for; (*chiedere indietro*): **~ qc** to ask for sth back; (*chiedere: per sapere*) to ask; (: *per avere*) to ask for; (*Amm: documenti*) to apply for; (*esigere*) to need, require; **essere molto richiesto** to be in great demand
richiˈesto, -a [riˈkjɛsto] *pp di* **richiedere** ■ *sf* (*domanda*) request; (*Amm*) application, request; (*esigenza*) demand, request; **a richiesta** on request
riciˈclaggio [ritʃiˈkladdʒo] *sm* (*fig*) laundering; **~ di materiale** recycling; **~ di denaro sporco** money laundering
riciˈclare [ritʃiˈklare] *vt* (*vetro, carta, bottiglie*) to recycle; (*fig: personale*) to retrain
ˈricino [ˈritʃino] *sm*: **olio di ~** castor oil
ricogniˈtore [rikoɲɲiˈtore] *sm* (*Aer*) reconnaissance aircraft
ricogniziˈone [rikoɲɲitˈtsjone] *sf* (*Mil*) reconnaissance; (*Dir*) recognition, acknowledgement
ricolleˈgare *vt* (*collegare nuovamente: gen*) to join again, link again; (*connettere: fatti*): **~ (a, con)** to connect (with); **ricollegarsi** *vr*: **ricollegarsi a** (*fatti connettersi*) to be connected to; (*persona: riferirsi*) to refer to
riˈcolmo, -a *ag*: **~ (di)** (*bicchiere*) full to the brim (with); (*stanza*) full (of)
ricominciˈare [rikominˈtʃare] *vt, vi* to start again, begin again; **~ a fare qc** to begin doing *o* to do sth again, start doing *o* to do sth again
ricomˈpensa *sf* reward
ricompenˈsare *vt* to reward
ricomˈporsi *vr* to compose o.s., regain one's composure
ricomˈposto, -a *pp di* **ricomporsi**
riconciliˈare [rikontʃiˈljare] *vt* to reconcile; **riconciliarsi** *vr* to be reconciled
riconciliaziˈone [rikontʃiliatˈtsjone] *sf* reconciliation
riconˈdotto, -a *pp di* **ricondurre**
riconˈdurre *vt* to bring (*o* take) back
riconˈferma *sf* reconfirmation
riconferˈmare *vt* to reconfirm
ricongiungiˈmento [rikondʒundʒiˈmento] *sm* (*di famiglia, coniugi*) reconciliation; **~ familiare** (*Dir: di immigrati*) family reunification

r

rico'no'scente [rikonoʃʃɛnte] *ag* grateful
riconoscenza [rikonoʃʃɛntsa] *sf* gratitude
rico'noscere [riko'noʃʃere] *vt* to recognize; (*Dir: figlio, debito*) to acknowledge; (*ammettere: errore*) to admit, acknowledge; **~ qn colpevole** to find sb guilty
riconosci'mento [rikonoʃʃi'mento] *sm* recognition; acknowledgement; (*identificazione*) identification; **come ~ dei servizi resi** in recognition of services rendered; **documento di ~** means of identification; **segno di ~** distinguishing mark; **programma per il ~ vocale** (*Inform*) voice recognition program
riconosci'uto, -a [rikonoʃʃuto] *pp di* **riconoscere**
riconquis'tare *vt* (*Mil*) to reconquer; (*libertà, stima*) to win back
rico'perto, -a *pp di* **ricoprire**
ricopi'are *vt* to copy
rico'prire *vt* to re-cover; (*coprire*) to cover; (*occupare: carica*) to hold
ricor'dare *vt* to remember, recall; (*richiamare alla memoria*): **~ qc a qn** to remind sb of sth; **ricordarsi** *vr*: **ricordarsi (di)** to remember; **ricordarsi di qc/di aver fatto** to remember sth/having done
ri'cordo *sm* memory; (*regalo*) keepsake, souvenir; (*di viaggio*) souvenir; **ricordi** *smpl* (*memorie*) memoirs
ricor'rente *ag* recurrent, recurring
ricor'renza [rikor'rɛntsa] *sf* recurrence; (*festività*) anniversary
ri'correre *vi* (*ripetersi*) to recur; **~ a** (*rivolgersi*) to turn to; (*Dir*) to appeal to; (*servirsi di*) to have recourse to; **~ in appello** to lodge an appeal
ri'corso, -a *pp di* **ricorrere** ■ *sm* recurrence; (*Dir*) appeal; **far ~ a** = **ricorrere a**
ricostitu'ente *ag* (*Med*): **cura ~** tonic treatment ■ *sm* (*Med*) tonic
ricostitu'ire *vt* (*società*) to build up again; (*governo, partito*) to re-form; **ricostituirsi** *vr* (*gruppo etc*) to re-form
ricostru'ire *vt* (*casa*) to rebuild; (*fatti*) to reconstruct
ricostruzi'one [rikostrut'tsjone] *sf* rebuilding *no pl*; reconstruction
ri'cotta *sf soft white unsalted cheese made from sheep's milk*
ricove'rare *vt* to give shelter to; **~ qn in ospedale** to admit sb to hospital
ricove'rato, -a *sm/f* patient
ri'covero *sm* shelter, refuge; (*Mil*) shelter; (*Med*) admission (to hospital); **~ antiaereo** air-raid shelter
ricre'are *vt* to recreate; (*rinvigorire*) to restore; (*fig: distrarre*) to amuse
ricrea'tivo, -a *ag* recreational
ricreazi'one [rikreat'tsjone] *sf* recreation, entertainment; (*Ins*) break
ri'credersi *vr* to change one's mind
ricupe'rare *vt* (*rientrare in possesso di*) to recover, get back; (*tempo perduto*) to make up for; (*Naut*) to salvage; (*: naufraghi*) to rescue; (*delinquente*) to rehabilitate; **~ lo svantaggio** (*Sport*) to close the gap
ri'cupero *sm* (*gen*) recovery; (*di relitto etc*) salvaging; **capacità di ~** resilience
ricu'sare *vt* to refuse
ridacchi'are [ridak'kjare] *vi* to snigger
ri'dare *vt* to return, give back
'ridda *sf* (*di ammiratori etc*) swarm; (*di pensieri*) jumble
ri'dente *ag* (*occhi, volto*) smiling; (*paesaggio*) delightful
'ridere *vi* to laugh; (*deridere, beffare*): **~ di** to laugh at, make fun of; **non c'è niente da ~, c'è poco da ~** it's not a laughing matter
rides'tare *vt* (*fig: ricordi, passioni*) to reawaken
ri'detto, -a *pp di* **ridire**
ridico'laggine [ridiko'laddʒine] *sf* (*di situazione*) absurdity; (*cosa detta o fatta*) nonsense *no pl*
ridicoliz'zare [ridikolid'dzare] *vt* to ridicule
ri'dicolo, -a *ag* ridiculous, absurd ■ *sm*: **cadere nel ~** to become ridiculous; **rendersi ~** to make a fool of o.s.
ridimensiona'mento *sm* reorganization; (*di fatto storico*) reappraisal
ridimensio'nare *vt* to reorganize; (*fig*) to see in the right perspective
ri'dire *vt* to repeat; (*criticare*) to find fault with; to object to; **trova sempre qualcosa da ~** he always manages to find fault
ridon'dante *ag* redundant
ri'dosso *sm*: **a ~ di** (*dietro*) behind; (*contro*) against
ri'dotto, -a *pp di* **ridurre**
ri'duco *etc vb vedi* **ridurre**
ri'durre *vt* (*anche Chim, Mat*) to reduce; (*prezzo, spese*) to cut, reduce; (*accorciare: opera letteraria*) to abridge; (*Radio, TV*) to adapt; **ridursi** *vr* (*diminuirsi*) to be reduced, shrink; **ridursi a** to be reduced to; **ridursi a pelle e ossa** to be reduced to skin and bone
ri'dussi *etc vb vedi* **ridurre**
ridut'tore *sm* (*Tecn, Chim, Elettr*) reducer
riduzi'one [ridut'tsjone] *sf* reduction; abridgement; adaptation
ri'ebbi *etc vb vedi* **riavere**
riecheg'giare [rieked'dʒare] *vi* to re-echo
riedu'care *vt* (*persona, arto*) to re-educate; (*malato*) to rehabilitate

rieducazi'one [riedukat'tsjone] *sf* re-education; rehabilitation; **centro di ~** rehabilitation centre
rie'leggere [rie'lɛddʒere] *vt* to re-elect
rie'letto, -a *pp di* **rieleggere**
riempi'mento *sm* filling (up)
riem'pire *vt* to fill (up); (*modulo*) to fill in *o* out; **riempirsi** *vr* to fill (up); (*mangiare troppo*) to stuff o.s.; **~ qc di** to fill sth (up) with
riempi'tivo, -a *ag* filling ■ *sm* (*anche fig*) filler
rien'tranza [rien'trantsa] *sf* recess; indentation
rien'trare *vi* (*entrare di nuovo*) to go (*o* come) back in; (*tornare*) to return; (*fare una rientranza*) to go in, curve inwards; to be indented; (*riguardare*): **~ in** to be included among, form part of; **~ (a casa)** to get back home; **non rientriamo nelle spese** we are not within our budget
ri'entro *sm* (*ritorno*) return; (*di astronave*) re-entry; **è iniziato il grande ~** (*estivo*) people are coming back from their (summer) holidays
riepilo'gare *vt* to summarize ■ *vi* to recapitulate
rie'pilogo, -ghi *sm* recapitulation; **fare un ~ di qc** to summarize sth
rie'same *sm* re-examination
riesami'nare *vt* to re-examine
ri'esco *etc vb vedi* **riuscire**
ri'essere *vi*: **ci risiamo!** (*fam*) we're back to this again!
rievo'care *vt* (*passato*) to recall; (*commemorare: figura, meriti*) to commemorate
rievocazi'one [rievokat'tsjone] *sf* (*vedi vt*) recalling; commemoration
rifaci'mento [rifatʃi'mento] *sm* (*di film*) remake; (*di opera letteraria*) rehashing
ri'fare *vt* to do again; (*ricostruire*) to make again; (*nodo*) to tie again, do up again; (*imitare*) to imitate, copy; **rifarsi** *vr* (*risarcirsi*): **rifarsi di** to make up for; (*vendicarsi*): **rifarsi di qc su qn** to get one's own back on sb for sth; (*riferirsi*): **rifarsi a** (*periodo, fenomeno storico*) to go back to; **~ il letto** to make the bed; **rifarsi una vita** to make a new life for o.s.
ri'fatto, -a *pp di* **rifare**
riferi'mento *sm* reference; **in** *o* **con ~ a** with reference to; **far ~ a** to refer to
rife'rire *vt* (*riportare*) to report; (*ascrivere*): **~ qc a** to attribute sth to ■ *vi* to do a report; **riferirsi** *vr*: **riferirsi a** to refer to; **riferirò** I'll pass on the message
rifi'lare *vt* (*tagliare a filo*) to trim; (*fam: affibbiare*): **~ qc a qn** to palm sth off on sb
rifi'nire *vt* to finish off, put the finishing touches to
rifini'tura *sf* finishing touch; **rifiniture** *sfpl* (*di mobile, auto*) finish *sg*
rifiu'tare *vt* to refuse; **~ di fare** to refuse to do
rifi'uto *sm* refusal; **rifiuti** *smpl* (*spazzatura*) rubbish *sg*, refuse *sg*; **rifiuti solidi urbani** solid urban waste *sg*
riflessi'one *sf* (*Fisica*) reflection; (*il pensare*) thought, reflection; (*osservazione*) remark
rifles'sivo, -a *ag* (*persona*) thoughtful, reflective; (*Ling*) reflexive
ri'flesso, -a *pp di* **riflettere** ■ *sm* (*di luce, su specchio*) reflection; (*Fisiol*) reflex; (*su capelli*) light; (*fig*) effect; **di** *o* **per ~** indirectly; **avere i riflessi pronti** to have quick reflexes
riflessolo'gia [riflessolo'dʒia] *sf*: **~ (plantare)** reflexology
ri'flettere *vt* to reflect ■ *vi* to think; **riflettersi** *vr* to be reflected; (*ripercuotersi*): **riflettersi su** to have repercussions on; **~ su** to think over
riflet'tore *sm* reflector; (*proiettore*) floodlight; (*Mil*) searchlight
ri'flusso *sm* flowing back; (*della marea*) ebb; **un'epoca di ~** an era of nostalgia
rifocil'larsi [rifotʃil'larsi] *vr* (*poetico*) to take refreshment
rifondazi'one [rifondat'tsjone] *sf* (*Pol*): **R~ Comunista** *hard left party, originating from former P.C.I.*
ri'fondere *vt* (*rimborsare*) to refund, repay; **~ le spese a qn** to refund sb's expenses; **~ i danni a qn** to compensate sb for damages
ri'forma *sf* reform; (*Mil*) declaration of unfitness for service; discharge; (*on health grounds*): **la R~** (*Rel*) the Reformation
rifor'mare *vt* to re-form; (*cambiare, innovare*) to reform; (*Mil: recluta*) to declare unfit for service; (*soldato*) to invalid out, discharge
riforma'tore, -'trice *ag* reforming ■ *sm/f* reformer
riforma'torio *sm* (*Dir*) community home (*Brit*), reformatory (*US*)
rifor'mista, -i, e *ag, sm/f* reformist
riforni'mento *sm* supplying, providing restocking; (*di carburante*) refuelling; **rifornimenti** *smpl* supplies, provisions; **fare ~ di** (*viveri*) to stock up with; (*benzina*) to fill up with; **posto di ~** filling *o* gas (*US*) station
rifor'nire *vt* (*provvedere*): **~ di** to supply *o* provide with; (*fornire di nuovo: casa etc*) to restock
ri'frangere [ri'frandʒere] *vt* to refract
ri'fratto, -a *pp di* **rifrangere**
rifrazi'one [rifrat'tsjone] *sf* refraction
rifug'gire [rifud'dʒire] *vi* to escape again; (*fig*): **~ da** to shun
rifugi'arsi [rifu'dʒarsi] *vr* to take refuge

r

rifugi'ato, -a [rifu'dʒato] *sm/f* refugee
ri'fugio [ri'fudʒo] *sm* refuge, shelter; (*in montagna*) shelter; **~ antiaereo** air-raid shelter
ri'fuso, -a *pp di* **rifondere**
'riga, -ghe *sf* line; (*striscia*) stripe; (*di persone, cose*) line, row; (*regolo*) ruler; (*scriminatura*) parting; **mettersi in ~** to line up; **a righe** (*foglio*) lined; (*vestito*) striped; **buttare giù due righe** (*note*) to jot down a few notes; **mandami due righe appena arrivi** drop me a line as soon as you arrive
ri'gagnolo [ri'gaɲɲolo] *sm* rivulet
ri'gare *vt* (*foglio*) to rule ■ *vi*: **~ diritto** (*fig*) to toe the line
rigassifica'tore *sm* regasification terminal
riga'toni *smpl* (*Cuc*) *short, ridged pasta shapes*
rigatti'ere *sm* junk dealer
riga'tura *sf* (*di pagina, quaderno*) lining, ruling; (*di fucile*) rifling
rigene'rare [ridʒene'rare] *vt* (*gen, Tecn*) to regenerate; (*forze*) to restore; (*gomma*) to retread; **rigenerarsi** *vr* (*gen*) to regenerate; (*ramo, tumore*) to regenerate, grow again; **gomma rigenerata** retread
rigenerazi'one [ridʒenerat'tsjone] *sf* regeneration
riget'tare [ridʒet'tare] *vt* (*gettare indietro*) to throw back; (*fig: respingere*) to reject; (*vomitare*) to bring *o* throw up
ri'getto [ri'dʒɛtto] *sm* (*anche Med*) rejection
ri'ghello [ri'gɛllo] *sm* ruler
righerò *etc* [rige'rɔ] *vb vedi* **rigare**
rigi'dezza [ridʒi'dettsa], **rigidità** [ridʒidi'ta] *sf* rigidity; stiffness; severity, rigours *pl* (*Brit*), rigors *pl* (*US*); strictness
'rigido, a ['ridʒido] *ag* rigid, stiff; (*membra etc: indurite*) stiff; (*Meteor*) harsh, severe; (*fig*) strict
rigi'rare [ridʒi'rare] *vt* to turn; **rigirarsi** *vr* to turn round; (*nel letto*) to turn over; **~ qc tra le mani** to turn sth over in one's hands; **~ il discorso** to change the subject
'rigo, -ghi *sm* line; (*Mus*) staff, stave
rigogli'oso, -a [rigoʎ'ʎoso] *ag* (*pianta*) luxuriant; (*fig: commercio, sviluppo*) thriving
rigonfia'mento *sm* (*Anat*) swelling; (*su legno, intonaco etc*) bulge
ri'gonfio, -a *ag* swollen; (*grembiule, sporta*): **~ di** bulging with
ri'gore *sm* (*Meteor*) harshness, rigours *pl* (*Brit*), rigors *pl* (*US*); (*fig*) severity, strictness; (*anche*: **calcio di rigore**) penalty; **di ~** compulsory; **"è di ~ l'abito da sera"** "evening dress"; **area di ~** (*Calcio*) penalty box (*Brit*); **a rigor di termini** strictly speaking
rigorosità *sf* strictness; rigour (*Brit*), rigor (*US*)
rigo'roso, -a *ag* (*severo: persona, ordine*) strict; (*preciso*) rigorous
rigover'nare *vt* to wash (up)
riguar'dare *vt* to look at again; (*considerare*) to regard, consider; (*concernere*) to regard, concern; **riguardarsi** *vr* (*aver cura di sé*) to look after o.s.; **per quel che mi riguarda** as far as I'm concerned; **sono affari che non ti riguardano** it's none of your business
rigu'ardo *sm* (*attenzione*) care; (*considerazione*) regard, respect; **~ a** concerning, with regard to; **per ~ a** out of respect for; **ospite/persona di ~** very important guest/person; **non aver riguardi nell'agire/nel parlare** to act/speak freely
riguar'doso, -a *ag* (*rispettoso*) respectful; (*premuroso*) considerate, thoughtful
rigurgi'tare [rigurdʒi'tare] *vi* (*liquido*): **~ da** to gush out from; (*recipiente: traboccare*): **~ di** to overflow with
ri'gurgito [ri'gurdʒito] *sm* (*Med*) regurgitation; (*fig: ritorno, risveglio*) revival
rilanci'are [rilan'tʃare] *vt* (*lanciare di nuovo: gen*) to throw again; (*moda*) to bring back; (*prodotto*) to re-launch; **~ un'offerta** (*asta*) to make a higher bid
ri'lancio [ri'lantʃo] *sm* (*Carte: di offerta*) raising
rilasci'are [rilaʃ'ʃare] *vt* (*rimettere in libertà*) to release; (*Amm: documenti*) to issue; (*intervista*) to give; **~ delle dichiarazioni** to make a statement
ri'lascio [ri'laʃʃo] *sm* release; issue
rilassa'mento *sm* (*gen, Med*) relaxation
rilas'sare *vt* to relax; **rilassarsi** *vr* to relax; (*fig: disciplina*) to become slack
rilassa'tezza [rilassa'tettsa] *sf* (*fig: di costumi, disciplina*) laxity
rilas'sato, -a *ag* (*persona, muscoli*) relaxed; (*disciplina, costumi*) lax
rile'gare *vt* (*libro*) to bind
rilega'tura *sf* binding
ri'leggere [ri'lɛddʒere] *vt* to reread, read again; (*rivedere*) to read over
ri'lento: **a ~** *av* slowly
ri'letto, -a *pp di* **rileggere**
rilet'tura *sf* (*vedi vt*) rereading; reading over
rileva'mento *sm* (*topografico, statistico*) survey; (*Naut*) bearing
rile'vante *ag* considerable; important
rile'vanza [rile'vantsa] *sf* importance
rile'vare *vt* (*ricavare*) to find; (*notare*) to notice; (*mettere in evidenza*) to point out; (*venire a conoscere: notizia*) to learn; (*raccogliere: dati*) to gather, collect; (*Topografia*) to survey; (*Mil*) to relieve; (*Comm*) to take over
rilevazi'one [rilevat'tsjone] *sf* survey

rili'evo *sm* (*Arte, Geo*) relief; (*fig: rilevanza*) importance; (*osservazione*) point, remark; (*Topografia*) survey; **dar ~ a** *o* **mettere in ~ qc** (*fig*) to bring sth out, highlight sth; **di poco/ nessun ~** (*fig*) of little/no importance; **un personaggio di ~** an important person
rilut'tante *ag* reluctant
rilut'tanza [rilut'tantsa] *sf* reluctance
'rima *sf* rhyme; (*verso*) verse; **far ~ con** to rhyme with; **rispondere a qn per le rime** to give sb tit for tat
riman'dare *vt* to send again; (*restituire, rinviare*) to send back, return; (*differire*): **~ qc (a)** to postpone sth *o* put sth off (till); (*fare riferimento*): **~ qn a** to refer sb to; **essere rimandato** (*Ins*) to have to resit one's exams
ri'mando *sm* (*rinvio*) return; (*dilazione*) postponement; (*riferimento*) cross-reference
rimaneggi'are [rimaned'dʒare] *vt* (*testo*) to reshape, recast; (*Pol*) to reshuffle
rima'nente *ag* remaining ■ *sm* rest, remainder; **i rimanenti** (*persone*) the rest of them, the others
rima'nenza [rima'nɛntsa] *sf* rest, remainder; **rimanenze** *sfpl* (*Comm*) unsold stock *sg*
rima'nere *vi* (*restare*) to remain, stay; (*avanzare*) to be left, remain; (*restare stupito*) to be amazed; (*restare, mancare*): **rimangono poche settimane a Pasqua** there are only a few weeks left till Easter; (*diventare*): **~ vedovo** to be left a widower; (*trovarsi*): **~ confuso/ sorpreso** to be confused/surprised; **rimane da vedere se** it remains to be seen whether
rimangi'are [riman'dʒare] *vt* to eat again; **rimangiarsi la parola/una promessa** (*fig*) to go back on one's word/one's promise
ri'mango *etc vb vedi* **rimanere**
ri'mare *vt, vi* to rhyme
rimargi'nare [rimardʒi'nare] *vt, vi*, **rimargi'narsi** to heal
ri'masto, -a *pp di* **rimanere**
rima'sugli [rima'suʎʎi] *smpl* leftovers
rimbal'zare [rimbal'tsare] *vi* to bounce back, rebound; (*proiettile*) to ricochet
rim'balzo [rim'baltso] *sm* rebound; ricochet
rimbam'bire *vi* to be in one's dotage; (*rincretinire*) to grow foolish
rimbam'bito, -a *ag* senile, gaga; (*fam*): **un vecchio ~** a doddering old man
rimbec'care *vt* (*persona*) to answer back; (*offesa*) to return
rimbecil'lire [rimbetʃil'lire] *vi*, **rimbecil'lirsi** *vr* to become stupid
rimboc'care *vt* (*orlo*) to turn up; (*coperta*) to tuck in; (*maniche, pantaloni*) to turn *o* roll up
rimbom'bare *vi* to resound; (*artiglieria*) to boom; (*tuono*) to rumble
rim'bombo *sm* (*vedi vi*) boom; rumble
rimbor'sare *vt* to pay back, repay; **~ qc a qn** to reimburse sb for sth
rim'borso *sm* repayment; (*di spese, biglietto*) refund; **~ d'imposta** tax rebate
rimboschi'mento [rimboski'mento] *sm* reafforestation
rimbos'chire [rimbos'kire] *vt* to reafforest
rimbrot'tare *vt* to reproach
rim'brotto *sm* reproach
rimedi'are *vi*: **~ a** to remedy ■ *vt* (*fam: procurarsi*) to get *o* scrape together; **~ da vivere** to scrape a living
ri'medio *sm* (*medicina*) medicine; (*cura: fig*) remedy, cure; **porre ~ a qc** to remedy sth; **non c'è ~** there's no way out, there's nothing to be done about it
rimesco'lare *vt* to mix well, stir well; (*carte*) to shuffle; **sentirsi ~ il sangue** (*per rabbia*) to feel one's blood boil
ri'messa *sf* (*locale: per veicoli*) garage; (*per aerei*) hangar; (*Comm: di merce*) consignment; (*di denaro*) remittance; (*Tennis*) return; (*Calcio: anche*: **rimessa in gioco**) throw-in
ri'messo, -a *pp di* **rimettere**
rimes'tare *vt* (*mescolare*) to mix well, stir well; (*fig: passato*) to drag up again
ri'mettere *vt* (*mettere di nuovo*) to put back; (*indossare di nuovo*): **~ qc** to put sth back on, put sth on again; (*restituire*) to return, give back; (*affidare*) to entrust; (*: decisione*) to refer; (*condonare*) to remit; (*Comm: merci*) to deliver; (*: denaro*) to remit; (*vomitare*) to bring up; (*perdere: anche*: **rimetterci**) to lose; **rimettersi** *vr*: **rimettersi a** (*affidarsi*) to trust; **~ a nuovo** (*casa etc*) to do up (*Brit*) *o* over (*US*); **rimetterci di tasca propria** to be out of pocket; **rimettersi al bello** (*tempo*) to clear up; **rimettersi in cammino** to set off again; **rimettersi al lavoro** to start working again; **rimettersi in salute** to get better, recover one's health
rimi'nese *ag* of (*o* from) Rimini
ri'misi *etc vb vedi* **rimettere**
'rimmel® *sm inv* mascara
rimoderna'mento *sm* modernization
rimoder'nare *vt* to modernize
ri'monta *sf* (*Sport: gen*) recovery
rimon'tare *vt* (*meccanismo*) to reassemble; (*tenda*) to put up again ■ *vi* (*salire di nuovo*): **~ in** (*macchina, treno*) to get back into; (*Sport*) to close the gap
rimorchi'are [rimor'kjare] *vt* to tow; (*fig: ragazza*) to pick up
rimorchia'tore [rimorkja'tore] *sm* (*Naut*) tug(boat)

ri'morchio [ri'mɔrkjo] *sm* tow; (*veicolo*) trailer; **andare a ~** to be towed; **prendere a ~** to tow; **cavo da ~** towrope; **autocarro con ~** articulated lorry (*Brit*) semi(trailer) (*US*)
ri'morso *sm* remorse; **avere il ~ di aver fatto qc** to deeply regret having done sth
ri'mosso, -a *pp di* **rimuovere**
rimos'tranza [rimos'trantsa] *sf* protest, complaint; **fare le proprie rimostranze a qn** to remonstrate with sb
rimozi'one [rimot'tsjone] *sf* removal; (*da un impiego*) dismissal; (*Psic*) repression; **"~ forzata"** "illegally parked vehicles will be removed at owner's expense"
rimpas'tare *vt* (*Pol*: *ministero*) to reshuffle
rim'pasto *sm* (*Pol*) reshuffle; **~ ministeriale** cabinet reshuffle
rimpatri'are *vi* to return home ■ *vt* to repatriate
rim'patrio *sm* repatriation
rimpi'angere [rim'pjandʒere] *vt* to regret; (*persona*) to miss; **~ di (non) aver fatto qc** to regret (not) having done sth
rimpi'anto, -a *pp di* **rimpiangere** ■ *sm* regret
rimpiat'tino *sm* hide-and-seek
rimpiaz'zare [rimpjat'tsare] *vt* to replace
rimpiccio'lire [rimpittʃo'lire] *vt* to make smaller ■ *vi* (*anche*: **rimpicciolirsi**) to become smaller
rimpin'zare [rimpin'tsare] *vt*: **~ di** to cram *o* stuff with
rimprove'rare *vt* to rebuke, reprimand
rim'provero *sm* rebuke, reprimand; **di ~** (*tono, occhiata*) reproachful; (*parole*) of reproach
rimugi'nare [rimudʒi'nare] *vt* (*fig*) to turn over in one's mind
rimune'rare *vt* (*retribuire*) to remunerate; (*ricompensare*: *sacrificio etc*) to reward; **un lavoro ben rimunerato** a well-paid job
rimunera'tivo, -a *ag* (*lavoro, attività*) remunerative, profitable
rimunerazi'one [rimunerat'tsjone] *sf* remuneration; (*premio*) reward
rimu'overe *vt* to remove; (*destituire*) to dismiss; (*fig*: *distogliere*) to dissuade
rinascimen'tale [rinaʃʃimen'tale] *ag* Renaissance *cpd*, of the Renaissance
Rinasci'mento [rinaʃʃi'mento] *sm*: **il ~** the Renaissance
ri'nascita [ri'naʃʃita] *sf* rebirth, revival
rincal'zare [rinkal'tsare] *vt* (*palo, albero*) to support, prop up; (*lenzuola*) to tuck in
rin'calzo [rin'kaltso] *sm* support, prop; (*rinforzo*) reinforcement; (*Sport*) reserve (player); **rincalzi** *smpl* (*Mil*) reserves
rinca'rare *vt* to increase the price of ■ *vi* to go up, become more expensive; **~ la dose** (*fig*) to pile it on
rin'caro *sm*: **~ (di)** (*prezzi, costo della vita*) increase (in); (*prodotto*) increase in the price (of)
rinca'sare *vi* to go home
rinchi'udere [rin'kjudere] *vt* to shut (*o* lock) up; **rinchiudersi** *vr*: **rinchiudersi in** to shut o.s. up in; **rinchiudersi in se stesso** to withdraw into o.s.
rinchi'uso, -a [rin'kjuso] *pp di* **rinchiudere**
rincitrul'lirsi [rintʃitrul'lirsi] *vr* to grow foolish
rin'correre *vt* to chase, run after
rin'corso, -a *pp di* **rincorrere** ■ *sf* short run
rin'crescere [rin'kreʃʃere] *vb impers*: **mi rincresce che/di non poter fare** I'm sorry that/I can't do, I regret that/being unable to do
rincresci'mento [rinkreʃʃi'mento] *sm* regret
rincresci'uto, -a [rinkreʃʃuto] *pp di* **rincrescere**
rincu'lare *vi* to draw back; (*arma*) to recoil
rinfacci'are [rinfat'tʃare] *vt* (*fig*): **~ qc a qn** to throw sth in sb's face
rinfoco'lare *vt* (*fig*: *odio, passioni*) to rekindle; (*risentimento, rabbia*) to stir up
rinfor'zare [rinfor'tsare] *vt* to reinforce, strengthen ■ *vi* (*anche*: **rinforzarsi**) to grow stronger
rin'forzo [rin'fɔrtso] *sm*: **mettere un ~ a** to strengthen; **rinforzi** *smpl* (*Mil*) reinforcements; **di ~** (*asse, sbarra*) strengthening; (*esercito*) supporting; (*personale*) extra, additional
rinfran'care *vt* to encourage, reassure
rinfres'cante *ag* (*bibita*) refreshing
rinfres'care *vt* (*atmosfera, temperatura*) to cool (down); (*abito, pareti*) to freshen up ■ *vi* (*tempo*) to grow cooler; **rinfrescarsi** *vr* (*ristorarsi*) to refresh o.s.; (*lavarsi*) to freshen up; **~ la memoria a qn** to refresh sb's memory
rin'fresco, -schi *sm* (*festa*) party; **rinfreschi** *smpl* (*cibi e bevande*) refreshments
rin'fusa *sf*: **alla ~** in confusion, higgledy-piggledy
ringhi'are [rin'gjare] *vi* to growl, snarl
ringhi'era [rin'gjɛra] *sf* railing; (*delle scale*) banister(s) (*pl*)
'ringhio ['ringjo] *sm* growl, snarl
ringhi'oso, -a [rin'gjoso] *ag* growling, snarling
ringiova'nire [rindʒova'nire] *vt* (*vestito, acconciatura etc*): **~ qn** to make sb look younger; (*vacanze etc*) to rejuvenate ■ *vi*

(*anche*: **ringiovanirsi**) to become (*o* look) younger
ringrazia'mento [ringrattsja'mento] *sm* thanks *pl*; **lettera/biglietto di** ~ thank you letter/card
ringrazi'are [ringrat'tsjare] *vt* to thank; **~ qn di qc** to thank sb for sth; **~ qn per aver fatto qc** to thank sb for doing sth
rinne'gare *vt* (*fede*) to renounce; (*figlio*) to disown, repudiate
rinne'gato, -a *sm/f* renegade
rinno'vabile *ag* (*contratto, energia*) renewable
rinnova'mento *sm* renewal; (*economico*) revival
rinno'vare *vt* to renew; (*ripetere*) to repeat, renew; **rinnovarsi** *vr* (*fenomeno*) to be repeated, recur
rin'novo *sm* (*di contratto*) renewal; **"chiuso per ~ (dei) locali"** (*negozio*) "closed for alterations"
rinoce'ronte [rinotʃe'ronte] *sm* rhinoceros
rino'mato, -a *ag* renowned, celebrated
rinsal'dare *vt* to strengthen
rinsa'vire *vi* to come to one's senses
rinsec'chito, -a [rinsek'kito] *ag* (*vecchio, albero*) thin, gaunt
rinta'narsi *vr* (*animale*) to go into its den; (*persona: nascondersi*) to hide
rintoc'care *vi* (*campana*) to toll; (*orologio*) to strike
rin'tocco, -chi *sm* toll
rintracci'are [rintrat'tʃare] *vt* to track down; (*persona scomparsa, documento*) to trace
rintro'nare *vi* to boom, roar ■ *vt* (*assordare*) to deafen; (*stordire*) to stun
rintuz'zare [rintut'tsare] *vt* (*fig: sentimento*) to check, repress; (*accusa*) to refute
ri'nuncia [ri'nuntʃa] *sf* renunciation; **~ a** (*carica*) resignation from; (*eredità*) relinquishment of; **~ agli atti del giudizio** (*Dir*) abandonment of a claim
rinunci'are [rinun'tʃare] *vi*: **~ a** to give up, renounce; **~ a fare qc** to give up doing sth
rinuncia'tario, -a [rinuntʃa'tarjo] *ag* defeatist
ri'nunzia *etc* [ri'nuntsja] = **rinuncia** *etc*
rinveni'mento *sm* (*ritrovamento*) recovery; (*scoperta*) discovery; (*Metallurgia*) tempering
rinve'nire *vt* to find, recover; (*scoprire*) to discover, find out ■ *vi* (*riprendere i sensi*) to come round; (*riprendere l'aspetto naturale*) to revive
rinve'nuto, -a *pp di* **rinvenire**
rinver'dire *vi* (*bosco, ramo*) to become green again
rinvi'are *vt* (*rimandare indietro*) to send back, return; (*differire*): **~ qc (a)** to postpone sth *o* put sth off (till); (*: seduta*) to adjourn sth (till); (*fare un rimando*): **~ qn a** to refer sb to; **~ a giudizio** (*Dir*) to commit for trial
rinvigo'rire *vt* to strengthen
rin'vio, -'vii *sm* (*rimando*) return; (*differimento*) postponement; (*di seduta*) adjournment; (*in un testo*) cross-reference; **~ a giudizio** (*Dir*) indictment
riò *etc vb vedi* **riavere**
'Rio de Ja'neiro ['riodedʒa'neiro] *sf* Rio de Janeiro
rio'nale *ag* (*mercato, cinema*) local, district *cpd*
ri'one *sm* district, quarter
riordina'mento *sm* (*di ente, azienda*) reorganization
riordi'nare *vt* (*rimettere in ordine*) to tidy; (*riorganizzare*) to reorganize
riorganiz'zare [riorganid'dzare] *vt* to reorganize
riorganizzazi'one [riorganiddzat'tsjone] *sf* reorganization
ripa'gare *vt* to repay
ripa'rare *vt* (*proteggere*) to protect, defend; (*correggere: male, torto*) to make up for; (*: errore*) to put right; (*aggiustare*) to repair ■ *vi* (*mettere rimedio*): **~ a** to make up for; **ripararsi** *vr* (*rifugiarsi*) to take refuge *o* shelter
ripa'rato, -a *ag* (*posto*) sheltered
riparazi'one [riparat'tsjone] *sf* (*di un torto*) reparation; (*di guasto, scarpe*) repairing *no pl*; repair; (*risarcimento*) compensation; (*Ins*): **esame di** ~ resit (*Brit*), test retake (*US*)
ri'paro *sm* (*protezione*) shelter, protection; (*rimedio*) remedy; **al ~ da** (*sole, vento*) sheltered from; **mettersi al** ~ to take shelter; **correre ai ripari** (*fig*) to take remedial action
ripar'tire *vt* (*dividere*) to divide up; (*distribuire*) to share out, distribute ■ *vi* to leave again; (*motore*) to start again
ripartizi'one [ripartit'tsjone] *sf* division sharing out, distribution; (*Amm: dipartimento*) department
ripas'sare *vi* to come (*o* go) back ■ *vt* (*scritto, lezione*) to go over (again)
ri'passo *sm* (*di lezione*) revision (*Brit*), review (*US*)
ripensa'mento *sm* second thoughts *pl* (*Brit*), change of mind; **avere un** ~ to have second thoughts, change one's mind
ripen'sare *vi* to think; (*cambiare idea*) to change one's mind; (*tornare col pensiero*): **~ a** to recall; **a ripensarci ...** on thinking it over ...
riper'correre *vt* (*itinerario*) to travel over again; (*strada*) to go along again; (*fig: ricordi, passato*) to go back over
riper'corso, -a *pp di* **ripercorrere**
riper'cosso, -a *pp di* **ripercuotersi**
ripercu'otersi *vr*: **~ su** (*fig*) to have repercussions on

ripercussi'one *sf* (*fig*): **avere una ~** *o* **delle ripercussioni su** to have repercussions on
ripes'care *vt* (*pesce*) to catch again; (*persona, cosa*) to fish out; (*fig: ritrovare*) to dig out
ripe'tente *sm/f* student repeating the year, repeater (US)
ri'petere *vt* to repeat; (*ripassare*) to go over
ripeti'tore *sm* (*Radio, TV*) relay
ripetizi'one [ripetit'tsjone] *sf* repetition; (*di lezione*) revision; **ripetizioni** *sfpl* (*Ins*) private tutoring *o* coaching *sg*; **fucile a ~** repeating rifle
ripetuta'mente *av* repeatedly, again and again
ripi'ano *sm* (*Geo*) terrace; (*di mobile*) shelf
ri'picca *sf*: **per ~** out of spite
'ripido, -a *ag* steep
ripiega'mento *sm* (*Mil*) retreat
ripie'gare *vt* to refold; (*piegare più volte*) to fold (up) ■ *vi* (*Mil*) to retreat, fall back; (*fig: accontentarsi*): **~ su** to make do with; **ripiegarsi** *vr* to bend
ripi'ego, -ghi *sm* expedient; **una soluzione di ~** a makeshift solution
ripi'eno, -a *ag* full; (*Cuc*) stuffed; (*panino*) filled ■ *sm* (*Cuc*) stuffing
ri'pone *vb vedi* **riporre**
ri'pongo *vb vedi* **riporre**
ri'porre *vt* (*porre al suo posto*) to put back, replace; (*mettere via*) to put away; (*fiducia, speranza*): **~ qc in qn** to place *o* put sth in sb
ripor'tare *vt* (*portare indietro*) to bring (*o* take) back; (*riferire*) to report; (*citare*) to quote; (*ricevere*) to receive, get; (*vittoria*) to gain; (*successo*) to have; (*Mat*) to carry; (*Comm*) to carry forward; **riportarsi** *vr*: **riportarsi a** (*anche fig*) to go back to; (*riferirsi a*) to refer to; **~ danni** to suffer damage; **ha riportato gravi ferite** he was seriously injured
ri'porto *sm* amount carried over; amount carried forward
ripo'sante *ag* (*gen*) restful; (*musica, colore*) soothing
ripo'sare *vt* (*bicchiere, valigia*) to put down; (*dare sollievo*) to rest ■ *vi* to rest; **riposarsi** *vr* to rest; **qui riposa …** (*su tomba*) here lies …
ripo'sato, -a *ag* (*viso, aspetto*) rested; (*mente*) fresh
ri'posi *etc vb vedi* **riporre**
ri'poso *sm* rest; (*Mil*): **~!** at ease!; **a ~** (*in pensione*) retired; **giorno di ~** day off; **"oggi ~"** (*Cine, Teat*) "no performance today"; (*ristorante*) "closed today"
ripos'tiglio [ripos'tiʎʎo] *sm* lumber room (*Brit*), storage room (*US*)
ri'posto, -a *pp di* **riporre** ■ *ag* (*fig: senso, significato*) hidden
ri'prendere *vt* (*prigioniero, fortezza*) to recapture; (*prendere indietro*) to take back; (*ricominciare: lavoro*) to resume; (*andare a prendere*) to fetch, come back for; (*assumere di nuovo: impiegati*) to take on again, re-employ; (*rimproverare*) to tell off; (*restringere: abito*) to take in; (*Cine*) to shoot; **riprendersi** *vr* to recover; (*correggersi*) to correct o.s.; **~ a fare qc** to start doing sth again; **~ il cammino** to set off again; **~ i sensi** to recover consciousness; **~ sonno** to go back to sleep
ripresen'tare *vt* (*certificato*) to submit again; (*domanda*) to put forward again; (*persona*) to introduce again; **ripresentarsi** *vr* (*ritornare: persona*) to come back; (*: occasione*) to arise again; **ripresentarsi a** (*esame*) to sit (*Brit*) *o* take (*US*) again; (*concorso*) to enter again; **ripresentarsi come candidato** (*Pol*) to stand (*Brit*) *o* run (*US*) again (as a candidate)
ri'preso, -a *pp di* **riprendere** ■ *sf* recapture; resumption; (*economica, da malattia, emozione*) recovery; (*Aut*) acceleration *no pl*; (*Teat, Cine*) rerun; (*Cine: presa*) shooting *no pl*; shot; (*Sport*) second half; (*Pugilato*) round; **a più riprese** on several occasions, several times
ripristi'nare *vt* to restore
ri'pristino *sm* (*gen*) restoration; (*di tradizioni*) revival
ripro'dotto, -a *pp di* **riprodurre**
ripro'durre *vt* to reproduce; **riprodursi** *vr* (*Biol*) to reproduce; (*riformarsi*) to form again
riprodut'tivo, -a *ag* reproductive
riprodut'tore, -'trice *ag* (*organo*) reproductive ■ *sm*: **~ acustico** pick-up; **~ a cassetta** cassette player
riproduzi'one [riprodut'tsjone] *sf* reproduction; **~ vietata** all rights reserved
ripro'messo, -a *pp di* **ripromettersi**
ripro'mettersi *vt* (*aspettarsi*): **~ qc da** to expect sth from; (*intendere*): **~ di fare qc** to intend to do sth
ripro'porre *vt*: **riproporsi di fare qc** to intend to do sth
ripro'posto, -a *pp di* **riproporre**
ri'prova *sf* confirmation; **a ~ di** as confirmation of
ripro'vare *vt* (*provare di nuovo: gen*) to try again; (*: vestito*) to try on again; (*: sensazione*) to experience again ■ *vi* (*tentare*): **~ (a fare qc)** to try (to do sth) again; **riproverò più tardi** I'll try again later
ripro'vevole *ag* reprehensible
ripudi'are *vt* to repudiate, disown
ri'pudio *sm* repudiation, disowning
ripu'gnante [ripuɲ'ɲante] *ag* disgusting, repulsive

ripu'gnanza [ripuɲ'ɲantsa] *sf* repugnance, disgust
ripu'gnare [ripuɲ'ɲare] *vi*: **~ a qn** to repel *o* disgust sb
ripu'lire *vt* to clean up; (*ladri*) to clean out; (*perfezionare*) to polish, refine
ripulsi'one *sf* (*Fisica, fig*) repulsion
ri'quadro *sm* square; (*Archit*) panel
RIS [ris] *sigla m* (= *Reparto Investigazioni Scientifiche*) ≈ CID, *branch of the Carabinieri*
ri'sacca, -che *sf* backwash
ri'saia *sf* paddy field
risa'lire *vi* (*ritornare in su*) to go back up; **~ a** (*ritornare con la mente*) to go back to; (*datare da*) to date back to, go back to
risa'lita *sf*: **mezzi di ~** (*Sci*) ski lifts
risal'tare *vi* (*fig: distinguersi*) to stand out; (*Archit*) to project, jut out
ri'salto *sm* prominence; (*sporgenza*) projection; **mettere** *o* **porre in ~ qc** to make sth stand out
risana'mento *sm* (*economico*) improvement; (*bonifica*) reclamation; **~ del bilancio** reorganization of the budget; **~ edilizio** building improvement
risa'nare *vt* (*guarire*) to heal, cure; (*palude*) to reclaim; (*economia*) to improve; (*bilancio*) to reorganize
risa'pere *vt*: **~ qc** to come to know of sth
risa'puto, -a *ag*: **è ~ che ...** everyone knows that ..., it's common knowledge that ...
risarci'mento [risartʃi'mento] *sm*: **~ (di)** compensation (for); **aver diritto al ~ dei danni** to be entitled to damages
risar'cire [risar'tʃire] *vt* (*cose*) to pay compensation for; (*persona*): **~ qn di qc** to compensate sb for sth; **~ i danni a qn** to pay sb damages
ri'sata *sf* laugh
riscalda'mento *sm* heating; **~ centrale** central heating
riscal'dare *vt* (*scaldare*) to heat; (*mani, persona*) to warm; (*minestra*) to reheat; **riscaldarsi** *vr* to warm up
ris'caldo *sm* (*fam*) (slight) inflammation
riscat'tare *vt* (*prigioniero*) to ransom, pay a ransom for; (*Dir*) to redeem; **riscattarsi** *vr* (*da disonore*) to redeem o.s.
ris'catto *sm* ransom; redemption
rischia'rare [riskja'rare] *vt* (*illuminare*) to light up; (*colore*) to make lighter; **rischiararsi** *vr* (*tempo*) to clear up; (*cielo*) to clear; (*fig: volto*) to brighten up; **rischiararsi la voce** to clear one's throat
rischi'are [ris'kjare] *vt* to risk ■ *vi*: **~ di fare qc** to risk *o* run the risk of doing sth
'rischio ['riskjo] *sm* risk; **a ~** (*zona, situazione*) at risk, vulnerable; **a proprio ~ e pericolo** at one's own risk; **correre il ~ di fare qc** to run the risk of doing sth; **~ del mestiere** occupational hazard
rischi'oso, -a [ris'kjoso] *ag* risky, dangerous
risciac'quare [riʃʃak'kware] *vt* to rinse
risci'acquo [riʃʃakkwo] *sm* rinse
riscon'trare *vt* (*confrontare: due cose*) to compare; (*esaminare*) to check, verify; (*rilevare*) to find
ris'contro *sm* comparison check, verification; (*Amm: lettera di risposta*) reply; **mettere a ~** to compare; **in attesa di un vostro cortese ~** we look forward to your reply
risco'perto, -a *pp di* **riscoprire**
risco'prire *vt* to rediscover
riscossi'one *sf* collection
ris'cosso, -a *pp di* **riscuotere** ■ *sf* (*riconquista*) recovery, reconquest
riscri'vibile *ag* (*CD, DVD*) rewritable
riscu'otere *vt* (*ritirare una somma dovuta*) to collect; (*stipendio*) to draw, collect; (*fig: successo etc*) to win, earn; **riscuotersi** *vr*: **riscuotersi (da)** to shake o.s. (out of), rouse o.s. (from); **~ un assegno** to cash a cheque
'rise *etc vb vedi* **ridere**
risenti'mento *sm* resentment
risen'tire *vt* to hear again; (*provare*) to feel ■ *vi*: **~ di** to feel (*o* show) the effects of; **risentirsi** *vr*: **risentirsi di** *o* **per** to take offence (*Brit*) *o* offense (*US*) at, resent
risen'tito, -a *ag* resentful
ri'serbo *sm* reserve
ri'serva *sf* reserve; (*di caccia, pesca*) preserve; (*restrizione, di indigeni*) reservation; (*Calcio*) substitute; **fare ~ di** (*cibo*) to get in a supply of; **tenere di ~** to keep in reserve; **con le dovute riserve** with certain reservations; **ha accettato con la ~ di potersi ritirare** he accepted with the proviso that he could pull out
riser'vare *vt* (*tenere in serbo*) to keep, put aside; (*prenotare*) to book, reserve; **riservarsi** *vr*: **riservarsi di fare qc** to intend to do sth; **riservarsi il diritto di fare qc** to reserve the right to do sth
riserva'tezza [riserva'tettsa] *sf* reserve
riser'vato, -a *ag* (*prenotato: fig: persona*) reserved; (*confidenziale*) confidential; (*lettera, informazione*) confidential
'risi *etc vb vedi* **ridere**
ri'sibile *ag* laughable
risi'cato, -a *ag* (*vittoria etc*) very narrow
risi'edere *vi*: **~ a** *o* **in** to reside in
'risma *sf* (*di carta*) ream; (*fig*) kind, sort
'riso[1], -a *pp di* **ridere** ■ *sm* (*pl(f)* **risa**) (*il ridere*): **un ~** a laugh; **il ~** laughter; **uno scoppio di risa** a burst of laughter
'riso[2] *sm* (*pianta*) rice

riso'lino *sm* snigger
risolle'vare *vt* (*sollevare di nuovo: testa*) to raise again, lift up again; (*fig: questione*) to raise again, bring up again; (*morale*) to raise; **risollevarsi** *vr* (*da terra*) to rise again; (*fig: da malattia*) to recover; **~ le sorti di qc** to improve the chances of sth
ri'solsi *etc vb vedi* **risolvere**
ri'solto, -a *pp di* **risolvere**
risolu'tezza [risolu'tettsa] *sf* determination
risolu'tivo, -a *ag* (*determinante*) decisive; (*che risolve*): **arrivare ad una formula risolutiva** to come up with a formula to resolve a situation
riso'luto, -a *ag* determined, resolute
risoluzi'one [risolut'tsjone] *sf* solving *no pl*; (*Mat*) solution; (*decisione, di immagine*) resolution; (*Dir: di contratto*) annulment, cancellation
ri'solvere *vt* (*difficoltà, controversia*) to resolve; (*problema*) to solve; (*decidere*): **~ di fare** to resolve to do; **risolversi** *vr* (*decidersi*): **risolversi a fare** to make up one's mind to do; (*andare a finire*): **risolversi in** to end up, turn out; **risolversi in nulla** to come to nothing
risol'vibile *ag* solvable
riso'nanza [riso'nantsa] *sf* resonance; **aver vasta ~** (*fig: fatto etc*) to be known far and wide; **~ magnetica** magnetic resonance
riso'nare *vt, vi* = **risuonare**
ri'sorgere [ri'sordʒere] *vi* to rise again
risorgimen'tale [risordʒimen'tale] *ag* of the Risorgimento
risorgi'mento [risordʒi'mento] *sm* revival; **il R~** (*Storia*) the Risorgimento; *see note*

Risorgimento

The *Risorgimento*, the period stretching from the early nineteenth century to 1861 and the proclamation of the Kingdom of Italy, saw considerable upheaval and change. Political and personal freedom took on new importance as the events of the French Revolution unfolded. The *Risorgimento* paved the way for the unification of Italy in 1871.

ri'sorsa *sf* expedient, resort; **risorse** *sfpl* (*naturali, finanziarie etc*) resources; **persona piena di risorse** resourceful person
ri'sorsi *etc vb vedi* **risorgere**
ri'sorto, -a *pp di* **risorgere**
ri'sotto *sm* (*Cuc*) risotto
risparmi'are *vt* to save; (*non uccidere*) to spare ■ *vi* to save; **~ qc a qn** to spare sb sth; **~ fatica/fiato** to save one's energy/breath; **risparmiati il disturbo** *o* **la fatica** (*anche ironico*) save yourself the trouble
risparmia'tore, -'trice *sm/f* saver
ris'parmio *sm* saving *no pl*; (*denaro*) savings *pl*
rispecchi'are [rispek'kjare] *vt* to reflect; **rispecchiarsi** *vr* to be reflected
rispe'dire *vt* to send back; **~ qc a qn** to send sth back to sb
rispet'tabile *ag* respectable; (*considerevole: somma*) sizeable, considerable
rispet'tare *vt* to respect; (*legge*) to obey, comply with, abide by; (*promessa*) to keep; **farsi ~** to command respect; **~ le distanze** to keep one's distance; **~ i tempi** to keep to schedule; **ogni medico che si rispetti** every self-respecting doctor
rispettiva'mente *av* respectively
rispet'tivo, -a *ag* respective
ris'petto *sm* respect; **rispetti** *smpl* (*saluti*) respects, regards; **~ a** (*in paragone a*) compared to; (*in relazione a*) as regards, as for; **~ (di** *o* **per)** (*norme, leggi*) observance (of), compliance (with); **portare ~ a qn/qc** to have *o* feel respect for sb/sth; **mancare di ~ a qn** to be disrespectful to sb; **con ~ parlando** with respect, if you will excuse my saying so; **(porga) i miei rispetti alla signora** (give) my regards to your wife
rispet'toso, -a *ag* respectful
risplen'dente *ag* (*giornata, sole*) bright, shining; (*occhi*) sparkling
ris'plendere *vi* to shine
rispon'dente *ag*: **~ a** in keeping *o* conformity with
rispon'denza [rispon'dɛntsa] *sf* correspondence
ris'pondere *vi* to answer, reply; (*freni*) to respond; **~ a** (*domanda*) to answer, reply to; (*persona*) to answer; (*invito*) to reply to; (*provocazione: veicolo, apparecchio*) to respond to; (*corrispondere a*) to correspond to; (*speranze, bisogno*) to answer; **~ a qn di qc** (*essere responsabile*) to be answerable to sb for sth
rispo'sarsi *vr* to get married again, remarry
ris'posto, -a *pp di* **rispondere** ■ *sf* answer, reply; **in risposta a** in reply to; **dare una risposta** to give an answer; **diamo risposta alla vostra lettera del ...** in reply to your letter of ...
'rissa *sf* brawl
ris'soso, -a *ag* quarrelsome
rist. *abbr* = **ristampa**
ristabi'lire *vt* to re-establish, restore; (*persona: riposo etc*) to restore to health; **ristabilirsi** *vr* to recover

rista'gnare [ristaɲ'ɲare] *vi* (*acqua*) to become stagnant; (*sangue*) to cease flowing; (*fig: industria*) to stagnate
ris'tagno [ris'taɲɲo] *sm* stagnation; **c'è un ~ delle vendite** business is slack
ris'tampa *sf* reprinting *no pl*; reprint
ristam'pare *vt* to reprint
risto'rante *sm* restaurant
risto'rare *vt* (*persona, forze*) to revive, refresh; **ristorarsi** *vr* (*rifocillarsi*) to have something to eat and drink; (*riposarsi*) to rest, have a rest
ristora'tore, -'trice *ag* refreshing, reviving ■ *sm* (*gestore di ristorante*) restaurateur
ris'toro *sm* (*bevanda, cibo*) refreshment; **posto di ~** (*Ferr*) buffet, snack bar; **servizio di ~** (*Ferr*) refreshments *pl*
ristret'tezza [ristret'tettsa] *sf* (*strettezza*) narrowness; (*fig: scarsezza*) scarcity, lack; (*: meschinità*) meanness; **ristrettezze** *sfpl* (*povertà*) poverty *sg*
ris'tretto, -a *pp di* **restringere** ■ *ag* (*racchiuso*) enclosed, hemmed in; (*angusto*) narrow; (*limitato*): **~ (a)** restricted *o* limited (to); (*Cuc: brodo*) thick; (*caffè*) extra strong
ristruttu'rare *vt* (*azienda*) to reorganize; (*edificio*) to restore; (*appartamento*) to alter; (*crema, balsamo*) to repair
ristrutturazi'one [ristrutturat'tsjone] *sf* reorganization; restoration; alteration
risucchi'are [risuk'kjare] *vt* to suck in
ri'succhio [ri'sukkjo] *sm* (*di acqua*) undertow, pull; (*di aria*) suction
risul'tare *vi* (*dimostrarsi*) to prove (to be), turn out (to be); (*riuscire*): **~ vincitore** to emerge as the winner; **~ da** (*provenire*) to result from, be the result of; **mi risulta che ...** I understand that ..., as far as I know ...; **(ne) risulta che ...** it follows that ...; **non mi risulta** not as far as I know
risul'tato *sm* result
risuo'nare *vi* (*rimbombare*) to resound
risurrezi'one [risurret'tsjone] *sf* (*Rel*) resurrection
risusci'tare [risuʃʃi'tare] *vt* to resuscitate, restore to life; (*fig*) to revive, bring back ■ *vi* to rise (from the dead)
risvegli'are [rizveʎ'ʎare] *vt* (*gen*) to wake up, waken; (*fig: interesse*) to stir up, arouse; (*curiosità*) to arouse; (*fig: dall'inerzia etc*): **~ qn (da)** to rouse sb (from); **risvegliarsi** *vr* to wake up, awaken; (*fig: interesse, curiosità*) to be aroused
ris'veglio [riz'veʎʎo] *sm* waking up; (*fig*) revival
ris'volto *sm* (*di giacca*) lapel; (*di pantaloni*) turn-up (*Brit*), cuff (*US*); (*di manica*) cuff; (*di tasca*) flap; (*di libro*) inside flap; (*fig*) implication
ritagli'are [ritaʎ'ʎare] *vt* (*tagliar via*) to cut out
ri'taglio [ri'taʎʎo] *sm* (*di giornale*) cutting, clipping; (*di stoffa etc*) scrap; **nei ritagli di tempo** in one's spare time
ritar'dare *vi* (*persona, treno*) to be late; (*orologio*) to be slow ■ *vt* (*rallentare*) to slow down; (*impedire*) to delay, hold up; (*differire*) to postpone, delay; **~ il pagamento** to defer payment
ritarda'tario, -a *sm/f* latecomer
ritar'dato, -a *ag* (*Psic*) retarded
ri'tardo *sm* delay; (*di persona aspettata*) lateness *no pl*; (*fig: mentale*) backwardness; **in ~** late
ri'tegno [ri'teɲɲo] *sm* restraint
ritem'prare *vt* (*forze, spirito*) to restore
rite'nere *vt* (*trattenere*) to hold back; (*: somma*) to deduct; (*giudicare*) to consider, believe
ri'tengo *vb vedi* **ritenere**
ri'tenni *vb vedi* **ritenere**
riten'tare *vt* to try again, make another attempt at
rite'nuta *sf* (*sul salario*) deduction; **~ d'acconto** advance deduction of tax; **~ alla fonte** (*Fisco*) taxation at source
riterrò *etc vb vedi* **ritenere**
ritiene *etc vb vedi* **ritenere**
riti'rare *vt* to withdraw; (*Pol: richiamare*) to recall; (*andare a prendere: pacco etc*) to collect, pick up; **ritirarsi** *vr* to withdraw; (*da un'attività*) to retire; (*stoffa*) to shrink; (*marea*) to recede; **gli hanno ritirato la patente** they disqualified him from driving (*Brit*), they took away his licence (*Brit*) *o* license (*US*); **ritirarsi a vita privata** to withdraw from public life
riti'rata *sf* (*Mil*) retreat; (*latrina*) lavatory
riti'rato, -a *ag* secluded; **fare vita ritirata** to live in seclusion
ri'tiro *sm* (*di truppe, candidati, soldi*) withdrawal; (*di pacchi*) collection; (*di passaporto*) confiscation; (*da attività*) retirement; (*luogo appartato*) retreat
rit'mato, -a *ag* rhythmic(al)
'ritmico, -a, ci, che *ag* rhythmic(al)
'ritmo *sm* rhythm; (*fig*) rate; (*della vita*) pace, tempo; **al ~ di** at a speed *o* rate of; **ballare al ~ di valzer** to waltz
'rito *sm* rite; **di ~** usual, customary
ritoc'care *vt* (*disegno, fotografia*) to touch up; (*testo*) to alter
ri'tocco, -chi *sm* touching up *no pl*; alteration
ri'torcere [ri'tɔrtʃere] *vt* (*filato*) to twist; (*fig: accusa, insulto*) to throw back; **ritorcersi** *vr* (*tornare a danno di*): **ritorcersi contro** to turn against
ritor'nare *vi* to return, go *o* come) back; (*ripresentarsi*) to recur; (*ridiventare*): **~ ricco** to

become rich again ■ *vt* (*restituire*) to return, give back

ritor'nello *sm* refrain

ri'torno *sm* return; **durante il (viaggio di) ~** on the return trip, on the way back; **al ~** (*tornando*) on the way back; **essere di ~** to be back; **far ~** to return; **avere un ~ di fiamma** (*Aut*) to backfire; (*fig: persona*) to be back in love again

ritorsi'one *sf* (*rappresaglia*) retaliation

ri'torto, -a *pp di* **ritorcere** ■ *ag* (*cotone, corda*) twisted

ri'trarre *vt* (*trarre indietro, via*) to withdraw; (*distogliere: sguardo*) to turn away; (*rappresentare*) to portray, depict; (*ricavare*) to get, obtain; **ritrarsi** *vr* to move back

ritrat'tare *vt* (*disdire*) to retract, take back; (*trattare nuovamente*) to deal with again

ritrattazi'one [ritrattat'tsjone] *sf* withdrawal

ritrat'tista, -i, e *sm/f* portrait painter

ri'tratto, -a *pp di* **ritrarre** ■ *sm* portrait

ritro'sia *sf* (*riluttanza*) reluctance, unwillingness; (*timidezza*) shyness

ri'troso, -a *ag* (*restio*): **~ (a)** reluctant (to); (*schivo*) shy; **andare a ~** to go backwards

ritrova'mento *sm* (*di cadavere, oggetto smarrito etc*) finding; (*oggetto ritrovato*) find

ritro'vare *vt* to find; (*salute*) to regain; (*persona*) to find; to meet again; **ritrovarsi** *vr* (*essere, capitare*) to find o.s.; (*raccapezzarsi*) to find one's way; (*con senso reciproco*) to meet (again)

ritro'vato *sm* discovery

ri'trovo *sm* meeting place; **~ notturno** night club

'ritto, -a *ag* (*in piedi*) standing, on one's feet; (*levato in alto*) erect, raised; (*capelli*) standing on end; (*posto verticalmente*) upright

ritu'ale *ag, sm* ritual

riuni'one *sf* (*adunanza*) meeting; (*riconciliazione*) reunion; **essere in ~** to be at a meeting

riu'nire *vt* (*ricongiungere*) to join (together); (*riconciliare*) to reunite, bring together (again); **riunirsi** *vr* (*adunarsi*) to meet; (*tornare a stare insieme*) to be reunited; **siamo qui riuniti per festeggiare il vostro anniversario** we are gathered here to celebrate your anniversary

riu'scire [riuʃʃire] *vi* (*uscire di nuovo*) to go out again, go back out; (*aver esito: fatti, azioni*) to go, turn out; (*aver successo*) to succeed, be successful; (*essere, apparire*) to be, prove; (*raggiungere il fine*) to manage, succeed; **~ a fare qc** to manage *o* be able to do sth; **questo mi riesce nuovo** this is new to me

riu'scita [riuʃʃita] *sf* (*esito*) result, outcome; (*buon esito*) success

riutiliz'zare [riutilid'dzare] *vt* to use again, re-use

'riva *sf* (*di fiume*) bank; (*di lago, mare*) shore; **in ~ al mare** on the (sea) shore

ri'vale *ag* rival *cpd* ■ *sm/f* rival; **non avere rivali** (*anche fig*) to be unrivalled

rivaleggi'are [rivaled'dʒare] *vi* to compete, vie

rivalità *sf* rivalry

ri'valsa *sf* (*rivincita*) revenge; (*risarcimento*) compensation; **prendersi una ~ su qn** to take revenge on sb

rivalu'tare *vt* (*Econ*) to revalue

rivalutazi'one [rivalutat'tsjone] *sf* (*Econ*) revaluation; (*fig*) re-evaluation

rivan'gare *vt* (*ricordi etc*) to dig up (again)

rive'dere *vt* to see again; (*ripassare*) to revise; (*verificare*) to check

rivedrò *etc vb vedi* **rivedere**

rive'lare *vt* to reveal; (*divulgare*) to reveal, disclose; (*dare indizio*) to reveal, show; **rivelarsi** *vr* (*manifestarsi*) to be revealed; **rivelarsi onesto** *etc* to prove to be honest *etc*

rivela'tore, -'trice *ag* revealing ■ *sm* (*Tecn*) detector; (*Fot*) developer

rivelazi'one [rivelat'tsjone] *sf* revelation

ri'vendere *vt* (*vendere: di nuovo*) to resell, sell again; (*al dettaglio*) to retail, sell retail

rivendi'care *vt* to claim, demand

rivendicazi'one [rivendikat'tsjone] *sf* claim; **rivendicazioni salariali** wage claims

ri'vendita *sf* (*bottega*) retailer's (shop); **~ di tabacchi** tobacconist's (shop)

rivendi'tore, -'trice *sm/f* retailer; **~ autorizzato** authorized dealer

riverbe'rare *vt* to reflect

ri'verbero *sm* (*di luce, calore*) reflection; (*di suono*) reverberation

rive'rente *ag* reverent, respectful

rive'renza [rive'rɛntsa] *sf* reverence; (*inchino*) bow; curtsey

rive'rire *vt* (*rispettare*) to revere; (*salutare*) to pay one's respects to

river'sare *vt* (*anche fig*) to pour; **riversarsi** *vr* (*fig: persone*) to pour out

rivesti'mento *sm* covering; coating

rives'tire *vt* to dress again; (*ricoprire*) to cover; (*con vernice*) to coat; (*fig: carica*) to hold; **rivestirsi** *vr* to get dressed again, to change (one's clothes); **~ di piastrelle** to tile

ri'vidi *etc vb vedi* **rivedere**

rivi'era *sf* coast; **la ~ italiana** the Italian Riviera

ri'vincita [ri'vintʃita] *sf* (*Sport*) return match; (*fig*) revenge; **prendersi la ~ (su qn)** to take *o* get one's revenge (on sb)

rivis'suto, -a *pp di* **rivivere**
ri'vista *sf* review; *(periodico)* magazine, review; *(Teat)* revue; variety show
ri'visto, -a *pp di* **rivedere**
rivitaliz'zante [rivitalid'dzante] *ag* revitalizing
rivitaliz'zare [rivitalid'dzare] *vt* to revitalize
ri'vivere *vi (riacquistare forza)* to come alive again; *(tornare in uso)* to be revived ■ *vt* to relive
'rivo *sm* stream
ri'volgere [ri'vɔldʒere] *vt (attenzione, sguardo)* to turn, direct; *(parole)* to address; **rivolgersi** *vr* to turn round; *(fig: dirigersi per informazioni)*: **rivolgersi a** to go and see, go and speak to; **~ un'accusa/una critica a qn** to accuse/criticize sb; **rivolgersi all'ufficio competente** to apply to the office concerned
rivolgi'mento [rivoldʒi'mento] *sm* upheaval
ri'volsi *etc vb vedi* **rivolgere**
ri'volta *sf* revolt, rebellion
rivol'tante *ag* revolting, disgusting
rivol'tare *vt* to turn over; *(con l'interno all'esterno)* to turn inside out; *(disgustare: stomaco)* to upset, turn; *(fig)* to revolt, disgust; **rivoltarsi** *vr (ribellarsi)*: **rivoltarsi (a)** to rebel (against)
rivol'tella *sf* revolver
ri'volto, -a *pp di* **rivolgere**
rivol'toso, -a *ag* rebellious ■ *sm/f* rebel
rivoluzio'nare [rivoluttsjo'nare] *vt* to revolutionize
rivoluzio'nario, a [rivoluttsjo'narjo] *ag, sm/f* revolutionary
rivoluzi'one [rivolut'tsjone] *sf* revolution
riz'zare [rit'tsare] *vt* to raise, erect; **rizzarsi** *vr* to stand up; *(capelli)* to stand on end; **rizzarsi in piedi** to stand up, get to one's feet
RN *sigla* = **Rimini**
RNA *sigla m* RNA (= *ribonucleic acid*)
RO *sigla* = **Rovigo**
'roba *sf* stuff, things *pl*; *(possessi, beni)* belongings *pl*, things *pl*, possessions *pl*; **~ da mangiare** things to eat, food; **~ da matti!** it's sheer madness *o* lunacy!
robi'vecchi [robi'vɛkki] *sm/f inv* junk dealer
'robot *sm inv* robot
ro'botica *sf* robotics *sg*
robus'tezza [robus'tettsa] *sf (di persona, pianta)* robustness, sturdiness; *(di edificio, ponte)* soundness
ro'busto, -a *ag* robust, sturdy; *(solido: catena)* strong; *(edificio, ponte)* sound, solid; *(vino)* full-bodied
'rocca, -che *sf* fortress
rocca'forte *sf* stronghold
roc'chetto [rok'ketto] *sm* reel, spool
'roccia, -ce ['rɔttʃa] *sf* rock; **fare ~** *(Sport)* to go rock climbing
roccia'tore, -'trice [rottʃa'tore] *sm/f* rock climber
rocci'oso, -a [rot'tʃoso] *ag* rocky; **le Montagne Rocciose** the Rocky Mountains
'roco, -a, chi, che *ag* hoarse
ro'daggio [ro'daddʒo] *sm* running *(Brit) o* breaking *(US)* in; **in ~** running *o* breaking in; **periodo di ~** *(fig)* period of adjustment
'Rodano *sm*: **il ~** the Rhone
ro'dare *vt (Aut, Tecn)* to run *(Brit) o* break *(US)* in
ro'deo *sm* rodeo
'rodere *vt* to gnaw (at); *(distruggere poco a poco)* to eat into
'Rodi *sf* Rhodes
rodi'tore *sm (Zool)* rodent
rodo'dendro *sm* rhododendron
'rogito ['rɔdʒito] *sm (Dir)* (notary's) deed
'rogna ['roɲɲa] *sf (Med)* scabies *sg*; *(di animale)* mange; *(fig)* bother, nuisance
ro'gnone [roɲ'ɲone] *sm (Cuc)* kidney
ro'gnoso, -a [roɲ'ɲoso] *ag (persona)* scabby; *(animale)* mangy; *(fig)* troublesome
'rogo, -ghi *sm (per cadaveri)* (funeral) pyre; *(supplizio)*: **il ~** the stake
rol'lare *vi (Naut, Aer)* to roll
rol'lino *sm* = **rullino**
rol'lio *sm* roll(ing)
'Roma *sf* Rome
roma'gnolo, -a [romaɲ'ɲɔlo] *ag* of (*o* from) Romagna
roma'nesco, -a, schi, sche *ag* Roman ■ *sm* Roman dialect
Roma'nia *sf*: **la ~** Romania
ro'manico, -a, ci, che *ag* Romanesque
ro'mano, -a *ag, sm/f* Roman; **fare alla romana** to go Dutch
romantiche'ria [romantike'ria] *sf* sentimentality
romanti'cismo [romanti'tʃizmo] *sm* romanticism
ro'mantico, -a, ci, che *ag* romantic
ro'manza [ro'mandza] *sf (Mus, Letteratura)* romance
roman'zare [roman'dzare] *vt* to romanticize
roman'zesco, -a, schi, sche [roman'dzesko] *ag (stile, personaggi)* fictional; *(fig)* storybook *cpd*
romanzi'ere [roman'dzjɛre] *sm* novelist
ro'manzo, -a [ro'mandzo] *ag (Ling)* romance *cpd* ■ *sm (medievale)* romance; *(moderno)* novel; **~ d'amore** love story; **~ d'appendice** serial (story); **~ cavalleresco** tale of chivalry; **~ poliziesco, ~ giallo** detective story; **~ rosa** romantic novel

rom'bare *vi* to rumble, thunder, roar
'rombo *sm* rumble, thunder, roar; (*Mat*) rhombus; (*Zool*) turbot
ro'meno, -a *ag, sm/f, sm* = **rumeno**
'rompere *vt* to break; (*conversazione, fidanzamento*) to break off ■ *vi* to break; **rompersi** *vr* to break; **mi rompe le scatole** (*fam*) he (*o* she) is a pain in the neck; **rompersi un braccio** to break an arm
rompi'capo *sm* worry, headache; (*indovinello*) puzzle; (*in enigmistica*) brain-teaser
rompi'collo *sm* daredevil
rompighi'accio [rompi'gjattʃo] *sm* (*Naut*) icebreaker
rompis'catole *sm/f inv* (*fam*) pest, pain in the neck
'ronda *sf* (*Mil*) rounds *pl*, patrol
ron'della *sf* (*Tecn*) washer
'rondine *sf* (*Zool*) swallow
ron'done *sm* (*Zool*) swift
ron'fare *vi* (*russare*) to snore
ron'zare [ron'dzare] *vi* to buzz, hum
ron'zino [ron'dzino] *sm* (*peg: cavallo*) nag
ron'zio, -ii [ron'dzio] *sm* buzzing, humming; **~ auricolare** (*Med*) tinnitus *sg*
'rosa *sf* rose; (*fig: gruppo*): **~ dei candidati** list of candidates ■ *ag inv, sm* pink
ro'saio *sm* (*pianta*) rosebush, rose tree; (*giardino*) rose garden
ro'sario *sm* (*Rel*) rosary
ro'sato, -a *ag* pink, rosy ■ *sm* (*vino*) rosé (wine)
ro'seo, -a *ag* (*anche fig*) rosy
ro'seto *sm* rose garden
ro'setta *sf* (*diamante*) rose-cut diamond; (*rondella*) washer
'rosi *vb vedi* **rodere**
rosicchi'are [rosik'kjare] *vt* to gnaw (at); (*mangiucchiare*) to nibble (at)
rosma'rino *sm* rosemary
'roso, -a *pp di* **rodere**
roso'lare *vt* (*Cuc*) to brown
roso'lia *sf* (*Med*) German measles *sg*, rubella
'rospo *sm* (*Zool*) toad; **mandar giù** *o* **ingoiare un** *o* **il ~** (*fig*) to swallow a bitter pill; **sputa il ~!** out with it!
ros'setto *sm* (*per labbra*) lipstick; (*per guance*) rouge
ros'siccio, -a, ci, ce [ros'sittʃo] *ag* reddish
'rosso, -a *ag, sm, sm/f* red; **diventare ~ (per la vergogna)** to blush *o* go red (with *o* for shame); **il mar R~** the Red Sea; **~ d'uovo** egg yolk
ros'sore *sm* flush, blush
rosticce'ria [rostittʃe'ria] *sf shop selling roast meat and other cooked food*
'rostro *sm* rostrum; (*becco*) beak
ro'tabile *ag* (*percorribile*): **strada ~** roadway; (*Ferr*): **materiale ~** rolling stock
ro'taia *sf* rut, track; (*Ferr*) rail
ro'tare *vt, vi* to rotate
rota'tivo, -a *ag* rotating, rotation *cpd*
rotazi'one [rotat'tsjone] *sf* rotation
rote'are *vt, vi* to whirl; **~ gli occhi** to roll one's eyes
ro'tella *sf* small wheel; (*di mobile*) castor
roto'calco, -chi *sm* (*Tip*) rotogravure; (*rivista*) illustrated magazine
roto'lare *vt, vi* to roll; **rotolarsi** *vr* to roll (about)
roto'lio *sm* rolling
'rotolo *sm* (*di carta, stoffa*) roll; (*di corda*) coil; **andare a rotoli** (*fig*) to go to rack and ruin; **mandare a rotoli** (*fig*) to ruin
ro'tondo, -a *ag* round ■ *sf* rotunda
ro'tore *sm* rotor
'rotta *sf* (*Aer, Naut*) course, route; (*Mil*) rout; **a ~ di collo** at breakneck speed; **essere in ~ con qn** to be on bad terms with sb; **fare ~ su** *o* **per** *o* **verso** to head for *o* towards; **cambiare ~** (*anche fig*) to change course; **in ~ di collisione** on a collision course; **ufficiale di ~** navigator, navigating officer
rotta'mare *vt to scrap old vehicles in return for incentives*
rottama'zione [rottamat'tsjone] *sf the scrapping of old vehicles in return for incentives*
rot'tame *sm* fragment, scrap, broken bit; **rottami** *smpl* (*di nave aereo etc*) wreckage *sg*; **rottami di ferro** scrap iron *sg*
'rotto, -a *pp di* **rompere** ■ *ag* broken; (*calzoni*) torn, split; (*persona: pratico, resistente*): **~ a** accustomed *o* inured to ■ *sm*: **per il ~ della cuffia** by the skin of one's teeth; **rotti** *smpl*: **20 euro e rotti** 20-odd euros
rot'tura *sf* (*azione*) breaking *no pl*; (*di rapporti*) breaking off; (*Med*) fracture, break
rou'lotte [ru'lɔt] *sf inv* caravan
ro'vente *ag* red-hot
'rovere *sm* oak
ro'vescia [ro'vɛʃʃa] *sf*: **alla ~** upside-down; inside-out; **oggi mi va tutto alla ~** everything is going wrong (for me) today
rovesci'are [roveʃ'ʃare] *vt* (*versare in giù*) to pour; (*accidentalmente*) to spill; (*capovolgere*) to turn upside down; (*gettare a terra*) to knock down; (*fig: governo*) to overthrow; (*piegare all'indietro: testa*) to throw back; **rovesciarsi** *vr* (*sedia, macchina*) to overturn; (*barca*) to capsize; (*liquido*) to spill; (*fig: situazione*) to be reversed
ro'vescio, sci [ro'vɛʃʃo] *sm* other side, wrong side; (*della mano*) back; (*di moneta*) reverse; (*pioggia*) sudden downpour; (*fig*) setback; (*Maglia*: *anche*: **punto rovescio**) purl (stitch);

(*Tennis*) backhand (stroke); **a ~** (*sottosopra*) upside-down; (*con l'esterno all'interno*) inside-out; **capire qc a ~** to misunderstand sth; **~ di fortuna** setback

ro'vina *sf* ruin; **rovine** *sfpl* ruins; **andare in ~** (*andare a pezzi*) to collapse; (*fig*) to go to rack and ruin; **mandare qc/qn in ~** to ruin sth/sb

rovi'nare *vi* to collapse, fall down ■ *vt* (*far cadere giù: casa*) to demolish; (*danneggiare: fig*) to ruin

rovi'nato, -a *ag* ruined, damaged; (*fig: persona*) ruined

rovi'noso, -a *ag* ruinous

rovis'tare *vt* (*casa*) to ransack; (*tasche*) to rummage in (*o* through)

'rovo *sm* (*Bot*) blackberry *o* bramble bush

roz'zezza [rod'dzettsa] *sf* roughness, coarseness

'rozzo, -a ['roddzo] *ag* rough, coarse

RP *sigla fpl vedi* **relazioni pubbliche**

R.R. *abbr* (*Posta*) = **ricevuta di ritorno**

Rr *abbr* (*Posta*) = **raccomandata con ricevuta di ritorno**

RSVP *abbr* (= *répondez s'il vous plaît*) RSVP

'ruba *sf*: **andare a ~** to sell like hot cakes

rubacu'ori *sm inv* ladykiller

ru'bare *vt* to steal; **~ qc a qn** to steal sth from sb

rubi'condo, -a *ag* ruddy

rubi'netto *sm* tap, faucet (*US*)

ru'bino *sm* ruby

ru'bizzo, -a [ru'bittso] *ag* lively, sprightly

'rublo *sm* rouble

ru'brica, -che *sf* (*di giornale: colonna*) column; (*: pagina*) page; (*quadernetto*) index book; (*per indirizzi*) address book

'rude *ag* tough, rough

'rudere *sm* (*rovina*) ruins *pl*

rudimen'tale *ag* rudimentary, basic

rudi'menti *smpl* rudiments; basic principles

ruffi'ano *sm* pimp

'ruga, -ghe *sf* wrinkle

'ruggine ['ruddʒine] *sf* rust

rug'gire [rud'dʒire] *vi* to roar

rug'gito [rud'dʒito] *sm* roar

rugi'ada [ru'dʒada] *sf* dew

ru'goso, -a *ag* wrinkled; (*scabro: superficie etc*) rough

rul'lare *vi* (*tamburo, nave*) to roll; (*aereo*) to taxi

rul'lino *sm* (*Fot*) roll of film, spool

rul'lio, -ii *sm* (*di tamburi*) roll

'rullo *sm* (*di tamburi*) roll; (*arnese cilindrico, Tip*) roller; **~ compressore** steam roller; **~ di pellicola** roll of film

rum *sm* rum

ru'meno, -a *ag, sm/f, sm* Romanian

rumi'nante *sm* (*Zool*) ruminant

rumi'nare *vt* (*Zool*) to ruminate; (*fig*) to ruminate on *o* over, chew over

ru'more *sm*: **un ~** a noise, a sound; **il ~** noise; **fare ~** to make a noise; **un ~ di passi** the sound of footsteps; **la notizia ha fatto molto ~** (*fig*) the news aroused great interest

rumoreggi'are [rumored'dʒare] *vi* (*tuono etc*) to rumble; (*fig: folla*) to clamour (*Brit*), clamor (*US*)

rumo'roso, -a *ag* noisy

ru'olo *sm* (*Teat, fig*) role, part; (*elenco*) roll, register, list; **di ~** permanent, on the permanent staff; **professore di ~** (*Ins*) ≈ lecturer with tenure; **fuori ~** (*personale, insegnante*) temporary

ru'ota *sf* wheel; **a ~** (*forma*) circular; **~ anteriore/posteriore** front/back wheel; **andare a ~ libera** to freewheel; **parlare a ~ libera** (*fig*) to speak freely; **~ di scorta** spare wheel

ruo'tare *vt, vi* = **rotare**

'rupe *sf* cliff, rock

ru'pestre *ag* rocky

ru'pia *sf* rupee

'ruppi *etc vb vedi* **rompere**

ru'rale *ag* rural, country *cpd*

ru'scello [ruʃʃɛllo] *sm* stream

'ruspa *sf* excavator

rus'pante *ag* (*pollo*) free-range

rus'sare *vi* to snore

'Russia *sf*: **la ~** Russia

'russo, -a *ag, sm/f, sm* Russian

'rustico, -a, ci, che *ag* country *cpd*, rural; (*arredamento*) rustic; (*fig*) rough, unrefined ■ *sm* (*fabbricato: per attrezzi*) shed; (*: per abitazione*) farm labourer's (*Brit*) *o* farmhand's cottage

'ruta *sf* (*Bot*) rue

rut'tare *vi* to belch

'rutto *sm* belch

'ruvido, -a *ag* rough, coarse

ruzzo'lare [ruttso'lare] *vi* to tumble down

ruzzo'lone [ruttso'lone] *sm* tumble, fall

ruzzo'loni [ruttso'loni] *av*: **cadere ~** to tumble down; **fare le scale ~** to tumble down the stairs

r

Ss

S, s [ˈɛsse] *sf o m* (*lettera*) S, s; **S come Savona** ≈ S for Sugar
s *abbr* (= *secondo*) sec.
S. *abbr* (= *sud*) S; (= *santo*) St
SA *sigla* = **Salerno** ■ *abbr* = **società anonima**
sa *vb vedi* **sapere**
sab. *abbr* (= *sabato*) Sat.
ˈsabato *sm* Saturday; *vedi anche* **martedì**
ˈsabbia *sf* sand; **sabbie mobili** quicksand(*s pl*)
sabbiaˈtura *sf* (*Med*) sand bath; (*Tecn*) sand-blasting; **fare le sabbiature** to take sand baths
sabbiˈoso, -a *ag* sandy
saboˈtaggio [saboˈtaddʒo] *sm* sabotage
saboˈtare *vt* to sabotage
sabotaˈtore, -ˈtrice *sm/f* saboteur
ˈsacca, -che *sf* bag; (*bisaccia*) haversack; (*insenatura*) inlet; **~ d'aria** air pocket; **~ da viaggio** travelling bag
saccaˈrina *sf* saccharin(e)
sacˈcente [satˈtʃɛnte] *sm/f* know-all (*Brit*), know-it-all (*US*)
saccheggiˈare [sakkedˈdʒare] *vt* to sack, plunder
sacˈcheggio [sakˈkeddʒo] *sm* sack(ing)
sacˈchetto [sakˈketto] *sm* (small) bag; (small) sack; **~ di carta/di plastica** paper/plastic bag
ˈsacco, -chi *sm* bag; (*per carbone etc*) sack; (*Anat, Biol*) sac; (*tela*) sacking; (*saccheggio*) sack(ing); (*fig: grande quantità*): **un ~ di** lots of, heaps of; **cogliere** *o* **prendere qn con le mani nel ~** to catch sb red-handed; **vuotare il ~** to confess, spill the beans; **mettere qn nel ~** to cheat sb; **colazione al ~** packed lunch; **~ a pelo** sleeping bag; **~ per i rifiuti** bin bag (*Brit*), garbage bag (*US*)
sacerˈdote [satʃerˈdɔte] *sm* priest
sacerˈdozio [satʃerˈdɔttsjo] *sm* priesthood
ˈSacra Coˈrona Uˈnita *sf the mafia in Puglia*
sacraˈmento *sm* sacrament
saˈcrario *sm* memorial chapel
sacresˈtano *sm* = **sagrestano**
sacresˈtia *sf* = **sagrestia**
sacrifiˈcare *vt* to sacrifice; **sacrificarsi** *vr* to sacrifice o.s.; (*privarsi di qc*) to make sacrifices
sacrifiˈcato, -a *ag* sacrificed; (*non valorizzato*) wasted; **una vita sacrificata** a life of sacrifice
sacriˈficio [sakriˈfitʃo] *sm* sacrifice
sacriˈlegio [sacriˈlɛdʒo] *sm* sacrilege
saˈcrilego, -a, ghi, ghe *ag* (*Rel*) sacrilegious
ˈsacro, -a *ag* sacred
sacroˈsanto, -a *ag* sacrosanct
ˈsadico, -a, ci, che *ag* sadistic ■ *sm/f* sadist
saˈdismo *sm* sadism
sadomasoˈchismo [sadomazoˈkismo] *sm* sadomasochism
saˈetta *sf* arrow; (*fulmine: anche fig*) thunderbolt
saˈfari *sm inv* safari
saˈgace [saˈgatʃe] *ag* shrewd, sagacious
saˈgacia [saˈgatʃa] *sf* sagacity, shrewdness
sagˈgezza [sadˈdʒettsa] *sf* wisdom
saggiˈare [sadˈdʒare] *vt* (*metalli*) to assay; (*fig*) to test
ˈsaggio, -a, gi, ge [ˈsaddʒo] *ag* wise ■ *sm* (*persona*) sage; (*operazione sperimentale*) test; (*: dell'oro*) assay; (*fig: prova*) proof; (*campione indicativo*) sample; (*scritto: letterario*) essay; (*: Ins*) written test; **dare ~ di** to give proof of; **in ~** as a sample
sagˈgistica [sadˈdʒistika] *sf* ≈ non-fiction
Sagitˈtario [sadʒitˈtarjo] *sm* Sagittarius; **essere del ~** to be Sagittarius
ˈsagoma *sf* (*profilo*) outline, profile; (*forma*) form, shape; (*Tecn*) template; (*bersaglio*) target; (*fig: persona*) character
ˈsagra *sf* festival
saˈgrato *sm* churchyard
sagresˈtano *sm* sacristan; sexton
sagresˈtia *sf* sacristy; (*culto protestante*) vestry
Saˈhara [saˈara] *sm*: **il (Deserto del) ~** the Sahara (Desert)
sahariˈana [saaˈrjana] *sf* bush jacket
ˈsai *vb vedi* **sapere**

'saio *sm* (*Rel*) habit

'sala *sf* hall; (*stanza*) room; (*Cine: di proiezione*) screen; **~ d'aspetto** waiting room; **~ da ballo** ballroom; **~ (dei) comandi** control room; **~ per concerti** concert hall; **~ per conferenze** (*Ins*) lecture hall; (*in aziende*) conference room; **~ corse** betting shop; **~ giochi** amusement arcade; **~ da gioco** gaming room; **~ macchine** (*Naut*) engine room; **~ operatoria** (*Med*) operating theatre (*Brit*) *o* room (*US*); **~ da pranzo** dining room; **~ per ricevimenti** banqueting hall; **~ delle udienze** (*Dir*) courtroom

sa'lace [sa'latʃe] *ag* (*spinto, piccante*) salacious, saucy; (*mordace*) cutting, biting

sala'mandra *sf* salamander

sa'lame *sm* salami *no pl*, salami sausage

sala'moia *sf* (*Cuc*) brine

sa'lare *vt* to salt

salari'ale *ag* wage *cpd*, pay *cpd*; **aumento ~** wage *o* pay increase (*Brit*) *o* raise (*US*)

salari'ato, -a *sm/f* wage-earner

sa'lario *sm* pay, wages *pl*; **~ base** basic wage; **~ minimo garantito** guaranteed minimum wage

salas'sare *vt* (*Med*) to bleed

sa'lasso *sm* (*Med*) bleeding, bloodletting; (*fig: forte spesa*) drain

sala'tino *sm* cracker, salted biscuit

sa'lato, -a *ag* (*sapore*) salty; (*Cuc*) salted, salt *cpd*; (*fig: discorso etc*) biting, sharp; (*: prezzi*) steep, stiff

sal'dare *vt* (*congiungere*) to join, bind; (*parti metalliche*) to solder; (*: con saldatura autogena*) to weld; (*conto*) to settle, pay

salda'tore *sm* (*operaio*) solderer; welder; (*utensile*) soldering iron

salda'trice [salda'tritʃe] *sf* (*macchina*) welder, welding machine; **~ ad arco** arc welder

salda'tura *sf* soldering; welding; (*punto saldato*) soldered joint; weld; **~ autogena** welding; **~ dolce** soft soldering

sal'dezza [sal'dettsa] *sf* firmness, strength

'saldo, -a *ag* (*resistente, forte*) strong, firm; (*fermo*) firm, steady, stable; (*fig*) firm, steadfast ▪ *sm* (*svendita*) sale; (*di conto*) settlement; (*Econ*) balance; **pagare a ~** to pay in full; **~ attivo** credit; **~ passivo** deficit; **~ da riportare** balance carried forward

'sale *sm* salt; (*fig*) wit; **sali** *smpl* (*Med: da annusare*) smelling salts; **sotto ~** salted; **restare di ~** (*fig*) to be dumbfounded; **ha poco ~ in zucca** he doesn't have much sense; **~ da cucina**, **~ grosso** cooking salt; **~ da tavola**, **~ fino** table salt; **sali da bagno** bath salts; **sali minerali** mineral salts; **sali e tabacchi** tobacconist's (shop)

sal'gemma [sal'dʒɛmma] *sm* rock salt

'salgo *etc vb vedi* **salire**

'salice ['salitʃe] *sm* willow; **~ piangente** weeping willow

sali'ente *ag* (*fig*) salient, main

sali'era *sf* salt cellar

sa'lino, -a *ag* saline ▪ *sf* saltworks *sg*

sa'lire *vi* to go (*o* come) up; (*aereo etc*) to climb, go up; (*passeggero*) to get on; (*sentiero, prezzi, livello*) to go up, rise ▪ *vt* (*scale, gradini*) to go (*o* come) up; **~ su** to climb (up); **~ sul treno/sull'autobus** to board the train/the bus; **~ in macchina** to get into the car; **~ a cavallo** to mount; **~ al potere** to rise to power; **~ al trono** to ascend the throne; **~ alle stelle** (*prezzi*) to rocket

sali'scendi [saliʃʃendi] *sm inv* latch

sa'lita *sf* climb, ascent; (*erta*) hill, slope; **in ~** uphill

sa'liva *sf* saliva

'salma *sf* corpse

sal'mastro, -a *ag* (*acqua*) salt *cpd*; (*sapore*) salty ▪ *sm* (*sapore*) salty taste; (*odore*) salty smell

salmì *sm* (*Cuc*) salmi; **lepre in ~** salmi of hare

'salmo *sm* psalm

sal'mone *sm* salmon

salmo'nella *sf* salmonella

Salo'mone: **le isole ~** *sfpl* the Solomon Islands

sa'lone *sm* (*stanza*) sitting room, lounge; (*in albergo*) lounge; (*di ricevimento*) reception room; (*su nave*) lounge, saloon; (*mostra*) show, exhibition; (*negozio: di parrucchiere*) hairdresser's (salon); **~ dell'automobile** motor show; **~ di bellezza** beauty salon

salo'pette [salɔ'pɛt] *sf inv* dungarees *pl*

salotti'ero, -a *ag* mundane

sa'lotto *sm* lounge, sitting room; (*mobilio*) lounge suite

sal'pare *vi* (*Naut*) to set sail; (*anche*: **salpare l'ancora**) to weigh anchor

'salsa *sf* (*Cuc*) sauce; **in tutte le salse** (*fig*) in all kinds of ways; **~ di pomodoro** tomato sauce

sal'sedine *sf* (*del mare, vento*) saltiness; (*incrostazione*) (dried) salt

sal'siccia, -ce [sal'sittʃa] *sf* pork sausage

salsi'era *sf* sauceboat (*Brit*), gravy boat

'salso *sm* saltiness

sal'tare *vi* to jump, leap; (*esplodere*) to blow up, explode; (*: valvola*) to blow; (*venir via*) to pop off; (*non aver luogo: corso etc*) to be cancelled ▪ *vt* to jump (over), leap (over); (*fig: pranzo, capitolo*) to skip, miss (out); (*Cuc*) to sauté; **far ~** to blow up; (*serratura: forzare*) to break; **far ~ il banco** (*Gioco*) to break the bank; **farsi ~ le cervella** to blow one's brains out; **ma che ti**

S

salta in mente? what are you thinking of?; **~ da un argomento all'altro** to jump from one subject to another; **~ addosso a qn** (*aggredire*) to attack sb; **~ fuori** to jump out, leap out; (*venire trovato*) to turn up; **~ fuori con** (*frase, commento*) to come out with; **~ giù da qc** to jump off sth, jump down from sth

saltel'lare *vi* to skip; to hop

sal'tello *sm* hop, little jump

saltim'banco, -chi *sm* acrobat

'salto *sm* jump; (*Sport*) jumping; (*dislivello*) drop; **fare un ~** to jump, leap; **fare un ~ da qn** to pop over to sb's (place); **~ in alto/lungo** high/long jump; **~ con l'asta** pole vaulting; **~ mortale** somersault; **un ~ di qualità** (*miglioramento*) significant improvement

saltu'ario, -a *ag* occasional, irregular

sa'lubre *ag* healthy, salubrious

sa'lume *sm* (*Cuc*) cured pork; **salumi** *smpl* (*insaccati*) cured pork meats

salume'ria *sf* delicatessen

salumi'ere, -a *sm/f* ≈ delicatessen owner

salumi'ficio [salumi'fitʃo] *sm* cured pork meat factory

salu'tare *ag* healthy; (*fig*) salutary, beneficial ■ *vt* (*per dire buon giorno, fig*) to greet; (*per dire addio*) to say goodbye to; (*Mil*) to salute; **mi saluti sua moglie** my regards to your wife

sa'lute *sf* health; **~!** (*a chi starnutisce*) bless you!; (*nei brindisi*) cheers!; **bere alla ~ di qn** to drink (to) sb's health; **la ~ pubblica** public welfare; **godere di buona ~** to be healthy, enjoy good health

sa'luto *sm* (*gesto*) wave; (*parola*) greeting; (*Mil*) salute; **gli ha tolto il ~** he no longer says hello to him; **cari saluti, tanti saluti** best regards; **vogliate gradire i nostri più distinti saluti** yours faithfully; **i miei saluti alla sua signora** my regards to your wife

'salva *sf* salvo

salvacon'dotto *sm* (*Mil*) safe-conduct

salvada'naio *sm* moneybox, piggy bank

salvado'regno, -a [salvado'reɲɲo] *ag, sm/f* Salvadorean

salva'gente [salva'dʒente] *sm* (*Naut*) lifebuoy; (*pl inv: stradale*) traffic island; **~ a ciambella** lifebelt; **~ a giubbotto** lifejacket (*Brit*), life preserver (*US*)

salvaguar'dare *vt* to safeguard

salvagu'ardia *sf* safeguard; **a ~ di** for the safeguard of

sal'vare *vt* to save; (*trarre da un pericolo*) to rescue; (*proteggere*) to protect; **salvarsi** *vr* to save o.s.; to escape; **~ la vita a qn** to save sb's life; **~ le apparenze** to keep up appearances; **si salvi chi può!** every man for himself!

salvas'chermo [salvas'kermo] *sm* (*Inform*) screen saver

salva'slip® *sm inv* panty liner

salva'taggio [salva'taddʒo] *sm* rescue

salva'tore, -'trice *sm/f* saviour (*Brit*), savior (*US*)

salvazi'one [salvat'tsjone] *sf* (*Rel*) salvation

'salve *escl* (*fam*) hi!

sal'vezza [sal'vettsa] *sf* salvation; (*sicurezza*) safety

'salvia *sf* (*Bot*) sage

salvi'etta *sf* napkin, serviette

'salvo, -a *ag* safe, unhurt, unharmed; (*fuori pericolo*) safe, out of danger ■ *sm*: **in ~** safe ■ *prep* (*eccetto*) except; **~ che** *cong* (*a meno che*) unless; (*eccetto che*) except (that); **mettere qc in ~** to put sth in a safe place; **mettersi in ~** to reach safety; **portare qn in ~** to lead sb to safety; **~ contrordini** barring instructions to the contrary; **~ errori e omissioni** errors and omissions excepted; **~ imprevisti** barring accidents

sam'buca *sf* (*liquore*) sambuca (*type of anisette*)

sam'buco *sm* elder (tree)

sa'nare *vt* to heal, cure; (*economia*) to put right

sana'toria *sf* (*Dir*) act of indemnity

sana'torio *sm* sanatorium (*Brit*), sanitarium (*US*)

san'cire [san'tʃire] *vt* to sanction

'sandalo *sm* (*Bot*) sandalwood; (*calzatura*) sandal

sang'ria [san'gria] *sf* (*bibita*) sangria

'sangue *sm* blood; **farsi cattivo ~** to fret, get worked up; **all'ultimo ~** (*duello, lotta*) to the death; **non corre buon ~ tra di loro** there's bad blood between them; **buon ~ non mente!** blood will out!; **~ freddo** (*fig*) sang-froid, calm; **a ~ freddo** in cold blood

sangu'igno, -a [san'gwiɲɲo] *ag* blood *cpd*; (*colore*) blood-red

sangui'nante *ag* bleeding

sangui'nare *vi* to bleed

sangui'nario, -a *ag* bloodthirsty

sangui'noso, -a *ag* bloody

sangui'suga, -ghe *sf* leech

sanità *sf* health; (*salubrità*) healthiness; **Ministero della S~** Department of Health; **~ mentale** sanity; **~ pubblica** public health

sani'tario, -a *ag* health *cpd*; (*condizioni*) sanitary ■ *sm* (*Amm*) doctor; **Ufficiale S~** Health Officer; **(impianti) sanitari** bathroom *o* sanitary fittings

San Ma'rino *sf*: **la Repubblica di ~** the Republic of San Marino

'sanno *vb vedi* **sapere**

'sano, -a *ag* healthy; (*denti, costituzione*) healthy, sound; (*integro*) whole, unbroken;

(*fig: politica, consigli*) sound; **~ di mente** sane; **di sana pianta** completely, entirely; **~ e salvo** safe and sound
San Silvestro [san sil'vestro] *sm* (*giorno*) New Year's Eve
Santi'ago *sf*: **~ (del Cile)** Santiago (de Chile)
santifi'care *vt* to sanctify; (*feste*) to observe
san'tino *sm* holy picture
san'tissimo, -a *ag*: **il S~ Sacramento** the Holy Sacrament; **il Padre S~** (*papa*) the Holy Father
santità *sf* sanctity; holiness; **Sua/Vostra ~** (*titolo di papa*) His/Your Holiness
'santo, -a *ag* holy; (*fig*) saintly; (*seguito da nome proprio: dav sm* **san** + *C*, **sant'** + *V*, **santo** + *s impura, gn, pn, ps, x, z; dav sf* **santa** + *C*, **sant'** + *V*) saint ■ *sm/f* saint; **parole sante!** very true!; **tutto il ~ giorno** the whole blessed day, all day long; **non c'è ~ che tenga!** that's no excuse!; **la Santa Sede** the Holy See
san'tone *sm* holy man
santu'ario *sm* sanctuary
sanzio'nare [santsjo'nare] *vt* to sanction
sanzi'one [san'tsjone] *sf* sanction; (*penale, civile*) sanction, penalty; **sanzioni economiche** economic sanctions
sa'pere *vt* to know; (*essere capace di*): **so nuotare** I know how to swim, I can swim ■ *vi*: **~ di** (*aver sapore*) to taste of; (*aver odore*) to smell of ■ *sm* knowledge; **far ~ qc a qn** to inform sb about sth, let sb know sth; **venire a ~ qc (da qn)** to find out *o* hear about sth (from sb); **non ne vuole più ~ di lei** he doesn't want to have anything more to do with her; **mi sa che non sia vero** I don't think that's true
sapi'ente *ag* (*dotto*) learned; (*che rivela abilità*) masterly ■ *sm/f* scholar
sapien'tone, -a *sm/f* (*peg*) know-all (*Brit*), know-it-all (*US*)
sapi'enza [sa'pjɛntsa] *sf* wisdom
sa'pone *sm* soap; **~ da barba** shaving soap; **~ da bucato** washing soap; **~ liquido** liquid soap; **~ in scaglie** soapflakes *pl*
sapo'netta *sf* cake *o* bar *o* tablet of soap
sa'pore *sm* taste, flavour (*Brit*), flavor (*US*)
sapo'rito, -a *ag* tasty; (*fig: arguto*) witty; (*: piccante*) racy
sappi'amo *vb vedi* **sapere**
saprò *etc vb vedi* **sapere**
sapu'tello, -a *sm/f* know-all (*Brit*), know-it-all (*US*)
sarà *etc vb vedi* **essere**
sara'banda *sf* (*fig*) uproar
saraci'nesca, -sche [saratʃi'neska] *sf* (*serranda*) rolling shutter
sar'casmo *sm* sarcasm *no pl*; sarcastic remark
sar'castico, -a, ci, che *ag* sarcastic
sarchi'are [sar'kjare] *vt* (*Agr*) to hoe
sar'cofago (*mpl* **sarcofagi** *o* **sarcofaghi**) *sm* sarcophagus
Sar'degna [sar'deɲɲa] *sf*: **la ~** Sardinia
sar'dina *sf* sardine
'sardo, -a *ag, sm/f* Sardinian
sar'donico, -a, ci, che *ag* sardonic
sa'rei *etc vb vedi* **essere**
SARS *sf* (= *severe acute respiratory syndrome*) SARS
'sarta *sf vedi* **sarto**
'sartia *sf* (*Naut*) stay
'sarto, -a *sm/f* tailor/dressmaker; **~ d'alta moda** couturier
sarto'ria *sf* tailor's (shop); dressmaker's (shop); (*casa di moda*) fashion house; (*arte*) couture
sassai'ola *sf* hail of stones
sas'sata *sf* blow with a stone; **tirare una ~ contro** *o* **a qc/qn** to throw a stone at sth/sb
'sasso *sm* stone; (*ciottolo*) pebble; (*masso*) rock; **restare** *o* **rimanere di ~** to be dumbfounded
sassofo'nista, -i, e *sm/f* saxophonist
sas'sofono *sm* saxophone
sas'sone *ag, sm/f, sm* Saxon
sas'soso, -a *ag* stony; pebbly
'Satana *sm* Satan
sa'tanico, -a, ci, che *ag* satanic, fiendish
sa'tellite *sm, ag* satellite
'satira *sf* satire
satireggi'are [satired'dʒare] *vt* to satirize ■ *vi* (*fare della satira*) to be satirical; (*scrivere satire*) to write satires
sa'tirico, -a, ci, che *ag* satiric(al)
sa'tollo, -a *ag* full, replete
satu'rare *vt* to saturate
saturazi'one [saturat'tsjone] *sf* saturation
'saturo, -a *ag* saturated; (*fig*): **~ di** full of; **~ d'acqua** (*terreno*) waterlogged
'SAUB *sigla f* (= *Struttura Amministrativa Unificata di Base*) *state welfare system*
'sauna *sf* sauna; **fare la ~** to have *o* take a sauna
sa'vana *sf* savannah
'savio, -a *ag* wise, sensible ■ *sm* wise man
Sa'voia *sf*: **la ~** Savoy
savoi'ardo, -a *ag* of Savoy, Savoyard ■ *sm* (*biscotto*) sponge finger
sazi'are [sat'tsjare] *vt* to satisfy, satiate; **saziarsi** *vr* (*riempirsi di cibo*): **saziarsi (di)** to eat one's fill (of); (*fig*): **saziarsi di** to grow tired *o* weary of
sazietà [sattsje'ta] *sf* satiety, satiation
'sazio, -a ['sattsjo] *ag*: **~ (di)** sated (with), full (of); (*fig: stufo*) fed up (with), sick (of)
sbada'taggine [zbada'taddʒine] *sf* (*sventatezza*) carelessness; (*azione*) oversight
sba'dato, -a *ag* careless, inattentive
sbadigli'are [zbadiʎ'ʎare] *vi* to yawn

sba'diglio [zba'diʎʎo] *sm* yawn; **fare uno ~** to yawn
'sbafo *sm*: **a ~** at somebody else's expense
sbagli'are [zbaʎ'ʎare] *vt* to make a mistake in, get wrong ■ *vi* (*fare errori*) to make a mistake (*o* mistakes), be mistaken; (*ingannarsi*) to be wrong; (*operare in modo non giusto*) to err; **sbagliarsi** *vr* to make a mistake, be mistaken, be wrong; **~ la mira/strada** to miss one's aim/take the wrong road; **scusi, ho sbagliato numero** (*Tel*) sorry, I've got the wrong number; **non c'è da sbagliarsi** there can be no mistake
sbagli'ato, -a [zbaʎ'ʎato] *ag* (*gen*) wrong; (*compito*) full of mistakes; (*conclusione*) erroneous
'sbaglio ['zbaʎʎo] *sm* mistake, error; (*morale*) error; **fare uno ~** to make a mistake
sbales'trato, -a *ag* (*persona: scombussolato*) unsettled
sbal'lare *vt* (*merce*) to unpack ■ *vi* (*nel fare un conto*) to overestimate; (*Droga: gergo*) to get high
sbal'lato, -a *ag* (*calcolo*) wrong; (*fam: ragionamento, persona*) screwy
'sballo *sm* (*Droga: gergo*) trip
sballot'tare *vt* to toss (about)
sbalor'dire *vt* to stun, amaze ■ *vi* to be stunned, be amazed
sbalordi'tivo, -a *ag* amazing; (*prezzo*) incredible, absurd
sbal'zare [zbal'tsare] *vt* to throw, hurl; (*fig: da una carica*) to remove, dismiss ■ *vi* (*balzare*) to bounce; (*saltare*) to leap, bound
'sbalzo ['zbaltso] *sm* (*spostamento improvviso*) jolt, jerk; **a sbalzi** jerkily; (*fig*) in fits and starts; **uno ~ di temperatura** a sudden change in temperature
sban'care *vt* (*nei giochi*) to break the bank at (*o* of); (*fig*) to ruin, bankrupt
sbanda'mento *sm* (*Naut*) list; (*Aut*) skid; (*fig: di persona*) confusion; **ha avuto un periodo di ~** he went off the rails for a bit
sban'dare *vi* (*Naut*) to list; (*Aut*) to skid; **sbandarsi** *vr* (*folla*) to disperse; (*truppe*) to scatter; (*fig: famiglia*) to break up
sban'data *sf* (*Aut*) skid; (*Naut*) list; **prendere una ~ per qn** (*fig*) to fall for sb
sban'dato, -a *sm/f* mixed-up person
sbandie'rare *vt* (*bandiera*) to wave; (*fig*) to parade, show off
'sbando *sm*: **essere allo ~** to drift
sbarac'care *vt* (*libri, piatti etc*) to clear (up)
sbaragli'are [zbaraʎ'ʎare] *vt* (*Mil*) to rout; (*in gare sportive etc*) to beat, defeat
sba'raglio [zba'raʎʎo] *sm*: **gettarsi allo ~** (*soldato*) to throw o.s. into the fray; (*fig*) to risk everything
sbaraz'zarsi [zbarat'tsarsi] *vr*: **~ di** to get rid of, rid o.s. of
sbaraz'zino, -a [zbarat'tsino] *ag* impish, cheeky
sbar'bare *vt*, **sbar'barsi** *vr* to shave
sbarba'tello *sm* novice, greenhorn
sbar'care *vt* (*passeggeri*) to disembark; (*merci*) to unload ■ *vi* to disembark
'sbarco *sm* disembarkation; unloading; (*Mil*) landing
'sbarra *sf* bar; (*di passaggio a livello*) barrier; (*Dir*): **mettere/presentarsi alla ~** to bring/appear before the court
sbarra'mento *sm* (*stradale*) barrier; (*diga*) dam, barrage; (*Mil*) barrage; (*Pol*) cut-off point (*level of support below which a political party is excluded from representation in Parliament*)
sbar'rare *vt* (*bloccare*) to block, bar; (*cancellare: assegno*) to cross (*Brit*); **~ il passo** to bar the way; **~ gli occhi** to open one's eyes wide
sbar'rato, -a *ag* (*porta*) barred; (*passaggio*) blocked, barred; (*strada*) blocked, obstructed; (*occhi*) staring; (*assegno*) crossed (*Brit*)
'sbattere *vt* (*porta*) to bang; (*tappeti, ali, Cuc*) to beat; (*urtare*) to knock, hit ■ *vi* (*porta, finestra*) to bang; (*agitarsi: ali, vele etc*) to flap; **~ qn fuori/in galera** to throw sb out/into prison; **me ne sbatto!** (*fam*) I don't give a damn!
sbat'tuto, -a *ag* (*viso, aria*) dejected, worn out; (*uovo*) beaten
sba'vare *vi* to dribble; (*colore*) to smear, smudge
sbava'tura *sf* (*di persone*) dribbling; (*di lumache*) slime; (*di rossetto, vernice*) smear
sbelli'carsi *vr*: **~ dalle risa** to split one's sides laughing
'sberla *sf* slap
sber'leffo *sm*: **fare uno ~ a qn** to make a face at sb
sbia'dire *vi* (*anche*: **sbiadirsi**) ■ *vt* to fade
sbia'dito, -a *ag* faded; (*fig*) colourless (*Brit*), colorless (*US*), dull
sbian'care *vt* to whiten; (*tessuto*) to bleach ■ *vi* (*impallidire*) to grow pale *o* white
sbi'eco, -a, chi, che *ag* (*storto*) squint, askew; **di ~**: **guardare qn di ~** (*fig*) to look askance at sb; **tagliare una stoffa di ~** to cut material on the bias
sbigot'tire *vt* to dismay, stun ■ *vi* (*anche*: **sbigottirsi**) to be dismayed
sbilanci'are [zbilan'tʃare] *vt* to throw off balance; **sbilanciarsi** *vr* (*perdere l'equilibrio*) to overbalance, lose one's balance; (*fig: compromettersi*) to compromise o.s.
sbi'lenco, -a, chi, che *ag* (*persona*) crooked, misshapen; (*fig: idea, ragionamento*) twisted

sbirci'are [zbir'tʃare] *vt* to cast sidelong glances at, eye
sbirci'ata [zbir'tʃata] *sf*: **dare una ~ a qc** to glance at sth, have a look at sth
'sbirro *sm* (*peg*) cop
sbizzar'rirsi [zbiddzar'rirsi] *vr* to indulge one's whims
sbloc'care *vt* to unblock, free; (*freno*) to release; (*prezzi, affitti*) to free from controls; **sbloccarsi** *vr* (*gen*) to become unblocked; (*passaggio, strada*) to clear, become unblocked; **la situazione si è sbloccata** things are moving again
'sblocco, -chi *sm* (*vedi vt*) unblocking, freeing; release
sboc'care *vi*: **~ in** (*fiume*) to flow into; (*strada*) to lead into; (*persona*) to come (out) into; (*fig: concludersi*) to end (up) in
sboc'cato, -a *ag* (*persona*) foul-mouthed; (*linguaggio*) foul
sbocci'are [zbot'tʃare] *vi* (*fiore*) to bloom, open (out)
'sbocco, -chi *sm* (*di fiume*) mouth; (*di strada*) end; (*di tubazione, Comm*) outlet; (*uscita: anche fig*) way out; **una strada senza ~** a dead end; **siamo in una situazione senza sbocchi** there's no way out of this for us
sbocconcel'lare [zbokkontʃel'lare] *vt*: **~ (qc)** to nibble (at sth)
sbollen'tare *vt* (*Cuc*) to parboil
sbol'lire *vi* (*fig*) to cool down, calm down
'sbornia *sf* (*fam*): **prendersi una ~** to get plastered
sbor'sare *vt* (*denaro*) to pay out
sbot'tare *vi*: **~ in una risata/per la collera** to burst out laughing/explode with anger
sbotto'nare *vt* to unbutton, undo
sbra'cato, -a *ag* slovenly
sbracci'arsi [zbrat'tʃarsi] *vr* to wave (one's arms about)
sbracci'ato, -a [zbrat'tʃato] *ag* (*camicia*) sleeveless; (*persona*) bare-armed
sbrai'tare *vi* to yell, bawl
sbra'nare *vt* to tear to pieces
sbricio'lare [zbritʃo'lare] *vt*, **sbricio'larsi** *vr* to crumble
sbri'gare *vt* to deal with, get through; (*cliente*) to attend to, deal with; **sbrigarsi** *vr* to hurry (up)
sbriga'tivo, -a *ag* (*persona, modo*) quick, expeditious; (*giudizio*) hasty
sbrina'mento *sm* defrosting
sbri'nare *vt* to defrost
sbrindel'lato, -a *ag* tattered, in tatters
sbrodo'lare *vt* to stain, dirty
sbron'zarsi [zbron'tsarsi] *vr* (*fam*) to get sozzled
'sbronzo, -a ['zbrontso] *ag* (*fam*) sozzled ■ *sf*: **prendersi una sbronza** to get sozzled
sbruf'fone, -a *sm/f* boaster, braggart
sbu'care *vi* (*apparire*) to pop out (*o* up)
sbucci'are [zbut'tʃare] *vt* (*arancia, patata*) to peel; (*piselli*) to shell; **sbucciarsi un ginocchio** to graze one's knee
sbucherò *etc* [zbuke'rɔ] *vb vedi* **sbucare**
sbudel'larsi *vr*: **~ dalle risa** to split one's sides laughing
sbuf'fare *vi* (*persona, cavallo*) to snort; (*: ansimare*) to puff, pant; (*treno*) to puff
'sbuffo *sm* (*di aria, fumo, vapore*) puff; **maniche a ~** puff(ed) sleeves
sc. *abbr* (*Teat*: = *scena*) sc.
'scabbia *sf* (*Med*) scabies *sg*
'scabro, -a *ag* rough, harsh; (*fig*) concise, terse
sca'broso, -a *ag* (*fig: difficile*) difficult, thorny; (*: imbarazzante*) embarrassing; (*: sconcio*) indecent
scacchi'era [skak'kjɛra] *sf* chessboard
scacchiere [skak'kjɛre] *sm* (*Mil*) sector; **S~** (*in Gran Bretagna*) Exchequer
scaccia'cani [skattʃa'kani] *sm o f inv* pistol with blanks
scacciapensi'eri [skattʃapen'sjɛri] *sm inv* (*Mus*) jew's-harp
scacci'are [skat'tʃare] *vt* to chase away *o* out, drive away *o* out; **~ qn di casa** to turn sb out of the house
'scacco, -chi *sm* (*pezzo del gioco*) chessman; (*quadretto di scacchiera*) square; (*fig*) setback, reverse; **scacchi** *smpl* (*gioco*) chess *sg*; **a scacchi** (*tessuto*) check(ed); **subire uno ~** (*fig: sconfitta*) to suffer a setback
scacco'matto *sm* checkmate; **dare ~ a qn** (*anche fig*) to checkmate sb
'scaddi *etc vb vedi* **scadere**
sca'dente *ag* shoddy, of poor quality
sca'denza [ska'dɛntsa] *sf* (*di cambiale, contratto*) maturity; (*di passaporto*) expiry date; **a breve/lunga ~** short-/long-term; **data di ~** expiry date; **~ a termine** fixed deadline
sca'dere *vi* (*contratto etc*) to expire; (*debito*) to fall due; (*valore, forze, peso*) to decline, go down
sca'fandro *sm* (*di palombaro*) diving suit; (*di astronauta*) spacesuit
scaffala'tura *sf* shelving, shelves *pl*
scaf'fale *sm* shelf; (*mobile*) set of shelves
sca'fista *sm* (*di immigrati*) people smuggler (*by boat*)
'scafo *sm* (*Naut, Aer*) hull
scagio'nare [skadʒo'nare] *vt* to exonerate, free from blame
'scaglia ['skaʎʎa] *sf* (*Zool*) scale; (*scheggia*) chip, flake

scagli'are [skaʎ'ʎare] *vt* (*lanciare: anche fig*) to hurl, fling; **scagliarsi** *vr*: **scagliarsi su** *o* **contro** to hurl *o* fling o.s. at; (*fig*) to rail at
scagliona'mento [skaʎʎona'mento] *sm* (*Mil*) arrangement in echelons
scaglio'nare [skaʎʎo'nare] *vt* (*pagamenti*) to space out, spread out; (*Mil*) to echelon
scagli'one [skaʎ'ʎone] *sm* (*Mil*) echelon; (*Geo*) terrace; **a scaglioni** in groups
sca'gnozzo [skaɲ'ɲɔttso] *sm* (*peg*) lackey
'Scala: **la ~** *see note*

LA SCALA

Milan's *la Scala* first opened its doors in 1778 with a performance of Salieri's opera, "L'Europa riconosciuta". Built on the site of the church of Santa Maria della Scala, the theatre suffered serious damage in the bombing campaigns of 1943 but reopened in 1946 with a concert conducted by Toscanini. Enjoying worldwide renown for its opera, *la Scala* also has a famous school of classical dance.

'scala *sf* (*a gradini etc*) staircase, stairs *pl*; (*a pioli, di corda*) ladder; (*Mus, Geo, di colori, valori, fig*) scale; **scale** *sfpl* (*scalinata*) stairs; **su larga** *o* **vasta ~** on a large scale; **su piccola ~, su ~ ridotta** on a small scale; **su ~ nazionale/mondiale** on a national/worldwide scale; **in ~ di 1 a 100.000** on a scale of 1 cm to 1 km; **riproduzione in ~** reproduction to scale; **~ a chiocciola** spiral staircase; **~ a libretto** stepladder; **~ di misure** system of weights and measures; **~ mobile** escalator; (*Econ*) sliding scale; **~ mobile (dei salari)** index-linked pay scale; **~ di sicurezza** (*antincendio*) fire escape
sca'lare *vt* (*Alpinismo, muro*) to climb, scale; (*debito*) to scale down, reduce; **questa somma vi viene scalata dal prezzo originale** this sum is deducted from the original price
sca'lata *sf* scaling *no pl*, climbing *no pl*; (*arrampicata, fig*) climb; **dare la ~ a** (*fig*) to make a bid for
scala'tore, -'trice *sm/f* climber
scalca'gnato, -a [skalkaɲ'ɲato] *ag* (*logoro*) worn; (*persona*) shabby
scalci'are [skal'tʃare] *vi* to kick
scalci'nato, -a [skaltʃi'nato] *ag* (*fig peg*) shabby
scalda'bagno [skalda'baɲɲo] *sm* water heater
scal'dare *vt* to heat; **scaldarsi** *vr* to warm up, heat up; (*al fuoco, al sole*) to warm o.s.; (*fig*) to get excited; **~ la sedia** (*fig*) to twiddle one's thumbs
scaldavi'vande *sm inv* dish warmer
scal'dino *sm* (*per mani*) hand-warmer; (*per piedi*) foot-warmer; (*per letto*) bedwarmer
scal'fire *vt* to scratch
scalfit'tura *sf* scratch
scali'nata *sf* staircase
sca'lino *sm* (*anche fig*) step; (*di scala a pioli*) rung
scal'mana *sf* (hot) flush
scalma'narsi *vr* (*affaticarsi*) to rush about, rush around; (*agitarsi, darsi da fare*) to get all hot and bothered; (*arrabbiarsi*) to get excited, get steamed up
scalma'nato, -a *sm/f* hothead
'scalo *sm* (*Naut*) slipway; (*: porto d'approdo*) port of call; (*Aer*) stopover; **fare ~ (a)** (*Naut*) to call (at), put in (at); (*Aer*) to land (at), make a stop (at); **volo senza ~** non-stop flight; **~ merci** (*Ferr*) goods (*Brit*) *o* freight yard
sca'logna [ska'loɲɲa] *sf* (*fam*) bad luck
scalo'gnato, -a [skaloɲ'ɲato] *ag* (*fam*) unlucky
scalop'pina *sf* (*Cuc*) escalope
scal'pello *sm* chisel
scalpi'tare *vi* (*cavallo*) to paw the ground; (*persona*) to stamp one's feet
scal'pore *sm* noise, row; **far ~** (*notizia*) to cause a sensation *o* a stir
'scaltro, -a *ag* cunning, shrewd
scal'zare [skal'tsare] *vt* (*albero*) to bare the roots of; (*muro: fig: autorità*) to undermine
'scalzo, -a ['skaltso] *ag* barefoot
scambi'are *vt* to exchange; (*confondere*): **~ qn/qc per** to take *o* mistake sb/sth for; **mi hanno scambiato il cappello** they've given me the wrong hat
scambi'evole *ag* mutual, reciprocal
'scambio *sm* exchange; (*Comm*) trade; (*Ferr*) points *pl*; **fare (uno) ~** to make a swap; **libero ~** free trade; **scambi con l'estero** foreign trade
scamosci'ato, -a [skamoʃʃato] *ag* suede
scampa'gnata [skampaɲ'ɲata] *sf* trip to the country
scampa'nare *vi* to peal
scam'pare *vt* (*salvare*) to rescue, save; (*evitare: morte, prigione*) to escape ■ *vi*: **~ (a qc)** to survive (sth), escape (sth); **scamparla bella** to have a narrow escape
'scampo *sm* (*salvezza*) escape; (*Zool*) prawn; **cercare ~ nella fuga** to seek safety in flight; **non c'è (via di) ~** there's no way out
'scampolo *sm* remnant
scanala'tura *sf* (*incavo*) channel, groove
scandagli'are [skandaʎ'ʎare] *vt* (*Naut*) to sound; (*fig*) to sound out; to probe

scanda'listico, -a, ci, che *ag* (*settimanale etc*) sensational
scandaliz'zare [skandalid'dzare] *vt* to shock, scandalize; **scandalizzarsi** *vr* to be shocked
'scandalo *sm* scandal; **dare ~** to cause a scandal
scanda'loso, -a *ag* scandalous, shocking
Scandi'navia *sf*: **la ~** Scandinavia
scandi'navo, -a *ag, sm/f* Scandinavian
scan'dire *vt* (*versi*) to scan; (*parole*) to articulate, pronounce distinctly; **~ il tempo** (*Mus*) to beat time
scan'nare *vt* (*animale*) to butcher, slaughter; (*persona*) to cut *o* slit the throat of
'scanner ['skanner] *sm inv* scanner
scanneriz'zare [skannerid'dzare] *vt* to scan
'scanno *sm* seat, bench
scansafa'tiche [skansafa'tike] *sm/f inv* idler, loafer
scan'sare *vt* (*rimuovere*) to move (aside), shift; (*schivare: schiaffo*) to dodge; (*sfuggire*) to avoid; **scansarsi** *vr* to move aside
scan'sia *sf* shelves *pl*; (*per libri*) bookcase
'scanso *sm*: **a ~ di** in order to avoid, as a precaution against; **a ~ di equivoci** to avoid (any) misunderstanding
scanti'nato *sm* basement
scanto'nare *vi* to turn the corner; (*svignarsela*) to sneak off
scanzo'nato, -a [skantso'nato] *ag* easy-going
scapacci'one [skapat'tʃone] *sm* clout, slap
scapes'trato, -a *ag* dissolute
'scapito *sm* (*perdita*) loss; (*danno*) damage, detriment; **a ~ di** to the detriment of
'scapola *sf* shoulder blade
'scapolo *sm* bachelor
scappa'mento *sm* (*Aut*) exhaust
scap'pare *vi* (*fuggire*) to escape; (*andare via in fretta*) to rush off; **~ di prigione** to escape from prison; **~ di mano** (*oggetto*) to slip out of one's hands; **~ di mente a qn** to slip sb's mind; **lasciarsi ~** (*occasione, affare*) to miss, let go by; (*dettaglio*) to overlook; (*parola*) to let slip; (*prigioniero*) to let escape; **mi scappò detto** I let it slip
scap'pata *sf* quick visit *o* call
scappa'tella *sf* escapade
scappa'toia *sf* way out
scara'beo *sm* beetle
scarabocchi'are [skarabok'kjare] *vt* to scribble, scrawl
scara'bocchio [skara'bɔkkjo] *sm* scribble, scrawl
scara'faggio [skara'faddʒo] *sm* cockroach
scaraman'zia [skaraman'tsia] *sf*: **per ~** for luck
scara'muccia, -ce [skara'muttʃa] *sf* skirmish
scaraven'tare *vt* to fling, hurl
scarce'rare [skartʃe'rare] *vt* to release (from prison)
scarcerazi'one [skartʃerat'tsjone] *sf* release (from prison)
scardi'nare *vt* to take off its hinges
'scarica, -che *sf* (*di più armi*) volley of shots; (*di sassi, pugni*) hail, shower; (*Elettr*) discharge; **~ di mitra** burst of machine-gun fire
scari'care *vt* (*merci, camion etc*) to unload; (*passeggeri*) to set down; (*da Internet*) to download; (*arma*) to unload; (*: sparare, Elettr*) to discharge; (*corso d'acqua*) to empty, pour; (*fig: liberare da un peso*) to unburden, relieve; **scaricarsi** *vr* (*orologio*) to run *o* wind down; (*batteria, accumulatore*) to go flat (*Brit*) *o* dead; (*fig: rilassarsi*) to unwind; (*: sfogarsi*) to let off steam; **~ le proprie responsabilità su qn** to off-load one's responsibilities onto sb; **~ la colpa addosso a qn** to blame sb; **il fulmine si scaricò su un albero** the lightning struck a tree
scarica'tore *sm* loader; (*di porto*) docker
'scarico, -a, chi, che *ag* unloaded; (*orologio*) run down; (*batteria, accumulatore*) dead, flat (*Brit*) ■ *sm* (*di merci, materiali*) unloading; (*di immondizie*) dumping, tipping (*Brit*); (*: luogo*) rubbish dump; (*Tecn: deflusso*) draining; (*: dispositivo*) drain; (*Aut*) exhaust; **~ del lavandino** waste outlet
scarlat'tina *sf* scarlet fever
scar'latto, -a *ag* scarlet
'scarno, -a *ag* thin, bony
'scarpa *sf* shoe; **fare le scarpe a qn** (*fig*) to double-cross sb; **scarpe da ginnastica** gym shoes; **scarpe coi tacchi (alti)** high-heeled shoes; **scarpe col tacco basso** low-heeled shoes; **scarpe senza tacco** flat shoes; **scarpe da tennis** tennis shoes
scar'pata *sf* escarpment
scarpi'era *sf* shoe rack
scar'pone *sm* boot; **scarponi da montagna** climbing boots; **scarponi da sci** ski-boots
scarroz'zare [skarrot'tsare] *vt* to drive around
scarseggi'are [skarsed'dʒare] *vi* to be scarce; **~ di** to be short of, lack
scar'sezza [skar'settsa] *sf* scarcity, lack
'scarso, -a *ag* (*insufficiente*) insufficient, meagre (*Brit*), meager (*US*); (*povero: annata*) poor, lean; (*Ins: voto*) poor; **~ di** lacking in; **3 chili scarsi** just under 3 kilos
scartabel'lare *vt* to skim through, glance through
scarta'faccio [skarta'fattʃo] *sm* notebook
scarta'mento *sm* (*Ferr*) gauge; **~ normale/ridotto** standard/narrow gauge

S

scar'tare *vt* (*pacco*) to unwrap; (*idea*) to reject; (*Mil*) to declare unfit for military service; (*carte da gioco*) to discard; (*Calcio*) to dodge (past) ■ *vi* to swerve

'scarto *sm* (*cosa scartata, anche Comm*) reject; (*di veicolo*) swerve; (*differenza*) gap, difference; **~ salariale** wage differential

scar'toffie *sfpl* (*peg*) papers *pl*

scas'sare *vt* (*fam: rompere*) to wreck

scassi'nare *vt* to break, force

'scasso *sm vedi* **furto**

scate'nare *vt* (*fig*) to incite, stir up; **scatenarsi** *vr* (*temporale*) to break; (*rivolta*) to break out; (*persona: infuriarsi*) to rage

scate'nato, -a *ag* wild

'scatola *sf* box; (*di latta*) tin (*Brit*), can; **cibi in ~** tinned (*Brit*) *o* canned foods; **una ~ di cioccolatini** a box of chocolates; **comprare qc a ~ chiusa** to buy sth sight unseen; **~ cranica** cranium

scato'lone *sm* box

scat'tante *ag* quick off the mark; (*agile*) agile

scat'tare *vt* (*fotografia*) to take ■ *vi* (*congegno, molla etc*) to be released; (*balzare*) to spring up; (*Sport*) to put on a spurt; (*fig: per l'ira*) to fly into a rage; (*legge, provvedimento*) to come into effect; **~ in piedi** to spring to one's feet; **far ~** to release

'scatto *sm* (*dispositivo*) release; (*: di arma da fuoco*) trigger mechanism; (*rumore*) click; (*balzo*) jump, start; (*Sport*) spurt; (*fig: di ira etc*) fit; (*: di stipendio*) increment; **di ~** suddenly; **serratura a ~** spring lock

scatu'rire *vi* to gush, spring

scaval'care *vt* (*ostacolo*) to pass (*o* climb) over; (*fig*) to get ahead of, overtake

sca'vare *vt* (*terreno*) to dig; (*legno*) to hollow out; (*pozzo, galleria*) to bore; (*città sepolta etc*) to excavate

scava'trice [skava'tritʃe] *sf* (*macchina*) excavator

scavezza'collo [skavettsa'kɔllo] *sm* daredevil

'scavo *sm* excavating *no pl*; excavation

scazzot'tare [skattsot'tare] *vt* (*fam*) to beat up, give a thrashing to

'scegliere ['ʃeʎʎere] *vt* (*gen*) to choose; (*candidato, prodotto*) to choose, select; **~ di fare** to choose to do

sce'icco, -chi [ʃe'ikko] *sm* sheik

'scelgo *etc* ['ʃelgo] *vb vedi* **scegliere**

scelle'rato, -a [ʃelle'rato] *ag* wicked, evil

scel'lino [ʃel'lino] *sm* shilling

'scelto, -a ['ʃelto] *pp di* **scegliere** ■ *ag* (*gruppo*) carefully selected; (*frutta, verdura*) choice, top quality; (*Mil: specializzato*) crack *cpd*, highly skilled ■ *sf* choice; (*selezione*) selection, choice; **frutta o formaggi a scelta** choice of fruit or cheese; **fare una scelta** to make a choice, choose; **non avere scelta** to have no choice *o* option; **di prima scelta** top grade *o* quality

sce'mare [ʃe'mare] *vt, vi* to diminish

sce'menza [ʃe'mɛntsa] *sf* stupidity *no pl*; stupid thing (to do *o* say)

'scemo, -a ['ʃemo] *ag* stupid, silly

'scempio ['ʃempjo] *sm* slaughter, massacre; (*fig*) ruin; **far ~ di** (*fig*) to play havoc with, ruin

'scena ['ʃɛna] *sf* (*gen*) scene; (*palcoscenico*) stage; **le scene** (*fig: teatro*) the stage; **andare in ~** to be staged *o* put on *o* performed; **mettere in ~** to stage; **uscire di ~** to leave the stage; (*fig*) to leave the scene; **fare una ~** (*fig*) to make a scene; **ha fatto ~ muta** (*fig*) he didn't open his mouth

sce'nario [ʃe'narjo] *sm* scenery; (*di film*) scenario

sce'nata [ʃe'nata] *sf* row, scene

'scendere ['ʃendere] *vi* to go (*o* come) down; (*strada, sole*) to go down; (*notte*) to fall; (*passeggero: fermarsi*) to get out, alight; (*fig: temperatura, prezzi*) to fall, drop ■ *vt* (*scale, pendio*) to go (*o* come) down; **~ dalle scale** to go (*o* come) down the stairs; **~ dal treno** to get off *o* out of the train; **~ dalla macchina** to get out of the car; **~ da cavallo** to dismount, get off one's horse; **~ ad un albergo** to put up *o* stay at a hotel

sceneggi'ato [ʃened'dʒato] *sm* television drama

sceneggia'tore, -'trice [ʃeneddʒa'tore] *sm/f* script-writer

sceneggia'tura [ʃeneddʒa'tura] *sf* (*Teat*) scenario; (*Cine*) screenplay, scenario

'scenico, -a, ci, che ['ʃɛniko] *ag* stage *cpd*

scenogra'fia [ʃenogra'fia] *sf* (*Teat*) stage design; (*Cine*) set design; (*elementi scenici*) scenery

sce'nografo, -a [ʃe'nɔgrafo] *sm/f* set designer

sce'riffo [ʃe'riffo] *sm* sheriff

scervel'larsi [ʃervel'larsi] *vr*: **~ (su qc)** to rack one's brains (over sth)

scervel'lato, -a [ʃervel'lato] *ag* featherbrained

'sceso, -a ['ʃeso] *pp di* **scendere**

scetti'cismo [ʃetti'tʃizmo] *sm* scepticism (*Brit*), skepticism (*US*)

'scettico, -a, ci, che ['ʃɛttiko] *ag* sceptical (*Brit*), skeptical (*US*)

'scettro ['ʃɛttro] *sm* sceptre (*Brit*), scepter (*US*)

'scheda ['skɛda] *sf* (index) card; (*TV, Radio*) (brief) report; **~ audio** (*Inform*) sound card; **~ bianca/nulla** (*Pol*) unmarked/spoiled ballot paper; **~ a circuito stampato** printed-circuit board; ~ **elettorale** ballot paper; ~ **madre** (*Inform*) motherboard; ~ **perforata** punch card; ~ **ricaricabile** (*Tel*) top-up card; ~ **telefonica** phone card; ~ **video** (*Inform*) video card

sche'dare [ske'dare] *vt* (*dati*) to file; (*libri*) to catalogue; (*registrare*: *anche Polizia*) to put on one's files

sche'dario [ske'darjo] *sm* file; (*mobile*) filing cabinet

sche'dato, -a [ske'dato] *ag* with a (police) record ■ *sm/f* person with a (police) record

sche'dina [ske'dina] *sf* ≈ pools coupon (*Brit*)

'scheggia, -ge ['skeddʒa] *sf* splinter, sliver; ~ **impazzita** (*fig*) maverick

sche'letrico, -a, ci, che [ske'lɛtriko] *ag* (*anche Anat*) skeletal; (*fig*: *essenziale*) skeleton *cpd*

'scheletro ['skɛletro] *sm* skeleton; **avere uno ~ nell'armadio** (*fig*) to have a skeleton in the cupboard

'schema, -i ['skɛma] *sm* (*diagramma*) diagram, sketch; (*progetto, abbozzo*) outline, plan; **ribellarsi agli schemi** to rebel against traditional values; **secondo gli schemi tradizionali** in accordance with traditional values

sche'matico, -a, ci, che [ske'matiko] *ag* schematic

schematiz'zare [skematid'dzare] *vt* to schematize

'scherma ['skerma] *sf* fencing

scher'maglia [sker'maʎʎa] *sf* (*fig*) skirmish

scher'mirsi [sker'mirsi] *vr* to defend o.s.

'schermo ['skermo] *sm* shield, screen; (*Cine, TV*) screen

schermogra'fia [skermogra'fia] *sf* X-rays *pl*

scher'nire [sker'nire] *vt* to mock, sneer at

'scherno ['skerno] *sm* mockery, derision; **farsi ~ di** to sneer at; **essere oggetto di ~** to be a laughing stock

scher'zare [sker'tsare] *vi* to joke

'scherzo ['skertso] *sm* joke; (*tiro*) trick; (*Mus*) scherzo; **è uno ~!** (*una cosa facile*) it's child's play!, it's easy!; **per ~** for a joke *o* a laugh; **fare un brutto ~ a qn** to play a nasty trick on sb; **scherzi a parte** seriously, joking apart

scher'zoso, -a [sker'tsoso] *ag* (*tono, gesto*) playful; (*osservazione*) facetious; **è un tipo ~** he likes a joke

schiaccia'noci [skjattʃa'notʃi] *sm inv* nutcracker

schiacci'ante [skjat'tʃante] *ag* overwhelming

schiacci'are [skjat'tʃare] *vt* (*dito*) to crush; (*noci*) to crack; ~ **un pisolino** to have a nap

schiaffeggi'are [skjaffed'dʒare] *vt* to slap

schi'affo ['skjaffo] *sm* slap; **prendere qn a schiaffi** to slap sb's face; **uno ~ morale** a slap in the face, a rebuff

schiamaz'zare [skjamat'tsare] *vi* to squawk, cackle

schia'mazzo [skja'mattso] *sm* (*fig*: *chiasso*) din, racket

schian'tare [skjan'tare] *vt* to break, tear apart; **schiantarsi** *vr* to break (up), shatter; **schiantarsi al suolo** (*aereo*) to crash (to the ground)

schi'anto ['skjanto] *sm* (*rumore*) crash; tearing sound; **è uno ~!** (*fam*) it's (*o* he's *o* she's) terrific!; **di ~** all of a sudden

schia'rire [skja'rire] *vt* to lighten, make lighter ■ *vi* (*anche*: **schiarirsi**) to grow lighter; (*tornar sereno*) to clear, brighten up; **schiarirsi la voce** to clear one's throat

schia'rita [skja'rita] *sf* (*Meteor*) bright spell; (*fig*) improvement, turn for the better

schiat'tare [skjat'tare] *vi* to burst; ~ **d'invidia** to be green with envy; ~ **di rabbia** to be beside o.s. with rage

schiavitù [skjavi'tu] *sf* slavery

schiaviz'zare [skjavid'dzare] *vt* to enslave

schi'avo, -a ['skjavo] *sm/f* slave

schi'ena ['skjɛna] *sf* (*Anat*) back

schie'nale [skje'nale] *sm* (*di sedia*) back

schi'era ['skjɛra] *sf* (*Mil*) rank; (*gruppo*) group, band; **villette a ~** ≈ terraced houses

schiera'mento [skjera'mento] *sm* (*Mil, Sport*) formation; (*fig*) alliance

schie'rare [skje'rare] *vt* (*esercito*) to line up, draw up, marshal; **schierarsi** *vr* to line up; (*fig*): **schierarsi con** *o* **dalla parte di/contro qn** to side with/oppose sb

schi'etto, -a ['skjɛtto] *ag* (*puro*) pure; (*fig*) frank, straightforward

schi'fare [ski'fare] *vt* to disgust

schi'fezza [ski'fettsa] *sf*: **essere una ~** (*cibo, bibita etc*) to be disgusting; (*film, libro*) to be dreadful

schifil'toso, -a [skifil'toso] *ag* fussy, difficult

'schifo ['skifo] *sm* disgust; **fare ~** (*essere fatto male, dare pessimi risultati*) to be awful; **mi fa ~** it makes me sick, it's disgusting; **quel libro è uno ~** that book's rotten

schi'foso, -a [ski'foso] *ag* disgusting, revolting; (*molto scadente*) rotten, lousy

schioc'care [skjok'kare] *vt* (*frusta*) to crack; (*dita*) to snap; (*lingua*) to click; ~ **le labbra** to smack one's lips

schioppet'tata [skjoppet'tata] *sf* gunshot

schi'oppo ['skjɔppo] *sm* rifle, gun

schi'udere ['skjudere] *vt*, **schi'udersi** *vr* to open

S

schi'uma ['skjuma] *sf* foam; (*di sapone*) lather; (*di latte*) froth
schiu'mare [skju'mare] *vt* to skim ▪ *vi* to foam
schi'uso, -a ['skjuso] *pp di* **schiudere**
schi'vare [ski'vare] *vt* to dodge, avoid
'schivo, -a ['skivo] *ag* (*ritroso*) stand-offish, reserved; (*timido*) shy
schizofre'nia [skiddzofre'nia] *sf* schizophrenia
schizo'frenico, -a, ci, che [skiddzo'frɛniko] *ag* schizophrenic
schiz'zare [skit'tsare] *vt* (*spruzzare*) to spurt, squirt; (*sporcare*) to splash, spatter; (*fig: abbozzare*) to sketch ▪ *vi* to spurt, squirt; (*saltar fuori*) to dart up (*o* off *etc*); **~ via** (*animale, persona*) to dart away; (*macchina, moto*) to accelerate away
schizzi'noso, -a [skittsi'noso] *ag* fussy, finicky
'schizzo ['skittso] *sm* (*di liquido*) spurt; splash, spatter; (*abbozzo*) sketch
sci [ʃi] *sm inv* (*attrezzo*) ski; (*attività*) skiing; **~ di fondo** cross-country skiing, ski touring (US); **~ nautico** water-skiing
'scia ['ʃia] (*pl* **scie**) *sf* (*di imbarcazione*) wake; (*di profumo*) trail
scià [ʃa] *sm inv* shah
sci'abola ['ʃabola] *sf* sabre (*Brit*), saber (US)
scia'callo [ʃa'kallo] *sm* jackal; (*fig peg: profittatore*) shark, profiteer; (*: ladro*) looter
sciac'quare [ʃak'kware] *vt* to rinse
scia'gura [ʃa'gura] *sf* disaster, calamity
sciagu'rato, -a [ʃagu'rato] *ag* unfortunate; (*malvagio*) wicked
scialac'quare [ʃalak'kware] *vt* to squander
scia'lare [ʃa'lare] *vi* to throw one's money around
sci'albo, -a ['ʃalbo] *ag* pale, dull; (*fig*) dull, colourless (*Brit*), colorless (US)
sci'alle ['ʃalle] *sm* shawl
sci'alo ['ʃalo] *sm* squandering, waste
scia'luppa [ʃa'luppa] *sf* (*Naut*) sloop; (*anche*: **scialuppa di salvataggio**) lifeboat
scia'mare [ʃa'mare] *vi* to swarm
sci'ame ['ʃame] *sm* swarm
scian'cato, -a [ʃan'kato] *ag* lame; (*mobile*) rickety
sci'are [ʃi'are] *vi* to ski; **andare a ~** to go skiing
sci'arpa ['ʃarpa] *sf* scarf; (*fascia*) sash
scia'tore, -'trice [ʃia'tore] *sm/f* skier
sciat'tezza [ʃat'tettsa] *sf* slovenliness
sci'atto, -a ['ʃatto] *ag* (*persona: nell'aspetto*) slovenly, unkempt; (*: nel lavoro*) sloppy, careless
'scibile ['ʃibile] *sm* knowledge
scien'tifico, -a, ci, che [ʃen'tifiko] *ag* scientific; **la (polizia) scientifica** the forensic department
sci'enza ['ʃɛntsa] *sf* science; (*sapere*) knowledge; **scienze** *sfpl* (*Ins*) science *sg*; **scienze naturali** natural sciences; **scienze politiche** political science *sg*
scienzi'ato, -a [ʃen'tsjato] *sm/f* scientist
'Scilly ['ʃilli]: **le isole ~** *sfpl* the Scilly Isles
'scimmia ['ʃimmja] *sf* monkey
scimmiot'tare [ʃimmjot'tare] *vt* to ape, mimic
scimpanzé [ʃimpan'tse] *sm inv* chimpanzee
scimu'nito, -a [ʃimu'nito] *ag* silly, idiotic
'scindere ['ʃindere] *vt*, **'scindersi** *vr* to split (up)
scin'tilla [ʃin'tilla] *sf* spark
scintil'lare [ʃintil'lare] *vi* to spark; (*acqua, occhi*) to sparkle
scintil'lio [ʃintil'lio] *sm* sparkling
scioc'care [ʃok'kare] *vt* to shock
scioc'chezza [ʃok'kettsa] *sf* stupidity *no pl*; stupid *o* foolish thing; **dire sciocchezze** to talk nonsense
sci'occo, -a, chi, che ['ʃɔkko] *ag* stupid, foolish
sci'ogliere ['ʃɔʎʎere] *vt* (*nodo*) to untie; (*capelli*) to loosen; (*persona, animale*) to untie, release; (*fig: persona*): **~ da** to release from; (*neve*) to melt; (*nell'acqua: zucchero etc*) to dissolve; (*fig: mistero*) to solve; (*porre fine a: contratto*) to cancel; (*: società, matrimonio*) to dissolve; (*: riunione*) to bring to an end; **sciogliersi** *vr* to loosen, come untied; to melt; to dissolve; (*assemblea, corteo, duo*) to break up; **~ i muscoli** to limber up; **~ il ghiaccio** (*fig*) to break the ice; **~ le vele** (*Naut*) to set sail; **sciogliersi dai legami** (*fig*) to free o.s. from all ties
sci'olgo *etc* ['ʃɔlgo] *vb vedi* **sciogliere**
sciol'tezza [ʃol'tettsa] *sf* agility; suppleness; ease
sci'olto, -a ['ʃɔlto] *pp di* **sciogliere** ▪ *ag* loose; (*agile*) agile, nimble; (*disinvolto*) free and easy; **essere ~ nei movimenti** to be supple; **versi sciolti** (*Poesia*) blank verse
sciope'rante [ʃope'rante] *sm/f* striker
sciope'rare [ʃope'rare] *vi* to strike, go on strike
sci'opero ['ʃɔpero] *sm* strike; **fare ~** to strike; **entrare in ~** to go on *o* come out on strike; **~ bianco** work-to-rule (*Brit*), slowdown (US); **~ della fame** hunger strike; **~ selvaggio** wildcat strike; **~ a singhiozzo** on-off strike; **~ di solidarietà** sympathy strike
sciori'nare [ʃori'nare] *vt* (*ostentare*) to show off, display
scio'via [ʃio'via] *sf* ski lift

sciovi'nismo [ʃovi'nizmo] *sm* chauvinism
sciovi'nista, -i, e [ʃovi'nista] *sm/f* chauvinist
sci'pito, -a [ʃi'pito] *ag* insipid
scip'pare [ʃip'pare] *vt*: **~ qn** to snatch sb's bag
scippa'tore [ʃippa'tore] *sm* bag-snatcher
'scippo ['ʃippo] *sm* bag-snatching
sci'rocco [ʃi'rɔkko] *sm* sirocco
sci'roppo [ʃi'rɔppo] *sm* syrup; **~ per la tosse** cough syrup, cough mixture
'scisma, -i ['ʃizma] *sm* (*Rel*) schism
scissi'one [ʃis'sjone] *sf* (*anche fig*) split, division; (*Fisica*) fission
'scisso, -a ['ʃisso] *pp di* **scindere**
sciu'pare [ʃu'pare] *vt* (*abito, libro, appetito*) to spoil, ruin; (*tempo, denaro*) to waste; **sciuparsi** *vr* to get spoilt *o* ruined; (*rovinarsi la salute*) to ruin one's health
scivo'lare [ʃivo'lare] *vi* to slide *o* glide along; (*involontariamente*) to slip, slide
'scivolo ['ʃivolo] *sm* slide; (*Tecn*) chute
scivo'loso, -a [ʃivo'loso] *ag* slippery
scle'rosi *sf* sclerosis
scoc'care *vt* (*freccia*) to shoot ■ *vi* (*guizzare*) to shoot up; (*battere: ora*) to strike
scoccherò *etc* [skokke'rɔ] *vb vedi* **scoccare**
scocci'are [skot'tʃare] *vt* to bother, annoy; **scocciarsi** *vr* to be bothered *o* annoyed
scoccia'tore, -'trice [skottʃa'tore] *sm/f* nuisance, pest (*fam*)
scoccia'tura [skottʃa'tura] *sf* nuisance, bore
sco'della *sf* bowl
scodinzo'lare [skodintso'lare] *vi* to wag its tail
scogli'era [skoʎ'ʎɛra] *sf* reef; (*rupe*) cliff
'scoglio ['skɔʎʎo] *sm* (*al mare*) rock; (*fig: ostacolo*) difficulty, stumbling block
scogli'oso, -a [skoʎ'ʎoso] *ag* rocky
scoi'attolo *sm* squirrel
scola'pasta *sm inv* colander
sco'lare *ag*: **età ~** school age ■ *vt* to drain ■ *vi* to drip
scola'resca *sf* schoolchildren *pl*, pupils *pl*
sco'laro, -a *sm/f* pupil, schoolboy(-girl)
sco'lastico, -a, ci, che *ag* (*gen*) scholastic; (*libro, anno, divisa*) school *cpd*
scol'lare *vt* (*staccare*) to unstick; **scollarsi** *vr* to come unstuck
scol'lato, -a *ag* (*vestito*) low-cut, low-necked; (*donna*) wearing a low-cut dress (*o* blouse *etc*)
scolla'tura *sf* neckline
'scolo *sm* drainage; (*sbocco*) drain; (*acqua*) waste water; **canale di ~** drain; **tubo di ~** drainpipe
scolo'rire *vt* to fade; to discolour (*Brit*) discolor (*US*) ■ *vi* (*anche*: **scolorirsi**) to fade, to become discolo(u)red; (*impallidire*) to turn pale
scol'pire *vt* to carve, sculpt
scombi'nare *vt* to mess up, upset
scombi'nato, -a *ag* confused, muddled
scombusso'lare *vt* to upset
scom'messo, -a *pp di* **scommettere** ■ *sf* bet, wager; **fare una scommessa** to bet
scom'mettere *vt, vi* to bet
scomo'dare *vt* to trouble, bother, disturb; (*fig: nome famoso*) to involve, drag in; **scomodarsi** *vr* to put o.s. out; **scomodarsi a fare** to go to the bother *o* trouble of doing
scomodità *sf inv* (*di sedia, letto etc*) discomfort; (*di orario, sistemazione etc*) inconvenience
'scomodo, -a *ag* uncomfortable; (*sistemazione, posto*) awkward, inconvenient
scompagi'nare [skompadʒi'nare] *vt* to upset, throw into disorder
scompag'nato, -a [skompaɲ'ɲato] *ag* (*calzini, guanti*) odd
scompa'rire *vi* (*sparire*) to disappear, vanish; (*fig*) to be insignificant
scom'parso, -a *pp di* **scomparire** ■ *sf* disappearance; (*fig: morte*) passing away, death
scomparti'mento *sm* (*Ferr*) compartment; (*sezione*) division
scom'parto *sm* compartment, division
scom'penso *sm* imbalance, lack of balance
scompigli'are [skompiʎ'ʎare] *vt* (*cassetto, capelli*) to mess up, disarrange; (*fig: piani*) to upset
scom'piglio [skom'piʎʎo] *sm* mess, confusion
scom'porre *vt* (*parola, numero*) to break up; (*Chim*) to decompose; **scomporsi** *vr* (*Chim*) to decompose; (*fig*) to get upset, lose one's composure; **senza scomporsi** unperturbed
scom'posto, -a *pp di* **scomporre** ■ *ag* (*gesto*) unseemly; (*capelli*) ruffled, dishevelled
sco'munica, -che *sf* excommunication
scomuni'care *vt* to excommunicate
sconcer'tante [skontʃer'tante] *ag* disconcerting
sconcer'tare [skontʃer'tare] *vt* to disconcert, bewilder
'sconcio, -a, ci, ce ['skontʃo] *ag* (*osceno*) indecent, obscene ■ *sm* (*cosa riprovevole, mal fatta*) disgrace
sconclusio'nato, -a *ag* incoherent, illogical
sconfes'sare *vt* to renounce, disavow; to repudiate
scon'figgere [skon'fiddʒere] *vt* to defeat, overcome
sconfi'nare *vi* to cross the border; (*in proprietà privata*) to trespass; (*fig*): **~ da** to stray *o* digress from

S

sconfi'nato, -a *ag* boundless, unlimited
scon'fitto, -a *pp di* **sconfiggere** ■ *sf* defeat
sconfor'tante, -a *ag* discouraging, disheartening
sconfor'tare *vt* to discourage, dishearten; **sconfortarsi** *vr* to become discouraged, become disheartened, lose heart
scon'forto *sm* despondency
sconge'lare [skondʒe'lare] *vt* to defrost
scongiu'rare [skondʒu'rare] *vt* (*implorare*) to beseech, implore; (*eludere: pericolo*) to ward off, avert
scongi'uro [skon'dʒuro] *sm* (*esorcismo*) exorcism; **fare gli scongiuri** to touch wood (*Brit*), knock on wood (*US*)
scon'nesso, -a *ag* (*fig: discorso*) incoherent, rambling
sconosci'uto, -a [skonoʃ'ʃuto] *ag* unknown; new, strange ■ *sm/f* stranger, unknown person
sconquas'sare *vt* to shatter, smash
scon'quasso *sm* (*danno*) damage; (*fig*) confusion
sconside'rato, -a *ag* thoughtless, rash
sconsigli'are [skonsiʎ'ʎare] *vt*: **~ qc a qn** to advise sb against sth; **~ qn dal fare qc** to advise sb not to do *o* against doing sth
sconso'lato, -a *ag* disconsolate
scon'tare *vt* (*Comm: detrarre*) to deduct; (*: debito*) to pay off; (*: cambiale*) to discount; (*pena*) to serve; (*colpa, errori*) to pay for, suffer for
scon'tato, -a *ag* (*previsto*) foreseen, taken for granted; (*prezzo, merce*) discounted, at a discount; **dare per ~ che** to take it for granted that
sconten'tare *vt* to displease, dissatisfy
sconten'tezza [skonten'tettsa] *sf* displeasure, dissatisfaction
scon'tento, -a *ag*: **~ (di)** discontented *o* dissatisfied (with) ■ *sm* discontent, dissatisfaction
'sconto *sm* discount; **fare** *o* **concedere uno ~** to give a discount; **uno ~ del 10%** a 10% discount
scon'trarsi *vr* (*treni etc*) to crash, collide; (*venire ad uno scontro, fig*) to clash; **~ con** to crash into, collide with
scon'trino *sm* ticket
'scontro *sm* (*Mil, fig*) clash; (*di veicoli*) crash, collision; **~ a fuoco** shoot-out
scon'troso, -a *ag* sullen, surly; (*permaloso*) touchy
sconveni'ente *ag* unseemly, improper
sconvol'gente [skonvol'dʒɛnte] *ag* (*notizia, brutta esperienza*) upsetting, disturbing; (*bellezza*) amazing; (*passione*) overwhelming
scon'volgere [skon'vɔldʒere] *vt* to throw into confusion, upset; (*turbare*) to shake, disturb, upset
scon'volto, -a *pp di* **sconvolgere** ■ *ag* (*persona*) distraught, very upset
'scopa *sf* broom; (*Carte*) *Italian card game*
sco'pare *vt* to sweep; (*fam!*) to bonk (*!*)
sco'pata *sf* (*fam!*) bonk (*!*)
scoperchi'are [skoper'kjare] *vt* (*pentola, vaso*) to take the lid off, uncover; (*casa*) to take the roof off
sco'perto, -a *pp di* **scoprire** ■ *ag* uncovered; (*capo*) uncovered, bare; (*macchina*) open; (*Mil*) exposed, without cover; (*conto*) overdrawn ■ *sf* discovery ■ *sm*: **allo ~** (*dormire etc*) out in the open; **assegno ~** uncovered cheque; **avere un conto ~** to be overdrawn
'scopo *sm* aim, purpose; **a che ~?** what for?; **adatto allo ~** fit for its purpose; **allo ~ di fare qc** in order to do sth; **a ~ di lucro** for gain *o* money; **senza ~** (*fare, cercare*) pointlessly
scoppi'are *vi* (*spaccarsi*) to burst; (*esplodere*) to explode; (*fig*) to break out; **~ in pianto** *o* **a piangere** to burst out crying; **~ dalle risa** *o* **dal ridere** to split one's sides laughing; **~ dal caldo** to be boiling; **~ di salute** to be the picture of health
scoppiet'tare *vi* to crackle
'scoppio *sm* explosion; (*di tuono, arma etc*) crash, bang; (*di pneumatico*) bang; (*fig: di guerra*) outbreak; **a ~ ritardato** delayed-action; **reazione a ~ ritardato** delayed *o* slow reaction; **uno ~ di risa** a burst of laughter; **uno ~ di collera** an explosion of anger
sco'prire *vt* to discover; (*liberare da ciò che copre*) to uncover; (*: monumento*) to unveil; **scoprirsi** *vr* to put on lighter clothes; (*fig*) to give o.s. away
scopri'tore, -'trice *sm/f* discoverer
scoraggi'are [skorad'dʒare] *vt* to discourage; **scoraggiarsi** *vr* to become discouraged, lose heart
scor'butico, -a, ci, che *ag* (*fig*) cantankerous
scorcia'toia [skortʃa'toja] *sf* short cut
'scorcio ['skortʃo] *sm* (*Arte*) foreshortening; (*di secolo, periodo*) end, close; **~ panoramico** vista
scor'dare *vt* to forget; **scordarsi** *vr*: **scordarsi di qc/di fare** to forget sth/to do
sco'reggia [sko'reddʒa] (*fam!*) *sf* fart (*!*)
scoreggi'are [skored'dʒare] (*fam!*) *vi* to fart (*!*)
'scorgere ['skɔrdʒere] *vt* to make out, distinguish, see
'sco'ria *sf* (*di metalli*) slag; (*vulcanica*) scoria; **scorie radioattive** (*Fisica*) radioactive waste *sg*

'**scorno** *sm* ignominy, disgrace
scorpacci'ata [skorpat'tʃata] *sf*: **fare una ~ (di)** to stuff o.s. (with), eat one's fill (of)
scorpi'one *sm* scorpion; *(dello zodiaco)*: **S~** Scorpio; **essere dello S~** to be Scorpio
'**scorporo** *sm* *(Pol) transfer of votes aimed at increasing the chances of representation for minority parties*
scorraz'zare [skorrat'tsare] *vi* to run about
'**scorrere** *vt* *(giornale, lettera)* to run *o* skim through ■ *vi* *(liquido, fiume)* to run, flow; *(fune)* to run; *(cassetto, porta)* to slide easily; *(tempo)* to pass (by)
scorre'ria *sf* raid, incursion
scorret'tezza [skorret'tettsa] *sf* incorrectness; lack of politeness, rudeness; unfairness; **commettere una ~** *(essere sleale)* to be unfair
scor'retto, -a *ag* *(sbagliato)* incorrect; *(sgarbato)* impolite; *(sconveniente)* improper; *(sleale)* unfair; *(gioco)* foul
scor'revole *ag* *(porta)* sliding; *(fig: stile)* fluent, flowing
scorri'banda *sf* *(Mil)* raid; *(escursione)* trip, excursion
'**scorsi** *etc vb vedi* **scorgere**
'**scorso, -a** *pp di* **scorrere** ■ *ag* last ■ *sf* quick look, glance; **lo ~ mese** last month
scor'soio, -a *ag*: **nodo ~** noose
'**scorta** *sf* *(di personalità, convoglio)* escort; *(provvista)* supply, stock; **sotto la ~ di due agenti** escorted by two policemen; **fare ~ di** to stock up with, get in a supply of; **di ~** *(materiali)* spare; **ruota di ~** spare wheel
scor'tare *vt* to escort
scor'tese *ag* discourteous, rude
scorte'sia *sf* discourtesy, rudeness; *(azione)* discourtesy
scorti'care *vt* to skin
'**scorto, -a** *pp di* **scorgere**
'**scorza** ['skɔrdza] *sf* *(di albero)* bark; *(di agrumi)* peel, skin
sco'sceso, -a [skoʃ'ʃeso] *ag* steep
'**scosso, -a** *pp di* **scuotere** ■ *ag* *(turbato)* shaken, upset ■ *sf* jerk, jolt, shake; *(Elettr, fig)* shock; **prendere la scossa** to get an electric shock; **scossa di terremoto** earth tremor
scos'sone *sm*: **dare uno ~ a qn** to give sb a shake; **procedere a scossoni** to jolt *o* jerk along
scos'tante *ag* *(fig)* off-putting *(Brit)*, unpleasant
scos'tare *vt* to move (away), shift; **scostarsi** *vr* to move away
scostu'mato, -a *ag* immoral, dissolute

scotch [skɔtʃ] *sm inv* *(whisky)* Scotch® *(nastro adesivo)* Scotch tape®, Sellotape®
scot'tante *ag* *(fig: urgente)* pressing; *(: delicato)* delicate
scot'tare *vt* *(ustionare)* to burn; *(: con liquido bollente)* to scald ■ *vi* to burn; *(caffè)* to be too hot
scotta'tura *sf* burn; scald
'**scotto, -a** *ag* overcooked ■ *sm* *(fig)*: **pagare lo ~ (di)** to pay the penalty (for)
sco'vare *vt* to drive out, flush out; *(fig)* to discover
'**Scozia** ['skɔttsja] *sf*: **la ~** Scotland
scoz'zese [skot'tsese] *ag* Scottish ■ *sm/f* Scot
screan'zato, -a [skrean'tsato] *ag* ill-mannered ■ *sm/f* boor
scredi'tare *vt* to discredit
scre'mare *vt* to skim
scre'mato, -a *ag* skimmed; **parzialmente ~** semi-skimmed
screpo'lare *vt*, **screpo'larsi** *vr* to crack
screpola'tura *sf* cracking *no pl*; crack
screzi'ato, -a [skret'tsjato] *ag* streaked
'**screzio** ['skrɛttsjo] *sm* disagreement
scribac'chino [skribak'kino] *sm* *(peg: impiegato)* penpusher; *(: scrittore)* hack
scricchio'lare [skrikkjo'lare] *vi* to creak, squeak
scricchio'lio [skrikkjo'lio] *sm* creaking
'**scricciolo** ['skrittʃolo] *sm* wren
'**scrigno** ['skriɲɲo] *sm* casket
scrimina'tura *sf* parting
'**scrissi** *etc vb vedi* **scrivere**
'**scritto, -a** *pp di* **scrivere** ■ *ag* written ■ *sm* writing; *(lettera)* letter, note ■ *sf* inscription; **scritti** *smpl* *(letterari etc)* work(s), writings; **per** *o* **in ~** in writing
scrit'toio *sm* writing desk
scrit'tore, -'trice *sm/f* writer
scrit'tura *sf* writing; *(Comm)* entry; *(contratto)* contract; *(Rel)*: **la Sacra S~** the Scriptures *pl*; **scritture** *sfpl* *(Comm)* accounts, books
scrittu'rare *vt* *(Teat, Cine)* to sign up, engage; *(Comm)* to enter
scriva'nia *sf* desk
scri'vano *sm* *(amanuense)* scribe; *(impiegato)* clerk
scri'vente *sm/f* writer
'**scrivere** *vt* to write; **come si scrive?** how is it spelt?, how do you write it?; **~ qc a qn** to write sth to sb; **~ qc a macchina** to type sth; **~ a penna/matita** to write in pen/pencil; **~ qc maiuscolo/minuscolo** to write sth in capital/small letters
scroc'care *vt* *(fam)* to scrounge, cadge
scroc'cone, -a *sm/f* scrounger

S

'scrofa *sf* (*Zool*) sow
scrol'lare *vt* to shake; **scrollarsi** *vr* (*anche fig*) to give o.s. a shake; **~ le spalle/il capo** to shrug one's shoulders/shake one's head; **scrollarsi qc di dosso** (*anche fig*) to shake sth off
scrol'lata *sf* shake; **~ di spalle** shrug (of one's shoulders)
scrosci'ante [skroʃʃante] *ag* (*pioggia*) pouring; (*fig: applausi*) thunderous
scrosci'are [skroʃʃare] *vi* (*pioggia*) to pour down, pelt down; (*torrente, fig: applausi*) to thunder, roar
'scroscio ['skrɔʃʃo] *sm* pelting; thunder, roar; (*di applausi*) burst
scros'tare *vt* (*intonaco*) to scrape off, strip; **scrostarsi** *vr* to peel off, flake off
'scrupolo *sm* scruple; (*meticolosità*) care, conscientiousness; **essere senza scrupoli** to be unscrupulous
scrupo'loso, -a *ag* scrupulous; conscientious
scru'tare *vt* to scrutinize; (*intenzioni, causa*) to examine, scrutinize
scruta'tore, -'trice *sm/f* (*Pol*) scrutineer
scruti'nare *vt* (*voti*) to count
scru'tinio *sm* (*votazione*) ballot; (*insieme delle operazioni*) poll; (*Ins*) *meeting for assignment of marks at end of a term or year*
scu'cire [sku'tʃire] *vt* (*orlo etc*) to unpick, undo; **scucirsi** *vr* to come unstitched
scude'ria *sf* stable
scu'detto *sm* (*Sport*) (championship) shield; (*distintivo*) badge
scu'discio [sku'diʃʃo] *sm* (riding) crop, (riding) whip
'scudo *sm* shield; **farsi ~ di** *o* **con qc** to shield o.s. with sth; **~ aereo/missilistico** air/missile defence (*Brit*) *o* defense (*US*); **~ termico** heat shield
sculacci'are [skulat'tʃare] *vt* to spank
sculacci'one [skulat'tʃone] *sm* spanking
scul'tore, -'trice *sm/f* sculptor
scul'tura *sf* sculpture
scu'ola *sf* school; **~ elementare** *o* **primaria** primary (*Brit*) *o* grade (*US*) school (*for children from 6 to 11 years of age*); **~ guida** driving school; **~ materna** *o* **dell'infanzia** nursery school (*for children aged 3 to 6*); **~ secondaria di primo grado** *first 3 years of secondary school, for children from 11 to 14 years of age*; **~ secondaria di secondo grado** secondary school (*for children aged 14 to 18*); **~ dell'obbligo** compulsory education; **~ privata/pubblica** private/state school; **scuole serali** evening classes, night school *sg*; **~ tecnica** technical college; *see note*

SCUOLA

Italian children first go to school at the age of three. They remain at the "scuola materna" until they are six, when they move on to the "scuola primaria" for another five years. After this come three years of "scuola secondaria di primo grado". Students who wish to continue their schooling attend "scuola secondaria di secondo grado", choosing between several types of institution which specialize in different subject areas.

scu'otere *vt* to shake; **scuotersi** *vr* to jump, be startled; (*fig: muoversi*) to rouse o.s., stir o.s.; (*: turbarsi*) to be shaken
'scure *sf* axe, ax (*US*)
scu'rire *vt* to darken, make darker
'scuro, -a *ag* dark; (*fig: espressione*) grim ■ *sm* darkness; dark colour (*Brit*) *o* color (*US*); (*imposta*) (window) shutter; **verde/rosso** *etc* **~** dark green/red *etc*
scur'rile *ag* scurrilous
'scusa *sf* excuse; **scuse** *sfpl* apology *sg*, apologies; **chiedere ~ a qn (per)** to apologize to sb (for); **chiedo ~** I'm sorry; (*disturbando etc*) excuse me; **vi prego di accettare le mie scuse** please accept my apologies
scu'sare *vt* to excuse; **scusarsi** *vr*: **scusarsi (di)** to apologize (for); **(mi) scusi** I'm sorry; (*per richiamare l'attenzione*) excuse me
S.C.V. *sigla* = **Stato della Città del Vaticano**
sdebi'tarsi *vt*: **~ (con qn di** *o* **per qc)** (*anche fig*) to repay (sb for sth)
sde'gnare [zdeɲ'ɲare] *vt* to scorn, despise; **sdegnarsi** *vr* (*adirarsi*) to get angry
sde'gnato, -a [zdeɲ'ɲato] *ag* indignant, angry
'sdegno ['zdeɲɲo] *sm* scorn, disdain
sdegnosa'mente [zdeɲɲosa'mente] *av* scornfully, disdainfully
sde'gnoso, -a [zdeɲ'ɲoso] *ag* scornful, disdainful
sdilin'quirsi *vr* (*illanguidirsi*) to become sentimental
sdoga'nare *vt* (*Comm*) to clear through customs
sdolci'nato, -a [zdoltʃi'nato] *ag* mawkish, oversentimental
sdoppia'mento *sm* (*Chim: di composto*) splitting; (*Psic*): **~ della personalità** split personality
sdoppi'are *vt* (*dividere*) to divide *o* split in two
sdrai'arsi *vr* to stretch out, lie down
'sdraio *sm*: **sedia a ~** deck chair

sdrammatiz'zare [zdrammatid'dzare] *vt* to play down, minimize
sdruccio'lare [zdruttʃo'lare] *vi* to slip, slide
sdruccio'levole [zdruttʃo'levole] *ag* slippery
sdru'cito, -a [zdru'tʃito] *ag* (*strappato*) torn; (*logoro*) threadbare

PAROLA CHIAVE

se *pron vedi* **si**
■ *cong* **1** (*condizionale, ipotetica*) if; **se nevica non vengo** I won't come if it snows; **se fossi in te** if I were you; **sarei rimasto se me l'avessero chiesto** I would have stayed if they'd asked me; **non puoi fare altro se non telefonare** all you can do is phone; **se mai** if, if ever; **siamo noi se mai che le siamo grati** it is we who should be grateful to you; **se no** (*altrimenti*) or (else), otherwise; **se non** (*anzi*) if not; (*tranne*) except; **se non altro** if nothing else, at least; **se solo** *o* **solamente** if only
2 (*in frasi dubitative, interrogative indirette*) if, whether; **non so se scrivere o telefonare** I don't know whether *o* if I should write or phone

S.E. *abbr* (= *sud-est*) SE; (= *Sua Eccellenza*) HE
sé *pron* (*gen*) oneself; (*esso, essa, lui, lei, loro*) itself; himself; herself; themselves; **sé stesso(a)** oneself; itself; himself; herself; **sé stessi(e)** (*pl*) themselves; **di per sé non è un problema** it's no problem in itself; **parlare tra sé e sé** to talk to oneself; **va da sé che ...** it goes without saying that ..., it's obvious that ..., it stands to reason that ...; **è un caso a sé** *o* **a sé stante** it's a special case; **un uomo che s'è fatto da sé** a self-made man
S.E.A.T.O. *sigla f* (= *Southeast Asia Treaty Organization*) SEATO
seb'bene *cong* although, though
'sebo *sm* sebum
sec. *abbr* (= *secolo*) c
'SECAM *sigla m* (= *séquentiel couleur à mémoire*) SECAM
'secca *sf vedi* **secco**
secca'mente *av* (*rispondere, rifiutare*) sharply, curtly
sec'care *vt* to dry; (*prosciugare*) to dry up; (*fig: importunare*) to annoy, bother ■ *vi* to dry; to dry up; **seccarsi** *vr* to dry; to dry up; (*fig*) to grow annoyed; **si è seccato molto** he was very annoyed
sec'cato, -a *ag* (*fig: infastidito*) bothered, annoyed; (*: stufo*) fed up
secca'tore, -'trice *sm/f* nuisance, bother
secca'tura *sf* (*fig*) bother *no pl*, trouble *no pl*

seccherò *etc* [sekke'rɔ] *vb vedi* **seccare**
'secchia ['sekkja] *sf* bucket, pail
secchi'ello [sek'kjɛllo] *sm* (*per bambini*) bucket, pail
'secchio ['sekkjo] *sm* bucket, pail; **~ della spazzatura** *o* **delle immondizie** dustbin (*Brit*), garbage can (*US*)
'secco, -a, chi, che *ag* dry; (*fichi, pesce*) dried; (*foglie, ramo*) withered; (*magro: persona*) thin, skinny; (*fig: risposta, modo di fare*) curt, abrupt; (*: colpo*) clean, sharp ■ *sm* (*siccità*) drought ■ *sf* (*del mare*) shallows *pl*; **restarci ~** (*fig: morire sul colpo*) to drop dead; **avere la gola secca** to feel dry, be parched; **lavare a ~** to dry-clean; **tirare a ~** (*barca*) to beach
secen'tesco, -a, schi, sche [setʃen'tesko] *ag* = **seicentesco**
se'cernere [se'tʃɛrnere] *vt* to secrete
seco'lare *ag* age-old, centuries-old; (*laico, mondano*) secular
'secolo *sm* century; (*epoca*) age
se'conda *sf vedi* **secondo**; **la S~ Repubblica** *see note*

SECONDA REPUBBLICA

Seconda Repubblica is the term used, especially by the Italian media, to refer to the government and the country in general since the 1994 elections. This is when the old party system collapsed, following the "Tangentopoli" scandals. New political parties were set up and the electoral system was reformed, a first-past-the-post element being introduced side by side with proportional representation.

secondaria'mente *av* secondly
secon'dario, -a *ag* secondary; **scuola/istruzione secondaria** secondary school/education
secon'dino *sm* prison officer, warder (*Brit*)
se'condo, -a *ag* second ■ *sm* second; (*di pranzo*) main course ■ *sf* (*Aut*) second (gear); (*Ferr*) second class ■ *prep* according to; (*nel modo prescritto*) in accordance with; **~ me** in my opinion, to my mind; **~ la legge/quanto si era deciso** in accordance with the law/the decision taken; **di seconda classe** second-class; **di seconda mano** second-hand; **viaggiare in seconda** to travel second-class; **comandante in seconda** second-in-command; **a seconda di** *prep* according to; in accordance with
secondo'genito, -a [sekondo'dʒɛnito] *sm/f* second-born

secrezi'one [sekret'tsjone] *sf* secretion
'sedano *sm* celery
se'dare *vt* (*dolore*) to soothe; (*rivolta*) to put down, suppress
seda'tivo, -a *ag, sm* sedative
'sede *sf* (*luogo di residenza*) (place of) residence; (*di ditta: principale*) head office; (*: secondaria*) branch (office); (*di organizzazione*) headquarters *pl*; (*di governo, parlamento*) seat; (*Rel*) see; **in ~ di** (*in occasione di*) during; **in altra ~** on another occasion; **in ~ legislativa** in legislative sitting; **prendere ~** to take up residence; **un'azienda con diverse sedi in città** a firm with several branches in the city; **~ centrale** head office; **~ sociale** registered office
seden'tario, -a *ag* sedentary
se'dere *vi* to sit, be seated; **sedersi** *vr* to sit down ■ *sm* (*deretano*) bottom; **posto a ~** seat
'sedia *sf* chair; **~ elettrica** electric chair; **~ a rotelle** wheelchair
sedi'cenne [sedi'tʃɛnne] *ag, sm/f* sixteen-year-old
sedi'cente [sedi'tʃɛnte] *ag* self-styled
sedi'cesimo, -a [sedi'tʃɛzimo] *num* sixteenth
'sedici ['seditʃi] *num* sixteen
se'dile *sm* seat; (*panchina*) bench
sedimen'tare *vi* to leave a sediment
sedi'mento *sm* sediment
sedizi'one [sedit'tsjone] *sf* revolt, rebellion
sedizi'oso, -a [sedit'tsjoso] *ag* seditious
se'dotto, -a *pp di* **sedurre**
sedu'cente [sedu'tʃɛnte] *ag* seductive; (*proposta*) very attractive
se'durre *vt* to seduce
se'duta *sf* session, sitting; (*riunione*) meeting; **essere in ~** to be in session, be sitting; **~ stante** (*fig*) immediately; **~ spiritica** seance
sedut'tore, -'trice *sm/f* seducer/seductress
seduzi'one [sedut'tsjone] *sf* seduction; (*fascino*) charm, appeal
SEeO *abbr* (*= salvo errori e omissioni*) E & OE
'sega, -ghe *sf* saw; **~ circolare** circular saw; **~ a mano** handsaw
'segale *sf* rye
se'gare *vt* to saw; (*recidere*) to saw off
sega'tura *sf* (*residuo*) sawdust
'seggio ['sɛddʒo] *sm* seat; **~ elettorale** polling station
'seggiola ['sɛddʒola] *sf* chair
seggio'lino [seddʒo'lino] *sm* seat; (*per bambini*) child's chair; **~ di sicurezza** (*Aut*) child safety seat
seggio'lone [seddʒo'lone] *sm* (*per bambini*) highchair
seggio'via [seddʒo'via] *sf* chairlift
seghe'ria [sege'ria] *sf* sawmill
segherò *etc* [sege'rɔ] *vb vedi* **segare**
seghet'tato, -a [seget'tato] *ag* serrated
se'ghetto [se'getto] *sm* hacksaw
seg'mento *sm* segment
segna'lare [seɲɲa'lare] *vt* (*essere segno di*) to indicate, be a sign of; (*avvertire*) to signal; (*menzionare*) to indicate; (*: fatto, risultato, aumento*) to report; (*: errore, dettaglio*) to point out; (*Aut*) to signal, indicate; **segnalarsi** *vr* (*distinguersi*) to distinguish o.s.; **~ qn a qn** (*per lavoro etc*) to bring sb to sb's attention
segnalazi'one [seɲɲalat'tsjone] *sf* (*azione*) signalling; (*segnale*) signal; (*annuncio*) report; (*raccomandazione*) recommendation
se'gnale [seɲ'ɲale] *sm* signal; (*cartello*): **~ stradale** road sign; **~ acustico** acoustic *o* sound signal; (*di segreteria telefonica*) tone; **~ d'allarme** alarm; (*Ferr*) communication cord; **~ di linea libera** (*Tel*) dialling (*Brit*) *o* dial (*US*) tone; **~ luminoso** light signal; **~ di occupato** (*Tel*) engaged tone (*Brit*), busy signal (*US*); **~ orario** (*Radio*) time signal
segna'letica [seɲɲa'lɛtika] *sf* signalling, signposting; **~ stradale** road signs *pl*
segna'libro [seɲɲa'libro] *sm* (*anche Inform*) bookmark
segna'punti [seɲɲa'punti] *sm/f inv* scorer, scorekeeper
se'gnare [seɲ'ɲare] *vt* to mark; (*prendere nota*) to note; (*indicare*) to indicate, mark; (*Sport: goal*) to score; **segnarsi** *vr* (*Rel*) to make the sign of the cross, cross o.s.
'segno ['seɲɲo] *sm* sign; (*impronta, contrassegno*) mark; (*bersaglio*) target; **fare ~ di sì/no** to nod (one's head)/shake one's head; **fare ~ a qn di fermarsi** to motion (to) sb to stop; **cogliere** *o* **colpire nel ~** (*fig*) to hit the mark; **in** *o* **come ~ d'amicizia** as a mark *o* token of friendship; **"segni particolari"** (*su documento etc*) "distinguishing marks"
segre'gare *vt* to segregate, isolate
segregazi'one [segregat'tsjone] *sf* segregation
se'greta *sf vedi* **segreto**
segre'tario, -a *sm/f* secretary; **~ comunale** town clerk; **~ del partito** party leader; **S~ di Stato** Secretary of State
segrete'ria *sf* (*di ditta, scuola*) (secretary's) office; (*d'organizzazione internazionale*) secretariat; (*Pol etc: carica*) office of Secretary; **~ telefonica** answering service
segre'tezza [segre'tettsa] *sf* secrecy; **notizie della massima ~** confidential information; **in tutta ~** in secret; (*confidenzialmente*) in confidence
se'greto, -a *ag* secret ■ *sm* secret ■ *sf* dungeon; **in ~** in secret, secretly; **il ~**

professionale professional secrecy; **un ~ professionale** a professional secret
segu'ace [se'gwatʃe] *sm/f* follower, disciple
segu'ente *ag* following, next; **nel modo ~** as follows, in the following way
se'gugio [se'gudʒo] *sm* hound, hunting dog; (*fig*) private eye, sleuth
segu'ire *vt* to follow; (*frequentare: corso*) to attend ■ *vi* to follow; (*continuare: testo*) to continue; **~ i consigli di qn** to follow *o* to take sb's advice; **~ gli avvenimenti di attualità** to follow *o* keep up with current events; **come segue** as follows; **"segue"** "to be continued"
segui'tare *vt* to continue, carry on with ■ *vi* to continue, carry on
'seguito *sm* (*scorta*) suite, retinue; (*discepoli*) followers *pl*; (*serie*) sequence, series *sg*; (*continuazione*) continuation; (*conseguenza*) result; **di ~** at a stretch, on end; **in ~** later on; **in ~ a, a ~ di** following; (*a causa di*) as a result of, owing to; **essere al ~ di qn** to be among sb's suite, be one of sb's retinue; **non aver ~** (*conseguenze*) to have no repercussions; **facciamo ~ alla lettera del ...** further to *o* in answer to your letter of ...
'sei *vb vedi* **essere** ■ *num* six
Sei'celle [sei'tʃɛlle] *sfpl*: **le ~** the Seychelles
seicen'tesco, -a, schi, sche [seitʃen'tesko] *ag* seventeenth-century
sei'cento [sei'tʃɛnto] *num* six hundred ■ *sm*: **il S~** the seventeenth century
sei'mila *num* six thousand
'selce ['seltʃe] *sf* flint, flintstone
selci'ato [sel'tʃato] *sm* cobbled surface
selet'tivo, -a *ag* selective
selet'tore *sm* (*Tecn*) selector
selezio'nare [selettsjo'nare] *vt* to select
selezi'one [selet'tsjone] *sf* selection; **fare una ~** to make a selection *o* choice
'sella *sf* saddle
sel'lare *vt* to saddle
sel'lino *sm* saddle
seltz *sm inv* soda (water)
'selva *sf* (*bosco*) wood; (*foresta*) forest
selvag'gina [selvad'dʒina] *sf* (*animali*) game
sel'vaggio, -a, gi, ge [sel'vaddʒo] *ag* wild; (*tribù*) savage, uncivilized; (*fig: brutale*) savage, brutal; (*: incontrollato: fenomeno, aumento etc*) uncontrolled ■ *sm/f* savage; **inflazione selvaggia** runaway inflation
sel'vatico, -a, ci, che *ag* wild
S.Em. *abbr* (= *Sua Eminenza*) HE
se'maforo *sm* (*Aut*) traffic lights *pl*
se'mantico, -a *ag* semantic ■ *sf* semantics *sg*
sembi'anza [sem'bjantsa] *sf* (*poetico: aspetto*) appearance; **sembianze** *sfpl* (*lineamenti*) features; (*fig: falsa apparenza*) semblance *sg*
sem'brare *vi* to seem ■ *vb impers*: **sembra che** it seems that; **mi sembra che** it seems to me that; (*penso che*) I think (that); **~ di essere** to seem to be; **non mi sembra vero!** I can't believe it!
'seme *sm* seed; (*sperma*) semen; (*Carte*) suit
se'mente *sf* seed
semes'trale *ag* (*che dura 6 mesi*) six-month *cpd*; (*che avviene ogni 6 mesi*) six-monthly
se'mestre *sm* half-year, six-month period
'semi ... *prefisso* semi ...
semi'cerchio [semi'tʃerkjo] *sm* semicircle
semicondut'tore *sm* semiconductor
semidetenzi'one [semideten'tsjone] *sf* *custodial sentence whereby individual must spend a minimum of 10 hours per day in prison*
semifi'nale *sf* semifinal
semi'freddo, -a *ag* (*Cuc*) chilled ■ *sm* ice-cream cake
semilibertà *sf* *custodial sentence which allows prisoner to study or work outside prison for part of the day*
'semina *sf* (*Agr*) sowing
semi'nare *vt* to sow
semi'nario *sm* seminar; (*Rel*) seminary
semi'nato *sm*: **uscire dal ~** (*fig*) to wander off the point
seminter'rato *sm* basement; (*appartamento*) basement flat (*Brit*) *o* apartment (*US*)
semi'ologo, -a, gi, ghe *sm/f* semiologist
semi'otica *sf* semiotics *sg*
se'mitico, -a, ci, che *ag* semitic
semivu'oto, -a *ag* half-empty
sem'mai = **se mai**
'semola *sf* bran; **~ di grano duro** durum wheat
semo'lato *ag*: **zucchero ~** caster sugar
semo'lino *sm* semolina
'semplice ['semplitʃe] *ag* simple; (*di un solo elemento*) single; **è una ~ formalità** it's a mere formality
semplice'mente [semplitʃe'mente] *av* simply
sempli'cistico, -a, ci, che [sempli'tʃistiko] *ag* simplistic
semplicità [semplitʃi'ta] *sf* simplicity
semplifi'care *vt* to simplify
semplificazi'one [semplifikat'tsjone] *sf* simplification; **fare una ~ di** to simplify
'sempre *av* always; (*ancora*) still; **posso ~ tentare** I can always *o* still try; **da ~** always; **per ~** forever; **una volta per ~** once and for all; **~ che** *cong* as long as, provided (that); **~ più** more and more; **~ meno** less and less; **va ~ meglio** things are getting better and better; **è ~ più giovane** she gets younger and

S

younger; **è ~ meglio che niente** it's better than nothing; **è (pur) ~ tuo fratello** he is still your brother (however); **c'è ~ la possibilità che ...** there's still a chance that ..., there's always the possibility that ...
sempre'verde *ag, sm o f (Bot)* evergreen
Sen. *abbr (= senatore)* Sen.
'senape *sf (Cuc)* mustard
se'nato *sm* senate; **il S~** *see note*

SENATO

The *Senato* is the upper house of the Italian parliament, with similar functions to the "Camera dei deputati". Candidates must be at least 40 years of age and electors must be 25 or over. Elections are held every five years. Former heads of state become senators for life, as do five distinguished members of the public who are chosen by the head of state for their scientific, social, artistic or literary achievements. the chamber is presided over by the "Presidente del Senato", who is elected by the senators.

sena'tore, -'trice *sm/f* senator
'Senegal *sm*: **il ~** Senegal
senega'lese *ag, sm/f* Senegalese *inv*
se'nese *ag* of (*o* from) Siena
se'nile *ag* senile
'Senna *sf*: **la ~** the Seine
'senno *sm* judgment, (common) sense; **col ~ di poi** with hindsight
sennò *av* = **se no**
'seno *sm (Anat: petto, mammella)* breast; *(: grembo, fig)* womb; *(: cavità)* sinus; *(Geo)* inlet, creek; *(Mat)* sine; **in ~ al partito/all'organizzazione** within the party/the organization
sen'sale *sm (Comm)* agent
sensa'tezza [sensa'tettsa] *sf* good sense, good judgment
sen'sato, -a *ag* sensible
sensazio'nale [sensattsjo'nale] *ag* sensational
sensazi'one [sensat'tsjone] *sf* feeling, sensation; **fare ~** to cause a sensation, create a stir; **avere la ~ che** to have a feeling that
sen'sibile *ag* sensitive; *(ai sensi)* perceptible; *(rilevante, notevole)* appreciable, noticeable; **~ a** sensitive to
sensibilità *sf* sensitivity
sensibiliz'zare [sensibilid'dzare] *vt (fig)* to make aware, awaken
'senso *sm (Fisiol, istinto)* sense; *(impressione, sensazione)* feeling, sensation; *(significato)* meaning, sense; *(direzione)* direction; **sensi** *smpl (coscienza)* consciousness *sg*; *(sensualità)* senses; **perdere/riprendere i sensi** to lose/regain consciousness; **avere ~ pratico** to be practical; **avere un sesto ~** to have a sixth sense; **fare ~ a** *(ripugnare)* to disgust, repel; **ciò non ha ~** that doesn't make sense; **senza** *o* **privo di ~** meaningless; **nel ~ che** in the sense that; **nel vero ~ della parola** in the true sense of the word; **nel ~ della lunghezza** lengthwise, lengthways; **nel ~ della larghezza** widthwise; **ho dato disposizioni in quel ~** I've given instructions to that end *o* effect; **~ comune** common sense; **~ del dovere** sense of duty; **in ~ opposto** in the opposite direction; **in ~ orario/antiorario** clockwise/anticlockwise; **~ dell'umorismo** sense of humour; **a ~ unico** one-way; **"~ vietato"** *(Aut)* "no entry"
sensu'ale *ag* sensual; sensuous
sensualità *sf* sensuality; sensuousness
sen'tenza [sen'tɛntsa] *sf (Dir)* sentence; *(massima)* maxim
sentenzi'are [senten'tsjare] *vi (Dir)* to pass judgment
senti'ero *sm* path
sentimen'tale *ag* sentimental; *(vita, avventura)* love *cpd*
senti'mento *sm* feeling
senti'nella *sf* sentry
sen'tire *vt (percepire al tatto, fig)* to feel; *(udire)* to hear; *(ascoltare)* to listen to; *(odore)* to smell; *(avvertire con il gusto, assaggiare)* to taste ■ *vi*: **~ di** *(avere sapore)* to taste of; *(avere odore)* to smell of; **sentirsi** *vr (uso reciproco)* to be in touch; **sentirsi bene/male** to feel well/unwell *o* ill; **sentirsi di fare qc** *(essere disposto)* to feel like doing sth; **~ la mancanza di qn** to miss sb; **ho sentito dire che ...** I have heard that ...; **a ~ lui ...** to hear him talk ...; **fatti ~** keep in touch; **intendo ~ il mio legale/il parere di un medico** I'm going to consult my lawyer/a doctor
sentita'mente *av* sincerely; **ringraziare ~** to thank sincerely
sen'tito, -a *ag (sincero)* sincere, warm; **per ~ dire** by hearsay
sen'tore *sm* rumour *(Brit)*, rumor *(US)*, talk; **aver ~ di qc** to hear about sth
'senza ['sɛntsa] *prep, cong* without; **~ dir nulla** without saying a word; **~ dire che ...** not to mention the fact that ...; **~ contare che ...** without considering that ...; **fare ~ qc** to do without sth; **~ di me** without me; **~ che io lo sapessi** without me *o* my knowing; **~ amici** friendless; **senz'altro** of course, certainly; **~ dubbio** no doubt; **~ scrupoli**

unscrupulous; **i ~ lavoro** the jobless, the unemployed; **i ~ tetto** the homeless

senza'tetto [sentsa'tetto] *sm/f inv* homeless person; **i** ~ the homeless

sepa'rare *vt* to separate; (*dividere*) to divide; (*tenere distinto*) to distinguish; **separarsi** *vr* (*coniugi*) to separate, part; (*amici*) to part; **separarsi da** (*coniuge*) to separate *o* part from; (*amico, socio*) to part company with; (*oggetto*) to part with

separata'mente *av* separately

sepa'rato, -a *ag* (*letti, conto etc*) separate; (*coniugi*) separated

separazi'one [separat'tsjone] *sf* separation; **~ dei beni** division of property

séparé [sepa're] *sm inv* screen

se'polcro *sm* sepulchre (*Brit*), sepulcher (*US*)

se'polto, -a *pp di* **seppellire**

sepol'tura *sf* burial; **dare ~ a qn** to bury sb

seppel'lire *vt* to bury

'seppi *etc vb vedi* **sapere**

'seppia *sf* cuttlefish ■ *ag inv* sepia

sep'pure *cong* even if

se'quela *sf* (*di avvenimenti*) series, sequence; (*di offese, ingiurie*) string

se'quenza [se'kwentsa] *sf* sequence

sequenzi'ale [sekwen'tsjale] *ag* sequential

seques'trare *vt* (*Dir*) to impound; (*rapire*) to kidnap; (*costringere in un luogo*) to keep, confine

se'questro *sm* (*Dir*) impoundment; **~ di persona** kidnapping

se'quoia *sf* sequoia

'sera *sf* evening; **di** ~ in the evening; **domani** ~ tomorrow evening, tomorrow night; **questa** ~ this evening, tonight

se'rale *ag* evening *cpd*; **scuola ~** evening classes *pl*, night school

se'rata *sf* evening; (*ricevimento*) party

ser'bare *vt* to keep; (*mettere da parte*) to put aside; **~ rancore/odio verso qn** to bear sb a grudge/hate sb

serba'toio *sm* tank; (*cisterna*) cistern

'serbo *ag* Serbian ■ *sm/f* Serbian, Serb ■ *sm* (*Ling*) Serbian; (*il serbare*): **mettere/tenere** *o* **avere in ~ qc** to put/keep sth aside

serbocro'ato, -a *ag, sm* Serbo-Croat

serena'mente *av* serenely, calmly

sere'nata *sf* (*Mus*) serenade

serenità *sf* serenity

se'reno, -a *ag* (*tempo, cielo*) clear; (*fig*) serene, calm ■ *sm* (*tempo*) good weather; **un fulmine a ciel ~** (*fig*) a bolt from the blue

serg. *abbr* (= *sergente*) Sgt.

ser'gente [ser'dʒɛnte] *sm* (*Mil*) sergeant

seri'ale *ag* (*Inform*) serial

seria'mente *av* (*con serietà, in modo grave*) seriously; **lavorare ~** to take one's job seriously

'serie *sf inv* (*successione*) series *inv*; (*gruppo, collezione di chiavi etc*) set; (*Sport*) division; league; (*Comm*): **modello di ~/fuori ~** standard/custom-built model; **in ~** in quick succession; (*Comm*) mass *cpd*; **tutta una ~ di problemi** a whole string *o* series of problems

serietà *sf* seriousness; reliability

'serio, -a *ag* serious; (*impiegato*) responsible, reliable; (*ditta, cliente*) reliable, dependable; **sul ~** (*davvero*) really, truly; (*seriamente*) seriously, in earnest; **dico sul ~** I'm serious; **faccio sul ~** I mean it; **prendere qc/qn sul ~** to take sth/sb, seriously

seri'oso, -a *ag* (*persona, modi*): **un po' ~** a bit too serious

ser'mone *sm* sermon

'serpe *sf* snake; (*fig peg*) viper

serpeggi'are [serped'dʒare] *vi* to wind; (*fig*) to spread

ser'pente *sm* snake; **~ a sonagli** rattlesnake

'serra *sf* greenhouse; hothouse; (*Geo*) sierra

serra'manico *sm*: **coltello a ~** jack-knife

ser'randa *sf* roller shutter

ser'rare *vt* to close, shut; (*a chiave*) to lock; (*stringere*) to tighten; (*premere: nemico*) to close in on; **~ i pugni/i denti** to clench one's fists/teeth; **~ le file** to close ranks

ser'rata *sf* (*Industria*) lockout

ser'rato, -a *ag* (*veloce*): **a ritmo ~** quickly, fast

serra'tura *sf* lock

'serva *sf vedi* **servo**

'server ['server] *sm inv* (*Inform*) server

ser'vigio [ser'vidʒo] *sm* favour (*Brit*), favor (*US*), service

ser'vire *vt* to serve; (*clienti: al ristorante*) to wait on; (*: al negozio*) to serve, attend to; (*fig: giovare*) to aid, help; (*Carte*) to deal ■ *vi* (*Tennis*) to serve; (*essere utile*): **~ a qn** to be of use to sb; **~ a qc/a fare** (*utensile etc*) to be used for sth/for doing; **~ (a qn) da** to serve as (for sb); **servirsi** *vr* (*usare*): **servirsi di** to use; (*prendere: cibo*): **servirsi (di)** to help o.s. (to); (*essere cliente abituale*): **servirsi da** to be a regular customer at, go to; **non mi serve più** I don't need it any more; **non serve che lei vada** you don't need to go

servitù *sf* servitude; slavery; (*personale di servizio*) servants *pl* domestic staff, domestic staff

servizi'evole [servit'tsjevole] *ag* obliging, willing to help

ser'vizio [ser'vittsjo] *sm* service; (*al ristorante: sul conto*) service (charge); (*Stampa, TV, Radio*) report; (*da tè, caffè etc*) set, service; **servizi** *smpl* (*di casa*) kitchen and bathroom; (*Econ*) services; **essere di ~** to be on duty; **fuori ~** (*telefono etc*) out of order; **~ compreso/**

S

escluso service included/not included; **entrata di ~** service *o* tradesman's (*Brit*) entrance; **casa con doppi servizi** house with two bathrooms; **~ assistenza clienti** after-sales service; **~ civile** ≈ community service; **~ in diretta** (*TV, Radio*) live coverage; **~ fotografico** (*Stampa*) photo feature; **~ militare** military service; **~ d'ordine** (*Polizia*) police patrol; (*di manifestanti*) team of stewards (*responsible for crowd control*); **servizi segreti** secret service *sg*; **servizi di sicurezza** security forces

'servo, a *sm/f* servant

servo'freno *sm* (*Aut*) servo brake

servos'terzo [servos'tɛrtso] *sm* (*Aut*) power steering

'sesamo *sm* (*Bot*) sesame

ses'santa *num* sixty

sessan'tenne *ag, sm/f* sixty-year-old

sessan'tesimo, -a *num* sixtieth

sessan'tina *sf*: **una ~ (di)** about sixty

sessantot'tino, -a *sm/f* *a person who took part in the events of 1968*

sessan'totto *sm* *see note*

SESSANTOTTO

Sessantotto refers to the year 1968, the year of student protests. Originating in France, unrest soon spread to other industrialized countries including Italy. What began as a purely student concern gradually came to include other parts of society and led to major political and social change. Among the changes that resulted from the protests were reform of schools and universities and the referendum on divorce.

sessi'one *sf* session

'sesso *sm* sex; **il ~ debole/forte** the weaker/ stronger sex

sessu'ale *ag* sexual, sex *cpd*

sessualità *sf* sexuality

sessu'ologo, -a, gi, ghe *sm/f* sexologist, sex specialist

ses'tante *sm* sextant

'sesto, -a *num* sixth ■ *sm*: **rimettere in ~** (*aggiustare*) to put back in order; (*fig: persona*) to put back on his (*o* her) feet; **rimettersi in ~** (*riprendersi*) to recover, get well; (*riassettarsi*) to tidy o.s. up

'seta *sf* silk

setacci'are [setat'tʃare] *vt* (*farina etc*) to sift, sieve; (*fig: zona*) to search, comb

se'taccio [se'tattʃo] *sm* sieve; **passare al ~** (*fig*) to search, comb

'sete *sf* thirst; **avere ~** to be thirsty; **~ di potere** thirst for power

seti'ficio [seti'fitʃo] *sm* silk factory

'setola *sf* bristle

sett. *abbr* (= *settembre*) Sept.

'setta *sf* sect

set'tanta *num* seventy

settan'tenne *ag, sm/f* seventy-year-old

settan'tesimo, -a *num* seventieth

settan'tina *sf*: **una ~ (di)** about seventy

'sette *num* seven

settecen'tesco, -a, schi, sche [settetʃen'tesko] *ag* eighteenth-century

sette'cento [sette'tʃɛnto] *num* seven hundred ■ *sm*: **il S~** the eighteenth century

set'tembre *sm* September; *vedi anche* **luglio**

sette'mila *num* seven thousand

settentrio'nale *ag* northern ■ *sm/f* northerner

settentri'one *sm* north

'settico, -a, ci, che *ag* (*Med*) septic

setti'mana *sf* week; **la ~ scorsa/prossima** last/next week; **a metà ~** in the middle of the week; **~ bianca** winter-sport holiday

settima'nale *ag, sm* weekly

'settimo, -a *num* seventh

set'tore *sm* sector; **~ privato/pubblico** private/public sector; **~ terziario** service industries *pl*

Se'ul *sf* Seoul

severità *sf* severity

se'vero, -a *ag* severe

sevizi'are [sevit'tsjare] *vt* to torture

se'vizie [se'vittsje] *sfpl* torture *sg*

'sexy ['seksi] *ag inv* sexy

sez. *abbr* = **sezione**

sezio'nare [settsjo'nare] *vt* to divide into sections; (*Med*) to dissect

sezi'one [set'tsjone] *sf* section; (*Med*) dissection

sfaccen'dato, -a [sfattʃen'dato] *ag* idle

sfaccetta'tura [sfattʃetta'tura] *sf* (*azione*) faceting; (*parte sfaccettata, fig*) facet

sfacchi'nare [sfakki'nare] *vi* (*fam*) to toil, drudge

sfacchi'nata [sfakki'nata] *sf* (*fam*) chore, drudgery *no pl*

sfaccia'taggine [sfattʃa'taddʒine] *sf* insolence, cheek

sfacci'ato, -a [sfat'tʃato] *ag* (*maleducato*) cheeky, impudent; (*vistoso*) gaudy

sfa'celo [sfa'tʃɛlo] *sm* (*fig*) ruin, collapse

sfal'darsi *vr* to flake (off)

sfal'sare *vt* to offset

sfa'mare *vt* (*nutrire*) to feed; (*soddisfare la fame*): **~ qn** to satisfy sb's hunger; **sfamarsi** *vr* to satisfy one's hunger, fill o.s. up

sfarfal'lio *sm* (*Cine, TV*) flickering
'sfarzo ['sfartso] *sm* pomp, splendour (*Brit*), splendor (*US*)
sfar'zoso, -a [sfar'tsoso] *ag* splendid, magnificent
sfasa'mento *sm* (*Elettr*) phase displacement; (*fig*) confusion, bewilderment
sfa'sato, -a *ag* (*Elettr, motore*) out of phase; (*fig: persona*) confused, bewildered
sfasci'are [sfaʃ'ʃare] *vt* (*ferita*) to unbandage; (*distruggere: porta*) to smash, shatter; **sfasciarsi** *vr* (*rompersi*) to smash, shatter
sfa'tare *vt* (*leggenda*) to explode
sfati'cato, -a *sm/f* idler, loafer
'sfatto, -a *ag* (*letto*) unmade; (*orlo etc*) undone; (*gelato, neve*) melted; (*frutta*) overripe; (*riso, pasta etc*) overdone, overcooked; (*fam: persona, corpo*) flabby
sfavil'lare *vi* to spark, send out sparks; (*risplendere*) to sparkle
sfa'vore *sm* disfavour (*Brit*), disfavor (*US*), disapproval
sfavo'revole *ag* unfavourable (*Brit*), unfavorable (*US*)
sfega'tato, -a *ag* fanatical
'sfera *sf* sphere
'sferico, -a, ci, che *ag* spherical
sfer'rare *vt* (*fig: colpo*) to land, deal; (*: attacco*) to launch
sfer'zante [sfer'tsante] *ag* (*critiche, parole*) stinging
sfer'zare [sfer'tsare] *vt* to whip; (*fig*) to lash out at
sfian'care *vt* to wear out, exhaust; **sfiancarsi** *vr* to exhaust o.s., wear o.s. out
sfia'tare *vi* to allow air (*o* gas *etc*) to escape
sfiata'toio *sm* blowhole; (*Tecn*) vent
sfi'brante *ag* exhausting, energy-sapping
sfi'brare *vt* (*indebolire*) to exhaust, enervate
sfi'brato, -a *ag* exhausted, worn out
'sfida *sf* challenge
sfi'dante *ag* challenging ■ *sm/f* challenger
sfi'dare *vt* to challenge; (*fig*) to defy, brave; **~ qn a fare qc** to challenge sb to do sth; **~ un pericolo** to brave a danger; **sfido che ...** I dare say (that) ...
sfi'ducia [sfi'dutʃa] *sf* distrust, mistrust; **avere ~ in qn/qc** to distrust sb/sth
sfiduci'ato, -a [sfidu'tʃato] *ag* lacking confidence
sfigato, -a (*fam*) *ag*: **essere ~** (*sfortunato*) to be unlucky ■ *sm/f* (*fallito, sfortunato*) loser; (*fuori moda*) dork
sfigu'rare *vt* (*persona*) to disfigure; (*quadro, statua*) to deface ■ *vi* (*far cattiva figura*) to make a bad impression
sfilacci'are [sfilat'tʃare] *vt, vi,* **sfilacci'arsi** *vr* to fray
sfi'lare *vt* (*ago*) to unthread; (*abito, scarpe*) to slip off ■ *vi* (*truppe*) to march past, parade; (*manifestanti*) to march; **sfilarsi** *vr* (*perle etc*) to come unstrung; (*orlo, tessuto*) to fray; (*calza*) to run, ladder
sfi'lata *sf* (*Mil*) parade; (*di manifestanti*) march; **~ di moda** fashion show
'sfilza ['sfiltsa] *sf* (*di case*) row; (*di errori*) series *inv*
'sfinge ['sfindʒe] *sf* sphinx
sfini'mento *sm* exhaustion
sfi'nito, -a *ag* exhausted
sfio'rare *vt* to brush (against); (*argomento*) to touch upon; **~ la velocità di 150 km/h** to touch 150 km/h
sfio'rire *vi* to wither, fade
'sfitto, -a *ag* vacant, empty
sfo'cato, -a *ag* (*Fot*) out of focus
sfoci'are [sfo'tʃare] *vi*: **~ in** to flow into; (*fig: malcontento*) to develop into
sfode'rato, -a *ag* (*vestito*) unlined
sfo'gare *vt* to vent, pour out; **sfogarsi** *vr* (*sfogare la propria rabbia*) to give vent to one's anger; (*confidarsi*): **sfogarsi (con)** to pour out one's feelings (to); **non sfogarti su di me!** don't take your bad temper out on me!
sfoggi'are [sfod'dʒare] *vt, vi* to show off
'sfoggio ['sfɔddʒo] *sm* show, display; **fare ~ di** to show off, display
sfogherò *etc* [sfoge'rɔ] *vb vedi* **sfogare**
'sfoglia ['sfɔʎʎa] *sf* sheet of pasta dough; **pasta ~** (*Cuc*) puff pastry
sfogli'are [sfoʎ'ʎare] *vt* (*libro*) to leaf through
'sfogo, -ghi *sm* outlet; (*eruzione cutanea*) rash; (*fig*) outburst; **dare ~ a** (*fig*) to give vent to
sfolgo'rante *ag* (*luce*) blazing; (*fig: vittoria*) brilliant
sfolgo'rare *vi* to blaze
sfolla'gente [sfolla'dʒɛnte] *sm inv* truncheon (*Brit*), billy (*US*)
sfol'lare *vt* to empty, clear ■ *vi* to disperse; **~ da** (*città*) to evacuate
sfol'lato, -a *ag* evacuated ■ *sm/f* evacuee
sfol'tire *vt,* **sfol'tirsi** *vr* to thin (out)
sfon'dare *vt* (*porta*) to break down; (*scarpe*) to wear a hole in; (*cesto, scatola*) to burst, knock the bottom out of; (*Mil*) to break through ■ *vi* (*riuscire*) to make a name for o.s.
sfon'dato, -a *ag* (*scarpe*) worn out; (*scatola*) burst; (*sedia*) broken, damaged; **essere ricco ~** to be rolling in it
'sfondo *sm* background
sfo'rare *vi* to overrun
sfor'mare *vt* to put out of shape, knock out of shape; **sformarsi** *vr* to lose shape, get out of shape

S

sfor'mato, -a *ag* (*che ha perso forma*) shapeless ■ *sm* (*Cuc*) *type of soufflé*
sfor'nare *vt* (*pane*) to take out of the oven; (*fig*) to churn out
sfor'nito, -a *ag*: **~ di** lacking in, without; (*negozio*) out of
sfor'tuna *sf* misfortune, ill luck *no pl*; **avere ~** to be unlucky; **che ~!** how unfortunate!
sfortu'nato, -a *ag* unlucky; (*impresa, film*) unsuccessful
sfor'zare [sfor'tsare] *vt* to force; (*voce, occhi*) to strain; **sforzarsi** *vr*: **sforzarsi di** *o* **a** *o* **per fare** to try hard to do
'sforzo ['sfɔrtso] *sm* effort; (*tensione eccessiva, Tecn*) strain; **fare uno ~** to make an effort; **essere sotto ~** (*motore, macchina, fig: persona*) to be under stress
'sfottere *vt* (*fam*) to tease
sfracel'lare [sfratʃel'lare] *vt*, **sfracel'larsi** *vr* to smash
sfrat'tare *vt* to evict
'sfratto *sm* eviction; **dare lo ~ a qn** to give sb notice to quit
sfrecci'are [sfret'tʃare] *vi* to shoot *o* flash past
sfre'gare *vt* (*strofinare*) to rub; (*graffiare*) to scratch; **sfregarsi le mani** to rub one's hands; **~ un fiammifero** to strike a match
sfregi'are [sfre'dʒare] *vt* to slash, gash; (*persona*) to disfigure; (*quadro*) to deface
'sfregio ['sfredʒo] *sm* gash; scar; (*fig*) insult
sfre'nato, -a *ag* (*fig*) unrestrained, unbridled
sfron'dare *vt* (*albero*) to prune, thin out; (*fig: discorso, scritto*) to prune (down)
sfronta'tezza [sfronta'tettsa] *sf* impudence, cheek
sfron'tato, -a *ag* impudent, cheeky
sfrutta'mento *sm* exploitation
sfrut'tare *vt* (*terreno*) to overwork, exhaust; (*miniera*) to exploit, work; (*fig: operai, occasione, potere*) to exploit
sfrutta'tore, -'trice *sm/f* exploiter
sfug'gente [sfud'dʒɛnte] *ag* (*fig: sguardo*) elusive; (*mento*) receding
sfug'gire [sfud'dʒire] *vi* to escape; **~ a** (*custode*) to escape (from); (*morte*) to escape; **~ a qn** (*dettaglio, nome*) to escape sb; **~ di mano a qn** to slip out of sb's hand (*o* hands); **lasciarsi ~ un'occasione** to let an opportunity go by; **~ al controllo** (*macchina*) to go out of control; (*situazione*) to be no longer under control
sfug'gita [sfud'dʒita] *sf*: **di ~** (*rapidamente, in fretta*) in passing
sfu'mare *vt* (*colori, contorni*) to soften, shade off ■ *vi* to shade (off), fade; (*fig: svanire*) to vanish, disappear; (*: speranze*) to come to nothing
sfuma'tura *sf* shading off *no pl*; (*tonalità*) shade, tone; (*fig*) touch, hint
sfuo'cato, -a *ag* = **sfocato**
sfuri'ata *sf* (*scatto di collera*) fit of anger; (*rimprovero*) sharp rebuke
'sfuso, -a *ag* (*caramelle etc*) loose, unpacked; (*vino*) unbottled; (*birra*) draught (*Brit*), draft (*US*)
sg. *abbr* = **seguente**
sga'bello *sm* stool
sgabuz'zino [zgabud'dzino] *sm* lumber room
sgambet'tare *vi* to kick one's legs about
sgam'betto *sm*: **far lo ~ a qn** to trip sb up; (*fig*) to oust sb
sganasci'arsi [zganaʃ'ʃarsi] *vr*: **~ dalle risa** to roar with laughter
sganci'are [zgan'tʃare] *vt* to unhook; (*chiusura*) to unfasten, undo; (*Ferr*) to uncouple; (*bombe: da aereo*) to release, drop; (*fig: fam: soldi*) to fork out; **sganciarsi** *vr* to come unhooked; to come unfastened, come undone; to uncouple; (*fig*): **sganciarsi (da)** to get away (from)
sganghe'rato, -a [zgange'rato] *ag* (*porta*) off its hinges; (*auto*) ramshackle; (*riso*) wild, boisterous
sgar'bato, -a *ag* rude, impolite
'sgarbo *sm*: **fare uno ~ a qn** to be rude to sb
sgargi'ante [zgar'dʒante] *ag* gaudy, showy
sgar'rare *vi* (*persona*) to step out of line; (*orologio: essere avanti*) to gain; (*: essere indietro*) to lose
'sgarro *sm* inaccuracy
sgattaio'lare *vi* to sneak away *o* off
sge'lare [zdʒe'lare] *vi*, *vt* to thaw
'sghembo, -a ['zgembo] *ag* (*obliquo*) slanting; (*storto*) crooked
sghignaz'zare [zgiɲɲat'tsare] *vi* to laugh scornfully
sghignaz'zata [zgiɲɲat'tsata] *sf* scornful laugh
sgob'bare *vi* (*fam: scolaro*) to swot; (*: operaio*) to slog
sgoccio'lare [zgottʃo'lare] *vt* (*vuotare*) to drain (to the last drop) ■ *vi* (*acqua*) to drip; (*recipiente*) to drain
'sgoccioli ['zgottʃoli] *smpl*: **essere agli ~** (*lavoro, provviste etc*) to be nearly finished; (*periodo*) to be nearly over; **siamo agli ~** we've nearly finished, the end is in sight
sgo'larsi *vr* to talk (*o* shout *o* sing) o.s. hoarse
sgomberare, sgomb(e)'rare *vt* to clear; (*andarsene da: stanza*) to vacate; (*evacuare*) to evacuate
'sgombero *sm vedi* **sgombro**
'sgombro, -a *ag*: **~ (di)** clear (of), free (from) ■ *sm* (*Zool*) mackerel; (*anche*: **sgombero**)

clearing; vacating; evacuation; (: *trasloco*) removal
sgomen'tare *vt* to dismay; **sgomentarsi** *vr* to be dismayed
sgo'mento, -a *ag* dismayed ■ *sm* dismay, consternation
sgomi'nare *vt* (*nemico*) to rout; (*avversario*) to defeat; (*fig: epidemia*) to overcome
sgonfi'are *vt* to let down, deflate; **sgonfiarsi** *vr* to go down
'sgonfio, -a *ag* (*pneumatico, pallone*) flat
'sgorbio *sm* blot; scribble
sgor'gare *vi* to gush (out)
sgoz'zare [zgot'tsare] *vt* to cut the throat of
sgra'devole *ag* unpleasant, disagreeable
sgra'dito, -a *ag* unpleasant, unwelcome
sgraffi'gnare [zgraffiɲ'ɲare] *vt* (*fam*) to pinch, swipe
sgrammati'cato, -a *ag* ungrammatical
sgra'nare *vt* (*piselli*) to shell; **~ gli occhi** to open one's eyes wide
sgran'chirsi [zgran'kirsi] *vr* to stretch; **~ le gambe** to stretch one's legs
sgranocchi'are [zgranok'kjare] *vt* to munch
sgras'sare *vt* to remove the grease from
'sgravio *sm*: **~ fiscale** *o* **contributivo** tax relief
sgrazi'ato, -a [zgrat'tsjato] *ag* clumsy, ungainly
sgreto'lare *vt* to cause to crumble; **sgretolarsi** *vr* to crumble
sgri'dare *vt* to scold
sgri'data *sf* scolding
sguai'ato, -a *ag* coarse, vulgar
sguai'nare *vt* to draw, unsheathe
sgual'cire [zgwal'tʃire] *vt* to crumple (up), crease
sgual'drina *sf* (*peg*) slut
sgu'ardo *sm* (*occhiata*) look, glance; (*espressione*) look (in one's eye); **dare uno ~ a qc** to glance at sth, cast a glance *o* an eye over sth; **alzare** *o* **sollevare lo ~** to raise one's eyes, look up; **cercare qc/qn con lo ~** to look around for sth/sb
'sguattero, -a *sm/f* scullery boy(-maid)
sguaz'zare [zgwat'tsare] *vi* (*nell'acqua*) to splash about; (*nella melma*) to wallow; **~ nell'oro** to be rolling in money
sguinzagli'are [zgwintsaʎ'ʎare] *vt* to let off the leash; (*fig: persona*): **~ qn dietro a qn** to set sb on sb
sgusci'are [zguʃ'ʃare] *vt* to shell ■ *vi* (*sfuggire di mano*) to slip; **~ via** to slip *o* slink away
'shaker ['ʃeikəʳ] *sm inv* (cocktail) shaker
'shampoo ['ʃampo] *sm inv* shampoo
'shiatzu ['tʃiatsu] *sm, ag inv* shiatsu
shoc'care [ʃok'kare] *vt* = **shockare**
shock [ʃɔk] *sm inv* shock
shoc'kare [ʃok'kare] *vt* to shock
SI *sigla* = **Siena**

 PAROLA CHIAVE

si (*dav lo, la, li, le, ne diventa* **se**) *pron* **1** (*riflessivo: maschile*) himself; (: *femminile*) herself; (: *neutro*) itself; (: *impersonale*) oneself; (: *pl*) themselves; **lavarsi** to wash (oneself); **si è tagliato** he has cut himself; **si credono importanti** they think a lot of themselves
2 (*con complemento oggetto*): **lavarsi le mani** to wash one's hands; **sporcarsi i pantaloni** to get one's trousers dirty; **si sta lavando i capelli** he (*o* she) is washing his (*o* her) hair
3 (*reciproco*) one another, each other; **si amano** they love one another *o* each other
4 (*passivo*): **si ripara facilmente** it is easily repaired; **affittasi camera** room to let
5 (*impersonale*): **si dice che ...** they *o* people say that ...; **si vede che è vecchio** one *o* you can see that it's old; **non si fa credito** we do not give credit; **ci si sbaglia facilmente** it's easy to make a mistake
6 (*noi*) we; **tra poco si parte** we're leaving soon

sì *av* yes ■ *sm*: **non mi aspettavo un sì** I didn't expect him (*o* her *etc*) to say yes; **per me è sì** I should think so, I expect so; **saranno stati sì e no in 20** there must have been about 20 of them; **uno sì e uno no** every other one; **un giorno sì e uno no** every other day; **dire di sì** to say yes; **spero/penso di sì** I hope/think so; **fece di sì col capo** he nodded (his head); **e sì che ...** and to think that ...
'sia *cong*: **~ ... ~** (*o ... o*): **~ che lavori, ~ che non lavori** whether he works or not; (*tanto ... quanto*): **verranno ~ Luigi ~ suo fratello** both Luigi and his brother will be coming
'sia *etc vb vedi* **essere**
SIAE *sigla f* = **Società Italiana Autori ed Editori**
Si'am *sm*: **il ~** Siam
sia'mese *ag, sm/f* siamese *inv*
si'amo *vb vedi* **essere**
Si'beria *sf*: **la ~** Siberia
siberi'ano, -a *ag, sm/f* Siberian
sibi'lare *vi* to hiss; (*fischiare*) to whistle
'sibilo *sm* hiss; whistle
si'cario *sm* hired killer
sicché [sik'ke] *cong* (*perciò*) so (that), therefore; (*e quindi*) (and) so
siccità [sittʃi'ta] *sf* drought
sic'come *cong* since, as

S

Si'cilia [si'tʃilja] *sf*: **la ~** Sicily
sicili'ano, -a [sitʃi'ljano] *ag, sm/f* Sicilian
sico'moro *sm* sycamore
'siculo, -a *ag, sm/f* Sicilian
si'cura *sf* (*di arma, spilla*) safety catch; (*di portiera*) safety lock
sicura'mente *av* certainly
sicu'rezza [siku'rettsa] *sf* safety; security; confidence; certainty; **di ~** safety *cpd*; **la ~ stradale** road safety; **avere la ~ di qc** to be sure *o* certain of sth; **lo so con ~** I am quite certain; **ha risposto con molta ~** he answered very confidently
si'curo, -a *ag* safe; (*ben difeso*) secure; (*fiducioso*) confident; (*certo*) sure, certain; (*notizia, amico*) reliable; (*esperto*) skilled ■ *av* (*anche*: **di sicuro**) certainly ■ *sm*: **andare sul ~** to play safe; **essere/mettere al ~** to be safe/put in a safe place; **~ di sé** self-confident, sure of o.s.; **sentirsi ~** to feel safe *o* secure; **essere ~ di/che** to be sure of/that; **da fonte sicura** from reliable sources
siderur'gia [siderur'dʒia] *sf* iron and steel industry
side'rurgico, -a, ci, che [side'rurdʒiko] *ag* iron and steel *cpd*
'sidro *sm* cider
si'edo *etc vb vedi* **sedere**
si'epe *sf* hedge
si'ero *sm* (*Med*) serum; **~ antivipera** snake bite serum; **~ del latte** whey
sieronegatività *sf inv* HIV-negative status
sieronega'tivo, -a *ag* HIV-negative ■ *sm/f* HIV-negative person
sieropositività *sf inv* HIV-positive status
sieroposi'tivo, -a *ag* HIV-positive ■ *sm/f* HIV-positive person
si'erra *sf* (*Geo*) sierra
Si'erra Le'one *sf*: **la ~** Sierra Leone
si'esta *sf* siesta, (afternoon) nap
si'ete *vb vedi* **essere**
si'filide *sf* syphilis
si'fone *sm* siphon
Sig. *abbr* (= *signore*) Mr
siga'retta *sf* cigarette
'sigaro *sm* cigar
Sigg. *abbr* (= *signori*) Messrs
sigil'lare [sidʒil'lare] *vt* to seal
si'gillo [si'dʒillo] *sm* seal
'sigla *sf* (*iniziali*) initials *pl*; (*abbreviazione*) acronym, abbreviation; **~ automobilistica** *abbreviation of province on vehicle number plate*; **~ musicale** signature tune
si'glare *vt* to initial
Sig.na *abbr* (= *signorina*) Miss
signifi'care [siɲɲifi'kare] *vt* to mean; **cosa significa?** what does this mean?
significa'tivo, -a [siɲɲifika'tivo] *ag* significant
signifi'cato [siɲɲifi'kato] *sm* meaning
si'gnora [siɲ'ɲora] *sf* lady; **la ~ X** Mrs X; **buon giorno S~/Signore/Signorina** good morning; (*deferente*) good morning Madam/Sir/Madam; (*quando si conosce il nome*) good morning Mrs/Mr/Miss X; **Gentile S~/Signore/Signorina** (*in una lettera*) Dear Madam/Sir/Madam; **Gentile** (*o* **Cara**) **S~ Rossi** Dear Mrs Rossi; **Gentile S~ Anna Rossi** (*sulle buste*) Mrs Anna Rossi; **il signor Rossi e ~** Mr Rossi and his wife; **signore e signori** ladies and gentlemen; **le presento la mia ~** may I introduce my wife?
si'gnore [siɲ'ɲore] *sm* gentleman; (*padrone*) lord, master; (*Rel*): **il S~** the Lord; **il signor X** Mr X; **signor Presidente** Mr Chairman; **Gentile** (*o* **Caro**) **Signor Rossi** (*in lettere*) Dear Mr Rossi; **Gentile Signor Paolo Rossi** (*sulle buste*) Mr Paolo Rossi; **i signori Bianchi** (*coniugi*) Mr and Mrs Bianchi; *vedi anche* **signora**
signo'ria [siɲɲo'ria] *sf* (*Storia*) seignory, signoria; **S~ Vostra** (*Amm*) you
signo'rile [siɲɲo'rile] *ag* refined
signorilità [siɲɲorili'ta] *sf* (*raffinatezza*) refinement; (*eleganza*) elegance
signo'rina [siɲɲo'rina] *sf* young lady; **la ~ X** Miss X; **Gentile** (*o* **Cara**) **S~ Rossi** (*in lettere*) Dear Miss Rossi; **Gentile S~ Anna Rossi** (*sulle buste*) Miss Anna Rossi; *vedi anche* **signora**
signo'rino [siɲɲo'rino] *sm* young master
Sig.ra *abbr* (= *signora*) Mrs
silenzia'tore [silentsja'tore] *sm* silencer
si'lenzio [si'lɛntsjo] *sm* silence; **fare ~** to be quiet, stop talking; **far passare qc sotto ~** to keep quiet about sth, hush sth up
silenzi'oso, -a [silen'tsjoso] *ag* silent, quiet
'silice ['silitʃe] *sf* silica
si'licio [si'litʃo] *sm* silicon; **piastrina di ~** silicon chip
sili'cone *sm* silicone
'sillaba *sf* syllable
silu'rare *vt* to torpedo; (*fig: privare del comando*) to oust
si'luro *sm* torpedo
SIM [sim] *sigla f inv* (*Tel*): **~ card** SIM card
simbi'osi *sf* (*Biol, fig*) symbiosis
simboleggi'are [simboled'dʒare] *vt* to symbolize
sim'bolico, -a, ci, che *ag* symbolic(al)
simbo'lismo *sm* symbolism
'simbolo *sm* symbol
simi'lare *ag* similar
'simile *ag* (*analogo*) similar; (*di questo tipo*): **un uomo ~** such a man, a man like this ■ *sm*

(*persona*) fellow man; **libri simili** such books; **~ a** similar to; **non ho mai visto niente di ~** I've never seen anything like that; **è insegnante o qualcosa di ~** he's a teacher or something like that; **vendono vasi e simili** they sell vases and things like that; **i suoi simili** one's fellow men; one's peers
simili'tudine *sf* (*Ling*) simile
simme'tria *sf* symmetry
sim'metrico, -a, ci, che *ag* symmetric(al)
simpa'tia *sf* (*qualità*) pleasantness; (*inclinazione*) liking; **avere ~ per qn** to like sb, have a liking for sb; **con ~** (*su lettera etc*) with much affection
sim'patico, -a, ci, che *ag* (*persona*) nice, pleasant, likeable; (*casa, albergo etc*) nice, pleasant
simpatiz'zante [simpatid'dzante] *sm/f* sympathizer
simpatiz'zare [simpatid'dzare] *vi*: **~ con** to take a liking to
sim'posio *sm* symposium
simu'lacro *sm* (*monumento, statua*) image; (*fig*) semblance
simu'lare *vt* to sham, simulate; (*Tecn*) to simulate
simulazi'one [simulat'tsjone] *sf* shamming; simulation
simul'taneo, -a *ag* simultaneous
sin. *abbr* (= *sinistra*) L
sina'goga, -ghe *sf* synagogue
sincera'mente [sintʃera'mente] *av* (*gen*) sincerely; (*francamente*) honestly, sincerely
since'rarsi [sintʃe'rarsi] *vr*: **~ (di qc)** to make sure (of sth)
sincerità [sintʃeri'ta] *sf* sincerity
sin'cero, -a [sin'tʃero] *ag* (*genuino*) sincere; (*onesto*) genuine
'sincope *sf* syncopation; (*Med*) blackout
sincro'nia *sf* (*di movimento*) synchronism
sin'cronico, -a, ci, che *ag* synchronic
sincroniz'zare [sinkronid'dzare] *vt* to synchronize
sinda'cale *ag* (trade-)union *cpd*
sindaca'lista, -i, e *sm/f* trade unionist
sinda'care *vt* (*controllare*) to inspect; (*fig: criticare*) to criticize
sinda'cato *sm* (*di lavoratori*) (trade) union; **~ dei datori di lavoro** employers' association
'sindaco, -ci *sm* mayor
'sindrome *sf* (*Med*) syndrome
siner'gia, -gie [siner'dʒia] *sf* (*anche fig*) synergy
sinfo'nia *sf* (*Mus*) symphony
sin'fonico, -a, ci, che *ag* symphonic; (*orchestra*) symphony *cpd*
singa'lese *ag, sm/f* Sin(g)halese *inv*
Singa'pore *sf* Singapore
singhioz'zare [singjot'tsare] *vi* to sob; to hiccup
singhi'ozzo [sin'gjottso] *sm* (*di pianto*) sob; (*Med*) hiccup; **avere il ~** to have the hiccups; **a ~** (*fig*) by fits and starts
singo'lare *ag* (*insolito*) remarkable, singular; (*Ling*) singular ■ *sm* (*Ling*) singular; (*Tennis*): **~ maschile/femminile** men's(-women's) singles
singolar'mente *av* (*separatamente*) individually, one at a time; (*in modo strano*) strangely, peculiarly, oddly
'singolo, -a *ag* single, individual ■ *sm* (*persona*) individual; (*Tennis*) = **singolare**; **ogni ~ individuo** each individual; **camera singola** single room
sinis'trato, -a *ag* damaged ■ *sm/f* disaster victim; **zona sinistrata** disaster area
si'nistro, -a *ag* left, left-hand; (*fig*) sinister ■ *sm* (*incidente*) accident ■ *sf* (*Pol*) left (wing); **a sinistra** on the left; (*direzione*) to the left; **a sinistra di** to the left of; **di sinistra** left-wing; **tenere la sinistra** to keep to the left; **guida a sinistra** left hand drive
'sino *prep* = **fino**
si'nonimo, -a *ag* synonymous ■ *sm* synonym; **~ di** synonymous with
sin'tassi *sf* syntax
sin'tattico, -a, ci, che *ag* syntactic
'sintesi *sf* synthesis; (*riassunto*) summary, résumé; **in ~** in brief, in short
sin'tetico, -a, ci, che *ag* synthetic; (*conciso*) brief, concise
sintetiz'zare [sintetid'dzare] *vt* to synthesize; (*riassumere*) to summarize
sintetizza'tore [sintetiddza'tore] *sm* (*Mus*) synthesizer; **~ di voce** voice synthesizer
sinto'matico, -a, ci, che *ag* symptomatic
'sintomo *sm* symptom
sinto'nia *sf* (*Radio*) tuning; **essere in ~ con qn** (*fig*) to be on the same wavelength as sb
sintoniz'zare [sintonid'dzare] *vt* to tune (in); **sintonizzarsi** *vr*: **sintonizzarsi su** to tune in to
sintonizza'tore [sintoniddza'tore] *sm* tuner
sinu'oso, -a *ag* (*strada*) winding
sinu'site *sf* sinusitis
SIP *sigla f* (= *Società Italiana per l'esercizio telefonico*) *former name of Italian telephone company*
si'pario *sm* (*Teat*) curtain
si'rena *sf* (*apparecchio*) siren; (*nella mitologia, fig*) siren, mermaid; **~ d'allarmo** (*per incendio*) fire alarm; (*per furto*) burglar alarm
'Siria *sf*: **la ~** Syria
siri'ano, -a *ag, sm/f* Syrian

S

si'ringa, -ghe *sf* syringe
'sisma, -i *sm* earthquake
'SISMI *sigla m* (*= Servizio per l'Informazione e la Sicurezza Militari*) *military security service*
'sismico, -a, ci, che *ag* seismic; (*zona*) earthquake *cpd*
sis'mografo *sm* seismograph
sissi'gnore [sissiɲ'ɲore] *av* (*a un superiore*) yes, sir; (*enfatico*) yes indeed, of course
sis'tema, -i *sm* system; (*metodo*) method, way; **trovare il ~ per fare qc** to find a way to do sth; **~ decimale/metrico** decimal/metric system; **~ operativo** (*Inform*) operating system; **~ solare** solar system; **~ di vita** way of life
siste'mare *vt* (*mettere a posto*) to tidy, put in order; (*risolvere: questione*) to sort out, settle; (*procurare un lavoro a*) to find a job for; (*dare un alloggio a*) to settle, find accommodation (*Brit*) *o* accommodations (*US*) for; **sistemarsi** *vr* (*problema*) to be settled; (*persona: trovare alloggio*) to find accommodation(s); (*: trovarsi un lavoro*) to get fixed up with a job; **ti sistemo io!** I'll soon sort you out!; **~ qn in un albergo** to fix sb up with a hotel
sistematica'mente *av* systematically
siste'matico, -a, ci, che *ag* systematic
sistemazi'one [sistemat'tsjone] *sf* arrangement, order; settlement; employment; accommodation (*Brit*), accommodations (*US*)
'sito, -a *ag* (*Amm*) situated ■ *sm* (*letterario*) place; **~ Internet** website
situ'are *vt* to site, situate
situ'ato, -a *ag*: **~ a/su** situated at/on
situazi'one [situat'tsjone] *sf* situation; **vista la sua ~ familiare** given your family situation *o* circumstances; **nella sua ~** in your position *o* situation; **mi trovo in una ~ critica** I'm in a very difficult situation *o* position
'skai® *sm* Leatherette®
ski-lift [ski'lift] *sm inv* ski lift
ski pass [ski'pɑːs] *sm inv* ski pass
slacci'are [zlat'tʃare] *vt* to undo, unfasten
slanci'arsi [zlan'tʃarsi] *vr* to dash, fling o.s.
slanci'ato, -a [zlan'tʃato] *ag* slender
'slancio ['zlantʃo] *sm* dash, leap; (*fig*) surge; **in uno ~ d'affetto** in a burst *o* rush of affection; **di ~** impetuously
sla'vato, -a *ag* faded, washed out; (*fig: viso, occhi*) pale, colourless (*Brit*), colorless (*US*)
sla'vina *sf* snowslide
'slavo, -a *ag* Slav(onic), Slavic
sle'ale *ag* disloyal; (*concorrenza etc*) unfair
slealtà *sf* disloyalty; unfairness
sle'gare *vt* to untie
slip *sm inv* (*mutandine*) briefs *pl*; (*da bagno: per uomo*) (swimming) trunks *pl*; (*: per donna*) bikini bottoms *pl*
'slitta *sf* sledge; (*trainata*) sleigh
slitta'mento *sm* slipping; skidding; postponement; **~ salariale** wage drift
slit'tare *vi* to slip, slide; (*Aut*) to skid; (*incontro, conferenza*) to be put off, be postponed
s.l.m. *abbr* (*= sul livello del mare*) a.s.l.
slo'gare *vt* (*Med*) to dislocate; (*: caviglia, polso*) to sprain
sloga'tura *sf* dislocation; sprain
sloggi'are [zlod'dʒare] *vt* (*inquilino*) to turn out; (*nemico*) to drive out, dislodge ■ *vi* to move out
Slo'vacchia [zlo'vakkja] *sf* Slovakia
slo'vacco, -a, ci, che *ag, sm/f* Slovak, Slovakian; **la Repubblica Slovacca** the Slovak Republic
Slo'venia *sf* Slovenia
slo'veno, -a *ag, sm/f* Slovene, Slovenian ■ *sm* (*Ling*) Slovene
S.M. *abbr* (*Mil*) = **Stato Maggiore**; (*= Sua Maestà*) HM
smac'cato, -a *ag* (*fig*) excessive
smacchi'are [zmak'kjare] *vt* to remove stains from
smacchia'tore [zmakkja'tore] *sm* stain remover
'smacco, -chi *sm* humiliating defeat
smagli'ante [zmaʎ'ʎante] *ag* brilliant, dazzling
smagli'are [zmaʎ'ʎare] *vt*, **smagli'arsi** *vr* (*calza*) to ladder
smaglia'tura [zmaʎʎa'tura] *sf* (*su maglia, calza*) ladder (*Brit*), run; (*Med: sulla pelle*) stretch mark
sma'grire *vt* to make thin ■ *vi* to get *o* grow thin, lose weight
sma'grito, -a *ag*: **essere ~** to have lost a lot of weight
smalizi'ato, -a [smalit'tsjato] *ag* shrewd, cunning
smal'tare *vt* to enamel; (*ceramica*) to glaze; (*unghie*) to varnish
smalti'mento *sm* (*di rifiuti*) disposal
smal'tire *vt* (*merce*) to sell off; (*rifiuti*) to dispose of; (*cibo*) to digest; (*peso*) to lose; (*rabbia*) to get over; **~ la sbornia** to sober up
'smalto *sm* (*anche di denti*) enamel; (*per ceramica*) glaze; **~ per unghie** nail varnish
smance'rie [zmantʃe'rie] *sfpl* mawkishness *sg*
'smania *sf* agitation, restlessness; (*fig*): **~ di** thirst for, craving for; **avere la ~ addosso** to have the fidgets; **avere la ~ di fare** to long *o* yearn to do

smani'are *vi* (*agitarsi*) to be restless *o* agitated; (*fig*): **~ di fare** to long *o* yearn to do

smantella'mento *sm* dismantling

smantel'lare *vt* to dismantle

smar'carsi *vr* (*Sport*) to get free of marking

smargi'asso [zmar'dʒasso] *sm* show-off

smarri'mento *sm* loss; (*fig*) bewilderment; dismay

smar'rire *vt* to lose; (*non riuscire a trovare*) to mislay; **smarrirsi** *vr* (*perdersi*) to lose one's way, get lost; (: *oggetto*) to go astray

smar'rito, -a *ag* (*oggetto*) lost; (*fig: confuso: persona*) bewildered, nonplussed; (: *sguardo*) bewildered; **ufficio oggetti smarriti** lost property office (*Brit*), lost and found (*US*)

smasche'rare [zmaske'rare] *vt* to unmask

SME *abbr* = **Stato Maggiore Esercito** ▪ *sigla m* (= *Sistema Monetario Europeo*) EMS (= *European Monetary System*)

smem'brare *vt* (*gruppo, partito etc*) to split; **smembrarsi** *vr* to split up

smemo'rato, -a *ag* forgetful

smen'tire *vt* (*negare*) to deny; (*testimonianza*) to refute; (*reputazione*) to give the lie to; **smentirsi** *vr* to be inconsistent

smen'tita *sf* denial; refutation

sme'raldo *sm, ag inv* emerald

smerci'are [zmer'tʃare] *vt* (*Comm*) to sell; (: *svendere*) to sell off

'smercio ['zmɛrtʃo] *sm* sale; **avere poco/molto ~** to have poor/good sales

smerigli'ato, -a [zmeriʎ'ʎato] *ag*: **carta smerigliata** emery paper; **vetro ~** frosted glass

sme'riglio [zme'riʎʎo] *sm* emery

'smesso, -a *pp di* **smettere** ▪ *ag*: **abiti smessi** cast-offs

'smettere *vt* to stop; (*vestiti*) to stop wearing ▪ *vi* to stop, cease; **~ di fare** to stop doing

smidol'lato, -a *ag* spineless ▪ *sm/f* spineless person

smilitarizzazi'one [zmilitariddzat'tsjone] *sf* demilitarization

'smilzo, -a ['zmiltso] *ag* thin, lean

sminu'ire *vt* to diminish, lessen; (*fig*) to belittle; **~ l'importanza di qc** to play sth down

sminuz'zare [zminut'tsare] *vt* to break into small pieces; to crumble

'smisi *etc vb vedi* **smettere**

smista'mento *sm* (*di posta*) sorting; (*Ferr*) shunting

smis'tare *vt* (*pacchi etc*) to sort; (*Ferr*) to shunt

smisu'rato, -a *ag* boundless, immeasurable; (*grandissimo*) immense, enormous

smitiz'zare [zmitid'dzare] *vt* to debunk

smobili'tare *vt* to demobilize

smobilitazi'one [zmobilitat'tsjone] *sf* demobilization

smobi'lizzo [zmobi'liddzo] *sm* (*Comm*) disinvestment

smo'dato, -a *ag* excessive, unrestrained

smode'rato, -a *ag* immoderate

smog [zmɔg] *sm inv* smog

'smoking ['smoukɪŋ] *sm inv* dinner jacket (*Brit*), tuxedo (*US*)

smon'tare *vt* (*mobile, macchina etc*) to take to pieces, dismantle; (*fig: scoraggiare*) to dishearten ▪ *vi* (*scendere: da cavallo*) to dismount; (: *da treno*) to get off; (*terminare il lavoro*) to stop (work); **smontarsi** *vr* to lose heart; to lose one's enthusiasm

'smorfia *sf* grimace; (*atteggiamento lezioso*) simpering; **fare smorfie** to make faces; to simper

smorfi'oso, -a *ag* simpering

'smorto, -a *ag* (*viso*) pale, wan; (*colore*) dull

smor'zare [zmor'tsare] *vt* (*suoni*) to deaden; (*colori*) to tone down; (*luce*) to dim; (*sete*) to quench; (*entusiasmo*) to dampen; **smorzarsi** *vr* (*suono, luce*) to fade; (*entusiasmo*) to dampen

'smosso, -a *pp di* **smuovere**

smotta'mento *sm* landslide

sms ['ɛsse'ɛmme'ɛsse] *sm inv* text (message)

'smunto, -a *ag* haggard, pinched

smu'overe *vt* to move, shift; (*fig: commuovere*) to move; (: *dall'inerzia*) to rouse, stir; **smuoversi** *vr* to move, shift

smus'sare *vt* (*angolo*) to round off, smooth; (*lama etc*) to blunt; **smussarsi** *vr* to become blunt

s.n. *abbr* = **senza numero**

snatu'rato, -a *ag* inhuman, heartless

snazionaliz'zare [znattsjonalid'dzare] *vt* to denationalize

snelli'mento *sm* (*di traffico*) speeding up; (*di procedura*) streamlining

snel'lire *vt* (*persona*) to make slim; (*traffico*) to speed up; (*procedura*) to streamline; **snellirsi** *vr* (*persona*) to (get) slim; (*traffico*) to speed up

'snello, -a *ag* (*agile*) agile; (*svelto*) slender, slim

sner'vante *ag* (*attesa, lavoro*) exasperating

sner'vare *vt* to enervate, wear out; **snervarsi** *vr* to become enervated

sni'dare *vt* to drive out, flush out

sniffare [znif'fare] *vt* (*fam: cocaina*) to snort

snob'bare *vt* to snub

sno'bismo *sm* snobbery

snoccio'lare [znottʃo'lare] *vt* (*frutta*) to stone; (*fig: orazioni*) to rattle off; (: *verità*) to blab, (: *fam: soldi*) to shell out

sno'dabile *ag* (*lampada*) adjustable; (*tubo, braccio*) hinged

S

sno'dare *vt* to untie, undo; (*rendere agile, mobile*) to loosen; **snodarsi** *vr* to come loose; (*articolarsi*) to bend; (*strada, fiume*) to wind
SO *sigla* = **Sondrio**
so *vb vedi* **sapere**
S.O. *abbr* (= *sudovest*) SW
so'ave *ag* (*voce, maniera*) gentle; (*volto*) delicate, sweet; (*musica*) soft, sweet; (*profumo*) delicate
soavità *sf* gentleness; delicacy; sweetness; softness
sobbal'zare [sobbal'tsare] *vi* to jolt, jerk; (*trasalire*) to jump, start
sob'balzo [sob'baltso] *sm* jerk, jolt; jump, start
sobbar'carsi *vr*: **~ a** to take on, undertake
sob'borgo, -ghi *sm* suburb
sobil'lare *vt* to stir up, incite
'sobrio, -a *ag* sober
Soc. *abbr* (= *società*) Soc.
socchi'udere [sok'kjudere] *vt* (*porta*) to leave ajar; (*occhi*) to half-close
socchi'uso, -a [sok'kjuso] *pp di* **socchiudere** ■ *ag* (*porta, finestra*) ajar; (*occhi*) half-closed
soc'combere *vi* to succumb, give way
soc'correre *vt* to help, assist
soccorri'tore, -'trice *sm/f* rescuer
soc'corso, -a *pp di* **soccorrere** ■ *sm* help, aid, assistance; **soccorsi** *smpl* relief *sg*, aid *sg*; **prestare ~ a qn** to help *o* assist sb; **venire in ~ di qn** to help sb, come to sb's aid; **operazioni di ~** rescue operations; **~ stradale** breakdown service
socialdemo'cratico, -a, ci, che [sotʃaldemo'kratiko] *sm/f* Social Democrat
soci'ale [so'tʃale] *ag* social; (*di associazione*) club *cpd*, association *cpd*
socia'lismo [sotʃa'lizmo] *sm* socialism
socia'lista, -i, e [sotʃa'lista] *ag, sm/f* socialist
socializ'zare [sotʃalid'dzare] *vi* to socialize
società [sotʃe'ta] *sf inv* society; (*sportiva*) club; (*Comm*) company; **in ~ con qn** in partnership with sb; **mettersi in ~ con qn** to go into business with sb; **l'alta ~** high society; **~ anonima** ≈ limited (*Brit*) *o* incorporated (*US*) company; **~ per azioni** joint-stock company; **~ di comodo** shell company; **~ fiduciaria** trust company; **~ di mutuo soccorso** friendly society (*Brit*), benefit society (*US*); **~ a responsabilità limitata** *type of limited liability company*
soci'evole [so'tʃevole] *ag* sociable
socievo'lezza [sotʃevo'lettsa] *sf* sociableness
'socio ['sɔtʃo] *sm* (*Dir, Comm*) partner; (*membro di associazione*) member
sociolo'gia [sotʃolo'dʒia] *sf* sociology
soci'ologo, -a, gi, ghe [so'tʃɔlogo] *sm/f* sociologist
'soda *sf* (*Chim*) soda; (*acqua gassata*) soda (water)
soda'lizio [soda'littsjo] *sm* association, society
soddisfa'cente [soddisfa'tʃɛnte] *ag* satisfactory
soddis'fare *vt, vi*: **~ a** to satisfy; (*impegno*) to fulfil; (*debito*) to pay off; (*richiesta*) to meet, comply with; (*offesa*) to make amends for
soddis'fatto, -a *pp di* **soddisfare** ■ *ag* satisfied, pleased; **essere ~ di** to be satisfied *o* pleased with
soddisfazi'one [soddisfat'tsjone] *sf* satisfaction
'sodio *sm* (*Chim*) sodium
'sodo, -a *ag* firm, hard ■ *sm*: **venire al ~** to come to the point ■ *av* (*picchiare, lavorare*) hard; **dormire ~** to sleep soundly
sofà *sm inv* sofa
soffe'renza [soffe'rɛntsa] *sf* suffering; (*Comm*): **in ~** unpaid
sof'ferto, -a *pp di* **soffrire** ■ *ag* (*vittoria*) hard-fought; (*distacco, decisione*) painful
soffi'are *vt* to blow; (*notizia, segreto*) to whisper ■ *vi* to blow; (*sbuffare*) to puff (and blow); **soffiarsi il naso** to blow one's nose; **~ qc/qn a qn** (*fig*) to pinch *o* steal sth/sb from sb; **~ via qc** to blow sth away
soffi'ata *sf* (*fam*) tip-off; **fare una ~ alla polizia** to tip off the police
'soffice ['sɔffitʃe] *ag* soft
soffi'etto *sm* (*Mus, per fuoco*) bellows *pl*; **porta a ~** folding door
'soffio *sm* (*di vento*) breath; (*di fumo*) puff; (*Med*) murmur
soffi'one *sm* (*Bot*) dandelion
sof'fitta *sf* attic
sof'fitto *sm* ceiling
soffo'cante *ag* suffocating, stifling
soffo'care *vi* (*anche*: **soffocarsi**) to suffocate, choke ■ *vt* to suffocate, choke; (*fig*) to stifle, suppress
soffocazi'one [soffokat'tsjone] *sf* suffocation
sof'friggere [sof'friddʒere] *vt* to fry lightly
sof'frire *vt* to suffer, endure; (*sopportare*) to bear, stand ■ *vi* to suffer; to be in pain; **~ (di) qc** (*Med*) to suffer from sth
sof'fritto, -a *pp di* **soffriggere** ■ *sm* (*Cuc*) *fried mixture of herbs, bacon and onions*
sof'fuso, -a *ag* (*di luce*) suffused
So'fia *sf* (*Geo*) Sofia
sofisti'care *vt* (*vino, cibo*) to adulterate
sofisti'cato, -a *ag* sophisticated; (*vino*) adulterated
sofisticazi'one [sofistikat'tsjone] *sf* adulteration
'software ['sɔftwɛə] *sm*: **~ applicativo** applications package

soggettivo, -a [soddʒet'tivo] *ag* subjective
sog'getto, -a [sod'dʒɛtto] *ag*: **~ a** (*sottomesso*) subject to; (*esposto: a variazioni, danni etc*) subject *o* liable to ■ *sm* subject; **~ a tassa** taxable; **recitare a ~** (*Teat*) to improvise
soggezi'one [soddʒet'tsjone] *sf* subjection; (*timidezza*) awe; **avere ~ di qn** to be ill at ease in sb's presence
sogghi'gnare [soggiɲ'ɲare] *vi* to sneer
sog'ghigno [sog'giɲɲo] *sm* sneer
soggia'cere [soddʒa'tʃere] *vi*: **~ a** to be subjected to
soggio'gare [soddʒo'gare] *vt* to subdue, subjugate
soggior'nare [soddʒor'nare] *vi* to stay
soggi'orno [sod'dʒorno] *sm* (*invernale, marino*) stay; (*stanza*) living room
soggi'ungere [sod'dʒundʒere] *vt* to add
soggi'unto, -a [sod'dʒunto] *pp di* **soggiungere**
'soglia ['sɔʎʎa] *sf* doorstep; (*anche fig*) threshold
'sogliola ['sɔʎʎola] *sf* (*Zool*) sole
so'gnante [soɲ'ɲante] *ag* dreamy
so'gnare [soɲ'ɲare] *vt, vi* to dream; **~ a occhi aperti** to daydream
sogna'tore, -'trice [soɲɲa'tore] *sm/f* dreamer
'sogno ['soɲɲo] *sm* dream
'soia *sf* (*Bot*) soya
sol *sm* (*Mus*) G; (*: solfeggiando la scala*) so(h)
so'laio *sm* (*soffitta*) attic
sola'mente *av* only, just
so'lare *ag* solar, sun *cpd*
sol'care *vt* (*terreno, fig: mari*) to plough (*Brit*), plow (*US*)
'solco, -chi *sm* (*scavo, fig: ruga*) furrow; (*incavo*) rut, track; (*di disco*) groove; (*scia*) wake
sol'dato *sm* soldier; **~ di leva** conscript; **~ semplice** private
'soldo *sm* (*fig*): **non avere un ~** to be penniless; **non vale un ~** it's not worth a penny; **soldi** *smpl* (*denaro*) money *sg*
'sole *sm* sun; (*luce*) sun(light); (*tempo assolato*) sun(shine); **prendere il ~** to sunbathe; **il S~ che ride** (*Pol*) *symbol of the Italian Green party*
soleggi'ato, -a [soled'dʒato] *ag* sunny
so'lenne *ag* solemn
solennità *sf* solemnity; (*festività*) holiday, feast day
so'lere *vt*: **~ fare qc** to be in the habit of doing sth ■ *vb impers*: **come suole accadere** as is usually the case, as usually happens; **come si suol dire** as they say
so'lerte *ag* diligent
so'lerzia [so'lɛrtsja] *sf* diligence
so'letta *sf* (*per scarpe*) insole
sol'fato *sm* sulphate (*Brit*), sulfate (*US*)
sol'forico, -a, ci, che *ag* sulphuric (*Brit*), sulfuric (*US*); **acido ~** sulphuric *o* sulfuric acid
sol'furo *sm* sulphur (*Brit*), sulfur (*US*)
soli'dale *ag* in agreement; **essere ~ con qn** (*essere d'accordo*) to be in agreement with sb; (*appoggiare*) to be behind sb
solidarietà *sf* solidarity
solidifi'care *vt, vi* (*anche*: **solidificarsi**) to solidify
solidità *sf* solidity
'solido, -a *ag* solid; (*forte, robusto*) sturdy, solid; (*fig: ditta*) sound, solid ■ *sm* (*Mat*) solid
soli'loquio *sm* soliloquy
so'lista, -i, e *ag* solo ■ *sm/f* soloist
solita'mente *av* usually, as a rule
soli'tario, -a *ag* (*senza compagnia*) solitary, lonely; (*solo, isolato*) solitary, lone; (*deserto*) lonely ■ *sm* (*gioiello, gioco*) solitaire
'solito, -a *ag* usual; **essere ~ fare** to be in the habit of doing; **di ~** usually; **più tardi del ~** later than usual; **come al ~** as usual; **siamo alle solite!** (*fam*) here we go again!
soli'tudine *sf* solitude
sollaz'zare [sollat'tsare] *vt* to entertain; **sollazzarsi** *vr* to amuse o.s.
sol'lazzo [sol'lattso] *sm* amusement
solleci'tare [solletʃi'tare] *vt* (*lavoro*) to speed up; (*persona*) to urge on; (*chiedere con insistenza*) to press for, request urgently; (*stimolare*): **~ qn a fare** to urge sb to do; (*Tecn*) to stress
sollecitazi'one [solletʃitat'tsjone] *sf* entreaty, request; (*fig*) incentive; (*Tecn*) stress; **lettera di ~** (*Comm*) reminder
sol'lecito, -a [sol'letʃito] *ag* prompt, quick ■ *sm* (*Comm*) reminder; **~ di pagamento** payment reminder
solleci'tudine [solletʃi'tudine] *sf* promptness, speed
solleti'care *vt* to tickle
sol'letico *sm* tickling; **soffrire il ~** to be ticklish
solleva'mento *sm* raising; lifting; (*ribellione*) revolt; **~ pesi** (*sport*) weight-lifting
solle'vare *vt* to lift, raise; (*fig: persona: alleggerire*): **~ (da)** to relieve (of); (*: dar conforto*) to comfort, relieve; (*: questione*) to raise; (*: far insorgere*) to stir (to revolt); **sollevarsi** *vr* to rise; (*fig: riprendersi*) to recover; (*: ribellarsi*) to rise up; **sollevarsi da terra** (*persona*) to get up from the ground; (*aereo*) to take off; **sentirsi sollevato** to feel relieved
solli'evo *sm* relief; (*conforto*) comfort; **con mio grande ~** to my great relief
'solo, -a *ag* alone; (*in senso spirituale: isolato*) lonely; (*unico*): **un ~ libro** only one book, a single book; (*con ag numerale*): **veniamo noi**

S

tre soli just *o* only the three of us are coming ■ *av* (*soltanto*) only, just; **~ che** *cong* but; **è il ~ proprietario** he's the sole proprietor; **l'incontrò due sole volte** he only met him twice; **non ~ ... ma anche** not only ... but also; **fare qc da ~** to do sth (all) by oneself; **vive (da) ~** he lives on his own; **possiamo vederci da soli?** can I see you in private?

sol'stizio [sol'stittsjo] *sm* solstice

sol'tanto *av* only

so'lubile *ag* (*sostanza*) soluble; **caffè ~** instant coffee

soluzi'one [solut'tsjone] *sf* solution; **senza ~ di continuità** uninterruptedly

sol'vente *ag, sm* solvent; **~ per unghie** nail polish remover; **~ per vernici** paint remover

sol'venza [sol'vεntsa] *sf* (*Comm*) solvency

'soma *sf* load, burden; **bestia da ~** beast of burden

So'malia *sf*: **la ~** Somalia

'somalo, -a *ag, sm/f, sm* Somali

so'maro *sm* ass, donkey

so'matico, -a, ci, che *ag* somatic

somigli'anza [somiʎ'ʎantsa] *sf* resemblance

somigli'are [somiʎ'ʎare] *vi*: **~ a** to be like, resemble; (*nell'aspetto fisico*) to look like; **somigliarsi** *vr* to be (*o* look) alike

'somma *sf* (*Mat*) sum; (*di denaro*) sum (of money); (*complesso di varie cose*) whole amount, sum total; **tirare le somme** (*fig*) to sum up; **tirate le somme** (*fig*) all things considered

som'mare *vt* to add up; (*aggiungere*) to add; **tutto sommato** all things considered

som'mario, -a *ag* (*racconto, indagine*) brief; (*giustizia*) summary ■ *sm* summary

som'mergere [som'mεrdʒere] *vt* to submerge

sommer'gibile [sommer'dʒibile] *sm* submarine

som'merso, -a *pp di* **sommergere**

som'messo, -a *ag* (*voce*) soft, subdued

somminis'trare *vt* to give, administer

sommità *sf inv* summit, top; (*fig*) height

'sommo, -a *ag* highest; (*rispetto*) highest, greatest; (*poeta, artista*) great, outstanding ■ *sm* (*fig*) height; **per sommi capi** in short, in brief

som'mossa *sf* uprising

sommozza'tore [sommottsa'tore] *sm* (deep-sea) diver; (*Mil*) frogman

so'naglio [so'naʎʎo] *sm* (*di mucche etc*) bell; (*per bambini*) rattle

so'nante *ag*: **denaro** *o* **moneta ~** (ready) cash

so'nare *etc* = **suonare** *etc*

'sonda *sf* (*Med, Meteor, Aer*) probe; (*Mineralogia*) drill ■ *ag inv*: **pallone ~** weather balloon

son'daggio [son'daddʒo] *sm* sounding; probe; boring, drilling; (*indagine*) survey; **~ d'opinioni** opinion poll

son'dare *vt* (*Naut*) to sound; (*atmosfera, piaga*) to probe; (*Mineralogia*) to bore, drill; (*fig: opinione etc*) to survey, poll

so'netto *sm* sonnet

son'nambulo, -a *sm/f* sleepwalker

sonnecchi'are [sonnek'kjare] *vi* to doze, nod

sonnel'lino *sm* nap

son'nifero *sm* sleeping drug (*o* pill)

'sonno *sm* sleep; **aver ~** to be sleepy; **prendere ~** to fall asleep

sonno'lento, -a *ag* sleepy, drowsy; (*movimenti*) sluggish

sonno'lenza [sonno'lεntsa] *sf* sleepiness, drowsiness

'sono *vb vedi* **essere**

sonoriz'zare [sonorid'dzare] *vt* (*Ling*) to voice; (*Cine*) to add a sound-track to

so'noro, -a *ag* (*ambiente*) resonant; (*voce*) sonorous, ringing; (*onde, film*) sound *cpd* ■ *sm*: **il ~** (*Cine*) the talkies *pl*

sontu'oso, -a *ag* sumptuous

so'pire *vt* (*fig: dolore, tensione*) to soothe

so'pore *sm* drowsiness

sopo'rifero, -a *ag* soporific

soppe'rire *vi*: **~ a** to provide for; **~ alla mancanza di qc** to make up for the lack of sth

soppe'sare *vt* to weigh in one's hand(s), feel the weight of; (*fig*) to weigh up

soppian'tare *vt* to supplant

soppi'atto *av*: **di ~** secretly; furtively

soppor'tabile *ag* tolerable, bearable

soppor'tare *vt* (*reggere*) to support; (*subire: perdita, spese*) to bear, sustain; (*soffrire: dolore*) to bear, endure; (*cosa: freddo*) to withstand; (*persona: freddo, vino*) to take; (*tollerare*) to put up with, tolerate

sopportazi'one [sopportat'tsjone] *sf* patience; **avere spirito di ~, avere capacità di ~** to be long-suffering

soppressi'one *sf* abolition; withdrawal; suppression; deletion; elimination, liquidation

sop'presso, -a *pp di* **sopprimere**

sop'primere *vt* (*carica, privilegi etc*) to abolish, do away with; (*servizio*) to withdraw; (*pubblicazione*) to suppress; (*parola, frase*) to delete; (*uccidere*) to eliminate, liquidate

'sopra *prep* (*gen*) on; (*al di sopra di, più in alto di*) above; over; (*riguardo a*) on, about ■ *av* on top; (*attaccato, scritto*) on it; (*al di sopra*) above; (*al piano superiore*) upstairs; **donne ~ i 30 anni** women over 30 (years of age); **100 metri ~ il livello del mare** 100 metres above sea level;

5 gradi ~ lo zero 5 degrees above zero; **abito di ~** I live upstairs; **essere al di ~ di ogni sospetto** to be above suspicion; **per i motivi ~ illustrati** for the above-mentioned reasons, for the reasons shown above; **dormirci ~** (*fig*) to sleep on it; **passar ~ a qc** (*anche fig*) to pass over sth

so'prabito *sm* overcoat

sopraccen'nato, -a [soprattʃen'nato] *ag* above-mentioned

soprac'ciglio [soprat'tʃiʎʎo] (*pl*(*f*) **sopracciglia**) *sm* eyebrow

sopracco'perta *sf* (*di letto*) bedspread; (*di libro*) jacket

soprad'detto, -a *ag* aforesaid

sopraf'fare *vt* to overcome, overwhelm

sopraf'fatto, -a *pp di* **sopraffare**

sopraffazi'one [sopraffat'tsjone] *sf* overwhelming, overpowering

sopraf'fino, -a *ag* (*pranzo, vino*) excellent; (*fig*) masterly

sopraggi'ungere [soprad'dʒundʒere] *vi* (*giungere all'improvviso*) to arrive (unexpectedly); (*accadere*) to occur (unexpectedly)

sopraggi'unto, -a [soprad'dʒunto] *pp di* **sopraggiungere**

sopral'lu'ogo, -ghi *sm* (*di esperti*) inspection; (*di polizia*) on-the-spot investigation

sopram'mobile *sm* ornament

soprannatu'rale *ag* supernatural

sopran'nome *sm* nickname

soprannomi'nare *vt* to nickname

sopran'numero *av*: **in ~** in excess

so'prano, -a *sm/f* (*persona*) soprano ■ *sm* (*voce*) soprano

soprappensi'ero *av* lost in thought

soprappiù *sm* surplus, extra; **in ~** extra, surplus; (*per giunta*) besides, in addition

sopras'salto *sm*: **di ~** with a start, with a jump

soprasse'dere *vi*: **~ a** to delay, put off

soprat'tassa *sf* surtax

soprat'tutto *av* (*anzitutto*) above all; (*specialmente*) especially

sopravvalu'tare *vt* (*persona, capacità*) to overestimate

sopravve'nire *vi* to arrive, appear; (*fatto*) to occur

soprav'vento *sm*: **avere/prendere il ~ su qn** to have/get the upper hand over sb

sopravvis'suto, -a *pp di* **sopravvivere** ■ *sm/f* survivor

sopravvi'venza [sopravvi'vɛntsa] *sf* survival

soprav'vivere *vi* to survive; (*continuare a vivere*): **~ (in)** to live on (in); **~ a** (*incidente etc*) to survive; (*persona*) to outlive

soprele'vata *sf* (*di strada, ferrovia*) elevated section

soprinten'dente *sm/f* supervisor; (*statale: di belle arti etc*) keeper

soprinten'denza [soprinten'dɛntsa] *sf* supervision; (*ente*): **~ alle Belle Arti** *government department responsible for monuments and artistic treasures*

soprin'tendere *vi*: **~ a** to superintend, supervise

soprin'teso, -a *pp di* **soprintendere**

so'pruso *sm* abuse of power; **subire un ~** to be abused

soq'quadro *sm*: **mettere a ~** to turn upside-down

sor'betto *sm* sorbet, water ice (*Brit*)

sor'bire *vt* to sip; (*fig*) to put up with

'sorcio ['sortʃo] *sm* mouse

'sordido, -a *ag* sordid; (*fig: gretto*) stingy

sor'dina *sf*: **in ~** softly; (*fig*) on the sly

sordità *sf* deafness

'sordo, -a *ag* deaf; (*rumore*) muffled; (*dolore*) dull; (*lotta*) silent, hidden; (*odio, rancore*) veiled ■ *sm/f* deaf person

sordo'muto, -a *ag* deaf-and-dumb ■ *sm/f* deaf-mute

so'rella *sf* sister

sorel'lastra *sf* stepsister; (*con genitore in comune*) half sister

sor'gente [sor'dʒɛnte] *sf* (*acqua che sgorga*) spring; (*di fiume, Fisica, fig*) source; **acqua di ~** spring water; **~ di calore** source of heat; **~ termale** thermal spring

'sorgere ['sordʒere] *vi* to rise; (*scaturire*) to spring, rise; (*fig: difficoltà*) to arise ■ *sm*: **al ~ del sole** at sunrise

sori'ano, -a *ag, sm/f* tabby

sormon'tare *vt* (*fig*) to overcome, surmount

sorni'one, -a *ag* sly

sorpas'sare *vt* (*Aut*) to overtake; (*fig*) to surpass; (*: eccedere*) to exceed, go beyond; **~ in altezza** to be higher than; (*persona*) to be taller than

sorpas'sato, -a *ag* (*metodo, moda*) outmoded, old-fashioned; (*macchina*) obsolete

sor'passo *sm* (*Aut*) overtaking

sorpren'dente *ag* surprising; (*eccezionale, inaspettato*) astonishing, amazing

sor'prendere *vt* (*cogliere: in flagrante etc*) to catch; (*stupire*) to surprise; **sorprendersi** *vr*: **sorprendersi (di)** to be surprised (at)

sor'preso, -a *pp di* **sorprendere** ■ *sf* surprise; **fare una sorpresa a qn** to give sb a surprise; **prendere qn di sorpresa** to take sb by surprise *o* unawares

sor'reggere [sor'rɛddʒere] *vt* to support, hold up; (*fig*) to sustain

sor'retto, -a *pp di* **sorreggere**
sor'ridere *vi* to smile
sor'riso, -a *pp di* **sorridere** ■ *sm* smile
sor'sata *sf* gulp; **bere a sorsate** to gulp
sorseggi'are [sorsed'dʒare] *vt* to sip
'sorsi *etc vb vedi* **sorgere**
'sorso *sm* sip; **d'un ~, in un ~ solo** at one gulp
'sorta *sf* sort, kind; **di ~** whatever, of any kind at all; **ogni ~ di** all sorts of; **di ogni ~** of every kind
'sorte *sf* (*fato*) fate, destiny; (*evento fortuito*) chance; **tirare a ~** to draw lots; **tentare la ~** to try one's luck
sorteggi'are [sorted'dʒare] *vt* to draw for
sor'teggio [sor'teddʒo] *sm* draw
sorti'legio [sorti'lɛdʒo] *sm* witchcraft *no pl*; (*incantesimo*) spell; **fare un ~ a qn** to cast a spell on sb
sor'tire *vt* (*ottenere*) to produce
sor'tita *sf* (*Mil*) sortie
'sorto, -a *pp di* **sorgere**
sorvegli'ante [sorveʎ'ʎante] *sm/f* (*di carcere*) guard, warder (*Brit*); (*di fabbrica etc*) supervisor
sorvegli'anza [sorveʎ'ʎantsa] *sf* watch; supervision; (*Polizia, Mil*) surveillance
sorvegli'are [sorveʎ'ʎare] *vt* (*bambino, bagagli, prigioniero*) to watch, keep an eye on; (*malato*) to watch over; (*territorio, casa*) to watch *o* keep watch over; (*lavori*) to supervise
sorvo'lare *vt* (*territorio*) to fly over ■ *vi*: **~ su** (*fig*) to skim over
S.O.S. *sigla m* mayday, SOS
'sosia *sm inv* double
sos'pendere *vt* (*appendere*) to hang (up); (*interrompere, privare di una carica*) to suspend; (*rimandare*) to defer; **~ un quadro al muro/ un lampadario al soffitto** to hang a picture on the wall/a chandelier from the ceiling; **~ qn dal suo incarico** to suspend sb from office
sospensi'one *sf* (*anche Chim, Aut*) suspension; deferment; **~ condizionale della pena** (*Dir*) suspended sentence
sos'peso, -a *pp di* **sospendere** ■ *ag* (*appeso*): **~ a** hanging on (*o* from); (*treno, autobus*) cancelled; **in ~** in abeyance; (*conto*) outstanding; **tenere in ~** (*fig*) to keep in suspense; **col fiato ~** with bated breath
sospet'tare *vt* to suspect ■ *vi*: **~ di** to suspect; (*diffidare*) to be suspicious of
sos'petto, -a *ag* suspicious ■ *sm* suspicion; **destare sospetti** to arouse suspicion
sospet'toso, -a *ag* suspicious
sos'pingere [sos'pindʒere] *vt* to drive, push
sos'pinto, -a *pp di* **sospingere**
sospi'rare *vi* to sigh ■ *vt* to long for, yearn for
sos'piro *sm* sigh; **~ di sollievo** sigh of relief
'sosta *sf* (*fermata*) stop, halt; (*pausa*) pause, break; **senza ~** non-stop, without a break
sostanti'vato, -a *ag* (*Ling*): **aggettivo ~** adjective used as a noun
sostan'tivo *sm* noun, substantive
sos'tanza [sos'tantsa] *sf* substance; **sostanze** *sfpl* (*ricchezze*) wealth *sg*, possessions; **in ~** in short, to sum up; **la ~ del discorso** the essence of the speech
sostanzi'ale [sostan'tsjale] *ag* substantial
sostanzi'oso, -a [sostan'tsjoso] *ag* (*cibo*) nourishing, substantial
sos'tare *vi* (*fermarsi*) to stop (for a while), stay; (*fare una pausa*) to take a break
sos'tegno [sos'teɲɲo] *sm* support; **a ~ di** in support of; **muro di ~** supporting wall
soste'nere *vt* to support; (*prendere su di sé*) to take on, bear; (*resistere*) to withstand, stand up to; (*affermare*): **~ che** to maintain that; **sostenersi** *vr* to hold o.s. up, support o.s.; (*fig*) to keep up one's strength; **~ qn** (*moralmente*) to be a support to sb; (*difendere*) to stand up for sb, take sb's part; **~ gli esami** to sit exams; **~ il confronto** to bear *o* stand comparison
soste'nibile *ag* (*tesi*) tenable; (*spese*) bearable; (*sviluppo*) sustainable
sosteni'tore, -'trice *sm/f* supporter
sostenta'mento *sm* maintenance, support; **mezzi di ~** means of support
soste'nuto, -a *ag* (*stile*) elevated; (*velocità, ritmo*) sustained; (*prezzo*) high ■ *sm/f*: **fare il(la) ~(a)** to be standoffish, keep one's distance
sostitu'ire *vt* (*mettere al posto di*): **~ qn/qc a** to substitute sb/sth for; (*prendere il posto di*) to replace, take the place of
sostitu'tivo, -a *ag* (*Amm*: *documento, certificato*) equivalent
sosti'tuto, -a *sm/f* substitute; **~ procuratore della Repubblica** (*Dir*) deputy public prosecutor
sostituzi'one [sostitut'tsjone] *sf* substitution; **in ~ di** as a substitute for, in place of
sotta'ceti [sotta'tʃeti] *smpl* pickles
sot'tana *sf* (*sottoveste*) underskirt; (*gonna*) skirt; (*Rel*) soutane, cassock
sot'tecchi [sot'tekki] *av*: **guardare di ~** to steal a glance at
sotter'fugio [sotter'fudʒo] *sm* subterfuge
sotter'raneo, -a *ag* underground ■ *sm* cellar
sotter'rare *vt* to bury
sottigli'ezza [sottiʎ'ʎettsa] *sf* thinness; slimness; (*fig*: *acutezza*) subtlety; shrewdness; **sottigliezze** *sfpl* (*pedanteria*) quibbles

sot'tile *ag* thin; (*figura, caviglia*) thin, slim, slender; (*fine: polvere, capelli*) fine; (*fig: leggero*) light; (*: vista*) sharp, keen; (*: olfatto*) fine, discriminating; (*: mente*) subtle; shrewd ■ *sm*: **non andare per il ~** not to mince matters

sottiliz'zare [sottilid'dzare] *vi* to split hairs

sottin'tendere *vt* (*intendere qc non espresso*) to understand; (*implicare*) to imply; **lasciare ~ che** to let it be understood that

sottin'teso, -a *pp di* **sottintendere** ■ *sm* allusion; **parlare senza sottintesi** to speak plainly

'sotto *prep* (*gen*) under; (*più in basso di*) below ■ *av* underneath, beneath; below; (*al piano inferiore*): **(al piano) di ~** downstairs; **~ il monte** at the foot of the mountain; **~ la pioggia/il sole** in the rain/sun(shine); **tutti quelli ~ i 18 anni** all those under 18 (years of age) (*Brit*) *o* under age 18 (*US*); **~ il livello del mare** below sea level; **~ il chilo** under *o* less than a kilo; **ha 5 impiegati ~ di sé** he has 5 clerks under him; **siamo ~ Natale/Pasqua** it's nearly Christmas/Easter; **~ un certo punto di vista** in a sense; **~ forma di** in the form of; **~ falso nome** under a false name; **~ terra** underground; **~ voce** in a low voice; **chiuso ~ vuoto** vacuum packed

sotto'banco *av* (*di nascosto: vendere, comprare*) under the counter; (*agire*) in an underhand way

sottobicchi'ere [sottobik'kjɛre] *sm* mat, coaster

sotto'bosco, -schi *sm* undergrowth *no pl*

sotto'braccio [sotto'brattʃo] *av* by the arm; **prendere qn ~** to take sb by the arm; **camminare ~ a qn** to walk arm in arm with sb

sottochi'ave [sotto'kjave] *av* under lock and key

sottoco'perta *av* (*Naut*) below deck

sotto'costo *av* below cost (price)

sottocu'taneo, -a *ag* subcutaneous

sottoes'posto, -a *ag* (*fotografia, pellicola*) underexposed

sotto'fondo *sm* background; **~ musicale** background music

sotto'gamba *av*: **prendere qc ~** not to take sth seriously

sotto'gonna *sf* underskirt

sottogo'verno *sm* political patronage

sotto'gruppo *sm* subgroup; (*di partito*) faction

sottoline'are *vt* to underline; (*fig*) to emphasize, stress

sot't'olio *av, ag inv* in oil

sotto'mano *av* (*a portata di mano*) within reach, to hand; (*di nascosto*) secretly

sottoma'rino, -a *ag* (*flora*) submarine; (*cavo, navigazione*) underwater ■ *sm* (*Naut*) submarine

sotto'messo, -a *pp di* **sottomettere** ■ *ag* submissive

sotto'mettere *vt* to subdue, subjugate; **sottomettersi** *vr* to submit

sottomissi'one *sf* submission

sottopas'saggio [sottopas'saddʒo] *sm* (*Aut*) underpass; (*pedonale*) subway, underpass

sotto'porre *vt* (*costringere*) to subject; (*fig: presentare*) to submit; **sottoporsi** *vr* to submit; **sottoporsi a** (*subire*) to undergo

sotto'posto, -a *pp di* **sottoporre**

sottopro'dotto *sm* by-product

sottoproduzi'one [sottoprodut'tsjone] *sf* underproduction

sottoproletari'ato *sm*: **il ~** the underprivileged class

sot'tordine *av*: **passare in ~** to become of minor importance

sottos'cala *sm inv* (*ripostiglio*) cupboard (*Brit*) *o* closet (*US*) under the stairs; (*stanza*) room under the stairs

sottos'critto, -a *pp di* **sottoscrivere** ■ *sm/f*: **io ~, il ~** the undersigned

sottos'crivere *vt* to sign ■ *vi*: **~ a** to subscribe to

sottoscrizi'one [sottoskrit'tsjone] *sf* signing; subscription

sottosegre'tario *sm*: **S~ di Stato** undersecretary of state (*Brit*), assistant secretary of state (*US*)

sotto'sopra *av* upside-down

sottos'tante *ag* (*piani*) lower; **nella valle ~** in the valley below

sottos'tare *vi*: **~ a** (*assoggettarsi a*) to submit to; (*: richieste*) to give in to; (*subire: prova*) to undergo

sottosu'olo *sm* subsoil

sottosvilup'pato, -a *ag* underdeveloped

sottosvi'luppo *sm* underdevelopment

sottote'nente *sm* (*Mil*) second lieutenant

sotto'terra *av* underground

sotto'tetto *sm* attic

sotto'titolo *sm* subtitle

sottovalu'tare *vt* (*persona, prova*) to underestimate, underrate

sotto'vento *av* (*Naut*) leeward(s) ■ *ag inv* (*lato*) leeward, lee

sotto'veste *sf* underskirt

sotto'voce [sotto'votʃe] *av* in a low voice

sottovu'oto *av*: **confezionare ~** to vacuum-pack ■ *ag*: **confezione ~** vacuum pack

sot'trarre *vt* (*Mat*) to subtract, take away; **sottrarsi** *vr*: **sottrarsi a** (*sfuggire*) to escape; (*evitare*) to avoid; **~ qn/qc a** (*togliere*) to

S

remove sb/sth from; (*salvare*) to save *o* rescue sb/sth from; ~ **qc a qn** (*rubare*) to steal sth from sb; **sottratte le spese** once expenses have been deducted
sot'tratto, -a *pp di* **sottrarre**
sottrazi'one [sottrat'tsjone] *sf* (*Mat*) subtraction; (*furto*) removal
sottuffici'ale [sottuffi'tʃale] *sm* (*Mil*) non-commissioned officer; (*Naut*) petty officer
soufflé [su'fle] *sm inv* (*Cuc*) soufflé
souve'nir [suv(ə)'nir] *sm inv* souvenir
so'vente *av* often
soverchi'are [sover'kjare] *vt* to overpower, overwhelm
soverchie'ria [soverkje'ria] *sf* (*prepotenza*) abuse (of power)
sovi'etico, -a, ci, che *ag* Soviet ■ *sm/f* Soviet citizen
sovrabbon'dante *ag* overabundant
sovrabbon'danza [sovrabbon'dantsa] *sf* overabundance; **in** ~ in excess
sovraccari'care *vt* to overload
sovrac'carico, -a, chi, che *ag*: ~ **(di)** overloaded (with) ■ *sm* excess load; ~ **di lavoro** extra work
sovraesposizi'one [sovraespozit'tsjone] *sf* (*Fot*) overexposure
sovraffol'lato, -a *ag* overcrowded
sovraimmagazzi'nare [sovraimmagaddzi'nare] *vt* to overstock
sovranità *sf* sovereignty; (*fig: superiorità*) supremacy
sovrannatu'rale *ag* = **soprannaturale**
so'vrano, -a *ag* sovereign; (*fig: sommo*) supreme ■ *sm/f* sovereign, monarch
sovrappopolazi'one [sovrappopolat'tsjone] *sf* overpopulation
sovrap'porre *vt* to place on top of, put on top of; (*Fot, Geom*) to superimpose; **sovrapporsi** *vr* (*fig: aggiungersi*) to be added; (*Fot*) to be superimposed
sovrapposizi'one [sovrapposit'tsjone] *sf* superimposition
sovrap'posto, -a *pp di* **sovrapporre**
sovrapproduzi'one [sovrapprodut'tsjone] *sf* overproduction
sovras'tante *ag* overhanging; (*fig*) imminent
sovras'tare *vt* (*vallata, fiume*) to overhang; (*fig*) to hang over, threaten
sovrastrut'tura *sf* superstructure
sovrecci'tare [sovrettʃi'tare] *vt* to overexcite
sovrimpressi'one *sf* (*Fot, Cine*) double exposure; **immagini in** ~ superimposed images
sovrinten'dente *etc* = **soprintendente** *etc*
sovru'mano, -a *ag* superhuman
sovve'nire *vi* (*venire in mente*): ~ **a** to occur to
sovvenzio'nare [sovventsjo'nare] *vt* to subsidize
sovvenzi'one [sovven'tsjone] *sf* subsidy, grant
sovver'sivo, -a *ag* subversive
sovverti'mento *sm* subversion, undermining
sovver'tire *vt* (*Pol: ordine, stato*) to subvert, undermine
'sozzo, -a ['sottso] *ag* filthy, dirty
SP *sigla* = **La Spezia**
S.P. *abbr* = **strada provinciale**; *vedi* **provinciale**
S.p.A. *abbr vedi* **società per azioni**
spac'care *vt* to split, break; (*legna*) to chop; (*fig*) to divide; **spaccarsi** *vr* to split, break
spacca'tura *sf* split
spaccherò *etc* [spakke'rɔ] *vb vedi* **spaccare**
spacci'are [spat'tʃare] *vt* (*vendere*) to sell (off); (*mettere in circolazione*) to circulate; (*droga*) to peddle, push; **spacciarsi** *vr*: **spacciarsi per** (*farsi credere*) to pass o.s. off as, pretend to be
spacci'ato, -a [spat'tʃato] *ag* (*fam: malato, fuggiasco*): **essere** ~ to be done for
spaccia'tore, -'trice [spattʃa'tore] *sm/f* (*di droga*) pusher; (*di denaro falso*) dealer
'spaccio ['spattʃo] *sm* (*di merce rubata, droga*): ~ **(di)** trafficking (in); (*di denaro falso*): ~ **(di)** passing (of); (*vendita*) sale; (*bottega*) shop
'spacco, -chi *sm* (*fenditura*) split, crack; (*strappo*) tear; (*di gonna*) slit
spac'cone *sm/f* boaster, braggart
'spada *sf* sword
spadroneggi'are [spadroned'dʒare] *vi* to swagger
spae'sato, -a *ag* disorientated, lost
spaghet'tata [spaget'tata] *sf* spaghetti meal
spa'ghetti [spa'getti] *smpl* (*Cuc*) spaghetti *sg*
'Spagna ['spaɲɲa] *sf*: **la** ~ Spain
spa'gnolo, -a [spaɲ'ɲɔlo] *ag* Spanish ■ *sm/f* Spaniard ■ *sm* (*Ling*) Spanish; **gli Spagnoli** the Spanish
'spago, -ghi *sm* string, twine; **dare** ~ **a qn** (*fig*) to let sb have his (*o* her) way
spai'ato, -a *ag* (*calza, guanto*) odd
spalan'care *vt*, **spalan'carsi** *vr* to open wide
spa'lare *vt* to shovel
'spalla *sf* shoulder; (*fig: Teat*) stooge; **spalle** *sfpl* (*dorso*) back; **di spalle** from behind; **seduto alle mie spalle** sitting behind me; **prendere/colpire qn alle spalle** to take/hit sb from behind; **mettere qn con le spalle al muro** (*fig*) to put sb with his (*o* her) back to the wall; **vivere alle spalle di qn** (*fig*) to live off sb
spal'lata *sf* (*urto*) shove *o* push with the shoulder; **dare una** ~ **a qc** to give sth a push *o* shove with one's shoulder

spalleggi'are [spalled'dʒare] *vt* to back up, support
spal'letta *sf* (*parapetto*) parapet
spalli'era *sf* (*di sedia etc*) back; (*di letto: da capo*) head(board); (*: da piedi*) foot(board); (*Ginnastica*) wall bars *pl*
spal'lina *sf* (*Mil*) epaulette; (*di sottoveste, maglietta*) strap; **senza spalline** strapless
spal'mare *vt* to spread
'spalti *smpl* (*di stadio*) terraces (*Brit*), ≈ bleachers (*US*)
spamming ['spammiŋ] *sm* (*Internet*) spamming
'spandere *vt* to spread; (*versare*) to pour (out); **spandersi** *vr* to spread; **~ lacrime** to shed tears
'spanto, -a *pp di* **spandere**
spa'rare *vt* to fire ■ *vi* (*far fuoco*) to fire; (*tirare*) to shoot; **~ a qn/qc** to shoot sb/sth, fire at sb/sth
spa'rato *sm* (*di camicia*) dicky
spara'tore *sm* gunman
spara'toria *sf* exchange of shots
sparecchi'are [sparek'kjare] *vt*: **~ (la tavola)** to clear the table
spa'reggio [spa'reddʒo] *sm* (*Sport*) play-off
'spargere ['spardʒere] *vt* (*sparpagliare*) to scatter; (*versare: vino*) to spill; (*: lacrime, sangue*) to shed; (*diffondere*) to spread; (*emanare*) to give off (*o* out); **spargersi** *vr* (*voce, notizia*) to spread; (*persone*) to scatter; **si è sparsa una voce sul suo conto** there is a rumour going round about him
spargi'mento [spardʒi'mento] *sm* scattering; spilling; shedding; **~ di sangue** bloodshed
spa'rire *vi* to disappear, vanish; **~ dalla circolazione** (*fig fam*) to lie low, keep a low profile
sparizi'one [sparit'tsjone] *sf* disappearance
spar'lare *vi*: **~ di** to run down, speak ill of
'sparo *sm* shot
sparpagli'are [sparpaʎ'ʎare] *vt*, **sparpagli'arsi** *vr* to scatter
'sparso, -a *pp di* **spargere** ■ *ag* scattered; (*sciolto*) loose; **in ordine ~** (*Mil*) in open order
sparti'acque *sm* (*Geo*) watershed
sparti'neve *sm inv* snowplough (*Brit*), snowplow (*US*)
spar'tire *vt* (*eredità, bottino*) to share out; (*avversari*) to separate
spar'tito *sm* (*Mus*) score
sparti'traffico *sm inv* (*Aut*) central reservation (*Brit*), median (strip) (*US*)
spartizi'one [spartit'tsjone] *sf* division
spa'ruto, -a *ag* (*viso etc*) haggard
sparvi'ero *sm* (*Zool*) sparrowhawk
spasi'mante *sm* suitor
spasi'mare *vi* to be in agony; **~ di fare** (*fig*) to yearn to do; **~ per qn** to be madly in love with sb
'spasimo *sm* pang
'spasmo *sm* (*Med*) spasm
spas'modico, -a, ci, che *ag* (*angoscioso*) agonizing; (*Med*) spasmodic
spas'sarsela *vi* to enjoy o.s., have a good time
spassio'nato, -a *ag* dispassionate, impartial
'spasso *sm* (*divertimento*) amusement, enjoyment; **andare a ~** to go out for a walk; **essere a ~** (*fig*) to be out of work; **mandare qn a ~** (*fig*) to give sb the sack
spas'soso, -a *ag* amusing, entertaining
'spastico, -a, ci, che *ag, sm/f* spastic
'spatola *sf* spatula
spau'racchio [spau'rakkjo] *sm* scarecrow
spau'rire *vt* to frighten, terrify
spavalde'ria *sf* boldness, arrogance
spa'valdo, -a *ag* arrogant, bold
spaventa'passeri *sm inv* scarecrow
spaven'tare *vt* to frighten, scare; **spaventarsi** *vr* to become frightened, become scared
spa'vento *sm* fear, fright; **far ~ a qn** to give sb a fright
spaven'toso, -a *ag* frightening, terrible; (*fig fam*) tremendous, fantastic
spazi'ale [spat'tsjale] *ag* (*volo, nave, tuta*) space *cpd*; (*Archit, Geom*) spatial
spazia'tura [spattsja'tura] *sf* (*Tip*) spacing
spazien'tire [spattsjen'tire] *vi* (*anche*: **spazientirsi**) to lose one's patience
'spazio ['spattsjo] *sm* space; (*posto*) room, space; **fare ~ per qc/qn** to make room for sth/sb; **nello ~ di un'ora** within an hour, in the space of an hour; **dare ~ a** (*fig*) to make room for; **~ aereo** airspace
spazi'oso, -a [spat'tsjoso] *ag* spacious
spazzaca'mino [spattsaka'mino] *sm* chimney sweep
spazza'neve [spattsa'neve] *sm inv* (*spartineve, Sci*) snowplough (*Brit*), snowplow (*US*)
spaz'zare [spat'tsare] *vt* to sweep; (*foglie etc*) to sweep up; (*cacciare*) to sweep away
spazza'tura [spattsa'tura] *sf* sweepings *pl*; (*immondizia*) rubbish
spaz'zino [spat'tsino] *sm* street sweeper
'spazzola ['spattsola] *sf* brush; **~ per abiti** clothesbrush; **~ da capelli** hairbrush
spazzo'lare [spattso'lare] *vt* to brush
spazzo'lino [spattso'lino] *sm* (small) brush; **~ da denti** toothbrush
specchi'arsi [spek'kjarsi] *vr* to look at o.s. in a mirror; (*riflettersi*) to be mirrored, be reflected
specchi'era [spek'kjɛra] *sf* large mirror; (*mobile*) dressing table
specchi'etto [spek'kjetto] *sm* (*tabella*) table, chart; **~ da borsetta** pocket mirror; **~ retrovisore** (*Aut*) rear-view mirror

S

'specchio ['spɛkkjo] *sm* mirror; (*tabella*) table, chart; **uno ~ d'acqua** a sheet of water
speci'ale [spe'tʃale] *ag* special; **in special modo** especially; **inviato ~** (*Radio, TV, Stampa*) special correspondent; **offerta ~** special offer; **poteri/leggi speciali** (*Pol*) emergency powers/legislation
specia'lista, -i, e [spetʃa'lista] *sm/f* specialist
specia'listico, -a, ci, che [spetʃa'listiko] *ag* (*conoscenza, preparazione*) specialized
specialità [spetʃali'ta] *sf inv* speciality; (*branca di studio*) special field, speciality
specializ'zare [spetʃalid'dzare] *vt* (*industria*) to make more specialized; **specializzarsi** *vr*: **specializzarsi (in)** to specialize (in)
specializ'zato, -a [spetʃalid'dzato] *ag* (*manodopera*) skilled; **operaio non ~** semiskilled worker; **essere ~ in** to be a specialist in
specializzazi'one [spetʃaliddzat'tsjone] *sf* specialization; **prendere la ~ in** to specialize in
special'mente [spetʃal'mente] *av* especially, particularly
'specie ['spɛtʃe] *sf inv* (*Biol, Bot, Zool*) species *inv*; (*tipo*) kind, sort ■ *av* especially, particularly; **una ~ di** a kind of; **fare ~ a qn** to surprise sb; **la ~ umana** mankind
spe'cifica, -che [spe'tʃifika] *sf* specification
specifi'care [spetʃifi'kare] *vt* to specify, state
specificata'mente [spetʃifikata'mente] *av* in detail
spe'cifico, -a, ci, che [spe'tʃifiko] *ag* specific
speck [ʃpɛk] *sm inv kind of smoked ham*
specu'lare *vi*: **~ su** (*Comm*) to speculate in; (*sfruttare*) to exploit; (*meditare*) to speculate on
specula'tore, -'trice *sm/f* (*Comm*) speculator
speculazi'one [spekulat'tsjone] *sf* speculation
spe'dire *vt* to send; (*Comm*) to dispatch, forward; **~ per posta** to post (*Brit*), mail (*US*); **~ per mare** to ship
spedita'mente *av* quickly; **camminare ~** to walk at a brisk pace
spe'dito, -a *ag* (*gen*) quick; **con passo ~** at a brisk pace
spedizi'one [spedit'tsjone] *sf* sending; (*collo*) consignment; (*scientifica etc*) expedition; (*Comm*) forwarding; shipping; **fare una ~** to send a consignment; **agenzia di ~** forwarding agency; **spese di ~** postal charges; (*Comm*) forwarding charges
spedizioni'ere [spedittsjo'njɛre] *sm* forwarding agent, shipping agent
'spegnere ['spɛɲɲere] *vt* (*fuoco, sigaretta*) to put out, extinguish; (*apparecchio elettrico*) to turn *o* switch off; (*gas*) to turn off; (*fig: suoni, passioni*) to stifle; (*debito*) to extinguish; **spegnersi** *vr* to go out; to go off; (*morire*) to pass away
speleolo'gia [speleolo'dʒia] *sf* (*studio*) speleology; (*pratica*) potholing (*Brit*), speleology
spele'ologo, -a, gi, ghe *sm/f* speleologist; potholer
spel'lare *vt* (*scuoiare*) to skin; (*scorticare*) to graze; **spellarsi** *vr* to peel
spendacci'one, -a [spendat'tʃone] *sm/f* spendthrift
'spendere *vt* to spend; **~ una buona parola per qn** (*fig*) to put in a good word for sb
'spengo *etc vb vedi* **spegnere**
spen'nare *vt* to pluck
'spensi *etc vb vedi* **spegnere**
spensiera'tezza [spensjera'tettsa] *sf* carefreeness, lightheartedness
spensie'rato, -a *ag* carefree
'spento, -a *pp di* **spegnere** ■ *ag* (*suono*) muffled; (*colore*) dull; (*sigaretta*) out; (*civiltà, vulcano*) extinct
spe'ranza [spe'rantsa] *sf* hope; **nella ~ di rivederti** hoping to see *o* in the hope of seeing you again; **pieno di speranze** hopeful; **senza ~** (*situazione*) hopeless; (*amare*) without hope
speran'zoso, -a [speran'tsoso] *ag* hopeful
spe'rare *vt* to hope for ■ *vi*: **~ in** to trust in; **~ che/di fare** to hope that/to do; **lo spero, spero di sì** I hope so; **tutto fa ~ per il meglio** everything leads one to hope for the best
sper'duto, -a *ag* (*isolato*) out-of-the-way; (*persona: smarrita, a disagio*) lost
spergi'uro, -a [sper'dʒuro] *sm/f* perjurer ■ *sm* perjury
sperico'lato, -a *ag* fearless, daring; (*guidatore*) reckless
sperimen'tale *ag* experimental; **fare qc in via ~** to try sth out
sperimen'tare *vt* to experiment with, test; (*fig*) to test, put to the test
sperimentazi'one [sperimentat'tsjone] *sf* experimentation
'sperma, -i *sm* (*Biol*) sperm
spermato'zoo, -i [spermatod'dzɔo] *sm* spermatozoon
spe'rone *sm* spur
sperpe'rare *vt* to squander
'sperpero *sm* (*di denaro*) squandering, waste; (*di cibo, materiali*) waste
'spesa *sf* (*soldi spesi*) expense; (*costo*) cost; (*acquisto*) purchase; (*fam: acquisto del cibo quotidiano*) shopping; **spese** *sfpl* expenses; (*Comm*) costs; charges; **ridurre le spese** (*gen*)

to cut down; (*Comm*) to reduce expenditure; **fare la ~** to do the shopping; **fare le spese di qc** (*fig*) to pay the price for sth; **a spese di** (*a carico di*) at the expense of; **con la modica ~ di 200 euro** for the modest sum *o* outlay of 200 euros; **~ pubblica** public expenditure; **spese accessorie** incidental expenses; **spese generali** overheads; **spese di gestione** operating expenses; **spese d'impianto** initial outlay; **spese legali** legal costs; **spese di manutenzione, spese di mantenimento** maintenance costs; **spese postali** postage *sg*; **spese di sbarco e sdoganamento** landing charges; **spese di trasporto** handling charge; **spese di viaggio** travelling (*Brit*) *o* traveling (*US*) expenses

spe'sare *vt*: **viaggio tutto spesato** all-expenses-paid trip

'speso, -a *pp di* **spendere**

'spesso, -a *ag* (*fitto*) thick; (*frequente*) frequent ■ *av* often; **spesse volte** frequently, often

spes'sore *sm* thickness; **ha uno ~ di 20 cm** it is 20 cm thick

Spett. *abbr vedi* **spettabile**

spet'tabile *ag* (*abbr*): **Spett.** (*in lettere*): **~ ditta X** Messrs X and Co; **avvertiamo la ~ clientela ...** we inform our customers ...

spettaco'lare *ag* spectacular

spet'tacolo *sm* (*rappresentazione*) performance, show; (*vista, scena*) sight; **dare ~ di sé** to make an exhibition *o* a spectacle of o.s.

spettaco'loso, -a *ag* spectacular

spet'tanza [spet'tantsa] *sf* (*competenza*) concern; **non è di mia ~** it's no concern of mine

spet'tare *vi*: **~ a** (*decisione*) to be up to; (*stipendio*) to be due to; **spetta a lei decidere** it's up to you to decide

spetta'tore, -'trice *sm/f* (*Cine, Teat*) member of the audience; (*di avvenimento*) onlooker, witness

spettego'lare *vi* to gossip

spetti'nare *vt*: **~ qn** to ruffle sb's hair; **spettinarsi** *vr* to get one's hair in a mess

spet'trale *ag* spectral, ghostly

'spettro *sm* (*fantasma*) spectre (*Brit*), specter (*US*); (*Fisica*) spectrum

'spezie ['spettsje] *sfpl* (*Cuc*) spices

spez'zare [spet'tsare] *vt* (*rompere*) to break; (*fig: interrompere*) to break up; **spezzarsi** *vr* to break

spezza'tino [spettsa'tino] *sm* (*Cuc*) stew

spez'zato, -a [spet'tsato] *ag* (*unghia, ramo, braccio*) broken ■ *sm* (*abito maschile*) coordinated jacket and trousers (*Brit*) *o* pants (*US*); **fare orario ~** to work a split shift

spezzet'tare [spettset'tare] *vt* to break up (*o* chop) into small pieces

spez'zino, -a [spet'tsino] *ag* of (*o* from) La Spezia

spez'zone [spet'tsone] *sm* (*Cine*) clip

'spia *sf* spy; (*confidente della polizia*) informer; (*Elettr*) indicating light; warning light; (*fessura*) peephole; (*fig: sintomo*) sign, indication; **~ dell'olio** (*Aut*) oil warning light

spiacci'care [spjattʃi'kare] *vt* to squash, crush

spia'cente [spja'tʃɛnte] *ag* sorry; **essere ~ di qc/di fare qc** to be sorry about sth/for doing sth; **siamo spiacenti di dovervi annunciare che ...** we regret to announce that ...

spia'cevole [spja'tʃevole] *ag* unpleasant, disagreeable

spi'aggia, -ge ['spjaddʒa] *sf* beach

spia'nare *vt* (*terreno*) to level, make level; (*edificio*) to raze to the ground; (*pasta*) to roll out; (*rendere liscio*) to smooth (out)

spi'ano *sm*: **a tutto ~** (*lavorare*) non-stop, without a break; (*spendere*) lavishly

spian'tato, -a *ag* penniless, ruined

spi'are *vt* to spy on; (*occasione etc*) to watch *o* wait for

spi'ata *sf* tip-off

spiattel'lare *vt* (*fam: verità, segreto*) to blurt out

spi'azzo ['spjattso] *sm* open space; (*radura*) clearing

spic'care *vt* (*assegno, mandato di cattura*) to issue ■ *vi* (*risaltare*) to stand out; **~ il volo** to fly off; (*fig*) to spread one's wings; **~ un balzo** to jump, leap

spic'cato, -a *ag* (*marcato*) marked, strong; (*notevole*) remarkable

spiccherò *etc* [spikke'rɔ] *vb vedi* **spiccare**

'spicchio ['spikkjo] *sm* (*di agrumi*) segment; (*di aglio*) clove; (*parte*) piece, slice

spicci'are [spit'tʃare] *vt* (*faccenda, impegno*) to finish off; **spicciarsi** *vr* (*fare in fretta*) to hurry up, get a move on

'spiccio, -a, ci, ce ['spittʃo] *ag* (*modi, mezzi*) quick; **andare per le spicce** to be quick off the mark, waste no time

spiccio'lata [spittʃo'lata] *av*: **alla ~** in dribs and drabs, a few at a time

'spicciolo, -a ['spittʃolo] *ag*: **moneta spicciola** small change; **spiccioli** *smpl* (small) change

'spicco, -chi *sm*: **fare ~** to stand out; **di ~** outstanding, prominent; (*tema*) main, principal

spie'dino *sm* (*utensile*) skewer; (*cibo*) kebab

spi'edo *sm* (*Cuc*) spit; **pollo allo ~** spit-roasted chicken

spiega'mento *sm* (*Mil*): **~ di forze** deployment of forces
spie'gare *vt* (*far capire*) to explain; (*tovaglia*) to unfold; (*vele*) to unfurl; **spiegarsi** *vr* to explain o.s., make o.s. clear; **~ qc a qn** to explain sth to sb; **il problema si spiega** one can understand the problem; **non mi spiego come ...** I can't understand how ...
spiegazi'one [spjegat'tsjone] *sf* explanation; **avere una ~ con qn** to have it out with sb
spiegaz'zare [spjegat'tsare] *vt* to crease, crumple
spiegherò *etc* [spjege'rɔ] *vb vedi* **spiegare**
spie'tato, -a *ag* ruthless, pitiless
spiffe'rare *vt* (*fam*) to blurt out, blab
'spiffero *sm* draught (Brit), draft (US)
'spiga, -ghe *sf* (*Bot*) ear
spigli'ato, -a [spiʎ'ʎato] *ag* self-possessed, self-confident
spigo'lare *vt* (*anche fig*) to glean
'spigolo *sm* corner; (*Geom*) edge
spigo'loso, -a *ag* (*mobile*) angular; (*persona, carattere*) difficult
'spilla *sf* brooch; (*da cravatta, cappello*) pin
spil'lare *vt* (*vino, fig*) to tap; **~ denaro/notizie a qn** to tap sb for money/information
'spillo *sm* pin; (*spilla*) brooch; **tacco a ~** stiletto heel (Brit), spike heel (US); **~ di sicurezza** *o* **da balia** safety pin; **~ di sicurezza** (*Mil*) (safety) pin
spilorce'ria [spilortʃe'ria] *sf* meanness, stinginess
spi'lorcio, -a, ci, ce [spi'lortʃo] *ag* mean, stingy
spilun'gone *sm/f* beanpole
'spina *sf* (*Bot*) thorn; (*Zool*) spine, prickle; (*di pesce*) bone; (*Elettr*) plug; (*di botte*) bunghole; **birra alla ~** draught beer; **stare sulle spine** (*fig*) to be on tenterhooks; **~ dorsale** (*Anat*) backbone
spi'nacio [spi'natʃo] *sm* spinach *no pl*; (*Cuc*): **spinaci** spinach *sg*
spi'nale *ag* (*Anat*) spinal
spi'nato, -a *ag* (*fornito di spine*): **filo ~** barbed wire; (*tessuto*) herringbone *cpd*
spi'nello *sm* (*Droga: gergo*) joint
'spingere ['spindʒere] *vt* to push; (*condurre: anche fig*) to drive; (*stimolare*): **~ qn a fare** to urge *o* press sb to do; **spingersi** *vr* (*inoltrarsi*) to push on, carry on; **spingersi troppo lontano** (*anche fig*) to go too far
'spino *sm* (*Bot*) thorn bush
spi'noso, -a *ag* thorny, prickly
'spinsi *etc vb vedi* **spingere**
spinte'rogeno [spinte'rɔdʒeno] *sm* (*Aut*) coil ignition
'spinto, -a *pp di* **spingere** ■ *sf* (*urto*) push; (*Fisica*) thrust; (*fig: stimolo*) incentive, spur; (*: appoggio*) string-pulling *no pl*; **dare una spinta a qn** (*fig*) to pull strings for sb
spinto'nare *vt* to shove, push
spin'tone *sm* push, shove
spio'naggio [spio'naddʒo] *sm* espionage, spying
spion'cino [spion'tʃino] *sm* peephole
spi'one, -a *sm/f* (*spia*) informer; (*ragazzino, collega*) telltale, sneak
spio'nistico, -a, ci, che *ag* (*organizzazione*) spy *cpd*; **rete spionistica** spy ring
spi'overe *vi* (*scorrere*) to flow down; (*ricadere*) to hang down, fall
'spira *sf* coil
spi'raglio [spi'raʎʎo] *sm* (*fessura*) chink, narrow opening; (*raggio di luce, fig*) glimmer, gleam
spi'rale *sf* spiral; (*contraccettivo*) coil; **a ~** spiral(-shaped); **~ inflazionistica** inflationary spiral
spi'rare *vi* (*vento*) to blow; (*morire*) to expire, pass away
spiri'tato, -a *ag* possessed; (*fig: persona, espressione*) wild
spiri'tismo *sm* spiritualism
'spirito *sm* (*Rel, Chim, disposizione d'animo, di legge etc, fantasma*) spirit; (*pensieri, intelletto*) mind; (*arguzia*) wit; (*umorismo*) humour, wit; **in buone condizioni di ~** in the right frame of mind; **è una persona di ~** he has a sense of humour (Brit) *o* humor (US); **battuta di ~** joke; **~ di classe** class consciousness; **non ha ~ di parte** he never takes sides; **lo S~ Santo** the Holy Spirit *o* Ghost
spirito'saggine [spirito'saddʒine] *sf* witticism; (*peg*) wisecrack
spiri'toso, -a *ag* witty
spiritu'ale *ag* spiritual
splen'dente *ag* (*giornata*) bright, sunny; (*occhi*) shining; (*pavimento*) shining, gleaming
'splendere *vi* to shine
'splendido, -a *ag* splendid; (*splendente*) shining; (*sfarzoso*) magnificent, splendid
splen'dore *sm* splendour (Brit), splendor (US); (*luce intensa*) brilliance, brightness
spodes'tare *vt* to deprive of power; (*sovrano*) to depose
'spoglia ['spɔʎʎa] *sf vedi* **spoglio**
spogli'are [spoʎ'ʎare] *vt* (*svestire*) to undress; (*privare, fig: depredare*): **~ qn di qc** to deprive sb of sth; (*togliere ornamenti: anche fig*): **~ qn/qc di** to strip sb/sth of; **spogliarsi** *vr* to undress, strip; **spogliarsi di** (*ricchezze etc*) to deprive o.s. of, give up; (*pregiudizi*) to rid o.s. of

spoglia'rello [spoʎʎa'rɛllo] *sm* striptease
spoglia'toio [spoʎʎa'tojo] *sm* dressing room; (*di scuola etc*) cloakroom; (*Sport*) changing room
'spoglio, -a ['spɔʎʎo] *ag* (*pianta, terreno*) bare; (*privo*): **~ di** stripped of; lacking in, without ■ *sm* (*di voti*) counting ■ *sf* (*Zool*) skin, hide; (*: di rettile*) slough; **spoglie** *sfpl* (*salma*) remains; (*preda*) spoils, booty *sg*
'spola *sf* shuttle; (*bobina*) spool; **fare la ~ (fra)** to go to and fro *o* shuttle (between)
spo'letta *sf* (*Cucito: bobina*) spool; (*di bomba*) fuse
spol'pare *vt* to strip the flesh off
spolve'rare *vt* (*anche Cuc*) to dust; (*con spazzola*) to brush; (*con battipanni*) to beat; (*fig: mangiare*) to polish off ■ *vi* to dust
spolve'rino *sm* (*soprabito*) dust coat
'sponda *sf* (*di fiume*) bank; (*di mare, lago*) shore; (*bordo*) edge
sponsoriz'zare [sponsorid'dzare] *vt* to sponsor
sponsorizzazi'one [sponsoriddzat'tsjone] *sf* sponsorship
spontanea'mente *av* (*comportarsi*) naturally; (*agire*) spontaneously; (*reagire*) instinctively, spontaneously
spon'taneo, -a *ag* spontaneous; (*persona*) unaffected, natural; **di sua spontanea volontà** of his own free will
spopo'lare *vt* to depopulate ■ *vi* (*attirare folla*) to draw the crowds; **spopolarsi** *vr* to become depopulated
spo'radico, -a, ci, che *ag* sporadic
sporcacci'one, -a [sporkat'tʃone] *sm/f* (*peg*) pig, filthy person
spor'care *vt* to dirty, make dirty; (*fig*) to sully, soil; **sporcarsi** *vr* to get dirty
spor'cizia [spor'tʃittsja] *sf* (*stato*) dirtiness; (*sudiciume*) dirt, filth; (*fig: cosa oscena*) obscenity
'sporco, -a, chi, che *ag* dirty, filthy; **avere la coscienza sporca** to have a guilty conscience
spor'genza [spor'dʒɛntsa] *sf* projection
'sporgere ['spɔrdʒere] *vt* to put out, stretch out ■ *vi* (*venire in fuori*) to stick out; **sporgersi** *vr* to lean out; **~ querela contro qn** (*Dir*) to take legal action against sb
'sporsi *etc vb vedi* **sporgere**
sport *sm inv* sport
'sporta *sf* shopping bag
spor'tello *sm* (*di treno, auto etc*) door; (*di banca, ufficio*) window, counter; **~ automatico** (*Banca*) cash dispenser, automated telling machine
spor'tivo, -a *ag* (*gara, giornale*) sports *cpd*; (*persona*) sporty; (*abito*) casual; (*spirito, atteggiamento*) sporting ■ *sm/f* sportsman(-woman); **campo ~** playing field; **giacca sportiva** sports (*Brit*) *o* sport (*US*) jacket
'sporto, -a *pp di* **sporgere**
'sposa *sf* bride; (*moglie*) wife; **abito** *o* **vestito da ~** wedding dress
sposa'lizio [spoza'littsjo] *sm* wedding
spo'sare *vt* to marry; (*fig: idea, fede*) to espouse; **sposarsi** *vr* to get married, marry; **sposarsi con qn** to marry sb, get married to sb
spo'sato, -a *ag* married
'sposo *sm* (bride)groom; (*marito*) husband; **gli sposi** the newlyweds
spos'sante *ag* exhausting
spossa'tezza [spossa'tettsa] *sf* exhaustion
spos'sato, -a *ag* exhausted, weary
sposta'mento *sm* movement, change of position
spos'tare *vt* to move, shift; (*cambiare: orario*) to change; **spostarsi** *vr* to move; **hanno spostato la partenza di qualche giorno** they postponed *o* put off their departure by a few days
spot [spɔt] *sm inv* (*faretto*) spotlight, spot; (*TV*) advert, commercial, ad
'spranga, -ghe *sf* (*sbarra*) bar; (*catenaccio*) bolt
spran'gare *vt* to bar; to bolt
spray ['spraɪ] *sm inv* (*dispositivo, sostanza*) spray ■ *ag inv* (*bombola, confezione*) spray *cpd*
'sprazzo ['sprattso] *sm* (*di sole etc*) flash; (*fig: di gioia etc*) burst
spre'care *vt* to waste; **sprecarsi** *vr* (*persona*) to waste one's energy
'spreco, -chi *sm* waste
spre'gevole [spre'dʒevole] *ag* contemptible, despicable
'spregio ['sprɛdʒo] *sm* scorn, disdain
spregiudi'cato, -a [spredʒudi'kato] *ag* unprejudiced, unbiased; (*peg*) unscrupulous
'spremere *vt* to squeeze; **spremersi le meningi** (*fig*) to rack one's brains
spre'muta *sf* fresh fruit juice; **~ d'arancia** fresh orange juice
sprez'zante [spret'tsante] *ag* scornful, contemptuous
'sprezzo ['sprɛttso] *sm* contempt, scorn, disdain
sprigio'nare [sprid3o'nare] *vt* to give off, emit; **sprigionarsi** *vr* to emanate; (*uscire con impeto*) to burst out
spriz'zare [sprit'tsare] *vt, vi* to spurt; **~ gioia/salute** to be bursting with joy/health
sprofon'dare *vi* to sink; (*casa*) to collapse; (*suolo*) to give way, subside; **sprofondarsi** *vr*: **sprofondarsi in** (*poltrona*) to sink into; (*fig*) to become immersed *o* absorbed in

S

sproloqui'are *vi* to ramble on
spro'loquio *sm* rambling speech
spro'nare *vt* to spur (on)
'sprone *sm* (*sperone, fig*) spur
sproporzio'nato, -a [sproportsjo'nato] *ag* disproportionate, out of all proportion
sproporzi'one [spropor'tsjone] *sf* disproportion
spropositato, -a *ag* (*lettera, discorso*) full of mistakes; (*fig: costo*) excessive, enormous
spro'posito *sm* blunder; **a ~** at the wrong time; (*rispondere, parlare*) irrelevantly
sprovve'duto, -a *ag* inexperienced, naïve
sprov'visto, -a *ag* (*mancante*): **~ di** lacking in, without; **ne siamo sprovvisti** (*negozio*) we are out of it (*o* them); **alla sprovvista** unawares
spruz'zare [sprut'tsare] *vt* (*a nebulizzazione*) to spray; (*aspergere*) to sprinkle; (*inzaccherare*) to splash
spruzza'tore [spruttsa'tore] *sm* (*per profumi*) spray, atomizer; (*per biancheria*) sprinkler, spray
'spruzzo ['spruttso] *sm* spray; splash; **verniciatura a ~** spray painting
spudora'tezza [spudora'tettsa] *sf* shamelessness
spudo'rato, -a *ag* shameless
'spugna ['spuɲɲa] *sf* (*Zool*) sponge; (*tessuto*) towelling
spu'gnoso, -a [spuɲ'ɲoso] *ag* spongy
spulci'are [spul'tʃare] *vt* (*animali*) to rid of fleas; (*fig: testo, compito*) to examine thoroughly
'spuma *sf* (*schiuma*) foam; (*bibita*) fizzy drink
spu'mante *sm* sparkling wine
spumeggi'ante [spumed'dʒante] *ag* (*vino, fig*) sparkling; (*birra, mare*) foaming
spu'mone *sm* (*Cuc*) mousse
spun'tare *sm*: **allo ~ del sole** at sunrise; **allo ~ del giorno** at daybreak ■ *vt* (*coltello*) to break the point of; (*capelli*) to trim; (*elenco*) to tick off (Brit), check off (US) ■ *vi* (*uscire: germogli*) to sprout; (*: capelli*) to begin to grow; (*: denti*) to come through; (*apparire*) to appear (suddenly); **spuntarsi** *vr* to become blunt, lose its point; **spuntarla** (*fig*) to make it, win through
spun'tino *sm* snack
'spunto *sm* (*Teat, Mus*) cue; (*fig*) starting point; **dare lo ~ a** to give rise to; **prendere ~ da qc** to take sth as one's starting point
spur'gare *vt* (*fogna*) to clean, clear; **spurgarsi** *vr* (*Med*) to expectorate
spu'tare *vt* to spit out; (*fig*) to belch (out) ■ *vi* to spit
'sputo *sm* spittle *no pl*, spit *no pl*
sputta'nare *vt* (*fam*) to bad-mouth
'squadra *sf* (*strumento*) (set) square; (*gruppo*) team, squad; (*di operai*) gang, squad; (*Mil*) squad; (*: Aer, Naut*) squadron; (*Sport*) team; **lavoro a squadre** teamwork; **~ mobile/del buon costume** (*Polizia*) flying/vice squad
squa'drare *vt* to square, make square; (*osservare*) to look at closely
squa'driglia [skwa'driʎʎa] *sf* (*Aer*) flight; (*Naut*) squadron
squa'drone *sm* squadron
squagli'arsi [skwaʎ'ʎarsi] *vr* to melt; (*fig*) to sneak off
squa'lifica, -che *sf* disqualification
squalifi'care *vt* to disqualify
'squallido, -a *ag* wretched, bleak
squal'lore *sm* wretchedness, bleakness
'squalo *sm* shark
'squama *sf* scale
squa'mare *vt* to scale; **squamarsi** *vr* to flake *o* peel (off)
squarcia'gola [skwartʃa'gola]: **a ~** *av* at the top of one's voice
squarci'are [skwar'tʃare] *vt* (*muro, corpo*) to rip open; (*tessuto*) to rip; (*fig: tenebre, silenzio*) to split; (*: nuvole*) to pierce
'squarcio ['skwartʃo] *sm* (*ferita*) gash; (*in lenzuolo, abito*) rip; (*in un muro*) breach; (*in una nave*) hole; (*brano*) passage, excerpt; **uno ~ di sole** a burst of sunlight
squar'tare *vt* to quarter, cut up; (*cadavere*) to dismember
squattri'nato, -a *ag* penniless ■ *sm/f* pauper
squili'brare *vt* to unbalance
squili'brato, -a *ag* (*Psic*) unbalanced ■ *sm/f* deranged person
squi'librio *sm* (*differenza, sbilancio*) imbalance; (*Psic*) derangement
squil'lante *ag* (*suono*) shrill, sharp; (*voce*) shrill
squil'lare *vi* (*campanello, telefono*) to ring (out); (*tromba*) to blare
'squillo *sm* ring, ringing *no pl*; blare ■ *sf inv* (*anche*: **ragazza squillo**) call girl
squi'sito, -a *ag* exquisite; (*cibo*) delicious; (*persona*) delightful
squit'tire *vi* (*uccello*) to squawk; (*topo*) to squeak
SR *sigla* = **Siracusa**
sradi'care *vt* to uproot; (*fig*) to eradicate
sragio'nare [zradʒo'nare] *vi* to talk nonsense, rave
sregola'tezza [zregola'tettsa] *sf* (*nel mangiare, bere*) lack of moderation; (*di vita*) dissoluteness, dissipation
srego'lato, -a *ag* (*senza ordine: vita*) disorderly; (*smodato*) immoderate; (*dissoluto*) dissolute

Sri 'Lanka [sri'lanka] *sm*: **lo ~** Sri Lanka
S.r.l. *abbr vedi* **società a responsabilità limitata**
sroto'lare *vt*, **sroto'larsi** *vr* to unroll
SS *sigla* = **Sassari**
S.S. *abbr* (*Rel*) = **Sua Santità**; **Santa Sede**; **santi, santissimo**; (*Aut*) = **strada statale**; *vedi* **statale**
S.S.N. *abbr* (= *Servizio Sanitario Nazionale*) ≈ NHS
sta *etc vb vedi* **stare**
'stabbio *sm* (*recinto*) pen, fold; (*di maiali*) pigsty; (*letame*) manure
'stabile *ag* stable, steady; (*tempo: non variabile*) settled; (*Teat: compagnia*) resident ■ *sm* (*edificio*) building; **teatro ~** civic theatre
stabili'mento *sm* (*edificio*) establishment; (*fabbrica*) plant, factory; **~ balneare** bathing establishment; **~ tessile** textile mill
stabi'lire *vt* to establish; (*fissare: prezzi, data*) to fix; (*decidere*) to decide; **stabilirsi** *vr* (*prendere dimora*) to settle; **resta stabilito che ...** it is agreed that ...
stabilità *sf* stability
stabiliz'zare [stabilid'dzare] *vt* to stabilize
stabilizza'tore [stabiliddza'tore] *sm* stabilizer; (*fig*) stabilizing force
stabilizzazi'one [stabiliddzat'tsjone] *sf* stabilization
stacano'vista, -i, e *sm/f* (*ironico*) eager beaver
stac'care *vt* (*levare*) to detach, remove; (*separare: anche fig*) to separate, divide; (*strappare*) to tear off (*o* out); (*scandire: parole*) to pronounce clearly; (*Sport*) to leave behind; **staccarsi** *vr* (*bottone etc*) to come off; (*scostarsi*): **staccarsi (da)** to move away (from); (*fig: separarsi*): **staccarsi da** to leave; **non ~ gli occhi da qn** not to take one's eyes off sb; **~ la televisione/il telefono** to disconnect the television/the phone; **~ un assegno** to write a cheque
staccio'nata [stattʃo'nata] *sf* (*gen*) fence; (*Ippica*) hurdle
'stacco, -chi *sm* (*intervallo*) gap; (*: tra due scene*) break; (*differenza*) difference; (*Sport: nel salto*) takeoff
sta'dera *sf* lever scales *pl*
'stadio *sm* (*Sport*) stadium; (*periodo, fase*) phase, stage
'staffa *sf* (*di sella, Tecn*) stirrup; **perdere le staffe** (*fig*) to fly off the handle
staf'fetta *sf* (*messo*) dispatch rider; (*Sport*) relay race
stagflazi'one [stagflat'tsjone] *sf* (*Econ*) stagflation
stagio'nale [stadʒo'nale] *ag* seasonal ■ *sm/f* seasonal worker
stagio'nare [stadʒo'nare] *vt* (*legno*) to season; (*formaggi, vino*) to mature
stagio'nato, -a [stadʒo'nato] *ag* (*vedi vb*) seasoned; matured; (*scherzoso: attempato*) getting on in years
stagi'one [sta'dʒone] *sf* season; **alta/bassa ~** high/low season
stagli'arsi [staʎ'ʎarsi] *vr* to stand out, be silhouetted
sta'gnante [staɲ'ɲante] *ag* stagnant
sta'gnare [staɲ'ɲare] *vt* (*vaso, tegame*) to tin-plate; (*barca, botte*) to make watertight; (*sangue*) to stop ■ *vi* to stagnate
sta'gnino [staɲ'ɲino] *sm* tinsmith
'stagno, -a ['staɲɲo] *ag* (*a tenuta d'acqua*) watertight; (*a tenuta d'aria*) airtight ■ *sm* (*acquitrino*) pond; (*Chim*) tin
sta'gnola [staɲ'ɲɔla] *sf* tinfoil
stalag'mite *sf* stalagmite
stalat'tite *sf* stalactite
stali'nismo *sm* (*Pol*) Stalinism
'stalla *sf* (*per bovini*) cowshed; (*per cavalli*) stable
stalli'ere *sm* groom, stableboy
'stallo *sm* stall, seat; (*Scacchi*) stalemate; (*Aer*) stall; **situazione di ~** (*fig*) stalemate
stal'lone *sm* stallion
sta'mani, stamat'tina *av* this morning
stam'becco, -chi *sm* ibex
stam'berga, -ghe *sf* hovel
stami'nale *ag*: **cellula ~** stem cell; **ricerca sulle cellule staminali** stem cell research
'stampa *sf* (*Tip, Fot: tecnica*) printing; (*impressione, copia fotografica*) print; (*insieme di quotidiani, giornalisti etc*): **la ~** the press; **andare in ~** to go to press; **mandare in ~** to pass for press; **errore di ~** printing error; **prova di ~** print sample; **libertà di ~** freedom of the press; **"stampe"** "printed matter"
stam'pante *sf* (*Inform*) printer; **~ seriale/termica** serial/thermal printer
stam'pare *vt* to print; (*pubblicare*) to publish; (*coniare*) to strike, coin; (*imprimere: anche fig*) to impress
stampa'tello *sm* block letters *pl*
stam'pato, -a *ag* printed ■ *sm* (*opuscolo*) leaflet; (*modulo*) form; **stampati** *smpl* printed matter *sg*
stam'pella *sf* crutch
stampigli'are [stampiʎ'ʎare] *vt* to stamp
stampiglia'tura [stampiʎʎa'tura] *sf* (*atto*) stamping; (*marchio*) stamp
'stampo *sm* mould; (*fig: indole*) type, kind, sort
sta'nare *vt* to drive out
stan'care *vt* to tire, make tired; (*annoiare*) to bore; (*infastidire*) to annoy; **stancarsi** *vr* to get tired, tire o.s. out; **stancarsi (di)** (*stufarsi*) to grow weary (of), grow tired (of)

S

stan'chezza [stan'kettsa] *sf* tiredness, fatigue
'stanco, -a, chi, che *ag* tired; **~ di** tired of, fed up with
stand [stand] *sm inv* (*in fiera*) stand
'standard ['standərd] *sm inv* (*livello*) standard
standardiz'zare [standardid'dzare] *vt* to standardize
stan'dista, -i, e *sm/f* (*in una fiera etc*) person responsible for a stand
'stanga, -ghe *sm* bar; (*di carro*) shaft
stan'gare *vt* (*fig*: *cliente*) to overcharge; (: *studente*) to fail
stan'gata *sf* (*colpo*: *anche fig*) blow; (*cattivo risultato*) poor result; (*Calcio*) shot
stan'ghetta [stan'getta] *sf* (*di occhiali*) leg; (*Mus, di scrittura*) bar
'stanno *vb vedi* **stare**
sta'notte *av* tonight; (*notte passata*) last night
'stante *prep* owing to, because of; **a sé ~** (*appartamento, casa*) independent, separate
stan'tio, -a, 'tii, 'tie *ag* stale; (*burro*) rancid; (*fig*) old
stan'tuffo *sm* piston
'stanza ['stantsa] *sf* room; (*Poesia*) stanza; **essere di ~ a** (*Mil*) to be stationed in; **~ da bagno** bathroom; **~ da letto** bedroom
stanzia'mento [stantsja'mento] *sm* allocation
stanzi'are [stan'tsjare] *vt* to allocate
stan'zino [stan'tsino] *sm* (*ripostiglio*) storeroom; (*spogliatoio*) changing room (*Brit*), locker room (*US*)
stap'pare *vt* to uncork; (*tappo a corona*) to uncap
star [star] *sf* (*attore, attrice etc*) star
'stare *vi* (*restare in un luogo*) to stay, remain; (*abitare*) to stay, live; (*essere situato*) to be, be situated; (*anche*: **stare in piedi**) to stand; (*essere, trovarsi*) to be; (*dipendere*): **se stesse in me** if it were up to me, if it depended on me; (*seguito da gerundio*): **sta studiando** he's studying; **~ per fare qc** to be about to do sth; **starci** (*esserci spazio*): **nel baule non ci sta più niente** there's no more room in the boot; (*accettare*): **ci stai?** is that okay with you?; **~ a** (*attenersi a*) to follow, stick to; (*seguito dall'infinito*): **~ a sentire** to listen; **staremo a vedere** let's wait and see; **stiamo a discutere** we're talking; (*toccare a*): **sta a te giocare** it's your turn to play; **sta a te decidere** it's up to you to decide; **~ a qn** (*abiti etc*) to fit sb; **queste scarpe mi stanno strette** these shoes are tight for me; **il rosso ti sta bene** red suits you; **come sta?** how are you?; **io sto bene/male** I'm very well/not very well; **~ fermo** to keep *o* stay still; **~ seduto** to sit, be sitting; **~ zitto** to keep quiet; **stando così le cose** given the situation; **stando a ciò che dice lui** according to him *o* to his version
starnaz'zare [starnat'tsare] *vi* to squawk
starnu'tire *vi* to sneeze
star'nuto *sm* sneeze
sta'sera *av* this evening, tonight
'stasi *sf* (*Med, fig*) stasis
sta'tale *ag* state *cpd*, government *cpd* ■ *sm/f* state employee; (*nell'amministrazione*) ≈ civil servant; **bilancio ~** national budget; **strada ~** ≈ trunk (*Brit*) *o* main road
stataliz'zare [statalid'dzare] *vt* to nationalize, put under state control
'statico, -a, ci, che *ag* (*Elettr, fig*) static
sta'tista, -i *sm* statesman
sta'tistico, -a, ci, che *ag* statistical ■ *sf* statistic; (*scienza*) statistics *sg*; **fare una statistica** to carry out a statistical examination
'stato, -a *pp di* **essere**; **stare** ■ *sm* (*condizione*) state, condition; (*Pol*) state; (*Dir*) status; **essere in ~ d'accusa** (*Dir*) to be committed for trial; **essere in ~ d'arresto** (*Dir*) to be under arrest; **essere in ~ interessante** to be pregnant; **~ d'assedio/d'emergenza** state of siege/emergency; **~ civile** (*Amm*) marital status; **~ di famiglia** (*Amm*) *certificate giving details of a household and its dependents*; **~ maggiore** (*Mil*) general staff; **~ patrimoniale** (*Comm*) statement of assets and liabilities; **gli Stati Uniti (d'America)** the United States (of America)
'statua *sf* statue
statuni'tense *ag* United States *cpd*, of the United States
sta'tura *sf* (*Anat*) height; (*fig*) stature; **essere alto/basso di ~** to be tall/short *o* small
sta'tuto *sm* (*Dir*) statute; **regione a ~ speciale** *Italian region with political autonomy in certain matters*; **~ della società** (*Comm*) articles *pl* of association
sta'volta *av* this time
staziona'mento [stattsjona'mento] *sm* (*Aut*) parking; (: *sosta*) waiting; **freno di ~** handbrake
stazio'nare [stattsjo'nare] *vi* (*veicoli*) to be parked
stazio'nario, a [stattsjo'narjo] *ag* stationary; (*fig*) unchanged
stazi'one [stat'tsjone] *sf* station; (*balneare, invernale etc*) resort; **~ degli autobus** bus station; **~ balneare** seaside resort; **~ climatica** health resort; **~ ferroviaria** railway (*Brit*) *o* railroad (*US*) station; **~ invernale** winter sports resort; **~ di lavoro** work station; **~ di polizia** police station (*in*

small town); ~ **di servizio** service *o* petrol (*Brit*) *o* filling station; ~ **termale** spa
'stazza ['stattsa] *sf* tonnage
st. civ. *abbr* = **stato civile**
'stecca, -che *sf* stick; (*di ombrello*) rib; (*di sigarette*) carton; (*Med*) splint; (*stonatura*): **fare una** ~ to sing (*o* play) a wrong note
stec'cato *sm* fence
stec'chito, -a [stek'kito] *ag* dried up; (*persona*) skinny; **lasciar** ~ **qn** (*fig*) to leave sb flabbergasted; **morto** ~ stone dead
'stella *sf* star; ~ **alpina** (*Bot*) edelweiss; ~ **cadente** *o* **filante** shooting star; ~ **di mare** (*Zool*) starfish; ~ **di Natale** (*Bot*) poinsettia
stel'lato, -a *ag* (*cielo, notte*) starry
'stelo *sm* stem; (*asta*) rod; **lampada a** ~ standard lamp (*Brit*), floor lamp
'stemma, -i *sm* coat of arms
'stemmo *vb vedi* **stare**
stempe'rare *vt* (*calce, colore*) to dissolve
stempi'ato, -a *ag* with a receding hairline
stempia'tura *sf* receding hairline
sten'dardo *sm* standard
'stendere *vt* (*braccia, gambe*) to stretch (out); (*tovaglia*) to spread (out); (*bucato*) to hang out; (*mettere a giacere*) to lay (down); (*spalmare: colore*) to spread; (*mettere per iscritto*) to draw up; **stendersi** *vr* (*coricarsi*) to stretch out, lie down; (*estendersi*) to extend, stretch
stendibianche'ria [stendibjanke'ria] *sm inv* clotheshorse
stendi'toio *sm* (*locale*) drying room; (*stendibiancheria*) clotheshorse
stenodattilogra'fia *sf* shorthand typing (*Brit*), stenography (*US*)
stenodatti'lografo, -a *sm/f* shorthand typist (*Brit*), stenographer (*US*)
stenogra'fare *vt* to take down in shorthand
stenogra'fia *sf* shorthand
ste'nografo, -a *sm/f* stenographer
sten'tare *vi*: ~ **a fare** to find it hard to do, have difficulty doing
sten'tato, -a *ag* (*compito, stile*) laboured (*Brit*), labored (*US*); (*sorriso*) forced
'stento *sm* (*fatica*) difficulty; **stenti** *smpl* (*privazioni*) hardship *sg*, privation *sg*; **a** ~ *av* with difficulty, barely
'steppa *sf* steppe
'sterco *sm* dung
'stereo *ag* stereo
stereofo'nia *sf* stereophony
stereo'fonico, -a, ci, che *ag* stereophonic
stereoti'pato, -a *ag* stereotyped
stere'otipo *sm* stereotype; **pensare per stereotipi** to think in clichés
'sterile *ag* sterile; (*terra*) barren; (*fig*) futile, fruitless
sterilità *sf* sterility
steriliz'zare [sterilid'dzare] *vt* to sterilize
sterilizzazi'one [steriliddzat'tsjone] *sf* sterilization
ster'lina *sf* pound (sterling)
stermi'nare *vt* to exterminate, wipe out
stermi'nato, -a *ag* immense, endless
ster'minio *sm* extermination, destruction; **campo di** ~ death camp
'sterno *sm* (*Anat*) breastbone
ster'paglia [ster'paʎʎa] *sf* brushwood
'sterpo *sm* dry twig
ster'rare *vt* to excavate
ster'zare [ster'tsare] *vt, vi* (*Aut*) to steer
'sterzo ['stɛrtso] *sm* steering; (*volante*) steering wheel
'steso, -a *pp di* **stendere**
'stessi *etc vb vedi* **stare**
'stesso, -a *ag* same; (*rafforzativo: in persona, proprio*): **il re** ~ the king himself *o* in person ■ *pron*: **lo(la)** ~**(a)** the same (one); **quello** ~ **giorno** that very day; **i suoi stessi avversari lo ammirano** even his enemies admire him; **fa lo** ~ it doesn't matter; **parto lo** ~ I'm going all the same; **per me è lo** ~ it's all the same to me, it doesn't matter to me; *vedi* **io**; **tu** *etc*
ste'sura *sf* (*azione*) drafting *no pl*, drawing up *no pl*; (*documento*) draft
stetos'copio *sm* stethoscope
'stetti *etc vb vedi* **stare**
'stia *sf* hutch
'stia *etc vb vedi* **stare**
'stigma, -i *sm* stigma
'stigmate *sfpl* (*Rel*) stigmata
sti'lare *vt* to draw up, draft
'stile *sm* style; (*classe*) style, class; (*Sport*): ~ **libero** freestyle; **mobili in** ~ period furniture; **in grande** ~ in great style; **è proprio nel suo** ~ (*fig*) it's just like him
sti'lismo *sm* concern for style
sti'lista, -i, e *sm/f* designer
sti'listico, -a, ci, che *ag* stylistic
stiliz'zato, -a [stilid'dzato] *ag* stylized
stil'lare *vi* (*trasudare*) to ooze; (*gocciolare*) to drip
stilli'cidio [stilli'tʃidjo] *sm* (*fig*) continual pestering (*o* moaning *etc*)
stilo'grafica, -che *sf* (*anche*: **penna stilografica**) fountain pen
Stim. *abbr* = **stimata**
'stima *sf* esteem; valuation; assessment, estimate; **avere** ~ **di qn** to have respect for sb; **godere della** ~ **di qn** to enjoy sb's respect; **fare la** ~ **di qc** to estimate the value of sth
sti'mare *vt* (*persona*) to esteem, hold in high regard; (*terreno, casa etc*) to value; (*stabilire in*

S

misura approssimativa) to estimate, assess; (*ritenere*): ~ **che** to consider that; **stimarsi fortunato** to consider o.s. (to be) lucky

Stim.ma *abbr* = **stimatissima**

stimo'lante *ag* stimulating ■ *sm* (*Med*) stimulant

stimo'lare *vt* to stimulate; (*incitare*): ~ **qn (a fare)** to spur sb on (to do)

stimolazi'one [stimolat'tsjone] *sf* stimulation

'stimolo *sm* (*anche fig*) stimulus

'stinco, -chi *sm* shin; shinbone

'stingere ['stindʒere] *vt, vi* (*anche*: **stingersi**) to fade

'stinto, -a *pp di* **stingere**

sti'pare *vt* to cram, pack; **stiparsi** *vr* (*accalcarsi*) to crowd, throng

stipendi'are *vt* (*pagare*) to pay (a salary to)

stipendi'ato, -a *ag* salaried ■ *sm/f* salaried worker

sti'pendio *sm* salary

'stipite *sm* (*di porta, finestra*) jamb

stipu'lare *vt* (*redigere*) to draw up

stipulazi'one [stipulat'tsjone] *sf* (*di contratto*: *stesura*) drafting; (: *firma*) signing

stiracchi'are [stirak'kjare] *vt* (*fig*: *significato di una parola*) to stretch, force; **stiracchiarsi** *vr* (*persona*) to stretch

stira'mento *sm* (*Med*) sprain

sti'rare *vt* (*abito*) to iron; (*distendere*) to stretch; (*strappare*: *muscolo*) to strain; **stirarsi** *vr* (*fam*) to stretch (o.s.)

stira'tura *sf* ironing

'stirpe *sf* birth, stock; descendants *pl*

stiti'chezza [stiti'kettsa] *sf* constipation

'stitico, -a, ci, che *ag* constipated

'stiva *sf* (*di nave*) hold

sti'vale *sm* boot

stiva'letto *sm* ankle boot

sti'vare *vt* to stow, load

'stizza ['stittsa] *sf* anger, vexation

stiz'zire [stit'tsire] *vt* to irritate ■ *vi*, **stizzirsi** *vr* to become irritated, become vexed

stiz'zoso, -a [stit'tsoso] *ag* (*persona*) quick-tempered, irascible; (*risposta*) angry

stocca'fisso *sm* stockfish, dried cod

Stoc'carda *sf* Stuttgart

stoc'cata *sf* (*colpo*) stab, thrust; (*fig*) gibe, cutting remark

Stoc'colma *sf* Stockholm

stock [stɔk] *sm inv* (*Comm*) stock

'stoffa *sf* material, fabric; (*fig*): **aver la ~ di** to have the makings of; **avere della ~** to have what it takes

stoi'cismo [stoi'tʃizmo] *sm* stoicism

'stoico, -a, ci, che *ag* stoic(al)

sto'ino *sm* doormat

'stola *sf* stole

stol'tezza [stol'tettsa] *sf* stupidity; (*azione*) foolish action

'stolto, -a *ag* stupid, foolish

'stomaco, -chi *sm* stomach; **dare di ~** to vomit, be sick

sto'nare *vt* to sing (*o* play) out of tune ■ *vi* to be out of tune, sing (*o* play) out of tune; (*fig*) to be out of place, jar; (: *colori*) to clash

sto'nato, -a *ag* (*persona*) off-key; (*strumento*) off-key, out of tune

stona'tura *sf* (*suono*) false note

stop *sm inv* (*Telegrafia*) stop; (*Aut*: *cartello*) stop sign; (: *fanalino d'arresto*) brake-light (*Brit*), stoplight

'stoppa *sf* tow

'stoppia *sf* (*Agr*) stubble

stop'pino *sm* (*di candela*) wick; (*miccia*) fuse

'storcere ['stɔrtʃere] *vt* to twist; **storcersi** *vr* to writhe, twist; **~ il naso** (*fig*) to turn up one's nose; **storcersi la caviglia** to twist one's ankle

stordi'mento *sm* (*gen*) dizziness; (*da droga*) stupefaction

stor'dire *vt* (*intontire*) to stun, daze; **stordirsi** *vr*: **stordirsi col bere** to dull one's senses with drink

stor'dito, -a *ag* stunned; (*sventato*) scatterbrained, heedless

'storia *sf* (*scienza, avvenimenti*) history; (*racconto, bugia*) story; (*faccenda, questione*) business *no pl*; (*pretesto*) excuse, pretext; **storie** *sfpl* (*smancerie*) fuss *sg*; **passare alla ~** to go down in history; **non ha fatto storie** he didn't make a fuss

storicità [storitʃi'ta] *sf* historical authenticity

'storico, -a, ci, che *ag* historic(al) ■ *sm/f* historian

storiogra'fia *sf* historiography

stori'one *sm* (*Zool*) sturgeon

stor'mire *vi* to rustle

'stormo *sm* (*di uccelli*) flock

stor'nare *vt* (*Comm*) to transfer

stor'nello *sm* *kind of folk song*

'storno *sm* starling

storpi'are *vt* to cripple, maim; (*fig*: *parole*) to mangle; (: *significato*) to twist

storpia'tura *sf* (*fig*: *di parola*) twisting, distortion

'storpio, -a *ag* crippled, maimed

'storsi *etc vb vedi* **storcere**

'storto, -a *pp di* **storcere** ■ *ag* (*chiodo*) twisted, bent; (*gamba, quadro*) crooked; (*fig*: *ragionamento*) false, wrong ■ *sf* (*distorsione*) sprain, twist; (*recipiente*) retort ■ *av*: **guardare ~ qn** (*fig*) to look askance at sb; **andar ~** to go wrong

sto'viglie [sto'viʎʎe] *sfpl* dishes *pl*, crockery
str. *abbr (Geo)* = **stretto**
'strabico, -a, ci, che *ag* squint-eyed; *(occhi)* squint
strabili'ante *ag* astonishing, amazing
strabili'are *vi* to astonish, amaze
stra'bismo *sm* squinting
strabuz'zare [strabud'dzare] *vt*: **~ gli occhi** to open one's eyes wide
stra'carico, -a, chi, che *ag* overloaded
strac'chino [strak'kino] *sm type of soft cheese*
stracci'are [strat'tʃare] *vt* to tear
'straccio, -a, ci, ce ['strattʃo] *ag*: **carta straccia** waste paper ▪ *sm* rag; *(per pulire)* cloth, duster
stracci'one, -a [strat'tʃone] *sm/f* ragamuffin
stracci'vendolo [strattʃi'vendolo] *sm* ragman
'stracco, -a, chi, che *ag*: **~ (morto)** exhausted, dead tired
stra'cotto, -a *ag* overcooked ▪ *sm (Cuc)* beef stew
'strada *sf* road; *(di città)* street; *(cammino, via, fig)* way; **~ facendo** on the way; **tre ore di ~ (a piedi)/(in macchina)** three hours' walk/ drive; **essere sulla buona ~** *(nella vita)* to be on the right road *o* path; *(con indagine etc)* to be on the right track; **essere fuori ~** *(fig)* to be on the wrong track; **fare ~ a qn** to show sb the way; **fare** *o* **farsi ~** *(fig: persona)* to get on in life; **portare qn sulla cattiva ~** to lead sb astray; **donna di ~** *(fig peg)* streetwalker; **ragazzo di ~** *(fig peg)* street urchin; **~ ferrata** railway *(Brit)*, railroad *(US)*; **~ principale** main road; **~ senza uscita** dead end, cul-de-sac
stra'dale *ag* road *cpd*; *(polizia, regolamento)* traffic *cpd*
stra'dario *sm* street guide
stra'dino *sm* road worker
strafalci'one [strafal'tʃone] *sm* blunder, howler
stra'fare *vi* to overdo it
stra'fatto, -a *pp di* **strafare**
stra'foro; **di ~** *av (di nascosto)* on the sly
strafot'tente *ag*: **è ~** he doesn't give a damn, he couldn't care less
strafot'tenza [strafot'tɛntsa] *sf* arrogance
'strage ['stradʒe] *sf* massacre, slaughter
stra'grande *ag*: **la ~ maggioranza** the overwhelming majority
stralci'are [stral'tʃare] *vt* to remove
'stralcio ['straltʃo] *sm (Comm)*: **vendere in ~** to sell off (at bargain prices) ▪ *ag inv*: **legge ~** abridged version of an act
stralu'nato, -a *ag (occhi)* rolling; *(persona)* beside o.s., very upset
stramaz'zare [stramat'tsare] *vi* to fall heavily
strambe'ria *sf* eccentricity
'strambo, -a *ag* strange, queer
strampa'lato, -a *ag* odd, eccentric
strana'mente *av* oddly, strangely; **e lui, ~, ha accettato** and surprisingly, he agreed
stra'nezza [stra'nettsa] *sf* strangeness
strango'lare *vt* to strangle; **strangolarsi** *vr* to choke
strani'ero, -a *ag* foreign ▪ *sm/f* foreigner
stra'nito, -a *ag* dazed
'strano, -a *ag* strange, odd
straordi'nario, -a *ag* extraordinary; *(treno etc)* special ▪ *sm (lavoro)* overtime
strapaz'zare [strapat'tsare] *vt* to ill-treat; **strapazzarsi** *vr* to tire o.s. out, overdo things
strapaz'zato, -a [strapat'tsato] *ag*: **uova strapazzate** scrambled eggs
stra'pazzo [stra'pattso] *sm* strain, fatigue; **da ~** *(fig)* third-rate
strapi'eno, -a *ag* full to overflowing
strapi'ombo *sm* overhanging rock; **a ~** overhanging
strapo'tere *sm* excessive power
strappa'lacrime *ag inv (fam)*: **romanzo** *(o* **film** *etc)* **~** tear-jerker
strap'pare *vt (gen)* to tear, rip; *(pagina etc)* to tear off, tear out; *(sradicare)* to pull up; *(togliere)*: **~ qc a qn** to snatch sth from sb; *(fig)* to wrest sth from sb; **strapparsi** *vr (lacerarsi)* to rip, tear; *(rompersi)* to break; **strapparsi un muscolo** to tear a muscle
strap'pato, -a *ag* torn, ripped
'strappo *sm (strattone)* pull, tug; *(lacerazione)* tear, rip; *(fig fam: passaggio)* lift *(Brit)*, ride *(US)*; **fare uno ~ alla regola** to make an exception to the rule; **~ muscolare** torn muscle
strapun'tino *sm* jump *o* foldaway seat
strari'pare *vi* to overflow
Stras'burgo *sf* Strasbourg
strasci'care [straʃʃi'kare] *vt* to trail; *(piedi)* to drag; **~ le parole** to drawl
'strascico, -chi ['straʃʃiko] *sm (di abito)* train; *(conseguenza)* after-effect
strata'gemma, -i [strata'dʒɛmma] *sm* stratagem
stra'tega, -ghi *sm* strategist
strate'gia, -'gie [strate'dʒia] *sf* strategy
stra'tegico, -a, ci, che [stra'tɛdʒiko] *ag* strategic
'strato *sm* layer; *(rivestimento)* coat, coating; *(Geo, fig)* stratum; *(Meteor)* stratus
stratos'fera *sf* stratosphere
strat'tone *sm* tug, jerk; **dare uno ~ a qc** to tug *o* jerk sth, give sth a tug *o* jerk
stravac'cato, -a *ag* sprawling

strava'gante *ag* odd, eccentric
strava'ganza [strava'gantsa] *sf* eccentricity
stra'vecchio, -a [stra'vɛkkjo] *ag* very old
strave'dere *vi*: **~ per qn** to dote on sb
stra'visto, -a *pp di* **stravedere**
stra'vizio [stra'vittsjo] *sm* excess
stra'volgere [stra'vɔldʒere] *vt* (*volto*) to contort; (*fig: animo*) to trouble deeply; (*: verità*) to twist, distort
stra'volto, -a *pp di* **stravolgere** ■ *ag* (*persona: per stanchezza etc*) in a terrible state; (*: per sofferenza*) distraught
strazi'ante [strat'tsjante] *ag* (*scena*) harrowing; (*urlo*) bloodcurdling; (*dolore*) excruciating
strazi'are [strat'tsjare] *vt* to torture, torment
'strazio ['strattsjo] *sm* torture; (*fig: cosa fatta male*): **essere uno ~** to be appalling; **fare ~ di** (*corpo, vittima*) to mutilate
'strega, -ghe *sf* witch
stre'gare *vt* to bewitch
stre'gone *sm* (*mago*) wizard; (*di tribù*) witch doctor
stregone'ria *sf* (*pratica*) witchcraft; **fare una ~** to cast a spell
'stregua *sf*: **alla ~ di** by the same standard as
stre'mare *vt* to exhaust
'stremo *sm*: **essere allo ~** to be at the end of one's tether
'strenna *sf*: **~ natalizia** (*regalo*) Christmas present; (*libro*) *book published for the Christmas market*
'strenuo, -a *ag* brave, courageous
strepi'tare *vi* to yell and shout
'strepito *sm* (*di voci, folla*) clamour (*Brit*), clamor (*US*); (*di catene*) clanking, rattling
strepi'toso, -a *ag* clamorous, deafening; (*fig: successo*) resounding
stres'sante *ag* stressful
stres'sare *vt* to put under stress
stres'sato, -a *ag* under stress
'stretta *sf vedi* **stretto**
stretta'mente *av* tightly; (*rigorosamente*) strictly
stret'tezza [stret'tettsa] *sf* narrowness; **strettezze** *sfpl* (*povertà*) poverty *sg*, straitened circumstances
'stretto, -a *pp di* **stringere** ■ *ag* (*corridoio, limiti*) narrow; (*gonna, scarpe, nodo, curva*) tight; (*intimo: parente, amico*) close; (*rigoroso: osservanza*) strict; (*preciso: significato*) precise, exact ■ *sm* (*braccio di mare*) strait ■ *sf* (*di mano*) grasp; (*finanziaria*) squeeze; (*fig: dolore, turbamento*) pang; **a denti stretti** with clenched teeth; **lo ~ necessario** the bare minimum; **una stretta di mano** a handshake; **una stretta al cuore** a sudden sadness; **essere alle strette** to have one's back to the wall
stret'toia *sf* bottleneck; (*fig*) tricky situation
stri'ato, -a *ag* streaked
stria'tura *sf* (*atto*) streaking; (*effetto*) streaks *pl*
stric'nina *sf* strychnine
'strida *sfpl* screaming *sg*
stri'dente *ag* strident
'stridere *vi* (*porta*) to squeak; (*animale*) to screech, shriek; (*colori*) to clash
'strido (*pl(f)* **strida**) *sm* screech, shriek
stri'dore *sm* screeching, shrieking
'stridulo, -a *ag* shrill
'striglia ['striʎʎa] *sf* currycomb
strigli'are [striʎ'ʎare] *vt* (*cavallo*) to curry
strigli'ata [striʎ'ʎata] *sf* (*di cavallo*) currying; (*fig*): **dare una ~ a qn** to give sb a scolding
stril'lare *vt, vi* to scream, shriek
'strillo *sm* scream, shriek
stril'lone *sm* newspaper seller
strimin'zito, -a [strimin'tsito] *ag* (*misero*) shabby; (*molto magro*) skinny
strimpel'lare *vt* (*Mus*) to strum
'stringa, -ghe *sf* lace; (*Inform*) string
strin'gare *vt* (*fig: discorso*) to condense
strin'gato, -a *ag* (*fig*) concise
'stringere ['strindʒere] *vt* (*avvicinare due cose*) to press (together), squeeze (together); (*tenere stretto*) to hold tight, clasp, clutch; (*pugno, mascella, denti*) to clench; (*labbra*) to compress; (*avvitare*) to tighten; (*abito*) to take in; (*scarpe*) to pinch, be tight for; (*fig: concludere: patto*) to make; (*: accelerare: passo*) to quicken ■ *vi* (*incalzare*) to be pressing; **stringersi** *vr* (*accostarsi*): **stringersi a** to press o.s. up against; **~ la mano a qn** to shake sb's hand; **~ gli occhi** to screw up one's eyes; **~ amicizia con qn** to make friends with sb; **stringi stringi** in conclusion; **il tempo stringe** time is short
'strinsi *etc vb vedi* **stringere**
'striscia, -sce ['striʃʃa] *sf* (*di carta, tessuto etc*) strip; (*riga*) stripe; **strisce (pedonali)** zebra crossing *sg*; **a strisce** striped
strisci'ante [striʃ'ʃante] *ag* (*fig peg*) unctuous; (*Econ: inflazione*) creeping
strisci'are [striʃ'ʃare] *vt* (*piedi*) to drag; (*muro, macchina*) to graze ■ *vi* to crawl, creep
'striscio ['striʃʃo] *sm* graze; (*Med*) smear; **colpire di ~** to graze
strisci'one [striʃ'ʃone] *sm* banner
strito'lare *vt* to grind
striz'zare [strit'tsare] *vt* (*arancia*) to squeeze; (*panni*) to wring (out); **~ l'occhio** to wink
striz'zata [strit'tsata] *sf*: **dare una ~ a qc** to give sth a wring; **una ~ d'occhio** a wink

'strofa *sf*, **'strofe** *sf inv* strophe

strofi'naccio [strofi'nattʃo] *sm* duster, cloth; (*per piatti*) dishcloth; (*per pavimenti*) floorcloth

strofi'nare *vt* to rub

stron'care *vt* to break off; (*fig: ribellione*) to suppress, put down; (*: film, libro*) to tear to pieces

'stronzo ['strontso] *sm* (*sterco*) turd; (*fig fam!: persona*) shit (*!*)

stropicci'are [stropit'tʃare] *vt* to rub

stroz'zare [strot'tsare] *vt* (*soffocare*) to choke, strangle; **strozzarsi** *vr* to choke

strozza'tura [strottsa'tura] *sf* (*restringimento*) narrowing; (*di strada etc*) bottleneck

stroz'zino, -a [strot'tsino] *sm/f* (*usuraio*) usurer; (*fig*) shark

struc'care *vt* to remove make-up from; **struccarsi** *vr* to remove one's make-up

'struggere ['struddʒere] *vt* (*fig*) to consume; **struggersi** *vr* (*fig*): **struggersi di** to be consumed with

struggi'mento [struddʒi'mento] *sm* (*desiderio*) yearning

strumen'tale *ag* (*Mus*) instrumental

strumentaliz'zare [strumentalid'dzare] *vt* to exploit, use to one's own ends

strumentalizzazi'one [strumentaliddzat-tsjone] *sf* exploitation

strumentazi'one [strumentat'tsjone] *sf* (*Mus*) orchestration; (*Tecn*) instrumentation

stru'mento *sm* (*arnese, fig*) instrument, tool; (*Mus*) instrument; **~ a corda** *o* **ad arco/a fiato** string(ed)/wind instrument

'strussi *etc vb vedi* **struggere**

'strutto *sm* lard

strut'tura *sf* structure

struttu'rare *vt* to structure

'struzzo ['struttso] *sm* ostrich; **fare lo ~, fare la politica dello ~** to bury one's head in the sand

stuc'care *vt* (*muro*) to plaster; (*vetro*) to putty; (*decorare con stucchi*) to stucco

stucca'tore, -'trice *sm/f* plasterer; (*artista*) stucco worker

stuc'chevole [stuk'kevole] *ag* nauseating; (*fig*) tedious, boring

'stucco, -chi *sm* plaster; (*da vetri*) putty; (*ornamentale*) stucco; **rimanere di ~** (*fig*) to be dumbfounded

stu'dente, -'essa *sm/f* student; (*scolaro*) pupil, schoolboy(-girl)

studen'tesco, -a, schi, sche *ag* student *cpd*

studi'are *vt* to study; **studiarsi** *vr* (*sforzarsi*): **studiarsi di fare** to try *o* endeavour (*Brit*) *o* endeavor (*US*) to do

studi'ato, -a *ag* (*modi, sorriso*) affected

'studio *sm* studying; (*ricerca, saggio, stanza*) study; (*di professionista*) office; (*di artista, Cine, TV, Radio*) studio; (*di medico*) surgery (*Brit*), office (*US*); **studi** *smpl* (*Ins*) studies; **alla fine degli studi** at the end of one's course (of studies); **secondo recenti studi, appare che ...** recent research indicates that ...; **la proposta è allo ~** the proposal is under consideration; **~ legale** lawyer's office

studi'oso, -a *ag* studious, hardworking ▪ *sm/f* scholar

'stufa *sf* stove; **~ elettrica** electric fire *o* heater; **~ a legna/carbone** wood-burning/coal stove

stu'fare *vt* (*Cuc*) to stew; (*fig fam*) to bore

stu'fato *sm* (*Cuc*) stew

'stufo, -a *ag* (*fam*): **essere ~ di** to be fed up with, be sick and tired of

stu'oia *sf* mat

stu'olo *sm* crowd, host

stupefa'cente [stupefa'tʃɛnte] *ag* stunning, astounding ▪ *sm* drug, narcotic

stupe'fare *vt* to stun, astound

stupe'fatto, -a *pp di* **stupefare**

stupefazi'one [stupefat'tsjone] *sf* astonishment

stu'pendo, -a *ag* marvellous, wonderful

stupi'daggine [stupi'daddʒine] *sf* stupid thing (to do *o* say)

stupidità *sf* stupidity

'stupido, -a *ag* stupid

stu'pire *vt* to amaze, stun ▪ *vi* (*anche*: **stupirsi**): **~ (di)** to be amazed (at), be stunned (by); **non c'è da stupirsi** that's not surprising

stu'pore *sm* amazement, astonishment

stu'prare *vt* to rape

stupra'tore *sm* rapist

'stupro *sm* rape

stu'rare *vt* (*lavandino*) to clear

stuzzica'denti [stuttsika'dɛnti] *sm* toothpick

stuzzi'cante [stuttsi'kante] *ag* (*gen*) stimulating; (*appetitoso*) appetizing

stuzzi'care [stuttsi'kare] *vt* (*ferita etc*) to poke (at), prod (at); (*fig*) to tease; (*: appetito*) to whet; (*: curiosità*) to stimulate; **~ i denti** to pick one's teeth

 PAROLA CHIAVE

su (*su + il* = **sul**, *su + lo* = **sullo**, *su + l'* = **sull'**, *su + la* = **sulla**, *su + i* = **sui**, *su + gli* = **sugli**, *su + le* = **sulle**) *prep* **1** (*gen*) on; (*moto*) on(to); (*in cima a*) on (top of); **mettilo sul tavolo** put it on the table; **salire sul treno** to get on the train; **un paesino sul mare** a village by the sea; **è sulla destra** it's on the right; **cento metri sul livello del mare** a hundred metres

above sea level; **fecero rotta su Palermo** they set out for Palermo; **sul vestito portava un golf rosso** she was wearing a red sweater over her dress
2 (*argomento*) about, on; **un libro su Cesare** a book on *o* about Caesar
3 (*circa*) about; **costerà sui 3 milioni** it will cost about 3 million; **una ragazza sui 17 anni** a girl of about 17 (years of age)
4: **su misura** made to measure; **su ordinazione** to order; **su richiesta** on request; **3 casi su dieci** 3 cases out of 10
■ *av* **1** (*in alto, verso l'alto*) up; **vieni su** come on up; **guarda su** look up; **andare su e giù** to go up and down; **su le mani!** hands up!; **in su** (*verso l'alto*) up(wards); (*in poi*) onwards; **vieni su da me?** are you going to come up?; **dai 20 anni in su** from the age of 20 onwards
2 (*addosso*) on; **cos'hai su?** what have you got on?
■ *escl* come on!; **su avanti, muoviti!** come on, hurry up!; **su coraggio!** come on, cheer up!

'sua *vedi* **suo**
sua'dente *ag* persuasive
sub *sm/f inv* skin-diver
su'bacqueo, -a *ag* underwater ■ *sm* skin-diver
subaffit'tare *vt* to sublet
subaf'fitto *sm* (*contratto*) sublet
subal'terno, -a *ag, sm* subordinate; (*Mil*) subaltern
subappal'tare *vt* to subcontract
subap'palto *sm* subcontract
sub'buglio [sub'buʎʎo] *sm* confusion, turmoil; **essere/mettere in ~** to be in/throw into a turmoil
sub'conscio, -a [sub'kɔnʃo] *ag, sm* subconscious
subcosci'ente [subkoʃ'ʃɛnte] *sm* subconscious
'subdolo, -a *ag* underhand, sneaky
suben'trare *vi*: **~ a qn in qc** to take over sth from sb; **sono subentrati altri problemi** other problems arose
su'bire *vt* to suffer, endure
subis'sare *vt* (*fig*): **~ di** to overwhelm with, load with
subi'taneo, -a *ag* sudden
'subito *av* immediately, at once, straight away
subli'mare *vt* (*Psic*) to sublimate; (*Chim*) to sublime
su'blime *ag* sublime
sublo'care *vt* to sublease
sublocazi'one [sublokat'tsjone] *sf* sublease
subnor'male *ag* subnormal ■ *sm/f* mentally handicapped person
subodo'rare *vt* (*insidia etc*) to smell, suspect
subordi'nare *vt* to subordinate
subordi'nato, -a *ag* subordinate; (*dipendente*): **~ a** dependent on, subject to
subordinazi'one [subordinat'tsjone] *sf* subordination
su'bordine *sm*: **in ~** secondarily
subur'bano, -a *ag* suburban
succe'daneo [suttʃe'daneo] *sm* substitute
suc'cedere [sut'tʃɛdere] *vi* (*prendere il posto di qn*): **~ a** to succeed; (*venire dopo*): **~ a** to follow; (*accadere*) to happen; **succedersi** *vr* to follow each other; **~ al trono** to succeed to the throne; **sono cose che succedono** these things happen
successi'one [suttʃes'sjone] *sf* succession; **tassa di ~** death duty (*Brit*), inheritance tax (*US*)
successiva'mente [suttʃessiva'mente] *av* subsequently
succes'sivo, -a [suttʃes'sivo] *ag* successive; **il giorno ~** the following day; **in un momento ~** subsequently
suc'cesso, -a [sut'tʃɛsso] *pp di* **succedere** ■ *sm* (*esito*) outcome; (*buona riuscita*) success; **di ~** (*libro, personaggio*) successful; **avere ~** (*persona*) to be successful; (*idea*) to be well received
succes'sore [suttʃes'sore] *sm* successor
succhi'are [suk'kjare] *vt* to suck (up)
succhi'otto [suk'kjɔtto] *sm* dummy (*Brit*), pacifier (*US*), comforter (*US*)
suc'cinto, -a [sut'tʃinto] *ag* (*discorso*) succinct; (*abito*) brief
'succo, -chi *sm* juice; (*fig*) essence, gist; **~ di frutta/pomodoro** fruit/tomato juice
suc'coso, -a *ag* juicy; (*fig*) pithy
'succube *sm/f* victim; **essere ~ di qn** to be dominated by sb
succur'sale *sf* branch (office)
sud *sm* south ■ *ag inv* south; (*regione*) southern; **verso ~** south, southwards; **l'Italia del S~** Southern Italy; **l'America del S~** South America
Su'dafrica *sm*: **il ~** South Africa
sudafri'cano, -a *ag, sm/f* South African
Suda'merica *sm*: **il ~** South America
sudameri'cano, -a *ag, sm/f* South American
Su'dan *sm*: **il ~** (the) Sudan
suda'nese *ag, sm/f* Sudanese *inv*
su'dare *vi* to perspire, sweat; **~ freddo** to come out in a cold sweat
su'dato, -a *ag* (*persona, mani*) sweaty; (*fig: denaro*) hard-earned ■ *sf* (*anche fig*) sweat; **una vittoria sudata** a hard-won victory;

ho fatto una bella sudata per finirlo in tempo it was a real sweat to get it finished in time
sud'detto, -a *ag* above-mentioned
suddi'tanza [suddi'tantsa] *sf* subjection; (*cittadinanza*) citizenship
sud'dito, -a *sm/f* subject
suddi'videre *vt* to subdivide
suddivisi'one *sf* subdivision
suddi'viso, -a *pp di* **suddividere**
su'dest *sm* south-east; **vento di ~** south-easterly wind; **il ~ asiatico** South-East Asia
sudice'ria [suditʃe'ria] *sf* (*qualità*) filthiness, dirtiness; (*cosa sporca*) dirty thing
'sudicio, -a, ci, ce ['suditʃo] *ag* dirty, filthy
sudici'ume [sudi'tʃume] *sm* dirt, filth
su'doku *sm inv* sudoku
su'dore *sm* perspiration, sweat
su'dovest *sm* south-west; **vento di ~** south-westerly wind
'sue *vedi* **suo**
'Suez ['suez] *sm*: **il Canale di ~** the Suez Canal
suffici'ente [suffi'tʃɛnte] *ag* enough, sufficient; (*borioso*) self-important; (*Ins*) satisfactory
sufficiente'mente [suffitʃente'mente] *av* sufficiently, enough; (*guadagnare, darsi da fare*) enough
suffici'enza [suffi'tʃɛntsa] *sf* (*Ins*) pass mark; **con un'aria di ~** (*fig*) with a condescending air; **a ~** enough; **ne ho avuto a ~!** I've had enough of this!
suf'fisso *sm* (*Ling*) suffix
suffra'gare *vt* to support
suf'fragio [suf'fradʒo] *sm* (*voto*) vote; **~ universale** universal suffrage
suggel'lare [suddʒel'lare] *vt* (*fig*) to seal
suggeri'mento [suddʒeri'mento] *sm* suggestion; (*consiglio*) piece of advice, advice *no pl*; **dietro suo ~** on his advice
sugge'rire [suddʒe'rire] *vt* (*risposta*) to tell; (*consigliare*) to advise; (*proporre*) to suggest; (*Teat*) to prompt; **~ a qn di fare qc** to suggest to sb that he (*o* she) do sth
suggeri'tore, -'trice [suddʒeri'tore] *sm/f* (*Teat*) prompter
suggestio'nare [suddʒestjo'nare] *vt* to influence
suggesti'one [suddʒes'tjone] *sf* (*Psic*) suggestion; (*istigazione*) instigation
sugges'tivo, -a [suddʒes'tivo] *ag* (*paesaggio*) evocative; (*teoria*) interesting, attractive
'sughero ['sugero] *sm* cork
'sugli ['suʎʎi] *prep+det vedi* **su**
'sugo, -ghi *sm* (*succo*) juice; (*di carne*) gravy; (*condimento*) sauce; (*fig*) gist, essence
su'goso, -a *ag* (*frutto*) juicy; (*fig: articolo etc*) pithy
'sui *prep+det vedi* **su**
sui'cida, -i, e [sui'tʃida] *ag* suicidal ■ *sm/f* suicide
suici'darsi [suitʃi'darsi] *vr* to commit suicide
sui'cidio [sui'tʃidjo] *sm* suicide
su'ino, -a *ag*: **carne suina** pork ■ *sm* pig; **suini** *smpl* swine *pl*
sul, sull', 'sulla, 'sulle, 'sullo *prep+det vedi* **su**
sulfa'midico, -a, ci, che *ag, sm* (*Med*) sulphonamide
sulta'nina *sf*: **(uva) ~** sultana
sul'tano, -a *sm/f* sultan/sultana
Su'matra *sf* Sumatra
'summit ['summit] *sm inv* summit
S.U.N.I.A. *sigla m* (*= sindacato unitario nazionale inquilini e assegnatari*) *national association of tenants*
sunnomi'nato, -a *ag* aforesaid *cpd*
'sunto *sm* summary
'suo, 'sua, 'sue, su'oi *det*: **il ~, la sua** *etc* (*di lui*) his; (*di lei*) her; (*di esso*) its; (*con valore indefinito*) one's, his/her; (*forma di cortesia*: *anche*: **Suo**) your *pron*: **il ~, la sua** *etc* his; hers; yours ■ *sm*: **ha speso del ~** he (*o* she *etc*) spent his (*o* her *etc*) own money ■ *sf*: **la sua** (*opinione*) his (*o* her *etc*) view; **i suoi** (*parenti*) his (*o* her *etc*) family; **un ~ amico** a friend of his (*o* hers *etc*); **è dalla sua** he's on his (*o* her *etc*) side; **anche lui ha avuto le sue** (*disavventure*) he's had his problems too; **sta sulle sue** he keeps himself to himself
su'ocero, -a ['swɔtʃero] *sm/f* father(-mother)-in-law; **i suoceri** (*pl*) father- and mother-in-law
su'oi *vedi* **suo**
su'ola *sf* (*di scarpa*) sole
su'olo *sm* (*terreno*) ground; (*terra*) soil
suo'nare *vt* (*Mus*) to play; (*campana*) to ring; (*ore*) to strike; (*clacson, allarme*) to sound ■ *vi* to play; (*telefono, campana*) to ring; (*ore*) to strike; (*clacson, fig: parole*) to sound
suo'nato, -a *ag* (*compiuto*): **ha cinquant'anni suonati** he is well over fifty
suona'tore, -'trice *sm/f* player; **~ ambulante** street musician
suone'ria *sf* (*di sveglia*) alarm; (*di telefono*) ringtone
su'ono *sm* sound
su'ora *sf* (*Rel*) nun; **Suor Maria** Sister Maria
'super *ag inv*: **(benzina) ~** ≈ four-star (petrol) (*Brit*), ≈ premium (*US*)
supera'mento *sm* (*di ostacolo*) overcoming; (*di montagna*) crossing
supe'rare *vt* (*oltrepassare: limite*) to exceed, surpass; (*attraversare: fiume*) to cross; (*sorpassare: veicolo*) to overtake; (*fig: essere più bravo di*) to surpass, outdo; (*: difficoltà*) to

S

overcome; (*: esame*) to get through; **~ qn in altezza/peso** to be taller/heavier than sb; **ha superato la cinquantina** he's over fifty (years of age); **~ i limiti di velocità** to exceed the speed limit; **stavolta ha superato se stesso** this time he has surpassed himself

supe'rato, -a *ag* outmoded

supe'rattico, -ci *sm* penthouse

su'perbia *sf* pride

su'perbo, -a *ag* proud; (*fig*) magnificent, superb

supercondut'tore *sm* superconductor

superena'lotto *sm* *Italian national lottery*

superfici'ale [superfi'tʃale] *ag* superficial

superficialità [superfitʃali'ta] *sf* superficiality

super'ficie, -ci [super'fitʃe] *sf* surface; **tornare in ~** (*a galla*) to return to the surface; (*fig: problemi etc*) to resurface; **~ alare** (*Aer*) wing area; **~ velica** (*Naut*) sail area

su'perfluo, -a *ag* superfluous

superi'ora *sf* (*Rel*: *anche*: **madre superiora**) mother superior

superi'ore *ag* (*piano, arto, classi*) upper; (*più elevato: temperatura, livello*): **~ (a)** higher (than); (*migliore*): **~ (a)** superior (to) ■ *sfpl*: **le superiori** (*Ins*) *vedi* **scuola media superiore**; **il corso ~ di un fiume** the upper reaches of a river; **scuola media ~** ≈ senior comprehensive school (*Brit*), ≈ senior high (school) (*US*)

superiorità *sf* superiority

superla'tivo, -a *ag, sm* superlative

superla'voro *sm* overwork

super'market [super'market] *sm inv* = **supermercato**

supermer'cato *sm* supermarket

super'nova *sf* supernova

superpo'tenza [superpo'tentsa] *sf* (*Pol*) superpower

super'sonico, -a, ci, che *ag* supersonic

su'perstite *ag* surviving ■ *sm/f* survivor

superstizi'one [superstit'tsjone] *sf* superstition

superstizi'oso, -a [superstit'tsjoso] *ag* superstitious

super'strada *sf* ≈ expressway

supervisi'one *sf* supervision

supervi'sore *sm* supervisor

su'pino, -a *ag* supine; **accettazione supina** (*fig*) blind acceptance

suppel'lettile *sf* furnishings *pl*

suppergiù [supper'dʒu] *av* more or less, roughly

suppl. *abbr* (*= supplemento*) supp(l)

supplemen'tare *ag* extra; (*treno*) relief *cpd*; (*entrate*) additional

supple'mento *sm* supplement

sup'plente *ag* temporary; (*insegnante*) supply *cpd* (*Brit*), substitute *cpd* (*US*) ■ *sm/f* temporary member of staff; supply (*o* substitute) teacher

supp'lenza [sup'plɛntsa] *sf*: **fare ~** to do supply (*Brit*) *o* substitute (*US*) teaching

supple'tivo, -a *ag* (*gen*) supplementary; (*sessione d'esami*) extra

'supplica, -che *sf* (*preghiera*) plea; (*domanda scritta*) petition, request

suppli'care *vt* to implore, beseech

suppli'chevole [suppli'kevole] *ag* imploring

sup'plire *vi*: **~ a** to make up for, compensate for

sup'plizio [sup'plittsjo] *sm* torture

sup'pongo, sup'poni *etc vb vedi* **supporre**

sup'porre *vt* to suppose; **supponiamo che ...** let's *o* just suppose that ...

sup'porto *sm* (*sostegno*) support

supposizi'one [suppozit'tsjone] *sf* supposition

sup'posta *sf* (*Med*) suppository

sup'posto, -a *pp di* **supporre**

suppu'rare *vi* to suppurate

suprema'zia [supremat'tsia] *sf* supremacy

su'premo, -a *ag* supreme; **Suprema Corte (di Cassazione)** Supreme Court

surclas'sare *vt* to outclass

surge'lare [surdʒe'lare] *vt* to (deep-)freeze

surge'lato, -a [surdʒe'lato] *ag* (deep-)frozen ■ *smpl*: **i surgelati** frozen food *sg*

surme'nage [syrmə'naʒ] *sm* (*fisico*) overwork; (*mentale*) mental strain; (*Sport*) overtraining

sur'plus *sm inv* (*Econ*) surplus; **~ di manodopera** overmanning

surre'ale *ag* surrealistic

surriscalda'mento *sm* (*gen, Tecn*) overheating

surriscal'dare *vt* to overheat

surro'gato *sm* substitute

suscet'tibile [suʃʃet'tibile] *ag* (*sensibile*) touchy, sensitive; (*soggetto*): **~ di miglioramento** that can be improved, open to improvement

suscettibilità [suʃʃettibili'ta] *sf* touchiness; **urtare la ~ di qn** to hurt sb's feelings

susci'tare [suʃʃi'tare] *vt* to provoke, arouse

su'sina *sf* plum

su'sino *sm* plum (tree)

susseguire *vt* to follow; **susseguirsi** *vr* to follow one another

sussidi'ario, -a *ag* subsidiary; (*treno*) relief *cpd*; (*fermata*) extra

sus'sidio *sm* subsidy; (*aiuto*) aid; **sussidi didattici/audiovisivi** teaching/audiovisual aids; **~ di disoccupazione** unemployment benefit (*Brit*) *o* benefits (*US*); **~ per malattia** sickness benefit

sussi'ego *sm* haughtiness; **con aria di ~** haughtily
sussis'tenza [sussis'tɛntsa] *sf* subsistence
sus'sistere *vi* to exist; (*essere fondato*) to be valid *o* sound
sussul'tare *vi* to shudder
sus'sulto *sm* start
sussur'rare *vt, vi* to whisper, murmur; **si sussurra che ...** it's rumoured (*Brit*) *o* rumored (*US*) that ...
sus'surro *sm* whisper, murmur
su'tura *sf* (*Med*) suture
sutu'rare *vt* to stitch up, suture
suv'via *escl* come on!
SV *sigla* = **Savona**
S.V. *abbr* = **Signoria Vostra**
sva'gare *vt* (*divertire*) to amuse; (*distrarre*): **~ qn** to take sb's mind off things; **svagarsi** *vr* to amuse o.s.; to take one's mind off things
sva'gato, -a *ag* (*persona*) absent-minded; (*scolaro*) inattentive
'**svago, -ghi** *sm* (*riposo*) relaxation; (*ricreazione*) amusement; (*passatempo*) pastime
svaligi'are [zvali'dʒare] *vt* to rob, burgle (*Brit*), burglarize (*US*)
svaligia'tore, -'trice [zvalidʒa'tore] *sm/f* (*di banca*) robber; (*di casa*) burglar
svalu'tare *vt* (*Econ*) to devalue; (*fig*) to belittle; **svalutarsi** *vr* (*Econ*) to be devalued
svalutazi'one [zvalutat'tsjone] *sf* devaluation
svam'pito, -a *ag* absent-minded ■ *sm/f* absent-minded person
sva'nire *vi* to disappear, vanish
sva'nito, -a *ag* (*fig: persona*) absent-minded
svantaggi'ato, -a [zvantad'dʒato] *ag* at a disadvantage
svan'taggio [zvan'taddʒo] *sm* disadvantage; (*inconveniente*) drawback, disadvantage; **tornerà a suo ~** it will work against you
svantaggi'oso, -a [zvantad'dʒoso] *ag* disadvantageous; **è un'offerta svantaggiosa per me** it's not in my interest to accept this offer; **è un prezzo ~** it is not an attractive price
svapo'rare *vi* to evaporate
svapo'rato, -a *ag* (*bibita*) flat
svari'ato, -a *ag* (*vario, diverso*) varied; (*numeroso*) various
'**svastica, -che** *sf* swastika
sve'dese *ag* Swedish ■ *sm/f* Swede ■ *sm* (*Ling*) Swedish
'**sveglia** ['zveʎʎa] *sf* waking up; (*orologio*) alarm (clock); **suonare la ~** (*Mil*) to sound the reveille; **~ telefonica** alarm call
svegli'are [zveʎ'ʎare] *vt* to wake up; (*fig*) to awaken, arouse; **svegliarsi** *vr* to wake up; (*fig*) to be revived, reawaken
'**sveglio, a** ['zveʎʎo] *ag* awake; (*fig*) alert, quick-witted
sve'lare *vt* to reveal
svel'tezza [zvel'tettsa] *sf* (*gen*) speed; (*mentale*) quick-wittedness
svel'tire *vt* (*gen*) to speed up; (*procedura*) to streamline
'**svelto, -a** *ag* (*passo*) quick; (*mente*) quick, alert; (*linea*) slim, slender; **alla svelta** quickly
'**svendere** *vt* to sell off, clear
'**svendita** *sf* (*Comm*) (clearance) sale
sve'nevole *ag* mawkish
'**svengo** *etc vb vedi* **svenire**
sveni'mento *sm* fainting fit, faint
sve'nire *vi* to faint
sven'tare *vt* to foil, thwart
sventa'tezza [zventa'tettsa] *sf* (*distrazione*) absent-mindedness; (*mancanza di prudenza*) rashness
sven'tato, -a *ag* (*distratto*) scatterbrained; (*imprudente*) rash
'**sventola** *sf* (*colpo*) slap; **orecchie a ~** sticking-out ears
svento'lare *vt, vi* to wave, flutter
sven'trare *vt* to disembowel
sven'tura *sf* misfortune
sventu'rato, -a *ag* unlucky, unfortunate
sve'nuto, -a *pp di* **svenire**
svergo'gnare [zvergoɲ'ɲare] *vt* to shame
svergo'gnato, -a [zvergoɲ'ɲato] *ag* shameless ■ *sm/f* shameless person
sver'nare *vi* to spend the winter
sverrò *etc vb vedi* **svenire**
sves'tire *vt* to undress; **svestirsi** *vr* to get undressed
'**Svezia** ['zvɛttsja] *sf*: **la ~** Sweden
svez'zare [zvet'tsare] *vt* to wean
svi'are *vt* to divert; (*fig*) to lead astray; **sviarsi** *vr* to go astray
svico'lare *vi* to slip down an alley; (*fig*) to sneak off
svi'gnarsela [zviɲ'ɲarsela] *vr* to slip away, sneak off
svili'mento *sm* debasement
svi'lire *vt* to debase
svilup'pare *vt*, **svilup'parsi** *vr* to develop
sviluppa'tore, -'trice (*Inform*) *sm/f* developer
svi'luppo *sm* development; (*di industria*) expansion; **in via di ~** in the process of development; **paesi in via di ~** developing countries
svinco'lare *vt* to free, release; (*merce*) to clear
'**svincolo** *sm* (*Comm*) clearance; (*stradale*) motorway (*Brit*) *o* expressway (*US*) intersection
svisce'rare [zviʃʃe'rare] *vt* (*fig: argomento*) to examine in depth

S

svisce'rato, -a [zviʃʃe'rato] *ag* (*amore, odio*) passionate
'svista *sf* oversight
svi'tare *vt* to unscrew
'Svizzera ['zvittsera] *sf*: **la ~** Switzerland
'svizzero, -a ['zvittsero] *ag, sm/f* Swiss
svoglia'tezza [zvoʎʎa'tettsa] *sf* listlessness; indolence
svogli'ato, -a [zvoʎ'ʎato] *ag* listless; (*pigro*) lazy, indolent
svolaz'zare [zvolat'tsare] *vi* to flutter
'svolgere ['zvɔldʒere] *vt* to unwind; (*srotolare*) to unroll; (*fig: argomento*) to develop; (*: piano, programma*) to carry out; **svolgersi** *vr* to unwind; to unroll; (*fig: aver luogo*) to take place; (*: procedere*) to go on; **tutto si è svolto secondo i piani** everything went according to plan
svolgi'mento [zvoldʒi'mento] *sm* development; carrying out; (*andamento*) course
'svolsi *etc vb vedi* **svolgere**
'svolta *sf* (*atto*) turning *no pl*; (*curva*) turn, bend; (*fig*) turning-point; **essere ad una ~ nella propria vita** to be at a crossroads in one's life
svol'tare *vi* to turn
'svolto, -a *pp di* **svolgere**
svuo'tare *vt* to empty (out)
'Swaziland ['swadziland] *sm*: **lo ~** Swaziland

Tt

T, t [ti] *sf o m inv* (*lettera*) T, t; **T come Taranto** ≈ T for Tommy
T *abbr* = **tabaccheria**
t *abbr* = **tara; tonnellata**
TA *sigla* = **Taranto**
tabac'caio, -a *sm/f* tobacconist
tabacche'ria [tabakke'ria] *sf* tobacconist's (shop)
tabacchi'era [tabak'kjɛra] *sf* snuffbox
ta'bacco, -chi *sm* tobacco
ta'bella *sf* (*tavola*) table; (*elenco*) list; **~ di marcia** schedule; **~ dei prezzi** price list
tabel'lone *sm* (*per pubblicità*) billboard; (*per informazioni*) notice board (*Brit*), bulletin board (*US*); (*: in stazione*) timetable board
taber'nacolo *sm* tabernacle
tabù *ag, sm inv* taboo
'tabula 'rasa *sf* tabula rasa; **fare ~** (*fig*) to make a clean sweep
tabu'lare *vt* to tabulate
tabu'lato *sm* (*Inform*) printout
tabula'tore *sm* tabulator
TAC *sigla f* (*Med*: = *Tomografia Assiale Computerizzata*) CAT
'tacca, -che *sf* notch, nick; **di mezza ~** (*fig*) mediocre
taccagne'ria [takkaɲɲe'ria] *sf* meanness, stinginess
tac'cagno, -a [tak'kaɲɲo] *ag* mean, stingy
tac'cheggio [tak'keddʒo] *sm* shoplifting
tac'chino [tak'kino] *sm* turkey
'taccia, -ce ['tattʃa] *sf* bad reputation
tacci'are [tat'tʃare] *vt*: **~ qn di** (*vigliaccheria etc*) to accuse sb of
'taccio *etc* ['tattʃo] *vb vedi* **tacere**
'tacco, -chi *sm* heel
taccu'ino *sm* notebook
ta'cere [ta'tʃere] *vi* to be silent *o* quiet; (*smettere di parlare*) to fall silent ■ *vt* to keep to oneself, say nothing about; **far ~ qn** to make sb be quiet; (*fig*) to silence sb; **mettere a ~ qc** to hush sth up
tachicar'dia [takikar'dia] *sf* (*Med*) tachycardia
ta'chimetro [ta'kimetro] *sm* speedometer
'tacito, -a ['tatʃito] *ag* silent; (*sottinteso*) tacit, unspoken
taci'turno, -a [tatʃi'turno] *ag* taciturn
taci'uto, -a [ta'tʃuto] *pp di* **tacere**
'tacqui *etc vb vedi* **tacere**
ta'fano *sm* horsefly
taffe'ruglio [taffe'ruʎʎo] *sm* brawl, scuffle
taffettà *sm* taffeta
'taglia ['taʎʎa] *sf* (*statura*) height; (*misura*) size; (*riscatto*) ransom; (*ricompensa*) reward; **taglie forti** (*Abbigliamento*) outsize
taglia'boschi [taʎʎa'bɔski] *sm inv* woodcutter
taglia'carte [taʎʎa'karte] *sm inv* paperknife
taglia'legna [taʎʎa'leɲɲa] *sm inv* woodcutter
tagli'ando [taʎ'ʎando] *sm* coupon
tagli'are [taʎ'ʎare] *vt* to cut; (*recidere, interrompere*) to cut off; (*intersecare*) to cut across, intersect; (*carne*) to carve; (*vini*) to blend ■ *vi* to cut; (*prendere una scorciatoia*) to take a short-cut; **~ la strada a qn** to cut across in front of sb; **~ corto** (*fig*) to cut short
taglia'telle [taʎʎa'tɛlle] *sfpl* tagliatelle *pl*
tagli'ato, -a [taʎ'ʎato] *ag*: **essere ~ per qc** (*fig*) to be cut out for sth
taglia'trice [taʎʎa'tritʃe] *sf* (*Tecn*) cutter
taglia'unghie [taʎʎa'ungje] *sm inv* nail clippers *pl*
taglieggi'are [taʎʎed'dʒare] *vt* to exact a tribute from
tagli'ente [taʎ'ʎɛnte] *ag* sharp
tagli'ere [taʎ'ʎɛre] *sm* chopping board; (*per il pane*) bread board
'taglio ['taʎʎo] *sm* (*anche fig*) cut; (*azione*) cutting *no pl*; (*di carne*) piece; (*di stoffa*) length; (*di vini*) blending; **di ~** on edge, edgeways; **banconote di piccolo/grosso ~** notes of small/large denomination; **un bel ~ di capelli** a nice haircut *o* hairstyle; **pizza al ~** pizza by the slice
tagli'ola [taʎ'ʎɔla] *sf* trap, snare

tagli'one [taʎ'ʎone] *sm*: **la legge del ~** the concept of an eye for an eye and a tooth for a tooth
tagliuz'zare [taʎʎut'tsare] *vt* to cut into small pieces
Ta'hiti [ta'iti] *sf* Tahiti
tailan'dese *ag, sm/f, sm* Thai
Tai'landia *sf*: **la ~** Thailand
tai'lleur [ta'jœr] *sm inv* lady's suit
'talamo *sm* (*poetico*) marriage bed
'talco *sm* talcum powder

 PAROLA CHIAVE

'tale *det* **1** (*simile, così grande*) such; **un(a) tale ...** such a ...; **non accetto tali discorsi** I won't allow such talk; **è di una tale arroganza** he is so arrogant; **fa una tale confusione!** he makes such a mess!
2 (*persona o cosa indeterminata*) such-and-such; **il giorno tale all'ora tale** on such-and-such a day at such-and-such a time; **la tal persona** that person; **ha telefonato una tale Giovanna** somebody called Giovanna phoned
3 (*nelle similitudini*): **tale ... tale** like ... like; **tale padre tale figlio** like father, like son; **hai il vestito tale quale il mio** your dress is just *o* exactly like mine
■ *pron* (*indefinito: persona*): **un(a) tale** someone; **quel** (*o* **quella**) **tale** that person, that man (*o* woman); **il tal dei tali** what's-his-name

tale'bano *sm* Taliban
ta'lento *sm* talent
talis'mano *sm* talisman
talk-'show [tɔlk'ʃo] *sm inv* talk *o* chat show
tallo'nare *vt* to pursue; **~ il pallone** (*Calcio, Rugby*) to heel the ball
tallon'cino [tallon'tʃino] *sm* counterfoil (*Brit*), stub; **~ del prezzo** (*di medicinali*) tear-off tag
tal'lone *sm* heel
tal'mente *av* so
ta'lora *av* = **talvolta**
'talpa *sf* (*anche fig*) mole
tal'volta *av* sometimes, at times
tambu'rello *sm* tambourine
tambu'rino *sm* drummer boy
tam'buro *sm* drum; **freni a ~** drum brakes; **pistola a ~** revolver; **a ~ battente** (*fig*) immediately, at once
Ta'migi [ta'midʒi] *sm*: **il ~** the Thames
tampona'mento *sm* (*Aut*) collision; **~ a catena** pile-up
tampo'nare *vt* (*otturare*) to plug; (*urtare: macchina*) to crash *o* ram into
tam'pone *sm* (*Med*) wad, pad; (*per timbri*) ink-pad; (*respingente*) buffer; **~ assorbente** tampon
'tamtam *sm inv* (*fig*) grapevine
'tana *sf* lair, den; (*fig*) den, hideout
'tanfo *sm* (*di muffa*) musty smell; (*puzza*) stench
tan'gente [tan'dʒɛnte] *ag* (*Mat*): **~ a** tangential to ■ *sf* tangent; (*quota*) share; (*denaro estorto*) rake-off (*fam*), cut
tangen'topoli [tandʒɛn'topoli] *sf* (*Pol, Media*) Bribesville; *see note*

TANGENTOPOLI

Tangentopoli refers to the corruption scandal of the early 1990s which involved a large number of politicians from all parties, including government ministers, as well as leading industrialists and business people. Subsequent investigations unearthed a complex series of illegal payments and bribes involving both public and private money. The scandal began in Milan, which came to be known as *Tangentopoli*, or "Bribesville".

tangenzi'ale [tandʒen'tsjale] *sf* (*strada*) bypass
'Tangeri ['tandʒeri] *sf* Tangiers
tan'gibile [tan'dʒibile] *ag* tangible
tangibil'mente [tandʒibilmente] *av* tangibly
'tango, -ghi *sm* tango
'tanica, -che *sf* jerry can
tan'nino *sm* tannin
tan'tino: **un tan'tino** *av* (*un po'*) a little, a bit; (*alquanto*) rather

 PAROLA CHIAVE

'tanto, -a *det* **1** (*molto: quantità*) a lot of, much; (*: numero*) a lot of, many; **tanto pane/latte** a lot of bread/milk; **tanto tempo** a lot of time, a long time; **tanti auguri!** all the best!; **tante grazie** many thanks; **tanto persone** a lot of people, many people; **tante volte** many times, often; **ogni tanti chilometri** every so many kilometres
2 (*così tanto: quantità*) so much, such a lot of; (*: numero*) so many, such a lot of; **tanta fatica per niente!** a lot of trouble for nothing!; **ha tanto coraggio che ...** he's got so much courage that ..., he's so brave that ...; **ho aspettato per tanto tempo** I waited so long *o* for such a long time
3: **tanto ... quanto** (*quantità*) as much ... as; (*numero*) as many ... as; **ho tanta pazienza**

quanta ne hai tu I have as much patience as you have *o* as you; **ha tanti amici quanti nemici** he has as many friends as he has enemies
■ *pron* **1** (*molto*) much, a lot; (*così tanto*) so much, such a lot; **tanti, e** many, a lot; so many; such a lot; **credevo ce ne fosse tanto** I thought there was (such) a lot, I thought there was plenty; **una persona come tante** a person just like any other; **è passato tanto** (*tempo*) it's been so long; **è tanto che aspetto** I've been waiting for a long time; **tanto di guadagnato!** so much the better!
2: **tanto quanto** (*denaro*) as much as; (*cioccolatini*) as many as; **ne ho tanto quanto basta** I have as much as I need; **due volte tanto** twice as much
3 (*indeterminato*) so much; **tanto per l'affitto, tanto per il gas** so much for the rent, so much for the gas; **costa un tanto al metro** it costs so much per metre; **di tanto in tanto, ogni tanto** every so often; **tanto vale che ...** I (*o* we *etc*) may as well ...; **tanto meglio!** so much the better!; **tanto peggio per lui!** so much the worse for him!; **se tanto mi dà tanto** if that's how things are; **guardare qc con tanto d'occhi** to gaze wide-eyed at sth
■ *av* **1** (*molto*) very; **vengo tanto volentieri** I'd be very glad to come; **non ci vuole tanto a capirlo** it doesn't take much to understand it
2 (*così tanto: con ag, av*) so; (*: con vb*) so much, such a lot; **è tanto bella!** she's so beautiful!; **non urlare tanto (forte)** don't shout so much; **sto tanto meglio adesso** I'm so much better now; **era tanto bella da non credere** she was incredibly beautiful; **tanto ... che** so ... (that); **tanto ... da** so ... as
3: **tanto ... quanto** as ... as; **conosco tanto Carlo quanto suo padre** I know both Carlo and his father; **non è poi tanto complicato quanto sembra** it's not as difficult as it seems; **è tanto bella quanto buona** she is as good as she is beautiful; **tanto più insisti, tanto più non mollerà** the more you insist, the more stubborn he'll be; **quanto più ... tanto meno** the more ... the less; **quanto più lo conosco tanto meno mi piace** the better I know him the less I like him
4 (*solamente*) just; **tanto per cambiare/scherzare** just for a change/a joke; **una volta tanto** for once
5 (*a lungo*) (for) long
■ *cong* after all; **non insistere, tanto è inutile** don't keep on, it's no use; **lascia stare, tanto è troppo tardi** forget it, it's too late

Tanza'nia [tandza'nia] *sf*: **la ~** Tanzania
tapi'oca *sf* tapioca
ta'piro *sm* (*Zool*) tapir
'tappa *sf* (*luogo di sosta, fermata*) stop, halt; (*parte di un percorso*) stage, leg; (*Sport*) lap; **a tappe** in stages; **bruciare le tappe** (*fig*) to be a whizz kid
tappa'buchi [tappa'buki] *sm inv* stopgap; **fare da ~** to act as a stopgap
tap'pare *vt* to plug, stop up; (*bottiglia*) to cork; **tapparsi il naso** to hold one's nose; **tapparsi le orecchie** to turn a deaf ear; **tapparsi gli occhi** to turn a blind eye
tappa'rella *sf* rolling shutter
tappe'tino *sm* (*per auto*) car mat; **~ antiscivolo** (*da bagno*) non-slip mat
tap'peto *sm* carpet; (*anche*: **tappetino**) rug; (*di tavolo*) cloth; (*Sport*): **andare al ~** to go down for the count; **mettere sul ~** (*fig*) to bring up for discussion
tappez'zare [tappet'tsare] *vt* (*con carta*) to paper; (*rivestire*): **~ qc (di)** to cover sth (with)
tappezze'ria [tappettse'ria] *sf* (*arredamento*) soft furnishings *pl*; (*carta da parati*) wall covering; (*di automobile*) upholstery; **far da ~** (*fig*) to be a wallflower
tappezzi'ere [tappet'tsjɛre] *sm* upholsterer
'tappo *sm* stopper; (*in sughero*) cork; **~ a corona** bottle top; **~ a vite** screw top
TAR *sigla m* = **Tribunale Amministrativo Regionale**
'tara *sf* (*peso*) tare; (*Med*) hereditary defect; (*difetto*) flaw
taran'tella *sf* tarantella
ta'rantola *sf* tarantula
ta'rare *vt* (*Comm*) to tare; (*Tecn*) to calibrate
ta'rato, -a *ag* (*Comm*) tared; (*Med*) with a hereditary defect
tara'tura *sf* (*Comm*) taring; (*Tecn*) calibration
tarchi'ato, -a [tar'kjato] *ag* stocky, thickset
tar'dare *vi* to be late ■ *vt* to delay; **~ a fare** to delay doing
'tardi *av* late; **più ~** later (on); **al più ~** at the latest; **sul ~** (*verso sera*) late in the day; **far ~** to be late; (*restare alzato*) to stay up late
tar'divo, -a *ag* (*primavera*) late; (*rimedio*) belated, tardy; (*fig: bambino*) retarded
'tardo, -a *ag* (*lento, fig: ottuso*) slow; (*tempo: avanzato*) late
tar'dona *sf* (*peg*): **essere una ~** to be mutton dressed as lamb
'targa, -ghe *sf* plate; (*Aut*) number (*Brit*) *o* license (*US*) plate; *vedi anche* **circolazione**
tar'gare *vt* (*Aut*) to register

t

targ'hetta [tar'getta] *sf* (*con nome: su porta*) nameplate; (*: su bagaglio*) name tag
ta'riffa *sf* (*gen*) rate, tariff; (*di trasporti*) fare; (*elenco*) price list; tariff; **la ~ in vigore** the going rate; **~ normale/ridotta** standard/ reduced rate; (*su mezzi di trasporto*) full/ concessionary fare; **~ salariale** wage rate; **~ unica** flat rate; **tariffe doganali** customs rates *o* tariff; **tariffe postali/telefoniche** postal/telephone charges
tarif'fario, -ii *ag*: **aumento ~** increase in charges *o* rates ■ *sm* tariff, table of charges
'tarlo *sm* woodworm
'tarma *sf* moth
tarmi'cida, -i [tarmi'tʃida] *ag, sm* moth-killer
ta'rocco, -chi *sm* tarot card; **tarocchi** *smpl* (*gioco*) tarot *sg*
tar'pare *vt* (*fig*): **~ le ali a qn** to clip sb's wings
tartagli'are [tartaʎ'ʎare] *vi* to stutter, stammer
'tartaro, -a *ag, sm* (*in tutti i sensi*) tartar
tarta'ruga, -ghe *sf* tortoise; (*di mare*) turtle; (*materiale*) tortoiseshell
tartas'sare *vt* (*fam*): **~ qn** to give sb the works; **~ qn a un esame** to give sb a grilling at an exam
tar'tina *sf* canapé
tar'tufo *sm* (*Bot*) truffle
'tasca, -sche *sf* pocket; **da ~** pocket *cpd*; **fare i conti in ~ a qn** (*fig*) to meddle in sb's affairs
tas'cabile *ag* (*libro*) pocket *cpd*
tasca'pane *sm* haversack
tas'chino [tas'kino] *sm* breast pocket
Tas'mania *sf*: **la ~** Tasmania
'tassa *sf* (*imposta*) tax; (*doganale*) duty; (*per iscrizione: a scuola etc*) fee; **~ di circolazione/di soggiorno** road/tourist tax
tas'sametro *sm* taximeter
tas'sare *vt* to tax; to levy a duty on
tassa'tivo, -a *ag* peremptory
tassazi'one [tassat'tsjone] *sf* taxation; **soggetto a ~** taxable
tas'sello *sm* (*di legno, pietra*) plug; (*assaggio*) wedge
tassì *sm inv* = **taxi**
tas'sista, -i, e *sm/f* taxi driver
'tasso *sm* (*di natalità, d'interesse etc*) rate; (*Bot*) yew; (*Zool*) badger; **~ di cambio/d'interesse** rate of exchange/interest; **~ di crescita** growth rate
tas'tare *vt* to feel; **~ il terreno** (*fig*) to see how the land lies
tasti'era *sf* keyboard
tastie'rino *sm*: **~ numerico** numeric keypad
'tasto *sm* key; (*tatto*) touch, feel; **toccare un ~ delicato** (*fig*) to touch on a delicate subject; **toccare il ~ giusto** (*fig*) to strike the right note; **~ funzione** (*Inform*) function key; **~ delle maiuscole** (*su macchina da scrivere etc*) shift key
tas'toni *av*: **procedere (a) ~** to grope one's way forward
'tata *sf* (*linguaggio infantile*) nanny
'tattico, -a, ci, che *ag* tactical ■ *sf* tactics *pl*
'tatto *sm* (*senso*) touch; (*fig*) tact; **duro al ~** hard to the touch; **aver ~** to be tactful, have tact
tatu'aggio [tatu'addʒo] *sm* tattooing; (*disegno*) tattoo
tatu'are *vt* to tattoo
tauma'turgico, -a, ci, che [tauma'turdʒiko] *ag* (*fig*) miraculous
TAV [tav] *sigla m o f inv* (= *treno alta velocità*) high-speed train; (*sistema*) high-speed rail system
ta'verna *sf* (*osteria*) tavern
'tavola *sf* table; (*asse*) plank, board; (*lastra*) tablet; (*quadro*) panel (painting); (*illustrazione*) plate; **~ calda** snack bar; **~ pieghevole** folding table
tavo'lata *sf* company at table
tavo'lato *sm* boarding; (*pavimento*) wooden floor
tavo'letta *sf* tablet, bar; **a ~** (*Aut*) flat out
tavo'lino *sm* small table; (*scrivania*) desk; **~ da tè/gioco** coffee/card table; **mettersi a ~** to get down to work; **decidere qc a ~** (*fig*) to decide sth on a theoretical level
'tavolo *sm* table; **~ da disegno** drawing board; **~ da lavoro** desk; (*Tecn*) workbench; **~ operatorio** (*Med*) operating table
tavo'lozza [tavo'lɔttsa] *sf* (*Arte*) palette
'taxi *sm inv* taxi
'tazza ['tattsa] *sf* cup; **~ da caffè/tè** coffee/tea cup; **una ~ di caffè/tè** a cup of coffee/tea
taz'zina [tat'tsina] *sf* coffee cup
TBC *abbr f* (= *tubercolosi*) TB
TCI *sigla m* = **Touring Club Italiano**
TE *sigla* = **Teramo**
te *pron* (*soggetto: in forme comparative, oggetto*) you
tè *sm inv* tea; (*trattenimento*) tea party
tea'trale *ag* theatrical
te'atro *sm* theatre; **~ comico** comedy; **~ di posa** film studio
'tecnico, -a, ci, che *ag* technical ■ *sm/f* technician ■ *sf* technique; (*tecnologia*) technology
tecnolo'gia [teknolo'dʒia] *sf* technology; **alta ~** high technology, hi-tech
tecno'logico, -a, ci, che [tekno'lɔdʒiko] *ag* technological
te'desco, -a, schi, sche *ag, sm/f, sm* German; **~ orientale/occidentale** East/West German
tedi'are *vt* (*infastidire*) to bother, annoy; (*annoiare*) to bore

'tedio *sm* tedium, boredom
tedi'oso, -a *ag* tedious, boring
te'game *sm* (*Cuc*) pan; **al ~** fried
'teglia ['teʎʎa] *sf* (*Cuc: per dolci*) (baking) tin (*Brit*), cake pan (*US*); (*: per arrosti*) (roasting) tin
'tegola *sf* tile
Teh'ran *sf* Tehran
tei'era *sf* teapot
te'ina *sf* (*Chim*) theine
tel. *abbr* (= *telefono*) tel
'tela *sf* (*tessuto*) cloth; (*per vele, quadri*) canvas; (*dipinto*) canvas, painting; **di ~** (*calzoni*) (heavy) cotton *cpd*; (*scarpe, borsa*) canvas *cpd*; **~ cerata** oilcloth; **~ di ragno** spider's web
te'laio *sm* (*apparecchio*) loom; (*struttura*) frame
Tel A'viv *sf* Tel Aviv
tele... *prefisso* tele...
teleabbo'nato *sm* television licence holder
tele'camera *sf* television camera
telecoman'dare *vt* to operate by remote control
teleco'mando *sm* remote control; (*dispositivo*) remote-control device
telecomunicazi'oni [telekomunikat'tsjoni] *sfpl* telecommunications
teleconfe'renza *sf* teleconferencing
tele'cronaca, -che *sf* television report
telecro'nista, -i, e *sm/f* (television) commentator
tele'ferica, -che *sf* cableway
tele'film *sm inv* television film
telefo'nare *vi* to telephone, ring; (*fare una chiamata*) to make a phone call ■ *vt* to telephone; **~ a qn** to telephone sb, phone *o* ring *o* call sb (up)
telefo'nata *sf* (telephone) call; **~ urbana/interurbana** local/long-distance call; **~ a carico del destinatario** reverse charge (*Brit*) *o* collect (*US*) call; **~ con preavviso** person-to-person call
telefonica'mente *av* by (tele)phone
tele'fonico, -a, ci, che *ag* (tele)phone *cpd*
telefo'nino *sm* (*cellulare*) mobile phone
telefo'nista, -i, e *sm/f* telephonist; (*d'impresa*) switchboard operator
te'lefono *sm* telephone; **essere al ~** to be on the (tele)phone; **~ a gettoni** ≈ pay phone; **~ azzurro** ≈ Childline; **~ interno** internal phone; **~ pubblico** public phone, call box (*Brit*); **~ rosa** ≈ rape crisis
telegior'nale [teledʒor'nale] *sm* television news (programme)
telegra'fare *vt, vi* to telegraph, cable
telegra'fia *sf* telegraphy
tele'grafico, -a, ci, che *ag* telegraph *cpd*, telegraphic
telegra'fista, -i, e *sm/f* telegraphist, telegraph operator
te'legrafo *sm* telegraph; (*ufficio*) telegraph office
tele'gramma, -i *sm* telegram
telela'voro *sm* teleworking
tele'matica *sf* data transmission; telematics *sg*
teleno'vela *sf* soap opera
teleobiet'tivo *sm* telephoto lens *sg*
telepa'tia *sf* telepathy
tele'quiz [tele'kwits] *sm inv* (*TV*) game show
teles'chermo [teles'kɛrmo] *sm* television screen
teles'copio *sm* telescope
telescri'vente *sf* teleprinter (*Brit*), teletypewriter (*US*)
teleselet'tivo, -a *ag*: **prefisso ~** dialling code (*Brit*), dial code (*US*)
teleselezi'one [teleselet'tsjone] *sf* direct dialling
telespetta'tore, -'trice *sm/f* (television) viewer
tele'text *sm inv* teletext
tele'vendita [tele'vendita] *sf* teleshopping
tele'video *sm videotext service*
televisi'one *sf* television; *see note*

TELEVISIONE

Three state-owned channels, RAI 1, 2 and 3, and a large number of private companies broadcast television programmes in Italy. Some of the latter function at purely local level, while others are regional; some form part of a network, while others remain independent. As a public corporation, RAI reports to the Post and Telecommunications Ministry. Both RAI and the private-sector channels compete for advertising revenues.

televi'sore *sm* television set
'telex *sm inv* telex
'telo *sm* length of cloth
te'lone *sm* (*per merci etc*) tarpaulin; (*sipario*) drop curtain
'tema, -i *sm* theme; (*Ins*) essay, composition
te'matica *sf* basic themes *pl*
teme'rario, -a *ag* rash, reckless
te'mere *vt* to fear, be afraid of; (*essere sensibile a: freddo, calore*) to be sensitive to ■ *vi* to be afraid; (*essere preoccupato*): **~ per** to worry about, fear for; **~ di/che** to be afraid of/that
'tempera *sf* (*pittura*) tempera; (*dipinto*) painting in tempera

t

temperama'tite *sm inv* pencil sharpener
tempera'mento *sm* temperament
tempe'rante *ag* moderate
tempe'rare *vt* (*aguzzare*) to sharpen; (*fig*) to moderate, control, temper
tempe'rato, -a *ag* moderate, temperate; (*clima*) temperate
tempera'tura *sf* temperature; **~ ambiente** room temperature
tempe'rino *sm* penknife
tem'pesta *sf* storm; **~ di sabbia/neve** sand/snowstorm
tempes'tare *vt* (*percuotere*): **~ qn di colpi** to rain blows on sb; (*bombardare*): **~ qn di domande** to bombard sb with questions; (*ornare*) to stud
tempestività *sf* timeliness
tempes'tivo, -a *ag* timely
tempes'toso, -a *ag* stormy
'tempia *sf* (*Anat*) temple
'tempio *sm* (*edificio*) temple
tem'pismo *sm* sense of timing
tem'pistiche [tem'pistike] *sfpl* (*Comm*) time and motion
'tempo *sm* (*Meteor*) weather; (*cronologico*) time; (*epoca*) time, times *pl*; (*di film, gioco: parte*) part; (*Mus*) time; (*: battuta*) beat; (*Ling*) tense; **un ~** once; **da ~** for a long time now; **~ fa** some time ago; **poco ~ dopo** not long after; **a ~ e luogo** at the right time and place; **ogni cosa a suo ~** we'll (*o* you'll *etc*) deal with it in due course; **al ~ stesso** *o* **a un ~** at the same time; **per ~** early; **per qualche ~** for a while; **trovare il ~ di fare qc** to find the time to do sth; **aver fatto il proprio ~** to have had its (*o* his *etc*) day; **primo/secondo ~** (*Teat*) first/second part; (*Sport*) first/second half; **rispettare i tempi** to keep to the timetable; **stringere i tempi** to speed things up; **con i tempi che corrono** these days; **in questi ultimi tempi** of late; **ai miei tempi** in my day; **~ di cottura** cooking time; **in ~ utile** in due time *o* course; **tempi di esecuzione** (*Comm*) time scale *sg*; **tempi di lavorazione** (*Comm*) throughput time *sg*; **tempi morti** (*Comm*) downtime *sg*, idle time *sg*
tempo'rale *ag* temporal ■ *sm* (*Meteor*) (thunder)storm
tempora'lesco, -a, schi, sche *ag* stormy
tempo'raneo, -a *ag* temporary
temporeggi'are [tempored'dʒare] *vi* to play for time, temporize
'tempra *sf* (*Tecn: atto*) tempering, hardening; (*: effetto*) temper; (*fig: costituzione fisica*) constitution; (*: intellettuale*) temperament
tem'prare *vt* to temper
te'nace [te'natʃe] *ag* strong, tough; (*fig*) tenacious
te'nacia [te'natʃa] *sf* tenacity
te'naglie [te'naʎʎe] *sfpl* pincers *pl*
'tenda *sf* (*riparo*) awning; (*di finestra*) curtain; (*per campeggio etc*) tent
ten'daggio [ten'daddʒo] *sm* curtaining, curtains *pl*, drapes *pl* (*US*)
ten'denza [ten'dɛntsa] *sf* tendency; (*orientamento*) trend; **avere ~ a** *o* **per qc** to have a bent for sth; **~ al rialzo/ribasso** (*Borsa*) upward/downward trend
tendenziosità [tendentsjosi'ta] *sf* tendentiousness
tendenzi'oso, -a [tenden'tsjoso] *ag* tendentious, bias(s)ed
'tendere *vt* (*allungare al massimo*) to stretch, draw tight; (*porgere: mano*) to hold out; (*fig: trappola*) to lay, set ■ *vi*: **~ a qc/a fare** to tend towards sth/to do; **tutti i nostri sforzi sono tesi a ...** all our efforts are geared towards ...; **~ l'orecchio** to prick up one's ears; **il tempo tende al caldo** the weather is getting hot; **un blu che tende al verde** a greenish blue
ten'dina *sf* curtain
'tendine *sm* tendon, sinew
ten'done *sm* (*da circo*) big top
ten'dopoli *sf inv* (large) camp
'tenebre *sfpl* darkness *sg*
tene'broso, -a *ag* dark, gloomy
te'nente *sm* lieutenant
te'nere *vt* to hold; (*conservare, mantenere*) to keep; (*ritenere, considerare*) to consider; (*spazio: occupare*) to take up, occupy; (*seguire: strada*) to keep to; (*dare: lezione, conferenza*) to give ■ *vi* to hold; (*colori*) to be fast; (*dare importanza*): **~ a** to care about; **~ a fare** to want to do, be keen to do; **tenersi** *vr* (*stare in una determinata posizione*) to stand; (*stimarsi*) to consider o.s.; (*aggrapparsi*): **tenersi a** to hold on to; (*attenersi*): **tenersi a** to stick to; **~ in gran conto** *o* **considerazione qn** to have a high regard for sb, think highly of sb; **~ conto di qc** to take sth into consideration; **~ presente qc** to bear sth in mind; **non ci sono scuse che tengano** I'll take no excuses; **tenersi per la mano** (*uso reciproco*) to hold hands; **tenersi in piedi** to stay on one's feet
tene'rezza [tene'rettsa] *sf* tenderness
'tenero, -a *ag* tender; (*pietra, cera, colore*) soft; (*fig*) tender, loving ■ *sm*: **tra quei due c'è del ~** there's a romance budding between those two
'tengo *etc vb vedi* **tenere**
'tenia *sf* tapeworm
'tenni *etc vb vedi* **tenere**
'tennis *sm* tennis; **~ da tavolo** table tennis

ten'nista, -i, e *sm/f* tennis player
te'nore *sm* (*tono*) tone; (*Mus*) tenor; **~ di vita** way of life; (*livello*) standard of living
tensi'one *sf* tension; **ad alta ~** (*Elettr*) high-voltage *cpd*, high-tension *cpd*
tentaco'lare *ag* tentacular; (*fig: città*) magnet-like
ten'tacolo *sm* tentacle
ten'tare *vt* (*indurre*) to tempt; (*provare*): **~ qc/di fare** to attempt *o* try sth/to do; **~ la sorte** to try one's luck
tenta'tivo *sm* attempt
tentazi'one [tentat'tsjone] *sf* temptation; **aver la ~ di fare** to be tempted to do
tentenna'mento *sm* (*fig*) hesitation, wavering; **dopo molti tentennamenti** after much hesitation
tenten'nare *vi* to shake, be unsteady; (*fig*) to hesitate, waver ■ *vt*: **~ il capo** to shake one's head
ten'toni *av*: **andare a ~** (*anche fig*) to grope one's way
'tenue *ag* (*sottile*) fine; (*colore*) soft; (*fig*) slender, slight
te'nuta *sf* (*capacità*) capacity; (*divisa*) uniform; (*abito*) dress; (*Agr*) estate; **a ~ d'aria** airtight; **~ di strada** roadholding power; **in ~ da lavoro** in one's working clothes; **in ~ da sci** in a skiing outfit
teolo'gia [teolo'dʒia] *sf* theology
teo'logico, -a, ci, che [teo'lɔdʒiko] *ag* theological
te'ologo, -gi *sm* theologian
teo'rema, -i *sm* theorem
teo'ria *sf* theory; **in ~** in theory, theoretically
te'orico, -a, ci, che *ag* theoretic(al) ■ *sm* theorist, theoretician; **a livello ~, in linea teorica** theoretically
teoriz'zare [teorid'dzare] *vt* to theorize
'tepido, -a *ag* = **tiepido**
te'pore *sm* warmth
'teppa *sf* mob, hooligans *pl*
tep'paglia [tep'paʎʎa] *sf* hooligans *pl*
tep'pismo *sm* hooliganism
tep'pista, -i *sm* hooligan
tera'peutico, -a, ci, che *ag* therapeutic
tera'pia *sf* therapy; **~ di gruppo** group therapy
tera'pista, -i, e *sm/f* therapist
tergicris'tallo [terdʒikris'tallo] *sm* windscreen (*Brit*) *o* windshield (*US*) wiper
tergiver'sare [terdʒiver'sare] *vi* to shilly-shally
'tergo *sm*: **a ~** behind; **vedi a ~** please turn over
'terital® *sm inv* Terylene®
ter'male *ag* thermal
'terme *sfpl* thermal baths
'termico, -a, ci, che *ag* thermal; **centrale termica** thermal power station
termi'nale *ag* (*fase, parte*) final; (*Med*) terminal ■ *sm* terminal; **tratto ~** (*di fiume*) lower reaches *pl*
termi'nare *vt* to end; (*lavoro*) to finish ■ *vi* to end
terminazi'one [terminat'tsjone] *sf* (*fine*) end; (*Ling*) ending; **terminazioni nervose** (*Anat*) nerve endings
'termine *sm* term; (*fine, estremità*) end; (*di territorio*) boundary, limit; **fissare un ~** to set a deadline; **portare a ~ qc** to bring sth to a conclusion; **contratto a ~** (*Comm*) forward contract; **a breve/lungo ~** short-/long-term; **ai termini di legge** by law; **in altri termini** in other words; **parlare senza mezzi termini** to talk frankly, not to mince one's words
terminolo'gia [terminolo'dʒia] *sf* terminology
'termite *sf* termite
termoco'perta *sf* electric blanket
ter'mometro *sm* thermometer
termonucle'are *ag* thermonuclear
'termos *sm inv* = **thermos**
termosi'fone *sm* radiator; **(riscaldamento a) ~** central heating
ter'mostato *sm* thermostat
'terna *sf* set of three; (*lista di tre nomi*) list of three candidates
'terno *sm* (*al lotto etc*) (set of) three winning numbers; **vincere un ~ al lotto** (*fig*) to hit the jackpot
'terra *sf* (*gen, Elettr*) earth; (*sostanza*) soil, earth; (*opposto al mare*) land *no pl*; (*regione, paese*) land; (*argilla*) clay; **terre** *sfpl* (*possedimento*) lands, land *sg*; **a** *o* **per ~** (*stato*) on the ground (*o* floor); (*moto*) to the ground, down; **mettere a ~** (*Elettr*) to earth; **essere a ~** (*fig: depresso*) to be at rock bottom; **via ~** (*viaggiare*) by land, overland; **strada in ~ battuta** dirt track; **~ di nessuno** no man's land; **la T~ Santa** the Holy Land; **~ di Siena** sienna; **~ ~** (*fig: persona, argomento*) prosaic, pedestrian
terra-'aria *ag inv* (*Mil*) ground-to-air
terra'cotta *sf* terracotta; **vasellame di ~** earthenware
terra'ferma *sf* dry land, terra firma; (*continente*) mainland
ter'raglia [ter'raʎʎa] *sf* pottery; **terraglie** *sfpl* (*oggetti*) crockery *sg*, earthenware *sg*
Terra'nova *sf*: **la ~** Newfoundland
terrapi'eno *sm* embankment, bank
'terra-'terra *ag inv* (*Mil*) surface-to-surface

ter'razza [ter'rattsa] *sf*, **ter'razzo** [ter'rattso] *sm* terrace
terremo'tato, -a *ag* (*zona*) devastated by an earthquake ■ *sm/f* earthquake victim
terre'moto *sm* earthquake
ter'reno, -a *ag* (*vita, beni*) earthly ■ *sm* (*suolo, fig*) ground; (*Comm*) land *no pl*, plot (of land); site; (*Sport, Mil*) field; **perdere ~** (*anche fig*) to lose ground; **un ~ montuoso** a mountainous terrain; **~ alluvionale** (*Geo*) alluvial soil
'terreo, -a *ag* (*viso, colorito*) wan
ter'restre *ag* (*superficie*) of the earth, earth's; (*di terra: battaglia, animale*) land *cpd*; (*Rel*) earthly, worldly
ter'ribile *ag* terrible, dreadful
ter'riccio [ter'rittʃo] *sm* soil
terri'ero, -a *ag*: **proprietà terriera** landed property; **proprietario ~** landowner
terrifi'cante *ag* terrifying
ter'rina *sf* (*zuppiera*) tureen
territori'ale *ag* territorial
terri'torio *sm* territory
ter'rone, -a *sm/f* *derogatory term used by Northern Italians to describe Southern Italians*
ter'rore *sm* terror; **avere il ~ di qc** to be terrified of sth
terro'rismo *sm* terrorism
terro'rista, -i, e *sm/f* terrorist
terroriz'zare [terrorid'dzare] *vt* to terrorize
'terso, -a *ag* clear
ter'zetto [ter'tsetto] *sm* (*Mus*) trio, terzetto; (*di persone*) trio
terzi'ario, -a [ter'tsjarjo] *ag* (*Geo, Econ*) tertiary
ter'zino [ter'tsino] *sm* (*Calcio*) fullback, back
'terzo, -a ['tɛrtso] *ag* third ■ *sm* (*frazione*) third; (*Dir*) third party ■ *sf* (*gen*) third; (*Aut*) third (gear); (*di trasporti*) third class; (*Scol: elementare*) *third year at primary school*; (*: media*) *third year at secondary school*; (*: superiore*) *sixth year at secondary school*; **terzi** *smpl* (*altri*) others, other people; **agire per conto di terzi** to act on behalf of a third party; **assicurazione contro terzi** third-party insurance (*Brit*), liability insurance (*US*); **la terza età** old age; **il ~ mondo** the Third World; **di terz'ordine** third rate; **la terza pagina** (*Stampa*) the Arts page
'tesa *sf* brim; **a larghe tese** wide-brimmed
'teschio ['tɛskjo] *sm* skull
'tesi *sf inv* thesis; **~ di laurea** degree thesis
'tesi *etc vb vedi* **tendere**
'teso, -a *pp di* **tendere** ■ *ag* (*tirato*) taut, tight; (*fig*) tense
tesore'ria *sf* treasury
tesori'ere *sm* treasurer
te'soro *sm* treasure; **il Ministero del T~** the Treasury; **far ~ dei consigli di qn** to take sb's advice to heart
'tessera *sf* (*documento*) card; (*di abbonato*) season ticket; (*di giornalista*) pass; **ha la ~ del partito** he's a party member; **~ elettorale** ballot paper
tesse'rare *vt* (*iscrivere*) to give a membership card to
tesse'rato, -a *sm/f* (*di società sportiva etc*) (fully paid-up) member; (*Pol*) (card-carrying) member
'tessere *vt* to weave; **~ le lodi di qn** (*fig*) to sing sb's praises
'tessile *ag, sm* textile
tessi'tore, -'trice *sm/f* weaver
tessi'tura *sf* weaving
tes'suto *sm* fabric, material; (*Biol*) tissue; (*fig*) web
'testa *sf* head; (*di cose: estremità, parte anteriore*) head, front; **50 euro a ~** 50 euros apiece *o* a head *o* per person; **a ~ alta** with one's head held high; **a ~ bassa** (*correre*) headlong; (*con aria dimessa*) with head bowed; **di ~** *ag* (*vettura etc*) front; **dare alla ~** to go to one's head; **fare di ~ propria** to go one's own way; **in ~** (*Sport*) in the lead; **essere in ~ alla classifica** (*corridore*) to be number one; (*squadra*) to be at the top of the league table; (*disco*) to be top of the charts, be number one; **essere alla ~ di qc** (*società*) to be the head of; (*esercito*) to be at the head of; **tenere ~ a qn** (*nemico etc*) to stand up to sb; **una ~ d'aglio** a bulb of garlic; **~ o croce?** heads or tails?; **avere la ~ dura** to be stubborn; **~ di serie** (*Tennis*) seed, seeded player
testa-'coda *sm inv* (*Aut*) spin
testamen'tario, -a *ag* (*Dir*) testamentary; **le sue disposizioni testamentarie** the provisions of his will
testa'mento *sm* (*atto*) will, testament; **l'Antico/il Nuovo T~** (*Rel*) the Old/New Testament
testar'daggine [testar'daddʒine] *sf* stubbornness, obstinacy
tes'tardo, -a *ag* stubborn, pig-headed
tes'tare *vt* to test
tes'tata *sf* (*parte anteriore*) head; (*intestazione*) heading; **missile a ~ nucleare** missile with a nuclear warhead
'teste *sm/f* witness
tes'ticolo *sm* testicle
testi'era *sf* (*del letto*) headboard; (*di cavallo*) headpiece
testi'mone *sm/f* (*Dir*) witness; **fare da ~ alle nozze di qn** to be a witness at sb's wedding; **~ oculare** eye witness

testimoni'anza [testimo'njantsa] *sf* (*atto*) deposition; (*effetto*) evidence; (*fig: prova*) proof; **accusare qn di falsa ~** to accuse sb of perjury; **rilasciare una ~** to give evidence

testimoni'are *vt* to testify; (*fig*) to bear witness to, testify to ■ *vi* to give evidence, testify; **~ il vero** to tell the truth; **~ il falso** to perjure o.s.

tes'tina *sf* (*di giradischi, registratore*) head

'testo *sm* text; **fare ~** (*opera, autore*) to be authoritative; (*fig: dichiarazione*) to carry weight

testoste'rone *sm* testosterone

testu'ale *ag* textual; **le sue parole testuali** his (*o* her) actual words

tes'tuggine [tes'tuddʒine] *sf* tortoise; (*di mare*) turtle

'tetano *sm* (*Med*) tetanus

'tetro, -a *ag* gloomy

'tetta *sf* (*fam*) boob, tit

tetta'rella *sf* teat

'tetto *sm* roof; **abbandonare il ~ coniugale** to desert one's family; **~ a cupola** dome

tet'toia *sf* roofing; canopy

'Tevere *sm*: **il ~** the Tiber

TG [tid'dʒi] *abbr m* (= *telegiornale*) TV news *sg*

'thermos® ['tɛrmos] *sm inv* vacuum *o* Thermos® flask

'thriller ['θrilə], **'thrilling** ['θriliŋ] *sm inv* thriller

ti *pron* (*dav lo, la, li, le, ne diventa* **te**) (*oggetto*) you; (*complemento di termine*) (to) you; (*riflessivo*) yourself; **ti aiuto?** can I give you a hand?; **te lo ha dato?** did he give it to you?; **ti sei lavato?** have you washed?

ti'ara *sf* (*Rel*) tiara

'Tibet *sm*: **il ~** Tibet

tibe'tano, -a *ag, sm/f* Tibetan

'tibia *sf* tibia, shinbone

tic *sm inv* tic, (nervous) twitch; (*fig*) mannerism

ticchet'tio [tikket'tio] *sm* (*di macchina da scrivere*) clatter; (*di orologio*) ticking; (*della pioggia*) patter

'ticchio ['tikkjo] *sm* (*ghiribizzo*) whim; (*tic*) tic, (nervous) twitch

'ticket *sm inv* (*Med*) prescription charge (*Brit*)

ti'ene *etc vb vedi* **tenere**

ti'epido, -a *ag* lukewarm, tepid

ti'fare *vi*: **~ per** to be a fan of; (*parteggiare*) to side with

'tifo *sm* (*Med*) typhus; (*fig*): **fare il ~ per** to be a fan of

tifoi'dea *sf* typhoid

ti'fone *sm* typhoon

ti'foso, -a *sm/f* (*Sport etc*) fan

tight ['tait] *sm inv* morning suit

tigì [tid'dʒi] *sm inv* TV news

'tiglio ['tiʎʎo] *sm* lime (tree), linden (tree)

'tigna ['tiɲɲa] *sf* (*Med*) ringworm

ti'grato, -a *ag* striped

'tigre *sf* tiger

tilt *sm*: **andare in ~** (*fig*) to go haywire

tim'ballo *sm* (*strumento*) kettledrum; (*Cuc*) timbale

tim'brare *vt* to stamp; (*annullare: francobolli*) to postmark; **~ il cartellino** to clock in

'timbro *sm* stamp; (*Mus*) timbre, tone

timi'dezza [timi'dettsa] *sf* shyness, timidity

'timido, -a *ag* shy, timid

'timo *sm* thyme

ti'mone *sm* (*Naut*) rudder

timoni'ere *sm* helmsman

timo'rato, -a *ag* conscientious; **~ di Dio** God-fearing

ti'more *sm* (*paura*) fear; (*rispetto*) awe; **avere ~ di qc/qn** (*paura*) to be afraid of sth/sb

timo'roso, -a *ag* timid, timorous

'timpano *sm* (*Anat*) eardrum; (*Mus*): **timpani** kettledrums, timpani

'tinca, -che *sf* (*Zool*) tench

ti'nello *sm* small dining room

'tingere ['tindʒere] *vt* to dye

'tino *sm* vat

ti'nozza [ti'nɔttsa] *sf* tub

'tinsi *etc vb vedi* **tingere**

'tinta *sf* (*materia colorante*) dye; (*colore*) colour (*Brit*), color (*US*), shade

tinta'rella *sf* (*fam*) (sun)tan

tintin'nare *vi* to tinkle

tintin'nio *sm* tinkling

'tinto, -a *pp di* **tingere**

tinto'ria *sf* (*officina*) dyeworks *sg*; (*lavasecco*) dry cleaner's (shop)

tin'tura *sf* (*operazione*) dyeing; (*colorante*) dye; **~ di iodio** tincture of iodine

'tipico, -a, ci, che *ag* typical

'tipo *sm* type; (*genere*) kind, type; (*fam*) chap, fellow; **vestiti di tutti i tipi** all kinds of clothes; **sul ~ di questo** of this sort; **sei un bel ~!** you're a fine one!

tipogra'fia *sf* typography

tipo'grafico, -a, ci, che *ag* typographic(al)

ti'pografo *sm* typographer

tip 'tap [tip'tap] *sm* (*ballo*) tap dancing

T.I.R. *sigla m* (= *Transports Internationaux Routiers*) *International Heavy Goods Vehicle*

'tira e 'molla *sm inv* tug-of-war

ti'raggio [ti'raddʒo] *sm* (*di camino etc*) draught (*Brit*), draft (*US*)

Ti'rana *sf* Tirana

tiranneggi'are [tiranned'dʒare] *vt* to tyrannize

tiran'nia *sf* tyranny

t

ti'ranno, -a *ag* tyrannical ■ *sm* tyrant
ti'rante *sm* (*Naut, di tenda etc*) guy; (*Edil*) brace
tirapi'edi *sm/f inv* hanger-on
tira'pugni [tira'puɲɲi] *sm inv* knuckle-duster
ti'rare *vt* (*gen*) to pull; (*estrarre*): **~ qc da** to take *o* pull sth out of; to get sth out of; to extract sth from; (*chiudere: tenda etc*) to draw, pull; (*tracciare, disegnare*) to draw, trace; (*lanciare: sasso, palla*) to throw; (*stampare*) to print; (*pistola, freccia*) to fire ■ *vi* (*pipa, camino*) to draw; (*vento*) to blow; (*abito*) to be tight; (*fare fuoco*) to fire; (*fare del tiro, Calcio*) to shoot; **~ qn da parte** to take *o* draw sb aside; **~ un sospiro (di sollievo)** to heave a sigh (of relief); **~ a indovinare** to take a guess; **~ sul prezzo** to bargain; **~ avanti** *vi* to struggle on ■ *vt* (*famiglia*) to provide for; (*ditta*) to look after; **~ fuori** to take out, pull out; **~ giù** to pull down; **~ su** to pull up; (*capelli*) to put up; (*fig: bambino*) to bring up; **tirarsi indietro** to move back; (*fig*) to back out; **tirarsi su** to pull o.s. up; (*fig*) to cheer o.s. up
ti'rato, -a *ag* (*teso*) taut; (*fig: teso, stanco*) drawn
tira'tore *sm* gunman; **un buon ~** a good shot; **~ scelto** marksman
tira'tura *sf* (*azione*) printing; (*di libro*) (print) run; (*di giornale*) circulation
tirchie'ria [tirkje'ria] *sf* meanness, stinginess
'tirchio, -a ['tirkjo] *ag* mean, stingy
tiri'tera *sf* drivel, hot air
'tiro *sm* shooting *no pl*, firing *no pl*; (*colpo, sparo*) shot; (*di palla: lancio*) throwing *no pl*; throw; (*fig*) trick; **essere a ~** to be in range; **giocare un brutto ~ o un ~ mancino a qn** to play a dirty trick on s.b.; **cavallo da ~** draught (*Brit*) *o* draft (*US*) horse; **~ a segno** target shooting; (*luogo*) shooting range
tiroci'nante [tirotʃi'nante] *ag, sm/f* apprentice *cpd*; trainee *cpd*
tiro'cinio [tiro'tʃinjo] *sm* apprenticeship; (*professionale*) training
ti'roide *sf* thyroid (gland)
tiro'lese *ag, sm/f* Tyrolean, Tyrolese *inv*
Ti'rolo *sm*: **il ~** the Tyrol
tir'rennico, -a, ci, che *ag* Tyrrhenian
Tir'reno *sm*: **il (mar) ~** the Tyrrhenian Sea
ti'sana *sf* herb tea
'tisi *sf* (*Med*) consumption
'tisico, -a, ci, che *ag* (*Med*) consumptive; (*fig: gracile*) frail ■ *sm/f* consumptive (person)
ti'tanico, -a, ci, che *ag* gigantic, enormous
ti'tano *sm* (*Mitologia, fig*) titan
tito'lare *ag* appointed; (*sovrano*) titular ■ *sm/f* incumbent; (*proprietario*) owner; (*Calcio*) regular player
tito'lato, -a *ag* (*persona*) titled
'titolo *sm* title; (*di giornale*) headline; (*diploma*) qualification; (*Comm*) security; (*: azione*) share; **a che ~?** for what reason?; **a ~ di amicizia** out of friendship; **a ~ di cronaca** for your information; **a ~ di premio** as a prize; **~ di credito** share; **~ obbligazionario** bond; **~ al portatore** bearer bond; **~ di proprietà** title deed; **titoli di stato** government securities; **titoli di testa** (*Cine*) credits
titu'bante *ag* hesitant, irresolute
tivù *sf inv* (*fam*) telly (*Brit*), TV
'tizio, a ['tittsjo] *sm/f* fellow, chap
tiz'zone [tit'tsone] *sm* brand
T.M.G. *abbr* (= *tempo medio di Greenwich*) GMT
TN *sigla* = **Trento**
TNT *sigla m* (= *trinitrotoluolo*) TNT
TO *sigla* = **Torino**
toast [toust] *sm inv* toasted sandwich
toc'cante *ag* touching
toc'care *vt* to touch; (*tastare*) to feel; (*fig: riguardare*) to concern; (*: commuovere*) to touch, move; (*: pungere*) to hurt, wound; (*: far cenno a: argomento*) to touch on, mention ■ *vi*: **~ a** (*accadere*) to happen to; (*spettare*) to be up to; **tocca a te difenderci** it's up to you to defend us; **a chi tocca?** whose turn is it?; **mi toccò pagare** I had to pay; **~ il fondo** (*in acqua*) to touch the bottom; (*fig*) to touch rock bottom; **~ con mano** (*fig*) to find out for o.s.; **~ qn sul vivo** to cut sb to the quick
tocca'sana *sm inv* cure-all, panacea
toccherò *etc* [tokke'rɔ] *vb vedi* **toccare**
'tocco, -chi *sm* touch; (*Arte*) stroke, touch
toe'letta *sf* = **toilette**
'toga, -ghe *sf* toga; (*di magistrato, professore*) gown
'togliere ['tɔʎʎere] *vt* (*rimuovere*) to take away (*o* off), remove; (*riprendere, non concedere più*) to take away, remove; (*Mat*) to take away, subtract; (*liberare*) to free; **~ qc a qn** to take sth (away) from sb; **ciò non toglie che ...** nevertheless ..., be that as it may ...; **togliersi il cappello** to take off one's hat
'Togo *sm*: **il ~** Togo
toilette [twa'lɛt] *sf inv* (*gabinetto*) toilet; (*cosmesi*) make-up; (*abbigliamento*) gown, dress; (*mobile*) dressing table; **fare ~** to get made up, make o.s. beautiful
'Tokyo *sf* Tokyo
to'letta *sf* = **toilette**
'tolgo *etc vb vedi* **togliere**
tolle'rante *ag* tolerant
tolle'ranza [tolle'rantsa] *sf* tolerance; **casa di ~** brothel
tolle'rare *vt* to tolerate; **non tollero repliche** I won't stand for objections; **non**

sono tollerati i ritardi lateness will not be tolerated
To'losa *sf* Toulouse
'tolsi *etc vb vedi* **togliere**
'tolto, -a *pp di* **togliere**
to'maia *sf (di scarpa)* upper
'tomba *sf* tomb
tom'bale *ag*: **pietra ~** tombstone, gravestone
tom'bino *sm* manhole cover
'tombola *sf (gioco)* tombola; *(ruzzolone)* tumble
'tomo *sm* volume
tomogra'fia *sf (Med)* tomography; **~ assiale computerizzata** computerized axial tomography
'tonaca, -che *sf (Rel)* habit
to'nare *vi* = **tuonare**
'tondo, -a *ag* round
'tonfo *sm* splash; *(rumore sordo)* thud; *(caduta)*: **fare un ~** to take a tumble
'tonico, -a, ci, che *ag* tonic ■ *sm* tonic; *(cosmetico)* toner
tonifi'cante *ag* invigorating, bracing
tonifi'care *vt (muscoli, pelle)* to tone up; *(irrobustire)* to invigorate, brace
ton'nara *sf* tuna-fishing nets *pl*
ton'nato, -a *ag (Cuc)*: **salsa tonnata** tuna fish sauce; **vitello ~** veal with tuna fish sauce
tonnel'laggio [tonnel'laddʒo] *sm (Naut)* tonnage
tonnel'lata *sf* ton
'tonno *sm* tuna (fish)
'tono *sm (gen, Mus)* tone; *(di colore)* shade, tone; **rispondere a ~** *(a proposito)* to answer to the point; *(nello stesso modo)* to answer in kind; *(per le rime)* to answer back
ton'silla *sf* tonsil
tonsil'lite *sf* tonsillitis
ton'sura *sf* tonsure
'tonto, -a *ag* dull, stupid ■ *sm/f* blockhead, dunce; **fare il finto ~** to play dumb
top [tɔp] *sm inv (vertice, camicetta)* top
to'paia *sf (di topo)* mousehole; *(di ratto)* rat's nest; *(fig: casa etc)* hovel, dump
to'pazio [to'pattsjo] *sm* topaz
topi'cida, -i [topi'tʃida] *sm* rat poison
'topless ['tɔplis] *sm inv* topless bathing costume
'topo *sm* mouse; **~ d'albergo** *(fig)* hotel thief; **~ di biblioteca** *(fig)* bookworm
topogra'fia *sf* topography
topog'rafico, -a, ci, che *ag* topographic, topographical
to'ponimo *sm* place name
'toppa *sf (serratura)* keyhole; *(pezza)* patch
to'race [to'ratʃe] *sm* chest
'torba *sf* peat
'torbido, -a *ag (liquido)* cloudy; *(: fiume)* muddy; *(fig)* dark; troubled ■ *sm*: **pescare nel ~** *(fig)* to fish in troubled waters
'torcere ['tɔrtʃere] *vt* to twist; *(biancheria)* to wring (out); **torcersi** *vr* to twist, writhe; **dare del filo da ~ a qn** to make life *o* things difficult for sb
torchi'are [tor'kjare] *vt* to press
'torchio ['tɔrkjo] *sm* press; **mettere qn sotto il ~** *(fig fam: interrogare)* to grill sb; **~ tipografico** printing press
'torcia, -ce ['tɔrtʃa] *sf* torch; **~ elettrica** torch *(Brit)*, flashlight *(US)*
torci'collo [tortʃi'kɔllo] *sm* stiff neck
'tordo *sm* thrush
to'rero *sm* bullfighter, toreador
tori'nese *ag* of (*o* from) Turin ■ *sm/f* person from Turin
To'rino *sf* Turin
tor'menta *sf* snowstorm
tormen'tare *vt* to torment; **tormentarsi** *vr* to fret, worry o.s.
tor'mento *sm* torment
torna'conto *sm* advantage, benefit
tor'nado *sm* tornado
tor'nante *sm* hairpin bend *(Brit) o* curve *(US)*
tor'nare *vi* to return, go (*o* come) back; *(ridiventare: anche fig)* to become (again); *(riuscire giusto, esatto: conto)* to work out; *(risultare)* to turn out (to be), prove (to be); **~ al punto di partenza** to start again; **~ a casa** to go (*o* come) home; **i conti tornano** the accounts balance; **~ utile** to prove *o* turn out (to be) useful
torna'sole *sm inv* litmus
tor'neo *sm* tournament
'tornio *sm* lathe
tor'nire *vt (Tecn)* to turn (on a lathe); *(fig)* to shape, polish
tor'nito, -a *ag (gambe, caviglie)* well-shaped
'toro *sm* bull; *(dello zodiaco)*: **T~** Taurus; **essere del T~** to be Taurus
tor'pedine *sf* torpedo
torpedini'era *sf* torpedo boat
tor'pore *sm* torpor
'torre *sf* tower; *(Scacchi)* rook, castle; **~ di controllo** *(Aer)* control tower
torrefazi'one [torrefat'tsjone] *sf* roasting
torreggi'are [torred'dʒare] *vi*: **~ (su)** to tower (over)
tor'rente *sm* torrent
torren'tizio, -a [torren'tittsjo] *ag* torrential
torrenzi'ale [torren'tsjale] *ag* torrential
tor'retta *sf* turret
'torrido, -a *ag* torrid
torri'one *sm* keep
tor'rone *sm* nougat

t

'torsi *etc vb vedi* **torcere**
torsi'one *sf* twisting; (*Tecn*) torsion
'torso *sm* torso, trunk; (*Arte*) torso; **a ~ nudo** bare-chested
'torsolo *sm* (*di cavolo etc*) stump; (*di frutta*) core
'torta *sf* cake
tortel'lini *smpl* (*Cuc*) tortellini
torti'era *sf* cake tin (*Brit*), cake pan (*US*)
'torto, -a *pp di* **torcere** ■ *ag* (*ritorto*) twisted; (*storto*) twisted, crooked ■ *sm* (*ingiustizia*) wrong; (*colpa*) fault; **a ~** wrongly; **a ~ o a ragione** rightly or wrongly; **aver ~** to be wrong; **fare un ~ a qn** to wrong sb; **essere/passare dalla parte del ~** to be/put o.s. in the wrong; **lui non ha tutti i torti** there's something in what he says
'tortora *sf* turtle dove
tortu'oso, -a *ag* (*strada*) twisting; (*fig*) tortuous
tor'tura *sf* torture
tortu'rare *vt* to torture
'torvo, -a *ag* menacing, grim
tosa'erba *sm o f inv* (lawn)mower
to'sare *vt* (*pecora*) to shear; (*cane*) to clip; (*siepe*) to clip, trim
tosa'tura *sf* (*di pecore*) shearing; (*di cani*) clipping; (*di siepi*) trimming, clipping
Tos'cana *sf*: **la ~** Tuscany
tos'cano, -a *ag, sm/f* Tuscan ■ *sm* (*anche*: **sigaro toscano**) *strong Italian cigar*
'tosse *sf* cough
tossicità [tossitʃi'ta] *sf* toxicity
'tossico, -a, ci, che *ag* toxic; (*Econ*): **titolo ~** toxic asset
tossicodipen'dente *sm/f* drug addict
tossicodipen'denza [tossikodipen'dɛntsa] *sf* drug addiction
tossi'comane *sm/f* drug addict
tossicoma'nia *sf* drug addiction
tos'sina *sf* toxin
tos'sire *vi* to cough
tosta'pane *sm inv* toaster
tos'tare *vt* to toast; (*caffè*) to roast
tosta'tura *sf* (*di pane*) toasting; (*di caffè*) roasting
'tosto, -a *ag*: **faccia tosta** cheek ■ *av* at once, immediately; **~ che** as soon as
to'tale *ag, sm* total
totalità *sf*: **la ~ di** all of, the total amount (*o* number) of; the whole *+ sg*
totali'tario, -a *ag* totalitarian; (*totale*) complete, total; **adesione totalitaria** complete support
totalita'rismo *sm* (*Pol*) totalitarianism
totaliz'zare [totalid'dzare] *vt* to total; (*Sport*: *punti*) to score
totalizza'tore [totaliddza'tore] *sm* (*Tecn*) totalizator; (*Ippica*) totalizator, tote (*fam*)
to'tip *sm gambling pool betting on horse racing*
toto'calcio [toto'kaltʃo] *sm gambling pool betting on football results*, ≈ (football) pools *pl* (*Brit*)
tou'pet [tu'pɛ] *sm inv* toupee
tour [tur] *sm inv* (*giro*) tour; (*Ciclismo*) tour de France
tour de 'force ['tur də 'fɔrs] *sm inv* (*Sport*: *anche fig*) tour de force
tour'née [tur'ne] *sf* tour; **essere in ~** to be on tour
to'vaglia [to'vaʎʎa] *sf* tablecloth
tovagli'olo [tovaʎ'ʎɔlo] *sm* napkin
'tozzo, -a ['tɔttso] *ag* squat ■ *sm*: **~ di pane** crust of bread
TP *sigla* = **Trapani**
TR *sigla* = **Terni**
Tr *abbr* (*Comm*) = **tratta**
tra *prep* (*di due persone, cose*) between; (*di più persone, cose*) among(st); (*tempo*: *entro*) within, in; **prendere qn ~ le braccia** to take sb in one's arms; **litigano ~ (di) loro** they're fighting amongst themselves; **~ 5 giorni** in 5 days' time; **~ breve** *o* **poco** soon; **~ sé e sé** (*parlare etc*) to oneself; **sia detto ~ noi ...** between you and me ...; **~ una cosa e l'altra** what with one thing and another
trabal'lante *ag* shaky
trabal'lare *vi* to stagger, totter
tra'biccolo *sm* (*peg*: *auto*) old banger (*Brit*), jalopy
traboc'care *vi* to overflow
traboc'chetto [trabok'ketto] *sm* (*fig*) trap ■ *ag inv* trap *cpd*; **domanda ~** trick question
traca'gnotto, -a [trakaɲ'ɲɔtto] *ag* dumpy ■ *sm/f* dumpy person
tracan'nare *vt* to gulp down
'traccia, -ce ['trattʃa] *sf* (*segno, striscia*) trail, track; (*orma*) tracks *pl*; (*residuo, testimonianza*) trace, sign; (*abbozzo*) outline; **essere sulle tracce di qn** to be on sb's trail
tracci'are [trat'tʃare] *vt* to trace, mark (out); (*disegnare*) to draw; (*fig*: *abbozzare*) to outline; **~ un quadro della situazione** to outline the situation
tracci'ato [trat'tʃato] *sm* (*grafico*) layout, plan; **~ di gara** (*Sport*) race route
tra'chea [tra'kɛa] *sf* windpipe, trachea
tra'colla *sf* shoulder strap; **portare qc a ~** to carry sth over one's shoulder; **borsa a ~** shoulder bag
tra'collo *sm* (*fig*) collapse, ruin; **~ finanziario** crash; **avere un ~** (*Med*) to have a setback; (*Comm*) to collapse
traco'tante *ag* overbearing, arrogant
traco'tanza [trako'tantsa] *sf* arrogance
trad. *abbr* = **traduzione**

tradi'mento *sm* betrayal; (*Dir, Mil*) treason; **a** ~ by surprise; **alto** ~ high treason
tra'dire *vt* to betray; (*coniuge*) to be unfaithful to; (*doveri: mancare*) to fail in; (*rivelare*) to give away, reveal; **ha tradito le attese di tutti** he let everyone down
tradi'tore, 'trice *sm/f* traitor
tradizio'nale [tradittsjo'nale] *ag* traditional
tradizi'one [tradit'tsjone] *sf* tradition
tra'dotto, -a *pp di* **tradurre** ■ *sf* (*Mil*) troop train
tra'durre *vt* to translate; (*spiegare*) to render, convey; (*Dir*): ~ **qn in carcere/tribunale** to take sb to prison/court; ~ **in cifre** to put into figures; ~ **in atto** (*fig*) to put into effect
tradut'tore, -'trice *sm/f* translator
traduzi'one [tradut'tsjone] *sf* translation; (*Dir*) transfer
'trae *vb vedi* **trarre**
tra'ente *sm/f* (*Econ*) drawer
trafe'lato, -a *ag* out of breath
traffi'cante *sm/f* dealer; (*peg*) trafficker
traffi'care *vi* (*commerciare*): ~ **(in)** to trade (in), deal (in); (*affaccendarsi*) to busy o.s. ■ *vt* (*peg*) to traffic in
traffi'cato, -a *ag* (*strada, zona*) busy
'traffico, -ci *sm* traffic; (*commercio*) trade, traffic; ~ **aereo/ferroviario** air/rail traffic; ~ **di droga** drug trafficking; ~ **stradale** traffic
tra'figgere [tra'fiddʒere] *vt* to run through, stab; (*fig*) to pierce
tra'fila *sf* procedure
trafi'letto *sm* (*di giornale*) short article
tra'fitto, -a *pp di* **trafiggere**
trafo'rare *vt* to bore, drill
tra'foro *sm* (*azione*) boring, drilling; (*galleria*) tunnel
trafu'gare *vt* to purloin
tra'gedia [tra'dʒɛdja] *sf* tragedy
'traggo *etc vb vedi* **trarre**
traghet'tare [traget'tare] *vt* to ferry
tra'ghetto [tra'getto] *sm* crossing; (*barca*) ferry(boat)
tragicità [tradʒitʃi'ta] *sf* tragedy
'tragico, -a, ci, che ['tradʒiko] *ag* tragic ■ *sm* (*autore*) tragedian; **prendere tutto sul** ~ (*fig*) to take everything far too seriously
tragi'comico, -a, ci, che [tradʒi'kɔmiko] *ag* tragicomic
tra'gitto [tra'dʒitto] *sm* (*passaggio*) crossing; (*viaggio*) journey
tragu'ardo *sm* (*Sport*) finishing line; (*fig*) goal, aim
'trai *etc vb vedi* **trarre**
traiet'toria *sf* trajectory
trai'nante *ag* (*cavo, fune*) towing; (*fig: persona, settore*) driving
trai'nare *vt* to drag, haul; (*rimorchiare*) to tow
'training ['trɛinin(g)] *sm inv* training
'traino *sm* (*carro*) wagon; (*slitta*) sledge; (*carico*) load
tralasci'are [tralaʃʃare] *vt* (*studi*) to neglect; (*dettagli*) to leave out, omit
'tralcio ['traltʃo] *sm* (*Bot*) shoot
tra'liccio [tra'littʃo] *sm* (*tela*) ticking; (*struttura*) trellis; (*Elettr*) pylon
tram *sm inv* tram (*Brit*), streetcar (*US*)
'trama *sf* (*filo*) weft, woof; (*fig: argomento, maneggio*) plot
traman'dare *vt* to pass on, hand down
tra'mare *vt* (*fig*) to scheme, plot
tram'busto *sm* turmoil
trames'tio *sm* bustle
tramez'zino [tramed'dzino] *sm* sandwich
tra'mezzo [tra'mɛddzo] *sm* partition
'tramite *prep* through ■ *sm* means *pl*; **agire/fare da** ~ to act as/be a go-between
tramon'tana *sf* (*Meteor*) north wind
tramon'tare *vi* to set, go down
tra'monto *sm* setting; (*del sole*) sunset
tramor'tire *vi* to faint ■ *vt* to stun
trampo'lino *sm* (*per tuffi*) springboard, diving board; (*per lo sci*) ski-jump
'trampolo *sm* stilt
tramu'tare *vt*: ~ **in** to change into
trance [trɑ:ns] *sf inv* (*di medium*) trance; **cadere in** ~ to fall into a trance
'trancia, -ce ['trantʃa] *sf* slice; (*cesoia*) shearing machine
tranci'are [tran'tʃare] *vt* (*Tecn*) to shear
'trancio ['trantʃo] *sm* slice
tra'nello *sm* trap; **tendere un ~ a qn** to set a trap for sb; **cadere in un** ~ to fall into a trap
trangugi'are [trangu'dʒare] *vt* to gulp down
'tranne *prep* except (for), but (for); ~ **che** *cong* unless; **tutti i giorni ~ il venerdì** every day except *o* with the exception of Friday
tranquil'lante *sm* (*Med*) tranquillizer
tranquillità *sf* calm, stillness; quietness; peace of mind
tranquilliz'zare [trankwillid'dzare] *vt* to reassure
tran'quillo, -a *ag* calm, quiet; (*bambino, scolaro*) quiet; (*sereno*) with one's mind at rest; **sta'** ~ don't worry
transat'lantico, -a, ci, che *ag* transatlantic ■ *sm* transatlantic liner; (*Pol*) *corridor used as a meeting place by members of the lower chamber of the Italian Parliament*; *see note*

TRANSATLANTICO

The *transatlantico* is a room in the Palazzo di Montecitorio which is used by "deputati" between parliamentary sessions for relaxation and conversation. It is also used for media interviews and press conferences.

tran'satto, -a *pp di* **transigere**
transazi'one [transat'tsjone] *sf* (*Dir*) settlement; (*Comm*) transaction, deal
tran'senna *sf* barrier
tran'setto *sm* transept
trans'genico, -a, ci, che [trans'dʒɛniko] *ag* genetically modified
transiberi'ano, -a *ag* trans-Siberian
tran'sigere [tran'sidʒere] *vi* (*Dir*) to reach a settlement; (*venire a patti*) to compromise, come to an agreement
tran'sistor *sm inv*, **transis'tore** *sm* transistor
transi'tabile *ag* passable
transi'tare *vi* to pass
transi'tivo, -a *ag* transitive
'transito *sm* transit; **di ~** (*merci*) in transit; (*stazione*) transit *cpd*; **"divieto di ~"** "no entry"; **"~ interrotto"** "road closed"
transi'torio, -a *ag* transitory, transient; (*provvisorio*) provisional
transizi'one [transit'tsjone] *sf* transition
tran 'tran *sm* routine; **il solito ~** the same old routine
tran'via *sf* tramway (*Brit*), streetcar line (*US*)
tranvi'ario, -a *ag* tram *cpd* (*Brit*), streetcar *cpd* (*US*); **linea tranviaria** tramline, streetcar line
tranvi'ere *sm* (*conducente*) tram driver (*Brit*), streetcar driver (*US*); (*bigliettaio*) tram *o* streetcar conductor
trapa'nare *vt* (*Tecn*) to drill
'trapano *sm* (*utensile*) drill; (*: Med*) trepan
trapas'sare *vt* to pierce
trapas'sato *sm* (*Ling*) past perfect
tra'passo *sm* passage; **~ di proprietà** (*di case*) conveyancing; (*di auto etc*) legal transfer
trape'lare *vi* to leak, drip; (*fig*) to leak out
tra'pezio [tra'pɛttsjo] *sm* (*Mat*) trapezium; (*attrezzo ginnico*) trapeze
trape'zista, -i, e [trapet'tsista] *sm/f* trapeze artist
trapian'tare *vt* to transplant
trapi'anto *sm* transplanting; (*Med*) transplant
'trappola *sf* trap
tra'punta *sf* quilt
'trarre *vt* to draw, pull; (*prendere, tirare fuori*) to take (out), draw; (*derivare*) to obtain; **~ beneficio** *o* **profitto da qc** to benefit from sth; **~ le conclusioni** to draw one's own conclusions; **~ esempio da qn** to follow sb's example; **~ guadagno** to make a profit; **~ qn d'impaccio** to get sb out of an awkward situation; **~ origine da qc** to have its origins *o* originate in sth; **~ in salvo** to rescue
trasa'lire *vi* to start, jump
trasan'dato, -a *ag* shabby
trasbor'dare *vt* to transfer; (*Naut*) to tran(s)ship ■ *vi* (*Naut*) to change ship; (*Aer*) to change plane; (*Ferr*) to change (trains)
trascenden'tale [traʃʃenden'tale] *ag* transcendental
tra'scendere [traʃʃendere] *vt* (*Filosofia, Rel*) to transcend; (*fig: superare*) to surpass, go beyond
tra'sceso, -a [traʃʃeso] *pp di* **trascendere**
trasci'nare [traʃʃi'nare] *vt* to drag; **trascinarsi** *vr* to drag o.s. along; (*fig*) to drag on
tras'correre *vt* (*tempo*) to spend, pass ■ *vi* to pass
tras'corso, -a *pp di* **trascorrere** ■ *ag* past ■ *sm* mistake
tras'critto, -a *pp di* **trascrivere**
tras'crivere *vt* to transcribe
trascrizi'one [traskrit'tsjone] *sf* transcription
trascu'rare *vt* to neglect; (*non considerare*) to disregard
trascura'tezza [traskura'tettsa] *sf* carelessness, negligence
trascu'rato, -a *ag* (*casa*) neglected; (*persona*) careless, negligent
traseco'lato, -a *ag* astounded, amazed
trasferi'mento *sm* transfer; (*trasloco*) removal, move
trasfe'rire *vt* to transfer; **trasferirsi** *vr* to move
tras'ferta *sf* transfer; (*indennità*) travelling expenses *pl*; (*Sport*) away game
trasfigu'rare *vt* to transfigure
trasfor'mare *vt* to transform, change
trasforma'tore *sm* transformer
trasformazi'one [trasformat'tsjone] *sf* transformation
trasfusi'one *sf* (*Med*) transfusion
trasgre'dire *vt* to break, infringe; (*ordini*) to disobey
trasgressi'one *sf* breaking, infringement; disobeying
trasgres'sivo, -a *ag* (*personaggio, atteggiamento*) rule-breaking
trasgres'sore, trasgredi'trice [trazgredi'tritʃe] *sm/f* (*Dir*) transgressor
tras'lato, -a *ag* metaphorical, figurative
traslo'care *vt* to move, transfer; **traslocarsi** *vr* to move
tras'loco, -chi *sm* removal
tras'messo, -a *pp di* **trasmettere**

tras'mettere *vt* (*passare*): **~ qc a qn** to pass sth on to sb; (*mandare*) to send; (*Tecn, Tel, Med*) to transmit; (*TV, Radio*) to broadcast
trasmetti'tore *sm* transmitter
trasmissi'one *sf* (*gen, Fisica, Tecn*) transmission; (*passaggio*) transmission, passing on; (*TV, Radio*) broadcast
trasmit'tente *sf* transmitting *o* broadcasting station
traso'gnato, -a [trasoɲ'ɲato] *ag* dreamy
traspa'rente *ag* transparent
traspa'renza [traspa'rɛntsa] *sf* transparency; **guardare qc in ~** to look at sth against the light
traspa'rire *vi* to show (through)
tras'parso, -a *pp di* **trasparire**
traspi'rare *vi* to perspire; (*fig*) to come to light, leak out
traspirazi'one [traspirat'tsjone] *sf* perspiration
tras'porre *vt* to transpose
traspor'tare *vt* to carry, move; (*merce*) to transport, convey; **lasciarsi ~ (da qc)** (*fig*) to let o.s. be carried away (by sth)
tras'porto *sm* transport; (*fig*) rapture, passion; **con ~** passionately; **compagnia di ~** carriers *pl*; (*per strada*) hauliers *pl* (*Brit*), haulers *pl* (*US*); **mezzi di ~** means of transport; **nave/aereo da ~** transport ship/ aircraft *inv*; **~ (funebre)** funeral procession; **~ marittimo/aereo** sea/air transport; **~ stradale** (road) haulage; **i trasporti pubblici** public transport
tras'posto, -a *pp di* **trasporre**
'trassi *etc vb vedi* **trarre**
trastul'lare *vt* to amuse; **trastullarsi** *vr* to amuse o.s.
tras'tullo *sm* game
trasu'dare *vi* (*filtrare*) to ooze; (*sudare*) to sweat ■ *vt* to ooze with
trasver'sale *ag* (*taglio, sbarra*) cross(-); (*retta*) transverse; **via ~** side street
trasvo'lare *vt* to fly over
'tratta *sf* (*Econ*) draft; (*di persone*): **la ~ delle bianche** the white slave trade; **~ documentaria** documentary bill of exchange
tratta'mento *sm* treatment; (*servizio*) service; **ricevere un buon ~** (*cliente*) to get good service; **~ di bellezza** beauty treatment; **~ di fine rapporto** (*Comm*) severance pay
trat'tare *vt* (*gen*) to treat; (*commerciare*) to deal in; (*svolgere: argomento*) to discuss, deal with; (*negoziare*) to negotiate ■ *vi*: **~ di** to deal with; **~ con** (*persona*) to deal with; **si tratta di ...** it's about ...; **si tratterebbe solo di poche ore** it would just be a matter of a few hours
tratta'tiva *sf* negotiation; **trattative** *sfpl* (*tra governi, stati*) talks; **essere in ~ con** to be in negotiation with
trat'tato *sm* (*testo*) treatise; (*accordo*) treaty; **~ commerciale** trade agreement; **~ di pace** peace treaty
trattazi'one [trattat'tsjone] *sf* treatment
tratteggi'are [tratted'dʒare] *vt* (*disegnare: a tratti*) to sketch, outline; (*: col tratteggio*) to hatch
trat'teggio [trat'teddʒo] *sm* hatching
tratte'nere *vt* (*far rimanere: persona*) to detain; (*tenere, frenare, reprimere*) to hold back, keep back; (*astenersi dal consegnare*) to hold, keep; (*detrarre: somma*) to deduct; **trattenersi** *vr* (*astenersi*) to restrain o.s., stop o.s.; (*soffermarsi*) to stay, remain; **sono stato trattenuto in ufficio** I was delayed at the office
tratteni'mento *sm* entertainment; (*festa*) party
tratte'nuta *sf* deduction
trat'tino *sm* dash; (*in parole composte*) hyphen
'tratto, -a *pp di* **trarre** ■ *sm* (*di penna, matita*) stroke; (*parte*) part, piece; (*di strada*) stretch; (*di mare, cielo*) expanse; (*di tempo*) period (of time); **tratti** *smpl* (*caratteristiche*) features; (*modo di*) ways, manners; **a un ~, d'un ~** suddenly
trat'tore *sm* tractor
tratto'ria *sf* (small) restaurant
'trauma, -i *sm* trauma; **~ cranico** concussion
trau'matico, -a, ci, che *ag* traumatic
traumatiz'zare [traumatid'dzare] *vt* (*Med*) to traumatize; (*fig: impressionare*) to shock
tra'vaglio [tra'vaʎʎo] *sm* (*angoscia*) pain, suffering; (*Med*) pains *pl*; **~ di parto** labour pains
trava'sare *vt* to pour; (*vino*) to decant
tra'vaso *sm* pouring; decanting
trava'tura *sf* beams *pl*
'trave *sf* beam
tra'veggole *sfpl*: **avere le ~** to be seeing things
tra'versa *sf* (*trave*) crosspiece; (*via*) sidestreet; (*Ferr*) sleeper (*Brit*), (railroad) tie (*US*); (*Calcio*) crossbar
traver'sare *vt* to cross
traver'sata *sf* crossing; (*Aer*) flight, trip
traver'sie *sfpl* mishaps, misfortunes
traver'sina *sf* (*Ferr*) sleeper (*Brit*), (railroad) tie (*US*)
tra'verso, -a *ag* oblique; **di ~** *ag* askew ■ *av* sideways; **andare di ~** (*cibo*) to go down the wrong way; **messo di ~** sideways on; **guardare di ~** to look askance at; **via traversa** side road; **ottenere qc per vie traverse** (*fig*) to obtain sth in an underhand way

travesti'mento *sm* disguise
traves'tire *vt* to disguise; **travestirsi** *vr* to disguise o.s.
traves'tito *sm* transvestite
travi'are *vt* (*fig*) to lead astray
travi'sare *vt* (*fig*) to distort, misrepresent
travol'gente [travol'dʒɛnte] *ag* overwhelming
tra'volgere [tra'vɔldʒere] *vt* to sweep away, carry away; (*fig*) to overwhelm
tra'volto, -a *pp di* **travolgere**
trazi'one [trat'tsjone] *sf* traction; ~ **anteriore/posteriore** (*Aut*) front-wheel/rear-wheel drive
tre *num* three
tre'alberi *sm inv* (*Naut*) three-master
'trebbia *sf* (*Agr*: *operazione*) threshing; (: *stagione*) threshing season
trebbi'are *vt* to thresh
trebbia'trice [trebbja'tritʃe] *sf* threshing machine
trebbia'tura *sf* threshing
'treccia, -ce ['trettʃa] *sf* plait, braid; **lavorato a trecce** (*pullover etc*) cable-knit
trecen'tesco, -a, schi, sche [tretʃen'tesko] *ag* fourteenth-century
tre'cento [tre'tʃɛnto] *num* three hundred ■ *sm*: **il T~** the fourteenth century
tredi'cenne [tredi'tʃɛnne] *ag, sm/f* thirteen-year-old
tredi'cesimo, -a [tredi'tʃɛzimo] *num* thirteenth ■ *sf* *Christmas bonus of a month's pay*
'tredici ['treditʃi] *num* thirteen ■ *sm inv*: **fare** ~ (*Totocalcio*) to win the pools (*Brit*)
'tregua *sf* truce; (*fig*) respite; **senza** ~ non-stop, without stopping, uninterruptedly
tre'mante *ag* trembling, shaking
tre'mare *vi* to tremble, shake; ~ **di** (*freddo etc*) to shiver *o* tremble with; (*paura, rabbia*) to shake *o* tremble with
trema'rella *sf* shivers *pl*
tremen'tina *sf* turpentine
tre'mila *num* three thousand
'tremito *sm* trembling *no pl*; shaking *no pl*; shivering *no pl*
tremo'lare *vi* to tremble; (*luce*) to flicker; (*foglie*) to quiver
tremo'lio *sm* (*vedi vi*) tremble; flicker; quiver
tre'more *sm* tremor
'treno *sm* train; (*Aut*): ~ **di gomme** set of tyres; ~ **locale/diretto/espresso** local/fast/express train; ~ **merci** goods (*Brit*) *o* freight train; ~ **rapido** express (train) (*for which supplement must be paid*); ~ **straordinario** special train; ~ **viaggiatori** passenger train; *see note*

TRENI

There are several different types of train in Italy. "Regionali" and "interregionali" are local trains which stop at every small town and village; the former operate within regional boundaries, while the latter may cross them. "Diretti" are ordinary trains for which passengers do not pay a supplement; the main difference from "espressi" is that the latter are long-distance and mainly run at night. "Intercity" and "eurocity" are faster and entail a supplement. "Rapidi" only contain first-class seats,and the high-speed "pendolino", which offers both first- and second-class travel, runs between the major cities.

'trenta *num* thirty ■ *sm inv* (*Ins*): ~ **e lode** full marks plus distinction *o* cum laude
tren'tenne *ag, sm/f* thirty-year-old
tren'tennio *sm* period of thirty years
tren'tesimo, -a *num* thirtieth
tren'tina *sf*: **una ~ (di)** thirty or so, about thirty
tren'tino, -a *ag* of (*o* from) Trento
trepi'dante *ag* anxious
trepi'dare *vi* to be anxious; ~ **per qn** to be anxious about sb
'trepido, -a *ag* anxious
treppi'ede *sm* tripod; (*Cuc*) trivet
tre'quarti *sm inv* three-quarter-length coat
'tresca, -sche *sf* (*fig*) intrigue; (: *relazione amorosa*) affair
'trespolo *sm* trestle
trevigi'ano, -a [trevi'dʒano] *ag* of (*o* from) Treviso
triango'lare *ag* triangular
tri'angolo *sm* triangle
tribo'lare *vi* (*patire*) to suffer; (*fare fatica*) to have a lot of trouble
tribolazi'one [tribolat'tsjone] *sf* suffering, tribulation
tri'bordo *sm* (*Naut*) starboard
tribù *sf inv* tribe
tri'buna *sf* (*podio*) platform; (*in aule etc*) gallery; (*di stadio*) stand; ~ **della stampa/riservata al pubblico** press/public gallery
tribu'nale *sm* court; **presentarsi** *o* **comparire in** ~ to appear in court; ~ **militare** military tribunal; ~ **supremo** supreme court
tribu'tare *vt* to bestow; ~ **gli onori dovuti a qn** to pay tribute to sb
tribu'tario, -a *ag* (*imposta*) fiscal, tax *cpd*; (*Geo*): **essere ~ di** to be a tributary of

tri'buto *sm* tax; (*fig*) tribute
tri'checo, -chi [tri'kɛko] *sm* (*Zool*) walrus
tri'ciclo [tri'tʃiklo] *sm* tricycle
trico'lore *ag* three-coloured (*Brit*), three-colored (*US*) ■ *sm* tricolo(u)r; (*bandiera italiana*) Italian flag
tri'dente *sm* trident
trien'nale *ag* (*che dura 3 anni*) three-year *cpd*; (*che avviene ogni 3 anni*) three-yearly
tri'ennio *sm* period of three years
tries'tino, -a *ag* of (*o* from) Trieste
tri'fase *ag* (*Elettr*) three-phase
tri'foglio [tri'fɔʎʎo] *sm* clover
trifo'lato, -a *ag* (*Cuc*) *cooked in oil, garlic and parsley*
'triglia ['triʎʎa] *sf* red mullet
trigonome'tria *sf* trigonometry
tril'lare *vi* (*Mus*) to trill
'trillo *sm* trill
tri'mestre *sm* period of three months; (*Ins*) term, quarter (*US*); (*Comm*) quarter
trimo'tore *sm* (*Aer*) three-engined plane
'trina *sf* lace
trin'cea [trin'tʃɛa] *sf* trench
trince'rare [trintʃe'rare] *vt* to entrench
trinci'are [trin'tʃare] *vt* to cut up
'Trinidad *sm*: **~ e Tobago** Trinidad and Tobago
Trinità *sf* (*Rel*) Trinity
'trio (*pl* **trii**) *sm* trio
trion'fale *ag* triumphal, triumphant
trion'fante *ag* triumphant
trion'fare *vi* to triumph, win; **~ su** to triumph over, overcome
tri'onfo *sm* triumph
tripli'care *vt* to triple
'triplice ['triplitʃe] *ag* triple; **in ~ copia** in triplicate
'triplo, -a *ag* triple, treble ■ *sm*: **il ~ (di)** three times as much (as); **la spesa è tripla** it costs three times as much
'tripode *sm* tripod
'Tripoli *sf* Tripoli
'trippa *sf* (*Cuc*) tripe
tri'pudio *sm* triumph, jubilation; (*fig: di colori*) galaxy
tris *sm inv* (*Carte*): **~ d'assi/di re** *etc* three aces/kings *etc*
'triste *ag* sad; (*luogo*) dreary, gloomy
tris'tezza [tris'tettsa] *sf* sadness; gloominess
'tristo, -a *ag* (*cattivo*) wicked, evil; (*meschino*) sorry, poor
trita'carne *sm inv* mincer, grinder (*US*)
trita'ghiaccio [trita'gjattʃo] *sm inv* ice crusher
tri'tare *vt* to mince, grind (*US*)
trita'tutto *sm inv* mincer, grinder (*US*)
'trito, -a *ag* (*tritato*) minced, ground (*US*); **~ e ritrito** (*idee, argomenti, frasi*) trite, hackneyed
tri'tolo *sm* trinitrotoluene
tri'tone *sm* (*Zool*) newt
'trittico, -ci *sm* (*Arte*) triptych
tritu'rare *vt* to grind
tri'vella *sf* drill
trivel'lare *vt* to drill
trivellazi'one [trivellat'tsjone] *sf* drilling; **torre di ~** derrick
trivi'ale *ag* vulgar, low
trivialità *sf inv* (*volgarità*) coarseness, crudeness; (*: osservazione*) coarse *o* crude remark
tro'feo *sm* trophy
'trogolo *sm* (*per maiali*) trough
'troia *sf* (*Zool*) sow; (*fig peg*) whore
'tromba *sf* (*Mus*) trumpet; (*Aut*) horn; **~ d'aria** whirlwind; **~ delle scale** stairwell
trombet'tista, -i, e *sm/f* trumpeter, trumpet (player)
trom'bone *sm* trombone
trom'bosi *sf* thrombosis
tron'care *vt* to cut off; (*spezzare*) to break off
'tronco, -a, chi, che *ag* cut off; broken off; (*Ling*) truncated ■ *sm* (*Bot, Anat*) trunk; (*fig: tratto*) section; (*: pezzo: di lancia*) stump; **licenziare qn in ~** (*fig*) to fire sb on the spot
troneggi'are [troned'dʒare] *vi*: **~ (su)** to tower (over)
'tronfio, -a *ag* conceited
'trono *sm* throne
tropi'cale *ag* tropical
'tropico, -ci *sm* tropic; **~ del Cancro/Capricorno** Tropic of Cancer/Capricorn; **i tropici** the tropics

PAROLA CHIAVE

'troppo, -a *det* (*in eccesso: quantità*) too much; (*: numero*) too many; **ho messo troppo zucchero** I put too much sugar in; **c'era troppa gente** there were too many people
■ *pron* (*in eccesso: quantità*) too much; (*: numero*) too many; **ne hai messo troppo** you've put in too much; **meglio troppi che pochi** better too many than too few
■ *av* (*eccessivamente: con ag, av*) too; (*: con vb*) too much; **troppo amaro/tardi** too bitter/late; **lavora troppo** he works too much; **troppo buono da parte tua!** (*anche ironico*) you're too kind!; **di troppo** too much; too many; **qualche tazza di troppo** a few cups too many; **5 euro di troppo** 5 euros too much; **essere di troppo** to be in the way

'trota *sf* trout
trot'tare *vi* to trot

trotterel'lare *vi* to trot along; (*bambino*) to toddle
'trotto *sm* trot
'trottola *sf* spinning top
tro'vare *vt* to find; (*giudicare*): **trovo che** I find *o* think that; **trovarsi** *vr* (*reciproco: incontrarsi*) to meet; (*essere, stare*) to be; (*arrivare, capitare*) to find o.s.; **andare a ~ qn** to go and see sb; **~ qn colpevole** to find sb guilty; **trovo giusto/sbagliato che ...** I think/don't think it's right that ...; **trovarsi bene/male** (*in un luogo, con qn*) to get on well/badly; **trovarsi d'accordo con qn** to be in agreement with sb
tro'vata *sf* good idea; **~ pubblicitaria** advertising gimmick
trova'tello, -a *sm/f* foundling
truc'care *vt* (*falsare*) to fake; (*attore etc*) to make up; (*travestire*) to disguise; (*Sport*) to fix; (*Aut*) to soup up; **truccarsi** *vr* to make up (one's face)
trucca'tore, -'trice *sm/f* (*Cine, Teat*) make-up artist
'trucco, -chi *sm* trick; (*cosmesi*) make-up; **i trucchi del mestiere** the tricks of the trade
'truce ['trutʃe] *ag* fierce
truci'dare [trutʃi'dare] *vt* to slaughter
'truciolo ['trutʃolo] *sm* shaving
'truffa *sf* fraud, swindle
truf'fare *vt* to swindle, cheat
truffa'tore, -'trice *sm/f* swindler, cheat
'truppa *sf* troop
TS *sigla* = **Trieste**
tu *pron* you; **tu stesso(a)** you yourself; **dare del tu a qn** to address sb as "tu"; **trovarsi a tu per tu con qn** to find o.s. face to face with sb
'tua *vedi* **tuo**
'tuba *sf* (*Mus*) tuba; (*cappello*) top hat
tu'bare *vi* to coo
tuba'tura *sf*, **tubazi'one** [tubat'tsjone] ■ *sf* piping *no pl*, pipes *pl*
tuberco'losi *sf* tuberculosis
'tubero *sm* (*Bot*) tuber
tu'betto *sm* tube
tu'bino *sm* (*cappello*) bowler (*Brit*), derby (*US*); (*abito da donna*) sheath dress
'tubo *sm* tube; (*per conduttore*) pipe; **~ digerente** (*Anat*) digestive tract; **~ di scappamento** (*Aut*) exhaust pipe
tubo'lare *ag* tubular ■ *sm* tubeless tyre (*Brit*) *o* tire (*US*)
'tue *vedi* **tuo**
tuf'fare *vt* to plunge; (*intingere*) to dip; **tuffarsi** *vr* to plunge, dive
tuffa'tore, -'trice *sm/f* (*Sport*) diver
'tuffo *sm* dive; (*breve bagno*) dip
tu'gurio *sm* hovel
tuli'pano *sm* tulip
'tulle *sm* (*tessuto*) tulle
tume'fare *vt* to cause to swell; **tumefarsi** *vr* to swell
'tumido, -a *ag* swollen
tu'more *sm* (*Med*) tumour (*Brit*), tumor (*US*)
tumulazi'one [tumulat'tsjone] *sf* burial
tu'multo *sm* uproar, commotion; (*sommossa*) riot; (*fig*) turmoil
tumultu'oso, -a *ag* rowdy, unruly; (*fig*) turbulent, stormy
tungs'teno *sm* tungsten
'tunica, -che *sf* tunic
'Tunisi *sf* Tunis
Tuni'sia *sf*: **la ~** Tunisia
tuni'sino, -a *ag, sm/f* Tunisian
'tunnel *sm inv* tunnel
'tuo, 'tua, tu'oi, 'tue *det*: **il ~, la tua** *etc* your *pron*: **il ~, la tua** *etc* yours ■ *sm*: **hai speso del ~?** did you spend your own money? ■ *sf*: **la tua** (*opinione*) your view; **i tuoi** (*genitori, famiglia*) your family; **una tua amica** a friend of yours; **è dalla tua** he is on your side; **alla tua!** (*brindisi*) your health!; **ne hai fatta una delle tue!** (*sciocchezze*) you've done it again!
tuo'nare *vi* to thunder; **tuona** it is thundering, there's some thunder
tu'ono *sm* thunder
tu'orlo *sm* yolk
tu'racciolo [tu'rattʃolo] *sm* cap, top; (*di sughero*) cork
tu'rare *vt* to stop, plug; (*con sughero*) to cork; **turarsi il naso** to hold one's nose
'turba *sf* (*folla*) crowd, throng; (*: peg*) mob; **turbe** *sfpl* disorder(s); **soffrire di turbe psichiche** to suffer from a mental disorder
turba'mento *sm* disturbance; (*di animo*) anxiety, agitation
tur'bante *sm* turban
tur'bare *vt* to disturb, trouble; **~ la quiete pubblica** (*Dir*) to disturb the peace
tur'bato, -a *ag* upset; (*preoccupato, ansioso*) anxious
tur'bina *sf* turbine
turbi'nare *vi* to whirl
'turbine *sm* whirlwind; **~ di neve** swirl of snow; **~ di polvere/sabbia** dust/sandstorm
turbi'noso, -a *ag* (*vento, danza etc*) whirling
turbo'lento, -a *ag* turbulent; (*ragazzo*) boisterous, unruly
turbo'lenza [turbo'lentsa] *sf* turbulence
turboreat'tore *sm* turbojet engine
tur'chese [tur'kese] *ag, sm, sf* turquoise
Tur'chia [tur'kia] *sf*: **la ~** Turkey
tur'chino, -a [tur'kino] *ag* deep blue

'turco, -a, chi, che *ag* Turkish ■ *sm/f* Turk/ Turkish woman ■ *sm* (*Ling*) Turkish; **parlare** ~ (*fig*) to talk double Dutch
'turgido, -a ['turdʒido] *ag* swollen
tu'rismo *sm* tourism
tu'rista, -i, e *sm/f* tourist
tu'ristico, -a, ci, che *ag* tourist *cpd*
tur'nista, -i, e *sm/f* shift worker
'turno *sm* turn; (*di lavoro*) shift; **di** ~ (*soldato, medico, custode*) on duty; **a** ~ (*rispondere*) in turn; (*lavorare*) in shifts; **fare a ~ a fare qc** to take turns to do sth; **è il suo** ~ it's your (*o* his *etc*) turn
'turpe *ag* filthy, vile
turpi'loquio *sm* obscene language
'tuta *sf* overalls *pl*; (*Sport*) tracksuit; ~ **mimetica** (*Mil*) camouflage clothing; ~ **spaziale** spacesuit; ~ **subacquea** wetsuit
tu'tela *sf* (*Dir: di minore*) guardianship; (*: protezione*) protection; (*difesa*) defence (*Brit*), defense (*US*); ~ **dell'ambiente** environmental protection; ~ **del consumatore** consumer protection
tute'lare *vt* to protect, defend ■ *ag* (*Dir*): **giudice** ~ *judge with responsibility for guardianship cases*
tutor ['tiutor] *sm inv* (*Auto*) *electronic camera system for measuring average speed on motorways*
tu'tore, -'trice *sm/f* (*Dir*) guardian
tutta'via *cong* nevertheless, yet

 PAROLA CHIAVE

'tutto, -a *det* **1** (*intero*) all; **tutto il latte** all the milk; **tutta la notte** all night, the whole night; **tutto il libro** the whole book; **tutta una bottiglia** a whole bottle; **in tutto il mondo** all over the world
2 (*pl, collettivo*) all; every; **tutti i libri** all the books; **tutte le notti** every night; **tutti i venerdì** every Friday; **tutti gli uomini** all the men; (*collettivo*) all men; **tutte le volte che** every time (that); **tutti e due** both *o* each of us (*o* them *o* you); **tutti e cinque** all five of us (*o* them *o* you)
3 (*completamente*): **era tutta sporca** she was all dirty; **tremava tutto** he was trembling all over; **è tutta sua madre** she's just *o* exactly like her mother
4: **a tutt'oggi** so far, up till now; **a tutta velocità** at full *o* top speed
■ *pron* **1** (*ogni cosa*) everything, all; (*qualsiasi cosa*) anything; **ha mangiato tutto** he's eaten everything; **dimmi tutto** tell me all about it; **tutto compreso** all included, all-in (*Brit*); **tutto considerato** all things considered; **con tutto che** (*malgrado*) although; **del tutto** completely; **100 euro in tutto** 100 euros in all; **in tutto eravamo 50** there were 50 of us in all; **in tutto e per tutto** completely; **il che è tutto dire** and that's saying a lot
2: **tutti, e** (*ognuno*) all, everybody; **vengono tutti** they are all coming, everybody's coming; **tutti sanno che** everybody knows that; **tutti quanti** all and sundry
■ *av* (*completamente*) entirely, quite; **è tutto il contrario** it's quite *o* exactly the opposite; **tutt'al più**: **saranno stati tutt'al più una cinquantina** there were about fifty of them at (the very) most; **tutt'al più possiamo prendere un treno** if the worst comes to the worst we can take a train; **tutt'altro** on the contrary; **è tutt'altro che felice** he's anything but happy; **tutt'intorno** all around; **tutt'a un tratto** suddenly ■ *sm*: **il tutto** the whole lot, all of it; **il tutto si è svolto senza incidenti** it all went off without incident; **il tutto le costerà due milioni** the whole thing will cost you two million

tutto'fare *ag inv*: **domestica** ~ general maid; **ragazzo** ~ office boy ■ *sm/f inv* handyman(-woman)
tut'tora *av* still
tutù *sm inv* tutu, ballet skirt
TV [ti'vu] *sf inv* (= *televisione*) TV ■ *sigla* = **Treviso**

t

Uu

U, u [u] *sf o m inv* (*lettera*) U, u; **U come Udine** ≈ U for Uncle; **inversione ad U** U-turn
ub'bia *sf* (*letterario*) irrational fear
ubbidi'ente *ag* obedient
ubbidi'enza [ubbi'djɛntsa] *sf* obedience
ubbi'dire *vi* to obey; **~ a** to obey; (*veicolo, macchina*) to respond to
ubicazi'one [ubikat'tsjone] *sf* site, location
ubiquità *sf*: **non ho il dono dell'~** I can't be everywhere at once
ubria'care *vt*: **~ qn** to get sb drunk; (*alcool*) to make sb drunk; (*fig*) to make sb's head spin *o* reel; **ubriacarsi** *vr* to get drunk; **ubriacarsi di** (*fig*) to become intoxicated with
ubria'chezza [ubria'kettsa] *sf* drunkenness
ubri'aco, -a, chi, che *ag, sm/f* drunk
ubria'cone *sm* drunkard
uccellagi'one [uttʃella'dʒone] *sf* bird catching
uccelli'era [uttʃel'ljɛra] *sf* aviary
uccel'lino [uttʃel'lino] *sm* baby bird, chick
uc'cello [ut'tʃɛllo] *sm* bird
uc'cidere [ut'tʃidere] *vt* to kill; **uccidersi** *vr* (*suicidarsi*) to kill o.s.; (*perdere la vita*) to be killed
uccisi'one [uttʃi'zjone] *sf* killing
uc'ciso, -a [ut'tʃizo] *pp di* **uccidere**
ucci'sore [uttʃi'zore] *sm* killer
U'craina *sf* Ukraine
u'craino, -a *ag, sm/f* Ukrainian
UD *sigla* = **Udine**
U.D.C. *sigla f* (*Pol: = Unione di Centro*) *centre party*
u'dente *sm/f*: **i non udenti** the hard of hearing
u'dibile *ag* audible
udi'enza [u'djɛntsa] *sf* audience; (*Dir*) hearing; **dare ~ (a)** to grant an audience (to); **~ a porte chiuse** hearing in camera
u'dire *vt* to hear
udi'tivo, -a *ag* auditory
u'dito *sm* (sense of) hearing
udi'tore, -'trice *sm/f* listener; (*Ins*) unregistered student (*attending lectures*)
udi'torio *sm* (*persone*) audience
U.E. *abbr* = **uso esterno**
UE *sigla f* (= *Unione Europea*) EU
UEFA *sigla f* UEFA (= *Union of European Football Associations*)
UEM *sigla f* (= *Unione economica e monetaria*) EMU
'uffa *escl* tut!
uffici'ale [uffi'tʃale] *ag* official ■ *sm* (*Amm*) official, officer; (*Mil*) officer; **pubblico ~** public official; **~ giudiziario** clerk of the court; **~ di marina** naval officer; **~ sanitario** health inspector; **~ di stato civile** registrar
ufficializ'zare [uffitʃalid'dzare] *vt* to make official
uf'ficio [uf'fitʃo] *sm* (*gen*) office; (*dovere*) duty; (*mansione*) task, function, job; (*agenzia*) agency, bureau; (*Rel*) service; **d'~** *ag* office *cpd*; official ■ *av* officially; **provvedere d'~** to act officially; **convocare d'~** (*Dir*) to summons; **difensore** *o* **avvocato d'~** (*Dir*) court-appointed counsel for the defence; **~ brevetti** patent office; **~ di collocamento** employment office; **~ informazioni** information bureau; **~ oggetti smarriti** lost property office (*Brit*), lost and found (*US*); **~ postale** post office; **~ vendite/del personale** sales/personnel department
uffici'oso, -a [uffi'tʃoso] *ag* unofficial
'UFO *sm inv* (= *unidentified flying object*) UFO
'ufo: **a ~** *av* free, for nothing
U'ganda *sf*: **l'~** Uganda
'uggia ['uddʒa] *sf* (*noia*) boredom; (*fastidio*) bore; **avere/prendere qn in ~** to dislike/take a dislike to sb
uggi'oso, -a [ud'dʒoso] *ag* tiresome; (*tempo*) dull
'ugola *sf* uvula
uguagli'anza [ugwaʎ'ʎantsa] *sf* equality
uguagli'are [ugwaʎ'ʎare] *vt* to make equal; (*essere uguale*) to equal, be equal to; (*livellare*) to level; **uguagliarsi** *vr*: **uguagliarsi a** *o* **con qn** (*paragonarsi*) to compare o.s. to sb

ugu'ale *ag* equal; (*identico*) identical, the same; (*uniforme*) level, even ■ *av*: **costano ~** they cost the same; **sono bravi ~** they're equally good
ugual'mente *av* equally; (*lo stesso*) all the same
U.I. *abbr* = **uso interno**
UIL *sigla f* (= *Unione Italiana del Lavoro*) *trade union federation*
'ulcera ['ultʃera] *sf* ulcer
ulcerazi'one [ultʃerat'tsjone] *sf* ulceration
u'liva *etc* = **oliva** *etc*
U'livo *sm* (*Pol*) centre-left coalition
ulteri'ore *ag* further
ultima'mente *av* lately, of late
ulti'mare *vt* to finish, complete
ulti'matum *sm inv* ultimatum
ulti'missime *sfpl* latest news *sg*
'ultimo, -a *ag* (*finale*) last; (*estremo*) farthest, utmost; (*recente*: *notizia, moda*) latest; (*fig*: *sommo, fondamentale*) ultimate ■ *sm/f* last (one); **fino all'~** to the last, until the end; **da ~, in ~** in the end; **per ~** (*entrare, arrivare*) last; **abitare all'~ piano** to live on the top floor; **in ultima pagina** (*di giornale*) on the back page; **negli ultimi tempi** recently; **all'~ momento** at the last minute; **... la vostra lettera del 7 aprile ~ scorso** ... your letter of April 7th last; **in ultima analisi** in the final *o* last analysis; **in ~ luogo** finally
ultrà *sm/f* ultra
ultrasi'nistra *sf* (*Pol*) extreme left
ultrasu'ono *sm* ultrasound
ultravio'letto, -a *ag* ultraviolet
ulu'lare *vi* to howl
ulu'lato *sm* howling *no pl*; howl
umana'mente *av* (*con umanità*) humanely; (*nei limiti delle capacità umane*) humanly
uma'nesimo *sm* humanism
umanità *sf* humanity
umani'tario, -a *ag* humanitarian
umaniz'zare [umanid'dzare] *vt* to humanize
u'mano, -a *ag* human; (*comprensivo*) humane
umbi'lico *sm* = **ombelico**
'umbro, -a *ag* of (*o* from) Umbria
umet'tare *vt* to dampen, moisten
umi'diccio, -a, ci, ce [umi'dittʃo] *ag* (*terreno*) damp; (*mano*) moist, clammy
umidifi'care *vt* to humidify
umidifica'tore *sm* humidifier
umidità *sf* dampness; moistness; humidity
'umido, -a *ag* damp; (*mano, occhi*) moist; (*clima*) humid ■ *sm* dampness, damp; **carne in ~** stew
'umile *ag* humble
umili'ante *ag* humiliating
umili'are *vt* to humiliate; **umiliarsi** *vr* to humble o.s.
umiliazi'one [umiljat'tsjone] *sf* humiliation
umiltà *sf* humility, humbleness
u'more *sm* (*disposizione d'animo*) mood; (*carattere*) temper; **di buon/cattivo ~** in a good/bad mood
umo'rismo *sm* humour (*Brit*), humor (*US*); **avere il senso dell'~** to have a sense of humo(u)r
umo'rista, -i, e *sm/f* humorist
umo'ristico, -a, ci, che *ag* humorous, funny
un, un', una *vedi* **uno**
u'nanime *ag* unanimous
unanimità *sf* unanimity; **all'~** unanimously
'una 'tantum *ag* one-off *cpd* ■ *sf* (*imposta*) one-off tax
unci'nato, -a [untʃi'nato] *ag* (*amo*) barbed; (*ferro*) hooked; **croce uncinata** swastika
unci'netto [untʃi'netto] *sm* crochet hook
un'cino [un'tʃino] *sm* hook
undi'cenne [undi'tʃɛnne] *ag, sm/f* eleven-year-old
undi'cesimo, -a [undi'tʃɛzimo] *ag* eleventh
'undici ['unditʃi] *num* eleven
U'NESCO *sigla f* (= *United Nations Educational, Scientific and Cultural Organization*) UNESCO
'ungere ['undʒere] *vt* to grease, oil; (*Rel*) to anoint; (*fig*) to flatter, butter up; **ungersi** *vr* (*sporcarsi*) to get covered in grease; **ungersi con la crema** to put on cream
unghe'rese [unge'rese] *ag, sm/f, sm* Hungarian
Unghe'ria [unge'ria] *sf*: **l'~** Hungary
'unghia ['ungja] *sf* (*Anat*) nail; (*di animale*) claw; (*di rapace*) talon; (*di cavallo*) hoof; **pagare sull'~** (*fig*) to pay on the nail
unghi'ata [un'gjata] *sf* (*graffio*) scratch
ungu'ento *sm* ointment
unica'mente *av* only
'UNICEF ['unitʃɛf] *sigla m* (= *United Nations International Children's Emergency Fund*) UNICEF
'unico, -a, ci, che *ag* (*solo*) only; (*ineguagliabile*) unique; (*singolo: binario*) single; **è figlio ~** he's an only child; **atto ~** (*Teat*) one-act play; **agente ~** (*Comm*) sole agent
uni'corno *sm* unicorn
unifi'care *vt* to unite, unify; (*sistemi*) to standardize
unificazi'one [unifikat'tsjone] *sf* unification; standardization
unifor'mare *vt* (*terreno, superficie*) to level; **uniformarsi** *vr*: **uniformarsi a** to conform to; **~ qc a** to adjust *o* relate sth to
uni'forme *ag* uniform; (*superficie*) even ■ *sf* (*divisa*) uniform; **alta ~** dress uniform
uniformità *sf* uniformity; evenness
unilate'rale *ag* one-sided; (*Dir, Pol*) unilateral

uninomiˈnale *ag* (*Pol: collegio, sistema*) single-candidate *cpd*
uniˈone *sf* union; (*fig: concordia*) unity, harmony; **l'U~** (*Pol*) *coalition of centre-left parties*; **U~ economica e monetaria** economic and monetary union; **U~ Europea** European Union; **l'U~ Sovietica** the Soviet Union
uˈnire *vt* to unite; (*congiungere*) to join, connect; (*: ingredienti, colori*) to combine; (*in matrimonio*) to unite, join together; **unirsi** *vr* to unite; (*in matrimonio*) to be joined together; **~ qc a** to unite sth with; to join *o* connect sth with; to combine sth with; **unirsi a** (*gruppo, società*) to join
uˈnisono *sm*: **all'~** in unison
unità *sf inv* (*unione, concordia*) unity; (*Mat, Mil, Comm, di misura*) unit; **~ centrale (di elaborazione)** (*Inform*) central processing unit; **~ disco** (*Inform*) disk drive; **~ monetaria** monetary unit
uniˈtario, -a *ag* unitary; **prezzo ~** price per unit
uˈnito, -a *ag* (*paese*) united; (*amici, famiglia*) close; **in tinta unita** plain, self-coloured (*Brit*), self-colored (*US*)
univerˈsale *ag* universal; general
universalità *sf* universality
universalˈmente *av* universally
università *sf inv* university
universiˈtario, -a *ag* university *cpd* ■ *sm/f* (*studente*) university student; (*insegnante*) academic, university lecturer
uniˈverso *sm* universe
uˈnivoco, -a, ci, che *ag* unambiguous

 PAROLA CHIAVE

ˈuno, -a (*dav sm* **un** + *C, V,* **uno** + *s impura, gn, pn, ps, x, z; dav sf* **un'** + *V,* **una** + *C*) *det* **1** a; (*dav vocale*) an; **un bambino** a child; **una strada** a street; **uno zingaro** a gypsy
2 (*intensivo*): **ho avuto una paura!** I got such a fright!
■ *pron* **1** one; **ce n'è uno qui** there's one here; **prendine uno** take one (of them); **l'uno o l'altro** either (of them); **l'uno e l'altro** both (of them); **aiutarsi l'un l'altro** to help one another *o* each other; **sono entrati l'uno dopo l'altro** they came in one after the other; **a uno a uno** one by one; **metà per uno** half each
2 (*un tale*) someone, somebody; **ho incontrato uno che ti conosce** I met somebody who knows you
3 (*con valore impersonale*) one, you; **se uno vuole** if one wants, if you want; **cosa fa uno in quella situazione?** what does one do in that situation?
■ *num* one; **una mela e due pere** one apple and two pears; **uno più uno fa due** one plus one equals two, one and one are two
■ *sf*: **è l'una** it's one (o'clock)

ˈunsi *etc vb vedi* **ungere**
ˈunto, -a *pp di* **ungere** ■ *ag* greasy, oily ■ *sm* grease
untuˈoso, -a *ag* greasy, oily
unziˈone [un'tsjone] *sf*: **l'Estrema U~** (*Rel*) Extreme Unction
uˈomo (*pl* **uomini**) *sm* man; **da ~** (*abito, scarpe*) men's, for men; **a memoria d'~** since the world began; **a passo d'~** at walking pace; **~ d'affari** businessman; **~ d'azione** man of action; **~ di fiducia** right-hand man; **~ di mondo** man of the world; **~ di paglia** stooge; **~ rana** frogman; **l'~ della strada** the man in the street
uˈopo *sm*: **all'~** if necessary
uˈovo (*pl(f)* **uova**) *sm* egg; **cercare il pelo nell'~** (*fig*) to split hairs; **~ affogato** *o* **in camicia** poached egg; **~ bazzotto/sodo** soft-/hard-boiled egg; **~ alla coque** boiled egg; **~ di Pasqua** Easter egg; **~ al tegame** *o* **all'occhio di bue** fried egg; **uova strapazzate** scrambled eggs
uraˈgano *sm* hurricane
Uˈrali *smpl*: **gli ~**: **i Monti ~** the Urals, the Ural Mountains
uˈranio *sm* uranium; **~ impoverito** depleted uranium
urbaˈnista, -i, e *sm/f* town planner
urbaˈnistica *sf* town planning
urbanità *sf* urbanity
urˈbano, -a *ag* urban, city *cpd*, town *cpd*; (*Tel: chiamata*) local; (*fig*) urbane
urˈgente [ur'dʒɛnte] *ag* urgent
urˈgenza [ur'dʒɛntsa] *sf* urgency; **in caso d'~** in (case of) an emergency; **d'~** *ag* emergency ■ *av* urgently, as a matter of urgency; **non c'è ~** there's no hurry; **questo lavoro va fatto con ~** this work is urgent
ˈurgere ['urdʒere] *vi* to be needed urgently
uˈrina *etc* = **orina** *etc*
urˈlare *vi* (*persona*) to scream, yell; (*animale, vento*) to howl ■ *vt* to scream, yell
ˈurlo (*pl(m)* **urli**, *pl(f)* **urla**) *sm* scream, yell; howl
ˈurna *sf* urn; (*elettorale*) ballot box; **andare alle urne** to go to the polls
URP [urp] *sigla m* (= *Ufficio Relazioni con il Pubblico*) PR Office
urrà *escl* hurrah!
U.R.S.S. *sigla f* = **Unione delle Repubbliche Socialiste Sovietiche**; **l'~** the USSR

ur'tare *vt* to bump into, knock against; (*fig: irritare*) to annoy ■ *vi*: **~ contro** *o* **in** to bump into, knock against; (*fig: imbattersi*) to come up against; **urtarsi** *vr* (*reciproco: scontrarsi*) to collide; (*: fig*) to clash; (*irritarsi*) to get annoyed
'urto *sm* (*colpo*) knock, bump; (*scontro*) crash, collision; (*fig*) clash; **terapia d'~** (*Med*) shock treatment
uruguai'ano, -a *ag, sm/f* Uruguayan
Urugu'ay *sm*: **l'~** Uruguay
u.s. *abbr* = **ultimo scorso**
'USA *smpl*: **gli ~** the USA
u'sanza [u'zantsa] *sf* custom; (*moda*) fashion
u'sare *vt* to use, employ ■ *vi* (*essere di moda*) to be fashionable; (*servirsi*): **~ di** to use; (*: diritto*) to exercise; (*essere solito*): **~ fare** to be in the habit of doing, be accustomed to doing ■ *vb impers*: **qui usa così** it's the custom round here; **~ la massima cura nel fare qc** to exercise great care when doing sth
u'sato, -a *ag* used; (*consumato*) worn; (*di seconda mano*) used, second-hand ■ *sm* second-hand goods *pl*
u'scente [uʃ'ʃɛnte] *ag* (*Amm*) outgoing
usci'ere [uʃ'ʃɛre] *sm* usher
'uscio ['uʃʃo] *sm* door
u'scire [uʃ'ʃire] *vi* (*gen*) to come out; (*partire, andare a passeggio, a uno spettacolo etc*) to go out; (*essere sorteggiato: numero*) to come up; **~ da** (*gen*) to leave; (*posto*) to go (*o* come) out of, leave; (*solco, vasca etc*) to come out of; (*muro*) to stick out of; (*competenza etc*) to be outside; (*infanzia, adolescenza*) to leave behind; (*famiglia nobile etc*) to come from; **~ da** *o* **di casa** to go out; (*fig*) to leave home; **~ in automobile** to go out in the car, go for a drive; **~ di strada** (*Aut*) to go off *o* leave the road
u'scita [uʃ'ʃita] *sf* (*passaggio, varco*) exit, way out; (*per divertimento*) outing; (*Econ: somma*) expenditure; (*fig: battuta*) witty remark; **"vietata l'~"** "no exit"; **~ di sicurezza** emergency exit
usi'gnolo [uziɲ'ɲɔlo] *sm* nightingale
'uso *sm* (*utilizzazione*) use; (*esercizio*) practice (*Brit*), practise (*US*); (*abitudine*) custom; **fare ~ di qc** to use sth; **con l'~** with practice; **a ~ di** for (the use of); **d'~** (*corrente*) in use; **fuori ~** out of use; **essere in ~** to be in common *o* current use
ustio'nare *vt* to burn; **ustionarsi** *vr* to burn o.s.
usti'one *sf* burn
usu'ale *ag* common, everyday
usufru'ire *vi*: **~ di** (*giovarsi di*) to take advantage of, make use of
usu'frutto *sm* (*Dir*) usufruct
u'sura *sf* usury; (*logoramento*) wear (and tear)
usu'raio *sm* usurer
usur'pare *vt* to usurp
usurpa'tore, -'trice *sm/f* usurper
uten'sile *sm* tool, implement ■ *ag*: **macchina ~** machine tool; **utensili da cucina** kitchen utensils
utensile'ria *sf* (*utensili*) tools *pl*; (*reparto*) tool room
u'tente *sm/f* user; (*di gas etc*) consumer; (*del telefono*) subscriber; **~ finale** end user
'utero *sm* uterus, womb; **~ in affitto** host womb
'utile *ag* useful ■ *sm* (*vantaggio*) advantage, benefit; (*Econ: profitto*) profit; **rendersi ~** to be helpful; **in tempo ~ per** in time for; **unire l'~ al dilettevole** to combine business with pleasure; **partecipare agli utili** (*Econ*) to share in the profits
utilità *sf* usefulness *no pl*; use; (*vantaggio*) benefit; **essere di grande ~** to be very useful
utili'tario, -a *ag* utilitarian ■ *sf* (*Aut*) economy car
utiliz'zare [utilid'dzare] *vt* to use, make use of, utilize
utilizzazi'one [utiliddzat'tsjone] *sf* utilization, use
uti'lizzo [uti'liddzo] *sm* (*Amm*) utilization; (*Banca: di credito*) availment
util'mente *av* usefully, profitably
uto'pia *sf* utopia; **è pura ~** that's sheer utopianism
uto'pistico, -a, ci, che *ag* utopian
UVA *abbr* (= *ultravioletto prossimo*) UVA
'uva *sf* grapes *pl*; **~ passa** raisins *pl*; **~ spina** gooseberry
UVB *abbr* (= *ultravioletto lontano*) UVB

V, v [vi, vu] *sf o m inv (lettera)* V, v; **V come Venezia** ≈ V for Victor
V *abbr (= volt)* V
v. *abbr (= vedi, verso, versetto)* v.
VA *sigla* = **Varese**
va, va' *vb vedi* **andare**
va'cante *ag* vacant
va'canza [va'kantsa] *sf (l'essere vacante)* vacancy; *(riposo, ferie)* holiday(s *pl*) (*Brit*), vacation (*US*); *(giorno di permesso)* day off, holiday; **vacanze** *sfpl (periodo di ferie)* holidays, vacation *sg*; **essere/andare in ~** to be/go on holiday *o* vacation; **far ~** to have a holiday; **vacanze estive** summer holiday(s) *o* vacation
'vacca, -che *sf* cow
vacci'nare [vattʃi'nare] *vt* to vaccinate; **farsi ~** to have a vaccination, get vaccinated
vaccinazi'one [vattʃinat'tsjone] *sf* vaccination
vac'cino [vat'tʃino] *sm (Med)* vaccine
vacil'lante [vatʃil'lante] *ag (edificio, vecchio)* shaky, unsteady; *(fiamma)* flickering; *(salute, memoria)* shaky, failing
vacil'lare [vatʃil'lare] *vi* to sway; *(fiamma)* to flicker; *(fig: memoria, coraggio)* to be failing, falter
'vacuo, -a *ag (fig)* empty, vacuous ■ *sm* vacuum
'vado *etc vb vedi* **andare**
vagabon'daggio [vagabon'daddʒo] *sm* wandering, roaming; *(Dir)* vagrancy
vagabon'dare *vi* to roam, wander
vaga'bondo, -a *sm/f* tramp, vagrant; *(fannullone)* idler, loafer
va'gare *vi* to wander
vagheggi'are [vaged'dʒare] *vt* to long for, dream of
vagherò *etc* [vage'rɔ] *vb vedi* **vagare**
va'ghezza [va'gettsa] *sf* vagueness
va'gina [va'dʒina] *sf* vagina
va'gire [va'dʒire] *vi* to whimper
va'gito [va'dʒito] *sm* cry, wailing
'vaglia ['vaʎʎa] *sm inv* money order; **~ cambiario** promissory note; **~ postale** postal order
vagli'are [vaʎ'ʎare] *vt* to sift; *(fig)* to weigh up
'vaglio ['vaʎʎo] *sm* sieve; **passare al ~** *(fig)* to examine closely
'vago, -a, ghi, ghe *ag* vague
va'gone *sm (Ferr: per passeggeri)* carriage (*Brit*), car (*US*); *(: per merci)* truck, wagon; **~ letto** sleeper, sleeping car; **~ ristorante** dining *o* restaurant car
'vai *vb vedi* **andare**
vai'olo *sm* smallpox
val. *abbr* = **valuta**
va'langa, -ghe *sf* avalanche
va'lente *ag* able, talented
va'lenza [va'lɛntsa] *sf (fig: significato)* content; *(Chim)* valency
va'lere *vi (avere forza, potenza)* to have influence; *(essere valido)* to be valid; *(avere vigore, autorità)* to hold, apply; *(essere capace: poeta, studente)* to be good, be able ■ *vt (prezzo, sforzo)* to be worth; *(corrispondere)* to correspond to; *(procurare)*: **~ qc a qn** to earn sb sth; **valersi** *vr*: **valersi di** to make use of, take advantage of; **far ~** *(autorità etc)* to assert; **far ~ le proprie ragioni** to make o.s. heard; **farsi ~** to make o.s. appreciated *o* respected; **vale a dire** that is to say; **~ la pena** to be worth the effort *o* worth it; **l'uno vale l'altro** the one is as good as the other, they amount to the same thing; **non vale niente** it's worthless; **valersi dei consigli di qn** to take *o* act upon sb's advice
valeri'ana *sf (Bot, Med)* valerian
va'levole *ag* valid
'valgo *etc vb vedi* **valere**
vali'care *vt* to cross
'valico, -chi *sm (passo)* pass
validità *sf* validity
'valido, -a *ag* valid; *(rimedio)* effective; *(persona)* worthwhile; **essere di ~ aiuto a qn** to be a great help to sb

valige'ria [validʒe'ria] *sf* (*assortimento*) leather goods *pl*; (*fabbrica*) leather goods factory; (*negozio*) leather goods shop

vali'getta [vali'dʒetta] *sf*: **~ ventiquattrore** overnight bag *o* case

va'ligia, -gie *o* **ge** [va'lidʒa] *sf* (suit)case; **fare le valigie** to pack (up); **~ diplomatica** diplomatic bag

val'lata *sf* valley

'valle *sf* valley; **a ~** (*di fiume*) downstream; **scendere a ~** to go downhill

val'letto *sm* valet

valligi'ano, -a [valli'dʒano] *sm/f* inhabitant of a valley

va'lore *sm* (*gen, Comm*) value; (*merito*) merit, worth; (*coraggio*) valour (*Brit*), valor (*US*), courage; (*Finanza: titolo*) security; **valori** *smpl* (*oggetti preziosi*) valuables; **crescere/ diminuire di ~** to go up/down in value, gain/ lose in value; **è di gran ~** it's worth a lot, it's very valuable; **privo di ~** worthless; **~ contabile** book value; **~ effettivo** real value; **~ nominale** *o* **facciale** nominal value; **~ di realizzo** break-up value; **~ di riscatto** surrender value; **valori bollati** (revenue) stamps

valoriz'zare [valorid'dzare] *vt* (*terreno*) to develop; (*fig*) to make the most of

valo'roso, -a *ag* courageous

'valso, -a *pp di* **valere**

va'luta *sf* currency, money; (*Banca*): **~ 15 gennaio** interest to run from January 15th; **~ estera** foreign currency

valu'tare *vt* (*casa, gioiello, fig*) to value; (*stabilire: peso, entrate, fig*) to estimate

valu'tario, -a *ag* (*Finanza: norme*) currency *cpd*

valutazi'one [valutat'tsjone] *sf* valuation; estimate

'valva *sf* (*Zool, Bot*) valve

'valvola *sf* (*Tecn, Anat*) valve; (*Elettr*) fuse; **~ a farfalla del carburatore** (*Aut*) throttle; **~ di sicurezza** safety valve

'valzer ['valtser] *sm inv* waltz

vam'pata *sf* (*di fiamma*) blaze; (*di calore*) blast; (*: al viso*) flush

vam'piro *sm* vampire

vana'gloria *sf* boastfulness

van'dalico, -a, ci, che *ag* vandal *cpd*; **atto ~** act of vandalism

vanda'lismo *sm* vandalism

'vandalo *sm* vandal

vaneggia'mento [vaneddʒa'mento] *sm* raving, delirium

vaneggi'are [vaned'dʒare] *vi* to rave

va'nesio, -a *ag* vain, conceited

'vanga, -ghe *sf* spade

van'gare *vt* to dig

van'gelo [van'dʒɛlo] *sm* gospel

vanifi'care *vt* to nullify

va'niglia [va'niʎʎa] *sf* vanilla

vanigli'ato, -a [vaniʎ'ʎato] *ag*: **zucchero ~** (*Cuc*) vanilla sugar

vanità *sf* vanity; (*di promessa*) emptiness; (*di sforzo*) futility

vani'toso, -a *ag* vain, conceited

'vanno *vb vedi* **andare**

'vano, -a *ag* vain ■ *sm* (*spazio*) space; (*apertura*) opening; (*stanza*) room; **il ~ della porta** the doorway; **il ~ portabagagli** (*Aut*) the boot (*Brit*), the trunk (*US*)

van'taggio [van'taddʒo] *sm* advantage; **trarre ~ da qc** to benefit from sth; **essere/ portarsi in ~** (*Sport*) to be in/take the lead

vantaggi'oso, -a [vantad'dʒoso] *ag* advantageous, favourable (*Brit*), favorable (*US*)

van'tare *vt* to praise, speak highly of; **vantarsi** *vr*: **vantarsi (di/di aver fatto)** to boast *o* brag (about/about having done)

vante'ria *sf* boasting

'vanto *sm* boasting; (*merito*) virtue, merit; (*gloria*) pride

'vanvera *sf*: **a ~** haphazardly; **parlare a ~** to talk nonsense

va'pore *sm* vapour (*Brit*), vapor (*US*); (*anche*: **vapore acqueo**) steam; (*nave*) steamer; **a ~** (*turbina etc*) steam *cpd*; **al ~** (*Cuc*) steamed

vapo'retto *sm* steamer

vapori'era *sf* (*Ferr*) steam engine

vaporiz'zare [vaporid'dzare] *vt* to vaporize

vaporizza'tore [vaporiddza'tore] *sm* spray

vaporizzazi'one [vaporiddzat'tsjone] *sf* vaporization

vapo'roso, -a *ag* (*tessuto*) filmy; (*capelli*) soft and full

va'rare *vt* (*Naut, fig*) to launch; (*Dir*) to pass

var'care *vt* to cross

'varco, -chi *sm* passage; **aprirsi un ~ tra la folla** to push one's way through the crowd

vare'china [vare'kina] *sf* bleach

vari'abile *ag* variable; (*tempo, umore*) changeable, variable ■ *sf* (*Mat*) variable

vari'ante *sf* (*gen*) variation, change; (*di piano*) modification; (*Ling*) variant; (*Sport*) alternative route

vari'are *vt, vi* to vary; **~ di opinione** to change one's mind

variazi'one [varjat'tsjone] *sf* variation, change; (*Mus*) variation; **una ~ di programma** a change of plan

va'rice [va'ritʃe] *sf* varicose vein

vari'cella [vari'tʃɛlla] *sf* chickenpox

vari'coso, -a *ag* varicose

varie'gato, -a *ag* variegated

varietà *sf inv* variety ■ *sm inv* variety show
ˈ**vario, -a** *ag* varied; (*parecchi: col sostantivo al pl*) various; (*mutevole: umore*) changeable; **varie** *sfpl*: **varie ed eventuali** (*nell'ordine del giorno*) any other business
varioˈpinto, -a *ag* multicoloured (*Brit*), multicolored (*US*)
ˈ**varo** *sm* (*Naut, fig*) launch; (*di leggi*) passing
varrò *etc vb vedi* **valere**
Varˈsavia *sf* Warsaw
vaˈsaio *sm* potter
ˈ**vasca, -sche** *sf* basin; (*anche*: **vasca da bagno**) bathtub, bath
vaˈscello [vaʃˈʃɛllo] *sm* (*Naut*) vessel, ship
vasˈchetta [vasˈketta] *sf* (*per gelato*) tub; (*per sviluppare fotografie*) dish
vaseˈlina *sf* vaseline
vaselˈlame *sm* (*stoviglie*) crockery; (: *di porcellana*) china; **~ d'oro/d'argento** gold/silver plate
ˈ**vaso** *sm* (*recipiente*) pot; (: *barattolo*) jar; (: *decorativo*) vase; (*Anat*) vessel; **~ da fiori** vase; (*per piante*) flowerpot
vasˈsallo *sm* vassal
vasˈsoio *sm* tray
vastità *sf* vastness
ˈ**vasto, -a** *ag* vast, immense; **di vaste proporzioni** (*incendio*) huge; (*fenomeno, rivolta*) widespread; **su vasta scala** on a vast *o* huge scale
Vatiˈcano *sm*: **il ~** the Vatican; **la Città del ~** the Vatican City
VB *sigla* = **Vibo Valenza**
VC *sigla* = **Vercelli**
VE *sigla* = **Venezia** ■ *abbr* = **Vostra Eccellenza**
ve *pron, av vedi* **vi**
vecchiˈaia [vekˈkjaja] *sf* old age
ˈ**vecchio, -a** [ˈvɛkkjo] *ag* old ■ *sm/f* old man(-woman); **i vecchi** the old; **è un mio ~ amico** he's an old friend of mine; **è un uomo ~ stile** *o* **stampo** he's an old-fashioned man; **è ~ del mestiere** he's an old hand at the job
ˈ**vece** [ˈvetʃe] *sf*: **in ~ di** in the place of, for; **fare le veci di qn** to take sb's place; **firma del padre o di chi ne fa le veci** signature of the father or guardian
veˈdere *vt, vi* to see; **vedersi** *vr* to meet, see one another; **~ di fare qc** to see (to it) that sth is done, make sure that sth is done; **avere a che ~ con** to have to do with; **far ~ qc a qn** to show sb sth; **farsi ~** to show o.s.; (*farsi vivo*) to show one's face; **farsi ~ da un medico** to go and see a doctor; **modo di ~** outlook, view of things; **vedi pagina 8** (*rimando*) see page 8; **è da ~ se ...** it remains to be seen whether ...; **non vedo la ragione di farlo** I can't see any reason to do it; **si era visto costretto a ...** he found himself forced to ...; **non (ci) si vede** (*è buio etc*) you can't see a thing; **ci vediamo domani!** see you tomorrow!; **non lo posso ~** (*fig*) I can't stand him
veˈdetta *sf* (*sentinella, posto*) look-out; (*Naut*) patrol boat
veˈdette [vəˈdɛt] *sf inv* (*attrice*) star
ˈ**vedovo, -a** *sm/f* widower/widow; **rimaner ~** to be widowed
vedrò *etc vb vedi* **vedere**
veˈduta *sf* view; **di larghe** *o* **ampie vedute** broad-minded; **di vedute limitate** narrow-minded
veeˈmente *ag* (*discorso, azione*) vehement; (*assalto*) vigorous; (*passione*) overwhelming
veeˈmenza [veeˈmɛntsa] *sf* vehemence; **con ~** vehemently
vegeˈtale [vedʒeˈtale] *ag, sm* vegetable
vegeˈtare [vedʒeˈtare] *vi* (*fig*) to vegetate
vegetariˈano, -a [vedʒetaˈrjano] *ag, sm/f* vegetarian
vegetaˈtivo, -a *ag* vegetative
vegetaziˈone [vedʒetatˈtsjone] *sf* vegetation
ˈ**vegeto, -a** [ˈvɛdʒeto] *ag* (*pianta*) thriving; (*persona*) strong, vigorous
vegˈgente [vedˈdʒɛnte] *sm/f* (*indovino*) clairvoyant
ˈ**veglia** [ˈveʎʎa] *sf* (*sorveglianza*) watch; (*trattenimento*) evening gathering; **tra la ~ e il sonno** half awake; **fare la ~ a un malato** to watch over a sick person; **~ funebre** wake
vegliˈardo, -a [veʎˈʎardo] *sm/f* venerable old man/woman
vegliˈare [veʎˈʎare] *vi* to stay *o* sit up; (*stare vigile*) to watch; to keep watch ■ *vt* (*malato, morto*) to watch over, sit up with
vegliˈone [veʎˈʎone] *sm* ball, dance
veˈicolo *sm* vehicle; **~ spaziale** spacecraft *inv*
ˈ**vela** *sf* (*Naut: tela*) sail; (*sport*) sailing; **tutto va a gonfie vele** (*fig*) everything is going perfectly
veˈlare *vt* to veil; **velarsi** *vr* (*occhi, luna*) to mist over; (*voce*) to become husky; **velarsi il viso** to cover one's face (with a veil)
veˈlato, -a *ag* veiled
velaˈtura *sf* (*Naut*) sails *pl*
veleggiˈare [veledˈdʒare] *vi* to sail; (*Aer*) to glide
veˈleno *sm* poison
veleˈnoso, -a *ag* poisonous
veˈletta *sf* (*di cappello*) veil
veliˈero *sm* sailing ship
veˈlina *sf*: **carta ~** (*per imballare*) tissue paper; (: *per copie*) flimsy paper; (*copia*) carbon copy
veˈlista, -i, e *sm/f* yachtsman(-woman)

ve'livolo *sm* aircraft
velleità *sf inv* vain ambition, vain desire
vellei'tario, -a *ag* unrealistic
'vello *sm* fleece
vellu'tato, -a *ag* (*stoffa, pesca, colore*) velvety; (*voce*) mellow
vel'luto *sm* velvet; **~ a coste** cord
'velo *sm* veil; (*tessuto*) voile
ve'loce [ve'lotʃe] *ag* fast, quick ▪ *av* fast, quickly
velo'cista, -i, e [velo'tʃista] *sm/f* (*Sport*) sprinter
velocità [velotʃi'ta] *sf* speed; **a forte ~** at high speed; **~ di crociera** cruising speed
ve'lodromo *sm* velodrome
ven. *abbr* (= *venerdì*) Fri.
'vena *sf* (*gen*) vein; (*filone*) vein, seam; (*fig*: *ispirazione*) inspiration; (: *umore*) mood; **essere in ~ di qc** to be in the mood for sth
ve'nale *ag* (*prezzo, valore*) market *cpd*; (*fig*) venal; mercenary
venalità *sf* venality
ve'nato, -a *ag* (*marmo*) veined, streaked; (*legno*) grained
vena'torio, -a *ag* hunting; **la stagione venatoria** the hunting season
vena'tura *sf* (*di marmo*) vein, streak; (*di legno*) grain
ven'demmia *sf* (*raccolta*) grape harvest; (*quantità d'uva*) grape crop, grapes *pl*; (*vino ottenuto*) vintage
vendemmi'are *vt* to harvest ▪ *vi* to harvest the grapes
'vendere *vt* to sell; **~ all'ingrosso/al dettaglio** *o* **minuto** to sell wholesale/retail; **~ all'asta** to auction, sell by auction; **"vendesi"** "for sale"
ven'detta *sf* revenge
vendi'care *vt* to avenge; **vendicarsi** *vr*: **vendicarsi (di)** to avenge o.s. (for); (*per rancore*) to take one's revenge (for); **vendicarsi su qn** to revenge o.s. on sb
vendica'tivo, -a *ag* vindictive
'vendita *sf* sale; **la ~** (*attività*) selling; (*smercio*) sales *pl*; **in ~** on sale; **mettere in ~** to put on sale; **in ~ presso** on sale at; **contratto di ~** sales agreement; **reparto vendite** sales department; **~ all'asta** sale by auction; **~ al dettaglio** *o* **minuto** retail; **~ all'ingrosso** wholesale
vendi'tore, -'trice *sm/f* seller, vendor; (*gestore di negozio*) trader, dealer
ven'duto, -a *ag* (*merce*) sold; (*fig*: *corrotto*) corrupt
ve'nefico, -a, ci, che *ag* poisonous
vene'rabile *ag*, **vene'rando, -a** ▪ *ag* venerable
vene'rare *vt* to venerate
venerazi'one [venerat'tsjone] *sf* veneration
venerdì *sm inv* Friday; **V~ Santo** Good Friday; *vedi anche* **martedì**
'Venere *sm, sf* Venus
ve'nereo, -a *ag* venereal
'veneto, -a *ag* of (*o* from) the Veneto
'veneto-giuli'ano, -a ['vɛnetodʒu'ljano] *ag* of (*o* from) Venezia-Giulia
Ve'nezia [ve'nɛttsja] *sf* Venice
venezi'ano, -a [venet'tsjano] *ag, sm/f* Venetian
Venezu'ela [venettsu'ela] *sm*: **il ~** Venezuela
venezue'lano, -a [venettsue'lano] *ag, sm/f* Venezuelan
'vengo *etc vb vedi* **venire**
veni'ale *ag* venial
ve'nire *vi* to come; (*riuscire*: *dolce, fotografia*) to turn out; (*come ausiliare*: *essere*): **viene ammirato da tutti** he is admired by everyone; **~ da** to come from; **quanto viene?** how much does it cost?; **far ~** (*mandare a chiamare*) to send for; (*medico*) to call, send for; **~ a capo di qc** to unravel sth, sort sth out; **~ al dunque** *o* **nocciolo** *o* **fatto** to come to the point; **~ fuori** to come out; **~ giù** to come down; **~ meno** (*svenire*) to faint; **~ meno a qc** not to fulfil sth; **~ su** to come up; **~ via** to come away; **~ a sapere qc** to learn sth; **~ a trovare qn** to come and see sb; **negli anni a ~** in the years to come, in future; **è venuto il momento di ...** the time has come to ...
'venni *etc vb vedi* **venire**
ven'taglio [ven'taʎʎo] *sm* fan
ven'tata *sf* gust (of wind)
venten'nale *ag* (*che dura 20 anni*) twenty-year *cpd*; (*che ricorre ogni 20 anni*) which takes place every twenty years
ven'tenne *ag, sm/f* twenty-year-old
ven'tennio *sm* period of twenty years; **il ~ fascista** the Fascist period
ven'tesimo, -a *num* twentieth
'venti *num* twenty
venti'lare *vt* (*stanza*) to air, ventilate; (*fig*: *idea, proposta*) to air
venti'lato, -a *ag* (*camera, zona*) airy; **poco ~** airless
ventila'tore *sm* fan; (*su parete, finestra*) ventilator, fan
ventilazi'one [ventilat'tsjone] *sf* ventilation
ven'tina *sf*: **una ~ (di)** around twenty, twenty or so
ventiquat'tr'ore *sfpl* (*periodo*) twenty-four hours ▪ *sf inv* (*Sport*) twenty-four-hour race; (*valigetta*) overnight case
venti'sette *num* twenty-seven; **il ~** (*giorno di paga*) (monthly) pay day

V

ventitré *num* twenty-three ■ *sfpl*: **portava il cappello sulle ~** he wore his hat at a jaunty angle
'vento *sm* wind; **c'è ~** it's windy; **un colpo di ~** a gust of wind; **contro ~** against the wind; **~ contrario** (*Naut*) headwind
'ventola *sf* (*Aut, Tecn*) fan
ven'tosa *sf* (*Zool*) sucker; (*di gomma*) suction pad
ven'toso, -a *ag* windy
ven'totto *num* twenty-eight
'ventre *sm* stomach
ven'triloquo *sm* ventriloquist
ven'tuno *num* twenty-one
ven'tura *sf*: **andare alla ~** to trust to luck; **soldato di ~** mercenary
ven'turo, -a *ag* next, coming
ve'nuto, -a *pp di* **venire** ■ *sm/f*: **il(la) primo(a) ~(a)** the first person who comes along ■ *sf* coming, arrival
ver. *abbr* = **versamento**
'vera *sf* wedding ring
ve'race [ve'ratʃe] *ag* (*testimone*) truthful; (*testimonianza*) accurate; (*cibi*) real, genuine
vera'mente *av* really
ve'randa *sf* veranda(h)
ver'bale *ag* verbal ■ *sm* (*di riunione*) minutes *pl*; **accordo ~** verbal agreement; **mettere a ~** to place in the minutes *o* on record
'verbo *sm* (*Ling*) verb; (*parola*) word; (*Rel*): **il V~** the Word
ver'boso, -a *ag* verbose, wordy
ver'dastro, -a *ag* greenish
'verde *ag, sm* green; **~ bottiglia/oliva** (*inv*) bottle/olive green; **benzina ~** lead-free *o* unleaded petrol; **i Verdi** (*Pol*) the Greens; **essere al ~** (*fig*) to be broke
verdeggi'ante [verded'dʒante] *ag* green, verdant
verde'rame *sm* verdigris
ver'detto *sm* verdict
ver'dura *sf* vegetables *pl*
vere'condia *sf* modesty
vere'condo, -a *ag* modest
'verga, -ghe *sf* rod
ver'gato, -a *ag* (*foglio*) ruled
vergi'nale [verdʒi'nale] *ag* virginal
'vergine ['verdʒine] *sf* virgin; (*dello zodiaco*): **V~** Virgo ■ *ag* virgin; (*ragazza*): **essere ~** to be a virgin; **essere della V~** (*dello zodiaco*) to be Virgo; **pura lana ~** pure new wool; **olio ~ d'oliva** unrefined olive oil
verginità [verdʒini'ta] *sf* virginity
ver'gogna [ver'goɲɲa] *sf* shame; (*timidezza*) shyness, embarrassment
vergo'gnarsi [vergoɲ'ɲarsi] *vr*: **~ (di)** to be *o* feel ashamed (of); to be shy (about), be embarrassed (about)
vergo'gnoso, -a [vergoɲ'ɲoso] *ag* ashamed; (*timido*) shy, embarrassed; (*causa di vergogna: azione*) shameful
veridicità [veriditʃi'ta] *sf* truthfulness
ve'ridico, -a, ci, che *ag* truthful
ve'rifica, -che *sf* checking *no pl*; check; **fare una ~ di** (*freni, testimonianza, firma*) to check; **~ contabile** (*Finanza*) audit
verifi'care *vt* (*controllare*) to check; (*confermare*) to confirm, bear out; (*Finanza*) to audit
verità *sf inv* truth; **a dire la ~, per la ~** truth to tell, actually
veriti'ero, -a *ag* (*che dice la verità*) truthful; (*conforme a verità*) true
'verme *sm* worm
vermi'celli [vermi'tʃɛlli] *smpl* vermicelli *sg*
ver'miglio [ver'miʎʎo] *sm* vermilion, scarlet
'vermut *sm inv* vermouth
ver'nacolo *sm* vernacular
ver'nice [ver'nitʃe] *sf* (*colorazione*) paint; (*trasparente*) varnish; (*pelle*) patent leather; **"~ fresca"** "wet paint"
vernici'are [verni'tʃare] *vt* to paint; to varnish
vernicia'tura [vernitʃa'tura] *sf* painting; varnishing
'vero, -a *ag* (*veridico: fatti, testimonianza*) true; (*autentico*) real ■ *sm* (*verità*) truth; (*realtà*) (real) life; **un ~ e proprio delinquente** a real criminal, an out and out criminal; **tant'è ~ che ...** so much so that ...; **a onor del ~, a dire il ~** to tell the truth
Ve'rona *sf* Verona
vero'nese *ag* of (*o* from) Verona
vero'simile *ag* likely, probable
verrò *etc vb vedi* **venire**
ver'ruca, -che *sf* wart
versa'mento *sm* (*pagamento*) payment; (*deposito di denaro*) deposit
ver'sante *sm* slopes *pl*, side
ver'sare *vt* (*fare uscire: vino, farina*) to pour (out); (*spargere: lacrime, sangue*) to shed; (*rovesciare*) to spill; (*Econ*) to pay; (*: depositare*) to deposit, pay in ■ *vi*: **~ in gravi difficoltà** to find o.s. with serious problems; **versarsi** *vr* (*rovesciarsi*) to spill; (*fiume, folla*): **versarsi (in)** to pour (into)
versa'tile *ag* versatile
versatilità *sf* versatility
ver'sato, -a *ag*: **~ in** to be (well-)versed in
ver'setto *sm* (*Rel*) verse
versi'one *sf* version; (*traduzione*) translation
'verso *sm* (*di poesia*) verse, line; (*di animale, uccello, venditore ambulante*) cry; (*direzione*) direction; (*modo*) way; (*di foglio di carta*) verso; (*di moneta*) reverse; **versi** *smpl* (*poesia*) verse *sg*; **per un ~ o per l'altro** one way or another;

prendere qn/qc per il ~ giusto to approach sb/sth the right way; **rifare il ~ a qn** (*imitare*) to mimic sb; **non c'è ~ di persuaderlo** there's no way of persuading him, he can't be persuaded ■ *prep* (*in direzione di*) toward(s); (*nei pressi di*) near, around (about); (*in senso temporale*) about, around; (*nei confronti di*) for; **~ di me** towards me; **~ l'alto** upwards; **~ il basso** downwards; **~ sera** towards evening
'vertebra *sf* vertebra
verte'brale *ag* vertebral; **colonna ~** spinal column, spine
verte'brato, -a *ag, sm* vertebrate
ver'tenza [ver'tɛntsa] *sf* (*lite*) lawsuit, case; (*sindacale*) dispute
'vertere *vi*: **~ su** to deal with, be about
verti'cale *ag, sf* vertical
'vertice ['vɛrtitʃe] *sm* summit, top; (*Mat*) vertex; **conferenza al ~** (*Pol*) summit conference
ver'tigine [ver'tidʒine] *sf* dizziness *no pl*; dizzy spell; (*Med*) vertigo; **avere le vertigini** to feel dizzy
vertigi'noso, -a [vertidʒi'noso] *ag* (*altezza*) dizzy; (*fig*) breathtakingly high (*o* deep *etc*)
'verza ['verdza] *sf* Savoy cabbage
ve'scica, -che [veʃʃika] *sf* (*Anat*) bladder; (*Med*) blister
vesco'vile *ag* episcopal
'vescovo *sm* bishop
'vespa *sf* wasp; (®: *veicolo*) (motor) scooter
ves'paio *sm* wasps' nest; **suscitare un ~** (*fig*) to stir up a hornets' nest
vespasi'ano *sm* urinal
'vespro *sm* (*Rel*) vespers *pl*
ves'sare *vt* to oppress
vessazi'one [vessat'tsjone] *sf* oppression
ves'sillo *sm* standard; (*bandiera*) flag
ves'taglia [ves'taʎʎa] *sf* dressing gown, robe (*US*)
'veste *sf* garment; (*rivestimento*) covering; (*qualità, facoltà*) capacity; **vesti** *sfpl* clothes, clothing *sg*; **in ~ ufficiale** (*fig*) in an official capacity; **in ~ di** in the guise of, as; **~ da camera** dressing gown, robe (*US*); **~ editoriale** layout
vesti'ario *sm* wardrobe, clothes *pl*; **capo di ~** article of clothing, garment
ves'tibolo *sm* (entrance) hall
ves'tigia [ves'tidʒa] *sfpl* (*tracce*) vestiges, traces; (*rovine*) ruins, remains
ves'tire *vt* (*bambino, malato*) to dress; (*avere indosso*) to have on, wear; **vestirsi** *vr* to dress, get dressed; **vestirsi da** (*negozio, sarto*) to buy *o* get one's clothes at
ves'tito, -a *ag* dressed ■ *sm* garment; (*da donna*) dress; (*da uomo*) suit; **vestiti** *smpl* (*indumenti*) clothes; **~ di bianco** dressed in white
Ve'suvio *sm*: **il ~** Vesuvius
vete'rano, -a *ag, sm/f* veteran
veteri'nario, -a *ag* veterinary ■ *sm* veterinary surgeon (*Brit*), veterinarian (*US*), vet ■ *sf* veterinary medicine
'veto *sm inv* veto; **porre il ~ a qc** to veto sth
ve'traio *sm* glassmaker; (*per finestre*) glazier
ve'trato, -a *ag* (*porta, finestra*) glazed; (*che contiene vetro*) glass *cpd* ■ *sf* glass door (*o* window); (*di chiesa*) stained glass window; **carta vetrata** sandpaper
vetre'ria *sf* (*stabilimento*) glassworks *sg*; (*oggetti di vetro*) glassware
ve'trina *sf* (*di negozio*) (shop) window; (*armadio*) display cabinet
vetri'nista, -i, e *sm/f* window dresser
ve'trino *sm* slide
vetri'olo *sm* vitriol
'vetro *sm* glass; (*per finestra, porta*) pane (of glass); **~ blindato** bulletproof glass; **~ infrangibile** shatterproof glass; **~ di sicurezza** safety glass; **i vetri di Murano** Murano glassware *sg*
ve'troso, -a *ag* vitreous
'vetta *sf* peak, summit, top
vet'tore *sm* (*Mat, Fisica*) vector; (*chi trasporta*) carrier
vetto'vaglie [vetto'vaʎʎe] *sfpl* supplies
vet'tura *sf* (*carrozza*) carriage; (*Ferr*) carriage (*Brit*), car (*US*); (*auto*) car (*Brit*), automobile (*US*); **~ di piazza** hackney carriage
vettu'rino *sm* coach driver, coachman
vezzeggi'are [vettsed'dʒare] *vt* to fondle, caress
vezzeggia'tivo [vettseddʒa'tivo] *sm* (*Ling*) term of endearment
'vezzo ['vettso] *sm* habit; **vezzi** *smpl* (*smancerie*) affected ways; (*leggiadria*) charms
vez'zoso, -a [vet'tsoso] *ag* (*grazioso*) charming, pretty; (*lezioso*) affected
V.F. *abbr* = **vigili del fuoco**
V.G. *abbr* = **Vostra Grazia**
VI *sigla* = **Vicenza**
vi (*dav lo, la, li, le, ne diventa* **ve**) *pron* (*oggetto*) you; (*complemento di termine*) (to) you; (*riflessivo*) yourselves; (*reciproco*) each other ■ *av* (*lì*) there; (*qui*) here; (*per questo/quel luogo*) through here/there; **vi è/sono** there is/are
'via *sf* (*gen*) way; (*strada*) street; (*sentiero, pista*) path, track; (*Amm: procedimento*) channels *pl* ■ *prep* (*passando per*) via, by way of ■ *av* away ■ *escl* go away!; (*suvvia*) come on!; (*Sport*) go! ■ *sm* (*Sport*) starting signal; **per ~ di** (*a causa di*) because of, on account of; **in** *o* **per ~** on the way; **in ~ di guarigione** (*fig*) on the road

V

to recovery; **per ~ aerea** by air; (*lettere*) by airmail; **~ satellite** by satellite; **andare/ essere ~** to go/be away; **~ ~** (*pian piano*) gradually; **~ ~ che** (*a mano a mano*) as; **e ~ dicendo, e ~ di questo passo** and so on (and so forth); **dare il ~** (*Sport*) to give the starting signal; **dare il ~ a un progetto** to give the green light to a project; **hanno dato il ~ ai lavori** they've begun *o* started work; **in ~ amichevole** in a friendly manner; **comporre una disputa in ~ amichevole** (*Dir*) to settle a dispute out of court; **in ~ eccezionale** as an exception; **in ~ privata** *o* **confidenziale** (*dire etc*) in confidence; **in ~ provvisoria** provisionally; **V~ lattea** (*Astr*) Milky Way; **~ di mezzo** middle course; **non c'è ~ di scampo** *o* **d'uscita** there's no way out; **vie di comunicazione** communication routes

viabilità *sf* (*di strada*) practicability; (*rete stradale*) roads *pl*, road network

via'dotto *sm* viaduct

viaggi'are [viad'dʒare] *vi* to travel; **le merci viaggiano via mare** the goods go by sea

viaggia'tore, -'trice [viaddʒa'tore] *ag* travelling (*Brit*), traveling (*US*) ■ *sm* traveller (*Brit*), traveler (*US*), passenger

vi'aggio [vi'addʒo] *sm* travel(ling); (*tragitto*) journey, trip; **buon ~!** have a good trip!; **~ d'affari** business trip; **~ di nozze** honeymoon; **~ organizzato** package tour *o* holiday

vi'ale *sm* avenue

vian'dante *sm/f* vagrant

vi'atico, -ci *sm* (*Rel*) viaticum; (*fig*) encouragement

via'vai *sm* coming and going, bustle

vi'brare *vi* to vibrate; (*agitarsi*): **~ (di)** to quiver (with)

vibra'tore *sm* vibrator

vibrazi'one [vibrat'tsjone] *sf* vibration

vi'cario *sm* (*apostolico etc*) vicar

'vice ['vitʃe] *sm/f* deputy ■ *prefisso* vice

vice'console [vitʃe'kɔnsole] *sm* vice-consul

vicediret'tore, -'trice [vitʃediret'tore] *sm/f* assistant manager(-manageress); (*di giornale etc*) deputy editor

vi'cenda [vi'tʃɛnda] *sf* event; **vicende** *sfpl* (*sorte*) fortunes; **a ~** in turn; **con alterne vicende** with mixed fortunes

vicen'devole [vitʃen'devole] *ag* mutual, reciprocal

vicen'tino, -a [vitʃen'tino] *ag* of (*o* from) Vicenza

vicepresi'dente [vitʃepresi'dɛnte] *sm* vice-president, vice-chairman

vice'versa [vitʃe'vɛrsa] *av* vice versa; **da Roma a Pisa e ~** from Rome to Pisa and back

vi'chingo, -a, ghi, ghe [vi'kingo] *ag, sm/f* Viking

vici'nanza [vitʃi'nantsa] *sf* nearness, closeness; **vicinanze** *sfpl* (*paraggi*) neighbourhood (*Brit*), neighborhood (*US*), vicinity

vici'nato [vitʃi'nato] *sm* neighbourhood (*Brit*), neighborhood (*US*); (*vicini*) neighbo(u)rs *pl*

vi'cino, -a [vi'tʃino] *ag* (*gen*) near; (*nello spazio*) near, nearby; (*accanto*) next; (*nel tempo*) near, close at hand ■ *sm/f* neighbour (*Brit*), neighbor (*US*) ■ *av* near, close; **da ~** (*guardare*) close up; (*esaminare, seguire*) closely; (*conoscere*) well, intimately; **~ a** *prep* near (to), close to; (*accanto a*) beside; **mi sono stati molto vicini** (*fig*) they were very supportive towards me; **~ di casa** neighbo(u)r

vicissi'tudini [vitʃissi'tudini] *sfpl* trials and tribulations

'vicolo *sm* alley; **~ cieco** blind alley

'video *sm inv* (*TV: schermo*) screen

video'camera *sf* camcorder

videocas'setta *sf* videocassette

videochia'mare [videokja'mare] *vt* to video call

videodipen'dente *sm/f* telly addict ■ *ag*: **un pigrone ~** a couch potato

videofo'nino *sm* video mobile

videogi'oco, -chi [video'dʒɔko] *sm* video game

videono'leggio [videono'leddʒo] *sm* video rental

videoregistra'tore [videoredʒistra'tore] *sm* (*apparecchio*) video (recorder)

video'teca, -che *sf* video shop

videote'lefono *sm* videophone

videotermi'nale *sm* visual display unit

'vidi *etc vb vedi* **vedere**

vidi'mare *vt* (*Amm*) to authenticate

vidimazi'one [vidimat'tsjone] *sf* (*Amm*) authentication

Vi'enna *sf* Vienna

vien'nese *ag, sm/f* Viennese *inv*

vie'tare *vt* to forbid; (*Amm*) to prohibit; (*libro*) to ban; **~ a qn di fare** to forbid sb to do; to prohibit sb from doing

vie'tato, -a *ag* (*vedi vb*) forbidden; prohibited; banned; **"~ fumare/l'ingresso"** "no smoking/admittance"; **~ ai minori di 14/18 anni** prohibited to children under 14/18; **"senso ~"** (*Aut*) "no entry"; **"sosta vietata"** (*Aut*) "no parking"

Viet'nam *sm*: **il ~** Vietnam

vietna'mita, -i, e *ag, sm/f, sm* Vietnamese *inv*

vi'eto, -a *ag* worthless

vi'gente [vi'dʒɛnte] *ag* in force

'**vigere** ['vidʒere] *vi* (*difettivo: si usa solo alla terza persona*) to be in force; **in casa mia vige l'abitudine di ...** at home we are in the habit of ...
vigi'lante [vidʒi'lante] *ag* vigilant, watchful
vigi'lanza [vidʒi'lantsa] *sf* vigilance; (*sorveglianza: di operai, alunni*) supervision; (: *di sospetti, criminali*) surveillance; **~ notturna** night-watchman service
vigi'lare [vidʒi'lare] *vt* to watch over, keep an eye on; **~ che** to make sure that, see to it that
vigi'lato, -a [vidʒi'lato] *sm/f* (*Dir*) person under police surveillance
vigila'trice [vidʒila'tritʃe] *sf*: **~ d'infanzia** nursery-school teacher; **~ scolastica** school health officer
'**vigile** ['vidʒile] *ag* watchful ■ *sm* (*anche:* **vigile urbano**) policeman (*in towns*); **~ del fuoco** fireman; *see note*

VIGILI URBANI

The *vigili urbani* are a municipal police force attached to the "Comune". Their duties involve everyday aspects of life such as traffic, public works and services, and commerce.

vigi'lessa [vidʒi'lessa] *sf* (traffic) policewoman
vi'gilia [vi'dʒilja] *sf* (*giorno antecedente*) eve; **la ~ di Natale** Christmas Eve
vigliacche'ria [viʎʎakke'ria] *sf* cowardice
vigli'acco, -a, chi, che [viʎ'ʎakko] *ag* cowardly ■ *sm/f* coward
'**vigna** ['viɲɲa] *sf*, **vi'gneto** [viɲ'ɲeto] *sm* vineyard
vi'gnetta [viɲ'ɲetta] *sf* cartoon; (*Auto; vignetta autostradale : tassa*) car tax (*for motorways*); (: *adesivo*) *sticker showing that this tax has been paid*
vi'gogna [vi'goɲɲa] *sf* vicuña
vi'gore *sm* vigour (*Brit*), vigor (*US*); (*Dir*): **essere/entrare in ~** to be in/come into force; **non è più in ~** it is no longer in force, it no longer applies
vigo'roso, -a *ag* vigorous
'**vile** *ag* (*spregevole*) low, mean, base; (*codardo*) cowardly
vili'pendere *vt* to despise, scorn
vili'pendio *sm* contempt, scorn
vili'peso, -a *pp di* **vilipendere**
'**villa** *sf* villa
vil'laggio [vil'laddʒo] *sm* village; **~ turistico** holiday village
villa'nia *sf* rudeness, lack of manners; **fare (o dire) una ~ a qn** to be rude to sb
vil'lano, -a *ag* rude, ill-mannered ■ *sm/f* boor
villeggi'ante [villed'dʒante] *sm/f* holiday-maker (*Brit*), vacationer (*US*)
villeggi'are [villed'dʒare] *vi* to holiday, spend one's holidays, vacation (*US*)
villeggia'tura [villeddʒa'tura] *sf* holiday(s *pl*) (*Brit*), vacation (*US*); **luogo di ~** (holiday) resort
vil'letta *sf*, **vil'lino** *sm* small house (with a garden), cottage
vil'loso, -a *ag* hairy
viltà *sf* cowardice *no pl*; (*gesto*) cowardly act
Vimi'nale *sm see note*

VIMINALE

The *Viminale*, which takes its name from one of the famous Seven Hills of Rome on which it stands, is home to the Ministry of the Interior.

'**vimine** *sm* wicker; **mobili di vimini** wicker furniture *sg*
vi'naio *sm* wine merchant
'**vincere** ['vintʃere] *vt* (*in guerra, al gioco, a una gara*) to defeat, beat; (*premio, guerra, partita*) to win; (*fig*) to overcome, conquer ■ *vi* to win; **~ qn in** (*abilità, bellezza*) to surpass sb in
'**vincita** ['vintʃita] *sf* win; (*denaro vinto*) winnings *pl*
vinci'tore, -'trice [vintʃi'tore] *sm/f* winner; (*Mil*) victor
vinco'lante *ag* binding
vinco'lare *vt* to bind; (*Comm: denaro*) to tie up
vinco'lato, -a *ag*: **deposito ~** (*Comm*) fixed deposit
'**vincolo** *sm* (*fig*) bond, tie; (*Dir*) obligation
vi'nicolo, -a *ag* wine *cpd*; **regione vinicola** wine-producing area
vinificazi'one [vinifikat'tsjone] *sf* wine-making
'**vino** *sm* wine; **~ bianco/rosso** white/red wine
'**vinsi** *etc vb vedi* **vincere**
'**vinto, -a** *pp di* **vincere** ■ *ag*: **darla vinta a qn** to let sb have his (*o* her) way; **darsi per ~** to give up, give in
vi'ola *sf* (*Bot*) violet; (*Mus*) viola ■ *ag, sm inv* (*colore*) purple
vio'lare *vt* (*chiesa*) to desecrate, violate; (*giuramento, legge*) to violate
violazi'one [violat'tsjone] *sf* desecration; violation; **~ di domicilio** (*Dir*) breaking and entering
violen'tare *vt* to use violence on; (*donna*) to rape
vio'lento, -a *ag* violent
vio'lenza [vio'lɛntsa] *sf* violence; **~ carnale** rape
vio'letto, -a *ag, sm* (*colore*) violet ■ *sf* (*Bot*) violet

V

violi'nista, -i, e *sm/f* violinist
vio'lino *sm* violin
violoncel'lista, -i, e [violontʃel'lista] *sm/f* cellist, cello player
violon'cello [violon'tʃɛllo] *sm* cello
vi'ottolo *sm* path, track
VIP *sm/f inv* (= *Very Important Person*) VIP
'vipera *sf* viper, adder
vi'raggio [vi'raddʒo] *sm* (*Naut, Aer*) turn; (*Fot*) toning
vi'rale *ag* viral
vi'rare *vi* (*Naut*) to come about; (*Aer*) to turn; (*Fot*) to tone; **~ di bordo** to change course
vi'rata *sf* coming about; turning; change of course
'virgola *sf* (*Ling*) comma; (*Mat*) point
virgo'lette *sfpl* inverted commas, quotation marks
vi'rile *ag* (*proprio dell'uomo*) masculine; (*non puerile, da uomo*) manly, virile
virilità *sf* masculinity; manliness; (*sessuale*) virility
virtù *sf inv* virtue; **in** *o* **per ~ di** by virtue of, by
virtu'ale *ag* virtual
virtu'oso, -a *ag* virtuous ■ *sm/f* (*Mus etc*) virtuoso
viru'lento, -a *ag* virulent
'virus *sm inv* virus
visa'gista, -i, e [viza'dʒista] *sm/f* beautician
visce'rale [viʃʃe'rale] *ag* (*Med*) visceral; (*fig*) profound, deep-rooted
'viscere ['viʃʃere] *sm* (*Anat*) internal organ ■ *sfpl* (*di animale*) entrails *pl*; (*fig*) depths *pl*, bowels *pl*
'vischio ['viskjo] *sm* (*Bot*) mistletoe; (*pania*) birdlime
vischi'oso, -a [vis'kjoso] *ag* sticky
viscidità [viʃʃidi'ta] *sf* sliminess
'viscido, -a ['viʃʃido] *ag* slimy
vis'conte, -'essa *sm/f* viscount/viscountess
viscosità *sf* viscosity
vis'coso, -a *ag* viscous
vi'sibile *ag* visible
visi'bilio *sm*: **andare in ~** to go into raptures
visibilità *sf* visibility
visi'era *sf* (*di elmo*) visor; (*di berretto*) peak
visio'nare *vt* (*gen*) to look at, examine; (*Cine*) to screen
visio'nario, -a *ag, sm/f* visionary
visi'one *sf* vision; **prendere ~ di qc** to examine sth, look sth over; **prima/seconda ~** (*Cine*) first/second showing
'visita *sf* visit; (*Med*) visit, call; (*: esame*) examination; **far ~ a qn, andare in ~ da qn** to visit sb, pay sb a visit; **in ~ ufficiale in Italia** on an official visit to Italy; **orario di visite** (*ospedale*) visiting hours; **~ di controllo** (*Med*) checkup; **~ a domicilio** house call; **~ guidata** guided tour; **~ sanitaria** sanitary inspection
visi'tare *vt* to visit; (*Med*) to visit, call on; (*: esaminare*) to examine
visita'tore, -'trice *sm/f* visitor
vi'sivo, -a *ag* visual
'viso *sm* face; **fare buon ~ a cattivo gioco** to make the best of things
vi'sone *sm* mink
vi'sore *sm* (*Fot*) viewer
'vispo, -a *ag* quick, lively
'vissi *etc vb vedi* **vivere**
vis'suto, -a *pp di* **vivere** ■ *ag* (*aria, modo di fare*) experienced
'vista *sf* (*facoltà*) (eye)sight; (*fatto di vedere*): **la ~ di** the sight of; (*veduta*) view; **con ~ sul lago** with a view over the lake; **sparare a ~** to shoot on sight; **pagabile a ~** payable on demand; **in ~** in sight; **avere in ~ qc** to have sth in view; **mettersi in ~** to draw attention to o.s.; (*peg*) to show off; **perdere qn di ~** to lose sight of sb; (*fig*) to lose touch with sb; **far ~ di fare** to pretend to do; **a ~ d'occhio** as far as the eye can see; (*fig*) before one's very eyes
vis'tare *vt* to approve; (*Amm: passaporto*) to visa
'visto, -a *pp di* **vedere** ■ *sm* visa; **~ che** *cong* seeing (that); **~ d'ingresso/di transito** entry/transit visa; **~ permanente/di soggiorno** permanent/tourist visa
vis'toso, -a *ag* gaudy, garish; (*ingente*) considerable
visu'ale *ag* visual
visualiz'zare [vizualid'dzare] *vt* to visualize
visualizza'tore [vizualiddza'tore] *sm* (*Inform*) visual display unit, VDU
visualizzazi'one [vizualiddzat'tsjone] *sf* (*Inform*) display
'vita *sf* life; (*Anat*) waist; **essere in ~** to be alive; **pieno di ~** full of life; **a ~** for life; **membro a ~** life member
vi'tale *ag* vital
vitalità *sf* vitality
vita'lizio, -a [vita'littsjo] *ag* life *cpd* ■ *sm* life annuity
vita'mina *sf* vitamin
'vite *sf* (*Bot*) vine; (*Tecn*) screw; **giro di ~** (*anche fig*) turn of the screw
vi'tello *sm* (*Zool*) calf; (*carne*) veal; (*pelle*) calfskin
vi'ticcio [vi'tittʃo] *sm* (*Bot*) tendril
viticol'tore *sm* wine grower
viticol'tura *sf* wine growing
'vitreo, -a *ag* vitreous; (*occhio, sguardo*) glassy
'vittima *sf* victim

vitti'mismo *sm* self-pity
'vitto *sm* food; *(in un albergo etc)* board; **~ e alloggio** board and lodging
vit'toria *sf* victory
vittori'ano, -a *ag* Victorian
vittori'oso, -a *ag* victorious
vitupe'rare *vt* to rail at *o* against
vi'uzza [vi'uttsa] *sf* *(in città)* alley
'viva *escl*: **~ il re!** long live the king!
vivacchi'are [vivak'kjare] *vi* to scrape a living
vi'vace [vi'vatʃe] *ag* *(vivo, animato)* lively; (: *mente*) lively, sharp; *(colore)* bright
vivacità [vivatʃi'ta] *sf* liveliness; brightness
vivaciz'zare [vivatʃid'dzare] *vt* to liven up
vi'vaio *sm* *(di pesci)* hatchery; *(Agr)* nursery
viva'mente *av* *(commuoversi)* deeply, profoundly; *(ringraziare etc)* sincerely, warmly
vi'vanda *sf* food; *(piatto)* dish
viva'voce [viva'votʃe] *sm inv* *(dispositivo)* loudspeaker ■ *ag inv*: **telefono ~** speakerphone; **mettere in ~** to switch on the loudspeaker
vi'vente *ag* living, alive; **i viventi** the living
'vivere *vi* to live ■ *vt* to live; *(passare: brutto momento)* to live through, go through; *(sentire: gioie, pene di qn)* to share ■ *sm* life; *(anche: **modo di vivere**)* way of life; **viveri** *smpl* food *sg*, provisions; **~ di** to live on
vi'veur [vi'vœr] *sm inv* pleasure-seeker
'vivido, -a *ag* *(colore)* vivid, bright
vivifi'care *vt* to enliven, give life to; *(piante etc)* to revive
vivisezi'one [viviset'tsjone] *sf* vivisection
'vivo, -a *ag* *(vivente)* alive, living; *(fig)* lively; (: *colore*) bright, brilliant ■ *sm*: **entrare nel ~ di una questione** to get to the heart of a matter; **i vivi** the living; **esperimenti su animali vivi** experiments on live *o* living animals; **~ e vegeto** hale and hearty; **farsi ~** *(fig)* to show one's face; to keep in touch; **con ~ rammarico** with deep regret; **congratulazioni vivissime** heartiest congratulations; **con i più vivi ringraziamenti** with deepest *o* warmest thanks; **ritrarre dal ~** to paint from life; **pungere qn nel ~** *(fig)* to cut sb to the quick
vivrò *etc vb vedi* **vivere**
vizi'are [vit'tsjare] *vt* *(bambino)* to spoil; *(corrompere moralmente)* to corrupt; *(Dir)* to invalidate
vizi'ato, -a [vit'tsjato] *ag* spoilt; *(aria, acqua)* polluted; *(Dir)* invalid, invalidated
'vizio ['vittsjo] *sm* *(morale)* vice; *(cattiva abitudine)* bad habit; *(imperfezione)* flaw, defect; *(errore)* fault, mistake; **~ di forma** legal flaw *o* irregularity; **~ procedurale** procedural error
vizi'oso, -a [vit'tsjoso] *ag* depraved; *(inesatto)* incorrect; **circolo ~** vicious circle
V.le *abbr* = **viale**
vocabo'lario *sm* *(dizionario)* dictionary; *(lessico)* vocabulary
vo'cabolo *sm* word
vo'cale *ag* vocal ■ *sf* vowel
vocazi'one [vokat'tsjone] *sf* vocation; *(fig)* natural bent
'voce ['votʃe] *sf* voice; *(diceria)* rumour *(Brit)*, rumor *(US)*; *(di un elenco: in bilancio)* item; *(di dizionario)* entry; **parlare a alta/bassa ~** to speak in a loud/low *o* soft voice; **fare la ~ grossa** to raise one's voice; **dar ~ a qc** to voice sth, give voice to sth; **a gran ~** in a loud voice, loudly; **te lo dico a ~** I'll tell you when I see you; **a una ~** unanimously; **aver ~ in capitolo** *(fig)* to have a say in the matter; **voci di corridoio** rumours
voci'are [vo'tʃare] *vi* to shout, yell
vocife'rante [votʃife'rante] *ag* noisy
vo'cio [vo'tʃio] *sm* shouting
'vodka *sf inv* vodka
'voga *sf* *(Naut)* rowing; *(usanza)*: **essere in ~** to be in fashion *o* in vogue
vo'gare *vi* to row
voga'tore, -'trice *sm/f* oarsman(-woman) ■ *sm* rowing machine
vogherò *etc* [voge'rɔ] *vb vedi* **vogare**
'voglia ['vɔʎʎa] *sf* desire, wish; *(macchia)* birthmark; **aver ~ di qc/di fare** to feel like sth/like doing; *(più forte)* to want sth/to do; **di buona ~** willingly
'voglio *etc* ['vɔʎʎo] *vb vedi* **volere**
vogli'oso, -a [voʎ'ʎoso] *ag* *(sguardo etc)* longing; *(più forte)* full of desire
'voi *pron* you; **~ stessi(e)** you yourselves
voi'altri *pron* you
vol. *abbr* (= *volume*) vol.
vo'lano *sm* *(Sport)* shuttlecock; *(Tecn)* flywheel
vo'lant [vɔ'l] *sm inv* frill
vo'lante *ag* flying ■ *sm* (steering) wheel ■ *sf* *(Polizia: anche: **squadra volante**)* flying squad
volanti'naggio [volanti'naddʒo] *sm* leafleting
volanti'nare *vt* *(distribuire volantini)* to leaflet, hand out leaflets
volan'tino *sm* leaflet
vo'lare *vi* *(uccello, aereo, fig)* to fly; *(cappello)* to blow away *o* off, fly away *o* off; **~ via** to fly away *o* off
vo'lata *sf* flight; *(d'uccelli)* flock, flight; *(corsa)* rush; *(Sport)* final sprint; **passare di ~ da qn** to drop in on sb briefly
vo'latile *ag* *(Chim)* volatile ■ *sm* *(Zool)* bird
volatiliz'zarsi [volatilid'dzarsi] *vr* *(Chim)* to volatilize; *(fig)* to vanish, disappear

vo'lente *ag*: **verrai ~ o nolente** you'll come whether you like it or not
volente'roso, -a *ag* willing, keen
volenti'eri *av* willingly; **"~"** "with pleasure", "I'd be glad to"

PAROLA CHIAVE

vo'lere *sm* will, wish(es); **contro il volere di** against the wishes of; **per volere di qn** in obedience to sb's will *o* wishes
■ *vt* **1** (*esigere, desiderare*) to want; **volere fare qc** to want to do sth; **volere che qn faccia qc** to want sb to do sth; **vorrei andarmene** I'd like to go; **vorrei che se ne andasse** I'd like him to go; **vorrei quello lì!** I'd like that one; **volevo parlartene** I meant to talk to you about it; **come vuoi** as you like; **la vogliono al telefono** there's a call for you; **che tu lo voglia o no** whether you like it or not; **vuoi un caffè?** would you like a coffee?; **senza volere** (*inavvertitamente*) without meaning to, unintentionally; **te la sei voluta** you asked for it; **la tradizione vuole che ...** custom requires that ...; **la leggenda vuole che ...** legend has it that ...
2 (*consentire*): **vogliate attendere, per piacere** please wait; **vogliamo andare?** shall we go?; **vuole essere così gentile da ...?** would you be so kind as to ...?; **non ha voluto ricevermi** he wouldn't see me
3: **volerci** (*essere necessario*: *materiale, attenzione*) to be needed; (*: tempo*) to take; **quanta farina ci vuole per questa torta?** how much flour do you need for this cake?; **ci vuole un'ora per arrivare a Venezia** it takes an hour to get to Venice; **è quel che ci vuole** it's just what is needed
4: **voler bene a qn** (*amore*) to love sb; (*affetto*) to be fond of sb, like sb very much; **voler male a qn** to dislike sb; **volerne a qn** to bear sb a grudge; **voler dire** to mean; **voglio dire ...** I mean ...; **volevo ben dire!** I thought as much!

vol'gare *ag* vulgar
volgarità *sf* vulgarity
volgariz'zare [volgarid'dzare] *vt* to popularize
volgar'mente *av* (*in modo volgare*) vulgarly, coarsely; (*del popolo*) commonly, popularly
'volgere ['vɔldʒere] *vt* to turn ■ *vi* to turn; (*tendere*): **~ a**: **il tempo volge al brutto/al bello** the weather is breaking/is setting fair; **un rosso che volge al viola** a red verging on purple; **volgersi** *vr* to turn; **~ al peggio** to take a turn for the worse; **~ al termine** to draw to an end
'volgo *sm* common people
voli'era *sf* aviary
voli'tivo, -a *ag* strong-willed
'volli *etc vb vedi* **volere**
'volo *sm* flight; **ci sono due ore di ~ da Londra a Milano** it's a two-hour flight between London and Milan; **al ~**: **colpire qc al ~** to hit sth as it flies past; **prendere al ~** (*autobus, treno*) to catch at the last possible moment; (*palla*) to catch as it flies past; (*occasione*) to seize; **capire al ~** to understand straight away; **veduta a ~ d'uccello** bird's-eye view; **~ di linea** scheduled flight
volontà *sf inv* will; **a ~** (*mangiare, bere*) as much as one likes; **buona/cattiva ~** goodwill/lack of goodwill; **le sue ultime ~** (*testamento*) his last will and testament *sg*
volontaria'mente *av* voluntarily
volontari'ato *sm* (*Mil*) voluntary service; (*lavoro*) voluntary work
volon'tario, -a *ag* voluntary ■ *sm* (*Mil*) volunteer
'volpe *sf* fox
vol'pino, -a *ag* (*pelo, coda*) fox's; (*aspetto, astuzia*) fox-like ■ *sm* (*cane*) Pomeranian
vol'pone, -a *sm/f* (*fig*) old fox
'volsi *etc vb vedi* **volgere**
volt *sm inv* (*Elettr*) volt
'volta *sf* (*momento, circostanza*) time; (*turno, giro*) turn; (*curva*) turn, bend; (*Archit*) vault; (*direzione*): **partire alla ~ di** to set off for; **a mia (*o* tua *etc*) ~** in turn; **una ~** once; **una ~ sola** only once; **c'era una ~** once upon a time there was; **le cose di una ~** the things of the past; **due volte** twice; **tre volte** three times; **una cosa per ~** one thing at a time; **una ~ o l'altra** one of these days; **una ~ per tutte** once and for all; **una ~ tanto** just for once; **lo facciamo un'altra ~** we'll do it another time *o* some other time; **a volte** at times, sometimes; **di ~ in ~** from time to time; **una ~ che** (*temporale*) once; (*causale*) since; **3 volte 4** 3 times 4; **ti ha dato di ~ il cervello?** have you gone out of your mind?
volta'faccia [volta'fattʃa] *sm inv* (*fig*) volte-face
vol'taggio [vol'taddʒo] *sm* (*Elettr*) voltage
vol'tare *vt* to turn; (*girare*: *moneta*) to turn over; (*rigirare*) to turn round ■ *vi* to turn; **voltarsi** *vr* to turn; to turn over; to turn round
voltas'tomaco *sm* nausea; (*fig*) disgust
volteggi'are [volted'dʒare] *vi* (*volare*) to circle; (*in equitazione*) to do trick riding; (*in ginnastica*) to vault
'volto, -a *pp di* **volgere** ■ *ag* (*inteso a*): **il mio discorso è ~ a spiegare ...** in my speech I intend to explain ... ■ *sm* face

vo'lubile *ag* changeable, fickle
vo'lume *sm* volume
volumi'noso, -a *ag* voluminous, bulky
vo'luta *sf* (*gen*) spiral; (*Archit*) volute
voluttà *sf* sensual pleasure *o* delight
voluttu'oso, -a *ag* voluptuous
vomi'tare *vt, vi* to vomit
'vomito *sm* vomit; **ho il ~** I feel sick
'vongola *sf* clam
vo'race [vo'ratʃe] *ag* voracious, greedy
voracità [voratʃi'ta] *sf* voracity, voraciousness
vo'ragine [vo'radʒine] *sf* abyss, chasm
vorrò *etc vb vedi* **volere**
'vortice ['vɔrtitʃe] *sm* whirl, vortex; (*fig*) whirl
vorti'coso, -a *ag* whirling
'vostro, -a *det*: **il(la) ~(a)** *etc* your ■ *pron*: **il(la) ~(a)** *etc* yours ■ *sm*: **avete speso del ~?** did you spend your own money? ■ *sf*: **la vostra** (*opinione*) your view; **i vostri** (*famiglia*) your family; **un ~ amico** a friend of yours; **è dei vostri, è dalla vostra** he's on your side; **l'ultima vostra** (*Comm: lettera*) your most recent letter; **alla vostra!** (*brindisi*) here's to you!, your health!
vo'tante *sm/f* voter
vo'tare *vi* to vote ■ *vt* (*sottoporre a votazione*) to take a vote on; (*approvare*) to vote for; (*Rel*): **~ qc a** to dedicate sth to; **votarsi** *vr* to devote o.s. to
votazi'one [votat'tsjone] *sf* vote, voting; **votazioni** *sfpl* (*Pol*) votes; (*Ins*) marks
'voto *sm* (*Pol*) vote; (*Ins*) mark (*Brit*), grade (*US*); (*Rel*) vow; (: *offerta*) votive offering; **aver voti belli/brutti** (*Ins*) to get good/bad marks *o* grades; **prendere i voti** to take one's vows; **~ di fiducia** vote of confidence
V.P. *abbr* (= *vicepresidente*) VP
VR *sigla* = **Verona**
v.r. *abbr* (= *vedi retro*) PTO
vs. *abbr* (= *vostro*) yr
v.s. *abbr* = **vedi sopra**
VT *sigla* = **Viterbo**
V.U. *abbr* = **vigile urbano**
vul'canico, -a, ci, che *ag* volcanic
vulcanizzazi'one [vulkaniddzat'tsjone] *sf* vulcanization
vul'cano *sm* volcano
vulne'rabile *ag* vulnerable
vulnerabilità *sf* vulnerability
vu'oi, vu'ole *vb vedi* **volere**
vuo'tare *vt*, **vuo'tarsi** *vr* to empty
vu'oto, -a *ag* empty; (*fig: privo*): **~ di** (*senso etc*) devoid of ■ *sm* empty space, gap; (*spazio in bianco*) blank; (*Fisica*) vacuum; (*fig: mancanza*) gap, void; **a mani vuote** empty-handed; **assegno a ~** dud cheque (*Brit*), bad check (*US*); **~ d'aria** air pocket; **"~ a perdere"** "no deposit"; **"~ a rendere"** "returnable bottle"

V

W, w ['dɔppjovu] *sf o m inv* (*lettera*) W, w; **W come Washington** ≈ W for William

W *abbr* = **viva, evviva**

'**wafer** ['vafer] *sm inv* (*Cuc, Elettr*) wafer

wagon-'lit [vagɔ̃'li] *sm inv* (*Ferr*) sleeping car

'**walkman®** ['wɔ:kmən] *sm inv* Walkman®

'**water 'closet** ['wɔ:tə'klɔzɪt] *sm inv* toilet, lavatory

watt [vat] *sm inv* (*Elettr*) watt

wat'tora [vat'tora] *sm inv* (*Elettr*) watt-hour

WC *sm inv* WC

web [web] *sm*: **il ~** the web; **cercare nel ~** to search the web ■ *ag inv*: **pagina ~** webpage

webcam [web'kam] *sf inv* (*Comput*) webcam

'**weekend** ['wi:kend] *sm inv* weekend

'**western** ['wɛstern] *ag* (*Cine*) cowboy *cpd* ■ *sm inv* western, cowboy film; **~ all'italiana** spaghetti western

'**whisky** ['wiski] *sm inv* whisky

Wi-Fi [uai'fai] (*Comput*) *nm* Wi-Fi ■ *ag inv* Wi-Fi

'**windsurf** ['windsə:f] *sm inv* (*tavola*) windsurfer, sailboard; (*sport*) windsurfing

'**würstel** ['vyrstəl] *sm inv* frankfurter

X, x [iks] *sf o m inv* *(lettera)* X, x; **X come Xeres** ≈ X for Xmas

xenofoˈbia [ksenofoˈbia] *sf* xenophobia

xeˈnofobo, -a [kseˈnɔfobo] *ag* xenophobic ■ *sm/f* xenophobe

ˈxeres [ˈksɛres] *sm inv* sherry

xeroˈcopia [kseroˈkɔpja] *sf* xerox®, photocopy

xerocopiˈare [kserokoˈpjare] *vt* to photocopy

xiˈlofono [ksiˈlɔfono] *sm* xylophone

Y, y ['ipsilon] *sf o m inv* (*lettera*) Y, y; **Y come Yacht** ≈ Y for Yellow (*Brit*), ≈ Y for Yoke (*US*)
yacht [jɔt] *sm inv* yacht
'**yankee** ['jæŋki] *sm/f inv* Yank, Yankee
Y.C.I. *abbr* = **Yacht Club d'Italia**
'**Yemen** ['jemen] *sm*: **lo** ~ Yemen
yen [jen] *sm inv* (*moneta*) yen
'**yiddish** ['jidiʃ] *ag inv, sm inv* Yiddish
'**yoga** ['jɔga] *ag inv, sm* yoga (*cpd*)
yogurt ['jɔgurt] *sm inv* yog(h)urt

Zz

Z, z ['dzɛta] *sf o m inv (lettera)* Z, z; **Z come Zara** ≈ Z for Zebra
zabai'one [dzaba'jone] *sm dessert made of egg yolks, sugar and marsala*
zaf'fata [tsaf'fata] *sf (tanfo)* stench
zaffe'rano [dzaffe'rano] *sm* saffron
zaf'firo [dzaf'firo] *sm* sapphire
'zagara ['dzagara] *sf* orange blossom
zai'netto [dzai'netto] *sm* (small) rucksack
'zaino ['dzaino] *sm* rucksack
Za'ire [dza'ire] *sm*: **lo ~** Zaire
'Zambia ['dzambja] *sm*: **lo ~** Zambia
'zampa ['tsampa] *sf (di animale: gamba)* leg; *(: piede)* paw; **a quattro zampe** on all fours; **zampe di gallina** *(calligrafia)* scrawl; *(rughe)* crow's feet
zam'pata [tsam'pata] *sf (di cane, gatto)* blow with a paw
zampet'tare [tsampet'tare] *vi* to scamper
zampil'lare [tsampil'lare] *vi* to gush, spurt
zam'pillo [tsam'pillo] *sm* gush, spurt
zam'pino [tsam'pino] *sm* paw; **qui c'è sotto il suo ~** *(fig)* he's had a hand in this
zam'pogna [tsam'poɲɲa] *sf instrument similar to bagpipes*
'zanna ['tsanna] *sf (di elefante)* tusk; *(di carnivori)* fang
zan'zara [dzan'dzara] *sf* mosquito
zanzari'era [dzandza'rjɛra] *sf* mosquito net
'zappa ['tsappa] *sf* hoe
zap'pare [tsap'pare] *vt* to hoe
zappa'tura [tsappa'tura] *sf (Agr)* hoeing
'zapping ['tsapɪŋ] *sm* (TV) channel-hopping
zar, za'rina [tsar, tsa'rina] *sm/f* tsar/tsarina
'zattera ['dzattera] *sf* raft
za'vorra [dza'vɔrra] *sf* ballast
'zazzera ['tsattsera] *sf* shock of hair
'zebra ['dzɛbra] *sf* zebra; **zebre** *sfpl (Aut)* zebra crossing *sg (Brit)*, crosswalk *sg (US)*
ze'brato, -a [dze'brato] *ag* with black and white stripes; **strisce zebrate, attraversamento ~** *(Aut)* zebra crossing *(Brit)*, crosswalk *(US)*
'zecca, -che ['tsekka] *sf (Zool)* tick; *(officina di monete)* mint
zec'chino [tsek'kino] *sm* gold coin; **oro ~** pure gold
ze'lante [dze'lante] *ag* zealous
'zelo ['dzɛlo] *sm* zeal
'zenit ['dzɛnit] *sm* zenith
'zenzero ['dzendzero] *sm* ginger
'zeppa ['tseppa] *sf* wedge
'zeppo, -a ['tseppo] *ag*: **~ di** crammed *o* packed with
zer'bino [dzer'bino] *sm* doormat
'zero ['dzɛro] *sm* zero, nought; **vincere per tre a ~** *(Sport)* to win three-nil
'zeta ['dzɛta] *sm o f* zed, (the letter) z
'zia ['tsia] *sf* aunt
zibel'lino [dzibel'lino] *sm* sable
zi'gano, -a [tsi'gano] *ag, sm/f* gypsy
'zigomo ['dzigomo] *sm* cheekbone
zigri'nare [dzigri'nare] *vt (gen)* to knurl; *(pellame)* to grain; *(monete)* to mill
zig'zag [dzig'dzag] *sm inv* zigzag; **andare a ~** to zigzag
Zim'babwe [tsim'babwe] *sm*: **lo ~** Zimbabwe
zim'bello [dzim'bɛllo] *sm (oggetto di burle)* laughing-stock
'zinco ['dzinko] *sm* zinc
zinga'resco, -a, schi, sche [dzinga'resko] *ag* gypsy *cpd*
'zingaro, -a ['dzingaro] *sm/f* gipsy
'zio ['tsio] *(pl* **zii**) *sm* uncle; **zii** *smpl (zio e zia)* uncle and aunt
zip'pare [dzip'pare] *vt (Inform)* to zip
zi'tella [dzi'tɛlla] *sf* spinster; *(peg)* old maid
zit'tire [tsit'tire] *vt* to silence, hush *o* shut up ▪ *vi* to hiss
'zitto, -a ['tsitto] *ag* quiet, silent; **sta' ~!** be quiet!
ziz'zania [dzid'dzanja] *sf (Bot)* darnel; *(fig)* discord; **gettare** *o* **seminare ~** to sow discord
'zoccolo ['tsɔkkolo] *sm (calzatura)* clog; *(di cavallo etc)* hoof; *(Archit)* plinth; *(di parete)* skirting (board); *(di armadio)* base

zodia'cale [dzodia'kale] *ag* zodiac *cpd*; **segno ~** sign of the zodiac
zo'diaco [dzo'diako] *sm* zodiac
zolfa'nello [tsolfa'nɛllo] *sm* (sulphur) match
'zolfo ['tsolfo] *sm* sulphur (*Brit*), sulfur (*US*)
'zolla ['dzolla] *sf* clod (of earth)
zol'letta [dzol'letta] *sf* sugar lump
'zona ['dzɔna] *sf* zone, area; **~ di depressione** (*Meteor*) trough of low pressure; **~ erogena** erogenous zone; **~ pedonale** pedestrian precinct; **~ verde** (*di abitato*) green area
'zonzo ['dzondzo]: **a ~** *av*: **andare a ~** to wander about, stroll about
'zoo ['dzɔo] *sm inv* zoo
zoolo'gia [dzoolo'dʒia] *sf* zoology
zoo'logico, -a, ci, che [dzoo'lɔdʒiko] *ag* zoological
zo'ologo, -a, gi, ghe [dzo'ɔlogo] *sm/f* zoologist
zoosa'fari [dzoosa'fari] *sm inv* safari park
zoo'tecnico, -a, ci, che [dzoo'tɛkniko] *ag* zootechnical; **il patrimonio ~ di un paese** a country's livestock resources
zoppi'care [tsoppi'kare] *vi* to limp; (*fig: mobile*) to be shaky, rickety
'zoppo, -a ['tsɔppo] *ag* lame; (*fig: mobile*) shaky, rickety
zoti'cone [dzoti'kone] *sm* lout
ZTL [dzetati'ɛlle] *sigla f* (= *Zona a Traffico Limitato*) *controlled traffic zone*
zu'ava [dzu'ava] *sf*: **pantaloni alla ~** knickerbockers
'zucca, -che ['tsukka] *sf* (*Bot*) marrow (*Brit*), vegetable marrow (*US*); pumpkin; (*scherzoso*) head
zucche'rare [tsukke'rare] *vt* to put sugar in
zucche'rato, -a [tsukke'rato] *ag* sweet, sweetened
zuccheri'era [tsukke'rjɛra] *sf* sugar bowl
zuccheri'ficio [tsukkeri'fitʃo] *sm* sugar refinery
zucche'rino, -a [tsukke'rino] *ag* sugary, sweet
'zucchero ['tsukkero] *sm* sugar; **~ di canna** cane sugar; **~ caramellato** caramel; **~ filato** candy floss, cotton candy (*US*); **~ a velo** icing sugar (*Brit*), confectioner's sugar (*US*)
zucche'roso, -a [tsukke'roso] *ag* sugary
zuc'china [tsuk'kina] *sf*, **zuc'chino** [tsuk'kino] *sm* courgette (*Brit*), zucchini (*US*)
zuc'cotto [tsuk'kɔtto] *sm* ice-cream sponge
'zuffa ['tsuffa] *sf* brawl
zufo'lare [tsufo'lare] *vt, vi* to whistle
'zufolo ['tsufolo] *sm* (*Mus*) flageolet
'zuppa ['tsuppa] *sf* soup; (*fig*) mixture, muddle; **~ inglese** (*Cuc*) *dessert made with sponge cake, custard and chocolate*, ≈ trifle (*Brit*)
zuppi'era [tsup'pjɛra] *sf* soup tureen
'zuppo, -a ['tsuppo] *ag*: **~ (di)** drenched (with), soaked (with)
Zu'rigo [dzu'rigo] *sf* Zurich

Aa

A, a [eɪ] *n* (*letter*) A, a *f or m inv* (*Scol: mark*) ≈ 10 (*ottimo*); (*Mus*): **A** la *m*; **A for Andrew**, (US) **A for Able** ≈ A come Ancona; **from A to Z** dall'A alla Z; **A road** *n* (*Brit Aut*) ≈ strada statale; **A shares** *npl* (*Brit Stock Exchange*) azioni *fpl* senza diritto di voto; **A to Z®** *n* stradario

KEYWORD

a [ə] (*before vowel or silent h: an*) *indef art* **1** un, uno (*+ s impure, gn, pn, ps, x, z*), una *f*, un' *+ vowel*; **a book** un libro; **a mirror** uno specchio; **an apple** una mela; **she's a doctor** è medico
2 (*instead of the number "one"*) un, una *f*; **a year ago** un anno fa; **a hundred/thousand pounds** cento/mille sterline
3 (*in expressing ratios, prices etc*) a, per; **3 a day/week** 3 al giorno/alla settimana; **10 km an hour** 10 km all'ora; **£5 a person** 5 sterline a persona *or* per persona

a. *abbr* = **acre**
A2 *n abbr* (*Brit: Scol*) *seconda parte del diploma di studi superiori chiamato "A level"*
AA *n abbr* (*Brit: = Automobile Association*) ≈ A.C.I. *m* (*= Automobile Club d'Italia*); (*US: = Associate in/of Arts*) *titolo di studio*; (*= Alcoholics Anonymous*) A.A. *f* (*= Anonima Alcolisti*); (*Mil*) = **anti-aircraft**
AAA *n abbr* (*= American Automobile Association*) ≈ A.C.I. *m* (*= Automobile Club d'Italia*); (*Brit*) = **Amateur Athletics Association**
A & R *n abbr* (*Mus*) = **artists and repertoire**; **~ man** talent scout *m inv*
AAUP *n abbr* (*= American Association of University Professors*) *associazione dei professori universitari*
AB *abbr* (*Brit*) = **able-bodied seaman**; (*Canada*) = **Alberta**
aback [ə'bæk] *adv*: **to be taken ~** essere sbalordito(-a)
abacus (*pl* **abaci**) ['æbəkəs, -saɪ] *n* pallottoliere *m*, abaco
abandon [ə'bændən] *vt* abbandonare ■ *n* abbandono; **to ~ ship** abbandonare la nave
abandoned [ə'bændənd] *adj* (*child, house etc*) abbandonato(-a); (*unrestrained: manner*) disinvolto(-a)
abase [ə'beɪs] *vt*: **to ~ o.s. (so far as to do)** umiliarsi *or* abbassarsi (al punto di fare)
abashed [ə'bæʃt] *adj* imbarazzato(-a)
abate [ə'beɪt] *vi* calmarsi
abatement [ə'beɪtmənt] *n* (*of pollution, noise*) soppressione *f*, eliminazione *f*; **noise ~ society** associazione *f* per la lotta contro i rumori
abattoir ['æbətwɑːʳ] *n* (*Brit*) mattatoio
abbey ['æbɪ] *n* abbazia, badia
abbot ['æbət] *n* abate *m*
abbreviate [ə'briːvɪeɪt] *vt* abbreviare
abbreviation [əbriːvɪ'eɪʃən] *n* abbreviazione *f*
ABC *n abbr* (*= American Broadcasting Company*) *rete televisiva americana*
abdicate ['æbdɪkeɪt] *vt* abdicare a ■ *vi* abdicare
abdication [æbdɪ'keɪʃən] *n* abdicazione *f*
abdomen ['æbdəmən] *n* addome *m*
abdominal [æb'dɔmɪnl] *adj* addominale
abduct [æb'dʌkt] *vt* rapire
abduction [æb'dʌkʃən] *n* rapimento
Aberdonian [æbə'dəunɪən] *adj* di Aberdeen ■ *n* abitante *m/f* di Aberdeen, originario(-a) di Aberdeen
aberration [æbə'reɪʃən] *n* aberrazione *f*
abet [ə'bɛt] *vt* *see* **aid**
abeyance [ə'beɪəns] *n*: **in ~** in sospeso
abhor [əb'hɔːʳ] *vt* aborrire
abhorrent [əb'hɔrənt] *adj* odioso(-a)
abide [ə'baɪd] *vt* sopportare
▸ **abide by** *vt fus* conformarsi a
abiding [ə'baɪdɪŋ] *adj* (*memory etc*) persistente, duraturo(-a)
ability [ə'bɪlɪtɪ] *n* abilità *f inv*; **to the best of my ~** con il massimo impegno
abject ['æbdʒɛkt] *adj* (*poverty*) abietto(-a); (*apology*) umiliante; (*coward*) indegno(-a), vile
ablaze [ə'bleɪz] *adj* in fiamme; **~ with light** risplendente di luce

able ['eɪbl] *adj* capace; **to be ~ to do sth** essere capace di fare qc, poter fare qc
able-bodied ['eɪbl'bɔdɪd] *adj* robusto(-a)
able-bodied seaman *n* (*Brit*) marinaio scelto
ably ['eɪblɪ] *adv* abilmente
ABM *n abbr* (= *anti-ballistic missile*) ABM *m*
abnormal [æb'nɔ:məl] *adj* anormale
abnormality [æbnɔ:'mælɪtɪ] *n* (*condition*) anormalità; (*instance*) anomalia
aboard [ə'bɔ:d] *adv* a bordo ■ *prep* a bordo di; **~ the train** in *or* sul treno
abode [ə'bəud] *n* (*old*) dimora; (*Law*) domicilio, dimora; **of no fixed ~** senza fissa dimora
abolish [ə'bɔlɪʃ] *vt* abolire
abolition [æbəu'lɪʃən] *n* abolizione *f*
abominable [ə'bɔmɪnəbl] *adj* abominevole
aborigine [æbə'rɪdʒɪnɪ] *n* aborigeno(-a)
abort [ə'bɔ:t] *vt* (*Med, fig*) abortire; (*Comput*) interrompere l'esecuzione di
abortion [ə'bɔ:ʃən] *n* aborto; **to have an ~** avere un aborto, abortire
abortionist [ə'bɔ:ʃənɪst] *n* abortista *m/f*
abortive [ə'bɔ:tɪv] *adj* abortivo(-a)
abound [ə'baund] *vi* abbondare; **to ~ in** abbondare di

KEYWORD

about [ə'baut] *adv* **1** (*approximately*) circa, quasi; **about a hundred/thousand** un centinaio/migliaio, circa cento/mille; **it takes about 10 hours** ci vogliono circa 10 ore; **at about 2 o'clock** verso le 2; **I've just about finished** ho quasi finito; **it's about here** è qui intorno, è qui vicino
2 (*referring to place*) qua e là, in giro; **to leave things lying about** lasciare delle cose in giro; **to run about** correre qua e là; **to walk about** camminare; **is Paul about?** (*Brit*) hai visto Paul in giro?; **it's the other way about** (*Brit*) è il contrario
3: **to be about to do sth** stare per fare qc; **I'm not about to do all that for nothing** non ho intenzione di fare tutto questo per niente
■ *prep* **1** (*relating to*) su, di; **a book about London** un libro su Londra; **what is it about?** di che si tratta?; (*book, film etc*) di cosa tratta?; **we talked about it** ne abbiamo parlato; **do something about it!** fai qualcosa!; **what** *or* **how about doing this?** che ne dici di fare questo?
2 (*referring to place*): **to walk about the town** camminare per la città; **her clothes were scattered about the room** i suoi vestiti erano sparsi *or* in giro per tutta la stanza

about-face [ə'baut'feɪs] *n*, **about-turn** [ə'baut'tə:n] *n* (*Mil*) dietro front *m inv*
above [ə'bʌv] *adv, prep* sopra; **mentioned ~** suddetto; **costing ~ £10** più caro di 10 sterline; **he's not ~ a bit of blackmail** non rifuggirebbe dal ricatto; **~ all** soprattutto
aboveboard [ə'bʌv'bɔ:d] *adj* aperto(-a); onesto(-a)
abrasion [ə'breɪʒən] *n* abrasione *f*
abrasive [ə'breɪzɪv] *adj* abrasivo(-a)
abreast [ə'brɛst] *adv* di fianco; **3 ~** per 3 di fronte; **to keep ~ of** tenersi aggiornato su
abridge [ə'brɪdʒ] *vt* ridurre
abroad [ə'brɔ:d] *adv* all'estero; **there is a rumour ~ that ...** (*fig*) si sente dire in giro che ..., circola la voce che ...
abrupt [ə'brʌpt] *adj* (*steep*) erto(-a); (*sudden*) improvviso(-a); (*gruff, blunt*) brusco(-a)
abscess ['æbsɪs] *n* ascesso
abscond [əb'skɔnd] *vi* scappare
absence ['æbsəns] *n* assenza; **in the ~ of** (*person*) in assenza di; (*thing*) in mancanza di
absent ['æbsənt] *adj* assente; **to be ~ without leave** (*Mil etc*) essere assente ingiustificato
absentee [æbsən'ti:] *n* assente *m/f*
absenteeism [æbsən'ti:ɪzəm] *n* assenteismo
absent-minded ['æbsənt'maɪndɪd] *adj* distratto(-a)
absent-mindedness ['æbsənt'maɪndɪdnɪs] *n* distrazione *f*
absolute ['æbsəlu:t] *adj* assoluto(-a)
absolutely [æbsə'lu:tlɪ] *adv* assolutamente
absolve [əb'zɔlv] *vt*: **to ~ sb (from)** (*sin etc*) assolvere qn (da); **to ~ sb from** (*oath*) sciogliere qn da
absorb [əb'sɔ:b] *vt* assorbire; **to be absorbed in a book** essere immerso(-a) in un libro
absorbent [əb'sɔ:bənt] *adj* assorbente
absorbent cotton *n* (*US*) cotone *m* idrofilo
absorbing [əb'sɔ:bɪŋ] *adj* avvincente, molto interessante
absorption [əb'sɔ:pʃən] *n* assorbimento
abstain [əb'steɪn] *vi*: **to ~ (from)** astenersi (da)
abstemious [əb'sti:mɪəs] *adj* astemio(-a)
abstention [əb'stɛnʃən] *n* astensione *f*
abstinence ['æbstɪnəns] *n* astinenza
abstract ['æbstrækt] *adj* astratto(-a) ■ *n* (*summary*) riassunto ■ *vt* [æb'strækt] estrarre
absurd [əb'sə:d] *adj* assurdo(-a)
absurdity [əb'sə:dɪtɪ] *n* assurdità *f inv*
ABTA ['æbtə] *n abbr* = **Association of British Travel Agents**
Abu Dhabi ['æbu:'dɑ:bɪ] *n* Abu Dhabi *f*
abundance [ə'bʌndəns] *n* abbondanza
abundant [ə'bʌndənt] *adj* abbondante

abuse *n* [ə'bju:s] abuso; (*insults*) ingiurie *fpl* ■ *vt* [ə'bju:z] abusare di; **open to ~** che si presta ad abusi
abusive [ə'bju:sɪv] *adj* ingiurioso(-a)
abysmal [ə'bɪzməl] *adj* spaventoso(-a)
abyss [ə'bɪs] *n* abisso
AC *n abbr* (*US*) = **athletic club**
a/c *abbr* (*Banking etc*: = *account, account current*) c
academic [ækə'dɛmɪk] *adj* accademico(-a); (*pej: issue*) puramente formale ■ *n* universitario(-a)
academic year *n* anno accademico
academy [ə'kædəmɪ] *n* (*learned body*) accademia; (*school*) scuola privata; **military/naval ~** scuola militare/navale; **~ of music** conservatorio
ACAS ['eɪkæs] *n abbr* (*Brit*: = *Advisory, Conciliation and Arbitration Service*) *comitato governativo per il miglioramento della contrattazione collettiva*
accede [æk'si:d] *vi*: **to ~ to** (*request*) accedere a; (*throne*) ascendere a
accelerate [æk'sɛləreɪt] *vt, vi* accelerare
acceleration [æksɛlə'reɪʃən] *n* accelerazione *f*
accelerator [æk'sɛləreɪtə[r]] *n* acceleratore *m*
accent ['æksɛnt] *n* accento
accentuate [æk'sɛntjueɪt] *vt* (*syllable*) accentuare; (*need, difference etc*) accentuare, mettere in risalto *or* in evidenza
accept [ək'sɛpt] *vt* accettare
acceptable [ək'sɛptəbl] *adj* accettabile
acceptance [ək'sɛptəns] *n* accettazione *f*; **to meet with general ~** incontrare il favore *or* il consenso generale
access ['æksɛs] *n* accesso ■ *vt* (*Comput*) accedere a; **to have ~ to** avere accesso a; **the burglars gained ~ through a window** i ladri sono riusciti a penetrare da *or* attraverso una finestra
accessible [æk'sɛsəbl] *adj* accessibile
accession [æk'sɛʃən] *n* (*addition*) aggiunta; (*to library*) accessione *f*, acquisto; (*of king*) ascesa *or* salita al trono
accessory [æk'sɛsərɪ] *n* accessorio; **toilet accessories** *npl* (*Brit*) articoli *mpl* da toilette
access road *n* strada d'accesso; (*to motorway*) raccordo di entrata
access time *n* (*Comput*) tempo di accesso
accident ['æksɪdənt] *n* incidente *m*; (*chance*) caso; **to meet with** *or* **to have an ~** avere un incidente; **accidents at work** infortuni *mpl* sul lavoro; **by ~** per caso
accidental [æksɪ'dɛntl] *adj* accidentale
accidentally [æksɪ'dɛntəlɪ] *adv* per caso
accident insurance *n* assicurazione *f* contro gli infortuni
accident-prone ['æksɪdənt'prəun] *adj*: **he's very ~** è un vero passaguai
acclaim [ə'kleɪm] *vt* acclamare ■ *n* acclamazione *f*
acclamation [æklə'meɪʃən] *n* (*approval*) acclamazione *f*; (*applause*) applauso
acclimatize [ə'klaɪmətaɪz], (*US*) **acclimate** [ə'klaɪmeɪt] *vt*: **to become acclimatized** acclimatarsi
accolade ['ækəleɪd] *n* encomio
accommodate [ə'kɔmədeɪt] *vt* alloggiare; (*oblige, help*) favorire; **this car accommodates 4 people comfortably** quest'auto può trasportare comodamente 4 persone
accommodating [ə'kɔmədeɪtɪŋ] *adj* compiacente
accommodation [əkɔmə'deɪʃən] *n*, (*US*) **accommodations** [əkɔmə'deɪʃənz] *npl* alloggio; **seating ~** (*Brit*) posti a sedere; **"~ to let"** (*Brit*) "camere in affitto"; **have you any ~?** avete posto?
accompaniment [ə'kʌmpənɪmənt] *n* accompagnamento
accompanist [ə'kʌmpənɪst] *n* (*Mus*) accompagnatore(-trice)
accompany [ə'kʌmpənɪ] *vt* accompagnare
accomplice [ə'kʌmplɪs] *n* complice *m/f*
accomplish [ə'kʌmplɪʃ] *vt* compiere; (*achieve*) ottenere
accomplished [ə'kʌmplɪʃt] *adj* (*person*) esperto(-a)
accomplishment [ə'kʌmplɪʃmənt] *n* compimento; (*thing achieved*) risultato; **accomplishments** *npl* (*skills*) doti *fpl*
accord [ə'kɔ:d] *n* accordo ■ *vt* accordare; **of his own ~** di propria iniziativa; **with one ~** all'unanimità, di comune accordo
accordance [ə'kɔ:dəns] *n*: **in ~ with** in conformità con
according [ə'kɔ:dɪŋ]: **~ to** *prep* secondo; **it went ~ to plan** è andata secondo il previsto
accordingly [ə'kɔ:dɪŋlɪ] *adv* in conformità
accordion [ə'kɔ:dɪən] *n* fisarmonica
accost [ə'kɔst] *vt* avvicinare
account [ə'kaunt] *n* (*Comm*) conto; (*report*) descrizione *f*; **accounts** *npl* (*Comm*) conti; **"~ payee only"** (*Brit*) "assegno non trasferibile"; **to keep an ~ of** tenere nota di; **to bring sb to ~ for sth/for having done sth** chiedere a qn di render conto di qc/per aver fatto qc; **by all accounts** a quanto si dice; **of little ~** di poca importanza; **on ~** in acconto; **to buy sth on ~** comprare qc a credito; **on no ~** per nessun motivo; **on ~ of** a causa di; **to take into ~, take ~ of** tener conto di
▸ **account for** *vt fus* (*explain*) spiegare; giustificare; **all the children were**

accounted for nessun bambino mancava all'appello
accountability [əˈkauntəˈbɪlɪtɪ] *n* responsabilità
accountable [əˈkauntəbl] *adj* responsabile; **to be held ~ for sth** dover rispondere di qc
accountancy [əˈkauntənsɪ] *n* ragioneria
accountant [əˈkauntənt] *n* ragioniere(-a)
accounting [əˈkauntɪŋ] *n* contabilità
accounting period *n* esercizio finanziario, periodo contabile
account number *n* numero di conto
account payable *n* conto passivo
account receivable *n* conto da esigere
accredited [əˈkrɛdɪtɪd] *adj* accreditato(-a)
accretion [əˈkriːʃən] *n* accrescimento
accrue [əˈkruː] *vi* (*mount up*) aumentare; **to ~ to** derivare a; **accrued charges** ratei *mpl* passivi; **accrued interest** interesse *m* maturato
accumulate [əˈkjuːmjuleɪt] *vt* accumulare ■ *vi* accumularsi
accumulation [əkjuːmjuˈleɪʃən] *n* accumulazione *f*
accuracy [ˈækjurəsɪ] *n* precisione *f*
accurate [ˈækjurɪt] *adj* preciso(-a)
accurately [ˈækjurɪtlɪ] *adv* precisamente
accusation [ækjuˈzeɪʃən] *n* accusa
accusative [əˈkjuːzətɪv] *n* (*Ling*) accusativo
accuse [əˈkjuːz] *vt* accusare
accused [əˈkjuːzd] *n* accusato(-a)
accuser [əˈkjuːzə^r] *n* accusatore(-trice)
accustom [əˈkʌstəm] *vt* abituare; **to ~ o.s. to sth** abituarsi a qc
accustomed [əˈkʌstəmd] *adj* (*usual*) abituale; **~ to** abituato(-a) a
AC/DC *abbr* (= *alternating current/direct current*) c.a./c.c.
ACE [eɪs] *n abbr* = **American Council on Education**
ace [eɪs] *n* asso; **within an ~ of** (*Brit*) a un pelo da
acerbic [əˈsəːbɪk] *adj* (*also fig*) acido(-a)
acetate [ˈæsɪteɪt] *n* acetato
ache [eɪk] *n* male *m*, dolore *m* ■ *vi* (*be sore*) far male, dolere; (*yearn*): **to ~ to do sth** morire dalla voglia di fare qc; **I've got stomach ~** *or* (*US*) **a stomach ~** ho mal di stomaco; **my head aches** mi fa male la testa; **I'm aching all over** mi duole dappertutto
achieve [əˈtʃiːv] *vt* (*aim*) raggiungere; (*victory, success*) ottenere; (*task*) compiere
achievement [əˈtʃiːvmənt] *n* compimento; successo
Achilles heel [əˈkɪliːz-] *n* tallone *m* d'Achille
acid [ˈæsɪd] *adj* acido(-a) ■ *n* acido
acidity [əˈsɪdɪtɪ] *n* acidità
acid rain *n* pioggia acida
acid test *n* (*fig*) prova del fuoco
acknowledge [əkˈnɔlɪdʒ] *vt* riconoscere; (*letter*: *also*: **acknowledge receipt of**) accusare ricevuta di
acknowledgement [əkˈnɔlɪdʒmənt] *n* riconoscimento; (*of letter*) conferma; **acknowledgements** *npl* (*in book*) ringraziamenti *mpl*
ACLU *n abbr* (= *American Civil Liberties Union*) *unione americana per le libertà civili*
acme [ˈækmɪ] *n* culmine *m*, acme *m*
acne [ˈæknɪ] *n* acne *f*
acorn [ˈeɪkɔːn] *n* ghianda
acoustic [əˈkuːstɪk] *adj* acustico(-a); *see also* **acoustics**
acoustic coupler [-ˈkʌplə^r] *n* (*Comput*) accoppiatore *m* acustico
acoustics [əˈkuːstɪks] *n, npl* acustica
acquaint [əˈkweɪnt] *vt*: **to ~ sb with sth** far sapere qc a qn; **to be acquainted with** (*person*) conoscere
acquaintance [əˈkweɪntəns] *n* conoscenza; (*person*) conoscente *m/f*; **to make sb's ~** fare la conoscenza di qn
acquiesce [ækwɪˈɛs] *vi* (*agree*): **to ~ (in)** acconsentire (a)
acquire [əˈkwaɪə^r] *vt* acquistare
acquired [əˈkwaɪəd] *adj* acquisito(-a); **it's an ~ taste** è una cosa che si impara ad apprezzare
acquisition [ækwɪˈzɪʃən] *n* acquisto
acquisitive [əˈkwɪzɪtɪv] *adj* a cui piace accumulare le cose
acquit [əˈkwɪt] *vt* assolvere; **to ~ o.s. well** comportarsi bene
acquittal [əˈkwɪtl] *n* assoluzione *f*
acre [ˈeɪkə^r] *n* acro (= *4047 m²*)
acreage [ˈeɪkərɪdʒ] *n* superficie *f* in acri
acrid [ˈækrɪd] *adj* (*smell*) acre, pungente; (*fig*) pungente
acrimonious [ækrɪˈməunɪəs] *adj* astioso(-a)
acrobat [ˈækrəbæt] *n* acrobata *m/f*
acrobatic [ækrəˈbætɪk] *adj* acrobatico(-a)
acrobatics [ækrəˈbætɪks] *n* acrobatica ■ *npl* acrobazie *fpl*
Acropolis [əˈkrɔpəlɪs] *n*: **the ~** l'Acropoli *f*
across [əˈkrɔs] *prep* (*on the other side*) dall'altra parte di; (*crosswise*) attraverso ■ *adv* dall'altra parte; in larghezza; **to walk ~ (the road)** attraversare (la strada); **to take sb ~ the road** far attraversare la strada a qn; **~ from** di fronte a; **the lake is 12 km ~** il lago ha una larghezza di 12 km *or* è largo 12 km; **to get sth ~ to sb** (*fig*) far capire qc a qn
acrylic [əˈkrɪlɪk] *adj* acrilico(-a) ■ *n* acrilico
ACT *n abbr* (= *American College Test*) *esame di ammissione a college*

act [ækt] *n* atto; (*in music-hall etc*) numero; (*Law*) decreto ■ *vi* agire; (*Theat*) recitare; (*pretend*) fingere ■ *vt* (*part*) recitare; **to catch sb in the ~** cogliere qn in flagrante *or* sul fatto; **it's only an ~** è tutta scena, è solo una messinscena; **~ of God** (*Law*) calamità *f inv* naturale; **to ~ Hamlet** (*Brit*) recitare la parte di Amleto; **to ~ the fool** (*Brit*) fare lo stupido; **to ~ as** agire da; **it acts as a deterrent** serve da deterrente; **acting in my capacity as chairman, I ...** in qualità di presidente, io ...
▸ **act on** *vt*: **to ~ on sth** agire in base a qc
▸ **act out** *vt* (*event*) ricostruire; (*fantasies*) dare forma concreta a

acting ['æktɪŋ] *adj* che fa le funzioni di ■ *n* (*of actor*) recitazione *f*; (*activity*): **to do some ~** fare del teatro (*or* del cinema); **he is the ~ manager** fa le veci del direttore

action ['ækʃən] *n* azione *f*; (*Mil*) combattimento; (*Law*) processo ■ *vt* (*Comm: request*) evadere; (*tasks*) portare a termine; **to take ~** agire; **to put a plan into ~** realizzare un piano; **out of ~** fuori combattimento; (*machine etc*) fuori servizio; **killed in ~** (*Mil*) ucciso in combattimento; **to bring an ~ against sb** (*Law*) intentare causa contro qn

action replay *n* (*Brit TV*) replay *m inv*

activate ['æktɪveɪt] *vt* (*mechanism*) fare funzionare; (*Chem, Physics*) rendere attivo(-a)

active ['æktɪv] *adj* attivo(-a); **to play an ~ part in** partecipare attivamente a

active duty *n* (*US Mil*) = **active service**

actively ['æktɪvlɪ] *adv* attivamente

active partner *n* (*Comm*) socio effettivo

active service *n* (*Brit Mil*): **to be on ~** prestar servizio in zona di operazioni

activist ['æktɪvɪst] *n* attivista *m/f*

activity [æk'tɪvɪtɪ] *n* attività *f inv*

activity holiday *n* vacanza attiva (*in bici, a cavallo, in barca, a vela ecc.*)

actor ['æktəʳ] *n* attore *m*

actress ['æktrɪs] *n* attrice *f*

actual ['æktjuəl] *adj* reale, vero(-a)

actually ['æktjuəlɪ] *adv* veramente; (*even*) addirittura

actuary ['æktjuərɪ] *n* attuario(-a)

actuate ['æktjueɪt] *vt* attivare

acuity [ə'kju:ɪtɪ] *n* acutezza

acumen ['ækjumən] *n* acume *m*; **business ~** fiuto negli affari

acupuncture ['ækjupʌŋktʃəʳ] *n* agopuntura

AD *adv abbr* (= *Anno Domini*) d. C. ■ *n abbr* (*US Mil*) = **active duty**

ad [æd] *n abbr* = **advertisement**

adamant ['ædəmənt] *adj* irremovibile

Adam's apple ['ædəmz-] *n* pomo di Adamo

adapt [ə'dæpt] *vt* adattare ■ *vi*: **to ~ (to)** adattarsi (a)

adaptability [ədæptə'bɪlɪtɪ] *n* adattabilità

adaptable [ə'dæptəbl] *adj* (*device*) adattabile; (*person*) che sa adattarsi

adaptation [ædæp'teɪʃən] *n* adattamento

adapter, adaptor [ə'dæptəʳ] *n* (*Elec*) adattatore *m*

add [æd] *vt* aggiungere; (*figures*) addizionare ■ *vi*: **to ~ to** (*increase*) aumentare ■ *n* (*Internet*): **thanks for the ~** grazie per avermi aggiunto (come amico)
▸ **add on** *vt* aggiungere
▸ **add up** *vt* (*figures*) addizionare ■ *vi* (*fig*): **it doesn't ~ up** non ha senso; **it doesn't ~ up to much** non è un granché

adder ['ædəʳ] *n* vipera

addict ['ædɪkt] *n* tossicomane *m/f*; (*fig*) fanatico(-a); **heroin ~** eroinomane *m/f*; **drug ~** tossicodipendente *m/f*, tossicomane *m/f*

addicted [ə'dɪktɪd] *adj*: **to be ~ to** (*drink etc*) essere dedito(-a) a; (*fig: football etc*) essere tifoso(-a) di

addiction [ə'dɪkʃən] *n* (*Med*) tossicomania

Addis Ababa ['ædɪs'æbəbə] *n* Addis Abeba *f*

addition [ə'dɪʃən] *n* addizione *f*; **in ~** inoltre; **in ~ to** oltre

additional [ə'dɪʃənl] *adj* supplementare

additive ['ædɪtɪv] *n* additivo

address [ə'drɛs] *n* (*gen, Comput*) indirizzo; (*talk*) discorso ■ *vt* indirizzare; (*speak to*) fare un discorso a; **form of ~** (*gen*) formula di cortesia; (*in letters*) formula d'indirizzo *or* di intestazione; **to ~ o.s. to sth** indirizzare le proprie energie verso qc

address book *n* rubrica

addressee [ædrɛ'si:] *n* destinatario(-a)

Aden ['eɪdən] *n*: **the Gulf of ~** il golfo di Aden

adenoids ['ædɪnɔɪdz] *npl* adenoidi *fpl*

adept ['ædɛpt] *adj*: **~ at** esperto(-a) in

adequate ['ædɪkwɪt] *adj* (*description, reward*) adeguato(-a); (*amount*) sufficiente; **to feel ~ to a task** sentirsi all'altezza di un compito

adequately ['ædɪkwɪtlɪ] *adv* adeguatamente; sufficientemente

adhere [əd'hɪəʳ] *vi*: **to ~ to** aderire a; (*fig: rule, decision*) seguire

adhesion [əd'hi:ʒən] *n* adesione *f*

adhesive [əd'hi:zɪv] *adj* adesivo(-a) ■ *n* adesivo; **~ tape** (*Brit: for parcels etc*) nastro adesivo; (*US: Med*) cerotto adesivo

ad hoc [æd'hɔk] *adj* (*decision*) ad hoc *inv*; (*committee*) apposito(-a)

ad infinitum ['ædɪnfɪ'naɪtəm] *adv* all'infinito

adjacent [ə'dʒeɪsənt] *adj* adiacente; **~ to** accanto a

adjective ['ædʒɛktɪv] *n* aggettivo
adjoin [ə'dʒɔɪn] *vt* essere contiguo(-a) *or* attiguo(-a) a
adjoining [ə'dʒɔɪnɪŋ] *adj* accanto *inv*, adiacente ■ *prep* accanto a
adjourn [ə'dʒə:n] *vt* rimandare, aggiornare; (*US: end*) sospendere ■ *vi* sospendere la seduta; (*Parliament*) sospendere i lavori; (*go*) spostarsi; **to ~ a meeting till the following week** aggiornare *or* rinviare un incontro alla settimana seguente; **they adjourned to the pub** (*col*) si sono trasferiti al pub
adjournment [ə'dʒə:nmənt] *n* rinvio, aggiornamento; sospensione *f*
Adjt *abbr* (*Mil*) = **adjutant**
adjudicate [ə'dʒu:dɪkeɪt] *vt* (*contest*) giudicare; (*claim*) decidere su
adjudication [ədʒu:dɪ'keɪʃən] *n* decisione *f*
adjust [ə'dʒʌst] *vt* aggiustare; (*Comm*) rettificare ■ *vi*: **to ~ (to)** adattarsi (a)
adjustable [ə'dʒʌstəbl] *adj* regolabile
adjuster [ə'dʒʌstə^r] *n see* **loss adjuster**
adjustment [ə'dʒʌstmənt] *n* adattamento; (*of prices, wages*) aggiustamento
adjutant ['ædʒətənt] *n* aiutante *m*
ad-lib [æd'lɪb] *vt, vi* improvvisare ■ *n* improvvisazione *f* ■ *adv*: **ad lib** a piacere, a volontà
adman ['ædmæn] *n* (*col*) pubblicitario
admin [æd'mɪn] *n abbr* (*col*) = **administration**
administer [əd'mɪnɪstə^r] *vt* amministrare; (*justice*) somministrare
administration [ədmɪnɪs'treɪʃən] *n* amministrazione *f*; **the A~** (*US*) il Governo
administrative [əd'mɪnɪstrətɪv] *adj* amministrativo(-a)
administrator [əd'mɪnɪstreɪtə^r] *n* amministratore(-trice)
admirable ['ædmərəbl] *adj* ammirevole
admiral ['ædmərəl] *n* ammiraglio
Admiralty ['ædmərəltɪ] *n* (*Brit: also:* **Admiralty Board**) Ministero della Marina
admiration [ædmə'reɪʃən] *n* ammirazione *f*
admirer [əd'maɪərə^r] *n* ammiratore(-trice)
admiring [əd'maɪərɪŋ] *adj* (*glance etc*) di ammirazione
admissible [əd'mɪsəbl] *adj* ammissibile
admission [əd'mɪʃən] *n* ammissione *f*; (*to exhibition, night club etc*) ingresso; (*confession*) confessione *f*; **by his own ~** per sua ammissione; **"~ free"**, **"free ~"** "ingresso gratuito"
admit [əd'mɪt] *vt* ammettere; far entrare; (*agree*) riconoscere; **"children not admitted"** "vietato l'ingresso ai bambini"; **this ticket admits two** questo biglietto è valido per due persone; **I must ~ that ...** devo ammettere *or* confessare che ...
▸ **admit of** *vt fus* lasciare adito a
▸ **admit to** *vt fus* riconoscere
admittance [əd'mɪtəns] *n* ingresso; **"no ~"** "vietato l'ingresso"
admittedly [əd'mɪtɪdlɪ] *adv* bisogna pur riconoscere (che)
admonish [əd'mɔnɪʃ] *vt* ammonire
ad nauseam [æd'nɔ:zɪæm] *adv* fino alla nausea, a non finire
ado [ə'du:] *n*: **without (any) more ~** senza più indugi
adolescence [ædəu'lɛsns] *n* adolescenza
adolescent [ædəu'lɛsnt] *adj, n* adolescente *m/f*
adopt [ə'dɔpt] *vt* adottare
adopted [ə'dɔptɪd] *adj* adottivo(-a)
adoption [ə'dɔpʃən] *n* adozione *f*
adore [ə'dɔ:^r] *vt* adorare
adoring [ə'dɔ:rɪŋ] *adj* adorante; **his ~ wife** sua moglie che lo adora
adoringly [ə'dɔ:rɪŋlɪ] *adv* con adorazione
adorn [ə'dɔ:n] *vt* ornare
adornment [ə'dɔ:nmənt] *n* ornamento
ADP *n abbr* = **automatic data processing**
adrenalin [ə'drɛnəlɪn] *n* adrenalina; **it gets the ~ going** ti dà una carica
Adriatic [eɪdrɪ'ætɪk], **Adriatic Sea** [eɪdrɪ'ætɪk-] *n* Adriatico
adrift [ə'drɪft] *adv* alla deriva; **to come ~** (*boat*) andare alla deriva
adroit [ə'drɔɪt] *adj* abile, destro(-a)
ADSL *n abbr* (= *asymmetric digital subscriber line*) ADSL *m*
ADT *abbr* (*US:* = *Atlantic Daylight Time*) *ora legale di New York*
adult ['ædʌlt] *n* adulto(-a)
adult education *n* scuola per adulti
adulterate [ə'dʌltəreɪt] *vt* adulterare
adulterer [ə'dʌltərə^r] *n* adultero
adulteress [ə'dʌltərɪs] *n* adultera
adultery [ə'dʌltərɪ] *n* adulterio
adulthood ['ædʌlthud] *n* età adulta
advance [əd'vɑ:ns] *n* avanzamento; (*money*) anticipo ■ *vt* avanzare; (*date, money*) anticipare ■ *vi* avanzare; **in ~** in anticipo; **to make advances to sb** (*gen*) fare degli approcci a qn; (*amorously*) fare delle avances a qn
advanced [əd'vɑ:nst] *adj* avanzato(-a); (*Scol: studies*) superiore; **~ in years** avanti negli anni
advancement [əd'vɑ:nsmənt] *n* avanzamento
advance notice *n* preavviso
advantage [əd'vɑ:ntɪdʒ] *n* (*also Tennis*) vantaggio; **to take ~ of** approfittarsi di; **it's to our ~** è nel nostro interesse, torna a nostro vantaggio

a

advantageous [ædvən'teɪdʒəs] *adj* vantaggioso(-a)
advent ['ædvənt] *n* avvento; **A~** (*Rel*) Avvento
Advent calendar *n* calendario dell'Avvento
adventure [əd'vɛntʃə^r] *n* avventura
adventure playground *n* *area attrezzata di giochi per bambini con funi, strutture in legno etc*
adventurous [əd'vɛntʃərəs] *adj* avventuroso(-a)
adverb ['ædvə:b] *n* avverbio
adversary ['ædvəsərɪ] *n* avversario(-a)
adverse ['ædvə:s] *adj* avverso(-a); **in ~ circumstances** nelle avversità; **~ to** contrario(-a) a
adversity [əd'və:sɪtɪ] *n* avversità
advert ['ædvə:t] *n abbr* (*Brit*) = **advertisement**
advertise ['ædvətaɪz] *vi, vt* fare pubblicità *or* réclame (a), fare un'inserzione (per vendere); **to ~ for** (*staff*) cercare tramite annuncio
advertisement [əd'və:tɪsmənt] *n* (*Comm*) réclame *f inv*, pubblicità *f inv*; (*in classified ads*) inserzione *f*
advertiser ['ædvətaɪzə^r] *n* azienda che reclamizza un prodotto; (*in newspaper*) inserzionista *m/f*
advertising ['ædvətaɪzɪŋ] *n* pubblicità
advertising agency *n* agenzia pubblicitaria *or* di pubblicità
advertising campaign *n* campagna pubblicitaria
advice [əd'vaɪs] *n* consigli *mpl*; (*notification*) avviso; **piece of ~** consiglio; **to ask (sb) for ~** chiedere il consiglio (di qn), chiedere un consiglio (a qn); **legal ~** consulenza legale
advice note *n* (*Brit*) avviso di spedizione
advisable [əd'vaɪzəbl] *adj* consigliabile
advise [əd'vaɪz] *vt* consigliare; **to ~ sb of sth** informare qn di qc; **to ~ sb against sth/against doing sth** sconsigliare qc a qn/a qn di fare qc; **you will be well/ill advised to go** fareste bene/male ad andare
advisedly [əd'vaɪzɪdlɪ] *adv* (*deliberately*) deliberatamente
adviser [əd'vaɪzə^r] *n* consigliere(-a); (*in business*) consulente *m/f*, consigliere(-a)
advisory [əd'vaɪzərɪ] *adj* consultivo(-a); **in an ~ capacity** in veste di consulente
advocate *n* ['ædvəkɪt] (*upholder*) sostenitore(-trice) ■ *vt* ['ædvəkeɪt] propugnare; **to be an ~ of** essere a favore di
advt. *abbr* = **advertisement**
AEA *n abbr* (*Brit*: = *Atomic Energy Authority*) *ente di controllo sulla ricerca e lo sviluppo dell'energia atomica*
AEC *n abbr* (*US*: = *Atomic Energy Commission*) *ente di controllo sulla ricerca e lo sviluppo dell'energia atomica*
Aegean [i:'dʒi:ən], **Aegean Sea** [i:'dʒi:ən-] *n* (mare *m*) Egeo
aegis ['i:dʒɪs] *n*: **under the ~ of** sotto gli auspici di
aeon ['i:ən] *n* eternità *f inv*
aerial ['ɛərɪəl] *n* antenna ■ *adj* aereo(-a)
aerobatics ['ɛərəu'bætɪks] *npl* acrobazia *sg* aerea; (*stunts*) acrobazie *fpl* aeree
aerobics [ɛə'rəubɪks] *n* aerobica
aerodrome ['ɛərədrəum] *n* (*Brit*) aerodromo
aerodynamic ['ɛərəudaɪ'næmɪk] *adj* aerodinamico(-a)
aeronautics [ɛərə'nɔ:tɪks] *n* aeronautica
aeroplane ['ɛərəpleɪn] *n* aeroplano
aerosol ['ɛərəsɔl] *n* aerosol *m inv*
aerospace industry ['ɛərəuspeɪs-] *n* industria aerospaziale
aesthetic [ɪs'θɛtɪk] *adj* estetico(-a)
afar [ə'fɑ:^r] *adv* lontano; **from ~** da lontano
AFB *n abbr* (*US*) = **Air Force Base**
AFDC *n abbr* (*US*: = *Aid to Families with Dependent Children*) ≈ A.F. (= *assegni familiari*)
affable ['æfəbl] *adj* affabile
affair [ə'fɛə^r] *n* affare *m*; (*also*: **love affair**) relazione *f* amorosa; **affairs** *npl* (*business*) affari; **the Watergate ~** il caso Watergate
affect [ə'fɛkt] *vt* toccare; (*feign*) fingere
affectation [æfɛk'teɪʃən] *n* affettazione *f*
affected [ə'fɛktɪd] *adj* affettato(-a)
affection [ə'fɛkʃən] *n* affetto
affectionate [ə'fɛkʃənɪt] *adj* affettuoso(-a)
affectionately [ə'fɛkʃənɪtlɪ] *adv* affettuosamente
affidavit [æfɪ'deɪvɪt] *n* (*Law*) affidavit *m inv*
affiliated [ə'fɪlɪeɪtɪd] *adj* affiliato(-a); **~ company** filiale *f*
affinity [ə'fɪnɪtɪ] *n* affinità *f inv*
affirm [ə'fə:m] *vt* affermare, asserire
affirmation [æfə'meɪʃən] *n* affermazione *f*
affirmative [ə'fə:mətɪv] *adj* affermativo(-a) ■ *n*: **in the ~** affermativamente
affix [ə'fɪks] *vt* apporre; attaccare
afflict [ə'flɪkt] *vt* affliggere
affliction [ə'flɪkʃən] *n* afflizione *f*
affluence ['æfluəns] *n* ricchezza
affluent ['æfluənt] *adj* ricco(-a); **the ~ society** la società del benessere
afford [ə'fɔ:d] *vt* permettersi; (*provide*) fornire; **I can't ~ the time** non ho veramente il tempo; **can we ~ a car?** possiamo permetterci un'automobile?
affordable [ə'fɔ:dəbl] *adj* (che ha un prezzo) abbordabile
affray [ə'freɪ] *n* (*Brit Law*) rissa
affront [ə'frʌnt] *n* affronto
affronted [ə'frʌntɪd] *adj* insultato(-a)
Afghan ['æfgæn] *adj, n* afgano(-a)

Afghanistan [æf'gænɪstɑ:n] *n* Afganistan *m*
afield [ə'fi:ld] *adv*: **far ~** lontano
AFL-CIO *n abbr* (*= American Federation of Labor and Congress of Industrial Organizations*) *confederazione sindacale*
afloat [ə'fləut] *adj, adv* a galla
afoot [ə'fut] *adv*: **there is something ~** si sta preparando qualcosa
aforementioned [ə'fɔ:mɛnʃənd] *adj* suddetto(-a)
aforesaid [ə'fɔ:sɛd] *adj* suddetto(-a), predetto(-a)
afraid [ə'freɪd] *adj* impaurito(-a); **to be ~ of** aver paura di; **to be ~ of doing** *or* **to do** aver paura di fare; **I am ~ that I'll be late** mi dispiace, ma farò tardi; **I'm ~ so!** ho paura di sì!, temo proprio di sì!; **I'm ~ not** no, mi dispiace, purtroppo no
afresh [ə'frɛʃ] *adv* di nuovo
Africa ['æfrɪkə] *n* Africa
African ['æfrɪkən] *adj, n* africano(-a)
Afrikaans [æfrɪ'kɑ:ns] *n* afrikaans *m*
Afrikaner [æfrɪ'kɑ:nə^r] *n* africander *m inv*
Afro-American ['æfrəuə'mɛrɪkən] *adj* afroamericano(-a)
Afro-Caribbean ['æfrəukærɪ'biə:n] *adj* afrocaraibico(-a)
AFT *n abbr* (*= American Federation of Teachers*) *sindacato degli insegnanti*
aft [ɑ:ft] *adv* a poppa, verso poppa
after ['ɑ:ftə^r] *prep, adv* dopo; **~ dinner** dopo cena; **the day ~ tomorrow** dopodomani; **what/who are you ~?** che/chi cerca?; **the police are ~ him** è ricercato dalla polizia; **~ you!** prima lei!, dopo di lei!; **~ all** dopo tutto
afterbirth ['ɑ:ftəbə:θ] *n* placenta
aftercare ['ɑ:ftəkɛə^r] *n* (*Brit Med*) assistenza medica post-degenza
after-effects ['ɑ:ftərɪfɛkts] *npl* conseguenze *fpl*; (*of illness*) postumi *mpl*
afterlife ['ɑ:ftəlaɪf] *n* vita dell'al di là
aftermath ['ɑ:ftəmæθ] *n* conseguenze *fpl*; **in the ~ of** nel periodo dopo
afternoon ['ɑ:ftə'nu:n] *n* pomeriggio; **good ~!** buon giorno!
afters ['ɑ:ftəz] *n* (*Brit col: dessert*) dessert *m inv*
after-sales service [ɑ:ftə'seɪlz-] *n* servizio assistenza clienti
after-shave ['ɑ:ftəʃeɪv], **after-shave lotion** ['ɑ:ftəʃeɪv-] *n* dopobarba *m inv*
aftershock ['ɑ:ftəʃɔk] *n* scossa di assestamento
aftersun ['ɑ:ftəsʌn] *adj*: **~ (lotion/cream)** (lozione *f* /crema) doposole *m inv*
aftertaste ['ɑ:ftəteɪst] *n* retrogusto
afterthought ['ɑ:ftəθɔ:t] *n*: **as an ~** come aggiunta
afterwards ['ɑ:ftəwədz] *adv* dopo
again [ə'gɛn] *adv* di nuovo; **to begin/see ~** ricominciare/rivedere; **he opened it ~** l'ha aperto di nuovo, l'ha riaperto; **not ... ~** non ... più; **~ and ~** ripetutamente; **now and ~** di tanto in tanto, a volte
against [ə'gɛnst] *prep* contro; **~ a blue background** su uno sfondo azzurro; **leaning ~ the desk** appoggiato alla scrivania; **(as) ~** (*Brit*) in confronto a, contro
age [eɪdʒ] *n* età *f inv* ■ *vt, vi* invecchiare; **what ~ is he?** quanti anni ha?; **he is 20 years of ~** ha 20 anni; **under ~** minorenne; **to come of ~** diventare maggiorenne; **it's been ages since ...** sono secoli che ...
aged ['eɪdʒd] *adj*: **~ 10** di 10 anni; ■ *npl* ['eɪdʒɪd]: **the ~** gli anziani
age group *n* generazione *f*; **the 40 to 50 ~** le persone fra i 40 e i 50 anni
ageing ['eɪdʒɪŋ] *adj* che diventa vecchio(-a); **an ~ film star** una diva stagionata
ageless ['eɪdʒlɪs] *adj* senza età
age limit *n* limite *m* d'età
agency ['eɪdʒənsɪ] *n* agenzia; **through** *or* **by the ~ of** grazie a
agenda [ə'dʒɛndə] *n* ordine *m* del giorno; **on the ~** all'ordine del giorno
agent ['eɪdʒənt] *n* agente *m*
aggravate ['ægrəveɪt] *vt* aggravare, peggiorare; (*annoy*) esasperare
aggravation [ægrə'veɪʃən] *n* peggioramento; esasperazione *f*
aggregate ['ægrɪgeɪt] *n* aggregato; **on ~** (*Sport*) con punteggio complessivo
aggression [ə'grɛʃən] *n* aggressione *f*
aggressive [ə'grɛsɪv] *adj* aggressivo(-a)
aggressiveness [ə'grɛsɪvnɪs] *n* aggressività
aggressor [ə'grɛsə^r] *n* aggressore *m*
aggrieved [ə'gri:vd] *adj* addolorato(-a)
aggro ['ægrəu] *n* (*col: behaviour*) aggressività *f inv*; (*: hassle*) rottura
aghast [ə'gɑ:st] *adj* sbigottito(-a)
agile ['ædʒaɪl] *adj* agile
agility [ə'dʒɪlɪtɪ] *n* agilità *f inv*
agitate ['ædʒɪteɪt] *vt* turbare; agitare ■ *vi*: **to ~ for** agitarsi per
agitator ['ædʒɪteɪtə^r] *n* agitatore(-trice)
AGM *n abbr* = **annual general meeting**
agnostic [æg'nɔstɪk] *adj, n* agnostico(-a)
ago [ə'gəu] *adv*: **2 days ~** 2 giorni fa; **not long ~** poco tempo fa; **as long ~ as 1960** già nel 1960; **how long ~?** quanto tempo fa?
agog [ə'gɔg] *adj*: **(all) ~ (for)** ansioso(-a) (di), impaziente (di)
agonize ['ægənaɪz] *vi*: **to ~ (over)** angosciarsi (per)
agonizing ['ægənaɪzɪŋ] *adj* straziante

agony ['ægənɪ] *n* agonia; **I was in ~** avevo dei dolori atroci
agony aunt *n* (*Brit col*) *chi tiene la rubrica della posta del cuore*
agony column *n* posta del cuore
agree [ə'gri:] *vt* (*price*) pattuire ■ *vi*: **to ~ (with)** essere d'accordo (con); (*Ling*) concordare (con); **to ~ to sth/to do sth** accettare qc/di fare qc; **to ~ that** (*admit*) ammettere che; **to ~ on sth** accordarsi su qc; **it was agreed that ...** è stato deciso (di comune accordo) che ...; **garlic doesn't ~ with me** l'aglio non mi va
agreeable [ə'gri:əbl] *adj* gradevole; (*willing*) disposto(-a); **are you ~ to this?** è d'accordo con questo?
agreed [ə'gri:d] *adj* (*time, place*) stabilito(-a); **to be ~** essere d'accordo
agreement [ə'gri:mənt] *n* accordo; **in ~** d'accordo; **by mutual ~** di comune accordo
agricultural [ægrɪ'kʌltʃərəl] *adj* agricolo(-a)
agriculture ['ægrɪkʌltʃə^r] *n* agricoltura
aground [ə'graund] *adv*: **to run ~** arenarsi
ahead [ə'hɛd] *adv* avanti; davanti; **~ of** davanti a; (*fig: schedule etc*) in anticipo su; **~ of time** in anticipo; **go ~!** avanti!; **go right** *or* **straight ~** tiri diritto; **they were (right) ~ of us** erano (proprio) davanti a noi
AI *n abbr* = **Amnesty International**; (*Comput*) = **artificial intelligence**
AIB *n abbr* (*Brit: = Accident Investigation Bureau*) *ufficio d'inchiesta per incidenti aerei e simili*
AID *n abbr* = **artificial insemination by donor**; (*US: = Agency for International Development*) A.I.D. *f*
aid [eɪd] *n* aiuto ■ *vt* aiutare; **with the ~ of** con l'aiuto di; **in ~ of** a favore di; **to ~ and abet** (*Law*) essere complice di
aide [eɪd] *n* (*person*) aiutante *m*
aide-de-camp ['eɪddə'kɔŋ] *n* (*Mil*) aiutante *m* di campo
AIDS [eɪdz] *n abbr* (= *acquired immune (or immuno-) deficiency syndrome*) A.I.D.S. *f*
AIH *n abbr* = **artificial insemination by husband**
ailing ['eɪlɪŋ] *adj* sofferente; (*fig: economy, industry etc*) in difficoltà
ailment ['eɪlmənt] *n* indisposizione *f*
aim [eɪm] *vt*: **to ~ sth at** (*gun*) mirare qc a, puntare qc a; (*camera, remark*) rivolgere qc a; (*missile*) lanciare qc contro; (*blow etc*) tirare qc a ■ *vi* (*also*: **to take aim**) prendere la mira ■ *n* mira; **to ~ at** mirare; **to ~ to do** aver l'intenzione di fare
aimless ['eɪmlɪs] *adj*, **aimlessly** ['eɪmlɪslɪ] *adv* senza scopo
ain't [eɪnt] (*col*) = **am not**; **aren't**; **isn't**
air [ɛə^r] *n* aria ■ *vt* (*room, bed*) arieggiare; (*clothes*) far prendere aria a; (*idea, grievance*) esprimere pubblicamente, manifestare; (*views*) far conoscere ■ *cpd* (*currents*) d'aria; (*attack*) aereo(-a); **by ~** (*travel*) in aereo; **to be on the ~** (*Radio, TV: station*) trasmettere; (: *programme*) essere in onda
air bag *n* airbag *m inv*
air base *n* base *f* aerea
airbed ['ɛəbɛd] *n* (*Brit*) materassino
airborne ['ɛəbɔ:n] *adj* (*plane*) in volo; (*troops*) aerotrasportato(-a); **as soon as the plane was ~** appena l'aereo ebbe decollato
air cargo *n* carico trasportato per via aerea
air-conditioned ['ɛəkən'dɪʃənd] *adj* con *or* ad aria condizionata
air conditioning *n* condizionamento d'aria
air-cooled ['ɛəku:ld] *adj* raffreddato(-a) ad aria
aircraft ['ɛəkrɑ:ft] *n pl inv* apparecchio
aircraft carrier *n* portaerei *f inv*
air cushion *n* cuscino gonfiabile; (*Tech*) cuscino d'aria
airfield ['ɛəfi:ld] *n* campo d'aviazione
Air Force *n* aviazione *f* militare
air freight *n* spedizione *f* di merci per via aerea; (*goods*) carico spedito per via aerea
airgun ['ɛəgʌn] *n* fucile *m* ad aria compressa
air hostess *n* hostess *f inv*
airily ['ɛərɪlɪ] *adv* con disinvoltura
airing ['ɛərɪŋ] *n*: **to give an ~ to** (*linen*) far prendere aria a; (*room*) arieggiare; (*fig: ideas etc*) ventilare
air letter *n* (*Brit*) aerogramma *m*
airlift ['ɛəlɪft] *n* ponte *m* aereo
airline ['ɛəlaɪn] *n* linea aerea
airliner ['ɛəlaɪnə^r] *n* aereo di linea
airlock ['ɛəlɔk] *n* cassa d'aria
air mail *n* posta aerea; **by ~** per via *or* posta aerea
air mattress *n* materassino gonfiabile
airplane ['ɛəpleɪn] *n* (*US*) aeroplano
air pocket *n* vuoto d'aria
airport ['ɛəpɔ:t] *n* aeroporto
air rage *n* *comportamento aggressivo dei passeggeri di un aereo*
air raid *n* incursione *f* aerea
air rifle *n* fucile *m* ad aria compressa
airsick ['ɛəsɪk] *adj*: **to be ~** soffrire di mal d'aereo
airspace ['ɛəspeɪs] *n* spazio aereo
airspeed ['ɛəspi:d] *n* velocità *f inv* di crociera (*Aer*)
airstrip ['ɛəstrɪp] *n* pista d'atterraggio
air terminal *n* air-terminal *m inv*
airtight ['ɛətaɪt] *adj* ermetico(-a)
air time *n* (*Radio*) spazio radiofonico; (*TV*) spazio televisivo

air traffic control *n* controllo del traffico aereo
air traffic controller *n* controllore *m* del traffico aereo
airway ['ɛəweɪ] *n* (*Aviat*) rotte *fpl* aeree; (*Anat*) vie *fpl* respiratorie
airy ['ɛərɪ] *adj* arioso(-a); (*manners*) noncurante
aisle [aɪl] *n* (*of church*) navata laterale; navata centrale; (*of plane*) corridoio
aisle seat *n* (*on plane*) posto sul corridoio
ajar [ə'dʒɑːʳ] *adj* socchiuso(-a)
AK *abbr* (US) = **Alaska**
aka *abbr* (= *also known as*) alias
akin [ə'kɪn] *prep*: **~ to** simile a
AL *abbr* (US) = **Alabama**
ALA *n abbr* = **American Library Association**
Ala. *abbr* (US) = **Alabama**
à la carte [ɑːlɑː'kɑːt] *adv* alla carta
alacrity [ə'lækrɪtɪ] *n*: **with ~** con prontezza
alarm [ə'lɑːm] *n* allarme *m* ■ *vt* allarmare
alarm clock *n* sveglia
alarmed [ə'lɑːmd] *adj* (*person*) allarmato(-a); (*house, car etc*) dotato(-a) di allarme
alarming [ə'lɑːmɪŋ] *adj* allarmante, preoccupante
alarmingly [ə'lɑːmɪŋlɪ] *adv* in modo allarmante; **~ close** pericolosamente vicino
alarmist [ə'lɑːmɪst] *n* allarmista *m/f*
alas [ə'læs] *excl* ohimè!, ahimè!
Alas. *abbr* (US) = **Alaska**
Alaska [ə'læskə] *n* Alasca
Albania [æl'beɪnɪə] *n* Albania
Albanian [æl'beɪnɪən] *adj* albanese ■ *n* albanese *m/f*; (*Ling*) albanese *m*
albatross ['ælbətrɔs] *n* albatro, albatros *m inv*
albeit [ɔːl'biːɪt] *conj* sebbene + *sub*, benché + *sub*
album ['ælbəm] *n* album *m inv*; (*L.P.*) 33 giri *m inv*, L.P. *m inv*
albumen ['ælbjumɪn] *n* albume *m*
alchemy ['ælkɪmɪ] *n* alchimia
alcohol ['ælkəhɔl] *n* alcool *m*
alcohol-free ['ælkəhɔl'friː] *adj* analcolico(-a)
alcoholic [ælkə'hɔlɪk] *adj* alcolico(-a) ■ *n* alcolizzato(-a)
alcoholism ['ælkəhɔlɪzəm] *n* alcolismo
alcove ['ælkəuv] *n* alcova
Ald. *abbr* = **alderman**
alderman ['ɔːldəmən] *n* consigliere *m* comunale
ale [eɪl] *n* birra
alert [ə'ləːt] *adj* vivo(-a); (*watchful*) vigile ■ *n* allarme *m* ■ *vt*: **to ~ sb (to sth)** avvisare qn (di qc), avvertire qn (di qc); **to ~ sb to the dangers of sth** mettere qn in guardia contro qc; **on the ~** all'erta
Aleutian Islands [ə'luːʃən-] *npl* isole *fpl* Aleutine
A level *n* (*Brit*) *diploma di studi superiori*
Alexandria [ælɪg'zændrɪə] *n* Alessandria (d'Egitto)
alfresco [æl'frɛskəu] *adj, adv* all'aperto
algebra ['ældʒɪbrə] *n* algebra
Algeria [æl'dʒɪərɪə] *n* Algeria
Algerian [æl'dʒɪərɪən] *adj, n* algerino(-a)
Algiers [æl'dʒɪəz] *n* Algeri *f*
algorithm ['ælgərɪðəm] *n* algoritmo
alias ['eɪlɪəs] *adv* alias ■ *n* pseudonimo, falso nome *m*
alibi ['ælɪbaɪ] *n* alibi *m inv*
alien ['eɪlɪən] *n* straniero(-a) ■ *adj*: **~ (to)** estraneo(-a) (a)
alienate ['eɪlɪəneɪt] *vt* alienare
alienation [eɪlɪə'neɪʃən] *n* alienazione *f*
alight [ə'laɪt] *adj* acceso(-a) ■ *vi* scendere; (*bird*) posarsi
align [ə'laɪn] *vt* allineare
alignment [ə'laɪnmənt] *n* allineamento; **out of ~ (with)** non allineato (con)
alike [ə'laɪk] *adj* simile ■ *adv* allo stesso modo; **to look ~** assomigliarsi; **winter and summer ~** sia d'estate che d'inverno
alimony ['ælɪmənɪ] *n* (*payment*) alimenti *mpl*
alive [ə'laɪv] *adj* vivo(-a); (*active*) attivo(-a); **~ with** pieno(-a) di; **~ to** conscio(-a) di
alkali ['ælkəlaɪ] *n* alcali *m inv*

 KEYWORD

all [ɔːl] *adj* tutto(-a); **all day** tutto il giorno; **all night** tutta la notte; **all men** tutti gli uomini; **all five girls** tutt'e cinque le ragazze; **all five came** sono venuti tutti e cinque; **all the books** tutti i libri; **all the food** tutto il cibo; **all the time** tutto il tempo; (*always*) sempre; **all his life** tutta la vita; **for all their efforts** nonostante tutti i loro sforzi
■ *pron* **1** tutto(-a); **is that all?** non c'è altro?; (*in shop*) basta così?; **all of them** tutti(-e); **all of it** tutto(-a); **I ate it all, I ate all of it** l'ho mangiato tutto; **all of us went** tutti noi siamo andati; **all of the boys went** tutti i ragazzi sono andati
2 (*in phrases*): **above all** soprattutto; **after all** dopotutto; **at all**: **not at all** (*in answer to question*) niente affatto; (*in answer to thanks*) prego!, di niente!, s'immagini!; **I'm not at all tired** non sono affatto stanco; **anything at all will do** andrà bene qualsiasi cosa; **all in all** tutto sommato
■ *adv*: **all alone** tutto(-a) solo(-a); **to be/feel all in** (*Brit col*) essere/sentirsi sfinito(-a) *or* distrutto(-a); **all out** *adv*: **to go all out** mettercela tutta; **it's not as hard as all**

that non è poi così difficile; **all the more/ the better** tanto più/meglio; **all but** quasi; **the score is two all** il punteggio è di due a due *or* è due pari

allay [ə'leɪ] *vt* (*fears*) dissipare
all clear *n* (*Mil*) cessato allarme *m inv*; (*fig*) okay *m*
allegation [ælɪ'geɪʃən] *n* asserzione *f*
allege [ə'lɛdʒ] *vt* asserire; **he is alleged to have said ...** avrebbe detto che ...
alleged [ə'lɛdʒd] *adj* presunto(-a)
allegedly [ə'lɛdʒɪdlɪ] *adv* secondo quanto si asserisce
allegiance [ə'li:dʒəns] *n* fedeltà
allegory ['ælɪgərɪ] *n* allegoria
all-embracing ['ɔ:lɪm'breɪsɪŋ] *adj* universale
allergic [ə'lə:dʒɪk] *adj*: **~ to** allergico(-a) a
allergy ['ælədʒɪ] *n* allergia
alleviate [ə'li:vɪeɪt] *vt* alleviare
alley ['ælɪ] *n* vicolo; (*in garden*) vialetto
alleyway ['ælɪweɪ] *n* vicolo
alliance [ə'laɪəns] *n* alleanza
allied ['ælaɪd] *adj* alleato(-a)
alligator ['ælɪgeɪtə^r] *n* alligatore *m*
all-important ['ɔ:lɪm'pɔ:tənt] *adj* importantissimo(-a)
all-in ['ɔ:lɪn] *adj, adv* (*Brit: charge*) tutto compreso
all-in wrestling *n* (*Brit*) lotta americana
alliteration [əlɪtə'reɪʃən] *n* allitterazione *f*
all-night ['ɔ:l'naɪt] *adj* aperto(-a) (*or* che dura) tutta la notte
allocate ['æləkeɪt] *vt* (*share out*) distribuire; (*duties, sum, time*): **to ~ sth to** assegnare qc a; **to ~ sth for** stanziare qc per
allocation [æləu'keɪʃən] *n*: **~ (of money)** stanziamento
allot [ə'lɔt] *vt* (*share out*) spartire; **to ~ sth to** (*time*) dare qc a; (*duties*) assegnare qc a; **in the allotted time** nel tempo fissato *or* prestabilito
allotment [ə'lɔtmənt] *n* (*share*) spartizione *f*; (*garden*) lotto di terra
all-out ['ɔ:laut] *adj* (*effort etc*) totale ■ *adv*: **to go all out for** mettercela tutta per
allow [ə'lau] *vt* (*practice, behaviour*) permettere; (*sum to spend etc*) accordare; (*sum, time estimated*) dare; (*concede*): **to ~ that** ammettere che; **to ~ sb to do** permettere a qn di fare; **he is allowed to (do it)** lo può fare; **smoking is not allowed** è vietato fumare, non è permesso fumare; **we must ~ 3 days for the journey** dobbiamo calcolare 3 giorni per il viaggio
▸ **allow for** *vt fus* tener conto di
allowance [ə'lauəns] *n* (*money received*) assegno; (*for travelling, accommodation*) indennità *f inv*; (*Tax*) detrazione *f* di imposta; **to make ~(s) for** tener conto di; (*person*) scusare
alloy ['ælɔɪ] *n* lega
all right *adv* (*feel, work*) bene; (*as answer*) va bene
all-round [ɔ:l'raund] *adj* completo(-a)
all-rounder [ɔ:l'raundə^r] *n* (*Brit*): **to be a good ~** essere bravo(-a) in tutto
allspice ['ɔ:lspaɪs] *n* pepe *m* della Giamaica
all-time ['ɔ:l'taɪm] *adj* (*record*) assoluto(-a)
allude [ə'lu:d] *vi*: **to ~ to** alludere a
alluring [ə'ljuərɪŋ] *adj* seducente
allusion [ə'lu:ʒən] *n* allusione *f*
alluvium [ə'lu:vɪəm] *n* materiale *m* alluvionale
ally *n* ['ælaɪ] alleato ■ *vt* [ə'laɪ]: **to ~ o.s. with** allearsi con
almighty [ɔ:l'maɪtɪ] *adj* onnipotente
almond ['ɑ:mənd] *n* mandorla
almost ['ɔ:lməust] *adv* quasi; **he ~ fell** per poco non è caduto
alms [ɑ:mz] *n* elemosina
aloft [ə'lɔft] *adv* in alto; (*Naut*) sull'alberatura
alone [ə'ləun] *adj, adv* solo(-a); **to leave sb ~** lasciare qn in pace; **to leave sth ~** lasciare stare qc; **let ~ ...** figuriamoci poi ..., tanto meno ...
along [ə'lɔŋ] *prep* lungo ■ *adv*: **is he coming ~?** viene con noi?; **he was hopping/ limping ~** veniva saltellando/zoppicando; **~ with** insieme con
alongside [ə'lɔŋ'saɪd] *prep* accanto a; lungo ■ *adv* accanto; (*Naut*) sottobordo; **we brought our boat ~** (*of a pier/shore etc*) abbiamo accostato la barca (al molo/alla riva *etc*
aloof [ə'lu:f] *adj* distaccato(-a) ■ *adv* a distanza, in disparte; **to stand ~** tenersi a distanza *or* in disparte
aloofness [ə'lu:fnɪs] *n* distacco, riserbo
aloud [ə'laud] *adv* ad alta voce
alphabet ['ælfəbɛt] *n* alfabeto
alphabetical [ælfə'bɛtɪkəl] *adj* alfabetico(-a); **in ~ order** in ordine alfabetico
alphanumeric [ælfənju:'mɛrɪk] *adj* alfanumerico(-a)
alpine ['ælpaɪn] *adj* alpino(-a); **~ hut** rifugio alpino; **~ pasture** pascolo alpestre; **~ skiing** sci alpino
Alps [ælps] *npl*: **the ~** le Alpi
already [ɔ:l'rɛdɪ] *adv* già
alright ['ɔ:l'raɪt] *adv* (*Brit*) = **all right**
Alsatian [æl'seɪʃən] *n* (*Brit: dog*) pastore *m* tedesco, (cane *m*) lupo
also ['ɔ:lsəu] *adv* anche
Alta. *abbr* (*Canada*) = **Alberta**

altar [ˈɔltəʳ] *n* altare *m*
alter [ˈɔltəʳ] *vt, vi* alterare
alteration [ɔltəˈreɪʃən] *n* modificazione *f*, alterazione *f*; **alterations** (*Sewing, Archit*) modifiche *fpl*; **timetable subject to ~** orario soggetto a variazioni
altercation [ɔːltəˈkeɪʃən] *n* alterco, litigio
alternate *adj* [ɔlˈtəːnɪt] alterno(-a) ■ *vi* [ˈɔltəːneɪt] alternare; **on ~ days** ogni due giorni
alternately [ɔlˈtəːnɪtlɪ] *adv* alternatamente
alternating current [ˈɔltəneɪtɪŋ-] *n* corrente *f* alternata
alternative [ɔlˈtəːnətɪv] *adj* (*solutions*) alternativo(-a); (*solution*) altro(-a) ■ *n* (*choice*) alternativa; (*other possibility*) altra possibilità
alternatively [ɔlˈtəːnətɪvlɪ] *adv* altrimenti, come alternativa
alternative medicine *n* medicina alternativa
alternator [ˈɔltəːneɪtəʳ] *n* (*Aut*) alternatore *m*
although [ɔːlˈðəu] *conj* benché *+sub*, sebbene *+sub*
altitude [ˈæltɪtjuːd] *n* altitudine *f*
alto [ˈæltəu] *n* contralto
altogether [ɔːltəˈgɛðəʳ] *adv* del tutto, completamente; (*on the whole*) tutto considerato; (*in all*) in tutto; **how much is that ~?** quant'è in tutto?
altruism [ˈæltruɪzəm] *n* altruismo
altruistic [æltruˈɪstɪk] *adj* altruistico(-a)
aluminium [æljuˈmɪnɪəm], (*US*) **aluminum** [əˈluːmɪnəm] *n* alluminio
always [ˈɔːlweɪz] *adv* sempre
Alzheimer's [ˈæltshaɪməz] *n* (*also:* **Alzheimer's disease**) morbo di Alzheimer
AM *abbr* (*= amplitude modulation*) AM ■ *n abbr* (*= Assembly Member*) deputato gallese
am [æm] *vb see* **be**
a.m. *adv abbr* (*= ante meridiem*) della mattina
AMA *n abbr* = **American Medical Association**
amalgam [əˈmælgəm] *n* amalgama *m*
amalgamate [əˈmælgəmeɪt] *vt* amalgamare ■ *vi* amalgamarsi
amalgamation [əmælgəˈmeɪʃən] *n* amalgamazione *f*; (*Comm*) fusione *f*
amass [əˈmæs] *vt* ammassare
amateur [ˈæmətəʳ] *n* dilettante *m/f* ■ *adj* (*Sport*) dilettante; **~ dramatics** *n* filodrammatica
amateurish [ˈæmətərɪʃ] *adj* (*pej*) da dilettante
amaze [əˈmeɪz] *vt* stupire; **to be amazed (at)** essere sbalordito(-a) (da)
amazement [əˈmeɪzmənt] *n* stupore *m*
amazing [əˈmeɪzɪŋ] *adj* sorprendente, sbalorditivo(-a); (*bargain, offer*) sensazionale
amazingly [əˈmeɪzɪŋlɪ] *adv* incredibilmente, sbalorditivamente
Amazon [ˈæməzən] *n* (*Mythology*) Amazzone *f*; (*river*): **the ~** il Rio delle Amazzoni ■ *cpd* (*basin, jungle*) amazzonico(-a)
Amazonian [æməˈzəunɪən] *adj* amazzonico(-a)
ambassador [æmˈbæsədəʳ] *n* ambasciatore(-trice)
amber [ˈæmbəʳ] *n* ambra; **at ~** (*Brit Aut*) giallo
ambidextrous [æmbɪˈdɛkstrəs] *adj* ambidestro(-a)
ambience [ˈæmbɪəns] *n* ambiente *m*
ambiguity [æmbɪˈgjuɪtɪ] *n* ambiguità *f inv*
ambiguous [æmˈbɪgjuəs] *adj* ambiguo(-a)
ambition [æmˈbɪʃən] *n* ambizione *f*; **to achieve one's ~** realizzare le proprie aspirazioni *or* ambizioni
ambitious [æmˈbɪʃəs] *adj* ambizioso(-a)
ambivalent [æmˈbɪvələnt] *adj* ambivalente
amble [ˈæmbl] *vi* (*also:* **to amble along**) camminare tranquillamente
ambulance [ˈæmbjuləns] *n* ambulanza
ambush [ˈæmbuʃ] *n* imboscata ■ *vt* fare un'imboscata a
ameba [əˈmiːbə] *n* (*US*) = **amoeba**
ameliorate [əˈmiːlɪəreɪt] *vt* migliorare
amen [ˈɑːˈmɛn] *excl* così sia, amen
amenable [əˈmiːnəbl] *adj*: **~ to** (*advice etc*) ben disposto(-a) a
amend [əˈmɛnd] *vt* (*law*) emendare; (*text*) correggere ■ *vi* emendarsi; **to make amends** fare ammenda
amendment [əˈmɛndmənt] *n* emendamento; correzione *f*
amenities [əˈmiːnɪtɪz] *npl* attrezzature *fpl* ricreative e culturali
amenity [əˈmiːnɪtɪ] *n* amenità *f inv*
America [əˈmɛrɪkə] *n* America
American [əˈmɛrɪkən] *adj, n* americano(-a)
americanize [əˈmɛrɪkənaɪz] *vt* americanizzare
amethyst [ˈæmɪθɪst] *n* ametista
Amex [ˈæmɛks] *n abbr* = **American Stock Exchange**
amiable [ˈeɪmɪəbl] *adj* amabile, gentile
amicable [ˈæmɪkəbl] *adj* amichevole
amicably [ˈæmɪkəblɪ] *adv*: **to part ~** lasciarsi senza rancori
amid [əˈmɪd], **amidst** [əˈmɪdst] *prep* fra, tra, in mezzo a
amiss [əˈmɪs] *adj, adv*: **there's something ~** c'è qualcosa che non va bene; **don't take it ~** non avertene a male
ammo [ˈæməu] *n abbr* (*col*) = **ammunition**
ammonia [əˈməunɪə] *n* ammoniaca
ammunition [æmjuˈnɪʃən] *n* munizioni *fpl*; (*fig*) arma
ammunition dump *n* deposito di munizioni

amnesia [æmˈni:zɪə] *n* amnesia
amnesty [ˈæmnɪstɪ] *n* amnistia; **to grant an ~ to** concedere l'amnistia a, amnistiare
Amnesty International *n* Amnesty International *f*
amoeba, (US) **ameba** [əˈmi:bə] *n* ameba
amok [əˈmɔk] *adv*: **to run ~** diventare pazzo(-a) furioso(-a)
among [əˈmʌŋ], **amongst** [əˈmʌŋst] *prep* fra, tra, in mezzo a
amoral [eɪˈmɔrəl] *adj* amorale
amorous [ˈæmərəs] *adj* amoroso(-a)
amorphous [əˈmɔ:fəs] *adj* amorfo(-a)
amortization [əmɔ:taɪˈzeɪʃən] *n* (*Comm*) ammortamento
amount [əˈmaunt] *n* (*sum of money*) somma; (*of bill etc*) importo; (*quantity*) quantità *f inv* ■ *vi*: **to ~ to** (*total*) ammontare a; (*be same as*) essere come; **this amounts to a refusal** questo equivale a un rifiuto
amp [ˈæmp], **ampère** [ˈæmpɛəʳ] *n* ampere *m inv*; **a 13 ~ plug** una spina con fusibile da 13 ampere
ampersand [ˈæmpəsænd] *n* e *f* commerciale
amphetamine [æmˈfɛtəmi:n] *n* anfetamina
amphibian [æmˈfɪbɪən] *n* anfibio
amphibious [æmˈfɪbɪəs] *adj* anfibio(-a)
amphitheatre, (US) **amphitheater** [ˈæmfɪθɪətəʳ] *n* anfiteatro
ample [ˈæmpl] *adj* ampio(-a); spazioso(-a); (*enough*): **this is ~** questo è più che sufficiente; **to have ~ time/room** avere assai tempo/posto
amplifier [ˈæmplɪfaɪəʳ] *n* amplificatore *m*
amplify [ˈæmplɪfaɪ] *vt* amplificare
amply [ˈæmplɪ] *adv* ampiamente
ampoule, (US) **ampule** [ˈæmpu:l] *n* (*Med*) fiala
amputate [ˈæmpjuteɪt] *vt* amputare
amputee [æmpjuˈti:] *n* mutilato(-a), chi ha subito un'amputazione
Amsterdam [æmstəˈdæm] *n* Amsterdam *f*
amt *abbr* = **amount**
amuck [əˈmʌk] *adv* = **amok**
amuse [əˈmju:z] *vt* divertire; **to ~ o.s. with sth/by doing sth** divertirsi con qc/a fare qc; **to be amused at** essere divertito da; **he was not amused** non l'ha trovato divertente
amusement [əˈmju:zmənt] *n* divertimento; **much to my ~** con mio grande spasso
amusement arcade *n* sala giochi (*solo con macchinette a gettoni*)
amusement park *n* luna park *m inv*
amusing [əˈmju:zɪŋ] *adj* divertente
an [æn, ən, n] *indef art see* **a**
ANA *n abbr* = **American Newspaper Association**; **American Nurses Association**
anachronism [əˈnækrənɪzəm] *n* anacronismo
anaemia [əˈni:mɪə] *n* anemia
anaemic [əˈni:mɪk] *adj* anemico(-a)
anaesthetic [ænɪsˈθɛtɪk] *adj* anestetico(-a) ■ *n* anestetico; **local/general ~** anestesia locale/totale; **under the ~** sotto anestesia
anaesthetist [æˈni:sθɪtɪst] *n* anestesista *m/f*
anagram [ˈænəgræm] *n* anagramma *m*
anal [ˈeɪnl] *adj* anale
analgesic [ænælˈdʒi:sɪk] *adj* analgesico(-a) ■ *n* analgesico
analog, analogue [ˈænəlɔg] *adj* (*watch, computer*) analogico(-a)
analogous [əˈnæləgəs] *adj*: **~ to** *or* **with** analogo(-a) a
analogy [əˈnælədʒɪ] *n* analogia; **to draw an ~ between** fare un'analogia tra
analyse [ˈænəlaɪz] *vt* (*Brit*) analizzare
analysis (*pl* **analyses**) [əˈnæləsɪs, -si:z] *n* analisi *f inv*; **in the last ~** in ultima analisi
analyst [ˈænəlɪst] *n* (*political analyst etc*) analista *m/f*; (US) (psic)analista *m/f*
analytic [ænəˈlɪtɪk], **analytical** [ænəˈlɪtɪkl] *adj* analitico(-a)
analyze [ˈænəlaɪz] *vt* (US) = **analyse**
anarchic [æˈnɑ:kɪk] *adj* anarchico(-a)
anarchist [ˈænəkɪst] *adj, n* anarchico(-a)
anarchy [ˈænəkɪ] *n* anarchia
anathema [əˈnæθɪmə] *n*: **it is ~ to him** non ne vuol neanche sentir parlare
anatomical [ænəˈtɔmɪkl] *adj* anatomico(-a)
anatomy [əˈnætəmɪ] *n* anatomia
ANC *n abbr* = **African National Congress**
ancestor [ˈænsɪstəʳ] *n* antenato(-a)
ancestral [ænˈsɛstrəl] *adj* avito(-a)
ancestry [ˈænsɪstrɪ] *n* antenati *mpl*; ascendenza
anchor [ˈæŋkəʳ] *n* ancora ■ *vi* (*also*: **to drop anchor**) gettare l'ancora ■ *vt* ancorare; **to weigh ~** salpare *or* levare l'ancora
anchorage [ˈæŋkərɪdʒ] *n* ancoraggio
anchor man *n* (*TV, Radio*) anchorman *m inv*
anchor woman *n* (*TV, Radio*) anchorwoman *f inv*
anchovy [ˈæntʃəvɪ] *n* acciuga
ancient [ˈeɪnʃənt] *adj* antico(-a); (*fig*) anziano(-a); **~ monument** monumento storico
ancillary [ænˈsɪlərɪ] *adj* ausiliario(-a)
and [ænd] *conj* e (*often 'ed' before vowel*); **~ so on** e così via; **try ~ do it** prova a farlo; **come ~ sit here** vieni a sedere qui; **better ~ better** sempre meglio; **more ~ more** sempre di più
Andes [ˈændi:z] *npl*: **the ~** le Ande
Andorra [ænˈdɔ:rə] *n* Andorra
anecdote [ˈænɪkdəut] *n* aneddoto
anemia *etc* [əˈni:mɪə] = **anaemia** *etc*
anemone [əˈnɛmənɪ] *n* (*Bot*) anemone *m*; (*sea anemone*) anemone *m* di mare, attinia

anesthetic *etc* [ænɪs'θɛtɪk] = **anaesthetic** *etc*
anew [ə'nju:] *adv* di nuovo
angel ['eɪndʒəl] *n* angelo
angel dust *n sedativo usato a scopo allucinogeno*
anger ['æŋgəʳ] *n* rabbia ■ *vt* arrabbiare
angina [æn'dʒaɪnə] *n* angina pectoris
angle ['æŋgl] *n* angolo ■ *vi*: **to ~ for** (*fig*) cercare di avere; **from their ~** dal loro punto di vista
angler ['æŋgləʳ] *n* pescatore *m* con la lenza
Anglican ['æŋglɪkən] *adj, n* anglicano(-a)
anglicize ['æŋglɪsaɪz] *vt* anglicizzare
angling ['æŋglɪŋ] *n* pesca con la lenza
Anglo- ['æŋgləu] *prefix* anglo...; **~Italian** *adj, n* italobritannico(-a)
Anglo-Saxon ['æŋgləu'sæksən] *adj, n* anglosassone *m/f*
Angola [æŋ'gəulə] *n* Angola
Angolan [æŋ'gəulən] *adj, n* angolano(-a)
angrily ['æŋgrɪlɪ] *adv* con rabbia
angry ['æŋgrɪ] *adj* arrabbiato(-a), furioso(-a); **to be ~ with sb/at sth** essere in collera con qn/per qc; **to get ~** arrabbiarsi; **to make sb ~** fare arrabbiare qn
anguish ['æŋgwɪʃ] *n* angoscia
anguished ['æŋgwɪʃt] *adj* angosciato(-a), pieno(-a) d'angoscia
angular ['æŋgjuləʳ] *adj* angolare
animal ['ænɪməl] *adj, n* animale *m*
animal rights *npl* diritti *mpl* degli animali
animate *vt* ['ænɪmeɪt] animare ■ *adj* ['ænɪmɪt] animato(-a)
animated ['ænɪmeɪtɪd] *adj* animato(-a)
animation [ænɪ'meɪʃən] *n* animazione *f*
animosity [ænɪ'mɔsɪtɪ] *n* animosità
aniseed ['ænɪsi:d] *n* semi *mpl* di anice
Ankara ['æŋkərə] *n* Ankara
ankle ['æŋkl] *n* caviglia
ankle socks *npl* calzini *mpl*
annex *n* ['ænɛks] (*Brit*: *also*: **annexe**) edificio annesso ■ *vt* [ə'nɛks] annettere
annexation [ænɛk'seɪʃən] *n* annessione *f*
annihilate [ə'naɪəleɪt] *vt* annientare
annihilation [ənaɪə'leɪʃən] *n* annientamento
anniversary [ænɪ'və:sərɪ] *n* anniversario
anniversary dinner *n* cena commemorativa
annotate ['ænəuteɪt] *vt* annotare
announce [ə'nauns] *vt* annunciare; **he announced that he wasn't going** ha dichiarato che non (ci) sarebbe andato
announcement [ə'naunsmənt] *n* annuncio; (*letter, card*) partecipazione *f*; **I'd like to make an ~** ho una comunicazione da fare
announcer [ə'naunsəʳ] *n* (*Radio, TV*: *between programmes*) annunciatore(-trice); (*: in a programme*) presentatore(-trice)
annoy [ə'nɔɪ] *vt* dare fastidio a; **to be annoyed (at sth/with sb)** essere seccato *or* irritato (per qc/con qn); **don't get annoyed!** non irritarti!
annoyance [ə'nɔɪəns] *n* fastidio; (*cause of annoyance*) noia
annoying [ə'nɔɪɪŋ] *adj* irritante, seccante
annual ['ænjuəl] *adj* annuale ■ *n* (*Bot*) pianta annua; (*book*) annuario
annual general meeting *n* (*Brit*) assemblea generale
annually ['ænjuəlɪ] *adv* annualmente
annual report *n* relazione *f* annuale
annuity [ə'nju:ɪtɪ] *n* annualità *f inv*; **life ~** vitalizio
annul [ə'nʌl] *vt* annullare; (*law*) rescindere
annulment [ə'nʌlmənt] *n* annullamento; rescissione *f*
annum ['ænəm] *n see* **per annum**
Annunciation [ənʌnsɪ'eɪʃən] *n* Annunciazione *f*
anode ['ænəud] *n* anodo
anoint [ə'nɔɪnt] *vt* ungere
anomalous [ə'nɔmələs] *adj* anomalo(-a)
anomaly [ə'nɔməlɪ] *n* anomalia
anon. [ə'nɔn] *abbr* = **anonymous**
anonymity [ænə'nɪmɪtɪ] *n* anonimato
anonymous [ə'nɔnɪməs] *adj* anonimo(-a); **to remain ~** mantenere l'anonimato
anorak ['ænəræk] *n* giacca a vento
anorexia [ænə'rɛksɪə] *n* (*also*: **anorexia nervosa**) anoressia
anorexic [ænə'rɛksɪk] *adj, n* anoressico(-a)
another [ə'nʌðəʳ] *adj*: **~ book** (*one more*) un altro libro, ancora un libro; (*a different one*) un altro libro ■ *pron* un altro/un'altra, ancora uno(-a); **~ drink?** ancora qualcosa da bere?; **in ~ 5 years** fra altri 5 anni; *see also* **one**
ANSI *n abbr* (*= American National Standards Institution*) *Istituto americano di standardizzazione*
answer ['ɑ:nsəʳ] *n* risposta; soluzione *f* ■ *vi* rispondere ■ *vt* (*reply to*) rispondere a; (*problem*) risolvere; (*prayer*) esaudire; **in ~ to your letter** in risposta alla sua lettera; **to ~ the phone** rispondere (al telefono); **to ~ the bell** rispondere al campanello; **to ~ the door** aprire la porta
▸ **answer back** *vi* ribattere
▸ **answer for** *vt fus* essere responsabile di
▸ **answer to** *vt fus* (*description*) corrispondere a
answerable ['ɑ:nsərəbl] *adj*: **~ (to sb/for sth)** responsabile (verso qn/di qc); **I am ~ to no-one** non devo rispondere a nessuno
answering machine ['ɑ:nsərɪŋ-] *n* segreteria (telefonica) automatica
ant [ænt] *n* formica
ANTA *n abbr* = **American National Theater and Academy**

antagonism [æn'tægənɪzəm] *n* antagonismo
antagonist [æn'tægənɪst] *n* antagonista *m/f*
antagonistic [æntægə'nɪstɪk] *adj* antagonistico(-a)
antagonize [æn'tægənaɪz] *vt* provocare l'ostilità di
Antarctic [ænt'ɑ:ktɪk] *n*: **the ~** l'Antartide *f* ■ *adj* antartico(-a)
Antarctica [ænt'ɑ:ktɪkə] *n* Antartide *f*
Antarctic Circle *n* Circolo polare antartico
Antarctic Ocean *n* Oceano antartico
ante ['æntɪ] *n* (*Cards, fig*): **to up the ~** alzare la posta in palio
ante... ['æntɪ] *prefix* anti..., ante..., pre...
anteater ['ænti:tə^r] *n* formichiere *m*
antecedent [æntɪ'si:dənt] *n* antecedente *m*, precedente *m*
antechamber ['æntɪtʃeɪmbə^r] *n* anticamera
antelope ['æntɪləup] *n* antilope *f*
antenatal ['æntɪ'neɪtl] *adj* prenatale
antenatal clinic *n* assistenza medica preparto
antenna (*pl* **antennae**) [æn'tɛnə, -ni:] *n* antenna
anthem ['ænθəm] *n* antifona; **national ~** inno nazionale
ant-hill ['ænthɪl] *n* formicaio
anthology [æn'θɔlədʒɪ] *n* antologia
anthropologist [ænθrə'pɔlədʒɪst] *n* antropologo(-a)
anthropology [ænθrə'pɔlədʒɪ] *n* antropologia
anti- ['æntɪ] *prefix* anti...
anti-aircraft ['æntɪ'ɛəkrɑ:ft] *adj* antiaereo(-a)
antiballistic ['æntɪbə'lɪstɪk] *adj* antibalistico(-a)
antibiotic ['æntɪbaɪ'ɔtɪk] *adj* antibiotico(-a) ■ *n* antibiotico
antibody ['æntɪbɔdɪ] *n* anticorpo
anticipate [æn'tɪsɪpeɪt] *vt* prevedere; pregustare; (*wishes, request*) prevenire; **as anticipated** come previsto; **this is worse than I anticipated** è peggio di quel che immaginavo *or* pensavo
anticipation [æntɪsɪ'peɪʃən] *n* anticipazione *f*; (*expectation*) aspettative *fpl*; **thanking you in ~** vi ringrazio in anticipo
anticlimax ['æntɪ'klaɪmæks] *n*: **it was an ~** fu una completa delusione
anticlockwise ['æntɪ'klɔkwaɪz] *adj* in senso antiorario
antics ['æntɪks] *npl* buffonerie *fpl*
anticyclone ['æntɪ'saɪkləun] *n* anticiclone *m*
antidote ['æntɪdəut] *n* antidoto
antifreeze ['æntɪfri:z] *n* anticongelante *m*
anti-globalization [æntɪgləubəlaɪ'zeɪʃən] *adj* antiglobalizzazione *inv*
antihistamine [æntɪ'hɪstəmɪn] *n* antistaminico
Antilles [æn'tɪli:z] *npl*: **the ~** le Antille
antipathy [æn'tɪpəθɪ] *n* antipatia
antiperspirant ['æntɪ'pə:spərənt] *adj* antitraspirante
Antipodean [æntɪpə'di:ən] *adj* degli Antipodi
Antipodes [æn'tɪpədi:z] *npl*: **the ~** gli Antipodi
antiquarian [æntɪ'kwɛərɪən] *adj*: **~ bookshop** libreria antiquaria ■ *n* antiquario(-a)
antiquated ['æntɪkweɪtɪd] *adj* antiquato(-a)
antique [æn'ti:k] *n* antichità *f inv* ■ *adj* antico(-a)
antique dealer *n* antiquario(-a)
antique shop *n* negozio d'antichità
antiquity [æn'tɪkwɪtɪ] *n* antichità *f inv*
anti-semitic ['æntɪsɪ'mɪtɪk] *adj* antisemitico(-a), antisemita
anti-semitism ['æntɪ'sɛmɪtɪzəm] *n* antisemitismo
antiseptic [æntɪ'sɛptɪk] *adj* antisettico(-a) ■ *n* antisettico
antisocial ['æntɪ'səuʃəl] *adj* asociale; (*against society*) antisociale
antitank [æntɪ'tæŋk] *adj* anticarro *inv*
antithesis (*pl* **antitheses**) [æn'tɪθɪsɪs, -si:z] *n* antitesi *f inv*; (*contrast*) carattere *m* antitetico
anti-trust [æntɪ'trʌst] *adj* (*Comm*): **~ legislation** legislazione *f* antitrust *inv*
antiviral [æntɪ'vaɪərəl] *adj* (*Med*) antivirale
antivirus [æntɪ'vaɪərəs] *adj* (*Comput*) antivirus *inv*; **~ software** antivirus *m inv*
antlers ['æntləz] *npl* palchi *mpl*
Antwerp ['æntwə:p] *n* Anversa
anus ['eɪnəs] *n* ano
anvil ['ænvɪl] *n* incudine *f*
anxiety [æŋ'zaɪətɪ] *n* ansia; (*keenness*): **~ to do** smania di fare
anxious ['æŋkʃəs] *adj* ansioso(-a), inquieto(-a); (*keen*): **~ to do/that** impaziente di fare/che + *sub*; **I'm very ~ about you** sono molto preoccupato *or* in pensiero per te
anxiously ['æŋkʃəslɪ] *adv* ansiosamente, con ansia

KEYWORD

any ['ɛnɪ] *adj* **1** (*in questions etc*): **have you any butter?** hai del burro?, hai un po' di burro?; **have you any children?** hai bambini?; **if there are any tickets left** se ci sono ancora (dei) biglietti, se c'è ancora qualche biglietto
2 (*with negative*): **I haven't any money/books** non ho soldi/libri; **without any difficulty** senza nessuna *or* alcuna difficoltà
3 (*no matter which*) qualsiasi, qualunque;

choose any book you like scegli un libro qualsiasi
4 (*in phrases*): **in any case** in ogni caso; **any day now** da un giorno all'altro; **at any moment** in qualsiasi momento, da un momento all'altro; **at any rate** ad ogni modo
■ *pron* **1** (*in questions, with negative*): **have you got any?** ne hai?; **can any of you sing?** qualcuno di voi sa cantare?; **I haven't any (of them)** non ne ho
2 (*no matter which one(s)*): **take any of those books (you like)** prendi uno qualsiasi di quei libri
■ *adv* **1** (*in questions etc*): **do you want any more soup/sandwiches?** vuoi ancora un po' di minestra/degli altri panini?; **are you feeling any better?** ti senti meglio?
2 (*with negative*): **I can't hear him any more** non lo sento più; **don't wait any longer** non aspettare più

anybody ['ɛnɪbɔdɪ] *pron* qualsiasi persona; (*in interrogative sentences*) qualcuno; (*in negative sentences*): **I don't see ~** non vedo nessuno
anyhow ['ɛnɪhau] *adv* in qualsiasi modo; (*haphazardly*) come capita; **I shall go ~** ci andrò lo stesso *or* comunque
anyone ['ɛnɪwʌn] *pron* = **anybody**
anyplace ['ɛnɪpleɪs] *adv* (*US col*) = **anywhere**
anything ['ɛnɪθɪŋ] *pron* qualsiasi cosa; (*in interrogative sentences*) qualcosa; (*in negative sentences*) non ... niente, non ... nulla; **~ else?** (*in shop*) basta (così)?; **it can cost ~ between £15 and £20** può costare qualcosa come 15 o 20 sterline
anytime ['ɛnɪtaɪm] *adv* in qualunque momento; quando vuole
anyway ['ɛnɪweɪ] *adv* in *or* ad ogni modo
anywhere ['ɛnɪwɛəʳ] *adv* da qualsiasi parte; (*in interrogative sentences*) da qualche parte; **I don't see him ~** non lo vedo da nessuna parte; **~ in the world** dovunque nel mondo
Anzac ['ænzæk] *n abbr* (= *Australia-New Zealand Army Corps*) A.N.Z.A.C. *m*; (*soldier*) soldato dell'A.N.Z.A.C.; *vedi nota*

ANZAC DAY

L' *Anzac Day* è una festa nazionale australiana e neozelandese che cade il 25 aprile e commemora il famoso sbarco delle forze armate congiunte dei due paesi a Gallipoli nel 1915, durante la prima guerra mondiale.

apart [ə'pɑːt] *adv* (*to one side*) a parte; (*separately*) separatamente; **with one's legs ~** con le gambe divaricate; **10 miles/a long way ~** a 10 miglia di distanza/molto lontani l'uno dall'altro; **they are living ~** sono separati; **~ from** *prep* a parte, eccetto
apartheid [ə'pɑːteɪt] *n* apartheid *f*
apartment [ə'pɑːtmənt] *n* (*US*) appartamento; **apartments** *npl* appartamento ammobiliato
apartment building *n* (*US*) stabile *m*, caseggiato
apathetic [æpə'θɛtɪk] *adj* apatico(-a)
apathy ['æpəθɪ] *n* apatia
APB *n abbr* (*US: = all points bulletin: police expression*) *espressione della polizia che significa "trovate e arrestate il sospetto"*
ape [eɪp] *n* scimmia ■ *vt* scimmiottare
Apennines ['æpənaɪnz] *npl*: **the ~** gli Apennini
aperitif [ə'pɛrɪtiːf] *n* aperitivo
aperture ['æpətʃjuəʳ] *n* apertura
APEX ['eɪpɛks] *n abbr* (*Aviat: = advance purchase excursion*) APEX *m inv*
apex ['eɪpɛks] *n* apice *m*
aphid ['æfɪd] *n* afide *f*
aphrodisiac [æfrəu'dɪzɪæk] *adj* afrodisiaco(-a) ■ *n* afrodisiaco
API *n abbr* = **American Press Institute**
apiece [ə'piːs] *adv* ciascuno(-a)
aplomb [ə'plɔm] *n* disinvoltura
APO *n abbr* (*US: = Army Post Office*) *ufficio postale dell'esercito*
apocalypse [ə'pɔkəlɪps] *n* apocalisse *f*
apolitical [eɪpə'lɪtɪkl] *adj* apolitico(-a)
apologetic [əpɔlə'dʒɛtɪk] *adj* (*tone, letter*) di scusa; **to be very ~ about** scusarsi moltissimo di
apologetically [əpɔlə'dʒɛtɪkəlɪ] *adv* per scusarsi
apologize [ə'pɔlədʒaɪz] *vi*: **to ~ (for sth to sb)** scusarsi (di qc a qn), chiedere scusa (a qn per qc)
apology [ə'pɔlədʒɪ] *n* scuse *fpl*; **please accept my apologies** la prego di accettare le mie scuse
apoplectic [æpə'plɛktɪk] *adj* (*Med*) apoplettico(-a); **~ with rage** (*col*) livido(-a) per la rabbia
apoplexy ['æpəplɛksɪ] *n* apoplessia
apostle [ə'pɔsl] *n* apostolo
apostrophe [ə'pɔstrəfɪ] *n* (*sign*) apostrofo
app *n abbr* (*Comput*) = **application**
appal [ə'pɔːl] *vt* atterrire; sgomentare
Appalachian Mountains [æpə'leɪʃən-] *npl*: **the ~** i Monti Appalachi
appalling [ə'pɔːlɪŋ] *adj* spaventoso(-a); **she's an ~ cook** è un disastro come cuoca
apparatus [æpə'reɪtəs] *n* apparato
apparel [ə'pærl] *n* (*US*) abbigliamento, confezioni *fpl*

apparent [ə'pærənt] *adj* evidente
apparently [ə'pærəntlɪ] *adv* evidentemente, a quanto pare
apparition [æpə'rɪʃən] *n* apparizione *f*
appeal [ə'pi:l] *vi* (*Law*) appellarsi alla legge ■ *n* (*Law*) appello; (*request*) richiesta; (*charm*) attrattiva; **to ~ for** chiedere (con insistenza); **to ~ to** (*person*) appellarsi a; (*thing*) piacere a; **to ~ to sb for mercy** chiedere pietà a qn; **it doesn't ~ to me** mi dice poco; **right of ~** diritto d'appello
appealing [ə'pi:lɪŋ] *adj* (*moving*) commovente; (*attractive*) attraente
appear [ə'pɪə^r] *vi* apparire; (*Law*) comparire; (*publication*) essere pubblicato(-a); (*seem*) sembrare; **it would ~ that** sembra che; **to ~ in Hamlet** recitare nell'Amleto; **to ~ on TV** presentarsi in televisione
appearance [ə'pɪərəns] *n* apparizione *f*; (*look, aspect*) aspetto; **to put in** *or* **make an ~** fare atto di presenza; **by order of ~** (*Theat*) in ordine di apparizione; **to keep up appearances** salvare le apparenze; **to all appearances** a giudicar dalle apparenze
appease [ə'pi:z] *vt* calmare, appagare
appeasement [ə'pi:zmənt] *n* (*Pol*) appeasement *m inv*
append [ə'pɛnd] *vt* (*Comput*) aggiungere in coda
appendage [ə'pɛndɪdʒ] *n* aggiunta
appendicitis [əpɛndɪ'saɪtɪs] *n* appendicite *f*
appendix (*pl* **appendices**) [ə'pɛndɪks, -si:z] *n* appendice *f*; **to have one's ~ out** operarsi *or* farsi operare di appendicite
appetite ['æpɪtaɪt] *n* appetito; **that walk has given me an ~** la passeggiata mi ha messo appetito
appetizer ['æpɪtaɪzə^r] *n* (*food*) stuzzichino; (*drink*) aperitivo
appetizing ['æpɪtaɪzɪŋ] *adj* appetitoso(-a)
applaud [ə'plɔ:d] *vt, vi* applaudire
applause [ə'plɔ:z] *n* applauso
apple ['æpl] *n* mela; (*also*: **apple tree**) melo; **the ~ of one's eye** la pupilla dei propri occhi
apple turnover *n* sfogliatella alle mele
appliance [ə'plaɪəns] *n* apparecchio; **electrical appliances** elettrodomestici *mpl*
applicable [ə'plɪkəbl] *adj* applicabile; **to be ~ to** essere valido per; **the law is ~ from January** la legge entrerà in vigore in gennaio
applicant ['æplɪkənt] *n* candidato(-a); (*Admin: for benefit etc*) chi ha fatto domanda *or* richiesta
application [æplɪ'keɪʃən] *n* applicazione *f*; (*for a job, a grant etc*) domanda; (*Comput*) applicazione *f*; **on ~** su richiesta
application form *n* modulo di domanda
application program *n* (*Comput*) programma applicativo
applications package *n* (*Comput*) software *m inv* applicativo
applied [ə'plaɪd] *adj* applicato(-a); **~ arts** arti *fpl* applicate
apply [ə'plaɪ] *vt*: **to ~ (to)** (*paint, ointment*) dare (a); (*theory, technique*) applicare (a) ■ *vi*: **to ~ to** (*ask*) rivolgersi a; (*be suitable for, relevant to*) riguardare, riferirsi a; **to ~ (for)** (*permit, grant, job*) fare domanda (per); **to ~ the brakes** frenare; **to ~ o.s. to** dedicarsi a
appoint [ə'pɔɪnt] *vt* nominare
appointee [əpɔɪn'ti:] *n* incaricato(-a)
appointment [ə'pɔɪntmənt] *n* nomina; (*arrangement to meet*) appuntamento; **by ~** su *or* per appuntamento; **to make an ~ with sb** prendere un appuntamento con qn; (*Press*): **"appointments (vacant)"** "offerte *fpl* di impiego"
apportion [ə'pɔ:ʃən] *vt* attribuire
appraisal [ə'preɪzl] *n* valutazione *f*
appraise [ə'preɪz] *vt* (*value*) valutare, fare una stima di; (*situation etc*) fare il bilancio di
appreciable [ə'pri:ʃəbl] *adj* apprezzabile
appreciably [ə'pri:ʃəblɪ] *adv* notevolmente, sensibilmente
appreciate [ə'pri:ʃɪeɪt] *vt* (*like*) apprezzare; (*be grateful for*) essere riconoscente di; (*be aware of*) rendersi conto di ■ *vi* (*Comm*) aumentare; **I appreciated your help** ti sono grato per l'aiuto
appreciation [əpri:ʃɪ'eɪʃən] *n* apprezzamento; (*Finance*) aumento del valore
appreciative [ə'pri:ʃɪətɪv] *adj* (*person*) sensibile; (*comment*) elogiativo(-a)
apprehend [æprɪ'hɛnd] *vt* (*arrest*) arrestare; (*understand*) comprendere
apprehension [æprɪ'hɛnʃən] *n* (*fear*) inquietudine *f*
apprehensive [æprɪ'hɛnsɪv] *adj* apprensivo(-a)
apprentice [ə'prɛntɪs] *n* apprendista *m/f* ■ *vt*: **to be apprenticed to** lavorare come apprendista presso
apprenticeship [ə'prɛntɪsʃɪp] *n* apprendistato; **to serve one's ~** fare il proprio apprendistato *or* tirocinio
appro. ['æprəu] *abbr* (*Brit Comm: col*) = **approval**
approach [ə'prəutʃ] *vi* avvicinarsi ■ *vt* (*come near*) avvicinarsi a; (*ask, apply to*) rivolgersi a; (*subject, passer-by*) avvicinare ■ *n* approccio; accesso; (*to problem*) modo di affrontare; **to ~ sb about sth** rivolgersi a qn per qc

approachable [ə'prəutʃəbl] *adj* accessibile
approach road *n* strada d'accesso
approbation [æprə'beɪʃən] *n* approvazione *f*, benestare *m*
appropriate *vt* [ə'prəuprɪeɪt] (*take*) appropriarsi di ■ *adj* [ə'prəuprɪɪt] appropriato(-a), adatto(-a); **it would not be ~ for me to comment** non sta a me fare dei commenti
appropriately [ə'prəuprɪɪtlɪ] *adv* in modo appropriato
appropriation [əprəuprɪ'eɪʃən] *n* stanziamento
approval [ə'pru:vəl] *n* approvazione *f*; **on ~** (*Comm*) in prova, in esame; **to meet with sb's ~** soddisfare qn, essere di gradimento di qn
approve [ə'pru:v] *vt*, *vi* approvare
▸ **approve of** *vt fus* approvare
approved school *n* (*Brit: old*) riformatorio
approvingly [ə'pru:vɪŋlɪ] *adv* in approvazione
approx. *abbr* = **approximately**
approximate *adj* [ə'prɔksɪmɪt] approssimativo(-a) ■ *vt* [ə'prɔksɪmeɪt] essere un'approssimazione di, avvicinarsi a
approximately [ə'prɔksɪmətlɪ] *adv* circa
approximation [əprɔksɪ'meɪʃən] *n* approssimazione *f*
apr *n abbr* (= *annual percentage rate*) tasso di percentuale annuo
Apr. *abbr* (= *April*) apr.
apricot ['eɪprɪkɔt] *n* albicocca
April ['eɪprəl] *n* aprile *m*; **~ fool!** pesce d'aprile!; *see also* **July**
April Fools' Day *n vedi nota*

APRIL FOOLS' DAY

April Fools' Day è il primo aprile, il giorno degli scherzi e delle burle. Il nome deriva dal fatto che, se una persona cade nella trappola che gli è stata tesa, fa la figura del fool, cioè dello sciocco. Di recente gli scherzi stanno diventando sempre più elaborati, e persino i giornalisti a volte inventano vicende incredibili per burlarsi dei lettori.

apron ['eɪprən] *n* grembiule *m*; (*Aviat*) area di stazionamento
apse [æps] *n* (*Archit*) abside *f*
APT *n abbr* (*Brit*: = *advanced passenger train*) *treno ad altissima velocità*
apt [æpt] *adj* (*suitable*) adatto(-a); (*able*) capace; (*likely*): **to be ~ to do** avere tendenza a fare
Apt. *abbr* = **apartment**
aptitude ['æptɪtju:d] *n* abilità *f inv*
aptitude test *n* test *m inv* attitudinale
aptly ['æptlɪ] *adv* appropriatamente, in modo adatto
aqualung ['ækwəlʌŋ] *n* autorespiratore *m*
aquarium [ə'kwɛərɪəm] *n* acquario
Aquarius [ə'kwɛərɪəs] *n* Acquario; **to be ~** essere dell'Acquario
aquatic [ə'kwætɪk] *adj* acquatico(-a)
aqueduct ['ækwɪdʌkt] *n* acquedotto
AR *abbr* (*US*) = **Arkansas**
ARA *n abbr* (*Brit*) = **Associate of the Royal Academy**
Arab ['ærəb] *adj*, *n* arabo(-a)
Arabia [ə'reɪbɪə] *n* Arabia
Arabian [ə'reɪbɪən] *adj* arabo(-a)
Arabian Desert *n* Deserto arabico
Arabian Sea *n* mare *m* Arabico
Arabic ['ærəbɪk] *adj* arabico(-a) ■ *n* arabo
Arabic numerals *npl* numeri *mpl* arabi, numerazione *f* araba
arable ['ærəbl] *adj* arabile
ARAM *n abbr* (*Brit*) = **Associate of the Royal Academy of Music**
arbiter ['ɑ:bɪtə^r] *n* arbitro
arbitrary ['ɑ:bɪtrərɪ] *adj* arbitrario(-a)
arbitrate ['ɑ:bɪtreɪt] *vi* arbitrare
arbitration [ɑ:bɪ'treɪʃən] *n* (*Law*) arbitrato; (*Industry*) arbitraggio
arbitrator ['ɑ:bɪtreɪtə^r] *n* arbitro
ARC *n abbr* (= *American Red Cross*) C.R.I. *f* (= *Croce Rossa Italiana*)
arc [ɑ:k] *n* arco
arcade [ɑ:'keɪd] *n* portico; (*passage with shops*) galleria
arch [ɑ:tʃ] *n* arco; (*of foot*) arco plantare ■ *vt* inarcare ■ *prefix*: **~(-)** grande (*before n*); per eccellenza
archaeological [ɑ:kɪə'lɔdʒɪkəl] *adj* archeologico(-a)
archaeologist [ɑ:kɪ'ɔlədʒɪst] *n* archeologo(-a)
archaeology [ɑ:kɪ'ɔlədʒɪ] *n* archeologia
archaic [ɑ:'keɪɪk] *adj* arcaico(-a)
archangel ['ɑ:keɪndʒəl] *n* arcangelo
archbishop [ɑ:tʃ'bɪʃəp] *n* arcivescovo
arched [ɑ:tʃt] *adj* arcuato(-a), ad arco
arch-enemy ['ɑ:tʃ'ɛnɪmɪ] *n* arcinemico(-a)
archeology *etc* [ɑ:kɪ'ɔlədʒɪ] = **archaeology** *etc*
archer ['ɑ:tʃə^r] *n* arciere *m*
archery ['ɑ:tʃərɪ] *n* tiro all'arco
archetypal ['ɑ:kɪtaɪpəl] *adj* tipico(-a)
archetype ['ɑ:kɪtaɪp] *n* archetipo
archipelago [ɑ:kɪ'pɛlɪgəu] *n* arcipelago
architect ['ɑ:kɪtɛkt] *n* architetto
architectural [ɑ:kɪ'tɛktʃərəl] *adj* architettonico(-a)
architecture ['ɑ:kɪtɛktʃə^r] *n* architettura

archive file *n* (*Comput*) file *m inv* di archivio
archives [ˈɑːkaɪvz] *npl* archivi *mpl*
archivist [ˈɑːkɪvɪst] *n* archivista *m/f*
archway [ˈɑːtʃweɪ] *n* arco
ARCM *n abbr* (*Brit*) = **Associate of the Royal College of Music**
Arctic [ˈɑːktɪk] *adj* artico(-a) ■ *n*: **the ~** l'Artico
Arctic Circle *n* Circolo polare artico
Arctic Ocean *n* Oceano artico
ARD *n abbr* (*US Med*) = **acute respiratory disease**
ardent [ˈɑːdənt] *adj* ardente
ardour, (*US*) **ardor** [ˈɑːdəʳ] *n* ardore *m*
arduous [ˈɑːdjuəs] *adj* arduo(-a)
are [ɑːʳ] *vb see* **be**
area [ˈɛərɪə] *n* (*Geom*) area; (*zone*) zona; (*: smaller*) settore *m*; **dining ~** zona pranzo; **the London ~** la zona di Londra
area code *n* (*US Tel*) prefisso
arena [əˈriːnə] *n* arena
aren't [ɑːnt] = **are not**
Argentina [ɑːdʒənˈtiːnə] *n* Argentina
Argentinian [ɑːdʒənˈtɪnɪən] *adj, n* argentino(-a)
arguable [ˈɑːgjuəbl] *adj* discutibile; **it is ~ whether ...** è una cosa discutibile se ... + *sub*
arguably [ˈɑːgjuəblɪ] *adv*: **it is ~ ...** si può sostenere che sia ...
argue [ˈɑːgjuː] *vi* (*quarrel*) litigare; (*reason*) ragionare ■ *vt* (*debate: case, matter*) dibattere; **to ~ that** sostenere che; **to ~ about sth (with sb)** litigare per *or* a proposito di qc (con qn)
argument [ˈɑːgjumənt] *n* (*reasons*) argomento; (*quarrel*) lite *f*; (*debate*) discussione *f*; **~ for/against** argomento a *or* in favore di/contro
argumentative [ɑːgjuˈmɛntətɪv] *adj* litigioso(-a)
aria [ˈɑːrɪə] *n* aria
ARIBA *n abbr* (*Brit*) = **Associate of the Royal Institute of British Architects**
arid [ˈærɪd] *adj* arido(-a)
aridity [əˈrɪdɪtɪ] *n* aridità
Aries [ˈɛərɪz] *n* Ariete *m*; **to be ~** essere dell'Ariete
arise (*pt* **arose**, *pp* **arisen**) [əˈraɪz, əˈrəuz, əˈrɪzn] *vi* alzarsi; (*opportunity, problem*) presentarsi; **to ~ from** risultare da; **should the need ~** dovesse presentarsi la necessità, in caso di necessità
aristocracy [ærɪsˈtɔkrəsɪ] *n* aristocrazia
aristocrat [ˈærɪstəkræt] *n* aristocratico(-a)
aristocratic [ærɪstəˈkrætɪk] *adj* aristocratico(-a)
arithmetic [əˈrɪθmətɪk] *n* aritmetica
arithmetical [ærɪθˈmɛtɪkəl] *adj* aritmetico(-a)
Ariz. *abbr* (*US*) = **Arizona**
ark [ɑːk] *n*: **Noah's A~** l'arca di Noè
Ark. *abbr* (*US*) = **Arkansas**
arm [ɑːm] *n* braccio; (*Mil: branch*) arma ■ *vt* armare; **~ in ~** a braccetto; *see also* **arms**
armaments [ˈɑːməmənts] *npl* (*weapons*) armamenti *mpl*
armband [ˈɑːmbænd] *n* bracciale *m*
armchair [ˈɑːmtʃɛəʳ] *n* poltrona
armed [ɑːmd] *adj* armato(-a)
armed forces *npl* forze *fpl* armate
armed robbery *n* rapina a mano armata
Armenia [ɑːˈmiːnɪə] *n* Armenia
Armenian [ɑːˈmiːnɪən] *adj* armeno(-a) ■ *n* armeno(-a); (*Ling*) armeno
armful [ˈɑːmful] *n* bracciata
armistice [ˈɑːmɪstɪs] *n* armistizio
armour, (*US*) **armor** [ˈɑːməʳ] *n* armatura; (*also*: **armour-plating**) corazza, blindatura; (*Mil: tanks*) mezzi *mpl* blindati
armoured car, (*US*) **armored car** *n* autoblinda *f inv*
armoury, (*US*) **armory** [ˈɑːmərɪ] *n* arsenale *m*
armpit [ˈɑːmpɪt] *n* ascella
armrest [ˈɑːmrɛst] *n* bracciolo
arms [ɑːmz] *npl* (*weapons*) armi *fpl*; (*Heraldry*) stemma *m*
arms control *n* controllo degli armamenti
arms race *n* corsa agli armamenti
army [ˈɑːmɪ] *n* esercito
aroma [əˈrəumə] *n* aroma
aromatherapy [ərəuməˈθɛrəpɪ] *n* aromaterapia
aromatic [ærəˈmætɪk] *adj* aromatico(-a)
arose [əˈrəuz] *pt of* **arise**
around [əˈraund] *adv* attorno, intorno ■ *prep* intorno a; (*fig: about*): **~ £5/3 o'clock** circa 5 sterline/le 3; **is he ~?** è in giro?
arousal [əˈrauzəl] *n* (*sexual etc*) eccitazione *f*; (*awakening*) risveglio
arouse [əˈrauz] *vt* (*sleeper*) svegliare; (*curiosity, passions*) suscitare
arrange [əˈreɪndʒ] *vt* sistemare; (*programme*) preparare ■ *vi*: **we have arranged for a taxi to pick you up** la faremo venire a prendere da un taxi; **it was arranged that ...** è stato deciso *or* stabilito che ...; **to ~ to do sth** mettersi d'accordo per fare qc
arrangement [əˈreɪndʒmənt] *n* sistemazione *f*; (*plans etc*); **arrangements** *npl* progetti *mpl*, piani *mpl*; **by ~** su richiesta; **to come to an ~ (with sb)** venire ad un accordo (con qn), mettersi d'accordo *or* accordarsi (con qn); **I'll make arrangements for you to be met** darò disposizioni *or* istruzioni perché ci sia qualcuno ad incontrarla
arrant [ˈærənt] *adj*: **~ nonsense** colossali sciocchezze *fpl*

array [ə'reɪ] *n* fila; (*Comput*) array *m inv*, insiemi *mpl*
arrears [ə'rɪəz] *npl* arretrati *mpl*; **to be in ~ with one's rent** essere in arretrato con l'affitto
arrest [ə'rɛst] *vt* arrestare; (*sb's attention*) attirare ■ *n* arresto; **under ~** in arresto
arresting [ə'rɛstɪŋ] *adj* (*fig*) che colpisce
arrival [ə'raɪvəl] *n* arrivo; (*person*) arrivato(-a); **new ~** nuovo venuto
arrive [ə'raɪv] *vi* arrivare
▸ **arrive at** *vt fus* arrivare a
arrogance ['ærəgəns] *n* arroganza
arrogant ['ærəgənt] *adj* arrogante
arrow ['ærəu] *n* freccia
arse [ɑːs] *n* (*Brit col!*) culo (*!*)
arsenal ['ɑːsɪnl] *n* arsenale *m*
arsenic ['ɑːsnɪk] *n* arsenico
arson ['ɑːsn] *n* incendio doloso
art [ɑːt] *n* arte *f*; (*craft*) mestiere *m*; **work of ~** opera d'arte; *see also* **arts**
artefact, (US) **artifact** ['ɑːtɪfækt] *n* manufatto
arterial [ɑː'tɪərɪəl] *adj* (*Anat*) arterioso(-a); (*road etc*) di grande comunicazione; **~ roads** le (grandi *or* principali) arterie
artery ['ɑːtərɪ] *n* arteria
artful ['ɑːtful] *adj* furbo(-a)
art gallery *n* galleria d'arte
arthritis [ɑː'θraɪtɪs] *n* artrite *f*
artichoke ['ɑːtɪtʃəuk] *n* carciofo; **Jerusalem ~** topinambur *m inv*
article ['ɑːtɪkl] *n* articolo; **articles** *npl* (*Brit Law: training*) contratto di tirocinio; **articles of clothing** indumenti *mpl*
articles of association *npl* (*Comm*) statuto sociale
articulate *adj* [ɑː'tɪkjulɪt] (*person*) che si esprime forbitamente; (*speech*) articolato(-a) ■ *vi* [ɑː'tɪkjuleɪt] articolare
articulated lorry *n* (*Brit*) autotreno
artifact ['ɑːtɪfækt] *n* (US) = **artefact**
artifice ['ɑːtɪfɪs] *n* (*cunning*) abilità, destrezza; (*trick*) artificio
artificial [ɑːtɪ'fɪʃəl] *adj* artificiale
artificial insemination [-ɪnsɛmɪ'neɪʃən] *n* fecondazione *f* artificiale
artificial intelligence *n* intelligenza artificiale
artificial respiration *n* respirazione *f* artificiale
artillery [ɑː'tɪlərɪ] *n* artiglieria
artisan ['ɑːtɪzæn] *n* artigiano(-a)
artist ['ɑːtɪst] *n* artista *m/f*
artistic [ɑː'tɪstɪk] *adj* artistico(-a)
artistry ['ɑːtɪstrɪ] *n* arte *f*
artless ['ɑːtlɪs] *adj* semplice, ingenuo(-a)
arts [ɑːts] *npl* (*Scol*) lettere *fpl*
art school *n* scuola d'arte
artwork ['ɑːtwəːk] *n* materiale *m* illustrativo
ARV *n abbr* (*= American Revised Version*) *traduzione della Bibbia*
AS *n abbr* (*US Scol: = Associate in Science*) *titolo di studio*

 KEYWORD

as [æz] *conj* **1** (*referring to time*) mentre; **as the years went by** col passare degli anni; **he came in as I was leaving** arrivò mentre stavo uscendo; **as from tomorrow** da domani
2 (*in comparisons*): **as big as** grande come; **twice as big as** due volte più grande di; **as much/many as** tanto quanto/tanti quanti; **as soon as possible** prima possibile
3 (*since, because*) dal momento che, siccome
4 (*referring to manner, way*) come; **big as it is** grande com'è; **much as I like them, ...** per quanto mi siano simpatici, ...; **do as you wish** fa' come vuoi; **as she said** come ha detto lei
5 (*concerning*): **as for** *or* **to that** per quanto riguarda *or* quanto a quello
6: **as if** *or* **though** come se; **he looked as if he was ill** sembrava stare male; *see also* **long**; **such**; **well**
■ *prep*: **he works as a driver** fa l'autista; **as chairman of the company, he ...** come presidente della compagnia, lui ...; **he gave me it as a present** me lo ha regalato

ASA *n abbr* (*= American Standards Association*) *associazione per la normalizzazione*; (*Brit: = Advertising Standards Association*) ≈ Istituto di Autodisciplina Pubblicitaria
a.s.a.p. *abbr* (*= as soon as possible*) prima possibile
asbestos [æz'bɛstəs] *n* asbesto, amianto
ASBO ['æzbəu] *n abbr* (*Brit: = antisocial behaviour order*) *provvedimento restrittivo per comportamento antisociale*
ascend [ə'sɛnd] *vt* salire
ascendancy [ə'sɛndənsɪ] *n* ascendente *m*
ascendant [ə'sɛndənt] *n*: **to be in the ~** essere in auge
ascension [ə'sɛnʃən] *n*: **the A~** (*Rel*) l'Ascensione *f*
Ascension Island *n* isola dell'Ascensione
ascent [ə'sɛnt] *n* salita
ascertain [æsə'teɪn] *vt* accertare
ascetic [ə'sɛtɪk] *adj* ascetico(-a)
asceticism [ə'sɛtɪsɪzəm] *n* ascetismo
ASCII ['æskiː] *n abbr* (*= American Standard Code*

for Information Interchange) ASCII *m*
ascribe [əˈskraɪb] *vt*: **to ~ sth to** attribuire qc a
ASCU *n abbr (US)* = **Association of State Colleges and Universities**
ASE *n abbr* = **American Stock Exchange**
ASH [æʃ] *n abbr (Brit: = Action on Smoking and Health) iniziativa contro il fumo*
ash [æʃ] *n (dust)* cenere *f*; **~ (tree)** frassino
ashamed [əˈʃeɪmd] *adj* vergognoso(-a); **to be ~ of** vergognarsi di; **to be ~ (of o.s.) for having done** vergognarsi di aver fatto
ashen [ˈæʃən] *adj (pale)* livido(-a)
ashore [əˈʃɔːʳ] *adv* a terra; **to go ~** sbarcare
ashtray [ˈæʃtreɪ] *n* portacenere *m*
Ash Wednesday *n* Mercoledì *m inv* delle Ceneri
Asia Minor *n* Asia minore
Asian [ˈeɪʃən] *adj, n* asiatico(-a)
Asiatic [eɪsɪˈætɪk] *adj* asiatico(-a)
aside [əˈsaɪd] *adv* da parte ■ *n* a parte *m*; **to take sb ~** prendere qn da parte; **~ from** *(as well as)* oltre a; *(except for)* a parte
ask [ɑːsk] *vt (request)* chiedere; *(question)* domandare; *(invite)* invitare; **to ~ about sth** informarsi su *or* di qc; **to ~ sb sth/sb to do sth** chiedere qc a qn/a qn di fare qc; **to ~ sb about sth** chiedere a qn di qc; **to ~ (sb) a question** fare una domanda (a qn); **to ~ sb the time** chiedere l'ora a qn; **to ~ sb out to dinner** invitare qn a mangiare fuori; **you should ~ at the information desk** dovreste rivolgersi all'ufficio informazioni
▸ **ask after** *vt fus* chiedere di
▸ **ask for** *vt fus* chiedere; **it's just asking for trouble** *or* **for it** è proprio (come) andarsele a cercare
askance [əˈskɑːns] *adv*: **to look ~ at sb** guardare qn di traverso
askew [əˈskjuː] *adv* di traverso, storto
asking price [ˈɑːskɪŋ-] *n* prezzo di partenza
asleep [əˈsliːp] *adj* addormentato(-a); **to be ~** dormire; **to fall ~** addormentarsi
ASLEF [ˈæzlɛf] *n abbr (Brit: = Associated Society of Locomotive Engineers and Firemen) sindacato dei conducenti dei treni e dei macchinisti*
AS level *n abbr (= Advanced Subsidiary level) prima parte del diploma di studi superiori chiamato "A level"*
asp [æsp] *n* cobra *m inv* egiziano
asparagus [əsˈpærəgəs] *n* asparagi *mpl*
asparagus tips *npl* punte *fpl* d'asparagi
ASPCA *n abbr (= American Society for the Prevention of Cruelty to Animals)* ≈ E.N.P.A. *m (= Ente Nazionale per la Protezione degli Animali)*
aspect [ˈæspɛkt] *n* aspetto
aspersions [əsˈpəːʃənz] *npl*: **to cast ~ on** diffamare
asphalt [ˈæsfælt] *n* asfalto
asphyxiate [æsˈfɪksɪeɪt] *vt* asfissiare
asphyxiation [æsfɪksɪˈeɪʃən] *n* asfissia
aspiration [æspəˈreɪʃən] *n* aspirazione *f*
aspire [əsˈpaɪəʳ] *vi*: **to ~ to** aspirare a
aspirin [ˈæsprɪn] *n* aspirina
aspiring [əsˈpaɪərɪŋ] *adj* aspirante
ass [æs] *n* asino; *(US col!)* culo *(!)*
assail [əˈseɪl] *vt* assalire
assailant [əˈseɪlənt] *n* assalitore *m*
assassin [əˈsæsɪn] *n* assassino
assassinate [əˈsæsɪneɪt] *vt* assassinare
assassination [əsæsɪˈneɪʃən] *n* assassinio
assault [əˈsɔːlt] *n (Mil)* assalto; *(gen: attack)* aggressione *f*; *(Law)*: **~ (and battery)** minacce e vie di fatto *fpl* ■ *vt* assaltare; aggredire; *(sexually)* violentare
assemble [əˈsɛmbl] *vt* riunire; *(Tech)* montare ■ *vi* riunirsi
assembly [əˈsɛmblɪ] *n (meeting)* assemblea; *(construction)* montaggio
assembly language *n (Comput)* linguaggio assemblativo
assembly line *n* catena di montaggio
assent [əˈsɛnt] *n* assenso, consenso ■ *vi* assentire; **to ~ (to sth)** approvare (qc)
assert [əˈsəːt] *vt* asserire; *(insist on)* far valere; **to ~ o.s.** farsi valere
assertion [əˈsəːʃən] *n* asserzione *f*
assertive [əˈsəːtɪv] *adj* che sa imporsi
assess [əˈsɛs] *vt* valutare
assessment [əˈsɛsmənt] *n* valutazione *f*; *(judgment)*: **~ (of)** giudizio (su)
assessor [əˈsɛsəʳ] *n* perito; funzionario del fisco
asset [ˈæsɛt] *n* vantaggio; *(person)* elemento prezioso; **assets** *npl (Comm)* beni *mpl*; disponibilità *fpl*; attivo
asset-stripping [ˈæsɛtˈstrɪpɪŋ] *n (Comm) acquisto di una società in fallimento con lo scopo di rivenderne le attività*
assiduous [əˈsɪdjuəs] *adj* assiduo(-a)
assign [əˈsaɪn] *vt*: **to ~ (to)** *(task)* assegnare (a); *(resources)* riservare (a); *(cause, meaning)* attribuire (a); **to ~ a date to sth** fissare la data di qc
assignment [əˈsaɪnmənt] *n* compito
assimilate [əˈsɪmɪleɪt] *vt* assimilare
assimilation [əsɪmɪˈleɪʃən] *n* assimilazione *f*
assist [əˈsɪst] *vt* assistere, aiutare
assistance [əˈsɪstəns] *n* assistenza, aiuto
assistant [əˈsɪstənt] *n* assistente *m/f*; *(Brit: also:* **shop assistant***)* commesso(-a)
assistant manager *n* vicedirettore *m*
assizes [əˈsaɪzɪz] *npl* assise *fpl*
associate [əˈsəuʃɪɪt] *adj* associato(-a); *(member)* aggiunto(-a) ■ *n* collega *m/f*;

a

(*in business*) socio(-a) ■ *vb* [ə'səuʃɪeɪt] *vt* associare ■ *vi*: **to ~ with sb** frequentare qn
associated company [ə'səusɪ'eɪtɪd-] *n* società collegata
associate director *n* amministratore *m* aggiunto
association [əsəusɪ'eɪʃən] *n* associazione *f*; **in ~ with** in collaborazione con
association football *n* (*Brit*) (gioco del) calcio
assorted [ə'sɔːtɪd] *adj* assortito(-a); **in ~ sizes** in diverse taglie
assortment [ə'sɔːtmənt] *n* assortimento
Asst. *abbr* = **assistant**
assuage [ə'sweɪdʒ] *vt* alleviare
assume [ə'sjuːm] *vt* supporre; (*responsibilities etc*) assumere; (*attitude, name*) prendere
assumed name *n* nome *m* falso
assumption [ə'sʌmpʃən] *n* supposizione *f*, ipotesi *f inv*; **on the ~ that ...** partendo dal presupposto che ...
assurance [ə'ʃuərəns] *n* assicurazione *f*; (*self-confidence*) fiducia in se stesso; **I can give you no assurances** non posso assicurarle *or* garantirle niente
assure [ə'ʃuəʳ] *vt* assicurare
assured [ə'ʃuəd] *adj* (*confident*) sicuro(-a); (*certain: promotion etc*) assicurato(-a)
AST *abbr* (*US*: = *Atlantic Standard Time*) *ora invernale di New York*
asterisk ['æstərɪsk] *n* asterisco
astern [ə'stəːn] *adv* a poppa
asteroid ['æstərɔɪd] *n* asteroide *m*
asthma ['æsmə] *n* asma
asthmatic [æs'mætɪk] *adj, n* asmatico(-a)
astigmatism [ə'stɪgmətɪzəm] *n* astigmatismo
astir [ə'stəːʳ] *adv* in piedi; (*excited*) in fermento
astonish [ə'stɔnɪʃ] *vt* stupire
astonishing [ə'stɔnɪʃɪŋ] *adj* sorprendente, stupefacente; **I find it ~ that ...** mi stupisce che ...
astonishingly [ə'stɔnɪʃɪŋlɪ] *adv* straordinariamente, incredibilmente
astonishment [ə'stɔnɪʃmənt] *n* stupore *m*; **to my ~** con mia gran meraviglia, con mio grande stupore
astound [ə'staund] *vt* sbalordire
astray [ə'streɪ] *adv*: **to go ~** smarrirsi; (*fig*) traviarsi; **to go ~ in one's calculations** sbagliare i calcoli
astride [ə'straɪd] *adv* a cavalcioni ■ *prep* a cavalcioni di
astringent [əs'trɪndʒənt] *adj, n* astringente *m*
astrologer [əs'trɔlədʒəʳ] *n* astrologo(-a)
astrology [əs'trɔlədʒɪ] *n* astrologia
astronaut ['æstrənɔːt] *n* astronauta *m/f*
astronomer [əs'trɔnəməʳ] *n* astronomo(-a)
astronomical [æstrə'nɔmɪkl] *adj* astronomico(-a)
astronomy [əs'trɔnəmɪ] *n* astronomia
astrophysics ['æstrəu'fɪzɪks] *n* astrofisica
astute [əs'tjuːt] *adj* astuto(-a)
asunder [ə'sʌndəʳ] *adv*: **to tear ~** strappare
ASV *n abbr* (= *American Standard Version*) *traduzione della Bibbia*
asylum [ə'saɪləm] *n* asilo; (*lunatic asylum*) manicomio; **to seek political ~** chiedere asilo politico
asymmetric [eɪsɪ'mɛtrɪk], **asymmetrical** [eɪsɪ'mɛtrɪkəl] *adj* asimmetrico(-a)

 KEYWORD

at [æt] *prep* **1** (*referring to position, direction*) a; **at the top** in cima; **at the desk** al banco, alla scrivania; **at home/school** a casa/scuola; **at Paolo's** da Paolo; **at the baker's** dal panettiere; **to look at sth** guardare qc; **to throw sth at sb** lanciare qc a qn
2 (*referring to time*) a; **at 4 o'clock** alle 4; **at night** di notte; **at Christmas** a Natale; **at times** a volte
3 (*referring to rates, speed etc*) a; **at £1 a kilo** a 1 sterlina al chilo; **two at a time** due alla volta, due per volta; **at 50 km/h** a 50 km/h; **at full speed** a tutta velocità
4 (*referring to manner*): **at a stroke** d'un solo colpo; **at peace** in pace
5 (*referring to activity*): **to be at work** essere al lavoro; **to play at cowboys** giocare ai cowboy; **to be good at sth/doing sth** essere bravo in qc/a fare qc
6 (*referring to cause*): **shocked/surprised/annoyed at sth** colpito da/sorpreso da/arrabbiato per qc; **I went at his suggestion** ci sono andato dietro suo consiglio
7 (*Comput: symbol*) chiocciola

ate [eɪt] *pt of* **eat**
atheism ['eɪθɪɪzəm] *n* ateismo
atheist ['eɪθɪɪst] *n* ateo(-a)
Athenian [ə'θiːnɪən] *adj, n* ateniese *m/f*
Athens ['æθɪnz] *n* Atene *f*
athlete ['æθliːt] *n* atleta *m/f*
athletic [æθ'lɛtɪk] *adj* atletico(-a)
athletics [æθ'lɛtɪks] *n* atletica
Atlantic [ət'læntɪk] *adj* atlantico(-a) ■ *n*: **the ~ (Ocean)** l'Atlantico, l'Oceano Atlantico
atlas ['ætləs] *n* atlante *m*
Atlas Mountains *npl*: **the ~** i Monti dell'Atlante
ATM *abbr* (= *automated telling machine*) cassa automatica prelievi, sportello automatico

atmosphere ['ætməsfɪəʳ] *n* atmosfera; (*air*) aria
atmospheric [ætməs'fɛrɪk] *adj* atmosferico(-a)
atmospherics [ætməs'fɛrɪks] *npl* (*Radio*) scariche *fpl*
atoll ['ætɔl] *n* atollo
atom ['ætəm] *n* atomo
atom bomb *n* bomba atomica
atomic [ə'tɔmɪk] *adj* atomico(-a)
atomic bomb *n* bomba atomica
atomizer ['ætəmaɪzəʳ] *n* atomizzatore *m*
atone [ə'təun] *vi*: **to ~ for** espiare
atonement [ə'təunmənt] *n* espiazione *f*
ATP *n abbr* = **Association of Tennis Professionals**
atrocious [ə'trəuʃəs] *adj* atroce, pessimo(-a)
atrocity [ə'trɔsɪtɪ] *n* atrocità *f inv*
atrophy ['ætrəfɪ] *n* atrofia ■ *vi* atrofizzarsi
attach [ə'tætʃ] *vt* attaccare; (*document, letter*) allegare; (*Mil: troops*) assegnare; **to be attached to sb/sth** (*to like*) essere affezionato(-a) a qn/qc; **the attached letter** la lettera acclusa *or* allegata
attaché [ə'tæʃeɪ] *n* addetto
attaché case *n* valigetta per documenti
attachment [ə'tætʃmənt] *n* (*tool*) accessorio; (*love*): **~ (to)** affetto (per); (*Comput*) allegato
attack [ə'tæk] *vt* attaccare; (*task etc*) iniziare; (*problem*) affrontare ■ *n* attacco; (*also*: **heart attack**) infarto
attacker [ə'tækəʳ] *n* aggressore *m*, assalitore(-trice)
attain [ə'teɪn] *vt* (*also*: **to attain to**) arrivare a, raggiungere
attainments [ə'teɪnmənts] *npl* cognizioni *fpl*
attempt [ə'tɛmpt] *n* tentativo ■ *vt* tentare; **attempted murder** (*Law*) tentato omicidio; **to make an ~ on sb's life** attentare alla vita di qn; **he made no ~ to help** non ha (neanche) tentato *or* cercato di aiutare
attend [ə'tɛnd] *vt* frequentare; (*meeting, talk*) andare a; (*patient*) assistere
▸ **attend to** *vt fus* (*needs, affairs etc*) prendersi cura di; (*customer*) occuparsi di
attendance [ə'tɛndəns] *n* (*being present*) presenza; (*people present*) gente *f* presente
attendant [ə'tɛndənt] *n* custode *m/f*; persona di servizio ■ *adj* concomitante
attention [ə'tɛnʃən] *n* attenzione *f*; **attentions** premure *fpl*, attenzioni *fpl*; **~!** (*Mil*) attenti!; **at ~** (*Mil*) sull'attenti; **for the ~ of** (*Admin*) per l'attenzione di; **it has come to my ~ that ...** sono venuto a conoscenza (del fatto) che ...
attentive [ə'tɛntɪv] *adj* attento(-a); (*kind*) premuroso(-a)
attentively [ə'tɛntɪvlɪ] *adv* attentamente
attenuate [ə'tɛnjueɪt] *vt* attenuare ■ *vi* attenuarsi
attest [ə'tɛst] *vi*: **to ~ to** attestare
attic ['ætɪk] *n* soffitta
attire [ə'taɪəʳ] *n* abbigliamento
attitude ['ætɪtju:d] *n* (*behaviour*) atteggiamento; (*posture*) posa; (*view*): **~ (to)** punto di vista (nei confronti di)
attorney [ə'tə:nɪ] *n* (*US: lawyer*) avvocato; (*having proxy*) mandatario; **power of ~** procura
Attorney General *n* (*Brit*) Procuratore *m* Generale; (*US*) Ministro della Giustizia
attract [ə'trækt] *vt* attirare
attraction [ə'trækʃən] *n* (*gen pl: pleasant things*) attrattiva; (*Physics, fig: towards sth*) attrazione *f*
attractive [ə'træktɪv] *adj* attraente; (*idea, offer, price*) allettante, interessante
attribute *n* ['ætrɪbju:t] attributo ■ *vt* [ə'trɪbju:t]: **to ~ sth to** attribuire qc a
attrition [ə'trɪʃən] *n*: **war of ~** guerra di logoramento
Atty. Gen. *abbr* = **Attorney General**
atypical [eɪ'tɪpɪkl] *adj* atipico(-a)
AU *n abbr* (= *African Union*) Unione Africana
aubergine ['əubəʒi:n] *n* melanzana
auburn ['ɔ:bən] *adj* tizianesco(-a)
auction ['ɔ:kʃən] *n* (*also*: **sale by auction**) asta ■ *vt* (*also*: **to sell by auction**) vendere all'asta; (*also*: **to put up for auction**) mettere all'asta
auctioneer [ɔ:kʃə'nɪəʳ] *n* banditore *m*
auction room *n* sala dell'asta
audacious [ɔ:'deɪʃəs] *adj* (*bold*) audace; (*impudent*) sfrontato(-a)
audacity [ɔ:'dæsɪtɪ] *n* audacia
audible ['ɔ:dɪbl] *adj* udibile
audience ['ɔ:dɪəns] *n* (*people*) pubblico; spettatori *mpl*; ascoltatori *mpl*; (*interview*) udienza
audio-typist ['ɔ:dɪəu'taɪpɪst] *n* dattilografo(-a) che trascrive da nastro
audiovisual [ɔ:dɪəu'vɪzjuəl] *adj* audiovisivo(-a); **~ aids** sussidi *mpl* audiovisivi
audit ['ɔ:dɪt] *n* revisione *f*, verifica ■ *vt* rivedere, verificare
audition [ɔ:'dɪʃən] *n* (*Theat*) audizione *f*; (*Cine*) provino ■ *vi* fare un'audizione (*or* un provino)
auditor ['ɔ:dɪtəʳ] *n* revisore *m*
auditorium [ɔ:dɪ'tɔ:rɪəm] *n* sala, auditorio
Aug. *abbr* (= *August*) ago., ag.
augment [ɔ:g'mɛnt] *vt, vi* aumentare
augur ['ɔ:gəʳ] *vt* (*be a sign of*) predire ■ *vi*: **it augurs well** promette bene
August ['ɔ:gəst] *n* agosto; *see also* **July**

august [ɔːˈgʌst] *adj* augusto(-a)
aunt [ɑːnt] *n* zia
auntie, aunty [ˈɑːntɪ] *n* zietta
au pair [ˈəuˈpɛə^r] *n* (*also*: **au pair girl**) (ragazza *f*) alla pari *inv*
aura [ˈɔːrə] *n* aura
auspices [ˈɔːspɪsɪz] *npl*: **under the ~ of** sotto gli auspici di
auspicious [ɔːsˈpɪʃəs] *adj* propizio(-a)
austere [ɔsˈtɪə^r] *adj* austero(-a)
austerity [ɔsˈtɛrɪtɪ] *n* austerità *f inv*
Australasia [ɔstrəˈleɪzɪə] *n* Australasia
Australia [ɔsˈtreɪlɪə] *n* Australia
Australian [ɔsˈtreɪlɪən] *adj, n* australiano(-a)
Austria [ˈɔstrɪə] *n* Austria
Austrian [ˈɔstrɪən] *adj, n* austriaco(-a)
AUT *n abbr* (*Brit*: = *Association of University Teachers*) *associazione dei docenti universitari*
authentic [ɔːˈθɛntɪk] *adj* autentico(-a)
authenticate [ɔːˈθɛntɪkeɪt] *vt* autenticare
authenticity [ɔːθɛnˈtɪsɪtɪ] *n* autenticità
author [ˈɔːθə^r] *n* autore(-trice)
authoritarian [ɔːθɔrɪˈtɛərɪən] *adj* autoritario(-a)
authoritative [ɔːˈθɔrɪtətɪv] *adj* (*account etc*) autorevole; (*manner*) autoritario(-a)
authority [ɔːˈθɔrɪtɪ] *n* autorità *f inv*; (*permission*) autorizzazione *f*; **the authorities** *npl* le autorità; **to have ~ to do sth** avere l'autorizzazione a fare *or* il diritto di fare qc
authorization [ɔːθəraɪˈzeɪʃən] *n* autorizzazione *f*
authorize [ˈɔːθəraɪz] *vt* autorizzare
authorized capital *n* capitale *m* nominale
authorship [ˈɔːθəʃɪp] *n* paternità (*letteraria etc*)
autistic [ɔːˈtɪstɪk] *adj* autistico(-a)
auto [ˈɔːtəu] *n* (*US*) auto *f inv*
autobiography [ɔːtəbaɪˈɔgrəfɪ] *n* autobiografia
autocratic [ɔːtəˈkrætɪk] *adj* autocratico(-a)
Autocue® [ˈɔːtəukjuː] *n* (*Brit*) gobbo (*TV*)
autograph [ˈɔːtəgrɑːf] *n* autografo ■ *vt* firmare
autoimmune [ɔːtəuɪˈmjuːn] *adj* autoimmune
automat [ˈɔːtəmæt] *n* (*US*) *tavola calda fornita esclusivamente di distributori automatici*
automated [ˈɔːtəmeɪtɪd] *adj* automatizzato(-a)
automatic [ɔːtəˈmætɪk] *adj* automatico(-a) ■ *n* (*gun*) arma automatica; (*car*) automobile *f* con cambio automatico; (*washing machine*) lavatrice *f* automatica
automatically [ɔːtəˈmætɪklɪ] *adv* automaticamente
automatic data processing *n* elaborazione *f* automatica dei dati
automation [ɔːtəˈmeɪʃən] *n* automazione *f*
automaton (*pl* **automata**) [ɔːˈtɔmətən, -tə] *n* automa *m*
automobile [ˈɔːtəməbiːl] *n* (*US*) automobile *f*
autonomous [ɔːˈtɔnəməs] *adj* autonomo(-a)
autopsy [ˈɔːtɔpsɪ] *n* autopsia
autumn [ˈɔːtəm] *n* autunno
auxiliary [ɔːgˈzɪlɪərɪ] *adj* ausiliario(-a) ■ *n* ausiliare *m/f*
AV *n abbr* (= *Authorized Version*) *traduzione inglese della Bibbia* ■ *abbr* = **audiovisual**
Av. *abbr* = **avenue**
avail [əˈveɪl] *vt*: **to ~ o.s. of** servirsi di; approfittarsi di ■ *n*: **to no ~** inutilmente
availability [əveɪləˈbɪlɪtɪ] *n* disponibilità
available [əˈveɪləbl] *adj* disponibile; **every ~ means** tutti i mezzi disponibili; **to make sth ~ to sb** mettere qc a disposizione di qn; **is the manager ~?** è libero il direttore?
avalanche [ˈævəlɑːnʃ] *n* valanga
avant-garde [ˈævɑ̃ŋˈgɑːd] *adj* d'avanguardia
avarice [ˈævərɪs] *n* avarizia
avaricious [ævəˈrɪʃəs] *adj* avaro(-a)
avdp. *abbr* (= *avoirdupoids*) *sistema ponderale anglosassone basato su libbra, oncia e multipli*
Ave. *abbr* = **avenue**
avenge [əˈvɛndʒ] *vt* vendicare
avenue [ˈævənjuː] *n* viale *m*
average [ˈævərɪdʒ] *n* media ■ *adj* medio(-a) ■ *vt* (*also*: **average out at**) aggirarsi in media su, essere in media di; **on ~** in media; **above/below (the) ~** sopra/sotto la media
averse [əˈvəːs] *adj*: **to be ~ to sth/doing** essere contrario(-a) a qc/a fare; **I wouldn't be ~ to a drink** non avrei nulla in contrario a bere qualcosa
aversion [əˈvəːʃən] *n* avversione *f*
avert [əˈvəːt] *vt* evitare, prevenire; (*one's eyes*) distogliere
avian flu [ˈeɪvɪən-] *n* influenza aviaria
aviary [ˈeɪvɪərɪ] *n* voliera, uccelliera
aviation [eɪvɪˈeɪʃən] *n* aviazione *f*
avid [ˈævɪd] *adj* avido(-a)
avidly [ˈævɪdlɪ] *adv* avidamente
avocado [ævəˈkɑːdəu] *n* (*Brit*: *also*: **avocado pear**) avocado *m inv*
avoid [əˈvɔɪd] *vt* evitare
avoidable [əˈvɔɪdəbl] *adj* evitabile
avoidance [əˈvɔɪdəns] *n* l'evitare *m*
avowed [əˈvaud] *adj* dichiarato(-a)
AVP *n abbr* (*US*) = **assistant vice-president**
AWACS [ˈeɪwæks] *n abbr* (= *airborne warning and control system*) *sistema di allarme e controllo in volo*
await [əˈweɪt] *vt* aspettare; **awaiting attention** (*Comm*: *letter*) in attesa di risposta; (: *order*) in attesa di essere evaso; **long awaited** tanto atteso(-a)

awake [ə'weɪk] *adj* sveglio(-a) ■ *vb* (*pt* **awoke**, *pp* **awoken** *or* **awaked**) *vt* svegliare ■ *vi* svegliarsi; **~ to** consapevole di
awakening [ə'weɪknɪŋ] *n* risveglio
award [ə'wɔ:d] *n* premio; (*Law*) decreto ■ *vt* assegnare; (*Law: damages*) decretare
aware [ə'wɛəʳ] *adj*: **~ of** (*conscious*) conscio(-a) di; (*informed*) informato(-a) di; **to become ~ of** accorgersi di; **politically/socially ~** politicamente/socialmente preparato; **I am fully ~ that ...** mi rendo perfettamente conto che ...
awareness [ə'wɛənɪs] *n* consapevolezza; coscienza; **to develop people's ~ (of)** sensibilizzare la gente (a)
awash [ə'wɔʃ] *adj*: **~ (with)** inondato(-a) (da)
away [ə'weɪ] *adj, adv* via; lontano(-a); **two kilometres ~** a due chilometri di distanza; **two hours ~ by car** a due ore di distanza in macchina; **the holiday was two weeks ~** mancavano due settimane alle vacanze; **~ from** lontano da; **he's ~ for a week** è andato via per una settimana; **he's ~ in Milan** è (andato) a Milano; **to take ~** *vt* portare via; **he was working/pedalling** *etc* **~** *la particella indica la continuità e l'energia dell'azione*, lavorava/pedalava *etc* più che poteva; **to fade/wither** *etc* **~** *la particella rinforza l'idea della diminuzione*
away game *n* (*Sport*) partita fuori casa
awe [ɔ:] *n* timore *m*
awe-inspiring ['ɔ:ɪnspaɪərɪŋ], **awesome** ['ɔ:səm] *adj* imponente
awestruck ['ɔ:strʌk] *adj* sgomento(-a)
awful ['ɔ:fəl] *adj* terribile; **an ~ lot of** (*people, cars, dogs*) un numero incredibile di; (*jam, flowers*) una quantità incredibile di
awfully ['ɔ:flɪ] *adv* (*very*) terribilmente
awhile [ə'waɪl] *adv* (per) un po'
awkward ['ɔ:kwəd] *adj* (*clumsy*) goffo(-a); (*inconvenient*) scomodo(-a); (*embarrassing*) imbarazzante; (*difficult*) delicato(-a), difficile
awkwardness ['ɔ:kwədnɪs] *n* goffaggine *f*; scomodità; imbarazzo; delicatezza, difficoltà
awl ['ɔ:l] *n* punteruolo
awning ['ɔ:nɪŋ] *n* (*of tent*) veranda; (*of shop, hotel etc*) tenda
awoke [ə'wəuk] *pt of* **awake**
awoken [ə'wəukən] *pp of* **awake**
AWOL ['eɪwɔl] *abbr* (*Mil etc*) = **absent without leave**
awry [ə'raɪ] *adv* di traverso ■ *adj* storto(-a); **to go ~** andare a monte
axe, (*US*) **ax** [æks] *n* scure *f* ■ *vt* (*project etc*) abolire; (*jobs*) sopprimere; **to have an ~ to grind** (*fig*) fare i propri interessi *or* il proprio tornaconto
axiom ['æksɪəm] *n* assioma *m*
axiomatic [æksɪəu'mætɪk] *adj* assiomatico(-a)
axis (*pl* **axes**) ['æksɪs, -si:z] *n* asse *m*
axle ['æksl] *n* (*also*: **axle-tree**) asse *m*
ay, aye [aɪ] *excl* (*yes*) sì
AYH *n abbr* = **American Youth Hostels**
AZ *abbr* (*US*) = **Arizona**
azalea [ə'zeɪlɪə] *n* azalea
Azerbaijan [æzəbaɪ'dʒɑ:n] *n* Azerbaigian *m*
Azerbaijani [æzəbaɪ'dʒɑ:nɪ], **Azeri** [ə'zɛərɪ] *adj, n* azerbaigiano(-a), azero(-a)
Azores [ə'zɔ:z] *npl*: **the ~** le Azzorre
AZT *n abbr* (= *azidothymidine*) AZT *m*
Aztec ['æztɛk] *adj, n* azteco(-a)
azure ['eɪʒəʳ] *adj* azzurro(-a)

Bb

B, b [bi:] *n* (*letter*) B, b *f or m inv*; (*Scol: mark*) ≈ 8 (*buono*); (*Mus*): **B** si *m*; **B for Benjamin**, (*US*) **B for Baker** ≈ B come Bologna; **B road** *n* (*Brit Aut*) ≈ strada secondaria

b. *abbr* = **born**

BA *n abbr* = **British Academy**; (*Scol*) = **Bachelor of Arts**

babble ['bæbl] *vi* cianciare; mormorare ■ *n* ciance *fpl* mormorio

babe [beɪb] *n* (*col*): **she's a real ~** è uno schianto di ragazza

baboon [bə'bu:n] *n* babbuino

baby ['beɪbɪ] *n* bambino(-a)

baby carriage *n* (*US*) carrozzina

baby grand *n* (*also*: **baby grand piano**) pianoforte *m* a mezza coda

babyhood ['beɪbɪhud] *n* prima infanzia

babyish ['beɪbɪɪʃ] *adj* infantile

baby-minder ['beɪbɪ'maɪndə^r] *n* (*Brit*) bambinaia (*che tiene i bambini mentre la madre lavora*)

baby-sit ['beɪbɪsɪt] *vi* fare il (*or* la) babysitter

baby-sitter ['beɪbɪsɪtə^r] *n* baby-sitter *m/f inv*

bachelor ['bætʃələ^r] *n* scapolo; **B~ of Arts/Science (BA/BSc)** ≈ laureato(-a) in lettere/scienze; **B~ of Arts/Science degree (BA/BSc)** *n* ≈ laurea in lettere/scienze; *vedi nota*

BACHELOR'S DEGREE

Il *Bachelor's degree* è il riconoscimento che viene conferito a chi ha completato un corso di laurea di tre o quattro anni all'università. I *Bachelor's degree* più importanti sono il "BA" (Bachelor of Arts), il "BSc" (Bachelor of Science), il "BEd" (Bachelor of Education), e il "LLB" (Bachelor of Laws); *vedi anche* "Master's degree", "doctorate".

bachelorhood ['bætʃələhud] *n* celibato

bachelor party *n* (*US*) festa di addio al celibato

back [bæk] *n* (*of person, horse*) dorso, schiena; (*of hand*) dorso; (*of house, car*) didietro; (*of train*) coda; (*of chair*) schienale *m*; (*of page*) rovescio; (*Football*) difensore *m*; **~ to front** all'incontrario; **to break the ~ of a job** (*Brit*) fare il grosso *or* il peggio di un lavoro; **to have one's ~ to the wall** (*fig*) essere *or* trovarsi con le spalle al muro ■ *vt* (*financially*) finanziare; (*candidate*: *also*: **back up**) appoggiare; (*horse*: *at races*) puntare su; (*car*) guidare a marcia indietro ■ *vi* indietreggiare; (*car etc*) fare marcia indietro ■ *adj* (*in compounds*) posteriore, di dietro; arretrato(-a); **~ seats/wheels** (*Aut*) sedili *mpl*/ruote *fpl* posteriori; **~ payments/rent** arretrati *mpl*; **~ garden/room** giardino/stanza sul retro (della casa); **to take a ~ seat** (*fig*) restare in secondo piano ■ *adv* (*not forward*) indietro; (*returned*): **he's ~** è tornato; **when will you be ~?** quando torni?; **he ran ~** tornò indietro di corsa; **throw the ball ~** (*restitution*) ritira la palla; **can I have it ~?** posso riaverlo?; **he called ~** (*again*) ha richiamato

▸ **back down** *vi* (*fig*) fare marcia indietro

▸ **back on to** *vt fus*: **the house backs on to the golf course** il retro della casa dà sul campo da golf

▸ **back out** *vi* (*of promise*) tirarsi indietro

▸ **back up** *vt* (*support*) appoggiare, sostenere; (*Comput*) fare una copia di riserva di

backache ['bækeɪk] *n* mal *m* di schiena

backbencher ['bæk'bɛntʃə^r] *n* (*Brit*) *parlamentare che non ha incarichi né al governo né all'opposizione*

back benches *npl posti in Parlamento occupati dai backbencher*; *vedi nota*

BACK BENCHES

Nella "House of Commons", una delle camere del Parlamento britannico, sono chiamati *back benches* gli scanni dove siedono i "backbenchers", parlamentari che non hanno incarichi né al governo né all'opposizione. Nelle file davanti ad essi siedono i "frontbencher"; *vedi anche* "front bench".

backbiting ['bækbaɪtɪŋ] *n* maldicenza
backbone ['bækbəun] *n* spina dorsale; **the ~ of the organization** l'anima dell'organizzazione
backchat ['bæktʃæt] *n* (*Brit col*) impertinenza
backcloth ['bækklɔθ] *n* (*Brit*) scena di sfondo
backcomb ['bækkəum] *vt* (*Brit*) cotonare
backdate [bæk'deɪt] *vt* (*letter*) retrodatare; **backdated pay rise** aumento retroattivo
backdrop ['bækdrɔp] *n* = **backcloth**
backer ['bækə^r] *n* sostenitore(-trice); (*Comm*) fautore *m*
backfire ['bæk'faɪə^r] *vi* (*Aut*) dar ritorni di fiamma; (*plans*) fallire
backgammon ['bækgæmən] *n* tavola reale
background ['bækgraund] *n* sfondo; (*of events, Comput*) background *m inv*; (*basic knowledge*) base *f*; (*experience*) esperienza ■ *cpd* (*noise, music*) di fondo; **~ reading** letture *fpl* sull'argomento; **family ~** ambiente *m* familiare
backhand ['bækhænd] *n* (*Tennis: also:* **backhand stroke**) rovescio
backhanded [bæk'hændɪd] *adj* (*fig*) ambiguo(-a)
backhander ['bækhændə^r] *n* (*Brit: bribe*) bustarella
backing [bækɪŋ] *n* (*Comm*) finanziamento; (*Mus*) accompagnamento; (*fig*) appoggio
backlash ['bæklæʃ] *n* contraccolpo, ripercussione *f*
backlog ['bæklɔg] *n*: **~ of work** lavoro arretrato
back number *n* (*of magazine etc*) numero arretrato
backpack ['bækpæk] *n* zaino
backpacker ['bækpækə^r] *n chi viaggia con zaino e sacco a pelo*
back pay *n* arretrato di paga
backpedal ['bækpɛdl] *vi* pedalare all'indietro; (*fig*) far marcia indietro
backseat driver ['bæksi:t-] *n passeggero che dà consigli non richiesti al guidatore*
backside [bæk'saɪd] *n* (*col*) sedere *m*
backslash ['bækslæʃ] *n* backslash *m inv*, barra obliqua inversa
backslide ['bækslaɪd] *vi* ricadere
backspace ['bækspeɪs] *vi* (*in typing*) battere il tasto di ritorno
backstage [bæk'steɪdʒ] *adv* nel retroscena
back street *n* vicolo
back-street ['bækstri:t] *adj*: **~ abortionist** praticante *m/f* di aborti clandestini
backstroke ['bækstrəuk] *n* nuoto sul dorso
backtrack ['bæktræk] *vi* = **backpedal**
backup ['bækʌp] *adj* (*train, plane*) supplementare; (*Comput*) di riserva ■ *n* (*support*) appoggio, sostegno; (*Comput: also:* **backup file**) file *m inv* di riserva
backward ['bækwəd] *adj* (*movement*) indietro *inv*; (*person*) tardivo(-a); (*country*) arretrato(-a); **~ and forward movement** movimento avanti e indietro
backwards ['bækwədz] *adv* indietro; (*fall, walk*) all'indietro; **to know sth ~** *or* (*US*) **~ and forwards** (*col*) sapere qc a menadito
backwater ['bækwɔ:tə^r] *n* (*fig*) posto morto
back yard *n* cortile *m* sul retro
bacon ['beɪkən] *n* pancetta
bacteria [bæk'tɪərɪə] *npl* batteri *mpl*
bacteriology [bæktɪərɪ'ɔlədʒɪ] *n* batteriologia
bad [bæd] *adj* cattivo(-a); (*child*) cattivello(-a); (*meat, food*) andato(-a) a male; **his ~ leg** la sua gamba malata; **to go ~** (*meat, food*) andare a male; **to have a ~ time of it** passarsela male; **I feel ~ about it** (*guilty*) mi sento un po' in colpa; **~ debt** credito difficile da recuperare; **~ faith** malafede *f*
baddie, baddy ['bædɪ] *n* (*col: Cine etc*) cattivo(-a)
bade [bæd] *pt of* **bid**
badge [bædʒ] *n* insegna; (*of policeman*) stemma *m*; (*stick-on*) adesivo
badger ['bædʒə^r] *n* tasso ■ *vt* tormentare
badly ['bædlɪ] *adv* (*work, dress etc*) male; **things are going ~** le cose vanno male; **~ wounded** gravemente ferito; **he needs it ~** ne ha gran bisogno; **~ off** *adj* povero(-a)
bad-mannered [bæd'mænəd] *adj* maleducato(-a), sgarbato(-a)
badminton ['bædmɪntən] *n* badminton *m*
bad-tempered [bæd'tɛmpəd] *adj* irritabile; (*in bad mood*) di malumore
baffle ['bæfl] *vt* (*puzzle*) confondere
baffling ['bæflɪŋ] *adj* sconcertante
bag [bæg] *n* sacco; (*handbag etc*) borsa; (*of hunter*) carniere *m*; bottino ■ *vt* (*col: take*) mettersi in tasca; prendersi; **bags of** (*col: lots of*) un sacco di; **to pack one's bags** fare le valigie; **bags under the eyes** borse sotto gli occhi
bagful ['bægful] *n* sacco (pieno)
baggage ['bægɪdʒ] *n* bagagli *mpl*
baggage allowance *n* peso bagaglio consentito
baggage car *n* (*US*) bagagliaio
baggage claim *n* ritiro bagagli
baggy ['bægɪ] *adj* largo(-a), sformato(-a)
Baghdad [bæg'dæd] *n* Bagdad *f*
bag lady *n* (*col*) stracciona, barbona

bagpipes ['bægpaɪps] *npl* cornamusa
bag-snatcher ['bægsnætʃəʳ] *n* (*Brit*) scippatore(-trice)
bag-snatching ['bægsnætʃɪŋ] *n* (*Brit*) scippo
Bahamas [bə'hɑːməz] *npl*: **the ~** le isole Bahama
Bahrain [bɑː'reɪn] *n* Bahrein *m*
bail [beɪl] *n* cauzione *f* ■ *vt* (*prisoner*: *also*: **to grant bail to**) concedere la libertà provvisoria su cauzione a; (*Naut*: *also*: **bail out**) *see* **bale out**; **to be released on ~** essere rilasciato(-a) su cauzione
▸ **bail out** *vt* (*prisoner*) ottenere la libertà provvisoria su cauzione di; (*fig*) tirare fuori dai guai ■ *vi see* **bale out**
bailiff ['beɪlɪf] *n* usciere *m*; fattore *m*
bait [beɪt] *n* esca ■ *vt* (*hook*) innescare; (*trap*) munire di esca; (*fig*) tormentare
bake [beɪk] *vt* cuocere al forno ■ *vi* cuocersi al forno
baked beans *npl* fagioli *mpl* all'uccelletto
baked potato *n* patata (con la buccia) cotta al forno
baker ['beɪkəʳ] *n* fornaio(-a), panettiere(-a)
bakery ['beɪkərɪ] *n* panetteria
baking ['beɪkɪŋ] *n* cottura (al forno)
baking powder *n* lievito in polvere
baking tin *n* stampo, tortiera
baking tray *n* teglia
balaclava [bælə'klɑːvə] *n* (*also*: **balaclava helmet**) passamontagna *m inv*
balance ['bæləns] *n* equilibrio; (*Comm*: *sum*) bilancio; (*scales*) bilancia ■ *vt* tenere in equilibrio; (*pros and cons*) soppesare; (*budget*) far quadrare; (*account*) pareggiare; (*compensate*) contrappesare; **~ of trade/payments** bilancia commerciale/dei pagamenti; **~ brought forward** saldo riportato; **~ carried forward** saldo da riportare; **to ~ the books** fare il bilancio
balanced ['bælənst] *adj* (*personality, diet*) equilibrato(-a)
balance sheet *n* bilancio
balcony ['bælkənɪ] *n* balcone *m*
bald [bɔːld] *adj* calvo(-a)
baldness ['bɔːldnɪs] *n* calvizie *f*
bale [beɪl] *n* balla
▸ **bale out** *vt* (*Naut*: *water*) vuotare; (: *boat*) aggottare ■ *vi* (*of a plane*) gettarsi col paracadute
Balearic Islands [bælɪ'ærɪk] *npl*: **the ~** le (isole) Baleari
baleful ['beɪlful] *adj* funesto(-a)
balk [bɔːlk] *vi*: **to ~ (at)** tirarsi indietro (davanti a); (*horse*) recalcitrare (davanti a)
Balkan ['bɔːlkən] *adj* balcanico(-a) ■ *n*: **the Balkans** i Balcani
ball [bɔːl] *n* palla; (*football*) pallone *m*; (*for golf*) pallina; (*dance*) ballo; **to play ~ (with sb)** giocare a palla (con qn); (*fig*) stare al gioco (di qn); **to be on the ~** (*fig*: *competent*) essere in gamba; (: *alert*) stare all'erta; **to start the ~ rolling** (*fig*) fare la prima mossa; **the ~ is in your court** (*fig*) a lei la prossima mossa; *see also* **balls**
ballad ['bæləd] *n* ballata
ballast ['bæləst] *n* zavorra
ball bearing *n* cuscinetto a sfere
ball cock *n* galleggiante *m*
ballerina [bælə'riːnə] *n* ballerina
ballet ['bæleɪ] *n* balletto
ballet dancer *n* ballerino(-a)
ballistic [bə'lɪstɪk] *adj* balistico(-a)
ballistics [bə'lɪstɪks] *n* balistica
balloon [bə'luːn] *n* pallone *m*; (*in comic strip*) fumetto ■ *vi* gonfiarsi
balloonist [bə'luːnɪst] *n* aeronauta *m/f*
ballot ['bælət] *n* scrutinio
ballot box *n* urna (per le schede)
ballot paper *n* scheda
ballpark ['bɔːlpɑːk] *n* (*US*) stadio di baseball
ballpark figure *n* (*col*) cifra approssimativa
ball-point pen ['bɔːlpɔɪnt-] *n* penna a sfera
ballroom ['bɔːlrum] *n* sala da ballo
balls [bɔːlz] *npl* (*col!*) coglioni *mpl* (*!*)
balm [bɑːm] *n* balsamo
balmy ['bɑːmɪ] *adj* (*breeze, air*) balsamico(-a); (*Brit col*) = **barmy**
BALPA ['bælpə] *n abbr* (= *British Airline Pilots' Association*) *sindacato dei piloti*
balsa ['bɔːlsə], **balsa wood** *n* (legno di) balsa
balsam ['bɔːlsəm] *n* balsamo
Baltic ['bɔːltɪk] *adj, n*: **the ~ Sea** il (mar) Baltico
balustrade [bæləs'treɪd] *n* balaustrata
bamboo [bæm'buː] *n* bambù *m*
bamboozle [bæm'buːzl] *vt* (*col*) infinocchiare
ban [bæn] *n* interdizione *f* ■ *vt* interdire; **he was banned from driving** (*Brit*) gli hanno ritirato la patente
banal [bə'nɑːl] *adj* banale
banana [bə'nɑːnə] *n* banana
band [bænd] *n* banda; (*at a dance*) orchestra; (*Mil*) fanfara
▸ **band together** *vi* collegarsi
bandage ['bændɪdʒ] *n* benda
Band-Aid® ['bændeɪd] *n* (*US*) cerotto
B & B *n abbr* = **bed and breakfast**
bandit ['bændɪt] *n* bandito
bandstand ['bændstænd] *n* palco dell'orchestra
bandwagon ['bændwægən] *n*: **to jump on the ~** (*fig*) seguire la corrente
bandy ['bændɪ] *vt* (*jokes, insults*) scambiare

▸ **bandy about** *vt* far circolare
bandy-legged ['bændɪ'lɛgɪd] *adj* dalle gambe storte
bane [beɪn] *n*: **it** (*or* **he** *etc*) **is the ~ of my life** è la mia rovina
bang [bæŋ] *n* botta; (*of door*) lo sbattere; (*blow*) colpo ▪ *vt* battere (violentemente); (*door*) sbattere ▪ *vi* scoppiare; sbattere; **to ~ at the door** picchiare alla porta; **to ~ into sth** sbattere contro qc ▪ *adv*: **to be ~ on time** (*Brit col*) spaccare il secondo; *see also* **bangs**
banger ['bæŋəʳ] *n* (*Brit*: *car*: *also*: **old banger**) macinino; (*Brit col*: *sausage*) salsiccia; (*firework*) mortaretto
Bangkok ['bæŋkɔk] *n* Bangkok *f*
Bangladesh [bɑːŋglə'dɛʃ] *n* Bangladesh *m*
bangle ['bæŋgl] *n* braccialetto
bangs [bæŋz] *npl* (*US*: *fringe*) frangia, frangetta
banish ['bænɪʃ] *vt* bandire
banister ['bænɪstə] *n*, **banisters** ['bænɪstəz] *npl* ringhiera
banjo (*pl* **banjoes** *or* **banjos**) ['bændʒəu] *n* banjo *m inv*
bank [bæŋk] *n* (*for money*) banca, banco; (*of river, lake*) riva, sponda; (*of earth*) banco ▪ *vi* (*Aviat*) inclinarsi in virata; (*Comm*): **they ~ with Pitt's** sono clienti di Pitt's
▸ **bank on** *vt fus* contare su
bank account *n* conto in banca
bank balance *n* saldo; **a healthy ~** un solido conto in banca
bank card *n* = **banker's card**
bank charges *npl* (*Brit*) spese *fpl* bancarie
bank draft *n* assegno circolare *or* bancario
banker ['bæŋkəʳ] *n* banchiere *m*; **~'s card** (*Brit*) carta *f* assegni *inv*; **~'s order** (*Brit*) ordine *m* di banca
bank giro *n* bancogiro
bank holiday *n* (*Brit*) *giorno di festa*; *vedi nota*

BANK HOLIDAY

Una *bank holiday*, in Gran Bretagna, è una giornata in cui le banche e molti negozi sono chiusi. Generalmente le *bank holiday* cadono di lunedì e molti ne approfittano per fare una breve vacanza fuori città. Di conseguenza, durante questi fine settimana lunghi ("*bank holiday weekend*") si verifica un notevole aumento del traffico sulle strade, negli aeroporti e nelle stazioni e molte località turistiche registrano il tutto esaurito.

banking ['bæŋkɪŋ] *n* attività bancaria; professione *f* di banchiere
banking hours *npl* orario di sportello
bank loan *n* prestito bancario
bank manager *n* direttore *m* di banca
banknote ['bæŋknəut] *n* banconota
bank rate *n* tasso bancario
bankrupt ['bæŋkrʌpt] *adj, n* fallito(-a); **to go ~** fallire
bankruptcy ['bæŋkrʌptsɪ] *n* fallimento
bank statement *n* estratto conto
banned substance *n* sostanza al bando (*nello sport*)
banner ['bænəʳ] *n* striscione *m*
bannister ['bænɪstə] *n*, **bannisters** ['bænɪstəz] *npl see* **banister**
banns [bænz] *npl* pubblicazioni *fpl* di matrimonio
banquet ['bæŋkwɪt] *n* banchetto
bantam-weight ['bæntəmweɪt] *n* peso gallo
banter ['bæntəʳ] *n* scherzi *mpl* bonari
baptism ['bæptɪzəm] *n* battesimo
Baptist ['bæptɪst] *adj, n* battista (*m/f*)
baptize [bæp'taɪz] *vt* battezzare
bar [bɑːʳ] *n* barra; (*of window etc*) sbarra; (*of chocolate*) tavoletta; (*fig*) ostacolo; restrizione *f*; (*pub*) bar *m inv*; (*counter*: *in pub*) banco; (*Mus*) battuta ▪ *vt* (*road, window*) sbarrare; (*person*) escludere; (*activity*) interdire; **~ of soap** saponetta; **the B~** (*Law*) l'Ordine *m* degli avvocati; **behind bars** (*prisoner*) dietro le sbarre; **~ none** senza eccezione
Barbados [bɑː'beɪdɔs] *n* Barbados *fsg*
barbaric [bɑː'bærɪk], **barbarous** ['bɑːbərəs] *adj* barbaro(-a), barbarico(-a)
barbecue ['bɑːbɪkjuː] *n* barbecue *m inv*
barbed wire ['bɑːbd-] *n* filo spinato
barber ['bɑːbəʳ] *n* barbiere *m*
barbiturate [bɑː'bɪtjurɪt] *n* barbiturico
Barcelona [bɑːsɪ'ləunə] *n* Barcellona
bar chart *n* diagramma *m* di frequenza
bar code *n* codice *m* a barre
bare [bɛəʳ] *adj* nudo(-a) ▪ *vt* scoprire, denudare; (*teeth*) mostrare; **the ~ essentials** lo stretto necessario
bareback ['bɛəbæk] *adv* senza sella
barefaced ['bɛəfeɪst] *adj* sfacciato(-a)
barefoot ['bɛəfut] *adj, adv* scalzo(-a)
bareheaded [bɛə'hɛdɪd] *adj, adv* a capo scoperto
barely ['bɛəlɪ] *adv* appena
Barents Sea ['bærənts-] *n*: **the ~** il mar di Barents
bargain ['bɑːgɪn] *n* (*transaction*) contratto; (*good buy*) affare *m* ▪ *vi* (*haggle*) tirare sul prezzo; (*trade*) contrattare; **into the ~** per giunta
▸ **bargain for** *vt fus* (*col*): **to ~ for sth** aspettarsi qc; **he got more than he bargained for** gli è andata peggio di quel che si aspettasse

bargaining [ˈbɑːɡənɪŋ] *n* contrattazione *f*
bargaining position *n*: **to be in a weak/strong ~** non avere/avere potere contrattuale
barge [bɑːdʒ] *n* chiatta
▸ **barge in** *vi* (*walk in*) piombare dentro; (*interrupt talk*) intromettersi a sproposito
▸ **barge into** *vt fus* urtare contro
baritone [ˈbærɪtəun] *n* baritono
barium meal [ˈbɛərɪəm-] *n* (pasto di) bario
bark [bɑːk] *n* (*of tree*) corteccia; (*of dog*) abbaio ■ *vi* abbaiare
barley [ˈbɑːlɪ] *n* orzo
barley sugar *n* zucchero d'orzo
barmaid [ˈbɑːmeɪd] *n* cameriera al banco
barman [ˈbɑːmən] *n* barista *m*
barmy [ˈbɑːmɪ] *adj* (*Brit col*) tocco(-a)
barn [bɑːn] *n* granaio; (*for animals*) stalla
barnacle [ˈbɑːnəkl] *n* cirripede *m*
barn owl *n* barbagianni *m inv*
barometer [bəˈrɔmɪtəʳ] *n* barometro
baron [ˈbærən] *n* barone *m*; (*fig*) magnate *m*; **the oil barons** i magnati del petrolio; **the press barons** i baroni della stampa
baroness [ˈbærənɪs] *n* baronessa
baronet [ˈbærənɪt] *n* baronetto
barrack [ˈbærək] *vt* (*Brit*): **to ~ sb** subissare qn di grida e fischi
barracking [ˈbærəkɪŋ] *n* (*Brit*): **to give sb a ~** subissare qn di grida e fischi
barracks [ˈbærəks] *npl* caserma
barrage [ˈbærɑːʒ] *n* (*Mil*) sbarramento; **a ~ of questions** una raffica di *or* un fuoco di fila di domande
barrel [ˈbærəl] *n* barile *m*; (*of gun*) canna
barrel organ *n* organetto a cilindro
barren [ˈbærən] *adj* sterile; (*soil*) arido(-a)
barricade [bærɪˈkeɪd] *n* barricata ■ *vt* barricare
barrier [ˈbærɪəʳ] *n* barriera; (*Brit*: *also*: **crash barrier**) guardrail *m inv*
barrier cream *n* (*Brit*) crema protettiva
barring [ˈbɑːrɪŋ] *prep* salvo
barrister [ˈbærɪstəʳ] *n* (*Brit*) avvocato; *vedi nota*

BARRISTER

Il *barrister* è un membro della più prestigiosa delle due branche della professione legale (l'altra è quella dei "*solicitor*"); la sua funzione è quella di rappresentare i propri clienti in tutte le corti ("*magistrates' court*", "*crown court*" e "*Court of Appeal*"), generalmente seguendo le istruzioni del caso preparate dai "*solicitor*".

barrow [ˈbærəu] *n* (*cart*) carriola
barstool [ˈbɑːstuːl] *n* sgabello
Bart. *abbr* (*Brit*) = **baronet**
bartender [ˈbɑːtɛndəʳ] *n* (*US*) barista *m*
barter [ˈbɑːtəʳ] *n* baratto ■ *vt*: **to ~ sth for** barattare qc con
base [beɪs] *n* base *f* ■ *adj* vile ■ *vt*: **to ~ sth on** basare qc su; **to ~ at** (*troops*) mettere di stanza a; **coffee-based** a base di caffè; **a Paris-based firm** una ditta con sede centrale a Parigi; **I'm based in London** sono di base *or* ho base a Londra
baseball [ˈbeɪsbɔːl] *n* baseball *m*
baseboard [ˈbeɪsbɔːd] *n* (*US*) zoccolo, battiscopa *m inv*
base camp *n* campo *m* base *inv*
Basel [bɑːl] *n* = **Basle**
baseline [ˈbeɪslaɪn] *n* (*Tennis*) linea di fondo
basement [ˈbeɪsmənt] *n* seminterrato; (*of shop*) sotterraneo
base rate *n* tasso di base
bases [ˈbeɪsiːz] *npl of* **basis**; [ˈbeɪsɪz] *npl of* **base**
bash [bæʃ] *vt* (*col*) picchiare ■ *n*: **I'll have a ~ (at it)** (*Brit col*) ci proverò; **bashed in** *adj* sfondato(-a)
▸ **bash up** *vt* (*col*: *car*) sfasciare; (: *Brit*: *person*) riempire di *or* prendere a botte
bashful [ˈbæʃful] *adj* timido(-a)
bashing [ˈbæʃɪŋ] *n*: **Paki-/queer-~** atti *mpl* di violenza contro i pachistani/gli omosessuali
BASIC [ˈbeɪsɪk] *n* (*Comput*) BASIC *m*
basic [ˈbeɪsɪk] *adj* (*principles, precautions, rules*) elementare; (*salary*) base *inv* (*after n*)
basically [ˈbeɪsɪklɪ] *adv* fondamentalmente, sostanzialmente
basic rate *n* (*of tax*) aliquota minima
basil [ˈbæzl] *n* basilico
basin [ˈbeɪsn] *n* (*vessel, also Geo*) bacino; (*also*: **washbasin**) lavabo; (*Brit*: *for food*) terrina
basis (*pl* **bases**) [ˈbeɪsɪs, -siːz] *n* base *f*; **on the ~ of what you've said** in base alle sue asserzioni
bask [bɑːsk] *vi*: **to ~ in the sun** crogiolarsi al sole
basket [ˈbɑːskɪt] *n* cesta; (*smaller*) cestino; (*with handle*) paniere *m*
basketball [ˈbɑːskɪtbɔːl] *n* pallacanestro *f*
basketball player *n* cestista *m/f*
Basle [bɑːl] *n* Basilea
basmati rice [bæzˈmætɪ-] *n* riso basmati
Basque [bæsk] *adj, n* basco(-a)
bass [beɪs] *n* (*Mus*) basso
bass clef *n* chiave *f* di basso
bassoon [bəˈsuːn] *n* fagotto
bastard [ˈbɑːstəd] *n* bastardo(-a); (*col!*) stronzo (*!*)

baste [beɪst] *vt* (*Culin*) ungere con grasso; (*Sewing*) imbastire
bastion ['bæstɪən] *n* bastione *m*; (*fig*) baluardo
bat [bæt] *n* pipistrello; (*for baseball etc*) mazza; (*Brit: for table tennis*) racchetta; **off one's own ~** di propria iniziativa ■ *vt*: **he didn't ~ an eyelid** non battè ciglio
batch [bætʃ] *n* (*of bread*) infornata; (*of papers*) cumulo; (*of applicants, letters*) gruppo; (*of work*) sezione *f*; (*of goods*) partita, lotto
batch processing *n* (*Comput*) elaborazione *f* a blocchi
bated ['beɪtɪd] *adj*: **with ~ breath** col fiato sospeso
bath (*pl* **baths**) [bɑ:θ, bɑ:ðz] *n* bagno; (*bathtub*) vasca da bagno ■ *vt* far fare il bagno a; **to have a ~** fare un bagno; *see also* **baths**
bathchair ['bɑ:θtʃɛəʳ] *n* (*Brit*) poltrona a rotelle
bathe [beɪð] *vi* fare il bagno ■ *vt* bagnare; (*wound etc*) lavare
bather ['beɪðəʳ] *n* bagnante *m/f*
bathing ['beɪðɪŋ] *n* bagni *mpl*
bathing cap *n* cuffia da bagno
bathing costume, (*US*) **bathing suit** *n* costume *m* da bagno
bathmat ['bɑ:θmæt] *n* tappetino da bagno
bathrobe ['bɑ:θrəub] *n* accappatoio
bathroom ['bɑ:θrum] *n* stanza da bagno
baths [bɑ:ðz] *npl* bagni *mpl* pubblici
bath towel *n* asciugamano da bagno
bathtub ['bɑ:θtʌb] *n* (vasca da) bagno
batman ['bætmən] *n* (*Brit Mil*) attendente *m*
baton ['bætən] *n* bastone *m*; (*Mus*) bacchetta
battalion [bə'tælɪən] *n* battaglione *m*
batten ['bætən] *n* (*Carpentry*) assicella, correntino; (*for flooring*) tavola per pavimenti; (*Naut*) serretta; (*: on sail*) stecca
▸**batten down** *vt* (*Naut*): **to ~ down the hatches** chiudere i boccaporti
batter ['bætəʳ] *vt* battere ■ *n* pastetta
battered ['bætəd] *adj* (*hat*) sformato(-a); (*pan*) ammaccato(-a); **~ wife/baby** consorte *f*/bambino(-a) maltrattato(-a)
battering ram ['bætərɪŋ-] *n* ariete *m*
battery ['bætərɪ] *n* batteria; (*of torch*) pila
battery charger *n* caricabatterie *m inv*
battle ['bætl] *n* battaglia ■ *vi* battagliare, lottare; **to fight a losing ~** (*fig*) battersi per una causa persa; **that's half the ~** (*col*) è già una mezza vittoria
battle dress *n* uniforme *f* da combattimento
battlefield ['bætlfi:ld] *n* campo di battaglia
battlements ['bætlmənts] *npl* bastioni *mpl*
battleship ['bætlʃɪp] *n* nave *f* da guerra
batty ['bætɪ] *adj* (*col: person*) svitato(-a), strambo(-a); (*behaviour, idea*) strampalato(-a)
bauble ['bɔ:bl] *n* ninnolo
baud [bɔ:d] *n* (*Comput*) baud *m inv*
baulk [bɔ:lk] *vi* = **balk**
bauxite ['bɔ:ksaɪt] *n* bauxite *f*
Bavaria [bə'vɛərɪə] *n* Bavaria
Bavarian [bə'vɛərɪən] *adj, n* bavarese (*m/f*)
bawdy ['bɔ:dɪ] *adj* piccante
bawl [bɔ:l] *vi* urlare
bay [beɪ] *n* (*of sea*) baia; (*Brit: for parking*) piazzola di sosta; (*: for loading*) piazzale *m* di (sosta e) carico; **to hold sb at ~** tenere qn a bada
bay leaf *n* foglia d'alloro
bayonet ['beɪənɪt] *n* baionetta
bay tree *n* alloro
bay window *n* bovindo
bazaar [bə'zɑ:ʳ] *n* bazar *m inv*; vendita di beneficenza
bazooka [bə'zu:kə] *n* bazooka *m inv*
BB *n abbr* (*Brit: = Boys' Brigade*) *organizzazione giovanile a fine educativo*
BBB *n abbr* (*US: = Better Business Bureau*) *organismo per la difesa dei consumatori*
BBC *n abbr* (*= British Broadcasting Corporation*) *vedi nota*

BBC

La BBC è l'azienda statale che fornisce il servizio radiofonico e televisivo in Gran Bretagna. Pur dovendo rispondere al Parlamento del proprio operato, la BBC non è soggetta al controllo dello stato per scelte e programmi, anche perché si autofinanzia con il ricavato dei canoni d'abbonamento. La BBC ha canali televisivi digitali e terrestri, oltre a diverse emittenti radiofoniche nazionali e locali. Fornisce un servizio di informazione internazionale, il "BBC World Service", trasmesso in tutto il mondo.

BBE *n abbr* (*US: = Benevolent and Protective Order of Elks*) *organizzazione filantropica*
BC *adv abbr* (*= before Christ*) a.C. ■ *abbr* (*Canada*) = **British Columbia**
BCG *n abbr* (*= Bacillus Calmette-Guérin*) *vaccino antitubercolare*
BD *n abbr* (*= Bachelor of Divinity*) *titolo di studio*
B/D *abbr* = **bank draft**
BDS *n abbr* (*= Bachelor of Dental Surgery*) *titolo di studio*

 KEYWORD

be [bi:] (*pt* **was, were**, *pp* **been**) *aux vb* **1** (*with present participle: forming continuous tenses*): **what are you doing?** che fai?, che stai facendo?; **they're coming tomorrow** vengono domani; **I've been waiting for her for hours** sono ore che l'aspetto
2 (*with pp: forming passives*) essere; **to be killed** essere *or* venire ucciso(-a); **the box had been opened** la scatola era stata aperta; **the thief was nowhere to be seen** il ladro non si trovava da nessuna parte
3 (*in tag questions*): **it was fun, wasn't it?** è stato divertente, no?; **he's good-looking, isn't he?** è un bell'uomo, vero?; **she's back, is she?** così è tornata, eh?
4 (*+ to + infinitive*): **the house is to be sold** abbiamo (*or* hanno *etc*) intenzione di vendere casa; **you're to be congratulated for all your work** dovremo farvi i complimenti per tutto il vostro lavoro; **am I to understand that ...?** devo dedurre che ...?; **he's not to open it** non deve aprirlo; **he was to have come yesterday** sarebbe dovuto venire ieri
■ *vb + complement* **1** (*gen*) essere; **I'm English** sono inglese; **I'm tired** sono stanco(-a); **I'm hot/cold** ho caldo/freddo; **he's a doctor** è medico; **2 and 2 are 4** 2 più 2 fa 4; **be careful!** sta attento!; **be good** sii buono; **if I were you ...** se fossi in te ...
2 (*of health*) stare; **how are you?** come sta?; **he's very ill** sta molto male
3 (*of age*): **how old are you?** quanti anni hai?; **I'm sixteen (years old)** ho sedici anni
4 (*cost*) costare; **how much was the meal?** quant'era *or* quanto costava il pranzo?; **that'll be £5, please** (sono) 5 sterline, per favore
■ *vi* **1** (*exist, occur etc*) essere, esistere; **the best singer that ever was** il migliore cantante mai esistito *or* di tutti tempi; **be that as it may** comunque sia, sia come sia; **so be it** sia pure, e sia
2 (*referring to place*) essere, trovarsi; **I won't be here tomorrow** non ci sarò domani; **Edinburgh is in Scotland** Edimburgo si trova in Scozia
3 (*referring to movement*): **where have you been?** dove sei stato?; **I've been to China** sono stato in Cina
■ *impers vb* **1** (*referring to time, distance*) essere; **it's 5 o'clock** sono le 5; **it's the 28th of April** è il 28 aprile; **it's 10 km to the village** di qui al paese sono 10 km
2 (*referring to the weather*) fare; **it's too hot/cold** fa troppo caldo/freddo; **it's windy** c'è vento
3 (*emphatic*): **it's me** sono io; **it's only me** sono solo io; **it was Maria who paid the bill** è stata Maria che ha pagato il conto

B/E *abbr* = **bill of exchange**
beach [bi:tʃ] *n* spiaggia ■ *vt* tirare in secco
beach buggy *n* dune buggy *f inv*
beachcomber ['bi:tʃkəuməʳ] *n* vagabondo (*che s'aggira sulla spiaggia*)
beachwear ['bi:tʃwɛəʳ] *n* articoli *mpl* da spiaggia
beacon ['bi:kən] *n* (*lighthouse*) faro; (*marker*) segnale *m*; (*also*: **radio beacon**) radiofaro
bead [bi:d] *n* perlina; (*of dew, sweat*) goccia; **beads** *npl* (*necklace*) collana
beady ['bi:dɪ] *adj*: **~ eyes** occhi *mpl* piccoli e penetranti
beagle ['bi:gl] *n* cane *m* da lepre
beak [bi:k] *n* becco
beaker ['bi:kəʳ] *n* coppa
beam [bi:m] *n* trave *f*; (*of light*) raggio; (*Radio*) fascio (d'onde) ■ *vi* brillare; (*smile*): **to ~ at sb** rivolgere un radioso sorriso a qn; **to drive on full** *or* **main ~** *or* (*US*) **high ~** guidare con gli abbaglianti accesi
beaming ['bi:mɪŋ] *adj* (*sun, smile*) raggiante
bean [bi:n] *n* fagiolo; (*coffee bean*) chicco
beanpole ['bi:npəul] *n* (*col*) spilungone(-a)
beansprouts ['bi:nsprauts] *npl* germogli *mpl* di soia
bear [bɛəʳ] *n* orso; (*Stock Exchange*) ribassista *m/f* ■ *vb* (*pt* **bore**, *pp* **borne**) [bɔ:ʳ, bɔ:n] *vt* (*gen*) portare; (*produce: fruit*) produrre, dare; (*: traces, signs*) mostrare; (*Comm: interest*) fruttare; (*endure*) sopportare ■ *vi*: **to ~ right/left** piegare a destra/sinistra; **to ~ the responsibility of** assumersi la responsabilità di; **to ~ comparison with** reggere al paragone con; **I can't ~ him** non lo posso soffrire *or* sopportare; **to bring pressure to ~ on sb** fare pressione su qn
▸ **bear out** *vt* (*theory, suspicion*) confermare, convalidare
▸ **bear up** *vi* farsi coraggio; **he bore up well under the strain** ha sopportato bene lo stress
▸ **bear with** *vt fus* (*sb's moods, temper*) sopportare (con pazienza); **~ with me a minute** solo un attimo, prego
bearable ['bɛərəbl] *adj* sopportabile
beard [bɪəd] *n* barba
bearded ['bɪədɪd] *adj* barbuto(-a)
bearer ['bɛərəʳ] *n* portatore *m*; (*of passport*) titolare *m/f*
bearing ['bɛərɪŋ] *n* portamento; (*connection*) rapporto; **bearings** *npl* (*also*: **ball bearings**) cuscinetti *mpl* a sfere; **to take a ~** fare un

rilevamento; **to find one's bearings** orientarsi

beast [bi:st] *n* bestia

beastly ['bi:stlɪ] *adj* meschino(-a); (*weather*) da cani

beat [bi:t] *n* colpo; (*of heart*) battito; (*Mus*) tempo; battuta; (*of policeman*) giro ■ *vt* (*pt* **~**, *pp* **beaten**) battere; **off the beaten track** fuori mano; **to ~ about the bush** menare il cane per l'aia; **to ~ time** battere il tempo; **that beats everything!** (*col*) questo è il colmo!

▸ **beat down** *vt* (*door*) abbattere, buttare giù; (*price*) far abbassare; (*seller*) far scendere ■ *vi* (*rain*) scrosciare; (*sun*) picchiare

▸ **beat off** *vt* respingere

▸ **beat up** *vt* (*col: person*) picchiare; (*eggs*) sbattere

beater ['bi:təʳ] *n* (*for eggs, cream*) frullino

beating ['bi:tɪŋ] *n* botte *fpl*; (*defeat*) batosta; **to take a ~** prendere una (bella) batosta

beat-up [bi:t'ʌp] *adj* (*col*) scassato(-a)

beautician [bju:'tɪʃən] *n* estetista *m/f*

beautiful ['bju:tɪful] *adj* bello(-a)

beautify ['bju:tɪfaɪ] *vt* abbellire

beauty ['bju:tɪ] *n* bellezza; (*concept*) bello; **the ~ of it is that ...** il bello è che ...

beauty contest *n* concorso di bellezza

beauty queen *n* miss *f inv*, reginetta di bellezza

beauty salon *n* istituto di bellezza

beauty sleep *n*: **to get one's ~** farsi un sonno ristoratore

beauty spot *n* neo; (*Brit Tourism*) luogo pittoresco

beaver ['bi:vəʳ] *n* castoro

becalmed [bɪ'kɑ:md] *adj* in bonaccia

became [bɪ'keɪm] *pt of* **become**

because [bɪ'kɔz] *conj* perché; **~ of** *prep* a causa di

beck [bɛk] *n*: **to be at sb's ~ and call** essere a completa disposizione di qn

beckon ['bɛkən] *vt* (*also*: **beckon to**) chiamare con un cenno

become [bɪ'kʌm] *vt* (*irreg: like* **come**) diventare; **to ~ fat/thin** ingrassarsi/dimagrire; **to ~ angry** arrabbiarsi; **it became known that ...** si è venuto a sapere che ...; **what has ~ of him?** che gli è successo?

becoming [bɪ'kʌmɪŋ] *adj* (*behaviour*) che si conviene; (*clothes*) grazioso(-a)

BECTU ['bɛktu:] *n abbr* (*Brit*) = **Broadcasting Entertainment Cinematographic and Theatre Union**

BEd *n abbr* (= *Bachelor of Education*) laurea con abilitazione all'insegnamento

bed [bɛd] *n* letto; (*of flowers*) aiuola; (*of coal, clay*) strato; (*of sea, lake*) fondo; **to go to ~** andare a letto

▸ **bed down** *vi* sistemarsi (per dormire)

bed and breakfast *n* (*terms*) camera con colazione; (*place*) ≈ pensione *f* familiare; *vedi nota*

BED AND BREAKFAST (B & B)

I *bed and breakfasts*, anche *B & Bs*, sono piccole pensioni a conduzione familiare, in case private o fattorie, dove si affittano camere e viene servita al mattino la tradizionale colazione all'inglese. Queste pensioni offrono un servizio di camera con prima colazione, appunto *bed and breakfast*, a prezzi più contenuti rispetto agli alberghi.

bedbug ['bɛdbʌg] *n* cimice *f*

bedclothes ['bɛdkləuðz] *npl* coperte e lenzuola *fpl*

bedcover ['bɛdkʌvəʳ] *n* copriletto

bedding ['bɛdɪŋ] *n* coperte e lenzuola *fpl*

bedevil [bɪ'dɛvl] *vt* (*person*) tormentare; (*plans*) ostacolare continuamente

bedfellow ['bɛdfɛləu] *n*: **they are strange bedfellows** (*fig*) fanno una coppia ben strana

bedlam ['bɛdləm] *n* baraonda

bedpan ['bɛdpæn] *n* padella

bedpost ['bɛdpəust] *n* colonnina del letto

bedraggled [bɪ'drægld] *adj* sbrindellato(-a); (*wet*) fradicio(-a)

bedridden ['bɛdrɪdən] *adj* costretto(-a) a letto

bedrock ['bɛdrɔk] *n* (*Geo*) basamento; (*fig*) fatti *mpl* di base

bedroom ['bɛdrum] *n* camera da letto

Beds *abbr* (*Brit*) = **Bedfordshire**

bed settee *n* divano *m* letto *inv*

bedside ['bɛdsaɪd] *n*: **at sb's ~** al capezzale di qn

bedside lamp *n* lampada da comodino

bedsit ['bɛdsɪt], **bedsitter** ['bɛdsɪtəʳ] *n* (*Brit*) monolocale *m*

bedspread ['bɛdsprɛd] *n* copriletto

bedtime ['bɛdtaɪm] *n*: **it's ~** è ora di andare a letto

bee [bi:] *n* ape *f*; **to have a ~ in one's bonnet (about sth)** avere la fissazione (di qc)

beech [bi:tʃ] *n* faggio

beef [bi:f] *n* manzo

▸ **beef up** *vt* (*col*) rinforzare

beefburger ['bi:fbə:gəʳ] *n* hamburger *m inv*

beefeater ['bi:fi:təʳ] *n* guardia della Torre di Londra

beehive ['bi:haɪv] *n* alveare *m*
bee-keeping ['bi:ki:pɪŋ] *n* apicoltura
beeline ['bi:laɪn] *n*: **to make a ~ for** buttarsi a capo fitto verso
been [bi:n] *pp of* **be**
beep [bi:p] *n* (*of horn*) colpo di clacson; (*of phone etc*) segnale *m* (acustico), bip *m inv* ■ *vi* suonare
beeper ['bi:pəʳ] *n* (*of doctor etc*) cercapersone *m inv*
beer [bɪəʳ] *n* birra
beer belly *n* (*col*) stomaco da bevitore
beer can *n* lattina di birra
beetle ['bi:tl] *n* scarafaggio; coleottero
beetroot ['bi:tru:t] *n* (*Brit*) barbabietola
befall [bɪ'fɔ:l] *vi, vt* (*irreg*: *like* **fall**) accadere (a)
befit [bɪ'fɪt] *vt* addirsi a
before [bɪ'fɔ:ʳ] *prep* (*in time*) prima di; (*in space*) davanti a ■ *conj* prima che + *sub*; prima di ■ *adv* prima; **~ going** prima di andare; **~ she goes** prima che vada; **the week ~** la settimana prima; **I've seen it ~** l'ho già visto; **I've never seen it ~** è la prima volta che lo vedo
beforehand [bɪ'fɔ:hænd] *adv* in anticipo
befriend [bɪ'frɛnd] *vt* assistere; mostrarsi amico a
befuddled [bɪ'fʌdld] *adj* confuso(-a)
beg [bɛg] *vi* chiedere l'elemosina ■ *vt* chiedere in elemosina; (*favour*) chiedere; (*entreat*) pregare; **I ~ your pardon** (*apologising*) mi scusi; (*not hearing*) scusi?; **this begs the question of ...** questo presuppone che sia già risolto il problema di ...
began [bɪ'gæn] *pt of* **begin**
beggar ['bɛgəʳ] *n* (*also*: **beggarman, beggarwoman**) mendicante *m/f*
begin (*pt* **began**, *pp* **begun**) [bɪ'gɪn, bɪ'gæn, bɪ'gʌn] *vt, vi* cominciare; **to ~ doing** *or* **to do sth** incominciare *or* iniziare a fare qc; **I can't ~ to thank you** non so proprio come ringraziarla; **to ~ with, I'd like to know ...** tanto per cominciare vorrei sapere ...; **beginning from Monday** a partire da lunedì
beginner [bɪ'gɪnəʳ] *n* principiante *m/f*
beginning [bɪ'gɪnɪŋ] *n* inizio, principio; **right from the ~** fin dall'inizio
begrudge [bɪ'grʌdʒ] *vt*: **to ~ sb sth** dare qc a qn a malincuore; invidiare qn per qc
beguile [bɪ'gaɪl] *vt* (*enchant*) incantare
beguiling [bɪ'gaɪlɪŋ] *adj* (*charming*) allettante; (*deluding*) ingannevole
begun [bɪ'gʌn] *pp of* **begin**
behalf [bɪ'hɑ:f] *n*: **on ~ of**, (*US*) **in ~ of** per conto di; a nome di
behave [bɪ'heɪv] *vi* comportarsi; (*well*: *also*: **behave o.s.**) comportarsi bene
behaviour, (*US*) **behavior** [bɪ'heɪvjəʳ] *n* comportamento, condotta
behead [bɪ'hɛd] *vt* decapitare
beheld [bɪ'hɛld] *pt, pp of* **behold**
behind [bɪ'haɪnd] *prep* dietro; (*followed by pronoun*) dietro di; (*time*) in ritardo con ■ *adv* dietro; in ritardo ■ *n* didietro; **we're ~ them in technology** siamo più indietro *or* più arretrati di loro nella tecnica; **~ the scenes** dietro le quinte; **to be ~ (schedule) with sth** essere indietro con qc; (*payments*) essere in arretrato con qc; **to leave sth ~** dimenticare di prendere qc
behold [bɪ'həuld] *vt* (*irreg*: *like* **hold**) vedere, scorgere
beige [beɪʒ] *adj* beige *inv*
Beijing [beɪ'dʒɪŋ] *n* Pechino *f*
being ['bi:ɪŋ] *n* essere *m*; **to come into ~** cominciare ad esistere
Beirut [beɪ'ru:t] *n* Beirut *f*
Belarus ['bɛlærus] *n* Bielorussia
Belarussian [bɛlə'rʌʃən] *adj* bielorusso(-a) ■ *n* bielorusso(-a); (*Ling*) bielorusso
belated [bɪ'leɪtɪd] *adj* tardo(-a)
belch [bɛltʃ] *vi* ruttare ■ *vt* (*gen*: *also*: **belch out**: *smoke etc*) eruttare
beleaguered [bɪ'li:gəd] *adj* (*city*) assediato(-a); (*army*) accerchiato(-a); (*fig*) assillato(-a)
Belfast ['bɛlfɑ:st] *n* Belfast *f*
belfry ['bɛlfrɪ] *n* campanile *m*
Belgian ['bɛldʒən] *adj, n* belga (*m/f*)
Belgium ['bɛldʒəm] *n* Belgio
Belgrade [bɛl'greɪd] *n* Belgrado *f*
belie [bɪ'laɪ] *vt* smentire; (*give false impression of*) nascondere
belief [bɪ'li:f] *n* (*opinion*) opinione *f*, convinzione *f*; (*trust, faith*) fede *f*; (*acceptance as true*) credenza; **in the ~ that** nella convinzione che; **it's beyond ~** è incredibile
believe [bɪ'li:v] *vt, vi* credere; **to ~ in** (*God*) credere in; (*ghosts*) credere a; (*method*) avere fiducia in; **I don't ~ in corporal punishment** sono contrario alle punizioni corporali; **he is believed to be abroad** si pensa (che) sia all'estero
believer [bɪ'li:vəʳ] *n* (*Rel*) credente *m/f*; (*in idea, activity*): **to be a ~ in** credere in
belittle [bɪ'lɪtl] *vt* sminuire
Belize [bɛ'li:z] *n* Belize *m*
bell [bɛl] *n* campana; (*small, on door, electric*) campanello; **that rings a ~** (*fig*) mi ricorda qualcosa
bell-bottoms ['bɛlbɔtəmz] *npl* calzoni *mpl* a zampa d'elefante

bellboy ['bɛlbɔɪ], (*US*) **bellhop** ['bɛlhɔp] *n* ragazzo d'albergo, fattorino d'albergo
belligerent [bɪ'lɪdʒərənt] *adj* (*at war*) belligerante; (*fig*) bellicoso(-a)
bellow ['bɛləu] *vi* muggire; (*cry*) urlare (a squarciagola) ■ *vt* (*orders*) urlare (a squarciagola)
bellows ['bɛləuz] *npl* soffietto
bell push *n* (*Brit*) pulsante *m* del campanello
belly ['bɛlɪ] *n* pancia
bellyache ['bɛlɪeɪk] *n* mal *m* di pancia ■ *vi* (*col*) mugugnare
bellybutton ['bɛlɪbʌtn] *n* ombelico
bellyful ['bɛlɪful] *n* (*col*): **to have had a ~ of** (*fig*) averne piene le tasche (di)
belong [bɪ'lɔŋ] *vi*: **to ~ to** appartenere a; (*club etc*) essere socio di; **this book belongs here** questo libro va qui
belongings [bɪ'lɔŋɪŋz] *npl* cose *fpl*, roba; **personal ~** effetti *mpl* personali
Belorussia [bɛləu'rʌʃə] *n* Bielorussia
Belorussian [bɛləu'rʌʃən] *adj*, *n* = **Belarussian**
beloved [bɪ'lʌvɪd] *adj* adorato(-a)
below [bɪ'ləu] *prep* sotto, al di sotto di ■ *adv* sotto, di sotto; giù; **see ~** vedi sotto *or* oltre; **temperatures ~ normal** temperature al di sotto del normale
belt [bɛlt] *n* cintura; (*Tech*) cinghia ■ *vt* (*thrash*) picchiare ■ *vi* (*Brit col*) filarsela; **industrial ~** zona industriale
▸ **belt out** *vt* (*song*) cantare a squarciagola
▸ **belt up** *vi* (*Brit col*) chiudere la boccaccia
beltway ['bɛltweɪ] *n* (*US Aut*) circonvallazione *f*; (: *motorway*) autostrada
bemoan [bɪ'məun] *vt* lamentare
bemused [bɪ'mju:zd] *adj* perplesso(-a), stupito(-a)
bench [bɛntʃ] *n* panca; (*in workshop*) banco; **the B~** (*Law*) la Corte
bench mark *n* banco di prova
bend [bɛnd] *vb* (*pt, pp* **bent**) [bɛnt] *vt* curvare; (*leg, arm*) piegare ■ *vi* curvarsi; piegarsi ■ *n* (*Brit: in road*) curva; (*in pipe, river*) gomito
▸ **bend down** *vi* chinarsi
▸ **bend over** *vi* piegarsi
bends [bɛndz] *npl* (*Med*) embolia
beneath [bɪ'ni:θ] *prep* sotto, al di sotto di; (*unworthy of*) indegno(-a) di ■ *adv* sotto, di sotto
benefactor ['bɛnɪfæktə[r]] *n* benefattore *m*
benefactress ['bɛnɪfæktrɪs] *n* benefattrice *f*
beneficial [bɛnɪ'fɪʃəl] *adj* che fa bene; vantaggioso(-a); **~ to** che giova a
beneficiary [bɛnɪ'fɪʃərɪ] *n* (*Law*) beneficiario(-a)
benefit ['bɛnɪfɪt] *n* beneficio, vantaggio; (*allowance of money*) indennità *f inv* ■ *vt* far bene a ■ *vi*: **he'll ~ from it** ne trarrà beneficio *or* profitto
benefit performance *n* spettacolo di beneficenza
Benelux ['bɛnɪlʌks] *n* Benelux *m*
benevolent [bɪ'nɛvələnt] *adj* benevolo(-a)
BEng *n abbr* (= *Bachelor of Engineering*) *laurea in ingegneria*
benign [bɪ'naɪn] *adj* benevolo(-a); (*Med*) benigno(-a)
bent [bɛnt] *pt, pp of* **bend** ■ *n* inclinazione *f* ■ *adj* (*wire, pipe*) piegato(-a), storto(-a); (*col: dishonest*) losco(-a); **to be ~ on** essere deciso(-a) a
bequeath [bɪ'kwi:ð] *vt* lasciare in eredità
bequest [bɪ'kwɛst] *n* lascito
bereaved [bɪ'ri:vd] *adj* in lutto ■ *npl*: **the ~** i familiari in lutto
bereavement [bɪ'ri:vmənt] *n* lutto
beret ['bɛreɪ] *n* berretto
Bering Sea ['bɛrɪŋ-] *n*: **the ~** il mar di Bering
berk [bə:k] *n* (*Brit col!*) coglione(-a) (!)
Berks *abbr* (*Brit*) = **Berkshire**
Berlin [bə:'lɪn] *n* Berlino *f*; **East/West ~** Berlino est/ovest
berm [bə:m] *n* (*US Aut*) corsia d'emergenza
Bermuda [bə:'mju:də] *n* le Bermude
Bermuda shorts *npl* bermuda *mpl*
Bern [bə:n] *n* Berna *f*
berry ['bɛrɪ] *n* bacca
berserk [bə'sə:k] *adj*: **to go ~** montare su tutte le furie
berth [bə:θ] *n* (*bed*) cuccetta; (*for ship*) ormeggio ■ *vi* (*in harbour*) entrare in porto; (*at anchor*) gettare l'ancora; **to give sb a wide ~** (*fig*) tenersi alla larga da qn
beseech (*pt, pp* **besought**) [bɪ'si:tʃ, bɪ'sɔ:t] *vt* implorare
beset (*pt, pp* **~**) [bɪ'sɛt] *vt* assalire ■ *adj*: **a policy ~ with dangers** una politica irta *or* piena di pericoli
besetting [bɪ'sɛtɪŋ] *adj*: **his ~ sin** il suo più grande difetto
beside [bɪ'saɪd] *prep* accanto a; (*compared with*) rispetto a, in confronto a; **to be ~ o.s. (with anger)** essere fuori di sé; **that's ~ the point** non c'entra
besides [bɪ'saɪdz] *adv* inoltre, per di più ■ *prep* oltre a; (*except*) a parte
besiege [bɪ'si:dʒ] *vt* (*town*) assediare; (*fig*) tempestare
besotted [bɪ'sɔtɪd] *adj* (*Brit*): **~ with** infatuato(-a) di
besought [bɪ'sɔ:t] *pt, pp of* **beseech**
bespectacled [bɪ'spɛktɪkld] *adj* occhialuto(-a)
bespoke [bɪ'spəuk] *adj* (*Brit: garment*) su misura; **~ tailor** sarto

best [bɛst] *adj* migliore ▪ *adv* meglio; **the ~ thing to do is ...** la cosa migliore da fare *or* farsi è ...; **the ~ part of** *(quantity)* la maggior parte di; **at ~** tutt'al più; **to make the ~ of sth** cavare il meglio possibile da qc; **to do one's ~** fare del proprio meglio; **to the ~ of my knowledge** per quel che ne so; **to the ~ of my ability** al massimo delle mie capacità; **he's not exactly patient at the ~ of times** non è mai molto paziente
best-before date *n (Comm)* data limite d'utilizzo *or* di consumo
best man *n* testimone *m* dello sposo
bestow [bɪ'stəu] *vt*: **to ~ sth on sb** conferire qc a qn
bestseller ['bɛst'sɛləʳ] *n* bestseller *m inv*
bet [bɛt] *n* scommessa ▪ *vt, vi (pt, pp* **~** *or* **betted**) scommettere; **it's a safe ~** *(fig)* è molto probabile
Bethlehem ['bɛθlɪhɛm] *n* Betlemme *f*
betray [bɪ'treɪ] *vt* tradire
betrayal [bɪ'treɪəl] *n* tradimento
better ['bɛtəʳ] *adj* migliore ▪ *adv* meglio ▪ *vt* migliorare ▪ *n*: **to get the ~ of** avere la meglio su; **you had ~ do it** è meglio che lo faccia; **he thought ~ of it** cambiò idea; **to get ~** migliorare; **a change for the ~** un cambiamento in meglio; **that's ~!** così va meglio!; **I had ~ go** dovrei andare; **~ off** *adj* più ricco(-a); *(fig)*: **you'd be ~ off this way** starebbe meglio così
betting ['bɛtɪŋ] *n* scommesse *fpl*
betting shop *n (Brit)* ufficio dell'allibratore
between [bɪ'twi:n] *prep* tra ▪ *adv* in mezzo, nel mezzo; **the road ~ here and London** la strada da qui a Londra; **we only had £5 ~ us** fra tutti e due avevamo solo 5 sterline
bevel ['bɛvl] *n (also:* **bevel(led) edge**) profilo smussato
beverage ['bɛvərɪdʒ] *n* bevanda
bevy ['bɛvɪ] *n*: **a ~ of** una banda di
bewail [bɪ'weɪl] *vt* lamentare
beware [bɪ'wɛəʳ] *vt, vi*: **to ~ (of)** stare attento(-a) (a)
bewildered [bɪ'wɪldəd] *adj* sconcertato(-a), confuso(-a)
bewildering [bɪ'wɪldərɪŋ] *adj* sconcertante, sbalorditivo(-a)
bewitching [bɪ'wɪtʃɪŋ] *adj* affascinante
beyond [bɪ'jɔnd] *prep (in space)* oltre; *(exceeding)* al di sopra di ▪ *adv* di là; **~ doubt** senza dubbio; **~ repair** irreparabile
b/f *abbr* = **brought forward**
BFPO *n abbr (= British Forces Post Office) recapito delle truppe britanniche all'estero*
bhp *n abbr (Aut: = brake horsepower)* c.v. (= *cavallo vapore)*
bi... [baɪ] *prefix* bi...
biannual [baɪ'ænjuəl] *adj* semestrale
bias ['baɪəs] *n (prejudice)* pregiudizio; *(preference)* preferenza
biased, biassed ['baɪəst] *adj* parziale; **to be bias(s)ed against** essere prevenuto(-a) contro
biathlon [baɪ'æθlən] *n* biathlon *m*
bib [bɪb] *n* bavaglino
Bible ['baɪbl] *n* Bibbia
bibliography [bɪblɪ'ɔgrəfɪ] *n* bibliografia
bicarbonate of soda [baɪ'kɑ:bənɪt-] *n* bicarbonato (di sodio)
bicentenary [baɪsɛn'ti:nərɪ], **bicentennial** [baɪsɛn'tɛnɪəl] *n* bicentenario
biceps ['baɪsɛps] *n* bicipite *m*
bicker ['bɪkəʳ] *vi* bisticciare
bicycle ['baɪsɪkl] *n* bicicletta
bicycle path *n*, **bicycle track** *n* sentiero ciclabile
bicycle pump *n* pompa della bicicletta
bid [bɪd] *n* offerta; *(attempt)* tentativo ▪ *vb (pt* **bade** *or* **~**, *pp* **bidden** *or* **~**) *vi* fare un'offerta ▪ *vt* fare un'offerta di; **to ~ sb good day** dire buon giorno a qn
bidder ['bɪdəʳ] *n*: **the highest ~** il maggior offerente
bidding ['bɪdɪŋ] *n* offerte *fpl*
bide [baɪd] *vt*: **to ~ one's time** aspettare il momento giusto
bidet ['bi:deɪ] *n* bidè *m inv*
bidirectional ['baɪdɪ'rɛkʃənl] *adj* bidirezionale
biennial [baɪ'ɛnɪəl] *adj* biennale ▪ *n* (pianta) biennale *f*
bier [bɪəʳ] *n* bara
bifocals [baɪ'fəuklz] *npl* occhiali *mpl* bifocali
big [bɪg] *adj* grande; grosso(-a); **my ~ brother** mio fratello maggiore; **to do things in a ~ way** fare le cose in grande
bigamy ['bɪgəmɪ] *n* bigamia
big dipper [-'dɪpəʳ] *n* montagne *fpl* russe, otto *m inv* volante
big end *n (Aut)* testa di biella
biggish ['bɪgɪʃ] *adj see* **big** piuttosto grande, piuttosto grosso(-a); **a ~ rent** un affitto piuttosto alto
bigheaded ['bɪg'hɛdɪd] *adj* presuntuoso(-a)
big-hearted ['bɪg'hɑ:tɪd] *adj* generoso(-a)
bigot ['bɪgət] *n* persona gretta
bigoted ['bɪgətɪd] *adj* gretto(-a)
bigotry ['bɪgətrɪ] *n* grettezza
big toe *n* alluce *m*
big top *n* tendone *m* del circo
big wheel *n (at fair)* ruota (panoramica)
bigwig ['bɪgwɪg] *n (col)* pezzo grosso
bike [baɪk] *n* bici *f inv*

bike lane *n* pista ciclabile
bikini [bɪ'kiːnɪ] *n* bikini *m inv*
bilateral [baɪ'lætərl] *adj* bilaterale
bile [baɪl] *n* bile *f*
bilingual [baɪ'lɪŋgwəl] *adj* bilingue
bilious ['bɪlɪəs] *adj* biliare; (*fig*) bilioso(-a)
bill [bɪl] *n* (*in hotel, restaurant*) conto; (*Comm*) fattura; (*for gas, electricity*) bolletta, conto; (*Pol*) atto; (*US: banknote*) banconota; (*notice*) avviso; (*Theat*): **on the ~** in cartellone; (*of bird*) becco ■ *vt* mandare il conto a; **may I have the ~ please?** posso avere il conto per piacere?; **"stick** *or* **post no bills"** "divieto di affissione"; **to fit** *or* **fill the ~** (*fig*) fare al caso; **~ of exchange** cambiale *f*, tratta; **~ of lading** polizza di carico; **~ of sale** atto di vendita
billboard ['bɪlbɔːd] *n* tabellone *m*
billet ['bɪlɪt] *n* alloggio ■ *vt* (*troops etc*) alloggiare
billfold ['bɪlfəuld] *n* (*US*) portafoglio
billiards ['bɪljədz] *n* biliardo
billion ['bɪljən] *n* (*Brit*) bilione *m*; (*US*) miliardo
billow ['bɪləu] *n* (*of smoke*) nuvola; (*of sail*) rigonfiamento ■ *vi* (*smoke*) alzarsi in volute; (*sail*) gonfiarsi
bills payable *npl* effetti *mpl* passivi
bills receivable *npl* effetti *mpl* attivi
billy goat ['bɪlɪgəut] *n* caprone *m*, becco
bimbo ['bɪmbəu] *n* (*col*) pollastrella, svampitella
bin [bɪn] *n* bidone *m*; (*Brit: also:* **dustbin**) pattumiera; (*: also:* **litter bin**) cestino
binary ['baɪnərɪ] *adj* binario(-a)
bind (*pt, pp* **bound**) [baɪnd, baund] *vt* legare; (*oblige*) obbligare
▸**bind over** *vt* (*Law*) dare la condizionale a
▸**bind up** *vt* (*wound*) fasciare, bendare; **to be bound up in** (*work, research etc*) essere completamente assorbito da; **to be bound up with** (*person*) dedicarsi completamente a
binder ['baɪndə^r] *n* (*file*) classificatore *m*
binding ['baɪndɪŋ] *n* (*of book*) legatura ■ *adj* (*contract*) vincolante
binge [bɪndʒ] *n* (*col*): **to go on a ~** fare baldoria
binge drinker *n persona che di norma beve troppo*
bingo ['bɪŋgəu] *n gioco simile alla tombola*
bin liner *n* sacchetto per l'immondizia
binoculars [bɪ'nɔkjuləz] *npl* binocolo
biochemistry [baɪəu'kɛmɪstrɪ] *n* biochimica
biodegradable ['baɪəudɪ'greɪdəbl] *adj* biodegradabile
biodiversity ['baɪəudaɪ'vəːsɪtɪ] *n* biodiversità *f inv*
biofuel ['baɪəufjuəl] *n* carburante *m* biologico
biographer [baɪ'ɔgrəfə^r] *n* biografo(-a)
biographic [baɪə'græfɪk], **biographical** [baɪə'græfɪkl] *adj* biografico(-a)
biography [baɪ'ɔgrəfɪ] *n* biografia
biological [baɪə'lɔdʒɪkl] *adj* biologico(-a)
biological clock *n* orologio biologico
biologist [baɪ'ɔlədʒɪst] *n* biologo(-a)
biology [baɪ'ɔlədʒɪ] *n* biologia
biometric [baɪəu'mɛtrɪk] *adj* biometrico(-a)
biophysics [baɪəu'fɪzɪks] *n* biofisica
biopic ['baɪəupɪk] *n* film *m inv* biografia *inv*
biopsy ['baɪɔpsɪ] *n* biopsia
biosphere ['baɪəusfɪə^r] *n* biosfera
biotechnology [baɪəutɛk'nɔlədʒɪ] *n* biotecnologia
bioterrorism [baɪəu'tɛrərɪzəm] *n* bioterrorismo
birch [bəːtʃ] *n* betulla
bird [bəːd] *n* uccello; (*Brit col: girl*) bambola
bird flu *n* influenza aviaria
bird of prey *n* (uccello) rapace *m*
bird's-eye view ['bəːdzaɪ-] *n* vista panoramica
bird watcher *n* ornitologo(-a) dilettante
Biro® ['baɪrəu] *n* biro® *f inv*
birth [bəːθ] *n* nascita; **to give ~ to** dare alla luce; (*fig*) dare inizio a
birth certificate *n* certificato di nascita
birth control *n* controllo delle nascite; contraccezione *f*
birthday ['bəːθdeɪ] *n* compleanno
birthmark ['bəːθmɑːk] *n* voglia
birthplace ['bəːθpleɪs] *n* luogo di nascita
birth rate *n* indice *m* di natalità
Biscay ['bɪskeɪ] *n*: **the Bay of ~** il golfo di Biscaglia
biscuit ['bɪskɪt] *n* (*Brit*) biscotto; (*US*) panino al latte
bisect [baɪ'sɛkt] *vt* tagliare in due (parti); (*Math*) bisecare
bisexual ['baɪ'sɛksjuəl] *adj, n* bisessuale (*m/f*)
bishop ['bɪʃəp] *n* vescovo; (*Chess*) alfiere *m*
bistro ['biːstrəu] *n* bistrò *m inv*
bit [bɪt] *pt of* **bite** ■ *n* pezzo; (*of tool*) punta; (*of horse*) morso; (*Comput*) bit *m inv*; (*US: coin*) ottavo di dollaro; **a ~ of** un po' di; **a ~ mad/dangerous** un po' matto/pericoloso; **~ by ~** a poco a poco; **to do one's ~** fare la propria parte; **to come to bits** (*break*) andare a pezzi; **bring all your bits and pieces** porta tutte le tue cose
bitch [bɪtʃ] *n* (*dog*) cagna; (*col!*) puttana (*!*)
bite [baɪt] *vt, vi* (*pt* **bit**, *pp* **bitten**) mordere ■ *n* morso; (*insect bite*) puntura; (*mouthful*) boccone *m*; **let's have a ~ (to eat)** mangiamo un boccone; **to ~ one's nails** mangiarsi le unghie

biting ['baɪtɪŋ] *adj* pungente
bit part *n* (*Theat*) particina
bitten ['bɪtn] *pp of* **bite**
bitter ['bɪtəʳ] *adj* amaro(-a); (*wind, criticism*) pungente; (*icy: weather*) gelido(-a) ■ *n* (*Brit: beer*) birra amara; **to the ~ end** a oltranza
bitterly ['bɪtəlɪ] *adv* (*disappoint, complain, weep*) amaramente; (*oppose, criticise*) aspramente; (*jealous*) profondamente; **it's ~ cold** fa un freddo gelido
bitterness ['bɪtənɪs] *n* amarezza; gusto amaro
bittersweet ['bɪtəswi:t] *adj* agrodolce
bitty ['bɪtɪ] *adj* (*Brit col*) frammentario(-a)
bitumen ['bɪtjumɪn] *n* bitume *m*
bivouac ['bɪvuæk] *n* bivacco
bizarre [bɪ'zɑ:ʳ] *adj* bizzarro(-a)
bk *abbr* = **bank; book**
BL *n abbr* (= *Bachelor of Law(s), Bachelor of Letters*) *titolo di studio*; (*US:* = *Bachelor of Literature*) *titolo di studio*
B/L *abbr* = **bill of lading**
blab [blæb] *vi* parlare troppo ■ *vt* (*also:* **blab out**) spifferare
black [blæk] *adj* nero(-a) ■ *n* nero; (*person*): **B~** negro(-a) ■ *vt* (*Brit Industry*) boicottare; **~ coffee** caffè *m inv* nero; **to give sb a ~ eye** fare un occhio nero a qn; **in the ~** (*in credit*) in attivo; **there it is in ~ and white** (*fig*) eccolo nero su bianco; **~ and blue** *adj* tutto(-a) pesto(-a)
▸ **black out** *vi* (*faint*) svenire
black belt *n* (*Sport*) cintura nera; (*US: area*): **the ~** *zona abitata principalmente da negri*
blackberry ['blækbərɪ] *n* mora
blackbird ['blækbə:d] *n* merlo
blackboard ['blækbɔ:d] *n* lavagna
black box *n* (*Aviat*) scatola nera
Black Country *n* (*Brit*): **the ~** *zona carbonifera del centro dell'Inghilterra*
blackcurrant [blæk'kʌrənt] *n* ribes *m inv*
black economy *n* (*Brit*) economia sommersa
blacken ['blækn] *vt* annerire
Black Forest *n*: **the ~** la Foresta Nera
blackhead ['blækhɛd] *n* punto nero, comedone *m*
black hole *n* (*Astron*) buco nero
black ice *n* strato trasparente di ghiaccio
blackjack ['blækdʒæk] *n* (*Cards*) ventuno; (*US: truncheon*) manganello
blackleg ['blæklɛg] *n* (*Brit*) crumiro
blacklist ['blæklɪst] *n* lista nera ■ *vt* mettere sulla lista nera
blackmail ['blækmeɪl] *n* ricatto ■ *vt* ricattare
blackmailer ['blækmeɪləʳ] *n* ricattatore(-trice)
black market *n* mercato nero
blackout ['blækaut] *n* oscuramento; (*fainting*) svenimento; (*TV*) interruzione *f* delle trasmissioni
black pepper *n* pepe *m* nero
Black Sea *n*: **the ~** il mar Nero
black sheep *n* pecora nera
blacksmith ['blæksmɪθ] *n* fabbro ferraio
black spot *n* (*Aut*) luogo famigerato per gli incidenti
bladder ['blædəʳ] *n* vescica
blade [bleɪd] *n* lama; (*of oar*) pala; **~ of grass** filo d'erba
blame [bleɪm] *n* colpa ■ *vt*: **to ~ sb/sth for sth** dare la colpa di qc a qn/qc; **who's to ~?** chi è colpevole?; **I'm not to ~** non è colpa mia
blameless ['bleɪmlɪs] *adj* irreprensibile
blanch [blɑ:ntʃ] *vi* (*person*) sbiancare in viso ■ *vt* (*Culin*) scottare
bland [blænd] *adj* mite; (*taste*) blando(-a)
blank [blæŋk] *adj* bianco(-a); (*look*) distratto(-a) ■ *n* spazio vuoto; (*cartridge*) cartuccia a salve; **to draw a ~** (*fig*) non aver nessun risultato
blank cheque, (*US*) **blank check** *n* assegno in bianco; **to give sb a ~ to do** (*fig*) dare carta bianca a qn per fare
blanket ['blæŋkɪt] *n* coperta ■ *adj* (*statement, agreement*) globale
blanket cover *n*: **to give ~** (*insurance policy*) coprire tutti i rischi
blare [blɛəʳ] *vi* strombettare; (*radio*) suonare a tutto volume
blasé ['blɑ:zeɪ] *adj* blasé *inv*
blasphemous ['blæsfɪməs] *adj* blasfemo(-a)
blasphemy ['blæsfɪmɪ] *n* bestemmia
blast [blɑ:st] *n* (*of wind*) raffica; (*of air, steam*) getto; (*bomb blast*) esplosione *f* ■ *vt* far saltare ■ *excl* (*Brit col*) mannaggia!; **(at) full ~** a tutta forza
▸ **blast off** *vi* (*Space*) essere lanciato(-a)
blast-off ['blɑ:stɔf] *n* (*Space*) lancio
blatant ['bleɪtənt] *adj* flagrante
blatantly ['bleɪtəntlɪ] *adv*: **it's ~ obvious** è lampante
blaze [bleɪz] *n* (*fire*) incendio; (*glow: of fire, sun etc*) bagliore *m*; (*fig*) vampata ■ *vi* (*fire*) ardere, fiammeggiare; (*fig*) infiammarsi ■ *vt*: **to ~ a trail** (*fig*) tracciare una via nuova; **in a ~ of publicity** circondato da grande pubblicità
blazer ['bleɪzəʳ] *n* blazer *m inv*
bleach [bli:tʃ] *n* (*also:* **household bleach**) varechina ■ *vt* (*material*) candeggiare
bleached ['bli:tʃt] *adj* (*hair*) decolorato(-a)
bleachers ['bli:tʃəz] *npl* (*US*) posti *mpl* di gradinata

bleak [bli:k] *adj (prospect, future)* tetro(-a); *(landscape)* desolato(-a); *(weather)* gelido(-a)
bleary-eyed ['blɪərɪ'aɪd] *adj* dagli occhi offuscati
bleat [bli:t] *vi* belare
bleed *(pt, pp* **bled***)* [bli:d, blɛd] *vt* dissanguare; *(brakes, radiator)* spurgare ■ *vi* sanguinare; **my nose is bleeding** mi viene fuori sangue dal naso
bleep [bli:p] *n* breve segnale *m* acustico, bip *m inv* ■ *vi* suonare ■ *vt (doctor)* chiamare con il cercapersone
bleeper ['bli:pəʳ] *n (of doctor etc)* cercapersone *m inv*
blemish ['blɛmɪʃ] *n* macchia
blend [blɛnd] *n* miscela ■ *vt* mescolare ■ *vi (colours etc)* armonizzare
blender ['blɛndəʳ] *n (Culin)* frullatore *m*
bless *(pt, pp* **blessed** *or* **blest***)* [blɛs, blɛst] *vt* benedire; **~ you!** *(sneezing)* salute!; **to be blessed with** godere di
blessed ['blɛsɪd] *adj (Rel: holy)* benedetto(-a); *(happy)* beato(-a); **every ~ day** tutti i santi giorni
blessing ['blɛsɪŋ] *n* benedizione *f*; fortuna; **to count one's blessings** ringraziare Iddio, ritenersi fortunato; **it was a ~ in disguise** in fondo è stato un bene
blest [blɛst] *pt, pp of* **bless**
blew [blu:] *pt of* **blow**
blight [blaɪt] *n (of plants)* golpe *f* ■ *vt (hopes etc)* deludere; *(life)* rovinare
blimey ['blaɪmɪ] *excl (Brit col)* accidenti!
blind [blaɪnd] *adj* cieco(-a) ■ *n (for window)* avvolgibile *m*; *(Venetian blind)* veneziana ■ *vt* accecare; **to turn a ~ eye (on** *or* **to)** chiudere un occhio (su)
blind alley *n* vicolo cieco
blind corner *n (Brit)* svolta cieca
blind date *n* appuntamento combinato *(tra due persone che non si conoscono)*
blinders ['blaɪndəz] *npl (US)* = **blinkers**
blindfold ['blaɪndfəuld] *n* benda ■ *adj, adv* bendato(-a) ■ *vt* bendare gli occhi a
blinding ['blaɪndɪŋ] *adj (flash, light)* accecante; *(pain)* atroce
blindly ['blaɪndlɪ] *adv* ciecamente
blindness ['blaɪndnɪs] *n* cecità
blind spot *n (Aut etc)* punto cieco; *(fig)* punto debole
bling [blɪŋ] *n gioielli vistosi*
blink [blɪŋk] *vi* battere gli occhi; *(light)* lampeggiare ■ *n*: **to be on the ~** *(col)* essere scassato(-a)
blinkers ['blɪŋkəz] *npl (Brit)* paraocchi *mpl*
blinking ['blɪŋkɪŋ] *adj (Brit col)*: **this ~ ...** questo(-a) maledetto(-a) ...
blip [blɪp] *n (on radar etc)* segnale *m* intermittente; *(on graph)* piccola variazione *f*; *(fig)* momentanea battuta d'arresto
bliss [blɪs] *n* estasi *f*
blissful ['blɪsfəl] *adj (event, day)* stupendo(-a), meraviglioso(-a); *(smile)* beato(-a); **in ~ ignorance** nella (più) beata ignoranza
blissfully ['blɪsfəlɪ] *adv (sigh, smile)* beatamente; **~ happy** magnificamente felice
blister ['blɪstəʳ] *n (on skin)* vescica; *(on paintwork)* bolla ■ *vi (paint)* coprirsi di bolle
BLit, BLitt *n abbr (= Bachelor of Literature) titolo di studio*
blithe [blaɪð] *adj* gioioso(-a), allegro(-a)
blithely ['blaɪðlɪ] *adv* allegramente
blithering ['blɪðərɪŋ] *adj (col)*: **this ~ idiot** questa razza d'idiota
blitz [blɪts] *n* blitz *m*; **to have a ~ on sth** *(fig)* prendere d'assalto qc
blizzard ['blɪzəd] *n* bufera di neve
bloated ['bləutɪd] *adj* gonfio(-a)
blob [blɔb] *n (drop)* goccia; *(stain, spot)* macchia
bloc [blɔk] *n (Pol)* blocco
block [blɔk] *n (gen, Comput)* blocco; *(in pipes)* ingombro; *(toy)* cubo; *(of buildings)* isolato ■ *vt (gen, Comput)* bloccare; **~ of flats** caseggiato; **3 blocks from here** a 3 isolati di distanza da qui; **mental ~** blocco mentale
▸ **block up** *vt* bloccare; *(pipe)* ingorgare, intasare
blockade [blɔ'keɪd] *n* blocco ■ *vt* assediare
blockage ['blɔkɪdʒ] *n* ostacolo
block and tackle *n (Tech)* paranco
block booking *n* prenotazione *f* in blocco
blockbuster ['blɔkbʌstəʳ] *n* libro *or* film *etc* sensazionale
block capitals *npl* stampatello
blockhead ['blɔkhɛd] *n* testa di legno
block letters *npl* stampatello
block vote *n (Brit)* voto per delega
blog [blɔg] *n* blog *m inv* ■ *vi* scrivere blog, bloggare
blogger [blɔgəʳ] *n (Comput)* blogger *m/f inv*
blogging [blɔgɪŋ] *n* blogging *m* ■ *adj*: **~ website** sito di blogging
bloke [bləuk] *n (Brit col)* tizio
blond, blonde [blɔnd] *n (man)* biondo; *(woman)* bionda ■ *adj* biondo(-a)
blood [blʌd] *n* sangue *m*; **new ~** *(fig)* nuova linfa
blood bank *n* banca del sangue
blood count *n* conteggio di globuli rossi e bianchi
bloodcurdling ['blʌdkə:dlɪŋ] *adj* raccapricciante, da far gelare il sangue
blood donor *n* donatore(-trice) di sangue

blood group *n* gruppo sanguigno
bloodhound ['blʌdhaund] *n* segugio
bloodless ['blʌdlɪs] *adj* (*pale*) smorto(-a), esangue; (*coup*) senza spargimento di sangue
bloodletting ['blʌdlɛtɪŋ] *n* (*Med*) salasso; (*fig*) spargimento di sangue
blood poisoning *n* setticemia
blood pressure *n* pressione *f* sanguigna; **to have high/low ~** avere la pressione alta/ bassa
bloodshed ['blʌdʃɛd] *n* spargimento di sangue
bloodshot ['blʌdʃɔt] *adj*: **~ eyes** occhi iniettati di sangue
bloodstained ['blʌdsteɪnd] *adj* macchiato(-a) di sangue
bloodstream ['blʌdstri:m] *n* flusso del sangue
blood test *n* analisi *f inv* del sangue
bloodthirsty ['blʌdθə:stɪ] *adj* assetato(-a) di sangue
blood transfusion *n* trasfusione *f* di sangue
blood type *n* gruppo sanguigno
blood vessel *n* vaso sanguigno
bloody ['blʌdɪ] *adj* sanguinoso(-a); (*Brit col!*): **this ~ ...** questo maledetto ...; **a ~ awful day** (*col!*) una giornata di merda (*!*); **~ good** (*col!*) maledettamente buono
bloody-minded ['blʌdɪ'maɪndɪd] *adj* (*Brit col*) indisponente
bloom [blu:m] *n* fiore *m* ▪ *vi* essere in fiore
blooming ['blu:mɪŋ] *adj* (*col*): **this ~ ...** questo(-a) dannato(-a) ...
blossom ['blɔsəm] *n* fiore *m*; (*with pl sense*) fiori *mpl* ▪ *vi* essere in fiore; **to ~ into** (*fig*) diventare
blot [blɔt] *n* macchia ▪ *vt* macchiare; **to be a ~ on the landscape** rovinare il paesaggio; **to ~ one's copy book** (*fig*) farla grossa
▸ **blot out** *vt* (*memories*) cancellare; (*view*) nascondere; (*nation, city*) annientare
blotchy ['blɔtʃɪ] *adj* (*complexion*) coperto(-a) di macchie
blotter ['blɔtə^r] *n* tampone *m* (di carta assorbente)
blotting paper ['blɔtɪŋ-] *n* carta assorbente
blotto ['blɔtəu] *adj* (*col*) sbronzo(-a)
blouse [blauz] *n* camicetta
blow [bləu] *n* colpo ▪ *vb* (*pt* **blew**, *pp* **blown**) *vi* soffiare ▪ *vt* (*fuse*) far saltare; **to come to blows** venire alle mani; **to ~ one's nose** soffiarsi il naso; **to ~ a whistle** fischiare
▸ **blow away** *vi* volare via ▪ *vt* portare via
▸ **blow down** *vt* abbattere
▸ **blow off** *vt* far volare via; **to ~ off course** far uscire di rotta
▸ **blow out** *vi* scoppiare
▸ **blow over** *vi* calmarsi
▸ **blow up** *vi* saltare in aria ▪ *vt* far saltare in aria; (*tyre*) gonfiare; (*Phot*) ingrandire
blow-dry ['bləudraɪ] *n* (*hairstyle*) messa in piega a föhn ▪ *vt* asciugare con il föhn
blowlamp ['bləulæmp] *n* (*Brit*) lampada a benzina per saldare
blown [bləun] *pp of* **blow**
blowout ['bləuaut] *n* (*of tyre*) scoppio; (*col: big meal*) abbuffata
blowtorch ['bləutɔ:tʃ] *n* lampada a benzina per saldare
blowzy ['blauzɪ] *adj* trasandato(-a)
BLS *n abbr* (*US*) = **Bureau of Labor Statistics**
blubber ['blʌbə^r] *n* grasso di balena ▪ *vi* (*pej*) piangere forte
bludgeon ['blʌdʒən] *vt* prendere a randellate
blue [blu:] *adj* azzurro(-a), celeste; (*darker*) blu *inv*; **~ film/joke** film/barzelletta pornografico(a); **(only) once in a ~ moon** a ogni morte di papa; **out of the ~** (*fig*) all'improvviso; *see also* **blues**
blue baby *n* neonato cianotico
bluebell ['blu:bɛl] *n* giacinto di bosco
bluebottle ['blu:bɔtl] *n* moscone *m*
blue cheese *n formaggio tipo gorgonzola*
blue-chip ['blu:tʃɪp] *adj*: **~ investment** investimento sicuro
blue-collar worker ['blu:kɔlə^r-] *n* operaio(-a)
blue jeans *npl* blue-jeans *mpl*
blueprint ['blu:prɪnt] *n* cianografia; (*fig*): **~ (for)** formula (di)
blues [blu:z] *npl*: **the ~** (*Mus*) il blues; **to have the ~** (*col: feeling*) essere a terra
bluff [blʌf] *vi* bluffare ▪ *n* bluff *m inv*; (*promontory*) promontorio scosceso ▪ *adj* (*person*) brusco(-a); **to call sb's ~** mettere alla prova il bluff di qn
blunder ['blʌndə^r] *n* abbaglio ▪ *vi* prendere un abbaglio; **to ~ into sb/sth** andare a sbattere contro qn/qc
blunt [blʌnt] *adj* (*edge*) smussato(-a); (*point*) spuntato(-a); (*knife*) che non taglia; (*person*) brusco(-a) ▪ *vt* smussare; spuntare; **this pencil is ~** questa matita non ha più la punta; **~ instrument** (*Law*) corpo contundente
bluntly ['blʌntlɪ] *adv* (*speak*) senza mezzi termini
bluntness ['blʌntnɪs] *n* (*of person*) brutale franchezza
blur [blə:^r] *n* cosa offuscata ▪ *vt* offuscare
blurb [blə:b] *n* trafiletto pubblicitario
blurred [blə:d] *adj* (*photo*) mosso(-a); (*TV*) sfuocato(-a)
blurt out [blə:t-] *vt* lasciarsi sfuggire
blush [blʌʃ] *vi* arrossire ▪ *n* rossore *m*

blusher ['blʌʃəʳ] *n* fard *m inv*

bluster ['blʌstəʳ] *n* spacconate *fpl*; (*threats*) vuote minacce *fpl* ■ *vi* fare lo spaccone; minacciare a vuoto

blustering ['blʌstərɪŋ] *adj* (*tone etc*) da spaccone

blustery ['blʌstərɪ] *adj* (*weather*) burrascoso(-a)

Blvd *abbr* = **boulevard**

BM *n abbr* = **British Museum**; (*Scol*: = *Bachelor of Medicine*) *titolo di studio*

BMA *n abbr* = **British Medical Association**

BMJ *n abbr* = **British Medical Journal**

BMus *n abbr* (= *Bachelor of Music*) *titolo di studio*

BMX *n abbr* (= *bicycle motocross*) BMX *f inv*; **~ bike** mountain bike *f inv* per cross

bn *abbr* = **billion**

BO *n abbr* (*col*: = *body odour*) odori *mpl* sgradevoli (del corpo); = **box office**

boar [bɔːʳ] *n* cinghiale *m*

board [bɔːd] *n* tavola; (*on wall*) tabellone *m*; (*for chess etc*) scacchiera; (*committee*) consiglio, comitato; (*in firm*) consiglio d'amministrazione; (*Naut, Aviat*): **on ~** a bordo ■ *vt* (*ship*) salire a bordo di; (*train*) salire su; **full ~** (*Brit*) pensione *f* completa; **half ~** (*Brit*) mezza pensione; **~ and lodging** vitto e alloggio; **above ~** (*fig*) regolare; **across the ~** (*fig*) *adv* per tutte le categorie; *adj* generale; **to go by the ~** venir messo(-a) da parte
▸ **board up** *vt* (*door*) chiudere con assi

boarder ['bɔːdəʳ] *n* pensionante *m/f*; (*Scol*) convittore(-trice)

board game *n* gioco da tavolo

boarding card ['bɔːdɪŋ-] *n* (*Aviat, Naut*) carta d'imbarco

boarding house *n* pensione *f*

boarding party *n* squadra di ispezione (*del carico di una nave*)

boarding pass *n* (*Brit*) = **boarding card**

boarding school *n* collegio

board meeting *n* riunione *f* di consiglio

board room *n* sala del consiglio

boardwalk ['bɔːdwɔːk] *n* (*US*) passeggiata a mare

boast [bəust] *vi*: **to ~ (about** *or* **of)** vantarsi (di) ■ *vt* vantare ■ *n* vanteria; vanto

boastful ['bəustful] *adj* vanaglorioso(-a)

boastfulness ['bəustfulnɪs] *n* vanagloria

boat [bəut] *n* nave *f*; (*small*) barca; **to go by ~** andare in barca *or* in nave; **we're all in the same ~** (*fig*) siamo tutti nella stessa barca

boater ['bəutəʳ] *n* (*hat*) paglietta

boating ['bəutɪŋ] *n* canottaggio

boat people *n* boat people *mpl*

boatswain ['bəusn] *n* nostromo

bob [bɔb] *vi* (*boat, cork on water*: *also*: **bob up and down**) andare su e giù ■ *n* (*Brit col*) = **shilling**
▸ **bob up** *vi* saltare fuori

bobbin ['bɔbɪn] *n* bobina; (*of sewing machine*) rocchetto

bobby ['bɔbɪ] *n* (*Brit col*) ≈ poliziotto

bobsleigh ['bɔbsleɪ] *n* bob *m inv*

bode [bəud] *vi*: **to ~ well/ill (for)** essere di buon/cattivo auspicio (per)

bodice ['bɔdɪs] *n* corsetto

bodily ['bɔdɪlɪ] *adj* (*comfort, needs*) materiale; (*pain*) fisico(-a) ■ *adv* (*carry*) in braccio; (*lift*) di peso

body ['bɔdɪ] *n* corpo; (*of car*) carrozzeria; (*of plane*) fusoliera; (*organization*) associazione *f*, organizzazione *f*; (*quantity*) quantità *f inv*; (*of speech, document*) parte *f* principale; (*also*: **body stocking**) body *m inv*; **in a ~** in massa; **ruling ~** direttivo; **a wine with ~** un vino corposo

body blow *n* (*fig*) duro colpo

body-building ['bɔdɪ'bɪldɪŋ] *n* culturismo

bodyguard ['bɔdɪgɑːd] *n* guardia del corpo

body language *n* linguaggio del corpo

body repairs *npl* (*Aut*) lavori *mpl* di carrozzeria

body search *n* perquisizione *f* personale; **to submit to** *or* **undergo a ~** essere sottoposto(-a) a perquisizione personale

bodywork ['bɔdɪwəːk] *n* carrozzeria

boffin ['bɔfɪn] *n* scienziato

bog [bɔg] *n* palude *f* ■ *vt*: **to get bogged down** (*fig*) impantanarsi

bogey ['bəugɪ] *n* (*worry*) spauracchio; (*also*: **bogey man**) babau *m inv*

boggle ['bɔgl] *vi*: **the mind boggles** è incredibile

Bogotá [bəugə'tɑː] *n* Bogotà *f*

bogus ['bəugəs] *adj* falso(-a); finto(-a)

Bohemia [bəu'hiːmɪə] *n* Boemia

Bohemian [bəu'hiːmɪən] *adj, n* boemo(-a)

boil [bɔɪl] *vt, vi* bollire ■ *n* (*Med*) foruncolo; **to come to the** *or* (*US*) **a ~** raggiungere l'ebollizione; **to bring to the** *or* (*US*) **a ~** portare a ebollizione; **boiled egg** uovo alla coque; **boiled potatoes** patate *fpl* bollite *or* lesse
▸ **boil down** *vi* (*fig*): **to ~ down to** ridursi a
▸ **boil over** *vi* traboccare (bollendo)

boiler ['bɔɪləʳ] *n* caldaia

boiler suit *n* (*Brit*) tuta

boiling ['bɔɪlɪŋ] *adj* bollente; **I'm ~ (hot)** (*col*) sto morendo di caldo

boiling point *n* punto di ebollizione

boil-in-the-bag [bɔɪlɪnðə'bæg] *adj* (*rice etc*) da bollire nel sacchetto

boisterous ['bɔɪstərəs] *adj* chiassoso(-a)

bold [bəuld] *adj* audace; (*child*) impudente; (*outline*) chiaro(-a); (*colour*) deciso(-a)

boldness ['bəuldnɪs] *n* audacia; impudenza
bold type *n* (*Typ*) neretto, grassetto
Bolivia [bə'lɪvɪə] *n* Bolivia
Bolivian [bə'lɪvɪən] *adj, n* boliviano(-a)
bollard ['bɔləd] *n* (*Naut*) bitta; (*Brit Aut*) colonnina luminosa
Bollywood ['bɔlɪwud] *n* Bollywood *f*
bolshy ['bɔlʃɪ] *adj* (*Brit col*) piantagrane, ribelle; **to be in a ~ mood** essere in vena di piantar grane
bolster ['bəulstəʳ] *n* capezzale *m*
▸ **bolster up** *vt* sostenere
bolt [bəult] *n* chiavistello; (*with nut*) bullone *m* ■ *adv*: **~ upright** diritto(-a) come un fuso ■ *vt* serrare; (*food*) mangiare in fretta ■ *vi* scappare via; **a ~ from the blue** (*fig*) un fulmine a ciel sereno
bomb [bɔm] *n* bomba ■ *vt* bombardare
bombard [bɔm'bɑːd] *vt* bombardare
bombardment [bɔm'bɑːdmənt] *n* bombardamento
bombastic [bɔm'bæstɪk] *adj* ampolloso(-a)
bomb disposal *n*: **~ expert** artificiere *m*; **~ unit** corpo degli artificieri
bomber ['bɔməʳ] *n* bombardiere *m*; (*terrorist*) dinamitardo(-a)
bombing ['bɔmɪŋ] *n* bombardamento
bomb scare *n* stato di allarme (*per sospetta presenza di una bomba*)
bombshell ['bɔmʃɛl] *n* (*fig*) notizia bomba
bomb site *n* luogo bombardato
bona fide ['bəunə'faɪdɪ] *adj* sincero(-a); (*offer*) onesto(-a)
bonanza [bə'nænzə] *n* cuccagna
bond [bɔnd] *n* legame *m*; (*binding promise, Finance*) obbligazione *f*; **in ~** (*of goods*) in attesa di sdoganamento
bondage ['bɔndɪdʒ] *n* schiavitù *f*
bonded warehouse ['bɔndɪd-] *n* magazzino doganale
bone [bəun] *n* osso; (*of fish*) spina, lisca ■ *vt* disossare; togliere le spine a
bone china *n* porcellana fine
bone-dry ['bəun'draɪ] *adj* asciuttissimo(-a)
bone idle *adj*: **to be ~** essere un(a) fannullone(-a)
bone marrow *n* midollo osseo
boner ['bəunəʳ] *n* (*US*) gaffe *f inv*
bonfire ['bɔnfaɪəʳ] *n* falò *m inv*
bonk [bɔŋk] *vt, vi* (*hum, col*) scopare (*!*)
bonkers ['bɔŋkəz] *adj* (*Brit col*) suonato(-a)
Bonn [bɔn] *n* Bonn *f*
bonnet ['bɔnɪt] *n* cuffia; (*Brit: of car*) cofano
bonny ['bɔnɪ] *adj* (*esp Scottish*) bello(-a), carino(-a)
bonus ['bəunəs] *n* premio; (*on wages*) gratifica
bony ['bəunɪ] *adj* (*thin: person*) ossuto(-a), angoloso(-a); (*arm, face, Med: tissue*) osseo(-a); (*meat*) pieno(-a) di ossi; (*fish*) pieno(-a) di spine
boo [buː] *excl* ba! ■ *vt* fischiare ■ *n* fischio
boob [buːb] *n* (*col: breast*) tetta; (*: Brit: mistake*) gaffe *f inv*
booby prize ['buːbɪ-] *n* premio per il peggior contendente
booby trap ['buːbɪ-] *n* trabocchetto; (*bomb*) congegno che esplode al contatto
booby-trapped ['buːbɪtræpt] *adj*: **a ~ car** una macchina con dell'esplosivo a bordo
book [buk] *n* libro; (*of stamps etc*) blocchetto ■ *vt* (*ticket, seat, room*) prenotare; (*driver*) multare; (*football player*) ammonire; **books** *npl* (*Comm*) conti *mpl*; **to keep the books** (*Comm*) tenere la contabilità; **by the ~** secondo le regole; **to throw the ~ at sb** incriminare qn seriamente *or* con tutte le aggravanti
▸ **book in** *vi* (*Brit: at hotel*) prendere una camera
▸ **book up** *vt* riservare, prenotare; **the hotel is booked up** l'albergo è al completo; **all seats are booked up** è tutto esaurito
bookable ['bukəbl] *adj*: **seats are ~** si possono prenotare i posti
bookcase ['bukkeɪs] *n* scaffale *m*
book ends *npl* reggilibri *mpl*
booking ['bukɪŋ] *n* (*Brit*) prenotazione *f*
booking office *n* (*Brit*) biglietteria
book-keeping ['buk'kiːpɪŋ] *n* contabilità
booklet ['buklɪt] *n* opuscolo, libretto
bookmaker ['bukmeɪkəʳ] *n* allibratore *m*
bookmark ['bukmɑːk] (*also Comput*) *n* segnalibro ■ *vt* (*Comput*) mettere un segnalibro a; (*internet*) aggiungere a "Preferiti"
bookseller ['buksɛləʳ] *n* libraio
bookshelf ['bukʃɛlf] *n* mensola (per libri); **bookshelves** *npl* (*bookcase*) libreria
bookshop ['bukʃɔp] *n* libreria
bookstall ['bukstɔːl] *n* bancarella di libri
bookstore ['bukstɔːʳ] *n* = **bookshop**
book token *n* buono *m* libri *inv*
book value *n* valore *m* contabile
bookworm ['bukwəːm] *n* (*fig*) topo di biblioteca
boom [buːm] *n* (*noise*) rimbombo; (*busy period*) boom *m inv* ■ *vi* rimbombare; andare a gonfie vele
boomerang ['buːməræŋ] *n* boomerang *m inv* ■ *vi* (*fig*) avere effetto contrario; **to ~ on sb** (*fig*) ritorcersi contro qn
boom town *n* città *f inv* in rapidissima espansione
boon [buːn] *n* vantaggio
boorish ['buərɪʃ] *adj* maleducato(-a)

boost [bu:st] *n* spinta ■ *vt* spingere; (*increase: sales, production*) incentivare; **to give a ~ to** (*morale*) tirar su; **it gave a ~ to his confidence** è stata per lui un'iniezione di fiducia
booster ['bu:stəʳ] *n* (*Elec*) amplificatore *m*; (*TV*) amplificatore *m* di segnale; (*also*: **booster rocket**) razzo vettore; (*Med*) richiamo
booster seat *n* (*Aut: for children*) seggiolino di sicurezza
boot [bu:t] *n* stivale *m*; (*ankle boot*) stivaletto; (*for hiking*) scarpone *m* da montagna; (*for football etc*) scarpa; (*Brit: of car*) portabagagli *m inv* ■ *vt* (*Comput*) inizializzare; **to ~** (*in addition*) per giunta, in più; **to give sb the ~** (*col*) mettere qn alla porta
booth [bu:ð] *n* (*at fair*) baraccone *m*; (*of cinema, telephone etc*) cabina; (*also*: **voting booth**) cabina (elettorale)
bootleg ['bu:tlɛg] *adj* di contrabbando; **~ record** registrazione *f* pirata *inv*
booty ['bu:tɪ] *n* bottino
booze [bu:z] (*col*) *n* alcool *m* ■ *vi* trincare
boozer ['bu:zəʳ] *n* (*col: person*) beone *m*; (*Brit col: pub*) osteria
border ['bɔ:dəʳ] *n* orlo; margine *m*; (*of a country*) frontiera; **the B~** *la frontiera tra l'Inghilterra e la Scozia*; **the Borders** *la zona di confine tra l'Inghilterra e la Scozia*
▸ **border on** *vt fus* confinare con
borderline ['bɔ:dəlaɪn] *n* (*fig*) linea di demarcazione ■ *adj*: **~ case** caso limite
bore [bɔ:ʳ] *pt of* **bear** ■ *vt* (*hole*) perforare; (*person*) annoiare ■ *n* (*person*) seccatore(-trice); (*of gun*) calibro; **he's bored to tears** *or* **bored to death** *or* **bored stiff** è annoiato a morte, si annoia da morire
boredom ['bɔ:dəm] *n* noia
boring ['bɔ:rɪŋ] *adj* noioso(-a)
born [bɔ:n] *adj*: **to be ~** nascere; **I was ~ in 1960** sono nato nel 1960; **~ blind** cieco dalla nascita; **a ~ comedian** un comico nato
born-again [bɔ:nə'gɛn] *adj*: **~ Christian** convertito(-a) alla chiesa evangelica
borne [bɔ:n] *pp of* **bear**
Borneo ['bɔ:nɪəu] *n* Borneo
borough ['bʌrə] *n* comune *m*
borrow ['bɔrəu] *vt*: **to ~ sth (from sb)** prendere in prestito qc (da qn); **may I ~ your car?** può prestarmi la macchina?
borrower ['bɔrəuəʳ] *n* (*gen*) chi prende a prestito; (*Econ*) mutuatario(-a)
borrowing ['bɔrəuɪŋ] *n* prestito
borstal ['bɔ:stl] *n* (*Brit*) riformatorio
Bosnia ['bɔznɪə] *n* Bosnia
Bosnia-Herzegovina ['bɔznɪəhɛrzə'gəuvi:nə] *n* (*also*: **Bosnia-Hercegovina**) Bosnia-Erzegovina
Bosnian ['bɔznɪən] *adj, n* bosniaco(-a)
bosom ['buzəm] *n* petto; (*fig*) seno
bosom friend *n* amico(-a) del cuore
boss [bɔs] *n* capo ■ *vt* (*also*: **boss about** *or* **around**) comandare a bacchetta; **stop bossing everyone about!** smettila di dare ordini a tutti!
bossy ['bɔsɪ] *adj* prepotente
bosun ['bəusn] *n* nostromo
botanical [bə'tænɪkl] *adj* botanico(-a)
botanist ['bɔtənɪst] *n* botanico(-a)
botany ['bɔtənɪ] *n* botanica
botch [bɔtʃ] *vt* fare un pasticcio di
both [bəuθ] *adj* entrambi(-e), tutt'e due ■ *pron*: **~ of them** entrambi(-e) ■ *adv*: **they sell ~ meat and poultry** vendono insieme la carne ed il pollame; **~ of us went, we ~ went** ci siamo andati tutt'e due
bother ['bɔðəʳ] *vt* (*worry*) preoccupare; (*annoy*) infastidire ■ *vi* (*gen: also*: **bother o.s.**) preoccuparsi ■ *n*: **it is a ~ to have to do** è una seccatura dover fare ■ *excl* uffa!, accidenti!; **to ~ doing sth** darsi la pena di fare qc; **I'm sorry to ~ you** mi dispiace disturbarla; **please don't ~** non si scomodi; **it's no ~** non c'è problema
Botswana [bɔt'swa:nə] *n* Botswana *m*
bottle ['bɔtl] *n* bottiglia; (*of perfume, shampoo etc*) flacone *m*; (*baby's*) biberon *m inv* ■ *vt* imbottigliare; **~ of wine/milk** bottiglia di vino/latte; **wine/milk ~** bottiglia da vino/del latte
▸ **bottle up** *vt* contenere
bottle bank *n* contenitore *m* per la raccolta del vetro
bottle-fed ['bɔtlfɛd] *adj* allattato(-a) artificialmente
bottleneck ['bɔtlnɛk] *n* ingorgo
bottle-opener ['bɔtləupnəʳ] *n* apribottiglie *m inv*
bottom ['bɔtəm] *n* fondo; (*of mountain, tree, hill*) piedi *mpl*; (*buttocks*) sedere *m* ■ *adj* più basso(-a), ultimo(-a); **at the ~ of** in fondo a; **to get to the ~ of sth** (*fig*) andare al fondo di *or* in fondo a qc
bottomless ['bɔtəmlɪs] *adj* senza fondo
bottom line *n*: **the ~ is ...** in ultima analisi ...
botulism ['bɔtjulɪzəm] *n* botulismo
bough [bau] *n* ramo
bought [bɔ:t] *pt, pp of* **buy**
boulder ['bəuldəʳ] *n* masso (tondeggiante)
boulevard ['bu:lva:d] *n* viale *m*
bounce [bauns] *vi* (*ball*) rimbalzare; (*cheque*) essere restituito(-a) ■ *vt* far rimbalzare ■ *n* (*rebound*) rimbalzo; **to ~ in** entrare di slancio

or con foga; **he's got plenty of ~** *(fig)* è molto esuberante
bouncer ['baunsəʳ] *n* buttafuori *m inv*
bouncy castle® ['baunsɪ-] *n grande castello gonfiabile per giocare*
bound [baund] *pt, pp of* **bind** ■ *n (gen pl)* limite *m*; *(leap)* salto ■ *vt (leap)* saltare; *(limit)* delimitare ■ *adj*: **to be ~ to do sth** *(obliged)* essere costretto(-a) a fare qc; **he's ~ to fail** *(likely)* è certo di fallire; **~ for** diretto(-a) a; **out of bounds** il cui accesso è vietato
boundary ['baundrɪ] *n* confine *m*
boundless ['baundlɪs] *adj* illimitato(-a)
bountiful ['bauntɪful] *adj (person)* munifico(-a); *(God)* misericordioso(-a); *(supply)* abbondante
bounty ['bauntɪ] *n (generosity)* liberalità, munificenza; *(reward)* taglia
bounty hunter *n* cacciatore *m* di taglie
bouquet ['bukeɪ] *n* bouquet *m inv*
bourbon ['buəbən] *n (US: also:* **bourbon whiskey**) bourbon *m inv*
bourgeois ['buəʒwɑː] *adj, n* borghese *(m/f)*
bout [baut] *n* periodo; *(of malaria etc)* attacco; *(Boxing etc)* incontro
boutique [buː'tiːk] *n* boutique *f inv*
bow[1] [bəu] *n* nodo; *(weapon)* arco; *(Mus)* archetto
bow[2] [bau] *n (with body)* inchino; *(Naut: also:* **bows**) prua ■ *vi* inchinarsi; *(yield)*: **to ~ to** *or* **before** sottomettersi a; **to ~ to the inevitable** rassegnarsi all'inevitabile
bowels [bauəlz] *npl* intestini *mpl*; *(fig)* viscere *fpl*
bowl [bəul] *n (for eating)* scodella; *(for washing)* bacino; *(ball)* boccia; *(of pipe)* fornello; *(US: stadium)* stadio ■ *vi (Cricket)* servire (la palla); *see also* **bowls**
▸ **bowl over** *vt (fig)* sconcertare
bow-legged ['bəu'lɛgɪd] *adj* dalle gambe storte
bowler ['bəuləʳ] *n* giocatore *m* di bocce; *(Cricket)* giocatore che serve la palla; *(Brit: also:* **bowler hat**) bombetta
bowling ['bəulɪŋ] *n (game)* gioco delle bocce; bowling *m*
bowling alley *n* pista da bowling
bowling green *n* campo di bocce
bowls [bəulz] *n* gioco delle bocce
bow tie *n* cravatta a farfalla
box [bɔks] *n* scatola; *(also:* **cardboard box**) (scatola di) cartone *m*; *(crate; also for money)* cassetta; *(Theat)* palco; *(Brit Aut)* area d'incrocio ■ *vi* fare pugilato ■ *vt* mettere in (una) scatola; *(Sport)* combattere contro
boxer ['bɔksəʳ] *n (person)* pugile *m*; *(dog)* boxer *m inv*
boxing ['bɔksɪŋ] *n (Sport)* pugilato
Boxing Day *n (Brit)* ≈ Santo Stefano; *vedi nota*

BOXING DAY

Il *Boxing Day* è il primo giorno infrasettimanale dopo Natale e cade il 26 di dicembre. Prende il nome dall'usanza di donare pacchi regalo natalizi, un tempo chiamati "Christmas boxes", a fornitori e dipendenti, ed è un giorno di festa

boxing gloves *npl* guantoni *mpl* da pugile
boxing ring *n* ring *m inv*
box number *n (for advertisements)* casella
box office *n* biglietteria
box room *n* ripostiglio
boy [bɔɪ] *n* ragazzo; *(small)* bambino; *(son)* figlio; *(servant)* servo
boy band *n gruppo pop di soli ragazzi maschi creato per far presa su un pubblico giovane*
boycott ['bɔɪkɔt] *n* boicottaggio ■ *vt* boicottare
boyfriend ['bɔɪfrɛnd] *n* ragazzo
boyish ['bɔɪɪʃ] *adj* di *or* da ragazzo
bp *abbr* = **bishop**
bra [brɑː] *n* reggipetto, reggiseno
brace [breɪs] *n* sostegno; *(on teeth)* apparecchio correttore; *(tool)* trapano; *(Typ: also:* **brace bracket**) graffa ■ *vt* rinforzare, sostenere; **to ~ o.s.** *(fig)* farsi coraggio; *see also* **braces**
bracelet ['breɪslɪt] *n* braccialetto
braces ['breɪsɪz] *npl (Brit)* bretelle *fpl*
bracing ['breɪsɪŋ] *adj* invigorante
bracken ['brækən] *n* felce *f*
bracket ['brækɪt] *n (Tech)* mensola; *(group)* gruppo; *(Typ)* parentesi *f inv* ■ *vt* mettere fra parentesi; *(fig: also:* **bracket together**) mettere insieme; **in brackets** tra parentesi; **round/square brackets** parentesi tonde/quadre; **income ~** fascia di reddito
brackish ['brækɪʃ] *adj (water)* salmastro(-a)
brag [bræg] *vi* vantarsi
braid [breɪd] *n (trimming)* passamano; *(of hair)* treccia
Braille [breɪl] *n* braille *m*
brain [breɪn] *n* cervello; **brains** *npl* cervella *fpl*; **he's got brains** è intelligente
brainchild ['breɪntʃaɪld] *n* creatura, creazione *f*
braindead ['breɪndɛd] *adj (Med)* che ha subito morte cerebrale; *(col)* cerebroleso(-a), deficiente
brainless ['breɪnlɪs] *adj* deficiente, stupido(-a)
brainstorm ['breɪnstɔːm] *n (fig)* attacco di pazzia; *(US)* = **brainwave**

brainwash ['breɪnwɔʃ] *vt* fare un lavaggio di cervello a
brainwave ['breɪnweɪv] *n* lampo di genio
brainy ['breɪnɪ] *adj* intelligente
braise [breɪz] *vt* brasare
brake [breɪk] *n* (*on vehicle*) freno ■ *vt, vi* frenare
brake light *n* (fanalino dello) stop *m inv*
brake pedal *n* pedale *m* del freno
bramble ['bræmbl] *n* rovo; (*fruit*) mora
bran [bræn] *n* crusca
branch [brɑːntʃ] *n* ramo; (*Comm*) succursale *f*, filiale *f* ■ *vi* diramarsi
▸ **branch out** *vi*: **to ~ out into** intraprendere una nuova attività nel ramo di
branch line *n* (*Rail*) linea secondaria
branch manager *n* direttore *m* di filiale
brand [brænd] *n* marca ■ *vt* (*cattle*) marcare (a ferro rovente); (*fig: pej*): **to ~ sb a communist** *etc* definire qn come comunista *etc*
brandish ['brændɪʃ] *vt* brandire
brand name *n* marca
brand-new ['brænd'njuː] *adj* nuovo(-a) di zecca
brandy ['brændɪ] *n* brandy *m inv*
brash [bræʃ] *adj* sfacciato(-a)
Brasilia [brə'zɪljə] *n* Brasilia
brass [brɑːs] *n* ottone *m*; **the ~** (*Mus*) gli ottoni
brass band *n* fanfara
brassière ['bræsɪəʳ] *n* reggipetto, reggiseno
brass tacks *npl*: **to get down to ~** (*col*) venire al sodo
brat [bræt] *n* (*pej*) marmocchio, monello(-a)
bravado [brə'vɑːdəu] *n* spavalderia
brave [breɪv] *adj* coraggioso(-a) ■ *n* guerriero *m* pellerossa *inv* ■ *vt* affrontare
bravery ['breɪvərɪ] *n* coraggio
bravo [brɑː'vəu] *excl* bravo!, bene!
brawl [brɔːl] *n* rissa ■ *vi* azzuffarsi
brawn [brɔːn] *n* muscolo; (*meat*) carne *f* di testa di maiale
brawny ['brɔːnɪ] *adj* muscoloso(-a)
bray [breɪ] *n* raglio ■ *vi* ragliare
brazen ['breɪzn] *adj* svergognato(-a) ■ *vt*: **to ~ it out** fare lo sfacciato
brazier ['breɪzɪəʳ] *n* braciere *m*
Brazil [brə'zɪl] *n* Brasile *m*
Brazilian [brə'zɪljən] *adj, n* brasiliano(-a)
Brazil nut *n* noce *f* del Brasile
breach [briːtʃ] *vt* aprire una breccia in ■ *n* (*gap*) breccia, varco; (*estrangement*) rottura; (*of duty*) abuso; (*breaking*): **~ of contract** rottura di contratto; **~ of the peace** violazione *f* dell'ordine pubblico; **~ of trust** abuso di fiducia
bread [bred] *n* pane *m*; (*col: money*) grana; **to earn one's daily ~** guadagnarsi il pane; **to know which side one's ~ is buttered on** saper fare i propri interessi; **~ and butter** *n* pane e burro; (*fig*) mezzi *mpl* di sussistenza
breadbin ['brɛdbɪn] *n* (*Brit*) cassetta *f* portapane *inv*
breadboard ['brɛdbɔːd] *n* tagliere *m* (*per il pane*); (*Comput*) pannello per esperimenti
breadbox ['brɛdbɔks] *n* (*US*) cassetta *f* portapane *inv*
breadcrumbs ['brɛdkrʌmz] *npl* briciole *fpl*; (*Culin*) pangrattato
breadline ['brɛdlaɪn] *n*: **to be on the ~** avere appena denaro per vivere
breadth [brɛtθ] *n* larghezza
breadwinner ['brɛdwɪnəʳ] *n chi guadagna il pane per tutta la famiglia*
break [breɪk] *vb* (*pt* **broke**, *pp* **broken**) *vt* rompere; (*law*) violare; (*promise*) mancare a ■ *vi* rompersi; (*weather*) cambiare ■ *n* (*gap*) breccia; (*fracture*) rottura; (*rest, also Scol*) intervallo; (*: short*) pausa; (*chance*) possibilità *f inv*; (*holiday*) vacanza; **to ~ one's leg** *etc* rompersi la gamba *etc*; **to ~ a record** battere un primato; **to ~ the news to sb** comunicare per primo la notizia a qn; **to ~ with sb** (*fig*) rompere con qn; **to ~ even** *vi* coprire le spese; **to ~ free** *or* **loose** liberarsi; **without a ~** senza una pausa; **to have** *or* **take a ~** (*few minutes*) fare una pausa; (*holiday*) prendere un po' di riposo; **a lucky ~** un colpo di fortuna
▸ **break down** *vt* (*figures, data*) analizzare; (*door etc*) buttare giù, abbattere; (*resistance*) stroncare ■ *vi* crollare; (*Med*) avere un esaurimento (nervoso); (*Aut*) guastarsi
▸ **break in** *vt* (*horse etc*) domare ■ *vi* (*burglar*) fare irruzione
▸ **break into** *vt fus* (*house*) fare irruzione in
▸ **break off** *vi* (*speaker*) interrompersi; (*branch*) troncarsi ■ *vt* (*talks, engagement*) rompere
▸ **break open** *vt* (*door etc*) sfondare
▸ **break out** *vi* evadere; **to ~ out in spots** coprirsi di macchie
▸ **break through** *vi*: **the sun broke through** il sole ha fatto capolino tra le nuvole ■ *vt* (*defences, barrier*) sfondare, penetrare in; (*crowd*) aprirsi un varco in *or* tra, aprirsi un passaggio in *or* tra
▸ **break up** *vi* (*partnership*) sciogliersi; (*friends*) separarsi; **the line's** *or* **you're breaking up** la linea è disturbata ■ *vt* fare in pezzi, spaccare; (*fight etc*) interrompere, far cessare; (*marriage*) finire
breakable ['breɪkəbl] *adj* fragile; **breakables** *npl* oggetti *mpl* fragili
breakage ['breɪkɪdʒ] *n* rottura; **to pay for breakages** pagare i danni

breakaway ['breɪkəweɪ] *adj* (*group etc*) scissionista, dissidente
break-dancing ['breɪkdɑːnsɪŋ] *n* breakdance *f*
breakdown ['breɪkdaun] *n* (*Aut*) guasto; (*in communications*) interruzione *f*; (*Med*: *also*: **nervous breakdown**) esaurimento nervoso; (*of payments etc*) resoconto
breakdown service *n* (*Brit*) servizio riparazioni
breakdown van *n* carro *m* attrezzi *inv*
breaker ['breɪkəʳ] *n* frangente *m*
breakeven ['breɪk'iːvn] *cpd*: **~ chart** diagramma *m* del punto di rottura *or* pareggio; **~ point** punto di rottura *or* pareggio
breakfast ['brɛkfəst] *n* colazione *f*
breakfast cereal *n* fiocchi *mpl* d'avena *or* di mais *etc*
break-in ['breɪkɪn] *n* irruzione *f*
breaking point ['breɪkɪŋ-] *n* punto di rottura
breakthrough ['breɪkθruː] *n* (*Mil*) breccia; (*fig*) passo avanti
break-up ['breɪkʌp] *n* (*of partnership, marriage*) rottura
break-up value *n* (*Comm*) valore *m* di realizzo
breakwater ['breɪkwɔːtəʳ] *n* frangiflutti *m inv*
breast [brɛst] *n* (*of woman*) seno; (*chest*) petto
breast-feed ['brɛstfiːd] *vt* (*irreg*: *like* **feed**) allattare (al seno)
breast pocket *n* taschino
breast-stroke ['brɛststrəuk] *n* nuoto a rana
breath [brɛθ] *n* fiato; **out of ~** senza fiato; **to go out for a ~ of air** andare a prendere una boccata d'aria
Breathalyser® ['brɛθəlaɪzəʳ] *n* alcoltest *m inv*
breathe [briːð] *vt, vi* respirare; **I won't ~ a word about it** non fiaterò
▸ **breathe in** *vi* inspirare ■ *vt* respirare
▸ **breathe out** *vt, vi* espirare
breather ['briːðəʳ] *n* attimo di respiro
breathing ['briːðɪŋ] *n* respiro, respirazione *f*
breathing space *n* (*fig*) attimo di respiro
breathless ['brɛθlɪs] *adj* senza fiato; (*with excitement*) con il fiato sospeso
breath-taking ['brɛθteɪkɪŋ] *adj* sbalorditivo(-a)
breath test *n* ≈ prova del palloncino
-bred [brɛd] *suffix*: **to be well/ill~** essere ben educato(-a)/maleducato(-a)
breed [briːd] *vb* (*pt, pp* **bred**) *vt* allevare; (*fig*: *hate, suspicion*) generare, provocare ■ *vi* riprodursi ■ *n* razza, varietà *f inv*
breeder ['briːdəʳ] *n* (*Physics*: *also*: **breeder reactor**) reattore *m* autofertilizzante
breeding ['briːdɪŋ] *n* riproduzione *f*; allevamento
breeze [briːz] *n* brezza
breeze block *n* (*Brit*) *mattone composto di scorie di coke*
breezy ['briːzɪ] *adj* arioso(-a); allegro(-a)
Breton ['brɛtən] *adj, n* brettone (*m/f*)
brevity ['brɛvɪtɪ] *n* brevità
brew [bruː] *vt* (*tea*) fare un infuso di; (*beer*) fare; (*plot*) tramare ■ *vi* (*tea*) essere in infusione; (*beer*) essere in fermentazione; (*fig*) bollire in pentola
brewer ['bruːəʳ] *n* birraio
brewery ['bruːərɪ] *n* fabbrica di birra
briar ['braɪəʳ] *n* (*thorny bush*) rovo; (*wild rose*) rosa selvatica
bribe [braɪb] *n* bustarella ■ *vt* comprare; **to ~ sb to do sth** pagare qn sottobanco perché faccia qc
bribery ['braɪbərɪ] *n* corruzione *f*
bric-a-brac ['brɪkəbræk] *n* bric-a-brac *m*
brick [brɪk] *n* mattone *m*
bricklayer ['brɪkleɪəʳ] *n* muratore *m*
brickwork ['brɪkwəːk] *n* muratura in mattoni
brickworks ['brɪkwəːks] *n* fabbrica di mattoni
bridal ['braɪdl] *adj* nuziale; **~ party** corteo nuziale
bride [braɪd] *n* sposa
bridegroom ['braɪdgruːm] *n* sposo
bridesmaid ['braɪdzmeɪd] *n* damigella d'onore
bridge [brɪdʒ] *n* ponte *m*; (*Naut*) ponte di comando; (*of nose*) dorso; (*Cards, Dentistry*) bridge *m inv* ■ *vt* (*river*) fare un ponte sopra; (*gap*) colmare
bridging loan ['brɪdʒɪŋ-] *n* (*Brit*) anticipazione *f* sul mutuo
bridle ['braɪdl] *n* briglia ■ *vt* tenere a freno; (*horse*) mettere la briglia a ■ *vi* (*in anger etc*) adombrarsi, adontarsi
bridle path *n* sentiero (per cavalli)
brief [briːf] *adj* breve ■ *n* (*Law*) comparsa ■ *vt* (*Mil etc*) dare istruzioni a; **in ~ ...** in breve ..., a farla breve ...; **to ~ sb (about sth)** mettere qn al corrente (di qc); *see also* **briefs**
briefcase ['briːfkeɪs] *n* cartella
briefing ['briːfɪŋ] *n* istruzioni *fpl*
briefly ['briːflɪ] *adv* (*speak, visit*) brevemente; (*glimpse*) di sfuggita
briefness ['briːfnɪs] *n* brevità
briefs [briːfs] *npl* mutande *fpl*
Brig. *abbr* = **brigadier**
brigade [brɪ'geɪd] *n* (*Mil*) brigata
brigadier [brɪgə'dɪəʳ] *n* generale *m* di brigata
bright [braɪt] *adj* luminoso(-a); (*person*) sveglio(-a); (*colour*) vivace; **to look on the ~ side** vedere il lato positivo delle cose
brighten ['braɪtn] (*also*: **brighten up**) *vt* (*room*)

rendere luminoso(-a); rallegrare ▪ *vi* schiarirsi; (*person*) rallegrarsi

brightly ['braɪtlɪ] *adv* (*shine*) vivamente, intensamente; (*smile*) radiosamente; (*talk*) con animazione

brill [brɪl] *excl* (*Brit col*) stupendo!, fantastico!

brilliance ['brɪljəns] *n* splendore *m*; (*fig: of person*) genialità, talento

brilliant ['brɪljənt] *adj* brillante; (*sunshine*) sfolgorante

brim [brɪm] *n* orlo

brimful ['brɪm'ful] *adj* pieno(-a) *or* colmo(-a) fino all'orlo; (*fig*) pieno(-a)

brine [braɪn] *n* acqua salmastra; (*Culin*) salamoia

bring (*pt, pp* **brought**) [brɪŋ, brɔːt] *vt* portare; **to ~ sth to an end** mettere fine a qc; **I can't ~ myself to sack him** non so risolvermi a licenziarlo

▸ **bring about** *vt* causare

▸ **bring back** *vt* riportare

▸ **bring down** *vt* (*lower*) far scendere; (*shoot down*) abbattere; (*government*) far cadere

▸ **bring forward** *vt* portare avanti; (*in time*) anticipare; (*Book-keeping*) riportare

▸ **bring in** *vt* (*person*) fare entrare; (*object*) portare; (*Pol: bill*) presentare; (*: legislation*) introdurre; (*Law: verdict*) emettere; (*produce: income*) rendere

▸ **bring off** *vt* (*task, plan*) portare a compimento; (*deal*) concludere

▸ **bring out** *vt* (*meaning*) mettere in evidenza; (*new product*) lanciare; (*book*) pubblicare, fare uscire

▸ **bring round** *or* **to** *vt* (*unconscious person*) far rinvenire

▸ **bring up** *vt* allevare; (*question*) introdurre

brink [brɪŋk] *n* orlo; **on the ~ of doing sth** sul punto di fare qc; **she was on the ~ of tears** era lì lì per piangere

brisk [brɪsk] *adj* (*person, tone*) spiccio(-a), sbrigativo(-a); (*: abrupt*) brusco(-a); (*wind*) fresco(-a); (*trade etc*) vivace, attivo(-a); **to go for a ~ walk** fare una camminata di buon passo; **business is ~** gli affari vanno bene

bristle ['brɪsl] *n* setola ▪ *vi* rizzarsi; **bristling with** irto(-a) di

bristly ['brɪslɪ] *adj* (*chin*) ispido(-a); (*beard, hair*) irsuto(-a), setoloso(-a)

Brit [brɪt] *n abbr* (*col: = British person*) britannico(-a)

Britain ['brɪtən] *n* Gran Bretagna

British ['brɪtɪʃ] *adj* britannico(-a); **the British** *npl* i Britannici; **the ~ Isles** *npl* le Isole Britanniche

British Summer Time *n* ora legale (*in Gran Bretagna*)

Briton ['brɪtən] *n* britannico(-a)

Brittany ['brɪtənɪ] *n* Bretagna

brittle ['brɪtl] *adj* fragile

Br(o) *abbr* (*Rel*) = **brother**

broach [brəutʃ] *vt* (*subject*) affrontare

broad [brɔːd] *adj* largo(-a); (*distinction*) generale; (*accent*) spiccato(-a) ▪ *n* (*US col*) bellona; **~ hint** allusione *f* esplicita; **in ~ daylight** in pieno giorno; **the ~ outlines** le grandi linee

broadband ['brɔːdbænd] *adj* (*Comput*) a banda larga ▪ *n* banda larga

broad bean *n* fava

broadcast ['brɔːdkɑːst] *n* trasmissione *f* ▪ *vb* (*pt, pp* **~**) *vt* trasmettere per radio (*or* per televisione) ▪ *vi* fare una trasmissione

broadcaster ['brɔːdkɑːstə^r] *n* annunciatore(-trice) radiotelevisivo(-a) (*or* radiofonico(-a))

broadcasting ['brɔːdkɑːstɪŋ] *n* radiodiffusione *f*; televisione *f*

broadcasting station *n* stazione *f* trasmittente

broaden ['brɔːdn] *vt* allargare ▪ *vi* allargarsi

broadly ['brɔːdlɪ] *adv* (*fig*) in generale

broad-minded ['brɔːd'maɪndɪd] *adj* di mente aperta

broadsheet ['brɔːdʃiːt] *n* (*Brit*) giornale *m* (*si contrappone al tabloid che è di formato più piccolo*)

broccoli ['brɔkəlɪ] *n* (*Bot*) broccolo; (*Culin*) broccoli *mpl*

brochure ['brəuʃjuə^r] *n* dépliant *m inv*

brogue [brəug] *n* (*shoe*) scarpa rozza in cuoio; (*accent*) accento irlandese

broil [brɔɪl] *vt* cuocere a fuoco vivo

broke [brəuk] *pt of* **break** ▪ *adj* (*col*) squattrinato(-a); **to go ~** fare fallimento

broken ['brəukən] *pp of* **break** ▪ *adj* (*gen*) rotto(-a); (*stick, promise, vow*) spezzato(-a); (*marriage*) fallito(-a); **he comes from a ~ home** i suoi sono divisi; **in ~ French/ English** in un francese/inglese stentato

broken-down ['brəukən'daun] *adj* (*car*) in panne, rotto(-a); (*machine*) guasto(-a), fuori uso; (*house*) abbandonato(-a), in rovina

broken-hearted ['brəukən'hɑːtɪd] *adj*: **to be ~** avere il cuore spezzato

broker ['brəukə^r] *n* agente *m*

brokerage ['brəukərɪdʒ] *n* (*Comm*) commissione *f* di intermediazione

brolly ['brɔlɪ] *n* (*Brit col*) ombrello

bronchitis [brɔŋ'kaɪtɪs] *n* bronchite *f*

bronze [brɔnz] *n* bronzo

bronzed [brɔnzd] *adj* abbronzato(-a)

brooch [brəutʃ] *n* spilla

brood [bruːd] *n* covata ▪ *vi* (*hen*) covare; (*person*) rimuginare

broody ['bru:dɪ] *adj (fig)* cupo(-a) e taciturno(-a)
brook [bruk] *n* ruscello
broom [brum] *n* scopa
broomstick ['brumstɪk] *n* manico di scopa
Bros. *abbr (Comm: = brothers)* F.lli *(= Fratelli)*
broth [brɔθ] *n* brodo
brothel ['brɔθl] *n* bordello
brother ['brʌðə^r] *n* fratello
brotherhood ['brʌðəhud] *n* fratellanza; confraternità *f inv*
brother-in-law ['brʌðərɪnlɔ:] *n* cognato
brotherly ['brʌðəlɪ] *adj* fraterno(-a)
brought [brɔ:t] *pt, pp of* **bring**
brought forward *adj (Comm)* riportato(-a)
brow [brau] *n* fronte *f*; *(rare, gen: also:* **eyebrow***)* sopracciglio; *(of hill)* cima
browbeat ['braubi:t] *vt* intimidire
brown [braun] *adj* bruno(-a), marrone; *(hair)* castano(-a) ■ *n (colour)* color *m* bruno *or* marrone ■ *vt (Culin)* rosolare; **to go ~** *(person)* abbronzarsi; *(leaves)* ingiallire
brown bread *n* pane *m* integrale, pane nero
brownie ['braunɪ] *n* giovane esploratrice *f*
brown paper *n* carta da pacchi *or* da imballaggio
brown rice *n* riso greggio
brown sugar *n* zucchero greggio
browse [brauz] *vi (animal)* brucare; *(in bookshop etc)* curiosare; *(Comput)* navigare (in Internet) ■ *vt*: **to ~ the web** navigare in Internet ■ *n*: **to have a ~ (around)** dare un'occhiata (in giro); **to ~ through a book** sfogliare un libro
browser [brauzə^r] *n (Comput)* browser *m inv*
bruise [bru:z] *n* ammaccatura; *(on person)* livido ■ *vt* ammaccare; *(leg etc)* farsi un livido a; *(fig: feelings)* urtare ■ *vi (fruit)* ammaccarsi
Brum [brʌm] *n abbr*, **Brummagem** ['brʌmədʒəm] *n (col)* = **Birmingham**
Brummie ['brʌmɪ] *n (col)* abitante *m/f* di Birmingham, originario(-a) di Birmingham
brunch [brʌntʃ] *n ricca colazione consumata in tarda mattinata*
brunette [bru:'nɛt] *n* bruna
brunt [brʌnt] *n*: **the ~ of** *(attack, criticism etc)* il peso maggiore di
brush [brʌʃ] *n* spazzola; *(quarrel)* schermaglia ■ *vt* spazzolare; *(gen: also:* **brush past, brush against***)* sfiorare; **to have a ~ with sb** *(verbally)* avere uno scontro con qn; *(physically)* venire a diverbio *or* alle mani con qn; **to have a ~ with the police** avere delle noie con la polizia
▸ **brush aside** *vt* scostare
▸ **brush up** *vt (knowledge)* rinfrescare
brushed [brʌʃt] *adj (Tech: steel, chrome etc)* sabbiato(-a); *(nylon, denim etc)* pettinato(-a)
brush-off ['brʌʃɔf] *n*: **to give sb the ~** dare il ben servito a qn
brushwood ['brʌʃwud] *n* macchia
brusque [bru:sk] *adj (person, manner)* brusco(-a); *(tone)* secco(-a)
Brussels ['brʌslz] *n* Bruxelles *f*
Brussels sprout *n* cavolo di Bruxelles
brutal ['bru:tl] *adj* brutale
brutality [bru:'tælɪtɪ] *n* brutalità
brutalize ['bru:təlaɪz] *vt (harden)* abbrutire; *(ill-treat)* brutalizzare
brute [bru:t] *n* bestia; **by ~ force** con la forza, a viva forza
brutish ['bru:tɪʃ] *adj* da bruto
BS *n abbr (US: = Bachelor of Science) titolo di studio*
bs *abbr* = **bill of sale**
BSA *n abbr (US)* = **Boy Scouts of America**
BSc *n abbr* = **Bachelor of Science**
BSE *n abbr (= bovine spongiform encephalopathy)* encefalite *f* bovina spongiforme
BSI *n abbr (= British Standards Institution) associazione per la normalizzazione*
BST *abbr (= British Summer Time) ora legale*
Bt. *abbr (Brit)* = **baronet**
btu *n abbr (= British thermal unit)* Btu *m (= 1054.2 joules)*
bubble ['bʌbl] *n* bolla ■ *vi* ribollire; *(sparkle, fig)* essere effervescente
bubble bath *n* bagno *m* schiuma *inv*
bubblejet printer ['bʌbldʒɛt-] *n* stampante *f* a getto d'inchiostro
bubbly ['bʌblɪ] *adj (also fig)* frizzante ■ *n (col: champagne)* spumante *m*
Bucharest [bu:kə'rɛst] *n* Bucarest *f*
buck [bʌk] *n* maschio *(di camoscio, caprone, coniglio etc)*; *(US col)* dollaro ■ *vi* sgroppare; **to pass the ~ (to sb)** scaricare (su di qn) la propria responsabilità
▸ **buck up** *vi (cheer up)* rianimarsi ■ *vt*: **to ~ one's ideas up** mettere la testa a partito
bucket ['bʌkɪt] *n* secchio ■ *vi (Brit col)*: **the rain is bucketing (down)** piove a catinelle
Buckingham Palace ['bʌkɪŋəm-] *n vedi nota*

BUCKINGHAM PALACE

Buckingham Palace è la residenza ufficiale a Londra del sovrano britannico. Costruita nel 1703 per il duca di Buckingham, fu acquistata nel 1762 dal re Giorgio III e ricostruita tra il 1821 e il 1838 sotto la guida dell'architetto John Nash. All'inizio del Novecento alcune sue parti sono state ulteriormente modificate.

buckle ['bʌkl] *n* fibbia ■ *vt* affibbiare; (*warp*) deformare
▸ **buckle down** *vi* mettersi sotto
Bucks [bʌks] *abbr* (*Brit*) = **Buckinghamshire**
bud [bʌd] *n* gemma; (*of flower*) boccio ■ *vi* germogliare; (*flower*) sbocciare
Budapest [bju:də'pɛst] *n* Budapest *f*
Buddha ['budə] *n* Budda *m*
Buddhism ['budɪzəm] *n* buddismo
Buddhist ['budɪst] *adj, n* buddista (*m/f*)
budding ['bʌdɪŋ] *adj* (*flower*) in boccio; (*poet etc*) in erba
buddy ['bʌdɪ] *n* (*US*) compagno
budge [bʌdʒ] *vt* scostare ■ *vi* spostarsi
budgerigar ['bʌdʒərɪgɑːʳ] *n* pappagallino
budget ['bʌdʒɪt] *n* bilancio preventivo ■ *vi*: **to ~ for sth** fare il bilancio per qc; **I'm on a tight ~** devo contare la lira; **she works out her ~ every month** fa il preventivo delle spese ogni mese
budgie ['bʌdʒɪ] *n* = **budgerigar**
Buenos Aires ['bweɪnɔs'aɪrɪz] *n* Buenos Aires *f*
buff [bʌf] *adj* color camoscio *inv* ■ *n* (*enthusiast*) appassionato(-a)
buffalo (*pl* ~ *or* **buffaloes**) ['bʌfələu] *n* bufalo; (*US*) bisonte *m*
buffer ['bʌfəʳ] *n* respingente *m*; (*Comput*) memoria tampone, buffer *m inv* ■ *vi* (*Comput*) fare il buffering, trasferire nella memoria tampone
buffering ['bʌfərɪŋ] *n* (*Comput*) buffering *m inv*, trasferimento nella memoria tampone
buffer state *n* stato cuscinetto
buffer zone *n* zona *f* cuscinetto *inv*
buffet *n* ['bufeɪ] (*food, Brit: bar*) buffet *m inv* ■ *vt* ['bʌfɪt] schiaffeggiare scuotere; urtare
buffet car *n* (*Brit Rail*) ≈ servizio ristoro
buffet lunch *n* pranzo in piedi
buffoon [bə'fu:n] *n* buffone *m*
bug [bʌg] *n* (*insect*) cimice *f*; (*: gen*) insetto; (*fig: germ*) virus *m inv*; (*spy device*) microfono spia; (*Comput*) bug *m inv*, errore *m* nel programma ■ *vt* mettere sotto controllo; (*room*) installare microfoni spia in; (*annoy*) scocciare; **I've got the travel ~** (*fig*) mi è presa la mania dei viaggi
bugbear ['bʌgbɛəʳ] *n* spauracchio
bugger ['bʌgəʳ] (*col!*) *n* bastardo (*!*) ■ *vb*: **~ off!** vaffanculo! (*!*); **~ (it)!** merda! (*!*)
bugle ['bju:gl] *n* tromba
build [bɪld] *n* (*of person*) corporatura ■ *vt* (*pt, pp* **built**) [bɪlt] costruire
▸ **build on** *vt fus* (*fig*) prendere il via da
▸ **build up** *vt* (*establish: business*) costruire; (*: reputation*) fare, consolidare; (*increase: production*) allargare, incrementare; **don't ~ your hopes up too soon** non sperarci troppo
builder ['bɪldəʳ] *n* costruttore *m*
building ['bɪldɪŋ] *n* costruzione *f*; edificio; (*also:* **building trade**) edilizia
building contractor *n* costruttore *m*, imprenditore *m* (edile)
building industry *n* industria edilizia
building site *n* cantiere *m* di costruzione
building society *n*; *vedi nota*

BUILDING SOCIETY

Le *building societies* sono società immobiliari e finanziarie che forniscono numerosi servizi bancari ai clienti che vi investono i risparmi, e in particolare concedono mutui per l'acquisto della casa.

building trade *n* = **building industry**
build-up ['bɪldʌp] *n* (*of gas etc*) accumulo; (*publicity*): **to give sb/sth a good ~** fare buona pubblicità a qn/qc
built [bɪlt] *pt, pp of* **build**; **well-~** robusto(-a)
built-in ['bɪlt'ɪn] *adj* (*cupboard*) a muro; (*device*) incorporato(-a)
built-up area ['bɪltʌp-] *n* abitato
bulb [bʌlb] *n* (*Bot*) bulbo; (*Elec*) lampadina
bulbous ['bʌlbəs] *adj* bulboso(-a)
Bulgaria [bʌl'gɛərɪə] *n* Bulgaria
Bulgarian [bʌl'gɛərɪən] *adj* bulgaro(-a) ■ *n* bulgaro(-a); (*Ling*) bulgaro
bulge [bʌldʒ] *n* rigonfiamento; (*in birth rate, sales*) punta ■ *vi* essere protuberante *or* rigonfio(-a); **to be bulging with** essere pieno(-a) *or* zeppo(-a) di
bulimia [bə'lɪmɪə] *n* bulimia
bulk [bʌlk] *n* massa, volume *m*; **the ~ of** il grosso di; **(to buy) in ~** (comprare) in grande quantità
bulk buying *n* acquisto di merce in grande quantità
bulk carrier *n* grossa nave *f* da carico
bulkhead ['bʌlkhɛd] *n* paratia
bulky ['bʌlkɪ] *adj* grosso(-a); voluminoso(-a)
bull [bul] *n* toro; (*Stock Exchange*) rialzista *m/f*; (*Rel*) bolla (papale)
bulldog ['buldɔg] *n* bulldog *m inv*
bulldoze ['buldəuz] *vt* aprire *or* spianare col bulldozer; **I was bulldozed into doing it** (*fig, col*) mi ci hanno costretto con la prepotenza
bulldozer ['buldəuzəʳ] *n* bulldozer *m inv*
bullet ['bulɪt] *n* pallottola
bulletin ['bulɪtɪn] *n* bollettino
bulletin board *n* (*Comput*) bulletin board *m inv*

bullet point *n* punto; **bullet points** elenco *sg* puntato
bullet-proof ['bulɪtpruːf] *adj* a prova di proiettile; **~ vest** giubbotto antiproiettile
bullfight ['bulfaɪt] *n* corrida
bullfighter ['bulfaɪtəʳ] *n* torero
bullfighting ['bulfaɪtɪŋ] *n* tauromachia
bullion ['buljən] *n* oro *or* argento in lingotti
bullock ['bulək] *n* giovenco
bullring ['bulrɪŋ] *n* arena (per corride)
bull's-eye ['bulzaɪ] *n* centro del bersaglio
bullshit ['bulʃɪt] (*col!*) *excl, n* stronzate *fpl* (*!*) ■ *vi* raccontare stronzate (*!*) ■ *vt* raccontare stronzate a (*!*)
bully ['bulɪ] *n* prepotente *m* ■ *vt* angariare; (*frighten*) intimidire
bullying ['bulɪɪŋ] *n* prepotenze *fpl*
bum [bʌm] *n* (*col: backside*) culo; (*tramp*) vagabondo(-a); (*US: idler*) fannullone(-a)
▸ **bum around** *vi* (*col*) fare il vagabondo
bumblebee ['bʌmblbiː] *n* (*Zool*) bombo
bumf [bʌmf] *n* (*col: forms etc*) scartoffie *fpl*
bump [bʌmp] *n* (*blow*) colpo; (*jolt*) scossa; (*noise*) botto; (*on road etc*) protuberanza; (*on head*) bernoccolo ■ *vt* battere; (*car*) urtare, sbattere
▸ **bump along** *vi* procedere sobbalzando
▸ **bump into** *vt fus* scontrarsi con; (*col: meet*) imbattersi in, incontrare per caso
bumper ['bʌmpəʳ] *n* (*Brit*) paraurti *m inv* ■ *adj*: **~ harvest** raccolto eccezionale
bumper cars *npl* (*US*) autoscontri *mpl*
bumph [bʌmf] *n* = **bumf**
bumptious ['bʌmpʃəs] *adj* presuntuoso(-a)
bumpy ['bʌmpɪ] *adj* (*road*) dissestato(-a); (*journey, flight*) movimentato(-a)
bun [bʌn] *n* focaccia; (*of hair*) crocchia
bunch [bʌntʃ] *n* (*of flowers, keys*) mazzo; (*of bananas*) ciuffo; (*of people*) gruppo; **~ of grapes** grappolo d'uva
bundle ['bʌndl] *n* fascio ■ *vt* (*also*: **bundle up**) legare in un fascio; (*put*): **to ~ sth/sb into** spingere qc/qn in
▸ **bundle off** *vt* (*person*) mandare via in gran fretta
▸ **bundle out** *vt* far uscire (senza tante cerimonie)
bun fight *n* (*Brit: col*) tè *m inv* (*ricevimento*)
bung [bʌŋ] *n* tappo ■ *vt* (*Brit: throw: also*: **bung into**) buttare; (*also*: **bung up**: *pipe, hole*) tappare, otturare; **my nose is bunged up** (*col*) ho il naso otturato
bungalow ['bʌŋgələu] *n* bungalow *m inv*
bungee jumping ['bʌndʒiː'dʒʌmpɪŋ] *n salto nel vuoto da ponti, grattacieli etc con un cavo fissato alla caviglia*
bungle ['bʌŋgl] *vt* abborracciare
bunion ['bʌnjən] *n* callo (al piede)
bunk [bʌŋk] *n* cuccetta
▸ **bunk off** *vi* (*Brit col*): **to ~ off school** marinare la scuola; **I'll ~ off at 3 this afternoon** oggi me la filo dal lavoro alle 3
bunk beds *npl* letti *mpl* a castello
bunker ['bʌŋkəʳ] *n* (*coal store*) ripostiglio per il carbone; (*Mil, Golf*) bunker *m inv*
bunny ['bʌnɪ] *n* (*also*: **bunny rabbit**) coniglietto
bunny girl *n* coniglietta
bunny hill *n* (*US Ski*) pista per principianti
bunting ['bʌntɪŋ] *n* pavesi *mpl*, bandierine *fpl*
buoy [bɔɪ] *n* boa
▸ **buoy up** *vt* tenere a galla; (*fig*) sostenere
buoyancy ['bɔɪənsɪ] *n* (*of ship*) galleggiabilità
buoyant ['bɔɪənt] *adj* galleggiante; (*fig*) vivace; (*Comm: market*) sostenuto(-a); (*: prices, currency*) stabile
burden ['bəːdn] *n* carico, fardello ■ *vt* caricare; (*oppress*) opprimere; **to be a ~ to sb** essere di peso a qn
bureau (*pl* **bureaux**) ['bjuərəu, -z] *n* (*Brit: writing desk*) scrivania; (*US: chest of drawers*) cassettone *m*; (*office*) ufficio, agenzia
bureaucracy [bjuə'rɔkrəsɪ] *n* burocrazia
bureaucrat ['bjuərəkræt] *n* burocrate *m/f*
bureaucratic [bjuərə'krætɪk] *adj* burocratico(-a)
burgeon ['bəːdʒən] *vi* svilupparsi rapidamente
burger ['bəːgəʳ] *n* hamburger *m inv*
burglar ['bəːgləʳ] *n* scassinatore *m*
burglar alarm *n* antifurto *m inv*
burglarize ['bəːgləraɪz] *vt* (*US*) svaligiare
burglary ['bəːglərɪ] *n* furto con scasso
burgle ['bəːgl] *vt* svaligiare
Burgundy ['bəːgəndɪ] *n* Borgogna
burial ['bɛrɪəl] *n* sepoltura
burial ground *n* cimitero
burly ['bəːlɪ] *adj* robusto(-a)
Burma ['bəːmə] *n* Birmania; *see* **Myanmar**
Burmese [bəː'miːz] *adj* birmano(-a) ■ *n* (*pl inv*) birmano(-a); (*Ling*) birmano
burn [bəːn] *vt, vi* (*pt, pp* **burned** *or* **burnt**) bruciare ■ *n* bruciatura, scottatura; (*Med*) ustione *f*; **I've burnt myself!** mi sono bruciato!; **the cigarette burnt a hole in her dress** si è fatta un buco nel vestito con la sigaretta
▸ **burn down** *vt* distruggere col fuoco
▸ **burn out** *vt* (*writer etc*): **to ~ o.s. out** esaurirsi
burner ['bəːnəʳ] *n* fornello
burning ['bəːnɪŋ] *adj* (*building, forest*) in fiamme; (*issue, question*) scottante
burnish ['bəːnɪʃ] *vt* brunire
Burns Night *n vedi nota*

Burns Night

Burns Night è la festa celebrata il 25 gennaio per commemorare il poeta scozzese Robert Burns (1759–1796). Gli scozzese festeggiano questa data con una cena a base de "haggis" e whisky, spesso al suono di una cornamusa durante la cena vengono recitate le poesie di Robert Burns e vengono letti discorsi alla sua memoria.

burnt [bə:nt] *pt, pp of* **burn**
burnt sugar *n* (*Brit*) caramello
burp [bə:p] (*col*) *n* rutto ■ *vi* ruttare
burrow ['bʌrəu] *n* tana ■ *vt* scavare
bursar ['bə:səʳ] *n* economo(-a); (*Brit: student*) borsista *m/f*
bursary ['bə:sərɪ] *n* (*Brit*) borsa di studio
burst [bə:st] *vb* (*pt, pp* **~**) *vt* far scoppiare *or* esplodere ■ *vi* esplodere; (*tyre*) scoppiare ■ *n* scoppio; (*also*: **burst pipe**) rottura nel tubo, perdita; **~ of energy/laughter** scoppio d'energia/di risa; **a ~ of applause** uno scroscio d'applausi; **a ~ of speed** uno scatto (di velocità); **~ blood vessel** rottura di un vaso sanguigno; **the river has ~ its banks** il fiume ha rotto gli argini *or* ha straripato; **to ~ into flames/tears** scoppiare in fiamme/lacrime; **to be bursting with** essere pronto a scoppiare di; **to ~ out laughing** scoppiare a ridere; **to ~ open** *vi* aprirsi improvvisamente; (*door*) spalancarsi
▸ **burst into** *vt fus* (*room etc*) irrompere in
▸ **burst out of** *vt fus* precipitarsi fuori da
bury ['bɛrɪ] *vt* seppellire; **to ~ one's face in one's hands** nascondere la faccia tra le mani; **to ~ one's head in the sand** (*fig*) fare (la politica del)lo struzzo; **to ~ the hatchet** (*fig*) seppellire l'ascia di guerra
bus (*pl* **buses**) [bʌs, 'bʌsɪz] *n* autobus *m inv*
bus boy *n* (*US*) aiuto *inv* cameriere(-a)
bush [buʃ] *n* cespuglio; (*scrub land*) macchia
bushed [buʃt] *adj* (*col*) distrutto(-a)
bushel ['buʃl] *n* staio
bushfire ['buʃfaɪəʳ] *n grande incendio in aperta campagna*
bushy ['buʃɪ] *adj* (*plant, tail, beard*) folto(-a); (*eyebrows*) irsuto(-a)
busily ['bɪzɪlɪ] *adv* con impegno, alacremente
business ['bɪznɪs] *n* (*matter*) affare *m*; (*trading*) affari *mpl*; (*firm*) azienda; (*job, duty*) lavoro; **to be away on ~** essere andato via per affari; **I'm here on ~** sono qui per affari; **to do ~ with sb** fare affari con qn; **he's in the insurance ~** lavora nel campo delle assicurazioni; **it's none of my ~** questo non mi riguarda; **he means ~** non scherza
business address *n* indirizzo di lavoro *or* d'ufficio
business card *n* biglietto da visita della ditta
businesslike ['bɪznɪslaɪk] *adj* serio(-a); efficiente
businessman ['bɪznɪsmən] *n* uomo d'affari
business trip *n* viaggio d'affari
businesswoman ['bɪznɪswumən] *n* donna d'affari
busker ['bʌskəʳ] *n* (*Brit*) suonatore(-trice) ambulante
bus lane *n* (*Brit*) corsia riservata agli autobus
bus shelter *n* pensilina (*alla fermata dell'autobus*)
bus station *n* stazione *f* delle autolinee, autostazione *f*
bus stop *n* fermata d'autobus
bust [bʌst] *n* (*Art*) busto; (*bosom*) seno ■ *adj* (*broken*) rotto(-a) ■ *vt* (*col: Police: arrest*) pizzicare, beccare; **to go ~** fallire
bustle ['bʌsl] *n* movimento, attività ■ *vi* darsi da fare
bustling ['bʌslɪŋ] *adj* (*person*) indaffarato(-a); (*town*) animato(-a)
bust-up ['bʌstʌp] *n* (*Brit col*) lite *f*
busty ['bʌstɪ] *adj* (*col*) tettone(-a)
busy ['bɪzɪ] *adj* occupato(-a); (*shop, street*) molto frequentato(-a) ■ *vt*: **to ~ o.s.** darsi da fare; **he's a ~ man** (*normally*) è un uomo molto occupato; (*temporarily*) ha molto da fare, è molto occupato
busybody ['bɪzɪbɔdɪ] *n* ficcanaso *m/f inv*
busy signal *n* (*US*) segnale *m* di occupato

KEYWORD

but [bʌt] *conj* ma; **I'd love to come, but I'm busy** vorrei tanto venire, ma ho da fare
■ *prep* (*apart from, except*) eccetto, tranne, meno; **nothing but** nient'altro che; **he was nothing but trouble** non dava altro che guai; **no-one but him** solo lui; **no-one but him can do it** nessuno può farlo tranne lui; **the last but one** (*Brit*) il/la penultimo(-a); **but for you/your help** se non fosse per te/per il tuo aiuto; **anything but that** tutto ma non questo; **anything but finished** tutt'altro che finito
■ *adv* (*just, only*) solo, soltanto; **she's but a child** è solo una bambina; **had I but known** se solo avessi saputo; **I can but try** tentar non nuoce; **all but finished** quasi finito

butane ['bju:teɪn] *n* (*also*: **butane gas**) butano
butch [butʃ] *adj* (*woman: pej*) mascolino(-a), (*man*) macho *inv*
butcher ['butʃəʳ] *n* macellaio ■ *vt* macellare; **~'s (shop)** macelleria

butler [ˈbʌtləʳ] *n* maggiordomo
butt [bʌt] *n* (*cask*) grossa botte *f*; (*thick end*) estremità *f inv* più grossa; (*of gun*) calcio; (*of cigarette*) mozzicone *m*; (*Brit fig: target*) oggetto ▪ *vt* cozzare
▸ **butt in** *vi* (*interrupt*) interrompere
butter [ˈbʌtəʳ] *n* burro ▪ *vt* imburrare
buttercup [ˈbʌtəkʌp] *n* ranuncolo
butter dish *n* burriera
butterfingers [ˈbʌtəfɪŋgəz] *n* (*col*) mani *fpl* di ricotta
butterfly [ˈbʌtəflaɪ] *n* farfalla; (*Swimming*: *also*: **butterfly stroke**) (nuoto a) farfalla
buttocks [ˈbʌtəks] *npl* natiche *fpl*
button [ˈbʌtn] *n* bottone *m* ▪ *vt* (*also*: **button up**) abbottonare ▪ *vi* abbottonarsi
buttonhole [ˈbʌtnhəul] *n* asola, occhiello ▪ *vt* (*person*) attaccar bottone a
buttress [ˈbʌtrɪs] *n* contrafforte *m*
buxom [ˈbʌksəm] *adj* formoso(-a)
buy [baɪ] *vt* (*pt, pp* **bought**) [bɔːt] comprare, acquistare ▪ *n*: **a good/bad ~** un buon/cattivo acquisto *or* affare; **to ~ sb sth/sth from sb** comprare qc per qn/qc da qn; **to ~ sb a drink** offrire da bere a qn
▸ **buy back** *vt* riprendersi, prendersi indietro
▸ **buy in** *vt* (*Brit: goods*) far provvista di
▸ **buy into** *vt fus* (*Brit Comm*) acquistare delle azioni di
▸ **buy off** *vt* (*col: bribe*) comprare
▸ **buy out** *vt* (*business*) rilevare
▸ **buy up** *vt* accaparrare
buyer [ˈbaɪəʳ] *n* compratore(-trice); **~'s market** mercato favorevole ai compratori
buy-out [ˈbaɪaut] *n* (*Comm*) *acquisto di una società da parte dei suoi dipendenti*
buzz [bʌz] *n* ronzio; (*col: phone call*) colpo di telefono ▪ *vi* ronzare ▪ *vt* (*call on intercom*) chiamare al citofono; (*: with buzzer*) chiamare col cicalino; (*Aviat: plane, building*) passare rasente; **my head is buzzing** mi gira la testa
▸ **buzz off** *vi* (*Brit col*) filare, levarsi di torno
buzzard [ˈbʌzəd] *n* poiana
buzzer [ˈbʌzəʳ] *n* cicalino
buzz word *n* (*col*) termine *m* in voga

 KEYWORD

by [baɪ] *prep* **1** (*referring to cause, agent*) da; **killed by lightning** ucciso da un fulmine; **surrounded by a fence** circondato da uno steccato; **a painting by Picasso** un quadro di Picasso
2 (*referring to method, manner, means*): **by bus/car/train** in autobus/macchina/treno, con l'autobus/la macchina/il treno; **to pay by cheque** pagare con (un) assegno; **by moonlight** al chiaro di luna; **by saving hard, he ...** risparmiando molto, lui ...
3 (*via, through*) per; **we came by Dover** siamo venuti via Dover
4 (*close to, past*) accanto a; **the house by the river** la casa sul fiume; **a holiday by the sea** una vacanza al mare; **she sat by his bed** si sedette accanto al suo letto; **she rushed by me** mi è passata accanto correndo; **I go by the post office every day** passo davanti all'ufficio postale ogni giorno
5 (*not later than*) per, entro; **by 4 o'clock** per *or* entro le 4; **by this time tomorrow** domani a quest'ora; **by the time I got here it was too late** quando sono arrivato era ormai troppo tardi
6 (*during*): **by day/night** di giorno/notte
7 (*amount*) a; **by the kilo** a chili; **paid by the hour** pagato all'ora; **to increase by the hour** aumentare di ora in ora; **one by one** uno per uno; **little by little** a poco a poco
8 (*Math, measure*): **to divide/multiply by 3** dividere/moltiplicare per 3; **a room 3 metres by 4** una stanza di 3 metri per 4; **it's broader by a metre** è un metro più largo, è più largo di un metro
9 (*according to*) per; **to play by the rules** attenersi alle regole; **it's all right by me** per me va bene
10: **(all) by oneself** (tutto(-a)) solo(-a); **he did it (all) by himself** lo ha fatto (tutto) da solo
11: **by the way** a proposito; **this wasn't my idea by the way** tra l'altro l'idea non è stata mia
▪ *adv* **1** *see* **go**; **pass** *etc*
2: **by and by** (*in past*) poco dopo; (*in future*) fra breve; **by and large** nel complesso

bye [ˈbaɪ], **bye-bye** [ˈbaɪˈbaɪ] *excl* ciao!, arrivederci!
bye-law [ˈbaɪlɔː] *n* legge *f* locale
by-election [ˈbaɪɪlɛkʃən] *n* (*Brit*) elezione *f* straordinaria; *vedi nota*

BY-ELECTION

Una *by-election* in Gran Bretagna e in alcuni paesi del Commonwealth è un'elezione che si tiene per coprire un posto in Parlamento resosi vacante, a governo ancora in carica. é importante in quanto serve a misurare il consenso degli elettori in vista delle successive elezioni politiche.

Byelorussia [bjɛləu'rʌʃə] *n* Bielorussia, Belorussia
Byelorussian [bjɛləu'rʌʃən] *adj, n* = **Belarussian**
bygone ['baɪgɔn] *adj* passato(-a) ■ *n*: **let bygones be bygones** mettiamoci una pietra sopra
by-law ['baɪlɔː] *n* legge *f* locale
bypass ['baɪpɑːs] *n* circonvallazione *f*; (*Med*) by-pass *m inv* ■ *vt* fare una deviazione intorno a
by-product ['baɪprɔdʌkt] *n* sottoprodotto; (*fig*) conseguenza secondaria
byre ['baɪə[r]] *n* (*Brit*) stalla
bystander ['baɪstændə[r]] *n* spettatore(-trice)
byte [baɪt] *n* (*Comput*) byte *m inv*
byway ['baɪweɪ] *n* strada secondaria
byword ['baɪwəːd] *n*: **to be a ~ for** essere sinonimo di
by-your-leave ['baɪjɔː'liːv] *n*: **without so much as a ~** senza nemmeno chiedere il permesso

b

Cc

C, c [si:] *n* (*letter*) C, c *f or m inv*; (*Scol: mark*) ≈ 6 (*sufficiente*); (*Mus*): **C** do; **C for Charlie** ≈ C come Como
C *abbr* (= *Celsius, centigrade*) C
c. *abbr* (= *century*) sec.; (= *circa*) c; (*US etc*) = **cent(s)**
CA *abbr* = **Central America**; (US) = **California** ▪ *n abbr* (*Brit*) = **chartered accountant**
ca. *abbr* (= *circa*) ca
c/a *abbr* = **capital account**; **credit account**; **current account**
CAA *n abbr* (*Brit*: = *Civil Aviation Authority*, *US*: = *Civil Aeronautics Authority*) *organismo di controllo e di sviluppo dell'aviazione civile*
CAB *n abbr* (*Brit*: = *Citizens' Advice Bureau*) *organizzazione per la tutela del consumatore*
cab [kæb] *n* taxi *m inv*; (*of train, truck*) cabina; (*horsedrawn*) carrozza
cabaret ['kæbəreɪ] *n* cabaret *m inv*
cabbage ['kæbɪdʒ] *n* cavolo
cabbie, cabby ['kæbɪ] *n* (*col*) tassista *m/f*
cab driver *n* tassista *m/f*
cabin ['kæbɪn] *n* capanna; (*on ship*) cabina
cabin cruiser *n* cabinato
cabinet ['kæbɪnɪt] *n* (*Pol*) consiglio dei ministri; (*furniture*) armadietto; (*also*: **display cabinet**) vetrinetta; **cocktail ~** mobile *m* bar *inv*
cabinet-maker ['kæbɪnɪt'meɪkə^r] *n* stipettaio
cabinet minister *n* ministro (*membro del Consiglio*)
cable ['keɪbl] *n* cavo; fune *f*; (*Tel*) cablogramma *m* ▪ *vt* telegrafare
cable-car ['keɪblkɑ:^r] *n* funivia
cablegram ['keɪblgræm] *n* cablogramma *m*
cable railway *n* funicolare *f*
cable television *n* televisione *f* via cavo
cache [kæʃ] *n* nascondiglio; **a ~ of food** *etc* un deposito segreto di viveri *etc*
cackle ['kækl] *vi* schiamazzare
cactus (*pl* **cacti**) ['kæktəs, -taɪ] *n* cactus *m inv*
CAD *n abbr* (= *computer-aided design*) progettazione *f* con l'ausilio dell'elaboratore
caddie ['kædɪ] *n* caddie *m inv*
cadet [kə'dɛt] *n* (*Mil*) cadetto; **police ~** allievo poliziotto
cadge [kædʒ] *vt* (*col*) scroccare; **to ~ a meal (off sb)** scroccare un pranzo (a qn)
cadre ['kædrɪ] *n* quadro
Caesarean, (US) **Cesarean** [si:'zɛərɪən] *adj*: **~ (section)** (taglio) cesareo
CAF *abbr* (*Brit*: = *cost and freight*) Caf *m*
café ['kæfeɪ] *n* caffè *m inv*
cafeteria [kæfɪ'tɪərɪə] *n* self-service *m inv*
caffein, caffeine ['kæfi:n] *n* caffeina
cage [keɪdʒ] *n* gabbia ▪ *vt* mettere in gabbia
cagey ['keɪdʒɪ] *adj* (*col*) chiuso(-a); guardingo(-a)
cagoule [kə'gu:l] *n* K-way® *m inv*
cahoots [kə'hu:ts] *n*: **to be in ~ (with sb)** essere in combutta (con qn)
CAI *n abbr* (= *computer-aided instruction*) istruzione *f* assistita dall'elaboratore
Cairo ['kaɪərəu] *n* il Cairo
cajole [kə'dʒəul] *vt* allettare
cake [keɪk] *n* torta; **~ of soap** saponetta; **it's a piece of ~** (*col*) è una cosa da nulla; **he wants to have his ~ and eat it (too)** (*fig*) vuole la botte piena e la moglie ubriaca
caked [keɪkt] *adj*: **~ with** incrostato(-a) di
cake shop *n* pasticceria
Cal. *abbr* (US) = **California**
calamitous [kə'læmɪtəs] *adj* disastroso(-a)
calamity [kə'læmɪtɪ] *n* calamità *f inv*
calcium ['kælsɪəm] *n* calcio
calculate ['kælkjuleɪt] *vt* calcolare; (*estimate: chances, effect*) valutare
▸ **calculate on** *vt fus*: **to ~ on sth/on doing sth** contare su qc/di fare qc
calculated ['kælkjuleɪtɪd] *adj* calcolato(-a), intenzionale; **a ~ risk** un rischio calcolato
calculating ['kælkjuleɪtɪŋ] *adj* calcolatore(-trice)
calculation [kælkju'leɪʃən] *n* calcolo
calculator ['kælkjuleɪtə^r] *n* calcolatrice *f*

calculus ['kælkjuləs] *n* calcolo; **integral/ differential** ~ calcolo integrale/ differenziale
calendar ['kæləndə^r] *n* calendario
calendar year *n* anno civile
calf (*pl* **calves**) [kɑ:f, kɑ:vz] *n* (*of cow*) vitello; (*of other animals*) piccolo; (*also*: **calfskin**) (pelle *f* di) vitello; (*Anat*) polpaccio
caliber ['kælɪbə^r] *n* (*US*) = **calibre**
calibrate ['kælɪbreɪt] *vt* (*gun etc*) calibrare; (*scale of measuring instrument*) tarare
calibre, (*US*) **caliber** ['kælɪbə^r] *n* calibro
calico ['kælɪkəu] *n* tela grezza, cotone *m* grezzo; (US) cotonina stampata
Calif. *abbr* (*US*) = **California**
California [kælɪ'fɔ:nɪə] *n* California
calipers ['kælɪpəz] *npl* (*US*) = **callipers**
call [kɔ:l] *vt* (*gen, also Tel*) chiamare; (*announce: flight*) annunciare; (*meeting, strike*) indire, proclamare ■ *vi* chiamare; (*visit: also*: **call in, call round**) passare ■ *n* (*shout*) grido, urlo; (*visit*) visita; (*summons: for flight etc*) chiamata; (*fig: lure*) richiamo; (*also*: **telephone call**) telefonata; **to be on** ~ essere a disposizione; **to make a** ~ telefonare, fare una telefonata; **please give me a ~ at 7** per piacere mi chiami alle 7; **to pay a ~ on sb** fare (una) visita a qn; **there's not much ~ for these items** non c'è molta richiesta di questi articoli; **she's called Jane** si chiama Jane; **who is calling?** (*Tel*) chi parla?; **London calling** (*Radio*) qui Londra
▸**call at** *vt fus* (*ship*) fare scalo a; (*train*) fermarsi a
▸**call back** *vi* (*return*) ritornare; (*Tel*) ritelefonare, richiamare ■ *vt* (*Tel*) ritelefonare a, richiamare
▸**call for** *vt fus* (*demand: action etc*) richiedere; (*collect: person*) passare a prendere; (*: goods*) ritirare
▸**call in** *vt* (*doctor, expert, police*) chiamare, far venire
▸**call off** *vt* (*meeting, race*) disdire; (*deal*) cancellare; (*dog*) richiamare; **the strike was called off** lo sciopero è stato revocato
▸**call on** *vt fus* (*visit*) passare da; (*request*): **to ~ on sb to do** chiedere a qn di fare
▸**call out** *vi* urlare ■ *vt* (*doctor, police, troops*) chiamare
▸**call up** *vt* (*Mil*) richiamare
Callanetics® [kælə'nɛtɪks] *nsg tipo di ginnastica basata sulla ripetizione di piccoli movimenti*
callbox ['kɔ:lbɔks] *n* (*Brit*) cabina telefonica
call centre *n* centro informazioni telefoniche
caller ['kɔ:lə^r] *n* persona che chiama; visitatore(-trice); **hold the line, ~!** (*Tel*) rimanga in linea, signore (*or* signora)!
call girl *n* ragazza *f* squillo *inv*
call-in ['kɔ:lɪn] *n* (*US*) = **phone-in**
calling ['kɔ:lɪŋ] *n* vocazione *f*
calling card *n* (*US*) biglietto da visita
callipers, (*US*) **calipers** ['kælɪpəz] *npl* (*Med*) gambale *m*; (*Math*) calibro
callous ['kæləs] *adj* indurito(-a), insensibile
callousness ['kæləsnɪs] *n* insensibilità
callow ['kæləu] *adj* immaturo(-a)
calm [kɑ:m] *adj* calmo(-a) ■ *n* calma ■ *vt* calmare
▸**calm down** *vi* calmarsi ■ *vt* calmare
calmly ['kɑ:mlɪ] *adv* con calma
calmness ['kɑ:mnɪs] *n* calma
Calor gas® ['kælə^r-] *n* (*Brit*) butano
calorie ['kælərɪ] *n* caloria; **low-~ product** prodotto a basso contenuto di calorie
calve [kɑ:v] *vi* figliare
calves [kɑ:vz] *npl of* **calf**
CAM *n abbr* (*= computer-aided manufacturing*) fabbricazione *f* con l'ausilio dell'elaboratore
camber ['kæmbə^r] *n* (*of road*) bombatura
Cambodia [kæm'bəudjə] *n* Cambogia
Cambodian [kæm'bəudɪən] *adj, n* cambogiano(-a)
Cambs *abbr* (*Brit*) = **Cambridgeshire**
camcorder ['kæmkɔ:də^r] *n* videocamera
came [keɪm] *pt of* **come**
camel ['kæməl] *n* cammello
cameo ['kæmɪəu] *n* cammeo
camera ['kæmərə] *n* macchina fotografica; (*Cine, TV*) telecamera; (*also*: **cinecamera, movie camera**) cinepresa; **in ~** a porte chiuse
cameraman ['kæmərəmæn] *n* cameraman *m inv*
camera phone *n* telefonino con fotocamera integrata
Cameroon, Cameroun ['kæməru:n] *n* Camerun *m*
camouflage ['kæməflɑ:ʒ] *n* camuffamento; (*Mil*) mimetizzazione *f* ■ *vt* camuffare; mimetizzare
camp [kæmp] *n* campeggio; (*Mil*) campo ■ *vi* campeggiare; accamparsi; **to go camping** andare in campeggio
campaign [kæm'peɪn] *n* (*Mil, Pol etc*) campagna ■ *vi*: **to ~ (for/against)** (*also fig*) fare una campagna (per/contro)
campaigner [kæm'peɪnə^r] *n*: **~ for** fautore(-trice) di; **~ against** oppositore(-trice) di
campbed ['kæmp'bɛd] *n* (*Brit*) brandina
camper ['kæmpə^r] *n* campeggiatore(-trice)
camping ['kæmpɪŋ] *n* campeggio

C

camp site, camping site *n* campeggio
campus ['kæmpəs] *n* campus *m inv*
camshaft ['kæmʃɑ:ft] *n* albero a camme
can¹ [kæn] *n* (*of milk*) scatola; (*of oil*) bidone *m*; (*of water*) tanica; (*tin*) scatola ■ *vt* mettere in scatola; **a ~ of beer** una lattina di birra; **to carry the ~** (*Brit col*) prendere la colpa

 KEYWORD

can² [kæn] (*negative* **cannot, can't,** *conditional and pt* **could**) *aux vb* **1** (*be able to*) potere; **I can't go any further** non posso andare oltre; **you can do it if you try** sei in grado di farlo – basta provarci; **I'll help you all I can** ti aiuterò come potrò; **I can't see you** non ti vedo; **can you hear me?** mi senti?, riesci a sentirmi?
2 (*know how to*) sapere, essere capace di; **I can swim** so nuotare; **can you speak French?** parla francese?
3 (*may*) potere; **could I have a word with you?** posso parlarle un momento?
4 (*expressing disbelief, puzzlement etc*): **it can't be true!** non può essere vero!; **what CAN he want?** cosa può mai volere?
5 (*expressing possibility, suggestion etc*): **he could be in the library** può darsi che sia in biblioteca; **they could have forgotten** potrebbero essersene dimenticati; **she could have been delayed** può aver avuto un contrattempo

Canada ['kænədə] *n* Canada *m*
Canadian [kə'neɪdɪən] *adj, n* canadese (*m/f*)
canal [kə'næl] *n* canale *m*
canary [kə'nɛərɪ] *n* canarino
Canary Islands, Canaries [kə'nɛərɪz] *npl*: **the ~** le (isole) Canarie
Canberra ['kænbərə] *n* Camberra
cancel ['kænsəl] *vt* annullare; (*train*) sopprimere; (*cross out*) cancellare
▸ **cancel out** *vt* (*Math*) semplificare; (*fig*) annullare; **they ~ each other out** (*also fig*) si annullano a vicenda
cancellation [kænsə'leɪʃən] *n* annullamento; soppressione *f*; cancellazione *f*; (*Tourism*) prenotazione *f* annullata
cancer ['kænsəʳ] *n* cancro; **C~** (*sign*) Cancro; **to be C~** essere del Cancro
cancerous ['kænsərəs] *adj* canceroso(-a)
cancer patient *n* malato(-a) di cancro
cancer research *n* ricerca sul cancro
C and F *abbr* (*Brit*: = *cost and freight*) Caf *m*
candid ['kændɪd] *adj* onesto(-a)
candidacy ['kændɪdəsɪ] *n* candidatura
candidate ['kændɪdeɪt] *n* candidato(-a)
candidature ['kændɪdətʃəʳ] *n* (*Brit*) = **candidacy**
candied ['kændɪd] *adj* candito(-a); **~ apple** (*US*) mela caramellata
candle ['kændl] *n* candela
candlelight ['kændl'laɪt] *n*: **by ~** a lume di candela
candlestick ['kændlstɪk] *n* (*also*: **candle holder**) bugia; (*bigger, ornate*) candeliere *m*
candour, (*US*) **candor** ['kændəʳ] *n* sincerità
C & W *n abbr* = **country and western (music)**
candy ['kændɪ] *n* zucchero candito; (*US*) caramella; caramelle *fpl*
candy-floss ['kændɪflɔs] *n* (*Brit*) zucchero filato
candy store *n* (*US*) ≈ pasticceria
cane [keɪn] *n* canna; (*for baskets, chairs etc*) bambù *m*; (*Scol*) verga; (*for walking*) bastone *m* (da passeggio) ■ *vt* (*Brit Scol*) punire a colpi di verga
canine ['kænaɪn] *adj* canino(-a)
canister ['kænɪstəʳ] *n* scatola metallica
cannabis ['kænəbɪs] *n* canapa indiana
canned ['kænd] *adj* (*food*) in scatola; (*col*: *recorded*: *music*) registrato(-a); (*Brit col*: *drunk*) sbronzo(-a); (*US col*: *worker*) licenziato(-a)
cannibal ['kænɪbəl] *n* cannibale *m/f*
cannibalism ['kænɪbəlɪzəm] *n* cannibalismo
cannon (*pl* **~** *or* **cannons**) ['kænən] *n* (*gun*) cannone *m*
cannonball ['kænənbɔ:l] *n* palla di cannone
cannon fodder *n* carne *f* da macello
cannot ['kænɔt] = **can not**
canny ['kænɪ] *adj* furbo(-a)
canoe [kə'nu:] *n* canoa; (*Sport*) canotto
canoeing [kə'nu:ɪŋ] *n* (*sport*) canottaggio
canoeist [kə'nu:ɪst] *n* canottiere *m*
canon ['kænən] *n* (*clergyman*) canonico; (*standard*) canone *m*
canonize ['kænənaɪz] *vt* canonizzare
can opener [-əupnəʳ] *n* apriscatole *m inv*
canopy ['kænəpɪ] *n* baldacchino
cant [kænt] *n* gergo ■ *vt* inclinare ■ *vi* inclinarsi
can't [kænt] = **can not**
Cantab. *abbr* (*Brit*: = *cantabrigiensis*) *of Cambridge*
cantankerous [kæn'tæŋkərəs] *adj* stizzoso(-a)
canteen [kæn'ti:n] *n* mensa; (*Brit*: *of cutlery*) portaposate *m inv*
canter ['kæntəʳ] *n* piccolo galoppo ■ *vi* andare al piccolo galoppo
cantilever ['kæntɪli:vəʳ] *n* trave *f* a sbalzo
canvas ['kænvəs] *n* tela; **under ~** (*camping*) sotto la tenda; (*Naut*) sotto la vela
canvass ['kænvəs] *vt* (*Comm*: *district*) fare un'indagine di mercato in; (: *citizens, opinions*)

fare un sondaggio di; (*Pol: district*) fare un giro elettorale di; (*: person*) fare propaganda elettorale a
canvasser ['kænvəsə^r] *n* (*Comm*) agente *m* viaggiatore, piazzista *m*; (*Pol*) propagandista *m/f* (elettorale)
canvassing ['kænvəsɪŋ] *n* sollecitazione *f*
canyon ['kænjən] *n* canyon *m inv*
CAP *n abbr* (= *Common Agricultural Policy*) PAC *f*
cap [kæp] *n* (*also Brit Football*) berretto; (*of pen*) coperchio; (*of bottle*) tappo; (*for swimming*) cuffia; (*Brit: contraceptive: also:* **Dutch cap**) diaframma *m* ■ *vt* tappare; (*outdo*) superare; **capped with** ricoperto(-a) di; **and to ~ it all, he ...** (*Brit*) e per completare l'opera, lui ...
capability [keɪpə'bɪlɪtɪ] *n* capacità *f inv*, abilità *f inv*
capable ['keɪpəbl] *adj* capace; **~ of** capace di; suscettibile di
capacious [kə'peɪʃəs] *adj* capace
capacity [kə'pæsɪtɪ] *n* capacità *f inv*; (*of lift etc*) capienza; **in his ~ as** nella sua qualità di; **to work at full ~** lavorare al massimo delle proprie capacità; **this work is beyond my ~** questo lavoro supera le mie possibilità; **filled to ~** pieno zeppo; **in an advisory ~** a titolo consultativo
cape [keɪp] *n* (*garment*) cappa; (*Geo*) capo
Cape of Good Hope *n* Capo di Buona Speranza
caper ['keɪpə^r] *n* (*Culin: also:* **capers**) cappero; (*leap*) saltello; (*escapade*) birichinata
Cape Town *n* Città del Capo
capita ['kæpɪtə] *see* **per capita**
capital ['kæpɪtl] *n* (*also:* **capital city**) capitale *f*; (*money*) capitale *m*; (*also:* **capital letter**) (lettera) maiuscola
capital account *n* conto capitale
capital allowance *n* ammortamento fiscale
capital assets *npl* capitale *m* fisso
capital expenditure *n* spese *fpl* in capitale
capital gains tax *n* imposta sulla plusvalenza
capital goods *n* beni *mpl* d'investimento, beni *mpl* capitali
capital-intensive ['kæpɪtlɪn'tɛnsɪv] *adj* ad alta intensità di capitale
capitalism ['kæpɪtəlɪzəm] *n* capitalismo
capitalist ['kæpɪtəlɪst] *adj, n* capitalista (*m/f*)
capitalize ['kæpɪtəlaɪz] *vt* (*provide with capital*) capitalizzare
▸ **capitalize on** *vt fus* (*fig*) trarre vantaggio da
capital punishment *n* pena capitale
capital transfer tax *n* (*Brit*) imposta sui trasferimenti di capitali
Capitol ['kæpɪtl] *n*: **the ~** il Campidoglio; *vedi nota*

CAPITOL

Il *Capitol* è l'edificio che ospita le riunioni del Congresso degli Stati Uniti. é situato sull'omonimo colle, "Capitol Hill", a Washington DC. In molti stati americani il termine Capitol viene usato per indicare l'edificio dove si riuniscono i rappresentanti dello stato.

capitulate [kə'pɪtjuleɪt] *vi* capitolare
capitulation [kəpɪtju'leɪʃən] *n* capitolazione *f*
capricious [kə'prɪʃəs] *adj* capriccioso(-a)
Capricorn ['kæprɪkɔːn] *n* Capricorno; **to be ~** essere del Capricorno
caps [kæps] *abbr* = **capital letters**
capsize [kæp'saɪz] *vt* capovolgere ■ *vi* capovolgersi
capstan ['kæpstən] *n* argano
capsule ['kæpsjuːl] *n* capsula
Capt. *abbr* (= *captain*) Cap.
captain ['kæptɪn] *n* capitano ■ *vt* capitanare
caption ['kæpʃən] *n* leggenda
captivate ['kæptɪveɪt] *vt* avvincere
captive ['kæptɪv] *adj, n* prigioniero(-a)
captivity [kæp'tɪvɪtɪ] *n* prigionia; **in ~** (*animal*) in cattività
captor ['kæptə^r] *n* (*lawful*) chi ha catturato; (*unlawful*) rapitore *m*
capture ['kæptʃə^r] *vt* catturare, prendere; (*attention*) attirare ■ *n* cattura; (*data capture*) registrazione *f or* rilevazione *f* di dati
car [kɑː^r] *n* macchina, automobile *f*; (*US Rail*) carrozza; **by ~** in macchina
Caracas [kə'rækəs] *n* Caracas *f*
carafe [kə'ræf] *n* caraffa
carafe wine *n* (*in restaurant*) ≈ vino sfuso
caramel ['kærəməl] *n* caramello
carat ['kærət] *n* carato; **18 ~ gold** oro a 18 carati
caravan ['kærəvæn] *n* roulotte *f inv*
caravan site *n* (*Brit*) campeggio per roulotte
caraway ['kærəweɪ] *n*: **~ seed** seme *m* di cumino
carbohydrates [kɑːbəu'haɪdreɪts] *npl* (*foods*) carboidrati *mpl*
carbolic acid [kɑː'bɔlɪk-] *n* acido fenico, fenolo
car bomb *n ordigno esplosivo collocato in una macchina*; **a ~ went off yesterday** ieri è esplosa un'autobomba
carbon ['kɑːbən] *n* carbonio
carbonated ['kɑːbəneɪtəd] *adj* (*drink*) gassato(-a)
carbon copy *n* copia *f* carbone *inv*

carbon dioxide [-daɪ'ɔksaɪd] *n* diossido di carbonio
carbon footprint *n* impronta di carbonio
carbon paper *n* carta carbone
carbon ribbon *n* nastro carbonato
car boot sale *n mercatino dell'usato dove la merce viene esposta nel bagagliaio delle macchine*
carburettor, (US) **carburetor** [kɑːbju'rɛtəʳ] *n* carburatore *m*
carcass ['kɑːkəs] *n* carcassa
carcinogenic [kɑːsɪnə'dʒɛnɪk] *adj* cancerogeno(-a)
card [kɑːd] *n* carta; (*thin cardboard*) cartoncino; (*visiting card etc*) biglietto; (*membership card*) tessera; (*Christmas card etc*) cartolina; **to play cards** giocare a carte
cardamom ['kɑːdəməm] *n* cardamomo
cardboard ['kɑːdbɔːd] *n* cartone *m*
cardboard box *n* (scatola di) cartone *m*
cardboard city *n luogo dove dormono in scatole di cartone emarginati senzatetto*
card-carrying member ['kɑːd'kærɪɪŋ-] *n* tesserato(-a)
card game *n* gioco di carte
cardiac ['kɑːdɪæk] *adj* cardiaco(-a)
cardigan ['kɑːdɪgən] *n* cardigan *m inv*
cardinal ['kɑːdɪnl] *adj, n* cardinale (*m*)
card index *n* schedario
cardphone ['kɑːdfəun] *n* telefono a scheda (magnetica)
cardsharp ['kɑːdʃɑːp] *n* baro
card vote *n* (*Brit*) voto (palese) per delega
CARE [kɛəʳ] *n abbr* = **Cooperative for American Relief Everywhere**
care [kɛəʳ] *n* cura, attenzione *f*; (*worry*) preoccupazione *f* ■ *vi*: **to ~ about** interessarsi di; **would you ~ to/for ...?** le piacerebbe ...?; **I wouldn't ~ to do it** non lo vorrei fare; **in sb's ~** alle cure di qn; **to take ~** fare attenzione; **to take ~ of** curarsi di; (*details, arrangements*) occuparsi di; **I don't ~** non me ne importa; **I couldn't ~ less** non me ne importa un bel niente; **~ of (c/o)** (*on letter*) presso; **"with ~"** "fragile"; **the child has been taken into ~** il bambino è stato preso in custodia
▸ **care for** *vt fus* aver cura di; (*like*) voler bene a
careen [kə'riːn] *vi* (*ship*) sbandare ■ *vt* carenare
career [kə'rɪəʳ] *n* carriera; (*occupation*) professione *f* ■ *vi* (*also*: **career along**) andare di (gran) carriera
career girl *n* donna dedita alla carriera
careers officer *n* consulente *m/f* d'orientamento professionale
carefree ['kɛəfriː] *adj* sgombro(-a) di preoccupazioni
careful ['kɛəful] *adj* attento(-a); (*cautious*) cauto(-a); **(be) ~!** attenzione!; **he's very ~ with his money** bada molto alle spese
carefully ['kɛəfəlɪ] *adv* con cura; cautamente
careless ['kɛəlɪs] *adj* negligente; (*remark*) privo(-a) di tatto
carelessly ['kɛəlɪslɪ] *adv* negligentemente; senza tatto; (*without thinking*) distrattamente
carelessness ['kɛəlɪsnɪs] *n* negligenza; mancanza di tatto
carer ['kɛərəʳ] *n chi si occupa di un familiare anziano o invalido*
caress [kə'rɛs] *n* carezza ■ *vt* accarezzare
caretaker ['kɛəteɪkəʳ] *n* custode *m*
caretaker government *n* (*Brit*) governo *m* ponte *inv*
car-ferry ['kɑːfɛrɪ] *n* traghetto
cargo (*pl* **cargoes**) ['kɑːgəu] *n* carico
cargo boat *n* cargo
cargo plane *n* aereo di linea da carico
car hire *n* (*Brit*) autonoleggio
Caribbean [kærɪ'biːən] *adj* caraibico(-a); **the ~ (Sea)** il Mar dei Caraibi
caricature ['kærɪkətjuəʳ] *n* caricatura
caring ['kɛərɪŋ] *adj* (*person*) premuroso(-a); (*society, organization*) umanitario(-a)
carnage ['kɑːnɪdʒ] *n* carneficina
carnal ['kɑːnl] *adj* carnale
carnation [kɑː'neɪʃən] *n* garofano
carnival ['kɑːnɪvəl] *n* (*public celebration*) carnevale *m*; (*US*: *funfair*) luna park *m inv*
carnivorous [kɑː'nɪvərəs] *adj* carnivoro(-a)
carol ['kærəl] *n*: **(Christmas) ~** canto di Natale
carouse [kə'rauz] *vi* far baldoria
carousel [kærə'sɛl] *n* (*US*) giostra
carp [kɑːp] *n* (*fish*) carpa
▸ **carp at** *vt fus* trovare a ridire su
car park *n* parcheggio
carpenter ['kɑːpɪntəʳ] *n* carpentiere *m*
carpentry ['kɑːpɪntrɪ] *n* carpenteria
carpet ['kɑːpɪt] *n* tappeto; (*Brit*: *fitted carpet*) moquette *f inv* ■ *vt* coprire con tappeto
carpet bombing *n* bombardamento a tappeto
carpet slippers *npl* pantofole *fpl*
carpet sweeper *n* scopatappeti *m inv*
car phone *n* telefonino per auto
car rental *n* (*US*) autonoleggio
carriage ['kærɪdʒ] *n* vettura; (*of goods*) trasporto; (*of typewriter*) carrello; (*bearing*) portamento; **~ forward** porto assegnato; **~ free** franco di porto; **~ paid** porto pagato
carriage return *n* (*on typewriter etc*) leva (*or* tasto) del ritorno a capo
carriageway ['kærɪdʒweɪ] *n* (*Brit*: *part of road*) carreggiata

carrier ['kærɪəʳ] *n* (*of disease*) portatore(-trice); (*Comm*) impresa di trasporti; (*Naut*) portaerei *f inv*
carrier bag *n* (*Brit*) sacchetto
carrier pigeon *n* colombo viaggiatore
carrion ['kærɪən] *n* carogna
carrot ['kærət] *n* carota
carry ['kærɪ] *vt* (*person*) portare; (*vehicle*) trasportare; (*a motion, bill*) far passare; (*involve: responsibilities etc*) comportare; (*Comm: goods*) tenere; (*: interest*) avere; (*Math: figure*) riportare ■ *vi* (*sound*) farsi sentire; **this loan carries 10% interest** questo prestito è sulla base di un interesse del 10%; **to be carried away** (*fig*) farsi trascinare
▸ **carry forward** *vt* (*Math, Comm*) riportare
▸ **carry on** *vi*: **to ~ on with sth/doing** continuare qc/a fare ■ *vt* mandare avanti
▸ **carry out** *vt* (*orders*) eseguire; (*investigation*) svolgere; (*accomplish etc: plan*) realizzare; (*perform, implement: idea, threat*) mettere in pratica
carrycot ['kærɪkɔt] *n* (*Brit*) culla portabile
carry-on [kærɪ'ɔn] *n* (*col: fuss*) casino, confusione *f*; (*: annoying behaviour*): **I've had enough of your ~!** mi hai proprio scocciato!
cart [kɑːt] *n* carro ■ *vt* (*col*) trascinare, scarrozzare
carte blanche ['kɑːt'blɔŋʃ] *n*: **to give sb ~** dare carta bianca a qn
cartel [kɑː'tɛl] *n* (*Comm*) cartello
cartilage ['kɑːtɪlɪdʒ] *n* cartilagine *f*
cartographer [kɑː'tɔgrəfəʳ] *n* cartografo(-a)
cartography [kɑː'tɔgrəfɪ] *n* cartografia
carton ['kɑːtən] *n* (*box*) scatola di cartone; (*of yogurt*) cartone *m*; (*of cigarettes*) stecca
cartoon [kɑː'tuːn] *n* (*in newspaper etc*) vignetta; (*Cine, TV*) cartone *m* animato; (*Art*) cartone
cartoonist [kɑː'tuːnɪst] *n* vignettista *m/f*; cartonista *m/f*
cartridge ['kɑːtrɪdʒ] *n* (*for gun, pen*) cartuccia; (*for camera*) caricatore *m*; (*music tape*) cassetta; (*of record player*) testina
cartwheel ['kɑːtwiːl] *n*: **to turn a ~** (*Sport etc*) fare la ruota
carve [kɑːv] *vt* (*meat*) trinciare; (*wood, stone*) intagliare
▸ **carve up** *vt* (*meat*) tagliare; (*fig: country*) suddividere
carving ['kɑːvɪŋ] *n* (*in wood etc*) scultura
carving knife *n* trinciante *m*
car wash *n* lavaggio auto
Casablanca [kæsə'blæŋkə] *n* Casablanca
cascade [kæs'keɪd] *n* cascata ■ *vi* scendere a cascata
case [keɪs] *n* caso; (*Law*) causa, processo; (*box*) scatola; (*also*: **suitcase**) valigia; (*Typ*): **lower/upper ~** (carattere *m*) minuscolo/maiuscolo; **to have a good ~** avere pretese legittime; **there's a strong ~ for reform** ci sono validi argomenti a favore della riforma; **in ~ of** in caso di; **in ~ he** caso mai lui; **just in ~** in caso di bisogno
case history *n* (*Med*) cartella clinica
case-sensitive ['keɪs'sɛnsɪtɪv] *adj* (*Comput*) sensibile alle maiuscole o minuscole
case study *n studio di un caso*
cash [kæʃ] *n* (*coins, notes*) soldi *mpl*, denaro; (*col: money*) quattrini *mpl* ■ *vt* incassare; **to pay (in) ~** pagare in contanti; **to be short of ~** essere a corto di soldi; **~ with order/on delivery (COD)** (*Comm*) pagamento all'ordinazione/alla consegna
▸ **cash in** *vt* (*insurance policy etc*) riscuotere, riconvertire
▸ **cash in on** *vt fus*: **to ~ in on sth** sfruttare qc
cash account *n* conto *m* cassa *inv*
cash-and-carry ['kæʃənd'kærɪ] *n* cash and carry *m inv*
cashbook ['kæʃbuk] *n* giornale *m* di cassa
cash box *n* cassetta per il denaro spicciolo
cash card *n* carta per prelievi automatici
cash desk *n* (*Brit*) cassa
cash discount *n* sconto per contanti
cash dispenser *n* sportello automatico
cashew [kæ'ʃuː] *n* (*also*: **cashew nut**) anacardio
cash flow *n* cash-flow *m inv*, liquidità *f inv*
cashier [kæ'ʃɪəʳ] *n* cassiere(-a) ■ *vt* (*esp Mil*) destituire
cashmere ['kæʃmɪəʳ] *n* cachemire *m*
cash payment *n* pagamento in contanti
cash price *n* prezzo per contanti
cash register *n* registratore *m* di cassa
cash sale *n* vendita per contanti
casing ['keɪsɪŋ] *n* rivestimento
casino [kə'siːnəu] *n* casinò *m inv*
cask [kɑːsk] *n* botte *f*
casket ['kɑːskɪt] *n* cofanetto; (*US: coffin*) bara
Caspian Sea ['kæspɪən-] *n*: **the ~** il mar Caspio
casserole ['kæsərəul] *n* casseruola; (*food*): **chicken ~** pollo in casseruola
cassette [kæ'sɛt] *n* cassetta
cassette deck *n* piastra di registrazione
cassette player *n* riproduttore *m* a cassette
cassette recorder *n* registratore *m* a cassette
cast [kɑːst] *vt* (*pt, pp* **~**) (*throw*) gettare; (*shed*) perdere; spogliarsi di; (*metal*) gettare, fondere; (*Theat*): **to ~ sb as Hamlet** scegliere qn per la parte di Amleto ■ *n* (*Theat*) complesso di attori; (*mould*) forma; (*also*: **plaster cast**) ingessatura; **to ~ one's vote** votare, dare il voto

C

▸ **cast aside** *vt* (*reject*) mettere da parte
▸ **cast off** *vi* (*Naut*) salpare; (*Knitting*) diminuire, calare ▪ *vt* (*Naut*) disormeggiare; (*Knitting*) diminuire, calare
▸ **cast on** (*Knitting*) *vt* avviare ▪ *vi* avviare (le maglie)
castanets [kæstə'nɛts] *npl* castagnette *fpl*
castaway ['kɑːstəwəɪ] *n* naufrago(-a)
caste [kɑːst] *n* casta
caster sugar ['kɑːstə-] *n* zucchero semolato
casting vote ['kɑːstɪŋ-] *n* (*Brit*) voto decisivo
cast iron *n* ghisa ▪ *adj*: **cast-iron** (*fig*: *will, alibi*) di ferro, d'acciaio
castle ['kɑːsl] *n* castello; (*fortified*) rocca
castor ['kɑːstə^r] *n* (*wheel*) rotella
castor oil *n* olio di ricino
castrate [kæs'treɪt] *vt* castrare
casual ['kæʒjul] *adj* (*by chance*) casuale, fortuito(-a); (*irregular*: *work etc*) avventizio(-a); (*unconcerned*) noncurante, indifferente; **~ wear** casual *m*
casual labour *n* manodopera avventizia
casually ['kæʒjulɪ] *adv* con disinvoltura; (*by chance*) casualmente
casualty ['kæʒjultɪ] *n* ferito(-a); (*dead*) morto(-a), vittima; **heavy casualties** grosse perdite *fpl*
casualty ward *n* (*Brit*) pronto soccorso
cat [kæt] *n* gatto
catacombs ['kætəkuːmz] *npl* catacombe *fpl*
catalogue, (*US*) **catalog** ['kætəlɔg] *n* catalogo ▪ *vt* catalogare
catalyst ['kætəlɪst] *n* catalizzatore *m*
catalytic converter [kætə'lɪtɪkkən'vəːtə^r] *n* marmitta catalitica, catalizzatore *m*
catapult ['kætəpʌlt] *n* catapulta; fionda
cataract ['kætərækt] *n* (*also Med*) cateratta
catarrh [kə'tɑː^r] *n* catarro
catastrophe [kə'tæstrəfɪ] *n* catastrofe *f*
catastrophic [kætə'strɔfɪk] *adj* catastrofico(-a)
catcall ['kætkɔːl] *n* (*at meeting etc*) fischio
catch [kætʃ] *vb* (*pt, pp* **caught**) [kɔːt] *vt* (*train, thief, cold*) acchiappare; (*ball*) afferrare; (*person*: *by surprise*) sorprendere; (*understand*) comprendere; (*get entangled*) impigliare ▪ *vi* (*fire*) prendere ▪ *n* (*fish etc caught*) retata, presa; (*trick*) inganno; (*Tech*) gancio (*pt, pp* **to ~ sb's attention** *or* **eye**) attirare l'attenzione di qn; **to ~ fire** prendere fuoco; **to ~ sight of** scorgere
▸ **catch on** *vi* (*become popular*) affermarsi, far presa; (*understand*): **to ~ on (to sth)** capire (qc)
▸ **catch out** *vt* (*Brit fig*: *with trick question*) cogliere in fallo
▸ **catch up** *vi* mettersi in pari ▪ *vt* (*also*: **catch up with**) raggiungere
catching ['kætʃɪŋ] *adj* (*Med*) contagioso(-a)
catchment area ['kætʃmənt-] *n* (*Brit Scol*) circoscrizione *f* scolare; (*Geo*) bacino pluviale
catch phrase *n* slogan *m inv*; frase *f* fatta
catch-22 ['kætʃtwɛntɪ'tuː] *n*: **it's a ~ situation** non c'è via d'uscita
catchy ['kætʃɪ] *adj* orecchiabile
catechism ['kætɪkɪzəm] *n* catechismo
categoric [kætɪ'gɔrɪk], **categorical** [kætɪ'gɔrɪkl] *adj* categorico(-a)
categorize ['kætɪgəraɪz] *vt* categorizzare
category ['kætɪgərɪ] *n* categoria
cater ['keɪtə^r] *vi*: **to ~ (for)** provvedere da mangiare (per)
▸ **cater for** *vt fus* (*Brit*: *needs*) provvedere a; (*: readers, consumers*) incontrare i gusti di
caterer ['keɪtərə^r] *n* fornitore *m*
catering ['keɪtərɪŋ] *n* approvvigionamento
catering trade *n* settore *m* ristoranti
caterpillar ['kætəpɪlə^r] *n* (*Zool*) bruco ▪ *cpd* (*vehicle*) cingolato(-a); **~ track** cingolo
cat flap *n* gattaiola
cathedral [kə'θiːdrəl] *n* cattedrale *f*, duomo
cathode ['kæθəud] *n* catodo
cathode ray tube *n* tubo a raggi catodici
catholic ['kæθəlɪk] *adj* universale; aperto(-a); eclettico(-a); **C~** *adj, n* (*Rel*) cattolico(-a)
CAT scanner [kæt-] *n* (*Med*: *= computerized axial tomography scanner*) (rilevatore *m* per la) TAC *f inv*
cat's-eye ['kæts'aɪ] *n* (*Brit Aut*) catarifrangente *m*
catsup ['kætsəp] *n* (*US*) ketchup *m inv*
cattle ['kætl] *npl* bestiame *m*, bestie *fpl*
catty ['kætɪ] *adj* maligno(-a), dispettoso(-a)
catwalk ['kætwɔːk] *n* passerella
Caucasian [kɔː'keɪzɪən] *adj, n* caucasico(-a)
Caucasus ['kɔːkəsəs] *n* Caucaso
caucus ['kɔːkəs] *n* (*US Pol*) (riunione *f* del) comitato elettorale; (*Brit Pol*: *group*) comitato di dirigenti; *vedi nota*

CAUCUS

Caucus è il termine usato, specialmente negli Stati Uniti, per indicare una riunione informale dei rappresentanti di spicco di un partito politico che precede una riunione ufficiale. Con uso estensivo, la parola indica il nucleo direttivo di un partito politico.

caught [kɔːt] *pt, pp of* **catch**
cauliflower ['kɔlɪflauə^r] *n* cavolfiore *m*
cause [kɔːz] *n* causa ▪ *vt* causare; **there is no ~ for concern** non c'è ragione di preoccuparsi; **to ~ sb to do sth** far fare qc a qn; **to ~ sth to be done** far fare qc

causeway ['kɔ:zweɪ] *n* strada rialzata
caustic ['kɔ:stɪk] *adj* caustico(-a)
caution ['kɔ:ʃən] *n* prudenza; (*warning*) avvertimento ■ *vt* ammonire
cautious ['kɔ:ʃəs] *adj* cauto(-a), prudente
cautiously ['kɔ:ʃəslɪ] *adv* prudentemente
cautiousness ['kɔ:ʃəsnɪs] *n* cautela
cavalier [kævə'lɪəʳ] *n* (*knight*) cavaliere *m* ■ *adj* (*pej: offhand*) brusco(-a)
cavalry ['kævəlrɪ] *n* cavalleria
cave [keɪv] *n* caverna, grotta ■ *vi*: **to go caving** fare speleologia
▸ **cave in** *vi* (*roof etc*) crollare
caveman ['keɪvmæn] *n* uomo delle caverne
cavern ['kævən] *n* caverna
caviar, caviare ['kævɪɑ:ʳ] *n* caviale *m*
cavity ['kævɪtɪ] *n* cavità *f inv*
cavity wall insulation *n* isolamento per pareti a intercapedine
cavort [kə'vɔ:t] *vi* far capriole
cayenne [keɪ'ɛn], **cayenne pepper** [keɪ'ɛn-] *n* pepe *m* di Caienna
CB *n abbr* (*Brit: = Companion (of the Order) of the Bath*) *titolo*; (*= Citizens' Band (Radio)*) C.B *m*; **CB radio (set)** baracchino
CBC *n abbr* = **Canadian Broadcasting Corporation**
CBE *n abbr* (*Brit: = Companion (of the Order) of the British Empire*) *titolo*
CBI *n abbr* (*= Confederation of British Industry*) ≈ CONFINDUSTRIA (*= Confederazione Generale dell'Industria Italiana*)
CBS *n abbr* (*US*) = **Columbia Broadcasting System**
CC *abbr* (*Brit*) = **county council**
cc *abbr* (*= cubic centimetre*) cc; (*on letter etc*) = **carbon copy**
CCA *n abbr* (*US: = Circuit Court of Appeals*) corte *f* d'appello itinerante
CCTV *n abbr* = **closed-circuit television**
CCU *n abbr* (*US: = coronary care unit*) unità coronarica
CD *n abbr* (*= compact disk*) compact disc *m inv*; **CD player** lettore *m* CD; (*Mil*) = **Civil Defence (Corps)** (*Brit*), **Civil Defense** (*US*) ■ *abbr* (*Brit: = Corps Diplomatique*) C.D.
CD burner *n* masterizzatore *m*
CDC *n abbr* (*US*) = **center for disease control**
CD-I® *n* CD-I *m inv*, compact disc *m inv* interattivo
Cdr. *abbr* (*= commander*) Com
CD-ROM ['si:'di:'rɔm] *n abbr* (*= compact disc read-only memory*) CD-ROM *m inv*
CDT *abbr* (*US: = Central Daylight Time*) *ora legale del centro*; (*Brit: Scol: = Craft, Design and Technology*) educazione tecnica
CDW *n abbr* = **collision damage waiver**
CD writer *n* masterizzatore *m*
cease [si:s] *vt, vi* cessare
ceasefire ['si:sfaɪəʳ] *n* cessate il fuoco *m inv*
ceaseless ['si:slɪs] *adj* incessante, continuo(-a)
CED *n abbr* (*US*) = **Committee for Economic Development**
cedar ['si:dəʳ] *n* cedro
cede [si:d] *vt* cedere
CEEB *n abbr* (*US: = College Entrance Examination Board*) *commissione per l'esame di ammissione al college*
ceilidh ['keɪlɪ] *n festa con musiche e danze popolari scozzesi o irlandesi*
ceiling ['si:lɪŋ] *n* soffitto; (*fig: upper limit*) tetto, limite *m* massimo
celebrate ['sɛlɪbreɪt] *vt, vi* celebrare
celebrated ['sɛlɪbreɪtɪd] *adj* celebre
celebration [sɛlɪ'breɪʃən] *n* celebrazione *f*
celebrity [sɪ'lɛbrɪtɪ] *n* celebrità *f inv*
celeriac [sə'lɛrɪæk] *n* sedano *m* rapa *inv*
celery ['sɛlərɪ] *n* sedano
celestial [sɪ'lɛstɪəl] *adj* celeste
celibacy ['sɛlɪbəsɪ] *n* celibato
cell [sɛl] *n* cella; (*Biol*) cellula; (*Elec*) elemento (di batteria)
cellar ['sɛləʳ] *n* sottosuolo, cantina
cellist ['tʃɛlɪst] *n* violoncellista *m/f*
cello ['tʃɛləu] *n* violoncello
cellophane® ['sɛləfeɪn] *n* cellophane® *m*
cellphone ['sɛlfəun] *n* cellulare *m*
cellular ['sɛljuləʳ] *adj* cellulare
celluloid ['sɛljulɔɪd] *n* celluloide *f*
cellulose ['sɛljuləus] *n* cellulosa
Celsius ['sɛlsɪəs] *adj* Celsius *inv*
Celt [kɛlt, sɛlt] *n* celta *m/f*
Celtic ['kɛltɪk, 'sɛltɪk] *adj* celtico(-a) ■ *n* (*Ling*) celtico
cement [sə'mɛnt] *n* cemento ■ *vt* cementare
cement mixer *n* betoniera
cemetery ['sɛmɪtrɪ] *n* cimitero
cenotaph ['sɛnətɑ:f] *n* cenotafio
censor ['sɛnsəʳ] *n* censore *m* ■ *vt* censurare
censorship ['sɛnsəʃɪp] *n* censura
censure ['sɛnʃəʳ] *vt* censurare
census ['sɛnsəs] *n* censimento
cent [sɛnt] *n* (*of dollar, euro*) centesimo; *see also* **per cent**
centenary [sɛn'ti:nərɪ], **centennial** [sɛn'tɛnɪəl] *n* centenario
center ['sɛntəʳ] *n, vt* (*US*) = **centre**
centigrade ['sɛntɪgreɪd] *adj* centigrado(-a)
centilitre, (*US*) **centiliter** ['sɛntɪli:təʳ] *n* centilitro
centimetre, (*US*) **centimeter** ['sɛntɪmi:təʳ] *n* centimetro

centipede ['sɛntɪpi:d] *n* centopiedi *m inv*
central ['sɛntrəl] *adj* centrale
Central African Republic *n* Repubblica centrafricana
Central America *n* America centrale
central heating *n* riscaldamento centrale
centralize ['sɛntrəlaɪz] *vt* accentrare
central processing unit *n* (*Comput*) unità *f inv* centrale di elaborazione
central reservation *n* (*Brit Aut*) banchina *f* spartitraffico *inv*
centre, (*US*) **center** ['sɛntə^r] *n* centro ■ *vt* (*concentrate*): **to ~ (on)** concentrare (su)
centrefold, (*US*) **centerfold** ['sɛntəfəuld] *n* (*Press*) poster *m* (all'interno di rivista)
centre-forward ['sɛntə'fɔ:wəd] *n* (*Sport*) centroavanti *m inv*
centre-half ['sɛntə'hɑ:f] *n* (*Sport*) centromediano
centrepiece, (*US*) **centerpiece** ['sɛntəpi:s] *n* centrotavola *m*; (*fig*) punto centrale
centre spread *n* (*Brit*) pubblicità a doppia pagina
centre-stage [sɛntə'steɪdʒ] *n*: **to take ~** porsi al centro dell'attenzione
centrifugal [sɛn'trɪfjugəl] *adj* centrifugo(-a)
centrifuge ['sɛntrɪfju:ʒ] *n* centrifuga
century ['sɛntjurɪ] *n* secolo; **in the twentieth ~** nel ventesimo secolo
CEO *n abbr* = **chief executive officer**
ceramic [sɪ'ræmɪk] *adj* ceramico(-a)
cereal ['si:rɪəl] *n* cereale *m*
cerebral ['sɛrɪbrəl] *adj* cerebrale
ceremonial [sɛrɪ'məunɪəl] *n* cerimoniale *m*; (*rite*) rito
ceremony ['sɛrɪmənɪ] *n* cerimonia; **to stand on ~** fare complimenti
cert [sə:t] *n* (*Brit col*): **it's a dead ~** non c'è alcun dubbio
certain ['sə:tən] *adj* certo(-a); **to make ~ of** assicurarsi di; **for ~** per certo, di sicuro
certainly ['sə:tənlɪ] *adv* certamente, certo
certainty ['sə:təntɪ] *n* certezza
certificate [sə'tɪfɪkɪt] *n* certificato; diploma *m*
certified letter ['sə:tɪfaɪd-] *n* (*US*) lettera raccomandata
certified public accountant ['sə:tɪfaɪd-] *n* (*US*) ≈ commercialista *m/f*
certify ['sə:tɪfaɪ] *vt* certificare ■ *vi*: **to ~ to** attestare a
cervical ['sə:vɪkl] *adj*: **~ cancer** cancro della cervice, tumore *m* al collo dell'utero; **~ smear** Pap-test *m inv*
cervix ['sə:vɪks] *n* cervice *f*
Cesarean [si:'zɛərɪən] *adj, n* (*US*) = **Caesarean**
cessation [sə'seɪʃən] *n* cessazione *f*; arresto
cesspit ['sɛspɪt] *n* pozzo nero
CET *abbr* (= *Central European Time*) *fuso orario*
Ceylon [sɪ'lɔn] *n* Ceylon *f*
cf. *abbr* (= *compare*) cfr
c/f *abbr* (*Comm*) = **carried forward**
CFC *n abbr* (= *chlorofluorocarbon*) CFC *m inv*
CG *n abbr* (*US*) = **coastguard**
cg *abbr* (= *centigram*) cg
CH *n abbr* (*Brit*: = *Companion of Honour*) *titolo*
ch. *abbr* (= *chapter*) cap
Chad [tʃæd] *n* Chad *m*
chafe [tʃeɪf] *vt* fregare, irritare ■ *vi* (*fig*): **to ~ against** scontrarsi con
chaffinch ['tʃæfɪntʃ] *n* fringuello
chagrin ['ʃægrɪn] *n* disappunto, dispiacere *m*
chain [tʃeɪn] *n* catena ■ *vt* (*also*: **chain up**) incatenare
chain reaction *n* reazione *f* a catena
chain-smoke ['tʃeɪnsməuk] *vi* fumare una sigaretta dopo l'altra
chain store *n* negozio a catena
chair [tʃɛə^r] *n* sedia; (*armchair*) poltrona; (*of university*) cattedra ■ *vt* (*meeting*) presiedere; **the ~** (*US*: *electric chair*) la sedia elettrica
chairlift ['tʃɛəlɪft] *n* seggiovia
chairman ['tʃɛəmən] *n* presidente *m*
chairperson ['tʃɛəpə:sn] *n* presidente(-essa)
chairwoman ['tʃɛəwumən] *n* presidentessa
chalet ['ʃæleɪ] *n* chalet *m inv*
chalice ['tʃælɪs] *n* calice *m*
chalk [tʃɔ:k] *n* gesso
▸ **chalk up** *vt* scrivere col gesso; (*fig*: *success*) ottenere; (: *victory*) riportare
challenge ['tʃælɪndʒ] *n* sfida ■ *vt* sfidare; (*statement, right*) mettere in dubbio; **to ~ sb to a fight/game** sfidare qn a battersi/ad una partita; **to ~ sb to do** sfidare qn a fare
challenger ['tʃælɪndʒə^r] *n* (*Sport*) sfidante *m/f*
challenging ['tʃælɪndʒɪŋ] *adj* sfidante; (*remark, look*) provocatorio(-a)
chamber ['tʃeɪmbə^r] *n* camera; **~ of commerce** camera di commercio
chambermaid ['tʃeɪmbəmeɪd] *n* cameriera
chamber music *n* musica da camera
chamberpot ['tʃeɪmbəpɔt] *n* vaso da notte
chameleon [kə'mi:lɪən] *n* camaleonte *m*
chamois ['ʃæmwɑ:] *n* camoscio
chamois leather ['ʃæmɪ-] *n* pelle *f* di camoscio
champagne [ʃæm'peɪn] *n* champagne *m inv*
champers ['ʃæmpəz] *nsg* (*col*) sciampagna
champion ['tʃæmpɪən] *n* campione(-essa); (*of cause*) difensore *m* ■ *vt* difendere, lottare per
championship ['tʃæmpɪənʃɪp] *n* campionato
chance [tʃɑ:ns] *n* caso; (*opportunity*) occasione *f*; (*likelihood*) possibilità *f inv* ■ *vt*: **to ~ it**

rischiare, provarci ■ *adj* fortuito(-a); **there is little ~ of his coming** è molto improbabile che venga; **to take a ~** rischiare; **by ~** per caso; **it's the ~ of a lifetime** è un'occasione unica; **the chances are that ...** probabilmente ..., è probabile che ... *+ sub*; **to ~ to do sth** (*formal*: *happen*) fare per caso qc
▸ **chance (up)on** *vt fus* (*person*) incontrare per caso, imbattersi in; (*thing*) trovare per caso
chancel ['tʃɑːnsəl] *n* coro
chancellor ['tʃɑːnsələʳ] *n* cancelliere *m*; (*of university*) rettore *m* (onorario); **C~ of the Exchequer** (*Brit*) Cancelliere *m* dello Scacchiere
chandelier [ʃændə'lɪəʳ] *n* lampadario
change [tʃeɪndʒ] *vt* cambiare; (*transform*): **to ~ sb into** trasformare qn in ■ *vi* cambiarsi; (*be transformed*): **to ~ into** trasformarsi in ■ *n* cambiamento; (*money*) resto; **to ~ one's mind** cambiare idea; **to ~ gear** (*Aut*) cambiare (marcia); **she changed into an old skirt** si è cambiata e ha messo una vecchia gonna; **a ~ of clothes** un cambio (di vestiti); **for a ~** tanto per cambiare; **small ~** spiccioli *mpl*, moneta; **keep the ~** tenga il resto; **can you give me ~ for £1?** mi può cambiare una sterlina?
changeable ['tʃeɪndʒəbl] *adj* (*weather*) variabile; (*person*) mutevole
change machine *n* distributore *m* automatico di monete
changeover ['tʃeɪndʒəuvəʳ] *n* cambiamento, passaggio
changing ['tʃeɪndʒɪŋ] *adj* che cambia; (*colours*) cangiante
changing room *n* (*Brit*: *in shop*) camerino; (*: Sport*) spogliatoio
channel ['tʃænl] *n* canale *m*; (*of river, sea*) alveo ■ *vt* canalizzare; (*fig*: *interest, energies*): **to ~ into** concentrare su, indirizzare verso; **through the usual channels** per le solite vie; **the (English) C~** la Manica; **green/red ~** (*Customs*) uscita "niente da dichiarare"/ "merci da dichiarare"
channel-hopping ['tʃænlhɔpɪŋ] *n* (*TV*) zapping *m*
Channel Islands *npl*: **the ~** le Isole Normanne
Channel Tunnel *n*: **the ~** il tunnel della Manica
chant [tʃɑːnt] *n* canto; salmodia; (*of crowd*) slogan *m inv* ■ *vt* cantare; salmodiare; **the demonstrators chanted their disapproval** i dimostranti lanciavano slogan di protesta
chaos ['keɪɔs] *n* caos *m*
chaos theory *n* teoria del caos
chaotic [keɪ'ɔtɪk] *adj* caotico(-a)
chap [tʃæp] *n* (*Brit col*: *man*) tipo ■ *vt* (*skin*) screpolare; **old ~** vecchio mio
chapel ['tʃæpl] *n* cappella
chaperone ['ʃæpərəun] *n* accompagnatore(-trice) ■ *vt* accompagnare
chaplain ['tʃæplɪn] *n* cappellano
chapped [tʃæpt] *adj* (*skin, lips*) screpolato(-a)
chapter ['tʃæptəʳ] *n* capitolo
char [tʃɑːʳ] *vt* (*burn*) carbonizzare ■ *vi* (*Brit*: *cleaner*) lavorare come domestica (a ore) ■ *n* (*Brit*) = **charlady**
character ['kærɪktəʳ] *n* (*gen, Comput*) carattere *m*; (*in novel, film*) personaggio; (*eccentric*) originale *m*; **a person of good ~** una persona a modo
character code *n* (*Comput*) codice *m* di carattere
characteristic ['kærɪktə'rɪstɪk] *adj* caratteristico(-a) ■ *n* caratteristica; **~ of** tipico(-a) di
characterize ['kærɪktəraɪz] *vt* caratterizzare; (*describe*): **to ~ (as)** descrivere (come)
charade [ʃə'rɑːd] *n* sciarada
charcoal ['tʃɑːkəul] *n* carbone *m* di legna
charge [tʃɑːdʒ] *n* accusa; (*cost*) prezzo; (*of gun, battery, Mil*: *attack*) carica ■ *vt* (*gun, battery, Mil*: *enemy*) caricare; (*customer*) fare pagare a; (*sum*) fare pagare; (*Law*): **to ~ sb (with)** accusare qn (di) ■ *vi* (*gen with*: *up, along etc*) lanciarsi; **charges** *npl*: **bank charges** commissioni *fpl* bancarie; **labour charges** costi *mpl* del lavoro; **to ~ in/out** precipitarsi dentro/fuori; **to ~ up/down** lanciarsi su/giù per; **is there a ~?** c'è da pagare?; **there's no ~** non c'è niente da pagare; **extra ~** supplemento; **to take ~ of** incaricarsi di; **to be in ~ of** essere responsabile per; **to have ~ of sb** aver cura di qn; **how much do you ~ for this repair?** quanto chiede per la riparazione?; **to ~ an expense (up) to sb** addebitare una spesa a qn; **~ it to my account** lo metta *or* addebiti sul mio conto
charge account *n* conto
charge card *n* carta di credito commerciale
chargé d'affaires ['ʃɑːʒeɪdæ'fɛəʳ] *n* incaricato d'affari
chargehand ['tʃɑːdʒhænd] *n* (*Brit*) caposquadra *m/f*
charger ['tʃɑːdʒəʳ] *n* (*also*: **battery charger**) caricabatterie *m inv*; (*old*: *warhorse*) destriero
chariot ['tʃærɪət] *n* carro
charitable ['tʃærɪtəbl] *adj* caritatevole
charity ['tʃærɪtɪ] *n* carità; (*organization*) opera pia
charlady ['tʃɑːleɪdɪ] *n* (*Brit*) domestica a ore
charlatan ['ʃɑːlətən] *n* ciarlatano
charm [tʃɑːm] *n* fascino; (*on bracelet*) ciondolo ■ *vt* affascinare, incantare

charm bracelet *n* braccialetto con ciondoli
charming ['tʃɑːmɪŋ] *adj* affascinante
chart [tʃɑːt] *n* tabella; grafico; (*map*) carta nautica; (*weather chart*) carta del tempo ■ *vt* fare una carta nautica di; (*sales, progress*) tracciare il grafico di; **to be in the charts** (*record, pop group*) essere in classifica
charter ['tʃɑːtə^r] *vt* (*plane*) noleggiare ■ *n* (*document*) carta; **on ~** a nolo
chartered accountant ['tʃɑːtəd-] *n* (*Brit*) ragioniere(-a) professionista
charter flight *n* volo *m* charter *inv*
charwoman ['tʃɑːwumən] *n* = **charlady**
chase [tʃeɪs] *vt* inseguire; (*also*: **chase away**) cacciare ■ *n* caccia
▸ **chase down** *vt* (US) = **chase up**
▸ **chase up** *vt* (*Brit*: *person*) scovare; (: *information*) scoprire, raccogliere
chasm ['kæzəm] *n* abisso
chassis ['ʃæsɪ] *n* telaio
chastened ['tʃeɪsnd] *adj* abbattuto(-a), provato(-a)
chastening ['tʃeɪsnɪŋ] *adj* che fa riflettere
chastise [tʃæs'taɪz] *vt* punire, castigare
chastity ['tʃæstɪtɪ] *n* castità
chat [tʃæt] *vi* (*also*: **have a chat**) chiacchierare; (*on the internet*) chattare ■ *n* chiacchierata
▸ **chat up** *vt* (*Brit col*: *girl*) abbordare
chatline ['tʃætlaɪn] *n* *servicio telefonico che permette a più utenti di conversare insieme*
chat room *n* chat line *f inv*
chat show *n* (*Brit*) talk show *m inv*, conversazione *f* televisiva
chattel ['tʃætl] *n* *see* **goods**
chatter ['tʃætə^r] *vi* (*person*) ciarlare ■ *n* ciarle *fpl*; **her teeth were chattering** batteva i denti
chatterbox ['tʃætəbɔks] *n* chiacchierone(-a)
chattering classes ['tʃætərɪŋ-] *npl*: **the ~** (*col, pej*) ≈ gli intellettuali da salotto
chatty ['tʃætɪ] *adj* (*style*) familiare; (*person*) chiacchierino(-a)
chauffeur ['ʃəufə^r] *n* autista *m*
chauvinism ['ʃəuvɪnɪzəm] *n* (*also*: **male chauvinism**) maschilismo; (*nationalism*) sciovinismo
chauvinist ['ʃəuvɪnɪst] *n* (*also*: **male chauvinist**) maschilista *m*; (*nationalist*) sciovinista *m/f*
chauvinistic [ʃəuvɪ'nɪstɪk] *adj* sciovinistico(-a)
chav [tʃæv] *n* (*Brit*: *pej*) *giovane della periferia urbana poco colto che indossa abiti sportivi di particolari marche*
ChE *abbr* = **chemical engineer**
cheap [tʃiːp] *adj* a buon mercato; (*reduced*: *fare, ticket*) ridotto(-a); (*joke*) grossolano(-a); (*poor quality*) di cattiva qualità ■ *adv* a buon mercato; **cheaper** meno caro; **~ day return** biglietto giornaliero ridotto di andata e ritorno; **~ money** denaro a basso tasso di interesse
cheapen ['tʃiːpn] *vt* ribassare; (*fig*) avvilire
cheaply ['tʃiːplɪ] *adv* a buon prezzo, a buon mercato
cheat [tʃiːt] *vi* imbrogliare; (*at school*) copiare ■ *vt* ingannare; (*rob*) defraudare ■ *n* imbroglione *m*; copione *m*; (*trick*) inganno; **he's been cheating on his wife** ha tradito sua moglie
cheating ['tʃiːtɪŋ] *n* imbrogliare *m*; copiare *m*
check [tʃɛk] *vt* verificare; (*passport, ticket*) controllare; (*halt*) fermare; (*restrain*) contenere ■ *vi* (*official etc*) informarsi ■ *n* verifica; controllo; (*curb*) freno; (*bill*) conto; (*pattern*: *gen pl*) quadretti *mpl*; (US) = **cheque** ■ *adj* (*also*: **checked**: *pattern, cloth*) a scacchi, a quadretti; **to ~ with sb** chiedere a qn; **to keep a ~ on sb/sth** controllare qn/qc, fare attenzione a qn/qc
▸ **check in** *vi* (*in hotel*) registrare; (*at airport*) presentarsi all'accettazione ■ *vt* (*luggage*) depositare
▸ **check off** *vt* segnare
▸ **check out** *vi* (*from hotel*) saldare il conto ■ *vt* (*luggage*) ritirare; (*investigate*: *story*) controllare, verificare; (: *person*) prendere informazioni su
▸ **check up** *vi*: **to ~ up (on sth)** investigare (qc); **to ~ up on sb** informarsi sul conto di qn
checkbook ['tʃɛkbuk] *n* (US) = **chequebook**
checkered ['tʃɛkəd] *adj* (US) = **chequered**
checkers ['tʃɛkəz] *n* (US) dama
check guarantee card *n* (US) carta *f* assegni *inv*
check-in ['tʃɛkɪn] *n* (*also*: **check-in desk**: *at airport*) check-in *m inv*, accettazione *f* (bagagli *inv*)
checking account ['tʃɛkɪŋ-] *n* (US) conto corrente
checklist ['tʃɛklɪst] *n* lista di controllo
checkmate ['tʃɛkmeɪt] *n* scaccomatto
checkout ['tʃɛkaut] *n* (*in supermarket*) cassa
checkpoint ['tʃɛkpɔɪnt] *n* posto di blocco
checkroom ['tʃɛkrum] *n* (US) deposito *m* bagagli *inv*
checkup ['tʃɛkʌp] *n* (*Med*) controllo medico
cheek [tʃiːk] *n* guancia; (*impudence*) faccia tosta
cheekbone ['tʃiːkbəun] *n* zigomo
cheeky ['tʃiːkɪ] *adj* sfacciato(-a)
cheep [tʃiːp] *n* (*of bird*) pigolio ■ *vi* pigolare
cheer [tʃɪə^r] *vt* applaudire; (*gladden*)

rallegrare ■ *vi* applaudire ■ *n* (*gen pl*) applausi *mpl*; evviva *mpl*; **cheers!** salute!
▸ **cheer on** *vt* (*person etc*) incitare
▸ **cheer up** *vi* rallegrarsi, farsi animo ■ *vt* rallegrare
cheerful ['tʃɪəful] *adj* allegro(-a)
cheerfulness ['tʃɪəfulnɪs] *n* allegria
cheerio ['tʃɪərɪ'əu] *excl* (*Brit*) ciao!
cheerleader ['tʃɪəli:dəʳ] *n* cheerleader *f inv*
cheerless ['tʃɪəlɪs] *adj* triste
cheese [tʃi:z] *n* formaggio
cheeseboard ['tʃi:zbɔ:d] *n* piatto del (*or* per il) formaggio
cheeseburger ['tʃi:zbə:gəʳ] *n* cheeseburger *m inv*
cheesecake ['tʃi:zkeɪk] *n specie di torta di ricotta, a volte con frutta*
cheetah ['tʃi:tə] *n* ghepardo
chef [ʃɛf] *n* capocuoco
chemical ['kɛmɪkl] *adj* chimico(-a) ■ *n* prodotto chimico
chemical engineering *n* ingegneria chimica
chemist ['kɛmɪst] *n* (*Brit: pharmacist*) farmacista *m/f*; (*scientist*) chimico(-a); **~'s shop** *n* (*Brit*) farmacia
chemistry ['kɛmɪstrɪ] *n* chimica
chemo ['ki:məu] *n* chemio *f inv*
chemotherapy [ki:məu'θɛrəpɪ] *n* chemioterapia
cheque, (*US*) **check** [tʃɛk] *n* assegno; **to pay by ~** pagare per assegno *or* con un assegno
chequebook, (*US*) **checkbook** ['tʃɛkbuk] *n* libretto degli assegni
cheque card *n* (*Brit*) carta *f* assegni *inv*
chequered, (*US*) **checkered** ['tʃɛkəd] *adj* (*fig*) movimentato(-a)
cherish ['tʃɛrɪʃ] *vt* aver caro; (*hope etc*) nutrire
cheroot [ʃə'ru:t] *n* sigaro spuntato
cherry ['tʃɛrɪ] *n* ciliegia
Ches *abbr* (*Brit*) = **Cheshire**
chess [tʃɛs] *n* scacchi *mpl*
chessboard ['tʃɛsbɔ:d] *n* scacchiera
chessman ['tʃɛsmæn] *n* pezzo degli scacchi
chessplayer ['tʃɛspleɪəʳ] *n* scacchista *m/f*
chest [tʃɛst] *n* petto; (*box*) cassa; **to get sth off one's ~** (*col*) sputare il rospo; **~ of drawers** cassettone *m*
chest measurement *n* giro *m* torace *inv*
chestnut ['tʃɛsnʌt] *n* castagna; (*also:* **chestnut tree**) castagno ■ *adj* castano(-a)
chesty ['tʃɛstɪ] *adj*: **~ cough** tosse *f* bronchiale
chew [tʃu:] *vt* masticare
chewing gum ['tʃu:ɪŋ-] *n* chewing gum *m*
chic [ʃi:k] *adj* elegante
chick [tʃɪk] *n* pulcino; (*US col*) pollastrella
chicken ['tʃɪkɪn] *n* pollo; (*col: coward*) coniglio
▸ **chicken out** *vi* (*col*) avere fifa; **to ~ out of sth** tirarsi indietro da qc per fifa *or* paura
chicken feed *n* (*fig*) miseria
chickenpox ['tʃɪkɪnpɔks] *n* varicella
chick flick *n* (*col*) filmetto rosa
chickpea ['tʃɪkpi:] *n* cece *m*
chicory ['tʃɪkərɪ] *n* cicoria
chide [tʃaɪd] *vt* rimproverare
chief [tʃi:f] *n* capo ■ *adj* principale; **C~ of Staff** (*Mil*) Capo di Stato Maggiore
chief constable *n* (*Brit*) ≈ questore *m*
chief executive, (*US*) **chief executive officer** *n* direttore *m* generale
chiefly ['tʃi:flɪ] *adv* per lo più, soprattutto
chief operating officer *n* direttore(-trice) operativo(-a)
chiffon ['ʃɪfɔn] *n* chiffon *m inv*
chilblain ['tʃɪlbleɪn] *n* gelone *m*
child (*pl* **children**) [tʃaɪld, 'tʃɪldrən] *n* bambino(-a)
child abuse *n* molestie *fpl* a minori
child abuser [-ə'bju:zəʳ] *n* molestatore(-trice) di bambini
child benefit *n* (*Brit*) ≈ assegni *mpl* familiari
childbirth ['tʃaɪldbə:θ] *n* parto
childhood ['tʃaɪldhud] *n* infanzia
childish ['tʃaɪldɪʃ] *adj* puerile
childless ['tʃaɪldlɪs] *adj* senza figli
childlike ['tʃaɪldlaɪk] *adj* fanciullesco(-a)
child minder *n* (*Brit*) bambinaia
child prodigy *n* bambino *m* prodigio *inv*
children ['tʃɪldrən] *npl of* **child**
children's home *n* istituto per l'infanzia
Chile ['tʃɪlɪ] *n* Cile *m*
Chilean ['tʃɪlɪən] *adj, n* cileno(-a)
chill [tʃɪl] *n* freddo; (*Med*) infreddatura ■ *adj* freddo(-a), gelido(-a) ■ *vt* raffreddare; (*Culin*) mettere in fresco; **"serve chilled"** "servire fresco"
▸ **chill out** *vi* (*esp US: col*) darsi una calmata
chilli, (*US*) **chili** ['tʃɪlɪ] *n* peperoncino
chilling ['tʃɪlɪŋ] *adj* agghiacciante; (*wind*) gelido(-a)
chilly ['tʃɪlɪ] *adj* freddo(-a), fresco(-a); (*sensitive to cold*) freddoloso(-a); **to feel ~** sentirsi infreddolito(-a)
chime [tʃaɪm] *n* carillon *m inv* ■ *vi* suonare, scampanare
chimney ['tʃɪmnɪ] *n* camino
chimney sweep *n* spazzacamino
chimpanzee [tʃɪmpæn'zi:] *n* scimpanzé *m inv*
chin [tʃɪn] *n* mento
China ['tʃaɪnə] *n* Cina
china ['tʃaɪnə] *n* porcellana
Chinese [tʃaɪ'ni:z] *adj* cinese ■ *n* (*pl inv*) cinese *m/f*; (*Ling*) cinese *m*
chink [tʃɪŋk] *n* (*opening*) fessura; (*noise*) tintinnio
chinwag ['tʃɪnwæg] *n* (*col*): **to have a ~** fare una chiacchierata

chip [tʃɪp] *n* (*gen pl: Culin*) patatina fritta; (*: US: also:* **potato chip**) patatina; (*of wood, glass, stone*) scheggia; (*in gambling*) fiche *f inv* (*Comput: microchip*) chip *m inv* ■ *vt* (*cup, plate*) scheggiare; **when the chips are down** (*fig*) al momento critico
▸ **chip in** *vi* (*col: contribute*) contribuire; (*: interrupt*) intromettersi
chip and PIN *n* sistema *m* chip e PIN; ~ **machine** lettore *m* di carte chip e PIN; ~ **card** carta chip e PIN
chipboard ['tʃɪpbɔːd] *n* agglomerato
chipmunk ['tʃɪpmʌŋk] *n* tamia *m* striato
chippings ['tʃɪpɪŋz] *npl*: **loose ~** brecciame *m*
chip shop *n* (*Brit*) *vedi nota*

CHIP SHOP

I *chip shops*, anche chiamati "fish-and-chip shops", sono friggitorie che vendono principalmente filetti di pesce impanati e patatine fritte che un tempo venivano serviti ai clienti avvolti in carta di giornale.

chiropodist [kɪ'rɔpədɪst] *n* (*Brit*) pedicure *m/f inv*
chiropody [kɪ'rɔpədɪ] *n* (*Brit*) mestiere *m* di callista
chirp [tʃəːp] *n* cinguettio; (*of crickets*) cri cri *m* ■ *vi* cinguettare
chirpy ['tʃəːpɪ] *adj* (*col*) frizzante
chisel ['tʃɪzl] *n* cesello
chitchat ['tʃɪttʃæt] *n* (*col*) chiacchiere *fpl*
chivalrous ['ʃɪvəlrəs] *adj* cavalleresco(-a)
chivalry ['ʃɪvəlrɪ] *n* cavalleria; cortesia
chives [tʃaɪvz] *npl* erba cipollina
chloride ['klɔːraɪd] *n* cloruro
chlorinate ['klɔrɪneɪt] *vt* clorare
chlorine ['klɔːriːn] *n* cloro
chock [tʃɔk] *n* zeppa
chock-a-block ['tʃɔkə'blɔk], **chockfull** ['tʃɔk'ful] *adj* pieno(-a) zeppo(-a)
chocolate ['tʃɔklɪt] *n* (*substance*) cioccolato, cioccolata; (*drink*) cioccolata; (*a sweet*) cioccolatino
choice [tʃɔɪs] *n* scelta ■ *adj* scelto(-a); **a wide ~** un'ampia scelta; **I did it by** *or* **from ~** l'ho fatto di mia volontà *or* per mia scelta
choir ['kwaɪəʳ] *n* coro
choirboy ['kwaɪəbɔɪ] *n* corista *m* fanciullo
choke [tʃəuk] *vi* soffocare ■ *vt* soffocare; (*block*) ingombrare ■ *n* (*Aut*) valvola dell'aria
cholera ['kɔlərə] *n* colera *m*
cholesterol [kə'lɛstərɔl] *n* colesterolo
choose (*pt* **chose**, *pp* **chosen**) [tʃuːz, tʃəuz, 'tʃəuzn] *vt* scegliere; **to ~ to do** decidere di fare; preferire fare; **to ~ between** scegliere tra; **to ~ from** scegliere da *or* tra
choosy ['tʃuːzɪ] *adj*: **(to be) ~** (fare lo/la) schizzinoso(-a)
chop [tʃɔp] *vt* (*wood*) spaccare; (*Culin: also:* **chop up**) tritare ■ *n* colpo netto; (*Culin*) costoletta; **to get the ~** (*Brit col: project*) essere bocciato(-a); (*: person: be sacked*) essere licenziato(-a); *see also* **chops**
▸ **chop down** *vt* (*tree*) abbattere
choppy ['tʃɔpɪ] *adj* (*sea*) mosso(-a)
chops [tʃɔps] *npl* (*jaws*) mascelle *fpl*
chopsticks ['tʃɔpstɪks] *npl* bastoncini *mpl* cinesi
choral ['kɔːrəl] *adj* corale
chord [kɔːd] *n* (*Mus*) accordo
chore [tʃɔːʳ] *n* faccenda; **household chores** faccende *fpl* domestiche
choreographer [kɔrɪ'ɔgrəfəʳ] *n* coreografo(-a)
choreography [kɔrɪ'ɔgrəfɪ] *n* coreografia
chorister ['kɔrɪstəʳ] *n* corista *m/f*
chortle ['tʃɔːtl] *vi* ridacchiare
chorus ['kɔːrəs] *n* coro; (*repeated part of song, also fig*) ritornello
chose [tʃəuz] *pt of* **choose**
chosen ['tʃəuzn] *pp of* **choose**
chowder ['tʃaudəʳ] *n* zuppa di pesce
Christ [kraɪst] *n* Cristo
christen ['krɪsn] *vt* battezzare
christening ['krɪsnɪŋ] *n* battesimo
Christian ['krɪstɪən] *adj, n* cristiano(-a)
Christianity [krɪstɪ'ænɪtɪ] *n* cristianesimo
Christian name *n* nome *m* di battesimo
Christmas ['krɪsməs] *n* Natale *m*; **happy** *or* **merry ~!** Buon Natale!
Christmas card *n* cartolina di Natale
Christmas Day *n* il giorno di Natale
Christmas Eve *n* la vigilia di Natale
Christmas Island *n* isola di Christmas
Christmas tree *n* albero di Natale
chrome [krəum] *n* = **chromium**
chromium ['krəumɪəm] *n* cromo; (*also:* **chromium plating**) cromatura
chromosome ['krəuməsəum] *n* cromosoma *m*
chronic ['krɔnɪk] *adj* cronico(-a); (*fig: liar, smoker*) incallito(-a)
chronicle ['krɔnɪkl] *n* cronaca
chronological [krɔnə'lɔdʒɪkl] *adj* cronologico(-a)
chrysanthemum [krɪ'sænθəməm] *n* crisantemo
chubby ['tʃʌbɪ] *adj* paffuto(-a)
chuck [tʃʌk] *vt* buttare, gettare; **to ~ (up** *or* **in)** (*Brit: job, person*) piantare
▸ **chuck out** *vt* buttar fuori
chuckle ['tʃʌkl] *vi* ridere sommessamente

chuffed [tʃʌft] *adj (col)*: **to be ~ about sth** essere arcicontento(-a) di qc
chug [tʃʌg] *vi (also*: **chug along**: *train)* muoversi sbuffando
chum [tʃʌm] *n* compagno(-a)
chump [tʃʌmp] *n (col)* idiota *m/f*
chunk [tʃʌŋk] *n* pezzo; *(of bread)* tocco
chunky [tʃʌŋkɪ] *adj (furniture etc)* basso(-a) e largo(-a); *(person)* ben piantato(-a); *(knitwear)* di lana grossa
Chunnel ['tʃʌnəl] *n* = **Channel Tunnel**
church [tʃə:tʃ] *n* chiesa; **the C~ of England** la Chiesa anglicana
churchyard ['tʃə:tʃjɑ:d] *n* sagrato
churlish ['tʃə:lɪʃ] *adj* rozzo(-a), sgarbato(-a)
churn [tʃə:n] *n (for butter)* zangola; *(also*: **milk churn**) bidone *m*
▸ **churn out** *vt* sfornare
chute [ʃu:t] *n* cascata; *(also*: **rubbish chute**) canale *m* di scarico; *(Brit: children's slide)* scivolo
chutney ['tʃʌtnɪ] *n* salsa piccante (di frutta, zucchero e spezie)
CIA *n abbr (US*: = *Central Intelligence Agency)* C.I.A. *f*
CID *n abbr (Brit)* = **Criminal Investigation Department**
cider ['saɪdə^r] *n* sidro
CIF *abbr (= cost, insurance, and freight)* C.I.F. *m*
cigar [sɪ'gɑ:^r] *n* sigaro
cigarette [sɪgə'rɛt] *n* sigaretta
cigarette case *n* portasigarette *m inv*
cigarette end *n* mozzicone *m*
cigarette holder *n* bocchino
C-in-C *abbr* = **commander-in-chief**
cinch [sɪntʃ] *n (col)*: **it's a ~** è presto fatto; *(sure thing)* è una cosa sicura
cinder ['sɪndə^r] *n* cenere *f*
Cinderella [sɪndə'rɛlə] *n* Cenerentola
cine-camera ['sɪnɪ'kæmərə] *n (Brit)* cinepresa
cine-film ['sɪnɪfɪlm] *n (Brit)* pellicola
cinema ['sɪnəmə] *n* cinema *m inv*
cine-projector ['sɪnɪprə'dʒɛktə^r] *n (Brit)* proiettore *m*
cinnamon ['sɪnəmən] *n* cannella
cipher ['saɪfə^r] *n* cifra; *(fig: faceless employee etc)* persona di nessun conto; **in ~** in codice
circa ['sə:kə] *prep* circa
circle ['sə:kl] *n* cerchio; *(of friends etc)* circolo; *(in cinema)* galleria ■ *vi* girare in circolo ■ *vt (surround)* circondare; *(move round)* girare intorno a
circuit ['sə:kɪt] *n* circuito
circuit board *n (Comput)* tavola dei circuiti
circuitous [sə:'kjuɪtəs] *adj* indiretto(-a)
circular ['sə:kjulə^r] *adj* circolare ■ *n (letter)* circolare *f*; *(as advertisement)* volantino pubblicitario
circulate ['sə:kjuleɪt] *vi* circolare; *(person: socially)* girare e andare un po' da tutti ■ *vt* far circolare
circulating capital ['sə:kjuleɪtɪŋ-] *n (Comm)* capitale *m* d'esercizio
circulation [sə:kju'leɪʃən] *n* circolazione *f*; *(of newspaper)* tiratura
circumcise ['sə:kəmsaɪz] *vt* circoncidere
circumference [sə'kʌmfərəns] *n* circonferenza
circumflex ['sə:kəmflɛks] *n (also*: **circumflex accent**) accento circonflesso
circumscribe ['sə:kəmskraɪb] *vt* circoscrivere; *(fig: limit)* limitare
circumspect ['sə:kəmspɛkt] *adj* circospetto(-a)
circumstances ['sə:kəmstənsɪz] *npl* circostanze *fpl*; *(financial condition)* condizioni *fpl* finanziarie; **in the ~** date le circostanze; **under no ~** per nessun motivo
circumstantial ['sə:kəm'stænʃəl] *adj (report, statement)* circostanziato(-a), dettagliato(-a); **~ evidence** prova indiretta
circumvent [sə:kəm'vɛnt] *vt (rule etc)* aggirare
circus ['sə:kəs] *n* circo; *(also*: **Circus**: *in place names)* piazza (di forma circolare)
cirrhosis [sɪ'rəusɪs] *n (also*: **cirrhosis of the liver**) cirrosi *f inv* (epatica)
CIS *n abbr (= Commonwealth of Independent States)* CSI *f*
cissy ['sɪsɪ] *n* = **sissy**
cistern ['sɪstən] *n* cisterna; *(in toilet)* serbatoio d'acqua
citation [saɪ'teɪʃən] *n* citazione *f*
cite [saɪt] *vt* citare
citizen ['sɪtɪzn] *n (Pol)* cittadino(-a); *(resident)*: **the citizens of this town** gli abitanti di questa città
Citizens' Advice Bureau *n (Brit) organizzazione di volontari che offre gratuitamente assistenza legale e finanziaria*
citizenship ['sɪtɪznʃɪp] *n* cittadinanza
citric acid ['sɪtrɪk] *n* acido citrico
citrus fruit ['sɪtrəs-] *n* agrume *m*
city ['sɪtɪ] *n* città *f inv*; **the C~** la Città di Londra *(centro commerciale)*
city centre *n* centro della città
City Hall *n (US)* ≈ Comune *m*
City Technology College *n (Brit)* istituto tecnico superiore *(finanziato dall'industria)*
civic ['sɪvɪk] *adj* civico(-a)
civic centre *n (Brit)* centro civico
civil ['sɪvɪl] *adj* civile; *(polite)* educato(-a), gentile

civil disobedience *n* disubbidienza civile
civil engineer *n* ingegnere *m* civile
civil engineering *n* ingegneria civile
civilian [sɪ'vɪlɪən] *adj, n* borghese (*m/f*)
civilization [sɪvɪlaɪ'zeɪʃən] *n* civiltà *f inv*
civilized ['sɪvɪlaɪzd] *adj* civilizzato(-a); (*fig*) cortese
civil law *n* codice *m* civile; (*study*) diritto civile
civil liberties *npl* libertà *fpl* civili
civil rights *npl* diritti *mpl* civili
civil servant *n* impiegato(-a) statale
Civil Service *n* amministrazione *f* statale
civil war *n* guerra civile
civvies ['sɪvɪz] *npl* (*col*): **in ~** in borghese
CJD *n abbr* (= *Creutzfeld-Jakob disease*) malattia di Creutzfeldt-Jakob
cl *abbr* (= *centilitre*) cl
clad [klæd] *adj*: **~ (in)** vestito(-a) (di)
claim [kleɪm] *vt* (*rights etc*) rivendicare; (*damages*) richiedere; (*assert*) sostenere, pretendere ■ *vi* (*for insurance*) fare una domanda d'indennizzo ■ *n* rivendicazione *f*; pretesa; (*right*) diritto; **to ~ that/to be** sostenere che/di essere; **(insurance) ~** domanda d'indennizzo; **to put in a ~ for sth** fare una richiesta di qc
claimant ['kleɪmənt] *n* (*Admin, Law*) richiedente *m/f*
claim form *n* (*gen*) modulo di richiesta; (*for expenses*) modulo di rimborso spese
clairvoyant [klɛə'vɔɪənt] *n* chiaroveggente *m/f*
clam [klæm] *n* vongola
▸ **clam up** *vi* (*col*) azzittirsi
clamber ['klæmbəʳ] *vi* arrampicarsi
clammy ['klæmɪ] *adj* (*weather*) caldo(-a) umido(-a); (*hands*) viscido(-a)
clamour, (*US*) **clamor** ['klæməʳ] *n* (*noise*) clamore *m*; (*protest*) protesta ■ *vi*: **to ~ for sth** chiedere a gran voce qc
clamp [klæmp] *n* pinza; morsa ■ *vt* ammorsare
▸ **clamp down** *vt fus* (*fig*): **to ~ down (on)** dare un giro di vite (a)
clampdown ['klæmpdaun] *n* stretta, giro di vite; **a ~ on sth/sb** un giro di vite a qc/qn
clan [klæn] *n* clan *m inv*
clandestine [klæn'dɛstɪn] *adj* clandestino(-a)
clang [klæŋ] *n* fragore *m*, suono metallico
clanger ['klæŋəʳ] *n*: **to drop a ~** (*Brit col*) fare una gaffe
clansman ['klænzmən] *n* membro di un clan
clap [klæp] *vi* applaudire ■ *vt*: **to ~ one's hands** battere le mani ■ *n*: **a ~ of thunder** un tuono
clapping ['klæpɪŋ] *n* applausi *mpl*
claptrap ['klæptræp] *n* (*col*) stupidaggini *fpl*
claret ['klærət] *n* vino di Bordeaux
clarification [klærɪfɪ'keɪʃən] *n* (*fig*) chiarificazione *f*, chiarimento
clarify ['klærɪfaɪ] *vt* chiarificare, chiarire
clarinet [klærɪ'nɛt] *n* clarinetto
clarity ['klærɪtɪ] *n* chiarezza
clash [klæʃ] *n* frastuono; (*fig*) scontro ■ *vi* (*Mil, fig: have an argument*) scontrarsi; (*colours*) stridere; (*dates, events*) coincidere
clasp [klɑːsp] *n* fermaglio, fibbia ■ *vt* stringere
class [klɑːs] *n* classe *f*; (*group, category*) tipo, categoria ■ *vt* classificare
class-conscious ['klɑːskɔnʃəs] *adj* che ha coscienza di classe
class consciousness *n* coscienza di classe
classic ['klæsɪk] *adj* classico(-a) ■ *n* classico
classical ['klæsɪkəl] *adj* classico(-a)
classics ['klæsɪks] *npl* (*Scol*) studi *mpl* umanistici
classification [klæsɪfɪ'keɪʃən] *n* classificazione *f*
classified ['klæsɪfaɪd] *adj* (*information*) segreto(-a), riservato(-a); **~ ads** annunci economici
classify ['klæsɪfaɪ] *vt* classificare
classless society ['klɑːslɪs-] *n* società *f inv* senza distinzioni di classe
classmate ['klɑːsmeɪt] *n* compagno(-a) di classe
classroom ['klɑːsrum] *n* aula
classroom assistant *n* assistente *m/f* in classe dell'insegnante
clatter ['klætəʳ] *n* acciottolio; scalpitio ■ *vi* acciottolare; scalpitare
clause [klɔːz] *n* clausola; (*Ling*) proposizione *f*
claustrophobia [klɔːstrə'fəubɪə] *n* claustrofobia
claustrophobic [klɔːstrə'fəubɪk] *adj* claustrofobico(-a)
claw [klɔː] *n* tenaglia; (*of bird of prey*) artiglio; (*of lobster*) pinza ■ *vt* graffiare; afferrare
clay [kleɪ] *n* argilla
clean [kliːn] *adj* pulito(-a); (*clear, smooth*) netto(-a) ■ *vt* pulire ■ *adv*: **he ~ forgot** si è completamente dimenticato; **to come ~** (*col: admit guilt*) confessare; **to have a ~ driving licence** *or* (*US*) **record** non aver mai preso contravvenzioni; **to ~ one's teeth** (*Brit*) lavarsi i denti
▸ **clean off** *vt* togliere
▸ **clean out** *vt* ripulire
▸ **clean up** *vi* far pulizia ■ *vt* (*also fig*) ripulire; (*fig: make profit*): **to ~ up on** fare una barca di soldi con

clean-cut ['kli:n'kʌt] *adj* (*man*) curato(-a); (*situation etc*) ben definito(-a)
cleaner ['kli:nəʳ] *n* (*person*) uomo/donna delle pulizie; (*also*: **dry cleaner**) tintore(-a); (*product*) smacchiatore *m*
cleaning ['kli:nɪŋ] *n* pulizia
cleaning lady *n* donna delle pulizie
cleanliness ['klɛnlɪnɪs] *n* pulizia
cleanly ['kli:nlɪ] *adv* in modo netto
cleanse [klɛnz] *vt* pulire; purificare
cleanser ['klɛnzəʳ] *n* detergente *m*; (*cosmetic*) latte *m* detergente
clean-shaven ['kli:n'ʃeɪvn] *adj* sbarbato(-a)
cleansing department ['klɛnzɪŋ-] *n* (*Brit*) nettezza urbana
clean sweep *n*: **to make a ~ (of)** fare piazza pulita (di)
clean-up ['kli:nʌp] *n* pulizia
clear [klɪəʳ] *adj* chiaro(-a); (*road, way*) libero(-a); (*profit, majority*) netto(-a) ■ *vt* sgombrare; liberare; (*site, woodland*) spianare; (*Comm: goods*) liquidare; (*Law: suspect*) discolpare; (*obstacle*) superare; (*cheque*) fare la compensazione di ■ *vi* (*weather*) rasserenarsi; (*fog*) andarsene ■ *adv*: **~ of** distante da ■ *n*: **to be in the ~** (*out of debt*) essere in attivo; (*out of suspicion*) essere a posto; (*out of danger*) essere fuori pericolo; **to ~ the table** sparecchiare (la tavola); **to ~ one's throat** schiarirsi la gola; **to ~ a profit** avere un profitto netto; **to make o.s. ~** spiegarsi bene; **to make it ~ to sb that ...** far capire a qn che ...; **I have a ~ day tomorrow** (*Brit*) non ho impegni domani; **to keep ~ of sb/sth** tenersi lontano da qn/qc, stare alla larga da qn/qc
▸ **clear off** *vi* (*col: leave*) svignarsela
▸ **clear up** *vi* schiarirsi ■ *vt* mettere in ordine; (*mystery*) risolvere
clearance ['klɪərəns] *n* (*removal*) sgombro; (*free space*) spazio; (*permission*) autorizzazione *f*, permesso
clearance sale *n* vendita di liquidazione
clear-cut ['klɪə'kʌt] *adj* ben delineato(-a), distinto(-a)
clearing ['klɪərɪŋ] *n* radura; (*Brit Banking*) clearing *m*
clearing bank *n* (*Brit*) *banca che fa uso della camera di compensazione*
clearing house *n* (*Comm*) camera di compensazione
clearly ['klɪəlɪ] *adv* chiaramente
clearway ['klɪəweɪ] *n* (*Brit*) strada con divieto di sosta
cleavage ['kli:vɪdʒ] *n* (*of woman*) scollatura
cleaver ['kli:vəʳ] *n* mannaia
clef [klɛf] *n* (*Mus*) chiave *f*
cleft [klɛft] *n* (*in rock*) crepa, fenditura
clemency ['klɛmənsɪ] *n* clemenza
clement ['klɛmənt] *adj* (*weather*) mite, clemente
clench [klɛntʃ] *vt* stringere
clergy ['klə:dʒɪ] *n* clero
clergyman ['klə:dʒɪmən] *n* ecclesiastico
clerical ['klɛrɪkl] *adj* d'impiegato; (*Rel*) clericale
clerk [klɑ:k, (*US*) klə:rk] *n* impiegato(-a); (*US: salesman/woman*) commesso(-a); **C~ of the Court** (*Law*) cancelliere *m*
clever ['klɛvəʳ] *adj* (*mentally*) intelligente; (*deft, skilful*) abile; (*device, arrangement*) ingegnoso(-a)
cleverly ['klɛvəlɪ] *adv* abilmente
clew [klu:] *n* (*US*) = **clue**
cliché ['kli:ʃeɪ] *n* cliché *m inv*
click [klɪk] *vi* scattare ■ *vt*: **to ~ one's tongue** schioccare la lingua; **to ~ one's heels** battere i tacchi
clickable ['klɪkəbl] *adj* cliccabile
client ['klaɪənt] *n* cliente *m/f*
clientele [kli:ɑ̃:n'tɛl] *n* clientela
cliff [klɪf] *n* scogliera scoscesa, rupe *f*
cliffhanger ['klɪfhæŋəʳ] *n* (*TV, fig*) episodio (*or* situazione *etc*) ricco(-a) di suspense
climactic [klaɪ'mæktɪk] *adj* culminante
climate ['klaɪmɪt] *n* clima *m*
climate change *n* cambiamenti *mpl* climatici
climax ['klaɪmæks] *n* culmine *m*; (*of play etc*) momento più emozionante; (*sexual climax*) orgasmo
climb [klaɪm] *vi* salire; (*clamber*) arrampicarsi; (*plane*) prendere quota ■ *vt* salire; (*Climbing*) scalare ■ *n* salita; arrampicata; scalata; **to ~ over a wall** scavalcare un muro
▸ **climb down** *vi* scendere; (*Brit fig*) far marcia indietro
climbdown ['klaɪmdaun] *n* (*Brit*) ritirata
climber ['klaɪməʳ] *n* (*also*: **rock climber**) rocciatore(-trice); alpinista *m/f*
climbing ['klaɪmɪŋ] *n* (*also*: **rock climbing**) alpinismo
clinch [klɪntʃ] *vt* (*deal*) concludere
clincher ['klɪntʃəʳ] *n* (*col*): **that was the ~** quello è stato il fattore decisivo
cling (*pt, pp* **clung**) [klɪŋ, klʌŋ] *vi*: **to ~ (to)** tenersi stretto(-a) (a); (*clothes*) aderire strettamente (a)
clingfilm ['klɪŋfɪlm] *n* pellicola trasparente (*per alimenti*)
clinic ['klɪnɪk] *n* clinica; (*session*) seduta, serie *f* di sedute
clinical ['klɪnɪkəl] *adj* clinico(-a); (*fig*) freddo(-a), distaccato(-a)

clink [klɪŋk] *vi* tintinnare
clip [klɪp] *n* (*for hair*) forcina; (*also*: **paper clip**) graffetta; (*Brit*: *also*: **bulldog clip**) fermafogli *m inv*; (*holding hose etc*) anello d'attacco ■ *vt* (*also*: **clip together**: *papers*) attaccare insieme; (*hair, nails*) tagliare; (*hedge*) tosare
clippers ['klɪpəz] *npl* macchinetta per capelli; (*also*: **nail clippers**) forbicine *fpl* per le unghie
clipping ['klɪpɪŋ] *n* (*from newspaper*) ritaglio
clique [kli:k] *n* cricca
cloak [kləuk] *n* mantello ■ *vt* avvolgere
cloakroom ['kləukrum] *n* (*for coats etc*) guardaroba *m inv*; (*Brit*: *W.C.*) gabinetti *mpl*
clock [klɔk] *n* orologio; (*of taxi*) tassametro; **around the ~** ventiquattr'ore su ventiquattro; **to sleep round the ~** *or* **the ~ round** dormire un giorno intero; **to work against the ~** lavorare in gara col tempo; **30,000 on the ~** (*Brit Aut*) 30.000 sul contachilometri
▸ **clock in, clock on** *vi* (*Brit*) timbrare il cartellino (all'entrata)
▸ **clock off, clock out** *vi* (*Brit*) timbrare il cartellino (all'uscita)
▸ **clock up** *vt* (*miles, hours etc*) fare
clockwise ['klɔkwaɪz] *adv* in senso orario
clockwork ['klɔkwə:k] *n* movimento *or* meccanismo a orologeria ■ *adj* (*toy, train*) a molla
clog [klɔg] *n* zoccolo ■ *vt* intasare ■ *vi* intasarsi, bloccarsi
cloister ['klɔɪstə^r] *n* chiostro
clone [kləun] *n* clone *m* ■ *vt* clonare
close[1] [kləus] *adj* vicino(-a); (*writing, texture*) fitto(-a); (*watch*) stretto(-a); (*examination*) attento(-a); (*weather*) afoso(-a) ■ *adv* vicino, dappresso; **~ to** *prep* vicino a; **~ by, ~ at hand** qui (*or* lì) vicino; **how ~ is Edinburgh to Glasgow?** quanto dista Edimburgo da Glasgow?; **a ~ friend** un amico intimo; **to have a ~ shave** (*fig*) scamparla bella; **at ~ quarters** da vicino
close[2] [kləuz] *vt* chiudere; (*bargain, deal*) concludere ■ *vi* (*shop etc*) chiudere; (*lid, door etc*) chiudersi; (*end*) finire ■ *n* (*end*) fine *f*; **to bring sth to a ~** terminare qc
▸ **close down** *vt* chiudere (definitivamente) ■ *vi* cessare (definitivamente)
▸ **close in** *vi* (*hunters*) stringersi attorno; (*evening, night, fog*) calare; **to ~ in on sb** accerchiare qn; **the days are closing in** le giornate si accorciano
▸ **close off** *vt* (*area*) chiudere
closed [kləuzd] *adj* chiuso(-a)
closed-circuit ['kləuzd'sə:kɪt] *adj*: **~ television** televisione *f* a circuito chiuso
closed shop *n azienda o fabbrica che impiega solo aderenti ai sindacati*
close-knit ['kləus'nɪt] *adj* (*family, community*) molto unito(-a)
closely ['kləuslɪ] *adv* (*examine, watch*) da vicino; **we are ~ related** siamo parenti stretti; **a ~ guarded secret** un assoluto segreto
close season ['kləuz-] *n* (*Football*) periodo di vacanza del campionato; (*Hunting*) stagione *f* di chiusura (*di caccia, pesca etc*)
closet ['klɔzɪt] *n* (*cupboard*) armadio
close-up ['kləusʌp] *n* primo piano
closing ['kləuzɪŋ] *adj* (*stages, remarks*) conclusivo(-a), finale; **~ price** (*Stock Exchange*) prezzo di chiusura
closing time *n* orario di chiusura
closure ['kləuʒə^r] *n* chiusura
clot [klɔt] *n* (*also*: **blood clot**) coagulo; (*col*: *idiot*) scemo(-a) ■ *vi* coagularsi
cloth [klɔθ] *n* (*material*) tessuto, stoffa; (*Brit*: *also*: **teacloth**) strofinaccio; (*also*: **tablecloth**) tovaglia
clothe [kləuð] *vt* vestire
clothes [kləuðz] *npl* abiti *mpl*, vestiti *mpl*; **to put one's ~ on** vestirsi; **to take one's ~ off** togliersi i vestiti, svestirsi
clothes brush *n* spazzola per abiti
clothes line *n* corda (per stendere il bucato)
clothes peg, (*US*) **clothes pin** *n* molletta
clothing ['kləuðɪŋ] *n* = **clothes**
clotted cream ['klɔtɪd-] *n* (*Brit*) panna rappresa
cloud [klaud] *n* nuvola; (*of dust, smoke, gas*) nube *f* ■ *vt* (*liquid*) intorbidire; **to ~ the issue** distogliere dal problema; **every ~ has a silver lining** (*proverb*) non tutto il male vien per nuocere
▸ **cloud over** *vi* rannuvolarsi; (*fig*) offuscarsi
cloudburst ['klaudbə:st] *n* acquazzone *m*
cloud-cuckoo-land ['klaud'kuku:'lænd] *n* (*Brit*) mondo dei sogni
cloudy ['klaudɪ] *adj* nuvoloso(-a); (*liquid*) torbido(-a)
clout [klaut] *n* (*blow*) colpo; (*fig*) influenza ■ *vt* dare un colpo a
clove [kləuv] *n* chiodo di garofano; **~ of garlic** spicchio d'aglio
clover ['kləuvə^r] *n* trifoglio
cloverleaf ['kləuvəli:f] *n* foglia di trifoglio; (*Aut*) raccordo (a quadrifoglio)
clown [klaun] *n* pagliaccio ■ *vi* (*also*: **clown about, clown around**) fare il pagliaccio
cloying ['klɔɪɪŋ] *adj* (*taste, smell*) nauseabondo(-a)
club [klʌb] *n* (*society*) club *m inv*, circolo; (*weapon, Golf*) mazza ■ *vt* bastonare ■ *vi*:

to ~ together associarsi; **clubs** *npl* (*Cards*) fiori *mpl*

club car *n* (*US Rail*) carrozza *or* vagone *m* ristorante

club class *n* (*Aviat*) classe *f* club

clubhouse ['klʌbhaus] *n* sede *f* del circolo

club soda *n* (*US*) = **soda**

cluck [klʌk] *vi* chiocciare

clue [klu:] *n* indizio; (*in crosswords*) definizione *f*; **I haven't a ~** non ho la minima idea

clued up, (*US*) **clued in** [klu:d-] *adj* (*col*) (ben) informato(-a)

clump [klʌmp] *n*: **~ of trees** folto d'alberi

clumsy ['klʌmzɪ] *adj* (*person*) goffo(-a), maldestro(-a); (*object*) malfatto(-a), mal costruito(-a)

clung [klʌŋ] *pt, pp of* **cling**

cluster ['klʌstəʳ] *n* gruppo ■ *vi* raggrupparsi

clutch [klʌtʃ] *n* (*grip, grasp*) presa, stretta; (*Aut*) frizione *f* ■ *vt* afferrare, stringere forte; **to ~ at** aggrapparsi a

clutter ['klʌtəʳ] *vt* (*also:* **clutter up**) ingombrare ■ *n* confusione *f*, disordine *m*

cm *abbr* (= *centimetre*) cm

CNAA *n abbr* (*Brit:* = *Council for National Academic Awards*) *organizzazione che conferisce premi accademici*

CND *n abbr* (*Brit*) = **Campaign for Nuclear Disarmament**

CO *n abbr* (= *commanding officer*) Com.; (*Brit*) = **Commonwealth Office** ■ *abbr* (*US*) = **Colorado**

Co. *abbr* = **county**; (= *company*) C., C.ia

c/o *abbr* (= *care of*) c/o

coach [kəutʃ] *n* (*bus*) pullman *m inv*; (*horse-drawn, of train*) carrozza; (*Sport*) allenatore(-trice) ■ *vt* allenare

coach trip *n* viaggio in pullman

coagulate [kəu'ægjuleɪt] *vt* coagulare ■ *vi* coagularsi

coal [kəul] *n* carbone *m*

coalface ['kəulfeɪs] *n* fronte *f*

coalfield ['kəulfi:ld] *n* bacino carbonifero

coalition [kəuə'lɪʃən] *n* coalizione *f*

coalman ['kəulmən] *n* negoziante *m* di carbone

coalmine ['kəulmaɪn] *n* miniera di carbone

coalminer ['kəulmaɪnəʳ] *n* minatore *m*

coalmining ['kəulmaɪnɪŋ] *n* estrazione *f* del carbone

coarse [kɔ:s] *adj* (*salt, sand etc*) grosso(-a); (*cloth, person*) rozzo(-a); (*vulgar: character, laugh*) volgare

coast [kəust] *n* costa ■ *vi* (*with cycle etc*) scendere a ruota libera

coastal ['kəustəl] *adj* costiero(-a)

coaster ['kəustəʳ] *n* (*Naut*) nave *f* da cabotaggio; (*for glass*) sottobicchiere *m*

coastguard ['kəustgɑ:d] *n* guardia costiera

coastline ['kəustlaɪn] *n* linea costiera

coat [kəut] *n* cappotto; (*of animal*) pelo; (*of paint*) mano *f* ■ *vt* coprire; **~ of arms** *n* stemma *m*

coat hanger *n* attaccapanni *m inv*

coating ['kəutɪŋ] *n* rivestimento

co-author ['kəu'ɔ:θəʳ] *n* coautore(-trice)

coax [kəuks] *vt* indurre (con moine)

cob [kɔb] *n see* **corn**

cobbler ['kɔbləʳ] *n* calzolaio

cobbles ['kɔblz], **cobblestones** ['kɔblstəunz] *npl* ciottoli *mpl*

COBOL ['kəubɔl] *n* COBOL *m*

cobra ['kəubrə] *n* cobra *m inv*

cobweb ['kɔbwɛb] *n* ragnatela

cocaine [kə'keɪn] *n* cocaina

cock [kɔk] *n* (*rooster*) gallo; (*male bird*) maschio ■ *vt* (*gun*) armare; **to ~ one's ears** (*fig*) drizzare le orecchie

cock-a-hoop [kɔkə'hu:p] *adj* euforico(-a)

cockerel ['kɔkərəl] *n* galletto

cock-eyed ['kɔkaɪd] *adj* (*fig*) storto(-a); strampalato(-a)

cockle ['kɔkl] *n* cardio

cockney ['kɔknɪ] *n* cockney *m/f inv* (*abitante dei quartieri popolari dell'East End di Londra*)

cockpit ['kɔkpɪt] *n* abitacolo

cockroach ['kɔkrəutʃ] *n* blatta

cocktail ['kɔkteɪl] *n* cocktail *m inv*; **prawn ~**, (*US*) **shrimp ~** cocktail *m inv* di gamberetti

cocktail cabinet *n* mobile *m* bar *inv*

cocktail party *n* cocktail *m inv*

cocktail shaker *n* shaker *m inv*

cocky ['kɔkɪ] *adj* spavaldo(-a), arrogante

cocoa ['kəukəu] *n* cacao

coconut ['kəukənʌt] *n* noce *f* di cocco

cocoon [kə'ku:n] *n* bozzolo

COD *abbr* = **cash on delivery**; (*US*) = **collect on delivery**

cod [kɔd] *n* merluzzo

code [kəud] *n* codice *m*; **~ of behaviour** regole *fpl* di condotta; **~ of practice** codice professionale

codeine ['kəudi:n] *n* codeina

codger ['kɔdʒəʳ] *n* (*Brit col*): **an old ~** un simpatico nonnetto

codicil ['kɔdɪsɪl] *n* codicillo

codify ['kəudɪfaɪ] *vt* codificare

cod-liver oil ['kɔdlɪvəʳ-] *n* olio di fegato di merluzzo

co-driver ['kəu'draɪvəʳ] *n* (*in race*) copilota *m*; (*of lorry*) secondo autista *m*

co-ed ['kəu'ɛd] *adj abbr* = **coeducational** ■ *n abbr* (*US: female student*) *studentessa presso un'università mista*; (*Brit: school*) scuola mista

coeducational [ˈkəuɛdjuˈkeɪʃənl] *adj* misto(-a)
coerce [kəuˈəːs] *vt* costringere
coercion [kəuˈəːʃən] *n* coercizione *f*
coexistence [ˈkəuɪgˈzɪstəns] *n* coesistenza
C. of C. *n abbr* = **chamber of commerce**
C of E *abbr* = **Church of England**
coffee [ˈkɔfɪ] *n* caffè *m inv*; **white ~**, (*US*) **~ with cream** caffellatte *m*
coffee bar *n* (*Brit*) caffè *m inv*
coffee bean *n* grano *or* chicco di caffè
coffee break *n* pausa per il caffè
coffeecake [ˈkɔfɪkeɪk] *n* (*US*) panino dolce all'uva
coffee cup *n* tazzina da caffè
coffeepot [ˈkɔfɪpɔt] *n* caffettiera
coffee table *n* tavolino da tè
coffin [ˈkɔfɪn] *n* bara
C of I *abbr* = **Church of Ireland**
C of S *abbr* = **Church of Scotland**
cog [kɔg] *n* dente *m*
cogent [ˈkəudʒənt] *adj* convincente
cognac [ˈkɔnjæk] *n* cognac *m inv*
cogwheel [ˈkɔgwiːl] *n* ruota dentata
cohabit [kəuˈhæbɪt] *vi* (*formal*): **to ~ (with sb)** coabitare (con qn)
coherent [kəuˈhɪərənt] *adj* coerente
cohesion [kəuˈhiːʒən] *n* coesione *f*
cohesive [kəuˈhiːsɪv] *adj* (*fig*) unificante, coesivo(-a)
COI *n abbr* (*Brit*) = **Central Office of Information**
coil [kɔɪl] *n* rotolo; (*one loop*) anello; (*Aut, Elec*) bobina; (*contraceptive*) spirale *f*; (*of smoke*) filo ▪ *vt* avvolgere
coin [kɔɪn] *n* moneta ▪ *vt* (*word*) coniare
coinage [ˈkɔɪnɪdʒ] *n* sistema *m* monetario
coin-box [ˈkɔɪnbɔks] *n* (*Brit*) cabina telefonica
coincide [kəuɪnˈsaɪd] *vi* coincidere
coincidence [kəuˈɪnsɪdəns] *n* combinazione *f*
coin-operated [ˈkɔɪnˈɔpəreɪtɪd] *adj* (*machine*) (che funziona) a monete
Coke® [kəuk] *n* (*Coca-Cola*) coca *f inv*
coke [kəuk] *n* coke *m*
Col. *abbr* = **colonel**; (*US*) = **Colorado**
COLA *n abbr* (*US*: = *cost-of-living adjustment*) ≈ scala mobile
colander [ˈkɔləndəʳ] *n* colino
cold [kəuld] *adj* freddo(-a) ▪ *n* freddo; (*Med*) raffreddore *m*; **it's ~** fa freddo; **to be ~** aver freddo; **to catch ~** prendere freddo; **to catch a ~** prendere un raffreddore; **in ~ blood** a sangue freddo; **to have ~ feet** avere i piedi freddi; (*fig*) aver la fifa; **to give sb the ~ shoulder** ignorare qn
cold-blooded [kəuldˈblʌdɪd] *adj* (*Zool*) a sangue freddo
cold call *n* chiamata pubblicitaria non richiesta
cold cream *n* crema emolliente
coldly [ˈkəuldlɪ] *adv* freddamente
cold sore *n* erpete *m*
cold sweat *n*: **to be in a ~ (about sth)** sudare freddo (per qc)
cold turkey *n* (*col*): **to go ~** avere la scimmia (*drogato*)
Cold War *n*: **the ~** la guerra fredda
coleslaw [ˈkəulslɔː] *n* *insalata di cavolo bianco*
colic [ˈkɔlɪk] *n* colica
colicky [ˈkɔlɪkɪ] *adj* che soffre di coliche
collaborate [kəˈlæbəreɪt] *vi* collaborare
collaboration [kəlæbəˈreɪʃən] *n* collaborazione *f*
collaborator [kəˈlæbəreɪtəʳ] *n* collaboratore(-trice)
collage [kɔˈlɑːʒ] *n* (*Art*) collage *m inv*
collagen [ˈkɔlədʒən] *n* collageno
collapse [kəˈlæps] *vi* (*gen*) crollare; (*government*) cadere; (*Med*) avere un collasso; (*plans*) fallire ▪ *n* crollo; caduta; collasso; fallimento
collapsible [kəˈlæpsəbl] *adj* pieghevole
collar [ˈkɔləʳ] *n* (*of coat, shirt*) colletto; (*for dog*) collare *m*; (*Tech*) anello, fascetta ▪ *vt* (*col*: *person, object*) beccare
collarbone [ˈkɔləbəun] *n* clavicola
collate [kɔˈleɪt] *vt* collazionare
collateral [kɔˈlætərəl] *n* garanzia
collation [kɔˈleɪʃən] *n* collazione *f*
colleague [ˈkɔliːg] *n* collega *m/f*
collect [kəˈlɛkt] *vt* (*gen*) raccogliere; (*as a hobby*) fare collezione di; (*Brit*: *call for*) prendere; (*money owed, pension*) riscuotere; (*donations, subscriptions*) fare una colletta di ▪ *vi* (*people*) adunarsi, riunirsi; (*rubbish etc*) ammucchiarsi ▪ *adv* (*US Tel*): **to call ~** fare una chiamata a carico del destinatario; **to ~ one's thoughts** raccogliere le idee; **~ on delivery** (*US Comm*) pagamento alla consegna
collected [kəˈlɛktɪd] *adj*: **~ works** opere *fpl* raccolte
collection [kəˈlɛkʃən] *n* collezione *f*; raccolta; (*for money*) colletta; (*Post*) levata
collective [kəˈlɛktɪv] *adj* collettivo(-a) ▪ *n* collettivo
collective bargaining *n* trattative *fpl* (sindacali) collettive
collector [kəˈlɛktəʳ] *n* collezionista *m/f*; (*of taxes*) esattore *m*; **~'s item** *or* **piece** pezzo da collezionista
college [ˈkɔlɪdʒ] *n* (*Scol*) college *m inv*; (*of technology, agriculture etc*) istituto superiore; (*body*) collegio; **~ of education** ≈ facoltà *f inv* di Magistero

collide [kə'laɪd] *vi*: **to ~ (with)** scontrarsi (con)
collie ['kɔlɪ] *n* (*dog*) collie *m inv*
colliery ['kɔlɪərɪ] *n* (*Brit*) miniera di carbone
collision [kə'lɪʒən] *n* collisione *f*, scontro; **to be on a ~ course** (*also fig*) essere in rotta di collisione
collision damage waiver *n* (*Insurance*) *copertura per i danni alla vettura*
colloquial [kə'ləukwɪəl] *adj* familiare
collusion [kə'luːʒən] *n* collusione *f*; **in ~ with** in accordo segreto con
Colo. *abbr* (*US*) = **Colorado**
Cologne [kə'ləun] *n* Colonia
cologne [kə'ləun] *n* (*also*: **eau de cologne**) acqua di colonia
Colombia [kə'lɔmbɪə] *n* Colombia
Colombian [kə'lɔmbɪən] *adj, n* colombiano(-a)
colon ['kəulən] *n* (*sign*) due punti *mpl*; (*Med*) colon *m inv*
colonel ['kəːnl] *n* colonnello
colonial [kə'ləunɪəl] *adj* coloniale
colonize ['kɔlənaɪz] *vt* colonizzare
colony ['kɔlənɪ] *n* colonia
color *etc* ['kʌlə^r] (*US*) = **colour** *etc*
Colorado beetle [kɔlə'rɑːdəu-] *n* dorifora
colossal [kə'lɔsl] *adj* colossale
colour, (*US*) **color** ['kʌlə^r] *n* colore *m* ■ *vt* colorare; (*tint, dye*) tingere; (*fig: affect*) influenzare ■ *vi* arrossire ■ *cpd* (*film, photograph, television*) a colori; **colours** *npl* (*of party, club*) emblemi *mpl*
colour bar, (*US*) **color bar** *n* discriminazione *f* razziale (*in locali etc*)
colour-blind, (*US*) **color-blind** ['kʌləblaɪnd] *adj* daltonico(-a)
coloured, (*US*) **colored** ['kʌləd] *adj* colorato(-a); (*photo*) a colori ■ *n*: **colo(u)reds** gente *f* di colore
colour film, (*US*) **color film** *n* (*for camera*) pellicola a colori
colourful, (*US*) **colorful** ['kʌləful] *adj* pieno(-a) di colore, a vivaci colori; (*personality*) colorato(-a)
colouring, (*US*) **coloring** ['kʌlərɪŋ] *n* colorazione *f*; (*complexion*) colorito
colour scheme, (*US*) **color scheme** combinazione *f* di colori
colour supplement *n* (*Brit Press*) supplemento a colori
colour television, (*US*) **color television** *n* televisione *f* a colori
colt [kəult] *n* puledro
column ['kɔləm] *n* colonna; (*fashion column, sports column etc*) rubrica; **the editorial ~** l'articolo di fondo
columnist ['kɔləmnɪst] *n* articolista *m/f*
coma ['kəumə] *n* coma *m inv*
comb [kəum] *n* pettine *m* ■ *vt* (*hair*) pettinare; (*area*) battere a tappeto
combat ['kɔmbæt] *n* combattimento ■ *vt* combattere, lottare contro
combination [kɔmbɪ'neɪʃən] *n* combinazione *f*
combination lock *n* serratura a combinazione
combine [kəm'baɪn] *vt* combinare; (*one quality with another*): **to ~ sth with sth** unire qc a qc ■ *vi* unirsi; (*Chem*) combinarsi ■ *n* ['kɔmbaɪn] lega; (*Econ*) associazione *f*; **a combined effort** uno sforzo collettivo
combine, combine harvester *n* mietitrebbia
combo ['kɔmbəu] *n* (*Jazz etc*) gruppo
combustible [kəm'bʌstɪbl] *adj* combustibile
combustion [kəm'bʌstʃən] *n* combustione *f*
come (*pt* **came**, *pp* **~**) [kʌm, keɪm] *vi* venire; (*arrive*) venire, arrivare; **~ with me** vieni con me; **we've just ~ from Paris** siamo appena arrivati da Parigi; **nothing came of it** non è saltato fuori niente; **to ~ into sight** *or* **view** apparire; **to ~ to** (*decision etc*) raggiungere; **to ~ undone/loose** slacciarsi/allentarsi; **coming!** vengo!; **if it comes to it** nella peggiore delle ipotesi
▸ **come about** *vi* succedere
▸ **come across** *vt fus* trovare per caso ■ *vi*: **to ~ across well/badly** fare una buona/cattiva impressione
▸ **come along** *vi* (*pupil, work*) fare progressi; **~ along!** avanti!, andiamo!, forza!
▸ **come apart** *vi* andare in pezzi; (*become detached*) staccarsi
▸ **come away** *vi* venire via; (*become detached*) staccarsi
▸ **come back** *vi* ritornare; (*reply: col*): **can I ~ back to you on that one?** possiamo riparlarne più tardi?
▸ **come by** *vt fus* (*acquire*) ottenere; procurarsi
▸ **come down** *vi* scendere; (*prices*) calare; (*buildings*) essere demolito(-a)
▸ **come forward** *vi* farsi avanti; presentarsi
▸ **come from** *vt fus* venire da; provenire da
▸ **come in** *vi* entrare
▸ **come in for** *vt fus* (*criticism etc*) ricevere
▸ **come into** *vt fus* (*money*) ereditare
▸ **come off** *vi* (*button*) staccarsi; (*stain*) andar via; (*attempt*) riuscire
▸ **come on** *vi* (*lights, electricity*) accendersi; (*pupil, undertaking*) fare progressi; **~ on!** avanti!, andiamo!, forza!
▸ **come out** *vi* uscire; (*strike*) entrare in sciopero

▸ **come over** *vt fus*: **I don't know what's ~ over him!** non so cosa gli sia successo!
▸ **come round** *vi* (*after faint, operation*) riprendere conoscenza, rinvenire
▸ **come through** *vi* (*survive*) sopravvivere, farcela; **the call came through** ci hanno passato la telefonata
▸ **come to** *vi* rinvenire ■ *vt* (*add up to: amount*): **how much does it ~ to?** quanto costa?, quanto viene?
▸ **come under** *vt fus* (*heading*) trovarsi sotto; (*influence*) cadere sotto, subire
▸ **come up** *vi* venire su
▸ **come up against** *vt fus* (*resistance, difficulties*) urtare contro
▸ **come up to** *vt fus* arrivare (fino) a; **the film didn't ~ up to our expectations** il film ci ha delusi
▸ **come up with** *vt fus*: **he came up with an idea** venne fuori con un'idea
▸ **come upon** *vt fus* trovare per caso
comeback ['kʌmbæk] *n* (*Theat etc*) ritorno; (*reaction*) reazione *f*; (*response*) risultato, risposta
comedian [kə'mi:dɪən] *n* comico
comedienne [kəmi:dɪ'ɛn] *n* attrice *f* comica
comedown ['kʌmdaun] *n* rovescio
comedy ['kɔmɪdɪ] *n* commedia
comet ['kɔmɪt] *n* cometa
comeuppance [kʌm'ʌpəns] *n*: **to get one's ~** ricevere ciò che si merita
comfort ['kʌmfət] *n* comodità *f inv*, benessere *m*; (*solace*) consolazione *f*, conforto ■ *vt* consolare, confortare; *see also* **comforts**
comfortable ['kʌmfətəbl] *adj* comodo(-a); (*income, majority*) più che sufficiente; **I don't feel very ~ about it** non mi sento molto tranquillo
comfortably ['kʌmfətəblɪ] *adv* (*sit*) comodamente; (*live*) bene
comforter ['kʌmfətə^r] *n* (*US*) trapunta
comforts ['kʌmfəts] *npl* comforts *mpl*, comodità *fpl*
comfort station *n* (*US*) gabinetti *mpl*
comic ['kɔmɪk] *adj* comico(-a) ■ *n* comico; (*magazine*) giornaletto
comical ['kɔmɪkl] *adj* divertente, buffo(-a)
comic strip *n* fumetto
coming ['kʌmɪŋ] *n* arrivo ■ *adj* (*next*) prossimo(-a); (*future*) futuro(-a); **in the ~ weeks** nelle prossime settimane
comings and goings *npl*, **coming and going** *n* andirivieni *m inv*
Comintern ['kɔmɪntə:n] *n* KOMINTERN *m*
comma ['kɔmə] *n* virgola
command [kə'mɑ:nd] *n* ordine *m*, comando; (*Mil: authority*) comando; (*mastery*) padronanza; (*Comput*) command *m inv*, comando ■ *vt* comandare; **to ~ sb to do** ordinare a qn di fare; **to have/take ~ of** avere/prendere il comando di; **to have at one's ~** (*money, resources etc*) avere a propria disposizione
command economy *n* = **planned economy**
commandeer [kɔmən'dɪə^r] *vt* requisire
commander [kə'mɑ:ndə^r] *n* capo; (*Mil*) comandante *m*
commander-in-chief [kə'mɑ:ndərɪn'tʃi:f] *n* (*Mil*) comandante *m* in capo
commanding [kə'mɑ:ndɪŋ] *adj* (*appearance*) imponente; (*voice, tone*) autorevole; (*lead, position*) dominante
commanding officer *n* comandante *m*
commandment [kə'mɑ:ndmənt] *n* (*Rel*) comandamento
command module *n* (*Space*) modulo di comando
commando [kə'mɑ:ndəu] *n* commando *m inv*; membro di un commando
commemorate [kə'mɛməreɪt] *vt* commemorare
commemoration [kəmɛmə'reɪʃən] *n* commemorazione *f*
commemorative [kə'mɛmərətɪv] *adj* commemorativo(-a)
commence [kə'mɛns] *vt, vi* cominciare
commend [kə'mɛnd] *vt* lodare; raccomandare
commendable [kə'mɛndəbl] *adj* lodevole
commendation [kɔmɛn'deɪʃən] *n* lode *f*; raccomandazione *f*; (*for bravery etc*) encomio
commensurate [kə'mɛnʃərɪt] *adj*: **~ with** proporzionato(-a) a
comment ['kɔmɛnt] *n* commento ■ *vi*: **to ~ (on)** fare commenti (su); **to ~ that** osservare che; **"no ~"** "niente da dire"
commentary ['kɔməntərɪ] *n* commentario; (*Sport*) radiocronaca; telecronaca
commentator ['kɔmənteɪtə^r] *n* commentatore(-trice); (*Sport*) radiocronista *m/f*; telecronista *m/f*
commerce ['kɔmə:s] *n* commercio
commercial [kə'mə:ʃəl] *adj* commerciale ■ *n* (*TV*: *also*: **commercial break**) pubblicità *f inv*
commercial bank *n* banca commerciale
commercial college *n* ≈ istituto commerciale
commercialism [kə'mə:ʃəlɪzəm] *n* affarismo
commercial television *n* televisione *f* commerciale
commercial traveller *n* commesso viaggiatore
commercial vehicle *n* veicolo commerciale
commiserate [kə'mɪzəreɪt] *vi*: **to ~ with**

condolersi con
commission [kə'mɪʃən] *n* commissione *f*; (*for salesman*) commissione, provvigione *f* ■ *vt* (*Mil*) nominare (al comando); (*work of art*) commissionare; **I get 10% ~** ricevo il 10% sulle vendite; **out of ~** (*Naut*) in disarmo; (*machine*) fuori uso; **to ~ sb to do sth** incaricare qn di fare qc; **to ~ sth from sb** (*painting etc*) commissionare qc a qn; **~ of inquiry** (*Brit*) commissione *f* d'inchiesta
commissionaire [kəmɪʃə'nɛəʳ] *n* (*Brit: at shop, cinema etc*) portiere *m* in livrea
commissioner [kə'mɪʃənəʳ] *n* commissionario; (*Police*) questore *m*
commit [kə'mɪt] *vt* (*act*) commettere; (*to sb's care*) affidare; **to ~ o.s. (to do)** impegnarsi (a fare); **to ~ suicide** suicidarsi; **to ~ sb for trial** rinviare qn a giudizio
commitment [kə'mɪtmənt] *n* impegno
committed [kə'mɪtɪd] *adj* (*writer*) impegnato(-a); (*Christian*) convinto(-a)
committee [kə'mɪtɪ] *n* comitato; **to be on a ~** far parte di un comitato *or* di una commissione
committee meeting *n* riunione *f* di comitato *or* di commissione
commodity [kə'mɔdɪtɪ] *n* prodotto, articolo; (*food*) derrata
commodity exchange *n* borsa *f* merci *inv*
common ['kɔmən] *adj* comune; (*pej*) volgare; (*usual*) normale ■ *n* terreno comune; **in ~** in comune; **in ~ use** di uso comune; **it's ~ knowledge that** è di dominio pubblico che; **to the ~ good** nell'interesse generale, per il bene comune; *see also* **Commons**
common cold *n*: **the ~** il raffreddore
common denominator *n* denominatore *m* comune
commoner ['kɔmənəʳ] *n* cittadino(-a) (non nobile)
common ground *n* (*fig*) terreno comune
common land *n* terreno di uso pubblico
common law *n* diritto consuetudinario
common-law ['kɔmənlɔː] *adj*: **~ wife** convivente *f* more uxorio
commonly ['kɔmənlɪ] *adv* comunemente, usualmente
Common Market *n* Mercato Comune
commonplace ['kɔmənpleɪs] *adj* banale, ordinario(-a)
commonroom ['kɔmənrum] *n* sala di riunione; (*Scol*) sala dei professori
Commons ['kɔmənz] *npl* (*Brit Pol*): **the (House of) ~** la Camera dei Comuni
common sense *n* buon senso
Commonwealth ['kɔmənwɛlθ] *n*: **the ~** il Commonwealth; *vedi nota*

COMMONWEALTH

Il *Commonwealth* è un'associazione di stati sovrani indipendenti e di alcuni territori annessi che facevano parte dell'antico Impero Britannico. Ancora oggi molti stati del Commonwealth riconoscono simbolicamente il sovrano brittanico come capo di stato, e i loro rappresentanti si riuniscono per discutere questioni di comune interesse.

commotion [kə'məuʃən] *n* confusione *f*, tumulto
communal ['kɔmjuːnl] *adj* (*life*) comunale; (*for common use*) pubblico(-a)
commune *n* ['kɔmjuːn] (*group*) comune *f* ■ *vi* [kə'mjuːn]: **to ~ with** mettersi in comunione con
communicate [kə'mjuːnɪkeɪt] *vt* comunicare, trasmettere ■ *vi*: **to ~ (with)** comunicare (con)
communication [kəmjuːnɪ'keɪʃən] *n* comunicazione *f*
communication cord *n* (*Brit*) segnale *m* d'allarme
communications network *n* rete *f* delle comunicazioni
communications satellite *n* satellite *m* per telecomunicazioni
communicative [kə'mjuːnɪkətɪv] *adj* (*gen*) loquace
communion [kə'mjuːnɪən] *n* (*also*: **Holy Communion**) comunione *f*
communiqué [kə'mjuːnɪkeɪ] *n* comunicato
communism ['kɔmjunɪzəm] *n* comunismo
communist ['kɔmjunɪst] *adj, n* comunista (*m/f*)
community [kə'mjuːnɪtɪ] *n* comunità *f inv*
community centre *n* circolo ricreativo
community chest *n* (*US*) fondo di beneficenza
community health centre *n* centro socio-sanitario
community home *n* (*Brit*) riformatorio
community service *n* (*Brit*) ≈ lavoro sostitutivo
community spirit *n* spirito civico
commutation ticket [kɔmju'teɪʃən-] *n* (*US*) biglietto di abbonamento
commute [kə'mjuːt] *vi* fare il pendolare ■ *vt* (*Law*) commutare
commuter [kə'mjuːtəʳ] *n* pendolare *m/f*
compact *adj* [kəm'pækt] compatto(-a) ■ *n* ['kɔmpækt] (*also*: **powder compact**) portacipria *m inv*
compact disc *n* compact disc *m inv*; **~ player** lettore *m* CD *inv*

companion [kəm'pænjən] *n* compagno(-a)
companionship [kəm'pænjənʃɪp] *n* compagnia
companionway [kəm'pænjənweɪ] *n* (*Naut*) scala
company ['kʌmpənɪ] *n* (*also Comm, Mil, Theat*) compagnia; **he's good ~** è di buona compagnia; **we have ~** abbiamo ospiti; **to keep sb ~** tenere compagnia a qn; **to part ~ with** separarsi da; **Smith and C~** Smith e soci
company car *n* macchina (di proprietà) della ditta
company director *n* amministratore *m*, consigliere *m* di amministrazione
company secretary *n* (*Brit Comm*) segretario(-a) generale
comparable ['kɔmpərəbl] *adj* comparabile
comparative [kəm'pærətɪv] *adj* (*freedom, cost*) relativo(-a); (*adjective, adverb etc*) comparativo(-a); (*literature*) comparato(-a)
comparatively [kəm'pærətɪvlɪ] *adv* relativamente
compare [kəm'pɛə^r] *vt*: **to ~ sth/sb with/to** confrontare qc/qn con/a ■ *vi*: **to ~ (with)** reggere il confronto (con); **compared with** *or* **to** a paragone di, rispetto a; **how do the prices ~?** che differenza di prezzo c'è?
comparison [kəm'pærɪsn] *n* confronto; **in ~ (with)** a confronto (di)
compartment [kəm'pɑ:tmənt] *n* compartimento; (*Rail*) scompartimento
compass ['kʌmpəs] *n* bussola; **(a pair of) compasses** (*Math*) compasso; **within the ~ of** entro i limiti di
compassion [kəm'pæʃən] *n* compassione *f*
compassionate [kəm'pæʃənɪt] *adj* compassionevole; **on ~ grounds** per motivi personali
compassionate leave *n* congedo straordinario (*per gravi motivi di famiglia*)
compatibility [kəmpætɪ'bɪlɪtɪ] *n* compatibilità
compatible [kəm'pætɪbl] *adj* compatibile
compel [kəm'pɛl] *vt* costringere, obbligare
compelling [kəm'pɛlɪŋ] *adj* (*fig: argument*) irresistibile
compendium [kəm'pɛndɪəm] *n* compendio
compensate ['kɔmpənseɪt] *vt* risarcire ■ *vi*: **to ~ for** compensare
compensation [kɔmpən'seɪʃən] *n* compensazione *f*; (*money*) risarcimento
compère ['kɔmpɛə^r] *n* presentatore(-trice)
compete [kəm'pi:t] *vi* (*take part*) concorrere; (*vie*): **to ~ (with)** fare concorrenza (a)
competence ['kɔmpɪtəns] *n* competenza
competent ['kɔmpɪtənt] *adj* competente
competing [kəm'pi:tɪŋ] *adj* (*theories, ideas*) opposto(-a); (*companies*) in concorrenza; **three ~ explanations (of)** tre spiegazioni contrastanti tra di loro (di)
competition [kɔmpɪ'tɪʃən] *n* gara, concorso; (*Sport*) gara; (*Econ*) concorrenza; **in ~ with** in concorrenza con
competitive [kəm'pɛtɪtɪv] *adj* (*sports*) agonistico(-a); (*person*) che ha spirito di competizione; (*Econ*) concorrenziale
competitive examination *n* concorso
competitor [kəm'pɛtɪtə^r] *n* concorrente *m/f*
compile [kəm'paɪl] *vt* compilare
complacency [kəm'pleɪsnsɪ] *n* compiacenza di sé
complacent [kəm'pleɪsnt] *adj* compiaciuto(-a) di sé
complain [kəm'pleɪn] *vi*: **to ~ (about)** lagnarsi (di); (*in shop etc*) reclamare (per)
▸ **complain of** *vt fus* (*Med*) accusare
complaint [kəm'pleɪnt] *n* lamento; reclamo; (*Med*) malattia
complement *n* ['kɔmplɪmənt] complemento; (*especially of ship's crew etc*) effettivo ■ *vt* ['kɔmplɪmɛnt] (*enhance*) accompagnarsi bene a
complementary [kɔmplɪ'mɛntərɪ] *adj* complementare
complete [kəm'pli:t] *adj* completo(-a) ■ *vt* completare; (*form*) riempire; **it's a ~ disaster** è un vero disastro
completely [kəm'pli:tlɪ] *adv* completamente
completion [kəm'pli:ʃən] *n* completamento; **to be nearing ~** essere in fase di completamento; **on ~ of contract** alla firma del contratto
complex ['kɔmplɛks] *adj* complesso(-a) ■ *n* (*Psych, buildings etc*) complesso
complexion [kəm'plɛkʃən] *n* (*of face*) carnagione *f*; (*of event etc*) aspetto
complexity [kəm'plɛksɪtɪ] *n* complessità *f inv*
compliance [kəm'plaɪəns] *n* acquiescenza; **in ~ with** (*orders, wishes etc*) in conformità con
compliant [kəm'plaɪənt] *adj* acquiescente, arrendevole
complicate ['kɔmplɪkeɪt] *vt* complicare
complicated ['kɔmplɪkeɪtɪd] *adj* complicato(-a)
complication [kɔmplɪ'keɪʃən] *n* complicazione *f*
compliment *n* ['kɔmplɪmənt] complimento ■ *vt* ['kɔmplɪmɛnt] fare un complimento a; **compliments** *npl* complimenti *mpl*; rispetti *mpl*; **to pay sb a ~** fare un complimento a qn; **to ~ sb (on sth/on doing sth)** congratularsi *or* complimentarsi con qn (per qc/per aver fatto qc)
complimentary [kɔmplɪ'mɛntərɪ] *adj*

complimentoso(-a), elogiativo(-a); (*free*) in omaggio
complimentary ticket *n* biglietto d'omaggio
compliments slip *n* cartoncino della società
comply [kəm'plaɪ] *vi*: **to ~ with** assentire a; conformarsi a
component [kəm'pəunənt] *adj, n* componente (*m*)
compose [kəm'pəuz] *vt* comporre; **to ~ o.s.** ricomporsi; **composed of** composto(-a) di
composed [kəm'pəuzd] *adj* calmo(-a)
composer [kəm'pəuzə[r]] *n* (*Mus*) compositore(-trice)
composite ['kɔmpəzɪt] *adj* composito(-a); (*Math*) composto(-a)
composition [kɔmpə'zɪʃən] *n* composizione *f*
compost ['kɔmpɔst] *n* composta, concime *m*
composure [kəm'pəuʒə[r]] *n* calma
compound ['kɔmpaund] *n* (*Chem, Ling*) composto; (*enclosure*) recinto ■ *adj* composto(-a) ■ *vt* [kəm'paund] (*fig: problem, difficulty*) peggiorare
compound fracture *n* frattura esposta
compound interest *n* interesse *m* composto
comprehend [kɔmprɪ'hɛnd] *vt* comprendere, capire
comprehension [kɔmprɪ'hɛnʃən] *n* comprensione *f*
comprehensive [kɔmprɪ'hɛnsɪv] *adj* comprensivo(-a)
comprehensive insurance policy *n* polizza multi-rischio *inv*
comprehensive (school) *n* (*Brit*) *scuola secondaria aperta a tutti*
compress *vt* [kəm'prɛs] comprimere ■ *n* ['kɔmprɛs] (*Med*) compressa
compression [kəm'prɛʃən] *n* compressione *f*
comprise [kəm'praɪz] *vt* (*also:* **be comprised of**) comprendere
compromise ['kɔmprəmaɪz] *n* compromesso ■ *vt* compromettere ■ *vi* venire a un compromesso ■ *cpd* (*decision, solution*) di compromesso
compulsion [kəm'pʌlʃən] *n* costrizione *f*; **under ~** sotto pressioni
compulsive [kəm'pʌlsɪv] *adj* (*Psych*) incontrollabile; **he's a ~ smoker** non riesce a controllarsi nel fumare
compulsory [kəm'pʌlsərɪ] *adj* obbligatorio(-a)
compulsory purchase *n* espropriazione *f*
compunction [kəm'pʌŋkʃən] *n* scrupolo; **to have no ~ about doing sth** non farsi scrupoli a fare qc
computer [kəm'pju:tə[r]] *n* computer *m inv*, elaboratore *m* elettronico
computer game *n* computer game *m inv*
computerization [kəmpju:tərai'zeɪʃən] *n* computerizzazione *f*
computerize [kəm'pju:təraɪz] *vt* computerizzare
computer language *n* linguaggio *m* macchina *inv*
computer literate *adj*: **to be ~** essere in grado di usare il computer
computer peripheral *n* unità periferica
computer program *n* programma *m* di computer
computer programmer *n* programmatore(-trice)
computer programming *n* programmazione *f* di computer
computer science *n* informatica
computer scientist *n* informatico(-a)
computing [kəm'pju:tɪŋ] *n* informatica
comrade ['kɔmrɪd] *n* compagno(-a)
comradeship ['kɔmrɪdʃɪp] *n* cameratismo
Comsat® ['kɔmsæt] *n abbr* = **communications satellite**
con [kɔn] *vt* (*col*) truffare ■ *n* truffa; **to ~ sb into doing sth** indurre qn a fare qc con raggiri
concave ['kɔn'keɪv] *adj* concavo(-a)
conceal [kən'si:l] *vt* nascondere
concede [kən'si:d] *vt* concedere ■ *vi* fare una concessione
conceit [kən'si:t] *n* presunzione *f*, vanità
conceited [kən'si:tɪd] *adj* presuntuoso(-a), vanitoso(-a)
conceivable [kən'si:vəbl] *adj* concepibile; **it is ~ that ...** può anche darsi che ...
conceivably [kən'si:vəblɪ] *adv*: **he may ~ be right** può anche darsi che abbia ragione
conceive [kən'si:v] *vt* concepire ■ *vi* concepire un bambino; **to ~ of sth/of doing sth** immaginare qc/di fare qc
concentrate ['kɔnsəntreɪt] *vi* concentrarsi ■ *vt* concentrare
concentration [kɔnsən'treɪʃən] *n* concentrazione *f*
concentration camp *n* campo di concentramento
concentric [kɔn'sɛntrɪk] *adj* concentrico(-a)
concept ['kɔnsɛpt] *n* concetto
conception [kən'sɛpʃən] *n* concezione *f*; (*idea*) idea, concetto
concern [kən'sə:n] *n* affare *m*; (*Comm*) azienda, ditta; (*anxiety*) preoccupazione *f* ■ *vt* riguardare; **to be concerned (about)** preoccuparsi (di); **to be concerned with** occuparsi di; **as far as I am concerned** per quanto mi riguarda; **"to whom it may ~"** "a tutti gli interessati"; **the department**

C

concerned (*under discussion*) l'ufficio in questione; (*relevant*) l'ufficio competente
concerning [kən'sə:nɪŋ] *prep* riguardo a, circa
concert ['kɔnsət] *n* concerto; **in ~** di concerto
concerted [kən'sə:tɪd] *adj* concertato(-a)
concert hall *n* sala da concerti
concertina [kɔnsə'ti:nə] *n* piccola fisarmonica ■ *vi* ridursi come una fisarmonica
concerto [kən'tʃə:təu] *n* concerto
concession [kən'sɛʃən] *n* concessione *f*
concessionaire [kənsɛʃə'nɛəʳ] *n* concessionario
concessionary [kən'sɛʃənərɪ] *adj* (*ticket, fare*) a prezzo ridotto
conciliation [kənsɪlɪ'eɪʃən] *n* conciliazione *f*
conciliatory [kən'sɪlɪətrɪ] *adj* conciliativo(-a)
concise [kən'saɪs] *adj* conciso(-a)
conclave ['kɔnkleɪv] *n* riunione *f* segreta; (*Rel*) conclave *m*
conclude [kən'klu:d] *vt* concludere ■ *vi* (*speaker*) concludere; (*events*): **to ~ (with)** concludersi (con)
concluding [kən'klu:dɪŋ] *adj* (*remarks etc*) conclusivo(-a), finale
conclusion [kən'klu:ʒən] *n* conclusione *f*; **to come to the ~ that ...** concludere che ..., arrivare alla conclusione che ...
conclusive [kən'klu:sɪv] *adj* conclusivo(-a)
concoct [kən'kɔkt] *vt* inventare
concoction [kən'kɔkʃən] *n* (*food, drink*) miscuglio
concord ['kɔŋkɔ:d] *n* (*harmony*) armonia, concordia; (*treaty*) accordo
concourse ['kɔŋkɔ:s] *n* (*hall*) atrio
concrete ['kɔŋkri:t] *n* calcestruzzo ■ *adj* concreto(-a); (*Constr*) di calcestruzzo
concrete mixer *n* betoniera
concur [kən'kə:ʳ] *vi* concordare
concurrently [kən'kʌrntlɪ] *adv* simultaneamente
concussion [kən'kʌʃən] *n* (*Med*) commozione *f* cerebrale
condemn [kən'dɛm] *vt* condannare
condemnation [kɔndɛm'neɪʃən] *n* condanna
condensation [kɔndɛn'seɪʃən] *n* condensazione *f*
condense [kən'dɛns] *vi* condensarsi ■ *vt* condensare
condensed milk *n* latte *m* condensato
condescend [kɔndɪ'sɛnd] *vi* condiscendere; **to ~ to do sth** degnarsi di fare qc
condescending [kɔndɪ'sɛndɪŋ] *adj* condiscendente
condition [kən'dɪʃən] *n* condizione *f*; (*disease*) malattia ■ *vt* condizionare, regolare; **in good/poor ~** in buone/cattive condizioni; **to have a heart ~** soffrire di (mal di) cuore; **weather conditions** condizioni meteorologiche; **on ~ that** a condizione che *+sub*, a condizione di
conditional [kən'dɪʃənl] *adj* condizionale; **to be ~ upon** dipendere da
conditioner [kən'dɪʃənəʳ] *n* (*for hair*) balsamo
condo ['kɔndəu] *n abbr* (*US col*) = **condominium**
condolences [kən'dəulənsɪz] *npl* condoglianze *fpl*
condom ['kɔndəm] *n* preservativo
condominium [kɔndə'mɪnɪəm] *n* (*US*) condominio
condone [kən'dəun] *vt* condonare
conducive [kən'dju:sɪv] *adj*: **~ to** favorevole a
conduct *n* ['kɔndʌkt] condotta ■ *vt* [kən'dʌkt] condurre; (*manage*) dirigere; amministrare; (*Mus*) dirigere; **to ~ o.s.** comportarsi
conductor [kən'dʌktəʳ] *n* (*of orchestra*) direttore *m* d'orchestra; (*on bus*) bigliettaio; (*US Rail*) controllore *m*; (*Elec*) conduttore *m*
conductress [kən'dʌktrɪs] *n* (*on bus*) bigliettaia
conduit ['kɔndɪt] *n* condotto; tubo
cone [kəun] *n* cono; (*Bot*) pigna
confectioner [kən'fɛkʃənəʳ] *n*: **~'s (shop)** ≈ pasticceria
confectionery [kən'fɛkʃənərɪ] *n* dolciumi *mpl*
confederate [kən'fɛdərɪt] *adj* confederato(-a) ■ *n* (*pej*) complice *m/f*; (*US Hist*) confederato
confederation [kənfɛdə'reɪʃən] *n* confederazione *f*
confer [kən'fə:ʳ] *vt*: **to ~ sth on** conferire qc a ■ *vi* conferire; **to ~ (with sb about sth)** consultarsi (con qn su qc)
conference ['kɔnfərns] *n* congresso; **to be in ~** essere in riunione
conference room *n* sala *f* conferenze *inv*
confess [kən'fɛs] *vt* confessare, ammettere ■ *vi* confessarsi
confession [kən'fɛʃən] *n* confessione *f*
confessional [kən'fɛʃənl] *n* confessionale *m*
confessor [kən'fɛsəʳ] *n* confessore *m*
confetti [kən'fɛtɪ] *n* coriandoli *mpl*
confide [kən'faɪd] *vi*: **to ~ in** confidarsi con
confidence ['kɔnfɪdns] *n* confidenza; (*trust*) fiducia; (*also*: **self-confidence**) sicurezza di sé; **to tell sb sth in strict ~** dire qc a qn in via strettamente confidenziale; **to have (every) ~ that ...** essere assolutamente certo(-a) che ...; **motion of no ~** mozione *f* di sfiducia
confidence trick *n* truffa
confident ['kɔnfɪdənt] *adj* sicuro(-a); (*also*: **self-confident**) sicuro(-a) di sé
confidential [kɔnfɪ'dɛnʃəl] *adj* riservato(-a); (*secretary*) particolare

confidentiality ['kɔnfıdɛnʃı'ælıtı] *n* riservatezza, carattere *m* confidenziale
configuration [kən'fıgju'reıʃən] *n* (*Comput*) configurazione *f*
confine [kən'faın] *vt* limitare; (*shut up*) rinchiudere; **to ~ o.s. to doing sth** limitarsi a fare qc; *see also* **confines**
confined [kən'faınd] *adj* (*space*) ristretto(-a)
confinement [kən'faınmənt] *n* prigionia; (*Mil*) consegna; (*Med*) parto
confines ['kɔnfaınz] *npl* confini *mpl*
confirm [kən'fə:m] *vt* confermare; (*Rel*) cresimare
confirmation [kɔnfə'meıʃən] *n* conferma; cresima
confirmed [kən'fə:md] *adj* inveterato(-a)
confiscate ['kɔnfıskeıt] *vt* confiscare
confiscation [kɔnfıs'keıʃən] *n* confisca
conflagration [kɔnflə'greıʃən] *n* conflagrazione *f*
conflict *n* ['kɔnflıkt] conflitto ■ *vi* [kən'flıkt] essere in conflitto
conflicting [kən'flıktıŋ] *adj* contrastante; (*reports, evidence, opinions*) contraddittorio(-a)
conform [kən'fɔ:m] *vi*: **to ~ (to)** conformarsi (a)
conformist [kən'fɔ:mıst] *n* conformista *m/f*
confound [kən'faund] *vt* confondere; (*amaze*) sconcertare
confounded [kən'faundıd] *adj* maledetto(-a)
confront [kən'frʌnt] *vt* confrontare; (*enemy, danger*) affrontare
confrontation [kɔnfrən'teıʃən] *n* scontro
confrontational [kɔnfrən'teıʃənəl] *adj* polemico(-a), aggressivo(-a)
confuse [kən'fju:z] *vt* imbrogliare; (*one thing with another*) confondere
confused [kən'fju:zd] *adj* confuso(-a); **to get ~** confondersi
confusing [kən'fju:zıŋ] *adj* che fa confondere
confusion [kən'fju:ʒən] *n* confusione *f*
congeal [kən'dʒi:l] *vi* (*blood*) congelarsi
congenial [kən'dʒi:nıəl] *adj* (*person*) simpatico(-a); (*place, work, company*) piacevole
congenital [kən'dʒɛnıtl] *adj* congenito(-a)
conger eel ['kɔngər-] *n* grongo
congested [kən'dʒɛstıd] *adj* congestionato(-a); (*telephone lines*) sovraccarico(-a)
congestion [kən'dʒɛstʃən] *n* congestione *f*
congestion charge *n pedaggio da pagare per poter circolare in automobile nel centro di alcune città, introdotto per la prima volta a Londra nel 2002*
conglomerate [kən'glɔmərıt] *n* (*Comm*) conglomerato
conglomeration [kənglɔmə'reıʃən] *n* conglomerazione *f*
Congo ['kɔŋgəu] *n* Congo
congratulate [kən'grætjuleıt] *vt*: **to ~ sb (on)** congratularsi con qn (per *or* di)
congratulations [kəngrætju'leıʃənz] *npl*: **~ (on)** congratulazioni *fpl* (per) ■ *excl* congratulazioni!, rallegramenti!
congregate ['kɔŋgrıgeıt] *vi* congregarsi, riunirsi
congregation [kɔŋgrı'geıʃən] *n* congregazione *f*
congress ['kɔŋgrɛs] *n* congresso; (*US Pol*): **C~** il Congresso; *vedi nota*

CONGRESS

Il *Congress* è l'assemblea statunitense che si riunisce a Washington D.C. nel "Capitol" per elaborare e discutere le leggi federali. é costituita dalla "House of Representatives" (435 membri, eletti nei vari stati in base al numero degli abitanti) e dal "Senate" (100 senatori, due per ogni stato). Sia i membri della "House of Representatives" che quelli del "Senate" sono eletti direttamente dal popolo.

congressman ['kɔŋgrɛsmən] *n* (*US*) membro del Congresso
congresswoman ['kɔŋgrɛswumən] *n* (*US*) (donna) membro del Congresso
conical ['kɔnıkl] *adj* conico(-a)
conifer ['kɔnıfə[r]] *n* conifero
coniferous [kə'nıfərəs] *adj* (*forest*) di conifere
conjecture [kən'dʒɛktʃə[r]] *n* congettura ■ *vt, vi* congetturare
conjoined twin [kən'dʒɔınd-] *n* fratello (*or* sorella) siamese
conjugal ['kɔndʒugl] *adj* coniugale
conjugate ['kɔndʒugeıt] *vt* coniugare
conjugation [kɔndʒə'geıʃən] *n* coniugazione *f*
conjunction [kən'dʒʌŋkʃən] *n* congiunzione *f*; **in ~ with** in accordo con, insieme con
conjunctivitis [kəndʒʌŋktı'vaıtıs] *n* congiuntivite *f*
conjure ['kʌndʒə[r]] *vi* fare giochi di prestigio
▸ **conjure up** *vt* (*ghost, spirit*) evocare; (*memories*) rievocare
conjurer ['kʌndʒərə[r]] *n* prestigiatore(-trice), prestidigitatore(-trice)
conjuring trick ['kʌndʒərıŋ-] *n* gioco di prestigio
conker ['kɔŋkə[r]] *n* (*Brit col*) castagna (d'ippocastano)
conk out [kɔŋk-] *vi* (*col*) andare in panne
conman ['kɔnmæn] *n* truffatore *m*
Conn. *abbr* (*US*) = **Connecticut**

connect [kə'nɛkt] *vt* connettere, collegare; (*Elec*) collegare; (*fig*) associare ■ *vi* (*train*): **to ~ with** essere in coincidenza con; **to be connected with** aver rapporti con; essere imparentato(-a) con; **I am trying to ~ you** (*Tel*) sto cercando di darle la linea
connection [kə'nɛkʃən] *n* relazione *f*, rapporto; (*Elec*) connessione *f*; (*Tel*) collegamento; (*train etc*) coincidenza; **in ~ with** con riferimento a, a proposito di; **what is the ~ between them?** in che modo sono legati?; **business connections** rapporti d'affari; **to miss/get one's ~** (*train etc*) perdere/prendere la coincidenza
connexion [kə'nɛkʃən] *n* (*Brit*) = **connection**
conning tower ['kɔnɪŋ-] *n* torretta di comando
connive [kə'naɪv] *vi*: **to ~ at** essere connivente in
connoisseur [kɔnɪ'sə:ʳ] *n* conoscitore(-trice)
connotation [kɔnə'teɪʃən] *n* connotazione *f*
connubial [kə'nju:bɪəl] *adj* coniugale
conquer ['kɔŋkəʳ] *vt* conquistare; (*feelings*) vincere
conqueror ['kɔŋkərəʳ] *n* conquistatore *m*
conquest ['kɔŋkwɛst] *n* conquista
cons [kɔnz] *npl see* **pro; convenience**
conscience ['kɔnʃəns] *n* coscienza; **in all ~** onestamente, in coscienza
conscientious [kɔnʃɪ'ɛnʃəs] *adj* coscienzioso(-a)
conscientious objector *n* obiettore *m* di coscienza
conscious ['kɔnʃəs] *adj* consapevole; (*Med*) conscio(-a); (*deliberate: insult, error*) intenzionale, voluto(-a); **to become ~ of sth/that** rendersi conto di qc/che
consciousness ['kɔnʃəsnɪs] *n* consapevolezza; (*Med*) coscienza; **to lose/regain ~** perdere/riprendere coscienza
conscript ['kɔnskrɪpt] *n* coscritto
conscription [kən'skrɪpʃən] *n* coscrizione *f*
consecrate ['kɔnsɪkreɪt] *vt* consacrare
consecutive [kən'sɛkjutɪv] *adj* consecutivo(-a); **on 3 ~ occasions** 3 volte di fila
consensus [kən'sɛnsəs] *n* consenso; **the ~ of opinion** l'opinione *f* unanime *or* comune
consent [kən'sɛnt] *n* consenso ■ *vi*: **to ~ (to)** acconsentire (a); **age of ~** età legale (per avere rapporti sessuali); **by common ~** di comune accordo
consenting adults [kən'sɛntɪŋ-] *npl* adulti *mpl* consenzienti
consequence ['kɔnsɪkwəns] *n* conseguenza, risultato; importanza; **in ~** di conseguenza
consequently ['kɔnsɪkwəntlɪ] *adv* di conseguenza, dunque
conservation [kɔnsə'veɪʃən] *n* conservazione *f*; (*also*: **nature conservation**) tutela dell'ambiente; **energy ~** risparmio energetico
conservationist [kɔnsə'veɪʃənɪst] *n* fautore(-trice) della tutela dell'ambiente
conservative [kən'sə:vətɪv] *adj* conservatore(-trice); (*cautious*) cauto(-a); **C~** *adj, n* (*Brit Pol*) conservatore(-trice); **the C~ Party** il partito conservatore
conservatory [kən'sə:vətrɪ] *n* (*greenhouse*) serra
conserve [kən'sə:v] *vt* conservare ■ *n* conserva
consider [kən'sɪdəʳ] *vt* considerare; (*take into account*) tener conto di; **to ~ doing sth** considerare la possibilità di fare qc; **all things considered** tutto sommato *or* considerato; **~ yourself lucky** puoi dirti fortunato
considerable [kən'sɪdərəbl] *adj* considerevole, notevole
considerably [kən'sɪdərəblɪ] *adv* notevolmente, decisamente
considerate [kən'sɪdərɪt] *adj* premuroso(-a)
consideration [kənsɪdə'reɪʃən] *n* considerazione *f*; (*reward*) rimunerazione *f*; **out of ~ for** per riguardo a; **under ~** in esame; **my first ~ is my family** il mio primo pensiero è per la mia famiglia
considered [kən'sɪdəd] *adj*: **it is my ~ opinion that ...** dopo lunga riflessione il mio parere è che ...
considering [kən'sɪdərɪŋ] *prep* in considerazione di; **~ (that)** se si considera (che)
consign [kən'saɪn] *vt* consegnare; (*send: goods*) spedire
consignee [kɔnsaɪ'ni:] *n* consegnatario(-a), destinatario(-a)
consignment [kən'saɪnmənt] *n* consegna; spedizione *f*
consignment note *n* (*Comm*) nota di spedizione
consignor [kən'saɪnəʳ] *n* mittente *m/f*
consist [kən'sɪst] *vi*: **to ~ of** constare di, essere composto(-a) di
consistency [kən'sɪstənsɪ] *n* consistenza; (*fig*) coerenza
consistent [kən'sɪstənt] *adj* coerente; (*constant*) costante; **~ with** compatibile con
consolation [kɔnsə'leɪʃən] *n* consolazione *f*
console *vt* [kən'səul] consolare ■ *n* ['kɔnsəul] quadro di comando
consolidate [kən'sɔlɪdeɪt] *vt* consolidare
consols ['kɔnsɔlz] *npl* (*Stock Exchange*) titoli *mpl* del debito consolidato

consommé [kən'sɔmeɪ] *n* consommé *m inv*, brodo ristretto
consonant ['kɔnsənənt] *n* consonante *f*
consort ['kɔnsɔ:t] *n* consorte *m/f*; **prince ~** principe *m* consorte ▪ *vi* [kən'sɔ:t] (*often pej*): **to ~ with sb** frequentare qn
consortium [kən'sɔ:tɪəm] *n* consorzio
conspicuous [kən'spɪkjuəs] *adj* cospicuo(-a); **to make o.s. ~** farsi notare
conspiracy [kən'spɪrəsɪ] *n* congiura, cospirazione *f*
conspiratorial [kənspɪrə'tɔ:rɪəl] *adj* cospiratorio(-a)
conspire [kən'spaɪəʳ] *vi* congiurare, cospirare
constable ['kʌnstəbl] *n* (*Brit*: *also*: **police constable**) ≈ poliziotto, agente *m* di polizia
constabulary [kən'stæbjulərɪ] *n* forze *fpl* dell'ordine
constant ['kɔnstənt] *adj* costante; continuo(-a)
constantly ['kɔnstəntlɪ] *adv* costantemente; continuamente
constellation [kɔnstə'leɪʃən] *n* costellazione *f*
consternation [kɔnstə'neɪʃən] *n* costernazione *f*
constipated ['kɔnstɪpeɪtɪd] *adj* stitico(-a)
constipation [kɔnstɪ'peɪʃən] *n* stitichezza
constituency [kən'stɪtjuənsɪ] *n* collegio elettorale; (*people*) elettori *mpl* (del collegio); *vedi nota*

CONSTITUENCY

Con il termine *constituency* viene indicato sia un collegio elettorale che i suoi elettori. In Gran Bretagna ogni collegio elegge un rappresentante che in seguito incontra regolarmente i propri elettori in riunioni chiamate "surgeries" per discutere questioni di interesse locale.

constituency party *n* sezione *f* locale (del partito)
constituent [kən'stɪtjuənt] *n* elettore(-trice); (*part*) elemento componente
constitute ['kɔnstɪtju:t] *vt* costituire
constitution [kɔnstɪ'tju:ʃən] *n* costituzione *f*
constitutional [kɔnstɪ'tju:ʃənl] *adj* costituzionale
constitutional monarchy *n* monarchia costituzionale
constrain [kən'streɪn] *vt* costringere
constrained [kən'streɪnd] *adj* costretto(-a)
constraint [kən'streɪnt] *n* (*restraint*) limitazione *f*, costrizione *f*; (*embarrassment*) imbarazzo, soggezione *f*
constrict [kən'strɪkt] *vt* comprimere; opprimere
construct [kən'strʌkt] *vt* costruire
construction [kən'strʌkʃən] *n* costruzione *f*; (*fig*: *interpretation*) interpretazione *f*; **under ~** in costruzione
construction industry *n* edilizia, industria edile
constructive [kən'strʌktɪv] *adj* costruttivo(-a)
construe [kən'stru:] *vt* interpretare
consul ['kɔnsl] *n* console *m*
consulate ['kɔnsjulɪt] *n* consolato
consult [kən'sʌlt] *vt*: **to ~ sb (about sth)** consultare qn (su *or* riguardo a qc)
consultancy [kən'sʌltənsɪ] *n* consulenza
consultancy fee *n* onorario di consulenza
consultant [kən'sʌltənt] *n* (*Med*) consulente *m* medico; (*other specialist*) consulente ▪ *cpd*: **~ engineer** *n* ingegnere *m* consulente; **~ paediatrician** *n* specialista *m/f* in pediatria; **legal/management ~** consulente legale/gestionale
consultation [kɔnsəl'teɪʃən] *n* consultazione *f*; (*Med, Law*) consulto; **in ~ with** consultandosi con
consultative [kən'sʌltətɪv] *adj* di consulenza
consulting room [kən'sʌltɪŋ-] *n* (*Brit*) ambulatorio
consume [kən'sju:m] *vt* consumare
consumer [kən'sju:məʳ] *n* consumatore(-trice); (*of electricity, gas etc*) utente *m/f*
consumer credit *n* credito al consumatore
consumer durables *npl* prodotti *mpl* di consumo durevole
consumer goods *npl* beni *mpl* di consumo
consumerism [kən'sju:mərɪzəm] *n* (*consumer protection*) tutela del consumatore; (*Econ*) consumismo
consumer society *n* società dei consumi
consumer watchdog *n* comitato di difesa dei consumatori
consummate ['kɔnsʌmeɪt] *vt* consumare
consumption [kən'sʌmpʃən] *n* consumo; (*Med*) consunzione *f*; **not fit for human ~** non commestibile
cont. *abbr* (= *continued*) segue
contact ['kɔntækt] *n* contatto; (*person*) conoscenza ▪ *vt* mettersi in contatto con; **to be in ~ with sb/sth** essere in contatto con qn/qc; **business contacts** contatti *mpl* d'affari
contact lenses *npl* lenti *fpl* a contatto
contagious [kən'teɪdʒəs] *adj* contagioso(-a)
contain [kən'teɪn] *vt* contenere; **to ~ o.s.** contenersi
container [kən'teɪnəʳ] *n* recipiente *m*; (*for shipping etc*) container *m*

containerize [kən'teɪnəraɪz] *vt* mettere in container
container ship *n* nave *f* container *inv*
contaminate [kən'tæmɪneɪt] *vt* contaminare
contamination [kəntæmɪ'neɪʃən] *n* contaminazione *f*
cont'd *abbr* (= *continued*) segue
contemplate ['kɔntəmpleɪt] *vt* contemplare; (*consider*) pensare a (*or* di)
contemplation [kɔntəm'pleɪʃən] *n* contemplazione *f*
contemporary [kən'tɛmpərərɪ] *adj* contemporaneo(-a); (*design*) moderno(-a) ■ *n* contemporaneo(-a); (*of the same age*) coetaneo(-a)
contempt [kən'tɛmpt] *n* disprezzo; **~ of court** (*Law*) oltraggio alla Corte
contemptible [kən'tɛmptəbl] *adj* spregevole, vergognoso(-a)
contemptuous [kən'tɛmptjuəs] *adj* sdegnoso(-a)
contend [kən'tɛnd] *vt*: **to ~ that** sostenere che ■ *vi*: **to ~ with** lottare contro; **he has a lot to ~ with** ha un sacco di guai
contender [kən'tɛndə^r] *n* contendente *m/f*; concorrente *m/f*
content [kən'tɛnt] *adj* contento(-a), soddisfatto(-a) ■ *vt* contentare, soddisfare ■ *n* ['kɔntɛnt] contenuto; **contents** *npl* contenuto; (*of barrel etc: capacity*) capacità *f inv*; **(table of) contents** indice *m*; **to be ~ with** essere contento di; **to ~ o.s. with sth/with doing sth** accontentarsi di qc/di fare qc
contented [kən'tɛntɪd] *adj* contento(-a), soddisfatto(-a)
contentedly [kən'tɛntɪdlɪ] *adv* con soddisfazione
contention [kən'tɛnʃən] *n* contesa; (*assertion*) tesi *f inv*; **bone of ~** pomo della discordia
contentious [kən'tɛnʃəs] *adj* polemico(-a)
contentment [kən'tɛntmənt] *n* contentezza
contest *n* ['kɔntɛst] lotta; (*competition*) gara, concorso ■ *vt* [kən'tɛst] contestare; (*Law*) impugnare; (*compete for*) contendere
contestant [kən'tɛstənt] *n* concorrente *m/f*; (*in fight*) avversario(-a)
context ['kɔntɛkst] *n* contesto; **in/out of ~** nel/fuori dal contesto
continent ['kɔntɪnənt] *n* continente *m*; **the C~** (*Brit*) l'Europa continentale; **on the C~** in Europa
continental [kɔntɪ'nɛntl] *adj* continentale ■ *n* (*Brit*) abitante *m/f* dell'Europa continentale
continental breakfast *n* colazione *f* all'europea
continental quilt *n* (*Brit*) piumino
contingency [kən'tɪndʒənsɪ] *n* eventualità *f inv*
contingency plan *n* misura d'emergenza
contingent [kən'tɪndʒənt] *n* contingenza ■ *adj*: **to be ~ upon** dipendere da
continual [kən'tɪnjuəl] *adj* continuo(-a)
continually [kən'tɪnjuəlɪ] *adv* di continuo
continuation [kəntɪnju'eɪʃən] *n* continuazione *f*; (*after interruption*) ripresa; (*of story*) seguito
continue [kən'tɪnju:] *vi* continuare ■ *vt* continuare; (*start again*) riprendere; **to be continued** (*story*) continua; **continued on page 10** segue *or* continua a pagina 10
continuing education [kən'tɪnjuɪŋ-] *n* corsi *mpl* per adulti
continuity [kɔntɪ'nju:ɪtɪ] *n* continuità; (*Cine*) (ordine *m* della) sceneggiatura
continuity girl *n* (*Cine*) segretaria di edizione
continuous [kən'tɪnjuəs] *adj* continuo(-a), ininterrotto(-a); **~ performance** (*Cine*) spettacolo continuato; **~ stationery** (*Comput*) carta a moduli continui
continuously [kən'tɪnjuəslɪ] *adv* (*repeatedly*) continuamente; (*uninterruptedly*) ininterrottamente
contort [kən'tɔ:t] *vt* contorcere
contortion [kən'tɔ:ʃən] *n* contorcimento; (*of acrobat*) contorsione *f*
contortionist [kən'tɔ:ʃənɪst] *n* contorsionista *m/f*
contour ['kɔntuə^r] *n* contorno, profilo; (*also*: **contour line**) curva di livello
contraband ['kɔntrəbænd] *n* contrabbando ■ *adj* di contrabbando
contraception [kɔntrə'sɛpʃən] *n* contraccezione *f*
contraceptive [kɔntrə'sɛptɪv] *adj* contraccettivo(-a) ■ *n* contraccettivo
contract *n* ['kɔntrækt] contratto ■ *cpd* ['kɔntrækt] (*price, date*) del contratto; (*work*) a contratto ■ *vi* [kən'trækt] (*Comm*): **to ~ to do sth** fare un contratto per fare qc; (*become smaller*) contrarre; **to be under ~ to do sth** aver stipulato un contratto per fare qc; **~ of employment** contratto di lavoro
▸ **contract in** *vi* impegnarsi (con un contratto); (*Brit Admin*) *scegliere di pagare i contributi per una pensione*
▸ **contract out** *vi*: **to ~ out (of)** ritirarsi (da); (*Brit Admin*) *(scegliere di) non pagare i contributi per una pensione*
contraction [kən'trækʃən] *n* contrazione *f*
contractor [kən'træktə^r] *n* imprenditore *m*
contractual [kən'træktjuəl] *adj* contrattuale
contradict [kɔntrə'dɪkt] *vt* contraddire
contradiction [kɔntrə'dɪkʃən] *n* contraddizione *f*; **to be in ~ with** discordare con

contradictory [kɔntrəˈdɪktərɪ] *adj* contradditorio(-a)
contralto [kənˈtræltəu] *n* contralto
contraption [kənˈtræpʃən] *n* (*pej*) aggeggio
contrary[1] [ˈkɔntrərɪ] *adj* contrario(-a); (*unfavourable*) avverso(-a), contrario(-a) ■ *n* contrario; **on the ~** al contrario; **unless you hear to the ~** a meno che non si disdica; **~ to what we thought** a differenza di *or* contrariamente a quanto pensavamo
contrary[2] [kənˈtrɛərɪ] (*perverse*) bisbetico(-a)
contrast *n* [ˈkɔntrɑːst] contrasto ■ *vt* [kənˈtrɑːst] mettere in contrasto; **in ~ to** *or* **with** a differenza di, contrariamente a
contrasting [kənˈtrɑːstɪŋ] *adj* contrastante, di contrasto
contravene [kɔntrəˈviːn] *vt* contravvenire
contravention [kɔntrəˈvɛnʃən] *n*: **~ (of)** contravvenzione *f* (a), infrazione *f* (di)
contribute [kənˈtrɪbjuːt] *vi* contribuire ■ *vt*: **to ~ £10/an article to** dare 10 sterline/un articolo a; **to ~ to** contribuire a; (*newspaper*) scrivere per; (*discussion*) partecipare a
contribution [kɔntrɪˈbjuːʃən] *n* contribuzione *f*
contributor [kənˈtrɪbjutə[r]] *n* (*to newspaper*) collaboratore(-trice)
contributory [kənˈtrɪbjutərɪ] *adj* (*cause*) che contribuisce; **it was a ~ factor in ...** quello ha contribuito a ...
contributory pension scheme *n* (*Brit*) *sistema di pensionamento finanziato congiuntamente dai contributi del lavoratore e del datore di lavoro*
contrite [ˈkɔntraɪt] *adj* contrito(-a)
contrivance [kənˈtraɪvəns] *n* congegno; espediente *m*
contrive [kənˈtraɪv] *vt* inventare; escogitare ■ *vi*: **to ~ to do** fare in modo di fare
control [kənˈtrəul] *vt* dominare; (*firm, operation etc*) dirigere; (*check*) controllare; (*disease, fire*) arginare, limitare ■ *n* controllo; **controls** *npl* comandi *mpl*; **to take ~ of** assumere il controllo di; **to be in ~ of** aver autorità su; essere responsabile di; controllare; **to ~ o.s.** controllarsi; **everything is under ~** tutto è sotto controllo; **the car went out of ~** la macchina non rispondeva ai comandi; **circumstances beyond our ~** circostanze *fpl* che non dipendono da noi
control key *n* (*Comput*) tasto di controllo
controlled substance [kənˈtrəuld-] *n* sostanza stupefacente
controller [kənˈtrəulə[r]] *n* controllore *m*
controlling interest [kənˈtrəulɪŋ-] *n* (*Comm*) maggioranza delle azioni
control panel *n* (*on aircraft, ship, TV etc*) quadro dei comandi
control point *n* punto di controllo
control room *n* (*Naut, Mil*) sala di comando; (*Radio, TV*) sala di regia
control tower *n* (*Aviat*) torre *f* di controllo
control unit *n* (*Comput*) unità *f inv* di controllo
controversial [kɔntrəˈvəːʃl] *adj* controverso(-a), polemico(-a)
controversy [ˈkɔntrəvəːsɪ] *n* controversia, polemica
conurbation [kɔnəːˈbeɪʃən] *n* conurbazione *f*
convalesce [kɔnvəˈlɛs] *vi* rimettersi in salute
convalescence [kɔnvəˈlɛsns] *n* convalescenza
convalescent [kɔnvəˈlɛsnt] *adj, n* convalescente (*m/f*)
convector [kənˈvɛktə[r]] *n* convettore *m*
convene [kənˈviːn] *vt* convocare; (*meeting*) organizzare ■ *vi* convenire, adunarsi
convenience [kənˈviːnɪəns] *n* comodità *f inv*; **at your ~** a suo comodo; **at your earliest ~** (*Comm*) appena possibile; **all modern conveniences**, (*Brit*) **all mod cons** tutte le comodità moderne
convenience foods *npl* cibi *mpl* precotti
convenient [kənˈviːnɪənt] *adj* conveniente, comodo(-a); **if it is ~ to you** se per lei va bene, se non la incomoda
conveniently [kənˈviːnɪəntlɪ] *adv* (*happen*) a proposito; (*situated*) in un posto comodo
convent [ˈkɔnvənt] *n* convento
convention [kənˈvɛnʃən] *n* convenzione *f*; (*meeting*) convegno
conventional [kənˈvɛnʃənl] *adj* convenzionale
convent school *n* scuola retta da suore
converge [kənˈvəːdʒ] *vi* convergere
conversant [kənˈvəːsnt] *adj*: **to be ~ with** essere al corrente di; essere pratico(-a) di
conversation [kɔnvəˈseɪʃən] *n* conversazione *f*
conversational [kɔnvəˈseɪʃənl] *adj* non formale; (*Comput*) conversazionale; **~ Italian** l'italiano parlato
conversationalist [kɔnvəˈseɪʃnəlɪst] *n* conversatore(-trice)
converse *n* [ˈkɔnvəːs] contrario, opposto ■ *vi* [kənˈvəːs]: **to ~ (with sb about sth)** conversare (con qn su qc)
conversely [kɔnˈvəːslɪ] *adv* al contrario, per contro
conversion [kənˈvəːʃən] *n* conversione *f*; (*Brit: of house*) trasformazione *f*, rimodernamento
conversion table *n* tavola di equivalenze
convert *vt* [kənˈvəːt] (*Rel, Comm*) convertire; (*alter*) trasformare ■ *n* [ˈkɔnvəːt] convertito(-a)
convertible [kənˈvəːtəbl] *n* macchina decappottabile

convex ['kɔnvɛks] *adj* convesso(-a)
convey [kən'veɪ] *vt* trasportare; (*thanks*) comunicare; (*idea*) dare
conveyance [kən'veɪəns] *n* (*of goods*) trasporto; (*vehicle*) mezzo di trasporto
conveyancing [kən'veɪənsɪŋ] *n* (*Law*) redazione *f* di transazioni di proprietà
conveyor belt *n* nastro trasportatore
convict *vt* [kən'vɪkt] dichiarare colpevole ■ *n* ['kɔnvɪkt] carcerato(-a)
conviction [kən'vɪkʃən] *n* condanna; (*belief*) convinzione *f*
convince [kən'vɪns] *vt*: **to ~ sb (of sth/that)** convincere qn (di qc/che), persuadere qn (di qc/che)
convincing [kən'vɪnsɪŋ] *adj* convincente
convincingly [kən'vɪnsɪŋlɪ] *adv* in modo convincente
convivial [kən'vɪvɪəl] *adj* allegro(-a)
convoluted ['kɔnvəlu:tɪd] *adj* (*shape*) attorcigliato(-a), avvolto(-a); (*argument*) involuto(-a)
convoy ['kɔnvɔɪ] *n* convoglio
convulse [kən'vʌls] *vt* sconvolgere; **to be convulsed with laughter** contorcersi dalle risa
convulsion [kən'vʌlʃən] *n* convulsione *f*
COO *n abbr* = **chief operating officer**
coo [ku:] *vi* tubare
cook [kuk] *vt* cucinare, cuocere; (*meal*) preparare ■ *vi* cuocere; (*person*) cucinare ■ *n* cuoco(-a)
▸ **cook up** *vt* (*col: excuse, story*) improvvisare, inventare
cookbook ['kukbuk] *n* = **cookery book**
cooker ['kukə^r] *n* fornello, cucina
cookery book *n* (*Brit*) libro di cucina
cookie ['kukɪ] *n* (US) biscotto; (*Comput*) cookie *m inv*
cooking ['kukɪŋ] *n* cucina ■ *cpd* (*apples, chocolate*) da cuocere; (*utensils, salt, foil*) da cucina
cookout ['kukaut] *n* (US) pranzo (cucinato) all'aperto
cool [ku:l] *adj* fresco(-a); (*not afraid*) calmo(-a); (*unfriendly*) freddo(-a); (*impertinent*) sfacciato(-a) ■ *vt* raffreddare, rinfrescare ■ *vi* raffreddarsi, rinfrescarsi; **it's ~** (*weather*) fa fresco; **to keep sth ~** *or* **in a ~ place** tenere qc in fresco
▸ **cool down** *vi* raffreddarsi; (*fig: person, situation*) calmarsi
coolant ['ku:lənt] *n* (liquido) refrigerante *m*
cool box, (US) **cooler** ['ku:lə^r] *n* borsa termica
cooling ['ku:lɪŋ] *adj* (*breeze*) fresco(-a)
cooling tower *n* torre *f* di raffreddamento
coolly ['ku:lɪ] *adv* (*calmly*) con calma, tranquillamente; (*audaciously*) come se niente fosse; (*unenthusiastically*) freddamente
coolness ['ku:lnɪs] *n* freschezza; sangue *m* freddo, calma
coop [ku:p] *n* stia ■ *vt*: **to ~ up** (*fig*) rinchiudere
co-op ['kəuɔp] *n abbr* (= *cooperative (society)*) coop *f*
cooperate [kəu'ɔpəreɪt] *vi* cooperare, collaborare
cooperation [kəuɔpə'reɪʃən] *n* cooperazione *f*, collaborazione *f*
cooperative [kəu'ɔpərətɪv] *adj* cooperativo(-a) ■ *n* cooperativa
coopt [kəu'ɔpt] *vt*: **to ~ sb into sth** cooptare qn per qc
coordinate *vt* [kəu'ɔ:dɪneɪt] coordinare ■ *n* [kəu'ɔ:dɪnət] (*Math*) coordinata; **coordinates** *npl* (*clothes*) coordinati *mpl*
coordination [kəuɔ:dɪ'neɪʃən] *n* coordinazione *f*
coot [ku:t] *n* folaga
co-ownership [kəu'əunəʃɪp] *n* comproprietà
cop [kɔp] *n* (*col*) sbirro
cope [kəup] *vi* farcela; **to ~ with** (*problems*) far fronte a
Copenhagen [kəupən'heɪgən] *n* Copenhagen *f*
copier ['kɔpɪə^r] *n* (*also*: **photocopier**) (foto)copiatrice *f*
co-pilot ['kəupaɪlət] *n* secondo pilota *m*
copious ['kəupɪəs] *adj* copioso(-a), abbondante
copper ['kɔpə^r] *n* rame *m*; (*col: policeman*) sbirro; **coppers** *npl* spiccioli *mpl*
coppice ['kɔpɪs], **copse** [kɔps] *n* bosco ceduo
copulate ['kɔpjuleɪt] *vi* accoppiarsi
copy ['kɔpɪ] *n* copia; (*book etc*) esemplare *m*; (*material: for printing*) materiale *m*, testo ■ *vt* (*gen, Comput*) copiare; (*imitate*) imitare; **rough/fair ~** brutta/bella (copia); **to make good ~** (*fig*) fare notizia
▸ **copy out** *vt* ricopiare, trascrivere
copycat ['kɔpɪkæt] *n* (*pej*) copione *m*
copyright ['kɔpɪraɪt] *n* diritto d'autore; **~ reserved** tutti i diritti riservati
copy typist *n* dattilografo(-a)
copywriter ['kɔpɪraɪtə^r] *n* redattore *m* pubblicitario
coral ['kɔrəl] *n* corallo
coral reef *n* barriera corallina
Coral Sea *n*: **the ~** il mar dei Coralli
cord [kɔ:d] *n* corda; (*Elec*) filo; (*fabric*) velluto a coste; **cords** *npl* (*trousers*) calzoni *mpl* (di velluto) a coste
cordial ['kɔ:dɪəl] *adj, n* cordiale (*m*)
cordless ['kɔ:dlɪs] *adj* senza cavo

cordon ['kɔːdn] *n* cordone *m*
▸ **cordon off** *vt* fare cordone intorno a
corduroy ['kɔːdərɔɪ] *n* fustagno
CORE [kɔːʳ] *n abbr (US)* = **Congress of Racial Equality**
core [kɔːʳ] *n (of fruit)* torsolo; *(Tech)* centro; *(of earth, nuclear reactor)* nucleo; *(of problem etc)* cuore *m*, nocciolo ▪ *vt* estrarre il torsolo da; **rotten to the ~** marcio fino al midollo
Corfu [kɔː'fuː] *n* Corfù *f*
coriander [kɔrɪ'ændəʳ] *n* coriandolo
cork [kɔːk] *n* sughero; *(of bottle)* tappo
corkage ['kɔːkɪdʒ] *n somma da pagare se il cliente porta il proprio vino*
corked [kɔːkt], *(US)* **corky** ['kɔːkɪ] *adj (wine)* che sa di tappo
corkscrew ['kɔːkskruː] *n* cavatappi *m inv*
cormorant ['kɔːmərnt] *n* cormorano
corn [kɔːn] *n (Brit: wheat)* grano; *(US: maize)* granturco; *(on foot)* callo; **~ on the cob** *(Culin)* pannocchia cotta
cornea ['kɔːnɪə] *n* cornea
corned beef ['kɔːnd-] *n* carne *f* di manzo in scatola
corner ['kɔːnəʳ] *n* angolo; *(Aut)* curva; *(Football: also:* **corner kick***)* corner *m inv*, calcio d'angolo ▪ *vt* intrappolare; mettere con le spalle al muro; *(Comm: market)* accaparrare ▪ *vi* prendere una curva; **to cut corners** *(fig)* prendere una scorciatoia
corner flag *n (Football)* bandierina d'angolo
corner kick *n (Football)* calcio d'angolo
cornerstone ['kɔːnəstəun] *n* pietra angolare
cornet ['kɔːnɪt] *n (Mus)* cornetta; *(Brit: of ice-cream)* cono
cornflakes ['kɔːnfleɪks] *npl* fiocchi *mpl* di granturco
cornflour ['kɔːnflauəʳ] *n (Brit)* ≈ fecola di patate
cornice ['kɔːnɪs] *n* cornicione *m*; cornice *f*
Cornish ['kɔːnɪʃ] *adj* della Cornovaglia
corn oil *n* olio di mais
cornstarch ['kɔːnstɑːtʃ] *n (US)* = **cornflour**
cornucopia [kɔːnju'kəupɪə] *n* grande abbondanza
Cornwall ['kɔːnwəl] *n* Cornovaglia
corny ['kɔːnɪ] *adj (col)* trito(-a)
corollary [kə'rɔlərɪ] *n* corollario
coronary ['kɔrənərɪ] *n*: **~ (thrombosis)** trombosi *f* coronaria
coronation [kɔrə'neɪʃən] *n* incoronazione *f*
coroner ['kɔrənəʳ] *n magistrato incaricato di indagare la causa di morte in circostanze sospette*
coronet ['kɔrənɪt] *n* diadema *m*
Corp *abbr* = **corporation**
corporal ['kɔːpərl] *n* caporalmaggiore *m* ▪ *adj*: **~ punishment** pena corporale
corporate ['kɔːpərɪt] *adj* comune; *(Comm)* costituito(-a) (in corporazione)
corporate hospitality *n* omaggi *mpl* ai clienti *(come biglietti per spettacoli, cene etc)*
corporate identity, corporate image *n (of organization)* immagine *f* di marca
corporation [kɔːpə'reɪʃən] *n (of town)* consiglio comunale; *(Comm)* ente *m*
corporation tax *n* ≈ imposta societaria
corps [kɔːʳ ʃ] *(pl* **~***)* [kɔːz] *n* corpo; **press ~** ufficio *m* stampa *inv*
corpse [kɔːps] *n* cadavere *m*
corpuscle ['kɔːpʌsl] *n* corpuscolo
corral [kə'rɑːl] *n* recinto
correct [kə'rɛkt] *adj (accurate)* corretto(-a), esatto(-a); *(proper)* corretto(-a) ▪ *vt* correggere; **you are ~** ha ragione
correction [kə'rɛkʃən] *n* correzione *f*
correlate ['kɔrɪleɪt] *vt* mettere in correlazione ▪ *vi*: **to ~ with** essere in rapporto con
correlation [kɔrɪ'leɪʃən] *n* correlazione *f*
correspond [kɔrɪs'pɔnd] *vi* corrispondere
correspondence [kɔrɪs'pɔndəns] *n* corrispondenza
correspondence course *n* corso per corrispondenza
correspondent [kɔrɪs'pɔndənt] *n* corrispondente *m/f*
corridor ['kɔrɪdɔːʳ] *n* corridoio
corroborate [kə'rɔbəreɪt] *vt* corroborare, confermare
corrode [kə'rəud] *vt* corrodere ▪ *vi* corrodersi
corrosion [kə'rəuʒən] *n* corrosione *f*
corrosive [kə'rəuzɪv] *adj* corrosivo(-a)
corrugated ['kɔrəgeɪtɪd] *adj* increspato(-a), ondulato(-a)
corrugated iron *n* lamiera di ferro ondulata
corrupt [kə'rʌpt] *adj* corrotto(-a) ▪ *vt* corrompere; **~ practices** *(dishonesty, bribery)* pratiche *fpl* illecite
corruption [kə'rʌpʃən] *n* corruzione *f*
corset ['kɔːsɪt] *n* busto
Corsica ['kɔːsɪkə] *n* Corsica
Corsican ['kɔːsɪkən] *adj, n* corso(-a)
cortège [kɔː'teɪʒ] *n* corteo
cortisone ['kɔːtɪzəun] *n* cortisone *m*
coruscating ['kɔrəskeɪtɪŋ] *adj* scintillante
cosh [kɔʃ] *n (Brit)* randello (corto)
cosignatory [kəu'sɪgnətərɪ] *n* cofirmatario(-a)
cosiness ['kəuzɪnɪs] *n* intimità
cos lettuce ['kɔs-] *n* lattuga romana
cosmetic [kɔz'mɛtɪk] *n* cosmetico ▪ *adj (preparation)* cosmetico(-a); *(surgery)* estetico(-a); *(fig: reforms)* ornamentale

cosmic ['kɔzmɪk] *adj* cosmico(-a)
cosmonaut ['kɔzmənɔ:t] *n* cosmonauta *m/f*
cosmopolitan [kɔzmə'pɔlɪtn] *adj* cosmopolita
cosmos ['kɔzmɔs] *n* cosmo
cosset ['kɔsɪt] *vt* vezzeggiare
cost [kɔst] *n* costo ■ *vb (pt, pp* **~**) *vi* costare ■ *vt* stabilire il prezzo di; **costs** *npl (Law)* spese *fpl*; **it costs £5/too much** costa 5 sterline/troppo; **it ~ him his life/job** gli costò la vita/il suo lavoro; **how much does it ~?** quanto costa?, quanto viene?; **what will it ~ to have it repaired?** quanto costerà farlo riparare?; **~ of living** costo della vita; **at all costs** a ogni costo
cost accountant *n* analizzatore *m* dei costi
co-star ['kəusta:ʳ] *n attore/trice della stessa importanza del protagonista*
Costa Rica ['kɔstə'ri:kə] *n* Costa Rica
cost centre *n* centro di costo
cost control *n* controllo dei costi
cost-effective ['kɔstɪ'fɛktɪv] *adj (gen)* conveniente, economico(-a); *(Comm)* redditizio(-a), conveniente
cost-effectiveness ['kɔstɪ'fɛktɪvnɪs] *n* convenienza
costing ['kɔstɪŋ] *n* (determinazione *f* dei) costi *mpl*
costly ['kɔstlɪ] *adj* costoso(-a), caro(-a)
cost-of-living ['kɔstəv'lɪvɪŋ] *adj*: **~ allowance** indennità *f inv* di contingenza; **~ index** indice *m* della scala mobile
cost price *n (Brit)* prezzo all'ingrosso
costume ['kɔstju:m] *n* costume *m*; *(lady's suit)* tailleur *m inv*; *(Brit: also:* **swimming costume**) costume da bagno
costume jewellery *n* bigiotteria
cosy, (US) **cozy** ['kəuzɪ] *adj* intimo(-a); *(room, atmosphere)* accogliente
cot [kɔt] *n (Brit: child's)* lettino; *(US: folding bed)* brandina
cot death *n improvvisa e inspiegabile morte nel sonno di un neonato*
Cotswolds ['kɔtswəuldz] *npl*: **the ~** *zona collinare del Gloucestershire*
cottage ['kɔtɪdʒ] *n* cottage *m inv*
cottage cheese *n* fiocchi *mpl* di latte magro
cottage industry *n industria artigianale basata sul lavoro a cottimo*
cottage pie *n piatto a base di carne macinata in sugo e purè di patate*
cotton ['kɔtn] *n* cotone *m*; **~ dress** *etc* vestito *etc* di cotone
▸ **cotton on** *vi (col)*: **to ~ on (to sth)** afferrare (qc)
cotton wool *n (Brit)* cotone *m* idrofilo
couch [kautʃ] *n* sofà *m inv*; *(in doctor's surgery)* lettino ■ *vt* esprimere
couchette [ku:'ʃɛt] *n* cuccetta
couch potato *n (col)* pigrone(-a) teledipendente
cough [kɔf] *vi* tossire ■ *n* tosse *f*
cough drop *n* pasticca per la tosse
cough mixture, cough syrup *n* sciroppo per la tosse
could [kud] *pt of* **can²**
couldn't ['kudnt] = **could not**
council ['kaunsl] *n* consiglio; **city** *or* **town ~** consiglio comunale; **C~ of Europe** Consiglio d'Europa
council estate *n (Brit)* quartiere *m* di case popolari
council house *n (Brit)* casa popolare
council housing *n* alloggi *mpl* popolari
councillor ['kaunsələʳ] *n* consigliere(-a)
council tax *n (Brit) tassa comunale sulla proprietà*
counsel ['kaunsl] *n* avvocato; consultazione *f* ■ *vt*: **to ~ sth/sb to do sth** consigliare qc/a qn di fare qc; **~ for the defence/the prosecution** avvocato difensore/di parte civile
counsellor, (US) **counselor** ['kaunsləʳ] *n* consigliere(-a); *(US: lawyer)* avvocato(-essa)
count [kaunt] *vt, vi* contare ■ *n* conto; *(nobleman)* conte *m*; **to ~ (up) to 10** contare fino a 10; **to ~ the cost of** calcolare il costo di; **not counting the children** senza contare i bambini; **10 counting him** 10 compreso lui; **~ yourself lucky** considerati fortunato; **it counts for very little** non conta molto, non ha molta importanza; **to keep ~ of sth** tenere il conto di qc
▸ **count on** *vt fus* contare su; **to ~ on doing sth** contare di fare qc
▸ **count up** *vt* addizionare
countdown ['kauntdaun] *n* conto alla rovescia
countenance ['kauntɪnəns] *n* volto, aspetto ■ *vt* approvare
counter ['kauntəʳ] *n* banco; *(position: in post office, bank)* sportello; *(in game)* gettone *m*; *(Tech)* contatore *m* ■ *vt* opporsi a; *(blow)* parare ■ *adv*: **~ to** contro; in opposizione a; **to buy under the ~** *(fig)* comperare sottobanco; **to ~ sth with sth/by doing sth** rispondere a qc con qc/facendo qc
counteract [kauntər'ækt] *vt* agire in opposizione a; *(poison etc)* annullare gli effetti di
counterattack ['kauntərətæk] *n* contrattacco ■ *vi* contrattaccare
counterbalance ['kauntəbæləns] *vt* contrappesare
counter-clockwise ['kauntə'klɔkwaɪz] *adv* in senso antiorario

counter-espionage [kauntər'ɛspɪənɑːʒ] *n* controspionaggio
counterfeit ['kauntəfɪt] *n* contraffazione *f*, falso ■ *vt* contraffare, falsificare ■ *adj* falso(-a)
counterfoil ['kauntəfɔɪl] *n* matrice *f*
counterintelligence ['kauntərɪn'tɛlɪdʒəns] *n* = **counter-espionage**
countermand ['kauntəmɑːnd] *vt* annullare
countermeasure ['kauntəmɛʒəʳ] *n* contromisura
counteroffensive ['kauntərə'fɛnsɪv] *n* controffensiva
counterpane ['kauntəpeɪn] *n* copriletto *m inv*
counterpart ['kauntəpɑːt] *n* (*of document etc*) copia; (*of person*) corrispondente *m/f*
counterproductive ['kauntəprə'dʌktɪv] *adj* controproducente
counterproposal ['kauntəprə'pəuzl] *n* controproposta
countersign ['kauntəsaɪn] *vt* controfirmare
countersink ['kauntəsɪŋk] *vt* (*hole*) svasare
counterterrorism ['kauntə'terərɪzəm] *n* antiterrorismo
countess ['kauntɪs] *n* contessa
countless ['kauntlɪs] *adj* innumerevole
countrified ['kʌntrɪfaɪd] *adj* rustico(-a), campagnolo(-a)
country ['kʌntrɪ] *n* paese *m*; (*native land*) patria; (*as opposed to town*) campagna; (*region*) regione *f*; **in the ~** in campagna; **mountainous ~** territorio montagnoso
country and western, country and western music *n* musica country e western, country *m*
country dancing *n* (*Brit*) danza popolare
country house *n* villa in campagna
countryman ['kʌntrɪmən] *n* (*national*) compatriota *m*; (*rural*) contadino
countryside ['kʌntrɪsaɪd] *n* campagna
country-wide ['kʌntrɪ'waɪd] *adj* diffuso(-a) in tutto il paese ■ *adv* in tutto il paese
county ['kauntɪ] *n* contea
county council *n* (*Brit*) consiglio di contea
county town *n* (*Brit*) capoluogo
coup (*pl* **coups**) [kuː, kuːz] *n* (*also*: **coup d'état**) colpo di Stato; (*triumph*) bel colpo
coupé [kuː'peɪ] *n* coupé *m inv*
couple ['kʌpl] *n* coppia ■ *vt* (*carriages*) agganciare; (*Tech*) accoppiare; (*ideas, names*) associare; **a ~ of** un paio di
couplet ['kʌplɪt] *n* distico
coupling ['kʌplɪŋ] *n* (*Rail*) agganciamento
coupon ['kuːpɔn] *n* (*voucher*) buono; (*Comm*) coupon *m inv*
courage ['kʌrɪdʒ] *n* coraggio
courageous [kə'reɪdʒəs] *adj* coraggioso(-a)
courgette [kuə'ʒɛt] *n* (*Brit*) zucchina
courier ['kurɪəʳ] *n* corriere *m*; (*for tourists*) guida
course [kɔːs] *n* corso; (*of ship*) rotta; (*for golf*) campo; (*part of meal*) piatto; **first ~** primo piatto; **of ~** *adv* senz'altro, naturalmente; **(no) of ~ not!** certo che no!, no di certo!; **in the ~ of the next few days** nel corso dei prossimi giorni; **in due ~** a tempo debito; **~ (of action)** modo d'agire; **the best ~ would be to ...** la cosa migliore sarebbe ...; **we have no other ~ but to ...** non possiamo far altro che ...; **~ of lectures** corso di lezioni; **a ~ of treatment** (*Med*) una cura
court [kɔːt] *n* corte *f*; (*Tennis*) campo ■ *vt* (*woman*) fare la corte a; (*fig: favour, popularity*) cercare di conquistare; (*: death, disaster*) sfiorare, rasentare; **out of ~** (*Law: settle*) in via amichevole; **to take to ~** citare in tribunale; **C~ of Appeal** corte d'appello
courteous ['kəːtɪəs] *adj* cortese
courtesan [kɔːtɪ'zæn] *n* cortigiana
courtesy ['kəːtəsɪ] *n* cortesia; **by ~ of** per gentile concessione di
courtesy bus *n* navetta gratuita (*di hotel, aeroporto*)
courtesy car *n* vettura sostitutiva
courtesy light *n* (*Aut*) luce *f* interna
court-house ['kɔːthaus] *n* (*US*) palazzo di giustizia
courtier ['kɔːtɪəʳ] *n* cortigiano(-a)
court martial (*pl* **courts martial**) *n* corte *f* marziale
courtroom ['kɔːtrum] *n* tribunale *m*
court shoe *n* scarpa *f* décolleté *inv*
courtyard ['kɔːtjɑːd] *n* cortile *m*
cousin ['kʌzn] *n* cugino(-a)
cove [kəuv] *n* piccola baia
covenant ['kʌvənənt] *n* accordo ■ *vt*: **to ~ to do sth** impegnarsi (per iscritto) a fare qc
Coventry ['kɔvəntrɪ] *n*: **to send sb to ~** (*fig*) dare l'ostracismo a qn
cover ['kʌvəʳ] *vt* (*gen*) coprire; (*distance*) coprire, percorrere; (*Press: report on*) fare un servizio su ■ *n* (*of pan*) coperchio; (*over furniture*) fodera; (*of book*) copertina; (*shelter*) riparo; (*Comm, Insurance*) copertura; **to take ~** mettersi al coperto; **under ~** al riparo; **under ~ of darkness** protetto dall'oscurità; **under separate ~** (*Comm*) a parte, in plico separato; **£10 will ~ everything** 10 sterline saranno sufficienti
▸ **cover up** *vt* (*child, object*): **to ~ up (with)** coprire (di); (*fig: hide: truth, facts*) nascondere ■ *vi*: **to ~ up for sb** (*fig*) coprire qn
coverage ['kʌvərɪdʒ] *n* (*Press, TV, Radio*): **to give full ~ to** fare un ampio servizio su
coveralls ['kʌvərɔːlz] *npl* (*US*) tuta

cover charge *n* coperto
covering ['kʌvərɪŋ] *n* copertura
covering letter, (*US*) **cover letter** *n* lettera d'accompagnamento
cover note *n* (*Insurance*) polizza (di assicurazione) provvisoria
cover price *n* prezzo di copertina
covert ['kʌvət] *adj* nascosto(-a); (*glance*) di sottecchi, furtivo(-a)
cover-up ['kʌvərʌp] *n* occultamento (di informazioni)
covet ['kʌvɪt] *vt* bramare
cow [kau] *n* vacca ■ *cpd* femmina ■ *vt* intimidire; ~ **elephant** *n* elefantessa
cowardice ['kauədɪs] *n* vigliaccheria
cowardly ['kauədlɪ] *adj* vigliacco(-a)
cowboy ['kaubɔɪ] *n* cow-boy *m inv*
cower ['kauə[r]] *vi* acquattarsi
cowshed ['kauʃɛd] *n* stalla
cowslip ['kauslɪp] *n* (*Bot*) primula (odorata)
coxswain ['kɔksn] *n* (*also*: **cox**) timoniere *m*
coy [kɔɪ] *adj* falsamente timido(-a)
coyote [kɔɪ'əutɪ] *n* coyote *m inv*
cozy ['kəuzɪ] *adj* (*US*) = **cosy**
CP *n abbr* (= *Communist Party*) P.C. *m*
cp. *abbr* (= *compare*) cfr.
CPA *n abbr* (*US*) = **certified public accountant**
CPI *n abbr* (*US*: = *Consumer Price Index*) *indice dei prezzi al consumo*
Cpl. *abbr* = **corporal**
CP/M *n abbr* (= *Control Program for Microcomputers*) CP/M *m*
c.p.s. *abbr* (= *characters per second*) c.p.s.
CPSA *n abbr* (*Brit*: = *Civil and Public Services Association*) *sindacato dei servizi pubblici*
CPU *n abbr* = **central processing unit**
cr. *abbr* = **credit**; **creditor**
crab [kræb] *n* granchio
crab apple *n* mela selvatica
crack [kræk] *n* (*split, slit*) fessura, crepa; incrinatura; (*noise*) schiocco; (*: of gun*) scoppio; (*joke*) battuta; (*col: attempt*): **to have a ~ at sth** tentare qc; (*Drugs*) crack *m inv* ■ *vt* spaccare; incrinare; (*whip*) schioccare; (*nut*) schiacciare; (*case, mystery: solve*) risolvere; (*code*) decifrare ■ *cpd* (*athlete*) di prim'ordine; **to ~ jokes** (*col*) dire battute, scherzare; **to get cracking** (*col*) darsi una mossa
▸ **crack down on** *vt fus* prendere serie misure contro, porre freno a
▸ **crack up** *vi* crollare
crackdown ['krækdaun] *n* repressione *f*
cracked [krækt] *adj* (*col*) matto(-a)
cracker ['krækə[r]] *n* cracker *m inv*; (*firework*) petardo; (*Christmas cracker*) mortaretto natalizio (con sorpresa); **a ~ of a ...** (*Brit col*) un(-a) ... formidabile; **he's crackers** (*Brit col*) è tocco
crackle ['krækl] *vi* crepitare
crackling ['kræklɪŋ] *n* crepitio; (*on radio, telephone*) disturbo; (*of pork*) cotenna croccante (*del maiale*)
crackpot ['krækpɔt] *n* (*col*) imbecille *m/f* con idee assurde, assurdo(-a)
cradle ['kreɪdl] *n* culla ■ *vt* (*child*) tenere fra le braccia; (*object*) reggere tra le braccia
craft [krɑːft] *n* mestiere *m*; (*cunning*) astuzia; (*boat*) naviglio
craftsman ['krɑːftsmən] *n* artigiano
craftsmanship ['krɑːftsmənʃɪp] *n* abilità
crafty ['krɑːftɪ] *adj* furbo(-a), astuto(-a)
crag [kræg] *n* roccia
cram [kræm] *vt* (*fill*): **to ~ sth with** riempire qc di; (*put*): **to ~ sth into** stipare qc in
cramming ['kræmɪŋ] *n* (*fig: pej*) sgobbare *m*
cramp [kræmp] *n* crampo ■ *vt* soffocare, impedire
cramped [kræmpt] *adj* ristretto(-a)
crampon ['kræmpən] *n* (*Climbing*) rampone *m*
cranberry ['krænbərɪ] *n* mirtillo
crane [kreɪn] *n* gru *f inv* ■ *vt, vi*: **to ~ forward, to ~ one's neck** allungare il collo
cranium (*pl* **crania**) ['kreɪnɪəm, 'kreɪnɪə] *n* cranio
crank [kræŋk] *n* manovella; (*person*) persona stramba
crankshaft ['krænkʃɑːft] *n* albero a gomiti
cranky ['kræŋkɪ] *adj* eccentrico(-a); (*bad-tempered*): **to be ~** avere i nervi
cranny ['krænɪ] *n see* **nook**
crap [kræp] *n* (*col!*) fesserie *fpl*; **to have a ~** cacare (*!*)
crappy ['kræpɪ] *adj* (*col*) di merda (*!*)
crash [kræʃ] *n* fragore *m*; (*of car*) incidente *m*; (*of plane*) caduta; (*of business*) fallimento; (*Stock Exchange*) crollo ■ *vt* fracassare ■ *vi* (*plane*) fracassarsi; (*car*) avere un incidente; (*two cars*) scontrarsi; (*fig*) fallire, andare in rovina; **to ~ into** scontrarsi con; **he crashed the car into a wall** andò a sbattere contro un muro con la macchina
crash barrier *n* (*Brit Aut*) guardrail *m inv*
crash course *n* corso intensivo
crash helmet *n* casco
crash landing *n* atterraggio di fortuna
crass [kræs] *adj* crasso(-a)
crate [kreɪt] *n* gabbia
crater ['kreɪtə[r]] *n* cratere *m*
cravat, cravate [krə'væt] *n* fazzoletto da collo
crave [kreɪv] *vi*: **to ~ for** desiderare ardentemente
craving ['kreɪvɪŋ] *n*: **~ (for)** (*for food, cigarettes etc*) (gran) voglia (di)

crawl [krɔːl] *vi* strisciare carponi; (*child*) andare a gattoni; (*vehicle*) avanzare lentamente ■ *n* (*Swimming*) crawl *m*; **to ~ to sb** (*col: suck up*) arruffianarsi qn
crawler lane ['krɔːləʳ-] *n* (*Brit Aut*) *corsia riservata al traffico lento*
crayfish ['kreɪfɪʃ] *n* (*pl inv*) gambero (d'acqua dolce)
crayon ['kreɪən] *n* matita colorata
craze [kreɪz] *n* mania
crazed [kreɪzd] *adj* (*look, person*) folle, pazzo(-a); (*pottery, glaze*) incrinato(-a)
crazy ['kreɪzɪ] *adj* matto(-a); **to go ~** uscir di senno, impazzire; **to be ~ about sb** (*col: keen*) essere pazzo di qn; **to be ~ about sth** andare matto per qc
crazy paving *n* (*Brit*) lastricato a mosaico irregolare
creak [kriːk] *vi* cigolare, scricchiolare
cream [kriːm] *n* crema; (*fresh*) panna ■ *adj* (*colour*) color crema *inv*; **whipped ~** panna montata
▸ **cream off** *vt* (*best talents, part of profits*) portarsi via
cream cake *n* torta alla panna
cream cheese *n* formaggio fresco
creamery ['kriːmərɪ] *n* (*shop*) latteria; (*factory*) caseificio
creamy ['kriːmɪ] *adj* cremoso(-a)
crease [kriːs] *n* grinza; (*deliberate*) piega ■ *vt* sgualcire ■ *vi* sgualcirsi
crease-resistant ['kriːsrɪzɪstənt] *adj* ingualcibile
create [kriː'eɪt] *vt* creare; (*fuss, noise*) fare
creation [kriː'eɪʃən] *n* creazione *f*
creative [kriː'eɪtɪv] *adj* creativo(-a)
creativity [kriːeɪ'tɪvɪtɪ] *n* creatività
creator [kriː'eɪtəʳ] *n* creatore(-trice)
creature ['kriːtʃəʳ] *n* creatura
crèche, creche [krɛʃ] *n* asilo infantile
credence ['kriːdns] *n* credenza, fede *f*
credentials [krɪ'dɛnʃlz] *npl* (*papers*) credenziali *fpl*; (*letters of reference*) referenze *fpl*
credibility [krɛdɪ'bɪlɪtɪ] *n* credibilità
credible ['krɛdɪbl] *adj* credibile; (*witness, source*) attendibile
credit ['krɛdɪt] *n* credito; onore *m*; (*Scol: esp US*) *certificato del compimento di una parte del corso universitario* ■ *vt* (*Comm*) accreditare; (*believe: also:* **give credit to**) credere, prestar fede a; **to ~ £5 to sb** accreditare 5 sterline a qn; **to ~ sb with sth** (*fig*) attribuire qc a qn; **on ~** a credito; **to one's ~** a proprio onore; **to take the ~ for** farsi il merito di; **to be in ~** (*person*) essere creditore(-trice); (*bank account*) essere coperto(-a); **he's a ~ to his family** fa onore alla sua famiglia; *see also* **credits**
creditable ['krɛdɪtəbl] *adj* che fa onore, degno(-a) di lode
credit account *n* conto di credito
credit agency *n* (*Brit*) agenzia di analisi di credito
credit balance *n* saldo attivo
credit bureau *n* (*US*) agenzia di analisi di credito
credit card *n* carta di credito
credit control *n* controllo dei crediti
credit crunch *n* improvvisa stretta di credito
credit facilities *npl* agevolazioni *fpl* creditizie
credit limit *n* limite *m* di credito
credit note *n* (*Brit*) nota di credito
creditor ['krɛdɪtəʳ] *n* creditore(-trice)
credits ['krɛdɪts] *npl* (*Cine*) titoli *mpl*
credit transfer *n* bancogiro, postagiro
creditworthy ['krɛdɪt'wəːðɪ] *adj* autorizzabile al credito
credulity [krɪ'djuːlɪtɪ] *n* credulità
creed [kriːd] *n* credo; dottrina
creek [kriːk] *n* insenatura; (*US*) piccolo fiume *m*
creel [kriːl] *n* cestino per il pesce; (*also:* **lobster creel**) nassa
creep [kriːp] *vi* (*pt, pp* **crept**) [krɛpt] avanzare furtivamente (*or* pian piano); (*plant*) arrampicarsi ■ *n* (*col*): **he's a ~** è un tipo viscido; **it gives me the creeps** (*col*) mi fa venire la pelle d'oca; **to ~ up on sb** avvicinarsi quatto quatto a qn; (*fig: old age etc*) cogliere qn alla sprovvista
creeper ['kriːpəʳ] *n* pianta rampicante
creepy ['kriːpɪ] *adj* (*frightening*) che fa accapponare la pelle
creepy-crawly ['kriːpɪ'krɔːlɪ] *n* (*col*) bestiolina, insetto
cremate [krɪ'meɪt] *vt* cremare
cremation [krɪ'meɪʃən] *n* cremazione *f*
crematorium (*pl* **crematoria**) [krɛmə'tɔːrɪəm, -'tɔːrɪə] *n* forno crematorio
creosote ['krɪəsəut] *n* creosoto
crêpe [kreɪp] *n* crespo
crêpe bandage *n* (*Brit*) fascia elastica
crêpe paper *n* carta crespa
crêpe sole *n* suola di para
crept [krɛpt] *pt, pp of* **creep**
crescendo [krɪ'ʃɛndəu] *n* crescendo
crescent ['krɛsnt] *n* (*shape*) mezzaluna; (*street*) strada semicircolare
cress [krɛs] *n* crescione *m*
crest [krɛst] *n* cresta; (*of helmet*) pennacchiera; (*of coat of arms*) cimiero
crestfallen ['krɛstfɔːlən] *adj* mortificato(-a)
Crete [kriːt] *n* Creta
crevasse [krɪ'væs] *n* crepaccio
crevice ['krɛvɪs] *n* fessura, crepa

crew [kru:] *n* equipaggio; (*Cine*) troupe *f inv*; (*gang*) banda, compagnia
crew-cut ['kru:kʌt] *n*: **to have a ~** avere i capelli a spazzola
crew-neck ['kru:nɛk] *n* girocollo
crib [krɪb] *n* culla; (*Rel*) presepio ■ *vt* (*col*) copiare
cribbage ['krɪbɪdʒ] *n tipo di gioco di carte*
crick [krɪk] *n* crampo; **~ in the neck** torcicollo
cricket ['krɪkɪt] *n* (*insect*) grillo; (*game*) cricket *m*
cricketer ['krɪkɪtəʳ] *n* giocatore *m* di cricket
crime [kraɪm] *n* (*in general*) criminalità; (*instance*) crimine *m*, delitto
crime wave *n* ondata di criminalità
criminal ['krɪmɪnl] *adj, n* criminale (*m/f*); **C~ Investigation Department (CID)** ≈ polizia giudiziaria
crimp [krɪmp] *vt* arricciare
crimson ['krɪmzn] *adj* color cremisi *inv*
cringe [krɪndʒ] *vi* acquattarsi; (*fig*) essere servile
crinkle ['krɪŋkl] *vt* arricciare, increspare
cripple ['krɪpl] *n* zoppo(-a) ■ *vt* azzoppare; (*ship, plane*) avariare; (*production, exports*) rovinare; **crippled with arthritis** sciancato(-a) per l'artrite
crippling ['krɪplɪŋ] *adj* (*taxes, debts*) esorbitante; (*disease*) molto debilitante
crisis (*pl* **crises**) ['kraɪsɪs, -si:z] *n* crisi *f inv*
crisp [krɪsp] *adj* croccante; (*fig*) frizzante, vivace; deciso(-a)
crisps [krɪsps] *npl* (*Brit*) patatine *fpl* fritte
criss-cross ['krɪskrɔs] *adj* incrociato(-a) ■ *vt* incrociarsi
criterion (*pl* **criteria**) [kraɪ'tɪərɪən, -'tɪərɪə] *n* criterio
critic ['krɪtɪk] *n* critico(-a)
critical ['krɪtɪkl] *adj* critico(-a); **to be ~ of sb/sth** criticare qn/qc, essere critico verso qn/qc
critically ['krɪtɪklɪ] *adv* criticamente; **~ ill** gravemente malato
criticism ['krɪtɪsɪzəm] *n* critica
criticize ['krɪtɪsaɪz] *vt* criticare
critique [krɪ'ti:k] *n* critica, saggio critico
croak [krəuk] *vi* gracchiare
Croat ['krəuæt] *adj, n* = **Croatian**
Croatia [krəu'eɪʃɪə] *n* Croazia
Croatian [krəu'eɪʃɪən] *adj* croato(-a) ■ *n* croato(-a); (*Ling*) croato
crochet ['krəuʃeɪ] *n* lavoro all'uncinetto
crock [krɔk] *n* coccio; (*col: person: also:* **old crock**) rottame *m*; (*: car etc*) caffettiera, rottame *m*
crockery ['krɔkərɪ] *n* vasellame *m*; (*plates, cups etc*) stoviglie *fpl*
crocodile ['krɔkədaɪl] *n* coccodrillo
crocus ['krəukəs] *n* croco
croft [krɔft] *n* (*Brit*) piccolo podere *m*
crofter ['krɔftəʳ] *n* (*Brit*) affittuario di un piccolo podere
crone [krəun] *n* strega
crony ['krəunɪ] *n* (*col*) amicone(-a)
crook [kruk] *n* truffatore *m*; (*of shepherd*) bastone *m*
crooked ['krukɪd] *adj* curvo(-a), storto(-a); (*person, action*) disonesto(-a)
crop [krɔp] *n* raccolto; (*produce*) coltivazione *f*; (*of bird*) gozzo, ingluvie *f* ■ *vt* (*cut: hair*) tagliare, rapare; (*animals: grass*) brucare
▸ **crop up** *vi* presentarsi
cropper ['krɔpəʳ] *n*: **to come a ~** (*col*) fare fiasco
crop spraying *n* spruzzatura di antiparassitari
croquet ['krəukeɪ] *n* croquet *m*
croquette [krə'kɛt] *n* crocchetta
cross [krɔs] *n* croce *f*; (*Biol*) incrocio ■ *vt* (*street etc*) attraversare; (*arms, legs, Biol*) incrociare; (*cheque*) sbarrare; (*thwart: person, plan*) contrastare, ostacolare ■ *vi*: **the boat crosses from ... to ...** la barca fa la traversata da ... a ... ■ *adj* di cattivo umore; **to ~ o.s.** fare il segno della croce, segnarsi; **we have a crossed line** (*Brit: on telephone*) c'è un'interferenza; **they've got their lines crossed** (*fig*) si sono fraintesi; **to be/get ~ with sb (about sth)** essere arrabbiato(-a)/arrabbiarsi con qn (per qc)
▸ **cross out** *vt* cancellare
▸ **cross over** *vi* attraversare
crossbar ['krɔsbɑ:ʳ] *n* traversa
crossbow ['krɔsbəu] *n* balestra
crossbreed ['krɔsbri:d] *n* incrocio
cross-Channel ferry ['krɔs'tʃænl-] *n* traghetto che attraversa la Manica
cross-check ['krɔstʃɛk] *n* controprova ■ *vi* fare una controprova
crosscountry [krɔs'kʌntrɪ], **crosscountry race** [krɔs'kʌntrɪ-] *n* cross-country *m inv*
cross-dressing [krɔs'drɛsɪŋ] *n* travestitismo
cross-examination ['krɔsɪgzæmɪ'neɪʃən] *n* (*Law*) controinterrogatorio
cross-examine ['krɔsɪg'zæmɪn] *vt* (*Law*) sottoporre a controinterrogatorio
cross-eyed ['krɔsaɪd] *adj* strabico(-a)
crossfire ['krɔsfaɪəʳ] *n* fuoco incrociato
crossing ['krɔsɪŋ] *n* incrocio; (*sea-passage*) traversata; (*also:* **pedestrian crossing**) passaggio pedonale
crossing point *n* valico di frontiera
cross-purposes ['krɔs'pə:pəsɪz] *npl*: **to be at ~ with sb** (*misunderstand*) fraintendere qn; **to talk at ~** fraintendersi

cross-question [krɔs'kwɛstʃən] *vt* (*Law*) = **cross-examine**; (*fig*) sottoporre ad un interrogatorio
cross-reference ['krɔs'rɛfərəns] *n* rinvio, rimando
crossroads ['krɔsrəudz] *n* incrocio
cross section *n* (*Biol*) sezione *f* trasversale; (*in population*) settore *m* rappresentativo
crosswalk ['krɔswɔ:k] *n* (*US*) strisce *fpl* pedonali, passaggio pedonale
crosswind ['krɔswɪnd] *n* vento di traverso
crosswise ['krɔswaɪz] *adv* di traverso
crossword ['krɔswə:d] *n* cruciverba *m inv*
crotch [krɔtʃ] *n* (*Anat*) inforcatura; (*of garment*) pattina
crotchet ['krɔtʃɪt] *n* (*Mus*) semiminima
crotchety ['krɔtʃɪtɪ] *adj* (*person*) burbero(-a)
crouch [krautʃ] *vi* acquattarsi; rannicchiarsi
croup [kru:p] *n* (*Med*) crup *m*
crouton ['kru:tɔn] *n* crostino
crow [krəu] *n* (*bird*) cornacchia; (*of cock*) canto del gallo ■ *vi* (*cock*) cantare; (*fig*) vantarsi; cantar vittoria
crowbar ['krəubɑ:ʳ] *n* piede *m* di porco
crowd [kraud] *n* folla ■ *vt* affollare, stipare ■ *vi* affollarsi; **crowds of people** un sacco di gente
crowded ['kraudɪd] *adj* affollato(-a); **~ with** stipato(-a) di
crowd scene *n* (*Cine, Theat*) scena di massa
crown [kraun] *n* corona; (*of head*) calotta cranica; (*of hat*) cocuzzolo; (*of hill*) cima ■ *vt* incoronare; (*tooth*) incapsulare; **and to ~ it all ...** (*fig*) e per giunta ..., e come se non bastasse ...; *vedi nota*

CROWN COURT

Nel sistema legale inglese, la *crown court* è un tribunale penale che si sposta da una città all'altra. È formata da una giuria locale ed è presieduta da un giudice che si sposta assieme alla "court". Vi si discutono i reati più gravi, mentre dei reati minori si occupano le "magistrates' courts", presiedute da un giudice di pace, ma senza giuria. è il giudice di pace che decide se passare o meno un caso alla *crown court*.

crowning ['kraunɪŋ] *adj* (*achievement, glory*) supremo(-a)
crown jewels *npl* gioielli *mpl* della Corona
crown prince *n* principe *m* ereditario
crow's-feet ['krəuzfi:t] *npl* zampe *fpl* di gallina
crow's-nest ['krəuznɛst] *n* (*on sailing-ship*) coffa
crucial ['kru:ʃl] *adj* cruciale, decisivo(-a); **~ to** essenziale per
crucifix ['kru:sɪfɪks] *n* crocifisso
crucifixion [kru:sɪ'fɪkʃən] *n* crocifissione *f*
crucify ['kru:sɪfaɪ] *vt* crocifiggere, mettere in croce; (*fig*) distruggere, fare a pezzi
crude [kru:d] *adj* (*materials*) greggio(-a); non raffinato(-a); (*fig: basic*) crudo(-a), primitivo(-a); (*: vulgar*) rozzo(-a), grossolano(-a)
crude, crude oil *n* (petrolio) greggio
cruel ['kruəl] *adj* crudele
cruelty ['kruəltɪ] *n* crudeltà *f inv*
cruet ['kru:ɪt] *n* ampolla
cruise [kru:z] *n* crociera ■ *vi* andare a velocità di crociera; (*taxi*) circolare
cruise missile *n* missile *m* cruise *inv*
cruiser ['kru:zəʳ] *n* incrociatore *m*
cruising speed ['kru:zɪŋ-] *n* velocità *f inv* di crociera
crumb [krʌm] *n* briciola
crumble ['krʌmbl] *vt* sbriciolare ■ *vi* sbriciolarsi; (*plaster etc*) sgretolarsi; (*land, earth*) franare; (*building, fig*) crollare
crumbly ['krʌmblɪ] *adj* friabile
crummy ['krʌmɪ] *adj* (*col: cheap*) di infima categoria; (*: depressed*) giù *inv*
crumpet ['krʌmpɪt] *n specie di frittella*
crumple ['krʌmpl] *vt* raggrinzare, spiegazzare
crunch [krʌntʃ] *vt* sgranocchiare; (*underfoot*) scricchiolare ■ *n* (*fig*) punto *or* momento cruciale
crunchy ['krʌntʃɪ] *adj* croccante
crusade [kru:'seɪd] *n* crociata ■ *vi* (*fig*): **to ~ for/against** fare una crociata per/contro
crusader [kru:'seɪdəʳ] *n* crociato; (*fig*): **~ (for)** sostenitore(-trice) (di)
crush [krʌʃ] *n* folla; (*love*): **to have a ~ on sb** avere una cotta per qn; (*drink*): **lemon ~** spremuta di limone ■ *vt* schiacciare; (*crumple*) sgualcire; (*grind, break up: garlic, ice*) tritare; (*: grapes*) pigiare
crush barrier *n* (*Brit*) transenna
crushing ['krʌʃɪŋ] *adj* schiacciante
crust [krʌst] *n* crosta
crustacean [krʌs'teɪʃən] *n* crostaceo
crusty ['krʌstɪ] *adj* (*bread*) croccante; (*person*) brontolone(-a); (*remark*) brusco(-a)
crutch [krʌtʃ] *n* (*Med*) gruccia; (*support*) sostegno; (*also:* **crotch**) pattina
crux [krʌks] *n* nodo
cry [kraɪ] *vi* piangere; (*shout: also:* **cry out**) urlare ■ *n* urlo, grido; (*of animal*) verso; **to ~ for help** gridare aiuto; **what are you crying**

about? perché piangi?; **she had a good ~** si è fatta un bel pianto; **it's a far ~ from ...** (*fig*) è tutt'un'altra cosa da ...
▸ **cry off** *vi* ritirarsi
crying ['kraɪɪŋ] *adj* (*fig*) palese; urgente
crypt [krɪpt] *n* cripta
cryptic ['krɪptɪk] *adj* ermetico(-a)
crystal ['krɪstl] *n* cristallo
crystal-clear ['krɪstl'klɪəʳ] *adj* cristallino(-a); (*fig*) chiaro(-a) (come il sole)
crystallize ['krɪstəlaɪz] *vi* cristallizzarsi ■ *vt* (*fig*) concretizzare, concretare; **crystallized fruits** (*Brit*) frutta candita
CSA *n abbr* (*US*) = **Confederate States of America**; (*Brit*: = *Child Support Agency*) *istituto a difesa dei figli di coppie separate, che si adopera affinché venga rispettato l'obbligo del mantenimento*
CSC *n abbr* (= *Civil Service Commission*) *commissione per il reclutamento dei funzionari statali*
CS gas *n* (*Brit*) *tipo di gas lacrimogeno*
CST *abbr* (*US*: = *Central Standard Time*) *fuso orario*
CT *abbr* (*US*) = **Connecticut**
ct *abbr* = **cent**; **court**
CTC *n abbr* (*Brit*: = *city technology college*) *istituto tecnico superiore*
cu. *abbr* = **cubic**
cub [kʌb] *n* cucciolo; (*also*: **cub scout**) lupetto
Cuba ['kju:bə] *n* Cuba
Cuban ['kju:bən] *adj, n* cubano(-a)
cubbyhole ['kʌbɪhəul] *n* angolino
cube [kju:b] *n* cubo ■ *vt* (*Math*) elevare al cubo
cube root *n* radice *f* cubica
cubic ['kju:bɪk] *adj* cubico(-a); **~ metre** *etc* metro *etc* cubo; **~ capacity** (*Aut*) cilindrata
cubicle ['kju:bɪkl] *n* scompartimento separato; cabina
cuckoo ['kuku:] *n* cucù *m inv*
cuckoo clock *n* orologio a cucù
cucumber ['kju:kʌmbəʳ] *n* cetriolo
cud [kʌd] *n*: **to chew the ~** ruminare
cuddle ['kʌdl] *vt* abbracciare, coccolare ■ *vi* abbracciarsi
cuddly ['kʌdlɪ] *adj* da coccolare
cudgel ['kʌdʒl] *n* randello ■ *vt*: **to ~ one's brains** scervellarsi, spremere le meningi
cue [kju:] *n* stecca; (*Theat etc*) segnale *m*
cuff [kʌf] *n* (*of shirt, coat etc*) polsino; (*US*: *on trousers*) = **turnup**; (*blow*) schiaffo ■ *vt* dare uno schiaffo a; **off the ~** *adv* improvvisando
cufflink ['kʌflɪŋk] *n* gemello
cu. ft. *abbr* = **cubic feet**
cu. in. *abbr* = **cubic inches**
cuisine [kwɪ'zi:n] *n* cucina
cul-de-sac ['kʌldəsæk] *n* vicolo cieco
culinary ['kʌlɪnərɪ] *adj* culinario(-a)
cull [kʌl] *vt* (*kill selectively*: *animals*) selezionare e abbattere
culminate ['kʌlmɪneɪt] *vi*: **to ~ in** culminare con
culmination [kʌlmɪ'neɪʃən] *n* culmine *m*
culottes [kju:'lɔts] *npl* gonna *f* pantalone *inv*
culpable ['kʌlpəbl] *adj* colpevole
culprit ['kʌlprɪt] *n* colpevole *m/f*
cult [kʌlt] *n* culto
cult figure *n* idolo
cultivate ['kʌltɪveɪt] *vt* (*also fig*) coltivare
cultivation [kʌltɪ'veɪʃən] *n* coltivazione *f*
cultural ['kʌltʃərəl] *adj* culturale
culture ['kʌltʃəʳ] *n* (*also fig*) cultura
cultured ['kʌltʃəd] *adj* colto(-a)
cumbersome ['kʌmbəsəm] *adj* ingombrante
cumin ['kʌmɪn] *n* (*spice*) cumino
cumulative ['kju:mjulətɪv] *adj* cumulativo(-a)
cunning ['kʌnɪŋ] *n* astuzia, furberia ■ *adj* astuto(-a), furbo(-a); (*clever*: *device, idea*) ingegnoso(-a)
cunt [kʌnt] *n* (*col!*) figa (*!*); (*insult*) stronzo(-a) (*!*)
cup [kʌp] *n* tazza; (*prize*) coppa; **a ~ of tea** una tazza di tè
cupboard ['kʌbəd] *n* armadio
cup final *n* (*Brit Football*) finale *f* di coppa
Cupid ['kju:pɪd] *n* Cupido; (*figurine*): **cupid** cupido
cupidity [kju:'pɪdɪtɪ] *n* cupidigia
cupola ['kju:pələ] *n* cupola
cuppa ['kʌpə] *n* (*Brit col*) tazza di tè
cup-tie ['kʌptaɪ] *n* (*Brit Football*) partita di coppa
curable ['kjuərəbl] *adj* curabile
curate ['kjuərɪt] *n* cappellano
curator [kjuə'reɪtəʳ] *n* direttore *m* (*di museo etc*)
curb [kə:b] *vt* tenere a freno; (*expenditure*) limitare ■ *n* freno; (*US*) = **kerb**
curd cheese [kə:d-] *n* cagliata
curdle ['kə:dl] *vi* cagliare
curds [kə:dz] *npl* latte *m* cagliato
cure [kjuəʳ] *vt* guarire; (*Culin*) trattare; affumicare; essiccare ■ *n* rimedio; **to be cured of sth** essere guarito(-a) da qc
cure-all ['kjuərɔ:l] *n* (*also fig*) panacea, toccasana *m inv*
curfew ['kə:fju:] *n* coprifuoco
curio ['kjuərɪəu] *n* curiosità *f inv*
curiosity [kjuərɪ'ɔsɪtɪ] *n* curiosità
curious ['kjuərɪəs] *adj* curioso(-a); **I'm ~ about him** m'incuriosisce
curiously ['kjuərɪəslɪ] *adv* con curiosità; (*strangely*) stranamente; **~ enough, ...** per quanto possa sembrare strano, ...
curl [kə:l] *n* riccio; (*of smoke etc*) anello ■ *vt* ondulare; (*tightly*) arricciare ■ *vi* arricciarsi
▸ **curl up** *vi* avvolgersi a spirale; rannicchiarsi

curler ['kəːləʳ] *n* bigodino; (*Sport*) giocatore(-trice) di curling
curlew ['kəːluː] *n* chiurlo
curling ['kəːlɪŋ] *n* (*Sport*) curling *m*
curling tongs, (*US*) **curling irons** *npl* (*for hair*) arricciacapelli *m inv*
curly ['kəːlɪ] *adj* ricciuto(-a)
currant ['kʌrnt] *n* uva passa
currency ['kʌrnsɪ] *n* moneta; **foreign ~** divisa estera; **to gain ~** (*fig*) acquistare larga diffusione
current ['kʌrnt] *adj* corrente; (*tendency, price, event*) attuale ■ *n* corrente *f*; **in ~ use** in uso corrente, d'uso comune; **the ~ issue of a magazine** l'ultimo numero di una rivista; **direct/alternating ~** (*Elec*) corrente continua/alternata
current account *n* (*Brit*) conto corrente
current affairs *npl* attualità *fpl*
current assets *npl* (*Comm*) attivo realizzabile e disponibile
current liabilities *npl* (*Comm*) passività *fpl* correnti
currently ['kʌrntlɪ] *adv* attualmente
curriculum (*pl* **curriculums** *or* **curricula**) [kə'rɪkjuləm, -lə] *n* curriculum *m inv*
curriculum vitae [-'viːtaɪ] *n* curriculum vitae *m inv*
curry ['kʌrɪ] *n* curry *m inv* ■ *vt*: **to ~ favour with** cercare di attirarsi i favori di; **chicken ~** pollo al curry
curry powder *n* curry *m*
curse [kəːs] *vt* maledire ■ *vi* bestemmiare ■ *n* maledizione *f*; bestemmia
cursor ['kəːsəʳ] *n* (*Comput*) cursore *m*
cursory ['kəːsərɪ] *adj* superficiale
curt [kəːt] *adj* secco(-a)
curtail [kəː'teɪl] *vt* (*visit etc*) accorciare; (*expenses etc*) ridurre, decurtare
curtain ['kəːtn] *n* tenda; (*Theat*) sipario; **to draw the curtains** (*together*) chiudere *or* tirare le tende; (*apart*) aprire le tende
curtain call *n* (*Theat*) chinata alla ribalta
curtsy, curtsey ['kəːtsɪ] *n* inchino, riverenza ■ *vi* fare un inchino *or* una riverenza
curvature ['kəːvətʃəʳ] *n* curvatura
curve [kəːv] *n* curva ■ *vt* curvare ■ *vi* curvarsi; (*road*) fare una curva
curved [kəːvd] *adj* curvo(-a)
cushion ['kuʃən] *n* cuscino ■ *vt* (*shock*) fare da cuscinetto a
cushy ['kuʃɪ] *adj* (*col*): **a ~ job** un lavoro di tutto riposo; **to have a ~ time** spassarsela
custard ['kʌstəd] *n* (*for pouring*) crema
custard powder *n* (*Brit*) crema pasticcera in polvere
custodial sentence [kʌs'təudɪəl-] *n* condanna a pena detentiva
custodian [kʌs'təudɪən] *n* custode *m/f*; (*of museum etc*) soprintendente *m/f*
custody ['kʌstədɪ] *n* (*of child*) custodia; (*for offenders*) arresto; **to take sb into ~** mettere qn in detenzione preventiva; **in the ~ of** alla custodia di
custom ['kʌstəm] *n* costume *m*, usanza; (*Law*) consuetudine *f*; (*Comm*) clientela; *see also* **customs**
customary ['kʌstəmərɪ] *adj* consueto(-a); **it is ~ to do** è consuetudine fare
custom-built ['kʌstəm'bɪlt] *adj see* **custom-made**
customer ['kʌstəməʳ] *n* cliente *m/f*; **he's an awkward ~** (*col*) è un tipo incontentabile
customer profile *n* profilo del cliente
customized ['kʌstəmaɪzd] *adj* personalizzato(-a); (*car*) fuoriserie *inv*
custom-made ['kʌstəm'meɪd] *adj* (*clothes*) fatto(-a) su misura; (*other goods: also*: **custom-built**) fatto(-a) su ordinazione
customs ['kʌstəmz] *npl* dogana; **to go through (the) ~** passare la dogana
Customs and Excise *n* (*Brit*) Ufficio Dazi e Dogana
customs officer *n* doganiere *m*
cut [kʌt] *vb* (*pt, pp* **~**) *vt* tagliare; (*shape, make*) intagliare; (*reduce*) ridurre; (*col: avoid: class, lecture, appointment*) saltare ■ *vi* tagliare; (*intersect*) tagliarsi ■ *n* taglio; (*in salary etc*) riduzione *f*; **cold cuts** *npl* (*US*) affettati *mpl*; **power ~** mancanza di corrente elettrica; **to ~ one's finger** tagliarsi un dito; **to get one's hair ~** farsi tagliare i capelli; **to ~ a tooth** mettere un dente; **to ~ sb/sth short** interrompere qn/qc; **to ~ sb dead** ignorare qn completamente
▸ **cut back** *vt* (*plants*) tagliare; (*production, expenditure*) ridurre
▸ **cut down** *vt* (*tree*) abbattere; (*consumption, expenses*) ridurre; **to ~ sb down to size** (*fig*) sgonfiare *or* ridimensionare qn
▸ **cut down on** *vt fus* ridurre
▸ **cut in** *vi*: **to ~ in (on)** (*interrupt conversation*) intromettersi (in); (*Aut*) tagliare la strada (a)
▸ **cut off** *vt* tagliare; (*fig*) isolare; **we've been ~ off** (*Tel*) è caduta la linea
▸ **cut out** *vt* tagliare; (*picture*) ritagliare
▸ **cut up** *vt* (*gen*) tagliare; (*chop: food*) sminuzzare
cut-and-dried ['kʌtən'draɪd] *adj* (*also*: **cut-and-dry**) assodato(-a)
cutaway ['kʌtəweɪ] *adj, n*: **~ (drawing)** spaccato
cutback ['kʌtbæk] *n* riduzione *f*

cute [kjuːt] *adj* grazioso(-a); (*clever*) astuto(-a)
cut glass *n* cristallo
cuticle ['kjuːtɪkl] *n* (*on nail*) pellicina, cuticola
cutlery ['kʌtlərɪ] *n* posate *fpl*
cutlet ['kʌtlɪt] *n* costoletta
cutoff ['kʌtɔf] *n* (*also*: **cutoff point**) limite *m*
cutoff switch *n* interruttore *m*
cutout ['kʌtaut] *n* (*switch*) interruttore *m*; (*paper, cardboard figure*) ritaglio
cut-price ['kʌt'praɪs], (US) **cut-rate** ['kʌt'reɪt] *adj* a prezzo ridotto
cutthroat ['kʌtθrəut] *n* assassino ▪ *adj*: ~ **competition** concorrenza spietata
cutting ['kʌtɪŋ] *adj* tagliente; (*fig*) pungente ▪ *n* (*Brit*: *Press*) ritaglio (di giornale); (: *Rail*) trincea; (*Cine*) montaggio
cutting edge *n* (*of knife*) taglio, filo; **on** *or* **at the ~ of sth** all'avanguardia di qc
cuttlefish ['kʌtlfɪʃ] *n* seppia
cut-up ['kʌtʌp] *adj* stravolto(-a)
CV *n abbr* = **curriculum vitae**
CWO *abbr* = **cash with order**
cwt. *abbr* = **hundredweight**
cyanide ['saɪənaɪd] *n* cianuro
cybercafé ['saɪbəkæfeɪ] *n* cybercaffè *m inv*
cybercrime ['saɪbəkraɪm] *n* delinquenza informatica
cybernetics [saɪbə'nɛtɪks] *n* cibernetica
cyberterrorism [saɪbə'tɛrərɪzəm] *n* ciberterrorismo
cyclamen ['sɪkləmən] *n* ciclamino
cycle ['saɪkl] *n* ciclo; (*bicycle*) bicicletta ▪ *vi* andare in bicicletta
cycle path *n* percorso ciclabile
cycle race *n* gara *or* corsa ciclistica
cycle rack *n* portabiciclette *m inv*
cycle track *n* percorso ciclabile; (*in velodrome*) pista
cycling ['saɪklɪŋ] *n* ciclismo; **to go on a ~ holiday** (*Brit*) fare una vacanza in bicicletta
cyclist ['saɪklɪst] *n* ciclista *m/f*
cyclone ['saɪkləun] *n* ciclone *m*
cygnet ['sɪgnɪt] *n* cigno giovane
cylinder ['sɪlɪndə[r]] *n* cilindro
cylinder capacity *n* cilindrata
cylinder head *n* testata
cylinder head gasket *n* guarnizione *f* della testata del cilindro
cymbals ['sɪmblz] *npl* cembali *mpl*
cynic ['sɪnɪk] *n* cinico(-a)
cynical ['sɪnɪkl] *adj* cinico(-a)
cynicism ['sɪnɪsɪzəm] *n* cinismo
cypress ['saɪprɪs] *n* cipresso
Cypriot ['sɪprɪət] *adj, n* cipriota (*m/f*)
Cyprus ['saɪprəs] *n* Cipro
cyst [sɪst] *n* cisti *f inv*
cystitis [sɪ'staɪtɪs] *n* cistite *f*
CZ *n abbr* (*US*: = *Canal Zone*) *zona del Canale di Panama*
czar [zɑː[r]] *n* zar *m inv*
Czech [tʃɛk] *adj* ceco(-a) ▪ *n* ceco(-a); (*Ling*) ceco; **the ~ Republic** la Repubblica Ceca
Czechoslovak [tʃɛkə'sləuvæk] *adj, n* = **Czechoslovakian**
Czechoslovakia [tʃɛkəslə'vækɪə] *n* Cecoslovacchia
Czechoslovakian [tʃɛkəslə'vækɪən] *adj, n* cecoslovacco(-a)

Dd

D, d [di:] *n* (*letter*) D, d *f or m inv*; (*Mus*): **D** re *m*; **D for David**, (*US*) **D for Dog** ≈ D come Domodossola

D *abbr* (*US Pol*) = **democrat(ic)**

d *abbr* (*Brit: old*) = **penny**

d. *abbr* = **died**

DA *n abbr* (*US*) = **district attorney**

dab [dæb] *vt* (*eyes, wound*) tamponare; (*paint, cream*) applicare (con leggeri colpetti); **a ~ of paint** un colpetto di vernice

dabble ['dæbl] *vi*: **to ~ in** occuparsi (da dilettante) di

Dacca ['dækə] *n* Dacca *f*

dachshund ['dækshund] *n* bassotto

dad [dæd], **daddy** ['dædı] *n* babbo, papà *m inv*

daddy-long-legs [dædı'lɔŋlɛgz] *n* tipula, zanzarone *m*

daffodil ['dæfədıl] *n* trombone *m*, giunchiglia

daft [dɑ:ft] *adj* sciocco(-a); **to be ~ about sb** perdere la testa per qn; **to be ~ about sth** andare pazzo per qc

dagger ['dægəʳ] *n* pugnale *m*

dahlia ['deıljə] *n* dalia

daily ['deılı] *adj* quotidiano(-a), giornaliero(-a) ■ *n* quotidiano; (*Brit: servant*) donna di servizio ■ *adv* tutti i giorni; **twice ~** due volte al giorno

dainty ['deıntı] *adj* delicato(-a), grazioso(-a)

dairy ['dɛərı] *n* (*shop*) latteria; (*on farm*) caseificio ■ *cpd* caseario(-a)

dairy cow *n* mucca da latte

dairy farm *n* caseificio

dairy produce *n* latticini *mpl*

dais ['deııs] *n* pedana, palco

daisy ['deızı] *n* margherita

daisy wheel *n* (*on printer*) margherita

daisy-wheel printer ['deızıwi:l-] *n* stampante *f* a margherita

Dakar ['dækəʳ] *n* Dakar *f*

dale [deıl] *n* valle *f*

dally ['dælı] *vi* trastullarsi

dalmatian [dæl'meıʃən] *n* (*dog*) dalmata *m*

dam [dæm] *n* diga; (*reservoir*) bacino artificiale ■ *vt* sbarrare; costruire dighe su

damage ['dæmıdʒ] *n* danno, danni *mpl*; (*fig*) danno ■ *vt* danneggiare; (*fig*) recar danno a; **~ to property** danni materiali

damages ['dæmıdʒız] *npl* (*Law*) danni *mpl*; **to pay £5000 in ~** pagare 5000 sterline di indennizzo

damaging ['dæmıdʒıŋ] *adj*: **~ (to)** nocivo(-a) (a)

Damascus [də'mɑ:skəs] *n* Damasco *f*

dame [deım] *n* (*title, US col*) donna; (*Theat*) vecchia signora (*ruolo comico di donna recitato da un uomo*)

damn [dæm] *vt* condannare; (*curse*) maledire ■ *n* (*col*): **I don't give a ~** non me ne importa un fico ■ *adj* (*col*): **this ~ ...** questo maledetto ...; **~ (it)!** accidenti!

damnable ['dæmnəbl] *adj* (*col: behaviour*) vergognoso(-a); (*: weather*) schifoso(-a)

damnation [dæm'neıʃən] *n* (*Rel*) dannazione *f* ■ *excl* (*col*) dannazione!, diavolo!

damning ['dæmıŋ] *adj* (*evidence*) schiacciante

damp [dæmp] *adj* umido(-a) ■ *n* umidità, umido ■ *vt* (*also:* **dampen**: *cloth, rag*) inumidire, bagnare; (*enthusiasm etc*) spegnere

dampcourse ['dæmpkɔ:s] *n* strato *m* isolante antiumido *inv*

damper ['dæmpəʳ] *n* (*Mus*) sordina; (*of fire*) valvola di tiraggio; **to put a ~ on sth** (*fig: atmosphere*) gelare; (*: enthusiasm*) far sbollire

dampness ['dæmpnıs] *n* umidità, umido

damson ['dæmzən] *n* susina damaschina

dance [dɑ:ns] *n* danza, ballo; (*ball*) ballo ■ *vi* ballare; **to ~ about** saltellare

dance hall *n* dancing *m inv*, sala da ballo

dancer ['dɑ:nsəʳ] *n* danzatore(-trice); (*professional*) ballerino(-a)

dancing ['dɑ:nsıŋ] *n* danza, ballo

D and C *n abbr* (*Med: = dilation and curettage*) raschiamento

dandelion ['dændılaıən] *n* dente *m* di leone

dandruff ['dændrəf] *n* forfora

D & T *n abbr* (*Brit: Scol*) = **design and technology**

dandy ['dændɪ] *n* dandy *m inv*, elegantone *m* ■ *adj* (*US col*) fantastico(-a)
Dane [deɪn] *n* danese *m/f*
danger ['deɪndʒəʳ] *n* pericolo; **there is a ~ of fire** c'è pericolo di incendio; **in ~** in pericolo; **out of ~** fuori pericolo; **he was in ~ of falling** rischiava di cadere
danger list *n* (*Med*): **on the ~** in prognosi riservata
dangerous ['deɪndʒrəs] *adj* pericoloso(-a)
dangerously ['deɪndʒrəslɪ] *adv*: **~ ill** in pericolo di vita
danger zone *n* area di pericolo
dangle ['dæŋgl] *vt* dondolare; (*fig*) far balenare ■ *vi* pendolare
Danish ['deɪnɪʃ] *adj* danese ■ *n* (*Ling*) danese *m*
Danish pastry *n* dolce *m* di pasta sfoglia
dank [dæŋk] *adj* freddo(-a) e umido(-a)
Danube ['dænju:b] *n*: **the ~** il Danubio
dapper ['dæpəʳ] *adj* lindo(-a)
Dardanelles [dɑ:də'nɛlz] *npl* Dardanelli *mpl*
dare [dɛəʳ] *vt*: **to ~ sb to do** sfidare qn a fare ■ *vi*: **to ~ (to) do sth** osare fare qc; **I daren't tell him** (*Brit*) non oso dirglielo; **I ~ say he'll turn up** immagino che spunterà
daredevil ['dɛədɛvl] *n* scavezzacollo *m/f*
Dar-es-Salaam ['dɑ:rɛssə'lɑ:m] *n* Dar-es-Salaam *f*
daring ['dɛərɪŋ] *adj* audace, ardito(-a)
dark [dɑ:k] *adj* (*night, room*) buio(-a), scuro(-a); (*colour, complexion*) scuro(-a); (*fig*) cupo(-a), tetro(-a), nero(-a) ■ *n*: **in the ~** al buio; **it is/is getting ~** è/si sta facendo buio; **in the ~ about** (*fig*) all'oscuro di; **after ~** a notte fatta; **~ chocolate** cioccolata amara
darken ['dɑ:kən] *vt* (*room*) oscurare; (*photo, painting*) far scuro(-a) ■ *vi* oscurarsi; imbrunirsi
dark glasses *npl* occhiali *mpl* scuri
dark horse *n* (*fig*) incognita
darkly ['dɑ:klɪ] *adv* (*gloomily*) cupamente, con aria cupa; (*in a sinister way*) minacciosamente
darkness ['dɑ:knɪs] *n* oscurità, buio
darkroom ['dɑ:kru:m] *n* camera oscura
darling ['dɑ:lɪŋ] *adj* caro(-a) ■ *n* tesoro
darn [dɑ:n] *vt* rammendare
dart [dɑ:t] *n* freccetta ■ *vi*: **to ~ towards** (*also*: **make a dart towards**) precipitarsi verso; **to ~ along** passare come un razzo; **to ~ away** guizzare via; *see also* **darts**
dartboard ['dɑ:tbɔ:d] *n* bersaglio (per freccette)
darts [dɑ:ts] *n* tiro al bersaglio (con freccette)
dash [dæʃ] *n* (*sign*) lineetta; (*small quantity*: *of liquid*) goccio, goccino; (: *of soda*) spruzzo ■ *vt* (*missile*) gettare; (*hopes*) infrangere ■ *vi*: **to ~ towards** (*also*: **make a dash towards**) precipitarsi verso
▸ **dash away** *vi* scappare via
dashboard ['dæʃbɔ:d] *n* cruscotto
dashing ['dæʃɪŋ] *adj* ardito(-a)
dastardly ['dæstədlɪ] *adj* vile
DAT *n abbr* (= *digital audio tape*) cassetta *f* digitale audio *inv*
data ['deɪtə] *npl* dati *mpl*
database ['deɪtəbeɪs] *n* database *m*, base *f* di dati
data capture *n* registrazione *f or* rilevazione *f* di dati
data processing *n* elaborazione *f* (elettronica) dei dati
data transmission *n* trasmissione *f* di dati
date [deɪt] *n* data; (*appointment*) appuntamento; (*fruit*) dattero ■ *vt* datare; (*col*: *girl etc*) uscire con; **what's the ~ today?** quanti ne abbiamo oggi?; **~ of birth** data di nascita; **closing ~** scadenza, termine *m*; **to ~** *adv* fino a oggi; **out of ~** scaduto(-a); (*old-fashioned*) passato(-a) di moda; **up to ~** moderno(-a), aggiornato(-a); **to bring up to ~** (*correspondence, information*) aggiornare; (*method*) modernizzare; (*person*) aggiornare, mettere al corrente; **dated the 13th** datato il 13; **thank you for your letter dated 5th July** *or* **July 5th** (*US*) la ringrazio per la sua lettera in data 5 luglio
dated ['deɪtɪd] *adj* passato(-a) di moda
dateline ['deɪtlaɪn] *n* linea del cambiamento di data
date rape *n* *stupro perpetrato da persona conosciuta*
date stamp *n* timbro datario
daub [dɔ:b] *vt* imbrattare
daughter ['dɔ:təʳ] *n* figlia
daughter-in-law ['dɔ:tərɪnlɔ:] *n* nuora
daunt [dɔ:nt] *vt* intimidire
daunting ['dɔ:ntɪŋ] *adj* non invidiabile
dauntless ['dɔ:ntlɪs] *adj* intrepido(-a)
dawdle ['dɔ:dl] *vi* bighellonare; **to ~ over one's work** gingillarsi con il lavoro
dawn [dɔ:n] *n* alba ■ *vi* (*day*) spuntare; (*fig*) venire in mente; **at ~** all'alba; **from ~ to dusk** dall'alba al tramonto; **it dawned on him that ...** gli è venuto in mente che ...
dawn chorus *n* (*Brit*) coro mattutino degli uccelli
day [deɪ] *n* giorno; (*as duration*) giornata; (*period of time, age*) tempo, epoca; **the ~ before** il giorno avanti *or* prima; **the ~ after, the following ~** il giorno dopo, il giorno seguente; **the ~ before yesterday** l'altroieri; **the ~ after tomorrow** dopodomani; **(on) that ~** quel giorno; **(on) the ~ that ...** il giorno che *or* in cui ...; **to work an 8-hour ~**

avere una giornata lavorativa di 8 ore; **by ~** di giorno; **~ by ~** giorno per giorno; **paid by the ~** pagato(-a) a giornata; **these days, in the present ~** di questi tempi, oggigiorno

daybook ['deɪbuk] *n* (*Brit*) brogliaccio

day boy *n* (*Scol*) alunno esterno

daybreak ['deɪbreɪk] *n* spuntar *m* del giorno

day care centre *n* scuola materna

daydream ['deɪdri:m] *n* sogno a occhi aperti ■ *vi* sognare a occhi aperti

day girl *n* (*Scol*) alunna esterna

daylight ['deɪlaɪt] *n* luce *f* del giorno

daylight robbery *n*: **it's ~!** (*Brit col*) è un vero furto!

Daylight Saving Time *n* (*US*) ora legale

day release *n*: **to be on ~** *avere un giorno di congedo alla settimana per formazione professionale*

day return, day return ticket *n* (*Brit*) biglietto giornaliero di andata e ritorno

day shift *n* turno di giorno

daytime ['deɪtaɪm] *n* giorno

day-to-day ['deɪtə'deɪ] *adj* (*routine*) quotidiano(-a); (*expenses*) giornaliero(-a); **on a ~ basis** a giornata

day trader *n* (*Stock Exchange*) day dealer *m/f inv*, *operatore che compra e vende titoli nel corso della stessa giornata*

day trip *n* gita (di un giorno)

day tripper *n* gitante *m/f*

daze [deɪz] *vt* (*drug*) inebetire; (*blow*) stordire ■ *n*: **in a ~** inebetito(-a), stordito(-a)

dazzle ['dæzl] *vt* abbagliare

dazzling ['dæzlɪŋ] *adj* (*light*) abbagliante; (*colour*) violento(-a); (*smile*) smagliante

dB *abbr* (= *decibel*) db

DC *abbr* (*Elec*: = *direct current*) c.c.; (*US*) = **District of Columbia**

DCC® *n abbr* = **digital compact cassette**

DD *n abbr* (= *Doctor of Divinity*) *titolo di studio*

dd. *abbr* (*Comm*) = **delivered**

DD *abbr* = **direct debit**

D-day ['di:deɪ] *n giorno dello sbarco alleato in Normandia*

DDS *n abbr* (*US*: = *Doctor of Dental Science, Doctor of Dental Surgery*) *titoli di studio*

DDT *n abbr* (= *dichlorodiphenyl trichloroethane*) D.D.T. *m*

DE *abbr* (*US*) = **Delaware**

deacon ['di:kən] *n* diacono

dead [dɛd] *adj* morto(-a); (*numb*) intirizzito(-a) ■ *adv* assolutamente, perfettamente; **the dead** *npl* i morti; **he was shot ~** fu colpito a morte; **~ on time** in perfetto orario; **~ tired** stanco(-a) morto(-a); **to stop ~** fermarsi in tronco; **the line has gone ~** (*Tel*) è caduta la linea

dead beat *adj* (*col*) stanco(-a) morto(-a)

deaden ['dɛdn] *vt* (*blow, sound*) ammortire; (*make numb*) intirizzire

dead end *n* vicolo cieco

dead-end ['dɛdɛnd] *adj*: **a ~ job** un lavoro senza sbocchi

dead heat *n* (*Sport*): **to finish in a ~** finire alla pari

dead-letter office [dɛd'lɛtə-] *n* ufficio della posta in giacenza

deadline ['dɛdlaɪn] *n* scadenza; **to work to a ~** avere una scadenza

deadlock ['dɛdlɔk] *n* punto morto

dead loss *n* (*col*): **to be a ~** (*person, thing*) non valere niente

deadly ['dɛdlɪ] *adj* mortale; (*weapon, poison*) micidiale ■ *adv*: **~ dull** di una noia micidiale

deadpan ['dɛdpæn] *adj* a faccia impassibile

Dead Sea *n*: **the ~** il mar Morto

deaf [dɛf] *adj* sordo(-a); **to turn a ~ ear to sth** fare orecchi da mercante a qc

deaf-aid ['dɛfeɪd] *n* apparecchio per la sordità

deaf-and-dumb ['dɛfən'dʌm] *adj* (*person*) sordomuto(-a); (*alphabet*) dei sordomuti

deafen ['dɛfn] *vt* assordare

deafening ['dɛfnɪŋ] *adj* fragoroso(-a), assordante

deaf-mute ['dɛfmju:t] *n* sordomuto(-a)

deafness ['dɛfnɪs] *n* sordità

deal [di:l] *n* accordo; (*business deal*) affare *m* ■ *vt* (*pt, pp* **dealt**) [dɛlt] (*blow, cards*) dare; **to strike a ~ with sb** fare un affare con qn; **it's a ~!** (*col*) affare fatto!; **he got a bad/fair ~ from them** l'hanno trattato male/bene; **a good ~ of, a great ~ of** molto(-a)

▸ **deal in** *vt fus* (*Comm*) occuparsi di

▸ **deal with** *vt fus* (*Comm*) fare affari con, trattare con; (*handle*) occuparsi di; (*be about*: *book etc*) trattare di

dealer ['di:ləʳ] *n* commerciante *m/f*

dealership ['di:ləʃɪp] *n* rivenditore *m*

dealings ['di:lɪŋz] *npl* rapporti *mpl*; (*in goods, shares*) transazioni *fpl*

dealt [dɛlt] *pt, pp of* **deal**

dean [di:n] *n* (*Rel*) decano; (*Scol*) preside *m* di facoltà (*or* di collegio)

dear [dɪəʳ] *adj* caro(-a) ■ *n*: **my ~** caro mio/cara mia; **~ me!** Dio mio!; **D~ Sir/Madam** (*in letter*) Egregio Signore/Egregia Signora; **D~ Mr/Mrs X** Gentile Signor/Signora X

dearly ['dɪəlɪ] *adv* (*love*) moltissimo; (*pay*) a caro prezzo

dear money *n* (*Comm*) denaro ad alto interesse

dearth [də:θ] *n* scarsità, carestia

death [dɛθ] *n* morte *f*; (*Admin*) decesso

deathbed ['dɛθbɛd] *n* letto di morte
death certificate *n* atto di decesso
death duty *n* (*Brit*) imposta *or* tassa di successione
deathly ['dɛθlɪ] *adj* di morte ■ *adv* come un cadavere
death penalty *n* pena di morte
death rate *n* indice *m* di mortalità
death row [-rəu] *n* (*US*): **to be on ~** essere nel braccio della morte
death sentence *n* condanna a morte
death squad *n* squadra della morte
deathtrap ['dɛθtræp] *n* trappola mortale
deb [dɛb] *n abbr* (*col*) = **debutante**
debacle [deɪ'bɑːkl] *n* (*defeat*) disfatta; (*collapse*) sfacelo
debar [dɪ'bɑːʳ] *vt*: **to ~ sb from a club** *etc* escludere qn da un club *etc*; **to ~ sb from doing** vietare a qn di fare
debase [dɪ'beɪs] *vt* (*currency*) adulterare; (*person*) degradare
debatable [dɪ'beɪtəbl] *adj* discutibile; **it is ~ whether ...** è in dubbio se ...
debate [dɪ'beɪt] *n* dibattito ■ *vt* dibattere, discutere ■ *vi* (*consider*): **to ~ whether** riflettere se
debauchery [dɪ'bɔːtʃərɪ] *n* dissolutezza
debenture [dɪ'bɛntʃəʳ] *n* (*Comm*) obbligazione *f*
debilitate [dɪ'bɪlɪteɪt] *vt* debilitare
debit ['dɛbɪt] *n* debito ■ *vt*: **to ~ a sum to sb** *or* **to sb's account** addebitare una somma a qn
debit balance *n* saldo debitore
debit note *n* nota di addebito
debonair [dɛbə'nɛəʳ] *adj* gioviale e disinvolto(-a)
debrief [diː'briːf] *vt* chiamare a rapporto (a operazione ultimata)
debriefing [diː'briːfɪŋ] *n* rapporto
debris ['dɛbriː] *n* detriti *mpl*
debt [dɛt] *n* debito; **to be in ~** essere indebitato(-a); **debts of £5000** debiti per 5000 sterline; **bad ~** debito insoluto
debt collector *n* agente *m* di recupero crediti
debtor ['dɛtəʳ] *n* debitore(-trice)
debug [diː'bʌg] *vt* (*Comput*) localizzare e rimuovere errori in
debunk [diː'bʌŋk] *vt* (*col: theory*) demistificare; (*: claim*) smentire; (*: person, institution*) screditare
debut ['deɪbjuː] *n* debutto
debutante ['dɛbjutɑːnt] *n* debuttante *f*
Dec. *abbr* (= *December*) dic.
decade ['dɛkeɪd] *n* decennio
decadence ['dɛkədəns] *n* decadenza
decadent ['dɛkədənt] *adj* decadente
de-caff ['diːkæf] *n* (*col*) decaffeinato
decaffeinated [dɪ'kæfɪneɪtɪd] *adj* decaffeinato(-a)
decamp [dɪ'kæmp] *vi* (*col*) filarsela, levare le tende
decant [dɪ'kænt] *vt* (*wine*) travasare
decanter [dɪ'kæntəʳ] *n* caraffa
decarbonize [diː'kɑːbənaɪz] *vt* (*Aut*) decarburare
decathlon [dɪ'kæθlən] *n* decathlon *m*
decay [dɪ'keɪ] *n* decadimento; imputridimento; (*fig*) rovina; (*also*: **tooth decay**) carie *f* ■ *vi* (*rot*) imputridire; (*fig*) andare in rovina
decease [dɪ'siːs] *n* decesso
deceased [dɪ'siːst] *n*: **the ~** il(la) defunto(a)
deceit [dɪ'siːt] *n* inganno
deceitful [dɪ'siːtful] *adj* ingannevole, perfido(-a)
deceive [dɪ'siːv] *vt* ingannare; **to ~ o.s.** illudersi, ingannarsi
decelerate [diː'sɛləreɪt] *vt, vi* rallentare
December [dɪ'sɛmbəʳ] *n* dicembre *m*; *see also* **July**
decency ['diːsənsɪ] *n* decenza
decent ['diːsənt] *adj* decente; **they were very ~ about it** si sono comportati da signori riguardo a ciò
decently ['diːsəntlɪ] *adv* (*respectably*) decentemente, convenientemente; (*kindly*) gentilmente
decentralization [diːsɛntrəlaɪ'zeɪʃən] *n* decentramento
decentralize [diː'sɛntrəlaɪz] *vt* decentrare
deception [dɪ'sɛpʃən] *n* inganno
deceptive [dɪ'sɛptɪv] *adj* ingannevole
decibel ['dɛsɪbɛl] *n* decibel *m inv*
decide [dɪ'saɪd] *vt* (*person*) far prendere una decisione a; (*question, argument*) risolvere, decidere ■ *vi* decidere, decidersi; **to ~ to do/that** decidere di fare/che; **to ~ on** decidere per; **to ~ against doing sth** decidere di non fare qc
decided [dɪ'saɪdɪd] *adj* (*resolute*) deciso(-a); (*clear, definite*) netto(-a), chiaro(-a)
decidedly [dɪ'saɪdɪdlɪ] *adv* indubbiamente; decisamente
deciding [dɪ'saɪdɪŋ] *adj* decisivo(-a)
deciduous [dɪ'sɪdjuəs] *adj* deciduo(-a)
decimal ['dɛsɪməl] *adj, n* decimale (*m*); **to 3 ~ places** al terzo decimale
decimalize ['dɛsɪməlaɪz] *vt* (*Brit*) convertire al sistema metrico decimale
decimal point *n* ≈ virgola
decimate ['dɛsɪmeɪt] *vt* decimare
decipher [dɪ'saɪfəʳ] *vt* decifrare
decision [dɪ'sɪʒən] *n* decisione *f*; **to make a ~** prendere una decisione
decisive [dɪ'saɪsɪv] *adj* (*victory, factor*) decisivo(-a); (*influence*) determinante;

(*manner, person*) risoluto(-a), deciso(-a); (*reply*) deciso(-a), categorico(-a)

deck [dɛk] *n* (*Naut*) ponte *m*; (*of cards*) mazzo; (*of bus*): **top ~** imperiale *m*; **to go up on ~** salire in coperta; **below ~** sotto coperta; **cassette ~** piastra (di registrazione); **record ~** piatto (giradischi)

deckchair ['dɛktʃɛəʳ] *n* sedia a sdraio

deck hand *n* marinaio

declaration [dɛklə'reɪʃən] *n* dichiarazione *f*

declare [dɪ'klɛəʳ] *vt* dichiarare

declassify [di:'klæsɪfaɪ] *vt* rendere accessibile al pubblico

decline [dɪ'klaɪn] *n* (*decay*) declino; (*lessening*) ribasso ■ *vt* declinare; rifiutare ■ *vi* declinare; diminuire; **~ in living standards** abbassamento del tenore di vita; **to ~ to do sth** rifiutar(si) di fare qc

declutch [di:'klʌtʃ] *vi* (*Brit*) premere la frizione

decode [di:'kəud] *vt* decifrare

decoder [di:'kəudəʳ] *n* (*Comput, TV*) decodificatore *m*

decompose [di:kəm'pəuz] *vi* decomporre

decomposition [di:kɔmpə'zɪʃən] *n* decomposizione *f*

decompression [di:kəm'prɛʃən] *n* decompressione *f*

decompression chamber *n* camera di decompressione

decongestant [di:kən'dʒɛstənt] *n* decongestionante *m*

decontaminate [di:kən'tæmɪneɪt] *vt* decontaminare

decontrol [di:kən'trəul] *vt* (*trade*) liberalizzare; (*prices*) togliere il controllo governativo a

decor ['deɪkɔ:ʳ] *n* decorazione *f*

decorate ['dɛkəreɪt] *vt* (*adorn, give a medal to*) decorare; (*paint and paper*) pitturare e tappezzare

decoration [dɛkə'reɪʃən] *n* decorazione *f*

decorative ['dɛkərətɪv] *adj* decorativo(-a)

decorator ['dɛkəreɪtəʳ] *n* decoratore(-trice)

decorum [dɪ'kɔ:rəm] *n* decoro

decoy ['di:kɔɪ] *n* zimbello; **they used him as a ~ for the enemy** l'hanno usato come esca per il nemico

decrease *n* ['di:kri:s] diminuzione *f* ■ *vt, vi* [di:'kri:s] diminuire; **to be on the ~** essere in diminuzione

decreasing [di:'kri:sɪŋ] *adj* sempre meno *inv*

decree [dɪ'kri:] *n* decreto ■ *vt*: **to ~ (that)** decretare (che + *sub*); **~ absolute** sentenza di divorzio definitiva; **~ nisi** [-'naɪsaɪ] sentenza provvisoria di divorzio

decrepit [dɪ'krɛpɪt] *adj* decrepito(-a); (*building*) cadente

decry [dɪ'kraɪ] *vt* condannare, deplorare

dedicate ['dɛdɪkeɪt] *vt* consacrare; (*book etc*) dedicare

dedicated ['dɛdɪkeɪtɪd] *adj* coscienzioso(-a); (*Comput*) specializzato(-a), dedicato(-a)

dedication [dɛdɪ'keɪʃən] *n* (*devotion*) dedizione *f*; (*in book*) dedica

deduce [dɪ'dju:s] *vt* dedurre

deduct [dɪ'dʌkt] *vt*: **to ~ sth (from)** dedurre qc (da); (*from wage etc*) trattenere qc (da)

deduction [dɪ'dʌkʃən] *n* (*deducting*) deduzione *f*; (*from wage etc*) trattenuta; (*deducing*) deduzione *f*, conclusione *f*

deed [di:d] *n* azione *f*, atto; (*Law*) atto; **~ of covenant** atto di donazione

deem [di:m] *vt* (*formal*) giudicare, ritenere; **to ~ it wise to do** ritenere prudente fare

deep [di:p] *adj* profondo(-a) ■ *adv*: **~ in snow** affondato(-a) nella neve; **spectators stood 20 ~** c'erano 20 file di spettatori; **knee-~ in water** in acqua fino alle ginocchia; **4 metres ~** profondo(a) 4 metri; **he took a ~ breath** fece un respiro profondo

deepen ['di:pn] *vt* (*hole*) approfondire ■ *vi* approfondirsi; (*darkness*) farsi più intenso(-a)

deep-freeze [di:p'fri:z] *n* congelatore *m* ■ *vt* congelare

deep-fry ['di:p'fraɪ] *vt* friggere in olio abbondante

deeply ['di:plɪ] *adv* profondamente; **to regret sth ~** rammaricarsi sinceramente di qc

deep-rooted ['di:p'ru:tɪd] *adj* (*prejudice*) profondamente radicato(-a); (*affection*) profondo(-a); (*habit*) inveterato(-a)

deep-sea diver ['di:p'si:-] *n* palombaro

deep-sea diving *n* immersione *f* in alto mare

deep-sea fishing *n* pesca d'alto mare

deep-seated ['di:p'si:tɪd] *adj* (*beliefs*) radicato(-a)

deep-set ['di:psɛt] *adj* (*eyes*) infossato(-a)

deep-vein thrombosis ['di:pveɪn-] *n* trombosi *f inv* venosa profonda

deer [dɪəʳ] *n* (*pl inv*): **the ~** i cervidi (*Zool*); **(red) ~** cervo; **(fallow) ~** daino; **(roe) ~** capriolo

deerskin ['dɪəskɪn] *n* pelle *f* di daino

deerstalker ['dɪəstɔ:kəʳ] *n* berretto da cacciatore

deface [dɪ'feɪs] *vt* imbrattare

defamation [dɛfə'meɪʃən] *n* diffamazione *f*

defamatory [dɪ'fæmətərɪ] *adj* diffamatorio(-a)

default [dɪ'fɔ:lt] *vi* (*Law*) essere contumace; (*gen*) essere inadempiente ■ *n* (*Comput*: *also*: **default value**) default *m inv*; **by ~** (*Law*) in contumacia; (*Sport*) per abbandono; **to ~ on a debt** non onorare un debito

defaulter [dɪ'fɔ:ltəʳ] *n* (*on debt*) inadempiente *m/f*

default option *n* (*Comput*) opzione *f* di default
defeat [dɪ'fi:t] *n* sconfitta ■ *vt* (*team, opponents*) sconfiggere; (*fig: plans, efforts*) frustrare
defeatism [dɪ'fi:tɪzəm] *n* disfattismo
defeatist [dɪ'fi:tɪst] *adj, n* disfattista (*m/f*)
defecate ['dɛfəkeɪt] *vi* defecare
defect *n* ['di:fɛkt] difetto ■ *vi* [dɪ'fɛkt]: **to ~ to the enemy/the West** passare al nemico/ all'Ovest; **physical ~** difetto fisico; **mental ~** anomalia mentale
defective [dɪ'fɛktɪv] *adj* difettoso(-a)
defector [dɪ'fɛktə^r] *n* rifugiato(-a) politico(-a)
defence, (*US*) **defense** [dɪ'fɛns] *n* difesa; **in ~ of** in difesa di; **the Ministry of D~**, (*US*) **the Department of Defense** il Ministero della Difesa; **witness for the ~** teste *m/f* a difesa
defenceless [dɪ'fɛnslɪs] *adj* senza difesa
defend [dɪ'fɛnd] *vt* difendere; (*decision, action*) giustificare; (*opinion*) sostenere
defendant [dɪ'fɛndənt] *n* imputato(-a)
defender [dɪ'fɛndə^r] *n* difensore(-a)
defending champion *n* (*Sport*) campione(-essa) in carica
defending counsel *n* (*Law*) avvocato difensore
defense [dɪ'fɛns] *n* (*US*) = **defence**
defensive [dɪ'fɛnsɪv] *adj* difensivo(-a) ■ *n* difensiva; **on the ~** sulla difensiva
defer [dɪ'fə:^r] *vt* (*postpone*) differire, rinviare ■ *vi* (*submit*): **to ~ to sb/sth** rimettersi a qn/qc
deference ['dɛfərəns] *n* deferenza; riguardo; **out of** *or* **in ~ to** per riguardo a
defiance [dɪ'faɪəns] *n* sfida; **in ~ of** a dispetto di
defiant [dɪ'faɪənt] *adj* (*attitude*) di sfida; (*person*) ribelle
defiantly [dɪ'faɪəntlɪ] *adv* con aria di sfida
deficiency [dɪ'fɪʃənsɪ] *n* deficienza; carenza; (*Comm*) ammanco
deficiency disease *n* malattia da carenza
deficient [dɪ'fɪʃənt] *adj* deficiente; insufficiente; **to be ~ in** mancare di
deficit ['dɛfɪsɪt] *n* disavanzo
defile [dɪ'faɪl] *vt* contaminare ■ *vi* sfilare ■ *n* ['di:faɪl] gola, stretta
define [dɪ'faɪn] *vt* (*gen, Comput*) definire
definite ['dɛfɪnɪt] *adj* (*fixed*) definito(-a), preciso(-a); (*clear, obvious*) ben definito(-a), esatto(-a); (*Ling*) determinativo(-a); **he was ~ about it** ne era sicuro
definitely ['dɛfɪnɪtlɪ] *adv* indubbiamente
definition [dɛfɪ'nɪʃən] *n* definizione *f*
definitive [dɪ'fɪnɪtɪv] *adj* definitivo(-a)
deflate [di:'fleɪt] *vt* sgonfiare; (*Econ*) deflazionare; (*pompous person*) fare abbassare la cresta a
deflation [di:'fleɪʃən] *n* (*Econ*) deflazione *f*
deflationary [di:'fleɪʃənrɪ] *adj* (*Econ*) deflazionistico(-a)
deflect [dɪ'flɛkt] *vt* deflettere, deviare
defog ['di:'fɔg] *vt* (*US Aut*) sbrinare
defogger ['di:'fɔgə^r] *n* (*US Aut*) sbrinatore *m*
deform [dɪ'fɔ:m] *vt* deformare
deformed [dɪ'fɔ:md] *adj* deforme
deformity [dɪ'fɔ:mɪtɪ] *n* deformità *f inv*
Defra *n abbr* (*Brit*) = **Department for Environment, Food and Rural Affairs**
defraud [dɪ'frɔ:d] *vt*: **to ~ (of)** defraudare (di)
defray [dɪ'freɪ] *vt*: **to ~ sb's expenses** sostenere le spese di qn
defrost [di:'frɔst] *vt* (*fridge*) disgelare; (*frozen food*) scongelare
deft [dɛft] *adj* svelto(-a), destro(-a)
defunct [dɪ'fʌŋkt] *adj* defunto(-a)
defuse [di:'fju:z] *vt* disinnescare; (*fig*) distendere
defy [dɪ'faɪ] *vt* sfidare; (*efforts etc*) resistere a; (*refuse to obey: person*) rifiutare di obbedire a
degenerate *vi* [dɪ'dʒɛnəreɪt] degenerare ■ *adj* [dɪ'dʒɛnərɪt] degenere
degradation [dɛgrə'deɪʃən] *n* degradazione *f*
degrade [dɪ'greɪd] *vt* degradare
degrading [dɪ'greɪdɪŋ] *adj* degradante
degree [dɪ'gri:] *n* grado; (*Scol*) laurea (universitaria); **10 degrees below freezing** 10 gradi sotto zero; **a (first) ~ in maths** una laurea in matematica; **a considerable ~ of risk** una grossa percentuale di rischio; **by degrees** (*gradually*) gradualmente, a poco a poco; **to some ~, to a certain ~** fino a un certo punto, in certa misura
dehydrated [di:haɪ'dreɪtɪd] *adj* disidratato(-a); (*milk, eggs*) in polvere
dehydration [di:haɪ'dreɪʃən] *n* disidratazione *f*
de-ice [di:'aɪs] *vt* (*windscreen*) disgelare
de-icer ['di:aɪsə^r] *n* sbrinatore *m*
deign [deɪn] *vi*: **to ~ to do** degnarsi di fare
deity ['di:ɪtɪ] *n* divinità *f inv*; dio/dea
déjà vu [deɪʒa:'vu:] *n* déjà vu *m inv*
dejected [dɪ'dʒɛktɪd] *adj* abbattuto(-a), avvilito(-a)
dejection [dɪ'dʒɛkʃən] *n* abbattimento, avvilimento
Del. *abbr* (*US*) = **Delaware**
delay [dɪ'leɪ] *vt* (*journey, operation*) ritardare, rinviare; (*travellers, trains*) ritardare; (*payment*) differire ■ *n* ritardo; **without ~** senza ritardo
delayed-action [dɪ'leɪd'ækʃən] *adj* a azione ritardata
delectable [dɪ'lɛktəbl] *adj* delizioso(-a)
delegate *n* ['dɛlɪgɪt] delegato(-a) ■ *vt*

['dɛlɪgeɪt] delegare; **to ~ sth to sb/sb to do sth** delegare qc a qn/qn a fare qc
delegation [dɛlɪ'geɪʃən] *n* delegazione *f*; (*of work etc*) delega
delete [dɪ'li:t] *vt* (*gen, Comput*) cancellare
Delhi ['dɛlɪ] *n* Delhi *f*
deli ['dɛlɪ] *n* = **delicatessen**
deliberate *adj* [dɪ'lɪbərɪt] (*intentional*) intenzionale; (*slow*) misurato(-a) ■ *vi* [dɪ'lɪbəreɪt] deliberare, riflettere
deliberately [dɪ'lɪbərɪtlɪ] *adv* (*on purpose*) deliberatamente
deliberation [dɪlɪbə'reɪʃən] *n* (*consideration*) riflessione *f*; (*discussion*) discussione *f*, deliberazione *f*
delicacy ['dɛlɪkəsɪ] *n* delicatezza
delicate ['dɛlɪkɪt] *adj* delicato(-a)
delicately ['dɛlɪkɪtlɪ] *adv* (*gen*) delicatamente; (*act, express*) con delicatezza
delicatessen [dɛlɪkə'tɛsn] *n* ≈ salumeria
delicious [dɪ'lɪʃəs] *adj* delizioso(-a), squisito(-a)
delight [dɪ'laɪt] *n* delizia, gran piacere *m* ■ *vt* dilettare; **it is a ~ to the eyes** è un piacere guardarlo; **to take ~ in** divertirsi a; **to be the ~ of** essere la gioia di
delighted [dɪ'laɪtɪd] *adj*: **~ (at** *or* **with sth)** contentissimo(-a) (di qc), felice (di qc); **to be ~ to do sth/that** essere felice di fare qc/che +*sub*; **I'd be ~** con grande piacere
delightful [dɪ'laɪtful] *adj* (*person, place, meal*) delizioso(-a); (*smile, manner*) incantevole
delimit [di:'lɪmɪt] *vt* delimitare
delineate [dɪ'lɪnɪeɪt] *vt* delineare
delinquency [dɪ'lɪŋkwənsɪ] *n* delinquenza
delinquent [dɪ'lɪŋkwənt] *adj, n* delinquente (*m/f*)
delirious [dɪ'lɪrɪəs] *adj* (*Med, fig*) delirante, in delirio; **to be ~** delirare; (*fig*) farneticare
delirium [dɪ'lɪrɪəm] *n* delirio
deliver [dɪ'lɪvəʳ] *vt* (*mail*) distribuire; (*goods*) consegnare; (*speech*) pronunciare; (*free*) liberare; (*Med*) far partorire; **to ~ a message** fare un'ambasciata; **to ~ the goods** (*fig*) partorire
deliverance [dɪ'lɪvrəns] *n* liberazione *f*
delivery [dɪ'lɪvərɪ] *n* distribuzione *f*; consegna; (*of speaker*) dizione *f*; (*Med*) parto; **to take ~ of** prendere in consegna
delivery note *n* bolla di consegna
delivery van, (*US*) **delivery truck** *n* furgoncino (per le consegne)
delta ['dɛltə] *n* delta *m*
delude [dɪ'lu:d] *vt* deludere, illudere
deluge ['dɛlju:dʒ] *n* diluvio ■ *vt* (*fig*): **to ~ (with)** subissare (di), inondare (di)
delusion [dɪ'lu:ʒən] *n* illusione *f*
de luxe [də'lʌks] *adj* di lusso
delve [dɛlv] *vi*: **to ~ into** frugare in; (*subject*) far ricerche in
Dem. *abbr* (*US Pol*) = **Democrat(ic)**
demagogue ['dɛməgɔg] *n* demagogo
demand [dɪ'mɑ:nd] *vt* richiedere ■ *n* richiesta; (*Econ*) domanda; **to ~ sth (from** *or* **of sb)** pretendere qc (da qn), esigere qc (da qn); **in ~** ricercato(-a), richiesto(-a); **on ~** a richiesta
demand draft *n* (*Comm*) tratta a vista
demanding [dɪ'mɑ:ndɪŋ] *adj* (*boss*) esigente; (*work*) impegnativo(-a)
demarcation [di:mɑ:'keɪʃən] *n* demarcazione *f*
demarcation dispute *n* (*Industry*) controversia settoriale (*or* di categoria)
demean [dɪ'mi:n] *vt*: **to ~ o.s.** umiliarsi
demeanour, (*US*) **demeanor** [dɪ'mi:nəʳ] *n* comportamento; contegno
demented [dɪ'mɛntɪd] *adj* demente, impazzito(-a)
demilitarized zone [di:'mɪlɪtəraɪzd-] *n* zona smilitarizzata
demise [dɪ'maɪz] *n* decesso
demist [di:'mɪst] *vt* (*Brit Aut*) sbrinare
demister [di:'mɪstəʳ] *n* (*Brit Aut*) sbrinatore *m*
demo ['dɛməu] *n abbr* (*col*) = **demonstration**
demobilize [di:'məubɪlaɪz] *vt* smobilitare
democracy [dɪ'mɔkrəsɪ] *n* democrazia
democrat ['dɛməkræt] *n* democratico(-a)
democratic [dɛmə'krætɪk] *adj* democratico(-a); **the D~ Party** (*US*) il partito democratico
demography [dɪ'mɔgrəfɪ] *n* demografia
demolish [dɪ'mɔlɪʃ] *vt* demolire
demolition [dɛmə'lɪʃən] *n* demolizione *f*
demon ['di:mən] *n* (*also fig*) demonio ■ *cpd*: **a ~ squash player** un mago dello squash; **a ~ driver** un guidatore folle
demonstrate ['dɛmənstreɪt] *vt* dimostrare, provare ■ *vi*: **to ~ (for/against)** dimostrare (per/contro), manifestare (per/contro)
demonstration [dɛmən'streɪʃən] *n* dimostrazione *f*; (*Pol*) manifestazione *f*, dimostrazione; **to hold a ~** (*Pol*) tenere una manifestazione, fare una dimostrazione
demonstrative [dɪ'mɔnstrətɪv] *adj* dimostrativo(-a)
demonstrator ['dɛmənstreɪtəʳ] *n* (*Pol*) dimostrante *m/f*; (*Comm: sales person*) dimostratore(-trice); (*: car, computer etc*) modello per dimostrazione
demoralize [dɪ'mɔrəlaɪz] *vt* demoralizzare
demote [dɪ'məut] *vt* far retrocedere
demotion [dɪ'məuʃən] *n* retrocessione *f*, degradazione *f*

demur [dɪ'mə:ʳ] *vi* (*formal*): **to ~ (at)** sollevare obiezioni (a *or* su) ■ *n*: **without ~** senza obiezioni
demure [dɪ'mjuəʳ] *adj* contegnoso(-a)
demurrage [dɪ'mʌrɪdʒ] *n* diritti *mpl* di immagazzinaggio; spese *fpl* di controstallia
den [dɛn] *n* tana, covo
denationalization ['di:næʃnəlaɪ'zeɪʃən] *n* denazionalizzazione *f*
denationalize [di:'næʃnəlaɪz] *vt* snazionalizzare
denial [dɪ'naɪəl] *n* diniego; rifiuto
denier ['dɛnɪəʳ] *n* denaro (*di filati, calze*)
denigrate ['dɛnɪgreɪt] *vt* denigrare
denim ['dɛnɪm] *n* tessuto di cotone ritorto; *see also* **denims**
denim jacket *n* giubbotto di jeans
denims ['dɛnɪmz] *npl* blue jeans *mpl*
denizen ['dɛnɪzən] *n* (*inhabitant*) abitante *m/f*; (*foreigner*) straniero(-a) naturalizzato(-a)
Denmark ['dɛnmɑ:k] *n* Danimarca
denomination [dɪnɔmɪ'neɪʃən] *n* (*of money*) valore *m*; (*Rel*) confessione *f*
denominator [dɪ'nɔmɪneɪtəʳ] *n* denominatore *m*
denote [dɪ'nəut] *vt* denotare
denounce [dɪ'nauns] *vt* denunciare
dense [dɛns] *adj* fitto(-a); (*stupid*) ottuso(-a), duro(-a)
densely ['dɛnslɪ] *adv*: **~ wooded** fittamente boscoso(-a); **~ populated** densamente popolato(-a)
density ['dɛnsɪtɪ] *n* densità *f inv*; **single/double ~ disk** (*Comput*) disco a singola/doppia densità di registrazione
dent [dɛnt] *n* ammaccatura ■ *vt* (*also*: **make a dent in**) ammaccare; (*fig*) intaccare
dental ['dɛntl] *adj* dentale
dental floss [-flɔs] *n* filo interdentale
dental surgeon *n* medico(-a) dentista
dentist ['dɛntɪst] *n* dentista *m/f*; **~'s surgery** (*Brit*) gabinetto dentistico
dentistry ['dɛntɪstrɪ] *n* odontoiatria
denture ['dɛntʃə] *n*, **dentures** ['dɛntʃəz] *npl* dentiera
denunciation [dɪnʌnsɪ'eɪʃən] *n* denuncia
deny [dɪ'naɪ] *vt* negare; (*refuse*) rifiutare; **he denies having said it** nega di averlo detto
deodorant [di:'əudərənt] *n* deodorante *m*
depart [dɪ'pɑ:t] *vi* partire; **to ~ from** (*leave*) allontanarsi da, partire da; (*fig*) deviare da
departed [dɪ'pɑ:tɪd] *adj* estinto(-a) ■ *n*: **the ~** il caro estinto/la cara estinta
department [dɪ'pɑ:tmənt] *n* (*Comm*) reparto; (*Scol*) sezione *f*, dipartimento; (*Pol*) ministero; **that's not my ~** (*also fig*) questo non è di mia competenza; **D~ of State** (*US*) Dipartimento di Stato
departmental [di:pɑ:t'mɛntl] *adj* (*dispute*) settoriale; (*meeting*) di sezione; **~ manager** caporeparto *m/f*
department store *n* grande magazzino
departure [dɪ'pɑ:tʃəʳ] *n* partenza; (*fig*): **~ from** deviazione *f* da; **a new ~** una novità
departure lounge *n* sala d'attesa
depend [dɪ'pɛnd] *vi*: **to ~ (up)on** dipendere da; (*rely on*) contare su; (*be dependent on*) dipendere (economicamente) da, essere a carico di; **it depends** dipende; **depending on the result ...** a seconda del risultato ...
dependable [dɪ'pɛndəbl] *adj* fidato(-a); (*car etc*) affidabile
dependant [dɪ'pɛndənt] *n* persona a carico
dependence [dɪ'pɛndəns] *n* dipendenza
dependent [dɪ'pɛndənt] *adj*: **to be ~ (on)** (*gen*) dipendere (da); (*child, relative*) essere a carico (di) ■ *n* = **dependant**
depict [dɪ'pɪkt] *vt* (*in picture*) dipingere; (*in words*) descrivere
depilatory [dɪ'pɪlətərɪ] *n* (*also*: **depilatory cream**) crema depilatoria
depleted [dɪ'pli:tɪd] *adj* diminuito(-a)
deplorable [dɪ'plɔ:rəbl] *adj* deplorevole, lamentevole
deplore [dɪ'plɔ:ʳ] *vt* deplorare
deploy [dɪ'plɔɪ] *vt* dispiegare
depopulate [di:'pɔpjuleɪt] *vt* spopolare
depopulation ['di:pɔpju'leɪʃən] *n* spopolamento
deport [dɪ'pɔ:t] *vt* deportare; espellere
deportation [di:pɔ:'teɪʃən] *n* deportazione *f*
deportation order *n* foglio di via obbligatorio
deportee [di:pɔ:'ti:] *n* deportato(-a)
deportment [dɪ'pɔ:tmənt] *n* portamento
depose [dɪ'pəuz] *vt* deporre
deposit [dɪ'pɔzɪt] *n* (*Comm, Geo*) deposito; (*of ore, oil*) giacimento; (*Chem*) sedimento; (*part payment*) acconto; (*for hired goods etc*) cauzione *f* ■ *vt* depositare; dare in acconto; (*luggage etc*) mettere *or* lasciare in deposito; **to put down a ~ of £50** versare una caparra di 50 sterline
deposit account *n* conto vincolato
depositor [dɪ'pɔzɪtəʳ] *n* depositante *m/f*
depository [dɪ'pɔzɪtərɪ] *n* (*person*) depositario(-a); (*place*) deposito
depot ['dɛpəu] *n* deposito
depraved [dɪ'preɪvd] *adj* depravato(-a)
depravity [dɪ'prævɪtɪ] *n* depravazione *f*
deprecate ['dɛprɪkeɪt] *vt* deprecare
deprecating ['dɛprɪkeɪtɪŋ] *adj* (*disapproving*) di biasimo; (*apologetic*): **a ~ smile** un sorriso di scusa
depreciate [dɪ'pri:ʃɪeɪt] *vt* svalutare ■ *vi* svalutarsi

depreciation [dɪpri:ʃɪ'eɪʃən] *n* svalutazione *f*
depress [dɪ'prɛs] *vt* deprimere; (*press down*) premere
depressant [dɪ'prɛsnt] *n* (*Med*) sedativo
depressed [dɪ'prɛst] *adj* (*person*) depresso(-a), abbattuto(-a); (*area*) depresso(-a); (*Comm: market, trade*) stagnante, in ribasso; **to get ~** deprimersi
depressing [dɪ'prɛsɪŋ] *adj* deprimente
depression [dɪ'prɛʃən] *n* depressione *f*
deprivation [dɛprɪ'veɪʃən] *n* privazione *f*; (*state*) indigenza; (*Psych*) carenza affettiva
deprive [dɪ'praɪv] *vt*: **to ~ sb of** privare qn di
deprived [dɪ'praɪvd] *adj* disgraziato(-a)
dept. *abbr* = **department**
depth [dɛpθ] *n* profondità *f inv*; **at a ~ of 3 metres** a una profondità di 3 metri, a 3 metri di profondità; **in the depths of** nel profondo di; nel cuore di; **in the depths of winter** in pieno inverno; **to study sth in ~** studiare qc in profondità; **to be out of one's ~** (*Brit: swimmer*) essere dove non si tocca; (*fig*) non sentirsi all'altezza della situazione
depth charge *n* carica di profondità
deputation [dɛpju'teɪʃən] *n* deputazione *f*, delegazione *f*
deputize ['dɛpjutaɪz] *vi*: **to ~ for** svolgere le funzioni di
deputy ['dɛpjutɪ] *n* (*replacement*) supplente *m/f*; (*second in command*) vice *m/f* ■ *cpd*: **~ chairman** vicepresidente *m*; **~ head** (*Scol*) vicepreside *m/f*; **~ leader** (*Brit Pol*) sottosegretario
derail [dɪ'reɪl] *vt* far deragliare; **to be derailed** deragliare
derailment [dɪ'reɪlmənt] *n* deragliamento
deranged [dɪ'reɪndʒd] *adj*: **to be (mentally) ~** essere pazzo(a)
derby ['də:bɪ] *n* (*US*) bombetta
deregulate [di:'rɛgjuleɪt] *vt* eliminare la regolamentazione di
deregulation ['di:rɛgju'leɪʃən] *n* eliminazione *f* della regolamentazione
derelict ['dɛrɪlɪkt] *adj* abbandonato(-a)
deride [dɪ'raɪd] *vt* deridere
derision [dɪ'rɪʒən] *n* derisione *f*
derisive [dɪ'raɪsɪv] *adj* di derisione
derisory [dɪ'raɪsərɪ] *adj* (*sum*) irrisorio(-a)
derivation [dɛrɪ'veɪʃən] *n* derivazione *f*
derivative [dɪ'rɪvətɪv] *n* derivato ■ *adj* derivato(-a)
derive [dɪ'raɪv] *vt*: **to ~ sth from** derivare qc da; trarre qc da ■ *vi*: **to ~ from** derivare da
dermatitis [də:mə'taɪtɪs] *n* dermatite *f*
dermatology [də:mə'tɔlədʒɪ] *n* dermatologia
derogatory [dɪ'rɔgətərɪ] *adj* denigratorio(-a)
derrick ['dɛrɪk] *n* gru *f inv*; (*for oil*) derrick *m inv*
derv [də:v] *n* (*Brit*) gasolio
desalination [di:sælɪ'neɪʃən] *n* desalinizzazione *f*, dissalazione *f*
descend [dɪ'sɛnd] *vt, vi* discendere, scendere; **to ~ from** discendere da; **in descending order of importance** in ordine decrescente d'importanza
▸ **descend on** *vt fus* (*enemy, angry person*) assalire, piombare su; (*misfortune*) arrivare addosso a; (*fig: gloom, silence*) scendere su; **visitors descended (up)on us** ci sono arrivate visite tra capo e collo
descendant [dɪ'sɛndənt] *n* discendente *m/f*
descent [dɪ'sɛnt] *n* discesa; (*origin*) discendenza, famiglia
describe [dɪs'kraɪb] *vt* descrivere
description [dɪs'krɪpʃən] *n* descrizione *f*; (*sort*) genere *m*, specie *f*; **of every ~** di ogni genere e specie
descriptive [dɪs'krɪptɪv] *adj* descrittivo(-a)
desecrate ['dɛsɪkreɪt] *vt* profanare
desert *n* ['dɛzət] deserto *vb* [dɪ'zə:t] *vt* lasciare, abbandonare ■ *vi* (*Mil*) disertare; *see also* **deserts**
deserter [dɪ'zə:tə[r]] *n* disertore *m*
desertion [dɪ'zə:ʃən] *n* diserzione *f*
desert island *n* isola deserta
deserts [dɪ'zə:ts] *npl*: **to get one's just ~** avere ciò che si merita
deserve [dɪ'zə:v] *vt* meritare
deservedly [dɪ'zə:vɪdlɪ] *adv* meritatamente, giustamente
deserving [dɪ'zə:vɪŋ] *adj* (*person*) meritevole, degno(-a); (*cause*) meritorio(-a)
desiccated ['dɛsɪkeɪtɪd] *adj* essiccato(-a)
design [dɪ'zaɪn] *n* (*sketch*) disegno; (*: of dress, car*) modello; (*layout, shape*) linea; (*pattern*) fantasia; (*Comm*) disegno tecnico; (*intention*) intenzione *f* ■ *vt* disegnare; progettare; **to have designs on** aver mire su; **well-designed** ben concepito; **industrial ~** disegno industriale
design and technology *n* (*Brit: Scol*) progettazione *f* e tecnologie *fpl*
designate *vt* ['dɛzɪgneɪt] designare ■ *adj* ['dɛzɪgnɪt] designato(-a)
designation [dɛzɪg'neɪʃən] *n* designazione *f*
designer [dɪ'zaɪnə[r]] *n* (*Tech*) disegnatore(-trice), progettista *m/f*; (*of furniture*) designer *m/f inv*; (*fashion designer*) disegnatore(-trice) di moda; (*of theatre sets*) scenografo(-a)
designer baby *n bambino progettato geneticamente prima della nascita*
desirability [dɪzaɪərə'bɪlɪtɪ] *n* desiderabilità; vantaggio
desirable [dɪ'zaɪərəbl] *adj* desiderabile; **it is ~ that** è opportuno che + *sub*

d

desire [dɪ'zaɪə^r] *n* desiderio, voglia ■ *vt* desiderare, volere; **to ~ sth/to do sth/that** desiderare qc/di fare qc/che + *sub*
desirous [dɪ'zaɪərəs] *adj*: **~ of** desideroso(-a) di
desk [dɛsk] *n* (*in office*) scrivania; (*for pupil*) banco; (*Brit: in shop, restaurant*) cassa; (*in hotel*) ricevimento; (*at airport*) accettazione *f*
desk job *n* lavoro d'ufficio
desktop computer ['dɛsktɔp-] *n* personal *m inv*, personal computer *m inv*
desktop publishing *n* desktop publishing *m*
desolate ['dɛsəlɪt] *adj* desolato(-a)
desolation [dɛsə'leɪʃən] *n* desolazione *f*
despair [dɪs'pɛə^r] *n* disperazione *f* ■ *vi*: **to ~ of** disperare di; **in ~** disperato(-a)
despatch [dɪs'pætʃ] *n, vt* = **dispatch**
desperate ['dɛspərɪt] *adj* disperato(-a); (*measures*) estremo(-a); (*fugitive*) capace di tutto; **we are getting ~** siamo sull'orlo della disperazione
desperately ['dɛspərɪtlɪ] *adv* disperatamente; (*very*) terribilmente, estremamente; **~ ill** in pericolo di vita
desperation [dɛspə'reɪʃən] *n* disperazione *f*; **in ~** per disperazione
despicable [dɪs'pɪkəbl] *adj* disprezzabile
despise [dɪs'paɪz] *vt* disprezzare, sdegnare
despite [dɪs'paɪt] *prep* malgrado, a dispetto di, nonostante
despondent [dɪs'pɔndənt] *adj* abbattuto(-a), scoraggiato(-a)
despot ['dɛspɔt] *n* despota *m*
dessert [dɪ'zə:t] *n* dolce *m*; frutta
dessertspoon [dɪ'zə:tspu:n] *n* cucchiaio da dolci
destabilize [di:'steɪbɪlaɪz] *vt* privare di stabilità; (*fig*) destabilizzare
destination [dɛstɪ'neɪʃən] *n* destinazione *f*
destine ['dɛstɪn] *vt* destinare
destined ['dɛstɪnd] *adj*: **to be ~ to do sth** essere destinato(a) a fare qc; **~ for London** diretto a Londra, con destinazione Londra
destiny ['dɛstɪnɪ] *n* destino
destitute ['dɛstɪtju:t] *adj* indigente, bisognoso(-a); **~ of** privo(a) di
destroy [dɪs'trɔɪ] *vt* distruggere
destroyer [dɪs'trɔɪə^r] *n* (*Naut*) cacciatorpediniere *m*
destruction [dɪs'trʌkʃən] *n* distruzione *f*
destructive [dɪs'trʌktɪv] *adj* distruttivo(-a)
desultory ['dɛsəltərɪ] *adj* (*reading*) disordinato(-a); (*conversation*) sconnesso(-a); (*contact*) saltuario(-a), irregolare
detach [dɪ'tætʃ] *vt* staccare, distaccare
detachable [dɪ'tætʃəbl] *adj* staccabile
detached [dɪ'tætʃt] *adj* (*attitude*) distante
detached house *n* villa
detachment [dɪ'tætʃmənt] *n* (*Mil*) distaccamento; (*fig*) distacco
detail ['di:teɪl] *n* particolare *m*, dettaglio; (*Mil*) piccolo distaccamento ■ *vt* dettagliare, particolareggiare; (*Mil*): **to ~ sb (for)** assegnare qn (a); **in ~** nei particolari; **to go into ~(s)** scendere nei particolari
detailed ['di:teɪld] *adj* particolareggiato(-a)
detain [dɪ'teɪn] *vt* trattenere; (*in captivity*) detenere
detainee [di:teɪ'ni:] *n* detenuto(-a)
detect [dɪ'tɛkt] *vt* scoprire, scorgere; (*Med, Police, Radar etc*) individuare
detection [dɪ'tɛkʃən] *n* scoperta; individuazione *f*; **crime ~** indagini *fpl* criminali; **to escape ~** (*criminal*) eludere le ricerche; (*mistake*) passare inosservato(-a)
detective [dɪ'tɛktɪv] *n* investigatore(-trice); **private ~** investigatore *m* privato
detective story *n* giallo
detector [dɪ'tɛktə^r] *n* rivelatore *m*
détente [deɪ'tɑ:nt] *n* distensione *f*
detention [dɪ'tɛnʃən] *n* detenzione *f*; (*Scol*) *permanenza forzata per punizione*
deter [dɪ'tə:^r] *vt* dissuadere
detergent [dɪ'tə:dʒənt] *n* detersivo
deteriorate [dɪ'tɪərɪəreɪt] *vi* deteriorarsi
deterioration [dɪtɪərɪə'reɪʃən] *n* deterioramento
determination [dɪtə:mɪ'neɪʃən] *n* determinazione *f*
determine [dɪ'tə:mɪn] *vt* determinare; **to ~ to do sth** decidere di fare qc
determined [dɪ'tə:mɪnd] *adj* (*person*) risoluto(-a), deciso(-a); **to be ~ to do sth** essere determinato *or* deciso a fare qc; **a ~ effort** uno sforzo di volontà
deterrence [dɪ'tɛrəns] *n* deterrenza
deterrent [dɪ'tɛrənt] *n* deterrente *m*; **to act as a ~** fungere da deterrente
detest [dɪ'tɛst] *vt* detestare
detestable [dɪ'tɛstəbl] *adj* detestabile, abominevole
detonate ['dɛtəneɪt] *vi* detonare ■ *vt* far detonare
detonator ['dɛtəneɪtə^r] *n* detonatore *m*
detour ['di:tuə^r] *n* deviazione *f*
detract [dɪ'trækt] *vt*: **to ~ from** detrarre da
detractor [dɪ'træktə^r] *n* detrattore(-trice)
detriment ['dɛtrɪmənt] *n*: **to the ~ of** a detrimento di; **without ~ to** senza danno a
detrimental [dɛtrɪ'mɛntl] *adj*: **~ to** dannoso(-a) a, nocivo(-a) a
deuce [dju:s] *n* (*Tennis*) quaranta pari *m inv*
devaluation [di:vælju'eɪʃən] *n* svalutazione *f*
devalue ['di:'vælju:] *vt* svalutare

devastate ['dɛvəsteɪt] *vt* devastare; **he was devastated by the news** la notizia fu per lui un colpo terribile
devastating ['dɛvəsteɪtɪŋ] *adj* devastatore(-trice)
devastation [dɛvə'steɪʃən] *n* devastazione *f*
develop [dɪ'vɛləp] *vt* sviluppare; (*habit*) prendere (gradualmente) ■ *vi* svilupparsi; (*facts, symptoms: appear*) manifestarsi, rivelarsi; **to ~ a taste for sth** imparare a gustare qc; **to ~ into** diventare
developer [dɪ'vɛləpəʳ] *n* (*Phot*) sviluppatore *m*; **property ~** costruttore *m* (edile)
developing country [dɪ'vɛləpɪŋ-] *n* paese *m* in via di sviluppo
development [dɪ'vɛləpmənt] *n* sviluppo
development area *n* area di sviluppo industriale
deviant ['di:vɪənt] *adj* deviante
deviate ['di:vɪeɪt] *vi*: **to ~ (from)** deviare (da)
deviation [di:vɪ'eɪʃən] *n* deviazione *f*
device [dɪ'vaɪs] *n* (*apparatus*) congegno; (*explosive device*) ordigno esplosivo
devil ['dɛvl] *n* diavolo; demonio
devilish ['dɛvlɪʃ] *adj* diabolico(-a)
devil-may-care ['dɛvlmeɪ'kɛəʳ] *adj* impudente
devil's advocate *n*: **to play ~** fare l'avvocato del diavolo
devious ['di:vɪəs] *adj* (*means*) indiretto(-a), tortuoso(-a); (*person*) subdolo(-a)
devise [dɪ'vaɪz] *vt* escogitare, concepire
devoid [dɪ'vɔɪd] *adj*: **~ of** privo(-a) di
devolution [di:və'lu:ʃən] *n* (*Pol*) decentramento
devolve [dɪ'vɔlv] *vi*: **to ~ (up)on** ricadere su
devote [dɪ'vəut] *vt*: **to ~ sth to** dedicare qc a
devoted [dɪ'vəutɪd] *adj* devoto(-a); **to be ~ to** essere molto attaccato(-a) a
devotee [dɛvəu'ti:] *n* (*Rel*) adepto(-a); (*Mus, Sport*) appassionato(-a)
devotion [dɪ'vəuʃən] *n* devozione *f*, attaccamento; (*Rel*) atto di devozione, preghiera
devour [dɪ'vauəʳ] *vt* divorare
devout [dɪ'vaut] *adj* pio(-a), devoto(-a)
dew [dju:] *n* rugiada
dexterity [dɛks'tɛrɪtɪ] *n* destrezza
dexterous, dextrous ['dɛkstrəs] *adj* (*skilful*) destro(-a), abile; (*movement*) agile
DfEE *n abbr* (*Brit: = Department for Education and Employment*) Ministero della pubblica istruzione e dell'occupazione
dg *abbr* (*= decigram*) dg
diabetes [daɪə'bi:ti:z] *n* diabete *m*
diabetic [daɪə'bɛtɪk] *adj* diabetico(-a); (*chocolate, jam*) per diabetici ■ *n* diabetico(-a)
diabolical [daɪə'bɔlɪkl] *adj* diabolico(-a); (*col: dreadful*) infernale, atroce
diaerisis [daɪ'ɛrɪsɪs] *n* dieresi *f inv*
diagnose [daɪəg'nəuz] *vt* diagnosticare
diagnosis (*pl* **diagnoses**) [daɪəg'nəusɪs, -si:z] *n* diagnosi *f inv*
diagonal [daɪ'ægənl] *adj, n* diagonale (*f*)
diagram ['daɪəgræm] *n* diagramma *m*
dial ['daɪəl] *n* quadrante *m*; (*on telephone*) disco combinatore ■ *vt* (*number*) fare; **to ~ a wrong number** sbagliare numero; **can I ~ London direct?** si può chiamare Londra in teleselezione?
dial. *abbr* = **dialect**
dialect ['daɪəlɛkt] *n* dialetto
dialling code ['daɪəlɪŋ-], (*US*) **area code** *n* prefisso
dialling tone ['daɪəlɪŋ-], (*US*) **dial tone** *n* segnale *m* di linea libera
dialogue ['daɪəlɔg] *n* dialogo
dialysis [daɪ'ælɪsɪs] *n* dialisi *f*
diameter [daɪ'æmɪtəʳ] *n* diametro
diametrically [daɪə'mɛtrɪklɪ] *adv*: **~ opposed (to)** diametralmente opposto(-a) (a)
diamond ['daɪəmənd] *n* diamante *m*; (*shape*) rombo; **diamonds** *npl* (*Cards*) quadri *mpl*
diamond ring *n* anello di brillanti; (*with one diamond*) anello con brillante
diaper ['daɪəpəʳ] *n* (*US*) pannolino
diaphragm ['daɪəfræm] *n* diaframma *m*
diarrhoea, (*US*) **diarrhea** [daɪə'ri:ə] *n* diarrea
diary ['daɪərɪ] *n* (*daily account*) diario; (*book*) agenda; **to keep a ~** tenere un diario
diatribe ['daɪətraɪb] *n* diatriba
dice [daɪs] *n* (*pl inv*) dado ■ *vt* (*Culin*) tagliare a dadini
dicey ['daɪsɪ] *adj* (*col*): **it's a bit ~** è un po' un rischio
dichotomy [daɪ'kɔtəmɪ] *n* dicotomia
dickhead ['dɪkhɛd] *n* (*Brit col!*) testa *m* di cazzo (*!*)
Dictaphone® ['dɪktəfəun] *n* dittafono
dictate *vt* [dɪk'teɪt] dettare ■ *vi*: **to ~ to** (*person*) dare ordini a, dettar legge a ■ *n* ['dɪkteɪt] dettame *m*; **I won't be dictated to** non ricevo ordini
dictation [dɪk'teɪʃən] *n* dettato; (*to secretary etc*) dettatura; **at ~ speed** a velocità di dettatura
dictator [dɪk'teɪtəʳ] *n* dittatore *m*
dictatorship [dɪk'teɪtəʃɪp] *n* dittatura
diction ['dɪkʃən] *n* dizione *f*
dictionary ['dɪkʃənrɪ] *n* dizionario
did [dɪd] *pt of* **do**
didactic [daɪ'dæktɪk] *adj* didattico(-a)
didn't = **did not**

d

die [daɪ] *n* (*pl* **dies**) conio; matrice *f*; stampo ■ *vi* morire; **to be dying** star morendo; **to be dying for sth/to do sth** morire dalla voglia di qc/di fare qc; **to ~ (of** *or* **from)** morire (di)
▸ **die away** *vi* spegnersi a poco a poco
▸ **die down** *vi* abbassarsi
▸ **die out** *vi* estinguersi
diehard ['daɪhɑːd] *n* reazionario(-a)
diesel ['diːzl] *n* diesel *m*
diesel engine *n* motore *m* diesel *inv*
diesel fuel, diesel oil *n* gasolio (per motori diesel)
diet ['daɪət] *n* alimentazione *f*; (*restricted food*) dieta ■ *vi* (*also*: **be on a diet**) stare a dieta; **to live on a ~ of** nutrirsi di
dietician [daɪə'tɪʃən] *n* dietologo(-a)
differ ['dɪfəʳ] *vi*: **to ~ from sth** differire da qc; essere diverso(-a) da qc; **to ~ from sb over sth** essere in disaccordo con qn su qc
difference ['dɪfrəns] *n* differenza; (*quarrel*) screzio; **it makes no ~ to me** per me è lo stesso; **to settle one's differences** risolvere la situazione
different ['dɪfrənt] *adj* diverso(-a)
differential [dɪfə'rɛnʃəl] *n* (*Aut, in wages*) differenziale *m*
differentiate [dɪfə'rɛnʃɪeɪt] *vi* differenziarsi; **to ~ between** discriminare fra, fare differenza fra
differently ['dɪfrəntlɪ] *adv* diversamente
difficult ['dɪfɪkəlt] *adj* difficile; **~ to understand** difficile da capire
difficulty ['dɪfɪkəltɪ] *n* difficoltà *f inv*; **to have difficulties with** (*police, landlord etc*) avere noie con; **to be in ~** essere *or* trovarsi in difficoltà
diffidence ['dɪfɪdəns] *n* mancanza di sicurezza
diffident ['dɪfɪdənt] *adj* sfiduciato(-a)
diffuse *adj* [dɪ'fjuːs] diffuso(-a) ■ *vt* [dɪ'fjuːz] diffondere, emanare
dig [dɪg] *vb* (*pt, pp* **dug**) [dʌg] *vt* (*hole*) scavare; (*garden*) vangare ■ *vi* scavare ■ *n* (*prod*) gomitata; (*fig*) frecciata; (*Archaeology*) scavo, scavi *mpl*; **to ~ into** (*snow, soil*) scavare; **to ~ into one's pockets for sth** frugarsi le tasche cercando qc; **to ~ one's nails into** conficcare le unghie in; *see also* **digs**
▸ **dig in** *vi* (*col*: *eat*) attaccare a mangiare; (*also*: **dig o.s. in**: *Mil*) trincerarsi; (: *fig*) insediarsi, installarsi ■ *vt* (*compost*) interrare; (*knife, claw*) affondare; **to ~ in one's heels** (*fig*) impuntarsi
▸ **dig out** *vt* (*survivors, car from snow*) tirar fuori (scavando), estrarre (scavando)
▸ **dig up** *vt* scavare; (*tree etc*) sradicare
digest [daɪ'dʒɛst] *vt* digerire
digestible [dɪ'dʒɛstəbl] *adj* digeribile
digestion [dɪ'dʒɛstʃən] *n* digestione *f*
digestive [dɪ'dʒɛstɪv] *adj* digestivo(-a); **~ system** apparato digerente
digit ['dɪdʒɪt] *n* cifra; (*finger*) dito
digital ['dɪdʒɪtəl] *adj* digitale
digital camera *n* fotocamera digitale
digital compact cassette *n* piastra digitale per CD
digital radio *n* radio digitale
digital TV *n* televisione *f* digitale
dignified ['dɪgnɪfaɪd] *adj* dignitoso(-a)
dignitary ['dɪgnɪtərɪ] *n* dignitario
dignity ['dɪgnɪtɪ] *n* dignità
digress [daɪ'grɛs] *vi*: **to ~ from** divagare da
digression [daɪ'grɛʃən] *n* digressione *f*
digs [dɪgz] *npl* (*Brit col*) camera ammobiliata
dilapidated [dɪ'læpɪdeɪtɪd] *adj* cadente
dilate [daɪ'leɪt] *vt* dilatare ■ *vi* dilatarsi
dilatory ['dɪlətərɪ] *adj* dilatorio(-a)
dilemma [daɪ'lɛmə] *n* dilemma *m*; **to be in a ~** essere di fronte a un dilemma
diligent ['dɪlɪdʒənt] *adj* diligente
dill [dɪl] *n* aneto
dilly-dally ['dɪlɪdælɪ] *vi* gingillarsi
dilute [daɪ'luːt] *vt* diluire; (*with water*) annacquare ■ *adj* diluito(-a)
dim [dɪm] *adj* (*light, eyesight*) debole; (*memory, outline*) vago(-a); (*stupid*) ottuso(-a) ■ *vt* (*light*: *also US Aut*) abbassare; **to take a ~ view of sth** non vedere di buon occhio qc
dime [daɪm] *n* (*US*) = **10 cents**
dimension [dɪ'mɛnʃən] *n* dimensione *f*
-dimensional [dɪ'mɛnʃənl] *adj suffix*: **two~** bi-dimensionale
diminish [dɪ'mɪnɪʃ] *vt, vi* diminuire
diminished [dɪ'mɪnɪʃt] *adj*: **~ responsibility** (*Law*) incapacità d'intendere e di volere
diminutive [dɪ'mɪnjutɪv] *adj* minuscolo(-a) ■ *n* (*Ling*) diminutivo
dimly ['dɪmlɪ] *adv* debolmente; indistintamente
dimmer ['dɪməʳ] *n* (*also*: **dimmer switch**) dimmer *m inv*, interruttore *m* a reostato; **dimmers** *npl* (*US Aut*) anabbaglianti *mpl*; (: *parking lights*) luci *fpl* di posizione
dimple ['dɪmpl] *n* fossetta
dim-witted ['dɪm'wɪtɪd] *adj* (*col*) sciocco(-a), stupido(-a)
din [dɪn] *n* chiasso, fracasso ■ *vt*: **to ~ sth into sb** (*col*) ficcare qc in testa a qn
dine [daɪn] *vi* pranzare
diner ['daɪnəʳ] *n* (*person*: *in restaurant*) cliente *m*; (*Rail*) carrozza *or* vagone *m* ristorante; (*US*: *eating place*) tavola calda
dinghy ['dɪŋgɪ] *n* battello pneumatico; (*also*: **sailing dinghy**) dinghy *m inv*

dingy ['dɪndʒɪ] *adj* grigio(-a)
dining area ['daɪnɪŋ-] *n* zona pranzo *inv*
dining car *n* vagone *m* ristorante
dining room *n* sala da pranzo
dinner ['dɪnəʳ] *n* pranzo; (*evening meal*) cena; (*public*) banchetto; **~'s ready!** a tavola!
dinner jacket *n* smoking *m inv*
dinner party *n* cena
dinner service *n* servizio da tavola
dinner time *n* ora di pranzo (*or* cena)
dinosaur ['daɪnəsɔːʳ] *n* dinosauro
dint [dɪnt] *n*: **by ~ of (doing) sth** a forza di (fare) qc
diocese ['daɪəsɪs] *n* diocesi *f inv*
dioxide [daɪ'ɔksaɪd] *n* biossido
dip [dɪp] *n* (*slope*) discesa; (*in sea*) bagno ■ *vt* immergere, bagnare; (*Brit Aut: lights*) abbassare ■ *vi* (*road*) essere in pendenza; (*bird, plane*) abbassarsi
Dip. *abbr* (*Brit*) = **diploma**
diphtheria [dɪf'θɪərɪə] *n* difterite *f*
diphthong ['dɪfθɔŋ] *n* dittongo
diploma [dɪ'pləumə] *n* diploma *m*
diplomacy [dɪ'pləuməsɪ] *n* diplomazia
diplomat ['dɪpləmæt] *n* diplomatico
diplomatic [dɪplə'mætɪk] *adj* diplomatico(-a); **to break off ~ relations** rompere le relazioni diplomatiche
diplomatic corps *n* corpo diplomatico
diplomatic immunity *n* immunità *f inv* diplomatica
dipstick ['dɪpstɪk] *n* (*Aut*) indicatore *m* di livello dell'olio
dipswitch ['dɪpswɪtʃ] *n* (*Brit Aut*) levetta dei fari
dire [daɪəʳ] *adj* terribile; estremo(-a)
direct [daɪ'rɛkt] *adj* diretto(-a); (*manner, person*) franco(-a), esplicito(-a) ■ *vt* dirigere; **to ~ sb to do sth** dare direttive a qn di fare qc; **can you ~ me to ...?** mi può indicare la strada per ...?
direct cost *n* (*Comm*) costo diretto
direct current *n* (*Elec*) corrente *f* continua
direct debit *n* (*Banking*) addebito effettuato per ordine di un cliente di banca
direct dialling *n* (*Tel*) ≈ teleselezione *f*
direct hit *n* (*Mil*) colpo diretto
direction [dɪ'rɛkʃən] *n* direzione *f*; (*of play, film, programme*) regia; **directions** *npl* (*advice*) chiarimenti *mpl*; (*instructions: to a place*) indicazioni *fpl*; **directions for use** istruzioni *fpl*; **to ask for directions** chiedere la strada; **sense of ~** senso dell'orientamento; **in the ~ of** in direzione di
directive [dɪ'rɛktɪv] *n* direttiva, ordine *m*; **a government ~** una disposizione governativa
direct labour *n* manodopera diretta
directly [dɪ'rɛktlɪ] *adv* (*in straight line*) direttamente; (*at once*) subito
direct mail *n* pubblicità diretta
direct mailshot *n* (*Brit*) materiale *m* pubblicitario ad approccio diretto
directness [daɪ'rɛktnɪs] *n* (*of person, speech*) franchezza
director [dɪ'rɛktəʳ] *n* direttore(-trice), amministratore(-trice); (*Theat, Cine, TV*) regista *m/f*; **D~ of Public Prosecutions** (*Brit*) ≈ Procuratore *m* della Repubblica
directory [dɪ'rɛktərɪ] *n* elenco; (*street directory*) stradario; (*trade directory*) repertorio del commercio; (*Comput*) directory *m inv*
directory enquiries, (*US*) **directory assistance** *n* (*Tel*) servizio informazioni, informazioni *fpl* elenco abbonati
dirt [dəːt] *n* sporcizia; immondizia; **to treat sb like ~** trattare qn come uno straccio
dirt-cheap ['dəːt'tʃiːp] *adj* da due soldi
dirt road *n* strada non asfaltata
dirty ['dəːtɪ] *adj* sporco(-a) ■ *vt* sporcare; **~ bomb** bomba convenzionale contenente materiale radioattivo; **~ story** storia oscena; **~ trick** brutto scherzo
disability [dɪsə'bɪlɪtɪ] *n* invalidità *f inv*; (*Law*) incapacità *f inv*
disability allowance *n* pensione *f* d'invalidità
disable [dɪs'eɪbl] *vt* (*illness, accident*) rendere invalido(-a); (*tank, gun*) mettere fuori uso
disabled [dɪs'eɪbld] *adj* invalido(-a); (*maimed*) mutilato(-a); (*through illness, old age*) inabile
disadvantage [dɪsəd'vɑːntɪdʒ] *n* svantaggio
disadvantaged [dɪsəd'vɑːntɪdʒd] *adj* (*person*) svantaggiato(-a)
disadvantageous [dɪsædvɑːn'teɪdʒəs] *adj* svantaggioso(-a)
disaffected [dɪsə'fɛktɪd] *adj*: **~ (to** *or* **towards)** scontento(-a) di, insoddisfatto(-a) di
disaffection [dɪsə'fɛkʃən] *n* malcontento, insoddisfazione *f*
disagree [dɪsə'griː] *vi* (*differ*) discordare; (*be against, think otherwise*): **to ~ (with)** essere in disaccordo (con), dissentire (da); **I ~ with you** non sono d'accordo con lei; **garlic disagrees with me** l'aglio non mi va
disagreeable [dɪsə'griːəbl] *adj* sgradevole; (*person*) antipatico(-a)
disagreement [dɪsə'griːmənt] *n* disaccordo; (*quarrel*) dissapore *m*; **to have a ~ with sb** litigare con qn
disallow ['dɪsə'lau] *vt* respingere; (*Brit Football: goal*) annullare
disappear [dɪsə'pɪəʳ] *vi* scomparire
disappearance [dɪsə'pɪərəns] *n* scomparsa

d

disappoint [dɪsə'pɔɪnt] *vt* deludere
disappointed [dɪsə'pɔɪntɪd] *adj* deluso(-a)
disappointing [dɪsə'pɔɪntɪŋ] *adj* deludente
disappointment [dɪsə'pɔɪntmənt] *n* delusione *f*
disapproval [dɪsə'pru:vəl] *n* disapprovazione *f*
disapprove [dɪsə'pru:v] *vi*: **to ~ of** disapprovare
disapproving [dɪsə'pru:vɪŋ] *adj* di disapprovazione
disarm [dɪs'ɑ:m] *vt* disarmare
disarmament [dɪs'ɑ:məmənt] *n* disarmo
disarming [dɪs'ɑ:mɪŋ] *adj* (*smile*) disarmante
disarray [dɪsə'reɪ] *n*: **in ~** (*troops*) in rotta; (*thoughts*) confuso(-a); (*clothes*) in disordine; **to throw into ~** buttare all'aria
disaster [dɪ'zɑ:stə^r] *n* disastro
disaster area *n* zona disastrata
disastrous [dɪ'zɑ:strəs] *adj* disastroso(-a)
disband [dɪs'bænd] *vt* sbandare; (*Mil*) congedare ■ *vi* sciogliersi
disbelief ['dɪsbə'li:f] *n* incredulità; **in ~** incredulo(-a)
disbelieve ['dɪsbə'li:v] *vt* (*person, story*) non credere a, mettere in dubbio; **I don't ~ you** vorrei poterle credere
disc [dɪsk] *n* disco
disc. *abbr* (*Comm*) = **discount**
discard [dɪs'kɑ:d] *vt* (*old things*) scartare; (*fig*) abbandonare
disc brake *n* freno a disco
discern [dɪ'sə:n] *vt* discernere, distinguere
discernible [dɪ'sə:nəbl] *adj* percepibile
discerning [dɪ'sə:nɪŋ] *adj* perspicace
discharge *vt* [dɪs'tʃɑ:dʒ] (*duties*) compiere; (*settle: debt*) pagare, estinguere; (*Elec, waste etc*) scaricare; (*Med*) emettere; (*patient*) dimettere; (*employee*) licenziare; (*soldier*) congedare; (*defendant*) liberare ■ *n* ['dɪstʃɑ:dʒ] (*Elec*) scarica; (*Med, of gas, chemicals*) emissione *f*; (*vaginal discharge*) perdite *fpl* (bianche); (*dismissal*) licenziamento; congedo; liberazione *f*; **to ~ one's gun** fare fuoco
discharged bankrupt [dɪs'tʃɑ:dʒd-] *n fallito cui il tribunale ha concesso la riabilitazione*
disciple [dɪ'saɪpl] *n* discepolo
disciplinary ['dɪsɪplɪnərɪ] *adj* disciplinare; **to take ~ action against sb** prendere un provvedimento disciplinare contro qn
discipline ['dɪsɪplɪn] *n* disciplina ■ *vt* disciplinare; (*punish*) punire; **to ~ o.s. to do sth** imporsi di fare qc
disc jockey *n* disc jockey *m inv*
disclaim [dɪs'kleɪm] *vt* negare, smentire
disclaimer [dɪs'kleɪmə^r] *n* smentita; **to issue a ~** pubblicare una smentita
disclose [dɪs'kləuz] *vt* rivelare, svelare
disclosure [dɪs'kləuʒə^r] *n* rivelazione *f*
disco ['dɪskəu] *n abbr* = **discothèque**
discolour, (US) **discolor** [dɪs'kʌlə^r] *vt* scolorire; (*sth white*) ingiallire ■ *vi* sbiadire, scolorirsi; (*sth white*) ingiallire
discolouration, (US) **discoloration** [dɪskʌlə'reɪʃən] *n* scolorimento
discoloured, (US) **discolored** [dɪs'kʌləd] *adj* scolorito(-a), ingiallito(-a)
discomfort [dɪs'kʌmfət] *n* disagio; (*lack of comfort*) scomodità *f inv*
disconcert [dɪskən'sə:t] *vt* sconcertare
disconnect [dɪskə'nɛkt] *vt* sconnettere, staccare; (*Elec, Radio*) staccare; (*gas, water*) chiudere
disconnected [dɪskə'nɛktɪd] *adj* (*speech, thought*) sconnesso(-a)
disconsolate [dɪs'kɔnsəlɪt] *adj* sconsolato(-a)
discontent [dɪskən'tɛnt] *n* scontentezza
discontented [dɪskən'tɛntɪd] *adj* scontento(-a)
discontinue [dɪskən'tɪnju:] *vt* smettere, cessare; **"discontinued"** (*Comm*) "sospeso"
discord ['dɪskɔ:d] *n* disaccordo; (*Mus*) dissonanza
discordant [dɪs'kɔ:dənt] *adj* discordante; dissonante
discothèque ['dɪskəutɛk] *n* discoteca
discount *n* ['dɪskaunt] sconto ■ *vt* [dɪs'kaunt] scontare; (*report etc*) non badare a; **at a ~** con uno sconto; **to give sb a ~ on sth** fare uno sconto a qn su qc; **~ for cash** sconto *m* cassa *inv*
discount house *n* (*Finance*) casa di sconto, discount house *f inv*; (*Comm: also:* **discount store**) discount *m inv*
discount rate *n* tasso di sconto
discourage [dɪs'kʌrɪdʒ] *vt* scoraggiare; (*dissuade, deter*) tentare di dissuadere
discouragement [dɪs'kʌrɪdʒmənt] *n* (*dissuasion*) disapprovazione *f*; (*depression*) scoraggiamento; **to act as a ~ to** ostacolare
discouraging [dɪs'kʌrɪdʒɪŋ] *adj* scoraggiante
discourteous [dɪs'kə:tɪəs] *adj* scortese
discover [dɪs'kʌvə^r] *vt* scoprire
discovery [dɪs'kʌvərɪ] *n* scoperta
discredit [dɪs'krɛdɪt] *vt* screditare; mettere in dubbio ■ *n* discredito
discreet [dɪ'skri:t] *adj* discreto(-a)
discreetly [dɪ'skri:tlɪ] *adv* con discrezione
discrepancy [dɪ'skrɛpənsɪ] *n* discrepanza
discretion [dɪ'skrɛʃən] *n* discrezione *f*; **use your own ~** giudichi lei
discretionary [dɪs'krɛʃənərɪ] *adj* (*powers*) discrezionale

discriminate [dɪ'skrɪmɪneɪt] *vi*: **to ~ between** distinguere tra; **to ~ against** discriminare contro
discriminating [dɪs'krɪmɪneɪtɪŋ] *adj* (*ear, taste*) fine, giudizioso(-a); (*person*) esigente; (*tax, duty*) discriminante
discrimination [dɪskrɪmɪ'neɪʃən] *n* discriminazione *f*; (*judgement*) discernimento; **racial/sexual ~** discriminazione razziale/sessuale
discus ['dɪskəs] *n* disco
discuss [dɪ'skʌs] *vt* discutere; (*debate*) dibattere
discussion [dɪ'skʌʃən] *n* discussione *f*; **under ~** in discussione
discussion forum *n* (*Comput*) forum *m inv* di discussione
disdain [dɪs'deɪn] *n* disdegno
disease [dɪ'zi:z] *n* malattia
diseased [dɪ'zi:zd] *adj* malato(-a)
disembark [dɪsɪm'bɑ:k] *vt, vi* sbarcare
disembarkation [dɪsɛmbɑ:'keɪʃən] *n* sbarco
disembodied [dɪsɪm'bɔdɪd] *adj* disincarnato(-a)
disembowel [dɪsɪm'bauəl] *vt* sbudellare, sventrare
disenchanted [dɪsɪn'tʃɑ:ntɪd] *adj* disincantato(-a); **~ (with)** deluso(-a) (da)
disenfranchise [dɪsɪn'fræntʃaɪz] *vt* privare del diritto di voto; (*Comm*) revocare una condizione di privilegio commerciale a
disengage [dɪsɪn'geɪdʒ] *vt* disimpegnare; (*Tech*) distaccare; (*Aut*) disinnestare
disentangle [dɪsɪn'tæŋgl] *vt* sbrogliare
disfavour, (*US*) **disfavor** [dɪs'feɪvə^r] *n* sfavore *m*; disgrazia
disfigure [dɪs'fɪgə^r] *vt* sfigurare
disgorge [dɪs'gɔ:dʒ] *vt* (*river*) riversare
disgrace [dɪs'greɪs] *n* vergogna; (*disfavour*) disgrazia ■ *vt* disonorare, far cadere in disgrazia
disgraceful [dɪs'greɪsful] *adj* scandaloso(-a), vergognoso(-a)
disgruntled [dɪs'grʌntld] *adj* scontento(-a), di cattivo umore
disguise [dɪs'gaɪz] *n* travestimento ■ *vt* travestire; (*voice*) contraffare; (*feelings etc*) mascherare; **to ~ o.s. as** travestirsi da; **in ~** travestito(-a); **there's no disguising the fact that ...** non si può nascondere (il fatto) che ...
disgust [dɪs'gʌst] *n* disgusto, nausea ■ *vt* disgustare, far schifo a
disgusting [dɪs'gʌstɪŋ] *adj* disgustoso(-a)
dish [dɪʃ] *n* piatto; **to do** *or* **wash the dishes** fare i piatti
▸ **dish out** *vt* (*food*) servire; (*advice*) elargire; (*money*) tirare fuori; (*exam papers*) distribuire
▸ **dish up** *vt* (*food*) servire; (*facts, statistics*) presentare
dishcloth ['dɪʃklɔθ] *n* strofinaccio dei piatti
dishearten [dɪs'hɑ:tn] *vt* scoraggiare
dishevelled, (*US*) **disheveled** [dɪ'ʃɛvəld] *adj* arruffato(-a), scapigliato(-a)
dishonest [dɪs'ɔnɪst] *adj* disonesto(-a)
dishonesty [dɪs'ɔnɪstɪ] *n* disonestà
dishonour, (*US*) **dishonor** [dɪs'ɔnə^r] *n* disonore *m*
dishonourable, (*US*) **dishonorable** [dɪs'ɔnərəbl] *adj* disonorevole
dish soap *n* (*US*) detersivo liquido (per stoviglie)
dishtowel ['dɪʃtauəl] *n* strofinaccio dei piatti
dishwasher ['dɪʃwɔʃə^r] *n* lavastoviglie *f inv*; (*person*) sguattero(-a)
dishy ['dɪʃɪ] *adj* (*Brit col*) figo(-a)
disillusion [dɪsɪ'lu:ʒən] *vt* disilludere, disingannare ■ *n* disillusione *f*; **to become disillusioned (with)** perdere le illusioni (su)
disillusionment [dɪsɪ'lu:ʒənmənt] *n* disillusione *f*
disincentive [dɪsɪn'sɛntɪv] *n*: **to act as a ~ (to)** agire da freno (su); **to be a ~ to** scoraggiare
disinclined [dɪsɪn'klaɪnd] *adj*: **to be ~ to do sth** essere poco propenso(-a) a fare qc
disinfect [dɪsɪn'fɛkt] *vt* disinfettare
disinfectant [dɪsɪn'fɛktənt] *n* disinfettante *m*
disinflation [dɪsɪn'fleɪʃən] *n* disinflazione *f*
disinformation [dɪsɪnfə'meɪʃən] *n* disinformazione *f*
disinherit [dɪsɪn'hɛrɪt] *vt* diseredare
disintegrate [dɪs'ɪntɪgreɪt] *vi* disintegrarsi
disinterested [dɪs'ɪntrəstɪd] *adj* disinteressato(-a)
disjointed [dɪs'dʒɔɪntɪd] *adj* sconnesso(-a)
disk [dɪsk] *n* (*Comput*) disco; **single-/double-sided ~** disco *m* monofaccia *inv* /a doppia faccia
disk drive *n* disk drive *m inv*, unità *f inv* a dischi magnetici
diskette [dɪs'kɛt] *n* (*Comput*) dischetto
disk operating system *n* sistema *m* operativo a disco
dislike [dɪs'laɪk] *n* antipatia, avversione *f* ■ *vt*: **he dislikes it** non gli piace; **I ~ the idea** l'idea non mi va; **to take a ~ to sb/sth** prendere in antipatia qn/qc
dislocate ['dɪsləkeɪt] *vt* (*Med*) slogare; (*fig*) disorganizzare; **he dislocated his shoulder** si è lussato una spalla
dislodge [dɪs'lɔdʒ] *vt* rimuovere, staccare; (*enemy*) sloggiare
disloyal [dɪs'lɔɪəl] *adj* sleale
dismal ['dɪzml] *adj* triste, cupo(-a)

dismantle [dɪs'mæntl] *vt* smantellare, smontare; (*fort, warship*) disarmare
dismast [dɪs'mɑ:st] *vt* disalberare
dismay [dɪs'meɪ] *n* costernazione *f* ■ *vt* sgomentare; **much to my ~** con mio gran stupore
dismiss [dɪs'mɪs] *vt* congedare; (*employee*) licenziare; (*idea*) scacciare; (*Law*) respingere ■ *vi* (*Mil*) rompere i ranghi
dismissal [dɪs'mɪsəl] *n* congedo; licenziamento
dismount [dɪs'maunt] *vi* scendere ■ *vt* (*rider*) disarcionare
disobedience [dɪsə'bi:dɪəns] *n* disubbidienza
disobedient [dɪsə'bi:dɪənt] *adj* disubbidiente
disobey [dɪsə'beɪ] *vt* disubbidire; (*rule*) trasgredire
disorder [dɪs'ɔ:dər] *n* disordine *m*; (*rioting*) tumulto; (*Med*) disturbo; **civil ~** disordini *mpl* interni
disorderly [dɪs'ɔ:dəlɪ] *adj* disordinato(-a), tumultuoso(-a)
disorderly conduct *n* (*Law*) comportamento atto a turbare l'ordine pubblico
disorganize [dɪs'ɔ:gənaɪz] *vt* disorganizzare
disorganized [dɪs'ɔ:gənaɪzd] *adj* (*person, life*) disorganizzato(-a); (*system, meeting*) male organizzato(-a)
disorientated [dɪs'ɔ:rɪɛnteɪtɪd] *adj* disorientato(-a)
disown [dɪs'əun] *vt* ripudiare
disparaging [dɪs'pærɪdʒɪŋ] *adj* spregiativo(-a), sprezzante; **to be ~ about sb/sth** denigrare qn/qc
disparate ['dɪspərɪt] *adj* disparato(-a)
disparity [dɪs'pærɪtɪ] *n* disparità *f inv*
dispassionate [dɪs'pæʃənət] *adj* calmo(-a), freddo(-a); imparziale
dispatch [dɪs'pætʃ] *vt* spedire, inviare; (*deal with: business*) sbrigare ■ *n* spedizione *f*, invio; (*Mil, Press*) dispaccio
dispatch department *n* reparto spedizioni
dispatch rider *n* (*Mil*) corriere *m*, portaordini *m inv*
dispel [dɪs'pɛl] *vt* dissipare, scacciare
dispensary [dɪs'pɛnsərɪ] *n* farmacia; (*in chemist's*) dispensario
dispense [dɪs'pɛns] *vt* distribuire, amministrare; (*medicine*) preparare e dare; **to ~ sb from** dispensare qn da
▸ **dispense with** *vt fus* fare a meno di; (*make unnecessary*) rendere superfluo(-a)
dispenser [dɪs'pɛnsər] *n* (*container*) distributore *m*
dispensing chemist *n* (*Brit*) farmacista *m/f*
dispersal [dɪs'pə:sl] *n* dispersione *f*
disperse [dɪs'pə:s] *vt* disperdere; (*knowledge*) disseminare ■ *vi* disperdersi
dispirited [dɪs'pɪrɪtɪd] *adj* scoraggiato(-a), abbattuto(-a)
displace [dɪs'pleɪs] *vt* spostare
displaced person *n* (*Pol*) profugo(-a)
displacement [dɪs'pleɪsmənt] *n* spostamento
display [dɪs'pleɪ] *n* mostra; esposizione *f*; (*of feeling etc*) manifestazione *f*; (*military display*) parata (militare); (*computer display*) display *m inv*; (*pej*) ostentazione *f* ■ *vt* mostrare; (*goods*) esporre; (*results*) affiggere; (*departure times*) indicare; **on ~** (*gen*) in mostra; (*goods*) in vetrina
display advertising *n* pubblicità tabellare
displease [dɪs'pli:z] *vt* dispiacere a, scontentare; **displeased with** scontento(-a) di
displeasure [dɪs'plɛʒər] *n* dispiacere *m*
disposable [dɪs'pəuzəbl] *adj* (*pack etc*) a perdere; (*income*) disponibile; **~ nappy** (*Brit*) pannolino di carta
disposal [dɪs'pəuzl] *n* (*of rubbish*) evacuazione *f*; distruzione *f*; (*of property etc: by selling*) vendita; (*: by giving away*) cessione *f*; **at one's ~** alla sua disposizione; **to put sth at sb's ~** mettere qc a disposizione di qn
dispose [dɪs'pəuz] *vt* disporre
▸ **dispose of** *vt fus* (*time, money*) disporre di; (*Comm: sell*) vendere; (*unwanted goods*) sbarazzarsi di; (*problem*) eliminare
disposed [dɪs'pəuzd] *adj*: **~ to do** disposto(-a) a fare
disposition [dɪspə'zɪʃən] *n* disposizione *f*; (*temperament*) carattere *m*
dispossess ['dɪspə'zɛs] *vt*: **to ~ sb (of)** spossessare qn (di)
disproportion [dɪsprə'pɔ:ʃən] *n* sproporzione *f*
disproportionate [dɪsprə'pɔ:ʃənət] *adj* sproporzionato(-a)
disprove [dɪs'pru:v] *vt* confutare
dispute [dɪs'pju:t] *n* disputa; (*also*: **industrial dispute**) controversia (sindacale) ■ *vt* contestare; (*matter*) discutere; (*victory*) disputare; **to be in** *or* **under ~** (*matter*) essere in discussione; (*territory*) essere oggetto di contesa
disqualification [dɪskwɔlɪfɪ'keɪʃən] *n* squalifica; **~ (from driving)** (*Brit*) ritiro della patente
disqualify [dɪs'kwɔlɪfaɪ] *vt* (*Sport*) squalificare; **to ~ sb from sth/from doing** rendere qn incapace a qc/a fare; squalificare qn da qc/da fare; **to ~ sb from driving** (*Brit*) ritirare la patente a qn
disquiet [dɪs'kwaɪət] *n* inquietudine *f*

disquieting [dɪsˈkwaɪətɪŋ] *adj* inquietante, allarmante
disregard [dɪsrɪˈgɑːd] *vt* non far caso a, non badare a ■ *n* (*indifference*): ~ **(for)** (*feelings*) insensibilità (a), indifferenza (verso); (*danger*) noncuranza (di); (*money*) disprezzo (di)
disrepair [dɪsrɪˈpɛəʳ] *n* cattivo stato; **to fall into ~** (*building*) andare in rovina; (*street*) deteriorarsi
disreputable [dɪsˈrɛpjutəbl] *adj* (*person*) di cattiva fama; (*area*) malfamato(-a), poco raccomandabile
disrepute [ˈdɪsrɪˈpjuːt] *n* disonore *m*, vergogna; **to bring into ~** rovinare la reputazione di
disrespectful [dɪsrɪˈspɛktful] *adj* che manca di rispetto
disrupt [dɪsˈrʌpt] *vt* (*meeting, lesson*) disturbare, interrompere; (*public transport*) creare scompiglio in; (*plans*) scombussolare
disruption [dɪsˈrʌpʃən] *n* disordine *m*; interruzione *f*
disruptive [dɪsˈrʌptɪv] *adj* (*influence*) negativo(-a), deleterio(-a); (*strike action*) paralizzante
dissatisfaction [dɪssætɪsˈfækʃən] *n* scontentezza, insoddisfazione *f*
dissatisfied [dɪsˈsætɪsfaɪd] *adj*: **~ (with)** scontento(a) *or* insoddisfatto(a) (di)
dissect [dɪˈsɛkt] *vt* sezionare; (*fig*) sviscerare
disseminate [dɪˈsɛmɪneɪt] *vt* disseminare
dissent [dɪˈsɛnt] *n* dissenso
dissenter [dɪˈsɛntəʳ] *n* (*Rel, Pol etc*) dissidente *m/f*
dissertation [dɪsəˈteɪʃən] *n* (*Scol*) tesi *f inv*, dissertazione *f*
disservice [dɪsˈsəːvɪs] *n*: **to do sb a ~** fare un cattivo servizio a qn
dissident [ˈdɪsɪdnt] *adj* dissidente; (*speech, voice*) di dissenso ■ *n* dissidente *m/f*
dissimilar [dɪˈsɪmɪləʳ] *adj*: **~ (to)** dissimile *or* diverso(a) (da)
dissipate [ˈdɪsɪpeɪt] *vt* dissipare
dissipated [ˈdɪsɪpeɪtɪd] *adj* dissipato(-a)
dissociate [dɪˈsəuʃɪeɪt] *vt* dissociare; **to ~ o.s. from** dichiarare di non avere niente a che fare con
dissolute [ˈdɪsəluːt] *adj* dissoluto(-a), licenzioso(-a)
dissolve [dɪˈzɔlv] *vt* dissolvere, sciogliere; (*Comm, Pol, marriage*) sciogliere ■ *vi* dissolversi, sciogliersi; (*fig*) svanire
dissuade [dɪˈsweɪd] *vt*: **to ~ sb (from)** dissuadere qn (da)
distaff side [ˈdɪstɑːf-] *n ramo femminile di una famiglia*
distance [ˈdɪstns] *n* distanza; **in the ~** in lontananza; **what's the ~ to London?** quanto dista Londra?; **it's within walking ~** ci si arriva a piedi; **at a ~ of 2 metres** a 2 metri di distanza
distant [ˈdɪstnt] *adj* lontano(-a), distante; (*manner*) riservato(-a), freddo(-a)
distaste [dɪsˈteɪst] *n* ripugnanza
distasteful [dɪsˈteɪstful] *adj* ripugnante, sgradevole
Dist. Atty. *abbr* (*US*) = **district attorney**
distemper [dɪsˈtɛmpəʳ] *n* (*paint*) tempera; (*of dogs*) cimurro
distend [dɪsˈtɛnd] *vt* dilatare ■ *vi* dilatarsi
distended [dɪsˈtɛndɪd] *adj* (*stomach*) dilatato(-a)
distil, (*US*) **distill** [dɪsˈtɪl] *vt* distillare
distillery [dɪsˈtɪlərɪ] *n* distilleria
distinct [dɪsˈtɪŋkt] *adj* distinto(-a); (*preference, progress*) definito(-a); **as ~ from** a differenza di
distinction [dɪsˈtɪŋkʃən] *n* distinzione *f*; (*in exam*) lode *f*; **to draw a ~ between** fare distinzione tra; **a writer of ~** uno scrittore di notevoli qualità
distinctive [dɪsˈtɪŋktɪv] *adj* distintivo(-a)
distinctly [dɪsˈtɪŋktlɪ] *adv* distintamente; (*remember*) chiaramente; (*unhappy, better*) decisamente
distinguish [dɪsˈtɪŋgwɪʃ] *vt* distinguere; discernere ■ *vi*: **to ~ (between)** distinguere (tra); **to ~ o.s.** distinguersi
distinguished [dɪsˈtɪŋgwɪʃt] *adj* (*eminent*) eminente; (*career*) brillante; (*refined*) distinto(-a), signorile
distinguishing [dɪsˈtɪŋgwɪʃɪŋ] *adj* (*feature*) distinto(-a), caratteristico(-a)
distort [dɪsˈtɔːt] *vt* (*also fig*) distorcere; (*account, news*) falsare; (*Tech*) deformare
distortion [dɪsˈtɔːʃən] *n* (*gen*) distorsione *f*; (*of truth etc*) alterazione *f*; (*of facts*) travisamento; (*Tech*) deformazione *f*
distract [dɪsˈtrækt] *vt* distrarre
distracted [dɪsˈtræktɪd] *adj* distratto(-a)
distraction [dɪsˈtrækʃən] *n* distrazione *f*; **to drive sb to ~** spingere qn alla pazzia
distraught [dɪsˈtrɔːt] *adj* stravolto(-a)
distress [dɪsˈtrɛs] *n* angoscia; (*pain*) dolore *m* ■ *vt* affliggere; **in ~** (*ship etc*) in pericolo, in difficoltà; **distressed area** (*Brit*) zona sinistrata
distressing [dɪsˈtrɛsɪŋ] *adj* doloroso(-a), penoso(-a)
distress signal *n* segnale *m* di pericolo
distribute [dɪsˈtrɪbjuːt] *vt* distribuire
distribution [dɪstrɪˈbjuːʃən] *n* distribuzione *f*
distribution cost *n* costo di distribuzione
distributor [dɪsˈtrɪbjutəʳ] *n* distributore *m*; (*Comm*) concessionario
district [ˈdɪstrɪkt] *n* (*of country*) regione *f*; (*of town*) quartiere *m*; (*Admin*) distretto

district attorney *n* (*US*) ≈ sostituto procuratore *m* della Repubblica
district council *n organo di amministrazione regionale*; *vedi nota*

DISTRICT COUNCIL

In Inghilterra e in Galles, il *district council* è l'organo responsabile dell'amministrazione dei paesi più piccoli e dei distretti di campagna. È finanziato tramite una tassa locale e riceve un contributo da parte del governo. I district councils vengono eletti a livello locale ogni quattro anni. L'organo amministrativo nelle città è invece il "city council".

district nurse *n* (*Brit*) infermiera di quartiere
distrust [dɪs'trʌst] *n* diffidenza, sfiducia ■ *vt* non aver fiducia in
distrustful [dɪs'trʌstful] *adj* diffidente
disturb [dɪs'tə:b] *vt* disturbare; (*inconvenience*) scomodare; **sorry to ~ you** scusi se la disturbo
disturbance [dɪs'tə:bəns] *n* disturbo; (*political etc*) tumulto; (*by drunks etc*) disordini *mpl*; **~ of the peace** disturbo della quiete pubblica; **to cause a ~** provocare disordini
disturbed [dɪs'tə:bd] *adj* turbato(-a); **to be emotionally ~** avere problemi emotivi; **to be mentally ~** essere malato(-a) di mente
disturbing [dɪs'tə:bɪŋ] *adj* sconvolgente
disuse [dɪs'ju:s] *n*: **to fall into ~** cadere in disuso
disused [dɪs'ju:zd] *adj* abbandonato(-a)
ditch [dɪtʃ] *n* fossa ■ *vt* (*col*) piantare in asso
dither ['dɪðər] *vi* vacillare
ditto ['dɪtəu] *adv* idem
divan [dɪ'væn] *n* divano
divan bed *n* divano letto *inv*
dive [daɪv] *n* tuffo; (*of submarine*) immersione *f*; (*Aviat*) picchiata; (*pej*) buco ■ *vi* tuffarsi
diver ['daɪvər] *n* tuffatore(-trice); (*deep-sea diver*) palombaro
diverge [daɪ'və:dʒ] *vi* divergere
divergent [daɪ'və:dʒənt] *adj* divergente
diverse [daɪ'və:s] *adj* vario(-a)
diversification [daɪvə:sɪfɪ'keɪʃən] *n* diversificazione *f*
diversify [daɪ'və:sɪfaɪ] *vt* diversificare
diversion [daɪ'və:ʃən] *n* (*Brit Aut*) deviazione *f*; (*distraction*) divertimento
diversionary tactics [daɪ'və:ʃənrɪ-] *npl* tattica *fsg* diversiva
diversity [daɪ'və:sɪtɪ] *n* diversità *f inv*, varietà *f inv*
divert [daɪ'və:t] *vt* (*traffic, river*) deviare; (*train, plane*) dirottare; (*amuse*) divertire
divest [daɪ'vɛst] *vt*: **to ~ sb of** spogliare qn di
divide [dɪ'vaɪd] *vt* dividere; (*separate*) separare ■ *vi* dividersi; **to ~ (between** *or* **among)** dividere (tra), ripartire (tra); **40 divided by 5** 40 diviso 5
▸ **divide out** *vt*: **to ~ out (between** *or* **among)** (*sweets etc*) distribuire (tra); (*tasks*) distribuire *or* ripartire (tra)
divided [dɪ'vaɪdɪd] *adj* (*country*) diviso(-a); (*opinions*) discordi
divided highway *n* (*US*) strada a doppia carreggiata
divided skirt *n* gonna *f* pantalone *inv*
dividend ['dɪvɪdɛnd] *n* dividendo
dividend cover *n* rapporto dividendo profitti
dividers [dɪ'vaɪdəz] *npl* compasso a punte fisse
divine [dɪ'vaɪn] *adj* divino(-a) ■ *vt* (*future*) divinare, predire; (*truth*) indovinare; (*water, metal*) individuare tramite radioestesia
diving ['daɪvɪŋ] *n* tuffo
diving board *n* trampolino
diving suit *n* scafandro
divinity [dɪ'vɪnɪtɪ] *n* divinità *f inv*; teologia
division [dɪ'vɪʒən] *n* divisione *f*; separazione *f*; (*Brit Football*) serie *f inv*; **~ of labour** divisione *f* del lavoro
divisive [dɪ'vaɪsɪv] *adj* che è causa di discordia
divorce [dɪ'vɔ:s] *n* divorzio ■ *vt* divorziare da
divorced [dɪ'vɔ:st] *adj* divorziato(-a)
divorcee [dɪvɔ:'si:] *n* divorziato(-a)
divot ['dɪvət] *n* (*Golf*) zolla di terra (*sollevata accidentalmente*)
divulge [daɪ'vʌldʒ] *vt* divulgare, rivelare
D.I.Y. *adj, n abbr* (*Brit*) = **do-it-yourself**
dizziness ['dɪzɪnɪs] *n* vertigini *fpl*
dizzy ['dɪzɪ] *adj* (*height*) vertiginoso(-a); **to make sb ~** far girare la testa a qn; **to feel ~** avere il capogiro; **I feel ~** mi gira la testa, ho il capogiro
DJ *n abbr* = **disc jockey**
dj *n abbr* = **dinner jacket**
Djakarta [dʒə'kɑ:tə] *n* Giakarta
DJIA *n abbr* (*US Stock Exchange: = Dow-Jones Industrial Average*) indice *m* Dow-Jones
dl *abbr* (= *decilitre*) dl
DLit, DLitt *n abbr* = **Doctor of Literature**; **Doctor of Letters**
dm *abbr* (= *decimetre*) dm
DMus *n abbr* = **Doctor of Music**
DMZ *n abbr* (= *demilitarized zone*) zona smilitarizzata
DNA *n abbr* (= *deoxyribonucleic acid*) DNA *m*; **~ test** test *m inv* del DNA

KEYWORD

do [du:] (*pt* **did**, *pp* **done**) *n* (*col: party etc*) festa; **it was rather a grand do** è stato un ricevimento piuttosto importante
■ *vb* **1** (*in negative constructions*) *non tradotto*; **I don't understand** non capisco
2 (*to form questions*) *non tradotto*; **didn't you know?** non lo sapevi?; **why didn't you come?** perché non sei venuto?
3 (*for emphasis, in polite expressions*): **she does seem rather late** sembra essere piuttosto in ritardo; **I DO wish I could ...** magari potessi ...; **but I DO like it!** sì che mi piace!; **do sit down** si accomodi la prego, prego si sieda; **do take care!** mi raccomando, stai attento!
4 (*used to avoid repeating vb*): **she swims better than I do** lei nuota meglio di me; **do you agree? — yes, I do/no, I don't** sei d'accordo? — sì/no; **she lives in Glasgow — so do I** lei vive a Glasgow — anch'io; **he asked me to help him and I did** mi ha chiesto di aiutarlo ed io l'ho fatto; **they come here often — do they?** vengono qui spesso — ah sì?, davvero?
5 (*in question tags*): **you like him, don't you?** ti piace, vero?; **I don't know him, do I?** non lo conosco, vero?
■ *vt* (*gen, carry out, perform etc*) fare; **what are you doing tonight?** che fai stasera?; **what can I do for you?** (*in shop*) desidera?; **I'll do all I can** farò tutto il possibile; **to do the cooking** cucinare; **to do the washing-up** fare i piatti; **to do one's teeth** lavarsi i denti; **to do one's hair/nails** farsi i capelli/le unghie; **the car was doing 100** la macchina faceva i 100 all'ora; **how do you like your steak done?** come preferisce la bistecca?; **well done** ben cotto(a)
■ *vi* **1** (*act, behave*) fare; **do as I do** faccia come me, faccia come faccio io; **what did he do with the cat?** che ne ha fatto del gatto?
2 (*get on, fare*) andare; **he's doing well/badly at school** va bene/male a scuola; **how do you do?** piacere!
3 (*suit*) andare bene; **this room will do** questa stanza va bene
4 (*be sufficient*) bastare; **will £10 do?** basteranno 10 sterline?; **that'll do** basta così; **that'll do!** (*in annoyance*) ora basta!; **to make do (with)** arrangiarsi (con)
▸ **do away with** *vt fus* (*kill*) far fuori; (*abolish*) abolire
▸ **do for** *vt fus* (*Brit col: clean for*) fare i servizi per
▸ **do out of** *vt fus*: **to do sb out of sth** fregare qc a qn
▸ **do up** *vt* (*laces*) allacciare; (*dress, buttons*) abbottonare; (*renovate: room, house*) rimettere a nuovo, rifare; **to do o.s. up** farsi bello(a)
▸ **do with** *vt fus* (*need*) aver bisogno di; **I could do with some help/a drink** un aiuto/un bicchierino non guasterebbe; **it could do with a wash** una lavata non gli farebbe male; (*be connected*): **what has it got to do with you?** e tu che c'entri?; **I won't have anything to do with it** non voglio avere niente a che farci; **it has to do with money** si tratta di soldi
▸ **do without** *vi* fare senza
■ *vt fus* fare a meno di

do. *abbr* = **ditto**
DOA *abbr* (= *dead on arrival*) morto(a) durante il trasporto
d.o.b. *abbr* = **date of birth**
doc [dɔk] *n* (*col*) dottore(-essa)
docile ['dəusaɪl] *adj* docile
dock [dɔk] *n* bacino; (*wharf*) molo; (*Law*) banco degli imputati ■ *vi* entrare in bacino ■ *vt* (*pay etc*) decurtare
dock dues *npl* diritti *mpl* di banchina
docker ['dɔkə^r] *n* scaricatore *m*
docket ['dɔkɪt] *n* (*on parcel etc*) etichetta, cartellino
dockyard ['dɔkjɑ:d] *n* cantiere *m* navale
doctor ['dɔktə^r] *n* medico, dottore(-essa); (*PhD etc*) dottore(-essa) ■ *vt* (*interfere with: food, drink*) adulterare; (*: text, document*) alterare, manipolare; **~'s office** (*US*) gabinetto medico, ambulatorio; **D~ of Philosophy (PhD)** dottorato di ricerca; (*person*) titolare *m/f* di un dottorato di ricerca
doctorate ['dɔktərɪt] *n* dottorato di ricerca; *vedi nota*

DOCTORATE

Il *doctorate* è il riconoscimento accademico più prestigioso in tutti i campi del sapere e viene conferito in seguito alla presentazione di una tesi originale di fronte ad una commissione di esperti. Generalmente tale tesi è un compendio del lavoro svolto durante più anni di studi; *vedi anche* "Bachelor's degree", "Master's degree".

doctrine ['dɔktrɪn] *n* dottrina
docudrama [dɔkju'drɑ:mə] *n* (*TV*) ricostruzione *f* filmata
document *n* ['dɔkjumənt] documento ■ *vt* ['dɔkjumɛnt] documentare
documentary [dɔkju'mɛntərɪ] *adj* documentario(-a); (*evidence*) documentato(-a) ■ *n* documentario

documentation [dɔkjumən'teɪʃən] *n* documentazione *f*
DOD *n abbr* (*US*) = **Department of Defense**
doddering ['dɔdərɪŋ] *adj* traballante
doddery ['dɔdərɪ] *adj* malfermo(-a)
doddle ['dɔdl] *n*: **it's a ~** (*col*) è un gioco da ragazzi
Dodecanese Islands [dəudɪkə'ni:z-] *npl* Isole *fpl* del Dodecanneso
dodge [dɔdʒ] *n* trucco; schivata ■ *vt* schivare, eludere ■ *vi* scansarsi; (*Sport*) fare una schivata; **to ~ out of the way** scansarsi; **to ~ through the traffic** destreggiarsi nel traffico
dodgems ['dɔdʒəmz] *npl* (*Brit*) autoscontri *mpl*
dodgy ['dɔdʒɪ] *adj* (*col: uncertain*) rischioso(-a); (*untrustworthy*) sospetto(-a)
DOE *n abbr* (*US*) = **Department of Energy**
doe [dəu] *n* (*deer*) femmina di daino; (*rabbit*) coniglia
does [dʌz] *see* **do**
doesn't ['dʌznt] = **does not**
dog [dɔg] *n* cane *m* ■ *vt* (*follow closely*) pedinare; (*fig: memory etc*) perseguitare; **to go to the dogs** (*person*) ridursi male, lasciarsi andare; (*nation etc*) andare in malora
dog biscuits *npl* biscotti *mpl* per cani
dog collar *n* collare *m* di cane; (*fig*) collarino
dog-eared ['dɔgɪəd] *adj* (*book*) con orecchie
dog food *n* cibo per cani
dogged ['dɔgɪd] *adj* ostinato(-a), tenace
doggie, doggy ['dɔgɪ] *n* (*col*) cane *m*, cagnolino
doggy bag *n* sacchetto per gli avanzi (*da portare a casa*)
dogma ['dɔgmə] *n* dogma *m*
dogmatic [dɔg'mætɪk] *adj* dogmatico(-a)
do-gooder [du:'gudə[r]] *n* (*col, pej*): **to be a ~** fare il filantropo
dogsbody ['dɔgzbɔdɪ] *n* (*Brit*) factotum *m inv*
doily ['dɔɪlɪ] *n* centrino di carta sottopiatto
doing ['du:ɪŋ] *n*: **this is your ~** è opera tua, sei stato tu
doings ['duɪŋz] *npl* attività *fpl*
do-it-yourself ['du:ɪtjɔ:'sɛlf] *n* il far da sé
doldrums ['dɔldrəmz] *npl* (*fig*): **to be in the ~** essere giù; (*business*) attraversare un momento difficile
dole [dəul] *n* (*Brit*) sussidio di disoccupazione; **to be on the ~** vivere del sussidio
▸**dole out** *vt* distribuire
doleful ['dəulful] *adj* triste, doloroso(-a)
doll [dɔl] *n* bambola
▸**doll up** *vt*: **to ~ o.s. up** farsi bello(a)
dollar ['dɔlə[r]] *n* dollaro
dollop ['dɔləp] *n* (*of food*) cucchiaiata
dolly ['dɔlɪ] *n* bambola
dolphin ['dɔlfɪn] *n* delfino
domain [də'meɪn] *n* dominio; (*fig*) campo, sfera
dome [dəum] *n* cupola
domestic [də'mɛstɪk] *adj* (*duty, happiness, animal*) domestico(-a); (*policy, affairs, flights*) nazionale; (*news*) dall'interno
domesticated [də'mɛstɪkeɪtɪd] *adj* addomesticato(-a); (*person*) casalingo(-a)
domesticity [dəumɛs'tɪsɪtɪ] *n* vita di famiglia
domestic servant *n* domestico(-a)
domicile ['dɔmɪsaɪl] *n* domicilio
dominant ['dɔmɪnənt] *adj* dominante
dominate ['dɔmɪneɪt] *vt* dominare
domination [dɔmɪ'neɪʃən] *n* dominazione *f*
domineering [dɔmɪ'nɪərɪŋ] *adj* dispotico(-a), autoritario(-a)
Dominican Republic [də'mɪnɪkən-] *n* Repubblica Dominicana
dominion [də'mɪnɪən] *n* dominio; sovranità; (*Brit Pol*) dominion *m inv*
domino (*pl* **dominoes**) ['dɔmɪnəu] *n* domino; **dominoes** *npl* (*game*) gioco del domino
don [dɔn] *n* (*Brit*) docente *m/f* universitario(-a) ■ *vt* indossare
donate [də'neɪt] *vt* donare
donation [də'neɪʃən] *n* donazione *f*
done [dʌn] *pp of* **do**
donkey ['dɔŋkɪ] *n* asino
donkey-work ['dɔŋkɪwə:k] *n* (*Brit col*) lavoro ingrato
donor ['dəunə[r]] *n* donatore(-trice)
donor card *n* tessera di donatore di organi
don't [dəunt] *vb* = **do not**
donut ['dəunʌt] *n* (*US*) = **doughnut**
doodle ['du:dl] *n* scarabocchio ■ *vi* scarabocchiare
doom [du:m] *n* destino; rovina ■ *vt*: **to be doomed (to failure)** essere predestinato(-a) (a fallire)
doomsday ['du:mzdeɪ] *n* il giorno del Giudizio
door [dɔ:[r]] *n* porta; (*of vehicle*) sportello, portiera; **from ~ to ~** di porta in porta
doorbell ['dɔ:bɛl] *n* campanello
door handle *n* maniglia
doorman ['dɔ:mæn] *n* (*in hotel*) portiere *m* in livrea; (*in block of flats*) portinaio
doormat ['dɔ:mæt] *n* stuoia della porta
doorstep ['dɔ:stɛp] *n* gradino della porta
door-to-door ['dɔ:tə'dɔ:[r]] *adj*: **~ selling** vendita porta a porta
doorway ['dɔ:weɪ] *n* porta; **in the ~** nel vano della porta

dope [dəup] *n* (*col: drugs*) roba; (*: information*) dati *mpl* ■ *vt* (*horse etc*) drogare
dopey ['dəupɪ] *adj* (*col*) inebetito(-a)
dormant ['dɔ:mənt] *adj* inattivo(-a); (*fig*) latente
dormer ['dɔ:məʳ] *n* (*also*: **dormer window**) abbaino
dormice ['dɔ:maɪs] *npl of* **dormouse**
dormitory ['dɔ:mɪtrɪ] *n* dormitorio; (*US: hall of residence*) casa dello studente
dormouse(*pl* **dormice**) ['dɔ:maus, -maɪs] *n* ghiro
DOS [dɔs] *n abbr* = **disk operating system**
dosage ['dəusɪdʒ] *n* (*on medicine bottle*) posologia
dose [dəus] *n* dose *f*; (*Brit: bout*) attacco ■ *vt*: **to ~ sb with sth** somministrare qc a qn; **a ~ of flu** una bella influenza
dosser ['dɔsəʳ] *n* (*Brit col*) barbone(-a)
doss house ['dɔs-] *n* (*Brit*) asilo notturno
dossier ['dɔsɪeɪ] *n* dossier *m inv*
DOT *n abbr* (*US*) = **Department of Transportation**
dot [dɔt] *n* punto; macchiolina ■ *vt*: **dotted with** punteggiato(a) di; **on the ~** in punto
dotcom [dɔt'kɔm] *n* azienda che opera in Internet
dot command *n* (*Comput*) dot command *m inv*
dote [dəut]: **to ~ on** *vt fus* essere infatuato(a) di
dot-matrix printer [dɔt'meɪtrɪks-] *n* stampante *f* a matrice a punti
dotted line ['dɔtɪd-] *n* linea punteggiata; **to sign on the ~** firmare (nell'apposito spazio); (*fig*) accettare
dotty ['dɔtɪ] *adj* (*col*) strambo(-a)
double ['dʌbl] *adj* doppio(-a) ■ *adv* (*fold*) in due, doppio; (*twice*): **to cost ~ sth** costare il doppio (di qc) ■ *n* sosia *m inv*; (*Cine*) controfigura ■ *vt* raddoppiare; (*fold*) piegare doppio *or* in due ■ *vi* raddoppiarsi; **spelt with a ~ "l"** scritto con due elle *or* con doppia elle; **~ five two six (5526)** (*Brit Tel*) cinque cinque due sei; **on the ~**, (*Brit*) **at the ~** a passo di corsa; **to ~ as** (*have two uses etc*) funzionare *or* servire anche da; *see also* **doubles**
▸ **double back** *vi* (*person*) tornare sui propri passi
▸ **double up** *vi* (*bend over*) piegarsi in due; (*share room*) dividere la stanza
double bass *n* contrabbasso
double bed *n* letto matrimoniale
double-breasted ['dʌbl'brɛstɪd] *adj* a doppio petto
double-check ['dʌbl'tʃɛk] *vt, vi* ricontrollare
double-clutch ['dʌbl'klʌtʃ] *vi* (*US*) fare la doppietta
double cream *n* (*Brit*) doppia panna
doublecross ['dʌbl'krɔs] *vt* fare il doppio gioco con
doubledecker ['dʌbl'dɛkəʳ] *n* autobus *m inv* a due piani
double declutch *vi* (*Brit*) fare la doppietta
double exposure *n* (*Phot*) sovrimpressione *f*
double glazing *n* (*Brit*) doppi vetri *mpl*
double-page ['dʌblpeɪdʒ] *adj*: **~ spread** pubblicità a doppia pagina
double parking *n* parcheggio in doppia fila
double room *n* camera per due
doubles ['dʌblz] *n* (*Tennis*) doppio
double time *n* tariffa doppia per lavoro straordinario
double whammy [-'wæmɪ] *n* doppia mazzata (*fig*)
doubly ['dʌblɪ] *adv* doppiamente
doubt [daut] *n* dubbio ■ *vt* dubitare di; **to ~ that** dubitare che + *sub*; **without (a) ~** senza dubbio; **beyond ~** fuor di dubbio; **I ~ it very much** ho i miei dubbi, nutro seri dubbi in proposito
doubtful ['dautful] *adj* dubbioso(-a), incerto(-a); (*person*) equivoco(-a); **to be ~ about sth** avere dei dubbi su qc, non essere convinto di qc; **I'm a bit ~** non ne sono sicuro
doubtless ['dautlɪs] *adv* indubbiamente
dough [dəu] *n* pasta, impasto; (*col: money*) grana
doughnut, (*US*) **donut** ['dəunʌt] *n* bombolone *m*
dour [duəʳ] *adj* arcigno(-a)
douse [daus] *vt* (*with water*) infradiciare; (*flames*) spegnere
dove [dʌv] *n* colombo(-a)
Dover ['dəuvəʳ] *n* Dover *f*
dovetail ['dʌvteɪl] *n*: **~ joint** incastro a coda di rondine ■ *vi* (*fig*) combaciare
dowager ['dauədʒəʳ] *n* vedova titolata
dowdy ['daudɪ] *adj* trasandato(-a), malvestito(-a)
Dow-Jones average ['dau'dʒəunz-] *n* (*US*) indice *m* Dow-Jones
down [daun] *n* (*fluff*) piumino; (*hill*) collina, colle *m* ■ *adv* giù, di sotto ■ *prep* giù per ■ *vt* (*col: drink*) scolarsi; **~ there** laggiù, là in fondo; **~ here** quaggiù; **I'll be ~ in a minute** scendo tra un minuto; **the price of meat is ~** il prezzo della carne è sceso; **I've got it ~ in my diary** ce l'ho sulla mia agenda; **to pay £2 ~** dare 2 sterline in acconto *or* di anticipo; **I've been ~ with flu** sono stato a letto con l'influenza; **England is two goals ~** l'Inghilterra sta perdendo per due goal; **to ~ tools** (*Brit*) incrociare le braccia; **~ with X!** abbasso X!

down-and-out ['daunəndaut] *n* (*tramp*) barbone *m*
down-at-heel ['daunət'hi:l] *adj* scalcagnato(-a); (*fig*) trasandato(-a)
downbeat ['daunbi:t] *n* (*Mus*) tempo in battere ■ *adj* (*col*) volutamente distaccato(-a)
downcast ['daunkɑ:st] *adj* abbattuto(-a)
downer ['daunəʳ] *n* (*col*: *drug*) farmaco depressivo; **to be on a ~** (*depressed*) essere giù
downfall ['daunfɔ:l] *n* caduta; rovina
downgrade ['daungreɪd] *vt* (*job, hotel*) declassare; (*employee*) degradare
downhearted [daun'hɑ:tɪd] *adj* scoraggiato(-a)
downhill ['daun'hɪl] *adv* verso il basso ■ *n* (*Ski*: *also*: **downhill race**) discesa libera; **to go ~** andare in discesa; (*business*) andare a rotoli
Downing Street ['daunɪŋ-] *n*: **10 ~** *residenza del primo ministro inglese*; *vedi nota*

Downing Street

Downing Street è la via di Westminster che porta da Whitehall al parco di St James dove, al numero 10, si trova la residenza del primo ministro inglese e, al numero 11, quella del Cancelliere dello Scacchiere. Spesso si usa *Downing Street* per indicare il governo britannico.

download ['daunləud] *vt* (*Comput*) scaricare ■ *n* (*Comput*) file *m inv* da scaricare
downloadable *adj* (*Comput*) scaricabile
down-market ['daun'mɑ:kɪt] *adj* rivolto(-a) ad una fascia di mercato inferiore
down payment *n* acconto
downplay ['daunpleɪ] *vt* (*US*) minimizzare
downpour ['daunpɔ:ʳ] *n* scroscio di pioggia
downright ['daunraɪt] *adj* franco(-a); (*refusal*) assoluto(-a)
Downs [daunz] *npl* (*Brit*): **the ~** *colline ricche di gesso nel sud-est dell'Inghilterra*
downsize ['daun'saɪz] *vt* (*workforce*) ridurre
Down's syndrome *n* sindrome *f* di Down
downstairs ['daun'stɛəz] *adv* di sotto; al piano inferiore; **to come ~**, **go ~** scendere giù
downstream ['daun'stri:m] *adv* a valle
downtime ['dauntaɪm] *n* (*Comm*) tempi *mpl* morti
down-to-earth ['dauntu'ə:θ] *adj* pratico(-a)
downtown ['daun'taun] *adv* in città ■ *adj* (*US*): **~ Chicago** il centro di Chicago
downtrodden ['dauntrɔdn] *adj* oppresso(-a)
down under *adv* agli antipodi
downward ['daunwəd] *adj* in giù, in discesa; **a ~ trend** una diminuzione progressiva ■ *adv* in giù, in discesa
downwards ['daunwədz] *adv* in giù, in discesa
dowry ['daurɪ] *n* dote *f*
doz. *abbr* = **dozen**
doze [dəuz] *vi* sonnecchiare
▸ **doze off** *vi* appisolarsi
dozen ['dʌzn] *n* dozzina; **a ~ books** una dozzina di libri; **80p a ~** 80 pence la dozzina; **dozens of times** centinaia *or* migliaia di volte
DPh, DPhil *n abbr* (= *Doctor of Philosophy*) ≈ dottorato di ricerca
DPP *n abbr* (*Brit*) = **Director of Public Prosecutions**
DPT *n abbr* (*Med*: = *diphtheria, pertussis, tetanus*) *vaccino*
Dr, Dr. *abbr* (= *doctor*) Dr, Dott./Dott.ssa
dr *abbr* (*Comm*) = **debtor**
Dr. *abbr* (*in street names*) = **drive**
drab [dræb] *adj* tetro(-a), grigio(-a)
draft [drɑ:ft] *n* abbozzo; (*Comm*) tratta; (*US Mil*) contingente *m*; (: *call-up*) leva ■ *vt* abbozzare; (*document, report*) stendere (in versione preliminare); *see also* **draught**
drag [dræg] *vt* trascinare; (*river*) dragare ■ *vi* trascinarsi ■ *n* (*Aviat, Naut*) resistenza (aerodinamica); (*col*: *person*) noioso(-a); (: *task*) noia; (*women's clothing*): **in ~** travestito (da donna)
▸ **drag away** *vt*: **to ~ away (from)** tirare via (da)
▸ **drag on** *vi* tirar avanti lentamente
dragnet ['drægnɛt] *n* giacchio; (*fig*) rastrellamento
dragon ['drægən] *n* drago
dragonfly ['drægənflaɪ] *n* libellula
dragoon [drə'gu:n] *n* (*cavalryman*) dragone *m* ■ *vt*: **to ~ sb into doing sth** (*Brit*) costringere qn a fare qc
drain [dreɪn] *n* canale *m* di scolo; (*for sewage*) fogna; (*on resources*) salasso ■ *vt* (*land, marshes*) prosciugare; (*vegetables*) scolare; (*reservoir etc*) vuotare ■ *vi* (*water*) defluire; **to feel drained** sentirsi svuotato(-a), sentirsi sfinito(-a)
drainage ['dreɪnɪdʒ] *n* prosciugamento; fognatura
draining board ['dreɪnɪŋ-], (*US*) **drainboard** ['dreɪnbɔ:d] *n* piano del lavello
drainpipe ['dreɪnpaɪp] *n* tubo di scarico
drake [dreɪk] *n* maschio dell'anatra
dram [dræm] *n* bicchierino (di whisky *etc*)
drama ['drɑ:mə] *n* (*art*) dramma *m*, teatro; (*play*) commedia; (*event*) dramma
dramatic [drə'mætɪk] *adj* drammatico(-a)
dramatically [drə'mætɪklɪ] *adv* in modo spettacolare

dramatist ['dræmətɪst] *n* drammaturgo(-a)
dramatize ['dræmətaɪz] *vt* (*events etc*) drammatizzare; (*adapt: novel: for TV*) ridurre *or* adattare per la televisione; (*: for cinema*) ridurre *or* adattare per lo schermo
drank [dræŋk] *pt of* **drink**
drape [dreɪp] *vt* drappeggiare; *see also* **drapes**
draper ['dreɪpəʳ] *n* (*Brit*) negoziante *m/f* di stoffe
drapes [dreɪps] *npl* (*US*) tende *fpl*
drastic ['dræstɪk] *adj* drastico(-a)
drastically ['dræstɪklɪ] *adv* drasticamente
draught, (US) **draft** [drɑːft] *n* corrente *f* d'aria; (*Naut*) pescaggio; **on ~** (*beer*) alla spina; *see also* **draughts**
draught beer *n* birra alla spina
draughtboard ['drɑːftbɔːd] *n* scacchiera
draughts [drɑːfts] *n* (*Brit*) (gioco della) dama
draughtsman, (US) **draftsman** ['drɑːftsmən] *n* disegnatore *m*
draughtsmanship, (US) **draftsmanship** ['drɑːftsmənʃɪp] *n* disegno tecnico; (*skill*) arte *f* del disegno
draw [drɔː] *vb* (*pt* **drew**, *pp* **drawn**) [druː, drɔːn] *vt* tirare; (*attract*) attirare; (*picture*) disegnare; (*line, circle*) tracciare; (*money*) ritirare; (*formulate: conclusion*) trarre, ricavare; (*: comparison, distinction*): **to ~ (between)** fare (tra) ■ *vi* (*Sport*) pareggiare ■ *n* (*Sport*) pareggio; (*in lottery*) estrazione *f*; (*attraction*) attrazione *f*; **to ~ to a close** avvicinarsi alla conclusione; **to ~ near** *vi* avvicinarsi
▸ **draw back** *vi*: **to ~ back (from)** indietreggiare (di fronte a), tirarsi indietro (di fronte a)
▸ **draw in** *vi* (*Brit: car*) accostarsi; (*: train*) entrare in stazione
▸ **draw on** *vt* (*resources*) attingere a; (*imagination, person*) far ricorso a
▸ **draw out** *vi* (*lengthen*) allungarsi ■ *vt* (*money*) ritirare
▸ **draw up** *vi* (*stop*) arrestarsi, fermarsi ■ *vt* (*document*) compilare; (*plans*) formulare
drawback ['drɔːbæk] *n* svantaggio, inconveniente *m*
drawbridge ['drɔːbrɪdʒ] *n* ponte *m* levatoio
drawee [drɔː'iː] *n* trattario
drawer [drɔːʳ] *n* cassetto; ['drɔːəʳ] (*of cheque*) riscuotitore(-trice)
drawing ['drɔːɪŋ] *n* disegno
drawing board *n* tavola da disegno
drawing pin *n* (*Brit*) puntina da disegno
drawing room *n* salotto
drawl [drɔːl] *n* pronuncia strascicata
drawn [drɔːn] *pp of* **draw** ■ *adj* (*haggard: with tiredness*) tirato(-a); (*: with pain*) contratto(-a) (dal dolore)
drawstring ['drɔːstrɪŋ] *n* laccio (*per stringere maglie, sacche etc*)
dread [drɛd] *n* terrore *m* ■ *vt* tremare all'idea di
dreadful ['drɛdful] *adj* terribile; **I feel ~!** (*ill*) mi sento uno straccio!; (*ashamed*) vorrei scomparire (dalla vergogna)!
dream [driːm] *n* sogno ■ *vt, vi* (*pt, pp* **dreamed** *or* **dreamt**) [drɛmt] sognare; **to have a ~ about sb/sth** fare un sogno su qn/qc; **sweet dreams!** sogni d'oro!
▸ **dream up** *vt* (*reason, excuse*) inventare; (*plan, idea*) escogitare
dreamer ['driːməʳ] *n* sognatore(-trice)
dreamt [drɛmt] *pt, pp of* **dream**
dreamy ['driːmɪ] *adj* (*look, voice*) sognante; (*person*) distratto(-a), sognatore(-trice)
dreary ['drɪərɪ] *adj* tetro(-a); monotono(-a)
dredge [drɛdʒ] *vt* dragare
▸ **dredge up** *vt* tirare alla superficie; (*fig: unpleasant facts*) rivangare
dredger ['drɛdʒəʳ] *n* draga; (*Brit: also:* **sugar dredger**) spargizucchero *m inv*
dregs [drɛgz] *npl* feccia
drench [drɛntʃ] *vt* inzuppare; **drenched to the skin** bagnato(a) fino all'osso, bagnato(a) fradicio(a)
dress [drɛs] *n* vestito; (*clothing*) abbigliamento ■ *vt* vestire; (*wound*) fasciare; (*food*) condire; preparare; (*shop window*) allestire ■ *vi* vestirsi; **to ~ o.s.**, **to get dressed** vestirsi; **she dresses very well** veste molto bene
▸ **dress up** *vi* vestirsi a festa; (*in fancy dress*) vestirsi in costume
dress circle *n* prima galleria
dress designer *n* disegnatore(-trice) di moda
dresser ['drɛsəʳ] *n* (*Theat*) assistente *m/f* del camerino; (*also:* **window dresser**) vetrinista *m/f*; (*furniture*) credenza
dressing ['drɛsɪŋ] *n* (*Med*) benda; (*Culin*) condimento
dressing gown *n* (*Brit*) vestaglia
dressing room *n* (*Theat*) camerino; (*Sport*) spogliatoio
dressing table *n* toilette *f inv*
dressmaker ['drɛsmeɪkəʳ] *n* sarta
dressmaking ['drɛsmeɪkɪŋ] *n* sartoria; confezioni *fpl* per donna
dress rehearsal *n* prova generale
dress shirt *n* camicia da sera
dressy ['drɛsɪ] *adj* (*col*) elegante
drew [druː] *pt of* **draw**
dribble ['drɪbl] *vi* gocciolare; (*baby*) sbavare; (*Football*) dribblare ■ *vt* dribblare
dried [draɪd] *adj* (*fruit, beans*) secco(-a); (*eggs, milk*) in polvere

drier ['draɪə^r] *n* = **dryer**
drift [drɪft] *n* (*of current etc*) direzione *f*; forza; (*of sand, snow*) cumulo; (*general meaning*) senso ■ *vi* (*boat*) essere trasportato(-a) dalla corrente; (*sand, snow*) ammucchiarsi; **to catch sb's ~** capire dove qn vuole arrivare; **to let things ~** lasciare che le cose vadano come vogliono; **to ~ apart** (*friends*) perdersi di vista; (*lovers*) allontanarsi l'uno dall'altro
drifter ['drɪftə^r] *n* *persona che fa una vita da zingaro*
driftwood ['drɪftwud] *n* resti *mpl* della mareggiata
drill [drɪl] *n* trapano; (*Mil*) esercitazione *f* ■ *vt* trapanare; (*soldiers*) esercitare, addestrare; (*pupils: in grammar*) fare esercitare ■ *vi* (*for oil*) fare trivellazioni
drilling ['drɪlɪŋ] *n* (*for oil*) trivellazione *f*
drilling rig *n* (*on land*) torre *f* di perforazione; (*at sea*) piattaforma (per trivellazioni subacquee)
drily ['draɪlɪ] *adv* = **dryly**
drink [drɪŋk] *n* bevanda, bibita ■ *vt, vi* (*pt* **drank**, *pp* **drunk**) [dræŋk, drʌŋk] bere; **to have a ~** bere qualcosa; **a ~ of water** un bicchier d'acqua; **would you like something to ~?** vuole qualcosa da bere?; **we had drinks before lunch** abbiamo preso l'aperitivo
▸**drink in** *vt* (*person: fresh air*) aspirare; (*: story*) ascoltare avidamente; (*: sight*) ammirare, bersi con gli occhi
drinkable ['drɪŋkəbl] *adj* (*not poisonous*) potabile; (*palatable*) bevibile
drink-driving ['drɪŋk'draɪvɪŋ] *n* guida in stato di ebbrezza
drinker ['drɪŋkə^r] *n* bevitore(-trice)
drinking ['drɪŋkɪŋ] *n* (*drunkenness*) il bere, alcoolismo
drinking fountain *n* fontanella
drinking water *n* acqua potabile
drip [drɪp] *n* goccia; (*dripping*) sgocciolio; (*Med*) fleboclisi *f inv*; (*col: spineless person*) lavativo ■ *vi* gocciolare; (*washing*) sgocciolare; (*wall*) trasudare
drip-dry ['drɪp'draɪ] *adj* (*shirt*) che non si stira
drip-feed ['drɪpfi:d] *vt* alimentare mediante fleboclisi
dripping ['drɪpɪŋ] *n* (*Culin*) grasso d'arrosto ■ *adj*: **~ wet** fradicio(a)
drive [draɪv] *n* passeggiata *or* giro in macchina; (*also*: **driveway**) viale *m* d'accesso; (*energy*) energia; (*Psych*) impulso; bisogno; (*push*) sforzo eccezionale; campagna; (*Sport*) drive *m inv*; (*Tech*) trasmissione *f*; (*Comput: also*: **disk drive**) disk drive *m inv*, unità *f inv* a dischi magnetici ■ *vb* (*pt* **drove**, *pp* **driven**) [drəuv, 'drɪvn] *vt* (*vehicle*) guidare; (*nail*) piantare; (*push*) cacciare, spingere; (*Tech: motor*) azionare; far funzionare ■ *vi* (*Aut: at controls*) guidare; (*: travel*) andare in macchina; **to go for a ~** andare a fare un giro in macchina; **it's 3 hours' ~ from London** è a 3 ore di macchina da Londra; **left-/right-hand ~** (*Aut*) guida a sinistra/destra; **front-/rear-wheel ~** (*Aut*) trazione *f* anteriore/posteriore; **to ~ sb to (do) sth** spingere qn a (fare) qc; **he drives a taxi** fa il tassista; **to ~ at 50 km an hour** guidare *or* andare a 50 km all'ora
▸**drive at** *vt fus* (*fig: intend, mean*) mirare a, voler dire
▸**drive on** *vi* proseguire, andare (più) avanti ■ *vt* (*incite, encourage*) sospingere, spingere
drive-by ['draɪvbaɪ] *n* (*also*: **drive-by shooting**) sparatoria dalla macchina; **he was killed in a ~ shooting** lo hanno ammazzato sparandogli da una macchina in corsa
drive-in ['draɪvɪn] *adj, n* (*esp US*) drive-in (*m inv*)
drive-in window *n* (*US*) sportello di drive-in
drivel ['drɪvl] *n* (*col: nonsense*) ciance *fpl*
driven ['drɪvn] *pp of* **drive**
driver ['draɪvə^r] *n* conducente *m/f*; (*of taxi*) tassista *m*; (*of bus*) autista *m*; (*Comput*) driver *m inv*
driver's license *n* (*US*) patente *f* di guida
driveway ['draɪvweɪ] *n* viale *m* d'accesso
driving ['draɪvɪŋ] *adj*: **~ rain** pioggia sferzante ■ *n* guida
driving force *n* forza trainante
driving instructor *n* istruttore(-trice) di scuola guida
driving lesson *n* lezione *f* di guida
driving licence *n* (*Brit*) patente *f* di guida
driving school *n* scuola *f* guida *inv*
driving test *n* esame *m* di guida
drizzle ['drɪzl] *n* pioggerella ■ *vi* piovigginare
droll [drəul] *adj* buffo(-a)
dromedary ['drɔmədərɪ] *n* dromedario
drone [drəun] *n* ronzio; (*male bee*) fuco ■ *vi* (*bee, aircraft, engine*) ronzare; (*also*: **drone on**: *person*) continuare a parlare (in modo monotono); (*: voice*) continuare a ronzare
drool [dru:l] *vi* sbavare; **to ~ over sb/sth** (*fig*) andare in estasi per qn/qc
droop [dru:p] *vi* abbassarsi; languire
drop [drɔp] *n* goccia; (*fall: in price*) calo, ribasso; (*: in salary*) riduzione *f*, taglio; (*also*: **parachute drop**) lancio; (*steep incline*) salto ■ *vt* lasciar cadere; (*voice, eyes, price*) abbassare; (*set down from car*) far scendere ■ *vi* cascare; (*decrease: wind, temperature, price, voice*)

calare; (*numbers, attendance*) diminuire; **drops** *npl* (*Med*) gocce *fpl*; **cough drops** pastiglie *fpl* per la tosse; **a ~ of 10%** un calo del 10%; **to ~ sb a line** mandare due righe a qn; **to ~ anchor** gettare l'ancora
▸ **drop in** *vi* (*col: visit*): **to ~ in (on)** fare un salto (da), passare (da)
▸ **drop off** *vi* (*sleep*) addormentarsi ▪ *vt*: **to ~ sb off** far scendere qn
▸ **drop out** *vi* (*withdraw*) ritirarsi; (*student etc*) smettere di studiare

droplet ['drɔplɪt] *n* gocciolina

dropout ['drɔpaut] *n* (*from society/university*) chi ha abbandonato (la società/gli studi)

dropper ['drɔpə^r] *n* (*Med*) contagocce *m inv*

droppings ['drɔpɪŋz] *npl* sterco

dross [drɔs] *n* scoria; scarto

drought [draut] *n* siccità *f inv*

drove [drəuv] *pt of* **drive** ▪ *n*: **droves of people** una moltitudine di persone

drown [draun] *vt* affogare; (*also*: **drown out**: *sound*) coprire ▪ *vi* affogare

drowse [drauz] *vi* sonnecchiare

drowsy ['drauzɪ] *adj* sonnolento(-a), assonnato(-a)

drudge [drʌdʒ] *n* (*person*) uomo/donna di fatica; (*job*) faticaccia

drudgery ['drʌdʒərɪ] *n* fatica improba; **housework is sheer ~** le faccende domestiche sono alienanti

drug [drʌg] *n* farmaco; (*narcotic*) droga ▪ *vt* drogare; **he's on drugs** si droga; (*Med*) segue una cura

drug abuser [-ə'bju:zə^r] *n* chi fa uso di droghe

drug addict *n* tossicomane *m/f*

druggist ['drʌgɪst] *n* (*US*) farmacista *m/f*

drug peddler *n* spacciatore(-trice) di droga

drugstore ['drʌgstɔ:^r] *n* (*US*) *negozio di generi vari e di articoli di farmacia con un bar*

drum [drʌm] *n* tamburo; (*for oil, petrol*) fusto ▪ *vt*: **to ~ one's fingers on the table** tamburellare con le dita sulla tavola; **drums** *npl* (*Mus*) batteria
▸ **drum up** *vt* (*enthusiasm, support*) conquistarsi

drummer ['drʌmə^r] *n* batterista *m/f*

drum roll *n* rullio di tamburi

drumstick ['drʌmstɪk] *n* (*Mus*) bacchetta; (*chicken leg*) coscia di pollo

drunk [drʌŋk] *pp of* **drink** ▪ *adj* ubriaco(-a), ebbro(-a) ▪ *n* ubriacone(-a); **to get ~** ubriacarsi, prendere una sbornia

drunkard ['drʌŋkəd] *n* ubriacone(-a)

drunken ['drʌŋkən] *adj* ubriaco(-a), da ubriaco; **~ driving** guida in stato di ebbrezza

drunkenness ['drʌŋkənnɪs] *n* ubriachezza; ebbrezza

dry [draɪ] *adj* secco(-a); (*day, clothes: fig: humour*) asciutto(-a); (*uninteresting: lecture, subject*) poco avvincente ▪ *vt* seccare; (*clothes, hair, hands*) asciugare ▪ *vi* asciugarsi; **on ~ land** sulla terraferma; **to ~ one's hands/hair/eyes** asciugarsi le mani/i capelli/gli occhi
▸ **dry up** *vi* seccarsi; (*source of supply*) esaurirsi; (*fig: imagination etc*) inaridirsi; (*fall silent: speaker*) azzittirsi

dry-clean [draɪ'kli:n] *vt* pulire *or* lavare a secco

dry-cleaner's [draɪ'kli:nəz] *n* lavasecco *m inv*

dry-cleaning [draɪ'kli:nɪŋ] *n* pulitura a secco

dry dock *n* (*Naut*) bacino di carenaggio

dryer ['draɪə^r] *n* (*for hair*) föhn *m inv*, asciugacapelli *m inv*; (*for clothes*) asciugabiancheria *m inv*

dry goods *npl* (*Comm*) tessuti *mpl* e mercerie *fpl*

dry goods store *n* (*US*) negozio di stoffe

dry ice *n* ghiaccio secco

dryly ['draɪlɪ] *adv* con fare asciutto

dryness ['draɪnɪs] *n* secchezza; (*of ground*) aridità

dry rot *n* fungo del legno

dry run *n* (*fig*) prova

dry ski slope *n* pista artificiale

DSc *n abbr* (= *Doctor of Science*) *titolo di studio*

DSS *n abbr* (*Brit*) = **Department of Social Security**; *see* **social security**

DST *abbr* = **Daylight Saving Time**

DTI *n abbr* (*Brit*) = **Department of Trade and Industry**; *see* **trade**

DTP *n abbr* = **desktop publishing**; (*Med*: = *diphtheria, tetanus, pertussis*) *vaccino*

DT's *n abbr* (*col*) = **delirium tremens**

dual ['djuəl] *adj* doppio(-a)

dual carriageway *n* (*Brit*) strada a doppia carreggiata

dual-control ['djuəlkən'trəul] *adj* con doppi comandi

dual nationality *n* doppia nazionalità

dual-purpose ['djuəl'pə:pəs] *adj* a doppio uso

dubbed [dʌbd] *adj* (*Cine*) doppiato(-a); (*nicknamed*) soprannominato(-a)

dubious ['dju:bɪəs] *adj* dubbio(-a); (*character, manner*) ambiguo(-a), equivoco(-a); **I'm very ~ about it** ho i miei dubbi in proposito

Dublin ['dʌblɪn] *n* Dublino *f*

Dubliner ['dʌblɪnə^r] *n* dublinese *m/f*

duchess ['dʌtʃɪs] *n* duchessa

duck [dʌk] *n* anatra ▪ *vi* abbassare la testa ▪ *vt* spingere sotto (acqua)

duckling ['dʌklɪŋ] *n* anatroccolo

duct [dʌkt] *n* condotto; (*Anat*) canale *m*

dud [dʌd] *n* (*shell*) proiettile *m* che fa cilecca; **it's a ~** (*object, tool*) è inutile, non funziona ▪ *adj* (*Brit: cheque*) a vuoto; (*note, coin*) falso(-a)

due [dju:] *adj* dovuto(-a); (*expected*) atteso(-a); (*fitting*) giusto(-a) ■ *n* dovuto ■ *adv*: **~ north** diritto verso nord; **dues** *npl* (*for club, union*) quota; (*in harbour*) diritti *mpl* di porto; **in ~ course** a tempo debito; finalmente; **~ to** dovuto a; a causa di; **the rent's ~ on the 30th** l'affitto scade il 30; **the train is ~ at 8** il treno è atteso per le 8; **she is ~ back tomorrow** dovrebbe essere di ritorno domani; **I am ~ 6 days' leave** mi spettano 6 giorni di ferie
due date *n* data di scadenza
duel ['djuəl] *n* duello
duet [dju:'ɛt] *n* duetto
duff [dʌf] *adj* (*Brit col*) barboso(-a)
duffelbag, duffle bag ['dʌflbæg] *n* sacca da viaggio di tela
duffelcoat, duffle coat ['dʌflkəut] *n* montgomery *m inv*
duffer ['dʌfə^r] *n* (*col*) schiappa
dug [dʌg] *pt, pp of* **dig**
dugout ['dʌgaut] *n* (*Football*) panchina
duke [dju:k] *n* duca *m*
dull [dʌl] *adj* (*boring*) noioso(-a); (*slow-witted*) ottuso(-a); (*sound, pain*) sordo(-a); (*weather, day*) fosco(-a), scuro(-a); (*blade*) smussato(-a) ■ *vt* (*pain, grief*) attutire; (*mind, senses*) intorpidire
duly ['dju:lɪ] *adv* (*on time*) a tempo debito; (*as expected*) debitamente
dumb [dʌm] *adj* muto(-a); (*stupid*) stupido(-a); **to be struck ~** (*fig*) ammutolire, restare senza parole
dumbbell ['dʌmbɛl] *n* (*Sport*) manubrio, peso
dumbfounded [dʌm'faundɪd] *adj* stupito(-a), stordito(-a)
dummy ['dʌmɪ] *n* (*tailor's model*) manichino; (*Sport*) finto; (*Brit: for baby*) tettarella ■ *adj* falso(-a), finto(-a)
dummy run *n* giro di prova
dump [dʌmp] *n* mucchio di rifiuti; (*place*) luogo di scarico; (*Mil*) deposito; (*Comput*) scaricamento, dump *m inv* ■ *vt* (*put down*) scaricare; mettere giù; (*get rid of*) buttar via; (*Comm: goods*) svendere; (*Comput*) scaricare; **to be (down) in the dumps** (*col*) essere giù di corda
dumping ['dʌmpɪŋ] *n* (*Econ*) dumping *m*; (*of rubbish*): **"no ~"** "vietato lo scarico"
dumpling ['dʌmplɪŋ] *n* *specie di gnocco*
dumpy ['dʌmpɪ] *adj* tracagnotto(-a)
dunce [dʌns] *n* asino
dune [dju:n] *n* duna
dung [dʌŋ] *n* concime *m*
dungarees [dʌŋgə'ri:z] *npl* tuta
dungeon ['dʌndʒən] *n* prigione *f* sotterranea
dunk [dʌŋk] *vt* inzuppare
duo ['dju:əu] *n* (*gen, Mus*) duo *m inv*
duodenal [dju:əu'di:nl] *adj* (*ulcer*) duodenale
duodenum [dju:əu'di:nəm] *n* duodeno
dupe [dju:p] *vt* gabbare, ingannare
duplex ['dju:plɛks] *n* (*US: also:* **duplex apartment**) appartamento su due piani
duplicate *n* ['dju:plɪkət] doppio; (*copy of letter etc*) duplicato ■ *vt* ['dju:plɪkeɪt] raddoppiare; (*on machine*) ciclostilare ■ *adj* (*copy*) conforme, esattamente uguale; **in ~** in duplice copia; **~ key** duplicato (della chiave)
duplicating machine ['dju:plɪkeɪtɪŋ-], **duplicator** ['dju:plɪkeɪtə^r] *n* duplicatore *m*
duplicity [dju:'plɪsɪtɪ] *n* doppiezza, duplicità
Dur. *abbr* (*Brit*) = **Durham**
durability [djuərə'bɪlɪtɪ] *n* durevolezza; resistenza
durable ['djuərəbl] *adj* durevole; (*clothes, metal*) resistente
duration [djuə'reɪʃən] *n* durata
duress [djuə'rɛs] *n*: **under ~** sotto costrizione
Durex® ['djuərɛks] *n* (*Brit*) preservativo
during ['djuərɪŋ] *prep* durante, nel corso di
dusk [dʌsk] *n* crepuscolo
dusky ['dʌskɪ] *adj* scuro(-a)
dust [dʌst] *n* polvere *f* ■ *vt* (*furniture*) spolverare; (*cake etc*): **to ~ with** cospargere con
▸ **dust off** *vt* rispolverare
dustbin ['dʌstbɪn] *n* (*Brit*) pattumiera
duster ['dʌstə^r] *n* straccio per la polvere
dust jacket *n* sopraccoperta
dustman ['dʌstmən] *n* (*Brit*) netturbino
dustpan ['dʌstpæn] *n* pattumiera
dusty ['dʌstɪ] *adj* polveroso(-a)
Dutch [dʌtʃ] *adj* olandese ■ *n* (*Ling*) olandese *m* ■ *adv*: **to go ~** *or* **dutch** fare alla romana; **the ~** gli Olandesi
Dutch auction *n* asta all'olandese
Dutchman ['dʌtʃmən] *n* olandese *m*
Dutchwoman ['dʌtʃwumən] *n* olandese *f*
dutiable ['dju:tɪəbl] *adj* soggetto(-a) a dazio
dutiful ['dju:tɪful] *adj* (*child*) rispettoso(-a); (*husband*) premuroso(-a); (*employee*) coscienzioso(-a)
duty ['dju:tɪ] *n* dovere *m*; (*tax*) dazio, tassa; **duties** *npl* mansioni *fpl*; **on ~** di servizio; (*Med: in hospital*) di guardia; **off ~** libero(a), fuori servizio; **to make it one's ~ to do sth** assumersi l'obbligo di fare qc; **to pay ~ on sth** pagare il dazio su qc
duty-free ['dju:tɪ'fri:] *adj* esente da dazio; **~ shop** duty free *m inv*
duty officer *n* (*Mil etc*) ufficiale *m* di servizio
duvet ['du:veɪ] *n* piumino, piumone *m*
DV *abbr* (= *Deo volente*) D.V.
DVD *n abbr* (= *digital versatile or video disc*) DVD *m inv*
DVD burner *n* masterizzatore *m* (di) DVD

DVD player *n* lettore *m* DVD
DVD writer *n* masterizzatore *m* (di) DVD
DVLA *n abbr* (*Brit: = Driver and Vehicle Licensing Agency*) ≈ I.M.C.T.C. *m* (= *Ispettorato Generale della Motorizzazione Civile e dei Trasporti in Concessione*)
DVM *n abbr* (*US: = Doctor of Veterinary Medicine*) *titolo di studio*
DVT *n abbr* = **deep-vein thrombosis**
dwarf [dwɔːf] *n* nano(-a) ■ *vt* far apparire piccolo
dwell (*pt, pp* **dwelt**) [dwɛl, dwɛlt] *vi* dimorare
▸ **dwell on** *vt fus* indugiare su
dweller ['dwɛləʳ] *n* abitante *m/f*; **city ~** cittadino(-a)
dwelling ['dwɛlɪŋ] *n* dimora
dwelt [dwɛlt] *pt, pp of* **dwell**
dwindle ['dwɪndl] *vi* diminuire, decrescere
dwindling ['dwɪndlɪŋ] *adj* (*strength, interest*) che si affievolisce; (*resources, supplies*) in diminuzione
dye [daɪ] *n* colore *m*; (*chemical*) colorante *m*, tintura ■ *vt* tingere; **hair ~** tinta per capelli
dyestuffs ['daɪstʌfs] *npl* coloranti *mpl*
dying ['daɪɪŋ] *adj* morente, moribondo(-a)
dyke [daɪk] *n* diga; (*channel*) canale *m* di scolo; (*causeway*) sentiero rialzato
dynamic [daɪ'næmɪk] *adj* dinamico(-a)
dynamics [daɪ'næmɪks] *n, npl* dinamica
dynamite ['daɪnəmaɪt] *n* dinamite *f* ■ *vt* far saltare con la dinamite
dynamo ['daɪnəməu] *n* dinamo *f inv*
dynasty ['dɪnəstɪ] *n* dinastia
dysentery ['dɪsntrɪ] *n* dissenteria
dyslexia [dɪs'lɛksɪə] *n* dislessia
dyslexic [dɪs'lɛksɪk] *adj, n* dislessico(-a)
dyspepsia [dɪs'pɛpsɪə] *n* dispepsia
dystrophy ['dɪstrəfɪ] *n* distrofia; **muscular ~** distrofia muscolare

Ee

E, e [iː] *n* (*letter*) E, e *f or m inv*; (*Mus*): **E** mi *m*; **E for Edward**, (US) **E for Easy** ≈ E come Empoli
E *abbr* (= *east*) E ■ *n abbr* (= *Ecstasy*) ecstasy *f inv*
e- [iː] *prefix* e-
E111 *n abbr* (*also*: **form E111**) E111 (*modulo UE per rimborso spese mediche*)
ea. *abbr* = **each**
each [iːtʃ] *adj* ogni, ciascuno(-a) ■ *pron* ciascuno(-a), ognuno(-a); **~ one** ognuno(a); **~ other** si (*or* ci *etc*); **they hate ~ other** si odiano (l'un l'altro); **you are jealous of ~ other** siete gelosi l'uno dell'altro; **~ day** ogni giorno; **they have 2 books ~** hanno 2 libri ciascuno; **they cost £5 ~** costano 5 sterline l'uno; **~ of us** ciascuno *or* ognuno di noi
eager ['iːgə^r] *adj* impaziente; desideroso(-a); ardente; (*keen: pupil*) appassionato(-a), attento(-a); **to be ~ to do sth** non veder l'ora di fare qc; essere desideroso di fare qc; **to be ~ for** essere desideroso di, aver gran voglia di
eagle ['iːgl] *n* aquila
E & OE *abbr* (= *errors and omissions excepted*) S.E.O.
ear [ɪə^r] *n* orecchio; (*of corn*) pannocchia; **up to the ears in debt** nei debiti fino al collo
earache ['ɪəreɪk] *n* mal *m* d'orecchi
eardrum ['ɪədrʌm] *n* timpano
earful ['ɪəful] *n*: **to give sb an ~** fare una ramanzina a qn
earl [əːl] *n* conte *m*
earlier ['əːlɪə^r] *adj* (*date etc*) anteriore; (*edition etc*) precedente, anteriore ■ *adv* prima; **I can't come any ~** non posso venire prima
early ['əːlɪ] *adv* presto, di buon'ora; (*ahead of time*) in anticipo ■ *adj* precoce; anticipato(-a); che si fa vedere di buon'ora; (*man*) primitivo(-a); (*Christians, settlers*) primo(-a); **~ in the morning/afternoon** nelle prime ore del mattino/del pomeriggio; **you're ~!** sei in anticipo!; **have an ~ night/start** vada a letto/parta presto; **in the ~** *or* **~ in the spring/19th century** all'inizio della primavera/dell'Ottocento; **she's in her ~ forties** ha appena passato la quarantina; **at your earliest convenience** (*Comm*) non appena possibile
early retirement *n* ritiro anticipato
early warning system *n* sistema *m* del preallarme
earmark ['ɪəmɑːk] *vt*: **to ~ sth for** destinare qc a
earn [əːn] *vt* guadagnare; (*rest, reward*) meritare; (*Comm: yield*) maturare; **to ~ one's living** guadagnarsi da vivere; **this earned him much praise, he earned much praise for this** si è attirato grandi lodi per questo
earned income *n* reddito da lavoro
earnest ['əːnɪst] *adj* serio(-a) ■ *n* (*also*: **earnest money**) caparra; **in ~** *adv* sul serio
earnings ['əːnɪŋz] *npl* guadagni *mpl*; (*of company etc*) proventi *mpl*; (*salary*) stipendio
ear, nose and throat specialist *n* otorinolaringoiatra *m/f*
earphones ['ɪəfəunz] *npl* cuffia
earplugs ['ɪəplʌgz] *npl* tappi *mpl* per le orecchie
earring ['ɪərɪŋ] *n* orecchino
earshot ['ɪəʃɔt] *n*: **out of/within ~** fuori portata/a portata d'orecchio
earth [əːθ] *n* (*gen also Brit: Elec*) terra; (*of fox etc*) tana ■ *vt* (*Brit Elec*) mettere a terra
earthenware ['əːθənwɛə^r] *n* terracotta; stoviglie *fpl* di terracotta ■ *adj* di terracotta
earthly ['əːθlɪ] *adj* terreno(-a); **~ paradise** paradiso terrestre; **there is no ~ reason to think ...** non vi è ragione di pensare ...
earthquake ['əːθkweɪk] *n* terremoto
earth-shattering ['əːθʃætərɪŋ] *adj* stupefacente
earth tremor *n* scossa sismica
earthworks ['əːθwəːks] *npl* lavori *mpl* di sterro
earthworm ['əːθwəːm] *n* lombrico
earthy ['əːθɪ] *adj* (*fig*) grossolano(-a)
earwax ['ɪəwæks] *n* cerume *m*
earwig ['ɪəwɪg] *n* forbicina
ease [iːz] *n* agio, comodo ■ *vt* (*soothe*) calmare; (*loosen*) allentare ■ *vi* (*situation*)

allentarsi, distendersi; **life of ~** vita comoda; **with ~** senza difficoltà; **at ~** a proprio agio; (*Mil*) a riposo; **to feel at ~/ill at ~** sentirsi a proprio agio/a disagio; **to ~ sth out/in** tirare fuori/infilare qc con delicatezza; facilitare l'uscita/l'entrata di qc
▸ **ease off, ease up** *vi* diminuire; (*slow down*) rallentarsi; (*fig*) rilassarsi
easel ['i:zl] *n* cavalletto
easily ['i:zɪlɪ] *adv* facilmente
easiness ['i:zɪnɪs] *n* facilità, semplicità; (*of manners*) disinvoltura
east [i:st] *n* est *m* ■ *adj* dell'est ■ *adv* a oriente; **the E~** l'Oriente *m*; (*Pol*) i Paesi dell'Est
Easter ['i:stə^r] *n* Pasqua ■ *adj* (*holidays*) pasquale, di Pasqua
Easter egg *n* uovo di Pasqua
Easter Island *n* isola di Pasqua
easterly ['i:stəlɪ] *adj* dall'est, d'oriente
Easter Monday *n* Pasquetta
eastern ['i:stən] *adj* orientale, d'oriente; **E~ Europe** l'Europa orientale; **the E~ bloc** (*Pol*) i Paesi dell'Est
Easter Sunday *n* domenica di Pasqua
East Germany *n* (*formerly*) Germania dell'Est
eastward ['i:stwəd], **eastwards** ['i:stwədz] *adv* verso est, verso levante
easy ['i:zɪ] *adj* facile; (*manner*) disinvolto(-a); (*carefree: life*) agiato(-a), tranquillo(-a) ■ *adv*: **to take it** *or* **things ~** prendersela con calma; **I'm ~** (*col*) non ho problemi; **easier said than done** tra il dire e il fare c'è di mezzo il mare; **payment on ~ terms** (*Comm*) facilitazioni *fpl* di pagamento
easy chair *n* poltrona
easy-going ['i:zɪ'gəuɪŋ] *adj* accomodante
eat (*pt* **ate**, *pp* **eaten**) [i:t, eɪt, 'i:tn] *vt* mangiare
▸ **eat away** *vt* (*sea*) erodere; (*acid*) corrodere
▸ **eat away at, eat into** *vt fus* rodere
▸ **eat out** *vi* mangiare fuori
▸ **eat up** *vt* (*meal etc*) finire di mangiare; **it eats up electricity** consuma un sacco di corrente
eatable ['i:təbl] *adj* mangiabile; (*safe to eat*) commestibile
eaten ['i:tn] *pp of* **eat**
eau de Cologne ['əudəkə'ləun] *n* acqua di colonia
eaves [i:vz] *npl* gronda
eavesdrop ['i:vzdrɔp] *vi*: **to ~ (on a conversation)** origliare (una conversazione)
ebb [ɛb] *n* riflusso ■ *vi* rifluire; (*fig: also:* **ebb away**) declinare; **~ and flow** flusso e riflusso; **to be at a low ~** (*fig: person, spirits*) avere il morale a terra; (*: business*) andar male
ebb tide *n* marea discendente
ebony ['ɛbənɪ] *n* ebano
ebullient [ɪ'bʌlɪənt] *adj* esuberante
ECB *n abbr* (= *European Central Bank*) BCE *f*
eccentric [ɪk'sɛntrɪk] *adj, n* eccentrico(-a)
ecclesiastic [ɪkli:zɪ'æstɪk] *n* ecclesiastico ■ *adj* ecclesiastico(-a)
ecclesiastical [ɪkli:zɪ'æstɪkəl] *adj* ecclesiastico(-a)
ECG *n abbr* = **electrocardiogram**
echo (*pl* **echoes**) ['ɛkəu] *n* eco *m or f* ■ *vt* ripetere; fare eco a ■ *vi* echeggiare; dare un eco
éclair ['eɪklɛə^r] *n* ≈ bignè *m inv*
eclipse [ɪ'klɪps] *n* eclissi *f inv* ■ *vt* eclissare
eco... ['i:kəu] *prefix* eco...
eco-friendly [i:kəu'frɛndlɪ] *adj* ecologico(-a)
ecological [i:kə'lɔdʒɪkəl] *adj* ecologico(-a)
ecologist [ɪ'kɔlədʒɪst] *n* ecologo(-a)
ecology [ɪ'kɔlədʒɪ] *n* ecologia
e-commerce [i:'kɔmə:s] *n* commercio elettronico, e-commerce *m inv*
economic [i:kə'nɔmɪk] *adj* economico(-a); (*profitable: price*) vantaggioso(-a); (*business*) che rende
economical [i:kə'nɔmɪkəl] *adj* economico(-a); (*person*) economo(-a)
economically [i:kə'nɔmɪklɪ] *adv* con economia; (*regarding economics*) dal punto di vista economico
economics [i:kə'nɔmɪks] *n* economia ■ *npl* aspetto *or* lato economico
economist [ɪ'kɔnəmɪst] *n* economista *m/f*
economize [ɪ'kɔnəmaɪz] *vi* risparmiare, fare economia
economy [ɪ'kɔnəmɪ] *n* economia; **economies of scale** (*Comm*) economie *fpl* di scala
economy class *n* (*Aviat etc*) classe *f* turistica
economy size *n* confezione *f* economica
ecosystem ['i:kəusɪstəm] *n* ecosistema *m*
eco-tourism [i:kəu'tuərɪzəm] *n* ecoturismo
ECSC *n abbr* (= *European Coal & Steel Community*) C.E.C.A. *f* (= *Comunità Europea del Carbone e dell'Acciaio*)
ecstasy ['ɛkstəsɪ] *n* estasi *f inv*; **to go into ecstasies over** andare in estasi davanti a; **E~** (*drug*) ecstasy *f inv*
ecstatic [ɛks'tætɪk] *adj* estatico(-a), in estasi
ECT *n abbr* = **electroconvulsive therapy**
ECU, ecu ['eɪkju:] *n abbr* (= *European Currency Unit*) ECU *f inv*, ecu *f inv*
Ecuador ['ɛkwədɔ:^r] *n* Ecuador *m*
ecumenical [i:kju'mɛnɪkl] *adj* ecumenico(-a)
eczema ['ɛksɪmə] *n* eczema *m*
eddy ['ɛdɪ] *n* mulinello
edge [ɛdʒ] *n* margine *m*; (*of table, plate, cup*) orlo; (*of knife etc*) taglio ■ *vt* bordare ■ *vi*:

e

to ~ away from sgattaiolare da; **to ~ past** passar rasente; **to ~ forward** avanzare a poco a poco; **on ~** (*fig*) = **edgy**; **to have the ~ on** essere in vantaggio su
edgeways ['ɛdʒweɪz] *adv* di fianco; **he couldn't get a word in ~** non riuscì a dire una parola
edging ['ɛdʒɪŋ] *n* bordo
edgy ['ɛdʒɪ] *adj* nervoso(-a)
edible ['ɛdɪbl] *adj* commestibile; (*meal*) mangiabile
edict ['iːdɪkt] *n* editto
edifice ['ɛdɪfɪs] *n* edificio
edifying ['ɛdɪfaɪɪŋ] *adj* edificante
Edinburgh ['ɛdɪnbərə] *n* Edimburgo *f*
edit ['ɛdɪt] *vt* curare; (*newspaper, magazine*) dirigere; (*Comput*) correggere e modificare, editare
edition [ɪ'dɪʃən] *n* edizione *f*
editor ['ɛdɪtə^r] *n* (*in newspaper*) redattore(-trice); redattore(-trice) capo; (*of sb's work*) curatore(-trice); (*film editor*) responsabile *m/f* del montaggio
editorial [ɛdɪ'tɔːrɪəl] *adj* redazionale, editoriale ■ *n* editoriale *m*; **the ~ staff** la redazione
EDP *n abbr* = **electronic data processing**
EDT *abbr* (*US:* = *Eastern Daylight Time*) *ora legale di New York*
educate ['ɛdjukeɪt] *vt* istruire; educare
educated guess ['ɛdjukeɪtɪd-] *n* ipotesi *f* ben fondata
education [ɛdju'keɪʃən] *n* (*teaching*) insegnamento; istruzione *f*; (*knowledge, culture*) cultura; (*Scol: subject etc*) pedagogia; **primary** *or* (*US*) **elementary/secondary ~** scuola primaria/secondaria
educational [ɛdju'keɪʃənl] *adj* pedagogico(-a); scolastico(-a); istruttivo(-a); **~ technology** tecnologie *fpl* applicate alla didattica
Edwardian [ɛd'wɔːdɪən] *adj* edoardiano(-a)
EE *abbr* = **electrical engineer**
EEG *n abbr* = **electroencephalogram**
eel [iːl] *n* anguilla
EENT *n abbr* (*US Med*) = **eye, ear, nose and throat**
EEOC *n abbr* (*US*) = **Equal Employment Opportunity Commission**
eerie ['ɪərɪ] *adj* che fa accapponare la pelle
EET *abbr* (= *Eastern European Time*) *fuso orario*
effect [ɪ'fɛkt] *n* effetto ■ *vt* effettuare; **to take ~** (*law*) entrare in vigore; (*drug*) fare effetto; **to have an ~ on sb/sth** avere *or* produrre un effetto su qn/qc; **to put into ~** (*plan*) attuare; **in ~** effettivamente; **his letter is to the ~ that ...** il contenuto della sua lettera è che ...; *see also* **effects**
effective [ɪ'fɛktɪv] *adj* efficace; (*striking: display, outfit*) che fa colpo; **~ date** data d'entrata in vigore; **to become ~** (*law*) entrare in vigore
effectively [ɪ'fɛktɪvlɪ] *adv* (*efficiently*) efficacemente; (*strikingly*) ad effetto; (*in reality*) di fatto; (*in effect*) in effetti
effectiveness [ɪ'fɛktɪvnɪs] *n* efficacia
effects [ɪ'fɛkts] *npl* (*Theat*) effetti *mpl* scenici; (*property*) effetti *mpl*
effeminate [ɪ'fɛmɪnɪt] *adj* effeminato(-a)
effervescent [ɛfə'vɛsnt] *adj* effervescente
efficacy ['ɛfɪkəsɪ] *n* efficacia
efficiency [ɪ'fɪʃənsɪ] *n* efficienza; rendimento effettivo
efficiency apartment *n* (*US*) miniappartamento
efficient [ɪ'fɪʃənt] *adj* efficiente; (*remedy, product, system*) efficace; (*machine, car*) che ha un buon rendimento
efficiently [ɪ'fɪʃəntlɪ] *adv* efficientemente; efficacemente
effigy ['ɛfɪdʒɪ] *n* effigie *f*
effluent ['ɛfluənt] *n* effluente *m*
effort ['ɛfət] *n* sforzo; **to make an ~ to do sth** sforzarsi di fare qc
effortless ['ɛfətlɪs] *adj* senza sforzo, facile
effrontery [ɪ'frʌntərɪ] *n* sfrontatezza
effusive [ɪ'fjuːsɪv] *adj* (*person*) espansivo(-a); (*welcome, letter*) caloroso(-a); (*thanks, apologies*) interminabile
EFL *n abbr* (*Scol*) = **English as a foreign language**
EFTA ['ɛftə] *n abbr* (= *European Free Trade Association*) E.F.T.A. *f*
e.g. *adv abbr* (= *exempli gratia: for example*) p.es.
egalitarian [ɪgælɪ'tɛərɪən] *adj* egualitario(-a)
egg [ɛg] *n* uovo
▸ **egg on** *vt* incitare
eggcup ['ɛgkʌp] *n* portauovo *m inv*
eggplant ['ɛgplɑːnt] *n* (*esp US*) melanzana
eggshell ['ɛgʃɛl] *n* guscio d'uovo ■ *adj* (*colour*) guscio d'uovo *inv*
egg-timer ['ɛgtaɪmə^r] *n* clessidra (*per misurare il tempo di cottura delle uova*)
egg white *n* albume *m*, bianco d'uovo
egg yolk *n* tuorlo, rosso (d'uovo)
ego ['iːgəu] *n* ego *m inv*
egoism ['ɛgəuɪzəm] *n* egoismo
egoist ['ɛgəuɪst] *n* egoista *m/f*
egotism ['ɛgəutɪzəm] *n* egotismo
egotist ['ɛgəutɪst] *n* egotista *m/f*
ego trip *n*: **to be on an ~** gasarsi
Egypt ['iːdʒɪpt] *n* Egitto
Egyptian [ɪ'dʒɪpʃən] *adj, n* egiziano(-a)
eiderdown ['aɪdədaun] *n* piumino

eight [eɪt] *num* otto
eighteen ['eɪ'tiːn] *num* diciotto
eighth [eɪtθ] *num* ottavo(-a)
eighty [eɪtɪ] *num* ottanta
Eire ['ɛərə] *n* Repubblica d'Irlanda
EIS *n abbr (= Educational Institute of Scotland) principale sindacato degli insegnanti in Scozia*
either ['aɪðə^r] *adj* l'uno(-a) o l'altro(-a); (*both, each*) ciascuno(-a); **on ~ side** su ciascun lato ■ *pron*: **~ (of them)** (o) l'uno(a) o l'altro(a); **I don't like ~** non mi piace né l'uno né l'altro ■ *adv* neanche; **no, I don't ~** no, neanch'io ■ *conj*: **~ good or bad** o buono o cattivo; **I haven't seen ~ one or the other** non ho visto né l'uno né l'altro
ejaculation [ɪdʒækju'leɪʃən] *n* (*Physiol*) eiaculazione *f*
eject [ɪ'dʒɛkt] *vt* espellere; lanciare ■ *vi* (*pilot*) catapultarsi
ejector seat [ɪ'dʒɛktə-] *n* sedile *m* eiettabile
eke [iːk]: **to ~ out** *vt* far durare; aumentare
EKG *n abbr* (*US*) = **electrocardiogram**
el [ɛl] *n abbr* (*US col*) = **elevated railroad**
elaborate *adj* [ɪ'læbərɪt] elaborato(-a), minuzioso(-a) ■ *vb* [ɪ'læbəreɪt] *vt* elaborare ■ *vi* entrare in dettagli
elapse [ɪ'læps] *vi* trascorrere, passare
elastic [ɪ'læstɪk] *adj* elastico(-a) ■ *n* elastico
elastic band *n* (*Brit*) elastico
elasticity [ɪlæs'tɪsɪtɪ] *n* elasticità
elated [ɪ'leɪtɪd] *adj* pieno(-a) di gioia
elation [ɪ'leɪʃən] *n* gioia
elbow ['ɛlbəu] *n* gomito ■ *vt*: **to ~ one's way through the crowd** farsi largo tra la folla a gomitate
elbow grease *n*: **to use a bit of ~** usare un po' di olio di gomiti
elbowroom ['ɛlbəurum] *n* spazio
elder ['ɛldə^r] *adj* maggiore, più vecchio(-a) ■ *n* (*tree*) sambuco; **one's elders** i più anziani
elderly ['ɛldəlɪ] *adj* anziano(-a) ■ *npl*: **the ~** gli anziani
elder statesman *n anziano uomo politico in pensione, ma ancora influente*; (*of company*) anziano(-a) consigliere(-a)
eldest ['ɛldɪst] *adj, n*: **the ~ (child)** il(la) maggiore (dei bambini)
elect [ɪ'lɛkt] *vt* eleggere; (*choose*): **to ~ to do** decidere di fare ■ *adj*: **the president ~** il presidente designato
election [ɪ'lɛkʃən] *n* elezione *f*; **to hold an ~** indire un'elezione
election campaign *n* campagna elettorale
electioneering [ɪlɛkʃə'nɪərɪŋ] *n* propaganda elettorale
elector [ɪ'lɛktə^r] *n* elettore(-trice)
electoral [ɪ'lɛktərəl] *adj* elettorale
electoral college *n* collegio elettorale
electoral roll *n* (*Brit*) registro elettorale
electoral system *n* sistema *m* elettorale
electorate [ɪ'lɛktərɪt] *n* elettorato
electric [ɪ'lɛktrɪk] *adj* elettrico(-a)
electrical [ɪ'lɛktrɪkəl] *adj* elettrico(-a)
electrical engineer *n* ingegnere *m* elettrotecnico
electrical failure *n* guasto all'impianto elettrico
electric blanket *n* coperta elettrica
electric chair *n* sedia elettrica
electric cooker *n* cucina elettrica
electric current *n* corrente *f* elettrica
electric fire *n* (*Brit*) stufa elettrica
electrician [ɪlɛk'trɪʃən] *n* elettricista *m*
electricity [ɪlɛk'trɪsɪtɪ] *n* elettricità; **to switch on/off the ~** attaccare/staccare la corrente
electricity board *n* (*Brit*) ente *m* regionale per l'energia elettrica
electric light *n* luce *f* elettrica
electric shock *n* scossa (elettrica)
electrify [ɪ'lɛktrɪfaɪ] *vt* (*Rail*) elettrificare; (*audience*) elettrizzare
electro... [ɪ'lɛktrəu] *prefix* elettro...
electrocardiogram [ɪ'lɛktrə'kɑːdɪəgræm] *n* elettrocardiogramma *m*
electroconvulsive therapy [ɪ'lɛktrəkən'vʌlsɪv-] *n* elettroshockterapia
electrocute [ɪ'lɛktrəkjuːt] *vt* fulminare
electrode [ɪ'lɛktrəud] *n* elettrodo
electroencephalogram [ɪ'lɛktrəuɛn'sɛfələgræm] *n* (*Med*) elettroencefalogramma *m*
electrolysis [ɪlɛk'trɔlɪsɪs] *n* elettrolisi *f*
electromagnetic [ɪ'lɛktrəumæg'nɛtɪk] *n* elettromagnetico(-a)
electron [ɪ'lɛktrɔn] *n* elettrone *m*
electronic [ɪlɛk'trɔnɪk] *adj* elettronico(-a); *see also* **electronics**
electronic data processing *n* elaborazione *f* elettronica di dati
electronic mail *n* posta elettronica
electronics [ɪlɛk'trɔnɪks] *n* elettronica
electron microscope *n* microscopio elettronico
electroplated [ɪ'lɛktrəu'pleɪtɪd] *adj* galvanizzato(-a)
electrotherapy [ɪ'lɛktrəu'θɛrəpɪ] *n* elettroterapia
elegance ['ɛlɪgəns] *n* eleganza
elegant ['ɛlɪgənt] *adj* elegante
element ['ɛlɪmənt] *n* elemento; (*of heater, kettle etc*) resistenza
elementary [ɛlɪ'mɛntərɪ] *adj* elementare
elementary school *n* (*US*) *vedi nota*

ELEMENTARY SCHOOL

Negli Stati Uniti e in Canada, i bambini frequentano la *elementary school* per almeno sei anni, a volte anche per otto. Negli Stati Uniti si chiama anche "grade school" o "grammar school".

elephant ['ɛlɪfənt] *n* elefante(-essa)
elevate ['ɛlɪveɪt] *vt* elevare
elevated railroad, el *n* (*US*) (ferrovia) soprelevata
elevation [ɛlɪ'veɪʃən] *n* elevazione *f*; (*height*) altitudine *f*
elevator ['ɛlɪveɪtəʳ] *n* elevatore *m*; (*US: lift*) ascensore *m*
eleven [ɪ'lɛvn] *num* undici
elevenses [ɪ'lɛvnzɪz] *npl* (*Brit*) caffè *m* a metà mattina
eleventh [ɪ'lɛvnθ] *adj* undicesimo(-a); **at the ~ hour** (*fig*) all'ultimo minuto
elf (*pl* **elves**) [ɛlf, ɛlvz] *n* elfo
elicit [ɪ'lɪsɪt] *vt*: **to ~ (from)** trarre (da), cavare fuori (da); **to ~ sth (from sb)** strappare qc (a qn)
eligible ['ɛlɪdʒəbl] *adj* eleggibile; (*for membership*) che ha i requisiti; **to be ~ for a pension** essere pensionabile
eliminate [ɪ'lɪmɪneɪt] *vt* eliminare
elimination [ɪlɪmɪ'neɪʃən] *n* eliminazione *f*; **by process of ~** per eliminazione
élite [eɪ'li:t] *n* élite *f inv*
elitist [eɪ'li:tɪst] *adj* (*pej*) elitario(-a)
elixir [ɪ'lɪksəʳ] *n* elisir *m inv*
Elizabethan [ɪlɪzə'bi:θən] *n* elisabettiano(-a)
ellipse [ɪ'lɪps] *n* ellisse *f*
elliptical [ɪ'lɪptɪkl] *adj* ellittico(-a)
elm [ɛlm] *n* olmo
elocution [ɛlə'kju:ʃən] *n* elocuzione *f*
elongated ['i:lɔŋgeɪtɪd] *adj* allungato(-a)
elope [ɪ'ləup] *vi* (*lovers*) scappare
elopement [ɪ'ləupmənt] *n* fuga romantica
eloquence ['ɛləkwəns] *n* eloquenza
eloquent ['ɛləkwənt] *adj* eloquente
else [ɛls] *adv* altro; **something ~** qualcos'altro; **somewhere ~** altrove; **everywhere ~** in qualsiasi altro luogo; **where ~?** in quale altro luogo?; **little ~** poco altro; **everyone ~** tutti gli altri; **nothing ~** nient'altro; **or ~** (*otherwise*) altrimenti; **is there anything ~ I can do?** posso fare qualcos'altro?
elsewhere [ɛls'wɛəʳ] *adv* altrove
ELT *n abbr* (*Scol*) = **English Language Teaching**
elucidate [ɪ'lu:sɪdeɪt] *vt* delucidare
elude [ɪ'lu:d] *vt* eludere
elusive [ɪ'lu:sɪv] *adj* elusivo(-a); (*answer*) evasivo(-a); **he is very ~** è proprio inafferrabile *or* irraggiungibile
elves [ɛlvz] *npl of* **elf**
emaciated [ɪ'meɪsɪeɪtɪd] *adj* emaciato(-a)
email ['i:meɪl] *n abbr* (= *electronic mail*) posta elettronica ■ *vt*: **to ~ sb** comunicare con qn mediante posta elettronica; **~ address** indirizzo di posta elettronica; **~ account** account *m inv* di posta elettronica
emanate ['ɛməneɪt] *vi*: **to ~ from** emanare da
emancipate [ɪ'mænsɪpeɪt] *vt* emancipare
emancipation [ɪmænsɪ'peɪʃən] *n* emancipazione *f*
emasculate [ɪ'mæskjuleɪt] *vt* (*fig*) rendere impotente
embalm [ɪm'bɑ:m] *vt* imbalsamare
embankment [ɪm'bæŋkmənt] *n* (*of road, railway*) massicciata; (*riverside*) argine *m*; (*dyke*) diga
embargo [ɪm'bɑ:gəu] *n* (*pl* **embargoes**) (*Comm, Naut*) embargo ■ *vt* mettere l'embargo su; **to put an ~ on sth** mettere l'embargo su qc
embark [ɪm'bɑ:k] *vi*: **to ~ (on)** imbarcarsi (su) ■ *vt* imbarcare; **to ~ on** (*fig*) imbarcarsi in; (*journey*) intraprendere
embarkation [ɛmbɑ:'keɪʃən] *n* imbarco
embarkation card *n* carta d'imbarco
embarrass [ɪm'bærəs] *vt* imbarazzare; **to be embarrassed** essere imbarazzato(-a)
embarrassing [ɪm'bærəsɪŋ] *adj* imbarazzante
embarrassment [ɪm'bærəsmənt] *n* imbarazzo
embassy ['ɛmbəsɪ] *n* ambasciata; **the Italian E~** l'ambasciata d'Italia
embed [ɪm'bɛd] *vt* conficcare; incastrare
embellish [ɪm'bɛlɪʃ] *vt* abbellire; **to ~ (with)** (*fig: story, truth*) infiorare (con)
embers ['ɛmbəz] *npl* braci *fpl*
embezzle [ɪm'bɛzl] *vt* appropriarsi indebitamente di
embezzlement [ɪm'bɛzlmənt] *n* appropriazione *f* indebita, malversazione *f*
embezzler [ɪm'bɛzləʳ] *n* malversatore(-trice)
embitter [ɪm'bɪtəʳ] *vt* amareggiare; inasprire
emblem ['ɛmbləm] *n* emblema *m*
embodiment [ɪm'bɔdɪmənt] *n* personificazione *f*, incarnazione *f*
embody [ɪm'bɔdɪ] *vt* (*features*) racchiudere, comprendere; (*ideas*) dar forma concreta a, esprimere
embolden [ɪm'bəuldn] *vt* incitare
embolism ['ɛmbəlɪzəm] *n* embolia
embossed [ɪm'bɔst] *adj* in rilievo; goffrato(-a); **~ with ...** con in rilievo ...

embrace [ɪmˈbreɪs] *vt* abbracciare; (*include*) comprendere ■ *vi* abbracciarsi ■ *n* abbraccio

embroider [ɪmˈbrɔɪdəʳ] *vt* ricamare; (*fig: story*) abbellire

embroidery [ɪmˈbrɔɪdərɪ] *n* ricamo

embroil [ɪmˈbrɔɪl] *vt*: **to become embroiled (in sth)** restare invischiato(a) (in qc)

embryo [ˈɛmbrɪəu] *n* (*also fig*) embrione *m*

emcee [ɛmˈsiː] *n abbr* = **master of ceremonies**

emend [ɪˈmɛnd] *vt* (*text*) correggere, emendare

emerald [ˈɛmərəld] *n* smeraldo

emerge [ɪˈməːdʒ] *vi* apparire, sorgere; **it emerges that** (*Brit*) risulta che

emergence [ɪˈməːdʒəns] *n* apparizione *f*; (*of nation*) nascita

emergency [ɪˈməːdʒənsɪ] *n* emergenza; **in an ~** in caso di emergenza; **to declare a state of ~** dichiarare lo stato di emergenza

emergency exit *n* uscita di sicurezza

emergency landing *n* atterraggio forzato

emergency lane *n* (*US Aut*) corsia d'emergenza

emergency road service *n* (*US*) servizio riparazioni

emergency service *n* servizio di pronto intervento

emergency stop *n* (*Brit Aut*) frenata improvvisa

emergent [ɪˈməːdʒənt] *adj*: **~ nation** paese *m* in via di sviluppo

emery board [ˈɛmərɪ-] *n* limetta di carta smerigliata

emery paper *n* carta smerigliata

emetic [ɪˈmɛtɪk] *n* emetico

emigrant [ˈɛmɪgrənt] *n* emigrante *m/f*

emigrate [ˈɛmɪgreɪt] *vi* emigrare

emigration [ɛmɪˈgreɪʃən] *n* emigrazione *f*

émigré [ˈɛmɪgreɪ] *n* emigrato(-a)

eminence [ˈɛmɪnəns] *n* eminenza

eminent [ˈɛmɪnənt] *adj* eminente

eminently [ˈɛmɪnəntlɪ] *adv* assolutamente, perfettamente

emirate [ɛˈmɪərɪt] *n* emirato

emission [ɪˈmɪʃən] *n* (*of gas, radiation*) emissione *f*

emit [ɪˈmɪt] *vt* emettere

emolument [ɪˈmɔljumənt] *n* (*often pl: formal*) emolumento

emoticon [ɪˈməutɪkən] *n* (*Comput*) faccina

emotion [ɪˈməuʃən] *n* emozione *f*; (*love, jealousy etc*) sentimento

emotional [ɪˈməuʃənl] *adj* (*person*) emotivo(-a); (*scene*) commovente; (*tone, speech*) carico(-a) d'emozione

emotionally [ɪˈməuʃnəlɪ] *adv* (*behave, be involved*) sentimentalmente; (*speak*) con emozione; **~ disturbed** con turbe emotive

emotive [ɪˈməutɪv] *adj* emotivo(-a); **~ power** capacità di commuovere

empathy [ˈɛmpəθɪ] *n* immedesimazione *f*; **to feel ~ with sb** immedesimarsi con i sentimenti di qn

emperor [ˈɛmpərəʳ] *n* imperatore *m*

emphasis (*pl* **emphases**) [ˈɛmfəsɪs, -siːz] *n* enfasi *f inv*; importanza; **to lay** *or* **place ~ on sth** (*fig*) mettere in risalto *or* in evidenza qc; **the ~ is on sport** si dà molta importanza allo sport

emphasize [ˈɛmfəsaɪz] *vt* (*word, point*) sottolineare; (*feature*) mettere in evidenza

emphatic [ɪmˈfætɪk] *adj* (*strong*) vigoroso(-a); (*unambiguous, clear*) netto(-a), categorico(-a)

emphatically [ɪmˈfætɪkəlɪ] *adv* vigorosamente; nettamente

emphysema [ɛmfɪˈsiːmə] *n* (*Med*) enfisema *m*

empire [ˈɛmpaɪəʳ] *n* impero

empirical [ɛmˈpɪrɪkl] *adj* empirico(-a)

employ [ɪmˈplɔɪ] *vt* (*make use of: thing, method, person*) impiegare, servirsi di; (*give job to*) dare lavoro a, impiegare; **he's employed in a bank** lavora in banca

employee [ɪmplɔɪˈiː] *n* impiegato(-a)

employer [ɪmˈplɔɪəʳ] *n* principale *m/f*, datore *m* di lavoro

employment [ɪmˈplɔɪmənt] *n* impiego; **to find ~** trovare impiego *or* lavoro; **without ~** disoccupato(a); **place of ~** posto di lavoro

employment agency *n* agenzia di collocamento

employment exchange *n* (*Brit*) ufficio *m* collocamento *inv*

empower [ɪmˈpauəʳ] *vt*: **to ~ sb to do** concedere autorità a qn di fare

empress [ˈɛmprɪs] *n* imperatrice *f*

emptiness [ˈɛmptɪnɪs] *n* vuoto

empty [ˈɛmptɪ] *adj* vuoto(-a); (*street, area*) deserto(-a); (*threat, promise*) vano(-a) ■ *n* (*bottle*) vuoto ■ *vt* vuotare ■ *vi* vuotarsi; (*liquid*) scaricarsi; **on an ~ stomach** a stomaco vuoto; **to ~ into** (*river*) gettarsi in

empty-handed [ɛmptɪˈhændɪd] *adj* a mani vuote

empty-headed [ɛmptɪˈhɛdɪd] *adj* sciocco(-a)

EMS *n abbr* (= *European Monetary System*) S.M.E. *m*

EMT *n abbr* (*US*) = **emergency medical technician**

EMU *n abbr* (= *European Monetary Union*) Unità *f* monetaria europea; (= *economic and monetary union*) UEM *f*

emulate [ˈɛmjuleɪt] *vt* emulare

emulsion [ɪˈmʌlʃən] *n* emulsione *f*; (*also*: **emulsion paint**) colore *m* a tempera

enable [ɪˈneɪbl] *vt*: **to ~ sb to do** permettere a qn di fare

enact [ɪ'nækt] *vt* (*law*) emanare; (*play, scene*) rappresentare
enamel [ɪ'næməl] *n* smalto
enamel paint *n* vernice *f* a smalto
enamoured [ɪ'næməd] *adj*: **~ of** innamorato(a) di
enc. *abbr* (*on letters etc*: = *enclosed, enclosure*) all., alleg.
encampment [ɪn'kæmpmənt] *n* accampamento
encased [ɪn'keɪst] *adj*: **~ in** racchiuso(a) in, rivestito(a) di
enchant [ɪn'tʃɑːnt] *vt* incantare; (*magic spell*) catturare
enchanting [ɪn'tʃɑːntɪŋ] *adj* incantevole, affascinante
encircle [ɪn'səːkl] *vt* accerchiare
encl. *abbr* (*on letters etc*: = *enclosed, enclosure*) all., alleg.
enclose [ɪn'kləuz] *vt* (*land*) circondare, recingere; (*letter etc*): **to ~ (with)** allegare (con); **please find enclosed** trovi qui accluso
enclosure [ɪn'kləuʒə^r] *n* recinto; (*Comm*) allegato
encoder [ɪn'kəudə^r] *n* (*Comput*) codificatore *m*
encompass [ɪn'kʌmpəs] *vt* comprendere
encore [ɔŋ'kɔː^r] *excl, n* bis (*m inv*)
encounter [ɪn'kauntə^r] *n* incontro ■ *vt* incontrare
encourage [ɪn'kʌrɪdʒ] *vt* incoraggiare; (*industry, growth etc*) favorire; **to ~ sb to do sth** incoraggiare qn a fare qc
encouragement [ɪn'kʌrɪdʒmənt] *n* incoraggiamento
encouraging [ɪn'kʌrɪdʒɪŋ] *adj* incoraggiante
encroach [ɪn'krəutʃ] *vi*: **to ~ (up)on** (*rights*) usurpare; (*time*) abusare di; (*land*) oltrepassare i limiti di
encrusted [ɪn'krʌstɪd] *adj*: **~ with** incrostato(a) di
encumbered [ɪn'kʌmbəd] *adj*: **to be ~ (with)** essere carico(a) di
encyclopedia, encyclopaedia [ɛnsaɪklə u'piːdɪə] *n* enciclopedia
end [ɛnd] *n* fine *f*; (*aim*) fine *m*; (*of table*) bordo estremo; (*of line, rope etc*) estremità *f inv*; (*of pointed object*) punta; (*of town*) parte *f* ■ *vt* finire; (*also*: **bring to an end, put an end to**) mettere fine a ■ *vi* finire; **from ~ to ~** da un'estremità all'altra; **to come to an ~** arrivare alla fine, finire; **to be at an ~** essere finito; **in the ~** alla fine; **at the ~ of the street** in fondo alla strada; **at the ~ of the day** (*Brit fig*) in fin dei conti; **on ~** (*object*) ritto(a); **to stand on ~** (*hair*) rizzarsi; **for 5 hours on ~** per 5 ore di fila; **for hours on ~** per ore e ore; **to this ~, with this ~ in view** a questo fine; **to ~ (with)** concludere (con)
▸ **end up** *vi*: **to ~ up in** finire in
endanger [ɪn'deɪndʒə^r] *vt* mettere in pericolo; **an endangered species** una specie in via di estinzione
endear [ɪn'dɪə^r] *vt*: **to ~ o.s. to sb** accattivarsi le simpatie di qn
endearing [ɪn'dɪərɪŋ] *adj* accattivante
endearment [ɪn'dɪəmənt] *n*: **to whisper endearments** sussurrare tenerezze; **term of ~** vezzeggiativo, parola affettuosa
endeavour, (*US*) **endeavor** [ɪn'dɛvə^r] *n* sforzo, tentativo ■ *vi*: **to ~ to do** cercare *or* sforzarsi di fare
endemic [ɛn'dɛmɪk] *adj* endemico(-a)
ending ['ɛndɪŋ] *n* fine *f*, conclusione *f*; (*Ling*) desinenza
endive ['ɛndaɪv] *n* (*curly*) indivia (riccia); (*smooth, flat*) indivia belga
endless ['ɛndlɪs] *adj* senza fine; (*patience, resources*) infinito(-a); (*possibilities*) illimitato(-a)
endorse [ɪn'dɔːs] *vt* (*cheque*) girare; (*approve*) approvare, appoggiare
endorsee [ɪndɔː'siː] *n* giratario(-a)
endorsement [ɪn'dɔːsmənt] *n* (*approval*) approvazione *f*; (*signature*) firma; (*Brit*: *on driving licence*) *contravvenzione registrata sulla patente*
endorser [ɪn'dɔːsə^r] *n* girante *m/f*
endow [ɪn'dau] *vt* (*prize*) istituire; (*hospital*) fondare; (*provide with money*) devolvere denaro a; (*equip*): **to ~ with** fornire di, dotare di
endowment [ɪn'daumənt] *n* istituzione *f*; fondazione *f*; (*amount*) donazione *f*
endowment mortgage *n mutuo che viene ripagato sotto forma di un'assicurazione a vita*
endowment policy *n* polizza-vita mista
end product *n* (*Industry*) prodotto finito; (*fig*) risultato
end result *n* risultato finale
endurable [ɪn'djuərəbl] *adj* sopportabile
endurance [ɪn'djuərəns] *n* resistenza; pazienza
endurance test *n* prova di resistenza
endure [ɪn'djuə^r] *vt* sopportare, resistere a ■ *vi* durare
enduring [ɪn'djuərɪŋ] *adj* duraturo(-a)
end user *n* (*Comput*) consumatore(-trice) effettivo(-a)
enema ['ɛnɪmə] *n* (*Med*) clistere *m*
enemy ['ɛnəmɪ] *adj, n* nemico(-a); **to make an ~ of sb** inimicarsi qn
energetic [ɛnə'dʒɛtɪk] *adj* energico(-a), attivo(-a)
energy ['ɛnədʒɪ] *n* energia; **Department of E~** (*US*) Ministero dell'Energia

energy crisis *n* crisi *f* energetica

energy-saving ['ɛnədʒɪ'seɪvɪŋ] *adj* (*policy*) del risparmio energetico; (*device*) che risparmia energia

enervating ['ɛnə:veɪtɪŋ] *adj* debilitante

enforce [ɪn'fɔ:s] *vt* (*Law*) applicare, far osservare

enforced [ɪn'fɔ:st] *adj* forzato(-a)

enfranchise [ɪn'fræntʃaɪz] *vt* (*give vote to*) concedere il diritto di voto a; (*set free*) affrancare

engage [ɪn'geɪdʒ] *vt* (*hire*) assumere; (*lawyer*) incaricare; (*attention, interest*) assorbire; (*Mil*) attaccare; (*Tech*): **to ~ gear/the clutch** innestare la marcia/la frizione ■ *vi* (*Tech*) ingranare; **to ~ in** impegnarsi in; **he is engaged in research/a survey** si occupa di ricerca/di un'inchiesta; **to ~ sb in conversation** attaccare conversazione con qn

engaged [ɪn'geɪdʒd] *adj* (*Brit: busy, in use*) occupato(-a); (*betrothed*) fidanzato(-a); **to get ~** fidanzarsi

engaged tone *n* (*Brit Tel*) segnale *m* di occupato

engagement [ɪn'geɪdʒmənt] *n* impegno, obbligo; appuntamento; (*to marry*) fidanzamento; (*Mil*) combattimento; **I have a previous ~** ho già un impegno

engagement ring *n* anello di fidanzamento

engaging [ɪn'geɪdʒɪŋ] *adj* attraente

engender [ɪn'dʒɛndə[r]] *vt* produrre, causare

engine ['ɛndʒɪn] *n* (*Aut*) motore *m*; (*Rail*) locomotiva

engine driver *n* (*Brit: of train*) macchinista *m*

engineer [ɛndʒɪ'nɪə[r]] *n* ingegnere *m*; (*Brit: for domestic appliances*) tecnico; (*US Rail*) macchinista *m*; **civil/mechanical ~** ingegnere civile/meccanico

engineering [ɛndʒɪ'nɪərɪŋ] *n* ingegneria ■ *cpd* (*works, factory, worker etc*) metalmeccanico(-a)

engine failure *n* guasto al motore

engine trouble *n* panne *f*

England ['ɪŋglənd] *n* Inghilterra

English ['ɪŋglɪʃ] *adj* inglese ■ *n* (*Ling*) inglese *m*; **the English** *npl* gli Inglesi; **to be an ~ speaker** essere anglofono(a)

English Channel *n*: **the ~** il Canale della Manica

Englishman ['ɪŋglɪʃmən] *n* inglese *m*

English-speaking ['ɪŋglɪʃspi:kɪŋ] *adj* di lingua inglese

Englishwoman ['ɪŋglɪʃwumən] *n* inglese *f*

engrave [ɪn'greɪv] *vt* incidere

engraving [ɪn'greɪvɪŋ] *n* incisione *f*

engrossed [ɪn'grəust] *adj*: **~ in** assorbito(a) da, preso(a) da

engulf [ɪn'gʌlf] *vt* inghiottire

enhance [ɪn'hɑ:ns] *vt* accrescere; (*position, reputation*) migliorare

enigma [ɪ'nɪgmə] *n* enigma *m*

enigmatic [ɛnɪg'mætɪk] *adj* enigmatico(-a)

enjoy [ɪn'dʒɔɪ] *vt* godere; (*have: success, fortune*) avere; (*have benefit of: health*) godere (di); **I ~ dancing** mi piace ballare; **to ~ o.s.** godersela, divertirsi

enjoyable [ɪn'dʒɔɪəbl] *adj* piacevole

enjoyment [ɪn'dʒɔɪmənt] *n* piacere *m*, godimento

enlarge [ɪn'lɑ:dʒ] *vt* ingrandire ■ *vi*: **to ~ on** (*subject*) dilungarsi su

enlarged [ɪn'lɑ:dʒd] *adj* (*edition*) ampliato(-a); (*Med: organ, gland*) ingrossato(-a)

enlargement [ɪn'lɑ:dʒmənt] *n* (*Phot*) ingrandimento

enlighten [ɪn'laɪtn] *vt* illuminare; dare chiarimenti a

enlightened [ɪn'laɪtnd] *adj* illuminato(-a)

enlightening [ɪn'laɪtnɪŋ] *adj* istruttivo(-a)

enlightenment [ɪn'laɪtnmənt] *n* progresso culturale; chiarimenti *mpl*; (*Hist*): **the E~** l'Illuminismo

enlist [ɪn'lɪst] *vt* arruolare; (*support*) procurare ■ *vi* arruolarsi; **enlisted man** (*US Mil*) soldato semplice

enliven [ɪn'laɪvn] *vt* (*people*) rallegrare; (*events*) ravvivare

enmity ['ɛnmɪtɪ] *n* inimicizia

ennoble [ɪ'nəubl] *vt* nobilitare; (*with title*) conferire un titolo nobiliare a

enormity [ɪ'nɔ:mɪtɪ] *n* enormità *f inv*

enormous [ɪ'nɔ:məs] *adj* enorme

enormously [ɪ'nɔ:məslɪ] *adv* enormemente

enough [ɪ'nʌf] *adj, n*: **~ time/books** assai tempo/libri; **have you got ~?** ne ha abbastanza *or* a sufficienza? ■ *adv*: **big ~** abbastanza grande; **he has not worked ~** non ha lavorato abbastanza; **~!** basta!; **it's hot ~ (as it is)!** fa abbastanza caldo così!; **will £5 be ~?** bastano 5 sterline?; **that's ~** basta; **I've had ~!** non ne posso più!; **he was kind ~ to lend me the money** è stato così gentile da prestarmi i soldi; **... which, funnily ~** ... che, strano a dirsi

enquire [ɪn'kwaɪə[r]] *vt, vi* = **inquire**

enrage [ɪn'reɪdʒ] *vt* fare arrabbiare

enrich [ɪn'rɪtʃ] *vt* arricchire

enrol, (*US*) **enroll** [ɪn'rəul] *vt* iscrivere; (*at university*) immatricolare ■ *vi* iscriversi

enrolment, (*US*) **enrollment** [ɪn'rəulmənt] *n* iscrizione *f*

en route [ɔn'ru:t] *adv*: **~ for/from/to** in viaggio per/da/a

ensconced [ɪn'skɔnst] *adj*: **~ in** ben sistemato(a) in

e

ensemble [ɑ̃:n'sɑ̃:mbl] *n* (*Mus*) ensemble *m inv*
enshrine [ɪn'ʃraɪn] *vt* conservare come una reliquia
ensign *n* (*Naut*) ['ɛnsən] bandiera; (*Mil*) ['ɛnsaɪn] portabandiera *m inv*
enslave [ɪn'sleɪv] *vt* fare schiavo
ensue [ɪn'sju:] *vi* seguire, risultare
ensure [ɪn'ʃuəʳ] *vt* assicurare; garantire; **to ~ that** assicurarsi che
ENT *n abbr* (*Med*: = *ear, nose and throat*) O.R.L.
entail [ɪn'teɪl] *vt* comportare
entangle [ɪn'tæŋgl] *vt* (*thread etc*) impigliare; **to become entangled in sth** (*fig*) rimanere impegolato in qc
enter ['ɛntəʳ] *vt* (*gen*) entrare in; (*club*) associarsi a; (*profession*) intraprendere; (*army*) arruolarsi in; (*competition*) partecipare a; (*sb for a competition*) iscrivere; (*write down*) registrare; (*Comput*: *data*) introdurre, inserire ■ *vi* entrare
▸ **enter for** *vt fus* iscriversi a
▸ **enter into** *vt fus* (*explanation*) cominciare a dare; (*debate*) partecipare a; (*agreement*) concludere; (*negotiations*) prendere parte a
▸ **enter (up)on** *vt fus* cominciare
enteritis [ɛntə'raɪtɪs] *n* enterite *f*
enterprise ['ɛntəpraɪz] *n* (*undertaking, company*) impresa; (*spirit*) iniziativa
enterprising ['ɛntəpraɪzɪŋ] *adj* intraprendente
entertain [ɛntə'teɪn] *vt* divertire; (*invite*) ricevere; (*idea, plan*) nutrire
entertainer [ɛntə'teɪnəʳ] *n* comico(-a)
entertaining [ɛntə'teɪnɪŋ] *adj* divertente ■ *n*: **to do a lot of ~** avere molti ospiti
entertainment [ɛntə'teɪnmənt] *n* (*amusement*) divertimento; (*show*) spettacolo
entertainment allowance *n* spese *fpl* di rappresentanza
enthral [ɪn'θrɔ:l] *vt* affascinare, avvincere
enthralled [ɪn'θrɔ:ld] *adj* affascinato(-a)
enthralling [ɪn'θrɔ:lɪŋ] *adj* avvincente
enthuse [ɪn'θu:z] *vi*: **to ~ (about** *or* **over)** entusiasmarsi (per)
enthusiasm [ɪn'θu:zɪæzəm] *n* entusiasmo
enthusiast [ɪn'θu:zɪæst] *n* entusiasta *m/f*; **a jazz** *etc* **~** un appassionato di jazz *etc*
enthusiastic [ɪnθu:zɪ'æstɪk] *adj* entusiasta, entusiastico(-a); **to be ~ about sth/sb** essere appassionato di qc/entusiasta di qn
entice [ɪn'taɪs] *vt* allettare, sedurre
enticing [ɪn'taɪsɪŋ] *adj* allettante
entire [ɪn'taɪəʳ] *adj* intero(-a)
entirely [ɪn'taɪəlɪ] *adv* completamente, interamente
entirety [ɪn'taɪərətɪ] *n*: **in its ~** nel suo complesso
entitle [ɪn'taɪtl] *vt* (*give right*): **to ~ sb to sth/to do** dare diritto a qn a qc/a fare
entitled [ɪn'taɪtld] *adj* (*book*) che si intitola; **to be ~ to sth/to do sth** avere diritto a qc/a fare qc
entity ['ɛntɪtɪ] *n* entità *f inv*
entrails ['ɛntreɪlz] *npl* interiora *fpl*
entrance *n* ['ɛntrns] entrata, ingresso; (*of person*) entrata ■ *vt* [ɪn'trɑ:ns] incantare, rapire; **to gain ~ to** (*university etc*) essere ammesso a
entrance examination *n* (*to school*) esame *m* di ammissione
entrance fee *n* tassa d'iscrizione; (*to museum etc*) prezzo d'ingresso
entrance ramp *n* (*US Aut*) rampa di accesso
entrancing [ɪn'trɑ:nsɪŋ] *adj* incantevole
entrant ['ɛntrnt] *n* partecipante *m/f*; concorrente *m/f*; (*Brit*: *in exam*) candidato(-a)
entreat [ɛn'tri:t] *vt* supplicare
entreaty [ɪn'tri:tɪ] *n* supplica, preghiera
entrée ['ɔntreɪ] *n* (*Culin*) prima portata
entrenched [ɛn'trɛntʃt] *adj* radicato(-a)
entrepreneur ['ɔntrəprə'nə:ʳ] *n* imprenditore *m*
entrepreneurial ['ɔntrəprə'nə:rɪəl] *adj* imprenditoriale
entrust [ɪn'trʌst] *vt*: **to ~ sth to** affidare qc a
entry ['ɛntrɪ] *n* entrata; (*way in*) entrata, ingresso; (*in dictionary*) voce *f*; (*in diary, ship's log*) annotazione *f*; (*in account book, ledger, list*) registrazione *f*; **"no ~"** "vietato l'ingresso"; (*Aut*) "divieto di accesso"; **single/double ~ book-keeping** partita semplice/doppia
entry form *n* modulo d'iscrizione
entry phone *n* (*Brit*) citofono
entwine [ɪn'twaɪn] *vt* intrecciare
E number *n sigla di additivo alimentare*
enumerate [ɪ'nju:məreɪt] *vt* enumerare
enunciate [ɪ'nʌnsɪeɪt] *vt* enunciare; pronunciare
envelop [ɪn'vɛləp] *vt* avvolgere, avviluppare
envelope ['ɛnvələup] *n* busta
enviable ['ɛnvɪəbl] *adj* invidiabile
envious ['ɛnvɪəs] *adj* invidioso(-a)
environment [ɪn'vaɪərənmənt] *n* ambiente *m*; **Department of the E~** (*Brit*) ≈ Ministero dell'Ambiente
environmental [ɪnvaɪərən'mɛntl] *adj* ecologico(-a); ambientale; **~ studies** (*in school etc*) ecologia
environmentalist [ɪn'vaɪərən'mɛntəlɪst] *n* studioso(-a) della protezione dell'ambiente
environmentally [ɪnvaɪərən'mɛntəlɪ] *adv*: **~ sound/friendly** che rispetta l'ambiente
Environmental Protection Agency *n* (*US*) ≈ Ministero dell'Ambiente

envisage [ɪn'vɪzɪdʒ] *vt* immaginare; prevedere
envision [ɪn'vɪʒən] *vt* concepire, prevedere
envoy ['ɛnvɔɪ] *n* inviato(-a)
envy ['ɛnvɪ] *n* invidia ■ *vt* invidiare; **to ~ sb sth** invidiare qn per qc
enzyme ['ɛnzaɪm] *n* enzima *m*
EPA *n abbr (US)* = **Environmental Protection Agency**
ephemeral [ɪ'fɛmərəl] *adj* effimero(-a)
epic ['ɛpɪk] *n* poema *m* epico ■ *adj* epico(-a)
epicentre, *(US)* **epicenter** ['ɛpɪsɛntəʳ] *n* epicentro
epidemic [ɛpɪ'dɛmɪk] *n* epidemia
epilepsy ['ɛpɪlɛpsɪ] *n* epilessia
epileptic [ɛpɪ'lɛptɪk] *adj, n* epilettico(-a)
epilogue ['ɛpɪlɔg] *n* epilogo
Epiphany [ɪ'pɪfənɪ] *n* Epifania
episcopal [ɪ'pɪskəpəl] *adj* episcopale
episode ['ɛpɪsəud] *n* episodio
epistle [ɪ'pɪsl] *n* epistola
epitaph ['ɛpɪtɑːf] *n* epitaffio
epithet ['ɛpɪθɛt] *n* epiteto
epitome [ɪ'pɪtəmɪ] *n* epitome *f*; quintessenza
epitomize [ɪ'pɪtəmaɪz] *vt (fig)* incarnare
epoch ['iːpɔk] *n* epoca
epoch-making ['iːpɔkmeɪkɪŋ] *adj* che fa epoca
eponymous [ɪ'pɔnɪməs] *adj* dello stesso nome
equable ['ɛkwəbl] *adj* uniforme; *(climate)* costante; *(character)* equilibrato(-a)
equal ['iːkwl] *adj, n* uguale *(m/f)* ■ *vt* uguagliare; **~ to** *(task)* all'altezza di
equality [iː'kwɔlɪtɪ] *n* uguaglianza
equalize ['iːkwəlaɪz] *vt, vi* pareggiare
equalizer ['iːkwəlaɪzəʳ] *n* punto del pareggio
equally ['iːkwəlɪ] *adv* ugualmente; **they are ~ clever** sono intelligenti allo stesso modo
Equal Opportunities Commission, *(US)* **Equal Employment Opportunity Commission** *n commissione contro discriminazioni sessuali o razziali nel mondo del lavoro*
equal sign, equals sign *n* segno d'uguaglianza
equanimity [ɛkwə'nɪmɪtɪ] *n* serenità
equate [ɪ'kweɪt] *vt*: **to ~ sth with** considerare qc uguale a; *(compare)* paragonare qc con; **to ~ A to B** mettere in equazione A e B
equation [ɪ'kweɪʃən] *n (Math)* equazione *f*
equator [ɪ'kweɪtəʳ] *n* equatore *m*
Equatorial Guinea [ɛkwə'tɔːrɪəl-] *n* Guinea Equatoriale
equestrian [ɪ'kwɛstrɪən] *adj* equestre ■ *n* cavaliere/amazzone
equilibrium [iːkwɪ'lɪbrɪəm] *n* equilibrio
equinox ['iːkwɪnɔks] *n* equinozio
equip [ɪ'kwɪp] *vt* equipaggiare, attrezzare; **to ~ sb/sth with** fornire qn/qc di; **equipped with** *(machinery etc)* dotato(a) di; **he is well equipped for the job** ha i requisiti necessari per quel lavoro
equipment [ɪ'kwɪpmənt] *n* attrezzatura; *(electrical etc)* apparecchiatura
equitable ['ɛkwɪtəbl] *adj* equo(-a), giusto(-a)
equities ['ɛkwɪtɪz] *npl (Brit Comm)* azioni *fpl* ordinarie
equity ['ɛkwɪtɪ] *n* equità
equity capital *n* capitale *m* azionario
equivalent [ɪ'kwɪvələnt] *adj, n* equivalente *(m)*; **to be ~ to** equivalere a
equivocal [ɪ'kwɪvəkl] *adj* equivoco(-a); *(open to suspicion)* dubbio(-a)
equivocate [ɪ'kwɪvəkeɪt] *vi* esprimersi in modo equivoco
equivocation [ɪkwɪvə'keɪʃən] *n* parole *fpl* equivoche
ER *abbr (Brit)* = **Elizabeth Regina**
ERA *n abbr (US Pol)* = **Equal Rights Amendment**
era ['ɪərə] *n* era, età *f inv*
eradicate [ɪ'rædɪkeɪt] *vt* sradicare
erase [ɪ'reɪz] *vt* cancellare
eraser [ɪ'reɪzəʳ] *n* gomma
erect [ɪ'rɛkt] *adj* eretto(-a) ■ *vt* costruire; *(monument, tent)* alzare
erection [ɪ'rɛkʃən] *n (also Physiol)* erezione *f*; *(of building)* costruzione *f*; *(of machinery)* montaggio
ergonomics [əːgə'nɔmɪks] *n* ergonomia
ERISA *n abbr (US: = Employee Retirement Income Security Act) legge relativa al pensionamento statale*
Eritrea [ɛrɪ'treɪə] *n* Eritrea
ERM *n abbr (= Exchange Rate Mechanism)* meccanismo dei tassi di cambio
ermine ['əːmɪn] *n* ermellino
ERNIE ['əːnɪ] *n abbr (Brit: = Electronic Random Number Indicator Equipment) sistema che seleziona i numeri vincenti di buoni del Tesoro*
erode [ɪ'rəud] *vt* erodere; *(metal)* corrodere
erogenous zone [ɪ'rɔdʒənəs-] *n* zona erogena
erosion [ɪ'rəuʒən] *n* erosione *f*
erotic [ɪ'rɔtɪk] *adj* erotico(-a)
eroticism [ɪ'rɔtɪsɪzəm] *n* erotismo
err [əːʳ] *vi* errare; *(Rel)* peccare
errand ['ɛrənd] *n* commissione *f*; *(also:* **to run errands***)* fare commissioni; **~ of mercy** atto di carità
errand boy *n* fattorino
erratic [ɪ'rætɪk] *adj* imprevedibile; *(person, mood)* incostante
erroneous [ɪ'rəunɪəs] *adj* erroneo(-a)
error ['ɛrəʳ] *n* errore *m*; **typing/spelling ~**

errore di battitura/di ortografia; **in ~** per errore; **errors and omissions excepted** salvo errori ed omissioni
error message *n* (*Comput*) messaggio di errore
erstwhile [ˈəːstwaɪl] *adv* allora, un tempo ■ *adj* di allora
erudite [ˈɛrjudaɪt] *adj* erudito(-a)
erupt [ɪˈrʌpt] *vi* erompere; (*volcano*) mettersi (*or* essere) in eruzione
eruption [ɪˈrʌpʃən] *n* eruzione *f*; (*of anger, violence*) esplosione *f*
ESA *n abbr* (= *European Space Agency*) ESA *f*
escalate [ˈɛskəleɪt] *vi* intensificarsi; (*costs*) salire
escalation [ɛskəˈleɪʃən] *n* escalation *f*; (*of prices*) aumento
escalation clause *n* clausola di revisione
escalator [ˈɛskəleɪtə^r] *n* scala mobile
escapade [ɛskəˈpeɪd] *n* scappatella; avventura
escape [ɪˈskeɪp] *n* evasione *f*; fuga; (*of gas etc*) fuga, fuoriuscita ■ *vi* fuggire; (*from jail*) evadere, scappare; (*fig*) sfuggire; (*leak*) uscire ■ *vt* sfuggire a; **to ~ from sb** sfuggire a qn; **to ~ to** (*another place*) fuggire in; (*freedom, safety*) fuggire verso; **to ~ notice** passare inosservato(a)
escape artist *n* mago della fuga
escape clause *n* clausola scappatoia
escapee [ɪskeɪˈpiː] *n* evaso(-a)
escape hatch *n* (*in submarine, space rocket*) portello di sicurezza
escape key *n* (*Comput*) tasto di escape, tasto per cambio di codice
escape route *n* percorso della fuga
escapism [ɪsˈkeɪpɪzəm] *n* evasione *f* (dalla realtà)
escapist [ɪsˈkeɪpɪst] *adj* d'evasione ■ *n* persona che cerca di evadere dalla realtà
escapologist [ɛskəˈpɔlədʒɪst] *n* (*Brit*) = **escape artist**
escarpment [ɪsˈkɑːpmənt] *n* scarpata
eschew [ɪsˈtʃuː] *vt* evitare
escort *n* [ˈɛskɔːt] scorta; (*to dance etc*): **her ~** il suo cavaliere; **his ~** la sua dama ■ *vt* [ɪˈskɔːt] scortare; accompagnare
escort agency *n* agenzia di hostess
Eskimo [ˈɛskɪməu] *adj* eschimese ■ *n* eschimese *m/f*; (*Ling*) eschimese *m*
ESL *n abbr* (*Scol*) = **English as a Second Language**
esophagus [iːˈsɔfəgəs] *n* (*US*) = **oesophagus**
esoteric [ɛsəuˈtɛrɪk] *adj* esoterico(-a)
ESP *n abbr* = **extrasensory perception**; (*Scol*) = **English for Specific (*or* Special) Purposes**
esp. *abbr* (= *especially*) spec.
especially [ɪˈspɛʃlɪ] *adv* specialmente; (*above all*) soprattutto; (*specifically*) espressamente; (*particularly*) particolarmente
espionage [ˈɛspɪənɑːʒ] *n* spionaggio
esplanade [ɛspləˈneɪd] *n* lungomare *m*
espouse [ɪˈspauz] *vt* abbracciare
Esquire [ɪˈskwaɪə^r] *n* (*Brit*): **J. Brown, Esquire** Signor J. Brown
essay [ˈɛseɪ] *n* (*Scol*) composizione *f*; (*Literature*) saggio
essence [ˈɛsns] *n* essenza; **in ~** in sostanza; **speed is of the ~** la velocità è di estrema importanza
essential [ɪˈsɛnʃəl] *adj* essenziale; (*basic*) fondamentale ■ *n* elemento essenziale; **it is ~ that** è essenziale che *+ sub*
essentially [ɪˈsɛnʃəlɪ] *adv* essenzialmente
EST *abbr* (*US*: = *Eastern Standard Time*) *fuso orario*
est. *abbr* = **established**; **estimate(d)**
establish [ɪˈstæblɪʃ] *vt* stabilire; (*business*) mettere su; (*one's power etc*) confermare; (*prove: fact, identity, sb's innocence*) dimostrare
establishment [ɪsˈtæblɪʃmənt] *n* stabilimento; (*business*) azienda; **the E~** la classe dirigente; l'establishment *m*; **a teaching ~** un istituto d'istruzione
estate [ɪˈsteɪt] *n* proprietà *f inv*; (*Law*) beni *mpl*, patrimonio; (*Brit*: *also*: **housing estate**) complesso edilizio
estate agency *n* (*Brit*) agenzia immobiliare
estate agent *n* (*Brit*) agente *m* immobiliare
estate car *n* (*Brit*) giardiniera
esteem [ɪˈstiːm] *n* stima ■ *vt* considerare; stimare; **I hold him in high ~** gode di tutta la mia stima
esthetic [ɪsˈθɛtɪk] *adj* (*US*) = **aesthetic**
estimate *n* [ˈɛstɪmət] stima; (*Comm*) preventivo ■ *vt* [ˈɛstɪmeɪt] stimare, valutare ■ *vi* (*Brit Comm*): **to ~ for** fare il preventivo per; **to give sb an ~ of** fare a qn una valutazione approssimativa (*or* un preventivo) di; **at a rough ~** approssimativamente
estimation [ɛstɪˈmeɪʃən] *n* stima; opinione *f*; **in my ~** a mio giudizio, a mio avviso
Estonia [ɛˈstəunɪə] *n* Estonia
Estonian [ɛˈstəunɪən] *adj* estone *inv* ■ *n* estone *m/f*; (*Ling*) estone *m*
estranged [ɪˈstreɪndʒd] *adj* separato(-a)
estrangement [ɪsˈtreɪndʒmənt] *n* alienazione *f*
estrogen [ˈiːstrəudʒən] *n* (*US*) = **oestrogen**
estuary [ˈɛstjuərɪ] *n* estuario
ET *abbr* (= *Eastern Time*) *fuso orario*; (*Brit*: = *Employment Training*) *corso di formazione professionale per disoccupati*
ETA *n abbr* (= *estimated time of arrival*) ora di arrivo prevista

e-tailer ['i:teɪləʳ] *n* venditore(-trice) in Internet
e-tailing ['i:teɪlɪŋ] *n* commercio in Internet
et al. *abbr (= et alii: and others)* ed altri
etc. *abbr (= et cetera)* ecc., etc.
etch [ɛtʃ] *vt* incidere all'acquaforte
etching ['ɛtʃɪŋ] *n* acquaforte *f*
ETD *n abbr (= estimated time of departure)* ora di partenza prevista
eternal [ɪ'tə:nl] *adj* eterno(-a)
eternity [ɪ'tə:nɪtɪ] *n* eternità
ether ['i:θəʳ] *n* etere *m*
ethereal [ɪ'θɪərɪəl] *adj* etereo(-a)
ethical ['ɛθɪkl] *adj* etico(-a), morale
ethics ['ɛθɪks] *n* etica ■ *npl* morale *f*
Ethiopia [i:θɪ'əupɪə] *n* Etiopia
Ethiopian [i:θɪ'əupɪən] *adj, n* etiope *(m/f)*
ethnic ['ɛθnɪk] *adj* etnico(-a)
ethnic cleansing [-'klɛnzɪŋ] *n* pulizia etnica
ethnic minority *n* minoranza etnica
ethnology [ɛθ'nɔlədʒɪ] *n* etnologia
ethos ['i:θɔs] *n (of culture, group)* norma di vita
e-ticket ['i:tɪkɪt] *n* e-ticket *m inv*, biglietto elettronico
etiquette ['ɛtɪkɛt] *n* etichetta
ETV *n abbr (US)* = **Educational Television**
etymology [ɛtɪ'mɔlədʒɪ] *n* etimologia
EU *n abbr (= European Union)* UE *f*
eucalyptus [ju:kə'lɪptəs] *n* eucalipto
eulogy ['ju:lədʒɪ] *n* elogio
euphemism ['ju:fəmɪzəm] *n* eufemismo
euphemistic [ju:fə'mɪstɪk] *adj* eufemistico(-a)
euphoria [ju:'fɔ:rɪə] *n* euforia
Eurasia [juə'reɪʃə] *n* Eurasia
Eurasian [juə'reɪʃən] *adj, n* eurasiano(-a)
Euratom [juə'rætəm] *n abbr (= European Atomic Energy Community)* EURATOM *f*
euro ['juərəu] *n (currency)* euro *m inv*
Euro- ['juərəu] *prefix* euro-
Eurocheque ['juərəutʃɛk] *n* eurochèque *m inv*
Eurocrat ['juərəukræt] *n* eurocrate *m/f*
Eurodollar ['juərəudɔləʳ] *n* eurodollaro
Euroland ['juərəulænd] *n* Eurolandia
Europe ['juərəp] *n* Europa
European [juərə'pi:ən] *adj, n* europeo(-a)
European Court of Justice *n* Corte *f* di Giustizia della Comunità Europea
Europol ['juərəupɔl] *n* Europol *f*
Euro-sceptic ['juərəuskɛptɪk] *n* euroscettico(-a)
Eurozone ['juərəuzəun] *n* zona euro
euthanasia [ju:θə'neɪzɪə] *n* eutanasia
evacuate [ɪ'vækjueɪt] *vt* evacuare
evacuation [ɪvækju'eɪʃən] *n* evacuazione *f*
evacuee [ɪvækju'i:] *n* sfollato(-a)
evade [ɪ'veɪd] *vt* eludere; *(duties etc)* sottrarsi a
evaluate [ɪ'væljueɪt] *vt* valutare
evangelist [ɪ'vændʒəlɪst] *n* evangelista *m*
evangelize [ɪ'vændʒəlaɪz] *vt* evangelizzare
evaporate [ɪ'væpəreɪt] *vi* evaporare ■ *vt* far evaporare
evaporated milk *n* latte *m* concentrato
evaporation [ɪvæpə'reɪʃən] *n* evaporazione *f*
evasion [ɪ'veɪʒən] *n* evasione *f*
evasive [ɪ'veɪsɪv] *adj* evasivo(-a)
eve [i:v] *n*: **on the ~ of** alla vigilia di
even ['i:vn] *adj* regolare; *(number)* pari *inv* ■ *adv* anche, perfino; **~ if, ~ though** anche se; **~ more** ancora di più; **he loves her ~ more** la ama anche di più; **~ faster** ancora più veloce; **~ so** ciò nonostante; **not ~ ...** nemmeno ...; **to break ~** finire in pari *or* alla pari; **to get ~ with sb** dare la pari a qn
▸ **even out** *vi* pareggiare
even-handed ['i:vn'hændɪd] *adj* imparziale, equo(-a)
evening ['i:vnɪŋ] *n* sera; *(as duration, event)* serata; **in the ~** la sera; **this ~** stasera, questa sera; **tomorrow/yesterday ~** domani/ieri sera
evening class *n* corso serale
evening dress *n (woman's)* abito da sera; **in ~** *(man)* in abito scuro; *(woman)* in abito lungo
evenly ['i:vənlɪ] *adv (distribute, space, spread)* uniformemente; *(divide)* in parti uguali
evensong ['i:vnsɔŋ] *n* ≈ vespro
event [ɪ'vɛnt] *n* avvenimento; *(Sport)* gara; **in the ~ of** in caso di; **at all events**, *(Brit)* **in any ~** in ogni caso; **in the ~** in realtà, di fatto; **in the course of events** nel corso degli eventi
eventful [ɪ'vɛntful] *adj* denso(-a) di eventi
eventing [ɪ'vɛntɪŋ] *n (Horseriding)* concorso ippico
eventual [ɪ'vɛntʃuəl] *adj* finale
eventuality [ɪvɛntʃu'ælɪtɪ] *n* possibilità *f inv*, eventualità *f inv*
eventually [ɪ'vɛntʃuəlɪ] *adv* finalmente
ever ['ɛvəʳ] *adv* mai; *(at all times)* sempre; **for ~** per sempre; **the best ~** il migliore che ci sia mai stato; **hardly ~** non ... quasi mai; **did you ~ meet him?** l'ha mai incontrato?; **have you ~ been there?** c'è mai stato?; **~ so pretty** così bello(a); **thank you ~ so much** grazie mille; **yours ~** *(Brit: in letters)* sempre tuo; **~ since** *adv* da allora ■ *conj* sin da quando
Everest ['ɛvərɪst] *n (also:* **Mount Everest***)* Everest *m*
evergreen ['ɛvəgri:n] *n* sempreverde *m*
everlasting [ɛvə'lɑ:stɪŋ] *adj* eterno(-a)
every ['ɛvrɪ] *adj* ogni; **~ day** tutti i giorni, ogni giorno; **~ other/third day** ogni due/tre giorni; **~ other car** una macchina su due; **~ now and then** ogni tanto, di quando in

quando; **I have ~ confidence in him** ho piena fiducia in lui
everybody ['ɛvrɪbɔdɪ] *pron* ognuno, tutti *pl*; **~ else** tutti gli altri; **~ knows about it** lo sanno tutti
everyday ['ɛvrɪdeɪ] *adj* quotidiano(-a); di ogni giorno; (*use, occurrence, experience*) comune; (*expression*) di uso corrente
everyone ['ɛvrɪwʌn] = **everybody**
everything ['ɛvrɪθɪŋ] *pron* tutto, ogni cosa; **~ is ready** è tutto pronto; **he did ~ possible** ha fatto tutto il possibile
everywhere ['ɛvrɪwɛəʳ] *adv* in ogni luogo, dappertutto; (*wherever*) ovunque; **~ you go you meet ...** ovunque si vada si trova ...
evict [ɪ'vɪkt] *vt* sfrattare
eviction [ɪ'vɪkʃən] *n* sfratto
eviction notice *n* avviso di sfratto
evidence ['ɛvɪdəns] *n* (*proof*) prova; (*of witness*) testimonianza; (*sign*): **to show ~ of** dare segni di; **to give ~** deporre; **in ~** (*obvious*) in evidenza; in vista
evident ['ɛvɪdənt] *adj* evidente
evidently ['ɛvɪdəntlɪ] *adv* evidentemente
evil ['i:vl] *adj* cattivo(-a), maligno(-a) ■ *n* male *m*
evince [ɪ'vɪns] *vt* manifestare
evocative [ɪ'vɔkətɪv] *adj* evocativo(-a)
evoke [ɪ'vəuk] *vt* evocare; (*admiration*) suscitare
evolution [i:və'lu:ʃən] *n* evoluzione *f*
evolve [ɪ'vɔlv] *vt* elaborare ■ *vi* svilupparsi, evolversi
ewe [ju:] *n* pecora
ex- [ɛks] *prefix* ex; (*out of*): **the price ~works** il prezzo franco fabbrica
exacerbate [ɪk'sæsəbeɪt] *vt* (*pain*) aggravare; (*fig: relations, situation*) esacerbare, esasperare
exact [ɪg'zækt] *adj* esatto(-a) ■ *vt*: **to ~ sth (from)** estorcere qc (da); esigere qc (da)
exacting [ɪg'zæktɪŋ] *adj* esigente; (*work*) faticoso(-a)
exactitude [ɪg'zæktɪtju:d] *n* esattezza, precisione *f*
exactly [ɪg'zæktlɪ] *adv* esattamente; **~!** esatto!
exaggerate [ɪg'zædʒəreɪt] *vt, vi* esagerare
exaggeration [ɪgzædʒə'reɪʃən] *n* esagerazione *f*
exalt [ɪg'zɔ:lt] *vt* esaltare; elevare
exalted [ɪg'zɔ:ltɪd] *adj* (*rank, person*) elevato(-a); (*elated*) esaltato(-a)
exam [ɪg'zæm] *n abbr* (*Scol*) = **examination**
examination [ɪgzæmɪ'neɪʃən] *n* (*Scol*) esame *m*; (*Med*) controllo; **to take** *or* **sit an ~** (*Brit*) sostenere *or* dare un esame; **the matter is under ~** la questione è all'esame
examine [ɪg'zæmɪn] *vt* esaminare; (*Scol: orally, Law: person*) interrogare; (*inspect: machine, premises*) ispezionare; (*luggage, passport*) controllare; (*Med*) visitare
examiner [ɪg'zæmɪnəʳ] *n* esaminatore(-trice)
example [ɪg'zɑ:mpl] *n* esempio; **for ~** ad *or* per esempio; **to set a good/bad ~** dare il buon/cattivo esempio
exasperate [ɪg'zɑ:spəreɪt] *vt* esasperare; **exasperated by** (*or* **at** *or* **with**) esasperato da
exasperating [ɪg'zɑ:spəreɪtɪŋ] *adj* esasperante
exasperation [ɪgzɑ:spə'reɪʃən] *n* esasperazione *f*
excavate ['ɛkskəveɪt] *vt* scavare
excavation [ɛkskə'veɪʃən] *n* escavazione *f*
excavator ['ɛkskəveɪtəʳ] *n* scavatore *m*, scavatrice *f*
exceed [ɪk'si:d] *vt* superare; (*one's powers, time limit*) oltrepassare
exceedingly [ɪk'si:dɪŋlɪ] *adv* eccessivamente
excel [ɪk'sɛl] *vi* eccellere ■ *vt* sorpassare; **to ~ o.s.** (*Brit*) superare se stesso
excellence ['ɛksələns] *n* eccellenza
Excellency ['ɛksələnsɪ] *n*: **His ~** Sua Eccellenza
excellent ['ɛksələnt] *adj* eccellente
except [ɪk'sɛpt] *prep* (*also*: **except for, excepting**) salvo, all'infuori di, eccetto ■ *vt* escludere; **~ if/when** salvo se/quando; **~ that** salvo che
exception [ɪk'sɛpʃən] *n* eccezione *f*; **to take ~ to** trovare a ridire su; **with the ~ of** ad eccezione di
exceptional [ɪk'sɛpʃənl] *adj* eccezionale
excerpt ['ɛksə:pt] *n* estratto
excess [ɪk'sɛs] *n* eccesso; **in ~ of** al di sopra di
excess baggage *n* bagaglio in eccedenza
excess fare *n* supplemento
excessive [ɪk'sɛsɪv] *adj* eccessivo(-a)
excess supply *n* eccesso di offerta
exchange [ɪks'tʃeɪndʒ] *n* scambio; (*also*: **telephone exchange**) centralino ■ *vt*: **to ~ (for)** scambiare (con); **in ~ for** in cambio di; **foreign ~** (*Comm*) cambio
exchange control *n* controllo sui cambi
exchange market *n* mercato dei cambi
exchange rate *n* tasso di cambio
Exchequer [ɪks'tʃɛkəʳ] *n*: **the ~** (*Brit*) lo Scacchiere, ≈ il ministero delle Finanze
excisable [ɪk'saɪzəbl] *adj* soggetto(-a) a dazio
excise *n* ['ɛksaɪz] imposta, dazio ■ *vt* [ɛk'saɪz] recidere
excise duties *npl* dazi *mpl*
excitable [ɪk'saɪtəbl] *adj* eccitabile
excite [ɪk'saɪt] *vt* eccitare; **to get excited** eccitarsi
excitement [ɪk'saɪtmənt] *n* eccitazione *f*; agitazione *f*

exciting [ɪk'saɪtɪŋ] *adj* avventuroso(-a); (*film, book*) appassionante
excl. *abbr* (= *excluding, exclusive (of)*) escl.
exclaim [ɪk'skleɪm] *vi* esclamare
exclamation [ɛksklə'meɪʃən] *n* esclamazione *f*
exclamation mark *n* punto esclamativo
exclude [ɪk'sklu:d] *vt* escludere
excluding [ɪk'sklu:dɪŋ] *prep*: **~ VAT** IVA esclusa
exclusion [ɪk'sklu:ʒən] *n* esclusione *f*; **to the ~ of** escludendo
exclusion clause *n* clausola di esclusione
exclusion zone *n* area interdetta
exclusive [ɪk'sklu:sɪv] *adj* esclusivo(-a); (*club*) selettivo(-a); (*district*) snob *inv* ■ *adv* (*Comm*) non compreso; **~ of VAT** IVA esclusa; **~ of postage** spese postali escluse; **~ of service** servizio escluso; **from 1st to 15th March ~** dal 1° al 15 marzo esclusi; **~ rights** *npl* (*Comm*) diritti *mpl* esclusivi
exclusively [ɪk'sklu:sɪvlɪ] *adv* esclusivamente
excommunicate [ɛkskə'mju:nɪkeɪt] *vt* scomunicare
excrement ['ɛkskrəmənt] *n* escremento
excruciating [ɪk'skru:ʃɪeɪtɪŋ] *adj* straziante, atroce
excursion [ɪk'skə:ʃən] *n* escursione *f*, gita
excursion ticket *n* biglietto a tariffa escursionistica
excusable [ɪk'skju:zəbl] *adj* scusabile
excuse *n* [ɪk'skju:s] scusa ■ *vt* [ɪk'skju:z] scusare; (*justify*) giustificare; **to make excuses for sb** trovare giustificazioni per qn; **to ~ sb from** (*activity*) dispensare qn da; **~ me!** mi scusi!; **now if you will ~ me, ...** ora, mi scusi ma ...; **to ~ o.s. (for (doing) sth)** giustificarsi (per (aver fatto) qc)
ex-directory ['ɛksdɪ'rɛktərɪ] *adj* (*Brit*): **~ (phone) number** numero non compreso nell'elenco telefonico
execrable ['ɛksɪkrəbl] *adj* (*gen*) pessimo(-a); (*manners*) esecrabile
execute ['ɛksɪkju:t] *vt* (*prisoner*) giustiziare; (*plan etc*) eseguire
execution [ɛksɪ'kju:ʃən] *n* esecuzione *f*
executioner [ɛksɪ'kju:ʃnə^r] *n* boia *m inv*
executive [ɪg'zɛkjutɪv] *n* (*Comm*) dirigente *m*; (*Pol*) esecutivo ■ *adj* esecutivo(-a); (*secretary*) di direzione; (*offices, suite*) della direzione; (*car, plane*) dirigenziale; (*position, job, duties*) direttivo(-a)
executive director *n* amministratore(-trice)
executor [ɪg'zɛkjutə^r] *n* esecutore(-trice) testamentario(-a)
exemplary [ɪg'zɛmplərɪ] *adj* esemplare
exemplify [ɪg'zɛmplɪfaɪ] *vt* esemplificare
exempt [ɪg'zɛmpt] *adj*: **~ (from)** (*person: from tax*) esentato(-a) (da); (*: from military service etc*) esonerato(-a) (da); (*goods*) esente (da) ■ *vt*: **to ~ sb from** esentare qn da
exemption [ɪg'zɛmpʃən] *n* esenzione *f*
exercise ['ɛksəsaɪz] *n* esercizio ■ *vt* esercitare; (*dog*) portar fuori ■ *vi* (*also*: **take exercise**) fare del movimento *or* moto
exercise bike *n* cyclette® *f inv*
exercise book *n* quaderno
exert [ɪg'zə:t] *vt* esercitare; (*strength, force*) impiegare; **to ~ o.s.** sforzarsi
exertion [ɪg'zə:ʃən] *n* sforzo
ex gratia ['ɛks'greɪʃə] *adj*: **~ payment** gratifica
exhale [ɛks'heɪl] *vt, vi* espirare
exhaust [ɪg'zɔ:st] *n* (*also*: **exhaust fumes**) scappamento; (*also*: **exhaust pipe**) tubo di scappamento ■ *vt* esaurire; **to ~ o.s.** sfiancarsi
exhausted [ɪg'zɔ:stɪd] *adj* esaurito(-a)
exhausting [ɪg'zɔ:stɪŋ] *adj* estenuante
exhaustion [ɪg'zɔ:stʃən] *n* esaurimento; **nervous ~** sovraffaticamento mentale
exhaustive [ɪg'zɔ:stɪv] *adj* esauriente
exhibit [ɪg'zɪbɪt] *n* (*Art*) oggetto esposto; (*Law*) documento *or* oggetto esibito ■ *vt* esporre; (*courage, skill*) dimostrare
exhibition [ɛksɪ'bɪʃən] *n* mostra, esposizione *f*; (*of rudeness etc*) spettacolo; **to make an ~ of o.s.** dare spettacolo di sé
exhibitionist [ɛksɪ'bɪʃənɪst] *n* esibizionista *m/f*
exhibitor [ɪg'zɪbɪtə^r] *n* espositore(-trice)
exhilarating [ɪg'zɪləreɪtɪŋ] *adj* esilarante; stimolante
exhilaration [ɪgzɪlə'reɪʃən] *n* esaltazione *f*, ebbrezza
exhort [ɪg'zɔ:t] *vt* esortare
exile ['ɛksaɪl] *n* esilio; (*person*) esiliato(-a) ■ *vt* esiliare; **in ~** in esilio
exist [ɪg'zɪst] *vi* esistere
existence [ɪg'zɪstəns] *n* esistenza; **to be in ~** esistere
existentialism [ɛgzɪs'tɛnʃəlɪzəm] *n* esistenzialismo
existing [ɪg'zɪstɪŋ] *adj* (*laws, regime*) attuale
exit ['ɛksɪt] *n* uscita ■ *vi* (*Comput, Theat*) uscire
exit poll *n* exit poll *m inv*, sondaggio all'uscita dei seggi
exit ramp *n* (*US Aut*) rampa di uscita
exit visa *n* visto d'uscita
exodus ['ɛksədəs] *n* esodo
ex officio ['ɛksə'fɪʃɪəu] *adj, adv* d'ufficio
exonerate [ɪg'zɔnəreɪt] *vt*: **to ~ from** discolpare da

e

exorbitant [ɪg'zɔ:bɪtənt] *adj* (*price*) esorbitante; (*demands*) spropositato(-a)
exorcize ['ɛksɔ:saɪz] *vt* esorcizzare
exotic [ɪg'zɔtɪk] *adj* esotico(-a)
expand [ɪk'spænd] *vt* (*chest, economy etc*) sviluppare; (*market, operations*) espandere; (*influence*) estendere; (*horizons*) allargare ■ *vi* svilupparsi; (*gas*) espandersi; (*metal*) dilatarsi; **to ~ on** (*notes, story etc*) ampliare
expanse [ɪk'spæns] *n* distesa, estensione *f*
expansion [ɪk'spænʃən] *n* (*gen*) espansione *f*; (*of town, economy*) sviluppo; (*of metal*) dilatazione *f*
expansionism [ɪk'spænʃənɪzəm] *n* espansionismo
expansionist [ɪk'spænʃənɪst] *adj* espansionistico(-a)
expatriate *n* [ɛks'pætrɪət] espatriato(-a) ■ *vt* [ɛks'pætrɪeɪt] espatriare
expect [ɪk'spɛkt] *vt* (*anticipate*) prevedere, aspettarsi, prevedere *or* aspettarsi che *+sub*; (*count on*) contare su; (*hope for*) sperare; (*require*) richiedere, esigere; (*suppose*) supporre; (*await, also baby*) aspettare ■ *vi*: **to be expecting** essere in stato interessante; **to ~ sb to do** aspettarsi che qn faccia; **to ~ to do sth** pensare *or* contare di fare qc; **as expected** come previsto; **I ~ so** credo di sì
expectancy [ɪk'spɛktənsɪ] *n* attesa; **life ~** probabilità *fpl* di vita
expectant [ɪk'spɛktənt] *adj* pieno(-a) di aspettative
expectantly [ɪk'spɛktəntlɪ] *adv* (*look, listen*) con un'aria d'attesa
expectant mother *n* gestante *f*
expectation [ɛkspɛk'teɪʃən] *n* aspettativa; speranza; **in ~ of** in previsione di; **against** *or* **contrary to all ~(s)** contro ogni aspettativa; **to come** *or* **live up to sb's expectations** rispondere alle attese di qn
expedience [ɪk'spi:dɪəns], **expediency** [ɪk'spi:dɪənsɪ] *n* convenienza; **for the sake of ~** per una questione di comodità
expedient [ɪk'spi:dɪənt] *adj* conveniente; vantaggioso(-a) ■ *n* espediente *m*
expedite ['ɛkspədaɪt] *vt* sbrigare; facilitare
expedition [ɛkspə'dɪʃən] *n* spedizione *f*
expeditionary force [ɛkspə'dɪʃənərɪ-] *n* corpo di spedizione
expeditious [ɛkspə'dɪʃəs] *adj* sollecito(-a), rapido(-a)
expel [ɪk'spɛl] *vt* espellere
expend [ɪk'spɛnd] *vt* spendere; (*use up*) consumare
expendable [ɪk'spɛndəbl] *adj* sacrificabile
expenditure [ɪk'spɛndɪtʃə^r^] *n* spesa; (*of time, effort*) dispendio
expense [ɪk'spɛns] *n* spesa; (*high cost*) costo; **expenses** *npl* (*Comm*) spese *fpl*, indennità *fpl*; **to go to the ~ of** sobbarcarsi la spesa di; **at great ~** con grande impiego di mezzi; **at the ~ of** a spese di
expense account *n* conto *m* spese *inv*
expensive [ɪk'spɛnsɪv] *adj* caro(-a), costoso(-a); **she has ~ tastes** le piacciono le cose costose
experience [ɪk'spɪərɪəns] *n* esperienza ■ *vt* (*pleasure*) provare; (*hardship*) soffrire; **to learn by ~** imparare per esperienza
experienced [ɪk'spɪərɪənst] *adj* che ha esperienza
experiment *n* [ɪk'spɛrɪmənt] esperimento, esperienza ■ *vi* [ɪk'spɛrɪmɛnt] fare esperimenti; **to perform** *or* **carry out an ~** fare un esperimento; **as an ~** a titolo di esperimento; **to ~ with a new vaccine** sperimentare un nuovo vaccino
experimental [ɪkspɛrɪ'mɛntl] *adj* sperimentale; **at the ~ stage** in via di sperimentazione
expert ['ɛkspə:t] *adj, n* esperto(a); **~ witness** (*Law*) esperto(-a); **~ in** *or* **at doing sth** esperto nel fare qc; **an ~ on sth** un esperto di qc
expertise [ɛkspə:'ti:z] *n* competenza
expire [ɪk'spaɪə^r^] *vi* (*period of time, licence*) scadere
expiry [ɪk'spaɪərɪ] *n* scadenza
explain [ɪk'spleɪn] *vt* spiegare
▸ **explain away** *vt* dar ragione di
explanation [ɛksplə'neɪʃən] *n* spiegazione *f*; **to find an ~ for sth** trovare la spiegazione di qc
explanatory [ɪk'splænətrɪ] *adj* esplicativo(-a)
expletive [ɪk'spli:tɪv] *n* imprecazione *f*
explicit [ɪk'splɪsɪt] *adj* esplicito(-a); (*definite*) netto(-a)
explode [ɪk'spləud] *vi* esplodere ■ *vt* (*fig: theory*) demolire; **to ~ a myth** distruggere un mito
exploit *n* ['ɛksplɔɪt] impresa ■ *vt* [ɪk'splɔɪt] sfruttare
exploitation [ɛksplɔɪ'teɪʃən] *n* sfruttamento
exploration [ɛksplə'reɪʃən] *n* esplorazione *f*
exploratory [ɪk'splɔrətrɪ] *adj* (*fig: talks*) esplorativo(-a); **~ operation** (*Med*) intervento d'esplorazione
explore [ɪk'splɔ:^r^] *vt* esplorare; (*possibilities*) esaminare
explorer [ɪk'splɔ:rə^r^] *n* esploratore(-trice)
explosion [ɪk'spləuʒən] *n* esplosione *f*
explosive [ɪk'spləusɪv] *adj* esplosivo(-a) ■ *n* esplosivo
exponent [ɪk'spəunənt] *n* esponente *m/f*
export *vt* [ɛk'spɔ:t] esportare ■ *n* ['ɛkspɔ:t]

esportazione *f*; articolo di esportazione ■ *cpd* d'esportazione
exportation [ɛkspɔː'teɪʃən] *n* esportazione *f*
exporter [ɪk'spɔːtəʳ] *n* esportatore *m*
export licence *n* licenza d'esportazione
expose [ɪk'spəuz] *vt* esporre; (*unmask*) smascherare; **to ~ o.s.** (*Law*) oltraggiare il pudore
exposed [ɪk'spəuzd] *adj* (*land, house*) esposto(-a); (*Elec: wire*) scoperto(-a); (*pipe, beam*) a vista
exposition [ɛkspə'zɪʃən] *n* esposizione *f*
exposure [ɪk'spəuʒəʳ] *n* esposizione *f*; (*Phot*) posa; (*Med*) assideramento; **to die of ~** morire assiderato(-a)
exposure meter *n* esposimetro
expound [ɪk'spaund] *vt* esporre; (*theory, text*) spiegare
express [ɪk'sprɛs] *adj* (*definite*) chiaro(-a), espresso(-a); (*Brit: letter etc*) espresso *inv* ■ *n* (*train*) espresso ■ *adv*: **to send sth ~** spedire qc per espresso ■ *vt* esprimere; **to ~ o.s.** esprimersi
expression [ɪk'sprɛʃən] *n* espressione *f*
expressionism [ɪk'sprɛʃənɪzəm] *n* espressionismo
expressive [ɪk'sprɛsɪv] *adj* espressivo(-a)
expressly [ɪk'sprɛslɪ] *adv* espressamente
expressway [ɪk'sprɛsweɪ] *n* (*US*) autostrada che attraversa la città
expropriate [ɛks'prəuprɪeɪt] *vt* espropriare
expulsion [ɪk'spʌlʃən] *n* espulsione *f*
exquisite [ɛk'skwɪzɪt] *adj* squisito(-a)
ex-serviceman ['ɛks'səːvɪsmən] *n* ex combattente *m*
ext. *abbr* (*Tel:* = *extension*) int. (= *interno*)
extemporize [ɪk'stɛmpəraɪz] *vi* improvvisare
extend [ɪk'stɛnd] *vt* (*visit*) protrarre; (*road, deadline*) prolungare; (*building*) ampliare; (*offer*) offrire, porgere; (*Comm: credit*) accordare ■ *vi* (*land*) estendersi
extension [ɪk'stɛnʃən] *n* (*of road, term*) prolungamento; (*of contract, deadline*) proroga; (*building*) annesso; (*to wire, table*) prolunga; (*telephone*) interno; (*: in private house*) apparecchio supplementare; **~ 3718** (*Tel*) interno 3718
extension cable *n* (*Elec*) prolunga
extensive [ɪk'stɛnsɪv] *adj* esteso(-a), ampio(-a); (*damage*) su larga scala; (*alterations*) notevole; (*inquiries*) esauriente; (*use*) grande
extensively [ɪk'stɛnsɪvlɪ] *adv* (*altered, damaged etc*) radicalmente; **he's travelled ~** ha viaggiato molto
extent [ɪk'stɛnt] *n* estensione *f*; (*of knowledge, activities, power*) portata; (*degree: of damage, loss*) proporzioni *fpl*; **to some ~** fino a un certo punto; **to a certain/large ~** in certa/larga misura; **to what ~?** fino a che punto?; **to such an ~ that ...** a tal punto che ...
extenuating [ɪk'stɛnjueɪtɪŋ] *adj*: **~ circumstances** attenuanti *fpl*
exterior [ɛk'stɪərɪəʳ] *adj* esteriore, esterno(-a) ■ *n* esteriore *m*, esterno; aspetto (esteriore)
exterminate [ɪk'stəːmɪneɪt] *vt* sterminare
extermination [ɪkstəːmɪ'neɪʃən] *n* sterminio
external [ɛk'stəːnl] *adj* esterno(-a), esteriore ■ *n*: **the externals** le apparenze; **for ~ use only** (*Med*) solo per uso esterno; **~ affairs** (*Pol*) affari *mpl* esteri
externally [ɛk'stəːnəlɪ] *adv* esternamente
extinct [ɪk'stɪŋkt] *adj* estinto(-a)
extinction [ɪk'stɪŋkʃən] *n* estinzione *f*
extinguish [ɪk'stɪŋgwɪʃ] *vt* estinguere
extinguisher [ɪk'stɪŋgwɪʃəʳ] *n* estintore *m*
extol, (*US*) **extoll** [ɪk'stəul] *vt* (*merits, virtues*) magnificare; (*person*) celebrare
extort [ɪk'stɔːt] *vt*: **to ~ sth from** estorcere qc (da)
extortion [ɪk'stɔːʃən] *n* estorsione *f*
extortionate [ɪk'stɔːʃənɪt] *adj* esorbitante
extra ['ɛkstrə] *adj* extra *inv*, supplementare ■ *adv* (*in addition*) di più ■ *n* supplemento; (*Theat*) comparso; **wine will cost ~** il vino è extra; **~ large sizes** taglie *fpl* forti
extra... ['ɛkstrə] *prefix* extra...
extract *vt* [ɪk'strækt] estrarre; (*money, promise*) strappare ■ *n* ['ɛkstrækt] estratto; (*passage*) brano
extraction [ɪk'strækʃən] *n* estrazione *f*; (*descent*) origine *f*
extractor fan [ɪk'stræktəʳ-] *n* aspiratore *m*
extracurricular [ɛkstrəkə'rɪkjuləʳ] *adj* (*Scol*) parascolastico(-a)
extradite ['ɛkstrədaɪt] *vt* estradare
extradition [ɛkstrə'dɪʃən] *n* estradizione *f*
extramarital [ɛkstrə'mærɪtl] *adj* extraconiugale
extramural [ɛkstrə'mjuərl] *adj* fuori dell'università
extraneous [ɛk'streɪnɪəs] *adj*: **~ to** estraneo(a) a
extraordinary [ɪk'strɔːdnrɪ] *adj* straordinario(-a); **the ~ thing is that ...** la cosa strana è che ...
extraordinary general meeting *n* assemblea straordinaria
extrapolation [ɪkstræpə'leɪʃən] *n* estrapolazione *f*
extrasensory perception [ɛkstrə'sɛnsərɪ-] *n* percezione *f* extrasensoriale
extra time *n* (*Football*) tempo supplementare
extravagance [ɪk'strævəgəns] *n* (*excessive spending*) sperpero; (*thing bought*) stravaganza

e

extravagant [ɪk'strævəgənt] *adj* stravagante; (*in spending: person*) prodigo(-a); (*: tastes*) dispendioso(-a)
extreme [ɪk'stri:m] *adj* estremo(-a) ■ *n* estremo; **extremes of temperature** eccessivi sbalzi *mpl* di temperatura; **the ~ left/right** (*Pol*) l'estrema sinistra/destra
extremely [ɪk'stri:mlɪ] *adv* estremamente
extremist [ɪk'stri:mɪst] *adj, n* estremista (*m/f*)
extremity [ɪk'strɛmɪtɪ] *n* estremità *f inv*
extricate ['ɛkstrɪkeɪt] *vt*: **to ~ sth from** districare qc (da)
extrovert ['ɛkstrəvə:t] *n* estroverso(-a)
exuberance [ɪg'zu:bərəns] *n* esuberanza
exuberant [ɪg'zju:bərənt] *adj* esuberante
exude [ɪg'zju:d] *vt* trasudare; (*fig*) emanare
exult [ɪg'zʌlt] *vi* esultare, gioire
exultant [ɪg'zʌltənt] *adj* (*person, smile*) esultante; (*shout, expression*) di giubilo
exultation [ɛgzʌl'teɪʃən] *n* giubilo; **in ~** per la gioia
eye [aɪ] *n* occhio; (*of needle*) cruna ■ *vt* osservare; **to keep an ~ on** tenere d'occhio; **in the public ~** esposto(a) al pubblico; **as far as the ~ can see** a perdita d'occhio; **with an ~ to doing sth** (*Brit*) con l'idea di far qc; **to have an ~ for sth** avere occhio per qc; **there's more to this than meets the ~** non è così semplice come sembra
eyeball ['aɪbɔ:l] *n* globo dell'occhio
eyebath ['aɪbɑ:θ] *n* occhino
eyebrow ['aɪbrau] *n* sopracciglio
eyebrow pencil *n* matita per le sopracciglia
eye-catching ['aɪkætʃɪŋ] *adj* che colpisce l'occhio
eye cup *n* (*US*) = **eyebath**
eyedrops ['aɪdrɔps] *npl* gocce *fpl* oculari, collirio
eyeful ['aɪful] *n*: **to get an ~ (of sth)** (*col*) avere l'occasione di dare una bella sbirciata (a qc)
eyeglass ['aɪglɑ:s] *n* monocolo
eyelash ['aɪlæʃ] *n* ciglio
eyelet ['aɪlɪt] *n* occhiello
eye-level ['aɪlɛvl] *adj* all'altezza degli occhi
eyelid ['aɪlɪd] *n* palpebra
eyeliner ['aɪlaɪnə^r] *n* eye-liner *m inv*
eye-opener ['aɪəupnə^r] *n* rivelazione *f*
eyeshadow ['aɪʃædəu] *n* ombretto
eyesight ['aɪsaɪt] *n* vista
eyesore ['aɪsɔ:^r] *n* pugno nell'occhio
eyestrain ['aɪstreɪn] *n*: **to get ~** stancarsi gli occhi
eye-tooth (*pl* **eye-teeth**) ['aɪtu:θ, -ti:θ] *n* canino superiore; **to give one's eye-teeth for sth/to do sth** (*fig*) dare non so che cosa per qc/per fare qc
eyewash ['aɪwɔʃ] *n* collirio; (*fig*) sciocchezze *fpl*
eye witness *n* testimone *m/f* oculare
eyrie ['ɪərɪ] *n* nido (d'aquila)

Ff

F, f [ɛf] *n* (*letter*) F, f *f or m inv*; (*Mus*): **F** fa *m*; **F for Frederick**, (*US*) **F for Fox** ≈ F come Firenze

F. *abbr* (= *Fahrenheit*) F

FA *n abbr* (*Brit*) = **Football Association**

FAA *n abbr* (*US*) = **Federal Aviation Administration**

fable ['feɪbl] *n* favola

fabric ['fæbrɪk] *n* stoffa, tessuto; (*Archit*) struttura

fabricate ['fæbrɪkeɪt] *vt* fabbricare

fabrication [fæbrɪ'keɪʃən] *n* fabbricazione *f*

fabric ribbon *n* (*for typewriter*) dattilonastro di tessuto

fabulous ['fæbjuləs] *adj* favoloso(-a); (*col: super*) favoloso(-a), fantastico(-a)

façade [fə'sɑːd] *n* facciata; (*fig*) apparenza

face [feɪs] *n* faccia, viso, volto; (*expression*) faccia; (*grimace*) smorfia; (*of clock*) quadrante *m*; (*of building*) facciata; (*side, surface*) faccia; (*of mountain, cliff*) parete *f* ■ *vt* fronteggiare; (*fig*) affrontare; **~ down** (*person*) bocconi; (*object*) a faccia in giù; **to lose/save ~** perdere/salvare la faccia; **to pull a ~** fare una smorfia; **in the ~ of** (*difficulties etc*) di fronte a; **on the ~ of it** a prima vista; **to ~ the fact that ...** riconoscere *or* ammettere che ...

▸ **face up to** *vt fus* affrontare, far fronte a

face cloth *n* (*Brit*) guanto di spugna

face cream *n* crema per il viso

faceless ['feɪslɪs] *adj* anonimo(-a)

face lift *n* lifting *m inv*; (*of façade etc*) ripulita

face powder *n* cipria

face-saving ['feɪs'seɪvɪŋ] *adj* che salva la faccia

facet ['fæsɪt] *n* faccetta, sfaccettatura; (*fig*) sfaccettatura

facetious [fə'siːʃəs] *adj* faceto(-a)

face-to-face ['feɪstə'feɪs] *adv* faccia a faccia

face value ['feɪs'væljuː] *n* (*of coin*) valore *m* facciale *or* nominale; **to take sth at ~** (*fig*) giudicare qc dalle apparenze

facia ['feɪʃɪə] *n* = **fascia**

facial ['feɪʃəl] *adj* facciale ■ *n* trattamento del viso

facile ['fæsaɪl] *adj* facile; superficiale

facilitate [fə'sɪlɪteɪt] *vt* facilitare

facility [fə'sɪlɪtɪ] *n* facilità; **facilities** *npl* attrezzature *fpl*; **credit facilities** facilitazioni *fpl* di credito

facing ['feɪsɪŋ] *n* (*of wall etc*) rivestimento; (*Sewing*) paramontura

facsimile [fæk'sɪmɪlɪ] *n* facsimile *m inv*

facsimile machine *n* telecopiatrice *f*

fact [fækt] *n* fatto; **in ~** infatti; **to know for a ~ that ...** sapere per certo che ...; **the ~ (of the matter) is that ...** la verità è che ...; **the facts of life** (*sex*) i fatti riguardanti la vita sessuale; (*fig*) le realtà della vita

fact-finding ['fæktfaɪndɪŋ] *adj*: **a ~ tour/mission** un viaggio/una missione d'inchiesta

faction ['fækʃən] *n* fazione *f*

factional ['fækʃənl] *adj*: **~ fighting** scontri *mpl* tra fazioni

factor ['fæktəʳ] *n* fattore *m*; (*Comm: company*) *organizzazione specializzata nell'incasso di crediti per conto terzi*; (*: agent*) agente *m* depositario ■ *vi* incassare crediti per conto terzi; **human ~** elemento umano; **safety ~** coefficiente *m* di sicurezza

factory ['fæktərɪ] *n* fabbrica, stabilimento

factory farming *n* (*Brit*) allevamento su scala industriale

factory floor *n*: **the ~** (*workers*) gli operai; (*area*) il reparto produzione; **on the ~** nel reparto produzione

factory ship *n* nave *f* fattoria *inv*

factual ['fæktjuəl] *adj* che si attiene ai fatti

faculty ['fækəltɪ] *n* facoltà *f inv*; (*US: teaching staff*) corpo insegnante

fad [fæd] *n* mania; capriccio

fade [feɪd] *vi* sbiadire, sbiadirsi; (*light, sound, hope*) attenuarsi, affievolirsi; (*flower*) appassire

▸ **fade in** *vt* (*picture*) aprire in dissolvenza; (*sound*) aumentare gradualmente d'intensità

▸**fade out** *vt* (*picture*) chiudere in dissolvenza; (*sound*) diminuire gradualmente d'intensità
faeces, (*US*) **feces** ['fi:si:z] *npl* feci *fpl*
fag [fæg] *n* (*Brit col: cigarette*) cicca; (*: chore*) sfacchinata; (*US col: homosexual*) frocio
fag end *n* (*Brit col*) mozzicone *m*
fagged out ['fægd-] *adj* (*Brit col*) stanco(-a) morto(-a)
fail [feɪl] *vt* (*exam*) non superare; (*candidate*) bocciare; (*courage, memory*) mancare a ▪ *vi* fallire; (*student*) essere respinto(-a); (*supplies*) mancare; (*eyesight, health, light: also:* **be failing**) venire a mancare; (*brakes*) non funzionare; **to ~ to do sth** (*neglect*) mancare di fare qc; (*be unable*) non riuscire a fare qc; **without ~** senza fallo; certamente
failing ['feɪlɪŋ] *n* difetto ▪ *prep* in mancanza di; **~ that** se questo non è possibile
failsafe ['feɪlseɪf] *adj* (*device etc*) di sicurezza
failure ['feɪljə^r^] *n* fallimento; (*person*) fallito(-a); (*mechanical etc*) guasto; (*in exam*) insuccesso, bocciatura; (*of crops*) perdita; **his ~ to come** il fatto che non sia venuto; **it was a complete ~** è stato un vero fiasco
faint [feɪnt] *adj* debole; (*recollection*) vago(-a); (*mark*) indistinto(-a); (*smell, breeze, trace*) leggero(-a) ▪ *vi* svenire; **to feel ~** sentirsi svenire
faintest ['feɪntɪst] *adj*: **I haven't the ~ idea** non ho la più pallida idea
faint-hearted [feɪnt'hɑ:tɪd] *adj* pusillanime
faintly ['feɪntlɪ] *adv* debolmente; vagamente
faintness ['feɪntnɪs] *n* debolezza
fair [fɛə^r^] *adj* (*person, decision*) giusto(-a), equo(-a); (*hair etc*) biondo(-a); (*skin, complexion*) bianco(-a); (*weather*) bello(-a), clemente; (*good enough*) assai buono(-a); (*sizeable*) bello(-a) ▪ *adv*: **to play ~** giocare correttamente ▪ *n* fiera; (*Brit: funfair*) luna park *m inv*; (*also:* **trade fair**) fiera campionaria; **it's not ~!** non è giusto!; **a ~ amount of** un bel po' di
fair copy *n* bella copia
fair game *n*: **to be ~** (*person*) essere bersaglio legittimo
fairground ['fɛəgraund] *n* luna park *m inv*
fair-haired [fɛə'hɛəd] *adj* (*person*) biondo(-a)
fairly ['fɛəlɪ] *adv* equamente; (*quite*) abbastanza
fairness ['fɛənɪs] *n* equità, giustizia; **in all ~** per essere giusti, a dire il vero
fair play *n* correttezza
fair trade *n* commercio equo e solidale
fairy ['fɛərɪ] *n* fata
fairy godmother *n* fata buona
fairy lights *npl* (*Brit*) lanternine *fpl* colorate
fairy tale *n* fiaba
faith [feɪθ] *n* fede *f*; (*trust*) fiducia; (*sect*) religione *f*, fede *f*; **to have ~ in sb/sth** avere fiducia in qn/qc
faithful ['feɪθful] *adj* fedele
faithfully ['feɪθfəlɪ] *adv* fedelmente; **yours ~** (*Brit: in letters*) distinti saluti
faith healer *n* guaritore(-trice)
fake [feɪk] *n* imitazione *f*; (*picture*) falso; (*person*) impostore(-a) ▪ *adj* falso(-a) ▪ *vt* (*accounts*) falsificare; (*illness*) fingere; (*painting*) contraffare; **his illness is a ~** fa finta di essere malato
falcon ['fɔ:lkən] *n* falco, falcone *m*
Falkland Islands ['fɔ:lklənd-] *npl*: **the ~** le isole Falkland
fall [fɔ:l] *n* caduta; (*decrease*) diminuzione *f*, calo; (*in temperature*) abbassamento; (*in price*) ribasso; (*US: autumn*) autunno ▪ *vi* (*pt* **fell**, *pp* **fallen**) [fɛl, 'fɔ:lən] cadere; (*temperature, price*) abbassare; **a ~ of earth** uno smottamento; **a ~ of snow** (*Brit*) una nevicata; **to ~ in love (with sb/sth)** innamorarsi (di qn/qc); **to ~ short of** (*sb's expectations*) non corrispondere a; **to ~ flat** *vi* (*on one's face*) cadere bocconi; (*joke*) fare cilecca; (*plan*) fallire; *see also* **falls**
▸**fall apart** *vi* cadere a pezzi
▸**fall back** *vi* indietreggiare; (*Mil*) ritirarsi
▸**fall back on** *vt fus* ripiegare su; **to have sth to ~ back on** avere qc di riserva
▸**fall behind** *vi* rimanere indietro; (*fig: with payments*) essere in arretrato
▸**fall down** *vi* (*person*) cadere; (*building, hopes*) crollare
▸**fall for** *vt fus* (*person*) prendere una cotta per; **to ~ for a trick (***or* **a story** *etc***)** cascarci
▸**fall in** *vi* crollare; (*Mil*) mettersi in riga
▸**fall in with** *vt fus* (*sb's plans etc*) trovarsi d'accordo con
▸**fall off** *vi* cadere; (*diminish*) diminuire, abbassarsi
▸**fall out** *vi* (*friends etc*) litigare
▸**fall over** *vi* cadere
▸**fall through** *vi* (*plan, project*) fallire
fallacy ['fæləsɪ] *n* errore *m*
fallback ['fɔ:lbæk] *adj*: **~ position** posizione *f* di ripiego
fallen ['fɔ:lən] *pp of* **fall**
fallible ['fælɪbl] *adj* fallibile
falling ['fɔ:lɪŋ] *adj*: **~ market** (*Comm*) mercato in ribasso
falling-off ['fɔ:lɪŋ'ɔf] *n* calo
fallopian tube [fə'ləupɪən-] *n* (*Anat*) tuba di Falloppio
fallout ['fɔ:laut] *n* fall-out *m*
fallout shelter *n* rifugio antiatomico
fallow ['fæləu] *adj* incolto(-a); a maggese

falls [fɔ:lz] *npl* (*waterfall*) cascate *fpl*
false [fɔ:ls] *adj* falso(-a); **under ~ pretences** con l'inganno
false alarm *n* falso allarme *m*
falsehood ['fɔ:lshud] *n* menzogna
falsely ['fɔ:lslɪ] *adv* (*accuse*) a torto
false teeth *npl* (*Brit*) denti *mpl* finti
falsify ['fɔ:lsɪfaɪ] *vt* falsificare; (*figures*) alterare
falter ['fɔ:ltə^r] *vi* esitare, vacillare
fame [feɪm] *n* fama, celebrità
familiar [fə'mɪlɪə^r] *adj* familiare; (*common*) comune; (*close*) intimo(-a); **to be ~ with** (*subject*) conoscere; **to make o.s. ~ with** familiarizzarsi con; **to be on ~ terms with** essere in confidenza con
familiarity [fəmɪlɪ'ærɪtɪ] *n* familiarità; intimità
familiarize [fə'mɪlɪəraɪz] *vt*: **to ~ sb with sth** far conoscere qc a qn
family ['fæmɪlɪ] *n* famiglia
family allowance *n* (*Brit*) assegni *mpl* familiari
family business *n* impresa familiare
family credit *n* (*Brit*) ≈ assegni *mpl* familiari
family doctor *n* medico di famiglia
family life *n* vita familiare
family man *n* padre *m* di famiglia
family planning clinic *n* consultorio familiare
family tree *n* albergo genealogico
famine ['fæmɪn] *n* carestia
famished ['fæmɪʃt] *adj* affamato(-a); **I'm ~!** (*col*) ho una fame da lupo!
famous ['feɪməs] *adj* famoso(-a)
famously ['feɪməslɪ] *adv* (*get on*) a meraviglia
fan [fæn] *n* (*folding*) ventaglio; (*machine*) ventilatore *m*; (*person*) ammiratore(-trice); (*Sport*) tifoso(-a) ■ *vt* far vento a; (*fire, quarrel*) alimentare
▸ **fan out** *vi* spargersi (a ventaglio)
fanatic [fə'nætɪk] *n* fanatico(-a)
fanatical [fə'nætɪkl] *adj* fanatico(-a)
fan belt *n* cinghia del ventilatore
fancied ['fænsɪd] *adj* immaginario(-a)
fanciful ['fænsɪful] *adj* fantasioso(-a); (*object*) di fantasia
fan club *n* fan club *m inv*
fancy ['fænsɪ] *n* immaginazione *f*, fantasia; (*whim*) capriccio ■ *cpd* (di) fantasia *inv* ■ *vt* (*feel like, want*) aver voglia di; (*imagine*) immaginare, credere; **to take a ~ to** incapricciarsi di; **it took** *or* **caught my ~** mi è piaciuto; **when the ~ takes him** quando ne ha voglia; **to ~ that** immaginare che; **he fancies her** gli piace
fancy dress *n* costume *m* (per maschera)
fancy-dress ball *n* ballo in maschera
fancy goods *npl* articoli *mpl* di ogni genere
fanfare ['fænfɛə^r] *n* fanfara
fanfold paper ['fænfəuld-] *n* carta a moduli continui
fang [fæŋ] *n* zanna; (*of snake*) dente *m*
fan heater *n* (*Brit*) stufa ad aria calda
fanlight ['fænlaɪt] *n* lunetta
fanny ['fænɪ] *n* (*Brit col!*) figa (*!*); (*US col*) culo (*!*)
fantasize ['fæntəsaɪz] *vi* fantasticare, sognare
fantastic [fæn'tæstɪk] *adj* fantastico(-a)
fantasy ['fæntəsɪ] *n* fantasia, immaginazione *f*; fantasticheria; chimera
fanzine ['fænzi:n] *n* rivista specialistica (*per appassionati*)
FAO *n abbr* (= *Food and Agriculture Organization*) FAO *f*
FAQ *abbr* (= *free alongside quay*) franco lungo banchina; (*Comput*: = *frequently asked question(s)*) FAQ
far [fɑ:^r] *adj*: **the ~ side/end** l'altra parte/ l'altro capo; **the ~ left/right** (*Pol*) l'estrema sinistra/destra ■ *adv* lontano; **is it ~ to London?** è lontana Londra?; **it's not ~ (from here)** non è lontano (da qui); **~ away, ~ off** lontano, distante; **~ better** assai migliore; **~ from** lontano da; **by ~** di gran lunga; **as ~ back as the 13th century** già nel duecento; **go as ~ as the farm** vada fino alla fattoria; **as ~ as I know** per quel che so; **as ~ as possible** nei limiti del possibile; **how ~ have you got with your work?** dov'è arrivato con il suo lavoro?
faraway ['fɑ:rəweɪ] *adj* lontano(-a); (*voice, look*) assente
farce [fɑ:s] *n* farsa
farcical ['fɑ:sɪkəl] *adj* farsesco(-a)
fare [fɛə^r] *n* (*on trains, buses*) tariffa; (*in taxi*) prezzo della corsa; (*food*) vitto, cibo ■ *vi* passarsela; **full ~** tariffa completa
Far East *n*: **the ~** l'Estremo Oriente *m*
farewell [fɛə'wɛl] *excl, n* addio ■ *cpd* (*party etc*) d'addio
far-fetched ['fɑ:'fɛtʃt] *adj* (*explanation*) stiracchiato(-a), forzato(-a); (*idea, scheme, story*) inverosimile
farm [fɑ:m] *n* fattoria, podere *m* ■ *vt* coltivare
▸ **farm out** *vt* (*work*) dare in consegna
farmer ['fɑ:mə^r] *n* coltivatore(-trice), agricoltore(-trice)
farmhand ['fɑ:mhænd] *n* bracciante *m* agricolo
farmhouse ['fɑ:mhaus] *n* fattoria
farming ['fɑ:mɪŋ] *n* agricoltura; **intensive ~** coltura intensiva; **sheep ~** allevamento di pecore

farm labourer *n* = **farmhand**
farmland ['fɑːmlænd] *n* terreno da coltivare
farm produce *n* prodotti *mpl* agricoli
farm worker *n* = **farmhand**
farmyard ['fɑːmjɑːd] *n* aia
Faroe Islands ['fɛərəu-],**Faroes** ['fɛərəuz] *npl*: **the ~** le isole Faeroer
far-reaching ['fɑː'riːtʃɪŋ] *adj* di vasta portata
far-sighted ['fɑː'saɪtɪd] *adj* presbite; (*fig*) lungimirante
fart [fɑːt] (*col!*) *n* scoreggia (*!*) ■ *vi* scoreggiare (*!*)
farther ['fɑːðə^r] *adv* più lontano ■ *adj* più lontano(-a)
farthest ['fɑːðɪst] *adv superlative of* **far**
FAS *abbr* (*Brit*: *= free alongside ship*) franco banchina nave
fascia ['feɪʃɪə] *n* (*Aut*) cruscotto; (*of mobile phone*) mascherina
fascinate ['fæsɪneɪt] *vt* affascinare
fascinating ['fæsɪneɪtɪŋ] *adj* affascinante
fascination [fæsɪ'neɪʃən] *n* fascino
fascism ['fæʃɪzəm] *n* fascismo
fascist ['fæʃɪst] *adj, n* fascista *m/f*
fashion ['fæʃən] *n* moda; (*manner*) maniera, modo ■ *vt* foggiare, formare; **in ~** alla moda; **out of ~** passato(a) di moda; **after a ~** (*finish, manage etc*) così così; **in the Greek ~** alla greca
fashionable ['fæʃənəbl] *adj* alla moda, di moda; (*writer*) di grido
fashion designer *n* disegnatore(-trice) di moda
fashionista [fæʃə'nɪstə] *n* fashionista *m/f*, maniaco(-a) della moda
fashion show *n* sfilata di moda
fast [fɑːst] *adj* rapido(-a), svelto(-a), veloce; (*clock*): **to be ~** andare avanti; (*dye, colour*) solido(-a) ■ *adv* rapidamente; (*stuck, held*) saldamente ■ *n* digiuno ■ *vi* digiunare; **~ asleep** profondamente addormentato; **as ~ as I can** più in fretta possibile; **my watch is 5 minutes ~** il mio orologio va avanti di 5 minuti
fasten ['fɑːsn] *vt* chiudere, fissare; (*coat*) abbottonare, allacciare ■ *vi* chiudersi, fissarsi; abbottonarsi, allacciarsi
▸ **fasten (up)on** *vt fus* (*idea*) cogliere al volo
fastener ['fɑːsnə^r],**fastening** ['fɑːsnɪŋ] *n* fermaglio, chiusura; (*Brit*: *zip fastener*) chiusura lampo
fast food *n* fast food *m inv*
fastidious [fæs'tɪdɪəs] *adj* esigente, difficile
fast lane *n* (*Aut*) ≈ corsia di sorpasso
fat [fæt] *adj* grasso(-a) ■ *n* grasso; **to live off the ~ of the land** vivere nel lusso, avere ogni ben di Dio
fatal ['feɪtl] *adj* fatale; mortale; disastroso(-a)
fatalism ['feɪtəlɪzəm] *n* fatalismo
fatality [fə'tælɪtɪ] *n* morto(-a), vittima
fatally ['feɪtəlɪ] *adv* a morte
fate [feɪt] *n* destino; (*of person*) sorte *f*; **to meet one's ~** trovare la morte
fated ['feɪtɪd] *adj* (*governed by fate*) destinato(-a); (*person, project etc*) destinato(-a) a finire male
fateful ['feɪtful] *adj* fatidico(-a)
fat-free ['fæt'friː] *adj* senza grassi
father ['fɑːðə^r] *n* padre *m*
Father Christmas *n* Babbo Natale
fatherhood ['fɑːðəhuːd] *n* paternità
father-in-law ['fɑːðərɪnlɔː] *n* suocero
fatherland ['fɑːðəlænd] *n* patria
fatherly ['fɑːðəlɪ] *adj* paterno(-a)
fathom ['fæðəm] *n* braccio (*= 1828 mm*) ■ *vt* (*mystery*) penetrare, sondare
fatigue [fə'tiːg] *n* stanchezza; (*Mil*) corvé *f*; **metal ~** fatica del metallo
fatness ['fætnɪs] *n* grassezza
fatten ['fætn] *vt, vi* ingrassare; **chocolate is fattening** la cioccolata fa ingrassare
fatty ['fætɪ] *adj* (*food*) grasso(-a) ■ *n* (*col*) ciccione(-a)
fatuous ['fætjuəs] *adj* fatuo(-a)
faucet ['fɔːsɪt] *n* (*US*) rubinetto
fault [fɔːlt] *n* colpa; (*Tennis*) fallo; (*defect*) difetto; (*Geo*) faglia ■ *vt* criticare; **it's my ~** è colpa mia; **to find ~ with** trovare da ridire su; **at ~** in fallo; **generous to a ~** eccessivamente generoso
faultless ['fɔːltlɪs] *adj* perfetto(-a); senza difetto; impeccabile
faulty ['fɔːltɪ] *adj* difettoso(-a)
fauna ['fɔːnə] *n* fauna
faux pas [fəu'pɑː] *n* gaffe *f inv*
favour, (*US*)**favor** ['feɪvə^r] *n* favore *m* ■ *vt* (*proposition*) favorire, essere favorevole a; (*pupil etc*) favorire; (*team, horse*) dare per vincente; **to do sb a ~** fare un favore *or* una cortesia a qn; **in ~ of** in favore di; **to be in ~ of sth/of doing sth** essere favorevole a qc/a fare qc; **to find ~ with sb** (*person*) entrare nelle buone grazie di qn; (*suggestion*) avere l'approvazione di qn
favourable, (*US*)**favorable** ['feɪvərəbl] *adj* favorevole
favourably, (*US*)**favorably** ['feɪvərəblɪ] *adv* favorevolmente
favourite, (*US*)**favorite** ['feɪvrɪt] *adj, n* favorito(-a)
favouritism, (*US*)**favoritism** ['feɪvrɪtɪzəm] *n* favoritismo
fawn [fɔːn] *n* daino ■ *adj* (*also*: **fawn-coloured**) marrone chiaro *inv* ■ *vi*: **to ~ (up)on** adulare servilmente

fax [fæks] *n* (*document, machine*) facsimile *m inv* ■ *vt* teletrasmettere, spedire in facsimile
FBI *n abbr* (*US*: = *Federal Bureau of Investigation*) FBI *f*
FCC *n abbr* (*US*) = **Federal Communications Commission**
FCO *n abbr* (*Brit*: = *Foreign and Commonwealth Office*) ≈ Ufficio affari esteri
FD *n abbr* (*US*) = **fire department**
FDA *n abbr* (*US*) = **Food and Drug Administration**
FE *n abbr* = **further education**
fear [fɪəʳ] *n* paura, timore *m* ■ *vt* aver paura di, temere ■ *vi*: **to ~ for** temere per, essere in ansia per; **~ of heights** vertigini *fpl*; **for ~ of** per paura di; **to ~ that** avere paura di (*or* che + *sub*), temere di (*or* che + *sub*)
fearful ['fɪəful] *adj* pauroso(-a); (*sight, noise*) terribile, spaventoso(-a); (*frightened*): **to be ~ of** temere
fearfully ['fɪəfəlɪ] *adv* (*timidly*) timorosamente; (*col*: *very*) terribilmente, spaventosamente
fearless ['fɪəlɪs] *adj* intrepido(-a), senza paura
fearsome ['fɪəsəm] *adj* (*opponent*) formidabile, terribile; (*sight*) terrificante
feasibility [fiːzə'bɪlɪtɪ] *n* praticabilità
feasibility study *n* studio delle possibilità di realizzazione
feasible ['fiːzəbl] *adj* fattibile, realizzabile
feast [fiːst] *n* festa, banchetto; (*Rel*: *also*: **feast day**) festa ■ *vi* banchettare; **to ~ on** godersi, gustare
feat [fiːt] *n* impresa, fatto insigne
feather ['fɛðəʳ] *n* penna ■ *cpd* (*mattress, bed, pillow*) di piume ■ *vt*: **to ~ one's nest** (*fig*) arricchirsi
feather-weight ['fɛðəweɪt] *n* peso *m* piuma *inv*
feature ['fiːtʃəʳ] *n* caratteristica; (*article*) articolo ■ *vt* (*film*) avere come protagonista ■ *vi* figurare; **features** *npl* (*of face*) fisionomia; **a (special) ~ on sth/sb** un servizio speciale su qc/qn; **it featured prominently in ...** ha avuto un posto di prima importanza in ...
feature film *n* film *m inv* principale
featureless ['fiːtʃəlɪs] *adj* anonimo(-a), senza caratteri distinti
Feb. [fɛb] *abbr* (= *February*) febb.
February ['fɛbruərɪ] *n* febbraio; *see also* **July**
feces ['fiːsiːz] *npl* (*US*) = **faeces**
feckless ['fɛklɪs] *adj* irresponsabile, incosciente
Fed [fɛd] *abbr* (*US*) = **federal; federation**
fed [fɛd] *pt, pp of* **feed**; **to be fed up** essere stufo(-a)
Fed. [fɛd] *n abbr* (*US col*) = **Federal Reserve Board**
federal ['fɛdərəl] *adj* federale
Federal Republic of Germany *n* Repubblica Federale Tedesca
Federal Reserve Board *n* (*US*) *organo di controllo del sistema bancario statunitense*
Federal Trade Commission *n* (*US*) *organismo di protezione contro le pratiche commerciali abusive*
federation [fɛdə'reɪʃən] *n* federazione *f*
fee [fiː] *n* pagamento; (*of doctor, lawyer*) onorario; (*for examination*) tassa d'esame; **school fees** tasse *fpl* scolastiche; **entrance ~, membership ~** quota d'iscrizione; **for a small ~** per una somma modesta
feeble ['fiːbl] *adj* debole
feeble-minded [fiːbl'maɪndɪd] *adj* deficiente
feed [fiːd] *n* (*of baby*) pappa ■ *vt* (*pt, pp* **fed**) [fɛd] nutrire; (*horse etc*) dare da mangiare a; (*fire, machine*) alimentare ■ *vi* (*baby, animal*) mangiare; **to ~ material into sth** introdurre materiale in qc; **to ~ data/information into sth** inserire dati/informazioni in qc
▸ **feed back** *vt* (*results*) riferire
▸ **feed on** *vt fus* nutrirsi di
feedback ['fiːdbæk] *n* feed-back *m*; (*from person*) reazioni *fpl*
feeder ['fiːdəʳ] *n* (*bib*) bavaglino
feeding bottle ['fiːdɪŋ-] *n* (*Brit*) biberon *m inv*
feel [fiːl] *n* sensazione *f*; (*sense of touch*) tatto; (*of substance*) consistenza ■ *vt* (*pt, pp* **felt**) [fɛlt] toccare; palpare; tastare; (*cold, pain, anger*) sentire; (*grief*) provare; (*think, believe*): **to ~ that** pensare che; **I ~ that you ought to do it** penso che dovreste farlo; **to ~ hungry/cold** aver fame/freddo; **to ~ lonely/better** sentirsi solo/meglio; **I don't ~ well** non mi sento bene; **to ~ sorry for** dispiacersi per; **it feels soft** è morbido al tatto; **it feels colder out here** sembra più freddo qui fuori; **it feels like velvet** sembra velluto (al tatto); **to ~ like** (*want*) aver voglia di; **to ~ about** *or* **around for** cercare a tastoni; **to ~ about** *or* **around in one's pocket for** frugarsi in tasca per cercare; **I'm still feeling my way** (*fig*) sto ancora tastando il terreno; **to get the ~ of sth** (*fig*) abituarsi a qc
feeler ['fiːləʳ] *n* (*of insect*) antenna; **to put out feelers** (*fig*) fare un sondaggio
feelgood ['fiːlgud] *adj* (*film, song*) allegro(-a) e a lieto fine
feeling ['fiːlɪŋ] *n* sensazione *f*; sentimento; (*impression*) senso, impressione *f*; **to hurt sb's feelings** offendere qn; **what are your feelings about the matter?** che cosa ne pensa?; **my ~ is that ...** ho l'impressione

che ...; **I got the ~ that ...** ho avuto l'impressione che ...; **feelings ran high about it** la cosa aveva provocato grande eccitazione

fee-paying school ['fi:peɪɪŋ-] *n* scuola privata

feet [fi:t] *npl of* **foot**

feign [feɪn] *vt* fingere, simulare

felicitous [fɪ'lɪsɪtəs] *adj* felice

fell [fɛl] *pt of* **fall** ■ *vt* (*tree*) abbattere; (*person*) atterrare ■ *adj*: **with one ~ blow** con un colpo terribile; **at one ~ swoop** in un colpo solo ■ *n* (*Brit*: *mountain*) monte *m*; (: *moorland*): **the fells** la brughiera

fellow ['fɛləu] *n* individuo, tipo; (*comrade*) compagno; (*of learned society*) membro; (*of university*) ≈ docente *m/f* ■ *cpd*: **their ~ prisoners/students** i loro compagni di prigione/studio

fellow citizen *n* concittadino(-a)

fellow countryman *n* compatriota *m*

fellow feeling *n* simpatia

fellow men *npl* simili *mpl*

fellowship ['fɛləuʃɪp] *n* associazione *f*; compagnia; (*Scol*) *specie di borsa di studio universitaria*

fellow traveller *n* compagno(-a) di viaggio; (*Pol*) simpatizzante *m/f*

fell-walking ['fɛlwɔ:kɪŋ] *n* (*Brit*) passeggiate *fpl* in montagna

felon ['fɛlən] *n* (*Law*) criminale *m/f*

felony ['fɛlənɪ] *n* (*Law*) reato, crimine *m*

felt [fɛlt] *pt, pp of* **feel** ■ *n* feltro

felt-tip pen ['fɛlttɪp-] *n* pennarello

female ['fi:meɪl] *n* (*Zool*) femmina; (*pej*: *woman*) donna, femmina ■ *adj* femminile; (*Biol, Elec*) femmina *inv*; **male and ~ students** studenti e studentesse

female impersonator *n* (*Theat*) *attore comico che fa parti da donna*

feminine ['fɛmɪnɪn] *adj, n* femminile (*m*)

femininity [fɛmɪ'nɪnɪtɪ] *n* femminilità

feminism ['fɛmɪnɪzəm] *n* femminismo

feminist ['fɛmɪnɪst] *n* femminista *m/f*

fen [fɛn] *n* (*Brit*): **the Fens** la regione delle Fen

fence [fɛns] *n* recinto; (*Sport*) ostacolo; (*col*: *person*) ricettatore(-trice) ■ *vt* (*also*: **fence in**) recingere ■ *vi* schermire; **to sit on the ~** (*fig*) rimanere neutrale

fencing ['fɛnsɪŋ] *n* (*Sport*) scherma

fend [fɛnd] *vi*: **to ~ for o.s.** arrangiarsi
▸ **fend off** *vt* (*attack, attacker*) respingere, difendersi da; (*blow*) parare; (*awkward question*) eludere

fender ['fɛndə^r] *n* parafuoco; (*US*) parafango; paraurti *m inv*

fennel ['fɛnl] *n* finocchio

ferment *vi* [fə'mɛnt] fermentare ■ *n* ['fə:mɛnt] agitazione *f*, eccitazione *f*

fermentation [fə:mɛn'teɪʃən] *n* fermentazione *f*

fern [fə:n] *n* felce *f*

ferocious [fə'rəuʃəs] *adj* feroce

ferocity [fə'rɔsɪtɪ] *n* ferocità

ferret ['fɛrɪt] *n* furetto
▸ **ferret about, ferret around** *vi* frugare
▸ **ferret out** *vt* (*person*) scovare, scoprire; (*secret, truth*) scoprire

ferry ['fɛrɪ] *n* (*small*) traghetto; (*large*: *also*: **ferryboat**) nave *f* traghetto *inv* ■ *vt* traghettare; **to ~ sth/sb across** *or* **over** traghettare qc/qn da una parte all'altra

ferryman ['fɛrɪmən] *n* traghettatore *m*

fertile ['fə:taɪl] *adj* fertile; (*Biol*) fecondo(-a); **~ period** periodo di fecondità

fertility [fə'tɪlɪtɪ] *n* fertilità; fecondità

fertility drug *n* farmaco fecondativo

fertilize ['fə:tɪlaɪz] *vt* fertilizzare; fecondare

fertilizer ['fə:tɪlaɪzə^r] *n* fertilizzante *m*

fervent ['fə:vənt] *adj* ardente, fervente

fervour, (*US*)**fervor** ['fə:və^r] *n* fervore *m*, ardore *m*

fester ['fɛstə^r] *vi* suppurare

festival ['fɛstɪvəl] *n* (*Rel*) festa; (*Art, Mus*) festival *m inv*

festive ['fɛstɪv] *adj* di festa; **the ~ season** (*Brit*: *Christmas*) il periodo delle feste

festivities [fɛs'tɪvɪtɪz] *npl* festeggiamenti *mpl*

festoon [fɛ'stu:n] *vt*: **to ~ with** ornare di; decorare con

fetch [fɛtʃ] *vt* andare a prendere; (*sell for*) essere venduto(-a) per; **how much did it ~?** a *or* per quanto lo ha venduto?
▸ **fetch up** *vi* (*Brit*) andare a finire

fetching ['fɛtʃɪŋ] *adj* attraente

fête [feɪt] *n* festa

fetid ['fɛtɪd] *adj* fetido(-a)

fetish ['fɛtɪʃ] *n* feticcio

fetter ['fɛtə^r] *vt* (*person*) incatenare; (*horse*) legare; (*fig*) ostacolare

fetters ['fɛtəz] *npl* catene *fpl*

fettle ['fɛtl] *n* (*Brit*): **in fine ~** in gran forma

fetus ['fi:təs] *n* (*US*) = **foetus**

feud [fju:d] *n* contesa, lotta ■ *vi* essere in lotta; **a family ~** una lite in famiglia

feudal ['fju:dl] *adj* feudale

feudalism ['fju:dəlɪzəm] *n* feudalesimo

fever ['fi:və^r] *n* febbre *f*; **he has a ~** ha la febbre

feverish ['fi:vərɪʃ] *adj* (*also fig*) febbrile; (*person*) febbricitante

few [fju:] *adj* pochi(-e) ■ *pron* alcuni(-e); **~ succeed** pochi ci riescono; **they were ~** erano pochi; **a ~ ...** qualche ...; **I know a ~**

ne conosco alcuni; **a good ~, quite a ~** parecchi; **in the next ~ days** nei prossimi giorni; **in the past ~ days** negli ultimi giorni, in questi ultimi giorni; **every ~ days/months** ogni due o tre giorni/mesi; **a ~ more days** qualche altro giorno

fewer ['fju:əʳ] *adj* meno *inv*; meno numerosi(-e) ■ *pron* meno; **they are ~ now** adesso ce ne sono di meno

fewest ['fju:ɪst] *adj* il minor numero di

FFA *n abbr* = **Future Farmers of America**

FH *abbr* (*Brit*) = **fire hydrant**

FHA *n abbr* (*US*) = **Federal Housing Administration**

fiancé [fɪ'ɑ̃:ŋseɪ] *n* fidanzato

fiancée [fɪ'ɑ̃:ŋseɪ] *n* fidanzata

fiasco [fɪ'æskəu] *n* fiasco

fib [fɪb] *n* piccola bugia

fibre, (*US*) **fiber** ['faɪbəʳ] *n* fibra

fibreboard, (*US*) **fiberboard** ['faɪbəbɔ:d] *n* pannello di fibre

fibre-glass, (*US*) **fiber-glass** ['faɪbəglɑ:s] *n* fibra di vetro

fibrositis [faɪbrə'saɪtɪs] *n* cellulite *f*

FICA *n abbr* (*US*) = **Federal Insurance Contributions Act**

fickle ['fɪkl] *adj* incostante, capriccioso(-a)

fiction ['fɪkʃən] *n* narrativa; (*sth made up*) finzione *f*

fictional ['fɪkʃənl] *adj* immaginario(-a)

fictionalize ['fɪkʃənəlaɪz] *vt* romanzare

fictitious [fɪk'tɪʃəs] *adj* fittizio(-a)

fiddle ['fɪdl] *n* (*Mus*) violino; (*cheating*) imbroglio; truffa ■ *vt* (*Brit: accounts*) falsificare, falsare; **tax ~** frode *f* fiscale; **to work a ~** fare un imbroglio
▸ **fiddle with** *vt fus* gingillarsi con

fiddler ['fɪdləʳ] *n* violinista *m/f*

fiddly ['fɪdlɪ] *adj* (*task*) da certosino; (*object*) complesso(-a)

fidelity [fɪ'dɛlɪtɪ] *n* fedeltà; (*accuracy*) esattezza

fidget ['fɪdʒɪt] *vi* agitarsi

fidgety ['fɪdʒɪtɪ] *adj* agitato(-a)

fiduciary [fɪ'du:ʃɪərɪ] *n* fiduciario

field [fi:ld] *n* (*gen, Comput*) campo; **to lead the ~** (*Sport, Comm*) essere in testa, essere al primo posto; **to have a ~ day** (*fig*) divertirsi, spassarsela

field glasses *npl* binocolo (da campagna)

field hospital *n* ospedale *m* da campo

field marshal *n* feldmaresciallo

fieldwork ['fi:ldwə:k] *n* ricerche *fpl* esterne; (*Archeology, Geo*) lavoro sul campo

fiend [fi:nd] *n* demonio

fiendish ['fi:ndɪʃ] *adj* demoniaco(-a)

fierce [fɪəs] *adj* (*look, fighting*) fiero(-a); (*wind*) furioso(-a); (*attack*) feroce; (*enemy*) acerrimo(-a)

fiery ['faɪərɪ] *adj* ardente; infocato(-a)

FIFA ['fi:fə] *n abbr* (= *Fédération Internationale de Football Association*) F.I.F.A. *f*

fifteen [fɪf'ti:n] *num* quindici

fifth [fɪfθ] *num* quinto(-a)

fiftieth ['fɪftɪɪθ] *num* cinquantesimo(-a)

fifty ['fɪftɪ] *num* cinquanta

fifty-fifty ['fɪftɪ'fɪftɪ] *adj, adv*: **to go ~ with sb** fare a metà con qn; **we have a ~ chance of success** abbiamo una probabilità su due di successo

fig [fɪg] *n* fico

fight [faɪt] *n* zuffa, rissa; (*Mil*) battaglia, combattimento; (*against cancer etc*) lotta ■ *vb* (*pt, pp* **fought**) [fɔ:t] *vt* combattere; (*cancer, alcoholism*) lottare contro, combattere; (*Law: case*) difendere ■ *vi* battersi, combattere; (*quarrel*): **to ~ (with sb)** litigare (con qn); (*fig*): **to ~ (for/against)** lottare (per/contro)
▸ **fight back** *vi* difendersi; (*Sport, after illness*) riprendersi ■ *vt* (*tears*) ricacciare
▸ **fight down** *vt* (*anger, anxiety*) vincere; (*urge*) reprimere
▸ **fight off** *vt* (*attack, attacker*) respingere; (*disease, sleep, urge*) lottare contro
▸ **fight out** *vt*: **to ~ it out** risolvere la questione a pugni

fighter ['faɪtəʳ] *n* combattente *m*; (*plane*) aeroplano da caccia

fighter-bomber ['faɪtəbɔməʳ] *n* cacciabombardiere *m*

fighter pilot *n* pilota *m* di caccia

fighting ['faɪtɪŋ] *n* combattimento; (*in streets*) scontri *mpl*

figment ['fɪgmənt] *n*: **a ~ of the imagination** un parto della fantasia

figurative ['fɪgjurətɪv] *adj* figurato(-a)

figure ['fɪgəʳ] *n* (*Drawing, Geom, person*) figura; (*number, cipher*) cifra; (*body, outline*) forma ■ *vi* (*appear*) figurare; (*US: make sense*) spiegarsi; essere logico(-a) ■ *vt* (*US: think, calculate*) pensare, immaginare; **public ~** personaggio pubblico; **~ of speech** figura retorica
▸ **figure on** *vt fus* (*US*) contare su
▸ **figure out** *vt* riuscire a capire; calcolare

figurehead ['fɪgəhɛd] *n* (*Naut*) polena; (*pej*) prestanome *m/f inv*

figure skating *n* pattinaggio artistico

Fiji ['fi:dʒi:] *n*, **Fiji Islands** *npl* le (isole) Figi

filament ['fɪləmənt] *n* filamento

filch [fɪltʃ] *vt* (*col: steal*) grattare

file [faɪl] *n* (*tool*) lima; (*for nails*) limetta; (*dossier*) incartamento; (*in cabinet*) scheda; (*folder*) cartellina; (*for loose leaf*) raccoglitore *m*; (*row*) fila; (*Comput*) archivio, file *m inv* ■ *vt*

(*nails, wood*) limare; (*papers*) archiviare; (*Law*: *claim*) presentare ■ *vi*: **to ~ in/out** entrare/ uscire in fila; **to ~ past** marciare in fila davanti a; **to ~ a suit against sb** intentare causa contro qn
file name *n* (*Comput*) nome *m* del file
filibuster ['fɪlɪbʌstə^r] (*esp US Pol*) *n* (*also*: **filibusterer**) ostruzionista *m/f* ■ *vi* fare ostruzionismo
filing ['faɪlɪŋ] *n* archiviare *m*; *see also* **filings**
filing cabinet *n* casellario
filing clerk *n* archivista *m/f*
filings ['faɪlɪŋz] *npl* limatura
Filipino [fɪlɪ'pi:nəu] *n* filippino(-a); (*Ling*) tagal *m*
fill [fɪl] *vt* riempire; (*tooth*) otturare; (*job*) coprire; (*supply*: *order, requirements, need*) soddisfare ■ *n*: **to eat one's ~** mangiare a sazietà; **we've already filled that vacancy** abbiamo già assunto qualcuno per quel posto
▸ **fill in** *vt* (*hole*) riempire; (*form*) compilare; (*details, report*) completare ■ *vi*: **to ~ in for sb** sostituire qn; **to ~ sb in on sth** (*col*) mettere qn al corrente di qc
▸ **fill out** *vt* (*form, receipt*) riempire
▸ **fill up** *vt* riempire ■ *vi* (*Aut*) fare il pieno; **~ it up, please** (*Aut*) mi faccia il pieno, per piacere
fillet ['fɪlɪt] *n* filetto
fillet steak *n* bistecca di filetto
filling ['fɪlɪŋ] *n* (*Culin*) impasto, ripieno; (*for tooth*) otturazione *f*
filling station *n* stazione *f* di rifornimento
fillip ['fɪlɪp] *n* incentivo, stimolo
filly ['fɪlɪ] *n* puledra
film [fɪlm] *n* (*Cine*) film *m inv*; (*Phot*) pellicola; (*thin layer*) velo ■ *vt* (*scene*) filmare
film script *n* copione *m*
film star *n* divo(-a) dello schermo
filmstrip ['fɪlmstrɪp] *n* filmina
film studio *n* studio cinematografico
Filofax ® ['faɪləufæks] *n* agenda ad anelli
filter ['fɪltə^r] *n* filtro ■ *vt* filtrare
▸ **filter in, filter through** *vi* (*news*) trapelare
filter coffee *n* caffè *m* da passare al filtro
filter lane *n* (*Brit Aut*) corsia di svincolo
filter tip *n* filtro
filth [fɪlθ] *n* sporcizia; (*fig*) oscenità
filthy ['fɪlθɪ] *adj* lordo(-a), sozzo(-a); (*language*) osceno(-a)
fin [fɪn] *n* (*of fish*) pinna
final ['faɪnl] *adj* finale, ultimo(-a); definitivo(-a) ■ *n* (*Sport*) finale *f*; **finals** *npl* (*Scol*) esami *mpl* finali; **~ demand** ingiunzione *f* di pagamento
finale [fɪ'nɑ:lɪ] *n* finale *m*
finalist ['faɪnəlɪst] *n* (*Sport*) finalista *m/f*
finality [faɪ'nælɪtɪ] *n* irrevocabilità; **with an air of ~** con risolutezza
finalize ['faɪnəlaɪz] *vt* mettere a punto
finally ['faɪnəlɪ] *adv* (*lastly*) alla fine; (*eventually*) finalmente; (*once and for all*) definitivamente
finance [faɪ'næns] *n* finanza; (*funds*) fondi *mpl*, capitale *m* ■ *vt* finanziare; **finances** *npl* finanze *fpl*
financial [faɪ'nænʃəl] *adj* finanziario(-a); **~ statement** estratto conto finanziario
financial adviser *n* consulente *m/f* finanziario(-a)
financially [faɪ'nænʃəlɪ] *adv* finanziariamente
financial year *n* anno finanziario, esercizio finanziario
financier [faɪ'nænsɪə^r] *n* finanziatore *m*
find [faɪnd] *vt* (*pt, pp* **found**) [faund] trovare; (*lost object*) ritrovare ■ *n* trovata, scoperta; **to ~ (some) difficulty in doing sth** trovare delle difficoltà nel fare qc; **to ~ sb guilty** (*Law*) giudicare qn colpevole
▸ **find out** *vt* informarsi di; (*truth, secret*) scoprire; (*person*) cogliere in fallo ■ *vi*: **to ~ out about** informarsi su; (*by chance*) venire a sapere
findings ['faɪndɪŋz] *npl* (*Law*) sentenza, conclusioni *fpl*; (*of report*) conclusioni
fine [faɪn] *adj* bello(-a); ottimo(-a); (*thin, subtle*) fine ■ *adv* (*well*) molto bene; (*small*) finemente ■ *n* (*Law*) multa ■ *vt* (*Law*) multare; **he's ~** sta bene; **the weather is ~** il tempo è bello; **you're doing ~** te la cavi benissimo; **to cut it ~** (*with time, money*) farcela per un pelo
fine arts *npl* belle arti *fpl*
finely ['faɪnlɪ] *adv* (*splendidly*) in modo stupendo; (*chop*) finemente; (*adjust*) con precisione
fine print *n*: **the ~** i caratteri minuti
finery ['faɪnərɪ] *n* abiti *mpl* eleganti
finesse [fɪ'nɛs] *n* finezza
fine-tooth comb ['faɪntu:θ-] *n*: **to go through sth with a ~** (*fig*) passare qc al setaccio
finger ['fɪŋgə^r] *n* dito ■ *vt* toccare, tastare
fingernail ['fɪŋgəneɪl] *n* unghia
fingerprint ['fɪŋgəprɪnt] *n* impronta digitale ■ *vt* (*person*) prendere le impronte digitali di
fingerstall ['fɪŋgəstɔ:l] *n* ditale *m*
fingertip ['fɪŋgətɪp] *n* punta del dito; **to have sth at one's fingertips** (*fig*) avere qc sulla punta delle dita
finicky ['fɪnɪkɪ] *adj* esigente, pignolo(-a); minuziosoa(-a)
finish ['fɪnɪʃ] *n* fine *f*; (*Sport*: *place*) traguardo;

(*polish etc*) finitura ■ *vt* finire; (*use up*) esaurire ■ *vi* finire; (*session*) terminare; **to ~ doing sth** finire di fare qc; **to ~ first/second** (*Sport*) arrivare primo/secondo; **she's finished with him** ha chiuso con lui
▸ **finish off** *vt* compiere; (*kill*) uccidere
▸ **finish up** *vi, vt* finire
finished ['fɪnɪʃt] *adj* (*product*) finito(-a); (*performance*) perfetto(-a); (*col: tired*) sfinito(-a)
finishing line ['fɪnɪʃɪŋ-] *n* linea d'arrivo
finishing school *n* scuola privata di perfezionamento (*per signorine*)
finishing touches *npl* ultimi ritocchi *mpl*
finite ['faɪnaɪt] *adj* limitato(-a); (*verb*) finito(-a)
Finland ['fɪnlənd] *n* Finlandia
Finn [fɪn] *n* finlandese *m/f*
Finnish ['fɪnɪʃ] *adj* finlandese ■ *n* (*Ling*) finlandese *m*
fiord [fjɔːd] *n* fiordo
fir [fəːʳ] *n* abete *m*
fire [faɪəʳ] *n* fuoco; incendio ■ *vt* (*discharge*): **to ~ a gun** scaricare un fucile; (*fig*) infiammare; (*dismiss*) licenziare ■ *vi* sparare, far fuoco; **on ~** in fiamme; **insured against ~** assicurato contro gli incendi; **electric/gas ~** stufa elettrica/a gas; **to set ~ to sth, set sth on ~** dar fuoco a qc, incendiare qc; **to be/come under ~ (from)** essere/finire sotto il fuoco *or* il tiro (di)
fire alarm *n* allarme *m* d'incendio
firearm ['faɪərɑːm] *n* arma da fuoco
fire brigade *n* (*Brit*) (corpo dei) pompieri *mpl*
fire chief *n* (*US*) = **fire master**
fire department *n* (*US*) = **fire brigade**
fire door *n* porta *f* rompifuoco *inv*
fire drill *n* esercitazione *f* antincendio
fire engine *n* autopompa
fire escape *n* scala di sicurezza
fire extinguisher *n* estintore *m*
fireguard ['faɪəgɑːd] *n* (*Brit*) parafuoco
fire hazard *n*: **that's a ~** comporta rischi in caso d'incendio
fire hydrant *n* idrante *m*
fire insurance *n* assicurazione *f* contro gli incendi
fireman ['faɪəmən] *n* pompiere *m*
fire master *n* (*Brit*) comandante *m* dei vigili del fuoco
fireplace ['faɪəpleɪs] *n* focolare *m*
fireplug ['faɪəplʌg] *n* (*US*) = **fire hydrant**
fire practice *n* = **fire drill**
fireproof ['faɪəpruːf] *adj* resistente al fuoco
fire regulations *npl* norme *fpl* antincendio
fire screen *n* parafuoco
fireside ['faɪəsaɪd] *n* angolo del focolare
fire station *n* caserma dei pompieri
firewall ['faɪəwɔːl] *n* firewall *m inv*
firewood ['faɪəwud] *n* legna
firework ['faɪəwəːk] *n* fuoco d'artificio
firing ['faɪərɪŋ] *n* (*Mil*) spari *mpl*, tiro
firing line *n* linea del fuoco; **to be in the ~** (*fig*) essere sotto tiro
firing squad *n* plotone *m* d'esecuzione
firm [fəːm] *adj* fermo(-a); (*offer, decision*) definitivo(-a) ■ *n* ditta, azienda; **to be a ~ believer in sth** credere fermamente in qc
firmly ['fəːmlɪ] *adv* fermamente
firmness ['fəːmnɪs] *n* fermezza
first [fəːst] *adj* primo(-a) ■ *adv* (*before others*) il primo, la prima; (*before other things*) per primo; (*for the first time*) per la prima volta; (*when listing reasons etc*) per prima cosa ■ *n* (*person: in race*) primo(-a); (*Brit Scol*) laurea con lode; (*Aut*) prima; **at ~** dapprima, all'inizio; **~ of all** prima di tutto; **in the ~ instance** prima di tutto, in primo luogo; **I'll do it ~ thing tomorrow** lo farò per prima cosa domani; **from the (very) ~** fin dall'inizio, fin dal primo momento; **the ~ of January** il primo (di) gennaio
first aid *n* pronto soccorso
first-aid kit ['fəːst'eɪd-] *n* cassetta pronto soccorso
first-class ['fəːst'klɑːs] *adj* di prima classe
first-class mail *n* ≈ espresso
first-hand ['fəːst'hænd] *adj* di prima mano; diretto(-a)
first lady *n* (*US*) moglie *f* del presidente
firstly ['fəːstlɪ] *adv* in primo luogo
first name *n* nome *m* di battesimo
first night *n* (*Theat*) prima
first-rate ['fəːst'reɪt] *adj* di prima qualità, ottimo(-a)
first-time buyer ['fəːsttaɪm-] *n* acquirente *m/f* di prima casa
First World War *n*: **the ~** la prima guerra mondiale
fir tree *n* abete *m*
fiscal ['fɪskəl] *adj* fiscale; **~ year** anno fiscale
fish [fɪʃ] *n* (*pl inv*) pesce *m* ■ *vt, vi* pescare; **to ~ a river** pescare in un fiume; **to go fishing** andare a pesca
▸ **fish out** *vt* (*from water*) ripescare; (*from box etc*) tirare fuori
fish-and-chip shop [fɪʃən'tʃɪp-] *n* ≈ friggitoria; *see* **chip shop**
fishbone ['fɪʃbəun] *n* lisca, spina
fisherman ['fɪʃəmən] *n* pescatore *m*
fishery ['fɪʃərɪ] *n* zona da pesca
fish factory *n* (*Brit*) fabbrica per la lavorazione del pesce
fish farm *n* vivaio
fish fingers *npl* (*Brit*) bastoncini *mpl* di pesce (surgelati)

fish hook *n* amo
fishing boat ['fɪʃɪŋ-] *n* barca da pesca
fishing industry *n* industria della pesca
fishing line *n* lenza
fishing net *n* rete *f* da pesca
fishing rod *n* canna da pesca
fishing tackle *n* attrezzatura da pesca
fish market *n* mercato del pesce
fishmonger ['fɪʃmʌŋgə^r] *n* pescivendolo; **~'s (shop)** pescheria
fish slice *n* (*Brit*) posata per servire il pesce
fish sticks *npl* (*US*) = **fish fingers**
fishy ['fɪʃɪ] *adj* (*fig*) sospetto(-a)
fission ['fɪʃən] *n* fissione *f*; **atomic/nuclear ~** fissione atomica/nucleare
fissure ['fɪʃə^r] *n* fessura
fist [fɪst] *n* pugno
fistfight ['fɪstfaɪt] *n* scazzottata
fit [fɪt] *adj* (*Med, Sport*) in forma; (*proper*) adatto(-a), appropriato(-a); conveniente ■ *vt* (*clothes*) stare bene a; (*match: facts etc*) concordare con; (*: description*) corrispondere a; (*adjust*) aggiustare; (*put in, attach*) mettere; installare; (*equip*) fornire, equipaggiare ■ *vi* (*clothes*) stare bene; (*parts*) andare bene, adattarsi; (*in space, gap*) entrare ■ *n* (*Med*) attacco; **~ to** in grado di; **~ for** adatto(a) a; degno(a) di; **to keep ~** tenersi in forma; **~ for work** (*after illness*) in grado di riprendere il lavoro; **do as you think** *or* **see ~** faccia come meglio crede; **this dress is a tight/good ~** questo vestito è stretto/sta bene; **~ of anger/enthusiasm** accesso d'ira/d'entusiasmo; **to have a ~** (*Med*) avere un attacco di convulsioni; (*col*) andare su tutte le furie; **by fits and starts** a sbalzi
▸ **fit in** *vi* accordarsi; adattarsi ■ *vt* (*object*) far entrare; (*fig: appointment, visitor*) trovare il tempo per; **to ~ in with sb's plans** adattarsi ai progetti di qn
▸ **fit out** *vt* (*Brit: also:* **fit up**) equipaggiare
fitful ['fɪtful] *adj* saltuario(-a)
fitment ['fɪtmənt] *n* componibile *m*
fitness ['fɪtnɪs] *n* (*Med*) forma fisica; (*of remark*) appropriatezza
fitted ['fɪtɪd] *adj*: **~ carpet** moquette *f inv*; **~ cupboards** armadi *mpl* a muro; **~ kitchen** (*Brit*) cucina componibile
fitter ['fɪtə^r] *n* aggiustatore *m or* montatore *m* meccanico; (*Dressmaking*) sarto(-a)
fitting ['fɪtɪŋ] *adj* appropriato(-a) ■ *n* (*of dress*) prova; (*of piece of equipment*) montaggio, aggiustaggio; *see also* **fittings**
fitting room *n* (*in shop*) camerino
fittings ['fɪtɪŋz] *npl* impianti *mpl*
five [faɪv] *num* cinque
five-day week ['faɪvdeɪ-] *n* settimana di 5 giorni (lavorativi)
fiver ['faɪvə^r] *n* (*col: Brit*) biglietto da cinque sterline; (*: US*) biglietto da cinque dollari
fix [fɪks] *vt* fissare; (*mend*) riparare; (*make ready: meal, drink*) preparare ■ *n*: **to be in a ~** essere nei guai; **the fight was a ~** (*col*) l'incontro è stato truccato
▸ **fix up** *vt* (*arrange: date, meeting*) fissare, stabilire; **to ~ sb up with sth** procurare qc a qn
fixation [fɪk'seɪʃən] *n* (*Psych, fig*) fissazione *f*, ossessione *f*
fixed [fɪkst] *adj* (*prices etc*) fisso(-a); **there's a ~ charge** c'è una quota fissa; **how are you ~ for money?** (*col*) a soldi come stai?
fixed assets *npl* beni *mpl* patrimoniali
fixed penalty, fixed penalty fine *n* contravvenzione *f* a importo fisso
fixture ['fɪkstʃə^r] *n* impianto (fisso); (*Sport*) incontro (del calendario sportivo)
fizz [fɪz] *vi* frizzare
fizzle ['fɪzl] *vi* frizzare; (*also:* **fizzle out**: *enthusiasm, interest*) smorzarsi, svanire; (*: plan*) fallire
fizzy ['fɪzɪ] *adj* frizzante; gassato(-a)
fjord [fjɔːd] *n* = **fiord**
FL, Fla. *abbr* (*US*) = **Florida**
flabbergasted ['flæbəgɑːstɪd] *adj* sbalordito(-a)
flabby ['flæbɪ] *adj* flaccido(-a)
flag [flæg] *n* bandiera; (*also:* **flagstone**) pietra da lastricare ■ *vi* stancarsi; affievolirsi; **~ of convenience** bandiera di convenienza
▸ **flag down** *vt* fare segno (di fermarsi) a
flagon ['flægən] *n* bottiglione *m*
flagpole ['flægpəul] *n* albero
flagrant ['fleɪgrənt] *adj* flagrante
flag stop *n* (*US: for bus*) fermata facoltativa, fermata a richiesta
flair [flɛə^r] *n* (*for business etc*) fiuto; (*for languages etc*) facilità
flak [flæk] *n* (*Mil*) fuoco d'artiglieria; (*col: criticism*) critiche *fpl*
flake [fleɪk] *n* (*of rust, paint*) scaglia; (*of snow, soap powder*) fiocco ■ *vi* (*also:* **flake off**) sfaldarsi
flaky ['fleɪkɪ] *adj* (*paintwork*) scrostato(-a); (*skin*) squamoso(-a); **~ pastry** (*Culin*) pasta sfoglia
flamboyant [flæm'bɔɪənt] *adj* sgargiante
flame [fleɪm] *n* fiamma; **old ~** (*col*) vecchia fiamma
flamingo [flə'mɪŋgəu] *n* fenicottero, fiammingo
flammable ['flæməbl] *adj* infiammabile
flan [flæn] *n* (*Brit*) flan *m inv*
Flanders ['flɑːndəz] *n* Fiandre *fpl*
flange [flændʒ] *n* flangia; (*on wheel*) suola

flank [flæŋk] *n* fianco
flannel ['flænl] *n* (*Brit*: *also*: **face flannel**) guanto di spugna; (*fabric*) flanella; **flannels** *npl* pantaloni *mpl* di flanella
flannelette [flænə'lɛt] *n* flanella di cotone
flap [flæp] *n* (*of pocket*) patta; (*of envelope*) lembo; (*Aviat*) flap *m inv* ■ *vt* (*wings*) battere ■ *vi* (*sail, flag*) sbattere; (*col*: *also*: **be in a flap**) essere in agitazione
flapjack ['flæpdʒæk] *n* (*US*: *pancake*) frittella; (*Brit*: *biscuit*) biscotto di avena
flare [flɛəʳ] *n* razzo; (*in skirt etc*) svasatura ▸ **flare up** *vi* andare in fiamme; (*fig*: *person*) infiammarsi di rabbia; (: *revolt*) scoppiare
flared ['flɛəd] *adj* (*trousers*) svasato(-a)
flash [flæʃ] *n* vampata; (*also*: **news flash**) notizia *f* lampo *inv*; (*Phot*) flash *m inv*; (*US*: *torch*) torcia elettrica, lampadina tascabile ■ *vt* accendere e spegnere; (*send*: *message*) trasmettere; (*flaunt*) ostentare ■ *vi* brillare; (*light on ambulance, eyes etc*) lampeggiare; **in a ~** in un lampo; **~ of inspiration** lampo di genio; **to ~ one's headlights** lampeggiare; **he flashed by** *or* **past** ci passò davanti come un lampo
flashback ['flæʃbæk] *n* flashback *m inv*
flashbulb ['flæʃbʌlb] *n* cubo *m* flash *inv*
flash card *n* (*Scol*) scheda didattica
flashcube ['flæʃkju:b] *n* flash *m inv*
flasher ['flæʃəʳ] *n* (*Aut*) lampeggiatore *m*
flashlight ['flæʃlaɪt] *n* (*torch*) lampadina tascabile
flashpoint ['flæʃpɔɪnt] *n* punto di infiammabilità; (*fig*) livello critico
flashy ['flæʃɪ] *adj* (*pej*) vistoso(-a)
flask [flɑ:sk] *n* fiasco; (*Chem*) beuta; (*also*: **vacuum flask**) thermos® *m inv*
flat [flæt] *adj* piatto(-a); (*tyre*) sgonfio(-a), a terra; (*battery*) scarico(-a); (*denial*) netto(-a); (*Mus*) bemolle *inv*; (: *voice*) stonato(-a); (: *instrument*) scordato(-a) ■ *n* (*Brit*: *rooms*) appartamento; (*Mus*) bemolle *m*; (*Aut*) pneumatico sgonfio ■ *adv*: **(to work) ~ out** (lavorare) a più non posso; **~ rate of pay** tariffa unica di pagamento
flat-footed ['flæt'futɪd] *adj*: **to be ~** avere i piedi piatti
flatly ['flætlɪ] *adv* categoricamente, nettamente
flatmate ['flætmeɪt] *n* (*Brit*): **he's my ~** divide l'appartamento con me
flatness ['flætnɪs] *n* (*of land*) assenza di rilievi
flat-pack ['flætpæk] *adj*: **~ furniture** mobili *mpl* in kit ■ *n*: **flat pack** kit *m inv*
flat-screen ['flætskri:n] *adj* a schermo piatto
flatten ['flætn] *vt* (*also*: **flatten out**) appiattire; (*house, city*) abbattere, radere al suolo
flatter ['flætəʳ] *vt* lusingare; (*show to advantage*) donare a
flatterer ['flætərəʳ] *n* adulatore(-trice)
flattering ['flætərɪŋ] *adj* lusinghiero(-a); (*clothes etc*) che dona, che abbellisce
flattery ['flætərɪ] *n* adulazione *f*
flatulence ['flætjuləns] *n* flatulenza
flaunt [flɔ:nt] *vt* fare mostra di
flavour, (*US*) **flavor** ['fleɪvəʳ] *n* gusto, sapore *m* ■ *vt* insaporire, aggiungere sapore a; **vanilla-flavoured** al gusto di vaniglia
flavouring, (*US*) **flavoring** ['fleɪvərɪŋ] *n* essenza (artificiale)
flaw [flɔ:] *n* difetto
flawless ['flɔ:lɪs] *adj* senza difetti
flax [flæks] *n* lino
flaxen ['flæksən] *adj* biondo(-a)
flea [fli:] *n* pulce *f*
flea market *n* mercato delle pulci
fleck [flɛk] *n* (*of mud, paint, colour*) macchiolina; (*of dust*) granello ■ *vt* (*with blood, mud etc*) macchiettare; **brown flecked with white** marrone screziato di bianco
fled [flɛd] *pt, pp of* **flee**
fledgeling, fledgling ['flɛdʒlɪŋ] *n* uccellino
flee (*pt, pp* **fled**) [fli:, flɛd] *vt* fuggire da ■ *vi* fuggire, scappare
fleece [fli:s] *n* vello; (*garment*) pile *m inv* ■ *vt* (*col*) pelare
fleecy ['fli:sɪ] *adj* (*blanket*) soffice; (*cloud*) come ovatta
fleet [fli:t] *n* flotta; (*of lorries etc*) convoglio; (*of cars*) parco
fleeting ['fli:tɪŋ] *adj* fugace, fuggitivo(-a); (*visit*) volante
Flemish ['flɛmɪʃ] *adj* fiammingo(-a) ■ *n* (*Ling*) fiammingo; **the Flemish** *npl* i Fiamminghi
flesh [flɛʃ] *n* carne *f*; (*of fruit*) polpa
flesh wound *n* ferita superficiale
flew [flu:] *pt of* **fly**
flex [flɛks] *n* filo (flessibile) ■ *vt* flettere; (*muscles*) contrarre
flexibility [flɛksɪ'bɪlɪtɪ] *n* flessibilità
flexible ['flɛksəbl] *adj* flessibile
flexitime ['flɛksɪtaɪm] *n* orario flessibile
flick [flɪk] *n* colpetto; *see also* **flicks** ▸ **flick through** *vt fus* sfogliare
flicker ['flɪkəʳ] *vi* tremolare ■ *n* tremolio; **a ~ of light** un breve bagliore
flick knife *n* (*Brit*) coltello a serramanico
flicks *npl*: **the ~** (*col*) il cine
flier ['flaɪəʳ] *n* aviatore *m*
flight [flaɪt] *n* volo; (*escape*) fuga; (*also*: **flight of steps**) scalinata; **to take ~** darsi alla fuga; **to put to ~** mettere in fuga
flight attendant *n* (*US*) steward *m*, hostess *f inv*

f

flight crew *n* equipaggio
flight deck *n* (*Aviat*) cabina di controllo; (*Naut*) ponte *m* di comando
flight path *n* (*of aircraft*) rotta di volo; (*of rocket, projectile*) traiettoria
flight recorder *n* registratore *m* di volo
flimsy ['flɪmzɪ] *adj* (*fabric*) inconsistente; (*excuse*) meschino(-a)
flinch [flɪntʃ] *vi* ritirarsi; **to ~ from** tirarsi indietro di fronte a
fling (*pt, pp* **flung**) [flɪŋ, flʌŋ] *vt* lanciare, gettare ■ *n* (*love affair*) avventura
flint [flɪnt] *n* selce *f*; (*in lighter*) pietrina
flip [flɪp] *n* colpetto ■ *vt* dare un colpetto a; (*US: pancake*) far saltare (in aria) ■ *vi*: **to ~ for sth** (*US*) fare a testa e croce per qc
▸ **flip through** *vt fus* (*book, records*) dare una scorsa a
flippant ['flɪpənt] *adj* senza rispetto, irriverente
flipper ['flɪpə^r] *n* pinna
flip side *n* (*of record*) retro
flirt [flə:t] *vi* flirtare ■ *n* civetta
flirtation [flə:'teɪʃən] *n* flirt *m inv*
flit [flɪt] *vi* svolazzare
float [fləut] *n* galleggiante *m*; (*in procession*) carro; (*sum of money*) somma ■ *vi* galleggiare; (*bather*) fare il morto; (*Comm: currency*) fluttuare ■ *vt* far galleggiare; (*loan, business*) lanciare; **to ~ an idea** ventilare un'idea
floating ['fləutɪŋ] *adj* a galla; **~ vote** voto oscillante; **~ voter** elettore *m* indeciso
flock [flɔk] *n* gregge *m*; (*of people*) folla; (*of birds*) stormo
floe [fləu] *n* (*also*: **ice floe**) banchisa
flog [flɔg] *vt* flagellare
flood [flʌd] *n* alluvione *f*; (*of words, tears etc*) diluvio ■ *vt* inondare, allagare; (*Aut: carburettor*) ingolfare; **in ~** in pieno; **to ~ the market** (*Comm*) inondare il mercato
flooding ['flʌdɪŋ] *n* inondazione *f*
floodlight ['flʌdlaɪt] *n* riflettore *m* ■ *vt* illuminare a giorno
floodlit ['flʌdlɪt] *pt, pp of* **floodlight** ■ *adj* illuminato(-a) a giorno
flood tide *n* alta marea, marea crescente
floodwater ['flʌdwɔ:tə^r] *n* acque *fpl* (*di inondazione*)
floor [flɔ:^r] *n* pavimento; (*storey*) piano; (*of sea, valley*) fondo; (*fig: at meeting*): **the ~** il pubblico ■ *vt* pavimentare; (*knock down*) atterrare; (*baffle*) confondere; (*silence*) far tacere; **on the ~** sul pavimento, per terra; **ground ~**, (*US*) **first ~** pianterreno; **first ~**, (*US*) **second ~** primo piano; **top ~** ultimo piano; **to have the ~** (*speaker*) prendere la parola
floorboard ['flɔ:bɔ:d] *n* tavellone *m* di legno
flooring ['flɔ:rɪŋ] *n* (*floor*) pavimento; (*material*) materiale *m* per pavimentazioni
floor lamp *n* (*US*) lampada a stelo
floor show *n* spettacolo di varietà
floorwalker ['flɔ:wɔ:kə^r] *n* (*esp US*) ispettore *m* di reparto
flop [flɔp] *n* fiasco ■ *vi* (*fail*) far fiasco
floppy ['flɔpɪ] *adj* floscio(-a), molle ■ *n* (*Comput*) = **floppy disk**; **~ hat** cappello floscio
floppy disk *n* floppy disk *m inv*
flora ['flɔ:rə] *n* flora
floral ['flɔ:rl] *adj* floreale
Florence ['flɔrəns] *n* Firenze *f*
Florentine ['flɔrəntaɪn] *adj* fiorentino(-a)
florid ['flɔrɪd] *adj* (*complexion*) florido(-a); (*style*) fiorito(-a)
florist ['flɔrɪst] *n* fioraio(-a); **at the ~'s (shop)** dal fioraio
flotation [fləu'teɪʃən] *n* (*Comm*) lancio
flounce [flauns] *n* balzo
▸ **flounce out** *vi* uscire stizzito(-a)
flounder ['flaundə^r] *vi* annaspare ■ *n* (*Zool*) passera di mare
flour ['flauə^r] *n* farina
flourish ['flʌrɪʃ] *vi* fiorire ■ *vt* brandire ■ *n* abbellimento; svolazzo; (*of trumpets*) fanfara
flourishing ['flʌrɪʃɪŋ] *adj* prosperoso(-a), fiorente
flout [flaut] *vt* (*order*) contravvenire a; (*convention*) sfidare
flow [fləu] *n* flusso; circolazione *f*; (*of river, also Elec*) corrente *f* ■ *vi* fluire; (*traffic, blood in veins*) circolare; (*hair*) scendere
flow chart *n* schema *m* di flusso
flow diagram *n* organigramma *m*
flower ['flauə^r] *n* fiore *m* ■ *vi* fiorire; **in ~** in fiore
flower bed *n* aiuola
flowerpot ['flauəpɔt] *n* vaso da fiori
flowery ['flauərɪ] *adj* fiorito(-a)
flown [fləun] *pp of* **fly**
flu [flu:] *n* influenza
fluctuate ['flʌktjueɪt] *vi* fluttuare, oscillare
fluctuation [flʌktju'eɪʃən] *n* fluttuazione *f*, oscillazione *f*
flue [flu:] *n* canna fumaria
fluency ['flu:ənsɪ] *n* facilità, scioltezza; **his ~ in English** la sua scioltezza nel parlare l'inglese
fluent ['flu:ənt] *adj* (*speech*) facile, sciolto(-a); **he's a ~ speaker/reader** si esprime/legge senza difficoltà; **he speaks ~ Italian, he's ~ in Italian** parla l'italiano correntemente
fluently ['flu:əntlɪ] *adv* con facilità; correntemente
fluff [flʌf] *n* lanugine *f*

fluffy [ˈflʌfɪ] *adj* lanuginoso(-a); (*toy*) di peluche
fluid [ˈflu:ɪd] *adj* fluido(-a) ■ *n* fluido; (*in diet*) liquido
fluid ounce *n* (*Brit*) = *0.028 l; 0.05 pints*
fluke [flu:k] *n* (*col*) colpo di fortuna
flummox [ˈflʌməks] *vt* rendere perplesso(-a)
flung [flʌŋ] *pt, pp of* **fling**
flunky [ˈflʌŋkɪ] *n* tirapiedi *m/f inv*
fluorescent [fluəˈrɛsnt] *adj* fluorescente
fluoride [ˈfluəraɪd] *n* fluoruro
fluorine [ˈfluəri:n] *n* fluoro
flurry [ˈflʌrɪ] *n* (*of snow*) tempesta; **a ~ of activity/excitement** una febbre di attività/un'improvvisa agitazione
flush [flʌʃ] *n* rossore *m*; (*fig*) ebbrezza ■ *vt* ripulire con un getto d'acqua; (*also*: **flush out**: *birds*) far alzare in volo; (: *animals, fig: criminal*) stanare ■ *vi* arrossire ■ *adj*: **~ with** a livello di, pari a; **~ against** aderente a; **hot flushes** (*Med*) vampate *fpl* di calore; **to ~ the toilet** tirare l'acqua
flushed [flʌʃt] *adj* tutto(-a) rosso(-a)
fluster [ˈflʌstə^r] *n* agitazione *f*
flustered [ˈflʌstəd] *adj* sconvolto(-a)
flute [flu:t] *n* flauto
flutter [ˈflʌtə^r] *n* agitazione *f*; (*of wings*) frullio ■ *vi* (*bird*) battere le ali
flux [flʌks] *n*: **in a state of ~** in continuo mutamento
fly [flaɪ] *n* (*insect*) mosca; (*on trousers*: *also*: **flies**) bracchetta ■ *vb* (*pt* **flew**, *pp* **flown**) [flu:, fləun] *vt* pilotare; (*passengers, cargo*) trasportare (in aereo); (*distances*) percorrere ■ *vi* volare; (*passengers*) andare in aereo; (*escape*) fuggire; (*flag*) sventolare; **to ~ open** spalancarsi all'improvviso; **to ~ off the handle** perdere le staffe, uscire dai gangheri
▸ **fly away** *vi* volar via
▸ **fly in** *vi* (*plane*) arrivare; (*person*) arrivare in aereo
▸ **fly off** *vi* volare via
▸ **fly out** *vi* (*plane*) partire; (*person*) partire in aereo
fly-fishing [ˈflaɪfɪʃɪŋ] *n* pesca con la mosca
flying [ˈflaɪɪŋ] *n* (*activity*) aviazione *f*; (*action*) volo ■ *adj*: **~ visit** visita volante; **with ~ colours** con risultati brillanti; **he doesn't like ~** non gli piace viaggiare in aereo
flying buttress *n* arco rampante
flying picket *n* picchetto (*proveniente da fabbriche non direttamente coinvolte nello sciopero*)
flying saucer *n* disco volante
flying squad *n* (*Police*) (squadra) volante *f*
flying start *n*: **to get off to a ~** partire come un razzo
flyleaf [ˈflaɪli:f] *n* risguardo
flyover [ˈflaɪəuvə^r] *n* (*Brit: bridge*) cavalcavia *m inv*
flypast [ˈflaɪpɑ:st] *n* esibizione *f* della pattuglia aerea
flysheet [ˈflaɪʃi:t] *n* (*for tent*) sopratetto
flyweight [ˈflaɪweɪt] *n* (*Sport*) peso *m* mosca *inv*
flywheel [ˈflaɪwi:l] *n* volano
FM *abbr* = **frequency modulation**; (*Brit Mil*) = **Field Marshal**
FMB *n abbr* (*US*) = **Federal Maritime Board**
FMCS *n abbr* (*US*: = *Federal Mediation and Conciliation Services*) *organismo di conciliazione in caso di conflitti sul lavoro*
FO *n abbr* (*Brit*) = **Foreign Office**
foal [fəul] *n* puledro
foam [fəum] *n* schiuma ■ *vi* schiumare
foam rubber *n* gommapiuma®
FOB *abbr* (= *free on board*) franco a bordo
fob [fɔb] *vt*: **to ~ sb off with** appioppare qn con; sbarazzarsi di qn con ■ *n* (*also*: **watch fob**: *chain*) catena per orologio; (: *band of cloth*) nastro per orologio
foc *abbr* (*Brit*) = **free of charge**
focal [ˈfəukəl] *adj* focale
focal point *n* punto focale
focus [ˈfəukəs] *n* (*pl* **focuses**) fuoco; (*of interest*) centro ■ *vt* (*field glasses etc*) mettere a fuoco; (*light rays*) far convergere ■ *vi*: **to ~ on** (*with camera*) mettere a fuoco; (*person*) fissare lo sguardo su; **in ~** a fuoco; **out of ~** sfocato(-a)
focus group *n* (*Pol*) gruppo di discussione, focus group *m inv*
fodder [ˈfɔdə^r] *n* foraggio
FOE *n abbr* (= *Friends of the Earth*) Amici *mpl* della Terra; (*US*: = *Fraternal Order of Eagles*) *organizzazione filantropica*
foe [fəu] *n* nemico
foetus, (*US*) **fetus** [ˈfi:təs] *n* feto
fog [fɔg] *n* nebbia
fogbound [ˈfɔgbaund] *adj* fermo(-a) a causa della nebbia
foggy [ˈfɔgɪ] *adj* nebbioso(-a); **it's ~** c'è nebbia
fog lamp, (*US*) **fog light** *n* (*Aut*) faro *m* antinebbia *inv*
foible [ˈfɔɪbl] *n* debolezza, punto debole
foil [fɔɪl] *vt* confondere, frustrare ■ *n* lamina di metallo; (*also*: **kitchen foil**) foglio di alluminio; (*Fencing*) fioretto; **to act as a ~ to** (*fig*) far risaltare
foist [fɔɪst] *vt*: **to ~ sth on sb** rifilare qc a qn
fold [fəuld] *n* (*bend, crease*) piega; (*Agr*) ovile *m*; (*fig*) gregge *m* ■ *vt* piegare; **to ~ one's arms** incrociare le braccia
▸ **fold up** *vi* (*map etc*) piegarsi; (*business*) crollare ■ *vt* (*map etc*) piegare, ripiegare

folder ['fəuldəʳ] *n* (*for papers*) cartella; cartellina; (*binder*) raccoglitore *m*
folding ['fəuldɪŋ] *adj* (*chair, bed*) pieghevole
foliage ['fəulɪɪdʒ] *n* fogliame *m*
folk [fəuk] *npl* gente *f* ■ *cpd* popolare; **folks** *npl* famiglia
folklore ['fəuklɔːʳ] *n* folclore *m*
folk music *n* musica folk *inv*
folk singer *n* cantante *m/f* folk *inv*
folksong ['fəuksɔŋ] *n* canto popolare
follow ['fɔləu] *vt* seguire ■ *vi* seguire; (*result*) conseguire, risultare; **to ~ sb's advice** seguire il consiglio di qn; **I don't quite ~ you** non ti capisco *or* seguo affatto; **to ~ in sb's footsteps** seguire le orme di qn; **it follows that ...** ne consegue che ...; **he followed suit** lui ha fatto lo stesso
▸ **follow on** *vi* (*continue*): **to ~ on from** seguire
▸ **follow out** *vt* (*implement: idea, plan*) eseguire, portare a termine
▸ **follow through** *vt* = **follow out**
▸ **follow up** *vt* (*victory*) sfruttare; (*letter, offer*) fare seguito a; (*case*) seguire
follower ['fɔləuəʳ] *n* seguace *m/f*, discepolo(-a)
following ['fɔləuɪŋ] *adj* seguente, successivo(-a) ■ *n* seguito, discepoli *mpl*
follow-up ['fɔləuʌp] *n* seguito
folly ['fɔlɪ] *n* pazzia, follia
fond [fɔnd] *adj* (*memory, look*) tenero(-a), affettuoso(-a); **to be ~ of** volere bene a; **she's ~ of swimming** le piace nuotare
fondle ['fɔndl] *vt* accarezzare
fondly ['fɔndlɪ] *adv* (*lovingly*) affettuosamente; (*naïvely*): **he ~ believed that ...** ha avuto l'ingenuità di credere che ...
fondness ['fɔndnɪs] *n* affetto; **~ (for sth)** predilezione *f* (per qc)
font [fɔnt] *n* (*Rel*) fonte *m* (battesimale); (*Typ*) stile *m* di carattere
food [fuːd] *n* cibo
food chain *n* catena alimentare
food mixer *n* frullatore *m*
food poisoning *n* intossicazione *f* alimentare
food processor *n* tritatutto *m inv* elettrico
food stamp *n* (*US*) *buono alimentare dato agli indigenti*
foodstuffs ['fuːdstʌfs] *npl* generi *fpl* alimentari
fool [fuːl] *n* sciocco(-a); (*Hist: of king*) buffone *m*; (*Culin*) frullato ■ *vt* ingannare ■ *vi* (*gen*): **~ around** fare lo sciocco; **to make a ~ of sb** prendere in giro qn; **to make a ~ of o.s.** coprirsi di ridicolo; **you can't ~ me** non mi inganna
▸ **fool about, fool around** *vi* (*waste time*) perdere tempo
foolhardy ['fuːlhɑːdɪ] *adj* avventato(-a)
foolish ['fuːlɪʃ] *adj* scemo(-a), stupido(-a); imprudente
foolishly ['fuːlɪʃlɪ] *adv* stupidamente
foolishness ['fuːlɪʃnɪs] *n* stupidità
foolproof ['fuːlpruːf] *adj* (*plan etc*) sicurissimo(-a)
foolscap ['fuːlskæp] *n* carta protocollo
foot [fut] *n* (*pl* **feet**) [fiːt] piede *m*; (*measure*) piede (*= 304 mm; = 12 inches*); (*of animal*) zampa; (*of page, stairs etc*) fondo ■ *vt* (*bill*) pagare; **on ~** a piedi; **to put one's ~ down** (*Aut*) schiacciare l'acceleratore; (*say no*) imporsi; **to find one's feet** ambientarsi
footage ['futɪdʒ] *n* (*Cine: length*) ≈ metraggio; (*: material*) sequenza
foot and mouth, foot and mouth disease *n* afta epizootica
football ['fuːtbɔːl] *n* pallone *m*; (*sport: Brit*) calcio; (*: US*) football *m* americano
footballer ['fuːtbɔːləʳ] *n* (*Brit*) = **football player**
football ground *n* campo di calcio
football match *n* (*Brit*) partita di calcio
football player *n* (*Brit*) calciatore *m*; (*US*) giocatore *m* di football americano
footbrake ['fuːtbreɪk] *n* freno a pedale
footbridge ['fuːtbrɪdʒ] *n* passerella
foothills ['fuːthɪlz] *npl* contrafforti *fpl*
foothold ['futhəuld] *n* punto d'appoggio
footing ['futɪŋ] *n* (*fig*) posizione *f*; **to lose one's ~** mettere un piede in fallo; **on an equal ~** in condizioni di parità
footlights ['futlaɪts] *npl* luci *fpl* della ribalta
footman ['futmən] *n* lacchè *m inv*
footnote ['futnəut] *n* nota (a piè di pagina)
footpath ['futpɑːθ] *n* sentiero; (*in street*) marciapiede *m*
footprint ['futprɪnt] *n* orma, impronta
footrest ['futrɛst] *n* poggiapiedi *m inv*
footsie ['futsɪ] *n* (*col*): **to play ~ with sb** fare piedino a qn
Footsie ['futsɪ], **Footsie index** ['futsɪ-] *n* (*col*) = **Financial Times Stock Exchange 100 Index**
footsore ['futsɔːʳ] *adj*: **to be ~** avere mal di piedi
footstep ['futstɛp] *n* passo
footwear ['futwɛəʳ] *n* calzatura
FOR *abbr* (*= free on rail*) franco vagone

for [fɔːʳ] *prep* **1** (*indicating destination, intention, purpose*) per; **the train for London** il treno

per Londra; **he went for the paper** è andato a prendere il giornale; **it's time for lunch** è ora di pranzo; **what's it for?** a che serve?; **what for?** (*why*) perché?
2 (*on behalf of, representing*) per; **to work for sb/sth** lavorare per qn/qc; **I'll ask him for you** glielo chiederò a nome tuo; **G for George** ≈ G come George
3 (*because of*) per, a causa di; **for this reason** per questo motivo
4 (*with regard to*) per; **it's cold for July** è freddo per luglio; **for everyone who voted yes, 50 voted no** per ogni voto a favore ce n'erano 50 contro
5 (*in exchange for*) per; **I sold it for £5** l'ho venduto per 5 sterline
6 (*in favour of*) per, a favore di; **are you for or against us?** sei con noi o contro di noi?; **I'm all for it** sono completamente a favore
7 (*referring to distance, time*) per; **there are roadworks for 5 km** ci sono lavori in corso per 5 km; **he was away for 2 years** è stato via per 2 anni; **she will be away for a month** starà via un mese; **it hasn't rained for 3 weeks** non piove da 3 settimane; **can you do it for tomorrow?** può farlo per domani?
8 (*with infinitive clauses*): **it is not for me to decide** non sta a me decidere; **it would be best for you to leave** sarebbe meglio che lei se ne andasse; **there is still time for you to do it** ha ancora tempo per farlo; **for this to be possible ...** perché ciò sia possibile ...
9 (*in spite of*) nonostante; **for all his complaints, he's very fond of her** nonostante tutte le sue lamentele, le vuole molto bene
■ *conj* (*since, as: formal*) dal momento che, poiché

forage ['fɔrɪdʒ] *vi* foraggiare
forage cap *n* bustina
foray ['fɔreɪ] *n* incursione *f*
forbad, forbade [fə'bæd] *pt of* **forbid**
forbearing [fɔː'bɛərɪŋ] *adj* paziente, tollerante
forbid (*pt* **forbad(e)**, *pp* **forbidden**) [fə'bɪd, -'bæd, -'bɪdn] *vt* vietare, interdire; **to ~ sb to do sth** proibire a qn di fare qc
forbidding [fə'bɪdɪŋ] *adj* arcigno(-a), d'aspetto minaccioso
force [fɔːs] *n* forza ■ *vt* forzare; (*obtain by force: smile, confession*) strappare; **the Forces** *npl* (*Brit*) le forze armate; **in ~** (*in large numbers*) in gran numero; (*law*) in vigore; **to come into ~** entrare in vigore; **a ~ 5 wind** un vento forza 5; **to join forces** unire le forze; **the sales ~** (*Comm*) l'effettivo dei rappresentanti; **to ~ sb to do sth** costringere qn a fare qc
▸ **force back** *vt* (*crowd, enemy*) respingere; (*tears*) ingoiare
▸ **force down** *vt* (*food*) sforzarsi di mangiare
forced [fɔːst] *adj* forzato(-a)
force-feed ['fɔːsfiːd] *vt* sottoporre ad alimentazione forzata
forceful ['fɔːsful] *adj* forte, vigoroso(-a)
forcemeat ['fɔːsmiːt] *n* (*Brit Culin*) ripieno
forceps ['fɔːsɪps] *npl* forcipe *m*
forcibly ['fɔːsəblɪ] *adv* con la forza; (*vigorously*) vigorosamente
ford [fɔːd] *n* guado ■ *vt* guadare
fore [fɔːʳ] *n*: **to the ~** in prima linea; **to come to the ~** mettersi in evidenza
forearm ['fɔːrɑːm] *n* avambraccio
forebear ['fɔːbɛəʳ] *n* antenato
foreboding [fɔː'bəudɪŋ] *n* presagio di male
forecast ['fɔːkɑːst] *n* previsione *f*; (*weather forecast*) previsioni *fpl* del tempo ■ *vt* (*irreg: like* **cast**) prevedere
foreclose [fɔː'kləuz] *vt* (*Law: also:* **foreclose on**) sequestrare l'immobile ipotecato di
foreclosure [fɔː'kləuʒəʳ] *n* sequestro di immobile ipotecato
forecourt ['fɔːkɔːt] *n* (*of garage*) corte *f* esterna
forefathers ['fɔːfɑːðəz] *npl* antenati *mpl*, avi *mpl*
forefinger ['fɔːfɪŋgəʳ] *n* (dito) indice *m*
forefront ['fɔːfrʌnt] *n*: **in the ~ of** all'avanguardia di
forego [fɔː'gəu] *vt* = **forgo**
foregoing ['fɔːgəuɪŋ] *adj* precedente
foregone ['fɔːgɔn] *pp of* **forego** ■ *adj*: **it's a ~ conclusion** è una conclusione scontata
foreground ['fɔːgraund] *n* primo piano ■ *cpd* (*Comput*) foreground *inv*, di primo piano
forehand ['fɔːhænd] *n* (*Tennis*) diritto
forehead ['fɔrɪd] *n* fronte *f*
foreign ['fɔrən] *adj* straniero(-a); (*trade*) estero(-a)
foreign body *n* corpo estraneo
foreign currency *n* valuta estera
foreigner ['fɔrənəʳ] *n* straniero(-a)
foreign exchange *n* cambio di valuta; (*currency*) valuta estera
foreign exchange market *n* mercato delle valute
foreign exchange rate *n* cambio
foreign investment *n* investimento all'estero
foreign minister *n* ministro degli Affari esteri
Foreign Office *n* (*Brit*) Ministero degli Esteri
foreign secretary *n* (*Brit*) ministro degli Affari esteri
foreleg ['fɔːlɛg] *n* zampa anteriore

foreman ['fɔːmən] *n* caposquadra *m*; (*Law: of jury*) portavoce *m* della giuria
foremost ['fɔːməust] *adj* principale; più in vista ■ *adv*: **first and ~** innanzitutto
forename ['fɔːneɪm] *n* nome *m* di battesimo
forensic [fə'rɛnsɪk] *adj*: **~ medicine** medicina legale; **~ expert** esperto della (polizia) scientifica
foreplay ['fɔːpleɪ] *n* preliminari *mpl*
forerunner ['fɔːrʌnə^r] *n* precursore *m*
foresee (*pt* **foresaw**, *pp* **foreseen**) [fɔː'siː, -'sɔː, -'siːn] *vt* prevedere
foreseeable [fɔː'siːəbl] *adj* prevedibile
foreseen [fɔː'siːn] *pp of* **foresee**
foreshadow [fɔː'ʃædəu] *vt* presagire, far prevedere
foreshorten [fɔː'ʃɔːtn] *vt* (*figure, scene*) rappresentare in scorcio
foresight ['fɔːsaɪt] *n* previdenza
foreskin ['fɔːskɪn] *n* (*Anat*) prepuzio
forest ['fɔrɪst] *n* foresta
forestall [fɔː'stɔːl] *vt* prevenire
forestry ['fɔrɪstrɪ] *n* silvicoltura
foretaste ['fɔːteɪst] *n* pregustazione *f*
foretell (*pt, pp* **foretold**) [fɔː'tɛl, -'təuld] *vt* predire
forethought ['fɔːθɔːt] *n* previdenza
foretold [fɔː'təuld] *pt, pp of* **foretell**
forever [fə'rɛvə^r] *adv* per sempre; (*fig*) sempre, di continuo
forewarn [fɔː'wɔːn] *vt* avvisare in precedenza
forewent [fɔː'wɛnt] *pt of* **forego**
foreword ['fɔːwəːd] *n* prefazione *f*
forfeit ['fɔːfɪt] *n* ammenda, pena ■ *vt* perdere; (*one's happiness, health*) giocarsi
forgave [fə'geɪv] *pt of* **forgive**
forge [fɔːdʒ] *n* fucina ■ *vt* falsificare; (*signature*) contraffare, falsificare; (*wrought iron*) fucinare, foggiare
▸ **forge ahead** *vi* tirare avanti
forger ['fɔːdʒə^r] *n* contraffattore *m*
forgery ['fɔːdʒərɪ] *n* falso; (*activity*) contraffazione *f*
forget (*pt* **forgot**, *pp* **forgotten**) [fə'gɛt, -'gɔt, -'gɔtn] *vt, vi* dimenticare
forgetful [fə'gɛtful] *adj* di corta memoria; **~ of** dimentico(a) di
forgetfulness [fə'gɛtfulnɪs] *n* smemoratezza; (*oblivion*) oblio
forget-me-not [fə'gɛtmɪnɔt] *n* nontiscordardimé *m inv*
forgive (*pt* **forgave**, *pp* **forgiven**) [fə'gɪv, -'geɪv, -'gɪvn] *vt* perdonare; **to ~ sb for sth/ for doing sth** perdonare qc a qn/a qn di aver fatto qc
forgiveness [fə'gɪvnɪs] *n* perdono
forgiving [fə'gɪvɪŋ] *adj* indulgente
forgo (*pt* **forwent**, *pp* **forgone**) [fɔː'gəu, -'wɛnt, -'gɔn] *vt* rinunciare a
forgot [fə'gɔt] *pt of* **forget**
forgotten [fə'gɔtn] *pp of* **forget**
fork [fɔːk] *n* (*for eating*) forchetta; (*for gardening*) forca; (*of roads*) bivio; (*of railways*) inforcazione *f* ■ *vi* (*road*) biforcarsi
▸ **fork out** (*col: pay*) *vt* sborsare ■ *vi* pagare
forked [fɔːkt] *adj* (*lightning*) a zigzag
fork-lift truck ['fɔːklɪft-] *n* carrello elevatore
forlorn [fə'lɔːn] *adj* (*person*) sconsolato(-a); (*deserted: cottage*) abbandonato(-a); (*desperate: attempt*) disperato(-a)
form [fɔːm] *n* forma; (*Scol*) classe *f*; (*questionnaire*) modulo ■ *vt* formare; (*circle, queue etc*) fare; **in the ~ of** a forma di, sotto forma di; **to be in good ~** (*Sport, fig*) essere in forma; **in top ~** in gran forma; **to ~ part of sth** far parte di qc
formal ['fɔːməl] *adj* (*offer, receipt*) vero(-a) e proprio(-a); (*person*) cerimonioso(-a); (*occasion, dinner*) formale, ufficiale; (*Art, Philosophy*) formale; **~ dress** abito da cerimonia; (*evening dress*) abito da sera
formality [fɔː'mælɪtɪ] *n* formalità *f inv*
formalize ['fɔːməlaɪz] *vt* rendere ufficiale
formally ['fɔːməlɪ] *adv* ufficialmente; formalmente; cerimoniosamente; **to be ~ invited** ricevere un invito ufficiale
format ['fɔːmæt] *n* formato ■ *vt* (*Comput*) formattare
formation [fɔː'meɪʃən] *n* formazione *f*
formative ['fɔːmətɪv] *adj*: **~ years** anni *mpl* formativi
former ['fɔːmə^r] *adj* vecchio(-a) (*before n*), ex *inv* (*before n*); **the ~ president** l'ex presidente; **the ~ ... the latter** quello ... questo; **the ~ Yugoslavia/Soviet Union** l'ex Jugoslavia/ Unione Sovietica
formerly ['fɔːməlɪ] *adv* in passato
form feed *n* (*on printer*) alimentazione *f* modulo
formidable ['fɔːmɪdəbl] *adj* formidabile
formula ['fɔːmjulə] *n* formula; **F~ One** (*Aut*) formula uno
formulate ['fɔːmjuleɪt] *vt* formulare
fornicate ['fɔːnɪkeɪt] *vi* fornicare
forsake (*pt* **forsook**, *pp* **forsaken**) [fə'seɪk, -'suk, -'seɪkən] *vt* abbandonare
fort [fɔːt] *n* forte *m*; **to hold the ~** (*fig*) prendere le redini (della situazione)
forte ['fɔːtɪ] *n* forte *m*
forth [fɔːθ] *adv* in avanti; **to go back and ~** andare avanti e indietro; **and so ~** e così via
forthcoming [fɔːθ'kʌmɪŋ] *adj* prossimo(-a); (*character*) aperto(-a), comunicativo(-a)
forthright ['fɔːθraɪt] *adj* franco(-a), schietto(-a)

forthwith [fɔːθ'wɪθ] *adv* immediatamente, subito
fortieth ['fɔːtɪɪθ] *num* quarantesimo(-a)
fortification [fɔːtɪfɪ'keɪʃən] *n* fortificazione *f*
fortified wine *n* vino ad alta gradazione alcolica
fortify ['fɔːtɪfaɪ] *vt* fortificare
fortitude ['fɔːtɪtjuːd] *n* forza d'animo
fortnight ['fɔːtnaɪt] *n* (*Brit*) quindici giorni *mpl*, due settimane *fpl*; **it's a ~ since ...** sono due settimane da quando ...
fortnightly ['fɔːtnaɪtlɪ] *adj* bimensile ■ *adv* ogni quindici giorni
FORTRAN ['fɔːtræn] *n* FORTRAN *m*
fortress ['fɔːtrɪs] *n* fortezza, rocca
fortuitous [fɔː'tjuːɪtəs] *adj* fortuito(-a)
fortunate ['fɔːtʃənɪt] *adj* fortunato(-a); **he is ~ to have ...** ha la fortuna di avere ...; **it is ~ that** è una fortuna che + *sub*
fortunately ['fɔːtʃənɪtlɪ] *adv* fortunatamente
fortune ['fɔːtʃən] *n* fortuna; **to make a ~** farsi una fortuna
fortuneteller ['fɔːtʃəntɛlə^r] *n* indovino(-a)
forty ['fɔːtɪ] *num* quaranta
forum ['fɔːrəm] *n* foro; (*fig*) luogo di pubblica discussione
forward ['fɔːwəd] *adj* (*movement, position*) in avanti; (*not shy*) sfacciato(-a); (*Comm: delivery, sales, exchange*) a termine ■ *adv* avanti ■ *n* (*Sport*) avanti *m inv* ■ *vt* (*letter*) inoltrare; (*parcel, goods*) spedire; (*fig*) promuovere, appoggiare; **to move ~** avanzare; **"please ~"** "si prega di inoltrare"; **~ planning** programmazione *f* in anticipo
forwards ['fɔːwədz] *adv* avanti
forwent [fɔː'wɛnt] *pt of* **forgo**
fossil ['fɔsl] *adj, n* fossile (*m*); **~ fuel** combustibile *m* fossile
foster ['fɔstə^r] *vt* incoraggiare, nutrire; (*child*) avere in affidamento
foster brother *n* fratellastro
foster child *n* bambino(-a) preso(-a) in affidamento
foster mother *n* madre *f* affidataria
fought [fɔːt] *pt, pp of* **fight**
foul [faul] *adj* (*smell, food*) cattivo(-a); (*weather*) brutto(-a), orribile; (*language*) osceno(-a); (*deed*) infame ■ *n* (*Football*) fallo ■ *vt* sporcare; (*football player*) commettere un fallo su; (*entangle: anchor, propeller*) impigliarsi in
foul play *n* (*Sport*) gioco scorretto; **~ is not suspected** si è scartata l'ipotesi del delitto (*or* dell'attentato *etc*)
found [faund] *pt, pp of* **find** ■ *vt* (*establish*) fondare
foundation [faun'deɪʃən] *n* (*act*) fondazione *f*; (*base*) base *f*; (*also*: **foundation cream**) fondo tinta; **foundations** *npl* (*of building*) fondamenta *fpl*; **to lay the foundations** gettare le fondamenta
foundation stone *n* prima pietra
founder ['faundə^r] *n* fondatore(-trice) ■ *vi* affondare
founding ['faundɪŋ] *adj*: **~ fathers** (*US*) padri *mpl* fondatori; **~ member** socio fondatore
foundry ['faundrɪ] *n* fonderia
fount [faunt] *n* fonte *f*; (*Typ*) stile *m* di carattere
fountain ['fauntɪn] *n* fontana
fountain pen *n* penna stilografica
four [fɔː^r] *num* quattro; **on all fours** a carponi
four-letter word ['fɔːlɛtə-] *n* parolaccia
four-poster ['fɔː'pəustə^r] *n* (*also*: **four-poster bed**) letto a quattro colonne
foursome ['fɔːsəm] *n* partita a quattro; uscita in quattro
fourteen ['fɔː'tiːn] *num* quattordici
fourth [fɔːθ] *num* quarto(-a) ■ *n* (*Aut*: *also*: **fourth gear**) quarta
four-wheel drive ['fɔːwiːl-] *n* (*Aut*): **with ~** con quattro ruote motrici
fowl [faul] *n* pollame *m*; volatile *m*
fox [fɔks] *n* volpe *f* ■ *vt* confondere
fox fur *n* volpe *f*, pelliccia di volpe
foxglove ['fɔksglʌv] *n* (*Bot*) digitale *f*
fox-hunting ['fɔkshʌntɪŋ] *n* caccia alla volpe
foyer ['fɔɪeɪ] *n* atrio; (*Theat*) ridotto
FPA *n abbr* (*Brit*: = *Family Planning Association*) ≈ A.I.E.D. *f* (= *Associazione Italiana Educazione Demografica*)
Fr. *abbr* (*Rel*) = **father**; **friar**
fr. *abbr* (= *franc*) fr.
fracas ['frækɑː] *n* rissa, lite *f*
fraction ['frækʃən] *n* frazione *f*
fractionally ['frækʃnəlɪ] *adv* un tantino, minimamente
fractious ['frækʃəs] *adj* irritabile
fracture ['fræktʃə^r] *n* frattura ■ *vt* fratturare
fragile ['frædʒaɪl] *adj* fragile
fragment ['frægmənt] *n* frammento
fragmentary ['frægməntərɪ] *adj* frammentario(-a)
fragrance ['freɪgrəns] *n* fragranza, profumo
fragrant ['freɪgrənt] *adj* fragrante, profumato(-a)
frail [freɪl] *adj* debole, delicato(-a)
frame [freɪm] *n* (*of building*) armatura; (*of human, animal*) ossatura, corpo; (*of picture*) cornice *f*; (*of door, window*) telaio; (*of spectacles*: *also*: **frames**) montatura ■ *vt* (*picture*)

f

incorniciare; **to ~ sb** *(col)* incastrare qn; **~ of mind** stato d'animo
framework ['freɪmwəːk] *n* struttura
France [frɑːns] *n* Francia
franchise ['fræntʃaɪz] *n* *(Pol)* diritto di voto; *(Comm)* concessione *f*
franchisee [fræntʃaɪ'ziː] *n* concessionaria
franchiser ['fræntʃaɪzəʳ] *n* concedente *m*
frank [fræŋk] *adj* franco(-a), aperto(-a) ■ *vt* *(letter)* affrancare
Frankfurt ['fræŋkfəːt] *n* Francoforte *f*
frankfurter ['fræŋkfəːtəʳ] *n* würstel *m inv*
franking machine ['frænkɪŋ-] *n* macchina affrancatrice
frankly ['fræŋklɪ] *adv* francamente, sinceramente
frankness ['fræŋknɪs] *n* franchezza
frantic ['fræntɪk] *adj* *(activity, pace)* frenetico(-a); *(desperate: need, desire)* pazzo(-a), sfrenato(-a); *(: search)* affannoso(-a); *(person)* fuori di sé
frantically ['fræntɪklɪ] *adv* freneticamente; affannosamente
fraternal [frə'təːnl] *adj* fraterno(-a)
fraternity [frə'təːnɪtɪ] *n* *(club)* associazione *f*; *(spirit)* fratellanza
fraternize ['frætənaɪz] *vi* fraternizzare
fraud [frɔːd] *n* truffa; *(Law)* frode *f*; *(person)* impostore(-a)
fraudulent ['frɔːdjulənt] *adj* fraudolento(-a)
fraught [frɔːt] *adj* *(tense)* teso(-a); **~ with** pieno(a) di, intriso(a) da
fray [freɪ] *n* baruffa ■ *vt* logorare ■ *vi* logorarsi; **to return to the ~** tornare nella mischia; **tempers were getting frayed** cominciavano ad innervosirsi; **her nerves were frayed** aveva i nervi a pezzi
FRB *n abbr* (US) = **Federal Reserve Board**
FRCM *n abbr* (Brit) = **Fellow of the Royal College of Music**
FRCO *n abbr* (Brit) = **Fellow of the Royal College of Organists**
FRCP *n abbr* (Brit) = **Fellow of the Royal College of Physicians**
FRCS *n abbr* (Brit) = **Fellow of the Royal College of Surgeons**
freak [friːk] *n* fenomeno, mostro; *(col: enthusiast)* fanatico(-a) ■ *adj* *(storm, conditions)* anormale; *(victory)* inatteso(-a)
▸ **freak out** *vi* *(col)* andare fuori di testa
freakish ['friːkɪʃ] *adj* *(result, appearance)* strano(-a), bizzarro(-a); *(weather)* anormale
freckle ['frɛkl] *n* lentiggine *f*
free [friː] *adj* libero(-a); *(gratis)* gratuito(-a); *(liberal)* generoso(-a) ■ *vt* *(prisoner, jammed person)* liberare; *(jammed object)* districare; **~ (of charge)** gratuitamente; **admission ~** entrata libera; **to give sb a ~ hand** dare carta bianca a qn; **~ and easy** rilassato
freebie ['friːbɪ] *n* *(col)*: **it's a ~** è in omaggio
freedom ['friːdəm] *n* libertà
freedom fighter *n* combattente *m/f* per la libertà
free enterprise *n* liberalismo economico
Freefone® ['friːfəun] *n* *(Brit)* ≈ numero verde
free-for-all ['friːfərɔːl] *n* parapiglia *m* generale
free gift *n* regalo, omaggio
freehold ['friːhəuld] *n* proprietà assoluta
free kick *n* *(Sport)* calcio libero
freelance ['friːlɑːns] *adj* indipendente; **~ work** collaborazione *f* esterna
freeloader ['friːləudəʳ] *n* *(pej)* scroccone(-a)
freely ['friːlɪ] *adv* liberamente; *(liberally)* liberalmente
free-market economy [friː'mɑːkɪt-] *n* economia di libero mercato
freemason ['friːmeɪsn] *n* massone *m*
freemasonry ['friːmeɪsnrɪ] *n* massoneria
freepost ['friːpəust] *n* affrancatura a carica del destinatario
free-range ['friː'reɪndʒ] *adj* *(eggs)* di gallina ruspante
free sample *n* campione *m* gratuito
free speech *n* libertà di parola
freestyle ['friːstaɪl] *n* *(in swimming)* stile *m* libero
free trade *n* libero scambio
freeway ['friːweɪ] *n* *(US)* superstrada
freewheel [friː'wiːl] *vi* andare a ruota libera
freewheeling [friː'wiːlɪŋ] *adj* a ruota libera
free will *n* libero arbitrio; **of one's own ~** di spontanea volontà
freeze [friːz] *vb* *(pt* **froze**, *pp* **frozen**) [frəuz, 'frəuzn] *vi* gelare ■ *vt* gelare; *(food)* congelare; *(prices, salaries)* bloccare ■ *n* gelo; blocco
▸ **freeze over** *vi* *(lake, river)* ghiacciarsi; *(windows, windscreen)* coprirsi di ghiaccio
▸ **freeze up** *vi* gelarsi
freeze-dried ['friːzdraɪd] *adj* liofilizzato(-a)
freezer ['friːzəʳ] *n* congelatore *m*
freezing ['friːzɪŋ] *adj*: **I'm ~** mi sto congelando ■ *n* *(also:* **freezing point**) punto di congelamento; **3 degrees below ~** 3 gradi sotto zero
freight [freɪt] *n* *(goods)* merce *f*, merci *fpl*; *(money charged)* spese *fpl* di trasporto; **~ forward** spese a carico del destinatario; **~ inward** spese di trasporto sulla merce in entrata
freight car *n* *(US)* carro *m* merci *inv*
freighter ['freɪtəʳ] *n* *(Naut)* nave *f* da carico

freight forwarder [-'fɔːwədə^r] *n* spedizioniere *m*
freight train *n* (*US*) treno *m* merci *inv*
French [frɛntʃ] *adj* francese ■ *n* (*Ling*) francese *m*; **the French** *npl* i Francesi
French bean *n* fagiolino
French Canadian *adj, n* franco-canadese (*m/f*)
French dressing *n* (*Culin*) condimento per insalata
French fried potatoes, (*US*) **French fries** *npl* patate *fpl* fritte
French Guiana [-gar'ænə] *n* Guiana francese
French loaf *n* ≈ filoncino
Frenchman ['frɛntʃmən] *n* francese *m*
French Riviera *n*: **the ~** la Costa Azzurra
French stick *n* baguette *f inv*
French window *n* portafinestra
Frenchwoman ['frɛntʃwumən] *n* francese *f*
frenetic [frə'nɛtɪk] *adj* frenetico(-a)
frenzy ['frɛnzɪ] *n* frenesia
frequency ['friːkwənsɪ] *n* frequenza
frequency modulation *n* modulazione *f* di frequenza
frequent *adj* ['friːkwənt] frequente ■ *vt* [frɪ'kwɛnt] frequentare
frequently ['friːkwəntlɪ] *adv* frequentemente, spesso
fresco ['frɛskəu] *n* affresco
fresh [frɛʃ] *adj* fresco(-a); (*new*) nuovo(-a); (*cheeky*) sfacciato(-a); **to make a ~ start** cominciare da capo
freshen ['frɛʃən] *vi* (*wind, air*) rinfrescare
▸ **freshen up** *vi* rinfrescarsi
freshener ['frɛʃnə^r] *n*: **skin ~** tonico rinfrescante; **air ~** deodorante *m* per ambienti
fresher ['frɛʃə^r] *n* (*Brit Scol: col*) = **freshman**
freshly ['frɛʃlɪ] *adv* di recente, di fresco
freshman ['frɛʃmən] *n* (*Scol*) matricola
freshness ['frɛʃnɪs] *n* freschezza
freshwater ['frɛʃwɔːtə^r] *adj* (*fish*) d'acqua dolce
fret [frɛt] *vi* agitarsi, affliggersi
fretful ['frɛtful] *adj* (*child*) irritabile
Freudian ['frɔɪdɪən] *adj* freudiano(-a); **~ slip** lapsus *m inv* freudiano
FRG *n abbr* = **Federal Republic of Germany**
Fri. *abbr* (= *Friday*) ven.
friar ['fraɪə^r] *n* frate *m*
friction ['frɪkʃən] *n* frizione *f*, attrito
friction feed *n* (*on printer*) trascinamento ad attrito
Friday ['fraɪdɪ] *n* venerdì *m inv*; *see also* **Tuesday**
fridge [frɪdʒ] *n* (*Brit*) frigo, frigorifero
fridge-freezer ['frɪdʒ'friːzə^r] *n* freezer *m inv*
fried [fraɪd] *pt, pp of* **fry** ■ *adj* fritto(-a); **~ egg** uovo fritto
friend [frɛnd] *n* amico(-a); **to make friends with** fare amicizia con ■ *vt* (*Internet*) aggiungere come amico
friendliness ['frɛndlɪnɪs] *n* amichevolezza
friendly ['frɛndlɪ] *adj* amichevole ■ *n* (*also*: **friendly match**) partita amichevole; **to be ~ with** essere amico di; **to be ~ to** essere cordiale con
friendly fire *n* fuoco amico
friendly society *n* società *f inv* di mutuo soccorso
friendship ['frɛndʃɪp] *n* amicizia
frieze [friːz] *n* fregio
frigate ['frɪgɪt] *n* (*Naut: modern*) fregata
fright [fraɪt] *n* paura, spavento; **to take ~** spaventarsi; **she looks a ~!** guarda com'è conciata!
frighten ['fraɪtn] *vt* spaventare, far paura a
▸ **frighten away, frighten off** *vt* (*birds, children etc*) scacciare (facendogli paura)
frightened ['fraɪtnd] *adj*: **to be ~ (of)** avere paura (di)
frightening ['fraɪtnɪŋ] *adj* spaventoso(-a), pauroso(-a)
frightful ['fraɪtful] *adj* orribile
frightfully ['fraɪtfulɪ] *adv* terribilmente; **I'm ~ sorry** mi dispiace moltissimo
frigid ['frɪdʒɪd] *adj* (*woman*) frigido(-a)
frigidity [frɪ'dʒɪdɪtɪ] *n* frigidità
frill [frɪl] *n* balza; **no frills** (*fig*) senza fronzoli
frilly ['frɪlɪ] *adj* (*clothes, lampshade*) pieno(-a) di fronzoli
fringe [frɪndʒ] *n* frangia; (*edge: of forest etc*) margine *m*; (*fig*): **on the ~** al margine
fringe benefits *npl* vantaggi *mpl*
fringe theatre *n* teatro d'avanguardia
Frisbee® ['frɪzbɪ] *n* frisbee® *m inv*
frisk [frɪsk] *vt* perquisire
frisky ['frɪskɪ] *adj* vivace, vispo(-a)
fritter ['frɪtə^r] *n* frittella
▸ **fritter away** *vt* sprecare
frivolity [frɪ'vɔlɪtɪ] *n* frivolezza
frivolous ['frɪvələs] *adj* frivolo(-a)
frizzy ['frɪzɪ] *adj* crespo(-a)
fro [frəu] *adv*: **to and ~** avanti e indietro
frock [frɔk] *n* vestito
frog [frɔg] *n* rana; **to have a ~ in one's throat** avere la voce rauca
frogman ['frɔgmən] *n* uomo *m* rana *inv*
frogmarch ['frɔgmɑːtʃ] *vt* (*Brit*): **to ~ sb in/out** portar qn dentro/fuori con la forza
frolic ['frɔlɪk] *vi* sgambettare

KEYWORD

from [frɔm] *prep* **1** (*indicating starting place, origin etc*) da; **where do you come from?, where**

are you from? da dove viene?, di dov'è?; **where has he come from?** da dove arriva?; **from London to Glasgow** da Londra a Glasgow; **a letter from my sister** una lettera da mia sorella; **tell him from me that ...** gli dica da parte mia che ...
2 (*indicating time*) da; **from one o'clock to** *or* **until** *or* **till two** dall'una alle due; **(as) from Friday** a partire da venerdì; **from January (on)** da gennaio, a partire da gennaio
3 (*indicating distance*) da; **the hotel is 1 km from the beach** l'albergo è a 1 km dalla spiaggia
4 (*indicating price, number etc*) da; **from a pound** da una sterlina in su; **prices range from £10 to £50** i prezzi vanno dalle 10 alle 50 sterline
5 (*indicating difference*) da; **he can't tell red from green** non sa distinguere il rosso dal verde
6 (*because of, on the basis of*): **from what he says** da quanto dice lui; **weak from hunger** debole per la fame

frond [frɔnd] *n* fronda
front [frʌnt] *n* (*of house, dress*) davanti *m inv*; (*of train*) testa; (*of book*) copertina; (*promenade*: *also*: **sea front**) lungomare *m*; (*Mil, Pol, Meteor*) fronte *m*; (*fig: appearances*) fronte *f* ■ *adj* primo(-a); anteriore, davanti *inv* ■ *vi*: **to ~ onto sth** dare su qc, guardare verso qc; **in ~ (of)** davanti (a)
frontage ['frʌntɪdʒ] *n* facciata
frontal ['frʌntl] *adj* frontale
front bench *n posti in Parlamento occupati dai frontbencher*; *vedi nota*

FRONT BENCH

Nel Parlamento britannico, si chiamano *front bench* gli scanni della "House of Commons" che si trovano alla sinistra e alla destra dello "Speaker" davanti ai "backbenches". I *front bench* sono occupati dai "frontbenchers", parlamentari che ricoprono una carica di governo o che fanno parte dello "shadow cabinet" dell'opposizione.

frontbencher ['frʌnt'bɛntʃəʳ] *n* (*Brit*) *parlamentare con carica al governo o all'opposizione*
front desk *n* (*US: in hotel*) reception *f inv*; (*: at doctor's*) accettazione *f*
front door *n* porta d'entrata; (*of car*) sportello anteriore
frontier ['frʌntɪəʳ] *n* frontiera
frontispiece ['frʌntɪspiːs] *n* frontespizio
front page *n* prima pagina
front room *n* (*Brit*) salotto
front runner *n* (*fig*) favorito(-a)
front-wheel drive ['frʌntwiːl-] *n* trasmissione *f* anteriore
frost [frɔst] *n* gelo; (*also*: **hoarfrost**) brina
frostbite ['frɔstbaɪt] *n* congelamento
frosted ['frɔstɪd] *adj* (*glass*) smerigliato(-a); (*US: cake*) glassato(-a)
frosting ['frɔstɪŋ] *n* (*US: on cake*) glassa
frosty ['frɔstɪ] *adj* (*window*) coperto(-a) di ghiaccio; (*welcome*) gelido(-a)
froth [frɔθ] *n* spuma; schiuma
frown [fraun] *n* cipiglio ■ *vi* accigliarsi
▸ **frown on** *vt fus* (*fig*) disapprovare
froze [frəuz] *pt of* **freeze**
frozen ['frəuzn] *pp of* **freeze** ■ *adj* (*food*) congelato(-a); (*Comm: assets*) bloccato(-a)
FRS *n abbr* (*Brit*) = **Fellow of the Royal Society**; (*US*: = *Federal Reserve System*) *sistema bancario degli Stati Uniti*
frugal ['fruːgəl] *adj* frugale; (*person*) economo(-a)
fruit [fruːt] *n* (*pl inv*) frutto; (*collectively*) frutta
fruiterer ['fruːtərəʳ] *n* fruttivendolo; **at the ~'s (shop)** dal fruttivendolo
fruit fly *n* mosca della frutta
fruitful ['fruːtful] *adj* fruttuoso(-a); (*plant*) fruttifero(-a); (*soil*) fertile
fruition [fruː'ɪʃən] *n*: **to come to ~** realizzarsi
fruit juice *n* succo di frutta
fruitless ['fruːtlɪs] *adj* (*fig*) vano(-a), inutile
fruit machine *n* (*Brit*) macchina *f* mangiasoldi *inv*
fruit salad *n* macedonia
frump [frʌmp] *n*: **to feel a ~** sentirsi infagottato (a)
frustrate [frʌs'treɪt] *vt* frustrare
frustrated [frʌs'treɪtɪd] *adj* frustrato(-a)
frustrating [frʌs'treɪtɪŋ] *adj* (*job*) frustrante; (*day*) disastroso(-a)
frustration [frʌs'treɪʃən] *n* frustrazione *f*
fry (*pt, pp* **fried**) [fraɪ, -d] *vt* friggere ■ *npl*: **the small ~** i pesci piccoli
frying pan ['fraɪɪŋ-] *n* padella
FT *n abbr* (*Brit*: = *Financial Times*) *giornale finanziario*; **the FT index** l'indice FT
ft. *abbr* = **foot; feet**
FTC *n abbr* (*US*) = **Federal Trade Commission**
FT-SE 100 Index *n abbr* = **Financial Times Stock Exchange 100 Index**
fuchsia ['fjuːʃə] *n* fucsia
fuck [fʌk] *vt, vi* (*col!*) fottere (*!*); **~ off!** vaffanculo! (*!*)
fuddled ['fʌdld] *adj* (*muddled*) confuso(-a); (*col: tipsy*) brillo(-a)
fuddy-duddy ['fʌdɪdʌdɪ] *n* (*pej*) parruccone *m*
fudge [fʌdʒ] *n* (*Culin*) *specie di caramella a base di latte, burro e zucchero* ■ *vt* (*issue, problem*) evitare

fuel [fjuəl] *n* (*for heating*) combustibile *m*; (*for propelling*) carburante *m* ■ *vt* (*furnace etc*) alimentare; (*aircraft, ship etc*) rifornire di carburante
fuel oil *n* nafta
fuel poverty *n* povertà energetica
fuel pump *n* (*Aut*) pompa del carburante
fuel tank *n* deposito *m* nafta *inv*; (*on vehicle*) serbatoio (della benzina)
fug [fʌg] *n* (*Brit*) aria viziata
fugitive ['fju:dʒɪtɪv] *n* fuggitivo(-a), profugo(-a); (*from prison*) evaso(-a)
fulfil, (*US*) **fulfill** [ful'fɪl] *vt* (*function*) compiere; (*order*) eseguire; (*wish, desire*) soddisfare, appagare
fulfilled [ful'fɪld] *adj* (*person*) realizzato(-a), soddisfatto(-a)
fulfilment, (*US*) **fulfillment** [ful'fɪlmənt] *n* (*of wishes*) soddisfazione *f*, appagamento
full [ful] *adj* pieno(-a); (*details, skirt*) ampio(-a); (*price*) intero(-a) ■ *adv*: **to know ~ well that** sapere benissimo che; **~ (up)** (*hotel etc*) al completo; **I'm ~ (up)** sono pieno; **a ~ two hours** due ore intere; **at ~ speed** a tutta velocità; **in ~** per intero; **to pay in ~** pagare tutto; **~ name** nome *m* e cognome *m*; **~ employment** piena occupazione
fullback ['fulbæk] *n* (*Rugby, Football*) terzino
full-blooded ['ful'blʌdɪd] *adj* (*vigorous: attack*) energico(-a); (*virile: male*) virile
full-cream ['ful'kri:m] *adj*: **~ milk** (*Brit*) latte *m* intero
full-grown ['ful'grəun] *adj* maturo(-a)
full-length ['ful'lɛŋθ] *adj* (*portrait*) in piedi; (*film*) a lungometraggio
full moon *n* luna piena
full-scale ['fulskeɪl] *adj* (*plan, model*) in grandezza naturale; (*search, retreat*) su vasta scala
full-sized ['ful'saɪzd] *adj* (*portrait etc*) a grandezza naturale
full stop *n* punto
full-time ['ful'taɪm] *adj, adv* (*work*) a tempo pieno ■ *n* (*Sport*) fine *f* partita
fully ['fulɪ] *adv* interamente, pienamente, completamente; (*at least*): **~ as big** almeno così grosso
fully-fledged ['fulɪ'flɛdʒd] *adj* (*bird*) adulto(-a); (*fig: teacher, member etc*) a tutti gli effetti
fulsome ['fulsəm] *adj* (*pej: praise*) esagerato(-a), eccessivo(-a); (*: manner*) insincero
fumble ['fʌmbl] *vi* brancolare, andare a tentoni ■ *vt* (*ball*) lasciarsi sfuggire
▸ **fumble with** *vt fus* trafficare
fume [fju:m] *vi* essere furioso(-a); **fumes** *npl* esalazioni *fpl*, vapori *mpl*
fumigate ['fju:mɪgeɪt] *vt* suffumicare
fun [fʌn] *n* divertimento, spasso; **to have ~** divertirsi; **for ~** per scherzo; **it's not much ~** non è molto divertente; **to make ~ of** prendersi gioco di
function ['fʌŋkʃən] *n* funzione *f*; cerimonia, ricevimento ■ *vi* funzionare; **to ~ as** fungere da, funzionare da
functional ['fʌŋkʃənl] *adj* funzionale
function key *n* (*Comput*) tasto di funzioni
fund [fʌnd] *n* fondo, cassa; (*source*) fondo; (*store*) riserva; **funds** *npl* (*money*) fondi *mpl*
fundamental [fʌndə'mɛntl] *adj* fondamentale; **fundamentals** *npl* basi *fpl*
fundamentalism [fʌndə'mɛntəlɪzəm] *n* fondamentalismo
fundamentalist [fʌndə'mɛntəlɪst] *n* fondamentalista *m/f*
fundamentally [fʌndə'mɛntəlɪ] *adv* essenzialmente, fondamentalmente
funding ['fʌndɪŋ] *n* finanziamento
fund-raising ['fʌndreɪzɪŋ] *n* raccolta di fondi
funeral ['fju:nərəl] *n* funerale *m*
funeral director *n* impresario di pompe funebri
funeral parlour *n* impresa di pompe funebri
funeral service *n* ufficio funebre
funereal [fju:'nɪərɪəl] *adj* funereo(-a), lugubre
fun fair *n* luna park *m inv*
fungus (*pl* **fungi**) ['fʌŋgəs, -gaɪ] *n* fungo; (*mould*) muffa
funicular [fju:'nɪkjulə[r]] *adj* (*also*: **funicular railway**) funicolare *f*
funky ['fʌŋkɪ] *adj* (*music*) funky *inv*; (*col: excellent*) figo(-a)
funnel ['fʌnl] *n* imbuto; (*of ship*) ciminiera
funnily ['fʌnɪlɪ] *adv* in modo divertente; (*oddly*) stranamente
funny ['fʌnɪ] *adj* divertente, buffo(-a); (*strange*) strano(-a), bizzarro(-a)
funny bone *n* osso cubitale
fun run *n* marcia non competitiva
fur [fə:[r]] *n* pelo; pelliccia; pelle *f*; (*Brit: in kettle etc*) deposito calcare
fur coat *n* pelliccia
furious ['fjuərɪəs] *adj* furioso(-a); (*effort*) accanito(-a); (*argument*) violento(-a)
furiously ['fjuərɪəslɪ] *adv* furiosamente; accanitamente
furl [fə:l] *vt* (*sail*) piegare
furlong ['fə:lɔŋ] *n* 201.17 *m* (*termine ippico*)
furlough ['fə:ləu] *n* (*US*) congedo, permesso
furnace ['fə:nɪs] *n* fornace *f*
furnish ['fə:nɪʃ] *vt* ammobiliare; (*supply*) fornire; **furnished flat** *or* (*US*) **apartment** appartamento ammobiliato

furnishings ['fə:nɪʃɪŋz] *npl* mobili *mpl*, mobilia
furniture ['fə:nɪtʃə^r] *n* mobili *mpl*; **piece of ~** mobile *m*
furore [fjuə'rɔ:rɪ] *n* (*protests*) scalpore *m*; (*enthusiasm*) entusiasmo
furrier ['fʌrɪə^r] *n* pellicciaio(-a)
furrow ['fʌrəu] *n* solco ■ *vt* (*forehead*) segnare di rughe
furry ['fə:rɪ] *adj* (*animal*) peloso(-a); (*toy*) di peluche
further ['fə:ðə^r] *adj* supplementare, altro(-a); nuovo(-a); più lontano(-a) ■ *adv* più lontano; (*more*) di più; (*moreover*) inoltre ■ *vt* favorire, promuovere; **until ~ notice** fino a nuovo avviso; **how much ~ is it?** quanto manca *or* dista?; **~ to your letter of ...** (*Comm*) con riferimento alla vostra lettera del ...; **to ~ one's interests** fare i propri interessi
further education *n* ≈ corsi *mpl* di formazione
furthermore [fə:ðə'mɔ:^r] *adv* inoltre, per di più
furthermost ['fə:ðəməust] *adj* più lontano(-a)
furthest ['fə:ðɪst] *adv superlative of* **far**
furtive ['fə:tɪv] *adj* furtivo(-a)
fury ['fjuərɪ] *n* furore *m*
fuse, (*US*) **fuze** [fju:z] *n* fusibile *m*; (*for bomb etc*) miccia, spoletta ■ *vt* fondere; (*Elec*): **to ~ the lights** far saltare i fusibili ■ *vi* fondersi; **a ~ has blown** è saltato un fusibile
fuse box *n* cassetta dei fusibili
fuselage ['fju:zəlɑ:ʒ] *n* fusoliera
fuse wire *n* filo (di fusibile)
fusillade [fju:zɪ'leɪd] *n* scarica di fucileria; (*fig*) fuoco di fila, serie *f inv* incalzante
fusion ['fju:ʒən] *n* fusione *f*
fuss [fʌs] *n* chiasso, trambusto, confusione *f*; (*complaining*) storie *fpl* ■ *vt* (*person*) infastidire, scocciare ■ *vi* agitarsi; **to make a ~** fare delle storie; **to make a ~ of sb** coprire qn di attenzioni
▸ **fuss over** *vt fus* (*person*) circondare di premure
fusspot ['fʌspɔt] *n* (*col*): **he's such a ~** fa sempre tante storie
fussy ['fʌsɪ] *adj* (*person*) puntiglioso(-a), esigente; che fa le storie; (*dress*) carico(-a) di fronzoli; (*style*) elaborato(-a); **I'm not ~** (*col*) per me è lo stesso
fusty ['fʌstɪ] *adj* (*pej*: *archaic*) stantio(-a); (: *smell*) che sa di stantio
futile ['fju:taɪl] *adj* futile
futility [fju:'tɪlɪtɪ] *n* futilità
futon ['fu:tɔn] *n* futon *m inv*, letto giapponese
future ['fju:tʃə^r] *adj* futuro(-a) ■ *n* futuro, avvenire *m*; (*Ling*) futuro; **in ~** in futuro; **in the near ~** in un prossimo futuro; **in the immediate ~** nell'immediato futuro
futures ['fju:tʃəz] *npl* (*Comm*) operazioni *fpl* a termine
futuristic [fju:tʃə'rɪstɪk] *adj* futuristico(-a)
fuze [fju:z] *n, vt, vi* (*US*) = **fuse**
fuzzy ['fʌzɪ] *adj* (*Phot*) indistinto(-a), sfocato(-a); (*hair*) crespo(-a)
fwd. *abbr* = **forward**
fwy *abbr* (*US*) = **freeway**
FY *abbr* = **fiscal year**
FYI *abbr* = **for your information**

Gg

G, g [dʒiː] *n* (*letter*) G, g *f or m inv*; (*Mus*): **G** sol *m*; **G for George** ≈ G come Genova
G *n abbr* (*Brit Scol*: *mark*: = *good*) ≈ buono; (*US Cine*: = *general audience*) per tutti
g *abbr* (= *gram, gravity*) g
G8 *n abbr* (*Pol*: = *Group of Eight*) G8 *m*
G20 *n abbr* (*Pol*: = *Group of Twenty*) G20 *m*
GA *abbr* (*US Post*) = **Georgia**
gab [gæb] *n* (*col*): **to have the gift of the ~** avere parlantina
gabble ['gæbl] *vi* borbottare; farfugliare
gaberdine [gæbə'diːn] *n* gabardine *m inv*
gable ['geɪbl] *n* frontone *m*
Gabon [gə'bɒn] *n* Gabon *m*
gad about [gæd-] *vi* (*col*) svolazzare (qua e là)
gadget ['gædʒɪt] *n* aggeggio
Gaelic ['geɪlɪk] *adj* gaelico(-a) ■ *n* (*language*) gaelico
gaffe [gæf] *n* gaffe *f inv*
gaffer ['gæfə^r] *n* (*Brit col*) capo
gag [gæg] *n* bavaglio; (*joke*) facezia, scherzo ■ *vt* (*prisoner etc*) imbavagliare ■ *vi* (*choke*) soffocare
gaga ['gɑːgɑː] *adj*: **to go ~** rimbambirsi
gage [geɪdʒ] *n, vt* (*US*) = **gauge**
gaiety ['geɪɪtɪ] *n* gaiezza
gaily ['geɪlɪ] *adv* allegramente
gain [geɪn] *n* guadagno, profitto ■ *vt* guadagnare ■ *vi* (*watch*) andare avanti; **to ~ in/by** aumentare di/con; **to ~ 3lbs (in weight)** aumentare di 3 libbre; **to ~ ground** guadagnare terreno
▸ **gain (up)on** *vt fus* accorciare le distanze da, riprendere
gainful ['geɪnful] *adj* profittevole, lucrativo(-a)
gainfully ['geɪnfəlɪ] *adv*: **to be ~ employed** avere un lavoro retribuito
gainsay [geɪn'seɪ] *vt* (*irreg*: *like* **say**) contraddire; negare
gait [geɪt] *n* andatura
gal. *abbr* = **gallon**
gala ['gɑːlə] *n* gala; **swimming ~** manifestazione *f* di nuoto
Galapagos Islands [gə'læpəgəs-] *npl*: **the ~** le isole Galapagos
galaxy ['gæləksɪ] *n* galassia
gale [geɪl] *n* vento forte; burrasca; **~ force 10** vento forza 10
gall [gɔːl] *n* (*Anat*) bile *f*; (*fig*: *impudence*) fegato, faccia ■ *vt* urtare (i nervi a)
gall. *abbr* = **gallon**
gallant ['gælənt] *adj* valoroso(-a); (*towards ladies*) galante, cortese
gallantry ['gæləntrɪ] *n* valore *m* militare; galanteria, cortesia
gall bladder ['gɔːl-] *n* cistifellea
galleon ['gælɪən] *n* galeone *m*
gallery ['gælərɪ] *n* galleria; loggia; (*for spectators*) tribuna; (*in theatre*) loggione *m*, balconata; (*also*: **art gallery**: *state-owned*) museo; (: *private*) galleria
galley ['gælɪ] *n* (*ship's kitchen*) cambusa; (*ship*) galea; (*also*: **galley proof**) bozza in colonna
Gallic ['gælɪk] *adj* gallico(-a); (*French*) francese
galling ['gɔːlɪŋ] *adj* irritante
gallon ['gælən] *n* gallone *m* (*Brit* = *4.543 l*; *8 pints*; *US* = *3.785 l*)
gallop ['gæləp] *n* galoppo ■ *vi* galoppare; **galloping inflation** inflazione *f* galoppante
gallows ['gæləuz] *n* forca
gallstone ['gɔːlstəun] *n* calcolo biliare
Gallup Poll ['gæləp-] *n* sondaggio a campione
galore [gə'lɔː^r] *adv* a iosa, a profusione
galvanize ['gælvənaɪz] *vt* galvanizzare; **to ~ sb into action** (*fig*) galvanizzare qn, spronare qn all'azione
Gambia ['gæmbɪə] *n* Gambia *m*
gambit ['gæmbɪt] *n* (*fig*): **(opening) ~** prima mossa
gamble ['gæmbl] *n* azzardo, rischio calcolato ■ *vt, vi* giocare; **to ~ on** (*fig*) giocare su; **to ~ on the Stock Exchange** giocare in Borsa
gambler ['gæmblə^r] *n* giocatore(-trice) d'azzardo
gambling ['gæmblɪŋ] *n* gioco d'azzardo
gambol ['gæmbəl] *vi* saltellare

game [geɪm] *n* gioco; (*event*) partita; (*Hunting*) selvaggina ■ *adj* coraggioso(-a); (*ready*): **to be ~ (for sth/to do)** essere pronto(-a) (a qc/a fare); **games** *npl* (*Scol*) attività *fpl* sportive; **big ~** selvaggina grossa
game bird *n* uccello selvatico
gamekeeper ['geɪmki:pəʳ] *n* guardacaccia *m inv*
gamely ['geɪmlɪ] *adv* coraggiosamente
gamer [geɪməʳ] *n chi gioca con i videogame*
game reserve *n* riserva di caccia
games console *n* console *f inv* dei videogame
gameshow ['geɪmʃəu] *n* gioco a premi
gamesmanship ['geɪmzmənʃɪp] *n* abilità
gaming ['geɪmɪŋ] *n* gioco d'azzardo; (*Comput*) *il giocare con i videogame*
gammon ['gæmən] *n* (*bacon*) quarto di maiale; (*ham*) prosciutto affumicato
gamut ['gæmət] *n* gamma
gang [gæŋ] *n* banda, squadra ■ *vi*: **to ~ up on sb** far combutta contro qn
Ganges ['gændʒi:z] *n*: **the ~** il Gange
gangland ['gæŋlænd] *adj* della malavita
gangling ['gæŋglɪŋ] *adj* allampanato(-a)
gangly ['gæŋglɪ] *adj* = **gangling**
gangplank ['gæŋplæŋk] *n* passerella
gangrene ['gæŋgri:n] *n* cancrena
gangster ['gæŋstəʳ] *n* gangster *m inv*
gangway ['gæŋweɪ] *n* passerella; (*Brit: of bus*) passaggio
gantry ['gæntrɪ] *n* (*for crane, railway signal*) cavalletto; (*for rocket*) torre *f* di lancio
gaol [dʒeɪl] *n, vt* (*Brit*) = **jail**
gap [gæp] *n* buco; (*in time*) intervallo; (*fig*) lacuna; vuoto
gape [geɪp] *vi* restare a bocca aperta
gaping ['geɪpɪŋ] *adj* (*hole*) squarciato(-a)
gap year *n anno di pausa preso prima di iniziare l'università, per lavorare o viaggiare*
garage ['gærɑ:ʒ] *n* garage *m inv*
garb [gɑ:b] *n* abiti *mpl*, veste *f*
garbage ['gɑ:bɪdʒ] *n* immondizie *fpl*, rifiuti *mpl*; (*fig: film, book*) porcheria, robaccia; (*: nonsense*) fesserie *fpl*
garbage can *n* (*US*) bidone *m* della spazzatura
garbage collector *n* (*US*) spazzino(-a)
garbage disposal unit *n* tritarifiuti *m inv*
garbage truck *n* (*US*) camion *m inv* della spazzatura
garbled ['gɑ:bld] *adj* deformato(-a); ingarbugliato(-a)
garden ['gɑ:dn] *n* giardino ■ *vi* lavorare nel giardino; **gardens** *npl* (*public*) giardini pubblici; (*private*) parco
garden centre *n* vivaio
garden city *n* (*Brit*) città *f inv* giardino *inv*
gardener ['gɑ:dnəʳ] *n* giardiniere(-a)
gardening ['gɑ:dnɪŋ] *n* giardinaggio
gargle ['gɑ:gl] *vi* fare gargarismi ■ *n* gargarismo
gargoyle ['gɑ:gɔɪl] *n* gargouille *f inv*
garish ['gɛərɪʃ] *adj* vistoso(-a)
garland ['gɑ:lənd] *n* ghirlanda; corona
garlic ['gɑ:lɪk] *n* aglio
garment ['gɑ:mənt] *n* indumento
garner ['gɑ:nəʳ] *vt* ammucchiare, raccogliere
garnish ['gɑ:nɪʃ] *vt* guarnire
garret ['gærɪt] *n* soffitta
garrison ['gærɪsn] *n* guarnigione *f* ■ *vt* guarnire
garrulous ['gærjuləs] *adj* ciarliero(-a), loquace
garter ['gɑ:təʳ] *n* giarrettiera; (*US: suspender*) gancio (di reggicalze)
garter belt *n* (*US*) reggicalze *m inv*
gas [gæs] *n* gas *m inv*; (*used as anaesthetic*) etere *m*; (*US: gasoline*) benzina ■ *vt* asfissiare con il gas; (*Mil*) gasare
gas cooker *n* (*Brit*) cucina a gas
gas cylinder *n* bombola del gas
gaseous ['gæsɪəs] *adj* gassoso(-a)
gas fire *n* (*Brit*) radiatore *m* a gas
gas-fired ['gæsfaɪəd] *adj* (alimentato(-a)) a gas
gash [gæʃ] *n* sfregio ■ *vt* sfregiare
gasket ['gæskɪt] *n* (*Aut*) guarnizione *f*
gas mask *n* maschera *f* antigas *inv*
gas meter *n* contatore *m* del gas
gasoline ['gæsəli:n] *n* (*US*) benzina
gasp [gɑ:sp] *vi* ansare, boccheggiare; (*in surprise*) restare senza fiato
▸ **gasp out** *vt* dire affannosamente
gas ring *n* fornello a gas
gas station *n* (*US*) distributore *m* di benzina
gas stove *n* cucina a gas
gassy ['gæsɪ] *adj* gassoso(-a)
gas tank *n* (*US Aut*) serbatoio (di benzina)
gas tap *n* (*on cooker*) manopola del gas; (*on pipe*) rubinetto del gas
gastric ['gæstrɪk] *adj* gastrico(-a)
gastric ulcer *n* ulcera gastrica
gastroenteritis ['gæstrəuɛntə'raɪtɪs] *n* gastroenterite *f*
gastronomy [gæs'trɔnəmɪ] *n* gastronomia
gasworks ['gæswə:ks] *n, npl* impianto di produzione del gas
gate [geɪt] *n* cancello; (*of castle, town*) porta; (*at airport*) uscita; (*at level crossing*) barriera
gâteau (*pl* **gâteaux**) ['gætəu, -z] *n* torta
gatecrash ['geɪtkræʃ] *vt* partecipare senza invito a
gatecrasher ['geɪtkræʃəʳ] *n* intruso(-a),

ospite *m/f* non invitato(-a)
gatehouse ['geɪthaus] *n* casetta del custode (*all'entrata di un parco*)
gateway ['geɪtweɪ] *n* porta
gather ['gæðəʳ] *vt* (*flowers, fruit*) cogliere; (*pick up*) raccogliere; (*assemble*) radunare; raccogliere; (*understand*) capire ▪ *vi* (*assemble*) radunarsi; (*dust*) accumularsi; (*clouds*) addensarsi; **to ~ speed** acquistare velocità; **to ~ (from/that)** comprendere (da/che), dedurre (da/che); **as far as I can ~** da quel che ho potuto capire
gathering ['gæðərɪŋ] *n* adunanza
GATT [gæt] *n abbr* (= *General Agreement on Tariffs and Trade*) G.A.T.T *m*
gauche [gəuʃ] *adj* goffo(-a), maldestro(-a)
gaudy ['gɔːdɪ] *adj* vistoso(-a)
gauge [geɪdʒ] *n* (*standard measure*) calibro; (*Rail*) scartamento; (*instrument*) indicatore *m* ▪ *vt* misurare; (*fig: sb's capabilities, character*) valutare, stimare; **to ~ the right moment** calcolare il momento giusto; **petrol ~**, (US) **gas ~** indicatore *m or* spia della benzina
gaunt [gɔːnt] *adj* scarno(-a); (*grim, desolate*) desolato(-a)
gauntlet ['gɔːntlɪt] *n* (*fig*): **to run the ~ through an angry crowd** passare sotto il fuoco di una folla ostile; **to throw down the ~** gettare il guanto
gauze [gɔːz] *n* garza
gave [geɪv] *pt of* **give**
gawky ['gɔːkɪ] *adj* goffo(-a), sgraziato(-a)
gawp [gɔːp] *vi*: **to ~ at** guardare a bocca aperta
gay [geɪ] *adj* (*person*) gaio(-a), allegro(-a); (*colour*) vivace, vivo(-a); (*col*) omosessuale
gaze [geɪz] *n* sguardo fisso ▪ *vi*: **to ~ at** guardare fisso
gazelle [gə'zɛl] *n* gazzella
gazette [gə'zɛt] *n* (*newspaper*) gazzetta; (*official publication*) gazzetta ufficiale
gazetteer [gæzə'tɪəʳ] *n* (*book*) dizionario dei nomi geografici; (*section of book*) indice *m* dei nomi geografici
gazump [gə'zʌmp] *vt* (Brit): **to ~ sb** *nella compravendita di immobili, venire meno all'impegno preso con un acquirente accettando un'offerta migliore fatta da altri*
GB *abbr* (= *Great Britain*) GB
GBH *n abbr* (*Brit Law: col*) = **grievous bodily harm**
GC *n abbr* (*Brit: = George Cross*) *decorazione al valore*
GCE *n abbr* (*Brit: = General Certificate of Education*) ≈ diploma *m* di maturità
GCHQ *n abbr* (*Brit: = Government Communications Headquarters*) *centro per l'intercettazione delle telecomunicazioni straniere*
GCSE *n abbr* (*Brit: = General Certificate of Secondary Education*) *diploma di istruzione secondaria conseguito a 16 anni in Inghilterra e Galles*
Gdns. *abbr* = **gardens**
GDP *n abbr* = **gross domestic product**
GDR *n abbr* (*Hist*) = **German Democratic Republic**
gear [gɪəʳ] *n* attrezzi *mpl*, equipaggiamento; (*belongings*) roba; (*Tech*) ingranaggio; (*Aut*) marcia ▪ *vt* (*fig: adapt*) adattare; **top** *or* **high/ low/bottom ~** (US) quarta (*or* quinta)/ seconda/prima; **in ~** in marcia; **out of ~** in folle; **our service is geared to meet the needs of the disabled** la nostra organizzazione risponde espressamente alle esigenze degli handicappati
▸ **gear up** *vi*: **to ~ up (to do)** prepararsi (a fare)
gear box *n* scatola del cambio
gear lever, (US)**gear shift** *n* leva del cambio
GED *n abbr* (*US Scol*) = **general educational development**
geese [giːs] *npl of* **goose**
geezer ['giːzəʳ] *n* (*Brit col*) tizio
Geiger counter ['gaɪgə-] *n* geiger *m inv*
gel [dʒɛl] *n* gel *m inv*
gelatin, gelatine ['dʒɛlətiːn] *n* gelatina
gelignite ['dʒɛlɪgnaɪt] *n* nitroglicerina
gem [dʒɛm] *n* gemma
Gemini ['dʒɛmɪnaɪ] *n* Gemelli *mpl*; **to be ~** essere dei Gemelli
gen [dʒɛn] *n* (*Brit col*): **to give sb the ~ on sth** mettere qn al corrente di qc
Gen. *abbr* (*Mil: = General*) Gen
gen. *abbr* (= *general, generally*) gen.
gender ['dʒɛndəʳ] *n* genere *m*
gene [dʒiːn] *n* (*Biol*) gene *m*
genealogy [dʒiːnɪ'ælədʒɪ] *n* genealogia
general ['dʒɛnərl] *n* generale *m* ▪ *adj* generale; **in ~** in genere; **the ~ public** il grande pubblico
general anaesthetic *n* anestesia totale
general delivery *n* (US) fermo posta *m*
general election *n* elezioni *fpl* generali
generalization ['dʒɛnrəlaɪ'zeɪʃən] *n* generalizzazione *f*
generalize ['dʒɛnrəlaɪz] *vi* generalizzare
generally ['dʒɛnrəlɪ] *adv* generalmente
general manager *n* direttore *m* generale
general practitioner *n* medico generico
general strike *n* sciopero generale
generate ['dʒɛnəreɪt] *vt* generare
generation [dʒɛnə'reɪʃən] *n* generazione *f*; (*of electricity etc*) produzione *f*
generator ['dʒɛnəreɪtəʳ] *n* generatore *m*
generic [dʒɪ'nɛrɪk] *adj* generico(-a)
generosity [dʒɛnə'rɔsɪtɪ] *n* generosità

generous ['dʒɛnərəs] *adj* generoso(-a); (*copious*) abbondante
genesis ['dʒɛnɪsɪs] *n* genesi *f*
genetic [dʒɪ'nɛtɪk] *adj* genetico(-a); **~ engineering** ingegneria genetica
genetically modified [dʒɪ'nɛtɪklɪ'mɔdɪfaɪd] *adj* geneticamente modificato(-a), transgenico(-a); **~ organism** organismo geneticamente modificato
genetic fingerprinting [-fɪŋgəprɪntɪŋ] *n* rilevamento delle impronte genetiche
genetics [dʒɪ'nɛtɪks] *n* genetica
Geneva [dʒɪ'ni:və] *n* Ginevra; **Lake ~** il lago di Ginevra
genial ['dʒi:nɪəl] *adj* geniale, cordiale
genitals ['dʒɛnɪtlz] *npl* genitali *mpl*
genitive ['dʒɛnɪtɪv] *n* genitivo
genius ['dʒi:nɪəs] *n* genio
Genoa ['dʒɛnəuə] *n* Genova
genocide ['dʒɛnəusaɪd] *n* genocidio
Genoese [dʒɛnəu'i:z] *adj, n* (*pl inv*) genovese (*m/f*)
genome ['dʒi:nəum] *n* (*Biol*) genoma *m*
gent [dʒɛnt] *n abbr* (*Brit col*) = **gentleman**
genteel [dʒɛn'ti:l] *adj* raffinato(-a), distinto(-a)
gentle ['dʒɛntl] *adj* delicato(-a); (*person*) dolce
gentleman ['dʒɛntlmən] *n* signore *m*; (*well-bred man*) gentiluomo; **~'s agreement** impegno sulla parola
gentlemanly ['dʒɛntlmənlɪ] *adj* da gentiluomo
gentleness ['dʒɛntlnɪs] *n* delicatezza; dolcezza
gently ['dʒɛntlɪ] *adv* delicatamente
gentry ['dʒɛntrɪ] *n* nobiltà minore
gents [dʒɛnts] *n* W.C *m* (per signori)
genuine ['dʒɛnjuɪn] *adj* autentico(-a), sincero(-a)
genuinely ['dʒɛnjuɪnlɪ] *adv* genuinamente
geographer [dʒɪ'ɔgrəfə^r] *n* geografo(-a)
geographic [dʒɪə'græfɪk], **geographical** [dʒɪə'græfɪkl] *adj* geografico(-a)
geography [dʒɪ'ɔgrəfɪ] *n* geografia
geological [dʒɪə'lɔdʒɪkl] *adj* geologico(-a)
geologist [dʒɪ'ɔlədʒɪst] *n* geologo(-a)
geology [dʒɪ'ɔlədʒɪ] *n* geologia
geometric [dʒɪə'mɛtrɪk], **geometrical** [dʒɪə'mɛtrɪkl] *adj* geometrico(-a)
geometry [dʒɪ'ɔmətrɪ] *n* geometria
Geordie ['dʒɔ:dɪ] *n* (*col*) abitante *m/f* del Tyneside; originario(-a) del Tyneside
Georgia ['dʒɔ:dʒə] *n* Georgia
Georgian ['dʒɔ:dʒən] *adj* georgiano(-a) ■ *n* georgiano(-a); (*Ling*) georgiano
geranium [dʒɪ'reɪnɪəm] *n* geranio
geriatric [dʒɛrɪ'ætrɪk] *adj* geriatrico(-a)
germ [dʒə:m] *n* (*Med*) microbo; (*Biol, fig*) germe *m*
German ['dʒə:mən] *adj* tedesco(-a) ■ *n* tedesco(-a); (*Ling*) tedesco
German Democratic Republic *n* Repubblica Democratica Tedesca
germane [dʒə:'meɪn] *adj* (*formal*): **to be ~ to sth** essere attinente a qc
German measles *n* rosolia
Germany ['dʒə:mənɪ] *n* Germania
germination [dʒə:mɪ'neɪʃən] *n* germinazione *f*
germ warfare *n* guerra batteriologica
gerrymandering ['dʒɛrɪmændərɪŋ] *n* manipolazione *f* dei distretti elettorali.
gestation [dʒɛs'teɪʃən] *n* gestazione *f*
gesticulate [dʒɛs'tɪkjuleɪt] *vi* gesticolare
gesture ['dʒɛstjə^r] *n* gesto; **as a ~ of friendship** in segno d'amicizia

KEYWORD

get [gɛt] (*pt, pp* **got**, (*US*) *pp* **gotten**) *vi*
1 (*become, be*) diventare, farsi; **to get drunk** ubriacarsi; **to get killed** venire *or* rimanere ucciso(-a); **it's getting late** si sta facendo tardi; **to get old** invecchiare; **to get paid** venire pagato(-a); **to get ready** prepararsi; **to get shaved** farsi la barba; **to get tired** stancarsi; **to get washed** lavarsi
2 (*go*): **to get to/from** andare a/da; **to get home** arrivare *or* tornare a casa; **how did you get here?** come sei venuto?; **he got across the bridge** ha attraversato il ponte; **he got under the fence** è passato sotto il recinto
3 (*begin*) mettersi a, cominciare a; **to get to know sb** incominciare a conoscere qn; **let's get going** *or* **started** muoviamoci
4 (*modal aux vb*): **you've got to do it** devi farlo
■ *vt* **1**: **to get sth done** (*do*) fare qc; (*have done*) far fare qc; **to get sth/sb ready** preparare qc/qn; **to get one's hair cut** tagliarsi *or* farsi tagliare i capelli; **to get sb to do sth** far fare qc a qn
2 (*obtain: money, permission, results*) ottenere; (*find: job, flat*) trovare; (*fetch: person, doctor*) chiamare; (: *object*) prendere; **to get sth for sb** prendere *or* procurare qc a qn; **get me Mr Jones, please** (*Tel*) mi passi il signor Jones, per favore; **can I get you a drink?** le posso offrire da bere?
3 (*receive: present, letter, prize*) ricevere; (*acquire: reputation*) farsi; **how much did you get for the painting?** quanto le hanno dato per il quadro?
4 (*catch*) prendere; (*hit: target etc*) colpire;

to get sb by the arm/throat afferrare qn per un braccio/alla gola; **get him!** prendetelo!; **he really gets me** (*fig: annoy*) mi dà proprio sui nervi
5 (*take, move*) portare; **to get sth to sb** far avere qc a qn; **do you think we'll get it through the door?** pensi che riusciremo a farlo passare per la porta?
6 (*catch, take: plane, bus etc*) prendere; **he got the last bus** ha preso l'ultimo autobus; **she got the morning flight to Milan** ha preso il volo per Milano del mattino
7 (*understand*) afferrare; (*hear*) sentire; **I've got it!** ci sono arrivato!, ci sono!; **I'm sorry, I didn't get your name** scusi, non ho capito (*or* sentito) come si chiama
8 (*have, possess*): **to have got** avere; **how many have you got?** quanti ne ha?
▸ **get about** *vi* muoversi; (*news*) diffondersi
▸ **get across** *vt*: **to get across (to)** (*message, meaning*) comunicare (a)
■ *vi*: **to get across to** (*subj: speaker*) comunicare con
▸ **get along** *vi* (*agree*) andare d'accordo; (*depart*) andarsene; (*manage*) = **get by**
▸ **get at** *vt fus* (*attack*) prendersela con; (*reach*) raggiungere, arrivare a; **what are you getting at?** dove vuoi arrivare?
▸ **get away** *vi* partire, andarsene; (*escape*) scappare
▸ **get away with** *vt fus*: **he'll never get away with it!** non riuscirà a farla franca!
▸ **get back** *vi* (*return*) ritornare, tornare
■ *vt* riottenere, riavere; **to get back to** (*start again*) ritornare a; (*contact again*) rimettersi in contatto con
▸ **get back at** *vt fus* (*col*): **to get back at sb (for sth)** rendere pan per focaccia a qn (per qc)
▸ **get by** *vi* (*pass*) passare; (*manage*) farcela; **I can get by in Dutch** mi arrangio in olandese
▸ **get down** *vi, vt fus* scendere
■ *vt* far scendere; (*depress*) buttare giù
▸ **get down to** *vt fus* (*work*) mettersi a (fare); **to get down to business** venire al dunque
▸ **get in** *vi* entrare; (*train*) arrivare; (*arrive home*) ritornare, tornare
■ *vt* (*bring in: harvest*) raccogliere; (*: coal, shopping, supplies*) fare provvista di; (*insert*) far entrare, infilare
▸ **get into** *vt fus* entrare in; **to get into a rage** incavolarsi; **to get into bed** mettersi a letto
▸ **get off** *vi* (*from train etc*) scendere; (*depart: person, car*) andare via; (*escape*) cavarsela
■ *vt* (*remove: clothes, stain*) levare; (*send off*) spedire; (*have as leave: days, time*): **we got 2 days off** abbiamo avuto 2 giorni liberi
■ *vt fus* (*train, bus*) scendere da; **to get off to a good start** (*fig*) cominciare bene
▸ **get on** *vi*: **how did you get on?** com'è andata?; **he got on quite well** ha fatto bene, (gli) è andata bene; **to get on (with sb)** andare d'accordo (con qn); **how are you getting on?** come va la vita?
■ *vt fus* montare in; (*horse*) montare su
▸ **get on to** *vt fus* (*Brit col: contact: on phone etc*) contattare, rintracciare; (*: deal with*) occuparsi di
▸ **get out** *vi* uscire; (*of vehicle*) scendere
■ *vt* tirar fuori, far uscire; **to get out (of)** (*money from bank etc*) ritirare (da)
▸ **get out of** *vt fus* uscire da; (*duty etc*) evitare; **what will you get out of it?** cosa ci guadagni?
▸ **get over** *vt fus* (*illness*) riaversi da; (*communicate: idea etc*) comunicare, passare; **let's get it over (with)** togliamoci il pensiero
▸ **get round** *vt fus* aggirare; (*fig: person*) rigirare
■ *vi*: **to get round to doing sth** trovare il tempo di fare qc
▸ **get through** *vi* (*Tel*) avere la linea
■ *vt fus* (*finish: work*) sbrigare; (*: book*) finire
▸ **get through to** *vt fus* (*Tel*) parlare a
▸ **get together** *vi* riunirsi
■ *vt* raccogliere; (*people*) adunare
▸ **get up** *vi* (*rise*) alzarsi
■ *vt fus* salire su per
▸ **get up to** *vt fus* (*reach*) raggiungere; (*prank etc*) fare

getaway [ˈgɛtəweɪ] *n* fuga
getaway car *n* macchina per la fuga
get-together [ˈgɛttəgɛðəʳ] *n* (piccola) riunione *f*; (*party*) festicciola
get-up [ˈgɛtʌp] *n* (*col: outfit*) tenuta
get-well card [gɛtˈwɛl-] *n* cartolina di auguri di pronta guarigione
geyser [ˈgiːzəʳ] *n* scaldabagno; (*Geo*) geyser *m inv*
Ghana [ˈgɑːnə] *n* Ghana *m*
Ghanaian [gɑːˈneɪən] *adj, n* ganaense (*m/f*)
ghastly [ˈgɑːstlɪ] *adj* orribile, orrendo(-a)
gherkin [ˈgəːkɪn] *n* cetriolino
ghetto blaster [-ˈblɑːstəʳ] *n* maxistereo portatile
ghost [gəust] *n* fantasma *m*, spettro ■ *vt* (*book*) fare lo scrittore ombra per
ghostly [ˈgəustlɪ] *adj* spettrale
ghostwriter [ˈgəustraɪtəʳ] *n* scrittore(-trice) ombra *inv*
ghoul [guːl] *n* vampiro che si nutre di cadaveri

g

ghoulish ['gu:lɪʃ] *adj* (*tastes etc*) macabro(-a)
GHQ *n abbr* (*Mil*: = *general headquarters*) ≈ comando di Stato maggiore
GI *n abbr* (*US col*: = *government issue*) G.I. *m*, soldato americano
giant ['dʒaɪənt] *n* gigante(-essa) ■ *adj* gigante, enorme; **~ (size) packet** confezione *f* gigante
giant killer *n* (*Sport*) *piccola squadra che riesce a batterne una importante*
gibber ['dʒɪbəʳ] *vi* (*monkey*) squittire confusamente; (*idiot*) farfugliare
gibberish ['dʒɪbərɪʃ] *n* parole *fpl* senza senso
gibe [dʒaɪb] *n* frecciata ■ *vi*: **to ~ at** lanciare frecciate a
giblets ['dʒɪblɪts] *npl* frattaglie *fpl*
Gibraltar [dʒɪ'brɔ:ltəʳ] *n* Gibilterra
giddiness ['gɪdɪnɪs] *n* vertigine *f*
giddy ['gɪdɪ] *adj* (*dizzy*): **to be ~** aver le vertigini; (*height*) vertiginoso(-a); **I feel ~** mi gira la testa
gift [gɪft] *n* regalo; (*donation, ability*) dono; (*Comm*: *also*: **free gift**) omaggio; **to have a ~ for sth** (*talent*) avere il dono di qc
gifted ['gɪftɪd] *adj* dotato(-a)
gift token, gift voucher *n* buono (acquisto)
gig [gɪg] *n* (*col*: *of musician*) serata
gigabyte [gi:gəbaɪt] *n* gigabyte *m inv*
gigantic [dʒaɪ'gæntɪk] *adj* gigantesco(-a)
giggle ['gɪgl] *vi* ridere scioccamente ■ *n* risolino (sciocco)
GIGO ['gaɪgəu] *abbr* (*Comput*: *col*: = *garbage in, garbage out*) qualità di input = qualità di output
gild [gɪld] *vt* dorare
gill [dʒɪl] *n* (*measure*) = *0.25 pints* (*Brit* = *0.148 l*; *US* = *0.118 l*)
gills [gɪlz] *npl* (*of fish*) branchie *fpl*
gilt [gɪlt] *n* doratura ■ *adj* dorato(-a)
gilt-edged ['gɪltɛdʒd] *adj* (*stocks, securities*) della massima sicurezza
gimlet ['gɪmlɪt] *n* succhiello
gimmick ['gɪmɪk] *n* trucco; **sales ~** trovata commerciale
gin [dʒɪn] *n* (*liquor*) gin *m inv*
ginger ['dʒɪndʒəʳ] *n* zenzero
▸ **ginger up** *vt* scuotere; animare
ginger ale, ginger beer *n* bibita gassosa allo zenzero
gingerbread ['dʒɪndʒəbrɛd] *n* pan *m* di zenzero
ginger group *n* (*Brit*) gruppo di pressione
ginger-haired ['dʒɪndʒə'hɛəd] *adj* rossiccio(-a)
gingerly ['dʒɪndʒəlɪ] *adv* cautamente
gingham ['gɪŋəm] *n* percalle *m* a righe (*or* quadretti)
ginseng ['dʒɪnsɛŋ] *n* ginseng *m*
gipsy ['dʒɪpsɪ] *n* zingaro(-a) ■ *adj* degli zingari
giraffe [dʒɪ'rɑ:f] *n* giraffa
girder ['gə:dəʳ] *n* trave *f*
girdle ['gə:dl] *n* (*corset*) guaina
girl [gə:l] *n* ragazza; (*young unmarried woman*) signorina; (*daughter*) figlia, figliola; **a little ~** una bambina
girl band *n gruppo pop di sole ragazze creato per far presa su un pubblico giovane*
girlfriend ['gə:lfrɛnd] *n* (*of girl*) amica; (*of boy*) ragazza
girlish ['gə:lɪʃ] *adj* da ragazza
Girl Scout *n* (*US*) Giovane Esploratrice *f*
Giro ['dʒaɪrəu] *n*: **the National ~** (*Brit*) ≈ la *or* il Bancoposta
giro ['dʒaɪrəu] *n* (*bank giro*) versamento bancario; (*post office giro*) postagiro
girth [gə:θ] *n* circonferenza; (*of horse*) cinghia
gist [dʒɪst] *n* succo
give [gɪv] *n* (*of fabric*) elasticità ■ *vb* (*pt* **gave**, *pp* **given**) [geɪv, 'gɪvn] *vt* dare ■ *vi* cedere; **to ~ sb sth, ~ sth to sb** dare qc a qn; **to ~ a cry/sigh** emettere un grido/sospiro; **how much did you ~ for it?** quanto (l')hai pagato?; **12 o'clock, ~ or take a few minutes** mezzogiorno, minuto più minuto meno; **to ~ way** *vi* cedere; (*Brit Aut*) dare la precedenza
▸ **give away** *vt* dare via; (*give free*) fare dono di; (*betray*) tradire; (*disclose*) rivelare; (*bride*) condurre all'altare
▸ **give back** *vt* rendere
▸ **give in** *vi* cedere ■ *vt* consegnare
▸ **give off** *vt* emettere
▸ **give out** *vt* distribuire; annunciare ■ *vi* (*be exhausted*: *supplies*) esaurirsi, venir meno; (*fail*: *engine*) fermarsi; (: *strength*) mancare
▸ **give up** *vi* rinunciare ■ *vt* rinunciare a; **to ~ up smoking** smettere di fumare; **to ~ o.s. up** arrendersi
give-and-take [gɪvən'teɪk] *n* (*col*) elasticità (da ambo le parti), concessioni *fpl* reciproche
giveaway ['gɪvəweɪ] *n* (*col*): **her expression was a ~** le si leggeva tutto in volto; **the exam was a ~!** l'esame è stato uno scherzo! ■ *cpd*: **~ prices** prezzi stracciati
given ['gɪvn] *pp of* **give** ■ *adj* (*fixed*: *time, amount*) dato(-a), determinato(-a) ■ *conj*: **~ (that) ...** dato che ...; **~ the circumstances ...** date le circostanze ...
glacial ['gleɪsɪəl] *adj* glaciale
glacier ['glæsɪəʳ] *n* ghiacciaio
glad [glæd] *adj* lieto(-a), contento(-a); **to be ~ about sth/that** essere contento *or* lieto di qc/che + *sub*; **I was ~ of his help** gli sono stato grato del suo aiuto

gladden ['glædn] *vt* rallegrare, allietare

glade [gleɪd] *n* radura

gladioli [glædɪ'əulaɪ] *npl* gladioli *mpl*

gladly ['glædlɪ] *adv* volentieri

glamorous ['glæmərəs] *adj* (*gen*) favoloso(-a); (*person*) affascinante, seducente; (*occasion*) brillante, elegante

glamour ['glæməʳ] *n* fascino

glance [glɑ:ns] *n* occhiata, sguardo ■ *vi*: **to ~ at** dare un'occhiata a

▸ **glance off** *vt fus* (*bullet*) rimbalzare su

glancing ['glɑ:nsɪŋ] *adj* (*blow*) che colpisce di striscio

gland [glænd] *n* ghiandola

glandular ['glændjuləʳ] *adj*: **~ fever** (*Brit*) mononucleosi *f*

glare [glɛəʳ] *n* riverbero, luce *f* abbagliante; (*look*) sguardo furioso ■ *vi* abbagliare; **to ~ at** guardare male

glaring ['glɛərɪŋ] *adj* (*mistake*) madornale

glasnost ['glæznɔst] *n* glasnost *f*

glass [glɑ:s] *n* (*substance*) vetro; (*tumbler*) bicchiere *m*; (*also*: **looking glass**) specchio; *see also* **glasses**

glass-blowing ['glɑ:sbləuɪŋ] *n* soffiatura del vetro

glass ceiling *n* (*fig*) barriera invisibile

glasses ['glɑ:sɪz] *npl* (*spectacles*) occhiali *mpl*

glass fibre *n* fibra di vetro

glasshouse ['glɑ:shaus] *n* serra

glassware ['glɑ:swɛəʳ] *n* vetrame *m*

glassy ['glɑ:sɪ] *adj* (*eyes*) vitreo(-a)

Glaswegian [glæs'wi:dʒən] *adj* di Glasgow ■ *n* abitante *m/f* di Glasgow, originario(-a) di Glasgow

glaze [gleɪz] *vt* (*door*) fornire di vetri; (*pottery*) smaltare; (*Culin*) glassare ■ *n* smalto; glassa

glazed ['gleɪzd] *adj* (*eye*) vitreo(-a); (*tiles, pottery*) smaltato(-a)

glazier ['gleɪzɪəʳ] *n* vetraio

gleam [gli:m] *n* barlume *m*; raggio ■ *vi* luccicare; **a ~ of hope** un barlume di speranza

gleaming ['gli:mɪŋ] *adj* lucente

glean [gli:n] *vt* (*information*) racimolare

glee [gli:] *n* allegrezza, gioia

gleeful ['gli:ful] *adj* allegro(-a), gioioso(-a)

glen [glɛn] *n* valletta

glib [glɪb] *adj* dalla parola facile; facile

glide [glaɪd] *vi* scivolare; (*Aviat, birds*) planare ■ *n* scivolata; planata

glider ['glaɪdəʳ] *n* (*Aviat*) aliante *m*

gliding ['glaɪdɪŋ] *n* (*Aviat*) volo a vela

glimmer ['glɪməʳ] *vi* luccicare ■ *n* barlume *m*

glimpse [glɪmps] *n* impressione *f* **fugace** ■ *vt* vedere di sfuggita; **to catch a ~ of** vedere di sfuggita

glint [glɪnt] *n* luccichio ■ *vi* luccicare

glisten ['glɪsn] *vi* luccicare

glitter ['glɪtəʳ] *vi* scintillare ■ *n* scintillio

glitz [glɪts] *n* (*col*) vistosità, chiassosità

gloat [gləut] *vi*: **to ~ (over)** gongolare di piacere (per)

global ['gləubl] *adj* globale; (*world-wide*) mondiale

globalization [gləubəlaɪ'zeɪʃən] *n* globalizzazione *f*

global warming *n* riscaldamento dell'atmosfera terrestre

globe [gləub] *n* globo, sfera

globetrotter ['gləubtrɔtəʳ] *n* giramondo *m/f inv*

globule ['glɔbju:l] *n* (*Anat*) globulo; (*of water etc*) gocciolina

gloom [glu:m] *n* oscurità, buio; (*sadness*) tristezza, malinconia

gloomy ['glu:mɪ] *adj* fosco(-a), triste; **to feel ~** sentirsi giù *or* depresso

glorification [glɔ:rɪfɪ'keɪʃən] *n* glorificazione *f*

glorify ['glɔ:rɪfaɪ] *vt* glorificare; celebrare, esaltare

glorious ['glɔ:rɪəs] *adj* glorioso(-a), magnifico(-a)

glory ['glɔ:rɪ] *n* gloria; splendore *m* ■ *vi*: **to ~ in** gloriarsi di *or* in

glory hole *n* (*col*) ripostiglio

Glos *abbr* (*Brit*) = **Gloucestershire**

gloss [glɔs] *n* (*shine*) lucentezza; (*also*: **gloss paint**) vernice *f* a olio

▸ **gloss over** *vt fus* scivolare su

glossary ['glɔsərɪ] *n* glossario

glossy ['glɔsɪ] *adj* lucente ■ *n* (*also*: **glossy magazine**) rivista di lusso

glove [glʌv] *n* guanto

glove compartment *n* (*Aut*) vano portaoggetti

glow [gləu] *vi* ardere; (*face*) essere luminoso(-a) ■ *n* bagliore *m*; (*of face*) colorito acceso

glower ['glauəʳ] *vi*: **to ~ (at sb)** guardare (qn) in cagnesco

glowing ['gləuɪŋ] *adj* (*fire*) ardente; (*complexion*) luminoso(-a); (*fig*: *report, description etc*) entusiasta

glow-worm ['gləuwə:m] *n* lucciola

glucose ['glu:kəus] *n* glucosio

glue [glu:] *n* colla ■ *vt* incollare

glue-sniffing ['glu:snɪfɪŋ] *n* sniffare *m* (colla)

glum [glʌm] *adj* abbattuto(-a)

glut [glʌt] *n* eccesso ■ *vt* saziare; (*market*) saturare

glutinous ['glu:tɪnəs] *adj* colloso(-a), appiccicoso(-a)

glutton ['glʌtn] *n* ghiottone(-a); **a ~ for work** un(-a) patito(-a) del lavoro
gluttonous ['glʌtənəs] *adj* ghiotto(-a), goloso(-a)
gluttony ['glʌtənɪ] *n* ghiottoneria; (*sin*) gola
glycerin, glycerine ['glɪsəri:n] *n* glicerina
GM *adj abbr* = **genetically modified**
gm *abbr* = **gram**
GMAT *n abbr* (*US*: = *Graduate Management Admissions Test*) *esame di ammissione all'ultimo biennio di scuola superiore*
GMB *n abbr* (*Brit*) = **General, Municipal, and Boilermakers (Union)**
GM-free [dʒi:ɛm'fri:] *adj* privo(-a) di OGM
GMO *n abbr* (= *genetically modified organism*) OGM *m inv*
GMT *abbr* (= *Greenwich Mean Time*) T.M.G
gnarled [nɑ:ld] *adj* nodoso(-a)
gnash [næʃ] *vt*: **to ~ one's teeth** digrignare i denti
gnat [næt] *n* moscerino
gnaw [nɔ:] *vt* rodere
gnome [nəum] *n* gnomo
GNP *n abbr* = **gross national product**
go [gəu] *vb* (*pt* **went**, *pp* **gone**) [wɛnt, gɔn] *vi* andare; (*depart*) partire, andarsene; (*work*) funzionare; (*break etc*) cedere; (*be sold*): **to go for £10** essere venduto per 10 sterline; (*fit, suit*): **to go with** andare bene con; (*become*): **to go pale** diventare pallido(-a); **to go mouldy** ammuffire ■ *n* (*pl* **goes**); **to have a go (at)** provare; **to be on the go** essere in moto; **whose go is it?** a chi tocca?; **to go by car/on foot** andare in macchina/a piedi; **he's going to do** sta per fare; **to go for a walk** andare a fare una passeggiata; **to go dancing/shopping** andare a ballare/fare la spesa; **to go looking for sb/sth** andare in cerca di qn/qc; **to go to sleep** addormentarsi; **to go and see sb, to go to see sb** andare a trovare qn; **how is it going?** come va (la vita)?; **how did it go?** com'è andato?; **to go round the back/by the shop** passare da dietro/davanti al negozio; **my voice has gone** m'è andata via la voce; **the cake is all gone** il dolce è finito tutto; **I'll take whatever is going** (*Brit*) prendo quello che c'è; **... to go** (*US*: *food*) ... da portar via; **the money will go towards our holiday** questi soldi li mettiamo per la vacanza
▸ **go about** *vi* (*also*: **go around**) aggirarsi; (*: rumour*) correre, circolare ■ *vt fus*: **how do I go about this?** qual è la prassi per questo?; **to go about one's business** occuparsi delle proprie faccende
▸ **go after** *vt fus* (*pursue*) correr dietro a, rincorrere; (*job, record etc*) mirare a
▸ **go against** *vt fus* (*be unfavourable to*) essere contro; (*be contrary to*) andare contro
▸ **go ahead** *vi* andare avanti; **go ahead!** faccia pure!
▸ **go along** *vi* andare, avanzare ■ *vt fus* percorrere; **to go along with** (*accompany*) andare con, accompagnare; (*agree with: idea*) sottoscrivere, appoggiare
▸ **go away** *vi* partire, andarsene
▸ **go back** *vi* tornare, ritornare; (*go again*) andare di nuovo
▸ **go back on** *vt fus* (*promise*) non mantenere
▸ **go by** *vi* (*years, time*) scorrere ■ *vt fus* attenersi a, seguire (alla lettera); prestar fede a
▸ **go down** *vi* scendere; (*ship*) affondare; (*sun*) tramontare ■ *vt fus* scendere; **that should go down well with him** dovrebbe incontrare la sua approvazione
▸ **go for** *vt fus* (*fetch*) andare a prendere; (*like*) andar matto(-a) per; (*attack*) attaccare; saltare addosso a
▸ **go in** *vi* entrare
▸ **go in for** *vt fus* (*competition*) iscriversi a; (*be interested in*) interessarsi di
▸ **go into** *vt fus* entrare in; (*investigate*) indagare, esaminare; (*embark on*) lanciarsi in
▸ **go off** *vi* partire, andar via; (*food*) guastarsi; (*explode*) esplodere, scoppiare; (*lights etc*) spegnersi; (*event*) passare ■ *vt fus*: **I've gone off chocolate** la cioccolata non mi piace più; **the gun went off** il fucile si scaricò; **the party went off well** la festa è andata *or* è riuscita bene; **to go off to sleep** addormentarsi
▸ **go on** *vi* continuare; (*happen*) succedere; (*lights*) accendersi ■ *vt fus* (*be guided by: evidence etc*) basarsi su, fondarsi su; **to go on doing** continuare a fare; **what's going on here?** che succede *or* che sta succedendo qui?
▸ **go on at** *vt fus* (*nag*) assillare
▸ **go on with** *vt fus* continuare, proseguire
▸ **go out** *vi* uscire; (*fire, light*) spegnersi; (*ebb: tide*) calare; **to go out with sb** uscire con qn
▸ **go over** *vi* (*ship*) ribaltarsi ■ *vt fus* (*check*) esaminare; **to go over sth in one's mind** pensare bene a qc
▸ **go round** *vi* (*circulate: news, rumour*) circolare; (*revolve*) girare; (*visit*): **to go round (to sb's)** passare (da qn); (*make a detour*): **to go round (by)** passare (per); (*suffice*) bastare (per tutti)
▸ **go through** *vt fus* (*town etc*) attraversare; (*search through*) frugare in; (*examine: list, book*) leggere da capo a fondo; (*perform*) fare
▸ **go through with** *vt fus* (*plan, crime*) mettere in atto, eseguire; **I couldn't go through with it** non sono riuscito ad andare fino in fondo

▸ **go under** *vi* (*sink: ship*) affondare, colare a picco; (*: person*) andare sotto; (*fig: business, firm*) fallire

▸ **go up** *vi* salire ■ *vt fus* salire su per; **to go up in flames** andare in fiamme

▸ **go without** *vt fus* fare a meno di

goad [gəud] *vt* spronare

go-ahead ['gəuəhɛd] *adj* intraprendente ■ *n*: **to give sb/sth the ~** dare l'okay a qn/qc

goal [gəul] *n* (*Sport*) gol *m*, rete *f*; (*: place*) porta; (*fig: aim*) fine *m*, scopo

goal difference *n* differenza *f* reti *inv*

goalie ['gəulɪ] *n* (*col*) portiere *m*

goalkeeper ['gəulki:pəʳ] *n* portiere *m*

goalpost ['gəulpəust] *n* palo (della porta)

goat [gəut] *n* capra

gobble ['gɔbl] *vt* (*also*: **gobble down**, **gobble up**) ingoiare

go-between ['gəubɪtwi:n] *n* intermediario(-a)

Gobi Desert ['gəubɪ-] *n*: **the ~** il Deserto dei Gobi

goblet ['gɔblɪt] *n* calice *m*, coppa

goblin ['gɔblɪn] *n* folletto

go-cart ['gəukɑ:t] *n* go-kart *m inv* ■ *cpd*: **~ racing** *n* kartismo

god [gɔd] *n* dio; **C~** Dio

god-awful [gɔd'ɔ:fəl] *adj* (*col*) di merda (*!*)

godchild ['gɔdtʃaɪld] *n* figlioccio(-a)

goddamn ['gɔddæm], **goddamned** ['gɔddæmd] (*esp US: col*) *excl*: **~!** porca miseria! ■ *adj* fottuto(-a) (*!*), maledetto(-a) ■ *adv* maledettamente

goddaughter ['gɔddɔ:təʳ] *n* figlioccia

goddess ['gɔdɪs] *n* dea

godfather ['gɔdfɑ:ðəʳ] *n* padrino

god-fearing ['gɔdfɪərɪŋ] *adj* timorato(-a) di Dio

god-forsaken ['gɔdfəseɪkən] *adj* desolato(-a), sperduto(-a)

godmother ['gɔdmʌðəʳ] *n* madrina

godparents ['gɔdpɛərənts] *npl*: **the ~** il padrino e la madrina

godsend ['gɔdsɛnd] *n* dono del cielo

godson ['gɔdsʌn] *n* figlioccio

goes [gəuz] *vb see* **go**

gofer ['gəufəʳ] *n* (*col*) tuttofare *m/f*, tirapiedi *m/f inv*

go-getter ['gəugɛtəʳ] *n* arrivista *m/f*

goggle ['gɔgl] *vi*: **to ~ (at)** stare con gli occhi incollati *or* appiccicati (a *or* addosso a)

goggles ['gɔglz] *npl* occhiali *mpl* (di protezione)

going ['gəuɪŋ] *n* (*conditions*) andare *m*, stato del terreno ■ *adj*: **the ~ rate** la tariffa in vigore; **a ~ concern** un'azienda avviata; **it was slow ~** si andava a rilento

going-over [gəuɪŋ'əuvəʳ] *n* (*col*) controllata; (*violent attack*) pestaggio

goings-on ['gəuɪŋz'ɔn] *npl* (*col*) fatti *mpl* strani, cose *fpl* strane

go-kart ['gəukɑ:t] *n* = **go-cart**

gold [gəuld] *n* oro ■ *adj* d'oro; (*reserves*) aureo(-a)

golden ['gəuldən] *adj* (*made of gold*) d'oro; (*gold in colour*) dorato(-a)

golden age *n* età d'oro

golden handshake *n* (*Brit*) gratifica di fine servizio

golden rule *n* regola principale

goldfish ['gəuldfɪʃ] *n* pesce *m* dorato *or* rosso

gold leaf *n* lamina d'oro

gold medal *n* (*Sport*) medaglia d'oro

goldmine ['gəuldmaɪn] *n* miniera d'oro

gold-plated ['gəuld'pleɪtɪd] *adj* placcato(-a) oro *inv*

goldsmith ['gəuldsmɪθ] *n* orefice *m*, orafo

gold standard *n* tallone *m* aureo

golf [gɔlf] *n* golf *m*

golf ball *n* pallina da golf

golf club *n* circolo di golf; (*stick*) bastone *m or* mazza da golf

golf course *n* campo di golf

golfer ['gɔlfəʳ] *n* giocatore(-trice) di golf

golfing ['gɔlfɪŋ] *n* il giocare a golf

gondola ['gɔndələ] *n* gondola

gondolier [gɔndə'lɪəʳ] *n* gondoliere *m*

gone [gɔn] *pp of* **go**

goner ['gɔnəʳ] *n* (*col*): **I thought you were a ~** pensavo che ormai fossi spacciato

gong [gɔŋ] *n* gong *m inv*

good [gud] *adj* buono(-a); (*kind*) buono(-a), gentile; (*child*) bravo(-a) ■ *n* bene *m*; **~!** bene!, ottimo!; **to be ~ at** essere bravo(-a) in; **it's ~ for you** fa bene; **it's a ~ thing you were there** meno male che c'era; **she is ~ with children/her hands** ci sa fare coi bambini/è abile nei lavori manuali; **to feel ~** sentirsi bene; **it's ~ to see you** che piacere vederla; **he's up to no ~** ne sta combinando qualcuna; **it's no ~ complaining** brontolare non serve a niente; **for the common ~** nell'interesse generale, per il bene comune; **for ~** (*for ever*) per sempre, definitivamente; **would you be ~ enough to ...?** avrebbe la gentilezza di ...?; **that's very ~ of you** è molto gentile da parte sua; **is this any ~?** (*will it do?*) va bene questo?; (*what's it like?*) com'è?; **a ~ deal (of)** molto(-a), una buona quantità (di); **a ~ many** molti(-e); **~ morning!** buon giorno!; **~ afternoon/evening!** buona sera!; **~ night!** buona notte!; *see also* **goods**

goodbye [gud'baɪ] *excl* arrivederci!; **to say ~ to** (*person*) salutare

good faith *n* buona fede
good-for-nothing ['gudfənʌθɪŋ] *n* buono(-a) a nulla, vagabondo(-a)
Good Friday *n* Venerdì Santo
good-humoured [gud'hju:məd] *adj* (*person*) di buon umore; (*remark, joke*) bonario(-a)
good-looking [gud'lukɪŋ] *adj* bello(-a)
good-natured [gud'neɪtʃəd] *adj* (*person*) affabile; (*discussion*) amichevole, cordiale
goodness ['gudnɪs] *n* (*of person*) bontà; **for ~ sake!** per amor di Dio!; **~ gracious!** santo cielo!, mamma mia!
goods [gudz] *npl* (*Comm etc*) merci *fpl*, articoli *mpl*; **~ and chattels** beni *mpl* e effetti *mpl*
goods train *n* (*Brit*) treno *m* merci *inv*
goodwill [gud'wɪl] *n* amicizia, benevolenza; (*Comm*) avviamento
goody-goody ['gudɪgudɪ] *n* (*pej*) santarellino(-a)
gooey ['gu:ɪ] *adj* (*Brit col: sticky*) appiccicoso(-a); (*cake, dessert*) troppo zuccherato(-a)
Google ® ['gu:gl] *n* Google® *m* ■ *vt* fare ricerche in Internet su
goose (*pl* **geese**) [gu:s, gi:s] *n* oca
gooseberry ['guzbərɪ] *n* uva spina; **to play ~** (*Brit*) tenere la candela
gooseflesh ['gu:sflɛʃ] *n*, **goosepimples** ['gu:spɪmplz] *npl* pelle *f* d'oca
goose step *n* (*Mil*) passo dell'oca
GOP *n abbr* (*US Pol: col:* = *Grand Old Party*) partito repubblicano
gopher ['gəufə^r] *n* = **gofer**
gore [gɔ:^r] *vt* incornare ■ *n* sangue *m* (coagulato)
gorge [gɔ:dʒ] *n* gola ■ *vt*: **to ~ o.s. (on)** ingozzarsi (di)
gorgeous ['gɔ:dʒəs] *adj* magnifico(-a)
gorilla [gə'rɪlə] *n* gorilla *m inv*
gormless ['gɔ:mlɪs] *adj* (*Brit col*) tonto(-a); (*: stronger*) deficiente
gorse [gɔ:s] *n* ginestrone *m*
gory ['gɔ:rɪ] *adj* sanguinoso(-a)
go-slow ['gəu'sləu] *n* (*Brit*) rallentamento dei lavori (*per agitazione sindacale*)
gospel ['gɔspl] *n* vangelo
gossamer ['gɔsəmə^r] *n* (*cobweb*) fili *mpl* della Madonna *or* di ragnatela; (*light fabric*) stoffa sottilissima
gossip ['gɔsɪp] *n* chiacchiere *fpl*; pettegolezzi *mpl*; (*person*) pettegolo(-a) ■ *vi* chiacchierare; (*maliciously*) pettegolare; **a piece of ~** un pettegolezzo
gossip column *n* cronaca mondana
got [gɔt] *pt, pp of* **get**
Gothic ['gɔθɪk] *adj* gotico(-a)
gotten ['gɔtn] (*US*) *pp of* **get**
gouge [gaudʒ] *vt* (*also*: **gouge out**: *hole etc*) scavare; (*: initials*) scolpire; (*: sb's eyes*) cavare
gourd [guəd] *n* zucca
gourmet ['guəmeɪ] *n* buongustaio(-a)
gout [gaut] *n* gotta
govern ['gʌvən] *vt* governare; (*Ling*) reggere
governess ['gʌvənɪs] *n* governante *f*
governing ['gʌvənɪŋ] *adj* (*Pol*) al potere, al governo; **~ body** consiglio di amministrazione
government ['gʌvnmənt] *n* governo; (*Brit: ministers*) ministero ■ *cpd* statale; **local ~** amministrazione *f* locale
governmental [gʌvn'mɛntl] *adj* governativo(-a)
government housing *n* (*US*) alloggi *mpl* popolari
government stock *n* titoli *mpl* di stato
governor ['gʌvənə^r] *n* (*of state, bank*) governatore *m*; (*of school, hospital*) amministratore *m*; (*Brit: of prison*) direttore(-trice)
Govt *abbr* = **government**
gown [gaun] *n* vestito lungo; (*of teacher, judge*) toga
GP *n abbr* (*Med*) = **general practitioner**; **who's your GP?** qual è il suo medico di fiducia?
GPMU *n abbr* (*Brit*) = **Graphical, Paper and Media Union**
GPO *n abbr* (*Brit: old*) = **General Post Office**; (*US:* = *Government Printing Office*) ≈ Poligrafici dello Stato
GPS *n abbr* (= *global positioning system*) GPS *m*
gr. *abbr* (*Comm*) = **gross**
grab [græb] *vt* afferrare, arraffare; (*property, power*) impadronirsi di ■ *vi*: **to ~ at** tentare disperatamente di afferrare
grace [greɪs] *n* grazia; (*graciousness*) garbo, cortesia ■ *vt* onorare; **5 days' ~** dilazione *f* di 5 giorni; **to say ~** dire il benedicite; **with a good/bad ~** volentieri/malvolentieri; **his sense of humour is his saving ~** il suo senso dell'umorismo è quello che lo salva
graceful ['greɪsful] *adj* elegante, aggraziato(-a)
gracious ['greɪʃəs] *adj* grazioso(-a), misericordioso(-a) ■ *excl*: **(good) ~!** madonna (mia)!
gradation [grə'deɪʃən] *n* gradazione *f*
grade [greɪd] *n* (*Comm*) qualità *f inv*; classe *f*; categoria; (*in hierarchy*) grado; (*US Scol*) voto; classe; (*gradient*) pendenza, gradiente *m* ■ *vt* classificare; ordinare; graduare; **to make the ~** (*fig*) farcela
grade crossing *n* (*US*) passaggio a livello
grade school *n* (*US*) scuola elementare *or* primaria

gradient ['greɪdɪənt] *n* pendenza, gradiente *m*
gradual ['grædjuəl] *adj* graduale
gradually ['grædjuəlɪ] *adv* man mano, a poco a poco
graduate *n* ['grædjuɪt] laureato(-a); (*US Scol*) diplomato(-a), licenziato(-a) ■ *vi* ['grædjueɪt] laurearsi
graduated pension ['grædjueɪtɪd-] *n pensione calcolata sugli ultimi stipendi*
graduation [grædju'eɪʃən] *n* cerimonia del conferimento della laurea; (*US Scol*) consegna dei diplomi
graffiti [grə'fi:tɪ] *npl* graffiti *mpl*
graft [grɑ:ft] *n* (*Agr, Med*) innesto ■ *vt* innestare; **hard ~** (*col*) duro lavoro
grain [greɪn] *n* (*no pl: cereals*) cereali *mpl*; (*US: corn*) grano; (*of sand*) granello; (*of wood*) venatura; **it goes against the ~** (*fig*) va contro la mia (*or* la sua *etc*) natura
gram [græm] *n* grammo
grammar ['græmə^r] *n* grammatica
grammar school *n* (*Brit*) ≈ liceo; (*US*) ≈ scuola elementare
grammatical [grə'mætɪkl] *adj* grammaticale
gramme [græm] *n* = **gram**
gramophone ['græməfəun] *n* (*Brit*) grammofono
granary ['grænərɪ] *n* granaio
grand [grænd] *adj* grande, magnifico(-a); grandioso(-a) ■ *n* (*col: thousand*) mille dollari *mpl* (*or* sterline *fpl*)
grandchild (*pl* **-children**) ['græntʃaɪld, -tʃɪldrən] *n* nipote *m*
granddad ['grændæd] *n* (*col*) nonno
granddaughter ['grændɔ:tə^r] *n* nipote *f*
grandeur ['grændjə^r] *n* (*of style, house*) splendore *m*; (*of occasion, scenery etc*) grandiosità, maestà
grandfather ['grændfɑ:ðə^r] *n* nonno
grandiose ['grændɪəus] *adj* grandioso(-a); (*pej*) pomposo(-a)
grand jury *n* (*US*) giuria (*formata da 12 a 23 membri*)
grandma ['grænmɑ:] *n* (*col*) nonna
grandmother ['grænmʌðə^r] *n* nonna
grandpa ['grænpɑ:] *n* (*col*) = **granddad**
grandparent ['grænpɛərənt] *n* nonno(-a)
grand piano *n* pianoforte *m* a coda
Grand Prix ['grɑ̃:'pri:] *n* (*Aut*) Gran Premio, Grand Prix *m inv*
grandson ['grænsʌn] *n* nipote *m*
grandstand ['grændstænd] *n* (*Sport*) tribuna
grand total *n* somma complessiva
granite ['grænɪt] *n* granito
granny ['grænɪ] *n* (*col*) nonna
grant [grɑ:nt] *vt* accordare; (*a request*) accogliere; (*admit*) ammettere, concedere ■ *n* (*Scol*) borsa; (*Admin*) sussidio, sovvenzione *f*; **to take sth for granted** dare qc per scontato
granulated ['grænjuleɪtɪd] *adj*: **~ sugar** zucchero cristallizzato
granule ['grænju:l] *n* granello
grape [greɪp] *n* chicco d'uva, acino; **a bunch of grapes** un grappolo d'uva
grapefruit ['greɪpfru:t] *n* pompelmo
grapevine ['greɪpvaɪn] *n* vite *f*; **I heard it on the ~** (*fig*) me l'ha detto l'uccellino
graph [grɑ:f] *n* grafico
graphic ['græfɪk] *adj* grafico(-a); (*vivid*) vivido(-a); *see also* **graphics**
graphic designer *n* grafico(-a)
graphic equalizer *n* equalizzatore *m* grafico
graphics ['græfɪks] *n* (*art, process*) grafica; (*pl: drawings*) illustrazioni *fpl*
graphite ['græfaɪt] *n* grafite *f*
graph paper *n* carta millimetrata
grapple ['græpl] *vi*: **to ~ with** essere alle prese con
grappling iron ['græplɪŋ-] *n* (*Naut*) grappino
grasp [grɑ:sp] *vt* afferrare ■ *n* (*grip*) presa; (*fig*) potere *m*; comprensione *f*; **to have sth within one's ~** avere qc a portata di mano; **to have a good ~ of** (*subject*) avere una buona padronanza di
▸ **grasp at** *vt fus* (*rope etc*) afferrarsi a, aggrapparsi a; (*fig: opportunity*) non farsi sfuggire, approfittare di
grasping ['grɑ:spɪŋ] *adj* avido(-a)
grass [grɑ:s] *n* erba; (*pasture*) pascolo, prato; (*Brit col: informer*) informatore(-trice); (*ex-terrorist*) pentito(-a)
grasshopper ['grɑ:shɔpə^r] *n* cavalletta
grassland ['grɑ:slænd] *n* prateria
grass roots *npl* (*fig*) base *f*
grass snake *n* natrice *f*
grassy ['grɑ:sɪ] *adj* erboso(-a)
grate [greɪt] *n* graticola (del focolare) ■ *vi* cigolare, stridere ■ *vt* (*Culin*) grattugiare
grateful ['greɪtful] *adj* grato(-a), riconoscente
gratefully ['greɪtfulɪ] *adv* con gratitudine
grater ['greɪtə^r] *n* grattugia
gratification [grætɪfɪ'keɪʃən] *n* soddisfazione *f*
gratify ['grætɪfaɪ] *vt* appagare; (*whim*) soddisfare
gratifying ['grætɪfaɪɪŋ] *adj* gradito(-a), soddisfacente
grating ['greɪtɪŋ] *n* (*iron bars*) grata ■ *adj* (*noise*) stridente, stridulo(-a)
gratitude ['grætɪtju:d] *n* gratitudine *f*
gratuitous [grə'tju:ɪtəs] *adj* gratuito(-a)
gratuity [grə'tju:ɪtɪ] *n* mancia
grave [greɪv] *n* tomba ■ *adj* grave, serio(-a)

gravedigger ['greɪvdɪgəʳ] *n* becchino
gravel ['grævl] *n* ghiaia
gravely ['greɪvlɪ] *adv* gravemente, solennemente; **~ ill** in pericolo di vita
gravestone ['greɪvstəun] *n* pietra tombale
graveyard ['greɪvjɑ:d] *n* cimitero
gravitate ['grævɪteɪt] *vi* gravitare
gravity ['grævɪtɪ] *n* (*all senses*) gravità
gravy ['greɪvɪ] *n* intingolo della carne; salsa
gravy boat *n* salsiera
gravy train *n*: **the ~** (*col*) l'albero della cuccagna
gray [greɪ] *adj* (*US*) = **grey**
graze [greɪz] *vi* pascolare, pascere ■ *vt* (*touch lightly*) sfiorare; (*scrape*) escoriare ■ *n* (*Med*) escoriazione *f*
grazing ['greɪzɪŋ] *n* pascolo
grease [gri:s] *n* (*fat*) grasso; (*lubricant*) lubrificante *m* ■ *vt* ingrassare; lubrificare; **to ~ the skids** (*US: fig*) spianare la strada
grease gun *n* ingrassatore *m*
greasepaint ['gri:speɪnt] *n* cerone *m*
greaseproof paper ['gri:spru:f-] *n* (*Brit*) carta oleata
greasy ['gri:sɪ] *adj* grasso(-a), untuoso(-a); (*Brit: road, surface*) scivoloso(-a); (*hands, clothes*) unto(-a)
great [greɪt] *adj* grande; (*pain, heat*) forte, intenso(-a); (*col*) magnifico(-a), meraviglioso(-a); **they're ~ friends** sono grandi amici; **the ~ thing is that ...** il bello è che ...; **it was ~!** è stato fantastico!; **we had a ~ time** ci siamo divertiti un mondo
Great Barrier Reef *n*: **the ~** la Grande Barriera Corallina
Great Britain *n* Gran Bretagna
great-grandchild (*pl* **-children**) [greɪt'græntʃaɪld, -tʃɪldrən] *n* pronipote *m/f*
great-grandfather [greɪt'grændfɑ:ðəʳ] *n* bisnonno
great-grandmother [greɪt'grænmʌðəʳ] *n* bisnonna
Great Lakes *npl*: **the ~** i Grandi Laghi
greatly ['greɪtlɪ] *adv* molto
greatness ['greɪtnɪs] *n* grandezza
Grecian ['gri:ʃən] *adj* greco(-a)
Greece [gri:s] *n* Grecia
greed [gri:d] *n* (*also*: **greediness**) avarizia; (*for food*) golosità, ghiottoneria
greedily ['gri:dɪlɪ] *adv* avidamente; golosamente
greedy ['gri:dɪ] *adj* avido(-a); goloso(-a), ghiotto(-a)
Greek [gri:k] *adj* greco(-a) ■ *n* greco(-a); (*Ling*) greco; **ancient/modern ~** greco antico/moderno
green [gri:n] *adj* (*also Pol*) verde; (*inexperienced*) inesperto(-a), ingenuo(-a) ■ *n* verde *m*; (*stretch of grass*) prato; (*also*: **village green**) ≈ piazza del paese; (*of golf course*) green *m inv*; **greens** *npl* (*vegetables*) verdura; **to have ~ fingers** *or* (*US*) **a ~ thumb** (*fig*) avere il pollice verde; **the G~ Party** (*Brit Pol*) i Verdi
green belt *n* (*round town*) cintura di verde
green card *n* (*Aut*) carta verde
greenery ['gri:nərɪ] *n* verde *m*
greenfly ['gri:nflaɪ] *n* afide *f*
greengage ['gri:ngeɪdʒ] *n* susina Regina Claudia
greengrocer ['gri:ngrəusəʳ] *n* (*Brit*) fruttivendolo(-a), erbivendolo(-a)
greenhouse ['gri:nhaus] *n* serra
greenhouse effect *n*: **the ~** l'effetto serra
greenhouse gas *n* gas *m inv* responsabile dell'effetto serra
greenish ['gri:nɪʃ] *adj* verdastro(-a)
Greenland ['gri:nlənd] *n* Groenlandia
Greenlander ['gri:nləndəʳ] *n* groenlandese *m/f*
green light *n*: **to give sb the ~** dare via libera a qn
green pepper *n* peperone *m* verde
greet [gri:t] *vt* salutare
greeting ['gri:tɪŋ] *n* saluto; **Christmas/birthday greetings** auguri *mpl* di Natale/di compleanno; **Season's greetings** Buone Feste
greeting card, greetings card *n* cartolina d'auguri
gregarious [grə'gɛərɪəs] *adj* gregario(-a), socievole
grenade [grə'neɪd] *n* (*also*: **hand grenade**) granata
grew [gru:] *pt of* **grow**
grey [greɪ] *adj* grigio(-a); **to go ~** diventar grigio
greyhound ['greɪhaund] *n* levriere *m*
grid [grɪd] *n* grata; (*Elec*) rete *f*; (*US Aut*) area d'incrocio
griddle ['grɪdl] *n* piastra
gridiron ['grɪdaɪən] *n* graticola
gridlock ['grɪdlɔk] *n* (*traffic jam*) paralisi *f inv* del traffico
grief [gri:f] *n* dolore *m*; **to come to ~** (*plan*) naufragare; (*person*) finire male
grievance ['gri:vəns] *n* doglianza, lagnanza; (*cause for complaint*) motivo di risentimento
grieve [gri:v] *vi* addolorarsi, soffrire ■ *vt* addolorare; **to ~ for sb** compiangere qn; (*dead person*) piangere qn
grievous bodily harm ['gri:vəs-] *n* (*Law*) aggressione *f*
grill [grɪl] *n* (*on cooker*) griglia ■ *vt* (*Brit*) cuocere ai ferri; (*question*) interrogare senza sosta; **grilled meat** carne *f* ai ferri *or* alla griglia; *see* **grillroom**

grille [grɪl] *n* grata; (*Aut*) griglia
grillroom ['grɪlrum], **grill** ['grɪl] *n* rosticceria
grim [grɪm] *adj* sinistro(-a), brutto(-a)
grimace [grɪ'meɪs] *n* smorfia ■ *vi* fare smorfie
grime [graɪm] *n* sudiciume *m*
grimy ['graɪmɪ] *adj* sudicio(-a)
grin [grɪn] *n* sorriso smagliante ■ *vi*: **to ~ (at)** sorridere (a), fare un gran sorriso (a)
grind [graɪnd] *vb* (*pt, pp* **ground**) [graund] *vt* macinare; (*US: meat*) tritare, macinare; (*make sharp*) arrotare; (*polish: gem, lens*) molare ■ *vi* (*car gears*) grattare ■ *n* (*work*) sgobbata; **to ~ one's teeth** digrignare i denti; **to ~ to a halt** (*vehicle*) arrestarsi con uno stridio di freni; (*fig: talks, scheme*) insabbiarsi; (*: work, production*) cessare del tutto; **the daily ~** (*col*) il trantran quotidiano
grinder ['graɪndəʳ] *n* (*machine: for coffee*) macinino
grindstone ['graɪndstəun] *n*: **to keep one's nose to the ~** darci sotto
grip [grɪp] *n* presa; (*holdall*) borsa da viaggio ■ *vt* afferrare; **to come to grips with** affrontare; cercare di risolvere; **to ~ the road** (*tyres*) far presa sulla strada; (*car*) tenere bene la strada; **to lose one's ~** perdere *or* allentare la presa; (*fig*) perdere la grinta
gripe [graɪp] *n* (*Med*) colica; (*col: complaint*) lagna ■ *vi* (*col*) brontolare
gripping ['grɪpɪŋ] *adj* avvincente
grisly ['grɪzlɪ] *adj* macabro(-a), orrido(-a)
grist [grɪst] *n* (*fig*): **it's (all) ~ to the mill** tutto aiuta
gristle ['grɪsl] *n* cartilagine *f*
grit [grɪt] *n* ghiaia; (*courage*) fegato ■ *vt* (*road*) coprire di sabbia; **to ~ one's teeth** stringere i denti; **I've got a piece of ~ in my eye** ho un bruscolino nell'occhio
grits [grɪts] *npl* (US) macinato grosso (di avena *etc*)
grizzle ['grɪzl] *vi* (*Brit*) piagnucolare
grizzly ['grɪzlɪ] *n* (*also*: **grizzly bear**) orso grigio, grizzly *m inv*
groan [grəun] *n* gemito ■ *vi* gemere
grocer ['grəusəʳ] *n* negoziante *m* di generi alimentari; **~'s (shop)** negozio di alimentari
groceries ['grəusərɪz] *npl* provviste *fpl*
grocery ['grəusərɪ] *n* (*shop*) (negozio di) alimentari
grog [grɔg] *n* grog *m inv*
groggy ['grɔgɪ] *adj* barcollante
groin [grɔɪn] *n* inguine *m*
groom [gru:m] *n* palafreniere *m*; (*also*: **bridegroom**) sposo ■ *vt* (*horse*) strigliare; (*fig*): **to ~ sb for** avviare qn a
groove [gru:v] *n* scanalatura, solco
grope [grəup] *vi* andare a tentoni; **to ~ for sth** cercare qc a tastoni
gross [grəus] *adj* grossolano(-a); (*Comm*) lordo(-a) ■ *n* (*pl inv: twelve dozen*) grossa ■ *vt* (*Comm*) incassare, avere un incasso lordo di
gross domestic product *n* prodotto interno lordo
grossly ['grəuslɪ] *adv* (*greatly*) molto
gross national product *n* prodotto nazionale lordo
grotesque [grəu'tɛsk] *adj* grottesco(-a)
grotto ['grɔtəu] *n* grotta
grotty ['grɔtɪ] *adj* (*Brit col*) squallido(-a)
grouch [grautʃ] (*col*) *vi* brontolare ■ *n* (*person*) brontolone(-a)
ground [graund] *pt, pp of* **grind** ■ *adj* (*coffee etc*) macinato(-a) ■ *n* suolo, terra; (*land*) terreno; (*Sport*) campo; (*reason: gen pl*) ragione *f*; (*US: also*: **ground wire**) (presa a) terra ■ *vt* (*plane*) tenere a terra; (*US Elec*) mettere la presa a terra a ■ *vi* (*ship*) arenarsi; **grounds** *npl* (*of coffee etc*) fondi *mpl*; (*gardens etc*) terreno, giardini *mpl*; **on/to the ~** per/a terra; **below ~** sottoterra; **common ~** terreno comune; **to gain/lose ~** guadagnare/perdere terreno; **he covered a lot of ~ in his lecture** ha toccato molti argomenti nel corso della conferenza
ground cloth *n* (*US*) = **groundsheet**
ground control *n* (*Aviat, Space*) base *f* di controllo
ground floor *n* pianterreno
grounding ['graundɪŋ] *n* (*in education*) basi *fpl*
groundless ['graundlɪs] *adj* infondato(-a)
groundnut ['graundnʌt] *n* arachide *f*
ground rent *n* (*Brit*) canone *m* di affitto di un terreno
ground rules *npl* regole *fpl* fondamentali
groundsheet ['graundʃi:t] *n* (*Brit*) telone *m* impermeabile
groundsman ['graundzmən], (*US*) **groundskeeper** ['graundzki:pəʳ] *n* (*Sport*) custode *m* (di campo sportivo)
ground staff *n* personale *m* di terra
groundswell ['graundswɛl] *n* maremoto; (*fig*) movimento
ground-to-air ['graundtu'ɛəʳ] *adj* terra-aria *inv*
ground-to-ground ['grauntə'graund] *adj*: **~ missile** missile *m* terra-terra
groundwork ['graundwə:k] *n* preparazione *f*
group [gru:p] *n* gruppo; (*Mus: pop group*) complesso, gruppo ■ *vt* raggruppare ■ *vi* raggrupparsi
groupie ['gru:pɪ] *n* groupie *m/f inv*, fan *m/f inv* scatenato(-a)
group therapy *n* terapia di gruppo
grouse [graus] *n* (*pl inv: bird*) tetraone *m* ■ *vi* (*complain*) brontolare

g

grove [grəuv] *n* boschetto
grovel ['grɔvl] *vi* (*fig*): **to ~ (before)** strisciare (di fronte a)
grow (*pt* **grew**, *pp* **grown**) [grəu, gru:, grəun] *vi* crescere; (*increase*) aumentare; (*become*): **to ~ rich/weak** arricchirsi/indebolirsi ■ *vt* coltivare, far crescere; **to ~ tired of waiting** stancarsi di aspettare
▸ **grow apart** *vi* (*fig*) estraniarsi
▸ **grow away from** *vt fus* (*fig*) allontanarsi da, staccarsi da
▸ **grow on** *vt fus*: **that painting is growing on me** quel quadro più lo guardo più mi piace
▸ **grow out of** *vt fus* (*clothes*) diventare troppo grande per indossare; (*habit*) perdere (col tempo); **he'll ~ out of it** gli passerà
▸ **grow up** *vi* farsi grande, crescere
grower ['grəuə^r] *n* coltivatore(-trice)
growing ['grəuɪŋ] *adj* (*fear, amount*) crescente; **~ pains** (*also fig*) problemi *mpl* di crescita
growl [graul] *vi* ringhiare
grown [grəun] *pp of* **grow** ■ *adj* adulto(-a), maturo(-a)
grown-up [grəun'ʌp] *n* adulto(-a), grande *m/f*
growth [grəuθ] *n* crescita, sviluppo; (*what has grown*) crescita; (*Med*) escrescenza, tumore *m*
growth rate *n* tasso di crescita
grub [grʌb] *n* larva; (*col: food*) roba (da mangiare)
grubby ['grʌbɪ] *adj* sporco(-a)
grudge [grʌdʒ] *n* rancore *m* ■ *vt*: **to ~ sb sth** dare qc a qn di malavoglia; invidiare qc a qn; **to bear sb a ~ (for)** serbar rancore a qn (per)
grudgingly ['grʌdʒɪŋlɪ] *adv* di malavoglia, di malincuore
gruelling, (*US*) **grueling** ['gruəlɪŋ] *adj* estenuante
gruesome ['gru:səm] *adj* orribile
gruff [grʌf] *adj* rozzo(-a)
grumble ['grʌmbl] *vi* brontolare, lagnarsi
grumpy ['grʌmpɪ] *adj* stizzito(-a)
grunge [grʌndʒ] *n* (*Mus*) grunge *m inv*; (*style*) moda *f* grunge *inv*
grunt [grʌnt] *vi* grugnire ■ *n* grugnito
G-string ['dʒi:strɪŋ] *n* (*garment*) tanga *m inv*
GT *abbr* (*Aut*: = *gran turismo*) GT
GU *abbr* (*US Post*) = **Guam**
guarantee [gærən'ti:] *n* garanzia ■ *vt* garantire; **he can't ~ (that) he'll come** non può garantire che verrà
guarantor [gærən'tɔ:^r] *n* garante *m/f*
guard [gɑ:d] *n* guardia; (*protection*) riparo, protezione *f*; (*Boxing*) difesa; (*one man*) guardia, sentinella; (*Brit Rail*) capotreno; (*safety device: on machine*) schermo protettivo; (*also*: **fire guard**) parafuoco ■ *vt* fare la guardia a; **to ~ (against** *or* **from)** proteggere (da), salvaguardare (da); **to be on one's ~** (*fig*) stare in guardia
▸ **guard against** *vi*: **to ~ against doing sth** guardarsi dal fare qc
guard dog *n* cane *m* da guardia
guarded ['gɑ:dɪd] *adj* (*fig*) cauto(-a), guardingo(-a)
guardian ['gɑ:dɪən] *n* custode *m*; (*of minor*) tutore(-trice)
guard's van *n* (*Brit Rail*) vagone *m* di servizio
Guatemala [gwɑ:tə'mɑ:lə] *n* Guatemala *m*
Guernsey ['gə:nzɪ] *n* Guernesey *f*
guerrilla [gə'rɪlə] *n* guerrigliero
guerrilla warfare *n* guerriglia
guess [gɛs] *vi* indovinare ■ *vt* indovinare; (*US*) credere, pensare ■ *n* congettura; **to take** *or* **have a ~** cercare di indovinare; **my ~ is that ...** suppongo che ...; **to keep sb guessing** tenere qn in sospeso *or* sulla corda; **I ~ you're right** mi sa che hai ragione
guesstimate ['gɛstɪmɪt] *n* (*col*) stima approssimativa
guesswork ['gɛswə:k] *n*: **I got the answer by ~** ho azzeccato la risposta
guest [gɛst] *n* ospite *m/f*; (*in hotel*) cliente *m/f*; **be my ~** (*col*) fai come (se fossi) a casa tua
guest-house ['gɛsthaus] *n* pensione *f*
guest room *n* camera degli ospiti
guff [gʌf] *n* (*col*) stupidaggini *fpl*, assurdità *fpl*
guffaw [gʌ'fɔ:] *n* risata sonora ■ *vi* scoppiare di una risata sonora
guidance ['gaɪdəns] *n* guida, direzione *f*; **marriage/vocational ~** consulenza matrimoniale/per l'avviamento professionale
guide [gaɪd] *n* (*person, book etc*) guida; (*also*: **girl guide**) giovane esploratrice *f* ■ *vt* guidare; **to be guided by sb/sth** farsi *or* lasciarsi guidare da qn/qc
guidebook ['gaɪdbuk] *n* guida
guided missile *n* missile *m* telecomandato
guide dog *n* (*Brit*) cane *m* guida *inv*
guidelines ['gaɪdlaɪnz] *npl* (*fig*) indicazioni *fpl*, linee *fpl* direttive
guild [gɪld] *n* arte *f*, corporazione *f*; associazione *f*
guildhall ['gɪldhɔ:l] *n* (*Brit*) palazzo municipale
guile [gaɪl] *n* astuzia
guileless ['gaɪllɪs] *adj* candido(-a)
guillotine ['gɪləti:n] *n* ghigliottina
guilt [gɪlt] *n* colpevolezza
guilty ['gɪltɪ] *adj* colpevole; **to feel ~ (about)**

sentirsi in colpa (per); **to plead ~/not ~** dichiararsi colpevole/innocente
Guinea ['gɪnɪ] *n*: **Republic of ~** Repubblica di Guinea
guinea ['gɪnɪ] *n* (*Brit*) ghinea (*= 21 shillings: valuta ora fuori uso*)
guinea pig *n* cavia
guise [gaɪz] *n* maschera
guitar [gɪ'tɑːʳ] *n* chitarra
guitarist [gɪ'tɑːrɪst] *n* chitarrista *m/f*
gulch [gʌltʃ] *n* (*US*) burrone *m*
gulf [gʌlf] *n* golfo; (*abyss*) abisso; **the (Persian) G~** il Golfo Persico
Gulf States *npl*: **the ~** i paesi del Golfo Persico
Gulf Stream *n*: **the ~** la corrente del Golfo
gull [gʌl] *n* gabbiano
gullet ['gʌlɪt] *n* gola
gullibility [gʌlɪ'bɪlɪtɪ] *n* semplicioneria
gullible ['gʌlɪbl] *adj* credulo(-a)
gully ['gʌlɪ] *n* burrone *m*; gola; canale *m*
gulp [gʌlp] *vi* deglutire; (*from emotion*) avere il nodo in gola ▪ *vt* (*also*: **gulp down**) tracannare, inghiottire ▪ *n* (*of liquid*) sorso; (*of food*) boccone *m*; **in** *or* **at one ~** in un sorso, d'un fiato
gum [gʌm] *n* (*Anat*) gengiva; (*glue*) colla; (*sweet*) gelatina di frutta; (*also*: **chewing-gum**) chewing-gum *m* ▪ *vt* incollare
▸ **gum up** *vt*: **to ~ up the works** (*col*) mettere il bastone tra le ruote
gumboil ['gʌmbɔɪl] *n* ascesso (dentario)
gumboots ['gʌmbuːts] *npl* (*Brit*) stivali *mpl* di gomma
gumption ['gʌmpʃən] *n* buon senso, senso pratico
gun [gʌn] *n* fucile *m*; (*small*) pistola, rivoltella; (*rifle*) carabina; (*shotgun*) fucile da caccia; (*cannon*) cannone *m* ▪ *vt* (*also*: **gun down**) abbattere a colpi di pistola *or* fucile; **to stick to one's guns** (*fig*) tener duro
gunboat ['gʌnbəut] *n* cannoniera
gun dog *n* cane *m* da caccia
gunfire ['gʌnfaɪəʳ] *n* spari *mpl*
gung-ho ['gʌŋ'həu] *adj* (*col*) stupidamente entusiasta
gunk [gʌŋk] *n* porcherie *fpl*
gunman ['gʌnmən] *n* bandito armato
gunner ['gʌnəʳ] *n* artigliere *m*
gunpoint ['gʌnpɔɪnt] *n*: **at ~** sotto minaccia di fucile
gunpowder ['gʌnpaudəʳ] *n* polvere *f* da sparo
gunrunner ['gʌnrʌnəʳ] *n* contrabbandiere d'armi
gunrunning ['gʌnrʌnɪŋ] *n* contrabbando d'armi
gunshot ['gʌnʃɔt] *n* sparo; **within ~** a portata di fucile
gunsmith ['gʌnsmɪθ] *n* armaiolo
gurgle ['gəːgl] *n* gorgoglio ▪ *vi* gorgogliare
guru ['guruː] *n* guru *m inv*
gush [gʌʃ] *n* fiotto, getto ▪ *vi* sgorgare; (*fig*) abbandonarsi ad effusioni
gushing ['gʌʃɪŋ] *adj* che fa smancerie, smorfioso(-a)
gusset ['gʌsɪt] *n* gherone *m*; (*in tights, pants*) rinforzo
gust [gʌst] *n* (*of wind*) raffica; (*of smoke*) buffata
gusto ['gʌstəu] *n* entusiasmo
gusty ['gʌstɪ] *adj* (*wind*) a raffiche; (*day*) tempestoso(-a)
gut [gʌt] *n* intestino, budello; (*Mus etc*) minugia; **guts** *npl* (*col: innards*) budella *fpl*; (*: of animals*) interiora *fpl*; (*courage*) fegato ▪ *vt* (*poultry, fish*) levare le interiora a, sventrare; (*building*) svuotare; (*: fire*) divorare l'interno di; **to hate sb's guts** odiare qn a morte
gut reaction *n* reazione *f* istintiva
gutsy ['gʌtsɪ] *adj* (*col: style*) che ha mordente; (*plucky*) coraggioso(-a)
gutted ['gʌtɪd] *adv* (*col: upset*) scioccato(-a)
gutter ['gʌtəʳ] *n* (*of roof*) grondaia; (*in street*) cunetta
gutter press *n*: **the ~** la stampa scandalistica
guttural ['gʌtərl] *adj* gutturale
guy [gaɪ] *n* (*also*: **guyrope**) cavo *or* corda di fissaggio; (*col: man*) tipo, elemento; (*figure*) *effigie di Guy Fawkes*
Guyana [gaɪ'ænə] *n* Guayana *f*
Guy Fawkes Night [-'fɔːks-] *n* (*Brit*) *vedi nota*

GUY FAWKES NIGHT

La sera del 5 novembre, in occasione della *Guy Fawkes Night*, altrimenti chiamata *Bonfire Night*, viene commemorato con falò e fuochi d'artificio il fallimento della Congiura delle Polveri contro Giacomo I nel 1605. La festa prende il nome dal principale congiurato della cospirazione, Guy Fawkes, la cui effigie viene bruciata durante i festeggiamenti.

guzzle ['gʌzl] *vi* gozzovigliare ▪ *vt* trangugiare
gym [dʒɪm] *n* (*also*: **gymnasium**) palestra; (*also*: **gymnastics**) ginnastica
gymkhana [dʒɪm'kɑːnə] *n* gimkana
gymnasium [dʒɪm'neɪzɪəm] *n* palestra
gymnast ['dʒɪmnæst] *n* ginnasta *m/f*
gymnastics [dʒɪm'næstɪks] *n, npl* ginnastica

gym shoes *npl* scarpe *fpl* da ginnastica
gym slip *n* (*Brit*) grembiule *m* da scuola (*per ragazze*)
gynaecologist, (*US*) **gynecologist** [gaɪnɪ'kɔlədʒɪst] *n* ginecologo(-a)
gynaecology, (*US*) **gynecology** [gaɪnə'kɔlədʒɪ] *n* ginecologia
gypsy ['dʒɪpsɪ] *n* = **gipsy**
gyrate [dʒaɪ'reɪt] *vi* girare
gyroscope ['dʒaɪərəskəup] *n* giroscopio

H, h [eɪtʃ] *n* (*letter*) H, h *f or m inv*; **H for Harry**, (*US*) **H for How** ≈ H come Hotel
habeas corpus ['heɪbɪəs'kɔ:pəs] *n* (*Law*) habeas corpus *m inv*
haberdashery ['hæbədæʃərɪ] *n* merceria
habit ['hæbɪt] *n* abitudine *f*; (*costume*) abito; (*Rel*) tonaca; **to get out of/into the ~ of doing sth** perdere/prendere l'abitudine di fare qc
habitable ['hæbɪtəbl] *adj* abitabile
habitat ['hæbɪtæt] *n* habitat *m inv*
habitation [hæbɪ'teɪʃən] *n* abitazione *f*
habitual [hə'bɪtjuəl] *adj* abituale; (*drinker, liar*) inveterato(-a)
habitually [hə'bɪtjuəlɪ] *adv* abitualmente, di solito
hack [hæk] *vt* tagliare, fare a pezzi ■ *n* (*cut*) taglio; (*blow*) colpo; (*old horse*) ronzino; (*pej: writer*) negro
hacker ['hækəʳ] *n* (*Comput*) pirata *m* informatico
hackles ['hæklz] *npl*: **to make sb's ~ rise** (*fig*) rendere qn furioso
hackney cab ['hæknɪ-] *n* carrozza a nolo
hackneyed ['hæknɪd] *adj* comune, trito(-a)
hacksaw ['hæksɔ:] *n* seghetto (per metallo)
had [hæd] *pt, pp of* **have**
haddock ['hædək] *n* eglefino
hadn't ['hædnt] = **had not**
haematology, (*US*) **hematology** [hi:mə'tɔlədʒɪ] *n* ematologia
haemoglobin, (*US*) **hemoglobin** [hi:məu'gləubɪn] *n* emoglobina
haemophilia, (*US*) **hemophilia** [hi:məu'fɪlɪə] *n* emofilia
haemorrhage, (*US*) **hemorrhage** ['hɛmərɪdʒ] *n* emorragia
haemorrhoids, (*US*) **hemorrhoids** ['hɛmərɔɪdz] *npl* emorroidi *fpl*
hag [hæg] *n* (*ugly*) befana; (*nasty*) megera; (*witch*) strega
haggard ['hægəd] *adj* sfinito(-a)
haggis ['hægɪs] *n* (*Scottish*) *insaccato a base di frattaglie di pecora e avena*
haggle ['hægl] *vi*: **to ~ (over)** contrattare (su); (*argue*) discutere (su)
haggling ['hæglɪŋ] *n* contrattazioni *fpl*
Hague [heɪg] *n*: **The ~** L'Aia
hail [heɪl] *n* grandine *f* ■ *vt* (*call*) chiamare; (*greet*) salutare ■ *vi* grandinare; **to ~ (as)** acclamare (come); **he hails from Scotland** viene dalla Scozia
hailstone ['heɪlstəun] *n* chicco di grandine
hailstorm ['heɪlstɔ:m] *n* grandinata
hair [hɛəʳ] *n* capelli *mpl*; (*single hair: on head*) capello; (*: on body*) pelo; **to do one's ~** pettinarsi
hairbrush ['hɛəbrʌʃ] *n* spazzola per capelli
haircut ['hɛəkʌt] *n* taglio di capelli; **I need a ~** devo tagliarmi i capelli
hairdo ['hɛədu:] *n* acconciatura, pettinatura
hairdresser ['hɛədrɛsəʳ] *n* parrucchiere(-a)
hair-dryer ['hɛədraɪəʳ] *n* asciugacapelli *m inv*
-haired [hɛəd] *suffix*: **fair/long~** dai capelli biondi/lunghi
hairgrip ['hɛəgrɪp] *n* forcina
hairline ['hɛəlaɪn] *n* attaccatura dei capelli
hairline fracture *n* incrinatura
hairnet ['hɛənɛt] *n* retina (per capelli)
hair oil *n* brillantina
hairpiece ['hɛəpi:s] *n* toupet *m inv*
hairpin ['hɛəpɪn] *n* forcina
hairpin bend, (*US*) **hairpin curve** *n* tornante *m*
hair-raising ['hɛəreɪzɪŋ] *adj* orripilante
hair remover *n* crema depilatoria
hair spray *n* lacca per capelli
hairstyle ['hɛəstaɪl] *n* pettinatura, acconciatura
hairy ['hɛərɪ] *adj* irsuto(-a); peloso(-a); (*col: frightening*) spaventoso(-a)
Haiti ['heɪtɪ] *n* Haiti *f*
hake (*pl* **~** *or* **hakes**) [heɪk] *n* nasello
halal [hə'lɑ:l] *n*: **~ meat** carne macellata secondo la legge mussulmana
halcyon ['hælsɪən] *adj* sereno(-a)
hale [heɪl] *adj*: **~ and hearty** che scoppia di salute

half [hɑːf] *n* (*pl* **halves**) [hɑːvz] mezzo, metà *f inv*; (*Sport: of match*) tempo; (*: of ground*) metà campo ■ *adj* mezzo(-a) ■ *adv* a mezzo, a metà; **~ an hour** mezz'ora; **~ a dozen** mezza dozzina; **~ a pound** mezza libbra; **two and a ~** due e mezzo; **a week and a ~** una settimana e mezza; **~ (of it)** la metà; **~ (of)** la metà di; **~ the amount of** la metà di; **to cut sth in ~** tagliare qc in due; **~ empty/closed** mezzo vuoto/chiuso, semivuoto/semichiuso; **~ past 3** le 3 e mezza; **to go halves (with sb)** fare a metà (con qn)
half-back ['hɑːfbæk] *n* (*Sport*) mediano
half-baked [hɑːf'beɪkt] *adj* (*col: idea, scheme*) mal combinato(-a), che non sta in piedi
half-breed ['hɑːfbriːd] *n* = **half-caste**
half-brother ['hɑːfbrʌðəʳ] *n* fratellastro
half-caste ['hɑːfkɑːst] *n* meticcio(-a)
half-hearted [hɑːf'hɑːtɪd] *adj* tiepido(-a)
half-hour [hɑːf'auəʳ] *n* mezz'ora
half-mast ['hɑːf'mɑːst] *n*: **at ~** (*flag*) a mezz'asta
halfpenny ['heɪpnɪ] *n* mezzo penny *m inv*
half-price ['hɑːf'praɪs] *adj* a metà prezzo ■ *adv* (*also*: **at half-price**) a metà prezzo
half term *n* (*Brit Scol*) vacanza a *or* di metà trimestre
half-time [hɑːf'taɪm] *n* (*Sport*) intervallo
halfway [hɑːf'weɪ] *adv* a metà strada; **to meet sb ~** (*fig*) arrivare a un compromesso con qn
halfway house *n* (*hostel*) *ostello dove possono alloggiare temporaneamente ex detenuti*; (*fig*) via di mezzo
half-wit ['hɑːfwɪt] *n* (*col*) idiota *m/f*
half-yearly [hɑːf'jɪəlɪ] *adv* semestralmente, ogni sei mesi ■ *adj* semestrale
halibut ['hælɪbət] *n* (*pl inv*) ippoglosso
halitosis [hælɪ'təusɪs] *n* alitosi *f*
hall [hɔːl] *n* sala, salone *m*; (*entrance way*) entrata; (*corridor*) corridoio; (*mansion*) grande villa, maniero; **~ of residence** *n* (*Brit*) casa dello studente
hallmark ['hɔːlmɑːk] *n* marchio di garanzia; (*fig*) caratteristica
hallo [hə'ləu] *excl* = **hello**
Halloween ['hæləu'iːn] *n* vigilia d'Ognissanti; *vedi nota*

HALLOWEEN

Secondo la tradizione anglosassone, durante la notte di *Halloween*, il 31 di ottobre, è possibile vedere le streghe e i fantasmi. I bambini, travestiti da fantasmi, streghe, mostri o simili, vanno di porta in porta e raccolgono dolci e piccoli doni.

hallucination [həluːsɪ'neɪʃən] *n* allucinazione *f*
hallucinogenic [həluːsɪnəu'dʒɛnɪk] *adj* allucinogeno(-a)
hallway ['hɔːlweɪ] *n* ingresso; corridoio
halo ['heɪləu] *n* (*of saint etc*) aureola; (*of sun*) alone *m*
halt [hɔːlt] *n* fermata ■ *vt* fermare ■ *vi* fermarsi; **to call a ~ (to sth)** (*fig*) mettere *or* porre fine (a qc)
halter ['hɔːltəʳ] *n* (*for horse*) cavezza
halterneck ['hɔːltənɛk] *adj* allacciato(-a) dietro il collo
halve [hɑːv] *vt* (*apple etc*) dividere a metà; (*expense*) ridurre di metà
halves [hɑːvz] *npl of* **half**
ham [hæm] *n* prosciutto; (*col: also*: **radio ham**) radioamatore(-trice); (*also*: **ham actor**) attore(-trice) senza talento
Hamburg ['hæmbəːg] *n* Amburgo *f*
hamburger ['hæmbəːgəʳ] *n* hamburger *m inv*
ham-fisted ['hæm'fɪstɪd], (*US*) **ham-handed** ['hæm'hændɪd] *adj* maldestro(-a)
hamlet ['hæmlɪt] *n* paesetto
hammer ['hæməʳ] *n* martello ■ *vt* martellare; (*fig*) sconfiggere duramente ■ *vi* (*at door*) picchiare; **to ~ a point home to sb** cacciare un'idea in testa a qn
▸ **hammer out** *vt* (*metal*) spianare (a martellate); (*fig: solution, agreement*) mettere a punto
hammock ['hæmək] *n* amaca
hamper ['hæmpəʳ] *vt* impedire ■ *n* cesta
hamster ['hæmstəʳ] *n* criceto
hamstring ['hæmstrɪŋ] *n* (*Anat*) tendine *m* del ginocchio
hand [hænd] *n* mano *f*; (*of clock*) lancetta; (*handwriting*) scrittura; (*at cards*) mano; (*: game*) partita; (*worker*) operaio(-a); (*measurement: of horse*) ≈ dieci centimetri ■ *vt* dare, passare; **to give sb a ~** dare una mano a qn; **at ~** a portata di mano; **in ~** a disposizione; (*work*) in corso; **we have the matter in ~** ci stiamo occupando della cosa; **we have the situation in ~** abbiamo la situazione sotto controllo; **to be on ~** (*person*) essere disponibile; (*emergency services*) essere pronto(-a) a intervenire; **to ~** (*information etc*) a portata di mano; **to force sb's ~** forzare la mano a qn; **to have a free ~** avere carta bianca; **to have in one's ~** (*also fig*) avere in mano *or* in pugno; **on the one ~ ..., on the other ~** da un lato ..., dall'altro
▸ **hand down** *vt* passare giù; (*tradition, heirloom*) tramandare; (*US: sentence, verdict*) emettere
▸ **hand in** *vt* consegnare

▸ **hand out** *vt* (*leaflets*) distribuire; (*advice*) elargire
▸ **hand over** *vt* passare; cedere
▸ **hand round** *vt* (*Brit: information, papers*) far passare; (*distribute: chocolates etc*) far girare; (*hostess*) offrire

handbag ['hændbæg] *n* borsetta
hand baggage *n* bagaglio a mano
handball ['hændbɔːl] *n* pallamano *f*
handbasin ['hændbeɪsn] *n* lavandino
handbook ['hændbuk] *n* manuale *m*
handbrake ['hændbreɪk] *n* freno a mano
hand cream *n* crema per le mani
handcuffs ['hændkʌfs] *npl* manette *fpl*
handful ['hændful] *n* manciata, pugno
hand-held ['hænd'hɛld] *adj* portatile
handicap ['hændɪkæp] *n* handicap *m inv* ■ *vt* handicappare; **to be mentally handicapped** essere un handicappato mentale; **to be physically handicapped** essere handicappato
handicraft ['hændɪkrɑːft] *n* lavoro d'artigiano
handiwork ['hændɪwəːk] *n* lavorazione *f* a mano; **this looks like his ~** (*pej*) qui c'è il suo zampino
handkerchief ['hæŋkətʃɪf] *n* fazzoletto
handle ['hændl] *n* (*of door etc*) maniglia; (*of cup etc*) ansa; (*of knife etc*) impugnatura; (*of saucepan*) manico; (*for winding*) manovella ■ *vt* toccare, maneggiare; manovrare; (*deal with*) occuparsi di; (*treat: people*) trattare; **"~ with care"** "fragile"
handlebar ['hændlbɑːʳ] *n*, **handlebars** ['hændlbɑːz] *npl* manubrio
handling ['hændlɪŋ] *n* (*Aut*) maneggevolezza; (*of issue*) modo di affrontare
handling charges *npl* commissione *f* per la prestazione; (*for goods*) spese *fpl* di trasporto; (*Banking*) spese *fpl* bancarie
hand-luggage ['hændlʌgɪdʒ] *n* bagagli *mpl* a mano
handmade [hænd'meɪd] *adj* fatto(-a) a mano; (*biscuits etc*) fatto(-a) in casa
handout ['hændaut] *n* (*leaflet*) volantino; (*press handout*) comunicato stampa
hand-picked [hænd'pɪkt] *adj* (*produce*) scelto(-a), selezionato(-a); (*staff etc*) scelto(-a)
handrail ['hændreɪl] *n* (*on staircase etc*) corrimano
handset ['hændsɛt] *n* (*Tel*) ricevitore *m*
hands-free ['hændzfriː] *adj* (*telephone*) con auricolare; (*microphone*) vivavoce
handshake ['hændʃeɪk] *n* stretta di mano; (*Comput*) colloquio
handsome ['hænsəm] *adj* bello(-a); (*reward*) generoso(-a); (*profit, fortune*) considerevole
hands-on ['hændz'ɔn] *adj*: **~ experience** esperienza diretta *or* pratica
handstand ['hændstænd] *n*: **to do a ~** fare la verticale
hand-to-mouth ['hændtə'mauθ] *adj* (*existence*) precario(-a)
handwriting ['hændraɪtɪŋ] *n* scrittura
handwritten ['hændrɪtn] *adj* scritto(-a) a mano, manoscritto(-a)
handy ['hændɪ] *adj* (*person*) bravo(-a); (*close at hand*) a portata di mano; (*convenient*) comodo(-a); (*useful: machine etc*) pratico(-a), utile; **to come in ~** servire
handyman ['hændɪmæn] *n* tuttofare *m inv*; **tools for the ~** arnesi per il fatelo-da-voi
hang (*pt, pp* **hung**) [hæŋ, hʌŋ] *vt* appendere; (*criminal*) (*pt, pp* **hanged**) impiccare ■ *vi* pendere; (*hair*) scendere; (*drapery*) cadere; **to get the ~ of (doing) sth** (*col*) cominciare a capire (come si fa) qc
▸ **hang about** *vi* bighellonare, ciondolare
▸ **hang back** *vi* (*hesitate*): **to ~ back (from doing)** essere riluttante (a fare)
▸ **hang on** *vi* (*wait*) aspettare ■ *vt fus* (*depend on: decision etc*) dipendere da; **to ~ on to** (*keep hold of*) aggrapparsi a, attaccarsi a; (*keep*) tenere
▸ **hang out** *vt* (*washing*) stendere (fuori); (*col: live*) stare ■ *vi* penzolare, pendere
▸ **hang together** *vi* (*argument etc*) stare in piedi
▸ **hang up** *vi* (*Tel*) riattaccare ■ *vt* appendere; **to ~ up on sb** (*Tel*) metter giù il ricevitore a qn

hangar ['hæŋəʳ] *n* hangar *m inv*
hangdog ['hæŋdɔg] *adj* (*guilty: look, expression*) da cane bastonato
hanger ['hæŋəʳ] *n* gruccia
hanger-on [hæŋər'ɔn] *n* parassita *m*
hang-glider ['hæŋglaɪdəʳ] *n* deltaplano
hang-gliding ['hæŋglaɪdɪŋ] *n* volo col deltaplano
hanging ['hæŋɪŋ] *n* (*execution*) impiccagione *f*
hangman ['hæŋmən] *n* boia *m*, carnefice *m*
hangover ['hæŋəuvəʳ] *n* (*after drinking*) postumi *mpl* di sbornia
hang-up ['hæŋʌp] *n* complesso
hank [hæŋk] *n* matassa
hanker ['hæŋkəʳ] *vi*: **to ~ after** bramare
hankering ['hæŋkərɪŋ] *n*: **to have a ~ for sth/to do sth** avere una gran voglia di qc/di fare qc
hankie, hanky ['hæŋkɪ] *n abbr* = **handkerchief**
Hants *abbr* (*Brit*) = **Hampshire**
haphazard [hæp'hæzəd] *adj* a casaccio, alla carlona
hapless ['hæplɪs] *adj* disgraziato(-a); (*unfortunate*) sventurato(-a)

happen ['hæpən] *vi* accadere, succedere; **she happened to be free** per caso era libera; **if anything happened to him** se dovesse succedergli qualcosa; **as it happens** guarda caso; **what's happening?** cosa succede?, cosa sta succedendo?
▸ **happen (up)on** *vt fus* capitare su
happening ['hæpnɪŋ] *n* avvenimento
happily ['hæpɪlɪ] *adv* felicemente; fortunatamente
happiness ['hæpɪnɪs] *n* felicità, contentezza
happy ['hæpɪ] *adj* felice, contento(-a); **~ with** (*arrangements etc*) soddisfatto(-a) di; **yes, I'd be ~ to** (certo,) con piacere, (ben) volentieri; **~ birthday!** buon compleanno!; **~ Christmas/New Year!** buon Natale/anno!
happy-go-lucky ['hæpɪgəu'lʌkɪ] *adj* spensierato(-a)
happy hour *n orario in cui i pub hanno prezzi ridotti*
harangue [hə'ræŋ] *vt* arringare
harass ['hærəs] *vt* molestare
harassed ['hærəst] *adj* assillato(-a)
harassment ['hærəsmənt] *n* molestia
harbour, (*US*) **harbor** ['hɑːbə^r] *n* porto ■ *vt* dare rifugio a; (*retain: grudge etc*) covare, nutrire
harbour dues, (*US*) **harbor dues** *npl* diritti *mpl* portuali
harbour master, (*US*) **harbor master** *n* capitano di porto
hard [hɑːd] *adj* duro(-a) ■ *adv* (*work*) sodo; (*think, try*) bene; **to look ~ at** guardare fissamente; esaminare attentamente; **to drink ~** bere forte; **~ luck!** peccato!; **no ~ feelings!** senza rancore!; **to be ~ of hearing** essere duro(-a) d'orecchio; **to be ~ on sb** essere severo con qn; **to be ~ done by** essere trattato(-a) ingiustamente; **I find it ~ to believe that ...** stento *or* faccio fatica a credere che ... + *sub*
hard-and-fast ['hɑːdən'fɑːst] *adj* ferreo(-a)
hardback ['hɑːdbæk] *n* libro rilegato
hardboard ['hɑːdbɔːd] *n* legno precompresso
hard-boiled egg ['hɑːd'bɔɪld-] *n* uovo sodo
hard cash *n* denaro in contanti
hard copy *n* (*Comput*) hard copy *f inv*, terminale *m* di stampa
hard-core ['hɑːd'kɔː^r] *adj* (*pornography*) hardcore *inv*; (*supporters*) irriducibile
hard court *n* (*Tennis*) campo in terra battuta
hard disk *n* (*Comput*) hard disk *m inv*, disco rigido
harden ['hɑːdn] *vt* indurire; (*steel*) temprare; (*fig: determination*) rafforzare ■ *vi* (*substance*) indurirsi
hardened ['hɑːdnd] *adj* (*criminal*) incallito(-a); **to be ~ to sth** essere (diventato) insensibile a qc
hard graft *n*: **by sheer ~** lavorando da matti
hard-headed ['hɑː'd'hɛdɪd] *adj* pratico(-a)
hard-hearted ['hɑː'd'hɑːtɪd] *adj* che non si lascia commuovere, dal cuore duro
hard-hitting ['hɑː'd'hɪtɪŋ] *adj* molto duro(-a); **a ~ documentary** un documentario *m* verità *inv*
hard labour *n* lavori forzati *mpl*
hardliner [hɑː'd'laɪnə^r] *n* fautore(-trice) della linea dura
hard-luck story [hɑː'd'lʌk-] *n* storia lacrimosa (*con un fine ben preciso*)
hardly ['hɑːdlɪ] *adv* (*scarcely*) appena, a mala pena; **it's ~ the case** non è proprio il caso; **~ anyone/anywhere** quasi nessuno/da nessuna parte; **I can ~ believe it** stento a crederci
hardness ['hɑːdnɪs] *n* durezza
hard-nosed ['hɑː'd'nəuzd] *adj* (*people*) con i piedi per terra
hard-pressed ['hɑː'd'prɛst] *adj* in difficoltà
hard sell *n* (*Comm*) intensa campagna promozionale
hardship ['hɑːdʃɪp] *n* avversità *f inv*; privazioni *fpl*
hard shoulder *n* (*Brit Aut*) corsia d'emergenza
hard-up [hɑː'd'ʌp] *adj* (*col*) al verde
hardware ['hɑːdwɛə^r] *n* ferramenta *fpl*; (*Comput*) hardware *m*
hardware shop *n* (negozio di) ferramenta *fpl*
hard-wearing [hɑː'd'wɛərɪŋ] *adj* resistente, robusto(-a)
hard-won ['hɑː'd'wʌn] *adj* sudato(-a)
hard-working [hɑː'd'wəːkɪŋ] *adj* lavoratore(-trice)
hardy ['hɑːdɪ] *adj* robusto(-a); (*plant*) resistente al gelo
hare [hɛə^r] *n* lepre *f*
hare-brained ['hɛəbreɪnd] *adj* folle; scervellato(-a)
harelip ['hɛəlɪp] *n* (*Med*) labbro leporino
harem [hɑː'riːm] *n* harem *m inv*
hark back [hɑːk-] *vi*: **to ~ back to** (*former days*) rievocare; (*earlier occasion*) ritornare a *or* su
harm [hɑːm] *n* male *m*; (*wrong*) danno ■ *vt* (*person*) fare male a; (*thing*) danneggiare; **to mean no ~** non avere l'intenzione d'offendere; **out of ~'s way** al sicuro; **there's no ~ in trying** tentar non nuoce
harmful ['hɑːmful] *adj* dannoso(-a)
harmless ['hɑːmlɪs] *adj* innocuo(-a); inoffensivo(-a)
harmonic [hɑː'mɔnɪk] *adj* armonico(-a)
harmonica [hɑː'mɔnɪkə] *n* armonica
harmonics [hɑː'mɔnɪks] *npl* armonia
harmonious [hɑː'məunɪəs] *adj* armonioso(-a)

harmonium [hɑːˈməunɪəm] *n* armonium *m inv*
harmonize [ˈhɑːmənaɪz] *vt, vi* armonizzare
harmony [ˈhɑːmənɪ] *n* armonia
harness [ˈhɑːnɪs] *n* bardatura, finimenti *mpl* ■ *vt* (*horse*) bardare; (*resources*) sfruttare
harp [hɑːp] *n* arpa ■ *vi*: **to ~ on about** insistere tediosamente su
harpist [ˈhɑːpɪst] *n* arpista *m/f*
harpoon [hɑːˈpuːn] *n* arpione *m*
harpsichord [ˈhɑːpsɪkɔːd] *n* clavicembalo
harrow [ˈhærəu] *n* (*Agr*) erpice *m*
harrowing [ˈhærəuɪŋ] *adj* straziante
harry [ˈhærɪ] *vt* (*Mil*) saccheggiare; (*person*) assillare
harsh [hɑːʃ] *adj* (*hard*) duro(-a); (*severe*) severo(-a); (*unpleasant: sound*) rauco(-a); (*: colour*) chiassoso(-a); violento(-a)
harshly [ˈhɑːʃlɪ] *adv* duramente; severamente
harshness [ˈhɑːʃnɪs] *n* durezza; severità
harvest [ˈhɑːvɪst] *n* raccolto; (*of grapes*) vendemmia ■ *vt* fare il raccolto di, raccogliere; vendemmiare ■ *vi* fare il raccolto; vendemmiare
harvester [ˈhɑːvɪstəʳ] *n* (*machine*) mietitrice *f*; (*also*: **combine harvester**) mietitrebbia; (*person*) mietitore(-trice)
has [hæz] *see* **have**
has-been [ˈhæzbiːn] *n* (*col: person*): **he's/she's a ~** ha fatto il suo tempo
hash [hæʃ] *n* (*Culin*) *specie di spezzatino fatto con carne già cotta*; (*fig: mess*) pasticcio ■ *n abbr* (*col*) = **hashish**
hashish [ˈhæʃɪʃ] *n* hascisc *m*
hasn't [ˈhæznt] = **has not**
hassle [ˈhæsl] *n* (*col*) sacco di problemi
haste [heɪst] *n* fretta
hasten [ˈheɪsn] *vt* affrettare ■ *vi* affrettarsi; **I ~ to add that ...** mi preme di aggiungere che ...
hastily [ˈheɪstɪlɪ] *adv* in fretta, precipitosamente
hasty [ˈheɪstɪ] *adj* affrettato(-a), precipitoso(-a)
hat [hæt] *n* cappello
hatbox [ˈhætbɔks] *n* cappelliera
hatch [hætʃ] *n* (*Naut: also*: **hatchway**) boccaporto; (*Brit: also*: **service hatch**) portello di servizio ■ *vi* schiudersi ■ *vt* covare; (*fig: scheme, plot*) elaborare, mettere a punto
hatchback [ˈhætʃbæk] *n* (*Aut*) tre (*or* cinque) porte *f inv*
hatchet [ˈhætʃɪt] *n* accetta
hatchet job *n* (*col*) attacco spietato; **to do a ~ on sb** fare a pezzi qn
hatchet man *n* (*col*) tirapiedi *m inv*, scagnozzo
hate [heɪt] *vt* odiare, detestare ■ *n* odio; **to ~ to do** *or* **doing** detestare fare; **I ~ to trouble you, but ...** mi dispiace disturbarla, ma ...
hateful [ˈheɪtful] *adj* odioso(-a), detestabile
hater [ˈheɪtəʳ] *n*: **cop- ~** persona che odia i poliziotti; **woman- ~** misogino(-a)
hatred [ˈheɪtrɪd] *n* odio
hat trick *n* (*Brit Sport, also fig*): **to get a ~** segnare tre punti consecutivi (*or* vincere per tre volte consecutive)
haughty [ˈhɔːtɪ] *adj* altero(-a), arrogante
haul [hɔːl] *vt* trascinare, tirare ■ *n* (*of fish*) pescata; (*of stolen goods etc*) bottino
haulage [ˈhɔːlɪdʒ] *n* trasporto; autotrasporto
haulage contractor *n* (*Brit: firm*) impresa di trasporti; (*: person*) autotrasportatore *m*
haulier [ˈhɔːlɪəʳ], (*US*) **hauler** [ˈhɔːləʳ] *n* autotrasportatore *m*
haunch [hɔːntʃ] *n* anca; **a ~ of venison** una coscia di cervo
haunt [hɔːnt] *vt* (*fear*) pervadere; (*: person*) frequentare ■ *n* rifugio; **a ghost haunts the house** la casa è abitata da un fantasma
haunted [ˈhɔːntɪd] *adj* (*castle etc*) abitato(-a) dai fantasmi *or* dagli spiriti; (*look*) ossessionato(-a), tormentato(-a)
haunting [ˈhɔːntɪŋ] *adj* (*sight, music*) ossessionante, che perseguita
Havana [həˈvænə] *n* l'Avana

 KEYWORD

have [hæv] (*pt, pp* **had**) *aux vb* **1** (*gen*) avere; essere; **to have arrived/gone** essere arrivato(-a)/andato(-a); **to have eaten/slept** avere mangiato/dormito; **he has been kind/promoted** è stato gentile/promosso; **having finished** *or* **when he had finished, he left** dopo aver finito, se n'è andato
2 (*in tag questions*): **you've done it, haven't you?** l'hai fatto, (non è) vero?; **he hasn't done it, has he?** non l'ha fatto, vero?
3 (*in short answers and questions*): **you've made a mistake – no I haven't/so I have** ha fatto un errore – ma no, niente affatto/sì, è vero; **we haven't paid – yes we have!** non abbiamo pagato – ma sì che abbiamo pagato!; **I've been there before, have you?** ci sono già stato, e lei?
■ *modal aux vb* (*be obliged*): **to have (got) to do sth** dover fare qc; **I haven't got** *or* **I don't have to wear glasses** non ho bisogno di portare gli occhiali; **I had better leave** è meglio che io vada
■ *vt* **1** (*possess, obtain*) avere; **he has (got) blue eyes/dark hair** ha gli occhi azzurri/i capelli scuri; **have you got** *or* **do you have a car/phone?** ha la macchina/il telefono?; **may I have your address?** potrebbe darmi il suo

h

indirizzo?; **you can have it for £5** te lo do per 5 sterline
2 (*+ noun: take, hold etc*): **to have a bath** fare un bagno; **to have breakfast** fare colazione; **to have a cigarette** fumare una sigaretta; **to have dinner** cenare; **to have a drink** bere qualcosa; **to have lunch** pranzare; **to have a party** dare *or* fare una festa; **to have an operation** avere *or* subire un'operazione; **to have a swim** fare una nuotata; **I'll have a coffee** prendo un caffè; **let me have a try** fammi *or* lasciami provare
3: **to have sth done** far fare qc; **to have one's hair cut** tagliarsi *or* farsi tagliare i capelli; **he had a suit made** si fece fare un abito; **to have sb do sth** far fare qc a qn; **he had me phone his boss** mi ha fatto telefonare al suo capo
4 (*experience, suffer*) avere; **to have a cold/flu** avere il raffreddore/l'influenza; **she had her bag stolen** le hanno rubato la borsa
5 (*phrases*): **you've been had!** ci sei cascato!; **I won't have it!** (*accept*) non mi sta affatto bene!; *see also* **haves**
▸ **have in** *vt*: **to have it in for sb** (*col*) avercela con qn
▸ **have on** *vt* (*garment*) avere addosso; (*be busy with*) avere da fare; **I don't have any money on me** non ho soldi con me; **have you anything on tomorrow?** (*Brit*) ha qualcosa in programma per domani?; **to have sb on** (*Brit col*) prendere in giro qn
▸ **have out** *vt*: **to have it out with sb** (*settle a problem etc*) mettere le cose in chiaro con qn

haven ['heɪvn] *n* porto; (*fig*) rifugio
haversack ['hævəsæk] *n* zaino
haves [hævz] *npl* (*col*): **the ~ and the have-nots** gli abbienti e i non abbienti
havoc ['hævək] *n* confusione *f*, subbuglio; **to play ~ with sth** scombussolare qc; **to wreak ~ on sth** mettere in subbuglio qc
Hawaii [hə'waɪː] *n* le Hawaii
Hawaiian [hə'waɪjən] *adj* hawaiano(-a) ■ *n* hawaiano(-a); (*Ling*) lingua hawaiana
hawk [hɔːk] *n* falco ■ *vt* (*goods for sale*) vendere per strada
hawker ['hɔːkəʳ] *n* venditore *m* ambulante
hawkish ['hɔːkɪʃ] *adj* violento(-a)
hawthorn ['hɔːθɔːn] *n* biancospino
hay [heɪ] *n* fieno
hay fever *n* febbre *f* da fieno
haystack ['heɪstæk] *n* pagliaio
haywire ['heɪwaɪəʳ] *adj* (*col*): **to go ~** perdere la testa; impazzire
hazard ['hæzəd] *n* (*chance*) azzardo; (*risk*) pericolo, rischio ■ *vt* (*one's life*) rischiare, mettere a repentaglio; (*remark*) azzardare; **to be a health/fire ~** essere pericoloso per la salute/in caso d'incendio; **to ~ a guess** tirare a indovinare
hazardous ['hæzədəs] *adj* pericoloso(-a), rischioso(-a)
hazard pay *n* (*US*) indennità di rischio
hazard warning lights *npl* (*Aut*) luci *fpl* di emergenza
haze [heɪz] *n* foschia
hazel ['heɪzl] *n* (*tree*) nocciolo ■ *adj* (*eyes*) (color) nocciola *inv*
hazelnut ['heɪzlnʌt] *n* nocciola
hazy ['heɪzɪ] *adj* fosco(-a); (*idea*) vago(-a); (*photograph*) indistinto(-a)
H-bomb ['eɪtʃbɔm] *n* bomba H
HD *abbr* (= *high definition*) HD, alta definizione
HDTV *abbr* (= *high definition television*) televisore *m* HD, TV *f inv* ad alta definizione
HE *abbr* = **high explosive**; (*Rel, Diplomacy*: = *His (or Her) Excellency*) S.E.
he [hiː] *pron* lui, egli; **it is he who ...** è lui che ...; **here he is** eccolo
head [hɛd] *n* testa, capo; (*leader*) capo; (*on tape recorder, computer etc*) testina ■ *vt* (*list*) essere in testa a; (*group*) essere a capo di; **heads (or tails)** testa (o croce), pari (o dispari); **~ first** a capofitto; **~ over heels in love** pazzamente innamorato(-a); **£10 a** *or* **per ~** 10 sterline a testa; **to sit at the ~ of the table** sedersi a capotavola; **to have a ~ for business** essere tagliato per gli affari; **to have no ~ for heights** soffrire di vertigini; **to lose/keep one's ~** perdere/non perdere la testa; **to come to a ~** (*fig: situation etc*) precipitare; **to ~ the ball** (*Sport*) dare di testa alla palla
▸ **head for** *vt fus* dirigersi verso
▸ **head off** *vt* (*threat, danger*) sventare
headache ['hɛdeɪk] *n* mal *m* di testa; **to have a ~** aver mal di testa
headband ['hɛdbænd] *n* fascia per i capelli
headboard ['hɛdbɔːd] *n* testiera (del letto)
headdress ['hɛddrɛs] *n* (*of Indian etc*) copricapo; (*of bride*) acconciatura
headed notepaper ['hɛdɪd-] *n* carta intestata
header ['hɛdəʳ] *n* (*Brit col: Football*) colpo di testa; (*: fall*) caduta di testa
head-first ['hɛd'fəːst] *adv* a testa in giù; (*fig*) senza pensare
headhunt ['hɛdhʌnt] *vt*: **to be headhunted** avere un'offerta di lavoro da un cacciatore di teste
headhunter ['hɛdhʌntəʳ] *n* cacciatore *m* di teste
heading ['hɛdɪŋ] *n* titolo; intestazione *f*
headlamp ['hɛdlæmp] *n* (*Brit*) = **headlight**
headland ['hɛdlənd] *n* promontorio
headlight ['hɛdlaɪt] *n* fanale *m*

headline ['hɛdlaɪn] *n* titolo
headlong ['hɛdlɔŋ] *adv* (*fall*) a capofitto; (*rush*) precipitosamente
headmaster [hɛd'mɑːstəʳ] *n* preside *m*
headmistress [hɛd'mɪstrɪs] *n* preside *f*
head office *n* sede *f* (centrale)
head-on [hɛd'ɔn] *adj* (*collision*) frontale
headphones ['hɛdfəunz] *npl* cuffia
headquarters [hɛd'kwɔːtəz] *npl* ufficio centrale; (*Mil*) quartiere *m* generale
head-rest ['hɛdrɛst] *n* poggiacapo
headroom ['hɛdrum] *n* (*in car*) altezza dell'abitacolo; (*under bridge*) altezza limite
headscarf ['hɛdskɑːf] *n* foulard *m inv*
headset ['hɛdsɛt] *n* = **headphones**
headstone ['hɛdstəun] *n* (*on grave*) lapide *f*, pietra tombale
headstrong ['hɛdstrɔŋ] *adj* testardo(-a)
head waiter *n* capocameriere *m*
headway ['hɛdweɪ] *n*: **to make ~** fare progressi *or* passi avanti
headwind ['hɛdwɪnd] *n* controvento
heady ['hɛdɪ] *adj* che dà alla testa; inebriante
heal [hiːl] *vt, vi* guarire
health [hɛlθ] *n* salute *f*; **Department of H~** ≈ Ministero della Sanità
health care *n* assistenza sanitaria
health centre *n* (*Brit*) poliambulatorio
health food *n*, **health foods** *npl* alimenti *mpl* integrali
health hazard *n* pericolo per la salute
Health Service *n*: **the ~** (*Brit*) ≈ il Servizio Sanitario Statale
healthy ['hɛlθɪ] *adj* (*person*) in buona salute; (*climate*) salubre; (*food*) salutare; (*attitude etc*) sano(-a); (*economy*) florido(-a); (*bank balance*) solido(-a)
heap [hiːp] *n* mucchio ■ *vt* ammucchiare; **heaps (of)** (*col: lots*) un sacco (di), un mucchio (di); **to ~ favours/praise/gifts** *etc* **on sb** ricolmare qn di favori/lodi/regali *etc*
hear (*pt, pp* **heard**) [hɪəʳ, həːd] *vt* sentire; (*news*) ascoltare; (*lecture*) assistere a; (*Law: case*) esaminare ■ *vi* sentire; **to ~ about** sentire parlare di; (*have news of*) avere notizie di; **did you ~ about the move?** ha sentito del trasloco?; **to ~ from sb** ricevere notizie da qn
▸ **hear out** *vt* ascoltare senza interrompere
hearing ['hɪərɪŋ] *n* (*sense*) udito; (*of witnesses*) audizione *f*; (*of a case*) udienza; **to give sb a ~** dare ascolto a qn
hearing aid *n* apparecchio acustico
hearsay ['hɪəseɪ] *n* dicerie *fpl*, chiacchiere *fpl*; **by ~** *adv* per sentito dire
hearse [həːs] *n* carro funebre
heart [hɑːt] *n* cuore *m*; **hearts** *npl* (*Cards*) cuori *mpl*; **at ~** in fondo; **by ~** (*learn, know*) a memoria; **to take ~** farsi coraggio *or* animo; **to lose ~** perdere coraggio, scoraggiarsi; **to have a weak ~** avere il cuore debole; **to set one's ~ on sth/on doing sth** tenere molto a qc/a fare qc; **the ~ of the matter** il nocciolo della questione
heartache ['hɑːteɪk] *n* pene *fpl*, dolori *mpl*
heart attack *n* attacco di cuore
heartbeat ['hɑːtbiːt] *n* battito del cuore
heartbreak ['hɑːtbreɪk] *n* immenso dolore *m*
heartbreaking ['hɑːtbreɪkɪŋ] *adj* straziante
heartbroken ['hɑːtbrəukən] *adj* affranto(-a); **to be ~** avere il cuore spezzato
heartburn ['hɑːtbəːn] *n* bruciore *m* di stomaco
-hearted ['hɑːtɪd] *suffix*: **a kind- person** una persona molto gentile
heartening ['hɑːtnɪŋ] *adj* incoraggiante
heart failure *n* (*Med*) arresto cardiaco
heartfelt ['hɑːtfɛlt] *adj* sincero(-a)
hearth [hɑːθ] *n* focolare *m*
heartily ['hɑːtɪlɪ] *adv* (*laugh*) di cuore; (*eat*) di buon appetito; (*agree*) in pieno, completamente; **to be ~ sick of** (*Brit*) essere veramente stufo di, essere arcistufo di
heartland ['hɑːtlænd] *n* zona centrale; **Italy's industrial ~** il cuore dell'industria italiana
heartless ['hɑːtlɪs] *adj* senza cuore, insensibile; crudele
heartstrings ['hɑːtstrɪŋz] *npl*: **to tug at sb's ~** toccare il cuore a qn, toccare qn nel profondo
heart-throb ['hɑːtθrɔb] *n* rubacuori *m inv*
heart-to-heart ['hɑːttə'hɑːt] *adj, adv* a cuore aperto
heart transplant *n* trapianto del cuore
heartwarming ['hɑːtwɔːmɪŋ] *adj* confortante, che scalda il cuore
hearty ['hɑːtɪ] *adj* caloroso(-a), robusto(-a), sano(-a); vigoroso(-a)
heat [hiːt] *n* calore *m*; (*fig*) ardore *m*; fuoco; (*Sport: also:* **qualifying heat**) prova eliminatoria; (*Zool*): **in** *or* (*Brit*) **on ~** in calore ■ *vt* scaldare
▸ **heat up** *vi* (*liquids*) scaldarsi; (*room*) riscaldarsi ■ *vt* riscaldare
heated ['hiːtɪd] *adj* riscaldato(-a); (*fig*) appassionato(-a); acceso(-a), eccitato(-a)
heater ['hiːtəʳ] *n* stufa; radiatore *m*
heath [hiːθ] *n* (*Brit*) landa
heathen ['hiːðn] *adj, n* pagano(-a)
heather ['hɛðəʳ] *n* erica
heating ['hiːtɪŋ] *n* riscaldamento
heat-resistant ['hiːtrɪzɪstənt] *adj* termoresistente

heat-seeking ['hi:tsi:kɪŋ] *adj* che cerca fonti di calore
heatstroke ['hi:tstrəuk] *n* colpo di sole
heatwave ['hi:tweɪv] *n* ondata di caldo
heave [hi:v] *vt* sollevare (con forza) ■ *vi* sollevarsi ■ *n* (*push*) grande spinta; **to ~ a sigh** emettere *or* mandare un sospiro
▸ **heave to** (*pt, pp* **hove**) *vi* (*Naut*) mettersi in cappa
heaven ['hɛvn] *n* paradiso, cielo; **~ forbid!** Dio ce ne guardi!; **for ~'s sake!** (*pleading*) per amor del cielo!, per carità!; (*protesting*) santo cielo!, in nome del cielo!; **thank ~!** grazie al cielo!
heavenly ['hɛvnlɪ] *adj* divino(-a), celeste
heavily ['hɛvɪlɪ] *adv* pesantemente; (*drink, smoke*) molto
heavy ['hɛvɪ] *adj* pesante; (*sea*) grosso(-a); (*rain*) forte; (*drinker, smoker*) gran (*before noun*); **it's ~ going** è una gran fatica; **~ industry** industria pesante
heavy cream *n* (*US*) doppia panna
heavy-duty ['hɛvɪ'dju:tɪ] *adj* molto resistente
heavy goods vehicle *n* (*Brit*) veicolo per trasporti pesanti
heavy-handed ['hɛvɪ'hændɪd] *adj* (*clumsy, tactless*) pesante
heavy metal *n* (*Mus*) heavy metal *m*
heavy-set ['hɛvɪ'sɛt] *adj* (*esp US*) tarchiato(-a)
heavyweight ['hɛvɪweɪt] *n* (*Sport*) peso massimo
Hebrew ['hi:bru:] *adj* ebreo(-a) ■ *n* (*Ling*) ebraico
Hebrides ['hɛbrɪdi:z] *npl*: **the ~** le Ebridi
heck [hɛk] (*col*) *excl*: **oh ~!** oh no! ■ *n*: **a ~ of a lot of** un gran bel po' di
heckle ['hɛkl] *vt* interpellare e dare noia a (*un oratore*)
heckler ['hɛklə^r] *n* agitatore(-trice)
hectare ['hɛktɑ:^{r}] *n* (*Brit*) ettaro
hectic ['hɛktɪk] *adj* movimentato(-a); (*busy*) frenetico(-a)
hector ['hɛktə^r] *vt* usare le maniere forti con
he'd [hi:d] = **he would; he had**
hedge [hɛdʒ] *n* siepe *f* ■ *vi* essere elusivo(-a); **as a ~ against inflation** per cautelarsi contro l'inflazione; **to ~ one's bets** (*fig*) coprirsi dai rischi
▸ **hedge in** *vt* recintare con una siepe
hedgehog ['hɛdʒhɔg] *n* riccio
hedgerow ['hɛdʒrəu] *n* siepe *f*
hedonism ['hi:dənɪzəm] *n* edonismo
heed [hi:d] *vt* (*also*: **take heed of**) badare a, far conto di ■ *n*: **to pay (no) ~ to, to take (no) ~ of** (non) ascoltare, (non) tener conto di
heedless ['hi:dlɪs] *adj* sbadato(-a)
heel [hi:l] *n* (*Anat*) calcagno; (*of shoe*) tacco ■ *vt* (*shoe*) rifare i tacchi a; **to bring to ~** addomesticare; **to take to one's heels** (*col*) darsela a gambe, alzare i tacchi
hefty ['hɛftɪ] *adj* (*person*) solido(-a); (*parcel*) pesante; (*piece, price*) grosso(-a)
heifer ['hɛfə^r] *n* giovenca
height [haɪt] *n* altezza; (*high ground*) altura; (*fig: of glory*) apice *m*; (*: of stupidity*) colmo; **what ~ are you?** quanto sei alto?; **of average ~** di statura media; **to be afraid of heights** soffrire di vertigini; **it's the ~ of fashion** è l'ultimo grido della moda
heighten ['haɪtn] *vt* innalzare; (*fig*) accrescere
heinous ['heɪnəs] *adj* nefando(-a), atroce
heir [ɛə^r] *n* erede *m*
heir apparent *n* erede *m/f* legittimo(-a)
heiress ['ɛərɛs] *n* erede *f*
heirloom ['ɛəlu:m] *n* mobile *m* (*or* gioiello *or* quadro) di famiglia
heist [haɪst] *n* (*US col*) rapina
held [hɛld] *pt, pp of* **hold**
helicopter ['hɛlɪkɔptə^r] *n* elicottero
heliport ['hɛlɪpɔ:t] *n* eliporto
helium ['hi:lɪəm] *n* elio
hell [hɛl] *n* inferno; **a ~ of a ...** (*col*) un(-a) maledetto(-a) ...; **oh ~!** (*col*) porca miseria!, accidenti!
he'll [hi:l] = **he will, he shall**
hell-bent [hɛl'bɛnt] *adj* (*col*): **to be ~ on doing sth** voler fare qc a tutti i costi
hellish ['hɛlɪʃ] *adj* infernale
hello [hə'ləu] *excl* buon giorno!; ciao! (*to sb one addresses as "tu"*); (*surprise*) ma guarda!
helm [hɛlm] *n* (*Naut*) timone *m*
helmet ['hɛlmɪt] *n* casco
helmsman ['hɛlmzmən] *n* timoniere *m*
help [hɛlp] *n* aiuto; (*charwoman*) donna di servizio; (*assistant etc*) impiegato(-a) ■ *vt* aiutare; **~!** aiuto!; **with the ~ of** con l'aiuto di; **to be of ~ to sb** essere di aiuto *or* essere utile a qn; **to ~ sb (to) do sth** aiutare qn a far qc; **can I ~ you?** (*in shop*) desidera?; **~ yourself (to bread)** si serva (del pane); **I can't ~ saying** non posso evitare di dire; **he can't ~ it** non ci può far niente
helper ['hɛlpə^r] *n* aiutante *m/f*, assistente *m/f*
helpful ['hɛlpful] *adj* di grande aiuto; (*useful*) utile
helping ['hɛlpɪŋ] *n* porzione *f*
helping hand *n*: **to give sb a ~** dare una mano a qn
helpless ['hɛlplɪs] *adj* impotente; debole; (*baby*) indifeso(-a)
helplessly ['hɛlplɪslɪ] *adv* (*watch*) senza poter fare nulla
helpline ['hɛlplaɪn] *n* ≈ telefono amico;

(*Comm*) servizio *m* informazioni *inv* (*a pagamento*)
Helsinki ['hɛlsɪŋkɪ] *n* Helsinki *f*
helter-skelter ['hɛltə'skɛltəʳ] *n* (*Brit: in funfair*) scivolo (a spirale)
hem [hɛm] *n* orlo ■ *vt* fare l'orlo a
▸ **hem in** *vt* cingere; **to feel hemmed in** (*fig*) sentirsi soffocare
he-man ['hi:mæn] *n* (*col*) fusto
hematology [hi:mə'tɔlədʒɪ] *n* (*US*) = **haematology**
hemisphere ['hɛmɪsfɪəʳ] *n* emisfero
hemlock ['hɛmlɔk] *n* cicuta
hemoglobin [hi:məu'gləubɪn] *n* (*US*) = **haemoglobin**
hemophilia [hi:məu'fɪlɪə] *n* (*US*) = **haemophilia**
hemorrhage ['hɛmərɪdʒ] *n* (*US*) = **haemorrhage**
hemorrhoids ['hɛmərɔɪdz] *npl* (*US*) = **haemorrhoids**
hemp [hɛmp] *n* canapa
hen [hɛn] *n* gallina; (*female bird*) femmina
hence [hɛns] *adv* (*therefore*) dunque; **2 years ~** di qui a 2 anni
henceforth [hɛns'fɔ:θ] *adv* d'ora in poi
henchman ['hɛntʃmən] *n* (*pej*) caudatario
henna ['hɛnə] *n* henna
hen night *n* (*col*) addio al nubilato
hen party *n* (*col*) festa di sole donne
henpecked ['hɛnpɛkt] *adj* dominato dalla moglie
hepatitis [hɛpə'taɪtɪs] *n* epatite *f*
her [hə:ʳ] *pron* (*direct*) la, l' + *vowel*; (*indirect*) le; (*stressed, after prep*) lei ■ *adj* il/la suo(-a), i/le suoi/sue; **I see ~** la vedo; **give ~ a book** le dia un libro; **after ~** dopo (di) lei
herald ['hɛrəld] *n* araldo ■ *vt* annunciare
heraldic [hɛ'rældɪk] *adj* araldico(-a)
heraldry ['hɛrəldrɪ] *n* araldica
herb [hə:b] *n* erba; **herbs** *npl* (*Culin*) erbette *fpl*
herbaceous [hə:'beɪʃəs] *adj* erbaceo(-a)
herbal ['hə:bəl] *adj* di erbe; **~ tea** tisana
herbicide ['hə:bɪsaɪd] *n* erbicida *m*
herd [hə:d] *n* mandria; (*of wild animals, swine*) branco ■ *vt* (*drive, gather: animals*) guidare; (*: people*) radunare; **herded together** ammassati (come bestie)
here [hɪəʳ] *adv* qui, qua ■ *excl* ehi!; **~!** (*at roll call*) presente!; **~ is, ~ are** ecco; **~'s my sister** ecco mia sorella; **~ she is** eccola; **~ she comes** eccola che viene; **come ~!** vieni qui!; **~ and there** qua e là
hereabouts ['hɪərəbauts] *adv* da queste parti
hereafter [hɪər'ɑ:ftəʳ] *adv* in futuro; dopo questo ■ *n*: **the ~** l'al di là *m*
hereby [hɪə'baɪ] *adv* (*in letter*) con la presente
hereditary [hɪ'rɛdɪtrɪ] *adj* ereditario(-a)
heredity [hɪ'rɛdɪtɪ] *n* eredità
heresy ['hɛrəsɪ] *n* eresia
heretic ['hɛrətɪk] *n* eretico(-a)
heretical [hɪ'rɛtɪkl] *adj* eretico(-a)
herewith [hɪə'wɪð] *adv* qui accluso
heritage ['hɛrɪtɪdʒ] *n* eredità; (*of country, nation*) retaggio; **our national ~** il nostro patrimonio nazionale
hermetically [hə:'mɛtɪklɪ] *adv* ermeticamente; **~ sealed** ermeticamente chiuso
hermit ['hə:mɪt] *n* eremita *m*
hernia ['hə:nɪə] *n* ernia
hero (*pl* **heroes**) ['hɪərəu] *n* eroe *m*
heroic [hɪ'rəuɪk] *adj* eroico(-a)
heroin ['hɛrəuɪn] *n* eroina (*droga*)
heroin addict *n* eroinomane *m/f*
heroine ['hɛrəuɪn] *n* eroina (*donna*)
heroism ['hɛrəuɪzəm] *n* eroismo
heron ['hɛrən] *n* airone *m*
hero worship *n* divismo
herring ['hɛrɪŋ] *n* aringa
hers [hə:z] *pron* il/la suo(-a), i/le suoi/sue; **a friend of ~** un suo amico; **this is ~** questo è (il) suo
herself [hə:'sɛlf] *pron* (*reflexive*) si; (*emphatic*) lei stessa; (*after prep*) se stessa, sé
Herts *abbr* (*Brit*) = **Hertfordshire**
he's [hi:z] = **he is; he has**
hesitant ['hɛzɪtənt] *adj* esitante, indeciso(-a); **to be ~ about doing sth** esitare a fare qc
hesitate ['hɛzɪteɪt] *vi*: **to ~ (about/to do)** esitare (su/a fare); **don't ~ to ask (me)** non aver timore *or* paura di chiedermelo
hesitation [hɛzɪ'teɪʃən] *n* esitazione *f*; **I have no ~ in saying (that) ...** non esito a dire che ...
hessian ['hɛsɪən] *n* tela di canapa
heterogeneous [hɛtərəu'dʒi:nɪəs] *adj* eterogeneo(-a)
heterosexual [hɛtərəu'sɛksjuəl] *adj, n* eterosessuale (*m/f*)
het up [hɛt'ʌp] *adj* agitato(-a)
HEW *n abbr* (*US: = Department of Health, Education, and Welfare*) *ministero della sanità, della pubblica istruzione e della previdenza sociale*
hew [hju:] *vt* tagliare (con l'accetta)
hex [hɛks] (*US*) *n* stregoneria ■ *vt* stregare
hexagon ['hɛksəgən] *n* esagono
hexagonal [hɛk'sægənl] *adj* esagonale
hey [heɪ] *excl* ehi!
heyday ['heɪdeɪ] *n*: **the ~ of** i bei giorni di, l'età d'oro di
HF *n abbr* (*= high frequency*) AF
HGV *n abbr* = **heavy goods vehicle**

HI *abbr* (US) = **Hawaii**
hi [haɪ] *excl* ciao!
hiatus [haɪ'eɪtəs] *n* vuoto; (*Ling*) iato
hibernate ['haɪbəneɪt] *vi* ibernare
hibernation [haɪbə'neɪʃən] *n* letargo, ibernazione *f*
hiccough, hiccup ['hɪkʌp] *vi* singhiozzare ■ *n* singhiozzo; **to have (the) hiccoughs** avere il singhiozzo
hick [hɪk] *n* (*US col*) buzzurro(-a)
hid [hɪd] *pt of* **hide**
hidden ['hɪdn] *pp of* **hide** ■ *adj* nascosto(-a); **there are no ~ extras** è veramente tutto compreso nel prezzo; **~ agenda** programma *m* occulto
hide [haɪd] *n* (*skin*) pelle *f* ■ *vb* (*pt* **hid**, *pp* **hidden**) [hɪd, 'hɪdn] *vt*: **to ~ sth (from sb)** nascondere qc (a qn) ■ *vi*: **to ~ (from sb)** nascondersi (da qn)
hide-and-seek ['haɪdən'si:k] *n* rimpiattino
hideaway ['haɪdəweɪ] *n* nascondiglio
hideous ['hɪdɪəs] *adj* laido(-a); orribile
hide-out ['haɪdaut] *n* nascondiglio
hiding ['haɪdɪŋ] *n* (*beating*) bastonata; **to be in ~** (*concealed*) tenersi nascosto(-a)
hiding place *n* nascondiglio
hierarchy ['haɪərɑ:kɪ] *n* gerarchia
hieroglyphic [haɪərə'glɪfɪk] *adj* geroglifico(-a); **hieroglyphics** *npl* geroglifici *mpl*
hi-fi ['haɪ'faɪ] *adj, n abbr* (= *high fidelity*) hi-fi (*m*) *inv*
higgledy-piggledy ['hɪgldɪ'pɪgldɪ] *adv* alla rinfusa
high [haɪ] *adj* alto(-a); (*speed, respect, number*) grande; (*wind*) forte; (*Brit Culin: meat, game*) frollato(-a); (*: spoilt*) andato(-a) a male; (*col: on drugs*) fatto(-a); (*: on drink*) su di giri ■ *adv* alto, in alto ■ *n*: **exports have reached a new ~** le esportazioni hanno toccato un nuovo record; **20m ~** alto(-a) 20m; **to pay a ~ price for sth** pagare (molto) caro qc
highball ['haɪbɔ:l] *n* (*US: drink*) whisky (*or* brandy) e soda con ghiaccio
highboy ['haɪbɔɪ] *n* (*US*) cassettone *m*
highbrow ['haɪbrau] *adj, n* intellettuale (*m/f*)
highchair ['haɪtʃɛə^r] *n* seggiolone *m*
high-class ['haɪ'klɑ:s] *adj* (*neighbourhood*) elegante; (*hotel*) di prim'ordine; (*person*) di gran classe; (*food*) raffinato(-a)
High Court *n* alta corte *f*; *vedi nota*

HIGH COURT

Nel sistema legale inglese e gallese, la *High Court* e la "Court of Appeal" compongono la "Supreme Court of Judicature", e si occupa di casi più importanti e complessi. In Scozia, invece, la *High Court* è la corte che si occupa dei reati più gravi e corrisponde alla "crown court" inglese.

higher ['haɪə^r] *adj* (*form of life, study etc*) superiore ■ *adv* più in alto, più in su
higher education *n* istruzione *f* superiore, istruzione universitaria
highfalutin [haɪfə'lu:tɪn] *adj* (*col*) pretenzioso(-a)
high finance *n* alta finanza
high-flier, high-flyer [haɪ'flaɪə^r] *n* (giovane) promessa (*fig*)
high-flying [haɪ'flaɪɪŋ] *adj* (*fig*) promettente
high-handed [haɪ'hændɪd] *adj* prepotente
high-heeled [haɪ'hi:ld] *adj* a tacchi alti
highjack ['haɪdʒæk] *vt, n* = **hijack**
high jump *n* (*Sport*) salto in alto
highlands ['haɪləndz] *npl* zona montuosa; **the H~** le Highlands scozzesi
high-level ['haɪlɛvl] *adj* (*talks etc, Comput*) ad alto livello
highlight ['haɪlaɪt] *n* (*fig: of event*) momento culminante ■ *vt* mettere in evidenza; **highlights** *npl* (*in hair*) colpi *mpl* di sole
highlighter ['haɪlaɪtə^r] *n* (*pen*) evidenziatore *m*
highly ['haɪlɪ] *adv* molto; **~ paid** pagato molto bene; **to speak ~ of** parlare molto bene di
highly-strung ['haɪlɪ'strʌŋ] *adj* teso(-a) di nervi, eccitabile
High Mass *n* messa cantata *or* solenne
highness ['haɪnɪs] *n* altezza; **Her H~** Sua Altezza
high-pitched [haɪ'pɪtʃt] *adj* acuto(-a)
high point *n*: **the ~** il momento più importante
high-powered ['haɪ'pauəd] *adj* (*engine*) molto potente, ad alta potenza; (*fig: person*) di prestigio
high-pressure ['haɪprɛʃə^r] *adj* ad alta pressione; (*fig*) aggressivo(-a)
high-rise block ['haɪraɪz-] *n* palazzone *m*
high school *n* (*Brit*) scuola secondaria; (*US*) istituto d'istruzione secondaria; *vedi nota*

HIGH SCHOOL

Negli Stati Uniti la *high school* è un istituto di istruzione secondaria. Si suddivide in "junior high school" (dal settimo al nono anno di corso) e "senior high school" (dal decimo al dodicesimo), dove vengono impartiti sia insegnamenti scolastici che di formazione professionale. In Gran Bretagna molte scuole secondarie si chiamano *high school*.

high season *n* (*Brit*) alta stagione
high spirits *npl* buonumore *m*, euforia; **to be in ~** essere euforico(-a)
high street *n* (*Brit*) strada principale
highway ['haɪweɪ] *n* strada maestra; **the information ~** l'autostrada telematica
Highway Code *n* (*Brit*) codice *m* della strada
highwayman ['haɪweɪmən] *n* bandito
hijack ['haɪdʒæk] *vt* dirottare ■ *n* dirottamento; (*also*: **hijacking**) pirateria aerea
hijacker ['haɪdʒækər] *n* dirottatore(-trice)
hike [haɪk] *vi* fare un'escursione a piedi ■ *n* escursione *f* a piedi; (*col*: *in prices etc*) aumento ■ *vt* (*col*) aumentare
hiker ['haɪkər] *n* escursionista *m/f*
hiking ['haɪkɪŋ] *n* escursioni *fpl* a piedi
hilarious [hɪ'lɛərɪəs] *adj* che fa schiantare dal ridere
hilarity [hɪ'lærɪtɪ] *n* ilarità
hill [hɪl] *n* collina, colle *m*; (*fairly high*) montagna; (*on road*) salita
hillbilly ['hɪlbɪlɪ] *n* (*US*) montanaro(-a) dal sud degli Stati Uniti; (*pej*) zotico(-a)
hillock ['hɪlək] *n* collinetta, poggio
hillside ['hɪlsaɪd] *n* fianco della collina
hill start *n* (*Aut*) partenza in salita
hill walking *n* escursioni *fpl* in montagna
hilly ['hɪlɪ] *adj* collinoso(-a), montagnoso(-a)
hilt [hɪlt] *n* (*of sword*) elsa; **to the ~** (*fig*: *support*) fino in fondo
him [hɪm] *pron* (*direct*) lo, l' + *vowel*; (*indirect*) gli; (*stressed, after prep*) lui; **I see ~** lo vedo; **give ~ a book** gli dia un libro; **after ~** dopo (di) lui
Himalayas [hɪmə'leɪəz] *npl*: **the ~** l'Himalaia *m*
himself [hɪm'sɛlf] *pron* (*reflexive*) si; (*emphatic*) lui stesso; (*after prep*) se stesso, sé
hind [haɪnd] *adj* posteriore ■ *n* cerva
hinder ['hɪndər] *vt* ostacolare; (*delay*) tardare; (*prevent*): **to ~ sb from doing** impedire a qn di fare
hindquarters ['haɪndkwɔːtəz] *npl* (*Zool*) posteriore *m*
hindrance ['hɪndrəns] *n* ostacolo, impedimento
hindsight ['haɪndsaɪt] *n* senno di poi; **with the benefit of ~** con il senno di poi
Hindu ['hɪnduː] *n* indù *m/f inv*
hinge [hɪndʒ] *n* cardine *m* ■ *vi* (*fig*): **to ~ on** dipendere da
hint [hɪnt] *n* accenno, allusione *f*; (*advice*) consiglio ■ *vt*: **to ~ that** lasciar capire che ■ *vi*: **to ~ at** accennare a; **to drop a ~** lasciar capire; **give me a ~** (*clue*) dammi almeno un'idea, dammi un'indicazione
hip [hɪp] *n* anca, fianco; (*Bot*) frutto della rosa canina
hip flask *n* fiaschetta da liquore tascabile
hip hop *n* hip-hop *m*
hippie ['hɪpɪ] *n* hippy *m/f inv*
hip pocket *n* tasca posteriore dei calzoni
hippopotamus (*pl* **hippopotamuses** *or* **hippopotami**) [hɪpə'pɔtəməs, -'pɔtəmaɪ] *n* ippopotamo
hippy ['hɪpɪ] *n* = **hippie**
hire ['haɪər] *vt* (*Brit*: *car, equipment*) noleggiare; (*worker*) assumere, dare lavoro a ■ *n* nolo, noleggio; **for ~** da nolo; (*taxi*) libero(-a); **on ~** a nolo
▸ **hire out** *vt* noleggiare, dare a nolo *or* noleggio, affittare
hire car, hired car *n* (*Brit*) macchina a nolo
hire purchase *n* (*Brit*) acquisto (*or* vendita) rateale; **to buy sth on ~** comprare qc a rate
his [hɪz] *adj, pron* il/la suo/sua, i/le suoi/sue; **this is ~** questo è (il) suo
hiss [hɪs] *vi* fischiare; (*cat, snake*) sibilare ■ *n* fischio; sibilo
histogram ['hɪstəgræm] *n* istogramma *m*
historian [hɪ'stɔːrɪən] *n* storico(-a)
historic [hɪ'stɔrɪk], **historical** [hɪ'stɔrɪkl] *adj* storico(-a)
history ['hɪstərɪ] *n* storia; **there's a long ~ of that illness in his family** ci sono molti precedenti (della malattia) nella sua famiglia
histrionics [hɪstrɪ'ɔnɪks] *n* istrionismo
hit [hɪt] *vt* (*pt, pp* **~**) colpire, picchiare; (*knock against*) battere; (*reach*: *target*) raggiungere; (*collide with*: *car*) urtare contro; (*fig*: *affect*) colpire; (*find*: *problem*) incontrare ■ *n* colpo; (*success, song*) successo; **to ~ the headlines** far titolo; **to ~ the road** (*col*) mettersi in cammino; **to ~ it off with sb** andare molto d'accordo con qn; **to get a ~/10,000 hits** (*Comput*) trovare una pagina Web/10.000 pagine Web; **our web page had 10,000 hits last month** lo scorso mese il nostro sito ha avuto 10.000 visitatori
▸ **hit back** *vi*: **to ~ back at sb** restituire il colpo a qn
▸ **hit out at** *vt fus* sferrare dei colpi contro; (*fig*) attaccare
▸ **hit (up)on** *vt fus* (*answer*) imbroccare, azzeccare; (*solution*) trovare (per caso)
hit-and-run driver ['hɪtænd'rʌn-] *n* pirata *m* della strada
hitch [hɪtʃ] *vt* (*fasten*) attaccare; (*also*: **hitch up**) tirare su ■ *n* (*difficulty*) intoppo, difficoltà *f inv*; **technical ~** difficoltà tecnica; **to ~ a lift** fare l'autostop
▸ **hitch up** *vt* (*horse, cart*) attaccare
hitch-hike ['hɪtʃhaɪk] *vi* fare l'autostop
hitch-hiker ['hɪtʃhaɪkər] *n* autostoppista *m/f*

hi-tech ['haɪ'tɛk] *adj* high-tech *inv*, a tecnologia avanzata
hitherto ['hɪðə'tuː] *adv* finora
hit list *n* libro nero
hitman ['hɪtmæn] *n* (*col*) sicario
hit-or-miss ['hɪtə'mɪs] *adj* casuale; **it's ~ whether ...** è in dubbio se ...; **the service in this hotel is very ~** il servizio dell'albergo lascia a desiderare
hit parade *n* hit-parade *f*
HIV *n abbr* (= *human immunodeficiency virus*) virus *m inv* di immunodeficienza; **~-negative/-positive** sieronegativo(-a)/sieropositivo(-a)
hive [haɪv] *n* alveare *m*; **the shop was a ~ of activity** (*fig*) c'era una grande attività nel negozio
▸ **hive off** *vt* (*col*) separare
hl *abbr* (= *hectolitre*) hl
HM *abbr* (= *His (or Her) Majesty*) S.M. (= *Sua Maestà*)
HMG *abbr* (*Brit*) = **His (***or* **Her) Majesty's Government**
HMI *n abbr* (*Brit Scol*: = *His (or Her) Majesty's Inspector*) ≈ ispettore *m* scolastico
HMO *n abbr* (*US*: = *Health Maintenance Organization*) *organo per la salvaguardia della salute pubblica*
HMS *abbr* (*Brit*) = **His (***or* **Her) Majesty's Ship**
HNC *n abbr* (*Brit*: = *Higher National Certificate*) *diploma di istituto tecnico o professionale*
HND *n abbr* (*Brit*: = *Higher National Diploma*) *diploma in materie tecniche equivalente ad una laurea*
hoard [hɔːd] *n* (*of food*) provviste *fpl*; (*of money*) gruzzolo ▪ *vt* ammassare
hoarding ['hɔːdɪŋ] *n* (*Brit*) tabellone *m* per affissioni
hoarfrost ['hɔːfrɔst] *n* brina
hoarse [hɔːs] *adj* rauco(-a)
hoax [həuks] *n* scherzo; falso allarme
hob [hɔb] *n* piastra (con fornelli)
hobble ['hɔbl] *vi* zoppicare
hobby ['hɔbɪ] *n* hobby *m inv*, passatempo
hobby-horse ['hɔbɪhɔːs] *n* cavallo a dondolo; (*fig*) chiodo fisso
hobnail boots ['hɔbneɪl-], **hobnailed boots** ['hɔbneɪld-] *n* scarponi *mpl* chiodati
hobnob ['hɔbnɔb] *vi*: **to ~ (with)** mescolarsi (con)
hobo ['həubəu] *n* (*US*) vagabondo
hock [hɔk] *n* (*Brit*: *wine*) vino del Reno; (*of animal*, *Culin*) garretto; (*col*): **to be in ~** avere debiti
hockey ['hɔkɪ] *n* hockey *m*
hocus-pocus ['həukəs'pəukəs] *n* (*trickery*) trucco; (*words*: *of magician*) abracadabra *m inv*; (*: jargon*) parolone *fpl*
hod [hɔd] *n* (*Tech*) cassetta per portare i mattoni
hodgepodge ['hɔdʒpɔdʒ] *n* = **hotchpotch**
hoe [həu] *n* zappa ▪ *vt* (*ground*) zappare
hog [hɔg] *n* maiale *m* ▪ *vt* (*fig*) arraffare; **to go the whole ~** farlo fino in fondo
Hogmanay [hɔgmə'neɪ] *n* (*Scottish*) ≈ San Silvestro
hogwash ['hɔgwɔʃ] *n* (*col*) stupidaggini *fpl*
hoist [hɔɪst] *n* paranco ▪ *vt* issare
hoity-toity [hɔɪtɪ'tɔɪtɪ] *adj* (*col*) altezzoso(-a)
hold [həuld] *vb* (*pt, pp* **held**) [hɛld] *vt* tenere; (*contain*) contenere; (*keep back*) trattenere; (*believe*) mantenere; considerare; (*possess*) avere, possedere; detenere ▪ *vi* (*withstand pressure*) tenere; (*be valid*) essere valido(-a) ▪ *n* presa; (*fig*) potere *m*; (*Naut*) stiva; **~ the line!** (*Tel*) resti in linea!; **to ~ office** (*Pol*) essere in carica; **to ~ sb responsible for sth** considerare *or* ritenere qn responsabile di qc; **to ~ one's own** (*fig*) difendersi bene; **he holds the view that ...** è del parere che ...; **to ~ firm** *or* **fast** resistere bene, tenere; **to catch** *or* **get (a) ~ of** afferrare; **to get ~ of** (*fig*) trovare; **to get ~ of o.s.** trattenersi
▸ **hold back** *vt* trattenere; (*secret*) tenere celato(-a); **to ~ sb back from doing sth** impedire a qn di fare qc
▸ **hold down** *vt* (*person*) tenere a terra; (*job*) tenere
▸ **hold forth** *vi* fare *or* tenere una concione
▸ **hold off** *vt* tener lontano ▪ *vi* (*rain*): **if the rain holds off** se continua a non piovere
▸ **hold on** *vi* tener fermo; (*wait*) aspettare; **~ on!** (*Tel*) resti in linea!
▸ **hold on to** *vt fus* tenersi stretto(-a) a; (*keep*) conservare
▸ **hold out** *vt* offrire ▪ *vi* (*resist*): **to ~ out (against)** resistere (a)
▸ **hold over** *vt* (*meeting etc*) rimandare, rinviare
▸ **hold up** *vt* (*raise*) alzare; (*support*) sostenere; (*delay*) ritardare; (*traffic*) rallentare; (*rob*: *bank*) assaltare
holdall ['həuldɔːl] *n* (*Brit*) borsone *m*
holder ['həuldər] *n* (*of ticket, title*) possessore/posseditrice; (*of office etc*) incaricato(-a); (*of passport, post*) titolare; (*of record*) detentore(-trice)
holding ['həuldɪŋ] *n* (*share*) azioni *fpl*, titoli *mpl*; (*farm*) podere *m*, tenuta
holding company *n* holding *f inv*
holdup ['həuldʌp] *n* (*robbery*) rapina a mano armata; (*delay*) ritardo; (*Brit*: *in traffic*) blocco
hole [həul] *n* buco, buca ▪ *vt* bucare; **~ in the heart** (*Med*) morbo blu; **to pick holes in** (*fig*) trovare da ridire su
▸ **hole up** *vi* nascondersi, rifugiarsi
holiday ['hɔlədɪ] *n* vacanza; (*from work*) ferie

fpl; (*day off*) giorno di vacanza; (*public*) giorno festivo; **to be on ~** essere in vacanza; **tomorrow is a ~** domani è festa
holiday camp *n* (*Brit: for children*) colonia (di villeggiatura); (*also*: **holiday centre**) ≈ villaggio (di vacanze)
holiday home *n* seconda casa (*per le vacanze*)
holiday-maker ['hɔlədɪmeɪkə^r] *n* (*Brit*) villeggiante *m/f*
holiday pay *n* stipendio delle ferie
holiday resort *n* luogo di villeggiatura
holiday season *n* stagione *f* delle vacanze
holiness ['həulɪnɪs] *n* santità
holistic [həu'lɪstɪk] *adj* olistico(-a)
Holland ['hɔlənd] *n* Olanda
holler ['hɔlə^r] *vi* gridare, urlare
hollow ['hɔləu] *adj* cavo(-a), vuoto(-a); (*fig*) falso(-a); vano(-a) ■ *n* cavità *f inv*; (*in land*) valletta, depressione *f*
▸ **hollow out** *vt* scavare
holly ['hɔlɪ] *n* agrifoglio
hollyhock ['hɔlɪhɔk] *n* malvone *m*
Hollywood ['hɔlɪwud] *n* Hollywood *f*
holocaust ['hɔləkɔːst] *n* olocausto
hologram ['hɔləgræm] *n* ologramma *m*
hols [hɔlz] *npl*: **the ~** le vacanze
holster ['həulstə^r] *n* fondina (di pistola)
holy ['həulɪ] *adj* santo(-a); (*bread*) benedetto(-a), consacrato(-a); (*ground*) consacrato(-a); **the H~ Father** il Santo Padre
Holy Communion *n* la Santa Comunione
Holy Ghost, Holy Spirit *n* Spirito Santo
Holy Land *n*: **the ~** la Terra Santa
holy orders *npl* ordini *mpl* (sacri)
homage ['hɔmɪdʒ] *n* omaggio; **to pay ~ to** rendere omaggio a
home [həum] *n* casa; (*country*) patria; (*institution*) casa, ricovero ■ *cpd* (*life*) familiare; (*cooking etc*) casalingo(-a); (*Econ, Pol*) nazionale, interno(-a); (*Sport: team*) di casa; (*: match, win*) in casa ■ *adv* a casa; in patria; (*right in: nail etc*) fino in fondo; **at ~** a casa; **to go (***or* **come) ~** tornare a casa (*or* in patria); **it's near my ~** è vicino a casa mia; **make yourself at ~** si metta a suo agio
▸ **home in on** *vt fus* (*missiles*) dirigersi (automaticamente) verso
home address *n* indirizzo di casa
home-brew [həum'bruː] *n* birra *or* vino fatto(-a) in casa
homecoming ['həumkʌmɪŋ] *n* ritorno
Home Counties *npl* contee *fpl* intorno a Londra
home economics *n* economia domestica
home ground *n* (*fig*): **to be on ~** essere sul proprio terreno
home-grown [həum'grəun] *adj* nostrano(-a), di produzione locale
home help *n* (*Brit*) *collaboratore familiare per persone bisognose stipendiato dal comune*
homeland ['həumlænd] *n* patria
homeless ['həumlɪs] *adj* senza tetto; spatriato(-a); **the homeless** *npl* i senzatetto
home loan *n* prestito con garanzia immobiliare
homely ['həumlɪ] *adj* semplice, alla buona; accogliente
home-made [həum'meɪd] *adj* casalingo(-a)
Home Office *n* (*Brit*) ministero degli Interni
homeopathy *etc* [həumɪ'ɔpəθɪ] (*US*) = **homoeopathy** *etc*
home page *n* (*Comput*) home page *f inv*
home rule *n* autogoverno
Home Secretary *n* (*Brit*) ministro degli Interni
homesick ['həumsɪk] *adj*: **to be ~** avere la nostalgia
homestead ['həumstɛd] *n* fattoria e terreni
home town *n* città *f inv* natale
home truth *n*: **to tell sb a few home truths** dire a qn qualche amara verità
homeward ['həumwəd] *adj* (*journey*) di ritorno ■ *adv* verso casa
homewards ['həumwədz] *adv* verso casa
homework ['həumwəːk] *n* compiti *mpl* (per casa)
homicidal [hɔmɪ'saɪdl] *adj* omicida
homicide ['hɔmɪsaɪd] *n* (*US*) omicidio
homily ['hɔmɪlɪ] *n* omelia
homing ['həumɪŋ] *adj* (*device, missile*) autocercante; **~ pigeon** piccione *m* viaggiatore
homoeopath, (*US*) **homeopath** ['həumɪəupæθ] *n* omeopatico
homoeopathic, (*US*) **homeopathic** ['həumɪəu'pæθɪk] *adj* omeopatico(-a)
homoeopathy, (*US*) **homeopathy** [həumɪ'ɔpəθɪ] *n* omeopatia
homogeneous [hɔməu'dʒiːnɪəs] *adj* omogeneo(-a)
homogenize [hə'mɔdʒənaɪz] *vt* omogenizzare
homosexual [hɔməu'sɛksjuəl] *adj, n* omosessuale (*m/f*)
Hon. *abbr* = **honourable; honorary**
Honduras [hɔn'djuərəs] *n* Honduras *m*
hone [həun] *vt* (*sharpen*) affilare; (*fig*) affinare
honest ['ɔnɪst] *adj* onesto(-a), sincero(-a); **to be quite ~ with you ...** se devo dirle la verità ...
honestly ['ɔnɪstlɪ] *adv* onestamente; sinceramente
honesty ['ɔnɪstɪ] *n* onestà
honey ['hʌnɪ] *n* miele *m*; (*US col*) tesoro *m*

h

honeycomb ['hʌnɪkəum] *n* favo ■ *vt* (*fig*): **honeycombed with tunnels** *etc* pieno(-a) di gallerie *etc*
honeymoon ['hʌnɪmu:n] *n* luna di miele, viaggio di nozze
honeysuckle ['hʌnɪsʌkl] *n* caprifoglio
Hong Kong ['hɔŋ'kɔŋ] *n* Hong Kong *f*
honk [hɔŋk] *n* (*Aut*) colpo di clacson ■ *vi* suonare il clacson
Honolulu [honə'lu:lu:] *n* Honolulu *f*
honorary ['ɔnərərɪ] *adj* onorario(-a); (*duty, title*) onorifico(-a)
honour, (*US*) **honor** ['ɔnə^r] *vt* onorare ■ *n* onore *m*; **in ~ of** in onore di
honourable, (*US*) **honorable** ['ɔnərəbl] *adj* onorevole
honour-bound, (*US*) **honor-bound** ['ɔnə'baund] *adj*: **to be hono(u)r-bound to do** dover fare per una questione di onore
honours degree *n* (*Scol*) *laurea (con corso di studi di 4 o 5 anni)*; *vedi nota*

HONOURS DEGREE

In Gran Bretagna esistono titoli universitari di diverso livello. Gli studenti che conseguono ottimi risultati e che approfondiscono una o più materie possono ottenere l'*honours degree*. Questo titolo, abbreviato in Hons., viene posto dopo il titolo ottenuto (ad esempio BA Hons); *vedi anche* "ordinary degree".

honours list *n* (*Brit*) *elenco ufficiale dei destinati al conferimento di onorificenze*; *vedi nota*

HONOURS LIST

La *honours list* è un elenco di cittadini britannici e del Commonwealth che si sono distinti in campo imprenditoria/e, militare, sportivo ecc, meritando il conferimento di un titolo o di una decorazione da parte del sovrano. Ogni anno vengono redatte dal primo ministro due *honours lists*, una a Capodanno e una in occasione del compleanno del sovrano.

Hons. [ɔnz] *abbr* (*Scol*) = **hono(u)rs degree**
hood [hud] *n* cappuccio; (*Brit Aut*) capote *f*; (*US Aut*) cofano; (*col*) malvivente *m/f*
hooded ['hudɪd] *adj* (*robber*) mascherato(-a)
hoodie ['hudɪ] *n* felpa con cappuccio
hoodlum ['hu:dləm] *n* malvivente *m/f*
hoodwink ['hudwɪŋk] *vt* infinocchiare
hoof (*pl* **hoofs** *or* **hooves**) [hu:f, hu:vz] *n* zoccolo
hook [huk] *n* gancio; (*for fishing*) amo ■ *vt* uncinare; (*dress*) agganciare; **to be hooked on** (*col*) essere fanatico di; **hooks and eyes** gancetti; **by ~ or by crook** in un modo o nell'altro
▸ **hook up** *vt* (*Radio, TV etc*) allacciare, collegare
hooligan ['hu:lɪgən] *n* giovinastro, teppista *m*
hooliganism ['hu:lɪgənɪzəm] *n* teppismo
hoop [hu:p] *n* cerchio
hoot [hu:t] *vi* (*Aut*) suonare il clacson; (*owl*) gufare ■ *n* colpo di clacson; **to ~ with laughter** farsi una gran risata
hooter ['hu:tə^r] *n* (*Aut*) clacson *m inv*; (*Naut, at factory*) sirena
hoover® ['hu:və^r] *n* (*Brit*) aspirapolvere *m inv* ■ *vt* pulire con l'aspirapolvere
hooves [hu:vz] *npl of* **hoof**
hop [hɔp] *vi* saltellare, saltare; (*on one foot*) saltare su una gamba ■ *n* salto; **hops** *npl* luppoli *mpl*
hope [həup] *vt, vi* sperare ■ *n* speranza; **I ~ so/not** spero di sì/no
hopeful ['həupful] *adj* (*person*) pieno(-a) di speranza; (*situation*) promettente; **I'm ~ that she'll manage to come** ho buone speranze che venga
hopefully ['həupfulɪ] *adv* con speranza; **~ he will recover** speriamo che si riprenda
hopeless ['həuplɪs] *adj* senza speranza, disperato(-a); (*useless*) inutile
hopelessly ['həuplɪslɪ] *adv* (*live etc*) senza speranza; (*involved, complicated*) spaventosamente; (*late*) disperatamente, irrimediabilmente; **I'm ~ confused/lost** sono completamente confuso/perso
hopper ['hɔpə^r] *n* (*chute*) tramoggia
hops [hɔps] *npl* luppoli *mpl*
horde [hɔ:d] *n* orda
horizon [hə'raɪzn] *n* orizzonte *m*
horizontal [hɔrɪ'zɔntl] *adj* orizzontale
hormone ['hɔ:məun] *n* ormone *m*
hormone replacement therapy *n* terapia ormonale (*usata in menopausa*)
horn [hɔ:n] *n* corno; (*Aut*) clacson *m inv*
horned [hɔ:nd] *adj* (*animal*) cornuto(-a)
hornet ['hɔ:nɪt] *n* calabrone *m*
horny ['hɔ:nɪ] *adj* corneo(-a); (*hands*) calloso(-a)
horoscope ['hɔrəskəup] *n* oroscopo
horrendous [hɔ'rɛndəs] *n* orrendo(-a)
horrible ['hɔrɪbl] *adj* orribile, tremendo(-a)
horrid ['hɔrɪd] *adj* orrido(-a); (*person*) antipatico(-a)
horrific [hɔ'rɪfɪk] *adj* (*accident*) spaventoso(-a); (*film*) orripilante
horrify ['hɔrɪfaɪ] *vt* lasciare inorridito(-a)

horrifying ['hɔrɪfaɪɪŋ] *adj* terrificante
horror ['hɔrəʳ] *n* orrore *m*
horror film *n* film *m inv* dell'orrore
horror-struck ['hɔrəstrʌk], **horror-stricken** ['hɔrəstrɪkn] *adj* inorridito(-a)
hors d'œuvre [ɔ:'də:vrə] *n* antipasto
horse [hɔ:s] *n* cavallo
horseback ['hɔ:sbæk]: **on ~** *adj, adv* a cavallo
horsebox ['hɔ:sbɔks] *n* carro *or* furgone *m* per il trasporto dei cavalli
horse chestnut *n* ippocastano
horse-drawn ['hɔ:sdrɔ:n] *adj* tirato(-a) da cavallo
horsefly ['hɔ:sflaɪ] *n* tafano, mosca cavallina
horseman ['hɔ:smən] *n* cavaliere *m*
horsemanship ['hɔ:smənʃɪp] *n* equitazione *f*
horseplay ['hɔ:spleɪ] *n* giochi *mpl* scatenati
horsepower ['hɔ:spauəʳ] *n* cavallo (vapore), c/v
horse-racing ['hɔ:sreɪsɪŋ] *n* ippica
horseradish ['hɔ:srædɪʃ] *n* rafano
horseshoe ['hɔ:sʃu:] *n* ferro di cavallo
horse show *n* concorso ippico, gare *fpl* ippiche
horse-trading ['hɔ:streɪdɪŋ] *n* mercanteggiamento
horse trials *npl* = **horse show**
horsewhip ['hɔ:swɪp] *vt* frustare
horsewoman ['hɔ:swumən] *n* amazzone *f*
horsey ['hɔ:sɪ] *adj* (*col: person*) che adora i cavalli; (*appearance*) cavallino(-a), da cavallo
horticulture ['hɔ:tɪkʌltʃəʳ] *n* orticoltura
hose [həuz] *n* (*also*: **hosepipe**) tubo; (*also*: **garden hose**) tubo per annaffiare
▸ **hose down** *vt* lavare con un getto d'acqua
hosepipe ['həuzpaɪp] *n see* **hose**
hosiery ['həuzɪərɪ] *n* (*in shop*) (reparto di) calze *fpl* e calzini *mpl*
hospice ['hɔspɪs] *n* ricovero, ospizio
hospitable [hɔ'spɪtəbl] *adj* ospitale
hospital ['hɔspɪtl] *n* ospedale *m*; **in ~**, (*US*) **in the ~** all'ospedale
hospitality [hɔspɪ'tælɪtɪ] *n* ospitalità
hospitalize ['hɔspɪtəlaɪz] *vt* ricoverare (in *or* all'ospedale)
host [həust] *n* ospite *m*; (*TV, Radio*) presentatore(-trice); (*Rel*) ostia; (*large number*): **a ~ of** una schiera di ■ *vt* (*TV programme, games*) presentare
hostage ['hɔstɪdʒ] *n* ostaggio(-a)
host country *n* paese *m* ospite, paese che ospita
hostel ['hɔstl] *n* ostello; (*for students, nurses etc*) pensionato; (*for homeless people*) ospizio, ricovero; (*also*: **youth hostel**) ostello della gioventù
hostelling ['hɔstəlɪŋ] *n*: **to go (youth) ~** passare le vacanze negli ostelli della gioventù
hostess ['həustɪs] *n* ospite *f*; (*Aviat*) hostess *f* *inv*; (*in nightclub*) entraineuse *f inv*
hostile ['hɔstaɪl] *adj* ostile
hostility [hɔ'stɪlɪtɪ] *n* ostilità *f inv*
hot [hɔt] *adj* caldo(-a); (*as opposed to only warm*) molto caldo(-a); (*spicy*) piccante; (*fig*) accanito(-a); ardente; violento(-a), focoso(-a); **to be ~** (*person*) aver caldo; (*thing*) essere caldo(-a); (*Meteor*) far caldo
▸ **hot up** (*Brit col*) *vi* (*situation*) farsi più teso(-a); (*party*) scaldarsi ■ *vt* (*pace*) affrettare; (*engine*) truccare
hot-air balloon [hɔt'ɛə-] *n* mongolfiera
hotbed ['hɔtbɛd] *n* (*fig*) focolaio
hotchpotch ['hɔtʃpɔtʃ] *n* (*Brit*) pot-pourri *m*
hot dog *n* hot dog *m inv*
hotel [həu'tɛl] *n* albergo
hotelier [həu'tɛljeɪ] *n* albergatore(-trice)
hotel industry *n* industria alberghiera
hotel room *n* camera d'albergo
hot flush *n* (*Brit*) scalmana, caldana
hotfoot ['hɔtfut] *adv* di gran carriera
hothead ['hɔthɛd] *n* (*fig*) testa calda
hotheaded [hɔt'hɛdɪd] *adj* focoso(-a), eccitabile
hothouse ['hɔthaus] *n* serra
hot line *n* (*Pol*) telefono rosso
hotly ['hɔtlɪ] *adv* violentemente
hotplate ['hɔtpleɪt] *n* fornello; piastra riscaldante
hotpot ['hɔtpɔt] *n* (*Brit Culin*) stufato
hot potato *n* (*Brit col*) patata bollente; **to drop sb/sth like a ~** mollare subito qn/qc
hot seat *n* (*fig*) posto che scotta
hotspot ['hɔtspɔt] *n* (*Comput: wireless hotspot*) hotspot *m inv* Wi-Fi
hot spot *n* (*fig*) zona calda
hot spring *n* sorgente *f* termale
hot-tempered [hɔt'tɛmpəd] *adj* irascibile
hot-water bottle [hɔt'wɔ:tə-] *n* borsa dell'acqua calda
hot-wire ['hɔtwaɪəʳ] *vt* (*col: car*) *avviare mettendo in contatto i fili dell'accensione*
hound [haund] *vt* perseguitare ■ *n* segugio
hour ['auəʳ] *n* ora; **at 30 miles an ~** a 30 miglia all'ora; **lunch ~** intervallo di pranzo; **to pay sb by the ~** pagare qn a ore
hourly ['auəlɪ] *adj* (ad) ogni ora; (*rate*) orario(-a) ■ *adv* ogni ora; **~ paid** *adj* pagato(-a) a ore
house *n* [haus] (*pl* **houses**) ['hauzɪz] casa; (*Pol*) camera; (*Theat*) sala; pubblico; spettacolo ■ *vt* [hauz] (*person*) ospitare; **at (*or* to) my ~** a casa mia; **the H~ (of Commons/Lords)** (*Brit*) la Camera dei Comuni/Lords; **the H~ (of Representatives)** (*US*) ≈ la Camera dei Deputati; **on the ~** (*fig*) offerto(-a) dalla casa

house arrest *n* arresti *mpl* domiciliari
houseboat ['hausbəut] *n* house boat *f inv*
housebound ['hausbaund] *adj* confinato(-a) in casa
housebreaking ['hausbreɪkɪŋ] *n* furto con scasso
house-broken ['hausbrəukn] *adj* (*US*) = **house-trained**
housecoat ['hauskəut] *n* vestaglia
household ['haushəuld] *n* famiglia, casa
householder ['haushəuldə^r] *n* padrone(-a) di casa; (*head of house*) capofamiglia *m/f*
household name *n* nome *m* che tutti conoscono
househunting ['haushʌntɪŋ] *n*: **to go ~** mettersi a cercar casa
housekeeper ['hauski:pə^r] *n* governante *f*
housekeeping ['hauski:pɪŋ] *n* (*work*) governo della casa; (*also*: **housekeeping money**) soldi *mpl* per le spese di casa; (*Comput*) ausilio
houseman ['hausmən] *n* (*Brit Med*) ≈ interno
house-owner ['hausəunə^r] *n* possessore *m/f* di casa
house plant *n* pianta da appartamento
house-proud ['hauspraud] *adj* che è maniaco(-a) della pulizia
house-to-house ['haustə'haus] *adj* (*collection*) di porta in porta; (*search*) casa per casa
house-train ['haustreɪn] *vt* (*Brit*: *pet animal*) addestrare a non sporcare in casa
house-trained ['haustreɪnd] *adj* (*Brit*: *animal*) che non sporca in casa
house-warming party ['hauswɔ:mɪŋ-] *n* festa per inaugurare la casa nuova
housewife ['hauswaɪf] *n* massaia, casalinga
housework ['hauswə:k] *n* faccende *fpl* domestiche
housing ['hauzɪŋ] *n* alloggio ■ *cpd* (*problem, shortage*) degli alloggi
housing association *n* cooperativa edilizia
housing benefit *n* (*Brit*) contributo abitativo (*ad affittuari e a coloro che comprano una casa*)
housing conditions *npl* condizioni *fpl* di abitazione
housing development, (*Brit*) **housing estate** *n* *zona residenziale con case popolari e/o private*
hovel ['hɔvl] *n* casupola
hover ['hɔvə^r] *vi* (*bird*) librarsi; (*helicopter*) volare a punto fisso; **to ~ round sb** aggirarsi intorno a qn
hovercraft ['hɔvəkrɑ:ft] *n* hovercraft *m inv*
hoverport ['hɔvəpɔ:t] *n* porto per hovercraft
how [hau] *adv* come; **~ are you?** come sta?; **~ do you do?** piacere!, molto lieto!; **~ far is it to ...?** quanto è lontano ...?; **~ long have you been here?** da quanto tempo sta qui?; **~ lovely!** che bello!; **~ many?** quanti(-e)?; **~ much?** quanto(-a)?; **~ many people/much milk?** quante persone/quanto latte?; **~ old are you?** quanti anni ha?; **~'s life?** (*col*) come va (la vita)?; **~ about a drink?** che ne diresti di andare a bere qualcosa?; **~ is it that ...?** com'è che ...? *+ sub*
however [hau'ɛvə^r] *adv* in qualsiasi modo *or* maniera che; (*+ adjective*) per quanto *+ sub*; (*in questions*) come ■ *conj* comunque, però
howitzer ['hauɪtsə^r] *n* (*Mil*) obice *m*
howl [haul] *n* ululato ■ *vi* ululare
howler ['haulə^r] *n* marronata
howling ['haulɪŋ] *adj*: **a ~ wind** *or* **gale** un vento terribile
HP *n abbr* (*Brit*) = **hire purchase**
hp *abbr* (*Aut*) = **horsepower**
HQ *n abbr* (= *headquarters*) Q.G.
HR *n abbr* (*US*) = **House of Representatives**; (= *human resources*: *department*) ufficio personale; (: *staff*) risorse umane
hr, hrs *abbr* (= *hour(s)*) h
HRH *abbr* (= *His* (*or Her*) *Royal Highness*) S.A.R.
HRT *n abbr* = **hormone replacement therapy**
HS *abbr* (*US*) = **high school**
HST *abbr* (= *Hawaiian Standard Time*) *fuso orario*
HT *abbr* (= *high tension*) A.T.
HTML *n abbr* (*Comput*: = *hypertext markup language*) HTML
hub [hʌb] *n* (*of wheel*) mozzo; (*fig*) fulcro
hubbub ['hʌbʌb] *n* baccano
hubcap ['hʌbkæp] *n* (*Aut*) coprimozzo
HUD *n abbr* (*US*) = **Department of Housing and Urban Development**
huddle ['hʌdl] *vi*: **to ~ together** rannicchiarsi l'uno contro l'altro
hue [hju:] *n* tinta; **~ and cry** *n* clamore *m*
huff [hʌf] *n*: **in a ~** stizzito(-a); **to take the ~** mettere il broncio
huffy ['hʌfɪ] *adj* (*col*) stizzito(-a), indispettito(-a)
hug [hʌg] *vt* abbracciare; (*shore, kerb*) stringere ■ *n* abbraccio, stretta; **to give sb a ~** abbracciare qn
huge [hju:dʒ] *adj* enorme, immenso(-a)
hulk [hʌlk] *n* carcassa
hulking ['hʌlkɪŋ] *adj*: **~ (great)** grosso(-a) e goffo(-a)
hull [hʌl] *n* (*of ship*) scafo
hullabaloo [hʌləbə'lu:] *n* (*col*: *noise*) fracasso
hullo [hə'ləu] *excl* = **hello**
hum [hʌm] *vt* (*tune*) canticchiare ■ *vi* canticchiare; (*insect, plane, tool*) ronzare ■ *n* (*also Elec*) ronzio; (*of traffic, machines*) rumore *m*; (*of voices etc*) mormorio, brusio
human ['hju:mən] *adj* umano(-a) ■ *n* (*also*: **human being**) essere *m* umano

humane [hju:'meɪn] *adj* umanitario(-a)
humanism ['hju:mənɪzəm] *n* umanesimo
humanitarian [hju:mænɪ'tɛərɪən] *adj* umanitario(-a)
humanity [hju:'mænɪtɪ] *n* umanità; **the humanities** gli studi umanistici
humanly ['hju:mənlɪ] *adv* umanamente
humanoid ['hju:mənɔɪd] *adj* che sembra umano(-a) ■ *n* umanoide *m/f*
human rights *npl* diritti *mpl* dell'uomo
humble ['hʌmbl] *adj* umile, modesto(-a) ■ *vt* umiliare
humbly ['hʌmblɪ] *adv* umilmente, modestamente
humbug ['hʌmbʌg] *n* inganno; sciocchezze *fpl*; (*Brit: sweet*) caramella alla menta
humdrum ['hʌmdrʌm] *adj* monotono(-a), tedioso(-a)
humid ['hju:mɪd] *adj* umido(-a)
humidifier [hju:'mɪdɪfaɪə^r] *n* umidificatore *m*
humidity [hju:'mɪdɪtɪ] *n* umidità
humiliate [hju:'mɪlɪeɪt] *vt* umiliare
humiliation [hju:mɪlɪ'eɪʃən] *n* umiliazione *f*
humility [hju:'mɪlɪtɪ] *n* umiltà
humorist ['hju:mərɪst] *n* umorista *m/f*
humorous ['hju:mərəs] *adj* umoristico(-a); (*person*) buffo(-a)
humour, (*US*) **humor** ['hju:mə^r] *n* umore *m* ■ *vt* (*person*) compiacere; (*sb's whims*) assecondare; **sense of ~** senso dell'umorismo; **to be in a good/bad ~** essere di buon/cattivo umore
humourless, (*US*) **humorless** ['hju:məlɪs] *adj* privo(-a) di umorismo
hump [hʌmp] *n* gobba
humpback ['hʌmpbæk] *n* schiena d'asino; (*Brit*: *also*: **humpback bridge**) ponte *m* a schiena d'asino
humus ['hju:məs] *n* humus *m*
hunch [hʌntʃ] *n* gobba; (*premonition*) intuizione *f*; **I have a ~ that** ho la vaga impressione che
hunchback ['hʌntʃbæk] *n* gobbo(-a)
hunched [hʌntʃt] *adj* incurvato(-a)
hundred ['hʌndrəd] *num* cento; **about a ~ people** un centinaio di persone; **hundreds of people** centinaia *fpl* di persone; **I'm a ~ per cent sure** sono sicuro al cento per cento
hundredweight ['hʌndrɪdweɪt] *n* (*Brit*) = *50.8 kg*; = *112 lb*; (*US*) = *45.3 kg*; = *100 lb*
hung [hʌŋ] *pt, pp of* **hang**
Hungarian [hʌŋ'gɛərɪən] *adj* ungherese ■ *n* ungherese *m/f*; (*Ling*) ungherese *m*
Hungary ['hʌŋgərɪ] *n* Ungheria
hunger ['hʌŋgə^r] *n* fame *f* ■ *vi*: **to ~ for** desiderare ardentemente
hunger strike *n* sciopero della fame
hungover [hʌŋ'əuvə^r] *adj* (*col*): **to be ~** avere i postumi della sbornia
hungrily ['hʌŋgrəlɪ] *adv* voracemente; (*fig*) avidamente
hungry ['hʌŋgrɪ] *adj* affamato(-a); **to be ~** aver fame; **~ for** (*fig*) assetato di
hung up *adj* (*col*) complessato(-a)
hunk [hʌŋk] *n* bel pezzo
hunt [hʌnt] *vt* (*seek*) cercare; (*Sport*) cacciare ■ *vi* andare a caccia ■ *n* caccia
▸ **hunt down** *vt* scovare
hunter ['hʌntə^r] *n* cacciatore *m*; (*Brit: horse*) cavallo da caccia
hunting ['hʌntɪŋ] *n* caccia
hurdle ['hə:dl] *n* (*Sport, fig*) ostacolo
hurl [hə:l] *vt* lanciare con violenza
hurling ['hə:lɪŋ] *n* (*Sport*) hurling *m*
hurly-burly ['hə:lɪ'bə:lɪ] *n* chiasso, baccano
hurrah [hu'rɑ:], **hurray** [hu'reɪ] *excl* urra!, evviva!
hurricane ['hʌrɪkən] *n* uragano
hurried ['hʌrɪd] *adj* affrettato(-a); (*work*) fatto(-a) in fretta
hurriedly ['hʌrɪdlɪ] *adv* in fretta
hurry ['hʌrɪ] *n* fretta ■ *vi* affrettarsi ■ *vt* (*person*) affrettare; (*work*) far in fretta; **to be in a ~** aver fretta; **to do sth in a ~** fare qc in fretta; **to ~ in/out** entrare/uscire in fretta; **to ~ back/home** affrettarsi a tornare indietro/a casa
▸ **hurry along** *vi* camminare in fretta
▸ **hurry away, hurry off** *vi* andarsene in fretta
▸ **hurry up** *vi* sbrigarsi
hurt [hə:t] *vb* (*pt, pp* **~**) *vt* (*cause pain to*) far male a; (*injure, fig*) ferire; (*business, interests etc*) colpire, danneggiare ■ *vi* far male ■ *adj* ferito(-a); **I ~ my arm** mi sono fatto male al braccio; **where does it ~?** dove ti fa male?
hurtful ['hə:tful] *adj* (*remark*) che ferisce
hurtle ['hə:tl] *vt* scagliare ■ *vi*: **to ~ past/down** passare/scendere a razzo
husband ['hʌzbənd] *n* marito
hush [hʌʃ] *n* silenzio, calma ■ *vt* zittire; **~!** zitto(-a)!
▸ **hush up** *vt* (*fact*) cercare di far passare sotto silenzio
hush-hush ['hʌʃ'hʌʃ] *adj* (*col*) segretissimo(-a)
husk [hʌsk] *n* (*of wheat*) cartoccio; (*of rice, maize*) buccia
husky ['hʌskɪ] *adj* roco(-a) ■ *n* cane *m* eschimese
hustings ['hʌstɪŋz] *npl* (*Brit Pol*) comizi *mpl* elettorali
hustle ['hʌsl] *vt* spingere, incalzare ■ *n* pigia pigia *m inv*; **~ and bustle** trambusto
hut [hʌt] *n* rifugio; (*shed*) ripostiglio

h

hutch [hʌtʃ] *n* gabbia
hyacinth ['haɪəsɪnθ] *n* giacinto
hybrid ['haɪbrɪd] *adj* ibrido(-a) ■ *n* ibrido
hydrant ['haɪdrənt] *n* (*also*: **fire hydrant**) idrante *m*
hydraulic [haɪ'drɔlɪk] *adj* idraulico(-a)
hydraulics [haɪ'drɔlɪks] *n* idraulica
hydrochloric [haɪdrə'klɔrɪk] *adj*: **~ acid** acido cloridrico
hydroelectric [haɪdrəuɪ'lɛktrɪk] *adj* idroelettrico(-a)
hydrofoil ['haɪdrəfɔɪl] *n* aliscafo
hydrogen ['haɪdrədʒən] *n* idrogeno
hydrogen bomb *n* bomba all'idrogeno
hydrophobia [haɪdrə'fəubɪə] *n* idrofobia
hydroplane ['haɪdrəupleɪn] *n* idrovolante *m*
hyena [haɪ'i:nə] *n* iena
hygiene ['haɪdʒi:n] *n* igiene *f*
hygienic [haɪ'dʒi:nɪk] *adj* igienico(-a)
hymn [hɪm] *n* inno; cantica
hype [haɪp] *n* (*col*) clamorosa pubblicità
hyperactive [haɪpər'æktɪv] *adj* iperattivo(-a)
hyperlink [haɪpəlɪŋk] *n* collegamento *o* link *m inv* ipertestuale
hypermarket ['haɪpəmɑ:kɪt] *n* (*Brit*) ipermercato
hypertension [haɪpə'tɛnʃən] *n* (*Med*) ipertensione *f*
hypertext ['haɪpətɛkst] *n* (*Comput*) ipertesto
hyphen ['haɪfn] *n* trattino
hypnosis [hɪp'nəusɪs] *n* ipnosi *f*
hypnotic [hɪp'nɔtɪk] *adj* ipnotico(-a)
hypnotism ['hɪpnətɪzəm] *n* ipnotismo
hypnotist ['hɪpnətɪst] *n* ipnotizzatore(-trice)
hypnotize ['hɪpnətaɪz] *vt* ipnotizzare
hypoallergenic [haɪpəuælə'dʒɛnɪk] *adj* ipoallergico(-a)
hypochondriac [haɪpə'kɔndrɪæk] *n* ipocondriaco(-a)
hypocrisy [hɪ'pɔkrɪsɪ] *n* ipocrisia
hypocrite ['hɪpəkrɪt] *n* ipocrita *m/f*
hypocritical [hɪpə'krɪtɪkl] *adj* ipocrita
hypodermic [haɪpə'də:mɪk] *adj* ipodermico(-a) ■ *n* (*syringe*) siringa ipodermica
hypotenuse [haɪ'pɔtɪnju:z] *n* ipotenusa
hypothermia [haɪpəu'θə:mɪə] *n* ipotermia
hypothesis (*pl* **hypotheses**) [haɪ'pɔθɪsɪs, -si:z] *n* ipotesi *f inv*
hypothetical [haɪpəu'θɛtɪkl] *adj* ipotetico(-a)
hysterectomy [hɪstə'rɛktəmɪ] *n* isterectomia
hysteria [hɪ'stɪərɪə] *n* isteria
hysterical [hɪ'stɛrɪkl] *adj* isterico(-a); **to become ~** avere una crisi isterica
hysterics [hɪ'stɛrɪks] *npl* accesso di isteria; (*laughter*) attacco di riso; **to have ~** avere una crisi isterica

I i

I, i [aɪ] *n* (*letter*) I, i *f or m inv*; **I for Isaac**, (*US*) **I for Item** ≈ I come Imola
I [aɪ] *pron* io ■ *abbr* (= *island, isle*) Is.
IA *abbr* (*US*) = **Iowa**
IAEA *n abbr* = **International Atomic Energy Agency**
ib. ['ɪb] *abbr* (= *ibidem: from the same source*) ibid
Iberian [aɪ'bɪərɪən] *adj* iberico(-a)
Iberian Peninsula *n*: **the ~** la Penisola iberica
IBEW *n abbr* (*US: = International Brotherhood of Electrical Workers*) *associazione internazionale degli elettrotecnici*
ibid. ['ɪbɪd] *abbr* (= *ibidem: from the same source*) ibid
i/c *abbr* (*Brit*) = **in charge**
ICBM *n abbr* (= *intercontinental ballistic missile*) ICBM *m inv*
ICC *n abbr* (= *International Chamber of Commerce*) C.C.I. *f*; (*US: = Interstate Commerce Commission*) *commissione per il commercio tra gli stati degli USA*
ice [aɪs] *n* ghiaccio; (*on road*) gelo ■ *vt* (*cake*) glassare; (*drink*) mettere in fresco ■ *vi* (*also*: **ice over**) ghiacciare; (*also*: **ice up**) gelare; **to keep sth on ~** (*fig: plan, project*) mettere da parte (per il momento), accantonare
Ice Age *n* era glaciale
ice axe *n* piccozza da ghiaccio
iceberg ['aɪsbəːg] *n* iceberg *m inv*; **tip of the ~** (*also fig*) punta dell'iceberg
icebox ['aɪsbɔks] *n* (*US*) frigorifero; (*Brit*) reparto ghiaccio; (*insulated box*) frigo portatile
icebreaker ['aɪsbreɪkə[r]] *n* rompighiaccio *m inv*
ice bucket *n* secchiello del ghiaccio
ice-cap ['aɪskæp] *n* calotta polare
ice-cold [aɪs'kəuld] *adj* gelato(-a)
ice cream *n* gelato
ice-cream soda *n* (gelato) affogato al seltz
ice cube *n* cubetto di ghiaccio
iced [aɪst] *adj* (*drink*) ghiacciato(-a); (*coffee, tea*) freddo(-a); (*cake*) glassato(-a)
ice hockey *n* hockey *m* su ghiaccio
Iceland ['aɪslənd] *n* Islanda
Icelander ['aɪsləndə[r]] *n* islandese *m/f*
Icelandic [aɪs'lændɪk] *adj* islandese ■ *n* (*Ling*) islandese *m*
ice lolly *n* (*Brit*) ghiacciolo
ice pick *n* piccone *m* per ghiaccio
ice rink *n* pista di pattinaggio
ice-skate ['aɪsskeɪt] *n* pattino da ghiaccio ■ *vi* pattinare sul ghiaccio
ice-skating ['aɪsskeɪtɪŋ] *n* pattinaggio sul ghiaccio
icicle ['aɪsɪkl] *n* ghiacciolo
icing ['aɪsɪŋ] *n* (*Aviat etc*) patina di ghiaccio; (*Culin*) glassa
icing sugar *n* zucchero a velo
ICJ *n abbr* = **International Court of Justice**
icon ['aɪkɔn] *n* icona; (*Comput*) immagine *f*
ICR *n abbr* (*US*) = **Institute for Cancer Research**
ICRC *n abbr* (= *International Committee of the Red Cross*) CICR *m*
ICT *n abbr* (*Brit: Scol: = Information and Communications Technology*) informatica
ICU *n abbr* = **intensive care unit**
icy ['aɪsɪ] *adj* ghiacciato(-a); (*weather, temperature*) gelido(-a)
ID *abbr* = **identification document**; (*US*) = **Idaho**
I'd [aɪd] = **I would; I had**
Ida. *abbr* (*US*) = **Idaho**
ID card *n* = **identity card**
IDD *n abbr* (*Brit Tel: = International direct dialling*) teleselezione *f* internazionale
idea [aɪ'dɪə] *n* idea; **good ~!** buon'idea!; **to have an ~ that ...** aver l'impressione che ...; **I haven't the least ~** non ne ho la minima idea
ideal [aɪ'dɪəl] *adj, n* ideale (*m*)
idealist [aɪ'dɪəlɪst] *n* idealista *m/f*
ideally [aɪ'dɪəlɪ] *adv* perfettamente, assolutamente; **~ the book should have ...** l'ideale sarebbe che il libro avesse ...
identical [aɪ'dɛntɪkl] *adj* identico(-a)
identification [aɪdɛntɪfɪ'keɪʃən] *n* identificazione *f*; **means of ~** carta d'identità

identify [aɪ'dɛntɪfaɪ] *vt* identificare ■ *vi*: **to ~ with** identificarsi con
Identikit® [aɪ'dɛntɪkɪt] *n*: **~ (picture)** identikit *m inv*
identity [aɪ'dɛntɪtɪ] *n* identità *f inv*
identity card *n* carta d'identità
identity parade *n* (*Brit*) confronto all'americana
identity theft *n* furto d'identità
ideological [aɪdɪə'lɔdʒɪkəl] *adj* ideologico(-a)
ideology [aɪdɪ'ɔlədʒɪ] *n* ideologia
idiocy ['ɪdɪəsɪ] *n* idiozia
idiom ['ɪdɪəm] *n* idioma *m*; (*phrase*) espressione *f* idiomatica
idiomatic [ɪdɪə'mætɪk] *adj* idiomatico(-a)
idiosyncrasy [ɪdɪəu'sɪŋkrəsɪ] *n* idiosincrasia
idiot ['ɪdɪət] *n* idiota *m/f*
idiotic [ɪdɪ'ɔtɪk] *adj* idiota
idle ['aɪdl] *adj* inattivo(-a); (*lazy*) pigro(-a), ozioso(-a); (*unemployed*) disoccupato(-a); (*question, pleasures*) ozioso(-a) ■ *vi* (*engine*) girare al minimo; **to lie ~** stare fermo, non funzionare
▸ **idle away** *vt* (*time*) sprecare, buttar via
idleness ['aɪdlnɪs] *n* ozio; pigrizia
idler ['aɪdlə^r] *n* ozioso(-a), fannullone(-a)
idle time *n* tempi *mpl* morti
idol ['aɪdl] *n* idolo
idolize ['aɪdəlaɪz] *vt* idoleggiare
idyllic [ɪ'dɪlɪk] *adj* idillico(-a)
i.e. *abbr* (= *id est: that is*) cioè
if [ɪf] *conj* se ■ *n*: **there are a lot of ifs and buts** ci sono molti se e ma; **I'd be pleased if you could do it** sarei molto contento se potesse farlo; **if necessary** se (è) necessario; **if only he were here** se solo fosse qui; **if only to show him my gratitude** se non altro per esprimergli la mia gratitudine
iffy ['ɪfɪ] *adj* (*col*) incerto(-a)
igloo ['ɪglu:] *n* igloo *m inv*
ignite [ɪg'naɪt] *vt* accendere ■ *vi* accendersi
ignition [ɪg'nɪʃən] *n* (*Aut*) accensione *f*; **to switch on/off the ~** accendere/spegnere il motore
ignition key *n* (*Aut*) chiave *f* dell'accensione
ignoble [ɪg'nəubl] *adj* ignobile
ignominious [ɪgnə'mɪnɪəs] *adj* vergognoso(-a), ignominioso(-a)
ignoramus [ɪgnə'reɪməs] *n* ignorante *m/f*
ignorance ['ɪgnərəns] *n* ignoranza; **to keep sb in ~ of sth** tenere qn all'oscuro di qc
ignorant ['ɪgnərənt] *adj* ignorante; **to be ~ of** (*subject*) essere ignorante in; (*events*) essere ignaro(-a) di
ignore [ɪg'nɔ:^r] *vt* non tener conto di; (*person, fact*) ignorare
ikon ['aɪkɔn] *n* = **icon**
IL *abbr* (*US*) = **Illinois**
ILA *n abbr* (*US: = International Longshoremen's Association*) *associazione internazionale degli scaricatori di porto*
ill [ɪl] *adj* (*sick*) malato(-a); (*bad*) cattivo(-a) ■ *n* male *m*; **to take** *or* **be taken ~** ammalarsi; **to feel ~** star male; **to speak/think ~ of sb** parlar/pensar male di qn
I'll [aɪl] = **I will**; **I shall**
Ill. *abbr* (*US*) = **Illinois**
ill-advised [ɪləd'vaɪzd] *adj* (*decision*) poco giudizioso(-a); (*person*) mal consigliato(-a)
ill-at-ease [ɪlət'i:z] *adj* a disagio
ill-considered [ɪlkən'sɪdəd] *adj* (*plan*) avventato(-a)
ill-disposed [ɪldɪs'pəuzd] *adj*: **to be ~ towards sb/sth** essere maldisposto(-a) verso qn/qc *or* nei riguardi di qn/qc
illegal [ɪ'li:gl] *adj* illegale
illegally [ɪ'li:gəlɪ] *adv* illegalmente
illegible [ɪ'lɛdʒɪbl] *adj* illeggibile
illegitimate [ɪlɪ'dʒɪtɪmət] *adj* illegittimo(-a)
ill-fated [ɪl'feɪtɪd] *adj* nefasto(-a)
ill-favoured, (*US*) **ill-favored** [ɪl'feɪvəd] *adj* sgraziato(-a), brutto(-a)
ill feeling *n* rancore *m*
ill-gotten ['ɪlgɔtn] *adj*: **~ gains** maltolto
ill health *n* problemi *mpl* di salute
illicit [ɪ'lɪsɪt] *adj* illecito(-a)
ill-informed [ɪlɪn'fɔ:md] *adj* (*judgement, speech*) pieno(-a) di inesattezze; (*person*) male informato(-a)
illiterate [ɪ'lɪtərət] *adj* analfabeta, illetterato(-a); (*letter*) scorretto(-a)
ill-mannered [ɪl'mænəd] *adj* maleducato(-a), sgarbato(-a)
illness ['ɪlnɪs] *n* malattia
illogical [ɪ'lɔdʒɪkl] *adj* illogico(-a)
ill-suited [ɪl'su:tɪd] *adj* (*couple*) mal assortito(-a); **he is ~ to the job** è inadatto a quel lavoro
ill-timed [ɪl'taɪmd] *adj* intempestivo(-a), inopportuno(-a)
ill-treat [ɪl'tri:t] *vt* maltrattare
ill-treatment [ɪl'tri:tmənt] *n* maltrattamenti *mpl*
illuminate [ɪ'lu:mɪneɪt] *vt* illuminare; **illuminated sign** insegna luminosa
illuminating [ɪ'lu:mɪneɪtɪŋ] *adj* chiarificatore(-trice)
illumination [ɪlu:mɪ'neɪʃən] *n* illuminazione *f*
illusion [ɪ'lu:ʒən] *n* illusione *f*; **to be under the ~ that** avere l'impressione che
illusive [ɪ'lu:sɪv], **illusory** [ɪ'lu:sərɪ] *adj* illusorio(-a)
illustrate ['ɪləstreɪt] *vt* illustrare

illustration [ɪlə'streɪʃən] *n* illustrazione *f*
illustrator ['ɪləstreɪtəʳ] *n* illustratore(-trice)
illustrious [ɪ'lʌstrɪəs] *adj* illustre
ill will *n* cattiva volontà
ILO *n abbr* (= *International Labour Organization*) OIL *f*
IM *n abbr* (= *instant messaging*) messaggeria istantanea
I'm [aɪm] = **I am**
image ['ɪmɪdʒ] *n* immagine *f*; (*public face*) immagine (pubblica)
imagery ['ɪmɪdʒərɪ] *n* immagini *fpl*
imaginable [ɪ'mædʒɪnəbl] *adj* immaginabile, che si possa immaginare
imaginary [ɪ'mædʒɪnərɪ] *adj* immaginario(-a)
imagination [ɪmædʒɪ'neɪʃən] *n* immaginazione *f*, fantasia
imaginative [ɪ'mædʒɪnətɪv] *adj* immaginoso(-a)
imagine [ɪ'mædʒɪn] *vt* immaginare
imbalance [ɪm'bæləns] *n* squilibrio
imbecile ['ɪmbəsiːl] *n* imbecille *m/f*
imbue [ɪm'bjuː] *vt*: **to ~ sth with** impregnare qc di
IMF *n abbr* = **International Monetary Fund**
imitate ['ɪmɪteɪt] *vt* imitare
imitation [ɪmɪ'teɪʃən] *n* imitazione *f*
imitator ['ɪmɪteɪtəʳ] *n* imitatore(-trice)
immaculate [ɪ'mækjulət] *adj* immacolato(-a); (*dress, appearance*) impeccabile
immaterial [ɪmə'tɪərɪəl] *adj* immateriale, indifferente; **it is ~ whether** poco importa se *or* che + *sub*
immature [ɪmə'tjuəʳ] *adj* immaturo(-a)
immaturity [ɪmə'tjuərɪtɪ] *n* immaturità, mancanza di maturità
immeasurable [ɪ'mɛʒərəbl] *adj* incommensurabile
immediacy [ɪ'miːdɪəsɪ] *n* immediatezza
immediate [ɪ'miːdɪət] *adj* immediato(-a)
immediately [ɪ'miːdɪətlɪ] *adv* (*at once*) subito, immediatamente; **~ next to** proprio accanto a
immense [ɪ'mɛns] *adj* immenso(-a); enorme
immensity [ɪ'mɛnsɪtɪ] *n* (*of size, difference*) enormità; (*of problem etc*) vastità
immerse [ɪ'məːs] *vt* immergere
immersion heater [ɪ'məːʃən-] *n* (*Brit*) scaldaacqua *m inv* a immersione
immigrant ['ɪmɪgrənt] *n* immigrante *m/f*; (*already established*) immigrato(-a)
immigration [ɪmɪ'greɪʃən] *n* immigrazione *f*
immigration authorities *npl* ufficio stranieri
immigration laws *npl* leggi *fpl* relative all'immigrazione
imminent ['ɪmɪnənt] *adj* imminente
immobile [ɪ'məubaɪl] *adj* immobile
immobilize [ɪ'məubɪlaɪz] *vt* immobilizzare
immobilizer [ɪ'məubɪlaɪzəʳ] *n* (*Aut*) immobilizer *m inv*, dispositivo di bloccaggio del motore
immoderate [ɪ'mɔdərɪt] *adj* (*person*) smodato(-a), sregolato(-a); (*opinion, reaction, demand*) eccessivo(-a)
immodest [ɪ'mɔdɪst] *adj* (*indecent*) indecente, impudico(-a); (*boasting*) presuntuoso(-a)
immoral [ɪ'mɔrl] *adj* immorale
immorality [ɪmɔ'rælɪtɪ] *n* immoralità
immortal [ɪ'mɔːtl] *adj, n* immortale (*m/f*)
immortalize [ɪ'mɔːtəlaɪz] *vt* rendere immortale
immovable [ɪ'muːvəbl] *adj* (*object*) non movibile; (*person*) irremovibile
immune [ɪ'mjuːn] *adj*: **~ (to)** immune (da)
immune system *n* sistema *m* immunitario
immunity [ɪ'mjuːnɪtɪ] *n* (*also fig: of diplomat*) immunità; **diplomatic ~** immunità diplomatica
immunization [ɪmjunaɪ'zeɪʃən] *n* immunizzazione *f*
immunize ['ɪmjunaɪz] *vt* immunizzare
imp [ɪmp] *n* folletto, diavoletto; (*child*) diavoletto
impact ['ɪmpækt] *n* impatto
impair [ɪm'pɛəʳ] *vt* danneggiare
impaired [ɪm'pɛəd] *adj* indebolito(-a)
-impaired [ɪm'pɛəd] *suffix*: **visually~** videoleso(-a)
impale [ɪm'peɪl] *vt* impalare
impart [ɪm'pɑːt] *vt* (*make known*) comunicare; (*bestow*) impartire
impartial [ɪm'pɑːʃl] *adj* imparziale
impartiality [ɪmpɑːʃɪ'ælɪtɪ] *n* imparzialità
impassable [ɪm'pɑːsəbl] *adj* insuperabile; (*road*) impraticabile
impasse [æm'pɑːs] *n* impasse *f inv*
impassioned [ɪm'pæʃənd] *adj* appassionato(-a)
impassive [ɪm'pæsɪv] *adj* impassibile
impatience [ɪm'peɪʃəns] *n* impazienza
impatient [ɪm'peɪʃənt] *adj* impaziente; **to get** *or* **grow ~** perdere la pazienza
impeach [ɪm'piːtʃ] *vt* accusare, attaccare; (*public official*) mettere sotto accusa
impeachment [ɪm'piːtʃmənt] *n* (*Law*) imputazione *f*
impeccable [ɪm'pɛkəbl] *adj* impeccabile
impecunious [ɪmpɪ'kjuːnɪəs] *adj* povero(-a)
impede [ɪm'piːd] *vt* impedire
impediment [ɪm'pɛdɪmənt] *n* impedimento; (*also*: **speech impediment**) difetto di pronuncia
impel [ɪm'pɛl] *vt* (*force*): **to ~ sb (to do sth)** costringere *or* obbligare qn (a fare qc)

impending [ɪm'pɛndɪŋ] *adj* imminente
impenetrable [ɪm'pɛnɪtrəbl] *adj* impenetrabile
imperative [ɪm'pɛrətɪv] *adj* imperativo(-a); necessario(-a), urgente; (*voice*) imperioso(-a) ■ *n* (*Ling*) imperativo
imperceptible [ɪmpə'sɛptɪbl] *adj* impercettibile
imperfect [ɪm'pə:fɪkt] *adj* imperfetto(-a); (*goods etc*) difettoso(-a) ■ *n* (*Ling*: *also*: **imperfect tense**) imperfetto
imperfection [ɪmpə:'fɛkʃən] *n* imperfezione *f*; (*flaw*) difetto
imperial [ɪm'pɪərɪəl] *adj* imperiale; (*measure*) legale
imperialism [ɪm'pɪərɪəlɪzəm] *n* imperialismo
imperil [ɪm'pɛrɪl] *vt* mettere in pericolo
imperious [ɪm'pɪərɪəs] *adj* imperioso(-a)
impersonal [ɪm'pə:sənl] *adj* impersonale
impersonate [ɪm'pə:səneɪt] *vt* impersonare; (*Theat*) imitare
impersonation [ɪmpə:sə'neɪʃən] *n* (*Law*) usurpazione *f* d'identità; (*Theat*) imitazione *f*
impersonator [ɪm'pə:səneɪtə[r]] *n* (*gen, Theat*) imitatore(-trice)
impertinence [ɪm'pə:tɪnəns] *n* impertinenza
impertinent [ɪm'pə:tɪnənt] *adj* impertinente
imperturbable [ɪmpə'tə:bəbl] *adj* imperturbabile
impervious [ɪm'pə:vɪəs] *adj* impermeabile; (*fig*): **~ to** insensibile a; impassibile di fronte a
impetuous [ɪm'pɛtjuəs] *adj* impetuoso(-a), precipitoso(-a)
impetus ['ɪmpətəs] *n* impeto
impinge [ɪm'pɪndʒ]: **to ~ on** *vt fus* (*person*) colpire; (*rights*) ledere
impish ['ɪmpɪʃ] *adj* malizioso(-a), birichino(-a)
implacable [ɪm'plækəbl] *adj* implacabile
implant [ɪm'plɑ:nt] *vt* (*Med*) innestare; (*fig*: *idea, principle*) inculcare
implausible [ɪm'plɔ:zɪbl] *adj* non plausibile
implement *n* ['ɪmplɪmənt] attrezzo; (*for cooking*) utensile *m* ■ *vt* ['ɪmplɪmɛnt] effettuare
implicate ['ɪmplɪkeɪt] *vt* implicare
implication [ɪmplɪ'keɪʃən] *n* implicazione *f*; **by ~** implicitamente
implicit [ɪm'plɪsɪt] *adj* implicito(-a); (*complete*) completo(-a)
implicitly [ɪm'plɪsɪtlɪ] *adv* implicitamente
implore [ɪm'plɔ:[r]] *vt* implorare
imply [ɪm'plaɪ] *vt* insinuare; suggerire
impolite [ɪmpə'laɪt] *adj* scortese
imponderable [ɪm'pɔndərəbl] *adj* imponderabile
import *vt* [ɪm'pɔ:t] importare ■ *n* ['ɪmpɔ:t] (*Comm*) importazione *f*; (*meaning*) significato, senso ■ *cpd* (*duty, licence etc*) d'importazione
importance [ɪm'pɔ:tns] *n* importanza; **to be of great/little ~** importare molto/poco, essere molto/poco importante
important [ɪm'pɔ:tnt] *adj* importante; **it's not ~** non ha importanza; **it is ~ that** è importante che *+ sub*
importantly [ɪm'pɔ:təntlɪ] *adv* (*pej*) con (un'aria d')importanza; **but, more ~, ...** ma, quel che più conta *or* importa, ...
importation [ɪmpɔ:'teɪʃən] *n* importazione *f*
imported [ɪm'pɔ:tɪd] *adj* importato(-a)
importer [ɪm'pɔ:tə[r]] *n* importatore(-trice)
impose [ɪm'pəuz] *vt* imporre ■ *vi*: **to ~ on sb** sfruttare la bontà di qn
imposing [ɪm'pəuzɪŋ] *adj* imponente
imposition [ɪmpə'zɪʃən] *n* imposizione *f*; **to be an ~ on** (*person*) abusare della gentilezza di
impossibility [ɪmpɔsə'bɪlɪtɪ] *n* impossibilità
impossible [ɪm'pɔsɪbl] *adj* impossibile; **it is ~ for me to leave now** mi è impossibile venir via adesso
impostor [ɪm'pɔstə[r]] *n* impostore(-a)
impotence ['ɪmpətns] *n* impotenza
impotent ['ɪmpətnt] *adj* impotente
impound [ɪm'paund] *vt* confiscare
impoverished [ɪm'pɔvərɪʃt] *adj* impoverito(-a)
impracticable [ɪm'præktɪkəbl] *adj* impraticabile
impractical [ɪm'præktɪkl] *adj* non pratico(-a)
imprecise [ɪmprɪ'saɪs] *adj* impreciso(-a)
impregnable [ɪm'prɛgnəbl] *adj* (*fortress*) inespugnabile; (*fig*) inoppugnabile; irrefutabile
impregnate ['ɪmprɛgneɪt] *vt* impregnare; (*fertilize*) fecondare
impresario [ɪmprɪ'sɑ:rɪəu] *n* impresario(-a)
impress [ɪm'prɛs] *vt* impressionare; (*mark*) imprimere, stampare; **to ~ sth on sb** far capire qc a qn
impression [ɪm'prɛʃən] *n* impressione *f*; **to be under the ~ that** avere l'impressione che; **to make a good/bad ~ on sb** fare una buona/cattiva impressione a *or* su qn
impressionable [ɪm'prɛʃnəbl] *adj* impressionabile
impressionist [ɪm'prɛʃənɪst] *n* impressionista *m/f*
impressive [ɪm'prɛsɪv] *adj* impressionante
imprint ['ɪmprɪnt] *n* (*Publishing*) sigla editoriale

imprinted [ɪm'prɪntɪd] *adj*: **~ on** impresso(-a) in
imprison [ɪm'prɪzn] *vt* imprigionare
imprisonment [ɪm'prɪznmənt] *n* imprigionamento
improbable [ɪm'prɔbəbl] *adj* improbabile; (*excuse*) inverosimile
impromptu [ɪm'prɔmptju:] *adj* improvvisato(-a) ■ *adv* improvvisando, così su due piedi
improper [ɪm'prɔpəʳ] *adj* scorretto(-a); (*unsuitable*) inadatto(-a), improprio(-a); sconveniente, indecente
impropriety [ɪmprə'praɪətɪ] *n* sconvenienza; (*of expression*) improprietà
improve [ɪm'pru:v] *vt* migliorare ■ *vi* migliorare; (*pupil etc*) fare progressi
▸ **improve (up)on** *vt fus* (*offer*) aumentare
improvement [ɪm'pru:vmənt] *n* miglioramento; progresso; **to make improvements to** migliorare, apportare dei miglioramenti a
improvisation [ɪmprəvaɪ'zeɪʃən] *n* improvvisazione *f*
improvise ['ɪmprəvaɪz] *vt, vi* improvvisare
imprudence [ɪm'pru:dns] *n* imprudenza
imprudent [ɪm'pru:dnt] *adj* imprudente
impudence ['ɪmpjudns] *n* impudenza
impudent ['ɪmpjudnt] *adj* impudente, sfacciato(-a)
impugn [ɪm'pju:n] *vt* impugnare
impulse ['ɪmpʌls] *n* impulso; **to act on ~** agire d'impulso *or* impulsivamente
impulse buy *n* acquisto fatto d'impulso
impulsive [ɪm'pʌlsɪv] *adj* impulsivo(-a)
impunity [ɪm'pju:nɪtɪ] *n*: **with ~** impunemente
impure [ɪm'pjuəʳ] *adj* impuro(-a)
impurity [ɪm'pjuərɪtɪ] *n* impurità *f inv*
IN *abbr* (*US*) = **Indiana**

 KEYWORD

in [ɪn] *prep* **1** (*indicating place, position*) in; **in the house/garden** in casa/giardino; **in the box** nella scatola; **in the fridge** nel frigorifero; **I have it in my hand** ce l'ho in mano; **in town/the country** in città/campagna; **in school** a scuola; **in here/there** qui/lì dentro
2 (*with place names: of town, region, country*): **in London** a Londra; **in England** in Inghilterra; **in the United States** negli Stati Uniti; **in Yorkshire** nello Yorkshire
3 (*indicating time: during, in the space of*) in; **in spring/summer** in primavera/estate; **in 1988** nel 1988; **in May** in *or* a maggio; **I'll see you in July** ci vediamo a luglio; **in the afternoon** nel pomeriggio; **at 4 o'clock in the afternoon** alle 4 del pomeriggio; **I did it in 3 hours/days** l'ho fatto in 3 ore/giorni; **I'll see you in 2 weeks** *or* **in 2 weeks' time** ci vediamo tra 2 settimane; **once in a hundred years** una volta ogni cento anni
4 (*indicating manner etc*) a; **in a loud/soft voice** a voce alta/bassa; **in pencil** a matita; **in English/French** in inglese/francese; **in writing** per iscritto; **the boy in the blue shirt** il ragazzo con la camicia blu
5 (*indicating circumstances*): **in the sun** al sole; **in the shade** all'ombra; **in the rain** sotto la pioggia; **a rise in prices** un aumento dei prezzi
6 (*indicating mood, state*): **in tears** in lacrime; **in anger** per la rabbia; **in despair** disperato(-a); **in good condition** in buono stato, in buone condizioni; **to live in luxury** vivere nel lusso
7 (*with ratios, numbers*): **1 in 10** 1 su 10; **20 pence in the pound** 20 pence per sterlina; **they lined up in twos** si misero in fila per due; **in hundreds** a centinaia
8 (*referring to people, works*) in; **the disease is common in children** la malattia è comune nei bambini; **in (the works of) Dickens** in Dickens, nelle opere di Dickens
9 (*indicating profession etc*) in; **to be in teaching** fare l'insegnante, insegnare; **to be in publishing** lavorare nell'editoria
10 (*after superlative*) di; **the best in the class** il migliore della classe
11 (*with present participle*): **in saying this** dicendo questo, nel dire questo
12: **in that** *conj* poiché
■ *adv*: **to be in** (*person: at home, work*) esserci; (*train, ship, plane*) essere arrivato(-a); (*in fashion*) essere di moda; **their party is in** il loro partito è al potere; **to ask sb in** invitare qn ad entrare; **to run/limp** *etc* **in** entrare di corsa/zoppicando *etc*
■ *n*: **the ins and outs of the problem** tutti gli aspetti del problema

in., ins *abbr* = **inch(es)**
inability [ɪnə'bɪlɪtɪ] *n* inabilità, incapacità; **~ to pay** impossibilità di pagare
inaccessible [ɪnək'sɛsɪbl] *adj* inaccessibile
inaccuracy [ɪn'ækjurəsɪ] *n* inaccuratezza; inesattezza; imprecisione *f*
inaccurate [ɪn'ækjurət] *adj* inaccurato(-a); (*figures*) inesatto(-a); (*translation*) impreciso(-a)
inaction [ɪn'ækʃən] *n* inazione *f*
inactivity [ɪnæk'tɪvɪtɪ] *n* inattività

inadequacy [ɪn'ædɪkwəsɪ] *n* insufficienza
inadequate [ɪn'ædɪkwət] *adj* insufficiente
inadmissible [ɪnəd'mɪsəbl] *adj* inammissibile
inadvertent [ɪnəd'vəːtənt] *adj* involontario(-a)
inadvertently [ɪnəd'vəːtntlɪ] *adv* senza volerlo
inadvisable [ɪnəd'vaɪzəbl] *adj* sconsigliabile
inane [ɪ'neɪn] *adj* vacuo(-a), stupido(-a)
inanimate [ɪn'ænɪmət] *adj* inanimato(-a)
inapplicable [ɪn'æplɪkəbl] *adj* inapplicabile
inappropriate [ɪnə'prəuprɪət] *adj* disadatto(-a); (*word, expression*) improprio(-a)
inapt [ɪn'æpt] *adj* maldestro(-a); fuori luogo
inaptitude [ɪn'æptɪtjuːd] *n* improprietà
inarticulate [ɪnɑː'tɪkjulət] *adj* (*person*) che si esprime male; (*speech*) inarticolato(-a)
inasmuch as [ɪnəz'mʌtʃæz] *adv* in quanto che; (*seeing that*) poiché
inattention [ɪnə'tɛnʃən] *n* mancanza di attenzione
inattentive [ɪnə'tɛntɪv] *adj* disattento(-a), distratto(-a); negligente
inaudible [ɪn'ɔːdɪbl] *adj* che non si riesce a sentire
inaugural [ɪ'nɔːgjurəl] *adj* inaugurale
inaugurate [ɪ'nɔːgjureɪt] *vt* inaugurare; (*president, official*) insediare
inauguration [ɪnɔːgju'reɪʃən] *n* inaugurazione *f*; insediamento in carica
inauspicious [ɪnɔːs'pɪʃəs] *adj* poco propizio(-a)
in-between [ɪnbɪ'twiːn] *adj* fra i (*or* le) due
inborn [ɪn'bɔːn] *adj* (*feeling*) innato(-a); (*defect*) congenito(-a)
inbred [ɪn'brɛd] *adj* innato(-a); (*family*) connaturato(-a)
inbreeding [ɪn'briːdɪŋ] *n* incrocio ripetuto di animali consanguinei; unioni *fpl* fra consanguinei
Inc. *abbr* = **incorporated**
Inca ['ɪŋkə] *adj* (*also*: **Incan**) inca *inv* ■ *n* inca *m/f inv*
incalculable [ɪn'kælkjuləbl] *adj* incalcolabile
incapability [ɪnkeɪpə'bɪlɪtɪ] *n* incapacità
incapable [ɪn'keɪpəbl] *adj*: **~ (of doing sth)** incapace (di fare qc)
incapacitate [ɪnkə'pæsɪteɪt] *vt*: **to ~ sb from doing** rendere qn incapace di fare
incapacitated [ɪnkə'pæsɪteɪtɪd] *adj* (*Law*) inabilitato(-a)
incapacity [ɪnkə'pæsɪtɪ] *n* incapacità
incarcerate [ɪn'kɑːsəreɪt] *vt* imprigionare
incarnate *adj* [ɪn'kɑːnɪt] incarnato(-a) ■ *vt* ['ɪnkɑːneɪt] incarnare
incarnation [ɪnkɑː'neɪʃən] *n* incarnazione *f*
incendiary [ɪn'sɛndɪərɪ] *adj* incendiario(-a) ■ *n* (*bomb*) bomba incendiaria
incense *n* ['ɪnsɛns] incenso ■ *vt* [ɪn'sɛns] (*anger*) infuriare
incense burner *n* incensiere *m*
incentive [ɪn'sɛntɪv] *n* incentivo
incentive scheme *n* piano di incentivazione
inception [ɪn'sɛpʃən] *n* inizio, principio
incessant [ɪn'sɛsnt] *adj* incessante
incessantly [ɪn'sɛsntlɪ] *adv* di continuo, senza sosta
incest ['ɪnsɛst] *n* incesto
inch [ɪntʃ] *n* pollice *m* (= *25 mm; 12 in a foot*); **within an ~ of** a un pelo da; **he wouldn't give an ~** (*fig*) non ha ceduto di un millimetro
▸ **inch forward** *vi* avanzare pian piano
inch tape *n* (*Brit*) metro a nastro (da sarto)
incidence ['ɪnsɪdns] *n* incidenza
incident ['ɪnsɪdnt] *n* incidente *m*; (*in book*) episodio
incidental [ɪnsɪ'dɛntl] *adj* accessorio(-a), d'accompagnamento; (*unplanned*) incidentale; **~ to** marginale a; **~ expenses** *npl* spese *fpl* accessorie
incidentally [ɪnsɪ'dɛntəlɪ] *adv* (*by the way*) a proposito
incidental music *n* sottofondo (musicale), musica di sottofondo
incident room *n* (*Police*) centrale *f* delle operazioni (*per indagini*)
incinerate [ɪn'sɪnəreɪt] *vt* incenerire
incinerator [ɪn'sɪnəreɪtə^r] *n* inceneritore *m*
incipient [ɪn'sɪpɪənt] *adj* incipiente
incision [ɪn'sɪʒən] *n* incisione *f*
incisive [ɪn'saɪsɪv] *adj* incisivo(-a); tagliante; acuto(-a)
incisor [ɪn'saɪzə^r] *n* incisivo
incite [ɪn'saɪt] *vt* incitare
incl. *abbr* = **including**; **inclusive (of)**
inclement [ɪn'klɛmənt] *adj* inclemente
inclination [ɪnklɪ'neɪʃən] *n* inclinazione *f*
incline *n* ['ɪnklaɪn] pendenza, pendio ■ *vt* [ɪn'klaɪn] inclinare ■ *vi*: **to ~ to** tendere a; **to be inclined to do** tendere a fare; essere propenso(-a) a fare; **to be well inclined towards sb** essere ben disposto(-a) verso qn
include [ɪn'kluːd] *vt* includere, comprendere; **the tip is/is not included** la mancia è compresa/esclusa
including [ɪn'kluːdɪŋ] *prep* compreso(-a), incluso(-a); **~ tip** mancia compresa, compresa la mancia
inclusion [ɪn'kluːʒən] *n* inclusione *f*
inclusive [ɪn'kluːsɪv] *adj* incluso(-a), compreso(-a); **£50, ~ of all surcharges** 50 sterline, incluse tutte le soprattasse

inclusive terms *npl* (*Brit*) prezzo tutto compreso
incognito [ɪnkɔg'ni:təu] *adv* in incognito
incoherent [ɪnkəu'hɪərənt] *adj* incoerente
income ['ɪnkʌm] *n* reddito; **gross/net ~** reddito lordo/netto; **~ and expenditure account** conto entrate ed uscite
income support *n* (*Brit*) sussidio di indigenza *or* povertà
income tax *n* imposta sul reddito
income tax inspector *n* ispettore *m* delle imposte dirette
income tax return *n* dichiarazione *f* annuale dei redditi
incoming ['ɪnkʌmɪŋ] *adj* (*passengers*) in arrivo; (*government, tenant*) subentrante; **~ tide** marea montante
incommunicado [ɪnkəmjunɪ'kɑ:dəu] *adj*: **to hold sb ~** tenere qn in segregazione
incomparable [ɪn'kɔmpərəbl] *adj* incomparabile
incompatible [ɪnkəm'pætɪbl] *adj* incompatibile
incompetence [ɪn'kɔmpɪtns] *n* incompetenza, incapacità
incompetent [ɪn'kɔmpɪtnt] *adj* incompetente, incapace
incomplete [ɪnkəm'pli:t] *adj* incompleto(-a)
incomprehensible [ɪnkɔmprɪ'hɛnsɪbl] *adj* incomprensibile
inconceivable [ɪnkən'si:vəbl] *adj* inimmaginabile
inconclusive [ɪnkən'klu:sɪv] *adj* improduttivo(-a); (*argument*) poco convincente
incongruous [ɪn'kɔŋgruəs] *adj* poco appropriato(-a); (*remark, act*) incongruo(-a)
inconsequential [ɪnkɔnsɪ'kwɛnʃl] *adj* senza importanza
inconsiderable [ɪnkən'sɪdərəbl] *adj*: **not ~** non trascurabile
inconsiderate [ɪnkən'sɪdərət] *adj* sconsiderato(-a)
inconsistency [ɪnkən'sɪstənsɪ] *n* (*of actions etc*) incongruenza; (*of work*) irregolarità; (*of statement etc*) contraddizione *f*
inconsistent [ɪnkən'sɪstnt] *adj* incoerente; poco logico(-a); contraddittorio(-a); **~ with** in contraddizione con
inconsolable [ɪnkən'səuləbl] *adj* inconsolabile
inconspicuous [ɪnkən'spɪkjuəs] *adj* incospicuo(-a); (*colour*) poco appariscente; (*dress*) dimesso(-a); **to make o.s. ~** cercare di passare inosservato(-a)
inconstant [ɪn'kɔnstnt] *adj* incostante; mutevole
incontinence [ɪn'kɔntɪnəns] *n* incontinenza
incontinent [ɪn'kɔntɪnənt] *adj* incontinente
incontrovertible [ɪnkɔntrə'və:təbl] *adj* incontrovertibile
inconvenience [ɪnkən'vi:njəns] *n* inconveniente *m*; (*trouble*) disturbo ■ *vt* disturbare; **to put sb to great ~** creare degli inconvenienti a qn; **don't ~ yourself** non si disturbi
inconvenient [ɪnkən'vi:njənt] *adj* scomodo(-a); **that time is very ~ for me** quell'ora mi è molto scomoda, non è un'ora adatta per me
incorporate [ɪn'kɔ:pəreɪt] *vt* incorporare; (*contain*) contenere
incorporated [ɪn'kɔ:pəreɪtɪd] *adj*: **~ company** (*US*) società *f inv* registrata
incorrect [ɪnkə'rɛkt] *adj* scorretto(-a); (*statement*) impreciso(-a)
incorrigible [ɪn'kɔrɪdʒəbl] *adj* incorreggibile
incorruptible [ɪnkə'rʌptɪbl] *adj* incorruttibile
increase *n* ['ɪnkri:s] aumento ■ *vi* [ɪn'kri:s] aumentare; **to be on the ~** essere in aumento; **an ~ of £5/10%** un aumento di 5 sterline/del 10%
increasing [ɪn'kri:sɪŋ] *adj* (*number*) crescente
increasingly [ɪn'kri:sɪŋlɪ] *adv* sempre più
incredible [ɪn'krɛdɪbl] *adj* incredibile
incredulous [ɪn'krɛdjuləs] *adj* incredulo(-a)
increment ['ɪnkrɪmənt] *n* aumento, incremento
incriminate [ɪn'krɪmɪneɪt] *vt* compromettere
incriminating [ɪn'krɪmɪneɪtɪŋ] *adj* incriminante
incubate ['ɪnkjubeɪt] *vt* (*eggs*) covare ■ *vi* (*egg*) essere in incubazione; (*disease*) avere un'incubazione
incubation [ɪnkju'beɪʃən] *n* incubazione *f*
incubation period *n* (periodo di) incubazione *f*
incubator ['ɪnkjubeɪtə[r]] *n* incubatrice *f*
inculcate ['ɪnkʌlkeɪt] *vt*: **to ~ sth in sb** inculcare qc a qn, instillare qc a qn
incumbent [ɪn'kʌmbənt] *adj*: **it is ~ on him to do ...** è suo dovere fare ... ■ *n* titolare *m/f*
incur [ɪn'kə:[r]] *vt* (*expenses*) incorrere; (*debt*) contrarre; (*loss*) subire; (*anger, risk*) esporsi a
incurable [ɪn'kjuərəbl] *adj* incurabile
incursion [ɪn'kə:ʃən] *n* incursione *f*
Ind. *abbr* (*US*) = **Indiana**
indebted [ɪn'dɛtɪd] *adj*: **to be ~ to sb (for)** essere obbligato(-a) verso qn (per)
indecency [ɪn'di:snsɪ] *n* indecenza
indecent [ɪn'di:snt] *adj* indecente
indecent assault *n* (*Brit*) aggressione *f* a scopo di violenza sessuale

indecent exposure *n* atti *mpl* osceni in luogo pubblico
indecipherable [ɪndɪ'saɪfərəbl] *adj* indecifrabile
indecision [ɪndɪ'sɪʒən] *n* indecisione *f*
indecisive [ɪndɪ'saɪsɪv] *adj* indeciso(-a); (*discussion*) non decisivo(-a)
indeed [ɪn'di:d] *adv* infatti; veramente; **yes ~!** certamente!
indefatigable [ɪndɪ'fætɪgəbl] *adj* infaticabile, instancabile
indefensible [ɪndɪ'fɛnsəbl] *adj* (*conduct*) ingiustificabile
indefinable [ɪndɪ'faɪnəbl] *adj* indefinibile
indefinite [ɪn'dɛfɪnɪt] *adj* indefinito(-a); (*answer*) vago(-a); (*period, number*) indeterminato(-a)
indefinitely [ɪn'dɛfɪnɪtlɪ] *adv* (*wait*) indefinitamente
indelible [ɪn'dɛlɪbl] *adj* indelebile
indelicate [ɪn'dɛlɪkɪt] *adj* (*tactless*) indelicato(-a), privo(-a) di tatto; (*not polite*) sconveniente
indemnify [ɪn'dɛmnɪfaɪ] *vt* indennizzare
indemnity [ɪn'dɛmnɪtɪ] *n* (*insurance*) assicurazione *f*; (*compensation*) indennità, indennizzo
indent [ɪn'dɛnt] *vt* (*Typ: text*) far rientrare dal margine
indentation [ɪndɛn'teɪʃən] *n* dentellatura; (*Typ*) rientranza; (*dent*) tacca
indented [ɪn'dɛntɪd] *adj* (*Typ*) rientrante
indenture [ɪn'dɛntʃə^r] *n* contratto *m* formazione *inv*
independence [ɪndɪ'pɛndns] *n* indipendenza
Independence Day *n* (*US*) *vedi nota*

INDEPENDENCE DAY

Negli Stati Uniti il 4 luglio si festeggia l'*Independence Day*, il giorno in cui è stata firmata, nel 1776, la Dichiarazione di Indipendenza con la quale tredici colonie britanniche dichiaravano la propria indipendenza dalla Gran Bretagna e la propria appartenenza agli Stati Uniti d'America.

independent [ɪndɪ'pɛndnt] *adj* indipendente
independently [ɪndɪ'pɛndntlɪ] *adv* indipendentemente; separatamente; **~ of** indipendentemente da
in-depth ['ɪn'dɛpθ] *adj* approfondito(-a)
indescribable [ɪndɪ'skraɪbəbl] *adj* indescrivibile
indestructible [ɪndɪ'strʌktəbl] *adj* indistruttibile
indeterminate [ɪndɪ'tə:mɪnɪt] *adj* indeterminato(-a)
index ['ɪndɛks] *n* (*pl* **indexes**) (*in book*) indice *m*; (*in library etc*) catalogo; (*pl* **indices**): (*ratio, sign*) indice *m*
index card *n* scheda
index finger *n* (dito) indice *m*
index-linked ['ɪndɛks'lɪŋkt], (*US*) **indexed** ['ɪndɛkst] *adj* legato(-a) al costo della vita
India ['ɪndɪə] *n* India
Indian ['ɪndɪən] *adj, n* indiano(-a)
Indian ink *n* inchiostro di china
Indian Ocean *n*: **the ~** l'Oceano Indiano
Indian Summer *n* (*fig*) estate *f* di San Martino
India paper *n* carta d'India, carta bibbia
India rubber *n* caucciù *m*
indicate ['ɪndɪkeɪt] *vt* indicare ■ *vi* (*Brit Aut*): **to ~ left/right** mettere la freccia a sinistra/a destra
indication [ɪndɪ'keɪʃən] *n* indicazione *f* segno
indicative [ɪn'dɪkətɪv] *adj* indicativo(-a) ■ *n* (*Ling*) indicativo; **to be ~ of sth** essere indicativo(-a) *or* un indice di qc
indicator ['ɪndɪkeɪtə^r] *n* (*sign*) segno; (*Aut*) indicatore *m* di direzione, freccia
indices ['ɪndɪsi:z] *npl of* **index**
indict [ɪn'daɪt] *vt* accusare
indictable [ɪn'daɪtəbl] *adj* passibile di pena; **~ offence** atto che costituisce reato
indictment [ɪn'daɪtmənt] *n* accusa
indifference [ɪn'dɪfrəns] *n* indifferenza
indifferent [ɪn'dɪfrənt] *adj* indifferente; (*poor*) mediocre
indigenous [ɪn'dɪdʒɪnəs] *adj* indigeno(-a)
indigestible [ɪndɪ'dʒɛstɪbl] *adj* indigeribile
indigestion [ɪndɪ'dʒɛstʃən] *n* indigestione *f*
indignant [ɪn'dɪgnənt] *adj*: **~ (at sth/with sb)** indignato(-a) (per qc/contro qn)
indignation [ɪndɪg'neɪʃən] *n* indignazione *f*
indignity [ɪn'dɪgnɪtɪ] *n* umiliazione *f*
indigo ['ɪndɪgəu] *adj, n* indaco (*inv*)
indirect [ɪndɪ'rɛkt] *adj* indiretto(-a)
indirectly [ɪndɪ'rɛktlɪ] *adv* indirettamente
indiscreet [ɪndɪ'skri:t] *adj* indiscreto(-a); (*rash*) imprudente
indiscretion [ɪndɪ'skrɛʃən] *n* indiscrezione *f*; imprudenza
indiscriminate [ɪndɪ'skrɪmɪnət] *adj* (*person*) che non sa discernere; (*admiration*) cieco(-a); (*killings*) indiscriminato(-a)
indispensable [ɪndɪ'spɛnsəbl] *adj* indispensabile
indisposed [ɪndɪ'spəuzd] *adj* (*unwell*) indisposto(-a)
indisposition [ɪndɪspə'zɪʃən] *n* (*illness*) indisposizione *f*

indisputable [ɪndɪ'spju:təbl] *adj* incontestabile, indiscutibile
indistinct [ɪndɪ'stɪŋkt] *adj* indistinto(-a); (*memory, noise*) vago(-a)
indistinguishable [ɪndɪ'stɪŋgwɪʃəbl] *adj* indistinguibile
individual [ɪndɪ'vɪdjuəl] *n* individuo ■ *adj* individuale; (*characteristic*) particolare, originale
individualist [ɪndɪ'vɪdjuəlɪst] *n* individualista *m/f*
individuality [ɪndɪvɪdju'ælɪtɪ] *n* individualità
individually [ɪndɪ'vɪdjuəlɪ] *adv* singolarmente, uno(-a) per uno(-a)
indivisible [ɪndɪ'vɪzɪbl] *adj* indivisibile
Indochina ['ɪndəu'tʃaɪnə] *n* Indocina
indoctrinate [ɪn'dɔktrɪneɪt] *vt* indottrinare
indoctrination [ɪndɔktrɪ'neɪʃən] *n* indottrinamento
indolent ['ɪndələnt] *adj* indolente
Indonesia [ɪndəu'ni:zɪə] *n* Indonesia
Indonesian [ɪndəu'ni:zɪən] *adj, n* indonesiano(-a); (*Ling*) indonesiano
indoor ['ɪndɔ:ʳ] *adj* da interno; (*plant*) d'appartamento; (*swimming pool*) coperto(-a); (*sport, games*) fatto(-a) al coperto
indoors [ɪn'dɔ:z] *adv* all'interno; (*at home*) in casa
indubitable [ɪn'dju:bɪtəbl] *adj* indubitabile
induce [ɪn'dju:s] *vt* persuadere; (*bring about*) provocare; **to ~ sb to do sth** persuadere qn a fare qc
inducement [ɪn'dju:smənt] *n* incitamento; (*incentive*) stimolo, incentivo
induct [ɪn'dʌkt] *vt* insediare; (*fig*) iniziare
induction [ɪn'dʌkʃən] *n* (*Med: of birth*) parto indotto
induction course *n* (*Brit*) corso di avviamento
indulge [ɪn'dʌldʒ] *vt* (*whim*) compiacere, soddisfare; (*child*) viziare ■ *vi*: **to ~ in sth** concedersi qc; abbandonarsi a qc
indulgence [ɪn'dʌldʒəns] *n* lusso (che uno si permette); (*leniency*) indulgenza
indulgent [ɪn'dʌldʒənt] *adj* indulgente
industrial [ɪn'dʌstrɪəl] *adj* industriale; (*injury*) sul lavoro; (*dispute*) di lavoro
industrial action *n* azione *f* rivendicativa
industrial estate *n* zona industriale
industrialist [ɪn'dʌstrɪəlɪst] *n* industriale *m*
industrialize [ɪn'dʌstrɪəlaɪz] *vt* industrializzare
industrial park *n* (*US*) zona industriale
industrial relations *npl* relazioni *fpl* industriali
industrial tribunal *n* (*Brit*) ≈ Tribunale *m* Amministrativo Regionale
industrial unrest *n* (*Brit*) agitazione *f* (sindacale)
industrious [ɪn'dʌstrɪəs] *adj* industrioso(-a), assiduo(-a)
industry ['ɪndəstrɪ] *n* industria; (*diligence*) operosità
inebriated [ɪ'ni:brɪeɪtɪd] *adj* ubriaco(-a)
inedible [ɪn'ɛdɪbl] *adj* immangiabile; non commestibile
ineffective [ɪnɪ'fɛktɪv] *adj* inefficace
ineffectual [ɪnɪ'fɛktʃuəl] *adj* inefficace; incompetente
inefficiency [ɪnɪ'fɪʃənsɪ] *n* inefficienza
inefficient [ɪnɪ'fɪʃənt] *adj* inefficiente
inelegant [ɪn'ɛlɪgənt] *adj* poco elegante
ineligible [ɪn'ɛlɪdʒɪbl] *adj* (*candidate*) ineleggibile; **to be ~ for sth** non avere il diritto a qc
inept [ɪ'nɛpt] *adj* inetto(-a)
ineptitude [ɪ'nɛptɪtju:d] *n* inettitudine *f*, stupidità
inequality [ɪnɪ'kwɔlɪtɪ] *n* ineguaglianza
inequitable [ɪn'ɛkwɪtəbl] *adj* iniquo(-a)
ineradicable [ɪnɪ'rædɪkəbl] *adj* inestirpabile
inert [ɪ'nə:t] *adj* inerte
inertia [ɪ'nə:ʃə] *n* inerzia
inertia-reel seat belt [ɪ'nə:ʃə'ri:l-] *n* cintura di sicurezza con arrotolatore
inescapable [ɪnɪ'skeɪpəbl] *adj* inevitabile
inessential [ɪnɪ'sɛnʃl] *adj* non essenziale
inestimable [ɪn'ɛstɪməbl] *adj* inestimabile, incalcolabile
inevitable [ɪn'ɛvɪtəbl] *adj* inevitabile
inevitably [ɪn'ɛvɪtəblɪ] *adv* inevitabilmente; **as ~ happens ...** come immancabilmente succede ...
inexact [ɪnɪg'zækt] *adj* inesatto(-a)
inexcusable [ɪnɪks'kju:zəbl] *adj* imperdonabile
inexhaustible [ɪnɪg'zɔ:stɪbl] *adj* inesauribile; (*person*) instancabile
inexorable [ɪn'ɛksərəbl] *adj* inesorabile
inexpensive [ɪnɪk'spɛnsɪv] *adj* poco costoso(-a)
inexperience [ɪnɪk'spɪərɪəns] *n* inesperienza
inexperienced [ɪnɪk'spɪərɪənst] *adj* inesperto(-a), senza esperienza; **to be ~ in sth** essere poco pratico di qc
inexplicable [ɪnɪk'splɪkəbl] *adj* inesplicabile
inexpressible [ɪnɪk'sprɛsəbl] *adj* inesprimibile
inextricable [ɪnɪk'strɪkəbl] *adj* inestricabile
infallibility [ɪnfælə'bɪlɪtɪ] *n* infallibilità
infallible [ɪn'fælɪbl] *adj* infallibile
infamous ['ɪnfəməs] *adj* infame
infamy ['ɪnfəmɪ] *n* infamia
infancy ['ɪnfənsɪ] *n* infanzia

infant [ˈɪnfənt] *n* bambino(-a)
infantile [ˈɪnfəntaɪl] *adj* infantile
infant mortality *n* mortalità infantile
infantry [ˈɪnfəntrɪ] *n* fanteria
infantryman [ˈɪnfəntrɪmən] *n* fante *m*
infant school *n* (*Brit*) scuola elementare (*per bambini dall'età di 5 a 7 anni*)
infatuated [ɪnˈfætjueɪtɪd] *adj*: **~ with** infatuato(-a) di; **to become ~ (with sb)** infatuarsi (di qn)
infatuation [ɪnfætjuˈeɪʃən] *n* infatuazione *f*
infect [ɪnˈfɛkt] *vt* infettare; **infected with** (*illness*) affetto(-a) da; **to become infected** (*wound*) infettarsi
infection [ɪnˈfɛkʃən] *n* infezione *f*
infectious [ɪnˈfɛkʃəs] *adj* (*disease*) infettivo(-a), contagioso(-a); (*person, laughter*) contagioso(-a)
infer [ɪnˈfəːʳ] *vt*: **to ~ (from)** dedurre (da), concludere (da)
inference [ˈɪnfərəns] *n* deduzione *f*, conclusione *f*
inferior [ɪnˈfɪərɪəʳ] *adj* inferiore; (*goods*) di qualità scadente ■ *n* inferiore *m/f*; (*in rank*) subalterno(-a); **to feel ~** sentirsi inferiore
inferiority [ɪnfɪərɪˈɔrətɪ] *n* inferiorità
inferiority complex *n* complesso di inferiorità
infernal [ɪnˈfəːnl] *adj* infernale
inferno [ɪnˈfəːnəu] *n* inferno
infertile [ɪnˈfəːtaɪl] *adj* sterile
infertility [ɪnfəːˈtɪlɪtɪ] *n* sterilità
infested [ɪnˈfɛstɪd] *adj*: **~ (with)** infestato(-a) (di)
infidelity [ɪnfɪˈdɛlɪtɪ] *n* infedeltà
in-fighting [ˈɪnfaɪtɪŋ] *n* lotte *fpl* intestine
infiltrate [ˈɪnfɪltreɪt] *vt* (*troops etc*) far penetrare; (*enemy line etc*) infiltrare ■ *vi* infiltrarsi
infinite [ˈɪnfɪnɪt] *adj* infinito(-a); **an ~ amount of time/money** un'illimitata quantità di tempo/denaro
infinitely [ˈɪnfɪnɪtlɪ] *adv* infinitamente
infinitesimal [ɪnfɪnɪˈtɛsɪməl] *adj* infinitesimale
infinitive [ɪnˈfɪnɪtɪv] *n* infinito
infinity [ɪnˈfɪnɪtɪ] *n* infinità; (*also Math*) infinito
infirm [ɪnˈfəːm] *adj* infermo(-a)
infirmary [ɪnˈfəːmərɪ] *n* ospedale *m*; (*in school, factory*) infermeria
infirmity [ɪnˈfəːmɪtɪ] *n* infermità *f inv*
inflamed [ɪnˈfleɪmd] *adj* infiammato(-a)
inflammable [ɪnˈflæməbl] *adj* infiammabile
inflammation [ɪnfləˈmeɪʃən] *n* infiammazione *f*
inflammatory [ɪnˈflæmətərɪ] *adj* (*speech*) incendiario(-a)
inflatable [ɪnˈfleɪtəbl] *adj* gonfiabile
inflate [ɪnˈfleɪt] *vt* (*tyre, balloon*) gonfiare; (*fig*) esagerare; gonfiare; **to ~ the currency** far ricorso all'inflazione
inflated [ɪnˈfleɪtɪd] *adj* (*style*) gonfio(-a); (*value*) esagerato(-a)
inflation [ɪnˈfleɪʃən] *n* (*Econ*) inflazione *f*
inflationary [ɪnˈfleɪʃənərɪ] *adj* inflazionistico(-a)
inflexible [ɪnˈflɛksɪbl] *adj* inflessibile, rigido(-a)
inflict [ɪnˈflɪkt] *vt*: **to ~ on** infliggere a
infliction [ɪnˈflɪkʃən] *n* inflizione *f*; afflizione *f*
in-flight [ˈɪnflaɪt] *adj* a bordo
inflow [ˈɪnfləu] *n* afflusso
influence [ˈɪnfluəns] *n* influenza ■ *vt* influenzare; **under the ~ of** sotto l'influenza di; **under the ~ of drink** sotto l'influenza *or* l'effetto dell'alcool
influential [ɪnfluˈɛnʃl] *adj* influente
influenza [ɪnfluˈɛnzə] *n* (*Med*) influenza
influx [ˈɪnflʌks] *n* afflusso
inform [ɪnˈfɔːm] *vt*: **to ~ sb (of)** informare qn (di) ■ *vi*: **to ~ on sb** denunciare qn; **to ~ sb about** mettere qn al corrente di
informal [ɪnˈfɔːml] *adj* (*person, manner*) alla buona, semplice; (*visit, discussion*) informale; (*announcement, invitation*) non ufficiale; **"dress ~"** "non è richiesto l'abito scuro"; **~ language** linguaggio colloquiale
informality [ɪnfɔːˈmælɪtɪ] *n* semplicità, informalità; carattere *m* non ufficiale
informally [ɪnˈfɔːməlɪ] *adv* senza cerimonie; (*invite*) in modo non ufficiale
informant [ɪnˈfɔːmənt] *n* informatore(-trice)
informatics [ɪnfəːˈmætɪks] *n* informatica
information [ɪnfəˈmeɪʃən] *n* informazioni *fpl*; particolari *mpl*; **to get ~ on** informarsi su; **a piece of ~** un'informazione; **for your ~** a titolo d'informazione, per sua informazione
information bureau *n* ufficio *m* informazioni *inv*
information processing *n* elaborazione *f* delle informazioni
information retrieval *n* ricupero delle informazioni
information superhighway *n* autostrada informatica
information technology *n* informatica
informative [ɪnˈfɔːmətɪv] *adj* istruttivo(-a)
informed [ɪnˈfɔːmd] *adj* (*observer*) (ben) informato(-a); **an ~ guess** un'ipotesi fondata
informer [ɪnˈfɔːməʳ] *n* informatore(-trice)
infra dig [ˈɪnfrəˈdɪg] *adj abbr* (*col*: = *infra dignitatem*: *beneath one's dignity*) indecoroso(-a)

infra-red [ɪnfrə'rɛd] *adj* infrarosso(-a)
infrastructure ['ɪnfrəstrʌktʃə^r] *n* infrastruttura
infrequent [ɪn'fri:kwənt] *adj* infrequente, raro(-a)
infringe [ɪn'frɪndʒ] *vt* infrangere ■ *vi*: **to ~ on** calpestare
infringement [ɪn'frɪndʒmənt] *n*: **~ (of)** infrazione *f* (di)
infuriate [ɪn'fjuərɪeɪt] *vt* rendere furioso(-a)
infuriating [ɪn'fjuərɪeɪtɪŋ] *adj* molto irritante
infuse [ɪn'fju:z] *vt* (*with courage, enthusiasm*): **to ~ sb with sth** infondere qc a qn, riempire qn di qc
infusion [ɪn'fju:ʒən] *n* (*tea etc*) infuso, infusione *f*
ingenious [ɪn'dʒi:njəs] *adj* ingegnoso(-a)
ingenuity [ɪndʒɪ'nju:ɪtɪ] *n* ingegnosità
ingenuous [ɪn'dʒɛnjuəs] *adj* ingenuo(-a)
ingot ['ɪŋgət] *n* lingotto
ingrained [ɪn'greɪnd] *adj* radicato(-a)
ingratiate [ɪn'greɪʃɪeɪt] *vt*: **to ~ o.s. with sb** ingraziarsi qn
ingratiating [ɪn'greɪʃɪeɪtɪŋ] *adj* (*smile, speech*) suadente, cattivante; (*person*) compiacente
ingratitude [ɪn'grætɪtju:d] *n* ingratitudine *f*
ingredient [ɪn'gri:dɪənt] *n* ingrediente *m*; elemento
ingrowing ['ɪngrəuɪŋ], **ingrown** ['ɪngrəun] *adj*: **~ (toe)nail** unghia incarnita
inhabit [ɪn'hæbɪt] *vt* abitare
inhabitable [ɪn'hæbɪtəbl] *adj* abitabile
inhabitant [ɪn'hæbɪtnt] *n* abitante *m/f*
inhale [ɪn'heɪl] *vt* inalare ■ *vi* (*in smoking*) aspirare
inhaler [ɪn'heɪlə^r] *n* inalatore *m*
inherent [ɪn'hɪərənt] *adj*: **~ (in** *or* **to)** inerente (a)
inherently [ɪn'hɪərəntlɪ] *adv* (*easy, difficult*) di per sé, di per se stesso(-a); **~ lazy** pigro di natura
inherit [ɪn'hɛrɪt] *vt* ereditare
inheritance [ɪn'hɛrɪtəns] *n* eredità
inhibit [ɪn'hɪbɪt] *vt* (*Psych*) inibire; **to ~ sb from doing** impedire a qn di fare
inhibited [ɪn'hɪbɪtɪd] *adj* (*person*) inibito(-a)
inhibiting [ɪn'hɪbɪtɪŋ] *adj* che inibisce
inhibition [ɪnhɪ'bɪʃən] *n* inibizione *f*
inhospitable [ɪnhɔs'pɪtəbl] *adj* inospitale
in-house ['ɪn'haus] *adj* effettuato(-a) da personale interno, interno(-a) ■ *adv* (*training*) all'interno dell'azienda
inhuman [ɪn'hju:mən] *adj* inumano(-a), disumano(-a)
inhumane [ɪnhju:'meɪn] *adj* inumano(-a), disumano(-a)
inimitable [ɪ'nɪmɪtəbl] *adj* inimitabile
iniquity [ɪ'nɪkwɪtɪ] *n* iniquità *f inv*
initial [ɪ'nɪʃl] *adj* iniziale ■ *n* iniziale *f* ■ *vt* siglare; **initials** *npl* iniziali *fpl*; (*as signature*) sigla
initialize [ɪ'nɪʃəlaɪz] *vt* (*Comput*) inizializzare
initially [ɪ'nɪʃəlɪ] *adv* inizialmente, all'inizio
initiate [ɪ'nɪʃɪeɪt] *vt* (*start*) avviare; intraprendere; iniziare; (*person*) iniziare; **to ~ sb into sth** iniziare qn a qc; **to ~ proceedings against sb** (*Law*) intentare causa a *or* contro qn
initiation [ɪnɪʃɪ'eɪʃən] *n* iniziazione *f*
initiative [ɪ'nɪʃətɪv] *n* iniziativa; **to take the ~** prendere l'iniziativa
inject [ɪn'dʒɛkt] *vt* (*liquid*) iniettare; (*person*) fare una puntura a; (*fig: money*): **to ~ into** immettere in
injection [ɪn'dʒɛkʃən] *n* iniezione *f*, puntura; **to have an ~** farsi fare un'iniezione *or* una puntura
injudicious [ɪndʒu'dɪʃəs] *adj* poco saggio(-a)
injunction [ɪn'dʒʌŋkʃən] *n* (*Law*) ingiunzione *f*, intimazione *f*
injure ['ɪndʒə^r] *vt* ferire; (*wrong*) fare male *or* torto a; (*damage: reputation etc*) nuocere a; (*feelings*) offendere; **to ~ o.s.** farsi male
injured ['ɪndʒəd] *adj* (*person, leg etc*) ferito(-a); (*tone, feelings*) offeso(-a); **~ party** (*Law*) parte *f* lesa
injurious [ɪn'dʒuərɪəs] *adj*: **~ (to)** nocivo(-a) (a), pregiudizievole (per)
injury ['ɪndʒərɪ] *n* ferita; (*wrong*) torto; **to escape without ~** rimanere illeso
injury time *n* (*Sport*) tempo di ricupero
injustice [ɪn'dʒʌstɪs] *n* ingiustizia; **you do me an ~** mi fa un torto, è ingiusto verso di me
ink [ɪŋk] *n* inchiostro
ink-jet printer ['ɪŋkdʒɛt-] *n* stampante *f* a getto d'inchiostro
inkling ['ɪŋklɪŋ] *n* sentore *m*, vaga idea
inkpad ['ɪŋkpæd] *n* tampone *m*, cuscinetto per timbri
inky ['ɪŋkɪ] *adj* macchiato(-a) *or* sporco(-a) d'inchiostro
inlaid ['ɪnleɪd] *adj* incrostato(-a); (*table etc*) intarsiato(-a)
inland *adj* ['ɪnlənd] interno(-a) ■ *adv* [ɪn'lænd] all'interno; **~ waterways** canali e fiumi *mpl* navigabili
Inland Revenue *n* (*Brit*) Fisco
in-laws ['ɪnlɔ:z] *npl* suoceri *mpl*; famiglia del marito (*or* della moglie)
inlet ['ɪnlɛt] *n* (*Geo*) insenatura, baia
inlet pipe *n* (*Tech*) tubo d'immissione
inmate ['ɪnmeɪt] *n* (*in prison*) carcerato(-a); (*in asylum*) ricoverato(-a)

inmost ['ɪnməust] *adj* più profondo(-a), più intimo(-a)
inn [ɪn] *n* locanda
innards ['ɪnədz] *npl* (*col*) interiora *fpl*, budella *fpl*
innate [ɪ'neɪt] *adj* innato(-a)
inner ['ɪnəʳ] *adj* interno(-a), interiore
inner city *n* centro di una zona urbana
innermost ['ɪnəməust] *adj* = **inmost**
inner tube *n* camera d'aria
innings ['ɪnɪŋz] *n* (*Cricket*) turno di battuta; (*Brit fig*): **he has had a good ~** ha avuto molto dalla vita
innocence ['ɪnəsns] *n* innocenza
innocent ['ɪnəsnt] *adj* innocente
innocuous [ɪ'nɔkjuəs] *adj* innocuo(-a)
innovation [ɪnəu'veɪʃən] *n* innovazione *f*
innuendo [ɪnju'ɛndəu] *n* (*pl* **innuendoes**) insinuazione *f*
innumerable [ɪ'nju:mrəbl] *adj* innumerevole
inoculate [ɪ'nɔkjuleɪt] *vt*: **to ~ sb with sth/ against sth** inoculare qc a qn/qn contro qc
inoculation [ɪnɔkju'leɪʃən] *n* inoculazione *f*
inoffensive [ɪnə'fɛnsɪv] *adj* inoffensivo(-a), innocuo(-a)
inopportune [ɪn'ɔpətju:n] *adj* inopportuno(-a)
inordinate [ɪ'nɔ:dɪnɪt] *adj* eccessivo(-a)
inordinately [ɪ'nɔ:dɪnətlɪ] *adv* smoderatamente
inorganic [ɪnɔ:'gænɪk] *adj* inorganico(-a)
in-patient ['ɪnpeɪʃənt] *n* ricoverato(-a)
input ['ɪnput] *n* (*Elec*) energia, potenza; (*of machine*) alimentazione *f*; (*of computer*) input *m* ■ *vt* (*Comput*) inserire, introdurre
inquest ['ɪnkwɛst] *n* inchiesta
inquire [ɪn'kwaɪəʳ] *vi* informarsi ■ *vt* domandare, informarsi di *or* su; **to ~ about** informarsi di *or* su, chiedere informazioni su; **to ~ when/where/whether** informarsi di quando/su dove/se
▶ **inquire after** *vt fus* (*person*) chiedere di; (*sb's health*) informarsi di
▶ **inquire into** *vt fus* indagare su, fare delle indagini *or* ricerche su
inquiring [ɪn'kwaɪərɪŋ] *adj* (*mind*) inquisitivo(-a)
inquiry [ɪn'kwaɪərɪ] *n* domanda; (*Law*) indagine *f*, investigazione *f*; **to hold an ~ into sth** fare un'inchiesta su qc
inquiry desk *n* (*Brit*) banco delle informazioni
inquiry office *n* (*Brit*) ufficio *m* informazioni *inv*
inquisition [ɪnkwɪ'zɪʃən] *n* inquisizione *f*, inchiesta; (*Rel*): **the I~** l'Inquisizione
inquisitive [ɪn'kwɪzɪtɪv] *adj* curioso(-a)
inroads ['ɪnrəudz] *npl*: **to make ~ into** (*savings, supplies*) intaccare (seriamente)
insane [ɪn'seɪn] *adj* matto(-a), pazzo(-a); (*Med*) alienato(-a)
insanitary [ɪn'sænɪtərɪ] *adj* insalubre
insanity [ɪn'sænɪtɪ] *n* follia; (*Med*) alienazione *f* mentale
insatiable [ɪn'seɪʃəbl] *adj* insaziabile
inscribe [ɪn'skraɪb] *vt* iscrivere; (*book etc*): **to ~ (to sb)** dedicare (a qn)
inscription [ɪn'skrɪpʃən] *n* iscrizione *f*; (*in book*) dedica
inscrutable [ɪn'skru:təbl] *adj* imperscrutabile
inseam ['ɪnsi:m] *n* (*US*): **~ measurement** lunghezza interna
insect ['ɪnsɛkt] *n* insetto
insect bite *n* puntura *or* morsicatura di insetto
insecticide [ɪn'sɛktɪsaɪd] *n* insetticida *m*
insect repellent *n* insettifugo
insecure [ɪnsɪ'kjuəʳ] *adj* malsicuro(-a); (*person*) insicuro(-a)
insecurity [ɪnsɪ'kjuərɪtɪ] *n* mancanza di sicurezza
insensible [ɪn'sɛnsɪbl] *adj* insensibile; (*unconscious*) privo(-a) di sensi
insensitive [ɪn'sɛnsɪtɪv] *adj* insensibile
insensitivity [ɪnsɛnsɪ'tɪvɪtɪ] *n* mancanza di sensibilità
inseparable [ɪn'sɛprəbl] *adj* inseparabile
insert *vt* [ɪn'sə:t] inserire, introdurre ■ *n* ['ɪnsə:t] inserto
insertion [ɪn'sə:ʃən] *n* inserzione *f*
in-service ['ɪn'sə:vɪs] *adj* (*course, training*) dopo l'assunzione
inshore [ɪn'ʃɔ:ʳ] *adj* costiero(-a) ■ *adv* presso la riva; verso la riva
inside ['ɪn'saɪd] *n* interno, parte *f* interiore; (*of road: Brit*) sinistra; (*: US, in Europe etc*) destra ■ *adj* interno(-a), interiore ■ *adv* dentro, all'interno ■ *prep* dentro, all'interno di; (*of time*): **~ 10 minutes** entro 10 minuti; **insides** *npl* (*col*) ventre *m*; **~ out** *adv* alla rovescia; **to turn sth ~ out** rivoltare qc; **to know sth ~ out** conoscere qc a fondo; **~ information** informazioni *fpl* riservate; **~ story** storia segreta
inside forward *n* (*Sport*) mezzala, interno
inside lane *n* (*Aut*) corsia di marcia
inside leg measurement *n* (*Brit*) lunghezza interna
insider [ɪn'saɪdəʳ] *n* uno(-a) che ha le mani in pasta
insider dealing, insider trading *n* (*Stock Exchange*) insider trading *m inv*
insidious [ɪn'sɪdɪəs] *adj* insidioso(-a)

insight ['ɪnsaɪt] *n* acume *m*, perspicacia; (*glimpse, idea*) percezione *f*; **to gain** *or* **get an ~ into sth** potersi render conto di qc
insignia [ɪn'sɪgnɪə] *npl* insegne *fpl*
insignificant [ɪnsɪg'nɪfɪknt] *adj* insignificante
insincere [ɪnsɪn'sɪəʳ] *adj* insincero(-a)
insincerity [ɪnsɪn'sɛrɪtɪ] *n* falsità, insincerità
insinuate [ɪn'sɪnjueɪt] *vt* insinuare
insinuation [ɪnsɪnju'eɪʃən] *n* insinuazione *f*
insipid [ɪn'sɪpɪd] *adj* insipido(-a), insulso(-a)
insist [ɪn'sɪst] *vi* insistere; **to ~ on doing** insistere per fare; **to ~ that** insistere perché *+sub*; (*claim*) sostenere che
insistence [ɪn'sɪstəns] *n* insistenza
insistent [ɪn'sɪstənt] *adj* insistente
insofar [ɪnsəu'fɑːʳ] *conj*: **~ as** in quanto
insole ['ɪnsəul] *n* soletta; (*fixed part of shoe*) tramezza
insolence ['ɪnsələns] *n* insolenza
insolent ['ɪnsələnt] *adj* insolente
insoluble [ɪn'sɔljubl] *adj* insolubile
insolvency [ɪn'sɔlvənsɪ] *n* insolvenza
insolvent [ɪn'sɔlvənt] *adj* insolvente
insomnia [ɪn'sɔmnɪə] *n* insonnia
insomniac [ɪn'sɔmnɪæk] *n* chi soffre di insonnia
inspect [ɪn'spɛkt] *vt* ispezionare; (*Brit: ticket*) controllare
inspection [ɪn'spɛkʃən] *n* ispezione *f*; controllo
inspector [ɪn'spɛktəʳ] *n* ispettore(-trice); controllore *m*
inspiration [ɪnspə'reɪʃən] *n* ispirazione *f*
inspire [ɪn'spaɪəʳ] *vt* ispirare
inspired [ɪn'spaɪəd] *adj* (*writer, book etc*) ispirato(-a); **in an ~ moment** in un momento d'ispirazione
inspiring [ɪn'spaɪərɪŋ] *adj* stimolante
inst. [ɪnst] *abbr* (*Brit Comm*: = *instant*) c.m. (= *corrente mese*)
instability [ɪnstə'bɪlɪtɪ] *n* instabilità
install [ɪn'stɔːl] *vt* installare
installation [ɪnstə'leɪʃən] *n* installazione *f*
installment plan *n* (*US*) acquisto a rate
instalment, (*US*) **installment** [ɪn'stɔːlmənt] *n* rata; (*of TV serial etc*) puntata; **to pay in instalments** pagare a rate
instance ['ɪnstəns] *n* esempio, caso; **for ~** per *or* ad esempio; **in that ~** in quel caso; **in the first ~** in primo luogo
instant ['ɪnstənt] *n* istante *m*, attimo ■ *adj* immediato(-a), urgente; (*coffee, food*) in polvere; **the 10th ~** il 10 corrente (mese)
instantaneous [ɪnstən'teɪnɪəs] *adj* istantaneo(-a)
instantly ['ɪnstəntlɪ] *adv* immediatamente, subito
instant messaging *n* messaggeria istantanea
instant replay *n* (*US TV*) replay *m inv*
instead [ɪn'stɛd] *adv* invece; **~ of** invece di; **~ of sb** al posto di qn
instep ['ɪnstɛp] *n* collo del piede; (*of shoe*) collo della scarpa
instigate ['ɪnstɪgeɪt] *vt* (*rebellion, strike, crime*) istigare a; (*new ideas etc*) promuovere
instigation [ɪnstɪ'geɪʃən] *n* istigazione *f*; **at sb's ~** per *or* in seguito al suggerimento di qn
instil [ɪn'stɪl] *vt*: **to ~ (into)** inculcare (in)
instinct ['ɪnstɪŋkt] *n* istinto
instinctive [ɪn'stɪŋktɪv] *adj* istintivo(-a)
instinctively [ɪn'stɪŋktɪvlɪ] *adv* per istinto
institute ['ɪnstɪtjuːt] *n* istituto ■ *vt* istituire, stabilire; (*inquiry*) avviare; (*proceedings*) iniziare
institution [ɪnstɪ'tjuːʃən] *n* istituzione *f*; istituto (d'istruzione); istituto (psichiatrico)
institutional [ɪnstɪ'tjuːʃənl] *adj* istituzionale; **~ care** assistenza presso un istituto
instruct [ɪn'strʌkt] *vt* istruire; **to ~ sb in sth** insegnare qc a qn; **to ~ sb to do** dare ordini a qn di fare
instruction [ɪn'strʌkʃən] *n* istruzione *f*; **instructions (for use)** istruzioni per l'uso
instruction book *n* libretto di istruzioni
instructive [ɪn'strʌktɪv] *adj* istruttivo(-a)
instructor [ɪn'strʌktəʳ] *n* istruttore(-trice); (*for skiing*) maestro(-a)
instrument ['ɪnstrumənt] *n* strumento
instrumental [ɪnstru'mɛntl] *adj* (*Mus*) strumentale; **to be ~ in sth/in doing sth** avere un ruolo importante in qc/nel fare qc
instrumentalist [ɪnstru'mɛntəlɪst] *n* strumentista *m/f*
instrument panel *n* quadro *m*, portastrumenti *inv*
insubordinate [ɪnsə'bɔːdənɪt] *adj* insubordinato(-a)
insubordination [ɪnsəbɔːdə'neɪʃən] *n* insubordinazione *f*
insufferable [ɪn'sʌfrəbl] *adj* insopportabile
insufficient [ɪnsə'fɪʃənt] *adj* insufficiente
insufficiently [ɪnsə'fɪʃəntlɪ] *adv* in modo insufficiente
insular ['ɪnsjuləʳ] *adj* insulare; (*person*) di mente ristretta
insulate ['ɪnsjuleɪt] *vt* isolare
insulating tape ['ɪnsjuleɪtɪŋ-] *n* nastro isolante
insulation [ɪnsju'leɪʃən] *n* isolamento
insulin ['ɪnsjulɪn] *n* insulina
insult *n* ['ɪnsʌlt] insulto, affronto ■ *vt* [ɪn'sʌlt] insultare

insulting [ɪn'sʌltɪŋ] *adj* offensivo(-a), ingiurioso(-a)
insuperable [ɪn'sju:prəbl] *adj* insormontabile, insuperabile
insurance [ɪn'ʃuərəns] *n* assicurazione *f*; **fire/life ~** assicurazione contro gli incendi/ sulla vita; **to take out ~ (against)** fare un'assicurazione (contro), assicurarsi (contro)
insurance agent *n* agente *m* d'assicurazioni
insurance broker *n* broker *m inv* d'assicurazioni
insurance policy *n* polizza d'assicurazione
insurance premium *n* premio assicurativo
insure [ɪn'ʃuəʳ] *vt* assicurare; **to ~ sb** *or* **sb's life** assicurare qn sulla vita; **to be insured for £5000** essere assicurato per 5000 sterline
insured [ɪn'ʃuəd] *n*: **the ~** l'assicurato(-a)
insurer [ɪn'ʃuərəʳ] *n* assicuratore(-trice)
insurgent [ɪn'sə:dʒənt] *adj* ribelle ▪ *n* insorto(-a), rivoltoso(-a)
insurmountable [ɪnsə'mauntəbl] *adj* insormontabile
insurrection [ɪnsə'rɛkʃən] *n* insurrezione *f*
intact [ɪn'tækt] *adj* intatto(-a)
intake ['ɪnteɪk] *n* (*Tech*) immissione *f*; (*of food*) consumo; (*of pupils etc*) afflusso
intangible [ɪn'tændʒɪbl] *adj* intangibile
integral ['ɪntɪgrəl] *adj* integrale; (*part*) integrante
integrate ['ɪntɪgreɪt] *vt* integrare
integrated circuit *n* (*Comput*) circuito integrato
integration [ɪntɪ'greɪʃən] *n* integrazione *f*; **racial ~** integrazione razziale
integrity [ɪn'tɛgrɪtɪ] *n* integrità
intellect ['ɪntəlɛkt] *n* intelletto
intellectual [ɪntə'lɛktjuəl] *adj*, *n* intellettuale (*m/f*)
intelligence [ɪn'tɛlɪdʒəns] *n* intelligenza; (*Mil etc*) informazioni *fpl*
intelligence quotient *n* quoziente *m* d'intelligenza
Intelligence Service *n* servizio segreto
intelligence test *n* test *m inv* d'intelligenza
intelligent [ɪn'tɛlɪdʒənt] *adj* intelligente
intelligible [ɪn'tɛlɪdʒɪbl] *adj* intelligibile
intemperate [ɪn'tɛmpərət] *adj* immoderato(-a); (*drinking too much*) intemperante nel bere
intend [ɪn'tɛnd] *vt* (*gift etc*): **to ~ sth for** destinare qc a; **to ~ to do** aver l'intenzione di fare
intended [ɪn'tɛndɪd] *adj* (*insult*) intenzionale; (*effect*) voluto(-a); (*journey, route*) progettato(-a)
intense [ɪn'tɛns] *adj* intenso(-a); (*person*) di forti sentimenti
intensely [ɪn'tɛnslɪ] *adv* intensamente; profondamente
intensify [ɪn'tɛnsɪfaɪ] *vt* intensificare
intensity [ɪn'tɛnsɪtɪ] *n* intensità
intensive [ɪn'tɛnsɪv] *adj* intensivo(-a)
intensive care *n* terapia intensiva; **~ unit** *n*, reparto terapia intensiva
intent [ɪn'tɛnt] *n* intenzione *f* ▪ *adj*: **~ (on)** intento(-a) (a), immerso(-a) (in); **to all intents and purposes** a tutti gli effetti; **to be ~ on doing sth** essere deciso a fare qc
intention [ɪn'tɛnʃən] *n* intenzione *f*
intentional [ɪn'tɛnʃənl] *adj* intenzionale, deliberato(-a)
intentionally [ɪn'tɛnʃənəlɪ] *adv* apposta
intently [ɪn'tɛntlɪ] *adv* attentamente
inter [ɪn'tə:ʳ] *vt* sotterrare
interact [ɪntər'ækt] *vi* agire reciprocamente, interagire
interaction [ɪntər'ækʃən] *n* azione *f* reciproca, interazione *f*
interactive [ɪntər'æktɪv] *adj* interattivo(-a)
intercede [ɪntə'si:d] *vi*: **to ~ (with sb/on behalf of sb)** intercedere (presso qn/a favore di qn)
intercept [ɪntə'sɛpt] *vt* intercettare; (*person*) fermare
interception [ɪntə'sɛpʃən] *n* intercettamento
interchange *n* ['ɪntətʃeɪndʒ] (*exchange*) scambio; (*on motorway*) incrocio pluridirezionale ▪ *vt* [ɪntə'tʃeɪndʒ] scambiare; sostituire l'uno(-a) per l'altro(-a)
interchangeable [ɪntə'tʃeɪndʒəbl] *adj* intercambiabile
intercity [ɪntə'sɪtɪ] *adj*: **~ (train)** ≈ (treno) rapido
intercom ['ɪntəkɔm] *n* interfono
interconnect [ɪntəkə'nɛkt] *vi* (*rooms*) essere in comunicazione
intercontinental ['ɪntəkɔntɪ'nɛntl] *adj* intercontinentale
intercourse ['ɪntəkɔ:s] *n* rapporti *mpl*; (*sexual intercourse*) rapporti sessuali
interdependent [ɪntədɪ'pɛndənt] *adj* interdipendente
interest ['ɪntrɪst] *n* interesse *m*; (*Comm: stake, share*) interessi *mpl* ▪ *vt* interessare; **compound/simple ~** interesse composto/ semplice; **business interests** attività *fpl* commerciali; **British interests in the Middle East** gli interessi (commerciali) britannici nel Medio Oriente
interested ['ɪntrɪstɪd] *adj* interessato(-a); **to be ~ in** interessarsi di
interest-free ['ɪntrɪst'fri:] *adj* senza interesse
interesting ['ɪntrɪstɪŋ] *adj* interessante

interest rate *n* tasso di interesse
interface ['ɪntəfeɪs] *n* (*Comput*) interfaccia
interfere [ɪntə'fɪəʳ] *vi*: **to ~ (in)** (*quarrel, other people's business*) immischiarsi (in); **to ~ with** (*object*) toccare; (*plans*) ostacolare; (*duty*) interferire con
interference [ɪntə'fɪərəns] *n* interferenza
interfering [ɪntə'fɪərɪŋ] *adj* invadente
interim ['ɪntərɪm] *adj* provvisorio(-a) ■ *n*: **in the ~** nel frattempo; **~ dividend** (*Comm*) acconto di dividendo
interior [ɪn'tɪərɪəʳ] *n* interno; (*of country*) entroterra ■ *adj* interiore, interno(-a)
interior decorator, interior designer *n* decoratore(-trice) (d'interni)
interjection [ɪntə'dʒɛkʃən] *n* interiezione *f*
interlock [ɪntə'lɔk] *vi* ingranarsi ■ *vt* ingranare
interloper ['ɪntələupəʳ] *n* intruso(-a)
interlude ['ɪntəlu:d] *n* intervallo; (*Theat*) intermezzo
intermarry [ɪntə'mærɪ] *vi* imparentarsi per mezzo di matrimonio; sposarsi tra parenti
intermediary [ɪntə'mi:dɪərɪ] *n* intermediario(-a)
intermediate [ɪntə'mi:dɪət] *adj* intermedio(-a); (*Scol: course, level*) medio(-a)
interment [ɪn'tə:mənt] *n* (*formal*) inumazione *f*
interminable [ɪn'tə:mɪnəbl] *adj* interminabile
intermission [ɪntə'mɪʃən] *n* pausa; (*Theat, Cine*) intermissione *f*, intervallo
intermittent [ɪntə'mɪtnt] *adj* intermittente
intermittently [ɪntə'mɪtntlɪ] *adv* a intermittenza
intern *vt* [ɪn'tə:n] internare ■ *n* ['ɪntə:n] (*US*) medico interno
internal [ɪn'tə:nl] *adj* interno(-a); **~ injuries** lesioni *fpl* interne
internally [ɪn'tə:nəlɪ] *adv* all'interno; **"not to be taken ~"** "per uso esterno"
Internal Revenue, Internal Revenue Service *n* (*US*) Fisco
international [ɪntə'næʃənl] *adj* internazionale ■ *n* (*Brit Sport*) partita internazionale
International Atomic Energy Agency *n* Agenzia Internazionale per l'Energia Atomica
International Court of Justice *n* Corte *f* Internazionale di Giustizia
international date line *n* linea del cambiamento di data
internationally [ɪntə'næʃnəlɪ] *adv* a livello internazionale
International Monetary Fund *n* Fondo monetario internazionale
international relations *npl* rapporti *mpl* internazionali
internecine [ɪntə'ni:saɪn] *adj* sanguinoso(-a)
internee [ɪntə:'ni:] *n* internato(-a)
internet ['ɪntənɛt] *n*: **the ~** Internet *f*
internment [ɪn'tə:nmənt] *n* internamento
interplay ['ɪntəpleɪ] *n* azione e reazione *f*
Interpol ['ɪntəpɔl] *n* Interpol *f*
interpret [ɪn'tə:prɪt] *vt* interpretare ■ *vi* fare da interprete
interpretation [ɪntə:prɪ'teɪʃən] *n* interpretazione *f*
interpreter [ɪn'tə:prɪtəʳ] *n* interprete *m/f*
interpreting [ɪn'tə:prɪtɪŋ] *n* (*profession*) interpretariato
interrelated [ɪntərɪ'leɪtɪd] *adj* correlato(-a)
interrogate [ɪn'tɛrəugeɪt] *vt* interrogare
interrogation [ɪntɛrəu'geɪʃən] *n* interrogazione *f*; (*of suspect etc*) interrogatorio
interrogative [ɪntə'rɔgətɪv] *adj* interrogativo(-a) ■ *n* (*Ling*) interrogativo
interrogator [ɪn'tɛrəgeɪtəʳ] *n* interrogante *m/f*
interrupt [ɪntə'rʌpt] *vt* interrompere
interruption [ɪntə'rʌpʃən] *n* interruzione *f*
intersect [ɪntə'sɛkt] *vt* intersecare ■ *vi* (*roads*) intersecarsi
intersection [ɪntə'sɛkʃən] *n* intersezione *f*; (*of roads*) incrocio
intersperse [ɪntə'spə:s] *vt*: **to ~ with** costellare di
intertwine [ɪntə'twaɪn] *vt* intrecciare ■ *vi* intrecciarsi
interval ['ɪntəvl] *n* intervallo; (*Brit Scol*) ricreazione *f*, intervallo; **bright intervals** (*in weather*) schiarite *fpl*; **at intervals** a intervalli
intervene [ɪntə'vi:n] *vi* (*time*) intercorrere; (*event, person*) intervenire
intervention [ɪntə'vɛnʃən] *n* intervento
interview ['ɪntəvju:] *n* (*Radio, TV etc*) intervista; (*for job*) colloquio ■ *vt* intervistare; avere un colloquio con
interviewee [ɪntəvju'i:] *n* (*TV*) intervistato(-a); (*for job*) chi si presenta ad un colloquio di lavoro
interviewer ['ɪntəvju:əʳ] *n* intervistatore(-trice)
intestate [ɪn'tɛsteɪt] *adj* intestato(-a)
intestinal [ɪn'tɛstɪnl] *adj* intestinale
intestine [ɪn'tɛstɪn] *n* intestino; **large/small ~** intestino crasso/tenue
intimacy ['ɪntɪməsɪ] *n* intimità
intimate *adj* ['ɪntɪmət] intimo(-a); (*knowledge*) profondo(-a) ■ *vt* ['ɪntɪmeɪt] lasciar capire
intimately ['ɪntɪmɪtlɪ] *adv* intimamente
intimation [ɪntɪ'meɪʃən] *n* annuncio

intimidate [ɪn'tɪmɪdeɪt] *vt* intimidire, intimorire
intimidation [ɪntɪmɪ'deɪʃən] *n* intimidazione *f*
into ['ɪntu] *prep* dentro, in; **come ~ the house** vieni dentro la casa; **~ pieces** a pezzi; **~ Italian** in italiano; **to change pounds ~ dollars** cambiare delle sterline in dollari
intolerable [ɪn'tɔlərəbl] *adj* intollerabile
intolerance [ɪn'tɔlərns] *n* intolleranza
intolerant [ɪn'tɔlərnt] *adj*: **~ (of)** intollerante (di)
intonation [ɪntəu'neɪʃən] *n* intonazione *f*
intoxicate [ɪn'tɔksɪkeɪt] *vt* inebriare
intoxicated [ɪn'tɔksɪkeɪtɪd] *adj* inebriato(-a)
intoxication [ɪntɔksɪ'keɪʃən] *n* ebbrezza
intractable [ɪn'træktəbl] *adj* intrattabile; (*illness*) difficile da curare; (*problem*) insolubile
intranet ['ɪntrənɛt] *n* Intranet *f*
intransigence [ɪn'trænsɪdʒəns] *n* intransigenza
intransigent [ɪn'trænsɪdʒənt] *adj* intransigente
intransitive [ɪn'trænsɪtɪv] *adj* intransitivo(-a)
intra-uterine device [ɪntrə'ju:təraɪn-] *n* dispositivo intrauterino
intravenous [ɪntrə'vi:nəs] *adj* endovenoso(-a)
in-tray ['ɪntreɪ] *n* raccoglitore *m* per le carte in arrivo
intrepid [ɪn'trɛpɪd] *adj* intrepido(-a)
intricacy ['ɪntrɪkəsɪ] *n* complessità *f inv*
intricate ['ɪntrɪkət] *adj* intricato(-a), complicato(-a)
intrigue [ɪn'tri:g] *n* intrigo ■ *vt* affascinare ■ *vi* complottare, tramare
intriguing [ɪn'tri:gɪŋ] *adj* affascinante
intrinsic [ɪn'trɪnsɪk] *adj* intrinseco(-a)
introduce [ɪntrə'dju:s] *vt* introdurre; **to ~ sb (to sb)** presentare qn (a qn); **to ~ sb to** (*pastime, technique*) iniziare qn a; **may I ~ ...?** permette che le presenti ...?
introduction [ɪntrə'dʌkʃən] *n* introduzione *f*; (*of person*) presentazione *f*; **a letter of ~** una lettera di presentazione
introductory [ɪntrə'dʌktərɪ] *adj* introduttivo(-a); **an ~ offer** un'offerta di lancio; **~ remarks** osservazioni *fpl* preliminari
introspection [ɪntrəu'spɛkʃən] *n* introspezione *f*
introspective [ɪntrəu'spɛktɪv] *adj* introspettivo(-a)
introvert ['ɪntrəuvə:t] *adj, n* introverso(-a)
intrude [ɪn'tru:d] *vi* (*person*) intromettersi; **to ~ on** (*person*) importunare; **~ on** *or* **into** (*conversation*) intromettersi in; **am I intruding?** disturbo?
intruder [ɪn'tru:də^r] *n* intruso(-a)
intrusion [ɪn'tru:ʒən] *n* intrusione *f*
intrusive [ɪn'tru:sɪv] *adj* importuno(-a)
intuition [ɪntju:'ɪʃən] *n* intuizione *f*
intuitive [ɪn'tju:ɪtɪv] *adj* intuitivo(-a); dotato(-a) di intuito
inundate ['ɪnʌndeɪt] *vt*: **to ~ with** inondare di
inure [ɪn'juə^r] *vt*: **to ~ (to)** assuefare (a)
invade [ɪn'veɪd] *vt* invadere
invader [ɪn'veɪdə^r] *n* invasore *m*
invalid *n* ['ɪnvəlɪd] malato(-a); (*with disability*) invalido(-a) ■ *adj* [ɪn'vælɪd] (*not valid*) invalido(-a), non valido(-a)
invalidate [ɪn'vælɪdeɪt] *vt* invalidare
invalid chair *n* (*Brit*) sedia a rotelle
invaluable [ɪn'væljuəbl] *adj* prezioso(-a), inestimabile
invariable [ɪn'vɛərɪəbl] *adj* costante, invariabile
invariably [ɪn'vɛərɪəblɪ] *adv* invariabilmente; **she is ~ late** è immancabilmente in ritardo
invasion [ɪn'veɪʒən] *n* invasione *f*
invective [ɪn'vɛktɪv] *n* invettiva
inveigle [ɪn'vi:gl] *vt*: **to ~ sb into (doing) sth** circuire qn per (fargli fare) qc
invent [ɪn'vɛnt] *vt* inventare
invention [ɪn'vɛnʃən] *n* invenzione *f*
inventive [ɪn'vɛntɪv] *adj* inventivo(-a)
inventiveness [ɪn'vɛntɪvnɪs] *n* inventiva
inventor [ɪn'vɛntə^r] *n* inventore *m*
inventory ['ɪnvəntrɪ] *n* inventario
inventory control *n* (*Comm*) controllo delle giacenze
inverse [ɪn'və:s] *adj* inverso(-a) ■ *n* inverso, contrario; **in ~ proportion (to)** in modo inversamente proporzionale (a)
inversely [ɪn'və:slɪ] *adv* inversamente
invert [ɪn'və:t] *vt* invertire; (*object*) rovesciare
invertebrate [ɪn'və:tɪbrɪt] *n* invertebrato
inverted commas [ɪn'və:tɪd-] *npl* (*Brit*) virgolette *fpl*
invest [ɪn'vɛst] *vt* investire; (*fig: time, effort*) impiegare; (*endow*): **to ~ sb with sth** investire qn di qc ■ *vi* fare investimenti; **to ~ in** investire in, fare (degli) investimenti in; (*acquire*) comprarsi
investigate [ɪn'vɛstɪgeɪt] *vt* investigare, indagare; (*crime*) fare indagini su
investigation [ɪnvɛstɪ'geɪʃən] *n* investigazione *f*; (*of crime*) indagine *f*
investigative [ɪn'vɛstɪgətɪv] *adj*: **~ journalism** giornalismo investigativo
investigator [ɪn'vɛstɪgeɪtə^r] *n* investigatore(-trice); **a private ~** un

investigatore privato, un detective
investiture [ɪn'vɛstɪtʃəʳ] *n* investitura
investment [ɪn'vɛstmənt] *n* investimento
investment income *n* reddito da investimenti
investment trust *n* fondo comune di investimento
investor [ɪn'vɛstəʳ] *n* investitore(-trice); (*shareholder*) azionista *m/f*
inveterate [ɪn'vɛtərət] *adj* inveterato(-a)
invidious [ɪn'vɪdɪəs] *adj* odioso(-a); (*task*) spiacevole
invigilate [ɪn'vɪdʒɪleɪt] *vt, vi* (*Brit Scol*) sorvegliare
invigilator [ɪn'vɪdʒɪleɪtəʳ] *n* (*Brit*) chi sorveglia agli esami
invigorating [ɪn'vɪgəreɪtɪŋ] *adj* stimolante; vivificante
invincible [ɪn'vɪnsɪbl] *adj* invincibile
inviolate [ɪn'vaɪələt] *adj* inviolato(-a)
invisible [ɪn'vɪzɪbl] *adj* invisibile
invisible assets *npl* (*Brit*) beni *mpl* immateriali
invisible ink *n* inchiostro simpatico
invisible mending *n* rammendo invisibile
invitation [ɪnvɪ'teɪʃən] *n* invito; **by ~ only** esclusivamente su *or* per invito; **at sb's ~** dietro invito di qn
invite [ɪn'vaɪt] *vt* invitare; (*opinions etc*) sollecitare; (*trouble*) provocare; **to ~ sb (to do)** invitare qn (a fare); **to ~ sb to dinner** invitare qn a cena
▸ **invite out** *vt* invitare fuori
▸ **invite over** *vt* invitare (a casa)
inviting [ɪn'vaɪtɪŋ] *adj* invitante, attraente
invoice ['ɪnvɔɪs] *n* fattura ▪ *vt* fatturare; **to ~ sb for goods** inviare a qn la fattura per le *or* delle merci
invoke [ɪn'vəuk] *vt* invocare
involuntary [ɪn'vɔləntrɪ] *adj* involontario(-a)
involve [ɪn'vɔlv] *vt* (*entail*) richiedere, comportare; (*associate*): **to ~ sb (in)** implicare qn (in); coinvolgere qn (in); **to ~ o.s. in sth** (*politics etc*) impegnarsi in qc
involved [ɪn'vɔlvd] *adj* involuto(-a), complesso(-a); **to feel ~** sentirsi coinvolto(-a); **to become ~ with sb** (*socially*) legarsi a qn; (*emotionally*) legarsi sentimentalmente a qn
involvement [ɪn'vɔlvmənt] *n* implicazione *f*; coinvolgimento; impegno; partecipazione *f*
invulnerable [ɪn'vʌlnərəbl] *adj* invulnerabile
inward ['ɪnwəd] *adj* (*movement*) verso l'interno; (*thought, feeling*) interiore, intimo(-a) ▪ *adv* verso l'interno
inwardly ['ɪnwədlɪ] *adv* (*feel, think etc*) nell'intimo, entro di sé
inwards ['ɪnwədz] *adv* verso l'interno
I/O *abbr* (*Comput: = input/output*) I/O
IOC *n abbr* (= *International Olympic Committee*) CIO *m* (= *Comitato Internazionale Olimpico*)
iodine ['aɪəudi:n] *n* iodio
IOM *abbr* (*Brit*) = **Isle of Man**
ion ['aɪən] *n* ione *m*
Ionian Sea [aɪ'əunɪən-] *n*: **the ~** il mare Ionio
ioniser ['aɪənaɪzəʳ] *n* ionizzatore *m*
iota [aɪ'əutə] *n* (*fig*) briciolo
IOU *n abbr* (= *I owe you*) pagherò *m inv*
IOW *abbr* (*Brit*) = **Isle of Wight**
IPA *n abbr* (= *International Phonetic Alphabet*) I.P.A. *m*
IP address *n* (*Comput*) indirizzo IP
iPod® ['aɪpɔd] *n* iPod® *m inv*, lettore *m* MP3
IQ *n abbr* = **intelligence quotient**
IRA *n abbr* (= *Irish Republican Army*) I.R.A. *f*; (*US*) = **individual retirement account**
Iran [ɪ'rɑ:n] *n* Iran *m*
Iranian [ɪ'reɪnɪən] *adj* iraniano(-a) ▪ *n* iraniano(-a); (*Ling*) iranico
Iraq [ɪ'rɑ:k] *n* Iraq *m*
Iraqi [ɪ'rɑ:kɪ] *adj* iracheno(-a) ▪ *n* iracheno(-a)
irascible [ɪ'ræsɪbl] *adj* irascibile
irate [aɪ'reɪt] *adj* irato(-a)
Ireland ['aɪələnd] *n* Irlanda; **Republic of ~** Repubblica d'Irlanda, Eire *f*
iris ['aɪrɪs, -ɪz] *n* (*pl* **irises**) iride *f*; (*Bot*) giaggiolo, iride
Irish ['aɪrɪʃ] *adj* irlandese ▪ *npl*: **the ~** gli Irlandesi
Irishman ['aɪrɪʃmən] *n* irlandese *m*
Irish Sea *n*: **the ~** il mar d'Irlanda
Irishwoman ['aɪrɪʃwumən] *n* irlandese *f*
irk [ə:k] *vt* seccare
irksome ['ə:ksəm] *adj* seccante
IRN *n abbr* (= *Independent Radio News*) *agenzia d'informazioni per la radio*
IRO *n abbr* (= *International Refugee Organization*) O.I.R. *f* (= *Organizzazione Internazionale per i Rifugiati*)
iron ['aɪən] *n* ferro; (*for clothes*) ferro da stiro ▪ *adj* di *or* in ferro ▪ *vt* (*clothes*) stirare; *see also* **irons**
▸ **iron out** *vt* (*crease*) appianare; (*fig*) spianare; far sparire
Iron Curtain *n*: **the ~** la cortina di ferro
iron foundry *n* fonderia
ironic [aɪ'rɔnɪk], **ironical** [aɪ'rɔnɪkl] *adj* ironico(-a)
ironically [aɪ'rɔnɪklɪ] *adv* ironicamente
ironing ['aɪənɪŋ] *n* (*act*) stirare *m*; (*clothes*) roba da stirare
ironing board *n* asse *f* da stiro
iron lung *n* (*Med*) polmone *m* d'acciaio

ironmonger ['aɪənmʌŋgəʳ] *n* (*Brit*) negoziante *m* in ferramenta; **~'s (shop)** *n* negozio di ferramenta
iron ore *n* minerale *m* di ferro
irons ['aɪənz] *npl* (*chains*) catene *fpl*
ironworks ['aɪənwə:ks] *n* ferriera
irony ['aɪrənɪ] *n* ironia
irrational [ɪ'ræʃənl] *adj* irrazionale; irragionevole; illogico(-a)
irreconcilable [ɪrɛkən'saɪləbl] *adj* irreconciliabile; (*opinion*): **~ with** inconciliabile con
irredeemable [ɪrɪ'di:məbl] *adj* (*Comm*) irredimibile
irrefutable [ɪrɪ'fju:təbl] *adj* irrefutabile
irregular [ɪ'rɛgjuləʳ] *adj* irregolare
irregularity [ɪrɛgju'lærɪtɪ] *n* irregolarità *f inv*
irrelevance [ɪ'rɛləvəns] *n* inappropriatezza
irrelevant [ɪ'rɛləvənt] *adj* non pertinente
irreligious [ɪrɪ'lɪdʒəs] *adj* irreligioso(-a)
irreparable [ɪ'rɛprəbl] *adj* irreparabile
irreplaceable [ɪrɪ'pleɪsəbl] *adj* insostituibile
irrepressible [ɪrɪ'prɛsəbl] *adj* irrefrenabile
irreproachable [ɪrɪ'prəutʃəbl] *adj* irreprensibile
irresistible [ɪrɪ'zɪstɪbl] *adj* irresistibile
irresolute [ɪ'rɛzəlu:t] *adj* irresoluto(-a), indeciso(-a)
irrespective [ɪrɪ'spɛktɪv]: **~ of** *prep* senza riguardo a
irresponsible [ɪrɪ'spɔnsɪbl] *adj* irresponsabile
irretrievable [ɪrɪ'tri:vəbl] *adj* (*object*) irrecuperabile; (*loss, damage*) irreparabile
irreverent [ɪ'rɛvərnt] *adj* irriverente
irrevocable [ɪ'rɛvəkəbl] *adj* irrevocabile
irrigate ['ɪrɪgeɪt] *vt* irrigare
irrigation [ɪrɪ'geɪʃən] *n* irrigazione *f*
irritable ['ɪrɪtəbl] *adj* irritabile
irritant ['ɪrɪtənt] *n* sostanza irritante
irritate ['ɪrɪteɪt] *vt* irritare
irritation [ɪrɪ'teɪʃən] *n* irritazione *f*
IRS *n abbr* (*US*) = **Internal Revenue Service**
is [ɪz] *vb see* **be**
ISA ['aɪsə] *n abbr* (= *individual savings account*) forma di investimento detassata
ISBN *n abbr* (= *International Standard Book Number*) ISBN *m*
ISDN *n abbr* (= *Integrated Services Digital Network*) ISDN *m*
Islam ['ɪzlɑ:m] *n* Islam *m*
island ['aɪlənd] *n* isola; (*also*: **traffic island**) salvagente *m*
islander ['aɪləndəʳ] *n* isolano(-a)
isle [aɪl] *n* isola
isn't ['ɪznt] = **is not**
isolate ['aɪsəleɪt] *vt* isolare
isolated ['aɪsəleɪtɪd] *adj* isolato(-a)
isolation [aɪsə'leɪʃən] *n* isolamento
isolationism [aɪsə'leɪʃənɪzəm] *n* isolazionismo
isotope ['aɪsəutəup] *n* isotopo
ISP *n abbr* (*Comput*: = *internet service provider*) ISP *m inv*
Israel ['ɪzreɪl] *n* Israele *m*
Israeli [ɪz'reɪlɪ] *adj, n* israeliano(-a)
issue ['ɪʃju:] *n* questione *f*, problema *m*; (*outcome*) esito, risultato; (*of banknotes etc*) emissione *f*; (*of newspaper etc*) numero; (*offspring*) discendenza ■ *vt* (*rations, equipment*) distribuire; (*orders*) dare; (*book*) pubblicare; (*banknotes, cheques, stamps*) emettere ■ *vi*: **to ~ (from)** uscire (da), venir fuori (da); **at ~** in gioco, in discussione; **to avoid the ~** evitare la discussione; **to take ~ with sb (over sth)** prendere posizione contro qn (riguardo a qc); **to confuse** *or* **obscure the ~** confondere le cose; **to make an ~ of sth** fare un problema di qc; **to ~ sth to sb, ~ sb with sth** consegnare qc a qn
Istanbul [ɪstæn'bu:l] *n* Istanbul *f*
isthmus ['ɪsməs] *n* istmo
IT *n abbr* = **information technology**

 KEYWORD

it [ɪt] *pron* **1** (*specific: subject*) esso(-a) (*mostly omitted in Italian*); (*: direct object*) lo/la, l'; (*: indirect object*) gli/le; **where's my book? — it's on the table** dov'è il mio libro? — è sulla tavola; **what is it?** che cos'è?; (*what's the matter?*) cosa c'è?; **where is it?** dov'è?; **I can't find it** non lo (*or* la) trovo; **give it to me** dammelo (*or* dammela); **about/from/of it** ne; **I spoke to him about it** gliene ho parlato; **what did you learn from it?** quale insegnamento ne hai tratto?; **I'm proud of it** ne sono fiero; **in/to/at it** ci; **put the book in it** mettici il libro; **did you go to it?** ci sei andato?; **I wasn't at it** non c'ero; **above/over it** sopra; **below/under it** sotto; **in front of/behind it** lì davanti/dietro
2 (*impers*): **it's raining** piove; **it's Friday tomorrow** domani è venerdì; **it's 6 o'clock** sono le 6; **it's 2 hours on the train** sono *or* ci vogliono 2 ore di treno; **who is it? — it's me** chi è? — sono io

ITA *n abbr* (*Brit*: = *initial teaching alphabet*) *alfabeto fonetico semplificato per insegnare a leggere*
Italian [ɪ'tæljən] *adj* italiano(-a) ■ *n* italiano(-a); (*Ling*) italiano; **the Italians** gli Italiani
italic [ɪ'tælɪk] *adj* corsivo(-a); **italics** *npl* corsivo

Italy ['ɪtəlɪ] *n* Italia
ITC *n abbr* (*Brit:* = *Independent Television Commission*) *organo di controllo sulle reti televisive*
itch [ɪtʃ] *n* prurito ■ *vi* (*person*) avere il prurito; (*part of body*) prudere; **to be itching to do** non veder l'ora di fare
itchy ['ɪtʃɪ] *adj* che prude; **my back is ~** ho prurito alla schiena
it'd ['ɪtd] = **it would; it had**
item ['aɪtəm] *n* articolo; (*on agenda*) punto; (*in programme*) numero; (*also:* **news item**) notizia; **items of clothing** capi *mpl* di abbigliamento
itemize ['aɪtəmaɪz] *vt* specificare, dettagliare
itemized bill ['aɪtəmaɪzd-] *n* conto dettagliato
itinerant [ɪ'tɪnərənt] *adj* ambulante
itinerary [aɪ'tɪnərərɪ] *n* itinerario
it'll ['ɪtl] = **it will; it shall**
ITN *n abbr* (*Brit:* = *Independent Television News*) *agenzia d'informazioni per la televisione*
its [ɪts] *adj, pron* il/la suo(-a), i/le suoi/sue
it's [ɪts] = **it is; it has**
itself [ɪt'sɛlf] *pron* (*emphatic*) esso(-a) stesso(-a); (*reflexive*) si
ITV *n abbr* (*Brit:* = *Independent Television*) *rete televisiva indipendente*; *vedi nota*

ITV

La ITV è un'azienda televisiva privata che comprende una serie di emittenti regionali, la prima delle quali è stata aperta nel 1955. Si autofinanzia tramite la pubblicità ed è sottoposta al controllo di un ente ufficiale, la "Ofcom" *vedi anche* "BBC".

IUD *n abbr* = **intra-uterine device**
I've [aɪv] = **I have**
ivory ['aɪvərɪ] *n* avorio
Ivory Coast *n* Costa d'Avorio
ivory tower *n* torre *f* d'avorio
ivy ['aɪvɪ] *n* edera
Ivy League *n* (*US*) *vedi nota*

IVY LEAGUE

Ivy League è il termine usato per indicare le otto università più prestigiose degli Stati Uniti nordorientali (Brown, Columbia, Cornell, Dartmouth College, Harvard, Princeton, University of Pennsylvania e Yale).

J, j [dʒeɪ] *n* (*letter*) J, j *f or m inv*; **J for Jack**, (*US*) **J for Jig** ≈ J come Jersey

JA *n abbr* = **judge advocate**

J/A *abbr* = **joint account**

jab [dʒæb] *vt*: **to ~ sth into** affondare *or* piantare qc dentro ■ *vi*: **to ~ at** dare colpi a ■ *n* colpo; (*Med*: *col*) puntura

jabber ['dʒæbə^r] *vt, vi* borbottare

jack [dʒæk] *n* (*Aut*) cricco; (*Bowls*) boccino, pallino; (*Cards*) fante *m*

▸**jack in** *vt* (*col*) mollare

▸**jack up** *vt* sollevare sul cricco; (*raise*: *prices etc*) alzare

jackal ['dʒækl] *n* sciacallo

jackass ['dʒækæs] *n* (*also fig*) asino, somaro

jackdaw ['dʒækdɔː] *n* taccola

jacket ['dʒækɪt] *n* giacca; (*of book*) copertura; **potatoes in their jackets** (*Brit*) patate *fpl* con la buccia

jacket potato *n patata cotta al forno con la buccia*

jack-in-the-box ['dʒækɪnðəbɔks] *n* scatola a sorpresa (con pupazzo a molla)

jack-knife ['dʒæknaɪf] *vi*: **the lorry jack-knifed** l'autotreno si è piegato su se stesso

jack-of-all-trades [dʒækəv'ɔːltreɪdz] *n* uno che fa un po' di tutto

jack plug *n* (*Brit*) jack plug *f inv*

jackpot ['dʒækpɔt] *n* primo premio (in denaro)

Jacuzzi® [dʒə'kuːzɪ] *n* vasca per idromassaggio Jacuzzi®

jade [dʒeɪd] *n* (*stone*) giada

jaded ['dʒeɪdɪd] *adj* sfinito(-a), spossato(-a)

jagged ['dʒægɪd] *adj* sbocconcellato(-a); (*cliffs etc*) frastagliato(-a)

jaguar ['dʒægjuə^r] *n* giaguaro

jail [dʒeɪl] *n* prigione *f* ■ *vt* mandare in prigione

jailbird ['dʒeɪlbəːd] *n* avanzo di galera

jailbreak ['dʒeɪlbreɪk] *n* evasione *f*

jailer ['dʒeɪlə^r] *n* custode *m* del carcere

jalopy [dʒə'lɔpɪ] *n* (*col*) macinino

jam [dʒæm] *n* marmellata; (*of shoppers etc*) ressa; (*also*: **traffic jam**) ingorgo ■ *vt* (*passage etc*) ingombrare, ostacolare; (*mechanism, drawer etc*) bloccare; (*Radio*) disturbare con interferenze ■ *vi* (*mechanism, sliding part*) incepparsi, bloccarsi; (*gun*) incepparsi; **to get sb out of a ~** tirare qn fuori dai pasticci; **to ~ sth into** forzare qc dentro; infilare qc a forza dentro; **the telephone lines are jammed** le linee sono sovraccariche

Jamaica [dʒə'meɪkə] *n* Giamaica

Jamaican [dʒə'meɪkən] *adj, n* giamaicano(-a)

jamb [dʒæm] *n* stipite *m*

jam-packed [dʒæm'pækt] *adj*: **~ (with)** pieno(-a) zeppo(-a) (di), strapieno(-a) (di)

jam session *n* improvvisazione *f* jazzistica

Jan. *abbr* (= *January*) gen., genn.

jangle ['dʒæŋgl] *vi* risuonare; (*bracelet*) tintinnare

janitor ['dʒænɪtə^r] *n* (*caretaker*) portiere *m*; (*Scol*) bidello

January ['dʒænjuərɪ] *n* gennaio; *see also* **July**

Japan [dʒə'pæn] *n* Giappone *m*

Japanese [dʒæpə'niːz] *adj* giapponese ■ *n* (*pl inv*) giapponese *m/f*; (*Ling*) giapponese *m*

jar [dʒɑː^r] *n* (*container*) barattolo, vasetto ■ *vi* (*sound*) stridere; (*colours etc*) stonare ■ *vt* (*shake*) scuotere

jargon ['dʒɑːgən] *n* gergo

jarring ['dʒɑːrɪŋ] *adj* (*sound, colour*) stonato(-a)

Jas. *abbr* = **James**

jasmin, jasmine ['dʒæzmɪn] *n* gelsomino

jaundice ['dʒɔːndɪs] *n* itterizia

jaundiced ['dʒɔːndɪst] *adj* (*fig*) invidioso(-a) e critico(-a)

jaunt [dʒɔːnt] *n* gita

jaunty ['dʒɔːntɪ] *adj* vivace; disinvolto(-a), spigliato(-a)

Java ['dʒɑːvə] *n* Giava

javelin ['dʒævlɪn] *n* giavellotto

jaw [dʒɔː] *n* mascella; **jaws** *npl* (*Tech*: *of vice etc*) morsa

jawbone ['dʒɔːbəun] *n* mandibola

jay [dʒeɪ] *n* ghiandaia

jaywalker ['dʒeɪwɔːkəʳ] *n* pedone(-a) indisciplinato(-a)
jazz [dʒæz] *n* jazz *m*
▸**jazz up** *vt* rendere vivace
jazz band *n* banda *f* jazz *inv*
jazzy ['dʒæzɪ] *adj* vistoso(-a), chiassoso(-a)
JCB® *n* scavatrice *f*
JCS *n abbr* (*US*) = **Joint Chiefs of Staff**
JD *n abbr* (*US: = Doctor of Laws*) *titolo di studio;* (*= Justice Department*) *ministero della Giustizia*
jealous ['dʒɛləs] *adj* geloso(-a)
jealously ['dʒɛləslɪ] *adv* (*enviously*) con gelosia; (*watchfully*) gelosamente
jealousy ['dʒɛləsɪ] *n* gelosia
jeans [dʒiːnz] *npl* (blue-)jeans *mpl*
Jeep® [dʒiːp] *n* jeep *m inv*
jeer [dʒɪəʳ] *vi*: **to ~ (at)** fischiare; beffeggiare; *see also* **jeers**
jeering ['dʒɪərɪŋ] *adj* (*crowd*) che urla e fischia ■ *n* fischi *mpl*; parole *fpl* di scherno
jeers ['dʒɪəz] *npl* fischi *mpl*
jelly ['dʒɛlɪ] *n* gelatina
jellyfish ['dʒɛlɪfɪʃ] *n* medusa
jeopardize ['dʒɛpədaɪz] *vt* mettere in pericolo
jeopardy ['dʒɛpədɪ] *n*: **in ~** in pericolo
jerk [dʒəːk] *n* sobbalzo, scossa; sussulto; (*col*) povero scemo ■ *vt* dare una scossa a ■ *vi* (*vehicles*) sobbalzare
jerkin ['dʒəːkɪn] *n* giubbotto
jerky ['dʒəːkɪ] *adj* a scatti; a sobbalzi
jerry-built ['dʒɛrɪbɪlt] *adj* fatto(-a) di cartapesta
jerry can ['dʒɛrɪ-] *n* tanica
Jersey ['dʒəːzɪ] *n* Jersey *m*
jersey ['dʒəːzɪ] *n* maglia, jersey *m*
Jerusalem [dʒə'ruːsələm] *n* Gerusalemme *f*
jest [dʒɛst] *n* scherzo; **in ~** per scherzo
jester ['dʒɛstəʳ] *n* (*Hist*) buffone *m*
Jesus ['dʒiːzəs] *n* Gesù *m*; **~ Christ** Gesù Cristo
jet [dʒɛt] *n* (*of gas, liquid*) getto; (*Aut*) spruzzatore *m*; (*Aviat*) aviogetto
jet-black ['dʒɛt'blæk] *adj* nero(-a) come l'ebano, corvino(-a)
jet engine *n* motore *m* a reazione
jet lag *n* (problemi *mpl* dovuti allo) sbalzo dei fusi orari
jetsam ['dʒɛtsəm] *n* relitti *mpl* di mare
jet-setter ['dʒɛtsɛtəʳ] *n* membro del jet set
jettison ['dʒɛtɪsn] *vt* gettare in mare
jetty ['dʒɛtɪ] *n* molo
Jew [dʒuː] *n* ebreo
jewel ['dʒuːəl] *n* gioiello
jeweller, (*US*) **jeweler** ['dʒuːələʳ] *n* orefice *m*, gioielliere(-a); **~'s shop** *n* oreficeria, gioielleria
jewellery, (*US*) **jewelry** ['dʒuːəlrɪ] *n* gioielli *mpl*
Jewess ['dʒuːɪs] *n* ebrea
Jewish ['dʒuːɪʃ] *adj* ebreo(-a), ebraico(-a)
JFK *n abbr* (*US*) = **John Fitzgerald Kennedy International Airport**
jib [dʒɪb] *n* (*Naut*) fiocco; (*of crane*) braccio ■ *vi* (*horse*) impennarsi; **to ~ at doing sth** essere restio a fare qc
jibe [dʒaɪb] *n* beffa
jiffy ['dʒɪfɪ] *n* (*col*): **in a ~** in un batter d'occhio
jig [dʒɪg] *n* (*dance, tune*) giga
jigsaw ['dʒɪgsɔː] *n* (*tool*) sega da traforo; (*also:* **jigsaw puzzle**) puzzle *m inv*
jilt [dʒɪlt] *vt* piantare in asso
jingle ['dʒɪŋgl] *n* (*advert*) sigla pubblicitaria ■ *vi* tintinnare, scampanellare
jingoism ['dʒɪŋgəuɪzəm] *n* sciovinismo
jinx [dʒɪŋks] *n* (*col*) iettatura; (*person*) iettatore(-trice)
jitters ['dʒɪtəz] *npl* (*col*): **to get the ~** aver fifa
jittery ['dʒɪtərɪ] *adj* (*col*) teso(-a), agitato(-a); **to be ~** aver fifa
jiujitsu [dʒuː'dʒɪtsuː] *n* jujitsu *m*
job [dʒɔb] *n* lavoro; (*employment*) impiego, posto; **a part-time/full-time ~** un lavoro a mezza giornata/a tempo pieno; **that's not my ~** non è compito mio; **he's only doing his ~** non fa che il suo dovere; **it's a good ~ that ...** meno male che ...; **just the ~!** proprio quello che ci vuole!
jobber ['dʒɔbəʳ] *n* (*Brit Stock Exchange*) *intermediario tra agenti di cambio*
jobbing ['dʒɔbɪŋ] *adj* (*Brit: workman*) a ore, a giornata
Jobcentre ['dʒɔbsɛntəʳ] *n* ufficio di collocamento
job creation scheme *n* progetto per la creazione di nuovi posti di lavoro
job description *n* caratteristiche *fpl* (di un lavoro)
jobless ['dʒɔblɪs] *adj* senza lavoro, disoccupato(-a) ■ *npl*: **the ~** i senza lavoro
job lot *n* partita di articoli disparati
job satisfaction *n* soddisfazione *f* nel lavoro
job security *n* sicurezza del posto di lavoro
job share *vi* fare un lavoro ripartito ■ *n* lavoro ripartito
job specification *n* caratteristiche *fpl* (di un lavoro)
Jock [dʒɔk] *n* (*col*) *termine colloquiale per chiamare uno scozzese*
jockey ['dʒɔkɪ] *n* fantino, jockey *m inv* ■ *vi*: **to ~ for position** manovrare per una posizione di vantaggio
jockey box *n* (*US Aut*) vano portaoggetti
jockstrap ['dʒɔkstræp] *n* conchiglia (*per atleti*)
jocular ['dʒɔkjuləʳ] *adj* gioviale; scherzoso(-a)

jog [dʒɔg] *vt* urtare ▪ *vi* (*Sport*) fare footing, fare jogging; **to ~ along** trottare; (*fig*) andare avanti pian piano; **to ~ sb's memory** stimolare la memoria di qn
jogger ['dʒɔgəʳ] *n* persona che fa footing *or* jogging
jogging ['dʒɔgɪŋ] *n* footing *m*, jogging *m*
john [dʒɔn] *n* (*US col*): **the ~** il gabinetto
join [dʒɔɪn] *vt* unire, congiungere; (*become member of*) iscriversi a; (*meet*) raggiungere; riunirsi a ▪ *vi* (*roads, rivers*) confluire ▪ *n* giuntura; **to ~ forces (with)** allearsi (con *or* a); (*fig*) mettersi insieme (a); **will you ~ us for dinner?** viene a cena con noi?; **I'll ~ you later** vi raggiungo più tardi
▸**join in** *vt fus* unirsi a, prendere parte a, partecipare a ▪ *vi* partecipare
▸**join up** *vi* arruolarsi
joiner ['dʒɔɪnəʳ] *n* falegname *m*
joinery ['dʒɔɪnərɪ] *n* falegnameria
joint [dʒɔɪnt] *n* (*Tech*) giuntura; giunto; (*Anat*) articolazione *f*, giuntura; (*Brit Culin*) arrosto; (*col: place*) locale *m* ▪ *adj* comune; (*responsibility*) collettivo(-a); (*committee*) misto(-a)
joint account *n* (*at bank etc*) conto in comune
jointly ['dʒɔɪntlɪ] *adv* in comune, insieme
joint ownership *n* comproprietà
joint-stock company ['dʒɔɪntstɔk-] *n* società *f inv* per azioni
joist [dʒɔɪst] *n* trave *f*
joke [dʒəuk] *n* scherzo; (*funny story*) barzelletta ▪ *vi* scherzare; **to play a ~ on** fare uno scherzo a
joker ['dʒəukəʳ] *n* buffone(-a), burlone(-a); (*Cards*) matta, jolly *m inv*
joking ['dʒəukɪŋ] *n* scherzi *mpl*
jollity ['dʒɔlɪtɪ] *n* allegria
jolly ['dʒɔlɪ] *adj* allegro(-a), gioioso(-a) ▪ *adv* (*Brit col*) veramente, proprio ▪ *vt* (*Brit*): **to ~ sb along** cercare di tenere qn su (di morale); **~ good!** (*Brit*) benissimo!
jolt [dʒəult] *n* scossa, sobbalzo ▪ *vt* urtare
Jordan ['dʒɔ:dən] *n* (*country*) Giordania; (*river*) Giordano
Jordanian [dʒɔ:'deɪnɪən] *adj, n* giordano(-a)
joss stick ['dʒɔs-] *n* bastoncino d'incenso
jostle ['dʒɔsl] *vt* spingere coi gomiti ▪ *vi* farsi spazio coi gomiti
jot [dʒɔt] *n*: **not one ~** nemmeno un po'
▸**jot down** *vt* annotare in fretta, buttare giù
jotter ['dʒɔtəʳ] *n* (*Brit*) quaderno; blocco
journal ['dʒə:nl] *n* (*newspaper*) giornale *m*; (*periodical*) rivista; (*diary*) diario
journalese [dʒə:nə'li:z] *n* (*pej*) stile *m* giornalistico
journalism ['dʒə:nəlɪzəm] *n* giornalismo
journalist ['dʒə:nəlɪst] *n* giornalista *m/f*
journey ['dʒə:nɪ] *n* viaggio; (*distance covered*) tragitto; **a 5-hour ~** un viaggio *or* un tragitto di 5 ore
jovial ['dʒəuvɪəl] *adj* gioviale, allegro(-a)
jowl [dʒaul] *n* mandibola; guancia
joy [dʒɔɪ] *n* gioia
joyful ['dʒɔɪful], **joyous** ['dʒɔɪəs] *adj* gioioso(-a), allegro(-a)
joyride ['dʒɔɪraɪd] *n*: **to go for a ~** rubare una macchina per farsi un giro
joyrider ['dʒɔɪraɪdəʳ] *n chi ruba una macchina per andare a farsi un giro*
joystick ['dʒɔɪstɪk] *n* (*Aviat*) barra di comando; (*Comput*) joystick *m inv*
JP *n abbr* = **Justice of the Peace**
Jr. *abbr* = **junior**
jubilant ['dʒu:bɪlnt] *adj* giubilante; trionfante
jubilation [dʒu:bɪ'leɪʃən] *n* giubilo
jubilee ['dʒu:bɪli:] *n* giubileo; **silver ~** venticinquesimo anniversario
judge [dʒʌdʒ] *n* giudice *m/f* ▪ *vt* giudicare; (*consider*) ritenere; (*estimate: weight, size etc*) calcolare, valutare ▪ *vi*: **judging** *or* **to ~ by his expression** a giudicare dalla sua espressione; **as far as I can ~** a mio giudizio; **I judged it necessary to inform him** ho ritenuto necessario informarlo
judge advocate *n* (*Mil*) magistrato militare
judgment, judgement ['dʒʌdʒmənt] *n* giudizio; (*punishment*) punizione *f*; **in my judg(e)ment** a mio giudizio; **to pass judg(e)ment (on)** (*Law*) pronunciare un giudizio (su); (*fig*) dare giudizi affrettati (su)
judicial [dʒu:'dɪʃl] *adj* giudiziale, giudiziario(-a)
judiciary [dʒu:'dɪʃɪərɪ] *n* magistratura
judicious [dʒu:'dɪʃəs] *adj* giudizioso(-a)
judo ['dʒu:dəu] *n* judo
jug [dʒʌg] *n* brocca, bricco
jugged hare [dʒʌgd-] *n* (*Brit*) lepre *f* in salmì
juggernaut ['dʒʌgənɔ:t] *n* (*Brit: huge truck*) bestione *m*
juggle ['dʒʌgl] *vi* fare giochi di destrezza
juggler ['dʒʌgləʳ] *n* giocoliere(-a)
Jugoslav ['ju:gəu'slɑ:v] *adj, n* = **Yugoslav**
jugular ['dʒʌgjuləʳ] *adj*: **~ (vein)** vena giugulare
juice [dʒu:s] *n* succo; (*of meat*) sugo; **we've run out of ~** (*col: petrol*) siamo rimasti a secco
juicy ['dʒu:sɪ] *adj* succoso(-a)
jukebox ['dʒu:kbɔks] *n* juke-box *m inv*
Jul. *abbr* (= *July*) lug., lu.
July [dʒu:'laɪ] *n* luglio; **the first of ~** il primo luglio; **(on) the eleventh of ~** l'undici luglio; **in the month of ~** nel mese di luglio;

at the beginning/end of ~ all'inizio/alla fine di luglio; **in the middle of ~** a metà luglio; **during ~** durante (il mese di) luglio; **in ~ of next year** a luglio dell'anno prossimo; **each** *or* **every ~** ogni anno a luglio; **~ was wet this year** ha piovuto molto a luglio quest'anno

jumble ['dʒʌmbl] *n* miscuglio ■ *vt* (*also:* **jumble up**, **jumble together**) mischiare, mettere alla rinfusa

jumble sale *n* ≈ vendita di beneficenza; *vedi nota*

JUMBLE SALE

La *jumble sale* è un mercatino dove vengono venduti vari oggetti, per lo più di seconda mano; viene organizzata in chiese, scuole o circoli ricreativi. I proventi delle vendite vengono devoluti in beneficenza o usati per una giusta causa.

jumbo ['dʒʌmbəu] *adj*: **~ jet** jumbo-jet *m inv*; **~ size** formato gigante

jump [dʒʌmp] *vi* saltare, balzare; (*start*) sobbalzare; (*increase*) rincarare ■ *vt* saltare ■ *n* salto, balzo; sobbalzo; (*Showjumping*) salto; (*fence*) ostacolo; **to ~ the queue** (*Brit*) passare davanti agli altri (*in una coda*)
▸ **jump about** *vi* fare salti, saltellare
▸ **jump at** *vt fus* (*fig*) cogliere *or* afferrare al volo; **he jumped at the offer** si affrettò ad accettare l'offerta
▸ **jump down** *vi* saltare giù
▸ **jump up** *vi* saltare in piedi

jumped-up ['dʒʌmptʌp] *adj* (*Brit pej*) presuntuoso(-a)

jumper ['dʒʌmpəʳ] *n* (*Brit: pullover*) maglia; (*US: pinafore dress*) scamiciato; (*Sport*) saltatore(-trice)

jump leads, (US) **jumper cables** *npl* cavi *mpl* per batteria

jump-start ['dʒʌmpstɑ:t] *vt* (*car*) far partire spingendo; (*fig*) dare una spinta a, rimettere in moto

jump suit *n* tuta

jumpy ['dʒʌmpɪ] *adj* nervoso(-a), agitato(-a)

Jun. *abbr* (= *June*) giu.

Jun., Junr *abbr* = **junior**

junction ['dʒʌŋkʃən] *n* (*Brit: of roads*) incrocio; (*of rails*) nodo ferroviario

juncture ['dʒʌŋktʃəʳ] *n*: **at this ~** in questa congiuntura

June [dʒu:n] *n* giugno; *see also* **July**

jungle ['dʒʌŋgl] *n* giungla

junior ['dʒu:nɪəʳ] *adj, n*: **he's ~ to me (by 2 years), he's my ~ (by 2 years)** è più giovane di me (di 2 anni); **he's ~ to me** (*seniority*) è al di sotto di me, ho più anzianità di lui

junior executive *n* giovane dirigente *m*

junior high school *n* (*US*) scuola media (*da 12 a 15 anni*)

junior minister *n* (*Brit Pol*) *ministro che non fa parte del Cabinet*

junior partner *n* socio meno anziano

junior school *n* (*Brit*) scuola elementare (*da 8 a 11 anni*)

junior sizes *npl* (*Comm*) taglie *fpl* per ragazzi

juniper ['dʒu:nɪpəʳ] *n*: **~ berry** bacca di ginepro

junk [dʒʌŋk] *n* (*rubbish*) chincaglia; (*ship*) giunca ■ *vt* disfarsi di

junk bond *n* (*Comm*) titolo *m* spazzatura *inv*

junk dealer *n* rigattiere *m*

junket ['dʒʌŋkɪt] *n* (*Culin*) giuncata; (*Brit col*): **to go on a ~** fare bisboccia

junk food *n* porcherie *fpl*, cibo a scarso valore nutritivo

junkie ['dʒʌŋkɪ] *n* (*col*) drogato(-a)

junk mail *n* posta *f* spazzatura *inv*

junk room *n* (*US*) ripostiglio

junk shop *n* chincaglieria

junta ['dʒʌntə] *n* giunta

Jupiter ['dʒu:pɪtəʳ] *n* (*planet*) Giove *m*

jurisdiction [dʒuərɪs'dɪkʃən] *n* giurisdizione *f*; **it falls** *or* **comes within/outside our ~** è/non è di nostra competenza

jurisprudence [dʒuərɪs'pru:dəns] *n* giurisprudenza

juror ['dʒuərəʳ] *n* giurato(-a)

jury ['dʒuərɪ] *n* giuria

jury box *n* banco della giuria

juryman ['dʒuərɪmən] *n* = **juror**

just [dʒʌst] *adj* giusto(-a) ■ *adv*: **he's ~ done it/left** lo ha appena fatto/è appena partito; **~ as I expected** proprio come me lo aspettavo; **~ right** proprio giusto; **~ 2 o'clock** le 2 precise; **we were ~ going** stavamo uscendo; **I was ~ about to phone** stavo proprio per telefonare; **~ as he was leaving** proprio mentre se ne stava andando; **it was ~ before/enough/here** era poco prima/appena assai/proprio qui; **it's ~ me** sono solo io; **it's ~ a mistake** non è che uno sbaglio; **~ missed/caught** appena perso/preso; **~ listen to this!** senta un po' questo!; **~ ask someone the way** basta che tu chieda la strada a qualcuno; **it's ~ as good** è altrettanto buono; **it's ~ as well you didn't go** per fortuna non ci sei andato; **not ~ now** non proprio adesso; **~ a minute!**, **~ one moment!** un attimo!

justice ['dʒʌstɪs] *n* giustizia; **Lord Chief J~** (*Brit*) presidente *m* della Corte d'Appello;

this photo doesn't do you ~ questa foto non ti fa giustizia
Justice of the Peace *n* giudice *m* conciliatore
justifiable [dʒʌstɪ'faɪəbl] *adj* giustificabile
justifiably [dʒʌstɪ'faɪəblɪ] *adv* legittimamente, con ragione
justification [dʒʌstɪfɪ'keɪʃən] *n* giustificazione *f*; (*Typ*) giustezza
justify ['dʒʌstɪfaɪ] *vt* giustificare; (*Typ etc*) allineare, giustificare; **to be justified in doing sth** avere ragione di fare qc
justly ['dʒʌstlɪ] *adv* giustamente
justness ['dʒʌstnɪs] *n* giustezza
jut [dʒʌt] *vi* (*also*: **jut out**) sporgersi
jute [dʒu:t] *n* iuta
juvenile ['dʒu:vənaɪl] *adj* giovane, giovanile; (*court*) dei minorenni; (*books*) per ragazzi ■ *n* giovane *m/f*, minorenne *m/f*
juvenile delinquency *n* delinquenza minorile
juvenile delinquent *n* delinquente *m/f* minorenne
juxtapose ['dʒʌkstəpəuz] *vt* giustapporre
juxtaposition [dʒʌkstəpə'zɪʃən] *n* giustapposizione *f*

Kk

K, k [keɪ] *n* (*letter*) K, k *f or m inv*; **K for King** = K come Kursaal
K *n abbr* (= *one thousand*) mille ■ *abbr* (*Brit*: = *Knight*) *titolo*; (= *kilobyte*) K
kaftan ['kæftæn] *n* caffettano
Kalahari Desert [kælə'hɑːrɪ-] *n* Deserto di Calahari
kale [keɪl] *n* cavolo verde
kaleidoscope [kə'laɪdəskəup] *n* caleidoscopio
kamikaze [kæmɪ'kɑːzɪ] *adj* da kamikaze
Kampala [kæm'pɑːlə] *n* Kampala *f*
Kampuchea [kæmpu'tʃɪə] *n* Kampuchea *f*
kangaroo [kæŋgə'ruː] *n* canguro
Kans. *abbr* (*US*) = **Kansas**
kaput [kə'put] *adj* (*col*) kaputt *inv*
karaoke [kɑːrə'əukɪ] *n* karaoke *m inv*
karate [kə'rɑːtɪ] *n* karate *m*
Kashmir [kæʃ'mɪəʳ] *n* Kashmir *m*
Kazakhstan [kæzæk'stɑːn] *n* Kazakistan *m*
KC *n abbr* (*Brit Law*: = *King's Counsel*) avvocato della Corona; *see also* **QC**
kebab [kə'bæb] *n* spiedino
keel [kiːl] *n* chiglia; **on an even ~** (*fig*) in uno stato normale
▸ **keel over** *vi* (*Naut*) capovolgersi; (*person*) crollare
keen [kiːn] *adj* (*interest, desire*) vivo(-a); (*eye, intelligence*) acuto(-a); (*competition*) serrato(-a); (*edge*) affilato(-a); (*eager*) entusiasta; **to be ~ to do** *or* **on doing sth** avere una gran voglia di fare qc; **to be ~ on sth** essere appassionato(-a) di qc; **to be ~ on sb** avere un debole per qn; **I'm not ~ on going** non mi va di andare
keenly ['kiːnlɪ] *adv* (*enthusiastically*) con entusiasmo; (*acutely*) vivamente; in modo penetrante
keenness ['kiːnnɪs] *n* (*eagerness*) entusiasmo
keep [kiːp] *vb* (*pt, pp* **kept**) [kɛpt] *vt* tenere; (*hold back*) trattenere; (*feed: one's family etc*) mantenere, sostentare; (*a promise*) mantenere; (*chickens, bees, pigs etc*) allevare ■ *vi* (*food*) mantenersi; (*remain: in a certain state or place*) restare ■ *n* (*of castle*) maschio; (*food etc*): **enough for his ~** abbastanza per vitto e alloggio; **to ~ doing sth** continuare a fare qc; fare qc di continuo; **to ~ sb from doing/ sth from happening** impedire a qn di fare/ che qc succeda; **to ~ sb busy/a place tidy** tenere qn occupato(-a)/un luogo in ordine; **to ~ sb waiting** far aspettare qn; **to ~ an appointment** andare ad un appuntamento; **to ~ a record** *or* **note of sth** prendere nota di qc; **to ~ sth to o.s.** tenere qc per sé; **to ~ sth (back) from sb** celare qc a qn; **to ~ time** (*clock*) andar bene; **~ the change** tenga il resto; *see also* **keeps**
▸ **keep away** *vt*: **to ~ sth/sb away from sb** tenere qc/qn lontano da qn ■ *vi*: **to ~ away (from)** stare lontano (da)
▸ **keep back** *vt* (*crowds, tears, money*) trattenere ■ *vi* tenersi indietro
▸ **keep down** *vt* (*control: prices, spending*) contenere, ridurre; (*retain: food*) trattenere, ritenere ■ *vi* tenersi giù, stare giù
▸ **keep in** *vt* (*invalid, child*) tenere a casa; (*Scol*) trattenere a scuola ■ *vi* (*col*): **to ~ in with sb** tenersi buono qn
▸ **keep off** *vt* (*dog, person*) tenere lontano da ■ *vi* stare alla larga; **~ your hands off!** non toccare!, giù le mani!; **"~ off the grass"** "non calpestare l'erba"
▸ **keep on** *vi* continuare; **to ~ on doing** continuare a fare
▸ **keep out** *vt* tener fuori ■ *vi* restare fuori; **"~ out"** "vietato l'accesso"
▸ **keep up** *vi* mantenersi ■ *vt* continuare, mantenere; **to ~ up with** tener dietro a, andare di pari passo con; (*work etc*) farcela a seguire; **to ~ up with sb** (*in race etc*) mantenersi al passo con qn
keeper ['kiːpəʳ] *n* custode *m/f*, guardiano(-a)
keep-fit [kiːp'fɪt] *n* ginnastica
keeping ['kiːpɪŋ] *n* (*care*) custodia; **in ~ with** in armonia con; in accordo con

keeps [kiːps] *n*: **for ~** (*col*) per sempre
keepsake ['kiːpseɪk] *n* ricordo
keg [kɛg] *n* barilotto
Ken. *abbr* (*US*) = **Kentucky**
kennel ['kɛnl] *n* canile *m*
Kenya ['kɛnjə] *n* Kenia *m*
Kenyan ['kɛnjən] *adj, n* Keniano(-a), Keniota (*m/f*)
kept [kɛpt] *pt, pp of* **keep**
kerb [kəːb] *n* (*Brit*) orlo del marciapiede
kerb crawler [-'krɔːləʳ] *n chi va in macchina in cerca di una prostituta*
kernel ['kəːnl] *n* nocciolo
kerosene ['kɛrəsiːn] *n* cherosene *m*
ketchup ['kɛtʃəp] *n* ketchup *m inv*
kettle ['kɛtl] *n* bollitore *m*
kettle drum *n* timpano
key [kiː] *n* (*gen, Mus*) chiave *f*; (*of piano, typewriter*) tasto; (*on map*) leg(g)enda ■ *cpd* (*vital: position, industry etc*) chiave *inv*
▸ **key in** *vt* (*text*) introdurre da tastiera
keyboard ['kiːbɔːd] *n* tastiera ■ *vt* (*text*) comporre su tastiera
keyboarder ['kiːbɔːdəʳ] *n* dattilografo(-a)
keyed up [kiːd'ʌp] *adj*: **to be ~** essere agitato(-a)
keyhole ['kiːhəul] *n* buco della serratura
keyhole surgery *n* chirurgia mininvasiva
keynote ['kiːnəut] *n* (*Mus*) tonica; (*fig*) nota dominante
keypad ['kiːpæd] *n* tastierino numerico
key ring *n* portachiavi *m inv*
keystroke ['kiːstrəuk] *n* battuta (di un tasto)
kg *abbr* (= *kilogram*) Kg
KGB *n abbr* KGB *m*
khaki ['kɑːkɪ] *adj, n* cachi (*m*)
kibbutz [kɪ'buts] *n* kibbutz *m inv*
kick [kɪk] *vt* calciare, dare calci a ■ *vi* (*horse*) tirar calci ■ *n* calcio; (*of rifle*) contraccolpo; (*thrill*): **he does it for kicks** lo fa giusto per il piacere di farlo
▸ **kick around** *vi* (*col*) essere in giro
▸ **kick off** *vi* (*Sport*) dare il primo calcio
kick-off ['kɪkɔf] *n* (*Sport*) calcio d'inizio
kick-start ['kɪkstɑːt] *n* (*also*: **kick-starter**) pedale *m* d'avviamento
kid [kɪd] *n* ragazzino(-a); (*animal, leather*) capretto ■ *vi* (*col*) scherzare ■ *vt* (*col*) prendere in giro
kid gloves *npl*: **to treat sb with ~** trattare qn coi guanti
kidnap ['kɪdnæp] *vt* rapire, sequestrare
kidnapper ['kɪdnæpəʳ] *n* rapitore(-trice)
kidnapping ['kɪdnæpɪŋ] *n* sequestro (di persona)
kidney ['kɪdnɪ] *n* (*Anat*) rene *m*; (*Culin*) rognone *m*
kidney bean *n* fagiolo borlotto
kidney machine *n* rene *m* artificiale
Kilimanjaro [kɪlɪmən'dʒɑːrəu] *n*: **Mount ~** il monte Kilimangiaro
kill [kɪl] *vt* uccidere, ammazzare; (*fig*) sopprimere; sopraffare; ammazzare ■ *n* uccisione *f*; **to ~ time** ammazzare il tempo
▸ **kill off** *vt* sterminare; (*fig*) eliminare, soffocare
killer ['kɪləʳ] *n* uccisore *m*, killer *m inv*; assassino(-a)
killer instinct *n*: **to have a/the ~** essere spietato(-a)
killing ['kɪlɪŋ] *n* assassinio; (*massacre*) strage *f*; (*col*): **to make a ~** fare un bel colpo
kill-joy ['kɪldʒɔɪ] *n* guastafeste *m/f inv*
kiln [kɪln] *n* forno
kilo ['kiːləu] *n abbr* (= *kilogram*) chilo
kilobyte ['kɪləbaɪt] *n* kilobyte *m inv*
kilogram, kilogramme ['kɪləugræm] *n* chilogrammo
kilometre, (*US*) **kilometer** ['kɪləmiːtəʳ] *n* chilometro
kilowatt ['kɪləuwɔt] *n* chilowatt *m inv*
kilt [kɪlt] *n* gonnellino scozzese
kilter ['kɪltəʳ] *n*: **out of ~** fuori fase
kimono [kɪ'məunəu] *n* chimono
kin [kɪn] *n see* **next of kin; kith**
kind [kaɪnd] *adj* gentile, buono(-a) ■ *n* sorta, specie *f*; (*species*) genere *m*; **to be two of a ~** essere molto simili; **would you be ~ enough to ...?, would you be so ~ as to ...?** sarebbe così gentile da ...?; **it's very ~ of you (to do)** è molto gentile da parte sua (di fare); **in ~** (*Comm*) in natura; (*fig*): **to repay sb in ~** ripagare qn della stessa moneta
kindergarten ['kɪndəgɑːtn] *n* giardino d'infanzia
kind-hearted [kaɪnd'hɑːtɪd] *adj* di buon cuore
kindle ['kɪndl] *vt* accendere, infiammare
kindling ['kɪndlɪŋ] *n* frasche *fpl*, ramoscelli *mpl*
kindly ['kaɪndlɪ] *adj* pieno(-a) di bontà, benevolo(-a) ■ *adv* con bontà, gentilmente; **will you ~ ...** vuole ... per favore; **he didn't take it ~** se l'è presa a male
kindness ['kaɪndnɪs] *n* bontà, gentilezza
kindred ['kɪndrɪd] *adj* imparentato(-a); **~ spirit** spirito affine
kinetic [kɪ'nɛtɪk] *adj* cinetico(-a)
king [kɪŋ] *n* re *m inv*
kingdom ['kɪŋdəm] *n* regno, reame *m*
kingfisher ['kɪŋfɪʃəʳ] *n* martin *m inv* pescatore
kingpin ['kɪŋpɪn] *n* (*Tech, fig*) perno
king-size ['kɪŋsaɪz], **king-sized** ['kɪŋsaɪzd] *adj* super *inv*; gigante; (*cigarette*) extra lungo(-a)

kink [kɪŋk] *n* (*of rope*) attorcigliamento; (*in hair*) ondina; (*fig*) aberrazione *f*
kinky ['kɪŋkɪ] *adj* (*fig*) eccentrico(-a); dai gusti particolari
kinship ['kɪnʃɪp] *n* parentela
kinsman ['kɪnzmən] *n* parente *m*
kinswoman ['kɪnzwumən] *n* parente *f*
kiosk ['ki:ɔsk] *n* edicola, chiosco; (*Brit: also*: **telephone kiosk**) cabina (telefonica); (*: also*: **newspaper kiosk**) edicola
kipper ['kɪpə^r] *n* aringa affumicata
Kirghizia [kə:'gɪzɪə] *n* Kirghizistan
kiss [kɪs] *n* bacio ■ *vt* baciare; **to ~ (each other)** baciarsi; **to ~ sb goodbye** congedarsi da qn con un bacio; **~ of life** (*Brit*) respirazione *f* bocca a bocca
kissagram ['kɪsəgræm] *n servizio di recapito a domicilio di messaggi e baci augurali*
kit [kɪt] *n* equipaggiamento, corredo; (*set of tools etc*) attrezzi *mpl*; (*for assembly*) scatola di montaggio; **tool ~** cassetta *or* borsa degli attrezzi
▸ **kit out** *vt* (*Brit*) attrezzare, equipaggiare
kitbag ['kɪtbæg] *n* zaino; sacco militare
kitchen ['kɪtʃɪn] *n* cucina
kitchen garden *n* orto
kitchen sink *n* acquaio
kitchen unit *n* (*Brit*) elemento da cucina
kitchenware ['kɪtʃɪnwεə^r] *n* stoviglie *fpl*; utensili *mpl* da cucina
kite [kaɪt] *n* (*toy*) aquilone *m*; (*Zool*) nibbio
kith [kɪθ] *n*: **~ and kin** amici e parenti *mpl*
kitten ['kɪtn] *n* gattino(-a), micino(-a)
kitty ['kɪtɪ] *n* (*money*) fondo comune
kiwi fruit ['ki:wi:-] *n* kiwi *m inv*
KKK *n abbr* (*US*) = **Ku Klux Klan**
Kleenex® ['kli:nεks] *n* fazzolettino di carta
kleptomaniac [klεptəu'meɪnɪæk] *n* cleptomane *m/f*
km *abbr* (= *kilometre*) km
km/h *abbr* (= *kilometres per hour*) km/h
knack [næk] *n*: **to have a ~ (for doing)** avere una pratica (per fare); **to have the ~ of** avere l'abilità di; **there's a ~ to doing this** c'è un trucco per fare questo
knackered ['nækəd] *adj* (*col*) fuso(-a)
knapsack ['næpsæk] *n* zaino, sacco da montagna
knave [neɪv] *n* (*Cards*) fante *m*
knead [ni:d] *vt* impastare
knee [ni:] *n* ginocchio
kneecap ['ni:kæp] *n* rotula ■ *vt* gambizzare
knee-deep ['ni:'di:p] *adj*: **the water was ~** l'acqua ci arrivava alle ginocchia
kneel [ni:l] *vi* (*pt, pp* **knelt**) [nεlt] inginocchiarsi
kneepad ['ni:pæd] *n* ginocchiera
knell [nεl] *n* rintocco
knelt [nεlt] *pt, pp of* **kneel**
knew [nju:] *pt of* **know**
knickers ['nɪkəz] *npl* (*Brit*) mutandine *fpl*
knick-knack ['nɪknæk] *n* ninnolo
knife [naɪf] *n* (*pl* **knives**) coltello ■ *vt* accoltellare, dare una coltellata a; **~, fork and spoon** coperto
knife edge *n*: **to be on a ~** (*fig*) essere appeso(-a) a un filo
knight [naɪt] *n* cavaliere *m*; (*Chess*) cavallo
knighthood ['naɪthud] *n* cavalleria; (*title*): **to get a ~** essere fatto cavaliere
knit [nɪt] *vt* fare a maglia; (*fig*): **to ~ together** unire ■ *vi* lavorare a maglia; (*broken bones*) saldarsi
knitted ['nɪtɪd] *adj* lavorato(-a) a maglia
knitting ['nɪtɪŋ] *n* lavoro a maglia
knitting machine *n* macchina per maglieria
knitting needle *n* ferro (da calza)
knitting pattern *n* modello (per maglia)
knitwear ['nɪtwεə^r] *n* maglieria
knives [naɪvz] *npl of* **knife**
knob [nɔb] *n* bottone *m*; manopola; (*Brit*): **a ~ of butter** una noce di burro
knobbly ['nɔblɪ], (*US*) **knobby** ['nɔbɪ] *adj* (*wood, surface*) nodoso(-a); (*knee*) ossuto(-a)
knock [nɔk] *vt* (*strike*) colpire; urtare; (*fig: col*) criticare ■ *vi* (*engine*) battere; (*at door etc*): **to ~ at/on** bussare a ■ *n* bussata; colpo, botta; **he knocked at the door** ha bussato alla porta; **to ~ a nail into sth** conficcare un chiodo in qc
▸ **knock down** *vt* abbattere; (*pedestrian*) investire; (*price*) abbassare
▸ **knock off** *vi* (*col: finish*) smettere (di lavorare) ■ *vt* (*strike off*) far cadere; (*col: steal*) sgraffignare, grattare; **to ~ off £10** fare uno sconto di 10 sterline
▸ **knock out** *vt* stendere; (*Boxing*) mettere K.O., mettere fuori combattimento
▸ **knock over** *vt* (*object*) far cadere; (*pedestrian*) investire
knockdown ['nɔkdaun] *adj* (*price*) fortemente scontato(-a)
knocker ['nɔkə^r] *n* (*on door*) battente *m*
knocking ['nɔkɪŋ] *n* colpi *mpl*
knock-kneed [nɔk'ni:d] *adj* che ha le gambe ad x
knockout ['nɔkaut] *n* (*Boxing*) knock out *m inv*
knockout competition *n* (*Brit*) gara ad eliminazione
knock-up ['nɔkʌp] *n* (*Tennis etc*) palleggio; **to have a ~** palleggiare
knot [nɔt] *n* nodo ■ *vt* annodare; **to tie a ~** fare un nodo
knotty ['nɔtɪ] *adj* (*fig*) spinoso(-a)

know [nəu] *vt* (*pt* **knew**, *pp* **known**) [njuː, nəun] sapere; (*person, author, place*) conoscere ■ *vi* sapere; **to ~ that ...** sapere che ...; **to ~ how to do** sapere fare; **to get to ~ sth** venire a sapere qc; **I ~ nothing about it** non ne so niente; **I don't ~ him** non lo conosco; **to ~ right from wrong** distinguere il bene dal male; **as far as I ~ ...** che io sappia ..., per quanto io ne sappia ...; **yes, I ~** sì, lo so; **I don't ~** non lo so

know-all ['nəuɔːl] *n* (*Brit pej*) sapientone(-a)

know-how ['nəuhau] *n* tecnica; pratica

knowing ['nəuɪŋ] *adj* (*look etc*) d'intesa

knowingly ['nəuɪŋlɪ] *adv* consapevolmente; di complicità

know-it-all ['nəuɪtɔːl] *n* (*US*) = **know-all**

knowledge ['nɔlɪdʒ] *n* consapevolezza; (*learning*) conoscenza, sapere *m*; **to have no ~ of** ignorare, non sapere; **not to my ~** che io sappia, no; **to have a working ~ of Italian** avere una conoscenza pratica dell'italiano; **without my ~** a mia insaputa; **it is common ~ that ...** è risaputo che ...; **it has come to my ~ that ...** sono venuto a sapere che ...

knowledgeable ['nɔlɪdʒəbl] *adj* ben informato(-a)

known [nəun] *pp of* **know** ■ *adj* (*thief, facts*) noto(-a); (*expert*) riconosciuto(-a)

knuckle ['nʌkl] *n* nocca

▸ **knuckle down** *vi* (*col*): **to ~ down to some hard work** mettersi sotto a lavorare

▸ **knuckle under** *vi* (*col*) cedere

knuckleduster ['nʌkldʌstə^r] *n* tirapugni *m inv*

KO *abbr* (= *knock out*) ■ *n* K.O. *m* ■ *vt* mettere K.O.

koala [kəu'ɑːlə] *n* (*also*: **koala bear**) koala *m inv*

kook [kuːk] *n* (*US col*) svitato(-a)

Koran [kɔ'rɑːn] *n* Corano

Korea [kə'riːə] *n* Corea; **North/South ~** Corea del Nord/Sud

Korean [kə'riːən] *adj, n* coreano(-a)

kosher ['kəuʃə^r] *adj* kasher *inv*

kowtow ['kau'tau] *vi*: **to ~ to sb** mostrarsi ossequioso(-a) verso qn

Kremlin ['krɛmlɪn] *n*: **the ~** il Cremlino

KS *abbr* (*US*) = **Kansas**

Kt *abbr* (*Brit*: = *Knight*) *titolo*

Kuala Lumpur ['kwɑːlə'lumpuə^r] *n* Kuala Lumpur *f*

kudos ['kjuːdɔs] *n* gloria, fama

Kurd [kəːd] *n* curdo(-a)

Kuwait [ku'weɪt] *n* Kuwait *m*

Kuwaiti [ku'weɪtɪ] *adj, n* kuwaitiano(-a)

kW *abbr* (= *kilowatt*) kw

KY, Ky. *abbr* (*US*) = **Kentucky**

L, l [ɛl] *n* (*letter*) L, l *f or m inv*; **L for Lucy**, (*US*) **L for Love** ≈ L come Livorno
L *abbr* (= *lake*) l; (= *large*) taglia grande; (= *left*) sin.; (*Brit Aut*) = **learner**
l *abbr* (= *litre*) l
LA *n abbr* (*US*) = **Los Angeles** ■ *abbr* (*US*) = **Louisiana**
La. *abbr* (*US*) = **Louisiana**
lab [læb] *n abbr* (= *laboratory*) laboratorio
Lab. *abbr* (*Canada*) = **Labrador**
label ['leɪbl] *n* etichetta, cartellino; (*brand: of record*) casa ■ *vt* etichettare; classificare
labor *etc* ['leɪbə^r] (*US*) = **labour** *etc*
laboratory [lə'bɔrətərɪ] *n* laboratorio
Labor Day *n* (*US*) festa del lavoro; *vedi nota*

LABOR DAY

Negli Stati Uniti e nel Canada il *Labor Day*, la festa del lavoro, cade il primo lunedì di settembre, contrariamente a quanto accade nella maggior parte dei paesi europei dove tale celebrazione ha luogo il primo maggio.

laborious [lə'bɔːrɪəs] *adj* laborioso(-a)
labor union *n* (*US*) sindacato
Labour ['leɪbə^r] *n* (*Brit Pol: also:* **the Labour Party**) il partito laburista, i laburisti
labour, (*US*) **labor** ['leɪbə^r] *n* (*task*) lavoro; (*workmen*) manodopera; (*Med*) travaglio del parto, doglie *fpl* ■ *vi*: **to ~ (at)** lavorare duro(a); **to be in ~** (*Med*) avere le doglie
labour camp, (*US*) **labor camp** *n* campo dei lavori forzati
labour cost, (*US*) **labor cost** *n* costo del lavoro
labour dispute, (*US*) **labor dispute** *n* conflitto tra lavoratori e datori di lavoro
laboured, (*US*) **labored** ['leɪbəd] *adj* (*breathing*) affaticato(-a), affannoso(-a); (*style*) elaborato(-a), pesante
labourer, (*US*) **laborer** ['leɪbərə^r] *n* manovale *m*; (*on farm*) lavoratore *m* agricolo
labour force, (*US*) **labor force** *n* manodopera
labour-intensive, (*US*) **labor-intensive** [leɪbərɪn'tɛnsɪv] *adj* che assorbe molta manodopera
labour market, (*US*) **labor market** *n* mercato del lavoro
labour pains, (*US*) **labor pains** *npl* doglie *fpl*
labour relations, (*US*) **labor relations** *npl* relazioni *fpl* industriali
labour-saving, (*US*) **labor-saving** ['leɪbə-seɪvɪŋ] *adj* che fa risparmiare fatica *or* lavoro
labour unrest, (*US*) **labor unrest** *n* agitazioni *fpl* degli operai
labyrinth ['læbɪrɪnθ] *n* labirinto
lace [leɪs] *n* merletto, pizzo; (*of shoe etc*) laccio ■ *vt* (*shoe*) allacciare; (*drink: fortify with spirits*) correggere
lacemaking ['leɪsmeɪkɪŋ] *n* fabbricazione *f* dei pizzi *or* dei merletti
laceration [læsə'reɪʃən] *n* lacerazione *f*
lace-up ['leɪsʌp] *adj* (*shoes etc*) con i lacci, con le stringhe
lack [læk] *n* mancanza, scarsità ■ *vt* mancare di; **through** *or* **for ~ of** per mancanza di; **to be lacking** mancare; **to be lacking in** mancare di
lackadaisical [lækə'deɪzɪkl] *adj* disinteressato(-a), noncurante
lackey ['lækɪ] *n* (*also fig*) lacchè *m inv*
lacklustre, (*US*) **lackluster** ['læklʌstə^r] *adj* (*surface*) opaco(-a); (*style*) scialbo(-a); (*eyes*) spento(-a)
laconic [lə'kɔnɪk] *adj* laconico(-a)
lacquer ['lækə^r] *n* lacca; **hair ~** lacca per (i) capelli
lacy ['leɪsɪ] *adj* (*like lace*) che sembra un pizzo
lad [læd] *n* ragazzo, giovanotto; (*Brit: in stable etc*) mozzo *or* garzone *m* di stalla
ladder ['lædə^r] *n* scala; (*Brit: in tights*) smagliatura ■ *vt* smagliare ■ *vi* smagliarsi
laden ['leɪdn] *adj*: **~ (with)** carico(-a) *or* caricato(-a) (di); **fully ~** (*truck, ship*) a pieno carico

ladle ['leɪdl] *n* mestolo
lady ['leɪdɪ] *n* signora; **L~ Smith** lady Smith; **the ladies' (toilets)** i gabinetti per signore; **a ~ doctor** una dottoressa
ladybird ['leɪdɪbə:d], (*US*) **ladybug** ['leɪdɪbʌg] *n* coccinella
lady-in-waiting ['leɪdɪɪn'weɪtɪŋ] *n* dama di compagnia
ladykiller ['leɪdɪkɪləʳ] *n* dongiovanni *m inv*
ladylike ['leɪdɪlaɪk] *adj* da signora, distinto(-a)
ladyship ['leɪdɪʃɪp] *n*: **your L~** signora contessa *etc*
lag [læg] *n* = **time lag** ■ *vi* (*also*: **lag behind**) trascinarsi ■ *vt* (*pipes*) rivestire di materiale isolante
lager ['lɑ:gəʳ] *n* lager *m inv*
lager lout *n* (*Brit col*) giovinastro ubriaco
lagging ['lægɪŋ] *n* rivestimento di materiale isolante
lagoon [lə'gu:n] *n* laguna
Lagos ['leɪgɔs] *n* Lagos *f*
laid [leɪd] *pt, pp of* **lay**
laid-back [leɪd'bæk] *adj* (*col*) rilassato(-a)
lain [leɪn] *pp of* **lie**
lair [lɛəʳ] *n* covo, tana
laissez-faire [lɛseɪ'fɛəʳ] *n* liberismo
laity ['leɪətɪ] *n* laici *mpl*
lake [leɪk] *n* lago
Lake District *n*: **the ~** (*Brit*) la regione dei laghi
lamb [læm] *n* agnello
lamb chop *n* cotoletta d'agnello
lambskin ['læmskɪn] *n* (pelle *f* d')agnello
lambswool ['læmzwul] *n* lamb's wool *m*
lame [leɪm] *adj* zoppo(-a); **~ duck** (*fig: person*) persona inetta; (*: firm*) azienda traballante
lamely ['leɪmlɪ] *adv* (*fig*) in modo poco convincente
lament [lə'mɛnt] *n* lamento ■ *vt* lamentare, piangere
lamentable ['læməntəbl] *adj* doloroso(-a); deplorevole
laminated ['læmɪneɪtɪd] *adj* laminato(-a)
lamp [læmp] *n* lampada
lamplight ['læmplaɪt] *n*: **by ~** a lume della lampada
lampoon [læm'pu:n] *n* satira
lamppost ['læmppəust] *n* lampione *m*
lampshade ['læmpʃeɪd] *n* paralume *m*
lance [lɑ:ns] *n* lancia ■ *vt* (*Med*) incidere
lance corporal *n* (*Brit*) caporale *m*
lancet ['lɑ:nsɪt] *n* (*Med*) bisturi *m inv*
Lancs [læŋks] *abbr* (*Brit*) = **Lancashire**
land [lænd] *n* (*as opposed to sea*) terra (ferma); (*country*) paese *m*; (*soil*) terreno; (*estate*) terreni *mpl*, terre *fpl* ■ *vi* (*from ship*) sbarcare; (*Aviat*) atterrare; (*fig: fall*) cadere ■ *vt* (*obtain*) acchiappare; (*passengers*) sbarcare; (*goods*) scaricare; **to go/travel by ~** andare/ viaggiare per via di terra; **to own ~** possedere dei terreni, avere delle proprietà (terriere); **to ~ on one's feet** cadere in piedi; (*fig: to be lucky*) cascar bene
▸ **land up** *vi* andare a finire
landed gentry ['lændɪd-] *n* proprietari *mpl* terrieri
landfill site ['lændfɪl-] *n* discarica dove i rifiuti vengono sepolti
landing ['lændɪŋ] *n* (*from ship*) sbarco; (*Aviat*) atterraggio; (*of staircase*) pianerottolo
landing card *n* carta di sbarco
landing craft *n* mezzo da sbarco
landing gear *n* (*Aviat*) carrello d'atterraggio
landing stage *n* pontile *m* da sbarco
landing strip *n* pista d'atterraggio
landlady ['lændleɪdɪ] *n* padrona *or* proprietaria di casa
landlocked ['lændlɔkt] *adj* senza sbocco sul mare
landlord ['lændlɔ:d] *n* padrone *m or* proprietario di casa; (*of pub etc*) oste *m*
landlubber ['lændlʌbəʳ] *n* marinaio d'acqua dolce
landmark ['lændmɑ:k] *n* punto di riferimento; (*fig*) pietra miliare
landowner ['lændəunəʳ] *n* proprietario(-a) terriero(-a)
landscape ['lænskeɪp] *n* paesaggio
landscape architect, landscape gardener *n* paesaggista *m/f*
landscape painting *n* (*Art*) paesaggistica
landslide ['lændslaɪd] *n* (*Geo*) frana; (*fig: Pol*) valanga
lane [leɪn] *n* (*in country*) viottolo; (*in town*) stradetta; (*Aut, in race*) corsia; **shipping ~** rotta (marittima)
language ['læŋgwɪdʒ] *n* lingua; (*way one speaks*) linguaggio; **bad ~** linguaggio volgare
language laboratory *n* laboratorio linguistico
language school *n* scuola di lingue
languid ['læŋgwɪd] *adj* languente, languido(-a)
languish ['læŋgwɪʃ] *vi* languire
lank [læŋk] *adj* (*hair*) liscio(-a) e opaco(-a)
lanky ['læŋkɪ] *adj* allampanato(-a)
lanolin, lanoline ['lænəlɪn] *n* lanolina
lantern ['læntn] *n* lanterna
Laos [lauz] *n* Laos *m*
lap [læp] *n* (*of track*) giro; (*of body*): **in** *or* **on one's ~** in grembo ■ *vt* (*also*: **lap up**) papparsi, leccare ■ *vi* (*waves*) sciabordare
▸ **lap up** *vt* (*fig: compliments, attention*) bearsi di
La Paz [læ'pæz] *n* La Paz *f*

lapdog ['læpdɔg] *n* cane *m* da grembo
lapel [lə'pɛl] *n* risvolto
Lapland ['læplænd] *n* Lapponia
Lapp [læp] *adj* lappone ■ *n* lappone *m/f*; (*Ling*) lappone *m*
lapse [læps] *n* lapsus *m inv*; (*longer*) caduta; (*fault*) mancanza; (*in behaviour*) scorrettezza ■ *vi* (*law, act*) cadere; (*ticket, passport*) scadere; **to ~ into bad habits** pigliare cattive abitudini; **~ of time** spazio di tempo; **a ~ of memory** un vuoto di memoria
laptop ['læptɔp] *n* (*also*: **laptop computer**) laptop *m inv*
larceny ['lɑːsənɪ] *n* furto
lard [lɑːd] *n* lardo
larder ['lɑːdə^r] *n* dispensa
large [lɑːdʒ] *adj* grande; (*person, animal*) grosso(-a) ■ *adv*: **by and ~** generalmente; **at ~** (*free*) in libertà; (*generally*) in generale; nell'insieme; **to make larger** ingrandire; **a ~ number of people** molta gente; **on a ~ scale** su vasta scala
largely ['lɑːdʒlɪ] *adv* in gran parte
large-scale ['lɑːdʒ'skeɪl] *adj* (*map, drawing etc*) in grande scala; (*reforms, business activities*) su vasta scala
lark [lɑːk] *n* (*bird*) allodola; (*joke*) scherzo, gioco
▸ **lark about** *vi* fare lo stupido
larva (*pl* **larvae**) ['lɑːvə, -iː] *n* larva
laryngitis [lærɪn'dʒaɪtɪs] *n* laringite *f*
larynx ['lærɪŋks] *n* laringe *f*
lasagne [lə'zænjə] *n* lasagne *fpl*
lascivious [lə'sɪvɪəs] *adj* lascivo(-a)
laser ['leɪzə^r] *n* laser *m*
laser beam *n* raggio *m* laser *inv*
laser printer *n* stampante *f* laser *inv*
lash [læʃ] *n* frustata; (*also*: **eyelash**) ciglio ■ *vt* frustare; (*tie*) legare
▸ **lash down** *vt* assicurare (con corde) ■ *vi* (*rain*) scrosciare
▸ **lash out** *vi*: **to ~ out (at** *or* **against sb/sth)** attaccare violentemente (qn/qc); **to ~ out (on sth)** (*col*: *spend*) spendere un sacco di soldi (per qc)
lashing ['læʃɪŋ] *n* (*beating*) frustata, sferzata; **lashings of** (*Brit col*) un mucchio di, una montagna di
lass [læs] *n* ragazza
lasso [læ'suː] *n* laccio ■ *vt* acchiappare con il laccio
last [lɑːst] *adj* ultimo(-a); (*week, month, year*) scorso(-a), passato(-a) ■ *adv* per ultimo ■ *vi* durare; **~ week** la settimana scorsa; **~ night** ieri sera, la notte scorsa; **at ~** finalmente, alla fine; **~ but one** penultimo(-a); **the ~ time** l'ultima volta; **it lasts (for) 2 hours** dura 2 ore
last-ditch ['lɑːst'dɪtʃ] *adj* ultimo(-a) e disperato(-a)
lasting ['lɑːstɪŋ] *adj* durevole
lastly ['lɑːstlɪ] *adv* infine, per finire, per ultimo
last-minute ['lɑːstmɪnɪt] *adj* fatto(-a) (*or* preso(-a) *etc*) all'ultimo momento
latch [lætʃ] *n* serratura a scatto
▸ **latch on to** *vt fus* (*cling to*: *person*) attaccarsi a, appiccicarsi a; (: *idea*) afferrare, capire
latchkey ['lætʃkiː] *n* chiave *f* di casa
late [leɪt] *adj* (*not on time*) in ritardo; (*far on in day etc*) tardi *inv*; tardo(-a); (*recent*) recente, ultimo(-a); (*former*) ex; (*dead*) defunto(-a) ■ *adv* tardi; (*behind time, schedule*) in ritardo; **to be (10 minutes) ~** essere in ritardo (di 10 minuti); **to work ~** lavorare fino a tardi; **~ in life** in età avanzata; **of ~** di recente; **in the ~ afternoon** nel tardo pomeriggio; **in ~ May** verso la fine di maggio; **the ~ Mr X** il defunto Signor X
latecomer ['leɪtkʌmə^r] *n* ritardatario(-a)
lately ['leɪtlɪ] *adv* recentemente
lateness ['leɪtnɪs] *n* (*of person*) ritardo; (*of event*) tardezza, ora tarda
latent ['leɪtnt] *adj* latente; **~ defect** vizio occulto
later ['leɪtə^r] *adj* (*date etc*) posteriore; (*version etc*) successivo(-a) ■ *adv* più tardi; **~ on today** oggi più tardi
lateral ['lætərl] *adj* laterale
latest ['leɪtɪst] *adj* ultimo(-a), più recente; **at the ~** al più tardi; **the ~ news** le ultime notizie
latex ['leɪtɛks] *n* latice *m*
lath [læθ] *n* (*pl* **laths**) [læðz] assicella
lathe [leɪð] *n* tornio
lather ['lɑːðə^r] *n* schiuma di sapone ■ *vt* insaponare ■ *vi* far schiuma
Latin ['lætɪn] *n* latino ■ *adj* latino(-a)
Latin America *n* America Latina
Latin American *adj* sudamericano(-a)
latitude ['lætɪtjuːd] *n* latitudine *f*; (*fig*: *freedom*) libertà d'azione
latrine [lə'triːn] *n* latrina
latter ['lætə^r] *adj* secondo(-a); più recente ■ *n*: **the ~** quest'ultimo, il secondo
latterly ['lætəlɪ] *adv* recentemente, negli ultimi tempi
lattice ['lætɪs] *n* traliccio; graticolato
lattice window *n* finestra con vetrata a losanghe
Latvia ['lætvɪə] *n* Lettonia
Latvian ['lætvɪən] *adj* lettone *inv* ■ *n* lettone *m/f*; (*Ling*) lettone *m*
laudable ['lɔːdəbl] *adj* lodevole
laudatory ['lɔːdətrɪ] *adj* elogiativo(-a)

laugh [lɑːf] *n* risata ■ *vi* ridere
▸ **laugh at** *vt fus* (*misfortune etc*) ridere di; **I laughed at his joke** la sua barzelletta mi fece ridere
▸ **laugh off** *vt* prendere alla leggera
laughable ['lɑːfəbl] *adj* ridicolo(-a)
laughing ['lɑːfɪŋ] *adj* (*face*) ridente; **this is no ~ matter** non è una cosa da ridere
laughing gas *n* gas *m* esilarante
laughing stock *n*: **the ~ of** lo zimbello di
laughter ['lɑːftə^r] *n* riso; risate *fpl*
launch [lɔːntʃ] *n* (*of rocket, product etc*) lancio; (*of new ship*) varo; (*boat*) scialuppa; (*also*: **motor launch**) lancia ■ *vt* (*rocket, product*) lanciare; (*ship, plan*) varare
▸ **launch out** *vi*: **to ~ out (into)** lanciarsi (in)
launching ['lɔːntʃɪŋ] *n* lancio; varo
launch pad, launching pad *n* rampa di lancio
launder ['lɔːndə^r] *vt* lavare e stirare
Launderette® [lɔːn'drɛt], (US) **Laundromat**® ['lɔːndrəmæt] *n* lavanderia (automatica)
laundry ['lɔːndrɪ] *n* lavanderia; (*clothes*) biancheria; **to do the ~** fare il bucato
laureate ['lɔːrɪət] *adj see* **poet laureate**
laurel ['lɔrl] *n* lauro, alloro; **to rest on one's laurels** riposare *or* dormire sugli allori
Lausanne [ləu'zæn] *n* Losanna
lava ['lɑːvə] *n* lava
lavatory ['lævətərɪ] *n* gabinetto
lavatory paper *n* (*Brit*) carta igienica
lavender ['lævəndə^r] *n* lavanda
lavish ['lævɪʃ] *adj* abbondante; sontuoso(-a); (*giving freely*): **~ with** prodigo(-a) di, largo(-a) in ■ *vt*: **to ~ sth on sb/sth** profondere qc a qn/qc
lavishly ['lævɪʃlɪ] *adv* (*give, spend*) generosamente; (*furnished*) sontuosamente, lussuosamente
law [lɔː] *n* legge *f*; **against the ~** contro la legge; **to study ~** studiare diritto; **to go to ~** (*Brit*) ricorrere alle vie legali; **civil/criminal ~** diritto civile/penale
law-abiding ['lɔːəbaɪdɪŋ] *adj* ubbidiente alla legge
law and order *n* l'ordine *m* pubblico
lawbreaker ['lɔːbreɪkə^r] *n* violatore(-trice) della legge
law court *n* tribunale *m*, corte *f* di giustizia
lawful ['lɔːful] *adj* legale
lawfully ['lɔːfəlɪ] *adv* legalmente
lawless ['lɔːlɪs] *adj* senza legge; illegale
Law Lords *npl* ≈ Corte *f* Suprema
lawmaker ['lɔːmeɪkə^r] *n* legislatore *m*
lawn [lɔːn] *n* tappeto erboso
lawnmower ['lɔːnməuə^r] *n* tosaerba *m or f inv*
lawn tennis *n* tennis *m* su prato
law school *n* facoltà *f inv* di legge
law student *n* studente(-essa) di legge
lawsuit ['lɔːsuːt] *n* processo, causa; **to bring a ~ against** intentare causa a
lawyer ['lɔːjə^r] *n* (*consultant, with company*) giurista *m/f*; (*for sales, wills etc*) ≈ notaio; (*partner, in court*) ≈ avvocato(-essa)
lax [læks] *adj* (*conduct*) rilassato(-a); (*person*: *careless*) negligente; (: *on discipline*) permissivo(-a)
laxative ['læksətɪv] *n* lassativo
laxity ['læksɪtɪ] *n* rilassatezza; negligenza
lay [leɪ] *pt of* **lie** ■ *adj* laico(-a); secolare ■ *vt* (*pt, pp* **laid**) [leɪd] posare, mettere; (*eggs*) fare; (*trap*) tendere; (*plans*) fare, elaborare; **to ~ the table** apparecchiare la tavola; **to ~ the facts/one's proposals before sb** presentare i fatti/delle proposte a qn; **to get laid** (*col!*) scopare (*!*), essere scopato(-a) (*!*)
▸ **lay aside, lay by** *vt* mettere da parte
▸ **lay down** *vt* mettere giù; **to ~ down the law** (*fig*) dettar legge
▸ **lay in** *vt* fare una scorta di
▸ **lay into** *vt fus* (*col*: *attack, scold*) aggredire
▸ **lay off** *vt* (*workers*) licenziare
▸ **lay on** *vt* (*water, gas*) installare, mettere; (*provide*: *meal etc*) fornire; (*paint*) applicare
▸ **lay out** *vt* (*design*) progettare; (*display*) presentare; (*spend*) sborsare
▸ **lay up** *vt* (*to store*) accumulare; (*ship*) mettere in disarmo; (*illness*) costringere a letto
layabout ['leɪəbaut] *n* sfaccendato(-a), fannullone(-a)
lay-by ['leɪbaɪ] *n* (*Brit*) piazzola (di sosta)
lay days *npl* (*Naut*) stallie *fpl*
layer ['leɪə^r] *n* strato
layette [leɪ'ɛt] *n* corredino (per neonato)
layman ['leɪmən] *n* laico; profano
lay-off ['leɪɔf] *n* sospensione *f*, licenziamento
layout ['leɪaut] *n* lay-out *m inv*, disposizione *f*; (*Press*) impaginazione *f*
laze [leɪz] *vi* oziare
laziness ['leɪzɪnɪs] *n* pigrizia
lazy ['leɪzɪ] *adj* pigro(-a)
lb. *abbr* (= *libra*: *pound*) lb.
lbw *abbr* (*Cricket*: = *leg before wicket*) *fallo dovuto al fatto che il giocatore ha la gamba davanti alla porta*
LC *n abbr* (US) = **Library of Congress**
lc *abbr* (*Typ*) = **lower case**
L/C *abbr* = **letter of credit**
LCD *n abbr* = **liquid crystal display**
Ld *abbr* (*Brit*: = *lord*) *titolo*
LDS *n abbr* (*Brit*: = *Licentiate in Dental Surgery*) *specializzazione dopo la laurea*; (= *Latter-day Saints*) *Chiesa di Gesù Cristo dei Santi dell'Ultimo Giorno*

LEA *n abbr* (*Brit*: = *local education authority*) ≈ Provveditorato degli Studi
lead[1] [li:d] *n* (*front position*) posizione *f* di testa; (*distance, time ahead*) vantaggio; (*clue*) indizio; (*Elec*) filo (elettrico); (*for dog*) guinzaglio; (*Theat*) parte *f* principale ■ *vb* (*pt, pp* **led**) [lɛd] *vt* menare, guidare, condurre; (*induce*) indurre; (*be leader of*) essere a capo di; (: *orchestra*: *Brit*) essere il primo violino di; (: *US*) dirigere; (*Sport*) essere in testa a ■ *vi* condurre, essere in testa; **to be in the ~** (*Sport*) essere in testa; **to take the ~** (*Sport*) passare in testa; (*fig*) prendere l'iniziativa; **to ~ to** menare a; condurre a; portare a; **to ~ astray** sviare; **to ~ sb to believe that ...** far credere a qn che ...; **to ~ sb to do sth** portare qn a fare qc
▸ **lead away** *vt* condurre via
▸ **lead back** *vt* riportare, ricondurre
▸ **lead off** *vt* portare ■ *vi* partire da
▸ **lead on** *vt* (*tease*) tenere sulla corda
▸ **lead on to** *vt* (*induce*) portare a
▸ **lead up to** *vt fus* portare a; (*fig*) preparare la strada per
lead[2] [lɛd] (*metal*) piombo; (*in pencil*) mina
leaded ['lɛdɪd] *adj* (*petrol*) con piombo; **~ windows** vetrate *fpl* (artistiche)
leaden ['lɛdn] *adj* di piombo
leader ['li:dəʳ] *n* capo; leader *m inv*; (*in newspaper*) articolo di fondo; **they are leaders in their field** (*fig*) sono all'avanguardia nel loro campo; **the L~ of the House** (*Brit*) il capo della maggioranza ministeriale
leadership ['li:dəʃɪp] *n* direzione *f*; **under the ~ of ...** sotto la direzione *or* guida di ...; **qualities of ~** qualità *fpl* di un capo
lead-free ['lɛdfri:] *adj* senza piombo
leading ['li:dɪŋ] *adj* primo(-a), principale; **a ~ question** una domanda tendenziosa; **~ role** ruolo principale
leading lady *n* (*Theat*) prima attrice
leading light *n* (*person*) personaggio di primo piano
leading man *n* (*Theat*) primo attore
lead pencil [lɛd-] *n* matita con la mina di grafite
lead poisoning [lɛd-] *n* saturnismo
lead time [li:d-] *n* (*Comm*) tempo di consegna
lead weight [lɛd-] *n* piombino, piombo
leaf [li:f] *n* (*pl* **leaves**) foglia; (*of table*) ribalta; **to turn over a new ~** (*fig*) cambiar vita; **to take a ~ out of sb's book** (*fig*) prendere esempio da qn
▸ **leaf through** *vt* (*book*) sfogliare
leaflet ['li:flɪt] *n* dépliant *m inv*; (*Pol, Rel*) volantino
leafy ['li:fɪ] *adj* ricco(-a) di foglie
league [li:g] *n* lega; (*Football*) campionato; **to be in ~ with** essere in lega con
league table *n* classifica
leak [li:k] *n* (*out*) fuga; (*in*) infiltrazione *f*; (*fig*: *of information*) fuga di notizie ■ *vi* (*roof, bucket*) perdere; (*liquid*) uscire; (*shoes*) lasciar passare l'acqua ■ *vt* (*liquid*) spandere; (*information*) divulgare
▸ **leak out** *vi* uscire; (*information*) trapelare
leakage ['li:kɪdʒ] *n* (*of water, gas etc*) perdita
leaky ['li:kɪ] *adj* (*pipe, bucket, roof*) che perde; (*shoe*) che lascia passare l'acqua; (*boat*) che fa acqua
lean [li:n] *adj* magro(-a) ■ *n* (*of meat*) carne *f* magra ■ *vb* (*pt, pp* **leaned** *or* **leant**) [lɛnt] *vt*: **to ~ sth on** appoggiare qc su ■ *vi* (*slope*) pendere; (*rest*): **to ~ against** appoggiarsi contro; essere appoggiato(-a) a; **to ~ on** appoggiarsi a
▸ **lean back** *vi* sporgersi indietro
▸ **lean forward** *vi* sporgersi in avanti
▸ **lean out** *vi*: **to ~ out (of)** sporgersi (da)
▸ **lean over** *vi* inclinarsi
leaning ['li:nɪŋ] *n*: **~ (towards)** propensione *f* (per) ■ *adj* inclinato(-a), pendente; **the L~ Tower of Pisa** la torre (pendente) di Pisa
leant [lɛnt] *pt, pp of* **lean**
lean-to ['li:ntu:] *n* (*roof*) tettoia; (*building*) *edificio con tetto appoggiato ad altro edificio*
leap [li:p] *n* salto, balzo ■ *vi* (*pt, pp* **leaped** *or* **leapt**) [lɛpt] saltare, balzare; **to ~ at an offer** afferrare al volo una proposta
▸ **leap up** *vi* (*person*) alzarsi d'un balzo, balzare su
leapfrog ['li:pfrɔg] *n* gioco della cavallina ■ *vi*: **to ~ over sb/sth** saltare (alla cavallina) qn/qc
leapt [lɛpt] *pt, pp of* **leap**
leap year *n* anno bisestile
learn (*pt, pp* **learned** *or* **learnt**) [lə:n, -t] *vt, vi* imparare; **to ~ how to do sth** imparare a fare qc; **to ~ that ...** apprendere che ...; **to ~ about sth** (*Scol*) studiare qc; (*hear*) apprendere qc; **we were sorry to ~ that it was closing down** la notizia della chiusura ci ha fatto dispiacere
learned ['lə:nɪd] *adj* erudito(-a), dotto(-a)
learner ['lə:nəʳ] *n* principiante *m/f*; apprendista *m/f*; **he's a ~ (driver)** (*Brit*) sta imparando a guidare
learning ['lə:nɪŋ] *n* erudizione *f*, sapienza
learnt [lə:nt] *pt, pp of* **learn**
lease [li:s] *n* contratto d'affitto ■ *vt* affittare; **on ~** in affitto
▸ **lease back** *vt* effettuare un lease-back *inv*
leaseback ['li:sbæk] *n* lease-back *m inv*

leasehold ['li:shəuld] *n* (*contract*) contratto di affitto (*a lungo termine con responsabilità simili a quelle di un proprietario*) ■ *adj* in affitto
leash [li:ʃ] *n* guinzaglio
least [li:st] *adj*: **the ~** (+*noun*) il/la più piccolo(-a), il/la minimo(-a); (*smallest amount of*) il/la meno ■ *adv*: **the ~** (+*adjective*): **the ~ beautiful girl** la ragazza meno bella; **the ~ expensive** il/la meno caro(-a); **I have the ~ money** ho meno denaro di tutti; **at ~** almeno; **not in the ~** affatto, per nulla
leather ['lɛðə^r] *n* (*soft*) pelle *f*; (*hard*) cuoio ■ *cpd* di *or* in pelle; di cuoio; **~ goods** pelletteria, pelletterie *fpl*
leave [li:v] *vb* (*pt, pp* **left**) [lɛft] *vt* lasciare; (*go away from*) partire da ■ *vi* partire, andarsene ■ *n* (*time off*) congedo; (*Mil*) licenza; **to be left** rimanere; **there's some milk left over** c'è rimasto del latte; **to take one's ~ of** congedarsi di; **he's already left for the airport** è già uscito per andare all'aeroporto; **to ~ school** finire la scuola; **~ it to me!** ci penso io!, lascia fare a me!; **on ~** in congedo; **on ~ of absence** in permesso; (*public employee*) in congedo; (*Mil*) in licenza
▸ **leave behind** *vt* (*also fig*) lasciare indietro; (*forget*) dimenticare
▸ **leave off** *vt* non mettere; (*Brit col: stop*): **to ~ off doing sth** smetterla *or* piantarla di fare qc
▸ **leave on** *vt* lasciare su; (*light, fire, cooker*) lasciare acceso(-a)
▸ **leave out** *vt* omettere, tralasciare
leaves [li:vz] *npl of* **leaf**
leavetaking ['li:vteɪkɪŋ] *n* commiato, addio
Lebanese [lɛbə'ni:z] *adj, n* (*pl inv*) libanese (*m/f*)
Lebanon ['lɛbənən] *n* Libano
lecherous ['lɛtʃərəs] *adj* lascivo(-a), lubrico(-a)
lectern ['lɛktə:n] *n* leggio
lecture ['lɛktʃə^r] *n* conferenza; (*Scol*) lezione *f* ■ *vi* fare conferenze; fare lezioni; (*reprove*) rimproverare, fare una ramanzina a; **to ~ on** fare una conferenza su; **to give a ~ (on)** (*Brit*) fare una conferenza (su); fare lezione (su)
lecture hall *n* aula magna
lecturer ['lɛktʃərə^r] *n* (*speaker*) conferenziere(-a); (*Brit: at university*) professore(-essa), docente *m/f*; **assistant ~** (*Brit*) ≈ professore(-essa) associato(-a); **senior ~** (*Brit*) ≈ professore(-essa) ordinario(-a)
lecture theatre *n* = **lecture hall**
LED *n abbr* (*Elec: = light-emitting diode*) diodo a emissione luminosa
led [lɛd] *pt, pp of* **lead'**
ledge [lɛdʒ] *n* (*of window*) davanzale *m*; (*on wall etc*) sporgenza; (*of mountain*) cornice *f*, cengia
ledger ['lɛdʒə^r] *n* libro maestro, registro
lee [li:] *n* lato sottovento; **in the ~ of** a ridosso di, al riparo di
leech [li:tʃ] *n* sanguisuga
leek [li:k] *n* porro
leer [lɪə^r] *vi*: **to ~ at sb** gettare uno sguardo voglioso (*or* maligno) su qn
leeward ['li:wəd] *adj* sottovento *inv* ■ *n* lato sottovento; **to ~** sottovento
leeway ['li:weɪ] *n* (*fig*): **to have some ~** avere una certa libertà di agire
left [lɛft] *pt, pp of* **leave** ■ *adj* sinistro(-a) ■ *adv* a sinistra ■ *n* sinistra; **on the ~, to the ~** a sinistra; **the L~** (*Pol*) la sinistra
left-click ['leftklɪk] *vi* (*Comput*): **to ~ on** fare clic con il pulsante sinistro del mouse su
left-hand drive ['lɛfthænd-] *n* (*Brit*) guida a sinistra
left-handed [lɛft'hændɪd] *adj* mancino(-a); **~ scissors** forbici *fpl* per mancini
left-hand side ['lɛfthænd-] *n* lato *or* fianco sinistro
leftie ['lɛftɪ] *n*: **a ~** (*col*) uno(-a) di sinistra
leftist ['lɛftɪst] *adj* (*Pol*) di sinistra
left-luggage [lɛft'lʌgɪdʒ], **left-luggage office** [lɛft'lʌgɪdʒ-] *n* deposito *m* bagagli *inv*
left-overs ['lɛftəuvəz] *npl* avanzi *mpl*, resti *mpl*
left wing *n* (*Mil, Sport*) ala sinistra; (*Pol*) sinistra ■ *adj*: **left-wing** (*Pol*) di sinistra
left-winger [lɛft'wɪŋə^r] *n* (*Pol*) uno(-a) di sinistra; (*Sport*) ala sinistra
lefty ['lɛftɪ] *n* = **leftie**
leg [lɛg] *n* gamba; (*of animal*) zampa; (*of furniture*) piede *m*; (*Culin: of chicken*) coscia; (*of journey*) tappa; **1st/2nd ~** (*Sport*) partita di andata/ritorno; **~ of lamb** (*Culin*) cosciotto d'agnello; **to stretch one's legs** sgranchirsi le gambe
legacy ['lɛgəsɪ] *n* eredità *f inv*; (*fig*) retaggio
legal ['li:gl] *adj* legale; **to take ~ action** *or* **proceedings against sb** intentare un'azione legale contro qn, far causa a qn
legal adviser *n* consulente *m/f* legale
legality [lɪ'gælɪtɪ] *n* legalità
legalize ['li:gəlaɪz] *vt* legalizzare
legally ['li:gəlɪ] *adv* legalmente; **~ binding** legalmente vincolante
legal tender *n* moneta legale
legation [lɪ'geɪʃən] *n* legazione *f*
legend ['lɛdʒənd] *n* leggenda
legendary ['lɛdʒəndərɪ] *adj* leggendario(-a)
-legged ['lɛgɪd] *suffix*: **two~** a due gambe (*or* zampe), bipede
leggings ['lɛgɪŋz] *npl* ghette *fpl*
leggy ['lɛgɪ] *adj* dalle gambe lunghe
legibility [lɛdʒɪ'bɪlɪtɪ] *n* leggibilità

legible ['lɛdʒəbl] *adj* leggibile
legibly ['lɛdʒəblɪ] *adv* in modo leggibile
legion ['li:dʒən] *n* legione *f*
legionnaire [li:dʒə'nɛə^r] *n* legionario; **~'s disease** morbo del legionario
legislate ['lɛdʒɪsleɪt] *vi* legiferare
legislation [lɛdʒɪs'leɪʃən] *n* legislazione *f*; **a piece of ~** una legge
legislative ['lɛdʒɪslətɪv] *adj* legislativo(-a)
legislator ['lɛdʒɪsleɪtə^r] *n* legislatore(-trice)
legislature ['lɛdʒɪslətʃə^r] *n* corpo legislativo
legitimacy [lɪ'dʒɪtɪməsɪ] *n* legittimità
legitimate [lɪ'dʒɪtɪmət] *adj* legittimo(-a)
legitimize [lɪ'dʒɪtɪmaɪz] *vt* (*gen*) legalizzare, rendere legale; (*child*) legittimare
legless ['lɛglɪs] *adj* (*Brit col*) sbronzo(-a), fatto(-a)
leg-room ['lɛgru:m] *n* spazio per le gambe
Leics *abbr* (*Brit*) = **Leicestershire**
leisure ['lɛʒə^r] *n* agio, tempo libero; ricreazioni *fpl*; **at ~** all'agio; a proprio comodo
leisure centre *n* centro di ricreazione
leisurely ['lɛʒəlɪ] *adj* tranquillo(-a), fatto(-a) con comodo *or* senza fretta
leisure suit *n* (*Brit*) tuta (da ginnastica)
lemon ['lɛmən] *n* limone *m*
lemonade [lɛmə'neɪd] *n* limonata
lemon cheese, lemon curd *n* crema di limone (*che si spalma sul pane etc*)
lemon juice *n* succo di limone
lemon squeezer *n* spremiagrumi *m inv*
lemon tea *n* tè *m inv* al limone
lend (*pt, pp* **lent**) [lɛnd, lɛnt] *vt*: **to ~ sth (to sb)** prestare qc (a qn); **to ~ a hand** dare una mano
lender ['lɛndə^r] *n* prestatore(-trice)
lending library ['lɛndɪŋ-] *n* biblioteca circolante
length [lɛŋθ] *n* lunghezza; (*section: of road, pipe etc*) pezzo, tratto; **~ of time** periodo (di tempo); **what ~ is it?** quant'è lungo?; **it is 2 metres in ~** è lungo 2 metri; **to fall full ~** cadere lungo disteso; **at ~** (*at last*) finalmente, alla fine; (*lengthily*) a lungo; **to go to any ~(s) to do sth** fare qualsiasi cosa pur di *or* per fare qc
lengthen ['lɛŋθən] *vt* allungare, prolungare ▪ *vi* allungarsi
lengthways ['lɛŋθweɪz] *adv* per il lungo
lengthy ['lɛŋθɪ] *adj* molto lungo(-a)
leniency ['li:nɪənsɪ] *n* indulgenza, clemenza
lenient ['li:nɪənt] *adj* indulgente, clemente
leniently ['li:nɪəntlɪ] *adv* con indulgenza
lens [lɛnz] *n* lente *f*; (*of camera*) obiettivo
Lent [lɛnt] *n* Quaresima
lent [lɛnt] *pt, pp of* **lend**
lentil ['lɛntl] *n* lenticchia
Leo ['li:əu] *n* Leone *m*; **to be ~** essere del Leone
leopard ['lɛpəd] *n* leopardo
leotard ['li:əta:d] *n* calzamaglia
leper ['lɛpə^r] *n* lebbroso(-a)
leper colony *n* lebbrosario
leprosy ['lɛprəsɪ] *n* lebbra
lesbian ['lɛzbɪən] *n* lesbica ▪ *adj* lesbico(-a)
lesion ['li:ʒən] *n* (*Med*) lesione *f*
Lesotho [lɪ'su:tu] *n* Lesotho *m*
less [lɛs] *adj, pron, adv* meno; **~ than you/ever** meno di lei/che mai; **~ than half** meno della metà; **~ and ~** sempre meno; **the ~ he works ...** meno lavora ...; **~ than £1/a kilo/3 metres** meno di una sterlina/un chilo/3 metri; **~ 5%** meno il 5%
lessee [lɛ'si:] *n* affittuario(-a), locatario(-a)
lessen ['lɛsn] *vi* diminuire, attenuarsi ▪ *vt* diminuire, ridurre
lesser ['lɛsə^r] *adj* minore, più piccolo(-a); **to a ~ extent** *or* **degree** in grado *or* misura minore
lesson ['lɛsn] *n* lezione *f*; **a maths ~** una lezione di matematica; **to give lessons in** dare *or* impartire lezioni di; **it taught him a ~** (*fig*) gli è servito di lezione
lessor ['lɛsɔ:^r, lɛ'sɔ:^r] *n* locatore(-trice)
lest [lɛst] *conj* per paura di + *infinitive*, per paura che + *sub*
let (*pt, pp* **~**) [lɛt] *vt* lasciare; (*Brit: lease*) dare in affitto; **to ~ sb do sth** lasciar fare qc a qn, lasciare che qn faccia qc; **to ~ sb know sth** far sapere qc a qn; **to ~ sb have sth** dare qc a qn; **he ~ me go** mi ha lasciato andare; **~ the water boil and ...** fate bollire l'acqua e ...; **~'s go** andiamo; **~ him come** lo lasci venire; **"to ~"** "affittasi"
▸ **let down** *vt* (*lower*) abbassare; (*dress*) allungare; (*hair*) sciogliere; (*disappoint*) deludere; (*Brit: tyre*) sgonfiare
▸ **let go** *vi* mollare ▪ *vt* mollare; (*allow to go*) lasciare andare
▸ **let in** *vt* lasciare entrare; (*visitor etc*) far entrare; **what have you ~ yourself in for?** in che guai *or* pasticci sei andato a cacciarti?
▸ **let off** *vt* (*allow to go*) lasciare andare; (*firework etc*) far partire; (*smell etc*) emettere; (*taxi driver, bus driver*) far scendere; **to ~ off steam** (*fig, col*) sfogarsi, scaricarsi
▸ **let on** *vi* (*col*): **to ~ on that ...** lasciar capire che ...
▸ **let out** *vt* lasciare uscire; (*dress*) allargare; (*scream*) emettere; (*rent out*) affittare, dare in affitto
▸ **let up** *vi* diminuire
let-down ['lɛtdaun] *n* (*disappointment*) delusione *f*

lethal ['li:θl] *adj* letale, mortale
lethargic [lɛ'θɑ:dʒɪk] *adj* letargico(-a)
lethargy ['lɛθədʒɪ] *n* letargia
letter ['lɛtəʳ] *n* lettera; **letters** *npl* (*Literature*) lettere; **small/capital ~** lettera minuscola/ maiuscola; **~ of credit** lettera di credito; **documentary ~ of credit** lettera di credito documentata
letter bomb *n* lettera esplosiva
letterbox ['lɛtəbɔks] *n* buca delle lettere
letterhead ['lɛtəhɛd] *n* intestazione *f*
lettering ['lɛtərɪŋ] *n* iscrizione *f*; caratteri *mpl*
letter-opener ['lɛtərəupnəʳ] *n* tagliacarte *m inv*
letterpress ['lɛtəprɛs] *n* (*method*) rilievografia
letter quality *n* (*of printer*) qualità di stampa
letters patent *npl* brevetto di invenzione
lettuce ['lɛtɪs] *n* lattuga, insalata
let-up ['lɛtʌp] *n* (*col*) interruzione *f*
leukaemia, (US) **leukemia** [lu:'ki:mɪə] *n* leucemia
level ['lɛvl] *adj* piatto(-a), piano(-a); orizzontale ■ *n* livello; (*also*: **spirit level**) livella (a bolla d'aria) ■ *vt* livellare, spianare; (*gun*) puntare (verso); (*accusation*): **to ~ (against)** lanciare (a *or* contro) ■ *vi* (*col*): **to ~ with sb** essere franco(-a) con qn; **to be ~ with** essere alla pari di; **a ~ spoonful** (*Culin*) un cucchiaio raso; **to draw ~ with** (*team*) mettersi alla pari di; (*runner, car*) affiancarsi a; **A levels** *npl* (*Brit*) ≈ esami *mpl* di maturità; **O levels** *npl* (*Brit: formerly*) *diploma di istruzione secondaria conseguito a 16 anni in Inghilterra e Galles, ora sostituito dal* GCSE; **on the ~** piatto(-a); (*fig*) onesto(-a)
▸ **level off, level out** *vi* (*prices etc*) stabilizzarsi; (*ground*) diventare pianeggiante; (*aircraft*) volare in quota
level crossing *n* (*Brit*) passaggio a livello
level-headed [lɛvl'hɛdɪd] *adj* equilibrato(-a)
levelling, (US) **leveling** ['lɛvlɪŋ] *adj* (*process, effect*) di livellamento
level playing field *n*: **to compete on a ~** (*fig*) competere ad armi pari
lever ['li:vəʳ] *n* leva ■ *vt*: **to ~ up/out** sollevare/estrarre con una leva
leverage ['li:vərɪdʒ] *n*: **~ (on** *or* **with)** ascendente *m* (su)
levity ['lɛvɪtɪ] *n* leggerezza, frivolità
levy ['lɛvɪ] *n* tassa, imposta ■ *vt* imporre
lewd [lu:d] *adj* osceno(-a), lascivo(-a)
lexicographer [lɛksɪ'kɔgrəfəʳ] *n* lessicografo(-a)
lexicography [lɛksɪ'kɔgrəfɪ] *n* lessicografia
LGV *n abbr* (*Brit*: = *Large Goods Vehicle*) automezzo pesante
LI *abbr* (US) = **Long Island**
liabilities [laɪə'bɪlətɪz] *npl* debiti *mpl*; (*on balance sheet*) passivo
liability [laɪə'bɪlətɪ] *n* responsabilità *f inv*; (*handicap*) peso
liable ['laɪəbl] *adj* (*subject*): **~ to** soggetto(-a) a; passibile di; (*responsible*): **~ (for)** responsabile (di); (*likely*): **~ to do** propenso(-a) a fare; **to be ~ to a fine** essere passibile di multa
liaise [li:'eɪz] *vi*: **to ~ (with)** mantenere i contatti (con)
liaison [li:'eɪzɔn] *n* relazione *f*; (*Mil*) collegamento
liar ['laɪəʳ] *n* bugiardo(-a)
libel ['laɪbl] *n* libello, diffamazione *f* ■ *vt* diffamare
libellous, (US) **libelous** ['laɪbləs] *adj* diffamatorio(-a)
liberal ['lɪbərl] *adj* liberale; (*generous*): **to be ~ with** distribuire liberalmente ■ *n* (*Pol*): **L~** liberale *m/f*
Liberal Democrat *n* liberaldemocratico(-a)
liberality [lɪbə'rælɪtɪ] *n* (*generosity*) generosità, liberalità
liberalize ['lɪbərəlaɪz] *vt* liberalizzare
liberal-minded [lɪbərl'maɪndɪd] *adj* tollerante
liberate ['lɪbəreɪt] *vt* liberare
liberation [lɪbə'reɪʃən] *n* liberazione *f*
liberation theology *n* teologia della liberazione
Liberia [laɪ'bɪərɪə] *n* Liberia
Liberian [laɪ'bɪərɪən] *adj, n* liberiano(-a)
liberty ['lɪbətɪ] *n* libertà *f inv*; **at ~ to do** libero(-a) di fare; **to take the ~ of** prendersi la libertà di, permettersi di
libido [lɪ'bi:dəu] *n* libido *f*
Libra ['li:brə] *n* Bilancia; **to be ~** essere della Bilancia
librarian [laɪ'brɛərɪən] *n* bibliotecario(-a)
library ['laɪbrərɪ] *n* biblioteca
library book *n* libro della biblioteca
libretto [lɪ'brɛtəu] *n* libretto
Libya ['lɪbɪə] *n* Libia
Libyan ['lɪbɪən] *adj, n* libico(-a)
lice [laɪs] *npl of* **louse**
licence, (US) **license** ['laɪsns] *n* autorizzazione *f*, permesso; (*Comm*) licenza; (*Radio, TV*) canone *m*, abbonamento; (*also*: **driving licence**, (US) **driver's license**) patente *f* di guida; (*excessive freedom*) licenza; **import ~** licenza di importazione; **produced under ~** prodotto su licenza
licence number *n* (*Brit Aut*) numero di targa
license ['laɪsns] *n* US = **licence** ■ *vt* dare una licenza a; (*car*) pagare la tassa di circolazione *or* il bollo di
licensed ['laɪsnst] *adj* (*for alcohol*) che ha la licenza di vendere bibite alcoliche

licensed trade *n* commercio di bevande alcoliche con licenza speciale
licensee [laɪsən'si:] *n* (*Brit: of pub*) detentore(-trice) di autorizzazione alla vendita di bevande alcoliche
license plate *n* (*esp US Aut*) targa (automobilistica)
licentious [laɪ'sɛnʃəs] *adj* licenzioso(-a)
lichen ['laɪkən] *n* lichene *m*
lick [lɪk] *vt* leccare; (*col: defeat*) suonarle a, stracciare ■ *n* leccata; **a ~ of paint** una passata di vernice
licorice ['lɪkərɪs] *n* = **liquorice**
lid [lɪd] *n* coperchio; **to take the ~ off sth** (*fig*) smascherare qc
lido ['laɪdəu] *n* piscina all'aperto; (*part of the beach*) lido, stabilimento balneare
lie [laɪ] *n* bugia, menzogna ■ *vi* mentire, dire bugie (*pt* **lay**, *pp* **lain**) [leɪ, leɪn] (*rest*) giacere, star disteso(-a); (*in grave*) giacere, riposare; (*object: be situated*) trovarsi, essere; **to tell lies** raccontare *or* dire bugie; **to ~ low** (*fig*) latitare
▸ **lie about, lie around** *vi* (*things*) essere in giro; (*person*) bighellonare
▸ **lie back** *vi* stendersi
▸ **lie down** *vi* stendersi, sdraiarsi
▸ **lie up** *vi* (*hide*) nascondersi
Liechtenstein ['lɪktənstaɪn] *n* Liechtenstein *m*
lie detector *n* macchina della verità
lie-down ['laɪdaun] *n* (*Brit*): **to have a ~** sdraiarsi, riposarsi
lie-in ['laɪɪn] *n* (*Brit*): **to have a ~** rimanere a letto
lieu [lu:] *n*: **in ~ of** invece di, al posto di
Lieut. *abbr* (= *lieutenant*) Ten.
lieutenant [lɛf'tɛnənt, (*US*) lu:'tɛnənt] *n* tenente *m*
lieutenant-colonel [lɛf'tɛnənt'kə:nl, (*US*) lu:'tɛnənt'kə:nl] *n* tenente colonnello
life [laɪf] *n* (*pl* **lives**) vita ■ *cpd* di vita; della vita; a vita; **country/city ~** vita di campagna/di città; **to be sent to prison for ~** essere condannato all'ergastolo; **true to ~** fedele alla realtà; **to paint from ~** dipingere dal vero
life annuity *n* rendita vitalizia
life assurance *n* (*Brit*) = **life insurance**
lifebelt ['laɪfbɛlt] *n* (*Brit*) salvagente *m*
lifeblood ['laɪfblʌd] *n* (*fig*) linfa vitale
lifeboat ['laɪfbəut] *n* scialuppa di salvataggio
life expectancy *n* durata media della vita
lifeguard ['laɪfgɑ:d] *n* bagnino
life imprisonment *n* ergastolo
life insurance *n* assicurazione *f* sulla vita
life jacket *n* giubbotto di salvataggio
lifeless ['laɪflɪs] *adj* senza vita
lifelike ['laɪflaɪk] *adj* che sembra vero(-a); rassomigliante
lifeline ['laɪflaɪn] *n* cavo di salvataggio
lifelong ['laɪflɔŋ] *adj* per tutta la vita
life preserver *n* (*US*) salvagente *m*; giubbotto di salvataggio; (*Brit*) sfollagente *m inv*
lifer ['laɪfə^r] *n* (*col*) ergastolano(-a)
life-raft ['laɪfrɑ:ft] *n* zattera di salvataggio
life-saver ['laɪfseɪvə^r] *n* bagnino
life sentence *n* (condanna all')ergastolo
life-sized ['laɪfsaɪzd] *adj* a grandezza naturale
life span *n* (durata della) vita
life style *n* stile *m* di vita
life support system *n* (*Med*) respiratore *m* automatico
lifetime ['laɪftaɪm] *n*: **in his ~** durante la sua vita; **in a ~** nell'arco della vita; in tutta la vita; **the chance of a ~** un'occasione unica
lift [lɪft] *vt* sollevare, levare; (*steal*) prendere, rubare ■ *vi* (*fog*) alzarsi ■ *n* (*Brit: elevator*) ascensore *m*; **to give sb a ~** (*Brit*) dare un passaggio a qn
▸ **lift off** *vt* togliere ■ *vi* (*rocket*) partire; (*helicopter*) decollare
▸ **lift out** *vt* tirar fuori; (*troops, evacuees etc*) far evacuare per mezzo di elicotteri (*or* aerei)
▸ **lift up** *vt* sollevare, alzare
lift-off ['lɪftɔf] *n* decollo
ligament ['lɪgəmənt] *n* legamento
light [laɪt] *n* luce *f*, lume *m*; (*daylight*) luce, giorno; (*lamp*) lampada; (*Aut: rear light*) luce di posizione; (*: headlamp*) fanale *m*; (*for cigarette etc*): **have you got a ~?** ha da accendere? ■ *vt* (*pt, pp* **lighted**, *pt, pp* **lit**) [lɪt] (*candle, cigarette, fire*) accendere; (*room*) illuminare ■ *adj* (*room, colour*) chiaro(-a); (*not heavy, also fig*) leggero(-a) ■ *adv* (*travel*) con poco bagaglio; **lights** *npl* (*Aut: traffic lights*) semaforo; **in the ~ of** alla luce di; **to turn the ~ on/off** accendere/spegnere la luce; **to come to ~** venire in luce; **to cast** *or* **shed** *or* **throw ~ on** gettare luce su; **to make ~ of sth** (*fig*) prendere alla leggera qc, non dar peso a qc
▸ **light up** *vi* illuminarsi ■ *vt* illuminare
light bulb *n* lampadina
lighten ['laɪtn] *vi* schiarirsi ■ *vt* (*give light to*) illuminare; (*make lighter*) schiarire; (*make less heavy*) alleggerire
lighter ['laɪtə^r] *n* (*also*: **cigarette lighter**) accendino; (*boat*) chiatta
light-fingered [laɪt'fɪŋgəd] *adj* lesto(-a) di mano
light-headed ['laɪt'hɛdɪd] *adj* stordito(-a)
light-hearted ['laɪt'hɑ:tɪd] *adj* gioioso(-a), gaio(-a)

l

lighthouse ['laɪthaus] *n* faro
lighting ['laɪtɪŋ] *n* illuminazione *f*
lighting-up time ['laɪtɪŋʌp-] *n* (*Brit*) *orario per l'accensione delle luci*
lightly ['laɪtlɪ] *adv* leggermente; **to get off ~** cavarsela a buon mercato
light meter *n* (*Phot*) esposimetro
lightness ['laɪtnɪs] *n* chiarezza; (*in weight*) leggerezza
lightning ['laɪtnɪŋ] *n* lampo, fulmine *m*; **a flash of ~** un lampo, un fulmine
lightning conductor, (*US*) **lightning rod** *n* parafulmine *m*
lightning strike *n* (*Brit*) sciopero *m* lampo *inv*
light pen *n* penna luminosa
lightship ['laɪtʃɪp] *n* battello *m* faro *inv*
lightweight ['laɪtweɪt] *adj* (*suit*) leggero(-a); (*boxer*) peso leggero *inv*
light year ['laɪtjɪəʳ] *n* anno *m* luce *inv*
Ligurian [lɪ'gjuərɪən] *adj, n* ligure (*m/f*)
like [laɪk] *vt* (*person*) volere bene a; (*activity, object, food*): **I ~ swimming/that book/chocolate** mi piace nuotare/quel libro/il cioccolato ■ *prep* come ■ *adj* simile, uguale ■ *n*: **the ~** uno(-a) uguale; **I would ~, I'd ~** mi piacerebbe, vorrei; **would you ~ a coffee?** gradirebbe un caffè?; **if you ~** se vuoi; **to be/look ~ sb/sth** somigliare a qn/qc; **what's he ~?** che tipo è?, com'è?; **what's the weather ~?** che tempo fa?; **that's just ~ him** è proprio da lui; **something ~ that** qualcosa del genere; **I feel ~ a drink** avrei voglia di bere qualcosa; **there's nothing ~ ...** non c'è niente di meglio di *or* niente come ...; **his likes and dislikes** i suoi gusti
likeable ['laɪkəbl] *adj* simpatico(-a)
likelihood ['laɪklɪhud] *n* probabilità; **in all ~** con ogni probabilità, molto probabilmente
likely ['laɪklɪ] *adj* probabile; plausibile; **he's ~ to leave** probabilmente partirà, è probabile che parta; **not ~!** (*col*) neanche per sogno!
like-minded ['laɪk'maɪndɪd] *adj* che pensa allo stesso modo
liken ['laɪkən] *vt*: **to ~ sth to** paragonare qc a
likeness ['laɪknɪs] *n* (*similarity*) somiglianza
likewise ['laɪkwaɪz] *adv* similmente, nello stesso modo
liking ['laɪkɪŋ] *n*: **~ (for)** simpatia (per); debole *m* (per); **to be to sb's ~** essere di gusto *or* gradimento di qn; **to take a ~ to sb** prendere qn in simpatia
lilac ['laɪlək] *n* lilla *m inv* ■ *adj* lilla *inv*
Lilo® ['laɪləu] *n* materassino gonfiabile
lilt [lɪlt] *n* cadenza
lilting ['lɪltɪŋ] *adj* melodioso(-a)
lily ['lɪlɪ] *n* giglio; **~ of the valley** mughetto
Lima ['li:mə] *n* Lima
limb [lɪm] *n* membro; **to be out on a ~** (*fig*) sentirsi spaesato *or* tagliato fuori
limber ['lɪmbəʳ]: **to ~ up** *vi* riscaldarsi i muscoli
limbo ['lɪmbəu] *n*: **to be in ~** (*fig*) essere lasciato(-a) nel dimenticatoio
lime [laɪm] *n* (*tree*) tiglio; (*fruit*) limetta; (*Geo*) calce *f*
lime juice *n* succo di limetta
limelight ['laɪmlaɪt] *n*: **in the ~** (*fig*) alla ribalta, in vista
limerick ['lɪmərɪk] *n* *poesiola umoristica di cinque versi*
limestone ['laɪmstəun] *n* pietra calcarea; (*Geo*) calcare *m*
limit ['lɪmɪt] *n* limite *m* ■ *vt* limitare; **weight/speed ~** limite di peso/di velocità; **within limits** entro certi limiti
limitation [lɪmɪ'teɪʃən] *n* limitazione *f*, limite *m*
limited ['lɪmɪtɪd] *adj* limitato(-a), ristretto(-a); **~ edition** edizione *f* a bassa tiratura
limited company, limited liability company *n* (*Brit*) ≈ società *f inv* a responsabilità limitata (S.r.l.)
limitless ['lɪmɪtlɪs] *adj* illimitato(-a)
limousine ['lɪməzi:n] *n* limousine *f inv*
limp [lɪmp] *n*: **to have a ~** zoppicare ■ *vi* zoppicare ■ *adj* floscio(-a), flaccido(-a)
limpet ['lɪmpɪt] *n* patella
limpid ['lɪmpɪd] *adj* (*poet*) limpido(-a)
linchpin ['lɪntʃpɪn] *n* acciarino, bietta; (*fig*) perno
Lincs *abbr* (*Brit*) = **Lincolnshire**
line [laɪn] *n* (*gen, Comm*) linea; (*rope*) corda; (*wire*) filo; (*of poem*) verso; (*row, series*) fila, riga; coda ■ *vt* (*clothes*): **to ~ (with)** foderare (di); (*box*): **to ~ (with)** rivestire *or* foderare (di); (*trees, crowd*) fiancheggiare; **to cut in ~** (*US*) passare avanti; **in his ~ of business** nel suo ramo (di affari); **on the right lines** sulla buona strada; **a new ~ in cosmetics** una nuova linea di cosmetici; **hold the ~ please** (*Brit Tel*) resti in linea per cortesia; **to be in ~ for sth** (*fig*) essere in lista per qc; **in ~ with** d'accordo con, in linea con; **to bring sth into ~ with sth** mettere qc al passo con qc; **to draw the ~ at (doing) sth** (*fig*) rifiutarsi di fare qc; **to take the ~ that ...** essere del parere che ...
▸ **line up** *vi* allinearsi, mettersi in fila ■ *vt* mettere in fila; **to have sth lined up** avere qc in programma; **to have sb lined up** avere qn in mente
linear ['lɪnɪəʳ] *adj* lineare
lined [laɪnd] *adj* (*paper*) a righe, rigato(-a); (*face*) rugoso(-a); (*clothes*) foderato(-a)

line feed *n* (*Comput*) avanzamento di una interlinea
linen ['lɪnɪn] *n* biancheria, panni *mpl*; (*cloth*) tela di lino
line printer *n* stampante *f* parallela
liner ['laɪnə^r] *n* nave *f* di linea; **dustbin ~** sacchetto per la pattumiera
linesman ['laɪnzmən] *n* guardalinee *m inv*, segnalinee *m inv*
line-up ['laɪnʌp] *n* allineamento, fila; (*also*: **police line-up**) confronto all'americana; (*Sport*) formazione *f* di gioco
linger ['lɪŋgə^r] *vi* attardarsi; indugiare; (*smell, tradition*) persistere
lingerie ['lænʒəri:] *n* biancheria intima (femminile)
lingering ['lɪŋgərɪŋ] *adj* lungo(-a), persistente; (*death*) lento(-a)
lingo ['lɪŋgəu] *n* (*pl* **lingoes**) (*pej*) gergo
linguist ['lɪŋgwɪst] *n* linguista *m/f*; poliglotta *m/f*
linguistic [lɪŋ'gwɪstɪk] *adj* linguistico(-a)
linguistics [lɪŋ'gwɪstɪks] *n* linguistica
lining ['laɪnɪŋ] *n* fodera; (*Tech*) rivestimento (interno); (*of brake*) guarnizione *f*
link [lɪŋk] *n* (*of a chain*) anello; (*connection*) legame *m*, collegamento; (*Comput*) link, collegamento ■ *vt* collegare, unire, congiungere; (*Comput*) creare un collegamento con ■ *vi* (*Comput*): **to ~ to a site** creare un collegamento con un sitio; **rail ~** collegamento ferroviario; *see also* **links**
▸ **link up** *vt* collegare, unire ■ *vi* riunirsi; associarsi
links [lɪŋks] *npl* pista *or* terreno da golf
link-up ['lɪŋkʌp] *n* legame *m*; (*of roads*) nodo; (*of spaceships*) aggancio; (*Radio, TV*) collegamento
linoleum [lɪ'nəulɪəm] *n* linoleum *m inv*
linseed oil ['lɪnsi:d-] *n* olio di semi di lino
lint [lɪnt] *n* garza
lintel ['lɪntl] *n* architrave *f*
lion ['laɪən] *n* leone *m*
lion cub *n* leoncino
lioness ['laɪənɪs] *n* leonessa
lip [lɪp] *n* labbro; (*of cup etc*) orlo; (*insolence*) sfacciataggine *f*
liposuction ['lɪpəusʌkʃən] *n* liposuzione *f*
lipread ['lɪpri:d] *vi* leggere sulle labbra
lip salve *n* burro di cacao
lip service *n*: **to pay ~ to sth** essere favorevole a qc solo a parole
lipstick ['lɪpstɪk] *n* rossetto
liquefy ['lɪkwɪfaɪ] *vt* liquefare ■ *vi* liquefarsi
liqueur [lɪ'kjuə^r] *n* liquore *m*
liquid ['lɪkwɪd] *n* liquido ■ *adj* liquido(-a)
liquid assets *npl* attività *fpl* liquide, crediti *mpl* liquidi
liquidate ['lɪkwɪdeɪt] *vt* liquidare
liquidation [lɪkwɪ'deɪʃən] *n* liquidazione *f*; **to go into ~** andare in liquidazione
liquidator ['lɪkwɪdeɪtə^r] *n* liquidatore *m*
liquid crystal display *n* visualizzazione *f* a cristalli liquidi
liquidity [lɪ'kwɪdɪtɪ] *n* (*Comm*) liquidità
liquidize ['lɪkwɪdaɪz] *vt* (*Brit Culin*) passare al frullatore
liquidizer ['lɪkwɪdaɪzə^r] *n* (*Brit Culin*) frullatore *m* (a brocca)
liquor ['lɪkə^r] *n* alcool *m*
liquorice ['lɪkərɪs] *n* liquirizia
Lisbon ['lɪzbən] *n* Lisbona
lisp [lɪsp] *n* difetto nel pronunciare le sibilanti
lissom ['lɪsəm] *adj* leggiadro(-a)
list [lɪst] *n* lista, elenco; (*of ship*) sbandamento ■ *vt* (*write down*) mettere in lista; fare una lista di; (*enumerate*) elencare; (*Comput*) stampare (un prospetto di) ■ *vi* (*ship*) sbandare; **shopping ~** lista *or* nota della spesa
listed building ['lɪstəd-] *n* (*Archit*) edificio sotto la protezione delle Belle Arti
listed company *n* società quotata in Borsa
listen ['lɪsn] *vi* ascoltare; **to ~ to** ascoltare
listener ['lɪsnə^r] *n* ascoltatore(-trice)
listeria [lɪs'tɪərɪə] *n* listeria
listing ['lɪstɪŋ] *n* (*Comput*) lista stampata
listless ['lɪstlɪs] *adj* svogliato(-a); apatico(-a)
listlessly ['lɪstlɪslɪ] *adv* svogliatamente; apaticamente
list price *n* prezzo di listino
lit [lɪt] *pt, pp of* **light**
litany ['lɪtənɪ] *n* litania
liter ['li:tə^r] *n* (*US*) = **litre**
literacy ['lɪtərəsɪ] *n* il sapere leggere e scrivere
literacy campaign *n* lotta contro l'analfabetismo
literal ['lɪtərl] *adj* letterale
literally ['lɪtərəlɪ] *adv* alla lettera, letteralmente
literary ['lɪtərərɪ] *adj* letterario(-a)
literate ['lɪtərɪt] *adj* che sa leggere e scrivere
literature ['lɪtərɪtʃə^r] *n* letteratura; (*brochures etc*) materiale *m*
lithe [laɪð] *adj* agile, snello(-a)
lithography [lɪ'θɔgrəfɪ] *n* litografia
Lithuania [lɪθju'eɪnɪə] *n* Lituania
Lithuanian [lɪθju'eɪnɪən] *adj* lituano(-a) ■ *n* lituano(-a); (*Ling*) lituano
litigate ['lɪtɪgeɪt] *vt* muovere causa a ■ *vi* litigare
litigation [lɪtɪ'geɪʃən] *n* causa
litmus ['lɪtməs] *n*: **~ paper** cartina di tornasole

litre, (US) **liter** ['liːtəʳ] *n* litro
litter ['lɪtəʳ] *n* (*rubbish*) rifiuti *mpl*; (*young animals*) figliata ■ *vt* sparpagliare; lasciare rifiuti in; **littered with** coperto(-a) di
litter bin *n* (*Brit*) cestino per rifiuti
litter lout, (US) **litterbug** ['lɪtəbʌg] *n persona che butta per terra le cartacce o i rifiuti*
little ['lɪtl] *adj* (*small*) piccolo(-a); (*not much*) poco(-a) ■ *adv* poco; **a ~** un po' (di); **a ~ milk** un po' di latte; **with ~ difficulty** senza fatica *or* difficoltà; **~ by ~** a poco a poco; **as ~ as possible** il meno possibile; **for a ~ while** per un po'; **to make ~ of** dare poca importanza a; **~ finger** mignolo
little-known ['lɪtl'nəun] *adj* poco noto(-a)
liturgy ['lɪtədʒɪ] *n* liturgia
live[1] [lɪv] *vi* vivere; (*reside*) vivere, abitare; **to ~ in London** abitare a Londra; **to ~ together** vivere insieme, convivere
▶ **live down** *vt* far dimenticare (alla gente)
▶ **live in** *vi* essere interno(-a); avere vitto e alloggio
▶ **live off** *vi* (*land, fish etc*) vivere di; (*pej: parents etc*) vivere alle spalle *or* a spese di
▶ **live on** *vt fus* (*food*) vivere di ■ *vi* sopravvivere, continuare a vivere; **to ~ on £50 a week** vivere con 50 sterline la settimana
▶ **live out** *vi* (*Brit: students*) essere esterno(-a) ■ *vt*: **to ~ out one's days** *or* **life** trascorrere gli ultimi anni
▶ **live up** *vt*: **to ~ it up** (*col*) fare la bella vita
▶ **live up to** *vt fus* tener fede a, non venir meno a
live[2] [laɪv] *adj* (*animal*) vivo(-a); (*issue*) scottante, d'attualità; (*wire*) sotto tensione; (*broadcast*) diretto(-a); (*ammunition: not blank*) carico(-a); (*unexploded*) inesploso(-a)
live-in ['lɪvɪn] *adj* (*col: partner*) convivente; (*servant*) che vive in casa; **he has a ~ girlfriend** la sua ragazza vive con lui
livelihood ['laɪvlɪhud] *n* mezzi *mpl* di sostentamento
liveliness ['laɪvlɪnəs] *n* vivacità
lively ['laɪvlɪ] *adj* vivace, vivo(-a)
liven up ['laɪvn-] *vt* (*room etc*) ravvivare; (*discussion, evening*) animare
liver ['lɪvəʳ] *n* fegato
liverish ['lɪvərɪʃ] *adj* che soffre di mal di fegato; (*fig*) scontroso(-a)
Liverpudlian [lɪvə'pʌdlɪən] *adj* di Liverpool ■ *n* abitante *m/f* di Liverpool; originario(-a) di Liverpool
livery ['lɪvərɪ] *n* livrea
lives [laɪvz] *npl of* **life**
livestock ['laɪvstɔk] *n* bestiame *m*
live wire [laɪv-] *n* (*col: fig*): **to be a ~** essere pieno(-a) di vitalità
livid ['lɪvɪd] *adj* livido(-a); (*furious*) livido(-a) di rabbia, furibondo(-a)
living ['lɪvɪŋ] *adj* vivo(-a), vivente ■ *n*: **to earn** *or* **make a ~** guadagnarsi la vita; **cost of ~** costo della vita, carovita *m*; **within ~ memory** a memoria d'uomo
living conditions *npl* condizioni *fpl* di vita
living expenses *npl* spese *fpl* di mantenimento
living room *n* soggiorno
living standards *npl* tenore *m* di vita
living wage *n* salario sufficiente per vivere
lizard ['lɪzəd] *n* lucertola
llama ['lɑːmə] *n* lama *m inv*
LLB *n abbr* (= *Bachelor of Laws*) ≈ laurea in legge
LLD *n abbr* (= *Doctor of Laws*) *titolo di studio*
LMT *abbr* (*US: = Local Mean Time*) tempo medio locale
load [ləud] *n* (*weight*) peso; (*Elec, Tech, thing carried*) carico ■ *vt*: **to ~ (with)** (*lorry, ship*) caricare (di); (*gun, camera*) caricare (con); **a ~ of, loads of** (*fig*) un sacco di; **to ~ a program** (*Comput*) caricare un programma
loaded ['ləudɪd] *adj* (*dice*) falsato(-a); (*question, word*) capzioso(-a); (*col: rich*) pieno(-a) di soldi
loading bay ['ləudɪŋ-] *n* piazzola di carico
loaf [ləuf] *n* (*pl* **loaves**) pane *m*, pagnotta ■ *vi* (*also:* **loaf about, loaf around**) bighellonare
loam [ləum] *n* terra di marna
loan [ləun] *n* prestito ■ *vt* dare in prestito; **on ~** in prestito
loan account *n* conto dei prestiti
loan capital *n* capitale *m* di prestito
loan shark *n* (*col: pej*) strozzino(-a)
loath [ləuθ] *adj*: **to be ~ to do** essere restio(-a) a fare
loathe [ləuð] *vt* detestare, aborrire
loathing ['ləuðɪŋ] *n* aborrimento, disgusto
loathsome ['ləuðsəm] *adj* (*gen*) ripugnante; (*person*) detestabile, odioso(-a)
loaves [ləuvz] *npl of* **loaf**
lob [lɔb] *vt* (*ball*) lanciare
lobby ['lɔbɪ] *n* atrio, vestibolo; (*Pol: pressure group*) gruppo di pressione ■ *vt* fare pressione su
lobbyist ['lɔbɪɪst] *n* appartenente *m/f* ad un gruppo di pressione
lobe [ləub] *n* lobo
lobster ['lɔbstəʳ] *n* aragosta
lobster pot *n* nassa per aragoste
local ['ləukl] *adj* locale ■ *n* (*Brit: pub*) ≈ bar *m inv* all'angolo; **the locals** *npl* la gente della zona
local anaesthetic *n* anestesia locale
local authority *n* autorità locale
local call *n* (*Tel*) telefonata urbana

local government *n* amministrazione *f* locale
locality [ləu'kælɪtɪ] *n* località *f inv*; (*position*) posto, luogo
localize ['ləukəlaɪz] *vt* localizzare
locally ['ləukəlɪ] *adv* da queste parti; nel vicinato
locate [ləu'keɪt] *vt* (*find*) trovare; (*situate*) collocare
location [ləu'keɪʃən] *n* posizione *f*; **on ~** (*Cine*) all'esterno
loch [lɔx] *n* lago
lock [lɔk] *n* (*of door, box*) serratura; (*of canal*) chiusa; (*of hair*) ciocca, riccio ■ *vt* (*with key*) chiudere a chiave; (*immobilize*) bloccare ■ *vi* (*door etc*) chiudersi; (*wheels*) bloccarsi, incepparsi; **~ stock and barrel** (*fig*) in blocco; **on full ~** (*Brit Aut*) a tutto sterzo
▸ **lock away** *vt* (*valuables*) tenere (rinchiuso(-a)) al sicuro; (*criminal*) metter dentro
▸ **lock out** *vt* chiudere fuori; **to ~ workers out** fare una serrata
▸ **lock up** *vi* chiudere tutto (a chiave)
locker ['lɔkəʳ] *n* armadietto
locket ['lɔkɪt] *n* medaglione *m*
lockjaw ['lɔkdʒɔː] *n* tetano
lockout ['lɔkaut] *n* (*Industry*) serrata
locksmith ['lɔksmɪθ] *n* magnano
lock-up ['lɔkʌp] *n* (*prison*) prigione *f*; (*cell*) guardina; (*also*: **lock-up garage**) box *m inv*
locomotive [ləukə'məutɪv] *n* locomotiva
locum ['ləukəm] *n* (*Med*) medico sostituto
locust ['ləukəst] *n* locusta
lodge [lɔdʒ] *n* casetta, portineria; (*Freemasonry*) loggia ■ *vi* (*person*): **to ~ (with)** essere a pensione (presso *or* da) ■ *vt* (*appeal etc*) presentare, fare; **to ~ a complaint** presentare un reclamo; **to ~ (itself) in/between** piantarsi dentro/fra
lodger ['lɔdʒəʳ] *n* affittuario(-a); (*with room and meals*) pensionante *m/f*
lodging ['lɔdʒɪŋ] *n* alloggio; *see also* **board**; **lodgings**
lodging house *n* (*Brit*) casa con camere in affitto
lodgings ['lɔdʒɪŋz] *npl* camera d'affitto; camera ammobiliata
loft [lɔft] *n* soffitta; (*Agr*) granaio; (*US*) appartamento ricavato da solaio, granaio *etc*
lofty ['lɔftɪ] *adj* alto(-a); (*haughty*) altezzoso(-a); (*sentiments, aims*) nobile
log [lɔg] *n* (*of wood*) ceppo; (*book*) = **logbook** ■ *n abbr* = **logarithm** ■ *vt* registrare
▸ **log in, log on** *vi* (*Comput*) aprire una sessione (*con codice di riconoscimento*)
▸ **log off, log out** *vi* (*Comput*) terminare una sessione
logarithm ['lɔgərɪðm] *n* logaritmo
logbook ['lɔgbuk] *n* (*Naut, Aviat*) diario di bordo; (*Aut*) libretto di circolazione; (*of lorry driver*) registro di viaggio; (*of events, movement of goods etc*) registro
log cabin *n* capanna di tronchi
log fire *n* fuoco di legna
logger ['lɔgəʳ] *n* boscaiolo, taglialegna *m inv*
loggerheads ['lɔgəhɛdz] *npl*: **at ~ (with)** ai ferri corti (con)
logic ['lɔdʒɪk] *n* logica
logical ['lɔdʒɪkəl] *adj* logico(-a)
logically ['lɔdʒɪkəlɪ] *adv* logicamente
login ['lɔgɪn] *n* (*Comput*) nome *m* utente *inv*
logistics [lɔ'dʒɪstɪks] *n* logistica
log jam ['lɔgdʒæm] *n*: **to break the ~** superare l'impasse
logo ['ləugəu] *n* logo *m inv*
loin [lɔɪn] *n* (*Culin*) lombata; **loins** *npl* reni *fpl*
loin cloth *n* perizoma *m*
loiter ['lɔɪtəʳ] *vi* attardarsi; **to ~ (about)** indugiare, bighellonare
lol *abbr* (*Internet, Tel: = laugh out loud*) lol (*morto dal ridere*)
loll [lɔl] *vi* (*also*: **loll about**) essere stravaccato(-a)
lollipop ['lɔlɪpɔp] *n* lecca lecca *m inv*
lollipop man, lollipop lady *n* (*Brit*) *vedi nota*

LOLLIPOP MAN, LOLLIPOP LADY

In Gran Bretagna il *lollipop man* e la *lollipop lady* sono persone incaricate di regolare il traffico in prossimità delle scuole e di aiutare i bambini ad attraversare la strada usando una paletta la cui forma ricorda quella di un lecca lecca, in inglese, appunto, "lollipop".

lollop ['lɔləp] *vi* (*Brit*) camminare (*or* correre) goffamente
lolly ['lɔlɪ] (*col*) *n* lecca lecca *m inv*; (*also*: **ice lolly**) ghiacciolo; (*money*) grana
Lombardy ['lɔmbədɪ] *n* Lombardia
London ['lʌndən] *n* Londra
Londoner ['lʌndənəʳ] *n* londinese *m/f*
lone [ləun] *adj* solitario(-a)
loneliness ['ləunlɪnɪs] *n* solitudine *f*, isolamento
lonely ['ləunlɪ] *adj* solitario(-a); (*place*) isolato(-a); **to feel ~** sentirsi solo(-a)
lonely hearts *adj*: **~ ads**, **~ column** messaggi *mpl* personali; **~ club** club *m inv* dei cuori solitari
lone parent *n* (*unmarried: mother*) ragazza madre; (*: father*) ragazzo padre; (*divorced*) genitore *m* divorziato(-a); (*widowed*) genitore rimasto vedovo

loner ['ləunəʳ] *n* solitario(-a)
lonesome ['ləunsəm] *adj* solo(-a)
long [lɔŋ] *adj* lungo(-a) ■ *adv* a lungo, per molto tempo ■ *n*: **the ~ and the short of it is that ...** *(fig)* a farla breve ... ■ *vi*: **to ~ for sth/to do** desiderare qc/di fare; non veder l'ora di aver qc/di fare; **he had ~ understood that ...** aveva capito da molto tempo che ...; **how ~ is this river/course?** quanto è lungo questo fiume/corso?; **6 metres ~** lungo 6 metri; **6 months ~** che dura 6 mesi, di 6 mesi; **all night ~** tutta la notte; **he no longer comes** non viene più; **~ before** molto tempo prima; **before ~** *(+ future)* presto, fra poco; *(+ past)* poco tempo dopo; **~ ago** molto tempo fa; **don't be ~!** faccia presto!; **I shan't be ~** non ne avrò per molto; **at ~ last** finalmente; **in the ~ run** alla fin fine; **so** *or* **as ~ as** sempre che *+ sub*
long-distance [lɔŋ'dɪstəns] *adj (race)* di fondo; *(call)* interurbano(-a)
long-haired ['lɔŋ'hɛəd] *adj (person)* dai capelli lunghi; *(animal)* dal pelo lungo
longhand ['lɔŋhænd] *n* scrittura normale
longing ['lɔŋɪŋ] *n* desiderio, voglia, brama ■ *adj* di desiderio; pieno(-a) di nostalgia
longingly ['lɔŋɪŋlɪ] *adv* con desiderio *(or* nostalgia)
longitude ['lɔŋgɪtju:d] *n* longitudine *f*
long johns [-dʒɔnz] *npl* mutande *fpl* lunghe
long jump *n* salto in lungo
long-lost ['lɔŋlɔst] *adj* perduto(-a) da tempo
long-playing ['lɔŋpleɪɪŋ] *adj*: **~ record (LP)** (disco) 33 giri *m inv*
long-range [lɔŋ'reɪndʒ] *adj* a lunga portata; *(weather forecast)* a lungo termine
longshoreman ['lɔŋʃɔ:mən] *n (US)* scaricatore *m* (di porto), portuale *m*
long-sighted [lɔŋ'saɪtɪd] *adj (Brit)* presbite; *(fig)* lungimirante
long-standing ['lɔŋstændɪŋ] *adj* di vecchia data
long-suffering [lɔŋ'sʌfərɪŋ] *adj* estremamente paziente; infinitamente tollerante
long-term ['lɔŋtə:m] *adj* a lungo termine
long wave *n (Radio)* onde *fpl* lunghe
long-winded [lɔŋ'wɪndɪd] *adj* prolisso(-a), interminabile
loo [lu:] *n (Brit col)* W.C. *m inv*, cesso
loofah ['lu:fə] *n* luffa
look [luk] *vi* guardare; *(seem)* sembrare, parere; *(building etc)*: **to ~ south/on to the sea** dare a sud/sul mare ■ *n* sguardo; *(appearance)* aspetto, aria; **looks** *npl* aspetto; bellezza; **to ~ like** assomigliare a; **to ~ ahead** guardare avanti; **it looks about 4 metres long** sarà lungo un 4 metri; **it looks all right to me** a me pare che vada bene; **to have a ~ at sth** dare un'occhiata a qc; **to have a ~ for sth** cercare qc
▸ **look after** *vt fus* occuparsi di, prendersi cura di; *(keep an eye on)* guardare, badare a
▸ **look around** *vi* guardarsi intorno
▸ **look at** *vt fus* guardare
▸ **look back** *vi*: **to ~ back at sth/sb** voltarsi a guardare qc/qn; **to ~ back on** *(event, period)* ripensare a
▸ **look down on** *vt fus (fig)* guardare dall'alto, disprezzare
▸ **look for** *vt fus* cercare
▸ **look forward to** *vt fus* non veder l'ora di; **I'm not looking forward to it** non ne ho nessuna voglia; **looking forward to hearing from you** *(in letter)* aspettando tue notizie
▸ **look in** *vi*: **to ~ in on sb** *(visit)* fare un salto da qn
▸ **look into** *vt fus (matter, possibility)* esaminare
▸ **look on** *vi* fare da spettatore
▸ **look out** *vi (beware)*: **to ~ out (for)** stare in guardia (per)
▸ **look out for** *vt fus* cercare; *(watch out for)*: **to ~ out for sb/sth** guardare se arriva qn/qc
▸ **look over** *vt (essay)* dare un'occhiata a, riguardare; *(town, building)* vedere; *(person)* esaminare
▸ **look round** *vi (turn)* girarsi, voltarsi; *(in shops)* dare un'occhiata; **to ~ round for sth** guardarsi intorno cercando qc
▸ **look through** *vt fus (papers, book)* scorrere; *(telescope)* guardare attraverso
▸ **look to** *vt fus* stare attento(-a) a; *(rely on)* contare su
▸ **look up** *vi* alzare gli occhi; *(improve)* migliorare ■ *vt (word)* cercare; *(friend)* andare a trovare
▸ **look up to** *vt fus* avere rispetto per
look-out ['lukaut] *n* posto d'osservazione; guardia; **to be on the ~ (for)** stare in guardia (per)
look-up table ['lukʌp-] *n (Comput)* tabella di consultazione
loom [lu:m] *n* telaio ■ *vi* sorgere; *(fig)* minacciare
loony ['lu:nɪ] *adj, n (col)* pazzo(-a)
loop [lu:p] *n* cappio; *(Comput)* anello
loophole ['lu:phəul] *n* via d'uscita; scappatoia
loose [lu:s] *adj (knot)* sciolto(-a); *(screw)* allentato(-a); *(stone)* cadente; *(clothes)* ampio(-a), largo(-a); *(animal)* in libertà, scappato(-a); *(life, morals)* dissoluto(-a); *(discipline)* allentato(-a); *(thinking)* poco

rigoroso(-a), vago(-a) ■ *vt* (*untie*) sciogliere; (*slacken*) allentare; (*free*) liberare; (*Brit: arrow*) scoccare; **~ connection** (*Elec*) filo che fa contatto; **to be at a ~ end** *or* (*US*) **at ~ ends** (*fig*) non saper che fare; **to tie up ~ ends** (*fig*) avere ancora qualcosa da sistemare
loose change *n* spiccioli *mpl*, moneta
loose-fitting ['lu:sfɪtɪŋ] *adj* ampio(-a)
loose-leaf ['lu:sli:f] *adj*: **~ binder** *or* **folder** raccoglitore *m*
loose-limbed [lu:s'lɪmd] *adj* snodato(-a), agile
loosely ['lu:slɪ] *adv* lentamente; approssimativamente
loosely-knit ['lu:slɪ'nɪt] *adj* non rigidamente strutturato(-a)
loosen ['lu:sn] *vt* sciogliere
▸ **loosen up** *vi* (*before game*) sciogliere i muscoli, scaldarsi; (*col: relax*) rilassarsi
loot [lu:t] *n* bottino ■ *vt* saccheggiare
looter ['lu:tə^r] *n* saccheggiatore(-trice)
looting ['lu:tɪŋ] *n* saccheggio
lop [lɔp] *vt* (*also*: **lop off**) tagliare via, recidere
lop-sided ['lɔp'saɪdɪd] *adj* non equilibrato(-a), asimmetrico(-a)
lord [lɔ:d] *n* signore *m*; **L~ Smith** lord Smith; **the L~** (*Rel*) il Signore; **the (House of) Lords** (*Brit*) la Camera dei Lord
lordly ['lɔ:dlɪ] *adj* nobile, maestoso(-a); (*arrogant*) altero(-a)
lordship ['lɔ:dʃɪp] *n* (*Brit*): **your L~** Sua Eccellenza
lore [lɔ:^r] *n* tradizioni *fpl*
lorry ['lɔrɪ] *n* (*Brit*) camion *m inv*
lorry driver *n* (*Brit*) camionista *m*
lose (*pt, pp* **lost**) [lu:z, lɔst] *vt* perdere; (*pursuers*) distanziare ■ *vi* perdere; **to ~ (time)** (*clock*) ritardare; **to ~ no time (in doing sth)** non perdere tempo (a fare qc); **to get lost** (*person*) perdersi, smarrirsi; (*object*) andare perso *or* perduto
loser ['lu:zə^r] *n* perdente *m/f*; **to be a good/bad ~** saper/non saper perdere
loss [lɔs] *n* perdita; **to cut one's losses** rimetterci il meno possibile; **to make a ~** subire una perdita; **to sell sth at a ~** vendere qc in perdita; **to be at a ~** essere perplesso(-a); **to be at a ~ to explain sth** non saper come fare a spiegare qc
loss adjuster *n* (*Insurance*) responsabile *m/f* della valutazione dei danni
loss leader *n* (*Comm*) articolo a prezzo ridottissimo per attirare la clientela
lost [lɔst] *pt, pp of* **lose** ■ *adj* perduto(-a); **~ in thought** immerso *or* perso nei propri pensieri; **~ and found property** *n* (*US*) oggetti *mpl* smarriti; **~ and found** *n* (*US*) ufficio oggetti smarriti
lost property *n* (*Brit*) oggetti *mpl* smarriti; **~ office** *or* **department** ufficio oggetti smarriti
lot [lɔt] *n* (*at auctions*) lotto; (*destiny*) destino, sorte *f*; **the ~** tutto(-a) quanto(-a); tutti(-e) quanti(-e); **a ~** molto; **a ~ of** una gran quantità di, un sacco di; **lots of** molto(-a); **to draw lots (for sth)** tirare a sorte (per qc)
lotion ['ləuʃən] *n* lozione *f*
lottery ['lɔtərɪ] *n* lotteria
loud [laud] *adj* forte, alto(-a); (*gaudy*) vistoso(-a), sgargiante ■ *adv* (*speak etc*) forte; **out ~** ad alta voce
loudhailer [laud'heɪlə^r] *n* (*Brit*) portavoce *m inv*
loudly ['laudlɪ] *adv* fortemente, ad alta voce
loudspeaker [laud'spi:kə^r] *n* altoparlante *m*
lounge [laundʒ] *n* salotto, soggiorno; (*of hotel*) salone *m*; (*of airport*) sala d'attesa ■ *vi* oziare; starsene colle mani in mano
lounge bar *n* bar *m inv* con servizio a tavolino
lounge suit *n* (*Brit*) completo da uomo
louse [laus] *n* (*pl* **lice**) pidocchio
▸ **louse up** *vt* (*col*) rovinare
lousy ['lauzɪ] *adj* (*fig*) orrendo(-a), schifoso(-a)
lout [laut] *n* zoticone *m*
louvre, (*US*) **louver** ['lu:və^r] *adj* (*door, window*) con apertura a gelosia
lovable ['lʌvəbl] *adj* simpatico(-a), carino(-a); amabile
love [lʌv] *n* amore *m* ■ *vt* amare; voler bene a; **to ~ to do**: **I ~ to do** mi piace fare; **I'd ~ to come** mi piacerebbe molto venire; **to be in ~ with** essere innamorato(-a) di; **to fall in ~ with** innamorarsi di; **to make ~** fare l'amore; **~ at first sight** amore a prima vista, colpo di fulmine; **to send one's ~ to sb** mandare i propri saluti a qn; **~ from Anne, ~, Anne** con affetto, Anne; **"15 ~"** (*Tennis*) "15 a zero"
love affair *n* relazione *f*
love child *n* figlio(-a) dell'amore
loved ones [lʌvd-] *npl*: **my ~** i miei cari
love-hate relationship ['lʌv'heɪt-] *n* rapporto amore-odio *inv*
love letter *n* lettera d'amore
love life *n* vita sentimentale
lovely ['lʌvlɪ] *adj* bello(-a); (*delicious: smell, meal*) buono(-a); **we had a ~ time** ci siamo divertiti molto
lover ['lʌvə^r] *n* amante *m/f*; (*amateur*): **a ~ of** un/un'amante di; un/un'appassionato(-a) di
lovesick ['lʌvsɪk] *adj* malato(-a) d'amore
lovesong ['lʌvsɔŋ] *n* canzone *f* d'amore

l

loving ['lʌvɪŋ] *adj* affettuoso(-a), amoroso(-a), tenero(-a)
low [ləu] *adj* basso(-a) ■ *adv* in basso ■ *n* (*Meteor*) depressione *f* ■ *vi* (*cow*) muggire; **to feel ~** sentirsi giù; **he's very ~** (*ill*) è molto debole; **to reach a new** *or* **an all-time ~** toccare il livello più basso *or* il minimo; **to turn (down) ~** *vt* abbassare
low-alcohol [ləu'ælkəhɔl] *adj* a basso contenuto alcolico
lowbrow ['ləubrau] *adj* (*person*) senza pretese intellettuali
low-calorie ['ləu'kælərɪ] *adj* a basso contenuto calorico
low-cut ['ləukʌt] *adj* (*dress*) scollato(-a)
low-down ['ləudaun] *adj* (*mean*) ignobile ■ *n* (*col*): **he gave me the ~ on it** mi ha messo al corrente dei fatti
lower ['ləuə^r] *adj, adv comparative of* **low** ■ *vt* (*gen*) calare; (*reduce: price*) abbassare, ridurre; (*resistance*) indebolire ■ *vi* ['lauə^r] (*person*): **to ~ (at sb)** dare un'occhiataccia (a qn); (*sky*) minacciare
lower case *n* minuscolo
low-fat ['ləu'fæt] *adj* magro(-a)
low-key ['ləu'ki:] *adj* moderato(-a); (*operation*) condotto(-a) con discrezione
lowland ['ləulənd] *n* bassopiano, pianura
low-level ['ləulɛvl] *adj* a basso livello; (*flying*) a bassa quota
low-loader ['ləuləudə^r] *n* camion *m* a pianale basso
lowly ['ləulɪ] *adj* umile, modesto(-a)
low-lying [ləu'laɪɪŋ] *adj* a basso livello
low-paid [ləu'peɪd] *adj* mal pagato(-a)
low-rise ['ləuraɪz] *adj* di altezza contenuta
low-tech ['ləu'tɛk] *adj* a basso contenuto tecnologico
loyal ['lɔɪəl] *adj* fedele, leale
loyalist ['lɔɪəlɪst] *n* lealista *m/f*
loyalty ['lɔɪəltɪ] *n* fedeltà, lealtà
loyalty card *n carta che offre sconti a clienti abituali*
lozenge ['lɔzɪndʒ] *n* (*Med*) pastiglia; (*Geom*) losanga
LP *n abbr* (= *long-playing record*) LP *m*
LPG *n abbr* (= *liquefied petroleum gas*) GPL (= *gas di petrolio liquefatto*)
L-plate *n* ≈ contrassegno P principiante; *vedi nota*

L-PLATE

Le *L-plates* sono delle tabelle bianche con una L rossa che in Gran Bretagna i guidatori principianti, "learners", in possesso di una "provisional licence", che corrisponde al nostro foglio rosa, devono applicare davanti e dietro alla loro autovettura finché non ottengono la patente.

LPN *n abbr* (*US: = Licensed Practical Nurse*) ≈ infermiera diplomata
LRAM *n abbr* (*Brit: = Licentiate of the Royal Academy of Music*) *specializzazione dopo la laurea*
LSD *n abbr* (= *lysergic acid diethylamide*) L.S.D. *m*; (*Brit: = pounds, shillings and pence*) *sistema monetario in vigore in Gran Bretagna fino al 1971*
LSE *n abbr* = **London School of Economics**
LT *abbr* (*Elec: = low tension*) B.T.
Lt. *abbr* (= *lieutenant*) Ten.
Ltd *abbr* (*Comm*) = **limited**
lubricant ['lu:brɪkənt] *n* lubrificante *m*
lubricate ['lu:brɪkeɪt] *vt* lubrificare
lucid ['lu:sɪd] *adj* lucido(-a)
lucidity [lu:'sɪdɪtɪ] *n* lucidità
luck [lʌk] *n* fortuna, sorte *f*; **bad ~** sfortuna, mala sorte; **good ~** (buona) fortuna; **to be in ~** essere fortunato(-a); **to be out of ~** essere sfortunato(-a)
luckily ['lʌkɪlɪ] *adv* fortunatamente, per fortuna
luckless ['lʌklɪs] *adj* sventurato(-a)
lucky ['lʌkɪ] *adj* fortunato(-a); (*number etc*) che porta fortuna
lucrative ['lu:krətɪv] *adj* lucrativo(-a), lucroso(-a), profittevole
ludicrous ['lu:dɪkrəs] *adj* ridicolo(-a), assurdo(-a)
ludo ['lu:dəu] *n* ≈ gioco dell'oca
lug [lʌg] *vt* trascinare
luggage ['lʌgɪdʒ] *n* bagagli *mpl*
luggage rack *n* portabagagli *m inv*
luggage van, (*US*) **luggage car** *n* (*Rail*) bagagliaio
lugubrious [lu'gu:brɪəs] *adj* lugubre
lukewarm ['lu:kwɔ:m] *adj* tiepido(-a)
lull [lʌl] *n* intervallo di calma ■ *vt* (*child*) cullare; (*person, fear*) acquietare, calmare
lullaby ['lʌləbaɪ] *n* ninnananna
lumbago [lʌm'beɪgəu] *n* lombaggine *f*
lumber ['lʌmbə^r] *n* roba vecchia ■ *vt* (*Brit col*): **to ~ sb with sth/sb** affibbiare *or* rifilare qc/qn a qn ■ *vi* (*also*: **lumber about, lumber along**) muoversi pesantemente
lumberjack ['lʌmbədʒæk] *n* boscaiolo
lumber room *n* (*Brit*) sgabuzzino
lumber yard *n* segheria
luminous ['lu:mɪnəs] *adj* luminoso(-a)
lump [lʌmp] *n* pezzo; (*in sauce*) grumo; (*swelling*) gonfiore *m* ■ *vt* (*also*: **lump together**) riunire, mettere insieme
lump sum *n* somma globale

lumpy ['lʌmpɪ] *adj* (*sauce*) grumoso(-a)
lunacy ['lu:nəsɪ] *n* demenza, follia, pazzia
lunar ['lu:nəʳ] *adj* lunare
lunatic ['lu:nətɪk] *adj, n* pazzo(-a), matto(-a)
lunatic asylum *n* manicomio
lunch [lʌntʃ] *n* pranzo, colazione *f*; **to invite sb to** *or* **for ~** invitare qn a pranzo *or* a colazione
lunch break *n* intervallo del pranzo
luncheon ['lʌntʃən] *n* pranzo
luncheon meat *n* ≈ mortadella
luncheon voucher *n* buono *m* pasto *inv*
lunch hour *n* = **lunch break**
lunchtime ['lʌntʃtaɪm] *n* ora di pranzo
lung [lʌŋ] *n* polmone *m*
lung cancer *n* cancro del polmone
lunge [lʌndʒ] *vi* (*also*: **lunge forward**) fare un balzo in avanti; **to ~ at sb** balzare su qn
lupin ['lu:pɪn] *n* lupino
lurch [lə:tʃ] *vi* vacillare, barcollare ■ *n* scatto improvviso; **to leave sb in the ~** piantare in asso qn
lure [luəʳ] *n* richiamo; lusinga ■ *vt* attirare (con l'inganno)
lurid ['luərɪd] *adj* sgargiante; (*details etc*) impressionante
lurk [lə:k] *vi* stare in agguato
luscious ['lʌʃəs] *adj* succulento(-a); delizioso(-a)
lush [lʌʃ] *adj* lussureggiante
lust [lʌst] *n* lussuria; cupidigia; desiderio; (*fig*): **~ for** sete *f* di
▸ **lust after** *vt fus* bramare, desiderare
luster ['lʌstəʳ] *n* (US) = **lustre**
lustful ['lʌstful] *adj* lascivo(-a), voglioso(-a)
lustre, (US) **luster** ['lʌstəʳ] *n* lustro, splendore *m*
lusty ['lʌstɪ] *adj* vigoroso(-a), robusto(-a)
lute [lu:t] *n* liuto
Luxembourg ['lʌksəmbə:g] *n* (*state*) Lussemburgo *m*; (*city*) Lussemburgo *f*
luxuriant [lʌg'zjuərɪənt] *adj* lussureggiante
luxurious [lʌg'zjuərɪəs] *adj* sontuoso(-a), di lusso
luxury ['lʌkʃərɪ] *n* lusso ■ *cpd* di lusso
LV *n abbr* (*Brit*) = **luncheon voucher**
LW *abbr* (*Radio*: = *long wave*) O.L.
Lycra® ['laɪkrə] *n* lycra® *f inv*
lying ['laɪɪŋ] *n* bugie *fpl*, menzogne *fpl* ■ *adj* (*statement, story*) falso(-a); (*person*) bugiardo(-a)
lynch [lɪntʃ] *vt* linciare
lynx [lɪŋks] *n* lince *f*
Lyons ['laɪənz] *n* Lione *f*
lyre ['laɪəʳ] *n* lira
lyric ['lɪrɪk] *adj* lirico(-a); **lyrics** *npl* (*of song*) parole *fpl*
lyrical ['lɪrɪkl] *adj* lirico(-a)
lyricism ['lɪrɪsɪzəm] *n* lirismo

Mm

M, m [ɛm] *n* (*letter*) M, m *f or m inv*; **M for Mary**, (*US*) **M for Mike** ≈ M come Milano
M *n abbr* (*Brit*) = **motorway**; **the M8** ≈ l'A8
■ *abbr* (= *medium*) taglia media
m *abbr* (= *metre*) m; = **mile**; **million**
MA *n abbr* (*Scol*) = **Master of Arts**; (*US*) = **military academy** ■ *abbr* (*US*) = **Massachusetts**
mac [mæk] *n* (*Brit*) impermeabile *m*
macabre [mə'kɑ:brə] *adj* macabro(-a)
macaroni [mækə'rəunɪ] *n* maccheroni *mpl*
macaroon [mækə'ru:n] *n* amaretto (*biscotto*)
mace [meɪs] *n* mazza; (*spice*) macis *m or f*
Macedonia [mæsɪ'dəunɪə] *n* Macedonia
Macedonian [mæsɪ'dəunɪən] *adj* macedone ■ *n* macedone *m/f*; (*Ling*) macedone *m*
machinations [mækɪ'neɪʃənz] *npl* macchinazioni *fpl*, intrighi *mpl*
machine [mə'ʃi:n] *n* macchina ■ *vt* (*dress etc*) cucire a macchina; (*Tech*) lavorare (a macchina)
machine code *n* (*Comput*) codice *m* di macchina, codice assoluto
machine gun *n* mitragliatrice *f*
machine language *n* (*Comput*) linguaggio *m* macchina *inv*
machine-readable [mə'ʃi:nri:dəbl] *adj* (*Comput*) leggibile dalla macchina
machinery [mə'ʃi:nərɪ] *n* macchinario, macchine *fpl*; (*fig*) macchina
machine shop *n* officina meccanica
machine tool *n* macchina utensile
machine washable *adj* lavabile in lavatrice
machinist [mə'ʃi:nɪst] *n* macchinista *m/f*
macho ['mætʃəu] *adj* macho *inv*
mackerel ['mækrəl] *n* (*pl inv*) sgombro
mackintosh ['mækɪntɔʃ] *n* impermeabile *m*
macro... ['mækrəu] *prefix* macro...
macroeconomics ['mækrəui:kə'nɔmɪks] *n* macroeconomia
mad [mæd] *adj* matto(-a), pazzo(-a); (*foolish*) sciocco(-a); (*angry*) furioso(-a); **to go ~** impazzire, diventar matto; **~ (at** *or* **with sb)** furibondo(-a) (con qn); **to be ~ (keen) about** *or* **on sth** (*col*) andar pazzo *or* matto per qc
madam ['mædəm] *n* signora; **M~ Chairman** Signora Presidentessa
madcap ['mædkæp] *adj* (*col*) senza senso, assurdo(-a)
mad cow disease *n* encefalite *f* bovina spongiforme
madden ['mædn] *vt* fare infuriare
maddening ['mædnɪŋ] *adj* esasperante
made [meɪd] *pt, pp of* **make**
Madeira [mə'dɪərə] *n* (*Geo*) Madera; (*wine*) madera *m*
made-to-measure ['meɪdtə'mɛʒə^r] *adj* (*Brit*) fatto(-a) su misura
madhouse ['mædhaus] *n* (*also fig*) manicomio
madly ['mædlɪ] *adv* follemente; (*love*) alla follia
madman ['mædmən] *n* pazzo, alienato
madness ['mædnɪs] *n* pazzia
Madrid [mə'drɪd] *n* Madrid *f*
Mafia ['mæfɪə] *n* mafia *f*
mag. [mæg] *n abbr* (*Brit col*) = **magazine** (*Press*)
magazine [mægə'zi:n] *n* (*Press*) rivista; (*Mil: store*) magazzino, deposito; (*of firearm*) caricatore *m*
maggot ['mægət] *n* baco, verme *m*
magic ['mædʒɪk] *n* magia ■ *adj* magico(-a)
magical ['mædʒɪkəl] *adj* magico(-a)
magician [mə'dʒɪʃən] *n* mago(-a)
magistrate ['mædʒɪstreɪt] *n* magistrato; giudice *m/f*
magistrates' court *n see* **crown court**
magnanimous [mæg'nænɪməs] *adj* magnanimo(-a)
magnate ['mægneɪt] *n* magnate *m*
magnesium [mæg'ni:zɪəm] *n* magnesio
magnet ['mægnɪt] *n* magnete *m*, calamita
magnetic [mæg'nɛtɪk] *adj* magnetico(-a)
magnetic disk *n* (*Comput*) disco magnetico
magnetic tape *n* nastro magnetico
magnetism ['mægnɪtɪzəm] *n* magnetismo

magnification [mægnɪfɪ'keɪʃən] *n* ingrandimento
magnificence [mæg'nɪfɪsns] *n* magnificenza
magnificent [mæg'nɪfɪsnt] *adj* magnifico(-a)
magnify ['mægnɪfaɪ] *vt* ingrandire
magnifying glass ['mægnɪfaɪɪŋ-] *n* lente *f* d'ingrandimento
magnitude ['mægnɪtju:d] *n* grandezza; importanza
magnolia [mæg'nəulɪə] *n* magnolia
magpie ['mægpaɪ] *n* gazza
mahogany [mə'hɔgənɪ] *n* mogano ■ *cpd* di *or* in mogano
maid [meɪd] *n* domestica; (*in hotel*) cameriera; **old ~** (*pej*) vecchia zitella
maiden ['meɪdn] *n* fanciulla ■ *adj* (*aunt etc*) nubile; (*speech, voyage*) inaugurale
maiden name *n* nome *m* nubile *or* da ragazza
mail [meɪl] *n* posta ■ *vt* spedire (per posta); **by ~** per posta
mailbox ['meɪlbɔks] *n* (*US*) cassetta delle lettere; (*Comput*) mailbox *f inv*
mailing list ['meɪlɪŋ-] *n* elenco d'indirizzi
mailman ['meɪlmæn] *n* (*US*) portalettere *m inv*, postino
mail-order ['meɪlɔ:dər] *n* vendita (*or* acquisto) per corrispondenza ■ *cpd*: **~ firm** *or* **house** ditta di vendita per corrispondenza
mailshot ['meɪlʃɔt] *n* mailing *m inv*
mail train *n* treno postale
mail truck *n* (*US Aut*) = **mail van**
mail van *n* (*Brit Aut*) furgone *m* postale; (: *Rail*) vagone *m* postale
maim [meɪm] *vt* mutilare
main [meɪn] *adj* principale ■ *n* (*pipe*) conduttura principale; **the mains** (*Elec*) la linea principale; **mains operated** *adj* che funziona a elettricità; **in the ~** nel complesso, nell'insieme
main course *n* (*Culin*) piatto principale, piatto forte
mainframe ['meɪnfreɪm] *n* (*also*: **mainframe computer**) mainframe *m inv*
mainland ['meɪnlənd] *n* continente *m*
mainline ['meɪnlaɪn] *adj* (*Rail*) della linea principale ■ *vb* (*drugs slang*) *vt* bucarsi di ■ *vi* bucarsi
main line *n* (*Rail*) linea principale
mainly ['meɪnlɪ] *adv* principalmente, soprattutto
main road *n* strada principale
mainstay ['meɪnsteɪ] *n* (*fig*) sostegno principale
mainstream ['meɪnstri:m] *n* (*fig*) corrente *f* principale
maintain [meɪn'teɪn] *vt* mantenere; (*affirm*) sostenere; **to ~ that ...** sostenere che ...
maintenance ['meɪntənəns] *n* manutenzione *f*; (*alimony*) alimenti *mpl*
maintenance contract *n* contratto di manutenzione
maintenance order *n* (*Law*) obbligo degli alimenti
maisonette [meɪzə'nɛt] *n* (*Brit*) appartamento a due piani
maize [meɪz] *n* granturco, mais *m*
Maj. *abbr* (*Mil*) = **major**
majestic [mə'dʒɛstɪk] *adj* maestoso(-a)
majesty ['mædʒɪstɪ] *n* maestà *f inv*
major ['meɪdʒər] *n* (*Mil*) maggiore *m* ■ *adj* (*greater, Mus*) maggiore; (*in importance*) principale, importante ■ *vi* (*US Scol*): **to ~ (in)** specializzarsi (in); **a ~ operation** (*Med*) una grossa operazione
Majorca [mə'jɔ:kə] *n* Maiorca
major general *n* (*Mil*) generale *m* di divisione
majority [mə'dʒɔrɪtɪ] *n* maggioranza ■ *cpd* (*verdict*) maggioritario(-a)
majority holding *n* (*Comm*): **to have a ~** essere maggiore azionista
make [meɪk] *vt* (*pt, pp* **made**) [meɪd] fare; (*manufacture*) fare, fabbricare; (*cause to be*): **to ~ sb sad** *etc* rendere qn triste *etc*; (*force*): **to ~ sb do sth** costringere qn a fare qc, far fare qc a qn; (*equal*): **2 and 2 ~ 4** 2 più 2 fa 4 ■ *n* fabbricazione *f*; (*brand*) marca; **to ~ it** (*in time etc*) arrivare; (*succeed*) farcela; **what time do you ~ it?** che ora fai?; **to ~ good** *vi* (*succeed*) aver successo ■ *vt* (*deficit*) colmare; (*losses*) compensare; **to ~ do with** arrangiarsi con
▸ **make for** *vt fus* (*place*) avviarsi verso
▸ **make off** *vi* svignarsela
▸ **make out** *vt* (*write out*) scrivere; (*understand*) capire; (*see*) distinguere; (: *numbers*) decifrare; (*claim, imply*): **to ~ out (that)** voler far credere (che); **to ~ out a case for sth** presentare delle valide ragioni in favore di qc
▸ **make over** *vt* (*assign*): **to ~ over (to)** passare (a), trasferire (a)
▸ **make up** *vt* (*invent*) inventare; (*parcel*) fare ■ *vi* conciliarsi; (*with cosmetics*) truccarsi; **to be made up of** essere composto di *or* formato da
▸ **make up for** *vt fus* compensare; ricuperare
make-believe ['meɪkbɪli:v] *n*: **a world of ~** un mondo di favole; **it's just ~** è tutta un'invenzione
makeover ['meɪkəuvər] *n* cambio di immagine; **to give sb a ~** far cambiare immagine a qn
maker ['meɪkər] *n* fabbricante *m*; creatore(-trice), autore(-trice)
makeshift ['meɪkʃɪft] *adj* improvvisato(-a)
make-up ['meɪkʌp] *n* trucco
make-up bag *n* borsa del trucco

m

make-up remover *n* struccatore *m*
making ['meɪkɪŋ] *n (fig)*: **in the ~** in formazione; **he has the makings of an actor** ha la stoffa dell'attore
maladjusted [mælə'dʒʌstɪd] *adj* disadattato(-a)
maladroit [mælə'drɔɪt] *adj* maldestro(-a)
malaise [mæ'leɪz] *n* malessere *m*
malaria [mə'lɛərɪə] *n* malaria
Malawi [mə'lɑːwɪ] *n* Malawi *m*
Malay [mə'leɪ] *adj* malese ■ *n* malese *m/f*; *(Ling)* malese *m*
Malaya [mə'leɪə] *n* Malesia
Malayan [mə'leɪən] *adj, n* = **Malay**
Malaysia [mə'leɪzɪə] *n* Malaysia
Malaysian [mə'leɪzɪən] *adj, n* malaysiano(-a)
Maldives ['mɔːldaɪvz] *npl*: **the ~** le (isole) Maldive
male [meɪl] *n (Bio, Elec)* maschio ■ *adj (gen, sex)* maschile; *(animal, child)* maschio(-a); **~ and female students** studenti e studentesse
male chauvinist *n* maschilista *m*
male nurse *n* infermiere *m*
malevolence [mə'lɛvələns] *n* malevolenza
malevolent [mə'lɛvələnt] *adj* malevolo(-a)
malfunction [mæl'fʌŋkʃən] *n* funzione *f* difettosa
malice ['mælɪs] *n* malevolenza
malicious [mə'lɪʃəs] *adj* malevolo(-a); *(Law)* doloso(-a)
malign [mə'laɪn] *vt* malignare su; calunniare
malignant [mə'lɪgnənt] *adj (Med)* maligno(-a)
malingerer [mə'lɪŋgərəʳ] *n* scansafatiche *m/f inv*
mall [mɔːl] *n (also:* **shopping mall***)* centro commerciale
malleable ['mælɪəbl] *adj* malleabile
mallet ['mælɪt] *n* maglio
malnutrition [mælnjuː'trɪʃən] *n* denutrizione *f*
malpractice [mæl'præktɪs] *n* prevaricazione *f*; negligenza
malt [mɔːlt] *n* malto ■ *cpd (whisky)* di malto
Malta ['mɔːltə] *n* Malta
Maltese [mɔːl'tiːz] *adj, n (pl inv)* maltese *(m/f)*; *(Ling)* maltese *m*
maltreat [mæl'triːt] *vt* maltrattare
mammal ['mæml] *n* mammifero
mammoth ['mæməθ] *n* mammut *m inv* ■ *adj* enorme, gigantesco(-a)
man [mæn] *n (pl* **men***)* uomo; *(Chess)* pezzo; *(Draughts)* pedina ■ *vt* fornire d'uomini; stare a; essere di servizio a
Man. *abbr (Canada)* = **Manitoba**
manacles ['mænəklz] *npl* manette *fpl*
manage ['mænɪdʒ] *vi* farcela ■ *vt (be in charge of)* occuparsi di; *(shop, restaurant)* gestire; **to ~ without sth/sb** fare a meno di qc/qn; **to ~ to do sth** riuscire a far qc
manageable ['mænɪdʒəbl] *adj* maneggevole; *(task etc)* fattibile
management ['mænɪdʒmənt] *n* amministrazione *f*, direzione *f*; gestione *f*; *(persons: of business, firm)* dirigenti *mpl*; *(: of hotel, shop, theatre)* direzione *f*; **"under new ~"** "sotto nuova gestione"
management accounting *n* contabilità di gestione
management buyout *n acquisto di una società da parte dei suoi dirigenti*
management consultant *n* consulente *m/f* aziendale
manager ['mænɪdʒəʳ] *n* direttore *m*; *(of shop, restaurant)* gerente *m*; *(of artist)* manager *m inv*; **sales ~** direttore *m* delle vendite
manageress [mænɪdʒə'rɛs] *n* direttrice *f*; gerente *f*
managerial [mænə'dʒɪərɪəl] *adj* dirigenziale
managing director ['mænɪdʒɪŋ-] *n* amministratore *m* delegato
Mancunian [mæŋ'kjuːnɪən] *adj* di Manchester ■ *n* abitante *m/f* di Manchester; originario(-a) di Manchester
mandarin ['mændərɪn] *n (person, fruit)* mandarino
mandate ['mændeɪt] *n* mandato
mandatory ['mændətərɪ] *adj* obbligatorio(-a); ingiuntivo(-a)
mandolin, mandoline ['mændəlɪn] *n* mandolino
mane [meɪn] *n* criniera
maneuver *etc* [mə'nuːvəʳ] *(US)* = **manoeuvre** *etc*
manful ['mænful] *adj* coraggioso(-a), valoroso(-a)
manfully ['mænfəlɪ] *adv* valorosamente
manganese [mæŋgə'niːz] *n* manganese *m*
mangetout ['mɔnʒ'tuː] *n* pisello dolce, taccola
mangle ['mæŋgl] *vt* straziare; mutilare ■ *n* strizzatoio
mango *(pl* **mangoes***)* ['mæŋgəu] *n* mango
mangrove ['mæŋgrəuv] *n* mangrovia
mangy ['meɪndʒɪ] *adj* rognoso(-a)
manhandle ['mænhændl] *vt (treat roughly)* malmenare; *(move by hand: goods)* spostare a mano
manhole ['mænhəul] *n* botola stradale
manhood ['mænhud] *n* età virile; virilità
man-hour ['mænauəʳ] *n* ora di lavoro
manhunt ['mænhʌnt] *n* caccia all'uomo
mania ['meɪnɪə] *n* mania
maniac ['meɪnɪæk] *n* maniaco(-a)
manic ['mænɪk] *adj* maniacale

manic-depressive ['mænɪkdɪ'prɛsɪv] *adj* maniaco-depressivo(-a) ■ *n* persona affetta da mania depressiva
manicure ['mænɪkjuəʳ] *n* manicure *f inv*
manicure set *n* trousse *f inv* della manicure
manifest ['mænɪfɛst] *vt* manifestare ■ *adj* manifesto(-a), palese ■ *n* (*Aviat, Naut*) manifesto
manifestation [mænɪfɛs'teɪʃən] *n* manifestazione *f*
manifesto [mænɪ'fɛstəu] *n* manifesto
manifold ['mænɪfəuld] *adj* molteplice ■ *n* (*Aut etc*): **exhaust ~** collettore *m* di scarico
Manila [mə'nɪlə] *n* Manila
manila, manilla [mə'nɪlə] *adj* (*paper, envelope*) manilla *inv*
manipulate [mə'nɪpjuleɪt] *vt* (*tool*) maneggiare; (*controls*) azionare; (*limb, facts*) manipolare
manipulation [mənɪpju'leɪʃən] *n* maneggiare *m*; capacità di azionare; manipolazione *f*
mankind [mæn'kaɪnd] *n* umanità, genere *m* umano
manliness ['mænlɪnɪs] *n* virilità
manly ['mænlɪ] *adj* virile; coraggioso(-a)
man-made ['mæn'meɪd] *adj* sintetico(-a); artificiale
manna ['mænə] *n* manna
mannequin ['mænɪkɪn] *n* (*dummy*) manichino; (*fashion model*) indossatrice *f*
manner ['mænəʳ] *n* maniera, modo; **manners** *npl* maniere *fpl*; **(good) manners** buona educazione *f*, buone maniere; **bad manners** maleducazione *f*; **all ~ of** ogni sorta di
mannerism ['mænərɪzəm] *n* vezzo, tic *m inv*
mannerly ['mænəlɪ] *adj* educato(-a), civile
manoeuvrable, (*US*) **maneuverable** [mə'nu:vrəbl] *adj* facile da manovrare; (*car*) maneggevole
manoeuvre, (*US*) **maneuver** [mə'nu:vəʳ] *vt* manovrare ■ *vi* far manovre ■ *n* manovra; **to ~ sb into doing sth** costringere abilmente qn a fare qc
manor ['mænəʳ] *n* (*also*: **manor house**) maniero
manpower ['mænpauəʳ] *n* manodopera
Manpower Services Commission *n* (*Brit*) *ente nazionale per l'occupazione*
manservant (*pl* **menservants**) ['mænsə:vənt, 'mɛn-] *n* domestico
mansion ['mænʃən] *n* casa signorile
manslaughter ['mænslɔ:təʳ] *n* omicidio preterintenzionale
mantelpiece ['mæntlpi:s] *n* mensola del caminetto
mantle ['mæntl] *n* mantello
man-to-man ['mæntə'mæn] *adj, adv* da uomo a uomo
Mantua ['mæntjuə] *n* Mantova
manual ['mænjuəl] *adj, n* manuale (*m*)
manual worker *n* manovale *m*
manufacture [mænju'fæktʃəʳ] *vt* fabbricare ■ *n* fabbricazione *f*, manifattura
manufactured goods *npl* manufatti *mpl*
manufacturer [mænju'fæktʃərəʳ] *n* fabbricante *m*
manufacturing industries [mænju'fæktʃərɪŋ-] *npl* industrie *fpl* manifatturiere
manure [mə'njuəʳ] *n* concime *m*
manuscript ['mænjuskrɪpt] *n* manoscritto
many ['mɛnɪ] *adj* molti(-e) ■ *pron* molti(-e), un gran numero; **a great ~** moltissimi(-e), un gran numero (di); **~ a ...** molti(-e) ..., più di un(-a) ...; **too ~ difficulties** troppe difficoltà; **twice as ~** due volte tanto; **how ~?** quanti(-e)?
Maori ['maurɪ] *adj, n* maori (*m/f*) *inv*
map [mæp] *n* carta (geografica) ■ *vt* fare una carta di
▸ **map out** *vt* tracciare un piano di; (*fig: career, holiday, essay*) pianificare
maple ['meɪpl] *n* acero
mar [mɑ:ʳ] *vt* sciupare
Mar. *abbr* (= *March*) mar.
marathon ['mærəθən] *n* maratona ■ *adj*: **a ~ session** una seduta fiume
marathon runner *n* maratoneta *m/f*
marauder [mə'rɔ:dəʳ] *n* saccheggiatore *m*; predatore *m*
marble ['mɑ:bl] *n* marmo; (*toy*) pallina, bilia; **marbles** *n* (*game*) palline, bilie
March [mɑ:tʃ] *n* marzo; *see also* **July**
march [mɑ:tʃ] *vi* marciare; sfilare ■ *n* marcia; (*demonstration*) dimostrazione *f*; **to ~ into a room** entrare a passo deciso in una stanza
marcher ['mɑ:tʃəʳ] *n* dimostrante *m/f*
marching ['mɑ:tʃɪŋ] *n*: **to give sb his ~ orders** (*fig*) dare il benservito a qn
march-past ['mɑ:tʃpɑ:st] *n* sfilata
mare [mɛəʳ] *n* giumenta
marg [mɑ:dʒ] *n abbr* (*col*) = **margarine**
margarine [mɑ:dʒə'ri:n] *n* margarina
marge [mɑ:dʒ] *n abbr* (*col*) = **margarine**
margin ['mɑ:dʒɪn] *n* margine *m*
marginal ['mɑ:dʒɪnl] *adj* marginale; **~ seat** (*Pol*) *seggio elettorale ottenuto con una stretta maggioranza*
marginally ['mɑ:dʒɪnəlɪ] *adv* (*bigger, better*) lievemente, di poco; (*different*) un po'
marigold ['mærɪgəuld] *n* calendola

m

marijuana [mærɪˈwɑːnə] *n* marijuana
marina [məˈriːnə] *n* marina
marinade *n* [mærɪˈneɪd] marinata ■ *vt* [ˈmærɪneɪd] = **marinate**
marinate [ˈmærɪneɪt] *vt* marinare
marine [məˈriːn] *adj* (*animal, plant*) marino(-a); (*forces, engineering*) marittimo(-a) ■ *n* fante *m* di marina; (*US*) marine *m inv*
marine insurance *n* assicurazione *f* marittima
marital [ˈmærɪtl] *adj* maritale, coniugale; **~ status** stato coniugale
maritime [ˈmærɪtaɪm] *adj* marittimo(-a)
maritime law *n* diritto marittimo
marjoram [ˈmɑːdʒərəm] *n* maggiorana
mark [mɑːk] *n* segno; (*stain*) macchia; (*of skid etc*) traccia; (*Brit Scol*) voto; (*Sport*) bersaglio; (*Hist: currency*) marco; (*Brit Tech*): **M~ 2/3** 1a/2a serie *f* ■ *vt* segnare; (*stain*) macchiare; (*Brit Scol*) dare un voto a; correggere; (*Sport: player*) marcare; **punctuation marks** segni di punteggiatura; **to be quick off the ~ (in doing)** (*fig*) non perdere tempo (per fare); **up to the ~** (*in efficiency*) all'altezza; **to ~ time** segnare il passo
▸ **mark down** *vt* (*reduce: prices, goods*) ribassare, ridurre
▸ **mark off** *vt* (*tick off*) spuntare, cancellare
▸ **mark out** *vt* delimitare
▸ **mark up** *vt* (*price*) aumentare
marked [mɑːkt] *adj* spiccato(-a), chiaro(-a)
markedly [ˈmɑːkɪdlɪ] *adv* visibilmente, notevolmente
marker [ˈmɑːkə^r] *n* (*sign*) segno; (*bookmark*) segnalibro
market [ˈmɑːkɪt] *n* mercato ■ *vt* (*Comm*) mettere in vendita; (*promote*) lanciare sul mercato; **to play the ~** giocare *or* speculare in borsa; **to be on the ~** essere (messo) in vendita *or* in commercio; **open ~** mercato libero
marketable [ˈmɑːkɪtəbl] *adj* commercializzabile
market analysis *n* analisi *f* di mercato
market day *n* giorno di mercato
market demand *n* domanda del mercato
market economy *n* economia di mercato
market forces *npl* forze *fpl* di mercato
market garden *n* (*Brit*) orto industriale
marketing [ˈmɑːkɪtɪŋ] *n* marketing *m*
marketplace [ˈmɑːkɪtpleɪs] *n* (piazza del) mercato; (*world of trade*) piazza, mercato
market price *n* prezzo di mercato
market research *n* indagine *f or* ricerca di mercato
market value *n* valore *m* di mercato
marking [ˈmɑːkɪŋ] *n* (*on animal*) marcatura di colore; (*on road*) segnaletica orizzontale
marksman [ˈmɑːksmən] *n* tiratore *m* scelto
marksmanship [ˈmɑːksmənʃɪp] *n* abilità nel tiro
mark-up [ˈmɑːkʌp] *n* (*Comm: margin*) margine *m* di vendita; (*: increase*) aumento
marmalade [ˈmɑːməleɪd] *n* marmellata d'arance
maroon [məˈruːn] *vt* (*fig*): **to be marooned (in** *or* **at)** essere abbandonato(-a) (in) ■ *adj* bordeaux *inv*
marquee [mɑːˈkiː] *n* padiglione *m*
marquess, marquis [ˈmɑːkwɪs] *n* marchese *m*
Marrakech, Marrakesh [mærəˈkɛʃ] *n* Marrakesh *f*
marriage [ˈmærɪdʒ] *n* matrimonio
marriage bureau *n* agenzia matrimoniale
marriage certificate *n* certificato di matrimonio
marriage guidance, (*US*) **marriage counseling** *n* consulenza matrimoniale
marriage of convenience *n* matrimonio di convenienza
married [ˈmærɪd] *adj* sposato(-a); (*life, love*) coniugale, matrimoniale
marrow [ˈmærəu] *n* midollo; (*vegetable*) zucca
marry [ˈmærɪ] *vt* sposare, sposarsi con; (*father, priest etc*) dare in matrimonio ■ *vi* (*also*: **get married**) sposarsi
Mars [mɑːz] *n* (*planet*) Marte *m*
Marseilles [mɑːˈseɪlz] *n* Marsiglia
marsh [mɑːʃ] *n* palude *f*
marshal [ˈmɑːʃl] *n* maresciallo; (*US: fire marshal*) capo; (*: police marshal*) capitano; (*for demonstration, meeting*) membro del servizio d'ordine ■ *vt* adunare
marshalling yard [ˈmɑːʃlɪŋ-] *n* scalo smistamento
marshmallow [mɑːʃˈmæləu] *n* (*Bot*) altea; (*sweet*) *caramella soffice e gommosa*
marshy [ˈmɑːʃɪ] *adj* paludoso(-a)
marsupial [mɑːˈsuːpɪəl] *adj, n* marsupiale (*m*)
martial [ˈmɑːʃl] *adj* marziale
martial arts *npl* arti *fpl* marziali
martial law *n* legge *f* marziale
Martian [ˈmɑːʃən] *n* marziano(-a)
martin [ˈmɑːtɪn] *n* (*also*: **house martin**) balestruccio
martyr [ˈmɑːtə^r] *n* martire *m/f* ■ *vt* martirizzare
martyrdom [ˈmɑːtədəm] *n* martirio
marvel [ˈmɑːvl] *n* meraviglia ■ *vi*: **to ~ (at)** meravigliarsi (di)

marvellous, (*US*) **marvelous** ['mɑːvələs] *adj* meraviglioso(-a)
Marxism ['mɑːksɪzəm] *n* marxismo
Marxist ['mɑːksɪst] *adj, n* marxista (*m/f*)
marzipan ['mɑːzɪpæn] *n* marzapane *m*
mascara [mæs'kɑːrə] *n* mascara *m inv*
mascot ['mæskət] *n* mascotte *f inv*
masculine ['mæskjulɪn] *adj* maschile ■ *n* genere *m* maschile
masculinity [mæskju'lɪnɪtɪ] *n* mascolinità
MASH [mæʃ] *n abbr* (*US Mil: = mobile army surgical hospital*) *ospedale di campo di unità mobile dell'esercito*
mash [mæʃ] *vt* (*Culin*) passare, schiacciare
mashed [mæʃt] *adj*: **~ potatoes** purè *m* di patate
mask [mɑːsk] *n* (*gen, Elec*) maschera ■ *vt* mascherare
masochism ['mæsəkɪzəm] *n* masochismo
masochist ['mæsəkɪst] *n* masochista *m/f*
mason ['meɪsn] *n* (*also*: **stonemason**) scalpellino; (*also*: **freemason**) massone *m*
masonic [mə'sɔnɪk] *adj* massonico(-a)
masonry ['meɪsnrɪ] *n* muratura
masquerade [mæskə'reɪd] *n* ballo in maschera; (*fig*) mascherata ■ *vi*: **to ~ as** farsi passare per
mass [mæs] *n* moltitudine *f*, massa; (*Physics*) massa; (*Rel*) messa ■ *vi* ammassarsi; **the masses** le masse; **to go to ~** andare a *or* alla messa
Mass. *abbr* (*US*) = **Massachusetts**
massacre ['mæsəkə^r] *n* massacro ■ *vt* massacrare
massage ['mæsɑːʒ] *n* massaggio ■ *vt* massaggiare
masseur [mæ'səː^r] *n* massaggiatore *m*
masseuse [mæ'səːz] *n* massaggiatrice *f*
massive ['mæsɪv] *adj* enorme, massiccio(-a)
mass market *n* mercato di massa
mass media *npl* mass media *mpl*
mass meeting *n* (*of everyone concerned*) riunione *f* generale; (*huge*) adunata popolare
mass-produce ['mæsprə'djuːs] *vt* produrre in serie
mass production *n* produzione *f* in serie
mast [mɑːst] *n* albero; (*Radio, TV*) pilone *m* (a traliccio)
mastectomy [mæs'tektəmɪ] *n* mastectomia
master ['mɑːstə^r] *n* padrone *m*; (*Art etc, teacher: in primary school*) maestro; (*: in secondary school*) professore *m*; (*title for boys*): **M~ X** Signorino X ■ *vt* domare; (*learn*) imparare a fondo; (*understand*) conoscere a fondo; **~ of ceremonies** *n* maestro di cerimonie; **M~'s degree** *n vedi nota*

MASTER'S DEGREE

Il *Master's degree* è il riconoscimento che viene conferito a chi segue un corso di specializzazione dopo aver conseguito un "Bachelor's degree". Vi sono diversi tipi di *Master's Degree*; i più comuni sono il "Master of Arts (MA)" e il "Master of Science (MSc)" che si ottengono dopo aver seguito un corso e aver presentato una tesi originale. Per il "Master of Letters (MLitt)" e il "Master of Philosophy (MPhil)" è invece sufficiente presentare la tesi; *vedi anche* "doctorate".

master disk *n* (*Comput*) disco *m* master *inv*, disco principale
masterful ['mɑːstəful] *adj* autoritario(-a), imperioso(-a)
master key *n* chiave *f* maestra
masterly ['mɑːstəlɪ] *adj* magistrale
mastermind ['mɑːstəmaɪnd] *n* mente *f* superiore ■ *vt* essere il cervello di
masterpiece ['mɑːstəpiːs] *n* capolavoro
master plan *n* piano generale
master stroke *n* colpo maestro
mastery ['mɑːstərɪ] *n* dominio; padronanza
mastiff ['mæstɪf] *n* mastino inglese
masturbate ['mæstəbeɪt] *vi* masturbare
masturbation [mæstə'beɪʃən] *n* masturbazione *f*
mat [mæt] *n* stuoia; (*also*: **doormat**) stoino, zerbino ■ *adj* = **matt**
match [mætʃ] *n* fiammifero; (*game*) partita, incontro; (*fig*) uguale *m/f*; matrimonio; partito ■ *vt* intonare; (*go well with*) andare benissimo con; (*equal*) uguagliare ■ *vi* intonarsi; **to be a good ~** andare bene
▸ **match up** *vt* intonare
matchbox ['mætʃbɔks] *n* scatola per fiammiferi
matching ['mætʃɪŋ] *adj* ben assortito(-a)
matchless ['mætʃlɪs] *adj* senza pari
mate [meɪt] *n* compagno(-a) di lavoro; (*col: friend*) amico(-a); (*animal*) compagno(-a); (*in merchant navy*) secondo ■ *vi* accoppiarsi ■ *vt* accoppiare
material [mə'tɪərɪəl] *n* (*substance*) materiale *m*, materia; (*cloth*) stoffa ■ *adj* materiale; (*important*) essenziale; **materials** *npl* (*equipment etc*) materiali *mpl*; occorrente *m*
materialistic [mətɪərɪə'lɪstɪk] *adj* materialistico(-a)
materialize [mə'tɪərɪəlaɪz] *vi* materializzarsi, realizzarsi
materially [mə'tɪərɪəlɪ] *adv* dal punto di vista materiale; sostanzialmente

m

maternal [mə'tə:nl] *adj* materno(-a)
maternity [mə'tə:nɪtɪ] *n* maternità ■ *cpd* di maternità; (*clothes*) pre-maman *inv*
maternity benefit *n* sussidio di maternità
maternity hospital *n* ≈ clinica ostetrica
matey ['meɪtɪ] *adj* (*Brit col*) amicone(-a)
math [mæθ] *n abbr* (US) = **mathematics**
mathematical [mæθə'mætɪkl] *adj* matematico(-a)
mathematician [mæθəmə'tɪʃən] *n* matematico(-a)
mathematics [mæθə'mætɪks] *n* matematica
maths [mæθs] *n abbr* (*Brit*) = **mathematics**
matinée ['mætɪneɪ] *n* matinée *f inv*
mating ['meɪtɪŋ] *n* accoppiamento
mating call *n* chiamata all'accoppiamento
mating season *n* stagione *f* degli amori
matriarchal [meɪtrɪ'ɑ:kl] *adj* matriarcale
matrices ['meɪtrɪsi:z] *npl of* **matrix**
matriculation [mətrɪkju'leɪʃən] *n* immatricolazione *f*
matrimonial [mætrɪ'məunɪəl] *adj* matrimoniale, coniugale
matrimony ['mætrɪmənɪ] *n* matrimonio
matrix (*pl* **matrices**) ['meɪtrɪks, 'meɪtrɪsi:z] *n* matrice *f*
matron ['meɪtrən] *n* (*in hospital*) capoinfermiera; (*in school*) infermiera
matronly ['meɪtrənlɪ] *adj* da matrona
matt [mæt] *adj* opaco(-a)
matted ['mætɪd] *adj* ingarbugliato(-a)
matter ['mætə^r] *n* questione *f*; (*Physics*) materia, sostanza; (*content*) contenuto; (*Med: pus*) pus *m* ■ *vi* importare; **it doesn't ~** non importa; (*I don't mind*) non fa niente; **what's the ~?** che cosa c'è?; **no ~ what** qualsiasi cosa accada; **that's another ~** quello è un altro affare; **as a ~ of course** come cosa naturale; **as a ~ of fact** in verità; **it's a ~ of habit** è una questione di abitudine; **printed ~** stampe *fpl*; **reading ~** (*Brit*) qualcosa da leggere
matter-of-fact [mætərəv'fækt] *adj* prosaico(-a)
matting ['mætɪŋ] *n* stuoia
mattress ['mætrɪs] *n* materasso
mature [mə'tjuə^r] *adj* maturo(-a); (*cheese*) stagionato(-a) ■ *vi* maturare; stagionare; (*Comm*) scadere
mature student *n studente universitario che ha più di 25 anni*
maturity [mə'tjuərɪtɪ] *n* maturità
maudlin ['mɔ:dlɪn] *adj* lacrimoso(-a)
maul [mɔ:l] *vt* lacerare
Mauritania [mɔrɪ'teɪnɪə] *n* Mauritania
Mauritius [mə'rɪʃəs] *n* Maurizio
mausoleum [mɔ:sə'lɪəm] *n* mausoleo
mauve [məuv] *adj* malva *inv*
maverick ['mævərɪk] *n* (*fig*) chi sta fuori del branco
mawkish ['mɔ:kɪʃ] *adj* sdolcinato(-a); insipido(-a)
max. *abbr* = **maximum**
maxim ['mæksɪm] *n* massima
maxima ['mæksɪmə] *npl of* **maximum**
maximize ['mæksɪmaɪz] *vt* (*profits etc*) massimizzare; (*chances*) aumentare al massimo
maximum ['mæksɪməm] *adj* massimo(-a) ■ *n* (*pl* **maxima**) massimo
May [meɪ] *n* maggio; *see also* **July**
may [meɪ] *vi* (*conditional*: **might**) (*indicating possibility*): **he ~ come** può darsi che venga; (*be allowed to*): **~ I smoke?** posso fumare?; **~ I sit here?** le dispiace se mi siedo qua?; (*wishes*): **~ God bless you!** Dio la benedica!; **he might be there** può darsi che ci sia; **he might come** potrebbe venire, può anche darsi che venga; **I might as well go** potrei anche andarmene; **you might like to try** forse le piacerebbe provare
maybe ['meɪbi:] *adv* forse, può darsi; **~ he'll ...** può darsi che lui ... + *sub*, forse lui ...; **~ not** forse no, può darsi di no
mayday ['meɪdeɪ] *n* S.O.S. *m*, mayday *m inv*
May Day *n* il primo maggio
mayhem ['meɪhɛm] *n* cagnara
mayonnaise [meɪə'neɪz] *n* maionese *f*
mayor [mɛə^r] *n* sindaco
mayoress ['mɛərɛs] *n* sindaco (*donna*); moglie *f* del sindaco
maypole ['meɪpəul] *n palo ornato di fiori attorno a cui si danza durante la festa di maggio*
maze [meɪz] *n* labirinto, dedalo
MB *abbr* (*Comput*) = **megabyte**; (*Canada*) = **Manitoba**
MBA *n abbr* (= *Master of Business Administration*) *titolo di studio*
MBE *n abbr* (*Brit*: = *Member of the Order of the British Empire*) *titolo*
MBO *n abbr* = **management buyout**
MC *n abbr* = **master of ceremonies**; (US: = *Member of Congress*) *membro del Congresso*
MCAT *n abbr* (US: = *Medical College Admissions Test*) *esame di ammissione a studi superiori di medicina*
MD *n abbr* (= *Doctor of Medicine*) *titolo di studio*; (*Comm*) = **managing director** ■ *abbr* (US) = **Maryland**
Md. *abbr* (US) = **Maryland**
MDT *abbr* (US: = *Mountain Daylight Time*) *ora legale delle Montagne Rocciose*
ME *abbr* (US) = **Maine** ■ *n abbr* (*Med*: = *myalgic encephalomyelitis*) sindrome *f* da affaticamento cronico; (US) = **medical examiner**

me [mi:] *pron* mi, m' *+vowel*; *(stressed, after prep)* me; **it's me** sono io; **it's for me** è per me
meadow ['mɛdəu] *n* prato
meagre, *(US)* **meager** ['mi:gəʳ] *adj* magro(-a)
meal [mi:l] *n* pasto; *(flour)* farina; **to go out for a ~** mangiare fuori
meals on wheels *n* *(Brit)* distribuzione *f* di pasti caldi a domicilio *(per persone malate o anziane)*
mealtime ['mi:ltaɪm] *n* l'ora di mangiare
mealy-mouthed ['mi:lɪmauðd] *adj* che parla attraverso eufemismi
mean [mi:n] *adj* *(with money)* avaro(-a), gretto(-a); *(unkind)* meschino(-a), maligno(-a); *(US: vicious: animal)* cattivo(-a); *(: person)* perfido(-a); *(average)* medio(-a) ■ *vt* *(pt, pp* **meant***)* [mɛnt] *(signify)* significare, voler dire; *(intend)*: **to ~ to do** aver l'intenzione di fare ■ *n* mezzo; *(Math)* media; **to be meant for** essere destinato(-a) a; **do you ~ it?** dice sul serio?; **what do you ~?** che cosa vuol dire?; *see also* **means**
meander [mɪ'ændəʳ] *vi* far meandri; *(fig)* divagare
meaning ['mi:nɪŋ] *n* significato, senso
meaningful ['mi:nɪŋful] *adj* significativo(-a); *(relationship)* valido(-a)
meaningless ['mi:nɪŋlɪs] *adj* senza senso
meanness ['mi:nnɪs] *n* avarizia; meschinità
means [mi:nz] *npl* mezzi *mpl*; **by ~ of** per mezzo di; *(person)* a mezzo di; **by all ~** ma certo, prego
means test *n* *(Admin)* accertamento dei redditi *(per una persona che ha chiesto un aiuto finanziario)*
meant [mɛnt] *pt, pp of* **mean**
meantime ['mi:ntaɪm], **meanwhile** ['mi:nwaɪl] *adv* *(also:* **in the meantime***)* nel frattempo
measles ['mi:zlz] *n* morbillo
measly ['mi:zlɪ] *adj* *(col)* miserabile
measurable ['mɛʒərəbl] *adj* misurabile
measure ['mɛʒəʳ] *vt, vi* misurare ■ *n* misura; *(ruler)* metro; **a litre ~** una misura da un litro; **some ~ of success** un certo successo; **to take measures to do sth** prendere provvedimenti per fare qc
▸ **measure up** *vi*: **to ~ up (to)** dimostrarsi *or* essere all'altezza (di)
measured ['mɛʒəd] *adj* misurato(-a)
measurement ['mɛʒəmənt] *n* *(act)* misurazione *f*; *(measure)* misura; **chest/hip ~** giro petto/fianchi; **to take sb's measurements** prendere le misure di qn
meat [mi:t] *n* carne *f*; **cold meats** *(Brit)* affettati *mpl*; **crab ~** polpa di granchio
meatball ['mi:tbɔ:l] *n* polpetta di carne
meat pie *n* *torta salata in pasta frolla con ripieno di carne*
meaty ['mi:tɪ] *adj* che sa di carne; *(fig)* sostanzioso(-a); *(person)* corpulento(-a); *(part of body)* carnoso(-a); **~ meal** pasto a base di carne
Mecca ['mɛkə] *n* La Mecca; *(fig)*: **a ~ (for)** la Mecca (di)
mechanic [mɪ'kænɪk] *n* meccanico; *see also* **mechanics**
mechanical [mɪ'kænɪkəl] *adj* meccanico(-a)
mechanical engineering *n* *(science)* ingegneria meccanica; *(industry)* costruzioni *fpl* meccaniche
mechanics [mə'kænɪks] *n* meccanica ■ *npl* meccanismo
mechanism ['mɛkənɪzəm] *n* meccanismo
mechanization [mɛkənaɪ'zeɪʃən] *n* meccanizzazione *f*
MEd *n abbr (= Master of Education) titolo di studio*
medal ['mɛdl] *n* medaglia
medallion [mɪ'dælɪən] *n* medaglione *m*
medallist, *(US)* **medalist** ['mɛdəlɪst] *n* *(Sport)* vincitore(-trice) di medaglia
meddle ['mɛdl] *vi*: **to ~ in** immischiarsi in, mettere le mani in; **to ~ with** toccare
meddlesome ['mɛdlsəm], **meddling** ['mɛdlɪŋ] *adj* *(interfering)* che mette il naso dappertutto; *(touching things)* che tocca tutto
media ['mi:dɪə] *npl* *(Press, Radio, TV)* media *mpl*
media circus *n* carrozzone *m* dell'informazione
mediaeval [mɛdɪ'i:vl] *adj* = **medieval**
median ['mi:dɪən] *n* *(US: also:* **median strip***)* banchina *f* spartitraffico *inv*
media research *n* sondaggio tra gli utenti dei mass media
mediate ['mi:dɪeɪt] *vi* interporsi; fare da mediatore(-trice)
mediation [mi:dɪ'eɪʃən] *n* mediazione *f*
mediator ['mi:dɪeɪtəʳ] *n* mediatore(-trice)
Medicaid ['mɛdɪkeɪd] *n* *(US) assistenza medica ai poveri*
medical ['mɛdɪkl] *adj* medico(-a); **~ (examination)** visita medica
medical certificate *n* certificato medico
medical examiner *n* *(US) medico incaricato di indagare la causa di morte in circostanze sospette*
medical student *n* studente(-essa) di medicina
Medicare ['mɛdɪkɛəʳ] *n* *(US) assistenza medica agli anziani*
medicated ['mɛdɪkeɪtɪd] *adj* medicato(-a)
medication [mɛdɪ'keɪʃən] *n* *(drugs etc)* medicinali *mpl*, farmaci *mpl*
medicinal [mɛ'dɪsɪnl] *adj* medicinale
medicine ['mɛdsɪn] *n* medicina

m

medicine chest *n* armadietto farmaceutico
medicine man *n* stregone *m*
medieval [mɛdɪ'i:vl] *adj* medievale
mediocre [mi:dɪ'əukəʳ] *adj* mediocre
mediocrity [mi:dɪ'ɔkrɪtɪ] *n* mediocrità
meditate ['mɛdɪteɪt] *vi*: **to ~ (on)** meditare (su)
meditation [mɛdɪ'teɪʃən] *n* meditazione *f*
Mediterranean [mɛdɪtə'reɪnɪən] *adj* mediterraneo(-a); **the ~ (Sea)** il (mare) Mediterraneo
medium ['mi:dɪəm] *adj* medio(-a) ■ *n* (*pl* **media**) (*means*) mezzo (*pl* **mediums**) (*person*) medium *m inv*; **the happy ~** una giusta via di mezzo; *see also* **media**
medium-dry ['mi:dɪəm'draɪ] *adj* demisec *inv*
medium-sized ['mi:dɪəmsaɪzd] *adj* (*tin etc*) di grandezza media; (*clothes*) di taglia media
medium wave *n* (*Radio*) onde *fpl* medie
medley ['mɛdlɪ] *n* selezione *f*
meek [mi:k] *adj* dolce, umile
meet (*pt, pp* **met**) [mi:t, mɛt] *vt* incontrare; (*for the first time*) fare la conoscenza di; (*fig*) affrontare; far fronte a; soddisfare; raggiungere ■ *vi* incontrarsi; (*in session*) riunirsi; (*join: objects*) unirsi ■ *n* (*Brit Hunting*) raduno (dei partecipanti alla caccia alla volpe); (*US Sport*) raduno (sportivo); **I'll ~ you at the station** verrò a prenderla alla stazione; **pleased to ~ you!** lieto di conoscerla!, piacere!
▸ **meet up** *vi*: **to ~ up with sb** incontrare qn
▸ **meet with** *vt fus* incontrare; **he met with an accident** ha avuto un incidente
meeting ['mi:tɪŋ] *n* incontro; (*session: of club etc*) riunione *f*; (*interview*) intervista; (*formal*) colloquio; (*Sport: rally*) raduno; **she's at a ~** (*Comm*) è in riunione; **to call a ~** convocare una riunione
meeting place *n* luogo d'incontro
megabyte ['mɛgəbaɪt] *n* megabyte *m inv*
megalomaniac [mɛgələu'meɪnɪæk] *n* megalomane *m/f*
megaphone ['mɛgəfəun] *n* megafono
megapixel ['mɛgəpɪksl] *n* megapixel *m inv*
megawatt ['mɛgəwɔt] *n* megawatt *m inv*
melancholy ['mɛlənkəlɪ] *n* malinconia ■ *adj* malinconico(-a)
mellow ['mɛləu] *adj* (*wine, sound*) ricco(-a); (*person, light*) dolce; (*colour*) caldo(-a); (*fruit*) maturo(-a) ■ *vi* (*person*) addolcirsi
melodious [mɪ'ləudɪəs] *adj* melodioso(-a)
melodrama ['mɛləudrɑ:mə] *n* melodramma *m*
melodramatic [mɛlədrə'mætɪk] *adj* melodrammatico(-a)
melody ['mɛlədɪ] *n* melodia
melon ['mɛlən] *n* melone *m*
melt [mɛlt] *vi* (*gen*) sciogliersi, struggersi; (*metals*) fondersi; (*fig*) intenerirsi ■ *vt* sciogliere, struggere; fondere; (*person*) commuovere; **melted butter** burro fuso
▸ **melt away** *vi* sciogliersi completamente
▸ **melt down** *vt* fondere
meltdown ['mɛltdaun] *n* melt-down *m inv*
melting point ['mɛltɪŋ-] *n* punto di fusione
melting pot ['mɛltɪŋ-] *n* (*fig*) crogiolo; **to be in the ~** essere ancora in discussione
member ['mɛmbəʳ] *n* membro; (*of club*) socio(-a), iscritto(-a); (*of political party*) iscritto(-a); **~ country/state** *n* paese *m*/stato membro; **M~ of Parliament (MP)** *n* (*Brit*) deputato; **M~ of the European Parliament** *n* eurodeputato; **M~ of the House of Representatives** *n* (*US*) membro della Camera dei Rappresentanti
membership ['mɛmbəʃɪp] *n* iscrizione *f*; (numero d')iscritti *mpl*, membri *mpl*
membership card *n* tessera (di iscrizione)
membrane ['mɛmbreɪn] *n* membrana
memento [mə'mɛntəu] *n* ricordo, souvenir *m inv*
memo ['mɛməu] *n* appunto; (*Comm etc*) comunicazione *f* di servizio
memoir ['mɛmwɑ:ʳ] *n* memoria; **memoirs** *npl* memorie *fpl*, ricordi *mpl*
memo pad *n* blocchetto per appunti
memorable ['mɛmərəbl] *adj* memorabile
memorandum (*pl* **memoranda**) [mɛmə'rændəm, -də] *n* appunto; (*Comm etc*) comunicazione *f* di servizio; (*Diplomacy*) memorandum *m inv*
memorial [mɪ'mɔ:rɪəl] *n* monumento commemorativo ■ *adj* commemorativo(-a)
Memorial Day *n* (*US*) *vedi nota*

MEMORIAL DAY

Negli Stati Uniti il *Memorial Day* è una festa nazionale per la commemorazione di tutti i soldati americani caduti in guerra. Le celebrazioni sono tenute ogni anno l'ultimo lunedì di maggio.

memorize ['mɛməraɪz] *vt* imparare a memoria
memory ['mɛmərɪ] *n* (*gen, Comput*) memoria; (*recollection*) ricordo; **in ~ of** in memoria di; **to have a good/bad ~** aver buona/cattiva memoria; **loss of ~** amnesia
memory card *n* (*for digital camera*) scheda di memoria *m inv* di memoria
memory stick *n* (*Comput*) stick *m inv* di memoria
men [mɛn] *npl of* **man**
menace ['mɛnɪs] *n* minaccia; (*col: nuisance*)

peste *f* ■ *vt* minacciare; **a public ~** un pericolo pubblico
menacing ['mɛnɪsɪŋ] *adj* minaccioso(-a)
menagerie [mɪ'nædʒərɪ] *n* serraglio
mend [mɛnd] *vt* aggiustare, riparare; (*darn*) rammendare ■ *n* rammendo; **on the ~** in via di guarigione
mending ['mɛndɪŋ] *n* rammendo; (*items to be mended*) roba da rammendare
menial ['mi:nɪəl] *adj* da servo, domestico(-a); umile
meningitis [mɛnɪn'dʒaɪtɪs] *n* meningite *f*
menopause ['mɛnəupɔ:z] *n* menopausa
menservants ['mɛnsə:vənts] *npl of* **manservant**
men's room *n*: **the ~** (*esp US*) la toilette degli uomini
menstruate ['mɛnstrueɪt] *vi* mestruare
menstruation [mɛnstru'eɪʃən] *n* mestruazione *f*
menswear ['mɛnzwɛə^r] *n* abbigliamento maschile
mental ['mɛntl] *adj* mentale; **~ illness** malattia mentale
mental hospital *n* ospedale *m* psichiatrico
mentality [mɛn'tælɪtɪ] *n* mentalità *f inv*
mentally ['mɛntlɪ] *adv*: **to be ~ handicapped** essere minorato psichico
menthol ['mɛnθɔl] *n* mentolo
mention ['mɛnʃən] *n* menzione *f* ■ *vt* menzionare, far menzione di; **don't ~ it!** non c'è di che!, prego!; **I need hardly ~ that …** inutile dire che …; **not to ~, without mentioning** per non parlare di, senza contare
mentor ['mɛntɔ:^r] *n* mentore *m*
menu ['mɛnju:] *n* (*set menu, Comput*) menù *m inv*; (*printed*) carta
menu-driven ['mɛnju:drɪvn] *adj* (*Comput*) guidato(-a) da menù
MEP *n abbr* = **Member of the European Parliament**
mercantile ['mə:kəntaɪl] *adj* mercantile; (*law*) commerciale
mercenary ['mə:sɪnərɪ] *adj* venale ■ *n* mercenario
merchandise ['mə:tʃəndaɪz] *n* merci *fpl* ■ *vt* commercializzare
merchandiser ['mə:tʃəndaɪzə^r] *n* merchandiser *m inv*
merchant ['mə:tʃənt] *n* (*trader*) commerciante *m*; (*shopkeeper*) negoziante *m*; **timber/wine ~** negoziante di legno/vino
merchant bank *n* (*Brit*) banca d'affari
merchantman ['mə:tʃəntmən] *n* mercantile *m*
merchant navy, (*US*) **merchant marine** *n* marina mercantile
merciful ['mə:sɪful] *adj* pietoso(-a), clemente
mercifully ['mə:sɪflɪ] *adv* con clemenza; (*fortunately*) per fortuna
merciless ['mə:sɪlɪs] *adj* spietato(-a)
mercurial [mə:'kjuərɪəl] *adj* (*unpredictable*) volubile
mercury ['mə:kjurɪ] *n* mercurio
mercy ['mə:sɪ] *n* pietà; (*Rel*) misericordia; **to have ~ on sb** aver pietà di qn; **at the ~ of** alla mercè di
mercy killing *n* eutanasia
mere [mɪə^r] *adj* semplice; **by a ~ chance** per mero caso
merely ['mɪəlɪ] *adv* semplicemente, non … che
merge [mə:dʒ] *vt* unire; (*Comput: files, text*) fondere ■ *vi* fondersi, unirsi; (*Comm*) fondersi
merger ['mə:dʒə^r] *n* (*Comm*) fusione *f*
meridian [mə'rɪdɪən] *n* meridiano
meringue [mə'ræŋ] *n* meringa
merit ['mɛrɪt] *n* merito, valore *m* ■ *vt* meritare
meritocracy [mɛrɪ'tɔkrəsɪ] *n* meritocrazia
mermaid ['mə:meɪd] *n* sirena
merriment ['mɛrɪmənt] *n* gaiezza, allegria
merry ['mɛrɪ] *adj* gaio(-a), allegro(-a); **M~ Christmas!** Buon Natale!
merry-go-round ['mɛrɪgəuraund] *n* carosello
mesh [mɛʃ] *n* maglia; rete *f* ■ *vi* (*gears*) ingranarsi; **wire ~** rete metallica
mesmerize ['mɛzməraɪz] *vt* ipnotizzare; affascinare
mess [mɛs] *n* confusione *f*, disordine *m*; (*fig*) pasticcio; (*Mil*) mensa; **to be (in) a ~** (*house, room*) essere in disordine (*or* molto sporco); (*fig: marriage, life*) essere un caos; **to be/get o.s. in a ~** (*fig*) essere/cacciarsi in un pasticcio
▶ **mess about, mess around** *vi* (*col*) trastullarsi
▶ **mess about** *or* **around with** *vt fus* (*col*) gingillarsi con; (*plans*) fare un pasticcio di
▶ **mess up** *vt* sporcare; fare un pasticcio di; rovinare
message ['mɛsɪdʒ] *n* messaggio; **to get the ~** (*fig, col*) capire l'antifona
message board *n* (*Comput*) bacheca elettronica
message switching *n* (*Comput*) smistamento messaggi
messenger ['mɛsɪndʒə^r] *n* messaggero(-a)
Messiah [mɪ'saɪə] *n* Messia *m*
Messrs, Messrs. ['mɛsəz] *abbr* (*on letters: = messieurs*) Spett.
messy ['mɛsɪ] *adj* sporco(-a); disordinato(-a); (*confused: situation etc*) ingarbugliato(-a)

Met [mɛt] *n abbr* (*US*) = **Metropolitan Opera**
met [mɛt] *pt, pp of* **meet** ▪ *adj abbr* = **meteorological**; **the M~ Office** l'Ufficio Meteorologico
metabolism [mɛ'tæbəlɪzəm] *n* metabolismo
metal ['mɛtl] *n* metallo ▪ *vt* massicciare
metallic [mɛ'tælɪk] *adj* metallico(-a)
metallurgy [mɛ'tælədʒɪ] *n* metallurgia
metalwork ['mɛtlwə:k] *n* (*craft*) lavorazione *f* del metallo
metamorphosis (*pl* **-phoses**) [mɛtə'mɔ:fəsɪs, -i:z] *n* metamorfosi *f inv*
metaphor ['mɛtəfə^r] *n* metafora
metaphysics [mɛtə'fɪzɪks] *n* metafisica
mete [mi:t]: **to ~ out** *vt fus* infliggere
meteor ['mi:tɪə^r] *n* meteora
meteoric [mi:tɪ'ɔrɪk] *adj* (*fig*) fulmineo(-a)
meteorite ['mi:tɪəraɪt] *n* meteorite *m*
meteorological [mi:tɪərə'lɔdʒɪkl] *adj* meteorologico(-a)
meteorology [mi:tɪə'rɔlədʒɪ] *n* meteorologia
meter ['mi:tə^r] *n* (*instrument*) contatore *m*; (*parking meter*) parchimetro; (*US*) = **metre**
methane ['mi:θeɪn] *n* metano
method ['mɛθəd] *n* metodo; **~ of payment** modo *or* modalità *f inv* di pagamento
methodical [mɪ'θɔdɪkl] *adj* metodico(-a)
Methodist ['mɛθədɪst] *adj, n* metodista (*m/f*)
methylated spirits ['mɛθɪleɪtɪd-] *n* (*Brit: also:* **meths**) alcool *m* denaturato
meticulous [mɛ'tɪkjuləs] *adj* meticoloso(-a)
metre, (*US*) **meter** ['mi:tə^r] *n* metro
metric ['mɛtrɪk] *adj* metrico(-a); **to go ~** adottare il sistema metrico decimale
metrical ['mɛtrɪkl] *adj* metrico(-a)
metrication [mɛtrɪ'keɪʃən] *n* conversione *f* al sistema metrico
metric system *n* sistema *m* metrico decimale
metric ton *n* tonnellata
metronome ['mɛtrənəum] *n* metronomo
metropolis [mɪ'trɔpəlɪs] *n* metropoli *f inv*
metropolitan [mɛtrə'pɔlɪtən] *adj* metropolitano(-a)
Metropolitan Police *n* (*Brit*): **the ~** la polizia di Londra
mettle ['mɛtl] *n* coraggio
mew [mju:] *vi* (*cat*) miagolare
mews [mju:z] *n* (*Brit*): **~ flat** *appartamentino ricavato da una vecchia scuderia*
Mexican ['mɛksɪkən] *adj, n* messicano(-a)
Mexico ['mɛksɪkəu] *n* Messico
Mexico City *n* Città del Messico
mezzanine ['mɛtsəni:n] *n* mezzanino
MFA *n abbr* (*US: = Master of Fine Arts*) *titolo di studio*
mfr *abbr* = **manufacture**; **manufacturer**
mg *abbr* (*= milligram*) mg
Mgr *abbr* (*= Monseigneur, Monsignor*) mons.; (*Comm*) = **manager**
MHR *n abbr* (*US*) = **Member of the House of Representatives**
MHz *abbr* (*= megahertz*) MHz
MI *abbr* (*US*) = **Michigan**
MI5 *n abbr* (*Brit: = Military Intelligence, section five*) *agenzia di controspionaggio*
MI6 *n abbr* (*Brit: = Military Intelligence, section six*) *agenzia di spionaggio*
MIA *abbr* = **missing in action**
miaow [mi:'au] *vi* miagolare
mice [maɪs] *npl of* **mouse**
Mich. *abbr* (*US*) = **Michigan**
microbe ['maɪkrəub] *n* microbio
microbiology [maɪkrəubaɪ'ɔlədʒɪ] *n* microbiologia
microchip ['maɪkrəutʃɪp] *n* microcircuito integrato, chip *m inv*
microcomputer [maɪkrəukəm'pju:tə^r] *n* microcomputer *m inv*
microcosm ['maɪkrəukɔzəm] *n* microcosmo
microeconomics [maɪkrəui:kə'nɔmɪks] *n* microeconomia
microfiche ['maɪkrəufi:ʃ] *n* microfiche *f inv*
microfilm ['maɪkrəufɪlm] *n* microfilm *m inv* ▪ *vt* microfilmare
microlight ['maɪkrəulaɪt] *n* aereo *m* biposto *inv*
micrometer [maɪ'krɔmɪtə^r] *n* micrometro, palmer *m inv*
microphone ['maɪkrəfəun] *n* microfono
microprocessor [maɪkrəu'prəusɛsə^r] *n* microprocessore *m*
micro-scooter ['maɪkrəusku:tə^r] *n* monopattino
microscope ['maɪkrəskəup] *n* microscopio; **under the ~** al microscopio
microscopic [maɪkrə'skɔpɪk] *adj* microscopico(-a)
microwavable, microwaveable ['maɪkrəuweɪvəbl] *adj* adatto(-a) al forno a microonde
microwave ['maɪkrəuweɪv] *n* (*also:* **microwave oven**) forno a microonde
mid [mɪd] *adj*: **~ May** metà maggio; **~ afternoon** metà pomeriggio; **in ~ air** a mezz'aria; **he's in his ~ thirties** avrà circa trentacinque anni
midday [mɪd'deɪ] *n* mezzogiorno
middle ['mɪdl] *n* mezzo; centro; (*waist*) vita ▪ *adj* di mezzo; **I'm in the ~ of reading it** sto proprio leggendolo ora; **in the ~ of the night** nel mezzo della notte
middle age *n* mezza età
middle-aged [mɪdl'eɪdʒd] *adj* di mezza età

Middle Ages *npl*: **the ~** il Medioevo
middle class *adj* (*also*: **middle-class**) ≈ borghese ■ *n*: **the ~(es)** ≈ la borghesia
Middle East *n*: **the ~** il Medio Oriente
middleman ['mɪdlmæn] *n* intermediario; agente *m* rivenditore
middle management *n* quadri *mpl* intermedi
middle name *n* secondo nome *m*
middle-of-the-road ['mɪdləvðə'rəud] *adj* moderato(-a)
middleweight ['mɪdlweɪt] *n* (*Boxing*) peso medio
middling ['mɪdlɪŋ] *adj* medio(-a)
midge [mɪdʒ] *n* moscerino
midget ['mɪdʒɪt] *n* nano(-a)
midi system ['mɪdɪ-] *n* (*hi-fi*) compatto
Midlands ['mɪdləndz] *npl contee del centro dell'Inghilterra*
midnight ['mɪdnaɪt] *n* mezzanotte *f*; **at ~** a mezzanotte
midriff ['mɪdrɪf] *n* diaframma *m*
midst [mɪdst] *n*: **in the ~ of** in mezzo a
midsummer [mɪd'sʌmə^r] *n* mezza *or* piena estate *f*
midway [mɪd'weɪ] *adj, adv*: **~ (between)** a mezza strada (fra)
midweek [mɪd'wi:k] *adv, adj* a metà settimana
midwife (*pl* **midwives**) ['mɪdwaɪf, -vz] *n* levatrice *f*
midwifery ['mɪdwɪfərɪ] *n* ostetrica
midwinter [mɪd'wɪntə^r] *n* pieno inverno
miffed [mɪft] *adj* (*col*) seccato(-a), stizzito(-a)
might [maɪt] *vb see* **may** ■ *n* potere *m*, forza
mighty ['maɪtɪ] *adj* forte, potente ■ *adv* (*col*) molto
migraine ['mi:greɪn] *n* emicrania
migrant ['maɪgrənt] *n* (*bird, animal*) migratore *m*; (*person*) migrante *m/f*; nomade *m/f* ■ *adj* migratore(-trice), nomade; (*worker*) emigrato(-a)
migrate [maɪ'greɪt] *vi* migrare
migration [maɪ'greɪʃən] *n* migrazione *f*
mike [maɪk] *n abbr* (= *microphone*) microfono
Milan [mɪ'læn] *n* Milano *f*
mild [maɪld] *adj* mite; (*person, voice*) dolce; (*flavour*) delicato(-a); (*illness*) leggero(-a) ■ *n* birra leggera
mildew ['mɪldju:] *n* muffa
mildly ['maɪldlɪ] *adv* mitemente; dolcemente; delicatamente; leggermente; **to put it ~** a dire poco
mildness ['maɪldnɪs] *n* mitezza; dolcezza; delicatezza; non gravità
mile [maɪl] *n* miglio; **to do 20 miles per gallon** ≈ usare 14 litri per cento chilometri
mileage ['maɪlɪdʒ] *n* distanza in miglia, ≈ chilometraggio
mileage allowance *n* rimborso per miglio
mileometer [maɪ'lɔmɪtə^r] *n* (*Brit*) = **milometer**
milestone ['maɪlstəun] *n* pietra miliare
milieu ['mi:ljə:] *n* ambiente *m*
militant ['mɪlɪtnt] *adj, n* militante (*m/f*)
militarism ['mɪlɪtərɪzəm] *n* militarismo
militaristic [mɪlɪtə'rɪstɪk] *adj* militaristico(-a)
military ['mɪlɪtərɪ] *adj* militare ■ *n*: **the ~** i militari, l'esercito
military service *n* servizio militare
militate ['mɪlɪteɪt] *vi*: **to ~ against** essere d'ostacolo a
militia [mɪ'lɪʃə] *n* milizia
milk [mɪlk] *n* latte *m* ■ *vt* (*cow*) mungere; (*fig*) sfruttare
milk chocolate *n* cioccolato al latte
milk float *n* (*Brit*) furgone *m* del lattaio
milking ['mɪlkɪŋ] *n* mungitura
milkman ['mɪlkmən] *n* lattaio
milk shake *n* frappé *m inv*
milk tooth *n* dente *m* di latte
milk truck *n* (*US*) = **milk float**
milky ['mɪlkɪ] *adj* lattiginoso(-a); (*colour*) latteo(-a)
Milky Way *n* Via Lattea
mill [mɪl] *n* mulino; (*small: for coffee, pepper etc*) macinino; (*factory*) fabbrica; (*spinning mill*) filatura ■ *vt* macinare ■ *vi* (*also*: **mill about**) formicolare
millennium (*pl* **millenniums** *or* **millennia**) [mɪ'lɛnɪəm, -'lɛnɪə] *n* millennio
millennium bug *n* baco di fine millennio
miller ['mɪlə^r] *n* mugnaio
millet ['mɪlɪt] *n* miglio
milli... ['mɪlɪ] *prefix* milli...
milligram, milligramme ['mɪlɪgræm] *n* milligrammo
millilitre, (*US*) **milliliter** ['mɪlɪli:tə^r] *n* millilitro
millimetre, (*US*) **millimeter** ['mɪlɪmi:tə^r] *n* millimetro
milliner ['mɪlɪnə^r] *n* modista
millinery ['mɪlɪnərɪ] *n* modisteria
million ['mɪljən] *n* milione *m*
millionaire [mɪljə'nɛə^r] *n* milionario, ≈ miliardario
millipede ['mɪlɪpi:d] *n* millepiedi *m inv*
millstone ['mɪlstəun] *n* macina
millwheel ['mɪlwi:l] *n* ruota di mulino
milometer [maɪ'lɔmɪtə^r] *n* ≈ contachilometri *m inv*
mime [maɪm] *n* mimo ■ *vt, vi* mimare
mimic ['mɪmɪk] *n* imitatore(-trice) ■ *vt* (*comedian*) imitare; (*animal, person*) scimmiottare

m

mimicry ['mɪmɪkrɪ] *n* imitazioni *fpl*; (*Zool*) mimetismo
Min. *abbr* (*Brit Pol*: = *ministry*) Min.
min. *abbr* (= *minute, minimum*) min.
minaret [mɪnə'rɛt] *n* minareto
mince [mɪns] *vt* tritare, macinare ■ *vi* (*in walking*) camminare a passettini ■ *n* (*Brit Culin*) carne *f* tritata *or* macinata; **he does not ~ (his) words** parla chiaro e tondo
mincemeat ['mɪnsmi:t] *n frutta secca tritata per uso in pasticceria*
mince pie *n specie di torta con frutta secca*
mincer ['mɪnsə^r] *n* tritacarne *m inv*
mincing ['mɪnsɪŋ] *adj* lezioso(-a)
mind [maɪnd] *n* mente *f* ■ *vt* (*attend to, look after*) badare a, occuparsi di; (*be careful*) fare attenzione a, stare attento(-a) a; (*object to*): **I don't ~ the noise** il rumore non mi dà alcun fastidio; **do you ~ if ...?** le dispiace se ...?; **I don't ~** non m'importa; **~ you, ...** sì, però va detto che ...; **never ~** non importa, non fa niente; **it is on my ~** mi preoccupa; **to change one's ~** cambiare idea; **to be in two minds about sth** essere incerto su qc; **to my ~** secondo me, a mio parere; **to be out of one's ~** essere uscito(-a) di mente; **to keep sth in ~** non dimenticare qc; **to bear sth in ~** tener presente qc; **to have sb/sth in ~** avere in mente qn/qc; **to have in ~ to do** aver l'intenzione di fare; **it went right out of my ~** mi è completamente passato di mente, me ne sono completamente dimenticato; **to bring** *or* **call sth to ~** riportare *or* richiamare qc alla mente; **to make up one's ~** decidersi; **"~ the step"** "attenzione allo scalino"
mind-boggling ['maɪndbɔglɪŋ] *adj* (*col*) sconcertante
-minded ['maɪndɪd] *adj*: **fair~** imparziale; **an industrially~ nation** una nazione orientata verso l'industria
minder ['maɪndə^r] *n* (*child minder*) bambinaia; (*bodyguard*) guardia del corpo
mindful ['maɪndful] *adj*: **~ of** attento(-a) a; memore di
mindless ['maɪndlɪs] *adj* idiota; (*violence, crime*) insensato(-a)
mine[1] [maɪn] *pron* il/la mio(-a); (*pl*) i/le miei/ mie; **this book is ~** questo libro è mio
mine[2] [maɪn] *n* miniera; (*explosive*) mina ■ *vt* (*coal*) estrarre; (*ship, beach*) minare
mine detector *n* rivelatore *m* di mine
minefield ['maɪnfi:ld] *n* campo minato
miner ['maɪnə^r] *n* minatore *m*
mineral ['mɪnərəl] *adj* minerale ■ *n* minerale *m*; **minerals** *npl* (*Brit: soft drinks*) bevande *fpl* gasate
mineralogy [mɪnə'rælədʒɪ] *n* mineralogia
mineral water *n* acqua minerale
minesweeper ['maɪnswi:pə^r] *n* dragamine *m inv*
mingle ['mɪŋgl] *vt* mescolare, mischiare ■ *vi*: **to ~ with** mescolarsi a, mischiarsi con
mingy ['mɪndʒɪ] *adj* (*col: amount*) misero(-a); (*: person*) spilorcio(-a)
miniature ['mɪnətʃə^r] *adj* in miniatura ■ *n* miniatura
minibus ['mɪnɪbʌs] *n* minibus *m inv*
minicab ['mɪnɪkæb] *n* (*Brit*) ≈ taxi *m inv*
minicomputer ['mɪnɪkəm'pju:tə^r] *n* minicomputer *m inv*
Minidisc® ['mɪnɪdɪsk] *n* minidisc *m inv*
minim ['mɪnɪm] *n* (*Mus*) minima
minima ['mɪnɪmə] *npl of* **minimum**
minimal ['mɪnɪml] *adj* minimo(-a)
minimalist ['mɪnɪməlɪst] *adj, n* minimalista (*m/f*)
minimize ['mɪnɪmaɪz] *vt* minimizzare
minimum ['mɪnɪməm] *n* (*pl* **minima**) minimo ■ *adj* minimo(-a); **to reduce to a ~** ridurre al minimo; **~ wage** salario minimo garantito
minimum lending rate *n* (*Brit*) ≈ tasso ufficiale di sconto
mining ['maɪnɪŋ] *n* industria mineraria ■ *adj* minerario(-a); di minatori
minion ['mɪnjən] *n* (*pej*) caudatario; favorito(-a)
mini-series ['mɪnɪsɪəri:z] *n* miniserie *f inv*
miniskirt ['mɪnɪskə:t] *n* minigonna
minister ['mɪnɪstə^r] *n* (*Brit Pol*) ministro; (*Rel*) pastore *m* ■ *vi*: **to ~ to sb** assistere qn; **to ~ to sb's needs** provvedere ai bisogni di qn
ministerial [mɪnɪs'tɪərɪəl] *adj* (*Brit Pol*) ministeriale
ministry ['mɪnɪstrɪ] *n* (*Brit Pol*) ministero; (*Rel*): **to go into the ~** diventare pastore
mink [mɪŋk] *n* visone *m*
mink coat *n* pelliccia di visone
Minn. *abbr* (*US*) = **Minnesota**
minnow ['mɪnəu] *n* pesciolino d'acqua dolce
minor ['maɪnə^r] *adj* minore, di poca importanza; (*Mus*) minore ■ *n* (*Law*) minorenne *m/f*
Minorca [mɪ'nɔ:kə] *n* Minorca
minority [maɪ'nɔrɪtɪ] *n* minoranza; **to be in a ~** essere in minoranza
minster ['mɪnstə^r] *n* cattedrale *f* (*annessa a monastero*)
minstrel ['mɪnstrəl] *n* giullare *m*, menestrello
mint [mɪnt] *n* (*plant*) menta; (*sweet*) pasticca di menta ■ *vt* (*coins*) battere; **the (Royal) M~**, (*US*) **the (US) M~** la Zecca; **in ~ condition** come nuovo(-a) di zecca
mint sauce *n* salsa di menta

minuet [mɪnju'ɛt] *n* minuetto
minus ['maɪnəs] *n* (*also*: **minus sign**) segno meno ▪ *prep* meno
minuscule ['mɪnəskju:l] *adj* minuscolo(-a)
minute[1] ['mɪnɪt] *n* minuto; (*official record*) processo verbale, resoconto sommario; **minutes** *npl* verbale *m*, verbali *mpl*; **it is 5 minutes past 3** sono le 3 e 5 (minuti); **wait a ~!** (aspetta) un momento!; **at the last ~** all'ultimo momento; **up to the ~** ultimissimo; modernissimo
minute[2] [maɪ'nju:t] *adj* minuscolo(-a); (*detail*) minuzioso(-a); **in ~ detail** minuziosamente
minute book *n* libro dei verbali
minute hand *n* lancetta dei minuti
minutely [maɪ'nju:tlɪ] *adv* (*by a small amount*) di poco; (*in detail*) minuziosamente
minutiae [mɪ'nju:ʃii:] *npl* minuzie *fpl*
miracle ['mɪrəkl] *n* miracolo
miraculous [mɪ'rækjuləs] *adj* miracoloso(-a)
mirage ['mɪrɑ:ʒ] *n* miraggio
mire ['maɪəʳ] *n* pantano, melma
mirror ['mɪrəʳ] *n* specchio ▪ *vt* rispecchiare, riflettere
mirror image *n* immagine *f* speculare
mirth [mə:θ] *n* gaiezza
misadventure [mɪsəd'vɛntʃəʳ] *n* disavventura; **death by ~** (*Brit*) morte *f* accidentale
misanthropist [mɪ'zænθrəpɪst] *n* misantropo(-a)
misapply [mɪsə'plaɪ] *vt* impiegare male
misapprehension ['mɪsæprɪ'hɛnʃən] *n* malinteso
misappropriate [mɪsə'prəuprɪeɪt] *vt* appropriarsi indebitamente di
misappropriation ['mɪsəprəuprɪ'eɪʃən] *n* appropriazione *f* indebita
misbehave [mɪsbɪ'heɪv] *vi* comportarsi male
misbehaviour, (US) **misbehavior** [mɪsbɪ'heɪvjəʳ] *n* comportamento scorretto
misc. *abbr* = **miscellaneous**
miscalculate [mɪs'kælkjuleɪt] *vt* calcolare male
miscalculation ['mɪskælkju'leɪʃən] *n* errore *m* di calcolo
miscarriage ['mɪskærɪdʒ] *n* (*Med*) aborto spontaneo; **~ of justice** errore *m* giudiziario
miscarry [mɪs'kærɪ] *vi* (*Med*) abortire; (*fail: plans*) andare a monte, fallire
miscellaneous [mɪsɪ'leɪnɪəs] *adj* (*items*) vario(-a); (*selection*) misto(-a); **~ expenses** spese varie
miscellany [mɪ'sɛlənɪ] *n* raccolta
mischance [mɪs'tʃɑ:ns] *n*: **by (some) ~** per sfortuna
mischief ['mɪstʃɪf] *n* (*naughtiness*) birichineria; (*harm*) male *m*, danno; (*maliciousness*) malizia
mischievous ['mɪstʃɪvəs] *adj* (*naughty*) birichino(-a); (*harmful*) dannoso(-a)
misconception [mɪskən'sɛpʃən] *n* idea sbagliata
misconduct [mɪs'kɔndʌkt] *n* cattiva condotta; **professional ~** reato professionale
misconstrue [mɪskən'stru:] *vt* interpretare male
miscount [mɪs'kaunt] *vt, vi* contare male
misdeed [mɪs'di:d] *n* (*old*) misfatto
misdemeanour, (US) **misdemeanor** [mɪsdɪ'mi:nəʳ] *n* misfatto; infrazione *f*
misdirect [mɪsdɪ'rɛkt] *vt* mal indirizzare
miser ['maɪzəʳ] *n* avaro
miserable ['mɪzərəbl] *adj* infelice; (*wretched*) miserabile; (*weather*) deprimente; **to feel ~** sentirsi avvilito *or* giù di morale
miserably ['mɪzərəblɪ] *adv* (*fail, live, pay*) miseramente; (*smile, answer*) tristemente
miserly ['maɪzəlɪ] *adj* avaro(-a)
misery ['mɪzərɪ] *n* (*unhappiness*) tristezza; (*pain*) sofferenza; (*wretchedness*) miseria
misfire [mɪs'faɪəʳ] *vi* far cilecca; (*car engine*) perdere colpi
misfit ['mɪsfɪt] *n* (*person*) spostato(-a)
misfortune [mɪs'fɔ:tʃən] *n* sfortuna
misgiving [mɪs'gɪvɪŋ] *n*, **misgivings** [mɪs'gɪvɪŋz] *npl* dubbi *mpl*, sospetti *mpl*; **to have misgivings about sth** essere diffidente *or* avere dei dubbi per quanto riguarda qc
misguided [mɪs'gaɪdɪd] *adj* sbagliato(-a); poco giudizioso(-a)
mishandle [mɪs'hændl] *vt* (*treat roughly*) maltrattare; (*mismanage*) trattare male
mishap ['mɪshæp] *n* disgrazia
mishear [mɪs'hɪəʳ] *vt, vi irreg* capire male
mishmash ['mɪʃmæʃ] *n* (*col*) minestrone *m*, guazzabuglio
misinform [mɪsɪn'fɔ:m] *vt* informare male
misinterpret [mɪsɪn'tə:prɪt] *vt* interpretare male
misinterpretation ['mɪsɪntə:prɪ'teɪʃən] *n* errata interpretazione *f*
misjudge [mɪs'dʒʌdʒ] *vt* giudicare male
mislay [mɪs'leɪ] *vt irreg* smarrire
mislead [mɪs'li:d] *vt irreg* sviare
misleading [mɪs'li:dɪŋ] *adj* ingannevole
misled [mɪs'lɛd] *pt, pp of* **mislead**
mismanage [mɪs'mænɪdʒ] *vt* gestire male; trattare male
mismanagement [mɪs'mænɪdʒmənt] *n* cattiva amministrazione *f*

m

misnomer [mɪsˈnəuməʳ] *n* termine *m* sbagliato *or* improprio
misogynist [mɪˈsɔdʒɪnɪst] *n* misogino
misplace [mɪsˈpleɪs] *vt* smarrire; collocare fuori posto; **to be misplaced** (*trust etc*) essere malriposto(-a)
misprint [ˈmɪsprɪnt] *n* errore *m* di stampa
mispronounce [mɪsprəˈnauns] *vt* pronunziare male
misquote [mɪsˈkwəut] *vt* citare erroneamente
misread [mɪsˈriːd] *vt irreg* leggere male
misrepresent [mɪsrɛprɪˈzɛnt] *vt* travisare
Miss [mɪs] *n* Signorina; **Dear ~ Smith** Cara Signorina; (*formal*) Gentile Signorina
miss [mɪs] *vt* (*fail to get*) perdere; (*appointment, class*) mancare a; (*escape, avoid*) evitare; (*notice loss of: money etc*) accorgersi di non avere più; (*regret the absence of*): **I ~ him/it** sento la sua mancanza, lui/esso mi manca ■ *vi* mancare ■ *n* (*shot*) colpo mancato; (*fig*): **that was a near ~** c'è mancato poco; **the bus just missed the wall** l'autobus per un pelo non è andato a finire contro il muro; **you're missing the point** non capisce
▸ **miss out** *vt* (*Brit*) omettere
▸ **miss out on** *vt fus* (*fun, party*) perdersi; (*chance, bargain*) lasciarsi sfuggire
Miss. *abbr* (*US*) = **Mississippi**
missal [ˈmɪsl] *n* messale *m*
misshapen [mɪsˈʃeɪpən] *adj* deforme
missile [ˈmɪsaɪl] *n* (*Aviat*) missile *m*; (*object thrown*) proiettile *m*
missile base *n* base *f* missilistica
missile launcher *n* lancia-missili *m inv*
missing [ˈmɪsɪŋ] *adj* perso(-a), smarrito(-a); **to go ~** sparire; **~ person** scomparso(-a), disperso(-a); **~ in action** (*Mil*) disperso(-a)
mission [ˈmɪʃən] *n* missione *f*; **on a ~ to sb** in missione da qn
missionary [ˈmɪʃənrɪ] *n* missionario(-a)
misspell [mɪsˈspɛl] *vt* (*irreg: like* **spell**) sbagliare l'ortografia di
misspent [mɪsˈspɛnt] *adj*: **his ~ youth** la sua gioventù sciupata
mist [mɪst] *n* nebbia, foschia ■ *vi* (*also:* **mist over, mist up**) annebbiarsi; (*Brit: windows*) appannarsi
mistake [mɪsˈteɪk] *n* sbaglio, errore *m* ■ *vt* (*irreg: like* **take**) sbagliarsi di; fraintendere; **to ~ for** prendere per; **by ~** per sbaglio; **to make a ~** (*in writing, calculating etc*) fare uno sbaglio *or* un errore; **to make a ~ about sb/sth** sbagliarsi sul conto di qn/su qc
mistaken [mɪsˈteɪkən] *pp of* **mistake** ■ *adj* (*idea etc*) sbagliato(-a); **to be ~** sbagliarsi
mistaken identity *n* errore *m* di persona
mistakenly [mɪsˈteɪkənlɪ] *adv* per errore
mister [ˈmɪstəʳ] *n* (*col*) signore *m*; *see* **Mr**
mistletoe [ˈmɪsltəu] *n* vischio
mistook [mɪsˈtuk] *pt of* **mistake**
mistranslation [mɪstrænsˈleɪʃən] *n* traduzione *f* errata
mistreat [mɪsˈtriːt] *vt* maltrattare
mistress [ˈmɪstrɪs] *n* padrona; (*lover*) amante *f*; (*Brit Scol*) insegnante *f*
mistrust [mɪsˈtrʌst] *vt* diffidare di ■ *n*: **~ (of)** diffidenza (nei confronti di)
mistrustful [mɪsˈtrʌstful] *adj*: **~ (of)** diffidente (nei confronti di)
misty [ˈmɪstɪ] *adj* nebbioso(-a), brumoso(-a)
misty-eyed [ˈmɪstɪˈaɪd] *adj* trasognato(-a)
misunderstand [mɪsʌndəˈstænd] *vt, vi irreg* capire male, fraintendere
misunderstanding [mɪsʌndəˈstændɪŋ] *n* malinteso, equivoco
misunderstood [mɪsʌndəˈstud] *pt, pp of* **misunderstand**
misuse *n* [mɪsˈjuːs] cattivo uso; (*of power*) abuso ■ *vt* [mɪsˈjuːz] far cattivo uso di; abusare di
MIT *n abbr* (*US*) = **Massachusetts Institute of Technology**
mite [maɪt] *n* (*small quantity*) briciolo; (*Brit: small child*): **poor ~!** povera creaturina!
miter [ˈmaɪtəʳ] *n* (*US*) = **mitre**
mitigate [ˈmɪtɪgeɪt] *vt* mitigare; (*suffering*) alleviare; **mitigating circumstances** circostanze *fpl* attenuanti
mitigation [mɪtɪˈgeɪʃən] *n* mitigazione *f*; alleviamento
mitre, (*US*) **miter** [ˈmaɪtəʳ] *n* mitra; (*Carpentry*) giunto ad angolo retto
mitt [ˈmɪt], **mitten** [ˈmɪtn] *n* mezzo guanto; manopola
mix [mɪks] *vt* mescolare ■ *vi* mescolarsi ■ *n* mescolanza; preparato; **to ~ sth with sth** mischiare qc a qc; **to ~ business with pleasure** unire l'utile al dilettevole; **cake ~** preparato per torta
▸ **mix in** *vt* (*eggs etc*) incorporare
▸ **mix up** *vt* mescolare; (*confuse*) confondere; **to be mixed up in sth** essere coinvolto in qc
mixed [mɪkst] *adj* misto(-a)
mixed-ability [ˈmɪkstəˈbɪlɪtɪ] *adj* (*class etc*) con alunni di capacità diverse
mixed bag *n* miscuglio, accozzaglia; **it's a ~** c'è un po' di tutto
mixed blessing *n*: **it's a ~** ha i suoi lati positivi e negativi
mixed doubles *npl* (*Sport*) doppio misto
mixed economy *n* economia mista
mixed grill *n* (*Brit*) misto alla griglia
mixed marriage *n* matrimonio misto

mixed-up [mɪkst'ʌp] *adj (confused)* confuso(-a)
mixer ['mɪksəʳ] *n (for food: electric)* frullatore *m*; (*: hand*) frullino; (*person*): **he is a good ~** è molto socievole
mixer tap *n* miscelatore *m*
mixture ['mɪkstʃəʳ] *n* mescolanza; (*blend: of tobacco etc*) miscela; (*Med*) sciroppo
mix-up ['mɪksʌp] *n* confusione *f*
MK *abbr* (*Brit Tech*) = **mark**
mk *abbr* (*Hist: currency*) = **mark**
mkt *abbr* = **market**
MLitt *n abbr* (*= Master of Literature, Master of Letters*) *titolo di studio*
MLR *n abbr* (*Brit*) = **minimum lending rate**
mm *abbr* (*= millimetre*) mm
MMS *n abbr* (*= multimedia messaging service*) mms *m inv* (*servizio*); **~ message** mms *m inv*
MN *abbr* (*Brit*) = **Merchant Navy**; (*US*) = **Minnesota**
MO *n abbr* = **medical officer**; (*US col: = modus operandi*) modo d'agire ■ *abbr* (*US*) = **Missouri**
m.o. *abbr* = **money order**
moan [məun] *n* gemito ■ *vi* gemere; (*col: complain*): **to ~ (about)** lamentarsi (di)
moaner ['məunəʳ] *n* (*col*) uno(-a) che si lamenta sempre
moaning ['məunɪŋ] *n* gemiti *mpl*
moat [məut] *n* fossato
mob [mɔb] *n* folla; (*disorderly*) calca; (*pej*): **the ~** la plebaglia ■ *vt* accalcarsi intorno a
mobile ['məubaɪl] *adj* mobile ■ *n* (*phone*) telefonino; (*Art*) mobile *m inv*; **applicants must be ~** (*Brit*) i candidati devono essere disposti a viaggiare
mobile home *n* grande roulotte *f inv* (*utilizzata come domicilio*)
mobile phone *n* telefonino
mobile shop *n* (*Brit*) negozio ambulante
mobility [məu'bɪlɪtɪ] *n* mobilità; (*of applicant*) disponibilità a viaggiare
mobilize ['məubɪlaɪz] *vt* mobilitare ■ *vi* mobilitarsi
moccasin ['mɔkəsɪn] *n* mocassino
mock [mɔk] *vt* deridere, burlarsi di ■ *adj* falso(-a)
mockery ['mɔkərɪ] *n* derisione *f*; **to make a ~ of** rendere ridicolo
mocking ['mɔkɪŋ] *adj* derisorio(-a)
mockingbird ['mɔkɪŋbə:d] *n* mimo (*uccello*)
mock-up ['mɔkʌp] *n* modello dimostrativo; abbozzo
MOD *n abbr* (*Brit*) = **Ministry of Defence**; *see* **defence**
mod cons ['mɔd'kɔnz] *npl abbr* (*Brit*) = **modern conveniences**
mode [məud] *n* modo; (*of transport*) mezzo; (*Comput*) modalità *f inv*
model ['mɔdl] *n* modello; (*person: for fashion*) indossatore(-trice); (*: for artist*) modello(-a) ■ *vt* modellare ■ *vi* fare l'indossatore (*or* l'indossatrice) ■ *adj* (*small-scale: railway etc*) in miniatura; (*child, factory*) modello *inv*; **to ~ clothes** presentare degli abiti; **to ~ sb/sth on** modellare qn/qc su
modem ['məudɛm] *n* modem *m inv*
moderate ['mɔdərɪt] *adj* moderato(-a) ■ *n* (*Pol*) moderato(-a) ■ *vi* ['mɔdəreɪt] moderarsi, placarsi ■ *vt* moderare
moderately ['mɔdərɪtlɪ] *adv* (*act*) con moderazione; (*expensive, difficult*) non troppo; (*pleased, happy*) abbastanza, discretamente; **~ priced** a prezzo modico
moderation [mɔdə'reɪʃən] *n* moderazione *f*, misura; **in ~** in quantità moderata, con moderazione
moderator ['mɔdəreɪtəʳ] *n* moderatore(-trice); (*Rel*) *moderatore in importanti riunioni ecclesiastiche*
modern ['mɔdən] *adj* moderno(-a); **~ conveniences** comodità *fpl* moderne; **~ languages** lingue *fpl* moderne
modernization [mɔdənaɪ'zeɪʃən] *n* rimodernamento, modernizzazione *f*
modernize ['mɔdənaɪz] *vt* modernizzare
modest ['mɔdɪst] *adj* modesto(-a)
modesty ['mɔdɪstɪ] *n* modestia
modicum ['mɔdɪkəm] *n*: **a ~ of** un minimo di
modification [mɔdɪfɪ'keɪʃən] *n* modificazione *f*; **to make modifications** fare *or* apportare delle modifiche
modify ['mɔdɪfaɪ] *vt* modificare
modish ['məudɪʃ] *adj* (*literary*) à la page *inv*
Mods [mɔdz] *n abbr* (*Brit: = (Honour) Moderations*) *esame all'università di Oxford*
modular ['mɔdjuləʳ] *adj* (*filing, unit*) modulare
modulate ['mɔdjuleɪt] *vt* modulare
modulation [mɔdju'leɪʃən] *n* modulazione *f*
module ['mɔdju:l] *n* modulo
Mogadishu [mɔgə'dɪʃu:] *n* Mogadiscio *f*
mogul ['məugl] *n* (*fig*) magnate *m*, pezzo grosso; (*Ski*) cunetta
MOH *n abbr* (*Brit: = Medical Officer of Health*) ≈ ufficiale *m* sanitario
mohair ['məuhɛəʳ] *n* mohair *m*
Mohammed [məu'hæmɪd] *n* Maometto
moist [mɔɪst] *adj* umido(-a)
moisten ['mɔɪsn] *vt* inumidire
moisture ['mɔɪstʃəʳ] *n* umidità; (*on glass*) goccioline *fpl* di vapore
moisturize ['mɔɪstʃəraɪz] *vt* (*skin*) idratare
moisturizer ['mɔɪstʃəraɪzəʳ] *n* idratante *f*
molar ['məuləʳ] *n* molare *m*
molasses [məu'læsɪz] *n* molassa
mold *etc* [məuld] (*US*) = **mould** *etc*

m

Moldavia [mɔl'deɪvɪə], **Moldova** [mɔl'dəuvə] *n* Moldavia
Moldavian [mɔl'deɪvɪən], **Moldovan** [mɔl'dəuvən] *adj* moldavo(-a)
mole [məul] *n* (*animal*) talpa; (*spot*) neo
molecule ['mɔlɪkju:l] *n* molecola
molehill ['məulhɪl] *n cumulo di terra sulla tana di una talpa*
molest [məu'lɛst] *vt* molestare
mollusc, (*US*) **mollusk** ['mɔləsk] *n* mollusco
mollycoddle ['mɔlɪkɔdl] *vt* coccolare, vezzeggiare
Molotov cocktail ['mɔlətɔf-] *n* (bottiglia) Molotov *f inv*
molt [məult] *vi* (*US*) = **moult**
molten ['məultən] *adj* fuso(-a)
mom [mɔm] *n* (*US*) = **mum**
moment ['məumənt] *n* momento, istante *m*; importanza; **at the ~** al momento, in questo momento; **for the ~** per il momento, per ora; **in a ~** tra un momento; **"one ~ please"** (*Tel*) "attenda, prego"
momentarily ['məuməntərɪlɪ] *adv* per un momento; (*US: very soon*) da un momento all'altro
momentary ['məuməntərɪ] *adj* momentaneo(-a), passeggero(-a)
momentous [məu'mɛntəs] *adj* di grande importanza
momentum [məu'mɛntəm] *n* velocità acquisita, slancio; (*Physics*) momento; **to gather ~** aumentare di velocità; (*fig*) prendere *or* guadagnare terreno
mommy ['mɔmɪ] *n* (*US*) mamma
Mon. *abbr* (= *Monday*) lun.
Monaco ['mɔnəkəu] *n* Monaco *f*
monarch ['mɔnək] *n* monarca *m*
monarchist ['mɔnəkɪst] *n* monarchico(-a)
monarchy ['mɔnəkɪ] *n* monarchia
monastery ['mɔnəstərɪ] *n* monastero
monastic [mə'næstɪk] *adj* monastico(-a)
Monday ['mʌndɪ] *n* lunedì *m inv*; *see also* **Tuesday**
Monegasque [mɔnə'gæsk] *adj, n* monegasco(-a)
monetarist ['mʌnɪtərɪst] *n* monetarista *m/f*
monetary ['mʌnɪtərɪ] *adj* monetario(-a)
money ['mʌnɪ] *n* denaro, soldi *mpl*; **to make ~** (*person*) fare (i) soldi; (*business*) rendere; **danger ~** (*Brit*) indennità di rischio; **I've got no ~ left** non ho più neanche una lira
moneyed ['mʌnɪd] *adj* ricco(-a)
moneylender ['mʌnɪlɛndə^r] *n* prestatore *m* di denaro
moneymaker ['mʌnɪmeɪkə^r] *n* (*Brit col: business*) affare *m* d'oro
moneymaking ['mʌnɪmeɪkɪŋ] *adj* che rende (bene *or* molto), lucrativo(-a)
money market *n* mercato monetario
money order *n* vaglia *m inv*
money-spinner ['mʌnɪspɪnə^r] *n* (*col*) miniera d'oro (*fig*)
money supply *n* liquidità monetaria
Mongol ['mɔŋgəl] *n* mongolo(-a); (*Ling*) mongolo
mongol ['mɔŋgəl] *adj, n* (*Med*) mongoloide (*m/f*)
Mongolia [mɔŋ'gəulɪə] *n* Mongolia
Mongolian [mɔŋ'gəulɪən] *adj* mongolico(-a) ▪ *n* mongolo(-a); (*Ling*) mongolo
mongoose ['mɔŋgu:s] *n* mangusta
mongrel ['mʌŋgrəl] *n* (*dog*) cane *m* bastardo
monitor ['mɔnɪtə^r] *n* (*Brit Scol*) capoclasse *m/f*; (*US Scol*) chi sorveglia agli esami; (*TV, Comput*) monitor *m inv* ▪ *vt* controllare; (*foreign station*) ascoltare le trasmissioni di
monk [mʌŋk] *n* monaco
monkey ['mʌŋkɪ] *n* scimmia
monkey business *n* (*col*) scherzi *mpl*
monkey nut *n* (*Brit*) nocciolina americana
monkey wrench *n* chiave *f* a rullino
mono ['mɔnəu] *adj* mono *inv*; (*broadcast*) in mono
mono... ['mɔnəu] *prefix* mono...
monochrome ['mɔnəkrəum] *adj* monocromo(-a)
monocle ['mɔnəkl] *n* monocolo
monogamous [mə'nɔgəməs] *adj* monogamo(-a)
monogamy [mə'nɔgəmɪ] *n* monogamia
monogram ['mɔnəgræm] *n* monogramma *m*
monolith ['mɔnəlɪθ] *n* monolito
monologue ['mɔnəlɔg] *n* monologo
monoplane ['mɔnəupleɪn] *n* monoplano
monopolize [mə'nɔpəlaɪz] *vt* monopolizzare
monopoly [mə'nɔpəlɪ] *n* monopolio; **Monopolies and Mergers Commission** (*Brit*) commissione *f* antimonopoli
monorail ['mɔnəureɪl] *n* monorotaia
monosodium glutamate [mɔnə'səudɪəm-'glu:təmeɪt] *n* glutammato di sodio
monosyllabic [mɔnəsɪ'læbɪk] *adj* monosillabico(-a); (*person*) che parla a monosillabi
monosyllable ['mɔnəsɪləbl] *n* monosillabo
monotone ['mɔnətəun] *n* pronunzia (*or* voce *f* monotona; **to speak in a ~** parlare con voce monotona
monotonous [mə'nɔtənəs] *adj* monotono(-a)
monotony [mə'nɔtənɪ] *n* monotonia
monoxide [mɔ'nɔksaɪd] *n*: **carbon ~** ossido di carbonio
monsoon [mɔn'su:n] *n* monsone *m*

monster ['mɔnstəʳ] *n* mostro
monstrosity [mɔn'strɔsɪtɪ] *n* mostruosità *f inv*
monstrous ['mɔnstrəs] *adj* mostruoso(-a)
Mont. *abbr* (*US*) = **Montana**
montage [mɔn'tɑːʒ] *n* montaggio
Mont Blanc [mɔ̃blɑ̃] *n* Monte *m* Bianco
month [mʌnθ] *n* mese *m*; **300 dollars a ~** 300 dollari al mese; **every ~** (*happen*) tutti i mesi; (*pay*) mensilmente, ogni mese
monthly ['mʌnθlɪ] *adj* mensile ■ *adv* al mese; ogni mese ■ *n* (*magazine*) rivista mensile; **twice ~** due volte al mese
monument ['mɔnjumənt] *n* monumento
monumental [mɔnju'mɛntl] *adj* monumentale; (*fig*) colossale
monumental mason *n* lapidario
moo [muː] *vi* muggire, mugghiare
mood [muːd] *n* umore *m*; **to be in a good/bad ~** essere di buon/cattivo umore; **to be in the ~ for** essere disposto(-a) a, aver voglia di
moody ['muːdɪ] *adj* (*variable*) capriccioso(-a), lunatico(-a); (*sullen*) imbronciato(-a)
moon [muːn] *n* luna
moonbeam ['muːnbiːm] *n* raggio di luna
moon landing *n* allunaggio
moonlight ['muːnlaɪt] *n* chiaro di luna ■ *vi* fare del lavoro nero
moonlighting ['muːnlaɪtɪŋ] *n* lavoro nero
moonlit ['muːnlɪt] *adj* illuminato(-a) dalla luna; **a ~ night** una notte rischiarata dalla luna
moonshot ['muːnʃɔt] *n* lancio sulla luna
moonstruck ['muːnstrʌk] *adj* lunatico(-a)
moony ['muːnɪ] *adj* (*eyes*) sognante
Moor [muəʳ] *n* moro(-a)
moor [muəʳ] *n* brughiera ■ *vt* (*ship*) ormeggiare ■ *vi* ormeggiarsi
moorings ['muərɪŋz] *npl* (*chains*) ormeggi *mpl*; (*place*) ormeggio
Moorish ['muərɪʃ] *adj* moresco(-a)
moorland ['muələnd] *n* brughiera
moose [muːs] *n* (*pl inv*) alce *m*
moot [muːt] *vt* sollevare ■ *adj*: **~ point** punto discutibile
mop [mɔp] *n* lavapavimenti *m inv*; (*also*: **mop of hair**) zazzera ■ *vt* lavare con lo straccio; **to ~ one's brow** asciugarsi la fronte
▸ **mop up** *vt* asciugare con uno straccio
mope [məup] *vi* fare il broncio
▸ **mope about, mope around** *vi* trascinarsi *or* aggirarsi con aria avvilita
moped ['məupɛd] *n* (*Brit*) ciclomotore *m*
MOR *adj abbr* (*Mus*) = **middle-of-the-road**; **~ music** musica leggera
moral ['mɔrəl] *adj* morale ■ *n* morale *f*; **morals** *npl* moralità
morale [mɔ'rɑːl] *n* morale *m*
morality [mə'rælɪtɪ] *n* moralità
moralize ['mɔrəlaɪz] *vi*: **to ~ (about)** fare il (*or* la) moralista (riguardo), moraleggiare (riguardo)
morally ['mɔrəlɪ] *adv* moralmente
moral victory *n* vittoria morale
morass [mə'ræs] *n* palude *f*, pantano
moratorium [mɔrə'tɔːrɪəm] *n* moratoria
morbid ['mɔːbɪd] *adj* morboso(-a)

 KEYWORD

more [mɔːʳ] *adj* **1** (*greater in number etc*) più; **more people/letters than we expected** più persone/lettere di quante ne aspettavamo; **I have more wine/money than you** ho più vino/soldi di te; **I have more wine than beer** ho più vino che birra
2 (*additional*) altro(-a), ancora; **do you want (some) more tea?** vuole dell'altro tè?, vuole ancora del tè?; **I have no** *or* **I don't have any more money** non ho più soldi
■ *pron* **1** (*greater amount*) più; **more than 10** più di 10; **it cost more than we expected** è costato più di quanto ci aspettassimo; **and what's more ...** e per di più ...
2 (*further or additional amount*) ancora; **is there any more?** ce n'è ancora?; **there's no more** non ce n'è più; **a little more** ancora un po'; **many/much more** molti(-e)/molto(-a) di più
■ *adv*: **more dangerous/easily (than)** più pericoloso/facilmente (di); **more and more** sempre di più; **more and more difficult** sempre più difficile; **more or less** più o meno; **more than ever** più che mai; **once more** ancora (una volta), un'altra volta; **no more, not any more** non ... più; **I have no more money, I haven't any more money** non ho più soldi

moreover [mɔː'rəuvəʳ] *adv* inoltre, di più
morgue [mɔːg] *n* obitorio
MORI ['mɔːrɪ] *n abbr* (*Brit*: = *Market & Opinion Research Institute*) *istituto di sondaggio*
moribund ['mɔrɪbʌnd] *adj* moribondo(-a)
morning ['mɔːnɪŋ] *n* mattina, mattino; (*duration*) mattinata; **in the ~** la mattina; **this ~** stamattina; **7 o'clock in the ~** le 7 di *or* della mattina
morning-after pill ['mɔːnɪŋ'ɑːftə-] *n* pillola del giorno dopo
morning sickness *n* nausee *fpl* mattutine
Moroccan [mə'rɔkən] *adj, n* marocchino(-a)
Morocco [mə'rɔkəu] *n* Marocco
moron ['mɔːrɔn] *n* deficiente *m/f*
moronic [mə'rɔnɪk] *adj* deficiente

m

morose [mə'rəus] *adj* cupo(-a), tetro(-a)
morphine ['mɔ:fi:n] *n* morfina
morris dancing ['mɔrɪs-] *n* (*Brit*) *antica danza tradizionale inglese*
Morse [mɔ:s] *n* (*also*: **Morse code**) alfabeto Morse
morsel ['mɔ:sl] *n* boccone *m*
mortal ['mɔ:tl] *adj, n* mortale (*m*)
mortality [mɔ:'tælɪtɪ] *n* mortalità
mortality rate *n* tasso di mortalità
mortar ['mɔ:tə^r] *n* (*Constr*) malta; (*dish*) mortaio
mortgage ['mɔ:gɪdʒ] *n* ipoteca; (*in house buying*) mutuo ipotecario ■ *vt* ipotecare; **to take out a ~** contrarre un mutuo (*or* un'ipoteca)
mortgage company *n* (*US*) società *f inv* immobiliare
mortgagee [mɔ:gɪ'dʒi:] *n* creditore *m* ipotecario
mortgagor ['mɔ:gɪdʒə^r] *n* debitore *m* ipotecario
mortician [mɔ:'tɪʃən] *n* (*US*) impresario di pompe funebri
mortified ['mɔ:tɪfaɪd] *adj* umiliato(-a)
mortise lock ['mɔ:tɪs-] *n* serratura incastrata
mortuary ['mɔ:tjuərɪ] *n* camera mortuaria; obitorio
mosaic [məu'zeɪɪk] *n* mosaico
Moscow ['mɔskəu] *n* Mosca
Moslem ['mɔzləm] *adj, n* = **Muslim**
mosque [mɔsk] *n* moschea
mosquito (*pl* **mosquitoes**) [mɔs'ki:təu] *n* zanzara
mosquito net *n* zanzariera
moss [mɔs] *n* muschio
mossy ['mɔsɪ] *adj* muscoso(-a)
most [məust] *adj* la maggior parte di; il più di ■ *pron* la maggior parte ■ *adv* più; (*work, sleep etc*) di più; (*very*) molto, estremamente; **the ~** (*also*: *+ adjective*) il/la più; **~ fish** la maggior parte dei pesci; **~ of** la maggior parte di; **~ of them** quasi tutti; **I saw ~** ho visto più io; **at the (very) ~** al massimo; **to make the ~ of** trarre il massimo vantaggio da
mostly ['məustlɪ] *adv* per lo più
MOT *n abbr* (*Brit*) = **Ministry of Transport**; **the ~ (test)** *revisione obbligatoria degli autoveicoli*
motel [məu'tɛl] *n* motel *m inv*
moth [mɔθ] *n* farfalla notturna; tarma
mothball ['mɔθbɔ:l] *n* pallina di naftalina
moth-eaten ['mɔθi:tn] *adj* tarmato(-a)
mother ['mʌðə^r] *n* madre *f* ■ *vt* (*care for*) fare da madre a
mother board *n* (*Comput*) scheda madre
motherhood ['mʌðəhud] *n* maternità
mother-in-law ['mʌðərɪnlɔ:] *n* suocera
mother-of-pearl [mʌðərəv'pə:l] *n* madreperla
mother's help *n* bambinaia
mother-to-be [mʌðətə'bi:] *n* futura mamma
mother tongue *n* madrelingua
mothproof ['mɔθpru:f] *adj* antitarmico(-a)
motif [məu'ti:f] *n* motivo
motion ['məuʃən] *n* movimento, moto; (*gesture*) gesto; (*at meeting*) mozione *f*; (*Brit*: *also*: **bowel motion**) evacuazione *f* ■ *vt, vi*: **to ~ (to) sb to do** fare cenno a qn di fare; **to be in ~** (*vehicle*) essere in moto; **to set in ~** avviare; **to go through the motions of doing sth** (*fig*) fare qc pro forma
motionless ['məuʃənlɪs] *adj* immobile
motion picture *n* film *m inv*
motivate ['məutɪveɪt] *vt* (*act, decision*) dare origine a, motivare; (*person*) spingere
motivated ['məutɪveɪtɪd] *adj* motivato(-a)
motivation [məutɪ'veɪʃən] *n* motivazione *f*
motive ['məutɪv] *n* motivo ■ *adj* motore(-trice); **from the best motives** con le migliori intenzioni
motley ['mɔtlɪ] *adj* eterogeneo(-a), molto vario(-a)
motor ['məutə^r] *n* motore *m*; (*Brit col*: *vehicle*) macchina ■ *adj* motore(-trice)
motorbike ['məutəbaɪk] *n* moto *f inv*
motorboat ['məutəbəut] *n* motoscafo
motorcade ['məutəkeɪd] *n* corteo di macchine
motorcar ['məutəkɑ:] *n* automobile *f*
motorcoach ['məutəkəutʃ] *n* (*Brit*) pullman *m inv*
motorcycle ['məutəsaɪkl] *n* motocicletta
motorcyclist ['məutəsaɪklɪst] *n* motociclista *m/f*
motoring ['məutərɪŋ] *n* (*Brit*) turismo automobilistico ■ *adj* (*accident*) d'auto, automobilistico(-a); (*offence*) di guida; **~ holiday** vacanza in macchina
motorist ['məutərɪst] *n* automobilista *m/f*
motorize ['məutəraɪz] *vt* motorizzare
motor oil *n* olio lubrificante
motor racing *n* (*Brit*) corse *fpl* automobilistiche
motor scooter *n* motorscooter *m inv*
motor vehicle *n* autoveicolo
motorway ['məutəweɪ] *n* (*Brit*) autostrada
mottled ['mɔtld] *adj* chiazzato(-a), marezzato(-a)
motto (*pl* **mottoes**) ['mɔtəu] *n* motto
mould, (*US*) **mold** [məuld] *n* forma, stampo; (*mildew*) muffa ■ *vt* formare; (*fig*) foggiare
moulder, (*US*) **molder** ['məuldə^r] *vi* (*decay*) ammuffire
moulding, (*US*) **molding** ['məuldɪŋ] *n* (*Archit*) modanatura

mouldy, (US) **moldy** ['məuldɪ] *adj* ammuffito(-a)
moult, (US) **molt** [məult] *vi* far la muta
mound [maund] *n* rialzo, collinetta
mount [maunt] *n* monte *m*, montagna; (*horse*) cavalcatura; (*for jewel etc*) montatura ■ *vt* montare; (*horse*) montare a; (*exhibition*) organizzare; (*attack*) sferrare, condurre; (*picture, stamp*) sistemare ■ *vi* salire; (*get on a horse*) montare a cavallo; (*also*: **mount up**) aumentare
mountain ['mauntɪn] *n* montagna ■ *cpd* di montagna; **to make a ~ out of a molehill** fare di una mosca un elefante
mountain bike *n* mountain bike *f inv*
mountaineer [mauntɪ'nɪə^r] *n* alpinista *m/f*
mountaineering [mauntɪ'nɪərɪŋ] *n* alpinismo; **to go ~** fare dell'alpinismo
mountainous ['mauntɪnəs] *adj* montagnoso(-a)
mountain range *n* catena montuosa
mountain rescue team *n* ≈ squadra di soccorso alpino
mountainside ['mauntɪnsaɪd] *n* fianco della montagna
mounted ['mauntɪd] *adj* a cavallo
mourn [mɔ:n] *vt* piangere, lamentare ■ *vi*: **to ~ (for sb)** piangere (la morte di qn)
mourner ['mɔ:nə^r] *n* parente *m/f* (*or* amico(-a)) del defunto
mourning ['mɔ:nɪŋ] *n* lutto ■ *cpd* (*dress*) da lutto; **in ~** in lutto
mouse (*pl* **mice**) [maus, maɪs] *n* topo; (*Comput*) mouse *m inv*
mousetrap ['maustræp] *n* trappola per i topi
moussaka [mu'sɑ:kə] *n* moussaka
mousse [mu:s] *n* mousse *f inv*
moustache [məs'tɑ:ʃ] *n* baffi *mpl*
mousy ['mausɪ] *adj* (*person*) timido(-a); (*hair*) né chiaro(-a) né scuro(-a)
mouth (*pl* **mouths**) [mauθ, -ðz] *n* bocca; (*of river*) bocca, foce *f*; (*opening*) orifizio
mouthful ['mauθful] *n* boccata
mouth organ *n* armonica
mouthpiece ['mauθpi:s] *n* (*Mus*) bocchino; (*Tel*) microfono; (*of breathing apparatus*) boccaglio; (*person*) portavoce *m/f*
mouth-to-mouth ['mauθtə'mauθ] *adj*: **~ resuscitation** respirazione *f* bocca a bocca
mouthwash ['mauθwɔʃ] *n* collutorio
mouth-watering ['mauθwɔ:tərɪŋ] *adj* che fa venire l'acquolina in bocca
movable ['mu:vəbl] *adj* mobile
move [mu:v] *n* (*movement*) movimento; (*in game*) mossa; (*: turn to play*) turno; (*change of house*) trasloco ■ *vt* muovere, spostare; (*emotionally*) commuovere; (*Pol: resolution etc*) proporre ■ *vi* (*gen*) muoversi, spostarsi; (*traffic*) circolare; (*also*: **move house**) cambiar casa, traslocare; **to ~ towards** andare verso; **to ~ sb to do sth** indurre *or* spingere qn a fare qc; **to get a ~ on** affrettarsi, sbrigarsi; **to be moved** (*emotionally*) essere commosso(-a)
▸ **move about, move around** *vi* (*fidget*) agitarsi; (*travel*) viaggiare
▸ **move along** *vi* muoversi avanti
▸ **move away** *vi* allontanarsi, andarsene
▸ **move back** *vi* indietreggiare; (*return*) ritornare
▸ **move forward** *vi* avanzare ■ *vt* avanzare, spostare in avanti; (*people*) far avanzare
▸ **move in** *vi* (*to a house*) entrare (*in una nuova casa*)
▸ **move off** *vi* partire
▸ **move on** *vi* riprendere la strada ■ *vt* (*onlookers*) far circolare
▸ **move out** *vi* (*of house*) sgombrare
▸ **move over** *vi* spostarsi
▸ **move up** *vi* avanzare
movement ['mu:vmənt] *n* (*gen*) movimento; (*gesture*) gesto; (*of stars, water, physical*) moto; **~ (of the bowels)** (*Med*) evacuazione *f*
mover ['mu:və^r] *n* proponente *m/f*
movie ['mu:vɪ] *n* film *m inv*; **the movies** il cinema
movie camera *n* cinepresa
moviegoer ['mu:vɪgəuə^r] *n* (*US*) frequentatore(-trice) di cinema
moving ['mu:vɪŋ] *adj* mobile; (*causing emotion*) commovente; (*instigating*) animatore(-trice)
mow (*pt* **mowed**, *pp* **mowed** *or* **mown**) [məu, -n] *vt* falciare; (*grass*) tagliare
▸ **mow down** *vt* falciare
mower ['məuə^r] *n* (*also*: **lawn mower**) tagliaerba *m inv*
mown [məun] *pp of* **mow**
Mozambique [məuzəm'bi:k] *n* Mozambico
MP *n abbr* = **Military Police**; (*Brit*) = **Member of Parliament**; (*Canada*) = **Mounted Police**
MP3 *n* MP3 *m inv*
MP3 player *n* lettore *m* MP3
mpg *n abbr* = **miles per gallon** (*30 mpg = 9.4 l. per 100 km*)
mph *n abbr* = **miles per hour** (*60 mph = 96 km/h*)
MPhil *n abbr* (*= Master of Philosophy*) *titolo di studio*
MPS *n abbr* (*Brit*) = **Member of the Pharmaceutical Society**
Mr, Mr. ['mɪstə^r] *n*: **Mr X** Signor X, Sig. X
MRC *n abbr* (*Brit: = Medical Research Council*) *ufficio governativo per la ricerca medica in Gran Bretagna e nel Commonwealth*
MRCP *n abbr* (*Brit*) = **Member of the Royal College of Physicians**

m

MRCS *n abbr* (*Brit*) = **Member of the Royal College of Surgeons**
MRCVS *n abbr* (*Brit*) = **Member of the Royal College of Veterinary Surgeons**
Mrs, Mrs. ['mɪsɪz] *n*: ~ **X** Signora X, Sig.ra X
MS *n abbr* (*US*: = *Master of Science*) *titolo di studio*; (= *manuscript*) ms; (*Med*) = **multiple sclerosis** ■ *abbr* (*US*) = **Mississippi**
Ms, Ms. [mɪz] *n* = **Miss** *or* **Mrs**; **Ms X** ≈ Signora X, ≈ Sig.ra X
MSA *n abbr* (*US*: = *Master of Science in Agriculture*) *titolo di studio*
MSc *n abbr* = **Master of Science**
MSG *abbr* = **monosodium glutamate**
MSP *n abbr* (*Brit*) = **Member of the Scottish Parliament**
MST *abbr* (*US*: = *Mountain Standard Time*) *ora invernale delle Montagne Rocciose*
MSW *n abbr* (*US*: = *Master of Social Work*) *titolo di studio*
MT *n abbr* = **machine translation** ■ *abbr* (*US*) = **Montana**
Mt *abbr* (*Geo*: = *mount*) M
mth *abbr* (= *month*) m
MTV *n abbr* = **music television**

KEYWORD

much [mʌtʃ] *adj, pron* molto(-a); **he's done so much work** ha lavorato così tanto; **I have as much money as you** ho tanti soldi quanti ne hai tu; **how much is it?** quant'è?; **it's not much** non è tanto; **it costs too much** costa troppo; **as much as you want** quanto vuoi
■ *adv* **1** (*greatly*) molto, tanto; **thank you very much** molte grazie; **I like it very/so much** mi piace moltissimo/così tanto; **much to my amazement** con mio enorme stupore; **he's very much the gentleman** è il vero gentiluomo; **I read as much as I can** leggo quanto posso; **as much as you** tanto quanto te
2 (*by far*) molto; **it's much the biggest company in Europe** è di gran lunga la più grossa società in Europa
3 (*almost*) grossomodo, praticamente; **they're much the same** sono praticamente uguali

muck [mʌk] *n* (*mud*) fango; (*dirt*) sporcizia
▸ **muck about, muck around** *vi* (*col*) fare lo stupido; (: *waste time*) gingillarsi; (*tinker*) armeggiare
▸ **muck in** *vi* (*Brit col*) mettersi insieme
▸ **muck out** *vt* (*stable*) pulire
▸ **muck up** *vt* (*col*: *dirty*) sporcare; (: *spoil*) rovinare

muckraking ['mʌkreɪkɪŋ] *n* (*fig, col*) caccia agli scandali ■ *adj* scandalistico(-a)
mucky ['mʌkɪ] *adj* (*dirty*) sporco(-a), lordo(-a)
mucus ['mju:kəs] *n* muco
mud [mʌd] *n* fango
muddle ['mʌdl] *n* confusione *f*, disordine *m*; pasticcio ■ *vt* (*also*: **muddle up**) mettere sottosopra; confondere; **to be in a ~** (*person*) non riuscire a raccapezzarsi; **to get in a ~** (*while explaining etc*) imbrogliarsi
▸ **muddle along** *vi* andare avanti a casaccio
▸ **muddle through** *vi* cavarsela alla meno peggio
muddle-headed [mʌdl'hɛdɪd] *adj* (*person*) confusionario(-a)
muddy ['mʌdɪ] *adj* fangoso(-a)
mud flats *npl* distesa fangosa
mudguard ['mʌdgɑ:d] *n* parafango
mudpack ['mʌdpæk] *n* maschera di fango
mud-slinging ['mʌdslɪŋɪŋ] *n* (*fig*) infangamento
muesli ['mju:zlɪ] *n* müsli *m inv*
muff [mʌf] *n* manicotto ■ *vt* (*shot, catch etc*) mancare, sbagliare; **to ~ it** sbagliare tutto
muffin ['mʌfɪn] *n specie di pasticcino soffice da tè*
muffle ['mʌfl] *vt* (*sound*) smorzare, attutire; (*against cold*) imbacuccare
muffled ['mʌfld] *adj* smorzato(-a), attutito(-a)
muffler ['mʌflər] *n* (*scarf*) sciarpa (pesante); (*US Aut*) marmitta; (*on motorbike*) silenziatore *m*
mufti ['mʌftɪ] *n*: **in ~** in borghese
mug [mʌg] *n* (*cup*) tazzone *m*; (*for beer*) boccale *m*; (*col*: *face*) muso; (: *fool*) scemo(-a) ■ *vt* (*assault*) assalire; **it's a ~'s game** (*Brit*) è proprio (una cosa) da fessi
▸ **mug up** *vt* (*Brit col*: *also*: **mug up on**) studiare bene
mugger ['mʌgər] *n* aggressore *m*
mugging ['mʌgɪŋ] *n* aggressione *f* (a scopo di rapina)
muggins ['mʌgɪnz] *n* (*col*) semplicione(-a), sprovveduto(-a)
muggy ['mʌgɪ] *adj* afoso(-a)
mug shot *n* (*col*) foto *f inv* segnaletica
mulatto (*pl* **mulattoes**) [mju:'lætəu] *n* mulatto(-a)
mulberry ['mʌlbərɪ] *n* (*fruit*) mora (di gelso); (*tree*) gelso, moro
mule [mju:l] *n* mulo
mull [mʌl]: **to ~ over** *vt* rimuginare
mulled [mʌld] *adj*: **~ wine** vino caldo
multi... ['mʌltɪ] *prefix* multi...
multi-access [mʌltɪ'æksɛs] *adj* (*Comput*) ad accesso multiplo
multicoloured, (*US*) **multicolored** ['mʌltɪkʌləd] *adj* multicolore, variopinto(-a)

multifarious [mʌltɪ'fɛərɪəs] *adj* molteplice, svariato(-a)
multilateral [mʌltɪ'lætərəl] *adj* (*Pol*) multilaterale
multi-level ['mʌltɪlɛvl] *adj* (*US*) = **multistorey**
multimillionaire [mʌltɪmɪljə'nɛəʳ] *n* multimiliardario(-a)
multinational [mʌltɪ'næʃənl] *adj, n* multinazionale (*f*)
multiple ['mʌltɪpl] *adj* multiplo(-a); molteplice ■ *n* multiplo; (*Brit*: *also*: **multiple store**) *grande magazzino che fa parte di una catena*
multiple choice *n* esercizi *mpl* a scelta multipla
multiple crash *n* serie *f inv* di incidenti a catena
multiple sclerosis *n* sclerosi *f* a placche
multiplex ['mʌltɪplɛks] *n* (*also*: **multiplex cinema**) cinema *m inv* multisale *inv*
multiplication [mʌltɪplɪ'keɪʃən] *n* moltiplicazione *f*
multiplication table *n* tavola pitagorica
multiplicity [mʌltɪ'plɪsɪtɪ] *n* molteplicità
multiply ['mʌltɪplaɪ] *vt* moltiplicare ■ *vi* moltiplicarsi
multiracial [mʌltɪ'reɪʃəl] *adj* multirazziale
multistorey ['mʌltɪ'stɔːrɪ] *adj* (*Brit*: *building, car park*) a più piani
multitude ['mʌltɪtjuːd] *n* moltitudine *f*
mum [mʌm] *n* (*Brit*) mamma ■ *adj*: **to keep ~** non aprire bocca; **~'s the word!** acqua in bocca!
mumble ['mʌmbl] *vt, vi* borbottare
mumbo jumbo ['mʌmbəu-] *n* (*col*) parole *fpl* incomprensibili
mummify ['mʌmɪfaɪ] *vt* mummificare
mummy ['mʌmɪ] *n* (*Brit*: *mother*) mamma; (*embalmed*) mummia
mumps [mʌmps] *n* orecchioni *mpl*
munch [mʌntʃ] *vt, vi* sgranocchiare
mundane [mʌn'deɪn] *adj* terra a terra *inv*
Munich ['mjuːnɪk] *n* Monaco *f* (di Baviera)
municipal [mjuː'nɪsɪpl] *adj* municipale
municipality [mjuːnɪsɪ'pælɪtɪ] *n* municipio
munitions [mjuː'nɪʃənz] *npl* munizioni *fpl*
mural ['mjuərəl] *n* dipinto murale
murder ['məːdəʳ] *n* assassinio, omicidio ■ *vt* assassinare; **to commit ~** commettere un omicidio
murderer ['məːdərəʳ] *n* omicida *m*, assassino
murderess ['məːdərɪs] *n* omicida *f*, assassina
murderous ['məːdərəs] *adj* micidiale
murk [məːk] *n* oscurità, buio
murky ['məːkɪ] *adj* tenebroso(-a), buio(-a)
murmur ['məːməʳ] *n* mormorio ■ *vt, vi* mormorare; **heart ~** (*Med*) soffio al cuore
MusB, MusBac *n abbr* (= *Bachelor of Music*) *titolo di studio*
muscle ['mʌsl] *n* muscolo
▸ **muscle in** *vi* immischiarsi
muscular ['mʌskjuləʳ] *adj* muscolare; (*person, arm*) muscoloso(-a)
muscular dystrophy *n* distrofia muscolare
MusD, MusDoc *n abbr* (= *Doctor of Music*) *titolo di studio*
muse [mjuːz] *vi* meditare, sognare ■ *n* musa
museum [mjuː'zɪəm] *n* museo
mush [mʌʃ] *n* pappa
mushroom ['mʌʃrum] *n* fungo ■ *vi* (*fig*) svilupparsi rapidamente
mushy ['mʌʃɪ] *adj* (*food*) spappolato(-a); (*sentimental*) sdolcinato(-a)
music ['mjuːzɪk] *n* musica
musical ['mjuːzɪkəl] *adj* musicale ■ *n* (*show*) commedia musicale
musical box *n* carillon *m inv*
musical chairs *n* gioco delle sedie (*in cui bisogna sedersi non appena cessa la musica*); (*fig*) scambio delle poltrone
musical instrument *n* strumento musicale
music box *n* carillon *m inv*
music centre *n* impianto *m* stereo *inv* monoblocco *inv*
music hall *n* teatro di varietà
musician [mjuː'zɪʃən] *n* musicista *m/f*
music stand *n* leggio
musk [mʌsk] *n* muschio
musket ['mʌskɪt] *n* moschetto
muskrat ['mʌskræt] *n* topo muschiato
musk rose *n* (*Bot*) rosa muschiata
Muslim ['mʌzlɪm] *adj, n* musulmano(-a)
muslin ['mʌzlɪn] *n* mussola
musquash ['mʌskwɔʃ] *n* (*fur*) rat musqué *m inv*
mussel ['mʌsl] *n* cozza
must [mʌst] *aux vb* (*obligation*): **I ~ do it** devo farlo; (*probability*): **he ~ be there by now** dovrebbe essere arrivato ormai; **I ~ have made a mistake** devo essermi sbagliato ■ *n*: **this programme/trip is a ~** è un programma/viaggio da non perdersi
mustache ['mʌstæʃ] *n* (*US*) = **moustache**
mustard ['mʌstəd] *n* senape *f*, mostarda
mustard gas *n* iprite *f*
muster ['mʌstəʳ] *vt* radunare; (*also*: **muster up**: *strength, courage*) fare appello a
mustiness ['mʌstɪnɪs] *n* odor di muffa *or* di stantio
mustn't ['mʌsnt] = **must not**
musty ['mʌstɪ] *adj* che sa di muffa *or* di rinchiuso
mutant ['mjuːtənt] *adj, n* mutante (*m*)
mutate [mjuː'teɪt] *vi* subire una mutazione

m

mutation [mju:'teɪʃən] *n* mutazione *f*
mute [mju:t] *adj*, *n* muto(-a)
muted ['mju:tɪd] *adj* (*noise*) attutito(-a), smorzato(-a); (*criticism*) attenuato(-a); (*Mus*) in sordina; (: *trumpet*) con sordina
mutilate ['mju:tɪleɪt] *vt* mutilare
mutilation [mju:tɪ'leɪʃən] *n* mutilazione *f*
mutinous ['mju:tɪnəs] *adj* (*troops*) ammutinato(-a); (*attitude*) ribelle
mutiny ['mju:tɪnɪ] *n* ammutinamento ■ *vi* ammutinarsi
mutter ['mʌtəʳ] *vt*, *vi* borbottare, brontolare
mutton ['mʌtn] *n* carne *f* di montone
mutual ['mju:tʃuəl] *adj* mutuo(-a), reciproco(-a)
mutually ['mju:tʃuəlɪ] *adv* reciprocamente
Muzak® ['mju:zæk] *n* (*often pej*) musica di sottofondo
muzzle ['mʌzl] *n* muso; (*protective device*) museruola; (*of gun*) bocca ■ *vt* mettere la museruola a
MV *abbr* (= *motor vessel*) M/N, m/n
MVP *n abbr* (*US Sport*: = *most valuable player*) *titolo ottenuto da sportivo*
MW *abbr* (*Radio*: = *medium wave*) O.M.; = **megawatt**
my [maɪ] *adj* il/la mio(-a); (*pl*) i/le miei/mie
Myanmar ['maɪænmɑ:ʳ] *n* Myanma
myopic [maɪ'ɔpɪk] *adj* miope
myriad ['mɪrɪəd] *n* miriade *f*
myself [maɪ'sɛlf] *pron* (*reflexive*) mi; (*emphatic*) io stesso(-a); (*after prep*) me
mysterious [mɪs'tɪərɪəs] *adj* misterioso(-a)
mystery ['mɪstərɪ] *n* mistero
mystery story *n* racconto del mistero
mystic ['mɪstɪk] *adj*, *n* mistico(-a)
mystical ['mɪstɪkəl] *adj* mistico(-a)
mystify ['mɪstɪfaɪ] *vt* mistificare; (*puzzle*) confondere
mystique [mɪs'ti:k] *n* fascino
myth [mɪθ] *n* mito
mythical ['mɪθɪkl] *adj* mitico(-a)
mythological [mɪθə'lɔdʒɪkl] *adj* mitologico(-a)
mythology [mɪ'θɔlədʒɪ] *n* mitologia

Nn

N, n [ɛn] *n (letter)* N, n *f or m inv*; **N for Nellie,** (US) **N for Nan** ≈ N come Napoli

N *abbr (= north)* N

NA *n abbr* (US: = *Narcotics Anonymous*) *associazione in aiuto dei tossicodipendenti*; (US) = **National Academy**

n/a *abbr (= not applicable)* non pertinente

NAACP *n abbr* (US) = **National Association for the Advancement of Colored People**

NAAFI ['næfɪ] *n abbr (Brit: = Navy, Army, & Air Force Institutes) organizzazione che gestisce negozi, mense ecc. per il personale militare*

nab [næb] *vt (col)* beccare, acchiappare

NACU *n abbr* (US) = **National Association of Colleges and Universities**

nadir ['neɪdɪəʳ] *n (Astronomy)* nadir *m*; *(fig)* punto più basso

nag [næg] *n (pej: horse)* ronzino; *(person)* brontolone(-a) ■ *vt* tormentare ■ *vi* brontolare in continuazione

nagging ['nægɪŋ] *adj (doubt, pain)* persistente ■ *n* brontolii *mpl*, osservazioni *fpl* continue

nail [neɪl] *n (human)* unghia; *(metal)* chiodo ■ *vt* inchiodare; **to ~ sb down to a date/price** costringere qn a un appuntamento/ad accettare un prezzo; **to pay cash on the ~** *(Brit)* pagare a tamburo battente

nailbrush ['neɪlbrʌʃ] *n* spazzolino da *or* per unghie

nailfile ['neɪlfaɪl] *n* lima da *or* per unghie

nail polish *n* smalto da *or* per unghie

nail polish remover *n* acetone *m*, solvente *m*

nail scissors *npl* forbici *fpl* da *or* per unghie

nail varnish *n (Brit)* = **nail polish**

Nairobi [naɪ'rəubɪ] *n* Nairobi *f*

naïve [naɪ'iːv] *adj* ingenuo(-a)

naïveté [nɑːiːv'teɪ], **naivety** [naɪ'iːvtɪ] *n* ingenuità *f inv*

naked ['neɪkɪd] *adj* nudo(-a); **with the ~ eye** a occhio nudo

nakedness ['neɪkɪdnɪs] *n* nudità

NAM *n abbr* (US) = **National Association of Manufacturers**

name [neɪm] *n* nome *m*; *(reputation)* nome, reputazione *f* ■ *vt (baby etc)* chiamare; *(person, object)* identificare; *(price, date)* fissare; **by ~** di nome; **she knows them all by ~** li conosce tutti per nome; **in the ~ of** in nome di; **what's your ~?** come si chiama?; **my ~ is Peter** mi chiamo Peter; **to take sb's ~ and address** prendere nome e indirizzo di qn; **to make a ~ for o.s.** farsi un nome; **to get (o.s.) a bad ~** farsi una cattiva fama *or* una brutta reputazione; **to call sb names** insultare qn

name dropping *n menzionare qualcuno per fare bella figura*

nameless ['neɪmlɪs] *adj* senza nome

namely ['neɪmlɪ] *adv* cioè

nameplate ['neɪmpleɪt] *n (on door etc)* targa

namesake ['neɪmseɪk] *n* omonimo

nan bread [nɑːn-] *n tipo di pane indiano poco lievitato di forma allungata*

nanny ['nænɪ] *n* bambinaia

nanny goat *n* capra

nap [næp] *n (sleep)* pisolino; *(of cloth)* peluria ■ *vi*: **to be caught napping** essere preso alla sprovvista; **to have a ~** schiacciare un pisolino

NAPA *n abbr* (US: = *National Association of Performing Artists*) *associazione nazionale degli artisti di palcoscenico*

napalm ['neɪpɑːm] *n* napalm *m*

nape [neɪp] *n*: **~ of the neck** nuca

napkin ['næpkɪn] *n* tovagliolo; *(Brit: for baby)* pannolino

Naples ['neɪplz] *n* Napoli *f*

Napoleonic [nəpəulɪ'ɔnɪk] *adj* napoleonico(-a)

nappy ['næpɪ] *n (Brit)* pannolino

nappy liner *n (Brit)* foglietttino igienico

narcissistic [nɑːsɪ'sɪstɪk] *adj* narcisistico(-a)

narcissus (*pl* **narcissi**) [nɑː'sɪsəs, -saɪ] *n* narciso

narcotic [nɑː'kɔtɪk] *n (Med)* narcotico; **narcotics** *npl (drugs)* narcotici, stupefacenti *mpl*

nark [nɑːk] *vt* (*Brit col*) scocciare
narrate [nəˈreɪt] *vt* raccontare, narrare
narration [nəˈreɪʃən] *n* narrazione *f*
narrative [ˈnærətɪv] *n* narrativa ■ *adj* narrativo(-a)
narrator [nəˈreɪtəʳ] *n* narratore(-trice)
narrow [ˈnærəu] *adj* stretto(-a); (*resources, means*) limitato(-a), modesto(-a); (*fig*): **to take a ~ view of** avere una visione limitata di ■ *vi* restringersi; **to have a ~ escape** farcela per un pelo; **to ~ sth down to** ridurre qc a
narrow gauge *adj* (*Rail*) a scartamento ridotto
narrowly [ˈnærəulɪ] *adv*: **Maria ~ escaped drowning** per un pelo Maria non è affogata; **he ~ missed hitting the cyclist** per poco non ha investito il ciclista
narrow-minded [nærəuˈmaɪndɪd] *adj* meschino(-a)
NAS *n abbr* (*US*) = **National Academy of Sciences**
NASA [ˈnæsə] *n abbr* (*US*: = *National Aeronautics and Space Administration*) N.A.S.A. *f*
nasal [ˈneɪzl] *adj* nasale
Nassau [ˈnæsɔː] *n* Nassau *f*
nastily [ˈnɑːstɪlɪ] *adv* con cattiveria
nastiness [ˈnɑːstɪnɪs] *n* (*of person, remark*) cattiveria; (: *spitefulness*) malignità
nasturtium [nəsˈtəːʃəm] *n* cappuccina, nasturzio (indiano)
nasty [ˈnɑːstɪ] *adj* (*person, remark*) cattivo(-a); (: *spiteful*) maligno(-a); (*smell, wound, situation*) brutto(-a); **to turn ~** (*situation*) mettersi male; (*weather*) guastarsi; (*person*) incattivirsi; **it's a ~ business** è una brutta faccenda, è un brutto affare
NAS/UWT *n abbr* (*Brit*: = *National Association of Schoolmasters/Union of Women Teachers*) *sindacato di insegnanti in Inghilterra e Galles*
nation [ˈneɪʃən] *n* nazione *f*
national [ˈnæʃənl] *adj* nazionale ■ *n* cittadino(-a)
national anthem *n* inno nazionale
National Curriculum *n* (*Brit*) ≈ programma *m* scolastico ministeriale (*in Inghilterra e Galles*)
national debt *n* debito pubblico
national dress *n* costume *m* nazionale
National Guard *n* (*US*) milizia nazionale (*volontaria, in ogni stato*)
National Health Service *n* (*Brit*) *servizio nazionale di assistenza sanitaria*, ≈ S.A.U.B. *f*
National Insurance *n* (*Brit*) ≈ Previdenza Sociale
nationalism [ˈnæʃnəlɪzəm] *n* nazionalismo
nationalist [ˈnæʃnəlɪst] *adj, n* nazionalista (*m/f*)
nationality [næʃəˈnælɪtɪ] *n* nazionalità *f inv*
nationalization [næʃnəlaɪˈzeɪʃən] *n* nazionalizzazione *f*
nationalize [ˈnæʃnəlaɪz] *vt* nazionalizzare
nationally [ˈnæʃnəlɪ] *adv* a livello nazionale
national park *n* parco nazionale
national press *n* stampa a diffusione nazionale
National Security Council *n* (*US*) consiglio nazionale di sicurezza
national service *n* (*Mil*) servizio militare
National Trust *n* sovrintendenza ai beni culturali e ambientali; *vedi nota*

NATIONAL TRUST

Fondato nel 1895, il *National Trust* è un'organizzazione che si occupa della tutela e salvaguardia di edifici e monumenti di interesse storico e di territori di interesse ambientale nel Regno Unito.

nation-wide [ˈneɪʃənwaɪd] *adj* diffuso(-a) in tutto il paese ■ *adv* in tutto il paese
native [ˈneɪtɪv] *n* abitante *m/f* del paese; (*in colonies*) indigeno(-a) ■ *adj* indigeno(-a); (*country*) natio(-a); (*ability*) innato(-a); **a ~ of Russia** un nativo della Russia; **a ~ speaker of French** una persona di madrelingua francese; **~ language** madrelingua
Native American *n discendente di tribù dell'America settentrionale*
Nativity [nəˈtɪvɪtɪ] *n* (*Rel*): **the ~** la Natività
nativity play *n* recita sulla Natività
NATO [ˈneɪtəu] *n abbr* (= *North Atlantic Treaty Organization*) N.A.T.O. *f*
natter [ˈnætəʳ] (*Brit col*) *vi* chiacchierare ■ *n* chiacchierata
natural [ˈnætʃrəl] *adj* naturale; (*ability*) innato(-a); (*manner*) semplice; **death from ~ causes** (*Law*) morte *f* per cause naturali
natural childbirth *n* parto indolore
natural gas *n* gas *m* metano
natural history *n* storia naturale
naturalist [ˈnætʃrəlɪst] *n* naturalista *m/f*
naturalization [nætʃrəlaɪˈzeɪʃən] *n* naturalizzazione *f*; acclimatazione *f*
naturalize [ˈnætʃrəlaɪz] *vt*: **to be naturalized** (*person*) naturalizzarsi; **to become naturalized** (*animal, plant*) acclimatarsi
naturally [ˈnætʃrəlɪ] *adv* naturalmente; (*by nature: gifted*) di natura
naturalness [ˈnætʃrəlnɪs] *n* naturalezza
natural resources *npl* risorse *fpl* naturali
natural selection *n* selezione *f* naturale

natural wastage *n* (*Industry*) diminuzione *f* di manodopera (*per pensionamento decesso etc*)
nature ['neɪtʃəʳ] *n* natura; (*character*) natura, indole *f*; **by ~** di natura; **documents of a confidential ~** documenti *mpl* di natura privata
-natured ['neɪtʃəd] *suffix*: **ill~** maldisposto(-a)
nature reserve *n* (*Brit*) parco naturale
nature trail *n percorso tracciato in parchi nazionali ecc con scopi educativi*
naturist ['neɪtʃərɪst] *n* naturista *m/f*, nudista *m/f*
naught [nɔːt] *n* = **nought**
naughtiness ['nɔːtɪnɪs] *n* cattiveria
naughty ['nɔːtɪ] *adj* (*child*) birichino(-a), cattivello(-a); (*story, film*) spinto(-a)
nausea ['nɔːsɪə] *n* (*Med*) nausea; (*fig: disgust*) schifo
nauseate ['nɔːsɪeɪt] *vt* nauseare; far schifo a
nauseating ['nɔːsɪeɪtɪŋ] *adj* nauseante; (*fig*) disgustoso(-a)
nauseous ['nɔːsɪəs] *adj* nauseabondo(-a); (*feeling sick*): **to be ~** avere la nausea
nautical ['nɔːtɪkl] *adj* nautico(-a)
nautical mile *n* miglio nautico *or* marino
naval ['neɪvl] *adj* navale
naval officer *n* ufficiale *m* di marina
nave [neɪv] *n* navata centrale
navel ['neɪvl] *n* ombelico
navigable ['nævɪgəbl] *adj* navigabile
navigate ['nævɪgeɪt] *vt* percorrere navigando ■ *vi* navigare; (*Aut*) fare da navigatore
navigation [nævɪ'geɪʃən] *n* navigazione *f*
navigator ['nævɪgeɪtəʳ] *n* (*Naut, Aviat*) ufficiale *m* di rotta; (*explorer*) navigatore *m*; (*Aut*) copilota *m/f*
navvy ['nævɪ] *n* manovale *m*
navy ['neɪvɪ] *n* marina; **Department of the N~** (*US*) Ministero della Marina ■ *adj* blu scuro *inv*
navy-blue ['neɪvɪ'bluː] *adj* blu scuro *inv*
Nazareth ['næzərɪθ] *n* Nazareth *f*
Nazi ['nɑːtsɪ] *adj, n* nazista (*m/f*)
NB *abbr* (= *nota bene*) N.B.; (*Canada*) = **New Brunswick**
NBA *n abbr* (*US*: = *National Basketball Association*) ≈ F.I.P. *f* (= *Federazione Italiana Pallacanestro*); = **National Boxing Association**
NBC *n abbr* (*US*: = *National Broadcasting Company*) *compagnia nazionale di radiodiffusione*
NBS *n abbr* (*US*: = *National Bureau of Standards*) *ufficio per la normalizzazione*
NC *abbr* (*Comm etc*: = *no charge*) gratis; (*US*) = **North Carolina**
NCC *n abbr* (*US*) = **National Council of Churches**
NCO *n abbr* = **non-commissioned officer**
ND, N. Dak. *abbr* (*US*) = **North Dakota**
NE *abbr* (*US*) = **Nebraska; New England**
NEA *n abbr* (*US*) = **National Education Association**
neap [niːp] *n* (*also*: **neaptide**) marea di quadratura
Neapolitan [nɪə'pɔlɪtən] *adj, n* napoletano(-a)
near [nɪəʳ] *adj* vicino(-a); (*relation*) prossimo(-a) ■ *adv* vicino ■ *prep* (*also*: **near to**) vicino a, presso; (*in time*) verso ■ *vt* avvicinarsi a; **to come ~** avvicinarsi; **~ here/ there** qui/lì vicino; **£25,000 or nearest offer** (*Brit*) 25.000 sterline trattabili; **in the ~ future** in un prossimo futuro; **the building is nearing completion** il palazzo è quasi terminato *or* ultimato
nearby [nɪə'baɪ] *adj* vicino(-a) ■ *adv* vicino
Near East *n*: **the ~** il Medio Oriente
nearer ['nɪərəʳ] *adj* più vicino(-a) ■ *adv* più vicino
nearly ['nɪəlɪ] *adv* quasi; **not ~** non ... affatto; **I ~ lost it** per poco non lo perdevo; **she was ~ crying** era lì lì per piangere
near miss *n*: **that was a ~** c'è mancato poco
nearness ['nɪənɪs] *n* vicinanza
nearside ['nɪəsaɪd] *n* (*right-hand drive*) lato sinistro; (*left-hand drive*) lato destro ■ *adj* sinistro(-a); destro(-a)
near-sighted [nɪə'saɪtɪd] *adj* miope
neat [niːt] *adj* (*person, room*) ordinato(-a); (*work*) pulito(-a); (*solution, plan*) ben indovinato(-a), azzeccato(-a); (*spirits*) liscio(-a)
neatly ['niːtlɪ] *adv* con ordine; (*skilfully*) abilmente
neatness ['niːtnɪs] *n* (*tidiness*) ordine *m*; (*skilfulness*) abilità
Nebr. *abbr* (*US*) = **Nebraska**
nebulous ['nɛbjuləs] *adj* nebuloso(-a); (*fig*) vago(-a)
necessarily ['nɛsɪsrɪlɪ] *adv* necessariamente; **not ~** non è detto, non necessariamente
necessary ['nɛsɪsrɪ] *adj* necessario(-a); **if ~** se necessario
necessitate [nɪ'sɛsɪteɪt] *vt* rendere necessario(-a)
necessity [nɪ'sɛsɪtɪ] *n* necessità *f inv*; **in case of ~** in caso di necessità
neck [nɛk] *n* collo; (*of garment*) colletto ■ *vi* (*col*) pomiciare, sbaciucchiarsi; **~ and ~** testa a testa; **to stick one's ~ out** (*col*) rischiare (forte)
necklace ['nɛklɪs] *n* collana
neckline ['nɛklaɪn] *n* scollatura
necktie ['nɛktaɪ] *n* (*esp US*) cravatta
nectar ['nɛktəʳ] *n* nettare *m*

n

nectarine ['nɛktərɪn] *n* nocepesca
née [neɪ] *adj*: **~ Scott** nata Scott
need [ni:d] *n* bisogno ■ *vt* aver bisogno di; **I ~ to do it** lo devo fare, bisogna che io lo faccia; **you don't ~ to go** non deve andare, non c'è bisogno che lei vada; **a signature is needed** occorre *or* ci vuole una firma; **to be in ~ of, have ~ of** aver bisogno di; **£10 will meet my immediate needs** 10 sterline mi basteranno per le necessità più urgenti; **in case of ~** in caso di bisogno *or* necessità; **there's no ~ for ...** non c'è bisogno *or* non occorre che ...; **there's no ~ to do ...** non occorre fare ...; **the needs of industry** le esigenze dell'industria
needle ['ni:dl] *n* ago; (*on record player*) puntina ■ *vt* punzecchiare
needlecord ['ni:dlkɔ:d] *n* (*Brit*) velluto a coste sottili
needless ['ni:dlɪs] *adj* inutile; **~ to say, ...** inutile dire che ...
needlessly ['ni:dlɪslɪ] *adv* inutilmente
needlework ['ni:dlwə:k] *n* cucito
needn't ['ni:dnt] = **need not**
needy ['ni:dɪ] *adj* bisognoso(-a)
negation [nɪ'geɪʃən] *n* negazione *f*
negative ['nɛgətɪv] *n* (*Phot*) negativa, negativo; (*Elec*) polo negativo; (*Ling*) negazione *f* ■ *adj* negativo(-a); **to answer in the ~** rispondere negativamente *or* di no
negative equity *n situazione in cui l'ammontare del mutuo su un immobile supera il suo valore sul mercato*
neglect [nɪ'glɛkt] *vt* trascurare ■ *n* (*of person, duty*) negligenza; **state of ~** stato di abbandono; **to ~ to do sth** trascurare *or* tralasciare di fare qc
neglected [nɪ'glɛktɪd] *adj* trascurato(-a)
neglectful [nɪ'glɛktful] *adj* (*gen*) negligente; **to be ~ of sb/sth** trascurare qn/qc
negligee ['nɛglɪʒeɪ] *n* néglígé *m inv*
negligence ['nɛglɪdʒəns] *n* negligenza
negligent ['nɛglɪdʒənt] *adj* negligente
negligently ['nɛglɪdʒəntlɪ] *adv* con negligenza
negligible ['nɛglɪdʒɪbl] *adj* insignificante, trascurabile
negotiable [nɪ'gəuʃɪəbl] *adj* negoziabile; (*cheque*) trasferibile; (*road*) transitabile
negotiate [nɪ'gəuʃɪeɪt] *vi* negoziare ■ *vt* (*Comm*) negoziare; (*obstacle*) superare; (*bend in road*) prendere; **to ~ with sb for sth** trattare con qn per ottenere qc
negotiating table [nɪ'gəuʃɪeɪtɪŋ-] *n* tavolo delle trattative
negotiation [nɪgəuʃɪ'eɪʃən] *n* trattativa; (*Pol*) negoziato; **to enter into negotiations with sb** entrare in trattative (*or* intavolare i negoziati) con qn
negotiator [nɪ'gəuʃɪeɪtə^r] *n* negoziatore(-trice)
Negress ['ni:grɪs] *n* negra
Negro ['ni:grəu] *adj, n* (*pl* **Negroes**) negro(-a)
neigh [neɪ] *vi* nitrire
neighbour, (*US*) **neighbor** ['neɪbə^r] *n* vicino(-a)
neighbourhood, (*US*) **neighborhood** ['neɪbəhud] *n* vicinato
neighbourhood watch *n* (*Brit*: *also*: **neighbourhood watch scheme**) *sistema di vigilanza reciproca in un quartiere*
neighbouring, (*US*) **neighboring** ['neɪbərɪŋ] *adj* vicino(-a)
neighbourly, (*US*) **neighborly** ['neɪbəlɪ] *adj*: **he is a neighbo(u)rly person** è un buon vicino
neither ['naɪðə^r] *adj, pron* né l'uno(-a) né l'altro(-a), nessuno(-a) dei/delle due ■ *conj* neanche, nemmeno, neppure ■ *adv*: **~ good nor bad** né buono né cattivo; **I didn't move and ~ did Claude** io non mi mossi e nemmeno Claude; **... ~ did I refuse ...**, ma non ho nemmeno rifiutato
neo... ['ni:əu] *prefix* neo...
neolithic [ni:əu'lɪθɪk] *adj* neolitico(-a)
neologism [nɪ'ɔlədʒɪzəm] *n* neologismo
neon ['ni:ɔn] *n* neon *m*
neon light *n* luce *f* al neon
neon sign *n* insegna al neon
Nepal [nɪ'pɔ:l] *n* Nepal *m*
nephew ['nɛvju:] *n* nipote *m*
nepotism ['nɛpətɪzəm] *n* nepotismo
nerd [nə:d] *n* (*col*) sfigato(-a), povero(-a) fesso(-a)
nerve [nə:v] *n* nervo; (*fig*) coraggio; (*impudence*) faccia tosta; **he gets on my nerves** mi dà ai nervi, mi fa venire i nervi; **a fit of nerves** una crisi di nervi; **to lose one's ~** (*self-confidence*) perdere fiducia in se stesso; **I lost my ~** (*courage*) mi è mancato il coraggio
nerve centre *n* (*Anat*) centro nervoso; (*fig*) cervello, centro vitale
nerve gas *n* gas *m* nervino
nerve-racking ['nə:vrækɪŋ] *adj* che spezza i nervi
nervous ['nə:vəs] *adj* nervoso(-a)
nervous breakdown *n* esaurimento nervoso
nervously ['nə:vəslɪ] *adv* nervosamente
nervousness ['nə:vəsnɪs] *n* nervosismo
nervous wreck *n*: **to be a ~** (*col*) essere nevrastenico(-a)
nervy ['nə:vɪ] *adj* agitato(-a), nervoso(-a)
nest [nɛst] *n* nido; **~ of tables** tavolini *mpl* cicogna *inv*

nest egg *n* (*fig*) gruzzolo
nestle ['nɛsl] *vi* accoccolarsi
nestling ['nɛslɪŋ] *n* uccellino di nido
net [nɛt] *n* rete *f*; (*fabric*) tulle *m*; **the N~** (*internet*) Internet *f* ■ *adj* netto(-a) ■ *vt* (*person*) ricavare un utile netto di; (*deal, sale*) dare un utile netto di; **~ of tax** netto, al netto di tasse; **he earns £10,000 ~ per year** guadagna 10.000 sterline nette all'anno
netball ['nɛtbɔ:l] *n specie di pallacanestro*
net curtains *npl* tende *fpl* di tulle
Netherlands ['nɛðələndz] *npl*: **the ~** i Paesi Bassi
netiquette ['nɛtɪkɛt] *n* netiquette *f inv*
net profit *n* utile *m* netto
nett [nɛt] *adj* = **net**
netting ['nɛtɪŋ] *n* (*for fence etc*) reticolato; (*fabric*) tulle *m*
nettle ['nɛtl] *n* ortica
network ['nɛtwə:k] *n* rete *f*
neuralgia [njuə'rældʒə] *n* nevralgia
neurological [njuərə'lɔdʒɪkl] *adj* neurologico(-a)
neurosis (*pl* **neuroses**) [njuə'rəusɪs, -si:z] *n* nevrosi *f inv*
neurotic [njuə'rɔtɪk] *adj, n* nevrotico(-a)
neuter ['nju:tə^r] *adj* neutro(-a) ■ *n* neutro ■ *vt* (*cat etc*) castrare
neutral ['nju:trəl] *adj* neutro(-a); (*person, nation*) neutrale ■ *n* (*Aut*): **in ~** in folle
neutrality [nju:'trælɪtɪ] *n* neutralità
neutralize ['nju:trəlaɪz] *vt* neutralizzare
neutron bomb ['nju:trɔn-] *n* bomba al neutrone
Nev. *abbr* (*US*) = **Nevada**
never ['nɛvə^r] *adv* (non...) mai; **~ again** mai più; **I'll ~ go there again** non ci vado più; **~ in my life** mai in vita mia; *see also* **mind**
never-ending [nɛvər'ɛndɪŋ] *adj* interminabile
nevertheless [nɛvəðə'lɛs] *adv* tuttavia, ciò nonostante, ciò nondimeno
new [nju:] *adj* nuovo(-a); (*brand new*) nuovo(-a) di zecca; **as good as ~** come nuovo
New Age *adj, n* New Age *f inv*
newbie ['nju:bɪ] *n* (*Comput, Tech*) utilizzatore(-trice) inesperto(-a); (*to a job or group*) nuovo(-a) arrivato(-a); (*to a hobby or experience*) neofita *m/f*
newborn ['nju:bɔ:n] *adj* neonato(-a)
newcomer ['nju:kʌmə^r] *n* nuovo(-a) venuto(-a)
new-fangled ['nju:fæŋgld] *adj* (*pej*) stramoderno(-a)
new-found ['nju:faund] *adj* nuovo(-a)
Newfoundland ['nju:fənlənd] *n* Terranova
New Guinea *n* Nuova Guinea
newly ['nju:lɪ] *adv* di recente
newly-weds ['nju:lɪwɛdz] *npl* sposini *mpl*, sposi *mpl* novelli
new moon *n* luna nuova
newness ['nju:nɪs] *n* novità
news [nju:z] *n* notizie *fpl*; (*Radio*) giornale *m* radio; (*TV*) telegiornale *m*; **a piece of ~** una notizia; **good/bad ~** buone/cattive notizie; **financial ~** (*Press*) pagina economica e finanziaria; (*Radio, TV*) notiziario economico
news agency *n* agenzia di stampa
newsagent ['nju:zeɪdʒənt] *n* (*Brit*) giornalaio
news bulletin *n* (*Radio, TV*) notiziario
newscaster ['nju:zkɑ:stə^r] *n* (*Radio, TV*) annunciatore(-trice)
newsdealer ['nju:zdi:lə^r] *n* (*US*) = **newsagent**
newsflash ['nju:zflæʃ] *n* notizia *f* lampo *inv*
newsletter ['nju:zlɛtə^r] *n* bollettino (*di ditta, associazione*)
newspaper ['nju:zpeɪpə^r] *n* giornale *m*; **daily ~** quotidiano; **weekly ~** settimanale *m*
newsprint ['nju:zprɪnt] *n* carta da giornale
newsreader ['nju:zri:də^r] *n* = **newscaster**
newsreel ['nju:zri:l] *n* cinegiornale *m*
newsroom ['nju:zrum] *n* (*Press*) redazione *f*; (*Radio, TV*) studio
news stand *n* edicola
newsworthy ['nju:zwə:ðɪ] *adj* degno(-a) di menzione (*per radio, TV ecc*); **to be ~** fare notizia
newt [nju:t] *n* tritone *m*
new town *n* (*Brit*) *nuovo centro urbano creato con fondi pubblici*
New Year *n* Anno Nuovo; **Happy ~!** Buon Anno!; **to wish sb a happy ~** augurare Buon Anno a qn
New Year's Day *n* il Capodanno
New Year's Eve *n* la vigilia di Capodanno
New York [-'jɔ:k] *n* New York *f*, Nuova York *f*; (*also*: **New York State**) stato di New York
New Zealand [-'zi:lənd] *n* Nuova Zelanda ■ *adj* neozelandese
New Zealander [-'zi:ləndə^r] *n* neozelandese *m/f*
next [nɛkst] *adj* prossimo(-a) ■ *adv* accanto; (*in time*) dopo; **~ to** *prep* accanto a; **~ to nothing** quasi niente; **~ time** *adv* la prossima volta; **~ week** la settimana prossima; **the ~ week** la settimana dopo *or* seguente; **the week after ~** fra due settimane; **the ~ day** il giorno dopo, l'indomani; **~ year** l'anno prossimo *or* venturo; **"turn to the ~ page"** "vedi pagina seguente"; **who's ~?** a chi tocca?; **when do we meet ~?** quando ci rincontriamo?
next door *adv* accanto
next of kin *n* parente *m/f* prossimo(-a)
NF *n abbr* (*Brit Pol*: = *National Front*) *partito di estrema destra* ■ *abbr* (*Canada*) = **Newfoundland**
NFL *n abbr* (*US*) = **National Football League**

n

Nfld. *abbr* (*Canada*) = **Newfoundland**
NG *abbr* (*US*) = **National Guard**
NGO *n abbr* = **non-governmental organization**
NH *abbr* (*US*) = **New Hampshire**
NHL *n abbr* (*US*: = *National Hockey League*) ≈ F.I.H.P. *f* (= *Federazione Italiana Hockey e Pattinaggio*)
NHS *n abbr* (*Brit*) = **National Health Service**
NI *abbr* = **Northern Ireland**; (*Brit*) = **National Insurance**
Niagara Falls [naɪ'ægərə-] *npl*: **the ~** le cascate del Niagara
nib [nɪb] *n* (*of pen*) pennino
nibble ['nɪbl] *vt* mordicchiare
Nicaragua [nɪkə'rægjuə] *n* Nicaragua *m*
Nicaraguan [nɪkə'rægjuən] *adj*, *n* nicaraguense (*m/f*)
Nice [ni:s] *n* Nizza
nice [naɪs] *adj* (*holiday, trip*) piacevole; (*flat, picture*) bello(-a); (*person*) simpatico(-a), gentile; (*taste, smell, meal*) buono(-a); (*distinction, point*) sottile
nice-looking ['naɪslukɪŋ] *adj* bello(-a)
nicely ['naɪslɪ] *adv* bene; **that will do ~** andrà benissimo
niceties ['naɪsɪtɪz] *npl* finezze *fpl*
nick [nɪk] *n* tacca ■ *vt* intaccare; tagliare; (*col*: *steal*) rubare; (: *Brit*: *arrest*) beccare; **in the ~ of time** appena in tempo; **in good ~** (*Brit col*) decente, in buono stato; **to ~ o.s.** farsi un taglietto
nickel ['nɪkl] *n* nichel *m*; (*US*) *moneta da cinque centesimi di dollaro*
nickname ['nɪkneɪm] *n* soprannome *m* ■ *vt* soprannominare
Nicosia [nɪkə'si:ə] *n* Nicosia
nicotine ['nɪkəti:n] *n* nicotina
nicotine patch *n* cerotto antifumo (*a base di nicotina*)
niece [ni:s] *n* nipote *f*
nifty ['nɪftɪ] *adj* (*col*: *car, jacket*) chic *inv*; (: *gadget, tool*) ingegnoso(-a)
Niger ['naɪdʒəʳ] *n* Niger *m*
Nigeria [naɪ'dʒɪərɪə] *n* Nigeria
Nigerian [naɪ'dʒɪərɪən] *adj*, *n* nigeriano(-a)
niggardly ['nɪgədlɪ] *adj* (*person*) tirchio(-a), spilorcio(-a); (*allowance, amount*) misero(-a)
nigger ['nɪgəʳ] *n* (*col!*) negro(-a)
niggle ['nɪgl] *vt* assillare ■ *vi* fare il/la pignolo(-a)
niggling ['nɪglɪŋ] *adj* pignolo(-a); (*detail*) insignificante; (*doubt, pain*) persistente
night [naɪt] *n* notte *f*; (*evening*) sera; **at ~** la notte; la sera; **by ~** di notte; **in the ~, during the ~** durante la notte; **the ~ before last** l'altro ieri notte; l'altro ieri sera
night-bird ['naɪtbə:d] *n* uccello notturno; (*fig*) nottambulo(-a)
nightcap ['naɪtkæp] *n* *bicchierino prima di andare a letto*
night club *n* locale *m* notturno
nightdress ['naɪtdrɛs] *n* camicia da notte
nightfall ['naɪtfɔ:l] *n* crepuscolo
nightie ['naɪtɪ] *n* camicia da notte
nightingale ['naɪtɪŋgeɪl] *n* usignolo
night life *n* vita notturna
nightly ['naɪtlɪ] *adj* di ogni notte *or* sera; (*by night*) notturno(-a) ■ *adv* ogni notte *or* sera
nightmare ['naɪtmɛəʳ] *n* incubo
night porter *n* portiere *m* di notte
night safe *n* cassa continua
night school *n* scuola serale
nightshade ['naɪtʃeɪd] *n*: **deadly ~** (*Bot*) belladonna
nightshift ['naɪtʃɪft] *n* turno di notte
night-time ['naɪttaɪm] *n* notte *f*
night watchman *n* guardiano notturno
nihilism ['naɪɪlɪzəm] *n* nichilismo
nil [nɪl] *n* nulla *m*; (*Sport*) zero
Nile [naɪl] *n*: **the ~** il Nilo
nimble ['nɪmbl] *adj* agile
nine [naɪn] *num* nove
9-11 *n* 11 settembre
nineteen [naɪn'ti:n] *num* diciannove
ninety ['naɪntɪ] *num* novanta
ninth [naɪnθ] *num* nono(-a)
nip [nɪp] *vt* pizzicare ■ *vi* (*Brit col*): **to ~ out/down/up** fare un salto fuori/giù/di sopra ■ *n* (*pinch*) pizzico; (*drink*) goccio, bicchierino
nipple ['nɪpl] *n* (*Anat*) capezzolo
nippy ['nɪpɪ] *adj* (*weather*) pungente; (*Brit*: *car, person*) svelto(-a)
nit [nɪt] *n* (*of louse*) lendine *m*; (*col*: *idiot*) cretino(-a), scemo(-a)
nit-pick ['nɪtpɪk] *vi* (*col*) cercare il pelo nell'uovo
nitrogen ['naɪtrədʒən] *n* azoto
nitroglycerin, nitroglycerine [naɪtrəu'glɪsəri:n] *n* nitroglicerina
nitty-gritty ['nɪtɪ'grɪtɪ] *n* (*col*): **to get down to the ~** venire al sodo
nitwit ['nɪtwɪt] *n* (*col*) scemo(-a)
NJ *abbr* (*US*) = **New Jersey**
NLF *n abbr* (= *National Liberation Front*) ≈ F.L.N. *m*
NLRB *n abbr* (*US*: = *National Labor Relations Board*) *organismo per la tutela dei lavoratori*
NM, N. Mex. *abbr* (*US*) = **New Mexico**

 KEYWORD

no [nəu] *adv* (*opposite of "yes"*) no; **are you coming? — no (I'm not)** viene? — no (non vengo); **would you like some more? — no**

thank you ne vuole ancora un po'? — no, grazie; **I have no more wine** non ho più vino ■ *adj* (*not any*) nessuno(-a); **I have no money/time/books** non ho soldi/tempo/libri; **no student would have done it** nessuno studente lo avrebbe fatto; **there is no reason to believe ...** non c'è nessuna ragione per credere ...; **"no parking"** "divieto di sosta"; **"no smoking"** "vietato fumare"; **"no entry"** "ingresso vietato"; **"no dogs"** "vietato l'accesso ai cani" ■ *n* (*pl* **noes**) no *m inv*; **I won't take no for an answer** non accetterò un rifiuto

no. *abbr* (= *number*) n.
nobble ['nɔbl] *vt* (*Brit col: bribe: person*) comprare, corrompere; (*: person to speak to, criminal*) bloccare, beccare; (*Racing: horse, dog*) drogare
Nobel prize [nəu'bɛl-] *n* premio Nobel
nobility [nəu'bɪlɪtɪ] *n* nobiltà
noble ['nəubl] *adj, n* nobile (*m*)
nobleman ['nəublmən] *n* nobile *m*, nobiluomo
nobly ['nəublɪ] *adv* (*selflessly*) generosamente
nobody ['nəubədɪ] *pron* nessuno
no-claims bonus ['nəukleɪmz-] *n* bonus malus *m inv*
nocturnal [nɔk'tə:nl] *adj* notturno(-a)
nod [nɔd] *vi* accennare col capo, fare un cenno; (*sleep*) sonnecchiare ■ *vt*: **to ~ one's head** fare di sì col capo ■ *n* cenno; **they nodded their agreement** accennarono di sì (col capo)
▸ **nod off** *vi* assopirsi
no-fly zone [nəu'flaɪ-] *n* zona di interdizione aerea
noise [nɔɪz] *n* rumore *m*; (*din, racket*) chiasso
noiseless ['nɔɪzlɪs] *adj* silenzioso(-a)
noisily ['nɔɪzɪlɪ] *adv* rumorosamente
noisy ['nɔɪzɪ] *adj* (*street, car*) rumoroso(-a); (*person*) chiassoso(-a)
nomad ['nəumæd] *n* nomade *m/f*
nomadic [nəu'mædɪk] *adj* nomade
no man's land *n* terra di nessuno
nominal ['nɔmɪnl] *adj* nominale
nominate ['nɔmɪneɪt] *vt* (*propose*) proporre come candidato; (*elect*) nominare
nomination [nɔmɪ'neɪʃən] *n* nomina; candidatura
nominee [nɔmɪ'ni:] *n* persona nominata; candidato(-a)
non... [nɔn] *prefix* non...
non-alcoholic ['nɔnælkə'hɔlɪk] *adj* analcolico(-a)
non-breakable [nɔn'breɪkəbl] *adj* infrangibile
nonce word ['nɔns-] *n* parola coniata per l'occasione
nonchalant ['nɔnʃələnt] *adj* incurante, indifferente
non-commissioned [nɔnkə'mɪʃnd] *adj*: **~ officer** sottufficiale *m*
non-committal [nɔnkə'mɪtl] *adj* evasivo(-a)
nonconformist [nɔnkən'fɔ:mɪst] *n* anticonformista *m/f*; (*Brit Rel*) dissidente *m/f* ■ *adj* anticonformista
non-contributory [nɔnkən'trɪbjutərɪ] *adj*: **~ pension scheme** *or* (*US*) **plan** *sistema di pensionamento con i contributi interamente a carico del datore di lavoro*
non-cooperation ['nɔnkəuɔpə'reɪʃən] *n* non cooperazione *f*, non collaborazione *f*
nondescript ['nɔndɪskrɪpt] *adj* qualunque *inv*
none [nʌn] *pron* (*not one thing*) niente; (*not one person*) nessuno(-a); **~ of you** nessuno(-a) di voi; **I have ~** non ne ho nemmeno uno; **I have ~ left** non ne ho più; **~ at all** proprio niente; (*not one*) nemmeno uno; **he's ~ the worse for it** non ne ha risentito
nonentity [nɔ'nɛntɪtɪ] *n* persona insignificante
non-essential [nɔnɪ'sɛnʃl] *adj* non essenziale ■ *n*: **non-essentials** superfluo, cose *fpl* superflue
nonetheless ['nʌnðə'lɛs] *adv* nondimeno
non-event [nɔnɪ'vɛnt] *n* delusione *f*
non-executive [nɔnɪg'zɛkjutɪv] *adj*: **~ director** direttore *m* senza potere esecutivo
non-existent [nɔnɪg'zɪstənt] *adj* inesistente
non-fiction [nɔn'fɪkʃən] *n* saggistica
non-flammable [nɔn'flæməbl] *adj* ininfiammabile
non-intervention ['nɔnɪntə'vɛnʃən] *n* non intervento
no-no ['nəunəu] *n*: **it's a ~!** (*undesirable*) è inaccettabile!; (*forbidden*) non si può fare!
non obst. *abbr* (*notwithstanding: = non obstante*) nonostante
no-nonsense [nəu'nɔnsəns] *adj* che va al sodo
non-payment [nɔn'peɪmənt] *n* mancato pagamento
nonplussed [nɔn'plʌst] *adj* sconcertato(-a)
non-profit-making [nɔn'prɔfɪtmeɪkɪŋ] *adj* senza scopo di lucro
nonsense ['nɔnsəns] *n* sciocchezze *fpl*; **~!** che sciocchezze!, che assurdità!; **it is ~ to say that ...** è un'assurdità *or* non ha senso dire che ...
nonsensical [nɔn'sɛnsɪkl] *adj* assurdo(-a), ridicolo(-a)
non-shrink [nɔn'ʃrɪŋk] *adj* (*Brit*) irrestringibile

non-skid [nɔn'skɪd] *adj* antisdrucciolo(-a)
non-smoker ['nɔn'sməukəʳ] *n* non fumatore(-trice)
non-starter [nɔn'stɑ:təʳ] *n*: **it's a ~** è fallito in partenza
non-stick ['nɔn'stɪk] *adj* antiaderente, antiadesivo(-a)
non-stop ['nɔn'stɔp] *adj* continuo(-a); (*train, bus*) direttissimo(-a) ■ *adv* senza sosta
non-taxable [nɔn'tæksəbl] *adj*: **~ income** reddito non imponibile
non-U [nɔn'ju:] *adj abbr* (*Brit col*) = **non-upper class**
non-volatile [nɔn'vɔlətaɪl] *adj*: **~ memory** (*Comput*) memoria permanente
non-voting [nɔn'vəutɪŋ] *adj*: **~ shares** azioni *fpl* senza diritto di voto
non-white ['nɔn'waɪt] *adj* di colore ■ *n* persona di colore
noodles ['nu:dlz] *npl* taglierini *mpl*
nook [nuk] *n*: **nooks and crannies** angoli *mpl*
noon [nu:n] *n* mezzogiorno
no one ['nəuwʌn] *pron* = **nobody**
noose [nu:s] *n* nodo scorsoio, cappio; (*hangman's*) cappio
nor [nɔ:ʳ] *conj* = **neither** ■ *adv see* **neither**
norm [nɔ:m] *n* norma
normal ['nɔ:ml] *adj* normale ■ *n*: **to return to ~** tornare alla normalità
normality [nɔ:'mælɪtɪ] *n* normalità
normally ['nɔ:məlɪ] *adv* normalmente
Normandy ['nɔ:məndɪ] *n* Normandia
north [nɔ:θ] *n* nord *m*, settentrione *m* ■ *adj* nord *inv*, del nord, settentrionale ■ *adv* verso nord
North Africa *n* Africa del Nord
North African *adj, n* nordafricano(-a)
North America *n* America del Nord
North American *adj, n* nordamericano(-a)
Northants [nɔ:'θænts] *abbr* (*Brit*) = **Northamptonshire**
northbound ['nɔ:θbaund] *adj* (*traffic*) diretto(-a) a nord; (*carriageway*) nord *inv*
north-east [nɔ:θ'i:st] *n* nord-est *m*
northerly ['nɔ:ðəlɪ] *adj* (*wind*) del nord; (*direction*) verso nord
northern ['nɔ:ðən] *adj* del nord, settentrionale
Northern Ireland *n* Irlanda del Nord
North Pole *n*: **the North** il Polo Nord
North Sea *n*: **the ~** il mare del Nord
North Sea oil *n* petrolio del mare del Nord
northward ['nɔ:θwəd], **northwards** ['nɔ:θwədz] *adv* verso nord
north-west [nɔ:θ'wɛst] *n* nord-ovest *m*
Norway ['nɔ:weɪ] *n* Norvegia
Norwegian [nɔ:'wi:dʒən] *adj* norvegese ■ *n* norvegese *m/f*; (*Ling*) norvegese *m*
nos. *abbr* (= *numbers*) nn.
nose [nəuz] *n* naso; (*of animal*) muso ■ *vi* (*also*: **nose one's way**) avanzare cautamente; **to pay through the ~ (for sth)** (*col*) pagare (qc) un occhio della testa
▸ **nose about, nose around** *vi* aggirarsi
nosebleed ['nəuzbli:d] *n* emorragia nasale
nose-dive ['nəuzdaɪv] *n* picchiata
nose drops *npl* gocce *fpl* per il naso
nosey ['nəuzɪ] *adj* curioso(-a)
nostalgia [nɔs'tældʒɪə] *n* nostalgia
nostalgic [nɔs'tældʒɪk] *adj* nostalgico(-a)
nostril ['nɔstrɪl] *n* narice *f*; (*of horse*) frogia
nosy ['nəuzɪ] *adj* = **nosey**
not [nɔt] *adv* non; **~ at all** niente affatto; (*after thanks*) prego, s'immagini; **you must ~** *or* **mustn't do this** non deve fare questo; **he isn't ...** egli non è ...; **I hope ~** spero di no
notable ['nəutəbl] *adj* notevole
notably ['nəutəblɪ] *adv* notevolmente; (*in particular*) in particolare
notary ['nəutərɪ] *n* (*also*: **notary public**) notaio
notation [nəu'teɪʃən] *n* notazione *f*
notch [nɔtʃ] *n* tacca
▸ **notch up** *vt* (*score, victory*) marcare, segnare
note [nəut] *n* nota; (*letter, banknote*) biglietto ■ *vt* prendere nota di; **to take ~ of** prendere nota di; **to take notes** prendere appunti; **to compare notes** (*fig*) scambiarsi le impressioni; **of ~** eminente, importante; **just a quick ~ to let you know ...** ti scrivo solo due righe per informarti ...
notebook ['nəutbuk] *n* taccuino; (*for shorthand*) bloc-notes *m inv*
note-case ['nəutkeɪs] *n* (*Brit*) portafoglio
noted ['nəutɪd] *adj* celebre
notepad ['nəutpæd] *n* bloc-notes *m inv*, blocchetto
notepaper ['nəutpeɪpəʳ] *n* carta da lettere
noteworthy ['nəutwə:ðɪ] *adj* degno(-a) di nota, importante
nothing ['nʌθɪŋ] *n* nulla *m*, niente *m*; **he does ~** non fa niente; **~ new** niente di nuovo; **for ~** (*free*) per niente; **~ at all** proprio niente
notice ['nəutɪs] *n* avviso; (*of leaving*) preavviso; (*Brit*: *review*: *of play etc*) critica, recensione *f* ■ *vt* notare, accorgersi di; **to take ~ of** fare attenzione a; **to bring sth to sb's ~** far notare qc a qn; **to give sb ~ of sth** avvisare qn di qc; **to give ~, hand in one's ~** (*employee*) licenziarsi; **without ~** senza preavviso; **at short ~** con un breve preavviso; **until further ~** fino a nuovo avviso; **advance ~** preavviso; **to escape** *or* **avoid ~**

passare inosservato; **it has come to my ~ that ...** sono venuto a sapere che ...
noticeable ['nəutɪsəbl] *adj* evidente
notice board *n* (*Brit*) tabellone *m* per affissi
notification [nəutɪfɪ'keɪʃən] *n* annuncio; notifica; denuncia
notify ['nəutɪfaɪ] *vt*: **to ~ sth to sb** notificare qc a qn; **to ~ sb of sth** avvisare qn di qc; (*police*) denunciare qc a qn
notion ['nəuʃən] *n* idea; (*concept*) nozione *f*
notions ['nəuʃənz] *npl* (*US: haberdashery*) merceria
notoriety [nəutə'raɪətɪ] *n* notorietà
notorious [nəu'tɔːrɪəs] *adj* famigerato(-a)
notoriously [nəu'tɔːrɪəslɪ] *adv* notoriamente
Notts [nɔts] *abbr* (*Brit*) = **Nottinghamshire**
notwithstanding [nɔtwɪθ'stændɪŋ] *adv* nondimeno ■ *prep* nonostante, malgrado
nougat ['nuːgɑː] *n* torrone *m*
nought [nɔːt] *n* zero
noun [naun] *n* nome *m*, sostantivo
nourish ['nʌrɪʃ] *vt* nutrire
nourishing ['nʌrɪʃɪŋ] *adj* nutriente
nourishment ['nʌrɪʃmənt] *n* nutrimento
Nov. *abbr* (= *November*) nov.
Nova Scotia ['nəuvə'skəuʃə] *n* Nuova Scozia
novel ['nɔvl] *n* romanzo ■ *adj* nuovo(-a)
novelist ['nɔvəlɪst] *n* romanziere(-a)
novelty ['nɔvəltɪ] *n* novità *f inv*
November [nəu'vɛmbəʳ] *n* novembre *m*; *see also* **July**
novice ['nɔvɪs] *n* principiante *m/f*; (*Rel*) novizio(-a)
NOW [nau] *n abbr* (*US:* = *National Organization for Women*) ≈ U.D.I. *f* (= *Unione Donne Italiane*)
now [nau] *adv* ora, adesso ■ *conj*: **~ (that)** adesso che, ora che; **right ~** subito; **by ~** ormai; **just ~**: **that's the fashion just ~** è la moda del momento; **I saw her just ~** l'ho vista proprio adesso; **I'll read it just ~** lo leggo subito; **~ and then, ~ and again** ogni tanto; **from ~ on** da ora in poi; **in 3 days from ~** fra 3 giorni; **between ~ and Monday** da qui a lunedì, entro lunedì; **that's all for ~** per ora basta
nowadays ['nauədeɪz] *adv* oggidì
nowhere ['nəuwɛəʳ] *adv* in nessun luogo, da nessuna parte; **~ else** in nessun altro posto
no-win situation [nəu'wɪn-] *n*: **to be in a ~** aver perso in partenza
noxious ['nɔkʃəs] *adj* nocivo(-a)
nozzle ['nɔzl] *n* (*of hose etc*) boccaglio
NP *n abbr* = **notary public**
NS *abbr* (*Canada*) = **Nova Scotia**
NSC *n abbr* (*US*) = **National Security Council**
NSF *n abbr* (*US*) = **National Science Foundation**
NSPCC *n abbr* (*Brit*) = **National Society for the Prevention of Cruelty to Children**
NSW *abbr* (*Australia*) = **New South Wales**
NT *n abbr* (= *New Testament*) N.T. ■ *abbr* (*Canada*) = **Northwest Territories**
nth [ɛnθ] *adj*: **for the ~ time** (*col*) per l'ennesima volta
nuance ['njuːɑ̃ːns] *n* sfumatura
nubile ['njuːbaɪl] *adj* nubile; (*attractive*) giovane e desiderabile
nuclear ['njuːklɪəʳ] *adj* nucleare; (*warfare*) atomico(-a)
nuclear disarmament *n* disarmo nucleare
nuclear family *n* famiglia nucleare
nuclear-free zone ['njuːklɪə'friː-] *n* zona denuclearizzata
nucleus (*pl* **nuclei**) ['njuːklɪəs, 'njuːklɪaɪ] *n* nucleo
NUCPS *n abbr* (*Brit*) = **National Union of Civil and Public Servants**
nude [njuːd] *adj* nudo(-a) ■ *n* (*Art*) nudo; **in the ~** tutto(-a) nudo(-a)
nudge [nʌdʒ] *vt* dare una gomitata a
nudist ['njuːdɪst] *n* nudista *m/f*
nudity ['njuːdɪtɪ] *n* nudità
nugget ['nʌgɪt] *n* pepita
nuisance ['njuːsns] *n*: **it's a ~** è una seccatura; **he's a ~** lui dà fastidio; **what a ~!** che seccatura!
NUJ *n abbr* (*Brit:* = *National Union of Journalists*) *sindacato nazionale dei giornalisti*
nuke [njuːk] *n* (*col*) bomba atomica
null [nʌl] *adj*: **~ and void** nullo(-a)
nullify ['nʌlɪfaɪ] *vt* annullare
NUM *n abbr* (*Brit:* = *National Union of Mineworkers*) *sindacato nazionale dei dipendenti delle miniere*
numb [nʌm] *adj* intorpidito(-a) ■ *vt* intorpidire; **~ with** (*fear*) paralizzato(-a) da; (*grief*) impietrito(-a) da; **~ with cold** intirizzito(-a) (dal freddo)
number ['nʌmbəʳ] *n* numero ■ *vt* numerare; (*include*) contare; **a ~ of** un certo numero di; **telephone ~** numero di telefono; **wrong ~** (*Tel*) numero sbagliato; **the staff numbers 20** gli impiegati sono in 20
numbered account ['nʌmbəd-] *n* (*in bank*) conto numerato
number plate *n* (*Brit Aut*) targa
Number Ten *n* (*Brit:* = *10 Downing Street*) *residenza del Primo Ministro del Regno Unito*
numbness ['nʌmnɪs] *n* intorpidimento; (*due to cold*) intirizzimento
numbskull ['nʌmskʌl] *n* (*col*) imbecille *m/f*, idiota *m/f*
numeral ['njuːmərəl] *n* numero, cifra
numerate ['njuːmərɪt] *adj* (*Brit*): **to be ~** saper far di conto

n

numerical [nju:'mɛrɪkl] *adj* numerico(-a)
numerous ['nju:mərəs] *adj* numeroso(-a)
nun [nʌn] *n* suora, monaca
nunnery ['nʌnərɪ] *n* convento
nuptial ['nʌpʃəl] *adj* nuziale
nurse [nə:s] *n* infermiere(-a); (*also*: **nursemaid**) bambinaia ■ *vt* (*patient, cold*) curare; (*baby*: *Brit*) cullare; (: *US*) allattare, dare il latte a; (*hope*) nutrire
nursery ['nə:sərɪ] *n* (*room*) camera dei bambini; (*institution*) asilo; (*for plants*) vivaio
nursery rhyme *n* filastrocca
nursery school *n* scuola materna
nursery slope *n* (*Brit Ski*) pista per principianti
nursing ['nə:sɪŋ] *n* (*profession*) professione *f* di infermiere (*or* di infermiera) ■ *adj* (*mother*) che allatta
nursing home *n* casa di cura
nurture ['nə:tʃə[r]] *vt* allevare; nutrire
NUS *n abbr* (*Brit*: = *National Union of Students*) *sindacato nazionale degli studenti*
NUT *n abbr* (*Brit*: = *National Union of Teachers*) *sindacato nazionale degli insegnanti*
nut [nʌt] *n* (*of metal*) dado; (*fruit*) noce *f* (*or* nocciola *or* mandorla *etc*) ■ *adj* (*chocolate etc*) alla nocciola *etc*; **he's nuts** (*col*) è matto
nutcase ['nʌtkeɪs] *n* (*col*) mattarello(-a)
nutcrackers ['nʌtkrækəz] *npl* schiaccianoci *m inv*
nutmeg ['nʌtmɛg] *n* noce *f* moscata
nutrient ['nju:trɪənt] *adj* nutriente ■ *n* sostanza nutritiva
nutrition [nju:'trɪʃən] *n* nutrizione *f*
nutritionist [nju:'trɪʃənɪst] *n* nutrizionista *m/f*
nutritious [nju:'trɪʃəs] *adj* nutriente
nutshell ['nʌtʃɛl] *n* guscio di noce; **in a ~** in poche parole
nutty ['nʌtɪ] *adj* di noce (*or* nocciola *or* mandorla *etc*); (*Brit col*) tocco(-a), matto(-a)
nuzzle ['nʌzl] *vi*: **to ~ up to** strofinare il muso contro
NV *abbr* (*US*) = **Nevada**
NWT *abbr* (*Canada*) = **Northwest Territories**
NY *abbr* (*US*) = **New York**
NYC *abbr* (*US*) = **New York City**
nylon ['naɪlɔn] *n* nailon *m*; **nylons** *npl* calze *fpl* di nailon
nymph [nɪmf] *n* ninfa
nymphomaniac [nɪmfəu'meɪnɪæk] *adj, n* ninfomane (*f*)
NYSE *abbr* (*US*) = **New York Stock Exchange**

Oo

O, o [əu] *n* (*letter*) O, o *f or m inv*; (*US Scol*: = *outstanding*) ≈ ottimo; (*number*: *Tel etc*) zero; **O for Oliver**, (US) **O for Oboe** ≈ O come Otranto
oaf [əuf] *n* zoticone *m*
oak [əuk] *n* quercia ■ *cpd* di quercia
OAP *n abbr* (*Brit*) = **old-age pensioner**
oar [ɔːʳ] *n* remo; **to put** *or* **shove one's ~ in** (*fig, col*) intromettersi
oarsman ['ɔːzmən], **oarswoman** ['ɔːzwumən] *n* rematore(-trice)
OAS *n abbr* (= *Organization of American States*) O.S.A. *f* (= *Organizzazione degli Stati Americani*)
oasis (*pl* **oases**) [əu'eɪsɪs, əu'eisiːz] *n* oasi *f inv*
oath [əuθ] *n* giuramento; (*swear word*) bestemmia; **to take the ~** giurare; **on ~** (*Brit*) *or* **under ~** sotto giuramento
oatmeal ['əutmiːl] *n* farina d'avena
oats [əuts] *npl* avena
obdurate ['ɔbdjurɪt] *adj* testardo(-a); incallito(-a); ostinato(-a), irremovibile
OBE *n abbr* (*Brit*: = *Order of the British Empire*) *titolo*
obedience [ə'biːdɪəns] *n* ubbidienza; **in ~ to** conformemente a
obedient [ə'biːdɪənt] *adj* ubbidiente; **to be ~ to sb/sth** ubbidire a qn/qc
obelisk ['ɔbɪlɪsk] *n* obelisco
obese [əu'biːs] *adj* obeso(-a)
obesity [əu'biːsɪtɪ] *n* obesità
obey [ə'beɪ] *vt* ubbidire a; (*instructions, regulations*) osservare ■ *vi* ubbidire
obituary [ə'bɪtjuərɪ] *n* necrologia
object *n* ['ɔbdʒɪkt] oggetto; (*purpose*) scopo, intento; (*Ling*) complemento oggetto ■ *vi* [əb'dʒɛkt]: **to ~ to** (*attitude*) disapprovare; (*proposal*) protestare contro, sollevare delle obiezioni contro; **I ~!** mi oppongo!; **he objected that ...** obiettò che ...; **do you ~ to my smoking?** la disturba se fumo?; **what's the ~ of doing that?** a che serve farlo?; **expense is no ~** non si bada a spese
objection [əb'dʒɛkʃən] *n* obiezione *f*; (*drawback*) inconveniente *m*; **if you have no ~** se non ha obiezioni; **to make** *or* **raise an ~** sollevare un'obiezione
objectionable [əb'dʒɛkʃənəbl] *adj* antipatico(-a); (*smell*) sgradevole; (*language*) scostumato(-a)
objective [əb'dʒɛktɪv] *n* obiettivo ■ *adj* obiettivo(-a)
objectivity [ɔbdʒɪk'tɪvɪtɪ] *n* obiettività
object lesson *n*: **~ (in)** dimostrazione *f* (di)
objector [əb'dʒɛktəʳ] *n* oppositore(-trice)
obligation [ɔblɪ'geɪʃən] *n* obbligo, dovere *m*; (*debt*) obbligo (di riconoscenza); **"without ~"** "senza impegno"; **to be under an ~ to sb/to do sth** essere in dovere verso qn/di fare qc
obligatory [ə'blɪgətərɪ] *adj* obbligatorio(-a)
oblige [ə'blaɪdʒ] *vt* (*force*): **to ~ sb to do** costringere qn a fare; (*do a favour*) fare una cortesia a; **to be obliged to sb for sth** essere grato a qn per qc; **anything to ~!** (*col*) questo e altro!
obliging [ə'blaɪdʒɪŋ] *adj* servizievole, compiacente
oblique [ə'bliːk] *adj* obliquo(-a); (*allusion*) indiretto(-a) ■ *n* (*Brit Typ*): **~ (stroke)** barra
obliterate [ə'blɪtəreɪt] *vt* cancellare
oblivion [ə'blɪvɪən] *n* oblio
oblivious [ə'blɪvɪəs] *adj*: **~ of** incurante di; inconscio(-a) di
oblong ['ɔblɔŋ] *adj* oblungo(-a) ■ *n* rettangolo
obnoxious [əb'nɔkʃəs] *adj* odioso(-a); (*smell*) disgustoso(-a), ripugnante
oboe ['əubəu] *n* oboe *m*
obscene [əb'siːn] *adj* osceno(-a)
obscenity [əb'sɛnɪtɪ] *n* oscenità *f inv*
obscure [əb'skjuəʳ] *adj* oscuro(-a) ■ *vt* oscurare; (*hide*: *sun*) nascondere
obscurity [əb'skjuərɪtɪ] *n* oscurità; (*obscure point*) punto oscuro; (*lack of fame*) anonimato
obsequious [əb'siːkwɪəs] *adj* ossequioso(-a)
observable [əb'zəːvəbl] *adj* osservabile; (*appreciable*) notevole
observance [əb'zəːvns] *n* osservanza; **religious observances** pratiche *fpl* religiose

observant [əb'zəːvnt] *adj* attento(-a)
observation [ɔbzə'veɪʃən] *n* osservazione *f*; (*by police etc*) sorveglianza
observation post *n* (*Mil*) osservatorio
observatory [əb'zəːvətrɪ] *n* osservatorio
observe [əb'zəːv] *vt* osservare
observer [əb'zəːvə[r]] *n* osservatore(-trice)
obsess [əb'sɛs] *vt* ossessionare; **to be obsessed by** *or* **with sb/sth** essere ossessionato da qn/qc
obsession [əb'sɛʃən] *n* ossessione *f*
obsessive [əb'sɛsɪv] *adj* ossessivo(-a)
obsolescence [ɔbsə'lɛsns] *n* obsolescenza; **built-in** *or* **planned ~** (*Comm*) obsolescenza programmata
obsolescent [ɔbsə'lɛsnt] *adj* obsolescente
obsolete ['ɔbsəliːt] *adj* obsoleto(-a); (*word*) desueto(-a)
obstacle ['ɔbstəkl] *n* ostacolo
obstacle race *n* corsa agli ostacoli
obstetrician [ɔbstə'trɪʃən] *n* ostetrico(-a)
obstetrics [ɔb'stɛtrɪks] *n* ostetrica
obstinacy ['ɔbstɪnəsɪ] *n* ostinatezza
obstinate ['ɔbstɪnɪt] *adj* ostinato(-a)
obstreperous [əb'strɛpərəs] *adj* turbolento(-a)
obstruct [əb'strʌkt] *vt* (*block*) ostruire, ostacolare; (*halt*) fermare; (*hinder*) impedire
obstruction [əb'strʌkʃən] *n* ostruzione *f*; ostacolo
obstructive [əb'strʌktɪv] *adj* ostruttivo(-a); che crea impedimenti
obtain [əb'teɪn] *vt* ottenere ■ *vi* essere in uso; **to ~ sth (for o.s.)** procurarsi qc
obtainable [əb'teɪnəbl] *adj* ottenibile
obtrusive [əb'truːsɪv] *adj* (*person*) importuno(-a); (*smell*) invadente; (*building etc*) imponente e invadente
obtuse [əb'tjuːs] *adj* ottuso(-a)
obverse ['ɔbvəːs] *n* opposto, inverso
obviate ['ɔbvɪeɪt] *vt* ovviare a, evitare
obvious ['ɔbvɪəs] *adj* ovvio(-a), evidente
obviously ['ɔbvɪəslɪ] *adv* ovviamente; **~!** certo!; **~ not!** certo che no!; **he was ~ not drunk** si vedeva che non era ubriaco; **he was not ~ drunk** non si vedeva che era ubriaco
OCAS *n abbr* = **Organization of Central American States**
occasion [ə'keɪʒən] *n* occasione *f*; (*event*) avvenimento ■ *vt* cagionare; **on that ~** in quell'occasione, quella volta; **to rise to the ~** mostrarsi all'altezza della situazione
occasional [ə'keɪʒənl] *adj* occasionale; **I smoke an ~ cigarette** ogni tanto fumo una sigaretta
occasionally [ə'keɪʒənəlɪ] *adv* ogni tanto; **very ~** molto raramente
occasional table *n* tavolino
occult [ɔ'kʌlt] *adj* occulto(-a) ■ *n*: **the ~** l'occulto
occupancy ['ɔkjupənsɪ] *n* occupazione *f*
occupant ['ɔkjupənt] *n* occupante *m/f*; (*of boat, car etc*) persona a bordo
occupation [ɔkju'peɪʃən] *n* occupazione *f*; (*job*) mestiere *m*, professione *f*; **unfit for ~** (*house*) inabitabile
occupational [ɔkju'peɪʃənl] *adj* (*disease*) professionale; (*hazard*) del mestiere; **~ accident** infortunio sul lavoro
occupational guidance *n* (*Brit*) orientamento professionale
occupational pension scheme *n sistema pensionistico programmato dal datore di lavoro*
occupational therapy *n* ergoterapia
occupier ['ɔkjupaɪə[r]] *n* occupante *m/f*
occupy ['ɔkjupaɪ] *vt* occupare; **to ~ o.s. by doing** occuparsi a fare; **to be occupied with sth/in doing sth** essere preso da qc/occupato a fare qc
occur [ə'kəː[r]] *vi* accadere; (*difficulty, opportunity*) capitare; (*phenomenon, error*) trovarsi; **to ~ to sb** venire in mente a qn
occurrence [ə'kʌrəns] *n* caso, fatto; presenza
ocean ['əuʃən] *n* oceano; **oceans of** (*col*) un sacco di
ocean bed *n* fondale *m* oceanico
ocean-going ['əuʃəngəuɪŋ] *adj* d'alto mare
Oceania [əuʃɪ'ɑːnɪə] *n* Oceania
ocean liner *n* transatlantico
ochre, (*US*) **ocher** ['əukə[r]] *adj* ocra *inv*
o'clock [ə'klɔk] *adv*: **it is one ~** è l'una; **it is 5 ~** sono le 5
OCR *n abbr* = **optical character reader; optical character recognition**
Oct. *abbr* (= *October*) ott.
octagonal [ɔk'tægənl] *adj* ottagonale
octane ['ɔkteɪn] *n* ottano; **high-~ petrol** *or* (*US*) **gas** benzina ad alto numero di ottani
octave ['ɔktɪv] *n* ottavo
October [ɔk'təubə[r]] *n* ottobre *m*; *see also* **July**
octogenarian [ɔktəudʒɪ'nɛərɪən] *n* ottuagenario(-a)
octopus ['ɔktəpəs] *n* polpo, piovra
odd [ɔd] *adj* (*strange*) strano(-a), bizzarro(-a); (*number*) dispari *inv*; (*left over*) in più; (*not of a set*) spaiato(-a); **60-~** 60 e oltre; **at ~ times** di tanto in tanto; **the ~ one out** l'eccezione *f*
oddball ['ɔdbɔːl] *n* (*col*) eccentrico(-a)
oddity ['ɔdɪtɪ] *n* bizzarria; (*person*) originale *m/f*
odd-job man [ɔd'dʒɔb-] *n* tuttofare *m inv*
odd jobs *npl* lavori *mpl* occasionali
oddly ['ɔdlɪ] *adv* stranamente
oddments ['ɔdmənts] *npl* (*Brit Comm*) rimanenze *fpl*

odds [ɔdz] *npl* (*in betting*) quota; **the ~ are against his coming** c'è poca probabilità che venga; **it makes no ~** non importa; **at ~** in contesa; **to succeed against all the ~** riuscire contro ogni aspettativa; **~ and ends** avanzi *mpl*
odds-on [ɔdz'ɔn] *adj* (*col*) probabile; **~ favourite** (*Racing*) favorito(-a)
ode [əud] *n* ode *f*
odious ['əudɪəs] *adj* odioso(-a), ripugnante
odometer [ɔ'dɔmɪtə^r] *n* odometro
odour, (US) **odor** ['əudə^r] *n* odore *m*
odourless, (US) **odorless** ['əudəlɪs] *adj* inodoro(-a)
OECD *n abbr* (= *Organization for Economic Cooperation and Development*) O.C.S.E. *f* (= *Organizzazione per la Cooperazione e lo Sviluppo Economico*)
oesophagus, (US) **esophagus** [iː'sɔfəgəs] *n* esofago
oestrogen, (US) **estrogen** ['iːstrəudʒən] *n* estrogeno

KEYWORD

of [ɔv, əv] *prep* **1** (*gen*) di; **a boy of 10** un ragazzo di 10 anni; **a friend of ours** un nostro amico; **that was kind of you** è stato molto gentile da parte sua
2 (*expressing quantity, amount, dates etc*) di; **a kilo of flour** un chilo di farina; **how much of this do you need?** quanto gliene serve?; **there were four of them** (*people*) erano in quattro; (*objects*) ce n'erano quattro; **three of us went** tre di noi sono andati; **the 5th of July** il 5 luglio; **a quarter of 4** (US) le 4 meno un quarto
3 (*from, out of*) di, in; **made of wood** (fatto) di *or* in legno

Ofcom ['ɔfkɔm] *n abbr* (*Brit*: = *Office of Communications*) *organismo di regolamentazione delle telecomunicazioni*

KEYWORD

off [ɔf] *adv* **1** (*distance, time*): **it's a long way off** è lontano; **the game is 3 days off** la partita è tra 3 giorni
2 (*departure, removal*) via; **to go off to Paris** andarsene a Parigi; **I must be off** devo andare via; **to take off one's coat** togliersi il cappotto; **the button came off** il bottone è venuto via *or* si è staccato; **10% off** con lo sconto del 10%
3 (*not at work*): **to have a day off** avere un giorno libero; **to be off sick** essere assente per malattia
■ *adj* (*engine*) spento(-a); (*tap*) chiuso(-a); (*cancelled*) sospeso(-a); (*Brit*: *food*) andato(-a) a male; **to be well/badly off** essere/non essere benestante; **the lid was off** non c'era il coperchio; **I'm afraid the chicken is off** (*Brit*: *not available*) purtroppo il pollo è finito; **on the off chance** nel caso; **to have an off day** non essere in forma; **that's a bit off, isn't it?** (*fig, col*) non è molto carino, vero?
■ *prep* **1** (*motion, removal etc*) da; (*distant from*) a poca distanza da; **a street off the square** una strada che parte dalla piazza; **5km off the road** a 5km dalla strada; **off the coast** al largo della costa; **a house off the main road** una casa che non è sulla strada principale
2: **to be off meat** non mangiare più la carne

offal ['ɔfl] *n* (*Culin*) frattaglie *fpl*
offbeat ['ɔfbiːt] *adj* eccentrico(-a)
off-centre, (US) **off-center** [ɔf'sɛntə^r] *adj* storto(-a), fuori centro
off-colour ['ɔf'kʌlə^r] *adj* (*Brit*: *ill*) malato(-a), indisposto(-a); **to feel ~** sentirsi poco bene
offence, (US) **offense** [ə'fɛns] *n* (*Law*) contravvenzione *f*; (: *more serious*) reato; **to give ~ to** offendere; **to take ~ at** offendersi per; **to commit an ~** commettere un reato
offend [ə'fɛnd] *vt* (*person*) offendere ■ *vi*: **to ~ against** (*law, rule*) trasgredire
offender [ə'fɛndə^r] *n* delinquente *m/f*; (*against regulations*) contravventore(-trice)
offending [ə'fɛndɪŋ] *adj* (*often humorous*): **the ~ word/object** la parola incriminata/l'oggetto incriminato
offense [ə'fɛns] *n* (US) = **offence**
offensive [ə'fɛnsɪv] *adj* offensivo(-a); (*smell etc*) sgradevole, ripugnante ■ *n* (*Mil*) offensiva
offer ['ɔfə^r] *n* offerta, proposta ■ *vt* offrire; **"on ~"** (*Comm*) "in offerta speciale"; **to make an ~ for sth** fare un'offerta per qc; **to ~ sth to sb, ~ sb sth** offrire qc a qn; **to ~ to do sth** offrirsi di fare qc
offering ['ɔfərɪŋ] *n* offerta
offhand [ɔf'hænd] *adj* disinvolto(-a), noncurante ■ *adv* all'impronto; **I can't tell you ~** non posso dirglielo su due piedi
office ['ɔfɪs] *n* (*place*) ufficio; (*position*) carica; **doctor's ~** (US) ambulatorio; **to take ~** entrare in carica; **through his good offices** con il suo prezioso aiuto; **O~ of Fair Trading** (*Brit*) *organismo di protezione contro le pratiche commerciali abusive*
office automation *n* automazione *f* d'ufficio, burotica
office bearer *n* (*of club etc*) membro dell'amministrazione

office block, (*US*) **office building** *n* complesso di uffici
office boy *n* garzone *m*
office hours *npl* orario d'ufficio; (*US Med*) orario di visite
office manager *n* capoufficio *m/f*
officer ['ɔfɪsəʳ] *n* (*Mil etc*) ufficiale *m*; (*of organization*) funzionario; (*also*: **police officer**) agente *m* di polizia
office work *n* lavoro d'ufficio
office worker *n* impiegato(-a) d'ufficio
official [ə'fɪʃl] *adj* (*authorized*) ufficiale ■ *n* ufficiale *m*; (*civil servant*) impiegato(-a) statale; funzionario
officialdom [ə'fɪʃəldəm] *n* burocrazia
officially [ə'fɪʃəlɪ] *adv* ufficialmente
official receiver *n* curatore *m* fallimentare
officiate [ə'fɪʃieɪt] *vi* (*Rel*) ufficiare; **to ~ as Mayor** esplicare le funzioni di sindaco; **to ~ at a marriage** celebrare un matrimonio
officious [ə'fɪʃəs] *adj* invadente
offing ['ɔfɪŋ] *n*: **in the ~** (*fig*) in vista
off-key [ɔf'ki:] *adj* stonato(-a) ■ *adv* fuori tono
off-licence ['ɔflaɪsns] *n* (*Brit*) spaccio di bevande alcoliche; *vedi nota*

OFF-LICENCE

In Gran Bretagna e in Irlanda, gli *off-licences* sono esercizi pubblici specializzati nella vendita strettamente regolamentata di bevande alcoliche, per la quale è necessario avere un'apposita licenza. In genere sono aperti fino a tarda sera.

off-limits [ɔf'lɪmɪts] *adj* (*esp US*) in cui vige il divieto d'accesso
off line *adj, adv* (*Comput*) off line *inv*, fuori linea; (*: switched off*) spento(-a)
off-load ['ɔfləud] *vt* scaricare
off-peak [ɔf'pi:k] *adj* (*ticket etc*) a tariffa ridotta; (*time*) non di punta
off-putting ['ɔfputɪŋ] *adj* (*Brit*) un po' scostante
off-season ['ɔfsi:zn] *adj, adv* fuori stagione
offset ['ɔfsɛt] *vt irreg* (*counteract*) controbilanciare, compensare ■ *n* (*also*: **offset printing**) offset *m*
offshoot ['ɔfʃu:t] *n* (*fig*) diramazione *f*
offshore [ɔf'ʃɔ:ʳ] *adj* (*breeze*) di terra; (*island*) vicino alla costa; (*fishing*) costiero(-a); **~ oilfield** giacimento petrolifero in mare aperto
offside ['ɔf'saɪd] *adj* (*Sport*) fuori gioco; (*Aut: with right-hand drive*) destro(-a); (*: with left-hand drive*) sinistro(-a) ■ *n* destra; sinistra
offspring ['ɔfsprɪŋ] *n* prole *f*, discendenza
offstage [ɔf'steɪdʒ] *adv* dietro le quinte
off-the-cuff [ɔfðə'kʌf] *adv* improvvisando
off-the-job ['ɔfðə'dʒɔb] *adj*: **~ training** addestramento fuori sede
off-the-peg ['ɔfðə'pɛg], (*US*) **off-the-rack** ['ɔfðə'ræk] *adv* prêt-à-porter
off-the-record ['ɔfðə'rɛkɔ:d] *adj* ufficioso(-a) ■ *adv* in via ufficiosa
off-white ['ɔfwaɪt] *adj* bianco sporco *inv*
Ofgem ['ɔfdʒɛm] *n abbr* (*Brit*: = *Office of Gas and Electricity Markets*) *organo indipendente di controllo per la tutela dei consumatori*
often ['ɔfn] *adv* spesso; **how ~ do you go?** quanto spesso ci va?; **as ~ as not** quasi sempre
Ofwat ['ɔfwɔt] *n abbr* (*Brit*: = *Office of Water Services*) *in Inghilterra e Galles, organo indipendente di controllo per la tutela dei consumatori*
ogle ['əugl] *vt* occhieggiare
ogre ['əugəʳ] *n* orco
OH *abbr* (*US*) = **Ohio**
oh [əu] *excl* oh!
OHMS *abbr* (*Brit*) = **On His (*or* Her) Majesty's Service**
oil [ɔɪl] *n* olio; (*petroleum*) petrolio; (*for central heating*) nafta ■ *vt* (*machine*) lubrificare
oilcan ['ɔɪlkæn] *n* oliatore *m* a mano; (*for storing*) latta da olio
oil change *n* cambio dell'olio
oilfield ['ɔɪlfi:ld] *n* giacimento, petrolifero
oil filter *n* (*Aut*) filtro dell'olio
oil-fired ['ɔɪlfaɪəd] *adj* a nafta
oil gauge *n* indicatore *m* del livello dell'olio
oil industry *n* industria del petrolio
oil level *n* livello dell'olio
oil painting *n* quadro a olio
oil refinery *n* raffineria di petrolio
oil rig *n* derrick *m inv*; (*at sea*) piattaforma per trivellazioni subacquee
oilskins ['ɔɪlskɪnz] *npl* indumenti *mpl* di tela cerata
oil slick *n* chiazza d'olio
oil tanker *n* petroliera
oil well *n* pozzo petrolifero
oily ['ɔɪlɪ] *adj* unto(-a), oleoso(-a); (*food*) untuoso(-a)
ointment ['ɔɪntmənt] *n* unguento
OK *abbr* (*US*) = **Oklahoma**
O.K., okay [əu'keɪ] *excl* d'accordo! ■ *vt* approvare ■ *n*: **to give sth one's O.K.** approvare qc ■ *adj*: **is it O.K.?, are you O.K.?** tutto bene?; **it's O.K. with *or* by me** per me va bene; **are you O.K. for money?** sei a posto coi soldi?
Okla. *abbr* (*US*) = **Oklahoma**
old [əuld] *adj* vecchio(-a); (*ancient*) antico(-a),

vecchio(-a); *(person)* vecchio(-a), anziano(-a); **how ~ are you?** quanti anni ha?; **he's 10 years ~** ha 10 anni; **older brother/sister** fratello/sorella maggiore; **any ~ thing will do** va bene qualsiasi cosa

old age *n* vecchiaia

old-age pensioner ['əuldeɪdʒ-] *n* (*Brit*) pensionato(-a)

old-fashioned ['əuld'fæʃnd] *adj* antiquato(-a), fuori moda; *(person)* all'antica

old maid *n* zitella

old people's home *n* ricovero per anziani

old-style ['əuldstaɪl] *adj* (di) vecchio stampo *inv*

old-time ['əuldtaɪm] *adj* di una volta

old-timer [əuld'taɪmər] *n* veterano(-a)

old wives' tale *n* vecchia superstizione *f*

O levels *npl* (*Brit: formerly*) *diploma di istruzione secondaria conseguito a 16 anni in Inghilterra e Galles, ora sostituito dal GCSE*

olive ['ɔlɪv] *n* (*fruit*) oliva; (*tree*) olivo ■ *adj* (*also:* **olive-green**) verde oliva *inv*

olive oil *n* olio d'oliva

Olympic [əu'lɪmpɪk] *adj* olimpico(-a); **the ~ Games, the Olympics** i giochi olimpici, le Olimpiadi

OM *n abbr* (*Brit:* = *Order of Merit*) *titolo*

Oman [əu'mɑːn] *n* Oman *m*

OMB *n abbr* (*US:* = *Office of Management and Budget*) *servizio di consulenza al Presidente in materia di bilancio*

omelet, omelette ['ɔmlɪt] *n* omelette *f inv*; **ham/cheese ~(te)** omelette al prosciutto/al formaggio

omen ['əumən] *n* presagio, augurio

ominous ['ɔmɪnəs] *adj* minaccioso(-a); (*event*) di malaugurio

omission [əu'mɪʃən] *n* omissione *f*

omit [əu'mɪt] *vt* omettere; **to ~ to do sth** tralasciare *or* trascurare di fare qc

omnivorous [ɔm'nɪvərəs] *adj* onnivoro(-a)

ON *abbr* (*Canada*) = **Ontario**

 KEYWORD

on [ɔn] *prep* **1** (*indicating position*) su; **on the wall** sulla parete; **on the left** a *or* sulla sinistra; **I haven't any money on me** non ho soldi con me

2 (*indicating means, method, condition etc*): **on foot** a piedi; **on the train/plane** in treno/aereo; **on the telephone** al telefono; **on the radio/television** alla radio/televisione; **to be on drugs** drogarsi; **on holiday** in vacanza; **he's on £16,000 a year** guadagna 16.000 sterline all'anno; **this round's on me** questo giro lo offro io

3 (*referring to time*): **on Friday** venerdì; **on Fridays** il *or* di venerdì; **on June 20th** il 20 giugno; **on Friday, June 20th** venerdì, 20 giugno; **a week on Friday** venerdì a otto; **on his arrival** al suo arrivo; **on seeing this** vedendo ciò

4 (*about, concerning*) su, di; **information on train services** informazioni sui collegamenti ferroviari; **a book on Goldoni/physics** un libro su Goldoni/di *or* sulla fisica

■ *adv* **1** (*referring to dress, covering*): **to have one's coat on** avere indosso il cappotto; **to put one's coat on** mettersi il cappotto; **what's she got on?** cosa indossa?; **she put her boots/gloves/hat on** si mise gli stivali/i guanti/il cappello; **screw the lid on tightly** avvita bene il coperchio

2 (*further, continuously*): **to walk on, go on** *etc* continuare, proseguire; **to read on** continuare a leggere; **on and off** ogni tanto; **from that day on** da quel giorno in poi; **it was well on in the evening** era sera inoltrata

■ *adj* **1** (*in operation: machine, TV, light*) acceso(-a); (*: tap*) aperto(-a); (*: brake*) inserito(-a); **is the meeting still on?** (*in progress*) la riunione è ancora in corso?; (*not cancelled*) è confermato l'incontro?; **there's a good film on at the cinema** danno un buon film al cinema; **when is the film on?** quando c'è questo film?; **my father's always on at me to get a job** (*col*) mio padre mi tormenta sempre perché trovi un lavoro

2 (*col*): **that's not on!** (*not acceptable*) non si fa così!; (*not possible*) non se ne parla neanche!

once [wʌns] *adv* una volta ■ *conj* non appena, quando; **~ he had left/it was done** dopo che se n'era andato/fu fatto; **at ~** subito; (*simultaneously*) a un tempo; **all at ~** (tutto) ad un tratto; **~ a week** una volta alla settimana; **~ more** ancora una volta; **I knew him ~** un tempo *or* in passato lo conoscevo; **~ and for all** una volta per sempre; **~ upon a time there was ...** c'era una volta ...

oncoming ['ɔnkʌmɪŋ] *adj* (*traffic*) che viene in senso opposto

 KEYWORD

one [wʌn] *num* uno(-a); **one hundred and fifty** centocinquanta; **one day** un giorno; **it's one (o'clock)** è l'una; **to be one up on sb** essere avvantaggiato(-a) rispetto a qn; **to be at one (with sb)** andare d'accordo (con qn)

■ *adj* **1** (*sole*) unico(-a); **the one book which** l'unico libro che; **the one man who** l'unico che

O

2 (*same*) stesso(-a); **they came in the one car** sono venuti nella stessa macchina ■ *pron* **1**: **this one** questo(-a); **that one** quello(-a); **which one do you want?** quale vuole?; **I've already got one/a red one** ne ho già uno/uno rosso; **one by one** uno per uno
2: **one another** l'un l'altro; **to look at one another** guardarsi; **to help one another** aiutarsi l'un l'altro *or* a vicenda
3 (*impersonal*) si; **one never knows** non si sa mai; **to cut one's finger** tagliarsi un dito; **to express one's opinion** esprimere la propria opinione; **one needs to eat** bisogna mangiare

one-armed bandit ['wʌnɑ:md-] *n* slot-machine *f inv*

one-day excursion ['wʌndeɪ-] *n* (*US*) biglietto giornaliero di andata e ritorno

One-hundred share index ['wʌnhʌndrəd-] *n* *indice borsistico del Financial Times*

one-man ['wʌn'mæn] *adj* (*business*) diretto(-a) *etc* da un solo uomo

one-man band *n* *suonatore ambulante con vari strumenti*

one-off [wʌn'ɔf] (*Brit col*) *n* fatto eccezionale ■ *adj* eccezionale

one-parent family ['wʌnpɛərənt-] *n* famiglia monogenitore

one-piece ['wʌnpi:s] *adj* (*bathing suit*) intero(-a)

onerous ['ɔnərəs] *adj* (*task, duty*) gravoso(-a); (*responsibility*) pesante

oneself [wʌn'sɛlf] *pron* si; (*after prep*) sé, se stesso(-a); **to do sth (by) ~** fare qc da sé

one-shot [wʌn'ʃɔt] *n* (*US*) = **one-off**

one-sided [wʌn'saɪdɪd] *adj* (*decision, view*) unilaterale; (*judgement, account*) parziale; (*game, contest*) impari *inv*

one-time ['wʌntaɪm] *adj* ex *inv*

one-to-one ['wʌntəwʌn] *adj* (*relationship*) univoco(-a)

one-upmanship [wʌn'ʌpmənʃɪp] *n*: **the art of ~** l'arte *f* di primeggiare

one-way ['wʌnweɪ] *adj* (*street, traffic*) a senso unico

ongoing ['ɔngəuɪŋ] *adj* in corso; in attuazione

onion ['ʌnjən] *n* cipolla

on line *adj* (*Comput*) on line *inv*, in linea; (*: switched on*) acceso(-a)

onlooker ['ɔnlukəʳ] *n* spettatore(-trice)

only ['əunlɪ] *adv* solo, soltanto ■ *adj* solo(-a), unico(-a) ■ *conj* solo che, ma; **an ~ child** un figlio unico; **not ~** non solo; **I ~ took one** ne ho preso soltanto uno, non ne ho preso che uno; **I saw her ~ yesterday** l'ho vista appena ieri; **I'd be ~ too pleased to help** sarei proprio felice di essere d'aiuto; **I would come, ~ I'm very busy** verrei volentieri, solo che sono molto occupato

ono *abbr* = **or nearest offer**; *see* **near**

onset ['ɔnsɛt] *n* inizio; (*of winter*) arrivo

onshore ['ɔnʃɔ:ʳ] *adj* (*wind*) di mare

onslaught ['ɔnslɔ:t] *n* attacco, assalto

Ont. *abbr* (*Canada*) = **Ontario**

on-the-job ['ɔnðə'dʒɔb] *adj*: **~ training** addestramento in sede

onto ['ɔntu] *prep* su, sopra

onus ['əunəs] *n* onere *m*, peso; **the ~ is upon him to prove it** sta a lui dimostrarlo

onward ['ɔnwəd], **onwards** ['ɔnwədz] *adv* (*move*) in avanti; **from this time ~(s)** d'ora in poi

onyx ['ɔnɪks] *n* onice *f*

oops [ups] *excl* ops! (*esprime rincrescimento per un piccolo contrattempo*); **~-a-daisy!** oplà!

ooze [u:z] *vi* stillare

opacity [əu'pæsɪtɪ] *n* opacità

opal ['əupl] *n* opale *m or f*

opaque [əu'peɪk] *adj* opaco(-a)

OPEC ['əupɛk] *n abbr* (= *Organization of Petroleum-Exporting Countries*) O.P.E.C. *f*

open ['əupn] *adj* aperto(-a); (*road*) libero(-a); (*meeting*) pubblico(-a); (*admiration*) evidente, franco(-a); (*question*) insoluto(-a); (*enemy*) dichiarato(-a) ■ *vt* aprire ■ *vi* (*eyes, door, debate*) aprirsi; (*flower*) sbocciare; (*shop, bank, museum*) aprire; (*book etc: commence*) cominciare; **in the ~ (air)** all'aperto; **the ~ sea** il mare aperto, l'alto mare; **~ ground** (*among trees*) radura; (*waste ground*) terreno non edificato; **to have an ~ mind (on sth)** non avere ancora deciso (su qc)
▸ **open on to** *vt fus* (*room, door*) dare su
▸ **open out** *vt* aprire ■ *vi* aprirsi
▸ **open up** *vt* aprire; (*blocked road*) sgombrare ■ *vi* aprirsi

open-air [əupn'ɛəʳ] *adj* all'aperto

open-and-shut ['əupnən'ʃʌt] *adj*: **~ case** caso indubbio

open day *n* (*Brit*) giornata di apertura al pubblico

open-ended [əupn'ɛndɪd] *adj* (*fig*) aperto(-a), senza limiti

opener ['əupnəʳ] *n* (*also*: **can opener, tin opener**) apriscatole *m inv*

open-heart [əupn'hɑ:t] *adj*: **~ surgery** chirurgia a cuore aperto

opening ['əupnɪŋ] *n* apertura; (*opportunity*) occasione *f*, opportunità *f inv*; sbocco; (*job*) posto vacante

opening night *n* (*Theat*) prima

open learning *n sistema educativo secondo il quale lo studente ha maggior controllo e gestione delle modalità di apprendimento*
openly ['əupnlı] *adv* apertamente
open-minded [əupn'maındıd] *adj* che ha la mente aperta
open-necked ['əupnnɛkt] *adj* col collo slacciato
openness ['əupnnıs] *n* (*frankness*) franchezza, sincerità
open-plan ['əupn'plæn] *adj* senza pareti divisorie
open prison *n istituto di pena dove viene data maggiore libertà ai detenuti*
open sandwich *n* canapè *m inv*
open shop *n fabbrica o ditta dove sono accolti anche operai non iscritti ai sindacati*
Open University *n* (*Brit*) *vedi nota*

OPEN UNIVERSITY

La *Open University* (OU), fondata in Gran Bretagna nel 1969, organizza corsi universitari per corrispondenza o via Internet, basati anche su lezioni che vengono trasmesse dalla BBC per radio e per televisione e su corsi estivi.

opera ['ɔpərə] *n* opera
opera glasses *npl* binocolo da teatro
opera house *n* opera
opera singer *n* cantante *m/f* d'opera *or* lirico(-a)
operate ['ɔpəreıt] *vt* (*machine*) azionare, far funzionare; (*system*) usare ▪ *vi* funzionare; (*drug, person*) agire; **to ~ on sb (for)** (*Med*) operare qn (di)
operatic [ɔpə'rætık] *adj* dell'opera, lirico(-a)
operating ['ɔpəreıtıŋ] *adj* (*Comm: costs etc*) di gestione; (*Med*) operatorio(-a)
operating room *n* (*US*) = **operating theatre**
operating system *n* (*Comput*) sistema *m* operativo
operating theatre *n* (*Med*) sala operatoria
operation [ɔpə'reıʃən] *n* operazione *f*; **to be in ~** (*machine*) essere in azione *or* funzionamento; (*system*) essere in vigore; **to have an ~ (for)** (*Med*) essere operato(-a) (di)
operational [ɔpə'reıʃənl] *adj* operativo(-a); (*Comm*) di gestione, d'esercizio; (*ready for use or action*) in attività, in funzione; **when the service is fully ~** quando il servizio sarà completamente in funzione
operative ['ɔpərətıv] *adj* (*measure*) operativo(-a) ▪ *n* (*in factory*) operaio(-a); **the ~ word** la parola chiave
operator ['ɔpəreıtə^r] *n* (*of machine*) operatore(-trice); (*Tel*) centralinista *m/f*
operetta [ɔpə'rɛtə] *n* operetta
ophthalmologist [ɔfθæl'mɔlədʒıst] *n* oftalmologo(-a)
opinion [ə'pınjən] *n* opinione *f*, parere *m*; **in my ~** secondo me, a mio avviso; **to seek a second ~** (*Med etc*) consultarsi con un altro medico *etc*
opinionated [ə'pınjəneıtıd] *adj* dogmatico(-a)
opinion poll *n* sondaggio di opinioni
opium ['əupıəm] *n* oppio
opponent [ə'pəunənt] *n* avversario(-a)
opportune ['ɔpətju:n] *adj* opportuno(-a)
opportunist [ɔpə'tju:nıst] *n* opportunista *m/f*
opportunity [ɔpə'tju:nıtı] *n* opportunità *f inv*, occasione *f*; **to take the ~ to do** *or* **of doing** cogliere l'occasione per fare
oppose [ə'pəuz] *vt* opporsi a; **opposed to** contrario(-a) a; **as opposed to** in contrasto con
opposing [ə'pəuzıŋ] *adj* opposto(-a); (*team*) avversario(-a)
opposite ['ɔpəzıt] *adj* opposto(-a); (*house etc*) di fronte ▪ *adv* di fronte, dirimpetto ▪ *prep* di fronte a ▪ *n* opposto, contrario; (*of word*) contrario; **"see ~ page"** "vedere pagina a fronte"
opposite number *n* controparte *f*, corrispondente *m/f*
opposite sex *n*: **the ~** l'altro sesso
opposition [ɔpə'zıʃən] *n* opposizione *f*
oppress [ə'prɛs] *vt* opprimere
oppression [ə'prɛʃən] *n* oppressione *f*
oppressive [ə'prɛsıv] *adj* oppressivo(-a)
opprobrium [ə'prəubrıəm] *n* (*formal*) obbrobrio
opt [ɔpt] *vi*: **to ~ for** optare per; **to ~ to do** scegliere di fare; **to ~ out of** (*Brit: of NHS*) scegliere di non far più parte di; (*of agreement, arrangement*) scegliere di non partecipare a
optical ['ɔptıkl] *adj* ottico(-a)
optical character reader *n* lettore *m* ottico
optical character recognition *n* lettura ottica di caratteri
optical fibre *n* fibra ottica
optician [ɔp'tıʃən] *n* ottico
optics ['ɔptıks] *n* ottica
optimism ['ɔptımızəm] *n* ottimismo
optimist ['ɔptımıst] *n* ottimista *m/f*
optimistic [ɔptı'mıstık] *adj* ottimistico(-a)
optimum ['ɔptıməm] *adj* ottimale
option ['ɔpʃən] *n* scelta; (*Scol*) materia facoltativa; (*Comm*) opzione *f*; **to keep one's options open** (*fig*) non impegnarsi; **I have no ~** non ho scelta

optional ['ɔpʃənl] *adj* facoltativo(-a); (*Comm*) a scelta; ~ **extra** optional *m inv*
opulence ['ɔpjuləns] *n* opulenza
opulent ['ɔpjulənt] *adj* opulento(-a)
OR *abbr* (*US*) = **Oregon**
or [ɔːʳ] *conj* o, oppure; (*with negative*): **he hasn't seen or heard anything** non ha visto né sentito niente; **or else** se no, altrimenti; oppure
oracle ['ɔrəkl] *n* oracolo
oral ['ɔːrəl] *adj* orale ■ *n* esame *m* orale
orange ['ɔrɪndʒ] *n* (*fruit*) arancia ■ *adj* arancione
orangeade [ɔrɪndʒ'eɪd] *n* aranciata
oration [ɔː'reɪʃən] *n* orazione *f*
orator ['ɔrətəʳ] *n* oratore(-trice)
oratorio [ɔrə'tɔːrɪəu] *n* oratorio
orb [ɔːb] *n* orbe *m*
orbit ['ɔːbɪt] *n* orbita ■ *vt* orbitare intorno a; **to be in/go into ~ (round)** essere/entrare in orbita (attorno a)
orbital ['ɔːbɪtl] *n* (*also*: **orbital motorway**) raccordo anulare
orchard ['ɔːtʃəd] *n* frutteto; **apple ~** meleto
orchestra ['ɔːkɪstrə] *n* orchestra; (*US: seating*) platea
orchestral [ɔː'kɛstrəl] *adj* orchestrale; (*concert*) sinfonico(-a)
orchestrate ['ɔːkɪstreɪt] *vt* (*Mus: fig*) orchestrare
orchid ['ɔːkɪd] *n* orchidea
ordain [ɔː'deɪn] *vt* (*Rel*) ordinare; (*decide*) decretare
ordeal [ɔː'diːl] *n* prova, travaglio
order ['ɔːdəʳ] *n* ordine *m*; (*Comm*) ordinazione *f* ■ *vt* ordinare; **to ~ sb to do** ordinare a qn di fare; **in ~** in ordine; (*document*) in regola; **in ~ of size** in ordine di grandezza; **in ~ to do** per fare; **in ~ that** affinché + *sub*; **a machine in working ~** una macchina che funziona bene; **to be out of ~** (*machine, toilets*) essere guasto(-a); (*telephone*) essere fuori servizio; **to place an ~ for sth with sb** ordinare qc a qn; **to the ~ of** (*Banking*) all'ordine di; **to be under orders to do sth** avere l'ordine di fare qc; **a point of ~** una questione di procedura; **to be on ~** essere stato ordinato; **made to ~** fatto su commissione; **the lower orders** (*pej*) i ceti inferiori
order book *n* copiacommissioni *m inv*
order form *n* modulo d'ordinazione
orderly ['ɔːdəlɪ] *n* (*Mil*) attendente *m* ■ *adj* (*room*) in ordine; (*mind*) metodico(-a); (*person*) ordinato(-a), metodico(-a)
order number *n* numero di ordinazione
ordinal ['ɔːdɪnl] *adj* (*number*) ordinale
ordinary ['ɔːdnrɪ] *adj* normale, comune; (*pej*) mediocre ■ *n*: **out of the ~** diverso dal solito, fuori dell'ordinario
ordinary degree *n* laurea; *vedi nota*

ORDINARY DEGREE

Il corso universitario di studi che porta al conferimento del Bachelor's degree può avere una durata diversa, a seconda del profitto dello studente. Chi non è interessato a proseguire gli studi oltre tre anni di corso può optare per l'*ordinary degree*; *vedi anche* "honours degree".

ordinary seaman *n* (*Brit*) marinaio semplice
ordinary shares *npl* azioni *fpl* ordinarie
ordination [ɔːdɪ'neɪʃən] *n* ordinazione *f*
ordnance ['ɔːdnəns] *n* (*Mil: unit*) (reparto di) sussistenza
Ordnance Survey map *n* (*Brit*) ≈ carta topografica dell'IGM
ore [ɔːʳ] *n* minerale *m* grezzo
Ore., Oreg. *abbr* (*US*) = **Oregon**
organ ['ɔːgən] *n* organo
organic [ɔː'gænɪk] *adj* organico(-a); (*food, produce*) biologico(-a)
organism ['ɔːgənɪzəm] *n* organismo
organist ['ɔːgənɪst] *n* organista *m/f*
organization [ɔːgənaɪ'zeɪʃən] *n* organizzazione *f*
organization chart *n* organigramma *m*
organize ['ɔːgənaɪz] *vt* organizzare; **to get organized** organizzarsi
organized crime ['ɔːgənaɪzd-] *n* criminalità organizzata
organized labour ['ɔːgənaɪzd-] *n* manodopera organizzata
organizer ['ɔːgənaɪzəʳ] *n* organizzatore(-trice)
orgasm ['ɔːgæzəm] *n* orgasmo
orgy ['ɔːdʒɪ] *n* orgia
Orient ['ɔːrɪənt] *n*: **the ~** l'Oriente *m*
oriental [ɔːrɪ'ɛntl] *adj, n* orientale (*m/f*)
orientate ['ɔːrɪənteɪt] *vt* orientare
orifice ['ɔrɪfɪs] *n* orifizio
origin ['ɔrɪdʒɪn] *n* origine *f*; **country of ~** paese *m* d'origine
original [ə'rɪdʒɪnl] *adj* originale; (*earliest*) originario(-a) ■ *n* originale *m*
originality [ərɪdʒɪ'nælɪtɪ] *n* originalità
originally [ə'rɪdʒɪnəlɪ] *adv* (*at first*) all'inizio
originate [ə'rɪdʒɪneɪt] *vi*: **to ~ from** venire da, essere originario(-a) di; (*suggestion*) provenire da; **to ~ in** nascere in; (*custom*) avere origine in
originator [ə'rɪdʒɪneɪtəʳ] *n* iniziatore(-trice)
Orkneys ['ɔːknɪz] *npl*: **the ~** (*also*: **the Orkney Islands**) le (isole) Orcadi

ornament ['ɔːnəmənt] *n* ornamento; (*trinket*) ninnolo
ornamental [ɔːnə'mɛntl] *adj* ornamentale
ornamentation [ɔːnəmɛn'teɪʃən] *n* decorazione *f*, ornamento
ornate [ɔː'neɪt] *adj* molto ornato(-a)
ornithologist [ɔːnɪ'θɔlədʒɪst] *n* ornitologo(-a)
ornithology [ɔːnɪ'θɔlədʒɪ] *n* ornitologia
orphan ['ɔːfn] *n* orfano(-a) ■ *vt*: **to be orphaned** diventare orfano
orphanage ['ɔːfənɪdʒ] *n* orfanotrofio
orthodox ['ɔːθədɔks] *adj* ortodosso(-a)
orthopaedic, (*US*) **orthopedic** [ɔːθə'piːdɪk] *adj* ortopedico(-a)
OS *abbr* (*Brit*: = *Ordnance Survey*) ≈ IGM *m* (= *Istituto Geografico Militare*); (: *Naut*) = **ordinary seaman**; (: *Dress*) = **outsize**
O.S. *abbr* = **out of stock**
Oscar ['ɔskəʳ] *n* Oscar *m inv*
oscillate ['ɔsɪleɪt] *vi* oscillare
OSHA *n abbr* (*US*: = *Occupational Safety and Health Administration*) *amministrazione per la sicurezza e la salute sul lavoro*
Oslo ['ɔzləu] *n* Oslo *f*
ostensible [ɔs'tɛnsɪbl] *adj* preteso(-a); apparente
ostensibly [ɔs'tɛnsɪblɪ] *adv* all'apparenza
ostentation [ɔstɛn'teɪʃən] *n* ostentazione *f*
ostentatious [ɔstɛn'teɪʃəs] *adj* pretenzioso(-a); ostentato(-a)
osteopath ['ɔstɪəpæθ] *n* specialista *m/f* di osteopatia
ostracize ['ɔstrəsaɪz] *vt* dare l'ostracismo a
ostrich ['ɔstrɪtʃ] *n* struzzo
OT *abbr* (= *Old Testament*) V.T.
OTB *n abbr* (*US*: = *off-track betting*) *puntate effettuate fuori dagli ippodromi*
OTE *abbr* (= *on-target earnings*) *stipendio compreso le commissioni*
other ['ʌðəʳ] *adj* altro(-a) ■ *pron*: **the ~** l'altro(-a); **the others** gli altri; **the ~ day** l'altro giorno; **some ~ people have still to arrive** (alcuni) altri devono ancora arrivare; **some actor or ~** un certo attore; **somebody or ~** qualcuno; **~ than** altro che; a parte; **the car was none ~ than Roberta's** la macchina era proprio di Roberta
otherwise ['ʌðəwaɪz] *adv, conj* altrimenti; **an ~ good piece of work** un lavoro comunque buono
OTT *abbr* (*col*) = **over the top**; *see* **top**
otter ['ɔtəʳ] *n* lontra
OU *n abbr* (*Brit*) = **Open University**
ouch [autʃ] *excl* ohi!, ahi!
ought (*pt* **~**) [ɔːt] *aux vb*: **I ~ to do it** dovrei farlo; **this ~ to have been corrected** questo avrebbe dovuto essere corretto; **he ~ to win** dovrebbe vincere; **you ~ to go and see it** dovreste andare a vederlo, fareste bene ad andarlo a vedere
ounce [auns] *n* oncia (= *28.35 g; 16 in a pound*)
our [auəʳ] *adj* il/la nostro(-a); (*pl*) i/le nostri(-e)
ours [auəz] *pron* il/la nostro(-a); (*pl*) i/le nostri(-e)
ourselves [auə'sɛlvz] *pron pl* (*reflexive*) ci; (*after preposition*) noi; (*emphatic*) noi stessi(-e); **we did it (all) by ~** l'abbiamo fatto (tutto) da soli
oust [aust] *vt* cacciare, espellere

 KEYWORD

out [aut] *adv* (*gen*) fuori; **out here/there** qui/là fuori; **to speak out loud** parlare forte; **to have a night out** uscire una sera; **to be out and about** *or* (*US*) **around again** essere di nuovo in piedi; **the boat was 10 km out** la barca era a 10 km dalla costa; **the journey out** l'andata; **3 days out from Plymouth** a 3 giorni da Plymouth
■ *adj*: **to be out** (*gen*) essere fuori; (*unconscious*) aver perso i sensi; (*style, singer*) essere fuori moda; **before the week was out** prima che la settimana fosse finita; **to be out to do sth** avere intenzione di fare qc; **he's out for all he can get** sta cercando di trarne il massimo profitto; **to be out in one's calculations** aver sbagliato i calcoli;
out of *prep* **1** (*outside, beyond*) fuori di; **to go out of the house** uscire di casa; **to look out of the window** guardare fuori dalla finestra
2 (*because of*) per; **out of pity** per pietà; **out of boredom** per noia
3 (*origin*) da; **made out of wood** (fatto) di *or* in legno; **to drink out of a cup** bere da una tazza
4 (*from among*): **out of 10** su 10
5 (*without*) senza; **out of petrol** senza benzina; **it's out of stock** (*Comm*) è esaurito

outage ['autɪdʒ] *n* (*esp US*: *power failure*) interruzione *f or* mancanza di corrente elettrica
out-and-out ['autəndaut] *adj* vero(-a) e proprio(-a)
outback ['autbæk] *n* zona isolata; (*in Australia*) interno, entroterra
outbid (*pt, pp* **~**) [aut'bɪd] *vt* fare un'offerta più alta di
outboard ['autbɔːd] *n*: **~ (motor)** (motore *m*) fuoribordo
outbound ['autbaund] *adj*: **~ (for** *or* **from)** in partenza (per *or* da)

O

outbreak ['autbreɪk] *n* scoppio; epidemia
outbuilding ['autbɪldɪŋ] *n* dipendenza
outburst ['autbə:st] *n* scoppio
outcast ['autkɑ:st] *n* esule *m/f*; (*socially*) paria *m inv*
outclass [aut'klɑ:s] *vt* surclassare
outcome ['autkʌm] *n* esito, risultato
outcrop ['autkrɔp] *n* affioramento
outcry ['autkraɪ] *n* protesta, clamore *m*
outdated [aut'deɪtɪd] *adj* (*custom, clothes*) fuori moda; (*idea*) sorpassato(-a)
outdistance [aut'dɪstəns] *vt* distanziare
outdo [aut'du:] *vt irreg* sorpassare
outdoor [aut'dɔ:ʳ] *adj* all'aperto
outdoors [aut'dɔ:z] *adv* fuori; all'aria aperta
outer ['autəʳ] *adj* esteriore; **~ suburbs** estrema periferia
outer space *n* spazio cosmico
outfit ['autfɪt] *n* equipaggiamento; (*clothes*) abito; (*col: organization*) organizzazione *f*
outfitter ['autfɪtəʳ] *n* (*Brit*): **"(gent's) outfitters"** "confezioni da uomo"
outgoing ['autgəuɪŋ] *adj* (*president, tenant*) uscente; (*means of transport*) in partenza; (*character*) socievole
outgoings ['autgəuɪŋz] *npl* (*Brit: expenses*) spese *fpl*
outgrow [aut'grəu] *vt irreg* (*clothes*) diventare troppo grande per
outhouse ['authaus] *n* costruzione *f* annessa
outing ['autɪŋ] *n* gita; escursione *f*
outlandish [aut'lændɪʃ] *adj* strano(-a)
outlast [aut'lɑ:st] *vt* sopravvivere a
outlaw ['autlɔ:] *n* fuorilegge *m/f* ■ *vt* (*person*) mettere fuori della legge; (*practice*) proscrivere
outlay ['autleɪ] *n* spesa
outlet ['autlɛt] *n* (*for liquid etc*) sbocco, scarico; (*for emotion*) sfogo; (*for goods*) sbocco, mercato; (*also*: **retail outlet**) punto di vendita; (*US Elec*) presa di corrente
outline ['autlaɪn] *n* contorno, profilo; (*summary*) abbozzo, grandi linee *fpl*
outlive [aut'lɪv] *vt* sopravvivere a
outlook ['autluk] *n* prospettiva, vista
outlying ['autlaɪɪŋ] *adj* periferico(-a)
outmanoeuvre, (*US*) **outmaneuver** [autmə'nu:vəʳ] *vt* (*rival etc*) superare in strategia
outmoded [aut'məudɪd] *adj* passato(-a) di moda; antiquato(-a)
outnumber [aut'nʌmbəʳ] *vt* superare in numero
out-of-court [autəv'kɔ:t] *adj* extragiudiziale ■ *adv* (*settle*) senza ricorrere al tribunale
out-of-date [autəv'deɪt] *adj* (*passport, ticket*) scaduto(-a); (*theory, idea*) sorpassato(-a), superato(-a); (*custom*) antiquato(-a); (*clothes*) fuori moda
out-of-the-way ['autəvðə'weɪ] *adj* (*remote*) fuori mano; (*unusual*) originale, insolito(-a)
outpatient ['autpeɪʃənt] *n* paziente *m/f* esterno(-a)
outpost ['autpəust] *n* avamposto
outpouring ['autpɔ:rɪŋ] *n* (*fig*) torrente *m*
output ['autput] *n* produzione *f*; (*Comput*) output *m inv* ■ *vt* emettere
outrage ['autreɪdʒ] *n* oltraggio; scandalo ■ *vt* oltraggiare
outrageous [aut'reɪdʒəs] *adj* oltraggioso(-a); scandaloso(-a)
outrider ['autraɪdəʳ] *n* (*on motorcycle*) battistrada *m inv*
outright *adv* [aut'raɪt] completamente; schiettamente; apertamente; sul colpo ■ *adj* ['autraɪt] completo(-a); schietto(-a) e netto(-a)
outrun [aut'rʌn] *vt irreg* superare (nella corsa)
outset ['autsɛt] *n* inizio
outshine [aut'ʃaɪn] *vt irreg* (*fig*) eclissare
outside [aut'saɪd] *n* esterno, esteriore *m* ■ *adj* esterno(-a), esteriore; (*remote, unlikely*): **an ~ chance** una vaga possibilità ■ *adv* fuori, all'esterno ■ *prep* fuori di, all'esterno di; **at the ~** (*fig*) al massimo; **~ left/right** *n* (*Football*) ala sinistra/destra
outside broadcast *n* (*Radio, TV*) trasmissione *f* in esterno
outside lane *n* (*Aut*) corsia di sorpasso
outside line *n* (*Tel*) linea esterna
outsider [aut'saɪdəʳ] *n* (*in race etc*) outsider *m inv*; (*stranger*) straniero(-a)
outsize ['autsaɪz] *adj* enorme; (*clothes*) per taglie forti
outskirts ['autskə:ts] *npl* sobborghi *mpl*
outsmart [aut'smɑ:t] *vt* superare in astuzia
outspoken [aut'spəukən] *adj* molto franco(-a)
outspread ['autsprɛd] *adj* (*wings*) aperto(-a), spiegato(-a)
outstanding [aut'stændɪŋ] *adj* eccezionale, di rilievo; (*unfinished*) non completo(-a); non evaso(-a); non regolato(-a); **your account is still ~** deve ancora saldare il conto
outstay [aut'steɪ] *vt*: **to ~ one's welcome** diventare un ospite sgradito
outstretched [aut'strɛtʃt] *adj* (*hand*) teso(-a); (*body*) disteso(-a)
outstrip [aut'strɪp] *vt* (*also fig*) superare
out-tray ['auttreɪ] *n* raccoglitore *m* per le carte da spedire
outvote [aut'vəut] *vt*: **to ~ sb (by)** avere la maggioranza rispetto a qn (per); **to ~ sth (by)** respingere qc (per)

outward ['autwəd] *adj* (*sign, appearances*) esteriore; (*journey*) d'andata
outwardly ['autwədlɪ] *adv* esteriormente; in apparenza
outweigh [aut'weɪ] *vt* avere maggior peso di
outwit [aut'wɪt] *vt* superare in astuzia
oval ['əuvl] *adj, n* ovale (*m*)
Oval Office *n* (US) *vedi nota*

OVAL OFFICE

L' *Oval Office* è una grande stanza di forma ovale nella White House, la Casa Bianca, dove ha sede l'ufficio del Presidente degli Stati Uniti. Spesso il termine è usato per indicare la stessa presidenza degli Stati Uniti.

ovarian [əu'vɛərɪən] *adj* ovarico(-a)
ovary ['əuvərɪ] *n* ovaia
ovation [əu'veɪʃən] *n* ovazione *f*
oven ['ʌvn] *n* forno
ovenproof ['ʌvnpru:f] *adj* da forno
oven-ready ['ʌvnrɛdɪ] *adj* pronto(-a) da infornare
ovenware ['ʌvnwɛəʳ] *n* vasellame *m* da mettere in forno
over ['əuvəʳ] *adv* al di sopra; (*excessively*) molto, troppo ■ *adj (or adv)* (*finished*) finito(-a), terminato(-a); (*too much*) troppo; (*remaining*) che avanza ■ *prep* su; sopra; (*above*) al di sopra di; (*on the other side of*) di là di; (*more than*) più di; (*during*) durante; **~ here** qui; **~ there** là; **all ~** (*everywhere*) dappertutto; (*finished*) tutto(-a) finito(-a); **~ and ~ (again)** più e più volte; **~ and above** oltre (a); **to ask ~** invitare qn (a passare); **now ~ to our Rome correspondent** diamo ora la linea al nostro corrispondente da Roma; **the world ~** in tutto il mondo; **she's not ~ intelligent** (*Brit*) non è troppo intelligente; **they fell out ~ money** litigarono per una questione di denaro
over... ['əuvəʳ] *prefix*: **overabundant** sovrabbondante
overact [əuvər'ækt] *vi* (*Theat*) esagerare *or* strafare la propria parte
overall *adj, n* ['əuvərɔ:l] ■ *adj* totale ■ *n* (*Brit*) grembiule *m* ■ *adv* [əuvər'ɔ:l] nell'insieme, complessivamente; **overalls** *npl* tuta (da lavoro)
overall majority *n* maggioranza assoluta
overanxious [əuvər'æŋkʃəs] *adj* troppo ansioso(-a)
overawe [əuvər'ɔ:] *vt* intimidire
overbalance [əuvə'bæləns] *vi* perdere l'equilibrio
overbearing [əuvə'bɛərɪŋ] *adj* imperioso(-a), prepotente
overboard ['əuvəbɔ:d] *adv* (*Naut*) fuori bordo, in acqua; **to go ~ for sth** (*fig*) impazzire per qc
overbook [əuvə'buk] *vt* sovrapprenotare
overcapitalize [əuvə'kæpɪtəlaɪz] *vt* sovraccapitalizzare
overcast ['əuvəkɑ:st] *adj* coperto(-a)
overcharge [əuvə'tʃɑ:dʒ] *vt*: **to ~ sb for sth** far pagare troppo caro a qn per qc
overcoat ['əuvəkəut] *n* soprabito, cappotto
overcome [əuvə'kʌm] *vt irreg* superare; sopraffare; **~ with grief** sopraffatto(-a) dal dolore
overconfident [əuvə'kɔnfɪdənt] *adj* troppo sicuro(-a) (di sé), presuntuoso(-a)
overcrowded [əuvə'kraudɪd] *adj* sovraffollato(-a)
overcrowding [əuvə'kraudɪŋ] *n* sovraffollamento; (*in bus*) calca
overdo [əuvə'du:] *vt irreg* esagerare; (*overcook*) cuocere troppo; **to ~ it, to ~ things** (*work too hard*) lavorare troppo
overdose ['əuvədəus] *n* dose *f* eccessiva
overdraft ['əuvədrɑ:ft] *n* scoperto (di conto)
overdrawn [əuvə'drɔ:n] *adj* (*account*) scoperto(-a)
overdrive ['əuvədraɪv] *n* (*Aut*) overdrive *m inv*
overdue [əuvə'dju:] *adj* in ritardo; (*recognition*) tardivo(-a); (*bill*) insoluto(-a); **that change was long ~** quel cambiamento ci voleva da tempo
overemphasis [əuvər'ɛmfəsɪs] *n*: **~ on sth** importanza eccessiva data a qc
overemphasize [əuvər'ɛmfəsaɪz] *vt* dare un'importanza eccessiva a
overestimate [əuvər'ɛstɪmeɪt] *vt* sopravvalutare
overexcited [əuvərɪk'saɪtɪd] *adj* sovraeccitato(-a)
overexertion [əuvərɪg'zə:ʃən] *n* logorio (fisico)
overexpose [əuvərɪk'spəuz] *vt* (*Phot*) sovraesporre
overflow *vi* [əuvə'fləu] traboccare ■ *n* ['əuvəfləu] eccesso; (*also*: **overflow pipe**) troppopieno
overfly [əuvə'flaɪ] *vt irreg* sorvolare
overgenerous [əuvə'dʒɛnərəs] *adj* troppo generoso(-a)
overgrown [əuvə'grəun] *adj* (*garden*) ricoperto(-a) di vegetazione; **he's just an ~ schoolboy** è proprio un bambinone
overhang [əuvə'hæŋ] *vt irreg* sporgere da ■ *vi* sporgere
overhaul *vt* [əuvə'hɔ:l] revisionare ■ *n* ['əuvəhɔ:l] revisione *f*

overhead *adv* [əuvə'hɛd] di sopra ■ *adj* ['əuvəhɛd] aereo(-a); (*lighting*) verticale ■ *n* (*US*) = **overheads**
overheads ['əuvəhɛdz] *npl* (*Brit*) spese *fpl* generali
overhear [əuvə'hɪəʳ] *vt irreg* sentire (per caso)
overheat [əuvə'hi:t] *vi* surriscaldarsi
overjoyed [əuvə'dʒɔɪd] *adj* pazzo(-a) di gioia
overkill ['əuvəkɪl] *n* (*fig*) strafare *m*
overland ['əuvəlænd] *adj*, *adv* per via di terra
overlap *vi* [əuvə'læp] sovrapporsi ■ *n* ['əuvəlæp] sovrapposizione *f*
overleaf [əuvə'li:f] *adv* a tergo
overload [əuvə'ləud] *vt* sovraccaricare
overlook [əuvə'luk] *vt* (*have view of*) dare su; (*miss*) trascurare; (*forgive*) passare sopra a
overlord ['əuvəlɔ:d] *n* capo supremo
overmanning [əuvə'mænɪŋ] *n* eccedenza di manodopera
overnight *adv* [əuvə'naɪt] (*happen*) durante la notte; (*fig*) tutto ad un tratto ■ *adj* ['əuvənaɪt] di notte; fulmineo(-a); **he stayed there ~** ci ha passato la notte; **if you travel ~...** se viaggia di notte ...; **he'll be away ~** passerà la notte fuori
overpass ['əuvəpɑ:s] *n* cavalcavia *m inv*
overpay [əuvə'peɪ] *vt*: **to ~ sb by £50** pagare 50 sterline in più a qn
overplay [əuvə'pleɪ] *vt* dare troppa importanza a; **to ~ one's hand** sopravvalutare la propria posizione
overpower [əuvə'pauəʳ] *vt* sopraffare
overpowering [əuvə'pauərɪŋ] *adj* irresistibile; (*heat, stench*) soffocante
overproduction ['əuvəprə'dʌkʃən] *n* sovrapproduzione *f*
overrate [əuvə'reɪt] *vt* sopravvalutare
overreach [əuvə'ri:tʃ] *vt*: **to ~ o.s.** volere strafare
overreact [əuvəri:'ækt] *vi* reagire in modo esagerato
override [əuvə'raɪd] *vt* (*irreg: like* **ride**) (*order, objection*) passar sopra a; (*decision*) annullare
overriding [əuvə'raɪdɪŋ] *adj* preponderante
overrule [əuvə'ru:l] *vt* (*decision*) annullare; (*claim*) respingere
overrun [əuvə'rʌn] *vt irreg* (*Mil: country etc*) invadere; (*time limit etc*) superare, andare al di là di ■ *vi* protrarsi; **the town is ~ with tourists** la città è invasa dai turisti
overseas [əuvə'si:z] *adv* oltremare; (*abroad*) all'estero ■ *adj* (*trade*) estero(-a); (*visitor*) straniero(-a)
oversee [əuvə'si:] *vt irreg* sorvegliare
overseer ['əuvəsɪəʳ] *n* (*in factory*) caposquadra *m*
overshadow [əuvə'ʃædəu] *vt* (*fig*) eclissare
overshoot [əuvə'ʃu:t] *vt irreg* superare
oversight ['əuvəsaɪt] *n* omissione *f*, svista; **due to an ~** per una svista
oversimplify [əuvə'sɪmplɪfaɪ] *vt* rendere troppo semplice
oversleep [əuvə'sli:p] *vi irreg* dormire troppo a lungo
overspend [əuvə'spɛnd] *vi irreg* spendere troppo; **we have overspent by 5000 dollars** abbiamo speso 5000 dollari di troppo
overspill ['əuvəspɪl] *n* eccedenza di popolazione
overstaffed [əuvə'stɑ:ft] *adj*: **to be ~** avere troppo personale
overstate [əuvə'steɪt] *vt* esagerare
overstatement [əuvə'steɪtmənt] *n* esagerazione *f*
overstay [əuvə'steɪ] *vt*: **to ~ one's welcome** trattenersi troppo a lungo (come ospite)
overstep [əuvə'stɛp] *vt*: **to ~ the mark** superare ogni limite
overstock [əuvə'stɔk] *vt* sovrapprovvigionare, sovraimmagazzinare
overstretched [əuvə'stretʃt] *adj* sovraccarico(-a); (*budget*) arrivato(-a) al limite
overstrike *n* ['əuvəstraɪk] (*on printer*) sovrapposizione *f* (di caratteri) ■ *vt* [əuvə'straɪk] *irreg* sovrapporre
overt [əu'və:t] *adj* palese
overtake [əuvə'teɪk] *vt irreg* sorpassare
overtaking [əuvə'teɪkɪŋ] *n* (*Aut*) sorpasso
overtax [əuvə'tæks] *vt* (*Econ*) imporre tasse eccessive a, tassare eccessivamente; (*fig: strength, patience*) mettere alla prova, abusare di; **to ~ o.s.** chiedere troppo alle proprie forze
overthrow [əuvə'θrəu] *vt irreg* (*government*) rovesciare
overtime ['əuvətaɪm] *n* (lavoro) straordinario; **to do** *or* **work ~** fare lo straordinario
overtime ban *n* rifiuto sindacale a fare gli straordinari
overtone ['əuvətəun] *n* (*also*: **overtones**) sfumatura
overture ['əuvətʃuəʳ] *n* (*Mus*) ouverture *f inv*; (*fig*) approccio
overturn [əuvə'tə:n] *vt* rovesciare ■ *vi* rovesciarsi
overview ['əuvəvju:] *n* visione *f* d'insieme
overweight [əuvə'weɪt] *adj* (*person*) troppo grasso(-a); (*luggage*) troppo pesante
overwhelm [əuvə'wɛlm] *vt* sopraffare; sommergere; schiacciare
overwhelming [əuvə'wɛlmɪŋ] *adj* (*victory, defeat*) schiacciante; (*desire*) irresistibile;

one's ~ impression is of heat l'impressione dominante è quella di caldo
overwhelmingly [əuvə'wɛlmɪŋlɪ] *adv* in massa
overwork [əuvə'wə:k] *vt* far lavorare troppo ■ *vi* lavorare troppo, strapazzarsi
overwrite [əuvə'raɪt] *vt* (*Comput*) ricoprire
overwrought [əuvə'rɔ:t] *adj* molto agitato(-a)
ovulation [ɔvju'leɪʃən] *n* ovulazione *f*
owe [əu] *vt* dovere; **to ~ sb sth, to ~ sth to sb** dovere qc a qn
owing to ['əuɪŋtu:] *prep* a causa di
owl [aul] *n* gufo
own [əun] *adj* proprio(-a) ■ *vt* possedere ■ *vi* (*Brit*): **to ~ to sth** ammettere qc; **to ~ to having done sth** ammettere di aver fatto qc; **a room of my ~** la mia propria camera; **to get one's ~ back** vendicarsi; **on one's ~** tutto(-a) solo(-a); **can I have it for my (very) ~?** posso averlo tutto per me?; **to come into one's ~** mostrare le proprie qualità
▸ **own up** *vi* confessare
own brand *n* (*Comm*) etichetta propria
owner ['əunə^r] *n* proprietario(-a)
owner-occupier ['əunər'ɔkjupaɪə^r] *n* *proprietario/a della casa in cui abita*
ownership ['əunəʃɪp] *n* possesso; **it's under new ~** ha un nuovo proprietario
own goal *n* (*also fig*) autogol *m inv*
ox (*pl* **oxen**) [ɔks, 'ɔksn] *n* bue *m*
Oxbridge ['ɔksbrɪdʒ] *n le università di Oxford e/o Cambridge; vedi nota*

OXBRIDGE

La parola *Oxbridge* deriva dalla fusione dei nomi Ox(ford) e (Cam)bridge e fa riferimento a queste due antiche università.

Oxfam ['ɔksfæm] *n abbr* (*Brit: = Oxford Committee for Famine Relief*) *organizzazione per aiuti al terzo mondo*
oxide ['ɔksaɪd] *n* ossido
Oxon. ['ɔksn] *abbr* (*Brit: of Oxford*) = **Oxoniensis**
oxtail ['ɔksteɪl] *n*: **~ soup** minestra di coda di bue
oxyacetylene ['ɔksɪə'sɛtɪli:n] *adj* ossiacetilenico(-a); **~ burner, ~ lamp** cannello ossiacetilenico
oxygen ['ɔksɪdʒən] *n* ossigeno
oxygen mask *n* maschera ad ossigeno
oxygen tent *n* tenda ad ossigeno
oyster ['ɔɪstə^r] *n* ostrica
oz. *abbr* = **ounce**
ozone ['əuzəun] *n* ozono
ozone-friendly ['əuzəun'frɛndlɪ] *adj* che non danneggia lo strato d'ozono

Pp

P, p [pi:] *n* (*letter*) P, p *f or m inv*; **P for Peter** ≈ P come Padova
P *abbr* = **president**; **prince**
p *abbr* (= *page*) p; (*Brit*) = **penny**; **pence**
PA *n abbr* = **personal assistant**; **public address system** ■ *abbr* (*US*) = **Pennsylvania**
pa [pɑ:] *n* (*col*) papà *m inv*, babbo
p.a. *abbr* = **per annum**
PAC *n abbr* (*US*) = **political action committee**
pace [peɪs] *n* passo; (*speed*) passo; velocità ■ *vi*: **to ~ up and down** camminare su e giù; **to keep ~ with** camminare di pari passo a; (*events*) tenersi al corrente di; **to put sb through his paces** (*fig*) mettere qn alla prova; **to set the ~** (*running*) fare l'andatura; (*fig*) dare il la *or* il tono
pacemaker ['peɪsmeɪkəʳ] *n* (*Med*) pacemaker *m inv*, stimolatore *m* cardiaco; (*Sport*) chi fa l'andatura
pacific [pə'sɪfɪk] *adj* pacifico(-a) ■ *n*: **the P~ (Ocean)** il Pacifico, l'Oceano Pacifico
pacification [pæsɪfɪ'keɪʃən] *n* pacificazione *f*
pacifier ['pæsɪfaɪəʳ] *n* (*US*: *dummy*) succhiotto, ciuccio (*col*)
pacifist ['pæsɪfɪst] *n* pacifista *m/f*
pacify ['pæsɪfaɪ] *vt* pacificare; (*soothe*) calmare
pack [pæk] *n* (*packet*) pacco; (*Comm*) confezione *f*; (*US*: *of cigarettes*) pacchetto; (*of goods*) balla; (*of hounds*) muta; (*of wolves*) branco; (*of thieves etc*) banda; (*of cards*) mazzo ■ *vt* (*goods*) impaccare, imballare; (*in suitcase etc*) mettere; (*box*) riempire; (*cram*) stipare, pigiare; (*press down*) tamponare; turare; (*Comput*) comprimere, impaccare ■ *vi*: **to ~ one's bags** fare la valigia; **to send sb packing** (*col*) spedire via qn
▸ **pack in** (*Brit col*) *vi* (*watch, car*) guastarsi ■ *vt* mollare, piantare; **~ it in!** piantala!
▸ **pack off** *vt* (*person*) spedire
▸ **pack up** *vi* (*Brit col*: *machine*) guastarsi; (: *person*) far fagotto ■ *vt* (*belongings, clothes*) mettere in una valigia; (*goods, presents*) imballare
package ['pækɪdʒ] *n* pacco; balla; (*also*: **package deal**) pacchetto; forfait *m inv* ■ *vt* (*goods*) confezionare
package holiday *n* (*Brit*) vacanza organizzata
package tour *n* viaggio organizzato
packaging ['pækɪdʒɪŋ] *n* confezione *f*, imballo
packed [pækt] *adj* (*crowded*) affollato(-a); **~ lunch** (*Brit*) pranzo al sacco
packer ['pækəʳ] *n* (*person*) imballatore(-trice)
packet ['pækɪt] *n* pacchetto
packet switching [-swɪtʃɪŋ] *n* (*Comput*) commutazione *f* di pacchetto
pack ice ['pækaɪs] *n* banchisa
packing ['pækɪŋ] *n* imballaggio
packing case *n* cassa da imballaggio
pact [pækt] *n* patto, accordo; trattato
pad [pæd] *n* blocco; (*for inking*) tampone *m*; (*col*: *flat*) appartamentino ■ *vt* imbottire ■ *vi*: **to ~ about/in** *etc* camminare/entrare *etc* a passi felpati
padded cell ['pædɪd-] *n* cella imbottita
padding ['pædɪŋ] *n* imbottitura; (*fig*) riempitivo
paddle ['pædl] *n* (*oar*) pagaia ■ *vi* sguazzare ■ *vt* (*boat*) fare andare a colpi di pagaia
paddle steamer *n* battello a ruote
paddling pool ['pædlɪŋ-] *n* piscina per bambini
paddock ['pædək] *n* recinto; paddock *m inv*
paddy ['pædɪ] *n* (*also*: **paddy field**) risaia
padlock ['pædlɔk] *n* lucchetto ■ *vt* chiudere con il lucchetto
padre ['pɑ:drɪ] *n* cappellano
Padua ['pædʒuə] *n* Padova
paediatrician, (*US*) **pediatrician** [pi:dɪə'trɪʃən] *n* pediatra *m/f*
paediatrics, (*US*) **pediatrics** [pi:dɪ'ætrɪks] *n* pediatria
paedophile, (*US*) **pedophile** ['pi:dəufaɪl] *adj*, *n* pedofilo(-a)
pagan ['peɪgən] *adj*, *n* pagano(-a)
page [peɪdʒ] *n* pagina; (*also*: **page boy**)

fattorino; (: *at wedding*) paggio ■ *vt* (*in hotel etc*) (far) chiamare
pageant ['pædʒənt] *n* spettacolo storico; grande cerimonia
pageantry ['pædʒəntrɪ] *n* pompa
page break *n* interruzione *f* di pagina
pager ['peɪdʒə^r] *n* cicalino, cercapersone *m*
paginate ['pædʒɪneɪt] *vt* impaginare
pagination [pædʒɪ'neɪʃən] *n* impaginazione *f*
pagoda [pə'gəudə] *n* pagoda
paid [peɪd] *pt, pp of* **pay** ■ *adj* (*work, official*) rimunerato(-a); **to put ~ to** (*Brit*) mettere fine a
paid-up ['peɪdʌp], (*US*) **paid in** ['peɪdɪn] *adj* (*member*) che ha pagato la sua quota; (*share*) interamente pagato(-a); **~ capital** capitale *m* interamente versato
pail [peɪl] *n* secchio
pain [peɪn] *n* dolore *m*; **to be in ~** soffrire, aver male; **to have a ~ in** aver male *or* un dolore a; **to take pains to do** mettercela tutta per fare; **on ~ of death** sotto pena di morte
pained [peɪnd] *adj* addolorato(-a), afflitto(-a)
painful ['peɪnful] *adj* doloroso(-a), che fa male; (*difficult*) difficile, penoso(-a)
painfully ['peɪnfəlɪ] *adv* (*fig: very*) fin troppo
painkiller ['peɪnkɪlə^r] *n* antalgico, antidolorifico
painstaking ['peɪnzteɪkɪŋ] *adj* sollecito(-a)
paint [peɪnt] *n* (*for house etc*) tinta, vernice *f*; (*Art*) colore *m* ■ *vt* (*Art: walls*) dipingere; (*door etc*) verniciare; **a tin of ~** un barattolo di tinta *or* vernice; **to ~ the door blue** verniciare la porta di azzurro; **to ~ in oils** dipingere a olio
paintbox ['peɪntbɔks] *n* scatola di colori
paintbrush ['peɪntbrʌʃ] *n* pennello
painter ['peɪntə^r] *n* (*artist*) pittore *m*; (*decorator*) imbianchino
painting ['peɪntɪŋ] *n* (*activity: of artist*) pittura; (: *of decorator*) imbiancatura; verniciatura; (*picture*) dipinto, quadro
paint-stripper ['peɪntstrɪpə^r] *n* prodotto sverniciante
paintwork ['peɪntwə:k] *n* (*Brit*) tinta; (: *of car*) vernice *f*
pair [pɛə^r] *n* (*of shoes, gloves etc*) paio; (*of people*) coppia; duo *m inv*; **a ~ of scissors/trousers** un paio di forbici/pantaloni
▸ **pair off** *vi*: **to ~ off (with sb)** fare coppia (con qn)
pajamas [pə'dʒɑ:məz] *npl* (*US*) pigiama *m*
Pakistan [pɑ:kɪ'stɑ:n] *n* Pakistan *m*
Pakistani [pɑ:kɪ'stɑ:nɪ] *adj, n* pakistano(-a)
pal [pæl] *n* (*col*) amico(-a), compagno(-a)
palace ['pæləs] *n* palazzo

palatable ['pælɪtəbl] *adj* gustoso(-a)
palate ['pælɪt] *n* palato
palatial [pə'leɪʃəl] *adj* sontuoso(-a), sfarzoso(-a)
palaver [pə'lɑ:və^r] *n* chiacchiere *fpl*; storie *fpl*
pale [peɪl] *adj* pallido(-a) ■ *vi* impallidire ■ *n*: **to be beyond the ~** aver oltrepassato ogni limite; **to grow** *or* **turn ~** (*person*) diventare pallido(-a), impallidire; **to ~ into insignificance (beside)** perdere d'importanza (nei confronti di); **~ blue** azzurro *or* blu pallido *inv*
paleness ['peɪlnɪs] *n* pallore *m*
Palestine ['pælɪstaɪn] *n* Palestina
Palestinian [pælɪs'tɪnɪən] *adj, n* palestinese (*m/f*)
palette ['pælɪt] *n* tavolozza
paling ['peɪlɪŋ] *n* (*stake*) palo; (*fence*) palizzata
palisade [pælɪ'seɪd] *n* palizzata
pall [pɔ:l] *n* (*of smoke*) cappa ■ *vi*: **to ~ (on)** diventare noioso(-a) (a)
pallet ['pælɪt] *n* (*for goods*) paletta
pallid ['pælɪd] *adj* pallido(-a), smorto(-a)
pallor ['pælə^r] *n* pallore *m*
pally ['pælɪ] *adj* (*col*) amichevole
palm [pɑ:m] *n* (*Anat*) palma, palmo; (*also*: **palm tree**) palma ■ *vt*: **to ~ sth off on sb** (*col*) rifilare qc a qn
palmist ['pɑ:mɪst] *n* chiromante *m/f*
Palm Sunday *n* Domenica delle Palme
palpable ['pælpəbl] *adj* palpabile
palpitation [pælpɪ'teɪʃən] *n* palpitazione *f*; **to have palpitations** avere le palpitazioni
paltry ['pɔ:ltrɪ] *adj* derisorio(-a), insignificante
pamper ['pæmpə^r] *vt* viziare, accarezzare
pamphlet ['pæmflət] *n* dépliant *m inv*; (*political etc*) volantino, manifestino
pan [pæn] *n* (*also*: **saucepan**) casseruola; (*also*: **frying pan**) padella ■ *vi* (*Cine*) fare una panoramica; **to ~ for gold** (lavare le sabbie aurifere per) cercare l'oro
panacea [pænə'sɪə] *n* panacea
panache [pə'næʃ] *n* stile *m*
Panama ['pænəmɑ:] *n* Panama *m*
Panama Canal *n* canale *m* di Panama
Panamanian [pænə'meɪnɪən] *adj, n* panamense (*m/f*)
pancake ['pænkeɪk] *n* frittella
Pancake Day *n* (*Brit*) martedì *m* grasso
pancake roll *n* *crêpe ripiena di verdure alla cinese*
pancreas ['pæŋkrɪəs] *n* pancreas *m inv*
panda ['pændə] *n* panda *m inv*
panda car *n* (*Brit*) auto *f* della polizia
pandemic [pændɛmɪk] *n* pandemia
pandemonium [pændɪ'məunɪəm] *n* pandemonio

pander ['pændəʳ] *vi*: **to ~ to** lusingare; concedere tutto a
p & h *abbr* (*US*: = *postage and handling*) affrancatura e trasporto
P & L *abbr* (= *profit and loss*) P.P.
p & p *abbr* (*Brit*: = *postage and packing*) affrancatura ed imballaggio
pane [peɪn] *n* vetro
panel ['pænl] *n* (*of wood, cloth etc*) pannello; (*Radio, TV*) giuria
panel game *n* (*Brit*) quiz *m inv* a squadre
panelling, (*US*) **paneling** ['pænəlɪŋ] *n* rivestimento a pannelli
panellist, (*US*) **panelist** ['pænəlɪst] *n* partecipante *m/f* (al quiz, alla tavola rotonda *etc*)
pang [pæŋ] *n*: **to feel pangs of remorse** essere torturato(-a) dal rimorso; **pangs of hunger** spasimi *mpl* della fame; **pangs of conscience** morsi *mpl* di coscienza
panhandler ['pænhændləʳ] *n* (*US col*) accattone(-a)
panic ['pænɪk] *n* panico ■ *vi* perdere il sangue freddo
panic buying [-baɪɪŋ] *n* accaparramento (*di generi alimentari etc*)
panicky ['pænɪkɪ] *adj* (*person*) pauroso(-a)
panic-stricken ['pænɪkstrɪkən] *adj* (*person*) preso(-a) dal panico, in preda al panico; (*look*) terrorizzato(-a)
pannier ['pænɪəʳ] *n* (*on animal*) bisaccia; (*on bicycle*) borsa
panorama [pænə'rɑːmə] *n* panorama *m*
panoramic [pænə'ræmɪk] *adj* panoramico(-a)
pansy ['pænzɪ] *n* (*Bot*) viola del pensiero, pensée *f inv*; (*col*) femminuccia
pant [pænt] *vi* ansare
pantechnicon [pæn'tɛknɪkən] *n* (*Brit*) grosso furgone *m* per traslochi
panther ['pænθəʳ] *n* pantera
panties ['pæntɪz] *npl* slip *m*, mutandine *fpl*
pantihose ['pæntɪhəuz] *n* (*US*) collant *m inv*
panto ['pæntəu] *n* (*Brit col*) *see* **pantomime**
pantomime ['pæntəmaɪm] *n* (*at Christmas*) spettacolo natalizio; (*tecnica*) pantomima; *vedi nota*

PANTOMIME

In Gran Bretagna la *pantomime* (abbreviata in *panto*) è una sorta di libera interpretazione delle favole più conosciute che vengono messe in scena nei teatri durante il periodo natalizio. Gli attori principali sono la dama, dame, che è un uomo vestito da donna, il protagonista, principal boy, che è una donna travestita da uomo, e il cattivo, villain . È uno spettacolo per tutta la famiglia, che prevede la partecipazione del pubblico.

pantry ['pæntrɪ] *n* dispensa
pants [pænts] *npl* (*Brit*) mutande *fpl*, slip *m*; (*US*: *trousers*) pantaloni *mpl*
pantsuit ['pæntsuːt] *n* (*US*) completo *m or* tailleur *m inv* pantalone *inv*
papacy ['peɪpəsɪ] *n* papato
papal ['peɪpəl] *adj* papale, pontificio(-a)
paparazzi [pæpə'rætsiː] *npl* paparazzi *mpl*
paper ['peɪpəʳ] *n* carta; (*also*: **wallpaper**) carta da parati, tappezzeria; (*also*: **newspaper**) giornale *m*; (*study, article*) saggio; (*exam*) prova scritta ■ *adj* di carta ■ *vt* tappezzare; **a piece of ~** (*odd bit*) un pezzo di carta; (*sheet*) un foglio (di carta); **to put sth down on ~** mettere qc per iscritto; *see also* **papers**
paper advance *n* (*on printer*) avanzamento della carta
paperback ['peɪpəbæk] *n* tascabile *m*; edizione *f* economica ■ *adj*: **~ edition** edizione *f* tascabile
paper bag *n* sacchetto di carta
paperboy ['peɪpəbɔɪ] *n* (*selling*) strillone *m*; (*delivering*) ragazzo che recapita i giornali
paper clip *n* graffetta, clip *f inv*
paper handkerchief *n* fazzolettino di carta
paper mill *n* cartiera
paper money *n* cartamoneta, moneta cartacea
paper profit *n* utile *m* teorico
papers ['peɪpəz] *npl* (*also*: **identity papers**) carte *fpl*, documenti *mpl*
paper shop *n* (*Brit*) giornalaio (*negozio*)
paperweight ['peɪpəweɪt] *n* fermacarte *m inv*
paperwork ['peɪpəwəːk] *n* lavoro amministrativo
papier-mâché ['pæpɪeɪ'mæʃeɪ] *n* cartapesta
paprika ['pæprɪkə] *n* paprica
Pap test, Pap smear ['pæp-] *n* (*Med*) pap-test *m inv*
par [pɑːʳ] *n* parità, pari *f*; (*Golf*) norma; **on a ~ with** alla pari con; **at/above/below ~** (*Comm*) alla/sopra la/sotto la pari; **above/below ~** (*gen, Golf*) al di sopra/al di sotto della norma; **to feel below** *or* **under** *or* **not up to ~** non sentirsi in forma
parable ['pærəbl] *n* parabola (*Rel*)
parabola [pə'ræbələ] *n* parabola (*Math*)
parachute ['pærəʃuːt] *n* paracadute *m inv* ■ *vi* scendere col paracadute
parachute jump *n* lancio col paracadute
parachutist ['pærəʃuːtɪst] *n* paracadutista *m/f*

parade [pəˈreɪd] *n* parata; (*inspection*) rivista, rassegna ▪ *vt* (*fig*) fare sfoggio di ▪ *vi* sfilare in parata; **a fashion ~** (*Brit*) una sfilata di moda
parade ground *n* piazza d'armi
paradise [ˈpærədaɪs] *n* paradiso
paradox [ˈpærədɔks] *n* paradosso
paradoxical [pærəˈdɔksɪkl] *adj* paradossale
paradoxically [pærəˈdɔksɪklɪ] *adv* paradossalmente
paraffin [ˈpærəfɪn] *n* (*Brit*): **~ (oil)** paraffina; **liquid ~** olio di paraffina
paraffin heater *n* (*Brit*) stufa al cherosene
paraffin lamp *n* (*Brit*) lampada al cherosene
paragon [ˈpærəgən] *n* modello di perfezione *or* di virtù
paragraph [ˈpærəgrɑːf] *n* paragrafo; **to begin a new ~** andare a capo
Paraguay [ˈpærəgwaɪ] *n* Paraguay *m*
Paraguayan [pærəˈgwaɪən] *adj, n* paraguaiano(-a)
parallel [ˈpærəlɛl] *adj* (*also Comput*) parallelo(-a); (*fig*) analogo(-a) ▪ *n* (*line*) parallela; (*fig, Geo*) parallelo; **~ (with** *or* **to)** parallelo(-a) (a)
paralysis (*pl* **paralyses**) [pəˈrælɪsɪs, -siːz] *n* paralisi *f inv*
paralytic [pærəˈlɪtɪk] *adj* paralitico(-a); (*Brit col: drunk*) ubriaco(-a) fradicio(-a)
paralyze [ˈpærəlaɪz] *vt* paralizzare
paramedic [pærəˈmɛdɪk] *n* paramedico
parameter [pəˈræmɪtəʳ] *n* parametro
paramilitary [pærəˈmɪlɪtərɪ] *adj* paramilitare
paramount [ˈpærəmaunt] *adj*: **of ~ importance** di capitale importanza
paranoia [pærəˈnɔɪə] *n* paranoia
paranoid [ˈpærənɔɪd] *adj* paranoico(-a)
paranormal [pærəˈnɔːml] *adj* paranormale
paraphernalia [pærəfəˈneɪlɪə] *n* attrezzi *mpl*, roba
paraphrase [ˈpærəfreɪz] *vt* parafrasare
paraplegic [pærəˈpliːdʒɪk] *n* paraplegico(-a)
parapsychology [pærəsaɪˈkɔlədʒɪ] *n* parapsicologia
parasite [ˈpærəsaɪt] *n* parassita *m*
parasol [ˈpærəsɔl] *n* parasole *m inv*
paratrooper [ˈpærətruːpəʳ] *n* paracadutista *m* (*soldato*)
parcel [ˈpɑːsl] *n* pacco, pacchetto ▪ *vt* (*also*: **parcel up**) impaccare
▸ **parcel out** *vt* spartire
parcel bomb *n* (*Brit*) pacchetto esplosivo
parcel post *n* servizio pacchi
parch [pɑːtʃ] *vt* riardere
parched [ˈpɑːtʃt] *adj* (*person*) assetato(-a)
parchment [ˈpɑːtʃmənt] *n* pergamena
pardon [ˈpɑːdn] *n* perdono; grazia ▪ *vt* perdonare; (*Law*) graziare; **~!** scusi!; **~ me!** mi scusi!; **I beg your ~!** scusi!; **(I beg your) ~?**, (*US*) **~ me?** prego?
pare [pɛəʳ] *vt* (*Brit: nails*) tagliarsi; (*: fruit etc*) sbucciare, pelare
parent [ˈpɛərənt] *n* padre *m* (*or* madre *f*); **parents** *npl* genitori *mpl*
parentage [ˈpɛərəntɪdʒ] *n* natali *mpl*; **of unknown ~** di genitori sconosciuti
parental [pəˈrɛntl] *adj* dei genitori
parent company *n* società madre *f inv*
parenthesis (*pl* **parentheses**) [pəˈrɛnθɪsɪs, -siːz] *n* parentesi *f inv*; **in parentheses** fra parentesi
parenthood [ˈpɛərənthud] *n* paternità *or* maternità
parenting [ˈpɛərəntɪŋ] *n* mestiere *m* di genitore
Paris [ˈpærɪs] *n* Parigi *f*
parish [ˈpærɪʃ] *n* parrocchia; (*civil*) ≈ municipio ▪ *adj* parrocchiale
parish council *n* (*Brit*) ≈ consiglio comunale
parishioner [pəˈrɪʃənəʳ] *n* parrocchiano(-a)
Parisian [pəˈrɪzɪən] *adj, n* parigino(-a)
parity [ˈpærɪtɪ] *n* parità
park [pɑːk] *n* parco; (*public*) giardino pubblico ▪ *vt, vi* parcheggiare
parka [ˈpɑːkə] *n* eskimo
parking [ˈpɑːkɪŋ] *n* parcheggio; **"no ~"** "sosta vietata"
parking lights *npl* luci *fpl* di posizione
parking lot *n* (*US*) posteggio, parcheggio
parking meter *n* parchimetro
parking offence *n* (*Brit*) infrazione *f* al divieto di sosta
parking place *n* posto di parcheggio
parking ticket *n* multa per sosta vietata
parking violation *n* (*US*) = **parking offence**
Parkinson's [ˈpɑːkɪnsənz] *n* (*also*: **Parkinson's disease**) morbo di Parkinson
parkway [ˈpɑːkweɪ] *n* (*US*) viale *m*
parlance [ˈpɑːləns] *n*: **in common/modern ~** nel gergo *or* linguaggio comune/moderno
parliament [ˈpɑːləmənt] *n* parlamento; *vedi nota*

PARLIAMENT

Nel Regno Unito il Parlamento, *Parliament*, è formato da due camere: la House of Commons, e la House of Lords. Nella House of Commons siedono 650 parlamentari, chiamati MPs, eletti per votazione diretta del popolo nelle rispettive circoscrizioni elettorali, le constituencies. Le sessioni del

P

Parlamento sono presiedute e moderate dal presidente della Camera, lo Speaker. Alla House of Lords, i cui poteri sono più limitati, in passato si accedeva per nomina o per carica ereditaria mentre ora le cariche ereditarie sono state ridotte e in futuro verranno abolite.

parliamentary [pɑːlə'mɛntərɪ] *adj* parlamentare
parlour, (*US*) **parlor** ['pɑːlə^r] *n* salotto
parlous ['pɑːləs] *adj* periglioso(-a)
Parmesan [pɑːmɪ'zæn] *n* (*also*: **Parmesan cheese**) parmigiano
parochial [pə'rəukɪəl] *adj* parrocchiale; (*pej*) provinciale
parody ['pærədɪ] *n* parodia
parole [pə'rəul] *n*: **on ~** in libertà per buona condotta
paroxysm ['pærəksɪzəm] *n* (*Med*) parossismo; (*of anger, laughter, coughing*) convulso; (*of grief*) attacco
parquet ['pɑːkeɪ] *n*: **~ floor(ing)** parquet *m*
parrot ['pærət] *n* pappagallo
parrot fashion *adv* in modo pappagallesco
parry ['pærɪ] *vt* parare
parsimonious [pɑːsɪ'məunɪəs] *adj* parsimonioso(-a)
parsley ['pɑːslɪ] *n* prezzemolo
parsnip ['pɑːsnɪp] *n* pastinaca
parson ['pɑːsn] *n* prete *m*; (*Church of England*) parroco
part [pɑːt] *n* parte *f*; (*of machine*) pezzo; (*Theat etc*) parte, ruolo; (*Mus*) voce *f*; parte ■ *adj* in parte ■ *adv* = **partly** ■ *vt* separare ■ *vi* (*people*) separarsi; (*roads*) dividersi; **to take ~ in** prendere parte a; **to take sb's ~** parteggiare per qn, prendere le parti di qn; **on his ~** da parte sua; **for my ~** per parte mia; **for the most ~** in generale; nella maggior parte dei casi; **for the better ~ of the day** per la maggior parte della giornata; **to be ~ and parcel of** essere parte integrante di; **to take sth in good/bad ~** prendere bene/male qc; **~ of speech** (*Ling*) parte del discorso
▸ **part with** *vt fus* separarsi da; rinunciare a
partake [pɑː'teɪk] *vi irreg* (*formal*): **to ~ of sth** consumare qc, prendere qc
part exchange *n* (*Brit*): **in ~** in pagamento parziale
partial ['pɑːʃl] *adj* parziale; **to be ~ to** avere un debole per
partially ['pɑːʃəlɪ] *adv* in parte, parzialmente
participant [pɑː'tɪsɪpənt] *n*: **~ (in)** partecipante *m/f* (a)
participate [pɑː'tɪsɪpeɪt] *vi*: **to ~ (in)** prendere parte (a), partecipare (a)
participation [pɑːtɪsɪ'peɪʃən] *n* partecipazione *f*
participle ['pɑːtɪsɪpl] *n* participio
particle ['pɑːtɪkl] *n* particella
particular [pə'tɪkjulə^r] *adj* particolare; speciale; (*fussy*) difficile; meticoloso(-a); **particulars** *npl* particolari *mpl*, dettagli *mpl*; (*information*) informazioni *fpl*; **in ~** in particolare, particolarmente; **to be very ~ about** essere molto pignolo(-a) su; **I'm not ~** per me va bene tutto
particularly [pə'tɪkjuləlɪ] *adv* particolarmente; in particolare
parting ['pɑːtɪŋ] *n* separazione *f*; (*Brit: in hair*) scriminatura ■ *adj* d'addio; **~ shot** (*fig*) battuta finale
partisan [pɑːtɪ'zæn] *n* partigiano(-a) ■ *adj* partigiano(-a); di parte
partition [pɑː'tɪʃən] *n* (*Pol*) partizione *f*; (*wall*) tramezzo
partly ['pɑːtlɪ] *adv* parzialmente; in parte
partner ['pɑːtnə^r] *n* (*Comm*) socio(-a); (*Sport*) compagno(-a); (*at dance*) cavaliere/dama
partnership ['pɑːtnəʃɪp] *n* associazione *f*; (*Comm*) società *f inv*; **to go into ~ (with)**, **form a ~ (with)** mettersi in società (con), associarsi (a)
part payment *n* acconto
partridge ['pɑːtrɪdʒ] *n* pernice *f*
part-time ['pɑː'taɪm] *adj, adv* a orario ridotto, part-time (*inv*)
part-timer ['pɑː'taɪmə^r] *n* (*also*: **part-time worker**) lavoratore(-trice) part-time
party ['pɑːtɪ] *n* (*Pol*) partito; (*team*) squadra; gruppo; (*Law*) parte *f*; (*celebration*) ricevimento; serata; festa; **dinner ~** cena; **to give** *or* **throw a ~** dare una festa *or* un party; **to be a ~ to a crime** essere coinvolto in un reato
party line *n* (*Pol*) linea del partito; (*Tel*) duplex *m inv*
party piece *n*: **to do one's ~** (*Brit col*) *esibirsi nel proprio pezzo forte a una festa, cena etc*
party political broadcast *n* comunicato radiotelevisivo di propaganda
pass [pɑːs] *vt* (*gen*) passare; (*place*) passare davanti a; (*exam*) passare, superare; (*candidate*) promuovere; (*overtake, surpass*) sorpassare, superare; (*approve*) approvare ■ *vi* passare; (*Scol*) essere promosso(-a) ■ *n* (*permit*) lasciapassare *m inv*; permesso; (*in mountains*) passo, gola; (*Sport*) passaggio; (*Scol: also*: **pass mark**): **to get a ~** prendere la sufficienza; **to ~ for** passare per; **could you ~ the vegetables round?** potrebbe far passare i contorni?; **to make a ~ at sb** (*col*) fare delle proposte *or* delle avances a qn;

things have come to a pretty ~ (*Brit*) ecco a cosa siamo arrivati
▸ **pass away** *vi* morire
▸ **pass by** *vi* passare ■ *vt* trascurare
▸ **pass down** *vt* (*customs, inheritance*) tramandare, trasmettere
▸ **pass on** *vi* (*die*) spegnersi, mancare ■ *vt* (*hand on*): **to ~ on (to)** (*news, information, object*) passare (a); (*cold, illness*) attaccare (a); (*benefits*) trasmettere (a); (*price rises*) riversare (su)
▸ **pass out** *vi* svenire; (*Brit Mil*) uscire dall'accademia
▸ **pass over** *vi* (*die*) spirare ■ *vt* lasciare da parte
▸ **pass up** *vt* (*opportunity*) lasciarsi sfuggire, perdere
passable ['pɑːsəbl] *adj* (*road*) praticabile; (*work*) accettabile
passage ['pæsɪdʒ] *n* (*gen*) passaggio; (*also:* **passageway**) corridoio; (*in book*) brano, passo; (*by boat*) traversata
passenger ['pæsɪndʒəʳ] *n* passeggero(-a)
passer-by [pɑːsə'baɪ] *n* passante *m/f*
passing ['pɑːsɪŋ] *adj* (*fig*) fuggevole; **to mention sth in ~** accennare a qc di sfuggita
passing place *n* (*Aut*) piazzola (di sosta)
passion ['pæʃən] *n* passione *f*; amore *m*; **to have a ~ for sth** aver la passione di *or* per qc
passionate ['pæʃənɪt] *adj* appassionato(-a)
passion fruit *n* frutto della passione
passion play *n* rappresentazione *f* della Passione di Cristo
passive ['pæsɪv] *adj* (*also Ling*) passivo(-a)
passive smoking *n* fumo passivo
passkey ['pɑːskiː] *n* passe-partout *m inv*
Passover ['pɑːsəuvəʳ] *n* Pasqua ebraica
passport ['pɑːspɔːt] *n* passaporto
passport control *n* controllo *m* passaporti *inv*
passport office *n* ufficio *m* passaporti *inv*
password ['pɑːswəːd] *n* parola d'ordine
past [pɑːst] *prep* (*further than*) oltre, di là di; dopo; (*later than*) dopo ■ *adv*: **to run ~** passare di corsa; **to walk ~** passare ■ *adj* passato(-a); (*president etc*) ex *inv* ■ *n* passato; **quarter/half ~ four** le quattro e un quarto/e mezzo; **ten/twenty ~ four** le quattro e dieci/venti; **he's ~ forty** ha più di quarant'anni; **it's ~ midnight** è mezzanotte passata; **for the ~ few days** da qualche giorno; in questi ultimi giorni; **for the ~ 3 days** negli ultimi 3 giorni; **in the ~** in *or* nel passato; (*Ling*) al passato; **I'm ~ caring** non me ne importa più nulla; **to be ~ it** (*Brit col: person*) essere finito(-a)
pasta ['pæstə] *n* pasta
paste [peɪst] *n* (*glue*) colla; (*Culin*) pâté *m inv*; pasta ■ *vt* collare; **tomato ~** concentrato di pomodoro
pastel ['pæstl] *adj* pastello *inv*
pasteurized ['pæstəraɪzd] *adj* pastorizzato(-a)
pastille ['pæstl] *n* pastiglia
pastime ['pɑːstaɪm] *n* passatempo
past master *n* (*Brit*): **to be a ~ at** essere molto esperto(-a) in
pastor ['pɑːstəʳ] *n* pastore *m*
pastoral ['pɑːstərl] *adj* pastorale
pastry ['peɪstrɪ] *n* pasta
pasture ['pɑːstʃəʳ] *n* pascolo
pasty *n* ['pæstɪ] pasticcio di carne ■ *adj* ['peɪstɪ] pastoso(-a); (*complexion*) pallido(-a)
pat [pæt] *vt* accarezzare, dare un colpetto (affettuoso) a ■ *n*: **a ~ of butter** un panetto di burro; **to give sb/o.s. a ~ on the back** (*fig*) congratularsi *or* compiacersi con qn/se stesso; **he knows it (off) ~**, (*US*) **he has it down ~** lo conosce *or* sa a menadito
patch [pætʃ] *n* (*of material*) toppa; (*spot*) macchia; (*of land*) pezzo ■ *vt* (*clothes*) rattoppare; **a bad ~** (*Brit*) un brutto periodo
▸ **patch up** *vt* rappezzare
patchwork ['pætʃwəːk] *n* patchwork *m*
patchy ['pætʃɪ] *adj* irregolare
pate [peɪt] *n*: **a bald ~** una testa pelata
pâté ['pæteɪ] *n* pâté *m inv*
patent ['peɪtnt] *n* brevetto ■ *vt* brevettare ■ *adj* patente, manifesto(-a)
patent leather *n* cuoio verniciato
patently ['peɪtntlɪ] *adv* palesemente
patent medicine *n* specialità *f inv* medicinale
patent office *n* ufficio brevetti
paternal [pə'təːnl] *adj* paterno(-a)
paternity [pə'təːnɪtɪ] *n* paternità
paternity suit *n* (*Law*) causa di riconoscimento della paternità
path [pɑːθ] *n* sentiero, viottolo; viale *m*; (*fig*) via, strada; (*of planet, missile*) traiettoria
pathetic [pə'θɛtɪk] *adj* (*pitiful*) patetico(-a); (*very bad*) penoso(-a)
pathological [pæθə'lɔdʒɪkl] *adj* patologico(-a)
pathologist [pə'θɔlədʒɪst] *n* patologo(-a)
pathology [pə'θɔlədʒɪ] *n* patologia
pathos ['peɪθɔs] *n* pathos *m*
pathway ['pɑːθweɪ] *n* sentiero, viottolo
patience ['peɪʃns] *n* pazienza; (*Brit Cards*) solitario; **to lose one's ~** spazientirsi
patient ['peɪʃnt] *n* paziente *m/f*; malato(-a) ■ *adj* paziente; **to be ~ with sb** essere paziente *or* aver pazienza con qn
patiently ['peɪʃntlɪ] *adv* pazientemente
patio ['pætɪəu] *n* terrazza

P

patriot ['peɪtrɪət] *n* patriota *m/f*
patriotic [pætrɪ'ɔtɪk] *adj* patriottico(-a)
patriotism ['pætrɪətɪzəm] *n* patriottismo
patrol [pə'trəul] *n* pattuglia ■ *vt* pattugliare; **to be on ~** fare la ronda; essere in ricognizione; essere in perlustrazione
patrol boat *n* guardacoste *m inv*
patrol car *n* autoradio *f inv* (della polizia)
patrolman [pə'trəulmən] *n* (*US*) poliziotto
patron ['peɪtrən] *n* (*in shop*) cliente *m/f*; (*of charity*) benefattore(-trice); **~ of the arts** mecenate *m/f*
patronage ['pætrənɪdʒ] *n* patronato
patronize ['pætrənaɪz] *vt* essere cliente abituale di; (*fig*) trattare con condiscendenza
patronizing ['pætrənaɪzɪŋ] *adj* condiscendente
patron saint *n* patrono
patter ['pætə[r]] *n* picchiettio; (*sales talk*) propaganda di vendita ■ *vi* picchiettare
pattern ['pætən] *n* modello; (*Sewing etc*) modello (di carta), cartamodello; (*design*) disegno, motivo; (*sample*) campione *m*; **behaviour patterns** tipi *mpl* di comportamento
patterned ['pætənd] *adj* a disegni, a motivi; (*material*) fantasia *inv*
paucity ['pɔːsɪtɪ] *n* scarsità
paunch [pɔːntʃ] *n* pancione *m*
pauper ['pɔːpə[r]] *n* indigente *m/f*; **~'s grave** fossa comune
pause [pɔːz] *n* pausa ■ *vi* fare una pausa, arrestarsi; **to ~ for breath** fermarsi un attimo per riprender fiato
pave [peɪv] *vt* pavimentare; **to ~ the way for** aprire la via a
pavement ['peɪvmənt] *n* (*Brit*) marciapiede *m*; (*US*) pavimentazione *f* stradale
pavilion [pə'vɪlɪən] *n* padiglione *m*; tendone *m*; (*Sport*) *edificio annesso ad un campo sportivo*
paving ['peɪvɪŋ] *n* pavimentazione *f*
paving stone *n* lastra di pietra
paw [pɔː] *n* zampa ■ *vt* dare una zampata a; (*person: pej*) palpare
pawn [pɔːn] *n* pegno; (*Chess*) pedone *m*; (*fig*) pedina ■ *vt* dare in pegno
pawnbroker ['pɔːnbrəukə[r]] *n* prestatore *m* su pegno
pawnshop ['pɔːnʃɔp] *n* monte *m* di pietà
pay [peɪ] *n* (*gen*) paga ■ *vb* (*pt, pp* **paid**) [peɪd] *vt* pagare; (*be profitable to: also fig*) convenire a ■ *vi* pagare; (*be profitable*) rendere; **to ~ attention (to)** fare attenzione (a); **I paid £5 for that record** quel disco l'ho pagato 5 sterline; **how much did you ~ for it?** quanto l'ha pagato?; **to ~ one's way** pagare la propria parte; (*company*) coprire le spese; **to ~ dividends** (*fig*) dare buoni frutti
▸ **pay back** *vt* rimborsare
▸ **pay for** *vt fus* pagare
▸ **pay in** *vt* versare
▸ **pay off** *vt* (*debts*) saldare; (*creditor*) pagare; (*mortgage*) estinguere; (*workers*) licenziare ■ *vi* (*scheme*) funzionare; (*patience*) dare dei frutti; **to ~ sth off in instalments** pagare qc a rate
▸ **pay out** *vt* (*money*) sborsare, tirar fuori; (*rope*) far allentare
▸ **pay up** *vt* saldare
payable ['peɪəbl] *adj* pagabile; **to make a cheque ~ to sb** intestare un assegno a (nome di) qn
pay-as-you-go ['peɪəzjə'gəu] *adj* (*mobile phone*) con scheda prepagata
pay award *n* aumento salariale
pay day *n* giorno di paga
PAYE *n abbr* (*Brit: = pay as you earn*) *pagamento di imposte tramite ritenute alla fonte*
payee [peɪ'iː] *n* beneficiario(-a)
pay envelope *n* (*US*) busta *f* paga *inv*
paying ['peɪɪŋ] *adj*: **~ guest** ospite *m/f* pagante, pensionante *m/f*
payload ['peɪləud] *n* carico utile
payment ['peɪmənt] *n* pagamento; **advance ~** (*part sum*) anticipo, acconto; (*total sum*) pagamento anticipato; **deferred ~, ~ by instalments** pagamento dilazionato *or* a rate; **in ~ for, in ~ of** in pagamento di; **on ~ of £5** dietro pagamento di 5 sterline
pay packet *n* (*Brit*) busta *f* paga *inv*
payphone ['peɪfəun] *n* cabina telefonica
payroll ['peɪrəul] *n* ruolo (organico); **to be on a firm's ~** far parte del personale di una ditta
pay slip *n* (*Brit*) foglio *m* paga *inv*
pay station *n* (*US*) cabina telefonica
PBS *n abbr* (*US: = Public Broadcasting Service*) *servizio che collabora alla realizzazione di programmi per la rete televisiva nazionale*
PBX *abbr* (*= private branch exchange*) *sistema telefonico con centralino*
PC *n abbr* = **personal computer**; (*Brit*) = **police constable** ■ *abbr* (*Brit*) = **Privy Councillor** ■ *adj abbr* = **politically correct**
pc *abbr* = **per cent**; (*= postcard*) C.P.
p/c *abbr* = **petty cash**
PCB *n abbr* = **printed circuit board**
pcm *abbr* = **per calendar month**
PD *n abbr* (*US*) = **police department**
pd *abbr* = **paid**
PDA *n abbr* (*= personal digital assistant*) PDA *m inv*
PDQ *abbr* (*col*) = **pretty damn quick**
PDSA *n abbr* (*Brit: = People's Dispensary for Sick Animals*) *assistenza veterinaria gratuita*
PDT *abbr* (*US: = Pacific Daylight Time*) *ora legale del Pacifico*

PE *n abbr* (= *physical education*) ed. fisica ■ *abbr* (*Canada*) = **Prince Edward Island**
pea [pi:] *n* pisello
peace [pi:s] *n* pace *f*; (*calm*) calma, tranquillità; **to be at ~ with sb/sth** essere in pace con qn/qc; **to keep the ~** (*policeman*) mantenere l'ordine pubblico; (*: citizen*) rispettare l'ordine pubblico
peaceable ['pi:səbl] *adj* pacifico(-a)
peaceful ['pi:sful] *adj* pacifico(-a), calmo(-a)
peacekeeping ['pi:ski:pɪŋ] *n* mantenimento della pace; **~ force** forza di pace
peace offering *n* (*fig*) dono in segno di riconciliazione
peach [pi:tʃ] *n* pesca
peacock ['pi:kɔk] *n* pavone *m*
peak [pi:k] *n* (*of mountain*) cima, vetta; (*mountain itself*) picco; (*fig*) massimo; (*: of career*) acme *f*
peak-hour ['pi:kauəʳ] *adj* (*traffic etc*) delle ore di punta
peak hours *npl* ore *fpl* di punta
peak period *n* periodo di punta
peak rate *n* tariffa massima
peaky ['pi:kɪ] *adj* (*Brit col*) sbattuto(-a)
peal [pi:l] *n* (*of bells*) scampanio, carillon *m inv*; **peals of laughter** scoppi *mpl* di risa
peanut ['pi:nʌt] *n* arachide *f*, nocciolina americana
peanut butter *n* burro di arachidi
pear [pɛəʳ] *n* pera
pearl [pə:l] *n* perla
peasant ['pɛznt] *n* contadino(-a)
peat [pi:t] *n* torba
pebble ['pɛbl] *n* ciottolo
peck [pɛk] *vt* (*also*: **peck at**) beccare; (*: food*) mangiucchiare ■ *n* colpo di becco; (*kiss*) bacetto
pecking order ['pɛkɪŋ-] *n* (*fig*) ordine *m* gerarchico
peckish ['pɛkɪʃ] *adj* (*Brit col*): **I feel ~** ho un languorino
peculiar [pɪ'kju:lɪəʳ] *adj* strano(-a), bizzarro(-a); (*particular: importance, qualities*) particolare; **~ to** tipico(-a) di, caratteristico(-a) di
peculiarity [pɪkju:lɪ'ærɪtɪ] *n* peculiarità *f inv*; (*oddity*) bizzarria
pecuniary [pɪ'kju:nɪərɪ] *adj* pecuniario(-a)
pedal ['pɛdl] *n* pedale *m* ■ *vi* pedalare
pedal bin *n* (*Brit*) pattumiera a pedale
pedantic [pɪ'dæntɪk] *adj* pedantesco(-a)
peddle ['pɛdl] *vt* (*goods*) andare in giro a vendere; (*drugs*) spacciare; (*gossip*) mettere in giro
peddler ['pɛdləʳ] *n* venditore *m* ambulante
pedestal ['pɛdəstl] *n* piedestallo
pedestrian [pɪ'dɛstrɪən] *n* pedone(-a) ■ *adj* pedonale; (*fig*) prosaico(-a), pedestre
pedestrian crossing *n* (*Brit*) passaggio pedonale
pedestrian mall *n* (*US*) zona pedonale
pedestrian precinct *n* (*Brit*) zona pedonale
pediatrics [pi:dɪ'ætrɪks] *n* (*US*) = **paediatrics**
pedigree ['pɛdɪgri:] *n* stirpe *f*; (*of animal*) pedigree *m inv* ■ *cpd* (*animal*) di razza
pedlar ['pɛdləʳ] *n* = **peddler**
pee [pi:] *vi* (*col*) pisciare
peek [pi:k] *vi* guardare furtivamente
peel [pi:l] *n* buccia; (*of orange, lemon*) scorza ■ *vt* sbucciare ■ *vi* (*paint etc*) staccarsi
▸ **peel back** *vt* togliere, levare
peeler [pi:ləʳ] *n*: **potato ~** sbucciapatate *m inv*
peelings ['pi:lɪŋz] *npl* bucce *fpl*
peep [pi:p] *n* (*Brit: look*) sguardo furtivo, sbirciata; (*sound*) pigolio ■ *vi* (*Brit*) guardare furtivamente
▸ **peep out** *vi* (*Brit*) mostrarsi furtivamente
peephole ['pi:phəul] *n* spioncino
peer [pɪəʳ] *vi*: **to ~ at** scrutare ■ *n* (*noble*) pari *m inv*; (*equal*) pari *m/f inv*, uguale *m/f*
peerage ['pɪərɪdʒ] *n* dignità di pari; pari *mpl*
peerless ['pɪəlɪs] *adj* impareggiabile, senza pari
peeved [pi:vd] *adj* stizzito(-a)
peevish ['pi:vɪʃ] *adj* stizzoso(-a)
peg [pɛg] *n* (*tent peg*) picchetto; (*for coat etc*) attaccapanni *m inv*; (*Brit: also*: **clothes peg**) molletta ■ *vt* (*clothes*) appendere con le mollette; (*Brit: groundsheet*) fissare con i picchetti; (*fig: prices, wages*) fissare, stabilizzare; **off the ~** confezionato(-a)
pejorative [pɪ'dʒɔrətɪv] *adj* peggiorativo(-a)
Pekin [pi:'kɪn], **Peking** [pi:'kɪŋ] *n* Pechino *f*
pekinese, pekingese [pi:kɪ'ni:z] *n* pechinese *m*
pelican ['pɛlɪkən] *n* pellicano
pelican crossing *n* (*Brit Aut*) *attraversamento pedonale con semaforo a controllo manuale*
pellet ['pɛlɪt] *n* pallottola, pallina
pell-mell ['pɛl'mɛl] *adv* disordinatamente, alla rinfusa
pelmet ['pɛlmɪt] *n* mantovana; cassonetto
pelt [pɛlt] *vt*: **to ~ sb (with)** bombardare qn (con) ■ *vi* (*rain*) piovere a dirotto ■ *n* pelle *f*
pelvis ['pɛlvɪs] *n* pelvi *f inv*, bacino
pen [pɛn] *n* penna; (*for sheep*) recinto; (*US col: prison*) galera; **to put ~ to paper** prendere la penna in mano
penal ['pi:nl] *adj* penale
penalize ['pi:nəlaɪz] *vt* punire; (*Sport*) penalizzare; (*fig*) svantaggiare

P

penal servitude [-'sə:vɪtju:d] *n* lavori *mpl* forzati
penalty ['pɛnltɪ] *n* penalità *f inv*; sanzione *f* penale; (*fine*) ammenda; (*Sport*) penalizzazione *f*; (*Football*: *also*: **penalty kick**) calcio di rigore
penalty area *n* (*Brit Sport*) area di rigore
penalty clause *n* penale *f*
penalty kick *n* (*Football*) calcio di rigore
penalty shoot-out [-'ʃu:taut] *n* (*Football*) rigori *mpl*; **to beat a team in a ~** battere una squadra ai rigori
penance ['pɛnəns] *n* penitenza
pence [pɛns] *npl* (*Brit*) *of* **penny**
penchant ['pɑ̃:ʃɑ̃:ŋ] *n* debole *m*
pencil ['pɛnsl] *n* matita ■ *vt* (*also*: **pencil in**) scrivere a matita
pencil case *n* astuccio per matite
pencil sharpener *n* temperamatite *m inv*
pendant ['pɛndnt] *n* pendaglio
pending ['pɛndɪŋ] *prep* in attesa di ■ *adj* in sospeso
pendulum ['pɛndjuləm] *n* pendolo
penetrate ['pɛnɪtreɪt] *vt* penetrare
penetrating ['pɛnɪtreɪtɪŋ] *adj* penetrante
penetration [pɛnɪ'treɪʃən] *n* penetrazione *f*
penfriend ['pɛnfrɛnd] *n* (*Brit*) corrispondente *m/f*
penguin ['pɛŋgwɪn] *n* pinguino
penicillin [pɛnɪ'sɪlɪn] *n* penicillina
peninsula [pə'nɪnsjulə] *n* penisola
penis ['pi:nɪs] *n* pene *m*
penitence ['pɛnɪtns] *n* penitenza
penitent ['pɛnɪtnt] *adj* penitente
penitentiary [pɛnɪ'tɛnʃərɪ] *n* (*US*) carcere *m*
penknife ['pɛnnaɪf] *n* temperino
Penn., Penna. *abbr* (*US*) = **Pennsylvania**
pen name *n* pseudonimo
pennant ['pɛnənt] *n* banderuola
penniless ['pɛnɪlɪs] *adj* senza un soldo
Pennines ['pɛnaɪnz] *npl*: **the ~** i Pennini
penny (*pl* **pennies** *or* **pence**) ['pɛnɪ, 'pɛnɪz, pɛns] *n* penny *m* (*pl* = *pence*); (*US*) centesimo
penpal ['pɛnpæl] *n* corrispondente *m/f*
penpusher ['pɛnpuʃəʳ] *n* (*pej*) scribacchino(-a)
pension ['pɛnʃən] *n* pensione *f*
▸ **pension off** *vt* mandare in pensione
pensionable ['pɛnʃənəbl] *adj* (*person*) che ha diritto a una pensione, pensionabile; (*age*) pensionabile
pensioner ['pɛnʃənəʳ] *n* (*Brit*) pensionato(-a)
pension fund *n* fondo pensioni
pensive ['pɛnsɪv] *adj* pensoso(-a)
pentagon ['pɛntəgən] *n* pentagono; **the P~** (*US Pol*) il Pentagono; *vedi nota*

PENTAGON

Il *Pentagon* è un edificio a pianta pentagonale che si trova ad Arlington, in Virginia, nel quale hanno sede gli uffici del Ministero della Difesa degli Stati Uniti. Il termine "Pentagon" è usato anche per indicare la dirigenza militare del paese.

Pentecost ['pɛntɪkɔst] *n* Pentecoste *f*
penthouse ['pɛnthaus] *n* appartamento (di lusso) nell'attico
pent-up ['pɛntʌp] *adj* (*feelings*) represso(-a)
penultimate [pɪ'nʌltɪmət] *adj* penultimo(-a)
penury ['pɛnjurɪ] *n* indigenza
people ['pi:pl] *npl* gente *f*; persone *fpl*; (*citizens*) popolo ■ *n* (*nation, race*) popolo ■ *vt* popolare; **old ~** i vecchi; **young ~** i giovani; **~ at large** il grande pubblico; **a man of the ~** un uomo del popolo; **4/several ~ came** 4/ parecchie persone sono venute; **the room was full of ~** la stanza era piena di gente; **~ say that ...** si dice *or* la gente dice che ...
PEP [pɛp] *n abbr* = **personal equity plan**
pep [pɛp] *n* (*col*) dinamismo
▸ **pep up** *vt* vivacizzare; (*food*) rendere più gustoso(-a)
pepper ['pɛpəʳ] *n* pepe *m*; (*vegetable*) peperone *m* ■ *vt* pepare
peppermint ['pɛpəmɪnt] *n* (*plant*) menta peperita; (*sweet*) pasticca di menta
pepperoni [pɛpə'rəunɪ] *n* salsiccia piccante
pepperpot ['pɛpəpɔt] *n* pepaiola
peptalk ['pɛptɔ:k] *n* (*col*) discorso di incoraggiamento
per [pə:ʳ] *prep* per; a; **~ hour** all'ora; **~ kilo** *etc* il chilo *etc*; **~ day** al giorno; **~ week** alla settimana; **~ person** a testa, a *or* per persona; **as ~ your instructions** secondo le vostre istruzioni
per annum *adv* all'anno
per capita *adj, adv* pro capite
perceive [pə'si:v] *vt* percepire; (*notice*) accorgersi di
per cent *adv* per cento; **a 20 ~ discount** uno sconto del 20 per cento
percentage [pə'sɛntɪdʒ] *n* percentuale *f*; **on a ~ basis** a percentuale
percentage point *n* punto percentuale
perceptible [pə'sɛptɪbl] *adj* percettibile
perception [pə'sɛpʃən] *n* percezione *f*; sensibilità; perspicacia
perceptive [pə'sɛptɪv] *adj* percettivo(-a); perspicace
perch [pə:tʃ] *n* (*fish*) pesce *m* persico; (*for bird*) sostegno, ramo ■ *vi* appollaiarsi

percolate ['pəːkəleɪt] *vt* filtrare
percolator ['pəːkəleɪtəʳ] *n* caffettiera a pressione; caffettiera elettrica
percussion [pə'kʌʃən] *n* percussione *f*; (*Mus*) strumenti *mpl* a percussione
peremptory [pə'rɛmptərɪ] *adj* perentorio(-a)
perennial [pə'rɛnɪəl] *adj* perenne ■ *n* pianta perenne
perfect ['pəːfɪkt] *adj* perfetto(-a) ■ *n* (*also*: **perfect tense**) perfetto, passato prossimo ■ *vt* [pə'fɛkt] perfezionare; mettere a punto; **he's a ~ stranger to me** mi è completamente sconosciuto
perfection [pə'fɛkʃən] *n* perfezione *f*
perfectionist [pə'fɛkʃənɪst] *n* perfezionista *m/f*
perfectly ['pəːfɪktlɪ] *adv* perfettamente; **I'm ~ happy with the situation** sono completamente soddisfatta della situazione; **you know ~ well** sa benissimo
perforate ['pəːfəreɪt] *vt* perforare
perforated ulcer ['pəːfəreɪtɪd-] *n* (*Med*) ulcera perforata
perforation [pəːfə'reɪʃən] *n* perforazione *f*; (*line of holes*) dentellatura
perform [pə'fɔːm] *vt* (*carry out*) eseguire, fare; (*symphony etc*) suonare; (*play, ballet*) dare; (*opera*) fare ■ *vi* suonare; recitare
performance [pə'fɔːməns] *n* esecuzione *f*; (*at theatre etc*) rappresentazione *f*, spettacolo; (*of an artist*) interpretazione *f*; (*of player etc*) performance *f*; (*of car, engine*) prestazione *f*; **the team put up a good ~** la squadra ha giocato una bella partita
performer [pə'fɔməʳ] *n* artista *m/f*
performing [pə'fɔːmɪŋ] *adj* (*animal*) ammaestrato(-a)
performing arts *npl*: **the ~** le arti dello spettacolo
perfume ['pəːfjuːm] *n* profumo ■ *vt* profumare
perfunctory [pə'fʌŋktərɪ] *adj* superficiale, per la forma
perhaps [pə'hæps] *adv* forse; **~ he'll come** forse verrà, può darsi che venga; **~ so/not** forse sì/no, può darsi di sì/di no
peril ['pɛrɪl] *n* pericolo
perilous ['pɛrɪləs] *adj* pericoloso(-a)
perilously ['pɛrɪləslɪ] *adv*: **they came ~ close to being caught** sono stati a un pelo dall'esser presi
perimeter [pə'rɪmɪtəʳ] *n* perimetro
perimeter wall *n* muro di cinta
period ['pɪərɪəd] *n* periodo; (*Hist*) epoca; (*Scol*) lezione *f*; (*full stop*) punto; (*US Football*) tempo; (*Med*) mestruazioni *fpl* ■ *adj* (*costume, furniture*) d'epoca; **for a ~ of three weeks** per un periodo di *or* per la durata di tre settimane; **the holiday ~** (*Brit*) il periodo delle vacanze
periodic [pɪərɪ'ɔdɪk] *adj* periodico(-a)
periodical [pɪərɪ'ɔdɪkl] *adj* periodico(-a) ■ *n* periodico
periodically [pɪərɪ'ɔdɪklɪ] *adv* periodicamente
period pains *npl* (*Brit*) dolori *mpl* mestruali
peripatetic [pɛrɪpə'tɛtɪk] *adj* (*salesman*) ambulante; (*Brit*: *teacher*) peripatetico(-a)
peripheral [pə'rɪfərəl] *adj* periferico(-a) ■ *n* (*Comput*) unità *f inv* periferica
periphery [pə'rɪfərɪ] *n* periferia
periscope ['pɛrɪskəup] *n* periscopio
perish ['pɛrɪʃ] *vi* perire, morire; (*decay*) deteriorarsi
perishable ['pɛrɪʃəbl] *adj* deperibile
perishables ['pɛrɪʃəblz] *npl* merci *fpl* deperibili
perishing ['pɛrɪʃɪŋ] *adj* (*Brit col*): **it's ~ (cold)** fa un freddo da morire
peritonitis [pɛrɪtə'naɪtɪs] *n* peritonite *f*
perjure ['pəːdʒəʳ] *vt*: **to ~ o.s.** spergiurare
perjury ['pəːdʒərɪ] *n* (*Law*: *in court*) falso giuramento; (*breach of oath*) spergiuro
perk [pəːk] *n* vantaggio
▸ **perk up** *vi* (*cheer up*) rianimarsi
perky ['pəːkɪ] *adj* (*cheerful*) vivace, allegro(-a)
perm [pəːm] *n* (*for hair*) permanente *f* ■ *vt*: **to have one's hair permed** farsi fare la permanente
permanence ['pəːmənəns] *n* permanenza
permanent ['pəːmənənt] *adj* permanente; (*job, position*) fisso(-a); (*dye, ink*) indelebile; **~ address** residenza fissa; **I'm not ~ here** non sono fisso qui
permanently ['pəːmənəntlɪ] *adv* definitivamente
permeable ['pəːmɪəbl] *adj* permeabile
permeate ['pəːmɪeɪt] *vi* penetrare ■ *vt* permeare
permissible [pə'mɪsɪbl] *adj* permissibile, ammissibile
permission [pə'mɪʃən] *n* permesso; **to give sb ~ to do sth** dare a qn il permesso di fare qc
permissive [pə'mɪsɪv] *adj* tollerante; **the ~ society** la società permissiva
permit *n* ['pəːmɪt] permesso; (*entrance pass*) lasciapassare *m* ■ *vt, vi* [pə'mɪt] permettere; **fishing ~** licenza di pesca; **to ~ sb to do** permettere a qn di fare, dare il permesso a qn di fare; **weather permitting** tempo permettendo
permutation [pəːmju'teɪʃən] *n* permutazione *f*
pernicious [pəː'nɪʃəs] *adj* pernicioso(-a), nocivo(-a)

P

pernickety [pəˈnɪkɪtɪ] *adj* (*col: person*) pignolo(-a); (*: task*) da certosino
perpendicular [pəːpənˈdɪkjuləʳ] *adj, n* perpendicolare (*f*)
perpetrate [ˈpəːpɪtreɪt] *vt* perpetrare, commettere
perpetual [pəˈpɛtjuəl] *adj* perpetuo(-a)
perpetuate [pəˈpɛtjueɪt] *vt* perpetuare
perpetuity [pəːpɪˈtjuːɪtɪ] *n*: **in ~** in perpetuo
perplex [pəˈplɛks] *vt* lasciare perplesso(-a)
perplexing [pəˈplɛksɪŋ] *adj* che lascia perplesso(-a)
perquisites [ˈpəːkwɪzɪts] *npl* (*also*: **perks**) benefici *mpl* collaterali
persecute [ˈpəːsɪkjuːt] *vt* perseguitare
persecution [pəːsɪˈkjuːʃən] *n* persecuzione *f*
perseverance [pəːsɪˈvɪərəns] *n* perseveranza
persevere [pəːsɪˈvɪəʳ] *vi* perseverare
Persia [ˈpəːʃə] *n* Persia
Persian [ˈpəːʃən] *adj* persiano(-a) ▪ *n* (*Ling*) persiano; **the (~) Gulf** il Golfo Persico
Persian cat *n* gatto persiano
persist [pəˈsɪst] *vi*: **to ~ (in doing)** persistere (nel fare); ostinarsi (a fare)
persistence [pəˈsɪstəns] *n* persistenza; ostinazione *f*
persistent [pəˈsɪstənt] *adj* persistente; ostinato(-a); (*lateness, rain*) continuo(-a); **~ offender** (*Law*) delinquente *m/f* abituale
persnickety [pəˈsnɪkɪtɪ] *adj* (*US col*) = **pernickety**
person [ˈpəːsn] *n* persona; **in ~** di *or* in persona, personalmente; **on** *or* **about one's ~** (*weapon*) su di sé; (*money*) con sé; **a ~ to ~ call** (*Tel*) una chiamata con preavviso
personable [ˈpəːsnəbl] *adj* di bell'aspetto
personal [ˈpəːsnl] *adj* personale; individuale; **~ belongings, ~ effects** oggetti *mpl* d'uso personale; **a ~ interview** un incontro privato
personal allowance *n* (*Tax*) quota del reddito non imponibile
personal assistant *n* segretaria personale
personal call *n* (*Tel*) chiamata con preavviso
personal column *n* messaggi *mpl* personali
personal computer *n* personal computer *m inv*
personal details *npl* dati *mpl* personali
personal equity plan *n* (*Finance*) *fondo di investimento azionario con agevolazioni fiscali destinato al piccolo risparmiatore*
personal identification number *n* (*Comput, Banking*) numero di codice segreto
personality [pəːsəˈnælɪtɪ] *n* personalità *f inv*
personally [ˈpəːsnəlɪ] *adv* personalmente
personal organizer *n* agenda; (*electronic*) agenda elettronica
personal property *n* beni *mpl* personali
personal stereo *n* walkman® *m inv*
personify [pəːˈsɔnɪfaɪ] *vt* personificare
personnel [pəːsəˈnɛl] *n* personale *m*
personnel department *n* ufficio del personale
personnel manager *n* direttore(-trice) del personale
perspective [pəˈspɛktɪv] *n* prospettiva; **to get sth into ~** ridimensionare qc
Perspex® [ˈpəːspɛks] *n* (*Brit*) *tipo di resina termoplastica*
perspicacity [pəːspɪˈkæsɪtɪ] *n* perspicacia
perspiration [pəːspɪˈreɪʃən] *n* traspirazione *f*, sudore *m*
perspire [pəˈspaɪəʳ] *vi* traspirare
persuade [pəˈsweɪd] *vt*: **to ~ sb to do sth** persuadere qn a fare qc; **to ~ sb of sth/that** persuadere qn di qc/che
persuasion [pəˈsweɪʒən] *n* persuasione *f*; (*creed*) convinzione *f*, credo
persuasive [pəˈsweɪsɪv] *adj* persuasivo(-a)
pert [pəːt] *adj* (*bold*) sfacciato(-a), impertinente; (*hat*) spiritoso(-a)
pertaining [pəːˈteɪnɪŋ]: **~ to** *prep* che riguarda
pertinent [ˈpəːtɪnənt] *adj* pertinente
perturb [pəˈtəːb] *vt* turbare
perturbing [pəˈtəːbɪŋ] *adj* inquietante
Peru [pəˈruː] *n* Perù *m*
perusal [pəˈruːzl] *n* attenta lettura
Peruvian [pəˈruːvjən] *adj, n* peruviano(-a)
pervade [pəˈveɪd] *vt* pervadere
pervasive [pəːˈveɪsɪv] *adj* (*smell*) penetrante; (*influence*) dilagante; (*gloom, feelings*) diffuso(-a)
perverse [pəˈvəːs] *adj* perverso(-a)
perversion [pəˈvəːʃən] *n* pervertimento, perversione *f*
perversity [pəˈvəːsɪtɪ] *n* perversità
pervert *n* [ˈpəːvəːt] pervertito(-a) ▪ *vt* [pəˈvəːt] pervertire
pessimism [ˈpɛsɪmɪzəm] *n* pessimismo
pessimist [ˈpɛsɪmɪst] *n* pessimista *m/f*
pessimistic [pɛsɪˈmɪstɪk] *adj* pessimistico(-a)
pest [pɛst] *n* animale *m* (*or* insetto) pestifero; (*fig*) peste *f*
pest control *n* disinfestazione *f*
pester [ˈpɛstəʳ] *vt* tormentare, molestare
pesticide [ˈpɛstɪsaɪd] *n* pesticida *m*
pestilence [ˈpɛstɪləns] *n* pestilenza
pestle [ˈpɛsl] *n* pestello
pet [pɛt] *n* animale *m* domestico; (*favourite*) favorito(-a) ▪ *vt* accarezzare ▪ *vi* (*col*) fare il petting; **~ lion** *etc* leone *m etc* ammaestrato
petal [ˈpɛtl] *n* petalo
peter [ˈpiːtəʳ]: **to ~ out** *vi* esaurirsi; estinguersi

petite [pə'ti:t] *adj* piccolo(-a) e aggraziato(-a)
petition [pə'tɪʃən] *n* petizione *f* ■ *vi* richiedere; **to ~ for divorce** presentare un'istanza di divorzio
pet name *n* (*Brit*) nomignolo
petrified ['pɛtrɪfaɪd] *adj* (*fig*) morto(-a) di paura
petrify ['pɛtrɪfaɪ] *vt* pietrificare; (*fig*) terrorizzare
petrochemical [pɛtrə'kɛmɪkl] *adj* petrolchimico(-a)
petrodollars ['pɛtrəudɔləz] *npl* petrodollari *mpl*
petrol ['pɛtrəl] *n* (*Brit*) benzina
petrol bomb *n* (*Brit*) (bottiglia) molotov *f inv*
petrol can *n* (*Brit*) tanica per benzina
petrol engine *n* (*Brit*) motore *m* a benzina
petroleum [pə'trəulɪəm] *n* petrolio
petroleum jelly *n* vaselina
petrol pump *n* (*Brit: in car, at garage*) pompa di benzina
petrol station *n* (*Brit*) stazione *f* di rifornimento
petrol tank *n* (*Brit*) serbatoio della benzina
petticoat ['pɛtɪkəut] *n* sottana
pettifogging ['pɛtɪfɔgɪŋ] *adj* cavilloso(-a)
pettiness ['pɛtɪnɪs] *n* meschinità
petty ['pɛtɪ] *adj* (*mean*) meschino(-a); (*unimportant*) insignificante
petty cash *n* piccola cassa
petty officer *n* sottufficiale *m* di marina
petulant ['pɛtjulənt] *adj* irritabile
pew [pju:] *n* panca (di chiesa)
pewter ['pju:tər] *n* peltro
Pfc *abbr* (*US Mil*) = **private first class**
PG *n abbr* (*Cine: = parental guidance*) *consenso dei genitori richiesto*
PG 13 *abbr* (*US: Cine: = Parental Guidance 13*) *vietato ai minori di 13 anni non accompagnati dai genitori*
PGA *n abbr* (*= Professional Golfers Association*) *associazione dei giocatori di golf professionisti*
PH *n abbr* (*US Mil: = Purple Heart*) *decorazione per ferite riportate in guerra*
PHA *n abbr* (*US: = Public Housing Administration*) *amministrazione per l'edilizia pubblica*
phallic ['fælɪk] *adj* fallico(-a)
phantom ['fæntəm] *n* fantasma *m*
Pharaoh ['fɛərəu] *n* faraone *m*
pharmaceutical [fɑ:mə'sju:tɪkl] *adj* farmaceutico(-a) ■ *n*: **pharmaceuticals** prodotti *mpl* farmaceutici
pharmacist ['fɑ:məsɪst] *n* farmacista *m/f*
pharmacy ['fɑ:məsɪ] *n* farmacia
phase [feɪz] *n* fase *f*, periodo ■ *vt*: **to ~ sth in/out** introdurre/eliminare qc progressivamente
PhD *n abbr* = **Doctor of Philosophy**
pheasant ['fɛznt] *n* fagiano
phenomenon (*pl* **phenomena**) [fə'nɔmɪnən, -nə] *n* fenomeno
phew [fju:] *excl* uff!
phial ['faɪəl] *n* fiala
philanderer [fɪ'lændərər] *n* donnaiolo
philanthropic [fɪlən'θrɔpɪk] *adj* filantropico(-a)
philanthropist [fɪ'lænθrəpɪst] *n* filantropo
philatelist [fɪ'lætəlɪst] *n* filatelico(-a)
philately [fɪ'lætəlɪ] *n* filatelia
Philippines ['fɪlɪpi:nz] *npl* (*also*: **Philippine Islands**): **the ~** le Filippine
philosopher [fɪ'lɔsəfər] *n* filosofo(-a)
philosophical [fɪlə'sɔfɪkl] *adj* filosofico(-a)
philosophy [fɪ'lɔsəfɪ] *n* filosofia
phlegm [flɛm] *n* flemma
phlegmatic [flɛg'mætɪk] *adj* flemmatico(-a)
phobia ['fəubjə] *n* fobia
phone [fəun] *n* telefono ■ *vt* telefonare a ■ *vi* telefonare; **to be on the ~** avere il telefono; (*be calling*) essere al telefono
▸ **phone back** *vt, vi* richiamare
phone book *n* guida del telefono, elenco telefonico
phone box, phone booth *n* cabina telefonica
phone call *n* telefonata
phonecard ['fəunkɑ:d] *n* scheda telefonica
phone-in ['fəunɪn] *n* (*Brit Radio, TV*) *trasmissione radiofonica o televisiva con intervento telefonico degli ascoltatori*
phone tapping [-tæpɪŋ] *n* intercettazioni *fpl* telefoniche
phonetics [fə'nɛtɪks] *n* fonetica
phoney ['fəunɪ] *adj* falso(-a), fasullo(-a) ■ *n* (*person*) ciarlatano
phonograph ['fəunəgrɑ:f] *n* (*US*) giradischi *m inv*
phony ['fəunɪ] *adj, n* = **phoney**
phosphate ['fɔsfeɪt] *n* fosfato
phosphorus ['fɔsfərəs] *n* fosforo
photo ['fəutəu] *n* foto *f inv*
photo... ['fəutəu] *prefix* foto...
photocall ['fəutəukɔ:l] *n convocazione di fotoreporter a scopo pubblicitario*
photocopier ['fəutəukɔpɪər] *n* fotocopiatrice *f*
photocopy ['fəutəukɔpɪ] *n* fotocopia ■ *vt* fotocopiare
photoelectric [fəutəuɪ'lɛktrɪk] *adj*: **~ cell** cellula fotoelettrica
Photofit® ['fəutəufɪt] *n* photofit *m inv*
photogenic [fəutəu'dʒɛnɪk] *adj* fotogenico(-a)
photograph ['fəutəgræf] *n* fotografia ■ *vt* fotografare; **to take a ~ of sb** fare una fotografia a *or* fotografare qn

P

photographer [fəˈtɔgrəfəʳ] *n* fotografo
photographic [fəutəˈgræfɪk] *adj* fotografico(-a)
photography [fəˈtɔgrəfɪ] *n* fotografia
photo opportunity *n opportunità di scattare delle foto ad un personaggio importante*
Photostat® [ˈfəutəustæt] *n* fotocopia
photosynthesis [fəutəuˈsɪnθəsɪs] *n* fotosintesi *f*
phrase [freɪz] *n* espressione *f*; (*Ling*) locuzione *f*; (*Mus*) frase *f* ■ *vt* esprimere; (*letter*) redigere
phrasebook [ˈfreɪzbuk] *n* vocabolarietto
physical [ˈfɪzɪkl] *adj* fisico(-a); **~ examination** visita medica; **~ education** educazione *f* fisica; **~ exercises** ginnastica
physically [fɪzɪklɪ] *adv* fisicamente
physician [fɪˈzɪʃən] *n* medico
physicist [ˈfɪzɪsɪst] *n* fisico
physics [ˈfɪzɪks] *n* fisica
physiological [fɪzɪəˈlɔdʒɪkəl] *adj* fisiologico(-a)
physiology [fɪzɪˈɔlədʒɪ] *n* fisiologia
physiotherapist [fɪzɪəuˈθɛrəpɪst] *n* fisioterapista *m/f*
physiotherapy [fɪzɪəuˈθɛrəpɪ] *n* fisioterapia
physique [fɪˈziːk] *n* fisico
pianist [ˈpiːənɪst] *n* pianista *m/f*
piano [pɪˈænəu] *n* pianoforte *m*
piano accordion *n* (*Brit*) fisarmonica (a tastiera)
piccolo [ˈpɪkələu] *n* ottavino
pick [pɪk] *n* (*tool: also*: **pick-axe**) piccone *m* ■ *vt* scegliere; (*gather*) cogliere; (*scab, spot*) grattarsi ■ *vi*: **to ~ and choose** scegliere con cura; **take your ~** scelga; **the ~ of** il fior fiore di; **to ~ one's nose** mettersi le dita nel naso; **to ~ one's teeth** stuzzicarsi i denti; **to ~ sb's brains** farsi dare dei suggerimenti da qn; **to ~ pockets** borseggiare; **to ~ a fight/quarrel with sb** attaccar rissa/briga con qn; **to ~ one's way through** attraversare stando ben attento a dove mettere i piedi
▸ **pick off** *vt* (*kill*) abbattere
▸ **pick on** *vt fus* (*person*) avercela con
▸ **pick out** *vt* scegliere; (*distinguish*) distinguere
▸ **pick up** *vi* (*improve*) migliorarsi ■ *vt* raccogliere; (*collect*) passare a prendere; (*Aut: give lift to*) far salire; (*learn*) imparare; (*Radio, TV, Tel*) captare; **to ~ o.s. up** rialzarsi; **to ~ up where one left off** riprendere dal punto in cui ci si era fermati; **to ~ up speed** acquistare velocità
pickaxe, (*US*) **pickax** [ˈpɪkæks] *n* piccone *m*
picket [ˈpɪkɪt] *n* (*in strike*) scioperante *m/f* che fa parte di un picchetto; picchetto ■ *vt* picchettare
picket line *n* cordone *m* degli scioperanti
pickings [ˈpɪkɪŋz] *npl* (*pilferings*): **there are good ~ to be had here** qui ci sono buone possibilità di intascare qualcosa sottobanco
pickle [ˈpɪkl] *n* (*also*: **pickles**: *as condiment*) sottaceti *mpl*; (*fig*): **in a ~** nei pasticci ■ *vt* mettere sottaceto; mettere in salamoia
pick-me-up [ˈpɪkmiːʌp] *n* tiramisù *m inv*
pickpocket [ˈpɪkpɔkɪt] *n* borsaiolo
pickup [ˈpɪkʌp] *n* (*Brit: on record player*) pick-up *m inv*; (*small truck: also*: **pickup truck**, **pickup van**) camioncino
picnic [ˈpɪknɪk] *n* picnic *m inv* ■ *vi* fare un picnic
picnicker [ˈpɪknɪkəʳ] *n* chi partecipa a un picnic
pictorial [pɪkˈtɔːrɪəl] *adj* illustrato(-a)
picture [ˈpɪktʃəʳ] *n* quadro; (*painting*) pittura; (*photograph*) foto(grafia); (*drawing*) disegno; (*TV*) immagine *f*; (*film*) film *m inv* ■ *vt* raffigurarsi; **the pictures** (*Brit*) il cinema; **to take a ~ of sb/sth** fare una foto a qn/di qc; **we get a good ~ here** (*TV*) la ricezione qui è buona; **the overall ~** il quadro generale; **to put sb in the ~** mettere qn al corrente
picture book *n* libro illustrato
picture messaging *n* picture messaging *m*, invio di messaggini con disegni
picturesque [pɪktʃəˈrɛsk] *adj* pittoresco(-a)
picture window *n* finestra panoramica
piddling [ˈpɪdlɪŋ] *adj* (*col*) insignificante
pidgin English [ˈpɪdʒɪn-] *n inglese semplificato misto ad elementi indigeni*
pie [paɪ] *n* torta; (*of meat*) pasticcio
piebald [ˈpaɪbɔːld] *adj* pezzato(-a)
piece [piːs] *n* pezzo; (*of land*) appezzamento; (*Draughts etc*) pedina; (*item*): **a ~ of furniture/advice** un mobile/consiglio ■ *vt*: **to ~ together** mettere insieme; **in pieces** (*broken*) in pezzi; (*not yet assembled*) smontato(-a); **to take to pieces** smontare; **~ by ~** poco alla volta; **a 10p ~** (*Brit*) una moneta da 10 pence; **a six-~ band** un complesso di sei strumentisti; **in one ~** (*object*) intatto; **to get back all in one ~** (*person*) tornare a casa incolume *or* sano e salvo; **to say one's ~** dire la propria
piecemeal [ˈpiːsmiːl] *adv* pezzo a pezzo, a spizzico
piece rate *n* tariffa a cottimo
piecework [ˈpiːswəːk] *n* (lavoro a) cottimo
pie chart *n* grafico a torta
Piedmont [ˈpiːdmɔnt] *n* Piemonte *m*
pier [pɪəʳ] *n* molo; (*of bridge etc*) pila
pierce [pɪəs] *vt* forare; (*with arrow etc*) trafiggere; **to have one's ears pierced** farsi fare i buchi per gli orecchini

piercing ['pɪəsɪŋ] *adj* (*cry*) acuto(-a)
piety ['paɪətɪ] *n* pietà, devozione *f*
piffling ['pɪflɪŋ] *adj* insignificante
pig [pɪg] *n* maiale *m*, porco
pigeon ['pɪdʒən] *n* piccione *m*
pigeonhole ['pɪdʒənhəul] *n* casella ■ *vt* classificare
pigeon-toed ['pɪdʒən'təud] *adj* che cammina con i piedi in dentro
piggy bank ['pɪgɪ-] *n* salvadanaio
pigheaded [pɪg'hɛdɪd] *adj* caparbio(-a), cocciuto(-a)
piglet ['pɪglɪt] *n* porcellino
pigment ['pɪgmənt] *n* pigmento
pigmentation [pɪgmən'teɪʃən] *n* pigmentazione *f*
pigmy ['pɪgmɪ] *n* = **pygmy**
pigskin ['pɪgskɪn] *n* cinghiale *m*
pigsty ['pɪgstaɪ] *n* porcile *m*
pigtail ['pɪgteɪl] *n* treccina
pike [paɪk] *n* (*spear*) picca; (*fish*) luccio
pilchard ['pɪltʃəd] *n* *specie di sardina*
pile [paɪl] *n* (*pillar, of books*) pila; (*heap*) mucchio; (*of carpet*) pelo ■ *vb* (*also*: **pile up**) *vt* ammucchiare ■ *vi* ammucchiarsi; **in a ~** ammucchiato; *see also* **piles**
▸ **pile on** *vt*: **to ~ it on** (*col*) esagerare, drammatizzare
piles [paɪlz] *npl* (*Med*) emorroidi *fpl*
pileup ['paɪlʌp] *n* (*Aut*) tamponamento a catena
pilfer ['pɪlfə^r] *vt* rubacchiare ■ *vi* fare dei furtarelli
pilfering ['pɪlfərɪŋ] *n* rubacchiare *m*
pilgrim ['pɪlgrɪm] *n* pellegrino(-a)
pilgrimage ['pɪlgrɪmɪdʒ] *n* pellegrinaggio
pill [pɪl] *n* pillola; **to be on the ~** prendere la pillola
pillage ['pɪlɪdʒ] *vt* saccheggiare
pillar ['pɪlə^r] *n* colonna
pillar box *n* (*Brit*) cassetta delle lettere (a colonnina)
pillion ['pɪljən] *n* (*of motor cycle*) sellino posteriore; **to ride ~** viaggiare dietro
pillory ['pɪlərɪ] *n* berlina ■ *vt* mettere alla berlina
pillow ['pɪləu] *n* guanciale *m*
pillowcase ['pɪləukeɪs], **pillowslip** ['pɪləuslɪp] *n* federa
pilot ['paɪlət] *n* pilota *m/f* ■ *cpd* (*scheme etc*) pilota *inv* ■ *vt* pilotare
pilot boat *n* pilotina
pilot light *n* fiammella di sicurezza
pimento [pɪ'mɛntəu] *n* peperoncino
pimp [pɪmp] *n* mezzano
pimple ['pɪmpl] *n* foruncolo
pimply ['pɪmplɪ] *adj* foruncoloso(-a)

PIN *n abbr* = **personal identification number**
pin [pɪn] *n* spillo; (*Tech*) perno; (*Brit: drawing pin*) puntina da disegno; (*Brit Elec: of plug*) spinotto ■ *vt* attaccare con uno spillo; **pins and needles** formicolio; **to ~ sb against/to** inchiodare qn contro/a; **to ~ sth on sb** (*fig*) addossare la colpa di qc a qn
▸ **pin down** *vt* (*fig*): **to ~ sb down** obbligare qn a pronunziarsi; **there's something strange here but I can't quite ~ it down** c'è qualcosa di strano qua ma non riesco a capire cos'è
pinafore ['pɪnəfɔː^r] *n* grembiule *m* (senza maniche)
pinafore dress *n* scamiciato
pinball ['pɪnbɔːl] *n* flipper *m inv*
pincers ['pɪnsəz] *npl* pinzette *fpl*
pinch [pɪntʃ] *n* pizzicotto, pizzico ■ *vt* pizzicare; (*col: steal*) grattare ■ *vi* (*shoe*) stringere; **at a ~** in caso di bisogno; **to feel the ~** (*fig*) trovarsi nelle ristrettezze
pinched [pɪntʃt] *adj* (*drawn*) dai lineamenti tirati; (*short*): **~ for money/space** a corto di soldi/di spazio; **~ with cold** raggrinzito dal freddo
pincushion ['pɪnkuʃən] *n* puntaspilli *m inv*
pine [paɪn] *n* (*also*: **pine tree**) pino ■ *vi*: **to ~ for** struggersi dal desiderio di
▸ **pine away** *vi* languire
pineapple ['paɪnæpl] *n* ananas *m inv*
pine cone *n* pigna
pine needles *npl* aghi *mpl* di pino
ping [pɪŋ] *n* (*noise*) tintinnio
Ping-Pong® ['pɪŋpɔŋ] *n* ping-pong® *m*
pink [pɪŋk] *adj* rosa *inv* ■ *n* (*colour*) rosa *m inv*; (*Bot*) garofano
pinking shears ['pɪŋkɪŋ-] *n* forbici *fpl* a zigzag
pin money *n* (*Brit*) denaro per le piccole spese
pinnacle ['pɪnəkl] *n* pinnacolo
pinpoint ['pɪnpɔɪnt] *vt* indicare con precisione
pinstripe ['pɪnstraɪp] *n* stoffa gessata; (*also*: **pinstripe suit**) gessato
pint [paɪnt] *n* pinta (*Brit* = 0.57 *l*; *US* = 0.47 *l*); (*Brit col: of beer*) ≈ birra piccola
pinup ['pɪnʌp] *n* pin-up girl *f inv*
pioneer [paɪə'nɪə^r] *n* pioniere(-a) ■ *vt* essere un pioniere in
pious ['paɪəs] *adj* pio(-a)
pip [pɪp] *n* (*seed*) seme *m*; (*time signal on radio*) segnale *m* orario
pipe [paɪp] *n* tubo; (*for smoking*) pipa; (*Mus*) piffero ■ *vt* portare per mezzo di tubazione; **pipes** *npl* (*also*: **bagpipes**) cornamusa (scozzese)
▸ **pipe down** *vi* (*col*) calmarsi

P

pipe cleaner *n* scovolino
piped music [paɪpt-] *n* musica di sottofondo
pipe dream *n* vana speranza
pipeline ['paɪplaɪn] *n* conduttura; (*for oil*) oleodotto; (*for natural gas*) metanodotto; **it is in the ~** (*fig*) è in arrivo
piper ['paɪpə^r] *n* piffero; suonatore(-trice) di cornamusa
pipe tobacco *n* tabacco da pipa
piping ['paɪpɪŋ] *adv*: **~ hot** bollente
piquant ['pi:kənt] *adj* (*sauce*) piccante; (*conversation*) stimolante
pique [pi:k] *n* picca
piracy ['paɪərəsɪ] *n* pirateria
pirate ['paɪərət] *n* pirata *m* ▪ *vt* (*record, video, book*) riprodurre abusivamente
pirate radio *n* (*Brit*) radio pirata *f inv*
pirouette [pɪru'ɛt] *n* piroetta ▪ *vi* piroettare
Pisces ['paɪsi:z] *n* Pesci *mpl*; **to be ~** essere dei Pesci
piss [pɪs] *vi* (*col!*) pisciare; **~ off!** vaffanculo! (*!*)
pissed [pɪst] *adj* (*Brit col: drunk*) ubriaco(-a) fradicio(-a)
pistol ['pɪstl] *n* pistola
piston ['pɪstən] *n* pistone *m*
pit [pɪt] *n* buca, fossa; (*also*: **coal pit**) miniera; (*also*: **orchestra pit**) orchestra ▪ *vt*: **to ~ sb against sb** opporre qn a qn; **pits** *npl* (*Aut*) box *m*; **to ~ o.s. against** opporsi a
pitapat ['pɪtə'pæt] *adv* (*Brit*): **to go ~** (*heart*) palpitare, battere forte; (*rain*) picchiettare
pitch [pɪtʃ] *n* (*throw*) lancia; (*Mus*) tono; (*of voice*) altezza; (*fig: degree*) grado, punto; (*also*: **sales pitch**) discorso di vendita, imbonimento; (*Brit Sport*) campo; (*Naut*) beccheggio; (*tar*) pece *f* ▪ *vt* (*throw*) lanciare ▪ *vi* (*fall*) cascare; (*Naut*) beccheggiare; **to ~ a tent** piantare una tenda; **at this ~** a questo ritmo
pitch-black [pɪtʃ'blæk] *adj* nero(-a) come la pece
pitched battle [pɪtʃt-] *n* battaglia campale
pitcher ['pɪtʃə^r] *n* brocca
pitchfork ['pɪtʃfɔ:k] *n* forcone *m*
piteous ['pɪtɪəs] *adj* pietoso(-a)
pitfall ['pɪtfɔ:l] *n* trappola
pith [pɪθ] *n* (*of plant*) midollo; (*of orange*) parte *f* interna della scorza; (*fig*) essenza, succo; vigore *m*
pithead ['pɪthɛd] *n* (*Brit*) imbocco della miniera
pithy ['pɪθɪ] *adj* conciso(-a); vigoroso(-a)
pitiable ['pɪtɪəbl] *adj* pietoso(-a)
pitiful ['pɪtɪful] *adj* (*touching*) pietoso(-a); (*contemptible*) miserabile
pitifully ['pɪtɪfəlɪ] *adv* pietosamente; **it's ~ obvious** è penosamente chiaro
pitiless ['pɪtɪlɪs] *adj* spietato(-a)
pittance ['pɪtns] *n* miseria, magro salario
pitted ['pɪtɪd] *adj*: **~ with** (*potholes*) pieno(-a) di; (*chickenpox*) butterato(-a) da
pity ['pɪtɪ] *n* pietà ▪ *vt* aver pietà di, compatire, commiserare; **to have** *or* **take ~ on sb** aver pietà di qn; **it is a ~ that you can't come** è un peccato che non possa venire; **what a ~!** che peccato!
pitying ['pɪtɪɪŋ] *adj* compassionevole
pivot ['pɪvət] *n* perno ▪ *vi* imperniarsi
pixel ['pɪksl] *n* (*Comput*) pixel *m inv*
pixie ['pɪksɪ] *n* folletto
pizza ['pi:tsə] *n* pizza
placard ['plækɑ:d] *n* affisso
placate [plə'keɪt] *vt* placare, calmare
placatory [plə'keɪtərɪ] *adj* conciliante
place [pleɪs] *n* posto, luogo; (*proper position, rank, seat*) posto; (*house*) casa, alloggio; (*home*): **at/to his ~** a casa sua; (*in street names*): **Laurel P~** via dei Lauri ▪ *vt* (*object*) posare, mettere; (*identify*) riconoscere; individuare; (*goods*) piazzare; **to take ~** aver luogo; succedere; **out of ~** (*not suitable*) inopportuno(-a); **I feel rather out of ~ here** qui mi sento un po' fuori posto; **in the first ~** in primo luogo; **to change places with sb** scambiare il posto con qn; **to put sb in his ~** (*fig*) mettere a posto qn, mettere qn al suo posto; **from ~ to ~** da un posto all'altro; **all over the ~** dappertutto; **he's going places** (*fig, col*) si sta facendo strada; **it is not my ~ to do it** non sta a me farlo; **how are you placed next week?** com'è messo la settimana prossima?; **to ~ an order with sb (for)** (*Comm*) fare un'ordinazione a qn (di)
placebo [plə'si:bəu] *n* placebo *m inv*
place mat *n* sottopiatto; (*in linen etc*) tovaglietta
placement ['pleɪsmənt] *n* collocamento; (*job*) lavoro
place name *n* toponimo
placenta [plə'sɛntə] *n* placenta
placid ['plæsɪd] *adj* placido(-a), calmo(-a)
placidity [plə'sɪdɪtɪ] *n* placidità
plagiarism ['pleɪdʒjərɪzəm] *n* plagio
plagiarist ['pleɪdʒjərɪst] *n* plagiario(-a)
plagiarize ['pleɪdʒjəraɪz] *vt* plagiare
plague [pleɪg] *n* peste *f* ▪ *vt* tormentare; **to ~ sb with questions** assillare qn di domande
plaice [pleɪs] *n* (*pl inv*) pianuzza
plaid [plæd] *n* plaid *m inv*
plain [pleɪn] *adj* (*clear*) chiaro(-a), palese; (*simple*) semplice; (*frank*) franco(-a), aperto(-a); (*not handsome*) bruttino(-a); (*without seasoning etc*) scondito(-a); naturale; (*in one colour*) tinta unita *inv* ▪ *adv* francamente, chiaramente ▪ *n* pianura;

to make sth ~ to sb far capire chiaramente qc a qn; **in ~ clothes** (*police*) in borghese
plain chocolate *n* cioccolato fondente
plainly ['pleɪnlɪ] *adv* chiaramente; (*frankly*) francamente
plainness ['pleɪnnɪs] *n* semplicità
plain speaking *n*: **there has been some ~ between the two leaders** i due leader si sono parlati chiaro
plaintiff ['pleɪntɪf] *n* attore(-trice)
plaintive ['pleɪntɪv] *adj* (*voice, song*) lamentoso(-a); (*look*) struggente
plait [plæt] *n* treccia ▪ *vt* intrecciare; **to ~ one's hair** farsi una treccia (*or* le trecce)
plan [plæn] *n* pianta; (*scheme*) progetto, piano ▪ *vt* (*think in advance*) progettare; (*prepare*) organizzare; (*intend*) avere in progetto ▪ *vi*: **to ~ (for)** far piani *or* progetti (per); **to ~ to do** progettare di fare, avere l'intenzione di fare; **how long do you ~ to stay?** quanto conta di restare?
plane [pleɪn] *n* (*Aviat*) aereo; (*tree*) platano; (*tool*) pialla; (*Art, Math etc*) piano ▪ *adj* piano(-a), piatto(-a) ▪ *vt* (*with tool*) piallare
planet ['plænɪt] *n* pianeta *m*
planetarium [plænɪ'tɛərɪəm] *n* planetario
plank [plæŋk] *n* tavola, asse *f*
plankton ['plæŋktən] *n* plancton *m*
planned economy [plænd-] *n* economia pianificata
planner ['plænə^r] *n* pianificatore(-trice); (*chart*) calendario; **town** *or* (*US*) **city ~** urbanista *m/f*
planning ['plænɪŋ] *n* progettazione *f*; (*Pol, Econ*) pianificazione *f*; **family ~** pianificazione delle nascite
planning permission *n* (*Brit*) permesso di costruzione
plant [plɑːnt] *n* pianta; (*machinery*) impianto; (*factory*) fabbrica ▪ *vt* piantare; (*bomb*) mettere
plantation [plæn'teɪʃən] *n* piantagione *f*
plant pot *n* (*Brit*) vaso (di fiori)
plaque [plæk] *n* placca
plasma ['plæzmə] *n* plasma *m*
plasma TV *n* TV *f inv* al plasma
plaster ['plɑːstə^r] *n* intonaco; (*also*: **plaster of Paris**) gesso; (*Brit*: *also*: **sticking plaster**) cerotto ▪ *vt* intonacare; ingessare; (*cover*): **to ~ with** coprire di; (*col*: *mud etc*) impiastricciare; **in ~** (*Brit*: *leg etc*) ingessato(-a)
plasterboard ['plɑːstəbɔːd] *n* lastra di cartone ingessato
plaster cast *n* (*Med*) ingessatura, gesso; (*model, statue*) modello in gesso
plastered ['plɑːstəd] *adj* (*col*) ubriaco(-a) fradicio(-a)
plasterer ['plɑːstərə^r] *n* intonacatore *m*
plastic ['plæstɪk] *n* plastica ▪ *adj* (*made of plastic*) di *or* in plastica; (*flexible*) plastico(-a), malleabile; (*art*) plastico(-a)
plastic bag *n* sacchetto di plastica
plastic bullet *n* pallottola di plastica
plastic explosive *n* esplosivo al plastico
plasticine® ['plæstɪsiːn] *n* plastilina®
plastic surgery *n* chirurgia plastica
plate [pleɪt] *n* (*dish*) piatto; (*sheet of metal*) lamiera; (*Phot*) lastra; (*Typ*) cliché *m inv*; (*in book*) tavola; (*on door*) targa, targhetta; (*Aut*: *number plate*) targa; (*dishes*): **gold ~** vasellame *m* d'oro; **silver ~** argenteria
plateau (*pl* **plateaus** *or* **plateaux**) ['plætəu, -z] *n* altipiano
plateful ['pleɪtful] *n* piatto
plate glass *n* vetro piano
platen ['plætən] *n* (*on typewriter, printer*) rullo
plate rack *n* scolapiatti *m inv*
platform ['plætfɔːm] *n* (*stage, at meeting*) palco; (*Brit*: *on bus*) piattaforma; (*Rail*) marciapiede *m*; **the train leaves from ~ 7** il treno parte dal binario 7
platform ticket *n* (*Brit*) biglietto d'ingresso ai binari
platinum ['plætɪnəm] *n* platino
platitude ['plætɪtjuːd] *n* luogo comune
platoon [plə'tuːn] *n* plotone *m*
platter ['plætə^r] *n* piatto
plaudits ['plɔːdɪts] *npl* plauso
plausible ['plɔːzɪbl] *adj* plausibile, credibile; (*person*) convincente
play [pleɪ] *n* gioco; (*Theat*) commedia ▪ *vt* (*game*) giocare a; (*team, opponent*) giocare contro; (*instrument, piece of music*) suonare; (*play, part*) interpretare ▪ *vi* giocare; suonare; recitare; **to bring** *or* **call into ~** (*plan*) mettere in azione; (*emotions*) esprimere; **~ on words** gioco di parole; **to ~ a trick on sb** fare uno scherzo a qn; **they're playing at soldiers** stanno giocando ai soldati; **to ~ for time** (*fig*) cercare di guadagnar tempo; **to ~ into sb's hands** (*fig*) fare il gioco di qn
▸ **play about, play around** *vi* (*person*) divertirsi; **to ~ about** *or* **around with** (*fiddle with*) giocherellare con; (*idea*) accarezzare
▸ **play along** *vi*: **to ~ along with** (*fig*: *person*) stare al gioco di; (: *plan, idea*) fingere di assecondare ▪ *vt* (*fig*): **to ~ sb along** tenere qn in sospeso
▸ **play back** *vt* riascoltare, risentire
▸ **play down** *vt* minimizzare
▸ **play on** *vt fus* (*sb's feelings, credulity*) giocare su; **to ~ on sb's nerves** dare sui nervi a qn
▸ **play up** *vi* (*cause trouble*) fare i capricci
playact ['pleɪækt] *vi* fare la commedia

playboy ['pleɪbɔɪ] *n* playboy *m inv*
played-out ['pleɪd'aut] *adj* spossato(-a)
player ['pleɪə^r] *n* giocatore(-trice); (*Theat*) attore(-trice); (*Mus*) musicista *m/f*
playful ['pleɪful] *adj* giocoso(-a)
playgoer ['pleɪgəuə^r] *n* assiduo(-a) frequentatore(-a) di teatri
playground ['pleɪgraund] *n* (*in school*) cortile *m* per la ricreazione; (*in park*) parco *m* giochi *inv*
playgroup ['pleɪgru:p] *n* giardino d'infanzia
playing card ['pleɪɪŋ-] *n* carta da gioco
playing field ['pleɪɪŋ-] *n* campo sportivo
playmaker ['pleɪmeɪkə^r] *n* (*Sport*) playmaker *m inv*
playmate ['pleɪmeɪt] *n* compagno(-a) di gioco
play-off ['pleɪɔf] *n* (*Sport*) bella
playpen ['pleɪpɛn] *n* box *m inv*
playroom ['pleɪru:m] *n* stanza dei giochi
plaything ['pleɪθɪŋ] *n* giocattolo
playtime ['pleɪtaɪm] *n* (*Scol*) ricreazione *f*
playwright ['pleɪraɪt] *n* drammaturgo(-a)
plc *abbr* (*Brit*) = **public limited company**
plea [pli:] *n* (*request*) preghiera, domanda; (*excuse*) scusa; (*Law*) (argomento di) difesa
plea bargaining *n* (*Law*) patteggiamento
plead [pli:d] *vt* patrocinare; (*give as excuse*) addurre a pretesto ■ *vi* (*Law*) perorare la causa; (*beg*): **to ~ with sb** implorare qn; **to ~ for sth** implorare qc; **to ~ guilty/not guilty** (*defendant*) dichiararsi colpevole/innocente
pleasant ['plɛznt] *adj* piacevole, gradevole
pleasantly ['plɛzntlɪ] *adv* piacevolmente
pleasantry ['plɛzntrɪ] *n* (*joke*) scherzo; (*polite remark*): **to exchange pleasantries** scambiarsi i convenevoli
please [pli:z] *vt* piacere a ■ *vi* (*think fit*): **do as you ~** faccia come le pare; **~!** per piacere!; **my bill, ~** il conto, per piacere; **~ yourself!** come ti (*or* le) pare!; **~ don't cry!** ti prego, non piangere!
pleased [pli:zd] *adj* (*happy*) felice, lieto(-a); **~ (with)** (*satisfied*) contento(-a) (di); **we are ~ to inform you that ...** abbiamo il piacere di informarla che ...; **~ to meet you!** piacere!
pleasing ['pli:zɪŋ] *adj* piacevole, che fa piacere
pleasurable ['plɛʒərəbl] *adj* molto piacevole, molto gradevole
pleasure ['plɛʒə^r] *n* piacere *m*; **with ~** con piacere, volentieri; **"it's a ~"** "prego"; **is this trip for business or ~?** è un viaggio d'affari o di piacere?
pleasure cruise *n* crociera
pleat [pli:t] *n* piega
plebiscite ['plɛbɪsɪt] *n* plebiscito
plebs [plɛbz] *npl* (*pej*) plebe *f*
plectrum ['plɛktrəm] *n* plettro
pledge [plɛdʒ] *n* pegno; (*promise*) promessa ■ *vt* impegnare; promettere; **to ~ support for sb** impegnarsi a sostenere qn; **to ~ sb to secrecy** far promettere a qn di mantenere il segreto
plenary ['pli:nərɪ] *adj* plenario(-a); **in ~ session** in seduta plenaria
plentiful ['plɛntɪful] *adj* abbondante, copioso(-a)
plenty ['plɛntɪ] *n* abbondanza; **~ of** tanto(-a), molto(-a); un'abbondanza di; **we've got ~ of time to get there** abbiamo un sacco di tempo per arrivarci
pleurisy ['pluərɪsɪ] *n* pleurite *f*
Plexiglas® ['plɛksɪglɑ:s] *n* (*US*) plexiglas® *m*
pliable ['plaɪəbl] *adj* flessibile; (*person*) malleabile
pliers ['plaɪəz] *npl* pinza
plight [plaɪt] *n* situazione *f* critica
plimsolls ['plɪmsəlz] *npl* (*Brit*) scarpe *fpl* da tennis
plinth [plɪnθ] *n* plinto; piedistallo
PLO *n abbr* (= *Palestine Liberation Organization*) O.L.P. *f*
plod [plɔd] *vi* camminare a stento; (*fig*) sgobbare
plodder ['plɔdə^r] *n* sgobbone *m*
plodding ['plɔdɪŋ] *adj* lento(-a) e pesante
plonk [plɔŋk] (*col*) *n* (*Brit*: *wine*) vino da poco ■ *vt*: **to ~ sth down** buttare giù qc bruscamente
plot [plɔt] *n* congiura, cospirazione *f*; (*of story, play*) trama; (*of land*) lotto ■ *vt* (*mark out*) fare la pianta di; rilevare; (: *diagram etc*) tracciare; (*conspire*) congiurare, cospirare ■ *vi* congiurare; **a vegetable ~** (*Brit*) un orticello
plotter ['plɔtə^r] *n* cospiratore(-trice); (*Comput*) plotter *m inv*, tracciatore *m* di curve
plough, (*US*) **plow** [plau] *n* aratro ■ *vt* (*earth*) arare
▸ **plough back** *vt* (*Comm*) reinvestire
▸ **plough through** *vt fus* (*snow etc*) procedere a fatica in
ploughing, (*US*) **plowing** ['plauɪŋ] *n* aratura
ploughman, (*US*) **plowman** ['plaumən] *n* aratore *m*; **~'s lunch** (*Brit*) *semplice pasto a base di pane e formaggio*
ploy [plɔɪ] *n* stratagemma *m*
pls *abbr* = **please**
pluck [plʌk] *vt* (*fruit*) cogliere; (*musical instrument*) pizzicare; (*bird*) spennare ■ *n* coraggio, fegato; **to ~ one's eyebrows** depilarsi le sopracciglia; **to ~ up courage** farsi coraggio
plucky ['plʌkɪ] *adj* coraggioso(-a)
plug [plʌg] *n* tappo; (*Elec*) spina; (*Aut*: *also*:

spark(ing) plug) candela ■ *vt* (*hole*) tappare; (*col*: *advertise*) spingere; **to give sb/sth a ~** fare pubblicità a qn/qc
▸ **plug in** (*Elec*) *vi* inserire la spina ■ *vt* attaccare a una presa
plughole ['plʌghəul] *n* (*Brit*) scarico
plum [plʌm] *n* (*fruit*) susina ■ *cpd*: **~ job** (*col*) impiego ottimo *or* favoloso
plumage ['plu:mɪdʒ] *n* piume *fpl*, piumaggio
plumb [plʌm] *adj* verticale ■ *n* piombo ■ *adv* (*exactly*) esattamente ■ *vt* sondare
▸ **plumb in** *vt* (*washing machine*) collegare all'impianto idraulico
plumber ['plʌməʳ] *n* idraulico
plumbing ['plʌmɪŋ] *n* (*trade*) lavoro di idraulico; (*piping*) tubature *fpl*
plumbline ['plʌmlaɪn] *n* filo a piombo
plume [plu:m] *n* piuma, penna; (*decorative*) pennacchio
plummet ['plʌmɪt] *vi* cadere a piombo
plump [plʌmp] *adj* grassoccio(-a) ■ *vt*: **to ~ sth (down) on** lasciar cadere qc di peso su
▸ **plump for** *vt fus* (*col*) decidersi per
▸ **plump up** *vt* sprimacciare
plunder ['plʌndəʳ] *n* saccheggio ■ *vt* saccheggiare
plunge [plʌndʒ] *n* tuffo ■ *vt* immergere ■ *vi* (*dive*) tuffarsi; (*fall*) cadere, precipitare; **to take the ~** (*fig*) saltare il fosso; **to ~ a room into darkness** far piombare una stanza nel buio
plunger ['plʌndʒəʳ] *n* (*for blocked sink*) sturalavandini *m inv*
plunging ['plʌndʒɪŋ] *adj* (*neckline*) profondo(-a)
pluperfect [plu:'pə:fɪkt] *n* piuccheperfetto
plural ['pluərl] *adj, n* plurale (*m*)
plus [plʌs] *n* (*also*: **plus sign**) segno più ■ *prep* più ■ *adj* (*Math, Elec*) positivo(-a); **ten/twenty ~** più di dieci/venti; **it's a ~** (*fig*) è un vantaggio
plus fours *npl* calzoni *mpl* alla zuava
plush [plʌʃ] *adj* lussuoso(-a) ■ *n* felpa
plutonium [plu:'təunɪəm] *n* plutonio
ply [plaɪ] *n* (*of wool*) capo; (*of wood*) strato ■ *vt* (*tool*) maneggiare; (*a trade*) esercitare ■ *vi* (*ship*) fare il servizio; **three ~ (wool)** lana a tre capi; **to ~ sb with drink** dare da bere continuamente a qn
plywood ['plaɪwud] *n* legno compensato
PM *n abbr* (*Brit*) = **prime minister**
p.m. *adv abbr* (= *post meridiem*) del pomeriggio
PMS *n abbr* (= *premenstrual syndrome*) sindrome *f* premestruale
PMT *n abbr* (= *premenstrual tension*) sindrome *f* premestruale
pneumatic [nju:'mætɪk] *adj* pneumatico(-a); **~ drill** martello pneumatico
pneumonia [nju:'məunɪə] *n* polmonite *f*
PO *n abbr* (= *Post Office*) ≈ P.T. (= *Poste e Telegrafi*) ■ *abbr* (*Naut*) = **petty officer**
po *abbr* = **postal order**
POA *n abbr* (*Brit*: = *Prison Officers' Association*) *sindacato delle guardie carcerarie*
poach [pəutʃ] *vt* (*cook*) affogare; (*steal*) cacciare (*or* pescare) di frodo ■ *vi* fare il bracconiere
poached [pəutʃt] *adj* (*egg*) affogato(-a)
poacher ['pəutʃəʳ] *n* bracconiere *m*
poaching ['pəutʃɪŋ] *n* caccia (*or* pesca) di frodo
PO box *n abbr* = **post office box**
pocket ['pɔkɪt] *n* tasca ■ *vt* intascare; **to be out of ~** rimetterci; **to be £5 in/out of ~** (*Brit*) trovarsi con 5 sterline in più/in meno; **air ~** vuoto d'aria
pocketbook ['pɔkɪtbuk] *n* (*wallet*) portafoglio; (*notebook*) taccuino; (*US*: *handbag*) busta
pocket knife *n* temperino
pocket money *n* paghetta, settimana
pockmarked ['pɔkmɑ:kt] *adj* (*face*) butterato(-a)
pod [pɔd] *n* guscio ■ *vt* sgusciare
podcast ['pɔdkɑ:st] *n* podcast *m inv*
podgy ['pɔdʒɪ] *adj* grassoccio(-a)
podiatrist [pɔ'di:ətrɪst] *n* (*US*) callista *m/f*, pedicure *m/f*
podiatry [pɔ'di:ətrɪ] *n* (*US*) mestiere *m* di callista
podium ['pəudɪəm] *n* podio
POE *n abbr* = **port of embarkation; port of entry**
poem ['pəuɪm] *n* poesia
poet ['pəuɪt] *n* poeta(-essa)
poetic [pəu'ɛtɪk] *adj* poetico(-a)
poet laureate *n* (*Brit*) poeta *m* laureato; *vedi nota*

POET LAUREATE

In Gran Bretagna il *poet laureate* è un poeta che riceve un vitalizio dalla casa reale britannica e che ha l'incarico di scrivere delle poesie commemorative in occasione delle festività ufficiali.

poetry ['pəuɪtrɪ] *n* poesia
poignant ['pɔɪnjənt] *adj* struggente
point [pɔɪnt] *n* (*gen*) punto; (*tip*: *of needle etc*) punta; (*Brit Elec*: *also*: **power point**) presa (di corrente); (*in time*) punto, momento; (*Scol*) voto; (*main idea, important part*) nocciolo; (*also*: **decimal point**): **2 ~ 3 (2.3)** 2 virgola 3 (2,3) ■ *vt* (*show*) indicare; (*gun etc*): **to ~ sth at** puntare qc contro ■ *vi* mostrare a dito; **points** *npl*

P

(*Aut*) puntine *fpl*; (*Rail*) scambio; **to ~ to** indicare; (*fig*) dimostrare; **to make a ~** fare un'osservazione; **to get the ~** capire; **to come to the ~** venire al fatto; **when it comes to the ~** quando si arriva al dunque; **to be on the ~ of doing sth** essere sul punto di *or* stare (proprio) per fare qc; **to be beside the ~** non entrarci; **to make a ~ of doing sth** non mancare di fare qc; **there's no ~ (in doing)** è inutile (fare); **in ~ of fact** a dire il vero; **that's the whole ~!** precisamente!, sta tutto lì!; **you've got a ~ there!** giusto!, ha ragione!; **the train stops at Carlisle and all points south** il treno ferma a Carlisle e in tutte le stazioni a sud di Carlisle; **good points** vantaggi *mpl*; (*of person*) qualità *fpl*; **~ of departure** (*also fig*) punto di partenza; **~ of order** mozione *f* d'ordine; **~ of sale** (*Comm*) punto di vendita; **~ of view** punto di vista
▸ **point out** *vt* far notare

point-blank ['pɔɪnt'blæŋk] *adv* (*also*: **at point-blank range**) a bruciapelo; (*fig*) categoricamente

point duty *n* (*Brit*): **to be on ~** dirigere il traffico

pointed ['pɔɪntɪd] *adj* (*shape*) aguzzo(-a), appuntito(-a); (*remark*) specifico(-a)

pointedly ['pɔɪntɪdlɪ] *adv* in maniera inequivocabile

pointer ['pɔɪntə^r] *n* (*stick*) bacchetta; (*needle*) lancetta; (*clue*) indizio; (*advice*) consiglio; (*dog*) pointer *m*, cane *m* da punta

pointless ['pɔɪntlɪs] *adj* inutile, vano(-a)

poise [pɔɪz] *n* (*balance*) equilibrio; (*of head, body*) portamento; (*calmness*) calma ■ *vt* tenere in equilibrio; **to be poised for** (*fig*) essere pronto(-a) a

poison ['pɔɪzn] *n* veleno ■ *vt* avvelenare

poisoning ['pɔɪznɪŋ] *n* avvelenamento

poisonous ['pɔɪznəs] *adj* velenoso(-a); (*fumes*) venefico(-a), tossico(-a); (*ideas, literature*) pernicioso(-a); (*rumours, individual*) perfido(-a)

poke [pəuk] *vt* (*fire*) attizzare; (*jab with finger, stick etc*) punzecchiare; (*put*): **to ~ sth in(to)** spingere qc dentro ■ *n* (*jab*) colpetto; (*with elbow*) gomitata; **to ~ one's head out of the window** mettere la testa fuori dalla finestra; **to ~ fun at sb** prendere in giro qn
▸ **poke about** *vi* frugare

poker ['pəukə^r] *n* attizzatoio; (*Cards*) poker *m*

poker-faced ['pəukə'feɪst] *adj* dal viso impassibile

poky ['pəukɪ] *adj* piccolo(-a) e stretto(-a)

Poland ['pəulənd] *n* Polonia

polar ['pəulə^r] *adj* polare

polar bear *n* orso bianco

polarize ['pəuləraɪz] *vt* polarizzare

Pole [pəul] *n* polacco(-a)

pole [pəul] *n* (*of wood*) palo; (*Elec, Geo*) polo

poleaxe, (*US*) **poleax** ['pəulæks] *vt* (*fig*) stendere

pole bean *n* (*US*) fagiolino

polecat ['pəulkæt] *n* puzzola; (*US*) moffetta

Pol. Econ. ['pɔlɪkɔn] *n abbr* = **political economy**

polemic [pɔ'lɛmɪk] *n* polemica

pole star *n* stella polare

pole vault *n* salto con l'asta

police [pə'li:s] *n* polizia ■ *vt* mantenere l'ordine in; (*streets, city, frontier*) presidiare; **a large number of ~ were hurt** molti poliziotti sono rimasti feriti

police car *n* macchina della polizia

police constable *n* (*Brit*) agente *m* di polizia

police department *n* (*US*) dipartimento di polizia

police force *n* corpo di polizia, polizia

policeman [pə'li:smən] *n* poliziotto, agente *m* di polizia

police officer *n* = **police constable**

police record *n*: **to have a ~** avere precedenti penali

police state *n* stato di polizia

police station *n* posto di polizia

policewoman [pə'li:swumən] *n* donna *f* poliziotto *inv*

policy ['pɔlɪsɪ] *n* politica; (*of newspaper, company*) linea di condotta, prassi *f inv*; (*also*: **insurance policy**) polizza (d'assicurazione); **to take out a ~** (*Insurance*) stipulare una polizza di assicurazione

policy holder *n* assicurato(-a)

policy-making ['pɔlɪsɪmeɪkɪŋ] *n* messa a punto di programmi

polio ['pəulɪəu] *n* polio *f*

Polish ['pəulɪʃ] *adj* polacco(-a) ■ *n* (*Ling*) polacco

polish ['pɔlɪʃ] *n* (*for shoes*) lucido; (*for floor*) cera; (*for nails*) smalto; (*shine*) lucentezza, lustro; (*fig: refinement*) raffinatezza ■ *vt* lucidare; (*fig: improve*) raffinare
▸ **polish off** *vt* (*work*) sbrigare; (*food*) mangiarsi

polished ['pɔlɪʃt] *adj* (*fig*) raffinato(-a)

polite [pə'laɪt] *adj* cortese; **it's not ~ to do that** non è educato *or* buona educazione fare questo

politely [pə'laɪtlɪ] *adv* cortesemente

politeness [pə'laɪtnɪs] *n* cortesia

politic ['pɔlɪtɪk] *adj* diplomatico(-a)

political [pə'lɪtɪkl] *adj* politico(-a)

political asylum *n* asilo politico

politically [pə'lɪtɪklɪ] *adv* politicamente

politically correct *adj* politicamente corretto(-a)
politician [pɔlɪˈtɪʃən] *n* politico
politics [ˈpɔlɪtɪks] *n* politica ■ *npl* idee *fpl* politiche
polka [ˈpɔlkə] *n* polca
polka dot *n* pois *m inv*
poll [pəul] *n* scrutinio; (*votes cast*) voti *mpl*; (*also*: **opinion poll**) sondaggio (d'opinioni) ■ *vt* ottenere; **to go to the polls** (*voters*) andare alle urne; (*government*) indire le elezioni
pollen [ˈpɔlən] *n* polline *m*
pollen count *n* tasso di polline nell'aria
pollination [pɔlɪˈneɪʃən] *n* impollinazione *f*
polling [ˈpəulɪŋ] *n* (*Brit Pol*) votazione *f*, votazioni *fpl*; (*Tel*) interrogazione *f* ciclica
polling booth *n* (*Brit*) cabina elettorale
polling day *n* (*Brit*) giorno delle elezioni
polling station *n* (*Brit*) sezione *f* elettorale
pollster [ˈpəulstəʳ] *n* chi esegue sondaggi d'opinione
poll tax *n* (*Brit*) *imposta locale sulla persona fisica* (*non più in vigore*)
pollutant [pəˈluːtənt] *n* sostanza inquinante
pollute [pəˈluːt] *vt* inquinare
pollution [pəˈluːʃən] *n* inquinamento
polo [ˈpəuləu] *n* polo
polo neck *n* collo alto; (*also*: **polo neck sweater**) dolcevita ■ *adj* a collo alto
poly [ˈpɔlɪ] *n abbr* (*Brit*) = **polytechnic**
poly bag *n* (*Brit col*) borsa di plastica
polyester [pɔlɪˈɛstəʳ] *n* poliestere *m*
polygamy [pəˈlɪgəmɪ] *n* poligamia
polygraph [ˈpɔlɪgrɑːf] *n* macchina della verità
Polynesia [pɔlɪˈniːzɪə] *n* Polinesia
Polynesian [pɔlɪˈniːzɪən] *adj, n* polinesiano(-a)
polyp [ˈpɔlɪp] *n* (*Med*) polipo
polystyrene [pɔlɪˈstaɪriːn] *n* polistirolo
polytechnic [pɔlɪˈtɛknɪk] *n* (*college*) *istituto superiore ad indirizzo tecnologico*
polythene [ˈpɔlɪθiːn] *n* politene *m*
polythene bag *n* borsa di plastica
polyurethane [pɔlɪˈjuərɪθeɪn] *n* poliuretano
pomegranate [ˈpɔmɪgrænɪt] *n* melagrana
pommel [ˈpɔml] *n* pomo ■ *vt* = **pummel**
pomp [pɔmp] *n* pompa, fasto
pompom [ˈpɔmpɔm] *n* pompon *m inv*
pompous [ˈpɔmpəs] *adj* pomposo(-a); (*person*) pieno(-a) di boria
pond [pɔnd] *n* stagno; (*in park*) laghetto
ponder [ˈpɔndəʳ] *vi* riflettere, meditare ■ *vt* ponderare, riflettere su
ponderous [ˈpɔndərəs] *adj* ponderoso(-a), pesante
pong [pɔŋ] (*Brit col*) *n* puzzo ■ *vi* puzzare
pontiff [ˈpɔntɪf] *n* pontefice *m*
pontificate [pɔnˈtɪfɪkeɪt] *vi* (*fig*): **to ~ (about)** pontificare (su)
pontoon [pɔnˈtuːn] *n* pontone *m*; (*Brit Cards*) ventuno
pony [ˈpəunɪ] *n* pony *m inv*
ponytail [ˈpəunɪteɪl] *n* coda di cavallo
pony trekking [-trɛkɪŋ] *n* (*Brit*) escursione *f* a cavallo
poodle [ˈpuːdl] *n* barboncino, barbone *m*
pooh-pooh [puːˈpuː] *vt* deridere
pool [puːl] *n* (*of rain*) pozza; (*pond*) stagno; (*artificial*) vasca; (*also*: **swimming pool**) piscina; (*sth shared*) fondo comune; (*Comm: consortium*) pool *m inv*; (*US: monopoly trust*) trust *m inv*; (*billiards*) *specie di biliardo a buca* ■ *vt* mettere in comune; **typing ~**, (*US*) **secretary ~** servizio comune di dattilografia; **to do the (football) pools** ≈ fare la schedina, ≈ giocare al totocalcio
poor [puəʳ] *adj* povero(-a); (*mediocre*) mediocre, cattivo(-a) ■ *npl*: **the ~** i poveri
poorly [ˈpuəlɪ] *adv* poveramente; (*badly*) male ■ *adj* indisposto(-a), malato(-a)
pop [pɔp] *n* (*noise*) schiocco; (*Mus*) musica pop; (*US col: father*) babbo; (*col: drink*) bevanda gasata ■ *vt* (*put*) mettere (in fretta) ■ *vi* scoppiare; (*cork*) schioccare; **she popped her head out** (*of the window*) sporse fuori la testa
▸ **pop in** *vi* passare
▸ **pop out** *vi* fare un salto fuori
▸ **pop up** *vi* apparire, sorgere
pop concert *n* concerto *m* pop *inv*
popcorn [ˈpɔpkɔːn] *n* pop-corn *m*
pope [pəup] *n* papa *m*
poplar [ˈpɔpləʳ] *n* pioppo
poplin [ˈpɔplɪn] *n* popeline *f*
popper [ˈpɔpəʳ] *n* (*Brit*) bottone *m* automatico, bottone a pressione
poppy [ˈpɔpɪ] *n* papavero
poppycock [ˈpɔpɪkɔk] *n* (*col*) scempiaggini *fpl*
Popsicle® [ˈpɔpsɪkl] *n* (*US*) ghiacciolo
populace [ˈpɔpjuləs] *n* popolo
popular [ˈpɔpjuləʳ] *adj* popolare; (*fashionable*) in voga; **to be ~ (with)** (*person*) essere benvoluto(-a) *or* ben visto(-a) (da); (*decision*) essere gradito(-a) (a); **a ~ song** una canzone di successo
popularity [pɔpjuˈlærɪtɪ] *n* popolarità
popularize [ˈpɔpjuləraɪz] *vt* divulgare; (*science*) volgarizzare
populate [ˈpɔpjuleɪt] *vt* popolare
population [pɔpjuˈleɪʃən] *n* popolazione *f*
population explosion *n* forte espansione *f* demografica
populous [ˈpɔpjuləs] *adj* popolato(-a)
pop-up menu [ˈpɔpʌp-] *n* (*Comput*) menu *m inv* a comparsa

P

porcelain ['pɔːslɪn] *n* porcellana
porch [pɔːtʃ] *n* veranda
porcupine ['pɔːkjupaɪn] *n* porcospino
pore [pɔːʳ] *n* poro ■ *vi*: **to ~ over** essere immerso(-a) in
pork [pɔːk] *n* carne *f* di maiale
pork chop *n* braciola *or* costoletta di maiale
porn [pɔːn] (*col*) *n* pornografia ■ *adj* porno *inv*
pornographic [pɔːnə'græfɪk] *adj* pornografico(-a)
pornography [pɔː'nɔgrəfɪ] *n* pornografia
porous ['pɔːrəs] *adj* poroso(-a)
porpoise ['pɔːpəs] *n* focena
porridge ['pɔrɪdʒ] *n* porridge *m*
port[1] [pɔːt] *n* porto; (*opening in ship*) portello; (*Naut: left side*) babordo; (*Comput*) porta; **to ~** (*Naut*) a babordo; **~ of call** (porto di) scalo
port[2] [pɔːt] *n* (*wine*) porto
portable ['pɔːtəbl] *adj* portatile
portal ['pɔːtl] *n* portale *m*
portcullis [pɔːt'kʌlɪs] *n* saracinesca
portent ['pɔːtɛnt] *n* presagio
porter ['pɔːtəʳ] *n* (*for luggage*) facchino, portabagagli *m inv*; (*doorkeeper*) portiere *m*, portinaio; (*US Rail*) addetto ai vagoni letto
portfolio [pɔːt'fəulɪəu] *n* (*Pol: office; Econ*) portafoglio; (*of artist*) raccolta dei propri lavori
porthole ['pɔːthəul] *n* oblò *m inv*
portico ['pɔːtɪkəu] *n* portico
portion ['pɔːʃən] *n* porzione *f*
portly ['pɔːtlɪ] *adj* corpulento(-a)
portrait ['pɔːtreɪt] *n* ritratto
portray [pɔː'treɪ] *vt* fare il ritratto di; (*character on stage*) rappresentare; (*in writing*) ritrarre
portrayal ['pɔːtreɪəl] *n* ritratto; rappresentazione *f*
Portugal ['pɔːtjugl] *n* Portogallo
Portuguese [pɔːtju'giːz] *adj* portoghese ■ *n* (*pl inv*) portoghese *m/f*; (*Ling*) portoghese *m*
Portuguese man-of-war [-mænəv'wɔːʳ] *n* (*jellyfish*) medusa
pose [pəuz] *n* posa ■ *vi* posare; (*pretend*): **to ~ as** atteggiarsi a, posare a ■ *vt* porre; **to strike a ~** mettersi in posa
poser ['pəuzəʳ] *n* domanda difficile; (*person*) = **poseur**
poseur [pəu'zəːʳ] *n* (*pej*) persona affettata
posh [pɔʃ] *adj* (*col*) elegante; (*family*) per bene ■ *adv* (*col*): **to talk ~** parlare in modo snob
position [pə'zɪʃən] *n* posizione *f*; (*job*) posto ■ *vt* mettere in posizione, collocare; **to be in a ~ to do sth** essere nella posizione di fare qc
positive ['pɔzɪtɪv] *adj* positivo(-a); (*certain*) sicuro(-a), certo(-a); (*definite*) preciso(-a); definitivo(-a)
posse ['pɔsɪ] *n* (*US*) drappello
possess [pə'zɛs] *vt* possedere; **like one possessed** come un ossesso; **whatever can have possessed you?** cosa ti ha preso?
possession [pə'zɛʃən] *n* possesso; (*object*) bene *m*; **to take ~ of sth** impossessarsi *or* impadronirsi di qc
possessive [pə'zɛsɪv] *adj* possessivo(-a)
possessiveness [pə'zɛsɪvnɪs] *n* possessività
possessor [pə'zɛsəʳ] *n* possessore/posseditrice
possibility [pɔsɪ'bɪlɪtɪ] *n* possibilità *f inv*; **he's a ~ for the part** è uno dei candidati per la parte
possible ['pɔsɪbl] *adj* possibile; **it is ~ to do it** è possibile farlo; **if ~** se possibile; **as big as ~** il più grande possibile; **as far as ~** nei limiti del possibile
possibly ['pɔsɪblɪ] *adv* (*perhaps*) forse; **if you ~ can** se le è possibile; **I cannot ~ come** proprio non posso venire
post [pəust] *n* (*Brit: mail, letters, delivery*) posta; (*: collection*) levata; (*job, situation*) posto; (*pole*) palo; (*trading post*) stazione *f* commerciale; (*on internet forum*) post *m inv*, commento ■ *vt* (*Brit: send by post*) impostare; (*Mil*) appostare; (*notice*) affiggere; (*to internet: video*) caricare; (*: comment*) mandare; (*Brit: appoint*): **to ~ to** assegnare a; **by ~** (*Brit*) per posta; **by return of ~** (*Brit*) a giro di posta; **to keep sb posted** tenere qn al corrente
post... [pəust] *prefix* post...; **post-1990** dopo il 1990
postage ['pəustɪdʒ] *n* affrancatura
postage stamp *n* francobollo
postal ['pəustəl] *adj* postale
postal order *n* vaglia *m inv* postale
postbag ['pəustbæg] *n* (*Brit*) sacco postale, sacco della posta
postbox ['pəustbɔks] *n* cassetta delle lettere
postcard ['pəustkɑːd] *n* cartolina
postcode ['pəustkəud] *n* (*Brit*) codice *m* (di avviamento) postale
postdate ['pəust'deɪt] *vt* (*cheque*) postdatare
poster ['pəustəʳ] *n* manifesto, affisso
poste restante [pəust'rɛstɑ̃ːnt] *n* (*Brit*) fermo posta *m*
posterior [pɔs'tɪərɪəʳ] *n* (*col*) deretano, didietro
posterity [pɔs'tɛrɪtɪ] *n* posterità
poster paint *n* tempera
post exchange *n* (*US Mil*) spaccio militare
post-free [pəust'friː] *adj, adv* (*Brit*) franco di porto
postgraduate ['pəust'grædjuət] *n laureato/a che continua gli studi*
posthumous ['pɔstjuməs] *adj* postumo(-a)
posthumously ['pɔstjuməslɪ] *adv* dopo la mia (*or sua etc*) morte
posting ['pəustɪŋ] *n* (*Brit*) incarico

postman ['pəustmən] *n* postino
postmark ['pəustmɑːk] *n* bollo *or* timbro postale
postmaster ['pəustmɑːstəʳ] *n* direttore *m* di un ufficio postale
Postmaster General *n* ≈ ministro delle Poste
postmistress ['pəustmɪstrɪs] *n* direttrice *f* di un ufficio postale
post-mortem [pəust'mɔːtəm] *n* autopsia; (*fig*) analisi *f inv* a posteriori
postnatal ['pəust'neɪtl] *adj* post-parto *inv*
post office *n* (*building*) ufficio postale; (*organization*) poste *fpl*
post office box *n* casella postale
post-paid ['pəust'peɪd] *adj* già affrancato(-a)
postpone [pəust'pəun] *vt* rinviare
postponement [pəust'pəunmənt] *n* rinvio
postscript ['pəustskrɪpt] *n* poscritto
postulate ['pɔstjuleɪt] *vt* postulare
posture ['pɔstʃəʳ] *n* portamento; (*pose*) posa, atteggiamento ■ *vi* posare
postwar ['pəust'wɔːʳ] *adj* del dopoguerra
posy ['pəuzɪ] *n* mazzetto di fiori
pot [pɔt] *n* (*for cooking*) pentola; casseruola; (*for plants, jam*) vaso; (*piece of pottery*) ceramica; (*col: marijuana*) erba ■ *vt* (*plant*) piantare in vaso; **to go to ~** (*col*) andare in malora; **pots of** (*Brit col*) un sacco di
potash ['pɔtæʃ] *n* potassa
potassium [pə'tæsɪəm] *n* potassio
potato (*pl* **potatoes**) [pə'teɪtəu] *n* patata
potato crisps, (*US*) **potato chips** *npl* patatine *fpl*
potato flour *n* fecola di patate
potato peeler *n* sbucciapatate *m inv*
potbellied ['pɔtbɛlɪd] *adj* (*from overeating*) panciuto(-a); (*from malnutrition*) dal ventre gonfio
potency ['pəutnsɪ] *n* potenza; (*of drink*) forza
potent ['pəutnt] *adj* potente, forte
potentate ['pəutnteɪt] *n* potentato
potential [pə'tɛnʃl] *adj* potenziale ■ *n* possibilità *fpl*; **to have ~** essere promettente
potentially [pə'tɛnʃəlɪ] *adv* potenzialmente
pothole ['pɔthəul] *n* (*in road*) buca; (*Brit: underground*) marmitta
potholer ['pɔthəuləʳ] *n* (*Brit*) speleologo(-a)
potholing ['pɔthəulɪŋ] *n* (*Brit*): **to go ~** fare la speleologia
potion ['pəuʃən] *n* pozione *f*
potluck [pɔt'lʌk] *n*: **to take ~** tentare la sorte
potpourri [pəu'puriː] *n* (*dried petals etc*) *miscuglio di petali essiccati profumati*; (*fig*) pot-pourri *m inv*
pot roast *n* brasato
potshot ['pɔtʃɔt] *n*: **to take potshots at** tirare a casaccio contro
potted ['pɔtɪd] *adj* (*food*) in conserva; (*plant*) in vaso; (*fig: shortened*) condensato(-a)
potter ['pɔtəʳ] *n* vasaio ■ *vi* (*Brit*): **to ~ around, ~ about** lavoracchiare; **to ~ round the house** sbrigare con calma le faccende di casa; **~'s wheel** tornio (da vasaio)
pottery ['pɔtərɪ] *n* ceramiche *fpl*; **a piece of ~** una ceramica
potty ['pɔtɪ] *adj* (*Brit col: mad*) tocco(-a) ■ *n* (*child's*) vasino
potty-trained ['pɔtɪtreɪnd] *adj* che ha imparato a farla nel vasino
pouch [pautʃ] *n* borsa; (*Zool*) marsupio
pouf, pouffe [puːf] *n* (*stool*) pouf *m inv*
poultice ['pəultɪs] *n* impiastro, cataplasma *m*
poultry ['pəultrɪ] *n* pollame *m*
poultry farm *n* azienda avicola
poultry farmer *n* pollicoltore(-trice)
pounce [pauns] *vi*: **to ~ (on)** balzare addosso (a), piombare (su) ■ *n* balzo
pound [paund] *n* (*weight*) libbra (*= 453g, 16 ounces*); (*money*) (lira) sterlina (*= 100 pence*); (*for dogs*) canile *m* municipale ■ *vt* (*beat*) battere; (*crush*) pestare, polverizzare ■ *vi* (*beat*) battere, martellare; **half a ~** mezza libbra; **a five-~ note** una banconota da cinque sterline
pounding ['paundɪŋ] *n*: **to take a ~** (*fig*) prendere una batosta
pound sterling *n* sterlina
pour [pɔːʳ] *vt* versare ■ *vi* riversarsi; (*rain*) piovere a dirotto
▸ **pour away, pour off** *vt* vuotare
▸ **pour in** *vi* (*people*) entrare in fiotto; **to come pouring in** (*water*) entrare a fiotti; (*letters*) arrivare a valanghe; (*cars, people*) affluire in gran quantità
▸ **pour out** *vi* (*people*) riversarsi fuori ■ *vt* vuotare; versare
pouring ['pɔːrɪŋ] *adj*: **~ rain** pioggia torrenziale
pout [paut] *vi* sporgere le labbra; fare il broncio
poverty ['pɔvətɪ] *n* povertà, miseria
poverty line *n* soglia di povertà
poverty-stricken ['pɔvətɪstrɪkən] *adj* molto povero(-a), misero(-a)
poverty trap *n* (*Brit*) circolo vizioso della povertà
POW *n abbr* = **prisoner of war**
powder ['paudəʳ] *n* polvere *f* ■ *vt* spolverizzare; (*face*) incipriare; **powdered milk** latte *m* in polvere; **to ~ one's nose** incipriarsi il naso; (*euphemism*) andare alla toilette
powder compact *n* portacipria *m inv*

P

powder keg *n* (*fig: area*) polveriera; (*: situation*) situazione *f* esplosiva
powder puff *n* piumino della cipria
powder room *n* toilette *f inv* (per signore)
powdery ['paudərɪ] *adj* polveroso(-a)
power ['pauə^r] *n* (*strength*) potenza, forza; (*ability, Pol: of party, leader*) potere *m*; (*Math*) potenza; (*Elec*) corrente *f* ■ *vt* fornire di energia; azionare; **to be in ~** essere al potere; **to do all in one's ~ to help sb** fare tutto quello che si può per aiutare qn; **the world powers** le grandi potenze; **mental powers** capacità *fpl* mentali
powerboat ['pauəbəut] *n* (*Brit*) motobarca, imbarcazione *f* a motore
power cut *n* (*Brit*) interruzione *f* or mancanza di corrente
powered ['pauəd] *adj*: **~ by** azionato(-a) da; **nuclear-~ submarine** sottomarino a propulsione atomica
power failure *n* guasto alla linea elettrica
powerful ['pauəful] *adj* potente, forte
powerhouse ['pauəhaus] *n* (*fig: person*) persona molto dinamica; **a ~ of ideas** una miniera di idee
powerless ['pauəlɪs] *adj* impotente, senza potere
power line *n* linea elettrica
power of attorney *n* procura
power point *n* (*Brit*) presa di corrente
power station *n* centrale *f* elettrica
power steering *n* (*Aut: also:* **power-assisted steering**) servosterzo
powwow ['pauwau] *n* riunione *f*
pp *abbr* (*= pages*) pp; (*= per procurationem: by proxy*): **pp J. Smith** per il Signor J. Smith
PPE *n abbr* (*Brit Scol: = philosophy, politics, and economics*) *corso di laurea*
PPS *n abbr* (*Brit: = parliamentary private secretary*) *parlamentare che assiste un ministro*; **= post postscriptum**
PQ *abbr* (*Canada*) = **Province of Quebec**
PR *n abbr* = **proportional representation**; **public relations** ■ *abbr* (*US*) = **Puerto Rico**
Pr. *abbr* = **prince**
practicability [præktɪkə'bɪlɪtɪ] *n* praticabilità
practicable ['præktɪkəbl] *adj* (*scheme*) praticabile
practical ['præktɪkl] *adj* pratico(-a)
practicality [præktɪ'kælɪtɪ] *n* (*of plan*) fattibilità; (*of person*) senso pratico; **practicalities** *npl* dettagli *mpl* pratici
practical joke *n* beffa
practically ['præktɪklɪ] *adv* (*almost*) quasi, praticamente
practice ['præktɪs] *n* pratica; (*of profession*) esercizio; (*at football etc*) allenamento; (*business*) gabinetto; clientela ■ *vt, vi* (*US*) = **practise**; **in ~** (*in reality*) in pratica; **out of ~** fuori esercizio; **2 hours' piano ~** 2 ore di esercizio al pianoforte; **it's common ~** è d'uso; **to put sth into ~** mettere qc in pratica; **target ~** pratica di tiro
practice match *n* partita di allenamento
practise, (*US*) **practice** ['præktɪs] *vt* (*work at: piano, one's backhand etc*) esercitarsi a; (*train for: skiing, running etc*) allenarsi a; (*a sport, religion*) praticare; (*method*) usare; (*profession*) esercitare ■ *vi* esercitarsi; (*train*) allenarsi; **to ~ for a match** allenarsi per una partita
practised ['præktɪst] *adj* (*Brit: person*) esperto(-a); (*: performance*) da virtuoso(-a); (*: liar*) matricolato(-a); **with a ~ eye** con occhio esperto
practising ['præktɪsɪŋ] *adj* (*Christian etc*) praticante; (*lawyer*) che esercita la professione; (*homosexual*) attivo(-a)
practitioner [præk'tɪʃənə^r] *n* professionista *m/f*; (*Med*) medico
pragmatic [præg'mætɪk] *adj* prammatico(-a)
Prague [prɑːg] *n* Praga
prairie ['prɛərɪ] *n* prateria
praise [preɪz] *n* elogio, lode *f* ■ *vt* elogiare, lodare
praiseworthy ['preɪzwəːðɪ] *adj* lodevole
pram [præm] *n* (*Brit*) carrozzina
prance [prɑːns] *vi* (*horse*) impennarsi
prank [præŋk] *n* burla
prat [præt] *n* (*Brit col*) cretino(-a)
prattle ['prætl] *vi* cinguettare
prawn [prɔːn] *n* gamberetto
pray [preɪ] *vi* pregare
prayer [prɛə^r] *n* preghiera
prayer book *n* libro di preghiere
pre... [priː] *prefix* pre...; **pre-1970** prima del 1970
preach [priːtʃ] *vt, vi* predicare; **to ~ at sb** fare la predica a qn
preacher ['priːtʃə^r] *n* predicatore(-trice); (*US: minister*) pastore *m*
preamble [prɪ'æmbl] *n* preambolo
prearranged [priːə'reɪndʒd] *adj* organizzato(-a) in anticipo
precarious [prɪ'kɛərɪəs] *adj* precario(-a)
precaution [prɪ'kɔːʃən] *n* precauzione *f*
precautionary [prɪ'kɔːʃənərɪ] *adj* (*measure*) precauzionale
precede [prɪ'siːd] *vt, vi* precedere
precedence ['prɛsɪdəns] *n* precedenza; **to take ~ over** avere la precedenza su
precedent ['prɛsɪdənt] *n* precedente *m*; **to establish** or **set a ~** creare un precedente
preceding [prɪ'siːdɪŋ] *adj* precedente

precept ['pri:sɛpt] *n* precetto
precinct ['pri:sɪŋkt] *n* (*round cathedral*) recinto; (*US: district*) circoscrizione *f*; **precincts** *npl* (*neighbourhood*) dintorni *mpl*, vicinanze *fpl*; **pedestrian ~** zona pedonale; **shopping ~** (*Brit*) centro commerciale
precious ['prɛʃəs] *adj* prezioso(-a) ■ *adv* (*col*): **~ little/few** ben poco/pochi; **your ~ dog** (*ironic*) il suo amatissimo cane
precipice ['prɛsɪpɪs] *n* precipizio
precipitate *adj* [prɪ'sɪpɪtɪt] (*hasty*) precipitoso(-a) ■ *vt* [prɪ'sɪpɪteɪt] accelerare
precipitation [prɪsɪpɪ'teɪʃən] *n* precipitazione *f*
precipitous [prɪ'sɪpɪtəs] *adj* (*steep*) erto(-a), ripido(-a)
précis (*pl* **~**) ['preɪsi:, -z] *n* riassunto
precise [prɪ'saɪs] *adj* preciso(-a)
precisely [prɪ'saɪslɪ] *adv* precisamente; **~!** appunto!
precision [prɪ'sɪʒən] *n* precisione *f*
preclude [prɪ'klu:d] *vt* precludere, impedire; **to ~ sb from doing** impedire a qn di fare
precocious [prɪ'kəuʃəs] *adj* precoce
preconceived [pri:kən'si:vd] *adj* (*idea*) preconcetto(-a)
preconception [pri:kən'sɛpʃən] *n* preconcetto
precondition [pri:kən'dɪʃən] *n* condizione *f* necessaria
precursor [pri:'kə:sə^r] *n* precursore *m*
predate [pri:'deɪt] *vt* (*precede*) precedere
predator ['prɛdətə^r] *n* predatore *m*
predatory ['prɛdətərɪ] *adj* predatore(-trice)
predecessor ['pri:dɪsɛsə^r] *n* predecessore(-a)
predestination [pri:dɛstɪ'neɪʃən] *n* predestinazione *f*
predetermine [pri:dɪ'tə:mɪn] *vt* predeterminare
predicament [prɪ'dɪkəmənt] *n* situazione *f* difficile
predicate ['prɛdɪkɪt] *n* (*Ling*) predicativo
predict [prɪ'dɪkt] *vt* predire
predictable [prɪ'dɪktəbl] *adj* prevedibile
predictably [prɪ'dɪktəblɪ] *adv* (*behave, react*) in modo prevedibile; **~ she didn't arrive** come era da prevedere, non è arrivata
prediction [prɪ'dɪkʃən] *n* predizione *f*
predispose [pri:dɪs'pəuz] *vt* predisporre
predominance [prɪ'dɔmɪnəns] *n* predominanza
predominant [prɪ'dɔmɪnənt] *adj* predominante
predominantly [prɪ'dɔmɪnəntlɪ] *adv* in maggior parte; soprattutto
predominate [prɪ'dɔmɪneɪt] *vi* predominare
pre-eminent [pri:'ɛmɪnənt] *adj* preminente
pre-empt [prɪ'ɛmpt] *vt* acquistare per diritto di prelazione; (*fig*) anticipare
pre-emptive [prɪ'ɛmptɪv] *adj*: **~ strike** azione *f* preventiva
preen [pri:n] *vt*: **to ~ itself** (*bird*) lisciarsi le penne; **to ~ o.s.** agghindarsi
prefab ['pri:fæb] *n* casa prefabbricata
prefabricated [pri:'fæbrikeɪtɪd] *adj* prefabbricato(-a)
preface ['prɛfəs] *n* prefazione *f*
prefect ['pri:fɛkt] *n* (*Brit: in school*) *studente/essa con funzioni disciplinari*; (*in Italy*) prefetto
prefer [prɪ'fə:^r] *vt* preferire; (*Law: charges, complaint*) sporgere; (*: action*) intentare; **to ~ coffee to tea** preferire il caffè al tè
preferable ['prɛfrəbl] *adj* preferibile
preferably ['prɛfrəblɪ] *adv* preferibilmente
preference ['prɛfrəns] *n* preferenza; **in ~ to sth** piuttosto che qc
preference shares *npl* (*Brit*) azioni *fpl* privilegiate
preferential [prɛfə'rɛnʃəl] *adj* preferenziale; **~ treatment** trattamento di favore
preferred stock [prɪ'fə:d-] *npl* (*US*) = **preference shares**
prefix ['pri:fɪks] *n* prefisso
pregnancy ['prɛgnənsɪ] *n* gravidanza
pregnancy test *n* test *m inv* di gravidanza
pregnant ['prɛgnənt] *adj* incinta *adj f*; (*animal*) gravido(-a); (*fig: remark, pause*) significativo(-a); **3 months ~** incinta di 3 mesi
prehistoric ['pri:hɪs'tɔrɪk] *adj* preistorico(-a)
prehistory [pri:'hɪstərɪ] *n* preistoria
prejudge [pri:'dʒʌdʒ] *vt* pregiudicare
prejudice ['prɛdʒudɪs] *n* pregiudizio; (*harm*) torto, danno ■ *vt* pregiudicare, ledere; (*bias*): **to ~ sb in favour of/against** disporre bene/male qn verso
prejudiced ['prɛdʒudɪst] *adj* (*person*) pieno(-a) di pregiudizi; (*view*) prevenuto(-a); **to be ~ against sb/sth** essere prevenuto contro qn/qc
prelate ['prɛlət] *n* prelato
preliminaries [prɪ'lɪmɪnərɪz] *npl* preliminari *mpl*
preliminary [prɪ'lɪmɪnərɪ] *adj* preliminare
prelude ['prɛlju:d] *n* preludio
premarital ['pri:'mærɪtl] *adj* prematrimoniale
premature ['prɛmətʃuə^r] *adj* prematuro(-a); (*arrival*) (molto) anticipato(-a); **you are being a little ~** è un po' troppo precipitoso
premeditated [pri:'mɛdɪteɪtɪd] *adj* premeditato(-a)
premeditation [pri:mɛdɪ'teɪʃən] *n* premeditazione *f*
premenstrual tension [pri:'mɛnstruəl-] *n* (*Med*) tensione *f* premestruale

P

premier ['prɛmɪəʳ] *adj* primo(-a) ■ *n* (*Pol*) primo ministro
première ['prɛmɪɛəʳ] *n* prima
premise ['prɛmɪs] *n* premessa
premises ['prɛmɪsɪz] *npl* locale *m*; **on the ~** sul posto; **business ~** locali commerciali
premium ['pri:mɪəm] *n* premio; **to be at a ~** (*fig: housing etc*) essere ricercatissimo; **to sell at a ~** (*shares*) vendere sopra la pari
premium bond *n* (*Brit*) obbligazione *f* a premio
premium deal *n* (*Comm*) offerta speciale
premium gasoline *n* (*US*) super *f*
premonition [prɛmə'nɪʃən] *n* premonizione *f*
preoccupation [pri:ɔkju'peɪʃən] *n* preoccupazione *f*
preoccupied [pri:'ɔkjupaɪd] *adj* preoccupato(-a)
prep [prɛp] *n abbr* (*Scol: = preparation*) studio ■ *adj abbr*: **~ school** = **preparatory school**
prepackaged [pri:'pækɪdʒd] *adj* già impacchettato(-a)
prepaid [pri:'peɪd] *adj* pagato(-a) in anticipo; (*envelope*) affrancato(-a)
preparation [prɛpə'reɪʃən] *n* preparazione *f*; **preparations** *npl* (*for trip, war*) preparativi *mpl*; **in ~ for sth** in vista di qc
preparatory [prɪ'pærətərɪ] *adj* preparatorio(-a); **~ to sth/to doing sth** prima di qc/di fare qc
preparatory school *n* (*Brit*) scuola elementare privata; (*US*) scuola superiore privata; *vedi nota*

PREPARATORY SCHOOL

In Gran Bretagna, la *prep(aratory) school* è una scuola privata frequentata da bambini dai 7 ai 13 anni in vista dell'iscrizione alla "public school". Negli Stati Uniti, invece, è una scuola superiore privata che prepara i ragazzi che si iscriveranno al "college".

prepare [prɪ'pɛəʳ] *vt* preparare ■ *vi*: **to ~ for** prepararsi a
prepared [prɪ'pɛəd] *adj*: **~ for** preparato(-a) a; **~ to** pronto(-a) a; **to be ~ to help sb** (*willing*) essere disposto *or* pronto ad aiutare qn
preponderance [prɪ'pɔndərns] *n* preponderanza
preposition [prɛpə'zɪʃən] *n* preposizione *f*
prepossessing [pri:pə'zɛsɪŋ] *adj* simpatico(-a), attraente
preposterous [prɪ'pɔstərəs] *adj* assurdo(-a)
prerecord ['pri:rɪ'kɔ:d] *vt* registrare in anticipo; **prerecorded broadcast** trasmissione *f* registrata; **prerecorded cassette** (musi)cassetta
prerequisite [pri:'rɛkwɪzɪt] *n* requisito indispensabile
prerogative [prɪ'rɔgətɪv] *n* prerogativa
presbyterian [prɛzbɪ'tɪərɪən] *adj, n* presbiteriano(-a)
presbytery ['prɛzbɪtərɪ] *n* presbiterio
preschool ['pri:'sku:l] *adj* (*age*) prescolastico(-a); (*child*) in età prescolastica
prescribe [prɪ'skraɪb] *vt* prescrivere; (*Med*) ordinare; **prescribed books** (*Brit Scol*) testi *mpl* in programma
prescription [prɪ'skrɪpʃən] *n* prescrizione *f*; (*Med*) ricetta; **to make up** *or* (*US*) **fill a ~** preparare *or* fare una ricetta; **"only available on ~"** "ottenibile solo dietro presentazione di ricetta medica"
prescription charges *npl* (*Brit*) ticket *m inv*
prescriptive [prɪ'skrɪptɪv] *adj* normativo(-a)
presence ['prɛzns] *n* presenza; **~ of mind** presenza di spirito
present ['prɛznt] *adj* presente; (*wife, residence, job*) attuale ■ *n* regalo; (*also:* **present tense**) tempo presente ■ *vt* [prɪ'zɛnt] presentare; (*give*): **to ~ sb with sth** offrire qc a qn; **to be ~ at** essere presente a; **those ~** i presenti; **at ~** al momento; **to make sb a ~ of sth** regalare qc a qn
presentable [prɪ'zɛntəbl] *adj* presentabile
presentation [prɛzn'teɪʃən] *n* presentazione *f*; (*gift*) regalo, dono; (*ceremony*) consegna ufficiale; **on ~ of the voucher** dietro presentazione del buono
present-day ['prɛzntdeɪ] *adj* attuale, d'oggigiorno
presenter [prɪ'zɛntəʳ] *n* (*Brit Radio, TV*) presentatore(-trice)
presently ['prɛzntlɪ] *adv* (*soon*) fra poco, presto; (*at present*) al momento; (*US: now*) adesso, ora
preservation [prɛzə'veɪʃən] *n* preservazione *f*, conservazione *f*
preservative [prɪ'zə:vətɪv] *n* conservante *m*
preserve [prɪ'zə:v] *vt* (*keep safe*) preservare, proteggere; (*maintain*) conservare; (*food*) mettere in conserva ■ *n* (*for game, fish*) riserva; (*often pl: jam*) marmellata; (*: fruit*) frutta sciroppata
preshrunk [pri:'ʃrʌŋk] *adj* irrestringibile
preside [prɪ'zaɪd] *vi* presiedere
presidency ['prɛzɪdənsɪ] *n* presidenza; (*US: of company*) direzione *f*
president ['prɛzɪdənt] *n* presidente *m*; (*US: of company*) direttore(-trice) generale
presidential [prɛzɪ'dɛnʃl] *adj* presidenziale
press [prɛs] *n* (*tool, machine*) pressa; (*for wine*) torchio; (*newspapers*) stampa; (*crowd*) folla

■ *vt* (*push*) premere, pigiare; (*doorbell*) suonare; (*squeeze*) spremere; (*: hand*) stringere; (*clothes: iron*) stirare; (*pursue*) incalzare; (*insist*): **to ~ sth on sb** far accettare qc da qn; (*urge, entreat*): **to ~ sb to do** *or* **into doing sth** fare pressione su qn affinché faccia qc ■ *vi* premere; accalcare; **to go to ~** (*newspaper*) andare in macchina; **to be in the ~** (*in the newspapers*) essere sui giornali; **we are pressed for time** ci manca il tempo; **to ~ for sth** insistere per avere qc; **to ~ sb for an answer** insistere perché qn risponda; **to ~ charges against sb** (*Law*) sporgere una denuncia contro qn

▸ **press ahead** *vi*: **to ~ ahead (with)** andare avanti (con)

▸ **press on** *vi* continuare

press agency *n* agenzia di stampa

press clipping *n* ritaglio di giornale

press conference *n* conferenza stampa

press cutting *n* = **press clipping**

press-gang ['prɛsgæŋ] *vt*: **to ~ sb into doing sth** costringere qn a viva forza a fare qc

pressing ['prɛsɪŋ] *adj* urgente ■ *n* stiratura

press officer *n* addetto(-a) stampa *inv*

press release *n* comunicato stampa

press stud *n* (*Brit*) bottone *m* a pressione

press-up ['prɛsʌp] *n* (*Brit*) flessione *f* sulle braccia

pressure ['prɛʃəʳ] *n* pressione *f* ■ *vt* = **to put pressure on**; **high/low ~** alta/bassa pressione; **to put ~ on sb** fare pressione su qn

pressure cooker *n* pentola a pressione

pressure gauge *n* manometro

pressure group *n* gruppo di pressione

pressurize ['prɛʃəraɪz] *vt* pressurizzare; (*fig*): **to ~ sb (into doing sth)** fare delle pressioni su qn (per costringerlo a fare qc)

pressurized ['prɛʃəraɪzd] *adj* pressurizzato(-a)

Prestel® ['prɛstɛl] *n* Videotel® *m inv*

prestige [prɛs'ti:ʒ] *n* prestigio

prestigious [prɛs'tɪdʒəs] *adj* prestigioso(-a)

presumably [prɪ'zju:məblɪ] *adv* presumibilmente; **~ he did it** penso *or* presumo che l'abbia fatto

presume [prɪ'zju:m] *vt* supporre; **to ~ to do** (*dare*) permettersi di fare

presumption [prɪ'zʌmpʃən] *n* presunzione *f*; (*boldness*) audacia

presumptuous [prɪ'zʌmpʃəs] *adj* presuntuoso(-a)

presuppose [pri:sə'pəuz] *vt* presupporre

pre-tax [pri:'tæks] *adj* al lordo d'imposta

pretence, (*US*) **pretense** [prɪ'tɛns] *n* (*claim*) pretesa; (*pretext*) pretesto, scusa; **to make a ~ of doing** far finta di fare; **on** *or* **under the ~ of doing sth** con il pretesto *or* la scusa di fare qc; **she is devoid of all ~** non si nasconde dietro false apparenze

pretend [prɪ'tɛnd] *vt* (*feign*) fingere ■ *vi* far finta; (*claim*): **to ~ to sth** pretendere a qc; **to ~ to do** far finta di fare

pretense [prɪ'tɛns] *n* (*US*) = **pretence**

pretension [prɪ'tɛnʃən] *n* (*claim*) pretesa; **to have no pretensions to sth/to being sth** non avere la pretesa di avere qc/di essere qc

pretentious [prɪ'tɛnʃəs] *adj* pretenzioso(-a)

preterite ['prɛtərɪt] *n* preterito

pretext ['pri:tɛkst] *n* pretesto; **on** *or* **under the ~ of doing sth** col pretesto di fare qc

pretty ['prɪtɪ] *adj* grazioso(-a), carino(-a) ■ *adv* abbastanza, assai

prevail [prɪ'veɪl] *vi* (*win, be usual*) prevalere; (*persuade*): **to ~ (up)on sb to do** persuadere qn a fare

prevailing [prɪ'veɪlɪŋ] *adj* dominante

prevalent ['prɛvələnt] *adj* (*belief*) predominante; (*customs*) diffuso(-a); (*fashion*) corrente; (*disease*) comune

prevarication [prɪværɪ'keɪʃən] *n* tergiversazione *f*

prevent [prɪ'vɛnt] *vt* prevenire; **to ~ sb from doing** impedire a qn di fare

preventable [prɪ'vɛntəbl] *adj* evitabile

preventative [prɪ'vɛntətɪv] *adj* preventivo(-a)

prevention [prɪ'vɛnʃən] *n* prevenzione *f*

preventive [prɪ'vɛntɪv] *adj* preventivo(-a)

preview ['pri:vju:] *n* (*of film*) anteprima

previous ['pri:vɪəs] *adj* precedente; anteriore; **I have a ~ engagement** ho già (preso) un impegno; **~ to doing** prima di fare

previously ['pri:vɪəslɪ] *adv* prima

prewar ['pri:'wɔ:ʳ] *adj* anteguerra *inv*

prey [preɪ] *n* preda ■ *vi*: **to ~ on** far preda di; **it was preying on his mind** gli rodeva la mente

price [praɪs] *n* prezzo; (*Betting: odds*) quotazione *f* ■ *vt* (*goods*) fissare il prezzo di; valutare; **what is the ~ of ...?** quanto costa ...?; **to go up** *or* **rise in ~** salire *or* aumentare di prezzo; **to put a ~ on sth** valutare *or* stimare qc; **he regained his freedom, but at a ~** ha riconquistato la sua libertà, ma a caro prezzo; **what ~ his promises now?** (*Brit*) a che valgono ora le sue promesse?; **to be priced out of the market** (*article*) essere così caro da diventare invendibile; (*producer, nation*) non poter sostenere la concorrenza

price control *n* controllo dei prezzi

price-cutting ['praɪskʌtɪŋ] *n* riduzione *f* dei prezzi

P

priceless ['praɪslɪs] *adj* di valore inestimabile; (*col: amusing*) impagabile, spassosissimo(-a)
price list *n* listino (dei) prezzi
price range *n* gamma di prezzi; **it's within my ~** rientra nelle mie possibilità
price tag *n* cartellino del prezzo
price war *n* guerra dei prezzi
pricey ['praɪsɪ] *adj* (*col*) caruccio(-a)
prick [prɪk] *n* puntura ■ *vt* pungere; **to ~ up one's ears** drizzare gli orecchi
prickle ['prɪkl] *n* (*of plant*) spina; (*sensation*) pizzicore *m*
prickly ['prɪklɪ] *adj* spinoso(-a); (*fig: person*) permaloso(-a)
prickly heat *n* sudamina
prickly pear *n* fico d'India
pride [praɪd] *n* orgoglio; superbia ■ *vt*: **to ~ o.s. on** essere orgoglioso(-a) di; vantarsi di; **to take (a) ~ in** tenere molto a; essere orgoglioso di; **to take a ~ in doing** andare orgoglioso di fare; **to have ~ of place** (*Brit*) essere al primo posto
priest [pri:st] *n* prete *m*, sacerdote *m*
priestess ['pri:stɪs] *n* sacerdotessa
priesthood ['pri:sthud] *n* sacerdozio
prig [prɪg] *n*: **he's a ~** è compiaciuto di se stesso
prim [prɪm] *adj* pudico(-a); contegnoso(-a)
primacy ['praɪməsɪ] *n* primato
prima facie ['praɪmə'feɪʃɪ] *adj*: **to have a ~ case** (*Law*) presentare una causa in apparenza fondata
primal ['praɪməl] *adj* primitivo(-a), originario(-a)
primarily ['praɪmərɪlɪ] *adv* principalmente, essenzialmente
primary ['praɪmərɪ] *adj* primario(-a); (*first in importance*) primo(-a) ■ *n* (*US: election*) primarie *fpl*; *vedi nota*

PRIMARY

Negli Stati Uniti, attraverso le *primaries* viene fatta una prima scrematura dei candidati dei partiti alle elezioni presidenziali. La scelta definitiva del candidato da presentare alla presidenza si basa sui risultati delle *primaries* e ha luogo durante le "Conventions" dei partiti, che si tengono in luglio e in agosto.

primary colour *n* colore *m* fondamentale
primary school *n* (*Brit*) scuola elementare; *vedi nota*

PRIMARY SCHOOL

In Gran Bretagna la *primary school* è la scuola elementare, frequentata dai bambini dai 5 agli 11 anni di età. È suddivisa in "infant school" (5-7 anni) e "junior school" (7-11 anni); *vedi anche* "secondary school".

primate *n* (*Rel*: ['praɪmɪt], *Zool*: ['praɪmeɪt]) primate *m*
prime [praɪm] *adj* primario(-a), fondamentale; (*excellent*) di prima qualità ■ *n*: **in the ~ of life** nel fiore della vita ■ *vt* (*gun*) innescare; (*pump*) adescare; (*fig*) mettere al corrente
prime minister *n* primo ministro
primer ['praɪmə^r] *n* (*book*) testo elementare; (*paint*) vernice *f* base *inv*
prime time *n* (*Radio, TV*) fascia di massimo ascolto
primeval [praɪ'mi:vl] *adj* primitivo(-a)
primitive ['prɪmɪtɪv] *adj* primitivo(-a)
primrose ['prɪmrəuz] *n* primavera
primus® ['praɪməs], **primus® stove** *n* (*Brit*) fornello a petrolio
prince [prɪns] *n* principe *m*
prince charming *n* principe *m* azzurro
princess [prɪn'sɛs] *n* principessa
principal ['prɪnsɪpl] *adj* principale ■ *n* (*of school, college etc*) preside *m/f*; (*money*) capitale *m*; (*in play*) protagonista *m/f*
principality [prɪnsɪ'pælɪtɪ] *n* principato
principally ['prɪnsɪplɪ] *adv* principalmente
principle ['prɪnsɪpl] *n* principio; **in ~** in linea di principio; **on ~** per principio
print [prɪnt] *n* (*mark*) impronta; (*letters*) caratteri *mpl*; (*fabric*) tessuto stampato; (*Art, Phot*) stampa ■ *vt* imprimere; (*publish*) stampare, pubblicare; (*write in capitals*) scrivere in stampatello; **out of ~** esaurito(-a)
▸ **print out** *vt* (*Comput*) stampare
printed circuit board [prɪntɪd-] *n* circuito stampato
printed matter [prɪntɪd-] *n* stampe *fpl*
printer ['prɪntə^r] *n* tipografo; (*machine*) stampante *m*
printhead ['prɪnthɛd] *n* testa di stampa
printing ['prɪntɪŋ] *n* stampa
printing press *n* macchina tipografica
print-out ['prɪntaut] *n* tabulato
print wheel *n* margherita
prior ['praɪə^r] *adj* precedente ■ *n* (*Rel*) priore *m*; **~ to doing** prima di fare; **without ~ notice** senza preavviso; **to have a ~ claim to sth** avere un diritto di precedenza su qc
priority [praɪ'ɔrɪtɪ] *n* priorità *f inv*,

precedenza; **to have** *or* **take ~ over sth** avere la precedenza su qc
priory ['praɪərɪ] *n* monastero
prise [praɪz] *vt*: **to ~ open** forzare
prism ['prɪzəm] *n* prisma *m*
prison ['prɪzn] *n* prigione *f*
prison camp *n* campo di prigionia
prisoner ['prɪznəʳ] *n* prigioniero(-a); **to take sb ~** far prigioniero qn; **the ~ at the bar** l'accusato, l'imputato; **~ of war** prigioniero(-a) di guerra
prissy ['prɪsɪ] *adj* per benino
pristine ['prɪsti:n] *adj* originario(-a); intatto(-a); puro(-a)
privacy ['prɪvəsɪ] *n* solitudine *f*, intimità
private ['praɪvɪt] *adj* privato(-a); personale ■ *n* soldato semplice; **"~"** (*on envelope*) "riservata"; **in ~** in privato; **in (his) ~ life** nella vita privata; **he is a very ~ person** è una persona molto riservata; **~ hearing** (*Law*) udienza a porte chiuse; **to be in ~ practice** essere medico non convenzionato (con la mutua)
private enterprise *n* iniziativa privata
private eye *n* investigatore *m* privato
private limited company *n* (*Brit*) *società per azioni non quotata in Borsa*
privately ['praɪvɪtlɪ] *adv* in privato; (*within o.s.*) dentro di sé
private parts *npl* (*Anat*) parti *fpl* intime
private property *n* proprietà privata
private school *n* scuola privata
privation [praɪ'veɪʃən] *n* (*state*) privazione *f*; (*hardship*) privazioni *fpl*, stenti *mpl*
privatize ['praɪvɪtaɪz] *vt* privatizzare
privet ['prɪvɪt] *n* ligustro
privilege ['prɪvɪlɪdʒ] *n* privilegio
privileged ['prɪvɪlɪdʒd] *adj* privilegiato(-a); **to be ~ to do sth** avere il privilegio *or* l'onore di fare qc
privy ['prɪvɪ] *adj*: **to be ~ to** essere al corrente di
Privy Council *n* (*Brit*) Consiglio della Corona; *vedi nota*

PRIVY COUNCIL

Il *Privy Council*, un gruppo di consiglieri del re, era il principale organo di governo durante il regno dei Tudor e degli Stuart. Col tempo ha perso la sua importanza e oggi è un organo senza potere effettivo formato da ministri e altre personalità politiche ed ecclesiastiche.

Privy Councillor *n* (*Brit*) Consigliere *m* della Corona
prize [praɪz] *n* premio ■ *adj* (*example, idiot*) perfetto(-a); (*bull, novel*) premiato(-a) ■ *vt* apprezzare, pregiare
prize-fighter ['praɪzfaɪtəʳ] *n* pugile *m* (*che si batte per conquistare un premio*)
prize giving *n* premiazione *f*
prize money *n* soldi *mpl* del premio
prizewinner ['praɪzwɪnəʳ] *n* premiato(-a)
prizewinning ['praɪzwɪnɪŋ] *adj* vincente; (*novel, essay etc*) premiato(-a)
PRO *n abbr* = **public relations officer**
pro [prəu] *n* (*Sport*) professionista *m/f*; **the pros and cons** il pro e il contro
pro- [prəu] *prefix* (*in favour of*) filo...; **~Soviet** *adj* filosovietico(-a)
pro-active [prəu'æktɪv] *adj*: **to be ~** agire d'iniziativa
probability [prɔbə'bɪlɪtɪ] *n* probabilità *f inv*; **in all ~** con ogni probabilità
probable ['prɔbəbl] *adj* probabile; **it is ~/ hardly ~ that ...** è probabile/poco probabile che ... + *sub*
probably ['prɔbəblɪ] *adv* probabilmente
probate ['prəubɪt] *n* (*Law*) omologazione *f* (*di un testamento*)
probation [prə'beɪʃən] *n* (*in employment*) periodo di prova; (*Law*) libertà vigilata; (*Rel*) probandato; **on ~** (*employee*) in prova; (*Law*) in libertà vigilata
probationary [prəu'beɪʃənərɪ] *adj*: **~ period** periodo di prova
probe [prəub] *n* (*Med, Space*) sonda; (*enquiry*) indagine *f*, investigazione *f* ■ *vt* sondare, esplorare; indagare
probity ['prəubɪtɪ] *n* probità
problem ['prɔbləm] *n* problema *m*; **to have problems with the car** avere dei problemi con la macchina; **what's the ~?** che cosa c'è?; **I had no ~ in finding her** non mi è stato difficile trovarla; **no ~!** ma certamente!, non c'è problema!
problematic [prɔblə'mætɪk] *adj* problematico(-a)
problem-solving ['prɔbləmsɔlvɪŋ] *n* risoluzione *f* di problemi
procedure [prə'si:dʒəʳ] *n* (*Admin, Law*) procedura; (*method*) metodo, procedimento
proceed [prə'si:d] *vi* (*go forward*) avanzare, andare avanti; (*go about it*) procedere; (*continue*): **to ~ (with)** continuare; **to ~ to** andare a; passare a; **to ~ to do** mettersi a fare; **to ~ against sb** (*Law*) procedere contro qn; **I am not sure how to ~** non so bene come fare
proceedings [prə'si:dɪŋz] *npl* misure *fpl*; (*Law*) procedimento; (*meeting*) riunione *f*; (*records*) rendiconti *mpl*; atti *mpl*

P

proceeds ['prəusi:dz] *npl* profitto, incasso
process ['prəusɛs] *n* processo; (*method*) metodo, sistema *m* ■ *vt* trattare; (*information*) elaborare ■ *vi* [prə'sɛs] (*Brit formal: go in procession*) sfilare, procedere in corteo; **we are in the ~ of moving to ...** stiamo per trasferirci a ...
processed cheese, (*US*) **process cheese** *n* formaggio fuso
processing ['prəusɛsɪŋ] *n* trattamento; elaborazione *f*
procession [prə'sɛʃən] *n* processione *f*, corteo; **funeral ~** corteo funebre
pro-choice [prəu'tʃɔɪs] *adj* per la libertà di scelta di gravidanza
proclaim [prə'kleɪm] *vt* proclamare, dichiarare
proclamation [prɔklə'meɪʃən] *n* proclamazione *f*
proclivity [prə'klɪvɪtɪ] *n* tendenza, propensione *f*
procrastination [prəukræstɪ'neɪʃən] *n* procrastinazione *f*
procreation [prəukrɪ'eɪʃən] *n* procreazione *f*
Procurator Fiscal ['prɔkjureɪtə-] *n* (*Scottish*) procuratore *m*
procure [prə'kjuə^r] *vt* (*for o.s.*) procurarsi; (*for sb*) procurare
procurement [prə'kjuəmənt] *n* approvvigionamento
prod [prɔd] *vt* dare un colpetto a ■ *n* (*push, jab*) colpetto
prodigal ['prɔdɪgl] *adj* prodigo(-a)
prodigious [prə'dɪdʒəs] *adj* prodigioso(-a)
prodigy ['prɔdɪdʒɪ] *n* prodigio
produce *n* ['prɔdju:s] (*Agr*) prodotto, prodotti *mpl* ■ *vt* [prə'dju:s] produrre; (*show*) esibire, mostrare; (*proof of identity*) produrre, fornire; (*cause*) cagionare, causare; (*Theat*) mettere in scena
producer [prə'dju:sə^r] *n* (*Theat*) direttore(-trice); (*Agr, Cine*) produttore *m*
product ['prɔdʌkt] *n* prodotto
production [prə'dʌkʃən] *n* produzione *f*; (*Theat*) messa in scena; **to put into ~** mettere in produzione
production agreement *n* (*US*) accordo sui tempi di produzione
production line *n* catena di lavorazione
production manager *n* production manager *m inv*, direttore *m* della produzione
productive [prə'dʌktɪv] *adj* produttivo(-a)
productivity [prɔdʌk'tɪvɪtɪ] *n* produttività
productivity agreement *n* (*Brit*) accordo sui tempi di produzione
productivity bonus *n* premio di produzione
Prof. *abbr* (= *professor*) Prof.
profane [prə'feɪn] *adj* profano(-a); (*language*) empio(-a)
profess [prə'fɛs] *vt* professare; **I do not ~ to be an expert** non pretendo di essere un esperto
professed [prə'fɛst] *adj* (*self-declared*) dichiarato(-a)
profession [prə'fɛʃən] *n* professione *f*; **the professions** le professioni liberali
professional [prə'fɛʃənl] *n* (*Sport*) professionista *m/f* ■ *adj* professionale; (*work*) da professionista; **he's a ~ man** è un professionista; **to take ~ advice** consultare un esperto
professionalism [prə'fɛʃnəlɪzəm] *n* professionismo
professionally [prə'fɛʃnəlɪ] *adv* professionalmente, in modo professionale; (*Sport: play*) come professionista; **I only know him ~** con lui ho solo rapporti di lavoro
professor [prə'fɛsə^r] *n* professore *m* (*titolare di una cattedra*); (*US: teacher*) professore(-essa)
professorship [prə'fɛsəʃɪp] *n* cattedra
proffer ['prɔfə^r] *vt* (*remark*) profferire; (*apologies*) porgere, presentare; (*one's hand*) porgere
proficiency [prə'fɪʃənsɪ] *n* competenza, abilità
proficient [prə'fɪʃənt] *adj* competente, abile
profile ['prəufaɪl] *n* profilo; **to keep a low ~** (*fig*) cercare di passare inosservato *or* di non farsi notare troppo; **to maintain a high ~** mettersi in mostra
profit ['prɔfɪt] *n* profitto; beneficio ■ *vi*: **to ~ (by** *or* **from)** approfittare (di); **~ and loss account** conto perdite e profitti; **to make a ~** realizzare un profitto; **to sell sth at a ~** vendere qc con un utile
profitability [prɔfɪtə'bɪlɪtɪ] *n* redditività
profitable ['prɔfɪtəbl] *adj* redditizio(-a); (*fig: beneficial*) vantaggioso(-a); (*: meeting, visit*) fruttuoso(-a)
profit centre *n* centro di profitto
profiteering [prɔfɪ'tɪərɪŋ] *n* (*pej*) affarismo
profit-making ['prɔfɪtmeɪkɪŋ] *adj* a scopo di lucro
profit margin *n* margine *m* di profitto
profit-sharing ['prɔfɪtʃɛərɪŋ] *n* compartecipazione *f* agli utili
profits tax *n* (*Brit*) imposta sugli utili
profligate ['prɔflɪgɪt] *adj* (*dissolute: behaviour*) dissipato(-a); (*: person*) debosciato(-a); (*extravagant*): **he's very ~ with his money** è uno che sperpera i suoi soldi
pro forma ['prəu'fɔ:mə] *adv*: **~ invoice** fattura proforma
profound [prə'faund] *adj* profondo(-a)
profuse [prə'fju:s] *adj* infinito(-a), abbondante

profusely [prəˈfjuːslɪ] *adv* con grande effusione
profusion [prəˈfjuːʒən] *n* profusione *f*, abbondanza
progeny [ˈprɔdʒɪnɪ] *n* progenie *f*; discendenti *mpl*
programme, (*US*) **program** [ˈprəugræm] *n* programma *m* ■ *vt* programmare
programmer, programer [ˈprəugræməʳ] *n* programmatore(-trice)
programming, programing [ˈprəugræmɪŋ] *n* programmazione *f*
programming language, programing language *n* linguaggio di programmazione
progress *n* [ˈprəugrɛs] progresso ■ *vi* [prəˈgrɛs] (*go forward*) avanzare, procedere; (*in time*) procedere; (*also*: **make progress**) far progressi; **in ~** in corso
progression [prəˈgrɛʃən] *n* progressione *f*
progressive [prəˈgrɛsɪv] *adj* progressivo(-a); (*person*) progressista
progressively [prəˈgrɛsɪvlɪ] *adv* progressivamente
progress report *n* (*Med*) bollettino medico; (*Admin*) rendiconto dei lavori
prohibit [prəˈhɪbɪt] *vt* proibire, vietare; **to ~ sb from doing sth** vietare *or* proibire a qn di fare qc; **"smoking prohibited"** "vietato fumare"
prohibition [prəuɪˈbɪʃən] *n* (*US*) proibizionismo
prohibitive [prəˈhɪbɪtɪv] *adj* (*price etc*) proibitivo(-a)
project *n* [ˈprɔdʒɛkt] (*plan*) piano; (*venture*) progetto; (*Scol*) studio, ricerca ■ *vt* [prəˈdʒɛkt] proiettare ■ *vi* (*stick out*) sporgere
projectile [prəˈdʒɛktaɪl] *n* proiettile *m*
projection [prəˈdʒɛkʃən] *n* proiezione *f*; sporgenza
projectionist [prəˈdʒɛkʃənɪst] *n* (*Cine*) proiezionista *m/f*
projection room *n* (*Cine*) cabina *or* sala di proiezione
projector [prəˈdʒɛktəʳ] *n* proiettore *m*
proletarian [prəulɪˈtɛərɪən] *adj, n* proletario(-a)
proletariat [prəulɪˈtɛərɪət] *n* proletariato
pro-life [prəuˈlaɪf] *adj* per il diritto alla vita
proliferate [prəˈlɪfəreɪt] *vi* proliferare
proliferation [prəlɪfəˈreɪʃən] *n* proliferazione *f*
prolific [prəˈlɪfɪk] *adj* prolifico(-a)
prologue, (*US*) **prolog** [ˈprəulɔg] *n* prologo
prolong [prəˈlɔŋ] *vt* prolungare
prom [prɔm] *n abbr* = **promenade**; **promenade concert**; (*US: ball*) ballo studentesco; *vedi nota*

PROM

In Gran Bretagna i *Proms* (= promenade concerts) sono concerti di musica classica, i più noti dei quali sono quelli eseguiti nella Royal Albert Hall a Londra. Prendono il nome dal fatto che in origine il pubblico li ascoltava stando in piedi o passeggiando. Negli Stati Uniti, invece, con *prom* si intende il ballo studentesco di un'università o di un college.

promenade [prɔməˈnɑːd] *n* (*by sea*) lungomare *m*
promenade concert *n* concerto (*con posti in piedi*)
promenade deck *n* (*Naut*) ponte *m* di passeggiata
prominence [ˈprɔmɪnəns] *n* prominenza; importanza
prominent [ˈprɔmɪnənt] *adj* (*standing out*) prominente; (*important*) importante; **he is ~ in the field of ...** è un'autorità nel campo di ....
prominently [ˈprɔmɪnəntlɪ] *adv* (*display, set*) ben in vista; **he figured ~ in the case** ha avuto una parte di primo piano nella faccenda
promiscuity [prɔmɪsˈkjuːɪtɪ] *n* (*sexual*) rapporti *mpl* multipli
promiscuous [prəˈmɪskjuəs] *adj* (*sexually*) di facili costumi
promise [ˈprɔmɪs] *n* promessa ■ *vt, vi* promettere; **to make sb a ~** fare una promessa a qn; **a young man of ~** un giovane promettente; **to ~ (sb) to do sth** promettere (a qn) di fare qc
promising [ˈprɔmɪsɪŋ] *adj* promettente
promissory note [ˈprɔmɪsərɪ-] *n* pagherò *m inv*
promontory [ˈprɔməntrɪ] *n* promontorio
promote [prəˈməut] *vt* promuovere; (*venture, event*) organizzare; (*product*) lanciare, reclamizzare; **the team was promoted to the second division** (*Brit Football*) la squadra è stata promossa in serie B
promoter [prəˈməutəʳ] *n* (*of sporting event*) organizzatore(-trice); (*of cause etc*) sostenitore(-trice)
promotion [prəˈməuʃən] *n* promozione *f*
prompt [prɔmpt] *adj* rapido(-a), svelto(-a); puntuale; (*reply*) sollecito(-a) ■ *adv* (*punctually*) in punto ■ *n* (*Comput*) guida ■ *vt* incitare; provocare; (*Theat*) suggerire a; **at 8 o'clock ~** alle 8 in punto; **to be ~ to do sth** essere sollecito nel fare qc; **to ~ sb to do** spingere qn a fare

P

prompter ['prɔmptəʳ] *n* (*Theat*) suggeritore *m*
promptly ['prɔmptlɪ] *adv* prontamente; puntualmente
promptness ['prɔmptnɪs] *n* prontezza; puntualità
prone [prəun] *adj* (*lying*) prono(-a); **~ to** propenso(-a) a, incline a; **to be ~ to illness** essere soggetto(-a) a malattie; **she is ~ to burst into tears if ...** può facilmente scoppiare in lacrime se ...
prong [prɔŋ] *n* rebbio, punta
pronoun ['prəunaun] *n* pronome *m*
pronounce [prə'nauns] *vt* pronunziare ■ *vi*: **to ~ (up)on** pronunziare su; **they pronounced him unfit to drive** lo hanno dichiarato inabile alla guida
pronounced [prə'naunst] *adj* (*marked*) spiccato(-a)
pronouncement [prə'naunsmənt] *n* dichiarazione *f*
pronunciation [prənʌnsɪ'eɪʃən] *n* pronunzia
proof [pru:f] *n* prova; (*of book*) bozza; (*Phot*) provino; (*of alcohol*): **70% ~** ≈ 40° in volume ■ *vt* (*tent, anorak*) impermeabilizzare ■ *adj*: **~ against** a prova di
proofreader ['pru:fri:dəʳ] *n* correttore(-trice) di bozze
prop [prɔp] *n* sostegno, appoggio ■ *vt* (*also*: **prop up**) sostenere, appoggiare; (*lean*): **to ~ sth against** appoggiare qc contro *or* a
Prop. *abbr* (*Comm*) = **proprietor**
propaganda [prɔpə'gændə] *n* propaganda
propagation [prɔpə'geɪʃən] *n* propagazione *f*
propel [prə'pɛl] *vt* spingere (in avanti), muovere
propeller [prə'pɛləʳ] *n* elica
propelling pencil [prə'pɛlɪŋ-] *n* (*Brit*) matita a mina
propensity [prə'pɛnsɪtɪ] *n* tendenza
proper ['prɔpəʳ] *adj* (*suited, right*) adatto(-a), appropriato(-a); (*seemly*) decente; (*authentic*) vero(-a); (*col: real*) 'n' + vero(-a) e proprio(-a); **to go through the ~ channels** (*Admin*) seguire la regolare procedura
properly ['prɔpəlɪ] *adv* decentemente; (*really, thoroughly*) veramente
proper noun *n* nome *m* proprio
property ['prɔpətɪ] *n* (*things owned*) beni *mpl*; (*land, building, Chem etc*) proprietà *f inv*
property developer *n* (*Brit*) costruttore *m* edile
property owner *n* proprietario(-a)
property tax *n* imposta patrimoniale
prophecy ['prɔfɪsɪ] *n* profezia
prophesy ['prɔfɪsaɪ] *vt* predire, profetizzare
prophet ['prɔfɪt] *n* profeta *m*
prophetic [prə'fɛtɪk] *adj* profetico(-a)
proportion [prə'pɔ:ʃən] *n* proporzione *f*; (*share*) parte *f* ■ *vt* proporzionare, commisurare; **to be in/out of ~ to** *or* **with sth** essere in proporzione/sproporzionato rispetto a qc; **to see sth in ~** (*fig*) dare il giusto peso a qc
proportional [prə'pɔ:ʃənl] *adj* proporzionale
proportional representation *n* rappresentanza proporzionale
proportionate [prə'pɔ:ʃənɪt] *adj* proporzionato(-a)
proposal [prə'pəuzl] *n* proposta; (*plan*) progetto; (*of marriage*) proposta di matrimonio
propose [prə'pəuz] *vt* proporre, suggerire ■ *vi* fare una proposta di matrimonio; **to ~ to do** proporsi di fare, aver l'intenzione di fare
proposer [prə'pəuzəʳ] *n* (*Brit: of motion*) proponente *m/f*
proposition [prɔpə'zɪʃən] *n* proposizione *f*; (*proposal*) proposta; **to make sb a ~** proporre qualcosa a qn
propound [prə'paund] *vt* proporre, presentare
proprietary [prə'praɪətərɪ] *adj*: **~ article** prodotto con marchio depositato; **~ brand** marchio di fabbrica
proprietor [prə'praɪətəʳ] *n* proprietario(-a)
propriety [prə'praɪətɪ] *n* (*seemliness*) decoro, rispetto delle convenienze sociali
propulsion [prə'pʌlʃən] *n* propulsione *f*
pro rata [prəu'rɑ:tə] *adv* in proporzione
prosaic [prəu'zeɪɪk] *adj* prosaico(-a)
Pros. Atty. *abbr* (*US*) = **prosecuting attorney**
proscribe [prə'skraɪb] *vt* proscrivere
prose [prəuz] *n* prosa; (*Scol: translation*) traduzione *f* dalla madrelingua
prosecute ['prɔsɪkju:t] *vt* intentare azione contro
prosecuting attorney ['prɔsɪkju:tɪŋ-] *n* (*US*) ≈ procuratore *m*
prosecution [prɔsɪ'kju:ʃən] *n* (*Law*) azione *f* giudiziaria; (*accusing side*) accusa
prosecutor ['prɔsɪkju:təʳ] *n* (*also*: **public prosecutor**) ≈ procuratore *m* della Repubblica
prospect *n* ['prɔspɛkt] prospettiva; (*hope*) speranza ■ *vt* [prə'spɛkt] esplorare ■ *vi*: **to ~ for gold** cercare l'oro; **there is every ~ of an early victory** tutto lascia prevedere una rapida vittoria; *see also* **prospects**
prospecting [prə'spɛktɪŋ] *n* prospezione *f*
prospective [prə'spɛktɪv] *adj* (*buyer*) probabile; (*legislation, son-in-law*) futuro(-a)
prospector [prə'spɛktəʳ] *n* prospettore *m*; **gold ~** cercatore *m* d'oro

prospects ['prɔspɛkts] *npl* (*for work etc*) prospettive *fpl*
prospectus [prə'spɛktəs] *n* prospetto, programma *m*
prosper ['prɔspəʳ] *vi* prosperare
prosperity [prɔ'spɛrɪtɪ] *n* prosperità
prosperous ['prɔspərəs] *adj* prospero(-a)
prostate ['prɔsteɪt] *n* (*also*: **prostate gland**) prostata, ghiandola prostatica
prostitute ['prɔstɪtju:t] *n* prostituta; **male ~** uomo che si prostituisce
prostitution [prɔstɪ'tju:ʃən] *n* prostituzione *f*
prostrate *adj* ['prɔstreɪt] prostrato(-a) ■ *vt* [prɔ'streɪt]: **to ~ o.s.** (*before sb*) prostrarsi
protagonist [prə'tægənɪst] *n* protagonista *m/f*
protect [prə'tɛkt] *vt* proteggere, salvaguardare
protection [prə'tɛkʃən] *n* protezione *f*; **to be under sb's ~** essere sotto la protezione di qn
protectionism [prə'tɛkʃənɪzəm] *n* protezionismo
protection racket *n* racket *m inv*
protective [prə'tɛktɪv] *adj* protettivo(-a); **~ custody** (*Law*) protezione *f*
protector [prə'tɛktəʳ] *n* protettore(-trice)
protégé ['prəutɪʒeɪ] *n* protetto
protégée ['prəutɪʒeɪ] *n* protetta
protein ['prəuti:n] *n* proteina
pro tem [prəu'tɛm] *adv abbr* (*for the time being*: = *pro tempore*) pro tempore
protest *n* ['prəutɛst] protesta ■ *vt, vi* [prə'tɛst] protestare; **to do sth under ~** fare qc protestando; **to ~ against/about** protestare contro/per
Protestant ['prɔtɪstənt] *adj, n* protestante (*m/f*)
protester, protestor [prə'tɛstəʳ] *n* (*in demonstration*) dimostrante *m/f*
protest march *n* marcia di protesta
protocol ['prəutəkɔl] *n* protocollo
prototype ['prəutətaɪp] *n* prototipo
protracted [prə'træktɪd] *adj* tirato(-a) per le lunghe
protractor [prə'træktəʳ] *n* (*Geom*) goniometro
protrude [prə'tru:d] *vi* sporgere
protuberance [prə'tju:bərəns] *n* sporgenza
proud [praud] *adj* fiero(-a), orgoglioso(-a); (*pej*) superbo(-a); **to be ~ to do sth** essere onorato(-a) di fare qc; **to do sb ~** non far mancare nulla a qn; **to do o.s. ~** trattarsi bene
proudly ['praudlɪ] *adv* con orgoglio, fieramente
prove [pru:v] *vt* provare, dimostrare ■ *vi*: **to ~ correct** *etc* risultare vero(-a) *etc*; **to ~ o.s.** mostrare le proprie capacità; **to ~ o.s./itself (to be) useful** *etc* mostrarsi *or* rivelarsi utile *etc*; **he was proved right in the end** alla fine i fatti gli hanno dato ragione
Provence [prɔvɑ̃s] *n* Provenza
proverb ['prɔvə:b] *n* proverbio
proverbial [prə'və:bɪəl] *adj* proverbiale
provide [prə'vaɪd] *vt* fornire, provvedere; **to ~ sb with sth** fornire *or* provvedere qn di qc; **to be provided with** essere dotato *or* munito di
▸ **provide for** *vt fus* provvedere a
provided [prə'vaɪdɪd] *conj*: **~ (that)** purché + *sub*, a condizione che + *sub*
Providence ['prɔvɪdəns] *n* Provvidenza
providing [prə'vaɪdɪŋ] *conj* purché + *sub*, a condizione che + *sub*
province ['prɔvɪns] *n* provincia
provincial [prə'vɪnʃəl] *adj* provinciale
provision [prə'vɪʒən] *n* (*supply*) riserva; (*supplying*) provvista; rifornimento; (*stipulation*) condizione *f*; **provisions** *npl* (*food*) provviste *fpl*; **to make ~ for** (*one's family, future*) pensare a; **there's no ~ for this in the contract** il contratto non lo prevede
provisional [prə'vɪʒənl] *adj* provvisorio(-a) ■ *n*: **P~** (*Irish Pol*) provisional *m inv*
provisional licence *n* (*Brit Aut*) ≈ foglio *m* rosa *inv*
provisionally [prə'vɪʒnəlɪ] *adv* provvisoriamente; (*appoint*) a titolo provvisorio
proviso [prə'vaɪzəu] *n* condizione *f*; **with the ~ that** a condizione che + *sub*, a patto che + *sub*
Provo ['prɔvəu] *n abbr* (*col*) = **Provisional**
provocation [prɔvə'keɪʃən] *n* provocazione *f*
provocative [prə'vɔkətɪv] *adj* (*aggressive*) provocatorio(-a); (*thought-provoking*) stimolante; (*seductive*) provocante
provoke [prə'vəuk] *vt* provocare; incitare; **to ~ sb to sth/to do** *or* **into doing sth** spingere qn a qc/a fare qc
provoking [prə'vəukɪŋ] *adj* irritante, esasperante
provost ['prɔvəst] *n* (*Brit*: *of university*) rettore *m*; (*Scottish*) sindaco
prow [prau] *n* prua
prowess ['prauɪs] *n* prodezza; **his ~ as a footballer** le sue capacità di calciatore
prowl [praul] *vi* (*also*: **prowl about, prowl around**) aggirarsi furtivamente ■ *n*: **on the ~** in cerca di preda
prowler ['prauləʳ] *n* tipo sospetto (*che s'aggira con l'intenzione di rubare, aggredire etc*)
proximity [prɔk'sɪmɪtɪ] *n* prossimità
proxy ['prɔksɪ] *n* procura; **by ~** per procura
PRP *n abbr* (= *performance related pay*) retribuzione *f* commensurata al rendimento

P

prude [pru:d] *n* puritano(-a)
prudence ['pru:dns] *n* prudenza
prudent ['pru:dnt] *adj* prudente
prudish ['pru:dɪʃ] *adj* puritano(-a)
prune [pru:n] *n* prugna secca ■ *vt* potare
pry [praɪ] *vi*: **to ~ into** ficcare il naso in
PS *n abbr* (= *postscript*) P.S.
psalm [sɑ:m] *n* salmo
PSAT® *n abbr* (US) = **Preliminary Scholastic Aptitude Test**
PSBR *n abbr* (*Brit*: = *public sector borrowing requirement*) *fabbisogno di prestiti per il settore pubblico*
pseud ['sju:d] *n* (*Brit col*: *intellectually*) intellettualoide *m/f*; (: *socially*) snob *m/f inv*
pseudo- ['sju:dəu] *prefix* pseudo...
pseudonym ['sju:dənɪm] *n* pseudonimo
PSHE *n abbr* (*Brit*: *Scol*: = *personal, social and health education*) *formazione di formazione sociale e sanitaria*
PST *abbr* (*US*: = *Pacific Standard Time*) *ora invernale del Pacifico*
psyche ['saɪkɪ] *n* psiche *f*
psychedelic [saɪkɪ'dɛlɪk] *adj* psichedelico(-a)
psychiatric [saɪkɪ'ætrɪk] *adj* psichiatrico(-a)
psychiatrist [saɪ'kaɪətrɪst] *n* psichiatra *m/f*
psychiatry [saɪ'kaɪətrɪ] *n* psichiatria
psychic ['saɪkɪk] *adj* (*also*: **psychical**) psichico(-a); (*person*) dotato(-a) di qualità telepatiche
psycho ['saɪkəu] *n* (*col*) folle *m/f*, psicopatico(-a)
psychoanalyse [saɪkəu'ænəlaɪz] *vt* psicanalizzare
psychoanalysis (*pl* **-ses**) [saɪkəuə'nælɪsɪs, -si:z] *n* psicanalisi *f inv*
psychoanalyst [saɪkəu'ænəlɪst] *n* psicanalista *m/f*
psychological [saɪkə'lɔdʒɪkl] *adj* psicologico(-a)
psychologist [saɪ'kɔlədʒɪst] *n* psicologo(-a)
psychology [saɪ'kɔlədʒɪ] *n* psicologia
psychopath ['saɪkəupæθ] *n* psicopatico(-a)
psychosis (*pl* **psychoses**) [saɪ'kəusɪs, -si:z] *n* psicosi *f inv*
psychosomatic [saɪkəusə'mætɪk] *adj* psicosomatico(-a)
psychotherapy [saɪkəu'θɛrəpɪ] *n* psicoterapia
psychotic [saɪ'kɔtɪk] *adj, n* psicotico(-a)
PT *n abbr* (*Brit*: = *physical training*) ed. fisica
pt *abbr* (= *pint, point*) pt
Pt. *abbr* (*in place names*: = *Point*) Pt.
PTA *n abbr* (= *Parent-Teacher Association*) *associazione genitori e insegnanti*
Pte. *abbr* (*Brit Mil*) = **private**
PTO *abbr* (= *please turn over*) v.r. (= *vedi retro*)
PTV *n abbr* (US) = **pay television**; **public television**
pub [pʌb] *n abbr* (= *public house*) pub *m inv*; *vedi nota*

PUB

In Gran Bretagna e in Irlanda i *pubs* sono locali dove vengono servite bibite alcoliche ed analcoliche e dove è anche possibile mangiare. Sono punti di ritrovo dove spesso si può giocare a biliardo, a freccette o guardare la televisione. Le leggi che regolano la vendita degli alcolici sono molto severe in Gran Bretagna e quindi gli orari di apertura e di chiusura vengono osservati scrupolosamente.

pub crawl *n*: **to go on a ~** (*Brit col*) fare il giro dei pub
puberty ['pju:bətɪ] *n* pubertà
pubic ['pju:bɪk] *adj* pubico(-a), del pube
public ['pʌblɪk] *adj* pubblico(-a) ■ *n* pubblico; **in ~** in pubblico; **the general ~** il pubblico; **to make sth ~** render noto *or* di pubblico dominio qc; **to be ~ knowledge** essere di dominio pubblico; **to go ~** (*Comm*) emettere le azioni sul mercato
public address system *n* impianto di amplificazione
publican ['pʌblɪkən] *n* (*Brit*) gestore *m* (*or* proprietario) di un pub
publication [pʌblɪ'keɪʃən] *n* pubblicazione *f*
public company *n* ≈ società *f inv* per azioni (*costituita tramite pubblica sottoscrizione*)
public convenience *n* (*Brit*) gabinetti *mpl*
public holiday *n* (*Brit*) giorno festivo, festa nazionale
public house *n* (*Brit*) pub *m inv*
publicity [pʌb'lɪsɪtɪ] *n* pubblicità
publicize ['pʌblɪsaɪz] *vt* fare (della) pubblicità a, reclamizzare
public limited company *n* ≈ società per azioni a responsabilità limitata (*quotata in Borsa*)
publicly ['pʌblɪklɪ] *adv* pubblicamente
public opinion *n* opinione *f* pubblica
public ownership *n* proprietà pubblica *or* sociale; **to be taken into ~** essere statalizzato(-a)
public prosecutor *n* pubblico ministero; **~'s office** ufficio del pubblico ministero
public relations *n* pubbliche relazioni *fpl*
public relations officer *n* addetto(-a) alle pubbliche relazioni
public school *n* (*Brit*) scuola privata; (*US*) scuola statale; *vedi nota*

PUBLIC SCHOOL

In Inghilterra le *public schools* sono scuole o collegi privati di istruzione secondaria, spesso di un certo prestigio. In Scozia e negli Stati Uniti, invece, le *public schools* sono scuole pubbliche gratuite amministrate dallo stato.

public sector *n* settore *m* pubblico
public service vehicle *n* (*Brit*) mezzo pubblico
public-spirited [pʌblɪk'spɪrɪtɪd] *adj* che ha senso civico
public transport, (*US*) **public transportation** *n* mezzi *mpl* pubblici
public utility *n* servizio pubblico
public works *npl* lavori *mpl* pubblici
publish ['pʌblɪʃ] *vt* pubblicare
publisher ['pʌblɪʃə^r] *n* editore *m*; (*firm*) casa editrice
publishing ['pʌblɪʃɪŋ] *n* (*industry*) editoria; (*of a book*) pubblicazione *f*
publishing company *n* casa *or* società editrice
pub lunch *n*: **to go for a ~** andare a mangiare al pub
puce [pju:s] *adj* color pulce *inv*
puck [pʌk] *n* (*Ice Hockey*) disco
pucker ['pʌkə^r] *vt* corrugare
pudding ['pudɪŋ] *n* budino; (*dessert*) dolce *m*; **black ~**, (*US*) **blood ~** sanguinaccio; **rice ~** budino di riso
puddle ['pʌdl] *n* pozza, pozzanghera
puerile ['pjuəraɪl] *adj* puerile
Puerto Rico ['pwə:təu'ri:kəu] *n* Portorico
puff [pʌf] *n* sbuffo; (*also*: **powder puff**) piumino ■ *vt* (*also*: **puff out**: *sails, cheeks*) gonfiare ■ *vi* uscire a sbuffi; (*pant*) ansare; **to ~ out smoke** mandar fuori sbuffi di fumo; **to ~ one's pipe** tirare sboccate di fumo
puffed [pʌft] *adj* (*col*: *out of breath*) senza fiato
puffin ['pʌfɪn] *n* puffino
puff pastry, (*US*) **puff paste** *n* pasta sfoglia
puffy ['pʌfɪ] *adj* gonfio(-a)
pugnacious [pʌg'neɪʃəs] *adj* combattivo(-a)
pull [pul] *n* (*tug*) strattone *m*, tirata; (*of moon, magnet, the sea etc*) attrazione *f*; (*fig*) influenza ■ *vt* tirare; (*muscle*) strappare, farsi uno strappo a ■ *vi* tirare; **to give sth a ~** tirare su qc; **to ~ a face** fare una smorfia; **to ~ to pieces** fare a pezzi; **to ~ one's punches** (*Boxing*) risparmiare l'avversario; **not to ~ one's punches** (*fig*) non avere peli sulla lingua; **to ~ one's weight** dare il proprio contributo; **to ~ o.s. together** ricomporsi, riprendersi; **to ~ sb's leg** prendere in giro qn; **to ~ strings (for sb)** muovere qualche pedina (per qn)
▸ **pull about** *vt* (*Brit*: *handle roughly*: *object*) strapazzare; (: *person*) malmenare
▸ **pull apart** *vt* (*break*) fare a pezzi
▸ **pull down** *vt* (*house*) demolire; (*tree*) abbattere
▸ **pull in** *vi* (*Aut*: *at the kerb*) accostarsi; (*Rail*) entrare in stazione
▸ **pull off** *vt* (*deal etc*) portare a compimento
▸ **pull out** *vi* partire; (*withdraw*) ritirarsi; (*Aut*: *come out of line*) spostarsi sulla mezzeria ■ *vt* staccare; far uscire; (*withdraw*) ritirare
▸ **pull over** *vi* (*Aut*) accostare
▸ **pull round** *vi* (*unconscious person*) rinvenire; (*sick person*) ristabilirsi
▸ **pull through** *vi* farcela
▸ **pull up** *vi* (*stop*) fermarsi ■ *vt* (*uproot*) sradicare; (*stop*) fermare
pulley ['pulɪ] *n* puleggia, carrucola
pull-out ['pulaut] *n* inserto ■ *cpd* staccabile
pullover ['puləuvə^r] *n* pullover *m inv*
pulp [pʌlp] *n* (*of fruit*) polpa; (*for paper*) pasta per carta; (*magazines, books*) stampa di qualità e di tono scadenti; **to reduce sth to ~** spappolare qc
pulpit ['pulpɪt] *n* pulpito
pulsate [pʌl'seɪt] *vi* battere, palpitare
pulse [pʌls] *n* polso; **to feel** *or* **take sb's ~** sentire *or* tastare il polso a qn
pulses ['pʌlsəz] *npl* (*Culin*) legumi *mpl*
pulverize ['pʌlvəraɪz] *vt* polverizzare
puma ['pju:mə] *n* puma *m inv*
pumice ['pʌmɪs], **pumice stone** ['pʌmɪs-] *n* (pietra) pomice *f*
pummel ['pʌml] *vt* dare pugni a
pump [pʌmp] *n* pompa; (*shoe*) scarpetta ■ *vt* pompare; (*fig*: *col*) far parlare; **to ~ sb for information** cercare di strappare delle informazioni a qn
▸ **pump up** *vt* gonfiare
pumpkin ['pʌmpkɪn] *n* zucca
pun [pʌn] *n* gioco di parole
punch [pʌntʃ] *n* (*blow*) pugno; (*fig*: *force*) forza; (*tool*) punzone *m*; (*drink*) ponce *m* ■ *vt* (*hit*): **to ~ sb/sth** dare un pugno a qn/qc; **to ~ a hole (in)** fare un buco (in)
▸ **punch in** *vi* (*US*) timbrare il cartellino (all'entrata)
▸ **punch out** *vi* (*US*) timbrare il cortellino (all'uscita)
punch card, punched card ['pʌntʃt-] *n* scheda perforata
punch-drunk ['pʌntʃdrʌŋk] *adj* (*Brit*) stordito(-a)
punch line *n* (*of joke*) battuta finale

P

punch-up ['pʌntʃʌp] *n* (*Brit col*) rissa
punctual ['pʌŋktjuəl] *adj* puntuale
punctuality [pʌŋktju'ælɪtɪ] *n* puntualità
punctually [pʌŋktjuəlɪ] *adv* puntualmente; **it will start ~ at 6** comincerà alle 6 precise *or* in punto
punctuate ['pʌŋktjueɪt] *vt* punteggiare
punctuation [pʌŋktju'eɪʃən] *n* interpunzione *f*, punteggiatura
punctuation mark *n* segno d'interpunzione
puncture ['pʌŋktʃəʳ] *n* (*Brit*) foratura ■ *vt* forare; **to have a ~** (*Aut*) forare (una gomma)
pundit ['pʌndɪt] *n* sapientone(-a)
pungent ['pʌndʒənt] *adj* piccante; (*fig*) mordace, caustico(-a)
punish ['pʌnɪʃ] *vt* punire; **to ~ sb for sth/for doing sth** punire qn per qc/per aver fatto qc
punishable ['pʌnɪʃəbl] *adj* punibile
punishing ['pʌnɪʃɪŋ] *adj* (*fig: exhausting*) sfiancante
punishment ['pʌnɪʃmənt] *n* punizione *f*; (*fig, col*): **to take a lot of ~** (*boxer*) incassare parecchi colpi; (*car*) essere messo(-a) a dura prova
punk [pʌŋk] *n* (*person: also:* **punk rocker**) punk *m/f inv*; (*music: also:* **punk rock**) musica punk, punk rock *m*; (*US col: hoodlum*) teppista *m*
punt [pʌnt] *n* (*boat*) barchino; (*Football*) colpo a volo; (*Irish*) sterlina irlandese ■ *vi* (*Brit: bet*) scommettere
punter ['pʌntəʳ] *n* (*Brit: gambler*) scommettitore(-trice)
puny ['pju:nɪ] *adj* gracile
pup [pʌp] *n* cucciolo(-a)
pupil ['pju:pl] *n* allievo(-a); (*Anat*) pupilla
puppet ['pʌpɪt] *n* burattino
puppet government *n* governo fantoccio
puppy ['pʌpɪ] *n* cucciolo(-a), cagnolino(-a)
purchase ['pə:tʃɪs] *n* acquisto, compera; (*grip*) presa ■ *vt* comprare; **to get a ~ on** (*grip*) trovare un appoggio su
purchase order *n* ordine *m* d'acquisto, ordinazione *f*
purchase price *n* prezzo d'acquisto
purchaser ['pə:tʃɪsəʳ] *n* compratore(-trice)
purchase tax *n* (*Brit*) tassa d'acquisto
purchasing power ['pə:tʃɪsɪŋ-] *n* potere *m* d'acquisto
pure [pjuəʳ] *adj* puro(-a); **a ~ wool jumper** un golf di pura lana; **it's laziness ~ and simple** è pura pigrizia
purebred ['pjuəbrɛd] *adj* di razza pura
purée ['pjuəreɪ] *n* purè *m inv*
purely ['pjuəlɪ] *adv* puramente
purge [pə:dʒ] *n* (*Med*) purga; (*Pol*) epurazione *f* ■ *vt* purgare; (*fig*) epurare
purification [pjuərɪfɪ'keɪʃən] *n* purificazione *f*
purify ['pjuərɪfaɪ] *vt* purificare
purist ['pjuərɪst] *n* purista *m/f*
puritan ['pjuərɪtən] *adj, n* puritano(-a)
puritanical [pjuərɪ'tænɪkl] *adj* puritano(-a)
purity ['pjuərɪtɪ] *n* purità
purl [pə:l] *n* punto rovescio ■ *vt* lavorare a rovescio
purloin [pə:'lɔɪn] *vt* rubare
purple ['pə:pl] *adj* di porpora; viola *inv*
purport [pə:'pɔ:t] *vi*: **to ~ to be/do** pretendere di essere/fare
purpose ['pə:pəs] *n* intenzione *f*, scopo; **on ~** apposta, di proposito; **for illustrative purposes** a titolo illustrativo; **for teaching purposes** per l'insegnamento; **for the purposes of this meeting** agli effetti di questa riunione; **to no ~** senza nessun risultato, inutilmente
purpose-built ['pə:pəs'bɪlt] *adj* (*Brit*) costruito(-a) allo scopo
purposeful ['pə:pəsful] *adj* deciso(-a), risoluto(-a)
purposely ['pə:pəslɪ] *adv* apposta
purr [pə:ʳ] *n* fusa *fpl* ■ *vi* fare le fusa
purse [pə:s] *n* borsellino; (*US: handbag*) borsetta, borsa ■ *vt* contrarre
purser ['pə:səʳ] *n* (*Naut*) commissario di bordo
purse snatcher [-'snætʃəʳ] *n* (*US*) scippatore *m*
pursue [pə'sju:] *vt* inseguire; essere alla ricerca di; (*inquiry, matter*) approfondire
pursuer [pə'sju:əʳ] *n* inseguitore(-trice)
pursuit [pə'sju:t] *n* inseguimento; (*occupation*) occupazione *f*, attività *f inv*; **in (the) ~ of sth** alla ricerca di qc; **scientific pursuits** ricerche *fpl* scientifiche
purveyor [pə'veɪəʳ] *n* fornitore(-trice)
pus [pʌs] *n* pus *m*
push [puʃ] *n* spinta; (*effort*) grande sforzo; (*drive*) energia ■ *vt* spingere; (*button*) premere; (*thrust*): **to ~ sth (into)** ficcare qc (in); (*fig*) fare pubblicità a ■ *vi* spingere; premere; **to ~ a door open/shut** aprire/chiudere una porta con una spinta *or* spingendola; **to be pushed for time/money** essere a corto di tempo/soldi; **she is pushing 50** (*col*) va per i 50; **to ~ for** (*better pay, conditions etc*) fare pressione per ottenere; **"~"** (*on door*) "spingere"; (*on bell*) "suonare"; **at a ~** (*Brit col*) in caso di necessità
▸ **push aside** *vt* scostare
▸ **push in** *vi* introdursi a forza
▸ **push off** *vi* (*col*) filare
▸ **push on** *vi* (*continue*) continuare
▸ **push over** *vt* far cadere
▸ **push through** *vt* (*measure*) far approvare
▸ **push up** *vt* (*total, prices*) far salire
push-bike ['puʃbaɪk] *n* (*Brit*) bicicletta

push-button ['puʃbʌtn] *adj* a pulsante
pushchair ['puʃtʃɛəʳ] *n* passeggino
pusher ['puʃəʳ] *n* (*also*: **drug pusher**) spacciatore(-trice) (di droga)
pushover ['puʃəuvəʳ] *n* (*col*): **it's a ~** è un lavoro da bambini
push-up ['puʃʌp] *n* (*US*) flessione *f* sulle braccia
pushy ['puʃɪ] *adj* (*pej*) troppo intraprendente
puss [pus], **pussy** ['pusɪ], **pussy-cat** ['pusɪkæt] *n* micio
put (*pt, pp* **~**) [put] *vt* mettere, porre; (*say*) dire, esprimere; (*a question*) fare; (*estimate*) stimare ■ *adv*: **to stay ~** non muoversi; **to ~ sb to bed** mettere qn a letto; **to ~ sb in a good/bad mood** mettere qn di buon/cattivo umore; **to ~ sb to a lot of trouble** scomodare qn; **to ~ a lot of time into sth** dedicare molto tempo a qc; **to ~ money on a horse** scommettere su un cavallo; **how shall I ~ it?** come dire?; **I ~ it to you that ...** (*Brit*) io sostengo che ...
▸ **put about** *vi* (*Naut*) virare di bordo ■ *vt* (*rumour*) diffondere
▸ **put across** *vt* (*ideas etc*) comunicare, far capire
▸ **put aside** *vt* (*lay down: book etc*) mettere da una parte, posare; (*save*) mettere da parte; (*in shop*) tenere da parte
▸ **put away** *vt* (*clothes, toys etc*) mettere via
▸ **put back** *vt* (*replace*) rimettere (a posto); (*postpone*) rinviare; (*delay*) ritardare; (*set back: watch, clock*) mettere indietro; **this will ~ us back 10 years** questo ci farà tornare indietro di 10 anni
▸ **put by** *vt* (*money*) mettere da parte
▸ **put down** *vt* (*parcel etc*) posare, mettere giù; (*pay*) versare; (*in writing*) mettere per iscritto; (*suppress: revolt etc*) reprimere, sopprimere; (*attribute*) attribuire
▸ **put forward** *vt* (*ideas*) avanzare, proporre; (*date*) anticipare
▸ **put in** *vt* (*application, complaint*) presentare
▸ **put in for** *vt fus* (*job*) far domanda per; (*promotion*) far domanda di
▸ **put off** *vt* (*postpone*) rimandare, rinviare; (*discourage*) dissuadere
▸ **put on** *vt* (*clothes, lipstick etc*) mettere; (*light etc*) accendere; (*play etc*) mettere in scena; (*concert, exhibition etc*) allestire, organizzare; (*extra bus, train etc*) mettere in servizio; (*food, meal*) servire; (*brake*) mettere; (*assume: accent, manner*) affettare; (*col: tease*) prendere in giro; (*inform, indicate*): **to ~ sb on to sb/sth** indicare qn/qc a qn; **to ~ on weight** ingrassare; **to ~ on airs** darsi delle arie
▸ **put out** *vt* mettere fuori; (*one's hand*) porgere; (*light etc*) spegnere; (*person: inconvenience*) scomodare; (*dislocate: shoulder, knee*) lussarsi; (*: back*) farsi uno strappo a ■ *vi* (*Naut*): **to ~ out to sea** prendere il largo; **to ~ out from Plymouth** partire da Plymouth
▸ **put through** *vt* (*caller*) mettere in comunicazione; (*call*) passare; **~ me through to Miss Blair** mi passi la signorina Blair
▸ **put together** *vt* mettere insieme, riunire; (*assemble: furniture*) montare; (*: meal*) improvvisare
▸ **put up** *vt* (*raise*) sollevare, alzare; (*pin up*) affiggere; (*hang*) appendere; (*build*) costruire, erigere; (*increase*) aumentare; (*accommodate*) alloggiare; (*incite*): **to ~ sb up to doing sth** istigare qn a fare qc; **to ~ sth up for sale** mettere in vendita qc
▸ **put upon** *vt fus*: **to be ~ upon** (*imposed on*) farsi mettere sotto i piedi
▸ **put up with** *vt fus* sopportare
putrid ['pju:trɪd] *adj* putrido(-a)
putt [pʌt] *vt* (*ball*) colpire leggermente ■ *n* colpo leggero
putter ['pʌtəʳ] *n* (*Golf*) putter *m inv* ■ *vi* (*US*) = **potter**
putting green ['pʌtɪŋ-] *n* green *m inv*; campo da putting
putty ['pʌtɪ] *n* stucco
put-up ['putʌp] *adj*: **~ job** montatura
puzzle ['pʌzl] *n* enigma *m*, mistero; (*jigsaw*) puzzle *m* ■ *vt* confondere, rendere perplesso(-a) ■ *vi* scervellarsi; **to be puzzled about sth** domandarsi il perché di qc; **to ~ over** (*sb's actions*) cercare di capire; (*mystery, problem*) cercare di risolvere
puzzling ['pʌzlɪŋ] *adj* (*question*) poco chiaro(-a); (*attitude, set of instructions*) incomprensibile
PVC *n abbr* (= *polyvinyl chloride*) P.V.C. *m*
Pvt. *abbr* (*US Mil*) = **private**
PW *n abbr* (*US*) = **prisoner of war**
pw *abbr* = **per week**
PX *n abbr* (*US Mil*) = **post exchange**
pygmy ['pɪgmɪ] *n* pigmeo(-a)
pyjamas, (*US*) **pajamas** [pə'dʒɑ:məz] *npl* pigiama *m*; **a pair of ~** un pigiama
pylon ['paɪlən] *n* pilone *m*
pyramid ['pɪrəmɪd] *n* piramide *f*
Pyrenean [pɪrə'ni:ən] *adj* pirenaico(-a)
Pyrenees [pɪrə'ni:z] *npl*: **the ~** i Pirenei
Pyrex® ['paɪrɛks] *n* Pirex® *m inv* ■ *cpd*: **~ dish** pirofila
python ['paɪθən] *n* pitone *m*

Qq

Q, q [kjuː] *n (letter)* Q, q *f or m inv*; **Q for Queen** ≈ Q come Quarto
Qatar [kæ'tɑːʳ] *n* Qatar *m*
QC *n abbr (Brit: = Queen's Counsel) avvocato della Corona*
QED *abbr (= quod erat demonstrandum)* qed
QM *n abbr* = **quartermaster**
q.t. *n abbr (col: = quiet)* **on the q.t.** di nascosto
qty *abbr* = **quantity**
quack [kwæk] *n (of duck)* qua qua *m inv*; *(pej: doctor)* ciarlatano(-a)
quad [kwɔd] *n abbr* = **quadrangle; quadruple; quadruplet**
quadrangle ['kwɔdræŋgl] *n (Math)* quadrilatero; *(courtyard)*: cortile *m*
quadruped ['kwɔdrupɛd] *n* quadrupede *m*
quadruple [kwɔ'drupl] *adj* quadruplo(-a) ■ *n* quadruplo ■ *vt* quadruplicare ■ *vi* quadruplicarsi
quadruplet [kwɔ'druːplɪt] *n* uno(-a) di quattro gemelli
quagmire ['kwægmaɪəʳ] *n* pantano
quail [kweɪl] *n (Zool)* quaglia ■ *vi*: **to ~ at** *or* **before** perdersi d'animo davanti a
quaint [kweɪnt] *adj* bizzarro(-a); *(old-fashioned)* antiquato(-a) e pittoresco(-a)
quake [kweɪk] *vi* tremare ■ *n abbr* = **earthquake**
Quaker ['kweɪkəʳ] *n* quacchero(-a)
qualification [kwɔlɪfɪ'keɪʃən] *n (degree etc)* qualifica, titolo; *(ability)* competenza, qualificazione *f*; *(limitation)* riserva, restrizione *f*; **what are your qualifications?** quali sono le sue qualifiche?
qualified ['kwɔlɪfaɪd] *adj* qualificato(-a); *(able)* competente, qualificato(-a); *(limited)* condizionato(-a); **~ for/to do** qualificato(-a) per/per fare; **he's not ~ for the job** non ha i requisiti necessari per questo lavoro; **it was a ~ success** è stato un successo parziale
qualify ['kwɔlɪfaɪ] *vt* abilitare; *(limit: statement)* modificare, precisare ■ *vi*: **to ~ (as)** qualificarsi (come); **to ~ (for)** acquistare i requisiti necessari (per); *(Sport)* qualificarsi (per *or* a); **to ~ as an engineer** diventare un perito tecnico
qualifying ['kwɔlɪfaɪɪŋ] *adj (exam)* di ammissione; *(round)* eliminatorio(-a)
qualitative ['kwɔlɪtətɪv] *adj* qualitativo(-a)
quality ['kwɔlɪtɪ] *n* qualità *f inv* ■ *cpd* di qualità; **of good ~** di buona qualità; **of poor ~** scadente; **~ of life** qualità della vita
quality control *n* controllo di qualità
quality papers *npl*, **quality press** *n (Brit)*: **the ~** la stampa d'informazione; *vedi nota*

QUALITY PAPERS

Il termine *quality press* si riferisce ai quotidiani o ai settimanali che offrono un'informazione seria ed approfondita. Questi giornali si differenziano da quelli popolari, i "tabloid", per formato e contenuti. Questa divisione tra tipi di giornali riflette il tradizionale divario tra classi sociali nella società britannica; *vedi anche* "tabloid press".

qualm [kwɑːm] *n* dubbio; scrupolo; **to have qualms about sth** avere degli scrupoli per qc
quandary ['kwɔndrɪ] *n*: **in a ~** in un dilemma
quango ['kwæŋgəu] *n abbr (Brit: = quasi-autonomous non-governmental organization) commissione consultiva di nomina governativa*
quantifiable ['kwɔntɪfaɪəbl] *adj* quantificabile
quantitative ['kwɔntɪtətɪv] *adj* quantitativo(-a)
quantity ['kwɔntɪtɪ] *n* quantità *f inv*; **in ~** in grande quantità
quantity surveyor *n (Brit)* geometra *m (specializzato nel calcolare la quantità e il costo del materiale da costruzione)*
quantum leap ['kwɔntəm-] *n (fig)* enorme cambiamento
quarantine ['kwɔrntiːn] *n* quarantena

quark [kwɑːk] *n* quark *m inv*
quarrel ['kwɔrl] *n* lite *f*, disputa ■ *vi* litigare; **to have a ~ with sb** litigare con qn; **I've no ~ with him** non ho niente contro di lui; **I can't ~ with that** non ho niente da ridire su questo
quarrelsome ['kwɔrəlsəm] *adj* litigioso(-a)
quarry ['kwɔrɪ] *n* (*for stone*) cava; (*animal*) preda ■ *vt* (*marble etc*) estrarre
quart [kwɔːt] *n* due pinte *fpl*, ≈ litro
quarter ['kwɔːtə^r] *n* quarto; (*of year*) trimestre *m*; (*district*) quartiere *m*; (*US, Canada: 25 cents*) quarto di dollaro, 25 centesimi ■ *vt* dividere in quattro; (*Mil*) alloggiare; **quarters** *npl* alloggio; (*Mil*) alloggi *mpl*, quadrato; **to pay by the ~** pagare trimestralmente; **a ~ of an hour** un quarto d'ora; **it's a ~ to 3**, (*US*) **it's a ~ of 3** sono le 3 meno un quarto, manca un quarto alle 3; **it's a ~ past 3**, (*US*) **it's a ~ after 3** sono le 3 e un quarto; **from all quarters** da tutte le parti *or* direzioni; **at close quarters** a distanza ravvicinata
quarterback ['kwɔːtəbæk] *n* (*US Football*) quarterback *m inv*
quarter-deck ['kwɔːtədɛk] *n* (*Naut*) cassero
quarter final *n* quarto di finale
quarterly ['kwɔːtəlɪ] *adj* trimestrale ■ *adv* trimestralmente ■ *n* periodico trimestrale
quartermaster ['kwɔːtəmɑːstə^r] *n* (*Mil*) furiere *m*
quartet, quartette [kwɔː'tɛt] *n* quartetto
quarto ['kwɔːtəu] *adj, n* in quarto (*m*) *inv*
quartz [kwɔːts] *n* quarzo ■ *cpd* di quarzo; (*watch, clock*) al quarzo
quash [kwɔʃ] *vt* (*verdict*) annullare
quasi- ['kweɪzaɪ] *prefix* quasi + *noun*; quasi, pressoché + *adjective*
quaver ['kweɪvə^r] *n* (*Brit Mus*) croma ■ *vi* tremolare
quay [kiː] *n* (*also*: **quayside**) banchina
Que. *abbr* (*Canada*) = **Quebec**
queasy ['kwiːzɪ] *adj* (*stomach*) delicato(-a); **to feel ~** aver la nausea
Quebec [kwɪ'bɛk] *n* Quebec *m*
queen [kwiːn] *n* (*gen*) regina; (*Cards etc*) regina, donna
queen mother *n* regina madre
Queen's speech *n* (*Brit*) *vedi nota*

Queen's speech

Durante la sessione di apertura del Parlamento britannico il sovrano legge un discorso redatto dal primo ministro, il *Queen's speech* (se si tratta della regina), che contiene le linee generali del nuovo programma politico.

queer [kwɪə^r] *adj* strano(-a), curioso(-a); (*suspicious*) dubbio(-a), sospetto(-a); (*Brit: sick*): **I feel ~** mi sento poco bene ■ *n* (*col*) finocchio
quell [kwɛl] *vt* domare
quench [kwɛntʃ] *vt* (*flames*) spegnere; **to ~ one's thirst** dissetarsi
querulous ['kwɛruləs] *adj* querulo(-a)
query ['kwɪərɪ] *n* domanda, questione *f*; (*doubt*) dubbio ■ *vt* mettere in questione; (*disagree with, dispute*) contestare
quest [kwɛst] *n* cerca, ricerca
question ['kwɛstʃən] *n* domanda, questione *f* ■ *vt* (*person*) interrogare; (*plan, idea*) mettere in questione *or* in dubbio; **to ask sb a ~, put a ~ to sb** fare una domanda a qn; **to bring** *or* **call sth into ~** mettere in dubbio qc; **the ~ is ...** il problema è ...; **it's a ~ of doing** si tratta di fare; **there's some ~ of doing** c'è chi suggerisce di fare; **beyond ~** fuori di dubbio; **out of the ~** fuori discussione, impossibile
questionable ['kwɛstʃənəbl] *adj* discutibile
questioner ['kwɛstʃənə^r] *n* interrogante *m/f*
questioning ['kwɛstʃənɪŋ] *adj* interrogativo(-a) ■ *n* interrogatorio
question mark *n* punto interrogativo
questionnaire [kwɛstʃə'nɛə^r] *n* questionario
queue [kjuː] *n* coda, fila ■ *vi* fare la coda; **to jump the ~** passare davanti agli altri (in una coda)
quibble ['kwɪbl] *vi* cavillare
quick [kwɪk] *adj* rapido(-a), veloce; (*reply*) pronto(-a); (*mind*) pronto(-a), acuto(-a) ■ *adv* rapidamente, presto ■ *n*: **cut to the ~** (*fig*) toccato(-a) sul vivo; **be ~!** fa presto!; **to be ~ to act** agire prontamente; **she was ~ to see that ...** ha visto subito che ...
quicken ['kwɪkn] *vt* accelerare, affrettare; (*rouse*) animare, stimolare ■ *vi* accelerare, affrettarsi
quick fix *n* soluzione *f* tampone *inv*
quicklime ['kwɪklaɪm] *n* calce *f* viva
quickly ['kwɪklɪ] *adv* rapidamente, velocemente; **we must act ~** dobbiamo agire tempestivamente
quickness ['kwɪknɪs] *n* rapidità; prontezza; acutezza
quicksand ['kwɪksænd] *n* sabbie *fpl* mobili
quickstep ['kwɪkstɛp] *n* *tipo di ballo simile al fox-trot*
quick-tempered [kwɪk'tɛmpəd] *adj* che si arrabbia facilmente
quick-witted [kwɪk'wɪtɪd] *adj* pronto(-a) d'ingegno
quid [kwɪd] *n* (*pl inv: Brit col*) sterlina
quid pro quo ['kwɪdprəu'kwəu] *n* contraccambio

q

quiet ['kwaɪət] *adj* tranquillo(-a), quieto(-a); (*reserved*) quieto(-a), taciturno(-a); (*ceremony*) semplice; (*not noisy: engine*) silenzioso(-a); (*not busy: day*) calmo(-a), tranquillo(-a); (*colour*) discreto(-a) ■ *n* tranquillità, calma ■ *vt, vi* (*US*) = **quieten**; **keep ~!** sta zitto!; **on the ~** di nascosto; **I'll have a ~ word with him** gli dirò due parole in privato; **business is ~ at this time of year** questa è la stagione morta

quieten ['kwaɪətn] (*Brit: also:* **quieten down**) *vi* calmarsi, chetarsi ■ *vt* calmare, chetare

quietly ['kwaɪətlɪ] *adv* tranquillamente, calmamente; silenziosamente

quietness ['kwaɪətnɪs] *n* tranquillità, calma; silenzio

quill [kwɪl] *n* penna d'oca

quilt [kwɪlt] *n* trapunta; **continental ~** piumino

quin [kwɪn] *n abbr* = **quintuplet**

quince [kwɪns] *n* (mela) cotogna; (*tree*) cotogno

quinine [kwɪ'ni:n] *n* chinino

quintet, quintette [kwɪn'tɛt] *n* quintetto

quintuplet [kwɪn'tju:plɪt] *n* uno(-a) di cinque gemelli

quip [kwɪp] *n* battuta di spirito

quire ['kwaɪə^r] *n* ventesima parte di una risma

quirk [kwə:k] *n* ghiribizzo; **by some ~ of fate** per un capriccio della sorte

quit (*pt, pp* **~** *or* **quitted**) [kwɪt] *vt* lasciare, partire da ■ *vi* (*give up*) mollare; (*resign*) dimettersi; **to ~ doing** smettere di fare; **~ stalling!** (*US col*) non tirarla per le lunghe!; **notice to ~** (*Brit*) preavviso (*dato all'inquilino*)

quite [kwaɪt] *adv* (*rather*) assai; (*entirely*) completamente, del tutto; **I ~ understand** capisco perfettamente; **~ a few of them** non pochi di loro; **~ (so)!** esatto!; **~ new** proprio nuovo; **that's not ~ right** non è proprio esatto; **she's ~ pretty** è piuttosto carina

Quito ['ki:təu] *n* Quito *m*

quits [kwɪts] *adj*: **~ (with)** pari (con); **let's call it ~** adesso siamo pari

quiver ['kwɪvə^r] *vi* tremare, fremere ■ *n* (*for arrows*) faretra

quiz [kwɪz] *n* (*game*) quiz *m inv*; indovinello ■ *vt* interrogare

quizzical ['kwɪzɪkəl] *adj* enigmatico(-a)

quoits [kwɔɪts] *npl* gioco degli anelli

quorum ['kwɔ:rəm] *n* quorum *m*

quota ['kwəutə] *n* quota

quotation [kwəu'teɪʃən] *n* citazione *f*; (*of shares etc*) quotazione *f*; (*estimate*) preventivo

quotation marks *npl* virgolette *fpl*

quote [kwəut] *n* citazione *f* ■ *vt* (*sentence*) citare; (*price*) dare, indicare, fissare; (*shares*) quotare ■ *vi*: **to ~ from** citare; **to ~ for a job** dare un preventivo per un lavoro; **quotes** *npl* (*col*) = **quotation marks**; **in quotes** tra virgolette; **~ ... unquote** (*in dictation*) aprire le virgolette ... chiudere le virgolette

quotient ['kwəuʃənt] *n* quoziente *m*

qv *abbr* (= *quod vide: which see*) v

qwerty keyboard ['kwə:tɪ-] *n* tastiera qwerty *inv*

Rr

R, r [ɑːʳ] *n* (*letter*) R, r *f or m inv*; **R for Robert**, (*US*) **R for Roger** ≈ R come Roma
R *abbr* (= *Réaumur (scale)*) R; (= *river*) F; (= *right*) D; (*US Cine*: = *restricted*) ≈ vietato; (*US Pol*) = **republican**; (*Brit*) = **Rex; Regina**
RA *n abbr* (*Brit*) = **Royal Academy**; **Royal Academician** ■ *abbr* = **rear admiral**
RAAF *n abbr* = **Royal Australian Air Force**
Rabat [rə'bɑːt] *n* Rabat *f*
rabbi ['ræbaɪ] *n* rabbino
rabbit ['ræbɪt] *n* coniglio ■ *vi*: **to ~ (on)** (*Brit*) blaterare
rabbit hole *n* tana di coniglio
rabbit hutch *n* conigliera
rabble ['ræbl] *n* (*pej*) canaglia, plebaglia
rabid ['ræbɪd] *adj* rabbioso(-a); (*fig*) fanatico(-a)
rabies ['reɪbiːz] *n* rabbia
RAC *n abbr* (*Brit*: = *Royal Automobile Club*) ≈ A.C.I. *m* (= *Automobile Club d'Italia*)
raccoon [rə'kuːn] *n* procione *m*
race [reɪs] *n* razza; (*competition, rush*) corsa ■ *vt* (*person*) gareggiare (in corsa) con; (*horse*) far correre; (*engine*) imballare ■ *vi* correre; **the human ~** la razza umana; **he raced across the road** ha attraversato la strada di corsa; **to ~ in/out** *etc* precipitarsi dentro/fuori *etc*
race car *n* (*US*) = **racing car**
race car driver *n* (*US*) = **racing driver**
racecourse ['reɪskɔːs] *n* campo di corse, ippodromo
racehorse ['reɪshɔːs] *n* cavallo da corsa
race relations *npl* rapporti razziali
racetrack ['reɪstræk] *n* pista
racial ['reɪʃl] *adj* razziale
racial discrimination *n* discriminazione *f* razziale
racialism ['reɪʃəlɪzəm] *n* razzismo
racialist ['reɪʃəlɪst] *adj, n* razzista *m/f*
racing ['reɪsɪŋ] *n* corsa
racing car *n* (*Brit*) macchina da corsa
racing driver *n* (*Brit*) corridore *m* automobilista
racism ['reɪsɪzəm] *n* razzismo
racist ['reɪsɪst] *adj, n* (*pej*) razzista *m/f*
rack [ræk] *n* rastrelliera; (*also*: **luggage rack**) rete *f* portabagagli *m inv*; (*also*: **roof rack**) portabagagli ■ *vt* torturare, tormentare; **magazine ~** portariviste *m inv*; **shoe ~** scarpiera; **toast ~** portatoast *m inv*; **to go to ~ and ruin** (*building*) andare in rovina; (*business*) andare in malora *or* a catafascio; **to ~ one's brains** scervellarsi
▸ **rack up** *vt* accumulare
racket ['rækɪt] *n* (*for tennis*) racchetta; (*noise*) fracasso, baccano; (*swindle*) imbroglio, truffa; (*organized crime*) racket *m inv*
racketeer [rækɪ'tɪəʳ] *n* (*US*) trafficante *m/f*
racoon [rə'kuːn] *n* = **raccoon**
racquet ['rækɪt] *n* racchetta
racy ['reɪsɪ] *adj* brioso(-a); piccante
RADA ['rɑːdə] *n abbr* (*Brit*) = **Royal Academy of Dramatic Art**
radar ['reɪdɑːʳ] *n* radar *m* ■ *cpd* radar *inv*
radar trap *n* controllo della velocità con radar
radial ['reɪdɪəl] *adj* (*also*: **radial-ply**) radiale
radiance ['reɪdɪəns] *n* splendore *m*, radiosità
radiant ['reɪdɪənt] *adj* raggiante; (*Physics*) radiante
radiate ['reɪdɪeɪt] *vt* (*heat*) irraggiare, irradiare ■ *vi* (*lines*) irradiarsi
radiation [reɪdɪ'eɪʃən] *n* irradiamento; (*radioactive*) radiazione *f*
radiation sickness *n* malattia da radiazioni
radiator ['reɪdɪeɪtəʳ] *n* radiatore *m*
radiator cap *n* tappo del radiatore
radiator grill *n* (*Aut*) mascherina, calandra
radical ['rædɪkl] *adj* radicale
radii ['reɪdɪaɪ] *npl of* **radius**
radio ['reɪdɪəu] *n* radio *f inv* ■ *vt* (*information*) trasmettere per radio; (*one's position*) comunicare via radio; (*person*) chiamare via radio ■ *vi*: **to ~ to sb** comunicare via radio con qn; **on the ~** alla radio
radio... ['reɪdɪəu] *prefix* radio...
radioactive ['reɪdɪəu'æktɪv] *adj* radioattivo(-a)

radioactivity ['reɪdɪəuæk'tɪvɪtɪ] *n* radioattività
radio announcer *n* annunciatore/trice della radio
radio-controlled ['reɪdɪəukən'trəuld] *adj* radiocomandato(-a), radioguidato(-a)
radiographer [reɪdɪ'ɔgrəfəʳ] *n* radiologo(-a); (*tecnico*)
radiography [reɪdɪ'ɔgrəfɪ] *n* radiografia
radiologist [reɪdɪ'ɔlədʒɪst] *n* radiologo(-a) (*medico*)
radiology [reɪdɪ'ɔlədʒɪ] *n* radiologia
radio station *n* stazione *f*, radio *inv*
radio taxi *n* radiotaxi *m inv*
radiotelephone ['reɪdɪəu'tɛlɪfəun] *n* radiotelefono
radiotherapist ['reɪdɪəu'θɛrəpɪst] *n* radioterapista *m/f*
radiotherapy ['reɪdɪəu'θɛrəpɪ] *n* radioterapia
radish ['rædɪʃ] *n* ravanello
radium ['reɪdɪəm] *n* radio
radius (*pl* **radii**) ['reɪdɪəs, -ɪaɪ] *n* raggio; (*Anat*) radio; **within a ~ of 50 miles** in un raggio di 50 miglia
RAF *n abbr* (*Brit*) = **Royal Air Force**
raffia ['ræfɪə] *n* rafia
raffish ['ræfɪʃ] *adj* dal look trasandato
raffle ['ræfl] *n* lotteria ■ *vt* (*object*) mettere in palio
raft [rɑːft] *n* zattera
rafter ['rɑːftəʳ] *n* trave *f*
rag [ræg] *n* straccio, cencio; (*pej: newspaper*) giornalaccio; (*for charity*) *iniziativa studentesca a scopo benefico* ■ *vt* (*Brit*) prendere in giro; **rags** *npl* stracci *mpl*, brandelli *mpl*; **in rags** stracciato
rag-and-bone man ['rægən'bəun-] *n* straccivendolo
ragbag ['rægbæg] *n* (*fig*) guazzabuglio
rag doll *n* bambola di pezza
rage [reɪdʒ] *n* (*fury*) collera, furia ■ *vi* (*person*) andare su tutte le furie; (*storm*) infuriare; **it's all the ~** fa furore; **to fly into a ~** andare *or* montare su tutte le furie
ragged ['rægɪd] *adj* (*edge*) irregolare; (*cuff*) logoro(-a); (*appearance*) pezzente
raging ['reɪdʒɪŋ] *adj* (*all senses*) furioso(-a); **in a ~ temper** su tutte le furie
rag trade *n* (*col*): **the ~** l'abbigliamento
rag week *n* (*Brit*) *vedi nota*

RAG WEEK

Durante il *rag week*, gli studenti universitari organizzano vari spettacoli e manifestazioni i cui proventi vengono devoluti in beneficenza.

raid [reɪd] *n* (*Mil*) incursione *f*; (*criminal*) rapina; (*by police*) irruzione *f* ■ *vt* fare un'incursione in; rapinare; fare irruzione in
raider ['reɪdəʳ] *n* rapinatore(-trice); (*plane*) aeroplano da incursione
rail [reɪl] *n* (*on stair*) ringhiera; (*on bridge, balcony*) parapetto; (*of ship*) battagliola; (*for train*) rotaia; **rails** *npl* binario, rotaie *fpl*; **by ~** per ferrovia, in treno
railcard ['reɪlkɑːd] *n* (*Brit*) tessera di riduzione ferroviaria
railing ['reɪlɪŋ] *n*, **railings** ['reɪlɪŋz] *npl* ringhiere *fpl*
railway ['reɪlweɪ], (*US*) **railroad** ['reɪlrəud] *n* ferrovia
railway engine *n* (*Brit*) locomotiva
railway line *n* (*Brit*) linea ferroviaria
railwayman ['reɪlweɪmən] *n* (*Brit*) ferroviere *m*
railway station *n* (*Brit*) stazione *f* ferroviaria
rain [reɪn] *n* pioggia ■ *vi* piovere; **in the ~** sotto la pioggia; **it's raining** piove; **it's raining cats and dogs** piove a catinelle
rainbow ['reɪnbəu] *n* arcobaleno
raincoat ['reɪnkəut] *n* impermeabile *m*
raindrop ['reɪndrɔp] *n* goccia di pioggia
rainfall ['reɪnfɔːl] *n* pioggia; (*measurement*) piovosità
rainforest ['reɪnfɔrɪst] *n* foresta pluviale *or* equatoriale
rainproof ['reɪnpruːf] *adj* impermeabile
rainstorm ['reɪnstɔːm] *n* pioggia torrenziale
rainwater ['reɪnwɔːtəʳ] *n* acqua piovana
rainy ['reɪnɪ] *adj* piovoso(-a)
raise [reɪz] *n* aumento ■ *vt* (*lift*) alzare, sollevare; (*build*) erigere; (*increase*) aumentare; (*a protest, doubt, question*) sollevare; (*cattle, family*) allevare; (*crop*) coltivare; (*army, funds*) raccogliere; (*loan*) ottenere; (*end: siege, embargo*) togliere; **to ~ one's voice** alzare la voce; **to ~ sb's hopes** accendere le speranze di qn; **to ~ one's glass to sb/sth** brindare a qn/qc; **to ~ a laugh/a smile** far ridere/sorridere
raisin ['reɪzn] *n* uva secca
Raj [rɑːdʒ] *n*: **the ~** l'impero britannico (*in India*)
rajah ['rɑːdʒə] *n* ragià *m inv*
rake [reɪk] *n* (*tool*) rastrello; (*person*) libertino ■ *vt* (*garden*) rastrellare; (*with machine gun*) spazzare ■ *vi*: **to ~ through** (*fig: search*) frugare tra
rake-off ['reɪkɔf] *n* (*col*) parte *f* percentuale, fetta
rakish ['reɪkɪʃ] *adj* dissoluto(-a); disinvolto(-a)
rally ['rælɪ] *n* (*Pol etc*) riunione *f*; (*Aut*) rally *m inv*; (*Tennis*) scambio ■ *vt* riunire, radunare ■ *vi* raccogliersi, radunarsi; (*sick person, Stock Exchange*) riprendersi

▸ **rally round** *vt fus* raggrupparsi intorno a; venire in aiuto di
rallying point ['rælɪɪŋ-] *n* (*Pol, Mil*) punto di riunione, punto di raduno
RAM [ræm] *n abbr* (*Comput*: = *random access memory*) RAM *f*
ram [ræm] *n* montone *m*, ariete *m*; (*device*) ariete ■ *vt* conficcare; (*crash into*) cozzare, sbattere contro; percuotere; speronare
ramble ['ræmbl] *n* escursione *f* ■ *vi* (*pej*: *also*: **ramble on**) divagare
rambler ['ræmbləʳ] *n* escursionista *m/f*; (*Bot*) rosa rampicante
rambling ['ræmblɪŋ] *adj* (*speech*) sconnesso(-a); (*Bot*) rampicante; (*house*) tutto(-a) nicchie e corridoi
rambunctious [ræm'bʌŋkʃəs] *adj* (*US*) = **rumbustious**
RAMC *n abbr* (*Brit*) = **Royal Army Medical Corps**
ramification [ræmɪfɪ'keɪʃən] *n* ramificazione *f*
ramp [ræmp] *n* rampa; (*Aut*) dosso artificiale
rampage [ræm'peɪdʒ] *n*: **to go on the ~** scatenarsi in modo violento ■ *vi*: **they went rampaging through the town** si sono scatenati in modo violento per la città
rampant ['ræmpənt] *adj* (*disease etc*) che infierisce
rampart ['ræmpɑːt] *n* bastione *m*
ram raiding [-reɪdɪŋ] *n il rapinare un negozio sfondandone la vetrina con un veicolo rubato*
ramshackle ['ræmʃækl] *adj* (*house*) cadente; (*car etc*) sgangherato(-a)
RAN *n abbr* = **Royal Australian Navy**
ran [ræn] *pt of* **run**
ranch [rɑːntʃ] *n* ranch *m inv*
rancher ['rɑːntʃəʳ] *n* (*owner*) proprietario di un ranch; (*ranch hand*) cowboy *m inv*
rancid ['rænsɪd] *adj* rancido(-a)
rancour, (*US*) **rancor** ['ræŋkəʳ] *n* rancore *m*
R & B *n abbr* = **rhythm and blues**
R & D *n abbr* = **research and development**
random ['rændəm] *adj* fatto(-a) *or* detto(-a) per caso; (*Comput, Math*) casuale ■ *n*: **at ~** a casaccio
random access *n* (*Comput*) accesso casuale
R & R *n abbr* (= *rest and recreation*) ricreazione *f*; (*US Mil*) *permesso per militari*
randy ['rændɪ] *adj* (*col*) arrapato(-a); lascivo(-a)
rang [ræŋ] *pt of* **ring**
range [reɪndʒ] *n* (*of mountains*) catena; (*of missile, voice*) portata; (*of products*) gamma; (*Mil*: *also*: **shooting range**) campo di tiro; (*also*: **kitchen range**) fornello, cucina economica ■ *vt* (*place*) disporre, allineare; (*roam*) vagare per ■ *vi*: **to ~ over** coprire; **to ~ from ... to** andare da ... a; **price ~** gamma di prezzi; **do you have anything else in this price ~?** ha nient'altro su *or* di questo prezzo?; **within (firing) ~** a portata di tiro; **ranged left/right** (*text*) allineato(-a) a destra/sinistra
ranger ['reɪndʒəʳ] *n* guardia forestale
Rangoon [ræŋ'guːn] *n* Rangun *f*
rank [ræŋk] *n* fila; (*Mil*) grado; (*Brit*: *also*: **taxi rank**) posteggio di taxi ■ *vi*: **to ~ among** essere nel numero di ■ *adj* (*smell*) puzzolente; (*hypocrisy, injustice*) vero(-a) e proprio(-a); **the ranks** (*Mil*) la truppa; **the ~ and file** (*fig*) la gran massa; **to close ranks** (*Mil, fig*) serrare i ranghi; **I ~ him sixth** gli do il sesto posto, lo metto al sesto posto
rankle ['ræŋkl] *vi*: **to ~ with sb** bruciare (a qn)
rank outsider *n* outsider *m/f inv*
ransack ['rænsæk] *vt* rovistare; (*plunder*) saccheggiare
ransom ['rænsəm] *n* riscatto; **to hold sb to ~** (*fig*) esercitare pressione su qn
rant [rænt] *vi* vociare
ranting ['ræntɪŋ] *n* vociare *m*
rap [ræp] *n* (*noise*) colpetti *mpl*; (*at a door*) bussata ■ *vt* dare dei colpetti a; bussare a
rape [reɪp] *n* violenza carnale, stupro ■ *vt* violentare
rape oil, rapeseed oil ['reɪpsiːd-] *n* olio di ravizzone
rapid ['ræpɪd] *adj* rapido(-a)
rapidity [rə'pɪdɪtɪ] *n* rapidità
rapidly ['ræpɪdlɪ] *adv* rapidamente
rapids ['ræpɪdz] *npl* (*Geo*) rapida
rapist ['reɪpɪst] *n* violentatore *m*
rapport [ræ'pɔːʳ] *n* rapporto
rapt [ræpt] *adj* (*attention*) rapito(-a), profondo(-a); **to be ~ in contemplation** essere in estatica contemplazione
rapture ['ræptʃəʳ] *n* estasi *f inv*; **to go into raptures over** andare in solluchero per
rapturous ['ræptʃərəs] *adj* estatico(-a)
rare [rɛəʳ] *adj* raro(-a); (*Culin*: *steak*) al sangue; **it is ~ to find that ...** capita di rado *or* raramente che ... + *sub*
rarebit ['rɛəbɪt] *n see* **Welsh rarebit**
rarefied ['rɛərɪfaɪd] *adj* (*air, atmosphere*) rarefatto(-a)
rarely ['rɛəlɪ] *adv* raramente
raring ['rɛərɪŋ] *adj*: **to be ~ to go** (*col*) non veder l'ora di cominciare
rarity ['rɛərɪtɪ] *n* rarità *f inv*
rascal ['rɑːskl] *n* mascalzone *m*
rash [ræʃ] *adj* imprudente, sconsiderato(-a) ■ *n* (*Med*) eruzione *f*; **to come out in a ~** avere uno sfogo

r

rasher ['ræʃəʳ] *n* fetta sottile (di lardo *or* prosciutto)
rasp [rɑːsp] *n* (*tool*) lima ■ *vt* (*speak*: *also*: **rasp out**) gracchiare
raspberry ['rɑːzbərɪ] *n* lampone *m*
raspberry bush *n* lampone *m* (*pianta*)
rasping ['rɑːspɪŋ] *adj* stridulo(-a)
Rastafarian [ræstə'fɛərɪən] *adj, n* rastafariano(-a)
rat [ræt] *n* ratto
ratable ['reɪtəbl] *adj* = **rateable**
ratchet ['rætʃɪt] *n*: **~ wheel** ruota dentata
rate [reɪt] *n* (*proportion*) tasso, percentuale *f*; (*speed*) velocità *f inv*; (*price*) tariffa ■ *vt* valutare; stimare; **to ~ sb/sth as** valutare qn/qc come; **to ~ sb/sth among** annoverare qn/qc tra; **to ~ sb/sth highly** stimare molto qn/qc; **at a ~ of 60 kph** alla velocità di 60 km all'ora; **~ of exchange** tasso di cambio; **~ of flow** flusso medio; **~ of growth** tasso di crescita; **~ of return** tasso di rendimento; **pulse ~** frequenza delle pulsazioni; *see also* **rates**
rateable value ['reɪtəbl-] *n* (*Brit*) valore *m* imponibile (agli effetti delle imposte comunali)
ratepayer ['reɪtpeɪəʳ] *n* (*Brit*) contribuente *m/f* (che paga le imposte comunali)
rates [reɪts] *npl* (*Brit*) imposte *fpl* comunali
rather ['rɑːðəʳ] *adv* piuttosto; (*somewhat*) abbastanza; (*to some extent*) un po'; **it's ~ expensive** è piuttosto caro; (*too much*) è un po' caro; **there's ~ a lot** ce n'è parecchio; **I would** *or* **I'd ~ go** preferirei andare; **I had ~ go** farei meglio ad andare; **I'd ~ not leave** preferirei non partire; **or ~** (*more accurately*) anzi, per essere (più) precisi; **I ~ think he won't come** credo proprio che non verrà
ratification [rætɪfɪ'keɪʃən] *n* ratificazione *f*
ratify ['rætɪfaɪ] *vt* ratificare
rating ['reɪtɪŋ] *n* classificazione *f*; punteggio di merito; (*Naut*: *category*) classe *f*; (: *sailor*: *Brit*) marinaio semplice
ratings ['reɪtɪŋz] *npl* (*Radio, TV*) indice *m* di ascolto
ratio ['reɪʃɪəu] *n* proporzione *f*; **in the ~ of 2 to 1** in rapporto di 2 a 1
ration ['ræʃən] *n* razione *f* ■ *vt* razionare
rational ['ræʃənl] *adj* razionale, ragionevole; (*solution, reasoning*) logico(-a)
rationale [ræʃə'nɑːl] *n* fondamento logico; giustificazione *f*
rationalization [ræʃnəlaɪ'zeɪʃən] *n* razionalizzazione *f*
rationalize ['ræʃnəlaɪz] *vt* razionalizzare
rationally ['ræʃnəlɪ] *adv* razionalmente; logicamente
rationing ['ræʃnɪŋ] *n* razionamento
ratpack ['rætpæk] *n* (*Brit col*) stampa scandalistica
rat poison *n* veleno per topi
rat race *n* carrierismo, corsa al successo
rattan [ræ'tæn] *n* malacca
rattle ['rætl] *n* tintinnio; (*louder*) rumore *m* di ferraglia; (*object*: *of baby*) sonaglino; (: *of sports fan*) raganella ■ *vi* risuonare, tintinnare; fare un rumore di ferraglia ■ *vt* agitare; far tintinnare; (*col*: *disconcert*) sconcertare
rattlesnake ['rætlsneɪk] *n* serpente *m* a sonagli
ratty ['rætɪ] *adj* (*col*) incavolato(-a)
raucous ['rɔːkəs] *adj* sguaiato(-a)
raucously ['rɔːkəslɪ] *adv* sguaiatamente
raunchy ['rɔːntʃɪ] *adj* (*col*: *person*) allupato(-a); (: *voice, song*) libidinoso(-a)
ravage ['rævɪdʒ] *vt* devastare
ravages ['rævɪdʒɪz] *npl* danni *mpl*
rave [reɪv] *vi* (*in anger*) infuriarsi; (*with enthusiasm*) andare in estasi; (*Med*) delirare ■ *n*: **a ~ (party)** un rave ■ *adj* (*scene, culture, music*) del fenomeno rave ■ *cpd*: **~ review** (*col*) critica entusiastica
raven ['reɪvən] *n* corvo
ravenous ['rævənəs] *adj* affamato(-a)
ravine [rə'viːn] *n* burrone *m*
raving ['reɪvɪŋ] *adj*: **~ lunatic** pazzo(-a) furioso(-a)
ravings ['reɪvɪŋz] *npl* vaneggiamenti *mpl*
ravioli [rævɪ'əulɪ] *n* ravioli *mpl*
ravish ['rævɪʃ] *vt* (*delight*) estasiare
ravishing ['rævɪʃɪŋ] *adj* incantevole
raw [rɔː] *adj* (*uncooked*) crudo(-a); (*not processed*) greggio(-a); (*sore*) vivo(-a); (*inexperienced*) inesperto(-a); **to get a ~ deal** (*col*: *bad bargain*) prendere un bidone; (: *harsh treatment*) venire trattato ingiustamente
Rawalpindi [rɔːl'pɪndɪ] *n* Rawalpindi *f*
raw material *n* materia prima
ray [reɪ] *n* raggio
rayon ['reɪɔn] *n* raion *m*
raze [reɪz] *vt* radere, distruggere; (*also*: **raze to the ground**) radere al suolo
razor ['reɪzəʳ] *n* rasoio
razor blade *n* lama di rasoio
razzle ['ræzl], **razzle-dazzle** ['ræzl'dæzl] *n* (*Brit col*): **to be/go on the ~(-dazzle)** darsi alla pazza gioia
razzmatazz ['ræzmə'tæz] *n* (*col*) clamore *m*
RC *abbr* = **Roman Catholic**
RCAF *n abbr* = **Royal Canadian Air Force**
RCMP *n abbr* = **Royal Canadian Mounted Police**
RCN *n abbr* = **Royal Canadian Navy**
RD *abbr* (*US Post*) = **rural delivery**

Rd *abbr* = **road**
RDC *n abbr* (*Brit*) = **rural district council**
RE *n abbr* (*Brit Mil*: = *Royal Engineers*) ≈ G.M. (= *Genio Militare*); (*Brit*) = **religious education**
re [riː] *prep* con riferimento a
reach [riːtʃ] *n* portata; (*of river etc*) tratto ■ *vt* raggiungere; arrivare a ■ *vi* stendersi; (*stretch out hand*: *also*: **reach down, reach over, reach across** *etc*) allungare una mano; **out of/within ~** (*object*) fuori/a portata di mano; **within easy ~ (of)** (*place*) a breve distanza (di), vicino (a); **to ~ sb by phone** contattare qn per telefono; **can I ~ you at your hotel?** la posso contattare al suo albergo?
▸ **reach out** *vi*: **to ~ out for** stendere la mano per prendere
react [riːˈækt] *vi* reagire
reaction [riːˈækʃən] *n* reazione *f*
reactionary [riːˈækʃənrɪ] *adj, n* reazionario(-a)
reactor [riːˈæktəʳ] *n* reattore *m*
read (*pt, pp* **read**) [riːd, rɛd] ■ *vi* leggere ■ *vt* leggere; (*understand*) intendere, interpretare; (*study*) studiare; **do you ~ me?** (*Tel*) mi ricevete?; **to take sth as ~** (*fig*) dare qc per scontato
▸ **read out** *vt* leggere ad alta voce
▸ **read over** *vt* rileggere attentamente
▸ **read through** *vt* (*quickly*) dare una scorsa a; (*thoroughly*) leggere da cima a fondo
▸ **read up** *vt*, **read up on** *vt fus* studiare bene
readable [ˈriːdəbl] *adj* leggibile; che si legge volentieri
reader [ˈriːdəʳ] *n* lettore(-trice); (*book*) libro di lettura; (*Brit*: *at university*) *professore con funzioni preminenti di ricerca*
readership [ˈriːdəʃɪp] *n* (*of paper etc*) numero di lettori
readily [ˈrɛdɪlɪ] *adv* volentieri; (*easily*) facilmente
readiness [ˈrɛdɪnɪs] *n* prontezza; **in ~** (*prepared*) pronto(-a)
reading [ˈriːdɪŋ] *n* lettura; (*understanding*) interpretazione *f*; (*on instrument*) indicazione *f*
reading lamp *n* lampada da studio
reading room *n* sala di lettura
readjust [riːəˈdʒʌst] *vt* raggiustare ■ *vi* (*person*): **to ~ (to)** riadattarsi (a)
ready [ˈrɛdɪ] *adj* pronto(-a); (*willing*) pronto(-a), disposto(-a); (*quick*) rapido(-a); (*available*) disponibile ■ *n*: **at the ~** (*Mil*) pronto a sparare; (*fig*) tutto(-a) pronto(-a); **~ for use** pronto per l'uso; **to be ~ to do sth** essere pronto a fare qc; **to get ~** *vi* prepararsi ■ *vt* preparare
ready cash *n* denaro in contanti
ready-cooked [rɛdɪˈkukt] *adj* già cotto(-a)
ready-made [rɛdɪˈmeɪd] *adj* prefabbricato(-a); (*clothes*) confezionato(-a)
ready reckoner [-ˈrɛkənəʳ] *n* (*Brit*) prontuario di calcolo
ready-to-wear [rɛdɪtəˈwɛəʳ] *adj* prêt-à-porter *inv*
reagent [riːˈeɪdʒənt] *n*: **chemical ~** reagente *m* chimico
real [rɪəl] *adj* reale; vero(-a) ■ *adv* (*US col*: *very*) veramente, proprio; **in ~ terms** in realtà; **in ~ life** nella realtà
real ale *n birra ad effervescenza naturale*
real estate *n* beni *mpl* immobili
realism [ˈrɪəlɪzəm] *n* (*Art*) realismo
realist [ˈrɪəlɪst] *n* realista *m/f*
realistic [rɪəˈlɪstɪk] *adj* realistico(-a)
reality [riːˈælɪtɪ] *n* realtà *f inv*; **in ~** in realtà, in effetti
reality TV *n* reality TV *f*
realization [rɪəlaɪˈzeɪʃən] *n* (*awareness*) presa di coscienza; (*of hopes, project etc*) realizzazione *f*
realize [ˈrɪəlaɪz] *vt* (*understand*) rendersi conto di; (*a project, Comm*: *asset*) realizzare; **I ~ that ...** mi rendo conto *or* capisco che ...
really [ˈrɪəlɪ] *adv* veramente, davvero
realm [rɛlm] *n* reame *m*
real time *n* (*Comput*) tempo reale
Realtor® [ˈrɪəltɔːʳ] *n* (*US*) agente *m* immobiliare
ream [riːm] *n* risma; **reams** (*fig, col*) pagine e pagine *fpl*
reap [riːp] *vt* mietere; (*fig*) raccogliere
reaper [ˈriːpəʳ] *n* (*machine*) mietitrice *f*
reappear [riːəˈpɪəʳ] *vi* ricomparire, riapparire
reappearance [riːəˈpɪərəns] *n* riapparizione *f*
reapply [riːəˈplaɪ] *vi*: **to ~ for** fare un'altra domanda per
reappraisal [riːəˈpreɪzl] *n* riesame *m*
rear [rɪəʳ] *adj* di dietro; (*Aut*: *wheel etc*) posteriore ■ *n* didietro, parte *f* posteriore ■ *vt* (*cattle, family*) allevare ■ *vi* (*also*: **rear up**: *animal*) impennarsi
rear admiral *n* contrammiraglio
rear-engined [ˈrɪərˈɛndʒɪnd] *adj* (*Aut*) con motore posteriore
rearguard [ˈrɪəgɑːd] *n* retroguardia
rearm [riːˈɑːm] *vt, vi* riarmare
rearmament [riːˈɑːməmənt] *n* riarmo
rearrange [riːəˈreɪndʒ] *vt* riordinare
rear-view mirror [ˈrɪəvjuː-] *n* (*Aut*) specchio retrovisivo
reason [ˈriːzn] *n* ragione *f*; (*cause, motive*) ragione, motivo ■ *vi*: **to ~ with sb** far ragionare qn; **to have ~ to think** avere motivi per pensare; **it stands to ~ that** è ovvio che; **the ~ for/why** la ragione *or*

r

il motivo di/per cui; **with good ~** a ragione; **all the more ~ why you should not sell it** ragione di più per non venderlo
reasonable ['ri:znəbl] *adj* ragionevole; (*not bad*) accettabile
reasonably ['ri:znəblɪ] *adv* ragionevolmente; **one can ~ assume that ...** uno può facilmente supporre che ...
reasoned ['ri:znd] *adj* (*argument*) ponderato(-a)
reasoning ['ri:znɪŋ] *n* ragionamento
reassemble [ri:ə'sɛmbl] *vt* riunire; (*machine*) rimontare
reassert [ri:ə'sə:t] *vt* riaffermare
reassurance [ri:ə'ʃuərəns] *n* rassicurazione *f*
reassure [ri:ə'ʃuə^r] *vt* rassicurare; **to ~ sb of** rassicurare qn di *or* su
reassuring [ri:ə'ʃuərɪŋ] *adj* rassicurante
reawakening [ri:ə'weɪknɪŋ] *n* risveglio
rebate ['ri:beɪt] *n* rimborso
rebel *n* ['rɛbl] ribelle *m/f* ■ *vi* [rɪ'bɛl] ribellarsi
rebellion [rɪ'bɛljən] *n* ribellione *f*
rebellious [rɪ'bɛljəs] *adj* ribelle
rebirth [ri:'bə:θ] *n* rinascita
rebound *vi* [rɪ'baund] (*ball*) rimbalzare ■ *n* ['ri:baund] rimbalzo
rebuff [rɪ'bʌf] *n* secco rifiuto ■ *vt* respingere
rebuild [ri:'bɪld] *vt irreg* ricostruire
rebuke [rɪ'bju:k] *n* rimprovero ■ *vt* rimproverare
rebut [rɪ'bʌt] *vt* rifiutare
rebuttal [rɪ'bʌtl] *n* rifiuto
recalcitrant [rɪ'kælsɪtrənt] *adj* recalcitrante
recall [rɪ'kɔ:l] *vt* (*gen, Comput*) richiamare; (*remember*) ricordare, richiamare alla mente ■ *n* ['ri:kɔl] richiamo; **beyond ~** irrevocabile
recant [rɪ'kænt] *vi* ritrattarsi; (*Rel*) fare abiura
recap ['ri:kæp] *n* ricapitolazione *f* ■ *vt* ricapitolare ■ *vi* riassumere
recapture [ri:'kæptʃə^r] *vt* riprendere; (*atmosphere*) ricreare
recd. *abbr* = **received**
recede [rɪ'si:d] *vi* allontanarsi; ritirarsi; calare
receding [rɪ'si:dɪŋ] *adj* (*forehead, chin*) sfuggente; **he's got a ~ hairline** è stempiato
receipt [rɪ'si:t] *n* (*document*) ricevuta; (*act of receiving*) ricevimento; **to acknowledge ~ of** accusare ricevuta di; **we are in ~ of ...** abbiamo ricevuto ...
receipts [rɪ'si:ts] *npl* (*Comm*) introiti *mpl*
receivable [rɪ'si:vəbl] *adj* (*Comm*) esigibile; (*: owed*) dovuto(-a)
receive [rɪ'si:v] *vt* ricevere; (*guest*) ricevere, accogliere; **"received with thanks"** (*Comm*) "per quietanza"
Received Pronunciation *n* (*Brit*) *vedi nota*

RECEIVED PRONUNCIATION

Si chiama *Received Pronunciation (RP)* l'accento dell'inglese parlato in alcune parti del sud-est dell'Inghilterra. In esso si identifica l'inglese "standard" delle classi colte, privo di inflessioni regionali e adottato tradizionalmente dagli annunciatori della BBC . È anche l'accento standard dell'inglese insegnato come lingua straniera.

receiver [rɪ'si:və^r] *n* (*Tel*) ricevitore *m*; (*Radio*) apparecchio ricevente; (*of stolen goods*) ricettatore(-trice); (*Law*) curatore *m* fallimentare
receivership [rɪ'si:vəʃɪp] *n* curatela; **to go into ~** andare in amministrazione controllata
recent ['ri:snt] *adj* recente; **in ~ years** negli ultimi anni
recently ['ri:sntlɪ] *adv* recentemente; **as ~ as ...** soltanto ...; **until ~** fino a poco tempo fa
receptacle [rɪ'sɛptɪkl] *n* recipiente *m*
reception [rɪ'sɛpʃən] *n* (*gen*) ricevimento; (*welcome*) accoglienza; (*TV etc*) ricezione *f*
reception centre *n* (*Brit*) centro di raccolta
reception desk *n* (*in hotel*) reception *f inv*; (*in hospital, at doctor's*) accettazione *f*; (*in large building, offices*) portineria
receptionist [rɪ'sɛpʃənɪst] *n* receptionist *m/f inv*
receptive [rɪ'sɛptɪv] *adj* ricettivo(-a)
recess [rɪ'sɛs] *n* (*in room*) alcova; (*Pol etc: holiday*) vacanze *fpl*; (*US Law: short break*) sospensione *f*; (*US Scol*) intervallo
recession [rɪ'sɛʃən] *n* (*Econ*) recessione *f*
recessionista [rɪsɛʃə'nɪstə] *n* recessionista *m/f*
recharge [ri:'tʃɑ:dʒ] *vt* (*battery*) ricaricare
rechargeable ['ri:'tʃɑ:dʒəbl] *adj* ricaricabile
recipe ['rɛsɪpɪ] *n* ricetta
recipient [rɪ'sɪpɪənt] *n* beneficiario(-a); (*of letter*) destinatario(-a)
reciprocal [rɪ'sɪprəkl] *adj* reciproco(-a)
reciprocate [rɪ'sɪprəkeɪt] *vt* ricambiare, contraccambiare
recital [rɪ'saɪtl] *n* recital *m inv*; concerto (di solista)
recite [rɪ'saɪt] *vt* (*poem*) recitare
reckless ['rɛkləs] *adj* (*driver etc*) spericolato(-a); (*spender*) incosciente
recklessly ['rɛkləslɪ] *adv* in modo spericolato; da incosciente
reckon ['rɛkən] *vt* (*count*) calcolare; (*consider*) considerare, stimare; (*think*): **I ~ that ...** penso che .. ■ *vi* contare, calcolare; **to ~ without sb/sth** non tener conto di qn/qc; **he is somebody to be reckoned with** è uno da non sottovalutare

▸**reckon on** *vt fus* contare su
reckoning ['rɛknɪŋ] *n* conto; stima; **the day of ~** il giorno del giudizio
reclaim [rɪ'kleɪm] *vt* (*land*) bonificare; (*demand back*) richiedere, reclamare
reclamation [rɛklə'meɪʃən] *n* bonifica
recline [rɪ'klaɪn] *vi* stare sdraiato(-a)
reclining [rɪ'klaɪnɪŋ] *adj* (*seat*) ribaltabile
recluse [rɪ'klu:s] *n* eremita *m*, recluso(-a)
recognition [rɛkəg'nɪʃən] *n* riconoscimento; **to gain ~** essere riconosciuto(-a); **in ~ of** in *or* come segno di riconoscimento per; **transformed beyond ~** irriconoscibile
recognizable ['rɛkəgnaɪzəbl] *adj*: **~ (by)** riconoscibile (a *or* da)
recognize ['rɛkəgnaɪz] *vt*: **to ~ (by/as)** riconoscere (a *or* da/come)
recoil [rɪ'kɔɪl] *vi* (*gun*) rinculare; (*spring*) balzare indietro; (*person*): **to ~ (from)** indietreggiare (davanti a) ■ *n* (*gun*) rinculo
recollect [rɛkə'lɛkt] *vt* ricordare
recollection [rɛkə'lɛkʃən] *n* ricordo; **to the best of my ~** per quello che mi ricordo
recommend [rɛkə'mɛnd] *vt* raccomandare; (*advise*) consigliare; **she has a lot to ~ her** ha molti elementi a suo favore
recommendation [rɛkəmɛn'deɪʃən] *n* raccomandazione *f*; consiglio
recommended retail price [rɛkə'mɛndɪd-] *n* (*Brit*) prezzo raccomandato al dettaglio
recompense ['rɛkəmpɛns] *vt* ricompensare; (*compensate*) risarcire ■ *n* ricompensa; risarcimento
reconcilable ['rɛkənsaɪləbl] *adj* conciliabile
reconcile ['rɛkənsaɪl] *vt* (*two people*) riconciliare; (*two facts*) conciliare, quadrare; **to ~ o.s. to** rassegnarsi a
reconciliation [rɛkənsɪlɪ'eɪʃən] *n* riconciliazione *f*; conciliazione *f*
recondite [rɪ'kɔndaɪt] *adj* recondito(-a)
recondition [ri:kən'dɪʃən] *vt* rimettere a nuovo; rifare
reconnaissance [rɪ'kɔnɪsns] *n* (*Mil*) ricognizione *f*
reconnoitre, (*US*) **reconnoiter** [rɛkə'nɔɪtə^r] (*Mil*) *vt* fare una ricognizione di ■ *vi* fare una ricognizione
reconsider [ri:kən'sɪdə^r] *vt* riconsiderare
reconstitute [ri:'kɔnstɪtju:t] *vt* ricostituire
reconstruct [ri:kən'strʌkt] *vt* ricostruire
reconstruction [ri:kən'strʌkʃən] *n* ricostruzione *f*
reconvene [ri:kən'vi:n] *vt* riconvocare ■ *vi* radunarsi
record *n* ['rɛkɔ:d] ricordo, documento; (*of meeting etc*) nota, verbale *m*; (*register*) registro; (*file*) pratica, dossier *m inv*; (*Comput*) record *m inv*, registrazione *f*; (*also*: **police record**) fedina penale sporca; (*Mus: disc*) disco; (*Sport*) record *m inv*, primato ■ *vt* [rɪ'kɔ:d] (*set down*) prendere nota di, registrare; (*relate*) raccontare; (*Comput, Mus: song etc*) registrare; **public records** archivi *mpl*; **Italy's excellent ~** i brillanti successi italiani; **in ~ time** a tempo di record; **to keep a ~ of** tener nota di; **to set the ~ straight** mettere le cose in chiaro; **off the ~** *adj* ufficioso(-a); *adv* ufficiosamente; **he is on ~ as saying that ...** ha dichiarato pubblicamente che ...
record card *n* (*in file*) scheda
recorded delivery letter [rɪ'kɔ:dɪd-] *n* (*Brit Post*) lettera raccomandata
recorder [rɪ'kɔ:də^r] *n* (*Law*) *avvocato che funge da giudice*; (*Mus*) flauto diritto
record holder *n* (*Sport*) primatista *m/f*
recording [rɪ'kɔ:dɪŋ] *n* (*Mus*) registrazione *f*
recording studio *n* studio di registrazione
record library *n* discoteca
record player *n* giradischi *m inv*
recount [rɪ'kaunt] *vt* raccontare, narrare
re-count *n* ['ri:kaunt] (*Pol: of votes*) nuovo conteggio ■ *vt* [ri:'kaunt] ricontare
recoup [rɪ'ku:p] *vt* ricuperare; **to ~ one's losses** ricuperare le perdite, rifarsi
recourse [rɪ'kɔ:s] *n*: **to have ~ to** ricorrere a
recover [rɪ'kʌvə^r] *vt* ricuperare ■ *vi* (*from illness*) rimettersi (in salute), ristabilirsi; (*country, person: from shock*) riprendersi
re-cover [ri:'kʌvə^r] *vt* (*chair etc*) ricoprire
recovery [rɪ'kʌvərɪ] *n* ricupero; ristabilimento; ripresa
recreate [ri:krɪ'eɪt] *vt* ricreare
recreation [rɛkrɪ'eɪʃən] *n* ricreazione *f*; svago
recreational [rɛkrɪ'eɪʃənəl] *adj* ricreativo(-a)
recreational drug *n droga usata saltuariamente*
recreational vehicle *n* (*US*) camper *m inv*
recrimination [rɪkrɪmɪ'neɪʃən] *n* recriminazione *f*
recruit [rɪ'kru:t] *n* recluta ■ *vt* reclutare
recruiting office [rɪ'kru:tɪŋ-] *n* ufficio di reclutamento
recruitment [rɪ'kru:tmənt] *n* reclutamento
rectangle ['rɛktæŋgl] *n* rettangolo
rectangular [rɛk'tæŋgjulə^r] *adj* rettangolare
rectify ['rɛktɪfaɪ] *vt* (*error*) rettificare; (*omission*) riparare
rector ['rɛktə^r] *n* (*Rel*) parroco (*anglicano*); (*in Scottish universities*) *personalità eletta dagli studenti per rappresentarli*
rectory ['rɛktərɪ] *n* presbiterio
rectum ['rɛktəm] *n* (*Anat*) retto
recuperate [rɪ'kju:pəreɪt] *vi* ristabilirsi
recur [rɪ'kə:^{r}] *vi* riaccadere; (*idea, opportunity*) riapparire; (*symptoms*) ripresentarsi

recurrence [rɪ'kʌrəns] *n* ripresentarsi *m*; riapparizione *f*
recurrent [rɪ'kʌrənt] *adj* ricorrente, periodico(-a)
recurring [rɪ'kʌrɪŋ] *adj* (*Math*) periodico(-a)
recycle [ri:'saɪkl] *vt* riciclare
red [rɛd] *n* rosso; (*Pol: pej*) rosso(-a) ■ *adj* rosso(-a); **in the ~** (*account*) scoperto; (*business*) in deficit
red alert *n* allarme *m* rosso
red-blooded ['rɛd'blʌdɪd] *adj* (*col*) gagliardo(-a)
red-brick university ['rɛdbrɪk-] *n* (*Brit*) *università di recente formazione*; *vedi nota*

RED-BRICK UNIVERSITY

In Gran Bretagna, con *red-brick university* (letteralmente, università di mattoni rossi) si indicano le università istituite tra la fine dell'Ottocento e i primi del Novecento, per contraddistinguerle dalle università più antiche, i cui edifici sono di pietra; *vedi anche* "Oxbridge".

red carpet treatment *n* cerimonia col gran pavese
Red Cross *n* Croce *f* Rossa
redcurrant ['rɛdkʌrənt] *n* ribes *m inv*
redden ['rɛdn] *vt* arrossare ■ *vi* arrossire
reddish ['rɛdɪʃ] *adj* rossiccio(-a)
redecorate [ri:'dɛkəreɪt] *vt* tinteggiare (e tappezzare) di nuovo
redeem [rɪ'di:m] *vt* (*debt*) riscattare; (*sth in pawn*) ritirare; (*fig, also Rel*) redimere
redeemable [rɪ'di:məbl] *adj* con diritto di riscatto; redimibile
redeeming [rɪ'di:mɪŋ] *adj* (*feature*) che salva
redefine [ri:dɪ'faɪn] *vt* ridefinire
redemption [rɪ'dɛmpʃən] *n* (*Rel*) redenzione *f*; (*also*: **past** *or* **beyond redemption**) irrecuperabile
redeploy [ri:dɪ'plɔɪ] *vt* (*Mil*) riorganizzare lo schieramento di; (*resources*) riorganizzare
redeployment [ri:dɪ'plɔɪmənt] *n* riorganizzazione *f*
redevelop [ri:dɪ'vɛləp] *vt* ristrutturare
redevelopment [ri:dɪ'vɛləpmənt] *n* ristrutturazione *f*
red-handed [rɛd'hændɪd] *adj*: **to be caught ~** essere preso(-a) in flagrante *or* con le mani nel sacco
redhead ['rɛdhɛd] *n* rosso(-a)
red herring *n* (*fig*) falsa pista
red-hot [rɛd'hɔt] *adj* arroventato(-a)
redirect [ri:daɪ'rɛkt] *vt* (*mail*) far seguire
redistribute [ri:dɪ'strɪbju:t] *vt* ridistribuire
red-letter day ['rɛdlɛtə-] *n* giorno memorabile
red light *n*: **to go through a ~** (*Aut*) passare col rosso
red-light district [rɛd'laɪt-] *n* quartiere *m* luce rossa *inv*
red meat *n* carne *f* rossa
redness ['rɛdnɪs] *n* rossore *m*; (*of hair*) rosso
redo [ri:'du:] *vt irreg* rifare
redolent ['rɛdələnt] *adj*: **~ of** che sa di; (*fig*) che ricorda
redouble [ri:'dʌbl] *vt*: **to ~ one's efforts** raddoppiare gli sforzi
redraft [ri:'drɑ:ft] *vt* fare una nuova stesura di
redress [rɪ'drɛs] *n* riparazione *f* ■ *vt* riparare; **to ~ the balance** ristabilire l'equilibrio
Red Sea *n*: **the ~** il mar Rosso
redskin ['rɛdskɪn] *n* pellerossa *m/f*
red tape *n* (*fig*) burocrazia
reduce [rɪ'dju:s] *vt* ridurre; (*lower*) ridurre, abbassare; **"~ speed now"** (*Aut*) "rallentare"; **to ~ sth by/to** ridurre qc di/a; **to ~ sb to silence/despair/tears** ridurre qn al silenzio/alla disperazione/in lacrime
reduced [rɪ'dju:st] *adj* (*decreased*) ridotto(-a); **at a ~ price** a prezzo ribassato *or* ridotto; **"greatly ~ prices"** "grandi ribassi"
reduction [rɪ'dʌkʃən] *n* riduzione *f*; (*of price*) ribasso; (*discount*) sconto
redundancy [rɪ'dʌndənsɪ] *n* licenziamento (per eccesso di personale); **compulsory ~** licenziamento; **voluntary ~** *forma di cassa integrazione volontaria*
redundancy payment *n* (*Brit*) indennità *f inv* di licenziamento
redundant [rɪ'dʌndnt] *adj* (*Brit: worker*) licenziato(-a); (*detail, object*) superfluo(-a); **to make ~** (*Brit*) licenziare (per eccesso di personale)
reed [ri:d] *n* (*Bot*) canna; (*Mus: of clarinet etc*) ancia
re-educate [ri:'edjukeɪt] *vt* rieducare
reedy ['ri:dɪ] *adj* (*voice, instrument*) acuto(-a)
reef [ri:f] *n* (*at sea*) scogliera; **coral ~** barriera corallina
reek [ri:k] *vi*: **to ~ (of)** puzzare (di)
reel [ri:l] *n* bobina, rocchetto; (*Tech*) aspo; (*Fishing*) mulinello; (*Cine*) rotolo ■ *vt* (*Tech*) annaspare; (*also*: **reel up**) avvolgere ■ *vi* (*sway*) barcollare, vacillare; **my head is reeling** mi gira la testa
▸ **reel off** *vt* snocciolare
re-election [ri:ɪ'lɛkʃən] *n* rielezione *f*
re-enter [ri:'ɛntə[r]] *vt* rientrare in
re-entry [ri:'ɛntrɪ] *n* rientro
re-export *vt* [ri:ɪk'spɔ:t] riesportare ■ *n*

[riːˈɛkspɔːt] merce *f* riesportata, riesportazione *f*
ref [rɛf] *n abbr* (*col: = referee*) arbitro
ref. *abbr* (*Comm: = with reference to*) sogg
refectory [rɪˈfɛktərɪ] *n* refettorio
refer [rɪˈfəːʳ] *vt*: **to ~ sth to** (*dispute, decision*) deferire qc a; **to ~ sb to** (*inquirer: for information*) indirizzare qn a; (*reader: to text*) rimandare qn a; **he referred me to the manager** mi ha detto di rivolgermi al direttore
▸ **refer to** *vt fus* (*allude to*) accennare a; (*apply to*) riferire a; (*consult*) rivolgersi a; **referring to your letter** (*Comm*) in riferimento alla Vostra lettera
referee [rɛfəˈriː] *n* arbitro; (*Tennis*) giudice *m* di gara; (*Brit: for job application*) referenza ■ *vt* arbitrare
reference [ˈrɛfrəns] *n* riferimento; (*mention*) menzione *f*, allusione *f*; (*for job application: letter*) referenza; lettera di raccomandazione; (*: person*) referenza; (*in book*) rimando; **with ~ to** riguardo a; (*Comm: in letter*) in *or* con riferimento a; **"please quote this ~"** (*Comm*) "si prega di far riferimento al numero di protocollo"
reference book *n* libro di consultazione
reference library *n* biblioteca per la consultazione
reference number *n* (*Comm*) numero di riferimento
referendum (*pl* **referenda**) [rɛfəˈrɛndəm, -də] *n* referendum *m inv*
referral [rɪˈfəːrəl] *n* deferimento; (*Med*) richiesta (di visita specialistica)
refill *vt* [riːˈfɪl] riempire di nuovo; (*pen, lighter etc*) ricaricare ■ *n* [ˈriːfɪl] (*for pen etc*) ricambio
refine [rɪˈfaɪn] *vt* raffinare
refined [rɪˈfaɪnd] *adj* raffinato(-a)
refinement [rɪˈfaɪnmənt] *n* (*of person*) raffinatezza
refinery [rɪˈfaɪnərɪ] *n* raffineria
refit *n* [ˈriːfɪt] (*Naut*) raddobbo ■ *vt* [riːˈfɪt] (*ship*) raddobbare
reflate [riːˈfleɪt] *vt* (*economy*) rilanciare
reflation [riːˈfleɪʃən] *n* rilancio
reflationary [riːˈfleɪʃənərɪ] *adj* nuovamente inflazionario(-a)
reflect [rɪˈflɛkt] *vt* (*light, image*) riflettere; (*fig*) rispecchiare ■ *vi* (*think*) riflettere, considerare
▸ **reflect on** *vt fus* (*discredit*) rispecchiarsi su
reflection [rɪˈflɛkʃən] *n* riflessione *f*; (*image*) riflesso; (*criticism*): **~ on** giudizio su; attacco a; **on ~** pensandoci sopra
reflector [rɪˈflɛktəʳ] *n* (*also Aut*) catarifrangente *m*
reflex [ˈriːflɛks] *adj* riflesso(-a) ■ *n* riflesso
reflexive [rɪˈflɛksɪv] *adj* (*Ling*) riflessivo(-a)
reform [rɪˈfɔːm] *n* riforma ■ *vt* riformare
reformat [riːˈfɔːmæt] *vt* (*Comput*) riformattare
Reformation [rɛfəˈmeɪʃən] *n*: **the ~** la Riforma
reformatory [rɪˈfɔːmətərɪ] *n* (*US*) riformatorio
reformed [rɪˈfɔːmd] *adj* cambiato(-a) (per il meglio)
reformer [rɪˈfɔːməʳ] *n* riformatore(-trice)
refrain [rɪˈfreɪn] *vi*: **to ~ from doing** trattenersi dal fare ■ *n* ritornello
refresh [rɪˈfrɛʃ] *vt* rinfrescare; (*food, sleep*) ristorare
refresher course [rɪˈfrɛʃə-] *n* (*Brit*) corso di aggiornamento
refreshing [rɪˈfrɛʃɪŋ] *adj* (*drink*) rinfrescante; (*sleep*) riposante, ristoratore(-trice); (*change etc*) piacevole; (*idea, point of view*) originale
refreshment [rɪˈfrɛʃmənt] *n* (*eating, resting etc*) ristoro; **~(s)** rinfreschi *mpl*
refrigeration [rɪfrɪdʒəˈreɪʃən] *n* refrigerazione *f*
refrigerator [rɪˈfrɪdʒəreɪtəʳ] *n* frigorifero
refuel [riːˈfjuəl] *vt* rifornire (di carburante) ■ *vi* far rifornimento (di carburante)
refuge [ˈrɛfjuːdʒ] *n* rifugio; **to take ~ in** rifugiarsi in
refugee [rɛfjuˈdʒiː] *n* rifugiato(-a), profugo(-a)
refugee camp *n* campo (di) profughi
refund *n* [ˈriːfʌnd] rimborso ■ *vt* [rɪˈfʌnd] rimborsare
refurbish [riːˈfəːbɪʃ] *vt* rimettere a nuovo
refurnish [riːˈfəːnɪʃ] *vt* ammobiliare di nuovo
refusal [rɪˈfjuːzəl] *n* rifiuto; **to have first ~ on sth** avere il diritto d'opzione su qc
refuse[1] [ˈrɛfjuːs] *n* rifiuti *mpl*
refuse[2] [rɪˈfjuːz] *vt, vi* rifiutare; **to ~ to do sth** rifiutare *or* rifiutarsi di fare qc
refuse collection *n* raccolta di rifiuti
refuse disposal *n* sistema *m* di scarico dei rifiuti
refusenik [rɪˈfjuːznɪk] *n ebreo a cui il governo sovietico impediva di lasciare il paese*
refute [rɪˈfjuːt] *vt* confutare
regain [rɪˈgeɪn] *vt* riguadagnare; riacquistare, ricuperare
regal [ˈriːgl] *adj* regale
regale [rɪˈgeɪl] *vt*: **to ~ sb with sth** intrattenere qn con qc
regalia [rɪˈgeɪlɪə] *n* insegne *fpl* reali
regard [rɪˈgɑːd] *n* riguardo, stima ■ *vt* considerare, stimare; **to give one's regards to** porgere i suoi saluti a; **(kind) regards** cordiali saluti; **as regards, with ~ to** riguardo a

r

regarding [rɪ'gɑːdɪŋ] *prep* riguardo a, per quanto riguarda
regardless [rɪ'gɑːdlɪs] *adv* lo stesso; **~ of** a dispetto di, nonostante
regatta [rɪ'gætə] *n* regata
regency ['riːdʒənsɪ] *n* reggenza
regenerate [rɪ'dʒɛnəreɪt] *vt* rigenerare; (*feelings, enthusiasm*) far rinascere ■ *vi* rigenerarsi; rinascere
regent ['riːdʒənt] *n* reggente *m*
reggae ['rɛgeɪ] *n* reggae *m*
régime [reɪ'ʒiːm] *n* regime *m*
regiment *n* ['rɛdʒɪmənt] reggimento ■ *vt* ['rɛdʒɪmɛnt] irreggimentare
regimental [rɛdʒɪ'mɛntl] *adj* reggimentale
regimentation [rɛdʒɪmɛn'teɪʃən] *n* irreggimentazione *f*
region ['riːdʒən] *n* regione *f*; **in the ~ of** (*fig*) all'incirca di
regional ['riːdʒənl] *adj* regionale
regional development *n* sviluppo regionale
register ['rɛdʒɪstəʳ] *n* registro; (*also*: **electoral register**) lista elettorale ■ *vt* registrare; (*vehicle*) immatricolare; (*luggage*) spedire assicurato(-a); (*letter*) assicurare; (*instrument*) segnare ■ *vi* iscriversi; (*at hotel*) firmare il registro; (*make impression*) entrare in testa; **to ~ a protest** fare un esposto; **to ~ for a course** iscriversi a un corso
registered ['rɛdʒɪstəd] *adj* (*design*) depositato(-a); (*Brit: letter*) assicurato(-a); (*student, voter*) iscritto(-a)
registered company *n* società iscritta al registro
registered nurse *n* (*US*) infermiere(-a) diplomato(-a)
registered office *n* sede *f* legale
registered trademark *n* marchio depositato
registrar ['rɛdʒɪstrɑːʳ] *n* ufficiale *m* di stato civile; segretario
registration [rɛdʒɪs'treɪʃən] *n* (*act*) registrazione *f*; iscrizione *f*; (*Aut: also*: **registration number**) numero di targa
registry ['rɛdʒɪstrɪ] *n* ufficio del registro
registry office *n* (*Brit*) anagrafe *f*; **to get married in a ~** ≈ sposarsi in municipio
regret [rɪ'grɛt] *n* rimpianto, rincrescimento ■ *vt* rimpiangere; **I ~ that I/he cannot help** mi rincresce di non poter aiutare/che lui non possa aiutare; **we ~ to inform you that ...** siamo spiacenti di informarla che ...
regretfully [rɪ'grɛtfəlɪ] *adv* con rincrescimento
regrettable [rɪ'grɛtəbl] *adj* deplorevole
regrettably [rɪ'grɛtəblɪ] *adv* purtroppo, sfortunatamente
regroup [riː'gruːp] *vt* raggruppare ■ *vi* raggrupparsi
regt *abbr* (= *regiment*) Reg
regular ['rɛgjuləʳ] *adj* regolare; (*usual*) abituale, normale; (*listener, reader*) fedele; (*soldier*) dell'esercito regolare; (*Comm: size*) normale ■ *n* (*client etc*) cliente *m/f* abituale
regularity [rɛgju'lærɪtɪ] *n* regolarità *f inv*
regularly ['rɛgjuləlɪ] *adv* regolarmente
regulate ['rɛgjuleɪt] *vt* regolare
regulation [rɛgju'leɪʃən] *n* (*rule*) regola, regolamento; (*adjustment*) regolazione *f* ■ *cpd* (*Mil*) di ordinanza
rehabilitate [riːə'bɪlɪteɪt] *vt* (*criminal, drug addict, invalid*) ricuperare, reinserire
rehabilitation ['riːəbɪlɪ'teɪʃən] *n* (*see vb*) ricupero, reinserimento
rehash [riː'hæʃ] *vt* (*col*) rimaneggiare
rehearsal [rɪ'həːsəl] *n* prova; **dress ~** prova generale
rehearse [rɪ'həːs] *vt* provare
rehouse [riː'hauz] *vt* rialloggiare
reign [reɪn] *n* regno ■ *vi* regnare
reigning ['reɪnɪŋ] *adj* (*monarch*) regnante; (*champion*) attuale
reimburse [riːɪm'bəːs] *vt* rimborsare
rein [reɪn] *n* (*for horse*) briglia; **to give sb free ~** (*fig*) lasciare completa libertà a qn
reincarnation [riːɪnkɑː'neɪʃən] *n* reincarnazione *f*
reindeer ['reɪndɪəʳ] *n pl inv* renna
reinforce [riːɪn'fɔːs] *vt* rinforzare
reinforced concrete [riːɪn'fɔːst-] *n* cemento armato
reinforcement [riːɪn'fɔːsmənt] *n* (*action*) rinforzamento; **reinforcements** *npl* (*Mil*) rinforzi *mpl*
reinstate [riːɪn'steɪt] *vt* reintegrare
reinstatement [riːɪn'steɪtmənt] *n* reintegrazione *f*
reissue [riː'ɪʃjuː] *vt* (*book*) ristampare, ripubblicare; (*film*) distribuire di nuovo
reiterate [riː'ɪtəreɪt] *vt* reiterare, ripetere
reject *n* ['riːdʒɛkt] (*Comm*) scarto ■ *vt* [rɪ'dʒɛkt] rifiutare, respingere; (*Comm: goods*) scartare
rejection [rɪ'dʒɛkʃən] *n* rifiuto
rejoice [rɪ'dʒɔɪs] *vi*: **to ~ (at** *or* **over)** provare diletto (in)
rejoinder [rɪ'dʒɔɪndəʳ] *n* (*retort*) replica
rejuvenate [rɪ'dʒuːvəneɪt] *vt* ringiovanire
rekindle [riː'kɪndl] *vt* riaccendere
relapse [rɪ'læps] *n* (*Med*) ricaduta
relate [rɪ'leɪt] *vt* (*tell*) raccontare; (*connect*) collegare ■ *vi*: **to ~ to** (*refer to*) riferirsi a; (*get on with*) stabilire un rapporto con
related [rɪ'leɪtɪd] *adj* imparentato(-a); collegato(-a), connesso(-a); **~ to** imparentato(-a) con; collegato(-a) *or* connesso(-a) con

relating [rɪ'leɪtɪŋ]: ~ **to** *prep* che riguarda, rispetto a
relation [rɪ'leɪʃən] *n* (*person*) parente *m/f*; (*link*) rapporto, relazione *f*; **in ~ to** con riferimento a; **diplomatic/international relations** rapporti diplomatici/internazionali; **to bear a ~ to** corrispondere a
relationship [rɪ'leɪʃənʃɪp] *n* rapporto; (*personal ties*) rapporti *mpl*, relazioni *fpl*; (*also*: **family relationship**) legami *mpl* di parentela; (*affair*) relazione *f*; **they have a good ~** vanno molto d'accordo
relative ['rɛlətɪv] *n* parente *m/f* ■ *adj* relativo(-a); (*respective*) rispettivo(-a)
relatively ['rɛlətɪvlɪ] *adv* relativamente; (*fairly, rather*) abbastanza
relax [rɪ'læks] *vi* rilasciarsi; (*person: unwind*) rilassarsi ■ *vt* rilasciare; (*mind, person*) rilassare; **~!** (*calm down*) calma!
relaxation [ri:læk'seɪʃən] *n* rilasciamento; rilassamento; (*entertainment*) ricreazione *f*, svago
relaxed [rɪ'lækst] *adj* rilasciato(-a); rilassato(-a)
relaxing [rɪ'læksɪŋ] *adj* rilassante
relay ['ri:leɪ] *n* (*Sport*) corsa a staffetta ■ *vt* (*message*) trasmettere
release [rɪ'li:s] *n* (*from prison*) rilascio; (*from obligation*) liberazione *f*; (*of gas etc*) emissione *f*; (*of film etc*) distribuzione *f*; (*record*) disco; (*device*) disinnesto ■ *vt* (*prisoner*) rilasciare; (*from obligation, wreckage etc*) liberare; (*book, film*) fare uscire; (*news*) rendere pubblico(-a); (*gas etc*) emettere; (*Tech: catch, spring etc*) disinnestare; (*let go*) rilasciare; lasciar andare; sciogliere; **to ~ one's grip** mollare la presa; **to ~ the clutch** (*Aut*) staccare la frizione
relegate ['rɛləgeɪt] *vt* relegare; (*Sport*): **to be relegated** essere retrocesso(-a)
relent [rɪ'lɛnt] *vi* cedere
relentless [rɪ'lɛntlɪs] *adj* implacabile
relevance ['rɛləvəns] *n* pertinenza; **~ of sth to sth** rapporto tra qc e qc
relevant ['rɛləvənt] *adj* pertinente; (*chapter*) in questione; **~ to** pertinente a
reliability [rɪlaɪə'bɪlɪtɪ] *n* (*of person*) serietà; (*of machine*) affidabilità
reliable [rɪ'laɪəbl] *adj* (*person, firm*) fidato(-a), che dà affidamento; (*method*) sicuro(-a); (*machine*) affidabile
reliably [rɪ'laɪəblɪ] *adv*: **to be ~ informed** sapere da fonti sicure
reliance [rɪ'laɪəns] *n*: **~ (on)** dipendenza (da)
reliant [rɪ'laɪənt] *adj*: **to be ~ on sth/sb** dipendere da qc/qn
relic ['rɛlɪk] *n* (*Rel*) reliquia; (*of the past*) resto
relief [rɪ'li:f] *n* (*from pain, anxiety*) sollievo; (*help, supplies*) soccorsi *mpl*; (*of guard*) cambio; (*Art, Geo*) rilievo; **by way of light ~** come diversivo
relief map *n* carta in rilievo
relief road *n* (*Brit*) circonvallazione *f*
relieve [rɪ'li:v] *vt* (*pain, patient*) sollevare; (*bring help*) soccorrere; (*take over from: gen*) sostituire; (*: guard*) rilevare; **to ~ sb of sth** (*load*) alleggerire qn di qc; **to ~ sb of his command** (*Mil*) esonerare qn dal comando; **to ~ o.s.** (*euphemism*) fare i propri bisogni
relieved [rɪ'li:vd] *adj* sollevato(-a); **to be ~ that ...** essere sollevato(-a) (dal fatto) che ...; **I'm ~ to hear it** mi hai tolto un peso con questa notizia
religion [rɪ'lɪdʒən] *n* religione *f*
religious [rɪ'lɪdʒəs] *adj* religioso(-a)
religious education *n* religione *f*
relinquish [rɪ'lɪŋkwɪʃ] *vt* abbandonare; (*plan, habit*) rinunziare a
relish ['rɛlɪʃ] *n* (*Culin*) condimento; (*enjoyment*) gran piacere *m* ■ *vt* (*food etc*) godere; **to ~ doing** adorare fare
relive [ri:'lɪv] *vt* rivivere
reload [ri:'ləud] *vt* ricaricare
relocate [ri:ləu'keɪt] *vt* (*business*) trasferire ■ *vi*: **to ~ in** trasferire la propria sede a
reluctance [rɪ'lʌktəns] *n* riluttanza
reluctant [rɪ'lʌktənt] *adj* riluttante, mal disposto(-a); **to be ~ to do sth** essere restio a fare qc
reluctantly [rɪ'lʌktəntlɪ] *adv* di mala voglia, a malincuore
rely [rɪ'laɪ]: **to ~ on** *vt fus* contare su; (*be dependent*) dipendere da
remain [rɪ'meɪn] *vi* restare, rimanere; **to ~ silent** restare in silenzio; **I ~, yours faithfully** (*Brit: in letters*) distinti saluti
remainder [rɪ'meɪndə^r] *n* resto; (*Comm*) rimanenza
remaining [rɪ'meɪnɪŋ] *adj* che rimane
remains [rɪ'meɪnz] *npl* resti *mpl*
remand [rɪ'mɑ:nd] *n*: **on ~** in detenzione preventiva ■ *vt*: **to ~ in custody** rinviare in carcere; trattenere a disposizione della legge
remand home *n* (*Brit*) riformatorio, casa di correzione
remark [rɪ'mɑ:k] *n* osservazione *f* ■ *vt* osservare, dire; (*notice*) notare ■ *vi*: **to ~ on sth** fare dei commenti su qc
remarkable [rɪ'mɑ:kəbl] *adj* notevole; eccezionale
remarry [ri:'mærɪ] *vi* risposarsi
remedial [rɪ'mi:dɪəl] *adj* (*tuition, classes*) di riparazione
remedy ['rɛmədɪ] *n*: **~ (for)** rimedio (per) ■ *vt* rimediare a

r

remember [rɪ'mɛmbəʳ] *vt* ricordare, ricordarsi di; **I ~ seeing it, I ~ having seen it** (mi) ricordo di averlo visto; **she remembered to do it** si è ricordata di farlo; **~ me to your wife and children!** saluti sua moglie e i bambini da parte mia!
remembrance [rɪ'mɛmbrəns] *n* memoria; ricordo
Remembrance Sunday *n* (*Brit*) *vedi nota*

REMEMBRANCE SUNDAY

Nel Regno Unito, la domenica più vicina all'11 di novembre, data in cui fu firmato l'armistizio con la Germania nel 1918, ricorre il *Remembrance Sunday*, giorno in cui vengono commemorati i caduti in guerra. In questa occasione molti portano un papavero di carta appuntato al petto in segno di rispetto.

remind [rɪ'maɪnd] *vt*: **to ~ sb of sth** ricordare qc a qn; **to ~ sb to do** ricordare a qn di fare; **that reminds me!** a proposito!
reminder [rɪ'maɪndəʳ] *n* richiamo; (*note etc*) promemoria *m inv*
reminisce [rɛmɪ'nɪs] *vi*: **to ~ (about)** abbandonarsi ai ricordi (di)
reminiscences [rɛmɪ'nɪsnsɪz] *npl* reminiscenze *fpl*, memorie *fpl*
reminiscent [rɛmɪ'nɪsnt] *adj*: **~ of** che fa pensare a, che richiama
remiss [rɪ'mɪs] *adj* negligente; **it was ~ of me** è stata una negligenza da parte mia
remission [rɪ'mɪʃən] *n* remissione *f*; (*of fee*) esonero
remit [rɪ'mɪt] *vt* rimettere
remittance [rɪ'mɪtəns] *n* rimessa
remnant ['rɛmnənt] *n* resto, avanzo; **remnants** *npl* (*Comm*) scampoli *mpl*; fine *f* serie
remonstrate ['rɛmənstreɪt] *vi* protestare; **to ~ with sb about sth** fare le proprie rimostranze a qn circa qc
remorse [rɪ'mɔːs] *n* rimorso
remorseful [rɪ'mɔːsful] *adj* pieno(-a) di rimorsi
remorseless [rɪ'mɔːslɪs] *adj* (*fig*) spietato(-a)
remote [rɪ'məut] *adj* remoto(-a), lontano(-a); (*person*) distaccato(-a); **there is a ~ possibility that ...** c'è una vaga possibilità che ... *+sub*
remote control *n* telecomando
remote-controlled [rɪ'məutkən'trəuld] *adj* telecomandato(-a)
remotely [rɪ'məutlɪ] *adv* remotamente; (*slightly*) vagamente
remoteness [rɪ'məutnɪs] *n* lontananza
remould ['riːməuld] *n* (*Brit: tyre*) gomma rivestita
removable [rɪ'muːvəbl] *adj* (*detachable*) staccabile
removal [rɪ'muːvəl] *n* (*taking away*) rimozione *f*; soppressione *f*; (*from house*) trasloco; (*from office: sacking*) destituzione *f*; (*Med*) ablazione *f*
removal man *n* (*Brit*) addetto ai traslochi
removal van *n* (*Brit*) furgone *m* per traslochi
remove [rɪ'muːv] *vt* togliere, rimuovere; (*employee*) destituire; (*stain*) far sparire; (*doubt, abuse*) sopprimere, eliminare; **first cousin once removed** cugino di secondo grado
remover [rɪ'muːvəʳ] *n* (*for paint*) prodotto sverniciante; (*for varnish*) solvente *m*; **make-up ~** struccatore *m*
remunerate [rɪ'mjuːnəreɪt] *vt* rimunerare
remuneration [rɪmjuːnə'reɪʃən] *n* rimunerazione *f*
Renaissance [rə'neɪsəns] *n*: **the ~** il Rinascimento
rename [riː'neɪm] *vt* ribattezzare
rend (*pt, pp* **rent**) [rɛnd, rɛnt] *vt* lacerare
render ['rɛndəʳ] *vt* rendere; (*Culin: fat*) struggere
rendering ['rɛndərɪŋ] *n* (*Mus etc*) interpretazione *f*
rendez-vous ['rɔndɪvuː] *n* appuntamento; (*place*) luogo d'incontro; (*meeting*) incontro ■ *vi* ritrovarsi; (*spaceship*) effettuare un rendez-vous
rendition [rɛn'dɪʃən] *n* (*Mus*) interpretazione *f*
renegade ['rɛnɪgeɪd] *n* rinnegato(-a)
renew [rɪ'njuː] *vt* rinnovare; (*negotiations*) riprendere
renewable [rɪ'njuːəbl] *adj* riutilizzabile; (*contract, energy*) rinnovabile; **~ energy, renewables** fonti *mpl* di energia rinnovabile
renewal [rɪ'njuːəl] *n* rinnovamento; ripresa
renounce [rɪ'nauns] *vt* rinunziare a; (*disown*) ripudiare
renovate ['rɛnəveɪt] *vt* rinnovare; (*art work*) restaurare
renovation [rɛnə'veɪʃən] *n* rinnovamento; restauro
renown [rɪ'naun] *n* rinomanza
renowned [rɪ'naund] *adj* rinomato(-a)
rent [rɛnt] *pt, pp of* **rend** ■ *n* affitto ■ *vt* (*take for rent*) prendere in affitto; (*car, TV*) noleggiare, prendere a noleggio; (*also:* **rent out**) dare in affitto; (*car, TV*) noleggiare, dare a noleggio
rental ['rɛntl] *n* (*cost: on TV, telephone*) abbonamento; (*: on car*) nolo, noleggio
rent boy *n* (*Brit col*) giovane prostituto

renunciation [rɪnʌnsɪ'eɪʃən] *n* rinnegamento; (*self-denial*) rinunzia
reopen [riː'əupən] *vt* riaprire
reopening [riː'əupnɪŋ] *n* riapertura
reorder [riː'ɔːdəʳ] *vt* ordinare di nuovo; (*rearrange*) riorganizzare
reorganize [riː'ɔːgənaɪz] *vt* riorganizzare
Rep *abbr* (*US Pol*) = **representative**; **Republican**
rep [rɛp] *n abbr* (*Comm*: = *representative*) rappresentante *m/f*; (*Theat*: *repertory*) teatro di repertorio
repair [rɪ'pɛəʳ] *n* riparazione *f* ■ *vt* riparare; **in good/bad ~** in buona/cattiva condizione; **under ~** in riparazione
repair kit *n* corredo per riparazioni
repair man *n* riparatore *m*
repair shop *n* (*Aut etc*) officina
repartee [rɛpɑː'tiː] *n* risposta pronta
repast [rɪ'pɑːst] *n* (*formal*) pranzo
repatriate [riː'pætrɪeɪt] *vt* rimpatriare
repay [riː'peɪ] *vt irreg* (*money, creditor*) rimborsare, ripagare; (*sb's efforts*) ricompensare
repayment [riː'peɪmənt] *n* rimborsamento; ricompensa
repeal [rɪ'piːl] *n* (*of law*) abrogazione *f*; (*of sentence*) annullamento ■ *vt* abrogare; annullare
repeat [rɪ'piːt] *n* (*Radio, TV*) replica ■ *vt* ripetere; (*pattern*) riprodurre; (*promise, attack, also Comm*: *order*) rinnovare ■ *vi* ripetere
repeatedly [rɪ'piːtɪdlɪ] *adv* ripetutamente, spesso
repeat order *n* (*Comm*): **to place a ~ (for)** rinnovare l'ordinazione (di)
repel [rɪ'pɛl] *vt* respingere
repellent [rɪ'pɛlənt] *adj* repellente ■ *n*: **insect ~** prodotto *m* anti-insetti *inv*; **moth ~** anti-tarmico
repent [rɪ'pɛnt] *vi*: **to ~ (of)** pentirsi (di)
repentance [rɪ'pɛntəns] *n* pentimento
repercussion [riːpə'kʌʃən] *n* (*consequence*) ripercussione *f*
repertoire ['rɛpətwɑːʳ] *n* repertorio
repertory ['rɛpətərɪ] *n* (*also*: **repertory theatre**) teatro di repertorio
repertory company *n* compagnia di repertorio
repetition [rɛpɪ'tɪʃən] *n* ripetizione *f*; (*Comm*: *of order etc*) rinnovo
repetitious [rɛpɪ'tɪʃəs] *adj* (*speech*) pieno(-a) di ripetizioni
repetitive [rɪ'pɛtɪtɪv] *adj* (*movement*) che si ripete; (*work*) monotono(-a); (*speech*) pieno(-a) di ripetizioni
replace [rɪ'pleɪs] *vt* (*put back*) rimettere a posto; (*take the place of*) sostituire; (*Tel*): **"~ the receiver"** "riattaccare"
replacement [rɪ'pleɪsmənt] *n* rimessa; sostituzione *f*; (*person*) sostituto(-a)
replacement part *n* pezzo di ricambio
replay ['riːpleɪ] *n* (*of match*) partita ripetuta; (*of tape, film*) replay *m inv*
replenish [rɪ'plɛnɪʃ] *vt* (*glass*) riempire; (*stock etc*) rifornire
replete [rɪ'pliːt] *adj*: **~ (with)** ripieno(-a) (di); (*well-fed*) sazio(-a) (di)
replica ['rɛplɪkə] *n* replica, copia
reply [rɪ'plaɪ] *n* risposta ■ *vi* rispondere; **in ~** in risposta; **there's no ~** (*Tel*) non risponde (nessuno)
reply coupon *n* buono di risposta
report [rɪ'pɔːt] *n* rapporto; (*Press etc*) cronaca; (*Brit*: *also*: **school report**) pagella ■ *vt* riportare; (*Press etc*) fare una cronaca su; (*bring to notice*: *occurrence*) segnalare; (: *person*) denunciare ■ *vi* (*make a report*) fare un rapporto (*or* una cronaca); (*present o.s.*): **to ~ (to sb)** presentarsi (a qn); **to ~ (on)** fare un rapporto (su); **it is reported that** si dice che; **it is reported from Berlin that ...** ci è stato riferito da Berlino che ....
report card *n* (*US, Scottish*) pagella
reportedly [rɪ'pɔːtɪdlɪ] *adv*: **she is ~ living in Spain** si dice che vive in Spagna
reported speech [rɪ'pɔːtɪd-] *n* (*Ling*) discorso indiretto
reporter [rɪ'pɔːtəʳ] *n* (*Press*) cronista *m/f*, reporter *m inv*; (*Radio*) radiocronista *m/f*; (*TV*) telecronista *m/f*
repose [rɪ'pəuz] *n*: **in ~** in riposo
repossess [riːpə'zɛs] *vt* rientrare in possesso di
repossession order [riːpə'zɛʃən-] *n* ordine *m* di espropriazione
reprehensible [rɛprɪ'hɛnsɪbl] *adj* riprensibile
represent [rɛprɪ'zɛnt] *vt* rappresentare
representation [rɛprɪzɛn'teɪʃən] *n* rappresentazione *f*; **representations** *npl* (*protest*) protesta
representative [rɛprɪ'zɛntətɪv] *n* rappresentativo(-a); (*Comm*) rappresentante *m* (di commercio); (*US*: *Pol*) deputato(-a) ■ *adj*: **~ (of)** rappresentativo(-a) (di)
repress [rɪ'prɛs] *vt* reprimere
repression [rɪ'prɛʃən] *n* repressione *f*
repressive [rɪ'prɛsɪv] *adj* repressivo(-a)
reprieve [rɪ'priːv] *n* (*Law*) sospensione *f* dell'esecuzione della condanna; (*fig*) dilazione *f* ■ *vt* sospendere l'esecuzione della condanna a; accordare una dilazione a
reprimand ['rɛprɪmɑːnd] *n* rimprovero ■ *vt* rimproverare, redarguire

r

reprint ['ri:prɪnt] *n* ristampa ■ *vt* ristampare
reprisal [rɪ'praɪzl] *n* rappresaglia; **to take reprisals** fare delle rappresaglie
reproach [rɪ'prəutʃ] *n* rimprovero ■ *vt*: **to ~ sb with sth** rimproverare qn di qc; **beyond ~** irreprensibile
reproachful [rɪ'prəutʃful] *adj* di rimprovero
reproduce [ri:prə'dju:s] *vt* riprodurre ■ *vi* riprodursi
reproduction [ri:prə'dʌkʃən] *n* riproduzione *f*
reproductive [ri:prə'dʌktɪv] *adj* riproduttore(-trice); riproduttivo(-a)
reproof [rɪ'pru:f] *n* riprovazione *f*
reprove [rɪ'pru:v] *vt* (*action*) disapprovare; (*person*): **to ~ (for)** biasimare (per)
reproving [rɪ'pru:vɪŋ] *adj* di disapprovazione
reptile ['rɛptaɪl] *n* rettile *m*
Repub. *abbr* (*US Pol*) = **Republican**
republic [rɪ'pʌblɪk] *n* repubblica
republican [rɪ'pʌblɪkən] *adj, n* repubblicano(-a)
repudiate [rɪ'pju:dɪeɪt] *vt* ripudiare
repugnant [rɪ'pʌgnənt] *adj* ripugnante
repulse [rɪ'pʌls] *vt* respingere
repulsion [rɪ'pʌlʃən] *n* ripulsione *f*
repulsive [rɪ'pʌlsɪv] *adj* ripugnante, ripulsivo(-a)
reputable ['rɛpjutəbl] *adj* di buona reputazione; (*occupation*) rispettabile
reputation [rɛpju'teɪʃən] *n* reputazione *f*; **he has a ~ for being awkward** ha la fama di essere un tipo difficile
repute [rɪ'pju:t] *n* reputazione *f*
reputed [rɪ'pju:tɪd] *adj* reputato(-a); **to be ~ to be rich/intelligent** *etc* essere ritenuto(-a) ricco(-a)/intelligente *etc*
reputedly [rɪ'pju:tɪdlɪ] *adv* secondo quanto si dice
request [rɪ'kwɛst] *n* domanda; (*formal*) richiesta ■ *vt*: **to ~ (of** *or* **from sb)** chiedere (a qn); **at the ~ of** su richiesta di; **"you are requested not to smoke"** "si prega di non fumare"
request stop *n* (*Brit: for bus*) fermata facoltativa *or* a richiesta
requiem ['rɛkwɪəm] *n* requiem *m or f inv*
require [rɪ'kwaɪə^r] *vt* (*need: person*) aver bisogno di; (*: thing, situation*) richiedere; (*want*) volere; esigere; (*order*) obbligare; **to ~ sb to do sth/sth of sb** esigere che qn faccia qc/qc da qn; **what qualifications are required?** che requisiti ci vogliono?; **required by law** prescritto dalla legge; **if required** in caso di bisogno
required [rɪ'kwaɪəd] *adj* richiesto(-a)
requirement [rɪ'kwaɪəmənt] *n* (*need*) esigenza; (*condition*) requisito; **to meet sb's requirements** soddisfare le esigenze di qn
requisite ['rɛkwɪzɪt] *n* cosa necessaria ■ *adj* necessario(-a); **toilet requisites** articoli *mpl* da toletta
requisition [rɛkwɪ'zɪʃən] *n*: **~ (for)** richiesta (di) ■ *vt* (*Mil*) requisire
reroute [ri:'ru:t] *vt* (*train etc*) deviare
resale ['ri:'seɪl] *n* rivendita
resale price maintenance *n* prezzo minimo di vendita imposto
rescind [rɪ'sɪnd] *vt* annullare; (*law*) abrogare; (*judgement*) rescindere
rescue ['rɛskju:] *n* salvataggio; (*help*) soccorso ■ *vt* salvare; **to come/go to sb's ~** venire/andare in aiuto a *or* di qn
rescue party *n* squadra di salvataggio
rescuer ['rɛskjuə^r] *n* salvatore(-trice)
research [rɪ'sə:tʃ] *n* ricerca, ricerche *fpl* ■ *vt* fare ricerche su ■ *vi*: **to ~ (into sth)** fare ricerca (su qc); **a piece of ~** un lavoro di ricerca; **~ and development** ricerca e sviluppo
researcher [rɪ'sə:tʃə^r] *n* ricercatore(-trice)
research work *n* ricerche *fpl*
resell [ri:'sɛl] *vt irreg* rivendere
resemblance [rɪ'zɛmbləns] *n* somiglianza; **to bear a strong ~ to** somigliare moltissimo a
resemble [rɪ'zɛmbl] *vt* assomigliare a
resent [rɪ'zɛnt] *vt* risentirsi di
resentful [rɪ'zɛntful] *adj* pieno(-a) di risentimento
resentment [rɪ'zɛntmənt] *n* risentimento
reservation [rɛzə'veɪʃən] *n* (*booking*) prenotazione *f*; (*doubt*) dubbio; (*protected area*) riserva; (*Brit Aut: also*: **central reservation**) spartitraffico *m inv*; **to make a ~ (in an hotel/a restaurant/on a plane)** prenotare (una camera/una tavola/un posto); **with reservations** (*doubts*) con le dovute riserve
reservation desk *n* (*US: in hotel*) reception *f inv*
reserve [rɪ'zə:v] *n* riserva ■ *vt* (*seats etc*) prenotare; **reserves** *npl* (*Mil*) riserve *fpl*; **in ~** in serbo
reserve currency *n* valuta di riserva
reserved [rɪ'zə:vd] *adj* (*shy*) riservato(-a); (*seat*) prenotato(-a)
reserve price *n* (*Brit*) prezzo di riserva, prezzo *m* base *inv*
reserve team *n* (*Brit Sport*) seconda squadra
reservist [rɪ'zə:vɪst] *n* (*Mil*) riservista *m*
reservoir ['rɛzəvwa:^r] *n* serbatoio; (*artificial lake*) bacino idrico
reset [ri:'sɛt] *vt* (*Comput*) azzerare

reshape [riːˈʃeɪp] *vt* (*policy*) ristrutturare

reshuffle [riːˈʃʌfl] *n*: **Cabinet ~** (*Pol*) rimpasto governativo

reside [rɪˈzaɪd] *vi* risiedere

residence [ˈrɛzɪdəns] *n* residenza; **to take up ~** prendere residenza; **in ~** (*queen etc*) in sede; (*doctor*) fisso

residence permit *n* (*Brit*) permesso di soggiorno

resident [ˈrɛzɪdənt] *n* (*gen, Comput*) residente *m/f*; (*in hotel*) cliente *m/f* fisso(-a) ■ *adj* residente

residential [rɛzɪˈdɛnʃəl] *adj* di residenza; (*area*) residenziale

residue [ˈrɛzɪdjuː] *n* resto; (*Chem, Physics*) residuo

resign [rɪˈzaɪn] *vt* (*one's post*) dimettersi da ■ *vi*: **to ~ (from)** dimettersi (da), dare le dimissioni (da); **to ~ o.s. to** rassegnarsi a

resignation [rɛzɪgˈneɪʃən] *n* dimissioni *fpl*; rassegnazione *f*; **to tender one's ~** dare le dimissioni

resilience [rɪˈzɪlɪəns] *n* (*of material*) elasticità, resilienza; (*of person*) capacità di recupero

resilient [rɪˈzɪlɪənt] *adj* elastico(-a); (*person*) che si riprende facilmente

resin [ˈrɛzɪn] *n* resina

resist [rɪˈzɪst] *vt* resistere a

resistance [rɪˈzɪstəns] *n* resistenza

resistant [rɪˈzɪstənt] *adj*: **~ (to)** resistente (a)

resolute [ˈrɛzəluːt] *adj* risoluto(-a)

resolution [rɛzəˈluːʃən] *n* (*resolve*) fermo proposito, risoluzione *f*; (*determination*) risolutezza; (*on screen*) risoluzione *f*; **to make a ~** fare un proposito

resolve [rɪˈzɔlv] *n* risoluzione *f* ■ *vi* (*decide*): **to ~ to do** decidere di fare ■ *vt* (*problem*) risolvere

resolved [rɪˈzɔlvd] *adj* risoluto(-a)

resonance [ˈrɛzənəns] *n* risonanza

resonant [ˈrɛzənənt] *adj* risonante

resort [rɪˈzɔːt] *n* (*town*) stazione *f*; (*place*) località *f inv*; (*recourse*) ricorso ■ *vi*: **to ~ to** far ricorso a; **seaside/winter sports ~** stazione *f* balneare/di sport invernali; **as a last ~** come ultima risorsa

resound [rɪˈzaund] *vi*: **to ~ (with)** risonare (di)

resounding [rɪˈzaundɪŋ] *adj* risonante

resource [rɪˈsɔːs] *n* risorsa; **resources** *npl* risorse *fpl*; **natural resources** risorse naturali; **to leave sb to his** (*or* **her**) **own resources** (*fig*) lasciare che qn si arrangi (per conto suo)

resourceful [rɪˈsɔːsful] *adj* pieno(-a) di risorse, intraprendente

resourcefulness [rɪˈsɔːsfəlnɪs] *n* intraprendenza

respect [rɪsˈpɛkt] *n* rispetto; (*point, detail*): **in some respects** sotto certi aspetti ■ *vt* rispettare; **respects** *npl* ossequi *mpl*; **to have** *or* **show ~ for** aver rispetto per; **out of ~ for** per rispetto *or* riguardo a; **with ~ to** rispetto a, riguardo a; **in ~ of** quanto a; **in this ~** per questo riguardo; **with (all) due ~ I ...** con rispetto parlando, io ...

respectability [rɪspɛktəˈbɪlɪtɪ] *n* rispettabilità

respectable [rɪsˈpɛktəbl] *adj* rispettabile; (*quite big: amount etc*) considerevole; (*quite good: player, result etc*) niente male *inv*

respectful [rɪsˈpɛktful] *adj* rispettoso(-a)

respective [rɪsˈpɛktɪv] *adj* rispettivo(-a)

respectively [rɪsˈpɛktɪvlɪ] *adv* rispettivamente

respiration [rɛspɪˈreɪʃən] *n* respirazione *f*

respirator [ˈrɛspɪreɪtə^r] *n* respiratore *m*

respiratory [ˈrɛspərətərɪ] *adj* respiratorio(-a)

respite [ˈrɛspaɪt] *n* respiro, tregua

resplendent [rɪsˈplɛndənt] *adj* risplendente

respond [rɪsˈpɔnd] *vi* rispondere

respondent [rɪsˈpɔndənt] *n* (*Law*) convenuto(-a)

response [rɪsˈpɔns] *n* risposta; **in ~ to** in risposta a

responsibility [rɪspɔnsɪˈbɪlɪtɪ] *n* responsabilità *f inv*; **to take ~ for sth/sb** assumersi *or* prendersi la responsabilità di qc/per qn

responsible [rɪsˈpɔnsɪbl] *adj* (*liable*): **~ (for)** responsabile (di); (*trustworthy*) fidato(-a); (*job*) di (grande) responsabilità; **to be ~ to sb (for sth)** dover rispondere a qn (di qc)

responsibly [rɪsˈpɔnsəblɪ] *adv* responsabilmente

responsive [rɪsˈpɔnsɪv] *adj* che reagisce

rest [rɛst] *n* riposo; (*stop*) sosta, pausa; (*Mus*) pausa; (*support*) appoggio, sostegno; (*remainder*) resto, avanzi *mpl* ■ *vi* riposarsi; (*remain*) rimanere, restare; (*be supported*): **to ~ on** appoggiarsi su ■ *vt* (*lean*): **to ~ sth on/against** appoggiare qc su/contro; **to set sb's mind at ~** tranquillizzare qn; **the ~ of them** gli altri; **to ~ one's eyes** *or* **gaze on** posare lo sguardo su; **~ assured that ...** stia tranquillo che ...; **it rests with him to decide** sta a lui decidere

restart [riːˈstɑːt] *vt* (*engine*) rimettere in marcia; (*work*) ricominciare

restaurant [ˈrɛstərɔŋ] *n* ristorante *m*

restaurant car *n* (*Brit*) vagone *m* ristorante

rest cure *n* cura del riposo

restful [ˈrɛstful] *adj* riposante

rest home *n* casa di riposo

restitution [rɛstɪˈtjuːʃən] *n* (*act*) restituzione *f*; (*reparation*) riparazione *f*

r

restive ['rɛstɪv] *adj* agitato(-a), impaziente; (*horse*) restio(-a)
restless ['rɛstlɪs] *adj* agitato(-a), irrequieto(-a); **to get ~** spazientirsi
restlessly ['rɛstlɪslɪ] *adv* in preda all'agitazione
restock [riː'stɔk] *vt* rifornire
restoration [rɛstə'reɪʃən] *n* restauro; restituzione *f*
restorative [rɪ'stɔrətɪv] *adj* corroborante, ristorativo(-a) ■ *n* ricostituente *m*
restore [rɪ'stɔːʳ] *vt* (*building*) restaurare; (*sth stolen*) restituire; (*peace, health*) ristorare
restorer [rɪs'tɔːrəʳ] *n* (*Art etc*) restauratore(-trice)
restrain [rɪs'treɪn] *vt* (*feeling*) contenere, frenare; (*person*): **to ~ (from doing)** trattenere (dal fare)
restrained [rɪs'treɪnd] *adj* (*style*) contenuto(-a), sobrio(-a); (*manner*) riservato(-a)
restraint [rɪs'treɪnt] *n* (*restriction*) limitazione *f*; (*moderation*) ritegno; **wage ~** restrizioni *fpl* salariali
restrict [rɪs'trɪkt] *vt* restringere, limitare
restricted area [rɪs'trɪktɪd-] *n* (*Aut*) zona a velocità limitata
restriction [rɪs'trɪkʃən] *n* restrizione *f*, limitazione *f*
restrictive [rɪs'trɪktɪv] *adj* restrittivo(-a)
restrictive practices *npl* (*Industry*) pratiche restrittive di produzione
rest room *n* (*US*) toletta
restructure [riː'strʌktʃəʳ] *vt* ristrutturare
result [rɪ'zʌlt] *n* risultato ■ *vi*: **to ~ in** avere per risultato; **as a ~ (of)** in *or* di conseguenza (a), in seguito (a); **to ~ (from)** essere una conseguenza (di), essere causato(-a) (da)
resultant [rɪ'zʌltənt] *adj* risultante, conseguente
resume [rɪ'zjuːm] *vt, vi* (*work, journey*) riprendere; (*sum up*) riassumere
résumé ['reɪzjuːmeɪ] *n* riassunto; (*US: curriculum vitae*) curriculum vitae *m inv*
resumption [rɪ'zʌmpʃən] *n* ripresa
resurgence [rɪ'səːdʒəns] *n* rinascita
resurrection [rɛzə'rɛkʃən] *n* risurrezione *f*
resuscitate [rɪ'sʌsɪteɪt] *vt* (*Med*) risuscitare
resuscitation [rɪsʌsɪ'teɪʃən] *n* rianimazione *f*
retail ['riːteɪl] *n* (vendita al) minuto ■ *cpd* al minuto ■ *vt* vendere al minuto ■ *vi*: **to ~ at** essere in vendita al pubblico al prezzo di
retailer ['riːteɪləʳ] *n* commerciante *m/f* al minuto, dettagliante *m/f*
retail outlet *n* punto di vendita al dettaglio
retail price *n* prezzo al minuto
retail price index *n* indice *m* dei prezzi al consumo
retain [rɪ'teɪn] *vt* (*keep*) tenere, serbare
retainer [rɪ'teɪnəʳ] *n* (*servant*) servitore *m*; (*fee*) onorario
retaliate [rɪ'tælɪeɪt] *vi*: **to ~ (against)** vendicarsi (di); **to ~ on sb** fare una rappresaglia contro qn
retaliation [rɪtælɪ'eɪʃən] *n* rappresaglie *fpl*; **in ~ for** per vendicarsi di
retaliatory [rɪ'tælɪətərɪ] *adj* di rappresaglia, di ritorsione
retarded [rɪ'tɑːdɪd] *adj* ritardato(-a); (*also*: **mentally retarded**) tardo(-a) (di mente)
retch [rɛtʃ] *vi* aver conati di vomito
retentive [rɪ'tɛntɪv] *adj* ritentivo(-a)
rethink ['riː'θɪŋk] *vt* ripensare
reticence ['rɛtɪsns] *n* reticenza
reticent ['rɛtɪsnt] *adj* reticente
retina ['rɛtɪnə] *n* retina
retinue ['rɛtɪnjuː] *n* seguito, scorta
retire [rɪ'taɪəʳ] *vi* (*give up work*) andare in pensione; (*withdraw*) ritirarsi, andarsene; (*go to bed*) andare a letto, ritirarsi
retired [rɪ'taɪəd] *adj* (*person*) pensionato(-a)
retirement [rɪ'taɪəmənt] *n* pensione *f*
retirement age *n* età del pensionamento
retiring [rɪ'taɪərɪŋ] *adj* (*person*) riservato(-a); (*departing: chairman*) uscente
retort [rɪ'tɔːt] *n* (*reply*) rimbecco; (*container*) storta ■ *vi* rimbeccare
retrace [riː'treɪs] *vt* ricostruire; **to ~ one's steps** tornare sui propri passi
retract [rɪ'trækt] *vt* (*statement*) ritrattare; (*claws, undercarriage, aerial*) ritrarre, ritirare ■ *vi* ritrarsi
retractable [rɪ'træktəbl] *adj* retrattile
retrain [riː'treɪn] *vt* (*worker*) riaddestrare
retraining [rɪ'treɪnɪŋ] *n* riaddestramento
retread *vt* [riː'trɛd] (*Aut: tyre*) rigenerare ■ *n* ['riːtrɛd] gomma rigenerata
retreat [rɪ'triːt] *n* ritirata; (*place*) rifugio ■ *vi* battere in ritirata; (*flood*) ritirarsi; **to beat a hasty ~** (*fig*) battersela
retrial [riː'traɪəl] *n* nuovo processo
retribution [rɛtrɪ'bjuːʃən] *n* castigo
retrieval [rɪ'triːvəl] *n* ricupero
retrieve [rɪ'triːv] *vt* (*sth lost*) ricuperare, ritrovare; (*situation, honour*) salvare; (*Comput*) ricuperare
retriever [rɪ'triːvəʳ] *n* cane *m* da riporto
retroactive [rɛtrəu'æktɪv] *adj* retroattivo(-a)
retrograde ['rɛtrəugreɪd] *adj* retrogrado(-a)
retrospect ['rɛtrəspɛkt] *n*: **in ~** guardando indietro
retrospective [rɛtrə'spɛktɪv] *adj* retrospettivo(-a); (*law*) retroattivo(-a) ■ *n* (*Art*) retrospettiva
return [rɪ'təːn] *n* (*going or coming back*) ritorno;

(*of sth stolen etc*) restituzione *f*; (*Comm*: *from land, shares*) profitto, reddito; (: *of merchandise*) resa; (*report*) rapporto; (*reward*): **in ~ (for)** in cambio (di) ■ *cpd* (*journey, match*) di ritorno; (*Brit*: *ticket*) di andata e ritorno ■ *vi* tornare, ritornare ■ *vt* rendere, restituire; (*bring back*) riportare; (*send back*) mandare indietro; (*put back*) rimettere; (*Pol*: *candidate*) eleggere; **returns** *npl* (*Comm*) incassi *mpl*; profitti *mpl*; **by ~ of post** a stretto giro di posta; **many happy returns (of the day)!** auguri!, buon compleanno!

returnable [rɪ'tə:nəbl] *adj*: **~ bottle** vuoto a rendere

returner [rɪ'tə:nə^r] *n* *donna che ritorna al lavoro dopo la maternità*

returning officer [rɪ'tə:nɪŋ-] *n* (*Brit Pol*) *funzionario addetto all'organizzazione delle elezioni in un distretto*

return key *n* (*Comput*) tasto di ritorno

reunion [ri:'ju:nɪən] *n* riunione *f*

reunite [ri:ju:'naɪt] *vt* riunire

rev [rɛv] *n abbr* (= *revolution*: *Aut*) giro ■ *vb* (*also*: **rev up**) *vt* imballare ■ *vi* imballarsi

revaluation [ri:vælju'eɪʃən] *n* rivalutazione *f*

revamp ['ri:'væmp] *vt* rinnovare; riorganizzare

Rev., Revd. *abbr* = **reverend**

rev counter *n* contagiri *m inv*

reveal [rɪ'vi:l] *vt* (*make known*) rivelare, svelare; (*display*) rivelare, mostrare

revealing [rɪ'vi:lɪŋ] *adj* rivelatore(-trice); (*dress*) scollato(-a)

reveille [rɪ'vælɪ] *n* (*Mil*) sveglia

revel ['rɛvl] *vi*: **to ~ in sth/in doing** dilettarsi di qc/a fare

revelation [rɛvə'leɪʃən] *n* rivelazione *f*

reveller ['rɛvlə^r] *n* festaiolo(-a)

revelry ['rɛvlrɪ] *n* baldoria

revenge [rɪ'vɛndʒ] *n* vendetta; (*in game etc*) rivincita ■ *vt* vendicare; **to take ~** vendicarsi; **to get one's ~ (for sth)** vendicarsi (di qc)

revengeful [rɪ'vɛndʒful] *adj* vendicatore(-trice); vendicativo(-a)

revenue ['rɛvənju:] *n* reddito

reverberate [rɪ'və:bəreɪt] *vi* (*sound*) rimbombare; (*light*) riverberarsi

reverberation [rɪvə:bə'reɪʃən] *n* (*of light, sound*) riverberazione *f*

revere [rɪ'vɪə^r] *vt* venerare

reverence ['rɛvərəns] *n* venerazione *f*, riverenza

Reverend ['rɛvərənd] *adj* (*in titles*) reverendo(-a)

reverent ['rɛvərənt] *adj* riverente

reverie ['rɛvərɪ] *n* fantasticheria

reversal [rɪ'və:sl] *n* capovolgimento

reverse [rɪ'və:s] *n* contrario, opposto; (*back*) rovescio; (*Aut*: *also*: **reverse gear**) marcia indietro ■ *adj* (*order*) inverso(-a); (*direction*) opposto(-a) ■ *vt* (*turn*) invertire, rivoltare; (*change*) capovolgere, rovesciare; (*Law*: *judgement*) cassare ■ *vi* (*Brit Aut*) fare marcia indietro; **in ~ order** in ordine inverso; **to go into ~** fare marcia indietro

reverse-charge call *n* (*Brit Tel*) telefonata con addebito al ricevente

reverse video *n* reverse video *m*

reversible [rɪ'və:səbl] *adj* (*garment*) double-face *inv*; (*procedure*) reversibile

reversing lights [rɪ'və:sɪŋ-] *npl* (*Brit Aut*) luci *fpl* per la retromarcia

reversion [rɪ'və:ʃən] *n* ritorno

revert [rɪ'və:t] *vi*: **to ~ to** tornare a

review [rɪ'vju:] *n* rivista; (*of book, film*) recensione *f* ■ *vt* passare in rivista; fare la recensione di; **to come under ~** essere preso in esame

reviewer [rɪ'vju:ə^r] *n* recensore(-a)

revile [rɪ'vaɪl] *vt* insultare

revise [rɪ'vaɪz] *vt* (*manuscript*) rivedere, correggere; (*opinion*) emendare, modificare; (*study*: *subject, notes*) ripassare; **revised edition** edizione riveduta

revision [rɪ'vɪʒən] *n* revisione *f*; ripasso; (*revised version*) versione riveduta e corretta

revitalize [ri:'vaɪtəlaɪz] *vt* ravvivare

revival [rɪ'vaɪvəl] *n* ripresa; ristabilimento; (*of faith*) risveglio

revive [rɪ'vaɪv] *vt* (*person*) rianimare; (*custom*) far rivivere; (*hope, courage*) ravvivare; (*play, fashion*) riesumare ■ *vi* (*person*) rianimarsi; (*hope*) ravvivarsi; (*activity*) riprendersi

revoke [rɪ'vəuk] *vt* revocare; (*promise, decision*) rinvenire su

revolt [rɪ'vəult] *n* rivolta, ribellione *f* ■ *vi* rivoltarsi, ribellarsi; **to ~ (against sb/sth)** ribellarsi (a qn/qc)

revolting [rɪ'vəultɪŋ] *adj* ripugnante

revolution [rɛvə'lu:ʃən] *n* rivoluzione *f*; (*of wheel etc*) rivoluzione, giro

revolutionary [rɛvə'lu:ʃənrɪ] *adj, n* rivoluzionario(-a)

revolutionize [rɛvə'lu:ʃənaɪz] *vt* rivoluzionare

revolve [rɪ'vɔlv] *vi* girare

revolver [rɪ'vɔlvə^r] *n* rivoltella

revolving [rɪ'vɔlvɪŋ] *adj* girevole

revolving door *n* porta girevole

revue [rɪ'vju:] *n* (*Theat*) rivista

revulsion [rɪ'vʌlʃən] *n* ripugnanza

reward [rɪ'wɔ:d] *n* ricompensa, premio ■ *vt*: **to ~ (for)** ricompensare (per)

r

rewarding [rɪ'wɔːdɪŋ] *adj* (*fig*) soddisfacente; **financially ~** conveniente dal punto di vista economico
rewind [riː'waɪnd] *vt irreg* (*watch*) ricaricare; (*ribbon etc*) riavvolgere
rewire [riː'waɪə[r]] *vt* (*house*) rifare l'impianto elettrico di
reword [riː'wəːd] *vt* formulare *or* esprimere con altre parole
rewritable [riː'raɪtəbl] *adj* (*CD, DVD*) riscrivibile
rewrite [riː'raɪt] *vt irreg* riscrivere
Reykjavik ['reɪkjəviːk] *n* Reykjavik *f*
RFD *abbr* (*US Post*) = **rural free delivery**
RGN *n abbr* (*Brit*: = *Registered General Nurse*) *infermiera diplomata (dopo corso triennale)*
Rh *abbr* (= *rhesus*) Rh
rhapsody ['ræpsədɪ] *n* (*Mus*) rapsodia; (*fig*) elogio stravagante
rhesus negative ['riːsəs-] *adj* (*Med*) Rh-negativo(-a)
rhesus positive *adj* (*Med*) Rh-positivo(-a)
rhetoric ['rɛtərɪk] *n* retorica
rhetorical [rɪ'tɔrɪkl] *adj* retorico(-a)
rheumatic [ruː'mætɪk] *adj* reumatico(-a)
rheumatism ['ruːmətɪzəm] *n* reumatismo
rheumatoid arthritis ['ruːmətɔɪd-] *n* artrite *f* reumatoide
Rhine [raɪn] *n*: **the ~** il Reno
rhinestone ['raɪnstəun] *n* diamante *m* falso
rhinoceros [raɪ'nɔsərəs] *n* rinoceronte *m*
Rhodes [rəudz] *n* Rodi *f*
Rhodesia [rəu'diːʒə] *n* Rhodesia
Rhodesian [rəu'diːʒən] *adj, n* Rhodesiano(-a)
rhododendron [rəudə'dɛndrn] *n* rododendro
Rhone [rəun] *n*: **the ~** il Rodano
rhubarb ['ruːbɑːb] *n* rabarbaro
rhyme [raɪm] *n* rima; (*verse*) poesia ■ *vi*: **to ~ (with)** fare rima (con); **without ~ or reason** senza capo né coda
rhythm ['rɪðm] *n* ritmo
rhythmic ['rɪðmɪk], **rhythmical** ['rɪðmɪkəl] *adj* ritmico(-a)
rhythmically ['rɪðmɪkəlɪ] *adv* con ritmo
rhythm method *n* metodo Ogino-Knauss
RI *abbr* (*US*) = **Rhode Island** ■ *n abbr* (*Brit*) = **religious instruction**
rib [rɪb] *n* (*Anat*) costola ■ *vt* (*tease*) punzecchiare
ribald ['rɪbəld] *adj* licenzioso(-a), volgare
ribbed [rɪbd] *adj* (*knitting*) a coste
ribbon ['rɪbən] *n* nastro; **in ribbons** (*torn*) a brandelli
rice [raɪs] *n* riso
ricefield ['raɪsfiːld] *n* risaia
rice pudding *n* budino di riso
rich [rɪtʃ] *adj* ricco(-a); (*clothes*) sontuoso(-a); **the ~** *npl* i ricchi; **riches** *npl* ricchezze *fpl*; **to be ~ in sth** essere ricco di qc
richly ['rɪtʃlɪ] *adv* riccamente; (*dressed*) sontuosamente; (*deserved*) pienamente
rickets ['rɪkɪts] *n* rachitismo
rickety ['rɪkɪtɪ] *adj* zoppicante
rickshaw ['rɪkʃɔː] *n* risciò *m inv*
ricochet ['rɪkəʃeɪ] *n* rimbalzo ■ *vi* rimbalzare
rid (*pt, pp* **~**) [rɪd] *vt*: **to ~ sb of** sbarazzare *or* liberare qn di; **to get ~ of** sbarazzarsi di
riddance ['rɪdns] *n*: **good ~!** che liberazione!
ridden ['rɪdn] *pp of* **ride**
riddle ['rɪdl] *n* (*puzzle*) indovinello ■ *vt*: **to be riddled with** essere crivellato(-a) di
ride [raɪd] *n* (*on horse*) cavalcata; (*outing*) passeggiata; (*distance covered*) cavalcata; corsa ■ *vb* (*pt* **rode**, *pp* **ridden**) [rəud, 'rɪdn] *vi* (*as sport*) cavalcare; (*go somewhere: on horse, bicycle*) andare (a cavallo *or* in bicicletta *etc*); (*journey: on bicycle, motorcycle, bus*) andare, viaggiare ■ *vt* (*a horse*) montare, cavalcare; **to go for a ~** andare a fare una cavalcata; andare a fare un giro; **can you ~ a bike?** sai andare in bicicletta?; **we rode all day/all the way** abbiamo cavalcato tutto il giorno/per tutto il tragitto; **to ~ a horse/bicycle/camel** montare a cavallo/in bicicletta/in groppa a un cammello; **to ~ at anchor** (*Naut*) essere alla fonda; **horse ~** cavalcata; **car ~** passeggiata in macchina; **to take sb for a ~** (*fig*) prendere in giro qn; fregare qn
▸ **ride out** *vt*: **to ~ out the storm** (*fig*) mantenersi a galla
rider ['raɪdə[r]] *n* cavalcatore(-trice); (*jockey*) fantino; (*on bicycle*) ciclista *m/f*; (*on motorcycle*) motociclista *m/f*; (*in document*) clausola addizionale, aggiunta
ridge [rɪdʒ] *n* (*of hill*) cresta; (*of roof*) colmo; (*of mountain*) giogo; (*on object*) riga (in rilievo)
ridicule ['rɪdɪkjuːl] *n* ridicolo ■ *vt* mettere in ridicolo; **to hold sb/sth up to ~** mettere in ridicolo qn/qc
ridiculous [rɪ'dɪkjuləs] *adj* ridicolo(-a)
riding ['raɪdɪŋ] *n* equitazione *f*
riding school *n* scuola d'equitazione
rife [raɪf] *adj* diffuso(-a); **to be ~ with** abbondare di
riffraff ['rɪfræf] *n* canaglia, gentaglia
rifle ['raɪfl] *n* carabina ■ *vt* vuotare
▸ **rifle through** *vt fus* frugare
rifle range *n* campo di tiro; (*at fair*) tiro a segno
rift [rɪft] *n* fessura, crepatura; (*fig: disagreement*) incrinatura
rig [rɪg] *n* (*also*: **oil rig**: *on land*) derrick *m inv*; (: *at sea*) piattaforma di trivellazione ■ *vt* (*election etc*) truccare

▸**rig out** *vt* (*Brit*) attrezzare; (*pej*) abbigliare, agghindare
▸**rig up** *vt* allestire
rigging ['rɪgɪŋ] *n* (*Naut*) attrezzatura
right [raɪt] *adj* giusto(-a); (*suitable*) appropriato(-a); (*not left*) destro(-a) ■ *n* (*title, claim*) diritto; (*not left*) destra ■ *adv* (*answer*) correttamente; (*not on the left*) a destra ■ *vt* raddrizzare; (*fig*) riparare ■ *excl* bene!; **the ~ time** l'ora esatta; **to be ~** (*person*) aver ragione; (*answer*) essere giusto(-a) *or* corretto(-a); **to get sth ~** far giusto qc; **you did the ~ thing** ha fatto bene; **let's get it ~ this time!** cerchiamo di farlo bene stavolta!; **to put a mistake ~** (*Brit*) correggere un errore; **~ now** proprio adesso; subito; **~ away** subito; **~ before/after** subito prima/dopo; **to go ~ to the end of sth** andare fino in fondo a qc; **~ against the wall** proprio contro il muro; **~ ahead** sempre diritto; proprio davanti; **~ in the middle** proprio nel mezzo; **by rights** di diritto; **on the ~, to the ~** a destra; **~ and wrong** il bene e il male; **to have a ~ to sth** aver diritto a qc; **film rights** diritti di riproduzione cinematografica; **~ of way** diritto di passaggio; (*Aut*) precedenza
right angle *n* angolo retto
right-click ['raɪtklɪk] *vi* (*Comput*): **to ~ on** fare click con il pulsante destro del mouse su
righteous ['raɪtʃəs] *adj* retto(-a), virtuoso(-a); (*anger*) giusto(-a), giustificato(-a)
righteousness ['raɪtʃəsnɪs] *n* rettitudine *f*, virtù *f*
rightful ['raɪtful] *adj* (*heir*) legittimo(-a)
rightfully ['raɪtfəlɪ] *adv* legittimamente
right-handed [raɪt'hændɪd] *adj* (*person*) che adopera la mano destra
right-hand man ['raɪthænd-] *n* braccio destro (*fig*)
right-hand side *n* lato destro
rightly ['raɪtlɪ] *adv* bene, correttamente; (*with reason*) a ragione; **if I remember ~** se mi ricordo bene
right-minded [raɪt'maɪndɪd] *adj* sensato(-a)
rights issue *n* (*Stock Exchange*) emissione *f* di azioni riservate agli azionisti
right wing *n* (*Mil, Sport*) ala destra; (*Pol*) destra ■ *adj*: **right-wing** (*Pol*) di destra
right-winger [raɪt'wɪŋə^r] *n* (*Pol*) uno(-a) di destra; (*Sport*) ala destra
rigid ['rɪdʒɪd] *adj* rigido(-a); (*principle*) rigoroso(-a)
rigidity [rɪ'dʒɪdɪtɪ] *n* rigidità
rigidly ['rɪdʒɪdlɪ] *adv* rigidamente
rigmarole ['rɪgmərəul] *n* tiritera; commedia
rigor ['rɪgə^r] *n* (*US*) = **rigour**
rigor mortis ['rɪgə'mɔːtɪs] *n* rigidità cadaverica
rigorous ['rɪgərəs] *adj* rigoroso(-a)
rigorously ['rɪgərəslɪ] *adv* rigorosamente
rigour, (*US*) **rigor** ['rɪgə^r] *n* rigore *m*
rig-out ['rɪgaut] *n* (*Brit col*) tenuta
rile [raɪl] *vt* irritare, seccare
rim [rɪm] *n* orlo; (*of spectacles*) montatura; (*of wheel*) cerchione *m*
rimless ['rɪmlɪs] *adj* (*spectacles*) senza montatura
rimmed [rɪmd] *adj* bordato(-a); cerchiato(-a)
rind [raɪnd] *n* (*of bacon*) cotenna; (*of lemon etc*) scorza
ring [rɪŋ] *n* anello; (*also*: **wedding ring**) fede *f*; (*of people, objects*) cerchio; (*of spies*) giro; (*of smoke etc*) spirale *f*; (*arena*) pista, arena; (*for boxing*) ring *m inv*; (*sound of bell*) scampanio; (*telephone call*) colpo di telefono ■ *vb* (*pt* **rang**, *pp* **rung**) [ræŋ, rʌŋ] *vi* (*person, bell, telephone*) suonare; (*also*: **ring out**: *voice, words*) risuonare; (*Tel*) telefonare ■ *vt* (*Brit Tel*: *also*: **ring up**) telefonare a; **to give sb a ~** (*Tel*) dare un colpo di telefono a qn; **that has the ~ of truth about it** questo ha l'aria d'essere vero; **to ~ the bell** suonare il campanello; **the name doesn't ~ a bell (with me)** questo nome non mi dice niente
▸**ring back** *vt, vi* (*Brit Tel*) richiamare
▸**ring off** *vi* (*Brit Tel*) mettere giù, riattaccare
ring binder *n* classificatore *m* a anelli
ring finger *n* anulare *m*
ringing ['rɪŋɪŋ] *n* (*of bell*) scampanio; (*: louder*) scampanellata; (*of telephone*) squillo; (*in ears*) fischio, ronzio
ringing tone *n* (*Brit Tel*) segnale *m* di libero
ringleader ['rɪŋliːdə^r] *n* (*of gang*) capobanda *m*
ringlets ['rɪŋlɪts] *npl* boccoli *mpl*
ring road *n* (*Brit*) raccordo anulare
ringtone *n* (*Tel*) suoneria
rink [rɪŋk] *n* (*also*: **ice rink**) pista di pattinaggio; (*for roller-skating*) pista di pattinaggio (a rotelle)
rinse [rɪns] *n* risciacquatura; (*hair tint*) cachet *m inv* ■ *vt* sciacquare
Rio ['riːəu], **Rio de Janeiro** ['riːəudədʒə'nɪərəu] *n* Rio de Janeiro *f*
riot ['raɪət] *n* sommossa, tumulto ■ *vi* tumultuare; **a ~ of colours** un'orgia di colori; **to run ~** creare disordine
rioter ['raɪətə^r] *n* dimostrante *m/f* (*durante dei disordini*)
riot gear *n*: **in ~** in assetto di guerra
riotous ['raɪətəs] *adj* tumultuoso(-a); che fa crepare dal ridere
riotously ['raɪətəslɪ] *adv*: **~ funny** che fa crepare dal ridere

r

riot police *n* ≈ la Celere
RIP *abbr* (= *requiescat or requiescant in pace*) R.I.P.
rip [rɪp] *n* strappo ■ *vt* strappare ■ *vi* strapparsi
▸ **rip up** *vt* stracciare
ripcord ['rɪpkɔːd] *n* cavo di spiegamento
ripe [raɪp] *adj* (*fruit*) maturo(-a); (*cheese*) stagionato(-a)
ripen ['raɪpən] *vt* maturare ■ *vi* maturarsi; stagionarsi
ripeness ['raɪpnɪs] *n* maturità
rip-off ['rɪpɔf] *n* (*col*): **it's a ~!** è un furto!
riposte [rɪ'pɔst] *n* risposta per le rime
ripple ['rɪpl] *n* increspamento, ondulazione *f*; mormorio ■ *vi* incresparsi ■ *vt* increspare
rise [raɪz] *n* (*slope*) salita, pendio; (*hill*) altura; (*increase: in wages*) aumento; (*: in prices, temperature*) rialzo, aumento; (*fig: to power etc*) ascesa ■ *vi* (*pt* **rose**, *pp* **risen**) [rəuz, 'rɪzn] alzarsi, levarsi; (*prices*) aumentare; (*waters, river*) crescere; (*sun, wind*) levarsi; (*also*: **rise up**: *rebel*) insorgere; ribellarsi; **to give ~ to** provocare, dare origine a; **to ~ to the occasion** dimostrarsi all'altezza della situazione
rising ['raɪzɪŋ] *adj* (*increasing: number*) sempre crescente; (*: prices*) in aumento; (*tide*) montante; (*sun, moon*) nascente, che sorge ■ *n* (*uprising*) sommossa
rising damp *n* infiltrazioni *fpl* d'umidità
rising star *n* (*also fig*) astro nascente
risk [rɪsk] *n* rischio ■ *vt* rischiare; **to take** *or* **run the ~ of doing** correre il rischio di fare; **at ~** in pericolo; **at one's own ~** a proprio rischio e pericolo; **fire/health ~** rischio d'incendio/per la salute; **I'll ~ it** ci proverò lo stesso
risk capital *n* capitale *m* di rischio
risky ['rɪskɪ] *adj* rischioso(-a)
risqué ['riːskeɪ] *adj* (*joke*) spinto(-a)
rissole ['rɪsəul] *n* crocchetta
rite [raɪt] *n* rito; **last rites** l'estrema unzione
ritual ['rɪtjuəl] *adj, n* rituale *m*
rival ['raɪvl] *n* rivale *m/f*; (*in business*) concorrente *m/f* ■ *adj* rivale; che fa concorrenza ■ *vt* essere in concorrenza con; **to ~ sb/sth in** competere con qn/qc in
rivalry ['raɪvəlrɪ] *n* rivalità; concorrenza
river ['rɪvəʳ] *n* fiume *m* ■ *cpd* (*port, traffic*) fluviale; **up/down ~** a monte/valle
riverbank ['rɪvəbæŋk] *n* argine *m*
riverbed ['rɪvəbɛd] *n* alveo (fluviale)
riverside ['rɪəsaɪd] *n* sponda del fiume
rivet ['rɪvɪt] *n* ribattino, rivetto ■ *vt* ribadire; (*fig*) concentrare, fissare
riveting ['rɪvɪtɪŋ] *adj* (*fig*) avvincente
Riviera [rɪvɪ'ɛərə] *n*: **the (French) ~** la Costa Azzurra; **the Italian ~** la Riviera
Riyadh [rɪ'jɑːd] *n* Riad *f*
RMT *n abbr* (= *National Union of Rail, Maritime and Transport Workers*) *sindacato dei Ferrovieri, Marittimi e Trasportatori*
RN *n abbr* (*Brit*) = **Royal Navy**; (*US*) = **registered nurse**
RNA *n abbr* (= *ribonucleic acid*) R.N.A. *m*
RNLI *n abbr* (*Brit*: = *Royal National Lifeboat Institution*) *associazione volontaria che organizza e dispone di scialuppe di salvataggio*
RNZAF *n abbr* = **Royal New Zealand Air Force**
RNZN *n abbr* = **Royal New Zealand Navy**
road [rəud] *n* strada; (*small*) cammino; (*in town*) via; **main ~** strada principale; **major/minor ~** strada con/senza diritto di precedenza; **it takes 4 hours by ~** sono 4 ore di macchina (*or* in camion *etc*); **on the ~ to success** sulla via del successo; **"~ up"** (*Brit*) "attenzione: lavori in corso"
road accident *n* incidente *m* stradale
roadblock ['rəudblɔk] *n* blocco stradale
road haulage *n* autotrasporti *mpl*
roadhog ['rəudhɔg] *n* pirata *m* della strada
road map *n* carta stradale
road rage *n* aggressività al volante
road safety *n* sicurezza sulle strade
roadside ['rəudsaɪd] *n* margine *m* della strada; **by the ~** a lato della strada
roadsign ['rəudsaɪn] *n* cartello stradale
roadsweeper ['rəudswiːpəʳ] *n* (*Brit: person*) spazzino
road user *n* utente *m/f* della strada
roadway ['rəudweɪ] *n* carreggiata
roadworks ['rəudwəːks] *npl* lavori *mpl* stradali
roadworthy ['rəudwəːðɪ] *adj* in buono stato di marcia
roam [rəum] *vi* errare, vagabondare ■ *vt* vagare per
roar [rɔːʳ] *n* ruggito; (*of crowd*) tumulto; (*of thunder, storm*) muggito ■ *vi* ruggire; tumultuare; muggire; **to ~ with laughter** scoppiare dalle risa
roaring ['rɔːrɪŋ] *adj*: **a ~ fire** un bel fuoco; **to do a ~ trade** fare affari d'oro; **a ~ success** un successo strepitoso
roast [rəust] *n* arrosto ■ *vt* (*meat*) arrostire
roast beef *n* arrosto di manzo
roasting ['rəustɪŋ] *n* (*col*): **to give sb a ~** dare una lavata di capo a qn
rob [rɔb] *vt* (*person*) rubare; (*bank*) svaligiare; **to ~ sb of sth** derubare qn di qc; (*fig: deprive*) privare qn di qc
robber ['rɔbəʳ] *n* ladro; (*armed*) rapinatore *m*
robbery ['rɔbərɪ] *n* furto; rapina
robe [rəub] *n* (*for ceremony etc*) abito; (*also*: **bathrobe**) accappatoio ■ *vt* vestire

robin ['rɔbɪn] *n* pettirosso
robot ['rəubɔt] *n* robot *m inv*
robotics ['rəubɔtɪks] *n* robotica
robust [rəu'bʌst] *adj* robusto(-a); (*material*) solido(-a)
rock [rɔk] *n* (*substance*) roccia; (*boulder*) masso; roccia; (*in sea*) scoglio; (*Brit: sweet*) zucchero candito ■ *vt* (*swing gently: cradle*) dondolare; (*: child*) cullare; (*shake*) scrollare, far tremare ■ *vi* dondolarsi; oscillare; **on the rocks** (*drink*) col ghiaccio; (*ship*) sugli scogli; (*marriage etc*) in crisi; **to ~ the boat** (*fig*) piantare grane
rock and roll *n* rock and roll *m*
rock-bottom ['rɔk'bɔtəm] *n* (*fig*) stremo; **to reach** *or* **touch ~** (*price*) raggiungere il livello più basso; (*person*) toccare il fondo
rock climber *n* rocciatore(-trice), scalatore(-trice)
rock climbing *n* roccia
rockery ['rɔkərɪ] *n* giardino roccioso
rocket ['rɔkɪt] *n* razzo; (*Mil*) razzo, missile *m* ■ *vi* (*prices*) salire alle stelle
rocket launcher [-lɔːntʃəʳ] *n* lanciarazzi *m inv*
rock face *n* parete *f* della roccia
rock fall *n* caduta di massi
rocking chair ['rɔkɪŋ-] *n* sedia a dondolo
rocking horse *n* cavallo a dondolo
rocky ['rɔkɪ] *adj* (*hill*) roccioso(-a); (*path*) sassoso(-a); (*unsteady: table*) traballante
Rocky Mountains *npl*: **the ~** le Montagne Rocciose
rod [rɔd] *n* (*metallic, Tech*) asta; (*wooden*) bacchetta; (*also*: **fishing rod**) canna da pesca
rode [rəud] *pt of* **ride**
rodent ['rəudnt] *n* roditore *m*
rodeo ['rəudɪəu] *n* rodeo
roe [rəu] *n* (*species: also*: **roe deer**) capriolo; (*of fish: also*: **hard roe**) uova *fpl* di pesce; **soft ~** latte *m* di pesce
roe deer *n* (*species*) capriolo; (*female deer: pl inv*) capriolo femmina
rogue [rəug] *n* mascalzone *m*
roguish ['rəugɪʃ] *adj* birbantesco(-a)
role [rəul] *n* ruolo
role model *n* modello (di comportamento)
role-play ['rəulpleɪ], **role-playing** ['rəulpleɪɪŋ] *n* il recitare un ruolo, role-playing *m inv*
roll [rəul] *n* rotolo; (*of banknotes*) mazzo; (*also*: **bread roll**) panino; (*register*) lista; (*sound: of drums etc*) rullo; (*movement: of ship*) rullio ■ *vt* rotolare; (*also*: **roll up**: *string*) aggomitolare; (*also*: **roll out**: *pastry*) stendere ■ *vi* rotolare; (*wheel*) girare; **cheese ~** panino al formaggio
▸ **roll about, roll around** *vi* rotolare qua e là; (*person*) rotolarsi
▸ **roll by** *vi* (*time*) passare
▸ **roll in** *vi* (*mail, cash*) arrivare a bizzeffe
▸ **roll over** *vi* rivoltarsi
▸ **roll up** *vi* (*col: arrive*) arrivare ■ *vt* (*carpet, cloth, map*) arrotolare; (*sleeves*) rimboccare; **to ~ o.s. up into a ball** raggomitolarsi
roll call *n* appello
rolled gold [rəuld-] *adj* d'oro laminato
roller ['rəuləʳ] *n* rullo; (*wheel*) rotella
rollerblades ['rəuləbleɪdz] *npl* pattini *mpl* in linea
roller blind *n* (*Brit*) avvolgibile *m*
roller coaster *n* montagne *fpl* russe
roller skates *npl* pattini *mpl* a rotelle
rollicking ['rɔlɪkɪŋ] *adj* allegro(-a) e chiassoso(-a); **to have a ~ time** divertirsi pazzamente
rolling ['rəulɪŋ] *adj* (*landscape*) ondulato(-a)
rolling mill *n* fabbrica di laminati
rolling pin *n* matterello
rolling stock *n* (*Rail*) materiale *m* rotabile
roll-on-roll-off ['rəulɔn'rəulɔf] *adj* (*Brit: ferry*) roll-on roll-off *inv*
roly-poly ['rəulɪ'pəulɪ] *n* (*Brit Culin*) *rotolo di pasta con ripieno di marmellata*
ROM [rɔm] *n abbr* (*Comput: = read-only memory*) ROM *f*
Roman ['rəumən] *adj, n* romano(-a)
Roman Catholic *adj, n* cattolico(-a)
romance [rə'mæns] *n* storia (*or* avventura *or* film *m inv*) romantico(-a); (*charm*) poesia; (*love affair*) idillio
Romanesque [rəumə'nɛsk] *adj* romanico(-a)
Romania [rəu'meɪnɪə] *n* Romania
Romanian [rəu'meɪnɪən] *adj* romeno(-a) ■ *n* romeno(-a); (*Ling*) romeno
Roman numeral *n* numero romano
romantic [rə'mæntɪk] *adj* romantico(-a); sentimentale
romanticism [rə'mæntɪsɪzəm] *n* romanticismo
Romany ['rɔmənɪ] *adj* zingaresco(-a) ■ *n* (*person*) zingaro(-a); (*Ling*) lingua degli zingari
Rome [rəum] *n* Roma
romp [rɔmp] *n* gioco chiassoso ■ *vi* (*also*: **romp about**) giocare chiassosamente; **to ~ home** (*horse*) vincere senza difficoltà, stravincere
rompers ['rɔmpəz] *npl* pagliaccetto
rondo ['rɔndəu] *n* (*Mus*) rondò *m inv*
roof [ruːf] *n* tetto; (*of tunnel, cave*) volta ■ *vt* coprire (con un tetto); **~ of the mouth** palato
roof garden *n* giardino pensile
roofing ['ruːfɪŋ] *n* materiale *m* per copertura
roof rack *n* (*Aut*) portabagagli *m inv*
rook [ruk] *n* (*bird*) corvo nero; (*Chess*) torre *f* ■ *vt* (*cheat*) truffare, spennare

r

rookie ['rukɪ] *n* (*col: esp Mil*) pivellino(-a)
room [ru:m] *n* (*in house*) stanza, camera; (*in school etc*) sala; (*space*) posto, spazio; **rooms** *npl* (*lodging*) alloggio; **"rooms to let"**, (US) **"rooms for rent"** "si affittano camere"; **is there ~ for this?** c'è spazio per questo?, ci sta anche questo?; **to make ~ for sb** far posto a qn; **there is ~ for improvement** si potrebbe migliorare
rooming house ['ru:mɪŋ-] *n* (US) *casa in cui si affittano camere o appartamentini ammobiliati*
roommate ['ru:mmeɪt] *n* compagno(-a) di stanza
room service *n* servizio da camera
room temperature *n* temperatura ambiente
roomy ['ru:mɪ] *adj* spazioso(-a); (*garment*) ampio(-a)
roost [ru:st] *n* appollaiato ■ *vi* appollaiarsi
rooster ['ru:stəʳ] *n* gallo
root [ru:t] *n* radice *f* ■ *vt* (*plant, belief*) far radicare; **to take ~** (*plant*) attecchire, prendere; (*idea*) far presa; **the ~ of the problem is that ...** il problema deriva dal fatto che ...
▸ **root about** *vi* (*fig*) frugare
▸ **root for** *vt fus* (*col*) fare il tifo per
▸ **root out** *vt* estirpare
root beer *n* (US) *bibita dolce a base di estratti di erbe e radici*
rope [rəup] *n* corda, fune *f*; (*Naut*) cavo ■ *vt* (*box*) legare; (*climbers*) legare in cordata; **to ~ sb in** (*fig*) coinvolgere qn; **to know the ropes** (*fig*) conoscere i trucchi del mestiere
rope ladder *n* scala di corda
ropey ['rəupɪ] *adj* (*col*) scadente, da quattro soldi; **to feel ~** (*ill*) sentirsi male
rosary ['rəuzərɪ] *n* rosario; roseto
rose [rəuz] *pt of* **rise** ■ *n* rosa; (*also:* **rose bush**) rosaio; (*on watering can*) rosetta ■ *adj* rosa *inv*
rosé ['rəuzeɪ] *n* vino rosato
rosebed ['rəuzbɛd] *n* roseto
rosebud ['rəuzbʌd] *n* bocciolo di rosa
rosebush ['rəuzbuʃ] *n* rosaio
rosemary ['rəuzmərɪ] *n* rosmarino
rosette [rəu'zɛt] *n* coccarda
ROSPA ['rɔspə] *n abbr* (*Brit: = Royal Society for the Prevention of Accidents*) ≈ E.N.P.I. *m* (*= Ente Nazionale Prevenzione Infortuni*)
roster ['rɔstəʳ] *n*: **duty ~** ruolino di servizio
rostrum ['rɔstrəm] *n* tribuna
rosy ['rəuzɪ] *adj* roseo(-a)
rot [rɔt] *n* (*decay*) putrefazione *f*; (*col: nonsense*) stupidaggini *fpl* ■ *vt, vi* imputridire, marcire; **dry/wet ~** *funghi parassiti del legno*; **to stop the ~** (*Brit fig*) salvare la situazione
rota ['rəutə] *n* tabella dei turni; **on a ~ basis** a turno
rotary ['rəutərɪ] *adj* rotante
rotate [rəu'teɪt] *vt* (*revolve*) far girare; (*change round: crops*) avvicendare; (*: jobs*) fare a turno ■ *vi* (*revolve*) girare
rotating [rəu'teɪtɪŋ] *adj* (*movement*) rotante
rotation [rəu'teɪʃən] *n* rotazione *f*; **in ~** a turno, in rotazione
rote [rəut] *n*: **to learn sth by ~** imparare qc a memoria
rotor ['rəutəʳ] *n* rotore *m*
rotten ['rɔtn] *adj* (*decayed*) putrido(-a), marcio(-a); (*: teeth*) cariato(-a); (*dishonest*) corrotto(-a); (*col: bad*) brutto(-a); (*: action*) vigliacco(-a); **to feel ~** (*ill*) sentirsi proprio male
rotting ['rɔtɪŋ] *adj* in putrefazione
rotund [rəu'tʌnd] *adj* grassoccio(-a); tondo(-a)
rouble, (US) **ruble** ['ru:bl] *n* rublo
rouge [ru:ʒ] *n* belletto
rough [rʌf] *adj* aspro(-a); (*person, manner: coarse*) rozzo(-a), aspro(-a); (*: violent*) brutale; (*district*) malfamato(-a); (*weather*) cattivo(-a); (*plan*) abbozzato(-a); (*guess*) approssimativo(-a) ■ *n* (*Golf*) macchia; **~ estimate** approssimazione *f*; **to ~ it** far vita dura; **to play ~** far il gioco pesante; **to sleep ~** (*Brit*) dormire all'addiaccio; **to feel ~** (*Brit*) sentirsi male; **to have a ~ time (of it)** passare un periodaccio; **the sea is ~ today** c'è mare grosso oggi
▸ **rough out** *vt* (*draft*) abbozzare
roughage ['rʌfɪdʒ] *n* alimenti *mpl* ricchi di cellulosa
rough-and-ready ['rʌfən'rɛdɪ] *adj* rudimentale
rough-and-tumble ['rʌfən'tʌmbl] *n* zuffa
roughcast ['rʌfkɑ:st] *n* intonaco grezzo
rough copy, rough draft *n* brutta copia
roughen ['rʌfn] *vt* (*a surface*) rendere ruvido(-a)
rough justice *n* giustizia sommaria
roughly ['rʌflɪ] *adv* (*handle*) rudemente, brutalmente; (*make*) grossolanamente; (*approximately*) approssimativamente; **~ speaking** grosso modo, ad occhio e croce
roughness ['rʌfnɪs] *n* asprezza; rozzezza; brutalità
roughshod ['rʌfʃɔd] *adv*: **to ride ~ over** (*person*) mettere sotto i piedi; (*objection*) passare sopra a
rough work *n* (*at school etc*) brutta copia
roulette [ru:'lɛt] *n* roulette *f*
Roumania *etc* [ru:'meɪnɪə] = **Romania** *etc*
round [raund] *adj* rotondo(-a) ■ *n* tondo, cerchio; (*Brit: of toast*) fetta; (*duty: of policeman, milkman etc*) giro; (*: of doctor*) visite *fpl*; (*game: of*

cards, in competition) partita; (*Boxing*) round *m inv*; (*of talks*) serie *f inv* ■ *vt* (*corner*) girare; (*bend*) prendere; (*cape*) doppiare ■ *prep* intorno a ■ *adv*: **right ~, all ~** tutt'attorno; **the long way ~** il giro più lungo; **all the year ~** tutto l'anno; **in ~ figures** in cifra tonda; **it's just ~ the corner** (*also fig*) è dietro l'angolo; **to ask sb ~** invitare qn (a casa propria); **I'll be ~ at 6 o'clock** ci sarò alle 6; **to go ~** fare il giro; **to go ~ to sb's (house)** andare da qn; **to go ~ an obstacle** aggirare un ostacolo; **go ~ the back** passi da dietro; **to go ~ a house** visitare una casa; **enough to go ~** abbastanza per tutti; **she arrived ~ (about) noon** è arrivata intorno a mezzogiorno; **~ the clock** 24 ore su 24; **to go the rounds** (*illness*) diffondersi; (*story*) circolare, passare di bocca in bocca; **the daily ~** (*fig*) la routine quotidiana; **~ of ammunition** cartuccia; **~ of applause** applausi *mpl*; **~ of drinks** giro di bibite; **~ of sandwiches** (*Brit*) sandwich *m inv*
▸ **round off** *vt* (*speech etc*) finire
▸ **round up** *vt* radunare; (*criminals*) fare una retata di; (*prices*) arrotondare

roundabout ['raundəbaut] *n* (*Brit Aut*) rotatoria; (*at fair*) giostra ■ *adj* (*route, means*) indiretto(-a)

rounded ['raundɪd] *adj* arrotondato(-a); (*style*) armonioso(-a)

rounders ['raundəz] *npl* (*game*) *gioco simile al baseball*

roundly ['raundlɪ] *adv* (*fig*) chiaro e tondo

round robin *n* (*Sport: also*: **round robin tournament**) ≈ torneo all'italiana

round-shouldered [raund'ʃəuldəd] *adj* dalle spalle tonde

round trip *n* (viaggio di) andata e ritorno

roundup ['raundʌp] *n* raduno; (*of criminals*) retata; **a ~ of the latest news** un sommario *or* riepilogo delle ultime notizie

rouse [rauz] *vt* (*wake up*) svegliare; (*stir up*) destare; provocare; risvegliare

rousing ['rauzɪŋ] *adj* (*speech, applause*) entusiastico(-a)

rout [raut] *n* (*Mil*) rotta ■ *vt* mettere in rotta

route [ruːt] *n* itinerario; (*of bus*) percorso; (*of trade, shipping*) rotta; **"all routes"** (*Aut*) "tutte le direzioni"; **the best ~ to London** la strada migliore per andare a Londra; **en ~ for** in viaggio verso; **en ~ from ... to** viaggiando da ... a

route map *n* (*Brit: for journey*) cartina di itinerario; (*for trains etc*) pianta dei collegamenti

routine [ruː'tiːn] *adj* (*work*) corrente, abituale; (*procedure*) solito(-a) ■ *n* (*pej*) routine *f*, tran tran *m*; (*Theat*) numero; (*Comput*) sottoprogramma *m*; **daily ~** orario quotidiano; **~ procedure** prassi *f*

roving ['rəuvɪŋ] *adj* (*life*) itinerante

roving reporter *n* reporter *m inv* volante

row[1] [rəu] *n* (*line*) riga, fila; (*Knitting*) ferro; (*behind one another: of cars, people*) fila ■ *vi* (*in boat*) remare; (*as sport*) vogare ■ *vt* (*boat*) manovrare a remi; **in a ~** (*fig*) di fila

row[2] [rau] *n* (*noise*) baccano, chiasso; (*dispute*) lite *f* ■ *vi* litigare; **to make a ~** far baccano; **to have a ~** litigare

rowboat ['rəubəut] *n* (*US*) barca a remi

rowdiness ['raudɪnɪs] *n* baccano; (*fighting*) zuffa

rowdy ['raudɪ] *adj* chiassoso(-a), turbolento(-a) ■ *n* teppista *m/f*

rowdyism ['raudɪɪzəm] *n* teppismo

rowing ['rəuɪŋ] *n* canottaggio

rowing boat *n* (*Brit*) barca a remi

rowlock ['rɔlək] *n* scalmo

royal ['rɔɪəl] *adj* reale

Royal Academy *n* (*Brit*) *vedi nota*

> **ROYAL ACADEMY**
>
> L'Accademia Reale d'Arte britannica, *Royal Academy (of the Arts)*, è un'istituzione fondata nel 1768 al fine di incoraggiare la pittura, la scultura e l'architettura. Ogni anno organizza una mostra estiva d'arte contemporanea.

Royal Air Force *n* (*Brit*) *aeronautica militare britannica*

royal blue *adj* blu reale *inv*

royalist ['rɔɪəlɪst] *adj, n* realista *m/f*

Royal Navy *n* (*Brit*) *marina militare britannica*

royalty ['rɔɪəltɪ] *n* (*royal persons*) (membri *mpl* della) famiglia reale; (*payment: to author*) diritti *mpl* d'autore; (*: to inventor*) diritti di brevetto

RP *n abbr* (*Brit: = received pronunciation*) pronuncia standard

RPI *abbr* (*Brit*) = **retail price index**

rpm *abbr* (*= revolutions per minute*) giri/min

RR *abbr* (*US: = railroad*) Ferr

RRP *n abbr* (*Brit*) = **recommended retail price**

RSA *n abbr* (*Brit*) = **Royal Society of Arts**; **Royal Scottish Academy**

RSI *n abbr* (*Med: = repetitive strain injury*) *lesione al braccio tipica di violinisti e terminalisti*

RSPB *n abbr* (*Brit: = Royal Society for the Protection of Birds*) ≈ L.I.P.U. *f* (*= Lega Italiana Protezione Uccelli*)

RSPCA *n abbr* (*Brit: = Royal Society for the Prevention of Cruelty to Animals*) ≈ E.N.P.A. *m* (*= Ente Nazionale per la Protezione degli Animali*)

RSVP *abbr* (= *répondez s'il vous plaît*) R.S.V.P.
RTA *n abbr* (= *road traffic accident*) incidente *m* stradale
Rt Hon. *abbr* (*Brit*: = *Right Honourable*) ≈ On. (= *Onorevole*)
Rt Rev. *abbr* (= *Right Reverend*) Rev
rub [rʌb] *n* (*with cloth*) fregata, strofinata; (*on person*) frizione *f*, massaggio ■ *vt* fregare, strofinare; frizionare; **to ~ sb up** *or* (*US*) **~ sb the wrong way** lisciare qn contro pelo
▸ **rub down** *vt* (*body*) strofinare, frizionare; (*horse*) strigliare
▸ **rub in** *vt* (*ointment*) far penetrare (massaggiando *or* frizionando)
▸ **rub off** *vi* andare via; **to ~ off on** lasciare una traccia su
▸ **rub out** *vt* cancellare ■ *vi* cancellarsi
rubber ['rʌbəʳ] *n* gomma
rubber band *n* elastico
rubber bullet *n* pallottola di gomma
rubber plant *n* ficus *m inv*
rubber ring *n* (*for swimming*) ciambella
rubber stamp *n* timbro di gomma
rubber-stamp [rʌbə'stæmp] *vt* (*fig*) approvare senza discussione
rubbery ['rʌbərɪ] *adj* gommoso(-a)
rubbish ['rʌbɪʃ] *n* (*from household*) immondizie *fpl*, rifiuti *mpl*; (*fig*: *pej*) cose *fpl* senza valore; robaccia; (*nonsense*) sciocchezze *fpl* ■ *vt* (*col*) sputtanare; **what you've just said is ~** quello che ha appena detto è una sciocchezza
rubbish bin *n* (*Brit*) pattumiera
rubbish dump *n* luogo di scarico
rubbishy ['rʌbɪʃɪ] *adj* (*Brit col*) scadente, che non vale niente
rubble ['rʌbl] *n* macerie *fpl*; (*smaller*) pietrisco
ruble ['ru:bl] *n* (*US*) = **rouble**
ruby ['ru:bɪ] *n* rubino
RUC *n abbr* (*Brit*: = *Royal Ulster Constabulary*) *forza di polizia dell'Irlanda del Nord*
rucksack ['rʌksæk] *n* zaino
ructions ['rʌkʃənz] *npl* putiferio, finimondo
rudder ['rʌdəʳ] *n* timone *m*
ruddy ['rʌdɪ] *adj* (*face*) fresco(-a); (*col*: *damned*) maledetto(-a)
rude [ru:d] *adj* (*impolite*: *person*) scortese, rozzo(-a); (: *word, manners*) grossolano(-a), rozzo(-a); (*shocking*) indecente; **to be ~ to sb** essere maleducato con qn
rudely ['ru:dlɪ] *adv* scortesemente; grossolanamente
rudeness ['ru:dnɪs] *n* scortesia; grossolanità
rudiment ['ru:dɪmənt] *n* rudimento
rudimentary [ru:dɪ'mɛntərɪ] *adj* rudimentale
rue [ru:] *vt* pentirsi amaramente di
rueful ['ru:ful] *adj* mesto(-a), triste
ruff [rʌf] *n* gorgiera
ruffian ['rʌfɪən] *n* briccone *m*, furfante *m*
ruffle ['rʌfl] *vt* (*hair*) scompigliare; (*clothes, water*) increspare; (*fig*: *person*) turbare
rug [rʌg] *n* tappeto; (*Brit*: *for knees*) coperta
rugby ['rʌgbɪ] *n* (*also*: **rugby football**) rugby *m*
rugged ['rʌgɪd] *adj* (*landscape*) aspro(-a); (*features, determination*) duro(-a); (*character*) brusco(-a)
rugger ['rʌgəʳ] *n* (*col*) rugby *m*
ruin ['ru:ɪn] *n* rovina ■ *vt* rovinare; (*spoil*: *clothes*) sciupare; **ruins** *npl* rovine *fpl*, ruderi *mpl*; **in ruins** in rovina
ruination [ru:ɪ'neɪʃən] *n* rovina
ruinous ['ru:ɪnəs] *adj* rovinoso(-a); (*expenditure*) inverosimile
rule [ru:l] *n* (*gen*) regola; (*regulation*) regolamento, regola; (*government*) governo; (*dominion etc*): **under British ~** sotto la sovranità britannica ■ *vt* (*country*) governare; (*person*) dominare; (*decide*) decidere ■ *vi* regnare; decidere; (*Law*) dichiarare; **to ~ against/in favour of/on** (*Law*) pronunciarsi a sfavore di/in favore di/su; **it's against the rules** è contro le regole *or* il regolamento; **by ~ of thumb** a lume di naso; **as a ~** normalmente, di regola
▸ **rule out** *vt* escludere; **murder cannot be ruled out** non si esclude che si tratti di omicidio
ruled [ru:ld] *adj* (*paper*) vergato(-a)
ruler ['ru:ləʳ] *n* (*sovereign*) sovrano(-a); (*leader*) capo (dello Stato); (*for measuring*) regolo, riga
ruling ['ru:lɪŋ] *adj* (*party*) al potere; (*class*) dirigente ■ *n* (*Law*) decisione *f*
rum [rʌm] *n* rum *m* ■ *adj* (*Brit col*) strano(-a)
Rumania *etc* [ru:'meɪnɪə] = **Romania** *etc*
rumble ['rʌmbl] *n* rimbombo; brontolio ■ *vi* rimbombare; (*stomach, pipe*) brontolare
rumbustious [rʌm'bʌstʃəs] *adj* (*person*): **to be ~** essere un terremoto
rummage ['rʌmɪdʒ] *vi* frugare
rumour, (*US*) **rumor** ['ru:məʳ] *n* voce *f* ■ *vt*: **it is rumoured that** corre voce che
rump [rʌmp] *n* (*of animal*) groppa
rumple ['rʌmpl] *vt* (*hair*) arruffare, scompigliare; (*clothes*) spiegazzare, sgualcire
rump steak *n* bistecca di girello
rumpus ['rʌmpəs] *n* (*col*) baccano; (: *quarrel*) rissa; **to kick up a ~** fare un putiferio
run [rʌn] *n* corsa; (*outing*) gita (in macchina); (*distance travelled*) percorso, tragitto; (*series*) serie *f inv*; (*Theat*) periodo di rappresentazione; (*Ski*) pista ■ *vb* (*pt* **ran**, *pp* **~**) [ræn, rʌn] *vt* (*operate*: *business*) gestire, dirigere; (: *competition, course*) organizzare; (: *hotel*) gestire; (: *house*) governare; (*Comput*:

program) eseguire; (*water, bath*) far scorrere; (*force through: rope, pipe*): **to ~ sth through** far passare qc attraverso; (*to pass: hand, finger*): **to ~ sth over** passare qc su ■ *vi* correre; (*pass: road etc*) passare; (*work: machine, factory*) funzionare, andare; (*bus, train: operate*) far servizio; (*: travel*) circolare; (*continue: play, contract*) durare; (*slide: drawer; flow: river, bath*) scorrere; (*colours, washing*) stemperarsi; (*in election*) presentarsi come candidato; **to go for a ~** andare a correre; (*in car*) fare un giro (in macchina); **to break into a ~** mettersi a correre; **a ~ of luck** un periodo di fortuna; **to have the ~ of sb's house** essere libero di andare e venire in casa di qn; **there was a ~ on ...** c'era una corsa a ...; **in the long ~** alla lunga; in fin dei conti; **in the short ~** sulle prime; **on the ~** in fuga; **to make a ~ for it** scappare, tagliare la corda; **I'll ~ you to the station** la porto alla stazione; **to ~ a risk** correre un rischio; **to ~ errands** andare a fare commissioni; **the train runs between Gatwick and Victoria** il treno collega Gatwick alla stazione Victoria; **the bus runs every 20 minutes** c'è un autobus ogni 20 minuti; **it's very cheap to ~** comporta poche spese; **to ~ on petrol** *or* (*US*) **gas/on diesel/ off batteries** andare a benzina/a diesel/a batterie; **to ~ for the bus** fare una corsa per prendere l'autobus; **to ~ for president** presentarsi come candidato per la presidenza; **their losses ran into millions** le loro perdite hanno raggiunto i milioni; **to be ~ off one's feet** (*Brit*) doversi fare in quattro

▸ **run about** *vi* (*children*) correre qua e là

▸ **run across** *vt fus* (*find*) trovare per caso

▸ **run away** *vi* fuggire

▸ **run down** *vi* (*clock*) scaricarsi ■ *vt* (*Aut*) investire; (*criticize*) criticare; (*Brit: reduce: production*) ridurre gradualmente; (*: factory, shop*) rallentare l'attività di; **to be ~ down** (*battery*) essere scarico(-a); (*person*) essere giù (di corda)

▸ **run in** *vt* (*Brit: car*) rodare, fare il rodaggio di

▸ **run into** *vt fus* (*meet: person*) incontrare per caso; (*: trouble*) incontrare, trovare; (*collide with*) andare a sbattere contro; **to ~ into debt** trovarsi nei debiti

▸ **run off** *vi* fuggire ■ *vt* (*water*) far defluire; (*copies*) fare

▸ **run out** *vi* (*person*) uscire di corsa; (*liquid*) colare; (*lease*) scadere; (*money*) esaurirsi

▸ **run out of** *vt fus* rimanere a corto di; **I've ~ out of petrol** *or* (*US*) **gas** sono rimasto senza benzina

▸ **run over** *vt* (*Aut*) investire, mettere sotto ■ *vt fus* (*revise*) rivedere

▸ **run through** *vt fus* (*instructions*) dare una scorsa a

▸ **run up** *vt* (*debt*) lasciar accumulare; **to ~ up against** (*difficulties*) incontrare

runaround ['rʌnəraund] *n* (*col*): **to give sb the ~** far girare a vuoto qn

runaway ['rʌnəweɪ] *adj* (*person*) fuggiasco(-a); (*horse*) in libertà; (*truck*) fuori controllo; (*inflation*) galoppante

rundown ['rʌndaun] *n* (*Brit: of industry etc*) riduzione *f* graduale dell'attività di

rung [rʌŋ] *pp of* **ring** ■ *n* (*of ladder*) piolo

run-in ['rʌnɪn] *n* (*col*) scontro

runner ['rʌnə^r] *n* (*in race*) corridore *m*; (*on sledge*) pattino; (*for drawer etc, carpet*) guida

runner bean *n* (*Brit*) fagiolino

runner-up [rʌnər'ʌp] *n* secondo(-a) arrivato(-a)

running ['rʌnɪŋ] *n* corsa; direzione *f*; organizzazione *f*; funzionamento ■ *adj* (*water*) corrente; (*commentary*) simultaneo(-a); **6 days ~** 6 giorni di seguito; **to be in/out of the ~ for sth** essere/non essere più in lizza per qc

running costs *npl* (*of business*) costi *mpl* d'esercizio; (*of car*) spese *fpl* di mantenimento

running head *n* (*Typ*) testata, titolo corrente

running mate *n* (*US Pol*) candidato alla vicepresidenza

runny ['rʌnɪ] *adj* che cola

run-off ['rʌnɔf] *n* (*in contest, election*) confronto definitivo; (*extra race*) spareggio

run-of-the-mill ['rʌnəvðə'mɪl] *adj* solito(-a), banale

runt [rʌnt] *n* omuncolo; (*Zool*) animale *m* più piccolo del normale

run-through ['rʌnθru:] *n* prova

run-up ['rʌnʌp] *n* (*Brit: also:* **run-up to sth**) periodo che precede qc

runway ['rʌnweɪ] *n* (*Aviat*) pista (di decollo)

rupture ['rʌptʃə^r] *n* (*Med*) ernia ■ *vt*: **to ~ o.s.** farsi venire un'ernia

rural ['ruərl] *adj* rurale

rural district council *n* (*Brit*) consiglio (amministrativo) di distretto rurale

ruse [ru:z] *n* trucco

rush [rʌʃ] *n* corsa precipitosa; (*of crowd*) afflusso; (*hurry*) furia, fretta; (*current*) flusso; (*Bot*) giunco ■ *vt* mandare *or* spedire velocemente; (*attack: town etc*) prendere d'assalto ■ *vi* precipitarsi; **is there any ~ for this?** è urgente?; **we've had a ~ of orders** abbiamo avuto una valanga di ordinazioni; **I'm in a ~ (to do)** ho fretta *or* premura (di fare); **gold ~** corsa all'oro; **to ~ sth off** spedire con urgenza qc; **don't ~ me!** non farmi fretta!

▸ **rush through** *vt* (*meal*) mangiare in fretta; (*book*) dare una scorsa frettolosa a; (*town*) attraversare in fretta; (*Comm: order*) eseguire d'urgenza ■ *vt fus* (*work*) sbrigare frettolosamente
rush hour *n* ora di punta
rush job *n* (*urgent*) lavoro urgente
rush matting *n* stuoia
rusk [rʌsk] *n* fetta biscottata
Russia ['rʌʃə] *n* Russia
Russian ['rʌʃən] *adj* russo(-a) ■ *n* russo(-a); (*Ling*) russo
rust [rʌst] *n* ruggine *f* ■ *vi* arrugginirsi
rustic ['rʌstɪk] *adj* rustico(-a) ■ *n* (*pej*) cafone(-a)
rustle ['rʌsl] *vi* frusciare ■ *vt* (*paper*) far frusciare; (*US: cattle*) rubare
rustproof ['rʌstpru:f] *adj* inossidabile
rustproofing ['rʌstpru:fɪŋ] *n* trattamento antiruggine
rusty ['rʌstɪ] *adj* arrugginito(-a)
rut [rʌt] *n* solco; (*Zool*) fregola; **to be in a ~** (*fig*) essersi fossilizzato(-a)
rutabaga [ru:tə'beɪgə] *n* (*US*) rapa svedese
ruthless ['ru:θlɪs] *adj* spietato(-a)
ruthlessness ['ru:θlɪsnɪs] *n* spietatezza
RV *abbr* (= *revised version*) *versione riveduta della Bibbia* ■ *n abbr* (*US*) = **recreational vehicle**
rye [raɪ] *n* segale *f*

Ss

S, s [ɛs] *n (letter)* S, s *f or m inv*; *(US Scol: = satisfactory)* ≈ sufficiente; **S for Sugar** ≈ S come Savona

S *abbr (= saint)* S.; *(= south)* S; *(on clothes)* = **small**

SA *abbr* = **South Africa; South America**

Sabbath ['sæbəθ] *n (Jewish)* sabato; *(Christian)* domenica

sabbatical [sə'bætɪkl] *adj*: **~ year** anno sabbatico

sabotage ['sæbətɑ:ʒ] *n* sabotaggio ■ *vt* sabotare

saccharin, saccharine ['sækərɪn] *n* saccarina

sachet ['sæʃeɪ] *n* bustina

sack [sæk] *n (bag)* sacco ■ *vt (dismiss)* licenziare, mandare a spasso; *(plunder)* saccheggiare; **to get the ~** essere mandato a spasso; **to give sb the ~** licenziare qn, mandare qn a spasso

sackful ['sækful] *n*: **a ~ of** un sacco di

sacking ['sækɪŋ] *n* tela di sacco; *(dismissal)* licenziamento

sacrament ['sækrəmənt] *n* sacramento

sacred ['seɪkrɪd] *adj* sacro(-a)

sacred cow *n (fig: person)* intoccabile *m/f*; *(: institution)* caposaldo; *(: idea, belief)* dogma *m*

sacrifice ['sækrɪfaɪs] *n* sacrificio ■ *vt* sacrificare; **to make sacrifices (for sb)** fare (dei) sacrifici (per qn)

sacrilege ['sækrɪlɪdʒ] *n* sacrilegio

sacrosanct ['sækrəusæŋkt] *adj* sacrosanto(-a)

sad [sæd] *adj* triste; *(deplorable)* deplorevole

sadden ['sædn] *vt* rattristare

saddle ['sædl] *n* sella ■ *vt (horse)* sellare; **to be saddled with sth** *(col)* avere qc sulle spalle

saddlebag ['sædlbæg] *n* bisaccia; *(on bicycle)* borsa

sadism ['seɪdɪzəm] *n* sadismo

sadist ['seɪdɪst] *n* sadico(-a)

sadistic [sə'dɪstɪk] *adj* sadico(-a)

sadly ['sædlɪ] *adv* tristemente; *(regrettably)* sfortunatamente; **~ lacking in** penosamente privo di

sadness ['sædnɪs] *n* tristezza

sadomasochism [seɪdəu'mæsəkɪzəm] *n* sadomasochismo

sae *abbr (Brit)* = **stamped addressed envelope**; *see* **stamp**

safari [sə'fɑ:rɪ] *n* safari *m inv*

safari park *n* zoosafari *m inv*

safe [seɪf] *adj* sicuro(-a); *(out of danger)* salvo(-a), al sicuro; *(cautious)* prudente ■ *n* cassaforte *f*; **~ from** al sicuro da; **~ and sound** sano(-a) e salvo(-a); **~ journey!** buon viaggio!; **(just) to be on the ~ side** per non correre rischi; **to play ~** giocare sul sicuro; **it is ~ to say that ...** si può affermare con sicurezza che ...

safe bet *n*: **it's a ~** è una cosa sicura

safe-breaker ['seɪfbreɪkə[r]] *n (Brit)* scassinatore *m*

safe-conduct [seɪf'kɒndʌkt] *n* salvacondotto

safe-cracker ['seɪfkrækə[r]] *n* = **safe-breaker**

safe-deposit ['seɪfdɪpɒzɪt] *n (vault)* caveau *m inv*; *(box)* cassetta di sicurezza

safeguard ['seɪfgɑ:d] *n* salvaguardia ■ *vt* salvaguardare

safe haven *n* zona sicura *or* protetta

safekeeping ['seɪf'ki:pɪŋ] *n* custodia

safely ['seɪflɪ] *adv* sicuramente; sano(-a) e salvo(-a) prudentemente; prudentemente; **I can ~ say ...** posso tranquillamente asserire ...

safe passage *n* passaggio sicuro

safe sex *n* sesso sicuro

safety ['seɪftɪ] *n* sicurezza; **~ first!** la prudenza innanzitutto!

safety belt *n* cintura di sicurezza

safety catch *n* sicura

safety net *n* rete *f* di protezione

safety pin *n* spilla di sicurezza

safety valve *n* valvola di sicurezza

saffron ['sæfrən] *n* zafferano

sag [sæg] *vi* incurvarsi; afflosciarsi

saga ['sɑːgə] *n* saga; (*fig*) odissea
sage [seɪdʒ] *n* (*herb*) salvia; (*man*) saggio
Sagittarius [sædʒɪ'tɛərɪəs] *n* Sagittario; **to be ~** essere del Sagittario
sago ['seɪgəu] *n* sagù *m*
Sahara [sə'hɑːrə] *n*: **the ~ Desert** il Deserto del Sahara
Sahel [sæ'hɛl] *n* Sahel *m*
said [sɛd] *pt, pp of* **say**
Saigon [saɪ'gɔn] *n* Saigon *f*
sail [seɪl] *n* (*on boat*) vela; (*trip*): **to go for a ~** fare un giro in barca a vela ■ *vt* (*boat*) condurre, governare ■ *vi* (*travel: ship*) navigare; (*: passenger*) viaggiare per mare; (*set off*) salpare; (*Sport*) fare della vela; **they sailed into Genoa** entrarono nel porto di Genova
▸ **sail through** *vt fus* (*fig*) superare senza difficoltà ■ *vi* farcela senza difficoltà
sailboat ['seɪlbəut] *n* (*US*) barca a vela
sailing ['seɪlɪŋ] *n* (*sport*) vela; **to go ~** fare della vela
sailing boat *n* barca a vela
sailing ship *n* veliero
sailor ['seɪlə^r] *n* marinaio
saint [seɪnt] *n* santo(-a)
saintly ['seɪntlɪ] *adj* da santo(-a); santo(-a)
sake [seɪk] *n*: **for the ~ of** per, per amore di; **for pity's ~** per pietà; **for the ~ of argument** tanto per fare un esempio; **art for art's ~** l'arte per l'arte
salad ['sæləd] *n* insalata; **tomato ~** insalata di pomodori
salad bowl *n* insalatiera
salad cream *n* (*Brit*) (tipo di) maionese *f*
salad dressing *n* condimento per insalata
salad oil *n* olio da tavola
salami [sə'lɑːmɪ] *n* salame *m*
salaried ['sælərɪd] *adj* stipendiato(-a)
salary ['sælərɪ] *n* stipendio
salary scale *n* scala dei salari
sale [seɪl] *n* vendita; (*at reduced prices*) svendita, liquidazione *f*; **"for ~"** "in vendita"; **on ~** in vendita; **on ~ or return** da vendere o rimandare; **a closing-down** *or* (US) **liquidation ~** una liquidazione; **~ and lease back** *n* lease back *m inv*
saleroom ['seɪlrum] *n* sala delle aste
sales assistant *n* (*Brit*) commesso(-a)
sales clerk *n* (*US*) commesso(-a)
sales conference *n* riunione *f* marketing e vendite
sales drive *n* campagna di vendita, sforzo promozionale
sales force *n* personale *m* addetto alle vendite
salesman ['seɪlzmən] *n* commesso; (*representative*) rappresentante *m*
sales manager *n* direttore *m* commerciale
salesmanship ['seɪlzmənʃɪp] *n* arte *f* del vendere
sales tax *n* (*US*) imposta sulle vendite
saleswoman ['seɪlzwumən] *n* commessa
salient ['seɪlɪənt] *adj* saliente
saline ['seɪlaɪn] *adj* salino(-a)
saliva [sə'laɪvə] *n* saliva
sallow ['sæləu] *adj* giallastro(-a)
sally forth, sally out ['sælɪ-] *vi* uscire di gran carriera
salmon ['sæmən] *n* (*pl inv*) salmone *m*
salmon trout *n* trota (di mare)
saloon [sə'luːn] *n* (*US*) saloon *m inv*, bar *m inv*; (*Brit Aut*) berlina; (*ship's lounge*) salone *m*
SALT [sɔːlt] *n abbr* (= *Strategic Arms Limitation Talks/Treaty*) S.A.L.T. *m*
salt [sɔːlt] *n* sale *m* ■ *vt* salare ■ *cpd* di sale; (*Culin*) salato(-a); **an old ~** un lupo di mare
▸ **salt away** *vt* ammucchiare, mettere via
salt cellar *n* saliera
salt-free ['sɔːlt'friː] *adj* senza sale
saltwater ['sɔːltwɔːtə^r] *adj* (*fish etc*) di mare
salty ['sɔːltɪ] *adj* salato(-a)
salubrious [sə'luːbrɪəs] *adj* salubre; (*fig: district etc*) raccomandabile
salutary ['sæljutərɪ] *adj* salutare
salute [sə'luːt] *n* saluto ■ *vt* salutare
salvage ['sælvɪdʒ] *n* (*saving*) salvataggio; (*things saved*) beni *mpl* salvati *or* recuperati ■ *vt* salvare, mettere in salvo
salvage vessel *n* scialuppa di salvataggio
salvation [sæl'veɪʃən] *n* salvezza
Salvation Army *n* Esercito della Salvezza
salver ['sælvə^r] *n* vassoio
salvo, salvoes ['sælvəu] *n* salva
Samaritan [sə'mærɪtən] *n*: **the Samaritans** (*organization*) ≈ telefono amico
same [seɪm] *adj* stesso(-a), medesimo(-a) ■ *pron*: **the ~** lo(la) stesso(-a), gli(le) stessi(-e); **the ~ book as** lo stesso libro di (*or* che); **on the ~ day** lo stesso giorno; **at the ~ time** allo stesso tempo; **all** *or* **just the ~** tuttavia; **to do the ~** fare la stessa cosa; **to do the ~ as sb** fare come qn; **the ~ again** (*in bar etc*) un altro; **they're one and the ~** (*person/thing*) sono la stessa persona/cosa; **and the ~ to you!** altrettanto a lei!; **~ here!** anch'io!
sample ['sɑːmpl] *n* campione *m* ■ *vt* (*food*) assaggiare; (*wine*) degustare; **to take a ~** prelevare un campione; **free ~** campione omaggio
sanatorium (*pl* **sanatoria**) [sænə'tɔːrɪəm, -rɪə] *n* sanatorio
sanctify ['sæŋktɪfaɪ] *vt* santificare
sanctimonious [sæŋktɪ'məunɪəs] *adj* bigotto(-a), bacchettone(-a)

sanction ['sæŋkʃən] *n* sanzione *f* ■ *vt* sancire, sanzionare; **to impose economic sanctions on** *or* **against** adottare sanzioni economiche contro
sanctity ['sæŋktɪtɪ] *n* santità
sanctuary ['sæŋktjuərɪ] *n* (*holy place*) santuario; (*refuge*) rifugio; (*for wildlife*) riserva
sand [sænd] *n* sabbia ■ *vt* cospargere di sabbia; (*also*: **sand down**: *wood etc*) cartavetrare; *see also* **sands**
sandal ['sændl] *n* sandalo
sandbag ['sændbæg] *n* sacco di sabbia
sandblast ['sændblɑːst] *vt* sabbiare
sandbox ['sændbɔks] *n* (US: *for children*) buca di sabbia
sandcastle ['sændkɑːsl] *n* castello di sabbia
sand dune *n* duna di sabbia
sander ['sændəʳ] *n* levigatrice *f*
sandpaper ['sændpeɪpəʳ] *n* carta vetrata
sandpit ['sændpɪt] *n* (Brit: *for children*) buca di sabbia
sands [sændz] *npl* spiaggia
sandstone ['sændstəun] *n* arenaria
sandstorm ['sændstɔːm] *n* tempesta di sabbia
sandwich ['sændwɪtʃ] *n* tramezzino, panino, sandwich *m inv* ■ *vt* (*also*: **sandwich in**) infilare; **cheese/ham ~** sandwich al formaggio/prosciutto; **to be sandwiched between** essere incastrato(-a) fra
sandwich board *n* cartello pubblicitario (*portato da un uomo sandwich*)
sandwich course *n* (Brit) corso di formazione professionale
sandwich man *n* uomo *m* sandwich *inv*
sandy ['sændɪ] *adj* sabbioso(-a); (*colour*) color sabbia *inv*, biondo(-a) rossiccio(-a)
sane [seɪn] *adj* (*person*) sano(-a) di mente; (*outlook*) sensato(-a)
sang [sæŋ] *pt of* **sing**
sanguine ['sæŋgwɪn] *adj* ottimista
sanitarium (*pl* **sanitaria**) [sænɪ'tɛərɪəm, -rɪə] *n* (US) = **sanatorium**
sanitary ['sænɪtərɪ] *adj* (*system, arrangements*) sanitario(-a); (*clean*) igienico(-a)
sanitary towel, (US) **sanitary napkin** *n* assorbente *m* (igienico)
sanitation [sænɪ'teɪʃən] *n* (*in house*) impianti *mpl* sanitari; (*in town*) fognature *fpl*
sanitation department *n* (US) nettezza urbana
sanity ['sænɪtɪ] *n* sanità mentale; (*common sense*) buon senso
sank [sæŋk] *pt of* **sink**
San Marino [sænmə'riːnəu] *n* San Marino *f*
Santa Claus [sæntə'klɔːz] *n* Babbo Natale
Santiago [sæntɪ'ɑːgəu] *n* (*also*: **Santiago de Chile**) Santiago (del Cile) *f*
sap [sæp] *n* (*of plants*) linfa ■ *vt* (*strength*) fiaccare
sapling ['sæplɪŋ] *n* alberello
sapphire ['sæfaɪəʳ] *n* zaffiro
sarcasm ['sɑːkæzm] *n* sarcasmo
sarcastic [sɑː'kæstɪk] *adj* sarcastico(-a); **to be ~** fare del sarcasmo
sarcophagus (*pl* **sarcophagi**) [sɑː'kɔfəgəs, -gaɪ] *n* sarcofago
sardine [sɑː'diːn] *n* sardina
Sardinia [sɑː'dɪnɪə] *n* Sardegna
Sardinian [sɑː'dɪnɪən] *adj, n* sardo(-a)
sardonic [sɑː'dɔnɪk] *adj* sardonico(-a)
sari ['sɑːrɪ] *n* sari *m inv*
SARS [sɑːz] *n abbr* (= *severe acute respiratory syndrome*) SARS *f*, polmonite atipica
sartorial [sɑː'tɔːrɪəl] *adj* di sartoria
SAS *n abbr* (*Brit Mil*: = *Special Air Service*) *reparto dell'esercito britannico specializzato in operazioni clandestine*
SASE *n abbr* (US: = *self-addressed stamped envelope*) *busta affrancata e con indirizzo*
sash [sæʃ] *n* fascia
sash window *n* finestra a ghigliottina
Sask. *abbr* (*Canada*) = **Saskatchewan**
SAT *n abbr* (US) = **Scholastic Aptitude Test**
sat [sæt] *pt, pp of* **sit**
Sat. *abbr* (= *Saturday*) sab.
Satan ['seɪtən] *n* Satana *m*
satanic [sə'tænɪk] *adj* satanico(-a)
satchel ['sætʃl] *n* cartella
sated ['seɪtɪd] *adj* soddisfatto(-a); sazio(-a)
satellite ['sætəlaɪt] *adj, n* satellite *m*
satellite television *n* televisione *f* via satellite
satiate ['seɪʃɪeɪt] *vt* saziare
satin ['sætɪn] *n* satin *m* ■ *adj* di *or* in satin; **with a ~ finish** satinato(-a)
satire ['sætaɪəʳ] *n* satira
satirical [sə'tɪrɪkl] *adj* satirico(-a)
satirist ['sætərɪst] *n* (*writer etc*) scrittore(-trice) *etc* satirico(-a); (*cartoonist*) caricaturista *m/f*
satirize ['sætɪraɪz] *vt* satireggiare
satisfaction [sætɪs'fækʃən] *n* soddisfazione *f*; **has it been done to your ~?** ne è rimasto soddisfatto?
satisfactory [sætɪs'fæktərɪ] *adj* soddisfacente
satisfied ['sætɪsfaɪd] *adj* (*customer*) soddisfatto(-a); **to be ~ (with sth)** essere soddisfatto(-a) (di qc)
satisfy ['sætɪsfaɪ] *vt* soddisfare; (*convince*) convincere; **to ~ the requirements** rispondere ai requisiti; **to ~ sb (that)** convincere qn (che), persuadere qn (che); **to ~ o.s. of sth** accertarsi di qc

S

satisfying [ˈsætɪsfaɪɪŋ] *adj* soddisfacente
SATs *n abbr (Brit: = standard assessment tasks or tests) esame di fine anno sostenuto dagli allievi delle scuole pubbliche inglesi a 7, 11 o 14 anni*
satsuma [sætˈsuːmə] *n agrume di provenienza giapponese*
saturate [ˈsætʃəreɪt] *vt*: **to ~ (with)** saturare (di)
saturated fat [ˈsætʃəreɪtɪd-] *n* grassi *mpl* saturi
saturation [sætʃəˈreɪʃən] *n* saturazione *f*
Saturday [ˈsætədɪ] *n* sabato; *see also* **Tuesday**
sauce [sɔːs] *n* salsa; (*containing meat, fish*) sugo
saucepan [ˈsɔːspən] *n* casseruola
saucer [ˈsɔːsəʳ] *n* piattino
saucy [ˈsɔːsɪ] *adj* impertinente
Saudi [ˈsaudɪ] *adj, n* saudita *m/f*
Saudi Arabia *n* Arabia Saudita
Saudi Arabian *adj, n* saudita *m/f*
sauna [ˈsɔːnə] *n* sauna
saunter [ˈsɔːntəʳ] *vi* andare a zonzo, bighellonare
sausage [ˈsɔsɪdʒ] *n* salsiccia; (*salami etc*) salame *m*
sausage roll *n rotolo di pasta sfoglia ripieno di salsiccia*
sauté [ˈsəuteɪ] *adj* (*Culin: potatoes*) saltato(-a); (*: onions*) soffritto(-a) ■ *vt* far saltare; far soffriggere
savage [ˈsævɪdʒ] *adj* (*cruel, fierce*) selvaggio(-a), feroce; (*primitive*) primitivo(-a) ■ *n* selvaggio(-a) ■ *vt* attaccare selvaggiamente
savagery [ˈsævɪdʒrɪ] *n* crudeltà, ferocia
save [seɪv] *vt* (*person, belongings, Comput*) salvare; (*money*) risparmiare, mettere da parte; (*time*) risparmiare; (*food*) conservare; (*avoid: trouble*) evitare ■ *vi* (*also*: **save up**) economizzare ■ *n* (*Sport*) parata ■ *prep* salvo, a eccezione di; **it will ~ me an hour** mi farà risparmiare un'ora; **to ~ face** salvare la faccia; **God ~ the Queen!** Dio salvi la Regina!
saving [ˈseɪvɪŋ] *n* risparmio ■ *adj*: **the ~ grace of** l'unica cosa buona di; **savings** *npl* risparmi *mpl*; **to make savings** fare economia
savings account *n* libretto di risparmio
savings bank *n* cassa di risparmio
saviour, (*US*) **savior** [ˈseɪvjəʳ] *n* salvatore *m*
savour, (*US*) **savor** [ˈseɪvəʳ] *n* sapore *m*, gusto ■ *vt* gustare
savoury, (*US*) **savory** [ˈseɪvərɪ] *adj* saporito(-a); (*dish: not sweet*) salato(-a)
savvy [ˈsævɪ] *n* (*col*) arguzia
saw [sɔː] *pt of* **see** ■ *n* (*tool*) sega ■ *vt* (*pt* **sawed**, *pp* **sawed** *or* **sawn**) [sɔːn] segare; **to ~ sth up** fare a pezzi qc con la sega
sawdust [ˈsɔːdʌst] *n* segatura
sawmill [ˈsɔːmɪl] *n* segheria
sawn [sɔːn] *pp of* **saw**
sawn-off [ˈsɔːnɔf], (*US*) **sawed-off** [ˈsɔːdɔf] *adj*: **~ shotgun** fucile *m* a canne mozze
saxophone [ˈsæksəfəun] *n* sassofono
say [seɪ] *n*: **to have one's ~** fare sentire il proprio parere; **to have a** *or* **some ~** avere voce in capitolo ■ *vt* (*pt, pp* **said**) [sɛd] dire; **could you ~ that again?** potrebbe ripeterlo?; **to ~ yes/no** dire di sì/di no; **she said (that) I was to give you this** ha detto di darle questo; **my watch says 3 o'clock** il mio orologio fa le 3; **shall we ~ Tuesday?** facciamo martedì?; **that doesn't ~ much for him** non torna a suo credito; **when all is said and done** a conti fatti; **there is something** *or* **a lot to be said for it** ha i suoi lati positivi; **that is to ~** cioè, vale a dire; **to ~ nothing of** per non parlare di; **~ that ...** mettiamo *or* diciamo che ...; **that goes without saying** va da sé
saying [ˈseɪɪŋ] *n* proverbio, detto
SBA *n abbr* (*US: = Small Business Administration*) *organismo ausiliario per piccole imprese*
SC *n abbr* (*US*) = **supreme court** ■ *abbr* (*US*) = **South Carolina**
s/c *abbr* (*= self-contained*) indipendente
scab [skæb] *n* crosta; (*pej*) crumiro(-a)
scabby [ˈskæbɪ] *adj* crostoso(-a)
scaffold [ˈskæfəuld] *n* impalcatura; (*gallows*) patibolo
scaffolding [ˈskæfəldɪŋ] *n* impalcatura
scald [skɔːld] *n* scottatura ■ *vt* scottare
scalding [ˈskɔːldɪŋ] *adj* (*also*: **scalding hot**) bollente
scale [skeɪl] *n* scala; (*of fish*) squama ■ *vt* (*mountain*) scalare; **pay ~** scala dei salari; **~ of charges** tariffa; **on a large ~** su vasta scala; **to draw sth to ~** disegnare qc in scala; **small-~ model** modello in scala ridotta; *see also* **scales**
▸**scale down** *vt* ridurre (proporzionalmente)
scaled-down [skeɪldˈdaun] *adj* su scala ridotta
scale drawing *n* disegno in scala
scale model *n* modello in scala
scales [skeɪlz] *npl* bilancia
scallion [ˈskæljən] *n* cipolla; (*US: shallot*) scalogna; (*: leek*) porro
scallop [ˈskɔləp] *n* pettine *m*
scalp [skælp] *n* cuoio capelluto ■ *vt* scotennare
scalpel [ˈskælpl] *n* bisturi *m inv*
scalper [ˈskælpəʳ] *n* (*US col: of tickets*) bagarino
scam [skæm] *n* (*col*) truffa
scamp [skæmp] *n* (*col: child*) peste *f*

scamper ['skæmpəʳ] *vi*: **to ~ away, ~ off** darsela a gambe
scampi ['skæmpɪ] *npl* scampi *mpl*
scan [skæn] *vt* scrutare; (*glance at quickly*) scorrere, dare un'occhiata a; (*poetry*) scandire; (*TV*) analizzare; (*Radar*) esplorare ■ *n* (*Med*) ecografia
scandal ['skændl] *n* scandalo; (*gossip*) pettegolezzi *mpl*
scandalize ['skændəlaɪz] *vt* scandalizzare
scandalous ['skændələs] *adj* scandaloso(-a)
Scandinavia [skændɪ'neɪvɪə] *n* Scandinavia
Scandinavian [skændɪ'neɪvɪən] *adj, n* scandinavo(-a)
scanner ['skænəʳ] *n* (*Radar, Med*) scanner *m inv*
scant [skænt] *adj* scarso(-a)
scantily ['skæntɪlɪ] *adv*: **~ clad** *or* **dressed** succintamente vestito(-a)
scanty ['skæntɪ] *adj* insufficiente; (*swimsuit*) ridotto(-a)
scapegoat ['skeɪpgəut] *n* capro espiatorio
scar [skɑːʳ] *n* cicatrice *f* ■ *vt* sfregiare
scarce [skɛəs] *adj* scarso(-a); (*copy, edition*) raro(-a)
scarcely ['skɛəslɪ] *adv* appena; **~ anybody** quasi nessuno; **I can ~ believe it** faccio fatica a crederci
scarcity ['skɛəsɪtɪ] *n* scarsità, mancanza
scarcity value *n* valore *m* di rarità
scare [skɛəʳ] *n* spavento, paura ■ *vt* spaventare, atterrire; **to ~ sb stiff** spaventare a morte qn; **bomb ~** evacuazione *f* per sospetta presenza di un ordigno esplosivo
▸ **scare away, scare off** *vt* mettere in fuga
scarecrow ['skɛəkrəu] *n* spaventapasseri *m inv*
scared [skɛəd] *adj*: **to be ~** aver paura
scaremonger ['skɛəmʌŋgəʳ] *n* allarmista *m/f*
scarf (*pl* **scarves**) [skɑːf, skɑːvz] *n* (*long*) sciarpa; (*square*) fazzoletto da testa, foulard *m inv*
scarlet ['skɑːlɪt] *adj* scarlatto(-a)
scarlet fever *n* scarlattina
scarper ['skɑːpəʳ] *vi* (*Brit col*) darsela a gambe
SCART socket ['skɑːt-] *n* presa *f* SCART *inv*
scarves [skɑːvz] *npl of* **scarf**
scary ['skɛərɪ] *adj* (*col*) che fa paura
scathing ['skeɪðɪŋ] *adj* aspro(-a); **to be ~ about sth** essere molto critico rispetto a qc
scatter ['skætəʳ] *vt* spargere; (*crowd*) disperdere ■ *vi* disperdersi
scatterbrained ['skætəbreɪnd] *adj* scervellato(-a), sbadato(-a)
scattered ['skætəd] *adj* sparso(-a), sparpagliato(-a)
scatty ['skætɪ] *adj* (*col*) scervellato(-a), sbadato(-a)
scavenge ['skævɪndʒ] *vi* (*person*): **to ~ (for)** frugare tra i rifiuti (alla ricerca di); (*hyenas etc*) nutrirsi di carogne
scavenger ['skævəndʒəʳ] *n* spazzino
SCE *n abbr* = **Scottish Certificate of Education**
scenario [sɪ'nɑːrɪəu] *n* (*Theat, Cine*) copione *m*; (*fig*) situazione *f*
scene [siːn] *n* (*Theat, fig etc*) scena; (*of crime, accident*) scena, luogo; (*sight, view*) vista, veduta; **behind the scenes** (*also fig*) dietro le quinte; **to appear** *or* **come on the ~** (*also fig*) entrare in scena; **the political ~ in Italy** il quadro politico in Italia; **to make a ~** (*col: fuss*) fare una scenata
scenery ['siːnərɪ] *n* (*Theat*) scenario; (*landscape*) panorama *m*
scenic ['siːnɪk] *adj* scenico(-a); panoramico(-a)
scent [sɛnt] *n* odore *m*, profumo; (*sense of smell*) olfatto, odorato; (*fig: track*) pista; **to put** *or* **throw sb off the ~** (*fig*) far perdere le tracce a qn, sviare qn
sceptic, (*US*) **skeptic** ['skɛptɪk] *n* scettico(-a)
sceptical, (*US*) **skeptical** ['skɛptɪkl] *adj* scettico(-a)
scepticism, (*US*) **skepticism** ['skɛptɪsɪzm] *n* scetticismo
sceptre, (*US*) **scepter** ['sɛptəʳ] *n* scettro
schedule ['ʃɛdjuːl, (*US*) 'skɛdjuːl] *n* programma *m*, piano; (*of trains*) orario; (*of prices etc*) lista, tabella ■ *vt* fissare; **as scheduled** come stabilito; **on ~** in orario; **to be ahead of/behind ~** essere in anticipo/ ritardo sul previsto; **we are working to a very tight ~** il nostro programma di lavoro è molto intenso; **everything went according to ~** tutto è andato secondo i piani *or* secondo il previsto
scheduled ['ʃɛdjuːld, (*US*) 'skɛdjuːld] *adj* (*date, time*) fissato(-a); (*visit, event*) programmato(-a); (*train, bus, stop*) previsto(-a) (sull'orario); **~ flight** volo di linea
schematic [skɪ'mætɪk] *adj* schematico(-a)
scheme [skiːm] *n* piano, progetto; (*method*) sistema *m*; (*dishonest plan, plot*) intrigo, trama; (*arrangement*) disposizione *f*, sistemazione *f* ■ *vt* progettare; (*plot*) ordire ■ *vi* fare progetti; (*intrigue*) complottare; **colour ~** combinazione *f* di colori
scheming ['skiːmɪŋ] *adj* intrigante ■ *n* intrighi *mpl*, macchinazioni *fpl*
schism ['skɪzəm] *n* scisma *m*
schizophrenia [skɪtsə'friːnɪə] *n* schizofrenia
schizophrenic [skɪtsə'frɛnɪk] *adj, n* schizofrenico(-a)
scholar ['skɔləʳ] *n* erudito(-a)
scholarly ['skɔləlɪ] *adj* dotto(-a), erudito(-a)

S

scholarship ['skɔləʃɪp] *n* erudizione *f*; (*grant*) borsa di studio
school [sku:l] *n* scuola; (*in university*) scuola, facoltà *f inv* ■ *cpd* scolare, scolastico(-a) ■ *vt* (*animal*) addestrare
school age *n* età scolare
schoolbook ['sku:lbuk] *n* libro scolastico
schoolboy ['sku:lbɔɪ] *n* scolaro
schoolchild (*pl* **-children**) ['sku:ltʃaɪld, -'tʃɪldrən] *n* scolaro(-a)
schooldays ['sku:ldeɪz] *npl* giorni *mpl* di scuola
schoolgirl ['sku:lgə:l] *n* scolara
schooling ['sku:lɪŋ] *n* istruzione *f*
school-leaver ['sku:lli:vəʳ] *n* (*Brit*) ≈ neodiplomato(-a)
schoolmaster ['sku:lmɑ:stəʳ] *n* (*primary*) maestro; (*secondary*) insegnante *m*
schoolmistress ['sku:lmɪstrɪs] *n* (*primary*) maestra; (*secondary*) insegnante *f*
school report *n* (*Brit*) pagella
schoolroom ['sku:lru:m] *n* classe *f*, aula
schoolteacher ['sku:lti:tʃəʳ] *n* insegnante *m/f*, docente *m/f*; (*primary*) maestro(-a)
schoolyard ['sku:ljɑ:d] *n* (*US*) cortile *m* della scuola
schooner ['sku:nəʳ] *n* (*ship*) goletta, schooner *m inv*; (*glass*) bicchiere *m* alto da sherry
sciatica [saɪ'ætɪkə] *n* sciatica
science ['saɪəns] *n* scienza; **the sciences** le scienze; (*Scol*) le materie scientifiche
science fiction *n* fantascienza
scientific [saɪən'tɪfɪk] *adj* scientifico(-a)
scientist ['saɪəntɪst] *n* scienziato(-a)
sci-fi ['saɪfaɪ] *n abbr* (*col*) = **science fiction**
Scilly Isles ['sɪlɪ'aɪlz] *npl*, **Scillies** ['sɪlɪz] *npl*: **the ~** le isole Scilly
scintillating ['sɪntɪleɪtɪŋ] *adj* scintillante; (*wit, conversation, company*) brillante
scissors ['sɪzəz] *npl* forbici *fpl*; **a pair of ~** un paio di forbici
sclerosis [sklɪ'rəusɪs] *n* sclerosi *f*
scoff [skɔf] *vt* (*Brit col: eat*) trangugiare, ingozzare ■ *vi*: **to ~ (at)** (*mock*) farsi beffe (di)
scold [skəuld] *vt* rimproverare
scolding ['skəuldɪŋ] *n* lavata di capo, sgridata
scone [skɔn] *n* focaccina da tè
scoop [sku:p] *n* mestolo; (*for ice cream*) cucchiaio dosatore; (*Press*) colpo giornalistico, notizia (in) esclusiva
▸ **scoop out** *vt* scavare
▸ **scoop up** *vt* tirare su, sollevare
scooter ['sku:təʳ] *n* (*motorcycle*) motoretta, scooter *m inv*; (*toy*) monopattino
scope [skəup] *n* (*capacity: of plan, undertaking*) portata; (*: of person*) capacità *fpl*; (*opportunity*) possibilità *fpl*; **to be within the ~ of** rientrare nei limiti di; **it's well within his ~ to ...** è perfettamente in grado di ...; **there is plenty of ~ for improvement** (*Brit*) ci sono notevoli possibilità di miglioramento
scorch [skɔ:tʃ] *vt* (*clothes*) strinare, bruciacchiare; (*earth, grass*) seccare, bruciare
scorched earth policy [skɔ:tʃt-] *n* tattica della terra bruciata
scorcher ['skɔ:tʃəʳ] *n* (*col: hot day*) giornata torrida
scorching ['skɔ:tʃɪŋ] *adj* cocente, scottante
score [skɔ:ʳ] *n* punti *mpl*, punteggio; (*Mus*) partitura, spartito; (*twenty*): **a ~** venti ■ *vt* (*goal, point*) segnare, fare; (*success*) ottenere; (*cut: leather, wood, card*) incidere ■ *vi* segnare; (*Football*) fare un goal; (*keep score*) segnare i punti; **on that ~** a questo riguardo; **to have an old ~ to settle with sb** (*fig*) avere un vecchio conto da saldare con qn; **scores of people** (*fig*) un sacco di gente; **to ~ 6 out of 10** prendere 6 su 10
▸ **score out** *vt* cancellare con un segno
scoreboard ['skɔ:bɔ:d] *n* tabellone *m* segnapunti
scorecard ['skɔ:kɑ:d] *n* cartoncino segnapunti
scoreline ['skɔ:laɪn] *n* (*Sport*) risultato
scorer ['skɔ:rəʳ] *n* marcatore(-trice); (*keeping score*) segnapunti *m inv*
scorn [skɔ:n] *n* disprezzo ■ *vt* disprezzare
scornful ['skɔ:nful] *adj* sprezzante
Scorpio ['skɔ:pɪəu] *n* Scorpione *m*; **to be ~** essere dello Scorpione
scorpion ['skɔ:pɪən] *n* scorpione *m*
Scot [skɔt] *n* scozzese *m/f*
Scotch [skɔtʃ] *n* whisky *m* scozzese, scotch *m*
scotch [skɔtʃ] *vt* (*rumour etc*) soffocare
Scotch tape® *n* scotch® *m*
scot-free ['skɔt'fri:] *adj* impunito(-a); **to get off ~** (*unpunished*) farla franca; (*unhurt*) uscire illeso(-a)
Scotland ['skɔtlənd] *n* Scozia
Scots [skɔts] *adj* scozzese
Scotsman ['skɔtsmən] *n* scozzese *m*
Scotswoman ['skɔtswumən] *n* scozzese *f*
Scottish ['skɔtɪʃ] *adj* scozzese; **the ~ National Party** il partito nazionalista scozzese; **the ~ Parliament** il Parlamento scozzese
scoundrel ['skaundrl] *n* farabutto(-a); (*child*) furfantello(-a)
scour ['skauəʳ] *vt* (*clean*) pulire strofinando; raschiare via; ripulire; (*search*) battere, perlustrare
scourer ['skauərəʳ] *n* (*pad*) paglietta; (*powder*) (detersivo) abrasivo
scourge [skə:dʒ] *n* flagello

scout [skaut] *n* (*Mil*) esploratore *m*; (*also*: **boy scout**) giovane esploratore, scout *m inv*
▸ **scout around** *vi* cercare in giro
scowl [skaul] *vi* accigliarsi, aggrottare le sopracciglia; **to ~ at** guardare torvo
scrabble ['skræbl] *vi* (*claw*): **to ~ (at)** graffiare, grattare; **to ~ about** *or* **around for sth** cercare affannosamente qc ■ *n*: **S~**® Scarabeo®
scraggy ['skrægɪ] *adj* scarno(-a), molto magro(-a)
scram [skræm] *vi* (*col*) filare via
scramble ['skræmbl] *n* arrampicata ■ *vi* inerpicarsi; **to ~ out** *etc* uscire *etc* in fretta; **to ~ for** azzuffarsi per; **to go scrambling** (*Sport*) fare il motocross
scrambled eggs *npl* uova *fpl* strapazzate
scrap [skræp] *n* pezzo, pezzetto; (*fight*) zuffa; (*also*: **scrap iron**) rottami *mpl* di ferro, ferraglia ■ *vt* demolire; (*fig*) scartare; **scraps** *npl* (*waste*) scarti *mpl*; **to sell sth for ~** vendere qc come ferro vecchio
scrapbook ['skræpbuk] *n* album *m inv* di ritagli
scrap dealer *n* commerciante *m* di ferraglia
scrape [skreɪp] *vt, vi* raschiare, grattare ■ *n*: **to get into a ~** cacciarsi in un guaio
▸ **scrape through** *vi* (*succeed*) farcela per un pelo, cavarsela ■ *vt fus* (*exam*) passare per miracolo, passare per il rotto della cuffia
scraper ['skreɪpə^r] *n* raschietto
scrap heap *n* mucchio di rottami; **to throw sth on the ~** (*fig*) mettere qc nel dimenticatoio
scrap merchant *n* (*Brit*) commerciante *m* di ferraglia
scrap metal *n* ferraglia
scrap paper *n* cartaccia
scrappy ['skræpɪ] *adj* frammentario(-a), sconnesso(-a)
scrap yard *n* deposito di rottami; (*for cars*) cimitero delle macchine
scratch [skrætʃ] *n* graffio ■ *cpd*: **~ team** squadra raccogliticcia ■ *vt* graffiare, rigare; (*Comput*) cancellare ■ *vi* grattare, graffiare; **to start from ~** cominciare *or* partire da zero; **to be up to ~** essere all'altezza
scratch pad *n* (US) notes *m inv*, blocchetto
scrawl [skrɔ:l] *n* scarabocchio ■ *vi* scarabocchiare
scrawny ['skrɔ:nɪ] *adj* scarno(-a), pelle e ossa *inv*
scream [skri:m] *n* grido, urlo ■ *vi* urlare, gridare; **to ~ at sb (to do sth)** gridare a qn (di fare qc); **it was a ~** (*fig, col*) era da crepar dal ridere; **he's a ~** (*fig, col*) è una sagoma, è uno spasso
scree [skri:] *n* ghiaione *m*
screech [skri:tʃ] *n* strido; (*of tyres, brakes*) stridore *m* ■ *vi* stridere
screen [skri:n] *n* schermo; (*fig*) muro, cortina, velo ■ *vt* schermare, fare schermo a; (*from the wind etc*) riparare; (*film*) proiettare; (*book*) adattare per lo schermo; (*candidates etc*) passare al vaglio; (*for illness*) sottoporre a controlli medici
screen editing [-ɛdɪtɪŋ] *n* (*Comput*) correzione *f* e modifica su schermo
screening ['skri:nɪŋ] *n* (*Med*) dépistage *m inv*; (*of film*) proiezione *f*; (*for security*) controlli *mpl* (di sicurezza)
screen memory *n* (*Comput*) memoria di schermo
screenplay ['skri:npleɪ] *n* sceneggiatura
screensaver *n* (*Comput*) screen saver *m inv*
screen test *n* provino (cinematografico)
screw [skru:] *n* vite *f*; (*propeller*) elica ■ *vt* avvitare; **to ~ sth to the wall** fissare qc al muro con viti
▸ **screw up** *vt* (*paper, material*) spiegazzare; (*col: ruin*) mandare a monte; **to ~ up one's face** fare una smorfia
screwdriver ['skru:draɪvə^r] *n* cacciavite *m*
screwed-up ['skru:d'ʌp] *adj* (*col*): **she's totally ~** è nel pallone
screwy ['skru:ɪ] *adj* (*col*) svitato(-a)
scribble ['skrɪbl] *n* scarabocchio ■ *vt* scribacchiare ■ *vi* scarabocchiare; **to ~ sth down** scribacchiare qc
scribe [skraɪb] *n* scriba *m*
script [skrɪpt] *n* (*Cine etc*) copione *m*; (*in exam*) elaborato *or* compito d'esame; (*writing*) scrittura
scripted ['skrɪptɪd] *adj* (*Radio, TV*) preparato(-a)
Scripture ['skrɪptʃə^r] *n* Sacre Scritture *fpl*
scriptwriter ['skrɪptraɪtə^r] *n* soggettista *m/f*
scroll [skrəul] *n* rotolo di carta ■ *vt* (*Comput*) scorrere
scroll bar *n* (*Comput*) barra di scorrimento
scrotum ['skrəutəm] *n* scroto
scrounge [skraundʒ] *vt* (*col*): **to ~ sth (off** *or* **from sb)** scroccare qc (a qn) ■ *vi*: **to ~ on sb** vivere alle spalle di qn
scrounger ['skraundʒə^r] *n* scroccone(-a)
scrub [skrʌb] *n* (*clean*) strofinata; (*land*) boscaglia ■ *vt* pulire strofinando; (*reject*) annullare
scrubbing brush ['skrʌbɪŋ-] *n* spazzolone *m*
scruff [skrʌf] *n*: **by the ~ of the neck** per la collottola
scruffy ['skrʌfɪ] *adj* sciatto(-a)
scrum ['skrʌm], **scrummage** ['skrʌmɪdʒ] *n* mischia

S

scruple ['skru:pl] *n* scrupolo; **to have no scruples about doing sth** non avere scrupoli a fare qc
scrupulous ['skru:pjuləs] *adj* scrupoloso(-a)
scrupulously ['skru:pjuləslı] *adv* scrupolosamente; **he tries to be ~ fair/honest** cerca di essere più imparziale/onesto che può
scrutinize ['skru:tınaız] *vt* scrutare, esaminare attentamente
scrutiny ['skru:tını] *n* esame *m* accurato; **under the ~ of sb** sotto la sorveglianza di qn
scuba ['sku:bə] *n* autorespiratore *m*
scuba diving *n* immersioni *fpl* subacquee
scuff [skʌf] *vt* (*shoes*) consumare strascicando
scuffle ['skʌfl] *n* baruffa, tafferuglio
scullery ['skʌlərı] *n* retrocucina *m or f*
sculptor ['skʌlptə^r] *n* scultore *m*
sculpture ['skʌlptʃə^r] *n* scultura
scum [skʌm] *n* schiuma; (*pej: people*) feccia
scupper ['skʌpə^r] *vt* (*Brit*) autoaffondare; (*fig*) far naufragare
scurrilous ['skʌrıləs] *adj* scurrile, volgare
scurry ['skʌrı] *vi* sgambare, affrettarsi
scurvy ['skə:vı] *n* scorbuto
scuttle ['skʌtl] *n* (*Naut*) portellino; (*also:* **coal scuttle**) secchio del carbone ■ *vt* (*ship*) autoaffondare ■ *vi* (*scamper*): **to ~ away, ~ off** darsela a gambe, scappare
scythe [saıð] *n* falce *f*
SD, S. Dak. *abbr* (US) = **South Dakota**
SDI *n abbr* (= *Strategic Defense Initiative*) S.D.I. *f*
SDLP *n abbr* (Brit Pol) = **Social Democratic and Labour Party**
sea [si:] *n* mare *m* ■ *cpd* marino(-a), del mare; (*ship, port*) marittimo(-a), di mare; **on the ~** (*boat*) in mare; (*town*) di mare; **to go by ~** andare per mare; **by** *or* **beside the ~** (*holiday*) al mare; (*village*) sul mare; **to look out to ~** guardare il mare; **(out) at ~** al largo; **heavy** *or* **rough ~(s)** mare grosso *or* agitato; **a ~ of faces** (*fig*) una marea di gente; **to be all at ~** (*fig*) non sapere che pesci pigliare
sea bed *n* fondo marino
sea bird *n* uccello di mare
seaboard ['si:bɔ:d] *n* costa
sea breeze *n* brezza di mare
seafarer ['si:fɛərə^r] *n* navigante *m*
seafaring ['si:fɛərıŋ] *adj* (*community*) marinaro(-a); (*life*) da marinaio
seafood ['si:fu:d] *n* frutti *mpl* di mare
sea front *n* lungomare *m*
seagoing ['si:gəuıŋ] *adj* (*ship*) d'alto mare
seagull ['si:gʌl] *n* gabbiano
seal [si:l] *n* (*animal*) foca; (*stamp*) sigillo; (*impression*) impronta del sigillo ■ *vt* sigillare; (*decide: sb's fate*) segnare; (*: bargain*) concludere; **~ of approval** beneplacito
▸**seal off** *vt* (*close*) sigillare; (*forbid entry to*) bloccare l'accesso a
sea level *n* livello del mare
sealing wax ['si:lıŋ-] *n* ceralacca
sea lion *n* leone *m* marino
sealskin ['si:lskın] *n* pelle *f* di foca
seam [si:m] *n* cucitura; (*of coal*) filone *m*; **the hall was bursting at the seams** l'aula era piena zeppa
seaman ['si:mən] *n* marinaio
seamanship ['si:mənʃıp] *n* tecnica di navigazione
seamless ['si:mlıs] *adj* senza cucitura
seamy ['si:mı] *adj* malfamato(-a); squallido(-a)
seance ['seıɔns] *n* seduta spiritica
seaplane ['si:pleın] *n* idrovolante *m*
seaport ['si:pɔ:t] *n* porto di mare
search [sə:tʃ] *n* (*for person, thing*) ricerca; (*of drawer, pockets*) esame *m* accurato; (*Law: at sb's home*) perquisizione *f* ■ *vt* perlustrare, frugare; (*scan, examine*) esaminare minuziosamente; (*Comput*) ricercare ■ *vi*: **to ~ for** ricercare; **in ~ of** alla ricerca di; **"~ and replace"** (*Comput*) "ricercare e sostituire"
▸**search through** *vt fus* frugare
search engine *n* (*Comput*) motore *m* di ricerca
searcher ['sə:tʃə^r] *n* chi cerca
searching ['sə:tʃıŋ] *adj* minuzioso(-a); penetrante; (*question*) pressante
searchlight ['sə:tʃlaıt] *n* proiettore *m*
search party *n* squadra di soccorso
search warrant *n* mandato di perquisizione
searing ['sıərıŋ] *adj* (*heat*) rovente; (*pain*) acuto(-a)
seashore ['si:ʃɔ:^r] *n* spiaggia; **on the ~** sulla riva del mare
seasick ['si:sık] *adj* che soffre il mal di mare; **to be ~** avere il mal di mare
seaside ['si:saıd] *n* spiaggia; **to go to the ~** andare al mare
seaside resort *n* stazione *f* balneare
season ['si:zn] *n* stagione *f* ■ *vt* condire, insaporire; **to be in/out of ~** essere di/fuori stagione; **the busy ~** (*for shops*) il periodo di punta; (*for hotels etc*) l'alta stagione; **the open ~** (*Hunting*) la stagione della caccia
seasonal ['si:zənl] *adj* stagionale
seasoned ['si:znd] *adj* (*wood*) stagionato(-a); (*fig: worker, actor, troops*) con esperienza; **a ~ campaigner** un veterano
seasoning ['si:znıŋ] *n* condimento
season ticket *n* abbonamento
seat [si:t] *n* sedile *m*; (*in bus, train: place*) posto; (*Parliament*) seggio; (*centre: of government etc, of infection*) sede *f*; (*buttocks*) didietro; (*of trousers*) fondo ■ *vt* far sedere; (*have room for*) avere *or* essere fornito(-a) di posti a sedere per; **are**

there any seats left? ci sono posti?; **to take one's ~** prendere posto; **to be seated** essere seduto(-a); **please be seated** accomodatevi per favore
seat belt *n* cintura di sicurezza
seating arrangements ['si:tɪŋ-] *npl* sistemazione *f or* disposizione *f* dei posti
seating capacity *n* posti *mpl* a sedere
SEATO ['si:təu] *n abbr* (= *Southeast Asia Treaty Organization*) SEATO *f*
sea water *n* acqua di mare
seaweed ['si:wi:d] *n* alghe *fpl*
seaworthy ['si:wə:ðɪ] *adj* atto(-a) alla navigazione
SEC *n abbr* (*US*: = *Securities and Exchange Commission*) *commissione di controllo sulle operazioni in Borsa*
sec. *abbr* = **second'**
secateurs [sɛkə'tə:z] *npl* forbici *fpl* per potare
secede [sɪ'si:d] *vi*: **to ~ (from)** ritirarsi (da)
secluded [sɪ'klu:dɪd] *adj* isolato(-a), appartato(-a)
seclusion [sɪ'klu:ʒən] *n* isolamento
second' ['sɛkənd] *num* secondo(-a) ▪ *adv* (*in race etc*) al secondo posto; (*Rail*) in seconda ▪ *n* (*unit of time*) secondo; (*in series, position*) secondo(-a); (*Brit Scol*) *laurea con punteggio discreto*; (*Aut*: *also*: **second gear**) seconda; (*Comm*: *imperfect*) scarto ▪ *vt* (*motion*) appoggiare; **Charles the S~** Carlo Secondo; **just a ~!** un attimo!; **~ floor** (*Brit*) secondo piano; (*US*) primo piano; **to ask for a ~ opinion** (*Med*) chiedere un altro *or* ulteriore parere; **to have ~ thoughts (about doing sth)** avere dei ripensamenti (quanto a fare qc); **on ~ thoughts** *or* (*US*) **thought** a ripensarci, ripensandoci bene
second² [sɪ'kɔnd] *vt* (*employee*) distaccare
secondary ['sɛkəndərɪ] *adj* secondario(-a)
secondary school *n* scuola secondaria; *vedi nota*

SECONDARY SCHOOL

In Gran Bretagna la *secondary school* è la scuola frequentata dai ragazzi dagli 11 ai 18 anni. Nel paese è obbligatorio andare a scuola fino a 16 anni; *vedi anche* "primary school".

second-best [sɛkənd'bɛst] *n* ripiego; **as a ~** in mancanza di meglio
second-class [sɛkənd'klɑ:s] *adj* di seconda classe ▪ *adv*: **to travel ~** viaggiare in seconda (classe); **to send sth ~** spedire qc per posta ordinaria; **~ citizen** cittadino di second'ordine
second cousin *n* cugino di secondo grado
seconder ['sɛkəndə^r] *n* sostenitore(-trice)
second-guess ['sɛkənd'gɛs] *vt* (*predict*) anticipare; (*after the event*) giudicare col senno di poi
second hand *n* (*on clock*) lancetta dei secondi
second-hand [sɛkənd'hænd] *adj* di seconda mano, usato(-a) ▪ *adv* (*buy*) di seconda mano; **to hear sth ~** venire a sapere qc da terze persone
second-in-command ['sɛkəndɪnkə'mɑ:nd] *n* (*Mil*) comandante *m* in seconda; (*Admin*) aggiunto
secondly ['sɛkəndlɪ] *adv* in secondo luogo
secondment [sɪ'kɔndmənt] *n* (*Brit*) distaccamento
second-rate [sɛkənd'reɪt] *adj* scadente
Second World War *n*: **the ~** la seconda guerra mondiale
secrecy ['si:krəsɪ] *n* segretezza
secret ['si:krɪt] *adj* segreto(-a) ▪ *n* segreto; **in ~** in segreto, segretamente; **to keep sth ~ (from sb)** tenere qc segreto (a qn), tenere qc nascosto (a qn); **keep it ~** che rimanga un segreto; **to make no ~ of sth** non far mistero di qc
secret agent *n* agente *m* segreto
secretarial [sɛkrɪ'tɛərɪəl] *adj* (*work*) da segretario(-a); (*college, course*) di segretariato
secretariat [sɛkrɪ'tɛərɪət] *n* segretariato
secretary ['sɛkrətrɪ] *n* segretario(-a); **S~ of State** (*US Pol*) ≈ Ministro degli Esteri; **S~ of State (for)** (*Brit*: *Pol*) ministro (di)
secretary-general ['sɛkrətrɪ'dʒɛnərl] *n* segretario generale
secrete [sɪ'kri:t] *vt* (*Med, Anat, Biol*) secernere; (*hide*) nascondere
secretion [sɪ'kri:ʃən] *n* secrezione *f*
secretive ['si:krətɪv] *adj* riservato(-a)
secretly ['si:krɪtlɪ] *adv* in segreto, segretamente
secret police *n* polizia segreta
secret service *n* servizi *mpl* segreti
sect [sɛkt] *n* setta
sectarian [sɛk'tɛərɪən] *adj* settario(-a)
section ['sɛkʃən] *n* sezione *f*; (*of document*) articolo ▪ *vt* sezionare, dividere in sezioni; **the business ~** (*Press*) la pagina economica
sector ['sɛktə^r] *n* settore *m*
secular ['sɛkjulə^r] *adj* secolare
secure [sɪ'kjuə^r] *adj* (*free from anxiety*) sicuro(-a); (*firmly fixed*) assicurato(-a), ben fermato(-a); (*in safe place*) al sicuro ▪ *vt* (*fix*) fissare, assicurare; (*get*) ottenere, assicurarsi; (*Comm*: *loan*) garantire; **to make sth ~** fissare bene qc; **to ~ sth for sb** procurare qc per *or* a qn

S

secured creditor [sɪ'kjuəd-] *n* creditore *m* privilegiato
security [sɪ'kjuərɪtɪ] *n* sicurezza; (*for loan*) garanzia; **securities** *npl* (*Stock Exchange*) titoli *mpl*; **to increase/tighten ~** aumentare/intensificare la sorveglianza; **~ of tenure** garanzia del posto di lavoro, garanzia di titolo *or* di godimento
Security Council *n*: **the ~** il Consiglio di Sicurezza
security forces *npl* forze *fpl* dell'ordine
security guard *n* guardia giurata
security risk *n* rischio per la sicurezza
secy. *abbr* = **secretary**
sedan [sə'dæn] *n* (*US Aut*) berlina
sedate [sɪ'deɪt] *adj* posato(-a); calmo(-a) ■ *vt* calmare
sedation [sɪ'deɪʃən] *n* (*Med*): **to be under ~** essere sotto l'azione di sedativi
sedative ['sɛdɪtɪv] *n* sedativo, calmante *m*
sedentary ['sɛdntrɪ] *adj* sedentario(-a)
sediment ['sɛdɪmənt] *n* sedimento
sedition [sɪ'dɪʃən] *n* sedizione *f*
seduce [sɪ'dju:s] *vt* sedurre
seduction [sɪ'dʌkʃən] *n* seduzione *f*
seductive [sɪ'dʌktɪv] *adj* seducente
see [si:] *vb* (*pt* **saw**, *pp* **seen**) [sɔ:, si:n] *vt* vedere; (*accompany*): **to ~ sb to the door** accompagnare qn alla porta ■ *vi* vedere; (*understand*) capire ■ *n* sede *f* vescovile; **to ~ that** (*ensure*) badare che + *sub*, fare in modo che + *sub*; **to go and ~ sb** andare a trovare qn; **~ you soon/later/tomorrow!** a presto/più tardi/domani!; **as far as I can ~** da quanto posso vedere; **there was nobody to be seen** non c'era anima viva; **let me ~** (*show me*) fammi vedere; (*let me think*) vediamo (un po'); **~ for yourself** vai a vedere con i tuoi occhi; **I don't know what she sees in him** non so che cosa ci trovi in lui
▸ **see about** *vt fus* (*deal with*) occuparsi di
▸ **see off** *vt* salutare alla partenza
▸ **see through** *vt* portare a termine ■ *vt fus* non lasciarsi ingannare da
▸ **see to** *vt fus* occuparsi di
seed [si:d] *n* seme *m*; (*fig*) germe *m*; (*Tennis*) testa di serie; **to go to ~** fare seme; (*fig*) scadere
seedless ['si:dlɪs] *adj* senza semi
seedling ['si:dlɪŋ] *n* piantina di semenzaio
seedy ['si:dɪ] *adj* (*shabby: person*) sciatto(-a); (*: place*) cadente
seeing ['si:ɪŋ] *conj*: **~ (that)** visto che
seek [si:k] (*pt*, **sought**) *vt* cercare; **to ~ advice/help from sb** chiedere consiglio/aiuto a qn
▸ **seek out** *vt* (*person*) andare a cercare
seem [si:m] *vi* sembrare, parere; **there seems to be ...** sembra che ci sia ...; **it seems (that) ...** sembra *or* pare che ... + *sub*; **what seems to be the trouble?** cosa c'è che non va?
seemingly ['si:mɪŋlɪ] *adv* apparentemente
seen [si:n] *pp of* **see**
seep [si:p] *vi* filtrare, trapelare
seer [sɪə^r] *n* profeta(-essa), veggente *m/f*
seersucker ['sɪəsʌkə^r] *n* cotone *m* indiano
seesaw ['si:sɔ:] *n* altalena a bilico
seethe [si:ð] *vi* ribollire; **to ~ with anger** fremere di rabbia
see-through ['si:θru:] *adj* trasparente
segment ['sɛgmənt] *n* segmento
segregate ['sɛgrɪgeɪt] *vt* segregare, isolare
segregation [sɛgrɪ'geɪʃən] *n* segregazione *f*
Seine [seɪn] *n* Senna
seismic ['saɪzmɪk] *adj* sismico(-a)
seize [si:z] *vt* (*grasp*) afferrare; (*take possession of*) impadronirsi di; (*Law*) sequestrare
▸ **seize up** *vi* (*Tech*) grippare
▸ **seize (up)on** *vt fus* ricorrere a
seizure ['si:ʒə^r] *n* (*Med*) attacco; (*Law*) confisca, sequestro
seldom ['sɛldəm] *adv* raramente
select [sɪ'lɛkt] *adj* scelto(-a); (*hotel, restaurant*) chic *inv*; (*club*) esclusivo(-a) ■ *vt* scegliere, selezionare; **a ~ few** pochi eletti *mpl*
selection [sɪ'lɛkʃən] *n* selezione *f*, scelta
selection committee *n* comitato di selezione
selective [sɪ'lɛktɪv] *adj* selettivo(-a)
selector [sɪ'lɛktə^r] *n* (*person*) selezionatore(-trice); (*Tech*) selettore *m*
self (*pl* **selves**) [sɛlf, sɛlvz] *n*: **the ~** l'io *m* ■ *prefix* auto...
self-addressed ['sɛlfə'drɛst] *adj*: **~ envelope** busta col proprio nome e indirizzo
self-adhesive [sɛlfəd'hi:zɪv] *adj* autoadesivo(-a)
self-assertive [sɛlfə'sə:tɪv] *adj* autoritario(-a)
self-assurance [sɛlfə'ʃuərəns] *n* sicurezza di sé
self-assured [sɛlfə'ʃuəd] *adj* sicuro(-a) di sé
self-catering [sɛlf'keɪtərɪŋ] *adj* (*Brit*) in cui ci si cucina da sé; **~ apartment** appartamento (per le vacanze)
self-centred, (*US*) **self-centered** [sɛlf'sɛntəd] *adj* egocentrico(-a)
self-cleaning [sɛlf'kli:nɪŋ] *adj* autopulente
self-confessed [sɛlfkən'fɛst] *adj* (*alcoholic etc*) dichiarato(-a)
self-confidence [sɛlf'kɔnfɪdəns] *n* sicurezza di sé
self-conscious [sɛlf'kɔnʃəs] *adj* timido(-a)

self-contained [sɛlfkən'teɪnd] *adj* (*Brit: flat*) indipendente
self-control [sɛlfkən'trəul] *n* autocontrollo
self-defeating [sɛlfdɪ'fi:tɪŋ] *adj* futile
self-defence, (*US*) **self-defense** [sɛlfdɪ'fɛns] *n* autodifesa; (*Law*) legittima difesa
self-discipline [sɛlf'dɪsɪplɪn] *n* autodisciplina
self-employed [sɛlfɪm'plɔɪd] *adj* che lavora in proprio
self-esteem [sɛlfɪ'sti:m] *n* amor proprio *m*
self-evident [sɛlf'ɛvɪdənt] *adj* evidente
self-explanatory [sɛlfɪk'splænətərɪ] *adj* ovvio(-a)
self-governing [sɛlf'gʌvənɪŋ] *adj* autonomo(-a)
self-help ['sɛlf'hɛlp] *n* iniziativa individuale
self-importance [sɛlfim'pɔ:tns] *n* sufficienza
self-indulgent [sɛlfɪn'dʌldʒənt] *adj* indulgente verso se stesso(-a)
self-inflicted [sɛlfɪn'flɪktɪd] *adj* autoinflitto(-a)
self-interest [sɛlf'ɪntrɪst] *n* interesse *m* personale
selfish ['sɛlfɪʃ] *adj* egoista
selfishly ['sɛlfɪʃlɪ] *adv* egoisticamente
selfishness ['sɛlfɪʃnɪs] *n* egoismo
selfless ['sɛlflɪs] *adj* altruista
selflessly ['sɛlflɪslɪ] *adv* altruisticamente
selflessness ['sɛlflɪsnɪs] *n* altruismo
self-made man ['sɛlfmeɪd-] *n* self-made man *m inv*, uomo che si è fatto da sé
self-pity [sɛlf'pɪtɪ] *n* autocommiserazione *f*
self-portrait [sɛlf'pɔ:trɪt] *n* autoritratto
self-possessed [sɛlfpə'zɛst] *adj* controllato(-a)
self-preservation ['sɛlfprɛzə'veɪʃən] *n* istinto di conservazione
self-raising [sɛlf'reɪzɪŋ], (*US*) **self-rising** [sɛlf'raɪzɪŋ] *adj*: **~ flour** miscela di farina e lievito
self-reliant [sɛlfrɪ'laɪənt] *adj* indipendente
self-respect [sɛlfrɪs'pɛkt] *n* rispetto di sé, amor proprio
self-respecting [sɛlfrɪs'pɛktɪŋ] *adj* che ha rispetto di sé
self-righteous [sɛlf'raɪtʃəs] *adj* soddisfatto(-a) di sé
self-rising [sɛlf'raɪzɪŋ] *adj* (*US*) = **self-raising**
self-sacrifice [sɛlf'sækrɪfaɪs] *n* abnegazione *f*
self-same ['sɛlfseɪm] *adj* stesso(-a)
self-satisfied [sɛlf'sætɪsfaɪd] *adj* compiaciuto(-a) di sé
self-sealing [sɛlf'si:lɪŋ] *adj* autosigillante
self-service [sɛlf'sə:vɪs] *n* autoservizio, self-service *m*
self-styled [sɛlf'staɪld] *adj* sedicente
self-sufficient [sɛlfsə'fɪʃənt] *adj* autosufficiente
self-supporting [sɛlfsə'pɔ:tɪŋ] *adj* economicamente indipendente
self-taught [sɛlf'tɔ:t] *adj* autodidatta
self-test ['sɛlftɛst] *n* (*Comput*) autoverifica
sell (*pt, pp* **sold**) [sɛl, səuld] *vt* vendere ■ *vi* vendersi; **to ~ at** *or* **for 100 euros** essere in vendita a 100 euro; **to ~ sb an idea** (*fig*) far accettare un'idea a qn
▸ **sell off** *vt* svendere, liquidare
▸ **sell out** *vi*: **to ~ out (to sb/sth)** (*Comm*) vendere (tutto) (a qn/qc) ■ *vt* esaurire; **the tickets are all sold out** i biglietti sono esauriti
▸ **sell up** *vi* vendere (tutto)
sell-by date ['sɛlbaɪ-] *n* scadenza
seller ['sɛlə[r]] *n* venditore(-trice); **~'s market** mercato favorevole ai venditori
selling price ['sɛlɪŋ-] *n* prezzo di vendita
Sellotape® ['sɛləuteɪp] *n* (*Brit*) nastro adesivo, scotch® *m*
sellout ['sɛlaut] *n* (*betrayal*) tradimento; (*of tickets*): **it was a ~** registrò un tutto esaurito
selves [sɛlvz] *npl of* **self**
semantic [sɪ'mæntɪk] *adj* semantico(-a)
semantics [sɪ'mæntɪks] *n* semantica
semaphore ['sɛməfɔ:[r]] *n* segnali *mpl* con bandiere; (*Rail*) semaforo
semblance ['sɛmbləns] *n* parvenza, apparenza
semen ['si:mən] *n* sperma *m*
semester [sɪ'mɛstə[r]] *n* (*US*) semestre *m*
semi... ['sɛmɪ] *prefix* semi... ■ *n*: **semi** = **semidetached (house)**
semi-breve ['sɛmɪbri:v] *n* (*Brit*) semibreve *f*
semicircle ['sɛmɪsə:kl] *n* semicerchio
semicircular ['sɛmɪ'sə:kjulə[r]] *adj* semicircolare
semicolon [sɛmɪ'kəulən] *n* punto e virgola
semiconductor [sɛmɪkən'dʌktə[r]] *n* semiconduttore *m*
semiconscious [sɛmɪ'kɔnʃəs] *adj* parzialmente cosciente
semidetached [sɛmɪdɪ'tætʃt], **semidetached house** [sɛmɪdɪ'tætʃt-] *n* (*Brit*) casa gemella
semifinal [sɛmɪ'faɪnl] *n* semifinale *f*
seminar ['sɛmɪnɑ:[r]] *n* seminario
seminary ['sɛmɪnərɪ] *n* (*Rel: for priests*) seminario
semiprecious [sɛmɪ'prɛʃəs] *adj* semiprezioso(-a)
semiquaver ['sɛmɪkweɪvə[r]] *n* (*Brit*) semicroma
semiskilled ['sɛmɪ'skɪld] *adj*: **~ worker** operaio(-a) non specializzato(-a)

S

semi-skimmed ['sɛmɪ'skɪmd] *adj* parzialmente scremato(-a)
semitone ['sɛmɪtəun] *n* (*Mus*) semitono
semolina [sɛmə'li:nə] *n* semolino
Sen., sen. *abbr* = **senator; senior**
senate ['sɛnɪt] *n* senato
senator ['sɛnɪtə^r] *n* senatore(-trice)
send [sɛnd] (*pt, pp* **sent**) *vt* mandare; **to ~ by post** *or* (*US*) **mail** spedire per posta; **to ~ sb for sth** mandare qn a prendere qc; **to ~ word that ...** mandare a dire che ...; **she sends (you) her love** ti saluta affettuosamente; **to ~ sb to Coventry** (*Brit*) dare l'ostracismo a qn; **to ~ sb to sleep/into fits of laughter** far addormentare/scoppiare dal ridere qn; **to ~ sth flying** far volare via qc
▸ **send away** *vt* (*letter, goods*) spedire; (*person*) mandare via
▸ **send away for** *vt fus* richiedere per posta, farsi spedire
▸ **send back** *vt* rimandare
▸ **send for** *vt fus* mandare a chiamare, far venire; (*by post*) ordinare per posta
▸ **send in** *vt* (*report, application, resignation*) presentare
▸ **send off** *vt* (*goods*) spedire; (*Brit Sport: player*) espellere
▸ **send on** *vt* (*Brit: letter*) inoltrare; (*luggage etc: in advance*) spedire in anticipo
▸ **send out** *vt* (*invitation*) diramare; (*emit: light, heat*) mandare, emanare; (*: signals*) emettere
▸ **send round** *vt* (*letter, document etc*) far circolare
▸ **send up** *vt* (*person, price*) far salire; (*Brit: parody*) mettere in ridicolo
sender ['sɛndə^r] *n* mittente *m/f*
send-off ['sɛndɔf] *n*: **to give sb a good ~** festeggiare la partenza di qn
Senegal [sɛnɪ'gɔ:l] *n* Senegal *m*
Senegalese [sɛnɪgə'li:z] *adj, n* senegalese *m/f*
senile ['si:naɪl] *adj* senile
senility [sɪ'nɪlɪtɪ] *n* senilità *f*
senior ['si:nɪə^r] *adj* (*older*) più vecchio(-a); (*of higher rank*) di grado più elevato ■ *n* persona più anziana; (*in service*) persona con maggiore anzianità; **P. Jones ~** P. Jones senior, P. Jones padre
senior citizen *n* anziano(-a)
senior high school *n* (*US*) ≈ liceo
seniority [si:nɪ'ɔrɪtɪ] *n* anzianità; (*in rank*) superiorità
sensation [sɛn'seɪʃən] *n* sensazione *f*; **to create a ~** fare scalpore
sensational [sɛn'seɪʃənl] *adj* sensazionale; (*marvellous*) eccezionale
sense [sɛns] *n* senso; (*feeling*) sensazione *f*, senso; (*meaning*) senso, significato; (*wisdom*) buonsenso ■ *vt* sentire, percepire; **senses** *npl* (*sanity*) ragione *f*; **it makes ~** ha senso; **there is no ~ in (doing) that** non ha senso (farlo); **~ of humour** (senso dell')umorismo; **to come to one's senses** (*regain consciousness*) riprendere i sensi; (*become reasonable*) tornare in sé; **to take leave of one's senses** perdere il lume *or* l'uso della ragione
senseless ['sɛnslɪs] *adj* sciocco(-a); (*unconscious*) privo(-a) di sensi
sensibilities [sɛnsɪ'bɪlɪtɪz] *npl* sensibilità *fsg*
sensible ['sɛnsɪbl] *adj* sensato(-a), ragionevole
sensitive ['sɛnsɪtɪv] *adj*: **~ (to)** sensibile (a); **he is very ~ about it** è un tasto che è meglio non toccare con lui
sensitivity [sɛnsɪ'tɪvɪtɪ] *n* sensibilità
sensual ['sɛnsjuəl] *adj* sensuale
sensuous ['sɛnsjuəs] *adj* sensuale
sent [sɛnt] *pt, pp of* **send**
sentence ['sɛntns] *n* (*Ling*) frase *f*; (*Law: judgement*) sentenza; (*: punishment*) condanna ■ *vt*: **to ~ sb to death/to 5 years** condannare qn a morte/a 5 anni; **to pass ~ on sb** condannare qn
sentiment ['sɛntɪmənt] *n* sentimento; (*opinion*) opinione *f*
sentimental [sɛntɪ'mɛntl] *adj* sentimentale
sentimentality [sɛntɪmɛn'tælɪtɪ] *n* sentimentalità, sentimentalismo
sentry ['sɛntrɪ] *n* sentinella
sentry duty *n*: **to be on ~** essere di sentinella
Seoul [səul] *n* Seul *f*
separable ['sɛprəbl] *adj* separabile
separate *adj* ['sɛprɪt] separato(-a) ■ *vb* ['sɛpəreɪt] *vt* separare ■ *vi* separarsi; **~ from** separato da; **under ~ cover** (*Comm*) in plico a parte; **to ~ into** dividere in; *see also* **separates**
separately ['sɛprɪtlɪ] *adv* separatamente
separates ['sɛprɪts] *npl* (*clothes*) coordinati *mpl*
separation [sɛpə'reɪʃən] *n* separazione *f*
Sept. *abbr* (= *September*) sett., set.
September [sɛp'tɛmbə^r] *n* settembre *m*; *see also* **July**
septic ['sɛptɪk] *adj* settico(-a); (*wound*) infettato(-a); **to go ~** infettarsi
septicaemia, (*US*) **septicemia** [sɛptɪ'si:mɪə] *n* setticemia
septic tank *n* fossa settica
sequel ['si:kwl] *n* conseguenza; (*of story*) seguito
sequence ['si:kwəns] *n* (*series*) serie *f inv*; (*order*) ordine *m*; **in ~** in ordine, di seguito; **~ of tenses** concordanza dei tempi

sequential [sɪ'kwɛnʃəl] *adj*: **~ access** (*Comput*) accesso sequenziale
sequin ['si:kwɪn] *n* lustrino, paillette *f inv*
Serb [sə:b] *adj, n* = **Serbian**
Serbia ['sə:bɪə] *n* Serbia
Serbian ['sə:bɪən] *adj* serbo(-a) ■ *n* serbo(-a); (*Ling*) serbo
Serbo-Croat ['sə:bəu'krəuæt] *n* (*Ling*) serbocroato
serenade [sɛrə'neɪd] *n* serenata ■ *vt* fare la serenata a
serene [sɪ'ri:n] *adj* sereno(-a), calmo(-a)
serenity [sɪ'rɛnɪtɪ] *n* serenità, tranquillità
sergeant ['sɑ:dʒənt] *n* sergente *m*; (*Police*) brigadiere *m*
sergeant major *n* maresciallo
serial ['sɪərɪəl] *n* (*Press*) romanzo a puntate; (*Radio, TV*) trasmissione *f* a puntate ■ *cpd* (*number*) di serie; (*Comput*) seriale
serialize ['sɪərɪəlaɪz] *vt* pubblicare a puntate; trasmettere a puntate
serial killer *n* serial killer *m inv*
serial number *n* numero di serie
series ['sɪəri:z] *n* (*pl inv*) serie *f inv*; (*Publishing*) collana
serious ['sɪərɪəs] *adj* serio(-a), grave; **are you ~ (about it)?** parla sul serio?
seriously ['sɪərɪəslɪ] *adv* seriamente; **he's ~ rich** (*col: extremely*) ha un casino di soldi; **to take sth/sb ~** prendere qc/qn sul serio
seriousness ['sɪərɪəsnɪs] *n* serietà, gravità
sermon ['sə:mən] *n* sermone *m*
serrated [sɪ'reɪtɪd] *adj* seghettato(-a)
serum ['sɪərəm] *n* siero
servant ['sə:vənt] *n* domestico(-a)
serve [sə:v] *vt* (*employer etc*) servire, essere a servizio di; (*purpose*) servire a; (*customer, food, meal*) servire; (*apprenticeship*) fare; (*prison term*) scontare ■ *vi* (*also Tennis*) servire; (*soldier etc*) prestare servizio; (*be useful*): **to ~ as/for/to do** servire da/per/per fare ■ *n* (*Tennis*) servizio; **are you being served?** la stanno servendo?; **to ~ on a committee/jury** far parte di un comitato/una giuria; **it serves him right** ben gli sta, se l'è meritata; **it serves my purpose** fa al caso mio, serve al mio scopo
▸ **serve out, serve up** *vt* (*food*) servire
server ['sə:vəʳ] *n* (*Comput*) server *m inv*
service ['sə:vɪs] *n* servizio; (*Aut: maintenance*) revisione *f*; (*Rel*) funzione *f* ■ *vt* (*car, washing machine*) revisionare; **the Services** *npl* le forze armate; **to be of ~ to sb, to do sb a ~** essere d'aiuto a qn; **to put one's car in for (a) ~** portare la macchina in officina per una revisione; **dinner ~** servizio da tavola
serviceable ['sə:vɪsəbl] *adj* pratico(-a), utile; (*usable, working*) usabile
service area *n* (*on motorway*) area di servizio
service charge *n* (*Brit*) servizio
service industries *npl* settore *m* terziario
serviceman ['sə:vɪsmən] *n* militare *m*
service provider *n* (*Comput*) provider *m inv*
service station *n* stazione *f* di servizio
serviette [sə:vɪ'ɛt] *n* (*Brit*) tovagliolo
servile ['sə:vaɪl] *adj* servile
session ['sɛʃən] *n* (*sitting*) seduta, sessione *f*; (*Scol*) anno scolastico (*or* accademico); **to be in ~** essere in seduta
session musician *n* musicista *m/f* di studio
set [sɛt] *n* serie *f inv*; (*Radio, TV*) apparecchio; (*Tennis*) set *m inv*; (*group of people*) mondo, ambiente *m*; (*Cine*) scenario; (*Theat: stage*) scene *fpl*; (*: scenery*) scenario; (*Math*) insieme *m*; (*Hairdressing*) messa in piega ■ *adj* (*fixed*) stabilito(-a), determinato(-a); (*ready*) pronto(-a) ■ *vb* (*pt, pp* **~**) *vt* (*place*) posare, mettere; (*fix*) fissare; (*assign: task, homework*) dare, assegnare; (*adjust*) regolare; (*decide: rules etc*) stabilire, fissare; (*Typ*) comporre ■ *vi* (*sun*) tramontare; (*jam, jelly*) rapprendersi; (*concrete*) fare presa; **to be ~ on doing** essere deciso a fare; **to be all ~ to do sth** essere pronto fare qc; **to be (dead) ~ against** essere completamente contrario a; **~ in one's ways** abitudinario; **a novel ~ in Rome** un romanzo ambientato a Roma; **to ~ to music** mettere in musica; **to ~ on fire** dare fuoco a; **to ~ free** liberare; **to ~ sth going** mettere in moto qc; **to ~ sail** prendere il mare; **a ~ phrase** una frase fatta; **a ~ of false teeth** una dentiera; **a ~ of dining-room furniture** una camera da pranzo
▸ **set about** *vt fus* (*task*) intraprendere, mettersi a; **to ~ about doing sth** mettersi a fare qc
▸ **set aside** *vt* mettere da parte
▸ **set back** *vt* (*progress*) ritardare; **to ~ back (by)** (*in time*) mettere indietro (di); **a house ~ back from the road** una casa a una certa distanza dalla strada
▸ **set in** *vi* (*infection*) svilupparsi; (*complications*) intervenire; **the rain has ~ in for the day** ormai pioverà tutto il giorno
▸ **set off** *vi* partire ■ *vt* (*bomb*) far scoppiare; (*cause to start*) mettere in moto; (*show up well*) dare risalto a
▸ **set out** *vi* partire; (*aim*): **to ~ out to do** proporsi di fare ■ *vt* (*arrange*) disporre; (*state*) esporre, presentare
▸ **set up** *vt* (*organization*) fondare, costituire; (*record*) stabilire; (*monument*) innalzare
setback ['sɛtbæk] *n* (*hitch*) contrattempo, inconveniente *m*; (*in health*) ricaduta
set menu *n* menù *m inv* fisso

S

set square *n* squadra
settee [sɛ'ti:] *n* divano, sofà *m inv*
setting ['sɛtɪŋ] *n* ambiente *m*; (*scenery*) sfondo; (*of jewel*) montatura
setting lotion *n* fissatore *m*
settle ['sɛtl] *vt* (*argument, matter*) appianare; (*problem*) risolvere; (*pay: bill, account*) regolare, saldare; (*Med: calm*) calmare; (*colonize: land*) colonizzare ■ *vi* (*bird, dust etc*) posarsi; (*sediment*) depositarsi; (*also:* **settle down**) sistemarsi, stabilirsi; (*become calmer*) calmarsi; **to ~ to sth** applicarsi a qc; **to ~ for sth** accontentarsi di qc; **to ~ on sth** decidersi per qc; **that's settled then** allora è deciso; **to ~ one's stomach** calmare il mal di stomaco
▸ **settle in** *vi* sistemarsi
▸ **settle up** *vi*: **to ~ up with sb** regolare i conti con qn
settlement ['sɛtlmənt] *n* (*payment*) pagamento, saldo; (*agreement*) accordo; (*colony*) colonia; (*village etc*) villaggio, comunità *f inv*; **in ~ of our account** (*Comm*) a saldo del nostro conto
settler ['sɛtləʳ] *n* colonizzatore(-trice)
setup ['sɛtʌp] *n* (*arrangement*) sistemazione *f*; (*situation*) situazione *f*; (*Comput*) setup *m inv*
seven ['sɛvn] *num* sette
seventeen [sɛvn'ti:n] *num* diciassette
seventh ['sɛvnθ] *num* settimo(-a)
seventy ['sɛvntɪ] *num* settanta
sever ['sɛvəʳ] *vt* recidere, tagliare; (*relations*) troncare
several ['sɛvərl] *adj, pron* alcuni(-e), diversi(-e); **~ of us** alcuni di noi; **~ times** diverse volte
severance ['sɛvərəns] *n* (*of relations*) rottura
severance pay *n* indennità di licenziamento
severe [sɪ'vɪəʳ] *adj* severo(-a); (*serious*) serio(-a), grave; (*hard*) duro(-a); (*plain*) semplice, sobrio(-a)
severely [sɪ'vɪəlɪ] *adv* (*gen*) severamente; (*wounded, ill*) gravemente
severity [sɪ'vɛrɪtɪ] *n* severità; gravità; (*of weather*) rigore *m*
sew (*pt* **sewed**, *pp* **sewn**) [səu, səud, səun] *vt, vi* cucire
▸ **sew up** *vt* ricucire; **it is all sewn up** (*fig*) è tutto apposto
sewage ['su:ɪdʒ] *n* acque *fpl* di scolo
sewage works *n* stabilimento per la depurazione dei liquami
sewer ['su:əʳ] *n* fogna
sewing ['səuɪŋ] *n* cucito
sewing machine *n* macchina da cucire
sewn [səun] *pp of* **sew**
sex [sɛks] *n* sesso; **to have ~ with** avere rapporti sessuali con
sex act *n* atto sessuale
sex appeal *n* sex appeal *m inv*
sex education *n* educazione *f* sessuale
sexism ['sɛksɪzəm] *n* sessismo
sexist ['sɛksɪst] *adj* sessista
sex life *n* vita sessuale
sex object *n* oggetto sessuale; **to be treated like a ~** (*woman*) essere trattata da donna oggetto
sextet [sɛks'tɛt] *n* sestetto
sexual ['sɛksjuəl] *adj* sessuale; **~ assault** violenza carnale; **~ harassment** molestie *fpl* sessuali; **~ intercourse** rapporti *mpl* sessuali
sexy ['sɛksɪ] *adj* provocante, sexy *inv*
Seychelles [seɪ'ʃɛlz] *npl*: **the ~** le Seicelle
SF *n abbr* = **science fiction**
SG *n abbr* (*US*) = **Surgeon General**
Sgt. *abbr* (= *sergeant*) serg.
shabbiness ['ʃæbɪnɪs] *n* trasandatezza; squallore *m*; meschinità
shabby ['ʃæbɪ] *adj* trasandato(-a); (*building*) squallido(-a), malandato(-a); (*behaviour*) meschino(-a)
shack [ʃæk] *n* baracca, capanna
shackles ['ʃæklz] *npl* ferri *mpl*, catene *fpl*
shade [ʃeɪd] *n* ombra; (*for lamp*) paralume *m*; (*of colour*) tonalità *f inv*; (*US: window shade*) veneziana; (*small quantity*): **a ~ of** un po' *or* un'ombra di ■ *vt* ombreggiare, fare ombra a; **shades** *npl* (*US: sunglasses*) occhiali *mpl* da sole; **in the ~** all'ombra; **a ~ smaller** un tantino più piccolo
shadow ['ʃædəu] *n* ombra ■ *vt* (*follow*) pedinare; **without** *or* **beyond a ~ of doubt** senz'ombra di dubbio
shadow cabinet *n* (*Brit Pol*) governo *m* ombra *inv*
shadowy ['ʃædəuɪ] *adj* ombreggiato(-a), ombroso(-a); (*dim*) vago(-a), indistinto(-a)
shady ['ʃeɪdɪ] *adj* ombroso(-a); (*fig: dishonest*) losco(-a), equivoco(-a)
shaft [ʃɑ:ft] *n* (*of arrow, spear*) asta; (*Aut, Tech*) albero; (*of mine*) pozzo; (*of lift*) tromba; (*of light*) raggio; **ventilator ~** condotto di ventilazione
shaggy ['ʃægɪ] *adj* ispido(-a)
shake [ʃeɪk] *vb* (*pt* **shook**, *pp* **shaken**) [ʃuk, 'ʃeɪkn] *vt* scuotere; (*bottle, cocktail*) agitare ■ *vi* tremare ■ *n* scossa; **to ~ one's head** scuotere la testa; **to ~ hands with sb** stringere *or* dare la mano a qn
▸ **shake off** *vt* scrollare (via); (*fig*) sbarazzarsi di
▸ **shake up** *vt* scuotere
shake-up ['ʃeɪkʌp] *n* riorganizzazione *f* drastica

shakily ['ʃeɪkɪlɪ] *adv* (*reply*) con voce tremante; (*walk*) con passo malfermo; (*write*) con mano tremante
shaky ['ʃeɪkɪ] *adj* (*hand, voice*) tremante; (*memory*) labile; (*knowledge*) incerto(-a); (*building*) traballante
shale [ʃeɪl] *n* roccia scistosa
shall [ʃæl] *aux vb*: **I ~ go** andrò
shallot [ʃə'lɔt] *n* (*Brit*) scalogna
shallow ['ʃæləu] *adj* poco profondo(-a); (*fig*) superficiale
sham [ʃæm] *n* finzione *f*, messinscena; (*jewellery, furniture*) imitazione *f* ■ *adj* finto(-a) ■ *vt* fingere, simulare
shambles ['ʃæmblz] *n* confusione *f*, baraonda, scompiglio; **the economy is (in) a complete ~** l'economia è nel caos più totale
shambolic [ʃæm'bɔlɪk] *adj* (*col*) incasinato(-a)
shame [ʃeɪm] *n* vergogna ■ *vt* far vergognare; **it is a ~ (that/to do)** è un peccato (che + *sub*/fare); **what a ~!** che peccato!; **to put sb/sth to ~** (*fig*) far sfigurare qn/qc
shamefaced ['ʃeɪmfeɪst] *adj* vergognoso(-a)
shameful ['ʃeɪmful] *adj* vergognoso(-a)
shameless ['ʃeɪmlɪs] *adj* sfrontato(-a); (*immodest*) spudorato(-a)
shampoo [ʃæm'pu:] *n* shampoo *m inv* ■ *vt* fare lo shampoo a; **~ and set** shampoo e messa in piega
shamrock ['ʃæmrɔk] *n* trifoglio (*simbolo nazionale dell'Irlanda*)
shandy ['ʃændɪ] *n* birra con gassosa
shan't [ʃɑ:nt] = **shall not**
shanty town ['ʃæntɪ-] *n* bidonville *f inv*
SHAPE [ʃeɪp] *n abbr* (= *Supreme Headquarters Allied Powers, Europe*) *supremo quartier generale delle Potenze Alleate in Europa*
shape [ʃeɪp] *n* forma ■ *vt* (*clay, stone*) dar forma a; (*fig: ideas, character*) formare; (*: course of events*) determinare, condizionare; (*statement*) formulare; (*sb's ideas*) condizionare ■ *vi* (*also*: **shape up**: *events*) andare, mettersi; (*: person*) cavarsela; **to take ~** prendere forma; **in the ~ of a heart** a forma di cuore; **to get o.s. into ~** rimettersi in forma; **I can't bear gardening in any ~ or form** detesto il giardinaggio d'ogni genere e specie
-shaped [ʃeɪpt] *suffix*: **heart~** a forma di cuore
shapeless ['ʃeɪplɪs] *adj* senza forma, informe
shapely ['ʃeɪplɪ] *adj* ben proporzionato(-a)
share [ʃɛə^r] *n* (*thing received, contribution*) parte *f*; (*Comm*) azione *f* ■ *vt* dividere; (*have in common*) condividere, avere in comune; **to ~ out (among** *or* **between)** dividere (tra); **to ~ in** partecipare a
share capital *n* capitale *m* azionario
share certificate *n* certificato azionario
shareholder ['ʃɛəhəuldə^r] *n* azionista *m/f*
share index *n* listino di Borsa
shark [ʃɑ:k] *n* squalo, pescecane *m*
sharp [ʃɑ:p] *adj* (*razor, knife*) affilato(-a); (*point*) acuto(-a), acuminato(-a); (*nose, chin*) aguzzo(-a); (*outline*) netto(-a); (*curve, bend*) stretto(-a), accentuato(-a); (*cold, pain*) pungente; (*voice*) stridulo(-a); (*person: quick-witted*) sveglio(-a); (*: unscrupulous*) disonesto(-a); (*Mus*): **C ~** do diesis ■ *n* (*Mus*) diesis *m inv* ■ *adv*: **at 2 o'clock ~** alle due in punto; **turn ~ left** giri tutto a sinistra; **to be ~ with sb** rimproverare qn; **look ~!** sbrigati!
sharpen ['ʃɑ:pən] *vt* affilare; (*pencil*) fare la punta a; (*fig*) aguzzare
sharpener ['ʃɑ:pnə^r] *n* (*also*: **pencil sharpener**) temperamatite *m inv*; (*also*: **knife sharpener**) affilacoltelli *m inv*
sharp-eyed [ʃɑ:p'aɪd] *adj* dalla vista acuta
sharpish ['ʃɑ:pɪʃ] *adv* (*Brit col: quickly*) subito
sharply ['ʃɑ:plɪ] *adv* (*abruptly*) bruscamente; (*clearly*) nettamente; (*harshly*) duramente, aspramente
sharp-tempered [ʃɑ:p'tɛmpəd] *adj* irascibile
shatter ['ʃætə^r] *vt* mandare in frantumi, frantumare; (*fig: upset*) distruggere; (*: ruin*) rovinare ■ *vi* frantumarsi, andare in pezzi
shattered ['ʃætəd] *adj* (*grief-stricken*) sconvolto(-a); (*exhausted*) a pezzi, distrutto(-a)
shatterproof ['ʃætəpru:f] *adj* infrangibile
shave [ʃeɪv] *vt* radere, rasare ■ *vi* radersi, farsi la barba ■ *n*: **to have a ~** farsi la barba
shaven ['ʃeɪvn] *adj* (*head*) rasato(-a), tonsurato(-a)
shaver ['ʃeɪvə^r] *n* (*also*: **electric shaver**) rasoio elettrico
shaving ['ʃeɪvɪŋ] *n* (*action*) rasatura; **shavings** *npl* (*of wood etc*) trucioli *mpl*
shaving brush *n* pennello da barba
shaving cream *n* crema da barba
shaving soap *n* sapone *m* da barba
shawl [ʃɔ:l] *n* scialle *m*
she [ʃi:] *pron* ella, lei; **there ~ is** eccola; **~-bear** orsa; **~-elephant** elefantessa; *for ships, countries follow the gender of your translation*
sheaf (*pl* **sheaves**) [ʃi:f, ʃi:vz] *n* covone *m*
shear [ʃɪə^r] *vt* (*pt* **sheared**, *pp* **sheared** *or* **shorn**) [ʃɔ:n] (*sheep*) tosare
▸ **shear off** *vi* (*break off*) spezzarsi
shears ['ʃɪəz] *npl* (*for hedge*) cesoie *fpl*
sheath [ʃi:θ] *n* fodero, guaina; (*contraceptive*) preservativo
sheathe [ʃi:ð] *vt* rivestire; (*sword*) rinfoderare
sheath knife *n* coltello (con fodero)

S

sheaves [ʃi:vz] *npl of* **sheaf**
shed [ʃɛd] *n* capannone *m* ■ *vt (pt, pp* **~**) (*leaves, fur etc*) perdere; (*tears*) versare; **to ~ light on** (*problem, mystery*) far luce su
she'd [ʃi:d] = **she had; she would**
sheen [ʃi:n] *n* lucentezza
sheep [ʃi:p] *n* (*pl inv*) pecora
sheepdog ['ʃi:pdɔg] *n* cane *m* da pastore
sheep farmer *n* allevatore *m* di pecore
sheepish ['ʃi:pɪʃ] *adj* vergognoso(-a), timido(-a)
sheepskin ['ʃi:pskɪn] *n* pelle *f* di pecora
sheepskin jacket *n* (giacca di) montone *m*
sheer [ʃɪə[r]] *adj* (*utter*) vero(-a) (e proprio(-a)); (*steep*) a picco, perpendicolare; (*transparent*) trasparente ■ *adv* a picco; **by ~ chance** per puro caso
sheet [ʃi:t] *n* (*on bed*) lenzuolo; (*of paper*) foglio; (*of glass*) lastra; (*of metal*) foglio, lamina
sheet feed *n* (*on printer*) alimentazione *f* di fogli
sheet lightning *n* lampo diffuso
sheet metal *n* lamiera
sheet music *n* fogli *mpl* di musica
sheik, sheikh [ʃeɪk] *n* sceicco
shelf (*pl* **shelves**) [ʃɛlf, ʃɛlvz] *n* scaffale *m*, mensola
shelf life *n* (*Comm*) durata di conservazione
shell [ʃɛl] *n* (*on beach*) conchiglia; (*of egg, nut etc*) guscio; (*explosive*) granata; (*of building*) scheletro, struttura ■ *vt* (*peas*) sgranare; (*Mil*) bombardare, cannoneggiare
▸ **shell out** *vi* (*col*): **to ~ out (for)** sganciare soldi (per)
she'll [ʃi:l] = **she will; she shall**
shellfish ['ʃɛlfɪʃ] *n* (*pl inv*) (*crab etc*) crostaceo; (*scallop etc*) mollusco; (*pl: as food*) crostacei; molluschi
shellsuit ['ʃɛlsu:t] *n* tuta di acetato
shelter ['ʃɛltə[r]] *n* riparo, rifugio ■ *vt* riparare, proteggere; (*give lodging to*) dare rifugio *or* asilo a ■ *vi* ripararsi, mettersi al riparo; **to take ~ (from)** mettersi al riparo (da)
sheltered ['ʃɛltəd] *adj* (*life*) ritirato(-a); (*spot*) riparato(-a), protetto(-a)
shelve [ʃɛlv] *vt* (*fig*) accantonare, rimandare
shelves [ʃɛlvz] *npl of* **shelf**
shelving ['ʃɛlvɪŋ] *n* scaffalature *fpl*
shepherd ['ʃɛpəd] *n* pastore *m* ■ *vt* (*guide*) guidare
shepherdess ['ʃɛpədɪs] *n* pastora
shepherd's pie *n timballo di carne macinata e purè di patate*
sherbet ['ʃə:bət] *n* (*Brit: powder*) *polvere effervescente al gusto di frutta*; (*US: water ice*) sorbetto
sheriff ['ʃɛrɪf] *n* sceriffo
sherry ['ʃɛrɪ] *n* sherry *m inv*
she's [ʃi:z] = **she is; she has**
Shetland ['ʃɛtlənd] *n* (*also*: **the Shetlands, the Shetland Isles**) le (isole) Shetland
Shetland pony *n* pony *m inv* delle Shetland
shield [ʃi:ld] *n* scudo ■ *vt*: **to ~ (from)** riparare (da), proteggere (da *or* contro)
shift [ʃɪft] *n* (*change*) cambiamento; (*of workers*) turno ■ *vt* spostare, muovere; (*remove*) rimuovere ■ *vi* spostarsi, muoversi; **~ in demand** (*Comm*) variazione *f* della domanda; **the wind has shifted to the south** il vento si è girato e soffia da sud
shift key *n* (*on typewriter*) tasto delle maiuscole
shiftless ['ʃɪftlɪs] *adj* fannullone(-a)
shift work *n* lavoro a squadre; **to do ~** fare i turni
shifty ['ʃɪftɪ] *adj* ambiguo(-a); (*eyes*) sfuggente
Shiite ['ʃi:aɪt] *adj, n* sciita *m/f*
shilling ['ʃɪlɪŋ] *n* (*Brit*) scellino (*12 old pence; 20 in a pound*)
shilly-shally ['ʃɪlɪʃælɪ] *vi* tentennare, esitare
shimmer ['ʃɪmə[r]] *vi* brillare, luccicare
shimmering ['ʃɪmərɪŋ] *adj* (*gen*) luccicante, scintillante; (*haze*) tremolante; (*satin etc*) cangiante
shin [ʃɪn] *n* tibia ■ *vi*: **to ~ up/down a tree** arrampicarsi in cima a/scivolare giù da un albero
shindig ['ʃɪndɪg] *n* (*col*) festa chiassosa
shine [ʃaɪn] *n* splendore *m*, lucentezza ■ *vb* (*pt, pp* **shone**) [ʃɔn] *vi* (ri)splendere, brillare ■ *vt* far brillare, far risplendere; (*torch*): **to ~ sth on** puntare qc verso
shingle ['ʃɪŋgl] *n* (*on beach*) ciottoli *mpl*; (*on roof*) assicella di copertura
shingles ['ʃɪŋglz] *n* (*Med*) herpes zoster *m*
shining ['ʃaɪnɪŋ] *adj* (*surface, hair*) lucente; (*light*) brillante
shiny ['ʃaɪnɪ] *adj* lucente, lucido(-a)
ship [ʃɪp] *n* nave *f* ■ *vt* trasportare (via mare); (*send*) spedire (via mare); (*load*) imbarcare, caricare; **on board ~** a bordo
shipbuilder ['ʃɪpbɪldə[r]] *n* costruttore *m* navale
shipbuilding ['ʃɪpbɪldɪŋ] *n* costruzione *f* navale
ship chandler [-'tʃɑ:ndlə[r]] *n* fornitore *m* marittimo
shipment ['ʃɪpmənt] *n* carico
shipowner ['ʃɪpəunə[r]] *n* armatore *m*
shipper ['ʃɪpə[r]] *n* spedizioniere *m* (marittimo)
shipping ['ʃɪpɪŋ] *n* (*ships*) naviglio; (*traffic*) navigazione *f*
shipping agent *n* agente *m* marittimo
shipping company *n* compagnia di navigazione

shipping lane *n* rotta (di navigazione)
shipping line *n* = **shipping company**
shipshape ['ʃɪpʃeɪp] *adj* in perfetto ordine
shipwreck ['ʃɪprɛk] *n* relitto; (*event*) naufragio ■ *vt*: **to be shipwrecked** naufragare, fare naufragio
shipyard ['ʃɪpjɑːd] *n* cantiere *m* navale
shire ['ʃaɪəʳ] *n* (*Brit*) contea
shirk [ʃəːk] *vt* sottrarsi a, evitare
shirt [ʃəːt] *n* (*man's*) camicia; **in ~ sleeves** in maniche di camicia
shirty ['ʃəːtɪ] *adj* (*Brit col*) incavolato(-a)
shit [ʃɪt] *excl* (*col!*) merda (*!*)
shiver ['ʃɪvəʳ] *n* brivido ■ *vi* rabbrividire, tremare
shoal [ʃəul] *n* (*of fish*) banco
shock [ʃɔk] *n* (*impact*) urto, colpo; (*Elec*) scossa; (*emotional*) colpo, shock *m inv*; (*Med*) shock ■ *vt* colpire, scioccare; scandalizzare; **to give sb a ~** far venire un colpo a qn; **to be suffering from ~** essere in stato di shock; **it came as a ~ to hear that ...** è stata una grossa sorpresa sentire che ...
shock absorber *n* ammortizzatore *m*
shocker ['ʃɔkəʳ] *n*: **it was a real ~** (*col*) è stata una vera bomba
shocking ['ʃɔkɪŋ] *adj* scioccante, traumatizzante; (*scandalous*) scandaloso(-a); (*very bad: weather, handwriting*) orribile; (*: results*) disastroso(-a)
shockproof ['ʃɔkpruːf] *adj* antiurto *inv*
shock therapy, shock treatment *n* (*Med*) shockterapia
shock wave *n* onda d'urto; (*fig: usually pl*) impatto *msg*
shod [ʃɔd] *pt, pp of* **shoe**
shoddy ['ʃɔdɪ] *adj* scadente
shoe [ʃuː] *n* scarpa; (*also*: **horseshoe**) ferro di cavallo; (*brake shoe*) ganascia (del freno) ■ *vt* (*pt, pp* **shod**) [ʃɔd] (*horse*) ferrare
shoebrush ['ʃuːbrʌʃ] *n* spazzola per le scarpe
shoehorn ['ʃuːhɔːn] *n* calzante *m*
shoelace ['ʃuːleɪs] *n* stringa
shoemaker ['ʃuːmeɪkəʳ] *n* calzolaio
shoe polish *n* lucido per scarpe
shoeshop ['ʃuːʃɔp] *n* calzoleria
shoestring ['ʃuːstrɪŋ] *n* stringa (delle scarpe); **on a ~** (*fig: do sth*) con quattro soldi
shoetree ['ʃuːtriː] *n* forma per scarpe
shone [ʃɔn] *pt, pp of* **shine**
shoo [ʃuː] *excl* sciò!, via! ■ *vt* (*also*: **shoo away, shoo off**) cacciare (via)
shook [ʃuk] *pt of* **shake**
shoot [ʃuːt] *n* (*on branch, seedling*) germoglio; (*shooting party*) partita di caccia; (*competition*) gara di tiro ■ *vb* (*pt, pp* **shot**) [ʃɔt] *vt* (*game: Brit*) cacciare, andare a caccia di; (*person*) sparare a; (*execute*) fucilare; (*film*) girare ■ *vi* (*with gun*): **to ~ (at)** sparare (a), fare fuoco (su); (*with bow*): **to ~ (at)** tirare (su); (*Football*) sparare, tirare (forte); **to ~ past sb** passare vicino a qn come un fulmine; **to ~ in/out** entrare/uscire come una freccia
▸**shoot down** *vt* (*plane*) abbattere
▸**shoot up** *vi* (*fig*) salire alle stelle
shooting ['ʃuːtɪŋ] *n* (*shots*) sparatoria; (*murder*) uccisione *f* (a colpi d'arma da fuoco); (*Hunting*) caccia; (*Cine*) riprese *fpl*
shooting range *n* poligono (di tiro), tirassegno
shooting star *n* stella cadente
shop [ʃɔp] *n* negozio; (*workshop*) officina ■ *vi* (*also*: **go shopping**) fare spese; **repair ~** officina di riparazione; **to talk ~** (*fig*) parlare di lavoro
▸**shop around** *vi* fare il giro dei negozi
shopaholic ['ʃɔpə'hɔlɪk] *n* (*col*) maniaco(-a) dello shopping
shop assistant *n* (*Brit*) commesso(-a)
shop floor *n* (*Brit: fig*) operai *mpl*, maestranze *fpl*
shopkeeper ['ʃɔpkiːpəʳ] *n* negoziante *m/f*, bottegaio(-a)
shoplift ['ʃɔplɪft] *vi* taccheggiare
shoplifter ['ʃɔplɪftəʳ] *n* taccheggiatore(-trice)
shoplifting ['ʃɔplɪftɪŋ] *n* taccheggio
shopper ['ʃɔpəʳ] *n* compratore(-trice)
shopping ['ʃɔpɪŋ] *n* (*goods*) spesa, acquisti *mpl*
shopping bag *n* borsa per la spesa
shopping centre *n* centro commerciale
shop-soiled ['ʃɔpsɔɪld] *adj* sciupato(-a) a forza di stare in vetrina
shop steward *n* (*Brit Industry*) rappresentante *m* sindacale
shop window *n* vetrina
shore [ʃɔːʳ] *n* (*of sea*) riva, spiaggia; (*of lake*) riva ■ *vt*: **to ~ (up)** puntellare; **on ~** a terra
shore leave *n* (*Naut*) franchigia
shorn [ʃɔːn] *pp of* **shear**
short [ʃɔːt] *adj* (*not long*) corto(-a); (*soon finished*) breve; (*person*) basso(-a); (*curt*) brusco(-a), secco(-a); (*insufficient*) insufficiente ■ *n* (*also*: **short film**) cortometraggio; **it is ~ for** è l'abbreviazione *or* il diminutivo di; **a ~ time ago** poco tempo fa; **in the ~ term** nell'immediato futuro; **to be ~ of sth** essere a corto di *or* mancare di qc; **to run ~ of sth** rimanere senza qc; **to be in ~ supply** scarseggiare; **I'm 3 ~** me ne mancano 3; **in ~** in breve; **~ of doing** a meno che non si faccia; **everything ~ of** tutto fuorché; **to cut ~** (*speech, visit*) accorciare, abbreviare; (*person*) interrompere; **to fall ~ of** venire meno a; non soddisfare; **to stop ~**

S

fermarsi di colpo; **to stop ~ of** non arrivare fino a; *see also* **shorts**
shortage ['ʃɔ:tɪdʒ] *n* scarsezza, carenza
shortbread ['ʃɔ:tbrɛd] *n* biscotto di pasta frolla
short-change [ʃɔ:t'tʃeɪndʒ] *vt*: **to ~ sb** imbrogliare qn sul resto
short-circuit [ʃɔ:t'sə:kɪt] *n* cortocircuito ■ *vt* cortocircuitare ■ *vi* fare cortocircuito
shortcoming ['ʃɔ:tkʌmɪŋ] *n* difetto
shortcrust pastry ['ʃɔ:tkrʌst-], **short pastry** *n* (*Brit*) pasta frolla
shortcut ['ʃɔ:tkʌt] *n* scorciatoia
shorten ['ʃɔ:tn] *vt* accorciare, ridurre
shortening ['ʃɔ:tnɪŋ] *n* grasso per pasticceria
shortfall ['ʃɔ:tfɔ:l] *n* deficienza
shorthand ['ʃɔ:thænd] *n* (*Brit*) stenografia; **to take sth down in ~** stenografare qc
shorthand notebook *n* (*Brit*) bloc-notes *m inv* per stenografia
shorthand typist *n* (*Brit*) stenodattilografo(-a)
short list *n* (*Brit: for job*) rosa dei candidati
short-lived [ʃɔ:t'lɪvd] *adj* effimero(-a), di breve durata
shortly ['ʃɔ:tlɪ] *adv* fra poco
shortness ['ʃɔ:tnɪs] *n* brevità; insufficienza
shorts [ʃɔ:ts] *npl* (*also*: **a pair of shorts**) i calzoncini
short-sighted [ʃɔ:t'saɪtɪd] *adj* (*Brit*) miope; (*fig*) poco avveduto(-a)
short-staffed [ʃɔ:t'stɑ:ft] *adj* a corto di personale
short story *n* racconto, novella
short-tempered [ʃɔ:t'tɛmpəd] *adj* irascibile
short-term ['ʃɔ:ttə:m] *adj* (*effect*) di *or* a breve durata
short time *n* (*Industry*): **to work ~, be on ~** essere *or* lavorare a orario ridotto
short wave *n* (*Radio*) onde *fpl* corte
shot [ʃɔt] *pt, pp of* **shoot** ■ *n* sparo, colpo; (*shotgun pellets*) pallottole *fpl*; (*person*) tiratore *m*; (*try*) prova; (*injection*) iniezione *f*; (*Phot*) foto *f inv*; **like a ~** come un razzo; (*very readily*) immediatamente; **to fire a ~ at sb/sth** sparare un colpo a qn/qc; **to have a ~ at sth/doing sth** provarci con qc/a fare qc; **a big ~** (*col*) un pezzo grosso, un papavero; **to get ~ of sb/sth** (*col*) sbarazzarsi di qn/qc
shotgun ['ʃɔtgʌn] *n* fucile *m* da caccia
should [ʃud] *aux vb*: **I ~ go now** dovrei andare ora; **he ~ be there now** dovrebbe essere arrivato ora; **I ~ go if I were you** se fossi in lei andrei; **I ~ like to** mi piacerebbe; **~ he phone ...** se telefonasse ...
shoulder ['ʃəuldə[r]] *n* spalla; (*Brit: of road*): **hard ~** corsia d'emergenza ■ *vt* (*fig*) addossarsi, prendere sulle proprie spalle; **to look over one's ~** guardarsi alle spalle; **to rub shoulders with sb** (*fig*) essere a contatto con qn; **to give sb the cold ~** (*fig*) trattare qn con freddezza
shoulder bag *n* borsa a tracolla
shoulder blade *n* scapola
shoulder strap *n* bretella, spallina
shouldn't ['ʃudnt] = **should not**
shout [ʃaut] *n* urlo, grido ■ *vt* gridare ■ *vi* urlare, gridare; **to give sb a ~** chiamare qn gridando
▸ **shout down** *vt* zittire gridando
shouting ['ʃautɪŋ] *n* urli *mpl*
shouting match *n* (*col*) vivace scambio di opinioni
shove [ʃʌv] *vt* spingere; (*col: put*): **to ~ sth in** ficcare qc in ■ *n* spintone *m*; **he shoved me out of the way** mi ha spinto da parte
▸ **shove off** *vi* (*Naut*) scostarsi
shovel ['ʃʌvl] *n* pala ■ *vt* spalare
show [ʃəu] *n* (*of emotion*) dimostrazione *f*, manifestazione *f*; (*semblance*) apparenza; (*exhibition*) mostra, esposizione *f*; (*Theat, Cine*) spettacolo; (*Comm, Tech*) salone *m*, fiera ■ *vb* (*pt* **showed**, *pp* **shown**) [ʃəun] *vt* far vedere, mostrare; (*courage etc*) dimostrare, dar prova di; (*exhibit*) esporre ■ *vi* vedersi, essere visibile; **to ~ sb to his seat/to the door** accompagnare qn al suo posto/alla porta; **to ~ a profit/loss** (*Comm*) registrare un utile/una perdita; **it just goes to ~ that ...** il che sta a dimostrare che ...; **to ask for a ~ of hands** chiedere che si voti per alzata di mano; **to be on ~** essere esposto; **it's just for ~** è solo per far scena; **who's running the ~ here?** (*col*) chi è il padrone qui?
▸ **show in** *vt* far entrare
▸ **show off** *vi* (*pej*) esibirsi, mettersi in mostra ■ *vt* (*display*) mettere in risalto; (*pej*) mettere in mostra
▸ **show out** *vt* accompagnare alla porta
▸ **show up** *vi* (*stand out*) essere ben visibile; (*col: turn up*) farsi vedere ■ *vt* mettere in risalto; (*unmask*) smascherare
showbiz ['ʃəubɪz] *n* (*col*) = **show business**
show business *n* industria dello spettacolo
showcase ['ʃəukeɪs] *n* vetrina, bacheca
showdown ['ʃəudaun] *n* prova di forza
shower ['ʃauə[r]] *n* doccia; (*rain*) acquazzone *m*; (*of stones etc*) pioggia; (*US: party*) *festa in cui si fanno regali alla persona festeggiata (di fidanzamento etc)* ■ *vi* fare la doccia ■ *vt*: **to ~ sb with** (*gifts, abuse etc*) coprire qn di; (*missiles*) lanciare contro qn una pioggia di; **to have** *or* **take a ~** fare la doccia
shower cap *n* cuffia da doccia

showerproof ['ʃauəpru:f] *adj* impermeabile
showery ['ʃauərɪ] *adj* (*weather*) con piogge intermittenti
showground ['ʃəugraund] *n* terreno d'esposizione
showing ['ʃəuɪŋ] *n* (*of film*) proiezione *f*
show jumping *n* concorso ippico (di salto ad ostacoli)
showman ['ʃəumən] *n* (*at fair, circus*) impresario; (*fig*) attore *m*
showmanship ['ʃəumənʃɪp] *n* abilità d'impresario
shown [ʃəun] *pp of* **show**
show-off ['ʃəuɔf] *n* (*col: person*) esibizionista *m/f*
showpiece ['ʃəupi:s] *n* (*of exhibition*) pezzo forte; **that hospital is a ~** è un ospedale modello
showroom ['ʃəurum] *n* sala d'esposizione
show trial *n* processo a scopo dimostrativo (*spesso ideologico*)
showy ['ʃəuɪ] *adj* vistoso(-a), appariscente
shrank [ʃræŋk] *pt of* **shrink**
shrapnel ['ʃræpnl] *n* shrapnel *m*
shred [ʃrɛd] *n* (*gen pl*) brandello; (*fig: of truth, evidence*) briciolo ■ *vt* fare a brandelli; (*Culin*) sminuzzare, tagliuzzare; (*documents*) distruggere, sminuzzare
shredder ['ʃrɛdə^r] *n* (*for documents, papers*) distruttore *m* di documenti, sminuzzatrice *f*
shrew [ʃru:] *n* (*Zool*) toporagno; (*fig: pej: woman*) strega
shrewd [ʃru:d] *adj* astuto(-a), scaltro(-a)
shrewdness ['ʃru:dnɪs] *n* astuzia
shriek [ʃri:k] *n* strillo ■ *vt, vi* strillare
shrift [ʃrɪft] *n*: **to give sb short ~** sbrigare qn
shrill [ʃrɪl] *adj* acuto(-a), stridulo(-a), stridente
shrimp [ʃrɪmp] *n* gamberetto
shrine [ʃraɪn] *n* reliquario; (*place*) santuario
shrink [ʃrɪŋk] *vb* (*pt* **shrank**, *pp* **shrunk**) [ʃræŋk, ʃrʌŋk] *vi* restringersi; (*fig*) ridursi ■ *vt* (*wool*) far restringere ■ *n* (*col: pej*) psicanalista *m/f*; **to ~ from doing sth** rifuggire dal fare qc
shrinkage ['ʃrɪnkɪdʒ] *n* restringimento
shrink-wrap ['ʃrɪŋkræp] *vt* confezionare con plastica sottile
shrivel ['ʃrɪvl] (*also:* **shrivel up**) *vt* raggrinzare, avvizzire ■ *vi* raggrinzirsi, avvizzire
shroud [ʃraud] *n* lenzuolo funebre ■ *vt*: **shrouded in mystery** avvolto(-a) nel mistero
Shrove Tuesday ['ʃrəuv-] *n* martedì *m* grasso
shrub [ʃrʌb] *n* arbusto
shrubbery ['ʃrʌbərɪ] *n* arbusti *mpl*
shrug [ʃrʌg] *n* scrollata di spalle ■ *vt, vi*: **to ~ (one's shoulders)** alzare le spalle, fare spallucce
▸ **shrug off** *vt* passare sopra a; (*cold, illness*) sbarazzarsi di
shrunk [ʃrʌŋk] *pp of* **shrink**
shrunken ['ʃrʌŋkən] *adj* rattrappito(-a)
shudder ['ʃʌdə^r] *n* brivido ■ *vi* rabbrividire
shuffle ['ʃʌfl] *vt* (*cards*) mescolare; **to ~ (one's feet)** strascicare i piedi
shun [ʃʌn] *vt* sfuggire, evitare
shunt [ʃʌnt] *vt* (*Rail: direct*) smistare; (*: divert*) deviare ■ *vi*: **to ~ (to and fro)** fare la spola
shunting yard *n* fascio di smistamento
shush [ʃuʃ] *excl* zitto(-a)!
shut (*pt, pp* **~**) [ʃʌt] *vt* chiudere ■ *vi* chiudersi, chiudere
▸ **shut down** *vt, vi* chiudere definitivamente
▸ **shut off** *vt* (*stop: power*) staccare; (*: water*) chiudere; (*: engine*) spegnere; (*isolate*) isolare
▸ **shut out** *vt* (*person, noise, cold*) non far entrare; (*block: view*) impedire, bloccare; (*: memory*) scacciare
▸ **shut up** *vi* (*col: keep quiet*) stare zitto(-a) ■ *vt* (*close*) chiudere; (*silence*) far tacere
shutdown ['ʃʌtdaun] *n* chiusura
shutter ['ʃʌtə^r] *n* imposta; (*Phot*) otturatore *m*
shuttle ['ʃʌtl] *n* spola, navetta; (*also:* **shuttle service**) servizio *m* navetta *inv* ■ *vi* (*vehicle, person*) fare la spola ■ *vt* (*to and fro: passengers*) portare (avanti e indietro)
shuttlecock ['ʃʌtlkɔk] *n* volano
shuttle diplomacy *n* frequenti mediazioni *fpl* diplomatiche
shy [ʃaɪ] *adj* timido(-a) ■ *vi*: **to ~ away from doing sth** (*fig*) rifuggire dal fare qc; **to fight ~ of** tenersi alla larga da; **to be ~ of doing sth** essere restio a fare qc
shyness ['ʃaɪnɪs] *n* timidezza
Siam [saɪ'æm] *n* Siam *m*
Siamese [saɪə'mi:z] *adj*: **~ cat** gatto siamese; **~ twins** fratelli *mpl* (*or* sorelle *fpl*) siamesi
Siberia [saɪ'bɪərɪə] *n* Siberia
sibling ['sɪblɪŋ] *n* (*formal*) fratello/sorella
Sicilian [sɪ'sɪlɪən] *adj, n* siciliano(-a)
Sicily ['sɪsɪlɪ] *n* Sicilia
sick [sɪk] *adj* (*ill*) malato(-a); (*vomiting*): **to be ~** vomitare; (*humour*) macabro(-a); **to feel ~** avere la nausea; **to be ~ of** (*fig*) averne abbastanza di; **a ~ person** un malato; **to be (off) ~** essere assente perché malato; **to fall** *or* **take ~** ammalarsi
sickbag ['sɪkbæg] *n* sacchetto (*da usarsi in caso di malessere*)
sick bay *n* infermeria
sick building syndrome *n malattia causata da mancanza di ventilazione e luce naturale*

sicken ['sɪkn] *vt* nauseare ▪ *vi*: **to be sickening for sth** (*cold, flu etc*) covare qc
sickening ['sɪknɪŋ] *adj* (*fig*) disgustoso(-a), rivoltante
sickle ['sɪkl] *n* falcetto
sick leave *n* congedo per malattia
sickle-cell anaemia ['sɪklsɛl-] *n* anemia drepanocitica
sickly ['sɪklɪ] *adj* malaticcio(-a); (*causing nausea*) nauseante
sickness ['sɪknɪs] *n* malattia; (*vomiting*) vomito
sickness benefit *n* indennità di malattia
sick pay *n* sussidio per malattia
sickroom ['sɪkru:m] *n* stanza di malato
side [saɪd] *n* (*gen*) lato; (*of person, animal*) fianco; (*of lake*) riva; (*face, surface: gen*) faccia; (*: of paper*) facciata; (*fig: aspect*) aspetto, lato; (*team: Sport*) squadra; (*: Pol etc*) parte *f* ▪ *cpd* (*door, entrance*) laterale ▪ *vi*: **to ~ with sb** parteggiare per qn, prendere le parti di qn; **by the ~ of** a fianco di; (*road*) sul ciglio di; **~ by ~** fianco a fianco; **to take sides (with)** schierarsi (con); **the right/wrong ~** il dritto/rovescio; **from ~ to ~** da una parte all'altra; **~ of beef** quarto di bue
sideboard ['saɪdbɔ:d] *n* credenza
sideboards ['saɪdbɔ:dz], (*Brit*) **sideburns** ['saɪdbə:nz] *npl* (*whiskers*) basette *fpl*
sidecar ['saɪdkɑ:ʳ] *n* sidecar *m inv*
side dish *n* contorno
side drum *n* (*Mus*) piccolo tamburo
side effect *n* (*Med*) effetto collaterale
sidekick ['saɪdkɪk] *n* (*col*) compagno(-a)
sidelight ['saɪdlaɪt] *n* (*Aut*) luce *f* di posizione
sideline ['saɪdlaɪn] *n* (*Sport*) linea laterale; (*fig*) attività secondaria
sidelong ['saɪdlɔŋ] *adj* obliquo(-a); **to give a ~ glance at sth** guardare qc con la coda dell'occhio
side plate *n* piattino
side road *n* strada secondaria
sidesaddle ['saɪdsædl] *adv* all'amazzone
side show *n* attrazione *f*
sidestep ['saɪdstɛp] *vt* (*question*) eludere; (*problem*) scavalcare ▪ *vi* (*Boxing etc*) spostarsi di lato
side street *n* traversa
sidetrack ['saɪdtræk] *vt* (*fig*) distrarre
sidewalk ['saɪdwɔ:k] *n* (*US*) marciapiede *m*
sideways ['saɪdweɪz] *adv* (*move*) di lato, di fianco; (*look*) con la coda dell'occhio
siding ['saɪdɪŋ] *n* (*Rail*) binario di raccordo
sidle ['saɪdl] *vi*: **to ~ up (to)** avvicinarsi furtivamente (a)
SIDS *n* (= *sudden infant death syndrome*) = **cot death**
siege [si:dʒ] *n* assedio; **to lay ~ to** porre l'assedio a
siege economy *n* economia da stato d'assedio
Sierra Leone [sɪ'ɛrəlɪ'əun] *n* Sierra Leone *f*
sieve [sɪv] *n* setaccio ▪ *vt* setacciare
sift [sɪft] *vt* passare al crivello; (*fig*) vagliare ▪ *vi*: **to ~ through** esaminare minuziosamente
sigh [saɪ] *n* sospiro ▪ *vi* sospirare
sight [saɪt] *n* (*faculty*) vista; (*spectacle*) spettacolo; (*on gun*) mira ▪ *vt* avvistare; **in ~** in vista; **out of ~** non visibile; **at first ~** a prima vista; **to catch ~ of sth/sb** scorgere qc/qn; **to lose ~ of sb/sth** perdere di vista qn/qc; **to set one's sights on sth/on doing sth** mirare a qc/a fare qc; **at ~** a vista; **I know her by ~** la conosco di vista
sighted ['saɪtɪd] *adj* che ha il dono della vista; **partially ~** parzialmente cieco
sightseeing ['saɪtsi:ɪŋ] *n* turismo; **to go ~** visitare una località
sightseer ['saɪtsi:əʳ] *n* turista *m/f*
sign [saɪn] *n* segno; (*with hand etc*) segno, gesto; (*notice*) insegna, cartello; (*road sign*) segnale *m* ▪ *vt* firmare; **as a ~ of** in segno di; **it's a good/bad ~** è buon/brutto segno; **to show signs/no ~ of doing sth** accennare/non accennare a fare qc; **plus/minus ~** segno del più/meno; **to ~ one's name** firmare, apporre la propria firma
▸ **sign away** *vt* (*rights etc*) cedere (con una firma)
▸ **sign in** *vi* firmare il registro (all'arrivo)
▸ **sign off** *vi* (*Radio, TV*) chiudere le trasmissioni
▸ **sign on** *vi* (*Mil etc: enlist*) arruolarsi; (*as unemployed*) iscriversi sulla lista (dell'ufficio di collocamento); (*begin work*) prendere servizio; (*enrol*): **to ~ on for a course** iscriversi a un corso
▸ **sign out** *vi* firmare il registro (alla partenza)
▸ **sign over** *vt*: **to ~ sth over to sb** cedere qc con scrittura legale a qn
▸ **sign up** (*Mil*) *vt* arruolare ▪ *vi* arruolarsi
signal ['sɪgnl] *n* segnale *m* ▪ *vt* (*person*) fare segno a; (*message*) comunicare per mezzo di segnali ▪ *vi*: **to ~ to sb (to do sth)** far segno a qn (di fare qc); **to ~ a left/right turn** (*Aut*) segnalare un cambiamento di direzione a sinistra/destra
signal box *n* (*Rail*) cabina di manovra
signalman ['sɪgnlmən] *n* (*Rail*) deviatore *m*
signatory ['sɪgnətərɪ] *n* firmatario(-a)
signature ['sɪgnətʃəʳ] *n* firma
signature tune *n* sigla musicale

signet ring ['sɪgnət-] *n* anello con sigillo
significance [sɪg'nɪfɪkəns] *n* (*of remark*) significato; (*of event*) importanza; **that is of no ~** ciò non ha importanza
significant [sɪg'nɪfɪkənt] *adj* (*improvement, amount*) notevole; (*discovery, event*) importante; (*evidence, smile*) significativo(-a); **it is ~ that ...** è significativo che ...
significantly [sɪg'nɪfɪkəntlɪ] *adv* (*smile*) in modo eloquente; (*improve, increase*) considerevolmente, decisamente
signify ['sɪgnɪfaɪ] *vt* significare
sign language *n* linguaggio dei muti
signpost ['saɪnpəust] *n* cartello indicatore
silage ['saɪlɪdʒ] *n* insilato
silence ['saɪlns] *n* silenzio ■ *vt* far tacere, ridurre al silenzio
silencer ['saɪlənsəʳ] *n* (*on gun, Brit Aut*) silenziatore *m*
silent ['saɪlnt] *adj* silenzioso(-a); (*film*) muto(-a); **to keep** *or* **remain ~** tacere, stare zitto(-a)
silently ['saɪlntlɪ] *adv* silenziosamente, in silenzio
silent partner *n* (*Comm*) socio accomandante
silhouette [sɪlu:'ɛt] *n* silhouette *f inv* ■ *vt*: **to be silhouetted against** stagliarsi contro
silicon ['sɪlɪkən] *n* silicio
silicon chip *n* chip *m inv* al silicio
silicone ['sɪlɪkəun] *n* silicone *m*
silk [sɪlk] *n* seta ■ *cpd* di seta
silky ['sɪlkɪ] *adj* di seta, come la seta
sill [sɪl] *n* (*windowsill*) davanzale *m*; (*Aut*) predellino
silly ['sɪlɪ] *adj* stupido(-a), sciocco(-a); **to do something ~** fare una sciocchezza
silo ['saɪləu] *n* silo
silt [sɪlt] *n* limo
silver ['sɪlvəʳ] *n* argento; (*money*) *monete da 5, 10, 20 o 50 pence*; (*also*: **silverware**) argenteria ■ *cpd* d'argento
silver foil, (*Brit*) **silver paper** *n* carta argentata, (carta) stagnola
silver-plated [sɪlvə'pleɪtɪd] *adj* argentato(-a)
silversmith ['sɪlvəsmɪθ] *n* argentiere *m*
silverware ['sɪlvəwɛəʳ] *n* argenteria, argento
silvery ['sɪlvərɪ] *adj* (*colour*) argenteo(-a); (*sound*) argentino(-a)
SIM card ['sɪm-] *n* (*Tel*: = *Subscriber Identity Module card*) SIM card *f inv*
similar ['sɪmɪləʳ] *adj*: **~ (to)** simile (a)
similarity [sɪmɪ'lærɪtɪ] *n* somiglianza, rassomiglianza
similarly ['sɪmɪləlɪ] *adv* (*in a similar way*) allo stesso modo; (*as is similar*) così pure
simile ['sɪmɪlɪ] *n* similitudine *f*
simmer ['sɪməʳ] *vi* cuocere a fuoco lento
▸ **simmer down** *vi* (*fig, col*) calmarsi
simper ['sɪmpəʳ] *vi* fare lo(la) smorfioso(-a)
simpering ['sɪmpərɪŋ] *adj* lezioso(-a), smorfioso(-a)
simple ['sɪmpl] *adj* semplice; **the ~ truth** la pura verità
simple interest *n* (*Math, Comm*) interesse *m* semplice
simple-minded [sɪmpl'maɪndɪd] *adj* sempliciotto(-a)
simpleton ['sɪmpltən] *n* semplicione(-a), sempliciotto(-a)
simplicity [sɪm'plɪsɪtɪ] *n* semplicità
simplification [sɪmplɪfɪ'keɪʃən] *n* semplificazione *f*
simplify ['sɪmplɪfaɪ] *vt* semplificare
simply ['sɪmplɪ] *adv* semplicemente
simulate ['sɪmjuleɪt] *vt* fingere, simulare
simulation [sɪmju'leɪʃən] *n* simulazione *f*
simultaneous [sɪməl'teɪnɪəs] *adj* simultaneo(-a)
simultaneously [sɪməl'teɪnɪəslɪ] *adv* simultaneamente, contemporaneamente
sin [sɪn] *n* peccato ■ *vi* peccare
Sinai ['saɪnaɪ] *n* Sinai *m*
since [sɪns] *adv* da allora ■ *prep* da ■ *conj* (*time*) da quando; (*because*) poiché, dato che; **~ then** da allora; **~ Monday** da lunedì; **(ever) ~ I arrived** (fin) da quando sono arrivato
sincere [sɪn'sɪəʳ] *adj* sincero(-a)
sincerely [sɪn'sɪəlɪ] *adv* sinceramente; **Yours ~** (*at end of letter*) distinti saluti
sincerity [sɪn'sɛrɪtɪ] *n* sincerità
sine [saɪn] *n* (*Math*) seno
sinew ['sɪnju:] *n* tendine *m*; **sinews** *npl* (*muscles*) muscoli *mpl*
sinful ['sɪnful] *adj* peccaminoso(-a)
sing (*pt* **sang**, *pp* **sung**) [sɪŋ, sæŋ, sʌŋ] *vt, vi* cantare
Singapore [sɪŋgə'pɔ:ʳ] *n* Singapore *f*
singe [sɪndʒ] *vt* bruciacchiare
singer ['sɪŋəʳ] *n* cantante *m/f*
Singhalese [sɪŋə'li:z] *adj* = **Sinhalese**
singing ['sɪŋɪŋ] *n* (*of person, bird*) canto; (*of kettle, bullet, in ears*) fischio
single ['sɪŋgl] *adj* solo(-a), unico(-a); (*unmarried: man*) celibe; (*: woman*) nubile; (*not double*) semplice ■ *n* (*Brit*: *also*: **single ticket**) biglietto di (sola) andata; (*record*) 45 giri *m inv*; **not a ~ one was left** non ne è rimasto nemmeno uno; **every ~ day** tutti i santi giorni; *see also* **singles**
▸ **single out** *vt* scegliere; (*distinguish*) distinguere
single bed *n* letto a una piazza
single-breasted ['sɪŋglbrɛstɪd] *adj* a un petto
Single European Market *n*: **the ~** il Mercato Unico

S

single file *n*: **in ~** in fila indiana
single-handed [sɪŋgl'hændɪd] *adv* senza aiuto, da solo(-a)
single-minded [sɪŋgl'maɪndɪd] *adj* tenace, risoluto(-a)
single parent *n* ragazzo padre/ragazza madre; genitore *m* separato; **~ family** famiglia monoparentale
single room *n* camera singola
singles ['sɪŋglz] *npl* (*Tennis*) singolo; (*US: single people*) single *m/fpl*
singles bar *n* (*esp US*) bar *m inv* per single
single-sex school ['sɪŋgl'sɛks-] *n* (*for boys*) scuola maschile; (*for girls*) scuola femminile
singlet ['sɪŋglɪt] *n* canottiera
singly ['sɪŋglɪ] *adv* separatamente
singsong ['sɪŋsɔŋ] *adj* (*tone*) cantilenante ■ *n* (*songs*): **to have a ~** farsi una cantata
singular ['sɪŋgjulə^r] *adj* (*Ling*) singolare; (*unusual*) strano(-a), singolare ■ *n* (*Ling*) singolare *m*; **in the feminine ~** al femminile singolare
singularly ['sɪŋgjuləlɪ] *adv* stranamente
Sinhalese [sɪnhə'li:z] *adj* singalese
sinister ['sɪnɪstə^r] *adj* sinistro(-a)
sink [sɪŋk] *n* lavandino, acquaio ■ *vb* (*pt* **sank**, *pp* **sunk**) [sæŋk, sʌŋk] *vt* (*ship*) (fare) affondare, colare a picco; (*foundations*) scavare; (*piles etc*): **to ~ sth into** conficcare qc in ■ *vi* affondare, andare a fondo; (*ground etc*) cedere, avvallarsi; **he sank into a chair/the mud** sprofondò in una poltrona/nel fango
▸ **sink in** *vi* penetrare; **it took a long time to ~ in** ci ho (*or* ha *etc*) messo molto a capirlo
sinking ['sɪŋkɪŋ] *adj*: **that ~ feeling** una stretta allo stomaco
sinking fund *n* (*Comm*) fondo d'ammortamento
sink unit *n* blocco lavello
sinner ['sɪnə^r] *n* peccatore(-trice)
Sinn Féin [ʃɪn'feɪn] *n movimento separatista irlandese*
sinuous ['sɪnjuəs] *adj* sinuoso(-a)
sinus ['saɪnəs] *n* (*Anat*) seno
sip [sɪp] *n* sorso ■ *vt* sorseggiare
siphon ['saɪfən] *n* sifone *m* ■ *vt* (*funds*) trasferire
▸ **siphon off** *vt* travasare (con un sifone)
sir [sə^r] *n* signore *m*; **S~ John Smith** Sir John Smith; **yes ~** sì, signore; **Dear S~** (*in letter*) Egregio signor (*followed by name*); **Dear Sirs** Spettabile ditta
siren ['saɪərn] *n* sirena
sirloin ['sə:lɔɪn] *n* controfiletto
sirloin steak *n* bistecca di controfiletto
sirocco [sɪ'rɔkəu] *n* scirocco
sisal ['saɪsəl] *n* sisal *f inv*
sissy ['sɪsɪ] *n* (*col*) femminuccia
sister ['sɪstə^r] *n* sorella; (*nun*) suora; (*nurse*) infermiera *f* caposala *inv* ■ *cpd*: **~ organization** organizzazione *f* affine; **~ ship** nave *f* gemella
sister-in-law ['sɪstərɪnlɔ:] *n* cognata
sit (*pt, pp* **sat**) [sɪt, sæt] *vi* sedere, sedersi; (*dress etc*) cadere; (*assembly*) essere in seduta ■ *vt* (*exam*) sostenere, dare; **to ~ on a committee** far parte di una commissione
▸ **sit about, sit around** *vi* star seduto(-a) (senza far nulla)
▸ **sit back** *vi* (*in seat*) appoggiarsi allo schienale
▸ **sit down** *vi* sedersi; **to be sitting down** essere seduto(-a)
▸ **sit in** *vi*: **to ~ in on a discussion** assistere ad una discussione
▸ **sit up** *vi* tirarsi su a sedere; (*not go to bed*) stare alzato(-a) fino a tardi
sitcom ['sɪtkɔm] *n abbr* (*TV*: = *situation comedy*) sceneggiato a episodi (*comico*)
sit-down ['sɪtdaun] *adj*: **~ strike** sciopero bianco (con occupazione della fabbrica); **a ~ meal** un pranzo
site [saɪt] *n* posto; (*also*: **building site**) cantiere *m*; (*Comput*) sito ■ *vt* situare
sit-in ['sɪtɪn] *n* (*demonstration*) sit-in *m inv*
siting ['saɪtɪŋ] *n* ubicazione *f*
sitter ['sɪtə^r] *n* (*for painter*) modello(-a); (*also*: **baby sitter**) babysitter *m/f inv*
sitting ['sɪtɪŋ] *n* (*of assembly etc*) seduta; (*in canteen*) turno
sitting member *n* (*Pol*) deputato(-a) in carica
sitting room *n* soggiorno
sitting tenant *n* (*Brit*) attuale affittuario
situate ['sɪtjueɪt] *vt* collocare
situated ['sɪtjueɪtɪd] *adj* situato(-a)
situation [sɪtju'eɪʃən] *n* situazione *f*; **"situations vacant/wanted"** (*Brit*) "offerte/domande di impiego"
situation comedy *n* (*Theat*) commedia di situazione
six [sɪks] *num* sei
six-pack ['sɪkspæk] *n* (*esp US*) confezione *f* da sei
sixteen [sɪks'ti:n] *num* sedici
sixth [sɪksθ] *num* sesto(-a) ■ *n*: **the upper/lower ~** (*Brit Scol*) l'ultimo/il penultimo anno di scuola superiore
sixty ['sɪkstɪ] *num* sessanta
size [saɪz] *n* dimensioni *fpl*; (*of clothing*) taglia, misura; (*of shoes*) numero; (*glue*) colla; **I take ~ 14 in a dress** ≈ porto la 44 di vestiti; **I'd like the small/large ~** (*of soap powder etc*) vorrei la confezione piccola/grande
▸ **size up** *vt* giudicare, farsi un'idea di

sizeable ['saɪzəbl] *adj* considerevole
sizzle ['sɪzl] *vi* sfrigolare
SK *abbr (Canada)* = **Saskatchewan**
skate [skeɪt] *n* pattino; *(fish: pl inv)* razza ■ *vi* pattinare
▸ **skate over, skate around** *vt (problem, issue)* prendere alla leggera, prendere sotto gamba
skateboard ['skeɪtbɔ:d] *n* skateboard *m inv*
skater ['skeɪtə^r] *n* pattinatore(-trice)
skating ['skeɪtɪŋ] *n* pattinaggio
skating rink *n* pista di pattinaggio
skeleton ['skɛlɪtn] *n* scheletro
skeleton key *n* passe-partout *m inv*
skeleton staff *n* personale *m* ridotto
skeptic *etc* ['skɛptɪk] *(US)* = **sceptic** *etc*
sketch [skɛtʃ] *n (drawing)* schizzo, abbozzo; *(Theat etc)* scenetta comica, sketch *m inv* ■ *vt* abbozzare, schizzare
sketch book *n* album *m inv* per schizzi
sketch pad *n* blocco per schizzi
sketchy ['skɛtʃɪ] *adj* incompleto(-a), lacunoso(-a)
skew [skju:] *n (Brit)*: **on the ~** di traverso
skewer ['skju:ə^r] *n* spiedo
ski [ski:] *n* sci *m inv* ■ *vi* sciare
ski boot *n* scarpone *m* da sci
skid [skɪd] *n* slittamento; *(sideways slip)* sbandamento ■ *vi* slittare; sbandare; **to go into a ~** slittare; sbandare
skid mark *n* segno della frenata
skier ['ski:ə^r] *n* sciatore(-trice)
skiing ['ski:ɪŋ] *n* sci *m*
ski instructor *n* maestro(-a) di sci
ski jump *n (ramp)* trampolino; *(event)* salto con gli sci
skilful, *(US)* **skillful** ['skɪlful] *adj* abile
skilfully, *(US)* **skillfully** ['skɪlfəlɪ] *adv* abilmente
ski lift *n* sciovia
skill [skɪl] *n* abilità *f inv*, capacità *f inv*; *(technique)* tecnica
skilled [skɪld] *adj* esperto(-a); *(worker)* qualificato(-a), specializzato(-a)
skillful ['skɪlful] *adj (US)* = **skilful**
skillfully ['skɪlfəlɪ] *adv (US)* = **skilfully**
skim [skɪm] *vt (milk)* scremare; *(soup)* schiumare; *(glide over)* sfiorare ■ *vi*: **to ~ through** *(fig)* scorrere, dare una scorsa a
skimmed milk *n* latte *m* scremato
skimp [skɪmp] *vi*: **to ~ on** *vt (work)* fare alla carlona; *(cloth etc)* lesinare
skimpy ['skɪmpɪ] *adj* misero(-a); striminzito(-a); frugale
skin [skɪn] *n* pelle *f*; *(of fruit, vegetable)* buccia; *(on pudding, paint)* crosta ■ *vt (fruit etc)* sbucciare; *(animal)* scuoiare, spellare; **wet** *or* **soaked to the ~** bagnato fino al midollo
skin cancer *n* cancro alla pelle
skin-deep [skɪn'di:p] *adj* superficiale
skin diver *n* subacqueo
skin diving *n* nuoto subacqueo
skinflint ['skɪnflɪnt] *n* taccagno(-a), tirchio(-a)
skin graft *n* innesto epidermico
skinhead ['skɪnhɛd] *n* skinhead *m/f inv*
skinny ['skɪnɪ] *adj* molto magro(-a), pelle e ossa *inv*
skin test *n* prova di reazione cutanea
skintight ['skɪntaɪt] *adj* aderente
skip [skɪp] *n* saltello, balzo; *(container)* benna ■ *vi* saltare; *(with rope)* saltare la corda ■ *vt (pass over)* saltare; **to ~ school** *(US)* marinare la scuola
ski pants *npl* pantaloni *mpl* da sci
ski pass *n* ski pass *m inv*
ski pole *n* racchetta (da sci)
skipper ['skɪpə^r] *n (Naut, Sport)* capitano
skipping rope ['skɪpɪŋ-] *n (Brit)* corda per saltare
ski resort *n* località *f inv* sciistica
skirmish ['skə:mɪʃ] *n* scaramuccia
skirt [skə:t] *n* gonna, sottana ■ *vt* fiancheggiare, costeggiare
skirting board ['skə:tɪŋ-] *n (Brit)* zoccolo
ski run *n* pista (da sci)
ski suit *n* tuta da sci
skit [skɪt] *n* parodia; scenetta satirica
ski tow *n* = **ski lift**
skittle ['skɪtl] *n* birillo; **skittles** *n (game)* (gioco dei) birilli *mpl*
skive [skaɪv] *vi (Brit col)* fare il lavativo
skulk [skʌlk] *vi* muoversi furtivamente
skull [skʌl] *n* cranio, teschio
skullcap ['skʌlkæp] *n (worn by Jews)* zucchetto; *(worn by Pope)* papalina
skunk [skʌŋk] *n* moffetta
sky [skaɪ] *n* cielo; **to praise sb to the skies** portare alle stelle qn
sky-blue [skaɪ'blu:] *adj* azzurro(-a), celeste
sky-diving ['skaɪdaɪvɪŋ] *n* caduta libera, paracadutismo acrobatico
sky-high [skaɪ'haɪ] *adv (throw)* molto in alto ■ *adj (col)* esorbitante; **prices have gone ~** *(col)* i prezzi sono saliti alle stelle
skylark ['skaɪlɑ:k] *n* allodola
skylight ['skaɪlaɪt] *n* lucernario
skyline ['skaɪlaɪn] *n (horizon)* orizzonte *m*; *(of city)* profilo
sky marshal *n* agente *m/f* a bordo
Skype® [skaɪp] *(Internet, Tel) n* Skype® *m* ■ *vt*: **to skype sb** chiamare qn con Skype
skyscraper ['skaɪskreɪpə^r] *n* grattacielo
slab [slæb] *n* lastra; *(of wood)* tavola; *(of meat, cheese)* pezzo

S

slack [slæk] *adj* (*loose*) allentato(-a); (*slow*) lento(-a); (*careless*) negligente; (*Comm: market*) stagnante; (*: demand*) scarso(-a); (*period*) morto(-a) ■ *n* (*in rope etc*) parte *f* non tesa; **business is ~** l'attività commerciale è scarsa; *see also* **slacks**
slacken ['slækn] (*also*: **slacken off**) *vi* rallentare, diminuire ■ *vt* allentare; (*pressure*) diminuire
slacks [slæks] *npl* pantaloni *mpl*
slag [slæg] *n* scorie *fpl*
slag heap *n* ammasso di scorie
slain [sleɪn] *pp of* **slay**
slake [sleɪk] *vt* (*one's thirst*) spegnere
slalom ['slɑːləm] *n* slalom *m*
slam [slæm] *vt* (*door*) sbattere; (*throw*) scaraventare; (*criticize*) stroncare ■ *vi* sbattere
slammer ['slæməʳ] *n*: **the ~** (*col*) la gattabuia
slander ['slɑːndəʳ] *n* calunnia; (*Law*) diffamazione *f* ■ *vt* calunniare; diffamare
slanderous ['slɑːndrəs] *adj* calunnioso(-a); diffamatorio(-a)
slang [slæŋ] *n* gergo, slang *m*
slanging match ['slæŋɪŋ-] *n* (*Brit col*) rissa verbale
slant [slɑːnt] *n* pendenza, inclinazione *f*; (*fig*) angolazione *f*, punto di vista
slanted ['slɑːntɪd] *adj* tendenzioso(-a)
slanting ['slɑːntɪŋ] *adj* in pendenza, inclinato(-a)
slap [slæp] *n* manata, pacca; (*on face*) schiaffo ■ *vt* dare una manata a; schiaffeggiare ■ *adv* (*directly*) in pieno; **it fell ~ in the middle** cadde proprio nel mezzo
slapdash ['slæpdæʃ] *adj* abborracciato(-a)
slaphead ['slæphɛd] *n* (*Brit col*) imbecille *m/f*
slapstick ['slæpstɪk] *n* (*comedy*) farsa grossolana
slap-up ['slæpʌp] *adj* (*Brit*): **a ~ meal** un pranzo (*or* una cena) coi fiocchi
slash [slæʃ] *vt* squarciare; (*face*) sfregiare; (*fig: prices*) ridurre drasticamente, tagliare
slat [slæt] *n* (*of wood*) stecca
slate [sleɪt] *n* ardesia ■ *vt* (*fig: criticize*) stroncare, distruggere
slaughter ['slɔːtəʳ] *n* (*of animals*) macellazione *f*; (*of people*) strage *f*, massacro ■ *vt* macellare; trucidare, massacrare
slaughterhouse ['slɔːtəhaus] *n* macello, mattatoio
Slav [slɑːv] *adj*, *n* slavo(-a)
slave [sleɪv] *n* schiavo(-a) ■ *vi* (*also*: **slave away**) lavorare come uno schiavo; **to ~ (away) at sth/at doing sth** ammazzarsi di fatica *or* sgobbare per qc/per fare qc
slave driver *n* (*col, pej*) schiavista *m/f*
slave labour *n* lavoro degli schiavi; (*fig*): **we're just ~ here** siamo solamente sfruttati qui dentro
slaver ['slævəʳ] *vi* (*dribble*) sbavare
slavery ['sleɪvərɪ] *n* schiavitù *f*
Slavic ['slævɪk] *adj* slavo(-a)
slavish ['sleɪvɪʃ] *adj* servile; pedissequo(-a)
slavishly ['sleɪvɪʃlɪ] *adv* (*copy*) pedissequamente
Slavonic [slə'vɔnɪk] *adj* slavo(-a)
slay (*pt* **slew**, *pp* **slain**) [sleɪ, sluː, sleɪn] *vt* (*formal*) uccidere
sleazy ['sliːzɪ] *adj* trasandato(-a)
sledge [slɛdʒ] *n* slitta
sledgehammer ['slɛdʒhæməʳ] *n* martello da fabbro
sleek [sliːk] *adj* (*hair, fur*) lucido(-a), lucente; (*car, boat*) slanciato(-a), affusolato(-a)
sleep [sliːp] *n* sonno ■ *vi* (*pt, pp* **slept**) [slɛpt] dormire ■ *vt*: **we can ~ 4** abbiamo 4 posti letto, possiamo alloggiare 4 persone; **to have a good night's ~** farsi una bella dormita; **to go to ~** addormentarsi; **to ~ lightly** avere il sonno leggero; **to put to ~** (*patient*) far addormentare; (*animal: euphemistic: kill*) abbattere; **to ~ with sb** (*euphemistic: have sex*) andare a letto con qn
▸ **sleep in** *vi* (*lie late*) alzarsi tardi; (*oversleep*) dormire fino a tardi
sleeper ['sliːpəʳ] *n* (*person*) dormiente *m/f*; (*Brit Rail: on track*) traversina; (*: train*) treno di vagoni letto
sleepily ['sliːpɪlɪ] *adv* con aria assonnata
sleeping ['sliːpɪŋ] *adj* addormentato(-a)
sleeping bag *n* sacco a pelo
sleeping car *n* vagone *m* letto *inv*, carrozza *f* letto *inv*
sleeping partner *n* (*Brit Comm*) = **silent partner**
sleeping pill *n* sonnifero
sleeping sickness *n* malattia del sonno
sleepless ['sliːplɪs] *adj* (*person*) insonne; **a ~ night** una notte in bianco
sleeplessness ['sliːplɪsnɪs] *n* insonnia
sleepover ['sliːpəuvəʳ] *n il dormire a casa di amici, usato in riferimento a bambini*
sleepwalk ['sliːpwɔːk] *vi* camminare nel sonno; (*as a habit*) essere sonnambulo(-a)
sleepwalker ['sliːpwɔːkəʳ] *n* sonnambulo(-a)
sleepy ['sliːpɪ] *adj* assonnato(-a), sonnolento(-a); (*fig*) addormentato(-a); **to be** *or* **feel ~** avere sonno
sleet [sliːt] *n* nevischio
sleeve [sliːv] *n* manica; (*of record*) copertina
sleeveless ['sliːvlɪs] *adj* (*garment*) senza maniche
sleigh [sleɪ] *n* slitta

sleight [slaɪt] *n*: **~ of hand** gioco di destrezza
slender ['slɛndəʳ] *adj* snello(-a), sottile; (*not enough*) scarso(-a), esiguo(-a)
slept [slɛpt] *pt, pp of* **sleep**
sleuth [slu:θ] *n* (*col*) segugio
slew [slu:] *vi* (*also*: **slew round**) girare ■ *pt of* **slay**
slice [slaɪs] *n* fetta ■ *vt* affettare, tagliare a fette; **sliced bread** pane *m* a cassetta
slick [slɪk] *adj* (*clever*) brillante; (*insincere*) untuoso(-a), falso(-a) ■ *n* (*also*: **oil slick**) chiazza di petrolio
slid [slɪd] *pt, pp of* **slide**
slide [slaɪd] *n* (*in playground*) scivolo; (*Phot*) diapositiva; (*microscope slide*) vetrino; (*Brit: also*: **hair slide**) fermaglio (per capelli); (*in prices*) caduta ■ *vb* (*pt, pp* **slid**) [slɪd] *vt* far scivolare ■ *vi* scivolare; **to let things ~** (*fig*) lasciare andare tutto, trascurare tutto
slide projector *n* proiettore *m* per diapositive
slide rule *n* regolo calcolatore
sliding ['slaɪdɪŋ] *adj* (*door*) scorrevole; **~ roof** (*Aut*) capotte *f inv*
sliding scale *n* scala mobile
slight [slaɪt] *adj* (*slim*) snello(-a), sottile; (*frail*) delicato(-a), fragile; (*trivial*) insignificante; (*small*) piccolo(-a) ■ *n* offesa, affronto ■ *vt* (*offend*) offendere, fare un affronto a; **the slightest** il minimo (*or* la minima); **not in the slightest** affatto, neppure per sogno
slightly ['slaɪtlɪ] *adv* lievemente, un po'; **~ built** esile
slim [slɪm] *adj* magro(-a), snello(-a) ■ *vi* dimagrire, fare *or* seguire) una dieta dimagrante
slime [slaɪm] *n* limo, melma; viscidume *m*
slimming ['slɪmɪŋ] *adj* (*diet, pills*) dimagrante
slimy ['slaɪmɪ] *adj* (*also fig: person*) viscido(-a); (*covered with mud*) melmoso(-a)
sling [slɪŋ] *n* (*Med*) benda al collo ■ *vt* (*pt, pp* **slung**) [slʌŋ] lanciare, tirare; **to have one's arm in a ~** avere un braccio al collo
slink (*pt, pp* **slunk**) [slɪŋk, slʌŋk] *vi*: **to ~ away, ~ off** svignarsela
slinky ['slɪŋkɪ] *adj* (*clothing*) aderente, attillato(-a)
slip [slɪp] *n* scivolata, scivolone *m*; (*mistake*) errore *m*, sbaglio; (*underskirt*) sottoveste *f*; (*paper*) bigliettino, talloncino ■ *vt* (*slide*) far scivolare ■ *vi* (*slide*) scivolare; (*move smoothly*): **to ~ into/out of** scivolare in/via da; (*decline*) declinare; **to give sb the ~** sfuggire qn; **a ~ of paper** un foglietto; **a ~ of the tongue** un lapsus linguae; **to ~ sth on/off** infilarsi/togliersi qc; **to let a chance ~ by** lasciarsi scappare un'occasione; **it slipped from her hand** le sfuggì di mano
▸ **slip away** *vi* svignarsela
▸ **slip in** *vt* introdurre casualmente
▸ **slip out** *vi* uscire furtivamente
slip-on ['slɪpɔn] *adj* (*gen*) comodo(-a) da mettere; (*shoes*) senza allacciatura
slipped disc ['slɪpt-] *n* spostamento delle vertebre
slipper ['slɪpəʳ] *n* pantofola
slippery ['slɪpərɪ] *adj* scivoloso(-a); **it's ~** si scivola
slip road *n* (*Brit: to motorway*) rampa di accesso
slipshod ['slɪpʃɔd] *adj* sciatto(-a), trasandato(-a)
slip-up ['slɪpʌp] *n* granchio (*fig*)
slipway ['slɪpweɪ] *n* scalo di costruzione
slit [slɪt] *n* fessura, fenditura; (*cut*) taglio; (*tear*) strappo ■ *vt* (*pt, pp* **~**) tagliare; **to ~ sb's throat** tagliare la gola a qn
slither ['slɪðəʳ] *vi* scivolare, sdrucciolare
sliver ['slɪvəʳ] *n* (*of glass, wood*) scheggia; (*of cheese, sausage*) fettina
slob [slɔb] *n* (*col*) sciattone(-a)
slog [slɔg] (*Brit*) *n* faticata ■ *vi* lavorare con accanimento, sgobbare
slogan ['sləugən] *n* motto, slogan *m inv*
slop [slɔp] *vi* (*also*: **slop over**) traboccare; versarsi ■ *vt* spandere; versare ■ *npl*: **slops** acqua sporca; sbobba
slope [sləup] *n* pendio; (*side of mountain*) versante *m*; (*of roof*) pendenza; (*of floor*) inclinazione *f* ■ *vi*: **to ~ down** declinare; **to ~ up** essere in salita
sloping ['sləupɪŋ] *adj* inclinato(-a)
sloppy ['slɔpɪ] *adj* (*work*) tirato(-a) via; (*appearance*) sciatto(-a); (*film etc*) sdolcinato(-a)
slosh [slɔʃ] *vi* (*col*): **to ~ about** *or* **around** (*person*) sguazzare; (*liquid*) guazzare
sloshed [slɔʃt] *adj* (*col: drunk*) sbronzo(-a)
slot [slɔt] *n* fessura; (*fig: in timetable, Radio, TV*) spazio ■ *vt*: **to ~ into** introdurre in una fessura
sloth [sləuθ] *n* (*vice*) pigrizia, accidia; (*Zool*) bradipo
slot machine *n* (*Brit: vending machine*) distributore *m* automatico; (*for amusement*) slot-machine *f inv*
slot meter *n* contatore *m* a gettoni
slouch [slautʃ] *vi* (*when walking*) camminare dinoccolato(-a); **she was slouched in a chair** era sprofondata in una poltrona
▸ **slouch about, slouch around** *vi* (*laze*) oziare
Slovak ['sləuvæk] *adj* slovacco(-a) ■ *n* slovacco(-a); (*Ling*) slovacco; **the ~ Republic** la Repubblica Slovacca
Slovakia [sləu'vækɪə] *n* Slovacchia

S

Slovakian [sləu'vækıən] *adj, n* = **Slovak**
Slovene ['sləuvi:n] *adj* sloveno(-a) ■ *n* sloveno(-a); (*Ling*) sloveno
Slovenia [sləu'vi:nıə] *n* Slovenia
Slovenian [sləu'vi:nıən] *adj, n* = **Slovene**
slovenly ['slʌvənlı] *adj* sciatto(-a), trasandato(-a)
slow [sləu] *adj* lento(-a); (*watch*): **to be ~** essere indietro ■ *adv* lentamente ■ *vt, vi* (*also*: **slow down, slow up**) rallentare; **"~"** (*road sign*) "rallentare"; **at a ~ speed** a bassa velocità; **to be ~ to act/decide** essere lento ad agire/a decidere; **my watch is 20 minutes ~** il mio orologio è indietro di 20 minuti; **business is ~** (*Comm*) gli affari procedono a rilento; **to go ~** (*driver*) andare piano; (*in industrial dispute*) fare uno sciopero bianco
slow-acting ['sləu'æktıŋ] *adj* che agisce lentamente, ad azione lenta
slowly ['sləulı] *adv* lentamente; **to drive ~** andare piano
slow motion *n*: **in ~** al rallentatore
slowness ['sləunıs] *n* lentezza
sludge [slʌdʒ] *n* fanghiglia
slug [slʌg] *n* lumaca; (*bullet*) pallottola
sluggish ['slʌgıʃ] *adj* lento(-a); (*business, market, sales*) stagnante, fiacco(-a)
sluice [slu:s] *n* chiusa ■ *vt*: **to ~ down** *or* **out** lavare (con abbondante acqua)
slum [slʌm] *n* catapecchia
slumber ['slʌmbə[r]] *n* sonno
slump [slʌmp] *n* crollo, caduta; (*economic*) depressione *f*, crisi *f inv* ■ *vi* crollare; **he was slumped over the wheel** era curvo sul volante
slung [slʌŋ] *pt, pp of* **sling**
slunk [slʌŋk] *pt, pp of* **slink**
slur [slə:[r]] *n* pronuncia indistinta; (*stigma*) diffamazione *f*, calunnia; (*Mus*) legatura; (*smear*): **~ (on)** macchia (su) ■ *vt* pronunciare in modo indistinto; **to cast a ~ on sb** calunniare qn
slurp [slə:p] *vt, vi* bere rumorosamente ■ *n* *rumore fatto bevendo*
slurred [slə:d] *adj* (*pronunciation*) inarticolato(-a), disarticolato(-a)
slush [slʌʃ] *n* neve *f* mista a fango
slush fund *n* fondi *mpl* neri
slushy ['slʌʃı] *adj* (*snow*) che si scioglie; (*Brit: fig*) sdolcinato(-a)
slut [slʌt] *n* donna trasandata, sciattona
sly [slaı] *adj* furbo(-a), scaltro(-a); **on the ~** di soppiatto
SM *n abbr* (= *sadomasochism*) sadomasochismo
smack [smæk] *n* (*slap*) pacca; (*on face*) schiaffo ■ *vt* schiaffeggiare; (*child*) picchiare ■ *vi*: **to ~ of** puzzare di; **to ~ one's lips** fare uno schiocco con le labbra
smacker ['smækə[r]] *n* (*col: kiss*) bacio; (*: Brit: pound note*) sterlina; (*: US: dollar bill*) dollaro
small [smɔ:l] *adj* piccolo(-a); (*in height*) basso(-a); (*letter*) minuscolo(-a) ■ *n*: **the ~ of the back** le reni; **to get** *or* **grow smaller** (*stain, town*) rimpicciolire; (*debt, organization, numbers*) ridursi; **to make smaller** (*amount, income*) ridurre; (*garden, object, garment*) rimpicciolire; **in the ~ hours** alle ore piccole; **a ~ shopkeeper** un piccolo negoziante
small ads *npl* (*Brit*) piccoli annunci *mpl*
small arms *npl* armi *fpl* portatili *or* leggere
small business *n* piccola impresa
small change *n* moneta, spiccioli *mpl*
smallholder ['smɔ:lhəuldə[r]] *n* (*Brit*) piccolo proprietario
smallholding ['smɔ:lhəuldıŋ] *n* (*Brit*) piccola tenuta
smallish ['smɔ:lıʃ] *adj* piccolino(-a)
small-minded [smɔ:l'maındıd] *adj* meschino(-a)
smallpox ['smɔ:lpɔks] *n* vaiolo
small print *n* caratteri *mpl* piccoli; (*on document*) parte scritta in piccolo
small-scale ['smɔ:lskeıl] *adj* (*map, model*) in scala ridotta; (*business, farming*) modesto(-a)
small talk *n* chiacchiere *fpl*
small-time ['smɔ:ltaım] *adj* (*col*) da poco; **a ~ thief** un ladro di polli
small-town ['smɔ:ltaun] *adj* (*pej*) provinciale, di paese
smarmy ['smɑ:mı] *adj* (*Brit pej*) untuoso(-a), strisciante
smart [smɑ:t] *adj* elegante; (*also fig: clever*) intelligente; (*quick*) sveglio(-a) ■ *vi* bruciare; **the ~ set** il bel mondo; **to look ~** essere elegante; **my eyes are smarting** mi bruciano gli occhi
smartcard ['smɑ:tkɑ:d] *n* smartcard *f inv*, carta intelligente
smarten up ['smɑ:tn-] *vi* farsi bello(-a) ■ *vt* (*people*) fare bello(-a); (*things*) abbellire
smash [smæʃ] *n* (*also*: **smash-up**) scontro, collisione *f*; (*sound*) fracasso ■ *vt* frantumare, fracassare; (*opponent*) annientare, schiacciare; (*hopes*) distruggere; (*Sport: record*) battere ■ *vi* frantumarsi, andare in pezzi
▸ **smash up** *vt* (*car*) sfasciare; (*room*) distruggere
smash-hit [smæʃ'hıt] *n* successone *m*
smashing ['smæʃıŋ] *adj* (*col*) favoloso(-a), formidabile
smattering ['smætərıŋ] *n*: **a ~ of** un'infarinatura di

SME *npl abbr (= small and medium-sized enterprises)* PMI *fpl inv (= Piccole e Medie Imprese)*
smear [smɪəʳ] *n* macchia; *(Med)* striscio; *(insult)* calunnia ■ *vt* ungere; *(fig)* denigrare, diffamare; **his hands were smeared with oil/ink** aveva le mani sporche di olio/ inchiostro
smear campaign *n* campagna diffamatoria
smear test *n (Brit Med)* Pap-test *m inv*
smell [smɛl] *n* odore *m*; *(sense)* olfatto, odorato ■ *vb (pt, pp* **smelt** *or* **smelled***)* [smɛlt, smɛld] *vt* sentire (l')odore di ■ *vi (food etc)*: **to ~ (of)** avere odore (di); *(pej)* puzzare, avere un cattivo odore; **it smells good** ha un buon odore
smelly ['smɛlɪ] *adj* puzzolente
smelt [smɛlt] *pt, pp of* **smell** ■ *vt (ore)* fondere
smile [smaɪl] *n* sorriso ■ *vi* sorridere
smiling ['smaɪlɪŋ] *adj* sorridente
smirk [smə:k] *n* sorriso furbo; sorriso compiaciuto
smith [smɪθ] *n* fabbro
smithy ['smɪðɪ] *n* fucina
smitten ['smɪtn] *adj*: **~ with** colpito(-a) da
smock [smɔk] *n* grembiule *m*, camice *m*
smog [smɔg] *n* smog *m*
smoke [sməuk] *n* fumo ■ *vt, vi* fumare; **to have a ~** fumarsi una sigaretta; **do you ~?** fumi?; **to go up in ~** *(house etc)* bruciare, andare distrutto dalle fiamme; *(fig)* andare in fumo
smoked [sməukt] *adj (bacon, glass)* affumicato(-a)
smokeless fuel ['sməuklɪs-] *n* carburante *m* che non da fumo
smokeless zone *n (Brit)* zona dove sono vietati gli scarichi di fumo
smoker ['sməukəʳ] *n (person)* fumatore(-trice); *(Rail)* carrozza per fumatori
smoke screen *n* cortina fumogena *or* di fumo; *(fig)* copertura
smoke shop *n (US)* tabaccheria
smoking ['sməukɪŋ] *n* fumo; **"no ~"** *(sign)* "vietato fumare"; **he's given up ~** ha smesso di fumare
smoking compartment, *(US)* **smoking car** *n* carrozza (per) fumatori
smoky ['sməukɪ] *adj* fumoso(-a); *(surface)* affumicato(-a)
smolder ['sməuldəʳ] *vi (US)* = **smoulder**
smoochy ['smu:tʃɪ] *adj (col)* romantico(-a)
smooth [smu:ð] *adj* liscio(-a); *(sauce)* omogeneo(-a); *(flavour, whisky)* amabile; *(cigarette)* leggero(-a); *(movement)* regolare; *(person)* mellifluo(-a); *(landing, takeoff, flight)* senza scosse ■ *vt* lisciare, spianare; *(also:* **smooth out**: *difficulties)* appianare
▸ **smooth over** *vt*: **to ~ things over** *(fig)* sistemare le cose
smoothly ['smu:ðlɪ] *adv (easily)* liscio; **everything went ~** tutto andò liscio
smother ['smʌðəʳ] *vt* soffocare
smoulder, *(US)* **smolder** ['sməuldəʳ] *vi* covare sotto la cenere
SMS *n abbr (= short message service)* SMS *m (servizio)*
smudge [smʌdʒ] *n* macchia; sbavatura ■ *vt* imbrattare, sporcare
smug [smʌg] *adj* soddisfatto(-a), compiaciuto(-a)
smuggle ['smʌgl] *vt* contrabbandare; **to ~ in/out** *(goods etc)* far entrare/uscire di contrabbando
smuggler ['smʌgləʳ] *n* contrabbandiere(-a)
smuggling ['smʌglɪŋ] *n* contrabbando
smut [smʌt] *n (grain of soot)* granello di fuliggine; *(mark)* segno nero; *(in conversation etc)* sconcezze *fpl*
smutty ['smʌtɪ] *adj (fig)* osceno(-a), indecente
snack [snæk] *n* spuntino; **to have a ~** fare uno spuntino
snack bar *n* tavola calda, snack bar *m inv*
snag [snæg] *n* intoppo, ostacolo imprevisto
snail [sneɪl] *n* chiocciola
snake [sneɪk] *n* serpente *m*
snap [snæp] *n (sound)* schianto, colpo secco; *(photograph)* istantanea; *(game)* rubamazzo ■ *adj* improvviso(-a) ■ *vt* (far) schioccare; *(break)* spezzare di netto; *(photograph)* scattare un'istantanea di ■ *vi* spezzarsi con un rumore secco; *(fig: person)* crollare; **to ~ at sb** rivolgersi a qn con tono brusco; *(dog)* cercare di mordere qn; **to ~ open/shut** aprirsi/ chiudersi di scatto; **to ~ one's fingers at** *(fig)* infischiarsi di; **a cold ~** *(of weather)* un'improvvisa ondata di freddo
▸ **snap off** *vt (break)* schiantare
▸ **snap up** *vt* afferrare
snap fastener *n* bottone *m* automatico
snappy ['snæpɪ] *adj* rapido(-a); **make it ~!** *(col: hurry up)* sbrigati!, svelto!
snapshot ['snæpʃɔt] *n* istantanea
snare [snɛəʳ] *n* trappola
snarl [snɑ:l] *vi* ringhiare ■ *vt*: **to get snarled up** *(wool, plans)* ingarbugliarsi; *(traffic)* intasarsi
snatch [snætʃ] *n (fig)* furto; *(Brit: small amount)*: **snatches of** frammenti *mpl* di ■ *vt* strappare (con violenza); *(steal)* rubare ■ *vi*: **don't ~!** non strappare le cose di mano!; **to ~ a sandwich** mangiarsi in fretta un panino; **to ~ some sleep** riuscire a dormire un po'
▸ **snatch up** *vt* raccogliere in fretta
snazzy ['snæzi] *adj (col: clothes)* sciccoso(-a)

S

sneak [sni:k] *vi*: **to ~ in/out** entrare/uscire di nascosto ■ *vt*: **to ~ a look at sth** guardare di sottecchi qc
sneakers ['sni:kəz] *npl* scarpe *fpl* da ginnastica
sneaking ['sni:kɪŋ] *adj*: **to have a ~ feeling/suspicion that ...** avere la vaga impressione/il vago sospetto che ...
sneaky ['sni:kɪ] *adj* falso(-a), disonesto(-a)
sneer [snɪəʳ] *n* ghigno, sogghigno ■ *vi* ghignare, sogghignare; **to ~ at sb/sth** farsi beffe di qn/qc
sneeze [sni:z] *n* starnuto ■ *vi* starnutire
snide [snaɪd] *adj* maligno(-a)
sniff [snɪf] *n* fiutata, annusata ■ *vi* fiutare, annusare; tirare su col naso; (*in contempt*) arricciare il naso ■ *vt* fiutare, annusare; (*glue, drug*) sniffare
▸ **sniff at** *vt fus*: **it's not to be sniffed at** non è da disprezzare
sniffer dog ['snɪfə-] *n* cane *m* poliziotto (*per stupefacenti o esplosivi*)
snigger ['snɪgəʳ] *n* riso represso ■ *vi* ridacchiare, ridere sotto i baffi
snip [snɪp] *n* pezzetto; (*bargain*) (buon) affare *m*, occasione *f* ■ *vt* tagliare
sniper ['snaɪpəʳ] *n* franco tiratore *m*, cecchino
snippet ['snɪpɪt] *n* frammento
snivelling ['snɪvlɪŋ] *adj* piagnucoloso(-a)
snob [snɔb] *n* snob *m/f inv*
snobbery ['snɔbərɪ] *n* snobismo
snobbish ['snɔbɪʃ] *adj* snob *inv*
snog [snɔg] *vi* (*col*) pomiciare
snooker ['snu:kəʳ] *n tipo di gioco del biliardo*
snoop [snu:p] *vi*: **to ~ on sb** spiare qn; **to ~ about** curiosare
snooper ['snu:pəʳ] *n* ficcanaso *m/f*
snooty ['snu:tɪ] *adj* borioso(-a), snob *inv*
snooze [snu:z] *n* sonnellino, pisolino ■ *vi* fare un sonnellino
snore [snɔ:ʳ] *vi* russare
snoring ['snɔ:rɪŋ] *n* russare *m*
snorkel ['snɔ:kl] *n* (*of swimmer*) respiratore *m* a tubo
snort [snɔ:t] *n* sbuffo ■ *vi* sbuffare ■ *vt* (*drugs slang*) sniffare
snotty ['snɔtɪ] *adj* moccioso(-a)
snout [snaut] *n* muso
snow [snəu] *n* neve *f* ■ *vi* nevicare ■ *vt*: **to be snowed under with work** essere sommerso di lavoro
snowball ['snəubɔ:l] *n* palla di neve
snowbound ['snəubaund] *adj* bloccato(-a) dalla neve
snow-capped ['snəukæpt] *adj* (*mountain*) con la cima coperta di neve; (*peak*) coperto(-a) di neve
snowdrift ['snəudrɪft] *n* cumulo di neve (*ammucchiato dal vento*)
snowdrop ['snəudrɔp] *n* bucaneve *m inv*
snowfall ['snəufɔ:l] *n* nevicata
snowflake ['snəufleɪk] *n* fiocco di neve
snowman ['snəumæn] *n* pupazzo di neve
snowplough, (*US*) **snowplow** ['snəuplau] *n* spazzaneve *m inv*
snowshoe ['snəuʃu:] *n* racchetta da neve
snowstorm ['snəustɔ:m] *n* tormenta
snowy ['snəuɪ] *adj* nevoso(-a)
SNP *n abbr* (*Brit Pol*) = **Scottish National Party**
snub [snʌb] *vt* snobbare ■ *n* offesa, affronto
snub-nosed [snʌb'nəuzd] *adj* dal naso camuso
snuff [snʌf] *n* tabacco da fiuto ■ *vt* (*also*: **snuff out**: *candle*) spegnere
snuff movie *n* (*col*) *film porno dove una persona viene uccisa realmente*
snug [snʌg] *adj* comodo(-a); (*room, house*) accogliente, comodo(-a); **it's a ~ fit** è attillato
snuggle ['snʌgl] *vi*: **to ~ down in bed** accovacciarsi a letto; **to ~ up to sb** stringersi a qn
snugly ['snʌglɪ] *adv* comodamente; **it fits ~** (*object in pocket etc*) entra giusto giusto; (*garment*) sta ben attillato
SO *abbr* (*Banking*) = **standing order**

 KEYWORD

so [səu] *adv* **1** (*thus, likewise*) così; **if so** se è così, quand'è così; **I didn't do it — you did so!** non l'ho fatto io — sì che l'hai fatto!; **so do I, so am I** anch'io; **it's 5 o'clock — so it is!** sono le 5 — davvero!; **I hope so** lo spero; **I think so** penso di sì; **quite so!** esattamente!; **even so** comunque; **so far** finora, fin qui; (*in past*) fino ad allora
2 (*in comparisons etc: to such a degree*) così; **so big (that)** così grande (che); **she's not so clever as her brother** lei non è (così) intelligente come suo fratello
3: **so much** *adj* tanto(-a)
■ *adv* tanto; **I've got so much work/money** ho tanto lavoro/tanti soldi; **I love you so much** ti amo tanto; **so many** tanti(-e)
4 (*phrases*): **10 or so** circa 10; **so long!** (*col: goodbye*) ciao!, ci vediamo!; **so to speak** per così dire; **so what?** (*col*) e allora?, e con questo?
■ *conj* **1** (*expressing purpose*): **so as to do** in modo *or* così da fare; **we hurried so as not to be late** ci affrettammo per non fare tardi; **so (that)** affinché + *sub*, perché + *sub*
2 (*expressing result*): **he didn't arrive so I left**

non è venuto così me ne sono andata; **so you see, I could have gone** vedi, sarei potuto andare; **so that's the reason!** allora è questo il motivo!, ecco perché!

soak [səuk] *vt* inzuppare; (*clothes*) mettere a mollo ▪ *vi* inzupparsi; (*clothes*) essere a mollo; **to be soaked through** essere fradicio
▸ **soak in** *vi* penetrare
▸ **soak up** *vt* assorbire
soaking ['səukɪŋ] *adj* (*also*: **soaking wet**) fradicio(-a)
so-and-so ['səuənsəu] *n* (*somebody*) un tale; **Mr/Mrs ~** signor/signora tal dei tali
soap [səup] *n* sapone *m*
soapbox ['səupbɔks] *n* palco improvvisato (*per orazioni pubbliche*)
soapflakes ['səupfleɪks] *npl* sapone *m* in scaglie
soap opera *n* soap opera *f inv*
soap powder *n* detersivo
soapsuds ['səupsʌdz] *npl* saponata
soapy ['səupɪ] *adj* insaponato(-a)
soar [sɔːʳ] *vi* volare in alto; (*price, morale, spirits*) salire alle stelle
sob [sɔb] *n* singhiozzo ▪ *vi* singhiozzare
s.o.b. *n abbr* (*US col!*: = *son of a bitch*) figlio di puttana (*!*)
sober ['səubəʳ] *adj* non ubriaco(-a); (*sedate*) serio(-a); (*moderate*) moderato(-a); (*colour, style*) sobrio(-a)
▸ **sober up** *vt* far passare la sbornia a ▪ *vi* farsi passare la sbornia
sobriety [səu'braɪətɪ] *n* (*not being drunk*) sobrietà; (*seriousness, sedateness*) sobrietà, pacatezza
sob story *n* (*col, pej*) storia lacrimosa
Soc. *abbr* (= *society*) Soc
so-called ['səu'kɔːld] *adj* cosiddetto(-a)
soccer ['sɔkəʳ] *n* calcio
soccer pitch *n* campo di calcio
soccer player *n* calciatore *m*
sociable ['səuʃəbl] *adj* socievole
social ['səuʃl] *adj* sociale ▪ *n* festa, serata
social climber *n* arrampicatore(-trice) sociale, arrivista *m/f*
social club *n* club *m inv* sociale
Social Democrat *n* socialdemocratico(-a)
social insurance *n* (US) assicurazione *f* sociale
socialism ['səuʃəlɪzəm] *n* socialismo
socialist ['səuʃəlɪst] *adj, n* socialista *m/f*
socialite ['səuʃəlaɪt] *n* persona in vista nel bel mondo
socialize ['səuʃəlaɪz] *vi* frequentare la gente; farsi degli amici; **to ~ with** socializzare con
social life *n* vita sociale
social network *n* social network *m inv*, rete *f* sociale
social networking *n* *il comunicare tramite social network*
socially ['səuʃəlɪ] *adv* socialmente, in società
social science *n* scienze *fpl* sociali
social security *n* previdenza sociale; **Department of Social Security** (*Brit*) ≈ Istituto di Previdenza Sociale
social services *npl* servizi *mpl* sociali
social welfare *n* assistenza sociale
social work *n* servizio sociale
social worker *n* assistente *m/f* sociale
society [sə'saɪətɪ] *n* società *f inv*; (*club*) società, associazione *f*; (*also*: **high society**) alta società ▪ *cpd* (*party, column*) mondano(-a)
socioeconomic ['səusɪəuiːkə'nɔmɪk] *adj* socio-economico(-a)
sociological [səusɪə'lɔdʒɪkl] *adj* sociologico(-a)
sociologist [səusɪ'ɔlədʒɪst] *n* sociologo(-a)
sociology [səusɪ'ɔlədʒɪ] *n* sociologia
sock [sɔk] *n* calzino ▪ *vt* (*hit*) dare un pugno a; **to pull one's socks up** (*fig*) darsi una regolata
socket ['sɔkɪt] *n* cavità *f inv*; (*of eye*) orbita; (*Elec*: *also*: **wall socket**) presa di corrente; (*: for light bulb*) portalampada *m inv*
sod [sɔd] *n* (*of earth*) zolla erbosa; (*Brit col!*) bastardo(-a) (*!*)
▸ **sod off** *vi*: **~ off!** (*Brit col!*) levati dalle palle! (*!*)
soda ['səudə] *n* (*Chem*) soda; (*also*: **soda water**) acqua di seltz; (*US*: *also*: **soda pop**) gassosa
sodden ['sɔdn] *adj* fradicio(-a)
sodium ['səudɪəm] *n* sodio
sodium chloride *n* cloruro di sodio
sofa ['səufə] *n* sofà *m inv*
Sofia ['səufɪə] *n* Sofia
soft [sɔft] *adj* (*not rough*) morbido(-a); (*not hard*) soffice; (*not loud*) sommesso(-a); (*kind*) gentile; (*: look, smile*) dolce; (*not strict*) indulgente; (*weak*) debole; (*stupid*) stupido(-a)
soft-boiled ['sɔftbɔɪld] *adj* (*egg*) alla coque
soft drink *n* analcolico
soft drugs *npl* droghe *fpl* leggere
soften ['sɔfn] *vt* ammorbidire; addolcire; attenuare ▪ *vi* ammorbidirsi; addolcirsi; attenuarsi
softener ['sɔfnəʳ] *n* ammorbidente *m*
soft furnishings *npl* tessuti *mpl* d'arredo
soft-hearted [sɔft'hɑːtɪd] *adj* sensibile
softly ['sɔftlɪ] *adv* dolcemente; morbidamente
softness ['sɔftnɪs] *n* dolcezza; morbidezza
soft option *n* soluzione *f* (più) facile
soft sell *n* persuasione *f* all'acquisto
soft target *n* obiettivo civile (*e quindi facile da colpire*)

soft touch *n* (*col*): **to be a ~** lasciarsi spillare facilmente denaro
soft toy *n* giocattolo di peluche
software ['sɔftwɛəʳ] *n* software *m*
software package *n* pacchetto di software
soft water *n* acqua non calcarea
soggy ['sɔgɪ] *adj* inzuppato(-a)
soil [sɔɪl] *n* (*earth*) terreno, suolo ■ *vt* sporcare; (*fig*) macchiare
soiled [sɔɪld] *adj* sporco(-a), sudicio(-a)
sojourn ['sɔdʒə:n] *n* (*formal*) soggiorno
solace ['sɔlɪs] *n* consolazione *f*
solar ['səuləʳ] *adj* solare
solarium (*pl* **solaria**) [sə'lɛərɪəm, -rɪə] *n* solarium *m inv*
solar plexus [-'plɛksəs] *n* (*Anat*) plesso solare
solar power *n* energia solare
sold [səuld] *pt, pp of* **sell**
solder ['səuldəʳ] *vt* saldare ■ *n* saldatura
soldier ['səuldʒəʳ] *n* soldato, militare *m*; *see* **to soldier on** perseverare; **toy ~** soldatino
sold out *adj* (*Comm*) esaurito(-a)
sole [səul] *n* (*of foot*) pianta (del piede); (*of shoe*) suola; (*fish: pl inv*) sogliola ■ *adj* solo(-a), unico(-a); (*exclusive*) esclusivo(-a)
solely ['səullɪ] *adv* solamente, unicamente; **I will hold you ~ responsible** la considererò il solo responsabile
solemn ['sɔləm] *adj* solenne; grave; serio(-a)
sole trader *n* (*Comm*) commerciante *m* in proprio
solicit [sə'lɪsɪt] *vt* (*request*) richiedere, sollecitare ■ *vi* (*prostitute*) adescare i passanti
solicitor [sə'lɪsɪtəʳ] *n* (*Brit: for wills etc*) ≈ notaio; (*in court*) ≈ avvocato; *vedi nota*

SOLICITOR

Il *solicitor* appartiene a una delle due branche della professione legale britannica (*vedi anche* "barrister"). È compito dei *solicitors* agire come consulenti in materia legale, redarre documenti legali, preparare i casi per i "barristers". Contrariamente a questi ultimi, i *solicitors* non sono qualificati a rappresentare una parte nelle corti investite della potestà di decidere sui reati più.

solid ['sɔlɪd] *adj* (*not hollow*) pieno(-a); (*strong, sound, reliable, not liquid*) solido(-a); (*meal*) sostanzioso(-a); (*line*) ininterrotto(-a); (*vote*) unanime ■ *n* solido; **to be on ~ ground** essere su terraferma; (*fig*) muoversi su terreno sicuro; **we waited 2 ~ hours** abbiamo aspettato due ore buone
solidarity [sɔlɪ'dærɪtɪ] *n* solidarietà
solid fuel *n* combustibile *m* solido
solidify [sə'lɪdɪfaɪ] *vi* solidificarsi ■ *vt* solidificare
solidity [sə'lɪdɪtɪ] *n* solidità
solid-state ['sɔlɪdsteɪt] *adj* (*Elec*) a transistor
soliloquy [sə'lɪləkwɪ] *n* soliloquio
solitaire [sɔlɪ'tɛəʳ] *n* (*game, gem*) solitario
solitary ['sɔlɪtərɪ] *adj* solitario(-a)
solitary confinement *n* (*Law*): **to be in ~** essere in cella d'isolamento
solitude ['sɔlɪtju:d] *n* solitudine *f*
solo ['səuləu] *n* (*Mus*) assolo
soloist ['səuləuɪst] *n* solista *m/f*
Solomon Islands ['sɔləmən-] *n*: **the ~** le isole Salomone
solstice ['sɔlstɪs] *n* solstizio
soluble ['sɔljubl] *adj* solubile
solution [sə'lu:ʃən] *n* soluzione *f*
solve [sɔlv] *vt* risolvere
solvency ['sɔlvənsɪ] *n* (*Comm*) solvenza, solvibilità
solvent ['sɔlvənt] *adj* (*Comm*) solvibile ■ *n* (*Chem*) solvente *m*
solvent abuse *n* abuso di colle e, solventi
Somali [sə'mɑ:lɪ] *adj* somalo(-a)
Somalia [səu'mɑ:lɪə] *n* Somalia
Somaliland [səu'mɑ:lɪlænd] *n* paesi *mpl* del corno d'Africa
sombre, (*US*) **somber** ['sɔmbəʳ] *adj* scuro(-a); (*mood, person*) triste

KEYWORD

some [sʌm] *adj* **1** (*a certain amount or number of*): **some tea/water/cream** del tè/dell'acqua/della panna; **there's some milk in the fridge** c'è (del) latte nel frigo; **some children/apples** dei bambini/delle mele; **after some time** dopo un po'; **at some length** a lungo
2 (*certain: in contrasts*) certo(-a); **some people say that ...** alcuni dicono che ..., certa gente dice che ...
3 (*unspecified*) un(-a) certo(-a), qualche; **some woman was asking for you** una tale chiedeva di lei; **some day** un giorno; **some day next week** un giorno della prossima settimana; **in some form or other** in una forma o nell'altra
■ *pron* **1** (*a certain number*) alcuni(-e), certi(-e); **I've got some** (*books etc*) ne ho alcuni; **some (of them) have been sold** alcuni sono stati venduti
2 (*a certain amount*) un po'; **I've got some** (*money, milk*) ne ho un po'; **I've read some of the book** ho letto parte del libro; **some**

(of it) was left ne è rimasto un po'; **could I have some of that cheese?** potrei avere un po' di quel formaggio?
■ *adv*: **some 10 people** circa 10 persone

somebody ['sʌmbədɪ] *pron* qualcuno; **~ or other** qualcuno
someday ['sʌmdeɪ] *adv* uno di questi giorni, un giorno o l'altro
somehow ['sʌmhau] *adv* in un modo o nell'altro, in qualche modo; (*for some reason*) per qualche ragione
someone ['sʌmwʌn] *pron* = **somebody**
someplace ['sʌmpleɪs] *adv* (*US*) = **somewhere**
somersault ['sʌməsɔ:lt] *n* capriola; (*in air*) salto mortale ■ *vi* fare una capriola (*or* un salto mortale); (*car*) cappottare
something ['sʌmθɪŋ] *pron* qualcosa; **~ interesting** qualcosa di interessante; **~ to do** qualcosa da fare; **he's ~ like me** mi assomiglia un po'; **it's ~ of a problem** è un bel problema
sometime ['sʌmtaɪm] *adv* (*in future*) una volta o l'altra; (*in past*): **~ last month** durante il mese scorso; **I'll finish it ~** lo finirò prima o poi
sometimes ['sʌmtaɪmz] *adv* qualche volta
somewhat ['sʌmwɔt] *adv* piuttosto
somewhere ['sʌmwɛəʳ] *adv* in *or* da qualche parte; **~ else** da qualche altra parte
son [sʌn] *n* figlio
sonar ['səunɑ:ʳ] *n* sonar *m*
sonata [sə'nɑ:tə] *n* sonata
song [sɔŋ] *n* canzone *f*
songbook ['sɔŋbuk] *n* canzoniere *m*
songwriter ['sɔŋraɪtəʳ] *n* compositore(-trice) di canzoni
sonic ['sɔnɪk] *adj* (*boom*) sonico(-a)
son-in-law ['sʌnɪnlɔ:] *n* genero
sonnet ['sɔnɪt] *n* sonetto
sonny ['sʌnɪ] *n* (*col*) ragazzo mio
soon [su:n] *adv* presto, fra poco; (*early*) presto; **~ afterwards** poco dopo; **very/quite ~** molto/abbastanza presto; **as ~ as possible** prima possibile; **I'll do it as ~ as I can** lo farò appena posso; **how ~ can you be ready?** fra quanto tempo sarà pronto?; **see you ~!** a presto!
sooner ['su:nəʳ] *adv* (*time*) prima; (*preference*): **I would ~ do** preferirei fare; **~ or later** prima o poi; **no ~ said than done** detto fatto; **the ~ the better** prima è meglio è; **no ~ had we left than ...** eravamo appena partiti, quando ...
soot [sut] *n* fuliggine *f*
soothe [su:ð] *vt* calmare
soothing ['su:ðɪŋ] *adj* (*ointment etc*) calmante; (*tone, words etc*) rassicurante
SOP *n abbr* = **standard operating procedure**
sop [sɔp] *n*: **that's only a ~** è soltanto un contentino
sophisticated [sə'fɪstɪkeɪtɪd] *adj* sofisticato(-a); raffinato(-a); (*film, mind*) sottile
sophistication [səfɪstɪ'keɪʃən] *n* raffinatezza; (*of machine*) complessità; (*of argument etc*) sottigliezza
sophomore ['sɔfəmɔ:ʳ] *n* (*US*) studente(-essa) del secondo anno
soporific [sɔpə'rɪfɪk] *adj* soporifero(-a)
sopping ['sɔpɪŋ] *adj* (*also*: **sopping wet**) bagnato(-a) fradicioa(-a)
soppy ['sɔpɪ] *adj* (*pej*) sentimentale
soprano [sə'prɑ:nəu] *n* (*voice*) soprano *m*; (*singer*) soprano *m/f*
sorbet ['sɔ:beɪ] *n* sorbetto
sorcerer ['sɔ:sərəʳ] *n* stregone *m*, mago
sordid ['sɔ:dɪd] *adj* sordido(-a)
sore [sɔ:ʳ] *adj* (*painful*) dolorante; (*col: offended*) offeso(-a) ■ *n* piaga; **my eyes are ~, I have ~ eyes** mi fanno male gli occhi; **~ throat** mal *m* di gola; **it's a ~ point** (*fig*) è un punto delicato
sorely ['sɔ:lɪ] *adv* (*tempted*) fortemente
sorrel ['sɔrəl] *n* acetosa
sorrow ['sɔrəu] *n* dolore *m*
sorrowful ['sɔrəuful] *adj* triste
sorry ['sɔrɪ] *adj* spiacente; (*condition, excuse*) misero(-a), pietoso(-a); (*sight, failure*) triste; **~!** scusa! (*or* scusi! *or* scusate!); **to feel ~ for sb** rincrescersi per qn; **I'm ~ to hear that ...** mi dispiace (sentire) che ...; **to be ~ about sth** essere dispiaciuto *or* spiacente di qc
sort [sɔ:t] *n* specie *f*, genere *m*; (*make: of coffee, car etc*) tipo ■ *vt* (*also*: **sort out**: *papers*) classificare; ordinare; (*: letters etc*) smistare; (*: problems*) risolvere; (*Comput*) ordinare; **what ~ of car?** che tipo di macchina?; **I shall do nothing of the ~!** nemmeno per sogno!; **it's ~ of awkward** (*col*) è piuttosto difficile
sortie ['sɔ:tɪ] *n* sortita
sorting office ['sɔ:tɪŋ-] *n* ufficio *m* smistamento *inv*
SOS *n abbr* S.O.S. *m inv*
so-so ['səusəu] *adv* così così
soufflé ['su:fleɪ] *n* soufflé *m inv*
sought [sɔ:t] *pt, pp of* **seek**
sought-after ['sɔ:tɑ:ftəʳ] *adj* richiesto(-a)
soul [səul] *n* anima; **the poor ~ had nowhere to sleep** il poveraccio non aveva dove dormire; **I didn't see a ~** non ho visto anima viva
soul-destroying ['səuldɪ'strɔɪɪŋ] *adj* demoralizzante

S

soulful ['səulful] *adj* pieno(-a) di sentimento
soulless ['səullıs] *adj* senz'anima, inumano(-a)
soul mate *n* anima gemella
soul-searching ['səulsəːtʃıŋ] *n*: **after much ~** dopo un profondo esame di coscienza
sound [saund] *adj* (*healthy*) sano(-a); (*safe, not damaged*) solido(-a), in buono stato; (*reliable, not superficial*) solido(-a); (*sensible*) giudizioso(-a), di buon senso; (*valid: argument, policy, claim*) valido(-a) ■ *adv*: **~ asleep** profondamente addormentato ■ *n* (*noise*) suono; rumore *m*; (*Geo*) stretto ■ *vt* (*alarm*) suonare; (*also*: **sound out**: *opinions*) sondare ■ *vi* suonare; (*fig: seem*) sembrare; **to be of ~ mind** essere sano di mente; **I don't like the ~ of it** (*fig: film etc*) non mi dice niente; (*: news*) è preoccupante; **it sounds as if ...** ho l'impressione che ...; **it sounds like French** somiglia al francese; **that sounds like them arriving** mi sembra di sentirli arrivare
▸ **sound off** *vi* (*col*): **to ~ off (about)** (*give one's opinions*) fare dei grandi discorsi (su)
sound barrier *n* muro del suono
soundbite ['saundbaıt] *n* frase *f* incisiva
sound effects *npl* effetti *mpl* sonori
sound engineer *n* tecnico del suono
sounding ['saundıŋ] *n* (*Naut etc*) scandagliamento
sounding board *n* (*Mus*) cassa di risonanza; (*fig*): **to use sb as a ~ for one's ideas** provare le proprie idee su qn
soundly ['saundlı] *adv* (*sleep*) profondamente; (*beat*) duramente
soundproof ['saundpruːf] *vt* insonorizzare, isolare acusticamente ■ *adj* insonorizzato(-a), isolato(-a) acusticamente
sound system *n* impianto *m*, audio *inv*
soundtrack ['saundtræk] *n* (*of film*) colonna sonora
soup [suːp] *n* minestra; (*clear*) brodo; (*thick*) zuppa; **in the ~** (*fig*) nei guai
soup course *n* minestra
soup kitchen *n* mensa per i poveri
soup plate *n* piatto fondo
soupspoon ['suːpspuːn] *n* cucchiaio da minestra
sour ['sauəʳ] *adj* aspro(-a); (*fruit*) acerbo(-a); (*milk*) acido(-a), fermentato(-a); (*fig*) acido(-a); **to go** *or* **turn ~** (*milk, wine*) inacidirsi; (*fig: relationship, plans*) guastarsi; **it's ~ grapes** (*fig*) è soltanto invidia
source [sɔːs] *n* fonte *f*, sorgente *f*; (*fig*) fonte; **I have it from a reliable ~ that ...** ho saputo da fonte sicura che ...
south [sauθ] *n* sud *m*, meridione *m*, mezzogiorno ■ *adj* del sud, sud *inv*, meridionale ■ *adv* verso sud; **(to the) ~ of** a sud di; **the S~ of France** il sud della Francia; **to travel ~** viaggiare verso sud
South Africa *n* Sudafrica *m*
South African *adj, n* sudafricano(-a)
South America *n* Sudamerica *m*, America del sud
South American *adj, n* sudamericano(-a)
southbound ['sauθbaund] *adj* (*gen*) diretto(-a) a sud; (*carriageway*) sud *inv*
south-east [sauθ'iːst] *n* sud-est *m*
South-East Asia *n* Asia sudorientale
southerly ['sʌðəlı] *adj* del sud
southern ['sʌðən] *adj* del sud, meridionale; (*wall*) esposto(-a) a sud; **the ~ hemisphere** l'emisfero australe
South Pole *n* Polo Sud
South Sea Islands *npl*: **the ~** le isole dei Mari del Sud
South Seas *npl*: **the ~** i Mari del Sud
South Vietnam *n* Vietnam *m* del Sud
southward ['sauθwəd], **southwards** ['sauθwədz] *adv* verso sud
south-west [sauθ'wɛst] *n* sud-ovest *m*
souvenir [suːvə'nıəʳ] *n* ricordo, souvenir *m inv*
sovereign ['sɔvrın] *adj, n* sovrano(-a)
sovereignty ['sɔvrəntı] *n* sovranità
soviet ['səuvıət] *adj* sovietico(-a)
Soviet Union *n*: **the ~** l'Unione *f* Sovietica
sow[1] [səu] (*pt* **sowed**, *pp* **sown**) [səun] *vt* seminare
sow[2] [sau] *n* scrofa
soya ['sɔıə], (*US*) **soy** [sɔı] *n*: **~ bean** seme *m* di soia; **~ sauce** salsa di soia
sozzled ['sɔzld] *adj* (*Brit col*) sbronzo(-a)
spa [spɑː] *n* (*resort*) stazione *f* termale; (*US*: *also*: **health spa**) centro di cure estetiche
space [speıs] *n* spazio; (*room*) posto; spazio; (*length of time*) intervallo ■ *cpd* spaziale ■ *vt* (*also*: **space out**) distanziare; **in a confined ~** in un luogo chiuso; **to clear a ~ for sth** fare posto per qc; **in a short ~ of time** in breve tempo; **(with)in the ~ of an hour/three generations** nell'arco di un'ora/di tre generazioni
space bar *n* (*on typewriter*) barra spaziatrice
spacecraft ['speıskrɑːft] *n* (*pl inv*) veicolo spaziale
spaceman ['speısmæn] *n* astronauta *m*, cosmonauta *m*
spaceship ['speısʃıp] *n* astronave *f*, navicella spaziale
space shuttle *n* shuttle *m inv*
spacesuit ['speıssuːt] *n* tuta spaziale
spacewoman ['speıswumən] *n* astronauta *f*, cosmonauta *f*

spacing ['speɪsɪŋ] *n* spaziatura; **single/double ~** (*Typ etc*) spaziatura singola/doppia
spacious ['speɪʃəs] *adj* spazioso(-a), ampio(-a)
spade [speɪd] *n* (*tool*) vanga; pala; (*child's*) paletta; **spades** *npl* (*Cards*) picche *fpl*
spadework ['speɪdwəːk] *n* (*fig*) duro lavoro preparatorio
spaghetti [spə'gɛtɪ] *n* spaghetti *mpl*
Spain [speɪn] *n* Spagna
spam [spæm] (*Comput*) *n* spamming *m* ■ *vt*: **to ~ sb** inviare a qn messaggi pubblicitari non richiesti via email
span [spæn] *n* (*of bird, plane*) apertura alare; (*of arch*) campata; (*in time*) periodo; durata ■ *vt* attraversare; (*fig*) abbracciare
Spaniard ['spænjəd] *n* spagnolo(-a)
spaniel ['spænjəl] *n* spaniel *m inv*
Spanish ['spænɪʃ] *adj* spagnolo(-a) ■ *n* (*Ling*) spagnolo; **the ~** *npl* gli Spagnoli; **~ omelette** *frittata di cipolle, pomodori e peperoni*
spank [spæŋk] *vt* sculacciare
spanner ['spænəʳ] *n* (*Brit*) chiave *f* inglese
spar [spɑːʳ] *n* asta, palo ■ *vi* (*Boxing*) allenarsi
spare [spɛəʳ] *adj* di riserva, di scorta; (*surplus*) in più, d'avanzo ■ *n* (*part*) pezzo di ricambio ■ *vt* (*do without*) fare a meno di; (*afford to give*) concedere; (*refrain from hurting, using*) risparmiare; **to ~** (*surplus*) d'avanzo; **there are 2 going ~** (*Brit*) ce ne sono 2 in più; **to ~ no expense** non badare a spese; **can you ~ the time?** ha tempo?; **I've a few minutes to ~** ho un attimino di tempo; **there is no time to ~** non c'è tempo da perdere; **can you ~ (me) £10?** puoi prestarmi 10 sterline?
spare part *n* pezzo di ricambio
spare room *n* stanza degli ospiti
spare time *n* tempo libero
spare tyre *n* (*Aut*) gomma di scorta
spare wheel *n* (*Aut*) ruota di scorta
sparing ['spɛərɪŋ] *adj* (*amount*) scarso(-a); (*use*) parsimonioso(-a); **to be ~ with** essere avaro(-a) di
sparingly ['spɛərɪŋlɪ] *adv* moderatamente
spark [spɑːk] *n* scintilla
sparkle ['spɑːkl] *n* scintillio, sfavillio ■ *vi* scintillare, sfavillare; (*bubble*) spumeggiare, frizzare
sparkler ['spɑːkləʳ] *n* fuoco d'artificio
sparkling ['spɑːklɪŋ] *adj* scintillante, sfavillante; (*wine*) spumante
spark plug *n* candela
sparring partner ['spɑːrɪŋ-] *n* sparring partner *m inv*; (*fig*) *interlocutore abituale in discussioni, dibattiti, tavole rotonde ecc*
sparrow ['spærəu] *n* passero
sparse [spɑːs] *adj* sparso(-a), rado(-a)
spartan ['spɑːtən] *adj* (*fig*) spartano(-a)
spasm ['spæzəm] *n* (*Med*) spasmo; (*fig*) accesso, attacco
spasmodic [spæz'mɔdɪk] *adj* spasmodico(-a); (*fig*) intermittente
spastic ['spæstɪk] *n* spastico(-a)
spat [spæt] *pt, pp of* **spit** ■ *n* (*US*) battibecco
spate [speɪt] *n* (*fig*): **~ of** diluvio *or* fiume *m* di; **in ~** (*river*) in piena
spatial ['speɪʃəl] *adj* spaziale
spatter ['spætəʳ] *vt, vi* schizzare
spatula ['spætjulə] *n* spatola
spawn [spɔːn] *vt* deporre; (*pej*) produrre ■ *vi* deporre le uova ■ *n* uova *fpl*
SPCA *n abbr* (US: = *Society for the Prevention of Cruelty to Animals*) ≈ E.N.P.A. *m* (= *Ente Nazionale per la Protezione degli Animali*)
SPCC *n abbr* (US) = **Society for the Prevention of Cruelty to Children**
speak (*pt* **spoke**, *pp* **spoken**) [spiːk, spəuk, 'spəukn] *vt* (*language*) parlare; (*truth*) dire ■ *vi* parlare; **to ~ to sb/of** *or* **about sth** parlare a qn/di qc; **~ up!** parli più forte!; **to ~ at a conference/in a debate** partecipare ad una conferenza/ad un dibattito; **speaking!** (*on telephone*) sono io!; **to ~ one's mind** dire quello che si pensa; **he has no money to ~ of** non si può proprio dire che sia ricco
▸ **speak for** *vt fus*: **to ~ for sb** parlare a nome di qn; **that picture is already spoken for** (*in shop*) quel quadro è già stato venduto
speaker ['spiːkəʳ] *n* (*in public*) oratore(-trice); (*also*: **loudspeaker**) altoparlante *m*; (*Pol*): **the S~** *il presidente della Camera dei Comuni or* (*US*) *dei Rappresentanti*; **are you a Welsh ~?** parla gallese?
speaking ['spiːkɪŋ] *adj* parlante; **Italian-~ people** persone che parlano italiano; **to be on ~ terms** parlarsi
spear [spɪəʳ] *n* lancia
spearhead ['spɪəhɛd] *n* punta di lancia; (*Mil*) reparto d'assalto ■ *vt* (*attack etc*) condurre
spearmint ['spɪəmɪnt] *n* (*Bot etc*) menta verde
spec [spɛk] *n* (*Brit col*): **on ~** sperando bene; **to buy sth on ~** comprare qc sperando di fare un affare
special ['spɛʃl] *adj* speciale ■ *n* (*train*) treno supplementare; **nothing ~** niente di speciale; **take ~ care** siate particolarmente prudenti
special agent *n* agente *m* segreto
special correspondent *n* inviato speciale
special delivery *n* (*Post*): **by ~** per espresso
special effects *npl* (*Cine*) effetti *mpl* speciali
specialist ['spɛʃəlɪst] *n* specialista *m/f*; **a heart ~** (*Med*) un cardiologo
speciality [spɛʃɪ'ælɪtɪ], (*esp US*) **specialty** *n* specialità *f inv*

S

specialize ['spɛʃəlaɪz] *vi*: **to ~ (in)** specializzarsi (in)
specially ['spɛʃəlɪ] *adv* specialmente, particolarmente
special offer *n* (*Comm*) offerta speciale
specialty ['spɛʃəltɪ] *n* (*esp US*) = **speciality**
species ['spi:ʃi:z] *n* (*pl inv*) specie *f inv*
specific [spə'sɪfɪk] *adj* specifico(-a); preciso(-a); **to be ~ to** avere un legame specifico con
specifically [spə'sɪfɪklɪ] *adv* (*explicitly: state, warn*) chiaramente, esplicitamente; (*especially: design, intend*) appositamente
specification [spɛsɪfɪ'keɪʃən] *n* specificazione *f*; **specifications** *npl* (*of car, machine*) dati *mpl* caratteristici; (*for building*) dettagli *mpl*
specify ['spɛsɪfaɪ] *vt* specificare, precisare; **unless otherwise specified** salvo indicazioni contrarie
specimen ['spɛsɪmən] *n* esemplare *m*, modello; (*Med*) campione *m*
specimen copy *n* campione *m*
specimen signature *n* firma depositata
speck [spɛk] *n* puntino, macchiolina; (*particle*) granello
speckled ['spɛkld] *adj* macchiettato(-a)
specs [spɛks] *npl* (*col*) occhiali *mpl*
spectacle ['spɛktəkl] *n* spettacolo; *see also* **spectacles**
spectacle case *n* (*Brit*) fodero per gli occhiali
spectacles ['spɛktəklz] *npl* (*Brit*) occhiali *mpl*
spectacular [spɛk'tækjulə^r] *adj* spettacolare ▪ *n* (*Cine etc*) film *m inv etc* spettacolare
spectator [spɛk'teɪtə^r] *n* spettatore(-trice)
spectator sport *n* sport *m inv* come spettacolo
spectra ['spɛktrə] *npl of* **spectrum**
spectre, (*US*) **specter** ['spɛktə^r] *n* spettro
spectrum (*pl* **spectra**) ['spɛktrəm, -rə] *n* spettro; (*fig*) gamma
speculate ['spɛkjuleɪt] *vi* speculare; (*try to guess*): **to ~ about** fare ipotesi su
speculation [spɛkju'leɪʃən] *n* speculazione *f*; congetture *fpl*
speculative ['spɛkjulətɪv] *adj* speculativo(-a)
speculator ['spɛkjuleɪtə^r] *n* speculatore(-trice)
sped [spɛd] *pt, pp of* **speed**
speech [spi:tʃ] *n* (*faculty*) parola; (*talk*) discorso; (*manner of speaking*) parlata; (*language*) linguaggio; (*enunciation*) elocuzione *f*
speech day *n* (*Brit Scol*) giorno della premiazione
speech impediment *n* difetto di pronuncia
speechless ['spi:tʃlɪs] *adj* ammutolito(-a), muto(-a)
speech therapy *n* cura dei disturbi del linguaggio
speed [spi:d] *n* velocità *f inv*; (*promptness*) prontezza; (*Aut: gear*) marcia ▪ *vi* (*pt, pp* **sped**) [spɛd]: **to ~ along** procedere velocemente; **the years sped by** gli anni sono volati; (*Aut: exceed speed limit*) andare a velocità eccessiva; **at ~** (*Brit*) velocemente; **at full** *or* **top ~** a tutta velocità; **at a ~ of 70 km/h** a una velocità di 70 km l'ora; **shorthand/typing speeds** numero di parole al minuto in stenografia/dattilografia; **a five-~ gearbox** un cambio a cinque marce
▸ **speed up** (*pt, pp* **speeded up**) *vi, vt* accelerare
speedboat ['spi:dbəut] *n* motoscafo; fuoribordo *m inv*
speed dating [-deɪtɪŋ] *n sistema di appuntamenti grazie al quale si possono incontrare in pochissimo tempo diverse persone e scegliere eventualmente chi frequentare*
speedily ['spi:dɪlɪ] *adv* velocemente; prontamente
speeding ['spi:dɪŋ] *n* (*Aut*) eccesso di velocità
speed limit *n* limite *m* di velocità
speedometer [spɪ'dɔmɪtə^r] *n* tachimetro
speed trap *n* (*Aut*) *tratto di strada sul quale la polizia controlla la velocità dei veicoli*
speedway ['spi:dweɪ] *n* (*Sport*) pista per motociclismo
speedy ['spi:dɪ] *adj* veloce, rapido(-a); (*reply*) pronto(-a)
speleologist [spɛlɪ'ɔlədʒɪst] *n* speleologo(-a)
spell [spɛl] *n* (*also*: **magic spell**) incantesimo; (*period of time*) (breve) periodo ▪ *vt* (*pt, pp* **spelt** *or* **spelled**) [spɛlt, spɛld] (*in writing*) scrivere (lettera per lettera); (*aloud*) dire lettera per lettera; (*fig*) significare; **to cast a ~ on sb** fare un incantesimo a qn; **he can't ~** fa errori di ortografia; **how do you ~ your name?** come si scrive il suo nome?; **can you ~ it for me?** me lo può dettare lettera per lettera?
spellbound ['spɛlbaund] *adj* incantato(-a), affascinato(-a)
spelling ['spɛlɪŋ] *n* ortografia
spelt [spɛlt] *pt, pp of* **spell**
spend (*pt, pp* **spent**) [spɛnd, spɛnt] *vt* (*money*) spendere; (*time, life*) passare; **to ~ time/money/effort on sth** dedicare tempo/soldi/energie a qc
spending ['spɛndɪŋ] *n*: **government ~** spesa pubblica
spending money *n* denaro per le piccole spese
spending power *n* potere *m* d'acquisto
spendthrift ['spɛndθrɪft] *n* spendaccione(-a)

spent [spɛnt] *pt, pp of* **spend** ■ *adj* (*patience*) esaurito(-a); (*cartridge, bullets, match*) usato(-a)
sperm [spəːm] *n* sperma *m*
sperm bank *n* banca dello sperma
sperm whale *n* capodoglio
spew [spjuː] *vt* vomitare
sphere [sfɪəʳ] *n* sfera
spherical ['sfɛrɪkl] *adj* sferico(-a)
sphinx [sfɪŋks] *n* sfinge *f*
spice [spaɪs] *n* spezia ■ *vt* aromatizzare
spick-and-span ['spɪkən'spæn] *adj* impeccabile
spicy ['spaɪsɪ] *adj* piccante
spider ['spaɪdəʳ] *n* ragno; **~'s web** ragnatela
spiel [spiːl] *n* (*col*) tiritera
spike [spaɪk] *n* punta; **spikes** *npl* (*Sport*) scarpe *fpl* chiodate
spike heel *n* (*US*) tacco a spillo
spiky ['spaɪkɪ] *adj* (*bush, branch*) spinoso(-a); (*animal*) ricoperto(-a) di aculei
spill (*pt, pp* **spilt** *or* **spilled**) [spɪl, -t, -d] *vt* versare, rovesciare ■ *vi* versarsi, rovesciarsi; **to ~ the beans** (*col*) vuotare il sacco
▸ **spill out** *vi* riversarsi fuori
▸ **spill over** *vi*: **to ~ over (into)** (*liquid*) versarsi (in); (*crowd*) riversarsi (in)
spillage ['spɪlɪdʒ] *n* (*event*) fuoriuscita; (*substance*) sostanza fuoriuscita
spin [spɪn] *n* (*revolution of wheel*) rotazione *f*; (*Aviat*) avvitamento; (*trip in car*) giretto ■ *vb* (*pt, pp* **spun**) [spʌn] *vt* (*wool etc*) filare; (*wheel*) far girare; (*Brit: clothes*) mettere nella centrifuga ■ *vi* girare; **to ~ a yarn** raccontare una storia; **to ~ a coin** (*Brit*) lanciare in aria una moneta
▸ **spin out** *vt* far durare
spina bifida ['spaɪnə'bɪfɪdə] *n* spina bifida
spinach ['spɪnɪtʃ] *n* spinacio; (*as food*) spinaci *mpl*
spinal ['spaɪnl] *adj* spinale
spinal column *n* colonna vertebrale, spina dorsale
spinal cord *n* midollo spinale
spindly ['spɪndlɪ] *adj* lungo(-a) e sottile, filiforme
spin doctor *n* (*col*) *esperto di comunicazioni responsabile dell'immagine di un partito politico*
spin-dry ['spɪn'draɪ] *vt* asciugare con la centrifuga
spin-dryer [spɪn'draɪəʳ] *n* (*Brit*) centrifuga
spine [spaɪn] *n* spina dorsale; (*thorn*) spina
spine-chilling ['spaɪntʃɪlɪŋ] *adj* agghiacciante
spineless ['spaɪnlɪs] *adj* invertebrato(-a), senza spina dorsale; (*fig*) smidollato(-a)
spinner ['spɪnəʳ] *n* (*of thread*) tessitore(-trice)
spinning ['spɪnɪŋ] *n* filatura
spinning top *n* trottola
spinning wheel *n* filatoio
spin-off ['spɪnɔf] *n* applicazione *f* secondaria
spinster ['spɪnstəʳ] *n* nubile *f*; zitella
spiral ['spaɪərl] *n* spirale *f* ■ *adj* a spirale ■ *vi* (*prices*) salire vertiginosamente; **the inflationary ~** la spirale dell'inflazione
spiral staircase *n* scala a chiocciola
spire ['spaɪəʳ] *n* guglia
spirit ['spɪrɪt] *n* (*soul*) spirito, anima; (*ghost*) spirito, fantasma *m*; (*mood*) stato d'animo, umore *m*; (*courage*) coraggio; **spirits** *npl* (*drink*) alcolici *mpl*; **in good spirits** di buon umore; **in low spirits** triste, abbattuto(-a); **community ~, public ~** senso civico
spirit duplicator *n* duplicatore *m* a spirito
spirited ['spɪrɪtɪd] *adj* vivace, vigoroso(-a); (*horse*) focoso(-a)
spirit level *n* livella a bolla (d'aria)
spiritual ['spɪrɪtjuəl] *adj* spirituale ■ *n* (*also*: **Negro spiritual**) spiritual *m inv*
spiritualism ['spɪrɪtjuəlɪzəm] *n* spiritismo
spit [spɪt] *n* (*for roasting*) spiedo; (*spittle*) sputo; (*saliva*) saliva ■ *vi* (*pt, pp* **spat**) [spæt] sputare; (*fire, fat*) scoppiettare
spite [spaɪt] *n* dispetto ■ *vt* contrariare, far dispetto a; **in ~ of** nonostante, malgrado
spiteful ['spaɪtful] *adj* dispettoso(-a); (*tongue, remark*) maligno(-a), velenoso(-a)
spitroast ['spɪt'rəust] *vt* cuocere allo spiedo
spitting ['spɪtɪŋ] *n*: **"~ prohibited"** "vietato sputare" ■ *adj*: **to be the ~ image of sb** essere il ritratto vivente *or* sputato di qn
spittle ['spɪtl] *n* saliva; sputo
spiv [spɪv] *n* (*Brit col*) imbroglione *m*
splash [splæʃ] *n* spruzzo; (*sound*) tonfo; (*of colour*) schizzo ■ *vt* spruzzare ■ *vi* (*also*: **splash about**) sguazzare; **to ~ paint on the floor** schizzare il pavimento di vernice
splashdown ['splæʃdaun] *n* ammaraggio
splay [spleɪ] *adj*: **~ footed** che ha i piedi piatti
spleen [spliːn] *n* (*Anat*) milza
splendid ['splɛndɪd] *adj* splendido(-a), magnifico(-a)
splendour, (*US*) **splendor** ['splɛndəʳ] *n* splendore *m*
splice [splaɪs] *vt* (*rope*) impiombare; (*wood*) calettare
splint [splɪnt] *n* (*Med*) stecca
splinter ['splɪntəʳ] *n* scheggia ■ *vi* scheggiarsi
splinter group *n* gruppo dissidente
split [splɪt] *n* spaccatura; (*fig: division, quarrel*) scissione *f* ■ *vb* (*pt, pp* **~**) *vt* spaccare; (*party*) dividere; (*work, profits*) spartire, ripartire ■ *vi* (*divide*) dividersi; **to do the splits** fare la spaccata; **to ~ the difference** dividersi la differenza

S

▸ **split up** *vi* (*couple*) separarsi, rompere; (*meeting*) sciogliersi
split-level ['splɪtlɛvl] *adj* (*house*) a piani sfalsati
split peas *npl* piselli *mpl* secchi spaccati
split personality *n* doppia personalità
split second *n* frazione *f* di secondo
splitting ['splɪtɪŋ] *adj*: **a ~ headache** un mal di testa da impazzire
splutter ['splʌtəʳ] *vi* farfugliare; sputacchiare
spoil (*pt, pp* **spoilt** *or* **spoiled**) [spɔɪl, -t, -d] *vt* (*damage*) rovinare, guastare; (*mar*) sciupare; (*child*) viziare; (*ballot paper*) rendere nullo(-a), invalidare; **to be spoiling for a fight** morire dalla voglia di litigare
spoils [spɔɪlz] *npl* bottino
spoilsport ['spɔɪlspɔːt] *n* guastafeste *m/f inv*
spoilt [spɔɪlt] *pt, pp of* **spoil** ■ *adj* (*child*) viziato(-a); (*ballot paper*) nullo(-a)
spoke [spəuk] *pt of* **speak** ■ *n* raggio
spoken ['spəukn] *pp of* **speak**
spokesman ['spəuksmən], **spokeswoman** [-wumən] *n* portavoce *m/f inv*
spokesperson ['spəukspəːsn] *n* portavoce *m/f*
sponge [spʌndʒ] *n* spugna; (*Culin: also:* **sponge cake**) pan *m* di Spagna ■ *vt* spugnare, pulire con una spugna ■ *vi*: **to ~ on** *or* (*US*) **off of** scroccare a
sponge bag *n* (*Brit*) nécessaire *m inv*
sponge cake *n* pan *m* di Spagna
sponger ['spʌndʒəʳ] *n* (*pej*) parassita *m/f*, scroccone(-a)
spongy ['spʌndʒɪ] *adj* spugnoso(-a)
sponsor ['spɔnsəʳ] *n* (*Radio, TV, Sport etc*) sponsor *m inv*; (*of enterprise, bill, for fund-raising*) promotore(-trice) ■ *vt* sponsorizzare; patrocinare; (*Pol: bill*) presentare; **I sponsored him at 3p a mile** (*in fund-raising race*) ho offerto in beneficenza 3 penny per ogni miglio che fa
sponsorship ['spɔnsəʃɪp] *n* sponsorizzazione *f*; patrocinio
spontaneity [spɔntə'neɪɪtɪ] *n* spontaneità
spontaneous [spɔn'teɪnɪəs] *adj* spontaneo(-a)
spoof [spuːf] *n* presa in giro, parodia
spooky ['spuːkɪ] *adj* che fa accapponare la pelle
spool [spuːl] *n* bobina
spoon [spuːn] *n* cucchiaio
spoon-feed ['spuːnfiːd] *vt* nutrire con il cucchiaio; (*fig*) imboccare
spoonful ['spuːnful] *n* cucchiaiata
sporadic [spə'rædɪk] *adj* sporadico(-a)
sport [spɔːt] *n* sport *m inv*; (*person*) persona di spirito; (*amusement*) divertimento ■ *vt* sfoggiare; **indoor/outdoor sports** sport *mpl* al chiuso/all'aria aperta; **to say sth in ~** dire qc per scherzo
sporting ['spɔːtɪŋ] *adj* sportivo(-a); **to give sb a ~ chance** dare a qn una possibilità (di vincere)
sport jacket *n* (*US*) = **sports jacket**
sports car *n* automobile *f* sportiva
sports ground *n* campo sportivo
sports jacket *n* giacca sportiva
sportsman ['spɔːtsmən] *n* sportivo
sportsmanship ['spɔːtsmənʃɪp] *n* spirito sportivo
sports page *n* pagina sportiva
sports utility vehicle *n* (*esp US*) fuoristrada *m inv*
sportswear ['spɔːtswɛəʳ] *n* abiti *mpl* sportivi
sportswoman ['spɔːtswumən] *n* sportiva
sporty ['spɔːtɪ] *adj* sportivo(-a)
spot [spɔt] *n* punto; (*mark*) macchia; (*dot: on pattern*) pallino; (*pimple*) foruncolo; (*place*) posto; (*also:* **spot advertisement**) spot *m inv*; (*small amount*): **a ~ of** un po' di ■ *vt* (*notice*) individuare, distinguere; **on the ~** sul posto; **to do sth on the ~** fare qc immediatamente *or* lì per lì; **to put sb on the ~** mettere qn in difficoltà; **to come out in spots** coprirsi di foruncoli
spot check *n* controllo senza preavviso
spotless ['spɔtlɪs] *adj* immacolato(-a)
spotlight ['spɔtlaɪt] *n* proiettore *m*; (*Aut*) faro ausiliario
spot-on [spɔt'ɔn] *adj* (*Brit*) esatto(-a)
spot price *n* (*Comm*) prezzo del pronto
spotted ['spɔtɪd] *adj* macchiato(-a); a puntini, a pallini; **~ with** punteggiato(-a) di
spotty ['spɔtɪ] *adj* (*face*) foruncoloso(-a)
spouse [spauz] *n* sposo(-a)
spout [spaut] *n* (*of jug*) beccuccio; (*of liquid*) zampillo, getto ■ *vi* zampillare
sprain [spreɪn] *n* storta, distorsione *f* ■ *vt*: **to ~ one's ankle** storcersi una caviglia
sprang [spræŋ] *pt of* **spring**
sprawl [sprɔːl] *vi* sdraiarsi (in modo scomposto) ■ *n*: **urban ~** sviluppo urbanistico incontrollato; **to send sb sprawling** mandare qn a gambe all'aria
spray [spreɪ] *n* spruzzo; (*container*) nebulizzatore *m*, spray *m inv*; (*of flowers*) mazzetto ■ *cpd* (*deodorant*) spray *inv* ■ *vt* spruzzare; (*crops*) irrorare
spread [sprɛd] *n* diffusione *f*; (*distribution*) distribuzione *f*; (*Press, Typ: two pages*) doppia pagina; (*: across columns*) articolo a più colonne; (*Culin*) pasta (da spalmare) ■ *vb* (*pt, pp* **~**) *vt* (*cloth*) stendere, distendere; (*butter etc*) spalmare; (*disease, knowledge*) propagare, diffondere ■ *vi* stendersi, distendersi;

spalmarsi; propagarsi, diffondersi; **middle-age ~** pancetta; **repayments will be ~ over 18 months** i versamenti saranno scaglionati lungo un periodo di 18 mesi
spread-eagled ['sprɛdi:gld] *adj*: **to be** *or* **lie ~** essere disteso(-a) a gambe e braccia aperte
spreadsheet ['sprɛdʃi:t] *n* (*Comput*) foglio elettronico
spree [spri:] *n*: **to go on a ~** fare baldoria
sprig [sprɪg] *n* ramoscello
sprightly ['spraɪtlɪ] *adj* vivace
spring [sprɪŋ] *n* (*leap*) salto, balzo; (*bounciness*) elasticità; (*coiled metal*) molla; (*season*) primavera; (*of water*) sorgente *f* ■ *vi* (*pt* **sprang**, *pp* **sprung**) [spræŋ, sprʌŋ] saltare, balzare ■ *vt*: **to ~ a leak** (*pipe etc*) cominciare a perdere; **to walk with a ~ in one's step** camminare con passo elastico; **in ~, in the ~** in primavera; **to ~ from** provenire da; **to ~ into action** entrare (rapidamente) in azione; **he sprang the news on me** mi ha sorpreso con quella notizia
▸ **spring up** *vi* (*problem*) presentarsi
springboard ['sprɪŋbɔ:d] *n* trampolino
spring-clean [sprɪŋ'kli:n] *n* (*also*: **spring-cleaning**) grandi pulizie *fpl* di primavera
spring onion *n* (*Brit*) cipollina
spring roll *n* *involtino fritto di verdure o carne tipico della cucina cinese*
springtime ['sprɪŋtaɪm] *n* primavera
springy ['sprɪŋɪ] *adj* elastico(-a)
sprinkle ['sprɪŋkl] *vt* spruzzare; spargere; **to ~ water** *etc* **on, ~ with water** *etc* spruzzare dell'acqua *etc* su; **to ~ sugar** *etc* **on, ~ with sugar** *etc* spolverizzare di zucchero *etc*; **sprinkled with** (*fig*) cosparso(-a) di
sprinkler ['sprɪŋklə^r^] *n* (*for lawn etc*) irrigatore *m*; (*for fire-fighting*) sprinkler *m inv*
sprinkling ['sprɪŋklɪŋ] *n* (*of water*) qualche goccia; (*of salt, sugar*) pizzico
sprint [sprɪnt] *n* scatto ■ *vi* scattare; **the 200-metres ~** i 200 metri piani
sprinter ['sprɪntə^r^] *n* velocista *m/f*
sprite [spraɪt] *n* elfo, folletto
spritzer ['sprɪtsə^r^] *n* spritz *m inv*
sprocket ['sprɔkɪt] *n* (*on printer etc*) dente *m*, rocchetto
sprout [spraut] *vi* germogliare
sprouts [sprauts] *npl* (*also*: **Brussels sprouts**) cavolini *mpl* di Bruxelles
spruce [spru:s] *n* abete *m* rosso ■ *adj* lindo(-a); azzimato(-a)
▸ **spruce up** *vt* (*tidy*) mettere in ordine; (*smarten up*: *room etc*) abbellire; **to ~ o.s. up** farsi bello(-a)
sprung [sprʌŋ] *pp of* **spring**
spry [spraɪ] *adj* arzillo(-a), sveglio(-a)
SPUC *n abbr* (= *Society for the Protection of Unborn Children*) *associazione anti-abortista*
spun [spʌn] *pt, pp of* **spin**
spur [spə:^r^] *n* sperone *m*; (*fig*) sprone *m*, incentivo ■ *vt* (*also*: **spur on**) spronare; **on the ~ of the moment** lì per lì
spurious ['spjuərɪəs] *adj* falso(-a)
spurn [spə:n] *vt* rifiutare con disprezzo, sdegnare
spurt [spə:t] *n* getto; (*of energy*) esplosione *f* ■ *vi* sgorgare; zampillare; **to put in** *or* **on a ~** (*runner*) fare uno scatto; (*fig*: *in work etc*) affrettarsi, sbrigarsi
sputter ['spʌtə^r^] *vi* = **splutter**
spy [spaɪ] *n* spia ■ *cpd* (*film, story*) di spionaggio ■ *vi*: **to ~ on** spiare ■ *vt* (*see*) scorgere
spying ['spaɪɪŋ] *n* spionaggio
Sq. *abbr* (*in address*) = **square**
sq. *abbr* (*Math etc*) = **square**
squabble ['skwɔbl] *n* battibecco ■ *vi* bisticciarsi
squad [skwɔd] *n* (*Mil*) plotone *m*; (*Police*) squadra; **flying ~** (*Police*) volante *f*
squad car *n* (*Brit Police*) automobile *f* della polizia
squaddie ['skwɔdɪ] *n* (*Mil*: *col*) burba
squadron ['skwɔdrn] *n* (*Mil*) squadrone *m*; (*Aviat, Naut*) squadriglia
squalid ['skwɔlɪd] *adj* sordido(-a)
squall [skwɔ:l] *n* burrasca
squalor ['skwɔlə^r^] *n* squallore *m*
squander ['skwɔndə^r^] *vt* dissipare
square [skwɛə^r^] *n* quadrato; (*in town*) piazza; (*US*: *block of houses*) blocco, isolato; (*instrument*) squadra ■ *adj* quadrato(-a); (*honest*) onesto(-a); (*col*: *ideas, person*) di vecchio stampo ■ *vt* (*arrange*) regolare; (*Math*) elevare al quadrato ■ *vi* (*agree*) accordarsi; **a ~ meal** un pasto abbondante; **2 metres ~** di 2 metri per 2; **1 ~ metre** 1 metro quadrato; **we're back to ~ one** (*fig*) siamo al punto di partenza; **all ~** pari; **to get one's accounts ~** mettere in ordine i propri conti; **I'll ~ it with him** (*col*) sistemo io le cose con lui; **can you ~ it with your conscience?** (*reconcile*) puoi conciliarlo con la tua coscienza?
▸ **square up** *vi* (*Brit*: *settle*) saldare, pagare; **to ~ up with sb** regolare i conti con qn
square bracket *n* (*Typ*) parentesi *f inv* quadra
squarely ['skwɛəlɪ] *adv* (*directly*) direttamente; (*honestly, fairly*) onestamente
square root *n* radice *f* quadrata
squash [skwɔʃ] *n* (*Brit*: *drink*): **lemon/orange ~** sciroppo di limone/arancia; (*vegetable*) zucca; (*Sport*) squash *m* ■ *vt* schiacciare

S

squat [skwɔt] *adj* tarchiato(-a), tozzo(-a) ■ *vi* accovacciarsi; (*on property*) occupare abusivamente
squatter ['skwɔtə^r] *n* occupante *m/f* abusivo(-a)
squawk [skwɔ:k] *vi* emettere strida rauche
squeak [skwi:k] *vi* squittire ■ *n* (*of hinge, wheel etc*) cigolio; (*of shoes*) scricchiolio; (*of mouse etc*) squittio
squeaky ['skwi:kɪ] *adj* (*col*) cigolante; **to be ~ clean** (*fig*) avere un'immagine pulita
squeal [skwi:l] *vi* strillare
squeamish ['skwi:mɪʃ] *adj* schizzinoso(-a); disgustato(-a)
squeeze [skwi:z] *n* pressione *f*; (*also Econ*) stretta; (*credit squeeze*) stretta creditizia ■ *vt* premere; (*hand, arm*) stringere ■ *vi* (*also*: **to squeeze in**) infilarsi; **to ~ past/under sth** passare vicino/sotto a qc con difficoltà; **a ~ of lemon** una spruzzata di limone
▸ **squeeze out** *vt* spremere
squelch [skwɛltʃ] *vi* fare ciac; sguazzare
squib [skwɪb] *n* petardo
squid [skwɪd] *n* calamaro
squint [skwɪnt] *vi* essere strabico(-a); (*in the sunlight*) strizzare gli occhi ■ *n*: **he has a ~** è strabico; **to ~ at sth** guardare qc di traverso; (*quickly*) dare un'occhiata a qc
squire ['skwaɪə^r] *n* (*Brit*) proprietario terriero
squirm [skwə:m] *vi* contorcersi
squirrel ['skwɪrəl] *n* scoiattolo
squirt [skwə:t] *n* schizzo ■ *vi* schizzare; zampillare
Sr *abbr* = **senior**; **sister** (*Rel*)
SRC *n abbr* (*Brit*: = *Students' Representative Council*) *comitato di rappresentanza studenti*
Sri Lanka [srɪ'læŋkə] *n* Sri Lanka *m*
SRO *abbr* (*US*: = *standing room only*) solo posti in piedi
SS *abbr* = **steamship**
SSA *n abbr* (*US*: = *Social Security Administration*) ≈ Previdenza Sociale
SST *n abbr* (*US*) = **supersonic transport**
ST *abbr* (*US*: = *Standard Time*) *ora ufficiale*
St *abbr* = **saint**; **street**
stab [stæb] *n* (*with knife etc*) pugnalata; (*col*: *try*): **to have a ~ at (doing) sth** provare a fare qc ■ *vt* pugnalare; **to ~ sb to death** uccidere qn a coltellate
stabbing ['stæbɪŋ] *n*: **there's been a ~** qualcuno è stato pugnalato ■ *adj* (*pain, ache*) lancinante
stability [stə'bɪlɪtɪ] *n* stabilità
stabilization [steɪbəlaɪ'zeɪʃən] *n* stabilizzazione *f*
stabilize ['steɪbəlaɪz] *vt* stabilizzare ■ *vi* stabilizzarsi
stabilizer ['steɪbəlaɪzə^r] *n* (*Aviat, Naut*) stabilizzatore *m*
stable ['steɪbl] *n* (*for horses*) scuderia; (*for cattle*) stalla ■ *adj* stabile; **riding stables** maneggio
staccato [stə'kɑ:təu] *adv* in modo staccato ■ *adj* (*Mus*) staccato(-a); (*sound*) scandito(-a)
stack [stæk] *n* catasta, pila; (*col*) mucchio, sacco ■ *vt* accatastare, ammucchiare; **there's stacks of time to finish it** (*Brit col*) abbiamo un sacco di tempo per finirlo
stadium ['steɪdɪəm] *n* stadio
staff [stɑ:f] *n* (*work force*: *gen*) personale *m*; (: *Brit*: *Scol*) personale insegnante; (: *servants*) personale di servizio; (*Mil*) stato maggiore; (*stick*) bastone *m* ■ *vt* fornire di personale
staffroom ['stɑ:fru:m] *n* sala dei professori
Staffs *abbr* (*Brit*) = **Staffordshire**
stag [stæg] *n* cervo; (*Brit Stock Exchange*) rialzista *m/f* su nuove emissioni
stage [steɪdʒ] *n* (*platform*) palco; (*in theatre*) palcoscenico; (*profession*): **the ~** il teatro, la scena; (*point*) fase *f*, stadio ■ *vt* (*play*) allestire, mettere in scena; (*demonstration*) organizzare; (*fig*: *perform*: *recovery etc*) effettuare; **in stages** per gradi; a tappe; **in the early/final stages** negli stadi iniziali/finali; **to go through a difficult ~** attraversare un periodo difficile
stagecoach ['steɪdʒkəutʃ] *n* diligenza
stage door *n* ingresso degli artisti
stage fright *n* paura del pubblico
stagehand ['steɪdʒhænd] *n* macchinista *m*
stage-manage ['steɪdʒmænɪdʒ] *vt* allestire le scene per; montare
stage manager *n* direttore *m* di scena
stagger ['stægə^r] *vi* barcollare ■ *vt* (*person*) sbalordire; (*hours, holidays*) scaglionare
staggering ['stægərɪŋ] *adj* (*amazing*) incredibile, sbalorditivo(-a)
staging post ['steɪdʒɪŋ-] *n* passaggio obbligato
stagnant ['stægnənt] *adj* stagnante
stagnate [stæg'neɪt] *vi* (*also fig*) stagnare
stagnation [stæg'neɪʃən] *n* stagnazione *f*, ristagno
stag night, stag party *n* festa di addio al celibato
staid [steɪd] *adj* posato(-a), serio(-a)
stain [steɪn] *n* macchia; (*colouring*) colorante *m* ■ *vt* macchiare; (*wood*) tingere
stained glass window ['steɪnd-] *n* vetrata
stainless ['steɪnlɪs] *adj* (*steel*) inossidabile
stain remover *n* smacchiatore *m*
stair [stɛə^r] *n* (*step*) gradino; **stairs** *npl* (*flight of stairs*) scale *fpl*, scala

staircase ['stɛəkeɪs], **stairway** ['stɛəweɪ] *n* scale *fpl*, scala
stairwell ['stɛəwɛl] *n* tromba delle scale
stake [steɪk] *n* palo, piolo; (*Betting*) puntata, scommessa ■ *vt* (*bet*) scommettere; (*risk*) rischiare; (*also*: **stake out**: *area*) delimitare con paletti; **to be at ~** essere in gioco; **to have a ~ in sth** avere un interesse in qc; **to ~ a claim (to sth)** rivendicare (qc)
stakeout ['steɪkaut] *n* sorveglianza
stalactite ['stæləktaɪt] *n* stalattite *f*
stalagmite ['stæləgmaɪt] *n* stalagmite *f*
stale [steɪl] *adj* (*bread*) raffermo(-a), stantio(-a); (*beer*) svaporato(-a); (*smell*) di chiuso
stalemate ['steɪlmeɪt] *n* stallo; (*fig*) punto morto
stalk [stɔ:k] *n* gambo, stelo ■ *vt* inseguire ■ *vi* camminare impettito(-a)
stall [stɔ:l] *n* (*Brit: in street, market etc*) bancarella; (*in stable*) box *m inv* di stalla ■ *vt* (*Aut*) far spegnere ■ *vi* (*Aut*) spegnersi, fermarsi; (*fig*) temporeggiare; **stalls** *npl* (*Brit: in cinema, theatre*) platea; **newspaper/flower ~** chiosco del giornalaio/del fioraio
stallholder ['stɔ:lhəuldə^r] *n* (*Brit*) bancarellista *m/f*
stallion ['stæljən] *n* stallone *m*
stalwart ['stɔ:lwət] *n* membro fidato
stamen ['steɪmɛn] *n* stame *m*
stamina ['stæmɪnə] *n* vigore *m*, resistenza
stammer ['stæmə^r] *n* balbuzie *f* ■ *vi* balbettare
stamp [stæmp] *n* (*postage stamp*) francobollo; (*implement*) timbro; (*mark, also fig*) marchio, impronta; (*on document*) bollo; timbro ■ *vi* (*also*: **stamp one's foot**) battere il piede ■ *vt* battere; (*letter*) affrancare; (*mark with a stamp*) timbrare; **stamped addressed envelope** busta affrancata per la risposta
▸ **stamp out** *vt* (*fire*) estinguere; (*crime*) eliminare; (*opposition*) soffocare
stamp album *n* album *m inv* per francobolli
stamp collecting *n* filatelia
stamp duty *n* (*Brit*) bollo
stampede [stæm'pi:d] *n* fuggi fuggi *m inv*; (*of cattle*) fuga precipitosa
stamp machine *n* distributore *m* automatico di francobolli
stance [stæns] *n* posizione *f*
stand [stænd] *n* (*position*) posizione *f*; (*Mil*) resistenza; (*structure*) supporto, sostegno; (*at exhibition*) stand *m inv*; (*at market*) bancarella; (*booth*) chiosco; (*Sport*) tribuna; (*also*: **music stand**) leggio *m* ■ *vb* (*pt, pp* **stood**) [stud] *vi* stare in piedi; (*rise*) alzarsi in piedi; (*be placed*) trovarsi ■ *vt* (*place*) mettere, porre; (*tolerate, withstand*) resistere, sopportare; **to make a ~** prendere posizione; **to take a ~ on an issue** prendere posizione su un problema; **to ~ for parliament** (*Brit*) presentarsi come candidato (per il parlamento); **to ~ guard** *or* **watch** (*Mil*) essere di guardia; **it stands to reason** è logico; **as things ~** stando così le cose; **to ~ sb a drink/meal** offrire da bere/un pranzo a qn; **I can't ~ him** non lo sopporto
▸ **stand aside** *vi* farsi da parte, scostarsi
▸ **stand by** *vi* (*be ready*) tenersi pronto(-a) ■ *vt fus* (*opinion*) sostenere
▸ **stand down** *vi* (*withdraw*) ritirarsi; (*Law*) lasciare il banco dei testimoni
▸ **stand for** *vt fus* (*signify*) rappresentare, significare; (*tolerate*) sopportare, tollerare
▸ **stand in for** *vt fus* sostituire
▸ **stand out** *vi* (*be prominent*) spiccare
▸ **stand up** *vi* (*rise*) alzarsi in piedi
▸ **stand up for** *vt fus* difendere
▸ **stand up to** *vt fus* tener testa a, resistere a
stand-alone ['stændələun] *adj* (*Comput*) stand-alone *inv*
standard ['stændəd] *n* modello, standard *m inv*; (*level*) livello; (*flag*) stendardo ■ *adj* (*size etc*) normale, standard *inv*; (*practice*) normale; (*model*) di serie; **standards** *npl* (*morals*) principi *mpl*, valori *mpl*; **to be** *or* **come up to ~** rispondere ai requisiti; **below** *or* **not up to ~** (*work*) mediocre; **to apply a double ~** usare metri diversi (nel giudicare *or* fare *etc*); **~ of living** livello di vita
standardization [stændədaɪ'zeɪʃən] *n* standardizzazione *f*
standardize ['stændədaɪz] *vt* normalizzare, standardizzare
standard lamp *n* (*Brit*) lampada a stelo
standard time *n* ora ufficiale
stand-by ['stændbaɪ] *n* riserva, sostituto; **to be on ~** (*gen*) tenersi pronto(-a); (*doctor*) essere di guardia; **a ~ ticket** un biglietto standby; **to fly ~** essere in lista d'attesa per un volo
stand-by generator *n* generatore *m* d'emergenza
stand-by passenger *n* (*Aviat*) passeggero(-a) in lista d'attesa
stand-by ticket *n* (*Aviat*) biglietto senza garanzia
stand-in ['stændɪn] *n* sostituto(-a); (*Cine*) controfigura
standing ['stændɪŋ] *adj* diritto(-a), in piedi; (*permanent: committee*) permanente; (*: rule*) fisso(-a); (*: army*) regolare; (*grievance*) continuo(-a) ■ *n* rango, condizione *f*, posizione *f*; (*duration*): **of 6 months' ~** che dura da 6 mesi; **it's a ~ joke** è diventato

S

proverbiale; **he was given a ~ ovation** tutti si alzarono per applaudirlo; **a man of some ~** un uomo di una certa importanza
standing committee *n* commissione *f* permanente
standing order *n* (*Brit: at bank*) ordine *m* di pagamento (permanente); **standing orders** *npl* (*Mil*) regolamento
standing room *n* posto all'impiedi
stand-off ['stændɔf] *n* (*esp US: stalemate*) situazione *f* di stallo
standoffish [stænd'ɔfɪʃ] *adj* scostante, freddo(-a)
standpat ['stændpæt] *adj* (*US*) irremovibile
standpipe ['stændpaɪp] *n* fontanella
standpoint ['stændpɔɪnt] *n* punto di vista
standstill ['stændstɪl] *n*: **at a ~** fermo(-a); (*fig*) a un punto morto; **to come to a ~** fermarsi; giungere a un punto morto
stank [stæŋk] *pt of* **stink**
stanza ['stænzə] *n* stanza (*poesia*)
staple ['steɪpl] *n* (*for papers*) graffetta; (*chief product*) prodotto principale ■ *adj* (*food etc*) di base; (*crop, industry*) principale ■ *vt* cucire
stapler ['steɪplə^r] *n* cucitrice *f*
star [stɑː^r] *n* stella; (*celebrity*) divo(-a); (*principal actor*) vedette *f inv* ■ *vi*: **to ~ (in)** essere il (*or* la) protagonista (di) ■ *vt* (*Cine*) essere interpretato(-a) da; **four-~ hotel** ≈ albergo di prima categoria; **2-~ petrol** (*Brit*) ≈ benzina normale; **4-~ petrol** (*Brit*) ≈ super *f*
star attraction *n* numero principale
starboard ['stɑːbəd] *n* dritta; **to ~** a dritta
starch [stɑːtʃ] *n* amido
starched ['stɑːtʃt] *adj* (*collar*) inamidato(-a)
starchy ['stɑːtʃɪ] *adj* (*food*) ricco(-a) di amido
stardom ['stɑːdəm] *n* celebrità
stare [stɛə^r] *n* sguardo fisso ■ *vi*: **to ~ at** fissare
starfish ['stɑːfɪʃ] *n* stella di mare
stark [stɑːk] *adj* (*bleak*) desolato(-a); (*simplicity, colour*) austero(-a); (*reality, poverty, truth*) crudo(-a) ■ *adv*: **~ naked** completamente nudo(-a)
starkers ['stɑːkəz] *adj*: **to be ~** (*Brit col*) essere nudo(-a) come un verme
starlet ['stɑːlɪt] *n* (*Cine*) stellina
starlight ['stɑːlaɪt] *n*: **by ~** alla luce delle stelle
starling ['stɑːlɪŋ] *n* storno
starlit ['stɑːlɪt] *adj* stellato(-a)
starry ['stɑːrɪ] *adj* stellato(-a)
starry-eyed [stɑːrɪ'aɪd] *adj* (*idealistic, gullible*) ingenuo(-a); (*from wonder*) meravigliato(-a)
Stars and Stripes *npl*: **the ~** la bandiera a stelle e strisce
star sign *n* segno zodiacale
star-studded ['stɑːstʌdɪd] *adj*: **a ~ cast** un cast di attori famosi
start [stɑːt] *n* inizio; (*of race*) partenza; (*sudden movement*) sobbalzo; (*advantage*) vantaggio ■ *vt* cominciare, iniziare; (*found: business, newspaper*) fondare, creare ■ *vi* cominciare; (*on journey*) partire, mettersi in viaggio; (*jump*) sobbalzare; **to ~ doing sth** (in)cominciare a fare qc; **at the ~** all'inizio; **for a ~** tanto per cominciare; **to make an early ~** partire di buon'ora; **to ~ (off) with ...** (*firstly*) per prima cosa ...; (*at the beginning*) all'inizio; **to ~ a fire** provocare un incendio
▸ **start off** *vi* cominciare; (*leave*) partire
▸ **start over** *vi* (US) ricominciare
▸ **start up** *vi* cominciare; (*car*) avviarsi ■ *vt* iniziare; (*car*) avviare
starter ['stɑːtə^r] *n* (*Aut*) motorino d'avviamento; (*Sport: official*) starter *m inv*; (*: runner, horse*) partente *m/f*; (*Brit Culin*) primo piatto
starting handle ['stɑːtɪŋ-] *n* (*Brit*) manovella d'avviamento
starting point *n* punto di partenza
starting price *n* prezzo *m* base *inv*
startle ['stɑːtl] *vt* far trasalire
startling ['stɑːtlɪŋ] *adj* sorprendente, sbalorditivo(-a)
star turn *n* (*Brit*) attrazione *f* principale
starvation [stɑː'veɪʃən] *n* fame *f*, inedia; **to die of ~** morire d'inedia
starve [stɑːv] *vi* morire di fame; soffrire la fame ■ *vt* far morire di fame, affamare; **I'm starving** muoio di fame
stash [stæʃ] *vt*: **to ~ sth away** (*col*) nascondere qc
state [steɪt] *n* stato; (*pomp*): **in ~** in pompa ■ *vt* dichiarare, affermare; annunciare; **to be in a ~** essere agitato(-a); **the ~ of the art** il livello di tecnologia (*or* cultura *etc*); **~ of emergency** stato di emergenza; **~ of mind** stato d'animo
state control *n* controllo statale
stated ['steɪtɪd] *adj* fissato(-a), stabilito(-a)
State Department *n* (US) Dipartimento di Stato, ≈ Ministero degli Esteri
state education *n* (*Brit*) istruzione *f* pubblica *or* statale
stateless ['steɪtlɪs] *adj* apolide
stately ['steɪtlɪ] *adj* maestoso(-a), imponente
stately home *n* residenza nobiliare (*d'interesse storico o artistico spesso aperta al pubblico*)
statement ['steɪtmənt] *n* dichiarazione *f*; (*Law*) deposizione *f*; (*Finance*) rendiconto; **official ~** comunicato ufficiale; **~ of account, bank ~** estratto conto

state-owned ['steɪt'əund] *adj* statalizzato(-a)
States [steɪts] *npl*: **the ~** (*USA*) gli Stati Uniti
state school *n* scuola statale
statesman ['steɪtsmən] *n* statista *m*
statesmanship ['steɪtsmənʃɪp] *n* abilità politica
static ['stætɪk] *n* (*Radio*) scariche *fpl* ■ *adj* statico(-a); **~ electricity** elettricità statica
station ['steɪʃən] *n* stazione *f*; (*rank*) rango, condizione *f* ■ *vt* collocare, disporre; **action stations** posti *mpl* di combattimento; **to be stationed in** (*Mil*) essere di stanza in
stationary ['steɪʃənərɪ] *adj* fermo(-a), immobile
stationer ['steɪʃənəʳ] *n* cartolaio(-a); **~'s shop** cartoleria
stationery ['steɪʃənərɪ] *n* articoli *mpl* di cancelleria; (*writing paper*) carta da lettere
station master *n* (*Rail*) capostazione *m*
station wagon *n* (*US*) giardinetta
statistic [stə'tɪstɪk] *n* statistica; *see also* **statistics**
statistical [stə'tɪstɪkəl] *adj* statistico(-a)
statistics [stə'tɪstɪks] *n* (*science*) statistica
statue ['stætjuː] *n* statua
statuesque [stætju'ɛsk] *adj* statuario(-a)
statuette [stætju'ɛt] *n* statuetta
stature ['stætʃəʳ] *n* statura
status ['steɪtəs] *n* posizione *f*, condizione *f* sociale; (*prestige*) prestigio; (*legal, marital*) stato
status quo [-'kwəu] *n*: **the ~** lo statu quo
status symbol *n* simbolo di prestigio
statute ['stætjuːt] *n* legge *f*; **statutes** *npl* (*of club etc*) statuto
statute book *n* codice *m*
statutory ['stætjutərɪ] *adj* stabilito(-a) dalla legge, statutario(-a); **~ meeting** (*Comm*) assemblea ordinaria
staunch [stɔːntʃ] *adj* fidato(-a), leale ■ *vt* (*flow*) arrestare; (*blood*) arrestare il flusso di
stave [steɪv] *n* (*Mus*) rigo ■ *vt*: **to ~ off** (*attack*) respingere; (*threat*) evitare
stay [steɪ] *n* (*period of time*) soggiorno, permanenza ■ *vi* rimanere; (*reside*) alloggiare, stare; (*spend some time*) trattenersi, soggiornare; **~ of execution** (*Law*) sospensione *f* dell'esecuzione; **to ~ put** non muoversi; **to ~ with friends** stare presso amici; **to ~ the night** passare la notte
▸ **stay behind** *vi* restare indietro
▸ **stay in** *vi* (*at home*) stare in casa
▸ **stay on** *vi* restare, rimanere
▸ **stay out** *vi* (*of house*) rimanere fuori (di casa); (*strikers*) continuare lo sciopero
▸ **stay up** *vi* (*at night*) rimanere alzato(-a)
staying power ['steɪɪŋ-] *n* capacità di resistenza

STD *n abbr* (*Brit*: = *subscriber trunk dialling*) teleselezione *f*; (= *sexually transmitted disease*) malattia venerea
stead [stɛd] *n* (*Brit*): **in sb's ~** al posto di qn; **to stand sb in good ~** essere utile a qn
steadfast ['stɛdfɑːst] *adj* fermo(-a), risoluto(-a)
steadily ['stɛdɪlɪ] *adv* continuamente; (*walk*) con passo sicuro
steady ['stɛdɪ] *adj* stabile, solido(-a), fermo(-a); (*regular*) costante; (*boyfriend etc*) fisso(-a); (*person*) calmo(-a), tranquillo(-a) ■ *vt* stabilizzare; calmare; **to ~ o.s.** ritrovare l'equilibrio
steak [steɪk] *n* (*meat*) bistecca; (*fish*) trancia
steakhouse ['steɪkhaus] *n* *ristorante specializzato in bistecche*
steal (*pt* **stole**, *pp* **stolen**) [stiːl, stəul, 'stəuln] *vt* rubare ■ *vi* (*thieve*) rubare
▸ **steal away, steal off** *vi* svignarsela, andarsene alla chetichella
stealth [stɛlθ] *n*: **by ~** furtivamente
stealthy ['stɛlθɪ] *adj* furtivo(-a)
steam [stiːm] *n* vapore *m* ■ *vt* trattare con vapore; (*Culin*) cuocere a vapore ■ *vi* fumare; (*ship*): **to ~ along** filare; **to let off ~** (*fig*) sfogarsi; **under one's own ~** (*fig*) da solo, con i propri mezzi; **to run out of ~** (*fig*: *person*) non farcela più
▸ **steam up** *vi* (*window*) appannarsi; **to get steamed up about sth** (*fig*) andare in bestia per qc
steam engine *n* macchina a vapore; (*Rail*) locomotiva a vapore
steamer ['stiːməʳ] *n* piroscafo, vapore *m*; (*Culin*) pentola a vapore
steam iron *n* ferro a vapore
steamroller ['stiːmrəuləʳ] *n* rullo compressore
steamship ['stiːmʃɪp] *n* piroscafo, vapore *m*
steamy ['stiːmɪ] *adj* pieno(-a) di vapore; (*window*) appannato(-a)
steed [stiːd] *n* (*literary*) corsiero, destriero
steel [stiːl] *n* acciaio ■ *cpd* di acciaio
steel band *n* banda di strumenti a percussione (*tipica dei Caribi*)
steel industry *n* industria dell'acciaio
steel mill *n* acciaieria
steelworks ['stiːlwəːks] *n* acciaieria
steely ['stiːlɪ] *adj* (*determination*) inflessibile; (*gaze*) duro(-a); (*eyes*) freddo(-a) come l'acciaio
steep [stiːp] *adj* ripido(-a), scosceso(-a); (*price*) eccessivo(-a) ■ *vt* inzuppare; (*washing*) mettere a mollo
steeple ['stiːpl] *n* campanile *m*
steeplechase ['stiːpltʃeɪs] *n* corsa a ostacoli, steeplechase *m inv*

S

steeplejack ['sti:pldʒæk] *n* chi ripara campanili e ciminiere
steer [stɪəʳ] *n* manzo ■ *vt* (*ship*) governare; (*car*) guidare ■ *vi* (*Naut: person*) governare; (*: ship*) rispondere al timone; (*car*) guidarsi; **to ~ clear of sb/sth** (*fig*) tenersi alla larga da qn/qc
steering ['stɪərɪŋ] *n* (*Aut*) sterzo
steering column *n* piantone *m* dello sterzo
steering committee *n* comitato direttivo
steering wheel *n* volante *m*
stem [stɛm] *n* (*of flower, plant*) stelo; (*of tree*) fusto; (*of glass*) gambo; (*of fruit, leaf*) picciolo ■ *vt* contenere, arginare
▸ **stem from** *vt fus* provenire da, derivare da
stem cell *n* cellula staminale
stench [stɛntʃ] *n* puzzo, fetore *m*
stencil ['stɛnsl] *n* (*of metal, cardboard*) stampino, mascherina; (*in typing*) matrice *f*
stenographer [stɛ'nɔgrəfəʳ] *n* (*US*) stenografo(-a)
stenography [stɛ'nɔgrəfɪ] *n* (*US*) stenografia
step [stɛp] *n* passo; (*stair*) gradino, scalino; (*action*) mossa, azione *f* ■ *vi*: **to ~ forward** fare un passo avanti; **steps** *npl* (*Brit*) = **stepladder**; **~ by ~** un passo dietro l'altro; (*fig*) poco a poco; **to be in/out of ~ with** (*also fig*) stare/non stare al passo con
▸ **step down** *vi* (*fig*) ritirarsi
▸ **step in** *vi* fare il proprio ingresso
▸ **step off** *vt fus* scendere da
▸ **step over** *vt fus* scavalcare
▸ **step up** *vt* aumentare; intensificare
step aerobics *n* step *m inv*
stepbrother ['stɛpbrʌðəʳ] *n* fratellastro
stepchild ['stɛptʃaɪld] *n* figliastro(-a)
stepdaughter ['stɛpdɔ:təʳ] *n* figliastra
stepfather ['stɛpfɑ:ðəʳ] *n* patrigno
stepladder ['stɛplædəʳ] *n* scala a libretto
stepmother ['stɛpmʌðəʳ] *n* matrigna
stepping stone ['stɛpɪŋ-] *n* pietra di un guado; (*fig*) trampolino
step Reebok® [-'ri:bɔk] *n* step *m inv*
stepsister ['stɛpsɪstəʳ] *n* sorellastra
stepson ['stɛpsʌn] *n* figliastro
stereo ['stɛrɪəu] *n* (*system*) sistema *m* stereofonico; (*record player*) stereo *m inv* ■ *adj* (*also*: **stereophonic**) stereofonico(-a); **in ~** in stereofonia
stereotype ['stɪərɪətaɪp] *n* stereotipo
sterile ['stɛraɪl] *adj* sterile
sterility [stɛ'rɪlɪtɪ] *n* sterilità
sterilization [stɛrɪlaɪ'zeɪʃən] *n* sterilizzazione *f*
sterilize ['stɛrɪlaɪz] *vt* sterilizzare
sterling ['stə:lɪŋ] *adj* (*gold, silver*) di buona lega; (*fig*) autentico(-a), genuino(-a) ■ *n* (*Econ*) (lira) sterlina; **a pound ~** una lira sterlina
sterling area *n* area della sterlina
stern [stə:n] *adj* severo(-a) ■ *n* (*Naut*) poppa
sternum ['stə:nəm] *n* sterno
steroid ['stɛrɔɪd] *n* steroide *m*
stethoscope ['stɛθəskəup] *n* stetoscopio
stevedore ['sti:vɪdɔ:ʳ] *n* scaricatore *m* di porto
stew [stju:] *n* stufato ■ *vt, vi* cuocere in umido; **stewed tea** *tè lasciato troppo in infusione*; **stewed fruit** frutta cotta
steward ['stju:əd] *n* (*Aviat, Naut, Rail*) steward *m inv*; (*in club etc*) dispensiere *m*; (*shop steward*) rappresentante *m/f* sindacale
stewardess ['stjuədɛs] *n* assistente *f* di volo, hostess *f inv*
stewardship ['stjuədʃɪp] *n* amministrazione *f*
stewing steak ['stju:ɪŋ-], (*US*) **stew meat** *n* carne *f* (di manzo) per stufato
St. Ex. *abbr* = **stock exchange**
stg *abbr* = **sterling**
stick [stɪk] *n* bastone *m*; (*of rhubarb, celery*) gambo ■ *vb* (*pt, pp* **stuck**) [stʌk] *vt* (*glue*) attaccare; (*thrust*): **to ~ sth into** conficcare *or* piantare *or* infiggere qc in; (*col: put*) ficcare; (*: tolerate*) sopportare ■ *vi* conficcarsi; tenere; (*remain*) restare, rimanere; (*get jammed: door, lift*) bloccarsi; **to ~ to** (*one's word, promise*) mantenere; (*principles*) tener fede a; **to get hold of the wrong end of the ~** (*fig*) capire male; **it stuck in my mind** mi è rimasto in mente
▸ **stick around** *vi* (*col*) restare, fermarsi
▸ **stick out, stick up** *vi* sporgere, spuntare ■ *vt*: **to ~ it out** (*col*) tener duro
▸ **stick up for** *vt fus* difendere
sticker ['stɪkəʳ] *n* cartellino adesivo
sticking plaster ['stɪkɪŋ-] *n* cerotto adesivo
sticking point *n* (*fig*) punto di stallo, impasse *f inv*
stick insect *n* insetto *m* stecco *inv*
stickleback ['stɪklbæk] *n* spinarello
stickler ['stɪkləʳ] *n*: **to be a ~ for** essere pignolo(-a) su, tenere molto a
stick-on ['stɪkɔn] *adj* (*label*) adesivo(-a)
stick shift *n* (*US Aut*) cambio manuale
stick-up ['stɪkʌp] *n* (*col*) rapina a mano armata
sticky ['stɪkɪ] *adj* attaccaticcio(-a), vischioso(-a); (*label*) adesivo(-a)
stiff [stɪf] *adj* rigido(-a), duro(-a); (*muscle*) legato(-a), indolenzito(-a); (*difficult*) difficile, arduo(-a); (*cold: manner etc*) freddo(-a), formale; (*strong*) forte; (*high: price*) molto alto(-a); **to be** *or* **feel ~** (*person*) essere *or* sentirsi indolenzito; **to have a ~ neck/back** avere il torcicollo/mal di schiena; **to keep a**

~ upper lip (*Brit fig*) conservare il sangue freddo
stiffen ['stɪfn] *vt* irrigidire; rinforzare ■ *vi* irrigidirsi; indurirsi
stiffness ['stɪfnɪs] *n* rigidità; indolenzimento; difficoltà; freddezza
stifle ['staɪfl] *vt* soffocare
stifling ['staɪflɪŋ] *adj* (*heat*) soffocante
stigma *n* (*Bot, Med*) (*pl* **stigmata**) (*fig*) (*pl* **stigmas**) ['stɪgmə, stɪg'mɑ:tə] ■ *n* stigma *m*
stigmata [stig'mɑ:tə] *npl* (*Rel*) stigmate *fpl*
stile [staɪl] *n* cavalcasiepe *m*; cavalcasteccato
stiletto [stɪ'lɛtəu] *n* (*also*: **stiletto heel**) tacco a spillo
still [stɪl] *adj* fermo(-a); (*quiet*) silenzioso(-a); (*orange juice etc*) non gassato(-a) ■ *adv* (*up to this time, even*) ancora; (*nonetheless*) tuttavia, ciò nonostante ■ *n* (*Cine*) fotogramma *m*; **keep ~!** stai fermo!; **he ~ hasn't arrived** non è ancora arrivato
stillborn ['stɪlbɔ:n] *adj* nato(-a) morto(-a)
still life *n* natura morta
stilt [stɪlt] *n* trampolo; (*pile*) palo
stilted ['stɪltɪd] *adj* freddo(-a), formale; artificiale
stimulant ['stɪmjulənt] *n* stimolante *m*
stimulate ['stɪmjuleɪt] *vt* stimolare
stimulating ['stɪmjuleɪtɪŋ] *adj* stimolante
stimulation [stɪmju'leɪʃən] *n* stimolazione *f*
stimulus (*pl* **stimuli**) ['stɪmjuləs, 'stɪmjulaɪ] *n* stimolo
sting [stɪŋ] *n* puntura; (*organ*) pungiglione *m*; (*col*) trucco ■ *vb* (*pt, pp* **stung**) [stʌŋ] *vt* pungere ■ *vi* bruciare; **my eyes are stinging** mi bruciano gli occhi
stingy ['stɪndʒɪ] *adj* spilorcio(-a), tirchio(-a)
stink [stɪŋk] *n* fetore *m*, puzzo ■ *vi* (*pt* **stank**, *pp* **stunk**) [stæŋk, stʌŋk] puzzare
stinker ['stɪŋkə^r] *n* (*col*) porcheria; (*person*) fetente *m/f*
stinking ['stɪŋkɪŋ] *adj* (*col*): **a ~ ...** uno schifo di ..., un(-a) maledetto(-a) ...; **~ rich** ricco(-a) da far paura
stint [stɪnt] *n* lavoro, compito ■ *vi*: **to ~ on** lesinare su
stipend ['staɪpɛnd] *n* stipendio, congrua
stipendiary [staɪ'pɛndɪərɪ] *adj*: **~ magistrate** magistrato stipendiato
stipulate ['stɪpjuleɪt] *vt* stipulare
stipulation [stɪpju'leɪʃən] *n* stipulazione *f*
stir [stə:^r] *n* agitazione *f*, clamore *m* ■ *vt* rimescolare; (*move*) smuovere, agitare ■ *vi* muoversi; **to give sth a ~** mescolare qc; **to cause a ~** fare scalpore
▸ **stir up** *vt* provocare, suscitare
stir-fry ['stə:'fraɪ] *vt* saltare in padella ■ *n* pietanza al salto
stirring ['stə:rɪŋ] *adj* eccitante; commovente
stirrup ['stɪrəp] *n* staffa
stitch [stɪtʃ] *n* (*Sewing*) punto; (*Knitting*) maglia; (*Med*) punto (di sutura); (*pain*) fitta ■ *vt* cucire, attaccare; suturare
stoat [stəut] *n* ermellino
stock [stɔk] *n* riserva, provvista; (*Comm*) giacenza, stock *m inv*; (*Agr*) bestiame *m*; (*Culin*) brodo; (*Finance*) titoli *mpl*, azioni *fpl*; (*Rail*: *also*: **rolling stock**) materiale *m* rotabile; (*descent, origin*) stirpe *f* ■ *adj* (*fig*: *reply etc*) consueto(-a), solito(-a), classico(-a); (*greeting*) usuale; (*Comm*: *goods, size*) standard *inv* ■ *vt* (*have in stock*) avere, vendere; **well-stocked** ben fornito(-a); **to have sth in ~** avere qc in magazzino; **out of ~** esaurito(-a); **to take ~** (*fig*) fare il punto; **stocks and shares** valori *mpl* di borsa; **government ~** titoli di Stato
▸ **stock up** *vi*: **to ~ up (with)** fare provvista (di)
stockade [stɔ'keɪd] *n* palizzata
stockbroker ['stɔkbrəukə^r] *n* agente *m* di cambio
stock control *n* gestione *f* magazzino
stock cube *n* (*Brit Culin*) dado
stock exchange *n* Borsa (valori)
stockholder ['stɔkhəuldə^r] *n* (*Finance*) azionista *m/f*
Stockholm ['stɔkhəum] *n* Stoccolma
stocking ['stɔkɪŋ] *n* calza
stock-in-trade ['stɔkɪn'treɪd] *n* (*fig*): **it's his ~** è la sua specialità
stockist ['stɔkɪst] *n* (*Brit*) fornitore *m*
stock market *n* (*Brit*) Borsa, mercato finanziario
stock phrase *n* cliché *m inv*
stockpile ['stɔkpaɪl] *n* riserva ■ *vt* accumulare riserve di
stockroom ['stɔkrum] *n* magazzino
stocktaking ['stɔkteɪkɪŋ] *n* (*Brit Comm*) inventario
stocky ['stɔkɪ] *adj* tarchiato(-a), tozzo(-a)
stodgy ['stɔdʒɪ] *adj* pesante, indigesto(-a)
stoic ['stəuɪk] *n* stoico(-a)
stoical ['stəuɪkəl] *adj* stoico(-a)
stoke [stəuk] *vt* alimentare
stoker ['stəukə^r] *n* fochista *m*
stole [stəul] *pt of* **steal** ■ *n* stola
stolen ['stəuln] *pp of* **steal**
stolid ['stɔlɪd] *adj* impassibile
stomach ['stʌmək] *n* stomaco; (*abdomen*) ventre *m* ■ *vt* sopportare, digerire
stomach ache *n* mal *m* di stomaco
stomach pump *n* pompa gastrica
stomach ulcer *n* ulcera allo stomaco
stomp [stɔmp] *vi*: **to ~ in/out** *etc* entrare/uscire *etc* con passo pesante

S

stone [stəun] *n* pietra; (*pebble*) sasso, ciottolo; (*in fruit*) nocciolo; (*Med*) calcolo; (*Brit: weight*) *6.348 kg., 14 libbre* ■ *cpd* di pietra ■ *vt* lapidare; **within a ~'s throw of the station** a due passi dalla stazione
Stone Age *n*: **the** ~ l'età della pietra
stone-cold [stəun'kəuld] *adj* gelido(-a)
stoned [stəund] *adj* (*col: drunk*) sbronzo(-a); (*on drugs*) fuori *inv*
stone-deaf [stəun'dɛf] *adj* sordo(-a) come una campana
stonemason ['stəunmeɪsn] *n* scalpellino
stonewall [stəun'wɔːl] *vi* fare ostruzionismo ■ *vt* ostacolare
stonework ['stəunwəːk] *n* muratura
stony ['stəunɪ] *adj* pietroso(-a), sassoso(-a)
stood [stud] *pt, pp of* **stand**
stooge [stuːdʒ] *n* (*col*) tirapiedi *m/f inv*
stool [stuːl] *n* sgabello
stoop [stuːp] *vi* (*also:* **have a stoop**) avere una curvatura; (*bend*) chinarsi, curvarsi; **to ~ to sth/doing sth** abbassarsi a qc/a fare qc
stop [stɔp] *n* arresto; (*stopping place*) fermata; (*in punctuation*) punto ■ *vt* arrestare, fermare; (*break off*) interrompere; (*also:* **put a stop to**) porre fine a; (*prevent*) impedire ■ *vi* fermarsi; (*rain, noise etc*) cessare, finire; **to ~ doing sth** cessare *or* finire di fare qc; **to ~ sb (from) doing sth** impedire a qn di fare qc; **to ~ dead** fermarsi di colpo; **~ it!** smettila!, basta!
▸ **stop by** *vi* passare, fare un salto
▸ **stop off** *vi* sostare brevemente
▸ **stop up** *vt* (*hole*) chiudere, turare
stopcock ['stɔpkɔk] *n* rubinetto di arresto
stopgap ['stɔpgæp] *n* (*person*) tappabuchi *m/f inv*; (*measure*) ripiego ■ *cpd* (*measures, solution*) di fortuna
stoplights ['stɔplaɪts] *npl* (*Aut*) stop *mpl*
stopover ['stɔpəuvəʳ] *n* breve sosta; (*Aviat*) scalo
stoppage ['stɔpɪdʒ] *n* arresto, fermata; (*of pay*) trattenuta; (*strike*) interruzione *f* del lavoro
stopper ['stɔpəʳ] *n* tappo
stop press *n* ultimissime *fpl*
stopwatch ['stɔpwɔtʃ] *n* cronometro
storage ['stɔːrɪdʒ] *n* immagazzinamento; (*Comput*) memoria
storage heater *n* (*Brit*) radiatore *m* elettrico che accumula calore
store [stɔːʳ] *n* provvista, riserva; (*depot*) deposito; (*Brit: department store*) grande magazzino; (*US: shop*) negozio ■ *vt* mettere da parte; conservare; (*grain, goods*) immagazzinare; (*Comput*) registrare; **to set great/little ~ by sth** dare molta/poca importanza a qc; **who knows what is in ~ for us?** chissà cosa ci riserva il futuro?
▸ **store up** *vt* mettere in serbo, conservare
storehouse ['stɔːhaus] *n* magazzino, deposito
storekeeper ['stɔːkiːpəʳ] *n* (*US*) negoziante *m/f*
storeroom ['stɔːrum] *n* dispensa
storey, (*US*) **story** ['stɔːrɪ] *n* piano
stork [stɔːk] *n* cicogna
storm [stɔːm] *n* tempesta; (*also:* **thunderstorm**) temporale *m*; (*fig*) infuriarsi ■ *vt* prendere d'assalto
storm cloud *n* nube *f* temporalesca
storm door *n* controporta
stormy ['stɔːmɪ] *adj* tempestoso(-a), burrascoso(-a)
story ['stɔːrɪ] *n* storia; racconto; (*Press*) articolo; (*US*) = **storey**
storybook ['stɔːrɪbuk] *n* libro di racconti
storyteller ['stɔːrɪtɛləʳ] *n* narratore(-trice)
stout [staut] *adj* solido(-a), robusto(-a); (*brave*) coraggioso(-a); (*fat*) corpulento(-a), grasso(-a) ■ *n* birra scura
stove [stəuv] *n* (*for cooking*) fornello; (*small*) fornelletto; (*for heating*) stufa; **gas/electric ~** cucina a gas/elettrica
stow [stəu] *vt* mettere via
stowaway ['stəuəweɪ] *n* passeggero(-a) clandestino(-a)
straddle ['strædl] *vt* stare a cavalcioni di
straggle ['strægl] *vi* crescere (*or* estendersi) disordinatamente; trascinarsi; rimanere indietro; **straggled along the coast** disseminati(-e) lungo la costa
straggler ['strægləʳ] *n* sbandato(-a)
straggling ['stræglɪŋ], **straggly** ['stræglɪ] *adj* (*hair*) in disordine
straight [streɪt] *adj* (*continuous, direct*) dritto(-a); (*frank*) onesto(-a), franco(-a); (*plain, uncomplicated*) semplice; (*Theat: part, play*) serio(-a); (*col: heterosexual*) eterosessuale ■ *adv* diritto; (*drink*) liscio ■ *n*: **the ~** la linea retta; (*Rail*) il rettilineo; (*Sport*) la dirittura d'arrivo; **to put** *or* **get ~** mettere in ordine, mettere ordine in; **to be (all) ~** (*tidy*) essere a posto, essere sistemato; (*clarified*) essere chiaro; **ten ~ wins** dieci vittorie di fila; **~ away, ~ off** (*at once*) immediatamente; **~ off, ~ out** senza esitare; **I went ~ home** sono andato direttamente a casa
straighten ['streɪtn] *vt* (*also:* **straighten out**) raddrizzare; **to ~ things out** mettere le cose a posto
straighteners ['streɪtnəz] *npl* (*for hair*) piastra *f* per capelli
straight-faced [streɪt'feɪst] *adj* impassibile, imperturbabile ■ *adv* con il viso serio
straightforward [streɪt'fɔːwəd] *adj* semplice; (*frank*) onesto(-a), franco(-a)

strain [streɪn] *n* (*Tech*) sollecitazione *f*; (*physical*) sforzo; (*mental*) tensione *f*; (*Med*) strappo; (*streak, trace*) tendenza; elemento; (*breed*) razza; (*of virus*) tipo ■ *vt* tendere; (*muscle*) slogare; (*ankle*) storcere; (*friendship, marriage*) mettere a dura prova; (*filter*) colare, filtrare ■ *vi* sforzarsi; **strains** *npl* (*Mus*) note *fpl*; **she's under a lot of ~** è molto tesa, è sotto pressione

strained [streɪnd] *adj* (*laugh etc*) forzato(-a); (*relations*) teso(-a)

strainer ['streɪnəʳ] *n* passino, colino

strait [streɪt] *n* (*Geo*) stretto; **to be in dire straits** (*fig*) essere nei guai

straitjacket ['streɪtdʒækɪt] *n* camicia di forza

strait-laced [streɪt'leɪst] *adj* puritano(-a)

strand [strænd] *n* (*of thread*) filo

strange [streɪndʒ] *adj* (*not known*) sconosciuto(-a); (*odd*) strano(-a), bizzarro(-a)

strangely ['streɪndʒlɪ] *adv* stranamente

stranger ['streɪndʒəʳ] *n* (*unknown*) sconosciuto(-a); (*from another place*) estraneo(-a); **I'm a ~ here** non sono del posto

strangle ['stræŋgl] *vt* strangolare

stranglehold ['stræŋglhəuld] *n* (*fig*) stretta (mortale)

strangulation [stræŋgju'leɪʃən] *n* strangolamento

strap [stræp] *n* cinghia; (*of slip, dress*) spallina, bretella ■ *vt* legare con una cinghia; (*child etc*) punire (con una cinghia)

straphanging ['stræphæŋɪŋ] *n* viaggiare *m* in piedi (*su mezzi pubblici reggendosi a un sostegno*)

strapless ['stræplɪs] *adj* (*bra, dress*) senza spalline

strapped [stræpt] *adj*: **~ for cash** a corto di soldi; **financially ~** finanziariamente a terra

strapping ['stræpɪŋ] *adj* ben piantato(-a)

Strasbourg ['stræzbə:g] *n* Strasburgo *f*

strata ['strɑ:tə] *npl of* **stratum**

stratagem ['strætɪdʒəm] *n* stratagemma *m*

strategic [strə'ti:dʒɪk] *adj* strategico(-a)

strategist ['strætɪdʒɪst] *n* stratega *m*

strategy ['strætɪdʒɪ] *n* strategia

stratosphere ['strætəsfɪəʳ] *n* stratosfera

stratum (*pl* **strata**) ['strɑ:təm, 'strɑ:tə] *n* strato

straw [strɔ:] *n* paglia; (*drinking straw*) cannuccia; **that's the last ~!** è la goccia che fa traboccare il vaso!

strawberry ['strɔ:bərɪ] *n* fragola

stray [streɪ] *adj* (*animal*) randagio(-a) ■ *vi* perdersi; allontanarsi, staccarsi (dal gruppo); **~ bullet** proiettile *m* vagante

streak [stri:k] *n* striscia; (*fig: of madness etc*): **a ~ of** una vena di ■ *vt* striare, screziare ■ *vi*: **to ~ past** passare come un fulmine; **to have streaks in one's hair** avere le mèche nei capelli; **a winning/losing ~** un periodo fortunato/sfortunato

streaker ['stri:kəʳ] *n* streaker *m/f inv*

streaky ['stri:kɪ] *adj* screziato(-a), striato(-a)

streaky bacon *n* (*Brit*) ≈ pancetta

stream [stri:m] *n* ruscello; corrente *f*; (*of people*) fiume *m* ■ *vt* (*Scol*) dividere in livelli di rendimento ■ *vi* scorrere; **to ~ in/out** entrare/uscire a fiotti; **against the ~** controcorrente; **on ~** (*new power plant etc*) in funzione, in produzione

streamer ['stri:məʳ] *n* (*of paper*) stella filante

stream feed *n* (*on photocopier etc*) alimentazione *f* continua

streamline ['stri:mlaɪn] *vt* dare una linea aerodinamica a; (*fig*) razionalizzare

streamlined ['stri:mlaɪnd] *adj* aerodinamico(-a), affusolato(-a); (*fig*) razionalizzato(-a)

street [stri:t] *n* strada, via; **the back streets** le strade secondarie; **to be on the streets** (*homeless*) essere senza tetto; (*as prostitute*) battere il marciapiede

streetcar ['stri:tkɑ:ʳ] *n* (*US*) tram *m inv*

street cred [-krɛd] *n* (*col*) credibilità presso i giovani

street lamp *n* lampione *m*

street lighting *n* illuminazione *f* stradale

street map, street plan *n* pianta (di una città)

street market *n* mercato all'aperto

streetwise ['stri:twaɪz] *adj* (*col*) esperto(-a) dei bassifondi

strength [strɛŋθ] *n* forza; (*of girder, knot etc*) resistenza, solidità; (*of chemical solution*) concentrazione *f*; (*of wine*) gradazione *f* alcolica; **on the ~ of** sulla base di, in virtù di; **below/at full ~** con gli effettivi ridotti/al completo

strengthen ['strɛŋθən] *vt* rinforzare; (*muscles*) irrobustire; (*economy, currency*) consolidare

strenuous ['strɛnjuəs] *adj* vigoroso(-a), energico(-a); (*tiring*) duro(-a), pesante

stress [strɛs] *n* (*force, pressure*) pressione *f*; (*mental strain*) tensione *f*; (*accent*) accento; (*emphasis*) enfasi *f* ■ *vt* insistere su, sottolineare; **to be under ~** essere sotto tensione; **to lay great ~ on sth** dare grande importanza a qc

stressful ['strɛsful] *adj* (*job*) difficile, stressante

stretch [strɛtʃ] *n* (*of sand etc*) distesa; (*of time*) periodo ■ *vi* stirarsi; (*extend*): **to ~ to** *or*

S

as far as estendersi fino a; (*be enough: money, food*): **to ~ (to)** bastare (per) ■ *vt* tendere, allungare; (*spread*) distendere; (*fig*) spingere (al massimo); **at a ~** ininterrottamente; **to ~ a muscle** tendere un muscolo; **to ~ one's legs** sgranchirsi le gambe
▸ **stretch out** *vi* allungarsi, estendersi ■ *vt* (*arm etc*) allungare, tendere; (*spread*) distendere; **to ~ out for sth** allungare la mano per prendere qc
stretcher ['strɛtʃəʳ] *n* barella, lettiga
stretcher-bearer ['strɛtʃəbɛərəʳ] *n* barelliere *m*
stretch marks *npl* smagliature *fpl*
strewn [stru:n] *adj*: **~ with** cosparso(-a) di
stricken ['strɪkən] *adj* provato(-a), affranto(-a); **~ with** colpito(-a) da
strict [strɪkt] *adj* (*severe*) rigido(-a), severo(-a); (*: order, rule*) rigoroso(-a); (*: supervision*) stretto(-a); (*precise*) preciso(-a), stretto(-a); **in ~ confidence** in assoluta confidenza
strictly ['strɪktlɪ] *adv* severamente; rigorosamente; strettamente; **~ confidential** strettamente confidenziale; **~ speaking** a rigor di termini; **~ between ourselves ...** detto fra noi ...
stride [straɪd] *n* passo lungo ■ *vi* (*pt* **strode**, *pp* **stridden**) [strəud, 'strɪdn] camminare a grandi passi; **to take in one's ~** (*fig: changes etc*) prendere con tranquillità
strident ['straɪdnt] *adj* stridente
strife [straɪf] *n* conflitto; litigi *mpl*
strike [straɪk] *n* sciopero; (*of oil etc*) scoperta; (*attack*) attacco ■ *vb* (*pt, pp* **struck**) [strʌk] *vt* colpire; (*oil etc*) scoprire, trovare; (*produce, make: coin, medal*) coniare; (*: agreement, deal*) concludere ■ *vi* far sciopero, scioperare; (*attack*) attaccare; (*clock*) suonare; **to go on** *or* **come out on ~** mettersi in sciopero; **to ~ a match** accendere un fiammifero; **to ~ a balance** (*fig*) trovare il giusto mezzo
▸ **strike back** *vi* (*Mil*) fare rappresaglie; (*fig*) reagire
▸ **strike down** *vt* (*fig*) atterrare
▸ **strike off** *vt* (*from list*) cancellare; (*: doctor etc*) radiare
▸ **strike out** *vt* depennare
▸ **strike up** *vt* (*Mus*) attaccare; **to ~ up a friendship with** fare amicizia con
strikebreaker ['straɪkbreɪkəʳ] *n* crumiro(-a)
striker ['straɪkəʳ] *n* scioperante *m/f*; (*Sport*) attaccante *m*
striking ['straɪkɪŋ] *adj* impressionante
Strimmer® ['strɪməʳ] *n* tagliabordi *m inv*
string [strɪŋ] *n* spago; (*row*) fila; sequenza; catena; (*Comput*) stringa, sequenza; (*Mus*) corda ■ *vt* (*pt, pp* **strung**) [strʌŋ]: **to ~ out** disporre di fianco; **to ~ together** mettere insieme; **the strings** *npl* (*Mus*) gli archi; **~ of pearls** filo di perle; **with no strings attached** (*fig*) senza vincoli, senza obblighi; **to get a job by pulling strings** ottenere un lavoro a forza di raccomandazioni
string bean *n* fagiolino
stringed instrument, string instrument *n* (*Mus*) strumento a corda
stringent ['strɪndʒənt] *adj* rigoroso(-a); (*reasons, arguments*) stringente, impellente
string quartet *n* quartetto d'archi
strip [strɪp] *n* striscia; (*Sport*): **wearing the Celtic ~** con la divisa del Celtic ■ *vt* spogliare; (*also*: **strip down**: *machine*) smontare ■ *vi* spogliarsi
strip cartoon *n* fumetto
stripe [straɪp] *n* striscia, riga
striped ['straɪpt] *adj* a strisce *or* righe
strip light *n* (*Brit*) tubo al neon
stripper ['strɪpəʳ] *n* spogliarellista
strip-search ['strɪpsə:tʃ] *vt*: **to ~ sb** perquisire qn facendolo(-a) spogliare ■ *n* perquisizione *f* (*facendo spogliare il perquisito*)
striptease ['strɪpti:z] *n* spogliarello
strive (*pt* **strove**, *pp* **striven**) [straɪv, strəuv, 'strɪvn] *vi*: **to ~ to do** sforzarsi di fare
strobe [strəub] *n* (*also*: **strobe light**) luce *f* stroboscopica
strode [strəud] *pt of* **stride**
stroke [strəuk] *n* colpo; (*of piston*) corsa; (*Med*) colpo apoplettico; (*Swimming: style*) nuoto; (*caress*) carezza ■ *vt* accarezzare; **at a ~** in un attimo; **on the ~ of 5** alle 5 in punto, allo scoccare delle 5; **a ~ of luck** un colpo di fortuna; **two-~ engine** motore a due tempi
stroll [strəul] *n* giretto, passeggiatina ■ *vi* andare a spasso; **to go for a ~, have** *or* **take a ~** andare a fare un giretto *or* due passi
stroller ['strəuləʳ] *n* (*US*) passeggino
strong [strɔŋ] *adj* (*gen*) forte; (*sturdy: table, fabric etc*) solido(-a); (*concentrated, intense: bleach, acid*) concentrato(-a); (*protest, letter, measures*) energico(-a) ■ *adv*: **to be going ~** (*company*) andare a gonfie vele; (*person*) essere attivo(-a); **they are 50 ~** sono in 50; **~ language** (*swearing*) linguaggio volgare
strong-arm ['strɔŋɑ:m] *adj* (*tactics, methods*) energico(-a)
strongbox ['strɔŋbɔks] *n* cassaforte *f*
stronghold ['strɔŋhəuld] *n* fortezza, roccaforte *f*
strongly ['strɔŋlɪ] *adv* fortemente, con forza; solidamente; energicamente; **to feel ~ about sth** avere molto a cuore qc
strongman ['strɔŋmæn] *n* personaggio di spicco

strongroom ['strɔŋrum] *n* camera di sicurezza
stroppy ['strɔpɪ] *adj* (*Brit col*) scontroso(-a), indisponente
strove [strəuv] *pt of* **strive**
struck [strʌk] *pt, pp of* **strike**
structural ['strʌktʃərəl] *adj* strutturale; (*Constr*) di costruzione; di struttura
structurally ['strʌktʃrəlɪ] *adv* dal punto di vista della struttura
structure ['strʌktʃə^r] *n* struttura; (*building*) costruzione *f*, fabbricato
struggle ['strʌgl] *n* lotta ■ *vi* lottare; **to have a ~ to do sth** avere dei problemi per fare qc
strum [strʌm] *vt* (*guitar*) strimpellare
strung [strʌŋ] *pt, pp of* **string**
strut [strʌt] *n* sostegno, supporto ■ *vi* pavoneggiarsi
strychnine ['strɪkni:n] *n* stricnina
stub [stʌb] *n* mozzicone *m*; (*of ticket etc*) matrice *f*, talloncino ■ *vt*: **to ~ one's toe (on sth)** urtare *or* sbattere il dito del piede (contro qc)
▸ **stub out** *vt*: **to ~ out a cigarette** spegnere una sigaretta
stubble ['stʌbl] *n* stoppia; (*on chin*) barba ispida
stubborn ['stʌbən] *adj* testardo(-a), ostinato(-a)
stubby ['stʌbɪ] *adj* tozzo(-a)
stucco ['stʌkəu] *n* stucco
stuck [stʌk] *pt, pp of* **stick** ■ *adj* (*jammed*) bloccato(-a); **to get ~** bloccarsi
stuck-up [stʌk'ʌp] *adj* presuntuoso(-a)
stud [stʌd] *n* bottoncino; borchia; (*of horses*) scuderia, allevamento di cavalli; (*also*: **stud horse**) stallone *m* ■ *vt* (*fig*): **studded with** tempestato(-a) di
student ['stju:dənt] *n* studente(-essa) ■ *cpd* studentesco(-a); universitario(-a); degli studenti; **a law/medical ~** uno studente di legge/di medicina
student driver *n* (*US*) conducente *m/f* principiante
students' union *n* (*Brit*: *association*) circolo universitario; (: *building*) sede *f* del circolo universitario
studied ['stʌdɪd] *adj* studiato(-a), calcolato(-a)
studio ['stju:dɪəu] *n* studio
studio flat, (*US*) **studio apartment** *n* appartamento monolocale
studious ['stju:dɪəs] *adj* studioso(-a); (*studied*) studiato(-a), voluto(-a)
studiously ['stju:dɪəslɪ] *adv* (*carefully*) deliberatamente, di proposito
study ['stʌdɪ] *n* studio ■ *vt* studiare; esaminare ■ *vi* studiare; **to make a ~ of sth** fare uno studio su qc; **to ~ for an exam** prepararsi a un esame
stuff [stʌf] *n* (*substance*) roba; (*belongings*) cose *fpl*, roba ■ *vt* imbottire; (*animal*: *for exhibition*) impagliare; (*Culin*) farcire; **my nose is stuffed up** ho il naso chiuso; **get stuffed!** (*col!*) va' a farti fottere! (*!*); **stuffed toy** giocattolo di peluche
stuffing ['stʌfɪŋ] *n* imbottitura; (*Culin*) ripieno
stuffy ['stʌfɪ] *adj* (*room*) mal ventilato(-a), senz'aria; (*ideas*) antiquato(-a)
stumble ['stʌmbl] *vi* inciampare; **to ~ across** (*fig*) imbattersi in
stumbling block ['stʌmblɪŋ-] *n* ostacolo, scoglio
stump [stʌmp] *n* ceppo; (*of limb*) moncone *m* ■ *vt*: **to be stumped for an answer** essere incapace di rispondere
stun [stʌn] *vt* stordire; (*amaze*) sbalordire
stung [stʌŋ] *pt, pp of* **sting**
stunk [stʌŋk] *pp of* **stink**
stunning ['stʌnɪŋ] *adj* (*piece of news etc*) sbalorditivo(-a); (*girl, dress*) favoloso(-a), stupendo(-a)
stunt [stʌnt] *n* bravata; trucco pubblicitario; (*Aviat*) acrobazia ■ *vt* arrestare
stunted ['stʌntɪd] *adj* stentato(-a), rachitico(-a)
stuntman ['stʌntmæn] *n* cascatore *m*
stupefaction [stju:pɪ'fækʃən] *n* stupefazione *f*, stupore *m*
stupefy ['stju:pɪfaɪ] *vt* stordire; intontire; (*fig*) stupire
stupendous [stju:'pɛndəs] *adj* stupendo(-a), meraviglioso(-a)
stupid ['stju:pɪd] *adj* stupido(-a)
stupidity [stju:'pɪdɪtɪ] *n* stupidità
stupidly ['stju:pɪdlɪ] *adv* stupidamente
stupor ['stju:pə^r] *n* torpore *m*
sturdy ['stə:dɪ] *adj* robusto(-a), vigoroso(-a), solido(-a)
sturgeon ['stə:dʒən] *n* storione *m*
stutter ['stʌtə^r] *n* balbuzie *f* ■ *vi* balbettare
Stuttgart ['ʃtutgart] *n* Stoccarda
sty [staɪ] *n* (*of pigs*) porcile *m*
stye [staɪ] *n* (*Med*) orzaiolo
style [staɪl] *n* stile *m*; (*distinction*) eleganza, classe *f*; (*hair style*) pettinatura; (*of dress etc*) modello, linea; **in the latest ~** all'ultima moda
styli ['staɪlaɪ] *npl of* **stylus**
stylish ['staɪlɪʃ] *adj* elegante
stylist ['staɪlɪst] *n*: **hair ~** parrucchiere(-a)
stylized ['staɪlaɪzd] *adj* stilizzato(-a)

S

stylus (*pl* **styluses** *or* **styli**) ['staɪləs, -laɪ] *n* (*of record player*) puntina
Styrofoam® ['staɪrəfəum] *n* (*US*) = **polystyrene** ■ *adj* (*cup*) di polistirene
suave [swɑ:v] *adj* untuoso(-a)
sub [sʌb] *n abbr* = **submarine**; **subscription**
sub... [sʌb] *prefix* sub..., sotto...
subcommittee ['sʌbkəmɪtɪ] *n* sottocomitato
subconscious [sʌb'kɔnʃəs] *adj, n* subcosciente *m*
subcontinent [sʌb'kɔntɪnənt] *n*: **the (Indian) ~** il subcontinente (indiano)
subcontract *n* [sʌb'kɔntrækt] subappalto ■ *vt* [sʌbkən'trækt] subappaltare
subcontractor ['sʌbkən'træktə^r] *n* subappaltatore(-trice)
subdivide [sʌbdɪ'vaɪd] *vt* suddividere
subdivision ['sʌbdɪvɪʒən] *n* suddivisione *f*
subdue [səb'dju:] *vt* sottomettere, soggiogare
subdued [səb'dju:d] *adj* pacato(-a); (*light*) attenuato(-a); (*person*) poco esuberante
sub-editor ['sʌb'ɛdɪtə^r] *n* (*Brit*) redattore(-a) aggiunto(-a)
subject ['sʌbdʒɪkt] *n* soggetto; (*citizen etc*) cittadino(-a); (*Scol*) materia ■ *adj* (*liable*): **~ to** soggetto(-a) a ■ *vt* [səb'dʒɛkt]: **to ~ to** sottomettere a; esporre a; **~ to confirmation in writing** a condizione di ricevere conferma scritta; **to change the ~** cambiare discorso
subjection [səb'dʒɛkʃən] *n* sottomissione *f*, soggezione *f*
subjective [səb'dʒɛktɪv] *adj* soggettivo(-a)
subject matter *n* argomento; contenuto
sub judice [sʌb'dʒu:dɪsɪ] *adj* (*Law*) sub iudice
subjugate ['sʌbdʒugeɪt] *vt* sottomettere, soggiogare
subjunctive [səb'dʒʌŋktɪv] *adj* congiuntivo(-a) ■ *n* congiuntivo
sublet [sʌb'lɛt] *vt, vi irreg* subaffittare
sublime [sə'blaɪm] *adj* sublime
subliminal [sʌb'lɪmɪnl] *adj* subliminale
submachine gun ['sʌbmə'ʃi:n-] *n* mitra *m inv*
submarine [sʌbmə'ri:n] *n* sommergibile *m*
submerge [səb'mə:dʒ] *vt* sommergere; immergere ■ *vi* immergersi
submersion [səb'mə:ʃən] *n* sommersione *f*; immersione *f*
submission [səb'mɪʃən] *n* sottomissione *f*; (*to committee etc*) richiesta, domanda
submissive [səb'mɪsɪv] *adj* remissivo(-a)
submit [səb'mɪt] *vt* sottomettere; (*proposal, claim*) presentare ■ *vi* sottomettersi
subnormal [sʌb'nɔ:məl] *adj* subnormale
subordinate [sə'bɔ:dɪnət] *adj, n* subordinato(-a)
subpoena [səb'pi:nə] *n* (*Law*) citazione *f*, mandato di comparizione ■ *vt* (*Law*) citare in giudizio
subroutine ['sʌbru:ti:n] *n* (*Comput*) sottoprogramma *m*
subscribe [səb'skraɪb] *vi* contribuire; **to ~ to** (*opinion*) approvare, condividere; (*fund*) sottoscrivere; (*newspaper*) abbonarsi a; essere abbonato(-a) a
subscriber [səb'skraɪbə^r] *n* (*to periodical, telephone*) abbonato(-a)
subscript ['sʌbskrɪpt] *n* deponente *m*
subscription [səb'skrɪpʃən] *n* sottoscrizione *f*; abbonamento; **to take out a ~ to** abbonarsi a
subsequent ['sʌbsɪkwənt] *adj* (*later*) successivo(-a); (*further*) ulteriore; **~ to** in seguito a
subsequently ['sʌbsɪkwəntlɪ] *adv* in seguito, successivamente
subservient [səb'sə:vɪənt] *adj*: **~ (to)** remissivo(-a) (a), sottomesso(-a) (a)
subside [səb'saɪd] *vi* cedere, abbassarsi; (*flood*) decrescere; (*wind*) calmarsi
subsidence [səb'saɪdns] *n* cedimento, abbassamento
subsidiarity [səbsɪdɪ'ærɪtɪ] *n* (*Pol*) *principio del decentramento del potere*
subsidiary [səb'sɪdɪərɪ] *adj* sussidiario(-a); accessorio(-a); (*Brit Scol: subject*) complementare ■ *n* filiale *f*
subsidize ['sʌbsɪdaɪz] *vt* sovvenzionare
subsidy ['sʌbsɪdɪ] *n* sovvenzione *f*
subsist [səb'sɪst] *vi*: **to ~ on sth** vivere di qc
subsistence [səb'sɪstəns] *n* esistenza; mezzi *mpl* di sostentamento
subsistence allowance *n* indennità *f inv* di trasferta
subsistence level *n* livello minimo di vita
substance ['sʌbstəns] *n* sostanza; (*fig*) essenza; **to lack ~** (*argument*) essere debole
substance abuse *n* abuso di sostanze tossiche
substandard [sʌb'stændəd] *adj* (*goods, housing*) di qualità scadente
substantial [səb'stænʃl] *adj* solido(-a); (*amount, progress etc*) notevole; (*meal*) sostanzioso(-a)
substantially [səb'stænʃəlɪ] *adv* sostanzialmente; **~ bigger** molto più grande
substantiate [səb'stænʃɪeɪt] *vt* comprovare
substitute ['sʌbstɪtju:t] *n* (*person*) sostituto(-a); (*thing*) succedaneo, surrogato ■ *vt*: **to ~ sth/sb for** sostituire qc/qn a
substitute teacher *n* (*US*) supplente *m/f*
substitution [sʌbstɪ'tju:ʃən] *n* sostituzione *f*
subterfuge ['sʌbtəfju:dʒ] *n* sotterfugio

subterranean [sʌbtə'reɪnɪən] *adj* sotterraneo(-a)
subtitle ['sʌbtaɪtl] *n* (*Cine*) sottotitolo
subtle ['sʌtl] *adj* sottile; (*flavour, perfume*) delicato(-a)
subtlety ['sʌtltɪ] *n* sottigliezza
subtly ['sʌtlɪ] *adv* sottilmente; delicatamente
subtotal [sʌb'təutl] *n* somma parziale
subtract [səb'trækt] *vt* sottrarre
subtraction [səb'trækʃən] *n* sottrazione *f*
suburb ['sʌbə:b] *n* sobborgo; **the suburbs** la periferia
suburban [sə'bə:bən] *adj* suburbano(-a)
suburbia [sə'bə:bɪə] *n* periferia, sobborghi *mpl*
subversion [səb'və:ʃən] *n* sovversione *f*
subversive [səb'və:sɪv] *adj* sovversivo(-a)
subway ['sʌbweɪ] *n* (*US: underground*) metropolitana; (*Brit: underpass*) sottopassaggio
subzero [sʌb'zɪərəu] *adj*: **~ temperatures** temperature *fpl* sotto zero
succeed [sək'si:d] *vi* riuscire, avere successo ■ *vt* succedere a; **to ~ in doing** riuscire a fare
succeeding [sək'si:dɪŋ] *adj* (*following*) successivo(-a); **~ generations** generazioni *fpl* future
success [sək'sɛs] *n* successo
successful [sək'sɛsful] *adj* (*venture*) coronato(-a) da successo, riuscito(-a); **to be ~ (in doing)** riuscire (a fare)
successfully [sək'sɛsfəlɪ] *adv* con successo
succession [sək'sɛʃən] *n* successione *f*; **in ~** di seguito
successive [sək'sɛsɪv] *adj* successivo(-a); consecutivo(-a); **on 3 ~ days** per 3 giorni consecutivi *or* di seguito
successor [sək'sɛsə^r] *n* successore *m*
succinct [sək'sɪŋkt] *adj* succinto(-a), breve
succulent ['sʌkjulənt] *adj* succulento(-a) ■ *n* (*Bot*): **succulents** piante *fpl* grasse
succumb [sə'kʌm] *vi* soccombere
such [sʌtʃ] *adj* tale; (*of that kind*): **~ a book** un tale libro, un libro del genere; **~ books** tali libri, libri del genere; (*so much*): **~ courage** tanto coraggio ■ *adv*: **~ a long trip** un viaggio così lungo; **~ good books** libri così buoni; **~ a lot of** talmente *or* così tanto(-a); **making ~ a noise that** facendo un rumore tale che; **~ a long time ago** tanto tempo fa; **~ as** (*like*) come; **a noise ~ as to** un rumore tale da; **~ books as I have** quei pochi libri che ho; **as ~** come *or* in quanto tale; **I said no ~ thing** non ho detto niente del genere
such-and-such ['sʌtʃənsʌtʃ] *adj* tale (*after noun*)
suchlike ['sʌtʃlaɪk] *pron* (*col*): **and ~** e così via
suck [sʌk] *vt* succhiare; (*baby*) poppare; (*pump, machine*) aspirare
sucker ['sʌkə^r] *n* (*Zool, Tech*) ventosa; (*Bot*) pollone *m*; (*col*) gonzo(-a), babbeo(-a)
suckle ['sʌkl] *vt* allattare
sucrose ['su:krəuz] *n* saccarosio
suction ['sʌkʃən] *n* succhiamento; (*Tech*) aspirazione *f*
suction pump *n* pompa aspirante
Sudan [su:'dɑ:n] *n* Sudan *m*
Sudanese [su:də'ni:z] *adj, n* sudanese *m/f*
sudden ['sʌdn] *adj* improvviso(-a); **all of a ~** improvvisamente, all'improvviso
sudden-death [sʌdn'dɛθ] *n* (*also*: **sudden-death playoff**: *Sport*) spareggio, bella
suddenly ['sʌdnlɪ] *adv* bruscamente, improvvisamente, di colpo
sudoku [su'dəuku:] *n* sudoku *m inv*
suds [sʌdz] *npl* schiuma (di sapone)
sue [su:] *vt* citare in giudizio ■ *vi*: **to ~ (for)** intentare causa (per); **to ~ for divorce** intentare causa di divorzio; **to ~ sb for damages** citare qn per danni
suede [sweɪd] *n* pelle *f* scamosciata ■ *cpd* scamosciato(-a)
suet ['suɪt] *n* grasso di rognone
Suez ['su:ɪz] *n*: **the ~ Canal** il Canale di Suez
suffer ['sʌfə^r] *vt* soffrire, patire; (*bear*) sopportare, tollerare; (*undergo: loss, setback*) subire ■ *vi* soffrire; **to ~ from** soffrire di; **to ~ from the effects of alcohol/a fall** risentire degli effetti dell'alcool/di una caduta
sufferance ['sʌfərəns] *n*: **he was only there on ~** era più che altro sopportato lì
sufferer ['sʌfərə^r] *n* (*Med*): **~ (from)** malato(-a) (di)
suffering ['sʌfərɪŋ] *n* sofferenza; (*hardship, deprivation*) privazione *f*
suffice [sə'faɪs] *vi* essere sufficiente, bastare
sufficient [sə'fɪʃənt] *adj* sufficiente; **~ money** abbastanza soldi
sufficiently [sə'fɪʃəntlɪ] *adv* sufficientemente, abbastanza
suffix ['sʌfɪks] *n* suffisso
suffocate ['sʌfəkeɪt] *vi* (*have difficulty breathing*) soffocare; (*die through lack of air*) asfissiare
suffocation [sʌfə'keɪʃən] *n* soffocamento; (*Med*) asfissia
suffrage ['sʌfrɪdʒ] *n* suffragio
suffuse [sə'fju:z] *vt*: **to ~ (with)** (*colour*) tingere (di); (*light*) soffondere (di); **her face was suffused with joy** la gioia si dipingeva sul suo volto
sugar ['ʃugə^r] *n* zucchero ■ *vt* zuccherare
sugar beet *n* barbabietola da zucchero
sugar bowl *n* zuccheriera

sugar cane *n* canna da zucchero
sugar-coated ['ʃugəkəutɪd] *adj* ricoperto(-a) di zucchero
sugar lump *n* zolletta di zucchero
sugar refinery *n* raffineria di zucchero
sugary ['ʃugərɪ] *adj* zuccherino(-a), dolce; (*fig*) sdolcinato(-a)
suggest [sə'dʒɛst] *vt* proporre, suggerire; (*indicate*) indicare; **what do you ~ I do?** cosa mi suggerisce di fare?
suggestion [sə'dʒɛstʃən] *n* suggerimento, proposta
suggestive [sə'dʒɛstɪv] *adj* suggestivo(-a); (*indecent*) spinto(-a), indecente
suicidal [suɪ'saɪdl] *adj* suicida *inv*; (*fig*) fatale, disastroso(-a)
suicide ['suɪsaɪd] *n* (*person*) suicida *m/f*; (*act*) suicidio; **to commit ~** suicidarsi
suicide attempt, suicide bid *n* tentato suicidio
suicide bomber *n* attentatore(-trice) suicida
suicide bombing *n* attentato suicida
suit [su:t] *n* (*man's*) completo; (*woman's*) completo, tailleur *m inv*; (*lawsuit*) causa; (*Cards*) seme *m*, colore *m* ■ *vt* andar bene a *or* per; essere adatto(-a) a *or* per; (*adapt*): **to ~ sth to** adattare qc a; **to be suited to sth** (*suitable for*) essere adatto a qc; **well suited** (*couple*) fatti l'uno per l'altro; **to bring a ~ against sb** intentare causa a qn; **to follow ~** (*fig*) fare altrettanto
suitable ['su:təbl] *adj* adatto(-a); appropriato(-a); **would tomorrow be ~?** andrebbe bene domani?; **we found somebody ~** abbiamo trovato la persona adatta
suitably ['su:təblɪ] *adv* (*dress*) in modo adatto; (*thank*) adeguatamente
suitcase ['su:tkeɪs] *n* valigia
suite [swi:t] *n* (*of rooms*) appartamento; (*Mus*) suite *f inv*; (*furniture*): **bedroom/dining room ~** arredo *or* mobilia per la camera da letto/ sala da pranzo; **a three-piece ~** un salotto comprendente un divano e due poltrone
suitor ['su:təʳ] *n* corteggiatore *m*, spasimante *m*
sulfate ['sʌlfeɪt] *n* (*US*) = **sulphate**
sulfur *etc* ['sʌlfəʳ] (*US*) = **sulphur** *etc*
sulk [sʌlk] *vi* fare il broncio
sulky ['sʌlkɪ] *adj* imbronciato(-a)
sullen ['sʌlən] *adj* scontroso(-a); cupo(-a)
sulphate, (*US*) **sulfate** ['sʌlfeɪt] *n* solfato; **copper ~** solfato di rame
sulphur, (*US*) **sulfur** ['sʌlfəʳ] *n* zolfo
sulphur dioxide *n* biossido di zolfo
sulphuric, (*US*) **sulfuric** [sʌl'fjuərɪk] *adj*: **~ acid** acido solforico
sultan ['sʌltən] *n* sultano
sultana [sʌl'tɑ:nə] *n* (*fruit*) uva (secca) sultanina
sultry ['sʌltrɪ] *adj* afoso(-a)
sum [sʌm] *n* somma; (*Scol etc*) addizione *f*
▸**sum up** *vt* riassumere; (*evaluate rapidly*) valutare, giudicare ■ *vi* riassumere
Sumatra [su'mɑ:trə] *n* Sumatra
summarize ['sʌməraɪz] *vt* riassumere, riepilogare
summary ['sʌmərɪ] *n* riassunto ■ *adj* (*justice*) sommario(-a)
summer ['sʌməʳ] *n* estate *f* ■ *cpd* d'estate, estivo(-a); **in (the) ~** d'estate
summer camp *n* (*US*) colonia (estiva)
summerhouse ['sʌməhaus] *n* (*in garden*) padiglione *m*
summertime ['sʌmətaɪm] *n* (*season*) estate *f*
summer time *n* (*by clock*) ora legale (estiva)
summery ['sʌmərɪ] *adj* estivo(-a)
summing-up [sʌmɪŋ'ʌp] *n* (*Law*) ricapitolazione *f* del processo
summit ['sʌmɪt] *n* cima, sommità; (*Pol*) vertice *m*
summit conference *n* conferenza al vertice
summon ['sʌmən] *vt* chiamare, convocare; **to ~ a witness** citare un testimone
▸**summon up** *vt* raccogliere, fare appello a
summons *n* ordine *m* di comparizione ■ *vt* citare; **to serve a ~ on sb** notificare una citazione a qn
sumo ['su:məu] *n* (*also*: **sumo wrestling**) sumo
sump [sʌmp] *n* (*Aut*) coppa dell'olio
sumptuous ['sʌmptjuəs] *adj* sontuoso(-a)
Sun. *abbr* (= *Sunday*) dom.
sun [sʌn] *n* sole *m*; **in the ~** al sole; **to catch the ~** prendere sole; **they have everything under the ~** hanno tutto ciò che possono desiderare
sunbathe ['sʌnbeɪð] *vi* prendere un bagno di sole
sunbeam ['sʌnbi:m] *n* raggio di sole
sunbed ['sʌnbɛd] *n* lettino solare
sunblock ['sʌnblɔk] *n* crema solare a protezione totale
sunburn ['sʌnbə:n] *n* (*tan*) abbronzatura; (*painful*) scottatura
sunburnt ['sʌnbə:nt], **sunburned** ['sʌnbə:nd] *adj* abbronzato(-a); (*painfully*) scottato(-a) dal sole
sun cream *n* crema solare
sundae ['sʌndeɪ] *n* coppa di gelato guarnita
Sunday ['sʌndɪ] *n* domenica; *see also* **Tuesday**
Sunday paper *n* giornale *m* della domenica; *vedi nota*

SUNDAY PAPERS

I *Sunday papers* sono i giornali che escono di domenica. Sono generalmente corredati da supplementi e riviste di argomento culturale, sportivo e di attualità ed hanno un'alta tiratura.

Sunday school *n* ≈ scuola di catechismo
sundial ['sʌndaɪəl] *n* meridiana
sundown ['sʌndaun] *n* tramonto
sundries ['sʌndrɪz] *npl* articoli diversi, cose diverse
sundry ['sʌndrɪ] *adj* vari(-e), diversi(-e); **all and ~** tutti quanti
sunflower ['sʌnflauəʳ] *n* girasole *m*
sung [sʌŋ] *pp of* **sing**
sunglasses ['sʌnglɑːsɪz] *npl* occhiali *mpl* da sole
sunk [sʌŋk] *pp of* **sink**
sunken ['sʌŋkən] *adj* sommerso(-a); (*eyes, cheeks*) infossato(-a); (*bath*) incassato(-a)
sunlamp ['sʌnlæmp] *n* lampada a raggi ultravioletti
sunlight ['sʌnlaɪt] *n* (luce *f* del) sole *m*
sunlit ['sʌnlɪt] *adj* assolato(-a), soleggiato(-a)
sunny ['sʌnɪ] *adj* assolato(-a), soleggiato(-a); (*fig*) allegro(-a), felice; **it is ~** c'è il sole
sunrise ['sʌnraɪz] *n* levata del sole, alba
sunroof ['sʌnruːf] *n* (*on building*) tetto a terrazzo; (*Aut*) tetto apribile
sunscreen ['sʌnskriːn] *n* crema solare protettiva
sunset ['sʌnset] *n* tramonto
sunshade ['sʌnʃeɪd] *n* parasole *m*
sunshine ['sʌnʃaɪn] *n* (luce *f* del) sole *m*
sunspot ['sʌnspɔt] *n* macchia solare
sunstroke ['sʌnstrəuk] *n* insolazione *f*, colpo di sole
suntan ['sʌntæn] *n* abbronzatura
suntanned ['sʌntænd] *adj* abbronzato(-a)
suntan oil *n* olio solare
suntrap ['sʌntræp] *n* luogo molto assolato, angolo pieno di sole
super ['suːpəʳ] *adj* (*col*) fantastico(-a)
superannuation [suːpərænju'eɪʃən] *n* contributi *mpl* pensionistici, pensione *f*
superb [suː'pəːb] *adj* magnifico(-a)
Super Bowl *n* (*US Sport*) Super Bowl *m inv*
supercilious [suːpə'sɪlɪəs] *adj* sprezzante, sdegnoso(-a)
superconductor [suːpəkən'dʌktəʳ] *n* superconduttore *m*
superficial [suːpə'fɪʃəl] *adj* superficiale
superficially [suːpə'fɪʃəlɪ] *adv* superficialmente
superfluous [su'pəːfluəs] *adj* superfluo(-a)
superglue ['suːpəgluː] *n* colla a presa rapida
superhighway ['suːpəhaɪweɪ] *n* (*US*) autostrada; **the information ~** l'autostrada telematica
superhuman [suːpə'hjuːmən] *adj* sovrumano(-a)
superimpose ['suːpərɪm'pəuz] *vt* sovrapporre
superintend [suːpərɪn'tɛnd] *vt* dirigere, sovraintendere
superintendent [suːpərɪn'tɛndənt] *n* direttore(-trice); (*Police*) ≈ commissario (capo)
superior [su'pɪərɪəʳ] *adj* superiore; (*Comm: goods, quality*) di prim'ordine, superiore; (*smug: person*) che fa il superiore ■ *n* superiore *m/f*; **Mother S~** (*Rel*) Madre *f* Superiora, Superiora
superiority [supɪərɪ'ɔrɪtɪ] *n* superiorità
superlative [su'pəːlətɪv] *adj* superlativo(-a), supremo(-a) ■ *n* (*Ling*) superlativo
superman ['suːpəmæn] *n* superuomo
supermarket ['suːpəmɑːkɪt] *n* supermercato
supermodel ['suːpəmɔdl] *n* top model *m/f inv*
supernatural [suːpə'nætʃərəl] *adj* soprannaturale
supernova [suːpə'nəuvə] *n* supernova
superpower ['suːpəpauəʳ] *n* (*Pol*) superpotenza
superscript ['suːpəskrɪpt] *n* esponente *m*
supersede [suːpə'siːd] *vt* sostituire, soppiantare
supersonic ['suːpə'sɔnɪk] *adj* supersonico(-a)
superstar ['suːpəstɑːʳ] *adj, n* superstar (*f*) *inv*
superstition [suːpə'stɪʃən] *n* superstizione *f*
superstitious [suːpə'stɪʃəs] *adj* superstizioso(-a)
superstore ['suːpəstɔːʳ] *n* (*Brit*) grande supermercato
supertanker ['suːpətæŋkəʳ] *n* superpetroliera
supertax ['suːpətæks] *n* soprattassa
supervise ['suːpəvaɪz] *vt* (*person etc*) sorvegliare; (*organization*) soprintendere a
supervision [suːpə'vɪʒən] *n* sorveglianza, supervisione *f*; **under medical ~** sotto controllo medico
supervisor ['suːpəvaɪzəʳ] *n* sorvegliante *m/f*, soprintendente *m/f*; (*in shop*) capocommesso(-a); (*at university*) relatore(-trice)
supervisory ['suːpəvaɪzərɪ] *adj* di sorveglianza
supine ['suːpaɪn] *adj* supino(-a)
supper ['sʌpəʳ] *n* cena; **to have ~** cenare
supplant [sə'plɑːnt] *vt* soppiantare
supple ['sʌpl] *adj* flessibile; agile

S

supplement *n* ['sʌplɪmənt] supplemento ■ *vt* [sʌplɪ'mɛnt] completare, integrare
supplementary [sʌplɪ'mɛntərɪ] *adj* supplementare
supplementary benefit *n* (*Brit*) *forma di indennità assistenziale*
supplier [sə'plaɪə^r] *n* fornitore *m*
supply [sə'plaɪ] *vt* (*goods*): **to ~ sth (to sb)** fornire qc (a qn); (*people, organization*): **to ~ sb (with sth)** fornire a qn (qc); (*system, machine*): **to ~ sth (with sth)** alimentare qc (con qc); (*a need*) soddisfare ■ *n* riserva, provvista; (*supplying*) approvvigionamento; (*Tech*) alimentazione *f*; **supplies** *npl* (*food*) viveri *mpl*; (*Mil*) sussistenza; **office supplies** forniture *fpl* per ufficio; **to be in short ~** scarseggiare, essere scarso(-a); **the electricity/water/gas ~** l'erogazione *f* di corrente/d'acqua/di gas; **~ and demand** la domanda e l'offerta; **the car comes supplied with a radio** l'auto viene fornita completa di radio
supply teacher *n* (*Brit*) supplente *m/f*
support [sə'pɔːt] *n* (*moral, financial etc*) sostegno, appoggio; (*Tech*) supporto ■ *vt* sostenere; (*financially*) mantenere; (*uphold*) sostenere, difendere; (*Sport: team*) fare il tifo per; **they stopped work in ~ (of)** hanno smesso di lavorare per solidarietà (con); **to ~ o.s.** (*financially*) mantenersi
supporter [sə'pɔːtə^r] *n* (*Pol etc*) sostenitore(-trice), fautore(-trice); (*Sport*) tifoso(-a)
supporting [sə'pɔːtɪŋ] *adj* (*wall*) di sostegno
supporting actor *n* attore *m* non protagonista
supporting actress *n* attrice *f* non protagonista
supporting role *n* ruolo non protagonista
supportive [sə'pɔːtɪv] *adj* d'appoggio; **I have a ~ wife/family** mia moglie/la mia famiglia mi appoggia
suppose [sə'pəuz] *vt, vi* supporre; immaginare; **to be supposed to do** essere tenuto(-a) a fare; **always supposing (that) he comes** ammesso e non concesso che venga; **I don't ~ she'll come** non credo che venga; **he's supposed to be an expert** dicono che sia un esperto, passa per un esperto
supposedly [sə'pəuzɪdlɪ] *adv* presumibilmente; (*seemingly*) apparentemente
supposing [sə'pəuzɪŋ] *conj* se, ammesso che *+sub*
supposition [sʌpə'zɪʃən] *n* supposizione *f*, ipotesi *f inv*
suppository [sə'pɔzɪtərɪ] *n* supposta, suppositorio
suppress [sə'prɛs] *vt* reprimere; sopprimere, tenere segreto(-a)
suppression [sə'prɛʃən] *n* repressione *f*; soppressione *f*
suppressor [sə'prɛsə^r] *n* (*Elec etc*) soppressore *m*
supremacy [su'prɛməsɪ] *n* supremazia
supreme [su'priːm] *adj* supremo(-a)
Supreme Court *n* (*US*) Corte *f* suprema; **~ of Judicature** *corte di giudizio suprema dell'Inghilterra e del Galles*
supremo [su'priːməu] *n* autorità *f inv* massima
Supt. *abbr* (*Police*) = **superintendent**
surcharge ['səːtʃɑːdʒ] *n* supplemento; (*extra tax*) soprattassa
sure [ʃuə^r] *adj* sicuro(-a); (*definite, convinced*) sicuro(-a), certo(-a) ■ *adv* (*col: US*): **that ~ is pretty, that's ~ pretty** è veramente *or* davvero carino; **~!** (*of course*) senz'altro!, certo!; **~ enough** infatti; **to make ~ of** assicurarsi di; **to be ~ of sth** essere sicuro di qc; **to be ~ of o.s.** essere sicuro di sé; **I'm not ~ how/why/when** non so bene come/perché/quando *+sub*
sure-fire ['ʃuəfaɪə^r] *adj* (*col*) infallibile
sure-footed [ʃuə'futɪd] *adj* dal passo sicuro
surely ['ʃuəlɪ] *adv* sicuramente; certamente; **~ you don't mean that!** non parlerà sul serio!
surety ['ʃuərətɪ] *n* garanzia; **to go** *or* **stand ~ for sb** farsi garante per qn
surf [səːf] *n* (*waves*) cavalloni *mpl*; (*foam*) spuma ■ *vt*: **to ~ the Net** navigare in Internet
surface ['səːfɪs] *n* superficie *f* ■ *vt* (*road*) asfaltare ■ *vi* risalire alla superficie; (*fig: person*) venire a galla, farsi vivo(-a); **on the ~ it seems that ...** (*fig*) superficialmente sembra che ...
surface area *n* superficie *f*
surface mail *n* posta ordinaria
surface-to-surface ['səːfɪstə'səːfɪs] *adj* (*Mil*) terra-terra *inv*
surfboard ['səːfbɔːd] *n* tavola per surfing
surfeit ['səːfɪt] *n*: **a ~ of** un eccesso di; un'indigestione di
surfer ['səːfə^r] *n* (*in sea*) surfista *m/f*; (*on the internet*) navigatore(-trice)
surfing ['səːfɪŋ] *n* surfing *m*
surge [səːdʒ] *n* (*strong movement*) ondata; (*of feeling*) impeto; (*Elec*) sovracorrente *f* transitoria ■ *vi* (*waves*) gonfiarsi; (*Elec: power*) aumentare improvvisamente; **to ~ forward** buttarsi avanti
surgeon ['səːdʒən] *n* chirurgo

Surgeon General *n* (*US*) ≈ Ministro della Sanità
surgery ['sə:dʒərɪ] *n* chirurgia; (*Brit Med: room*) studio *or* gabinetto medico, ambulatorio; (*: session*) visita ambulatoriale; (*Brit: of MP etc*) incontri *mpl* con gli elettori; **to undergo ~** subire un intervento chirurgico
surgery hours *npl* (*Brit*) orario delle visite *or* di consultazione
surgical ['sə:dʒɪkl] *adj* chirurgico(-a)
surgical spirit *n* (*Brit*) alcool denaturato
surly ['sə:lɪ] *adj* scontroso(-a), burbero(-a)
surmise [sə:'maɪz] *vt* supporre, congetturare
surmount [sə:'maunt] *vt* sormontare
surname ['sə:neɪm] *n* cognome *m*
surpass [sə:'pɑ:s] *vt* superare
surplus ['sə:pləs] *n* eccedenza; (*Econ*) surplus *m inv* ■ *adj* eccedente, d'avanzo; **it is ~ to our requirements** eccede i nostri bisogni; **~ stock** merce *f* in sovrappiù
surprise [sə'praɪz] *n* sorpresa; (*astonishment*) stupore *m* ■ *vt* sorprendere; stupire; **to take by ~** (*person*) cogliere di sorpresa; (*Mil: town, fort*) attaccare di sorpresa
surprising [sə'praɪzɪŋ] *adj* sorprendente, stupefacente
surprisingly [se'praɪzɪŋlɪ] *adv* sorprendentemente; **(somewhat) ~, he agreed** cosa (alquanto) sorprendente, ha accettato
surrealism [sə'rɪəlɪzəm] *n* surrealismo
surrealist [sə'rɪəlɪst] *adj, n* surrealista *m/f*
surrender [sə'rɛndə^r] *n* resa, capitolazione *f* ■ *vi* arrendersi ■ *vt* (*claim, right*) rinunciare a
surrender value *n* (*Comm*) valore *m* di riscatto
surreptitious [sʌrəp'tɪʃəs] *adj* furtivo(-a)
surrogate ['sʌrəgɪt] *n* (*Brit: substitute*) surrogato ■ *adj* surrogato(-a)
surrogate mother *n* madre *f* sostitutiva
surround [sə'raund] *vt* circondare; (*Mil etc*) accerchiare
surrounding [sə'raundɪŋ] *adj* circostante
surroundings [sə'raundɪŋz] *npl* dintorni *mpl*; (*fig*) ambiente *m*
surtax ['sə:tæks] *n* soprattassa
surveillance [sə:'veɪləns] *n* sorveglianza, controllo
survey *n* ['sə:veɪ] (*comprehensive view: of situation, development*) quadro generale; (*study*) indagine *f*, studio; (*in housebuying etc*) perizia; (*of land*) rilevamento, rilievo topografico ■ *vt* [sə:'veɪ] osservare; esaminare; (*Surveying: building*) fare una perizia di; (*: land*) fare il rilevamento di
surveying [sə'veɪɪŋ] *n* (*of land*) agrimensura
surveyor [sə'veɪə^r] *n* perito; (*of land*) agrimensore *m*
survival [sə'vaɪvl] *n* sopravvivenza; (*relic*) reliquia, vestigio
survival course *n* corso di sopravvivenza
survival kit *n* equipaggiamento di prima necessità
survive [sə'vaɪv] *vi* sopravvivere ■ *vt* sopravvivere a
survivor [sə'vaɪvə^r] *n* superstite *m/f*, sopravvissuto(-a)
susceptible [sə'sɛptəbl] *adj*: **~ (to)** sensibile (a); (*disease*) predisposto(-a) (a)
suspect ['sʌspɛkt] *adj* sospetto(-a) ■ *n* persona sospetta ■ *vt* [səs'pɛkt] sospettare; (*think likely*) supporre; (*doubt*) dubitare di
suspected [səs'pɛktɪd] *adj* presunto(-a); **to have a ~ facture** avere una sospetta frattura
suspend [səs'pɛnd] *vt* sospendere
suspended animation *n*: **in a state of ~** in stato comatoso
suspended sentence *n* condanna con la condizionale
suspender belt [səs'pɛndə^r-] *n* (*Brit*) reggicalze *m inv*
suspenders [sə'spɛndəz] *npl* (*Brit*) giarrettiere *fpl*; (*US*) bretelle *fpl*
suspense [səs'pɛns] *n* apprensione *f*; (*in film etc*) suspense *m*
suspension [səs'pɛnʃən] *n* (*gen, Aut*) sospensione *f*; (*of driving licence*) ritiro temporaneo
suspension bridge *n* ponte *m* sospeso
suspicion [səs'pɪʃən] *n* sospetto; **to be under ~** essere sospettato; **arrested on ~ of murder** arrestato come presunto omicida
suspicious [səs'pɪʃəs] *adj* (*suspecting*) sospettoso(-a); (*causing suspicion*) sospetto(-a); **to be ~ of** *or* **about sb/sth** nutrire sospetti nei riguardi di qn/qc
suss out *vt* (*Brit col*): **I've sussed it/him out** ho capito come stanno le cose/che tipo è
sustain [səs'teɪn] *vt* sostenere; sopportare; (*suffer*) subire
sustainable [səs'teɪnəbl] *adj* sostenibile
sustained [sə'steɪnd] *adj* (*effort*) prolungato(-a)
sustenance ['sʌstɪnəns] *n* nutrimento; mezzi *mpl* di sostentamento
suture ['su:tʃə^r] *n* sutura
SUV *n abbr* = **sports utility vehicle**
SW *abbr* (*Radio*: = *short wave*) O.C.
swab [swɔb] *n* (*Med*) tampone *m* ■ *vt* (*Naut: also*: **swab down**) radazzare
swagger ['swægə^r] *vi* pavoneggiarsi
swallow ['swɔləu] *n* (*bird*) rondine *f*; (*of food*) boccone *m*; (*of drink*) sorso ■ *vt* inghiottire; (*fig: story*) bere
▸ **swallow up** *vt* inghiottire

S

swam [swæm] *pt of* **swim**
swamp [swɔmp] *n* palude *f* ■ *vt* sommergere
swampy ['swɔmpɪ] *adj* palludoso(-a), pantanoso(-a)
swan [swɔn] *n* cigno
swank [swæŋk] *vi* (*col: talk boastfully*) fare lo spaccone; (*: show off*) mettersi in mostra
swan song *n* (*fig*) canto del cigno
swap [swɔp] *n* scambio ■ *vt*: **to ~ (for)** scambiare (con)
SWAPO ['swɑːpəu] *n abbr* = **South-West Africa People's Organization**
swarm [swɔːm] *n* sciame *m* ■ *vi* formicolare; (*bees*) sciamare
swarthy ['swɔːðɪ] *adj* di carnagione scura
swashbuckling ['swɔʃbʌklɪŋ] *adj* (*role, hero*) spericolato(-a)
swastika ['swɔstɪkə] *n* croce *f* uncinata, svastica
SWAT [swɔt] *n abbr* (*US*: = *Special Weapons and Tactics*) *reparto speciale di polizia*; (= *a SWAT team*) uno squadrone del reparto speciale (di polizia)
swat [swɔt] *vt* schiacciare ■ *n* (*Brit: also*: **fly swat**) ammazzamosche *m inv*
swathe [sweɪð] *n* fascio ■ *vt*: **to ~ in** (*bandages, blankets*) avvolgere in
swatter ['swɔtəʳ] *n* (*also*: **fly swatter**) ammazzamosche *m inv*
sway [sweɪ] *vi* (*building*) oscillare; (*tree*) ondeggiare; (*person*) barcollare ■ *vt* (*influence*) influenzare ■ *n* (*rule, power*): **~ (over)** influenza (su); **to hold ~ over sb** dominare qn
Swaziland ['swɑːzɪlænd] *n* Swaziland *m*
swear (*pt* **swore**, *pp* **sworn**) [swɛəʳ, swɔːʳ, swɔːn] *vi* (*witness etc*) giurare; (*curse*) bestemmiare, imprecare ■ *vt*: **to ~ an oath** prestare giuramento; **to ~ to sth** giurare qc
▸ **swear in** *vt* prestare giuramento a
swearword ['swɛəwəːd] *n* parolaccia
sweat [swɛt] *n* sudore *m*, traspirazione *f* ■ *vi* sudare; **in a ~** in un bagno di sudore
sweatband ['swɛtbænd] *n* (*Sport*) fascia elastica (per assorbire il sudore)
sweater ['swɛtəʳ] *n* maglione *m*
sweatshirt ['swɛtʃəːt] *n* maglione *m* in cotone felpato
sweatshop ['swɛtʃɔp] *n azienda o fabbrica dove i dipendenti sono sfruttati*
sweaty ['swɛtɪ] *adj* sudato(-a); bagnato(-a) di sudore
Swede [swiːd] *n* svedese *m/f*
swede [swiːd] *n* (*Brit*) rapa svedese
Sweden ['swiːdn] *n* Svezia
Swedish ['swiːdɪʃ] *adj* svedese ■ *n* (*Ling*) svedese *m*
sweep [swiːp] *n* spazzata; (*curve*) curva; (*expanse*) distesa; (*range*) portata; (*also*: **chimney sweep**) spazzacamino ■ *vb* (*pt, pp* **swept**) [swɛpt] *vt* spazzare, scopare; (*fashion, craze*) invadere ■ *vi* camminare maestosamente; precipitarsi, lanciarsi; (e)stendersi
▸ **sweep away** *vt* spazzare via; trascinare via
▸ **sweep past** *vi* sfrecciare accanto; passare accanto maestosamente
▸ **sweep up** *vt, vi* spazzare
sweeper ['swiːpəʳ] *n* (*person*) spazzino(-a); (*machine*) spazzatrice *f*; (*Football*) libero
sweeping ['swiːpɪŋ] *adj* (*gesture*) ampio(-a); (*changes, reforms*) ampio(-a), radicale; **a ~ statement** un'affermazione generica
sweepstake ['swiːpsteɪk] *n* lotteria (*spesso abbinata alle corse dei cavalli*)
sweet [swiːt] *n* (*Brit*) dolce *m*; (*candy*) caramella ■ *adj* dolce; (*fresh*) fresco(-a); (*kind*) gentile; (*cute*) carino(-a) ■ *adv*: **to smell/taste ~** avere un odore/sapore dolce; **~ and sour** *adj* agrodolce
sweetbread ['swiːtbrɛd] *n* animella
sweetcorn ['swiːtkɔːn] *n* granturco dolce
sweeten ['swiːtn] *vt* addolcire; zuccherare
sweetener ['swiːtnəʳ] *n* (*Culin*) dolcificante *m*
sweetheart ['swiːthɑːt] *n* innamorato(-a)
sweetly ['swiːtlɪ] *adv* dolcemente
sweetness ['swiːtnɪs] *n* sapore *m* dolce; dolcezza
sweet pea *n* pisello odoroso
sweet potato *n* patata americana, patata dolce
sweetshop ['swiːtʃɔp] *n* (*Brit*) ≈ pasticceria
sweet tooth *n*: **to have a ~** avere un debole per i dolci
swell [swɛl] *n* (*of sea*) mare *m* lungo ■ *adj* (*col: excellent*) favoloso(-a) ■ *vb* (*pt* **swelled**, *pp* **swollen, swelled**) ['swəulən] *vt* gonfiare, ingrossare; (*numbers, sales etc*) aumentare ■ *vi* gonfiarsi, ingrossarsi; (*sound*) crescere; (*Med*) gonfiarsi
swelling ['swɛlɪŋ] *n* (*Med*) tumefazione *f*, gonfiore *m*
sweltering ['swɛltərɪŋ] *adj* soffocante
swept [swɛpt] *pt, pp of* **sweep**
swerve [swəːv] *vi* deviare; (*driver*) sterzare; (*boxer*) scartare
swift [swɪft] *n* (*bird*) rondone *m* ■ *adj* rapido(-a), veloce
swiftly ['swɪftlɪ] *adv* rapidamente, velocemente
swiftness ['swɪftnɪs] *n* rapidità, velocità
swig [swɪg] *n* (*col: drink*) sorsata

swill [swɪl] *n* broda ■ *vt* (*also*: **swill out, swill down**) risciacquare
swim [swɪm] *n*: **to go for a ~** andare a fare una nuotata ■ *vb* (*pt* **swam**, *pp* **swum**) [swæm, swʌm] *vi* nuotare; (*Sport*) fare del nuoto; (*head, room*) girare ■ *vt* (*river, channel*) attraversare *or* percorrere a nuoto; **to go swimming** andare a nuotare; **to ~ a length** fare una vasca (a nuoto)
swimmer ['swɪmə^r] *n* nuotatore(-trice)
swimming ['swɪmɪŋ] *n* nuoto
swimming baths *npl* (*Brit*) piscina
swimming cap *n* cuffia
swimming costume *n* (*Brit*) costume *m* da bagno
swimmingly ['swɪmɪŋlɪ] *adv*: **to go ~** (*wonderfully*) andare a gonfie vele
swimming pool *n* piscina
swimming trunks *npl* costume *m* da bagno (per uomo)
swimsuit ['swɪmsu:t] *n* costume *m* da bagno
swindle ['swɪndl] *n* truffa ■ *vt* truffare
swindler ['swɪndlə^r] *n* truffatore(-trice)
swine [swaɪn] *n* (*pl inv*) maiale *m*, porco; (*col!*) porco (*!*)
swine flu *n* influenza suina
swing [swɪŋ] *n* altalena; (*movement*) oscillazione *f*; (*Mus*) ritmo; (*also*: **swing music**) swing *m* ■ *vb* (*pt, pp* **swung**) [swʌŋ] *vt* dondolare, far oscillare; (*also*: **swing round**) far girare ■ *vi* oscillare, dondolare; (*also*: **swing round**: *object*) roteare; (*: person*) girarsi, voltarsi; **to be in full ~** (*activity*) essere in piena attività; (*party etc*) essere nel pieno; **a ~ to the left** (*Pol*) una svolta a sinistra; **to get into the ~ of things** entrare nel pieno delle cose; **the road swings south** la strada prende la direzione sud
swing bridge *n* ponte *m* girevole
swing door *n* (*Brit*) porta battente
swingeing ['swɪndʒɪŋ] *adj* (*Brit: defeat*) violento(-a); (*: price increase*) enorme
swinging ['swɪŋɪŋ] *adj* (*step*) cadenzato(-a), ritmico(-a); (*rhythm, music*) trascinante; **~ door** (*US*) porta battente
swipe [swaɪp] *n* forte colpo; schiaffo ■ *vt* (*hit*) colpire con forza; dare uno schiaffo a; (*col: steal*) sgraffignare; (*credit card etc*) far passare (nell'apposita macchinetta)
swirl [swə:l] *n* turbine *m*, mulinello ■ *vi* turbinare, far mulinello
swish [swɪʃ] *adj* (*col: smart*) all'ultimo grido, alla moda ■ *n* (*sound: of whip*) sibilo; (*: of skirts, grass*) fruscio ■ *vi* sibilare
Swiss [swɪs] *adj, n* (*pl inv*) svizzero(-a)
Swiss French *adj* svizzero(-a) francese
Swiss German *adj* svizzero(-a) tedesco(-a)
switch [swɪtʃ] *n* (*for light, radio etc*) interruttore *m*; (*change*) cambiamento ■ *vt* (*also*: **switch round, switch over**) cambiare; scambiare
▸ **switch off** *vt* spegnere
▸ **switch on** *vt* accendere; (*engine, machine*) mettere in moto, avviare; (*Aut: ignition*) inserire; (*Brit: water supply*) aprire
switchblade ['swɪtʃbleɪd] *n* (*also*: **switchblade knife**) coltello a scatto
switchboard ['swɪtʃbɔ:d] *n* centralino
switchboard operator *n* centralinista *m/f*
Switzerland ['swɪtsələnd] *n* Svizzera
swivel ['swɪvl] *vi* (*also*: **swivel round**) girare
swollen ['swəulən] *pp of* **swell** ■ *adj* (*ankle etc*) gonfio(-a)
swoon [swu:n] *vi* svenire
swoop [swu:p] *n* (*by police etc*) incursione *f*; (*of bird etc*) picchiata ■ *vi* (*also*: **swoop down**) scendere in picchiata; (*police*): **to ~ (on)** fare un'incursione (in)
swop [swɔp] *n, vt* = **swap**
sword [sɔ:d] *n* spada
swordfish ['sɔ:dfɪʃ] *n* pesce *m* spada *inv*
swore [swɔ:^r] *pt of* **swear**
sworn [swɔ:n] *pp of* **swear**
swot [swɔt] *vt* sgobbare su ■ *vi* sgobbare
swum [swʌm] *pp of* **swim**
swung [swʌŋ] *pt, pp of* **swing**
sycamore ['sɪkəmɔ:^r] *n* sicomoro
sycophant ['sɪkəfənt] *n* leccapiedi *m/f*
sycophantic [sɪkə'fæntɪk] *adj* ossequioso(-a), adulatore(-trice)
Sydney ['sɪdnɪ] *n* Sydney *f*
syllable ['sɪləbl] *n* sillaba
syllabus ['sɪləbəs] *n* programma *m*; **on the ~** in programma d'esame
symbol ['sɪmbl] *n* simbolo
symbolic [sɪm'bɔlɪk], **symbolical** [sɪm'bɔlɪkl] *adj* simbolico(-a); **to be ~(al) of sth** simboleggiare qc
symbolism ['sɪmbəlɪzəm] *n* simbolismo
symbolize ['sɪmbəlaɪz] *vt* simbolizzare
symmetrical [sɪ'mɛtrɪkl] *adj* simmetrico(-a)
symmetry ['sɪmɪtrɪ] *n* simmetria
sympathetic [sɪmpə'θɛtɪk] *adj* (*showing pity*) compassionevole; (*kind*) comprensivo(-a); **~ towards** ben disposto(-a) verso; **to be ~ to a cause** (*well-disposed*) simpatizzare per una causa
sympathetically [sɪmpə'θɛtɪklɪ] *adv* in modo compassionevole; con comprensione
sympathize ['sɪmpəθaɪz] *vi*: **to ~ with sb** compatire qn; partecipare al dolore di qn; (*understand*) capire qn
sympathizer ['sɪmpəθaɪzə^r] *n* (*Pol*) simpatizzante *m/f*

sympathy ['sɪmpəθɪ] *n* compassione *f*; **in ~ with** d'accordo con; (*strike*) per solidarietà con; **with our deepest ~** con le nostre più sincere condoglianze
symphonic [sɪm'fɔnɪk] *adj* sinfonico(-a)
symphony ['sɪmfənɪ] *n* sinfonia
symphony orchestra *n* orchestra sinfonica
symposium [sɪm'pəuzɪəm] *n* simposio
symptom ['sɪmptəm] *n* sintomo; indizio
symptomatic [sɪmptə'mætɪk] *adj*: **~ (of)** sintomatico(-a) (di)
synagogue ['sɪnəgɔg] *n* sinagoga
sync [sɪŋk] *n* (*col*): **in/out of ~** in/fuori sincronia; (*fig: people*): **they are in ~** sono in sintonia
synchromesh [sɪŋkrəu'mɛʃ] *n* cambio sincronizzato
synchronize ['sɪŋkrənaɪz] *vt* sincronizzare ■ *vi*: **to ~ with** essere contemporaneo(-a) a
synchronized swimming *n* nuoto sincronizzato
syncopated ['sɪŋkəpeɪtɪd] *adj* sincopato(-a)
syndicate ['sɪndɪkɪt] *n* sindacato; (*Press*) agenzia di stampa
syndrome ['sɪndrəum] *n* sindrome *f*
synonym ['sɪnənɪm] *n* sinonimo
synonymous [sɪ'nɔnɪməs] *adj*: **~ (with)** sinonimo(-a) (di)
synopsis (*pl* **synopses**) [sɪ'nɔpsɪs, -si:z] *n* sommario, sinossi *f inv*
syntax ['sɪntæks] *n* sintassi *f inv*
synthesis (*pl* **syntheses**) ['sɪnθəsɪs, -si:z] *n* sintesi *f inv*
synthesizer ['sɪnθəsaɪzə^r^] *n* (*Mus*) sintetizzatore *m*
synthetic [sɪn'θɛtɪk] *adj* sintetico(-a) ■ *n* prodotto sintetico; (*Textiles*) fibra sintetica
syphilis ['sɪfɪlɪs] *n* sifilide *f*
syphon ['saɪfən] *n, vb* = **siphon**
Syria ['sɪrɪə] *n* Siria
Syrian ['sɪrɪən] *adj, n* siriano(-a)
syringe [sɪ'rɪndʒ] *n* siringa
syrup ['sɪrəp] *n* sciroppo; (*also*: **golden syrup**) melassa raffinata
syrupy ['sɪrəpɪ] *adj* sciropposo(-a)
system ['sɪstəm] *n* sistema *m*; (*network*) rete *f*; (*Anat*) apparato; **it was a shock to his ~** è stato uno shock per il suo organismo
systematic [sɪstə'mætɪk] *adj* sistematico(-a)
system disk *n* (*Comput*) disco del sistema
systems analyst *n* analista *m/f* di sistemi

Tt

T, t [ti:] *n* (*letter*) T, t *m or f inv*; **T for Tommy** ≈ T come Taranto
TA *n abbr* (*Brit*) = **Territorial Army**
ta [tɑ:] *excl* (*Brit col*) grazie!
tab [tæb] *n abbr* = **tabulator** ■ *n* (*loop: on coat etc*) laccetto; (*label*) etichetta; **to keep tabs on**; (*fig*) tenere d'occhio
tabby ['tæbɪ] *n* (*also*: **tabby cat**) (gatto) soriano, gatto tigrato
tabernacle ['tæbənækl] *n* tabernacolo
table ['teɪbl] *n* tavolo, tavola; (*chart*) tabella ■ *vt* (*motion etc*) presentare; **to lay** *or* **set the ~** apparecchiare *or* preparare la tavola; **to clear the ~** sparecchiare; **league ~** (*Football, Rugby*) classifica; **~ of contents** indice *m*
tablecloth ['teɪblklɔθ] *n* tovaglia
table d'hôte [tɑ:bl'dəut] *adj* (*meal*) a prezzo fisso
table lamp *n* lampada da tavolo
tablemat ['teɪblmæt] *n* sottopiatto
table salt *n* sale *m* fino *or* da tavola
tablespoon ['teɪblspu:n] *n* cucchiaio da tavola; (*also*: **tablespoonful**: *as measurement*) cucchiaiata
tablet ['tæblɪt] *n* (*Med*) compressa; (: *for sucking*) pastiglia; (*for writing*) blocco; (*of stone*) targa; **~ of soap** (*Brit*) saponetta
table tennis *n* tennis *m* da tavolo, ping-pong® *m*
table wine *n* vino da tavola
tabloid ['tæblɔɪd] *n* (*newspaper*) tabloid *m inv* (*giornale illustrato di formato ridotto*); **the tabloids, the ~ press** i giornali popolari; *vedi nota*

TABLOID PRESS

Il termine *tabloid press* si riferisce ai quotidiani o ai settimanali popolari che, rispetto ai "quality papers" hanno un formato ridotto e presentano le notizie in modo più sensazionalistico e meno approfondito; *vedi anche* "quality press".

taboo [tə'bu:] *adj, n* tabù *m inv*
tabulate ['tæbjuleɪt] *vt* (*data, figures*) tabulare, disporre in tabelle
tabulator ['tæbjuleɪtə^r] *n* tabulatore *m*
tachograph ['tækəgrɑ:f] *n* tachigrafo
tachometer [tæ'kɔmɪtə^r] *n* tachimetro
tacit ['tæsɪt] *adj* tacito(-a)
taciturn ['tæsɪtə:n] *adj* taciturno(-a)
tack [tæk] *n* (*nail*) bulletta; (*stitch*) punto d'imbastitura; (*Naut*) bordo, bordata ■ *vt* imbullettare; imbastire ■ *vi* bordeggiare; **to change ~** virare di bordo; **on the wrong ~** (*fig*) sulla strada sbagliata; **to ~ sth on to (the end of) sth** (*of letter, book*) aggiungere qc alla fine di qc
tackle ['tækl] *n* (*equipment*) attrezzatura, equipaggiamento; (*for lifting*) paranco; (*Rugby*) placcaggio; (*Football*) contrasto ■ *vt* (*difficulty*) affrontare; (*Rugby*) placcare; (*Football*) contrastare
tacky ['tækɪ] *adj* colloso(-a), appiccicaticcio(-a); ancora bagnato(-a); (*col: shabby*) scadente
tact [tækt] *n* tatto
tactful ['tæktful] *adj* delicato(-a), discreto(-a); **to be ~** avere tatto
tactfully ['tæktfəlɪ] *adv* con tatto
tactical ['tæktɪkl] *adj* tattico(-a)
tactical voting *n* voto tattico
tactician [tæk'tɪʃən] *n* tattico(-a)
tactics ['tæktɪks] *n, npl* tattica
tactless ['tæktlɪs] *adj* che manca di tatto
tactlessly ['tæktlɪslɪ] *adv* senza tatto
tadpole ['tædpəul] *n* girino
taffy ['tæfɪ] *n* (*US*) caramella *f* mou *inv*
tag [tæg] *n* etichetta; **price/name ~** etichetta del prezzo/con il nome
▸ **tag along** *vi* seguire
Tahiti [tə'hi:ti] *n* Tahiti *f*
tail [teɪl] *n* coda; (*of shirt*) falda ■ *vt* (*follow*) seguire, pedinare; **to turn ~** voltare la schiena; *see also* **head**
▸ **tail away, tail off** *vi* (*in size, quality etc*) diminuire gradatamente

tailback ['teɪlbæk] *n* (*Brit*) ingorgo
tail coat *n* marsina
tail end *n* (*of train, procession etc*) coda; (*of meeting etc*) fine *f*
tailgate ['teɪlgeɪt] *n* (*Aut*) portellone *m* posteriore
tail light *n* (*Aut*) fanalino di coda
tailor ['teɪlə^r] *n* sarto ■ *vt*: **to ~ sth (to)** adattare qc (alle esigenze di); **~'s (shop)** sartoria (da uomo)
tailoring ['teɪlərɪŋ] *n* (*cut*) taglio
tailor-made ['teɪlə'meɪd] *adj* (*also fig*) fatto(-a) su misura
tailwind ['teɪlwɪnd] *n* vento di coda
taint [teɪnt] *vt* (*meat, food*) far avariare; (*fig: reputation*) infangare
tainted ['teɪntɪd] *adj* (*food*) guasto(-a); (*water, air*) infetto(-a); (*fig*) corrotto(-a)
Taiwan [taɪ'wɑːn] *n* Taiwan *m*
Tajikistan [tɑːdʒɪkɪ'stɑːn] *n* Tagikistan *m*
take [teɪk] *vb* (*pt* **took**, *pp* **taken**) [tuk, 'teɪkn] *vt* prendere; (*gain: prize*) ottenere, vincere; (*require: effort, courage*) occorrere, volerci; (*tolerate*) accettare, sopportare; (*hold: passengers etc*) contenere; (*accompany*) accompagnare; (*bring, carry*) portare; (*conduct: meeting*) condurre; (*exam*) sostenere, presentarsi a ■ *vi* (*dye, fire etc*) prendere; (*injection*) fare effetto; (*plant*) attecchire ■ *n* (*Cine*) ripresa; **I ~ it that** suppongo che; **to ~ for a walk** (*child, dog*) portare a fare una passeggiata; **to ~ sb's hand** prendere qn per mano; **to ~ it upon o.s. to do sth** prendersi la responsabilità di fare qc; **to be taken ill** avere un malore; **to be taken with sb/sth** (*attracted*) essere tutto preso da qn/qc; **it won't ~ long** non ci vorrà molto tempo; **it takes a lot of time/courage** occorre *or* ci vuole molto tempo/coraggio; **it will ~ at least 5 litres** contiene almeno 5 litri; **~ the first on the left** prenda la prima a sinistra; **to ~ Russian at university** fare russo all'università; **I took him for a doctor** l'ho preso per un dottore
▸ **take after** *vt fus* assomigliare a
▸ **take apart** *vt* smontare
▸ **take away** *vt* portare via; togliere; **to ~ away (from)** sottrarre (da)
▸ **take back** *vt* (*return*) restituire; riportare; (*one's words*) ritirare
▸ **take down** *vt* (*building*) demolire; (*dismantle: scaffolding*) smontare; (*letter etc*) scrivere
▸ **take in** *vt* (*lodger*) prendere, ospitare; (*orphan*) accogliere; (*stray dog*) raccogliere; (*Sewing*) stringere; (*deceive*) imbrogliare, abbindolare; (*understand*) capire; (*include*) comprendere, includere
▸ **take off** *vi* (*Aviat*) decollare ■ *vt* (*remove*) togliere; (*imitate*) imitare
▸ **take on** *vt* (*work*) accettare, intraprendere; (*employee*) assumere; (*opponent*) sfidare, affrontare
▸ **take out** *vt* portare fuori; (*remove*) togliere; (*licence*) prendere, ottenere; **to ~ sth out of** tirare qc fuori da; estrarre qc da; **don't ~ it out on me!** non prendertela con me!
▸ **take over** *vt* (*business*) rilevare ■ *vi*: **to ~ over from sb** prendere le consegne *or* il controllo da qn
▸ **take to** *vt fus* (*person*) prendere in simpatia; (*activity*) prendere gusto a; (*form habit of*): **to ~ to doing sth** prendere *or* cominciare a fare qc
▸ **take up** *vt* (*one's story*) riprendere; (*dress*) accorciare; (*absorb: liquids*) assorbire; (*accept: offer, challenge*) accettare; (*occupy: time, space*) occupare; (*engage in: hobby etc*) mettersi a; **to ~ up with sb** fare amicizia con qn
takeaway ['teɪkəweɪ] *adj* (*Brit: food*) da portar via
take-home pay ['teɪkhəum-] *n* stipendio netto
taken ['teɪkn] *pp of* **take**
takeoff ['teɪkɔf] *n* (*Aviat*) decollo
takeout ['teɪkaut] *adj* (*US*) = **takeaway**
takeover ['teɪkəuvə^r] *n* (*Comm*) assorbimento
takeover bid *n* offerta di assorbimento
takings ['teɪkɪŋz] *npl* (*Comm*) incasso
talc [tælk] *n* (*also*: **talcum powder**) talco
tale [teɪl] *n* racconto, storia; (*pej*) fandonia; **to tell tales** fare la spia
talent ['tælənt] *n* talento
talented ['tæləntɪd] *adj* di talento
talent scout *n* talent scout *m/f inv*
talisman ['tælɪzmən] *n* talismano
talk [tɔːk] *n* discorso; (*gossip*) chiacchiere *fpl*; (*conversation*) conversazione *f*; (*interview*) discussione *f* ■ *vi* parlare; (*chatter*) chiacchierare; **to give a ~** tenere una conferenza; **to ~ about** parlare di; (*converse*) discorrere *or* conversare su; **to ~ sb out of/into doing** dissuadere qn da/convincere qn a fare; **to ~ shop** parlare del lavoro *or* degli affari; **talking of films, have you seen ...?** a proposito di film, ha visto ...?
▸ **talk over** *vt* discutere
talkative ['tɔːkətɪv] *adj* loquace, ciarliero(-a)
talking point ['tɔːkɪŋ-] *n* argomento di conversazione
talking-to ['tɔːkɪŋtuː] *n*: **to give sb a good ~** fare una bella paternale a qn
talk show *n* (*TV, Radio*) intervista (informale), talk show *m inv*
tall [tɔːl] *adj* alto(-a); **to be 6 feet ~** ≈ essere

alto 1 metro e 80; **how ~ are you?** quanto è alto?
tallboy ['tɔ:lbɔɪ] *n* (*Brit*) cassettone *m* alto
tallness ['tɔ:lnɪs] *n* altezza
tall story *n* panzana, frottola
tally ['tælɪ] *n* conto, conteggio ■ *vi*: **to ~ (with)** corrispondere (a); **to keep a ~ of sth** tener il conto di qc
talon ['tælən] *n* artiglio
tambourine [tæmbə'ri:n] *n* tamburello
tame [teɪm] *adj* addomesticato(-a); (*fig: story, style*) insipido(-a), scialbo(-a)
Tamil ['tæmɪl] *adj* tamil *inv* ■ *n* tamil *m/f inv*; (*Ling*) tamil *m*
tamper ['tæmpə^r] *vi*: **to ~ with** manomettere
tampon ['tæmpɔn] *n* tampone *m*
tan [tæn] *n* (*also*: **suntan**) abbronzatura ■ *vt* abbronzare ■ *vi* abbronzarsi ■ *adj* (*colour*) marrone rossiccio *inv*; **to get a ~** abbronzarsi
tandem ['tændəm] *n* tandem *m inv*
tandoori [tæn'duərɪ] *adj nella cucina indiana, detto di carni o verdure cucinate allo spiedo in particolari forni*
tang [tæŋ] *n* odore *m* penetrante; sapore *m* piccante
tangent ['tændʒənt] *n* (*Math*) tangente *f*; **to go off at a ~** (*fig*) partire per la tangente
tangerine [tændʒə'ri:n] *n* mandarino
tangible ['tændʒəbl] *adj* tangibile; **~ assets** patrimonio reale
Tangier [tæn'dʒɪə^r] *n* Tangeri *f*
tangle ['tæŋgl] *n* groviglio ■ *vt* aggrovigliare; **to get in(to) a ~** finire in un groviglio
tango ['tæŋgəu] *n* tango
tank [tæŋk] *n* serbatoio; (*for processing*) vasca; (*for fish*) acquario; (*Mil*) carro armato
tankard ['tæŋkəd] *n* boccale *m*
tanker ['tæŋkə^r] *n* (*ship*) nave *f* cisterna *inv*; (*for oil*) petroliera; (*truck*) autobotte *f*, autocisterna
tankini [tæn'ki:nɪ] *n* tankini *m inv*
tanned [tænd] *adj* abbronzato(-a)
tannin ['tænɪn] *n* tannino
tanning ['tænɪŋ] *n* (*of leather*) conciatura
tannoy® ['tænɔɪ] *n* (*Brit*) altoparlante *m*; **over the ~** per altoparlante
tantalizing ['tæntəlaɪzɪŋ] *adj* allettante
tantamount ['tæntəmaunt] *adj*: **~ to** equivalente a
tantrum ['tæntrəm] *n* accesso di collera; **to throw a ~** fare le bizze
Tanzania [tænzə'nɪə] *n* Tanzania
Tanzanian [tænzə'nɪən] *adj, n* tanzaniano(-a)
tap [tæp] *n* (*on sink etc*) rubinetto; (*gentle blow*) colpetto ■ *vt* dare un colpetto a; (*resources*) sfruttare, utilizzare; (*telephone conversation*) intercettare; (*telephone*) mettere sotto controllo; **on ~** (*beer*) alla spina; (*fig: resources*) a disposizione
tap-dancing ['tæpdɑ:nsɪŋ] *n* tip tap *m*
tape [teɪp] *n* nastro; (*also*: **magnetic tape**) nastro (magnetico) ■ *vt* (*record*) registrare (su nastro); **on ~** (*song etc*) su nastro
tape deck *n* piastra di registrazione
tape measure *n* metro a nastro
taper ['teɪpə^r] *n* candelina ■ *vi* assottigliarsi
tape recorder *n* registratore *m* (a nastro)
tape recording *n* registrazione *f*
tapered ['teɪpəd], **tapering** ['teɪpərɪŋ] *adj* affusolato(-a)
tapestry ['tæpɪstrɪ] *n* arazzo; tappezzeria
tape-worm ['teɪpwə:m] *n* tenia, verme *m* solitario
tapioca [tæpɪ'əukə] *n* tapioca
tappet ['tæpɪt] *n* punteria
tar [tɑ:^r] *n* catrame *m*; **low-/middle-~ cigarettes** sigarette a basso/medio contenuto di nicotina
tarantula [tə'ræntjulə] *n* tarantola
tardy ['tɑ:dɪ] *adj* tardo(-a); tardivo(-a)
target ['tɑ:gɪt] *n* bersaglio; (*fig: objective*) obiettivo; **to be on ~** (*project*) essere nei tempi (di lavorazione)
target practice *n* tiro al bersaglio
tariff ['tærɪf] *n* tariffa
tarmac ['tɑ:mæk] *n* (*Brit: on road*) macadam *m* al catrame; (*Aviat*) pista di decollo ■ *vt* (*Brit*) macadamizzare
tarnish ['tɑ:nɪʃ] *vt* offuscare, annerire; (*fig*) macchiare
tarot ['tærəu] *n* tarocco
tarpaulin [tɑ:'pɔ:lɪn] *n* tela incatramata
tarragon ['tærəgən] *n* dragoncello
tart [tɑ:t] *n* (*Culin*) crostata; (*Brit col: pej: woman*) sgualdrina ■ *adj* (*flavour*) aspro(-a), agro(-a)
▸ **tart up** *vt* (*col*): **to ~ o.s. up** farsi bello(-a); (*pej*) agghindarsi
tartan ['tɑ:tn] *n* tartan *m inv*
tartar ['tɑ:tə^r] *n* (*on teeth*) tartaro
tartar sauce *n* salsa tartara
task [tɑ:sk] *n* compito; **to take to ~** rimproverare
task force *n* (*Mil, Police*) unità operativa
taskmaster ['tɑ:skmɑ:stə^r] *n*: **he's a hard ~** è un vero tiranno
Tasmania [tæz'meɪnɪə] *n* Tasmania
tassel ['tæsl] *n* fiocco
taste [teɪst] *n* gusto; (*flavour*) sapore *m*, gusto; (*fig: glimpse, idea*) idea ■ *vt* gustare; (*sample*) assaggiare ■ *vi*: **to ~ of** (*fish etc*) sapere di, avere sapore di; **what does it ~ like?** che

t

sapore *or* gusto ha?; **it tastes like fish** sa di pesce; **you can ~ the garlic (in it)** (ci) si sente il sapore dell'aglio; **can I have a ~ of this wine?** posso assaggiare un po' di questo vino?; **to have a ~ of sth** assaggiare qc; **to have a ~ for sth** avere un'inclinazione per qc; **to be in bad** *or* **poor ~** essere di cattivo gusto

taste bud *n* papilla gustativa

tasteful ['teɪstful] *adj* di buon gusto

tastefully ['teɪstfəlɪ] *adv* con gusto

tasteless ['teɪstlɪs] *adj* (*food*) insipido(-a); (*remark*) di cattivo gusto

tasty ['teɪstɪ] *adj* saporito(-a), gustoso(-a)

tattered ['tætəd] *adj see* **tatters**

tatters ['tætəz] *npl*: **in ~** (*also*: **tattered**) a brandelli, sbrindellato(-a)

tattoo [tə'tu:] *n* tatuaggio; (*spectacle*) parata militare ■ *vt* tatuare

tatty ['tætɪ] *adj* (*Brit col*) malandato(-a)

taught [tɔ:t] *pt, pp of* **teach**

taunt [tɔ:nt] *n* scherno ■ *vt* schernire

Taurus ['tɔ:rəs] *n* Toro; **to be ~** essere del Toro

taut [tɔ:t] *adj* teso(-a)

tavern ['tævən] *n* taverna

tawdry ['tɔ:drɪ] *adj* pacchiano(-a)

tawny ['tɔ:nɪ] *adj* fulvo(-a)

tax [tæks] *n* imposta, tassa; (*on income*) imposte *fpl*, tasse *fpl* ■ *vt* tassare; (*fig: strain: patience etc*) mettere alla prova; **free of ~** esentasse *inv*, esente da imposte; **before/ after ~** al lordo/netto delle tasse

taxable ['tæksəbl] *adj* imponibile

tax allowance *n* detrazione *f* d'imposta

taxation [tæk'seɪʃən] *n* tassazione *f*; tasse *fpl*, imposte *fpl*; **system of ~** sistema *m* fiscale

tax avoidance *n l'evitare legalmente il pagamento di imposte*

tax collector *n* esattore *m* delle imposte

tax disc *n* (*Brit Aut*) ≈ bollo

tax evasion *n* evasione *f* fiscale

tax exemption *n* esenzione *f* fiscale

tax exile *n chi ripara all'estero per evadere le imposte*

tax-free [tæks'fri:] *adj* esente da imposte

tax haven *n* paradiso fiscale

taxi ['tæksɪ] *n* taxi *m inv* ■ *vi* (*Aviat*) rullare

taxidermist ['tæksɪdə:mɪst] *n* tassidermista *m/f*

taxi driver *n* tassista *m/f*

tax inspector *n* (*Brit*) ispettore *m* delle tasse

taxi rank, (*US*) **taxi stand** *n* posteggio dei taxi

tax payer *n* contribuente *m/f*

tax rebate *n* rimborso fiscale

tax relief *n* sgravio fiscale

tax return *n* dichiarazione *f* dei redditi

tax shelter *n* paradiso fiscale

tax year *n* anno fiscale

TB *n abbr* (= *tuberculosis*) TBC *f*

tbc *abbr* (= *to be confirmed*) da confermarsi

TD *n abbr* (*US*) = **Treasury Department**; (: *Football*) = **touchdown**

tea [ti:] *n* tè *m inv*; (*Brit: snack: for children*) merenda; **high ~** (*Brit*) cena leggera (*presa nel tardo pomeriggio*)

tea bag *n* bustina di tè

tea break *n* (*Brit*) intervallo per il tè

teacake ['ti:keɪk] *n* (*Brit*) panino dolce all'uva

teach (*pt, pp* **taught**) [ti:tʃ, tɔ:t] *vt*: **to ~ sb sth, ~ sth to sb** insegnare qc a qn ■ *vi* insegnare; **it taught him a lesson** (*fig*) gli è servito da lezione

teacher ['ti:tʃə^r] *n* (*gen*) insegnante *m/f*; (*in secondary school*) professore(-essa); (*in primary school*) maestro(-a); **French ~** insegnante di francese

teacher training college *n* (*for primary schools*) ≈ istituto magistrale; (*for secondary schools*) *scuola universitaria per l'abilitazione all'insegnamento nelle medie superiori*

teaching ['ti:tʃɪŋ] *n* insegnamento

teaching aids *npl* materiali *mpl* per l'insegnamento

teaching hospital *n* (*Brit*) clinica universitaria

teaching staff *n* (*Brit*) insegnanti *mpl*, personale *m* insegnante

tea cosy *n* copriteiera *m inv*

teacup ['ti:kʌp] *n* tazza da tè

teak [ti:k] *n* teak *m*

tea leaves *npl* foglie *fpl* di tè

team [ti:m] *n* squadra; (*of animals*) tiro

▸ **team up** *vi*: **to ~ up (with)** mettersi insieme (a)

team games *npl* giochi *mpl* di squadra

teamwork ['ti:mwə:k] *n* lavoro di squadra

tea party *n* tè *m inv* (*ricevimento*)

teapot ['ti:pɔt] *n* teiera

tear¹ [tɪə^r] *n* lacrima; **in tears** in lacrime; **to burst into tears** scoppiare in lacrime

tear² [tɛə^r] *n* strappo ■ *vb* (*pt* **tore**, *pp* **torn**) [tɔ:^r, tɔ:n] *vt* strappare ■ *vi* strapparsi; **to ~ to pieces** *or* **to bits** *or* **to shreds** (*also fig*) fare a pezzi *or* a brandelli

▸ **tear along** *vi* (*rush*) correre all'impazzata

▸ **tear apart** *vt* (*also fig*) distruggere

▸ **tear away** *vt*: **to ~ o.s. away (from sth)** (*fig*) staccarsi (da qc)

▸ **tear out** *vt* (*sheet of paper, cheque*) staccare

▸ **tear up** *vt* (*sheet of paper etc*) strappare

tearaway ['tɛərəweɪ] *n* (*col*) monello(-a)

teardrop ['tɪədrɔp] *n* lacrima

tearful ['tɪəful] *adj* piangente, lacrimoso(-a)

tear gas *n* gas *m* lacrimogeno

tearoom ['ti:ru:m] *n* sala da tè
tease [ti:z] *vt* canzonare; (*unkindly*) tormentare
tea set *n* servizio da tè
teashop ['ti:ʃɔp] *n* (*Brit*) sala da tè
Teasmaid® ['ti:zmeɪd] *n* macchinetta per fare il tè
teaspoon ['ti:spu:n] *n* cucchiaino da tè; (*also*: **teaspoonful**: *as measurement*) cucchiaino
tea strainer *n* colino da tè
teat [ti:t] *n* capezzolo; (*of bottle*) tettarella
teatime ['ti:taɪm] *n* ora del tè
tea towel *n* (*Brit*) strofinaccio (per i piatti)
tea urn *n* bollitore *m* per il tè
tech [tɛk] *n abbr* (*col*) = **technical college**; **technology**
technical ['tɛknɪkl] *adj* tecnico(-a)
technical college *n* ≈ istituto tecnico
technicality [tɛknɪ'kælɪtɪ] *n* tecnicità; (*detail*) dettaglio tecnico; **on a legal ~** grazie a un cavillo legale
technically ['tɛknɪklɪ] *adv* dal punto di vista tecnico
technician [tɛk'nɪʃən] *n* tecnico(-a)
technique [tɛk'ni:k] *n* tecnica
techno ['tɛknəu] *n* (*Mus*) techno *f inv*
technocrat ['tɛknəkræt] *n* tecnocrate *m/f*
technological [tɛknə'lɔdʒɪkl] *adj* tecnologico(-a)
technologist [tɛk'nɔlədʒɪst] *n* tecnologo(-a)
technology [tɛk'nɔlədʒɪ] *n* tecnologia
teddy ['tɛdɪ], **teddy bear** ['tɛdɪ-] *n* orsacchiotto
tedious ['ti:dɪəs] *adj* noioso(-a), tedioso(-a)
tedium ['ti:dɪəm] *n* noia, tedio
tee [ti:] *n* (*Golf*) tee *m inv*
teem [ti:m] *vi* abbondare, brulicare; **to ~ with** brulicare di; **it is teeming (with rain)** piove a dirotto
teenage ['ti:neɪdʒ] *adj* (*fashions etc*) per giovani, per adolescenti
teenager ['ti:neɪdʒə^r] *n* adolescente *m/f*
teens [ti:nz] *npl*: **to be in one's ~** essere adolescente
tee-shirt ['ti:ʃə:t] *n* = **T-shirt**
teeter ['ti:tə^r] *vi* barcollare, vacillare
teeth [ti:θ] *npl of* **tooth**
teethe [ti:ð] *vi* mettere i denti
teething ring ['ti:ðɪŋ-] *n* dentaruolo
teething troubles *npl* (*fig*) difficoltà *fpl* iniziali
teetotal ['ti:'təutl] *adj* astemio(-a)
teetotaller, (*US*) **teetotaler** ['ti:'təutlə^r] *n* astemio(-a)
TEFL ['tɛfl] *n abbr* = **Teaching of English as a Foreign Language**
Teflon® ['tɛflɔn] *n* teflon® *m*
Tehran [tɛə'rɑ:n] *n* Tehran *f*
tel. *abbr* (= *telephone*) tel
Tel Aviv ['tɛlə'vi:v] *n* Tel Aviv *f*
telecast ['tɛlɪkɑ:st] *vt, vi* teletrasmettere
telecommunications ['tɛlɪkəmju:nɪ'keɪʃənz] *n* telecomunicazioni *fpl*
teleconferencing ['tɛlɪkɔnfərnsɪŋ] *n* teleconferenza
telegram ['tɛlɪgræm] *n* telegramma *m*
telegraph ['tɛlɪgrɑ:f] *n* telegrafo
telegraphic [tɛlɪ'græfɪk] *adj* telegrafico(-a)
telegraph pole *n* palo del telegrafo
telegraph wire *n* filo del telegrafo
telepathic [tɛlɪ'pæθɪk] *adj* telepatico(-a)
telepathy [tə'lɛpəθɪ] *n* telepatia
telephone ['tɛlɪfəun] *n* telefono ▪ *vt* (*person*) telefonare a; (*message*) telefonare; **to have a ~**, (*Brit*) **to be on the ~** (*subscriber*) avere il telefono; **to be on the ~** (*be speaking*) essere al telefono
telephone booth, (*Brit*) **telephone box** *n* cabina telefonica
telephone call *n* telefonata
telephone directory *n* elenco telefonico
telephone exchange *n* centralino telefonico
telephone number *n* numero di telefono
telephone operator *n* centralinista *m/f*
telephone tapping *n* intercettazione *f* telefonica
telephonist [tə'lɛfənɪst] *n* (*Brit*) telefonista *m/f*
telephoto lens ['tɛlɪfəutəu-] *n* teleobiettivo
teleprinter ['tɛlɪprɪntə^r] *n* telescrivente *f*
Teleprompter® ['tɛlɪprɔmptə^r] *n* (*US*) gobbo
telesales ['tɛlɪseɪlz] *n* televendita
telescope ['tɛlɪskəup] *n* telescopio ▪ *vi* chiudersi a telescopio; (*fig: vehicles*) accartocciarsi
telescopic [tɛlɪs'kɔpɪk] *adj* telescopico(-a); (*umbrella*) pieghevole
Teletext® ['tɛlɪtɛkst] *n* (*system*) teletext *m inv*; (*in Italy*) televideo
telethon ['tɛlɪθɔn] *n* maratona televisiva
televise ['tɛlɪvaɪz] *vt* teletrasmettere
television ['tɛlɪvɪʒən] *n* televisione *f*; **on ~** alla televisione
television licence *n* (*Brit*) abbonamento alla televisione
television programme *n* programma *m* televisivo
television set *n* televisore *m*
teleworking ['tɛlɪwə:kɪŋ] *n* telelavoro
telex ['tɛlɛks] *n* telex *m inv* ▪ *vt* trasmettere per telex ▪ *vi* mandare un telex; **to ~ sb (about sth)** informare qn via telex (di qc)
tell (*pt, pp* **told**) [tɛl, təuld] *vt* dire; (*relate: story*) raccontare; (*distinguish*): **to ~ sth from**

distinguere qc da ■ *vi* (*have effect*) farsi sentire, avere effetto; **to ~ sb to do** dire a qn di fare; **to ~ sb about sth** dire a qn di qc; raccontare qc a qn; **to ~ the time** leggere l'ora; **can you ~ me the time?** può dirmi l'ora?; **(I) ~ you what ...** so io che cosa fare ...; **I couldn't ~ them apart** non riuscivo a distinguerli

▸ **tell off** *vt* rimproverare, sgridare

▸ **tell on** *vt fus* (*inform against*) denunciare

teller ['tɛlər] *n* (*in bank*) cassiere(-a)

telling ['tɛlɪŋ] *adj* (*remark, detail*) rivelatore(-trice)

telltale ['tɛlteɪl] *adj* (*sign*) rivelatore(-trice) ■ *n* malalingua, pettegolo(-a)

telly ['tɛlɪ] *n abbr* (*Brit col: = television*) tivù *f inv*

temerity [tə'mɛrɪtɪ] *n* temerarietà

temp [tɛmp] *abbr* (*Brit col*) = **temporary** ■ *n* impiegato(-a) straordinarioa(-a) ■ *vi* lavorare come impiegato(-a) straordinario(-a)

temper ['tɛmpər] *n* (*nature*) carattere *m*; (*mood*) umore *m*; (*fit of anger*) collera ■ *vt* (*moderate*) temperare, moderare; **to be in a ~** essere in collera; **to keep one's ~** restare calmo; **to lose one's ~** andare in collera

temperament ['tɛmprəmənt] *n* temperamento

temperamental [tɛmprə'mɛntl] *adj* capriccioso(-a)

temperance ['tɛmpərns] *n* moderazione *f*; (*in drinking*) temperanza nel bere

temperate ['tɛmprət] *adj* moderato(-a); (*climate*) temperato(-a)

temperature ['tɛmprətʃər] *n* temperatura; **to have** *or* **run a ~** avere la febbre

tempered ['tɛmpəd] *adj* (*steel*) temprato(-a)

tempest ['tɛmpɪst] *n* tempesta

tempestuous [tɛm'pɛstjuəs] *adj* (*relationship, meeting*) burrascoso(-a)

tempi ['tɛmpi:] *npl of* **tempo**

template, (*US*) **templet** ['tɛmplɪt] *n* sagoma

temple ['tɛmpl] *n* (*building*) tempio; (*Anat*) tempia

templet ['tɛmplɪt] *n* (*US*) = **template**

tempo (*pl* **tempos, tempi**) ['tɛmpəu] *n* tempo; (*fig: of life etc*) ritmo

temporal ['tɛmpərl] *adj* temporale

temporarily ['tɛmpərərɪlɪ] *adv* temporaneamente

temporary ['tɛmpərərɪ] *adj* temporaneo(-a); (*job, worker*) avventizio(-a), temporaneo(-a); **~ secretary** segretaria temporanea; **~ teacher** supplente *m/f*

temporize ['tɛmpəraɪz] *vi* temporeggiare

tempt [tɛmpt] *vt* tentare; **to ~ sb into doing** indurre qn a fare; **to be tempted to do sth** essere tentato di fare qc

temptation [tɛmp'teɪʃən] *n* tentazione *f*

tempting ['tɛmptɪŋ] *adj* allettante, seducente

ten [tɛn] *num* dieci ■ *n* dieci; **tens of thousands** decine di migliaia

tenable ['tɛnəbl] *adj* sostenibile

tenacious [tə'neɪʃəs] *adj* tenace

tenacity [tə'næsɪtɪ] *n* tenacia

tenancy ['tɛnənsɪ] *n* affitto; condizione *f* di inquilino

tenant ['tɛnənt] *n* inquilino(-a)

tend [tɛnd] *vt* badare a, occuparsi di; (*sick etc*) prendersi cura di ■ *vi*: **to ~ to do** tendere a fare; (*colour*): **to ~ to** tendere a

tendency ['tɛndənsɪ] *n* tendenza

tender ['tɛndər] *adj* tenero(-a); (*sore*) sensibile; (*fig: subject*) delicato(-a) ■ *n* (*Comm: offer*) offerta; (*money*): **legal ~** valuta (a corso legale) ■ *vt* offrire; **to put in a ~ (for)** fare un'offerta (per); **to put work out to ~** (*Brit*) dare lavoro in appalto; **to ~ one's resignation** presentare le proprie dimissioni

tenderize ['tɛndəraɪz] *vt* (*Culin*) far intenerire

tenderly ['tɛndəlɪ] *adv* teneramente

tenderness ['tɛndənɪs] *n* tenerezza; sensibilità

tendon ['tɛndən] *n* tendine *m*

tenement ['tɛnəmənt] *n* casamento

Tenerife [tɛnə'ri:f] *n* Tenerife *f*

tenet ['tɛnət] *n* principio

Tenn. *abbr* (*US*) = **Tennessee**

tenner ['tɛnər] *n* (*Brit col*) (banconota da) dieci sterline *fpl*

tennis ['tɛnɪs] *n* tennis *m*

tennis ball *n* palla da tennis

tennis court *n* campo da tennis

tennis elbow *n* (*Med*) gomito del tennista

tennis match *n* partita di tennis

tennis player *n* tennista *m/f*

tennis racket *n* racchetta da tennis

tennis shoes *npl* scarpe *fpl* da tennis

tenor ['tɛnər] *n* (*Mus, of speech etc*) tenore *m*

tenpin bowling ['tɛnpɪn-] *n* (*Brit*) bowling *m*

tense [tɛns] *adj* teso(-a) ■ *n* (*Ling*) tempo ■ *vt* (*tighten: muscles*) tendere

tenseness ['tɛnsnɪs] *n* tensione *f*

tension ['tɛnʃən] *n* tensione *f*

tent [tɛnt] *n* tenda

tentacle ['tɛntəkl] *n* tentacolo

tentative ['tɛntətɪv] *adj* esitante, incerto(-a); (*conclusion*) provvisorio(-a)

tenterhooks ['tɛntəhuks] *npl*: **on ~** sulle spine

tenth [tɛnθ] *num* decimo(-a)

tent peg *n* picchetto da tenda

tent pole *n* palo da tenda, montante *m*

tenuous ['tɛnjuəs] *adj* tenue

tenure ['tɛnjuəʳ] *n* (*of property*) possesso; (*of job*) incarico; (*guaranteed employment*): **to have ~** essere di ruolo

tepid ['tɛpɪd] *adj* tiepido(-a)

Ter. *abbr* = **terrace**

term [tə:m] *n* (*limit*) termine *m*; (*word*) vocabolo, termine; (*Scol*) trimestre *m*; (*Law*) sessione *f* ■ *vt* chiamare, definire; **terms** *npl* (*conditions*) condizioni *fpl*; (*Comm*) prezzi *mpl*, tariffe *fpl*; **~ of imprisonment** periodo di prigionia; **during his ~ of office** durante il suo incarico; **in the short/long ~** a breve/lunga scadenza; **"easy terms"** (*Comm*) "facilitazioni di pagamento"; **to be on good terms with** essere in buoni rapporti con; **to come to terms with** (*person*) arrivare a un accordo con; (*problem*) affrontare

terminal ['tə:mɪnl] *adj* finale, terminale; (*disease*) nella fase terminale ■ *n* (*Elec, Comput*) terminale *m*; (*Aviat, for oil, ore etc*) terminal *m inv*; (*Brit*: *also*: **coach terminal**) capolinea *m*

terminate ['tə:mɪneɪt] *vt* mettere fine a ■ *vi*: **to ~ in** finire in *or* con

termination [tə:mɪ'neɪʃən] *n* fine *f*; (*of contract*) rescissione *f*; **~ of pregnancy** (*Med*) interruzione *f* della gravidanza

termini ['tə:mɪnaɪ] *npl of* **terminus**

terminology [tə:mɪ'nɔlədʒɪ] *n* terminologia

terminus (*pl* **termini**) ['tə:mɪnəs, 'tə:mɪnaɪ] *n* (*for buses*) capolinea *m*; (*for trains*) stazione *f* terminale

termite ['tə:maɪt] *n* termite *f*

term paper *n* (*US University*) *saggio scritto da consegnare a fine trimestre*

Terr. *abbr* = **terrace**

terrace ['tɛrəs] *n* terrazza; (*Brit*: *row of houses*) fila di case a schiera; **the terraces** *npl* (*Brit Sport*) le gradinate

terraced ['tɛrɪst] *adj* (*garden*) a terrazze; (*in a row*: *house, cottage etc*) a schiera

terrain [tɛ'reɪn] *n* terreno

terrible ['tɛrɪbl] *adj* terribile; (*weather*) bruttissimo(-a); (*performance, report*) pessimo(-a)

terribly ['tɛrəblɪ] *adv* terribilmente; (*very badly*) malissimo

terrier ['tɛrɪəʳ] *n* terrier *m inv*

terrific [tə'rɪfɪk] *adj* incredibile, fantastico(-a); (*wonderful*) formidabile, eccezionale

terrify ['tɛrɪfaɪ] *vt* terrorizzare; **to be terrified** essere atterrito(-a)

territorial [tɛrɪ'tɔ:rɪəl] *adj* territoriale

territorial waters *npl* acque *fpl* territoriali

territory ['tɛrɪtərɪ] *n* territorio

terror ['tɛrəʳ] *n* terrore *m*

terror attack *n* attentato terroristico

terrorism ['tɛrərɪzəm] *n* terrorismo

terrorist ['tɛrərɪst] *n* terrorista *m/f*

terrorize ['tɛrəraɪz] *vt* terrorizzare

terse [tə:s] *adj* (*style*) conciso(-a); (*reply*) laconico(-a)

tertiary ['tə:ʃərɪ] *adj* (*gen*) terziario(-a); **~ education** (*Brit*) educazione *f* superiore post-scolastica

Terylene® ['tɛrəli:n] *n* (*Brit*) terital® *m*, terilene® *m*

TESL ['tɛsl] *n abbr* = **Teaching of English as a Second Language**

TESSA ['tɛsə] *n abbr* (*Brit*: = *Tax Exempt Special Savings Account*) *deposito a risparmio esente da tasse*

test [tɛst] *n* (*trial, check*) prova; (*: of goods in factory*) controllo, collaudo; (*Med*) esame *m*; (*Chem*) analisi *f inv*; (*exam*: *of intelligence etc*) test *m inv*; (*: in school*) compito in classe; (*also*: **driving test**) esame *m* di guida ■ *vt* provare; controllare, collaudare; esaminare; analizzare; sottoporre ad esame; **to put sth to the ~** mettere qc alla prova; **to ~ sth for sth** analizzare qc alla ricerca di qc; **to ~ sb in history** esaminare qn in storia

testament ['tɛstəmənt] *n* testamento; **the Old/New T~** il Vecchio/Nuovo testamento

test ban *n* (*also*: **nuclear test ban**) divieto di esperimenti nucleari

test case *n* (*Law, fig*) caso che farà testo

testes ['tɛsti:z] *npl* testicoli *mpl*

test flight *n* volo di prova

testicle ['tɛstɪkl] *n* testicolo

testify ['tɛstɪfaɪ] *vi* (*Law*) testimoniare, deporre; **to ~ to sth** (*Law*) testimoniare qc; (*gen*) comprovare *or* dimostrare qc; (*be sign of*) essere una prova di qc

testimonial [tɛstɪ'məunɪəl] *n* (*Brit*: *reference*) benservito; (*gift*) testimonianza di stima

testimony ['tɛstɪmənɪ] *n* (*Law*) testimonianza, deposizione *f*

testing ['tɛstɪŋ] *adj* (*difficult*: *time*) duro(-a)

test match *n* (*Cricket, Rugby*) partita internazionale

testosterone [tɛs'tɔstərəun] *n* testosterone *m*

test paper *n* (*Scol*) interrogazione *f* scritta

test pilot *n* pilota *m* collaudatore

test tube *n* provetta

test-tube baby ['tɛsttju:b-] *n* bambino(-a) concepito(-a) in provetta

testy ['tɛstɪ] *adj* irritabile

tetanus ['tɛtənəs] *n* tetano

tetchy ['tɛtʃɪ] *adj* irritabile, irascibile

tether ['tɛðəʳ] *vt* legare ■ *n*: **at the end of one's ~** al limite (della pazienza)

t

Tex. *abbr (US)* = **Texas**
text [tɛkst] *n* testo; (*Tel*) messaggino, sms *m inv* ■ *vt* mandare un sms a ■ *vi* messaggiarsi
textbook ['tɛkstbuk] *n* libro di testo
textile ['tɛkstaɪl] *n* tessile *m*; **textiles** *npl* tessuti *mpl*
texting ['tɛkstɪŋ] *n* invio di sms
text message *n* (*Tel*) messaggino, sms *m inv*
textual ['tɛkstjuəl] *adj* testuale, del testo
texture ['tɛkstʃəʳ] *n* tessitura; (*of skin, paper etc*) struttura
TGIF *abbr* (*col*) = **thank God it's Friday**
TGWU *n abbr* (*Brit*: = *Transport and General Workers' Union*) *sindacato degli operai dei trasporti e non specializzati*
Thai [taɪ] *adj* tailandese ■ *n* tailandese *m/f*; (*Ling*) tailandese *m*
Thailand ['taɪlænd] *n* Tailandia
thalidomide® [θə'lɪdəmaɪd] *n* talidomide® *m*
Thames [tɛmz] *n*: **the ~** il Tamigi
than [ðæn, ðən] *conj* che; (*with numerals, pronouns, proper names*): **more ~ 10/me/Maria** più di 10/me/Maria; **you know her better ~ I do** la conosce meglio di me *or* di quanto non la conosca io; **she has more apples ~ pears** ha più mele che pere; **it is better to phone ~ to write** è meglio telefonare che scrivere; **no sooner did he leave ~ the phone rang** non appena uscì il telefono suonò
thank [θæŋk] *vt* ringraziare; **~ you (very much)** grazie (tante); **~ heavens/God!** grazie al cielo/a Dio!; *see also* **thanks**
thankful ['θæŋkful] *adj*: **~ (for)** riconoscente (per); **~ for/that** (*relieved*) sollevato(a) da/dal fatto che
thankfully ['θænkfəlɪ] *adv* con riconoscenza; con sollievo; **~ there were few victims** grazie al cielo ci sono state poche vittime
thankless ['θæŋklɪs] *adj* ingrato(-a)
thanks [θæŋks] *npl* ringraziamenti *mpl*, grazie *fpl* ■ *excl* grazie!; **~ to** *prep* grazie a
Thanksgiving ['θæŋksgɪvɪŋ], **Thanksgiving Day** ['θæŋksgɪvɪŋ-] *n* (*US*) giorno del ringraziamento; *vedi nota*

THANKSGIVING (DAY)

Negli Stati Uniti il quarto giovedì di novembre ricorre il *Thanksgiving (Day)*, festa nazionale in ricordo della celebrazione con cui i Padri Pellegrini, i puritani inglesi che fondarono la colonia di Plymouth nel Massachusetts, ringraziarono Dio del buon raccolto del 1621.

that [ðæt ʃ] (*pl* **those**) *adj* (*demonstrative*) quel(quell', quello) *m*; quella(quell') *f*; **that man/woman/book** quell'uomo/quella donna/quel libro; (*not "this"*) quell'uomo/quella donna/quel libro là; **that one** quello(-a) là
■ *pron* **1** (*demonstrative*) ciò; (*not "this one"*) quello(-a); **who's that?** chi è quello là?; **what's that?** cos'è quello?; **is that you?** sei tu?; **I prefer this to that** preferisco questo a quello; **that's what he said** questo è ciò che ha detto; **after that** dopo; **what happened after that?** che è successo dopo?; **that is (to say)** cioè; **at** *or* **with that she ...** con ciò lei ...; **do it like that** fallo così
2 (*relative: direct*) che; (*: indirect*) cui; **the book (that) I read** il libro che ho letto; **the box (that) I put it in** la scatola in cui l'ho messo; **the people (that) I spoke to** le persone con cui *or* con le quali ho parlato; **not that I know of** non che io sappia
3 (*relative: of time*) in cui; **the day (that) he came** il giorno in cui è venuto
■ *conj* che; **he thought that I was ill** pensava che io fossi malato
■ *adv* (*demonstrative*) così; **I can't work that much** non posso lavorare (così) tanto; **that high** così alto; **the wall's about that high and that thick** il muro è alto circa così e spesso circa così

thatched [θætʃt] *adj* (*roof*) di paglia; **~ cottage** cottage *m inv* col tetto di paglia
Thatcherism ['θætʃərɪzəm] *n* thatcherismo
thaw [θɔ:] *n* disgelo ■ *vi* (*ice*) sciogliersi; (*food*) scongelarsi ■ *vt* (*food*) (fare) scongelare; **it's thawing** (*weather*) sta sgelando

KEYWORD

the [ði:, ðə] *def art* **1** (*gen*) il(lo, l') *m*, la(l') *f*, I(gli) *mpl*; le *fpl*; **the boy/girl/ink** il ragazzo/la ragazza/l'inchiostro; **the books/pencils** i libri/le matite; **the history of the world** la storia del mondo; **give it to the postman** dallo al postino; **I haven't the time/money** non ho tempo/soldi; **the rich and the poor** i ricchi e i poveri; **1.5 euros to the dollar** 1.5 euro per un dollaro; **paid by the hour** pagato a ore
2 (*in titles*): **Elizabeth the First** Elisabetta prima; **Peter the Great** Pietro il Grande
3 (*in comparisons*): **the more he works, the more he earns** più lavora più guadagna; **the sooner the better** prima è meglio è

theatre, (*US*) **theater** ['θɪətəʳ] *n* teatro

theatre-goer ['θɪətəgəuəʳ] *n* frequentatore(-trice) di teatri

theatrical [θɪ'ætrɪkl] *adj* teatrale

theft [θɛft] *n* furto

their [ðɛəʳ] *adj* il(la) loro *pl* i(le) loro

theirs [ðɛəz] *pron* il(la) loro *pl* i(le) loro; **it is ~** è loro; **a friend of ~** un loro amico

them [ðɛm, ðəm] *pron* (*direct*) li(le); (*indirect*) gli, loro (*after vb*); (*stressed, after prep: people*) loro; (*: people, things*) essi(-e); **I see ~** li vedo; **give ~ the book** dà loro *or* dagli il libro; **give me a few of ~** dammene un po' *or* qualcuno

theme [θi:m] *n* tema *m*

theme park *n* parco dei divertimenti a soggetto

theme song, theme tune *n* tema musicale

themselves [ðəm'sɛlvz] *pl pron* (*reflexive*) si; (*emphatic*) loro stessi(-e); (*after prep*) se stessi(-e); **between ~** tra (di) loro

then [ðɛn] *adv* (*at that time*) allora; (*next*) poi, dopo; (*and also*) e poi ■ *conj* (*therefore*) perciò, dunque, quindi ■ *adj*: **the ~ president** il presidente di allora; **from ~ on** da allora in poi; **until ~** fino ad allora; **and ~ what?** e poi?, e allora?; **what do you want me to do ~?** allora cosa vuole che faccia?

theologian [θɪə'ləudʒən] *n* teologo(-a)

theological [θɪə'lɔdʒɪkl] *adj* teologico(-a)

theology [θɪ'ɔlədʒɪ] *n* teologia

theorem ['θɪərəm] *n* teorema *m*

theoretical [θɪə'rɛtɪkl] *adj* teorico(-a)

theorize ['θɪəraɪz] *vi* teorizzare

theory ['θɪərɪ] *n* teoria; **in ~** in teoria

therapeutic [θɛrə'pju:tɪk], **therapeutical** [θɛrə'pju:tɪkl] *adj* terapeutico(-a)

therapist ['θɛrəpɪst] *n* terapista *m/f*

py ['θɛrəpɪ] *n* terapia

KEYWORD

there [ðɛəʳ] *adv* **1**: **there is, there are** c'è, ci sono; **there are 3 of them** (*people*) sono in 3; (*things*) ce ne sono 3; **there is no-one here** non c'è nessuno qui; **there has been an accident** c'è stato un incidente

2 (*referring to place*) là, lì; **it's there** è là *or* lì; **up/in/down there** lassù/là dentro/laggiù; **back there** là dietro; **on there** lassù; **over there** là; **through there** di là; **he went there on Friday** ci è andato venerdì; **it takes two hours to go there and back** ci vogliono due ore per andare e tornare; **I want that book there** voglio quel libro là *or* lì; **there he is!** eccolo!

3: **there, there** (*esp to child*) su, su

thereabouts ['ðɛərəbauts] *adv* (*place*) nei pressi, da quelle parti; (*amount*) giù di lì, all'incirca

thereafter [ðɛər'ɑ:ftəʳ] *adv* da allora in poi

thereby [ðɛə'baɪ] *adv* con ciò

therefore ['ðɛəfɔ:ʳ] *adv* perciò, quindi

there's [ðɛəz] = **there is; there has**

thereupon [ðɛərə'pɔn] *adv* (*at that point*) a quel punto; (*formal: on that subject*) in merito

thermal ['θə:ml] *adj* (*currents, spring*) termale; (*underwear, printer*) termico(-a); (*paper*) termosensibile

thermodynamics [θə:məudaɪ'næmɪks] *n* termodinamica

thermometer [θə'mɔmɪtəʳ] *n* termometro

thermonuclear ['θə:məu'nju:klɪəʳ] *adj* termonucleare

Thermos® ['θə:məs] *n* (*also*: **Thermos flask**) thermos® *m inv*

thermostat ['θə:məstæt] *n* termostato

thesaurus [θɪ'sɔ:rəs] *n* dizionario dei sinonimi

these [ði:z] *pl pron, adj* questi(-e)

thesis (*pl* **theses**) ['θi:sɪs, 'θi:si:z] *n* tesi *f inv*

they [ðeɪ] *pl pron* essi(esse); (*people only*) loro; **~ say that ...** (*it is said that*) si dice che ...

they'd [ðeɪd] = **they would; they had**

they'll [ðeɪl] = **they will; they shall**

they're [ðɛəʳ] = **they are**

they've [ðeɪv] = **they have**

thick [θɪk] *adj* spesso(-a); (*crowd*) compatto(-a); (*stupid*) ottuso(-a), lento(-a) ■ *n*: **in the ~ of** nel folto di; **it's 20 cm ~** ha uno spessore di 20 cm

thicken ['θɪkən] *vi* ispessire ■ *vt* (*sauce etc*) ispessire, rendere più denso(-a)

thicket ['θɪkɪt] *n* boscaglia

thickly ['θɪklɪ] *adv* (*spread*) a strati spessi; (*cut*) a fette grosse; (*populated*) densamente

thickness ['θɪknɪs] *n* spessore *m*

thickset [θɪk'sɛt] *adj* tarchiato(-a), tozzo(-a)

thickskinned [θɪk'skɪnd] *adj* (*fig*) insensibile

thief (*pl* **thieves**) [θi:f, θi:vz] *n* ladro(-a)

thieving ['θi:vɪŋ] *n* furti *mpl*

thigh [θaɪ] *n* coscia

thighbone ['θaɪbəun] *n* femore *m*

thimble ['θɪmbl] *n* ditale *m*

thin [θɪn] *adj* sottile; (*person*) magro(-a); (*soup*) poco denso(-a); (*hair, crowd*) rado(-a); (*fog*) leggero(-a) ■ *vt* (*hair*) sfoltire ■ *vi* (*fog*) diradarsi; (*also*: **thin out**: *crowd*) disperdersi; **to ~ (down)** (*sauce, paint*) diluire; **his hair is thinning** sta perdendo i capelli

thing [θɪŋ] *n* cosa; (*object*) oggetto; (*contraption*) aggeggio; **things** *npl* (*belongings*) cose *fpl*; **for one ~** tanto per cominciare; **the best ~ would be to** la cosa migliore sarebbe

t

di; **the ~ is ...** il fatto è che ...; **the main ~ is to ...** la cosa più importante è di ...; **first ~ (in the morning)** come *or* per prima cosa (di mattina); **last ~ (at night)** come *or* per ultima cosa (di sera); **poor ~** poveretto(-a); **she's got a ~ about mice** è terrorizzata dai topi; **how are things?** come va?

think (*pt, pp* **thought**) [θɪŋk, θɔːt] *vi* pensare, riflettere ■ *vt* pensare, credere; (*imagine*) immaginare; **to ~ of** pensare a; **what did you ~ of them?** cosa ne ha pensato?; **to ~ about sth/sb** pensare a qc/qn; **I'll ~ about it** ci penserò; **to ~ of doing** pensare di fare; **I ~ so** penso *or* credo di sì; **to ~ well of** avere una buona opinione di; **to ~ aloud** pensare ad alta voce; **~ again!** rifletti!, pensaci su!

▸**think out** *vt* (*plan*) elaborare; (*solution*) trovare

▸**think over** *vt* riflettere su; **I'd like to ~ things over** vorrei pensarci su

▸**think through** *vt* riflettere a fondo su

▸**think up** *vt* ideare

thinking ['θɪŋkɪŋ] *n*: **to my (way of) ~** a mio parere

think tank *n* gruppo di esperti

thinly ['θɪnlɪ] *adv* (*cut*) a fette sottili; (*spread*) in uno strato sottile

thinness ['θɪnnɪs] *n* sottigliezza; magrezza

third [θəːd] *n* terzo(-a) ■ *n* terzo(-a); (*fraction*) terzo, terza parte *f*; (*Brit Scol: degree*) *laurea col minimo dei voti*

third-degree burns ['θəːddɪ'griː-] *npl* ustioni *fpl* di terzo grado

thirdly ['θəːdlɪ] *adv* in terzo luogo

third party insurance *n* (*Brit*) assicurazione *f* contro terzi

third-rate [θəːd'reɪt] *adj* di qualità scadente

Third World *n*: **the ~** il Terzo Mondo

thirst [θəːst] *n* sete *f*

thirsty ['θəːstɪ] *adj* (*person*) assetato(-a), che ha sete; **to be ~** aver sete

thirteen [θəː'tiːn] *num* tredici

thirtieth ['θəːtɪɪθ] *num* trentesimo(-a)

thirty ['θəːtɪ] *num* trenta

 KEYWORD

this [ðɪs ʃ] (*pl* **these**) *adj* (*demonstrative*) questo(-a); **this man/woman/book** quest'uomo/questa donna/questo libro; (*not "that"*) quest'uomo/questa donna/questo libro qui; **this one** questo(-a) qui; **this time** questa volta; **this time last year** l'anno scorso in questo periodo; **this way** (*in this direction*) da questa parte; (*in this fashion*) così
■ *pron* (*demonstrative*) questo(-a); (*not "that one"*) questo(-a) qui; **who/what is this?** chi è/che cos'è questo?; **I prefer this to that** preferisco questo a quello; **this is where I live** io abito qui; **this is what he said** questo è ciò che ha detto; **they were talking of this and that** stavano parlando del più e del meno; **this is Mr Brown** (*in introductions, photo*) questo è il signor Brown; (*on telephone*) sono il signor Brown
■ *adv* (*demonstrative*): **this high/long** *etc* alto/lungo *etc* così; **it's about this high** è alto circa così; **I didn't know things were this bad** non sapevo andasse così male

thistle ['θɪsl] *n* cardo

thong [θɔŋ] *n* cinghia

thorn [θɔːn] *n* spina

thorny ['θɔːnɪ] *adj* spinoso(-a)

thorough ['θʌrə] *adj* (*person*) preciso(-a), accurato(-a); (*search*) minuzioso(-a); (*knowledge, research*) approfondito(-a), profondo(-a); (*cleaning*) a fondo

thoroughbred ['θʌrəbrɛd] *n* (*horse*) purosangue *m/f inv*

thoroughfare ['θʌrəfɛə[r]] *n* strada transitabile; **"no ~"** (*Brit*) "divieto di transito"

thoroughgoing ['θʌrəgəuɪŋ] *adj* (*analysis*) approfondito(-a); (*reform*) totale

thoroughly ['θʌrəlɪ] *adv* accuratamente; minuziosamente, in profondità; a fondo; **he ~ agreed** fu completamente d'accordo

thoroughness ['θʌrənɪs] *n* precisione *f*

those [ðəuz] *pl pron* quelli(-e) ■ *pl adj* quei(quegli) *mpl*; quelle *fpl*

though [ðəu] *conj* benché, sebbene ■ *adv* comunque, tuttavia; **even ~** anche se; **it's not so easy, ~** tuttavia non è così facile

thought [θɔːt] *pt, pp of* **think** ■ *n* pensiero; (*opinion*) opinione *f*; (*intention*) intenzione *f*; **after much ~** dopo molti ripensamenti; **I've just had a ~** mi è appena venuta un'idea; **to give sth some ~** prendere qc in considerazione, riflettere su qc

thoughtful ['θɔːtful] *adj* pensieroso(-a), pensoso(-a); ponderato(-a); (*considerate*) premuroso(-a)

thoughtfully ['θɔːtfəlɪ] *adv* (*pensively*) con aria pensierosa

thoughtless ['θɔːtlɪs] *adj* sconsiderato(-a); (*behaviour*) scortese

thoughtlessly ['θɔːtlɪslɪ] *adv* sconsideratamente; scortesemente

thought-provoking ['θɔːtprəvəukɪŋ] *adj* stimolante

thousand ['θauzənd] *num* mille; **one ~** mille; **thousands of** migliaia di

thousandth ['θauzəntθ] *num* millesimo(-a)

thrash [θræʃ] *vt* picchiare; bastonare; (*defeat*) battere
▸ **thrash about** *vi* dibattersi
▸ **thrash out** *vt* dibattere, sviscerare
thrashing [ˈθræʃɪŋ] *n*: **to give sb a ~** = **to thrash sb**
thread [θrɛd] *n* filo; (*of screw*) filetto ■ *vt* (*needle*) infilare; **to ~ one's way between** infilarsi tra
threadbare [ˈθrɛdbɛəʳ] *adj* consumato(-a), logoro(-a)
threat [θrɛt] *n* minaccia; **to be under ~ of** (*closure, extinction*) rischiare di; (*exposure*) essere minacciato(-a) di
threaten [ˈθrɛtn] *vi* (*storm*) minacciare ■ *vt*: **to ~ sb with sth/to do** minacciare qn, con qc/di fare
threatening [ˈθrɛtnɪŋ] *adj* minaccioso(-a)
three [θriː] *num* tre
three-dimensional [θriːdaɪˈmɛnʃənl] *adj* tridimensionale
three-piece [ˈθriːpiːs]: **~ suit** *n* completo (con gilè); **~ suite** *n* salotto comprendente un divano e due poltrone
three-ply [θriːˈplaɪ] *adj* (*wood*) a tre strati; (*wool*) a tre fili
three-quarters [θriːˈkwɔːtəz] *npl* tre quarti *mpl*; **~ full** pieno per tre quarti
three-wheeler [θriːˈwiːləʳ] *n* (*car*) veicolo a tre ruote
thresh [θrɛʃ] *vt* (*Agr*) trebbiare
threshing machine [ˈθrɛʃɪŋ-] *n* trebbiatrice *f*
threshold [ˈθrɛʃhəuld] *n* soglia; **to be on the ~ of** (*fig*) essere sulla soglia di
threshold agreement *n* (*Econ*) ≈ scala mobile
threw [θruː] *pt of* **throw**
thrift [θrɪft] *n* parsimonia
thrifty [ˈθrɪftɪ] *adj* economico(-a), parsimonioso(-a)
thrill [θrɪl] *n* brivido ■ *vi* eccitarsi, tremare ■ *vt* (*audience*) elettrizzare; **I was thrilled to get your letter** la tua lettera mi ha fatto veramente piacere
thriller [ˈθrɪləʳ] *n* film *m inv* (*or* dramma *m or* libro) del brivido
thrilling [ˈθrɪlɪŋ] *adj* (*book, play etc*) pieno(-a) di suspense; (*news, discovery*) entusiasmante
thrive (*pt* **thrived** *or* **throve**, *pp* **thrived** *or* **thriven**) [θraɪv, θrəuv, ˈθrɪvn] *vi* crescere *or* svilupparsi bene; (*business*) prosperare; **he thrives on it** gli fa bene, ne gode
thriving [ˈθraɪvɪŋ] *adj* (*industry etc*) fiorente
throat [θrəut] *n* gola; **to have a sore ~** avere (un *or* il) mal di gola
throb [θrɔb] *n* (*of heart*) battito; (*of engine*) vibrazione *f*; (*of pain*) fitta ■ *vi* (*heart*) palpitare; (*engine*) vibrare; (*with pain*) pulsare; **my head is throbbing** mi martellano le tempie
throes [θrəuz] *npl*: **in the ~ of** alle prese con; in preda a; **in the ~ of death** in agonia
thrombosis [θrɔmˈbəusɪs] *n* trombosi *f*
throne [θrəun] *n* trono
throng [θrɔŋ] *n* moltitudine *f* ■ *vt* affollare
throttle [ˈθrɔtl] *n* (*Aut*) valvola a farfalla; (*on motorcycle*) (manopola del) gas ■ *vt* strangolare
through [θruː] *prep* attraverso; (*time*) per, durante; (*by means of*) per mezzo di; (*owing to*) a causa di ■ *adj* (*ticket, train, passage*) diretto(-a) ■ *adv* attraverso; **(from) Monday ~ Friday** (*US*) da lunedì a venerdì; **I am halfway ~ the book** sono a metà libro; **to let sb ~** lasciar passare qn; **to put sb ~ to sb** (*Tel*) passare qn a qn; **to be ~** (*Tel*) ottenere la comunicazione; (*have finished*) avere finito; **"no ~ traffic"** (*US*) "divieto d'accesso"; **"no ~ road"** (*Brit*) "strada senza sbocco"
throughout [θruːˈaut] *prep* (*place*) dappertutto in; (*time*) per *or* durante tutto(-a) ■ *adv* dappertutto; sempre
throughput [ˈθruːput] *n* (*of goods, materials*) materiale *m* in lavorazione; (*Comput*) volume *m* di dati immessi
throve [θrəuv] *pt of* **thrive**
throw [θrəu] *n* tiro, getto; (*Sport*) lancio ■ *vt* (*pt* **threw**, *pp* **thrown**) [θruː, θrəun] tirare, gettare; (*Sport*) lanciare; (*rider*) disarcionare; (*fig*) confondere; (*pottery*) formare al tornio; **to ~ a party** dare una festa; **to ~ open** (*doors, windows*) spalancare; (*house, gardens etc*) aprire al pubblico; (*competition, race*) aprire a tutti
▸ **throw about, throw around** *vt* (*litter etc*) spargere
▸ **throw away** *vt* gettare *or* buttare via
▸ **throw off** *vt* sbarazzarsi di
▸ **throw out** *vt* buttare fuori; (*reject*) respingere
▸ **throw together** *vt* (*clothes, meal etc*) mettere insieme; (*essay*) buttar giù
▸ **throw up** *vi* vomitare
throwaway [ˈθrəuəweɪ] *adj* da buttare
throwback [ˈθrəubæk] *n*: **it's a ~ to** (*fig*) ciò risale a
throw-in [ˈθrəuɪn] *n* (*Sport*) rimessa in gioco
thrown [θrəun] *pp of* **throw**
thru [θruː] *prep, adj, adv* (*US*) = **through**
thrush [θrʌʃ] *n* (*Zool*) tordo; (*Med: esp in children*) mughetto; (*: Brit: in women*) candida
thrust [θrʌst] *n* (*Tech*) spinta ■ *vt* (*pt, pp* **~**) spingere con forza; (*push in*) conficcare
thrusting [ˈθrʌstɪŋ] *adj* (troppo) intraprendente
thud [θʌd] *n* tonfo

t

thug [θʌg] *n* delinquente *m*
thumb [θʌm] *n* (*Anat*) pollice *m* ■ *vt* (*book*) sfogliare; **to ~ a lift** fare l'autostop; **to give sb/sth the thumbs up/down** approvare/ disapprovare qn/qc
thumb index *n* indice *m* a rubrica
thumbnail ['θʌmneɪl] *n* unghia del pollice
thumbnail sketch *n* descrizione *f* breve
thumbtack ['θʌmtæk] *n* (*US*) puntina da disegno
thump [θʌmp] *n* colpo forte; (*sound*) tonfo ■ *vt* battere su ■ *vi* picchiare, battere
thunder ['θʌndəʳ] *n* tuono ■ *vi* tuonare; (*train etc*): **to ~ past** passare con un rombo
thunderbolt ['θʌndəbəult] *n* fulmine *m*
thunderclap ['θʌndəklæp] *n* rombo di tuono
thunderous ['θʌndərəs] *adj* fragoroso(-a)
thunderstorm ['θʌndəstɔ:m] *n* temporale *m*
thunderstruck ['θʌndəstrʌk] *adj* (*fig*) sbigottito(-a)
thundery ['θʌndərɪ] *adj* temporalesco(-a)
Thur., Thurs. *abbr* (= *Thursday*) gio.
Thursday ['θə:zdɪ] *n* giovedì *m inv*; *see also* **Tuesday**
thus [ðʌs] *adv* così
thwart [θwɔ:t] *vt* contrastare
thyme [taɪm] *n* timo
thyroid ['θaɪrɔɪd] *n* tiroide *f*
tiara [tɪ'ɑ:rə] *n* (*woman's*) diadema *m*
Tiber ['taɪbəʳ] *n*: **the ~** il Tevere
Tibet [tɪ'bɛt] *n* Tibet *m*
Tibetan [tɪ'bɛtən] *adj* tibetano(-a) ■ *n* (*person*) tibetano(-a); (*Ling*) tibetano
tibia ['tɪbɪə] *n* tibia
tic [tɪk] *n* tic *m inv*
tick [tɪk] *n* (*sound: of clock*) tic tac *m inv*; (*mark*) segno; spunta; (*Zool*) zecca; (*Brit col*): **in a ~** in un attimo; (*Brit col: credit*): **to buy sth on ~** comprare qc a credito ■ *vi* fare tic tac ■ *vt* spuntare; **to put a ~ against sth** fare un segno di fianco a qc
▸ **tick off** *vt* spuntare; (*person*) sgridare
▸ **tick over** *vi* (*Brit: engine*) andare al minimo
ticker tape ['tɪkə-] *n* nastro di telescrivente; (*US: in celebrations*) stelle *fpl* filanti
ticket ['tɪkɪt] *n* biglietto; (*in shop: on goods*) etichetta; (*: from cash register*) scontrino; (*for library*) scheda; (*US Pol*) lista dei candidati; **to get a (parking) ~** (*Aut*) prendere una multa (per sosta vietata)
ticket agency *n* (*Theat*) agenzia di vendita di biglietti
ticket collector *n* bigliettaio
ticket holder *n* persona munita di biglietto
ticket inspector *n* controllore *m*
ticket office *n* biglietteria
tickle ['tɪkl] *n* solletico ■ *vt* fare il solletico a, solleticare; (*fig*) stuzzicare; piacere a; far ridere
ticklish ['tɪklɪʃ] *adj* che soffre il solletico; (*which tickles: blanket, cough*) che provoca prurito
tidal ['taɪdl] *adj* di marea
tidal wave *n* onda anomala
tidbit ['tɪdbɪt] *n* (*US*) = **titbit**
tiddlywinks ['tɪdlɪwɪŋks] *n* gioco della pulce
tide [taɪd] *n* marea; (*fig: of events*) corso ■ *vt*: **will £20 ~ you over till Monday?** ti basteranno 20 sterline fino a lunedì?; **high/ low ~** alta/bassa marea; **the ~ of public opinion** l'orientamento dell'opinione pubblica
tidily ['taɪdɪlɪ] *adv* in modo ordinato; **to arrange ~** sistemare; **to dress ~** vestirsi per benino
tidiness ['taɪdɪnɪs] *n* ordine *m*
tidy ['taɪdɪ] *adj* (*room*) ordinato(-a), lindo(-a); (*dress, work*) curato(-a), in ordine; (*person*) ordinato(-a); (*mind*) organizzato(-a) ■ *vt* (*also*: **tidy up**) riordinare, mettere in ordine; **to ~ o.s. up** rassettarsi
tie [taɪ] *n* (*string etc*) legaccio; (*Brit: also*: **necktie**) cravatta; (*fig: link*) legame *m*; (*Sport: draw*) pareggio; (*: match*) incontro; (*US Rail*) traversina ■ *vt* (*parcel*) legare; (*ribbon*) annodare ■ *vi* (*Sport*) pareggiare; **"black/ white ~"** "smoking/abito di rigore"; **family ties** legami familiari; **to ~ sth in a bow** annodare qc; **to ~ a knot in sth** fare un nodo a qc
▸ **tie down** *vt* fissare con una corda; (*fig*): **to ~ sb down to** costringere qn ad accettare
▸ **tie in** *vi*: **to ~ in (with)** (*correspond*) corrispondere (a)
▸ **tie on** *vt* (*Brit: label etc*) attaccare
▸ **tie up** *vt* (*parcel, dog*) legare; (*boat*) ormeggiare; (*arrangements*) concludere; **to be tied up** (*busy*) essere occupato *or* preso
tie-break ['taɪbreɪk], **tie-breaker** ['taɪbreɪkəʳ] *n* (*Tennis*) tie-break *m inv*; (*in quiz*) spareggio
tie-on ['taɪɔn] *adj* (*Brit: label*) volante
tie-pin ['taɪpɪn] *n* (*Brit*) fermacravatta *m inv*
tier [tɪəʳ] *n* fila; (*of cake*) piano, strato
Tierra del Fuego [tɪ'ɛrədɛl'fweɪgəu] *n* Terra del Fuoco
tie tack *n* (*US*) fermacravatta *m inv*
tiff [tɪf] *n* battibecco
tiger ['taɪgəʳ] *n* tigre *f*
tight [taɪt] *adj* (*rope*) teso(-a), tirato(-a); (*clothes*) stretto(-a); (*budget, programme, bend*) stretto(-a); (*control*) severo(-a), fermo(-a); (*col: drunk*) sbronzo(-a) ■ *adv* (*squeeze*) fortemente; (*shut*) ermeticamente; **to be packed ~**

(*suitcase*) essere pieno zeppo; (*people*) essere pigiati; **everybody hold ~!** tenetevi stretti!; *see also* **tights**
tighten ['taɪtn] *vt* (*rope*) tendere; (*screw*) stringere; (*control*) rinforzare ■ *vi* tendersi; stringersi
tight-fisted [taɪt'fɪstɪd] *adj* avaro(-a)
tight-lipped ['taɪt'lɪpt] *adj*: **to be ~** essere reticente; (*angry*) tenere le labbra serrate
tightly ['taɪtlɪ] *adv* (*grasp*) bene, saldamente
tightrope ['taɪtrəup] *n* corda (da acrobata)
tightrope walker *n* funambolo(-a)
tights [taɪts] *npl* (*Brit*) collant *m inv*
tigress ['taɪgrɪs] *n* tigre *f* (femmina)
tilde ['tɪldə] *n* tilde *f*
tile [taɪl] *n* (*on roof*) tegola; (*on floor*) mattonella; (*on wall*) piastrella ■ *vt* (*floor, bathroom etc*) piastrellare
tiled [taɪld] *adj* rivestito(-a) di tegole; a mattonelle; a piastrelle
till [tɪl] *n* registratore *m* di cassa ■ *vt* (*land*) coltivare ■ *prep, conj* = **until**
tiller ['tɪlə^r] *n* (*Naut*) barra del timone
tilt [tɪlt] *vt* inclinare, far pendere ■ *vi* inclinarsi, pendere ■ *n* (*slope*) pendio; **to wear one's hat at a ~** portare il cappello sulle ventitrè; **(at) full ~** a tutta velocità
timber ['tɪmbə^r] *n* (*material*) legname *m*; (*trees*) alberi *mpl* da legname
time [taɪm] *n* tempo; (*epoch: often pl*) epoca, tempo; (*by clock*) ora; (*moment*) momento; (*occasion, also Math*) volta; (*Mus*) tempo ■ *vt* (*race*) cronometrare; (*programme*) calcolare la durata di; (*remark etc*): **to ~ sth well/badly** scegliere il momento più/meno opportuno per qc; **a long ~** molto tempo; **for the ~ being** per il momento; **from ~ to ~** ogni tanto; **~ after ~, ~ and again** mille volte; **in ~** (*soon enough*) in tempo; (*after some time*) col tempo; (*Mus*) a tempo; **at times** a volte; **to take one's ~** prenderla con calma; **in a week's ~** fra una settimana; **in no ~** in un attimo; **on ~** puntualmente; **to be 30 minutes behind/ahead of ~** avere 30 minuti di ritardo/anticipo; **by the ~ he arrived** quando è arrivato; **5 times 5** 5 volte 5, 5 per 5; **what ~ is it?** che ora è?, che ore sono?; **what ~ do you make it?** che ora fa?; **to have a good ~** divertirsi; **they had a hard ~ of it** è stato duro per loro; **~'s up!** è (l')ora!; **to be behind the times** vivere nel passato; **I've no ~ for it** (*fig*) non ho tempo da perdere con cose del genere; **he'll do it in his own (good) ~** (*without being hurried*) lo farà quando avrà (un minuto di) tempo; **he'll do it in** *or* (*US*) **on his own ~** (*out of working hours*) lo farà nel suo tempo libero; **the bomb was timed to explode 5 minutes later** la bomba era stata regolata in modo da esplodere 5 minuti più tardi
time-and-motion study ['taɪmənd'məuʃən-] *n* analisi *f inv* dei tempi e dei movimenti
time bomb *n* bomba a orologeria
time card *n* cartellino (da timbrare)
time clock *n* orologio *m* marcatempo *inv*
time-consuming ['taɪmkənsju:mɪŋ] *adj* che richiede molto tempo
time difference *n* differenza di fuso orario
time frame *n* tempi *mpl*
time-honoured, (*US*) **time-honored** ['taɪmɔnəd] *adj* consacrato(-a) dal tempo
timekeeper ['taɪmki:pə^r] *n* (*Sport*) cronometrista *m/f*
time lag *n* intervallo, ritardo; (*in travel*) differenza di fuso orario
timeless ['taɪmlɪs] *adj* eterno(-a)
time limit *n* limite *m* di tempo
timely ['taɪmlɪ] *adj* opportuno(-a)
time off *n* tempo libero
timer ['taɪmə^r] *n* (*in kitchen*) contaminuti *m inv*; (*Tech*) timer *m inv*, temporizzatore *m*
time-saving ['taɪmseɪvɪŋ] *adj* che fa risparmiare tempo
time scale *n* tempi *mpl* d'esecuzione
time-sharing ['taɪmʃeərɪŋ] *n* (*Comput*) divisione *f* di tempo
time sheet *n* = **time card**
time signal *n* segnale *m* orario
time switch *n* interruttore *m* a tempo
timetable ['taɪmteɪbl] *n* orario; (*programme of events etc*) programma *m*
time zone *n* fuso orario
timid ['tɪmɪd] *adj* timido(-a); (*easily scared*) pauroso(-a)
timidity [tɪ'mɪdɪtɪ] *n* timidezza
timing ['taɪmɪŋ] *n* sincronizzazione *f*; (*fig*) scelta del momento opportuno, tempismo; (*Sport*) cronometraggio
timing device *n* (*on bomb*) timer *m inv*
timpani ['tɪmpənɪ] *npl* timpani *mpl*
tin [tɪn] *n* stagno; (*also*: **tin plate**) latta; (*Brit*: *can*) barattolo (di latta), lattina, scatola; (*for baking*) teglia; **a ~ of paint** un barattolo di tinta *or* vernice
tin foil *n* stagnola
tinge [tɪndʒ] *n* sfumatura ■ *vt*: **tinged with** tinto(-a) di
tingle ['tɪŋgl] *vi* (*cheeks, skin: from cold*) pungere, pizzicare; (*: from bad circulation*) formicolare
tinker ['tɪŋkə^r] *n* stagnino ambulante; (*gipsy*) zingaro(-a)
▸ **tinker with** *vt fus* armeggiare intorno a; cercare di riparare

t

tinkle ['tɪŋkl] *vi* tintinnare ■ *n* (*col*): **to give sb a ~** dare un colpo di telefono a qn
tin mine *n* miniera di stagno
tinned [tɪnd] *adj* (*Brit: food*) in scatola
tinnitus [tɪ'naɪtəs] *n* (*Med*) ronzio auricolare
tinny ['tɪnɪ] *adj* metallico(-a)
tin-opener ['tɪnəupnə[r]] *n* (*Brit*) apriscatole *m inv*
tinsel ['tɪnsl] *n* decorazioni *fpl* natalizie (*argentate*)
tint [tɪnt] *n* tinta; (*for hair*) shampoo *m inv* colorante ■ *vt* (*hair*) fare uno shampoo colorante a
tinted ['tɪntɪd] *adj* (*hair*) tinto(-a); (*spectacles, glass*) colorato(-a)
tiny ['taɪnɪ] *adj* minuscolo(-a)
tip [tɪp] *n* (*end*) punta; (*protective: on umbrella etc*) puntale *m*; (*gratuity*) mancia; (*for coal*) discarica; (*for rubbish*) immondezzaio; (*advice*) suggerimento ■ *vt* (*waiter*) dare la mancia a; (*tilt*) inclinare; (*overturn: also*: **tip over**) capovolgere; (*empty: also*: **tip out**) scaricare; (*predict: winner*) pronosticare; (*: horse*) dare vincente; **he tipped out the contents of the box** ha rovesciato il contenuto della scatola
▸ **tip off** *vt* fare una soffiata a
tip-off ['tɪpɔf] *n* (*hint*) soffiata
tipped ['tɪpt] *adj* (*Brit: cigarette*) col filtro; **steel-~** con la punta d'acciaio
Tipp-Ex® ['tɪpɛks] *n* (*Brit*) liquido correttore
tipple ['tɪpl] (*Brit*) *vi* sbevazzare ■ *n*: **to have a ~** prendere un bicchierino
tipster ['tɪpstə[r]] *n* (*Racing*) *chi vende informazioni sulle corse e altre manifestazioni oggetto di*
tipsy ['tɪpsɪ] *adj* brillo(-a)
tiptoe ['tɪptəu] *n*: **on ~** in punta di piedi
tiptop ['tɪptɔp] *adj*: **in ~ condition** in ottime condizioni
tirade [taɪ'reɪd] *n* filippica
tire ['taɪə[r]] *vt* stancare ■ *vi* stancarsi ■ *n* (*US*) = **tyre**
▸ **tire out** *vt* sfinire, spossare
tired ['taɪəd] *adj* stanco(-a); **to be/feel/look ~** essere/sentirsi/sembrare stanco; **to be ~ of** essere stanco *or* stufo di
tiredness ['taɪədnɪs] *n* stanchezza
tireless ['taɪəlɪs] *adj* instancabile
tiresome ['taɪəsəm] *adj* noioso(-a)
tiring ['taɪərɪŋ] *adj* faticoso(-a)
tissue ['tɪʃu:] *n* tessuto; (*paper handkerchief*) fazzolettino di carta
tissue paper *n* carta velina
tit [tɪt] *n* (*bird*) cinciallegra; (*col: breast*) tetta; **to give ~ for tat** rendere pan per focaccia
titanium [tɪ'teɪnɪəm] *n* titanio
titbit ['tɪtbɪt], (*US*) **tidbit** ['tɪdbɪt] *n* (*food*) leccornia; (*news*) notizia, ghiotta
titillate ['tɪtɪleɪt] *vt* titillare
titivate ['tɪtɪveɪt] *vt* agghindare
title ['taɪtl] *n* titolo; (*Law: right*): **~ (to)** diritto (a)
title deed *n* (*Law*) titolo di proprietà
title page *n* frontespizio
title role *n* ruolo *or* parte *f* principale
titter ['tɪtə[r]] *vi* ridere scioccamente
tittle-tattle ['tɪtltætl] *n* chiacchiere *fpl*, pettegolezzi *mpl*
titular ['tɪtjulə[r]] *adj* (*in name only*) nominale
tizzy ['tɪzɪ] *n* (*col*): **to be in a ~** essere in agitazione
T-junction ['ti:'dʒʌŋkʃən] *n* incrocio a T
TM *n abbr* (= *transcendental meditation*) M.T. *f*; (*Comm*) = **trademark**
TN *abbr* (*US*) = **Tennessee**
TNT *n abbr* (= *trinitrotoluene*) T.N.T. *m*

KEYWORD

to [tu:, tə] *prep* **1** (*direction*) a; **to go to France/London/school** andare in Francia/a Londra/a scuola; **to go to town** andare in città; **to go to Paul's/the doctor's** andare da Paul/dal dottore; **the road to Edinburgh** la strada per Edimburgo; **to the left/right** a sinistra/destra
2 (*as far as*) (fino) a; **from here to London** da qui a Londra; **to count to 10** contare fino a 10; **from 40 to 50 people** da 40 a 50 persone
3 (*with expressions of time*): **a quarter to 5** le 5 meno un quarto; **it's twenty to 3** sono le 3 meno venti
4 (*for, of*): **the key to the front door** la chiave della porta d'ingresso; **a letter to his wife** una lettera per la moglie
5 (*expressing indirect object*) a; **to give sth to sb** dare qc a qn; **give it to me** dammelo; **to talk to sb** parlare a qn; **it belongs to him** gli appartiene, è suo; **to be a danger to sb/sth** rappresentare un pericolo per qn/qc
6 (*in relation to*) a; **3 goals to 2** 3 goal a 2; **30 miles to the gallon** ≈ 11 chilometri con un litro; **4 apples to the kilo** 4 mele in un chilo
7 (*purpose, result*): **to come to sb's aid** venire in aiuto a qn; **to sentence sb to death** condannare a morte qn; **to my surprise** con mia sorpresa
■ *with vb* **1** (*simple infinitive*): **to go/eat** *etc* andare/mangiare *etc*
2 (*following another vb*): **to want/try/start to do** volere/cercare di/cominciare a fare
3 (*with vb omitted*): **I don't want to** non voglio (farlo); **you ought to** devi (farlo)
4 (*purpose, result*) per; **I did it to help you** l'ho fatto per aiutarti

5 (*equivalent to relative clause*): **I have things to do** ho da fare; **the main thing is to try** la cosa più importante è provare
6 (*after adjective etc*): **ready to go** pronto(-a) a partire; **too old/young to ...** troppo vecchio(-a)/giovane per ...
■ *adv*: **to push the door to** accostare la porta; **to go to and fro** andare e tornare

toad [təud] *n* rospo
toadstool ['təudstu:l] *n* fungo (velenoso)
toady ['təudɪ] *vi* adulare
toast [təust] *n* (*Culin*) toast *m*, pane *m* abbrustolito; (*drink, speech*) brindisi *m inv* ■ *vt* (*Culin*) abbrustolire; (*drink to*) brindare a; **a piece** *or* **slice of ~** una fetta di pane abbrustolito
toaster ['təustə^r] *n* tostapane *m inv*
toastmaster ['təustmɑ:stə^r] *n* direttore *m* dei brindisi
toast rack *n* portatoast *m inv*
tobacco [tə'bækəu] *n* tabacco; **pipe ~** tabacco da pipa
tobacconist [tə'bækənɪst] *n* tabaccaio(-a); **~'s (shop)** tabaccheria
Tobago [tə'beɪgəu] *n see* **Trinidad and Tobago**
toboggan [tə'bɔgən] *n* toboga *m inv*; (*child's*) slitta
today [tə'deɪ] *adv, n* (*also fig*) oggi *m inv*; **what day is it ~?** che giorno è oggi?; **what date is it ~?** quanti ne abbiamo oggi?; **~ is the 4th of March** (oggi) è il 4 di marzo; **~'s paper** il giornale di oggi; **a fortnight ~** quindici giorni a oggi
toddler ['tɔdlə^r] *n* bambino(-a) che impara a camminare
toddy ['tɔdɪ] *n* grog *m inv*
to-do [tə'du:] *n* (*fuss*) storie *fpl*
toe [təu] *n* dito del piede; (*of shoe*) punta ■ *vt*: **to ~ the line** (*fig*) stare in riga, conformarsi; **big ~** alluce *m*; **little ~** mignolino
TOEFL ['təufl] *n abbr* = **Test(ing) of English as a Foreign Language**
toehold ['təuhəuld] *n* punto d'appoggio
toenail ['təuneɪl] *n* unghia del piede
toffee ['tɔfɪ] *n* caramella
toffee apple *n* (*Brit*) mela caramellata
tofu ['təufu:] *n* tofu *m* (*latte di soia non fermentato*)
toga ['təugə] *n* toga
together [tə'geðə^r] *adv* insieme; (*at same time*) allo stesso tempo; **~ with** insieme a
togetherness [tə'geðənɪs] *n* solidarietà; intimità
toggle switch ['tɔgl-] *n* (*Comput*) tasto bistabile
Togo ['təugəu] *n* Togo
togs [tɔgz] *npl* (*col: clothes*) vestiti *mpl*
toil [tɔɪl] *n* travaglio, fatica ■ *vi* affannarsi; sgobbare
toilet ['tɔɪlət] *n* (*Brit: lavatory*) gabinetto ■ *cpd* (*soap etc*) da toletta; **to go to the ~** andare al gabinetto *or* al bagno
toilet bag *n* (*Brit*) nécessaire *m inv* da toilette
toilet bowl *n* vaso *or* tazza del gabinetto
toilet paper *n* carta igienica
toiletries ['tɔɪlɪtrɪz] *npl* articoli *mpl* da toletta
toilet roll *n* rotolo di carta igienica
toilet water *n* acqua di colonia
to-ing and fro-ing ['tu:ɪŋən'frəuɪŋ] *n* (*Brit*) andirivieni *m inv*
token ['təukən] *n* (*sign*) segno; (*voucher*) buono ■ *cpd* (*fee, strike*) simbolico(-a); **book/record ~** (*Brit*) buono-libro/-disco; **by the same ~** (*fig*) per lo stesso motivo
tokenism ['təukənɪzəm] *n* (*Pol*) concessione *f* pro forma *inv*
Tokyo ['təukjəu] *n* Tokyo *f*
told [təuld] *pt, pp of* **tell**
tolerable ['tɔlərəbl] *adj* (*bearable*) tollerabile; (*fairly good*) passabile
tolerably ['tɔlərəblɪ] *adv* (*good, comfortable*) abbastanza
tolerance ['tɔlərns] *n* (*also Tech*) tolleranza
tolerant ['tɔlərnt] *adj*: **~ (of)** tollerante (nei confronti di)
tolerate ['tɔləreɪt] *vt* sopportare; (*Med, Tech*) tollerare
toleration [tɔlə'reɪʃən] *n* tolleranza
toll [təul] *n* (*tax, charge*) pedaggio ■ *vi* (*bell*) suonare; **the accident ~ on the roads** il numero delle vittime della strada
tollbridge ['təulbrɪdʒ] *n* ponte *m* a pedaggio
toll call *n* (*US Tel*) (telefonata) interurbana
toll-free ['təul'fri:] (*US*) *adj* senza addebito, gratuito(-a) ■ *adv* gratuitamente; **~ number** ≈ numero verde
tomato (*pl* **tomatoes**) [tə'mɑ:təu] *n* pomodoro
tomb [tu:m] *n* tomba
tombola [tɔm'bəulə] *n* tombola
tomboy ['tɔmbɔɪ] *n* maschiaccio
tombstone ['tu:mstəun] *n* pietra tombale
tomcat ['tɔmkæt] *n* gatto
tomorrow [tə'mɔrəu] *adv, n* (*also fig*) domani *m inv*; **the day after ~** dopodomani; **a week ~** domani a otto; **~ morning** domani mattina
ton [tʌn] *n* tonnellata (*Brit = 1016 kg; 20 cwt; US = 907 kg; metric = 1000 kg*); (*Naut: also*: **register ton**) tonnellata di stazza (*= 2.83 cu.m; 100 cu.ft*); **tons of** (*col*) un mucchio *or* sacco di
tonal ['təunl] *adj* tonale
tone [təun] *n* tono; (*of musical instrument*) timbro ■ *vi* intonarsi

▸ **tone down** *vt* (*colour, criticism, sound*) attenuare
▸ **tone up** *vt* (*muscles*) tonificare
tone-deaf [təun'dɛf] *adj* che non ha orecchio (musicale)
toner ['təunəʳ] *n* (*for photocopier*) colorante *m* organico, toner *m*
Tonga ['tɔŋgə] *n* isole *fpl* Tonga
tongs [tɔŋz] *npl* tenaglie *fpl*; (*for coal*) molle *fpl*; (*for hair*) arricciacapelli *m inv*
tongue [tʌŋ] *n* lingua; **~ in cheek** (*fig*) ironicamente
tongue-tied ['tʌŋtaɪd] *adj* (*fig*) muto(-a)
tongue-twister ['tʌŋtwɪstəʳ] *n* scioglilingua *m inv*
tonic ['tɔnɪk] *n* (*Med*) ricostituente *m*; (*skin tonic*) tonico; (*Mus*) nota tonica; (*also*: **tonic water**) acqua tonica
tonight [tə'naɪt] *adv* stanotte; (*this evening*) stasera ■ *n* questa notte; questa sera; **I'll see you ~** ci vediamo stasera
tonnage ['tʌnɪdʒ] *n* (*Naut*) tonnellaggio, stazza
tonne [tʌn] *n* (*Brit*: *metric ton*) tonnellata
tonsil ['tɔnsl] *n* tonsilla; **to have one's tonsils out** farsi operare di tonsille
tonsillitis [tɔnsɪ'laɪtɪs] *n* tonsillite *f*; **to have ~** avere la tonsillite
too [tu:] *adv* (*excessively*) troppo; (*also*) anche; **it's ~ sweet** è troppo dolce; **I went ~** ci sono andato anch'io; **~ much** *adv* troppo *adj* troppo(-a); **~ many** *adj* troppi(-e); **~ bad!** tanto peggio!; peggio così!
took [tuk] *pt of* **take**
tool [tu:l] *n* utensile *m* attrezzo; (*fig*: *person*) strumento ■ *vt* lavorare con un attrezzo
tool box *n* cassetta *f* portautensili *inv*
tool kit *n* cassetta di attrezzi
toot [tu:t] *vi* suonare; (*with car horn*) suonare il clacson
tooth (*pl* **teeth**) [tu:θ, ti:θ] *n* (*Anat, Tech*) dente *m*; **to clean one's teeth** lavarsi i denti; **to have a ~ out** *or* (*US*) **pulled** farsi togliere un dente; **by the skin of one's teeth** per il rotto della cuffia
toothache ['tu:θeɪk] *n* mal *m* di denti; **to have ~** avere il mal di denti
tooth fairy *n*: **the ~** *fatina che porta soldini in regalo a un bimbo quando perde un dentino di latte*, ≈ topolino
toothpaste ['tu:θpeɪst] *n* dentifricio
toothpick ['tu:θpɪk] *n* stuzzicadenti *m inv*
tooth powder *n* dentifricio in polvere
top [tɔp] *n* (*of mountain, page, ladder*) cima; (*of box, cupboard, table*) sopra *m inv*, parte *f* superiore; (*lid*: *of box, jar*) coperchio; (: *of bottle*) tappo; (*toy*) trottola; (*Dress*: *blouse etc*) camicia (*or* maglietta *etc*); (*of pyjamas*) giacca ■ *adj* più alto(-a); (*in rank*) primo(-a); (*best*) migliore ■ *vt* (*exceed*) superare; (*be first in*) essere in testa a; **on ~ of** sopra, in cima a; (*in addition to*) oltre a; **from ~ to toe** (*Brit*) dalla testa ai piedi; **at the ~ of the stairs/page/street** in cima alle scale/alla pagina/alla strada; **the ~ of the milk** (*Brit*) la panna; **at ~ speed** a tutta velocità; **at the ~ of one's voice** (*fig*) a squarciagola; **over the ~** (*col*: *behaviour etc*) eccessivo(-a); **to go over the ~** esagerare
▸ **top up,** (*US*) **top off** *vt* riempire
topaz ['təupæz] *n* topazio
top-class ['tɔp'klɑ:s] *adj* di prim'ordine
topcoat ['tɔpkəut] *n* soprabito
topflight ['tɔpflaɪt] *adj* di primaria importanza
top floor *n* ultimo piano
top hat *n* cilindro
top-heavy [tɔp'hɛvɪ] *adj* (*object*) con la parte superiore troppo pesante
topic ['tɔpɪk] *n* argomento
topical ['tɔpɪkəl] *adj* d'attualità
topless ['tɔplɪs] *adj* (*bather etc*) col seno scoperto; **~ swimsuit** topless *m inv*
top-level ['tɔplɛvl] *adj* (*talks*) ad alto livello
topmost ['tɔpməust] *adj* il(la) più alto(-a)
top-notch ['tɔp'nɔtʃ] *adj* (*col*: *player, performer*) di razza; (: *school, car*) eccellente
topography [tə'pɔgrəfɪ] *n* topografia
topping ['tɔpɪŋ] *n* (*Culin*) guarnizione *f*
topple ['tɔpl] *vt* rovesciare, far cadere ■ *vi* cadere; traballare
top-ranking ['tɔp'ræŋkɪŋ] *adj* di massimo grado
top-secret ['tɔp'si:krɪt] *adj* segretissimo(-a)
top-security ['tɔpsɪ'kjuərɪtɪ] *adj* (*Brit*) di massima sicurezza
topsy-turvy ['tɔpsɪ'tə:vɪ] *adj, adv* sottosopra *inv*
top-up ['tɔpʌp] *n* (*for mobile phone*: *also*: **top-up card**) ricarica; **would you like a ~?** vuole che le riempia il bicchiere (*or* la tazza *etc*)?
top-up loan *n* (*Brit*) prestito integrativo
torch [tɔ:tʃ] *n* torcia; (*Brit*: *electric*) lampadina tascabile
tore [tɔ:ʳ] *pt of* **tear²**
torment *n* ['tɔ:mɛnt] tormento ■ *vt* [tɔ:'mɛnt] tormentare; (*fig*: *annoy*) infastidire
torn [tɔ:n] *pp of* **tear²** ■ *adj*: **~ between** (*fig*) combattuto(-a) tra
tornado (*pl* **tornadoes**) [tɔ:'neɪdəu] *n* tornado
torpedo (*pl* **torpedoes**) [tɔ:'pi:dəu] *n* siluro
torpedo boat *n* motosilurante *f*
torpor ['tɔ:pəʳ] *n* torpore *m*
torrent ['tɔrnt] *n* torrente *m*

torrential [tɔ'rɛnʃl] *adj* torrenziale
torrid ['tɔrɪd] *adj* torrido(-a); (*fig*) denso(-a) di passione
torso ['tɔːsəu] *n* torso
tortoise ['tɔːtəs] *n* tartaruga
tortoiseshell ['tɔːtəʃɛl] *adj* di tartaruga
tortuous ['tɔːtjuəs] *adj* tortuoso(-a)
torture ['tɔːtʃə^r] *n* tortura ■ *vt* torturare
torturer ['tɔːtʃərə^r] *n* torturatore(-trice)
Tory ['tɔːrɪ] *adj* tory *inv*, conservatore(-trice) ■ *n* tory *m/f inv*, conservatore(-trice)
toss [tɔs] *vt* gettare, lanciare; (*Brit*: *pancake*) far saltare; (*head*) scuotere ■ *n* (*movement*: *of head etc*) movimento brusco; (*of coin*) lancio; **to win/lose the ~** vincere/perdere a testa o croce; (*Sport*) vincere/perdere il sorteggio; **to ~ a coin** fare a testa o croce; **to ~ up for sth** fare a testa o croce per qc; **to ~ and turn** (*in bed*) girarsi e rigirarsi
tot [tɔt] *n* (*Brit*: *drink*) bicchierino; (*child*) bimbo(-a)
▸ **tot up** *vt* (*Brit*: *figures*) sommare
total ['təutl] *adj* totale ■ *n* totale *m* ■ *vt* (*add up*) sommare; (*amount to*) ammontare a; **in ~** in tutto
totalitarian [təutælɪ'tɛərɪən] *adj* totalitario(-a)
totality [təu'tælɪtɪ] *n* totalità
totally ['təutəlɪ] *adv* completamente
tote bag ['təut-] *n* sporta
totem pole ['təutəm-] *n* totem *m inv*
totter ['tɔtə^r] *vi* barcollare; (*object*, *government*) vacillare
touch [tʌtʃ] *n* tocco; (*sense*) tatto; (*contact*) contatto; (*Football*) fuori gioco *m* ■ *vt* toccare; **a ~ of** (*fig*) un tocco di; un pizzico di; **to get in ~ with** mettersi in contatto con; **to lose ~** (*friends*) perdersi di vista; **I'll be in ~** mi farò sentire; **to be out of ~ with events** essere tagliato fuori; **the personal ~** una nota personale; **to put the finishing touches to sth** dare gli ultimi ritocchi a qc
▸ **touch on** *vt fus* (*topic*) sfiorare, accennare a
▸ **touch up** *vt* (*improve*) ritoccare
touch-and-go ['tʌtʃən'gəu] *adj* incerto(-a); **it was ~ with the sick man** il malato era tra la vita e la morte
touchdown ['tʌtʃdaun] *n* atterraggio; (*on sea*) ammaraggio; (*US Football*) meta
touched [tʌtʃt] *adj* commosso(-a); (*col*) tocco(-a), toccato(-a)
touching ['tʌtʃɪŋ] *adj* commovente
touchline ['tʌtʃlaɪn] *n* (*Sport*) linea laterale
touch screen ['tʌtʃskriːn] *n* (*Tech*) schermo touch screen; **touch-screen mobile** telefono touch screen; **touch-screen technology** tecnologia touch screen
touch-sensitive ['tʌtʃsɛnsɪtɪv] *adj* sensibile al tatto
touch-type ['tʌtʃtaɪp] *vi* dattilografare (senza guardare i tasti)
touchy ['tʌtʃɪ] *adj* (*person*) suscettibile
tough [tʌf] *adj* duro(-a); (*resistant*) resistente; (*meat*) duro(-a), tiglioso(-a); (*journey*) faticoso(-a), duro(-a); (*person*: *rough*) violento(-a), brutale ■ *n* (*gangster etc*) delinquente *m/f*; **~ luck!** che sfortuna!
toughen ['tʌfn] *vt* indurire, rendere più resistente
toughness ['tʌfnɪs] *n* durezza; resistenza
toupee ['tuːpeɪ] *n* parrucchino
tour [tuə^r] *n* viaggio; (*also*: **package tour**) viaggio organizzato *or* tutto compreso; (*of town*, *museum*) visita; (*by artist*) tournée *f inv* ■ *vt* visitare; **to go on a ~ of** (*region*, *country*) fare il giro di; (*museum*, *castle*) visitare; **to go on ~** andare in tournée
tour guide *n* accompagnatore(-trice) turistico(-a)
touring ['tuərɪŋ] *n* turismo
tourism ['tuərɪzəm] *n* turismo
tourist ['tuərɪst] *n* turista *m/f* ■ *adv* (*travel*) in classe turistica ■ *cpd* turistico(-a); **the ~ trade** il turismo
tourist class *n* (*Aviat*) classe *f* turistica
tourist office *n* pro loco *f inv*
tournament ['tuənəmənt] *n* torneo
tourniquet ['tuənɪkeɪ] *n* (*Med*) laccio emostatico, pinza emostatica
tour operator *n* (*Brit*) operatore *m* turistico
tousled ['tauzld] *adj* (*hair*) arruffato(-a)
tout [taut] *vi*: **to ~ for** procacciare, raccogliere; cercare clienti per ■ *n* (*Brit*: *also*: **ticket tout**) bagarino; **to ~ sth (around)** (*Brit*) cercare di (ri)vendere qc
tow [təu] *vt* rimorchiare ■ *n* rimorchio; **"on ~"**, (*US*) **"in ~ "** (*Aut*) "veicolo rimorchiato"; **to give sb a ~** rimorchiare qn
toward [tə'wɔːd], **towards** [tə'wɔːdz] *prep* verso; (*of attitude*) nei confronti di; (*of purpose*) per; **~(s) noon/the end of the year** verso mezzogiorno/la fine dell'anno; **to feel friendly ~(s) sb** provare un sentimento d'amicizia per qn
towel ['tauəl] *n* asciugamano; (*also*: **tea towel**) strofinaccio; **to throw in the ~** (*fig*) gettare la spugna
towelling ['tauəlɪŋ] *n* (*fabric*) spugna
towel rail, (*US*) **towel rack** *n* portasciugamano
tower ['tauə^r] *n* torre *f* ■ *vi* (*building*, *mountain*) innalzarsi; **to ~ above** *or* **over sb/sth** sovrastare qn/qc
tower block *n* (*Brit*) palazzone *m*
towering ['tauərɪŋ] *adj* altissimo(-a), imponente

town [taun] *n* città *f inv*; **to go to ~** andare in città; (*fig*) mettercela tutta; **in (the) ~** in città; **to be out of ~** essere fuori città
town centre *n* centro (città)
town clerk *n* segretario comunale
town council *n* consiglio comunale
town crier [-'kraɪə^r] *n* (*Brit*) banditore(-trice)
town hall *n* ≈ municipio
townie ['taunɪ] *n* (*Brit col*) uno(-a) di città
town plan *n* pianta della città
town planner *n* urbanista *m/f*
town planning *n* urbanistica
township ['taunʃɪp] *n* township *f inv*
townspeople ['taunzpi:pl] *npl* cittadinanza, cittadini *mpl*
towpath ['təupɑ:θ] *n* alzaia
towrope ['təurəup] *n* (cavo da) rimorchio
tow truck *n* (*US*) carro *m* attrezzi *inv*
toxic ['tɔksɪk] *adj* tossico(-a)
toxic asset *n* (*Econ*) titolo tossico
toxic bank *n* (*Econ*) banca cattiva (*che investe in titoli tossici*)
toxin ['tɔksɪn] *n* tossina
toy [tɔɪ] *n* giocattolo
▸ **toy with** *vt fus* giocare con; (*idea*) accarezzare, trastullarsi con
toyshop ['tɔɪʃɔp] *n* negozio di giocattoli
trace [treɪs] *n* traccia ■ *vt* (*draw*) tracciare; (*follow*) seguire; (*locate*) rintracciare; **without ~** (*disappear*) senza lasciare traccia; **there was no ~ of it** non ne restava traccia
trace element *n* oligoelemento
trachea [trə'kɪə] *n* (*Anat*) trachea
tracing paper ['treɪsɪŋ-] *n* carta da ricalco
track [træk] *n* (*mark*: *of person, animal*) traccia; (*on tape, Sport*; *path*: *gen*) pista; (: *of suspect, animal*) pista, tracce *fpl*; (*Rail*) binario, rotaie *fpl*; (*Comput*) traccia, pista ■ *vt* seguire le tracce di; **to keep ~ of** seguire; **to be on the right ~** (*fig*) essere sulla buona strada
▸ **track down** *vt* (*prey*) scovare; snidare; (*sth lost*) rintracciare
tracker dog ['trækə-] *n* (*Brit*) cane *m* poliziotto *inv*
track events *npl* (*Sport*) prove *fpl* su pista
tracking station ['trækɪŋ-] *n* (*Space*) osservatorio spaziale
track meet *n* (*US*) meeting *m inv* di atletica
track record *n*: **to have a good ~** (*fig*) avere un buon curriculum
tracksuit ['træksu:t] *n* tuta sportiva
tract [trækt] *n* (*Geo*) tratto, estensione *f*; (*pamphlet*) opuscolo, libretto; **respiratory ~** (*Anat*) apparato respiratorio
traction ['trækʃən] *n* trazione *f*
tractor ['træktə^r] *n* trattore *m*
trade [treɪd] *n* commercio; (*skill, job*) mestiere *m*; (*industry*) industria, settore *m* ■ *vi* commerciare; **to ~ with/in** commerciare con/in; **foreign ~** commercio estero; **Department of T~ and Industry** (*Brit*) ≈ Ministero del Commercio
▸ **trade in** *vt* (*old car etc*) dare come pagamento parziale
trade barrier *n* barriera commerciale
trade deficit *n* bilancio commerciale in deficit
Trade Descriptions Act *n* (*Brit*) legge *f* a tutela del consumatore
trade discount *n* sconto sul listino
trade fair *n* fiera campionaria
trade-in ['treɪdɪn] *n*: **to take as a ~** accettare in permuta
trade-in price *n* prezzo di permuta
trademark ['treɪdmɑ:k] *n* marchio di fabbrica
trade mission *n* missione *f* commerciale
trade name *n* marca, nome *m* depositato
trade-off ['treɪdɔf] *n* compromesso, accomodamento
trader ['treɪdə^r] *n* commerciante *m/f*
trade secret *n* segreto di fabbricazione
tradesman ['treɪdzmən] *n* fornitore *m*; (*shopkeeper*) negoziante *m*
trade union *n* sindacato
trade unionist [-'ju:njənɪst] *n* sindacalista *m/f*
trade wind *n* aliseo
trading ['treɪdɪŋ] *n* commercio
trading estate *n* (*Brit*) zona industriale
trading stamp *n* bollo premio
tradition [trə'dɪʃən] *n* tradizione *f*; **traditions** *npl* tradizioni, usanze *fpl*
traditional [trə'dɪʃənl] *adj* tradizionale
traffic ['træfɪk] *n* traffico ■ *vi*: **to ~ in** (*pej*: *liquor, drugs*) trafficare in
traffic calming [-'kɑ:mɪŋ] *n uso di accorgimenti per rallentare il traffico in zone abitate*
traffic circle *n* (*US*) isola rotatoria
traffic island *n* salvagente *m*, isola *f*, spartitraffico *inv*
traffic jam *n* ingorgo (del traffico)
trafficker ['træfɪkə^r] *n* trafficante *m/f*
traffic lights *npl* semaforo
traffic offence *n* (*Brit*) infrazione *f* al codice stradale
traffic sign *n* cartello stradale
traffic violation *n* (*US*) = **traffic offence**
traffic warden *n* addetto(-a) al controllo del traffico e del parcheggio
tragedy ['trædʒədɪ] *n* tragedia
tragic ['trædʒɪk] *adj* tragico(-a)
trail [treɪl] *n* (*tracks*) tracce *fpl*, pista; (*path*) sentiero; (*of smoke etc*) scia ■ *vt* trascinare, strascicare; (*follow*) seguire ■ *vi* essere al traino; (*dress etc*) strusciare; (*plant*)

arrampicarsi; strusciare; **to be on sb's ~** essere sulle orme di qn
▸ **trail away, trail off** *vi* (*sound*) affievolirsi; (*interest, voice*) spegnersi a poco a poco
▸ **trail behind** *vi* essere al traino
trailer ['treɪlə^r] *n* (*Aut*) rimorchio; (*US*) roulotte *f inv*; (*Cine*) prossimamente *m inv*
trailer truck *n* (*US*) autoarticolato
train [treɪn] *n* treno; (*of dress*) coda, strascico; (*Brit*: *series*): **~ of events** serie *f* di avvenimenti a catena ▪ *vt* (*apprentice, doctor etc*) formare; (*sportsman*) allenare; (*dog*) addestrare; (*memory*) esercitare; (*point*: *gun etc*): **to ~ sth on** puntare qc contro ▪ *vi* formarsi; allenarsi; (*learn a skill*) fare pratica, fare tirocinio; **to go by ~** andare in *or* col treno; **one's ~ of thought** il filo dei propri pensieri; **to ~ sb to do sth** preparare qn a fare qc
train attendant *n* (*US*) addetto(-a) ai vagoni letto
trained [treɪnd] *adj* qualificato(-a); allenato(-a), addestrato(-a)
trainee [treɪ'niː] *n* allievo(-a); (*in trade*) apprendista *m/f*; **he's a ~ teacher** sta facendo tirocinio come insegnante
trainer ['treɪnə^r] *n* (*Sport*) allenatore(-trice); (*of dogs etc*) addestratore(-trice); **trainers** *npl* (*shoes*) scarpe *fpl* da ginnastica
training ['treɪnɪŋ] *n* formazione *f*; allenamento; addestramento; **in ~** (*Sport*) in allenamento; (*fit*) in forma
training college *n* istituto professionale
training course *n* corso di formazione professionale
train wreck *n* (*fig*) persona distrutta; (*: pej*) rottame (*m*); **he's a complete ~** è completamente distrutto, è un rottame
traipse [treɪps] *vi*: **to ~ in/out** *etc* entrare/uscire *etc* trascinandosi
trait [treɪt] *n* tratto
traitor ['treɪtə^r] *n* traditore(-trice)
trajectory [trə'dʒɛktərɪ] *n* traiettoria
tram [træm] *n* (*Brit*: *also*: **tramcar**) tram *m inv*
tramline ['træmlaɪn] *n* linea tranviaria
tramp [træmp] *n* (*person*) vagabondo(-a); (*col*: *pej*: *woman*) sgualdrina ▪ *vi* camminare con passo pesante
trample ['træmpl] *vt*: **to ~ (underfoot)** calpestare
trampoline ['træmpəliːn] *n* trampolino
trance [trɑːns] *n* trance *f inv*; (*Med*) catalessi *f inv*; **to go into a ~** cadere in trance
tranquil ['træŋkwɪl] *adj* tranquillo(-a)
tranquillity, (*US*) **tranquility** [træŋ'kwɪlɪtɪ] *n* tranquillità
tranquillizer, (*US*) **tranquilizer** ['træŋkwɪlaɪzə^r] *n* (*Med*) tranquillante *m*
transact [træn'zækt] *vt* (*business*) trattare
transaction [træn'zækʃən] *n* transazione *f*; **transactions** *npl* (*minutes*) atti *mpl*; **cash ~** operazione *f* in contanti
transatlantic ['trænzət'læntɪk] *adj* transatlantico(-a)
transcend [træn'sɛnd] *vt* trascendere; (*excel over*) superare
transcendental [trænsɛn'dɛntl] *adj*: **~ meditation** meditazione *f* trascendentale
transcribe [træn'skraɪb] *vt* trascrivere
transcript ['trænskrɪpt] *n* trascrizione *f*
transcription [træn'skrɪpʃən] *n* trascrizione *f*
transept ['trænsɛpt] *n* transetto
transfer *n* ['trænsfə^r] (*gen, also Sport*) trasferimento; (*Pol*: *of power*) passaggio; (*picture, design*) decalcomania; (*stick-on*) autoadesivo ▪ *vt* [træns'fəː^r] trasferire; passare; decalcare; **by bank ~** tramite trasferimento bancario; **to ~ the charges** (*Brit Tel*) telefonare con addebito al ricevente
transferable [træns'fəːrəbl] *adj* trasferibile; **not ~** non cedibile, personale
transfix [træns'fɪks] *vt* trafiggere; (*fig*): **transfixed with fear** paralizzato dalla paura
transform [træns'fɔːm] *vt* trasformare
transformation [trænsfə'meɪʃən] *n* trasformazione *f*
transformer [træns'fɔːmə^r] *n* (*Elec*) trasformatore *m*
transfusion [træns'fjuːʒən] *n* trasfusione *f*
transgress [træns'grɛs] *vt* (*go beyond*) infrangere; (*violate*) trasgredire, infrangere
tranship [træn'ʃɪp] *vt* trasbordare
transient ['trænzɪənt] *adj* transitorio(-a), fugace
transistor [træn'zɪstə^r] *n* (*Elec*) transistor *m inv*; (*also*: **transistor radio**) radio *f inv* a transistor
transit ['trænzɪt] *n*: **in ~** in transito
transit camp *n* campo (di raccolta) profughi
transition [træn'zɪʃən] *n* passaggio, transizione *f*
transitional [træn'zɪʃənl] *adj* di transizione
transitive ['trænzɪtɪv] *adj* (*Ling*) transitivo(-a)
transit lounge *n* (*Aviat*) sala di transito
transitory ['trænzɪtərɪ] *adj* transitorio(-a)
translate [trænz'leɪt] *vt* tradurre; **to ~ (from/into)** tradurre (da/in)
translation [trænz'leɪʃən] *n* traduzione *f*; (*Scol*: *as opposed to prose*) versione *f*
translator [trænz'leɪtə^r] *n* traduttore(-trice)
translucent [trænz'luːsnt] *adj* traslucido(-a)
transmission [trænz'mɪʃən] *n* trasmissione *f*
transmit [trænz'mɪt] *vt* trasmettere
transmitter [trænz'mɪtə^r] *n* trasmettitore *m*
transparency [træns'pɛərnsɪ] *n* (*Phot*) diapositiva

t

transparent [træns'pærnt] *adj* trasparente
transpire [træns'paɪəʳ] *vi* (*happen*) succedere; **it finally transpired that ...** alla fine si è venuto a sapere che ...
transplant *vt* [træns'plɑːnt] trapiantare ■ *n* ['trænsplɑːnt] trapianto; **to have a heart ~** subire un trapianto cardiaco
transport *n* ['trænspɔːt] trasporto ■ *vt* [træns'pɔːt] trasportare; **public ~** mezzi *mpl* pubblici; **Department of T~** (*Brit*) Ministero dei Trasporti
transportation ['trænspɔː'teɪʃən] *n* (mezzo di) trasporto; (*of prisoners*) deportazione *f*; **Department of T~** (*US*) Ministero dei Trasporti
transport café *n* (*Brit*) trattoria per camionisti
transpose [træns'pəuz] *vt* trasporre
transsexual [trænz'sɛksjuəl] *adj, n* transessuale *m/f*
transverse ['trænzvəːs] *adj* trasversale
transvestite [trænz'vɛstaɪt] *n* travestito(-a)
trap [træp] *n* (*snare, trick*) trappola; (*carriage*) calesse *m* ■ *vt* prendere in trappola, intrappolare; (*immobilize*) bloccare; (*jam*) chiudere, schiacciare; **to set** *or* **lay a ~ (for sb)** tendere una trappola (a qn); **to ~ one's finger in the door** chiudersi il dito nella porta; **shut your ~!** (*col*) chiudi quella boccaccia!
trap door *n* botola
trapeze [trə'piːz] *n* trapezio
trapper ['træpəʳ] *n* cacciatore *m* di animali da pelliccia
trappings ['træpɪŋz] *npl* ornamenti *mpl*; indoratura, sfarzo
trash [træʃ] *n* (*pej: goods*) ciarpame *m*; (*: nonsense*) sciocchezze *fpl*; (*US: rubbish*) rifiuti *mpl*, spazzatura
trash can *n* (*US*) secchio della spazzatura
trashy ['træʃɪ] *adj* (*col*) scadente
trauma ['trɔːmə] *n* trauma *m*
traumatic [trɔː'mætɪk] *adj* (*Psych: fig*) traumatico(-a), traumatizzante
travel ['trævl] *n* viaggio; viaggi *mpl* ■ *vi* viaggiare; (*move*) andare, spostarsi ■ *vt* (*distance*) percorrere; **this wine doesn't ~ well** questo vino non resiste agli spostamenti
travel agency *n* agenzia (di) viaggi
travel agent *n* agente *m* di viaggio
travel brochure *n* dépliant *m* di viaggi
traveller, (*US*) **traveler** ['trævləʳ] *n* viaggiatore(-trice); (*Comm*) commesso viaggiatore
traveller's cheque, (*US*) **traveler's check** *n* assegno turistico
travelling, (*US*) **traveling** ['trævlɪŋ] *n* viaggi *mpl* ■ *adj* (*circus, exhibition*) itinerante ■ *cpd* (*bag, clock*) da viaggio; (*expenses*) di viaggio
travelling salesman, (*US*) **traveling salesman** *n* commesso viaggiatore
travelogue ['trævəlɔg] *n* (*book, film*) diario *or* documentario di viaggio; (*talk*) conferenza sui viaggi
travel sickness *n* mal *m* d'auto (*or* di mare *or* d'aria)
traverse ['trævəs] *vt* traversare, attraversare
travesty ['trævəstɪ] *n* parodia
trawler ['trɔːləʳ] *n* peschereccio (a strascico)
tray [treɪ] *n* (*for carrying*) vassoio; (*on desk*) vaschetta
treacherous ['trɛtʃərəs] *adj* traditore(-trice); **road conditions today are ~** oggi il fondo stradale è pericoloso
treachery ['trɛtʃərɪ] *n* tradimento
treacle ['triːkl] *n* melassa
tread [trɛd] *n* passo; (*sound*) rumore *m* di passi; (*of tyre*) battistrada *m inv* ■ *vi* (*pt* **trod**, *pp* **trodden**) [trɔd, 'trɔdn] camminare
▸ **tread on** *vt fus* calpestare
treadle ['trɛdl] *n* pedale *m*
treas. *abbr* = **treasurer**
treason ['triːzn] *n* tradimento
treasure ['trɛʒəʳ] *n* tesoro ■ *vt* (*value*) tenere in gran conto, apprezzare molto; (*store*) custodire gelosamente
treasure hunt *n* caccia al tesoro
treasurer ['trɛʒərəʳ] *n* tesoriere(-a)
treasury ['trɛʒərɪ] *n* tesoreria; (*Pol*): **the T~**, (*US*) **the T~ Department** ≈ il Ministero del Tesoro
treasury bill *n* buono del tesoro
treat [triːt] *n* regalo ■ *vt* trattare; (*Med*) curare; (*consider*) considerare; **it was a ~** mi (*or* ci *etc*) ha fatto veramente piacere; **to ~ sb to sth** offrire qc a qn; **to ~ sth as a joke** considerare qc uno scherzo
treatise ['triːtɪz] *n* trattato
treatment ['triːtmənt] *n* trattamento; **to have ~ for sth** (*Med*) farsi curare qc
treaty ['triːtɪ] *n* patto, trattato
treble [trɛbl] *adj* triplo(-a), triplice ■ *n* (*Mus*) soprano *m/f* ■ *vt* triplicare ■ *vi* triplicarsi
treble clef *n* chiave *f* di violino
tree [triː] *n* albero
tree-lined ['triːlaɪnd] *adj* fiancheggiato(-a) da alberi
treetop ['triːtɔp] *n* cima di un albero
tree trunk *n* tronco d'albero
trek [trɛk] *n* (*hike*) spedizione *f*; (*tiring walk*) camminata sfiancante ■ *vi* (*as holiday*) fare dell'escursionismo
trellis ['trɛlɪs] *n* graticcio, pergola

tremble ['trɛmbl] *vi* tremare; (*machine*) vibrare
trembling ['trɛmblɪŋ] *n* tremito ■ *adj* tremante
tremendous [trɪ'mɛndəs] *adj* (*enormous*) enorme; (*excellent*) meraviglioso(-a), formidabile
tremendously [trɪ'mɛndəslɪ] *adv* incredibilmente; **he enjoyed it ~** gli è piaciuto da morire
tremor [trɛmə^r] *n* tremore *m*, tremito; (*also*: **earth tremor**) scossa sismica
trench [trɛntʃ] *n* trincea
trench coat *n* trench *m inv*
trench warfare *n* guerra di trincea
trend [trɛnd] *n* (*tendency*) tendenza; (*of events*) corso; (*fashion*) moda; **~ towards/away from** tendenza a/ad allontanarsi da; **to set the ~** essere all'avanguardia; **to set a ~** lanciare una moda
trendy ['trɛndɪ] *adj* (*idea*) di moda; (*clothes*) all'ultima moda
trepidation [trɛpɪ'deɪʃən] *n* trepidazione *f*, agitazione *f*
trespass ['trɛspəs] *vi*: **to ~ on** entrare abusivamente in; (*fig*) abusare di; **"no trespassing"** "proprietà privata", "vietato l'accesso"
trespasser ['trɛspəsə^r] *n* trasgressore *m*; **"trespassers will be prosecuted"** "i trasgressori saranno puniti secondo i termini di legge"
trestle ['trɛsl] *n* cavalletto
trestle table *n* tavola su cavalletti
trial ['traɪəl] *n* (*Law*) processo; (*test: of machine etc*) collaudo; (*hardship*) prova, difficoltà *f inv*; (*worry*) cruccio; **trials** *npl* (*Athletics*) prove *fpl* di qualificazione; **horse trials** concorso ippico; **to be on ~** essere sotto processo; **~ by jury** processo penale con giuria; **to be sent for ~** essere rinviato a giudizio; **to bring sb to ~ (for a crime)** portare qn in giudizio (per un reato); **by ~ and error** a tentoni
trial balance *n* (*Comm*) bilancio di verifica
trial basis *n*: **on a ~** in prova
trial run *n* periodo di prova
triangle ['traɪæŋgl] *n* (*Math, Mus*) triangolo
triangular [traɪ'æŋgjulə^r] *adj* triangolare
triathlon [traɪ'æθlən] *n* triathlon *m inv*
tribal ['traɪbəl] *adj* tribale
tribe [traɪb] *n* tribù *f inv*
tribesman ['traɪbzmən] *n* membro della tribù
tribulation [trɪbju'leɪʃən] *n* tribolazione *f*
tribunal [traɪ'bju:nl] *n* tribunale *m*
tributary ['trɪbju:tərɪ] *n* (*river*) tributario, affluente *m*
tribute ['trɪbju:t] *n* tributo, omaggio; **to pay ~ to** rendere omaggio a
trice [traɪs] *n*: **in a ~** in un attimo
trick [trɪk] *n* trucco; (*clever act*) stratagemma *m*; (*joke*) tiro; (*Cards*) presa ■ *vt* imbrogliare, ingannare; **to play a ~ on sb** giocare un tiro a qn; **it's a ~ of the light** è un effetto ottico; **that should do the ~** (*col*) vedrai che funziona; **to ~ sb into doing sth** convincere qn a fare qc con l'inganno; **to ~ sb out of sth** fregare qc a qn
trickery ['trɪkərɪ] *n* inganno
trickle ['trɪkl] *n* (*of water etc*) rivolo; gocciolio ■ *vi* gocciolare; **to ~ in/out** (*people*) entrare/uscire alla spicciolata
trick question *n* domanda *f* trabocchetto *inv*
trickster ['trɪkstə^r] *n* imbroglione(-a)
tricky ['trɪkɪ] *adj* difficile, delicato(-a)
tricycle ['traɪsɪkl] *n* triciclo
trifle ['traɪfl] *n* sciocchezza; (*Brit Culin*) ≈ zuppa inglese ■ *adv*: **a ~ long** un po' lungo ■ *vi*: **to ~ with** prendere alla leggera
trifling ['traɪflɪŋ] *adj* insignificante
trigger ['trɪgə^r] *n* (*of gun*) grilletto
▸**trigger off** *vt* dare l'avvio a
trigonometry [trɪgə'nɔmətrɪ] *n* trigonometria
trilby ['trɪlbɪ] *n* (*Brit: also*: **trilby hat**) cappello floscio di feltro
trill [trɪl] *n* (*of bird, Mus*) trillo
trilogy ['trɪlədʒɪ] *n* trilogia
trim [trɪm] *adj* ordinato(-a); (*house, garden*) ben tenuto(-a); (*figure*) snello(-a) ■ *n* (*haircut etc*) spuntata, regolata; (*embellishment*) finiture *fpl*; (*on car*) guarnizioni *fpl* ■ *vt* spuntare; (*decorate*): **to ~ (with)** decorare (con); (*Naut: a sail*) orientare; **to keep in (good) ~** mantenersi in forma
trimmings ['trɪmɪŋz] *npl* decorazioni *fpl*; (*extras: gen Culin*) guarnizione *f*
Trinidad and Tobago ['trɪnɪdæd-] *n* Trinidad e Tobago *m*
Trinity ['trɪnɪtɪ] *n*: **the ~** la Trinità
trinket ['trɪŋkɪt] *n* gingillo; (*piece of jewellery*) ciondolo
trio ['tri:əu] *n* trio
trip [trɪp] *n* viaggio; (*excursion*) gita, escursione *f*; (*stumble*) passo falso ■ *vi* inciampare; (*go lightly*) camminare con passo leggero; **on a ~** in viaggio
▸**trip up** *vi* inciampare ■ *vt* fare lo sgambetto a
tripartite [traɪ'pɑ:taɪt] *adj* (*agreement*) tripartito(-a); (*talks*) a tre
tripe [traɪp] *n* (*Culin*) trippa; (*pej: rubbish*) sciocchezze *fpl*, fesserie *fpl*
triple ['trɪpl] *adj* triplo(-a) ■ *adv*: **~ the**

distance/the speed tre volte più lontano/ più veloce
triple jump *n* triplo salto
triplets ['trɪplɪts] *npl* bambini(-e) trigemini(-e)
triplicate ['trɪplɪkət] *n*: **in ~** in triplice copia
tripod ['traɪpɔd] *n* treppiede *m*
Tripoli ['trɪpəlɪ] *n* Tripoli *f*
tripper ['trɪpəʳ] *n* (*Brit*) gitante *m/f*
tripwire ['trɪpwaɪəʳ] *n* *filo in tensione che fa scattare una trappola, allarme etc*
trite [traɪt] *adj* banale, trito(-a)
triumph ['traɪʌmf] *n* trionfo ■ *vi*: **to ~ (over)** trionfare (su)
triumphal [traɪ'ʌmfl] *adj* trionfale
triumphant [traɪ'ʌmfənt] *adj* trionfante
trivia ['trɪvɪə] *npl* banalità *fpl*
trivial ['trɪvɪəl] *adj* (*matter*) futile; (*excuse, comment*) banale; (*amount*) irrisorio(-a); (*mistake*) di poco conto
triviality [trɪvɪ'ælɪtɪ] *n* frivolezza; (*trivial detail*) futilità
trivialize ['trɪvɪəlaɪz] *vt* sminuire
trod [trɔd] *pt of* **tread**
trodden ['trɔdn] *pp of* **tread**
trolley ['trɔlɪ] *n* carrello; (*in hospital*) lettiga
trolley bus *n* filobus *m inv*
trollop ['trɔləp] *n* prostituta
trombone [trɔm'bəun] *n* trombone *m*
troop [tru:p] *n* gruppo; (*Mil*) squadrone *m*; **troops** *npl* (*Mil*) truppe *fpl*; **trooping the colour** (*Brit*: *ceremony*) sfilata della bandiera
▸**troop in** *vi* entrare a frotte
▸**troop out** *vi* uscire a frotte
troop carrier *n* (*plane*) aereo per il trasporto (di) truppe; (*Naut*: *also*: **troopship**) nave *f* per il trasporto (di) truppe
trooper ['tru:pəʳ] *n* (*Mil*) soldato di cavalleria; (*US*: *policeman*) poliziotto (della polizia di stato)
troopship ['tru:pʃɪp] *n* nave *f* per il trasporto (di) truppe
trophy ['trəufɪ] *n* trofeo
tropic ['trɔpɪk] *n* tropico; **in the tropics** ai tropici; **T~ of Cancer/Capricorn** tropico del Cancro/Capricorno
tropical ['trɔpɪkəl] *adj* tropicale
trot [trɔt] *n* trotto ■ *vi* trottare; **on the ~** (*Brit fig*) di fila, uno(-a) dopo l'altro(-a)
▸**trot out** *vt* (*excuse, reason*) tirar fuori; (*names, facts*) recitare di fila
trouble ['trʌbl] *n* (*problems*) difficoltà *fpl*, problemi *mpl*; (*worry*) preoccupazione *f*; (*bother, effort*) sforzo; (*with sth mechanical*) noie *fpl*; (*Pol*) conflitti *mpl*, disordine *m*; (*Med*): **stomach** *etc* **~** disturbi *mpl* gastrici *etc* ■ *vt* disturbare; (*worry*) preoccupare ■ *vi*: **to ~ to do** disturbarsi a fare; **troubles** *npl* (*Pol etc*) disordini *mpl*; **to be in ~** avere dei problemi; (*for doing wrong*) essere nei guai; **to go to the ~ of doing** darsi la pena di fare; **it's no ~!** di niente!; **what's the ~?** cosa c'è che non va?; **the ~ is ...** c'è che ..., il guaio è che ...; **to have ~ doing sth** avere delle difficoltà a fare qc; **please don't ~ yourself** non si disturbi
troubled ['trʌbld] *adj* (*person*) preoccupato(-a), inquieto(-a); (*epoch, life*) agitato(-a), difficile
trouble-free ['trʌblfri:] *adj* senza problemi
troublemaker ['trʌblmeɪkəʳ] *n* elemento disturbatore, agitatore(-trice)
troubleshooter ['trʌblʃu:təʳ] *n* (*in conflict*) conciliatore *m*
troublesome ['trʌblsəm] *adj* fastidioso(-a), seccante
trouble spot *n* zona calda
troubling ['trʌblɪŋ] *adj* (*thought*) preoccupante; **these are ~ times** questi sono tempi difficili
trough [trɔf] *n* (*also*: **drinking trough**) abbeveratoio; (*also*: **feeding trough**) trogolo, mangiatoia; (*channel*) canale *m*; **~ of low pressure** (*Meteor*) depressione *f*
trounce [trauns] *vt* (*defeat*) sgominare
troupe [tru:p] *n* troupe *f inv*
trouser press *n* stirapantaloni *m inv*
trousers ['trauzəz] *npl* pantaloni *mpl*, calzoni *mpl*; **short ~** (*Brit*) calzoncini *mpl*
trouser suit *n* (*Brit*) completo *m or* tailleur *m inv* pantalone *inv*
trousseau (*pl* **trousseaux** *or* **trousseaus**) ['tru:səu, -z] *n* corredo da sposa
trout [traut] *n* (*pl inv*) trota
trowel ['trauəl] *n* cazzuola
truant ['truənt] *n*: **to play ~** (*Brit*) marinare la scuola
truce [tru:s] *n* tregua
truck [trʌk] *n* autocarro, camion *m inv*; (*Rail*) carro merci aperto; (*for luggage*) carrello *m* portabagagli *inv*
truck driver, (*US*) **trucker** ['trʌkəʳ] *n* camionista *m/f*
truck farm *n* (*US*) orto industriale
trucking ['trʌkɪŋ] *n* (*esp US*) autotrasporto
trucking company *n* (*esp US*) impresa di trasporti
truculent ['trʌkjulənt] *adj* aggressivo(-a), brutale
trudge [trʌdʒ] *vi* trascinarsi pesantemente
true [tru:] *adj* vero(-a); (*accurate*) accurato(-a), esatto(-a); (*genuine*) reale; (*faithful*) fedele; (*wall, beam*) a piombo; (*wheel*) centrato(-a); **to come ~** avverarsi; **~ to life** verosimile
truffle ['trʌfl] *n* tartufo
truly ['tru:lɪ] *adv* veramente; (*truthfully*)

sinceramente; (*faithfully*) fedelmente; **yours ~** (*in letter-writing*) distinti saluti
trump [trʌmp] *n* (*Cards*) atout *m inv*; **to turn up trumps** (*fig*) fare miracoli
trump card *n* atout *m inv*; (*fig*) asso nella manica
trumped-up [trʌmpt'ʌp] *adj* inventato(-a)
trumpet ['trʌmpɪt] *n* tromba
truncated [trʌŋ'keɪtɪd] *adj* tronco(-a)
truncheon ['trʌntʃən] *n* sfollagente *m inv*
trundle ['trʌndl] *vt, vi*: **to ~ along** rotolare rumorosamente
trunk [trʌŋk] *n* (*of tree, person*) tronco; (*of elephant*) proboscide *f*; (*case*) baule *m*; (*US Aut*) bagagliaio
trunk call *n* (*Brit Tel*) (telefonata) interurbana
trunk road *n* (*Brit*) strada principale
trunks [trʌŋks] *npl* (*also*: **swimming trunks**) calzoncini *mpl* da bagno
truss [trʌs] *n* (*Med*) cinto erniario ■ *vt*: **to ~ (up)** (*Culin*) legare
trust [trʌst] *n* fiducia; (*Law*) amministrazione *f* fiduciaria; (*Comm*) trust *m inv* ■ *vt* (*have confidence in*) fidarsi di; (*rely on*) contare su; (*entrust*): **to ~ sth to sb** affidare qc a qn; (*hope*): **to ~ (that)** sperare (che); **you'll have to take it on ~** deve credermi sulla parola; **in ~** (*Law*) in amministrazione fiduciaria
trust company *n* trust *m inv*
trusted ['trʌstɪd] *adj* fidato(-a)
trustee [trʌs'ti:] *n* (*Law*) amministratore(-a) fiduciario(-a); (*of school etc*) amministratore(-trice)
trustful ['trʌstful] *adj* fiducioso(-a)
trust fund *n* fondo fiduciario
trusting ['trʌstɪŋ] *adj* = **trustful**
trustworthy ['trʌstwə:ðɪ] *adj* fidato(-a), degno(-a) di fiducia
trusty ['trʌstɪ] *adj* fidato(-a)
truth (*pl* **truths**) [tru:θ, tru:ðz] *n* verità *f inv*
truthful ['tru:θful] *adj* (*person*) sincero(-a); (*description*) veritiero(-a), esatto(-a)
truthfully ['tru:θfəlɪ] *adv* sinceramente
truthfulness ['tru:θfəlnɪs] *n* veracità
try [traɪ] *n* prova, tentativo; (*Rugby*) meta ■ *vt* (*Law*) giudicare; (*test: sth new*) provare; (*strain: patience, person*) mettere alla prova ■ *vi* provare; **to ~ to do** provare a fare; (*seek*) cercare di fare; **to give sth a ~** provare qc; **to ~ one's (very) best** *or* **one's (very) hardest** mettercela tutta
▸**try on** *vt* (*clothes*) provare, mettere alla prova; **to ~ it on** (*fig*) cercare di farla
▸**try out** *vt* provare, mettere alla prova
trying ['traɪɪŋ] *adj* (*day, experience*) logorante, pesante; (*child*) difficile, insopportabile
tsar [zɑ:ʳ] *n* zar *m inv*
T-shirt ['ti:ʃə:t] *n* maglietta
TSO *n abbr* (*Brit*: = *The Stationery Office*) ≈ Poligrafici *mpl* dello Stato
T-square ['ti:skwɛəʳ] *n* riga a T
tsunami [tsu'nɑ:mɪ] *n* tsunami *m inv*
TT *adj abbr* (*Brit col*) = **teetotal** ■ *abbr* (*US*) = **Trust Territory**
tub [tʌb] *n* tinozza; mastello; (*bath*) bagno
tuba ['tju:bə] *n* tuba
tubby ['tʌbɪ] *adj* grassoccio(-a)
tube [tju:b] *n* tubo; (*Brit: underground*) metropolitana; (*for tyre*) camera d'aria; (*col: television*): **the ~** la tele
tubeless ['tju:blɪs] *adj* (*tyre*) senza camera d'aria
tuber ['tju:bəʳ] *n* (*Bot*) tubero
tuberculosis [tjubə:kju'ləusɪs] *n* tubercolosi *f*
tube station *n* (*Brit*) stazione *f* del metrò
tubing ['tju:bɪŋ] *n* tubazione *f*; **a piece of ~** un tubo
tubular ['tju:bjuləʳ] *adj* tubolare
TUC *n abbr* (*Brit*: = *Trades Union Congress*) confederazione *f* dei sindacati britannici
tuck [tʌk] *n* (*Sewing*) piega ■ *vt* (*put*) mettere
▸**tuck away** *vt* riporre
▸**tuck in** *vt* mettere dentro; (*child*) rimboccare ■ *vi* (*eat*) mangiare di buon appetito; abbuffarsi
▸**tuck up** *vt* (*child*) rimboccare
tuck shop *n* negozio di pasticceria (*in una scuola*)
Tue., Tues. *abbr* (= *Tuesday*) mar.
Tuesday ['tju:zdɪ] *n* martedì *m inv*; **(the date) today is ~ 23rd March** oggi è martedì 23 marzo; **on ~** martedì; **on Tuesdays** di martedì; **every ~** tutti i martedì; **every other ~** ogni due martedì; **last/next ~** martedì scorso/prossimo; **~ next** martedì prossimo; **the following ~** (*in past*) il martedì successivo; (*in future*) il martedì dopo; **a week/fortnight on ~, ~ week/fortnight** martedì fra una settimana/quindici giorni; **the ~ before last** martedì di due settimane fa; **the ~ after next** non questo martedì ma il prossimo; **~ morning/lunchtime/afternoon/evening** martedì mattina/all'ora di pranzo/pomeriggio/sera; **~ night** martedì sera; (*overnight*) martedì notte; **~'s newspaper** il giornale di martedì
tuft [tʌft] *n* ciuffo
tug [tʌg] *n* (*ship*) rimorchiatore *m* ■ *vt* tirare con forza
tug-of-love [tʌgəv'lʌv] *n* contesa per la custodia dei figli; **~ children** bambini *mpl* coinvolti nella contesa per la custodia

tug-of-war [tʌgəv'wɔːʳ] *n* tiro alla fune
tuition [tjuː'ɪʃən] *n* (*Brit: lessons*) lezioni *fpl*; (*US: fees*) tasse *fpl* scolastiche (*or* universitarie)
tulip ['tjuːlɪp] *n* tulipano
tumble ['tʌmbl] *n* (*fall*) capitombolo ■ *vi* capitombolare, ruzzolare; (*somersault*) fare capriole ■ *vt* far cadere; **to ~ to sth** (*col*) realizzare qc
tumbledown ['tʌmbldaun] *n* cadente, diroccato(-a)
tumble dryer *n* (*Brit*) asciugatrice *f*
tumbler ['tʌmbləʳ] *n* bicchiere *m* senza stelo
tummy ['tʌmɪ] *n* (*col*) pancia
tumour, (US) **tumor** ['tjuːməʳ] *n* tumore *m*
tumult ['tjuːmʌlt] *n* tumulto
tumultuous [tjuː'mʌltjuəs] *adj* tumultuoso(-a)
tuna ['tjuːnə] *n* (*pl inv*: *also*: **tuna fish**) tonno
tune [tjuːn] *n* (*melody*) melodia, aria ■ *vt* (*Mus*) accordare; (*Radio, TV, Aut*) regolare, mettere a punto; **to be in/out of ~** (*instrument*) essere accordato(-a)/scordato(-a); (*singer*) essere intonato(-a)/stonato(-a); **to the ~ of** (*fig: amount*) per la modesta somma di; **in ~ with** (*fig*) in accordo con
▸ **tune in** *vi* (*Radio, TV*): **to ~ in (to)** sintonizzarsi (su)
▸ **tune up** *vi* (*musician*) accordare lo strumento
tuneful ['tjuːnful] *adj* melodioso(-a)
tuner ['tjuːnəʳ] *n* (*radio set*) sintonizzatore *m*; **piano ~** accordatore(-trice) di pianoforte
tuner amplifier *n* amplificatore *m* di sintonia
tungsten ['tʌŋstn] *n* tungsteno
tunic ['tjuːnɪk] *n* tunica
tuning ['tjuːnɪŋ] *n* messa a punto
tuning fork *n* diapason *m inv*
Tunis ['tjuːnɪs] *n* Tunisi *f*
Tunisia [tjuː'nɪzɪə] *n* Tunisia
Tunisian [tjuː'nɪzɪən] *adj, n* tunisino(-a)
tunnel ['tʌnl] *n* galleria ■ *vi* scavare una galleria
tunnel vision *n* (*Med*) riduzione *f* del campo visivo; (*fig*) visuale *f* ristretta
tunny ['tʌnɪ] *n* tonno
turban ['təːbən] *n* turbante *m*
turbid ['təːbɪd] *adj* torbido(-a)
turbine ['təːbaɪn] *n* turbina
turbo ['təːbəu] *n* turbo *m inv*
turbojet ['təːbəu'dʒɛt] *n* turboreattore *m*
turboprop ['təːbəu'prɔp] *n* turboelica *m inv*
turbot ['təːbət] *n* (*pl inv*) rombo gigante
turbulence ['təːbjuləns] *n* turbolenza
turbulent ['təːbjulənt] *adj* turbolento(-a); (*sea*) agitato(-a)
tureen [tə'riːn] *n* zuppiera
turf [təːf] *n* terreno erboso; (*clod*) zolla ■ *vt* coprire di zolle erbose; **the T~** l'ippodromo
▸ **turf out** *vt* (*col*) buttar fuori
turf accountant *n* (*Brit*) allibratore *m*
turgid ['təːdʒɪd] *adj* (*speech*) ampolloso(-a), pomposo(-a)
Turin [tjuə'rɪn] *n* Torino *f*
Turk [təːk] *n* turco(-a)
Turkey ['təːkɪ] *n* Turchia
turkey ['təːkɪ] *n* tacchino
Turkish ['təːkɪʃ] *adj* turco(-a) ■ *n* (*Ling*) turco
Turkish bath *n* bagno turco
Turkish delight *n gelatine ricoperte di zucchero a velo*
turmeric ['təːmərɪk] *n* curcuma
turmoil ['təːmɔɪl] *n* confusione *f*, tumulto
turn [təːn] *n* giro; (*in road*) curva; (*tendency: of mind, events*) tendenza; (*performance*) numero; (*Med*) crisi *f inv*, attacco ■ *vt* girare, voltare; (*milk*) far andare a male; (*shape: wood, metal*) tornire; (*change*): **to ~ sth into** trasformare qc in ■ *vi* girare; (*person: look back*) girarsi, voltarsi; (*reverse direction*) girarsi indietro; (*change*) cambiare; (*become*) diventare; **to ~ into** trasformarsi in; **a good ~** un buon servizio; **a bad ~** un brutto tiro; **it gave me quite a ~** mi ha fatto prendere un bello spavento; **"no left ~"** (*Aut*) "divieto di svolta a sinistra"; **it's your ~** tocca a lei; **in ~** a sua volta; a turno; **to take turns (at sth)** fare (qc) a turno; **at the ~ of the year/century** alla fine dell'anno/del secolo; **to take a ~ for the worse** (*situation, events*) volgere al peggio; (*patient, health*) peggiorare; **to ~ left/right** girare a sinistra/destra
▸ **turn about** *vi* girarsi indietro
▸ **turn away** *vi* girarsi (dall'altra parte) ■ *vt* (*reject: person*) mandar via; (*: business*) rifiutare
▸ **turn back** *vi* ritornare, tornare indietro
▸ **turn down** *vt* (*refuse*) rifiutare; (*reduce*) abbassare; (*fold*) ripiegare
▸ **turn in** *vi* (*col: go to bed*) andare a letto ■ *vt* (*fold*) voltare in dentro
▸ **turn off** *vi* (*from road*) girare, voltare ■ *vt* (*light, radio, engine etc*) spegnere
▸ **turn on** *vt* (*light, radio etc*) accendere; (*engine*) avviare
▸ **turn out** *vt* (*light, gas*) chiudere, spegnere; (*produce: goods*) produrre; (*: novel, good pupils*) creare ■ *vi* (*appear, attend: troops, doctor etc*) presentarsi; **to ~ out to be ...** rivelarsi ..., risultare ...
▸ **turn over** *vi* (*person*) girarsi; (*car etc*) capovolgersi ■ *vt* girare
▸ **turn round** *vi* girare; (*person*) girarsi
▸ **turn up** *vi* (*person*) arrivare, presentarsi;

(*lost object*) saltar fuori ■ *vt* (*collar, sound, gas etc*) alzare
turnabout ['tə:nəbaut], **turnaround** ['tə:nəraund] *n* (*fig*) dietrofront *m inv*
turncoat ['tə:nkəut] *n* voltagabbana *m/f inv*
turned-up ['tə:ndʌp] *adj* (*nose*) all'insù
turning ['tə:nɪŋ] *n* (*in road*) curva; (*side road*) strada laterale; **the first ~ on the right** la prima a destra
turning circle *n* (*Brit*) diametro di sterzata
turning point *n* (*fig*) svolta decisiva
turning radius *n* (*US*) = **turning circle**
turnip ['tə:nɪp] *n* rapa
turnout ['tə:naut] *n* presenza, affluenza
turnover ['tə:nəuvə^r] *n* (*Comm*: *amount of money*) giro di affari; (: *of goods*) smercio; (*Culin*): **apple** *etc* **~** sfogliatella alle mele *etc*; **there is a rapid ~ in staff** c'è un ricambio molto rapido di personale
turnpike ['tə:npaɪk] *n* (*US*) autostrada a pedaggio
turnstile ['tə:nstaɪl] *n* tornella
turntable ['tə:nteɪbl] *n* (*on record player*) piatto
turn-up ['tə:nʌp] *n* (*Brit*: *on trousers*) risvolto
turpentine ['tə:pəntaɪn] *n* (*also*: **turps**) acqua ragia
turquoise [tə:kwɔɪz] *n* (*stone*) turchese *m* ■ *adj* color turchese; di turchese
turret ['tʌrɪt] *n* torretta
turtle ['tə:tl] *n* testuggine *f*
turtleneck ['tə:tlnɛk], **turtleneck sweater** ['tə:tlnɛk-] *n* maglione *m* con il collo alto
Tuscan ['tʌskən] *adj, n* toscano(-a)
Tuscany ['tʌskənɪ] *n* Toscana
tusk [tʌsk] *n* zanna
tussle ['tʌsl] *n* baruffa, mischia
tutor ['tju:tə^r] *n* (*in college*) docente *m/f* (*responsabile di un gruppo di studenti*); (*private teacher*) precettore *m*
tutorial [tju:'tɔ:rɪəl] *n* (*Scol*) lezione *f* con discussione (*a un gruppo limitato*)
tuxedo [tʌk'si:dəu] *n* (*US*) smoking *m inv*
TV [ti:'vi:] *n abbr* (= *television*) tivù *f inv*
TV dinner *n* pasto *m* pronto
twaddle ['twɔdl] *n* scemenze *fpl*
twang [twæŋ] *n* (*of instrument*) suono vibrante; (*of voice*) accento nasale ■ *vi* vibrare ■ *vt* (*guitar*) pizzicare le corde di
tweak [twi:k] *vt* (*nose*) pizzicare; (*ear, hair*) tirare
tweed [twi:d] *n* tweed *m inv*
tweezers ['twi:zəz] *npl* pinzette *fpl*
twelfth [twɛlfθ] *num* dodicesimo(-a)
Twelfth Night *n* la notte dell'Epifania
twelve [twɛlv] *num* dodici; **at ~** alle dodici, a mezzogiorno; (*midnight*) a mezzanotte
twentieth ['twɛntɪɪθ] *num* ventesimo(-a)
twenty ['twɛntɪ] *num* venti
twerp [twə:p] *n* (*col*) idiota *m/f*
twice [twaɪs] *adv* due volte; **~ as much** due volte tanto; **~ a week** due volte alla settimana; **she is ~ your age** ha il doppio dei suoi anni
twiddle ['twɪdl] *vt, vi*: **to ~ (with) sth** giocherellare con qc; **to ~ one's thumbs** (*fig*) girarsi i pollici
twig [twɪg] *n* ramoscello ■ *vt, vi* (*col*) capire
twilight ['twaɪlaɪt] *n* (*evening*) crepuscolo; (*morning*) alba; **in the ~** nella penombra
twin [twɪn] *adj, n* gemello(-a)
twin beds *npl* letti *mpl* gemelli
twin-bedded room ['twɪn'bɛdɪd-] *n* stanza con letti gemelli
twin-carburettor ['twɪnkɑ:bju'rɛtə^r] *adj* a doppio carburatore
twine [twaɪn] *n* spago, cordicella ■ *vi* (*plant*) attorcigliarsi; (*road*) serpeggiare
twin-engined ['twɪn'ɛndʒɪnd] *adj* a due motori; **~ aircraft** bimotore *m*
twinge [twɪndʒ] *n* (*of pain*) fitta; **a ~ of conscience/regret** un rimorso/rimpianto
twinkle ['twɪŋkl] *n* scintillio ■ *vi* scintillare; (*eyes*) brillare
twin room *n* stanza con letti gemelli
twin town *n* città *f inv* gemella
twirl [twə:l] *n* piroetta ■ *vt* far roteare ■ *vi* roteare
twist [twɪst] *n* torsione *f*; (*in wire, flex*) storta; (*in story*) colpo di scena; (*bend*) svolta, piega ■ *vt* attorcigliare; (*weave*) intrecciare; (*roll around*) arrotolare; (*fig*) deformare ■ *vi* attorcigliarsi; arrotolarsi; (*road*) serpeggiare; **to ~ one's ankle/wrist** (*Med*) slogarsi la caviglia/il polso
twisted ['twɪstɪd] *adj* (*wire, rope*) attorcigliato(-a); (*ankle, wrist*) slogato(-a); (*fig*: *logic, mind*) contorto(-a)
twit [twɪt] *n* (*col*) minchione(-a)
twitch [twɪtʃ] *n* tiratina; (*nervous*) tic *m inv* ■ *vi* contrarsi; avere un tic
Twitter® [twɪtə^r] *n* Twitter® *m* ■ *vi* connettersi a Twitter, scrivere su Twitter
two [tu:] *num* due; **~ by ~**, **in twos** a due a due; **to put ~ and ~ together** (*fig*) trarre le conclusioni
two-bit [tu:'bɪt] *adj* (*esp US*: *col, pej*) da quattro soldi
two-door [tu:'dɔ:^{r}] *adj* (*Aut*) a due porte
two-faced ['tu:'feɪst] *adj* (*pej*: *person*) falso(-a)
twofold ['tu:fəuld] *adv*: **to increase ~** aumentare del doppio ■ *adj* (*increase*) doppio(-a); (*reply*) in due punti
two-piece ['tu:'pi:s] *n* (*also*: **two-piece suit**) due pezzi *m inv*; (*also*: **two-piece swimsuit**) (costume *m* da bagno a) due pezzi *m inv*

t

two-seater ['tuː'siːtəʳ] *n* (*plane*) biposto; (*car*) macchina a due posti
twosome ['tuːsəm] *n* (*people*) coppia
two-stroke ['tuːstrəuk] *n* (*engine*) due tempi *m inv* ■ *adj* a due tempi
two-tone ['tuːtəun] *adj* (*colour*) bicolore
two-way ['tuːweɪ] *adj* (*traffic*) a due sensi; ~ **radio** radio *f inv* ricetrasmittente
TX *abbr* (*US*) = **Texas**
tycoon [taɪ'kuːn] *n*: **(business)** ~ magnate *m*
type [taɪp] *n* (*category*) genere *m*; (*model*) modello; (*example*) tipo; (*Typ*) tipo, carattere *m* ■ *vt* (*letter etc*) battere (a macchina), dattilografare; **what ~ do you want?** che tipo vuole?; **in bold/italic ~** in grassetto/corsivo
type-cast ['taɪpkɑːst] *adj* (*actor*) a ruolo fisso
typeface ['taɪpfeɪs] *n* carattere *m* tipografico
typescript ['taɪpskrɪpt] *n* dattiloscritto
typeset ['taɪpsɛt] *vt* comporre
typesetter ['taɪpsɛtəʳ] *n* compositore *m*
typewriter ['taɪpraɪtəʳ] *n* macchina da scrivere
typewritten ['taɪprɪtn] *adj* dattiloscritto(-a), battuto(-a) a macchina
typhoid ['taɪfɔɪd] *n* tifoidea
typhoon [taɪ'fuːn] *n* tifone *m*
typhus ['taɪfəs] *n* tifo
typical ['tɪpɪkl] *adj* tipico(-a)
typify ['tɪpɪfaɪ] *vt* essere tipico(-a) di
typing ['taɪpɪŋ] *n* dattilografia
typing error *n* errore *m* di battitura
typing pool *n* ufficio *m*, dattilografia *inv*
typist ['taɪpɪst] *n* dattilografo(-a)
typo ['taɪpəu] *n abbr* (*col*: = *typographical error*) refuso
typography [taɪ'pɔgrəfɪ] *n* tipografia
tyranny ['tɪrənɪ] *n* tirannia
tyrant ['taɪərnt] *n* tiranno
tyre, (*US*) **tire** ['taɪəʳ] *n* pneumatico, gomma
tyre pressure *n* pressione *f* (delle gomme)
Tyrol [tɪ'rəul] *n* Tirolo
Tyrolean [tɪrə'liːən], **Tyrolese** [tɪrə'liːz] *adj, n* tirolese *m/f*
Tyrrhenian Sea [tɪ'riːnɪən-] *n*: **the ~** il mar Tirreno

Uu

U, u [ju:] *n (letter)* U, u *m or f inv*; **U for Uncle** ≈ U come Udine
U *n abbr (Brit Cine: = universal)* per tutti
UAW *n abbr (US: = United Automobile Workers) sindacato degli operai automobilistici*
UB40 *n abbr (Brit: = unemployment benefit form 40) modulo per la richiesta del sussidio di disoccupazione*
U-bend ['ju:bɛnd] *n (in pipe)* sifone *m*
ubiquitous [ju:'bɪkwɪtəs] *adj* onnipresente
UCAS ['ju:kæs] *n abbr (Brit)* = **Universities and Colleges Admissions Service**
UDA *n abbr (Brit: = Ulster Defence Association) organizzazione paramilitare protestante*
UDC *n abbr (Brit)* = **Urban District Council**
udder ['ʌdəʳ] *n* mammella
UDI *abbr (Brit Pol)* = **unilateral declaration of independence**
UDR *n abbr (Brit: = Ulster Defence Regiment) reggimento dell'esercito britannico in Irlanda del Nord*
UEFA [ju:'eɪfə] *n abbr (= Union of European Football Associations)* U.E.F.A. *f*
UFO ['ju:fəu] *n abbr (= unidentified flying object)* UFO *m inv*
Uganda [ju:'gændə] *n* Uganda
Ugandan [ju:'gændən] *adj, n* ugandese *m/f*
UGC *n abbr (Brit: = University Grants Committee) organo che autorizza sovvenzioni alle università*
ugh [ə:h] *excl* puah!
ugliness ['ʌglɪnɪs] *n* bruttezza
ugly ['ʌglɪ] *adj* brutto(-a)
UHF *abbr* = **ultra-high frequency**
UHT *adj abbr* = **ultra heat treated**; **~ milk** latte *m* UHT
UK *n abbr* = **United Kingdom**
Ukraine [ju:'kreɪn] *n* Ucraina
Ukrainian [ju:'kreɪnɪən] *adj* ucraino(-a) ■ *n (person)* ucraino(-a); *(Ling)* ucraino
ulcer ['ʌlsəʳ] *n* ulcera; **mouth ~** afta
Ulster ['ʌlstəʳ] *n* Ulster *m*
ulterior [ʌl'tɪərɪəʳ] *adj* ulteriore; **~ motive** secondo fine *m*
ultimata [ʌltɪ'meɪtə] *npl of* **ultimatum**
ultimate ['ʌltɪmɪt] *adj* ultimo(-a), finale; *(authority)* massimo(-a), supremo(-a) ■ *n*: **the ~ in luxury** il non plus ultra del lusso
ultimately ['ʌltɪmɪtlɪ] *adv* alla fine; in definitiva, in fin dei conti
ultimatum (*pl* **ultimatums** *or* **ultimata**) [ʌltɪ'meɪtəm, -tə] *n* ultimatum *m inv*
ultrasonic [ʌltrə'sɔnɪk] *adj* ultrasonico(-a)
ultrasound [ʌltrə'saund] *n (Med)* ecografia
ultraviolet ['ʌltrə'vaɪəlɪt] *adj* ultravioletto(-a)
umbilical [ʌm'bɪlɪkl] *adj*: **~ cord** cordone *m* ombelicale
umbrage ['ʌmbrɪdʒ] *n*: **to take ~** offendersi, impermalirsi
umbrella [ʌm'brɛlə] *n* ombrello; **under the ~ of** *(fig)* sotto l'egida di
umlaut ['umlaut] *n* Umlaut *m inv*
umpire ['ʌmpaɪəʳ] *n* arbitro
umpteen [ʌmp'ti:n] *adj* non so quanti(-e); **for the umpteenth time** per l'ennesima volta
UMW *n abbr (= United Mineworkers of America) unione dei minatori d'America*
UN *n abbr* = **United Nations**
unabashed [ʌnə'bæʃt] *adj* imperturbato(-a)
unabated [ʌnə'beɪtɪd] *adj* non diminuito(-a)
unable [ʌn'eɪbl] *adj*: **to be ~ to** non potere, essere nell'impossibilità di; *(not to know how to)* essere incapace di, non sapere
unabridged [ʌnə'brɪdʒd] *adj* integrale
unacceptable [ʌnək'sɛptəbl] *adj (proposal, behaviour)* inaccettabile; *(price)* impossibile
unaccompanied [ʌnə'kʌmpənɪd] *adj (child, lady)* non accompagnato(-a); *(singing, song)* senza accompagnamento
unaccountably [ʌnə'kauntəblɪ] *adv* inesplicabilmente
unaccounted [ʌnə'kauntɪd] *adj*: **two passengers are ~ for** due passeggeri mancano all'appello
unaccustomed [ʌnə'kʌstəmd] *adj* insolito(-a); **to be ~ to sth** non essere abituato(-a) a qc
unacquainted [ʌnə'kweɪntɪd] *adj*: **to be ~ with** *(facts)* ignorare, non essere al corrente di

unadulterated [ʌnəˈdʌltəreɪtɪd] *adj (gen)* puro(-a); *(wine)* non sofisticato(-a)
unaffected [ʌnəˈfɛktɪd] *adj (person, behaviour)* naturale, spontaneo(-a); *(emotionally)*: **to be ~ by** non essere toccato(-a) da
unafraid [ʌnəˈfreɪd] *adj*: **to be ~** non aver paura
unaided [ʌnˈeɪdɪd] *adv* senza aiuto
unanimity [juːnəˈnɪmɪtɪ] *n* unanimità
unanimous [juːˈnænɪməs] *adj* unanime
unanimously [juːˈnænɪməslɪ] *adv* all'unanimità
unanswered [ʌnˈɑːnsəd] *adj (question, letter)* senza risposta; *(criticism)* non confutato(-a)
unappetizing [ʌnˈæpɪtaɪzɪŋ] *adj* poco appetitoso(-a)
unappreciative [ʌnəˈpriːʃɪətɪv] *adj* che non apprezza
unarmed [ʌnˈɑːmd] *adj (person)* disarmato(-a); *(combat)* senz'armi
unashamed [ʌnəˈʃeɪmd] *adj* sfacciato(-a), senza vergogna
unassisted [ʌnəˈsɪstɪd] *adj, adv* senza nessun aiuto
unassuming [ʌnəˈsjuːmɪŋ] *adj* modesto(-a), senza pretese
unattached [ʌnəˈtætʃt] *adj* senza legami, libero(-a)
unattended [ʌnəˈtɛndɪd] *adj (car, child, luggage)* incustodito(-a)
unattractive [ʌnəˈtræktɪv] *adj* privo(-a) di attrattiva, poco attraente
unauthorized [ʌnˈɔːθəraɪzd] *adj* non autorizzato(-a)
unavailable [ʌnəˈveɪləbl] *adj (article, room, book)* non disponibile; *(person)* impegnato(-a)
unavoidable [ʌnəˈvɔɪdəbl] *adj* inevitabile
unavoidably [ʌnəˈvɔɪdəblɪ] *adv (detained)* per cause di forza maggiore
unaware [ʌnəˈwɛəʳ] *adj*: **to be ~ of** non sapere, ignorare
unawares [ʌnəˈwɛəz] *adv* di sorpresa, alla sprovvista
unbalanced [ʌnˈbælənst] *adj* squilibrato(-a)
unbearable [ʌnˈbɛərəbl] *adj* insopportabile
unbeatable [ʌnˈbiːtəbl] *adj* imbattibile
unbeaten [ʌnˈbiːtn] *adj (team, army)* imbattuto(-a); *(record)* insuperato(-a)
unbecoming [ʌnbɪˈkʌmɪŋ] *adj (unseemly: language, behaviour)* sconveniente; *(unflattering: garment)* che non dona
unbeknown [ʌnbɪˈnəun], **unbeknownst** [ʌnbɪˈnəunst] *adv*: **~(st) to** all'insaputa di
unbelief [ʌnbɪˈliːf] *n* incredulità
unbelievable [ʌnbɪˈliːvəbl] *adj* incredibile
unbelievingly [ʌnbɪˈliːvɪŋlɪ] *adv* con aria incredula
unbend [ʌnˈbɛnd] *vb (irreg) vi* distendersi ■ *vt (wire)* raddrizzare
unbending [ʌnˈbɛndɪŋ] *adj (fig)* inflessibile, rigido(-a)
unbiased, unbiassed [ʌnˈbaɪəst] *adj* obiettivo(-a), imparziale
unblemished [ʌnˈblɛmɪʃt] *adj* senza macchia
unblock [ʌnˈblɔk] *vt (pipe, road)* sbloccare
unborn [ʌnˈbɔːn] *adj* non ancora nato(-a)
unbounded [ʌnˈbaundɪd] *adj* sconfinato(-a), senza limite
unbreakable [ʌnˈbreɪkəbl] *adj* infrangibile
unbridled [ʌnˈbraɪdld] *adj* sbrigliato(-a)
unbroken [ʌnˈbrəukən] *adj (intact)* intero(-a); *(continuous)* continuo(-a); *(record)* insuperato(-a)
unbuckle [ʌnˈbʌkl] *vt* slacciare
unburden [ʌnˈbəːdn] *vt*: **to ~ o.s.** sfogarsi
unbutton [ʌnˈbʌtn] *vt* sbottonare
uncalled-for [ʌnˈkɔːldfɔːʳ] *adj (remark)* fuori luogo *inv*; *(action)* ingiustificato(-a)
uncanny [ʌnˈkænɪ] *adj* misterioso(-a), strano(-a)
unceasing [ʌnˈsiːsɪŋ] *adj* incessante
unceremonious [ʌnsɛrɪˈməunɪəs] *adj (abrupt, rude)* senza tante cerimonie
uncertain [ʌnˈsəːtn] *adj* incerto(-a); **it's ~ whether ...** non è sicuro se ...; **in no ~ terms** chiaro e tondo, senza mezzi termini
uncertainty [ʌnˈsəːtntɪ] *n* incertezza
unchallenged [ʌnˈtʃælɪndʒd] *adj* incontestato(-a); **to go ~** non venire contestato, non trovare opposizione
unchanged [ʌnˈtʃeɪndʒd] *adj* immutato(-a)
uncharitable [ʌnˈtʃærɪtəbl] *adj* duro(-a), severo(-a)
uncharted [ʌnˈtʃɑːtɪd] *adj* inesplorato(-a)
unchecked [ʌnˈtʃɛkt] *adj* incontrollato(-a)
uncivilized [ʌnˈsɪvɪlaɪzd] *adj (gen)* selvaggio(-a); *(fig)* incivile, barbaro(-a)
uncle [ˈʌŋkl] *n* zio
unclear [ʌnˈklɪəʳ] *adj* non chiaro(-a); **I'm still ~ about what I'm supposed to do** non ho ancora ben capito cosa dovrei fare
uncoil [ʌnˈkɔɪl] *vt* srotolare ■ *vi* srotolarsi, svolgersi
uncomfortable [ʌnˈkʌmfətəbl] *adj* scomodo(-a); *(uneasy)* a disagio, agitato(-a); *(situation)* sgradevole
uncomfortably [ʌnˈkʌmfətəblɪ] *adv* scomodamente; *(uneasily: say)* con voce inquieta; *(: think)* con inquietudine
uncommitted [ʌnkəˈmɪtɪd] *adj (attitude, country)* neutrale
uncommon [ʌnˈkɔmən] *adj* raro(-a), insolito(-a), non comune
uncommunicative [ʌnkəˈmjuːnɪkətɪv] *adj*

poco comunicativo(-a), chiuso(-a)
uncomplicated [ʌn'kɔmplɪkeɪtɪd] *adj* semplice, poco complicato(-a)
uncompromising [ʌn'kɔmprəmaɪzɪŋ] *adj* intransigente, inflessibile
unconcerned [ʌnkən'sə:nd] *adj* (*unworried*) tranquillo(-a); **to be ~ about** non darsi pensiero di, non preoccuparsi di *or* per
unconditional [ʌn'kən'dɪʃənl] *adj* incondizionato(-a), senza condizioni
uncongenial [ʌnkən'dʒi:nɪəl] *adj* (*work, surroundings*) poco piacevole
unconnected [ʌnkə'nɛktɪd] *adj* (*unrelated*) senza connessione, senza rapporto; **to be ~ with** essere estraneo(-a) a
unconscious [ʌn'kɔnʃəs] *adj* privo(-a) di sensi, svenuto(-a); (*unaware*) inconsapevole, inconscio(-a) ■ *n*: **the ~** l'inconscio; **to knock sb ~** far perdere i sensi a qn con un pugno
unconsciously [ʌn'kɔnʃəslɪ] *adv* inconsciamente
unconstitutional [ʌnkɔnstɪ'tju:ʃənl] *adj* incostituzionale
uncontested [ʌnkən'tɛstɪd] *adj* (*champion*) incontestato(-a); (*Pol: seat*) non disputato(-a)
uncontrollable [ʌnkən'trəuləbl] *adj* incontrollabile, indisciplinato(-a)
uncontrolled [ʌnkən'trəuld] *adj* (*child, dog, emotion*) sfrenato(-a); (*inflation, price rises*) che sfugge al controllo
unconventional [ʌnkən'vɛnʃənl] *adj* poco convenzionale
unconvinced [ʌnkən'vɪnst] *adj*: **to be** *or* **remain ~** non essere convinto(-a)
unconvincing [ʌnkən'vɪnsɪŋ] *adj* non convincente, poco persuasivo(-a)
uncork [ʌn'kɔ:k] *vt* stappare
uncorroborated [ʌnkə'rɔbəreɪtɪd] *adj* non convalidato(-a)
uncouth [ʌn'ku:θ] *adj* maleducato(-a), grossolano(-a)
uncover [ʌn'kʌvə^r] *vt* scoprire
unctuous ['ʌŋktjuəs] *adj* untuoso(-a)
undamaged [ʌn'dæmɪdʒd] *adj* (*goods*) in buono stato; (*fig: reputation*) intatto(-a)
undaunted [ʌn'dɔ:ntɪd] *adj* intrepido(-a)
undecided [ʌndɪ'saɪdɪd] *adj* indeciso(-a)
undelivered [ʌndɪ'lɪvəd] *adj* non recapitato(-a); **if ~ return to sender** in caso di mancato recapito rispedire al mittente
undeniable [ʌndɪ'naɪəbl] *adj* innegabile, indiscutibile
under ['ʌndə^r] *prep* sotto; (*less than*) meno di; al disotto di; (*according to*) secondo, in conformità a ■ *adv* (al) disotto; **from ~ sth** da sotto a *or* dal disotto di qc; **~ there** là sotto; **in ~ 2 hours** in meno di 2 ore; **~ anaesthetic** sotto anestesia; **~ discussion** in discussione; **~ repair** in riparazione; **~ the circumstances** date le circostanze
under ... ['ʌndə^r] *prefix* sotto..., sub...
under-age [ʌndər'eɪdʒ] *adj* minorenne
underarm ['ʌndərɑ:m] *n* ascella ■ *adj* ascellare ■ *adv* da sotto in su
undercapitalized [ʌndə'kæpɪtəlaɪzd] *adj* carente di capitali
undercarriage ['ʌndəkærɪdʒ] *n* (*Brit Aviat*) carrello (d'atterraggio)
undercharge [ʌndə'tʃɑ:dʒ] *vt* far pagare di meno a
underclass ['ʌndəklɑ:s] *n* sottoproletariato
underclothes ['ʌndəkləuðz] *npl* biancheria (intima)
undercover ['ʌndəkʌvə^r] *adj* segreto(-a), clandestino(-a)
undercurrent ['ʌndəkʌrənt] *n* corrente *f* sottomarina
undercut [ʌndə'kʌt] *vt irreg* vendere a prezzo minore di
underdeveloped ['ʌndədɪ'vɛləpt] *adj* sottosviluppato(-a)
underdog ['ʌndədɔg] *n* oppresso(-a)
underdone [ʌndə'dʌn] *adj* (*Culin*) poco cotto(-a)
under-employment [ʌndərɪm'plɔɪmənt] *n* sottoccupazione *f*
underestimate [ʌndər'ɛstɪmeɪt] *vt* sottovalutare
underexposed [ʌndərɪks'pəuzd] *adj* (*Phot*) sottoesposto(-a)
underfed [ʌndə'fɛd] *adj* denutrito(-a)
underfoot [ʌndə'fut] *adv* sotto i piedi
under-funded ['ʌndə'fʌndɪd] *adj* insufficientemente sovvenzionato(-a)
undergo [ʌndə'gəu] *vt irreg* subire; (*treatment*) sottoporsi a; **the car is undergoing repairs** la macchina è in riparazione
undergraduate [ʌndə'grædjuɪt] *n* studente(-essa) universitario(-a) ■ *cpd*: **~ courses** corsi *mpl* di laurea
underground ['ʌndəgraund] *n* metropolitana; (*Pol*) movimento clandestino ■ *adj* sotterraneo(-a); (*fig*) clandestino(-a); (*Art, Cine*) underground *inv* ■ *adv* sottoterra; clandestinamente
undergrowth ['ʌndəgrəuθ] *n* sottobosco
underhand [ʌndə'hænd], **underhanded** [ʌndə'hændɪd] *adj* (*fig*) furtivo(-a), subdolo(-a)
underinsured [ʌndərɪn'ʃuəd] *adj* non sufficientemente assicurato(-a)
underlie [ʌndə'laɪ] *vt irreg* essere alla base di; **the underlying cause** il motivo di fondo

underline [ʌndəˈlaɪn] *vt* sottolineare
underling [ˈʌndəlɪŋ] *n* (*pej*) subalterno(-a), tirapiedi *m/f inv*
undermanning [ʌndəˈmænɪŋ] *n* carenza di personale
undermentioned [ʌndəˈmɛnʃənd] *adj* (riportato(-a)) qui sotto *or* qui di seguito
undermine [ʌndəˈmaɪn] *vt* minare
underneath [ʌndəˈni:θ] *adv* sotto, disotto ■ *prep* sotto, al di sotto di
undernourished [ʌndəˈnʌrɪʃt] *adj* denutrito(-a)
underpaid [ʌndəˈpeɪd] *adj* mal pagato(-a)
underpants [ˈʌndəpænts] *npl* (*Brit*) mutande *fpl*, slip *m inv*
underpass [ˈʌndəpɑ:s] *n* (*Brit*) sottopassaggio
underpin [ʌndəˈpɪn] *vt* puntellare; (*argument, case*) corroborare
underplay [ʌndəˈpleɪ] *vt* minimizzare
underpopulated [ʌndəˈpɔpjuleɪtɪd] *adj* scarsamente popolato(-a), sottopopolato(-a)
underprice [ʌndəˈpraɪs] *vt* vendere a un prezzo inferiore al dovuto
underprivileged [ʌndəˈprɪvɪlɪdʒd] *adj* svantaggiato(-a)
underrate [ʌndəˈreɪt] *vt* sottovalutare
underscore [ʌndəˈskɔ:ʳ] *vt* sottolineare
underseal [ˈʌndəsi:l] *vt* rendere stagno il fondo di
undersecretary [ʌndəˈsɛkrətrɪ] *n* sottosegretario
undersell [ˈʌndəˈsɛl] *vt irreg* (*competitors*) vendere a prezzi più bassi di
undershirt [ˈʌndəʃə:t] *n* (*US*) maglietta
undershorts [ˈʌndəʃɔ:ts] *npl* (*US*) mutande *fpl*, slip *m inv*
underside [ˈʌndəsaɪd] *n* disotto
undersigned [ˈʌndəsaɪnd] *adj, n* sottoscritto(-a)
underskirt [ˈʌndəskə:t] *n* sottoveste *f*
understaffed [ʌndəˈstɑ:ft] *adj* a corto di personale
understand [ʌndəˈstænd] *vb* (*irreg: like* **stand**) *vt, vi* capire, comprendere; **I ~ that ...** sento che ...; credo di capire che ...; **to make o.s. understood** farsi capire
understandable [ʌndəˈstændəbl] *adj* comprensibile
understanding [ʌndəˈstændɪŋ] *adj* comprensivo(-a) ■ *n* comprensione *f*; (*agreement*) accordo; **on the ~ that ...** a patto che *or* a condizione che ...; **to come to an ~ with sb** giungere ad un accordo con qn
understate [ʌndəˈsteɪt] *vt* minimizzare, sminuire
understatement [ʌndəˈsteɪtmənt] *n*: **that's an ~!** a dire poco!
understood [ʌndəˈstud] *pt, pp of* **understand** ■ *adj* inteso(-a); (*implied*) sottinteso(-a)
understudy [ˈʌndəstʌdɪ] *n* sostituto(-a), attore(-trice) supplente
undertake [ʌndəˈteɪk] *vt irreg* intraprendere; **to ~ to do sth** impegnarsi a fare qc
undertaker [ˈʌndəteɪkəʳ] *n* impresario di pompe funebri
undertaking [ʌndəˈteɪkɪŋ] *n* impresa; (*promise*) promessa
undertone [ˈʌndətəun] *n* (*low voice*) tono sommesso; (*of criticism etc*) vena, sottofondo; **in an ~** sottovoce
undervalue [ʌndəˈvælju:] *vt* svalutare, sottovalutare
underwater [ʌndəˈwɔ:təʳ] *adv* sott'acqua ■ *adj* subacqueo(-a)
underwear [ˈʌndəwɛəʳ] *n* biancheria (intima)
underweight [ʌndəˈweɪt] *adj* al di sotto del giusto peso; (*person*) sottopeso *inv*
underworld [ˈʌndəwə:ld] *n* (*of crime*) malavita
underwrite [ˈʌndəraɪt] *vt* (*Finance*) sottoscrivere; (*Insurance*) assicurare
underwriter [ˈʌndəraɪtəʳ] *n* sottoscrittore(-trice); assicuratore(-trice)
undeserving [ʌndɪˈzə:vɪŋ] *adj*: **to be ~ of** non meritare, non essere degno di
undesirable [ʌndɪˈzaɪərəbl] *adj* indesiderabile, sgradito(-a)
undeveloped [ʌndɪˈvɛləpt] *adj* (*land, resources*) non sfruttato(-a)
undies [ˈʌndɪz] *npl* (*col*) robina, biancheria intima da donna
undiluted [ʌndaɪˈlu:tɪd] *adj* non diluito(-a)
undiplomatic [ʌndɪpləˈmætɪk] *adj* poco diplomatico(-a)
undischarged [ˈʌndɪsˈtʃɑ:dʒd] *adj*: **~ bankrupt** fallito non riabilitato
undisciplined [ʌnˈdɪsɪplɪnd] *adj* indisciplinato(-a)
undisguised [ʌndɪsˈgaɪzd] *adj* (*dislike, amusement etc*) palese
undisputed [ʌndɪsˈpju:tɪd] *adj* indiscusso(-a)
undistinguished [ʌndɪsˈtɪŋgwɪʃt] *adj* mediocre, qualunque
undisturbed [ʌndɪsˈtə:bd] *adj* tranquillo(-a); **to leave sth ~** lasciare qc così com'è
undivided [ʌndɪˈvaɪdɪd] *adj*: **I want your ~ attention** esigo tutta la sua attenzione
undo [ʌnˈdu:] *vt irreg* disfare
undoing [ʌnˈdu:ɪŋ] *n* rovina, perdita
undone [ʌnˈdʌn] *pp of* **undo**; **to come ~** slacciarsi
undoubted [ʌnˈdautɪd] *adj* sicuro(-a), certo(-a)
undoubtedly [ʌnˈdautɪdlɪ] *adv* senza alcun dubbio

undress [ʌn'drɛs] *vi* spogliarsi
undrinkable [ʌn'drɪŋkəbl] *adj* (*unpalatable*) imbevibile; (*poisonous*) non potabile
undue [ʌn'dju:] *adj* eccessivo(-a)
undulating ['ʌndjuleɪtɪŋ] *adj* ondeggiante, ondulato(-a)
unduly [ʌn'dju:lɪ] *adv* eccessivamente
undying [ʌn'daɪɪŋ] *adj* imperituro(-a)
unearned [ʌn'ə:nd] *adj* (*praise, respect*) immeritato(-a); **~ income** rendita
unearth [ʌn'ə:θ] *vt* dissotterrare; (*fig*) scoprire
unearthly [ʌn'ə:θlɪ] *adj* soprannaturale; (*hour*) impossibile
uneasy [ʌn'i:zɪ] *adj* a disagio; (*worried*) preoccupato(-a); **to feel ~ about doing sth** non sentirsela di fare qc
uneconomic ['ʌni:kə'nɔmɪk], **uneconomical** ['ʌni:kə'nɔmɪkl] *adj* non economico(-a), antieconomico(-a)
uneducated [ʌn'ɛdjukeɪtɪd] *adj* senza istruzione, incolto(-a)
unemployed [ʌnɪm'plɔɪd] *adj* disoccupato(-a) ■ *npl*: **the ~** i disoccupati
unemployment [ʌnɪm'plɔɪmənt] *n* disoccupazione *f*
unemployment benefit, (US) **unemployment compensation** *n* sussidio di disoccupazione
unending [ʌn'ɛndɪŋ] *adj* senza fine
unenviable [ʌn'ɛnvɪəbl] *adj* poco invidiabile
unequal [ʌn'i:kwəl] *adj* (*length, objects*) disuguale; (*amounts*) diverso(-a); (*division of labour*) ineguale
unequalled, (US) **unequaled** [ʌn'i:kwəld] *adj* senza pari, insuperato(-a)
unequivocal [ʌnɪ'kwɪvəkəl] *adj* (*answer*) inequivocabile; (*person*) esplicito(-a), chiaro(-a).
unerring [ʌn'ə:rɪŋ] *adj* infallibile
UNESCO [ju:'nɛskəu] *n abbr* (= *United Nations Educational, Scientific and Cultural Organization*) U.N.E.S.C.O *f*
unethical [ʌn'ɛθɪkəl] *adj* (*methods*) poco ortodosso(-a), non moralmente accettabile; (*doctor's behaviour*) contrario(-a) all'etica professionale
uneven [ʌn'i:vn] *adj* ineguale; (*ground*) disuguale, accidentato(-a); (*heartbeat*) irregolare
uneventful [ʌnɪ'vɛntful] *adj* senza sorprese, tranquillo(-a)
unexceptional [ʌnɪk'sɛpʃənl] *adj* che non ha niente d'eccezionale
unexciting [ʌnɪk'saɪtɪŋ] *adj* (*news*) poco emozionante; (*film, evening*) poco interessante
unexpected [ʌnɪk'spɛktɪd] *adj* inatteso(-a), imprevisto(-a)
unexpectedly [ʌnɪk'spɛktɪdlɪ] *adv* inaspettatamente
unexplained [ʌnɪk'spleɪnd] *adj* inspiegato(-a)
unexploded [ʌnɪk'spləudɪd] *adj* inesploso(-a)
unfailing [ʌn'feɪlɪŋ] *adj* (*supply, energy*) inesauribile; (*remedy*) infallibile
unfair [ʌn'fɛə^r] *adj*: **~ (to)** ingiusto(-a) (nei confronti di); **it's ~ that ...** non è giusto che ... + *sub*
unfair dismissal *n* licenziamento ingiustificato
unfairly [ʌn'fɛəlɪ] *adv* ingiustamente
unfaithful [ʌn'feɪθful] *adj* infedele
unfamiliar [ʌnfə'mɪlɪə^r] *adj* sconosciuto(-a), strano(-a); **to be ~ with sth** non essere pratico di qc, non avere familiarità con qc
unfashionable [ʌn'fæʃnəbl] *adj* (*clothes*) fuori moda *inv*; (*district*) non alla moda
unfasten [ʌn'fɑ:sn] *vt* slacciare; sciogliere
unfathomable [ʌn'fæðəməbl] *adj* insondabile
unfavourable, (US) **unfavorable** [ʌn'feɪvərəbl] *adj* sfavorevole
unfavourably, (US) **unfavorably** [ʌn'feɪvərəblɪ] *adv*: **to look ~ upon** vedere di malocchio
unfeeling [ʌn'fi:lɪŋ] *adj* insensibile, duro(-a)
unfinished [ʌn'fɪnɪʃt] *adj* incompiuto(-a)
unfit [ʌn'fɪt] *adj* inadatto(-a); (*ill*) non in forma; (*incompetent*): **~ (for)** incompetente (in); (*: work, Mil*) inabile (a); **~ for habitation** inabitabile
unflagging [ʌn'flægɪŋ] *adj* instancabile
unflappable [ʌn'flæpəbl] *adj* calmo(-a), composto(-a)
unflattering [ʌn'flætərɪŋ] *adj* (*dress, hairstyle*) che non dona
unflinching [ʌn'flɪntʃɪŋ] *adj* che non indietreggia, risoluto(-a)
unfold [ʌn'fəuld] *vt* spiegare; (*fig*) rivelare ■ *vi* (*view*) distendersi; (*story*) svelarsi
unforeseeable ['ʌnfɔ:'si:əbl] *adj* imprevedibile
unforeseen [ʌnfɔ:'si:n] *adj* imprevisto(-a)
unforgettable [ʌnfə'gɛtəbl] *adj* indimenticabile
unforgivable [ʌnfə'gɪvəbl] *adj* imperdonabile
unformatted [ʌn'fɔ:mætɪd] *adj* (*disk, text*) non formattato(-a)
unfortunate [ʌn'fɔ:tʃnɪt] *adj* sfortunato(-a); (*event, remark*) infelice
unfortunately [ʌn'fɔ:tʃnɪtlɪ] *adv* sfortunatamente, purtroppo

unfounded [ʌn'faundɪd] *adj* infondato(-a)
unfriendly [ʌn'frɛndlɪ] *adj* poco amichevole, freddo(-a)
unfulfilled [ʌnful'fɪld] *adj* (*ambition*) non realizzato(-a); (*prophecy*) che non si è avverato(-a); (*desire*) insoddisfatto(-a); (*promise*) non mantenuto(-a); (*terms of contract*) non rispettato(-a); (*person*) frustrato(-a)
unfurl [ʌn'fəːl] *vt* spiegare
unfurnished [ʌn'fəːnɪʃt] *adj* non ammobiliato(-a)
ungainly [ʌn'geɪnlɪ] *adj* goffo(-a), impacciato(-a)
ungodly [ʌn'gɔdlɪ] *adj* empio(-a); **at an ~ hour** a un'ora impossibile
ungrateful [ʌn'greɪtful] *adj* ingrato(-a)
unguarded [ʌn'gɑːdɪd] *adj*: **in an ~ moment** in un momento di distrazione
unhappily [ʌn'hæpɪlɪ] *adv* (*unfortunately*) purtroppo, sfortunatamente
unhappiness [ʌn'hæpɪnɪs] *n* infelicità
unhappy [ʌn'hæpɪ] *adj* infelice; **~ with** (*arrangements etc*) insoddisfatto(-a) di
unharmed [ʌn'hɑːmd] *adj* incolume, sano(-a) e salvo(-a)
UNHCR *n abbr* (= *United Nations High Commission for Refugees*) Alto Commissariato delle Nazioni Unite per Rifugiati
unhealthy [ʌn'hɛlθɪ] *adj* (*gen*) malsano(-a); (*person*) malaticcio(-a)
unheard-of [ʌn'həːdɔv] *adj* inaudito(-a), senza precedenti
unhelpful [ʌn'hɛlpful] *adj* poco disponibile
unhesitating [ʌn'hɛzɪteɪtɪŋ] *adj* (*loyalty*) che non vacilla; (*reply, offer*) pronto(-a), immediato(-a)
unholy [ʌn'həulɪ] *adj*: **an ~ alliance** un'alleanza nefasta; **he returned at an ~ hour** è tornato ad un'ora indecente
unhook [ʌn'huk] *vt* sganciare; sfibbiare
unhurt [ʌn'həːt] *adj* incolume, sano(-a) e salvo(-a)
unhygienic [ʌnhaɪ'dʒiːnɪk] *adj* non igienico(-a)
UNICEF ['juːnɪsɛf] *n abbr* (= *United Nations International Children's Emergency Fund*) U.N.I.C.E.F. *m*
unicorn ['juːnɪkɔːn] *n* unicorno
unidentified [ʌnaɪ'dɛntɪfaɪd] *adj* non identificato(-a)
uniform ['juːnɪfɔːm] *n* uniforme *f*, divisa ■ *adj* uniforme
uniformity [juːnɪ'fɔːmɪtɪ] *n* uniformità
unify ['juːnɪfaɪ] *vt* unificare
unilateral [juːnɪ'lætərəl] *adj* unilaterale
unimaginable [ʌnɪ'mædʒɪnəbl] *adj* inimmaginabile, inconcepibile
unimaginative [ʌnɪ'mædʒɪnətɪv] *adj* privo(-a) di fantasia, a corto di idee
unimpaired [ʌnɪm'pɛəd] *adj* intatto(-a), non danneggiato(-a)
unimportant [ʌnɪm'pɔːtənt] *adj* senza importanza, di scarsa importanza
unimpressed [ʌnɪm'prɛst] *adj* niente affatto impressionato(-a)
uninhabited [ʌnɪn'hæbɪtɪd] *adj* disabitato(-a)
uninhibited [ʌnɪn'hɪbɪtɪd] *adj* senza inibizioni; senza ritegno
uninjured [ʌn'ɪndʒəd] *adj* incolume
uninspiring [ʌnɪn'spaɪərɪŋ] *adj* banale
uninstall [ʌnɪn'stɔːl] *vt* (*Comput*) disinstallare
unintelligent [ʌnɪn'tɛlɪdʒənt] *adj* poco intelligente
unintentional [ʌnɪn'tɛnʃənəl] *adj* involontario(-a)
unintentionally [ʌnɪn'tɛnʃnəlɪ] *adv* senza volerlo, involontariamente
uninvited [ʌnɪn'vaɪtɪd] *adj* non invitato(-a)
uninviting [ʌnɪn'vaɪtɪŋ] *adj* (*place, food*) non invitante, poco invitante; (*offer*) poco allettante
union ['juːnjən] *n* unione *f*; (*also*: **trade union**) sindacato ■ *cpd* sindacale; **the U~** (*US*) gli stati dell'Unione
unionize ['juːnjənaɪz] *vt* sindacalizzare, organizzare in sindacato
Union Jack *n bandiera nazionale britannica*
Union of Soviet Socialist Republics *n* (*Hist*) Unione *f* delle Repubbliche Socialiste Sovietiche
union shop *n stabilimento in cui tutti gli operai sono tenuti ad aderire ad un sindacato*
unique [juː'niːk] *adj* unico(-a)
unisex ['juːnɪsɛks] *adj* unisex *inv*
Unison ['juːnɪsn] *n* (*trade union*) *sindacato generale dei funzionari*
unison ['juːnɪsn] *n*: **in ~** all'unisono
unit ['juːnɪt] *n* unità *f inv*; (*section*: *of furniture etc*) elemento; (*team, squad*) reparto, squadra; **production ~** reparto *m*, produzione *inv*; **sink ~** blocco *m* lavello *inv*
unit cost *n* costo unitario
unite [juː'naɪt] *vt* unire ■ *vi* unirsi
united [juː'naɪtɪd] *adj* unito(-a); (*efforts*) congiunto(-a)
United Arab Emirates *npl* Emirati *mpl* Arabi Uniti
United Kingdom *n* Regno Unito
United Nations, United Nations Organization *n* (Organizzazione *f* delle) Nazioni Unite
United States, United States of America *n* Stati *mpl* Uniti (d'America)

unit price *n* prezzo unitario
unit trust *n* (*Brit Comm*) fondo d'investimento
unity ['ju:nɪtɪ] *n* unità
Univ. *abbr* = **university**
universal [ju:nɪ'və:sl] *adj* universale
universe ['ju:nɪvə:s] *n* universo
university [ju:nɪ'və:sɪtɪ] *n* università *f inv*
▪ *cpd* (*student, professor, education*) universitario(-a); (*year*) accademico(-a)
university degree *n* laurea
unjust [ʌn'dʒʌst] *adj* ingiusto(-a)
unjustifiable ['ʌndʒʌstɪ'faɪəbl] *adj* ingiustificabile
unjustified [ʌn'dʒʌstɪfaɪd] *adj* ingiustificato(-a); (*Typ*) non allineato(-a)
unkempt [ʌn'kɛmpt] *adj* trasandato(-a); spettinato(-a)
unkind [ʌn'kaɪnd] *adj* poco gentile, villano(-a)
unkindly [ʌn'kaɪndlɪ] *adv* (*speak*) in modo sgarbato; (*treat*) male
unknown [ʌn'nəun] *adj* sconosciuto(-a); **~ to me ...** a mia insaputa ...; **~ quantity** (*Math: fig*) incognita
unladen [ʌn'leɪdn] *adj* (*ship, weight*) a vuoto
unlawful [ʌn'lɔ:ful] *adj* illecito(-a), illegale
unleaded ['ʌn'lɛdɪd] *adj* senza piombo; **~ petrol** benzina verde *or* senza piombo
unleash [ʌn'li:ʃ] *vt* sguinzagliare; (*fig*) scatenare
unleavened [ʌn'lɛvnd] *adj* non lievitato(-a), azzimo(-a)
unless [ʌn'lɛs] *conj* a meno che (non) + *sub*; **~ otherwise stated** salvo indicazione contraria; **~ I am mistaken** se non mi sbaglio
unlicensed [ʌn'laɪsənst] *adj* (*Brit*) senza licenza per la vendita di alcolici
unlike [ʌn'laɪk] *adj* diverso(-a) ▪ *prep* a differenza di, contrariamente a
unlikelihood [ʌn'laɪklɪhud] *n* improbabilità
unlikely [ʌn'laɪklɪ] *adj* improbabile; (*explanation*) inverosimile
unlimited [ʌn'lɪmɪtɪd] *adj* illimitato(-a)
unlisted [ʌn'lɪstɪd] *adj* (*US Tel*): **to be ~** non essere sull'elenco; (*Stock Exchange*) non quotato(-a)
unlit [ʌn'lɪt] *adj* (*room*) senza luce; (*road*) non illuminato(-a)
unload [ʌn'ləud] *vt* scaricare
unlock [ʌn'lɔk] *vt* aprire
unlucky [ʌn'lʌkɪ] *adj* sfortunato(-a); (*object, number*) che porta sfortuna, di malaugurio; **to be ~** (*person*) essere sfortunato, non avere fortuna
unmanageable [ʌn'mænɪdʒəbl] *adj* (*tool, vehicle*) poco maneggevole; (*situation*) impossibile
unmanned [ʌn'mænd] *adj* (*spacecraft*) senza equipaggio
unmannerly [ʌn'mænəlɪ] *adj* maleducato(-a)
unmarked [ʌn'mɑ:kt] *adj* (*unstained*) pulito(-a), senza macchie; **~ police car** civetta della polizia
unmarried [ʌn'mærɪd] *adj* non sposato(-a); (*man only*) scapolo, celibe; (*woman only*) nubile
unmarried mother *n* ragazza *f* madre *inv*
unmask [ʌn'mɑ:sk] *vt* smascherare
unmatched [ʌn'mætʃt] *adj* senza uguali
unmentionable [ʌn'mɛnʃnəbl] *adj* (*vice, topic*) innominabile; (*word*) irripetibile
unmerciful [ʌn'mə:sɪful] *adj* spietato(-a)
unmistakable [ʌnmɪs'teɪkəbl] *adj* indubbio(-a), facilmente riconoscibile
unmitigated [ʌn'mɪtɪgeɪtɪd] *adj* (*disaster etc*) totale, assoluto(-a)
unnamed [ʌn'neɪmd] *adj* (*nameless*) senza nome; (*anonymous*) anonimo(-a)
unnatural [ʌn'nætʃrəl] *adj* innaturale; contro natura
unnecessary [ʌn'nɛsəsərɪ] *adj* inutile, superfluo(-a)
unnerve [ʌn'nə:v] *vt* (*accident*) sgomentare; (*hostile attitude*) bloccare; (*long wait, interview*) snervare
unnoticed [ʌn'nəutɪst] *adj*: **to go** *or* **pass ~** passare inosservato(-a)
UNO ['ju:nəu] *n abbr* = **United Nations Organization**
unobservant [ʌnəb'zə:vənt] *adj*: **to be ~** non avere spirito di osservazione
unobtainable [ʌnəb'teɪnəbl] *adj* (*Tel*) non ottenibile
unobtrusive [ʌnəb'tru:sɪv] *adj* discreto(-a)
unoccupied [ʌn'ɔkjupaɪd] *adj* (*house*) vuoto(-a); (*seat, Mil: zone*) libero(-a), non occupato(-a)
unofficial [ʌnə'fɪʃl] *adj* non ufficiale; (*strike*) non dichiarato(-a) dal sindacato
unopened [ʌn'əupənd] *adj* (*letter*) non aperto(-a); (*present*) ancora incartato(-a)
unopposed [ʌnə'pəuzd] *adj* senza incontrare opposizione
unorthodox [ʌn'ɔ:θədɔks] *adj* non ortodosso(-a)
unpack [ʌn'pæk] *vi* disfare la valigia (*or* le valigie)
unpaid [ʌn'peɪd] *adj* (*holiday*) non pagato(-a); (*work*) non retribuito(-a); (*bill, debt*) da pagare
unpalatable [ʌn'pælətəbl] *adj* (*food*) immangiabile; (*drink*) imbevibile; (*truth*) sgradevole
unparalleled [ʌn'pærəlɛld] *adj* incomparabile, impareggiabile

U

unpatriotic ['ʌnpætrɪ'ɔtɪk] *adj* (*person*) poco patriottico(-a); (*speech, attitude*) antipatriottico(-a)
unplanned [ʌn'plænd] *adj* (*visit*) imprevisto(-a); (*baby*) non previsto(-a)
unpleasant [ʌn'plɛznt] *adj* spiacevole; (*person, remark*) antipatico(-a); (*day, experience*) brutto(-a)
unplug [ʌn'plʌg] *vt* staccare
unpolluted [ʌnpə'lu:tɪd] *adj* non inquinato(-a)
unpopular [ʌn'pɔpjulə^r] *adj* impopolare; **to make o.s. ~ (with)** rendersi antipatico (a); (*politician etc*) alienarsi le simpatie (di)
unprecedented [ʌn'prɛsɪdəntɪd] *adj* senza precedenti
unpredictable [ʌnprɪ'dɪktəbl] *adj* imprevedibile
unprejudiced [ʌn'prɛdʒudɪst] *adj* (*not biased*) obiettivo(-a), imparziale; (*having no prejudices*) senza pregiudizi
unprepared [ʌnprɪ'pɛəd] *adj* (*person*) impreparato(-a); (*speech*) improvvisato(-a)
unprepossessing [ʌnpri:pə'zɛsɪŋ] *adj* insulso(-a)
unpretentious [ʌnprɪ'tɛnʃəs] *adj* senza pretese
unprincipled [ʌn'prɪnsɪpld] *adj* senza scrupoli
unproductive [ʌnprə'dʌktɪv] *adj* improduttivo(-a); (*discussion*) sterile
unprofessional ['ʌnprə'fɛʃənl] *adj*: **~ conduct** scorrettezza professionale
unprofitable [ʌn'prɔfɪtəbl] *adj* (*financially*) non redditizio(-a); (*job, deal*) poco lucrativo(-a)
UNPROFOR ['ʌnprəfɔ:^r] *n abbr* (= *United Nations Protection Force*) reparto di protezione dell'ONU
unprotected ['ʌnprə'tɛktɪd] *adj* (*sex*) non protetto(-a)
unprovoked [ʌnprə'vəukt] *adj* non provocato(-a)
unpunished [ʌn'pʌnɪʃt] *adj*: **to go ~** restare impunito(-a)
unqualified [ʌn'kwɔlɪfaɪd] *adj* (*worker*) non qualificato(-a); (*in professions*) non abilitato(-a); (*success*) assoluto(-a), senza riserve
unquestionably [ʌn'kwɛstʃənəblɪ] *adv* indiscutibilmente
unquestioning [ʌn'kwɛstʃənɪŋ] *adj* (*obedience, acceptance*) cieco(-a)
unravel [ʌn'rævl] *vt* dipanare, districare
unreal [ʌn'rɪəl] *adj* irreale
unrealistic [ʌnrɪə'lɪstɪk] *adj* (*idea*) illusorio(-a); (*estimate*) non realistico(-a)
unreasonable [ʌn'ri:znəbl] *adj* irragionevole; **to make ~ demands on sb** voler troppo da qn
unrecognizable [ʌn'rɛkəgnaɪzəbl] *adj* irriconoscibile
unrecognized [ʌn'rɛkəgnaɪzd] *adj* (*talent, genius*) misconosciuto(-a); (*Pol: regime*) non ufficialmente riconosciuto(-a)
unrecorded [ʌnrɪ'kɔ:dɪd] *adj* non documentato(-a), non registrato(-a)
unrefined [ʌnrɪ'faɪnd] *adj* (*sugar, petroleum*) greggio(-a); (*person*) rozzo(-a)
unrehearsed [ʌnrɪ'hə:st] *adj* (*Theat etc*) improvvisato(-a); (*spontaneous*) imprevisto(-a)
unrelated [ʌnrɪ'leɪtɪd] *adj*: **~ (to)** senza rapporto (con); (*by family*) non imparentato(-a) (con)
unrelenting [ʌnrɪ'lɛntɪŋ] *adj* implacabile; accanito(-a)
unreliable [ʌnrɪ'laɪəbl] *adj* (*person, machine*) che non dà affidamento; (*news, source of information*) inattendibile
unrelieved [ʌnrɪ'li:vd] *adj* (*monotony*) uniforme
unremitting [ʌnrɪ'mɪtɪŋ] *adj* incessante, infaticabile
unrepeatable [ʌnrɪ'pi:təbl] *adj* (*offer*) unico(-a)
unrepentant [ʌnrɪ'pɛntənt] *adj* impenitente
unrepresentative [ʌnrɛprɪ'zɛntətɪv] *adj* atipico(-a), poco rappresentativo(-a)
unreserved [ʌnrɪ'zə:vd] *adj* (*seat*) non prenotato(-a), non riservato(-a); (*approval, admiration*) senza riserve
unresponsive [ʌnrɪs'pɔnsɪv] *adj* che non reagisce
unrest [ʌn'rɛst] *n* agitazione *f*
unrestricted [ʌnrɪ'strɪktɪd] *adj* (*power, time*) illimitato(-a); (*access*) libero(-a)
unrewarded [ʌnrɪ'wɔ:dɪd] *adj* non ricompensato(-a)
unripe [ʌn'raɪp] *adj* acerbo(-a)
unrivalled, (US) **unrivaled** [ʌn'raɪvəld] *adj* senza pari
unroll [ʌn'rəul] *vt* srotolare
unruffled [ʌn'rʌfld] *adj* (*person*) calmo(-a) e tranquillo(-a), imperturbato(-a); (*hair*) a posto
unruly [ʌn'ru:lɪ] *adj* indisciplinato(-a)
unsafe [ʌn'seɪf] *adj* pericoloso(-a), rischioso(-a); **~ to drink** non potabile; **~ to eat** non commestibile
unsaid [ʌn'sɛd] *adj*: **to leave sth ~** passare qc sotto silenzio
unsaleable, (US) **unsalable** [ʌn'seɪləbl] *adj* invendibile

unsatisfactory ['ʌnsætɪs'fæktərɪ] *adj* che lascia a desiderare, insufficiente
unsavoury, (*US*) **unsavory** [ʌn'seɪvərɪ] *adj* (*fig: person*) losco(-a); (*: reputation, subject*) disgustoso(-a), ripugnante
unscathed [ʌn'skeɪðd] *adj* incolume
unscientific ['ʌnsaɪən'tɪfɪk] *adj* poco scientifico(-a)
unscrew [ʌn'skru:] *vt* svitare
unscrupulous [ʌn'skru:pjuləs] *adj* senza scrupoli
unseat [ʌn'si:t] *vt* (*rider*) disarcionare; (*fig: an official*) spodestare
unsecured [ʌnsɪ'kjuəd] *adj*: **~ creditor** creditore *m* chirografario
unseeded [ʌn'si:dɪd] *adj* (*Sport*) che non è una testa di serie
unseemly [ʌn'si:mlɪ] *adj* sconveniente
unseen [ʌn'si:n] *adj* (*person*) inosservato(-a); (*danger*) nascosto(-a)
unselfish [ʌn'sɛlfɪʃ] *adj* (*person*) altruista; (*act*) disinteressato(-a)
unsettled [ʌn'sɛtld] *adj* (*person, future*) incerto(-a); (*question*) non risolto(-a); (*weather, market*) instabile; **to feel ~** sentirsi disorientato(-a)
unsettling [ʌn'sɛtlɪŋ] *adj* inquietante
unshakable, unshakeable [ʌn'ʃeɪkəbl] *adj* irremovibile
unshaven [ʌn'ʃeɪvn] *adj* non rasato(-a)
unsightly [ʌn'saɪtlɪ] *adj* brutto(-a), sgradevole a vedersi
unskilled [ʌn'skɪld] *adj*: **~ worker** manovale *m*
unsociable [ʌn'səuʃəbl] *adj* (*person*) poco socievole; (*behaviour*) antipatico(-a)
unsocial [ʌn'səuʃəl] *adj*: **~ hours** orario sconveniente
unsold [ʌn'səuld] *adj* invenduto(-a)
unsolicited [ʌnsə'lɪsɪtɪd] *adj* non richiesto(-a)
unsophisticated [ʌnsə'fɪstɪkeɪtɪd] *adj* semplice, naturale
unsound [ʌn'saund] *adj* (*health*) debole, cagionevole; (*in construction: floor, foundations*) debole, malsicuro(-a); (*policy, advice*) poco sensato(-a); (*judgment, investment*) poco sicuro(-a)
unspeakable [ʌn'spi:kəbl] *adj* (*bad*) abominevole
unspoken [ʌn'spəukən] *adj* (*words*) non detto(-a); (*agreement, approval*) tacito(-a)
unsteady [ʌn'stɛdɪ] *adj* instabile, malsicuro(-a)
unstinting [ʌn'stɪntɪŋ] *adj* (*support*) incondizionato(-a); (*generosity*) illimitato(-a); (*praise*) senza riserve
unstuck [ʌn'stʌk] *adj*: **to come ~** scollarsi; (*fig*) fare fiasco
unsubscribe [ʌnsʌb'skraɪb] *vi* (*Comput*) disdire l'abbonamento
unsubstantiated [ʌnsəb'stænʃɪeɪtɪd] *adj* (*rumour, accusation*) infondato(-a)
unsuccessful [ʌnsək'sɛsful] *adj* (*writer, proposal*) che non ha successo; (*marriage, attempt*) mal riuscito(-a), fallito(-a); **to be ~** (*in attempting sth*) non riuscire; non avere successo; (*application*) non essere considerato(-a)
unsuccessfully [ʌnsək'sɛsfəlɪ] *adv* senza successo
unsuitable [ʌn'su:təbl] *adj* inadatto(-a); (*moment*) inopportuno(-a)
unsuited [ʌn'su:tɪd] *adj*: **to be ~ for** *or* **to** non essere fatto(-a) per
unsung ['ʌn'sʌŋ] *adj*: **an ~ hero** un eroe misconosciuto
unsupported [ʌnsə'pɔ:tɪd] *adj* (*claim*) senza fondamento; (*theory*) non dimostrato(-a)
unsure [ʌn'ʃuə^r] *adj*: **~ (of** *or* **about)** incerto(-a) (su); **to be ~ of o.s.** essere insicuro(-a)
unsuspecting [ʌnsə'spɛktɪŋ] *adj* che non sospetta niente
unsweetened [ʌn'swi:tnd] *adj* senza zucchero
unswerving [ʌn'swə:vɪŋ] *adj* fermo(-a)
unsympathetic ['ʌnsɪmpə'θɛtɪk] *adj* (*attitude*) poco incoraggiante; (*person*) antipatico(-a); **~ (to)** non solidale (verso)
untangle [ʌn'tæŋgl] *vt* sbrogliare
untapped [ʌn'tæpt] *adj* (*resources*) non sfruttato(-a)
untaxed [ʌn'tækst] *adj* (*goods*) esente da imposte; (*income*) non imponibile
unthinkable [ʌn'θɪŋkəbl] *adj* impensabile, inconcepibile
unthinkingly ['ʌn'θɪŋkɪŋlɪ] *adv* senza pensare
untidy [ʌn'taɪdɪ] *adj* (*room*) in disordine; (*appearance, work*) trascurato(-a); (*person, writing*) disordinato(-a)
untie [ʌn'taɪ] *vt* (*knot, parcel*) disfare; (*prisoner, dog*) slegare
until [ʌn'tɪl] *prep* fino a; (*after negative*) prima di ■ *conj* finché, fino a quando; (*in past, after negative*) prima che + *sub*, prima di + *infinitive*; **~ now** finora; **~ then** fino ad allora; **from morning ~ night** dalla mattina alla sera
untimely [ʌn'taɪmlɪ] *adj* intempestivo(-a), inopportuno(-a); (*death*) prematuro(-a)
untold [ʌn'təuld] *adj* incalcolabile; indescrivibile

untouched [ʌn'tʌtʃt] *adj* *(not used etc)* non toccato(-a), intatto(-a); *(safe: person)* incolume; *(unaffected)*: ~ **by** insensibile a
untoward [ʌntə'wɔ:d] *adj* sfortunato(-a), sconveniente
untrained ['ʌn'treɪnd] *adj* *(worker)* privo(-a) di formazione professionale; *(troops)* privo(-a) di addestramento; **to the ~ eye** ad un occhio inesperto
untrammelled [ʌn'træmld] *adj* illimitato(-a)
untranslatable [ʌntrænz'leɪtəbl] *adj* intraducibile
untrue [ʌn'tru:] *adj* *(statement)* falso(-a), non vero(-a)
untrustworthy [ʌn'trʌstwə:ðɪ] *adj* di cui non ci si può fidare
unusable [ʌn'ju:zəbl] *adj* inservibile, inutilizzabile
unused[1] [ʌn'ju:zd] *adj* *(new)* nuovo(-a); *(not made use of)* non usato(-a), non utilizzato(-a)
unused[2] [ʌn'ju:st] *adj*: **to be ~ to sth/to doing sth** non essere abituato(-a) a qc/a fare qc
unusual [ʌn'ju:ʒuəl] *adj* insolito(-a), eccezionale raro(-a)
unusually [ʌn'ju:ʒuəlɪ] *adv* insolitamente
unveil [ʌn'veɪl] *vt* scoprire, svelare
unwanted [ʌn'wɔntɪd] *adj* non desiderato(-a)
unwarranted [ʌn'wɔrəntɪd] *adj* ingiustificato(-a)
unwary [ʌn'wɛərɪ] *adj* incauto(-a)
unwavering [ʌn'weɪvərɪŋ] *adj* fermo(-a), incrollabile
unwelcome [ʌn'wɛlkəm] *adj* *(gen)* non gradito(-a); **to feel ~** sentire che la propria presenza non è gradita
unwell [ʌn'wɛl] *adj* indisposto(-a); **to feel ~** non sentirsi bene
unwieldy [ʌn'wi:ldɪ] *adj* poco maneggevole
unwilling [ʌn'wɪlɪŋ] *adj*: **to be ~ to do** non voler fare
unwillingly [ʌn'wɪlɪŋlɪ] *adv* malvolentieri
unwind [ʌn'waɪnd] *vb* *(irreg)* *vt* svolgere, srotolare ■ *vi* *(relax)* rilassarsi
unwise [ʌn'waɪz] *adj* *(decision, act)* avventato(-a)
unwitting [ʌn'wɪtɪŋ] *adj* involontario(-a)
unworkable [ʌn'wə:kəbl] *adj* *(plan etc)* inattuabile
unworthy [ʌn'wə:ðɪ] *adj* indegno(-a); **to be ~ of sth/to do sth** non essere degno di qc/di fare qc
unwrap [ʌn'ræp] *vt* disfare; *(present)* aprire
unwritten [ʌn'rɪtn] *adj* *(agreement)* tacito(-a)
unzip [ʌn'zɪp] *vt* aprire (la chiusura lampo di); *(Comput)* dezippare

 KEYWORD

up [ʌp] *prep* su; **he went up the stairs/the hill** è salito su per le scale/sulla collina; **the cat was up a tree** il gatto era su un albero; **they live further up the street** vivono un po' più su nella stessa strada
■ *adv* **1** *(upwards, higher)* su, in alto; **up in the sky/the mountains** su nel cielo/in montagna; **up there** lassù; **up above** su in alto; **up with Leeds United!** viva il Leeds United!
2: **to be up** *(out of bed)* essere alzato(-a); *(prices, level)* essere salito(-a); *(building)* essere terminato(-a); *(tent)* essere piantato(-a); *(curtains, shutters, wallpaper)* essere su; **"this side up"** "alto"; **to be up (by)** *(in price, value)* essere salito(-a) *or* aumentato(-a) (di); **when the year was up** *(finished)* finito l'anno; **time's up** il tempo è scaduto; **he's well up in** *or* **on politics** *(Brit)* è molto informato di *or* sulla politica
3: **up to** *(as far as)* fino a; **up to now** finora
4: **to be up to** *(depending on)*: **it's up to you** sta a lei, dipende da lei; *(equal to)*: **he's not up to it** *(job, task etc)* non ne è all'altezza; *(col: be doing)*: **what is he up to?** cosa sta combinando?; **what's up?** *(col: wrong)* che c'è?; **what's up with him?** che ha?, che gli prende?
■ *n*: **ups and downs** alti e bassi *mpl*
■ *vi* *(col)*: **she upped and left** improvvisamente se ne andò

up-and-coming ['ʌpənd'kʌmɪŋ] *adj* pieno(-a) di promesse, promettente
upbeat ['ʌpbi:t] *n* *(Mus)* tempo in levare; *(in economy, prosperity)* incremento ■ *adj* *(col)* ottimistico(-a)
upbraid [ʌp'breɪd] *vt* rimproverare
upbringing ['ʌpbrɪŋɪŋ] *n* educazione *f*
upcoming ['ʌpkʌmɪŋ] *adj* imminente, prossimo(-a)
update [ʌp'deɪt] *vt* aggiornare
upend [ʌp'ɛnd] *vt* rovesciare
upfront [ʌp'frʌnt] *adj* *(col)* franco(-a), aperto(-a) ■ *adv* *(pay)* subito
upgrade [ʌp'greɪd] *vt* promuovere; *(job)* rivalutare; *(Comput)* far passare a potenza superiore
upheaval [ʌp'hi:vl] *n* sconvolgimento; tumulto
uphill [ʌp'hɪl] *adj* in salita; *(fig: task)* difficile ■ *adv*: **to go ~** andare in salita, salire
uphold [ʌp'həuld] *vt irreg* approvare; sostenere
upholstery [ʌp'həulstərɪ] *n* tappezzeria

upkeep ['ʌpki:p] *n* manutenzione *f*
up-market [ʌp'mɑ:kɪt] *adj* (*product*) che si rivolge ad una fascia di mercato superiore
upon [ə'pɔn] *prep* su
upper ['ʌpə^r] *adj* superiore ■ *n* (*of shoe*) tomaia; **the ~ class** ≈ l'alta borghesia
upper case *n* maiuscolo
upper-class [ʌpə'klɑ:s] *adj* dell'alta borghesia; (*district*) signorile; (*accent*) aristocratico(-a); (*attitude*) snob *inv*
uppercut ['ʌpəkʌt] *n* uppercut *m inv*, montante *m*
upper hand *n*: **to have the ~** avere il coltello dalla parte del manico
Upper House *n*: **the ~** (*in Britain*) la Camera Alta, la Camera dei Lords; (*in US etc*) il Senato
uppermost ['ʌpəməust] *adj* il(la) più alto(-a); predominante; **it was ~ in my mind** è stata la mia prima preoccupazione
Upper Volta [-'vɔltə] *n* Alto Volta *m*
upright ['ʌpraɪt] *adj* diritto(-a); verticale; (*fig*) diritto(-a), onesto(-a) ■ *n* montante *m*
uprising ['ʌpraɪzɪŋ] *n* insurrezione *f*, rivolta
uproar ['ʌprɔ:^r] *n* tumulto, clamore *m*
uproarious [ʌp'rɔ:rɪəs] *adj* clamoroso(-a); (*hilarious*) esilarante; **~ laughter** risata sonora
uproot [ʌp'ru:t] *vt* sradicare
upset *n* ['ʌpsɛt] turbamento ■ *vt* [ʌp'sɛt] (*irreg: like* **set**) (*glass etc*) rovesciare; (*plan, stomach*) scombussolare; (*person: offend*) contrariare; (*: grieve*) addolorare; sconvolgere ■ *adj* [ʌp'sɛt] contrariato(-a); addolorato(-a); (*stomach*) scombussolato(-a), disturbato(-a); **to have a stomach ~** (*Brit*) avere lo stomaco in disordine *or* scombussolato; **to get ~** contrariarsi; addolorarsi
upset price *n* (*US, Scottish*) prezzo di riserva
upsetting [ʌp'sɛtɪŋ] *adj* (*saddening*) sconvolgente; (*offending*) offensivo(-a); (*annoying*) fastidioso(-a)
upshot ['ʌpʃɔt] *n* risultato; **the ~ of it all was that ...** la conclusione è stata che ...
upside down ['ʌpsaɪd-] *adv* sottosopra; **to turn ~** capovolgere; (*fig*) mettere sottosopra
upstage ['ʌp'steɪdʒ] *vt*: **to ~ sb** rubare la scena a qn
upstairs [ʌp'stɛəz] *adv, adj* di sopra, al piano superiore ■ *n* piano di sopra
upstart ['ʌpstɑ:t] *n* parvenu *m inv*
upstream [ʌp'stri:m] *adv* a monte
upsurge ['ʌpsə:dʒ] *n* (*of enthusiasm etc*) ondata
uptake ['ʌpteɪk] *n*: **he is quick/slow on the ~** è pronto/lento di comprendonio
uptight [ʌp'taɪt] *adj* (*col*) teso(-a)
up-to-date ['ʌptə'deɪt] *adj* moderno(-a); aggiornato(-a)
upturn ['ʌptə:n] *n* (*in luck*) svolta favorevole; (*in value of currency*) rialzo
upturned ['ʌptə:nd] *adj* (*nose*) all'insù
upward ['ʌpwəd] *adj* ascendente; verso l'alto ■ *adv* in su, verso l'alto
upwardly-mobile ['ʌpwədlɪ'məubaɪl] *n*: **to be ~** salire nella scala sociale
upwards ['ʌpwədz] *adv* in su, verso l'alto
URA *n abbr* (*US: = Urban Renewal Administration*) *amministrazione per il rinnovamento urbano*
Ural Mountains ['juərəl-] *npl*: **the ~** (*also*: **the Urals**) gli Urali, i Monti Urali
uranium [juə'reɪnɪəm] *n* uranio
Uranus [juə'reɪnəs] *n* (*planet*) Urano
urban ['ə:bən] *adj* urbano(-a)
urbane [ə:'beɪn] *adj* civile, urbano(-a), educato(-a)
urbanization [ə:bənaɪ'zeɪʃən] *n* urbanizzazione *f*
urchin ['ə:tʃɪn] *n* monello; **sea ~** riccio di mare
Urdu ['uədu:] *n* urdu *m inv*
urge [ə:dʒ] *n* impulso, stimolo ■ *vt* (*caution etc*) raccomandare vivamente; **to ~ sb to do** esortare qn a fare, spingere qn a fare; raccomandare a qn di fare
▸ **urge on** *vt* spronare
urgency ['ə:dʒənsɪ] *n* urgenza; (*of tone*) insistenza
urgent ['ə:dʒənt] *adj* urgente; (*earnest, persistent: plea*) pressante; (*: tone*) insistente, incalzante
urgently ['ə:dʒəntlɪ] *adv* d'urgenza, urgentemente; con insistenza
urinal ['juərɪnl] *n* (*Brit: building*) vespasiano; (*: vessel*) orinale *m*, pappagallo
urinate ['juərɪneɪt] *vi* orinare
urine ['juərɪn] *n* orina
URL *n abbr* (*= uniform resource locator*) URL *m inv*
urn [ə:n] *n* urna; (*also*: **tea urn**) bollitore *m* per il tè
Uruguay ['juərəgwaɪ] *n* Uruguay *m*
Uruguayan [juərə'gwaɪən] *adj, n* uruguaiano(-a)
US *n abbr* = **United States**
us [ʌs] *pron* ci; (*stressed, after prep*) noi
USA *n abbr* (*Geo*) = **United States of America**; (*Mil*) = **United States Army**
usable ['ju:zəbl] *adj* utilizzabile, usabile
USAF *n abbr* = **United States Air Force**
usage ['ju:zɪdʒ] *n* uso
USCG *n abbr* = **United States Coast Guard**
USDA *n abbr* = **United States Department of Agriculture**
USDAW ['ʌzdɔ:] *n abbr* (*Brit: = Union of Shop, Distributive and Allied Workers*) *sindacato dei dipendenti di negozi, reti di distribuzione e simili*

u

USDI *n abbr* = **United States Department of the Interior**
use *n* [ju:s] uso; impiego, utilizzazione *f* ■ *vt* [ju:z] usare, utilizzare, servirsi di; **she used to do it** lo faceva (una volta), era solita farlo; **in ~** in uso; **out of ~** fuori uso; **to be of ~** essere utile, servire; **to make ~ of sth** far uso di qc, utilizzare qc; **ready for ~** pronto per l'uso; **it's no ~** non serve, è inutile; **to have the ~ of** poter usare; **what's this used for?** a che serve?; **to be used to** avere l'abitudine di; **to get used to** abituarsi a, fare l'abitudine a ▸ **use up** *vt* finire; (*supplies*) dare fondo a; (*left-overs*) utilizzare
used [ju:zd] *adj* (*car*) d'occasione
useful ['ju:sful] *adj* utile; **to come in ~** fare comodo, tornare utile
usefulness ['ju:sfəlnɪs] *n* utilità
useless ['ju:slɪs] *adj* inutile; (*unusable: object*) inservibile
user ['ju:zəʳ] *n* utente *m/f*; (*of petrol, gas etc*) consumatore(-trice)
user-friendly ['ju:zə'frɛndlɪ] *adj* orientato(-a) all'utente
USES *n abbr* = **United States Employment Service**
usher ['ʌʃəʳ] *n* usciere *m*; (*in cinema*) maschera ■ *vt*: **to ~ sb in** far entrare qn
usherette [ʌʃə'rɛt] *n* (*in cinema*) maschera
USIA *n abbr* = **United States Information Agency**
USM *n abbr* = **United States Mint; United States Mail**
USN *n abbr* = **United States Navy**
USP *n abbr* = **unique selling point** *or* **proposition**
USPHS *n abbr* = **United States Public Health Service**
USPO *n abbr* = **United States Post Office**
USS *abbr* = **United States Ship (***or* **Steamer)**
USSR *n abbr* (*Hist*) = **Union of Soviet Socialist Republics**
usu. *abbr* = **usually**
usual ['ju:ʒuəl] *adj* solito(-a); **as ~** come al solito, come d'abitudine
usually ['ju:ʒuəlɪ] *adv* di solito
usurer ['ju:ʒərəʳ] *n* usuraio(-a)
usurp [ju:'zə:p] *vt* usurpare
UT *abbr* (*US*) = **Utah**
utensil [ju:'tɛnsl] *n* utensile *m*
uterus ['ju:tərəs] *n* utero
utilitarian [ju:tɪlɪ'tɛərɪən] *adj* utilitario(-a)
utility [ju:'tɪlɪtɪ] *n* utilità; (*also*: **public utility**) servizio pubblico
utility room *n* *locale adibito alla stiratura dei panni etc*
utilization [ju:tɪlaɪ'zeɪʃən] *n* utilizzazione *f*
utilize ['ju:tɪlaɪz] *vt* utilizzare; sfruttare
utmost ['ʌtməust] *adj* estremo(-a) ■ *n*: **to do one's ~** fare il possibile *or* di tutto; **of the ~ importance** della massima importanza; **it is of the ~ importance that ...** è estremamente importante che ... *+ sub*
utter ['ʌtəʳ] *adj* assoluto(-a), totale ■ *vt* pronunciare, proferire; emettere
utterance ['ʌtərəns] *n* espressione *f*; parole *fpl*
utterly ['ʌtəlɪ] *adv* completamente, del tutto
U-turn ['ju:tə:n] *n* inversione *f* a U; (*fig*) voltafaccia *m inv*
Uzbekistan [ʌzbɛkɪ'stɑ:n] *n* Uzbekistan

Vv

V, v [viː] *n* (*letter*) V, v *m or f inv*; **V for Victor** ≈ V come Venezia
v *abbr* (= *verse*) v.; (= *vide*: *see*) v.; (= *volt*) V.; (= *versus*) contro
VA, Va. *abbr* (*US*) = **Virginia**
vac [væk] *n abbr* (*Brit col*) = **vacation**
vacancy ['veɪkənsɪ] *n* (*job*) posto libero; (*room*) stanza libera; **"no vacancies"** "completo"; **have you any vacancies?** (*office*) avete bisogno di personale?; (*hotel*) avete una stanza?
vacant ['veɪkənt] *adj* (*job, seat etc*) libero(-a); (*expression*) assente
vacant lot *n* terreno non occupato; (*for sale*) terreno in vendita
vacate [və'keɪt] *vt* lasciare libero(-a)
vacation [və'keɪʃən] *n* (*esp US*) vacanze *fpl*; **to take a ~** prendere una vacanza, prendere le ferie; **on ~** in vacanza, in ferie
vacation course *n* corso estivo
vaccinate ['væksɪneɪt] *vt* vaccinare
vaccination [væksɪ'neɪʃən] *n* vaccinazione *f*
vaccine ['væksiːn] *n* vaccino
vacuum ['vækjum] *n* vuoto
vacuum bottle *n* (*US*) = **vacuum flask**
vacuum cleaner *n* aspirapolvere *m inv*
vacuum flask *n* (*Brit*) thermos® *m inv*
vacuum-packed ['vækjum'pækt] *adj* confezionato(-a) sottovuoto
vagabond ['vægəbɔnd] *n* vagabondo(-a)
vagary ['veɪgərɪ] *n* capriccio
vagina [və'dʒaɪnə] *n* vagina
vagrancy ['veɪgrənsɪ] *n* vagabondaggio
vagrant ['veɪgrənt] *n* vagabondo(-a)
vague [veɪg] *adj* vago(-a); (*blurred*: *photo, memory*) sfocato(-a); **I haven't the vaguest idea** non ho la minima *or* più pallida idea
vaguely ['veɪglɪ] *adv* vagamente
vain [veɪn] *adj* (*useless*) inutile, vano(-a); (*conceited*) vanitoso(-a); **in ~** inutilmente, invano
valance ['væləns] *n* volant *m inv*, balza
valedictory [vælɪ'dɪktərɪ] *adj* di commiato
valentine ['væləntaɪn] *n* (*also*: **valentine card**) cartolina *or* biglietto di San Valentino
valet ['vælɪt] *n* cameriere *m* personale
valet parking *n* *parcheggio effettuato da un dipendente (dell'albergo etc)*
valet service *n* (*for clothes*) servizio di lavanderia; (*for car*) servizio completo di lavaggio
valiant ['vælɪənt] *adj* valoroso(-a), coraggioso(-a)
valid ['vælɪd] *adj* valido(-a), valevole; (*excuse*) valido(-a)
validate ['vælɪdeɪt] *vt* (*contract, document*) convalidare; (*argument, claim*) comprovare
validity [və'lɪdɪtɪ] *n* validità
valise [və'liːz] *n* borsa da viaggio
valley ['vælɪ] *n* valle *f*
valour, (*US*) **valor** ['vælə[r]] *n* valore *m*
valuable ['væljuəbl] *adj* (*jewel*) di (grande) valore; (*time*) prezioso(-a); **valuables** *npl* oggetti *mpl* di valore
valuation [vælju'eɪʃən] *n* valutazione *f*, stima
value ['væljuː] *n* valore *m* ■ *vt* (*fix price*) valutare, dare un prezzo a; (*cherish*) apprezzare, tenere a; **to be of great ~ to sb** avere molta importanza per qn; **to lose (in) ~** (*currency*) svalutarsi; (*property*) perdere (di) valore; **to gain (in) ~** (*currency*) guadagnare; (*property*) aumentare di valore; **you get good ~ (for money) in that shop** si compra bene in quel negozio
value added tax *n* (*Brit*) imposta sul valore aggiunto
valued ['væluːd] *adj* (*appreciated*) stimato(-a), apprezzato(-a)
valuer ['væljuə[r]] *n* stimatore(-trice)
valve [vælv] *n* valvola
vampire ['væmpaɪə[r]] *n* vampiro
van [væn] *n* (*Aut*) furgone *m*; (*Brit Rail*) vagone *m*
V and A *n abbr* (*Brit*) = **Victoria and Albert Museum**

vandal ['vændl] *n* vandalo(-a)
vandalism ['vændəlɪzəm] *n* vandalismo
vandalize ['vændəlaɪz] *vt* vandalizzare
vanguard ['vængɑːd] *n* avanguardia
vanilla [və'nɪlə] *n* vaniglia ■ *cpd* (*ice cream*) alla vaniglia
vanish ['vænɪʃ] *vi* svanire, scomparire
vanity ['vænɪtɪ] *n* vanità
vanity case *n* valigetta per cosmetici
vantage ['vɑːntɪdʒ] *n*: **~ point** posizione *f or* punto di osservazione; (*fig*) posizione vantaggiosa
vaporize ['veɪpəraɪz] *vt* vaporizzare ■ *vi* vaporizzarsi
vapour, (*US*) **vapor** ['veɪpə^r] *n* vapore *m*
variable ['vɛərɪəbl] *adj* variabile; (*mood*) mutevole ■ *n* fattore *m* variabile, variabile *f*
variance ['vɛərɪəns] *n*: **to be at ~ (with)** essere in disaccordo (con); (*facts*) essere in contraddizione (con)
variant ['vɛərɪənt] *n* variante *f*
variation [vɛərɪ'eɪʃən] *n* variazione *f*; (*in opinion*) cambiamento
varicose ['værɪkəus] *adj*: **~ veins** varici *fpl*
varied ['vɛərɪd] *adj* vario(-a), diverso(-a)
variety [və'raɪətɪ] *n* varietà *f inv*; (*quantity*): **a wide ~ of ...** una vasta gamma di ...; **for a ~ of reasons** per una serie di motivi
variety show *n* spettacolo di varietà
various ['vɛərɪəs] *adj* vario(-a), diverso(-a); (*several*) parecchi(-e), molti(-e); **at ~ times** in momenti diversi; (*several*) diverse volte
varnish ['vɑːnɪʃ] *n* vernice *f*; (*for nails*) smalto ■ *vt* verniciare; **to ~ one's nails** mettersi lo smalto sulle unghie
vary ['vɛərɪ] *vt, vi* variare, mutare; **to ~ (with** *or* **according to)** variare (con *or* a seconda di)
varying ['vɛərɪɪŋ] *adj* variabile
vase [vɑːz] *n* vaso
vasectomy [væ'sɛktəmɪ] *n* vasectomia
Vaseline® ['væsɪliːn] *n* vaselina
vast [vɑːst] *adj* vasto(-a); (*amount, success*) enorme
vastly ['vɑːstlɪ] *adv* enormemente
vastness ['vɑːstnɪs] *n* vastità
VAT [væt] *n abbr* (*Brit*) = **value added tax**
vat [væt] *n* tino
Vatican ['vætɪkən] *n*: **the ~** il Vaticano
vatman ['vætmæn] *n* (*Brit col*): **the ~** ≈ l'ispettore *m* dell'IVA
vault [vɔːlt] *n* (*of roof*) volta; (*tomb*) tomba; (*in bank*) camera blindata; (*jump*) salto ■ *vt* (*also*: **vault over**) saltare (d'un balzo)
vaunted ['vɔːntɪd] *adj*: **much-~** tanto celebrato(-a)
VC *n abbr* (*Brit*: = *Victoria Cross*) *medaglia al coraggio*; = **vice-chairman**
VCR *n abbr* = **video cassette recorder**
VD *n abbr* = **venereal disease**
VDU *n abbr* = **visual display unit**
veal [viːl] *n* vitello
veer [vɪə^r] *vi* girare; virare
veg. [vɛdʒ] *n abbr* (*Brit col*: = *vegetable(s)*) ≈ contorno
vegan ['viːgən] *n* (*Brit*) vegetaliano(-a)
vegeburger, veggieburger ['vɛdʒɪbəːgə^r] *n* hamburger *m inv* vegetariano
vegetable ['vɛdʒtəbl] *n* verdura, ortaggio ■ *adj* vegetale
vegetable garden *n* orto
vegetarian [vɛdʒɪ'tɛərɪən] *adj, n* vegetariano(-a)
vegetate ['vɛdʒɪteɪt] *vi* vegetare
vegetation [vɛdʒɪ'teɪʃən] *n* vegetazione *f*
vegetative ['vɛdʒɪtətɪv] *adj* (*also Bot*) vegetativo(-a)
vehemence ['viːɪməns] *n* veemenza, violenza
vehement ['viːɪmənt] *adj* veemente, violento(-a); profondo(-a)
vehicle ['viːɪkl] *n* veicolo; (*fig*) mezzo
vehicular [vɪ'hɪkjulə^r] *adj*: **"no ~ traffic"** "chiuso al traffico di veicoli"
veil [veɪl] *n* velo ■ *vt* velare; **under a ~ of secrecy** (*fig*) protetto da una cortina di segretezza
veiled [veɪld] *adj* (*also fig*) velato(-a)
vein [veɪn] *n* vena; (*on leaf*) nervatura; (*fig*: *mood*) vena, umore *m*
Velcro® ['vɛlkrəu] *n* velcro® *m inv*
vellum ['vɛləm] *n* (*writing paper*) carta patinata
velocity [vɪ'lɔsɪtɪ] *n* velocità *f inv*
velour [və'luə^r] *n* velours *m inv*
velvet ['vɛlvɪt] *n* velluto
vending machine ['vɛndɪŋ-] *n* distributore *m* automatico
vendor ['vɛndə^r] *n* venditore(-trice); **street ~** venditore ambulante
veneer [və'nɪə^r] *n* impiallacciatura; (*fig*) vernice *f*
venerable ['vɛnərəbl] *adj* venerabile
venereal disease [vɪ'nɪərɪəl-] *n* malattia venerea
Venetian [vɪ'niːʃən] *adj, n* veneziano(-a)
Venetian blind *n* (tenda alla) veneziana
Venezuela [vɛnɪ'zweɪlə] *n* Venezuela *m*
Venezuelan [vɛnɪ'zweɪlən] *adj, n* venezuelano(-a)
vengeance ['vɛndʒəns] *n* vendetta; **with a ~** (*fig*) davvero; furiosamente
vengeful ['vɛndʒful] *adj* vendicativo(-a)
Venice ['vɛnɪs] *n* Venezia
venison ['vɛnɪsn] *n* carne *f* di cervo
venom ['vɛnəm] *n* veleno

venomous ['vɛnəməs] *adj* velenoso(-a)
vent [vɛnt] *n* foro, apertura; (*in dress, jacket*) spacco ■ *vt* (*fig: one's feelings*) sfogare, dare sfogo a
ventilate ['vɛntɪleɪt] *vt* (*room*) dare aria a, arieggiare
ventilation [vɛntɪ'leɪʃən] *n* ventilazione *f*
ventilation shaft *n* condotto di aerazione
ventilator ['vɛntɪleɪtə'] *n* ventilatore *m*
ventriloquist [vɛn'trɪləkwɪst] *n* ventriloquo(-a)
venture ['vɛntʃə'] *n* impresa (rischiosa) ■ *vt* rischiare, azzardare ■ *vi* arrischiarsi, azzardarsi; **a business ~** un'iniziativa commerciale; **to ~ to do sth** azzardarsi a fare qc
venture capital *n* capitale *m* di rischio
venue ['vɛnju:] *n* luogo di incontro; (*Sport*) luogo (designato) per l'incontro
Venus ['vi:nəs] *n* (*planet*) Venere *m*
veracity [və'ræsɪtɪ] *n* veridicità
veranda, verandah [və'rændə] *n* veranda
verb [və:b] *n* verbo
verbal ['və:bəl] *adj* verbale; (*translation*) letterale
verbally ['və:bəlɪ] *adv* a voce
verbatim [və:'beɪtɪm] *adv, adj* parola per parola
verbose [və:'bəus] *adj* verboso(-a)
verdict ['və:dɪkt] *n* verdetto; (*opinion*) giudizio, parere *m*; **~ of guilty/not guilty** verdetto di colpevolezza/non colpevolezza
verge [və:dʒ] *n* bordo, orlo; **"soft verges"** (*Brit*) "banchina cedevole"; **on the ~ of doing** sul punto di fare
▸ **verge on** *vt fus* rasentare
verger ['və:dʒə'] *n* (*Rel*) sagrestano
verification [vɛrɪfɪ'keɪʃən] *n* verifica
verify ['vɛrɪfaɪ] *vt* verificare; (*prove the truth of*) confermare
veritable ['vɛrɪtəbl] *adj* vero(-a)
vermin ['və:mɪn] *npl* animali *mpl* nocivi; (*insects*) insetti *mpl* parassiti
vermouth ['və:məθ] *n* vermut *m inv*
vernacular [və'nækjulə'] *n* vernacolo
versatile ['və:sətaɪl] *adj* (*person*) versatile; (*machine, tool etc*) (che si presta) a molti usi
verse [və:s] *n* (*of poem*) verso; (*stanza*) stanza, strofa; (*in bible*) versetto; (*no pl: poetry*) versi *mpl*; **in ~** in versi
versed [və:st] *adj*: **(well-)~ in** versato(-a) in
version ['və:ʃən] *n* versione *f*
versus ['və:səs] *prep* contro
vertebra (*pl* **vertebrae**) ['və:tɪbrə, -bri:] *n* vertebra
vertebrate ['və:tɪbrɪt] *n* vertebrato
vertical ['və:tɪkl] *adj, n* verticale (*m*)
vertically ['və:tɪklɪ] *adv* verticalmente
vertigo ['və:tɪgəu] *n* vertigine *f*; **to suffer from ~** soffrire di vertigini
verve [və:v] *n* brio; entusiasmo
very ['vɛrɪ] *adv* molto ■ *adj*: **the ~ book which** proprio il libro che; **~ much** moltissimo; **~ well** molto bene; **~ little** molto poco; **at the ~ end** proprio alla fine; **the ~ last** proprio l'ultimo; **at the ~ least** almeno; **the ~ thought (of it) alarms me** il solo pensiero mi spaventa, sono spaventato solo al pensiero
vespers ['vɛspəz] *npl* vespro
vessel ['vɛsl] *n* (*Anat*) vaso; (*Naut*) nave *f*; (*container*) recipiente *m*
vest [vɛst] *n* (*Brit*) maglia; (*: sleeveless*) canottiera; (*US: waistcoat*) gilè *m inv* ■ *vt*: **to ~ sb with sth, to ~ sth in sb** conferire qc a qn
vested interest *n*: **to have a ~ in doing** avere tutto l'interesse a fare; **vested interests** *npl* (*Comm*) diritti *mpl* acquisiti
vestibule ['vɛstɪbju:l] *n* vestibolo
vestige ['vɛstɪdʒ] *n* vestigio
vestment ['vɛstmənt] *n* (*Rel*) paramento liturgico
vestry ['vɛstrɪ] *n* sagrestia
Vesuvius [vɪ'su:vɪəs] *n* Vesuvio
vet [vɛt] *n abbr* (*= veterinary surgeon*) veterinario; (*US: col*) = **veteran** ■ *vt* esaminare minuziosamente; (*text*) rivedere; **to ~ sb for a job** raccogliere delle informazioni dettagliate su qn prima di offrirgli un posto
veteran ['vɛtərn] *n* veterano; (*also:* **war veteran**) reduce *m* ■ *adj*: **she's a ~ campaigner for ...** lotta da sempre per ...
veteran car *n* auto *f inv* d'epoca (*anteriore al 1919*)
veterinarian [vɛtrɪ'nɛərɪən] *n* (*US*) = **veterinary surgeon**
veterinary ['vɛtrɪnərɪ] *adj* veterinario(-a)
veterinary surgeon *n* (*Brit*) veterinario
veto (*pl* **vetoes**) ['vi:təu] *n* veto ■ *vt* opporre il veto a; **to put a ~ on** opporre il veto a
vetting ['vɛtɪŋ] *n*: **positive ~** *indagine per accertare l'idoneità di un aspirante ad una carica ufficiale*
vex [vɛks] *vt* irritare, contrariare
vexed [vɛkst] *adj* (*question*) controverso(-a), dibattuto(-a)
VFD *n abbr* (*US*) = **voluntary fire department**
VG *abbr* (*Brit: Scol etc: = very good*) ottimo
VHF *abbr* (*= very high frequency*) VHF
VI *abbr* (*US*) = **Virgin Islands**
via ['vaɪə] *prep* (*by way of*) via; (*by means of*) tramite
viability [vaɪə'bɪlɪtɪ] *n* attuabilità
viable ['vaɪəbl] *adj* attuabile; vitale

viaduct ['vaɪədʌkt] *n* viadotto
vial ['vaɪəl] *n* fiala
vibes [vaɪbz] *npl* (*col*): **I got good/bad ~** ho trovato simpatica/antipatica l'atmosfera
vibrant ['vaɪbrənt] *adj* (*sound*) vibrante; (*colour*) vivace, vivo(-a)
vibraphone ['vaɪbrəfəun] *n* vibrafono
vibrate [vaɪ'breɪt] *vi*: **to ~ (with)** vibrare (di); (*resound*) risonare (di)
vibration [vaɪ'breɪʃən] *n* vibrazione *f*
vibrator [vaɪ'breɪtə^r] *n* vibratore *m*
vicar ['vɪkə^r] *n* pastore *m*
vicarage ['vɪkərɪdʒ] *n* presbiterio
vicarious [vɪ'kɛərɪəs] *adj* sofferto(-a) al posto di un altro; **to get ~ pleasure out of sth** trarre piacere indirettamente da qc
vice [vaɪs] *n* (*evil*) vizio; (*Tech*) morsa
vice- [vaɪs] *prefix* vice ...
vice-chairman [vaɪs'tʃɛəmən] *n* vicepresidente *m*
vice-chancellor [vaɪs'tʃɑ:nsələ^r] *n* (*Brit Scol*) rettore *m* (*per elezione*)
vice-president [vaɪs'prɛzɪdənt] *n* vicepresidente *m*
viceroy ['vaɪsrɔɪ] *n* viceré *m inv*
vice squad *n* (squadra del) buon costume *f*
vice versa ['vaɪsɪ'və:sə] *adv* viceversa
vicinity [vɪ'sɪnɪtɪ] *n* vicinanze *fpl*
vicious ['vɪʃəs] *adj* (*remark*) maligno(-a), cattivo(-a); (*blow*) violento(-a); **a ~ circle** un circolo vizioso
viciousness ['vɪʃəsnɪs] *n* malignità, cattiveria; ferocia
vicissitudes [vɪ'sɪsɪtju:dz] *npl* vicissitudini *fpl*
victim ['vɪktɪm] *n* vittima; **to be the ~ of** essere vittima di
victimization [vɪktɪmaɪ'zeɪʃən] *n* persecuzione *f*; rappresaglie *fpl*
victimize ['vɪktɪmaɪz] *vt* perseguitare; compiere delle rappresaglie contro
victor ['vɪktə^r] *n* vincitore *m*
Victorian [vɪk'tɔ:rɪən] *adj* vittoriano(-a)
victorious [vɪk'tɔ:rɪəs] *adj* vittorioso(-a)
victory ['vɪktərɪ] *n* vittoria; **to win a ~ over sb** riportare una vittoria su qn
video ['vɪdɪəu] *cpd* video... ■ *n* (*video film*) video *m inv*; (*also*: **video cassette**) videocassetta; (*also*: **video cassette recorder**) videoregistratore *m*
video call *n* videochiamata
video camera *n* videocamera
video cassette *n* videocassetta
video cassette recorder *n* videoregistratore *m*
videodisc ['vɪdɪəudɪsk] *n* disco ottico
video game *n* videogioco
video nasty *n* *video estremamente violento o porno*
videophone ['vɪdɪəufəun] *n* videotelefono
video recorder *n* videoregistratore *m*
video recording *n* registrazione *f* su video
video tape *n* videotape *m inv*
vie [vaɪ] *vi*: **to ~ with** competere con, rivaleggiare con
Vienna [vɪ'ɛnə] *n* Vienna
Vietnam, Viet Nam [vjɛt'næm] *n* Vietnam *m*
Vietnamese [vjɛtnə'mi:z] *adj* vietnamita ■ *n* vietnamita *m/f*; (*Ling*) vietnamita *m*
view [vju:] *n* vista, veduta; (*opinion*) opinione *f* ■ *vt* (*situation*) considerare; (*house*) visitare; **on ~** (*in museum etc*) esposto(-a); **to be in** *or* **within ~ (of sth)** essere in vista (di qc); **in full ~ of sb** sotto gli occhi di qn; **an overall ~ of the situation** una visione globale della situazione; **in my ~** a mio avviso, secondo me; **in ~ of the fact that** considerato che; **to take** *or* **hold the ~ that ...** essere dell'opinione che ...; **with a ~ to doing sth** con l'intenzione di fare qc
viewdata ['vju:deɪtə] *n* (*Brit*) *sistema di televideo*
viewer ['vju:ə^r] *n* (*viewfinder*) mirino; (*small projector*) visore *m*; (TV) telespettatore(-trice)
viewfinder ['vju:faɪndə^r] *n* mirino
viewpoint ['vju:pɔɪnt] *n* punto di vista
vigil ['vɪdʒɪl] *n* veglia; **to keep ~** vegliare
vigilance ['vɪdʒɪləns] *n* vigilanza
vigilant ['vɪdʒɪlənt] *adj* vigile
vigilante [vɪdʒɪ'læntɪ] *n* *cittadino che si fa giustizia da solo*
vigorous ['vɪgərəs] *adj* vigoroso(-a)
vigour, (US) **vigor** [vɪgə^r] *n* vigore *m*
vile [vaɪl] *adj* (*action*) vile; (*smell*) disgustoso(-a), nauseante; (*temper*) pessimo(-a)
vilify ['vɪlɪfaɪ] *vt* diffamare
villa ['vɪlə] *n* villa
village ['vɪlɪdʒ] *n* villaggio
villager ['vɪlɪdʒə^r] *n* abitante *m/f* di villaggio
villain ['vɪlən] *n* (*scoundrel*) canaglia; (*criminal*) criminale *m*; (*in novel etc*) cattivo
VIN *n abbr* (US) = **vehicle identification number**
vinaigrette [vɪneɪ'grɛt] *n* vinaigrette *f inv*
vindicate ['vɪndɪkeɪt] *vt* comprovare; giustificare
vindication [vɪndɪ'keɪʃən] *n*: **in ~ of** per giustificare; a discolpa di
vindictive [vɪn'dɪktɪv] *adj* vendicativo(-a)
vine [vaɪn] *n* vite *f*; (*climbing plant*) rampicante *m*
vinegar ['vɪnɪgə^r] *n* aceto
vine grower *n* viticoltore *m*
vine-growing ['vaɪngrəuɪŋ] *adj* viticolo(-a) ■ *n* viticoltura

vineyard ['vɪnjɑːd] *n* vigna, vigneto
vintage ['vɪntɪdʒ] *n* (*year*) annata, produzione *f*; **the 1970 ~** il vino del 1970
vintage car *n* auto *f inv* d'epoca
vintage wine *n* vino d'annata
vinyl ['vaɪnl] *n* vinile *m*
viola [vɪ'əulə] *n* viola
violate ['vaɪəleɪt] *vt* violare
violation [vaɪə'leɪʃən] *n* violazione *f*; **in ~ of sth** violando qc
violence ['vaɪələns] *n* violenza; (*Pol etc*) incidenti *mpl* violenti
violent [vaɪələnt] *adj* violento(-a); **a ~ dislike of sb/sth** una violenta avversione per qn/qc
violently ['vaɪələntlɪ] *adv* violentemente; (*ill, angry*) terribilmente
violet ['vaɪələt] *adj* (*colour*) viola *inv*, violetto(-a) ■ *n* (*plant*) violetta
violin [vaɪə'lɪn] *n* violino
violinist [vaɪə'lɪnɪst] *n* violinista *m/f*
VIP *n abbr* (= *very important person*) V.I.P. *m/f inv*
viper ['vaɪpəʳ] *n* vipera
viral ['vaɪərəl] *adj* virale
virgin ['vəːdʒɪn] *n* vergine *f* ■ *adj* vergine *inv*; **she is a ~** lei è vergine; **the Blessed V~** la Beatissima Vergine
virginity [vəː'dʒɪnɪtɪ] *n* verginità
Virgo ['vəːgəu] *n* (*sign*) Vergine *f*; **to be ~** essere della Vergine
virile ['vɪraɪl] *adj* virile
virility [vɪ'rɪlɪtɪ] *n* virilità
virtual ['vəːtjuəl] *adj* effettivo(-a), vero(-a); (*Comput, Physics*) virtuale; (*in effect*): **it's a ~ impossibility** è praticamente impossibile; **the ~ leader** il capo all'atto pratico
virtually ['vəːtjuəlɪ] *adv* (*almost*) praticamente; **it is ~ impossible** è praticamente impossibile
virtual reality *n* realtà *f inv* virtuale
virtue ['vəːtjuː] *n* virtù *f inv*; (*advantage*) pregio, vantaggio; **by ~ of** grazie a
virtuosity [vəːtju'ɔsɪtɪ] *n* virtuosismo
virtuoso [vəːtju'əuzəu] *n* virtuoso
virtuous ['vəːtjuəs] *adj* virtuoso(-a)
virulent ['vɪrulənt] *adj* virulento(-a)
virus ['vaɪərəs] *n* virus *m inv*
visa ['viːzə] *n* visto
vis-à-vis [viːzə'viː] *prep* rispetto a, nei riguardi di
viscount ['vaɪkaunt] *n* visconte *m*
viscous ['vɪskəs] *adj* viscoso(-a)
vise [vaɪs] *n* (*US Tech*) = **vice**
visibility [vɪzɪ'bɪlɪtɪ] *n* visibilità
visible ['vɪzəbl] *adj* visibile; **~ exports/imports** esportazioni *fpl*/importazioni *fpl* visibili
visibly ['vɪzəblɪ] *adv* visibilmente
vision ['vɪʒən] *n* (*sight*) vista; (*foresight, in dream*) visione *f*
visionary ['vɪʒənərɪ] *n* visionario(-a)
visit ['vɪzɪt] *n* visita; (*stay*) soggiorno ■ *vt* (*person*) andare a trovare; (*place*) visitare; **to pay a ~ to** (*person*) fare una visita a; (*place*) andare a visitare; **on a private/official ~** in visita privata/ufficiale
visiting ['vɪzɪtɪŋ] *adj* (*speaker, professor, team*) ospite
visiting card *n* biglietto da visita
visiting hours *npl* orario delle visite
visitor ['vɪzɪtəʳ] *n* visitatore(-trice); (*guest*) ospite *m/f*
visitors' book *n* libro d'oro; (*in hotel*) registro
visor ['vaɪzəʳ] *n* visiera
VISTA ['vɪstə] *n abbr* (= *Volunteers in Service to America*) *volontariato in zone depresse degli Stati Uniti*
vista ['vɪstə] *n* vista, prospettiva
visual ['vɪzjuəl] *adj* visivo(-a); visuale; ottico(-a)
visual aid *n* sussidio visivo
visual arts *npl* arti *fpl* figurative
visual display unit *n* unità *f inv* di visualizzazione
visualize ['vɪzjuəlaɪz] *vt* immaginare, figurarsi; (*foresee*) prevedere
visually ['vɪzjuəlɪ] *adv*: **~ appealing** piacevole a vedersi; **~ handicapped** con una menomazione della vista
vital ['vaɪtl] *adj* vitale; **of ~ importance (to sb/sth)** di vitale importanza (per qn/qc)
vitality [vaɪ'tælɪtɪ] *n* vitalità
vitally ['vaɪtəlɪ] *adv* estremamente
vital statistics *npl* (*of population*) statistica demografica; (*col: woman's*) misure *fpl*
vitamin ['vɪtəmɪn] *n* vitamina
vitiate ['vɪʃɪeɪt] *vt* viziare
vitreous ['vɪtrɪəs] *adj* (*rock*) vetroso(-a); (*china, enamel*) vetrificato(-a)
vitriolic [vɪtrɪ'ɔlɪk] *adj* (*fig*) caustico(-a)
viva ['vaɪvə] *n* (*also*: **viva voce**) (esame *m*) orale
vivacious [vɪ'veɪʃəs] *adj* vivace
vivacity [vɪ'væsɪtɪ] *n* vivacità
vivid ['vɪvɪd] *adj* vivido(-a)
vividly ['vɪvɪdlɪ] *adv* (*describe*) vividamente; (*remember*) con precisione
vivisection [vɪvɪ'sɛkʃən] *n* vivisezione *f*
vixen ['vɪksn] *n* volpe *f* femmina; (*pej: woman*) bisbetica
viz *abbr* (= *vide licet: namely*) cioè
VLF *abbr* (= *very low frequency*) bassissima frequenza
V-neck ['viːnɛk] *n* maglione *m* con lo collo a V

VOA *n abbr* (= *Voice of America*) voce *f* dell'America (*alla radio*)
vocabulary [vəu'kæbjulərɪ] *n* vocabolario
vocal ['vəukl] *adj* (*Mus*) vocale; (*communication*) verbale; (*noisy*) rumoroso(-a)
vocal cords *npl* corde *fpl* vocali
vocalist ['vəukəlɪst] *n* cantante *m/f* (*in un gruppo*)
vocation [vəu'keɪʃən] *n* vocazione *f*
vocational [vəu'keɪʃənl] *adj* professionale; **~ guidance** orientamento professionale; **~ training** formazione *f* professionale
vociferous [və'sɪfərəs] *adj* rumoroso(-a)
vodka ['vɔdkə] *n* vodka *f inv*
vogue [vəug] *n* moda; (*popularity*) popolarità, voga; **to be in ~, be the ~** essere di moda
voice [vɔɪs] *n* voce *f* ■ *vt* (*opinion*) esprimere; **in a loud/soft ~** a voce alta/bassa; **to give ~ to** esprimere
voice mail *n* servizio di segreteria telefonica
voice-over ['vɔɪsəuvə^r] *n* voce *f* fuori campo *inv*
void [vɔɪd] *n* vuoto ■ *adj*: **~ of** privo(-a) di
voile [vɔɪl] *n* voile *m*
vol. *abbr* (= *volume*) vol.
volatile ['vɔlətaɪl] *adj* volatile; (*fig*) volubile
volcanic [vɔl'kænɪk] *adj* vulcanico(-a)
volcano (*pl* **volcanoes**) [vɔl'keɪnəu] *n* vulcano
volition [və'lɪʃən] *n*: **of one's own ~** di propria volontà
volley ['vɔlɪ] *n* (*of gunfire*) salva; (*of stones etc*) raffica, gragnola; (*Tennis etc*) volata
volleyball ['vɔlɪbɔːl] *n* pallavolo *f*
volt [vəult] *n* volt *m inv*
voltage ['vəultɪdʒ] *n* tensione *f*, voltaggio; **high/low ~** alta/bassa tensione
voluble ['vɔljubl] *adj* loquace, ciarliero(-a)
volume ['vɔljuːm] *n* volume *m*; (*of tank*) capacità *f inv*; **~ one/two** (*of book*) volume primo/secondo; **his expression spoke volumes** la sua espressione lasciava capire tutto
volume control *n* (*Radio, TV*) regolatore *m* or manopola del volume
volume discount *n* (*Comm*) vantaggio sul volume di vendita
voluminous [və'luːmɪnəs] *adj* voluminoso(-a); (*notes etc*) abbondante
voluntarily ['vɔləntrɪlɪ] *adv* volontariamente; gratuitamente
voluntary ['vɔləntərɪ] *adj* volontario(-a); (*unpaid*) gratuito(-a), non retribuito(-a)
voluntary liquidation *n* (*Comm*) liquidazione *f* volontaria
volunteer [vɔlən'tɪə^r] *n* volontario(-a) ■ *vi* (*Mil*) arruolarsi volontario; **to ~ to do** offrire (volontariamente) di fare
voluptuous [və'lʌptjuəs] *adj* voluttuoso(-a)
vomit ['vɔmɪt] *n* vomito ■ *vt, vi* vomitare
voracious [və'reɪʃəs] *adj* (*appetite*) smisurato(-a); (*reader*) avido(-a)
vote [vəut] *n* voto, suffragio; (*cast*) voto; (*franchise*) diritto di voto ■ *vi* votare ■ *vt* (*gen*) votare; (*sum of money etc*) votare a favore di; **to ~ to do sth** votare a favore di fare qc; **he was voted secretary** è stato eletto segretario; **to put sth to the ~, to take a ~ on sth** mettere qc ai voti; **~ for/against** voto a favore/contrario; **to pass a ~ of confidence/no confidence** dare il voto di fiducia/sfiducia; **~ of thanks** discorso di ringraziamento
voter ['vəutə^r] *n* elettore(-trice)
voting ['vəutɪŋ] *n* scrutinio
voting paper *n* (*Brit*) scheda elettorale
voting right *n* diritto di voto
vouch [vautʃ]: **to ~ for** *vt fus* farsi garante di
voucher ['vautʃə^r] *n* (*for meal, petrol*) buono; (*receipt*) ricevuta; **travel ~** voucher *m inv*, tagliando
vow [vau] *n* voto, promessa solenne ■ *vi* giurare; **to take** *or* **make a ~ to do sth** fare voto di fare qc
vowel ['vauəl] *n* vocale *f*
voyage ['vɔɪɪdʒ] *n* viaggio per mare, traversata
voyeur [vwɑː'jəː^r] *n* guardone(-a)
VP *n abbr* (= *vice-president*) V.P.
vs *abbr* (= *versus*) contro
VSO *n abbr* (*Brit*: = *Voluntary Service Overseas*) *servizio volontario in paesi sottosviluppati*
VT, Vt. *abbr* (*US*) = **Vermont**
vulgar ['vʌlgə^r] *adj* volgare
vulgarity [vʌl'gærɪtɪ] *n* volgarità
vulnerability [vʌlnərə'bɪlɪtɪ] *n* vulnerabilità
vulnerable ['vʌlnərəbl] *adj* vulnerabile
vulture ['vʌltʃə^r] *n* avvoltoio

W, w ['dʌblju:] *n* (*letter*) W, w *m or f inv*; **W for William** ≈ W come Washington
W *abbr* (= *west*) O; (*Elec*: = *watt*) w
WA *abbr* (*US*) = **Washington**
wad [wɔd] *n* (*of cotton wool, paper*) tampone *m*; (*of banknotes etc*) fascio
wadding ['wɔdɪŋ] *n* imbottitura
waddle ['wɔdl] *vi* camminare come una papera
wade [weɪd] *vi*: **to ~ through** camminare a stento in ■ *vt* guadare
wafer ['weɪfəʳ] *n* (*Culin*) cialda; (*Rel*) ostia; (*Comput*) wafer *m inv*
wafer-thin ['weɪfə'θɪn] *adj* molto sottile
waffle ['wɔfl] *n* (*Culin*) cialda; (*col*) ciance *fpl*; riempitivo ■ *vi* cianciare; parlare a vuoto
waffle iron *n* stampo per cialde
waft [wɔft] *vt* portare ■ *vi* diffondersi
wag [wæg] *vt* agitare, muovere ■ *vi* agitarsi; **the dog wagged its tail** il cane scodinzolò
wage [weɪdʒ] *n* (*also*: **wages**) salario, paga ■ *vt*: **to ~ war** fare la guerra; **a day's wages** un giorno di paga
wage claim *n* rivendicazione *f* salariale
wage differential *n* differenza di salario
wage earner *n* salariato(-a)
wage freeze *n* blocco dei salari
wage packet *n* (*Brit*) busta *f* paga *inv*
wager ['weɪdʒəʳ] *n* scommessa
waggle ['wægl] *vt* dimenare, agitare ■ *vi* dimenarsi, agitarsi
wagon, waggon ['wægən] *n* (*horse-drawn*) carro; (*truck*) furgone *m*; (*Brit Rail*) vagone *m* (merci)
wail [weɪl] *n* gemito; (*of siren*) urlo ■ *vi* gemere; urlare
waist [weɪst] *n* vita, cintola
waistcoat ['weɪskəut] *n* panciotto, gilè *m inv*
waistline ['weɪstlaɪn] *n* (giro di) vita
wait [weɪt] *n* attesa ■ *vi* aspettare, attendere; **to ~ for** aspettare; **to keep sb waiting** far aspettare qn; **~ a moment!** (aspetti) un momento!; **"repairs while you ~"** "riparazioni lampo"; **I can't ~ to ...** (*fig*) non vedo l'ora di ...; **to lie in ~ for** stare in agguato a
▸ **wait behind** *vi* rimanere (ad aspettare)
▸ **wait on** *vt fus* servire
▸ **wait up** *vi* restare alzato(-a) (ad aspettare); **don't ~ up for me** non rimanere alzato per me
waiter ['weɪtəʳ] *n* cameriere *m*
waiting ['weɪtɪŋ] *n*: **"no ~"** (*Brit Aut*) "divieto di sosta"
waiting list *n* lista d'attesa
waiting room *n* sala d'aspetto *or* d'attesa
waitress ['weɪtrɪs] *n* cameriera
waive [weɪv] *vt* rinunciare a, abbandonare
waiver ['weɪvəʳ] *n* rinuncia
wake [weɪk] *vb* (*pt* **woke, waked**, *pp* **woken, waked**) [wəuk, 'wəukn] *vt* (*also*: **wake up**) svegliare ■ *vi* (*also*: **wake up**) svegliarsi ■ *n* (*for dead person*) veglia funebre; (*Naut*) scia; **to ~ up to sth** (*fig*) rendersi conto di qc; **in the ~ of** sulla scia di; **to follow in sb's ~** (*fig*) seguire le tracce di qn
waken ['weɪkn] *vt, vi* = **wake**
Wales [weɪlz] *n* Galles *m*
walk [wɔ:k] *n* passeggiata; (*short*) giretto; (*gait*) passo, andatura; (*path*) sentiero; (*in park etc*) sentiero, vialetto ■ *vi* camminare; (*for pleasure, exercise*) passeggiare ■ *vt* (*distance*) fare *or* percorrere a piedi; (*dog*) accompagnare, portare a passeggiare; **10 minutes' ~ from** 10 minuti di cammino *or* a piedi da; **to go for a ~** andare a fare quattro passi; andare a fare una passeggiata; **from all walks of life** di tutte le condizioni sociali; **to ~ in one's sleep** essere sonnambulo(-a); **I'll ~ you home** ti accompagno a casa
▸ **walk out** *vi* (*go out*) uscire; (*as protest*) uscire (in segno di protesta); (*strike*) scendere in sciopero; **to ~ out on sb** piantare in asso qn
walkabout ['wɔ:kəbaut] *n*: **to go (on a) ~** avere incontri informali col pubblico (*durante una visita ufficiale*)

walker ['wɔːkəʳ] *n* (*person*) camminatore(-trice)
walkie-talkie ['wɔːkɪ'tɔːkɪ] *n* walkie-talkie *m inv*
walking ['wɔːkɪŋ] *n* camminare *m*; **it's within ~ distance** ci si arriva a piedi
walking holiday *n* vacanza fatta di lunghe camminate
walking shoes *npl* scarpe *fpl* da passeggio
walking stick *n* bastone *m* da passeggio
Walkman® ['wɔːkmən] *n* walkman® *m inv*
walk-on ['wɔːkɔn] *adj* (*Theat: part*) da comparsa
walkout ['wɔːkaut] *n* (*of workers*) sciopero senza preavviso *or* a sorpresa
walkover ['wɔːkəuvəʳ] *n* (*col*) vittoria facile, gioco da ragazzi
walkway ['wɔːkweɪ] *n* passaggio pedonale
wall [wɔːl] *n* muro; (*internal, of tunnel, cave*) parete *f*; **to go to the ~** (*fig: firm etc*) fallire
▸ **wall in** *vt* (*garden etc*) circondare con un muro
wall cupboard *n* pensile *m*
walled [wɔːld] *adj* (*city*) fortificato(-a)
wallet ['wɔlɪt] *n* portafoglio
wallflower ['wɔːlflauəʳ] *n* violacciocca; **to be a ~** (*fig*) fare da tappezzeria
wall hanging *n* tappezzeria
wallop ['wɔləp] *vt* (*col*) pestare
wallow ['wɔləu] *vi* sguazzare, rotolarsi; **to ~ in one's grief** crogiolarsi nel proprio dolore
wallpaper ['wɔːlpeɪpəʳ] *n* carta da parati; (*Comput*) sfondo
wall-to-wall ['wɔːltə'wɔːl] *adj*: **~ carpeting** moquette *f*
walnut ['wɔːlnʌt] *n* noce *f*; (*tree*) noce *m*
walrus (*pl* **~** *or* **walruses**) ['wɔːlrəs] *n* tricheco
waltz [wɔːlts] *n* valzer *m inv* ■ *vi* ballare il valzer
wan [wɔn] *adj* pallido(-a), smorto(-a); triste
wand [wɔnd] *n* (*also:* **magic wand**) bacchetta (magica)
wander ['wɔndəʳ] *vi* (*person*) girare senza meta, girovagare; (*thoughts*) vagare; (*river*) serpeggiare
wanderer ['wɔndərəʳ] *n* vagabondo(-a)
wandering ['wɔndrɪŋ] *adj* (*tribe*) nomade; (*minstrel, actor*) girovago(-a); (*path, river*) tortuoso(-a); (*glance, mind*) distratto(-a)
wane [weɪn] *vi* (*moon*) calare; (*reputation*) declinare
wangle ['wæŋgl] (*Brit col*) *vt* procurare (con l'astuzia) ■ *n* astuzia
wanker ['wæŋkəʳ] *n* (*col!*) segaiolo (*!*); (*as insult*) coglione (*!*) *m*
want [wɔnt] *vt* volere; (*need*) aver bisogno di; (*lack*) mancare di ■ *n* (*poverty*) miseria, povertà; **wants** *npl* (*needs*) bisogni *mpl*; **for ~ of** per mancanza di; **to ~ to do** volere fare; **to ~ sb to do** volere che qn faccia; **you're wanted on the phone** la vogliono al telefono; **"cook wanted"** "cercasi cuoco"
want ads *npl* (*US*) piccoli annunci *mpl*
wanting ['wɔntɪŋ] *adj*: **to be ~ (in)** mancare (di); **to be found ~** non risultare all'altezza
wanton ['wɔntn] *adj* sfrenato(-a); senza motivo
war [wɔːʳ] *n* guerra; **to go to ~** entrare in guerra
warble ['wɔːbl] *n* (*of bird*) trillo ■ *vi* trillare
war cry *n* grido di guerra
ward [wɔːd] *n* (*in hospital: room*) corsia; (*: section*) reparto; (*Pol*) circoscrizione *f*; (*Law: child*) pupillo(-a)
▸ **ward off** *vt* parare, schivare
warden ['wɔːdn] *n* (*of institution*) direttore(-trice); (*of park, game reserve*) guardiano(-a); (*Brit: also:* **traffic warden**) addetto(-a) al controllo del traffico e del parcheggio
warder ['wɔːdəʳ] *n* (*Brit*) guardia carceraria
wardrobe ['wɔːdrəub] *n* (*cupboard*) guardaroba *m inv*, armadio; (*clothes*) guardaroba; (*Theat*) costumi *mpl*
warehouse ['wɛəhaus] *n* magazzino
wares [wɛəz] *npl* merci *fpl*
warfare ['wɔːfɛəʳ] *n* guerra
war game *n* war game *m inv*
warhead ['wɔːhɛd] *n* (*Mil*) testata, ogiva
warily ['wɛərɪlɪ] *adv* cautamente, con prudenza
warlike ['wɔːlaɪk] *adj* guerriero(-a)
warm [wɔːm] *adj* caldo(-a); (*welcome, applause*) caloroso(-a); (*person, greeting*) cordiale; (*heart*) d'oro; (*supporter*) convinto(-a); **it's ~** fa caldo; **I'm ~** ho caldo; **to keep sth ~** tenere qc al caldo; **with my warmest thanks** con i miei più sentiti ringraziamenti
▸ **warm up** *vi* scaldarsi, riscaldarsi; (*athlete, discussion*) riscaldarsi ■ *vt* scaldare, riscaldare; (*engine*) far scaldare
warm-blooded ['wɔːm'blʌdɪd] *adj* a sangue caldo
war memorial *n* monumento ai caduti
warm-hearted [wɔːm'hɑːtɪd] *adj* affettuoso(-a)
warmly ['wɔːmlɪ] *adv* caldamente; calorosamente; vivamente
warmonger ['wɔːmʌŋgəʳ] *n* guerrafondaio
warmongering ['wɔːmʌŋgrɪŋ] *n* bellicismo
warmth [wɔːmθ] *n* calore *m*
warm-up ['wɔːmʌp] *n* (*Sport*) riscaldamento
warn [wɔːn] *vt* avvertire, avvisare; **to ~ sb not to do sth** *or* **against doing sth** avvertire qn di non fare qc

warning ['wɔ:nɪŋ] *n* avvertimento; (*notice*) avviso; **without (any)** ~ senza preavviso; **gale** ~ avviso di burrasca
warning light *n* spia luminosa
warning triangle *n* (*Aut*) triangolo
warp [wɔ:p] *n* (*Textiles*) ordito ▪ *vi* deformarsi ▪ *vt* deformare; (*fig*) corrompere
warpath ['wɔ:pɑ:θ] *n*: **to be on the** ~ (*fig*) essere sul sentiero di guerra
warped [wɔ:pt] *adj* (*wood*) curvo(-a); (*fig: character, sense of humour etc*) contorto(-a)
warrant ['wɔrnt] *n* (*Law: to arrest*) mandato di cattura; (*: to search*) mandato di perquisizione ▪ *vt* (*justify, merit*) giustificare
warrant officer *n* sottufficiale *m*
warranty ['wɔrəntɪ] *n* garanzia; **under** ~ (*Comm*) in garanzia
warren ['wɔrən] *n* (*of rabbits*) tana
warring ['wɔ:rɪŋ] *adj* (*interests etc*) opposto(-a), in lotta; (*nations*) in guerra
warrior ['wɔrɪəʳ] *n* guerriero(-a)
Warsaw ['wɔ:sɔ:] *n* Varsavia
warship ['wɔ:ʃɪp] *n* nave *f* da guerra
wart [wɔ:t] *n* verruca
wartime ['wɔ:taɪm] *n*: **in** ~ in tempo di guerra
wary ['wɛərɪ] *adj* prudente; **to be** ~ **about** *or* **of doing sth** andare cauto nel fare qc
was [wɔz] *pt of* **be**
wash [wɔʃ] *vt* lavare; (*sweep, carry: sea etc*) portare, trascinare ▪ *vi* lavarsi ▪ *n*: **to give sth a** ~ lavare qc, dare una lavata a qc; **to have a** ~ lavarsi; **he was washed overboard** fu trascinato in mare (dalle onde)
▸ **wash away** *vt* (*stain*) togliere lavando; (*river etc*) trascinare via
▸ **wash down** *vt* lavare
▸ **wash off** *vi* andare via con il lavaggio
▸ **wash up** *vi* lavare i piatti; (*US: have a wash*) lavarsi
Wash. *abbr* (*US*) = **Washington**
washable ['wɔʃəbl] *adj* lavabile
washbasin ['wɔʃbeɪsn] *n* lavabo
washcloth ['wɔʃklɔθ] *n* (*US*) pezzuola (per lavarsi)
washer ['wɔʃəʳ] *n* (*Tech*) rondella
washing ['wɔʃɪŋ] *n* (*Brit: linen etc*) bucato; **dirty** ~ biancheria da lavare
washing line *n* (*Brit*) corda del bucato
washing machine *n* lavatrice *f*
washing powder *n* (*Brit*) detersivo (in polvere)
Washington ['wɔʃɪŋtən] *n* Washington *f*
washing-up [wɔʃɪŋ'ʌp] *n* (*dishes*) piatti *mpl* sporchi; **to do the** ~ lavare i piatti, rigovernare
washing-up liquid *n* (*Brit*) detersivo liquido (per stoviglie)
wash-out ['wɔʃaut] *n* (*col*) disastro
washroom ['wɔʃrum] *n* gabinetto
wasn't ['wɔznt] = **was not**
Wasp, WASP [wɔsp] *n abbr* (*US: = White Anglo-Saxon Protestant*) W.A.S.P. *m* (*protestante bianco anglosassone*)
wasp [wɔsp] *n* vespa
waspish ['wɔspɪʃ] *adj* litigioso(-a)
wastage ['weɪstɪdʒ] *n* spreco; (*in manufacturing*) scarti *mpl*
waste [weɪst] *n* spreco; (*of time*) perdita; (*rubbish*) rifiuti *mpl* ▪ *adj* (*material*) di scarto; (*food*) avanzato(-a); (*energy, heat*) sprecato(-a); (*land, ground: in city*) abbandonato(-a); (*: in country*) incolto(-a) ▪ *vt* sprecare; (*time, opportunity*) perdere; **wastes** *npl* distesa desolata; **it's a** ~ **of money** sono soldi sprecati; **to go to** ~ andare sprecato; **to lay** ~ devastare
▸ **waste away** *vi* deperire
wastebasket ['weɪstbɑ:skɪt] *n* = **wastepaper basket**
waste disposal, waste disposal unit *n* (*Brit*) eliminatore *m* di rifiuti
wasteful ['weɪstful] *adj* sprecone(-a); (*process*) dispendioso(-a)
waste ground *n* (*Brit*) terreno incolto *or* abbandonato
wasteland ['weɪstlænd] *n* terra desolata
wastepaper basket ['weɪstpeɪpə-] *n* cestino per la carta straccia
waste pipe *n* tubo di scarico
waste products *npl* (*Industry*) materiali *mpl* di scarto
waster ['weɪstəʳ] *n* (*col*) buono(-a) a nulla
watch [wɔtʃ] *n* (*wristwatch*) orologio; (*act of watching*) sorveglianza; (*guard: Mil, Naut*) guardia; (*Naut: spell of duty*) quarto ▪ *vt* (*look at*) osservare; (*: match, programme*) guardare; (*spy on, guard*) sorvegliare, tenere d'occhio; (*be careful of*) fare attenzione a ▪ *vi* osservare, guardare; (*keep guard*) fare *or* montare la guardia; **to keep a close** ~ **on sb/sth** tener bene d'occhio qn/qc; ~ **how you drive/what you're doing** attento a come guidi/quel che fai
▸ **watch out** *vi* fare attenzione
watchband ['wɔtʃbænd] *n* (*US*) cinturino da orologio
watchdog ['wɔtʃdɔg] *n* cane *m* da guardia; (*fig*) sorvegliante *m/f*
watchful ['wɔtʃful] *adj* attento(-a), vigile
watchmaker ['wɔtʃmeɪkəʳ] *n* orologiaio(-a)
watchman ['wɔtʃmən] *n* guardiano; (*also:* **night watchman**) guardiano notturno
watch stem *n* (*US*) corona di carica
watch strap *n* cinturino da orologio

watchword ['wɔtʃwəːd] *n* parola d'ordine
water [wɔːtə^r] *n* acqua ■ *vt* (*plant*) annaffiare ■ *vi* (*eyes*) piangere; **in British waters** nelle acque territoriali britanniche; **I'd like a drink of ~** vorrei un bicchier d'acqua; **to pass ~** orinare; **to make sb's mouth ~** far venire l'acquolina in bocca a qn
▸ **water down** *vt* (*milk*) diluire; (*fig*: *story*) edulcorare
water closet *n* (*Brit*) W.C. *m inv*, gabinetto
watercolour, (*US*) **watercolor** ['wɔːtəkʌlə^r] *n* (*picture*) acquerello; **watercolours** *npl* colori *mpl* per acquerelli
water-cooled ['wɔːtəkuːld] *adj* raffreddato(-a) ad acqua
watercress ['wɔːtəkrɛs] *n* crescione *m*
waterfall ['wɔːtəfɔːl] *n* cascata
waterfront ['wɔːtəfrʌnt] *n* (*seafront*) lungomare *m*; (*at docks*) banchina
water heater *n* scaldabagno
water hole *n* pozza d'acqua
water ice *n* (*Brit*) sorbetto
watering can ['wɔːtərɪŋ-] *n* annaffiatoio
water level *n* livello dell'acqua; (*of flood*) livello delle acque
water lily *n* ninfea
waterline ['wɔːtəlaɪn] *n* (*Naut*) linea di galleggiamento
waterlogged ['wɔːtəlɔgd] *adj* saturo(-a) d'acqua; imbevuto(-a) d'acqua; (*football pitch etc*) allagato(-a)
watermark ['wɔːtəmɑːk] *n* (*on paper*) filigrana
watermelon ['wɔːtəmɛlən] *n* anguria, cocomero
water polo *n* pallanuoto *f*
waterproof ['wɔːtəpruːf] *adj* impermeabile
water-repellent ['wɔːtərɪ'pɛlənt] *adj* idrorepellente
watershed ['wɔːtəʃɛd] *n* (*Geo*, *fig*) spartiacque *m*
water-skiing ['wɔːtəskiːɪŋ] *n* sci *m* acquatico
water softener *n* addolcitore *m*; (*substance*) anti-calcare *m*
water tank *n* serbatoio d'acqua
watertight ['wɔːtətaɪt] *adj* stagno(-a)
water vapour *n* vapore *m* acqueo
waterway ['wɔːtəweɪ] *n* corso d'acqua navigabile
waterworks ['wɔːtəwəːks] *npl* impianto idrico
watery ['wɔːtərɪ] *adj* (*colour*) slavato(-a); (*coffee*) acquoso(-a)
watt [wɔt] *n* watt *m inv*
wattage ['wɔtɪdʒ] *n* wattaggio
wattle ['wɔtl] *n* graticcio
wave [weɪv] *n* onda; (*of hand*) gesto, segno; (*in hair*) ondulazione *f*; (*fig*: *of enthusiasm, strikes etc*) ondata ■ *vi* fare un cenno con la mano; (*flag*) sventolare ■ *vt* (*handkerchief*) sventolare; (*stick*) brandire; (*hair*) ondulare; **short/medium/long ~** (*Radio*) onde corte/medie/lunghe; **the new ~** (*Cine, Mus*) la new wave; **to ~ sb goodbye, to ~ goodbye to sb** fare un cenno d'addio a qn; **he waved us over to his table** ci invitò con un cenno al suo tavolo
▸ **wave aside, wave away** *vt* (*person*): **to ~ sb aside** fare cenno a qn di spostarsi; (*fig*: *suggestion, objection*) respingere, rifiutare; (: *doubts*) scacciare
waveband ['weɪvbænd] *n* gamma di lunghezze d'onda
wavelength ['weɪvlɛŋθ] *n* lunghezza d'onda
waver ['weɪvə^r] *vi* vacillare; (*voice*) tremolare
wavy ['weɪvɪ] *adj* ondulato(-a); ondeggiante
wax [wæks] *n* cera ■ *vt* dare la cera a; (*car*) lucidare ■ *vi* (*moon*) crescere
waxworks ['wækswəːks] *npl* cere *fpl*; museo delle cere
way [weɪ] *n* via, strada; (*path, access*) passaggio; (*distance*) distanza; (*direction*) parte *f*, direzione *f*; (*manner*) modo, stile *m*; (*habit*) abitudine *f*; (*condition*) condizione *f*; **which ~? — this ~** da che parte *or* in quale direzione? — da questa parte *or* per di qua; **to crawl one's ~ to ...** raggiungere ... strisciando; **he lied his ~ out of it** se l'è cavata mentendo; **to lose one's ~** perdere la strada; **on the ~** (*en route*) per strada; (*expected*) in arrivo; **you pass it on your ~ home** ci passi davanti andando a casa; **to be on one's ~** essere in cammino *or* sulla strada; **to be in the ~** bloccare il passaggio; (*fig*) essere tra i piedi *or* d'impiccio; **to keep out of sb's ~** evitare qn; **it's a long ~ away** è molto lontano da qui; **the village is rather out of the ~** il villaggio è abbastanza fuori mano; **to go out of one's ~ to do** (*fig*) mettercela tutta *or* fare di tutto per fare; **to be under ~** (*work, project*) essere in corso; **to make ~ (for sb/sth)** far strada (a qn/qc); (*fig*) lasciare il posto *or* far largo (a qn/qc); **to get one's own ~** fare come si vuole; **put it the right ~ up** (*Brit*) mettilo in piedi dalla parte giusta; **to be the wrong ~ round** essere al contrario; **he's in a bad ~** è ridotto male; **in a ~** in un certo senso; **in some ways** sotto certi aspetti; **in the ~ of** come; **by ~ of** (*through*) attraverso; (*as a sort of*) come; **"~ in"** "entrata", "ingresso"; **"~ out"** "uscita"; **the ~ back** la via del ritorno; **this ~ and that** di qua e di là; **"give ~"** (*Brit Aut*) "dare la precedenza"; **no ~!** (*col*) assolutamente no!
waybill ['weɪbɪl] *n* (*Comm*) bolla di accompagnamento

waylay [weɪ'leɪ] *vt irreg* tendere un agguato a; attendere al passaggio; (*fig*): **I got waylaid** ho avuto un contrattempo
wayside ['weɪsaɪd] *n* bordo della strada; **to fall by the ~** (*fig*) perdersi lungo la strada
way station *n* (*US Rail*) stazione *f* secondaria; (*fig*) tappa
wayward ['weɪwəd] *adj* capriccioso(-a); testardo(-a)
WC *n abbr* (*Brit*: = *water closet*) W.C. *m inv*, gabinetto
WCC *n abbr* (= *World Council of Churches*) Consiglio Ecumenico delle Chiese
we [wi:] *pl pron* noi; **here we are** eccoci
weak [wi:k] *adj* debole; (*health*) precario(-a); (*beam etc*) fragile; (*tea, coffee*) leggero(-a); **to grow ~(er)** indebolirsi
weaken ['wi:kən] *vi* indebolirsi ■ *vt* indebolire
weak-kneed ['wi:k'ni:d] *adj* (*fig*) debole, codardo(-a)
weakling ['wi:klɪŋ] *n* smidollato(-a); debole *m/f*
weakly ['wi:klɪ] *adj* deboluccio(-a), gracile ■ *adv* debolmente
weakness ['wi:knɪs] *n* debolezza; (*fault*) punto debole, difetto
wealth [wɛlθ] *n* (*money, resources*) ricchezza, ricchezze *fpl*; (*of details*) abbondanza, profusione *f*
wealth tax *n* imposta sul patrimonio
wealthy ['wɛlθɪ] *adj* ricco(-a)
wean [wi:n] *vt* svezzare
weapon ['wɛpən] *n* arma; **weapons of mass destruction** armi di distruzione di massa
wear [wɛə^r] *n* (*use*) uso; (*deterioration through use*) logorio, usura; (*clothing*): **sports/baby ~** abbigliamento sportivo/per neonati ■ *vb* (*pt* **wore**, *pp* **worn**) [wɔ:^r, wɔ:n] *vt* (*clothes*) portare; mettersi; (*look, smile, beard etc*) avere; (*damage*: *through use*) consumare ■ *vi* (*last*) durare; (*rub etc through*) consumarsi; **~ and tear** usura, consumo; **town/evening ~** abiti *mpl or* tenuta da città/sera; **to ~ a hole in sth** bucare qc a furia di usarlo
▸ **wear away** *vt* consumare; erodere ■ *vi* consumarsi; essere eroso(-a)
▸ **wear down** *vt* consumare; (*strength*) esaurire
▸ **wear off** *vi* sparire lentamente
▸ **wear on** *vi* passare
▸ **wear out** *vt* consumare; (*person, strength*) esaurire
wearable ['wɛərəbl] *adj* indossabile
wearily ['wɪərɪlɪ] *adv* stancamente
weariness ['wɪərɪnɪs] *n* stanchezza
wearisome ['wɪərɪsəm] *adj* (*tiring*) estenuante; (*boring*) noioso(-a)
weary ['wɪərɪ] *adj* stanco(-a); (*tiring*) faticoso(-a) ■ *vt* stancare ■ *vi*: **to ~ of** stancarsi di
weasel ['wi:zl] *n* (*Zool*) donnola
weather ['wɛðə^r] *n* tempo ■ *vt* (*wood*) stagionare; (*storm, crisis*) superare; **what's the ~ like?** che tempo fa?; **under the ~** (*fig*: *ill*) poco bene
weather-beaten ['wɛðəbi:tn] *adj* (*person*) segnato(-a) dalle intemperie; (*building*) logorato(-a) dalle intemperie
weather forecast *n* previsioni *fpl* del tempo, bollettino meteorologico
weatherman ['wɛðəmæn] *n* meteorologo
weatherproof ['wɛðəpru:f] *adj* (*garment*) impermeabile
weather report *n* bollettino meteorologico
weather vane *n* = **weather cock**
weave (*pt* **wove**, *pp* **woven**) [wi:v, wəuv, 'wəuvn] *vt* (*cloth*) tessere; (*basket*) intrecciare ■ *vi* (*fig*) (*pt, pp* **weaved**) (*move in and out*) zigzagare
weaver ['wi:və^r] *n* tessitore(-trice)
weaving ['wi:vɪŋ] *n* tessitura
web [wɛb] *n* (*of spider*) ragnatela; (*on foot*) palma; (*fabric, also fig*) tessuto; **the (World Wide) W~** la Rete
web address *n* indirizzo Internet
webbed [wɛbd] *adj* (*foot*) palmato(-a)
webbing ['wɛbɪŋ] *n* (*on chair*) cinghie *fpl*
webcam ['wɛbkæm] *n* webcam *f inv*
web page *n* (*Comput*) pagina *f* web *inv*
website ['wɛbsaɪt] *n* (*Comput*) sito
wed [wɛd] *vt* (*pt, pp* **wedded**) sposare ■ *n*: **the newly-weds** gli sposi novelli
Wed. *abbr* (= *Wednesday*) mer.
we'd [wi:d] = **we had; we would**
wedded ['wɛdɪd] *pt, pp of* **wed**
wedding ['wɛdɪŋ] *n* matrimonio; **silver/golden ~** nozze *fpl* d'argento/d'oro
wedding anniversary *n* anniversario di matrimonio
wedding day *n* giorno delle nozze *or* del matrimonio
wedding dress *n* abito nuziale
wedding present *n* regalo di nozze
wedding ring *n* fede *f*
wedge [wɛdʒ] *n* (*of wood etc*) cuneo; (*under door etc*) zeppa; (*of cake*) spicchio, fetta ■ *vt* mettere una zeppa sotto (*or* in); **to ~ a door open** tenere aperta una porta con un fermo
wedge-heeled shoes ['wɛdʒhi:ld-] *npl* scarpe *fpl* con tacco a zeppa
wedlock ['wɛdlɔk] *n* vincolo matrimoniale
Wednesday ['wɛdnzdɪ] *n* mercoledì *m inv*; *see also* **Tuesday**
wee [wi:] *adj* (*Scottish*) piccolo(-a)

W

weed [wi:d] *n* erbaccia ■ *vt* diserbare
▸ **weed out** *vt* fare lo spoglio di
weed-killer ['wi:dkɪləʳ] *n* diserbante *m*
weedy ['wi:dɪ] *adj* (*man*) allampanato
week [wi:k] *n* settimana; **once/twice a ~** una volta/due volte alla settimana; **in 2 weeks' time** fra 2 settimane, fra 15 giorni; **Tuesday ~, a ~ on Tuesday** martedì a otto
weekday ['wi:kdeɪ] *n* giorno feriale; (*Comm*) giornata lavorativa; **on weekdays** durante la settimana
weekend [wi:k'ɛnd] *n* fine settimana *m or f inv*, weekend *m inv*
weekend case *n* borsa da viaggio
weekly ['wi:klɪ] *adv* ogni settimana, settimanalmente ■ *adj, n* settimanale (*m*)
weep (*pt, pp* **wept**) [wi:p, wɛpt] *vi* (*person*) piangere; (*Med: wound etc*) essudare
weeping willow ['wi:pɪŋ-] *n* salice *m* piangente
weepy ['wi:pɪ] *n* (*col*) film *m inv or* storia strappalacrime
weft [wɛft] *n* (*Textiles*) trama
weigh [weɪ] *vt, vi* pesare; **to ~ anchor** salpare *or* levare l'ancora; **to ~ the pros and cons** valutare i pro e i contro
▸ **weigh down** *vt* (*branch*) piegare; (*fig: with worry*) opprimere, caricare
▸ **weigh out** *vt* (*goods*) pesare
▸ **weigh up** *vt* valutare
weighbridge ['weɪbrɪdʒ] *n* bascula
weighing machine ['weɪɪŋ-] *n* pesa
weight [weɪt] *n* peso; **sold by ~** venduto(-a) a peso; **weights and measures** pesi e misure; **to put on/lose ~** ingrassare/dimagrire
weighting ['weɪtɪŋ] *n*: **~ allowance** indennità *f inv* speciale (*per carovita etc*)
weightlessness ['weɪtlɪsnɪs] *n* mancanza di peso
weightlifter ['weɪtlɪftəʳ] *n* pesista *m*
weight training *n*: **to do ~** allenarsi con i pesi
weighty ['weɪtɪ] *adj* pesante; (*fig*) importante, grave
weir [wɪəʳ] *n* diga
weird [wɪəd] *adj* strano(-a), bizzarro(-a); (*eerie*) soprannaturale
weirdo ['wɪədəu] *n* (*col*) tipo(-a) allucinante
welcome ['wɛlkəm] *adj* benvenuto(-a) ■ *n* accoglienza, benvenuto ■ *vt* accogliere cordialmente; (*also*: **bid welcome**) dare il benvenuto a; (*be glad of*) rallegrarsi di; **to be ~** essere il/la benvenuto(-a); **to make sb ~** accogliere bene qn; **you're ~** (*after thanks*) prego; **you're ~ to try** provi pure
welcoming ['wɛlkəmɪŋ] *adj* accogliente
weld [wɛld] *n* saldatura ■ *vt* saldare
welder ['wɛldəʳ] *n* (*person*) saldatore *m*
welding ['wɛldɪŋ] *n* saldatura (autogena)
welfare ['wɛlfɛəʳ] *n* benessere *m*
welfare state *n* stato sociale
welfare work *n* assistenza sociale
well [wɛl] *n* pozzo ■ *adv* bene ■ *adj*: **to be ~** (*person*) stare bene ■ *excl* allora!; ma!; ebbene!; **~ done!** bravo(-a)!; **get ~ soon!** guarisci presto!; **to do ~ in sth** riuscire in qc; **to be doing ~** stare bene; **to think ~ of sb** avere una buona opinione di qn; **I don't feel ~** non mi sento bene; **as ~** (*in addition*) anche; **X as ~ as Y** sia X che Y; **he did as ~ as he could** ha fatto come meglio poteva; **you might as ~ tell me** potresti anche dirmelo; **it would be as ~ to ask** sarebbe bene chiedere; **~, as I was saying ...** dunque, come stavo dicendo ...
▸ **well up** *vi* (*tears, emotions*) sgorgare
we'll [wi:l] = **we will; we shall**
well-behaved ['wɛlbɪ'heɪvd] *adj* ubbidiente
well-being ['wɛl'bi:ɪŋ] *n* benessere *m*
well-bred ['wɛl'brɛd] *adj* educato(-a), beneducato(-a)
well-built ['wɛl'bɪlt] *adj* (*person*) ben fatto(-a)
well-chosen ['wɛl'tʃəuzn] *adj* (*remarks, words*) ben scelto(-a), appropriato(-a)
well-developed ['wɛldɪ'vɛləpt] *adj* sviluppato(-a)
well-disposed ['wɛldɪs'pəuzd] *adj*: **~ to(wards)** bendisposto(-a) verso
well-dressed ['wɛl'drɛst] *adj* ben vestito(-a), vestito(-a) bene
well-earned ['wɛl'ə:nd] *adj* (*rest*) meritato(-a)
well-groomed ['wɛl'gru:md] *adj* curato(-a), azzimato(-a)
well-heeled ['wɛl'hi:ld] *adj* (*col: wealthy*) agiato(-a), facoltoso(-a)
well-informed ['welɪn'fɔ:md] *adj* ben informato(-a)
Wellington ['wɛlɪŋtən] *n* Wellington *f*
wellingtons ['wɛlɪŋtənz] *npl* (*also*: **wellington boots**) stivali *mpl* di gomma
well-kept ['wɛl'kɛpt] *adj* (*house, grounds, secret*) ben tenuto(-a); (*hair, hands*) ben curato(-a)
well-known ['wɛl'nəun] *adj* noto(-a), famoso(-a)
well-mannered ['wɛl'mænəd] *adj* ben educato(-a)
well-meaning ['wɛl'mi:nɪŋ] *adj* ben intenzionato(-a)
well-nigh ['wɛl'naɪ] *adv*: **~ impossible** quasi impossibile
well-off ['wɛl'ɔf] *adj* benestante, danaroso(-a)
well-read ['wɛl'rɛd] *adj* colto(-a)
well-spoken ['wɛl'spəukn] *adj* che parla bene
well-stocked ['wɛl'stɔkt] *adj* (*shop, larder*) ben fornito(-a)

well-timed ['wɛl'taɪmd] *adj* opportuno(-a)
well-to-do ['wɛltə'du:] *adj* abbiente, benestante
well-wisher ['wɛlwɪʃəʳ] *n* ammiratore(-trice); **letters from well-wishers** lettere *fpl* di incoraggiamento
well-woman clinic ['wɛlwumən-] *n* ≈ consultorio (familiare)
Welsh [wɛlʃ] *adj* gallese ■ *n* (*Ling*) gallese *m*; **the ~** *npl* i gallesi; **the ~ National Assembly** il Parlamento gallese
Welshman ['wɛlʃmən], **Welshwoman** ['wɛlʃwumən] *n* gallese *m/f*
Welsh rarebit *n* crostino al formaggio
welter ['wɛltəʳ] *n* massa, mucchio
went [wɛnt] *pt of* **go**
wept [wɛpt] *pt, pp of* **weep**
were [wə:ʳ] *pt of* **be**
we're [wɪəʳ] = **we are**
weren't [wə:nt] = **were not**
werewolf (*pl* **-wolves**) ['wɪəwulf, -wulvz] *n* licantropo, lupo mannaro (*col*)
west [wɛst] *n* ovest *m*, occidente *m*, ponente *m* ■ *adj* (a) ovest *inv*, occidentale ■ *adv* verso ovest; **the W~** l'Occidente
westbound ['wɛstbaund] *adj* (*traffic*) diretto(-a) a ovest; (*carriageway*) ovest *inv*
West Country *n*: **the ~** il sud-ovest dell'Inghilterra
westerly ['wɛstəlɪ] *adj* (*wind*) occidentale, da ovest
western ['wɛstən] *adj* occidentale, dell'ovest ■ *n* (*Cine*) western *m inv*
westerner ['wɛstənəʳ] *n* occidentale *m/f*
westernized ['wɛstənaɪzd] *adj* occidentalizzato(-a)
West German *adj, n* (*formerly*) tedesco(-a) occidentale
West Germany *n* (*formerly*) Germania Occidentale
West Indian *adj* delle Indie Occidentali ■ *n* abitante *m/f* (*or* originario(-a)) delle Indie Occidentali
West Indies [-'ɪndɪz] *npl*: **the ~** le Indie Occidentali
Westminster ['wɛstmɪnstəʳ] *n* il parlamento (britannico)
westward ['wɛstwəd], **westwards** ['wɛstwədz] *adv* verso ovest
wet [wɛt] *adj* umido(-a), bagnato(-a); (*soaked*) fradicio(-a); (*rainy*) piovoso(-a) ■ *vt*: **to ~ one's pants** *or* **o.s.** farsi la pipì addosso; **to get ~** bagnarsi; **"~ paint"** "vernice fresca"
wet blanket *n* (*fig*) guastafeste *m/f inv*
wetness ['wɛtnɪs] *n* umidità
wet suit *n* tuta da sub
we've [wi:v] = **we have**
whack [wæk] *vt* picchiare, battere
whacked [wækt] *adj* (*col: tired*) sfinito(-a), a pezzi
whale [weɪl] *n* (*Zool*) balena
whaler ['weɪləʳ] *n* (*ship*) baleniera
whaling ['weɪlɪŋ] *n* caccia alla balena
wharf (*pl* **wharves**) [wɔ:f, wɔ:vz] *n* banchina

 KEYWORD

what [wɔt] *adj* **1** (*in direct/indirect questions*) che; quale; **what size is it?** che taglia è?; **what colour is it?** di che colore è?; **what books do you want?** quali *or* che libri vuole?; **for what reason?** per quale motivo?
2 (*in exclamations*) che; **what a mess!** che disordine!
■ *pron* **1** (*interrogative*) che cosa, cosa, che; **what's in there?** cosa c'è lì dentro?; **what is his address?** qual è il suo indirizzo?; **what will it cost?** quanto costerà?; **what are you doing?** che *or* (che) cosa fai?; **what are you talking about?** di che cosa parli?; **what's happening?** che *or* (che) cosa succede?; **what is it called?** come si chiama?; **what about me?** e io?; **what about doing ...?** e se facessimo ...?
2 (*relative*) ciò che, quello che; **I saw what you did** ho visto quello che hai fatto; **I saw what was on the table** ho visto cosa c'era sul tavolo; **what I want is a cup of tea** ciò che voglio adesso è una tazza di tè
3 (*indirect use*) (che) cosa; **he asked me what she had said** mi ha chiesto che cosa avesse detto; **tell me what you're thinking about** dimmi a cosa stai pensando; **I don't know what to do** non so cosa fare
■ *excl* (*disbelieving*) cosa!, come!

whatever [wɔt'ɛvəʳ] *adj*: **~ book** qualunque *or* qualsiasi libro + *sub* ■ *pron*: **do ~ is necessary/you want** faccia qualunque *or* qualsiasi cosa sia necessaria/lei voglia; **~ happens** qualunque cosa accada; **no reason ~** *or* **whatsoever** nessuna ragione affatto *or* al mondo; **~ it costs** costi quello che costi
whatsoever [wɔtsəu'ɛvəʳ] *adj, pron* = **whatever**
wheat [wi:t] *n* grano, frumento
wheatgerm ['wi:tdʒə:m] *n* germe *m* di grano
wheatmeal ['wi:tmi:l] *n* farina integrale di frumento
wheedle ['wi:dl] *vt*: **to ~ sb into doing sth** convincere qn a fare qc (con lusinghe); **to ~ sth out of sb** ottenere qc da qn (con lusinghe)

wheel [wi:l] *n* ruota; (*Aut*: *also*: **steering wheel**) volante *m*; (*Naut*) (ruota del) timone *m* ■ *vt* spingere ■ *vi* (*also*: **wheel round**) girare
wheelbarrow ['wi:lbærəu] *n* carriola
wheelbase ['wi:lbeɪs] *n* interasse *m*
wheelchair ['wi:ltʃɛə^r] *n* sedia a rotelle
wheel clamp *n* (*Aut*) morsetto *m* bloccaruota *inv*
wheeler-dealer ['wi:lə'di:lə^r] *n* trafficone *m*, maneggione *m*
wheelie-bin ['wi:lɪbɪn] *n* (*Brit*) bidone *m* (della spazzatura) a rotelle
wheeling ['wi:lɪŋ] *n*: **~ and dealing** maneggi *mpl*
wheeze [wi:z] *n* respiro affannoso ■ *vi* ansimare
wheezy ['wi:zɪ] *adj* (*person*) che respira con affanno; (*breath*) sibilante

 KEYWORD

when [wɛn] *adv* quando; **when did it happen?** quando è successo?
■ *conj* **1** (*at, during, after the time that*) quando; **she was reading when I came in** quando sono entrato lei leggeva; **that was when I needed you** era allora che avevo bisogno di te
2 (*on, at which*): **on the day when I met him** il giorno in cui l'ho incontrato; **one day when it was raining** un giorno che pioveva
3 (*whereas*) quando, mentre; **you said I was wrong when in fact I was right** mi hai detto che avevo torto, quando in realtà avevo ragione

whenever [wɛn'ɛvə^r] *adv* quando mai ■ *conj* quando; (*every time that*) ogni volta che; **I go ~ I can** ci vado ogni volta che posso
where [wɛə^r] *adv, conj* dove; **this is ~** è qui che; **~ are you from?** di dov'è?; **~ possible** quando è possibile, se possibile
whereabouts ['wɛərəbauts] *adv* dove ■ *n*: **sb's ~** luogo dove qn si trova
whereas [wɛər'æz] *conj* mentre
whereby [wɛə'baɪ] *adv* (*formal*) per cui
whereupon [wɛərə'pɔn] *adv* al che
wherever [wɛər'ɛvə^r] *adv* dove mai ■ *conj* dovunque + *sub*; **sit ~ you like** si sieda dove vuole
wherewithal ['wɛəwɪðɔ:l] *n*: **the ~ (to do sth)** i mezzi (per fare qc)
whet [wɛt] *vt* (*tool*) affilare; (*appetite etc*) stimolare
whether ['wɛðə^r] *conj* se; **I don't know ~ to accept or not** non so se accettare o no; **it's doubtful ~** è poco probabile che; **~ you go or not** che lei vada o no
whey [weɪ] *n* siero

 KEYWORD

which [wɪtʃ] *adj* **1** (*interrogative*: *direct, indirect*) quale; **which picture do you want?** quale quadro vuole?; **which one?** quale?; **which one of you did it?** chi di voi lo ha fatto?; **tell me which one you want** mi dica quale vuole
2: **in which case** nel qual caso; **by which time** e a quel punto
■ *pron* **1** (*interrogative*) quale; **which (of these) are yours?** quali di questi sono suoi?; **which of you are coming?** chi di voi viene?
2 (*relative*) che; (: *indirect*) cui, il/la quale; **the apple which you ate/which is on the table** la mela che hai mangiato/che è sul tavolo; **the chair on which you are sitting** la sedia sulla quale *or* su cui sei seduto; **the book of which we were speaking** il libro del quale stavamo parlando; **he said he knew, which is true** ha detto che lo sapeva, il che è vero; **I don't mind which** non mi importa quale; **after which** dopo di che

whichever [wɪtʃ'ɛvə^r] *adj*: **take ~ book you prefer** prenda qualsiasi libro che preferisce; **~ book you take** qualsiasi libro prenda; **~ way you ...** in qualunque modo lei ... + *sub*
whiff [wɪf] *n* odore *m*; **to catch a ~ of sth** sentire l'odore di qc
while [waɪl] *n* momento ■ *conj* mentre; (*as long as*) finché; (*although*) sebbene + *sub*; **for a ~** per un po'; **in a ~** tra poco; **all the ~** tutto il tempo; **we'll make it worth your ~** faremo in modo che le valga la pena
▸ **while away** *vt* (*time*) far passare
whilst [waɪlst] *conj* = **while**
whim [wɪm] *n* capriccio
whimper ['wɪmpə^r] *n* piagnucolio ■ *vi* piagnucolare
whimsical ['wɪmzɪkl] *adj* (*person*) capriccioso(-a); (*look*) strano(-a)
whine [waɪn] *n* gemito ■ *vi* gemere; uggiolare; piagnucolare
whip [wɪp] *n* frusta; (*for riding*) frustino; (*Pol*: *person*) capogruppo; *vedi nota* ■ *vt* frustare; (*Culin*: *cream etc*) sbattere; (*snatch*) sollevare (*or* estrarre) bruscamente
▸ **whip up** *vt* (*cream*) montare, sbattere; (*col*: *meal*) improvvisare; (: *stir up*: *support, feeling*) suscitare, stimolare

WHIP

Nel Parlamento britannico i *whips* sono parlamentari incaricati di mantenere la disciplina tra i deputati del loro partito durante le votazioni e di verificare la loro presenza in aula.

whiplash ['wɪplæʃ] *n* (*Med*: *also*: **whiplash injury**) colpo di frusta
whipped cream ['wɪpt-] *n* panna montata
whipping boy ['wɪpɪŋ-] *n* (*fig*) capro espiatorio
whip-round ['wɪpraund] *n* (*Brit*) colletta
whirl [wəːl] *n* turbine *m* ■ *vt* (far) girare rapidamente; (far) turbinare ■ *vi* turbinare; (*dancers*) volteggiare; (*leaves, dust*) sollevarsi in un vortice
whirlpool ['wəːlpuːl] *n* mulinello
whirlwind ['wəːlwɪnd] *n* turbine *m*
whirr [wəːʳ] *vi* ronzare
whisk [wɪsk] *n* (*Culin*) frusta; frullino ■ *vt* sbattere, frullare; **to ~ sb away** *or* **off** portar via qn a tutta velocità
whiskers ['wɪskəz] *npl* (*of animal*) baffi *mpl*; (*of man*) favoriti *mpl*
whisky, (*Irish, US*) **whiskey** ['wɪskɪ] *n* whisky *m inv*
whisper ['wɪspəʳ] *n* bisbiglio, sussurro; (*rumour*) voce *f* ■ *vt, vi* bisbigliare, sussurrare; **to ~ sth to sb** bisbigliare qc a qn
whispering ['wɪspərɪŋ] *n* bisbiglio
whist [wɪst] *n* (*Brit*) whist *m*
whistle ['wɪsl] *n* (*sound*) fischio; (*object*) fischietto ■ *vi, vt* fischiare; **to ~ a tune** fischiettare un motivetto
whistle-stop ['wɪslstɔp] *adj*: **~ tour** (*Pol, fig*) rapido giro
Whit [wɪt] *n* Pentecoste *f*
white [waɪt] *adj* bianco(-a); (*with fear*) pallido(-a) ■ *n* bianco; (*person*) bianco(-a); **to turn** *or* **go ~** (*person*) sbiancare; (*hair*) diventare bianco; **the whites** (*washing*) i capi bianchi; **tennis whites** completo da tennis
whitebait ['waɪtbeɪt] *n* bianchetti *mpl*
whiteboard ['waɪtbɔːd] *n* lavagna bianca; **interactive ~** lavagna interattiva
white-collar worker ['waɪtkɔlə-] *n* impiegato(-a)
white elephant *n* (*fig*) oggetto (*or* progetto) costoso ma inutile
white goods *npl* (*appliances*) elettrodomestici *mpl*; (*linens*) biancheria per la casa
white-hot [waɪt'hɔt] *adj* (*metal*) incandescente
White House *n*: **the ~** la Casa Bianca; *vedi nota*

WHITE HOUSE

La *White House* è la residenza ufficiale del presidente degli Stati Uniti e ha sede a Washington DC. Spesso il termine viene usato per indicare l'esecutivo del governo statunitense.

white lie *n* bugia pietosa
whiteness ['waɪtnɪs] *n* bianchezza
white noise *n* rumore *m* bianco
white paper *n* (*Pol*) libro bianco
whitewash ['waɪtwɔʃ] *n* (*paint*) bianco di calce ■ *vt* imbiancare; (*fig*) coprire
whiting ['waɪtɪŋ] *n* (*pl inv*) merlango
Whit Monday *n* lunedì *m inv* di Pentecoste
Whitsun ['wɪtsn] *n* Pentecoste *f*
whittle ['wɪtl] *vt*: **to ~ away**, **~ down** ridurre, tagliare
whizz [wɪz] *vi* passare sfrecciando
whizz kid *n* (*col*) prodigio
WHO *n abbr* (= *World Health Organization*) O.M.S. *f* (= *Organizzazione mondiale della sanità*)

KEYWORD

who [huː] *pron* **1** (*interrogative*) chi; **who is it?, who's there?** chi è?
2 (*relative*) che; **the man who spoke to me** l'uomo che ha parlato con me; **those who can swim** quelli che sanno nuotare

whodunit [huː'dʌnɪt] *n* (*col*) giallo
whoever [huː'ɛvəʳ] *pron*: **~ finds it** chiunque lo trovi; **ask ~ you like** lo chieda a chiunque vuole; **~ told you that?** chi mai glielʼha detto?
whole [həul] *adj* (*complete*) tutto(-a), completo(-a); (*not broken*) intero(-a), intatto(-a) ■ *n* (*total*) totale *m*; (*sth not broken*) tutto; **the ~ lot (of it)** tutto; **the ~ lot (of them)** tutti; **the ~ of the time** tutto il tempo; **the ~ of the town** la città intera; **on the ~, as a ~** nel complesso, nell'insieme; **~ villages were destroyed** interi paesi furono distrutti
wholehearted [həul'hɑːtɪd] *adj* sincero(-a)
wholemeal ['həulmiːl] *adj* (*Brit: flour, bread*) integrale
whole note *n* (*US*) semibreve *f*
wholesale ['həulseɪl] *n* commercio *or* vendita all'ingrosso ■ *adj* all'ingrosso; (*destruction*) totale
wholesaler ['həulseɪləʳ] *n* grossista *m/f*
wholesome ['həulsəm] *adj* sano(-a); (*climate*) salubre
wholewheat ['həulwiːt] *adj* = **wholemeal**

W

wholly ['həulɪ] *adv* completamente, del tutto

whom [hu:m] *pron* **1** (*interrogative*) chi; **whom did you see?** chi hai visto?; **to whom did you give it?** a chi lo hai dato?
2 (*relative*) che, *prep* + il/la quale; **the man whom I saw** l'uomo che ho visto; **the man to whom I spoke** l'uomo al *or* con il quale ho parlato; **those to whom I spoke** le persone alle *or* con le quali ho parlato

whooping cough ['hu:pɪŋ-] *n* pertosse *f*
whoops [wu:ps] *excl*: **~-a-daisy!** ops!
whoosh [wuʃ] *n*: **it came out with a ~** (*sauce etc*) è uscito di getto; (*air*) è uscito con un sibilo
whopper ['wɔpə^r] *n* (*col: lie*) balla; (*: large thing*) cosa enorme
whopping ['wɔpɪŋ] *adj* (*col: big*) enorme
whore [hɔ:^r] *n* (*pej*) puttana

whose [hu:z] *adj* **1** (*possessive: interrogative*) di chi; **whose book is this?, whose is this book?** di chi è questo libro?; **whose daughter are you?** di chi sei figlia?; **whose pencil have you taken?** di chi è la matita che hai preso?
2 (*possessive: relative*): **the man whose son you rescued** l'uomo il cui figlio hai salvato *or* a cui hai salvato il figlio; **the girl whose sister you were speaking to** la ragazza alla cui sorella stavi parlando
■ *pron* di chi; **whose is this?** di chi è questo?; **I know whose it is** so di chi è

Who's Who ['hu:z'hu:] *n elenco di personalità*
why [waɪ] *adv, conj* perché ■ *excl* (*surprise*) ma guarda un po'!; (*remonstrating*) ma (via)!; (*explaining*) ebbene!; **~ not?** perché no?; **~ not do it now?** perché non farlo adesso?; **the reason ~** il motivo per cui
whyever [waɪ'ɛvə^r] *adv* perché mai
WI *n abbr* (*Brit*: = *Women's Institute*) circolo femminile ■ *abbr* (*Geo*) = **West Indies**; (*US*) = **Wisconsin**
wick [wɪk] *n* lucignolo, stoppino
wicked ['wɪkɪd] *adj* cattivo(-a), malvagio(-a); (*mischievous*) malizioso(-a)
wicker ['wɪkə^r] *n* vimine *m*; (*also*: **wickerwork**) articoli *mpl* di vimini
wicket ['wɪkɪt] *n* (*Cricket*) porta; area tra le due porte
wicket keeper *n* (*Cricket*) ≈ portiere *m*
wide [waɪd] *adj* largo(-a); (*region, knowledge*) vasto(-a); (*choice*) ampio(-a) ■ *adv*: **to open ~** spalancare; **to shoot ~** tirare a vuoto *or* fuori bersaglio; **it is 3 metres ~** è largo 3 metri
wide-angle lens ['waɪdæŋgl-] *n* grandangolare *m*
wide-awake [waɪdə'weɪk] *adj* completamente sveglio(-a)
wide-eyed [waɪd'aɪd] *adj* con gli occhi spalancati
widely ['waɪdlɪ] *adv* (*different*) molto, completamente; (*believed*) generalmente; **~ spaced** molto distanziati(-e); **to be ~ read** (*author*) essere molto letto; (*reader*) essere molto colto
widen ['waɪdn] *vt* allargare, ampliare
wideness ['waɪdnɪs] *n* larghezza; vastità; ampiezza
wide open *adj* spalancato(-a)
wide-ranging [waɪd'reɪndʒɪŋ] *adj* (*survey, report*) vasto(-a); (*interests*) svariato(-a)
widescreen ['waɪdskri:n] *adj* (*television*) a schermo panoramico
widespread ['waɪdsprɛd] *adj* (*belief etc*) molto *or* assai diffuso(-a)
widget ['wɪdʒɪt] *n* (*Comput*) widget *m inv*
widow ['wɪdəu] *n* vedova
widowed ['wɪdəud] *adj* (che è rimasto(-a)) vedovo(-a)
widower ['wɪdəuə^r] *n* vedovo
width [wɪdθ] *n* larghezza; **it's 7 metres in ~** è largo 7 metri
widthways ['wɪdθweɪz] *adv* trasversalmente
wield [wi:ld] *vt* (*sword*) maneggiare; (*power*) esercitare
wife (*pl* **wives**) [waɪf, waɪvz] *n* moglie *f*
Wi-Fi ['waɪfaɪ] *n* WiFi *m*
wig [wɪg] *n* parrucca
wigging ['wɪgɪŋ] *n* (*Brit col*) lavata di capo
wiggle ['wɪgl] *vt* dimenare, agitare ■ *vi* (*loose screw etc*) traballare; (*worm*) torcersi
wiggly ['wɪglɪ] *adj* (*line*) ondulato(-a), sinuoso(-a)
wild [waɪld] *adj* (*animal, plant*) selvatico(-a); (*countryside, appearance*) selvaggio(-a); (*sea*) tempestoso(-a); (*idea, life*) folle; (*col: angry*) arrabbiato(-a), furibondo(-a); (*enthusiastic*): **to be ~ about** andar pazzo(-a) per ■ *n*: **the ~** la natura; **wilds** *npl* regione *f* selvaggia
wild card *n* (*Comput*) carattere *m* jolly *inv*
wildcat ['waɪldkæt] *n* gatto(-a) selvatico(-a)
wildcat strike *n* ≈ sciopero selvaggio
wilderness ['wɪldənɪs] *n* deserto
wildfire ['waɪldfaɪə^r] *n*: **to spread like ~** propagarsi rapidamente
wild-goose chase [waɪld'gu:s-] *n* (*fig*) pista falsa

wildlife ['waɪldlaɪf] *n* natura
wildly ['waɪldlɪ] *adv* (*applaud*) freneticamente; (*hit, guess*) a casaccio; (*happy*) follemente
wiles [waɪlz] *npl* astuzie *fpl*
wilful, (*US*) **willful** ['wɪlful] *adj* (*person*) testardo(-a); ostinato(-a); (*action*) intenzionale; (*crime*) premeditato(-a)

KEYWORD

will [wɪl] *aux vb* **1** (*forming future tense*): **I will finish it tomorrow** lo finirò domani; **I will have finished it by tomorrow** lo finirò entro domani; **will you do it? — yes I will/ no I won't** lo farai? — sì (lo farò)/no (non lo farò); **the car won't start** la macchina non parte
2 (*in conjectures, predictions*): **he will** *or* **he'll be there by now** dovrebbe essere arrivato a quest'ora; **that will be the postman** sarà il postino
3 (*in commands, requests, offers*): **will you be quiet!** vuoi stare zitto?; **will you sit down?** (*politely*) prego, si accomodi; (*angrily*) vuoi metterti seduto?; **will you come?** vieni anche tu?; **will you help me?** mi aiuti?, mi puoi aiutare?; **you won't lose it, will you?** non lo perderai, vero?; **will you have a cup of tea?** vorrebbe una tazza di tè?; **I won't put up with it!** non lo accetterò!
■ *vt* (*pt, pp* **willed**); **to will sb to do** pregare tra sé perché qn faccia; **he willed himself to go on** continuò grazie a un grande sforzo di volontà
■ *n* **1** (*desire*) volontà; **against sb's will** contro la volontà *or* il volere di qn; **to do sth of one's own free will** fare qc di propria volontà
2 (*Law*) testamento; **to make a/one's will** fare testamento

willful ['wɪlful] *adj* (*US*) = **wilful**
willing ['wɪlɪŋ] *adj* volonteroso(-a) ■ *n*: **to show ~** dare prova di buona volontà; **~ to do** disposto(-a) a fare
willingly ['wɪlɪŋlɪ] *adv* volentieri
willingness ['wɪlɪŋnɪs] *n* buona volontà
will-o'-the-wisp [wɪləðə'wɪsp] *n* (*also fig*) fuoco fatuo
willow ['wɪləu] *n* salice *m*
will power *n* forza di volontà
willy-nilly ['wɪlɪ'nɪlɪ] *adv* volente o nolente
wilt [wɪlt] *vi* appassire
Wilts [wɪlts] *abbr* (*Brit*) = **Wiltshire**
wily ['waɪlɪ] *adj* furbo(-a)
wimp [wɪmp] *n* (*col*) mezza calzetta
win [wɪn] *n* (*in sports etc*) vittoria ■ *vb* (*pt, pp* **won**) [wʌn] *vt* (*battle, prize*) vincere; (*money*) guadagnare; (*popularity*) conquistare; (*contract*) aggiudicarsi ■ *vi* vincere
▸ **win over** (*Brit*), **win round** *vt* convincere
wince [wɪns] *n* trasalimento, sussulto ■ *vi* trasalire
winch [wɪntʃ] *n* verricello, argano
Winchester disk ['wɪntʃɪstə-] *n* (*Comput*) disco Winchester
wind¹ [wɪnd] *n* vento; (*Med*) flatulenza, ventosità ■ *vt* (*take breath away*) far restare senza fiato; **the ~(s)** (*Mus*) i fiati; **into** *or* **against the ~** controvento; **to get ~ of sth** venire a sapere qc; **to break ~** scoreggiare (*col*)
wind² (*pt, pp* **wound**) [waɪnd, waund] *vt* attorcigliare; (*wrap*) avvolgere; (*clock, toy*) caricare ■ *vi* (*road, river*) serpeggiare
▸ **wind down** *vt* (*car window*) abbassare; (*fig: production, business*) diminuire
▸ **wind up** *vt* (*clock*) caricare; (*debate*) concludere
windbreak ['wɪndbreɪk] *n* frangivento
windcheater ['wɪndtʃiːtəʳ], (*US*) **windbreaker** ['wɪndbreɪkəʳ] *n* giacca a vento
winder ['waɪndəʳ] *n* (*Brit: on watch*) corona di carica
windfall ['wɪndfɔːl] *n* colpo di fortuna
wind farm *n* centrale *f* eolica
winding ['waɪndɪŋ] *adj* (*road*) serpeggiante; (*staircase*) a chiocciola
wind instrument *n* (*Mus*) strumento a fiato
windmill ['wɪndmɪl] *n* mulino a vento
window ['wɪndəu] *n* (*gen, Comput*) finestra; (*in car, train*) finestrino; (*in shop etc*) vetrina; (*also:* **window pane**) vetro
window box *n* cassetta da fiori
window cleaner *n* (*person*) pulitore *m* di finestre
window dressing *n* allestimento della vetrina
window envelope *n* busta a finestra
window frame *n* telaio di finestra
window ledge *n* davanzale *m*
window pane *n* vetro
window-shopping ['wɪndəuʃɔpɪŋ] *n*: **to go ~** andare a vedere le vetrine
windowsill ['wɪndəusɪl] *n* davanzale *m*
windpipe ['wɪndpaɪp] *n* trachea
wind power *n* energia eolica
windscreen ['wɪndskriːn], (*US*) **windshield** ['wɪndʃiːld] *n* parabrezza *m inv*
windscreen washer *n* lavacristallo
windscreen wiper *n* tergicristallo
windshield ['wɪndʃiːld] *n* (*US*) = **windscreen**
windsurfing ['wɪndsəːfɪŋ] *n* windsurf *m inv*
windswept ['wɪndswɛpt] *adj* spazzato(-a) dal vento

W

wind tunnel *n* galleria aerodinamica *or* del vento
windy ['wɪndɪ] *adj* ventoso(-a); **it's ~** c'è vento
wine [waɪn] *n* vino ■ *vt*: **to ~ and dine sb** offrire un ottimo pranzo a qn
wine bar *n* enoteca
wine cellar *n* cantina
wine glass *n* bicchiere *m* da vino
wine list *n* lista dei vini
wine merchant *n* commerciante *m* di vino
wine tasting *n* degustazione *f* dei vini
wine waiter *n* sommelier *m inv*
wing [wɪŋ] *n* ala; **wings** *npl* (*Theat*) quinte *fpl*
winger ['wɪŋəʳ] *n* (*Sport*) ala
wing mirror *n* (*Brit*) specchietto retrovisore esterno
wing nut *n* galletto
wingspan ['wɪŋspæn], **wingspread** ['wɪŋsprɛd] *n* apertura alare, apertura d'ali
wink [wɪŋk] *n* occhiolino, strizzatina d'occhi ■ *vi* ammiccare, fare l'occhiolino
winkle ['wɪŋkl] *n* litorina
winner ['wɪnəʳ] *n* vincitore(-trice)
winning ['wɪnɪŋ] *adj* (*team*) vincente; (*goal*) decisivo(-a); (*charming*) affascinante; *see also* **winnings**
winning post *n* traguardo
winnings ['wɪnɪŋz] *npl* vincite *fpl*
winsome ['wɪnsəm] *adj* accattivante
winter ['wɪntəʳ] *n* inverno; **in ~** d'inverno, in inverno
winter sports *npl* sport *mpl* invernali
wintry ['wɪntrɪ] *adj* invernale
wipe [waɪp] *n* pulita, passata ■ *vt* pulire (strofinando); (*dishes*) asciugare; **to give sth a ~** dare una pulita *or* una passata a qc; **to ~ one's nose** soffiarsi il naso
▸ **wipe off** *vt* cancellare; (*stains*) togliere strofinando
▸ **wipe out** *vt* (*debt*) pagare, liquidare; (*memory*) cancellare; (*destroy*) annientare
▸ **wipe up** *vt* asciugare
wire ['waɪəʳ] *n* filo; (*Elec*) filo elettrico; (*Tel*) telegramma *m* ■ *vt* (*Elec*: *house*) fare l'impianto elettrico di; (: *circuit*) installare; (*also*: **wire up**) collegare, allacciare
wire brush *n* spazzola metallica
wire cutters [-kʌtəz] *npl* tronchese *m or f*
wireless ['waɪəlɪs] *n* (*Brit*) telegrafia senza fili; (*set*) (apparecchio *m*) radio *f inv* ■ *adj* (*technology*) wireless *inv*, senza fili
wire netting *n* rete *f* metallica
wire service *n* (*US*) = **news agency**
wire-tapping ['waɪə'tæpɪŋ] *n* intercettazione *f* telefonica
wiring ['waɪərɪŋ] *n* (*Elec*) impianto elettrico
wiry ['waɪərɪ] *adj* magro(-a) e nerboruto(-a)
Wis., Wisc. *abbr* (*US*) = **Wisconsin**
wisdom ['wɪzdəm] *n* saggezza; (*of action*) prudenza
wisdom tooth *n* dente *m* del giudizio
wise [waɪz] *adj* saggio(-a); (*advice, remark*) prudente; **I'm none the wiser** ne so come prima
▸ **wise up** *vi* (*col*): **to ~ up to** divenire più consapevole di
...wise [waɪz] *suffix*: **timewise** per quanto riguarda il tempo, in termini di tempo
wisecrack ['waɪzkræk] *n* battuta spiritosa
wish [wɪʃ] *n* (*desire*) desiderio; (*specific desire*) richiesta ■ *vt* desiderare, volere; **best wishes** (*on birthday etc*) i migliori auguri; **with best wishes** (*in letter*) cordiali saluti, con i migliori saluti; **give her my best wishes** le faccia i migliori auguri da parte mia; **to ~ sb goodbye** dire arrivederci a qn; **he wished me well** mi augurò di riuscire; **to ~ to do/sb to do** desiderare *or* volere fare/che qn faccia; **to ~ for** desiderare; **to ~ sth on sb** rifilare qc a qn
wishbone ['wɪʃbəun] *n* forcella
wishful ['wɪʃful] *adj*: **it's ~ thinking** è prendere i desideri per realtà
wishy-washy ['wɪʃɪ'wɔʃɪ] *adj* insulso(-a)
wisp [wɪsp] *n* ciuffo, ciocca; (*of smoke, straw*) filo
wistful ['wɪstful] *adj* malinconico(-a); (*nostalgic*) nostalgico(-a)
wit [wɪt] *n* (*gen pl*) intelligenza; presenza di spirito; (*wittiness*) spirito, arguzia; (*person*) bello spirito; **to be at one's wits' end** (*fig*) non sapere più cosa fare; **to have** *or* **keep one's wits about one** avere presenza di spirito; **to ~** *adv* cioè
witch [wɪtʃ] *n* strega
witchcraft ['wɪtʃkrɑːft] *n* stregoneria
witch doctor *n* stregone *m*
witch-hunt ['wɪtʃhʌnt] *n* (*fig*) caccia alle streghe

with [wɪð, wɪθ] *prep* **1** (*in the company of*) con; **I was with him** ero con lui; **we stayed with friends** siamo stati da amici; **I'll be with you in a minute** vengo subito
2 (*descriptive*) con; **a room with a view** una camera con vista (sul mare *or* sulle montagne *etc*); **the man with the grey hat/blue eyes** l'uomo con il cappello grigio/gli occhi blu
3 (*indicating manner, means, cause*): **with tears in her eyes** con le lacrime agli occhi; **red**

with anger rosso(-a) dalla rabbia; **to shake with fear** tremare di paura; **covered with snow** coperto(-a) di neve
4: **I'm with you** (*I understand*) la seguo; **I'm not really with it today** (*col*) oggi sono un po' fuori

withdraw [wɪθ'drɔ:] *vb irreg vt* ritirare; (*money from bank*) ritirare, prelevare ■ *vi* ritirarsi; **to ~ into o.s.** chiudersi in se stesso
withdrawal [wɪθ'drɔ:əl] *n* ritiro; prelievo; (*of army*) ritirata; (*Med*) stato di privazione
withdrawal symptoms *npl* crisi *f* di astinenza
withdrawn [wɪθ'drɔ:n] *pp of* **withdraw** ■ *adj* distaccato(-a)
wither ['wɪðə^r] *vi* appassire
withered ['wɪðəd] *adj* appassito(-a); (*limb*) atrofizzato(-a)
withhold [wɪθ'həuld] *vt irreg* (*money*) trattenere; (*permission*): **to ~ (from)** rifiutare (a); (*information*): **to ~ (from)** nascondere (a)
within [wɪð'ɪn] *prep* all'interno di; (*in time, distances*) entro ■ *adv* all'interno, dentro; **~ sight of** in vista di; **~ a mile of** entro un miglio da; **~ the week** prima della fine della settimana; **~ an hour from now** da qui a un'ora; **to be ~ the law** restare nei limiti della legge
without [wɪð'aut] *prep* senza; **to go** *or* **do ~ sth** fare a meno di qc; **~ anybody knowing** senza che nessuno lo sappia
withstand [wɪθ'stænd] *vt irreg* resistere a
witness ['wɪtnɪs] *n* (*person*) testimone *m/f* ■ *vt* (*event*) essere testimone di; (*document*) attestare l'autenticità di ■ *vi*: **to ~ to sth/ having seen sth** testimoniare qc/di aver visto qc; **to bear ~ to sth** testimoniare qc; **~ for the prosecution/defence** testimone a carico/discarico
witness box, (*US*) **witness stand** *n* banco dei testimoni
witticism ['wɪtɪsɪzəm] *n* spiritosaggine *f*
witty ['wɪtɪ] *adj* spiritoso(-a)
wives [waɪvz] *npl of* **wife**
wizard ['wɪzəd] *n* mago
wizened ['wɪznd] *adj* raggrinzito(-a)
wk *abbr* = **week**
Wm. *abbr* = **William**
WMD *n abbr see* **weapons of mass destruction**
WO *n abbr see* **warrant officer**
wobble ['wɔbl] *vi* tremare; (*chair*) traballare
wobbly ['wɔblɪ] *adj* (*hand, voice*) tremante; (*table, chair*) traballante; (*object about to fall*) che oscilla pericolosamente
woe [wəu] *n* dolore *m*; disgrazia
woeful ['wəuful] *adj* (*sad*) triste; (*deplorable*) deplorevole
wok [wɔk] *n* wok *m inv* (*padella concava usata nella cucina cinese*)
woke [wəuk] *pt of* **wake**
woken ['wəukn] *pp of* **wake**
wolf (*pl* **wolves**) [wulf, wulvz] *n* lupo
woman (*pl* **women**) ['wumən, 'wɪmɪn] *n* donna ■ *cpd*: **~ doctor** *n* dottoressa; **~ friend** *n* amica; **~ teacher** *n* insegnante *f*; **women's page** *n* (*Press*) rubrica femminile
womanize ['wumənaɪz] *vi* essere un donnaiolo
womanly ['wumənlɪ] *adj* femminile
womb [wu:m] *n* (*Anat*) utero
women ['wɪmɪn] *npl of* **woman**
Women's Movement, Women's Liberation Movement *n* (*also*: **Women's Lib**) Movimento per la Liberazione della Donna
won [wʌn] *pt, pp of* **win**
wonder ['wʌndə^r] *n* meraviglia ■ *vi*: **to ~ whether** domandarsi se; **to ~ at** essere sorpreso(-a) di; meravigliarsi di; **to ~ about** domandarsi di; pensare a; **it's no ~ that** c'è poco *or* non c'è da meravigliarsi che *+ sub*
wonderful ['wʌndəful] *adj* meraviglioso(-a)
wonderfully ['wʌndəfəlɪ] *adv* (*+ adjective*) meravigliosamente; (*+ verb*) a meraviglia
wonky ['wɔŋkɪ] *adj* (*Brit col*) traballante
wont [wəunt] *n*: **as is his/her ~** com'è solito/ a fare
won't [wəunt] = **will not**
woo [wu:] *vt* (*woman*) fare la corte a
wood [wud] *n* legno; (*timber*) legname *m*; (*forest*) bosco ■ *cpd* di bosco, silvestre
wood carving *n* scultura in legno, intaglio
wooded ['wudɪd] *adj* boschivo(-a); boscoso(-a)
wooden ['wudn] *adj* di legno; (*fig*) rigido(-a); inespressivo(-a)
woodland ['wudlənd] *n* zona boscosa
woodpecker ['wudpɛkə^r] *n* picchio
wood pigeon *n* colombaccio, palomba
woodwind ['wudwɪnd] *npl* (*Mus*): **the ~** i legni
woodwork ['wudwə:k] *n* parti *fpl* in legno; (*craft, subject*) falegnameria
woodworm ['wudwə:m] *n* tarlo del legno
woof [wuf] *n* (*of dog*) bau bau *m* ■ *vi* abbaiare; **~, ~!** bau bau!
wool [wul] *n* lana; **to pull the ~ over sb's eyes** (*fig*) fargliela a qn
woollen, (*US*) **woolen** ['wulən] *adj* di lana ■ *n*: **woollens** indumenti *mpl* di lana
woolly, (*US*) **wooly** ['wulɪ] *adj* lanoso(-a); (*fig: ideas*) confuso(-a)
woozy ['wu:zɪ] *adj* (*col*) stordito(-a)

word [wəːd] *n* parola; (*news*) notizie *fpl* ■ *vt* esprimere, formulare; **~ for ~** parola per parola, testualmente; **what's the ~ for "pen" in Italian?** come si dice "pen" in italiano?; **to put sth into words** esprimere qc a parole; **in other words** in altre parole; **to have a ~ with sb** scambiare due parole con qn; **to have words with sb** (*quarrel with*) avere un diverbio con qn; **to break/keep one's ~** non mantenere/mantenere la propria parola; **I'll take your ~ for it** la crederò sulla parola; **to send ~ of** avvisare di; **to leave ~ (with** *or* **for sb) that ...** lasciare detto (a qn) che ...
wording ['wəːdɪŋ] *n* formulazione *f*
word of mouth *n* passaparola *m*; **I learned it by** *or* **through ~** lo so per sentito dire
word-perfect ['wəːd'pəfɪkt] *adj* (*speech etc*) imparato(-a) a memoria
word processing *n* word processing *m*, elaborazione *f* testi
word processor *n* word processor *m inv*
wordwrap ['wəːdræp] *n* (*Comput*) ritorno carrello automatico
wordy ['wəːdɪ] *adj* verboso(-a), prolisso(-a)
wore [wɔːʳ] *pt of* **wear**
work [wəːk] *n* lavoro; (*Art, Literature*) opera ■ *vi* lavorare; (*mechanism, plan etc*) funzionare; (*medicine*) essere efficace ■ *vt* (*clay, wood etc*) lavorare; (*mine etc*) sfruttare; (*machine*) far funzionare; **to be at ~ (on sth)** lavorare (a qc); **to set to ~, to start ~** mettersi all'opera; **to go to ~** andare al lavoro; **to be out of ~** essere disoccupato(-a); **to ~ one's way through a book** riuscire a leggersi tutto un libro; **to ~ one's way through college** lavorare per pagarsi gli studi; **to ~ hard** lavorare sodo; **to ~ loose** allentarsi; *see also* **works**
▸ **work on** *vt fus* lavorare a; (*principle*) basarsi su; **he's working on the car** sta facendo dei lavori alla macchina
▸ **work out** *vi* (*plans etc*) riuscire, andare bene; (*Sport*) allenarsi ■ *vt* (*problem*) risolvere; (*plan*) elaborare; **it works out at £100** fa 100 sterline
workable ['wəːkəbl] *adj* (*solution*) realizzabile
workaholic [wəːkə'hɔlɪk] *n* stacanovista *m/f*
workbench ['wəːkbɛntʃ] *n* banco (da lavoro)
worked up *adj*: **to get ~** andare su tutte le furie; eccitarsi
worker ['wəːkəʳ] *n* lavoratore(-trice); (*esp Agr, Industry*) operaio(-a); **office ~** impiegato(-a)
work force *n* forza lavoro
work-in ['wəːkɪn] *n* (*Brit*) sciopero alla rovescia
working ['wəːkɪŋ] *adj* (*day*) feriale; (*tools, conditions*) di lavoro; (*clothes*) da lavoro; (*wife*) che lavora; (*partner*) attivo(-a); **in ~ order** funzionante; **~ knowledge** conoscenza pratica
working capital *n* (*Comm*) capitale *m* d'esercizio
working class *n* classe *f* operaia *or* lavoratrice ■ *adj*: **working-class** operaio(-a)
working man *n* lavoratore *m*
working party *n* (*Brit*) commissione *f*
working week *n* settimana lavorativa
work-in-progress ['wəːkɪn'prəugrɛs] *n* (*products*) lavoro in corso; (*value*) valore *m* del manufatto in lavorazione
workload ['wəːkləud] *n* carico di lavoro
workman ['wəːkmən] *n* operaio
workmanship ['wəːkmənʃɪp] *n* (*of worker*) abilità; (*of thing*) fattura
workmate ['wəːkmeɪt] *n* collega *m/f*
workout ['wəːkaut] *n* (*Sport*) allenamento
work permit *n* permesso di lavoro
works [wəːks] *n* (*Brit: factory*) fabbrica ■ *npl* (*of clock, machine*) meccanismo; **road ~** opere stradali
works council *n* consiglio aziendale
work sheet *n* (*Comput*) foglio col programma di lavoro
workshop ['wəːkʃɔp] *n* officina
work station *n* stazione *f* di lavoro
work study *n* studio di organizzazione del lavoro
worktop ['wəːktɔp] *n* piano di lavoro
work-to-rule ['wəːktə'ruːl] *n* (*Brit*) sciopero bianco
world [wəːld] *n* mondo ■ *cpd* (*tour*) del mondo; (*record, power, war*) mondiale; **all over the ~** in tutto il mondo; **to think the ~ of sb** pensare un gran bene di qn; **out of this ~** (*fig*) formidabile; **what in the ~ is he doing?** che cavolo sta facendo?; **to do sb a ~ of good** fare un gran bene a qn; **W~ War One/Two** la prima/seconda guerra mondiale
world champion *n* campione(-essa) mondiale
World Cup *n* (*Football*) Coppa del Mondo
world-famous [wəːld'feɪməs] *adj* di fama mondiale
worldly ['wəːldlɪ] *adj* di questo mondo
world music *n* musica etnica
World Series *n*: **the ~** (*US Baseball*) la finalissima di baseball
world-wide ['wəːld'waɪd] *adj* universale
worm [wəːm] *n* verme *m*
worn [wɔːn] *pp of* **wear** ■ *adj* usato(-a)
worn-out ['wɔːnaut] *adj* (*object*) consumato(-a), logoro(-a); (*person*) sfinito(-a)

worried ['wʌrɪd] *adj* preoccupato(-a); **to be ~ about sth** essere preoccupato per qc
worrier ['wʌrɪəʳ] *n* ansioso(-a)
worrisome ['wʌrɪsəm] *adj* preoccupante
worry ['wʌrɪ] *n* preoccupazione *f* ■ *vt* preoccupare ■ *vi* preoccuparsi; **to ~ about** *or* **over sth/sb** preoccuparsi di qc/per qn
worrying ['wʌrɪɪŋ] *adj* preoccupante
worse [wəːs] *adj* peggiore ■ *adv, n* peggio; **a change for the ~** un peggioramento; **to get ~, to grow ~** peggiorare; **he is none the ~ for it** non ha avuto brutte conseguenze; **so much the ~ for you!** tanto peggio per te!
worsen ['wəːsn] *vt, vi* peggiorare
worse off *adj* in condizioni (economiche) peggiori; *(fig)*: **you'll be ~ this way** così sarà peggio per lei; **he is now ~ than before** ora è in condizioni peggiori di prima
worship ['wəːʃɪp] *n* culto ■ *vt* *(God)* adorare, venerare; *(person)* adorare; **Your W~** *(to mayor)* signor sindaco; *(to judge)* signor giudice
worshipper ['wəːʃɪpəʳ] *n* adoratore(-trice); *(in church)* fedele *m/f*, devoto(-a)
worst [wəːst] *adj* il/la peggiore ■ *adv, n* peggio; **at ~** al peggio, per male che vada; **to come off ~** avere la peggio; **if the ~ comes to the ~** nel peggior dei casi
worst-case ['wəːst'keɪs] *adj*: **the ~ scenario** la peggiore delle ipotesi
worsted ['wustɪd] *n*: **(wool) ~** lana pettinata
worth [wəːθ] *n* valore *m* ■ *adj*: **to be ~** valere; **how much is it ~?** quanto vale?; **it's ~ it** ne vale la pena; **it's not ~ the trouble** non ne vale la pena; **50 pence ~ of apples** 50 pence di mele
worthless ['wəːθlɪs] *adj* di nessun valore
worthwhile ['wəːθ'waɪl] *adj* *(activity)* utile; *(cause)* lodevole; **a ~ book** un libro che vale la pena leggere
worthy ['wəːðɪ] *adj* *(person)* degno(-a); *(motive)* lodevole; **~ of** degno di

 KEYWORD

would [wud] *aux vb* **1** *(conditional tense)*: **if you asked him he would do it** se glielo chiedesse lo farebbe; **if you had asked him he would have done it** se glielo avesse chiesto lo avrebbe fatto
2 *(in offers, invitations, requests)*: **would you like a biscuit?** vorrebbe *or* vuole un biscotto?; **would you ask him to come in?** lo faccia entrare, per cortesia; **would you open the window please?** apra la finestra, per favore
3 *(in indirect speech)*: **I said I would do it** ho detto che l'avrei fatto
4 *(emphatic)*: **it WOULD have to snow today!** doveva proprio nevicare oggi!
5 *(insistence)*: **she wouldn't do it** non ha voluto farlo
6 *(conjecture)*: **it would have been midnight** sarà stata mezzanotte; **it would seem so** sembrerebbe proprio di sì
7 *(indicating habit)*: **he would go there on Mondays** andava lì ogni lunedì

would-be ['wudbiː] *adj* *(pej)* sedicente
wound¹ [wuːnd] *n* ferita ■ *vt* ferire; **wounded in the leg** ferito(-a) alla gamba
wound² [waund] *pt, pp of* **wind²**
wove [wəuv] *pt of* **weave**
WP *abbr (Brit col: = weather permitting)* tempo permettendo ■ *n abbr* = **word processing; word processor**
WPC *n abbr (Brit: = woman police constable)* donna poliziotto
wpm *abbr (= words per minute)* p.p.m.
WRAC *n abbr (Brit: = Women's Royal Army Corps) ausiliarie dell'esercito*
WRAF *n abbr (Brit: = Women's Royal Air Force) ausiliarie dell'aeronautica militare*
wrangle ['ræŋgl] *n* litigio ■ *vi* litigare
wrap [ræp] *n* *(stole)* scialle *m*; *(cape)* mantellina ■ *vt* *(also:* **wrap up***)* avvolgere; *(parcel)* incartare; **under wraps** segreto
wrapper ['ræpəʳ] *n* *(of book)* copertina; *(on chocolate)* carta
wrapping paper ['ræpɪŋ-] *n* carta da pacchi; *(for gift)* carta da regali
wrath [rɔθ] *n* collera, ira
wreak [riːk] *vt* *(destruction)* portare, causare; **to ~ vengeance on** vendicarsi su; **to ~ havoc on** portare scompiglio in
wreath *(pl* **wreaths***)* [riːθ, riːðz] *n* corona
wreck [rɛk] *n* *(sea disaster)* naufragio; *(ship)* relitto; *(pej: person)* rottame *m* ■ *vt* demolire; *(ship)* far naufragare; *(fig)* rovinare
wreckage ['rɛkɪdʒ] *n* rottami *mpl*; *(of building)* macerie *fpl*; *(of ship)* relitti *mpl*
wrecker ['rɛkəʳ] *n* *(US: breakdown van)* carro *m* attrezzi *inv*
WREN [rɛn] *n abbr (Brit) membro del WRNS*
wren [rɛn] *n* *(Zool)* scricciolo
wrench [rɛntʃ] *n* *(Tech)* chiave *f*; *(tug)* torsione *f* brusca; *(fig)* strazio ■ *vt* strappare; storcere; **to ~ sth from** strappare qc a *or* da
wrest [rɛst] *vt*: **to ~ sth from sb** strappare qc a qn
wrestle ['rɛsl] *vi*: **to ~ (with sb)** lottare (con qn); **to ~ with** *(fig)* combattere *or* lottare contro
wrestler ['rɛsləʳ] *n* lottatore(-trice)
wrestling ['rɛslɪŋ] *n* lotta; *(also:* **all-in wrestling***: Brit)* catch *m*, lotta libera

W

wrestling match *n* incontro di lotta (*or* lotta libera)
wretch [rɛtʃ] *n* disgraziato(-a), sciagurato(-a); **little ~!** (*often humorous*) birbante!
wretched ['rɛtʃɪd] *adj* disgraziato(-a); (*col: weather, holiday*) orrendo(-a), orribile; (*: child, dog*) pestifero(-a)
wriggle ['rɪgl] *n* contorsione *f* ■ *vi* dimenarsi; (*snake, worm*) serpeggiare, muoversi serpeggiando
wring (*pt, pp* **wrung**) [rɪŋ, rʌŋ] *vt* torcere; (*wet clothes*) strizzare; (*fig*): **to ~ sth out of** strappare qc a
wringer ['rɪŋər] *n* strizzatoio (manuale)
wringing ['rɪŋɪŋ] *adj* (*also*: **wringing wet**) bagnato(-a) fradicio(-a)
wrinkle ['rɪŋkl] *n* (*on skin*) ruga; (*on paper etc*) grinza ■ *vt* corrugare; raggrinzire ■ *vi* corrugarsi; raggrinzirsi
wrinkled ['rɪŋkld], **wrinkly** ['rɪŋklɪ] *adj* (*fabric, paper*) stropicciato(-a); (*surface*) corrugato(-a), increspato(-a); (*skin*) rugoso(-a)
wrist [rɪst] *n* polso
wristband ['rɪstbænd] *n* (*of shirt*) polsino; (*of watch*) cinturino
wrist watch *n* orologio da polso
writ [rɪt] *n* ordine *m*; mandato; **to issue a ~ against sb, serve a ~ on sb** notificare un mandato di comparizione a qn
write (*pt* **wrote**, *pp* **written**) [raɪt, rəut, 'rɪtn] *vt, vi* scrivere; **to ~ sb a letter** scrivere una lettera a qn
▸ **write away** *vi*: **to ~ away for** (*information*) richiedere per posta; (*goods*) ordinare per posta
▸ **write down** *vt* annotare; (*put in writing*) mettere per iscritto
▸ **write off** *vt* (*debt*) cancellare; (*depreciate*) deprezzare; (*smash up: car*) distruggere
▸ **write out** *vt* scrivere; (*copy*) ricopiare
▸ **write up** *vt* redigere
write-off ['raɪtɔf] *n* perdita completa; **the car is a ~** la macchina va bene per il demolitore
write-protect ['raɪtprə'tɛkt] *vt* (*Comput*) proteggere contro scrittura
writer ['raɪtər] *n* autore(-trice), scrittore(-trice)
write-up ['raɪtʌp] *n* (*review*) recensione *f*
writhe [raɪð] *vi* contorcersi
writing ['raɪtɪŋ] *n* scrittura; (*of author*) scritto, opera; **in ~** per iscritto; **in my own ~** scritto di mio pugno
writing case *n* nécessaire *m inv* per la corrispondenza
writing desk *n* scrivania, scrittoio
writing paper *n* carta da scrivere
written ['rɪtn] *pp of* **write**
WRNS *n abbr* (*Brit: = Women's Royal Naval Service*) *ausiliarie della marina militare*
wrong [rɔŋ] *adj* sbagliato(-a); (*not suitable*) inadatto(-a); (*wicked*) cattivo(-a); (*unfair*) ingiusto(-a) ■ *adv* in modo sbagliato, erroneamente ■ *n* (*evil*) male *m*; (*injustice*) torto ■ *vt* fare torto a; **to be ~** (*answer*) essere sbagliato; (*in doing, saying*) avere torto; **you are ~ to do it** ha torto a farlo; **you are ~ about that, you've got it ~** si sbaglia; **to be in the ~** avere torto; **what's ~?** cosa c'è che non va?; **there's nothing ~** va tutto bene; **what's ~ with the car?** cos'ha la macchina che non va?; **to go ~** (*person*) sbagliarsi; (*plan*) fallire, non riuscire; (*machine*) guastarsi; **it's ~ to steal, stealing is ~** è male rubare
wrongdoer ['rɔŋdu:ər] *n* malfattore(-trice)
wrong-foot [rɔŋ'fut] *vt* (*Sport; also fig*) prendere in contropiede
wrongful ['rɔŋful] *adj* illegittimo(-a); ingiusto(-a); **~ dismissal** licenziamento ingiustificato
wrongly ['rɔŋlɪ] *adv* (*accuse, dismiss*) a torto; (*answer, do, count*) erroneamente; (*treat*) ingiustamente
wrong number *n*: **you have the ~** (*Tel*) ha sbagliato numero
wrong side *n* (*of cloth*) rovescio
wrote [rəut] *pt of* **write**
wrought [rɔ:t] *adj*: **~ iron** ferro battuto
wrung [rʌŋ] *pt, pp of* **wring**
WRVS *n abbr* (*Brit*) = **Women's Royal Voluntary Service**
wry [raɪ] *adj* storto(-a)
wt. *abbr* = **weight**
WV, W. Va. *abbr* (*US*) = **West Virginia**
WY, Wyo. *abbr* (*US*) = **Wyoming**
WYSIWYG ['wɪzɪwɪg] *abbr* (*Comput*) = **what you see is what you get**

X, x [ɛks] *n* (*letter*) X, x *f or m inv*; (*Brit Cine*: *old*) ≈ film vietato ai minori di 18 anni; **X for Xmas** ≈ X come Xeres

Xerox® ['zɪərɔks] *n* (*also*: **Xerox machine**) fotocopiatrice *f*; (*photocopy*) fotocopia ■ *vt* fotocopiare

XL *abbr* = **extra large**

Xmas ['ɛksməs] *n abbr* = **Christmas**

X-rated ['ɛks'reɪtɪd] *adj* (*US*: *film*) ≈ vietato ai minori di 18 anni

X-ray ['ɛks'reɪ] *n* raggio X; (*photograph*) radiografia ■ *vt* radiografare; **to have an ~** farsi fare una radiografia

xylophone ['zaɪləfəun] *n* xilofono

Y, y [waɪ] *n* (*letter*) Y, y *f or m inv*; **Y for Yellow**, (*US*) **Y for Yoke** ≈ Y come Yacht
yacht [jɔt] *n* panfilo, yacht *m inv*
yachting ['jɔtɪŋ] *n* yachting *m*, sport *m* della vela
yachtsman ['jɔtsmən] *n* yachtsman *m inv*
yam [jæm] *n* igname *m*; (*sweet potato*) patata dolce
Yank [jæŋk], **Yankee** ['jæŋkɪ] *n* (*pej*) yankee *m/f inv*, nordamericano(-a)
yank [jæŋk] *n* strattone *m* ■ *vt* tirare, dare uno strattone a
yap [jæp] *vi* (*dog*) guaire
yard [jɑːd] *n* (*of house etc*) cortile *m*; (*US: garden*) giardino; (*measure*) iarda (= *914 mm; 3 feet*); **builder's ~** deposito di materiale da costruzione
yardstick ['jɑːdstɪk] *n* (*fig*) misura, criterio
yarn [jɑːn] *n* filato; (*tale*) lunga storia
yawn [jɔːn] *n* sbadiglio ■ *vi* sbadigliare
yawning ['jɔːnɪŋ] *adj* (*gap*) spalancato(-a)
yd. *abbr* = **yard**
yeah [jɛə] *adv* (*col*) sì
year [jɪəʳ] *n* (*gen, Scol*) anno; (*referring to harvest, wine etc*) annata; **every ~** ogni anno, tutti gli anni; **this ~** quest'anno; **~ in, ~ out** anno dopo anno; **she's three years old** ha tre anni; **a** *or* **per ~** all'anno
yearbook ['jɪəbuk] *n* annuario
yearly ['jɪəlɪ] *adj* annuale ■ *adv* annualmente; **twice-~** semestrale
yearn [jəːn] *vi*: **to ~ for sth/to do** desiderare ardentemente qc/di fare
yearning ['jəːnɪŋ] *n* desiderio intenso
yeast [jiːst] *n* lievito
yell [jɛl] *n* urlo ■ *vi* urlare
yellow ['jɛləu] *adj* giallo(-a)
yellow fever *n* febbre *f* gialla
yellowish ['jɛləuɪʃ] *adj* giallastro(-a), giallognolo(-a)
Yellow Pages® *npl* pagine *fpl* gialle
Yellow Sea *n*: **the ~** il mar Giallo
yelp [jɛlp] *n* guaito, uggiolio ■ *vi* guaire, uggiolare
Yemen ['jɛmən] *n* Yemen *m*
yen [jɛn] *n* (*currency*) yen *m inv*; (*craving*): **~ for/to do** gran voglia di/di fare
yeoman ['jəumən] *n*: **Y~ of the Guard** guardiano della Torre di Londra
yes [jɛs] *adv, n* sì (*m inv*); **to say ~ (to)** dire di sì (a), acconsentire (a)
yesterday ['jɛstədɪ] *adv, n* ieri (*m inv*); **~ morning/evening** ieri mattina/sera; **the day before ~** l'altro ieri; **all day ~** ieri tutto il giorno
yet [jɛt] *adv* ancora; già ■ *conj* ma, tuttavia; **it is not finished ~** non è ancora finito; **the best ~** il migliore finora; **as ~** finora; **~ again** di nuovo; **must you go just ~?** deve andarsene di già?; **a few days ~** ancora qualche giorno
yew [juː] *n* tasso (*albero*)
Y-fronts® ['waɪfrʌnts] *npl* (*Brit*) slip *m inv* da uomo
YHA *n abbr* (*Brit*: = *Youth Hostels Association*) Y.H.A. *f*
Yiddish ['jɪdɪʃ] *n* yiddish *m*
yield [jiːld] *n* resa; (*of crops etc*) raccolto ■ *vt* produrre, rendere; (*surrender*) cedere ■ *vi* cedere; (*US Aut*) dare la precedenza; **a ~ of 5%** un profitto *or* un interesse del 5%
YMCA *n abbr* (= *Young Men's Christian Association*) Y.M.C.A. *m*
yob ['jɔb], **yobbo** ['jɔbəu] *n* (*Brit col*) bullo
yodel ['jəudl] *vi* cantare lo jodel *or* alla tirolese
yoga ['jəugə] *n* yoga *m*
yogourt, yoghourt ['jəugət] *n* iogurt *m inv*
yoke [jəuk] *n* giogo ■ *vt* (*also*: **yoke together**: *oxen*) aggiogare
yolk [jəuk] *n* tuorlo, rosso d'uovo
yonder ['jɔndəʳ] *adv* là
yonks [jɔŋks] *npl*: **for ~** (*col*) da una vita
Yorks [jɔːks] *abbr* (*Brit*) = **Yorkshire**

 KEYWORD

you [juː] *pron* **1** (*subject*) tu; (*: polite form*) lei; (*: pl*) voi; (*: formal*) loro; **you Italians enjoy**

your food a voi italiani piace mangiare bene; **you and I will go** andiamo io e te (*or* lei ed io); **if I was** *or* **were you** se fossi in te (*or* lei *etc*)
2 (*object: direct*) ti; la; vi; loro (*after vb*); (*: indirect*) ti; le; vi; loro (*after vb*); **I know you** ti (*or* la *or* vi) conosco; **I'll see you tomorrow** ci vediamo domani; **I gave it to you** te l'ho dato; gliel'ho dato; ve l'ho dato; l'ho dato loro
3 (*stressed, after prep, in comparisons*) te; lei; voi; loro; **I told YOU to do it** ho detto a TE (*or* a LEI *etc*) di farlo; **she's younger than you** è più giovane di te (*or* lei *etc*)
4 (*impers: one*) si; **fresh air does you good** l'aria fresca fa bene; **you never know** non si sa mai

you'd [ju:d] = **you had; you would**
you'll [ju:l] = **you will; you shall**
young [jʌŋ] *adj* giovane ■ *npl* (*of animal*) piccoli *mpl*; (*people*): **the ~** i giovani, la gioventù; **a ~ man** un giovanotto; **a ~ lady** una signorina; **a ~ woman** una giovane donna; **the younger generation** la nuova generazione; **my younger brother** il mio fratello minore
youngish ['jʌŋɪʃ] *adj* abbastanza giovane
youngster ['jʌŋstəʳ] *n* giovanotto(-a); (*child*) bambino(-a)
your [jɔ:ʳ] *adj* il/la tuo(-a); (*pl*) i/le tuoi/tue; (*polite form*) il/la suo(-a); (*pl*) i/le suoi/sue; (*pl*) il/la vostro(-a); (*pl*) i/le vostri(-e); (*: formal*) il/la loro; (*pl*) i/le loro
you're [juəʳ] = **you are**
yours [jɔ:z] *pron* il/la tuo(-a); (*pl*) i/le tuoi/tue; (*polite form*) il/la suo(-a); (*pl*) i/le suoi/sue; (*pl*) il/la vostro(-a); (*pl*) i/le vostri(-e); (*: formal*) il/la loro; (*pl*) i/le loro; **~ sincerely/faithfully** (*in letter*) cordiali/distinti saluti; **a friend of ~** un tuo (*or* suo *etc*) amico; **is it ~?** è tuo (*or* suo *etc*)?
yourself [jɔ:'sɛlf] *pron* (*reflexive*) ti; (*: polite form*) si; (*after prep*) te; se; (*emphatic*) tu stesso(-a); lei stesso(-a); **you ~ told me** me l'hai detto proprio tu, tu stesso me l'hai detto
yourselves [jɔ:'sɛlvz] *pl pron* (*reflexive*) vi; (*: polite form*) si; (*after prep*) voi; loro; (*emphatic*) voi stessi(-e); loro stessi(-e)
youth [ju:θ] *n* gioventù *f*; (*young man*): (*pl* **youths**) [ju:ðz] giovane *m*, ragazzo; **in my ~** da giovane, quando ero giovane
youth club *n* centro giovanile
youthful ['ju:θful] *adj* giovane; da giovane; giovanile
youthfulness ['ju:θfəlnɪs] *n* giovinezza
youth hostel *n* ostello della gioventù
youth movement *n* movimento giovanile
you've [ju:v] = **you have**
yowl [jaul] *n* (*of dog, person*) urlo; (*of cat*) miagolio ■ *vi* urlare; miagolare
yr *abbr* = **year**
YT *abbr* (*Canada*) = **Yukon Territory**
Yugoslav ['ju:gəuslɑ:v] *adj, n* (*formerly*) jugoslavo(-a)
Yugoslavia [ju:gəu'slɑ:vɪə] *n* (*formerly*) Jugoslavia
Yugoslavian [ju:gəu'slɑ:vɪən] *adj, n* (*formerly*) jugoslavo(-a)
Yule log [ju:l-] *n ceppo nel caminetto a Natale*
yuppie ['jʌpɪ] *adj, n* (*col*) yuppie (*m o f*) *inv*
YWCA *n abbr* (= *Young Women's Christian Association*) Y.W.C.A. *m*

Zz

Z, z [zɛd, (US) zi:] *n* (*letter*) Z, z *f or m inv*; **Z for Zebra** ≈ Z come Zara
Zaire [zɑ:'ɪəʳ] *n* Zaire *m*
Zambia ['zæmbɪə] *n* Zambia *m*
Zambian ['zæmbɪən] *adj, n* zambiano(-a)
zany ['zeɪnɪ] *adj* un po' pazzo(-a)
zap [zæp] *vt* (*Comput*) cancellare
zeal [zi:l] *n* zelo; entusiasmo
zealot ['zɛlət] *n* zelota *m/f*
zealous ['zɛləs] *adj* zelante; premuroso(-a)
zebra ['zi:brə] *n* zebra
zebra crossing *n* (*Brit*) (passaggio pedonale a) strisce *fpl*, zebre *fpl*
zenith ['zɛnɪθ] *n* zenit *m inv*; (*fig*) culmine *m*
zero ['zɪərəu] *n* zero; **5° below ~** 5° sotto zero
zero hour *n* l'ora zero
zero option *n* (*Pol*) opzione *f* zero
zero-rated ['zɪərəu'reɪtɪd] *adj* (*Brit*) ad aliquota zero
zest [zɛst] *n* gusto; (*Culin*) buccia
zigzag ['zɪgzæg] *n* zigzag *m inv* ■ *vi* zigzagare
Zimbabwe [zɪm'bɑ:bwɪ] *n* Zimbabwe *m*
Zimbabwean [zɪm'bɑ:bwɪən] *adj* dello Zimbabwe
Zimmer® ['zɪməʳ] *n* (*also*: **Zimmer frame**) deambulatore *m*
zinc [zɪŋk] *n* zinco
Zionism ['zaɪənɪzəm] *n* sionismo
Zionist ['zaɪənɪst] *adj* sionistico(-a) ■ *n* sionista *m/f*
zip [zɪp] *n* (*also*: **zip fastener**, *US* **zipper**) chiusura *f* or cerniera *f* lampo *inv*; (*energy*) energia, forza ■ *vt* (*Comput*) zippare; (*also*: **zip up**) chiudere con una cerniera lampo
zip code *n* (*US*) codice *m* di avviamento postale
zither ['zɪðəʳ] *n* cetra
zodiac ['zəudɪæk] *n* zodiaco
zombie ['zɔmbɪ] *n* (*fig*): **like a ~** come un morto che cammina
zone [zəun] *n* zona
zoo [zu:] *n* zoo *m inv*
zoological [zuə'lɔdʒɪkl] *adj* zoologico(-a)
zoologist [zu:'ɔlədʒɪst] *n* zoologo(-a)
zoology [zu:'ɔlədʒɪ] *n* zoologia
zoom [zu:m] *vi*: **to ~ past** sfrecciare; **to ~ in (on sb/sth)** (*Phot, Cine*) zumare (su qn/qc)
zoom lens *n* zoom *m inv*, obiettivo a focale variabile
zucchini [zu:'ki:nɪ] *n* (*pl inv*: *US*) zucchina
Zulu ['zu:lu:] *adj, n* zulù (*m o f*) *inv*
Zürich ['zjuərɪk] *n* Zurigo *f*

Grammar
Grammatica

Using the grammar

The Grammar section deals systematically and comprehensively with all the information you will need in order to communicate accurately in Italian. The user-friendly layout explains the grammar point on a left-hand page, leaving the facing page free for illustrative examples. The numbers, → ① etc, direct you to the relevant example in every case.

The Grammar section also provides invaluable guidance on the danger of translating English structures by identical structures in Italian. Use of Numbers and Punctuation are important areas covered towards the end of the section. Finally, the index lists the main words and grammatical terms in both English and Italian.

Italic letters in Italian words show where stress does not follow the usual rules.

Abbreviations

fem.	*feminine*
infin.	*infinitive*
masc.	*masculine*
perf.	*perfect*
plur.	*plural*
sing.	*singular*
qc	qualcosa
qn	qualcuno
sb	somebody
sth	something

Contents

Simple Tenses: Formation

In English, tenses are either simple, which means they consist of one word, e.g. *I work*, or compound, which means they consist of more than one word, e.g. *I have worked, I have been working*. The same is true in Italian.

In Italian the simple tenses are:

- Present → 1
- Imperfect → 2
- Future → 3
- Present Conditional → 4
- Past Historic → 5
- Present Subjunctive → 6
- Imperfect Subjunctive → 7

They are formed by adding endings to a verb stem. The endings show the number and person of the subject of the verb → 8

The stem and endings of regular verbs are totally predictable. The following sections show all the patterns for regular verbs. For irregular verbs see page 80 onwards.

Regular Verbs

There are three regular verb patterns (called conjugations), each identifiable by the ending of the infinitive:

First conjugation verbs end in **-are** e.g. **parlare** to speak

Second conjugation verbs end in **-ere** e.g. **credere** to believe

Third conjugation verbs end in **-ire** e.g. **finire** to finish

These three conjugations are treated in order on the following pages.

Examples

1	parlo	I speak I am speaking
	parlo?	do I speak?
2	parlavo	I spoke I was speaking I used to speak
3	parlerò	I shall/will/'ll speak
4	parlerei	I should/would/'d speak
5	parlai	I spoke
6	(che) parli	that I speak
7	(che) parlassi	that I should speak
8	parlo parliamo parlerei parleremmo	I speak we speak I'd speak we'd speak

Simple Tenses: First Conjugation

The stem is formed by taking the **-are** ending off the infinitive. The stem of **parlare** is **parl-** .

Add the following endings to the stem:

		❶ PRESENT	❷ IMPERFECT	❸ FUTURE
	1st person	**-o**	**-avo**	**-erò**
sing.	2nd person	**-i**	**-avi**	**-erai**
	3rd person	**-a**	**-ava**	**-erà**
	1st person	**-iamo**	**-avamo**	**-eremo**
plur.	2nd person	**-ate**	**-avate**	**-erete**
	3rd person	**-ano**	**-avano**	**-eranno**

		❹ PRESENT CONDITIONAL	❺ PAST HISTORIC
	1st person	**-erei**	**-ai**
sing.	2nd person	**-eresti**	**-asti**
	3rd person	**-erebbe**	**-ò**
	1st person	**-eremmo**	**-ammo**
plur.	2nd person	**-ereste**	**-aste**
	3rd person	**-erebbero**	**-arono**

		❻ PRESENT SUBJUNCTIVE	❼ IMPERFECT SUBJUNCTIVE
sing.	1st, 2nd person	**-i**	**-assi**
	3rd person	**-i**	**-asse**
	1st person	**-iamo**	**-assimmo**
plur.	2nd person	**-iate**	**-aste**
	3rd person	**-ino**	**-assero**

Examples

1 PRESENT
parl**o**
parl**i**
parl**a**
parl**iamo**
parl**ate**
parl**ano**

2 IMPERFECT
parl**avo**
parl**avi**
parl**ava**
parl**avamo**
parl**avate**
parl**avano**

3 FUTURE
parl**erò**
parl**erai**
parl**erà**
parl**eremo**
parl**erete**
parl**eranno**

4 PRESENT CONDITIONAL
parl**erei**
parl**eresti**
parl**erebbe**
parl**eremmo**
parl**ereste**
parl**erebbero**

5 PAST HISTORIC
parl**ai**
parl**asti**
parl**ò**
parl**ammo**
parl**aste**
parl**arono**

6 PRESENT SUBJUNCTIVE
parl**i**
parl**i**
parl**i**
parl**iamo**
parl**iate**
parl**ino**

7 IMPERFECT SUBJUNCTIVE
parl**assi**
parl**assi**
parl**asse**
parl**assimo**
parl**aste**
parl**assero**

Simple Tenses: Second Conjugation

The stem is formed by taking the **-ere** ending off the infinitive. The stem of **credere** is **cred-** .

Add the following endings to the stem:

		1 PRESENT	2 IMPERFECT	3 FUTURE
	1st person	**-o**	**-evo**	**-erò**
sing.	2nd person	**-i**	**-evi**	**-erai**
	3rd person	**-e**	**-eva**	**-erà**
	1st person	**-iamo**	**-evamo**	**-eremo**
plur.	2nd person	**-ete**	**-evate**	**-erete**
	3rd person	**-ono**	**-evano**	**-eranno**

		4 PRESENT CONDITIONAL	5 PAST HISTORIC
	1st person	**-erei**	**-ei** *or* **-etti**
sing.	2nd person	**-eresti**	**-esti**
	3rd person	**-erebbe**	**-ette**
	1st person	**-eremmo**	**-emmo**
plur.	2nd person	**-ereste**	**-este**
	3rd person	**-erebbero**	**-ettero**

		6 PRESENT SUBJUNCTIVE	7 IMPERFECT SUBJUNCTIVE
sing.	1st, 2nd persons	**-a**	**-essi**
	3rd person	**-a**	**-esse**
	1st person	**-iamo**	**-essimmo**
plur.	2nd person	**-iate**	**-este**
	3rd person	**-ano**	**-essero**

Examples

❶ PRESENT

cred**o**
cred**i**
cred**e**
cred**iamo**
cred**ete**
cr*e*d**ono**

❷ IMPERFECT

cred**evo**
cred**evi**
cred**eva**
cred**evamo**
cred**evate**
cred***e*****vano**

❸ FUTURE

cred**erò**
cred**erai**
cred**erà**
cred**eremo**
cred**erete**
cred**eranno**

❹ PRESENT CONDITIONAL

cred**erei**
cred**eresti**
cred**erebbe**
cred**eremmo**
cred**ereste**
cred**er*e*bbero**

❺ PAST HISTORIC

cred**ei** *or* cred**etti**
cred**esti**
cred**ette**
cred**emmo**
cred**este**
cred***e*****ttero**

❻ PRESENT SUBJUNCTIVE

cred**a**
cred**a**
cred**a**
cred**iamo**
cred**iate**
cr*e*d**ano**

❼ IMPERFECT SUBJUNCTIVE

cred**essi**
cred**essi**
cred**esse**
cred**essimo**
cred**este**
cred***e*****ssero**

Simple Tenses: Third Conjugation

Generally, the stem is formed by taking the **-ire** ending off the infinitive. The stem for most tenses of **finire** is **fin-**.

However, in the present tense and present subjunctive, **-isc-** is added to the basic stem (except for the 1st and 2nd person plural):

EXCEPTIONS: **servire** to serve, **dormire** to sleep, **soffrire** to suffer, **coprire** to cover, **sentire** to feel, **partire** to leave, **offrire** to offer, **aprire** to offer

The present tenses of **finire** and **dormire** are as follows:

	1st person	fin**isc**o	dormo
sing.	2nd person	fin**isc**i	dormi
	3rd person	fin**isc**e	dorme
	1st person	finiamo	dormiamo
plur.	2nd person	finite	dormite
	3rd person	fin**isc**ono	dormono

Both types of verb take the following endings:

		❶ PRESENT	❷ IMPERFECT	❸ FUTURE
	1st person	**-o**	**-ivo**	**-irò**
sing.	2nd person	**-i**	**-ivi**	**-irai**
	3rd person	**-e**	**-iva**	**-irà**
	1st person	**-iamo**	**-ivamo**	**-iremo**
plur.	2nd person	**-ite**	**-ivate**	**-irete**
	3rd person	**-ono**	**-ivano**	**-iranno**

		❹ PRESENT CONDITIONAL	❺ PAST HISTORIC
	1st person	**-irei**	**-iì**
sing.	2nd person	**-iresti**	**-isti**
	3rd person	**-irebbe**	**-ì**
	1st person	**-iremmo**	**-immo**
plur.	2nd person	**-ireste**	**-iste**
	3rd person	**-irebbero**	**-irono**

Examples

		6 PRESENT SUBJUNCTIVE	7 IMPERFECT SUBJUNCTIVE
sing.	1st, 2nd persons	-a	-issi
	3rd person	-a	-isse
	1st person	-iamo	-issimmo
plur.	2nd person	-iate	-iste
	3rd person	-ano	-issero

1 PRESENT
fin**isco**
fin**isci**
fin**isce**
fin**iamo**
fin**ite**
fin***iscono***

2 IMPERFECT
fin**ivo**
fin**ivi**
fin**iva**
fin**ivamo**
fin**ivate**
fin***ivano***

3 FUTURE
fin**irò**
fin**irai**
fin**irà**
fin**iremo**
fin**irete**
fin**iranno**

4 PRESENT SUBJUNCTIVE
fin**irei**
fin**iresti**
fin**irebbe**
fin**iremmo**
fin**ireste**
fin***irebbero***

5 PAST HISTORIC
fin**iì**
fin**isti**
fin**ì**
fin**immo**
fin**iste**
fin***irono***

6 PRESENT SUBJUNCTIVE
fin**isca**
fin**isca**
fin**isca**
fin**iamo**
fin**iate**
fin***iscano***

7 IMPERFECT SUBJUNCTIVE
fin**issi**
fin**issi**
fin**isse**
fin**issimo**
fin**iste**
fin***issero***

First Conjugation Spelling Irregularities

Before certain endings, the stems of some **-are** verbs may change slightly.

Verbs ending: **-care**
Change: **c** becomes **ch** before **e** or **i**
Tenses affected: Present, Future, Conditional, Present Subjunctive
Model: **cercare** to look for → 1

Why the change occurs: **h** is added to keep the **c** sound hard *k*.

Verbs ending: **-gare**
Change: **g** becomes **gh** before **e** or **i**
Tenses affected: Present, Future, Conditional, Present Subjunctive
Model: **pagare** to pay → 2

Why the change occurs: **h** is added to keep the **g** sound hard *g*.

Examples

1 INFINITIVE
cercare

PRESENT
cerco
cerchi
cerca
cerchiamo
cercate
c*e*rcano

FUTURE
cercherò
cercherai
cercherà
cercheremo
cercherete
cercheranno

CONDITIONAL
cercherei
cercheresti
cercherebbe
cercheremmo
cerchereste
cercher*e*bbero

PRESENT SUBJUNCTIVE
cerchi
cerchi
cerchi
cerchiamo
cerchiate
c*e*rchino

2 INFINITIVE
pagare

PRESENT
pago
paghi
paga
paghiamo
pagate
p*a*gano

FUTURE
pagherò
pagherai
pagherà
pagheremo
pagherete
pagheranno

CONDITIONAL
pagherei
pagheresti
pagherebbe
pagheremmo
paghereste
pagher*e*bbero

PRESENT SUBJUNCTIVE
paghi
paghi
paghi
paghiamo
paghiate
p*a*ghino

First Conjugation Spelling Irregularities *continued*

Verbs ending: **-ciare**
Change: **i** is dropped before **e** or **i**
Tenses affected: Present, Future, Conditional, Present Subjunctive
Model: **annunciare** to announce → 1

Why the change occurs: the **i** of the infinitive is needed to keep **c** soft *tʃ* before **a** (before **e** and **i**, **c** is soft, so the **i** is unnecessary).

Verbs ending: **-giare**
Change: **i** is dropped before **e** or **i**
Tenses affected: Present, Future, Conditional, Present Subjunctive
Model: **mangiare** to eat → 2

Why the change occurs: the **i** of the infinitive is needed to keep **g** soft *dʒ* before **a** (before **e** and **i**, **g** is soft, so the **i** is unnecessary).

Examples

1 INFINITIVE
annunciare

PRESENT
ann*u*ncio
annunci
ann*u*ncia
annunciamo
annunciate
ann*u*nciano

FUTURE
annuncerò
annuncerai
annuncerà
annunceremo
annuncerete
annunceranno

CONDITIONAL
annuncerei
annunceresti
annuncerebbe
annunceremmo
annuncereste
annuncer*e*bbero

PRESENT SUBJUNCTIVE
annunci
annunci
annunci
annunciamo
annunciate
ann*u*ncino

2 INFINITIVE
mangiare

PRESENT
m*a*ngio
mangi
m*a*ngia
mangiamo
mangiate
m*a*ngiano

FUTURE
mangerò
mangerai
mangerà
mangeremo
mangerete
mangeranno

CONDITIONAL
mangerei
mangeresti
mangerebbe
mangeremmo
mangereste
manger*e*bbero

PRESENT SUBJUNCTIVE
mangi
mangi
mangi
mangiamo
mangiate
m*a*ngino

First Conjugation Spelling Irregularities *continued*

Verbs ending: **-iare**
Change: **i** is not dropped before another **i**, which is what usually happens
Tenses affected: Present, Present Subjunctive
Model: **inviare** to send, **sciare** to ski → 1

Why the change occurs: The **i** has to be retained in forms where it is the stressed vowel.

Verbs ending: **-gliare**
Change: **i** is dropped before endings beginning with **-i**
Tenses affected: Present, Present subjunctive, Imperfect Subjunctive, Imperative
Model: **consigliare** to advise, **svegliare** to wake up → 2

Why the change occurs: There is no need to retain the **i**.

Examples

① INFINITIVE	② INFINITIVE
inviare	**svegliare**
PRESENT	PRESENT
invio	sveglio
invii	**svegli**
invia	sv*e*glia
inviamo	svegliamo
inviate	svegliate
inv*i*ano	sv*e*gliano

The Imperative

The imperative is the form of the verb used to give commands or instructions. It can be used politely, as in English 'Please take a seat'. In Italian, the polite imperative is the 3rd person form, either singular or plural. The 1st person plural (we) is used to make suggestions, as in 'Let's go'.

The imperative is formed by adding endings to the stem of the verb. The endings for the 1st and 2nd persons plural are the same as those for the present tense, the others are different. → 1

		FIRST	SECOND	THIRD
sing.	2nd person	**-a**	**-i**	**-i**
	3rd person	**-i**	**-a**	**-a**
plur.	1st person	**-iamo**	**-iamo**	**-iamo**
	2nd person	**-ate**	**-ete**	**-ite**
	3rd person	**-ino**	**-ano**	**-ano**

NB Third conjugation verbs which add **isc** to the stem in the present tense also do so in the imperative → 2

The imperative of irregular verbs is given in the verb tables page 80.

Position of object and reflexive pronouns with the imperative:
- they follow imperatives in the 2nd person and the **-iamo** form, and are joined on to make one word → 3
- they precede 3rd person polite imperatives, and are not joined on to them → 4

Changes to pronouns following the imperative:
- the first letter of the pronoun is doubled when the imperative is one syllable: **mi** becomes **mmi**, **ti** becomes **tti**, **lo** becomes **llo** etc → 5
- When the pronouns **mi**, **ti**, **ci** and **vi** are followed by another pronoun they become **-me**, **-te**, **-ce** and **-ve**, and **gli** and **le** become **glie-** → 6

Negative imperatives:
- **non** precedes the imperative to make it negative (except in the 2nd person singular) → 7
- **non** precedes the infinitive in the 2nd person singular) → 8
- in 2nd person singular negative commands, **non** is used with the infinitive instead of the imperative. Pronouns may be joined onto the infinitive, or precede it → 8

Examples

1. Compare:

Aspetti, Maria?	Are you waiting, Maria?
and: Aspetta Maria!	Wait Maria!
Prende l'autobus	He gets the bus
and: Prenda l'autobus, signora!	Get the bus, madam!

2.

Finisci l'esercizio, Marco!	Finish the exercise, Marco!
Finisca tutto, signore!	Finish it all, sir!
Finiamo tutto	Let's finish it all
Finite i compiti, ragazzi!	Finish your homework, children!
Finiscano tutto signori!	Finish it all, ladies and gentlemen!

3.

Guardami, mamma!	Look at me, mum!
Aspettateli!	Wait for them!
Proviamolo!	Let's try it!

4.

Mi dia un chilo d'uva, per favore	Give me a kilo of grapes please
Si accomodi!	Take a seat!
La prenda, signore	Take it, sir

5.

Dimmi!	Tell me!
Fallo subito!	Do it immediately!

6.

Mandameli	Send me them
Daglielo	Give it to him
Mandiamogliela!	Let's send it to them!

7.

Non dimentichiamo	Don't let's forget
Non si preoccupi, signore	Don't worry, sir

8.

Non dire bugie Andrea!	Don't tell lies Andrea!
Non dimenticare!	Don't forget!
Non toccarlo! *or* Non lo toccare!	Don't touch it!
Non glielo dire! *or* Non dirglielo	Don't tell him about it!
Non preoccuparti! *or* Non ti preoccupare!	Don't worry!

Compound Tenses

Continuous tenses

The simple tense of an Italian verb, e.g. **piove**, can have two meanings: 'it rains', or 'it's raining'; the continuous tense, **sta piovendo** is an alternative way of expressing the English present continuous (it's raining).

The Present Continuous is used less in Italian than in English. It is formed with the present tense of the verb **stare**, plus the gerund → 1

The Past Continuous is formed with the imperfect tense of **stare**, and the gerund → 2

For information on how to form the gerund, see page 52.

The Past Continuous is also less used in Italian than in English, as the imperfect tense can be used to express this meaning.

Examples

1. | | |
|---|---|
| Ci sto pensando | I'm thinking about it |
| Stanno arrivando | They're coming |
| Cosa stai facendo? | What are you doing? |

2. | | |
|---|---|
| Stavo studiando | I was studying |
| Stava morendo | He was dying |
| St*a*vano lavorando | They were working |

Compound Tenses *continued*

Formed with the past participle

These are:

Perfect → ①
Pluperfect → ②
Future Perfect → ③
Perfect Conditional → ④
Past Anterior → ⑤
Perfect Subjunctive → ⑥
Pluperfect Subjunctive → ⑦

They consist of the past past participle and an auxiliary verb. Most verbs take the auxiliary **avere**, but some take ***essere*** (see page 30).

These tenses are formed in the same way for regular and irregular verbs, the only difference being that an irregular verb may have an irregular past participle.

The Past Participle

The past participle of regular verbs is formed as follows:

First conjugation: replace the **-are** of the infinitive with **-ato** → ⑧

Second conjugation: replace the **-ere** of the infinitive with **-uto** → ⑨

Third conjugation: replace the **-ire** of the infinitive with **-ito** → ⑩

Examples

	with **avere**	with **essere**
1	ho parlato I spoke, have spoken	sono andato I went, have gone
2	avevo parlato I had spoken	ero andato I had gone
3	avrò parlato I will have spoken	sarò andato I will have gone
4	avrei parlato I would have spoken	sarei andato I would have gone
5	ebbi parlato I had spoken	fui andato I had gone
6	*a*bbia parlato I spoke, have spoken	sia andato I went, have gone
7	avessi parlato I had spoken	fossi andato I had gone

8. parlare to speak → parlato spoken
9. cr*e*dere to believe → creduto believed
10. finire to finish → finito finished

Compound Tenses *continued*

Verbs taking the auxiliary avere

PERFECT TENSE
The present tense of **avere** plus the past participle → 1

PLUPERFECT TENSE
The imperfect tense of **avere** plus the past participle → 2

FUTURE PERFECT
The future tense of **avere** plus the past participle → 3

PERFECT CONDITIONAL
The conditional of **avere** plus the past participle → 4

PAST ANTERIOR
The past historic of **avere** plus the past participle → 5

PERFECT SUBJUNCTIVE
The present subjunctive of **avere** plus the past participle → 6

PLUPERFECT SUBJUNCTIVE
The imperfect subjunctive of **avere** plus the past participle → 7

For how to form the past participle of regular verbs see page 24. The past participle of irregular verbs is given for each verb in the verb tables, page 80 onwards.

The past participle agrees in number and gender with a preceding direct object when it is **lo, la, li** or **le**, e.g.

Le matite? Le ho comprate ieri	The pencils? I bought them yesterday

Examples

❶ PERFECT

ho parlato	abbiamo parlato
hai parlato	avete parlato
ha parlato	hanno parlato

❷ PLUPERFECT

avevo parlato	avevamo parlato
avevi parlato	avevate parlato
aveva parlato	avevano parlato

❸ FUTURE PERFECT

avrò parlato	avremo parlato
avrai parlato	avrete parlato
avrà parlato	avranno parlato

❹ PERFECT CONDITIONAL

avrei parlato	avremmo parlato
avresti parlato	avreste parlato
avrebbe parlato	avrebbero parlato

❺ PAST ANTERIOR

ebbi parlato	avemmo parlato
avesti parlato	aveste parlato
ebbe parlato	ebbero parlato

❻ PERFECT SUBJUNCTIVE

abbia parlato	abbiamo parlato
abbia parlato	abbiate parlato
abbia parlato	abbiano parlato

❼ PLUPERFECT SUBJUNCTIVE

avessi parlato	avessimo parlato
avessi parlato	aveste parlato
avesse parlato	avessero parlato

Compound Tenses *continued*

Verbs taking the auxiliary *essere*

PERFECT TENSE
The present tense of **essere** plus the past participle → 1

PLUPERFECT TENSE
The imperfect tense of **essere** plus the past participle → 2

FUTURE PERFECT
The future tense of **essere** plus the past participle → 3

PERFECT CONDITIONAL
The conditional of **essere** plus the past participle → 4

PAST ANTERIOR
The past historic of **essere** plus the past participle → 5

PERFECT SUBJUNCTIVE
The present subjunctive of **essere** plus the past participle → 6

PLUPERFECT SUBJUNCTIVE
The imperfect subjunctive of **essere** plus the past participle → 7

For how to form the past participle of regular verbs see page 24. The past participle of irregular verbs is given for each verb in the verb tables, page 80 onwards.

For agreement of past participles see page 56.

For a list of verbs and verb types that take the auxiliary **essere**, see page 30.

Examples

1. PERFECT

sono andato(a)	siamo andati(e)
sei andato(a)	siete andati(e)
è andato(a)	sono andati(e)

2. PLUPERFECT

ero andato(a)	eravamo andati(e)
eri andato(a)	eravate andati(e)
era andato(a)	erano andati(e)

3. FUTURE PERFECT

sarò andato(a)	saremo andati(e)
sarai andato(a)	sarete andati(e)
sarà andato(a)	saranno andati(e)

4. PERFECT CONDITIONAL

sarei andato(a)	saremmo andati(e)
saresti andato(a)	sareste andati(e)
sarebbe andato(a)	sarebbero andati(e)

5. PAST ANTERIOR

fui andato(a)	fummo andati(e)
fosti andato(a)	foste andati(e)
fu andato(a)	furono andati(e)

6. PERFECT SUBJUNCTIVE

sia andato(a)	siamo andati(e)
sia andato(a)	siate andati(e)
sia andato(a)	siano andati(e)

7. PLUPERFECT SUBJUNCTIVE

fossi andato(a)	fossimo andati(e)
fossi andato(a)	foste andati(e)
fosse andato(a)	fossero andati(e)

Compound Tenses *continued*

The following verbs take the auxiliary *essere*

Reflexive verbs (see page 32) → 1

Many intransitive verbs (i.e. verbs not taking a direct object), including the following:

andare to go
apparire to appear
arrivare to arrive → 2
bastare to be enough
cadere to fall
costare to cost → 3
dipendere to depend
divenire to become
diventare to become
durare to last
entrare to come in
esistere to exist
essere to be
fuggire to escape
intervenire to intervene
morire to die
nascere to be born
partire to leave
restare to stay
rimanere to stay
ritornare to return → 4
riuscire to succeed/manage → 5
salire to go up/get on
scadere to expire
scappare to get away
scendere to go down
scivolare to slip
sparire to disappear → 6
stare to be/stay
succedere to happen
tornare to come back
venire to come
uscire to go out

The following verbs, often used in impersonal constructions:

bisognare
convenire
dispiacere
importare
mancare → 7
occorrere
parere → 8
piacere → 9
sembrare

Verbs that can be used both transitively and intransitively take the auxiliary ***essere*** when intransitive and **avere** when transitive → 10

Impersonal verbs which describe the weather are used with both **essere** and **avere** → 11

ⓘ Note that the past participle agrees in gender and number with the subject of verbs conjugated with **essere**.

Examples

1	Mi sono fatto male	I've hurt *or* I hurt myself
	Si è rotta la gamba	She's broken *or* She broke her leg
	Vi siete divertiti?	Did you have *or* Have you had a nice time?
	Si sono addormentati	They've gone *or* They went to sleep
2	È arrivata	She's arrived *or* She arrived
3	È costato parecchio	It cost a lot *or* It has cost a lot
4	Siamo ritornati	We've returned *or* We returned
5	Sei riuscito?	Did you succeed? *or* Have you succeeded?
6	Sono spariti	They've disappeared
7	Ti sono mancata?	Did you miss me?
8	Mi è parso strano	It seemed strange to me
9	Vi è piaciuta la musica?	Did you like the music?
10	**passare**	
	Intransitive	
	Sono passati molti anni	Many years have passed
	Transitive	
	Ho passato l'esame	I've passed the exam
	saltare	
	Intransitive	
	Il gatto è saltato sul tavolo	The cat jumped on the table
	Transitive	
	Ho saltato il pranzo	I skipped lunch
11	Ha piovuto *or*	
	È piovuto molto	It rained a lot
	Ha nevicato! *or*	
	È nevicato!	It's snowed!

Reflexive Verbs

A reflexive verb is one accompanied by a reflexive pronoun, e.g. **divertirsi** to enjoy oneself; **annoiarsi** to get bored.
The reflexive pronouns are:

	SINGULAR	PLURAL
1st person	**mi**	**ci**
2nd person	**ti**	**vi**
3rd person	**si**	**si**

The Italian reflexive pronoun is often not translated in English → 1

Plural reflexive pronouns can sometimes be translated as 'each other' → 2

Simple tenses of reflexive verbs are conjugated in exactly the same way as other verbs, except that the reflexive pronoun is always used. Compound tenses are conjugated with the auxiliary ***essere***. A sample reflexive verb is conjugated in full on pages 36 and 37.

Position of Reflexive Pronouns

The pronoun generally comes before the verb → 3

However, in positive 2nd person commands the pronoun is joined onto the end of the imperative → 4

In the infinitive, the final **e** is dropped and replaced by the reflexive pronoun → 5

When the infinitive is used with **non** in negative commands, the reflexive pronoun **ti** either comes first, as a separate word, or is joined on at the end → 6

Two alternatives also exist

- when the infinitive is used after another verb, the pronoun either goes before the main verb or joins onto the infinitive → 7
- in continuous tenses the pronoun either goes before the main verb or joins onto the gerund → 8

Examples

1 Mi annoio	I'm getting bored
Ti fidi di lui?	Do you trust him?
Si vergogna	He's embarrassed
Non vi preoccupate!	Don't worry!
2 Si odiano	They hate each other
3 Mi diverto	I'm enjoying myself
Ci prepariamo	We're getting ready
Si accomodi!	Take a seat!
4 Svegliati!	Wake up!
Divertitevi!	Enjoy yourselves!
5 Compare:	
ordinary infinitive	reflexive infinitive
lavare to wash	lavarsi to get washed, wash oneself
divertire to amuse	divertirsi to enjoy oneself
6 Non ti bruciare! *or* Non bruciarti!	Don't burn yourself!
Non ti preoccupare! *or* Non preoccuparti!	Don't worry!
Mi voglio abbronzare *or* Voglio abbronzarmi	I want to get a tan
Ti devi alzare *or* Devi alzarti	You must get up
Vi dovreste preparare *or* Dovreste prepararvi	You ought to get ready
7 Ti stai annoiando? *or* Stai annoiandoti?	Are you getting bored?
Si stanno alzando? *or* Stanno alzandosi?	Are they getting up?

Reflexive Verbs *continued*

Past Participle Agreement

The past participle used in compound tenses of reflexive verbs generally agrees with the subject of the verb → 1

Here are some common reflexive verbs:

accomodarsi to sit down/take a seat
addormentarsi to go to sleep
alzarsi to get up
annoiarsi to get bored/be bored
arrabbiarsi to get angry
cambiarsi to get changed
chiamarsi to be called
chiedersi to wonder
divertirsi to enjoy oneself/have fun
farsi male to hurt oneself
fermarsi to stop
lavarsi to wash/get washed
perdersi to get lost
pettinarsi to comb one's hair
preoccuparsi to worry
prepararsi to get ready
ricordarsi to remember
sbrigarsi to hurry
sedersi to sit
svegliarsi to wake up
vestirsi to dress/get dressed

Examples

1 Si è lavato le mani — He washed his hands
Si è lavata le mani — She washed her hands
I ragazzi si sono lavati le mani — The boys washed their hands
Le ragazze si sono lavate le mani — The girls washed their hands

Reflexive Verbs *continued*

Conjugation of: **divertirsi** to enjoy oneself – SIMPLE TENSES

PRESENT

mi diverto	ci divertiamo
ti diverti	vi divertite
si diverte	si divertono

IMPERFECT

mi divertivo	ci divertivamo
ti divertivi	vi divertivate
si divertiva	si divertivano

FUTURE

mi divertirò	ci divertiremo
ti divertirai	vi divertirete
si divertirà	si divertiranno

CONDITIONAL

mi divertirei	ci divertiremmo
ti divertiresti	vi divertireste
si divertirebbe	si divertirebbero

PAST HISTORIC

mi divertiì	ci divertimmo
ti divertisti	vi divertiste
si divertì	si divertirono

PRESENT SUBJUNCTIVE

mi diverta	ci divertiamo
ti diverta	vi divertiate
si diverta	si divertano

IMPERFECT SUBJUNCTIVE

mi divertissi	ci divertissimo
ti divertissi	vi divertiste
si divertisse	si divertissero

Conjugation of: **divertirsi** to enjoy oneself – COMPOUND TENSES

PRESENT CONTINUOUS

mi sto divertendo *or*	ci stiamo divertendo *or*
sto divertendomi	stiamo divertendoci
ti stai divertendo *or*	vi state divertendo *or*
stai divertendoti	state divertendovi
si sta divertendo *or*	si stanno divertendo *or*
sta divertendosi	stanno divertendosi

PERFECT

mi sono divertito(a)	ci siamo divertiti(e)
ti sei divertito(a)	vi siete divertiti(e)
si è divertito(a)	si sono divertiti(e)

PLUPERFECT

mi ero divertito(a)	ci eravamo divertiti(e)
ti eri divertito(a)	vi eravate divertiti(e)
si era divertito(a)	si erano divertiti(e)

FUTURE PERFECT

mi sarò divertito(a)	ci saremo divertiti(e)
ti sarai divertito(a)	vi sarete divertiti(e)
si sarà divertito(a)	si saranno divertiti(e)

PERFECT CONDITIONAL

mi sarei divertito(a)	ci saremmo divertiti(e)
ti saresti divertito(a)	vi sareste divertiti(e)
si sarebbe divertito(a)	si sarebbero divertiti(e)

PAST ANTERIOR

mi fui divertito(a)	ci fummo divertiti(e)
ti fosti divertito(a)	vi foste divertiti(e)
si fu divertito(a)	si furono divertiti(e)

PERFECT SUBJUNCTIVE

mi sia divertito(a)	ci siamo divertiti(e)
ti sia divertito(a)	vi siate divertiti(e)
si sia divertito(a)	si siano divertiti(e)

PLUPERFECT SUBJUNCTIVE

mi fossi divertito(a)	ci fossimo divertiti(e)
ti fossi divertito(a)	vi foste divertiti(e)
si fosse divertito(a)	si fossero divertiti(e)

The Passive

In the passive, the subject *receives* the action (e.g. I was hit) as opposed to *performing* it (e.g. I hit him). In English the passive is formed with the verb 'to be' and the past participle, and in Italian the passive is formed in exactly the same way, i.e. a tense of **essere** + *past participle*.

The past participle agrees in gender and number with the subject → 1

A sample verb is conjugated in the passive on pages 40 and 41.

In English it is possible to make the indirect object of an active sentence into the subject of a passive sentence, e.g. Someone told me → I was told.

This is not possible in Italian; instead a 3rd person plural can be used → 2

The passive is used less overall in Italian. The following alternatives are used:

- active constructions → 3
- the **si passivante** (preceding an active verb with **si**, to make it passive → 4
- an impersonal construction with **si** → 5

Examples

1	È stato costretto a ritirarsi dalla gara	He was forced to withdraw from the competition
	L'elettricità è stata tagliata ieri	The electricity was cut off yesterday
	La partita è stata rinviata	The match has been postponed
	Siamo invitati ad una festa a casa loro	We're invited to a party at their house
	I ladri sono stati catturati	The thieves have been caught
	Le finestre saranno riparate domani	The windows will be repaired tomorrow
2	Mi hanno dato una chiave	I've been given a key
	Gli diranno tutto	He'll be told everything
3	Due persone sono morte	Two people were killed
	Mi hanno rubato la macchina la settimana scorsa	My car was stolen last week
	C'erano delle microspie nella stanza	The room was bugged
	Dicono che sia molto ambizioso	He's said to be very ambitious
4	Dove si trovano i vini migliori?	Where are the best wines to be found?
	Non si accettano assegni	Cheques are not accepted
	Queste parole non si usano più	These words are no longer used
	Questo vino si beve a temperatura ambiente	This wine should be drunk at room temperature
5	Non si fa così	That's not how it's done
	Si raccomanda la massima discrezione	The utmost discretion is called for

The Passive *continued*

Conjugation of: **invitare** to invite

PRESENT

sono invitato(a) | siamo invitati(e)
sei invitato(a) | siete invitati(e)
è invitato(a) | sono invitati(e)

IMPERFECT

ero invitato(a) | ervamo invitati(e)
eri invitato(a) | eravate invitati(e)
era invitato(a) | erano invitati(e)

FUTURE

sarò invitato(a) | saremo invitati(e)
sarai invitato(a) | sarete invitati(e)
sarà invitato(a) | saranno invitati(e)

CONDITIONAL

sarei invitato(a) | saremmo invitati(e)
saresti invitato(a) | sareste invitati(e)
sarebbe invitato(a) | sarebbero invitati(e)

PAST HISTORIC

fui invitato(a) | fummo invitati(e)
fosti invitato(a) | foste invitati(e)
fu invitato(a) | furono invitati(e)

PRESENT SUBJUNCTIVE

sia invitato(a) | siamo invitati(e)
sia invitato(a) | siate invitati(e)
sia invitato(a) | siano invitati(e)

IMPERFECT SUBJUNCTIVE

fossi invitato(a) | fossimo invitati(e)
fossi invitato(a) | foste invitati(e)
fosse invitato(a) | fossero invitati(e)

The Passive *continued*

Conjugation of: **invitare** to invite

PERFECT

sono stato(a) invitato(a)	siamo stati(e) invitati(e)
sei stato(a) invitato(a)	siete stati(e) invitati(e)
è stato(a) invitato(a)	sono stati(e) invitati(e)

PLUPERFECT

ero stato(a) invitato(a)	eravamo stati(e) invitati(e)
eri stato(a) invitato(a)	eravate stati(e) invitati(e)
era stato(a) invitato(a)	erano stati(e) invitati(e)

FUTURE PERFECT

sarò stato(a) invitato(a)	saremo stati(e) invitati(e)
sarai stato(a) invitato(a)	sarete stati(e) invitati(e)
sarà stato(a) invitato(a)	saranno stati(e) invitati(e)

PERFECT CONDITIONAL

sarei stato(a) invitato(a)	saremmo stati(e) invitati(e)
saresti stato(a) invitato(a)	sareste stati(e) invitati(e)
sarebbe stato(a) invitato(a)	sarebbero stati(e) invitati(e)

PAST ANTERIOR

fui stato(a) invitato(a)	fummo stati(e) invitati(e)
fosti stato(a) invitato(a)	foste stati(e) invitati(e)
fu stato(a) invitato(a)	furono stati(e) invitati(e)

PERFECT SUBJUNCTIVE

sia stato(a) invitato(a)	siamo stati(e) invitati(e)
sia stato(a) invitato(a)	siate stati(e) invitati(e)
sia stato(a) invitato(a)	siano stati(e) invitati(e)

PLUPERFECT SUBJUNCTIVE

fossi stato(a) invitato(a)	fossimo stati(e) invitati(e)
fossi stato(a) invitato(a)	foste stati(e) invitati(e)
fosse stato(a) invitato(a)	fossero stati(e) invitati(e)

Impersonal Verbs

Any verb can be made impersonal by the use of **si** → 1

si is often used to make the following verbs impersonal:

dire	**si dice che** → 2 it's said that
potere	**si può** → 3 it's possible to/you can
trattarsi	**si tratta di** → 4 it's about/it's a matter of

Impersonal verbs are used only in the infinitive, with a gerund and in third person singular simple tenses. No pronoun is used in Italian.

e.g.	**Ha iniziato a piovere.**	It started to rain.
	Sta piovendo?	Is it raining?
	Nevicava da due giorni.	It had been snowing for two days.
	È facile capire che...	It's easy to see that...

Common impersonal verbs are:

diluviare	**diluvia**	it's pouring
gelare	**gela**	it's freezing
grandinare	**grandina**	it's hailing
nevicare	**nevica**	it's snowing
piovere	**piove**	it's raining
tuonare	**tuona**	it's thundering

Other verbs are often used impersonally:

bastare	**basta**	that's enough
importare	**non importa**	it doesn't matter

Examples

1	In quel ristorante si m*a*ngia bene e si spende poco	In that restaurant the food's good and it doesn't cost much
2	Si dice che sia una persona strana	It's said that he's a strange person
3	Si può visitare il castello tutti i giorni dell'anno	You can visit the castle every day of the year
4	Di cosa si tratta? Si tratta di poche ore	What's it about? It's a matter of a few hours

Impersonal Verbs *continued*

The following verbs are used in impersonal constructions:

INFINITIVE	CONSTRUCTIONS
bastare	**basta** + *infinitive* → ❶ you just have to
bisognare	**bisogna** + *infinitive* → ❷ you have to
convenire	*indirect pronoun* + **conviene** + *infinitive* → ❸ it's best to
essere	**è** + *noun to do with time/season* → ❹
sono	+ *plural times of the clock* → ❺ it is **è** + *adjective* + *infinitive* → ❻ **è** + *adjective* + **che** → ❼ it is
fare	**fa** + *adjective describing weather* → ❽ it is **fa** + *noun to do with weather, time of day*
occorrere	**occorre** + *infinitive* → ❾ it would be best to
parere	**pare** + **di** + **sì/no** → ❿ it seems so/not **pare** + **che** → ⓫ it seems/apparently
sembrare	**sembra** + **che** → ⓬ it seems

Examples

1	Basta chi*e*dere a qualcuno	You just have to ask someone
2	Bisogna prenotare?	Do you have to book?
	Bisogna arrivare un'ora prima	You have to get there an hour before
3	Conviene partire presto	It's best to set off early
4	È tardi.	It's late
	Era presto	It was early
	Era Pasqua	It was Easter
	È mezzogiorno	It's midday
5	Sono le otto	It's eight o'clock
6	È stato st*u*pido buttarli via	It was stupid to throw them away
	Sarebbe bello andarci	It would be nice to go there
7	È vero che sono stato impaziente	It's true that I've been impatient
	È poss*i*bile che *a*bbia sbagliato tu	Maybe you made a mistake
8	Fa caldo	It's hot
	Fa freddo	It's cold
	Faceva bel tempo	It was good weather *or* The weather was good
	Fa sempre brutto tempo	The weather's always bad
	Si sta facendo buio	It's getting dark
9	Occorre farlo s*u*bito	It would be best to do it immediately
10	Sono contenti? – Pare di sì.	Are they happy? – It seems so.
	L'ha creduto? – Pare di no.	Did he believe it? – Apparently not.
11	Pare che sia stato lui	Apparently it was him
12	Sembra che tu *a*bbia ragione	It seems you're right

The Infinitive

The infinitive is the form of the verb found in dictionary entries, e.g. **parlare** to speak; **finire** to finish. The infinitive sometimes drops its final **-e**.

All regular verbs have infinitives ending in **-are**, **-ere**, or **-ire**.

A few irregular verbs have infinitives ending in **-rre**, e.g.

comporre	to compose	**condurre**	to lead
porre	to put	**produrre**	to produce
proporre	to propose	**ridurre**	to reduce
supporre	to suppose	**tradurre**	to translate

In Italian the infinitive is used in the following ways:

- after adjectives and nouns that are followed by **di** → 1
- after another verb → 2
- to give instructions and orders → 3
- in 2nd person negative imperatives → 4

See page 20 for negative imperatives

- after prepositions → 5

See pages 190-197 for prepositions

- as the subject or object of a sentence → 6

There are three main types of constructions when the infinitive follows another verb:

- no linking preposition → 7
- linking preposition **a** (see also pages 70-78) → 8
- linking preposition **di** (see also pages 70-78) → 9

Examples

1	Sono contento di vederti	I'm glad to see you
	Sono sorpreso di vederti qui	I'm surprised to see you here
	Sono stufo di studiare	I'm fed up of studying
	Non c'è bisogno di prenotare	There's no need to book
2	Non devi mangiare se non vuoi	You don't have to eat if you don't want to
	Posso entrare?	Can I come in?
	Cosa ti piacerebbe fare?	What would you like to do?
3	Rallentare	Slow down
	Spi*n*gere	Push
4	Non fare sciocchezze!	Don't do anything silly!
	Non toccarlo!	Don't touch it!
5	È andato via senza dire niente	He went away without saying anything
6	Camminare fa bene	Walking is good for you
	Mi piace cavalcare	I like riding
7	Devi aspettare	You must wait
8	Hanno cominciato a *r*idere	They started to laugh
9	Quando sono entrato hanno smesso di parlare	When I came in they stopped talking

The Infinitive *continued*

Verbs followed by the infinitive with no linking preposition

dovere, potere, sapere, volere (i.e. modal auxiliary verbs: page 58).

verbs of seeing and hearing, e.g. **vedere** to see; **sentire** to hear → 1

Verbs used impersonally such as **piacere**, **dispiacere**, **occorrere** and **convenire** → 2

fare → 3

lasciare to let, allow → 4

The following common verbs:

bisognare → 5	to be necessary
detestare	to hate
desiderare → 6	to want
odiare → 7	to hate
preferire → 8	to prefer

Examples

1	Ci ha visto arrivare Ti ho sentito cantare	He saw us arriving I heard you singing
2	Mi piace andare in bici Ci dispiace andar via Occorre farlo s*u*bito Ti conviene partire presto	I like cycling We're sorry to be leaving It should be done immediately You'd best set off early
3	Non mi far r*i*dere!	Don't make me laugh!
4	L*a*scia fare a me	Let me do it
5	Bisogna prenotare	You need to book
6	Desiderava migliorare il suo inglese	He wanted to improve his English
7	Odio alzarmi presto al mattino	I hate getting up early in the morning
8	Preferisco non parlarne	I prefer not to talk about it

The Infinitive *continued*

Set expressions

The following are set in Italian with the meaning shown:

far entrare to let in → 1
far sapere to inform/let someone know → 2
far fare to have done → 3
farsi fare to have done → 4
lasciare stare to leave alone → 5
sentir dire che to hear that → 6
sentir parlare di to hear about → 7
voler dire to mean → 8

The Perfect Infinitive

The perfect infinitive is formed using the auxiliary verb **avere** or **essere** (as appropriate) with the past participle of the verb → 9

The perfect infinitive is found:

- after modal verbs → 10
- after prepositions → 11

Examples

1	Non mi hanno fatto entrare	They wouldn't let me in
2	Ti far*ò* sapere prima poss*i*bile	I'll let you know as soon as possible
3	Ho fatto riparare la m*a*cchina	I had the car repaired
4	Mi sono fatta tagliare i capelli	I had my hair cut
5	L*a*scia stare mia sorella!	Leave my sister alone!
6	Ho sentito dire che è stato licenziato	I heard he's been sacked
7	Non ho più sentito parlare di loro	I haven't heard any more about them
8	Non so che cosa vuol dire	I don't know what it means
9	aver(e) visto *e*ssere partito *e*ssersi fatto male	to have seen to have gone to have hurt oneself
10	Può aver avuto un incidente Dev'*e*ssere successo ieri	He may have had an accident It must have happened yesterday
11	senza aver dato un esame dopo *e*ssere rimasto chiuso	without having done an exam after having been closed

The Gerund

Formation

First conjugation:

Replace the **-are** of the infinitive with **-ando** → 1

Second and Third conjugations:

Replace the **-ere**, or **-ire** of the infinitive with **-endo** → 2

Exceptions to these rules are:

fare and verbs made by adding a prefix to **fare** → 3
dire and verbs made by adding a prefix to **dire** → 4
porre and verbs made by adding a prefix to **porre** → 5
verbs with infinitives ending in **-durre** → 6

The gerund is invariable.*

*A word that is invariable never changes its ending.

Examples

1. parlare **to speak** → parlando **speaking**
   andare **to go** → andando **going**
   dare **to give** → dando **giving**

2. cr*e*dere **to believe** → credendo **believing**
   *e*ssere **to be** → essendo **being**
   dovere **to have to** → dovendo **having to**
   finire **to finish** → finendo **finishing**
   dormire **to sleep** → dormendo **sleeping**

3. fare **to do** → facendo **doing**
   rifare **to redo** → rifacendo **redoing**

4. dire **to say** → dicendo **saying**
   contraddire **to contradict** → contraddicendo **contradicting**

5. porre **to put** → ponendo **putting**
   comporre **to compose** → componendo **composing**
   supporre **to suppose** → supponendo **supposing**

6. condurre **to lead** → conducendo **leading**
   produrre **to produce** → producendo **producing**
   ridurre **to reduce** → riducendo **reducing**

The Gerund *continued*

Uses

The gerund is used with the present tense of **stare** to make the present continuous tense → 1

The gerund is used with the imperfect tense of **stare** to make the past continuous tense → 2

ⓘ Note that the Italian past participle is sometimes used with the verbs **stare** or ***essere*** to make a continuous tense, e.g.

essere *or* **stare disteso**	to be lying → 3
essere *or* **stare seduto**	to be sitting → 3
essere *or* **stare appoggiato**	to be leaning → 3

The gerund can used adverbially, to indicate when or why something happens → 4

Pronouns are usually joined onto the end of the gerund → 5

When the gerund is part of a continuous tense the pronoun can either come before **stare** or be joined onto the gerund → 6

Examples

1	Sto lavorando Cosa stai facendo?	I'm working What are you doing?
2	Il bambino stava piangendo Stavo lavando i piatti	The little boy was crying I was washing the dishes
3	Era disteso sul divano Stava seduta accanto a me La scala era appoggiata al muro	He was lying on the sofa She was sitting next to me The ladder was leaning against the wall
4	Entrando ho sentito odore di pesce Ripens*a*ndoci, credo che non fosse colpa sua Ved*e*ndolo solo, è venuta a parlargli Sent*e*ndomi male, sono andato a letto Volendo, potremmo comprarne un altro	When I came in I could smell fish Thinking back on it, I reckon it wasn't his fault Seeing that he was on his own, she came to speak to him Because I felt ill I went to bed If we wanted to, we could buy another
5	Ved*e*ndoli è scoppiata in l*a*crime Mi sono addormentato ascolt*a*ndolo Sbagliando si impara	When she saw them she burst into tears As I listened to him I fell asleep You learn by making mistakes
6	Ti sto parlando *or* Sto parl*a*ndoti Si sta vestendo *or* Sta vest*e*ndosi Me lo stavano mostrando *or* Stavano mostr*a*ndomelo	 I'm talking to you He's getting dressed They were showing me it

Past Participle Agreement

For the formation of the past participle, see page 24.

Note that many Italian verbs have irregular past participles → 1

Past participles are sometimes like adjectives, and change their endings. For the rules of agreement, see below:

		MASCULINE	FEMININE
SING.	1st conj	**andato**	**andata**
SING.	2nd conj	**caduto**	**caduta**
SING.	3rd conj	**uscito**	**uscita**
PLUR.	1st conj	**andati**	**andate**
PLUR.	2nd conj	**caduti**	**cadute**
PLUR.	3rd conj	**usciti**	**uscite**

Rules of Agreement in Compound Tenses

When the auxiliary verb is **avere**:

The past participle generally remains in the masculine singular form → 2

EXCEPTION: When the object of the verb is **la** (*feminine*: her/it), **li** (*masculine plural*: them) or **le** (*feminine plural*: them), the participle agrees with **la**, **li** or **le** → 3

When the auxiliary verb is **essere**:

The past participle agrees in number and gender with the subject → 4

For the agreement of the past participle with reflexive verbs, see page 34.

The Past Participle as an adjective

When a past participles is used as an adjective it agrees in the normal way → 5

Examples

❶ crescere to grow	cresciuto grown
dire to say	detto said
fare to do	fatto done
porre to put	posto put
❷ Mio fratello ha comprato una macchina	My brother has bought a car
Mia sorella ha comprato una macchina	My sister has bought a car
I ragazzi hanno comprato dei gelati	The children bought ice creams
❸ Dov'è Marco? L'hai visto?	Where's Marco? Have you seen him?
Dov'è Silvia? L'hai vista?	Where's Silvia? Have you seen her?
Dove sono i ragazzi? Li hai visti?	Where are the boys? Have you seen them?
Dove sone le ragazze? Le hai viste?	Where are the girls? Have you seen them?
❹ È andato a casa	He's gone home
È andata a casa	She's gone home
I ragazzi sono usciti	The boys have gone out
Le ragazze sono uscite	The girls have gone out
Si è fatto male?	Has he hurt himself?
Si è fatta male?	Has she hurt herself?
Vi siete fatti male, ragazzi?	Have you hurt yourselves, boys?
Vi siete fatte male, ragazze?	Have you hurt yourselves, girls?
❺ È chiuso il supermercato?	Is the supermarket closed?
È chiusa la banca?	Is the bank closed?
Sono chiuse le finestre?	Are the windows closed?

Modal Auxiliary Verbs

In Italian, the modal auxiliary verbs (i verbi servili) are: **dovere, potere, sapere** and **volere**.

They are followed by the infinitive (without a connecting preposition) and have the following meanings:

dovere to have to, must → 1
to be going to, to be supposed to → 2
in the present conditional/perfect conditional:
should/should have, ought/ought to have → 3

potere to be able to, can → 4
to be allowed to, can, may → 5
indicating possibility: may/might/could → 6

sapere to know how to, can → 7

volere to want/wish to → 8
with negative won't/wouldn't → 9
in polite phrases → 10

Compound Tenses of dovere and potere

dovere and **potere** are conjugated with **avere** if the following verb is conjugated with **avere**, e.g. **dare**, **risolvere** → 11

dovere and **potere** are generally conjugated with **essere** if the following verb is conjugated with **essere**, e.g. **andare**, **partire**, **alzarsi** → 12

EXCEPTION: **avere** is used in compound tenses of **dovere** and **potere** when followed by **essere**, e.g. **Avrebbe dovuto essere più freddo** It should have been colder

Examples

1	Devi farlo proprio adesso?	Do you have to do it right now?
	È dovuta partire	She had to leave
	Dev'essere caro	It must be expensive
2	Deve scendere qui?	Are you going to get off here?
	Dovevo venire, ma poi non ho avuto tempo	I was going to come, but then I didn't have time
	Dovevano arrivare ieri sera	They were supposed to arrive yesterday evening
3	Dovresti parlargli	You should speak to him
	Avrei dovuto stare più attento	I should have been more careful
4	Non potrò venire domani	I won't be able to come tomorrow
	Cosa posso dire?	What can I say?
5	Posso entrare?	May I come in?
	Non si può parcheggiare qui	You can't park here
6	Può anche essere vero	It may/might even be true
	Potrebbe piovere	It may/might/could rain
7	Sai guidare?	Can you drive?
	Non so fare gli gnocchi	I don't know how to make gnocchi
8	Vuole rimanere ancora un giorno	He wants to stay another day
9	Non vuole aiutarci	She won't help us
	Non voleva ascoltarmi	He wouldn't listen to me
10	Vuole bere qualcosa?	Would you like something to drink?
11	Ho dovuto darglielo	I had to give it to him
	Ho potuto risolvere il problema	I was able to sort out the problem
12	È dovuta partire subito	She had to leave immediately
	Siamo dovuti alzarci presto	We had to get up early
	Lara è potuta venire	Lara was able to come
	Non sono potuti decidersi	They couldn't decide
	Si sarebbero potuti sbagliare	They could have been mistaken

Use of Tenses

The Present

The Italian simple present can be used to translate both the English simple present, e.g. I work, and the English present continuous, e.g. I'm working → 1

The Italian present continuous tense is also used for continuous actions → 2

Italian uses the present tense with the preposition **da** to describe an action that *has been continuing for* some time, or *has continued since* some time in the past → 3

The Italian present is also used

- for the immediate future → 4
- for offers → 5
- for arrangements → 6
- for predictions → 7
- when asking for suggestions → 8

The Future

The future is generally used as in English, but note the following:

the future tense is used after **quando**, if the verb in the main clause is in the future → 9

The Future Perfect

It is used as in English to mean 'shall/will have done' → 10

It is also used in time clauses relating to the future, where English uses the perfect → 11

Examples

1	Dove *a*bitano?	Where do they live?
	Dove *a*bitano adesso?	Where are they living now?
	Piove molto qui	It rains a lot here
	Ora piove	It's raining now
2	Cosa stai facendo? *or* Cosa fai?	What are you doing?
	Sta piovendo *or* Piove	It's raining
3	St*u*dio italiano da due anni	I've been learning Italian for two years
	Aspettiamo da un'ora	We've been waiting for an hour
	Lavora qui da settembre	She's been working here since September
	Non lo vedo da un pezzo	I haven't seen him for a while
	Vivono qui dal 2006	They've lived here since 2006
4	Prendo un espresso	I'll have an espresso
	È rotto, lo butto via	It's broken, I'm going to throw it away
5	Pago io!	I'll pay!
	Devo tornare a casa – Ti porto io!	I need to go home – I'll take you!
6	Parto alle due	I'm leaving at two
	Domani gioco a tennis	I'm playing tennis tomorrow
7	Se fai così lo rompi	If you do that you'll break it
	Se piove non viene nessuno	If it rains nobody will come
8	Dove lo metto?	Where shall I put it?
	Cosa facciamo?	What shall we do?
9	Quando finirò, verrò da te *or* Quando finisco, vengo da te	When I finish I'll come to yours
	Lo comprerò quando avrò abbastanza soldi	I'll buy it when I've got enough money
	Quando verrà saremo già in vacanza	When he comes we'll be on holiday
10	Avrò finito fra un'ora	I'll have finished in an hour
11	Quando l'avrai letto rit*o*rnamelo	When you've read it let me have it back
	Partirò quando avrò finito	I'll leave when I've finished

Use of Tenses *continued*

The Imperfect

The imperfect describes:

- an action (or state) in the past without definite time limits → 1
- habitual action(s) in the past (often translated by 'would' or 'used to') → 2

Italian uses the imperfect tense with the preposition **da** to describe an action that *had been continuing for* some time, or *had continued since* some time in the past → 3

The Perfect

The Italian perfect tense corresponds to both the English perfect tense and the English simple past → 4

The Past Historic

The past historic, used mainly in written Italian, and in the south of Italy, corresponds to the English simple past → 5

The Past Anterior

This tense is used instead of the pluperfect when a verb in another part of the sentence is in the past historic → 6

The Perfect Conditional

The perfect conditional, not the present conditional, is used in reported speech → 7

Examples

1	Avevo la febbre	I had a temperature
	Non ne sapeva niente	He didn't know anything about it
	Guardavo la tivù	I was watching TV
2	Ti prend*e*vano in giro, vero?	They used to tease you, didn't they?
	Facevamo lungh*i*ssime passeggiate	We would go for very long walks
	Mi raccontava delle belle st*o*rie	She used to tell me lovely stories
3	Studiavo italiano da due anni	I had been learning Italian for two years
	Aspettavamo da molto tempo	We had been waiting for a long time
	Lavorava a Roma dal 2000	She'd been working in Rome since 2000
	Non lo vedevo da un pezzo	I hadn't seen him for a while
4	Non l'ho mai visto	I've never seen it
	Non l'ho visto ieri	I didn't see it yesterday
	Sono stata in città	I've been to town
	Stamattina sono stata in città	I went to town this morning
5	Dormimmo profondamente e ci svegliammo riposati	We slept soundly and awoke refreshed
6	Mi addormentai dopo che se ne f*u*rono andati	I went to sleep after they had gone
7	Ha detto che mi avrebbe aiutato	He said he would help me
	Ho detto che avrei pagato la met*à*	I said I'd pay half
	Hanno promesso che sar*e*bbero venuti	They promised they would come

The Subjunctive

When to use it

For how to form the subjunctive see page 8 onwards.

The subjunctive follows the conjunction **che**:

- when used with verbs expressing belief or hope, such as **credere, pensare** and **sperare** → 1
- when used with verbs and expressions expressing uncertainty → 2
- when it is used with **volere**. The Italian subjunctive + **che** corresponds to the infinitive construction in English → 3
- following impersonal verbs → 4
- after impersonal constructions which express necessity, possibility etc:

è meglio che	it's better (that) → 5
è possibile che	it's possible (that) → 6
è facile che	it's likely (that) → 7
può darsi che	it's possible (that) → 8
non è che	it's not that → 9
sembra che	it seems (that) → 10

Examples

1	Penso che sia giusto	I think it's fair
	Credo che p*a*rtano domani	I think they're leaving tomorrow
	Spero che Luca arrivi in tempo	I hope Luca arrives in time
2	Non so se sia la risposta giusta	I don't know if it's the right answer
	Non sono sicura che tu *a*bbia ragione	I'm not sure you're right
3	V*o*glio che i miei ragazzi s*i*ano felici	I want my children to be happy
	Vuole che la aiuti	She wants me to help her
	Non v*o*glio che mi p*a*rlino	I don't want them to speak to me
4	Mi dispiace che non s*i*ano qui	I'm sorry they're not here
5	È meglio che tu te ne vada	You'd better leave
6	È possibile che s*i*ano stranieri	It's possible they're foreigners
7	È f*a*cile che sc*e*lgano quelli rossi	They'll probably choose those red ones
8	Può darsi che non venga	It's possible that he won't come
9	Non è che si debba sempre dire la verit*à*	You don't always have to tell the truth
10	Sembra che *a*bbiano vinto	It seems they've won

The Subjunctive *continued*

The subjunctive is used:

- after the following conjunctions:

prima che	before → 1
affinché	so that → 2
a meno che	unless → 3
benché	although → 4
nel caso che	in case → 5
nonostante	even though → 6
perché	so (that) → 7
per quanto	however → 8
purché	as long as → 9
sebbene	even though → 10

- after superlatives → 11
  la più grande che ci sia the biggest there is

- after:
  chiunque whoever → 12
  qualunque + *noun* whatever → 13
  per quanto however → 14

Note that **che** is not always followed by the subjunctive.

The indicative follows **che** when it is used with positive uses of **sapere** to know, and with other expressions indicating certainty, such as **Sono sicuro** *I'm sure* → 15

Examples

1	Vuoi parlargli prima che parta?	Do you want to speak to him before he goes?
2	Ti do venti euro affinché tu possa comprarlo	I'll give you twenty euros so that you can buy it
3	Lo prendo io, a meno che lo voglia tu	I'll take it, unless you want it
4	Mi aiutò a fare i compiti benché fosse molto stanca	She helped me do my homework she was very tired
5	Vi do il mio numero di telefono nel caso che veniate a Roma	I'll give you my phone number in case you come to Rome
6	Vuole alzarsi, nonostante sia ancora malato	He wants to get up even though he's still ill
7	Lo metto qui perché tutti possano usarlo	I'll put it here so everyone can use it
8	Per quanto mi sforzi non riesco a capire	I can't understand, however hard I try
9	Vengo anch'io, purché possa pagare la mia parte	I'll come too as long as I can pay my share
10	Mi prestò il denaro sebbene non ne avesse molto	She lent me the money even though she hadn't got much
11	È la persona più simpatica che conosca	He's the nicest person I know
12	Chiunque sia, digli che non ci sono	Whoever it is, tell them I'm not here
13	qualunque cosa accada	whatever happens
14	per quanto bello sia	however nice it may be
15	So che non è suo Sai che ti piace Sono sicura che l'ha preso lui Sei sicuro che verranno?	I know it's not hers You know you like it I'm sure he took it Are you sure they're coming?

The Subjunctive *continued*

The Perfect Subjunctive

The perfect subjunctive follows the conjunction **che**
- when it follows verbs such as **credere**, **pensare** and **sperare** relating to something in the past → 1
- when it follows an impersonal expression → 2
- when it follows a superlative → 3
- when it follows a conjunction ending in **che** → 4

The Imperfect Subjunctive

The imperfect subjunctive is used:
- following **che**, and other conjunctions, as above → 5
- with past tenses of **volere** + **che** → 6
- following **se** in conditional clauses describing hypothetical situations → 7

The Pluperfect Subjunctive

The pluperfect subjunctive is used:
- after **che**, in the same way as other tenses of the subjunctive → 8
- after other conjunctions → 9
- following **se** in conditional clauses describing past hypothetical situations → 10

Examples

1	Penso che sia stata una buona idea	I think it was a good idea
	Spero che non si sia fatta male	I hope she didn't hurt herself
	Spero che *a*bbia detto la verit*à*	I hope you told the truth
2	È poss*i*bile che *a*bbiano cambiato idea	It's possible they've changed their minds
	Mi dispiace che*a*bbia fatto brutto tempo	I'm sorry the weather was bad
3	la più bella che *a*bbia mai visto	the most beautiful one I've ever seen
4	Sarà qui fra poco, a meno che *a*bbia perso l'*au*tobus	He'll be here soon, unless he's missed the bus
5	Voleva alzarsi nonostante fosse ancora malato	He wanted to get up, even though he was still ill
6	Voleva che fossimo pronti alle otto	He wanted us to be ready at eight
	Vol*e*vano che tutto fosse in *o*rdine	They wanted everything to be tidy
	Volevo che andasse più veloce	I wanted him to go faster
	Non volevo che mi parl*a*ssero	I didn't want them to speak to me
7	Se tu ne avessi bisogno, te lo darei	If you needed it I'd give it to you
	Se potessi dormirei fino a tardi	If I could I'd have a lie-in
	Se lo sapesse sarebbe molto deluso	If he knew he'd be very disappointed
	Se solo avessi più denaro!	If only I had more money!
8	Non pensavo che l'avesse fatto	I didn't think he'd done it
	Credevo che f*o*ssero partiti	I thought they had left
	Ero sicuro che avesse perso il treno	I was sure he'd missed the train
	la più bella che avessi mai visto	the most beautiful one I had ever seen
9	Non ha detto niente nonostante si fosse fatto male	He didn't say anything even though he'd hurt himself
10	Se avessi saputo non l'avrei mai fatto	If I had known, I'd never have done it
	Se fosse stato più furbo non avrebbe detto niente	If he'd had more sense he wouldn't have said anything
	Se l'avessi visto mi crederesti	If you'd seen, it you'd believe me
	Se solo mi avessi creduto!	If only you'd believed me!

Verbs governing a and di

The following list (pages 70 to 78) contain common verbal constructions using the prepositions **a** and **di**

Note the following abbreviations:

infin.	*infinitive*
perf. infin.	*perfect infinitive*
qc	qualcosa
qn	qualcuno
sb	somebody
sth	something

Verbs governing **a** may be followed by the stressed pronouns **me, te, lui, lei, noi, voi** and **loro** → 1

More often, however, they are preceded by an unstressed indirect pronoun, without **a** → 2

For stressed and unstressed pronouns see page 162.

abituarse qn a qc/a + *infin.*	to accustom sb to sth/to doing
abituarsi a + *infin.*	to get used to doing → 3
acconsentire a qc/a + *infin.*	to agree to sth/to do → 4
accorgersi di qc	to notice sth → 5
accusare qn di qc/di + *(perf.) infin.*	to accuse sb of sth/of doing, having done → 6
affrettarsi a + *infin.*	to hurry to do
aiutare qn a + *infin.*	to help sb to do → 7
andare a + *infin.*	to go to do
approfittare di qc/di + *infin.*	to take advantage of sth/of doing
aspettarsi di + *infin.*	to expect to do → 8
assistere a qc	to attend sth, be at sth
assomigliare a qn/qc	to look/be like sb/sth → 9
aver bisogno di qc /di + *infin.*	to need sth/to do sth
aver paura di qc/di + *infin.*	to be afraid to do/of doing
aver voglia di qc/di + *infin.*	to want sth/to do
avvicinarsi a qn/qc	to approach sb/sth → 10
badare a qc/qn	to look after sth/sb
cambiarsi di qc	to change sth → 11
cercare di + *infin.*	to try to do → 12

Examples

1	Assomigli a lui, non a lei	You look like him, not like her
2	Gli ho chiesto i soldi	I asked him for the money
3	Si è abituato a bere di meno	He got used to drinking less
4	Non hanno acconsentito a vende**rl**o	They haven't agreed to sell it
5	Non si è accorto del mio errore	He didn't notice my mistake
6	Mi ha accusato d'aver mentito	He accused me of lying
7	Aiut*a*temi a portare queste val*i*gie	Help me to carry these cases
8	Si aspettava di vederlo?	Was she expecting to see him?
9	Sara assomiglia molto a sua madre	Sara looks very like her mother
10	Si è avvicinata a me	She came up to me
11	Mi sono cambiato d'abito	I changed my clothes
12	Ho cercato di capirla	I tried to understand her

Verbs governing a and di *continued*

cessare di + *infin.*	to stop doing → 1
chiedere qc a qn	to ask sb sth/for sth → 2
chiedere a qn di + *infin.*	to ask sb to do → 3
cominciare a + *infin.*	to begin to do, to start to do → 4
comprare qc a qn	to buy sth from sb/for sb → 5
consentire qc a qn	to allow sb sth
consentire a qn di + *infin.*	to allow sb to do
consigliare a qn di+ *infin.*	to advise sb to do → 6
continuare a + *infin.*	to continue to do
convincere qn a + *infin.*	to persuade sb to do → 7
dare la colpa a qn di qc	to blame sb for sth
decidere di + *infin.*	to decide to → 8
decidersi a + *infin.*	to resolve to do, to make up one's mind to do
diffidare di qn	to distrust sb
dimenticare di + *infin.*	to forget to do → 9
dire a qn di + *infin.*	to tell sb to do → 10
discutere di qc	to discuss sth
disobbedire a qn	to disobey sb → 11
dispiacere a qn	to displease sb → 12
divertirsi a + *infin.*	to enjoy doing
domandare qc a qn	to ask sb sth/for sth
dubitare di qc	to doubt sth
esitare a + *infin.*	to hesitate to do
evitare di + *infin.*	to avoid doing → 13
far male a qn	to hurt sb
farcela a + *infin.*	to manage to do
fare a meno di qc	to do/go without sth → 14
fare finta di + *infin.*	to pretend to do → 15
fidarsi di qn	to trust sb → 16
fingere di + *infin.*	to pretend to do → 17
finire di + *infin.*	to finish doing → 18
forzare qn a + *infin.*	to force sb to do
giocare a (+ *sports, games*)	to play → 19
giurare di + *infin.*	to swear to do
godere di qc	to enjoy sth → 20

Examples

1 Ha cessato di piovere?	Has it stopped raining?
2 Ho chiesto a Paola che ora fosse	I asked Paola what time it was
3 Chiedi a Francesca di farlo	Ask Francesca to do it
4 Comincia a nevicare	It's starting to snow
5 Cristina ha comprato a Paolo due biglietti	Cristina bought two tickets for Paolo
6 Ha consigliato a Paolo di aspettare	He advised Paolo to wait
7 Ci ha convinto a restare	She persuaded us to stay
8 Cosa avete deciso di fare?	What have you decided to do?
9 Non dimenticarti di prendere l'ombrello	Don't forget to take your umbrella
10 Dì a Gigi di stare zitto	Tell Gigi to be quiet
11 Disobbediscono spesso ai genitori	They often disobey their parents
12 A me non dispiace il loro modo di fare	I quite like their attitude
13 Evita di parlarle	He avoids speaking to her
14 Ho fatto a meno dell'elettricità per diversi giorni	I did without electricity for several days
15 Ho fatto finta di non vederlo	I pretended not to see him
16 Non mi fido di quella gente	I don't trust those people
17 Finge di dormire	She's pretending to be asleep
18 Ha finito di leggere questo giornale?	Have you finished reading this newspaper?
19 Gioca a tennis	She plays tennis
20 Gode di buona salute	He enjoys good health

Verbs governing a and di *continued*

imparare a + *infin.*	to learn to do → 1
impedire a qn di + *infin.*	to prevent sb from doing → 2
impegnarsi a + *infin.*	to undertake to do
incaricarsi di qc/di + *infin.*	to see to sth/undertake to do
incoraggiare qn a + *infin.*	to encourage sb to do → 3
iniziare a + *infin.*	to begin to do
insegnare qc a qn	to teach sb sth
insegnare a qn a + *infin.*	to teach sb to do → 4
intendersi di qc	to know about sth
interessarsi a qn/qc	to be interested in sb/sth → 5
invitare qn a + *infin.*	to invite sb to do → 6
lagnarsi di qc	to complain about sth
lamentarsi di qc	to complain about sth
mancare a qn	to be missed by sb → 7
mancare di qc	to lack sth
mancare di + *infin.*	to fail to do → 8
meritare di + *infin.*	to deserve to do → 9
mettersi a + *infin.*	to begin to do
minacciare di + *infin.*	to threaten to do → 10
nascondere qc a qn	to hide sth from sb → 11
nuocere a qc	to harm sth, to damage sth → 12
obbligare qn a + *infin.*	to oblige/force sb to do → 13
occuparsi di qc/qn	to look after sth/sb → 14
offrirsi di + *infin.*	to offer to do → 15
omettere di + *infin.*	to fail to do
ordinare a qn di + *infin.*	to order sb to do → 16
partecipare a qc	to take part in sth
pensare a qn/qc	to think about sb/sth → 17
pentirsi di + *(perf.) infin.*	to regret doing, having done → 18
perdonare qc a qn	to forgive sb for sth
perdonare a qn di + *perf. infin.*	to forgive sb for doing → 19
permettere qc a qn	to allow sb sth
permettere a qn di + *infin.*	to allow sb to do → 20

Examples

1 Sta imparando a *le*ggere	She's learning to read
2 Il rumore mi impedisce di lavorare	The noise is preventing me from working
3 Incor*a*ggia i figli ad *e*ssere indipendenti	She encourages her children to be independent
4 Gli sto insegnando a nuotare	I'm teaching him to swim
5 Si interessa molto di sport	She's very interested in sport
6 Mi ha invitato a cenare da lui	He invited me for dinner at his house
7 Manchi molto ai tuoi genitori	Your parents miss you very much
8 Non mancherò di d*i*rglielo	I'll be sure to tell him about it
9 M*e*ritano di avere la promozione	They deserve to be promoted
10 Ha minacciato di dare le dimissioni	She threatened to resign
11 Nasc*o*ndile il regalo!	Hide the present from her!
12 Il fumo nuoce alla salute di tutti	Smoking damages everybody's health
13 Li ha obbligati a farlo	He forced them to do it
14 Mi *o*ccupo di mia nipote	I'm looking after my niece
15 Marco si è offerto di venire con noi	Marco has offered to go with us
16 Ha ordinato loro di sparare	He ordered them to shoot
17 Penso spesso a te	I often think about you
18 Mi pento di av*e*rglielo detto	I'm sorry I told him
19 Hai perdonato Carlo di averti mentito?	Have you forgiven Carlo for lying to you?
20 Permett*e*temi di continuare, per favore	Allow me to go on, please

Verbs governing a and di *continued*

persuadere qn a + *infin.*	to persuade sb to do
piacere a qn	to please sb → 1
portare via qc a qn	to take sth away from sb
pregare qn a + *infin.*	to beg sb to do
prendere qc a qn	to take sth from sb → 2
prendersi gioco di qn/qc	to make fun of sb/sth
preparare qn a + *infin.*	to prepare sb to do
prepararsi a + *infin.*	to get ready to do
proibire a qn di + *infin.*	to forbid sb to do → 3
promettere qc a qn	to promise sb sth
promettere a qn di + *infin.*	to promise sb to do → 4
proporre di + *infin.*	to suggest doing → 5
provare a + *infin.*	to try to do
rammaricarsi di + *(perf.) infin.*	to regret doing, having done
resistere a qc	to resist sth → 6
ricordarsi di qn/qc/di + *(perf.) infin.*	to remember sb/sth/doing, having done → 7
ridere di qn/qc	to laugh at sb/sth
rifiutarsi di + *infin.*	to refuse to do → 8
rimpiangere di + *(perf.) infin.*	to regret doing, having done
rimproverare qc a qn	to reproach sb with/for sth → 9
ringraziare qn di qc/di + *(perf.) infin.*	to thank sb for sth/for doing, having done → 10
rinunciare a qc/a + *infin.*	to give up sth /give up doing
rischiare di + *infin.*	to risk doing → 11
rispondere a qn	to answer sb
riuscire a + *infin.*	to manage to do → 12
rivolgersi a qn	to ask sb
rubare qc a qn	to steal sth from sb
scordare di + *infin.*	to forget to do
scordarsi di + *infin.*	to forget to do
scusarsi di qc/di + *(perf.) infin.*	to apologize for sth/for doing, having done → 13
servire a qc/a + *infin.*	to be used for sth/for doing → 14
servirsi di qc	to use sth → 15
sforzarsi di + *infin.*	to make an effort to do
smettere di + *infin.*	to stop doing → 16
sognare di + *infin.*	to dream of doing

Examples

1	A lui piace questo genere di film	He likes this kind of film
2	Gli ho preso il cellulare	I took his mobile phone from him
3	Ho proibito loro di uscire	I've forbidden them to go out
4	Hanno promesso a Luca di venire	They promised Luca they would come
5	Ho proposto a mio fratello di invitarli	I suggested to my brother that he should invite them
6	Come riesci a resistere alla tentazione?	How do you manage to resist the temptation?
7	Vi ricordate di Luciana? Non si ricorda di averlo perso	Do you remember Luciana? He doesn't remember losing it
8	Si è rifiutato di cooperare	He has refused to cooperate
9	Rimproverano alla figlia la sua mancanza d'entusiasmo	They reproach their daughter for her lack of enthusiasm
10	Li abbiamo ringraziati della loro gentilezza	We thanked them for their kindness
11	Rischiate di perdere soldi	You risk losing money
12	Siete riusciti a convincermi	You've managed to convince me
13	Mi scuso del ritardo	I'm sorry I'm late
14	Questo pulsante serve a regolare il volume	This button is for adjusting the volume
15	Si è servito di un cacciavite per aprirlo	He used a screwdriver to open it
16	Smettete di fare rumore!	Stop making so much noise!

Verbs governing a and di *continued*

somigliare a qn/qc	to look/be like sb/sth
sopravvivere a qn	to outlive sb → 1
spicciarsi a + *infin.*	to hurry to do
spingere qn a + *infin.*	to urge sb to do
strappare via qc a qn	to snatch sth from sb → 2
stufarsi di qc/qn	to be fed up with sth/sb
stupirsi di qc	to be amazed at sth
succedere a qn	to succeed sb
tardare a + *infin.*	to delay doing → 3
telefonare a qn	to phone sb
tendere a + *infin.*	to tend to do
tenere a + *infin.*	to be keen to do → 4
tentare di + *infin.*	to try to do → 5
togliere qc a qn	to take sth away from sb
trattare di qc	to be about sth
ubbidire a qn	to obey sb
vantarsi di qc	to boast about sth
venire a + *infin.*	to come to do
vietare a qn di + *infin.*	to forbid sb to do → 6
vivere di qc	to live on sth

Verbs followed by a preposition in Engish but not in Italian.

ascoltare qc/qn	to listen to sth/sb → 7
aspettare qc/qn	to wait for sth/sb → 8
cercare qc/qn	to look for sth/sb → 9
chiedere qc	to ask for sth → 10
guardare qc/qn	to look at sth/sb → 11
pagare qc/qn	to pay for sth/sb → 12

Examples

1	È sopravvissuta a suo marito	She outlived her husband
2	Il ladro le ha strappato via la borsa	The thief snatched her bag
3	Non ha tardato a prendere una decisione	He didn't take long to make a decision
4	Ci tiene a farlo da sola	She's keen to do it by herself
5	Ho tentato di darlo ad Alessia	I tried to give it to Alessia
6	Ha vietato ai bambini di giocare con i fiammiferi	He's forbidden the children to play with matches
7	Mi stai ascoltando?	Are you listening to me?
8	Aspettami!	Wait for me!
9	Sto cercando la chiave	I'm looking for my key
10	Ha chiesto qualcosa da mangiare	He asked for something to eat
11	Guarda la sua faccia	Look at his face
12	Ho già pagato il biglietto	I've already paid for my ticket

Introduction

The Verb Tables in the following section contain tables of Italian verbs (some regular and some irregular) in alphabetical order. Each table shows you the following forms: Present, Present Subjunctive, Perfect, Imperfect, Future, Conditional, Past Historic, Pluperfect, Imperative and the Past Participle and Gerund.

In Italian there are regular verbs (their forms follow the regular patterns of **-are**, **-ere** or **-ire** verbs), and irregular verbs (their forms do not follow the normal rules). Examples of regular verbs in these tables are:

parlare (regular **-are** verb)
credere (regular **-ere** verb)
capire (regular **-ire** verb)

Some irregular verbs are irregular in most of their forms, while others may only have a couple of irregular forms.

acc*o*rgersi (to realize)

PRESENT

io	mi accorgo
tu	ti accorgi
lui/lei/Lei	si accorge
noi	ci accorgiamo
voi	vi accorgete
loro	si acc*o*rgono

IMPERFECT

io	mi accorgevo
tu	ti accorgevi
lui/lei/Lei	si accorgeva
noi	ci accorgevamo
voi	vi accorgevate
loro	si accorg*e*vano

FUTURE

io	mi accorger*ò*
tu	ti accorgerai
lui/lei/Lei	si accorger*à*
noi	ci accorgeremo
voi	vi accorgerete
loro	si accorgeranno

CONDITIONAL

io	mi accorgerei
tu	ti accorgeresti
lui/lei/Lei	si accorgerebbe
noi	ci accorgeremmo
voi	vi accorgereste
loro	si accorger*e*bbero

PRESENT SUBJUNCTIVE

io	mi accorga
tu	ti accorga
lui/lei/Lei	si accorga
noi	ci accorgiamo
voi	vi accorgiate
loro	si acc*o*rgano

PAST HISTORIC

io	mi accorsi
tu	ti accorgesti
lui/lei/Lei	si accorse
noi	ci accorgemmo
voi	vi accorgeste
loro	si acc*o*rsero

PAST PARTICIPLE

accorto

IMPERATIVE

accorgiti
accorgi*a*moci
accorg*e*tevi

GERUND

accorg*e*ndosi

AUXILIARY

essere

addormentarsi (to go to sleep)

	PRESENT		IMPERFECT
io	mi addormento	io	mi addormentavo
tu	ti addormenti	tu	ti addormentavi
lui/lei/Lei	si addormenta	lui/lei/Lei	si addormentava
noi	ci addormentiamo	noi	ci addormentavamo
voi	vi addormentate	voi	vi addormentavate
loro	si addormentano	loro	si addormentavano

	FUTURE		CONDITIONAL
io	mi addormenterò	io	mi addormenterei
tu	ti addormenterai	tu	ti addormenteresti
lui/lei/Lei	si addormenterà	lui/lei/Lei	si addormenterebbe
noi	ci addormenteremo	noi	ci addormenteremmo
voi	vi addormenterete	voi	vi addormentereste
loro	si addormenteranno	loro	si addormenterebbero

	PRESENT SUBJUNCTIVE		PAST HISTORIC
io	mi addormenti	io	mi addormentai
tu	ti addormenti	tu	ti addormentasti
lui/lei/Lei	si addormenti	lui/lei/Lei	si addormentò
noi	ci addormentiamo	noi	ci addormentammo
voi	vi addormentiate	voi	vi addormentaste
loro	si addormentino	loro	si addormentarono

PAST PARTICIPLE
addormentato

IMPERATIVE
addormentati
addormentiamoci
addormentatevi

GERUND
addormentandosi

AUXILIARY
essere

andare (to go)

	PRESENT		IMPERFECT
io	vado	io	andavo
tu	vai	tu	andavi
lui/lei/Lei	va	lui/lei/Lei	andava
noi	andiamo	noi	andavamo
voi	andate	voi	andavate
loro	vanno	loro	and*a*vano

	FUTURE		CONDITIONAL
io	andr*ò*	io	andrei
tu	andrai	tu	andresti
lui/lei/Lei	andr*à*	lui/lei/Lei	andrebbe
noi	andremo	noi	andremmo
voi	andrete	voi	andreste
loro	andranno	loro	andr*e*bbero

	PRESENT SUBJUNCTIVE		PAST HISTORIC
io	vada	io	andai
tu	vada	tu	andasti
lui/lei/Lei	vada	lui/lei/Lei	and*ò*
noi	andiamo	noi	andammo
voi	andiate	voi	andaste
loro	v*a*dano	loro	and*a*rono

PAST PARTICIPLE
andato

IMPERATIVE
vai
andiamo
andate

GERUND
andando

AUXILIARY
essere

aprire (to open)

	PRESENT		IMPERFECT
io	apro	io	aprivo
tu	apri	tu	aprivi
lui/lei/Lei	apre	lui/lei/Lei	apriva
noi	apriamo	noi	aprivamo
voi	aprite	voi	aprivate
loro	*a*prono	loro	apri*v*ano

	FUTURE		CONDITIONAL
io	aprir*ò*	io	aprirei
tu	aprirai	tu	apriresti
lui/lei/Lei	aprir*à*	lui/lei/Lei	aprirebbe
noi	apriremo	noi	apriremmo
voi	aprirete	voi	aprireste
loro	apriranno	loro	aprir*e*bbero

	PRESENT SUBJUNCTIVE		PAST HISTORIC
io	apra	io	aprii
tu	apra	tu	apristi
lui/lei/Lei	apra	lui/lei/Lei	aprì
noi	apriamo	noi	aprimmo
voi	apriate	voi	apriste
loro	*a*prano	loro	apr*i*rono

PAST PARTICIPLE
aperto

IMPERATIVE
apri
apriamo
aprite

GERUND
aprendo

AUXILIARY
avere

assumere (to take on, to employ)

	PRESENT		IMPERFECT
io	assumo	io	assumevo
tu	assumi	tu	assumevi
lui/lei/Lei	assume	lui/lei/Lei	assumeva
noi	assumiamo	noi	assumevamo
voi	assumete	voi	assumevate
loro	ass*u*mono	loro	assum*e*vano

	FUTURE		CONDITIONAL
io	assumer*ò*	io	assumerei
tu	assumerai	tu	assumeresti
lui/lei/Lei	assumer*à*	lui/lei/Lei	assumerebbe
noi	assumeremo	noi	assumeremmo
voi	assumerete	voi	assumereste
loro	assumeranno	loro	assumer*e*bbero

	PRESENT SUBJUNCTIVE		PAST HISTORIC
io	assuma	io	assunsi
tu	assuma	tu	assumesti
lui/lei/Lei	assuma	lui/lei/Lei	assunse
noi	assumiamo	noi	assumemmo
voi	assumiate	voi	assumeste
loro	ass*u*mano	loro	ass*u*nsero

PAST PARTICIPLE
assunto

IMPERATIVE
assumi
assumiamo
assumete

GERUND
assumendo

AUXILIARY
avere

avere (to have)

PRESENT

io	ho
tu	hai
lui/lei/Lei	ha
noi	abbiamo
voi	avete
loro	hanno

IMPERFECT

io	avevo
tu	avevi
lui/lei/Lei	aveva
noi	avevamo
voi	avevate
loro	av*e*vano

FUTURE

io	avr*ò*
tu	avrai
lui/lei/Lei	avr*à*
noi	avremo
voi	avrete
loro	avranno

CONDITIONAL

io	avrei
tu	avresti
lui/lei/Lei	avrebbe
noi	avremmo
voi	avreste
loro	avr*e*bbero

PRESENT SUBJUNCTIVE

io	abbia
tu	abbia
lui/lei/Lei	abbia
noi	abbiamo
voi	abbiate
loro	*a*bbiano

PAST HISTORIC

io	ebbi
tu	avesti
lui/lei/Lei	ebbe
noi	avemmo
voi	aveste
loro	*e*bbero

PAST PARTICIPLE
avuto

IMPERATIVE
abbi
abbiamo
abbiate

GERUND
avendo

AUXILIARY
avere

bere (to drink)

	PRESENT		IMPERFECT
io	bevo	io	bevevo
tu	bevi	tu	bevevi
lui/lei/Lei	beve	lui/lei/Lei	beveva
noi	beviamo	noi	bevevamo
voi	bevete	voi	bevevate
loro	b*e*vono	loro	bev*e*vano

	FUTURE		CONDITIONAL
io	berrò	io	berrei
tu	berrai	tu	berresti
lui/lei/Lei	berrà	lui/lei/Lei	berrebbe
noi	berremo	noi	berremmo
voi	berrete	voi	berreste
loro	berranno	loro	berr*e*bbero

	PRESENT SUBJUNCTIVE		PAST HISTORIC
io	beva	io	bevvi
tu	beva	tu	bevesti
lui/lei/Lei	beva	lui/lei/Lei	bevve
noi	beviamo	noi	bevemmo
voi	beviate	voi	beveste
loro	b*e*vano	loro	b*e*vvero

PAST PARTICIPLE
bevuto

IMPERATIVE
bevi
beviamo
bevete

GERUND
bevendo

AUXILIARY
avere

cadere (to fall)

PRESENT

io	cado
tu	cadi
lui/lei/Lei	cade
noi	cadiamo
voi	cadete
loro	c*a*dono

FUTURE

io	cadr*ò*
tu	cadrai
lui/lei/Lei	cadr*à*
noi	cadremo
voi	cadrete
loro	cadranno

PRESENT SUBJUNCTIVE

io	cada
tu	cada
lui/lei/Lei	cada
noi	cadiamo
voi	cadiate
loro	c*a*dano

IMPERFECT

io	cadevo
tu	cadevi
lui/lei/Lei	cadeva
noi	cadevamo
voi	cadevate
loro	cad*e*vano

CONDITIONAL

io	cadrei
tu	cadresti
lui/lei/Lei	cadrebbe
noi	cadremmo
voi	cadreste
loro	cadr*e*bbero

PAST HISTORIC

io	caddi
tu	cadesti
lui/lei/Lei	cadde
noi	cademmo
voi	cadeste
loro	c*a*ddero

PAST PARTICIPLE
caduto

GERUND
cadendo

IMPERATIVE
cadi
cadiamo
cadete

AUXILIARY
essere

capire (to understand)

PRESENT		IMPERFECT	
io	capisco	io	capivo
tu	capisci	tu	capivi
lui/lei/Lei	capisce	lui/lei/Lei	capiva
noi	capiamo	noi	capivamo
voi	capite	voi	capivate
loro	cap*i*scono	loro	cap*i*vano

FUTURE		CONDITIONAL	
io	capir*ò*	io	capirei
tu	capirai	tu	capiresti
lui/lei/Lei	capir*à*	lui/lei/Lei	capirebbe
noi	capiremo	noi	capiremmo
voi	capirete	voi	capireste
loro	capiranno	loro	capir*e*bbero

PRESENT SUBJUNCTIVE		PAST HISTORIC	
io	capisca	io	capii
tu	capisca	tu	capisti
lui/lei/Lei	capisca	lui/lei/Lei	capì
noi	capiamo	noi	capimmo
voi	capiate	voi	capiste
loro	cap*i*scano	loro	cap*i*rono

PAST PARTICIPLE
capito

IMPERATIVE
capisci
capiamo
capite

GERUND
capendo

AUXILIARY
avere

cercare (to look for)

PRESENT

io	cerco
tu	cerchi
lui/lei/Lei	cerca
noi	cerchiamo
voi	cercate
loro	c*e*rcano

IMPERFECT

io	cercavo
tu	cercavi
lui/lei/Lei	cercava
noi	cercavamo
voi	cercavate
loro	cerc*a*vano

FUTURE

io	cercher*ò*
tu	cercherai
lui/lei/Lei	cercher*à*
noi	cercheremo
voi	cercherete
loro	cercheranno

CONDITIONAL

io	cercherei
tu	cercheresti
lui/lei/Lei	cercherebbe
noi	cercheremmo
voi	cerchereste
loro	cercher*e*bbero

PRESENT SUBJUNCTIVE

io	cerchi
tu	cerchi
lui/lei/Lei	cerchi
noi	cerchiamo
voi	cerchiate
loro	c*e*rchino

PAST HISTORIC

io	cercai
tu	cercasti
lui/lei/Lei	cerc*ò*
noi	cercammo
voi	cercaste
loro	cerc*a*rono

PAST PARTICIPLE
cercato

IMPERATIVE
cerca
cerchiamo
cercate

GERUND
cercando

AUXILIARY
avere

chi*u*dere (to close)

	PRESENT		IMPERFECT
io	chiudo	io	chiudevo
tu	chiudi	tu	chiudevi
lui/lei/Lei	chiude	lui/lei/Lei	chiudeva
noi	chiudiamo	noi	chiudevamo
voi	chiudete	voi	chiudevate
loro	chi*u*dono	loro	chiud*e*vano

	FUTURE		CONDITIONAL
io	chiuder*ò*	io	chiuderei
tu	chiuderai	tu	chiuderesti
lui/lei/Lei	chiuder*à*	lui/lei/Lei	chiuderebbe
noi	chiuderemo	noi	chiuderemmo
voi	chiuderete	voi	chiudereste
loro	chiuderanno	loro	chiuder*e*bbero

	PRESENT SUBJUNCTIVE		PAST HISTORIC
io	chiuda	io	chiusi
tu	chiuda	tu	chiudesti
lui/lei/Lei	chiuda	lui/lei/Lei	chiuse
noi	chiudiamo	noi	chiudemmo
voi	chiudiate	voi	chiudeste
loro	chi*u*dano	loro	chi*u*sero

PAST PARTICIPLE
chiuso

IMPERATIVE
chiudi
chiudiamo
chiudete

GERUND
chiudendo

AUXILIARY
avere

correre (to run)

	PRESENT		IMPERFECT
io	corro	io	correvo
tu	corri	tu	correvi
lui/lei/Lei	corre	lui/lei/Lei	correva
noi	corriamo	noi	correvamo
voi	correte	voi	correvate
loro	corrono	loro	correvano

	FUTURE		CONDITIONAL
io	correrò	io	correrei
tu	correrai	tu	correresti
lui/lei/Lei	correrà	lui/lei/Lei	correrebbe
noi	correremo	noi	correremmo
voi	correrete	voi	correreste
loro	correranno	loro	correrebbero

	PRESENT SUBJUNCTIVE		PAST HISTORIC
io	corra	io	corsi
tu	corra	tu	corresti
lui/lei/Lei	corra	lui/lei/Lei	corse
noi	corriamo	noi	corremmo
voi	corriate	voi	correste
loro	corrano	loro	corsero

PAST PARTICIPLE
corso

IMPERATIVE
corri
corriamo
correte

GERUND
correndo

AUXILIARY
avere

cr*e*dere (to believe)

	PRESENT
io	credo
tu	credi
lui/lei/Lei	crede
noi	crediamo
voi	credete
loro	cr*e*dono

	IMPERFECT
io	credevo
tu	credevi
lui/lei/Lei	credeva
noi	credevamo
voi	credevate
loro	cred*e*vano

	FUTURE
io	crederò
tu	crederai
lui/lei/Lei	crederà
noi	crederemo
voi	crederete
loro	crederanno

	CONDITIONAL
io	crederei
tu	crederesti
lui/lei/Lei	crederebbe
noi	crederemmo
voi	credereste
loro	crederebbero

	PRESENT SUBJUNCTIVE
io	creda
tu	creda
lui/lei/Lei	creda
noi	crediamo
voi	crediate
loro	cr*e*dano

	PAST HISTORIC
io	credetti *or* credei
tu	credesti
lui/lei/Lei	credette
noi	credemmo
voi	credeste
loro	cred*e*ttero

PAST PARTICIPLE
creduto

IMPERATIVE
credi
crediamo
credete

GERUND
credendo

AUXILIARY
avere

crescere (to grow)

	PRESENT		IMPERFECT
io	cresco	io	crescevo
tu	cresci	tu	crescevi
lui/lei/Lei	cresce	lui/lei/Lei	cresceva
noi	cresciamo	noi	crescevamo
voi	crescete	voi	crescevate
loro	crescono	loro	crescevano

	FUTURE		CONDITIONAL
io	crescerò	io	crescerei
tu	crescerai	tu	cresceresti
lui/lei/Lei	crescerà	lui/lei/Lei	crescerebbe
noi	cresceremo	noi	cresceremmo
voi	crescerete	voi	crescereste
loro	cresceranno	loro	crescerebbero

	PRESENT SUBJUNCTIVE		PAST HISTORIC
io	cresca	io	crebbi
tu	cresca	tu	crescesti
lui/lei/Lei	cresca	lui/lei/Lei	crebbe
noi	cresciamo	noi	crescemmo
voi	cresciate	voi	cresceste
loro	crescano	loro	crebbero

PAST PARTICIPLE
cresciuto

IMPERATIVE
cresci
cresciamo
crescete

GERUND
crescendo

AUXILIARY
essere

dare (to give)

	PRESENT		IMPERFECT
io	do	io	davo
tu	dai	tu	davi
lui/lei/Lei	dà	lui/lei/Lei	dava
noi	diamo	noi	davamo
voi	date	voi	davate
loro	danno	loro	davano

	FUTURE		CONDITIONAL
io	darò	io	darei
tu	darai	tu	daresti
lui/lei/Lei	darà	lui/lei/Lei	darebbe
noi	daremo	noi	daremmo
voi	darete	voi	dareste
loro	daranno	loro	darebbero

	PRESENT SUBJUNCTIVE		PAST HISTORIC
io	dia	io	diedi *or* detti
tu	dia	tu	desti
lui/lei/Lei	dia	lui/lei/Lei	diede *or* detti
noi	diamo	noi	demmo
voi	diate	voi	deste
loro	diano	loro	diedero *or* dettero

PAST PARTICIPLE
dato

IMPERATIVE
dai *or* da'
diamo
date

GERUND
dando

AUXILIARY
avere

dire (to say)

PRESENT

io	dico
tu	dici
lui/lei/Lei	dice
noi	diciamo
voi	dite
loro	d*i*cono

IMPERFECT

io	dicevo
tu	dicevi
lui/lei/Lei	diceva
noi	dicevamo
voi	dicevate
loro	dic*e*vano

FUTURE

io	dir*ò*
tu	dirai
lui/lei/Lei	dir*à*
noi	diremo
voi	direte
loro	diranno

CONDITIONAL

io	direi
tu	diresti
lui/lei/Lei	direbbe
noi	diremmo
voi	direste
loro	dir*e*bbero

PRESENT SUBJUNCTIVE

io	dica
tu	dica
lui/lei/Lei	dica
noi	diciamo
voi	diciate
loro	d*i*cano

PAST HISTORIC

io	dissi
tu	dicesti
lui/lei/Lei	disse
noi	dicemmo
voi	diceste
loro	d*i*ssero

PAST PARTICIPLE
detto

IMPERATIVE
di'
diciamo
dite

GERUND
dicendo

AUXILIARY
avere

dirigere (to direct)

	PRESENT		IMPERFECT
io	dirigo	io	dirigevo
tu	dirigi	tu	dirigevi
lui/lei/Lei	dirige	lui/lei/Lei	dirigeva
noi	dirigiamo	noi	dirigevamo
voi	dirigete	voi	dirigevate
loro	dirigono	loro	dirigevano

	FUTURE		CONDITIONAL
io	dirigerò	io	dirigerei
tu	dirigerai	tu	dirigeresti
lui/lei/Lei	dirigerà	lui/lei/Lei	dirigerebbe
noi	dirigeremo	noi	dirigeremmo
voi	dirigerete	voi	dirigereste
loro	dirigeranno	loro	dirigerebbero

	PRESENT SUBJUNCTIVE		PAST HISTORIC
io	diriga	io	diressi
tu	diriga	tu	dirigesti
lui/lei/Lei	diriga	lui/lei/Lei	diresse
noi	dirigiamo	noi	dirigemmo
voi	dirigiate	voi	dirigeste
loro	dirigano	loro	diressero

PAST PARTICIPLE
diretto

IMPERATIVE
dirigi
dirigiamo
dirigete

GERUND
dirigendo

AUXILIARY
avere

dormire (to sleep)

PRESENT

io	dormo
tu	dormi
lui/lei/Lei	dorme
noi	dormiamo
voi	dormite
loro	d*o*rmono

FUTURE

io	dormir*ò*
tu	dormirai
lui/lei/Lei	dormir*à*
noi	dormiremo
voi	dormirete
loro	dormiranno

PRESENT SUBJUNCTIVE

io	dorma
tu	dorma
lui/lei/Lei	dorma
noi	dormiamo
voi	dormiate
loro	d*o*rmano

IMPERFECT

io	dormivo
tu	dormivi
lui/lei/Lei	dormiva
noi	dormivamo
voi	dormivate
loro	dorm*i*vano

CONDITIONAL

io	dormirei
tu	dormiresti
lui/lei/Lei	dormirebbe
noi	dormiremmo
voi	dormireste
loro	dormir*e*bbero

PAST HISTORIC

io	dormii
tu	dormisti
lui/lei/Lei	dorm*ì*
noi	dormimmo
voi	dormiste
loro	dorm*i*rono

PAST PARTICIPLE

dormito

GERUND

dormendo

IMPERATIVE

dormi
dormiamo
dormite

AUXILIARY

avere

dovere (to have to)

	PRESENT		IMPERFECT
io	devo	io	dovevo
tu	devi	tu	dovevi
lui/lei/Lei	deve	lui/lei/Lei	doveva
noi	dobbiamo	noi	dovevamo
voi	dovete	voi	dovevate
loro	devono	loro	dovevano

	FUTURE		CONDITIONAL
io	dovrò	io	dovrei
tu	dovrai	tu	dovresti
lui/lei/Lei	dovrà	lui/lei/Lei	dovrebbe
noi	dovremo	noi	dovremmo
voi	dovrete	voi	dovreste
loro	dovranno	loro	dovrebbero

	PRESENT SUBJUNCTIVE		PAST HISTORIC
io	debba	io	dovetti
tu	debba	tu	dovesti
lui/lei/Lei	debba	lui/lei/Lei	dovette
noi	dobbiamo	noi	dovemmo
voi	dobbiate	voi	doveste
loro	debbano	loro	dovettero

PAST PARTICIPLE
dovuto

IMPERATIVE
–

GERUND
dovendo

AUXILIARY
avere

essere (to be)

	PRESENT		IMPERFECT
io	sono	io	ero
tu	sei	tu	eri
lui/lei/Lei	è	lui/lei/Lei	era
noi	siamo	noi	eravamo
voi	siete	voi	eravate
loro	sono	loro	*e*rano

	FUTURE		CONDITIONAL
io	sar*ò*	io	sarei
tu	sarai	tu	saresti
lui/lei/Lei	sar*à*	lui/lei/Lei	sarebbe
noi	saremo	noi	saremmo
voi	sarete	voi	sareste
loro	saranno	loro	sar*e*bbero

	PRESENT SUBJUNCTIVE		PAST HISTORIC
io	sia	io	fui
tu	sia	tu	fosti
lui/lei/Lei	sia	lui/lei/Lei	fu
noi	siamo	noi	fummo
voi	siate	voi	foste
loro	s*i*ano	loro	f*u*rono

PAST PARTICIPLE
stato

IMPERATIVE
sii
siamo
siate

GERUND
essendo

AUXILIARY
essere

fare (to do, to make)

PRESENT

io	f*a*ccio
tu	fai
lui/lei/Lei	fa
noi	facciamo
voi	fate
loro	fanno

IMPERFECT

io	facevo
tu	facevi
lui/lei/Lei	faceva
noi	facevamo
voi	facevate
loro	fac*e*vano

FUTURE

io	far*ò*
tu	farai
lui/lei/Lei	far*à*
noi	faremo
voi	farete
loro	faranno

CONDITIONAL

io	farei
tu	faresti
lui/lei/Lei	farebbe
noi	faremmo
voi	fareste
loro	far*e*bbero

PRESENT SUBJUNCTIVE

io	f*a*ccia
tu	f*a*ccia
lui/lei/Lei	f*a*ccia
noi	facciamo
voi	facciate
loro	f*a*cciano

PAST HISTORIC

io	feci
tu	facesti
lui/lei/Lei	fece
noi	facemmo
voi	faceste
loro	f*e*cero

PAST PARTICIPLE

fatto

IMPERATIVE

fai *or* fa'
facciamo
fate

GERUND

facendo

AUXILIARY

avere

leggere (to read)

	PRESENT		IMPERFECT
io	leggo	io	leggevo
tu	leggi	tu	leggevi
lui/lei/Lei	legge	lui/lei/Lei	leggeva
noi	leggiamo	noi	leggevamo
voi	leggete	voi	leggevate
loro	leggono	loro	leggevano

	FUTURE		CONDITIONAL
io	leggerò	io	leggerei
tu	leggerai	tu	leggeresti
lui/lei/Lei	leggerà	lui/lei/Lei	leggerebbe
noi	leggeremo	noi	leggeremmo
voi	leggerete	voi	leggereste
loro	leggeranno	loro	leggerebbero

	PRESENT SUBJUNCTIVE		PAST HISTORIC
io	legga	io	lessi
tu	legga	tu	leggesti
lui/lei/Lei	legga	lui/lei/Lei	lesse
noi	leggiamo	noi	leggemmo
voi	leggiate	voi	leggeste
loro	leggano	loro	lessero

PAST PARTICIPLE
letto

IMPERATIVE
leggi
leggiamo
leggete

GERUND
leggendo

AUXILIARY
avere

mettere (to put)

	PRESENT		IMPERFECT
io	metto	io	mettevo
tu	metti	tu	mettevi
lui/lei/Lei	mette	lui/lei/Lei	metteva
noi	mettiamo	noi	mettevamo
voi	mettete	voi	mettevate
loro	mettono	loro	mettevano

	FUTURE		CONDITIONAL
io	metterò	io	metterei
tu	metterai	tu	metteresti
lui/lei/Lei	metterà	lui/lei/Lei	metterebbe
noi	metteremo	noi	metteremmo
voi	metterete	voi	mettereste
loro	metteranno	loro	metterebbero

	PRESENT SUBJUNCTIVE		PAST HISTORIC
io	metta	io	misi
tu	metta	tu	mettesti
lui/lei/Lei	metta	lui/lei/Lei	mise
noi	mettiamo	noi	mettemmo
voi	mettiate	voi	metteste
loro	mettano	loro	misero

PAST PARTICIPLE
messo

IMPERATIVE
metti
mettiamo
mettete

GERUND
mettendo

AUXILIARY
avere

morire (to die)

	PRESENT		IMPERFECT
io	mu*o*io	io	morivo
tu	muori	tu	morivi
lui/lei/Lei	muore	lui/lei/Lei	moriva
noi	moriamo	noi	morivamo
voi	morite	voi	morivate
loro	mu*o*iono	loro	mor*i*vano

	FUTURE		CONDITIONAL
io	morir*ò*	io	morirei
tu	morirai	tu	moriresti
lui/lei/Lei	morir*à*	lui/lei/Lei	morirebbe
noi	moriremo	noi	moriremmo
voi	morirete	voi	morireste
loro	moriranno	loro	morir*e*bbero

	PRESENT SUBJUNCTIVE		PAST HISTORIC
io	mu*o*ia	io	morii
tu	mu*o*ia	tu	moristi
lui/lei/Lei	mu*o*ia	lui/lei/Lei	mor*ì*
noi	moriamo	noi	morimmo
voi	moriate	voi	moriste
loro	mu*o*iano	loro	mor*i*rono

PAST PARTICIPLE
morto

IMPERATIVE
muori
moriamo
morite

GERUND
morendo

AUXILIARY
essere

muovere (to move)

	PRESENT		IMPERFECT
io	muovo	io	muovevo
tu	muovi	tu	muovevi
lui/lei/Lei	muove	lui/lei/Lei	muoveva
noi	muoviamo	noi	muovevamo
voi	muovete	voi	muovevate
loro	muovono	loro	muovevano

	FUTURE		CONDITIONAL
io	muoverò	io	muoverei
tu	muoverai	tu	muoveresti
lui/lei/Lei	muoverà	lui/lei/Lei	muoverebbe
noi	muoveremo	noi	muoveremmo
voi	muoverete	voi	muovereste
loro	muoveranno	loro	muoverebbero

	PRESENT SUBJUNCTIVE		PAST HISTORIC
io	muova	io	mossi
tu	muova	tu	muovesti
lui/lei/Lei	muova	lui/lei/Lei	mosse
noi	muoviamo	noi	muovemmo
voi	muoviate	voi	muoveste
loro	muovano	loro	mossero

PAST PARTICIPLE
mosso

IMPERATIVE
muovi
muoviamo
muovete

GERUND
muovendo

AUXILIARY
avere

n*a*scere (to be born)

	PRESENT
io	nasco
tu	nasci
lui/lei/Lei	nasce
noi	nasciamo
voi	nascete
loro	n*a*scono

	IMPERFECT
io	nascevo
tu	nascevi
lui/lei/Lei	nasceva
noi	nascevamo
voi	nascevate
loro	nasc*e*vano

	FUTURE
io	nascer*ò*
tu	nascerai
lui/lei/Lei	nascer*à*
noi	nasceremo
voi	nascerete
loro	nasceranno

	CONDITIONAL
io	nascerei
tu	nasceresti
lui/lei/Lei	nascerebbe
noi	nasceremmo
voi	nascereste
loro	nascer*e*bbero

	PRESENT SUBJUNCTIVE
io	nasca
tu	nasca
lui/lei/Lei	nasca
noi	nasciamo
voi	nasciate
loro	n*a*scano

	PAST HISTORIC
io	nacqui
tu	nascesti
lui/lei/Lei	nacque
noi	nascemmo
voi	nasceste
loro	n*a*cquero

PAST PARTICIPLE
nato

IMPERATIVE
nasci
nasciamo
nascete

GERUND
nascendo

AUXILIARY
essere

parlare (to speak)

PRESENT

io	parlo
tu	parli
lui/lei/Lei	parla
noi	parliamo
voi	parlate
loro	p*a*rlano

IMPERFECT

io	parlavo
tu	parlavi
lui/lei/Lei	parlava
noi	parlavamo
voi	parlavate
loro	parl*a*vano

FUTURE

io	parler*ò*
tu	parlerai
lui/lei/Lei	parler*à*
noi	parleremo
voi	parlerete
loro	parleranno

CONDITIONAL

io	parlerei
tu	parleresti
lui/lei/Lei	parlerebbe
noi	parleremmo
voi	parlereste
loro	parler*e*bbero

PRESENT SUBJUNCTIVE

io	parli
tu	parli
lui/lei/Lei	parli
noi	parliamo
voi	parliate
loro	p*a*rlino

PAST HISTORIC

io	parlai
tu	parlasti
lui/lei/Lei	parl*ò*
noi	parlammo
voi	parlaste
loro	parl*a*rono

PAST PARTICIPLE

parlato

IMPERATIVE

parla
parliamo
parlate

GERUND

parlando

AUXILIARY

avere

piacere (to be pleasing)

	PRESENT		IMPERFECT
io	pi*a*ccio	io	piacevo
tu	piaci	tu	piacevi
lui/lei/Lei	piace	lui/lei/Lei	piaceva
noi	piacciamo	noi	piacevamo
voi	piacete	voi	piacevate
loro	pi*a*cciono	loro	piac*e*vano

	FUTURE		CONDITIONAL
io	piacer*ò*	io	piacerei
tu	piacerai	tu	piaceresti
lui/lei/Lei	piacer*à*	lui/lei/Lei	piacerebbe
noi	piaceremo	noi	piaceremmo
voi	piacerete	voi	piacereste
loro	piaceranno	loro	piacer*e*bbero

	PRESENT SUBJUNCTIVE		PAST HISTORIC
io	pi*a*ccia	io	piacqui
tu	pi*a*ccia	tu	piacesti
lui/lei/Lei	pi*a*ccia	lui/lei/Lei	piacque
noi	piacciamo	noi	piacemmo
voi	piacciate	voi	piaceste
loro	pi*a*cciano	loro	pi*a*cquero

PAST PARTICIPLE
piaciuto

IMPERATIVE
piaci
piacciamo
piacciate

GERUND
piacendo

AUXILIARY
essere

piovere (to rain)

PRESENT
piove

IMPERFECT
pioveva

FUTURE
pioverà

CONDITIONAL
pioverebbe

PRESENT SUBJUNCTIVE
piova

PAST HISTORIC
piovve

PAST PARTICIPLE
piovuto

IMPERATIVE
–

GERUND
piovendo

AUXILIARY
essere

potere (to be able)

	PRESENT		IMPERFECT
io	posso	io	potevo
tu	puoi	tu	potevi
lui/lei/Lei	può	lui/lei/Lei	poteva
noi	possiamo	noi	potevamo
voi	potete	voi	potevate
loro	possono	loro	potevano

	FUTURE		CONDITIONAL
io	potrò	io	potrei
tu	potrai	tu	potresti
lui/lei/Lei	potrà	lui/lei/Lei	potrebbe
noi	potremo	noi	potremmo
voi	potrete	voi	potreste
loro	potranno	loro	potrebbero

	PRESENT SUBJUNCTIVE		PAST HISTORIC
io	possa	io	potei
tu	possa	tu	potesti
lui/lei/Lei	possa	lui/lei/Lei	poté
noi	possiamo	noi	potemmo
voi	possiate	voi	poteste
loro	possano	loro	poterono

PAST PARTICIPLE
potuto

IMPERATIVE
–

GERUND
potendo

AUXILIARY
avere

prendere (to take)

	PRESENT		IMPERFECT
io	prendo	io	prendevo
tu	prendi	tu	prendevi
lui/lei/Lei	prende	lui/lei/Lei	prendeva
noi	prendiamo	noi	prendevamo
voi	prendete	voi	prendevate
loro	prendono	loro	prendevano

	FUTURE		CONDITIONAL
io	prenderò	io	prenderei
tu	prenderai	tu	prenderesti
lui/lei/Lei	prenderà	lui/lei/Lei	prenderebbe
noi	prenderemo	noi	prenderemmo
voi	prenderete	voi	prendereste
loro	prenderanno	loro	prenderebbero

	PRESENT SUBJUNCTIVE		PAST HISTORIC
io	prenda	io	presi
tu	prenda	tu	prendesti
lui/lei/Lei	prenda	lui/lei/Lei	prese
noi	prendiamo	noi	prendemmo
voi	prendiate	voi	prendeste
loro	prendano	loro	presero

PAST PARTICIPLE
preso

IMPERATIVE
prendi
prendiamo
prendete

GERUND
prendendo

AUXILIARY
avere

rompere (to break)

	PRESENT		IMPERFECT
io	rompo	io	rompevo
tu	rompi	tu	rompevi
lui/lei/Lei	rompe	lui/lei/Lei	rompeva
noi	rompiamo	noi	rompevamo
voi	rompete	voi	rompevate
loro	rompono	loro	rompevano

	FUTURE		CONDITIONAL
io	romperò	io	romperei
tu	romperai	tu	romperesti
lui/lei/Lei	romperà	lui/lei/Lei	romperebbe
noi	romperemo	noi	romperemmo
voi	romperete	voi	rompereste
loro	romperanno	loro	romperebbero

	PRESENT SUBJUNCTIVE		PAST HISTORIC
io	rompa	io	ruppi
tu	rompa	tu	rompesti
lui/lei/Lei	rompa	lui/lei/Lei	ruppe
noi	rompiamo	noi	rompemmo
voi	rompiate	voi	rompeste
loro	rompano	loro	ruppero

PAST PARTICIPLE
rotto

IMPERATIVE
rompi
rompiamo
rompete

GERUND
rompendo

AUXILIARY
avere

salire (to go up)

PRESENT

io	salgo
tu	sali
lui/lei/Lei	sale
noi	saliamo
voi	salite
loro	s*a*lgono

IMPERFECT

io	salivo
tu	salivi
lui/lei/Lei	saliva
noi	salivamo
voi	salivate
loro	sal*i*vano

FUTURE

io	salir*ò*
tu	salirai
lui/lei/Lei	salir*à*
noi	saliremo
voi	salirete
loro	saliranno

CONDITIONAL

io	salirei
tu	saliresti
lui/lei/Lei	salirebbe
noi	saliremmo
voi	salireste
loro	salir*e*bbero

PRESENT SUBJUNCTIVE

io	salga
tu	salga
lui/lei/Lei	salga
noi	saliamo
voi	saliate
loro	s*a*lgano

PAST HISTORIC

io	salii
tu	salisti
lui/lei/Lei	salì
noi	salimmo
voi	saliste
loro	sal*i*rono

PAST PARTICIPLE
salito

IMPERATIVE
sali
saliamo
salite

GERUND
salendo

AUXILIARY
essere

sapere (to know)

PRESENT

io	so
tu	sai
lui/lei/Lei	sa
noi	sappiamo
voi	sapete
loro	sanno

IMPERFECT

io	sapevo
tu	sapevi
lui/lei/Lei	sapeva
noi	sapevamo
voi	sapevate
loro	sap*e*vano

FUTURE

io	sapr*ò*
tu	saprai
lui/lei/Lei	sapr*à*
noi	sapremo
voi	saprete
loro	sapranno

CONDITIONAL

io	saprei
tu	sapresti
lui/lei/Lei	saprebbe
noi	sapremmo
voi	sapreste
loro	sapr*e*bbero

PRESENT SUBJUNCTIVE

io	s*a*ppia
tu	s*a*ppia
lui/lei/Lei	s*a*ppia
noi	sappiamo
voi	sappiate
loro	s*a*ppiano

PAST HISTORIC

io	seppi
tu	sapesti
lui/lei/Lei	seppe
noi	sapemmo
voi	sapeste
loro	s*e*ppero

PAST PARTICIPLE
saputo

IMPERATIVE
sappi
sappiamo
sappiate

GERUND
sapendo

AUXILIARY
avere

scr*i*vere (to write)

PRESENT

io	scrivo
tu	scrivi
lui/lei/Lei	scrive
noi	scriviamo
voi	scrivete
loro	scr*i*vono

IMPERFECT

io	scrivevo
tu	scrivevi
lui/lei/Lei	scriveva
noi	scrivevamo
voi	scrivevate
loro	scriv*e*vano

FUTURE

io	scriver*ò*
tu	scriverai
lui/lei/Lei	scriver*à*
noi	scriveremo
voi	scriverete
loro	scriveranno

CONDITIONAL

io	scriverei
tu	scriveresti
lui/lei/Lei	scriverebbe
noi	scriveremmo
voi	scrivereste
loro	scriver*e*bbero

PRESENT SUBJUNCTIVE

io	scriva
tu	scriva
lui/lei/Lei	scriva
noi	scriviamo
voi	scriviate
loro	scrivano

PAST HISTORIC

io	scrissi
tu	scrivesti
lui/lei/Lei	scrisse
noi	scrivemmo
voi	scriveste
loro	scr*i*ssero

PAST PARTICIPLE
scritto

GERUND
scrivendo

IMPERATIVE
scrivi
scriviamo
scrivete

AUXILIARY
avere

sedere (to sit)

	PRESENT		IMPERFECT
io	siedo	io	sedevo
tu	siedi	tu	sedevi
lui/lei/Lei	siede	lui/lei/Lei	sedeva
noi	sediamo	noi	sedevamo
voi	sedete	voi	sedevate
loro	si*e*dono	loro	sed*e*vano

	FUTURE		CONDITIONAL
io	seder*ò*	io	sederei
tu	sederai	tu	sederesti
lui/lei/Lei	seder*à*	lui/lei/Lei	sederebbe
noi	sederemo	noi	sederemmo
voi	sederete	voi	sedereste
loro	sederanno	loro	seder*e*bbero

	PRESENT SUBJUNCTIVE		PAST HISTORIC
io	sieda	io	sedetti
tu	sieda	tu	sedesti
lui/lei/Lei	sieda	lui/lei/Lei	sedette
noi	sediamo	noi	sedemmo
voi	sediate	voi	sedeste
loro	si*e*dano	loro	sed*e*ttero

PAST PARTICIPLE
seduto

IMPERATIVE
siedi
sediamo
sedete

GERUND
sedendo

AUXILIARY
essere

stare (to be)

PRESENT

io	sto
tu	stai
lui/lei/Lei	sta
noi	stiamo
voi	state
loro	stanno

IMPERFECT

io	stavo
tu	stavi
lui/lei/Lei	stava
noi	stavamo
voi	stavate
loro	st*a*vano

FUTURE

io	star*ò*
tu	starai
lui/lei/Lei	star*à*
noi	staremo
voi	starete
loro	staranno

CONDITIONAL

io	starei
tu	staresti
lui/lei/Lei	starebbe
noi	staremmo
voi	stareste
loro	star*e*bbero

PRESENT SUBJUNCTIVE

io	stia
tu	stia
lui/lei/Lei	stia
noi	stiamo
voi	stiate
loro	st*i*ano

PAST HISTORIC

io	stetti
tu	stesti
lui/lei/Lei	stette
noi	stemmo
voi	steste
loro	st*e*ttero

PAST PARTICIPLE

stato

IMPERATIVE

stai
stiamo
state

GERUND

stando

AUXILIARY

essere

succedere (to happen)

	PRESENT		IMPERFECT
sing.	succede	*sing.*	succedeva
plur.	succedono	*plur.*	succedevano

	FUTURE		CONDITIONAL
sing.	succederà	*sing.*	succederebbe
plur.	succederanno	*plur.*	succederebbero

	PRESENT SUBJUNCTIVE		PAST HISTORIC
sing.	succeda	*sing.*	successe
plur.	succedano	*plur.*	successero

PAST PARTICIPLE
successo

IMPERATIVE
–

GERUND
succedendo

AUXILIARY
essere

tenere (to hold)

	PRESENT		IMPERFECT
io	tengo	io	tenevo
tu	tieni	tu	tenevi
lui/lei/Lei	tiene	lui/lei/Lei	teneva
noi	teniamo	noi	tenevamo
voi	tenete	voi	tenevate
loro	tengono	loro	tenevano

	FUTURE		CONDITIONAL
io	terrò	io	terrei
tu	terrai	tu	terresti
lui/lei/Lei	terrà	lui/lei/Lei	terrebbe
noi	terremo	noi	terremmo
voi	terrete	voi	terreste
loro	terranno	loro	terrebbero

	PRESENT SUBJUNCTIVE		PAST HISTORIC
io	tenga	io	tenni
tu	tenga	tu	tenesti
lui/lei/Lei	tenga	lui/lei/Lei	tenne
noi	teniamo	noi	tenemmo
voi	teniate	voi	teneste
loro	tengano	loro	tennero

PAST PARTICIPLE
tenuto

IMPERATIVE
tieni
teniamo
tenete

GERUND
tenendo

AUXILIARY
avere

uscire (to go out)

PRESENT		IMPERFECT	
io	esco	io	uscivo
tu	esci	tu	uscivi
lui/lei/Lei	esce	lui/lei/Lei	usciva
noi	usciamo	noi	uscivamo
voi	uscite	voi	uscivate
loro	*e*scono	loro	usc*i*vano

FUTURE		CONDITIONAL	
io	uscir*ò*	io	uscirei
tu	uscirai	tu	usciresti
lui/lei/Lei	uscir*à*	lui/lei/Lei	uscirebbe
noi	usciremo	noi	usciremmo
voi	uscirete	voi	uscireste
loro	usciranno	loro	usci*r*ebbero

PRESENT SUBJUNCTIVE		PAST HISTORIC	
io	esca	io	uscii
tu	esca	tu	uscisti
lui/lei/Lei	esca	lui/lei/Lei	uscì
noi	usciamo	noi	uscimmo
voi	usciate	voi	usciste
loro	*e*scano	loro	usc*i*rono

PAST PARTICIPLE
uscito

IMPERATIVE
esci
usciamo
uscite

GERUND
uscendo

AUXILIARY
essere

vedere (to see)

	PRESENT
io	vedo
tu	vedi
lui/lei/Lei	vede
noi	vediamo
voi	vedete
loro	*ve*dono

	IMPERFECT
io	vedevo
tu	vedevi
lui/lei/Lei	vedeva
noi	vedevamo
voi	vedevate
loro	ved*e*vano

	FUTURE
io	vedr*ò*
tu	vedrai
lui/lei/Lei	vedr*à*
noi	vedremo
voi	vedrete
loro	vedranno

	CONDITIONAL
io	vedrei
tu	vedresti
lui/lei/Lei	vedrebbe
noi	vedremmo
voi	vedreste
loro	vedr*e*bbero

	PRESENT SUBJUNCTIVE
io	veda
tu	veda
lui/lei/Lei	veda
noi	vediamo
voi	vediate
loro	*ve*dano

	PAST HISTORIC
io	vidi
tu	vedesti
lui/lei/Lei	vide
noi	vedemmo
voi	vedeste
loro	*vi*dero

PAST PARTICIPLE
visto

IMPERATIVE
vedi
vediamo
vedete

GERUND
vedendo

AUXILIARY
avere

venire (to come)

	PRESENT
io	vengo
tu	vieni
lui/lei/Lei	viene
noi	veniamo
voi	venite
loro	v*e*ngono

	IMPERFECT
io	venivo
tu	venivi
lui/lei/Lei	veniva
noi	venivamo
voi	venivate
loro	ven*i*vano

	FUTURE
io	verr*ò*
tu	verrai
lui/lei/Lei	verr*à*
noi	verremo
voi	verrete
loro	verranno

	CONDITIONAL
io	verrei
tu	verresti
lui/lei/Lei	verrebbe
noi	verremmo
voi	verreste
loro	verr*e*bbero

	PRESENT SUBJUNCTIVE
io	venga
tu	venga
lui/lei/Lei	venga
noi	veniamo
voi	veniate
loro	v*e*ngano

	PAST HISTORIC
io	venni
tu	venisti
lui/lei/Lei	venne
noi	venimmo
voi	veniste
loro	v*e*nnero

PAST PARTICIPLE
venuto

IMPERATIVE
vieni
veniamo
venite

GERUND
venendo

AUXILIARY
essere

v*i*ncere (to defeat)

PRESENT

io	vinco
tu	vinci
lui/lei/Lei	vince
noi	vinciamo
voi	vincete
loro	v*i*ncono

IMPERFECT

io	vincevo
tu	vincevi
lui/lei/Lei	vinceva
noi	vincevamo
voi	vincevate
loro	vinc*e*vano

FUTURE

io	vincer*ò*
tu	vincerai
lui/lei/Lei	vincer*à*
noi	vinceremo
voi	vincerete
loro	vinceranno

CONDITIONAL

io	vincerei
tu	vinceresti
lui/lei/Lei	vincerebbe
noi	vinceremmo
voi	vincereste
loro	vincer*e*bbero

PRESENT SUBJUNCTIVE

io	vinca
tu	vinca
lui/lei/Lei	vinca
noi	vinciamo
voi	vinciate
loro	v*i*ncano

PAST HISTORIC

io	vinsi
tu	vincesti
lui/lei/Lei	vinse
noi	vincemmo
voi	vinceste
loro	v*i*nsero

PAST PARTICIPLE

vinto

IMPERATIVE

vinci
vinciamo
vincete

GERUND

vincendo

AUXILIARY

avere

vivere (to live)

	PRESENT		IMPERFECT
io	vivo	io	vivevo
tu	vivi	tu	vivevi
lui/lei/Lei	vive	lui/lei/Lei	viveva
noi	viviamo	noi	vivevamo
voi	vivete	voi	vivevate
loro	vivono	loro	vi*ve*vano

	FUTURE		CONDITIONAL
io	vivr*ò*	io	vivrei
tu	vivrai	tu	vivresti
lui/lei/Lei	vivr*à*	lui/lei/Lei	vivrebbe
noi	vivremo	noi	vivremmo
voi	vivrete	voi	vivreste
loro	vivranno	loro	vivr*e*bbero

	PRESENT SUBJUNCTIVE		PAST HISTORIC
io	viva	io	vissi
tu	viva	tu	vivesti
lui/lei/Lei	viva	lui/lei/Lei	visse
noi	viviamo	noi	vivemmo
voi	viviate	voi	viveste
loro	vivano	loro	vissero

PAST PARTICIPLE
vissuto

IMPERATIVE
vivi
viviamo
vivete

GERUND
vivendo

AUXILIARY
avere

volere (to want)

PRESENT

io	v*o*glio
tu	vuoi
lui/lei/Lei	vuole
noi	vogliamo
voi	volete
loro	v*o*gliono

IMPERFECT

io	volevo
tu	volevi
lui/lei/Lei	voleva
noi	volevamo
voi	volevate
loro	vol*e*vano

FUTURE

io	vorr*ò*
tu	vorrai
lui/lei/Lei	vorr*à*
noi	vorremo
voi	vorrete
loro	vorranno

CONDITIONAL

io	vorrei
tu	vorresti
lui/lei/Lei	vorrebbe
noi	vorremmo
voi	vorreste
loro	vorr*e*bbero

PRESENT SUBJUNCTIVE

io	v*o*glia
tu	v*o*glia
lui/lei/Lei	v*o*glia
noi	vogliamo
voi	vogliate
loro	v*o*gliano

PAST HISTORIC

io	volli
tu	volesti
lui/lei/Lei	volle
noi	volemmo
voi	voleste
loro	v*o*llero

PAST PARTICIPLE
voluto

IMPERATIVE
–

GERUND
volendo

AUXILIARY
avere

The Gender of Nouns

In Italian, all nouns are either masculine or feminine, whether they denote people, animals or things.

The gender of a noun is often indicated by its final letter. Here are some guidelines to help you determine what gender a noun is:

Nearly all nouns ending in **-o** are masculine, e.g.
il treno the train
l'uomo the man
un topo a mouse
un gatto a (tom)cat
un italiano an Italian (man)

EXCEPTIONS:
la mano the hand
una foto a photo
la radio the radio
una moto a motorbike

Very many nouns ending in **-a** are feminine, e.g.
la casa the house
una donna a woman
una gatta a (she) cat
un'italiana an Italian woman

There are, however, numerous exceptions, e.g.
il dramma the drama
il papa the pope
il problema the problem

A few nouns ending in **-a** are feminine, but can refer to a man or a woman, e.g.
una guida a guide (male or female)
una persona a person (male or female)
una vittima a victim (male or female)

Nouns ending in **-ista** denoting people, can be masculine or feminine, e.g.
un giornalista a (male) journalist
una giornalista a (female) journalist

The Gender of Nouns *continued*

un pessimista a (male) pessimist
una pessimista a (female) pessimist

Nearly all words ending in **-à**, **-sione** and **-zione** are feminine, e.g.
una difficoltà a difficulty
un'occasione an opportunity
una conversazione a conversation

Nouns ending in a consonant are nearly always masculine, e.g.
un film a film
un computer a computer
un box a garage

EXCEPTIONS:
una jeep a jeep
una star a star

Nouns ending in **-e** or **-i** can be masculine or feminine, e.g.
un mese a month
la mente the mind
un brindisi a toast
una crisi a crisis

The names of languages, and all months, are masculine, whether they end in **-o** or **-e**, e.g.
il tedesco German
il francese French
lo scorso febbraio last February
il prossimo dicembre next December

Suffixes that differentiate between male and female are shown on page 128.

Some words have different meanings depending on their gender, e.g.

il fine the objective	**la fine** the end
un posto a place	**la posta** the mail
il manico the handle	**la manica** the sleeve
un modo a way	**la moda** the fashion
un mostro a monster	**una mostra** an exhibition
il capitale capital (money)	**una capitale** a capital city

The Formation of Feminines

As in English, male and female are sometimes differentiated by the use of quite different words, e.g.

un fratello a brother
una sorella a sister
un toro a bull
una mucca a cow

More often, however, words in Italian show gender by their ending:

Many Italian nouns ending in **-o** can be made feminine by changing the ending to **-a** → 1

Some nouns ending in **-e** also change the ending to **-a** for the feminine → 2

Some nouns ending in **-a** or **-e** have no change of ending for the feminine → 3

Nouns ending in **-ese** that describe nationality are the same for masculine and feminine → 4

Nouns ending in **-ante** are the same for masculine and feminine → 5

Nouns ending in **-tore** make the the feminine by substituting the ending **-trice** → 6

Some nouns ending in **-e** have feminine forms ending in **-essa** → 7

Examples

1	un cuoco	a (*male*) cook
	una cuoca	a (*female*) cook
	uno zio	an uncle
	una zia	an aunt
	una ragazzo	a boy
	una ragazza	a girl
	un italiano	an Italian (man)
	un'italiana	an Italian (woman)
2	un signore	a gentleman
	una signora	a lady
	un infirmiere	a (*male*) nurse
	un'infirmiera	a (*female*) nurse
	un parrucchiere	a (*male*) hairdresser
	una parrucchiere	a (*female*) hairdresser
3	un collega	a (*male*) colleague
	una collega	a (*female*) colleague
	il mio dentista	my dentist (*male*)
	la mia dentista	my dentist (*female*)
	un nipote	a grandson
	una nipote	a granddaughter
4	un irlandese	an Irishman
	un'irlandese	an Irishwoman
	uno scozzese	a Scotsman
	una scozzese	a Scotswoman
5	un cantante	a (*male*) singer
	una cantante	a (*female*) singer
	un amante	a (*male*) lover
	un'amante	a (*female*) lover
	un principiante	a (*male*) beginner
	una principiante	a (*female*) beginner
6	un attore	an actor
	un'attrice	a (*female*) actor
	un pittore	a (*male*) painter
	una pittrice	a (*female*) painter
7	il professore	the (*male*) teacher
	la professoressa	the (*female*) teacher
	uno studente	a (*male*) student
	una studentessa	a (*female*) student

The Formation of Plurals

Masculine nouns, whether they end in **-o, -a** or **-e,** nearly always take the ending **-i** in the plural → ❶

Feminine nouns ending in **-a** take the ending **-e** in the plural → ❷

Feminine nouns ending in **-e** take the ending **-i** in the plural → ❸

Nouns that have no change of ending in the plural

Nouns ending in an accented vowel do not change the ending in the plural → ❹

Nouns ending in **-i** and **-ie** do not change in the plural → ❺

Words ending with a consonant remain unchanged in the plural → ❻

Other common words that do not change in the plural are:

il *ci*nema cinema	**i *ci*nema**
la *ra*dio radio	**le *ra*dio**
la moto motorbike	**le moto**
l'auto car	**le auto**
la foto photo	**le foto**

Examples

1	un anno	one year
	due anni	two years
	un ragazzo	a boy
	i ragazzi	the boys
	un ciclista	a (*male*) cyclist
	due ciclisti	two cyclists
	un problema	a problem
	molti problemi	lots of problems
	un mese	one month
	due mesi	two months
	un francese	a Frenchman
	due francesi	two Frenchmen
2	una settimana	one week
	due settimane	two weeks
	una ragazza	one girl
	due ragazze	two girls
3	un'inglese	an Englishwoman
	due inglesi	two Englishwomen
	la vite	the vine
	le viti	the vines
4	la citt*à*	the city
	le citt*à*	the cities
	la loro universit*à*	their university
	le loro universit*à*	their universities
	un caff*è*	a coffee
	due caff*è*	two coffees
	una virt*ù*	a virtue
	le sue virt*ù*	her virtues
5	un'*a*nalisi	an analysis
	delle *a*nalisi	analyses
	una s*e*rie	a series
	due s*e*rie	two series
	una sp*e*cie	a sort
	v*a*rie sp*e*cie	various sorts
6	il film	the film
	i film	the films
	il m*a*nager	the manager
	i m*a*nager	the managers
	il computer	the computer
	i computer	the computers
	la jeep	the jeep
	le jeep	the jeeps

Irregular Plural Forms

Some masculine nouns become feminine in the plural, and take the ending **-a** → ❶

The plural of **uomo** man is ***uomini***. The plural of **la mano** hand is **le mani.**

Nouns ending in **-ca** and **-ga** add an **h** before the plural ending, to keep the sound of the **c** and **g** hard → ❷

Some nouns ending in **-co** and **-go** also add an **h** before the plural ending, to keep the sound of the **c** and **g** hard → ❸

There are numerous exceptions. You can check the plural of such nouns in the dictionary.

EXCEPTIONS:
amico friend (*plural* **amici**)
nemico enemy (*plural* **nemici**)
psicologo psychologist (*plural* **psicologi**)
geologo geologist (*plural* **geologi**)

The plurals of compound nouns such as **pescespada** (*swordfish*), **capolavoro** (*masterpiece*), or **apriscatole** (*tin opener*) do not always follow the usual rules. You can find them in the dictionary.

Examples

1	il dito	the finger
	le dita	the fingers
	un uovo	an egg
	le uova	the eggs
	il lenzuolo	the sheet
	le lenzuola	the sheets
2	amica	(*female*) friend
	amiche	(*female*) friends
	buca	hole
	buche	holes
	riga	line
	righe	lines
	casalinga	housewife
	casalinghe	housewives
3	gioco	game
	giochi	games
	fuoco	fire
	fuochi	fires
	luogo	place
	luoghi	places
	borgo	district
	borghi	districts

The Definite Article

il (l')/lo, la(l'), i/gli;le

	MASCULINE	FEMININE
SING.	**il**	**la**
	lo	
	l'	**l'**
PLUR.	**i**	**le**
	gli	

The form of the Italian article depends on the gender and number of the noun it accompanies. It also depends on the letter the noun starts with.

il is used with masculine nouns starting with most consonants, except for **z**, **gn**, **pn**, **ps**, **x**, **y** and impure **s***; **lo** is used with these. **l'** is used before vowels → 1

i is used with masculine plural nouns starting with most consonants; **gli** is used before vowels and **z**, **gn**, **pn**, **ps**, **x**, **y** and impure **s***. → 2

la is used before feminine singular nouns beginning with a consonant, and **l'** is used before a vowel → 3

le is used with all feminine plural nouns → 4

If the article is separated from the noun by an adjective, the first letter of the adjective determines the choice of article → 5

For uses of the definite article see page 138.

*Impure **s** means **s** + another consonant.

Examples

1

il ragazzo	the boy
il cellulare	the mobile phone
lo zio	the uncle
lo studente	the student
lo pneum*a*tico	the tyre
lo psichiatra	the psychiatrist
lo yogurt	the yoghurt
l'ospedale	the hospital
l'albergo	the hotel

2

i fratelli	the brothers
i cellulari	the mobile phones
gli studenti	the students
gli zii	the uncles
gli gnocchi	the gnocchi
gli pneum*a*tici	the tyres
gli yogurt	the yoghurts
gli amici	the friends
gli orari	the timetables

3

la ragazza	the girl
la m*a*cchina	the car
l'amica	the (girl) friend
l'ar*a*ncia	the orange

4

le ragazze	the girls
le amiche	the (girl) friends

5

l'amico the friend	il migliore amico the best friend
lo studente the student	il migliore studente the best student
gli studenti the students	i migliori studenti the best students

The Definite Article *continued*

The prepositions **a, da, di, in** and **su** combine with the article to form one word.

a + article → ①

SING.	**a + il = al**	**a + la = alla**
	a + l' = all'	**a + l' = all'**
	a + lo = allo	
PLUR.	**a + i = ai**	**a+ le = alle**
	a + gli = agli	

da + article → ②

SING.	**da + il = dal**	**da + la = dalla**
	da + l' = dall'	**da + l' = dall'**
	da + lo = dallo	
PLUR.	**da + i = dai**	**da+ le = dalle**
	da + gli = dagli	

di + article → ③

SING.	**di + il = del**	**di + la = della**
	di + l' = dell'	**di + l' = dell'**
	di + lo = dello	
PLUR.	**di + i = dei**	**di+ le = delle**
	di + gli = degli	

in + article → ④

SING.	**in + il = nel**	**in + la = nella**
	in + l' = nell'	**in + l' = nell'**
	in + lo = nello	
PLUR.	**in + i = nei**	**in+ le = nelle**
	in + gli = negli	

su + article → ⑤

SING.	**su + il = sul**	**su + la = sulla**
	su + l' = sull'	**su + l' = sull'**
	su + lo = sullo	
PLUR.	**su + i = sui**	**su + le = sulle**
	su + gli = sugli	

Examples

① al c*i*nema	to the cinema
allo st*a*dio	at *or* to the stadium
ai concerti	at *or* to the concerts
alle partite	at *or* to the matches
② dall'albergo	from the hotel
dalla stazione	from the station
dagli aerop*o*rti	from the airports
della squadra	of the team
degli studenti	of the students
③ nel giardino	in the garden
nell'appartamento	in the flat
④ nei dintorni	in the surroundings
⑤ sullo sc*o*glio	on the rock
sulla spi*a*ggia	on the beach

The Definite Article *continued*

Uses of the Definite Article

The definite article is used much more in Italian than it is in English. It generally translates the English definite article, but is also used in many contexts where English has no article:

with possessive pronouns → ❶

with plurals and uncountable* nouns → ❷

in generalizations → ❸

with the names of regions and countries → ❹
EXCEPTIONS: no article with countries following the Italian preposition **in** *in/to* → ❺

with parts of the body, replacing the English possessive adjective → ❻

'Ownership' of parts of the body, and of clothes, is often indicated by an indirect object pronoun or a reflexive pronoun → ❼

with the time, dates and years → ❽

in expressions of quantity/rate/price → ❾

with titles, ranks, professions followed by a proper name, and colloquially, with female names → ❿

* An uncountable noun is one which cannot be used in the plural or with an indefinite article, e.g. *milk*.

Examples

1	la mia casa	my house
	le sue f*i*glie	her daughters
	i vostri amici	your friends
2	I bambini s*o*ffrono	Children are suffering
	Mi pi*a*cciono gli animali	I like animals
	Le cose vanno m*e*glio	Things are going better
	Il nuoto è il mio sport preferito	Swimming is my favourite sport
	Non mi piace il riso	I don't like rice
3	Lo z*u*cchero non fa bene	Sugar isn't good for you
	La povert*à* è un grande problema	Poverty is a big problem
4	L'Austr*a*lia è molto grande	Australia is very big
	La Cal*a*bria è bella	Calabria is beautiful
5	Vado in Fr*a*ncia a giugno	I'm going to France in June
	Lav*o*rano in Germ*a*nia	They work in Germany
6	Dammi la mano	Give me your hand
	Attento alla testa!	Mind your head!
7	Mi fa male il piede	My foot is hurting
	S*o*ffiati il naso!	Blow your nose!
	Si è tolto il cappotto	He took off his coat
	Mettiti le scarpe	Put your shoes on
8	all'una	at one o'clock
	alle due	at two o'clock
	Era l'una	It was one o'clock
	Sono le due	It's two o'clock
	Sono nata il primo m*a*ggio 1990	I was born on May 1, 1990
	Verranno nel 2011	They're coming in 2011
9	Costano 3 euro al chilo	They cost 3 euro a kilo
	70 km all'ora	70 km an hour
	50.000 d*o*llari al mese	50,000 dollars per month
	due volte alla settimana	twice a week
10	La signora Rossi è qui	Mrs. Rossi is here
	Il dott*o*r Gentile	Doctor Gentile
	la regina Elisabetta	Queen Elizabeth
	Ecco la Silvia!	Here's Silvia!

The Partitive Article

The partitive article has the sense of 'some' or 'any', although the Italian is not always translated in English.

Forms of the partitive

	WITH MASC. NOUN	WITH FEM. NOUN
SING.	**del**	**della**
	dell'	**dell'**
	dello	
PLUR.	**dei**	**delle**
	degli	

Examples

del burro	some butter
dell'olio	some oil
della carta	some paper
dei fiammiferi	some matches
delle uova	some eggs
Hanno rotto dei bicchieri	They broke some glasses
Mi ha fatto vedere delle foto	He showed me some photos
Ci vuole del sale	It needs (some) salt
Aggiungi della farina	Add (some) flour

The Indefinite Article

MASCULINE	FEMININE
un	**una**
uno	**un'**

The form of the indefinite article depends on the gender of the noun it accompanies. It also depends on the letter the noun starts with.

un is used with masculine nouns starting with vowels and most consonants, except for **z**, **gn**, **pn**, **ps**, **x**, **y** and impure **s*** → 1

uno is used with these → 2

una is used before feminine nouns beginning with a consonant, and **un'** is used before a vowel → 3

If the article is separated from the noun by an adjective, the first letter of the adjective determines the choice of article → 4

The indefinite article is used in Italian largely as it is in English except: → 5

- with the words **cento** and **mille**
- when translating *a few* or *a lot*
- in exclamations with **che**

The indefinite article is not used when speaking of someone's profession – either the verb ***essere*** is used, with no article, or **fare** is used with the definite article → 6

* impure **s** means **s** + another consonant.

Examples

1	un cellulare	a mobile phone
	un uomo	a man
2	uno studente	a student
	uno zio	an uncle
	uno psichiatra	a psychiatrist
3	una ragazza	a girl
	una mela	an apple
	un'ora	an hour
	un'amica	a (girl) friend
	un albergo	a hotel
4	uno splendido albergo	a magnificent hotel
	uno scultore	a sculptor
	un bravo scultore	a good sculptor
5	cento volte	a hundred times
	mille sterline	a thousand pounds
	qualche parola	a few words
	molti soldi	a lot of money
	Che sorpresa!	What a surprise!
	Che peccato!	What a pity!
6	È medico	He's a doctor
	Sono professori	They're teachers
	Faccio l'ingegnere	I'm an engineer
	Fa l'avvocato	She's a lawyer

The formation of feminines and plurals

Most adjectives agree in number and gender with the noun or pronoun.

The formation of feminines

If the masculine singular form of the adjective ends in **-o**, the feminine ends in **-a** → ❶

If the adjective ends in **-e**, the ending does not change for the feminine → ❷

The formation of plurals

If the masculine singular of the adjective ends in **-o**, the ending changes to **-i** for the masculine plural, and to **-e** for the feminine plural → ❸

If the adjective ends in **-e**, the ending changes to **-i** for both masculine and feminine plural → ❹

Invariable adjectives

Some adjectives have no change of ending either for the feminine or the plural → ❺

Examples

❶ un ragazzo alto	a tall boy
una ragazza alta	a tall girl
un film italiano	an Italian film
una squadra italiana	an Italian team
❷ un libro inglese	an English book
una famiglia inglese	an English family
un treno veloce	a fast train
una macchina veloce	a fast car
❸ un fiore rosso	a red flower
dei fiori rossi	red flowers
un computer nuovo	a new computer
dei computer nuovi	new computers
una strada pericolosa	a dangerous road
delle strade pericolose	dangerous roads
una moto nera	a black motorbike
delle moto nere	black motorbikes
❹ un esercizio difficile	a difficult exercise
degli esercizi difficili	difficult exercises
un sito web interessante	an interesting website
dei siti web interessanti	interesting websites
una storia triste	a sad story
delle storie tristi	sad stories
una valigia pesante	a heavy case
delle valigie pesanti	heavy cases
❺ un calzino rosa	a pink sock
una maglietta rosa	a pink T-shirt
un paio di guanti rosa	a pair of pink gloves
un tappeto blu	a blue rug
una macchina blu	a blue car
delle tende blu	blue curtains
un gruppo pop	a pop group
la musica pop	pop music
dei gruppi pop	pop groups

Irregular Adjectives

When **bello** *beautiful* is used in front of a masculine noun it has different forms depending on which letter follows it.

MASC. SING.	MASC. PLUR.	EXAMPLES
bel	**bei**	before most consonants → 1
bell'	**begli**	before vowels → 2
bello	**begli**	before **z**, **gn**, **pn**, **ps**, **x** and impure **s*** → 3

When used after a verb, **bello** has the same endings as any other adjective ending in **-o** → 4

buono good is becomes **buon** when used before a masculine singular noun, unless the noun starts with **z**, **gn**, **pn**, **ps**, **x** or impure **s*** → 5

grande big, great is often shortened to **gran** when it comes before a singular noun starting with a consonant → 6

*Impure **s** means **s** + another consonant.

Examples

1	bel tempo bei nomi	beautiful weather beautiful names
2	un bell'*a*lbero dei begli *a*lberi	a beautiful tree beautiful trees
3	un bello strumento dei begli strumenti	a beautiful instrument beautiful instruments
4	Il tempo era bello I fiori sono belli	The weather was beautiful The flowers are beautiful
5	Buon vi*a*ggio! un buon uomo un buono studente	Have a good journey! a good man a good student
6	la Gran Bretagna un gran n*u*mero di m*a*cchine	Great Britain a large number of cars

Comparatives and Superlatives

Comparatives are formed using the following constructions:

più ... (di) more ... (than) → 1
meno ... (di) less ... (than) → 2
(così) .... come as ... as → 3
(tanto) .... quanto as ... as → 4

Superlatives are formed using the following constructions:

il/la/i/le più ... (che) the most ... (that) → 5
il/la/i/le meno ... (che) the least ... (that) → 6

After a superlative the preposition **di** is often translated as 'in' → 7

If a clause follows a superlative the verb is in the subjunctive → 8

Adjectives with irregular comparatives/superlatives

ADJECTIVE	COMPARATIVE	SUPERLATIVE
buono	**migliore**	**il migliore**
good	better	the best
cattivo	**peggiore**	**il peggiore**
bad	worse	worst
grande	**maggiore**	**il maggiore**
big	bigger/older	the biggest/oldest
piccolo	**minore**	**il minore**
small	smaller/younger	the smallest/youngest
alto	**superiore**	**il superiore**
high	higher	the highest
basso	**inferiore**	**l'inferiore**
low	lower	the lowest

The above words also have regular comparatives/superlatives → 9

Emphatic adjectives

For added emphasis, the final vowel of an adjective can be replaced with the ending **-issimo**, or **-issima** → 10

Examples

1	una m*a*cchina più grande	a bigger car
	Sono più alto di te	I'm taller than you
2	un computer meno caro	a less expensive computer
	i suoi film meno interessanti	his less interesting films
	Quello verde è meno caro del nero	The green one is less expensive than the black one
3	È alta come sua sorella	She's as tall as her sister
	La mia borsa non è pesante come la tua	My bag's not as heavy as yours
	Non è così lontano come credi	It's not as far as you think
4	Sono stanca quanto te	I'm just as tired as you are
	Ha tanto lavoro quanto ne hai tu	He's got as much work as you have
	Non ho tanti soldi quanti ne hai tu	I haven't got as much money as you
5	il più alto	the tallest
	Queste sono le scarpe più c*o*mode	These shoes are the most comfortable
6	il meno interessante	the least interesting
	Gianni è il meno ambizioso	Gianni is the least ambitious
7	lo st*a*dio più grande d'It*a*lia	the biggest stadium in Italy
	il ristorante più caro della citt*à*	the most expensive restaurant in the town
8	la persona più pigra che conosca	the laziest person I know
	È una delle cose più belle che ci siano	It's one of the nicest things there is
9	Il libro è migliore del film	The book is better than the film
	Questo è più buono	This one's better
	la loro sorella minore	their younger sister
	il loro fratello più piccolo	their younger brother
10	Il tempo era bell*i*ssimo	The weather was really beautiful
	Anna è sempre elegant*i*ssima	Anna is always terribly smart
	Sono educat*i*ssimi	They're extremely polite

Demonstrative Adjectives

questo/questa/questi/queste → 1

	MASCULINE	FEMININE	
SING.	**questo**	**questa**	this
PLUR.	**questi**	**queste**	these

quello has different forms, depending on the gender of the following noun, and the letter it starts with.

	MASCULINE	FEMININE	
SING.	**quel**	**quella**	that
	quello		
	quell'	**quell'**	
PLUR.	**quei**	**quelle**	those
	quegli		

quel is used before most consonants, except for **z**, **gn**, **pn**, **ps**, **x** and impure **s**. **quello** is used before these letters. **quell'** is used before vowels. **quei** is used before most consonants; **quegli** is used before vowels and **z**, **gn**, **pn**, **ps**, **x** and impure **s***.

quella is used before feminine singular nouns beginning with a consonant, with **quell'** used before a vowel → 2

*Impure **s** means **s** + another consonant.

Examples

1. Questa gonna è troppo stretta — This skirt is too tight
   Questi pantaloni mi piacciono — I like these trousers
   Queste scarpe sono comode — These shoes are comfortable

2. quel ragazzo — that boy
   quello zaino — that rucksack
   quello studente — that student
   quell'albero — that tree
   quei cani — those dogs
   quegli uomini — those men
   quegli studenti — those students
   quella ragazza — that girl
   quell'amica — that friend
   quelle macchine — those cars

Interrogative Adjectives

che? what?

che is invariable → ❶

quale/quali? → ❷

	MASCULINE/FEMININE	
SING.	**quale**	what?; which?
PLUR.	**quali**	what?; which?

quanto/quanta/quanti/quante? → ❸

	MASCULINE	FEMININE	
SING.	**quanto**	**quanta**	how much?
PLUR.	**quanti**	**quante**	how many?

Interrogative adjectives are often preceded by prepositions → ❹

Exclamatory Adjectives

che and **quanto** are used with nouns in exclamations → ❺

che is also used with other adjectives → ❻

Examples

❶ Che giorno è oggi?	What day is it today?
Che ore sono?	What time is it?
Che gusto preferisci?	Which flavour do you like best?
Che film hai visto?	Which film did you see?
Che programmi hai?	What plans have you got?
❷ Quale tipo vuoi?	What kind do you want?
❸ Quanto pane hai comprato?	How much bread did you buy?
Quanta minestra vuoi?	How much soup do you want?
Quanti bicchieri ci sono?	How many glasses are there?
Quante uova vuoi?	How many eggs do you want?
❹ A che ora ti alzi?	What time do you get up?
Di che colore è?	What colour is it?
Per quale squadra tifi?	Which team do you support?
❺ Che peccato!	What a pity!
Che disordine!	What a mess!
Che bella giornata!	What a lovely day!
Che brutto tempo!	What awful weather!
Quanto tempo sprecato!	What a waste of time!
Quanta gente!	What a lot of people!
Quanti soldi!	What a lot of money!
Quante storie!	What a fuss!
❻ Che carino!	Isn't he sweet!
Che brutti!	They're horrible!

Possessive Adjectives

WITH SING. NOUN		WITH PLUR. NOUN		
MASC.	FEM.	MASC.	FEM.	
il mio	**la mia**	**i miei**	**le mie**	my
il tuo	**la tua**	**i tuoi**	**le tue**	your
il suo	**la sua**	**i suoi**	**le sue**	his; her; its; your
il nostro	**la nostra**	**i nostri**	**le nostre**	our
il vostro	**la vostra**	**i vostri**	**le vostre**	your
il loro	**la loro**	**i loro**	**le loro**	their

Possessive adjectives are generally preceded by the article → 1

Possessive adjectives agree in number and gender with the noun they describe (i.e. the thing which is owned), not with the owner → 2

il suo/la sua/i suoi/le sue can mean either 'his' or 'her'. To make clear which is meant, **di lui** can be used for 'his', and **di lei** for 'her' → 3

The article is not used with any possessive adjective except loro when referring to singular family members → 4

EXCEPTIONS: **mamma**, **babbo** and **papà**

Examples

1	Dove sono le mie chiavi?	Where are my keys?
	Luca ha perso il suo portafoglio	Luca has lost his wallet
	Ecco i nostri passaporti	Here are our passports
	Qual è la vostra camera?	Which is your room?
	Il tuo amico ti aspetta	Your friend is waiting for you
2	Anna ha perso il suo cellulare	Anna has lost her mobile phone
	Le ragazze hanno i loro biglietti	The girls have got their tickets
3	Le scarpe di lui sono eleganti	His shoes are smart
	Le scarpe di lei non mi piacciono	I don't like her shoes
4	con mia madre	with my mother
	Dov'è tuo padre?	Where's your father?
	lei e suo marito	she and her husband
	È sua moglie	She's his wife
	mia sorella ed io	my sister and I
	Non è il loro padre	He's not their father
	Maria e il suo papà	Maria and her dad

Position of Adjectives

Italian adjectives usually follow the noun → 1

Adjectives of colour or nationality *always* follow the noun → 2

As in English, demonstrative, possessive, numerical and interrogative adjectives precede the noun → 3

The adjectives **ogni**, **qualche** and **nessuno** always precede the noun → 4

The following common adjectives can precede the noun:

ottimo very good	**pessimo** very bad
bello beautiful	**brutto** bad, ugly
bravo good	**buono** good
prossimo next	**ultimo** last
povero poor	**grande** big, great
nuovo new	**vecchio** old
breve short	**piccolo** small

The meaning of the following adjectives can be affected by their position:

	AFTER NOUN	BEFORE NOUN
grande	big	great → 5
povero	poor	unfortunate → 6
vecchio	old	long-standing → 7

Adjectives following the noun are linked by **e** → 8

Examples

1	un gesto spont*a*neo	a spontaneous gesture
	una partita importante	an important match
2	capelli biondi	blonde hair
	pantaloni neri	black trousers
	una parola italiana	an Italian word
3	questo cellulare	this mobile phone
	la mia mamma	my mum
	il primo piano	the first floor
	Quale gusto?	What flavour?
4	ogni giorno	every day
	qualche volta	some times
	Non c'è nessun bisogno di andarci	There's no need to go
5	un uomo grande	a big man
	una grande sorpresa	a great surprise
6	gente p*o*vera	poor people
	P*o*vera Anna!	Poor Anna!
7	una casa v*e*cchia	an old house
	un mio v*e*cchio amico	an old friend of mine
8	un libro lungo e noioso	a long, boring book
	ragazze antip*a*tiche e maleducate	nasty rude girls

Personal Pronouns

	SUBJECT PRONOUNS	
	SINGULAR	PLURAL
1st person	**io** I	**noi** we
2nd person	**tu** you	**voi** you
3rd person (*masc.*)	**lui** he	**loro** they
(*fem.*)	**lei** she	
(*used as polite 'you'*)	**lei/Lei** you	

Italian verbs are frequently used without subject pronouns → 1

tu/lei
Lei, as well as being the 3rd person singular feminine, is used when addressing someone politely. As a general rule, use **tu** only when addressing a friend, a child, a fellow student, someone you know very well, or when invited to do so. In other cases use **lei,** which is occasionally spelled with a capital when used to mean *you* 2

loro
Loro is used only to refer to people, not to things → 3

Loro is occasionally used as a very formal alternative to **voi** → 4

Examples

1	Conosci Paolo?	Do you know Paul?
	Parlo italiano	I speak Italian
	Costa troppo	It costs too much
2	Tu cara, cosa prendi?	What are you going to have, dear?
	Lei, signora, cosa prende?	What are you going to have, madam?
3	Loro chi sono?	Who are they?
	Cosa sono? – Sono noci.	What are they? – They're walnuts.
4	Loro cosa prendono?	What will you have, ladies and gentlemen?

Personal Pronouns *continued*

3rd Person Pronouns

lui, lei and **loro** are the subject pronouns normally used in spoken Italian. In older written Italian you may find **egli** (masc. sing.), **ella** (fem. sing.), **essi** (masc. plur.) and **esse** (fem. plur.).

esso and **essa** are subject pronouns meaning *it*, but they are very rarely used. In Italian there is normally no pronoun corresponding to *it* at the start of a sentence → 1

Subject pronouns often follow the verb → 2

Subject pronouns are used:

- to add emphasis, for clarity, or to attract someone's attention → 3
- after **anche** *too*, **neanche** *neither* and **pure** *as well* → 4
- when the verb in Italian is understood → 5

	UNSTRESSED DIRECT OBJECT PRONOUNS	
	SINGULAR	PLURAL
1st person	**mi** me	**ci** us
2nd person	**ti** you	**vi** you
3rd person (*masc.*)	**lo (l')** him; it	**li** them
(*fem.*)	**la (l')** her; it	**le** them
(*used as polite 'you'*)	**la/La (l')** you	**le** you

mi, **ti**, **ci** and **vi** can (but do not have to) become **m'**, **t'**, **c'** and **v'** before a vowel or mute **h** → 6

lo and **la** change to **l'** before a vowel or mute **h** → 7

For information on past participle agreement see page 56.

lo/la /li/le
lo means *him*, or *it*, when the object referred to is masculine → 8

la means *her*, or *it*, when the object referred to is feminine → 9

li refers to people, or objects that are masculine → 10

le refers to females, or objects that are feminine → 11

Examples

1	Fa caldo Sono le tre È tardi	It's hot It's three o'clock It's late
2	Pago io Ci pensiamo noi	I'll pay We'll see to it
3	Tu cosa dici? No, l'ha fatto lui Lei, signore, cosa prende?	What do <u>you</u> think? No, <u>he</u> did it And you sir, what will you have?
4	Prendi un gelato anche tu? Non so perché. – Neanch'io È venuto pure lui	Are you going to have an ice cream too? I don't know why. – Neither do I He came as well
5	Chi è il più bravo? – Lui. Viene lui, ma lei no	Who's the best? – He is. He's coming, but she isn't
6	Non c'hanno visto *or* Non ci hanno visto	They didn't see us
7	Non l'ho visto più L'ho incontrata ieri	I didn't see him again I met her yesterday
8	Gianni? Non lo vedo mai Dov'è il mio cellulare? Non lo vedo	Gianni? I never see him Where's my mobile phone? I can't see it
9	Chiara? Non la vedo mai La birra? Non la bevo mai.	Chiara? I never see her Beer? I never drink it.
10	Marco e Sara – li conosci? Hai i biglietti? Sì, li ho nel portafoglio	Marco and Sara – do you know them? Have you got the tickets? Yes, I've got them in my wallet
11	Le sue sorelle? Non le conosco Hai le chiavi? Sì, le ho in tasca	His sisters? I don't know them Have you got the keys? Yes, I've got them in my pocket

Personal Pronouns *continued*

Position of unstressed direct object pronouns

The pronoun generally comes before the verb → 1

Unstressed direct pronouns come after the verb

- in imperatives, with the pronoun joined onto the verb → 2

ⓘ If the verb consists of a single syllable, the initial consonant of the pronoun is doubled, except in the case of **gli** → 3

- in infinitive constructions, when the final **-e** of the infinitive is dropped, and replaced by the pronoun → 4

Stressed direct object pronouns

	STRESSED DIRECT OBJECT PRONOUNS	
	SINGULAR	PLURAL
1st person	**me**	**noi**
2nd person	**te**	**voi**
3rd person (*masc.*)	**lui**	**loro**
(*fem.*)	**lei**	**loro**
(*used as polite 'you'*)	**lei/Lei**	**loro**

Stressed direct object pronouns are used:

- for emphasis or contrast → 5
- after prepositions → 6
- in comparisons → 7

For further information, see Order of Object Pronouns, page 166.

Reflexive Pronouns

These are dealt with under reflexive verbs, page 32.

Examples

	Italian	English
1	Ti amo	I love you
	Lo invito alla festa	I'm inviting him to the party
	Non lo mangio	I'm not going to eat it
	La guardava	He was looking at her
	Vi cercavo	I was looking for you
	Li conosciamo	We know them
2	Aiutami!	Help me!
	Lasciala stare	Leave her alone
3	Fallo subito!	Do it right away!
4	Potresti venire a prendermi?	Could you come and get me?
	Non posso aiutarvi	I can't help you
	Devo proprio farlo?	Do I really have to do it?
5	Amo solo te	I love only you
	Invito lui alla festa, ma lei no	I'm inviting him to the party but not her
	Non guardava me, guardava lei	He wasn't looking at me, he was looking at her
6	Vengo con te	I'll come with you
	Sono arrivati dopo di noi	They arrived after us
7	Sei più alto di me	You're taller than me
	Sono più ricchi di lui	They're richer than him

Personal Pronouns *continued*

	UNSTRESSED INDIRECT OBJECT PRONOUNS	
	SINGULAR	PLURAL
1st person	**mi**	**ci**
2nd person	**ti**	**vi**
3rd person (*masc.*)	**gli**	**gli** *or* **loro**
(*fem.*)	**le**	**gli** *or* **loro**
(*used as polite 'you'*)	**le**	**loro**

The pronouns in the above table replace the preposition **a** + *noun*, where the noun is a person or an animal → 1

Indirect object pronouns are used with verbs governing **a** → 2

Unstressed indirect pronouns are also used with impersonal verbs which govern **a** → 3

Position of unstressed indirect object pronouns

Unstressed indirect pronouns generally come before the verb → 4

Unstressed indirect pronouns come after the verb:
- in imperatives, with the pronoun joined onto the verb → 5

ⓘ If the verb consists of a single syllable, the initial consonant of the pronoun is doubled, except in the case of **gli** → 6

- in infinitive constructions. The final **-e** of the infinitive is dropped, and replaced by the pronoun → 7

Examples

➊ Ho detto la verità a Paola	I told Paola the truth
Le ho detto la verità	I told her the truth
Hai dato del latte al gatto?	Have you given the cat some milk?
Gli hai dato del latte?	Have you given him some milk?
Potresti dare qualche consiglio ai signori?	Could you give the lady and gentleman some advice?
Potresti dar loro *or* dargli qualche consiglio?	Could you give them some advice?
➋ telefonare a qn	to phone sb
Non le ho telefonato	I didn't phone her
promettere qc a qn	to promise sb sth
Mi ha promesso un regalo	He promised me a present
consigliare a qn di fare qc	to advise sb to do sth
Ci ha consigliato di aspettare	He advised us to wait
➌ Le piacciono i gatti	She likes cats
Non gli importa il prezzo, sono ricchi	They don't care about the price, they're rich
Se gli interessa può venire con me	If he's interested he can come with me
➍ Mi assomiglia?	Does she look like me?
Ti piace?	Do you like it?
➎ Rispondigli!	Answer him!
Mandami un SMS	Send me a text
➏ Dimmi dov'è	Tell me where it is
Dacci una mano	Give us a hand
➐ Dovresti scriverle	You ought to write to her
Luigi? Non voglio parlargli	Luigi? I don't want to talk to him

Personal Pronouns *continued*

Stressed Indirect Pronouns

	STRESSED INDIRECT OBJECT PRONOUNS	
	SINGULAR	PLURAL
1st person	**a me**	**a noi**
2nd person	**a te**	**a voi**
3rd person (*masc.*)	**a lui**	**a loro**
(*fem.*)	**a lei**	**a loro**
(*used as polite 'you'*)	**a lei**	**a loro**

The above forms are used for special emphasis, either before or after the verb → 1

For further information, see Order of Object Pronouns, below.

Reflexive Pronouns

These are dealt with under reflexive verbs, page 32.

Order of Object Pronouns

If direct and indirect unstressed pronouns occur together, the indirect pronoun always comes first .

mi/ti/ci/vi when followed by a direct object pronoun become **me**, **te**, **ce** and **ve** → 2

gli and **le** when followed by a direct object pronoun both become **glie-**, and add the pronoun to make one word: **glielo**, **gliela**, **glieli** or **gliele** → 3

When an indirect pronoun and a direct pronoun follow an imperative, or an infinitive, they join on to it to make one word → 4

When a stressed indirect object pronoun and an unstressed direct object pronoun occur together the above rules do not apply → 5

Examples

1	Ho scritto a lei, a lui no	I wrote to her, but not to him
	A me piace, ma Luca preferisce l'altro	I like it, but Luca would rather have the other one
2	Me la dai?	Will you give me it?
	È mia – non te la do	It's mine, I'm not going to give it to you
	Ce l'hanno promesso	They promised it to us
	Ve lo mando domani	I'll send it to you tomorrow
3	Glieli hai promessi	You promised them to her
	Gliel'ha spedite	He sent them to them
	Carlo? Glielo dir*ò* domani	Carlo? I'll tell him tomorrow
4	Mi pi*a*cciono, ma non vuole compr*a*rmeli	I like them but she won't buy me them
	Ecco la l*e*ttera di Rita, puoi d*a*rgliela?	Here's Rita's letter, can you give it to her?
	Ecco le chiavi. D*a*gliele	Here are the keys. Give them to her.
	Non abbiamo i biglietti – può mand*a*rceli?	We haven't got the tickets – can you send us them?
5	M*a*ndale a lui, non a me	Send them to him, not to me

The pronoun ne

ne replaces the preposition **di** + *noun* → 1

There may be no preposition in the English translation of verbal constructions with **di/ne** → 2

ne also replaces the partitive article (English = some, any) + *noun* → 3

When used with amounts or numbers, **ne** represents the noun → 4

Position: **ne** always follows another pronoun and comes before all verbs except imperatives and infinitives -> 5

Pronouns which precede **ne** change their form:
mi/ti/si/ci/vi before **ne** become **me/te/se/ce/ve** → 6

ne follows the imperative and joins onto to it to make one word → 7

ne joins onto the infinitive, which drops the final **-e** → 8

Pronouns which come between the imperative or infinitive and **ne** change their form: **mi**, **ti**, **ci**, **vi** become **me**, **te**, **ce** and **ve**.
gli and **le** become **glie** → 9

Examples

	Italian	English
1	Sono conscio del pericolo	I'm aware of the danger
	Ne sono conscio	I'm aware of it
	Sono sicura del fatto	I'm sure of the fact
	Ne sono sicura	I'm sure of it
	Ha scritto della guerra sul giornale	She's written about the war in the paper
	Ne ha scritto sul giornale	She's written about it in the paper
	Parliamo del futuro. – Sì, parliamone.	Let's talk about the future. – Yes, let's talk about it.
2	accorgersi di qc	to realize sth
	Non se ne accorge	He doesn't realize it
	aver bisogno di qc	to need sth
	Hai bisogno della chiave? – No, non ne ho più bisogno.	Do you need the key? – No, I don't need it any more.
3	Perché non prendi delle fragole?	Why aren't you having any strawberries?
	Perché non ne prendi?	Why aren't you having any?
	Vuoi del pane?	Would you like some bread?
	Ne vuoi?	Would you like some?
4	Hai due figli? – No, ne ho tre.	Have you got two children? – No, I've got three.
	Hai dello zucchero? – Ne ho un poco.	Have you got any sugar? – I've got a bit.
5	Ne hai paura?	Are you afraid of it?
6	Ti ricordi di quel giorno?	Do you remember that day?
	Te ne ricordi?	Do you remember it?
	Non si accorge degli errori	He doesn't notice mistakes
	Non se ne accorge	He doesn't notice them
7	Assaggiane un po'	Try a bit
8	Non voglio parlarne	I don't want to talk about it
9	Dammene uno per favore	Give me one of them please
	Dagliene due rossi	Give him two red ones
	Non posso dartene uno	I can't give you one
	Non posso dargliene due rossi	I can't give him two red ones

The pronoun ci

ci replaces the preposition **a** + *noun* → 1

There may be no preposition in the English translation of verbal constructions with **a/ci** → 2

Position: like **ne**, **ci** comes before the verb, unless it is an imperative, infinitive, or the gerund → 3

For **ci** as a personal pronoun see page 164.

Note that **ci** is also an adverb meaning 'there' → 4

Examples

❶ Credi ai fantasmi?	Do you believe in ghosts?
Ci credi?	Do you believe in them?
Non pensa al futuro	She doesn't think about the future
Non ci pensa	She doesn't think about it
❷ far caso a qc	to notice sth
Non ci ho fatto caso	I didn't notice it
avvicinarsi a qc	to approach sth
Ci si avvicinò	He approached it
❸ Ci penso io	I'll see to it
BUT	
P*e*nsaci un po'	Think about it a bit
Non so che farci	I don't know what to do about it
Ripens*a*ndoci mi sono pentito	When I thought it over I was sorry
❹ Non v*o*glio andarci	I don't want to go there
Ci sono molti turisti	There are a lot of tourists

Indefinite Pronouns

The following are indefinite pronouns:

alcuni(e) some → ❶

altro(a, i, e) the other one; another one; other people → ❷

chiunque anyone → ❸

ciascuno(a) each → ❹

molto(a, i, e) a lot, lots → ❺

nessuno(a) nobody, anybody; none → ❻

niente nothing → ❼

nulla nothing → ❽

ognuno(a) each → ❾

parecchio, parecchia, parecchi, parecchie quite a lot → ❿

poco, poca, pochi, poche not much, not many → ⓫

qualcosa something, anything → ⓬

qualcuno(a) somebody; any → ⓭

tanto(a, i, e) lots, so much, so many → ⓮

troppo(a, i, e) too much, too many → ⓯

tutti(e) everybody, all → ⓰

tutto everything, all → ⓱

uno(a) somebody → ⓲

Examples

1	Ci sono posti liberi? – Sì, alcuni.	Are there any empty seats? – Yes, some.
	Ci sono ancora delle fragole? – Sì, alcune.	Are there any strawberries left? – Yes, some.
2	L'altro è meno caro	The other one is cheaper
	Non m'interessa quello che dicono gli altri	I don't care what other people say
	Prendine un altro	Take another one
3	Attacca discorso con chiunque	She'll talk to anyone
4	Ne avevamo uno per ciascuno	We had one each
	Le torte costano due euro ciascuna	The cakes cost two euros each
5	Ne ha molto	He's got lots
	molti di noi	a lot of us
6	Non è venuto nessuno	Nobody came
	Nessuna delle ragazze è venuta	None of the girls came
7	Cosa c'è? – Niente.	What's wrong? – Nothing.
8	Che cos'hai comprato? – Nulla.	What did you buy? – Nothing.
9	ognuno di voi	each of you
10	C'e ancora del pane? – Sì, parecchio.	Is there any bread left? – Yes, quite a lot.
	Avete avuto problemi? – Sì, parecchi.	Did you have problems? – Yes, a lot.
11	C'è pane? – Poco.	Is there any bread? – Not much.
	Ci sono turisti? – Pochi.	Are there any tourists? – Not many.
12	Ho qualcosa da dirti	I've got something to tell you
	Ha bisogno di qualcosa?	Do you need anything?
13	Ha telefonato qualcuno	Somebody phoned
	Conosci qualcuna delle ragazze?	Do you know any of the girls?
14	Hai mangiato? – Sì, tanto!	Have you eaten? – Yes, lots!
15	Ci sono errori? – Sì, troppi.	Are there any mistakes? – Yes, too many.
16	Vengono tutti	Everybody is coming
	Sono arrivate tutte	They've all arrived
17	Va tutto bene?	Is everything okay?
	L'ho finito tutto	I've finished it all
18	Ho incontrato uno che ti conosce	I met somebody who knows you

Relative Pronouns

che who; whom; which; that
che is an invariable pronoun that can be the subject or object of a relative clause, and can refer to people or things → 1

The Italian object pronoun cannot be omitted, though it need not be translated in English → 2

After a preposition use **cui** → 3

il che which
This is used to refer to a fact or situation that's just been mentioned → 4

il quale, **la quale**, **i quali**, **le quali** who; whom; which; that
These are more formal relative pronouns, which agree in number and gender with the noun → 5

il quale, **la quale**, **i quali** and **le quali** are used most often with prepositions.
The prepositions **di**, **da**, **a**, **in** and **su** combine with the articles **il**, **la**, **i** and **le** → 6

Article + preposition combinations are dealt with on page 136

il cui, **la cui**, **i cui**, **le cui** whose
These agree in number and gender with the thing possessed → 7

Use **cui** instead of **che** with a preposition → 8

quello che, **ciò che** what, the thing which

These can be used as the subject or object of a relative clause. Literally they mean 'that which' → 9

In combination with **di**, **quello** *or* **ciò che** become **quello di cui** *or* **ciò di cui** → 10

Examples

1	quella signora che ha un p*i*ccolo cane nero	that lady who has a little black dog
	una persona che detesto	a person whom I detest
	l'uomo che hanno arrestato	the man that they've arrested
	la squadra che ha vinto	the team which won
2	la persona che ammiro di più	the person (whom) I admire most
	il dolce che hai fatto	the pudding (that) you made
3	la ragazza di cui ti ho parlato	the girl that I told you about
	gli amici con cui andiamo in vacanza	the friends we go on holiday with
	la persona a cui si riferiva	the person he was referring to
	il quartiere in cui *a*bito	the area in which I live
4	Non p*a*gano nulla, il che non mi sembra giusto	They don't pay anything, which doesn't seem fair to me
	Dice che non è colpa sua, il che è vero	She says it's not her fault, which is true
5	suo padre, il quale è avvocato	his father, who is a lawyer
	le sue sorelle, le quali st*u*diano a Roma	his sisters, who study in Rome
6	l'albergo nel quale ci siamo fermati	the hotel that we stayed at
	la borsa di st*u*dio sulla quale contava	the grant he was counting on
	gli amici dai quali ho avuto questo regalo	the friends I had this present from
	la medicina della quale ho bisogno	the medicine I need
7	una persona il cui nome me sfugge	a person whose name escapes me
	la persona i cui bagagli sono qui	the person whose bags are here
8	È quello con cui parlavo	He's the one I was talking to
9	Ho visto quello *or* ciò che c'era sul t*a*volo	I saw what was on the table
	Quello *or* ciò che mi preoccupa è che…	The thing which worries me is that…
	Quello *or* ciò che dici non ha senso	What you say doesn't make sense
	Ho fatto quello *or* ciò che potevo	I did what I could
10	Non è quello *or* ciò di cui si tratta	That's not what it's about
	Non è quello *or* ciò di cui mi aspettavo	That's not what I was expecting

Interrogative Pronouns

These pronouns are used in direct questions:

chi? who? whom?
che? what?
cosa? what?
che cosa? what?

These pronouns are invariable, and can be the subject or object of the verb → 1

che cos'è/cos'è? what is it?
This is used to ask for something to be explained or identified → 2

Prepositions come before the interrogative pronoun, and never at the end of the question → 3

di chi? whose → 4

quale? which? which one? what?
quale is the singular form (**qual** before a vowel), and **quali** the plural → 5

qual è?/quali sono? what is/what are?
These are used to ask about a particular detail, name, number etc → 6

quanto(a)? How much? → 7

quanti(e)? How many? → 8

All the pronouns used in direct questions can be used in indirect questions → 9

Examples

1	Chi è?	Who is it?
	Chi cerca?	Who(m) are you looking for?
	Che vuoi?	What do you want?
	Cosa vuole?	What does he want?
	Che cosa v*o*gliono?	What do they want?
2	Che cos'è? – È un regalo.	What is it? – It's a present.
3	A chi l'hai dato?	Who did you give it to?
	Con chi parlavi?	Who were you talking to?
	Di che cosa hai bisogno?	What do you need?
	A cosa ti aspettavi?	What were you expecting?
4	Di chi è questa borsa?	Whose is this bag?
	Di chi sono queste chiavi?	Whose are these keys?
5	Conosco sua sorella. – Quale?	I know his sister. – Which one?
	Ho rotto dei bicchieri. – Quali?	I broke some glasses. – Which ones?
6	Qual è il suo indirizzo?	What's her address?
	Qual è la capitale della Finl*a*ndia?	What's the capital of Finland?
	Quali sono i loro nomi?	What are their names?
7	Farina? Quanta ce ne vuole?	Flour? How much is needed?
8	Quante di loro p*a*ssano la sera a l*e*ggere?	How many of them spend the evening reading?
9	Dimmi chi è	Tell me who it is
	Non so cosa vuol dire	I don't know what it means
	Ho chiesto di chi era	I asked whose it was
	Può dirmi di che cosa si tratta?	Can you tell me what it's about?

Possessive Pronouns

Singular:

MASCULINE	FEMININE	
il mio	**la mia**	mine
il tuo	**la tua**	yours
il suo	**la sua**	his; hers; its; yours
il nostro	**la nostra**	ours
il vostro	**la vostra**	yours
il loro	**la loro**	theirs

Plural:

MASCULINE	FEMININE	
i miei	**le mie**	mine
i tuoi	**le tue**	yours
i suoi	**le sue**	his; hers; its; yours
i nostri	**le nostre**	ours
i vostri	**le vostre**	yours
i loro	**le loro**	theirs

The pronoun agrees in number and gender with the noun it replaces, not with the owner → ❶

di/da/a/su/in + *possessive pronoun*
These prepositions combine with the article → ❷

Examples

1	Paolo, questa borsa non è la mia, è la tua	Paolo, this bag's not mine, it's yours
	La nostra casa è p*i*ccola, la vostra è grande	Our house is small, yours is big
	I miei genitori e i suoi si conoscono	My parents and hers know each other
2	La mia m*a*cchina è più v*e*cchia della sua	My car is older than his
	Preferisco il nostro giardino al loro	I prefer our garden to theirs

Demonstrative Pronouns

questo/questa/questi/queste
quello/quella/quelli/quelle

	MASCULINE	FEMININE	
SING.	**questo**	**questa**	this, this one
	quello	**quella**	that, that one, that man/that woman
PLUR.	**questi**	**queste**	these, these ones
	quelli	**quelle**	those, those ones, those people

The pronoun agrees in number and gender with the noun it replaces → 1

quello/a used to mean that man/woman is pejorative → 2

quello(a, i, e) che the one(s) who/which → 3

quello(a, i, e) di the one(s) belonging to/the one(s) of
This use is often translated by apostrophe s ('s), or s apostrophe (s') → 4

questo(a, i, e) qui/qua
qui or **qua** can be used with **questo** for emphasis or to distinguish between two things → 5

quello(a, i, e) lì/là
lì or **là** can be used with **quello** for emphasis or to distinguish between two things → 6

Examples

1	Questo è mio marito	This is my husband
	Questa è *ca*mera mia	This is my bedroom
	Questi sono i miei fratelli	These are my brothers
	Quali scarpe ti metti? – Queste	Which shoes are you going to wear? – These ones
	Qual è la sua borsa? – Quella	Which bag is yours? – That one
	Quelli quanto *co*stano?	How much do those cost?
2	Dice sempre bugie quello	That man is always telling lies
	Quelle non sono mai contente	Those women are never happy
3	È quello che preferisco	That's the one (that) I prefer
	È quella che parla di più	She's the one who talks most
	Sono quelli che sono partiti senza pagare	They're the ones who left without paying
	Queste scarpe sono quelle che ha ordinato	These shoes are the ones (that) you ordered
4	Questo giardino è più grande di quello di Giulia	This garden is bigger than Giulia's
	Preferisco la mia *ma*cchina a quella di mio marito	I prefer my car to my husband's
	Le mie scarpe sono più belle di quelle di Lucia	My shoes are nicer than Lucia's
	i miei genitori e quelli delle mie amiche	my parents and those of my friends
	le montagne della Svizzera e quelle della Sc*o*zia	the mountains of Switzerland and those of Scotland
5	Non quello, questo qui	Not that one, this one here
	V*o*glio queste qua	I want these ones here
6	Questa gonna non ti sta bene, prova quella là	This skirt doesn't look good on you, try that one
	Quali prendi? – Quelli lì	Which ones are you going to have? – Those over there

Formation

Some adverbs are formed by adding **-mente** to an adjective.

-mente is added to the feminine form, (which ends in **-a**) of an adjective ending in **-o** → ❶

-mente is added to the basic form when an adjective ends in **-e** for both masculine and feminine → ❷

Adjectives ending in **-le** and **-re** drop the final **e** → ❸

Irregular Adverbs

ADJECTIVE	ADVERB
buono good	**bene** well → ❹
cattivo bad	**male** badly → ❺
migliore better	**meglio** better → ❻
peggiore worse	**peggio** worse → ❼

Adjectives used as adverbs

Certain adjectives are used adverbially. These include: **giusto**, **vicino**, **diritto**, **certo**, **solo**, **forte**, **molto**, **poco** → ❽

Examples

1	MASC./FEM. ADJECTIVE lento/lenta slow fortunato/fortunata lucky	ADVERB lentamente slowly fortunatamente luckily
2	MASC./FEM. ADJECTIVE veloce quick, fast corrente fluent	ADVERB velocemente quickly, fast correntemente fluently
3	**-le/-re** ADJECTIVE facile easy particolare particular	ADVERB facilmente easily particolarmente particularly
4	Parlano bene l'italiano	They speak Italian well
5	Ho giocato male	I played badly
6	Sto meglio	I'm better
7	Mi sento peggio	I'm feeling worse
8	Ha risposto giusto Abitano vicino Siamo andati sempre diritto Vieni stasera? – Certo!	She answered correctly They live nearby We kept straight on Are you coming tonight? – Of course!
	L'ho incontrata solo due volte Correva forte Quel quadro mi piace molto Vengo in ufficio poco spesso	I've only met her twice He was running fast I like that picture a lot I don't come into the office very often

Position of Adverbs

When the adverb accompanies a verb in a simple tense, it generally follows the verb → ❶

For emphasis the adverb can come at the beginning of the sentence → ❷

When adverbs such as **mai**, **sempre**, **già** and **appena** accompany a verb in a compound tense, they come between the auxilary verb and the past participle → ❸

When the adverb accompanies an adjective or another adverb it generally precedes the adjective/adverb → ❹

Comparatives of Adverbs

These are formed as follows:

più ... (di) more ... (than) → ❺
meno ... (di) less ... (than) → ❻

sempre più is used with the adjective to mean *more and more* → ❼

Superlatives of Adverbs

più ... and **meno ...** are also used to express the superlative → ❽
più ... di tutti/meno di tutti can be used to emphasize the superlative → ❾

Examples

1	Viene sempre	He always comes
	Parli bene l'italiano	You speak Italian well
2	Ora non posso	I can't do it just now
	Prima non lo sapevo	I didn't know that before
3	Non sono mai stata a Milano	I've never been to Milan
	È sempre venuto con me	He always came with me
	L'ho già letto	I've already read it
	Se n'è appena andato	He's just left
4	Fa troppo freddo	It's too cold
	Vai più piano	Go more slowly
5	più spesso	more often
	più lentamente	more slowly
	Correva più forte di me	He was running faster than me
6	meno velocemente	less quickly
	Costa meno	It costs less
	Vengo meno spesso di lui	I come less often than he does
7	Le cose vanno sempre meglio	Things are going better and better
	Mio nonno sta sempre peggio	My grandfather's getting worse and worse
	Cammina sempre più lento	He's walking slower and slower
8	È Carlo che viene più spesso	It's Carlo who comes most often
	Sono loro che lavorano meno volontieri	They're the ones who work least willingly
9	Cammina più piano di tutti	She walks the slowest (of all)
	L'ha fatto meno volentieri di tutti	He did it the least willingly

Adverbs with irregular comparatives/superlatives

ADVERB	COMPARATIVE/SUPERLATIVE
bene well	**meglio** better/best
male badly	**peggio** worse/worst
molto a lot	**più** more/most
poco not much	**meno** less/least

Emphatic Adverbs

For added emphasis the ending **-issimamente** can be used. It replaces the endings **-amente**, **-emente** or **-mente** → 1

bene and **male** have irregular emphatic forms: **benissimo** and **malissimo** → 2

Adverbial phrases

di più and **di meno** are used to say what you do most/least → 3

Examples

1	lentamente	slowly
	lentissimamente	very slowly
	velocemente	quickly
	velocissimamente	very quickly
2	Hai fatto benissimo	You did very well
3	la cosa che temeva di più	the thing she feared most
	quello che mi piace di meno	the one I like least
	Sono quelli che guad*a*gnano di meno	They're the ones who earn least

Some common adverbs and their usage

Some common adverbs:

abbastanza quite; enough → 1

anche too → 2

ancora still; yet → 3

appena just; only just → 4

certo certainly; of course → 5

così so; like this; like that → 6

ecco here → 7

forse perhaps, maybe → 8

già already → 9

mai never; ever → 10

molto very; very much; much → 11

piuttosto quite; rather → 12

poco not very; not at all → 13

presto soon; early → 14

quasi nearly → 15

spesso often → 16

tanto so; so much → 17

troppo too; too much → 18

Examples

1	È abbastanza alta Non st*u*dia abbastanza	She's quite tall He doesn't study enough
2	È venuta anche mia sorella	My sister came too
3	Sei ancora a letto? S*i*lvia non è ancora arrivata	Are you still in bed? Silvia's not here yet
4	L'ho appena fatto L'indirizzo ere appena legg*i*bile	I've just done it The address was only just legible
5	Certo che puoi Certo che sì	Of course you can Certainly
6	È così simp*a*tica! Si apre così Non si fa così	She's so nice! It opens like this You don't do it like that
7	Ecco l'*au*tobus! Dov'è Carla? – *E*ccola!	Here's the bus! Where's Carla? – Here she is!
8	Forse hanno ragione	Maybe they're right
9	Te l'ho già detto	I've already told you
10	Non sono mai stato in Am*e*rica Sei mai stato in Am*e*rica?	I've never been to America Have you ever been to America?
11	Sono molto stanca Ti piace? – Sì, molto. Ora mi sento molto m*e*glio	I'm very tired Do you like it? – Yes, very much I feel much better now
12	Fa piuttosto caldo oggi È piuttosto lontano	It's quite warm today It's rather a long way
13	Mi sento poco bene Mi pi*a*cciono poco	I don't feel at all well I don't like them at all
14	Arriver*à* presto Mi alzo sempre presto	He'll be here soon I always get up early
15	Sono quasi pronta	I'm nearly ready
16	Vanno spesso in centro	They often go into town
17	Questo libro è tanto noioso Mi manchi tanto	This book is so boring I miss you so much
18	È troppo caro P*a*rlano troppo	It's too expensive They talk too much

Prepositions

On the following pages you will find some of the most frequent uses of prepositions in Italian. Particular attention is paid to cases where usage differs greatly from English. It is often difficult to give an English equivalent for Italian prepositions, since usage varies so much between the two languages.

In the list below, the broad meaning of the preposition is given on the left, with examples of usage following.

Prepositions are given in alphabetical order, except for **a**, **di**, **da** and **in**. These prepositions, shown first, combine with the definite article to make one word.

For combinations of **a**, **di**, **da**, **in** and **su** with the definite article, see page 136.

a

at	**alla porta** at the door **a casa** at home **alla prossima fermata** at the next stop **a 50 chilometri all'ora** at 50 km an hour
in	**a Londra** in London **al sole** in the sun **Sta a letto** He's in bed
on	**al terzo piano** on the third floor **alla radio** on the radio
to	**Andiamo al cinema?** Shall we go to the cinema? **Vai a letto?** Are you going to bed? **Sei mai stato a New York?** Have you ever been to New York? **dare qc a qn** to give sth to sb **A chi l'hai dato?** Who did you give it to? **promettere qc a qn** to promise sth to sb **il primo/l'ultimo a fare qc** the first/last to do sth
from	**comprare qc a qn** to buy sth from sb

	nascondere qc a qn to hide sth from sb **prendere qc a qn** to take sth from sb **rubare qc a qn** to steal sth from sb
see you	**a presto** see you soon **a domani** see you tomorrow
manner	**a piedi** on foot **a mano** by hand **a poco a poco** little by little **all'antica** in the old-fashioned way **alla milanese** in the Milanese way
(made) with	**un gelato alla fragola** a strawberry ice cream **una torta al cioccolato** a chocolate cake **gli spaghetti al pomodoro** spaghetti with tomato sauce
time: at	**alle due** at two o'clock **a mezzanotte** at midnight **a Pasqua** at Easter
with month: in	**a maggio** in May
distance	**a tre chilometri da qui** three kilometres from here **a due ore di distanza in macchina** two hours away by car
purpose	**Sono uscita a fare due passi** I went out for a little walk **Sono andati a fare il bagno** They've gone to have a swim
after certain verbs	See pages 70-79

di

of, belonging to	**un amico di famiglia** a friend of the family **il padre di Marco** Marco's father **la casa dei miei amici** my friends' house **Di chi è?** Whose is it? **il periodo delle vacanze** the holiday season **il professore di francese** the French teacher **il campione del mondo** the world champion
(made) by	**un quadro di Picasso** a picture by Picasso **una commedia di Shakespeare** a play by Shakespeare
from	**È di Firenze** He's from Florence **Di dove sei?** Where are you from?
comparisons	**È più alto di me** He's taller than me **È più brava di lui** She's better than him
in (*after superlative*)	**il più grande del mondo** the biggest in the world **il migliore d'Italia** the best in Italy
time	**di domenica** on Sundays **di notte** at night **d'inverno** in winter
contents, composition, material, colour	**una bottiglia di vino** a bottle of wine **un gruppo di turisti** a group of tourists **una maglietta di cotone** a cotton T-shirt **Di che colore è?** What colour is it?
manner	**di rado** rarely **di solito** usually
after certain numbers	**un milione di dollari** a million dollars **un migliaio di persone** about a thousand people **una ventina di macchine** about twenty cars

after certain adjectives	**Le arance sono ricche di vitamina C** Oranges are rich in vitamin C **Era pieno di gente** It was full of people
after certain verbs	see pages 70-79

da

from	**a tre chilometri da qui** three kilometres from here **Viene da Roma** He comes from Rome **da cima a fondo** from top to bottom
off, out of	**Isobel è scesa dal treno** Isobel got off the train **È scesa dalla macchina** She got out of the car
at/to the home of	**Sono da Anna** I'm at Anna's house **Andiamo da Gabriele?** Shall we go to Gabriele's house?
at/to (*shop, workplace*)	**Laura è dal parrucchiere** Laura's at the hairdresser's **È andato dal dentista** He's gone to the dentist's
for	**Vivo qui da un anno** I've been living here for a year (*note tense*)
since	**da allora** since then **Ti aspetto dalle tre** I've been waiting for you since three o'clock (*note tense*)
by (*with passive agent*)	**dipinto da un grande artista** painted by a great artist **Sono stati catturati dalla polizia** They were caught by the police
to (*with infinitive*)	**C'è molto da fare** There's lots to do **È un film da vedere** It's a film that you've got to see
as	**Da bambino avevo paura del buio** As a child I was afraid of the dark

descriptive	**una ragazza dagli occhi azurri** a girl with blue eyes **un vestito da cento euro** a dress costing a hundred euros
purpose/use	**un nuovo paio di scarpe da corsa** a new pair of running shoes **Non ho il costume da bagno** I haven't got my swimming costume

in

to, in (*place*)	**in centro** in/to the town centre **in Italia** in/to Italy
into	**Su! Sali in macchina** Come on! get into the car
on, at (*state*)	**in vacanza** on holiday **in pace** at peace
in (*years, seasons, months*)	**nel duemilasei** in two thousand and six **in estate** in summer **in ottobre** in October
in (*time taken*)	**L'ha fatto in sei mesi** He did it in six months
transport	**in treno** by train **in bici** by bike
language	**in italiano** in Italian

con

with	**Con chi sei stata?** Who were you with?
to	**Hai parlato con lui?** Have you spoken to him?
manner	**con calma** without hurrying **con la forza** by force

davanti a

in front of	**Erano seduti davanti a me nell' *au*tobus** They were sitting in front of me in the bus
opposite	**la casa davanti alla mia** the house opposite mine

dopo

after	**dopo cena** after dinner
+ *pronoun* (add **di**)	**dopo di loro** after them

fra/tra

in (*time*)	**Torno fra** *or* **tra un'ora** I'll be back in an hour
between	**fra** *or* **tra la cucina ed il soggiorno** between the kitchen and the living room
+ *pronoun* (add **di**)	**fra** *or* **tra di noi** between/among us

per

for	**Questo è per te** This is for you **È troppo difficile per lui** It's too difficult for him **L'ho comprato per trenta cent*e*simi** I bought it for thirty cents **Ho guidato per trecento chil*o*metri** I drove for three hundred kilometres **una c*a*mera per due notti** a room for two nights **Parte per Milano** She's leaving for Milan
(going) to	**il volo per Londra** the flight to London **il treno per Roma** the train to Rome
through	**I ladri sono entrati per la finestra** The burglars got in through the window **Siamo passati per Crewe** We went through Crewe

by (means of)	**per posta** by post **per via aerea** by airmail **per posta elettronica** by email **per ferrovia** by rail **per telefono** by phone **per errore** by mistake
(so as) to	**L'ho fatto per aiutarti** I did it to help you **Si è chinato per prenderlo** He bent down to get it
out of	**Ci sono andato per abitudine** I went out of habit **Non l'ho fatto per pigrizia** I didn't do it out of laziness
distribution	**uno per uno** one by one **giorno per giorno** day by day **una per volta** one at a time **due per tre** two times three

prima di

before (+*noun*, *pronoun*)	**prime delle sette** before seven **prima di me** before me
+ *infin*	**prima di cominciare** before starting
until	**Non sarà pronto prima delle otto** It won't be ready until eight o'clock

senza

without	**Esci senza cappotto?** Are you going out without a coat?
+ *pronoun* (add **di**)	**senza di te** without you
+ *infinitive*	**È uscito senza dire niente** He went out without saying anything

sopra

over	**le donne sopra i sessant'anni** women over sixty
above	**cento metri sopra il livello del mare** a hundred metres above sea level
on top of	**sopra l'armadio** on top of the cupboard

su*

on	**sul pavimento** on the floor **sulla sinistra** on the left **un libro sugli animali** a book on animals
in	**sul giornale** in the paper
out of (*ratio*)	**in tre casi su dieci** in three cases out of ten **due giorni su tre** two days out of three
approximation	**sui cinquecento euro** around five hundred euros **È sulla trentina** She's about thirty

* **su** combines with the definite article to make one word

verso

towards (*place*)	**Correva verso l'uscita** He was running towards the exit
about	**Arriverò verso le sette** I'll arrive about seven

Conjunctions

Some conjunctions introduce a main clause, e.g. **e** (and), **ma** (but), **o** (or). Others introduce subordinate clauses, e.g. **perché** (because), **mentre** (while), **quando** (when), **se** (if). Conjunctions also link single words. Most are used in much the same way as in English, but note the following:

e and
When followed by a vowel, **e** often becomes **ed** → ❶

> Some Italian conjunctions have to be followed by the subjunctive, see page 66
>
> Some conjunctions are split in Italian, like 'both ... and', 'either ... or' in English.
> **o ... o** either ... or → ❷
> **né ... né** neither ... nor, either ... or → ❸
> **sia ... che** both ... and → ❹

In Italian, sentences with split conjunctions can have a singular or a plural verb → ❺

che that
- is followed by the indicative in statements → ❻
- is followed by the subjunctive after verbs expressing uncertainty, see page 64

perché because, so that
When **perché** means 'because' it is followed by the indicative → ❼
When it means 'so that', it is followed by the subjunctive → ❽

Note that **perché?** can also be used as an adverb with the meaning 'why?'

se if, whether
When used in conditional clauses **se** is followed by the subjunctive → ❾
Followed by the infinitive, **se** means 'whether to' → ❿
Followed by the indicative **se** expresses doubt → ⓫

Conjunctions are sometimes used in phrases where a verb is understood → ⓬

Examples

1	mia sorella ed io	my sister and I
	È venuto qui ed è rimasto mezzora	He came here and stayed for half an hour
2	o oggi o domani	either today or tomorrow
3	Non mi hanno chiamato né Cl*a*udio né Luca	Neither Claudio nor Luca has phoned me
	Non avevo né guanti né scarponi	I didn't have either gloves or boots
4	Verrano sia Luigi che suo fratello	Both Luigi and his brother are coming
5	Non v*e*ngono *or* Non viene né lui né sua m*o*glie	Neither he nor his wife is coming
6	Ha detto che far*à* tardi	He said that he'll be late
7	Sono uscita perch*é* faceva bel tempo	I went out because it was nice weather
8	Gliel'ho dato perch*é* lo leggesse	I gave it him so that he could read it
9	se fosse qui	if he was here
	Se avessi studiato avresti passato l'esame	If you'd worked you would have passed the exam
10	Non so se andarci o no	I don't know whether to go or not
11	Mi chiedo se avresti accettato	I wonder if you would have accepted
12	Ti dispiace? – Ma no!	Do you mind? – Of course I don't!
	Ho fame. – Anch'io!	I'm hungry. – So am I!
	Sì, lo so – strano per*ò*	Yes, I know – it's odd though

Word Order

Word order in Italian is very flexible, but:

- unstressed object pronouns always come before the verb, except when attached to the end of an infinitive or an imperative → 1
For details see pages 166

- most adjectives come after the noun → 2
For details see pages 156

- Adverbs of frequency accompanying verbs in a simple tense usually follow the verb, and those used with a compound tense follow the auxiliary verb → 3
For details see pages 184

Other parts of speech, however, may be positioned to give emphasis, or make a contrast:

- the noun which is the object of a verb generally follows the verb, but for emphasis it may come first → 4

- a question word generally comes first, but for emphasis, a noun subject or object can precede it → 5

- adjectives generally follow the verb ***essere***, but may precede it for emphasis → 6

- unstressed object pronouns generally precede the verb, but stressed pronouns can be used instead, and these follow the verb → 7
For details see pages 166

- subject pronouns are not normally used, but when added for emphasis they may come before or after the verb → 8

Examples

1 Li vedo! — I can see them!
Me l'ha dato — He gave it to me

2 la squadra italiana — the Italian team
un vino rosso — a red wine

3 Ci vado spesso — I often go there
Non ci sono mai stato — I've never been there

4 Normal order:
Non posso soffrire quel cane — I can't stand that dog
Emphatic order:
Quel cane non lo posso soffrire
note object pronoun added before the verb

5 Normal order:
Dov'*è* Lidia? — Where's Lidia?
Di chi sono queste scarpe? — Whose are these shoes?
Dove metto questa borsa? — Where shall I put this bag?
Emphatic order:
Lidia, dov'*è*?
Queste scarpe di chi sono?
Questa borsa dove la metto?
note added object pronoun

6 Normal order
Sono belli — They're lovely
Sei pazza — You're mad
Emphatic order:
Belli sono! — They're lovely!
Pazza sei! — You're mad!

7 Order with unstressed pronoun:
Me l'ha dato — He gave it to me
Order with stressed pronoun:
L'ha dato a me (non a te) — He gave it to me (not to you)

8 Unemphatic:
Cosa pensi? — What do you think?
Emphatic:
Tu cosa pensi?/Cosa pensi tu?

Negatives

In Italian, sentences are generally made negative by adding **non** before the verb → 1

di no is used after verbs such as **dire**, **credere**, **pensare** and **sperare** → 2

o no? is used to mean 'or not' → 3

noun/pronoun + **no**
no is used when making a distinction between people or things → 4

non is used in combination with other negative words such as **niente** *nothing*, **nessuno** *nobody*, **mai** *never* → 5

When **mai** is used with a compound tense, it usually comes between the auxiliary verb and the past participle → 6

When **niente** or **nessuno** are the subject of the verb they can come first, or they can follow the verb. If they come first, **non** is not used → 7

More than one negative word can follow a negative verb → 8

nessuno, nessuna no
These negative adjectives change their endings according to the letter that follows them, like the indefinite article **uno** → 9

non … né …. né neither … nor/not … either … or
A plural verb is required if there are two subjects → 10

Examples

1 Non posso venire	I can't come
Non l'ho visto	I didn't see it
Non è qui	It's not here
2 Ha detto di no	He said not
Credo di no	I don't think so
Pensa di no	He doesn't think so
Speriamo di no	Let's hope not
3 Vieni o no?	Are you coming or not?
che ti piaccia o no	whether you like it or not
4 Invito lui, lei no	I'm going to invite him, but not her
Loro hanno finito, noi no	They've finished, but we haven't
Lei è brava, io no	She's good, but I'm not
Prendo un dolce, il caffè no	I'll have a sweet, but not a coffee
5 Non ho niente	I haven't got anything/I've got nothing
Non l'ho detto a nessuno	I haven't told anyone/I've told nobody
Non ci vado mai	I never go there
6 Non l'ho mai vista	I've never seen her
Non ci siamo mai stati	We've never been there
7 Niente è cambiato	Nothing has changed
BUT	
Non è cambiato niente	
Nessuno vuole andarci	Nobody wants to go
BUT	
Non vuole andarci nessuno	
8 Non fanno mai niente	They never do anything
Non si confida mai con nessuno	He never confides in anyone
Non vendiamo più niente	We no longer sell anything
9 Nessun tipo di pianta può viverci	No type of plant can live there
Non ho nessuna voglia di farlo	I have no desire to do it
Non hanno fatto nessuno sforzo	They didn't make any effort
10 Non verranno né Anna né Maria	Neither Anna nor Maria is coming
BUT	
Non invito né Anna né Maria	I'm not inviting either Anna or Maria

Question Forms

In Italian, questions differ from statements in intonation, or the use of a question mark in writing. Unlike in English, the verb forms in questions are no different from those in statements → 1

Word order

When the subject of the question is a noun, it comes either before or after the verb → 2

When the object of the question is a noun, it either comes after the verb, or comes first. In this case an object pronoun agreeing with the noun is added before the verb → 3

A subject pronoun may also be added at the end of a question, for special emphasis → 4

When answering a question, either say **sì** or **no**, or **sì** or **no** with a full statement. There is no Italian equivalent for short answers such as Yes I do, or No I don't → 5

Question words such as **dove?** *where*?, **chi?** *who*? **cosa?** *what*? generally come first → 6

However, note the following:

- a noun subject can either follow the verb, or precede the question word → 7
- a noun object can follow the verb, or precede the question word. In this case an object pronoun agreeing with the noun is added before the verb → 8
- prepositions such as **di**, **con** and **a**, must precede question words → 9

Examples

	STATEMENT	QUESTION
1	Basta That's enough	Basta? Is that enough?
	Sono di qui They're from here	Sono di qui? Are they from here?
	L'ha fatto lui He did it	L'ha fatto lui? Did he do it?
	Va bene That's okay	Va bene? Is that okay?
2	Tua sorella è partita? *or* È partita tua sorella?	Has your sister gone?
	La Cal*a*bria è bella? *or* È bella la Cal*a*bria?	Is Calabria beautiful?
	Gli spaghetti sono buoni? *or* Sono buoni gli spaghetti?	Is the spaghetti nice?
3	Vuoi un gelato? *or* Un gelato lo vuoi?	Do you want an ice cream?
	Vuoi del latte *or* Un po' di latte lo vuoi?	Do you want some milk?
4	Contrast	
	Fai il bucato?	Are you doing the washing?
	with	
	Il bucato lo fai tu?	Will you do the washing?
5	Piove? Sì *or* Sì, piove	Is it raining? Yes *or* Yes, it's raining
	Capisci? No *or* No, non capisco	Do you understand? No *or* No, I don't
6	Dove vai?	Where are you going?
	Chi parla?	Who's speaking?
7	Quanto c*o*stano queste scarpe? *or* Queste scarpe, quanto c*o*stano?	How much are these shoes?
	Chi è quella signora? *or* Quella signora, chi è?	Who is that lady?
8	Chi pagher*à* il conto? *or* Il conto, chi lo pagherà?	Who will pay the bill?
9	Di che colore è?	What colour is it?
	Con chi parlavi?	Who were you talking to?
	A cosa stai pensando?	What are you thinking about?

Question Forms *continued*

no?, vero?
no? or **vero?** is used to check that what you've said is correct, like 'isn't it?' or 'haven't you?' in English → ➊

vero is used to check a negative statement → ➋

Indirect Questions

Word order in Italian indirect questions is no different from that of statements → ➌

Tenses in indirect questions are generally the same as in English, except for the use of the perfect conditional where the present conditional is used in English → ➍

Examples

1	Hai finito, no?	You've finished, haven't you?
	Questa è la tua m*a*cchina, vero?	This is your car, isn't it?
2	Non sono partiti, vero?	They haven't gone, have they?
	Non fa molto male, vero?	It doesn't hurt much, does it?
3	Vorrei sapere quanto costa	I'd like to know how much it costs
	Mi domando cosa p*e*nsano	I wonder what they think
4	Ha detto che non era colpa sua	He said it wasn't his fault
	Ha detto che verr*à*	He said he'll come
	Aveva detto che sarebbe venuto	He'd said he'd come

Use of numbers

Cardinal (one, two *etc*)		Ordinal (first, second *etc*)	
zero	0		
uno (una, un)	1	primo	1º
due	2	secondo	2º
tre	3	terzo	3º
quattro	4	quarto	4º
cinque	5	quinto	5º
sei	6	sesto	6º
sette	7	settimo	7º
otto	8	ottavo	8º
nove	9	nono	9º
dieci	10	decimo	10º
undici	11	undicesimo	11º
dodici	12	dodicesimo	12º
tredici	13	tredicesimo	13º
quattordici	14	quattordicesimo	14º
quindici	15	quindicesimo	15º
sedici	16	sedicesimo	16º
diciassette	17	diciassettesimo	17º
diciotto	18	diciottesimo	18º
diciannove	19	diciannovesimo	19º
venti	20	ventesimo	20º
ventuno	21	ventunesimo	21º
ventidue	22	ventiduesimo	22º
ventitré	23	ventitreesimo	23º
trenta	30	trentesimo	30º
quaranta	40	quarantesimo	40º
cinquanta	50	cinquantesimo	50º
sessanta	60	sessantesimo	60º
settanta	70	settantesimo	70º
ottanta	80	ottantesimo	80º
novanta	90	novantesimo	90º
novantanove	99	novantanovesimo	99º

Use of numbers

Cardinal		Ordinal	
cento	100	**centesimo**	100°
centouno (**centouna, centoun**)	101	**centunesimo**	101°
centodue	102	**centoduesimo**	102°
centotré	103	**centotreesimo**	103°
centodieci	110	**centodecimo**	110°
centoquarantadue	142	**centoquarantaduesimo**	142°
duecento	200	**duecentesimo**	200°
duecentouno	201	**duecentunesimo**	201°
duecentotré	203	**duecentotreesimo**	203°
trecento	300	**trecentesimo**	300°
quattrocento	400	**quattrocentesimo**	400°
cinquecento	500	**cinquecentesimo**	500°
seicento	600	**seicentesimo**	600°
settecento	700	**settecentesimo**	700°
ottocento	800	**ottocentesimo**	800°
novecento	900	**novecentesimo**	900°
mille	1000	**millesimo**	1000°
milleuno	1001	**millunesimo**	1001°
milleduecentodue	1202	**milleduecentoduesimo**	1202°
duemila	2000	**duemillesimo**	2000°
cinquemilatrecento	5300	**cinquemilatrecentesimo**	5300°
un milione	1.000.000	**milionesimo**	1.000.000°
due milioni	2.000.000	**duemilionesimo**	2.000.000°

Ordinal numbers are adjectives which tell you the order in which the noun occurs (first, third, etc). They end with either **o**, or **a**, depending on whether the noun is masculine or feminine:

il 15° piano	the 15th floor	**la 24ª giornata**	the 24th day

Fractions		Other numerical expressions	
un mezzo	a half	**zero virgola cinque (0,5)**	0.5
un terzo	a third	**uno virgola tre (1,3)**	1.3
due terzi	two thirds	**dieci per cento**	10%
un quarto	a quarter	**sei più due**	6 + 2
tre quarti	three quarters	**sei meno due**	6 – 2
un quinto	a fifth	**due volte sei**	2 × 6
un sesto	a sixth	**sei diviso due**	6 ÷ 2

ⓘ Note the use of commas in decimal numbers, and full stops with millions.

Other Uses

Approximate numbers

- ending in **-ina**

una ventina di DVD	about twenty DVDs
Eravamo una trentina	There were about thirty of us
È sulla quarantina	He's about forty
gente sulla cinquantina	people of around fifty

- ending in **-aio**

un centinaio di persone	about a hundred people
centinaia di volte	hundreds of times
un migliaio di casi	about a thousand cases
due migliaia di m*a*cchine	about two thousand cars

Measurements

venti metri quadri	20 square metres
venti metri cubi	20 cubic metres
un ponte lungo cento metri	a bridge 100 metres long
*e*ssere largo/alto tre metri	to be 3 metres wide/long

Miscellaneous

*A*bitano al numero dieci	They live at number 10
nel cap*i*tolo sei	in chapter 6
Sono a p*a*gina tre	They're on page 3
*A*bitano al terzo piano	They live on the 3rd floor
Sono arrivata seconda nella gara	I came second in the competition
su una scala da uno a dieci	on a scale of one to ten

Telephone numbers

The digits in a telephone number are spoken individually:

zero zero tre nove zero sei quattro due otto uno sette sei zero due (0039 0642817602)

tre quattro sette sette zero tre quattro nove zero cinque (3477034905)

Calendar

Che data è oggi?/ Quanti ne abbiamo oggi?	What's the date today?
È il primo m*a*ggio	It's May 1st
È il due m*a*ggio	It's May 2nd
È il ventotto febbraio	It's February 28th
Arr*i*vano il diciannove l*u*glio	They're arriving on July 19th

ⓘ Use cardinal numbers except for the first of the month.

Years

È nata nel 1993	She was born in 1993
il d*o*dici febbraio duemilaotto	(on) 12th February 2008

Other expressions

negli anni sessanta	in the sixties
nel ventun*e*simo s*e*colo	in the twenty-first century
in *or* a m*a*ggio	in May
lunedì (qu*i*ndici)	on Monday (the fifteenth)
di lunedì	on Mondays
fra *or* tra dieci giorni	in 10 days' time
otto giorni fa	8 days ago

The time

Che ore sono?	What time is it?
È l'una	It's one o'clock
Sono le due	It's two o'clock

ⓘ Use **sono** for all times except one o'clock.

00.00	mezzanotte midnight, twelve o'clock
00.10	mezzanotte e dieci ten past midnight
00.15	mezzanotte e un quarto, mezzanotte e quindici
00.30	mezzanotte e mezza, mezzanotte e trenta
00.45	l'una meno un quarto, l'una meno qu*i*ndici, mezzanotte e quarantacinque
01.00	l'una di mattina one a.m., one o'clock in the morning
01.10	l'una e dieci (di mattina)
01.15	l'una e un quarto, l'una e qu*i*ndici
01.30	l'una e mezza, l'una e trenta
01.45	l'una e quarantacinque; le due meno un quarto, le due meno quindici
01.50	l'una e cinquanta, le due meno dieci
01.59	l'una e cinquantanove, le due meno un minuto
12.00	mezzogiorno, le dodici noon, twelve o'clock
12.30	mezzogiorno e mezza, mezzogiorno e trenta, le dododici e mezza
13.00	l'una (del pomer*i*ggio), le tr*e*dici, le ore tr*e*dici
01.30	l'una e mezza/trenta (del pomer*i*ggio), le tr*e*dici e trenta, le ore tr*e*dici e trenta
19.00	le sette (di sera), le diciannove, le ore diciannove
19.30	le sette e mezza/trenta, le diciannove e trenta, le ore diciannove e trenta

ⓘ The twenty-four hour clock is widely used in Italy.

alle diciannove *or*	at nineteen hours
alle ore diciannove	at nineteen hundred hours

A che ora venite? – Alle sette	What time are you coming? – At seven
L'ufficio è chiuso da mezzogiorno alle due	The office is closed from twelve to two
alle due di notte/del pomeriggio	at two o'clock in the morning/ afternoon; at two a.m./p.m.
alle otto di sera	at eight in the evening; at eight p.m.
alle cinque in punto	at five o'clock sharp
verso le nove	at around nine
poco dopo mezzogiorno	shortly after noon
fra le otto e le nove	between eight and nine o'clock
Erano le tre e mezza passate	It was after half past three
Devi esserci entro le nove	You have to be there by nine
Ci vogliono tre ore	It takes three hours
Ci metto una mezz'ora	It takes me half an hour
È rimasta in bagno per un'ora	She was in the bathroom for an hour
Li aspetto da quaranta minuti	I've been waiting for them for forty minutes
Sono partiti qualche minuto fa	They left a few minutes ago
L'ho fatto in venti minuti	I did it in twenty minutes
Il treno arriva fra un quarto d'ora	The train arrives in a quarter of an hour
Per quanto tempo dovremo aspettare?	How long will we have to wait?

Translation problems

Beware of translating word for word. The following are examples of where Italian tends to differ from English:

English phrasal verbs (i.e. verbs such as 'to look for'; 'to fall down') are often translated by one word in Italian → 1

English verbs often require a preposition where there is none in Italian, or vice versa → 2

Different English prepositions may be translated by the one Italian preposition → 3

A word which is singular in English may be plural in Italian, or vice versa → 4

There is no Italian equivalent for the apostrophe s and s apostrophe possessive → 5

See also at/in/to, page 220.

The following pages look at some specific problems.

Examples

1	scappare	to run away
	cadere	to fall down
	rendere	to give back
2	pagare qc	to pay for sth
	guardare qc/qn	to look at sth/sb
	ascoltare qc/qn	to listen to sth/sb
	dire a qn	to tell sb
	ubbedire a qn	to obey sb
	ricordarsi di qc/qn	to remember sth/sb
3	meravigliarsi di	to be surprised at
	stufo di	fed up of/with
	rubare qc a	to steal sth from
	restio a	reluctant to
4	gli affari	business
	i suoi capelli	his/her hair
	Le lasagne sono ...	Lasagne is...
	i bagagli	luggage
5	la macchina di mia sorella	my sister's car (*literally*: ... of my sister)
	la camera delle ragazze	the girls' bedroom (*literally*... of the girls)

-ing

This is translated by the gerund in Italian:

'to be ...-ing' is sometimes translated by **stare** + *gerund*, when the verb describes something at the moment, but a simple tense is often used. A simple tense must be used when the verb refers to the future. → 1

The past participle, not the gerund, is used for physical positions such as lying and sitting → 2

to see/hear sb ...-ing, use an infinitive or **che** + *verb* → 3

'-ing' can also be translated by:

- an infinitive, see page 46 → 4
- a perfect infinitive, see page 50 → 5
- the gerund, when used abverbially, see page 52 → 6
- a noun → 7

to be

'to be' is generally translated by **essere** → 8

Examples

1	Che fai *or* stai facendo?	What are you doing?
	Che fai domani sera?	What are you doing tomorrow evening?
	P*a*rtono *or* Stanno partendo	They're leaving
	P*a*rtono alle sette	They're leaving at seven
2	Erano seduti in prima fila	They were sitting in the front row
	Era sdraiata sulla s*a*bbia	She was lying on the sand
3	L'ho visto partire	I saw him leaving
	L'ho visto che partiva	
	L'ho sentita pi*a*ngere	I heard her crying
	L'ho sentita che piangeva	
4	Mi piace cucinare	I like cooking
	invece di risp*o*ndere	instead of answering
	prima di partire	before leaving
	Inizi*ò* a piovere	It started raining
5	dopo aver perso molti soldi	after losing a lot of money
6	Essendo più t*i*mida di me, non ha gli ha parlato	Being shyer than me, she didn't speak to him
7	Il fumo fa molto male	Smoking is very bad for you
8	È tardi	It's late
	Sono loro	It's them
	Siamo stanchi	We're tired

stare is used

- with the gerund to make continuous tenses → 1
- in perfect and pluperfect tenses of ***essere***, which consist of the present/imperfect tense of ***essere*** + past participle of **stare** → 2
- interchangeably with ***essere*** when talking about locations → 3
- when talking about health → 4

In various set expressions **avere** is used (with the final **e** dropped):

aver caldo/freddo	to be hot/cold
aver fame/sete	to be hungry/thirsty
aver paura	to be afraid
aver torto/ragione	to be wrong/right

fare is used to talk about the weather → 5

avere is used for ages → 6

it is, it's

These are never translated by a pronoun in Italian → 7

In expressions of time, use **sono**, except for one o'clock → 8

To describe the weather, see above.

When 'it's' is followed by a pronoun, such as 'me', 'her' or 'them', the form of ***essere*** agrees with the person referred to → 9

can, be able

Ability is generally expressed by **potere** → 10

If the meaning is 'to know how to' use **sapere** → 11

'can' with verbs of seeing and hearing is not translated in Italian → 12

Examples

1 Ci sto pensando	I'm thinking about it
Stavano chiacchierando	They were chatting
2 Non ci sono mai stata	I've never been there
Ero stato malato	I had been ill
3 La casa sta *or* è sulla collina	The house is on the hill
Sta *or* è fuori	It's outside
4 Sto bene, grazie	I'm fine thanks
Sta male	He's not well
5 Che tempo fa?	What's the weather like?
Fa caldo/freddo	It's hot/cold
Fa bel/brutto tempo	It's nice/bad weather
6 Quanti anni hai?	How old are you?
Ho quindici anni	I'm fifteen
7 Dammelo, è mio	Give it me, it's mine
È molto lontano	It's a long way
8 Sono le nove	It's nine o'clock
È l'una meno un quarto	It's a quarter to one
9 Sono io	It's me
È lei	It's her
Sono loro	It's them
10 Puoi venire?	Can you come?
11 Non so come spiegarlo	I can't explain it
12 Si vede il mare	You can see the sea
Non ti sento	I can't hear you

to like

piacere, the Italian verb used to translate 'to like', means 'to be pleasing', so **Mi piace l'Italia** literally means 'Italy is pleasing to me', and **Gli animali piacciono ai bambini** means 'Animals are pleasing to children'.

Remember the following when using **piacere**:

- the thing(s) liked is/are the subject of the Italian verb → ①
- if the thing liked is singular, the verb is singular (**piace/è piaciuto** etc): if the things liked are plural, the verb is plural (**piacciono/sono piaciuti** etc) → ②
- **piacere** is used with **a**, or an indirect object pronoun → ③

to

'to' is often translated by **a**, see page 190 → ④

When telling the time, e.g. ten to six, use **meno** → ⑤

When the meaning is 'in order to' use **per** → ⑥

When 'to' is part of the infinitive following an adjective such as 'easy', 'difficult', 'impossible', use the Italian infinitive with **da** → ⑦

unless the infinitive has an object → ⑧

at/in/to

For 'in' or 'to' + a country, use the Italian preposition **in** → ⑨

For 'in' or 'to' + a town, use the Italian preposition **a** → ⑩

When the meaning is 'to'/'at' + someone's house/place of business use **da** → ⑪

Examples

1	Il cane piace a mio figlio I cani piacciono a mio figlio	My son likes the dog My son likes dogs
2	Il concerto è piaciuto a tutti I cioccolatini piaceranno a tutti	Everyone liked the concert Everyone will like the chocolates
3	A mia madre piace molto il giardinaggio Ti piace questa canzone? Non gli piacciono i pomodori	My mother likes gardening very much Do you like this song? He doesn't like tomatoes
4	Dallo a Patrizia	Give it to Patrizia
5	le sei meno un quarto l'una meno tre minuti	a quarter to six three minutes to one
6	L'ho fatto per rassicurarti Si è fermato per guardarlo	I did it to reassure you He stopped to look at it
7	facile da capire impossibile da dimenticare	easy to understand impossible to forget
8	È facile capirlo È impossibile crederci	It's easy to understand it It's impossible to believe it
9	Abitano negli Stati Uniti Andiamo in Germania il quattro maggio una città in Cina	They live in the United States We're going to Germany on May 4 a city in China
10	È andato a Parigi Vive a Bologna	He's gone to Paris He lives in Bologna
11	Andiamo da Anna È dal parucchiere	Let's go to Anna's house She's at the hairdresser's

General Points

Vowels and consonants are always clearly pronounced in Italian, and each syllable of a word is audible, unlike in English, where letters, and sometimes whole syllables, are often not pronounced. Compare, for example:
lettera (both **e**s are equally clear, audible **r**)
letter (2nd **e** indistinct, **r** usually not pronounced)
interessante, (5 syllables)
interesting (3 syllables)

Diphthongs

A diphthong is a glide between two vowel sounds in the same syllable. The vowels in 'say', 'go' and 'might' are diphthongs. Diphthongs are very common in English, but much less so in Italian, where most vowels are a single sound, as they are in English words such as 'top', 'back' and 'set' The diphthongs found in Italian are vowels preceded by a **y**, or a **w** sound:

ia [ja] - **chiaro**
ie [je] - **pieno**
io [jo] - **pioggia**
iu [ju] - **chiuso**
ua [wa] - **sguardo**
ue [we] - **guerra**
ui [wi] - **guidare**
uo [wo] - **fuoco**

Stress

Italian words are generally stressed on the next to the last syllable, (so two-syllable words are stressed on the first syllable, three-syllable words on the second syllable, and so on):

ca sa
ra **gaz** zo
set ti **ma** na
ge ne ral **men** te

For more details see page 180.

If the stress comes on the last vowel of a word with more than one syllable, the vowel is always written with an accent:
per **ché**
par le **rò**
un i ver si **tà**

For more details see page 180.

Pronunciation

Pronunciation of Consonants

Most consonants are pronounced as in English, except that they are always clear, and double consonants are audible. Thus, in **sabbia** *sand*, for example, the **b** sound ending the first syllable carries on to start the second syllable: sab-bya.

Note the following:

		PRONOUNCED	EXAMPLES
c before a, o, u	[k]	like k in kiss	camera, come, cubo
c before e or i	[tʃ]	like ch in China	certo, cinese
ch	[k]	like k in kiss	chiesa
g before a, o, u	[g]	like g in good	gara, largo, gusto
g before e or i	[dʒ]	like g in rage	gelato, giro
gh	[g]	like g in good	laghi, ghiaccio
gl before i	[ʎ]	like ll in million	meglio, gli
gl before other vowels	[gl]	like gl in piglet	sigla
gn	[ɲ]	like ny in canyon	gnocchi, ragno
h is not pronounced		like h in honest	hanno
r	[r]	like r in zero	raro, rapido
sc before e or i	[ʃ]	like sh in ship	scena, sci
z	[dz]	like ds in lids	zanzarra
z	[ts]	like ts in bits	ragazzo

Pronunciation of Vowels

		PRONOUNCED	EXAMPLES
a	[a]	like a in apple	animale
e	[ɛ]	like e in set	schema
e	[e]	like ay in day	stella
i	[i]	like ee in sheep	clima
i before a vowel often	[j]	like y in yoghurt	Lidia, negozio
o	[o]	like o in pot	ora
u	[u]	like oo in soot	puro
u before a vowel often	[w]	like w in win	usuale

Stress: Cases where the normal rule does not apply

In cases where the last syllable of a word is stressed, this is shown by an accent. Most of these are:

- nouns ending in **-tà**, many of which have counterparts in English ending in -ty, such as 'reality' and 'university'

re al t*à*	reality	u ni ver si t*à*	university
fe li ci t*à*	happiness, felicity	fe del t*à*	fidelity
cu rio si t*à*	curiosity	fa col t*à*	faculty
bon t*à*	goodness	cit t*à*	city
cru del t*à*	cruelty	e t*à*	age
me t*à*	half		

- 1st and 3rd person singular future verbs , and 3rd person singular past historics:

sa r*ò*	I will be
fi ni r*à*	it will finish
as pet te r*à*	she'll wait
par l*ò*	he spoke
an d*ò*	she went

- adverbs and conjunctions such as

perch*é*	why
per*ò*	however
cos*ì*	so

In cases where the stress is on an unexpected syllable other than the last, there is no accent to show this. In this book, such vowels are shown in italics, e.g.

m*a*cchina	car
*u*tile	useful
port*a*tile	laptop

Stress in present tense verb forms

All present tense forms except the 3rd person plural follow the rule, and stress the next to the last syllable, e.g. p*a*rlo I speak; cons*i*dera he considers

In the 3rd person plural form the stress is not on the next to the last syllable, but matches that of the 1st person singular:

1st person singular		3rd person plural	
p*a*r lo	I speak	p*a*r la no	they speak
con s*i* de ro	I consider	con s*i* de ra no	they consider
mi al l*e* no	I'm training	si al l*e* na no	they're training

Stress in 2nd conjugation infinitives

Stress is regular for the infinitives of all 1st and 3rd. and many 2nd conjugation verbs, e.g. **parlare** *to speak*, **finire** *to finish*, **vedere** *to see*. However, there are also many 2nd conjugation infinitives which do not stress the 1st **e** of the **-ere** ending, eg:

***e*ssere** *to be*, **v*e*ndere** *to sell*, **perm*e*ttere** *to allow*, **div*i*dere** *to divide*.

When learning 2nd conjugation verbs, note which syllable of the infinitive is stressed.

From Sounds to Spelling

Apart from the occasional problem of unexpected stress, the way Italian is spelled is a good guide to how it should be pronounced. See page 180.

It is also easy to know how to spell words, if the following points are remembered:

-care/-gare verbs

Verbs with infinitives ending **-care**, or **-gare**, for example **cercare** and **pagare**, add an **h** to keep the **c** or **g** hard in front of endings starting with **e** or **i**:

Vowel that follows **c/g**	Present of **cercare**		Present of **pagare**	
o	cerco	I look for	pago	I pay
i	cerchi	you look for	paghi	you pay
a	cerca	he/she looks for	paga	he/she pays
i	cerchiamo	we look for	paghiamo	we pay
a	cercate	you look for	pagate	you pay
a	cercano	they look for	pagano	they pay

Vowel that follows **c/g**	Future of **cercare**		Future of **pagare**	
e	cercherò	I'll look for	pagherò	I'll pay
e	cercherai	you'll look for	pagherai	you'll pay
e	cercherà	he/she will look for	pagherà	he/she will pay
e	cercheremo	we'll look for	pagheremo	we'll pay
e	cercherete	you'll look for	pagherete	you'll pay
e	cercheranno	they'll look for	pagheranno	they'll pay

-ca/-ga nouns and adjectives

Nouns and adjectives ending in **-ca** and **-ga** always keep the hard sound of the consonant in the plural, so **h** is added before the plural ending **-e**:

Singular		Plural	
amica	friend	**amiche**	friends
riga	line	**righe**	lines
ricca	rich	**ricche**	rich
lunga	long	**lunghe**	long

-co/-go nouns and adjectives

Some nouns and adjectives ending in **-co** and **-go** keep the hard sound of the consonant in the plural, so **h** is added before the plural ending **-i**, e.g.:

Singular		Plural	
fuoco	fire	**fuochi**	fires
albergo	hotel	**alberghi**	hotels
ricco	rich	**ricchi**	rich
lungo	long	**lunghi**	long

Other nouns nouns and adjectives ending in **-co** and **-go** change the sound of the consonant in the plural from hard [k] or [g] to soft [tʃ] or [dʒ], so no **h** is added, e.g.:

Singular		Plural	
amico	friend	**amici**	friends
astrologo	astrologer	**astrologi**	astrologers
greco	Greek	**greci**	Greek
psicologico	psychological	**psicologici**	psychological

-io nouns

The plural of nouns ending **-io** is spelled **-ii** if the **i** of the **-io** ending is a stressed vowel, e.g. **zio** *uncle* plural: **zii**, and **invio** *dispatch* plural: **invii**.

In cases where the **i** of the **-io** is not a stressed vowel, but is pronounced [j], the plural is spelled with a single **i**, e.g. **occhio** *eye* plural **occhi**; **figlio** *son* plural: **figli**.

-cia/-gia nouns

Generally, if the **i** of the **-cia/-gia** ending of a noun is a stressed vowel, the **i** is retained in the plural, eg **farmacia** *chemist* plural: **farmacie**; **bugia** *lie* plural: **bugie**. If the **i** of the ending serves to keep the **c/g** soft, and is not pronounced as a vowel, there is no **i** in the plural: **faccia** *face*, plural: **facce**; **spiaggia** *beach*, plural: **spiagge**.

Accents

Use an accent when a word is stressed on the final syllable, e.g. **città**, **cercherò**, **università**. See page 180.

Accents are also used on certain one- syllable words to distinguish them from words that are spelled the same (homophones):

da	from	**dà**	he/she gives
e	and	**è**	is
la	the/it	**là**	there
li	them	**lì**	there
ne	of it/them	**né**	neither
se	if	**sé**	himself
si	himself/herself/one	**sì**	yes
te	you	**tè**	tea

The grave accent (à, è, ì, ò ,ù) is used on most words. The acute accent is used to spell conjunctions ending in **che**, such as **benché** *although*, and **perché** *because*. It is also used on **né** and **sé** (except in the phrases **se stesso** and **se stessa** *himself; herself*).

può, **già**, **ciò**, **più** and **giù** are spelled with an accent, for no obvious reason.

The Alphabet

A,a	a	J,j	[i'lunga]	S,s	['ɛsse]
B,b	[bi]	K,k	['kappa]	T,t	[ti]
C,c	[tʃi]	L,l	['ɛlle]	U,u	u
D,d	[di]	M,m	['ɛmme]	V,v	[vi, vu]
E,e	e	N,n	['ɛnne]	W,w	['dɔppjovu]
F,f	['ɛffe]	O,o	[ɔ]	X,x	[iks]
G,g	[dʒi]	P,p	[pi]	Y,y	['ipsilon]
H,h	['akka]	Q,q	[ku]	Z,z	[dzɛta]
I,i	i	R,r	['ɛrre]		

Capital letters are used as in English except for the following:

adjectives of nationality

e.g. una città tedesca — a German town

una scrittrice italiana — an Italian writer

languages

e.g. Parla inglese? — Do you speak English?

Parlo francese ed italiano — I speak French and Italian

days of the week:

lunedì Monday
martedì Tuesday
mercoledì Wednesday
giovedì Thursday
venerdì Friday
sabato Saturday
domenica Sunday

months of the year:

gennaio January
febbraio February
marzo March
aprile April
maggio May
giugno June
luglio July
agosto August
settembre September
ottobre October
novembre November
dicembre December

Index

The following index lists comprehensively both grammatical terms and key words in English and Italian.